NASB-NIV PARALLEL NEW TESTAMENT

NASB-NIV PARALLEL NEW TESTAMENT IN GREEK AND ENGLISH

WITH INTERLINEAR TRANSLATION BY

Alfred Marshall

NASB-NIV PARALLEL NEW TESTAMENT IN GREEK AND ENGLISH

Published by special arrangement with Samuel Bagster, Ltd., London, and the Lockman Foundation.

REGENCY REFERENCE LIBRARY
is an imprint of
Zondervan Publishing House
1415 Lake Drive S.E.
Grand Rapids, Michigan 49506

Library of Congress Cataloging in Publication Data

Bible. N.T. English. New American Standard. 1986.
NASB–NIV parallel New Testament in Greek and English.

Includes Greek text and literal interlinear English translation of the New Testament.
1. Bible. N.T.—Interlinear translations, English. I. Marshall, Alfred. II. Bible. N.T. English. New International. 1986. III. Bible. N.T. Greek. 1986.

BS1965 1986 225.4'8 86–28273

ISBN 0–310–34670–3

Printed in the United States of America

90 91 92 93 94 95 / BB / 12 11 10 9 8 7 6 5

Introduction to the Interlinear Greek Text and Translation

The Greek Text

The text of the Greek New Testament has come down to us in various manuscripts, printing not being invented until the fifteenth century and Erasmus not publishing his Greek New Testament until 1516. Some of these manuscripts are more important than others (age not necessarily being indicative of importance). The study of the various manuscript copies, and the assessment of their individual value in attempting to reconstruct the original as nearly as possible, constitutes the science of textual criticism. For those who wish to study this seriously there are many books available; it is sufficient to say here that, after Erasmus, a great number of scholars have, over a long period, applied themselves to the task of constructing a reliable text out of the mass of various readings that have arisen from copying and making copies from copies of the old manuscripts (scholars such as Mill, Stephens, Griesbach, Lachmann, Tischendorf, Tregelles, and Alford).

The Greek text used in this book is that of the 21st edition of Eberhard Nestle's *Novum Testamentum Graece,* based on the study and critical research of generations of scholars, except that John 7:53–8:11 is not in that text but is relegated to the foot of the page as a critical note. It is here retained in the text. The critical notes of Nestle's work, which enable students to follow the reasons for variations in the text, have been omitted as being outside the scope of this publication. The student who requires these critical notes is referred to the Greek edition published in Great Britain by the British and Foreign Bible Society and in Germany (Stuttgart) by Privilegierte Württembergische Bibelanstalt, by whose permission this recension is used.

Square brackets are found in certain places in the Greek text.

These indicate only that, according to Nestle, some editors include and others omit the word or words so enclosed. Translation has been made here in the usual way.

Avoiding interpretation, then, we give some details of how we have proceeded in the matter of a literal translation. These should be studied and understood if proper use is to be made of this attempt to promote an intelligent reading of the Greek New Testament.

The English Translation

The Wording in General

The relationship between the Greek text and the interlinear English is as follows: Greek words not required in the translation into English are (*a*) represented by a short dash, as for example the definite article with proper names. Alternatively (*b*) italic type is used to show that words or even in some cases letters are not really needed for an idiomatic English rendering. For example, "man" is sometimes redundant (as in Matt. 20:1; Acts 2:22). On the other hand, words supplied in English for which there is no Greek equivalent are placed in square brackets [. . .]. Naturally, there will be differences of judgment as to this practice in the passages involved.

The modern form for the third person singular of verbs (present indicative) has been used (loves) in place of the now obsolete -(e)th (loveth); but the older "ye" has been retained for the nominative ("you" for the oblique cases) of the second person plural pronoun; and "thou" (thee), not "you," for the second person singular. It is a loss that in modern English these differences have disappeared; so unaccustomed are we now to them that even the average reader of the Authorized Version misses the point of Luke 22:31. The loss is even more to be regretted when God is addressed as "You."

Where some word other than the strictly literal one seems to be needed in the translation, the former is printed in parentheses immediately after the latter—e.g., Matthew 10:17, "beware from (of) men."

Occasionally it is not feasible to give a literal rendering without undue explanation; some idiomatic word or phrase has to be used. There are only a few of such passages, and they are indicated by the mark †.

There are a number of Greek phrases, other than where † is used, which are to be taken as a whole, not word for word:

ἐπὶ τὸ αὐτό = "on the same" = "together"
διὰ τοῦτο = "because-of this" = "therefore"
ἵνα μή = "in-order-that not" = "lest"
καθ' ὑπερβολήν = "by-way-of excess" = "excessively"

Εὐαγγελίζω. This and its cognate noun have been anglicized (evangelize, evangel). But while we can "evangelize" a city, we do not "evangelize" a person or a subject; so we must speak of "preaching (good tidings) to" a person or of "preaching" a subject. We can, of course, speak of "evangelizing" absolutely as in 1 Corinthians 1:17. Ellicott on 1 Thessalonians 3:6 has some useful information for the student.

Verbs

The ending of a Greek verb normally indicates the person (1st, 2nd, or 3rd, sing. or pl.). If the pronoun is separately expressed, this can be clearly seen in the interlinear translation.

Where there is more than one subject of a verb, Greek will often put the verb in the singular to agree with the nearest subject. This is not in accordance with English grammar, which requires a plural verb if there is more than one subject. In Revelation 9:2, "sun" and "air" call for the plural "were darkened," as in the Authorized Version. But the Greek verb is in the singular. It is sometimes typographically possible to indicate the difference of grammatical usage.

A peculiarity of Greek construction is that a neuter plural subject may take a singular verb; but this is by no means invariable, and there appears to be no rule to go by. In translating, the position is sometimes shown by the use of an italic letter for the ending of the verb ([they] commit*s*); at other times the alternative is given in parenthesis (is(are)). But there are places where neither course is possible without taking up too much space, and the matter is left to the intelligence of the reader.

The subjunctive mood is dying out in English, and no attempt has been made to represent consistently the Greek mood, except by the use of the analytic form "I may . . . ," with its related optative (of which latter there are only thirty-seven examples in the New Testament, fifteen of these being the familiar γένοιτο = "may it be"). But such words as ἵνα and compounds of ἄν (ὅταν, ἐάν), etc., introducing a subjective or hypothetical element into a verbal idea, must be followed by the subjunctive mood.

The Greek perfect can generally be taken as represented by an English present—a past action continuing in its effect down to the present, in contrast to an action wholly in the past. But in a literal translation the English perfect has been retained. In John 11:27, the Authorized Version is idiomatically correct, but the Revised Version is literally so (*πεπίστευκα* = "I have believed"); compare 2 Timothy 1:12, where the Authorized Version adopts the literal equivalent. So, for example, *τετέλεσται* = "it has been finished" = "it is finished." In participles, italics show that the auxiliary verbs may be dispensed with in English.

The interlinear translation has introduced a comma after "Behold" in a number of places. The reason for this is as follows. The Greek *ἰδού* (or other form), properly an imperative of the defective verb *ὁράω*, is used as an exclamation, as is its English equivalent. That is to say, it is not then an active verb taking a direct object in the accusative case; it is simply exclamatory and is followed by a noun in the nominative, with its predicate or complement understood. For example, in John 1:29, there is no command to behold the Lamb of God; instead, the idea is, "Look! [there goes]. . . ." The position is different in such passages as Matthew 28:6 and Romans 11:22, where there is a command.

Greek will often use a preposition in a compound verb and then repeat it (or use one similar) before a noun in the same sentence; in such passages the preposition would not be used twice in English. But in such a phrase as *εἰσέρχεσθαι εἰς οἶκον* we can say "to enter into a house" (the counterpart in French being *entrer dans une maison*). We can indeed say simply "to enter a house." Another exception would be *ἀπέρχεσθαι ἀπό* ("to go away from"). But *διαφέρειν διὰ τοῦ ἱεροῦ* means "to carry *through* through the temple" (e.g., Mark 11:16).

Necessity or compulsion is most frequently expressed by the use of an impersonal verb (or a verb used impersonally), with the person concerned in the accusative as the object of the verb (*δεῖ με* = "it behoves me" = "I must").

Participles

Greek is "a participle-loving language," said the late A. T. Robertson, and it uses this part of speech much more frequently than we do, and in different ways.

To begin with, it is absolutely essential to grasp the distinction between *continuous, momentary,* and *completed* action. The first is commonly, but wrongly, spoken of as a present participle, the second as an aorist (which does not mean "past"), and the third as a perfect. (There is a rare future participle—continuous in the future.)

1. A participle may be used as an adjective qualifying a noun,

just as in English (e.g., 1 Thess. 1:9—"a living God"; Heb. 7:8—"dying men"). This is so simple as not to need further remark.

2. A participle may be used, again as in English, as a verb to describe some action (e.g., Acts 9:39—"all the widows stood by . . . weeping and showing. . .").

3. A participle may be used, with the definite article, with, say, "one" understood, where we should use a noun or a relative phrase (e.g., frequently, ὁ πιστεύων = "the [one] believing" = "the believer" *or* "he who believes"). Here the participle is continuous; in Luke 1:45, it is momentary (and, naturally, feminine in gender, referring to Mary's one act of faith at the Annunciation). If two participles are used with but one definite article, as in John 5:24, the meaning is that one person is doubly described, not two persons doing two things. This feature has been preserved in our translation.

4. Very frequently indeed, where in English we use two or more finite verbs to describe associated actions, Greek will use participles and only one finite verb for the main action. But here judgment is necessary to distinguish two (or more) simultaneous actions from consecutive ones; and as we have no aorist participle in English the matter is not always free from difficulty. In Acts 10:34 ("Peter opening his mouth said") the two actions were obviously simultaneous! Likewise, Acts 1:24 ("Praying they said"). But sometimes one action must be completed before another could begin (e.g., Luke 22:17—"having given thanks, he said . . ."). Here the act of giving thanks to God would be complete before Jesus addressed His disciples; therefore the aorist participle must be represented in English by the analytic "having given thanks." That this is not unimportant is shown by Matthew 26:30 ("having sung a hymn they went out"). To translate the aorist participle here by "singing a hymn" would certainly convey the idea that the singing occurred as they went out. In Acts 21:14, it is not easy to see how the keeping silence and the saying could be contemporaneous ("Having said, The will of the Lord be done, we kept silence"). These few examples should, we think, suffice to show the principles involved.

Negatives

As the negatives οὐ(κ) (categorical) and μή (hypothetical) are easily recognizable, it has not been thought necessary always to render them separately, but they are included with any verb with which they may be used. But whereas in English the negative follows the verb, in Greek it precedes (e.g., Matt. 3:11). If such a phrase happens to be broken at the end of a line, this course has not been feasible.

The double negative οὐ μή has been consistently rendered "by no means."

Incidentally, though of importance, these two negative particles, or their compounds, when introducing questions, expect different answers. οὐ appeals to the fact, anticipating "Yes, it is so" (e.g., John 11:9, "Are there not twelve hours of the day?"). The answer would be "Yes, there are." On the contrary, μή denies the suggestion and expects the reply "No, it is not so"; or, if not so explicit as that, doubts whether it is so (e.g., John 18:35). The form of the question in the Authorized Version and the Revised Version indicates that Pilate was asking for information, whereas he was rejecting the idea with scorn and contempt—"I am not a Jew [am I]?" The answer, if any, would be—"No, certainly not." This distinction is largely overlooked in the English Versions. To assist to the correct nuance of thought, in such places the latter negative in the interlinear translation is italicized, and the reader must read into the original what is intended; the result is sometimes surprising. An article in *The Bible Translator* for January 1953 may be consulted.

While on the subject of negatives, Greek favors the use of two such, one strengthening the other. In such sentences the second negative has to be replaced in English by a positive (e.g., Matt. 22:46).

Nouns

In familiar proper names there will appear some inconsistency, a compromise between the actual spellings preferred by Nestle and the Authorized Version; but this is of no great importance.

In Greek, gender belongs to the word and not necessarily to what is indicated by the word; whereas, of course, in English we keep the ideas of masculine, feminine, and neuter to men, women, and inanimate things respectively—English, by the way, being the only great modern language to do so. Allowance must be made for this in translating; sometimes it is possible to transfer the idea from one language to another. The note to Revelation 13:1 may be consulted.

It has not been considered necessary always to indicate the order of a noun and its adjective; a knowledge of English is sufficient for this. But where there is any risk of ambiguity, small superior figures indicate the order in which the words should be read.

Adjectives

The construction of the demonstrative adjectives is peculiar in Greek. The definite article is used as well as the demonstrative adjective in one of two possible positions: either—

οὗτος ὁ οἶκος
this *the* house

or—

ὁ οἶκος οὗτος
the house this

The definite article is of course not wanted in English, and the proper translation of the phrase is obvious—"this house." Similarly ἐκεῖνος ("that"). It is sometimes possible typographically to treat the three-word phrase as a whole, with the idiomatic translation underneath.

There is no indefinite article in Greek. The use of it in translation is a matter of individual judgment. The numeral "one" is sometimes found; whether this means that just one, and no more, is to be understood is again open to argument (e.g., Matt. 21:19; 26:69). We have inserted "a" or "an" as a matter of course where it seems called for.

The definite article must sometimes be rendered by a pronoun or a possessive adjective. This is particularly so where parts of the body are indicated (e.g., Matt. 8:3). Sometimes it is used "pronominally"—that is, it must be rendered "he" (or otherwise according to the gender) or "they" (e.g., Mark 10:4).

Similarly, the definite article is used in Greek with a possessive adjective, as in Matthew 18:20—

εἰς τὸ ἐμὸν ὄνομα
in *the* my name

or, alternatively, the construction may be, say—

εἰς τὸ ὄνομα τὸ ἐμόν
in *the* name *the* my

This remark applies only to the first and second persons, singular and plural, not to the third, where the only possible construction in this respect would be "in the name of him/her/them." This has been followed literally, as the reader can always make the necessary English construction for himself. Occasionally such a construction as "in the name of me" will be found, meaning the same thing.

The neuter form of an adjective may be used as an adverb. In John 19:35, ἀληθῆ is the neuter of ἀληθής ("true") and must be rendered "truly." So πρῶτον ("firstly"), though "first" is quite often used in English as an adverb. Conversely, an adverb may be used as an adjective (e.g., νῦν, "now" = "present").

The word ταῦτα ("these things," neuter plural) might be rendered by the singular "this," as in the common phrase μετὰ ταῦτα ("after this"); but this liberty has not been taken in the present literal translation.

The gender of an adjective may demand "man," "woman," or "thing" to be supplied (e.g., Matt. 9:27—"two blind men").

There is the *genitive of quality,* of which there are many examples in the New Testament. If in English we say "a man of courage" or "an act of kindness," this is equivalent to "a courageous man" or "a kind act" respectively. We have translated literally, with an occasional footnote where this construction is not generally recognized.

As "first" is used as an adverb as well as "firstly," it has not been thought necessary always to print "first*ly*"; the matter is of no great importance.

Particles

A number of Greek particles are said to be "post-positive"—that is to say, they cannot stand as the first word in a sentence but are found in the second, third, or even the fourth place. Such words must of course be taken first in English; but it has not been thought necessary to show this, as the construction is sufficiently obvious. They include γάρ ("for"), δέ ("and, but, now"), οὖν ("therefore," which can be post-positive in English), τις (a certain), μέν (indeed), and γε ("really"—generally too subtle to be reproduced in English).

μέν . . . δέ. These two particles, in contrasted clauses, are not translatable literally, unless "indeed . . . but" be used, as we have done in some places. But by adopting the phrases "on the one hand . . . on the other" the contrast is brought out. These particles are, in fact, somewhat elusive as to their force. See John 19:24, 32, where μέν has been left untranslated—an example of the difficulty of rendering it satisfactorily in a literal translation.

The word ὅτι as a conjunction, when meaning "that," is used to introduce spoken words as recorded; it is then known as the "recitative ὅτι." In English the original present tense of any verb would in such a construction ("indirect speech") be changed to the past—e.g., "He said that the man was a liar." But Greek retains the original tense as actually used. What the speaker really said was "The man is a liar." The conjunction thus becomes superfluous and the reported words would in modern usage be put within quotation marks, as above. These, however, are not used in this translation (e.g., Matt. 21:3).

Strictly speaking, ἵνα is a "telic" particle—that is, it denotes purpose (τέλος, "an end"); hence a full translation is "in order that." But inasmuch as in New Testament times there was a tendency to use it where ὅτι would be expected, it sometimes means no more than the conjunction "that" (e.g., Matt. 5:29). Sometimes, then, where there may be room for difference of opinion as to its precise force, or even where there is none, "*in order* that" will be found in the literal translation.

Idiomatic constructions

There are five idiomatic Greek constructions that, being of frequent occurrence, call for explanation.

a. The *genitive absolute*. This is made up of a participle and a noun or pronoun, both in the genitive case and agreeing otherwise as well but having no grammatical relation to the context. It is used to indicate time during which, at which, or connected with which something takes place. The close of such a Greek phrase is shown by the superior letter [a] (e.g., Luke 3:1). There are variations of this. In Luke 12:36, two participles are used with no noun; it has to be supplied from the context. So also 2 Corinthians 7:15, and see the note on Romans 9:11 under "Notes on Particular Passages" below.

b. The *accusative* (or other case) *and infinitive*. Here what is in English the subject of the verb (the doer of the action) is put in the accusative (or other) case, and the verb itself is put in the infinitive. A superior letter [b] closes such a phrase (e.g., Luke 1:21).

c. The *dative of possession*. The possessor is put in the dative case. The idea may be grasped by comparing our English way of saying that a thing "belongs to so-and-so." The superior letter [c] shows this idiom (e.g., Luke 1:5, 7, 14).

d. The *genitive of purpose* or *result*. The infinitive of a verb is in the genitive case, as shown by the preceding definite article. The article itself can be ignored. Again the appropriate letter [d] shows the existence of the idiom (e.g., Matt. 2:13). The same idea can be shown without any article (e.g., Matt. 4:1).

e. The *dative of time*. This shows a point of time "in" or "at" which a thing happens (ἐν may or may not be used). The letter [e] indicates this (e.g., Luke 2:43; 18:35).

The constructions b and e can sometimes be combined (e.g., Luke 1:8).

Notes on Particular Passages

Mark 10:11—An article by Dr. Nigel Turner in *The Bible Translator* for October 1956 gives good reasons for understanding the verse thus, *αὐτήν* referring to the last woman mentioned (*ἄλλην*).

Mark 14:6—The *ἐν* here is somewhat puzzling. The parallel in Matthew (26:10) has *εἰς*, which would mean "to," "toward," or "for"; and Mark's *ἐν* must then be taken as equivalent in meaning to *εἰς*. This may throw light on 1 John 4:16.

Luke 7:14—It does not seem right to insist here on the passive voice of *ἐγέρθητι* (cf. 8:54 and, in another connection, 11:8). But our Lord "was raised," as are the dead generally; they do not "rise"; (see 1 Cor. 15, etc.).

John 8:25—"The answer of Jesus is one of the most disputed passages in the Gospel" (Godet). Nestle punctuates as a question; hence we have given what appears to be a reasonable rendering interrogatively.

Acts 7:46—The word *οἴκῳ* is a manuscript variant for *θεῷ*. There is some uncertainty as to how this reading arose; see the Authorized Version. Has Psalm 24:6, text and margin, any bearing on the matter?

Acts 18:10—The words *λαὸς πολύς* must not be understood as meaning "many persons." *λαός* is the regular word for the chosen people, Israel (almost without exception). Here in Corinth was to be a new community, taking the place of the Jewish population. So translate it "a great people."

Romans 1:12—This refers to their faith (= "confidence") in one another—Paul and his readers. "Mutual" is correct in Authorized Version, but it is generally misunderstood as being equivalent to "common," which it is not.

Romans 9:11—There is no noun agreeing with the two participles. But it is nevertheless a "genitive absolute" construction. The Authorized Version supplies the subject.

2 Corinthians 11:28—There is another view of Paul's words here. The word *ἐπίστασις* occurs in the New Testament only here and in Acts 24:12. The related noun *ἐπιστάτης* ("one standing over,"

''superintendent,'' ''master'') is peculiar to Luke (six times in his Gospel). Then there is a variant reading in our verse, μου instead of μοι. So the meaning may be—''my daily superintendence *or* attention.'' This would bring it into line with the remainder of the verse.

Philippians 3:16—This is, according to Burton, the only certain use in the New Testament of the ''imperatival infinitive,'' Romans 12:15 being a probable example. Moulton thinks it highly probable in Titus 2:1–10. The epistolary χαίρειν (Acts 15:23; 23:26; James 1:1) is said to be the same in origin, though a verb of bidding may be assumed, as in fact we do find in 2 John 10, 11. Compare the French warning in railway carriages—*Ne pas se pencher au dehors*. In English we have such a full expression as ''You are 'to do' so and so'' (e.g., 2 Thess. 3:14). If Nestle's text is accepted here, it is an additional instance to those given under Philippians 3:16 above, though with a negative as a prohibition. (Textus Receptus, etc., give a plain imperative.) But perhaps we may insert ''so as'' (''mark this man, so as not to mix with him'').

2 Timothy 4:3—The construction of the last three words of this verse is difficult. ''Having itching ears'' may be a workable paraphrase, but it cannot be said to represent literally the actual Greek. There is no word for ''having''; and there is nothing corresponding to ''itching'' as a participial adjective qualifying ''ears.'' τὴν ἀκοήν is accusative singular, the object of a verb—and the only verb is the participle that precedes. This is masculine plural, agreeing with διδασκάλους, and, while this latter is accusative, whereas the participle is nominative, this must be taken as an example of rational rather than grammatical concord. It is the teachers who ''tickle'' the ears of those concerned.

Hebrews 2:10—That is, it is God who perfected Jesus Christ (the author, or captain, of our salvation) by means of sufferings, whose work it is to lead many sons to glory; ἀγαγόντα (''leading,'' referring to Jesus) agrees with ἀρχηγόν, not with αὐτῷ (''him,'' i.e., God). Besides, there is a parallel between Joshua and Jesus, as both leaders of their peoples. In fine, it is the function of a captain to lead, and Jesus is the leader here.

Hebrews 9:16–17—We are aware of the problem in regard to διαθήκη in this passage; but this translation is no place for purporting to settle a question that has divided commentators. It must suffice to say that we have translated the word consistently as ''covenant''; the idea of a legatee receiving something on the death of a testator by reason of the latter's having made a "testament" or "will" is, so far as we can see, quite non-biblical. The covenant victim, then, is "the one making covenant," unless the person establishing the covenant is to be understood as identifying himself with it; and the covenant is in fact ratified over the dead body or bodies. But other views are taken of the matter.

James 2:1—This is an example of two genitives in apposition. There are other instances of such a construction. In Colossians 1:18, the meaning must be "of the body (,) *of* the church"—the body is the church, as verse 24 says. Colossians 2:2 has "of God, of Christ." For Romans 11:17, see the note at that place. Regarding John 8:44 ("of the father (,) *of* the devil"), their father was the Devil.

Revelation 16:14—The word "Almighty" is not an adjective but another noun in apposition.

NOTE on Matthew 16:3; 27:65; Luke 12:56; Acts 21:37; 1 Thessalonians 4:4; 1 Timothy 3:5; James 4:17; 2 Peter 2:9—As in French, so in the Greek of the New Testament, we have the idea of "to know (how) to do" a thing as being the same as "to be able to do" it. But while the French use only *savoir*, not *connaître,* in this way, both *γινώσκω* and *οἶδα* have this meaning in the New Testament. In fact, it is the former in Matthew 16:3 and the latter in the parallel in Luke (12:56). So, in French, *Savez-vous nager?* = Know you to swim? = Can you swim? In all the above passages this seems to be the meaning. It may be noted that the Authorized Version so renders the verbs in some passages, in others giving "know how." The instance in James 4:17 may be arguable. Philippians 4:12 also may be considered, and Matthew 7:11 = Luke 11:13.

The New American Standard Bible

Scriptural Promise

"The grass withers, the flower fades, but the word of our God stands forever." Isaiah 40:8

Foreword

The New American Standard Bible has been produced with the conviction that the words of Scripture as originally penned in the Hebrew, Aramaic, and Greek were inspired by God. Since they are the eternal Word of God, the Holy Scriptures speak with fresh power to each generation, to give wisdom that leads to salvation, that men may serve Christ to the glory of God.

The Editorial Board had a twofold purpose in making this translation: to adhere as closely as possible to the original languages of the Holy Scriptures, and to make the translation in a fluent and readable style according to current English usage.

The Fourfold Aim of The Lockman Foundation

1. These publications shall be true to the original Hebrew, Aramaic, and Greek.
2. They shall be grammatically correct.
3. They shall be understandable to the masses.
4. They shall give the Lord Jesus Christ His proper place, the place which the Word gives Him; therefore, no work will ever be personalized.

Preface to the New American Standard Bible

In the history of English Bible translations, the King James Version is the most prestigious. This time-honored version of 1611, itself a revision of the Bishops' Bible of 1568, became the basis for the English Revised Version appearing in 1881 (New Testament) and 1885 (Old Testament). The American counterpart of this last work was published in 1901 as the American Standard Version. Recognizing the values of the American Standard Version, the Lockman Foundation felt an urgency to update it by incorporating recent discoveries of Hebrew and Greek textual sources and by rendering it into more current English. Therefore, in 1959 a new translation project was launched, based on the ASV. The result is the New American Standard Bible.

The American Standard Version (1901) has been highly regarded for its scholarship and accuracy. A product of both British and American scholarship, it has frequently been used as a standard for other translations. It is still recognized as a valuable tool for study of the Scriptures. The New American Standard Bible has sought to preserve these and other lasting values of the ASV.

Furthermore, in the preparation of this work numerous other translations have been consulted along with the linguistic tools and literature of biblical scholarship. Decisions about English renderings were made by consensus of a team composed of educators and pastors. Subsequently, review and evaluation by other Hebrew and Greek scholars outside the Editorial Board were sought and carefully considered.

The Editorial Board has continued to function since publication of the complete Bible in 1971. Minor revisions and refinements, recommended over the last several years, are presented in this edition.

Principles of Translation

Modern English Usage: The attempt has been made to render the grammar and terminology in contemporary English. When it was felt that the word-for-word literalness was unacceptable to the modern reader, a change was made in the direction of a more current English idiom. In the instances where this has been done, the more literal rendering has been indicated in the notes.

Alternative Readings: In addition to the more literal renderings, notations have been made to include alternate translations, readings of variant manuscripts and explanatory equivalents of the text. Only such notations have been used as have been felt justified in assisting the reader's comprehension of the terms used by the original author.

GREEK TEXT: Consideration was given to the latest available manuscripts with a view to determining the best Greek text. In most instances the 23rd edition of Eberhard Nestle's NOVUM TESTAMENTUM GRAECE was followed.

GREEK TENSES: A careful distinction has been made in the treatment of the Greek aorist tense (usually translated as the English past, "He did") and the Greek imperfect tense (rendered either as English past progressive, "He was doing"; or, if inceptive, as "He *began* to do" or "He started to do"; or else if customary past, as "He used to do"). "Began" is italicized if it renders an imperfect tense, in order to distinguish it from the Greek verb for "begin."

On the other hand, not all aorists have been rendered as English pasts ("He did"), for some of them are clearly to be rendered as English perfects ("He has done"), or even as past perfects ("He had done"), judging from the context in which they occur. Such aorists have been rendered as perfects or past perfects in this translation.

As for the distinction between aorist and present imperatives, the translators have usually rendered these imperatives in the customary manner, rather than attempting any such fine distinction as "Begin to do!" (for the aorist imperative) or "Continually do!" (for the present imperative).

As for sequence of tenses, the translators took care to follow English rules rather than Greek in translating Greek presents, imperfects, and aorists. Thus, where English says, "We knew that he was doing," Greek puts it, "We knew that he does"; similarly, "We knew that he had done" is the Greek, "We knew that he did." Likewise, the English, "When he had come, they met him," is represented in Greek by: "When he came, they met him." In all cases a consistent transfer has been made from the Greek tense in the subordinate clause to the appropriate tense in English.

In the rendering of negative questions introduced by the particle **mē** (which always expects the answer "No") the wording has been altered from a mere, "Will he not do this?" to a more accurate, "He will not do this, will he?"

Explanation of GENERAL FORMAT

FOOTNOTES are used only where the text especially requires them for clarification. Marginal notes and cross references have been deleted from this edition.

PARAGRAPHS are designated by bold face numbers or letters.

QUOTATION MARKS are used in the text in accordance with modern English usage.

"THOU," "THEE," and "THY" are not used in this translation except in the language of prayer when addressing Deity.

PERSONAL PRONOUNS are capitalized when pertaining to Deity.

ITALICS are used in the text to indicate words which are not found in the original Hebrew, Aramaic, or Greek but implied by it. Italics are used in the footnotes to signify alternate readings for the text.

SMALL CAPS in the New Testament are used in the text to indicate Old Testament quotations or obvious allusions to Old Testament texts. Variations of Old Testament wording are found in New Testament citations depending on whether the New Testament writer translated from a Hebrew text, used existing Greek or Aramaic translations, or paraphrased the material. It should be noted that modern rules for the indication of direct quotation were not used in biblical times, thus allowing freedom for omissions or insertions without specific indication of these.

ASTERISKS are used to mark verbs that are historical presents in the Greek which have been translated with an English past tense in order to conform to modern usage. The translators recognized that in some contexts the present tense seems more unexpected and unjustified to the English reader than a past tense would have been. But Greek authors frequently used the present tense for the sake of heightened vividness, thereby transporting their readers in imagination to the actual scene at the time of occurrence. However, the translators felt that it would be wise to change these historical presents to English past tenses.

ABBREVIATIONS AND SPECIAL MARKINGS

Aram. = Aramaic
Gr. = Greek translation of O.T. (Septuagint, or LXX) or Greek text of N.T.
Lit. = A literal translation
Or = An alternate translation justified by the Hebrew, Aramaic, or Greek
[ ] = In text, brackets indicate words probably not in the original writings
cf. = compare
ms., mss. = manuscript, manuscripts
v., vv. = verse, verses

The New International Version

The New International Version of the New Testament, first published in 1973, is a completely new translation made by many scholars working directly from the Greek. The Greek text used in the work of translation was an eclectic one. Where existing texts differ, the translators made their choice of readings in accord with sound principles of textual criticism. Footnotes call attention to places where there was uncertainty about what constituted the original text. These have been introduced by the phrase "Some MSS add (*or* omit *or* read)."

As in all translations of the Scriptures, the precise meaning of the original text could not in every case be determined. In important instances of this kind, footnotes introduced by "Or" suggest an alternate rendering of the text. In the translation itself, brackets were occasionally used to indicate words or phrases supplied for clarification.

Certain convictions and aims guided the translators. They were all committed to the full authority and complete trustworthiness of the Scriptures. Therefore, their first concern was the accuracy of the translation and its fidelity to the thought of the New Testament writers. While they weighed the significance of the lexical and grammatical details of the Greek text, they strove for more than a word-for-word translation. Because thought patterns and syntax differ from language to language, faithful communication of the meaning of the writers of the New Testament demanded frequent modifications in sentence structure and constant regard for the contextual meanings of words.

Concern for clarity of style—that it should be idiomatic without being idiosyncratic, contemporary without being dated—also motivated the translators and their consultants. They consistently aimed at simplicity of expression, with sensitive attention to the connotation and sound of the chosen word. At the same time, they endeavored to avoid a sameness of style in order to reflect the varied styles and moods of the New Testament writers.

As for the omission of the pronouns "thou," "thee," and

"thine" in reference to the Deity, the translators felt that to retain these archaisms (along with the strange verb forms, such as *doest, wouldest,* and *hadst*) would have violated their aim of faithful translation. The Greek text uses no special pronouns to express reverence for God and Christ. Scripture is not enhanced by keeping, as a special mode of addressing Deity, forms that in the day of the King James Bible were simply the regular pronouns and verbs used in everyday speech, whether referring to God or to man.

The Greek Alphabet

Α	α	Alpha	a	
Β	β	Beta	b	
Γ	γ	Gamma	g	hard, as in be*g*in[1]
Δ	δ	Delta	d	
Ε	ε	Epsilon	e	short, as in m*e*t
Ζ	ζ	Zeta	z	
Η	η	Eta	e	long, as in sc*e*ne
Θ	θ	Theta	th	as in *th*in
Ι	ι	Iota	i	
Κ	κ	Kappa	k	
Λ	λ	Lambda	l	
Μ	μ	Mu	m	
Ν	ν	Nu	n	
Ξ	ξ	Xi	x	
Ο	ο	Omicron	o	short, as in l*o*t
Π	π	Pi	p	
Ρ	ρ	Rho	r	
Σ	σ, *final s*	Sigma	s[2]	
Τ	τ	Tau	t	
Υ	υ	Upsilon	u	
Φ	φ	Phi	ph	
Χ	χ	Chi	ch	hard, as in lo*ch*
Ψ	ψ	Psi	ps	
Ω	ω	Omega	o	long, as in thr*o*ne

[1] Except that before κ, χ or another γ, it is nasal—ng, as in a*nch*or.
[2] Sharp as in thi*s*, but flat before β or μ, as in a*s*bestos, di*s*mal.

The left-hand column contains the NASB text, the right-hand column, the NIV text.

Chapter 1

Genealogy of Jesus Christ

THE book of the genealogy of Jesus Christ, the son of David, the son of Abraham.

2To Abraham was born Isaac; and to Isaac, Jacob; and to Jacob, [a]Judah and his brothers;

3and to Judah were born Perez and Zerah by Tamar; and to Perez was born Hezron; and to Hezron, Ram;

4and to Ram was born Amminadab; and to Amminadab, Nahshon; and to Nahshon, Salmon;

5and to Salmon was born Boaz by Rahab; and to Boaz was born Obed by Ruth; and to Obed, Jesse;

6and to Jesse was born David the king.

And to David was born Solomon by her *who had been the wife* of Uriah;

7and to Solomon was born Rehoboam; and to Rehoboam, Abijah; and to Abijah, Asa;

8and to Asa was born Jehoshaphat; and to Jehoshaphat, Joram; and to Joram, Uzziah;

9and to Uzziah was born Jotham; and to Jotham, Ahaz; and to Ahaz, Hezekiah;

10and to Hezekiah was born Manasseh; and to Manasseh, Amon; and to Amon, Josiah;

11and to Josiah were born Jeconiah and his brothers, at the time of the deportation to Babylon.

12And after the deportation to Babylon, to Jeconiah was born Shealtiel; and to Shealtiel, Zerubbabel;

13and to Zerubbabel was born Abiud; and to Abiud, Eliakim; and to Eliakim,

[a]Gr., *Judas*. Names of Old Testament characters will be given in their Old Testament form.

---

1 *Βίβλος γενέσεως Ἰησοῦ Χριστοῦ*
[The] book of [the] generation of Jesus Christ
υἱοῦ Δαυὶδ υἱοῦ Ἀβραάμ.
son of David son of Abraham.

2 *Ἀβραὰμ ἐγέννησεν τὸν Ἰσαάκ, Ἰσαὰκ δὲ*
Abraham begat – Isaac, and Isaac
ἐγέννησεν τὸν Ἰακώβ, Ἰακὼβ δὲ ἐγέννησεν τὸν
begat – Jacob, and Jacob begat –
Ἰούδαν καὶ τοὺς ἀδελφοὺς αὐτοῦ, 3 *Ἰούδας δὲ*
Judas and the brothers of him, and Judas
ἐγέννησεν τὸν Φάρες καὶ τὸν Ζάρα ἐκ τῆς
begat – Phares and – Zara out of –
Θαμάρ, Φάρες δὲ ἐγέννησεν τὸν Ἑσρώμ,
Thamar, and Phares begat – Esrom,
Ἑσρὼμ δὲ ἐγέννησεν τὸν Ἀράμ, 4 *Ἀρὰμ δὲ*
and Esrom begat – Aram, and Aram
ἐγέννησεν τὸν Ἀμιναδάβ, Ἀμιναδὰβ δὲ
begat – Aminadab, and Aminadab
ἐγέννησεν τὸν Ναασσών, Ναασσὼν δὲ ἐγέννησεν
begat – Naasson, and Naasson begat
τὸν Σαλμών, 5 *Σαλμὼν δὲ ἐγέννησεν τὸν Βόες*
– Salmon, and Salmon begat – Booz
ἐκ τῆς Ῥαχάβ, Βόες δὲ ἐγέννησεν τὸν Ἰωβὴδ
out of – Rachab, and Booz begat – Obed
ἐκ τῆς Ῥούθ, Ἰωβὴδ δὲ ἐγέννησεν τὸν Ἰεσσαί,
out of – Ruth, and Obed begat – Jesse,
6 *Ἰεσσαὶ δὲ ἐγέννησεν τὸν Δαυὶδ τὸν βασιλέα.*
and Jesse begat – David the king.
Δαυὶδ δὲ ἐγέννησεν τὸν Σολομῶνα ἐκ τῆς
And David begat – Solomon out of the
τοῦ Οὐρίου, 7 *Σολομὼν δὲ ἐγέννησεν*
[one who had been the wife] – of Uriah, and Solomon begat
τὸν Ῥοβοάμ, Ῥοβοὰμ δὲ ἐγέννησεν τὸν
– Roboam, and Roboam begat –
Ἀβιά, Ἀβιὰ δὲ ἐγέννησεν τὸν Ἀσάφ, 8 *Ἀσὰφ*
Abia, and Abia begat – Asaph, and Asaph
δὲ ἐγέννησεν τὸν Ἰωσαφάτ, Ἰωσαφὰτ δὲ
begat – Josaphat, and Josaphat
ἐγέννησεν τὸν Ἰωράμ, Ἰωρὰμ δὲ ἐγέννησεν τὸν
begat – Joram, and Joram begat –
Ὀζίαν, 9 *Ὀζίας δὲ ἐγέννησεν τὸν Ἰωαθάμ,*
Ozias, and Ozias begat – Joatham,
Ἰωαθὰμ δὲ ἐγέννησεν τὸν Ἀχάζ, Ἀχὰζ δὲ
and Joatham begat – Achaz, and Achaz
ἐγέννησεν τὸν Ἑζεκίαν, 10 *Ἑζεκίας δὲ*
begat – Hezekias, and Hezekias
ἐγέννησεν τὸν Μανασσῆ, Μανασσῆς δὲ ἐγέννησεν
begat – Manasses, and Manasses begat
τὸν Ἀμώς, Ἀμὼς δὲ ἐγέννησεν τὸν Ἰωσίαν,
– Amos, and Amos begat – Josias,
11 *Ἰωσίας δὲ ἐγέννησεν τὸν Ἰεχονίαν καὶ*
and Josias begat – Jechonias and
τοὺς ἀδελφοὺς αὐτοῦ ἐπὶ τῆς μετοικεσίας
the brothers of him at the deportation
Βαβυλῶνος. 12 *Μετὰ δὲ τὴν μετοικεσίαν*
of Babylon. And after the deportation
Βαβυλῶνος Ἰεχονίας ἐγέννησεν τὸν Σαλαθιήλ,
of Babylon Jechonias begat – Salathiel,
Σαλαθιὴλ δὲ ἐγέννησεν τὸν Ζοροβαβέλ,
and Salathiel begat – Zorobabel,
13 *Ζοροβαβὲλ δὲ ἐγέννησεν τὸν Ἀβιούδ,*
and Zorobabel begat – Abiud,
Ἀβιοὺδ δὲ ἐγέννησεν τὸν Ἐλιακίμ, Ἐλιακὶμ δὲ
and Abiud begat – Eliakim, and Eliakim

Chapter 1

The Genealogy of Jesus

A RECORD of the genealogy of Jesus Christ the son of David, the son of Abraham:

2Abraham was the father of Isaac,
Isaac the father of Jacob,
Jacob the father of Judah and his brothers,
3Judah the father of Perez and Zerah, whose mother was Tamar,
Perez the father of Hezron,
Hezron the father of Ram,
4Ram the father of Amminadab,
Amminadab the father of Nahshon,
Nahshon the father of Salmon,
5Salmon the father of Boaz, whose mother was Rahab,
Boaz the father of Obed, whose mother was Ruth,
Obed the father of Jesse,
6and Jesse the father of King David.

David was the father of Solomon, whose mother had been Uriah's wife,
7Solomon the father of Rehoboam,
Rehoboam the father of Abijah,
Abijah the father of Asa,
8Asa the father of Jehoshaphat,
Jehoshaphat the father of Jehoram,
Jehoram the father of Uzziah,
9Uzziah the father of Jotham,
Jotham the father of Ahaz,
Ahaz the father of Hezekiah,
10Hezekiah the father of Manasseh,
Manasseh the father of Amon,
Amon the father of Josiah,
11and Josiah the father of Jeconiah[a] and his brothers at the time of the exile to Babylon.

12After the exile to Babylon:
Jeconiah was the father of Shealtiel,
Shealtiel the father of Zerubbabel,
13Zerubbabel the father of Abiud,
Abiud the father of Eliakim,
Eliakim the father of

[a]*11* That is, Jehoiachin; also in verse 12

Azor;
14and to Azor was born Zadok; and to Zadok, Achim; and to Achim, Eliud;
15and to Eliud was born Eleazar; and to Eleazar, Matthan; and to Matthan, Jacob;
16and to Jacob was born Joseph the husband of Mary, by whom was born Jesus, who is called Christ.
17Therefore all the generations from Abraham to David are fourteen generations; and from David to the deportation to Babylon fourteen generations; and from the deportation to Babylon to *the time of* Christ fourteen generations.

Conception and Birth of Jesus

18Now the birth of Jesus Christ was as follows. When His mother Mary had been betrothed to Joseph, before they came together she was found to be with child by the Holy Spirit.
19And Joseph her husband, being a righteous man, and not wanting to disgrace her, desired [b]to put her away secretly.
20But when he had considered this, behold, an angel of the Lord appeared to him in a dream, saying, "Joseph, son of David, do not be afraid to take Mary as your wife; for that which has been [c]conceived in her is of the Holy Spirit.
21"And she will bear a Son; and you shall call His name Jesus, for it is He who will save His people from their sins."
22Now all this took place that what was spoken by the Lord through the prophet might be fulfilled, saying,
23"BEHOLD, THE VIRGIN SHALL BE WITH CHILD, AND SHALL BEAR A SON, AND

[b]Or, *to divorce her*
[c]Lit., *begotten*

ἐγέννησεν τὸν Ἀζώρ, **14** Ἀζὼρ δὲ ἐγέννησεν
begat – Azor, and Azor begat
τὸν Σαδώκ, Σαδὼκ δὲ ἐγέννησεν τὸν Ἀχίμ,
– Sadoc, and Sadoc begat – Achim,
Ἀχὶμ δὲ ἐγέννησεν τὸν Ἐλιούδ, **15** Ἐλιοὺδ δὲ
and Achim begat – Eliud, and Eliud
ἐγέννησεν τὸν Ἐλεαζάρ, Ἐλεαζὰρ δὲ ἐγέννησεν
begat – Eleazar, and Eleazar begat
τὸν Μαθθάν, Μαθθὰν δὲ ἐγέννησεν τὸν Ἰακώβ,
– Matthan, and Matthan begat – Jacob,
16 Ἰακὼβ δὲ ἐγέννησεν τὸν Ἰωσὴφ τὸν ἄνδρα
and Jacob begat – Joseph the husband
Μαρίας, ἐξ ἧς ἐγεννήθη Ἰησοῦς ὁ λεγόμενος
of Mary, of whom was born Jesus the [one] called
Χριστός.
Christ.
17 Πᾶσαι οὖν αἱ γενεαὶ ἀπὸ Ἀβραὰμ
Therefore all the generations from Abraham
ἕως Δαυὶδ γενεαὶ δεκατέσσαρες, καὶ ἀπὸ
until David generations fourteen, and from
Δαυὶδ ἕως τῆς μετοικεσίας Βαβυλῶνος γενεαὶ
David until the deportation of Babylon generations
δεκατέσσαρες, καὶ ἀπὸ τῆς μετοικεσίας Βαβυ-
fourteen, and from the deportation of Baby-
λῶνος ἕως τοῦ Χριστοῦ γενεαὶ δεκατέσσαρες.
lon until the Christ generations fourteen.
18 Τοῦ δὲ Ἰησοῦ Χριστοῦ ἡ γένεσις
– Now [3]of Jesus [4]Christ [1]the [2]birth
οὕτως ἦν. μνηστευθείσης τῆς μητρὸς αὐτοῦ
[6]thus [5]was. Being betrothed the mother of him
=When his mother Mary was betrothed
Μαρίας τῷ Ἰωσήφ, πρὶν ἢ συνελθεῖν αὐτοὺς
Mary[a] – to Joseph, before to come together them[b]
=before they came together
εὑρέθη ἐν γαστρὶ ἔχουσα ἐκ πνεύματος
[1]she was found [3]in [4]womb [2]having of(by) [the] Spirit
= she was pregnant
ἁγίου. **19** Ἰωσὴφ δὲ ὁ ἀνὴρ αὐτῆς,
Holy. Now Joseph the husband of her,
δίκαιος ὢν καὶ μὴ θέλων αὐτὴν δειγμα-
[2]just [1]being and not wishing her to hold up as an
τίσαι, ἐβουλήθη λάθρα ἀπολῦσαι αὐτήν.
example, resolved secretly to dismiss her.
20 ταῦτα δὲ αὐτοῦ ἐνθυμηθέντος, ἰδοὺ
But these things him thinking on,[a] behold
=while he thought on these things,
ἄγγελος κυρίου κατ' ὄναρ ἐφάνη
an angel of [the] Lord by a dream appeared
αὐτῷ λέγων· Ἰωσὴφ υἱὸς Δαυίδ, μὴ
to him saying: Joseph son of David, [2]not
φοβηθῇς παραλαβεῖν Μαρίαν τὴν
[1]fear thou to take Mary the
γυναῖκά σου· τὸ γὰρ ἐν αὐτῇ γεννηθὲν
wife of thee: for the thing in her begotten
ἐκ πνεύματός ἐστιν ἁγίου. **21** τέξεται δὲ
[2]of [3][the] [5]Spirit [1]is [4]Holy. And she will bear
υἱόν, καὶ καλέσεις τὸ ὄνομα αὐτοῦ
a son, and thou shalt call the name of him
Ἰησοῦν· αὐτὸς γὰρ σώσει τὸν λαὸν
Jesus; for he will save the people
αὐτοῦ ἀπὸ τῶν ἁμαρτιῶν αὐτῶν. **22** Τοῦτο δὲ
of him from the sins of them. Now [2]this
ὅλον γέγονεν ἵνα πληρωθῇ τὸ ῥηθὲν
[1]all has occurred in order that might be fulfilled the [thing] spoken
ὑπὸ κυρίου διὰ τοῦ προφήτου λέγοντος·
by [the] Lord through the prophet saying:
23 ἰδοὺ ἡ παρθένος ἐν γαστρὶ ἕξει
Behold the virgin [2]in [3]womb [1]will have

Azor,
14Azor the father of Zadok,
Zadok the father of Akim,
Akim the father of Eliud,
15Eliud the father of Eleazar,
Eleazar the father of Matthan,
Matthan the father of Jacob,
16and Jacob the father of Joseph, the husband of Mary, of whom was born Jesus, who is called Christ.

17Thus there were fourteen generations in all from Abraham to David, fourteen from David to the exile to Babylon, and fourteen from the exile to the Christ.[b]

The Birth of Jesus Christ

18This is how the birth of Jesus Christ came about: His mother Mary was pledged to be married to Joseph, but before they came together, she was found to be with child through the Holy Spirit.
19Because Joseph her husband was a righteous man and did not want to expose her to public disgrace, he had in mind to divorce her quietly.
20But after he had considered this, an angel of the Lord appeared to him in a dream and said, "Joseph son of David, do not be afraid to take Mary home as your wife, because what is conceived in her is from the Holy Spirit.
21She will give birth to a son, and you are to give him the name Jesus,[c] because he will save his people from their sins."
22All this took place to fulfill what the Lord had said through the prophet:
23"The virgin will be with child and will give birth to a son, and they will call

[b]17 Or *Messiah*. "The Christ" (Greek) and "the Messiah" (Hebrew) both mean "the Anointed One."
[c]21 *Jesus* is the Greek form of *Joshua*, which means *the LORD saves*.

THEY SHALL CALL HIS NAME
IMMANUEL,'' which trans-
lated means, ''GOD WITH
US.''
24And Joseph arose from
his sleep, and did as the angel of the Lord commanded
him, and took *her* as his
wife,
25and [d]kept her a virgin
until she gave birth to a
Son; and he called His
name Jesus.

καὶ τέξεται υἱόν, καὶ καλέσουσιν τὸ
and will bear a son, and they will call the
ὄνομα αὐτοῦ Ἐμμανουήλ, ὅ ἐστιν
name of him Emmanuel, which is
μεθερμηνευόμενον μεθ' ἡμῶν ὁ θεός.
being interpreted with us – God.
24 ἐγερθεὶς δὲ [ὁ] Ἰωσὴφ ἀπὸ τοῦ
Then [2]being raised – [1]Joseph from the(his)
ὕπνου ἐποίησεν ὡς προσέταξεν αὐτῷ ὁ
sleep did as bade him the
ἄγγελος κυρίου, καὶ παρέλαβεν τὴν
angel of [the] Lord, and took the
γυναῖκα αὐτοῦ· 25 καὶ οὐκ ἐγίνωσκεν
wife of him; and knew not
αὐτὴν ἕως [οὗ] ἔτεκεν υἱόν· καὶ ἐκάλεσεν
her until she bore a son; and he called
τὸ ὄνομα αὐτοῦ Ἰησοῦν.
the name of him Jesus.

him Immanuel''[d]—which
means, ''God with us.''
24When Joseph woke up,
he did what the angel of the
Lord had commanded him
and took Mary home as his
wife. 25But he had no union
with her until she gave birth
to a son. And he gave him
the name Jesus.

Chapter 2

Visit of the Wise Men

NOW after Jesus was
born in Bethlehem of
Judea in the days of Herod
the king, behold, [e]magi
from the east arrived in
Jerusalem, saying,
2''Where is He who has
been born King of the
Jews? For we saw His star
in the east, and have come
to worship Him.''
3And when Herod the
king heard it, he was troubled, and all Jerusalem
with him.
4And gathering together
all the chief priests and
scribes of the people, he
began to inquire of them
where the Christ was to be
born.
5And they said to him,
''In Bethlehem of Judea,
for so it has been written by
the prophet,
6 'AND YOU, BETH-
LEHEM, LAND OF
JUDAH,
ARE BY NO MEANS
LEAST AMONG THE
LEADERS OF JUDAH;
FOR OUT OF YOU SHALL
COME FORTH A RULER,
WHO WILL SHEPHERD
MY PEOPLE ISRAEL.' ''
7Then Herod secretly
called the magi, and ascertained from them the time
the star appeared.
8And he sent them to
Bethlehem, and said, ''Go

2 Τοῦ δὲ Ἰησοῦ γεννηθέντος ἐν Βηθλέεμ
– Now Jesus having been born[a] in Bethlehem
=when Jesus was born
τῆς Ἰουδαίας ἐν ἡμέραις Ἡρῴδου τοῦ
– of Judæa in [the] days of Herod the
βασιλέως, ἰδοὺ μάγοι ἀπὸ ἀνατολῶν
king, behold magi from [the] east
παρεγένοντο εἰς Ἱεροσόλυμα 2 λέγοντες·
arrived in Jerusalem saying:
ποῦ ἐστιν ὁ τεχθεὶς βασιλεὺς τῶν
Where is the [one] born king of the
Ἰουδαίων; εἴδομεν γὰρ αὐτοῦ τὸν ἀστέρα
Jews? for we saw of him the star
ἐν τῇ ἀνατολῇ, καὶ ἤλθομεν προσκυνῆσαι
in the east, and came to worship
αὐτῷ. 3 ἀκούσας δὲ ὁ βασιλεὺς Ἡρῴδης
him. Now hearing [this] the king Herod
ἐταράχθη, καὶ πᾶσα Ἱεροσόλυμα μετ'
was troubled, and all Jerusalem with
αὐτοῦ, 4 καὶ συναγαγὼν πάντας τοὺς
him, and having assembled all the
ἀρχιερεῖς καὶ γραμματεῖς τοῦ λαοῦ
chief priests and scribes of the people
ἐπυνθάνετο παρ' αὐτῶν ποῦ ὁ χριστὸς
he inquired from them where the Christ
γεννᾶται. 5 οἱ δὲ εἶπαν αὐτῷ· ἐν
is being born. And they told him: In
Βηθλέεμ τῆς Ἰουδαίας· οὕτως γὰρ
Bethlehem – of Judæa; for thus
γέγραπται διὰ τοῦ προφήτου· 6 καὶ
it has been written through the prophet: And
σὺ Βηθλέεμ, γῆ Ἰούδα, οὐδαμῶς ἐλαχίστη
thou Bethlehem, land of Juda, [2]not at all [3]least
εἶ ἐν τοῖς ἡγεμόσιν Ἰούδα. ἐκ σοῦ γὰρ
[1]art among the governors of Juda. For out of thee
ἐξελεύσεται ἡγούμενος, ὅστις ποιμανεῖ
will come forth a governor, who will shepherd
τὸν λαόν μου τὸν Ἰσραήλ.
the people of me – Israel.
7 Τότε Ἡρῴδης λάθρα καλέσας τοὺς
Then Herod secretly calling the
μάγους ἠκρίβωσεν παρ' αὐτῶν τὸν
magi inquired carefully from them the
χρόνον τοῦ φαινομένου ἀστέρος, 8 καὶ
time of the appearing star, and
πέμψας αὐτοὺς εἰς Βηθλέεμ εἶπεν·
sending them to Bethlehem said:

Chapter 2

The Visit of the Magi

AFTER Jesus was born in
Bethlehem in Judea,
during the time of King
Herod, Magi[e] from the
east came to Jerusalem
2and asked, ''Where is the
one who has been born king
of the Jews? We saw his
star in the east[f] and have
come to worship him.''
3When King Herod heard
this he was disturbed, and
all Jerusalem with him.
4When he had called to-
gether all the people's chief
priests and teachers of the
law, he asked them where
the Christ[g] was to be born.
5''In Bethlehem in Judea,''
they replied, ''for this is
what the prophet has written:

6'' 'But you, Bethlehem,
in the land of Judah,
are by no means least
among the rulers of
Judah;
for out of you will come
a ruler
who will be the
shepherd of my
people Israel.'[h]''

7Then Herod called the
Magi secretly and found
out from them the exact
time the star had appeared.
8He sent them to Bethle-
hem and said, ''Go and

[d] Lit., *was not knowing her*
[e] Pronounced may-ji, a caste of wise men specializing in astrology, medicine and natural science

[d]23 Isaiah 7:14
[e]1 Traditionally *Wise Men*
[f]2 Or *star when it rose*
[g]4 Or *Messiah*
[h]6 Micah 5:2

and make careful search for
the Child; and when you
have found *Him,* report to
me, that I too may come
and worship Him."
9And having heard the
king, they went their way;
and lo, the star, which they
had seen in the east, went
on before them, until it
came and stood over where
the Child was.
10And when they saw the
star, they rejoiced exceedingly with great joy.
11And they came into the
house and saw the Child
with Mary His mother; and
they fell down and wor-
shiped Him; and opening
their treasures they
presented to Him gifts of
gold and frankincense and
myrrh.
12And having been
warned *by God* in a dream
not to return to Herod, they
departed for their own
country by another way.

The Flight to Egypt

13Now when they had departed, behold, an angel of
the Lord *appeared to Jo-
seph in a dream, saying,
"Arise and take the Child
and His mother, and flee to
Egypt, and remain there
until I tell you; for Herod is
going to search for the
Child to destroy Him."
14And he arose and took
the Child and His mother
by night, and departed for
Egypt;
15and was there until the
death of Herod, that what
was spoken by the Lord
through the prophet might
be fulfilled, saying, "OUT
OF EGYPT DID I CALL MY
SON."

Herod Slaughters Babies

16Then when Herod saw
that he had been tricked by
the magi, he became very
enraged, and sent and slew
all the male children who

πορευθέντες ἐξετάσατε ἀκριβῶς περὶ τοῦ
Going question ye carefully concerning the
παιδίου· ἐπὰν δὲ εὕρητε, ἀπαγγείλατέ
child; and when ye find, report
μοι, ὅπως κἀγὼ ἐλθὼν προσκυνήσω αὐτῷ.
to me, so that I also coming may worship him.
9 οἱ δὲ ἀκούσαντες τοῦ βασιλέως ἐπορεύθησαν·
So they hearing the king went;
καὶ ἰδοὺ ὁ ἀστήρ, ὃν εἶδον ἐν τῇ
and behold the star, which they saw in the
ἀνατολῇ, προῆγεν αὐτοὺς ἕως ἐλθὼν
east, went before them until coming
ἐστάθη ἐπάνω οὗ ἦν τὸ παιδίον. 10 ἰδόντες
it stood over where was the child. [2]seeing
δὲ τὸν ἀστέρα ἐχάρησαν χαρὰν μεγάλην
[1]And the star they rejoiced [with] a joy great
σφόδρα. 11 καὶ ἐλθόντες εἰς τὴν οἰκίαν
exceedingly. And coming into the house
εἶδον τὸ παιδίον μετὰ Μαρίας τῆς μητρὸς
they saw the child with Mary the mother
αὐτοῦ, καὶ πεσόντες προσεκύνησαν αὐτῷ,
of him, and falling they worshipped him,
καὶ ἀνοίξαντες τοὺς θησαυροὺς αὐτῶν
and opening the treasures of them
προσήνεγκαν αὐτῷ δῶρα, χρυσὸν καὶ
they offered to him gifts, gold and
λίβανον καὶ σμύρναν. 12 καὶ χρηματισθέντες
frankincense and myrrh. And having been warned
κατ' ὄναρ μὴ ἀνακάμψαι πρὸς Ἡρῴδην,
by a dream not to return to Herod,
δι' ἄλλης ὁδοῦ ἀνεχώρησαν εἰς τὴν
by another way they departed to the
χώραν αὐτῶν.
country of them.
13 Ἀναχωρησάντων δὲ αὐτῶν, ἰδοὺ
Now having departed them,* behold
= when they had departed,
ἄγγελος κυρίου φαίνεται κατ' ὄναρ τῷ
an angel of [the] Lord appears by a dream –
Ἰωσὴφ λέγων· ἐγερθεὶς παράλαβε τὸ
to Joseph saying: Rising take thou the
παιδίον καὶ τὴν μητέρα αὐτοῦ, καὶ φεῦγε
child and the mother of him, and flee
εἰς Αἴγυπτον, καὶ ἴσθι ἐκεῖ ἕως ἂν εἴπω
into Egypt, and be there until I tell
σοι· μέλλει γὰρ Ἡρῴδης ζητεῖν τὸ παιδίον τοῦ
thee; for [2]is about [1]Herod to seek the child –
ἀπολέσαι αὐτό. 14 ὁ δὲ ἐγερθεὶς παρέλαβεν
to destroy[d] him. So he rising took
τὸ παιδίον καὶ τὴν μητέρα αὐτοῦ
the child and the mother of him
νυκτὸς καὶ ἀνεχώρησεν εἰς Αἴγυπτον,
of(by) night and departed to Egypt,
15 καὶ ἦν ἐκεῖ ἕως τῆς τελευτῆς Ἡρῴδου·
and was there until the death of Herod;
ἵνα πληρωθῇ τὸ ῥηθὲν ὑπὸ κυρίου
in order that might be fulfilled the [thing] spoken by [the] Lord
διὰ τοῦ προφήτου λέγοντος· ἐξ
through the prophet saying: Out of
Αἰγύπτου ἐκάλεσα τὸν υἱόν μου.
Egypt I called the son of me.
16 Τότε Ἡρῴδης ἰδὼν ὅτι ἐνεπαίχθη
Then Herod seeing that he was mocked
ὑπὸ τῶν μάγων ἐθυμώθη λίαν, καὶ
by the magi was angered exceedingly, and
ἀποστείλας ἀνεῖλεν πάντας τοὺς παῖδας
sending killed all the boy-children

make a careful search for
the child. As soon as you
find him, report to me, so
that I too may go and worship him."
9After they had heard the
king, they went on their
way, and the star they had
seen in the east[i] went
ahead of them until it
stopped over the place
where the child was.
10When they saw the star,
they were overjoyed. 11On
coming to the house, they
saw the child with his
mother Mary, and they
bowed down and wor-
shiped him. Then they
opened their treasures and
presented him with gifts of
gold and of incense and of
myrrh. 12And having been
warned in a dream not to go
back to Herod, they re-
turned to their country by
another route.

The Escape to Egypt

13When they had gone, an
angel of the Lord appeared
to Joseph in a dream. "Get
up," he said, "take the
child and his mother and
escape to Egypt. Stay there
until I tell you, for Herod is
going to search for the child
to kill him."
14So he got up, took the
child and his mother during
the night and left for Egypt,
15where he stayed until the
death of Herod. And so
was fulfilled what the Lord
had said through the prophet: "Out of Egypt I called
my son."[j]
16When Herod realized
that he had been outwitted
by the Magi, he was furi-
ous, and he gave orders to
kill all the boys in Bethle-

[i]9 Or *seen when it rose*
[j]15 Hosea 11:1

were in Bethlehem and in
all its environs, from two
years old and under, ac-
cording to the time which
he had ascertained from the
magi.
17Then that which was
spoken through Jeremiah
the prophet was fulfilled,
saying,
18"A VOICE WAS HEARD IN
RAMAH,
WEEPING AND GREAT
MOURNING,
RACHEL WEEPING FOR
HER CHILDREN;
AND SHE REFUSED TO BE
COMFORTED,
BECAUSE THEY WERE
NO MORE."
19But when Herod was
dead, behold, an angel of
the Lord *appeared in a
dream to Joseph in Egypt,
saying,
20"Arise and take the
Child and His mother, and
go into the land of Israel;
for those who sought the
Child's life are dead."
21And he arose and took
the Child and His mother,
and came into the land of
Israel.
22But when he heard that
Archelaus was reigning
over Judea in place of his
father Herod, he was afraid
to go there. And being
warned *by God* in a dream,
he departed for the regions
of Galilee,
23and came and resided in
a city called Nazareth, that
what was spoken through
the prophets might be fulfilled, "He shall be called a
Nazarene."

τοὺς ἐν Βηθλέεμ καὶ ἐν πᾶσι τοῖς
– in Bethlehem and in all the
ὁρίοις αὐτῆς ἀπὸ διετοῦς καὶ κατωτέρω,
districts of it from two years and under,
κατὰ τὸν χρόνον ὃν ἠκρίβωσεν παρὰ τῶν
according to the time which he strictly inquired from the
μάγων. 17 τότε ἐπληρώθη τὸ ῥηθὲν διὰ
magi. Then was fulfilled the [thing] spoken through
Ἰερεμίου τοῦ προφήτου λέγοντος· 18 φωνὴ
Jeremiah the prophet saying: A voice
ἐν Ῥαμὰ ἠκούσθη, κλαυθμὸς καὶ ὀδυρμὸς
in Rama was heard, weeping and mourning
πολύς· Ῥαχὴλ κλαίουσα τὰ τέκνα αὐτῆς,
much; Rachel weeping for the children of her,
καὶ οὐκ ἤθελεν παρακληθῆναι, ὅτι
and would not *to* be comforted, because
οὐκ εἰσίν.
they are not.
19 Τελευτήσαντος δὲ τοῦ Ἡρῴδου, ἰδοὺ
But dying – Herod,[a] behold
= Herod having died,
ἄγγελος κυρίου φαίνεται κατ' ὄναρ τῷ
an angel of [the] Lord appears by a dream
Ἰωσὴφ ἐν Αἰγύπτῳ 20 λέγων· ἐγερθεὶς
to Joseph in Egypt saying: Rising
παράλαβε τὸ παιδίον καὶ τὴν μητέρα
take thou the child and the mother
αὐτοῦ, καὶ πορεύου εἰς γῆν Ἰσραήλ·
of him, and go into [the] land of Israel;
τεθνήκασιν γὰρ οἱ ζητοῦντες τὴν ψυχὴν
for have died the [ones] seeking the life
τοῦ παιδίου. 21 ὁ δὲ ἐγερθεὶς παρέλαβεν
of the child. So he rising took
τὸ παιδίον καὶ τὴν μητέρα αὐτοῦ καὶ
the child and the mother of him and
εἰσῆλθεν εἰς γῆν Ἰσραήλ. 22 ἀκούσας δὲ
entered into [the] land of Israel. But hearing
ὅτι Ἀρχέλαος βασιλεύει τῆς Ἰουδαίας
that Archelaus reigns over – Judæa
ἀντὶ τοῦ πατρὸς αὐτοῦ Ἡρῴδου ἐφοβήθη
instead of the father of him Herod he feared
ἐκεῖ ἀπελθεῖν· χρηματισθεὶς δὲ κατ'
there to go; and being warned by
ὄναρ ἀνεχώρησεν εἰς τὰ μέρη τῆς
a dream he departed into the parts –
Γαλιλαίας, 23 καὶ ἐλθὼν κατῴκησεν εἰς
of Galilee, and coming dwelt in
πόλιν λεγομένην Ναζαρέθ· ὅπως πληρωθῇ
a city called Nazareth; so that was fulfilled
τὸ ῥηθὲν διὰ τῶν προφητῶν ὅτι
the [thing] spoken through the prophets[,] –
Ναζωραῖος κληθήσεται.
A Nazarene he shall be called.

hem and its vicinity who
were two years old and under, in accordance with the
time he had learned from
the Magi. 17Then what was
said through the prophet
Jeremiah was fulfilled:

18"A voice is heard in
Ramah,
weeping and great
mourning,
Rachel weeping for her
children
and refusing to be
comforted,
because they are no
more."[k]

The Return to Nazareth

19After Herod died, an
angel of the Lord appeared
in a dream to Joseph in
Egypt 20and said, "Get up,
take the child and his mother and go to the land of Israel, for those who were trying to take the child's life
are dead."
21So he got up, took the
child and his mother and
went to the land of Israel.
22But when he heard that
Archelaus was reigning in
Judea in place of his father
Herod, he was afraid to go
there. Having been warned
in a dream, he withdrew to
the district of Galilee, 23and
he went and lived in a town
called Nazareth. So was
fulfilled what was said
through the prophets: "He
will be called a Nazarene."

Chapter 3

John the Baptist Preaches

NOW in those days John
the Baptist *came,
preaching in the wilderness
of Judea, saying,
2"Repent, for the king-
dom of heaven is at hand."
3For this is the one re-
ferred to by Isaiah the
prophet, saying,
"THE VOICE OF ONE CRY-

3 Ἐν δὲ ταῖς ἡμέραις ἐκείναις παραγίνεται
Now in – days those arrives
Ἰωάννης ὁ βαπτιστὴς κηρύσσων ἐν τῇ
John the Baptist proclaiming in the
ἐρήμῳ τῆς Ἰουδαίας, 2 λέγων· μετανοεῖτε·
wilderness – of Judæa, saying: Repent ye;
ἤγγικεν γὰρ ἡ βασιλεία τῶν οὐρανῶν.
for has come near the kingdom of the heavens.
3 οὗτος γάρ ἐστιν ὁ ῥηθεὶς διὰ Ἠσαΐου
For this is the [one] spoken [of] through Isaiah
τοῦ προφήτου λέγοντος· φωνὴ βοῶντος
the prophet saying: A voice of [one] crying

Chapter 3

John the Baptist Prepares the Way

IN those days John the
Baptist came, preaching
in the Desert of Judea 2and
saying, "Repent, for the
kingdom of heaven is
near." 3This is he who was
spoken of through the
prophet Isaiah:

"A voice of one calling

[k]*18* Jer. 31:15

ING IN THE WILDERNESS,
'MAKE READY THE WAY OF THE LORD,
MAKE HIS PATHS STRAIGHT!' "
4Now John himself had a garment of camel's hair, and a leather belt about his waist; and his food was locusts and wild honey.
5Then Jerusalem was going out to him, and all Judea, and all the district around the Jordan;
6and they were being baptized by him in the Jordan River, as they confessed their sins.
7But when he saw many of the Pharisees and Sadducees coming for baptism, he said to them, "You brood of vipers, who warned you to flee from the wrath to come?
8"Therefore bring forth fruit in keeping with repentance;
9and do not suppose that you can say to yourselves, 'We have Abraham for our father'; for I say to you, that God is able from these stones to raise up children to Abraham.
10"And the axe is already laid at the root of the trees; every tree therefore that does not bear good fruit is cut down and thrown into the fire.
11"As for me, I baptize you [f]with water for repentance, but He who is coming after me is mightier than I, and I am not fit to remove His sandals; He will baptize you with the Holy Spirit and fire.
12"And His winnowing fork is in His hand, and He will thoroughly clear His threshing floor; and He will gather His wheat into the barn, but He will burn up

[f]The Gr. here can be translated *in*, *with* or *by*

ἐν τῇ ἐρήμῳ· ἑτοιμάσατε τὴν ὁδὸν
in the wilderness: Prepare ye the way
κυρίου, εὐθείας ποιεῖτε τὰς τρίβους
of [the] Lord, straight make the paths
αὐτοῦ. **4** Αὐτὸς δὲ ὁ Ἰωάννης εἶχεν
of him. Now [2]himself – [1]John had
τὸ ἔνδυμα αὐτοῦ ἀπὸ τριχῶν καμήλου
the raiment of him from hairs of a camel
καὶ ζώνην δερματίνην περὶ τὴν ὀσφὺν
and a girdle leathern round the loin[s]
αὐτοῦ· ἡ δὲ τροφὴ ἦν αὐτοῦ ἀκρίδες
of him; and the food [2]was [1]of him locusts
καὶ μέλι ἄγριον. **5** Τότε ἐξεπορεύετο πρὸς
and honey wild. Then went out to
αὐτὸν Ἱεροσόλυμα καὶ πᾶσα ἡ Ἰουδαία
him Jerusalem and all – Judæa
καὶ πᾶσα ἡ περίχωρος τοῦ Ἰορδάνου,
and all the neighbourhood of the Jordan,
6 καὶ ἐβαπτίζοντο ἐν τῷ Ἰορδάνῃ ποταμῷ
and were baptized in the Jordan river
ὑπ' αὐτοῦ ἐξομολογούμενοι τὰς ἁμαρτίας
by him confessing the sins
αὐτῶν. **7** Ἰδὼν δὲ πολλοὺς τῶν
of them. And seeing many of the
Φαρισαίων καὶ Σαδδουκαίων ἐρχομένους
Pharisees and Sadducees coming
ἐπὶ τὸ βάπτισμα εἶπεν αὐτοῖς· γεννήματα
to the baptism he said to them: Offspring
ἐχιδνῶν, τίς ὑπέδειξεν ὑμῖν φυγεῖν ἀπὸ
of vipers, who warned you to flee from
τῆς μελλούσης ὀργῆς; **8** ποιήσατε οὖν
the coming wrath? Produce therefore
καρπὸν ἄξιον τῆς μετανοίας· **9** καὶ
fruit worthy – of repentance; and
μὴ δόξητε λέγειν ἐν ἑαυτοῖς· πατέρα
think not to say among [your]selves: [2][as] father
ἔχομεν τὸν Ἀβραάμ· λέγω γὰρ ὑμῖν ὅτι
[1]We have – [3]Abraham; for I tell you that
δύναται ὁ θεὸς ἐκ τῶν λίθων τούτων
[2]is able – [1]God out of – stones these
ἐγεῖραι τέκνα τῷ Ἀβραάμ. **10** ἤδη δὲ
to raise children – to Abraham. And already
ἡ ἀξίνη πρὸς τὴν ῥίζαν τῶν δένδρων
the axe at the root of the trees
κεῖται· πᾶν οὖν δένδρον μὴ ποιοῦν
is laid; therefore every tree not producing
καρπὸν καλὸν ἐκκόπτεται καὶ εἰς πῦρ
fruit good is cut down and into [the] fire
βάλλεται. **11** ἐγὼ μὲν ὑμᾶς βαπτίζω
is cast. I indeed you baptize
ἐν ὕδατι εἰς μετάνοιαν· ὁ δὲ
in water to repentance; but the [one]
ὀπίσω μου ἐρχόμενος ἰσχυρότερός μού
after me coming [2]stronger [3][than] [4]I
ἐστιν, οὗ οὐκ εἰμὶ ἱκανὸς τὰ ὑποδήματα
[1]is, of whom I am not worthy the sandals
βαστάσαι· αὐτὸς ὑμᾶς βαπτίσει ἐν πνεύματι
to bear; he [2]you [1]will baptize in [the] Spirit
ἁγίῳ καὶ πυρί· **12** οὗ τὸ πτύον ἐν τῇ
Holy and fire; of whom the fan [is] in the
χειρὶ αὐτοῦ, καὶ διακαθαριεῖ τὴν ἅλωνα
hand of him, and he will thoroughly cleanse the threshing-floor
αὐτοῦ, καὶ συνάξει τὸν σῖτον αὐτοῦ
of him, and will gather the wheat of him
εἰς τὴν ἀποθήκην, τὸ δὲ ἄχυρον κατα-
into the barn, but the chaff he will

in the desert,
'Prepare the way for the Lord,
make straight paths for him.' "[l]
4John's clothes were made of camel's hair, and he had a leather belt around his waist. His food was locusts and wild honey. 5People went out to him from Jerusalem and all Judea and the whole region of the Jordan. 6Confessing their sins, they were baptized by him in the Jordan River.
7But when he saw many of the Pharisees and Sadducees coming to where he was baptizing, he said to them: "You brood of vipers! Who warned you to flee from the coming wrath? 8Produce fruit in keeping with repentance. 9And do not think you can say to yourselves, 'We have Abraham as our father.' I tell you that out of these stones God can raise up children for Abraham. 10The ax is already at the root of the trees, and every tree that does not produce good fruit will be cut down and thrown into the fire.
11"I baptize you with[m] water for repentance. But after me will come one who is more powerful than I, whose sandals I am not fit to carry. He will baptize you with the Holy Spirit and with fire. 12His winnowing fork is in his hand, and he will clear his threshing floor, gathering his wheat into the barn and burning up the chaff with

[l]*3* Isaiah 40:3
[m]*11* Or *in*

the chaff with unquench-
able fire."

The Baptism of Jesus

13 Then Jesus *arrived
from Galilee at the Jordan
coming to John, to be baptized by him.
14 But John tried to pre-
vent Him, saying, "I have
need to be baptized by
You, and do You come to
me?"
15 But Jesus answering
said to him, "Permit *it* at
this time; for in this way it
is fitting for us to fulfill all
righteousness." Then he
*permitted Him.
16 And after being bap-
tized, Jesus went up
immediately from the
water; and behold, the
heavens were opened, and
he saw the Spirit of God descending as a dove, *and*
coming upon Him,
17 and behold, a voice out
of the heavens, saying,
"This is [g]My beloved Son,
in whom I am well-
pleased."

καύσει πυρὶ ἀσβέστῳ.
consume with fire unquenchable.

13 Τότε παραγίνεται ὁ Ἰησοῦς ἀπὸ τῆς
Then arrives – Jesus from –

Γαλιλαίας ἐπὶ τὸν Ἰορδάνην πρὸς τὸν
Galilee at the Jordan to –

Ἰωάννην τοῦ βαπτισθῆναι ὑπ' αὐτοῦ.
John – to be baptized[d] by him.

14 ὁ δὲ διεκώλυεν αὐτὸν λέγων· ἐγὼ
But he forbade him saying: I

χρείαν ἔχω ὑπὸ σοῦ βαπτισθῆναι, καὶ σὺ
[2]need [1]have [4]by [5]thee [3]to be baptized, and thou

ἔρχῃ πρός μέ; 15 ἀποκριθεὶς δὲ ὁ
comest to me? But answering –

Ἰησοῦς εἶπεν αὐτῷ· ἄφες ἄρτι· οὕτως γὰρ
Jesus said to him: Permit now; for thus

πρέπον ἐστὶν ἡμῖν πληρῶσαι πᾶσαν
[2]fitting [1]it is to us to fulfil all

δικαιοσύνην. τότε ἀφίησιν αὐτόν.
righteousness. Then he permits him.

16 βαπτισθεὶς δὲ ὁ Ἰησοῦς εὐθὺς ἀνέβη
And having been baptized – Jesus immediately went up

ἀπὸ τοῦ ὕδατος· καὶ ἰδοὺ ἠνεῴχθησαν
from the water; and behold [3]were opened

οἱ οὐρανοί, καὶ εἶδεν πνεῦμα θεοῦ
[1]the [2]heavens, and he saw [the] Spirit of God

καταβαῖνον ὡσεὶ περιστεράν, ἐρχόμενον ἐπ'
coming down as a dove, coming upon

αὐτόν· 17 καὶ ἰδοὺ φωνὴ ἐκ τῶν
him; and behold a voice out of the

οὐρανῶν λέγουσα· οὗτός ἐστιν ὁ υἱός
heavens saying: This is the son

μου ὁ ἀγαπητός, ἐν ᾧ εὐδόκησα.
of me the beloved, in whom I was well pleased.

unquenchable fire."

The Baptism of Jesus

13 Then Jesus came from
Galilee to the Jordan to be
baptized by John. 14 But
John tried to deter him,
saying, "I need to be baptized by you, and do you
come to me?"
15 Jesus replied, "Let it be
so now; it is proper for us to
do this to fulfill all righteousness." Then John con-
sented.
16 As soon as Jesus was
baptized, he went up out of
the water. At that moment
heaven was opened, and he
saw the Spirit of God de-
scending like a dove and
lighting on him. 17 And a
voice from heaven said,
"This is my Son, whom I
love; with him I am well
pleased."

Chapter 4

Temptation of Jesus

THEN Jesus was led up
by the Spirit into the
wilderness to be tempted
by the devil.
2 And after He had fasted
forty days and forty nights,
He [h]then became hungry.
3 And the tempter came
and said to Him, "If You
are the Son of God, com-
mand that these stones
become bread."
4 But He answered and
said, "It is written, 'MAN
SHALL NOT LIVE ON BREAD
ALONE, BUT ON EVERY WORD
THAT PROCEEDS OUT OF THE
MOUTH OF GOD.' "
5 Then the devil *took
Him into the holy city; and
he had Him stand on the
pinnacle of the temple,
6 and *said to Him, "If

4 Τότε ὁ Ἰησοῦς ἀνήχθη εἰς τὴν
Then – Jesus was led up into the

ἔρημον ὑπὸ τοῦ πνεύματος πειρασθῆναι
wilderness by the Spirit to be tempted

ὑπὸ τοῦ διαβόλου. 2 καὶ νηστεύσας ἡμέρας
by the devil. And having fasted days

τεσσεράκοντα καὶ τεσσεράκοντα νύκτας
forty and forty nights

ὕστερον ἐπείνασεν. 3 καὶ προσελθὼν ὁ
afterward he hungered. And approaching the

πειράζων εἶπεν αὐτῷ· εἰ υἱὸς εἶ τοῦ
tempting [one] said to him: If Son thou art –

θεοῦ, εἰπὲ ἵνα οἱ λίθοι οὗτοι ἄρτοι
of God, say *in order* that – stones these [2]loaves

γένωνται. 4 ὁ δὲ ἀποκριθεὶς εἶπεν·
[1]may become. But he answering said:

γέγραπται· οὐκ ἐπ' ἄρτῳ μόνῳ ζήσεται
It has been written: Not on bread only shall live

ὁ ἄνθρωπος, ἀλλ' ἐπὶ παντὶ ῥήματι
– man, but on every word

ἐκπορευομένῳ διὰ στόματος θεοῦ. 5 Τότε
proceeding through [the] mouth of God. Then

παραλαμβάνει αὐτὸν ὁ διάβολος εἰς τὴν
takes him the devil into the

ἁγίαν πόλιν, καὶ ἔστησεν αὐτὸν ἐπὶ τὸ
holy city, and stood him on the

πτερύγιον τοῦ ἱεροῦ, 6 καὶ λέγει αὐτῷ·
wing of the temple, and says to him:

Chapter 4

The Temptation of Jesus

THEN Jesus was led by
the Spirit into the des-
ert to be tempted by the
devil. 2 After fasting forty
days and forty nights, he
was hungry. 3 The tempter
came to him and said, "If
you are the Son of God, tell
these stones to become
bread."
4 Jesus answered, "It is
written: 'Man does not live
on bread alone, but on every word that comes from
the mouth of God.'[n]"
5 Then the devil took him
to the holy city and had him
stand on the highest point
of the temple. 6 "If you are

[g] Lit., *My Son, the Beloved*
[h] Lit., *later, afterward*

[n] 4 Deut. 8:3

You are the Son of God
throw Yourself down; for it
is written,

'HE WILL GIVE HIS ANGELS CHARGE CONCERNING YOU';
and
'ON *their* HANDS THEY WILL BEAR YOU UP,
LEST YOU STRIKE YOUR FOOT AGAINST A STONE.' "

7Jesus said to him, "On
the other hand, it is written,
'YOU SHALL NOT [i]PUT THE
LORD YOUR GOD TO THE
TEST.' "

8Again, the devil *took
Him to a very high mountain, and *showed Him all
the kingdoms of the world,
and their glory;

9and he said to Him,
"All these things will I give
You, if You fall down and
worship me."

10Then Jesus *said to
him, "Begone, Satan! For
it is written, 'YOU SHALL
WORSHIP THE LORD YOUR
GOD, AND SERVE HIM
ONLY.' "

11Then the devil *left
Him; and behold, angels
came and *began* to minister
to Him.

Jesus Begins His Ministry

12Now when He heard
that John had been taken
into custody, He withdrew
into Galilee;

13and leaving Nazareth,
He came and settled in
Capernaum, which is by
the sea, in the region of
Zebulun and Naphtali.

14*This was* to fulfill what
was spoken through Isaiah
the prophet, saying,

15"THE LAND OF ZEBULUN AND THE LAND OF NAPHTALI,
BY THE WAY OF THE SEA, BEYOND THE JORDAN, GALILEE OF THE [j]GENTILES—

16"THE PEOPLE WHO WERE SITTING IN DARKNESS SAW A GREAT LIGHT,
AND TO THOSE WHO WERE SITTING IN THE LAND AND SHADOW OF DEATH,
UPON THEM A LIGHT DAWNED."

17From that time Jesus
began to preach and say,
"Repent, for the kingdom
of heaven is at hand."

[i] Or, *tempt . . . God*
[j] Or, *nations*

εἰ υἱὸς εἶ τοῦ θεοῦ, βάλε σεαυτὸν
If Son thou art – of God, cast thyself

κάτω· γέγραπται γὰρ ὅτι τοῖς ἀγγέλοις
down; for it has been written[,] – To the angels

αὐτοῦ ἐντελεῖται περὶ σοῦ καὶ ἐπὶ χειρῶν
of him he will give command concerning thee and on hands

ἀροῦσίν σε, μήποτε προσκόψῃς πρὸς
they will bear thee, lest thou strike against

λίθον τὸν πόδα σου. 7 ἔφη αὐτῷ ὁ
a stone the foot of thee. Said to him –

Ἰησοῦς· πάλιν γέγραπται· οὐκ ἐκπειράσεις
Jesus: Again it has been written: Not overtempt shalt thou

κύριον τὸν θεόν σου. 8 Πάλιν παρα-
[the] Lord the God of thee. Again

λαμβάνει αὐτὸν ὁ διάβολος εἰς ὄρος
takes him the devil to a mountain

ὑψηλὸν λίαν, καὶ δείκνυσιν αὐτῷ πάσας
high exceedingly, and shows him all

τὰς βασιλείας τοῦ κόσμου καὶ τὴν
the kingdoms of the world and the

δόξαν αὐτῶν, 9 καὶ εἶπεν αὐτῷ· ταῦτά
glory of them, and said to him: These things

σοι πάντα δώσω, ἐὰν πεσὼν προσκυνήσῃς
to thee all I will give, if falling thou wilt worship

μοι. 10 τότε λέγει αὐτῷ ὁ Ἰησοῦς·
me. Then says to him – Jesus:

ὕπαγε, σατανᾶ· γέγραπται γάρ· κύριον
Go, Satan; for it has been written: [The] Lord

τὸν θεόν σου προσκυνήσεις καὶ αὐτῷ
the God of thee thou shalt worship and him

μόνῳ λατρεύσεις. 11 Τότε ἀφίησιν αὐτὸν
only thou shalt serve. Then leaves him

ὁ διάβολος, καὶ ἰδοὺ ἄγγελοι προσῆλθον
the devil, and behold angels approached

καὶ διηκόνουν αὐτῷ.
and ministered to him.

12 Ἀκούσας δὲ ὅτι Ἰωάννης παρεδόθη
Now hearing that John was delivered up

ἀνεχώρησεν εἰς τὴν Γαλιλαίαν. 13 καὶ
he departed to – Galilee. And

καταλιπὼν τὴν Ναζαρὰ ἐλθὼν κατῴκησεν
leaving – Nazareth coming he dwelt

εἰς Καφαρναοὺμ τὴν παραθαλασσίαν ἐν
in Capernaum – beside the sea in [the]

ὁρίοις Ζαβουλὼν καὶ Νεφθαλίμ· 14 ἵνα
districts of Zebulon and Naphthali; in order that

πληρωθῇ τὸ ῥηθὲν διὰ Ἠσαΐου
might be fulfilled the [thing] spoken through Isaiah

τοῦ προφήτου λέγοντος· 15 γῆ Ζαβουλὼν
the prophet saying: Land of Zebulon

καὶ γῆ Νεφθαλίμ, ὁδὸν θαλάσσης,
and land of Naphthali, way of [the] sea,

πέραν τοῦ Ἰορδάνου, Γαλιλαία τῶν ἐθνῶν,
beyond the Jordan, Galilee of the nations,

16 ὁ λαὸς ὁ καθήμενος ἐν σκοτίᾳ φῶς
the people – sitting in darkness [3]light

εἶδεν μέγα, καὶ τοῖς καθημένοις ἐν
[1]saw [2]a great, and to the [ones] sitting in

χώρᾳ καὶ σκιᾷ θανάτου, φῶς ἀνέτειλεν
a land and shadow of death, light sprang up

αὐτοῖς.
to them.

17 Ἀπὸ τότε ἤρξατο ὁ Ἰησοῦς κηρύσσειν
From then began – Jesus to proclaim

καὶ λέγειν· μετανοεῖτε· ἤγγικεν γὰρ
and to say: Repent ye; for has drawn near

the Son of God," he said,
"throw yourself down. For
it is written:

" 'He will command his angels concerning you,
and they will lift you up in their hands,
so that you will not strike your foot against a stone.'[o]"

7Jesus answered him, "It
is also written: 'Do not put
the Lord your God to the
test.'[p]"

8Again, the devil took
him to a very high mountain and showed him all the
kingdoms of the world and
their splendor.
9"All this I
will give you," he said, "if
you will bow down and
worship me."

10Jesus said to him,
"Away from me, Satan!
For it is written: 'Worship
the Lord your God, and
serve him only.'[q]"

11Then the devil left him,
and angels came and attended him.

Jesus Begins to Preach

12When Jesus heard that
John had been put in prison, he returned to Galilee.

13Leaving Nazareth, he
went and lived in Capernaum, which was by the lake
in the area of Zebulun and
Naphtali—
14to fulfill what
was said through the
prophet Isaiah:

15"Land of Zebulun and land of Naphtali,
the way to the sea, along the Jordan,
Galilee of the Gentiles—
16the people living in darkness
have seen a great light;
on those living in the land of the shadow of death
a light has dawned."[r]

17From that time on Jesus
began to preach, "Repent,
for the kingdom of heaven
is near."

[o] 6 Psalm 91:11,12
[p] 7 Deut. 6:16
[q] 10 Deut. 6:13
[r] 16 Isaiah 9:1,2

The First Disciples

18And walking by the Sea
of Galilee, He saw two
brothers, Simon who was
called Peter, and Andrew
his brother, casting a net
into the sea; for they were
fishermen.
19And He *said to them,
"Follow Me, and I will
make you fishers of men."
20And they immediately
left the nets, and followed
Him.
21And going on from
there He saw two other
brothers, James the *son* of
Zebedee, and John his
brother, in the boat with
Zebedee their father,
mending their nets; and He
called them.
22And they immediately
left the boat and their father, and followed Him.

Ministry in Galilee

23And *Jesus* was going
about in all Galilee, teaching in their synagogues,
and proclaiming the gospel
of the kingdom, and healing
every kind of disease and
every kind of sickness
among the people.
24And the news about
Him went out into all Syria;
and they brought to Him all
who were ill, taken with
various diseases and pains,
demoniacs, epileptics,
paralytics; and He healed
them.
25And great multitudes
followed Him from Galilee
and Decapolis and Jerusa-
lem and Judea and *from*
beyond the Jordan.

ἡ βασιλεία τῶν οὐρανῶν.
the kingdom of the heavens.
18 Περιπατῶν δὲ παρὰ τὴν θάλασσαν
And walking beside the sea
τῆς Γαλιλαίας εἶδεν δύο ἀδελφούς, Σίμωνα
– of Galilee he saw two brothers, Simon
τὸν λεγόμενον Πέτρον καὶ Ἀνδρέαν τὸν
– called Peter and Andrew the
ἀδελφὸν αὐτοῦ, βάλλοντας ἀμφίβληστρον εἰς
brother of him, casting a net into
τὴν θάλασσαν· ἦσαν γὰρ ἁλεεῖς. **19** καὶ
the sea; for they were fishers. And
λέγει αὐτοῖς· δεῦτε ὀπίσω μου, καὶ
he says to them: Come after me, and
ποιήσω ὑμᾶς ἁλεεῖς ἀνθρώπων. **20** οἱ
I will make you fishers of men. [2]they
δὲ εὐθέως ἀφέντες τὰ δίκτυα ἠκολούθη-
[1]And immediately leaving the nets fol-
σαν αὐτῷ. **21** Καὶ προβὰς ἐκεῖθεν εἶδεν
lowed him. And going on thence he saw
ἄλλους δύο ἀδελφούς, Ἰάκωβον τὸν τοῦ
other two brothers, James the [son] –
Ζεβεδαίου καὶ Ἰωάννην τὸν ἀδελφὸν
of Zebedee and John the brother
αὐτοῦ, ἐν τῷ πλοίῳ μετὰ Ζεβεδαίου τοῦ
of him, in the boat with Zebedee the
πατρὸς αὐτῶν καταρτίζοντας τὰ δίκτυα
father of them mending the nets
αὐτῶν· καὶ ἐκάλεσεν αὐτούς. **22** οἱ δὲ
of them; and he called them. And they
εὐθέως ἀφέντες τὸ πλοῖον καὶ τὸν
immediately leaving the boat and the
πατέρα αὐτῶν ἠκολούθησαν αὐτῷ.
father of them followed him.
23 Καὶ περιῆγεν ἐν ὅλῃ τῇ Γαλιλαίᾳ,
And he went about in all – Galilee,
διδάσκων ἐν ταῖς συναγωγαῖς αὐτῶν
teaching in the synagogues of them
καὶ κηρύσσων τὸ εὐαγγέλιον τῆς βασιλείας
and proclaiming the gospel of the kingdom
καὶ θεραπεύων πᾶσαν νόσον καὶ πᾶσαν
and healing every disease and every
μαλακίαν ἐν τῷ λαῷ. **24** καὶ ἀπῆλθεν ἡ
illness among the people. And went the
ἀκοὴ αὐτοῦ εἰς ὅλην τὴν Συρίαν· καὶ
report of him into all – Syria; and
προσήνεγκαν αὐτῷ πάντας τοὺς κακῶς
they brought to him all the [ones] [8]ill
=those who were ill
ἔχοντας ποικίλαις νόσοις καὶ βασάνοις
[7]having [2]various [3]diseases [4]and [5]tortures
συνεχομένους, δαιμονιζομένους καὶ σεληνιαζ-
[1]suffering from, demon-possessed and luna-
ομένους καὶ παραλυτικούς, καὶ ἐθεράπευσεν
tics and paralysed, and he healed
αὐτούς. **25** καὶ ἠκολούθησαν αὐτῷ ὄχλοι
them. And [3]followed [4]him [2]crowds
πολλοὶ ἀπὸ τῆς Γαλιλαίας καὶ Δεκαπόλεως
[1]many from – Galilee and Decapolis
καὶ Ἱεροσολύμων καὶ Ἰουδαίας καὶ πέραν
and Jerusalem and Judæa and beyond
τοῦ Ἰορδάνου.
the Jordan.

The Calling of the First Disciples

18As Jesus was walking
beside the Sea of Galilee,
he saw two brothers, Si-
mon called Peter and his
brother Andrew. They
were casting a net into the
lake, for they were fishermen. 19"Come, follow
me," Jesus said, "and I
will make you fishers of
men." 20At once they left
their nets and followed
him.
21Going on from there, he
saw two other brothers,
James son of Zebedee and
his brother John. They
were in a boat with their father Zebedee, preparing
their nets. Jesus called
them, 22and immediately
they left the boat and their
father and followed him.

Jesus Heals the Sick

23Jesus went throughout
Galilee, teaching in their
synagogues, preaching the
good news of the kingdom,
and healing every disease
and sickness among the
people. 24News about him
spread all over Syria, and
people brought to him all
who were ill with various
diseases, those suffering
severe pain, the demon-
possessed, those having
seizures, and the para-
lyzed, and he healed them.
25Large crowds from Gali-
lee, the Decapolis,[s] Jerusalem, Judea and the region
across the Jordan followed
him.

Chapter 5

The Sermon on the Mount
The Beatitudes

AND when He saw the
multitudes, He went

5 Ἰδὼν δὲ τοὺς ὄχλους ἀνέβη εἰς
And seeing the crowds he went up into

Chapter 5

The Beatitudes

NOW when he saw the
crowds, he went up

[s]25 That is, the Ten Cities

up on the mountain; and after He sat down, His disciples came to Him.
2And opening His mouth
He *began* to teach them,
saying,
3"Blessed are the poor
in spirit, for theirs is the
kingdom of heaven.
4"Blessed are those who
mourn, for they shall be
comforted.
5"Blessed are the [k]gen-
tle, for they shall inherit the
earth.
6"Blessed are those who
hunger and thirst for righteousness, for they shall be
satisfied.
7"Blessed are the merci-
ful, for they shall receive
mercy.
8"Blessed are the pure in
heart, for they shall see
God.
9"Blessed are the peace-
makers, for they shall be
called sons of God.
10"Blessed are those who
have been persecuted for
the sake of righteousness,
for theirs is the kingdom of
heaven.
11"Blessed are you when
men cast insults at you, and
persecute you, and say all
kinds of evil against you
falsely, on account of Me.
12"Rejoice, and be glad,
for your reward in heaven
is great, for so they persecuted the prophets who
were before you.

Disciples and the World

13"You are the salt of the
earth; but if the salt has
become tasteless, how will
it be made salty *again*? It is
good for nothing anymore,
except to be thrown out
and trampled under foot by
men.
14"You are the light of the
world. A city set on a hill
cannot be hidden.
15"Nor do *men* light a
lamp, and put it under the
peck-measure, but on the
lampstand; and it gives
light to all who are in the

[k]Or, *humble, meek*

τὸ ὄρος· καὶ καθίσαντος αὐτοῦ προσῆλθαν
the mountain; and sitting him[a] [4]approached
=when he sat
αὐτῷ οἱ μαθηταὶ αὐτοῦ· 2 καὶ ἀνοίξας τὸ
[b]*to* him [1]the [2]disciples [3]of him; and opening the
στόμα αὐτοῦ ἐδίδασκεν αὐτοὺς λέγων·
mouth of him he taught them saying:
3 Μακάριοι οἱ πτωχοὶ τῷ πνεύματι,
Blessed [are] the poor – in spirit,
ὅτι αὐτῶν ἐστιν ἡ βασιλεία τῶν οὐρανῶν.
for of them is the kingdom of the heavens.
4 μακάριοι οἱ πενθοῦντες, ὅτι αὐτοὶ
Blessed [are] the mourning [ones], for they
παρακληθήσονται. 5 μακάριοι οἱ πραεῖς,
shall be comforted. Blessed [are] the meek,
ὅτι αὐτοὶ κληρονομήσουσιν τὴν γῆν.
for they shall inherit the earth.
6 μακάριοι οἱ πεινῶντες καὶ διψῶντες
Blessed [are] the hungering and thirsting [ones] [after]
τὴν δικαιοσύνην, ὅτι αὐτοὶ χορτασ-
– righteousness, for they shall be
θήσονται. 7 μακάριοι οἱ ἐλεήμονες, ὅτι
satisfied. Blessed [are] the merciful, for
αὐτοὶ ἐλεηθήσονται. 8 μακάριοι οἱ καθαροὶ
they shall obtain mercy. Blessed [are] the clean
τῇ καρδίᾳ, ὅτι αὐτοὶ τὸν θεὸν ὄψονται.
– in heart, for they – [2]God [1]shall see.
9 μακάριοι οἱ εἰρηνοποιοί, ὅτι [αὐτοὶ]
Blessed [are] the peacemakers, for they
υἱοὶ θεοῦ κληθήσονται. 10 μακάριοι οἱ
sons of God shall be called. Blessed [are] the [ones]
δεδιωγμένοι ἕνεκεν δικαιοσύνης, ὅτι αὐτῶν
having been persecuted for the sake of righteousness, for of them
ἐστιν ἡ βασιλεία τῶν οὐρανῶν. 11 μακάριοί
is the kingdom of the heavens. Blessed
ἐστε ὅταν ὀνειδίσωσιν ὑμᾶς καὶ διώξωσιν
are ye when they reproach you and persecute
καὶ εἴπωσιν πᾶν πονηρὸν καθ' ὑμῶν
and say all evil against you
ψευδόμενοι ἕνεκεν ἐμοῦ. 12 χαίρετε
lying for the sake of me. Rejoice
καὶ ἀγαλλιᾶσθε, ὅτι ὁ μισθὸς ὑμῶν
and be glad, because the reward of you [is]
πολὺς ἐν τοῖς οὐρανοῖς· οὕτως γὰρ
much in the heavens; for thus
ἐδίωξαν τοὺς προφήτας τοὺς πρὸ
they persecuted the prophets – before
ὑμῶν.
you.
13 Ὑμεῖς ἐστε τὸ ἅλας τῆς γῆς· ἐὰν δὲ
Ye are the salt of the earth; but if
τὸ ἅλας μωρανθῇ, ἐν τίνι ἁλισθήσεται;
the salt be tainted, by what shall it be salted?
εἰς οὐδὲν ἰσχύει ἔτι εἰ μὴ βληθὲν ἔξω
for nothing is it strong longer except being cast out
καταπατεῖσθαι ὑπὸ τῶν ἀνθρώπων. 14 Ὑμεῖς
to be trodden down by – men. Ye
ἐστε τὸ φῶς τοῦ κόσμου. οὐ δύναται
are the light of the world. [6]Not [5]can
πόλις κρυβῆναι ἐπάνω ὄρους κειμένη·
[1]a city [7]*to* be hid [3]on [4]a mountain [2]set;
15 οὐδὲ καίουσιν λύχνον καὶ τιθέασιν
nor do they light a lamp and place
αὐτὸν ὑπὸ τὸν μόδιον, ἀλλ' ἐπὶ τὴν
it under the bushel, but on the
λυχνίαν, καὶ λάμπει πᾶσιν τοῖς ἐν τῇ
lampstand, and it lightens all the [ones] in the

on a mountainside and sat
down. His disciples came
to him, 2and he began to
teach them, saying:

3"Blessed are the poor in
spirit,
for theirs is the
kingdom of heaven.
4Blessed are those who
mourn,
for they will be
comforted.
5Blessed are the meek,
for they will inherit the
earth.
6Blessed are those who
hunger and thirst for
righteousness,
for they will be filled.
7Blessed are the merciful,
for they will be shown
mercy.
8Blessed are the pure in
heart,
for they will see God.
9Blessed are the
peacemakers,
for they will be called
sons of God.
10Blessed are those who
are persecuted
because of
righteousness,
for theirs is the
kingdom of heaven.

11"Blessed are you when
people insult you, perse-
cute you and falsely say all
kinds of evil against you because of me. 12Rejoice and
be glad, because great is
your reward in heaven, for
in the same way they persecuted the prophets who
were before you.

Salt and Light

13"You are the salt of the
earth. But if the salt loses
its saltiness, how can it be
made salty again? It is no
longer good for anything,
except to be thrown out
and trampled by men.
14"You are the light of the
world. A city on a hill cannot be hidden. 15Neither do
people light a lamp and put
it under a bowl. Instead
they put it on its stand, and
it gives light to everyone in

house.
16"Let your light shine
before men in such a way
that they may see your
good works, and glorify
your Father who is in
heaven.
17"Do not think that I
came to abolish the Law or
the Prophets; I did not
come to abolish, but to fulfill.
18"For truly I say to you,
until heaven and earth pass
away, not the smallest letter or stroke shall pass
away from the Law, until
all is accomplished.
19"Whoever then annuls
one of the least of these
commandments, and so
teaches others, shall be
called least in the kingdom
of heaven; but whoever
keeps and teaches *them,* he
shall be called great in the
kingdom of heaven.
20"For I say to you, that
unless your righteousness
surpasses *that* of the
scribes and Pharisees, you
shall not enter the kingdom
of heaven.

Personal Relationships

21"You have heard that
the ancients were told,
'YOU SHALL NOT COMMIT
MURDER' and 'Whoever
commits murder shall be
[l]liable to the court.'
22"But I say to you that
everyone who is angry with
his brother[m] shall be guilty
before the court; and whoever shall say to his brother, '[n]Raca,' shall be guilty
before [o]the supreme court;
and whoever shall say,
'You fool,' shall be guilty
enough to go into the [p]fiery
hell.
23"If therefore you are
presenting your offering at
the altar, and there remember that your brother has
something against you,

[l]Or, *guilty before*
[m]Some mss. insert here: *without cause*
[n]Aramaic for *empty-head* or, *good for nothing*
[o]Lit., *the Sanhedrin*
[p]Lit., *Gehenna of fire*

οἰκίᾳ. **16** οὕτως λαμψάτω τὸ φῶς ὑμῶν
house. Thus let shine the light of you
ἔμπροσθεν τῶν ἀνθρώπων, ὅπως ἴδωσιν
before – men, so that they may see
ὑμῶν τὰ καλὰ ἔργα καὶ δοξάσωσιν
of you the good works and may glorify
τὸν πατέρα ὑμῶν τὸν ἐν τοῖς οὐρανοῖς.
the Father of you – in the heavens.
17 Μὴ νομίσητε ὅτι ἦλθον καταλῦσαι
Think not that I came to destroy
τὸν νόμον ἢ τοὺς προφήτας· οὐκ ἦλθον
the law or the prophets; I came not
καταλῦσαι ἀλλὰ πληρῶσαι. **18** ἀμὴν γὰρ
to destroy but to fulfil. For truly
λέγω ὑμῖν, ἕως ἂν παρέλθῃ ὁ οὐρανὸς
I say to you, until pass away the heaven
καὶ ἡ γῆ, ἰῶτα ἓν ἢ μία κεραία οὐ
and the earth, iota one or one point by no
μὴ παρέλθῃ ἀπὸ τοῦ νόμου, ἕως ἂν
means shall pass away from the law, until
πάντα γένηται. **19** ὃς ἐὰν οὖν λύσῃ
all things come to pass. Whoever therefore breaks
μίαν τῶν ἐντολῶν τούτων τῶν ἐλαχίστων
one – commandments of these the least
καὶ διδάξῃ οὕτως τοὺς ἀνθρώπους, ἐλάχιστος
and teaches thus – men, least
κληθήσεται ἐν τῇ βασιλείᾳ τῶν οὐρανῶν·
he shall be called in the kingdom of the heavens;
ὃς δ' ἂν ποιήσῃ καὶ διδάξῃ, οὗτος
but whoever does and teaches, this [one]
μέγας κληθήσεται ἐν τῇ βασιλείᾳ τῶν
great shall be called in the kingdom of the
οὐρανῶν. **20** λέγω γὰρ ὑμῖν ὅτι ἐὰν μὴ
heavens. For I tell you that except
περισσεύσῃ ὑμῶν ἡ δικαιοσύνη πλεῖον
shall exceed of you the righteousness more [than] [that]
τῶν γραμματέων καὶ Φαρισαίων, οὐ μὴ
of the scribes and Pharisees, by no means
εἰσέλθητε εἰς τὴν βασιλείαν τῶν οὐρανῶν.
shall ye enter into the kingdom of the heavens.
21 Ἠκούσατε ὅτι ἐρρέθη τοῖς ἀρχαίοις·
Ye heard that it was said to the ancients:
οὐ φονεύσεις· ὃς δ' ἂν φονεύσῃ,
Thou shalt not kill; and whoever kills,
ἔνοχος ἔσται τῇ κρίσει. **22** ἐγὼ δὲ
liable shall be to the judgment. But I
λέγω ὑμῖν ὅτι πᾶς ὁ ὀργιζόμενος τῷ
tell you that everyone being angry with the
ἀδελφῷ αὐτοῦ ἔνοχος ἔσται τῇ κρίσει·
brother of him liable shall be to the judgment;
ὃς δ' ἂν εἴπῃ τῷ ἀδελφῷ αὐτοῦ ῥακά,
and whoever says to the brother of him[,] Raca,
ἔνοχος ἔσται τῷ συνεδρίῳ· ὃς δ' ἂν εἴπῃ
liable shall be to the council; and whoever says[,]
μωρέ, ἔνοχος ἔσται εἰς τὴν γέενναν
Fool, liable shall be to the gehenna
τοῦ πυρός. **23** ἐὰν οὖν προσφέρῃς τὸ
– of fire. Therefore if thou bringest the
δῶρόν σου ἐπὶ τὸ θυσιαστήριον κἀκεῖ
gift of thee to the altar and there
μνησθῇς ὅτι ὁ ἀδελφός σου ἔχει τι
rememberest that the brother of thee has something
κατὰ σοῦ, **24** ἄφες ἐκεῖ τὸ δῶρόν σου
against thee, leave there the gift of thee
ἔμπροσθεν τοῦ θυσιαστηρίου, καὶ ὕπαγε
before the altar, and go

the house. 16In the same
way, let your light shine before men, that they may see
your good deeds and praise
your Father in heaven.

The Fulfillment of the Law

17"Do not think that I
have come to abolish the
Law or the Prophets; I have
not come to abolish them
but to fulfill them. 18I tell
you the truth, until heaven
and earth disappear, not
the smallest letter, not the
least stroke of a pen, will by
any means disappear from
the Law until everything is
accomplished. 19Anyone
who breaks one of the least
of these commandments
and teaches others to do
the same will be called least
in the kingdom of heaven,
but whoever practices and
teaches these commands
will be called great in the
kingdom of heaven. 20For I
tell you that unless your
righteousness surpasses
that of the Pharisees and
the teachers of the law, you
will certainly not enter the
kingdom of heaven.

Murder

21"You have heard that it
was said to the people long
ago, 'Do not murder,[t] and
anyone who murders will
be subject to judgment.'
22But I tell you that anyone
who is angry with his brother[u] will be subject to judgment. Again, anyone who
says to his brother,
'Raca,[v]' is answerable to
the Sanhedrin. But anyone
who says, 'You fool!' will
be in danger of the fire of
hell.
23"Therefore, if you are
offering your gift at the altar and there remember
that your brother has something against you, 24leave

[t]*21* Exodus 20:13
[u]*22* Some manuscripts *brother without cause*
[v]*22* An Aramaic term of contempt

24leave your offering there before the altar, and go your way; first be reconciled to your brother, and then come and present your offering.

25"Make friends quickly with your opponent at law while you are with him on the way, in order that your opponent may not deliver you to the judge, and the judge to the officer, and you be thrown into prison.

26"Truly I say to you, you shall not come out of there, until you have paid up the last [q]cent.

27"You have heard that it was said, 'YOU SHALL NOT COMMIT ADULTERY';

28but I say to you, that everyone who looks on a woman to lust for her has committed adultery with her already in his heart.

29"And if your right eye makes you stumble, tear it out, and throw it from you; for it is better for you that one of the parts of your body perish, than for your whole body to be thrown into hell.

30"And if your right hand makes you stumble, cut it off, and throw it from you; for it is better for you that one of the parts of your body perish, than for your whole body to go into hell.

31"And it was said, 'WHOEVER SENDS HIS WIFE AWAY, LET HIM GIVE HER A CERTIFICATE OF DIVORCE';

32but I say to you that everyone who divorces his wife, except for *the* cause of unchastity, makes her commit adultery; and whoever marries a divorced woman commits adultery.

33"Again, you have heard that the ancients were told, 'YOU SHALL NOT MAKE FALSE VOWS, BUT SHALL FULFILL YOUR VOWS TO THE LORD.'

34"But I say to you, make no oath at all, either by heaven, for it is the throne of God,

πρῶτον διαλλάγηθι τῷ ἀδελφῷ σου, καὶ
first be reconciled to the brother of thee, and
τότε ἐλθὼν πρόσφερε τὸ δῶρόν σου.
then coming offer the gift of thee.
25 ἴσθι εὐνοῶν τῷ ἀντιδίκῳ σου
Be well disposed to the opponent of thee
ταχὺ ἕως ὅτου εἶ μετ' αὐτοῦ ἐν τῇ
quickly while thou art with him in the
ὁδῷ· μήποτέ σε παραδῷ ὁ ἀντίδικος τῷ
way; lest [4]thee [3]deliver [1]the [2]opponent to the
κριτῇ καὶ ὁ κριτὴς τῷ ὑπηρέτῃ, καὶ
judge and the judge to the attendant, and
εἰς φυλακὴν βληθήσῃ· 26 ἀμὴν λέγω
into prison thou be cast; truly I say
σοι, οὐ μὴ ἐξέλθῃς ἐκεῖθεν ἕως ἂν
to thee, by no means shalt thou come out thence until
ἀποδῷς τὸν ἔσχατον κοδράντην.
thou repayest the last farthing.
27 Ἠκούσατε ὅτι ἐρρέθη· οὐ μοιχεύσεις.
Ye heard that it was said: Thou shalt not commit adultery.
28 ἐγὼ δὲ λέγω ὑμῖν ὅτι πᾶς ὁ βλέπων
But I tell you that everyone seeing
γυναῖκα πρὸς τὸ ἐπιθυμῆσαι [αὐτὴν]
a woman with a view – to desire her
ἤδη ἐμοίχευσεν αὐτὴν ἐν τῇ καρδίᾳ
already committed adultery with her in the heart
αὐτοῦ. 29 εἰ δὲ ὁ ὀφθαλμός σου ὁ δεξιὸς
of him. So if the [2]eye [3]of thee – [1]right
σκανδαλίζει σε, ἔξελε αὐτὸν καὶ βάλε
[4]causes [6]to stumble [5]thee, pluck out it and cast
ἀπὸ σοῦ· συμφέρει γάρ σοι ἵνα ἀπόληται
from thee; for it is expedient for thee that [5]perish
ἓν τῶν μελῶν σου καὶ μὴ ὅλον τὸ
[1]one [2]of the [3]members [4]of thee and not all the
σῶμά σου βληθῇ εἰς γέενναν. 30 καὶ
body of thee be cast into gehenna. And
εἰ ἡ δεξιά σου χεὶρ σκανδαλίζει σε, ἔκκοψον
if the [1]right [3]of thee [2]hand [4]causes [6]to stumble [5]thee, cut out
αὐτὴν καὶ βάλε ἀπὸ σοῦ· συμφέρει γάρ
it and cast from thee; for it is expedient
σοι ἵνα ἀπόληται ἓν τῶν μελῶν σου
for thee that [5]perish [1]one [2]of the [3]members [4]of thee
καὶ μὴ ὅλον τὸ σῶμά σου εἰς γέενναν
and not all the body of thee into gehenna
ἀπέλθῃ. 31 Ἐρρέθη δέ· ὃς ἂν ἀπολύσῃ
go away. And it was said: Whoever dismisses
τὴν γυναῖκα αὐτοῦ, δότω αὐτῇ ἀποστάσιον.
the wife of him, let him give her a bill of divorce.
32 ἐγὼ δὲ λέγω ὑμῖν ὅτι πᾶς ὁ ἀπολύων
But I tell you that everyone dismissing
τὴν γυναῖκα αὐτοῦ παρεκτὸς λόγου
the wife of him apart from a matter
πορνείας ποιεῖ αὐτὴν μοιχευθῆναι,
of fornication makes her *to* commit adultery,
καὶ ὃς ἐὰν ἀπολελυμένην γαμήσῃ,
and whoever [2]a dismissed [woman] [1]marries,
μοιχᾶται. 33 Πάλιν ἠκούσατε ὅτι ἐρρέθη
commits adultery. Again ye heard that it was said
τοῖς ἀρχαίοις· οὐκ ἐπιορκήσεις, ἀποδώσεις
to the ancients: Thou shalt not perjure, [2]shalt repay
δὲ τῷ κυρίῳ τοὺς ὅρκους σου. 34 ἐγὼ δὲ
[1]but to the Lord the oaths of thee. But I
λέγω ὑμῖν μὴ ὀμόσαι ὅλως· μήτε ἐν τῷ
tell you not to swear at all; neither by the
οὐρανῷ, ὅτι θρόνος ἐστὶν τοῦ θεοῦ·
heaven, because [the] throne it is – of God;

your gift there in front of the altar. First go and be reconciled to your brother; then come and offer your gift.

25"Settle matters quickly with your adversary who is taking you to court. Do it while you are still with him on the way, or he may hand you over to the judge, and the judge may hand you over to the officer, and you may be thrown into prison.
26I tell you the truth, you will not get out until you have paid the last penny.[w]

Adultery

27"You have heard that it was said, 'Do not commit adultery.'[x] 28But I tell you
that anyone who looks at a woman lustfully has already committed adultery with her in his heart. 29If
your right eye causes you to sin, gouge it out and throw it away. It is better for you to lose one part of your body than for your whole body to be thrown into hell. 30And if your right
hand causes you to sin, cut it off and throw it away. It is better for you to lose one part of your body than for your whole body to go into hell.

Divorce

31"It has been said, 'Anyone who divorces his wife must give her a certificate of divorce.'[y] 32But I tell
you that anyone who divorces his wife, except for marital unfaithfulness, causes her to become an adulteress, and anyone who marries the divorced woman commits adultery.

Oaths

33"Again, you have heard that it was said to the people long ago, 'Do not break your oath, but keep the oaths you have made to the Lord.' 34But I tell you, Do
not swear at all: either by heaven, for it is God's throne; 35or by the earth,

[q] Lit., *quadrans* (equaling two lepta or mites), i.e., 1/64 of a denarius

[w] *26* Greek *kodrantes*
[x] *27* Exodus 20:14
[y] *31* Deut. 24:1

35or by the earth, for it is the footstool of His feet, or by Jerusalem, for it is THE CITY OF THE GREAT KING.

36"Nor shall you make an oath by your head, for you cannot make one hair white or black.

37"But let your statement be, 'Yes, yes' *or* 'No, no'; and anything beyond these is of evil.

38"You have heard that it was said, 'AN EYE FOR AN EYE, AND A TOOTH FOR A TOOTH.'

39"But I say to you, do not resist him who is evil; but whoever slaps you on your right cheek, turn to him the other also.

40"And if anyone wants to sue you, and take your [r]shirt, let him have your [s]coat also.

41"And whoever shall force you to go one mile, go with him two.

42"Give to him who asks of you, and do not turn away from him who wants to borrow from you.

43"You have heard that it was said, 'YOU SHALL LOVE YOUR NEIGHBOR, and hate your enemy.'

44"But I say to you, love your enemies, and pray for those who persecute you

45in order that you may be sons of your Father who is in heaven; for He causes His sun to rise on *the* evil and *the* good, and sends rain on *the* righteous and *the* unrighteous.

46"For if you love those who love you, what reward have you? Do not even the tax-gatherers do the same?

47"And if you greet your brothers only, what do you do more *than others*? Do

[r]Or, *tunic;* i.e., garment worn next to the body
[s]Or, *cloak;* i.e., outer garment

35 μήτε ἐν τῇ γῇ, ὅτι ὑποπόδιόν
nor by the earth, because footstool
ἐστιν τῶν ποδῶν αὐτοῦ· μήτε εἰς
it is of the feet of him; nor by
Ἱεροσόλυμα, ὅτι πόλις ἐστὶν τοῦ μεγάλου
Jerusalem, because city it is of the great
βασιλέως· **36** μήτε ἐν τῇ κεφαλῇ σου
King; nor by the head of thee
ὀμόσῃς, ὅτι οὐ δύνασαι μίαν τρίχα
swear, because thou canst not one hair
λευκὴν ποιῆσαι ἢ μέλαιναν. **37** ἔστω
white *to* make or black. [3]let [4]be
δὲ ὁ λόγος ὑμῶν ναὶ ναί, οὒ οὔ·
[1]But [2]the [4]word [5]of you Yes yes, No no;
τὸ δὲ περισσὸν τούτων ἐκ τοῦ πονηροῦ
for the excess of these of – evil
ἐστιν. **38** Ἠκούσατε ὅτι ἐρρέθη· ὀφθαλμὸν
is. Ye heard that it was said: An eye
ἀντὶ ὀφθαλμοῦ καὶ ὀδόντα ἀντὶ ὀδόντος.
instead of an eye and a tooth instead of a tooth.
39 ἐγὼ δὲ λέγω ὑμῖν μὴ ἀντιστῆναι
But I tell you not to oppose
τῷ πονηρῷ· ἀλλ' ὅστις σε ῥαπίζει εἰς
– evil; but who thee strikes on
τὴν δεξιὰν σιαγόνα [σου], στρέψον αὐτῷ
the right cheek of thee, turn to him
καὶ τὴν ἄλλην· **40** καὶ τῷ θέλοντί
also the other; and to the [one] wishing
σοι κριθῆναι καὶ τὸν χιτῶνά σου λαβεῖν,
thee to judge and the tunic of thee to take,
ἄφες αὐτῷ καὶ τὸ ἱμάτιον· **41** καὶ
allow him also the [outer] garment; and
ὅστις σε ἀγγαρεύσει μίλιον ἕν, ὕπαγε
who [2]thee [1]shall impress [4]mile [3]one, go
μετ' αὐτοῦ δύο. **42** τῷ αἰτοῦντί
with him two. To the [one] asking
σε δός, καὶ τὸν θέλοντα ἀπὸ σοῦ
thee give, and the [one] wishing from thee
δανείσασθαι μὴ ἀποστραφῇς. **43** Ἠκούσατε
to borrow turn not away. Ye heard
ὅτι ἐρρέθη· ἀγαπήσεις τὸν πλησίον σου
that it was said: Thou shalt love the neighbour of thee
καὶ μισήσεις τὸν ἐχθρόν σου. **44** ἐγὼ
and thou shalt hate the enemy of thee. [2]I
δὲ λέγω ὑμῖν· ἀγαπᾶτε τοὺς ἐχθροὺς
[1]But tell you: Love ye the enemies
ὑμῶν καὶ προσεύχεσθε ὑπὲρ τῶν
of you and pray ye for the [ones]
διωκόντων ὑμᾶς· **45** ὅπως γένησθε υἱοὶ
persecuting you; so that ye may become sons
τοῦ πατρὸς ὑμῶν τοῦ ἐν οὐρανοῖς,
of the Father of you – in heavens,
ὅτι τὸν ἥλιον αὐτοῦ ἀνατέλλει ἐπὶ
because the sun of him he makes to rise on
πονηροὺς καὶ ἀγαθοὺς καὶ βρέχει ἐπὶ
evil men and good and rains on
δικαίους καὶ ἀδίκους. **46** ἐὰν γὰρ
just men and unjust. For if
ἀγαπήσητε τοὺς ἀγαπῶντας ὑμᾶς, τίνα
ye love the [ones] loving you, what
μισθὸν ἔχετε; οὐχὶ καὶ οἱ τελῶναι τὸ
reward have ye? [2]not [3]even [4]the [5]tax-collectors [6]the
αὐτὸ ποιοῦσιν; **47** καὶ ἐὰν ἀσπάσησθε
[7]same [1]do? and if ye greet
τοὺς ἀδελφοὺς ὑμῶν μόνον, τί περισσὸν
the brothers of you only, what excess

for it is his footstool; or by
Jerusalem, for it is the city
of the Great King. 36And do
not swear by your head, for
you cannot make even one
hair white or black. 37Sim-
ply let your 'Yes' be 'Yes,'
and your 'No,' 'No'; any-
thing beyond this comes
from the evil one.

An Eye for an Eye

38"You have heard that it
was said, 'Eye for eye, and
tooth for tooth.'[z] 39But I
tell you, Do not resist an
evil person. If someone
strikes you on the right
cheek, turn to him the other
also. 40And if someone
wants to sue you and take
your tunic, let him have
your cloak as well. 41If
someone forces you to go
one mile, go with him two
miles. 42Give to the one
who asks you, and do not
turn away from the one
who wants to borrow from
you.

Love for Enemies

43"You have heard that it
was said, 'Love your
neighbor[a] and hate your
enemy.' 44But I tell you:
Love your enemies[b] and
pray for those who perse-
cute you, 45that you may be
sons of your Father in
heaven. He causes his sun
to rise on the evil and the
good, and sends rain on the
righteous and the unrighteous. 46If you love those
who love you, what reward
will you get? Are not even
the tax collectors doing
that? 47And if you greet
only your brothers, what
are you doing more than
others? Do not even pagans

[z]*38* Exodus 21:24; Lev. 24:20; Deut. 19:21
[a]*43* Lev. 19:18
[b]*44* Some late manuscripts *enemies, bless those who curse you, do good to those who hate you*

not even the Gentiles do the same?
48"Therefore you are to be perfect, as your heavenly Father is perfect.

Chapter 6

Concerning Alms and Prayer

"BEWARE of practicing your righteousness before men to be noticed by them; otherwise you have no reward with your Father who is in heaven.
2"When therefore you give alms, do not sound a trumpet before you, as the hypocrites do in the synagogues and in the streets, that they may be honored by men. Truly I say to you, they have their reward in full.
3"But when you give alms, do not let your left hand know what your right hand is doing
4that your alms may be in secret; and your Father who sees in secret will repay you.
5"And when you pray, you are not to be as the hypocrites; for they love to stand and pray in the synagogues and on the street corners, in order to be seen by men. Truly I say to you, they have their reward in full.
6"But you, when you pray, go into your inner room, and when you have shut your door, pray to your Father who is in secret, and your Father who sees in secret will repay you.
7"And when you are praying, do not use meaningless repetition, as the Gentiles do, for they suppose that they will be heard for their many words.

ποιεῖτε; οὐχὶ καὶ οἱ ἐθνικοὶ τὸ αὐτὸ
do ye? [2]not [3]even [4]the [5]gentiles [6]the [7]same

ποιοῦσιν; 48 Ἔσεσθε οὖν ὑμεῖς τέλειοι
[1]do? Be therefore ye perfect

ὡς ὁ πατὴρ ὑμῶν ὁ οὐράνιος τέλειός
as the [2]Father [3]of you – [1]heavenly perfect

ἐστιν.
is.

6 Προσέχετε δὲ τὴν δικαιοσύνην ὑμῶν
And take ye heed the righteousness of you

μὴ ποιεῖν ἔμπροσθεν τῶν ἀνθρώπων πρὸς
not to do in front of – men with a view to

τὸ θεαθῆναι αὐτοῖς· εἰ δὲ μή γε, μισθὸν
– to be seen by them; otherwise, reward

οὐκ ἔχετε παρὰ τῷ πατρὶ ὑμῶν τῷ
ye have not with the Father of you –

ἐν τοῖς οὐρανοῖς. 2 Ὅταν οὖν ποιῇς
in the heavens. [2]When [1]therefore thou doest

ἐλεημοσύνην, μὴ σαλπίσῃς ἔμπροσθέν σου,
alms, sound not a trumpet before thee,

ὥσπερ οἱ ὑποκριταὶ ποιοῦσιν ἐν ταῖς
as the hypocrites do in the

συναγωγαῖς καὶ ἐν ταῖς ῥύμαις, ὅπως
synagogues and in the streets, so that

δοξασθῶσιν ὑπὸ τῶν ἀνθρώπων· ἀμὴν
they may be glorified by – men; truly

λέγω ὑμῖν, ἀπέχουσιν τὸν μισθὸν αὐτῶν.
I tell you, they have the reward of them.

3 σοῦ δὲ ποιοῦντος ἐλεημοσύνην μὴ
But thee doing* alms not
= when thou doest

γνώτω ἡ ἀριστερά σου τί ποιεῖ ἡ
let know the left [hand] of thee what does the

δεξιά σου, 4 ὅπως ᾖ σου ἡ ἐλεημοσύνη
right of thee, so that [4]may be [3]of thee [1]the [2]alms

ἐν τῷ κρυπτῷ· καὶ ὁ πατήρ σου
in – secret; and the Father of thee

ὁ βλέπων ἐν τῷ κρυπτῷ ἀποδώσει σοι.
the [one] seeing in – secret will repay thee.

5 Καὶ ὅταν προσεύχησθε, οὐκ ἔσεσθε
And when ye pray, be not ye

ὡς οἱ ὑποκριταί· ὅτι φιλοῦσιν ἐν ταῖς
as the hypocrites; because they love in the

συναγωγαῖς καὶ ἐν ταῖς γωνίαις τῶν
synagogues and in the corners of the

πλατειῶν ἑστῶτες προσεύχεσθαι, ὅπως
open streets standing to pray, so that

φανῶσιν τοῖς ἀνθρώποις· ἀμὴν λέγω
they may appear – to men; truly I tell

ὑμῖν, ἀπέχουσιν τὸν μισθὸν αὐτῶν. 6 σὺ
you, they have the reward of them. [2]thou

δὲ ὅταν προσεύχῃ, εἴσελθε εἰς τὸ ταμιεῖόν
[1]But [3]when [4]prayest, enter into the private room

σου καὶ κλείσας τὴν θύραν σου πρόσευξαι
of thee and having shut the door of thee pray

τῷ πατρί σου τῷ ἐν τῷ κρυπτῷ·
to the Father of thee the [one] in – secret;

καὶ ὁ πατήρ σου ὁ βλέπων ἐν τῷ
and the Father of thee the [one] seeing in –

κρυπτῷ ἀποδώσει σοι. 7 Προσευχόμενοι δὲ
secret will repay thee. But praying

μὴ βατταλογήσητε ὥσπερ οἱ ἐθνικοί·
do not utter empty words as the gentiles;

δοκοῦσιν γὰρ ὅτι ἐν τῇ πολυλογίᾳ αὐτῶν
for they think that in the much speaking of them

do that? 48Be perfect, therefore, as your heavenly Father is perfect.

Chapter 6

Giving to the Needy

"BE careful not to do your 'acts of righteousness' before men, to be seen by them. If you do, you will have no reward from your Father in heaven.
2"So when you give to the needy, do not announce it with trumpets, as the hypocrites do in the synagogues and on the streets, to be honored by men. I tell you the truth, they have received their reward in full.
3But when you give to the needy, do not let your left hand know what your right hand is doing, 4so that your giving may be in secret. Then your Father, who sees what is done in secret, will reward you.

Prayer

5"And when you pray, do not be like the hypocrites, for they love to pray standing in the synagogues and on the street corners to be seen by men. I tell you the truth, they have received their reward in full. 6But when you pray, go into your room, close the door and pray to your Father, who is unseen. Then your Father, who sees what is done in secret, will reward you. 7And when you pray, do not keep on babbling like pagans, for they think they will be heard because of their many words. 8Do

8"Therefore do not be like them; for your Father knows what you need, before you ask Him.
9"Pray, then, in this way:
'Our Father who art in heaven,
Hallowed be Thy name.
10 'Thy kingdom come.
Thy will be done,
On earth as it is in heaven.
11 'Give us this day our daily bread.
12 'And forgive us our debts, as we also have forgiven our debtors.
13 'And do not lead us into temptation, but deliver us from evil. [For Thine is the kingdom, and the power, and the glory, forever. Amen.]'
14"For if you forgive men for their transgressions, your heavenly Father will also forgive you.
15"But if you do not forgive men, then your Father will not forgive your transgressions.

Concerning Fasting
True Treasure Mammon

16"And whenever you fast, do not put on a gloomy face as the hypocrites *do,* for they neglect their appearance in order to be seen fasting by men. Truly I say to you, they have their reward in full.
17"But you, when you fast, anoint your head, and wash your face
18so that you may not be seen fasting by men, but by your Father who is in secret; and your Father who sees in secret will repay you.
19"Do not lay up for yourselves treasures upon earth, where moth and rust destroy, and where thieves break in and steal.
20"But lay up for your-

εἰσακουσθήσονται. **8** μὴ οὖν ὁμοιωθῆτε
they will be heard. Not therefore be ye like
αὐτοῖς· οἶδεν γὰρ [ὁ θεὸς] ὁ πατὴρ
them; for [5]knows – [1]God [2]the [3]Father
ὑμῶν ὧν χρείαν ἔχετε πρὸ τοῦ ὑμᾶς
[4]of you of what things [2]need [1]ye have before – you
αἰτῆσαι αὐτόν. **9** οὕτως οὖν προσεύχεσθε
to ask[b] him. [2]Thus [1]therefore pray
ὑμεῖς· Πάτερ ἡμῶν ὁ ἐν τοῖς οὐρανοῖς·
ye: Father of us the [one] in the heavens:
Ἁγιασθήτω τὸ ὄνομά σου· **10** ἐλθάτω
Let it be hallowed the name of thee; let it come
ἡ βασιλεία σου· γενηθήτω τὸ θέλημά σου,
the kingdom of thee; let it come about the will of thee,
ὡς ἐν οὐρανῷ καὶ ἐπὶ γῆς· **11** Τὸν
as in heaven also on earth; The
ἄρτον ἡμῶν τὸν ἐπιούσιον δὸς ἡμῖν
[3]bread [2]of us – [1]daily give to us
σήμερον· **12** καὶ ἄφες ἡμῖν τὰ ὀφειλή-
to-day; and forgive us the debts
ματα ἡμῶν, ὡς καὶ ἡμεῖς ἀφήκαμεν
of us, as indeed we forgave
τοῖς ὀφειλέταις ἡμῶν· **13** καὶ μὴ εἰσενέγκῃς
the debtors of us; and not bring
ἡμᾶς εἰς πειρασμόν, ἀλλὰ ῥῦσαι ἡμᾶς ἀπὸ
us into temptation, but rescue us from
τοῦ πονηροῦ. **14** Ἐὰν γὰρ ἀφῆτε τοῖς
– evil. For if ye forgive –
ἀνθρώποις τὰ παραπτώματα αὐτῶν, ἀφήσει
men the trespasses of them, will forgive
καὶ ὑμῖν ὁ πατὴρ ὑμῶν ὁ οὐράνιος·
also you the [2]Father [3]of you – [1]heavenly;
15 ἐὰν δὲ μὴ ἀφῆτε τοῖς ἀνθρώποις,
but if ye forgive not – men,
οὐδὲ ὁ πατὴρ ὑμῶν ἀφήσει τὰ παραπτώ-
neither the Father of you will forgive the tres-
ματα ὑμῶν. **16** Ὅταν δὲ νηστεύητε,
passes of you. And when ye fast,
μὴ γίνεσθε ὡς οἱ ὑποκριταὶ σκυθρωποί·
be not as the hypocrites gloomy;
ἀφανίζουσιν γὰρ τὰ πρόσωπα αὐτῶν
for they disfigure the faces of them
ὅπως φανῶσιν τοῖς ἀνθρώποις νηστεύοντες·
so that they may appear – to men fasting;
ἀμὴν λέγω ὑμῖν, ἀπέχουσιν τὸν μισθὸν
truly I tell you, they have the reward
αὐτῶν. **17** σὺ δὲ νηστεύων ἄλειψαί σου
of them. But thou fasting anoint of thee
τὴν κεφαλὴν καὶ τὸ πρόσωπόν σου νίψαι,
the head and the face of thee wash,
18 ὅπως μὴ φανῇς τοῖς ἀνθρώποις νηστεύων
so that thou appearest not – to men fasting
ἀλλὰ τῷ πατρί σου τῷ ἐν τῷ κρυφαίῳ·
but to the Father of thee the [one] in – secret;
καὶ ὁ πατήρ σου ὁ βλέπων ἐν τῷ
and the Father of thee the [one] seeing in –
κρυφαίῳ ἀποδώσει σοι.
secret will repay thee.
19 Μὴ θησαυρίζετε ὑμῖν θησαυροὺς
Do not lay up *treasure* for you treasures
ἐπὶ τῆς γῆς, ὅπου σὴς καὶ βρῶσις
on the earth, where moth and rust
ἀφανίζει, καὶ ὅπου κλέπται διορύσσουσιν
removes, and where thieves dig through
καὶ κλέπτουσιν· **20** θησαυρίζετε δὲ ὑμῖν
and steal; but lay up *treasure* for you

not be like them, for your Father knows what you need before you ask him.
9"This, then, is how you should pray:
" 'Our Father in heaven,
hallowed be your name,
10your kingdom come,
your will be done
on earth as it is in heaven.
11Give us today our daily bread.
12Forgive us our debts,
as we also have forgiven our debtors.
13And lead us not into temptation,
but deliver us from the evil one.[c]'
14For if you forgive men when they sin against you, your heavenly Father will also forgive you.
15But if you do not forgive men their sins, your Father will not forgive your sins.

Fasting

16"When you fast, do not look somber as the hypocrites do, for they disfigure their faces to show men they are fasting. I tell you the truth, they have received their reward in full.
17But when you fast, put oil on your head and wash your face,
18so that it will not be obvious to men that you are fasting, but only to your Father, who is unseen; and your Father, who sees what is done in secret, will reward you.

Treasures in Heaven

19"Do not store up for yourselves treasures on earth, where moth and rust destroy, and where thieves break in and steal.
20But store up for yourselves

[c]*13* Or *from evil*; some late manuscripts *one, / for yours is the kingdom and the power and the glory forever. Amen.*

selves treasures in heaven,
where neither moth nor
rust destroys, and where
thieves do not break in or
steal;
21for where your treasure
is, there will your heart be
also.
22"The lamp of the body
is the eye; if therefore your
eye is clear, your whole
body will be full of light.
23"But if your eye is bad,
your whole body will be full
of darkness. If therefore
the light that is in you is
darkness, how great is the
darkness!
24"No one can serve two
masters; for either he will
hate the one and love the
other, or he will hold to one
and despise the other. You
cannot serve God and
[t] mammon.

The Cure for Anxiety

25"For this reason I say
to you, do not be anxious
for your life, *as to* what you
shall eat, or what you shall
drink; nor for your body, *as*
to what you shall put on. Is
not life more than food, and
the body than clothing?
26"Look at the birds of
the air, that they do not
sow, neither do they reap,
nor gather into barns, and
yet your heavenly Father
feeds them. Are you not
worth much more than
they?
27"And which of you by
being anxious can add a
single cubit to his life's
span?
28"And why are you anxious about clothing? Observe how the lilies of the
field grow; they do not toil
nor do they spin,
29yet I say to you that
even Solomon in all his
glory did not clothe himself
like one of these.
30"But if God so arrays

[t] Or, *riches*

θησαυροὺς ἐν οὐρανῷ, ὅπου οὔτε σὴς
treasures in heaven, where neither moth
οὔτε βρῶσις ἀφανίζει, καὶ ὅπου κλέπται
nor rust removes, and where thieves
οὐ διορύσσουσιν οὐδὲ κλέπτουσιν· 21 ὅπου
do not dig through nor steal; [2]where
γάρ ἐστιν ὁ θησαυρός σου, ἐκεῖ
[1]for is the treasure of thee, there
ἔσται καὶ ἡ καρδία σου. 22 Ὁ λύχνος
will be also the heart of thee. The lamp
τοῦ σώματός ἐστιν ὁ ὀφθαλμός. ἐὰν οὖν
of the body is the eye. [2]If [1]therefore
ᾖ ὁ ὀφθαλμός σου ἁπλοῦς, ὅλον τὸ σῶμά
[4]be [1]the [2]eye [3]of thee single, all the body
σου φωτεινὸν ἔσται· 23 ἐὰν δὲ ὁ
of thee shining will be; but if the
ὀφθαλμός σου πονηρὸς ᾖ, ὅλον τὸ σῶμά
eye of thee evil be, all the body
σου σκοτεινὸν ἔσται. εἰ οὖν τὸ φῶς
of thee dark will be. [2]If [1]therefore the light
τὸ ἐν σοὶ σκότος ἐστίν, τὸ σκότος
– in thee darkness is, the darkness
πόσον. 24 Οὐδεὶς δύναται δυσὶ κυρίοις
how great. No one can two lords
δουλεύειν· ἢ γὰρ τὸν ἕνα μισήσει καὶ
to serve; for either the one he will hate and
τὸν ἕτερον ἀγαπήσει, ἢ ἑνὸς ἀνθέξεται
the other he will love, or one he will hold to
καὶ τοῦ ἑτέρου καταφρονήσει. οὐ δύνασθε
and the other he will despise. Ye cannot
θεῷ δουλεύειν καὶ μαμωνᾷ. 25 Διὰ
God *to* serve and mammon. There-
τοῦτο λέγω ὑμῖν· μὴ μεριμνᾶτε τῇ
fore I say to you: Be not anxious for the
ψυχῇ ὑμῶν τί φάγητε [ἢ τί πίητε],
life of you[,] what ye may eat or what ye may drink,
μηδὲ τῷ σώματι ὑμῶν τί ἐνδύσησθε.
nor for the body of you[,] what ye may put on.
οὐχὶ ἡ ψυχὴ πλεῖόν ἐστιν τῆς τροφῆς καὶ τὸ
[2]not [3]the [4]life [5]more [1]Is [than] the food and the
σῶμα τοῦ ἐνδύματος; 26 ἐμβλέψατε εἰς
body [than] the raiment? Look ye at
τὰ πετεινὰ τοῦ οὐρανοῦ, ὅτι οὐ σπείρουσιν
the birds – of heaven, that they sow not
οὐδὲ θερίζουσιν οὐδὲ συνάγουσιν εἰς
nor reap nor gather into
ἀποθήκας, καὶ ὁ πατὴρ ὑμῶν ὁ οὐράνιος
barns, and the [2]Father [3]of you – [1]heavenly
τρέφει αὐτά· οὐχ ὑμεῖς μᾶλλον διαφέρετε
feeds them; do not ye more excel
αὐτῶν; 27 τίς δὲ ἐξ ὑμῶν μεριμνῶν
them? But who of you being anxious
δύναται προσθεῖναι ἐπὶ τὴν ἡλικίαν αὐτοῦ
can *to* add to the stature of him
πῆχυν ἕνα; 28 καὶ περὶ ἐνδύματος τί
cubit one? and concerning clothing why
μεριμνᾶτε; καταμάθετε τὰ κρίνα τοῦ ἀγροῦ,
be ye anxious? consider the lilies of the field,
πῶς αὐξάνουσιν· οὐ κοπιῶσιν οὐδὲ
how they grow; they labour not nor
νήθουσιν· 29 λέγω δὲ ὑμῖν ὅτι οὐδὲ Σολομὼν
spin; but I tell you that not Solomon
ἐν πάσῃ τῇ δόξῃ αὐτοῦ περιεβάλετο ὡς
in all the glory of him was clothed as
ἓν τούτων. 30 εἰ δὲ τὸν χόρτον τοῦ
one of these. But if the grass of the

treasures in heaven, where
moth and rust do not de-
stroy, and where thieves do
not break in and steal.
21For where your treasure
is, there your heart will be
also.
22"The eye is the lamp of
the body. If your eyes are
good, your whole body will
be full of light. 23But if your
eyes are bad, your whole
body will be full of darkness. If then the light within
you is darkness, how great
is that darkness!
24"No one can serve two
masters. Either he will hate
the one and love the other,
or he will be devoted to the
one and despise the other.
You cannot serve both God
and Money.

Do Not Worry

25"Therefore I tell you,
do not worry about your
life, what you will eat or
drink; or about your body,
what you will wear. Is not
life more important than
food, and the body more
important than clothes?
26Look at the birds of the
air; they do not sow or reap
or store away in barns, and
yet your heavenly Father
feeds them. Are you not
much more valuable than
they? 27Who of you by worrying can add a single hour
to his life[d]?
28"And why do you wor-
ry about clothes? See how
the lilies of the field grow.
They do not labor or spin.
29Yet I tell you that not
even Solomon in all his
splendor was dressed like
one of these. 30If that is

[d]27 Or *single cubit to his height*

the grass of the field, which
is *alive* today and tomorrow is thrown into the furnace, *will He* not much
more *do so for* you, O men
of little faith?
31"Do not be anxious
then, saying, 'What shall
we eat?' or 'What shall we
drink?' or 'With what shall
we clothe ourselves?'
32"For all these things the
Gentiles eagerly seek; for
your heavenly Father
knows that you need all
these things.
33"But seek first His
kingdom and His righteousness; and all these things
shall be added to you.
34"Therefore do not be
anxious for tomorrow; for
tomorrow will care for itself. *Each* day has enough
trouble of its own.

ἀγροῦ σήμερον ὄντα καὶ αὔριον εἰς
field to-day being and to-morrow into
κλίβανον βαλλόμενον ὁ θεὸς οὕτως
an oven being thrown – God thus
ἀμφιέννυσιν, οὐ πολλῷ μᾶλλον ὑμᾶς,
clothes, not much more you,
ὀλιγόπιστοι; **31** μὴ οὖν μεριμνήσητε
little-faiths? Therefore be ye not anxious
λέγοντες· τί φάγωμεν; ἤ· τί
saying: What may we eat? or: What
πίωμεν; ἤ· τί περιβαλώμεθα; **32** πάντα
may we drink? or: What may we put on? [2]all
γὰρ ταῦτα τὰ ἔθνη ἐπιζητοῦσιν· οἶδεν
[1]for these things the nations seek after; [6]knows
γὰρ ὁ πατὴρ ὑμῶν ὁ οὐράνιος ὅτι
[1]for [2]the [4]Father [5]of you – [3]heavenly that
χρῄζετε τούτων ἁπάντων. **33** ζητεῖτε δὲ
ye need these things *of* all. But seek ye
πρῶτον τὴν βασιλείαν καὶ τὴν δικαιοσύνην
first the kingdom and the righteousness
αὐτοῦ, καὶ ταῦτα πάντα προστεθήσεται
of him, and these things all shall be added
ὑμῖν. **34** μὴ οὖν μεριμνήσητε εἰς τὴν
to you. Therefore be ye not anxious for the
αὔριον, ἡ γὰρ αὔριον μεριμνήσει
morrow, for the morrow will be anxious
ἑαυτῆς· ἀρκετὸν τῇ ἡμέρᾳ ἡ κακία αὐτῆς.
of itself; sufficient to the day the evil of it.

how God clothes the grass
of the field, which is here
today and tomorrow is
thrown into the fire, will he
not much more clothe you,
O you of little faith? 31So do
not worry, saying, 'What
shall we eat?' or 'What
shall we drink?' or 'What
shall we wear?' 32For the
pagans run after all these
things, and your heavenly
Father knows that you
need them. 33But seek first
his kingdom and his righteousness, and all these
things will be given to you
as well. 34Therefore do not
worry about tomorrow, for
tomorrow will worry about
itself. Each day has enough
trouble of its own.

Chapter 7

Concerning Judging Others

"DO not judge lest
you be judged.
2"For in the way you
judge, you will be judged;
and by your standard of
measure, it will be mea-
sured to you.
3"And why do you look
at the speck that is in your
brother's eye, but do not
notice the log that is in your
own eye?
4"Or how can you say to
your brother, 'Let me take
the speck out of your eye,'
and behold, the log is in
your own eye?
5"You hypocrite, first
take the log out of your own
eye, and then you will see
clearly to take the speck
out of your brother's eye.
6"Do not give what is
holy to dogs, and do not
throw your pearls before
swine, lest they trample
them under their feet, and
turn and tear you to pieces.

Encouragement to Pray

7"Ask, and it shall be

7 Μὴ κρίνετε, ἵνα μὴ κριθῆτε· **2** ἐν ᾧ
Judge not, lest ye be judged; [3]with [2]what
γὰρ κρίματι κρίνετε κριθήσεσθε, καὶ
[1]for judgment ye judge ye shall be judged, and
ἐν ᾧ μέτρῳ μετρεῖτε μετρηθήσεται ὑμῖν.
with what measure ye measure it shall be measured to you.
3 τί δὲ βλέπεις τὸ κάρφος τὸ ἐν
And why seest thou the chip – in
τῷ ὀφθαλμῷ τοῦ ἀδελφοῦ σου, τὴν
the eye of the brother of thee, [2]the
δὲ ἐν τῷ σῷ ὀφθαλμῷ δοκὸν οὐ κατα-
[1]but [4]in – [5]thine [6]eye [3]beam thou consider-
νοεῖς; **4** ἢ πῶς ἐρεῖς τῷ ἀδελφῷ σου·
est not? or how wilt thou say to the brother of thee:
ἄφες ἐκβάλω τὸ κάρφος ἐκ τοῦ ὀφθαλμοῦ
Allow [that] I may pluck *out* the chip out of the eye
σου, καὶ ἰδοὺ ἡ δοκὸς ἐν τῷ ὀφθαλμῷ
of thee, and behold the beam in the eye
σου; **5** ὑποκριτά, ἔκβαλε πρῶτον ἐκ τοῦ
of thee? hypocrite, pluck *out* first out of the
ὀφθαλμοῦ σου τὴν δοκόν, καὶ τότε
eye of thee the beam, and then
διαβλέψεις ἐκβαλεῖν τὸ κάρφος ἐκ
thou wilt see clearly to pluck *out* the chip out of
τοῦ ὀφθαλμοῦ τοῦ ἀδελφοῦ σου. **6** Μὴ
the eye of the brother of thee. not
δῶτε τὸ ἅγιον τοῖς κυσίν, μηδὲ βάλητε
Give the holy to the dogs, neither cast
τοὺς μαργαρίτας ὑμῶν ἔμπροσθεν τῶν
the pearls of you before the
χοίρων, μήποτε καταπατήσουσιν αὐτοὺς
pigs, lest they will trample them
ἐν τοῖς ποσὶν αὐτῶν καὶ στραφέντες
with the feet of them and turning
ῥήξωσιν ὑμᾶς. **7** Αἰτεῖτε, καὶ δοθήσεται
may rend you. Ask, and it shall be given

Chapter 7

Judging Others

"DO not judge, or you
too will be judged.
2For in the same way you
judge others, you will be
judged, and with the mea-
sure you use, it will be measured to you.
3"Why do you look at the
speck of sawdust in your
brother's eye and pay no
attention to the plank in
your own eye? 4How can
you say to your brother,
'Let me take the speck out
of your eye,' when all the
time there is a plank in your
own eye? 5You hypocrite,
first take the plank out of
your own eye, and then you
will see clearly to remove
the speck from your brother's eye.
6"Do not give dogs what
is sacred; do not throw
your pearls to pigs. If you
do, they may trample them
under their feet, and then
turn and tear you to pieces.

Ask, Seek, Knock

7"Ask and it will be given

given to you; seek, and you shall find; knock, and it shall be opened to you.

8“For everyone who asks receives, and he who seeks finds, and to him who knocks it shall be opened.

9“Or what man is there among you, when his son shall ask him for a loaf, will give him a stone?

10“Or if he shall ask for a fish, he will not give him a snake, will he?

11“If you then, being evil, know how to give good gifts to your children, how much more shall your Father who is in heaven give what is good to those who ask Him!

12“Therefore, however you want people to treat you, so treat them, for this is the Law and the Prophets.

Ways Contrasted
Fruits Contrasted

13“Enter by the narrow gate; for the gate is wide, and the way is broad that leads to destruction, and many are those who enter by it.

14“For the gate is small, and the way is narrow that leads to life, and few are those who find it.

15“Beware of the false prophets, who come to you in sheep's clothing, but inwardly are ravenous wolves.

16“You will know them by their fruits. Grapes are not gathered from thorn *bushes,* nor figs from thistles, are they?

17“Even so, every good tree bears good fruit; but the bad tree bears bad fruit.

18“A good tree cannot produce bad fruit, nor can a bad tree produce good fruit.

ὑμῖν· ζητεῖτε, καὶ εὑρήσετε· κρούετε,
to you; seek, and ye shall find; knock,
καὶ ἀνοιγήσεται ὑμῖν. **8** πᾶς γὰρ ὁ αἰτῶν
and it shall be opened to you. For every asking [one]
λαμβάνει, καὶ ὁ ζητῶν εὑρίσκει, καὶ
receives, and the seeking [one] finds, and
τῷ κρούοντι ἀνοιγήσεται. **9** ἢ τίς ἐστιν
to the knocking [one] it shall be opened. Or [1]what [2]is there
ἐξ ὑμῶν ἄνθρωπος, ὃν αἰτήσει ὁ υἱὸς
[4]of [5]you [3]man, whom [4]will ask [1]the [2]son
αὐτοῦ ἄρτον, μὴ λίθον ἐπιδώσει αὐτῷ;
[3]of him [5]a loaf, *not* a stone he will give him?
10 ἢ καὶ ἰχθὺν αἰτήσει, μὴ ὄφιν ἐπιδώσει
or also a fish he will ask, *not* a serpent he will give
αὐτῷ; **11** εἰ οὖν ὑμεῖς πονηροὶ ὄντες
him? If therefore ye [2]evil [1]being
οἴδατε δόματα ἀγαθὰ διδόναι τοῖς τέκνοις
know [3]gifts [2]good [1]to give to the children
ὑμῶν, πόσῳ μᾶλλον ὁ πατὴρ ὑμῶν ὁ
of you, how much more the Father of you –
ἐν τοῖς οὐρανοῖς δώσει ἀγαθὰ τοῖς
in the heavens will give good things to the [ones]
αἰτοῦσιν αὐτόν. **12** Πάντα οὖν ὅσα ἐὰν
asking him. All things therefore as many soever as
θέλητε ἵνα ποιῶσιν ὑμῖν οἱ ἄνθρωποι,
ye wish that may do to you – men,
οὕτως καὶ ὑμεῖς ποιεῖτε αὐτοῖς· οὗτος
thus also ye do to them; [2]this
γάρ ἐστιν ὁ νόμος καὶ οἱ προφῆται.
[1]for is the law and the prophets.
13 Εἰσέλθατε διὰ τῆς στενῆς πύλης·
Enter ye in through the narrow gate;
ὅτι πλατεῖα [ἡ πύλη] καὶ εὐρύχωρος
because wide the gate and broad
ἡ ὁδὸς ἡ ἀπάγουσα εἰς τὴν ἀπώλειαν,
the way – leading away to – destruction,
καὶ πολλοί εἰσιν οἱ εἰσερχόμενοι δι'
and many are the [ones] going in through
αὐτῆς· **14** ὅτι στενὴ ἡ πύλη καὶ τεθλιμ-
it; because strait the gate and made
μένη ἡ ὁδὸς ἡ ἀπάγουσα εἰς τὴν ζωήν,
narrow the way – leading away to – life,
καὶ ὀλίγοι εἰσὶν οἱ εὑρίσκοντες αὐτήν.
and few are the [ones] finding it.
15 Προσέχετε ἀπὸ τῶν ψευδοπροφητῶν,
Beware from(of) – false prophets,
οἵτινες ἔρχονται πρὸς ὑμᾶς ἐν ἐνδύμασι
who come to you in clothes
προβάτων, ἔσωθεν δέ εἰσιν λύκοι ἅρπαγες.
of sheep, but within are wolves greedy.
16 ἀπὸ τῶν καρπῶν αὐτῶν ἐπιγνώσεσθε
From the fruits of them ye will know
αὐτούς. μήτι συλλέγουσιν ἀπὸ ἀκανθῶν σταφυλὰς
them. They do not gather from thorns grapes
ἢ ἀπὸ τριβόλων σῦκα; **17** οὕτως πᾶν
or from thistles figs? So [1]every
δένδρον ἀγαθὸν καρποὺς καλοὺς ποιεῖ,
[3]tree [2]good [6]fruits [5]good [4]produces,
τὸ δὲ σαπρὸν δένδρον καρποὺς πονηροὺς
but the corrupt tree fruits evil
ποιεῖ. **18** οὐ δύναται δένδρον ἀγαθὸν
produces. [3]Cannot [2]tree [1]a good
καρποὺς πονηροὺς ἐνεγκεῖν, οὐδὲ δένδρον
[6]fruits [5]evil [4]*to* bear, nor [2]tree
σαπρὸν καρποὺς καλοὺς ἐνεγκεῖν. **19** πᾶν
[1]a corrupt [5]fruits [4]good [3]*to* bear. Every

to you; seek and you will find; knock and the door will be opened to you. 8For everyone who asks receives; he who seeks finds; and to him who knocks, the door will be opened.

9“Which of you, if his son asks for bread, will give him a stone? 10Or if he asks for a fish, will give him a snake? 11If you, then, though you are evil, know how to give good gifts to your children, how much more will your Father in heaven give good gifts to those who ask him! 12So in everything, do to others what you would have them do to you, for this sums up the Law and the Prophets.

The Narrow and Wide Gates

13“Enter through the narrow gate. For wide is the gate and broad is the road that leads to destruction, and many enter through it. 14But small is the gate and narrow the road that leads to life, and only a few find it.

A Tree and Its Fruit

15“Watch out for false prophets. They come to you in sheep's clothing, but inwardly they are ferocious wolves. 16By their fruit you will recognize them. Do people pick grapes from thornbushes, or figs from thistles? 17Likewise every good tree bears good fruit, but a bad tree bears bad fruit. 18A good tree cannot bear bad fruit, and a bad tree cannot bear good fruit.

19"Every tree that does
not bear good fruit is cut
down and thrown into the
fire.
20"So then, you will
know them by their fruits.
21"Not everyone who
says to Me, 'Lord, Lord,'
will enter the kingdom of
heaven; but he who does
the will of My Father who
is in heaven.
22"Many will say to Me
on that day, 'Lord, Lord,
did we not prophesy in
Your name, and in Your
name cast out demons, and
in Your name perform
many miracles?'
23"And then I will declare
to them, 'I never knew you;
DEPART FROM ME, YOU WHO
PRACTICE LAWLESSNESS.'

The Two Foundations

24"Therefore everyone
who hears these words of
Mine, and acts upon them,
may be compared to a wise
man, who built his house
upon the rock.
25"And the rain descend-
ed, and the floods came,
and the winds blew, and
burst against that house;
and *yet* it did not fall, for it
had been founded upon the
rock.
26"And everyone who
hears these words of Mine,
and does not act upon
them, will be like a foolish
man, who built his house
upon the sand.
27"And the rain descend-
ed, and the floods came,
and the winds blew, and
burst against that house;
and it fell, and great was its
fall."
28The result was that
when Jesus had finished

δένδρον μὴ ποιοῦν καρπὸν καλὸν ἐκκόπτεται
tree not producing fruit good is cut down
καὶ εἰς πῦρ βάλλεται. **20** ἄρα γε ἀπὸ
and into fire is cast. Therefore from
τῶν καρπῶν αὐτῶν ἐπιγνώσεσθε αὐτούς.
the fruits of them ye will know them.
21 Οὐ πᾶς ὁ λέγων μοι κύριε κύριε,
Not everyone saying to me Lord[,] Lord,
εἰσελεύσεται εἰς τὴν βασιλείαν τῶν οὐρανῶν,
will enter into the kingdom of the heavens,
ἀλλ' ὁ ποιῶν τὸ θέλημα τοῦ πατρός
but the [one] doing the will of the Father
μου τοῦ ἐν τοῖς οὐρανοῖς. **22** πολλοὶ
of me – in the heavens. Many
ἐροῦσίν μοι ἐν ἐκείνῃ τῇ ἡμέρᾳ· κύριε
will say to me in that – day· Lord[,]
κύριε, οὐ τῷ σῷ ὀνόματι ἐπροφητεύσαμεν,
Lord, not – in thy name we prophesied,
καὶ τῷ σῷ ὀνόματι δαιμόνια ἐξεβάλομεν,
and – in thy name demons we expelled,
καὶ τῷ σῷ ὀνόματι δυνάμεις πολλὰς
and – in thy name mighty works many
ἐποιήσαμεν; **23** καὶ τότε ὁμολογήσω
did? and then I will declare
αὐτοῖς ὅτι οὐδέποτε ἔγνων ὑμᾶς· ἀπο-
to them[,] – Never I knew you; de-
χωρεῖτε ἀπ' ἐμοῦ οἱ ἐργαζόμενοι τὴν
part from me the [ones] working –
ἀνομίαν.
lawlessness.

24 Πᾶς οὖν ὅστις ἀκούει μου τοὺς
Everyone therefore who hears of me –
λόγους τούτους καὶ ποιεῖ αὐτούς,
words these and does them,
ὁμοιωθήσεται ἀνδρὶ φρονίμῳ, ὅστις ᾠκοδό-
shall be likened man to a prudent, who built
μησεν αὐτοῦ τὴν οἰκίαν ἐπὶ τὴν πέτραν.
of him the house on the rock.
25 καὶ κατέβη ἡ βροχὴ καὶ ἦλθον οἱ
And came down the rain and came the
ποταμοὶ καὶ ἔπνευσαν οἱ ἄνεμοι καὶ
rivers and blew the winds and
προσέπεσαν τῇ οἰκίᾳ ἐκείνῃ, καὶ οὐκ
fell against – house that, and not
ἔπεσεν· τεθεμελίωτο γὰρ ἐπὶ τὴν
it fell; for it had been founded on the
πέτραν. **26** καὶ πᾶς ὁ ἀκούων μου
rock. And everyone hearing of me
τοὺς λόγους τούτους καὶ μὴ ποιῶν
– words these and not doing
αὐτοὺς ὁμοιωθήσεται ἀνδρὶ μωρῷ, ὅστις
them shall be likened man to a foolish, who
ᾠκοδόμησεν αὐτοῦ τὴν οἰκίαν ἐπὶ τὴν
built of him the house on the
ἄμμον. **27** καὶ κατέβη ἡ βροχὴ καὶ
sand. And came down the rain and
ἦλθον οἱ ποταμοὶ καὶ ἔπνευσαν οἱ
came the rivers and blew the
ἄνεμοι καὶ προσέκοψαν τῇ οἰκίᾳ ἐκείνῃ,
winds and beat against – house that,
καὶ ἔπεσεν, καὶ ἦν ἡ πτῶσις αὐτῆς
and it fell, and was the fall of it
μεγάλη.
great.

28 Καὶ ἐγένετο ὅτε ἐτέλεσεν ὁ Ἰησοῦς
And it came to pass when finished – Jesus

19Every tree that does not
bear good fruit is cut down
and thrown into the fire.
20Thus, by their fruit you
will recognize them.
21"Not everyone who
says to me, 'Lord, Lord,'
will enter the kingdom of
heaven, but only he who
does the will of my Father
who is in heaven. 22Many
will say to me on that day,
'Lord, Lord, did we not
prophesy in your name,
and in your name drive out
demons and perform many
miracles?' 23Then I will tell
them plainly, 'I never knew
you. Away from me, you
evildoers!'

The Wise and Foolish Builders

24"Therefore everyone
who hears these words of
mine and puts them into
practice is like a wise man
who built his house on the
rock. 25The rain came
down, the streams rose,
and the winds blew and
beat against that house; yet
it did not fall, because it
had its foundation on the
rock. 26But everyone who
hears these words of mine
and does not put them into
practice is like a foolish
man who built his house on
sand. 27The rain came
down, the streams rose,
and the winds blew and
beat against that house,
and it fell with a great
crash."
28When Jesus had fin-

these words, the multitudes were amazed at His teaching;

[29]for He was teaching them as *one* having authority, and not as their scribes.

τοὺς λόγους τούτους, ἐξεπλήσσοντο οἱ
– words these, were astounded the
ὄχλοι ἐπὶ τῇ διδαχῇ αὐτοῦ· 29 ἦν γὰρ
crowds at the teaching of him; for he was
διδάσκων αὐτοὺς ὡς ἐξουσίαν ἔχων, καὶ
teaching them as authority having, and
οὐχ ὡς οἱ γραμματεῖς αὐτῶν.
not as the scribes of them.

ished saying these things,
the crowds were amazed at
his teaching, [29]because he
taught as one who had au-
thority, and not as their
teachers of the law.

Chapter 8

Jesus Cleanses a Leper
The Centurion's Faith

AND when He had come down from the mountain, great multitudes followed Him.

[2]And behold, a leper came to Him, and bowed down to Him, saying, "Lord, if You are willing, You can make me clean."

[3]And He stretched out His hand and touched him, saying, "I am willing; be cleansed." And immediately his leprosy was cleansed.

[4]And Jesus *said to him, "See that you tell no one; but go, show yourself to the priest, and present the offering that Moses commanded, for a testimony to them."

[5]And when He had entered Capernaum, a centurion came to Him, entreating Him,

[6]and saying, "Lord, my servant is lying paralyzed at home, suffering great pain."

[7]And He *said to him, "I will come and heal him."

[8]But the centurion answered and said, "Lord, I am not worthy for You to come under my roof, but just say the word, and my servant will be healed.

[9]"For I, too, am a man under authority, with soldiers under me; and I say to this one, 'Go!' and he goes, and to another, 'Come!' and he comes, and to my slave, 'Do this!' and he does *it*."

[10]Now when Jesus heard *this*, He marveled, and said to those who were following, "Truly I say to you, I

8 Καταβάντος δὲ αὐτοῦ ἀπὸ τοῦ ὄρους
And coming down him[a] from the mountain
=as he came down
ἠκολούθησαν αὐτῷ ὄχλοι πολλοί. 2 καὶ
followed him crowds many. And
ἰδοὺ λεπρὸς προσελθὼν προσεκύνει αὐτῷ
behold a leper approaching worshipped him
λέγων· κύριε, ἐὰν θέλῃς, δύνασαί με
saying: Lord, if thou art willing, thou art able me
καθαρίσαι. 3 καὶ ἐκτείνας τὴν χεῖρα
to cleanse. And stretching out the(his) hand
ἥψατο αὐτοῦ λέγων· θέλω, καθαρίσθητι.
he touched him saying: I am willing, be thou cleansed.
καὶ εὐθέως ἐκαθαρίσθη αὐτοῦ ἡ λέπρα.
And immediately was cleansed of him the leprosy.
4 καὶ λέγει αὐτῷ ὁ Ἰησοῦς· ὅρα μηδενὶ
And says to him – Jesus: See *to* no one
εἴπῃς, ἀλλὰ ὕπαγε σεαυτὸν δεῖξον τῷ
thou tellest, but go thyself show to the
ἱερεῖ καὶ προσένεγκον τὸ δῶρον ὃ
priest and offer the gift which
προσέταξεν Μωϋσῆς, εἰς μαρτύριον αὐτοῖς.
commanded Moses, for a testimony to them.
5 Εἰσελθόντος δὲ αὐτοῦ εἰς Καφαρναοὺμ
And entering him[a] into Capernaum,
=as he entered
προσῆλθεν αὐτῷ ἑκατόνταρχος παρακαλῶν
approached *to* him a centurion beseeching
αὐτὸν 6 καὶ λέγων· κύριε, ὁ παῖς μου
him and saying: Lord, the boy of me
βέβληται ἐν τῇ οἰκίᾳ παραλυτικός,
has been laid [aside] in the house a paralytic,
δεινῶς βασανιζόμενος. 7 λέγει αὐτῷ·
terribly *being* tortured. He says to him:
ἐγὼ ἐλθὼν θεραπεύσω αὐτόν. 8 ἀποκριθεὶς
I coming will heal him. answering
δὲ ὁ ἑκατόνταρχος ἔφη· κύριε, οὐκ εἰμὶ
But the centurion said: Lord, I am not
ἱκανὸς ἵνα μου ὑπὸ τὴν στέγην εἰσέλθῃς·
worthy that of me under the roof thou mayest enter;
ἀλλὰ μόνον εἰπὲ λόγῳ, καὶ ἰαθήσεται ὁ παῖς
but only say in a word, and will be healed the boy
μου. 9 καὶ γὰρ ἐγὼ ἄνθρωπός εἰμι
of me. [3]also [1]For [2]I [5]a man [4]am
ὑπὸ ἐξουσίαν, ἔχων ὑπ' ἐμαυτὸν στρατιώτας,
under authority, having under myself soldiers,
καὶ λέγω τούτῳ· πορεύθητι, καὶ πορεύεται,
and I say to this: Go, and he goes,
καὶ ἄλλῳ· ἔρχου, καὶ ἔρχεται, καὶ τῷ
and to another: Come, and he comes, and to the
δούλῳ μου· ποίησον τοῦτο, καὶ ποιεῖ.
slave of me: Do this, and he does [it].
10 ἀκούσας δὲ ὁ Ἰησοῦς ἐθαύμασεν
And hearing – Jesus marvelled
καὶ εἶπεν τοῖς ἀκολουθοῦσιν· ἀμὴν λέγω
and said to the [ones] following: Truly I tell

Chapter 8

The Man With Leprosy

WHEN he came down
from the mountain-
side, large crowds followed
him. [2]A man with leprosy[e]
came and knelt before him
and said, "Lord, if you are
willing, you can make me
clean."
[3]Jesus reached out his
hand and touched the man.
"I am willing," he said.
"Be clean!" Immediately
he was cured[f] of his leprosy. [4]Then Jesus said to him,
"See that you don't tell
anyone. But go, show
yourself to the priest and
offer the gift Moses com-
manded, as a testimony to
them."

The Faith of the Centurion

[5]When Jesus had entered
Capernaum, a centurion
came to him, asking for
help. [6]"Lord," he said,
"my servant lies at home
paralyzed and in terrible
suffering."
[7]Jesus said to him, "I will
go and heal him."
[8]The centurion replied,
"Lord, I do not deserve to
have you come under my
roof. But just say the word,
and my servant will be
healed. [9]For I myself am a
man under authority, with
soldiers under me. I tell this
one, 'Go,' and he goes; and
that one, 'Come,' and he
comes. I say to my servant,
'Do this,' and he does it."
[10]When Jesus heard this,
he was astonished and said
to those following him, "I
tell you the truth, I have not

[e]2 The Greek word was used for various diseases affecting the skin—not necessarily leprosy.
[f]3 Greek *made clean*

have not found such great
faith with anyone in Israel.
11"And I say to you, that
many shall come from east
and west, and [a]recline *at*
the table with Abraham,
and Isaac, and Jacob, in the
kingdom of heaven;
12but the sons of the kingdom shall be cast out into
the outer darkness; in that
place there shall be weeping and gnashing of teeth."
13And Jesus said to the
centurion, "Go your way;
let it be done to you as you
have believed." And the
servant was healed that
very hour.

Peter's Mother-in-law Healed
Many Healed

14And when Jesus had
come to Peter's home, He
saw his mother-in-law lying
sick in bed with a fever.
15And He touched her
hand, and the fever left her;
and she arose, and waited
on Him.
16And when evening had
come, they brought to Him
many who were demon-
possessed; and He cast out
the spirits with a word, and
healed all who were ill
17in order that what was
spoken through Isaiah the
prophet might be fulfilled,
saying, "HE HIMSELF TOOK
OUR INFIRMITIES, AND CAR-
RIED AWAY OUR DISEASES."

Discipleship Tested

18Now when Jesus saw a
crowd around Him, He
gave orders to depart to the
other side.
19And a certain scribe
came and said to Him,
"Teacher, I will follow
You wherever You go."
20And Jesus *said to him,
"The foxes have holes, and
the birds of the air *have*
nests; but the Son of Man

ὑμῖν, παρ' οὐδενὶ τοσαύτην πίστιν ἐν τῷ
you, from no one such faith in –
Ἰσραὴλ εὗρον. 11 λέγω δὲ ὑμῖν ὅτι
Israel I found. And I tell you that
πολλοὶ ἀπὸ ἀνατολῶν καὶ δυσμῶν ἥξουσιν
many from east and west will come
καὶ ἀνακλιθήσονται μετὰ Ἀβραὰμ καὶ
and will recline with Abraham and
Ἰσαὰκ καὶ Ἰακὼβ ἐν τῇ βασιλείᾳ τῶν
Isaac and Jacob in the kingdom of the
οὐρανῶν· 12 οἱ δὲ υἱοὶ τῆς βασιλείας
heavens; but the sons of the kingdom
ἐκβληθήσονται εἰς τὸ σκότος τὸ ἐξώτερον·
will be cast out into the darkness – outer;
ἐκεῖ ἔσται ὁ κλαυθμὸς καὶ ὁ βρυγμὸς
there will be the weeping and the gnashing
τῶν ὀδόντων. 13 καὶ εἶπεν ὁ Ἰησοῦς τῷ
of the teeth. And said – Jesus to the
ἑκατοντάρχῃ· ὕπαγε, ὡς ἐπίστευσας γενη-
centurion: Go, as thou believedst let it
θήτω σοι. καὶ ἰάθη ὁ παῖς ἐν τῇ
be to thee. And was healed the boy in –
ὥρᾳ ἐκείνῃ.
hour that.

14 Καὶ ἐλθὼν ὁ Ἰησοῦς εἰς τὴν οἰκίαν
And coming – Jesus into the house
Πέτρου εἶδεν τὴν πενθερὰν αὐτοῦ βεβλη-
of Peter he saw the mother-in-law of him *having been*
μένην καὶ πυρέσσουσαν· 15 καὶ ἥψατο
laid [aside] and fever-stricken; and he touched
τῆς χειρὸς αὐτῆς, καὶ ἀφῆκεν αὐτὴν ὁ
the hand of her, and left her the
πυρετός· καὶ ἠγέρθη, καὶ διηκόνει αὐτῷ.
fever; and she arose, and ministered to him.

16 Ὀψίας δὲ γενομένης προσήνεγκαν
And evening coming[a] they brought
= when evening came
αὐτῷ δαιμονιζομένους πολλούς· καὶ ἐξέβαλεν
to him *being* demon-possessed many; and he expelled
τὰ πνεύματα λόγῳ, καὶ πάντας τοὺς
the spirits with a word, and all the [ones]
= those
κακῶς ἔχοντας ἐθεράπευσεν· 17 ὅπως
ill having he healed; so that
who were ill
πληρωθῇ τὸ ῥηθὲν διὰ Ἠσαΐου τοῦ
was fulfilled the [thing] spoken through Isaiah the
προφήτου λέγοντος· αὐτὸς τὰς ἀσθενείας
prophet saying: He the weaknesses
ἡμῶν ἔλαβεν καὶ τὰς νόσους ἐβάστασεν.
of us took and the diseases he bore.

18 Ἰδὼν δὲ ὁ Ἰησοῦς ὄχλον περὶ
But [2]seeing – [1]Jesus a crowd around
αὐτὸν ἐκέλευσεν ἀπελθεῖν εἰς τὸ πέραν.
him commanded to go away to the other side.
19 Καὶ προσελθὼν εἷς γραμματεὺς εἶπεν
And approaching one scribe said
αὐτῷ· διδάσκαλε, ἀκολουθήσω σοι
to him: Teacher, I will follow thee
ὅπου ἐὰν ἀπέρχῃ. 20 καὶ λέγει αὐτῷ
wherever thou mayest go. And says to him
ὁ Ἰησοῦς· αἱ ἀλώπεκες φωλεοὺς ἔχουσιν
– Jesus: The foxes holes have
καὶ τὰ πετεινὰ τοῦ οὐρανοῦ κατα-
and the birds of the heaven nests,
σκηνώσεις, ὁ δὲ υἱὸς τοῦ ἀνθρώπου
but the Son – of man

found anyone in Israel with
such great faith. 11I say to
you that many will come
from the east and the west,
and will take their places at
the feast with Abraham,
Isaac and Jacob in the kingdom of heaven. 12But the
subjects of the kingdom
will be thrown outside, into
the darkness, where there
will be weeping and gnashing of teeth."
13Then Jesus said to the
centurion, "Go! It will be
done just as you believed it
would." And his servant
was healed at that very
hour.

Jesus Heals Many

14When Jesus came into
Peter's house, he saw Pe-
ter's mother-in-law lying in
bed with a fever. 15He
touched her hand and the
fever left her, and she got
up and began to wait on
him.
16When evening came,
many who were demon-
possessed were brought to
him, and he drove out the
spirits with a word and
healed all the sick. 17This
was to fulfill what was spoken through the prophet
Isaiah:

"He took up our
infirmities
and carried our
diseases."[g]

The Cost of Following Jesus

18When Jesus saw the
crowd around him, he gave
orders to cross to the other
side of the lake. 19Then a
teacher of the law came to
him and said, "Teacher, I
will follow you wherever
you go."
20Jesus replied, "Foxes
have holes and birds of the
air have nests, but the Son
of Man has no place to lay

[a]Or, *dine*

[g]*17* Isaiah 53:4

has nowhere to lay His
head.''
21And another of the dis-
ciples said to Him, ''Lord,
permit me first to go and
bury my father.''
22But Jesus *said to him,
''Follow Me; and allow the
dead to bury their own
dead.''
23And when He got into
the boat, His disciples followed Him.
24And behold, there arose
a great storm in the sea, so
that the boat was covered
with the waves; but He
Himself was asleep.
25And they came to *Him,*
and awoke Him, saying,
''Save *us,* Lord; we are
perishing!''
26And He *said to them,
''Why are you timid, you
men of little faith?'' Then
He arose, and rebuked the
winds and the sea; and it
became perfectly calm.
27And the men marveled,
saying, ''What kind of a
man is this, that even the
winds and the sea obey
Him?''

Jesus Casts Out Demons

28And when He had come
to the other side into the
country of the Gadarenes,
two men who were demon-
possessed met Him as they
were coming out of the
tombs; *they were* so ex-
ceedingly violent that no
one could pass by that
road.
29And behold, they cried
out, saying, ''What do we
have to do with You, Son of
God? Have You come here
to torment us before the
time?''
30Now there was at a dis-
tance from them a herd of
many swine feeding.
31And the demons *began*
to entreat Him, saying, ''If
You are *going to* cast us
out, send us into the herd of

οὐκ ἔχει ποῦ τὴν κεφαλὴν κλίνῃ.
has not where the(his) head he may lay.
21 ἕτερος δὲ τῶν μαθητῶν εἶπεν
And another of the disciples said
αὐτῷ· κύριε, ἐπίτρεψόν μοι πρῶτον
to him: Lord, allow me first
ἀπελθεῖν καὶ θάψαι τὸν πατέρα μου.
to go away and bury the father of me.
22 ὁ δὲ Ἰησοῦς λέγει αὐτῷ· ἀκολούθει
– But Jesus says to him: Follow thou
μοι, καὶ ἄφες τοὺς νεκροὺς θάψαι τοὺς
me, and leave the dead to bury the
ἑαυτῶν νεκρούς.
of themselves dead.
23 Καὶ ἐμβάντι αὐτῷ εἰς τὸ πλοῖον,
And embarking him[e] in the ship,
=as he embarked
ἠκολούθησαν αὐτῷ οἱ μαθηταὶ αὐτοῦ.
followed him the disciples of him.
24 καὶ ἰδοὺ σεισμὸς μέγας ἐγένετο ἐν
And behold storm a great there was in
τῇ θαλάσσῃ, ὥστε τὸ πλοῖον καλύπτ-
the sea, so as the ship to be en-
εσθαι ὑπὸ τῶν κυμάτων· αὐτὸς δὲ ἐκάθευδεν.
veloped by the waves; but he was sleeping.
25 καὶ προσελθόντες ἤγειραν αὐτὸν λέγοντες·
And approaching they roused him saying:
κύριε, σῶσον, ἀπολλύμεθα. **26** καὶ λέγει
Lord, save, we are perishing. And he says
αὐτοῖς· τί δειλοί ἐστε, ὀλιγόπιστοι;
to them: Why fearful are ye, little-faiths?
τότε ἐγερθεὶς ἐπετίμησεν τοῖς ἀνέμοις καὶ
Then rising he rebuked the winds and
τῇ θαλάσσῃ, καὶ ἐγένετο γαλήνη μεγάλη.
the sea, and there was calm a great.
27 οἱ δὲ ἄνθρωποι ἐθαύμασαν λέγοντες·
And the men marvelled saying:
ποταπός ἐστιν οὗτος, ὅτι καὶ οἱ ἄνεμοι
Of what sort is this [man], that even the winds
καὶ ἡ θάλασσα αὐτῷ ὑπακούουσιν;
and the sea him obey?
28 Καὶ ἐλθόντος αὐτοῦ εἰς τὸ πέραν εἰς
And coming him[a] to the other side into
=when he came
τὴν χώραν τῶν Γαδαρηνῶν ὑπήντησαν
the country of the Gadarenes met
αὐτῷ δύο δαιμονιζόμενοι ἐκ τῶν μνημείων
him two demon-possessed out of the tombs
ἐξερχόμενοι, χαλεποὶ λίαν, ὥστε μὴ
coming *out,* dangerous exceedingly, so as not
ἰσχύειν τινὰ παρελθεῖν διὰ τῆς ὁδοῦ
to be able anyone[b] to pass through – way
ἐκείνης. **29** καὶ ἰδοὺ ἔκραξαν λέγοντες·
that. And behold they cried out saying:
τί ἡμῖν καὶ σοί, υἱὲ τοῦ θεοῦ; ἦλθες
What to us and to thee, Son – of God? camest thou
ὧδε πρὸ καιροῦ βασανίσαι ἡμᾶς; **30** ἦν
here before [the] time to torture us? there was
δὲ μακρὰν ἀπ' αὐτῶν ἀγέλη χοίρων
Now far off from them a herd pigs
πολλῶν βοσκομένη. **31** οἱ δὲ δαίμονες
of many feeding. And the demons
παρεκάλουν αὐτὸν λέγοντες· εἰ ἐκβάλλεις
besought him saying: If thou expellest
ἡμᾶς, ἀπόστειλον ἡμᾶς εἰς τὴν ἀγέλην
us, send us into the herd

his head.''
21Another disciple said to
him, ''Lord, first let me go
and bury my father.''
22But Jesus told him,
''Follow me, and let the
dead bury their own dead.''

Jesus Calms the Storm

23Then he got into the
boat and his disciples followed him. 24Without
warning, a furious storm
came up on the lake, so that
the waves swept over the
boat. But Jesus was sleeping. 25The disciples went
and woke him, saying,
''Lord, save us! We're going to drown!''
26He replied, ''You of little faith, why are you so
afraid?'' Then he got up
and rebuked the winds and
the waves, and it was completely calm.
27The men were amazed
and asked, ''What kind of
man is this? Even the winds
and the waves obey him!''

The Healing of Two
Demon-possessed Men

28When he arrived at the
other side in the region of
the Gadarenes,[h] two de-
mon-possessed men com-
ing from the tombs met
him. They were so violent
that no one could pass that
way. 29''What do you want
with us, Son of God?'' they
shouted. ''Have you come
here to torture us before
the appointed time?''
30Some distance from
them a large herd of pigs
was feeding. 31The demons
begged Jesus, ''If you drive
us out, send us into the
herd of pigs.''

[h]28 Some manuscripts *Gergesenes;* others *Gerasenes*

swine."
32And He said to them, "Begone!" And they came out, and went into the swine, and behold, the whole herd rushed down the steep bank into the sea and perished in the waters.
33And the herdsmen ran away, and went to the city, and reported everything, including the *incident* of the demoniacs.
34And behold, the whole city came out to meet Jesus; and when they saw Him, they entreated *Him* to depart from their region.

Chapter 9

A Paralytic Cured

AND getting into a boat, He crossed over, and came to His own city.
2And behold, they were bringing to Him a paralytic, lying on a bed; and Jesus seeing their faith said to the paralytic, "Take courage, My son, your sins are forgiven."
3And behold, some of the scribes said to themselves, "This *fellow* blasphemes."
4And Jesus knowing their thoughts said, "Why are you thinking evil in your hearts?
5"For which is easier, to say, 'Your sins are forgiven,' or to say, 'Rise, and walk'?
6"But in order that you may know that the Son of Man has authority on earth to forgive sins"—then, He *said to the paralytic—"Rise, take up your bed, and go home."
7And he rose, and went home.
8But when the multitudes saw *this*, they were filled with awe, and glorified God, who had given such authority to men.

τῶν χοίρων. 32 καὶ εἶπεν αὐτοῖς·
of the pigs. And he said to them:
ὑπάγετε. οἱ δὲ ἐξελθόντες ἀπῆλθον εἰς
Go ye. So the coming out [ones] went away into
τοὺς χοίρους· καὶ ἰδοὺ ὥρμησεν πᾶσα ἡ
the pigs; and behold rushed all the
ἀγέλη κατὰ τοῦ κρημνοῦ εἰς τὴν θάλασσαν,
herd down the precipice into the sea,
καὶ ἀπέθανον ἐν τοῖς ὕδασιν. 33 οἱ
and died in the waters. the
δὲ βόσκοντες ἔφυγον, καὶ ἀπελθόντες
But feeding [ones] fled, and going away
εἰς τὴν πόλιν ἀπήγγειλαν πάντα καὶ
into the city reported all things and
τὰ τῶν δαιμονιζομένων. 34 καὶ ἰδοὺ
the [things] of the demon-possessed [ones]. And behold
πᾶσα ἡ πόλις ἐξῆλθεν εἰς ὑπάντησιν
all the city came out with a view to a meeting [with]
τῷ Ἰησοῦ, καὶ ἰδόντες αὐτὸν παρεκάλεσαν
– Jesus, and seeing [2]him [1]besought
ὅπως μεταβῇ ἀπὸ τῶν ὁρίων αὐτῶν.
so that he might remove from the borders of them.

9 Καὶ ἐμβὰς εἰς πλοῖον διεπέρασεν,
And embarking in a ship he crossed over,
καὶ ἦλθεν εἰς τὴν ἰδίαν πόλιν. 2 Καὶ
and came into the(his) own city. And
ἰδοὺ προσέφερον αὐτῷ παραλυτικὸν ἐπὶ
behold they brought to him a paralytic on
κλίνης βεβλημένον. καὶ ἰδὼν ὁ Ἰησοῦς
a mattress *having been* laid. And [2]seeing – [1]Jesus
τὴν πίστιν αὐτῶν εἶπεν τῷ παραλυτικῷ
the faith of them said to the paralytic:
θάρσει, τέκνον, ἀφίενταί σου αἱ ἁμαρτίαι.
Be of good cheer, child, are forgiven of thee the sins.
3 καὶ ἰδού τινες τῶν γραμματέων εἶπαν
And behold some of the scribes said
ἐν ἑαυτοῖς· οὗτος βλασφημεῖ. 4 καὶ
among themselves: This [man] blasphemes. And
εἰδὼς ὁ Ἰησοῦς τὰς ἐνθυμήσεις αὐτῶν
[2]knowing – [1]Jesus the thoughts of them
εἶπεν· ἱνατί ἐνθυμεῖσθε πονηρὰ ἐν ταῖς
said: Why think ye evil things in the
καρδίαις ὑμῶν; 5 τί γάρ ἐστιν εὐκοπώ-
hearts of you? for which is easier,
τερον, εἰπεῖν· ἀφίενταί σου αἱ ἁμαρτίαι, ἢ
to say: [4]are forgiven [3]of thee [1]The [2]sins, or
εἰπεῖν· ἔγειρε καὶ περιπάτει; 6 ἵνα δὲ
to say: Rise and walk? But in order that
εἰδῆτε ὅτι ἐξουσίαν ἔχει ὁ υἱὸς τοῦ
ye may know that authority has the Son –
ἀνθρώπου ἐπὶ τῆς γῆς ἀφιέναι ἁμαρτίας
of man on the earth to forgive sins—
τότε λέγει τῷ παραλυτικῷ· ἔγειρε ἆρόν
then he says to the paralytic: Rise[,] take
σου τὴν κλίνην καὶ ὕπαγε εἰς τὸν οἶκόν
of thee the mattress and go to the house
σου. 7 καὶ ἐγερθεὶς ἀπῆλθεν εἰς τὸν
of thee. And rising he went away to the
οἶκον αὐτοῦ. 8 ἰδόντες δὲ οἱ ὄχλοι
house of him. But seeing the crowds
ἐφοβήθησαν καὶ ἐδόξασαν τὸν θεὸν τὸν
feared and glorified – God the [one]
δόντα ἐξουσίαν τοιαύτην τοῖς ἀνθρώποις.
giving [2]authority [1]such – to men.

32He said to them, "Go!"
So they came out and went
into the pigs, and the whole
herd rushed down the steep
bank into the lake and died
in the water. 33Those tending the pigs ran off, went
into the town and reported
all this, including what had
happened to the demon-
possessed men. 34Then the
whole town went out to
meet Jesus. And when they
saw him, they pleaded with
him to leave their region.

Chapter 9

Jesus Heals a Paralytic

JESUS stepped into a
boat, crossed over and
came to his own town.
2Some men brought to him
a paralytic, lying on a mat.
When Jesus saw their faith,
he said to the paralytic,
"Take heart, son; your sins
are forgiven."
3At this, some of the
teachers of the law said to
themselves, "This fellow is
blaspheming!"
4Knowing their thoughts,
Jesus said, "Why do you
entertain evil thoughts in
your hearts? 5Which is easier: to say, 'Your sins are
forgiven,' or to say, 'Get up
and walk'? 6But so that you
may know that the Son of
Man has authority on earth
to forgive sins. . . ." Then
he said to the paralytic,
"Get up, take your mat and
go home." 7And the man
got up and went home.
8When the crowd saw this,
they were filled with awe;
and they praised God, who
had given such authority to
men.

Matthew Called

9And as Jesus passed on
from there, He saw a man,
called Matthew, sitting in
the tax office; and He *said
to him, "Follow Me!" And
he rose, and followed Him.
10And it happened that as
He was reclining *at the table* in the house, behold
many tax-gatherers and
sinners came and were dining with Jesus and His disciples.
11And when the Pharisees
saw *this,* they said to His
disciples, "Why is your
Teacher eating with the
tax-gatherers and sin-
ners?"
12But when He heard
this, He said, "*It is* not
those who are healthy who
need a physician, but those
who are sick.
13"But go and learn what
this means, 'I DESIRE COM-
PASSION, [v]AND NOT SACRI-
FICE,' for I did not come to
call the righteous, but sinners."
14Then the disciples of
John *came to Him, say-
ing, "Why do we and the
Pharisees fast, but Your
disciples do not fast?"
15And Jesus said to them,
"The attendants of the
bridegroom cannot mourn
as long as the bridegroom is
with them, can they? But
the days will come when
the bridegroom is taken
away from them, and then
they will fast.
16"But no one puts a
patch of unshrunk cloth on
an old garment; for the
patch pulls away from the
garment, and a worse tear
results.
17"Nor do *men* put new
wine into old wineskins;
otherwise the wineskins

v I.e., more than

9 Καὶ παράγων ὁ Ἰησοῦς ἐκεῖθεν εἶδεν
And [2]passing by – [1]Jesus thence saw
ἄνθρωπον καθήμενον ἐπὶ τὸ τελώνιον,
a man sitting at the custom house,
Μαθθαῖον λεγόμενον, καὶ λέγει αὐτῷ·
Matthew named, and says to him:
ἀκολούθει μοι. καὶ ἀναστὰς ἠκολούθησεν
Follow me. And rising up he followed
αὐτῷ. 10 Καὶ ἐγένετο αὐτοῦ ἀνακει-
him. And it came to pass him reclin-
=as he was reclining
μένου ἐν τῇ οἰκίᾳ, καὶ ἰδοὺ πολλοὶ
ing[a] in the house, and behold many
τελῶναι καὶ ἁμαρτωλοὶ ἐλθόντες συνανέκειντο
tax-collectors and sinners coming reclined at table with
τῷ Ἰησοῦ καὶ τοῖς μαθηταῖς αὐτοῦ.
– Jesus and the disciples of him.
11 καὶ ἰδόντες οἱ Φαρισαῖοι ἔλεγον τοῖς
And [3]seeing [1]the [2]Pharisees said to the
μαθηταῖς αὐτοῦ· διὰ τί μετὰ τῶν τελωνῶν
disciples of him: Why with – tax-collectors
καὶ ἁμαρτωλῶν ἐσθίει ὁ διδάσκαλος ὑμῶν;
and sinners eats the teacher of you?
12 ὁ δὲ ἀκούσας εἶπεν· οὐ χρείαν
But he hearing said: Not need
ἔχουσιν οἱ ἰσχύοντες ἰατροῦ ἀλλ' οἱ
have the [ones] being strong of a physician but the [ones]
=those
κακῶς ἔχοντες. 13 πορευθέντες δὲ μάθετε
ill having. But going learn ye
who are ill.
τί ἐστιν· ἔλεος θέλω καὶ οὐ θυσίαν· οὐ
what it is: Mercy I desire and not sacrifice; not
γὰρ ἦλθον καλέσαι δικαίους ἀλλὰ
for I came to call righteous [people] but
ἁμαρτωλούς.
sinners.
14 Τότε προσέρχονται αὐτῷ οἱ μαθηταὶ
Then approach *to* him the disciples
Ἰωάννου λέγοντες· διὰ τί ἡμεῖς καὶ οἱ
of John saying: Why we and the
Φαρισαῖοι νηστεύομεν, οἱ δὲ μαθηταί
Pharisees fast, but the disciples
σου οὐ νηστεύουσιν; 15 καὶ εἶπεν
of thee fast not? And said
αὐτοῖς ὁ Ἰησοῦς· μὴ δύνανται οἱ
to them – Jesus: *not* Can the
υἱοὶ τοῦ νυμφῶνος πενθεῖν, ἐφ' ὅσον
sons of the bridechamber *to* mourn, so long as
μετ' αὐτῶν ἐστιν ὁ νυμφίος; ἐλεύσονται
with them is the bridegroom? [3]will come
δὲ ἡμέραι ὅταν ἀπαρθῇ ἀπ' αὐτῶν ὁ
[1]but [2]days when is taken away from them the
νυμφίος, καὶ τότε νηστεύσουσιν. 16 οὐδεὶς
bridegroom, and then they will fast. no one
δὲ ἐπιβάλλει ἐπίβλημα ῥάκους ἀγνάφου
Now puts *on* a patch cloth of unfulled
ἐπὶ ἱματίῳ παλαιῷ· αἴρει γὰρ τὸ
on garment an old; for takes away the
πλήρωμα αὐτοῦ ἀπὸ τοῦ ἱματίου, καὶ
fullness of it from the garment, and
χεῖρον σχίσμα γίνεται. 17 οὐδὲ
a worse rent becomes. Neither
βάλλουσιν οἶνον νέον εἰς ἀσκοὺς
do they put wine new into wineskins
παλαιούς· εἰ δὲ μή γε, ῥήγνυνται
old; otherwise, are burst

The Calling of Matthew

9As Jesus went on from
there, he saw a man named
Matthew sitting at the tax
collector's booth. "Follow
me," he told him, and Matthew got up and followed
him.
10While Jesus was having
dinner at Matthew's house,
many tax collectors and
"sinners" came and ate
with him and his disciples.
11When the Pharisees saw
this, they asked his disciples, "Why does your
teacher eat with tax collectors and 'sinners'?"
12On hearing this, Jesus
said, "It is not the healthy
who need a doctor, but the
sick. 13But go and learn
what this means: 'I desire
mercy, not sacrifice.'[i] For
I have not come to call the
righteous, but sinners."

Jesus Questioned About Fasting

14Then John's disciples
came and asked him,
"How is it that we and the
Pharisees fast, but your
disciples do not fast?"
15Jesus answered, "How
can the guests of the bridegroom mourn while he is
with them? The time will
come when the bridegroom
will be taken from them;
then they will fast.
16"No one sews a patch
of unshrunk cloth on an old
garment, for the patch will
pull away from the gar-
ment, making the tear
worse. 17Neither do men
pour new wine into old
wineskins. If they do, the
skins will burst, the wine

i 13 Hosea 6:6

burst, and the wine pours
out, and the wineskins are
ruined; but they put new
wine into fresh wineskins,
and both are preserved."

Miracles of Healing

18 While He was saying
these things to them, be-
hold, there came a *syna-
gogue* official, and bowed
down before Him, saying,
"My daughter has just
died; but come and lay
Your hand on her, and she
will live."
19 And Jesus rose and *began* to follow him, and *so
did* His disciples.
20 And behold, a woman
who had been suffering
from a hemorrhage for
twelve years, came up be-
hind Him and touched the
fringe of His cloak;
21 for she was saying to
herself, "If I only touch
His garment, I shall get
well."
22 But Jesus turning and
seeing her said, "Daughter,
take courage; your faith has
made you well." And at
once the woman was made
well.
23 And when Jesus came
into the official's house,
and saw the flute-players,
and the crowd in noisy disorder,
24 He *began* to say, "Depart; for the girl has not
died, but is asleep." And
they *began* laughing at
Him.
25 But when the crowd
had been put out, He en-
tered and took her by the
hand; and the girl arose.
26 And this news went out
into all that land.
27 And as Jesus passed on
from there, two blind men
followed Him, crying out,
and saying, "Have mercy
on us, Son of David!"
28 And after He had come

οἱ ἀσκοί, καὶ ὁ οἶνος ἐκχεῖται καὶ
the wineskins, and the wine is poured out and
οἱ ἀσκοὶ ἀπόλλυνται. ἀλλὰ βάλλουσιν
the wineskins are destroyed. But they put
οἶνον νέον εἰς ἀσκοὺς καινούς, καὶ
wine new into wineskins fresh, and
ἀμφότεροι συντηροῦνται.
both are preserved.
18 Ταῦτα αὐτοῦ λαλοῦντος αὐτοῖς,
These things him speaking[a] to them,
=As he was speaking these things
ἰδοὺ ἄρχων [εἷς] προσελθὼν προσ-
behold ruler one approaching wor-
εκύνει αὐτῷ λέγων ὅτι ἡ θυγάτηρ
shipped him saying[,] – The daughter
μου ἄρτι ἐτελεύτησεν· ἀλλὰ ἐλθὼν
of me just now died; but coming
ἐπίθες τὴν χεῖρά σου ἐπ' αὐτήν,
lay *on* the hand of thee on her,
καὶ ζήσεται. 19 καὶ ἐγερθεὶς ὁ Ἰησοῦς
and she will live. And rising – Jesus
ἠκολούθει αὐτῷ καὶ οἱ μαθηταὶ αὐτοῦ.
followed him[,] also the disciples of him.
20 Καὶ ἰδοὺ γυνὴ αἱμορροοῦσα
And behold a woman suffering from a flow of blood
δώδεκα ἔτη προσελθοῦσα ὄπισθεν ἥψατο
twelve years approaching behind touched
τοῦ κρασπέδου τοῦ ἱματίου αὐτοῦ·
the fringe of the garment of him;
21 ἔλεγεν γὰρ ἐν ἑαυτῇ· ἐὰν μόνον
for she was saying in herself: If only
ἅψωμαι τοῦ ἱματίου αὐτοῦ, σωθήσομαι.
I may touch the garment of him, I shall be healed.
22 ὁ δὲ Ἰησοῦς στραφεὶς καὶ ἰδὼν
– And Jesus turning and seeing
αὐτὴν εἶπεν· θάρσει, θύγατερ· ἡ
her said: Be of good cheer, daughter; the
πίστις σου σέσωκέν σε. καὶ ἐσώθη
faith of thee has healed thee. And was healed
ἡ γυνὴ ἀπὸ τῆς ὥρας ἐκείνης. 23 Καὶ
the woman from – hour that. And
ἐλθὼν ὁ Ἰησοῦς εἰς τὴν οἰκίαν τοῦ ἄρχοντος
coming – Jesus into the house of the ruler
καὶ ἰδὼν τοὺς αὐλητὰς καὶ τὸν ὄχλον
and seeing the flute-players and the crowd
θορυβούμενον 24 ἔλεγεν· ἀναχωρεῖτε· οὐ
terrified he said: Depart ye; not
γὰρ ἀπέθανεν τὸ κοράσιον ἀλλὰ καθεύδει.
for died the girl but sleeps.
καὶ κατεγέλων αὐτοῦ. 25 ὅτε δὲ
And they ridiculed him. But when
ἐξεβλήθη ὁ ὄχλος, εἰσελθὼν ἐκράτησεν
was put out the crowd, entering he took hold of
τῆς χειρὸς αὐτῆς, καὶ ἠγέρθη τὸ κορα-
the hand of her, and was raised the girl.
σιον. 26 καὶ ἐξῆλθεν ἡ φήμη αὕτη
And went out – report this
εἰς ὅλην τὴν γῆν ἐκείνην. 27 Καὶ
into all – land that. And
παράγοντι ἐκεῖθεν τῷ Ἰησοῦ ἠκολούθησαν
passing by thence – Jesus[e] followed
=as Jesus passed by thence
δύο τυφλοὶ κράζοντες καὶ λέγοντες· ἐλέησον
two blind men crying out and saying: Pity
ἡμᾶς, υἱὸς Δαυίδ. 28 ἐλθόντι δὲ εἰς
us, son of David. And coming[e] into
=when he came

will run out and the wineskins will be ruined. No,
they pour new wine into
new wineskins, and both
are preserved."

A Dead Girl and a Sick Woman

18 While he was saying
this, a ruler came and knelt
before him and said, "My
daughter has just died. But
come and put your hand on
her, and she will live."
19 Jesus got up and went
with him, and so did his disciples.
20 Just then a woman who
had been subject to bleeding for twelve years came
up behind him and touched
the edge of his cloak. 21 She
said to herself, "If I only
touch his cloak, I will be
healed."
22 Jesus turned and saw
her. "Take heart, daugh-
ter," he said, "your faith
has healed you." And the
woman was healed from
that moment.
23 When Jesus entered the
ruler's house and saw the
flute players and the noisy
crowd, 24 he said, "Go
away. The girl is not dead
but asleep." But they
laughed at him. 25 After the
crowd had been put out-
side, he went in and took
the girl by the hand, and
she got up. 26 News of this
spread through all that region.

Jesus Heals the Blind and Mute

27 As Jesus went on from
there, two blind men fol-
lowed him, calling out,
"Have mercy on us, Son of
David!"
28 When he had gone in-
doors, the blind men came

into the house, the blind men came up to Him, and Jesus *said to them, "Do you believe that I am able to do this?" They *said to Him, "Yes, Lord."

29 Then He touched their eyes, saying, "Be it done to you according to your faith."

30 And their eyes were opened. And Jesus sternly warned them, saying, "See *here,* let no one know *about this!*"

31 But they went out, and spread the news about Him in all that land.

32 And as they were going out, behold, a dumb man, demon-possessed, was brought to Him.

33 And after the demon was cast out, the dumb man spoke; and the multitudes marveled, saying, "Nothing like this was ever seen in Israel."

34 But the Pharisees were saying, "He casts out the demons by the ruler of the demons."

35 And Jesus was going about all the cities and the villages, teaching in their synagogues, and proclaiming the gospel of the kingdom, and healing every kind of disease and every kind of sickness.

36 And seeing the multitudes, He felt compassion for them, because they were distressed and downcast like sheep without a shepherd.

37 Then He *said to His disciples, "The harvest is plentiful, but the workers are few.

38 "Therefore beseech the Lord of the harvest to send out workers into His harvest."

τὴν οἰκίαν προσῆλθον αὐτῷ οἱ τυφλοί,
the house approached *to* him the blind men,
καὶ λέγει αὐτοῖς ὁ Ἰησοῦς· πιστεύετε
and says to them – Jesus: Believe ye
ὅτι δύναμαι τοῦτο ποιῆσαι; λέγουσιν
that I can this *to* do? They say
αὐτῷ· ναί, κύριε. **29** τότε ἥψατο τῶν
to him: Yes, Lord. Then he touched the
ὀφθαλμῶν αὐτῶν λέγων· κατὰ τὴν
eyes of them saying: According to the
πίστιν ὑμῶν γενηθήτω ὑμῖν. **30** καὶ
faith of you let it be to you. And
ἠνεῴχθησαν αὐτῶν οἱ ὀφθαλμοί. καὶ
were opened of them the eyes. And
ἐνεβριμήθη αὐτοῖς ὁ Ἰησοῦς λέγων·
sternly admonished them – Jesus saying:
ὁρᾶτε μηδεὶς γινωσκέτω. **31** οἱ δὲ
See [2]no one [1]let [3]know. But they
ἐξελθόντες διεφήμισαν αὐτὸν ἐν ὅλῃ
going out spread about him in all
τῇ γῇ ἐκείνῃ. **32** Αὐτῶν δὲ ἐξερχομένων,
– land that. And them going out,[a]
=as they were going out,
ἰδοὺ προσήνεγκαν αὐτῷ κωφὸν δαι-
behold they brought to him a dumb man *being*
μονιζόμενον. **33** καὶ ἐκβληθέντος τοῦ
demon-possessed. And being expelled the
=when the demon was expelled
δαιμονίου ἐλάλησεν ὁ κωφός. καὶ ἐθαύμασαν
demon[a] spoke the dumb man. And marvelled
οἱ ὄχλοι λέγοντες· οὐδέποτε ἐφάνη οὕτως
the crowds saying: Never it appeared thus
ἐν τῷ Ἰσραήλ. **34** οἱ δὲ Φαρισαῖοι
in – Israel. But the Pharisees
ἔλεγον· ἐν τῷ ἄρχοντι τῶν δαιμονίων
said: By the ruler of the demons
ἐκβάλλει τὰ δαιμόνια.
he expels the demons.

35 Καὶ περιῆγεν ὁ Ἰησοῦς τὰς
And went about – Jesus the
πόλεις πάσας καὶ τὰς κώμας, διδάσκων
cities all and the villages, teaching
ἐν ταῖς συναγωγαῖς αὐτῶν καὶ κηρύσσων
in the synagogues of them and proclaiming
τὸ εὐαγγέλιον τῆς βασιλείας καὶ θεραπεύων
the gospel of the kingdom and healing
πᾶσαν νόσον καὶ πᾶσαν μαλακίαν.
every disease and every illness.
36 Ἰδὼν δὲ τοὺς ὄχλους ἐσπλαγχνίσθη
And seeing the crowds he was filled with tenderness
περὶ αὐτῶν, ὅτι ἦσαν ἐσκυλμένοι καὶ
concerning them, because they were distressed and
ἐρριμμένοι ὡσεὶ πρόβατα μὴ ἔχοντα
prostrate as sheep not having
ποιμένα. **37** τότε λέγει τοῖς μαθηταῖς
a shepherd. Then he says to the disciples
αὐτοῦ· ὁ μὲν θερισμὸς πολύς, οἱ δὲ
of him: Indeed the harvest [is] much, but the
ἐργάται ὀλίγοι· **38** δεήθητε οὖν τοῦ κυρίου
workmen few; pray ye therefore the Lord
τοῦ θερισμοῦ ὅπως ἐκβάλῃ
of the harvest so that he may thrust forth
ἐργάτας εἰς τὸν θερισμὸν αὐτοῦ. **10** Καὶ
workmen into the harvest of him. And

to him, and he asked them, "Do you believe that I am able to do this?"

"Yes, Lord," they replied.

29 Then he touched their eyes and said, "According to your faith will it be done to you"; 30 and their sight was restored. Jesus warned them sternly, "See that no one knows about this."
31 But they went out and spread the news about him all over that region.

32 While they were going out, a man who was demon-possessed and could not talk was brought to Jesus. 33 And when the demon was driven out, the man who had been mute spoke. The crowd was amazed and said, "Nothing like this has ever been seen in Israel."

34 But the Pharisees said, "It is by the prince of demons that he drives out demons."

The Workers Are Few

35 Jesus went through all the towns and villages, teaching in their synagogues, preaching the good news of the kingdom and healing every disease and sickness. 36 When he saw the crowds, he had compassion on them, because they were harassed and helpless, like sheep without a shepherd. 37 Then he said to his disciples, "The harvest is plentiful but the workers are few. 38 Ask the Lord of the harvest, therefore, to send out workers into his harvest field."

Chapter 10

The Twelve Disciples
Instructions for Service

AND having summoned His twelve disciples, He gave them authority over unclean spirits, to cast them out, and to heal every kind of disease and every kind of sickness.

2Now the names of the twelve apostles are these: The first, Simon, who is called Peter, and Andrew his brother; and James the *son* of Zebedee, and John his brother;

3Philip and Bartholomew; Thomas and Matthew the tax-gatherer; James the *son* of Alphaeus, and Thaddaeus;

4Simon the Zealot, and Judas Iscariot, the one who betrayed Him.

5These twelve Jesus sent out after instructing them, saying, "Do not go in *the* way of *the* Gentiles, and do not enter *any* city of the Samaritans;

6but rather go to the lost sheep of the house of Israel.

7"And as you go, preach, saying, 'The kingdom of heaven is at hand.'

8"Heal *the* sick, raise *the* dead, cleanse *the* lepers, cast out demons; freely you received, freely give.

9"Do not acquire gold, or silver, or copper for your money belts,

10or a bag for *your* journey, or even two tunics, or sandals, or a staff; for the worker is worthy of his support.

11"And into whatever city or village you enter, inquire who is worthy in it; and abide there until you go away.

προσκαλεσάμενος τοὺς δώδεκα μαθητὰς
calling forward the twelve disciples
αὐτοῦ ἔδωκεν αὐτοῖς ἐξουσίαν πνευμάτων
of him he gave to them authority of(over) spirits
ἀκαθάρτων ὥστε ἐκβάλλειν αὐτά, καὶ
unclean so as to expel them, and
θεραπεύειν πᾶσαν νόσον καὶ πᾶσαν μαλα-
to heal every disease and every ill-
κίαν. **2** Τῶν δὲ δώδεκα ἀποστόλων
ness. Now of the twelve apostles
τὰ ὀνόματά ἐστιν ταῦτα· πρῶτος Σίμων
the names is(are) these: first Simon
ὁ λεγόμενος Πέτρος καὶ Ἀνδρέας ὁ
the [one] named Peter and Andrew the
ἀδελφὸς αὐτοῦ, καὶ Ἰάκωβος ὁ τοῦ
brother of him, and James the [son] –
Ζεβεδαίου καὶ Ἰωάννης ὁ ἀδελφὸς αὐτοῦ,
of Zebedee and John the brother of him,
3 Φίλιππος καὶ Βαρθολομαῖος, Θωμᾶς
Philip and Bartholomew, Thomas
καὶ Μαθθαῖος ὁ τελώνης, Ἰάκωβος
and Matthew the tax-collector, James
ὁ τοῦ Ἁλφαίου καὶ Θαδδαῖος, **4** Σίμων
the [son] – of Alphæus and Thaddæus, Simon
ὁ Καναναῖος καὶ Ἰούδας ὁ Ἰσκαριώτης
the Cananæan and Judas – Iscariot
ὁ καὶ παραδοὺς αὐτόν. **5** Τούτους
the [one] also betraying him. These
τοὺς δώδεκα ἀπέστειλεν ὁ Ἰησοῦς
– twelve sent forth – Jesus
παραγγείλας αὐτοῖς λέγων·
giving charge to them saying:
Εἰς ὁδὸν ἐθνῶν μὴ ἀπέλθητε, καὶ
Into [the] way of [the] nations go ye not, and
εἰς πόλιν Σαμαριτῶν μὴ εἰσέλθητε·
into a city of Samaritans enter not;
6 πορεύεσθε δὲ μᾶλλον πρὸς τὰ πρόβατα
but go rather unto the sheep
τὰ ἀπολωλότα οἴκου Ἰσραήλ. **7** πορευ-
the lost of [the] house of Israel. And
όμενοι δὲ κηρύσσετε λέγοντες ὅτι ἤγγικεν
going proclaim ye saying[,] – has drawn near
ἡ βασιλεία τῶν οὐρανῶν. **8** ἀσθενοῦντας
The kingdom of the heavens. Ailing [ones]
θεραπεύετε, νεκροὺς ἐγείρετε, λεπροὺς
heal ye, dead [ones] raise, lepers
καθαρίζετε, δαιμόνια ἐκβάλλετε· δωρεὰν
cleanse, demons expel; freely
ἐλάβετε, δωρεὰν δότε. **9** Μὴ κτήσησθε
ye received, freely give. Do not provide
χρυσὸν μηδὲ ἄργυρον μηδὲ χαλκὸν εἰς
gold nor silver nor brass in
τὰς ζώνας ὑμων, **10** μὴ πήραν εἰς ὁδὸν
the girdles of you, not a wallet for [the] way
μηδὲ δύο χιτῶνας μηδὲ ὑποδήματα μηδὲ
nor two tunics nor sandals nor
ῥάβδον· ἄξιος γὰρ ὁ ἐργάτης τῆς
a staff; for worthy [is] the workman of the
τροφῆς αὐτοῦ. **11** εἰς ἣν δ' ἂν πόλιν
food of him. And into whatever city
ἢ κώμην εἰσέλθητε, ἐξετάσατε τίς ἐν
or village ye may enter, inquire who in
αὐτῇ ἄξιός ἐστιν· κἀκεῖ μείνατε ἕως ἂν
it worthy is; and there remain until

Chapter 10

Jesus Sends Out the Twelve

HE called his twelve disciples to him and gave them authority to drive out evil[j] spirits and to heal every disease and sickness.

2These are the names of
the twelve apostles: first,
Simon (who is called Peter)
and his brother Andrew;
James son of Zebedee, and
his brother John; 3Philip
and Bartholomew; Thomas
and Matthew the tax col-
lector; James son of Al-
phaeus, and Thaddaeus;
4Simon the Zealot and Ju-
das Iscariot, who betrayed
him.

5These twelve Jesus sent
out with the following instructions: "Do not go
among the Gentiles or enter
any town of the Samari-
tans. 6Go rather to the lost
sheep of Israel. 7As you go,
preach this message: 'The
kingdom of heaven is near.'
8Heal the sick, raise the
dead, cleanse those who
have leprosy,[k] drive out
demons. Freely you have
received, freely give. 9Do
not take along any gold or
silver or copper in your
belts; 10take no bag for the
journey, or extra tunic, or
sandals or a staff; for the
worker is worth his keep.

11"Whatever town or vil-
lage you enter, search for
some worthy person there
and stay at his house until

j1 Greek *unclean*
k8 The Greek word was used for various diseases affecting the skin—not necessarily leprosy.

12“And as you enter the
house, give it your greeting.
13“And if the house is
worthy, let your *greeting of*
peace come upon it; but if it
is not worthy, let your
greeting of peace return to
you.
14“And whoever does not
receive you, nor heed your
words, as you go out of that
house or that city, shake off
the dust of your feet.
15“Truly I say to you, it
will be more tolerable for
the land of Sodom and
Gomorrah in the day of
judgment, than for that
city.

A Hard Road before Them

16“Behold, I send you out
as sheep in the midst of
wolves; therefore be
shrewd as serpents, and innocent as doves.
17“But beware of men;
for they will deliver you up
to *the* courts, and scourge
you in their synagogues;
18and you shall even be
brought before governors
and kings for My sake, as a
testimony to them and to
the Gentiles.
19“But when they deliver
you up, do not become anxious about how or what you
will speak; for it shall be
given you in that hour what
you are to speak.
20“For it is not you who
speak, but *it is* the Spirit of
your Father who speaks in
you.
21“And brother will de-
liver up brother to death,
and a father *his* child; and
children will rise up against
parents, and cause them to
be put to death.
22“And you will be hated
by all on account of My
name, but it is the one who
has endured to the end who
will be saved.
23“But whenever they

ἐξέλθητε. **12** εἰσερχόμενοι δὲ εἰς τὴν
ye may go out. And entering into the
οἰκίαν ἀσπάσασθε αὐτήν· **13** καὶ ἐὰν μὲν
house greet it; and if indeed
ᾖ ἡ οἰκία ἀξία, ἐλθάτω ἡ εἰρήνη ὑμῶν
be the house worthy, let come the peace of you
ἐπ' αὐτήν· ἐὰν δὲ μὴ ᾖ ἀξία, ἡ εἰρήνη
on it; but if it be not worthy, the peace
ὑμῶν πρὸς ὑμᾶς ἐπιστραφήτω. **14** καὶ
of you unto you let return. And
ὃς ἂν μὴ δέξηται ὑμᾶς μηδὲ ἀκούσῃ
whoever may not receive you nor hear
τοὺς λόγους ὑμῶν, ἐξερχόμενοι ἔξω
the words of you, going *out* outside
τῆς οἰκίας ἢ τῆς πόλεως ἐκείνης ἐκτινά-
– house or – city that shake
ξατε τὸν κονιορτὸν τῶν ποδῶν ὑμῶν.
off the dust of the feet of you.
15 ἀμὴν λέγω ὑμῖν, ἀνεκτότερον ἔσται
Truly I tell you, more tolerable it will be [for]
γῇ Σοδόμων καὶ Γομόρρων ἐν ἡμέρᾳ κρίσεως
[the] land of Sodom and Gomorra in [the] day of judgment
ἢ τῇ πόλει ἐκείνῃ. **16** Ἰδοὺ ἐγὼ
than [for] – city that. Behold I
ἀποστέλλω ὑμᾶς ὡς πρόβατα ἐν μέσῳ
send forth you as sheep in [the] midst
λύκων· γίνεσθε οὖν φρόνιμοι ὡς οἱ
of wolves; be ye therefore prudent as –
ὄφεις καὶ ἀκέραιοι ὡς αἱ περιστεραί.
serpents and harmless as – doves.
17 Προσέχετε δὲ ἀπὸ τῶν ἀνθρώπων·
And beware from(of) – men;
παραδώσουσιν γὰρ ὑμᾶς εἰς συνέδρια,
for they will deliver up you to councils,
καὶ ἐν ταῖς συναγωγαῖς αὐτῶν μαστιγώ-
and in the synagogues of them they will
σουσιν ὑμᾶς· **18** καὶ ἐπὶ ἡγεμόνας δὲ καὶ
scourge you; and before leaders and also
βασιλεῖς ἀχθήσεσθε ἕνεκεν ἐμοῦ, εἰς
kings ye will be led for the sake of me, for
μαρτύριον αὐτοῖς καὶ τοῖς ἔθνεσιν.
a testimony to them and to the nations.
19 ὅταν δὲ παραδῶσιν ὑμᾶς, μὴ μεριμνή-
But when they deliver up you, do not be
σητε πῶς ἢ τί λαλήσητε· δοθήσεται
anxious how or what ye may say; [2]it will be given
γὰρ ὑμῖν ἐν ἐκείνῃ τῇ ὥρᾳ τί λαλήσητε·
[1]for to you in that – hour what ye may say;
20 οὐ γὰρ ὑμεῖς ἐστε οἱ λαλοῦντες,
for not ye are the [ones] speaking,
ἀλλὰ τὸ πνεῦμα τοῦ πατρὸς ὑμῶν τὸ
but the Spirit of the Father of you the [one]
λαλοῦν ἐν ὑμῖν. **21** παραδώσει δὲ
speaking in you. And [2]will deliver up
ἀδελφὸς • ἀδελφὸν εἰς θάνατον καὶ πατὴρ
[1]brother brother to death and father
τέκνον, καὶ ἐπαναστήσονται τέκνα ἐπὶ
child, and will stand up children against
γονεῖς καὶ θανατώσουσιν αὐτούς. **22** καὶ
parents and put to death them. And
ἔσεσθε μισούμενοι ὑπὸ πάντων διὰ
ye will be *being* hated by all men on account of
τὸ ὄνομά μου· ὁ δὲ ὑπομείνας εἰς
the name of me; but the [one] enduring to
τέλος, οὗτος σωθήσεται. **23** ὅταν δὲ
[the] end, this will be saved. But when

you leave. 12As you enter
the home, give it your
greeting. 13If the home is
deserving, let your peace
rest on it; if it is not, let
your peace return to you.
14If anyone will not wel-
come you or listen to your
words, shake the dust off
your feet when you leave
that home or town. 15I tell
you the truth, it will be
more bearable for Sodom
and Gomorrah on the day
of judgment than for that
town. 16I am sending you
out like sheep among
wolves. Therefore be as
shrewd as snakes and as innocent as doves.
17“Be on your guard
against men; they will hand
you over to the local councils and flog you in their
synagogues. 18On my ac-
count you will be brought
before governors and kings
as witnesses to them and to
the Gentiles. 19But when
they arrest you, do not
worry about what to say or
how to say it. At that time
you will be given what to
say, 20for it will not be you
speaking, but the Spirit of
your Father speaking
through you.
21“Brother will betray
brother to death, and a father his child; children will
rebel against their parents
and have them put to death.
22All men will hate you because of me, but he who
stands firm to the end will
be saved. 23When you are

persecute you in this city,
flee to the next; for truly I
say to you, you shall not
finish *going through* the
cities of Israel, until the
Son of Man comes.

The Meaning of Discipleship

24"A disciple is not above
his teacher, nor a slave
above his master.
25"It is enough for the
disciple that he become as
his teacher, and the slave
as his master. If they have
called the head of the house
Beelzebul, how much more
the members of his house-
hold!
26"Therefore do not fear
them, for there is nothing
covered that will not be revealed, and hidden that will
not be known.
27"What I tell you in the
darkness, speak in the
light; and what you hear
whispered in *your* ear, proclaim upon the housetops.
28"And do not fear those
who kill the body, but are
unable to kill the soul; but
rather fear Him who is able
to destroy both soul and
body in hell.
29"Are not two sparrows
sold for a [w]cent? And *yet*
not one of them will fall to
the ground apart from your
Father.
30"But the very hairs of
your head are all num-
bered.
31"Therefore do not fear;
you are of more value than
many sparrows.
32"Everyone therefore
who shall confess Me be-
fore men, I will also confess him before My Father
who is in heaven.
33"But whoever shall
deny Me before men, I will
also deny him before My

[w] Gr., *assarion*, the smallest copper coin

διώκωσιν ὑμᾶς ἐν τῇ πόλει ταύτῃ,
they persecute you in – city this,
φεύγετε εἰς τὴν ἑτέραν· ἀμὴν γὰρ
flee ye to – [an]other; for truly
λέγω ὑμῖν, οὐ μὴ τελέσητε τὰς πόλεις
I tell you, by no means ye will complete the cities
[τοῦ] Ἰσραὴλ ἕως ἔλθῃ ὁ υἱὸς τοῦ ἀν-
– of Israel until comes the Son – of
θρώπου. 24 Οὐκ ἔστιν μαθητὴς ὑπὲρ
man. not is A disciple above
τὸν διδάσκαλον οὐδὲ δοῦλος ὑπὲρ τὸν
the teacher nor a slave above the
κύριον αὐτοῦ. 25 ἀρκετὸν τῷ μαθητῇ
lord of him. Enough for the disciple
ἵνα γένηται ὡς ὁ διδάσκαλος αὐτοῦ,
that he be as the teacher of him,
καὶ ὁ δοῦλος ὡς ὁ κύριος αὐτοῦ. εἰ
and the slave as the lord of him. If
τὸν οἰκοδεσπότην Βεεζεβοὺλ ἐπεκάλεσαν,
the housemaster Beelzebub they called,
πόσῳ μᾶλλον τοὺς οἰκιακοὺς αὐτοῦ.
how much more the members of [the] household of him.
26 μὴ οὖν φοβηθῆτε αὐτούς· οὐδὲν γάρ
Therefore fear ye not them; for nothing
ἐστιν κεκαλυμμένον ὃ οὐκ ἀποκαλυφ-
is *having been* veiled which will not be un-
θήσεται, καὶ κρυπτὸν ὃ οὐ γνωσθήσεται.
veiled, and hidden which will not be made known.
27 ὃ λέγω ὑμῖν ἐν τῇ σκοτίᾳ, εἴπατε
What I say to you in the darkness, say ye
ἐν τῷ φωτί· καὶ ὃ εἰς τὸ οὖς ἀκούετε,
in the light; and what in the ear ye hear,
κηρύξατε ἐπὶ τῶν δωμάτων. 28 καὶ
proclaim on the housetops. And
μὴ φοβεῖσθε ἀπὸ τῶν ἀποκτεννόντων
do not fear – the [ones] killing
τὸ σῶμα, τὴν δὲ ψυχὴν μὴ δυναμένων
the body, but the soul not *being* able
ἀποκτεῖναι· φοβεῖσθε δὲ μᾶλλον τὸν
to kill; but fear ye rather the [one]
δυνάμενον καὶ ψυχὴν καὶ σῶμα ἀπολέσαι
being able both soul and body to destroy
ἐν γεέννῃ. 29 οὐχὶ δύο στρουθία ἀσσα-
in gehenna. Not two sparrows of(for) a
ρίου πωλεῖται; καὶ ἓν ἐξ αὐτῶν οὐ
farthing are sold? and one of them not
πεσεῖται ἐπὶ τὴν γῆν ἄνευ τοῦ πατρὸς
will fall on the earth without the Father
ὑμῶν. 30 ὑμῶν δὲ καὶ αἱ τρίχες τῆς
of you. But of you even the hairs of the
κεφαλῆς πᾶσαι ἠριθμημέναι εἰσίν. 31 μὴ
head all *having been* numbered are. not
οὖν φοβεῖσθε· πολλῶν στρουθίων διαφέρετε
Therefore fear ye; [3]many [4]sparrows [2]excel
ὑμεῖς. 32 Πᾶς οὖν ὅστις ὁμολογήσει
[1]ye. Everyone therefore who shall confess
ἐν ἐμοὶ ἔμπροσθεν τῶν ἀνθρώπων,
– me before – men,
ὁμολογήσω κἀγὼ ἐν αὐτῷ ἔμπροσθεν
will confess I also – him before
τοῦ πατρός μου τοῦ ἐν τοῖς οὐρανοῖς·
the Father of me – in the heavens;
33 ὅστις δ' ἂν ἀρνήσηται με ἔμπροσθεν
and whoever denies me before
τῶν ἀνθρώπων, ἀρνήσομαι κἀγὼ αὐτὸν
– men, will deny I also him

persecuted in one place,
flee to another. I tell you
the truth, you will not finish
going through the cities of
Israel before the Son of
Man comes.
24"A student is not above
his teacher, nor a servant
above his master. 25It is
enough for the student to
be like his teacher, and the
servant like his master. If
the head of the house has
been called Beelzebub,[l]
how much more the mem-
bers of his household!
26"So do not be afraid of
them. There is nothing concealed that will not be disclosed, or hidden that will
not be made known.
27What I tell you in the
dark, speak in the daylight;
what is whispered in your
ear, proclaim from the
roofs. 28Do not be afraid of
those who kill the body but
cannot kill the soul. Rather, be afraid of the One who
can destroy both soul and
body in hell. 29Are not two
sparrows sold for a pen-
ny[m]? Yet not one of them
will fall to the ground apart
from the will of your Fa-
ther. 30And even the very
hairs of your head are all
numbered. 31So don't be
afraid; you are worth more
than many sparrows.
32"Whoever acknowl-
edges me before men, I will
also acknowledge him be-
fore my Father in heaven.
33But whoever disowns me
before men, I will disown

[l]25 Greek *Beezeboul* or *Beelzeboul*
[m]29 Greek *an assarion*

Father who is in heaven.
34"Do not think that I
came to bring peace on the
earth; I did not come to
bring peace, but a sword.
35"For I came to SET A
MAN AGAINST HIS FATHER,
AND A DAUGHTER AGAINST
HER MOTHER, AND A DAUGH-
TER-IN-LAW AGAINST HER
MOTHER-IN-LAW;
36and A MAN'S ENEMIES
WILL BE THE MEMBERS OF HIS
HOUSEHOLD.
37"He who loves father
or mother more than Me is
not worthy of Me; and he
who loves son or daughter
more than Me is not worthy
of Me.
38"And he who does not
take his cross and follow after Me is not worthy of Me.
39"He who has found his
life shall lose it, and he who
has lost his life for My sake
shall find it.
40"He who receives you
receives Me, and he who
receives Me receives Him
who sent Me.
41"He who receives a
prophet in *the* name of
a prophet shall receive a
prophet's reward; and he
who receives a righteous
man in the name of a righteous man shall receive a
righteous man's reward.
42"And whoever in the
name of a disciple gives to
one of these little ones even
a cup of cold water to
drink, truly I say to you he
shall not lose his reward."

ἔμπροσθεν τοῦ πατρός μου τοῦ ἐν
before the Father of me – in
τοῖς οὐρανοῖς. **34** Μὴ νομίσητε ὅτι
the heavens. Do not suppose that
ἦλθον βαλεῖν εἰρήνην ἐπὶ τὴν γῆν· οὐκ ἦλθον
I came to bring peace on the earth; I came not
βαλεῖν εἰρήνην ἀλλὰ μάχαιραν. **35** ἦλθον γὰρ
to bring peace but a sword. For I came
διχάσαι ἄνθρωπον κατὰ τοῦ πατρὸς
to make hostile a man against the father
αὐτοῦ καὶ θυγατέρα κατὰ τῆς μητρὸς
of him and a daughter against the mother
αὐτῆς καὶ νύμφην κατὰ τῆς πενθερᾶς
of her and a bride against the mother-in-law
αὐτῆς, **36** καὶ ἐχθροὶ τοῦ ἀνθρώπου οἱ
of her, and [the] enemies – of a man the
οἰκιακοὶ αὐτοῦ. **37** Ὁ φιλῶν πατέρα
members of [the] household of him. The [one] loving father
ἢ μητέρα ὑπὲρ ἐμὲ οὐκ ἔστιν μου ἄξιος·
or mother beyond me is not of me worthy;
καὶ ὁ φιλῶν υἱὸν ἢ θυγατέρα ὑπὲρ
and the [one] loving son or daughter beyond
ἐμὲ οὐκ ἔστιν μου ἄξιος· **38** καὶ ὃς
me is not of me worthy; and [he] who
οὐ λαμβάνει τὸν σταυρὸν αὐτοῦ καὶ
takes not the cross of him and
ἀκολουθεῖ ὀπίσω μου, οὐκ ἔστιν μου
follows after me, is not of me
ἄξιος. **39** ὁ εὑρὼν τὴν ψυχὴν αὐτοῦ
worthy. The [one] finding the life of him
ἀπολέσει αὐτήν, καὶ ὁ ἀπολέσας τὴν
will lose it, and the [one] losing the
ψυχὴν αὐτοῦ ἕνεκεν ἐμοῦ εὑρήσει αὐτήν.
life of him for the sake of me will find it.
40 Ὁ δεχόμενος ὑμᾶς ἐμὲ δέχεται, καὶ
The [one] receiving you me receives, and
ὁ ἐμὲ δεχόμενος δέχεται τὸν
the [one] me receiving receives the [one]
ἀποστείλαντά με. **41** ὁ δεχόμενος προ-
having sent me. The [one] receiving a pro-
φήτην εἰς ὄνομα προφήτου μισθὸν
phet in [the] name of a prophet [the] reward
προφήτου λήμψεται, καὶ ὁ δεχόμενος
of a prophet will receive, and the [one] receiving
δίκαιον εἰς ὄνομα δικαίου μισθὸν
a righteous man in [the] name of a righteous man [the] reward
δικαίου λήμψεται. **42** καὶ ὃς ἐὰν ποτίσῃ
of a righteous man will receive. And whoever gives to drink
ἕνα τῶν μικρῶν τούτων ποτήριον ψυχροῦ
one – of these little [ones] a cup of cold water
μόνον εἰς ὄνομα μαθητοῦ, ἀμὴν λέγω ὑμῖν,
only in [the] name of a disciple, truly I tell you,
οὐ μὴ ἀπολέσῃ τὸν μισθὸν αὐτοῦ.
on no account will he lose the reward of him.

him before my Father in
heaven.
34"Do not suppose that I
have come to bring peace
to the earth. I did not come
to bring peace, but a sword.
35For I have come to turn

" 'a man against his
father,
a daughter against her
mother,
a daughter-in-law against
her mother-in-law—
36 a man's enemies will
be the members of
his own
household.'[n]

37"Anyone who loves his
father or mother more than
me is not worthy of me;
anyone who loves his son
or daughter more than me
is not worthy of me; 38and
anyone who does not take
his cross and follow me is
not worthy of me. 39Who-
ever finds his life will lose
it, and whoever loses his
life for my sake will find it.
40"He who receives you
receives me, and he who
receives me receives the
one who sent me. 41Anyone
who receives a prophet because he is a prophet will
receive a prophet's reward,
and anyone who receives a
righteous man because he
is a righteous man will receive a righteous man's reward. 42And if anyone
gives even a cup of cold water to one of these little
ones because he is my disciple, I tell you the truth, he
will certainly not lose his
reward."

Chapter 11

John's Questions

AND it came about that when Jesus had finished giving instructions to His twelve disciples, He departed from there to teach and preach in their cities.

11 Καὶ ἐγένετο ὅτε ἐτέλεσεν ὁ
And it came to pass when ended –
Ἰησοῦς διατάσσων τοῖς δώδεκα μαθηταῖς
Jesus giving charge to the twelve disciples
αὐτοῦ, μετέβη ἐκεῖθεν τοῦ διδάσκειν
of him, he removed thence – to teach[d]
καὶ κηρύσσειν ἐν ταῖς πόλεσιν αὐτῶν.
and to proclaim[d] in the cities of them.

Chapter 11

Jesus and John the Baptist

AFTER Jesus had finished instructing his twelve disciples, he went on from there to teach and preach in the towns of Galilee.[o]

[n]36 Micah 7:6
[o]1 Greek *in their towns*

2 Now when John in pris-
on heard of the works of
Christ, he sent *word* by his
disciples,
3 and said to Him, "Are
You the Expected One, or
shall we look for someone
else?"
4 And Jesus answered
and said to them, "Go and
report to John what you
hear and see:
5 *the* BLIND RECEIVE SIGHT
and *the* lame walk, *the* lepers are cleansed and *the*
deaf hear, and *the* dead are
raised up, and *the* POOR
HAVE THE GOSPEL PREACHED
TO THEM.
6 "And blessed is he who
keeps from stumbling over
Me."

Jesus' Tribute to John

7 And as these were going
away, Jesus began to speak
to the multitudes about
John, "What did you go out
into the wilderness to look
at? A reed shaken by the
wind?
8 "But what did you go
out to see? A man dressed
in soft *clothing*? Behold,
those who wear soft *clothing* are in kings' palaces.
9 "But why did you go
out? To see a prophet? Yes,
I say to you, and one who is
more than a prophet.
10 "This is the one about
whom it is written,
'BEHOLD, I SEND MY MESSENGER BEFORE YOUR FACE,
WHO WILL PREPARE YOUR WAY BEFORE YOU.'
11 "Truly, I say to you,
among those born of
women there has not arisen
anyone greater than John
the Baptist; yet he who is
least in the kingdom of
heaven is greater than he.
12 "And from the days of
John the Baptist until now
the kingdom of heaven suffers violence, and violent
men take it by force.
13 "For all the prophets
and the Law prophesied

2 Ὁ δὲ Ἰωάννης ἀκούσας ἐν τῷ
– But John hearing in the
δεσμωτηρίῳ τὰ ἔργα τοῦ Χριστοῦ,
prison the works – of Christ,
πέμψας διὰ τῶν μαθητῶν αὐτοῦ 3 εἶπεν
sending through the disciples of him said
αὐτῷ· σὺ εἶ ὁ ἐρχόμενος, ἢ ἕτερον
to him: Thou art the coming [one], or another
προσδοκῶμεν; 4 καὶ ἀποκριθεὶς ὁ
may we expect? And answering –
Ἰησοῦς εἶπεν αὐτοῖς· πορευθέντες ἀπαγ-
Jesus said to them: Going report
γείλατε Ἰωάννῃ ἃ ἀκούετε καὶ βλέπετε·
ye to John [the things] which ye hear and see:
5 τυφλοὶ ἀναβλέπουσιν καὶ χωλοὶ
blind men see again and lame men
περιπατοῦσιν, λεπροὶ καθαρίζονται καὶ κωφοὶ
walk, lepers are cleansed and deaf men
ἀκούουσιν, καὶ νεκροὶ ἐγείρονται καὶ
hear, and dead men are raised and
πτωχοὶ εὐαγγελίζονται· 6 καὶ μακάριός
poor men are evangelized; and blessed
ἐστιν ὃς ἐὰν μὴ σκανδαλισθῇ ἐν ἐμοί.
is whoever is not offended in me.
7 Τούτων δὲ πορευομένων ἤρξατο ὁ
And these going* began –
= as these were going
Ἰησοῦς λέγειν τοῖς ὄχλοις περὶ Ἰωάννου·
Jesus to say to the crowds concerning John:
τί ἐξήλθατε εἰς τὴν ἔρημον θεάσασθαι;
What went ye out into the wilderness to see?
κάλαμον ὑπὸ ἀνέμου σαλευόμενον; 8 ἀλλὰ
a reed by wind being shaken? But
τί ἐξήλθατε ἰδεῖν; ἄνθρωπον ἐν μαλακοῖς
what went ye out to see? a man in soft material
ἠμφιεσμένον; ἰδοὺ οἱ τὰ μαλακὰ
having been clothed? Behold[,] the [ones] – soft material
φοροῦντες ἐν τοῖς οἴκοις τῶν βασιλέων. 9 ἀλλὰ
wearing [are] in the houses – of kings. But
τί ἐξήλθατε; προφήτην ἰδεῖν; ναὶ λέγω
why went ye out? a prophet to see? Yes[,] I tell
ὑμῖν, καὶ περισσότερον προφήτου. 10 οὗτός
you, and more [than] a prophet. This
ἐστιν περὶ οὗ γέγραπται· ἰδοὺ ἐγὼ
is he concerning whom it has been written: Behold[,] I
ἀποστέλλω τὸν ἄγγελόν μου πρὸ προσώπου
send forth the messenger of me before [the] face
σου, ὃς κατασκευάσει τὴν ὁδόν σου
of thee, who will prepare the way of thee
ἔμπροσθέν σου. 11 ἀμὴν λέγω ὑμῖν,
before thee. Truly I tell you,
οὐκ ἐγήγερται ἐν γεννητοῖς γυναικῶν
there has not arisen among [those] born of women
μείζων Ἰωάννου τοῦ βαπτιστοῦ· ὁ δὲ
a greater [than] John the Baptist; but the
μικρότερος ἐν τῇ βασιλείᾳ τῶν οὐρανῶν
lesser in the kingdom of the heavens
μείζων αὐτοῦ ἐστιν. 12 ἀπὸ δὲ τῶν
greater [than] he is. And from the
ἡμερῶν Ἰωάννου τοῦ βαπτιστοῦ ἕως
days of John the Baptist until
ἄρτι ἡ βασιλεία τῶν οὐρανῶν βιάζεται,
now the kingdom of the heavens is forcibly treated,
καὶ βιασταὶ ἁρπάζουσιν αὐτήν. 13 πάντες γὰρ
and forceful men seize it. For all
οἱ προφῆται καὶ ὁ νόμος ἕως
the prophets and the law until

2 When John heard in prison what Christ was doing,
he sent his disciples 3 to ask
him, "Are you the one who
was to come, or should we
expect someone else?"
4 Jesus replied, "Go back
and report to John what
you hear and see: 5 The
blind receive sight, the
lame walk, those who have
leprosy[p] are cured, the
deaf hear, the dead are
raised, and the good news
is preached to the poor.
6 Blessed is the man who
does not fall away on ac-
count of me."
7 As John's disciples were
leaving, Jesus began to
speak to the crowd about
John: "What did you go out
into the desert to see? A
reed swayed by the wind?
8 If not, what did you go out
to see? A man dressed in
fine clothes? No, those
who wear fine clothes are
in kings' palaces. 9 Then
what did you go out to see?
A prophet? Yes, I tell you,
and more than a prophet.
10 This is the one about
whom it is written:
"'I will send my messenger ahead of you,
who will prepare your way before you.'[q]
11 I tell you the truth:
Among those born of wom-
en there has not risen anyone greater than John the
Baptist; yet he who is least
in the kingdom of heaven is
greater than he. 12 From the
days of John the Baptist until now, the kingdom of
heaven has been forcefully
advancing, and forceful
men lay hold of it. 13 For all
the Prophets and the Law
prophesied until John.

p5 The Greek word was used for various diseases affecting the skin—not necessarily leprosy.
q10 Mal. 3:1

until John.
14"And if you care to ac-
cept *it,* he himself is Elijah,
who was to come.
15"He who has ears to
hear, let him hear.
16"But to what shall I
compare this generation? It
is like children sitting in the
market places, who call out
to the other *children,*
17and say, 'We played the
flute for you, and you did
not dance; we sang a dirge,
and you did not mourn.'
18"For John came neither
eating nor drinking, and
they say, 'He has a de-
mon!'
19"The Son of Man came
eating and drinking, and
they say, 'Behold, a gluttonous man and a drunk-
ard, a friend of tax-gatherers and sinners!' Yet wisdom is vindicated by her
deeds."

The Unrepenting Cities

20Then He began to re-
proach the cities in which
most of His miracles were
done, because they did not
repent.
21"Woe to you, Chora-
zin! Woe to you, Beth-
saida! For if the miracles
had occurred in Tyre and
Sidon which occurred in
you, they would have re-
pented long ago in sack-
cloth and ashes.
22"Nevertheless I say to
you, it shall be more tolerable for Tyre and Sidon in
the day of judgment, than
for you.
23"And you, Capernaum,
will not be exalted to
heaven, will you? You shall
descend to Hades; for if the
miracles had occurred in
Sodom which occurred in
you, it would have re-
mained to this day.
24"Nevertheless I say to
you that it shall be more tolerable for the land of
Sodom in *the* day of judgment, than for you."

Come to Me

25At that time Jesus an-
swered and said, "I praise

Ἰωάννου ἐπροφήτευσαν· **14** καὶ εἰ θέλετε
John prophesied; and if ye are willing
δέξασθαι, αὐτός ἐστιν Ἡλίας ὁ μέλλων
to receive [it *or* him], he is Elias the [one] about
ἔρχεσθαι. **15** ὁ ἔχων ὦτα ἀκουέτω.
to come. The [one] having ears let him hear.
16 Τίνι δὲ ὁμοιώσω τὴν γενεὰν ταύτην;
But to what shall I liken – generation this?
ὁμοία ἐστὶν παιδίοις καθημένοις ἐν ταῖς
Like it is to children sitting in the
ἀγοραῖς ἃ προσφωνοῦντα τοῖς ἑτέροις
marketplaces who calling to the others
17 λέγουσιν· ηὐλήσαμεν ὑμῖν καὶ οὐκ
say: We piped to you and not
ὠρχήσασθε· ἐθρηνήσαμεν καὶ οὐκ ἐκόψασθε.
ye did dance; we lamented and ye did not mourn.
18 ἦλθεν γὰρ Ἰωάννης μήτε ἐσθίων μήτε
For came John neither eating nor
πίνων, καὶ λέγουσιν· δαιμόνιον ἔχει.
drinking, and they say: a demon He has.
19 ἦλθεν ὁ υἱὸς τοῦ ἀνθρώπου ἐσθίων καὶ
Came the Son – of man eating and
πίνων, καὶ λέγουσιν· ἰδοὺ ἄνθρωπος
drinking, and they say: Behold[,] a man
φάγος καὶ οἰνοπότης, τελωνῶν φίλος καὶ
gluttonous and a wine-drinker, of tax-collectors a friend and
ἁμαρτωλῶν. καὶ ἐδικαιώθη ἡ σοφία ἀπὸ
of sinners. And was(is) justified – wisdom from(by)
τῶν ἔργων αὐτῆς.
the works of her.
20 Τότε ἤρξατο ὀνειδίζειν τὰς πόλεις
Then he began to reproach the cities
ἐν αἷς ἐγένοντο αἱ πλεῖσται δυνάμεις
in which happened the very many powerful deeds
αὐτοῦ, ὅτι οὐ μετενόησαν· **21** οὐαί σοι,
of him, because they repented not: Woe to thee,
Χοραζίν· οὐαί σοι, Βηθσαϊδά· ὅτι εἰ
Chorazin; woe to thee, Bethsaida; because if
ἐν Τύρῳ καὶ Σιδῶνι ἐγένοντο αἱ δυνάμεις
in Tyre and Sidon happened the powerful deeds
αἱ γενόμεναι ἐν ὑμῖν, πάλαι ἂν
– having happened in you, long ago –
ἐν σάκκῳ καὶ σποδῷ μετενόησαν.
in sackcloth and ashes they would have repented.
22 πλὴν λέγω ὑμῖν, Τύρῳ καὶ Σιδῶνι
However I tell you, For Tyre and for Sidon
ἀνεκτότερον ἔσται ἐν ἡμέρᾳ κρίσεως ἢ
more tolerable it will be in [the] day of judgment than
ὑμῖν. **23** καὶ σύ, Καφαρναούμ, μὴ
for you. And thou, Capernaum, *not*
ἕως οὐρανοῦ ὑψωθήσῃ; ἕως ᾅδου
as far as heaven wast thou exalted? as far as hades
καταβήσῃ· ὅτι εἰ ἐν Σοδόμοις ἐγενήθησαν
thou shalt descend; because if in Sodom happened
αἱ δυνάμεις αἱ γενόμεναι ἐν σοί,
the powerful deeds – having happened in thee,
ἔμεινεν ἂν μέχρι τῆς σήμερον. **24** πλὴν
it would have remained until – to-day. However
λέγω ὑμῖν ὅτι γῇ Σοδόμων ἀνεκτότερον
I tell you that for [the] land of Sodom more tolerable
ἔσται ἐν ἡμέρᾳ κρίσεως ἢ σοί.
it will be in [the] day of judgment than for thee.
25 Ἐν ἐκείνῳ τῷ καιρῷ ἀποκριθεὶς
At that – time answering
ὁ Ἰησοῦς εἶπεν· ἐξομολογοῦμαί σοι,
– Jesus said: I give thanks to thee,

14And if you are willing to
accept it, he is the Elijah
who was to come. 15He
who has ears, let him hear.
16"To what can I com-
pare this generation? They
are like children sitting in
the marketplaces and calling out to others:
17" 'We played the flute
for you,
and you did not dance;
we sang a dirge,
and you did not
mourn.'
18For John came neither
eating nor drinking, and
they say, 'He has a de-
mon.' 19The Son of Man
came eating and drinking,
and they say, 'Here is a
glutton and a drunkard, a
friend of tax collectors and
"sinners." ' But wisdom is
proved right by her ac-
tions."

Woe on Unrepentant Cities

20Then Jesus began to de-
nounce the cities in which
most of his miracles had
been performed, because
they did not repent.
21"Woe to you, Korazin!
Woe to you, Bethsaida! If
the miracles that were performed in you had been
performed in Tyre and Si-
don, they would have re-
pented long ago in sack-
cloth and ashes. 22But I tell
you, it will be more bearable for Tyre and Sidon on
the day of judgment than
for you. 23And you, Capernaum, will you be lifted up
to the skies? No, you will
go down to the depths.[r] If
the miracles that were performed in you had been
performed in Sodom, it
would have remained to
this day. 24But I tell you
that it will be more bearable
for Sodom on the day of
judgment than for you."

Rest for the Weary

25At that time Jesus said,
"I praise you, Father, Lord

r23 Greek *Hades*

Thee, O Father, Lord of
heaven and earth, that
Thou didst hide these
things from *the* wise and intelligent and didst reveal
them to babes.
26"Yes, Father, for thus
it was well-pleasing in Thy
sight.
27"All things have been
handed over to Me by My
Father; and no one knows
the Son, except the Father;
nor does anyone know the
Father, except the Son,
and anyone to whom the
Son wills to reveal *Him*.
28"Come to Me, all who
are weary and heavy-laden,
and I will give you rest.
29"Take My yoke upon
you, and learn from Me, for
I am gentle and humble in
heart; and YOU SHALL FIND
REST FOR YOUR SOULS.
30"For My yoke is easy,
and My load is light."

πάτερ, κύριε τοῦ οὐρανοῦ καὶ τῆς γῆς,
Father, lord of the heaven and of the earth,
ὅτι ἔκρυψας ταῦτα ἀπὸ σοφῶν καὶ συνε-
because thou hiddest these things from wise and intel-
τῶν, καὶ ἀπεκάλυψας αὐτὰ νηπίοις·
ligent men, and didst reveal them to infants;
26 ναί, ὁ πατήρ, ὅτι οὕτως εὐδοκία
yes, – Father, because thus good pleasure
ἐγένετο ἔμπροσθέν σου. 27 Πάντα μοι
it was before thee. All things to me
παρεδόθη ὑπὸ τοῦ πατρός μου, καὶ
were delivered by the Father of me, and
οὐδεὶς ἐπιγινώσκει τὸν υἱὸν εἰ μὴ ὁ
no one fully knows the Son except the
πατήρ, οὐδὲ τὸν πατέρα τις ἐπιγινώσκει
Father, neither the Father anyone fully knows
εἰ μὴ ὁ υἱὸς καὶ ᾧ ἐὰν βούληται ὁ
except the Son and [he] to whom if wills the
υἱὸς ἀποκαλύψαι. 28 Δεῦτε πρός με
Son to reveal. Come unto me
πάντες οἱ κοπιῶντες καὶ πεφορτισμένοι,
all the [ones] labouring and *having been* burdened,
κἀγὼ ἀναπαύσω ὑμᾶς. 29 ἄρατε τὸν
and I will rest you. Take the
ζυγόν μου ἐφ' ὑμᾶς καὶ μάθετε ἀπ'
yoke of me on you and learn from
ἐμοῦ, ὅτι πραΰς εἰμι καὶ ταπεινὸς τῇ
me, because meek I am and lowly –
καρδίᾳ, καὶ εὑρήσετε ἀνάπαυσιν ταῖς
in heart, and ye will find rest to the
ψυχαῖς ὑμῶν· 30 ὁ γὰρ ζυγός μου
souls of you; for the yoke of me
χρηστὸς καὶ τὸ φορτίον μου ἐλαφρόν
gentle and the burden of me light
ἐστιν.
is.

of heaven and earth, be-
cause you have hidden
these things from the wise
and learned, and revealed
them to little children.
26Yes, Father, for this was
your good pleasure.
27"All things have been
committed to me by my Fa-
ther. No one knows the
Son except the Father, and
no one knows the Father
except the Son and those to
whom the Son chooses to
reveal him.
28"Come to me, all you
who are weary and bur-
dened, and I will give you
rest. 29Take my yoke upon
you and learn from me, for
I am gentle and humble in
heart, and you will find rest
for your souls. 30For my
yoke is easy and my burden
is light."

Chapter 12

Sabbath Questions

AT that time Jesus went
on the Sabbath
through the grainfields, and
His disciples became hun-
gry and began to pick the
heads *of grain* and eat.
2But when the Pharisees
saw it, they said to Him,
"Behold, Your disciples do
what is not lawful to do on a
Sabbath."
3But He said to them,
"Have you not read what
David did, when he became
hungry, he and his companions;
4how he entered the
house of God, and they ate
the consecrated bread,
which was not lawful for
him to eat, nor for those
with him, but for the priests
alone?
5"Or have you not read

12 Ἐν ἐκείνῳ τῷ καιρῷ ἐπορεύθη ὁ
At that – time went –
Ἰησοῦς τοῖς σάββασιν διὰ τῶν σπορίμων·
Jesus on the sabbath through the cornfields;
οἱ δὲ μαθηταὶ αὐτοῦ ἐπείνασαν, καὶ
and the disciples of him hungered, and
ἤρξαντο τίλλειν στάχυας καὶ ἐσθίειν.
began to pluck ears [of corn] and to eat.
2 οἱ δὲ Φαρισαῖοι ἰδόντες εἶπαν αὐτῷ·
But the Pharisees seeing said to him:
ἰδοὺ οἱ μαθηταί σου ποιοῦσιν ὃ οὐκ
Behold[,] the disciples of thee are doing what not
ἔξεστιν ποιεῖν ἐν σαββάτῳ. 3 ὁ δὲ
it is lawful to do on a sabbath. And he
εἶπεν αὐτοῖς· οὐκ ἀνέγνωτε τί ἐποίησεν
said to them: Did ye not read what did
Δαυίδ, ὅτε ἐπείνασεν καὶ οἱ μετ'
David, when he hungered and the [ones] with
αὐτοῦ; 4 πῶς εἰσῆλθεν εἰς τὸν οἶκον
him? how he entered into the house
τοῦ θεοῦ καὶ τοὺς ἄρτους τῆς προ-
– of God and the loaves of the set-
θέσεως ἔφαγον, ὃ οὐκ ἐξὸν ἦν αὐτῷ
ting forth ate, which not lawful it was for him
φαγεῖν οὐδὲ τοῖς μετ' αὐτοῦ, εἰ μὴ
to eat neither the [ones] with him, except
τοῖς ἱερεῦσιν μόνοις; 5 ἢ οὐκ ἀνέγνωτε
for the priests only? or did ye not read

Chapter 12

Lord of the Sabbath

AT that time Jesus went
through the grain-
fields on the Sabbath. His
disciples were hungry and
began to pick some heads
of grain and eat them.
2When the Pharisees saw
this, they said to him,
"Look! Your disciples are
doing what is unlawful on
the Sabbath."
3He answered, "Haven't
you read what David did
when he and his compan-
ions were hungry? 4He en-
tered the house of God, and
he and his companions ate
the consecrated bread—
which was not lawful for
them to do, but only for the
priests. 5Or haven't you

in the Law, that on the Sabbath the priests in the temple break the Sabbath, and
are innocent?
6 "But I say to you, that
something greater than the
temple is here.
7 "But if you had known
what this means, 'I DESIRE
COMPASSION, AND NOT A SAC-
RIFICE,' you would not have
condemned the innocent.

Lord of the Sabbath

8 "For the Son of Man is
Lord of the Sabbath."
9 And departing from
there, He went into their
synagogue.
10 And behold, *there was* a
man with a withered hand.
And they questioned Him,
saying, "Is it lawful to heal
on the Sabbath?"—in order
that they might accuse
Him.
11 And He said to them,
"What man shall there be
among you, who shall have
one sheep, and if it falls into
a pit on the Sabbath, will he
not take hold of it, and lift it
out?
12 "Of how much more
value then is a man than a
sheep! So then, it is lawful
to do good on the Sab-
bath."
13 Then He *said to the
man, "Stretch out your
hand!" And he stretched it
out, and it was restored to
normal, like the other.
14 But the Pharisees went
out, and counseled to-
gether against Him, *as to*
how they might destroy
Him.
15 But Jesus, aware of
this, withdrew from there.
And many followed Him,
and He healed them all,
16 and warned them not to
make Him known,
17 in order that what was
spoken through Isaiah the
prophet, might be fulfilled,
saying,
18 "BEHOLD, MY SERVANT
WHOM I HAVE CHOSEN;
MY BELOVED IN WHOM
MY SOUL IS WELL-
PLEASED;
I WILL PUT MY SPIRIT
UPON HIM,

ἐν τῷ νόμῳ ὅτι τοῖς σάββασιν οἱ
in the law that on the sabbaths the
ἱερεῖς ἐν τῷ ἱερῷ τὸ σάββατον βεβηλοῦ-
priests in the temple the sabbath pro-
σιν καὶ ἀναίτιοί εἰσιν; **6** λέγω δὲ
fane and guiltless are? And I tell
ὑμῖν ὅτι τοῦ ἱεροῦ μεῖζόν ἐστιν ὧδε.
you that [than] the temple a greater [thing] is here.
7 εἰ δὲ ἐγνώκειτε τί ἐστιν· ἔλεος
But if ye had known what it is: Mercy
θέλω καὶ οὐ θυσίαν, οὐκ ἂν κατε-
I desire and not sacrifice, ye would not have
δικάσατε τοὺς ἀναιτίους. **8** κύριος γάρ
condemned the guiltless. For Lord
ἐστιν τοῦ σαββάτου ὁ υἱὸς τοῦ ἀνθρώπου.
is of the sabbath the Son – of man.
9 Καὶ μεταβὰς ἐκεῖθεν ἦλθεν εἰς τὴν
And removing thence he came into the
συναγωγὴν αὐτῶν. **10** καὶ ἰδοὺ ἄνθρωπος
synagogue of them. And behold[,] a man
χεῖρα ἔχων ξηράν· καὶ ἐπηρώτησαν αὐτὸν
[2][this] hand [1]having [3]withered; and they questioned him
λέγοντες· εἰ ἔξεστιν τοῖς σάββασιν
saying: If it is lawful on the sabbaths
θεραπεῦσαι; ἵνα κατηγορήσωσιν αὐτοῦ.
to heal? in order that they might accuse him.
11 ὁ δὲ εἶπεν αὐτοῖς· τίς ἔσται ἐξ
So he said to them: [1]What [3]will there be [4]of
ὑμῶν ἄνθρωπος ὃς ἕξει πρόβατον ἕν,
[5]you [2]man who will have sheep one,
καὶ ἐὰν ἐμπέσῃ τοῦτο τοῖς σάββασιν
and if [2]fall *in* [1]this on the sabbaths
εἰς βόθυνον, οὐχὶ κρατήσει αὐτὸ καὶ
into a ditch, will he not lay hold of it and
ἐγερεῖ; **12** πόσῳ οὖν διαφέρει ἄνθρωπος
raise? By how much then surpasses a man
προβάτου. ὥστε ἔξεστιν τοῖς σάββασιν
a sheep. So that it is lawful on the sabbaths
καλῶς ποιεῖν. **13** τότε λέγει τῷ ἀνθρώπῳ·
well to do. Then he says to the man:
ἔκτεινόν σου τὴν χεῖρα. καὶ ἐξέτεινεν,
Stretch forth of thee the hand. And he stretched forth,
καὶ ἀπεκατεστάθη ὑγιὴς ὡς ἡ ἄλλη.
and it was restored healthy as the other.
14 ἐξελθόντες δὲ οἱ Φαρισαῖοι συμβούλιον
And going out the Pharisees counsel
ἔλαβον κατ' αὐτοῦ, ὅπως αὐτὸν ἀπολέ-
took against him, so as him they might
σωσιν. **15** Ὁ δὲ Ἰησοῦς γνοὺς ἀνε-
destroy. – But Jesus knowing de-
χώρησεν ἐκεῖθεν. καὶ ἠκολούθησαν αὐτῷ
parted thence. And followed him
πολλοί, καὶ ἐθεράπευσεν αὐτοὺς πάντας,
many, and he healed them all,
16 καὶ ἐπετίμησεν αὐτοῖς ἵνα μὴ φανερὸν
and warned them that [3]not [4]manifest
αὐτὸν ποιήσωσιν· **17** ἵνα πληρωθῇ τὸ
[5]him [1]they [2]should [6]make; that might be fulfilled the [thing]
ῥηθὲν διὰ Ἠσαΐου τοῦ προφήτου
spoken through Isaiah the prophet
λέγοντος· **18** ἰδοὺ ὁ παῖς μου ὃν
saying: Behold[,] the servant of me whom
ᾑρέτισα, ὁ ἀγαπητός μου ὃν εὐδόκησεν
I chose, the beloved of me [with] whom was well pleased
ἡ ψυχή μου· θήσω τὸ πνεῦμά μου ἐπ'
the soul of me; I will put the spirit of me on

read in the Law that on the
Sabbath the priests in the
temple desecrate the day
and yet are innocent? 6 I tell
you that one[s] greater than
the temple is here. 7 If you
had known what these
words mean, 'I desire mercy, not sacrifice,'[t] you
would not have condemned
the innocent. 8 For the Son
of Man is Lord of the Sabbath."
9 Going on from that
place, he went into their
synagogue, 10 and a man
with a shriveled hand was
there. Looking for a reason
to accuse Jesus, they asked
him, "Is it lawful to heal on
the Sabbath?"
11 He said to them, "If any
of you has a sheep and it
falls into a pit on the Sabbath, will you not take hold
of it and lift it out? 12 How
much more valuable is a
man than a sheep! There-
fore it is lawful to do good
on the Sabbath."
13 Then he said to the
man, "Stretch out your
hand." So he stretched it
out and it was completely
restored, just as sound as
the other. 14 But the Pharisees went out and plotted
how they might kill Jesus.

God's Chosen Servant

15 Aware of this, Jesus
withdrew from that place.
Many followed him, and he
healed all their sick,
16 warning them not to tell
who he was. 17 This was to
fulfill what was spoken
through the prophet Isaiah:

18 "Here is my servant
whom I have
chosen,
the one I love, in
whom I delight;
I will put my Spirit on
him,

[s]6 Or *something*; also in verses 41 and 42
[t]7 Hosea 6:6

AND HE SHALL PROCLAIM JUSTICE TO THE
GENTILES.
19 "HE WILL NOT QUARREL,
NOR CRY OUT;
NOR WILL ANYONE
HEAR HIS VOICE IN
THE STREETS.
20 "A BATTERED REED HE
WILL NOT BREAK OFF,
AND A SMOLDERING
WICK HE WILL NOT
PUT OUT,
UNTIL HE LEADS JUSTICE TO VICTORY.
21 "AND IN HIS NAME
THE GENTILES WILL
HOPE."

The Pharisees Rebuked

22 Then there was brought
to Him a demon-possessed
man *who was* blind and
dumb, and He healed him,
so that the dumb man
spoke and saw.
23 And all the multitudes
were amazed, and *began* to
say, "This *man* cannot be
the Son of David, can he?"
24 But when the Pharisees
heard it, they said, "This
man casts out demons only
by Beelzebul the ruler of
the demons."
25 And knowing their
thoughts He said to them,
"Any kingdom divided
against itself is laid waste;
and any city or house divided against itself shall not
stand.
26 "And if Satan casts out
Satan, he is divided against
himself; how then shall his
kingdom stand?
27 "And if I by Beelzebul
cast out demons, by whom
do your sons cast them out?
Consequently they shall be
your judges.
28 "But if I cast out demons by the Spirit of God,
then the kingdom of God
has come upon you.
29 "Or how can anyone
enter the strong man's
house and carry off his

αὐτόν, καὶ κρίσιν τοῖς ἔθνεσιν ἀπαγγελεῖ.
him, and judgment to the nations he will announce.
19 οὐκ ἐρίσει οὐδὲ κραυγάσει, οὐδὲ
He will not strive nor *will* shout, nor
ἀκούσει τις ἐν ταῖς πλατείαις τὴν
will hear anyone in the streets the
φωνὴν αὐτοῦ. 20 κάλαμον συντετριμμένον
voice of him. A reed *having been* bruised
οὐ κατεάξει καὶ λίνον τυφόμενον οὐ
he will not break and flax smoking not
σβέσει, ἕως ἂν ἐκβάλῃ εἰς νῖκος τὴν
he will quench, until he put forth to victory –
κρίσιν. 21 καὶ τῷ ὀνόματι αὐτοῦ ἔθνη
judgment. And in the name of him nations
ἐλπιοῦσιν.
will hope.

22 Τότε προσηνέχθη αὐτῷ δαιμονιζ-
Then was brought to him a demon-
όμενος τυφλὸς καὶ κωφός· καὶ ἐθεράπευσεν
possessed man blind and dumb; and he healed
αὐτόν, ὥστε τὸν κωφὸν λαλεῖν καὶ
him, so as the dumb to speak and
βλέπειν. 23 καὶ ἐξίσταντο πάντες οἱ
to see[b]. And were astonished all the
ὄχλοι καὶ ἔλεγον· μήτι οὗτός ἐστιν ὁ
crowds and said: *not* This is the
υἱὸς Δαυίδ; 24 οἱ δὲ Φαρισαῖοι ἀκού-
son of David? But the Pharisees hear-
σαντες εἶπον· οὗτος οὐκ ἐκβάλλει τὰ
ing said: This man does not expel the
δαιμόνια εἰ μὴ ἐν τῷ Βεεζεβοὺλ ἄρχοντι
demons except by – Beelzebub ruler
τῶν δαιμονίων. 25 εἰδὼς δὲ τὰς ἐνθυμήσεις
of the demons. But knowing the thoughts
αὐτῶν εἶπεν αὐτοῖς· πᾶσα βασιλεία
of them he said to them: Every kingdom
μερισθεῖσα καθ' ἑαυτῆς ἐρημοῦται,
divided against itself is brought to desolation,
καὶ πᾶσα πόλις ἢ οἰκία μερισθεῖσα καθ'
and every city or house divided against
ἑαυτῆς οὐ σταθήσεται. 26 καὶ εἰ
itself will not stand. And if
ὁ σατανᾶς τὸν σατανᾶν ἐκβάλλει, ἐφ'
– Satan – ²Satan ¹expels, against
ἑαυτὸν ἐμερίσθη· πῶς οὖν σταθή-
himself he was(is) divided; how therefore will
σεται ἡ βασιλεία αὐτοῦ; 27 καὶ εἰ
stand the kingdom of him? And if
ἐγὼ ἐν Βεεζεβοὺλ ἐκβάλλω τὰ δαιμόνια,
I by Beelzebub expel the demons,
οἱ υἱοὶ ὑμῶν ἐν τίνι ἐκβάλλουσιν;
the sons of you by what do they expel?
διὰ τοῦτο αὐτοὶ κριταὶ ἔσονται ὑμῶν.
therefore they judges shall be of you.
28 εἰ δὲ ἐν πνεύματι θεοῦ ἐγὼ
But if by [the] Spirit of God I
ἐκβάλλω τὰ δαιμόνια, ἄρα ἔφθασεν
expel the demons, then came
ἐφ' ὑμᾶς ἡ βασιλεία τοῦ θεοῦ. 29 ἢ
upon you the kingdom – of God. Or
πῶς δύναταί τις εἰσελθεῖν εἰς τὴν
how can anyone *to* enter into the
οἰκίαν τοῦ ἰσχυροῦ καὶ τὰ σκεύη αὐτοῦ
house of the strong man and the vessels of him

and he will proclaim
justice to the
nations.
19 He will not quarrel or
cry out;
no one will hear his
voice in the streets.
20 A bruised reed he will
not break,
and a smoldering wick
he will not snuff out,
till he leads justice to
victory.
21 In his name the nations
will put their
hope."[u]

Jesus and Beelzebub

22 Then they brought him
a demon-possessed man
who was blind and mute,
and Jesus healed him, so
that he could both talk and
see. 23 All the people were
astonished and said,
"Could this be the Son of
David?"
24 But when the Pharisees
heard this, they said, "It is
only by Beelzebub,[v] the
prince of demons, that this
fellow drives out demons."
25 Jesus knew their
thoughts and said to them,
"Every kingdom divided
against itself will be ruined,
and every city or household divided against itself
will not stand. 26 If Satan
drives out Satan, he is divided against himself. How
then can his kingdom
stand? 27 And if I drive out
demons by Beelzebub, by
whom do your people drive
them out? So then, they
will be your judges. 28 But if
I drive out demons by the
Spirit of God, then the
kingdom of God has come
upon you.
29 "Or again, how can
anyone enter a strong
man's house and carry off

[u] *21* Isaiah 42:1-4
[v] *24* Greek *Beezeboul* or *Beelzeboul*; also in verse 27

property, unless he first binds the strong *man*? And then he will plunder his house.

The Unpardonable Sin

30"He who is not with Me is against Me; and he who does not gather with Me scatters.

31"Therefore I say to you, any sin and blasphemy shall be forgiven men, but blasphemy against the Spirit shall not be forgiven.

32"And whoever shall speak a word against the Son of Man, it shall be forgiven him; but whoever shall speak against the Holy Spirit, it shall not be forgiven him, either in this age, or in the *age* to come.

Words Reveal Character

33"Either make the tree good, and its fruit good; or make the tree bad, and its fruit bad; for the tree is known by its fruit.

34"You brood of vipers, how can you, being evil, speak what is good? For the mouth speaks out of that which fills the heart.

35"The good man out of *his* good treasure brings forth what is good; and the evil man out of *his* evil treasure brings forth what is evil.

36"And I say to you, that every careless word that men shall speak, they shall render account for it in the day of judgment.

37"For by your words you shall be justified, and by your words you shall be condemned."

The Desire for Signs

38Then some of the scribes and Pharisees answered Him, saying, "Teacher, we want to see a sign from You."

ἁρπάσαι, ἐὰν μὴ πρῶτον δήσῃ τὸν
to seize, if not first he binds the
ἰσχυρόν; καὶ τότε τὴν οἰκίαν αὐτοῦ
strong man? and then the house of him
διαρπάσει. 30 ὁ μὴ ὢν μετ᾽ ἐμοῦ
he will plunder. The [one] not being with me
κατ᾽ ἐμοῦ ἐστιν, καὶ ὁ μὴ συνάγων μετ᾽
against me is, and the [one] not gathering with
ἐμοῦ σκορπίζει. 31 Διὰ τοῦτο λέγω
me scatters. Therefore I tell
ὑμῖν, πᾶσα ἁμαρτία καὶ βλασφημία
you, all sin and blasphemy
ἀφεθήσεται τοῖς ἀνθρώποις, ἡ δὲ τοῦ
will be forgiven – to men, but the of the
πνεύματος βλασφημία οὐκ ἀφεθήσεται.
Spirit blasphemy will not be forgiven.
32 καὶ ὃς ἐὰν εἴπῃ λόγον κατὰ τοῦ
And whoever speaks a word against the
υἱοῦ τοῦ ἀνθρώπου, ἀφεθήσεται αὐτῷ·
Son – of man, it will be forgiven *to* him;
ὃς δ᾽ ἂν εἴπῃ κατὰ τοῦ πνεύματος
but whoever speaks against the Spirit
τοῦ ἁγίου, οὐκ ἀφεθήσεται αὐτῷ
– Holy, it will not be forgiven *to* him
οὔτε ἐν τούτῳ τῷ αἰῶνι οὔτε ἐν τῷ
neither in this – age nor in the [one]
μέλλοντι. 33 Ἢ ποιήσατε τὸ δένδρον
coming. Either make the tree
καλὸν καὶ τὸν καρπὸν αὐτοῦ καλόν,
good and the fruit of it good,
ἢ ποιήσατε τὸ δένδρον σαπρὸν καὶ τὸν
or make the tree bad and the
καρπὸν αὐτοῦ σαπρόν· ἐκ γὰρ τοῦ
fruit of it bad; for of(by) the
καρποῦ τὸ δένδρον γινώσκεται. 34 γεννή-
fruit the tree is known. Off-
ματα ἐχιδνῶν, πῶς δύνασθε ἀγαθὰ λαλεῖν
spring of vipers, how can ye good things *to* speak
πονηροὶ ὄντες; ἐκ γὰρ τοῦ περισ-
[2]evil [1]being? for out of the abund-
σεύματος τῆς καρδίας τὸ στόμα λαλεῖ.
ance of the heart the mouth speaks.
35 ὁ ἀγαθὸς ἄνθρωπος ἐκ τοῦ ἀγαθοῦ
The good man out of the good
θησαυροῦ ἐκβάλλει ἀγαθά, καὶ ὁ πονηρὸς
treasure puts forth good things, and the evil
ἄνθρωπος ἐκ τοῦ πονηροῦ θησαυροῦ
man out of the evil treasure
ἐκβάλλει πονηρά. 36 λέγω δὲ
puts forth evil things. But I tell
ὑμῖν ὅτι πᾶν ῥῆμα ἀργὸν ὃ λαλήσουσιν
you that every word idle which will speak
οἱ ἄνθρωποι, ἀποδώσουσιν περὶ αὐτοῦ
– men, they will render concerning it
λόγον ἐν ἡμέρᾳ κρίσεως· 37 ἐκ γὰρ
account in [the] day of judgment; for of(by)
τῶν λόγων σου δικαιωθήσῃ, καὶ ἐκ
the words of thee thou wilt be justified, and of(by)
τῶν λόγων σου καταδικασθήσῃ.
the words of thee thou wilt be condemned.
38 Τότε ἀπεκρίθησαν αὐτῷ τινες τῶν
Then answered him some of the
γραμματέων καὶ Φαρισαίων λέγοντες·
scribes and Pharisees saying:
διδάσκαλε, θέλομεν ἀπὸ σοῦ σημεῖον ἰδεῖν.
Teacher, we wish from thee a sign to see.

his possessions unless he
first ties up the strong man?
Then he can rob his house.
30"He who is not with me
is against me, and he who
does not gather with me
scatters. 31And so I tell
you, every sin and blasphemy will be forgiven men,
but the blasphemy against
the Spirit will not be forgiv-
en. 32Anyone who speaks a
word against the Son of
Man will be forgiven, but
anyone who speaks against
the Holy Spirit will not be
forgiven, either in this age
or in the age to come.
33"Make a tree good and
its fruit will be good, or
make a tree bad and its fruit
will be bad, for a tree is recognized by its fruit. 34You
brood of vipers, how can
you who are evil say any-
thing good? For out of the
overflow of the heart the
mouth speaks. 35The good
man brings good things out
of the good stored up in
him, and the evil man
brings evil things out of the
evil stored up in him. 36But
I tell you that men will have
to give account on the day
of judgment for every careless word they have spo-
ken. 37For by your words
you will be acquitted, and
by your words you will be
condemned."

The Sign of Jonah

38Then some of the Pharisees and teachers of the law said to him, "Teacher, we want to see a miraculous sign from you."

39But He answered and said to them, "An evil and adulterous generation craves for a sign; and *yet* no sign shall be given to it but the sign of Jonah the prophet;

40for just as JONAH WAS THREE DAYS AND THREE NIGHTS IN THE BELLY OF THE SEA MONSTER, so shall the Son of Man be three days and three nights in the heart of the earth.

41"The men of Nineveh shall stand up with this generation at the judgment, and shall condemn it because they repented at the preaching of Jonah; and behold, something greater than Jonah is here.

42"*The* Queen of *the* South shall rise up with this generation at the judgment and shall condemn it, because she came from the ends of the earth to hear the wisdom of Solomon; and behold, something greater than Solomon is here.

43"Now when the unclean spirit goes out of a man, it passes through waterless places, seeking rest, and does not find *it*.

44"Then it says, 'I will return to my house from which I came'; and when it comes, it finds it unoccupied, swept, and put in order.

45"Then it goes, and takes along with it seven other spirits more wicked than itself, and they go in and live there; and the last state of that man becomes worse than the first. That is the way it will also be with this evil generation."

Changed Relationships

46While He was still speaking to the multitudes,

39 ὁ δὲ ἀποκριθεὶς εἶπεν αὐτοῖς·
But he answering said to them:
γενεὰ πονηρὰ καὶ μοιχαλὶς σημεῖον
generation An evil and adulterous a sign
ἐπιζητεῖ, καὶ σημεῖον οὐ δοθήσεται
seeks, and a sign shall not be given
αὐτῇ εἰ μὴ τὸ σημεῖον Ἰωνᾶ τοῦ
to it except the sign of Jonas the
προφήτου. 40 ὥσπερ γὰρ ἦν Ἰωνᾶς
prophet. For as was Jonas
ἐν τῇ κοιλίᾳ τοῦ κήτους τρεῖς ἡμέρας
in the belly of the sea monster three days
καὶ τρεῖς νύκτας, οὕτως ἔσται ὁ υἱὸς
and three nights, so will be the Son
τοῦ ἀνθρώπου ἐν τῇ καρδίᾳ τῆς γῆς
– of man in the heart of the earth
τρεῖς ἡμέρας καὶ τρεῖς νύκτας. 41 ἄνδρες
three days and three nights. Men
Νινευῖται ἀναστήσονται ἐν τῇ κρίσει
Ninevites will stand up in the judgment
μετὰ τῆς γενεᾶς ταύτης καὶ κατα-
with – generation this and will
κρινοῦσιν αὐτήν· ὅτι μετενόησαν εἰς τὸ
condemn it; because they repented at the
κήρυγμα Ἰωνᾶ, καὶ ἰδοὺ πλεῖον Ἰωνᾶ
proclamation of Jonas, and behold a greater thing [than] Jonas
ὧδε. 42 βασίλισσα νότου ἐγερθήσεται
[is] here. [The] queen of [the] south will be raised
ἐν τῇ κρίσει μετὰ τῆς γενεᾶς ταύτης
in the judgment with – generation this
καὶ κατακρινεῖ αὐτήν· ὅτι ἦλθεν ἐκ
and will condemn it; because she came out of
τῶν περάτων τῆς γῆς ἀκοῦσαι τὴν σοφίαν
the limits of the earth to hear the wisdom
Σολομῶνος, καὶ ἰδοὺ πλεῖον Σολομῶνος
of Solomon, and behold a greater thing [than] Solomon
ὧδε. 43 Ὅταν δὲ τὸ ἀκάθαρτον πνεῦμα
[is] here. Now when the unclean spirit
ἐξέλθῃ ἀπὸ τοῦ ἀνθρώπου, διέρχεται δι'
goes out from – a man, he goes through
ἀνύδρων τόπων ζητοῦν ἀνάπαυσιν, καὶ
dry places seeking rest, and
οὐχ εὑρίσκει. 44 τότε λέγει· εἰς τὸν
finds not. Then he says: Into the
οἶκόν μου ἐπιστρέψω ὅθεν ἐξῆλθον·
house of me I will return whence I came out;
καὶ ἐλθὸν εὑρίσκει σχολάζοντα [καὶ]
and coming he finds [it] standing empty and
σεσαρωμένον καὶ κεκοσμημένον. 45 τότε
having been swept and *having been* furnished. Then
πορεύεται καὶ παραλαμβάνει μεθ' ἑαυτοῦ
he goes and takes with him*self*
ἑπτὰ ἕτερα πνεύματα πονηρότερα ἑαυτοῦ,
seven other spirits more evil [than] himself,
καὶ εἰσελθόντα κατοικεῖ ἐκεῖ· καὶ
and entering dwells there; and
γίνεται τὰ ἔσχατα τοῦ ἀνθρώπου ἐκείνου
becomes the last things – man of that
χείρονα τῶν πρώτων. οὕτως ἔσται
worse [than] the first. Thus it will be
καὶ τῇ γενεᾷ ταύτῃ τῇ πονηρᾷ.
also – [3]generation [1]to this – [2]evil.
46 Ἔτι αὐτοῦ λαλοῦντος τοῖς ὄχλοις,
Yet him speaking* to the crowds,
=While he was still speaking

39He answered, "A wick-
ed and adulterous genera-
tion asks for a miraculous
sign! But none will be given
it except the sign of the
prophet Jonah. 40For as Jonah was three days and
three nights in the belly of a
huge fish, so the Son of
Man will be three days and
three nights in the heart of
the earth. 41The men of
Nineveh will stand up at
the judgment with this generation and condemn it; for
they repented at the
preaching of Jonah, and
now one[w] greater than Jonah is here. 42The Queen of
the South will rise at the
judgment with this generation and condemn it; for she
came from the ends of the
earth to listen to Solomon's
wisdom, and now one
greater than Solomon is
here.
43"When an evil[x] spirit
comes out of a man, it goes
through arid places seeking
rest and does not find it.
44Then it says, 'I will return
to the house I left.' When it
arrives, it finds the house
unoccupied, swept clean
and put in order. 45Then it
goes and takes with it seven
other spirits more wicked
than itself, and they go in
and live there. And the final
condition of that man is
worse than the first. That is
how it will be with this
wicked generation."

Jesus' Mother and Brothers

46While Jesus was still
talking to the crowd, his

[w]41 Or *something*; also in verse 42
[x]43 Greek *unclean*

behold, His mother and
brothers were standing outside, seeking to speak to
Him.
47And someone said to
Him, "Behold, Your
mother and Your brothers
are standing outside seeking to speak to You."
48But He answered the
one who was telling Him
and said, "Who is My
mother and who are My
brothers?"
49And stretching out His
hand toward His disciples,
He said, "Behold, My
mother and My brothers!
50"For whoever does the
will of My Father who is in
heaven, he is My brother
and sister and mother."

Chapter 13

Jesus Teaches in Parables

ON that day Jesus went
out of the house, and
was sitting by the sea.
2And great multitudes
gathered to Him, so that He
got into a boat and sat
down, and the whole multitude was standing on the
beach.
3And He spoke many
things to them in parables,
saying, "Behold, the sower
went out to sow;
4and as he sowed, some
seeds fell beside the road,
and the birds came and ate
them up.
5"And others fell upon
the rocky places, where
they did not have much
soil; and immediately they
sprang up, because they
had no depth of soil.
6"But when the sun had
risen, they were scorched;
and because they had no
root, they withered away.
7"And others fell among
the thorns, and the thorns

ἰδοὺ ἡ μήτηρ καὶ οἱ ἀδελφοὶ αὐτοῦ
behold the mother and the brothers of him
εἱστήκεισαν ἔξω ζητοῦντες αὐτῷ λαλῆσαι.
stood outside seeking to him to speak.
47 [εἶπεν δέ τις αὐτῷ· ἰδοὺ ἡ μήτηρ
And said someone to him: Behold[,] the mother
σου καὶ οἱ ἀδελφοί σου ἔξω ἑστήκασιν
of thee and the brothers of thee outside are standing
ζητοῦντές σοι λαλῆσαι.] **48** ὁ δὲ
seeking to thee to speak. And he
ἀποκριθεὶς εἶπεν τῷ λέγοντι αὐτῷ· τίς
answering said to the [one] saying to him: Who
ἐστιν ἡ μήτηρ μου, καὶ τίνες εἰσὶν οἱ
is the mother of me, and who are the
ἀδελφοί μου; **49** καὶ ἐκτείνας τὴν
brothers of me? And stretching forth the
χεῖρα [αὐτοῦ] ἐπὶ τοὺς μαθητὰς αὐτοῦ
hand of him on the disciples of him
εἶπεν· ἰδοὺ ἡ μήτηρ μου καὶ οἱ ἀδελφοί
he said: Behold[,] the mother of me and the brothers
μου. **50** ὅστις γὰρ ἂν ποιήσῃ τὸ θέλημα
of me. For whoever does the will
τοῦ πατρός μου τοῦ ἐν οὐρανοῖς, αὐτός
of the Father of me – in heavens, he
μου ἀδελφὸς καὶ ἀδελφὴ καὶ μήτηρ ἐστίν.
of me brother and sister and mother is.

13 Ἐν τῇ ἡμέρᾳ ἐκείνῃ ἐξελθὼν ὁ
On – day that [a]going out *of* –
Ἰησοῦς τῆς οἰκίας ἐκάθητο παρὰ τὴν
[1]Jesus of the house sat beside the
θάλασσαν· **2** καὶ συνήχθησαν πρὸς αὐτὸν
sea; and were assembled to him
ὄχλοι πολλοί, ὥστε αὐτὸν εἰς πλοῖον
crowds many, so as him in a ship
=so that embarking in a ship he sat,
ἐμβάντα καθῆσθαι, καὶ πᾶς ὁ ὄχλος
embarking to sit[b], and all the crowd
ἐπὶ τὸν αἰγιαλὸν εἱστήκει. **3** καὶ ἐλάλησεν
on the beach stood. And he spoke
αὐτοῖς πολλὰ ἐν παραβολαῖς λέγων·
to them many things in parables saying:
Ἰδοὺ ἐξῆλθεν ὁ σπείρων τοῦ σπείρειν.
Behold went out the [one] sowing – to sow[d].
4 καὶ ἐν τῷ σπείρειν αὐτὸν ἃ μὲν
And in the to sow him[e] some indeed
=as he sowed
ἔπεσεν παρὰ τὴν ὁδόν, καὶ ἐλθόντα τὰ
fell beside the way, and coming the
πετεινὰ κατέφαγεν αὐτά. **5** ἄλλα δὲ
birds devoured them. But others
ἔπεσεν ἐπὶ τὰ πετρώδη ὅπου οὐκ
fell on the rocky places where not
εἶχεν γῆν πολλήν, καὶ εὐθέως ἐξανέτειλεν
it had earth much, and immediately it sprang up
διὰ τὸ μὴ ἔχειν βάθος γῆς· **6** ἡλίου
on account of the not to have depth of earth; [the] sun
=because it had not
δὲ ἀνατείλαντος ἐκαυματίσθη, καὶ διὰ
But having risen[a] it was scorched, and on account of
=when the sun rose =because
τὸ μὴ ἔχειν ῥίζαν ἐξηράνθη. **7** ἄλλα δὲ
the not to have root it was dried up. But others
it had not
ἔπεσεν ἐπὶ τὰς ἀκάνθας, καὶ ἀνέβησαν
fell on the thorns, and came up

mother and brothers stood
outside, wanting to speak
to him. 47Someone told
him, "Your mother and
brothers are standing outside, wanting to speak to
you."[y]
48He replied to him,
"Who is my mother, and
who are my brothers?"
49Pointing to his disciples,
he said, "Here are my
mother and my brothers.
50For whoever does the will
of my Father in heaven is
my brother and sister and
mother."

Chapter 13

The Parable of the Sower

THAT same day Jesus
went out of the house
and sat by the lake. 2Such
large crowds gathered
around him that he got into
a boat and sat in it, while all
the people stood on the
shore. 3Then he told them
many things in parables,
saying: "A farmer went out
to sow his seed. 4As he was
scattering the seed, some
fell along the path, and the
birds came and ate it up.
5Some fell on rocky places,
where it did not have much
soil. It sprang up quickly,
because the soil was shal-
low. 6But when the sun
came up, the plants were
scorched, and they with-
ered because they had no
root. 7Other seed fell
among thorns, which grew

[y]47 Some manuscripts do not have verse 47.

came up and choked them
out.
8 "And others fell on the
good soil, and *yielded a
crop, some a hundredfold,
some sixty, and some
thirty.
9 "He who has ears, let
him hear."

An Explanation

10 And the disciples came
and said to Him, "Why do
You speak to them in parables?"
11 And He answered and
said to them, "To you it has
been granted to know the
mysteries of the kingdom
of heaven, but to them it
has not been granted.
12 "For whoever has, to
him shall *more* be given,
and he shall have an abundance; but whoever does
not have, even what he has
shall be taken away from
him.
13 "Therefore I speak to
them in parables; because
while seeing they do not
see, and while hearing they
do not hear, nor do they understand.
14 "And in their case the
prophecy of Isaiah is being
fulfilled, which says,

'YOU WILL KEEP ON HEARING, BUT WILL NOT UNDERSTAND;
AND YOU WILL KEEP ON SEEING, BUT WILL NOT PERCEIVE;
15 FOR THE HEART OF THIS PEOPLE HAS BECOME DULL,
AND WITH THEIR EARS THEY SCARCELY HEAR,
AND THEY HAVE CLOSED THEIR EYES
LEST THEY SHOULD SEE WITH THEIR EYES,
AND HEAR WITH THEIR EARS,
AND UNDERSTAND WITH THEIR HEART AND RETURN,
AND I SHOULD HEAL THEM.'

16 "But blessed are your
eyes, because they see; and
your ears, because they
hear.
17 "For truly I say to you,
that many prophets and
righteous men desired to
see what you see, and did
not see *it*; and to hear what
you hear, and did not hear
it.

αἱ ἄκανθαι καὶ ἀπέπνιξαν αὐτά. **8** ἄλλα δὲ
the thorns and choked them. And others
ἔπεσεν ἐπὶ τὴν γῆν τὴν καλὴν καὶ
fell on the earth – good and
ἐδίδου καρπόν, ὃ μὲν ἑκατόν, ὃ δὲ
gave fruit, the one a hundred, the other
ἑξήκοντα, ὃ δὲ τριάκοντα. **9** ὁ ἔχων
sixty, the other thirty. The [one] having
ὦτα ἀκουέτω. **10** Καὶ προσελθόντες οἱ
ears let him hear. And approaching the
μαθηταὶ εἶπαν αὐτῷ· διὰ τί ἐν παρα-
disciples said to him: Why in par-
βολαῖς λαλεῖς αὐτοῖς; **11** ὁ δὲ
ables speakest thou to them? And he
ἀποκριθεὶς εἶπεν· ὅτι ὑμῖν δέδοται
answering said: Because to you it has been given
γνῶναι τὰ μυστήρια τῆς βασιλείας τῶν
to know the mysteries of the kingdom of the
οὐρανῶν, ἐκείνοις δὲ οὐ δέδοται. **12** ὅστις
heavens, but to those it has not been given. [he] who
γὰρ ἔχει, δοθήσεται αὐτῷ καὶ περισ-
For has, it will be given to him and he will
σευθήσεται· ὅστις δὲ οὐκ ἔχει, καὶ
have abundance; but [he] who has not, even
ὃ ἔχει ἀρθήσεται ἀπ' αὐτοῦ. **13** διὰ
what he has will be taken from him. There-
τοῦτο ἐν παραβολαῖς αὐτοῖς λαλῶ, ὅτι
fore in parables to them I speak, because
βλέποντες οὐ βλέπουσιν καὶ ἀκούοντες
seeing they see not and hearing
οὐκ ἀκούουσιν οὐδὲ συνιοῦσιν. **14** καὶ
they hear not neither understand. And
ἀναπληροῦται αὐτοῖς ἡ προφητεία Ἠσαΐου
is fulfilled in them the prophecy of Isaiah
ἡ λέγουσα· ἀκοῇ ἀκούσετε καὶ οὐ μὴ
– saying: In hearing ye will hear and by no means
συνῆτε, καὶ βλέποντες βλέψετε
understand, and seeing ye will see
καὶ οὐ μὴ ἴδητε. **15** ἐπαχύνθη γὰρ
and by no means perceive. For waxed gross
ἡ καρδία τοῦ λαοῦ τούτου, καὶ τοῖς
the heart – people of this, and with the
ὠσὶν βαρέως ἤκουσαν, καὶ τοὺς ὀφθαλμοὺς
ears heavily they heard, and the eyes
αὐτῶν ἐκάμμυσαν· μήποτε ἴδωσιν τοῖς
of them they closed; lest they see with the
ὀφθαλμοῖς καὶ τοῖς ὠσὶν ἀκούσωσιν
eyes and with the ears hear
καὶ τῇ καρδίᾳ συνῶσιν καὶ ἐπιστρέψωσιν,
and with the heart understand and turn back,
καὶ ἰάσομαι αὐτούς. **16** ὑμῶν δὲ μακάριοι
and I will heal them. But of you blessed
οἱ ὀφθαλμοὶ ὅτι βλέπουσιν, καὶ τὰ
the eyes because they see, and the
ὦτα [ὑμῶν] ὅτι ἀκούουσιν. **17** ἀμὴν
ears of you because they hear. truly
γὰρ λέγω ὑμῖν ὅτι πολλοὶ προφῆται καὶ
For I say to you that many prophets and
δίκαιοι ἐπεθύμησαν ἰδεῖν ἃ
righteous men desired to see [the things] which
βλέπετε καὶ οὐκ εἶδαν, καὶ ἀκοῦσαι
ye see and did not see, and to hear
ἃ ἀκούετε καὶ οὐκ ἤκουσαν.
[the things] which ye hear and did not hear.

up and choked the plants.
8 Still other seed fell on
good soil, where it pro-
duced a crop—a hundred,
sixty or thirty times what
was sown. 9 He who has
ears, let him hear."
10 The disciples came to
him and asked, "Why do
you speak to the people in
parables?"
11 He replied, "The
knowledge of the secrets of
the kingdom of heaven has
been given to you, but not
to them. 12 Whoever has
will be given more, and he
will have an abundance.
Whoever does not have,
even what he has will be
taken from him. 13 This is
why I speak to them in parables:

"Though seeing, they do not see;
though hearing, they do not hear or understand.

14 In them is fulfilled the
prophecy of Isaiah:

" 'You will be ever hearing but never understanding;
you will be ever seeing but never perceiving.
15 For this people's heart has become calloused;
they hardly hear with their ears,
and they have closed their eyes.
Otherwise they might see with their eyes,
hear with their ears,
understand with their hearts
and turn, and I would heal them.'[z]

16 But blessed are your eyes
because they see, and your
ears because they hear.
17 For I tell you the truth,
many prophets and right-
eous men longed to see
what you see but did not
see it, and to hear what you
hear but did not hear it.

[z] *15* Isaiah 6:9,10

The Sower Explained

[18]"Hear then the parable of the sower.

[19]"When anyone hears the word of the kingdom, and does not understand it, the evil *one* comes and snatches away what has been sown in his heart. This is the one on whom seed was sown beside the road.

[20]"And the one on whom seed was sown on the rocky places, this is the man who hears the word, and immediately receives it with joy;

[21]yet he has no *firm* root in himself, but is *only* temporary, and when affliction or persecution arises because of the word, immediately he falls away.

[22]"And the one on whom seed was sown among the thorns, this is the man who hears the word, and the worry of the world, and the deceitfulness of riches choke the word, and it becomes unfruitful.

[23]"And the one on whom seed was sown on the good soil, this is the man who hears the word and understands it; who indeed bears fruit, and brings forth, some a hundredfold, some sixty, and some thirty."

Tares among Wheat

[24]He presented another parable to them, saying, "The kingdom of heaven may be compared to a man who sowed good seed in his field.

[25]"But while men were sleeping, his enemy came and sowed [x]tares also among the wheat, and went away.

[26]"But when the wheat sprang up and bore grain, then the tares became evident also.

[27]"And the slaves of the landowner came and said

[x]Or, *darnel*, a weed resembling wheat

18 Ὑμεῖς οὖν ἀκούσατε τὴν παραβολὴν
[2]Ye [3]therefore [1]hear the parable

τοῦ σπείραντος. **19** Παντὸς ἀκούοντος
of the sowing [one]. Everyone hearing[a]
=When anyone hears

τὸν λόγον τῆς βασιλείας καὶ μὴ συνιέντος
the word of the kingdom and not understanding[a]
=does not understand

ἔρχεται ὁ πονηρὸς καὶ ἁρπάζει τὸ
comes the evil one and seizes the [thing]

ἐσπαρμένον ἐν τῇ καρδίᾳ αὐτοῦ· οὗτός
having been sown in the heart of him; this

ἐστιν ὁ παρὰ τὴν ὁδὸν σπαρείς. **20** ὁ
is the [word] by the way sown. the [word]

δὲ ἐπὶ τὰ πετρώδη σπαρείς, οὗτός ἐστιν
And on the rocky places sown, this is

ὁ τὸν λόγον ἀκούων καὶ εὐθὺς μετὰ
the [one] [2]the [3]word [1]hearing and immediately with

χαρᾶς λαμβάνων αὐτόν· **21** οὐκ ἔχει δὲ
joy receiving it; but he has not

ῥίζαν ἐν ἑαυτῷ ἀλλὰ πρόσκαιρός ἐστιν,
root in himself but short-lived is,

γενομένης δὲ θλίψεως ἢ διωγμοῦ
and occurring tribulation or persecution[a]
=when tribulation or persecution occurs

διὰ τὸν λόγον εὐθὺς σκανδαλίζεται.
on account of the word immediately he is offended.

22 ὁ δὲ εἰς τὰς ἀκάνθας σπαρείς, οὗτός
But the [word] in the thorns sown, this

ἐστιν ὁ τὸν λόγον ἀκούων, καὶ ἡ
is the [one] [2]the [3]word [1]hearing, and the

μέριμνα τοῦ αἰῶνος καὶ ἡ ἀπάτη
anxiety of the age and the deceit

τοῦ πλούτου συμπνίγει τὸν λόγον, καὶ
– of riches chokes the word, and

ἄκαρπος γίνεται. **23** ὁ δὲ ἐπὶ τὴν
unfruitful it becomes. And the [word] on the

καλὴν γῆν σπαρείς, οὗτός ἐστιν ὁ
good earth sown, this is the [one]

τὸν λόγον ἀκούων καὶ συνιείς, ὃς
[4]the [5]word [1]hearing [2]and [3]understanding, who

δὴ καρποφορεῖ καὶ ποιεῖ ὃ μὲν ἑκατόν,
indeed bears fruit and produces one indeed a hundred,

ὃ δὲ ἑξήκοντα, ὃ δὲ τριάκοντα.
the other sixty, the other thirty.

24 Ἄλλην παραβολὴν παρέθηκεν αὐτοῖς
Another parable he set before them

λέγων· ὡμοιώθη ἡ βασιλεία τῶν
saying: was(is) likened The kingdom of the

οὐρανῶν ἀνθρώπῳ σπείραντι καλὸν σπέρμα
heavens to a man sowing good seed

ἐν τῷ ἀγρῷ αὐτοῦ. **25** ἐν δὲ τῷ
in the field of him. But in the
=while men slept

καθεύδειν τοὺς ἀνθρώπους ἦλθεν αὐτοῦ
to sleep – men[e] came of him

ὁ ἐχθρὸς καὶ ἐπέσπειρεν ζιζάνια ἀνὰ μέσον
the enemy and oversowed tares in between

τοῦ σίτου καὶ ἀπῆλθεν. **26** ὅτε δὲ
the wheat and went away. But when

ἐβλάστησεν ὁ χόρτος καὶ καρπὸν
sprouted the grass and fruit

ἐποίησεν, τότε ἐφάνη καὶ τὰ ζιζάνια.
produced, then appeared also the tares.

27 προσελθόντες δὲ οἱ δοῦλοι τοῦ οἰκο-
So approaching the slaves of the house-

[18]"Listen then to what
the parable of the sower
means: [19]When anyone
hears the message about
the kingdom and does not
understand it, the evil one
comes and snatches away
what was sown in his heart.
This is the seed sown along
the path. [20]The one who received the seed that fell on
rocky places is the man
who hears the word and at
once receives it with joy.
[21]But since he has no root,
he lasts only a short time.
When trouble or persecu-
tion comes because of the
word, he quickly falls
away. [22]The one who re-
ceived the seed that fell
among the thorns is the
man who hears the word,
but the worries of this life
and the deceitfulness of
wealth choke it, making it
unfruitful. [23]But the one
who received the seed that
fell on good soil is the man
who hears the word and understands it. He produces a
crop, yielding a hundred,
sixty or thirty times what
was sown."

The Parable of the Weeds

[24]Jesus told them another
parable: "The kingdom of
heaven is like a man who
sowed good seed in his
field. [25]But while everyone
was sleeping, his enemy
came and sowed weeds
among the wheat, and went
away. [26]When the wheat
sprouted and formed
heads, then the weeds also
appeared.
[27]"The owner's servants
came to him and said, 'Sir,

to him, 'Sir, did you not
sow good seed in your
field? How then does it
have tares?'
28"And he said to them,
'An enemy has done this!'
And the slaves *said to
him, 'Do you want us,
then, to go and gather them
up?'
29"But he *said, 'No; lest
while you are gathering up
the tares, you may root up
the wheat with them.
30'Allow both to grow to-
gether until the harvest;
and in the time of the harvest I will say to the reapers, "First gather up the
tares and bind them in bundles to burn them up; but
gather the wheat into my
barn." ' "

The Mustard Seed

31He presented another
parable to them, saying,
"The kingdom of heaven is
like a mustard seed, which
a man took and sowed in
his field;
32and this is smaller than
all *other* seeds; but when it
is full grown, it is larger
than the garden plants, and
becomes a tree, so that THE
BIRDS OF THE AIR come and
NEST IN ITS BRANCHES."

The Leaven

33He spoke another para-
ble to them, "The kingdom
of heaven is like leaven,
which a woman took, and
hid in three pecks of meal,
until it was all leavened."
34All these things Jesus
spoke to the multitudes in
parables, and He did not
speak to them without a
parable,
35so that what was
spoken through the prophet
might be fulfilled, saying,
"I WILL OPEN MY MOUTH
IN PARABLES;

δεσπότου εἶπον αὐτῷ· κύριε, οὐχὶ καλὸν
master said to him: Lord, not good
σπέρμα ἔσπειρας ἐν τῷ σῷ ἀγρῷ;
seed sowedst thou in – thy field?
πόθεν οὖν ἔχει ζιζάνια; **28** ὁ δὲ ἔφη
whence then has it tares? And he said
αὐτοῖς· ἐχθρὸς ἄνθρωπος τοῦτο ἐποίησεν.
to them: An enemy *man* this did.
οἱ δὲ δοῦλοι αὐτῷ λέγουσιν· θέλεις
So the slaves to him say: Willest thou
οὖν ἀπελθόντες συλλέξωμεν αὐτά; **29** ὁ
then going away we may collect them? he
δέ φησιν· οὔ, μήποτε συλλέγοντες τὰ
But says: No, lest collecting the
ζιζάνια ἐκριζώσητε ἅμα αὐτοῖς τὸν
tares ye should root up together with them the
σῖτον. **30** ἄφετε συναυξάνεσθαι ἀμφότερα
wheat. Leave to grow together both
ἕως τοῦ θερισμοῦ· καὶ ἐν καιρῷ τοῦ
until the harvest; and in time of the
θερισμοῦ ἐρῶ τοῖς θερισταῖς· συλλέξατε
harvest I will say to the reapers: Collect ye
πρῶτον τὰ ζιζάνια καὶ δήσατε αὐτὰ
first the tares and bind them
εἰς δέσμας πρὸς τὸ κατακαῦσαι αὐτά,
in bundles – – to burn them,
τὸν δὲ σῖτον συναγάγετε εἰς τὴν ἀποθήκην
but the wheat gather ye into the barn
μου. **31** Ἄλλην παραβολὴν παρέθηκεν
of me. Another parable he set before
αὐτοῖς λέγων· ὁμοία ἐστὶν ἡ βασιλεία
them saying: Like is the kingdom
τῶν οὐρανῶν κόκκῳ σινάπεως, ὃν
of the heavens to a grain of mustard, which
λαβὼν ἄνθρωπος ἔσπειρεν ἐν τῷ ἀγρῷ
[2]taking [1]a man sowed in the field
αὐτοῦ· **32** ὃ μικρότερον μέν ἐστιν
of him; which less indeed is
πάντων τῶν σπερμάτων, ὅταν δὲ
[than] all the seeds, but when
αὐξηθῇ, μεῖζον τῶν λαχάνων ἐστὶν
it grows, greater [than] the herbs it is
καὶ γίνεται δένδρον, ὥστε ἐλθεῖν τὰ
and becomes a tree, so as to come the
πετεινὰ τοῦ οὐρανοῦ καὶ κατασκηνοῦν
birds of the heaven and dwell
ἐν τοῖς κλάδοις αὐτοῦ. **33** Ἄλλην
in the branches of it. Another
παραβολὴν ἐλάλησεν αὐτοῖς· ὁμοία
parable he spoke to them: Like
ἐστὶν ἡ βασιλεία τῶν οὐρανῶν ζύμῃ,
is the kingdom of the heavens to leaven,
ἣν λαβοῦσα γυνὴ ἐνέκρυψεν εἰς ἀλεύρου
which [2]taking [1]a woman hid in [3]of meal
σάτα τρία, ἕως οὗ ἐζυμώθη ὅλον.
[2]measures [1]three, until was leavened [the] whole.
34 Ταῦτα πάντα ἐλάλησεν ὁ Ἰησοῦς ἐν
These things all spoke – Jesus in
παραβολαῖς τοῖς ὄχλοις, καὶ χωρὶς παραβολῆς
parables to the crowds, and without a parable
οὐδὲν ἐλάλει αὐτοῖς· **35** ὅπως πληρωθῇ
nothing he spoke to them; so that was fulfilled
τὸ ῥηθὲν διὰ τοῦ προφήτου λέγοντος·
the [thing] spoken through the prophet saying:
ἀνοίξω ἐν παραβολαῖς τὸ στόμα μου,
I will open in parables the mouth of me,

didn't you sow good seed in
your field? Where then did
the weeds come from?'
28" 'An enemy did this,'
he replied.
"The servants asked him,
'Do you want us to go and
pull them up?'
29" 'No,' he answered,
'because while you are
pulling the weeds, you may
root up the wheat with
them. 30Let both grow to-
gether until the harvest. At
that time I will tell the harvesters: First collect the
weeds and tie them in bundles to be burned; then
gather the wheat and bring
it into my barn.' "

The Parables of the Mustard Seed and the Yeast

31He told them another
parable: "The kingdom of
heaven is like a mustard
seed, which a man took and
planted in his field.
32Though it is the smallest
of all your seeds, yet when
it grows, it is the largest of
garden plants and becomes
a tree, so that the birds of
the air come and perch in
its branches."
33He told them still another parable: "The kingdom
of heaven is like yeast that
a woman took and mixed
into a large amount[a] of
flour until it worked all
through the dough."
34Jesus spoke all these
things to the crowd in parables; he did not say any-
thing to them without using
a parable. 35So was fulfilled
what was spoken through
the prophet:

"I will open my mouth
in parables,

[a]33 Greek *three satas* (probably about 1/2 bushel or 22 liters)

I WILL UTTER THINGS HIDDEN SINCE THE FOUNDATION OF THE WORLD.''

The Tares Explained

36 Then He left the multitudes, and went into the
house. And His disciples
came to Him, saying, ''Explain to us the parable of
the tares of the field.''
37 And He answered and
said, ''The one who sows
the good seed is the Son of
Man,
38 and the field is the
world; and *as for* the good
seed, these are the sons of
the kingdom; and the tares
are the sons of the evil *one;*
39 and the enemy who
sowed them is the devil,
and the harvest is the end of
the age; and the reapers are
angels.
40 ''Therefore just as the
tares are gathered up and
burned with fire, so shall it
be at the end of the age.
41 ''The Son of Man will
send forth His angels, and
they will gather out of His
kingdom all stumbling
blocks, and those who
commit lawlessness,
42 and will cast them into
the furnace of fire; in that
place there shall be weeping and gnashing of teeth.
43 ''Then THE RIGHTEOUS
WILL SHINE FORTH AS THE
SUN in the kingdom of their
Father. He who has ears,
let him hear.

Hidden Treasure

44 ''The kingdom of

ἐρεύξομαι κεκρυμμένα ἀπὸ καταβολῆς.
I will utter things having been hidden from [the] foundation.

36 Τότε ἀφεὶς τοὺς ὄχλους ἦλθεν
Then sending away the crowds he came

εἰς τὴν οἰκίαν. Καὶ προσῆλθον αὐτῷ
into the house. And approached *to* him

οἱ μαθηταὶ αὐτοῦ λέγοντες· διασάφησον
the disciples of him saying: Explain thou

ἡμῖν τὴν παραβολὴν τῶν ζιζανίων τοῦ
to us the parable of the tares of the

ἀγροῦ. 37 ὁ δὲ ἀποκριθεὶς εἶπεν· ὁ
field. And he answering said: The [one]

σπείρων τὸ καλὸν σπέρμα ἐστὶν ὁ
sowing the good seed is the

υἱὸς τοῦ ἀνθρώπου· 38 ὁ δὲ ἀγρός
Son – of man; and the field

ἐστιν ὁ κόσμος· τὸ δὲ καλὸν σπέρμα,
is the world; and the good seed,

οὗτοί εἰσιν οἱ υἱοὶ τῆς βασιλείας· τὰ δὲ
these are the sons of the kingdom; and the

ζιζάνιά εἰσιν οἱ υἱοὶ τοῦ πονηροῦ, 39 ὁ
tares are the sons of the evil [one], the

δὲ ἐχθρὸς ὁ σπείρας αὐτά ἐστιν ὁ
and enemy the [one] sowing them is the

διάβολος· ὁ δὲ θερισμὸς συντέλεια
devil; and the harvest [the] completion

αἰῶνός ἐστιν, οἱ δὲ θερισταὶ ἄγγελοί
of [the] age is, and the reapers angels

εἰσιν. 40 ὥσπερ οὖν συλλέγεται τὰ
are. As therefore are collected the

ζιζάνια καὶ πυρὶ κατακαίεται, οὕτως
tares and with fire are consumed, thus

ἔσται ἐν τῇ συντελείᾳ τοῦ αἰῶνος·
it will be at the completion of the age;

41 ἀποστελεῖ ὁ υἱὸς τοῦ ἀνθρώπου
will send forth the Son – of man

τοὺς ἀγγέλους αὐτοῦ, καὶ συλλέξουσιν
the angels of him, and they will collect

ἐκ τῆς βασιλείας αὐτοῦ πάντα
out of the kingdom of him all

τὰ σκάνδαλα καὶ τοὺς ποιοῦντας
the things leading to sin and the [ones] doing

τὴν ἀνομίαν, 42 καὶ βαλοῦσιν αὐτοὺς εἰς
– lawlessness, and will cast them into

τὴν κάμινον τοῦ πυρός· ἐκεῖ ἔσται ὁ
the furnace – of fire; there will be the

κλαυθμὸς καὶ ὁ βρυγμὸς τῶν ὀδόντων.
wailing and the gnashing of the teeth.

43 τότε οἱ δίκαιοι ἐκλάμψουσιν ὡς ὁ
Then the righteous will shine forth as the

ἥλιος ἐν τῇ βασιλείᾳ τοῦ πατρὸς
sun in the kingdom of the Father

αὐτῶν. ὁ ἔχων ὦτα ἀκουέτω.
of them. The [one] having ears let him hear.

44 Ὁμοία ἐστὶν ἡ βασιλεία τῶν
Like is the kingdom of the

οὐρανῶν θησαυρῷ κεκρυμμένῳ ἐν τῷ
heavens to treasure *having been* hidden in the

ἀγρῷ, ὃν εὑρὼν ἄνθρωπος ἔκρυψεν, καὶ
field, which [2]finding [1]a man hid, and

ἀπὸ τῆς χαρᾶς αὐτοῦ ὑπάγει καὶ πωλεῖ
from the joy of him goes and sells

ὅσα ἔχει καὶ ἀγοράζει τὸν ἀγρὸν
what things he has and buys – field

ἐκεῖνον. 45 Πάλιν ὁμοία ἐστὶν ἡ
that. Again like is the

I will utter things
hidden since the
creation of the
world.''[b]

The Parable of the Weeds Explained

36 Then he left the crowd
and went into the house.
His disciples came to him
and said, ''Explain to us
the parable of the weeds in
the field.''
37 He answered, ''The one
who sowed the good seed is
the Son of Man. 38 The field
is the world, and the good
seed stands for the sons of
the kingdom. The weeds
are the sons of the evil one,
39 and the enemy who sows
them is the devil. The harvest is the end of the age,
and the harvesters are angels.
40 ''As the weeds are
pulled up and burned in the
fire, so it will be at the end
of the age. 41 The Son of
Man will send out his an-
gels, and they will weed out
of his kingdom everything
that causes sin and all who
do evil. 42 They will throw
them into the fiery furnace,
where there will be weep-
ing and gnashing of teeth.
43 Then the righteous will
shine like the sun in the
kingdom of their Father.
He who has ears, let him
hear.

The Parables of the Hidden Treasure and the Pearl

44 ''The kingdom of heav-

[b] *35* Psalm 78:2

heaven is like a treasure hidden in the field, which a man found and hid; and from joy over it he goes and sells all that he has, and buys that field.

A Costly Pearl

45"Again, the kingdom of heaven is like a merchant seeking fine pearls,

46and upon finding one pearl of great value, he went and sold all that he had, and bought it.

A Dragnet

47"Again, the kingdom of heaven is like a dragnet cast into the sea, and gathering *fish* of every kind;

48and when it was filled, they drew it up on the beach; and they sat down, and gathered the good *fish* into containers, but the bad they threw away.

49"So it will be at the end of the age; the angels shall come forth, and take out the wicked from among the righteous,

50and will cast them into the furnace of fire; there shall be weeping and gnashing of teeth.

51"Have you understood all these things?" They *said to Him, "Yes."

52And He said to them, "Therefore every scribe who has become a disciple of the kingdom of heaven is like a head of a household, who brings forth out of his treasure things new and old."

Jesus Revisits Nazareth

53And it came about that when Jesus had finished these parables, He departed from there.

54And coming to His home town He *began* teaching them in their synagogue, so that they became astonished, and said, "Where *did* this man *get* this wisdom, and *these* miraculous powers?

55"Is not this the carpenter's son? Is not His mother called Mary, and His brothers, James and Joseph and

βασιλεία τῶν οὐρανῶν ἐμπόρῳ ζητοῦντι
kingdom of the heavens to a merchant seeking

καλοὺς μαργαρίτας· **46** εὑρὼν δὲ ἕνα πολύτιμον
beautiful pearls; and finding one valuable

μαργαρίτην ἀπελθὼν πέπρακεν πάντα
pearl going away sold all things

ὅσα εἶχεν καὶ ἠγόρασεν αὐτόν.
what he had and bought it.

47 Πάλιν ὁμοία ἐστὶν ἡ βασιλεία τῶν
Again like is the kingdom of the

οὐρανῶν σαγήνῃ βληθείσῃ εἰς τὴν θάλασσαν
heavens to a net cast into the sea

καὶ ἐκ παντὸς γένους συναγαγούσῃ·
and of every kind gathering;

48 ἣν ὅτε ἐπληρώθη ἀναβιβάσαντες ἐπὶ
which when it was filled bringing up onto

τὸν αἰγιαλὸν καὶ καθίσαντες συνέλεξαν
the shore and sitting collected

τὰ καλὰ εἰς ἄγγη, τὰ δὲ σαπρὰ ἔξω
the good into vessels, but the bad out

ἔβαλον. **49** οὕτως ἔσται ἐν τῇ συντελείᾳ
cast. Thus it will be at the completion

τοῦ αἰῶνος· ἐξελεύσονται οἱ ἄγγελοι καὶ
of the age: will go forth the angels and

ἀφοριοῦσιν τοὺς πονηροὺς ἐκ μέσου
will separate the evil men from [the] midst

τῶν δικαίων, **50** καὶ βαλοῦσιν αὐτοὺς
of the righteous, and will cast them

εἰς τὴν κάμινον τοῦ πυρός· ἐκεῖ
into the furnace – of fire; there

ἔσται ὁ κλαυθμὸς καὶ ὁ βρυγμὸς τῶν
will be the wailing and the gnashing of the

ὀδόντων. **51** Συνήκατε ταῦτα πάντα;
teeth. Did ye understand [2]these things [1]all?

λέγουσιν αὐτῷ· ναί. **52** ὁ δὲ εἶπεν
They say to him: Yes. So he said

αὐτοῖς· διὰ τοῦτο πᾶς γραμματεὺς
to them: Therefore every scribe

μαθητευθεὶς τῇ βασιλείᾳ τῶν οὐρανῶν
made a disciple to the kingdom of the heavens

ὅμοιός ἐστιν ἀνθρώπῳ οἰκοδεσπότῃ,
like is to *a man* a housemaster,

ὅστις ἐκβάλλει ἐκ τοῦ θησαυροῦ
who puts forth out of the treasure

αὐτοῦ καινὰ καὶ παλαιά.
of him new and old things.

53 Καὶ ἐγένετο ὅτε ἐτέλεσεν ὁ
And it came to pass when ended –

Ἰησοῦς τὰς παραβολὰς ταύτας, μετῆρεν
Jesus – parables these, he removed

ἐκεῖθεν. **54** καὶ ἐλθὼν εἰς τὴν πατρίδα
thence. And coming into the native town

αὐτοῦ ἐδίδασκεν αὐτοὺς ἐν τῇ συνα-
of him he taught them in the syna-

γωγῇ αὐτῶν, ὥστε ἐκπλήσσεσθαι αὐτοὺς
gogue of them, so as to be astounded them
=so that they were astounded

καὶ λέγειν· πόθεν τούτῳ ἡ σοφία αὕτη
and to say[b]: Whence to this man – wisdom this
and said:

καὶ αἱ δυνάμεις; **55** οὐχ οὗτός ἐστιν
and the powerful deeds? not this man is

ὁ τοῦ τέκτονος υἱός; οὐχ ἡ μήτηρ
the of the carpenter son? not the mother

αὐτοῦ λέγεται Μαριὰμ καὶ οἱ ἀδελφοὶ
of him called Mary and the brothers

αὐτοῦ Ἰάκωβος καὶ Ἰωσὴφ καὶ Σίμων
of him James and Joseph and Simon

en is like treasure hidden in
a field. When a man found
it, he hid it again, and then
in his joy went and sold all
he had and bought that
field.
45"Again, the kingdom of
heaven is like a merchant
looking for fine pearls.
46When he found one of
great value, he went away
and sold everything he had
and bought it.

The Parable of the Net

47"Once again, the kingdom of heaven is like a net
that was let down into the
lake and caught all kinds of
fish. 48When it was full, the
fishermen pulled it up on
the shore. Then they sat
down and collected the
good fish in baskets, but
threw the bad away. 49This
is how it will be at the end
of the age. The angels will
come and separate the
wicked from the righteous
50and throw them into the
fiery furnace, where there
will be weeping and gnashing of teeth.
51"Have you understood
all these things?" Jesus
asked.
"Yes," they replied.
52He said to them,
"Therefore every teacher
of the law who has been instructed about the kingdom
of heaven is like the owner
of a house who brings out
of his storeroom new treasures as well as old."

A Prophet Without Honor

53When Jesus had finished these parables, he
moved on from there.
54Coming to his hometown,
he began teaching the people in their synagogue, and
they were amazed. "Where
did this man get this wisdom and these miraculous
powers?" they asked.
55"Isn't this the carpenter's son? Isn't his mother's name Mary, and aren't
his brothers James, Joseph,

Simon and Judas?

56"And His sisters, are they not all with us? Where then *did* this man *get* all these things?"

57And they took offense at Him. But Jesus said to them, "A prophet is not without honor except in his home town, and in his *own* household."

58And He did not do many miracles there because of their unbelief.

καὶ Ἰούδας; **56** καὶ αἱ ἀδελφαὶ αὐτοῦ
and Judas? and the sisters of him
οὐχὶ πᾶσαι πρὸς ἡμᾶς εἰσιν; πόθεν
not all with us are? Whence
οὖν τούτῳ ταῦτα πάντα; **57** καὶ
then to this man these things all? And
ἐσκανδαλίζοντο ἐν αὐτῷ. ὁ δὲ Ἰησοῦς
they were offended in him. – But Jesus
εἶπεν αὐτοῖς· οὐκ ἔστιν προφήτης
said to them: [3]not [2]is [1]A prophet
ἄτιμος εἰ μὴ ἐν τῇ πατρίδι καὶ
unhonoured except in the(his) native town and
ἐν τῇ οἰκίᾳ αὐτοῦ. **58** καὶ οὐκ ἐποίησεν ἐκεῖ
in the house of him. And not he did there
δυνάμεις πολλὰς διὰ τὴν ἀπιστίαν αὐτῶν.
powerful deeds many because of the unbelief of them.

Simon and Judas? 56Aren't all his sisters with us? Where then did this man get all these things?" 57And they took offense at him.

But Jesus said to them, "Only in his hometown and in his own house is a prophet without honor."

58And he did not do many miracles there because of their lack of faith.

Chapter 14

John the Baptist Beheaded

At that time Herod the tetrarch heard the news about Jesus,

2and said to his servants, "This is John the Baptist; he has risen from the dead; and that is why miraculous powers are at work in him."

3For when Herod had John arrested, he bound him, and put him in prison on account of Herodias, the wife of his brother Philip.

4For John had been saying to him, "It is not lawful for you to have her."

5And although he wanted to put him to death, he feared the multitude, because they regarded him as a prophet.

6But when Herod's birthday came, the daughter of Herodias danced before *them* and pleased Herod.

7Thereupon he promised with an oath to give her whatever she asked.

8And having been prompted by her mother, she *said, "Give me here on a platter the head of John the Baptist."

9And although he was grieved, the king commanded *it* to be given because of his oaths, and because of his dinner guests.

10And he sent and had

14 Ἐν ἐκείνῳ τῷ καιρῷ ἤκουσεν
At that – time heard
Ἡρῴδης ὁ τετραάρχης τὴν ἀκοὴν Ἰησοῦ,
Herod the tetrarch the report of Jesus,
2 καὶ εἶπεν τοῖς παισὶν αὐτοῦ· οὗτός
and said to the servants of him: This
ἐστιν Ἰωάννης ὁ βαπτιστής· αὐτὸς
is John the Baptist; he
ἠγέρθη ἀπὸ τῶν νεκρῶν, καὶ διὰ τοῦτο
was raised from the dead, and therefore
αἱ δυνάμεις ἐνεργοῦσιν ἐν αὐτῷ.
the powerful deeds operate in him.
3 Ὁ γὰρ Ἡρῴδης κρατήσας τὸν Ἰωάννην
– For Herod seizing – John
ἔδησεν καὶ ἐν φυλακῇ ἀπέθετο διὰ
bound and in prison put away on account of
Ἡρῳδιάδα τὴν γυναῖκα Φιλίππου τοῦ
Herodias the wife of Philip the
ἀδελφοῦ αὐτοῦ· **4** ἔλεγεν γὰρ ὁ Ἰωάννης
brother of him; for said – John
αὐτῷ· οὐκ ἔξεστίν σοι ἔχειν αὐτήν.
to him: It is not lawful for thee to have her.
5 καὶ θέλων αὐτὸν ἀποκτεῖναι ἐφοβήθη
And wishing him to kill he feared
τὸν ὄχλον, ὅτι ὡς προφήτην αὐτὸν
the crowd, because as a prophet him
εἶχον. **6** γενεσίοις δὲ γενομένοις τοῦ
they had. Now on the birthday occurring° –
Ἡρῴδου ὠρχήσατο ἡ θυγάτηρ τῆς
of Herod danced the daughter –
Ἡρῳδιάδος ἐν τῷ μέσῳ καὶ ἤρεσεν
of Herodias in the midst and pleased
τῷ Ἡρῴδῃ, **7** ὅθεν μεθ' ὅρκου ὡμολόγησεν
– Herod, whence with an oath he promised
αὐτῇ δοῦναι ὃ ἐὰν αἰτήσηται. **8** ἡ δὲ
[2]her [1]to give whatever she might ask. So she
προβιβασθεῖσα ὑπὸ τῆς μητρὸς αὐτῆς·
being instructed by the mother of her:
δός μοι, φησίν, ὧδε ἐπὶ πίνακι τὴν
Give me, she says, here on a platter the
κεφαλὴν Ἰωάννου τοῦ βαπτιστοῦ. **9** καὶ
head of John the Baptist. And
λυπηθεὶς ὁ βασιλεὺς διὰ τοὺς
being grieved the king on account of the
ὅρκους καὶ τοὺς συνανακειμένους
oaths and the [ones] reclining at table with [him]
ἐκέλευσεν δοθῆναι, **10** καὶ πέμψας
he commanded to be given, and sending

Chapter 14

John the Baptist Beheaded

At that time Herod the tetrarch heard the reports about Jesus, 2and he said to his attendants, "This is John the Baptist; he has risen from the dead! That is why miraculous powers are at work in him."

3Now Herod had arrested John and bound him and put him in prison because of Herodias, his brother Philip's wife, 4for John had been saying to him: "It is not lawful for you to have her." 5Herod wanted to kill John, but he was afraid of the people, because they considered him a prophet.

6On Herod's birthday the daughter of Herodias danced for them and pleased Herod so much 7that he promised with an oath to give her whatever she asked. 8Prompted by her mother, she said, "Give me here on a platter the head of John the Baptist." 9The king was distressed, but because of his oaths and his dinner guests, he ordered that her request be granted 10and had John

John beheaded in the prison.
11And his head was
brought on a platter and
given to the girl; and she
brought *it* to her mother.
12And his disciples came
and took away the body
and buried it; and they went
and reported to Jesus.

Five Thousand Fed

13Now when Jesus heard
it, He withdrew from there
in a boat, to a lonely place
by Himself; and when the
multitudes heard *of this,*
they followed Him on foot
from the cities.
14And when He went
ashore, He saw a great multitude, and felt compassion
for them, and healed their
sick.
15And when it was eve-
ning, the disciples came to
Him, saying, "The place is
desolate, and the time is already past; so send the multitudes away, that they may
go into the villages and buy
food for themselves."
16But Jesus said to them,
"They do not need to go
away; you give them *something* to eat!"
17And they *said to Him,
"We have here only five
loaves and two fish."
18And He said, "Bring
them here to Me."
19And ordering the multi-
tudes to recline on the
grass, He took the five
loaves and the two fish, and
looking up toward heaven,
He blessed *the food,* and
breaking the loaves He
gave them to the disciples,
and the disciples *gave* to
the multitudes,
20and they all ate, and
were satisfied. And they
picked up what was left

ἀπεκεφάλισεν Ἰωάννην ἐν τῇ φυλακῇ.
beheaded John in the prison.
11 καὶ ἠνέχθη ἡ κεφαλὴ αὐτοῦ ἐπὶ
And was brought the head of him on
πίνακι καὶ ἐδόθη τῷ κορασίῳ, καὶ
a platter and was given to the maid, and
ἤνεγκεν τῇ μητρὶ αὐτῆς. 12 καὶ
she brought [it] to the mother of her. And
προσελθόντες οἱ μαθηταὶ αὐτοῦ ἦραν τὸ
[4]approaching [1]the [2]disciples [3]of him took the
πτῶμα καὶ ἔθαψαν αὐτόν, καὶ ἐλθόντες
corpse and buried him, and coming
ἀπήγγειλαν τῷ Ἰησοῦ. 13 Ἀκούσας δὲ
reported – to Jesus. And [2]hearing
ὁ Ἰησοῦς ἀνεχώρησεν ἐκεῖθεν ἐν
– [1]Jesus departed thence in
πλοίῳ εἰς ἔρημον τόπον κατ' ἰδίαν·
a ship to a desert place privately;
καὶ ἀκούσαντες οἱ ὄχλοι ἠκολούθησαν
and [3]hearing [1]the [2]crowds followed
αὐτῷ πεζῇ ἀπὸ τῶν πόλεων. 14 Καὶ
him afoot from the cities. And
ἐξελθὼν εἶδεν πολὺν ὄχλον, καὶ
going forth he saw a much crowd, and
ἐσπλαγχνίσθη ἐπ' αὐτοῖς καὶ
was filled with tenderness over them and
ἐθεράπευσεν τοὺς ἀρρώστους αὐτῶν.
healed the sick of them.
15 ὀψίας δὲ γενομένης προσῆλθον αὐτῷ
Now evening coming on* approached to him
=when evening came on
οἱ μαθηταὶ λέγοντες· ἔρημός ἐστιν ὁ
the disciples saying: Desert is the
τόπος καὶ ἡ ὥρα ἤδη παρῆλθεν·
place and the hour already passed;
ἀπόλυσον οὖν τοὺς ὄχλους, ἵνα ἀπελθόντες
dismiss therefore the crowds, that going away
εἰς τὰς κώμας ἀγοράσωσιν ἑαυτοῖς
into the villages they may buy for themselves
βρώματα. 16 ὁ δὲ Ἰησοῦς εἶπεν αὐτοῖς·
foods. – But Jesus said to them:
οὐ χρείαν ἔχουσιν ἀπελθεῖν· δότε
Not need they have to go away; give
αὐτοῖς ὑμεῖς φαγεῖν. 17 οἱ δὲ λέγουσιν
them ye to eat. But they say
αὐτῷ· οὐκ ἔχομεν ὧδε εἰ μὴ πέντε
to him: We have not here except five
ἄρτους καὶ δύο ἰχθύας. 18 ὁ δὲ εἶπεν·
loaves and two fishes. And he said:
φέρετέ μοι ὧδε αὐτούς. 19 καὶ κελεύσας
Bring to me here them. And having commanded
τοὺς ὄχλους ἀνακλιθῆναι ἐπὶ τοῦ χόρτου,
the crowds to recline on the grass,
λαβὼν τοὺς πέντε ἄρτους καὶ τοὺς δύο
taking the five loaves and the two
ἰχθύας, ἀναβλέψας εἰς τὸν οὐρανὸν
fishes, looking up to – heaven
εὐλόγησεν, καὶ κλάσας ἔδωκεν τοῖς
he blessed, and breaking gave to the
μαθηταῖς τοὺς ἄρτους, οἱ δὲ μαθηταὶ
disciples the loaves, and the disciples
τοῖς ὄχλοις. 20 καὶ ἔφαγον πάντες καὶ
to the crowds, And ate all and
ἐχορτάσθησαν· καὶ ἦραν τὸ περισσεῦον
were satisfied; and they took the excess

beheaded in the prison.
11His head was brought in
on a platter and given to the
girl, who carried it to her
mother. 12John's disciples
came and took his body and
buried it. Then they went
and told Jesus.

Jesus Feeds the Five Thousand

13When Jesus heard what
had happened, he withdrew
by boat privately to a solitary place. Hearing of this,
the crowds followed him on
foot from the towns.
14When Jesus landed and
saw a large crowd, he had
compassion on them and
healed their sick.
15As evening ap-
proached, the disciples
came to him and said,
"This is a remote place,
and it's already getting late.
Send the crowds away, so
they can go to the villages
and buy themselves some
food."
16Jesus replied, "They do
not need to go away. You
give them something to
eat."
17"We have here only
five loaves of bread and
two fish," they answered.
18"Bring them here to
me," he said. 19And he directed the people to sit
down on the grass. Taking
the five loaves and the two
fish and looking up to heav-
en, he gave thanks and
broke the loaves. Then he
gave them to the disciples,
and the disciples gave them
to the people. 20They all ate
and were satisfied, and the
disciples picked up twelve

over of the broken pieces,
twelve full baskets.
21And there were about
five thousand men who ate,
aside from women and children.

Jesus Walks on the Water

22And immediately He
made the disciples get into
the boat, and go ahead of
Him to the other side, while
He sent the multitudes
away.
23And after He had sent
the multitudes away, He
went up to the mountain by
Himself to pray; and when
it was evening, He was
there alone.
24But the boat was al-
ready many [y]stadia away
from the land, battered by
the waves; for the wind was
contrary.
25And in the [z]fourth
watch of the night He came
to them, walking on the
sea.
26And when the disciples
saw Him walking on the
sea, they were frightened,
saying, "It is a ghost!" And
they cried out for fear.
27But immediately Jesus
spoke to them, saying,
"Take courage, it is I; do
not be afraid."
28And Peter answered
Him and said, "Lord, if it is
You, command me to come
to You on the water."
29And He said, "Come!"
And Peter got out of the
boat, and walked on the
water and came toward
Jesus.
30But seeing the wind, he
became afraid, and begin-
ning to sink, he cried out,
saying, "Lord, save me!"
31And immediately Jesus
stretched out His hand and
took hold of him, and *said
to him, "O you of little

[y] A stadion was about 600 feet
[z] I.e., 3–6 a.m.

τῶν κλασμάτων, δώδεκα κοφίνους πλήρεις.
of the fragments, twelve baskets full.
21 οἱ δὲ ἐσθίοντες ἦσαν ἄνδρες ὡσεὶ
And the [ones] eating were men about
πεντακισχίλιοι χωρὶς γυναικῶν καὶ
five thousand apart from women and
παιδίων. 22 Καὶ [εὐθέως] ἠνάγκασεν
children. And immediately he constrained
τοὺς μαθητὰς ἐμβῆναι εἰς τὸ πλοῖον
the disciples to embark in the ship
καὶ προάγειν αὐτὸν εἰς τὸ πέραν,
and to go before him to the other side,
ἕως οὗ ἀπολύσῃ τοὺς ὄχλους. 23 Καὶ
until he should dismiss the crowds. And
ἀπολύσας τοὺς ὄχλους ἀνέβη εἰς τὸ
having dismissed the crowds he went up into the
ὄρος κατ' ἰδίαν προσεύξασθαι. ὀψίας
mountain privately to pray. evening
—And when
δὲ γενομένης μόνος ἦν ἐκεῖ. 24 τὸ δὲ
And coming on[a] alone he was there. But the
evening came on
πλοῖον ἤδη σταδίους πολλοὺς ἀπὸ τῆς
ship now furlongs many from the
γῆς ἀπεῖχεν, βασανιζόμενον ὑπὸ τῶν
land was away, being distressed by the
κυμάτων, ἦν γὰρ ἐναντίος ὁ ἄνεμος.
waves, [4]was [1]for [5]contrary [2]the [3]wind.
25 τετάρτῃ δὲ φυλακῇ τῆς νυκτὸς
Now in [the] fourth watch of the night
ἦλθεν πρὸς αὐτοὺς περιπατῶν ἐπὶ τὴν
he came toward them walking on the
θάλασσαν. 26 οἱ δὲ μαθηταὶ ἰδόντες
sea. And the disciples seeing
αὐτὸν ἐπὶ τῆς θαλάσσης περιπατοῦντα
him on the sea walking
ἐταράχθησαν λέγοντες ὅτι φάντασμά
were troubled saying[,] – A phantasm
ἐστιν, καὶ ἀπὸ τοῦ φόβου ἔκραξαν.
it is, and from – fear they cried out.
27 εὐθὺς δὲ ἐλάλησεν [ὁ Ἰησοῦς]
But immediately spoke – Jesus
αὐτοῖς λέγων· θαρσεῖτε, ἐγώ εἰμι·
to them saying: Be of good cheer, I am;
μὴ φοβεῖσθε. 28 ἀποκριθεὶς δὲ αὐτῷ ὁ
do not fear. And answering him –
Πέτρος εἶπεν· κύριε, εἰ σὺ εἶ, κέλευσόν
Peter said: Lord, if thou art, command
με ἐλθεῖν πρὸς σὲ ἐπὶ τὰ ὕδατα. 29 ὁ
me to come to thee on the waters. he
δὲ εἶπεν· ἐλθέ. καὶ καταβὰς ἀπὸ τοῦ
And said: Come. And going down from the
πλοίου Πέτρος περιεπάτησεν ἐπὶ τὰ ὕδατα
ship Peter walked on the waters
καὶ ἦλθεν πρὸς τὸν Ἰησοῦν. 30 βλέπων δὲ
and came toward – Jesus. But seeing
τὸν ἄνεμον ἐφοβήθη, καὶ ἀρξάμενος
the wind he was afraid, and beginning
καταποντίζεσθαι ἔκραξεν λέγων·
to sink he cried out saying:
κύριε, σῶσόν με. 31 εὐθέως δὲ ὁ
Lord, save me. And immediately –
Ἰησοῦς ἐκτείνας τὴν χεῖρα ἐπελάβετο
Jesus stretching out the(his) hand took hold
αὐτοῦ, καὶ λέγει αὐτῷ· ὀλιγόπιστε,
of him, and says to him: Little-faith,

basketfuls of broken pieces
that were left over. 21The
number of those who ate
was about five thousand
men, besides women and
children.

Jesus Walks on the Water

22Immediately Jesus
made the disciples get into
the boat and go on ahead of
him to the other side, while
he dismissed the crowd.
23After he had dismissed
them, he went up on a
mountainside by himself to
pray. When evening came,
he was there alone, 24but
the boat was already a considerable distance[c] from
land, buffeted by the waves
because the wind was
against it.
25During the fourth watch
of the night Jesus went out
to them, walking on the
lake. 26When the disciples
saw him walking on the
lake, they were terrified.
"It's a ghost," they said,
and cried out in fear.
27But Jesus immediately
said to them: "Take cour-
age! It is I. Don't be
afraid."
28"Lord, if it's you," Peter replied, "tell me to
come to you on the water."
29"Come," he said.
Then Peter got down out
of the boat, walked on the
water and came toward
Jesus. 30But when he saw
the wind, he was afraid
and, beginning to sink,
cried out, "Lord, save
me!"
31Immediately Jesus
reached out his hand and
caught him. "You of little

[c]24 Greek *many stadia*

faith, why did you doubt?"
32And when they got into
the boat, the wind stopped.
33And those who were in
the boat worshiped Him,
saying, "You are certainly
God's Son!"
34And when they had
crossed over, they came to
land at Gennesaret.
35And when the men of
that place recognized Him,
they sent into all that surrounding district and
brought to Him all who
were sick;
36and they *began* to en-
treat Him that they might
just touch the fringe of His
cloak; and as many as
touched *it* were cured.

εἰς τί ἐδίστασας; 32 καὶ ἀναβάντων
why didst thou doubt? And going up =as they went up
αὐτῶν εἰς τὸ πλοῖον ἐκόπασεν ὁ ἄνεμος.
them* into the ship ceased the wind.
33 οἱ δὲ ἐν τῷ πλοίῳ προσεκύνησαν αὐτῷ
And the [ones] in the ship worshipped him
λέγοντες· ἀληθῶς θεοῦ υἱὸς εἶ. 34 Καὶ
saying: Truly of God Son thou art. And
διαπεράσαντες ἦλθον ἐπὶ τὴν γῆν εἰς
crossing over they came onto the land to
Γεννησαρέτ. 35 καὶ ἐπιγνόντες αὐτὸν
Gennesaret. And recognizing him
οἱ ἄνδρες τοῦ τόπου ἐκείνου ἀπέστειλαν
the men – place of that sent
εἰς ὅλην τὴν περίχωρον ἐκείνην, καὶ
into all – neighbourhood that, and
προσήνεγκαν αὐτῷ πάντας τοὺς κακῶς
brought to him all the [ones] ill =those who were ill,
ἔχοντας, 36 καὶ παρεκάλουν αὐτὸν ἵνα
having, and besought him that
μόνον ἅψωνται τοῦ κρασπέδου τοῦ
only they might touch the fringe of the
ἱματίου αὐτοῦ· καὶ ὅσοι ἥψαντο διεσώθησαν.
garment of him; and as many as touched were completely healed.

faith," he said, "why did
you doubt?"
32And when they climbed
into the boat, the wind died
down. 33Then those who
were in the boat worshiped
him, saying, "Truly you
are the Son of God."
34When they had crossed
over, they landed at Gen-
nesaret. 35And when the
men of that place recog-
nized Jesus, they sent word
to all the surrounding country. People brought all their
sick to him 36and begged
him to let the sick just
touch the edge of his cloak,
and all who touched him
were healed.

Chapter 15

Tradition and Commandment

THEN some Pharisees
and scribes *came to
Jesus from Jerusalem, saying,
2"Why do Your disci-
ples transgress the tradition
of the elders? For they do
not wash their hands when
they eat bread."
3And He answered and
said to them, "And why do
you yourselves transgress
the commandment of God
for the sake of your tradition?
4"For God said, 'HONOR
YOUR FATHER AND MOTHER,'
and, 'HE WHO SPEAKS EVIL
OF FATHER OR MOTHER, LET
HIM BE PUT TO DEATH.'
5"But you say, 'Who-
ever shall say to *his* father
or mother, "Anything of
mine you might have been
helped by has been given *to
God*,"
6he is not to honor his
father [a]or his mother[b].'
And *thus* you invalidated
the word of God for the
sake of your tradition.
7"You hypocrites, right-
ly did Isaiah prophesy of
you, saying,
8 'THIS PEOPLE HONORS

15 Τότε προσέρχονται τῷ Ἰησοῦ
Then approach – to Jesus
ἀπὸ Ἱεροσολύμων Φαρισαῖοι καὶ γραμματεῖς
from Jerusalem Pharisees and scribes
λέγοντες· 2 διὰ τί οἱ μαθηταί σου
saying: Why the disciples of thee
παραβαίνουσιν τὴν παράδοσιν τῶν
transgress the tradition of the
πρεσβυτέρων; οὐ γὰρ νίπτονται τὰς χεῖρας
elders? for not they wash the(ir) hands
ὅταν ἄρτον ἐσθίωσιν. 3 ὁ δὲ ἀπο-
whenever bread they eat. And he answer-
κριθεὶς εἶπεν αὐτοῖς· διὰ τί καὶ ὑμεῖς
ing said to them: Why indeed ye
παραβαίνετε τὴν ἐντολὴν τοῦ θεοῦ
transgress the commandment – of God
διὰ τὴν παράδοσιν ὑμῶν; 4 ὁ γὰρ
on account of the tradition of you? – For
θεὸς εἶπεν· τίμα τὸν πατέρα καὶ τὴν
God said: Honour the father and the
μητέρα, καί· ὁ κακολογῶν πατέρα
mother, and: The [one] speaking evil of father
ἢ μητέρα θανάτῳ τελευτάτω. 5 ὑμεῖς δὲ
or mother by death let him die. But ye
λέγετε· ὃς ἂν εἴπῃ τῷ πατρὶ ἤ
say: Whoever says to the(his) father or
τῇ μητρί· δῶρον ὃ ἐὰν ἐξ ἐμοῦ
to the(his) mother: A gift whatever by me
ὠφελήθῃς, 6 οὐ μὴ τιμήσει τὸν
thou mightest be owed, by no means shall he honour the
πατέρα αὐτοῦ ἢ τὴν μητέρα αὐτοῦ·
father of him or the mother of him;
καὶ ἠκυρώσατε τὸν λόγον τοῦ θεοῦ
and ye annulled the word – of God
διὰ τὴν παράδοσιν ὑμῶν. 7 ὑποκρι-
on account of the tradition of you. Hypocrites,
ταί, καλῶς ἐπροφήτευσεν περὶ ὑμῶν
well prophesied concerning you
Ἠσαΐας λέγων· 8 ὁ λαὸς οὗτος τοῖς
Isaiah saying: This people with the

Chapter 15

Clean and Unclean

THEN some Pharisees
and teachers of the law
came to Jesus from Jerusalem and asked, 2"Why do
your disciples break the
tradition of the elders?
They don't wash their
hands before they eat!"
3Jesus replied, "And why
do you break the command
of God for the sake of your
tradition? 4For God said,
'Honor your father and
mother'[d] and 'Anyone
who curses his father or
mother must be put to
death.'[e] 5But you say that
if a man says to his father or
mother, 'Whatever help
you might otherwise have
received from me is a gift
devoted to God,' 6he is not
to 'honor his father'[f] with
it. Thus you nullify the
word of God for the sake of
your tradition. 7You hypocrites! Isaiah was right
when he prophesied about
you:
8" 'These people honor

[a] Many mss. do not contain *or his mother*
[b] I.e., by supporting them with it

[d] 4 Exodus 20:12; Deut. 5:16
[e] 4 Exodus 21:17; Lev. 20:9
[f] 6 Some manuscripts *father or his mother*

ME WITH THEIR LIPS,
BUT THEIR HEART IS
FAR AWAY FROM ME.
9 'BUT IN VAIN DO THEY
WORSHIP ME,
TEACHING AS DOC-
TRINES THE PRECEPTS
OF MEN.' "
10 And after He called the
multitude to Him, He said
to them, "Hear, and understand.
11 "Not what enters into
the mouth defiles the man,
but what proceeds out of
the mouth, this defiles the
man."
12 Then the disciples
*came and *said to Him,
"Do You know that the
Pharisees were offended
when they heard this
statement?"
13 But He answered and
said, "Every plant which
My heavenly Father did
not plant shall be rooted
up.
14 "Let them alone; they
are blind guides [c]of the
blind. And if a blind man
guides a blind man, both
will fall into a pit."

The Heart of Man

15 And Peter answered
and said to Him, "Explain
the parable to us."
16 And He said, "Are you
still lacking in understanding also?
17 "Do you not under-
stand that everything that
goes into the mouth passes
into the stomach, and is
eliminated?
18 "But the things that
proceed out of the mouth
come from the heart, and
those defile the man.
19 "For out of the heart
come evil thoughts, mur-
ders, adulteries, fornications, thefts, false witness,
slanders.
20 "These are the things
which defile the man; but to
eat with unwashed hands
does not defile the man."

The Syrophoenician Woman

21 And Jesus went away
from there, and withdrew

[c] Some mss. do not contain *of the blind*

χείλεσίν με τιμᾷ, ἡ δὲ καρδία αὐτῶν
lips me honours, but the heart of them
πόρρω ἀπέχει ἀπ' ἐμοῦ· 9 μάτην δὲ
far is away from me; and vainly
σέβονταί με, διδάσκοντες διδασκαλίας
they worship me, teaching teachings
ἐντάλματα ἀνθρώπων. 10 Καὶ προσκαλε-
ordinances of men. And calling
σάμενος τὸν ὄχλον εἶπεν αὐτοῖς·
forward the crowd he said to them:
ἀκούετε καὶ συνίετε· 11 οὐ τὸ εἰσερχ-
Hear ye and understand: Not the [thing] enter-
όμενον εἰς τὸ στόμα κοινοῖ τὸν ἄνθρωπον,
ing into the mouth defiles the man,
ἀλλὰ τὸ ἐκπορευόμενον ἐκ τοῦ στόματος,
but the [thing] coming forth out of the mouth,
τοῦτο κοινοῖ τὸν ἄνθρωπον. 12 Τότε
this defiles the man. Then
προσελθόντες οἱ μαθηταὶ λέγουσιν αὐτῷ·
approaching the disciples say to him:
οἶδας ὅτι οἱ Φαρισαῖοι ἀκούσαντες τὸν
Dost thou know that the Pharisees hearing the
λόγον ἐσκανδαλίσθησαν; 13 ὁ δὲ ἀπο-
saying were offended? And he answer-
κριθεὶς εἶπεν· πᾶσα φυτεία ἣν οὐκ
ing said: Every plant which not
ἐφύτευσεν ὁ πατήρ μου ὁ οὐράνιος ἐκριζω-
planted the Father of me – heavenly shall be
θήσεται. 14 ἄφετε αὐτούς· τυφλοί εἰσιν
uprooted. Leave them; blind they are
ὁδηγοὶ τυφλῶν· τυφλὸς δὲ τυφλὸν
leaders of blind; [3]a blind man [1]and [5]a blind man
ἐὰν ὁδηγῇ, ἀμφότεροι εἰς βόθυνον πεσοῦνται.
[2]if [4]leads, both into a ditch will fall.
15 Ἀποκριθεὶς δὲ ὁ Πέτρος εἶπεν αὐτῷ·
And answering – Peter said to him:
φράσον ἡμῖν τὴν παραβολήν. 16 ὁ δὲ
Explain to us the parable. So he
εἶπεν· ἀκμὴν καὶ ὑμεῖς ἀσύνετοί
said: Thus also ye unintelligent
ἐστε; 17 οὐ νοεῖτε ὅτι πᾶν τὸ
are? Do ye not understand that everything
εἰσπορευόμενον εἰς τὸ στόμα εἰς τὴν
entering into the mouth into the
κοιλίαν χωρεῖ καὶ εἰς ἀφεδρῶνα ἐκβάλλεται;
stomach goes and into a drain is cast out?
18 τὰ δὲ ἐκπορευόμενα ἐκ τοῦ
but the things coming forth out of the
στόματος ἐκ τῆς καρδίας ἐξέρχεται,
mouth out of the heart comes forth,
κἀκεῖνα κοινοῖ τὸν ἄνθρωπον. 19 ἐκ
and those defiles the man. out of
γὰρ τῆς καρδίας ἐξέρχονται διαλογισμοὶ
For the heart come forth thoughts
πονηροί, φόνοι, μοιχεῖαι, πορνεῖαι, κλοπαί,
evil, murders, adulteries, fornications, thefts,
ψευδομαρτυρίαι, βλασφημίαι. 20 ταῦτά
false witnessings, blasphemies. These things
ἐστιν τὰ κοινοῦντα τὸν ἄνθρωπον·
is(are) the [ones] defiling the man;
τὸ δὲ ἀνίπτοις χερσὶν φαγεῖν οὐ
– but with unwashed hands to eat not
κοινοῖ τὸν ἄνθρωπον.
defiles the man.
21 Καὶ ἐξελθὼν ἐκεῖθεν ὁ Ἰησοῦς
And going forth thence – Jesus

me with their lips,
but their hearts are far
from me.
9 They worship me in
vain;
their teachings are but
rules taught by
men.'[g]"
10 Jesus called the crowd
to him and said, "Listen
and understand. 11 What
goes into a man's mouth
does not make him 'un-
clean,' but what comes out
of his mouth, that is what
makes him 'unclean.' "
12 Then the disciples came
to him and asked, "Do you
know that the Pharisees
were offended when they
heard this?"
13 He replied, "Every
plant that my heavenly Father has not planted will be
pulled up by the roots.
14 Leave them; they are
blind guides.[h] If a blind
man leads a blind man,
both will fall into a pit."
15 Peter said, "Explain the
parable to us."
16 "Are you still so dull?"
Jesus asked them.
17 "Don't you see that
whatever enters the mouth
goes into the stomach and
then out of the body? 18 But
the things that come out of
the mouth come from the
heart, and these make a
man 'unclean.' 19 For out of
the heart come evil
thoughts, murder, adul-
tery, sexual immorality,
theft, false testimony, slander. 20 These are what make
a man 'unclean'; but eating
with unwashed hands does
not make him 'unclean.' "

The Faith of the Canaanite Woman

21 Leaving that place,
Jesus withdrew to the re-

[g]9 Isaiah 29:13
[h]14 Some manuscripts *guides of the blind*

into the district of Tyre and
Sidon.
22 And behold, a Canaan-
ite woman came out from
that region, and *began* to
cry out, saying, "Have
mercy on me, O Lord,
Son of David; my daugh-
ter is cruelly demon-pos-
sessed."
23 But He did not answer
her a word. And His disciples came to *Him* and kept
asking Him, saying, "Send
her away, for she is shouting out after us."
24 But He answered and
said, "I was sent only to
the lost sheep of the house
of Israel."
25 But she came and *be-
gan* to bow down before
Him, saying, "Lord, help
me!"
26 And He answered and
said, "It is not good to take
the children's bread and
throw it to the dogs."
27 But she said, "Yes,
Lord; but even the dogs
feed on the crumbs which
fall from their masters' table."
28 Then Jesus answered
and said to her, "O woman,
your faith is great; be it
done for you as you wish."
And her daughter was
healed at once.

Healing Multitudes

29 And departing from
there, Jesus went along by
the Sea of Galilee, and having gone up to the moun-
tain, He was sitting there.
30 And great multitudes
came to Him, bringing with
them *those who were* lame,
crippled, blind, dumb, and
many others, and they laid
them down at His feet; and
He healed them,
31 so that the multitude
marveled as they saw the
dumb speaking, the crip-

ἀνεχώρησεν εἰς τὰ μέρη Τύρου καὶ
departed into the parts of Tyre and
Σιδῶνος. **22** καὶ ἰδοὺ γυνὴ Χαναναία
Sidon. And behold woman a Canaanite
ἀπὸ τῶν ὁρίων ἐκείνων ἐξελθοῦσα
from – borders those coming forth
ἔκραζεν λέγουσα· ἐλέησόν με, κύριε
cried out saying: Pity me, Lord[,]
υἱὸς Δαυίδ· ἡ θυγάτηρ μου κακῶς
son of David; the daughter of me badly
δαιμονίζεται. **23** ὁ δὲ οὐκ ἀπεκρίθη
is demon-possessed. But he answered not
αὐτῇ λόγον. καὶ προσελθόντες οἱ μαθηταὶ
her a word. And approaching the disciples
αὐτοῦ ἠρώτων αὐτὸν λέγοντες· ἀπόλυσον
of him besought him saying: Dismiss
αὐτήν, ὅτι κράζει ὄπισθεν ἡμῶν. **24** ὁ
her, because she is crying out behind us. he
δὲ ἀποκριθεὶς εἶπεν· οὐκ ἀπεστάλην
But answering said: I was not sent
εἰ μὴ εἰς τὰ πρόβατα τὰ ἀπολωλότα
except to the sheep – lost
οἴκου Ἰσραήλ. **25** ἡ δὲ ἐλθοῦσα
of [the] house of Israel. But she coming
προσεκύνει αὐτῷ λέγουσα· κύριε, βοήθει
worshipped him saying: Lord, help
μοι. **26** ὁ δὲ ἀποκριθεὶς εἶπεν· οὐκ
me. But he answering said: not
ἔστιν καλὸν λαβεῖν τὸν ἄρτον τῶν τέκνων
It is good to take the bread of the children
καὶ βαλεῖν τοῖς κυναρίοις. **27** ἡ δὲ
and to throw to the dogs. And she
εἶπεν· ναί, κύριε· καὶ γὰρ τὰ κυνάρια
said: Yes, Lord; but even the dogs
ἐσθίει ἀπὸ τῶν ψιχίων τῶν πιπτόντων
eat*s* from the crumbs – falling
ἀπὸ τῆς τραπέζης τῶν κυρίων αὐτῶν.
from the table of the masters of them.
28 τότε ἀποκριθεὶς ὁ Ἰησοῦς εἶπεν αὐτῇ·
Then answering – Jesus said to her:
ὦ γύναι, μεγάλη σου ἡ πίστις· γενηθήτω
O woman, great of thee the faith; let it be
σοι ὡς θέλεις. καὶ ἰάθη ἡ
to thee as thou desirest. And was healed the
θυγάτηρ αὐτῆς ἀπὸ τῆς ὥρας ἐκείνης.
daughter of her from – hour that.
29 Καὶ μεταβὰς ἐκεῖθεν ὁ Ἰησοῦς
And removing thence – Jesus
ἦλθεν παρὰ τὴν θάλασσαν τῆς Γαλιλαίας,
came by the sea – of Galilee,
καὶ ἀναβὰς εἰς τὸ ὄρος ἐκάθητο ἐκεῖ.
and going up into the mountain he sat there.
30 καὶ προσῆλθον αὐτῷ ὄχλοι πολλοὶ ἔχοντες
And approached *to* him crowds many having
μεθ' ἑαυτῶν χωλούς, κυλλούς, τυφλούς,
with them*selves* lame, maimed, blind,
κωφούς, καὶ ἑτέρους πολλούς, καὶ ἔρριψαν
dumb, and others many, and cast
αὐτοὺς παρὰ τοὺς πόδας αὐτοῦ· καὶ
them at the feet of him; and
ἐθεράπευσεν αὐτούς· **31** ὥστε τὸν ὄχλον
he healed them; so as the crowd
=so that the crowd marvelled
θαυμάσαι βλέποντας κωφοὺς λαλοῦντας,
to marvel[b] seeing dumb men speaking,

gion of Tyre and Sidon. 22 A
Canaanite woman from
that vicinity came to him,
crying out, "Lord, Son of
David, have mercy on me!
My daughter is suffering
terribly from demon-pos-
session."
23 Jesus did not answer a
word. So his disciples came
to him and urged him,
"Send her away, for she
keeps crying out after us."
24 He answered, "I was
sent only to the lost sheep
of Israel."
25 The woman came and
knelt before him. "Lord,
help me!" she said.
26 He replied, "It is not
right to take the children's
bread and toss it to their
dogs."
27 "Yes, Lord," she said,
"but even the dogs eat the
crumbs that fall from their
masters' table."
28 Then Jesus answered,
"Woman, you have great
faith! Your request is granted." And her daughter was
healed from that very hour.

Jesus Feeds the Four Thousand

29 Jesus left there and
went along the Sea of Galilee. Then he went up on a
mountainside and sat
down. 30 Great crowds
came to him, bringing the
lame, the blind, the crippled, the mute and many
others, and laid them at his
feet; and he healed them.
31 The people were amazed
when they saw the mute
speaking, the crippled

pled restored, and the lame walking, and the blind seeing; and they glorified the God of Israel.

Four Thousand Fed

32And Jesus called His disciples to Him, and said, "I feel compassion for the multitude, because they have remained with Me now three days and have nothing to eat; and I do not wish to send them away hungry, lest they faint on the way."

33And the disciples *said to Him, "Where would we get so many loaves in a desolate place to satisfy such a great multitude?"

34And Jesus *said to them, "How many loaves do you have?" And they said, "Seven, and a few small fish."

35And He directed the multitude to sit down on the ground;

36and He took the seven loaves and the fish; and giving thanks, He broke them and started giving them to the disciples, and the disciples *in turn,* to the multitudes.

37And they all ate, and were satisfied, and they picked up what was left over of the broken pieces, seven large baskets full.

38And those who ate were four thousand men, besides women and children.

39And sending away the multitudes, He got into the boat, and came to the region of Magadan.

κυλλοὺς ὑγιεῖς καὶ χωλοὺς περιπατοῦντας
maimed whole and lame walking

καὶ τυφλοὺς βλέποντας· καὶ ἐδόξασαν
and blind seeing; and they glorified

τὸν θεὸν Ἰσραήλ. **32** Ὁ δὲ Ἰησοῦς
the God of Israel. – And Jesus

προσκαλεσάμενος τοὺς μαθητὰς αὐτοῦ
calling forward the disciples of him

εἶπεν· σπλαγχνίζομαι ἐπὶ τὸν ὄχλον,
said: I am filled with tenderness over the crowd,

ὅτι ἤδη ἡμέραι τρεῖς προσμένουσίν
because now days three they remain

μοι καὶ οὐκ ἔχουσιν τί φάγωσιν·
with me and have not anything they may eat;

καὶ ἀπολῦσαι αὐτοὺς νήστεις οὐ θέλω,
and to dismiss them without food I am not willing,

μήποτε ἐκλυθῶσιν ἐν τῇ ὁδῷ. **33** καὶ
lest they fail in the way. And

λέγουσιν αὐτῷ οἱ μαθηταί· πόθεν
say to him the disciples: Whence

ἡμῖν ἐν ἐρημίᾳ ἄρτοι τοσοῦτοι ὥστε
to us in a desert loaves so many so as

χορτάσαι ὄχλον τοσοῦτον; **34** καὶ λέγει
to satisfy a crowd so great? And says

αὐτοῖς ὁ Ἰησοῦς· πόσους ἄρτους ἔχετε;
to them – Jesus: How many loaves have ye?

οἱ δὲ εἶπαν· ἑπτά, καὶ ὀλίγα ἰχθύδια.
And they said: Seven, and a few fishes.

35 καὶ παραγγείλας τῷ ὄχλῳ ἀναπεσεῖν
And having enjoined the crowd to recline

ἐπὶ τὴν γῆν **36** ἔλαβεν τοὺς ἑπτὰ
on the ground he took the seven

ἄρτους καὶ τοὺς ἰχθύας καὶ εὐχαριστήσας
loaves and the fishes and giving thanks

ἔκλασεν καὶ ἐδίδου τοῖς μαθηταῖς, οἱ δὲ
he broke and gave to the disciples, and the

μαθηταὶ τοῖς ὄχλοις. **37** καὶ ἔφαγον πάντες
disciples to the crowds. And ate all

καὶ ἐχορτάσθησαν, καὶ τὸ περισσεῦον τῶν
and were satisfied, and the excess of the

κλασμάτων ἦραν, ἑπτὰ σπυρίδας πλήρεις.
fragments they took, seven baskets full.

38 οἱ δὲ ἐσθίοντες ἦσαν τετρακισχίλιοι
And the [ones] eating were four thousand

ἄνδρες χωρὶς γυναικῶν καὶ παιδίων.
men apart from women and children.

39 Καὶ ἀπολύσας τοὺς ὄχλους ἐνέβη εἰς
And having dismissed the crowds he embarked in

τὸ πλοῖον, καὶ ἦλθεν εἰς τὰ ὅρια Μαγαδάν.
the ship, and came into the borders of Magadan.

made well, the lame walking and the blind seeing. And they praised the God of Israel.

32Jesus called his disciples to him and said, "I have compassion for these people; they have already been with me three days and have nothing to eat. I do not want to send them away hungry, or they may collapse on the way."

33His disciples answered, "Where could we get enough bread in this remote place to feed such a crowd?"

34"How many loaves do you have?" Jesus asked.

"Seven," they replied, "and a few small fish."

35He told the crowd to sit down on the ground. 36Then he took the seven loaves and the fish, and when he had given thanks, he broke them and gave them to the disciples, and they in turn to the people. 37They all ate and were satisfied. Afterward the disciples picked up seven basketfuls of broken pieces that were left over. 38The number of those who ate was four thousand, besides women and children. 39After Jesus had sent the crowd away, he got into the boat and went to the vicinity of Magadan.

Chapter 16

Pharisees Test Jesus

AND the Pharisees and Sadducees came up, and testing Him asked Him to show them a sign from heaven.

2But He answered and said to them, "When it is evening, you say, '*It will be* fair weather, for the sky is red.'

3"And in the morning, '*There will be* a storm today, for the sky is red and

16 Καὶ προσελθόντες οἱ Φαρισαῖοι καὶ
And approaching the Pharisees and

Σαδδουκαῖοι πειράζοντες ἐπηρώτησαν αὐτὸν
Sadducees tempting asked him

σημεῖον ἐκ τοῦ οὐρανοῦ ἐπιδεῖξαι
a sign out of *the* heaven to show

αὐτοῖς. **2** ὁ δὲ ἀποκριθεὶς εἶπεν αὐτοῖς·
to them. But he answering said to them:

[ὀψίας γενομένης λέγετε· εὐδία,
Evening coming on[a] ye say: Fair weather,
=When evening comes on

πυρράζει γὰρ ὁ οὐρανός· **3** καὶ πρωΐ·
for is red the heaven(sky); and in the morning:

σήμερον χειμών, πυρράζει γὰρ στυγνάζων
To-day stormy weather, for is red being overcast

Chapter 16

The Demand for a Sign

THE Pharisees and Sadducees came to Jesus and tested him by asking him to show them a sign from heaven.

2He replied,[i] "When evening comes, you say, 'It will be fair weather, for the sky is red,' 3and in the

[i]2 Some early manuscripts do not have the rest of verse 2 and all of verse 3.

threatening.' Do you know
how to discern the appearance of the sky, but cannot
discern the signs of the
times?
4"An evil and adulterous
generation seeks after a
sign; and a sign will not be
given it, except the sign of
Jonah." And He left them,
and went away.
5And the disciples came
to the other side and had
forgotten to take bread.
6And Jesus said to them,
"Watch out and beware of
the leaven of the Pharisees
and Sadducees."
7And they began to dis-
cuss among themselves,
saying, "*It is* because we
took no bread."
8But Jesus, aware of
this, said, "You men of little faith, why do you discuss among yourselves that
you have no bread?
9"Do you not yet under-
stand or remember the five
loaves of the five thousand,
and how many baskets you
took up?
10"Or the seven loaves of
the four thousand, and how
many large baskets you
took up?
11"How is it that you do
not understand that I did
not speak to you concern-
ing bread? But beware of
the leaven of the Pharisees
and Sadducees."
12Then they understood
that He did not say to
beware of the leaven of
bread, but of the teaching
of the Pharisees and Sad-
ducees.

Peter's Confession of Christ

13Now when Jesus came
into the district of Caesarea
Philippi, He *began* asking
His disciples, saying,
"Who do people say that
the Son of Man is?"
14And they said, "Some
say John the Baptist; and
others, Elijah; but still others, Jeremiah, or one of the
prophets."

ὁ οὐρανός. τὸ μὲν πρόσωπον τοῦ
the heaven(sky). The – face of the
οὐρανοῦ γινώσκετε διακρίνειν, τὰ δὲ
heaven(sky) ye know* to discern, but the
σημεῖα τῶν καιρῶν οὐ δύνασθε;] 4 γενεὰ
signs of the times can ye not? A generation
πονηρὰ καὶ μοιχαλὶς σημεῖον ἐπιζητεῖ,
evil and adulterous a sign seeks,
καὶ σημεῖον οὐ δοθήσεται αὐτῇ εἰ μὴ
and a sign shall not be given to it except
τὸ σημεῖον Ἰωνᾶ. καὶ καταλιπὼν αὐτοὺς
the sign of Jonah. And leaving them
ἀπῆλθεν. 5 Καὶ ἐλθόντες οἱ μαθηταὶ εἰς
he went away. And coming the disciples to
τὸ πέραν ἐπελάθοντο ἄρτους λαβεῖν.
the other side they forgot loaves to take.
ὁ δὲ Ἰησοῦς εἶπεν αὐτοῖς· 6 ὁρᾶτε καὶ
– And Jesus said to them: Beware and
προσέχετε ἀπὸ τῆς ζύμης τῶν Φαρισαίων
take heed from the leaven of the Pharisees
καὶ Σαδδουκαίων. 7 οἱ δὲ διελογίζοντο
and Sadducees. But they reasoned
ἐν ἑαυτοῖς λέγοντες ὅτι ἄρτους οὐκ
among themselves saying[:] – Loaves not
ἐλάβομεν. 8 γνοὺς δὲ ὁ Ἰησοῦς εἶπεν·
we took. But knowing – Jesus said:
τί διαλογίζεσθε ἐν ἑαυτοῖς, ὀλιγόπιστοι,
Why reason ye among yourselves, little-faiths,
ὅτι ἄρτους οὐκ ἔχετε; 9 οὔπω νοεῖτε,
because loaves ye have not? Do ye not yet understand,
οὐδὲ μνημονεύετε τοὺς πέντε ἄρτους τῶν
neither remember ye the five loaves of the
πεντακισχιλίων καὶ πόσους κοφίνους
five thousand and how many baskets
ἐλάβετε; 10 οὐδὲ τοὺς ἑπτὰ ἄρτους τῶν
ye took? Neither the seven loaves of the
τετρακισχιλίων καὶ πόσας σπυρίδας
four thousand and how many baskets
ἐλάβετε; 11 πῶς οὐ νοεῖτε ὅτι οὐ
ye took? How do ye not understand that not
περὶ ἄρτων εἶπον ὑμῖν; προσέχετε δὲ ἀπὸ
concerning loaves I said to you? But take heed from
τῆς ζύμης τῶν Φαρισαίων καὶ Σαδ-
the leaven of the Pharisees and Sad-
δουκαίων. 12 τότε συνῆκαν ὅτι οὐκ
ducees. Then they understood that not
εἶπεν προσέχειν ἀπὸ τῆς ζύμης [τῶν
he said to take heed from the leaven of the
ἄρτων], ἀλλὰ ἀπὸ τῆς διδαχῆς τῶν
loaves, but from the teaching of the
Φαρισαίων καὶ Σαδδουκαίων.
Pharisees and Sadducees.
13 Ἐλθὼν δὲ ὁ Ἰησοῦς εἰς τὰ μέρη
And coming – Jesus into the parts
Καισαρείας τῆς Φιλίππου ἠρώτα τοὺς
of Cæsarea – of Philip he questioned the
μαθητὰς αὐτοῦ λέγων· τίνα λέγουσιν οἱ
disciples of him saying: Whom say –
ἄνθρωποι εἶναι τὸν υἱὸν τοῦ ἀνθρώπου;
men to be the Son – of man?
14 οἱ δὲ εἶπαν· οἱ μὲν Ἰωάννην τὸν
And they said: Some indeed John the
βαπτιστήν, ἄλλοι δὲ Ἠλίαν, ἕτεροι δὲ
Baptist, and others Elias, and others
Ἰερεμίαν ἢ ἕνα τῶν προφητῶν. 15 λέγει
Jeremias or one of the prophets. He says

*** See note on page xviii. Note the use in the next line of δύνασθε.**

morning, 'Today it will be
stormy, for the sky is red
and overcast.' You know
how to interpret the ap-
pearance of the sky, but
you cannot interpret the
signs of the times. 4A wicked and adulterous genera-
tion looks for a miraculous
sign, but none will be given
it except the sign of Jo-
nah." Jesus then left them
and went away.

The Yeast of the Pharisees and Sadducees

5When they went across
the lake, the disciples forgot to take bread. 6"Be
careful," Jesus said to
them. "Be on your guard
against the yeast of the
Pharisees and Sadducees."
7They discussed this
among themselves and
said, "It is because we
didn't bring any bread."
8Aware of their discus-
sion, Jesus asked, "You of
little faith, why are you
talking among yourselves
about having no bread? 9Do
you still not understand?
Don't you remember the
five loaves for the five
thousand, and how many
basketfuls you gathered?
10Or the seven loaves for
the four thousand, and how
many basketfuls you gath-
ered? 11How is it you don't
understand that I was not
talking to you about bread?
But be on your guard
against the yeast of the
Pharisees and Sadducees."
12Then they understood
that he was not telling them
to guard against the yeast
used in bread, but against
the teaching of the Pharisees and Sadducees.

Peter's Confession of Christ

13When Jesus came to the
region of Caesarea Philippi,
he asked his disciples,
"Who do people say the
Son of Man is?"
14They replied, "Some
say John the Baptist; others
say Elijah; and still others,
Jeremiah or one of the
prophets."

15He *said to them, "But
who do you say that I am?"
16And Simon Peter an-
swered and said, "Thou art
the Christ, the Son of the
living God."
17And Jesus answered
and said to him, "Blessed
are you, Simon Barjona,
because flesh and blood did
not reveal *this* to you, but
My Father who is in
heaven.
18"And I also say to you
that you are Peter, and
upon this rock I will build
My church; and the gates of
Hades shall not overpower
it.
19"I will give you the
keys of the kingdom of
heaven; and whatever you
shall bind on earth shall be
bound in heaven, and whatever you shall loose on
earth shall be loosed in
heaven."
20Then He warned the
disciples that they should
tell no one that He was the
Christ.

Jesus Foretells His Death

21From that time Jesus
Christ began to show His
disciples that He must go to
Jerusalem, and suffer many
things from the elders and
chief priests and scribes,
and be killed, and be raised
up on the third day.
22And Peter took Him
aside and began to rebuke
Him, saying, "God forbid
it, Lord! This shall never
happen to You."
23But He turned and said
to Peter, "Get behind Me,
Satan! You are a stumbling
block to Me; for you are not
setting your mind on God's
interests, but man's."

Discipleship Is Costly

24Then Jesus said to His
disciples, "If anyone

αὐτοῖς· ὑμεῖς δὲ τίνα με λέγετε εἶναι;
to them: But [3]ye [1]whom [4]me [2]say to be?
16 ἀποκριθεὶς δὲ Σίμων Πέτρος εἶπεν·
And answering Simon Peter said:
17 σὺ εἶ ὁ χριστὸς ὁ υἱὸς τοῦ θεοῦ
Thou art the Christ the Son – *of* God
τοῦ ζῶντος. ἀποκριθεὶς δὲ ὁ Ἰησοῦς
of the living. And answering – Jesus
εἶπεν αὐτῷ· μακάριος εἶ, Σίμων
said to him: Blessed art thou, Simon
Βαριωνά, ὅτι σὰρξ καὶ αἷμα οὐκ ἀπεκά-
Barjonas, because flesh and blood did not
λυψέν σοι ἀλλ' ὁ πατήρ μου ὁ ἐν
reveal to thee but the Father of me – in
τοῖς οὐρανοῖς. 18 κἀγὼ δέ σοι λέγω
the heavens. And I also to thee say[,]
ὅτι σὺ εἶ Πέτρος, καὶ ἐπὶ ταύτῃ τῇ
– Thou art Peter, and on this –
πέτρᾳ οἰκοδομήσω μου τὴν ἐκκλησίαν,
rock I will build of me the church,
καὶ πύλαι ᾅδου οὐ κατισχύσουσιν
and [the] gates of hades will not prevail against
αὐτῆς. 19 δώσω σοι τὰς κλεῖδας τῆς
it. I will give thee the keys of the
βασιλείας τῶν οὐρανῶν, καὶ ὃ ἐὰν
kingdom of the heavens, and whatever
δήσῃς ἐπὶ τῆς γῆς ἔσται δεδεμένον ἐν τοῖς
thou bindest on the earth shall be *having been* bound in the
οὐρανοῖς, καὶ ὃ ἐὰν λύσῃς ἐπὶ τῆς
heavens, and whatever thou loosest on the
γῆς ἔσται λελυμένον ἐν τοῖς οὐρανοῖς.
earth shall be *having been* loosed in the heavens.
20 τότε ἐπετίμησεν τοῖς μαθηταῖς ἵνα
Then he warned the disciples that
μηδενὶ εἴπωσιν ὅτι αὐτός ἐστιν ὁ
to no one they should tell that he is the
χριστός.
Christ.

21 Ἀπὸ τότε ἤρξατο Ἰησοῦς Χριστὸς
From then began Jesus Christ
δεικνύειν τοῖς μαθηταῖς αὐτοῦ ὅτι δεῖ
to show to the disciples of him that it behoves
αὐτὸν εἰς Ἱεροσόλυμα ἀπελθεῖν καὶ
him to Jerusalem to go and
πολλὰ παθεῖν ἀπὸ τῶν πρεσβυτέρων καὶ
many things to suffer from the elders and
ἀρχιερέων καὶ γραμματέων καὶ ἀποκτανθῆναι
chief priests and scribes and to be killed
καὶ τῇ τρίτῃ ἡμέρᾳ ἐγερθῆναι. 22 καὶ
and on the third day to be raised. And
προσλαβόμενος αὐτὸν ὁ Πέτρος ἤρξατο
taking him – Peter began
ἐπιτιμᾶν αὐτῷ λέγων· ἵλεώς σοι,
to rebuke him saying: Propitious to thee,
=May God help thee,
κύριε· οὐ μὴ ἔσται σοι τοῦτο. 23 ὁ δὲ
Lord: by no means shall be to thee this. But he
στραφεὶς εἶπεν τῷ Πέτρῳ· ὕπαγε ὀπίσω
turning said to Peter: Go behind
μου, σατανᾶ· σκάνδαλον εἶ ἐμοῦ,
me, Satan; an offence thou art of me,
ὅτι οὐ φρονεῖς τὰ τοῦ θεοῦ
because thou thinkest not the things – of God
ἀλλὰ τὰ τῶν ἀνθρώπων. 24 Τότε ὁ
but the things – of men. Then –
Ἰησοῦς εἶπεν τοῖς μαθηταῖς αὐτοῦ· εἴ
Jesus said to the disciples of him: If

15"But what about you?"
he asked. "Who do you say
I am?"
16Simon Peter answered,
"You are the Christ,[j] the
Son of the living God."
17Jesus replied, "Blessed
are you, Simon son of Jo-
nah, for this was not re-
vealed to you by man, but
by my Father in heaven.
18And I tell you that you are
Peter,[k] and on this rock I
will build my church, and
the gates of Hades[l] will not
overcome it.[m] 19I will give
you the keys of the king-
dom of heaven; whatever
you bind on earth will be[n]
bound in heaven, and whatever you loose on earth will
be[n] loosed in heaven."
20Then he warned his disciples not to tell anyone that
he was the Christ.

Jesus Predicts His Death

21From that time on Jesus
began to explain to his disciples that he must go to Jerusalem and suffer many
things at the hands of the
elders, chief priests and
teachers of the law, and
that he must be killed and
on the third day be raised to
life.
22Peter took him aside
and began to rebuke him.
"Never, Lord!" he said.
"This shall never happen
to you!"
23Jesus turned and said to
Peter, "Get behind me, Satan! You are a stumbling
block to me; you do not
have in mind the things of
God, but the things of
men."
24Then Jesus said to his
disciples, "If anyone

[j]16 Or *Messiah*; also in verse 20
[k]18 *Peter* means *rock.*
[l]18 Or *hell*
[m]18 Or *not prove stronger than it*
[n]19 Or *have been*

wishes to come after Me,
let him deny himself, and
take up his cross, and follow Me.
25"For whoever wishes
to save his life shall lose it;
but whoever loses his life
for My sake shall find it.
26"For what will a man be
profited, if he gains the
whole world, and forfeits
his soul? Or what will a man
give in exchange for his
soul?
27"For the Son of Man is
going to come in the glory
of His Father with His angels; and WILL THEN RECOM-
PENSE EVERY MAN ACCORD-
ING TO HIS DEEDS.
28"Truly I say to you,
there are some of those
who are standing here who
shall not taste death until
they see the Son of Man
coming in His kingdom."

τις θέλει ὀπίσω μου ἐλθεῖν, ἀπαρνησάσθω
anyone wishes after me to come, let him deny
ἑαυτὸν καὶ ἀράτω τὸν σταυρὸν αὐτοῦ,
himself and let him take the cross of him,
καὶ ἀκολουθείτω μοι. 25 ὃς γὰρ ἐὰν
and let him follow me. For whoever
θέλῃ τὴν ψυχὴν αὐτοῦ σῶσαι, ἀπολέσει
wishes the life of him to save, he will lose
αὐτήν· ὃς δ' ἂν ἀπολέσῃ τὴν ψυχὴν
it; and whoever loses the life
αὐτοῦ ἕνεκεν ἐμοῦ, εὑρήσει αὐτήν. 26 τί
of him for the sake of me, he will find it. what
γὰρ ὠφεληθήσεται ἄνθρωπος, ἐὰν τὸν
For will be benefited a man, if the
κόσμον ὅλον κερδήσῃ, τὴν δὲ ψυχὴν
world whole he should gain, but the soul
αὐτοῦ ζημιωθῇ; ἢ τί δώσει ἄνθρωπος
of him loses? or what will give a man
ἀντάλλαγμα τῆς ψυχῆς αὐτοῦ; 27 μέλλει
an exchange of the soul of him? is about
γὰρ ὁ υἱὸς τοῦ ἀνθρώπου ἔρχεσθαι ἐν τῇ
For the Son – of man to come in the
δόξῃ τοῦ πατρὸς αὐτοῦ μετὰ τῶν ἀγγέλων
glory of the Father of him with the angels
αὐτοῦ, καὶ τότε ἀποδώσει ἑκάστῳ
of him, and then he will reward *to* each man
κατὰ τὴν πρᾶξιν αὐτοῦ. 28 ἀμὴν λέγω
according to the conduct of him. Truly I say
ὑμῖν ὅτι εἰσίν τινες τῶν ὧδε ἑστώτων
to you[,] – There are some of the [ones] here standing
οἵτινες οὐ μὴ γεύσωνται θανάτου ἕως ἂν
who by no means may taste of death until
ἴδωσιν τὸν υἱὸν τοῦ ἀνθρώπου ἐρχόμενον
they see the Son – of man coming
ἐν τῇ βασιλείᾳ αὐτοῦ.
in the kingdom of him.

would come after me, he
must deny himself and take
up his cross and follow me.
25For whoever wants to
save his life[a] will lose it,
but whoever loses his life
for me will find it. 26What
good will it be for a man if
he gains the whole world,
yet forfeits his soul? Or
what can a man give in exchange for his soul? 27For
the Son of Man is going to
come in his Father's glory
with his angels, and then he
will reward each person according to what he has
done. 28I tell you the truth,
some who are standing
here will not taste death before they see the Son of
Man coming in his king-
dom."

Chapter 17

The Transfiguration

AND six days later Jesus
*took with Him Peter
and James and John his
brother, and *brought them
up to a high mountain by
themselves.
2And He was trans-
figured before them; and
His face shone like the sun,
and His garments became
as white as light.
3And behold, Moses and
Elijah appeared to them,
talking with Him.
4And Peter answered
and said to Jesus, "Lord, it
is good for us to be here; if
You wish, I will make three
tabernacles here, one for
You, and one for Moses,
and one for Elijah."
5While he was still

17 Καὶ μεθ' ἡμέρας ἓξ παραλαμβάνει ὁ
And after days six takes –
Ἰησοῦς τὸν Πέτρον καὶ Ἰάκωβον καὶ
Jesus – Peter and James and
Ἰωάννην τὸν ἀδελφὸν αὐτοῦ, καὶ ἀναφέρει
John the brother of him, and leads up
αὐτοὺς εἰς ὄρος ὑψηλὸν κατ' ἰδίαν. 2 καὶ
them to mountain a high privately. And
μετεμορφώθη ἔμπροσθεν αὐτῶν, καὶ
he was transfigured before them, and
ἔλαμψεν τὸ πρόσωπον αὐτοῦ ὡς ὁ ἥλιος,
shone the face of him as the sun,
τὰ δὲ ἱμάτια αὐτοῦ ἐγένετο λευκὰ ὡς
and the garments of him became white as
τὸ φῶς. 3 καὶ ἰδοὺ ὤφθη αὐτοῖς Μωϋσῆς
the light. And behold was seen by them Moses
καὶ Ἠλίας συλλαλοῦντες μετ' αὐτοῦ.
and Elias conversing with him.
4 ἀποκριθεὶς δὲ ὁ Πέτρος εἶπεν τῷ
And answering – Peter said –
Ἰησοῦ· κύριε, καλόν ἐστιν ἡμᾶς ὧδε
to Jesus: Lord, good it is us here
εἶναι· εἰ θέλεις, ποιήσω ὧδε τρεῖς
to be; if thou willest, I will make here three
σκηνάς, σοὶ μίαν καὶ Μωϋσεῖ
tents, for thee one and for Moses
μίαν καὶ Ἠλίᾳ μίαν. 5 ἔτι αὐτοῦ
one and for Elias one. Yet him
=While he was yet

Chapter 17

The Transfiguration

AFTER six days Jesus
took with him Peter,
James and John the brother
of James, and led them up a
high mountain by them-
selves. 2There he was
transfigured before them.
His face shone like the sun,
and his clothes became as
white as the light. 3Just
then there appeared before
them Moses and Elijah,
talking with Jesus.
4Peter said to Jesus,
"Lord, it is good for us to
be here. If you wish, I will
put up three shelters—one
for you, one for Moses and
one for Elijah."
5While he was still speak-

[a]25 The Greek word means either *life* or *soul*; also in verse 26.

speaking, behold, a bright
cloud overshadowed them;
and behold, a voice out of
the cloud, saying, "This is
My beloved Son, with
whom I am well-pleased;
listen to Him!"
6And when the disciples
heard *this*, they fell on their
faces and were much
afraid.
7And Jesus came to *them*
and touched them and said,
"Arise, and do not be
afraid."
8And lifting up their
eyes, they saw no one, except Jesus Himself alone.
9And as they were com-
ing down from the moun-
tain, Jesus commanded
them, saying, "Tell the vision to no one until the Son
of Man has risen from the
dead."
10And His disciples asked
Him, saying, "Why then
do the scribes say that Elijah must come first?"
11And He answered and
said, "Elijah is coming and
will restore all things;
12but I say to you, that
Elijah already came, and
they did not recognize him,
but did to him whatever
they wished. So also the
Son of Man is going to suffer at their hands."
13Then the disciples un-
derstood that He had
spoken to them about John
the Baptist.

The Demoniac

14And when they came to
the multitude, a man came
up to Him, falling on his
knees before Him, and saying,
15"Lord, have mercy on
my son, for he is a lunatic,
and is very ill; for he often
falls into the fire, and often
into the water.
16"And I brought him to
Your disciples, and they

λαλοῦντος, ἰδοὺ νεφέλη φωτεινὴ ἐπεσκίασεν
speaking[a], behold cloud a bright overshadowed
[a]speaking,
αὐτούς, καὶ ἰδοὺ φωνὴ ἐκ τῆς νεφέλης
them, and behold a voice out of the cloud
λέγουσα· οὗτός ἐστιν ὁ υἱός μου ὁ
saying: This is the son of me the
ἀγαπητός, ἐν ᾧ εὐδόκησα· ἀκούετε
beloved, in whom I was well pleased; hear ye
αὐτοῦ. **6** καὶ ἀκούσαντες οἱ μαθηταὶ
him. And hearing the disciples
ἔπεσαν ἐπὶ πρόσωπον αὐτῶν καὶ
fell on [the] face[s] of them and
ἐφοβήθησαν σφόδρα. **7** καὶ προσῆλθεν ὁ
feared exceedingly. And approached –
Ἰησοῦς καὶ ἁψάμενος αὐτῶν εἶπεν·
Jesus and touching them said:
ἐγέρθητε καὶ μὴ φοβεῖσθε. **8** ἐπάραντες δὲ
Rise and do not fear. And lifting up
τοὺς ὀφθαλμοὺς αὐτῶν οὐδένα εἶδον εἰ
the eyes of them no one they saw ex-
μὴ αὐτὸν Ἰησοῦν μόνον. **9** Καὶ κατα-
cept himself Jesus only. And com-
=as
βαινόντων αὐτῶν ἐκ τοῦ ὄρους ἐνετείλατο
ing down them[a] out of the mountain enjoined
they were coming down
αὐτοῖς ὁ Ἰησοῦς λέγων· μηδενὶ εἴπητε
them – Jesus saying: To no one tell
τὸ ὅραμα ἕως οὗ ὁ υἱὸς τοῦ ἀνθρώπου
the vision until the Son – of man
ἐκ νεκρῶν ἐγερθῇ. **10** Καὶ ἐπηρώτησαν
out of dead be raised. And questioned
αὐτὸν οἱ μαθηταὶ λέγοντες· τί οὖν
him the disciples saying: Why then
οἱ γραμματεῖς λέγουσιν ὅτι Ἠλίαν δεῖ
the scribes say that [a]Elias [1]it behoves
ἐλθεῖν πρῶτον; **11** ὁ δὲ ἀποκριθεὶς εἶπεν·
to come first? And he answering said:
Ἠλίας μὲν ἔρχεται καὶ ἀποκαταστήσει
Elias indeed is coming and will restore
πάντα· **12** λέγω δὲ ὑμῖν ὅτι Ἠλίας
all things; but I tell you that Elias
ἤδη ἦλθεν, καὶ οὐκ ἐπέγνωσαν
already came, and they did not recognize
αὐτόν, ἀλλ' ἐποίησαν ἐν αὐτῷ ὅσα
him, but did by him whatever things
ἠθέλησαν· οὕτως καὶ ὁ υἱὸς τοῦ ἀνθρώπου
they wished; thus also the Son – of man
μέλλει πάσχειν ὑπ' αὐτῶν. **13** τότε
is about to suffer by them. Then
συνῆκαν οἱ μαθηταὶ ὅτι περὶ
understood the disciples that concerning
Ἰωάννου τοῦ βαπτιστοῦ εἶπεν αὐτοῖς.
John the Baptist he spoke to them.
14 Καὶ ἐλθόντων πρὸς τὸν ὄχλον προσ-
And [they] coming to the crowd ap-
ῆλθεν αὐτῷ ἄνθρωπος γονυπετῶν αὐτὸν
proached *to* him a man falling on knees to him
15 καὶ λέγων· κύριε, ἐλέησόν μου τὸν
and saying: Lord, pity of me the
υἱόν, ὅτι σεληνιάζεται καὶ κακῶς ἔχει·
son, because he is moonstruck and ill has;
=is ill;
πολλάκις γὰρ πίπτει εἰς τὸ πῦρ καὶ
for often he falls into the fire and
πολλάκις εἰς τὸ ὕδωρ. **16** καὶ προσήνεγκα
often into the water. And I brought
αὐτὸν τοῖς μαθηταῖς σου, καὶ οὐκ
him to the disciples of thee, and not

ing, a bright cloud enveloped them, and a voice
from the cloud said, "This
is my Son, whom I love;
with him I am well pleased.
Listen to him!"
6When the disciples
heard this, they fell face-
down to the ground, terrified. 7But Jesus came and
touched them. "Get up,"
he said. "Don't be afraid."
8When they looked up,
they saw no one except
Jesus.
9As they were coming
down the mountain, Jesus
instructed them, "Don't
tell anyone what you have
seen, until the Son of Man
has been raised from the
dead."
10The disciples asked
him, "Why then do the
teachers of the law say that
Elijah must come first?"
11Jesus replied, "To be
sure, Elijah comes and will
restore all things. 12But I
tell you, Elijah has already
come, and they did not recognize him, but have done
to him everything they
wished. In the same way
the Son of Man is going to
suffer at their hands."
13Then the disciples understood that he was talking to
them about John the Bap-
tist.

The Healing of a Boy With a Demon

14When they came to the
crowd, a man approached
Jesus and knelt before him.
15"Lord, have mercy on
my son," he said. "He has
seizures and is suffering
greatly. He often falls into
the fire or into the water.
16I brought him to your disciples, but they could not

could not cure him."

17 And Jesus answered and said, "O unbelieving and perverted generation, how long shall I be with you? How long shall I put up with you? Bring him here to Me."

18 And Jesus rebuked him, and the demon came out of him, and the boy was cured at once.

19 Then the disciples came to Jesus privately and said, "Why could we not cast it out?"

20 And He *said to them, "Because of the littleness of your faith; for truly I say to you, if you have faith as a mustard seed, you shall say to this mountain, 'Move from here to there,' and it shall move; and nothing shall be impossible to you.

21 ["[d]But this kind does not go out except by prayer and fasting."]

22 And while they were gathering together in Galilee, Jesus said to them, "The Son of Man is going to be delivered into the hands of men;

23 and they will kill Him, and He will be raised on the third day." And they were deeply grieved.

The Tribute Money

24 And when they had come to Capernaum, those who collected the [e]two-drachma *tax* came to Peter, and said, "Does your teacher not pay the [e]two-drachma *tax*?"

25 He *said, "Yes." And when he came into the house, Jesus spoke to him first, saying, "What do you think, Simon? From whom do the kings of the earth collect customs or poll-tax, from their sons or from strangers?"

[d]Many mss. do not contain this verse

[e]Equivalent to two denarii or two days' wages paid as a temple tax

ἠδυνήθησαν αὐτὸν θεραπεῦσαι. **17** ἀπο-
they were able him to heal. an-
κριθεὶς δὲ ὁ Ἰησοῦς εἶπεν· ὦ γενεὰ
swering And – Jesus said: O generation
ἄπιστος καὶ διεστραμμένη, ἕως πότε
unbelieving and *having been* perverted, until when
μεθ' ὑμῶν ἔσομαι; ἕως πότε
with you shall I be? until when
ἀνέξομαι ὑμῶν; φέρετέ μοι αὐτὸν
shall I endure you? bring to me him
ὧδε. **18** καὶ ἐπετίμησεν αὐτῷ ὁ Ἰησοῦς,
here. And rebuked it – Jesus,
καὶ ἐξῆλθεν ἀπ' αὐτοῦ τὸ δαιμόνιον,
and came out from him the demon,
καὶ ἐθεραπεύθη ὁ παῖς ἀπὸ τῆς ὥρας
and was healed the boy from – hour
ἐκείνης. **19** Τότε προσελθόντες οἱ μαθηταὶ
that. Then [3]approaching [1]the [2]disciples
τῷ Ἰησοῦ κατ' ἰδίαν εἶπον· διὰ
– *to* Jesus privately said: Why
τί ἡμεῖς οὐκ ἠδυνήθημεν ἐκβαλεῖν αὐτό;
we were not able to expel it?
20 ὁ δὲ λέγει αὐτοῖς· διὰ τὴν ὀλιγο-
And he says to them: Because of the little
πιστίαν ὑμῶν· ἀμὴν γὰρ λέγω ὑμῖν, ἐὰν
faith of you; for truly I say to you, if
ἔχητε πίστιν ὡς κόκκον σινάπεως,
ye have faith as a grain of mustard,
ἐρεῖτε τῷ ὄρει τούτῳ· μετάβα
ye will say – mountain to this: Remove
ἔνθεν ἐκεῖ, καὶ μεταβήσεται, καὶ οὐδὲν
hence there, and it will be removed, and nothing
ἀδυνατήσει ὑμῖν. ‡
will be impossible to you.
22 Συστρεφομένων δὲ αὐτῶν ἐν τῇ
And strolling them[a] in –
=as they were strolling
Γαλιλαίᾳ εἶπεν αὐτοῖς ὁ Ἰησοῦς· μέλλει
Galilee said to them – Jesus: is about
ὁ υἱὸς τοῦ ἀνθρώπου παραδίδοσθαι εἰς
The Son – of man to be delivered into
χεῖρας ἀνθρώπων, **23** καὶ ἀποκτενοῦσιν
[the] hands of men, and they will kill
αὐτόν, καὶ τῇ τρίτῃ ἡμέρᾳ ἐγερθήσεται.
him, and on the third day he will be raised.
καὶ ἐλυπήθησαν σφόδρα.
And they were grieved exceedingly.
24 Ἐλθόντων δὲ αὐτῶν εἰς Καφαρναοὺμ
And coming them[a] to Capernaum
=when they came
προσῆλθον οἱ τὰ δίδραχμα λαμβάνοντες
approached the [ones] the didrachmæ receiving
τῷ Πέτρῳ καὶ εἶπαν· ὁ διδάσκαλος
– Peter and said: The teacher
ὑμῶν οὐ τελεῖ δίδραχμα; λέγει· ναί.
of you not pays drachmae? He says: Yes.
25 καὶ ἐλθόντα εἰς τὴν οἰκίαν προ-
And [4]coming [5]into [6]the [7]house [2]pre-
έφθασεν αὐτὸν ὁ Ἰησοῦς λέγων· τί σοι
ceded [3]him – [1]Jesus saying: What to thee
δοκεῖ, Σίμων; οἱ βασιλεῖς τῆς γῆς
seems it, Simon? the kings of the earth
ἀπὸ τίνων λαμβάνουσιν τέλη ἢ κῆνσον;
from whom do they take toll or poll-tax?
ἀπὸ τῶν υἱῶν αὐτῶν ἢ ἀπὸ τῶν ἀλλοτρίων;
from the sons of them or from – strangers?

‡ Verse 21 omitted by Nestle; *cf.* NIV

heal him."

17 "O unbelieving and perverse generation," Jesus replied, "how long shall I stay with you? How long shall I put up with you? Bring the boy here to me."

18 Jesus rebuked the demon, and it came out of the boy, and he was healed from that moment.

19 Then the disciples came to Jesus in private and asked, "Why couldn't we drive it out?"

20 He replied, "Because you have so little faith. I tell you the truth, if you have faith as small as a mustard seed, you can say to this mountain, 'Move from here to there' and it will move. Nothing will be impossible for you.[p]"

22 When they came to-
gether in Galilee, he said to
them, "The Son of Man is
going to be betrayed into
the hands of men. 23 They
will kill him, and on the
third day he will be raised
to life." And the disciples
were filled with grief.

The Temple Tax

24 After Jesus and his disciples arrived in Capernaum, the collectors of the two-drachma tax came to Peter and asked, "Doesn't your teacher pay the temple tax[q]?"

25 "Yes, he does," he replied.

When Peter came into the house, Jesus was the first to speak. "What do you think, Simon?" he asked. "From whom do the kings of the earth collect duty and taxes—from their own sons or from others?"

[p]20 Some manuscripts *you.* 21 *But this kind does not go out except by prayer and fasting.*

[q]24 Greek *the two drachmas*

[26]And upon his saying,
"From strangers," Jesus
said to him, "Consequently
the sons are exempt.
[27]"But, lest we give them
offense, go to the sea, and
throw in a hook, and take
the first fish that comes up;
and when you open its
mouth, you will find a
[f]stater. Take that and give
it to them for you and Me."

26 εἰπόντος δέ· ἀπὸ τῶν ἀλλο-
and [he] saying[a]: From – strangers,
=when he said :
τρίων, ἔφη αὐτῷ ὁ Ἰησοῦς· ἄρα γε
said to him – Jesus: Then
ἐλεύθεροί εἰσιν οἱ υἱοί. 27 ἵνα δὲ μὴ
free are the sons. But lest
σκανδαλίσωμεν αὐτούς, πορευθεὶς εἰς
we should offend them, going to
θάλασσαν βάλε ἄγκιστρον καὶ τὸν
[the] sea cast a hook and the
ἀναβάντα πρῶτον ἰχθὺν ἆρον, καὶ ἀνοίξας
[3]coming up [2]first [1]fish take, and opening
τὸ στόμα αὐτοῦ εὑρήσεις στατῆρα·
the mouth of it thou wilt find a stater;
ἐκεῖνον λαβὼν δὸς αὐτοῖς ἀντὶ ἐμοῦ καὶ
that taking give them for me and
σοῦ.
thee.

[26]"From others," Peter
answered.
"Then the sons are ex-
empt," Jesus said to him.
[27]"But so that we may not
offend them, go to the lake
and throw out your line.
Take the first fish you
catch; open its mouth and
you will find a four-drach-
ma coin. Take it and give it
to them for my tax and
yours."

Chapter 18

Rank in the Kingdom

AT that time the disciples
came to Jesus, saying,
"Who then is greatest in
the kingdom of heaven?"
[2]And He called a child to
Himself and set him before
them,
[3]and said, "Truly I say
to you, unless you are converted and become like
children, you shall not enter the kingdom of heaven.
[4]"Whoever then hum-
bles himself as this child,
he is the greatest in the
kingdom of heaven.
[5]"And whoever receives
one such child in My name
receives Me;
[6]but whoever causes one
of these little ones who believe in Me to stumble, it is
better for him that a heavy
millstone be hung around
his neck, and that he be
drowned in the depth of the
sea.

Stumbling Blocks

[7]"Woe to the world be-
cause of *its* stumbling
blocks! For it is inevitable
that stumbling blocks
come; but woe to that man
through whom the stum-
bling block comes!
[8]"And if your hand or
your foot causes you to
stumble, cut it off and

18 Ἐν ἐκείνῃ τῇ ὥρᾳ προσῆλθον οἱ
In that – hour approached the
μαθηταὶ τῷ Ἰησοῦ λέγοντες· τίς ἄρα
disciples – *to* Jesus saying: Who then
μείζων ἐστὶν ἐν τῇ βασιλείᾳ τῶν οὐρανῶν;
greater is in the kingdom of the heavens?
2 καὶ προσκαλεσάμενος παιδίον ἔστησεν
And calling forward a child he set
αὐτὸ ἐν μέσῳ αὐτῶν 3 καὶ εἶπεν· ἀμὴν
him in [the] midst of them and said: Truly
λέγω ὑμῖν, ἐὰν μὴ στραφῆτε καὶ
I say to you, except ye turn and
γένησθε ὡς τὰ παιδία, οὐ μὴ
become as – children, by no means
εἰσέλθητε εἰς τὴν βασιλείαν τῶν
may ye enter into the kingdom of the
οὐρανῶν. 4 ὅστις οὖν ταπεινώσει ἑαυτὸν
heavens. [2][he] who [1]Therefore will humble himself
ὡς τὸ παιδίον τοῦτο, οὗτός ἐστιν ὁ
as – child this, this [one] is the
μείζων ἐν τῇ βασιλείᾳ τῶν οὐρανῶν.
greater in the kingdom of the heavens.
5 καὶ ὃς ἐὰν δέξηται ἓν παιδίον
And whoever receives one child
τοιοῦτο ἐπὶ τῷ ὀνόματί μου, ἐμὲ δέχεται·
such on(in) the name of me, me receives;
6 ὃς δ' ἂν σκανδαλίσῃ ἕνα τῶν
and whoever offends one –
μικρῶν τούτων τῶν πιστευόντων εἰς ἐμέ,
little [ones] of these – believing in me,
συμφέρει αὐτῷ ἵνα κρεμασθῇ μύλος
it is expedient for him that be hanged an upper
ὀνικὸς περὶ τὸν τράχηλον αὐτοῦ καὶ
millstone round the neck of him and
καταποντισθῇ ἐν τῷ πελάγει τῆς θαλάσσης.
he be drowned in the depth of the sea.
7 Οὐαὶ τῷ κόσμῳ ἀπὸ τῶν σκανδάλων·
Woe to the world from – offences;
ἀνάγκη γὰρ ἐλθεῖν τὰ σκάνδαλα, πλὴν
for [it is] a necessity to come – offences, but
οὐαὶ τῷ ἀνθρώπῳ δι' οὗ τὸ σκάνδαλον
woe to the man through whom the offence
ἔρχεται. 8 Εἰ δὲ ἡ χείρ σου ἢ ὁ
comes. Now if the hand of thee or the
πούς σου σκανδαλίζει σε, ἔκκοψον αὐτὸν
foot of thee offends thee, cut off it

Chapter 18

The Greatest in the Kingdom of Heaven

AT that time the disciples
came to Jesus and
asked, "Who is the great-
est in the kingdom of heav-
en?"
[2]He called a little child
and had him stand among
them. [3]And he said: "I tell
you the truth, unless you
change and become like little children, you will never
enter the kingdom of heav-
en. [4]Therefore, whoever
humbles himself like this
child is the greatest in the
kingdom of heaven.
[5]"And whoever wel-
comes a little child like this
in my name welcomes me.
[6]But if anyone causes one
of these little ones who believe in me to sin, it would
be better for him to have a
large millstone hung
around his neck and to be
drowned in the depths of
the sea.
[7]"Woe to the world be-
cause of the things that
cause people to sin! Such
things must come, but woe
to the man through whom
they come! [8]If your hand or
your foot causes you to sin
cut it off and throw it away.

[f]Or, *shekel*, worth four drachmas

throw it from you; it is better for you to enter life crippled or lame, than having two hands or two feet, to be cast into the eternal fire.

9"And if your eye causes you to stumble, pluck it out, and throw it from you. It is better for you to enter life with one eye, than having two eyes, to be cast into the fiery hell.

10"See that you do not despise one of these little ones, for I say to you, that their angels in heaven continually behold the face of My Father who is in heaven.

11["[g]For the Son of Man has come to save that which was lost.]

Ninety-nine Plus One

12"What do you think? If any man has a hundred sheep, and one of them has gone astray, does he not leave the ninety-nine on the mountains and go and search for the one that is straying?

13"And if it turns out that he finds it, truly I say to you, he rejoices over it more than over the ninety-nine which have not gone astray.

14"Thus it is not *the* will of your Father who is in heaven that one of these little ones perish.

Discipline and Prayer

15"And if your brother sins[h], go and reprove him in private; if he listens to you, you have won your brother.

16"But if he does not listen *to you,* take one or two more with you, so that BY THE MOUTH OF TWO OR THREE WITNESSES EVERY FACT MAY BE CONFIRMED.

17"And if he refuses to listen to them, tell it to the

[g] Most ancient mss. do not contain this verse

[h] Many mss. add here: *against you*

καὶ βάλε ἀπὸ σοῦ· καλόν σοί ἐστιν
and cast from thee; good for thee it is

εἰσελθεῖν εἰς τὴν ζωὴν κυλλὸν ἢ χωλόν,
to enter into – life maimed or lame,

ἢ δύο χεῖρας ἢ δύο πόδας ἔχοντα βληθῆναι
than two hands or two feet having to be cast

εἰς τὸ πῦρ τὸ αἰώνιον. **9** καὶ εἰ ὁ
into the fire – eternal. And if the

ὀφθαλμός σου σκανδαλίζει σε, ἔξελε αὐτὸν
eye of thee offends thee, pluck out it

καὶ βάλε ἀπὸ σοῦ· καλόν σοί ἐστιν
and cast from thee; good for thee it is

μονόφθαλμον εἰς τὴν ζωὴν εἰσελθεῖν, ἢ
one-eyed into *the* life to enter, than

δύο ὀφθαλμοὺς ἔχοντα βληθῆναι εἰς
two eyes having to be cast into

τὴν γέενναν τοῦ πυρός. **10** Ὁρᾶτε μὴ
the gehenna – of fire. See [that] not

καταφρονήσητε ἑνὸς τῶν μικρῶν τούτων·
ye despise one – little [ones] of these;

λέγω γὰρ ὑμῖν ὅτι οἱ ἄγγελοι αὐτῶν
for I tell you that the angels of them

ἐν οὐρανοῖς διὰ παντὸς βλέπουσι τὸ
in heaven*s* always see the

πρόσωπον τοῦ πατρός μου τοῦ ἐν οὐρανοῖς.‡
face of the Father of me – in heaven*s*.

12 Τί ὑμῖν δοκεῖ; ἐὰν γένηταί τινι
What to you seems it? if there be to any
=any man has

ἀνθρώπῳ ἑκατὸν πρόβατα καὶ πλανηθῇ
man[c] a hundred sheep and wanders

ἓν ἐξ αὐτῶν, οὐχὶ ἀφήσει τὰ ἐνενήκοντα
one of them, will he not leave the ninety-

ἐννέα ἐπὶ τὰ ὄρη καὶ πορευθεὶς ζητεῖ τὸ
nine on the mountains and going seeks the

πλανώμενον; **13** καὶ ἐὰν γένηται
wandering [one]? And if he happens

εὑρεῖν αὐτό, ἀμὴν λέγω ὑμῖν ὅτι
to find it, truly I say to you that

χαίρει ἐπ' αὐτῷ μᾶλλον ἢ ἐπὶ τοῖς
he rejoices over it more than over the

ἐνενήκοντα ἐννέα τοῖς μὴ πεπλανημένοις.
ninety-nine – not having wandered.

14 οὕτως οὐκ ἔστιν θέλημα ἔμπροσθεν
So it is not [the] will before

τοῦ πατρὸς ὑμῶν τοῦ ἐν οὐρανοῖς ἵνα
the Father of you – in heaven*s* that

ἀπόληται ἓν τῶν μικρῶν τούτων.
should perish one – little [ones] of these.

15 Ἐὰν δὲ ἁμαρτήσῃ ὁ ἀδελφός σου,
Now if sins the brother of thee,

ὕπαγε ἔλεγξον αὐτὸν μεταξὺ σοῦ καὶ
go reprove him between thee and

αὐτοῦ μόνου. ἐάν σου ἀκούσῃ, ἐκέρδησας
him alone. If thee he hears, thou gainedst

τὸν ἀδελφόν σου· **16** ἐὰν δὲ μὴ
the brother of thee; but if not

ἀκούσῃ, παράλαβε μετὰ σοῦ ἔτι ἕνα ἢ
he hears, take with thee more one or

δύο, ἵνα ἐπὶ στόματος δύο μαρτύρων
two, that on(by) [the] mouth of two witnesses

ἢ τριῶν σταθῇ πᾶν ῥῆμα· **17** ἐὰν δὲ
or three may be established every word; but if

παρακούσῃ αὐτῶν, εἰπὸν τῇ ἐκκλησίᾳ
he refuses to hear them, tell *to* the church;

‡ Ver. 11 omitted by Nestle; *cf.* NIV note.

It is better for you to enter
life maimed or crippled
than to have two hands or
two feet and be thrown into
eternal fire. 9And if your
eye causes you to sin,
gouge it out and throw it
away. It is better for you to
enter life with one eye than
to have two eyes and be
thrown into the fire of hell.

The Parable of the Lost Sheep

10"See that you do not
look down on one of these
little ones. For I tell you
that their angels in heaven
always see the face of my
Father in heaven.[r]
12"What do you think? If
a man owns a hundred
sheep, and one of them
wanders away, will he not
leave the ninety-nine on the
hills and go to look for the
one that wandered off?
13And if he finds it, I tell
you the truth, he is happier
about that one sheep than
about the ninety-nine that
did not wander off. 14In the
same way your Father in
heaven is not willing that
any of these little ones
should be lost.

A Brother Who Sins Against You

15"If your brother sins
against you,[s] go and show
him his fault, just between
the two of you. If he listens
to you, you have won your
brother over. 16But if he
will not listen, take one or
two others along, so that
'every matter may be es-
tablished by the testimony
of two or three wit-
nesses.'[t] 17If he refuses to
listen to them, tell it to the

[r] *10* Some manuscripts *heaven. 11The Son of Man came to save what was lost.*

[s] *15* Some manuscripts do not have *against you.*

[t] *16* Deut. 19:15

church; and if he refuses to
listen even to the church,
let him be to you as a Gentile and a tax-gatherer.
18"Truly I say to you,
whatever you shall bind on
earth shall be bound in
heaven; and whatever you
loose on earth shall be
loosed in heaven.
19"Again I say to you,
that if two of you agree on
earth about anything that
they may ask, it shall be
done for them by My Fa-
ther who is in heaven.
20"For where two or
three have gathered to-
gether in My name, there I
am in their midst."

Forgiveness

21Then Peter came and
said to Him, "Lord, how
often shall my brother sin
against me and I forgive
him? Up to seven times?"
22Jesus *said to him, "I
do not say to you, up to
seven times, but up to seventy times seven.
23"For this reason the
kingdom of heaven may be
compared to a certain king
who wished to settle ac-
counts with his slaves.
24"And when he had
begun to settle *them,* there
was brought to him one
who owed him [i]ten thou-
sand talents.
25"But since he did not
have *the means* to repay,
his lord commanded him to
be sold, along with his wife
and children and all that he
had, and repayment to be
made.
26"The slave therefore
falling down, prostrated
himself before him, saying,
'Have patience with me,
and I will repay you everything.'
27"And the lord of that
slave felt compassion and
released him and forgave

ἐὰν δὲ καὶ τῆς ἐκκλησίας παρακούσῃ,
and if even the church he refuses to hear,
ἔστω σοι ὥσπερ ὁ ἐθνικὸς καὶ
let him be to thee as the gentile and
ὁ τελώνης. **18** Ἀμὴν λέγω ὑμῖν,
the tax-collector. Truly I say to you,
ὅσα ἐὰν δήσητε ἐπὶ τῆς γῆς ἔσται
whatever things ye bind on the earth shall be
δεδεμένα ἐν οὐρανῷ, καὶ ὅσα ἐὰν
having been bound in heaven, and whatever things
λύσητε ἐπὶ τῆς γῆς ἔσται λελυμένα
ye loose on the earth shall be *having been* loosed
ἐν οὐρανῷ. **19** Πάλιν [ἀμὴν] λέγω
in heaven. Again truly I say
ὑμῖν ὅτι ἐὰν δύο συμφωνήσωσιν ἐξ
to you that if two agree of
ὑμῶν ἐπὶ τῆς γῆς περὶ παντὸς πράγ-
you on the earth concerning every
ματος οὗ ἐὰν αἰτήσωνται, γενήσεται
thing whatever they ask, it shall be
αὐτοῖς παρὰ τοῦ πατρός μου τοῦ ἐν
to them from the Father of me – in
οὐρανοῖς. **20** οὗ γάρ εἰσιν δύο ἢ τρεῖς
heavens. For where are two or three
συνηγμένοι εἰς τὸ ἐμὸν ὄνομα, ἐκεῖ εἰμι
having been assembled in – my name, there I am
ἐν μέσῳ αὐτῶν.
in [the] midst of them.
21 Τότε προσελθὼν ὁ Πέτρος εἶπεν
Then approaching – Peter said
αὐτῷ· κύριε, ποσάκις ἁμαρτήσει εἰς
to him: Lord, how often will sin against
ἐμὲ ὁ ἀδελφός μου καὶ ἀφήσω αὐτῷ;
me the brother of me and I will forgive him?
ἕως ἑπτάκις; **22** λέγει αὐτῷ ὁ Ἰησοῦς·
until seven times? says to him – Jesus:
οὐ λέγω σοι ἕως ἑπτάκις, ἀλλὰ
I tell not *to* thee until seven times, but
ἕως ἑβδομηκοντάκις ἑπτά. **23** Διὰ τοῦτο
until seventy times seven. Therefore
ὡμοιώθη ἡ βασιλεία τῶν οὐρανῶν
was(is) likened the kingdom of the heavens
ἀνθρώπῳ βασιλεῖ, ὃς ἠθέλησεν συνᾶραι
to *a man* a king, who wished to take
λόγον μετὰ τῶν δούλων αὐτοῦ. **24** ἀρξα-
account with the slaves of him. And
μένου δὲ αὐτοῦ συναίρειν, προσήχθη
beginning him[a] to take, [5]was brought forward
=as he began
εἷς αὐτῷ ὀφειλέτης μυρίων ταλάντων.
[1]one [6]to him [2]debtor [3]of ten thousand [4]talents.
25 μὴ ἔχοντος δὲ αὐτοῦ ἀποδοῦναι, ἐκέλευσεν
And not having him[a] to repay, commanded
=as he had not
αὐτὸν ὁ κύριος πραθῆναι καὶ τὴν
him the lord to be sold and the(his)
γυναῖκα καὶ τὰ τέκνα καὶ πάντα ὅσα
wife and – children and all things whatever
ἔχει, καὶ ἀποδοθῆναι. **26** πεσὼν οὖν ὁ
he has, and to be repaid. Falling therefore the
δοῦλος προσεκύνει αὐτῷ λέγων· μακρο-
slave did obeisance to him saying: Defer
θύμησον ἐπ' ἐμοί, καὶ πάντα ἀποδώσω
anger over me, and all things I will repay
σοι. **27** σπλαγχνισθεὶς δὲ ὁ κύριος τοῦ
thee. And filled with tenderness the lord –
δούλου ἐκείνου ἀπέλυσεν αὐτόν, καὶ τὸ
slave of that released him, and the

church; and if he refuses to
listen even to the church,
treat him as you would a
pagan or a tax collector.
18"I tell you the truth,
whatever you bind on earth
will be[u] bound in heaven,
and whatever you loose on
earth will be[u] loosed in
heaven.
19"Again, I tell you that if
two of you on earth agree
about anything you ask for,
it will be done for you by
my Father in heaven. 20For
where two or three come
together in my name, there
am I with them."

The Parable of the
Unmerciful Servant

21Then Peter came to
Jesus and asked, "Lord,
how many times shall I forgive my brother when he
sins against me? Up to sev-
en times?"
22Jesus answered, "I tell
you, not seven times, but
seventy-seven times.[v]
23"Therefore, the king-
dom of heaven is like a king
who wanted to settle ac-
counts with his servants.
24As he began the settle-
ment, a man who owed him
ten thousand talents[w] was
brought to him. 25Since he
was not able to pay, the
master ordered that he and
his wife and his children
and all that he had be sold
to repay the debt.
26"The servant fell on his
knees before him. 'Be pa-
tient with me,' he begged,
'and I will pay back everything.' 27The servant's
master took pity on him,

[i] About $10,000,000 in silver content but worth much more in buying power

[u] 18 Or *have been*
[v] 22 Or *seventy times seven*
[w] 24 That is, millions of dollars

him the debt.

28"But that slave went out and found one of his fellow slaves who owed him a hundred [j]denarii; and he seized him and *began* to choke *him*, saying, 'Pay back what you owe.'

29"So his fellow slave fell down and *began* to entreat him, saying, 'Have patience with me and I will repay you.'

30"He was unwilling however, but went and threw him in prison until he should pay back what was owed.

31"So when his fellow slaves saw what had happened, they were deeply grieved and came and reported to their lord all that had happened.

32"Then summoning him, his lord *said to him, 'You wicked slave, I forgave you all that debt because you entreated me.

33'Should you not also have had mercy on your fellow slave, even as I had mercy on you?'

34"And his lord, moved with anger, handed him over to the torturers until he should repay all that was owed him.

35"So shall My heavenly Father also do to you, if each of you does not forgive his brother from your heart."

δάνειον ἀφῆκεν αὐτῷ. **28** ἐξελθὼν δὲ
loan forgave him. But going out
ὁ δοῦλος ἐκεῖνος εὗρεν ἕνα τῶν
– slave that found one of the
συνδούλων αὐτοῦ, ὃς ὤφειλεν αὐτὸν ἑκατὸν
fellow-slaves of him, who owed him a hundred
δηνάρια, καὶ κρατήσας αὐτὸν ἔπνιγεν
denarii, and seizing him throttled
λέγων· ἀπόδος εἴ τι ὀφείλεις.
saying: Repay if something thou owest.
29 πεσὼν οὖν ὁ σύνδουλος αὐτοῦ παρε-
Falling therefore the fellow-slave of him be-
κάλει αὐτὸν λέγων· μακροθύμησον ἐπ᾽
sought him saying: Defer anger over
ἐμοί, καὶ ἀποδώσω σοι. **30** ὁ δὲ οὐκ
me, and I will repay thee. But he not
ἤθελεν, ἀλλὰ ἀπελθὼν ἔβαλεν αὐτὸν εἰς
wished, but going away threw him into
φυλακὴν ἕως ἀποδῷ τὸ ὀφειλόμενον.
prison until he should repay the thing owing.
31 ἰδόντες οὖν οἱ σύνδουλοι αὐτοῦ τὰ
Seeing therefore the fellow-slaves of him the things
γενόμενα ἐλυπήθησαν σφόδρα, καὶ
having taken place they were grieved exceedingly, and
ἐλθόντες διεσάφησαν τῷ κυρίῳ ἑαυτῶν
coming explained to the lord of them*selves*
πάντα τὰ γενόμενα. **32** τότε προσ-
all the things having taken place. Then ¹call-
καλεσάμενος αὐτὸν ὁ κύριος αὐτοῦ λέγει
ing ³forward ²him the lord of him says
αὐτῷ· δοῦλε πονηρέ, πᾶσαν τὴν ὀφειλὴν
to him: ²Slave ¹wicked, all – debt
ἐκείνην ἀφῆκά σοι, ἐπεὶ παρεκάλεσάς με·
that I forgave thee, since thou besoughtest me;
33 οὐκ ἔδει καὶ σὲ ἐλεῆσαι τὸν
did it not behove also thee to pity the
σύνδουλόν σου, ὡς κἀγὼ σὲ ἠλέησα;
fellow-slave of thee, as I also thee pitied?
34 καὶ ὀργισθεὶς ὁ κύριος αὐτοῦ
And being angry the lord of him
παρέδωκεν αὐτὸν τοῖς βασανισταῖς ἕως οὗ
delivered him to the tormentors until
ἀποδῷ πᾶν τὸ ὀφειλόμενον αὐτῷ.
he should repay all the thing owing to him.
35 Οὕτως καὶ ὁ πατήρ μου ὁ οὐράνιος
Thus also the Father of me – heavenly
ποιήσει ὑμῖν, ἐὰν μὴ ἀφῆτε ἕκαστος
will do to you, unless ye forgive each one
τῷ ἀδελφῷ αὐτοῦ ἀπὸ τῶν καρδιῶν
the brother of him from the hearts
ὑμῶν.
of you.

canceled the debt and let him go.

28"But when that servant went out, he found one of his fellow servants who owed him a hundred denarii.[x] He grabbed him and began to choke him. 'Pay back what you owe me!' he demanded.

29"His fellow servant fell to his knees and begged him, 'Be patient with me, and I will pay you back.'

30"But he refused. Instead, he went off and had the man thrown into prison until he could pay the debt.
31When the other servants saw what had happened, they were greatly distressed and went and told their master everything that had happened.

32"Then the master called the servant in. 'You wicked servant,' he said, 'I canceled all that debt of yours because you begged me to.
33Shouldn't you have had mercy on your fellow servant just as I had on you?'
34In anger his master turned him over to the jailers to be tortured, until he should pay back all he owed.

35"This is how my heavenly Father will treat each of you unless you forgive your brother from your heart."

Chapter 19

Concerning Divorce

AND it came about that when Jesus had finished these words, He departed from Galilee, and came into the region of Judea beyond the Jordan;

2and great multitudes followed Him, and He healed them there.

19 Καὶ ἐγένετο ὅτε ἐτέλεσεν ὁ
And it came to pass when ended –
Ἰησοῦς τοὺς λόγους τούτους, μετῆρεν
Jesus – words these, he removed
ἀπὸ τῆς Γαλιλαίας καὶ ἦλθεν εἰς τὰ
from – Galilee and came into the
ὅρια τῆς Ἰουδαίας πέραν τοῦ Ἰορδάνου.
borders – of Judæa across the Jordan.
2 καὶ ἠκολούθησαν αὐτῷ ὄχλοι πολλοί,
And followed him crowds many,
καὶ ἐθεράπευσεν αὐτοὺς ἐκεῖ.
and he healed them there.

Chapter 19

Divorce

WHEN Jesus had fin-
ished saying these
things, he left Galilee and
went into the region of Judea to the other side of the
Jordan. 2Large crowds followed him, and he healed
them there.

[j]The denarius was equivalent to one day's wage

[x]28 That is, a few dollars

3And *some* Pharisees
came to Him, testing Him,
and saying, "Is it lawful *for*
a man to divorce his wife
for any cause at all?"
4And He answered and
said, "Have you not read,
that He who created *them*
from the beginning MADE
THEM MALE AND FEMALE,
5and said, 'FOR THIS
CAUSE A MAN SHALL LEAVE
HIS FATHER AND MOTHER,
AND SHALL CLEAVE TO HIS
WIFE; AND THE TWO SHALL
BECOME ONE FLESH'?
6"Consequently they are
no longer two, but one
flesh. What therefore God
has joined together, let no
man separate."
7They *said to Him,
"Why then did Moses com-
mand to GIVE HER A CERTIFI-
CATE OF DIVORCE AND SEND
her AWAY?"
8He *said to them, "Be-
cause of your hardness of
heart, Moses permitted you
to divorce your wives; but
from the beginning it has
not been this way.
9"And I say to you, who-
ever divorces his wife, except for immorality, and
marries another woman
commits adultery."
10The disciples *said to
Him, "If the relationship of
the man with his wife is like
this, it is better not to
marry."
11But He said to them,
"Not all men *can* accept
this statement, but *only*
those to whom it has been
given.
12"For there are eunuchs
who were born that way
from their mother's womb;
and there are eunuchs who
were made eunuchs by
men; and there are *also* eunuchs who made them-
selves eunuchs for the sake
of the kingdom of heaven.
He who is able to accept
this, let him accept *it*."

3 Καὶ προσῆλθον αὐτῷ Φαρισαῖοι
And approached *to* him Pharisees
πειράζοντες αὐτὸν καὶ λέγοντες· εἰ ἔξεστιν
tempting him and saying: If it is lawful
ἀπολῦσαι τὴν γυναῖκα αὐτοῦ κατὰ πᾶσαν
to dismiss the wife of him for every
αἰτίαν; 4 ὁ δὲ ἀποκριθεὶς εἶπεν· οὐκ
cause? And he answering said: not
ἀνέγνωτε ὅτι ὁ κτίσας ἀπ'
Did ye read that the [one] creating from
ἀρχῆς ἄρσεν καὶ θῆλυ ἐποίησεν αὐτούς;
[the] beginning male and female made them?
5 καὶ εἶπεν· ἕνεκα τούτου καταλείψει
And he said: For the sake of this shall leave
ἄνθρωπος τὸν πατέρα καὶ τὴν μητέρα
a man the(his) father and the(his) mother
καὶ κολληθήσεται τῇ γυναικὶ αὐτοῦ,
and shall cleave to the wife of him,
καὶ ἔσονται οἱ δύο εἰς σάρκα μίαν·
and [3]shall be [1]the [2]two [4]in [6]flesh [5]one;
6 ὥστε οὐκέτι εἰσὶν δύο ἀλλὰ σὰρξ μία.
so as no longer are they two but flesh one.
ὃ οὖν ὁ θεὸς συνέζευξεν, ἄνθρωπος
What therefore – God yoked together, a man
μὴ χωριζέτω. 7 λέγουσιν αὐτῷ· τί οὖν
let not separate. They say to him: Why then
Μωϋσῆς ἐνετείλατο δοῦναι βιβλίον ἀπο-
[2]Moses [1]did [3]enjoin to give a document of
στασίου καὶ ἀπολῦσαι; 8 λέγει αὐτοῖς·
divorce and to dismiss? He says to them:
ὅτι Μωϋσῆς πρὸς τὴν σκληροκαρδίαν
– Moses in view of the obduracy
ὑμῶν ἐπέτρεψεν ὑμῖν ἀπολῦσαι τὰς
of you allowed you to dismiss the
γυναῖκας ὑμῶν· ἀπ' ἀρχῆς δὲ οὐ
wives of you; but from [the] beginning not
γέγονεν οὕτως. 9 λέγω δὲ ὑμῖν ὅτι
it has been so. But I say to you that
ὃς ἂν ἀπολύσῃ τὴν γυναῖκα αὐτοῦ
whoever dismisses the wife of him
μὴ ἐπὶ πορνείᾳ καὶ γαμήσῃ ἄλλην,
not of(for) fornication and marries another,
μοιχᾶται. 10 λέγουσιν αὐτῷ οἱ μαθηταί·
commits adultery. Say to him the disciples:
εἰ οὕτως ἐστὶν ἡ αἰτία τοῦ ἀνθρώπου
If so is the cause of the man
μετὰ τῆς γυναικός, οὐ συμφέρει γαμῆσαι.
with the wife, it is not expedient to marry.
11 ὁ δὲ εἶπεν αὐτοῖς· οὐ πάντες χωροῦσιν
And he said to them: Not all men grasp
τὸν λόγον τοῦτον, ἀλλ' οἷς δέδοται.
– saying this, but [those] to whom it has been given.
12 εἰσὶν γὰρ εὐνοῦχοι οἵτινες ἐκ κοιλίας
For there are eunuchs who from [the] womb
μητρὸς ἐγεννήθησαν οὕτως, καὶ εἰσὶν
of a mother were born so, and there are
εὐνοῦχοι οἵτινες εὐνουχίσθησαν ὑπὸ τῶν
eunuchs who were made eunuchs by –
ἀνθρώπων, καὶ εἰσὶν εὐνοῦχοι οἵτινες
men, and there are eunuchs who
εὐνούχισαν ἑαυτοὺς διὰ τὴν
made eunuchs themselves on account of the
βασιλείαν τῶν οὐρανῶν. ὁ δυνάμενος
kingdom of the heavens. The [one] *being* able
χωρεῖν χωρείτω.
to grasp [it] let him grasp.

3Some Pharisees came to
him to test him. They
asked, "Is it lawful for a
man to divorce his wife for
any and every reason?"
4"Haven't you read," he
replied, "that at the beginning the Creator 'made
them male and female,'[y]
5and said, 'For this reason
a man will leave his father
and mother and be united
to his wife, and the two will
become one flesh'[z]? 6So
they are no longer two, but
one. Therefore what God
has joined together, let man
not separate."
7"Why then," they
asked, "did Moses com-
mand that a man give his
wife a certificate of divorce
and send her away?"
8Jesus replied, "Moses
permitted you to divorce
your wives because your
hearts were hard. But it
was not this way from the
beginning. 9I tell you that
anyone who divorces his
wife, except for marital unfaithfulness, and marries
another woman commits
adultery."
10The disciples said to
him, "If this is the situation
between a husband and
wife, it is better not to marry."
11Jesus replied, "Not ev-
eryone can accept this
word, but only those to
whom it has been given.
12For some are eunuchs because they were born that
way; others were made that
way by men; and others
have renounced marriage[a]
because of the kingdom of
heaven. The one who can
accept this should accept
it."

[y]4 Gen. 1:27
[z]5 Gen. 2:24
[a]12 Or *have made themselves eunuchs*

Jesus Blesses Little Children

13 Then *some* children
were brought to Him so
that He might lay His hands
on them and pray; and the
disciples rebuked them.
14 But Jesus said, "Let the
children alone, and do not
hinder them from coming
to Me; for the kingdom of
heaven belongs to such as
these."
15 And after laying His
hands on them, He de-
parted from there.

The Rich Young Ruler

16 And behold, one came
to Him and said, "Teacher,
what good thing shall I do
that I may obtain eternal
life?"
17 And He said to him,
"Why are you asking Me
about what is good? There
is *only* One who is good;
but if you wish to enter into
life, keep the command-
ments."
18 He *said to Him,
"Which ones?" And Jesus
said, "YOU SHALL NOT COM-
MIT MURDER; YOU SHALL NOT
COMMIT ADULTERY; YOU
SHALL NOT STEAL; YOU
SHALL NOT BEAR FALSE WIT-
NESS;
19 HONOR YOUR FATHER
AND MOTHER; and YOU
SHALL LOVE YOUR NEIGHBOR
AS YOURSELF."
20 The young man *said to
Him, "All these things I
have kept; what am I still
lacking?"
21 Jesus said to him, "If
you wish to be complete,
go *and* sell your possessions and give to *the* poor,
and you shall have treasure
in heaven; and come, fol-
low Me."
22 But when the young
man heard this statement,
he went away grieved; for
he was one who owned
much property.
23 And Jesus said to His
disciples, "Truly I say to
you, it is hard for a rich
man to enter the kingdom
of heaven.
24 "And again I say to
you, it is easier for a camel
to go through the eye of a

13 Τότε προσηνέχθησαν αὐτῷ παιδία,
Then were brought to him children,
ἵνα τὰς χεῖρας ἐπιθῇ αὐτοῖς καὶ
that the(his) hands he should put on them and
προσεύξηται· οἱ δὲ μαθηταὶ ἐπετίμησαν
pray; but the disciples rebuked
αὐτοῖς. 14 ὁ δὲ Ἰησοῦς εἶπεν· ἄφετε
them. – But Jesus said: Permit
τὰ παιδία καὶ μὴ κωλύετε αὐτὰ ἐλθεῖν
the children and do not prevent them to come
πρός με· τῶν γὰρ τοιούτων ἐστὶν ἡ
unto me; – for of such is the
βασιλεία τῶν οὐρανῶν. 15 καὶ ἐπιθεὶς
kingdom of the heavens. And putting on
τὰς χεῖρας αὐτοῖς ἐπορεύθη ἐκεῖθεν.
the(his) hands *on* them he went thence.
16 Καὶ ἰδοὺ εἷς προσελθὼν αὐτῷ εἶπεν·
And behold one approaching *to* him said:
διδάσκαλε, τί ἀγαθὸν ποιήσω ἵνα
Teacher, what good thing may I do that
σχῶ ζωὴν αἰώνιον; ὁ δὲ εἶπεν αὐτῷ·
I may have life eternal? And he said to him:
17 τί με ἐρωτᾷς περὶ τοῦ ἀγαθοῦ;
Why me questionest thou concerning the good?
εἷς ἐστιν ὁ ἀγαθός· εἰ δὲ θέλεις εἰς
one is the good; but if thou wishest into
τὴν ζωὴν εἰσελθεῖν, τήρει τὰς ἐντολάς.
– life to enter, keep the commandments.
18 λέγει αὐτῷ· ποίας; ὁ δὲ Ἰησοῦς
He says to him: Which? – And Jesus
ἔφη· τὸ οὐ φονεύσεις, οὐ μοιχεύσεις,
said: – Thou shalt not kill, Thou shalt not commit adultery,
οὐ κλέψεις, οὐ ψευδομαρτυρήσεις,
Thou shalt not steal, Thou shalt not bear false witness,
19 τίμα τὸν πατέρα καὶ τὴν μητέρα,
Honour the(thy) father and the(thy) mother,
καὶ ἀγαπήσεις τὸν πλησίον σου ὡς
and Thou shalt love the neighbour of thee as
σεαυτόν. 20 λέγει αὐτῷ ὁ νεανίσκος·
thyself. Says to him the young man:
ταῦτα πάντα ἐφύλαξα· τί ἔτι ὑστερῶ;
These things all I kept; what yet do I lack?
21 ἔφη αὐτῷ ὁ Ἰησοῦς· εἰ θέλεις τέλειος
Said to him – Jesus: If thou wishest perfect
εἶναι, ὕπαγε πώλησόν σου τὰ ὑπάρχοντα
to be, go sell of thee the belongings
καὶ δὸς πτωχοῖς, καὶ ἕξεις
and give to [the] poor, and thou shalt have
θησαυρὸν ἐν οὐρανοῖς, καὶ δεῦρο ἀκολούθει
treasure in heavens, and come follow
μοι. 22 ἀκούσας δὲ ὁ νεανίσκος τὸν
me. But hearing the young man –
λόγον [τοῦτον] ἀπῆλθεν λυπούμενος·
word this went away grieving;
ἦν γὰρ ἔχων κτήματα πολλά. 23 Ὁ
for he was having possessions many. –
δὲ Ἰησοῦς εἶπεν τοῖς μαθηταῖς αὐτοῦ·
So Jesus said to the disciples of him:
ἀμὴν λέγω ὑμῖν ὅτι πλούσιος δυσκόλως
Truly I tell you that a rich man hardly
εἰσελεύσεται εἰς τὴν βασιλείαν τῶν
will enter into the kingdom of the
οὐρανῶν. 24 πάλιν δὲ λέγω ὑμῖν,
heavens. And again I tell you,
εὐκοπώτερόν ἐστιν κάμηλον διὰ τρήματος
easier it is a camel through [the] eye

The Little Children and Jesus

13 Then little children
were brought to Jesus for
him to place his hands on
them and pray for them.
But the disciples rebuked
those who brought them.
14 Jesus said, "Let the little children come to me,
and do not hinder them, for
the kingdom of heaven be-
longs to such as these."
15 When he had placed his
hands on them, he went on
from there.

The Rich Young Man

16 Now a man came up to
Jesus and asked, "Teach-
er, what good thing must I
do to get eternal life?"
17 "Why do you ask me
about what is good?" Jesus
replied. "There is only One
who is good. If you want to
enter life, obey the com-
mandments."
18 "Which ones?" the
man inquired.
Jesus replied, " 'Do not
murder, do not commit
adultery, do not steal, do
not give false testimony,
19 honor your father and
mother,'[b] and 'love your
neighbor as yourself.'[c]"
20 "All these I have
kept," the young man said.
"What do I still lack?"
21 Jesus answered, "If
you want to be perfect, go,
sell your possessions and
give to the poor, and you
will have treasure in heav-
en. Then come, follow
me."
22 When the young man
heard this, he went away
sad, because he had great
wealth.
23 Then Jesus said to his
disciples, "I tell you the
truth, it is hard for a rich
man to enter the kingdom
of heaven. 24 Again I tell
you, it is easier for a camel
to go through the eye of a

b *19* Exodus 20:12-16; Deut. 5:16-20
c *19* Lev. 19:18

needle, than for a rich man to enter the kingdom of God."

25And when the disciples heard *this*, they were very astonished and said, "Then who can be saved?"

26And looking upon *them* Jesus said to them, "With men this is impossible, but with God all things are possible."

The Disciples' Reward

27Then Peter answered and said to Him, "Behold, we have left everything and followed You; what then will there be for us?"

28And Jesus said to them, "Truly I say to you, that you who have followed Me, in the regeneration when the Son of Man will sit on His glorious throne, you also shall sit upon twelve thrones, judging the twelve tribes of Israel.

29"And everyone who has left houses or brothers or sisters or father or mother[k] or children or farms for My name's sake, shall receive many times as much, and shall inherit eternal life.

30"But many *who are* first will be last; and *the* last, first.

Chapter 20

Laborers in the Vineyard

"FOR the kingdom of heaven is like a landowner who went out early in the morning to hire laborers for his vineyard.

2"And when he had agreed with the laborers for a [l]denarius for the day, he sent them into his vineyard.

3"And he went out about the [m]third hour and saw others standing idle in the market place;

4and to those he said,

ῥαφίδος εἰσελθεῖν ἢ πλούσιον εἰς τὴν
of a needle to enter than a rich man into the
βασιλείαν τοῦ θεοῦ. 25 ἀκούσαντες δὲ
kingdom – of God. And hearing
οἱ μαθηταὶ ἐξεπλήσσοντο σφόδρα
the disciples were astounded exceedingly
λέγοντες· τίς ἄρα δύναται σωθῆναι;
saying: Who then can *to* be saved?
26 ἐμβλέψας δὲ ὁ Ἰησοῦς εἶπεν
And looking upon – Jesus said
αὐτοῖς· παρὰ ἀνθρώποις τοῦτο ἀδύνατόν
to them: With men this impossible
ἐστιν, παρὰ δὲ θεῷ πάντα δυνατά.
is, but with God all things [are] possible.
27 Τότε ἀποκριθεὶς ὁ Πέτρος εἶπεν αὐτῷ·
Then answering – Peter said to him:
ἰδοὺ ἡμεῖς ἀφήκαμεν πάντα καὶ
Behold we left all things and
ἠκολουθήσαμέν σοι· τί ἄρα ἔσται
followed thee; what then shall be =shall we have?
ἡμῖν; 28 ὁ δὲ Ἰησοῦς εἶπεν αὐτοῖς·
to us[c]? – And Jesus said to them:
ἀμὴν λέγω ὑμῖν ὅτι ὑμεῖς οἱ ἀκολουθή-
Truly I tell you that ye the [ones] having
σαντές μοι, ἐν τῇ παλιγγενεσίᾳ, ὅταν
followed me, in the regeneration, when
καθίσῃ ὁ υἱὸς τοῦ ἀνθρώπου ἐπὶ θρόνου
sits the Son – of man on [the] throne
δόξης αὐτοῦ, καθήσεσθε καὶ αὐτοὶ ἐπὶ
of glory of him, ye will sit also [your]selves on
δώδεκα θρόνους κρίνοντες τὰς δώδεκα
twelve thrones judging the twelve
φυλὰς τοῦ Ἰσραήλ. 29 καὶ πᾶς ὅστις
tribes – of Israel. And everyone who
ἀφῆκεν οἰκίας ἢ ἀδελφοὺς ἢ ἀδελφὰς ἢ
left houses or brothers or sisters or
πατέρα ἢ μητέρα ἢ τέκνα ἢ ἀγροὺς
father or mother or children or fields
ἕνεκεν τοῦ ἐμοῦ ὀνόματος, πολλαπλα-
for the sake of – my name, mani-
σίονα λήμψεται καὶ ζωὴν αἰώνιον
fold will receive and life eternal
κληρονομήσει. 30 Πολλοὶ δὲ ἔσονται πρῶτοι
will inherit. But many [2]will be [1]first
ἔσχατοι καὶ ἔσχατοι πρῶτοι.
[3]last and last first.

20 Ὁμοία γάρ ἐστιν ἡ βασιλεία τῶν
For like is the kingdom of the
οὐρανῶν ἀνθρώπῳ οἰκοδεσπότῃ, ὅστις
heavens to *a man* a housemaster, who
ἐξῆλθεν ἅμα πρωῒ μισθώσασθαι
went out early in the morning to hire
ἐργάτας εἰς τὸν ἀμπελῶνα αὐτοῦ. 2 συμ-
workmen in the vineyard of him. And
φωνήσας δὲ μετὰ τῶν ἐργατῶν ἐκ δηναρίου
agreeing with the workmen out of(for) a denarius
τὴν ἡμέραν ἀπέστειλεν αὐτοὺς εἰς τὸν
the day he sent them into the
ἀμπελῶνα αὐτοῦ. 3 καὶ ἐξελθὼν περὶ
vineyard of him. And going out about
τρίτην ὥραν εἶδεν ἄλλους ἑστῶτας
[the] third hour he saw others standing
ἐν τῇ ἀγορᾷ ἀργούς, 4 καὶ ἐκείνοις
in the marketplace idle, and to those

needle than for a rich man to enter the kingdom of God."

25When the disciples heard this, they were greatly astonished and asked, "Who then can be saved?"

26Jesus looked at them and said, "With man this is impossible, but with God all things are possible."

27Peter answered him, "We have left everything to follow you! What then will there be for us?"

28Jesus said to them, "I tell you the truth, at the renewal of all things, when the Son of Man sits on his glorious throne, you who have followed me will also sit on twelve thrones, judging the twelve tribes of Israel. 29And everyone who has left houses or brothers or sisters or father or mother[d] or children or fields for my sake will receive a hundred times as much and will inherit eternal life. 30But many who are first will be last, and many who are last will be first.

Chapter 20

The Parable of the Workers in the Vineyard

"FOR the kingdom of heaven is like a landowner who went out early in the morning to hire men to work in his vineyard. 2He agreed to pay them a denarius for the day and sent them into his vineyard.

3"About the third hour he went out and saw others standing in the marketplace doing nothing. 4He told them, 'You also go and

[k] Many mss. add here, *or wife*
[l] The denarius was equivalent to one day's wage
[m] I.e., 9 a.m.

[d] 29 Some manuscripts *mother or wife*

'You too go into the vineyard, and whatever is right
I will give you.' And *so*
they went.
5"Again he went out
about the [n]sixth and the
ninth hour, and did the
same thing.
6"And about the [o]elev-
enth *hour* he went out, and
found others standing; and
he *said to them, 'Why
have you been standing
here idle all day long?'
7"They *said to him,
'Because no one hired us.'
He *said to them, 'You too
go into the vineyard.'
8"And when evening
had come, the owner of the
vineyard *said to his foreman, 'Call the laborers and
pay them their wages, be-
ginning with the last *group*
to the first.'
9"And when those *hired*
about the eleventh hour
came, each one received a
[p]denarius.
10"And when those *hired*
first came, they thought
that they would receive
more; and they also re-
ceived each one a [p]denari-
us.
11"And when they re-
ceived it, they grumbled at
the landowner,
12saying, 'These last men
have worked *only* one
hour, and you have made
them equal to us who have
borne the burden and the
scorching heat of the day.'
13"But he answered and
said to one of them,
'Friend, I am doing you no
wrong; did you not agree
with me for a [p]denarius?
14'Take what is yours and
go your way, but I wish to
give to this last man the
same as to you.
15'Is it not lawful for me
to do what I wish with what
is my own? Or is your eye
envious because I am gen-
erous?'

εἶπεν· ὑπάγετε καὶ ὑμεῖς εἰς τὸν
said: Go also ye into the

ἀμπελῶνα, καὶ ὃ ἐὰν ᾖ δίκαιον δώσω
vineyard, and whatever may be just I will give

ὑμῖν. οἱ δὲ ἀπῆλθον. 5 πάλιν [δὲ]
you. And they went. And again

ἐξελθὼν περὶ ἕκτην καὶ ἐνάτην ὥραν
going out about [the] sixth and [the] ninth hour

ἐποίησεν ὡσαύτως. 6 περὶ δὲ τὴν
he did similarly. And about the

ἑνδεκάτην ἐξελθὼν εὗρεν ἄλλους ἑστῶτας,
eleventh going out he found others standing,

καὶ λέγει αὐτοῖς· τί ὧδε ἑστήκατε
and says to them: Why here stand ye

ὅλην τὴν ἡμέραν ἀργοί; 7 λέγουσιν αὐτῷ·
all the day idle? They say to him:

ὅτι οὐδεὶς ἡμᾶς ἐμισθώσατο. λέγει αὐτοῖς·
Because no one us hired. He says to them:

ὑπάγετε καὶ ὑμεῖς εἰς τὸν ἀμπελῶνα.
Go also ye into the vineyard.

8 ὀψίας δὲ γενομένης λέγει ὁ κύριος
And evening having come[a] says the lord
= when evening had come

τοῦ ἀμπελῶνος τῷ ἐπιτρόπῳ αὐτοῦ·
of the vineyard to the steward of him:

κάλεσον τοὺς ἐργάτας καὶ ἀπόδος τὸν
Call the workmen and pay the

μισθόν, ἀρξάμενος ἀπὸ τῶν ἐσχάτων
wage, beginning from the last ones

ἕως τῶν πρώτων. 9 ἐλθόντες δὲ οἱ
until the first. And coming the [ones]

περὶ τὴν ἑνδεκάτην ὥραν ἔλαβον ἀνὰ
about the eleventh hour received each

δηνάριον. 10 καὶ ἐλθόντες οἱ πρῶτοι
a denarius. And coming the first

ἐνόμισαν ὅτι πλεῖον λήμψονται· καὶ
supposed that more they will receive; and

ἔλαβον τὸ ἀνὰ δηνάριον καὶ αὐτοί.
they received the [2]each [1]denarius also [them]selves.

11 λαβόντες δὲ ἐγόγγυζον κατὰ τοῦ
And receiving they grumbled against the

οἰκοδεσπότου λέγοντες· 12 οὗτοι οἱ ἔσχατοι
housemaster saying: These – last

μίαν ὥραν ἐποίησαν, καὶ ἴσους αὐτοὺς
one hour wrought, and equal them

ἡμῖν ἐποίησας τοῖς βαστάσασι τὸ
to us thou madest the [ones] having borne the

βάρος τῆς ἡμέρας καὶ τὸν καύσωνα.
burden of the day and the heat.

13 ὁ δὲ ἀποκριθεὶς ἑνὶ αὐτῶν εἶπεν·
But he answering one of them said:

ἑταῖρε, οὐκ ἀδικῶ σε· οὐχὶ
Comrade, I do not injure thee; not

δηναρίου συνεφώνησάς μοι; 14 ἆρον
of(for) a denarius thou didst agree with me? take

τὸ σὸν καὶ ὕπαγε· θέλω δὲ
the thine and go; but I wish
= that which is thine

τούτῳ τῷ ἐσχάτῳ δοῦναι ὡς καὶ
to this – last man to give as also

σοί· 15 οὐκ ἔξεστίν μοι ὃ θέλω
to thee; is it not lawful to me what I wish

ποιῆσαι ἐν τοῖς ἐμοῖς; ἢ ὁ
to do among *the* my things? or the

ὀφθαλμός σου πονηρός ἐστιν ὅτι ἐγὼ
eye of thee evil is because I

work in my vineyard, and I
will pay you whatever is
right.' 5So they went.
"He went out again about
the sixth hour and the ninth
hour and did the same
thing. 6About the eleventh
hour he went out and found
still others standing
around. He asked them,
'Why have you been stand-
ing here all day long doing
nothing?'
7" 'Because no one has
hired us,' they answered.
"He said to them, 'You
also go and work in my
vineyard.'
8"When evening came,
the owner of the vineyard
said to his foreman, 'Call
the workers and pay them
their wages, beginning with
the last ones hired and going on to the first.'
9"The workers who were
hired about the eleventh
hour came and each re-
ceived a denarius. 10So
when those came who were
hired first, they expected to
receive more. But each one
of them also received a denarius. 11When they re-
ceived it, they began to
grumble against the land-
owner. 12'These men who
were hired last worked
only one hour,' they said,
'and you have made them
equal to us who have borne
the burden of the work and
the heat of the day.'
13"But he answered one
of them, 'Friend, I am not
being unfair to you. Didn't
you agree to work for a denarius? 14Take your pay
and go. I want to give the
man who was hired last the
same as I gave you. 15Don't
I have the right to do what I
want with my own money?
Or are you envious because
I am generous?'

[n] I.e., Noon and 3 p.m.
[o] I.e., 5 p.m.
[p] The denarius was equivalent to one day's wage

[16]"Thus the last shall be
first, and the first last."

Death, Resurrection Foretold

[17]And as Jesus was about
to go up to Jerusalem, He
took the twelve *disciples*
aside by themselves, and
on the way He said to them,
[18]"Behold, we are going
up to Jerusalem; and the
Son of Man will be de-
livered to the chief priests
and scribes, and they will
condemn Him to death,
[19]and will deliver Him to
the Gentiles to mock and
scourge and crucify *Him*,
and on the third day He will
be raised up."

Preferment Asked

[20]Then the mother of the
sons of Zebedee came to
Him with her sons, bowing
down, and making a re-
quest of Him.
[21]And He said to her,
"What do you wish?" She
*said to Him, "Command
that in Your kingdom these
two sons of mine may sit,
one on Your right and one
on Your left."
[22]But Jesus answered and
said, "You do not know
what you are asking for.
Are you able to drink the
cup that I am about to
drink?" They *said to Him,
"We are able."
[23]He *said to them, "My
cup you shall drink; but to
sit on My right and on *My*
left, this is not Mine to give,
but it is for those for whom
it has been prepared by My
Father."
[24]And hearing *this*, the
ten became indignant with
the two brothers.
[25]But Jesus called them to
Himself, and said, "You
know that the rulers of the
Gentiles lord it over them,

ἀγαθός εἰμι; **16** Οὕτως ἔσονται οἱ ἔσχατοι
good am? Thus will be the last [ones]
πρῶτοι καὶ οἱ πρῶτοι ἔσχατοι.
first and the first last.
17 Μέλλων δὲ ἀναβαίνειν Ἰησοῦς εἰς
And being about to go up Jesus to
Ἱεροσόλυμα παρέλαβεν τοὺς δώδεκα κατ᾽
Jerusalem he took the twelve private-
ἰδίαν, καὶ ἐν τῇ ὁδῷ εἶπεν αὐτοῖς·
ly, and in the way said to them:
18 ἰδοὺ ἀναβαίνομεν εἰς Ἱεροσόλυμα, καὶ
Behold we are going up to Jerusalem, and
ὁ υἱὸς τοῦ ἀνθρώπου παραδοθήσεται τοῖς
the Son – of man will be delivered to the
ἀρχιερεῦσιν καὶ γραμματεῦσιν, καὶ κατα-
chief priests and scribes, and they will
κρινοῦσιν αὐτὸν εἰς θάνατον, **19** καὶ
condemn him to death, and
παραδώσουσιν αὐτὸν τοῖς ἔθνεσιν εἰς
they will deliver him to the nations *for*
τὸ ἐμπαῖξαι καὶ μαστιγῶσαι καὶ
– to mock and to scourge and
σταυρῶσαι, καὶ τῇ τρίτῃ ἡμέρᾳ ἐγερθή-
to crucify, and on the third day he will be
σεται.
raised.
20 Τότε προσῆλθεν αὐτῷ ἡ μήτηρ τῶν
Then approached *to* him the mother of the
υἱῶν Ζεβεδαίου μετὰ τῶν υἱῶν αὐτῆς
sons of Zebedee with the sons of her
προσκυνοῦσα καὶ αἰτοῦσά τι ἀπ᾽ αὐτοῦ.
doing obeisance and asking something from him.
21 ὁ δὲ εἶπεν αὐτῇ· τί θέλεις; λέγει
And he said to her: What wishest thou? She says
αὐτῷ· εἰπὲ ἵνα καθίσωσιν οὗτοι οἱ
to him: Say that may sit these the
δύο υἱοί μου εἷς ἐκ δεξιῶν καὶ εἷς
two sons of me one on [the] right and one
ἐξ εὐωνύμων σου ἐν τῇ βασιλείᾳ
on [the] left of thee in the kingdom
σου. **22** ἀποκριθεὶς δὲ ὁ Ἰησοῦς
of thee. And answering – Jesus
εἶπεν· οὐκ οἴδατε τί αἰτεῖσθε.
said: Ye know not what ye ask.
δύνασθε πιεῖν τὸ ποτήριον ὃ ἐγὼ
Can ye *to* drink the cup which I
μέλλω πίνειν; λέγουσιν αὐτῷ· δυνάμεθα.
am about to drink? They say to him: We can.
23 λέγει αὐτοῖς· τὸ μὲν ποτήριόν μου
He says to them: Indeed the cup of me
πίεσθε, τὸ δὲ καθίσαι ἐκ δεξιῶν
ye shall drink, – but to sit on [the] right
μου καὶ ἐξ εὐωνύμων οὐκ ἔστιν
of me and on [the] left is not
ἐμὸν τοῦτο δοῦναι, ἀλλ᾽ οἷς ἡτοί-
mine this to give, but to whom it has
μασται ὑπὸ τοῦ πατρός μου. **24** καὶ
been prepared by the Father of me. And
ἀκούσαντες οἱ δέκα ἠγανάκτησαν περὶ
hearing the ten were incensed about
τῶν δύο ἀδελφῶν. **25** ὁ δὲ Ἰησοῦς
the two brothers. – So Jesus
προσκαλεσάμενος αὐτοῖς εἶπεν· οἴδατε
calling forward them said: Ye know
ὅτι οἱ ἄρχοντες τῶν ἐθνῶν κατακυριεύουσιν
that the rulers of the nations lord it over

[16]"So the last will be first,
and the first will be last."

Jesus Again Predicts His Death

[17]Now as Jesus was going
up to Jerusalem, he took
the twelve disciples aside
and said to them, [18]"We
are going up to Jerusalem,
and the Son of Man will be
betrayed to the chief
priests and the teachers of
the law. They will condemn
him to death [19]and will turn
him over to the Gentiles to
be mocked and flogged and
crucified. On the third day
he will be raised to life!"

A Mother's Request

[20]Then the mother of
Zebedee's sons came to
Jesus with her sons and,
kneeling down, asked a favor of him.
[21]"What is it you want?"
he asked.
She said, "Grant that one
of these two sons of mine
may sit at your right and the
other at your left in your
kingdom."
[22]"You don't know what
you are asking," Jesus said
to them. "Can you drink
the cup I am going to
drink?"
"We can," they an-
swered.
[23]Jesus said to them,
"You will indeed drink
from my cup, but to sit at
my right or left is not for me
to grant. These places belong to those for whom
they have been prepared by
my Father."
[24]When the ten heard
about this, they were indignant with the two brothers.
[25]Jesus called them together and said, "You know
that the rulers of the Gentiles lord it over them, and

and *their* great men exercise authority over them.
26"It is not so among you,
but whoever wishes to
become great among you
shall be your servant,
27and whoever wishes to
be first among you shall be
your slave;
28just as the Son of Man
did not come to be served,
but to serve, and to give
His life a ransom for
many."

Sight for the Blind

29And as they were going
out from Jericho, a great
multitude followed Him.
30And behold, two blind
men sitting by the road,
hearing that Jesus was
passing by, cried out, saying, "Lord, have mercy on
us, Son of David!"
31And the multitude
sternly told them to be quiet; but they cried out all the
more, saying, "Lord, have
mercy on us, Son of Da-
vid!"
32And Jesus stopped and
called them, and said,
"What do you want Me to
do for you?"
33They *said to Him,
"Lord, *we want* our eyes to
be opened."
34And moved with com-
passion, Jesus touched
their eyes; and immediately
they regained their sight
and followed Him.

αὐτῶν καὶ οἱ μεγάλοι κατεξουσιάζουσιν
them and the great ones have authority over
αὐτῶν. 26 οὐχ οὕτως ἐστὶν ἐν ὑμῖν·
them. Not thus is it among you;
ἀλλ' ὃς ἐὰν θέλῃ ἐν ὑμῖν μέγας γενέσθαι,
but whoever wishes among you great to become,
ἔσται ὑμῶν διάκονος, 27 καὶ ὃς ἂν
will be of you servant, and whoever
θέλῃ ἐν ὑμῖν εἶναι πρῶτος, ἔσται ὑμῶν
wishes among you to be first, he shall be of you
δοῦλος· 28 ὥσπερ ὁ υἱὸς τοῦ ἀνθρώπου
slave; as the Son – of man
οὐκ ἦλθεν διακονηθῆναι, ἀλλὰ διακο-
came not to be served, but to
νῆσαι καὶ δοῦναι τὴν ψυχὴν αὐτοῦ
serve and to give the life of him
λύτρον ἀντὶ πολλῶν.
a ransom instead of many.
29 Καὶ ἐκπορευομένων αὐτῶν ἀπὸ Ἰεριχὼ
And going out them* from Jericho
=as they were going out
ἠκολούθησεν αὐτῷ ὄχλος πολύς. 30 καὶ
followed him crowd a much. And
ἰδοὺ δύο τυφλοὶ καθήμενοι παρὰ τὴν
behold two blind men sitting beside the
ὁδόν, ἀκούσαντες ὅτι Ἰησοῦς παράγει,
way, hearing that Jesus is passing by,
ἔκραξαν λέγοντες· κύριε, ἐλέησον ἡμᾶς,
cried out saying: Lord, pity us,
υἱὸς Δαυίδ. 31 ὁ δὲ ὄχλος ἐπετίμησεν
son of David. But the crowd rebuked
αὐτοῖς ἵνα σιωπήσωσιν· οἱ δὲ μεῖζον
them that they should be silent; but they more
ἔκραξαν λέγοντες· κύριε, ἐλέησον ἡμᾶς,
cried out saying: Lord, pity us,
υἱὸς Δαυίδ. 32 καὶ στὰς ὁ Ἰησοῦς
son of David. And standing – Jesus
ἐφώνησεν αὐτοὺς καὶ εἶπεν· τί θέλετε
called them and said: What wish ye
ποιήσω ὑμῖν; 33 λέγουσιν αὐτῷ· κύριε,
I may do to you? They say to him: Lord,
ἵνα ἀνοιγῶσιν οἱ ὀφθαλμοὶ ἡμῶν.
that may be opened the eyes of us.
34 σπλαγχνισθεὶς δὲ ὁ Ἰησοῦς ἥψατο
And being filled with tenderness – Jesus touched
τῶν ὀμμάτων αὐτῶν, καὶ εὐθέως ἀνέβλεψαν
the eyes of them, and immediately they saw again
καὶ ἠκολούθησαν αὐτῷ.
and followed him.

their high officials exercise
authority over them. 26Not
so with you. Instead, whoever wants to become great
among you must be your
servant, 27and whoever
wants to be first must be
your slave— 28just as the
Son of Man did not come to
be served, but to serve, and
to give his life as a ransom
for many."

Two Blind Men Receive Sight

29As Jesus and his disci-
ples were leaving Jericho, a
large crowd followed him.
30Two blind men were sit-
ting by the roadside, and
when they heard that Jesus
was going by, they shout-
ed, "Lord, Son of David,
have mercy on us!"
31The crowd rebuked
them and told them to be
quiet, but they shouted all
the louder, "Lord, Son of
David, have mercy on us!"
32Jesus stopped and
called them. "What do you
want me to do for you?" he
asked.
33"Lord," they an-
swered, "we want our
sight."
34Jesus had compassion
on them and touched their
eyes. Immediately they received their sight and followed him.

Chapter 21

The Triumphal Entry

AND when they had ap-
proached Jerusalem
and had come to Beth-
phage, to the Mount of Olives, then Jesus sent two
disciples,
2saying to them, "Go
into the village opposite
you, and immediately you
will find a donkey tied *there*
and a colt with her; untie
them, and bring *them* to
Me.
3"And if anyone says
something to you, you shall

21 Καὶ ὅτε ἤγγισαν εἰς Ἱεροσόλυμα
And when they drew near to Jerusalem
καὶ ἦλθον εἰς Βηθφαγὴ εἰς τὸ ὄρος τῶν
and came to Bethphage to the mount of the
ἐλαιῶν, τότε Ἰησοῦς ἀπέστειλεν δύο
olives, then Jesus sent two
μαθητὰς 2 λέγων αὐτοῖς· πορεύεσθε εἰς
disciples telling them: Go ye into
τὴν κώμην τὴν κατέναντι ὑμῶν, καὶ εὐθὺς
the village – opposite you, and at once
εὑρήσετε ὄνον δεδεμένην καὶ πῶλον μετ'
ye will find an ass *having been* tied and a colt with
αὐτῆς· λύσαντες ἀγάγετέ μοι. 3 καὶ ἐάν
her/it; loosening bring to me. And if
τις ὑμῖν εἴπῃ τι, ἐρεῖτε ὅτι ὁ
anyone to you says anything, ye shall say[,] – The

Chapter 21

The Triumphal Entry

AS they approached Jeru-
salem and came to
Bethphage on the Mount of
Olives, Jesus sent two disciples, 2saying to them,
"Go to the village ahead of
you, and at once you will
find a donkey tied there,
with her colt by her. Untie
them and bring them to me.
3If anyone says anything to
you, tell him that the Lord

say, 'The Lord has need of
them,' and immediately he
will send them.''
4Now this took place
that what was spoken
through the prophet might
be fulfilled, saying,
5''SAY TO THE DAUGHTER
OF ZION,
'BEHOLD YOUR KING IS
COMING TO YOU,
GENTLE, AND MOUNTED
ON A DONKEY,
EVEN ON A COLT, THE
FOAL OF A BEAST OF
BURDEN.' ''
6And the disciples went
and did just as Jesus had
directed them,
7and brought the donkey
and the colt, and laid on
them their garments, on
which He sat.
8And most of the multitude
spread their garments
in the road, and others
were cutting branches from
the trees, and spreading
them in the road.
9And the multitudes going
before Him, and those
who followed after were
crying out, saying,
''Hosanna to the Son of
David;
BLESSED IS HE WHO
COMES IN THE NAME OF
THE LORD;
Hosanna in the highest!''
10And when He had entered
Jerusalem, all the city
was stirred, saying, ''Who
is this?''
11And the multitudes
were saying, ''This is the
prophet Jesus, from Nazareth
in Galilee.''

Cleansing the Temple

12And Jesus entered the
temple and cast out all
those who were buying and
selling in the temple, and
overturned the tables of the
moneychangers and the
seats of those who were
selling doves.
13And He *said to them,
''It is written, 'MY HOUSE
SHALL BE CALLED A HOUSE OF
PRAYER'; but you are making
it a ROBBERS' DEN.''
14And *the* blind and *the*
lame came to Him in the

κύριος αὐτῶν χρείαν ἔχει· εὐθὺς δὲ
Lord of them need has; and immediately
ἀποστελεῖ αὐτούς. **4** Τοῦτο δὲ γέγονεν
he will send them. Now this has happened
ἵνα πληρωθῇ τὸ ῥηθὲν διὰ τοῦ
that might be fulfilled the thing spoken through the
προφήτου λέγοντος· **5** εἴπατε τῇ θυγατρὶ
prophet saying: Tell ye the daughter
Σιών· ἰδοὺ ὁ βασιλεύς σου ἔρχεταί σοι
of Zion: Behold[,] the king of thee comes to thee
πραῢς καὶ ἐπιβεβηκὼς ἐπὶ ὄνον καὶ ἐπὶ
meek and having mounted on an ass and on
πῶλον υἱὸν ὑποζυγίου. **6** πορευθέντες δὲ
a colt son(foal) of an ass. And going
οἱ μαθηταὶ καὶ ποιήσαντες καθὼς συνέταξεν
the disciples and doing as directed
αὐτοῖς ὁ Ἰησοῦς **7** ἤγαγον τὴν ὄνον καὶ
them – Jesus they brought the ass and
τὸν πῶλον, καὶ ἐπέθηκαν ἐπ' αὐτῶν
the colt, and put *on* on them
τὰ ἱμάτια, καὶ ἐπεκάθισεν ἐπάνω αὐτῶν.
the(ir) garments, and he sat *on* on them.
8 ὁ δὲ πλεῖστος ὄχλος ἔστρωσαν ἑαυτῶν
And the very large crowd strewed of them*selves*
τὰ ἱμάτια ἐν τῇ ὁδῷ, ἄλλοι δὲ ἔκοπτον
the garments in the way, and others cut
κλάδους ἀπὸ τῶν δένδρων καὶ ἐστρών-
branches from the trees and strewed
νυον ἐν τῇ ὁδῷ. **9** οἱ δὲ ὄχλοι οἱ
in the way. And the crowds the [ones]
προάγοντες αὐτὸν καὶ οἱ ἀκολουθοῦντες
going before him and the [ones] following
ἔκραζον λέγοντες· ὡσαννὰ τῷ υἱῷ Δαυίδ·
cried out saying: Hosanna to the son of David;
εὐλογημένος ὁ ἐρχόμενος ἐν ὀνόματι
blessed the [one] coming in [the] name
κυρίου· ὡσαννὰ ἐν τοῖς ὑψίστοις. **10** καὶ
of [the] Lord; hosanna in the highest [places]. And
εἰσελθόντος αὐτοῦ εἰς Ἱεροσόλυμα ἐσείσθη
entering him[a] into Jerusalem was shaken
=as he entered
πᾶσα ἡ πόλις λέγουσα· τίς ἐστιν οὗτος;
all the city saying: Who is this?
11 οἱ δὲ ὄχλοι ἔλεγον· οὗτός ἐστιν ὁ
And the crowds said: This is the
προφήτης Ἰησοῦς ὁ ἀπὸ Ναζαρὲθ τῆς
prophet Jesus the [one] from Nazareth –
Γαλιλαίας.
of Galilee.
12 Καὶ εἰσῆλθεν Ἰησοῦς εἰς τὸ ἱερὸν
And entered Jesus into the temple
καὶ ἐξέβαλεν πάντας τοὺς πωλοῦντας καὶ
and cast out all the [ones] selling and
ἀγοράζοντας ἐν τῷ ἱερῷ, καὶ τὰς τραπέζας
buying in the temple, and the tables
τῶν κολλυβιστῶν κατέστρεψεν καὶ τὰς
of the money-changers he overturned and the
καθέδρας τῶν πωλούντων τὰς περιστεράς,
seats of the [ones] selling the doves,
13 καὶ λέγει αὐτοῖς· γέγραπται· ὁ οἶκός
and says to them: It has been written: The house
μου οἶκος προσευχῆς κληθήσεται, ὑμεῖς
of me a house of prayer shall be called, [2]ye
δὲ αὐτὸν ποιεῖτε σπήλαιον λῃστῶν. **14** Καὶ
[1]but [4]it [3]are making a den of robbers. And
προσῆλθον αὐτῷ τυφλοὶ καὶ χωλοὶ ἐν τῷ
approached *to* him blind and lame [ones] in the

needs them, and he will
send them right away.''
4This took place to fulfill
what was spoken through
the prophet:
5''Say to the Daughter of
Zion,
'See, your king comes
to you,
gentle and riding on a
donkey,
on a colt, the foal of a
donkey.' ''[e]
6The disciples went and
did as Jesus had instructed
them. 7They brought the
donkey and the colt, placed
their cloaks on them, and
Jesus sat on them. 8A very
large crowd spread their
cloaks on the road, while
others cut branches from
the trees and spread them
on the road. 9The crowds
that went ahead of him and
those that followed shouted,
''Hosanna[f] to the Son of
David!''
''Blessed is he who
comes in the name
of the Lord!''[g]
''Hosanna[f] in the
highest!''
10When Jesus entered Jerusalem,
the whole city
was stirred and asked,
''Who is this?''
11The crowds answered,
''This is Jesus, the prophet
from Nazareth in Galilee.''

Jesus at the Temple

12Jesus entered the temple
area and drove out all
who were buying and selling
there. He overturned
the tables of the money
changers and the benches
of those selling doves. 13''It
is written,'' he said to
them, '' 'My house will be
called a house of prayer,'[h]
but you are making it a 'den
of robbers.'[i]''
14The blind and the lame
came to him at the temple,

[e] *5* Zech. 9:9
[f] *9* A Hebrew expression meaning ''Save!'' which became an exclamation of praise; also in verse 15
[g] *9* Psalm 118:26
[h] *13* Isaiah 56:7
[i] *13* Jer. 7:11

temple, and He healed them.

15But when the chief priests and the scribes saw the wonderful things that He had done, and the children who were crying out in the temple and saying, "Hosanna to the Son of David," they became indignant,

16and said to Him, "Do You hear what these are saying?" And Jesus *said to them, "Yes; have you never read, 'OUT OF THE MOUTH OF INFANTS AND NURSING BABES THOU HAST PREPARED PRAISE FOR THYSELF'?"

17And He left them and went out of the city to Bethany, and lodged there.

The Barren Fig Tree

18Now in the morning, when He returned to the city, He became hungry.

19And seeing a lone fig tree by the road, He came to it, and found nothing on it except leaves only; and He *said to it, "No longer shall there ever be *any* fruit from you." And at once the fig tree withered.

20And seeing *this*, the disciples marveled, saying, "How did the fig tree wither at once?"

21And Jesus answered and said to them, "Truly I say to you, if you have faith, and do not doubt, you shall not only do what was done to the fig tree, but even if you say to this mountain, 'Be taken up and cast into the sea,' it shall happen.

22"And all things you ask in prayer, believing, you shall receive."

Authority Challenged

23And when He had come into the temple, the chief priests and the elders of the people came to Him as He was teaching, and said, "By what authority are You doing these things, and who gave You this authority?"

ἱερῷ, καὶ ἐθεράπευσεν αὐτούς. **15** ἰδόντες
temple, and he healed them. [7]seeing
δὲ οἱ ἀρχιερεῖς καὶ οἱ γραμματεῖς τὰ
[1]But [2]the [3]chief priests [4]and [5]the [6]scribes the
θαυμάσια ἃ ἐποίησεν καὶ τοὺς παῖδας
marvels which he did and the children
τοὺς κράζοντας ἐν τῷ ἱερῷ καὶ λέγοντας·
– crying out in the temple and saying:
ὡσαννὰ τῷ υἱῷ Δαυίδ, ἠγανάκτησαν, **16** καὶ
Hosanna to the son of David, they were incensed, and
εἶπαν αὐτῷ· ἀκούεις τί οὗτοι λέγουσιν;
said to him: Hearest thou what these are saying?
ὁ δὲ Ἰησοῦς λέγει αὐτοῖς· ναί· οὐδέποτε
– And Jesus says to them: Yes; never
ἀνέγνωτε ὅτι ἐκ στόματος νηπίων καὶ
did ye read[,] – Out of [the] mouth of infants and
θηλαζόντων κατηρτίσω αἶνον; **17** Καὶ
sucking [ones] thou didst prepare praise? And
καταλιπὼν αὐτοὺς ἐξῆλθεν ἔξω τῆς
leaving them he went forth outside the
πόλεως εἰς Βηθανίαν, καὶ ηὐλίσθη ἐκεῖ.
city to Bethany, and lodged there.
18 Πρωῒ δὲ ἐπαναγαγὼν εἰς τὴν πόλιν
Now early going up to the city
ἐπείνασεν. **19** καὶ ἰδὼν συκῆν μίαν ἐπὶ τῆς
he hungered. And seeing fig-tree one on the
ὁδοῦ ἦλθεν ἐπ' αὐτήν, καὶ οὐδὲν εὗρεν
way he went up(to) it, and nothing found
ἐν αὐτῇ εἰ μὴ φύλλα μόνον, καὶ λέγει
in it except leaves only, and says
αὐτῇ· οὐ μηκέτι ἐκ σοῦ καρπὸς γένηται
to it: Never of thee fruit may be
εἰς τὸν αἰῶνα. καὶ ἐξηράνθη παραχρῆμα
to the age. And was dried up instantly
ἡ συκῆ. **20** καὶ ἰδόντες οἱ μαθηταὶ
the fig-tree. And seeing the disciples
ἐθαύμασαν λέγοντες· πῶς παραχρῆμα
marvelled saying: How instantly
ἐξηράνθη ἡ συκῆ; **21** ἀποκριθεὶς δὲ ὁ
was withered the fig-tree? And answering –
Ἰησοῦς εἶπεν αὐτοῖς· ἀμὴν λέγω ὑμῖν,
Jesus said to them: Truly I say to you,
ἐὰν ἔχητε πίστιν καὶ μὴ διακριθῆτε,
If ye have faith and do not doubt,
οὐ μόνον τὸ τῆς συκῆς ποιήσετε, ἀλλὰ
not only the* of the fig-tree ye will do, but
κἂν τῷ ὄρει τούτῳ εἴπητε· ἄρθητι
also if – mountain to this ye say: Be thou taken
καὶ βλήθητι εἰς τὴν θάλασσαν, γενήσεται·
and cast into the sea, it shall be;
22 καὶ πάντα ὅσα ἂν αἰτήσητε ἐν τῇ
and all things whatever ye may ask in –
προσευχῇ πιστεύοντες λήμψεσθε.
prayer believing ye shall receive.
23 Καὶ ἐλθόντος αὐτοῦ εἰς τὸ ἱερὸν
And coming him* into the temple
=as he came
προσῆλθον αὐτῷ διδάσκοντι οἱ ἀρχιερεῖς
approached *to* him teaching* the chief priests
=while he taught
καὶ οἱ πρεσβύτεροι τοῦ λαοῦ λέγοντες·
and the elders of the people saying:
ἐν ποίᾳ ἐξουσίᾳ ταῦτα ποιεῖς; καὶ
By what authority these things doest thou? and
τίς σοι ἔδωκεν τὴν ἐξουσίαν ταύτην;
who thee gave – authority this?

and he healed them. 15But
when the chief priests and
the teachers of the law saw
the wonderful things he did
and the children shouting in
the temple area, "Hosanna
to the Son of David," they
were indignant.
16"Do you hear what
these children are saying?"
they asked him.
"Yes," replied Jesus,
"have you never read,

" 'From the lips of
children and infants
you have ordained
praise'[j]?"

17And he left them and
went out of the city to Bethany, where he spent the
night.

The Fig Tree Withers

18Early in the morning, as
he was on his way back to
the city, he was hungry.
19Seeing a fig tree by the
road, he went up to it but
found nothing on it except
leaves. Then he said to it,
"May you never bear fruit
again!" Immediately the
tree withered.
20When the disciples saw
this, they were amazed.
"How did the fig tree wither so quickly?" they asked.
21Jesus replied, "I tell
you the truth, if you have
faith and do not doubt, not
only can you do what was
done to the fig tree, but also
you can say to this mountain, 'Go, throw yourself
into the sea,' and it will be
done. 22If you believe, you
will receive whatever you
ask for in prayer."

The Authority of Jesus Questioned

23Jesus entered the temple courts, and, while he
was teaching, the chief
priests and the elders of the
people came to him. "By
what authority are you doing these things?" they
asked. "And who gave you
this authority?"

j16 Psalm 8:2

24And Jesus answered
and said to them, "I will
ask you one thing too,
which if you tell Me, I will
also tell you by what au-
thority I do these things.

25"The baptism of John
was from what *source,*
from heaven or from
men?" And they *began*
reasoning among them-
selves, saying, "If we say,
'From heaven,' He will say
to us, 'Then why did you
not believe him?'

26"But if we say, 'From
men,' we fear the multi-
tude; for they all hold John
to be a prophet."

27And answering Jesus,
they said, "We do not
know." He also said to
them, "Neither will I tell
you by what authority I do
these things.

Parable of Two Sons

28"But what do you
think? A man had two sons,
and he came to the first and
said, 'Son, go work today
in the vineyard.'

29"And he answered and
said, 'I will, sir'; and he did
not go.

30"And he came to the
second and said the same
thing. But he answered and
said, 'I will not'; *yet* he afterward regretted *it* and
went.

31"Which of the two did
the will of his father?"
They *said, "The latter."
Jesus *said to them, "Truly
I say to you that the tax-
gatherers and harlots will
get into the kingdom of God
before you.

32"For John came to you
in the way of righteousness
and you did not believe
him; but the tax-gatherers
and harlots did believe him;
and you, seeing this, did
not even feel remorse afterward so as to believe him.

Parable of the Landowner

33"Listen to another par-
able. There was a landown-

24 ἀποκριθεὶς δὲ ὁ Ἰησοῦς εἶπεν αὐτοῖς·
And answering – Jesus said to them:
ἐρωτήσω ὑμᾶς κἀγὼ λόγον ἕνα, ὃν
will question you I also word one, which
ἐὰν εἴπητέ μοι, κἀγὼ ὑμῖν ἐρῶ ἐν ποίᾳ
if ye tell me, I also you will tell by what
ἐξουσίᾳ ταῦτα ποιῶ· **25** τὸ βάπτισμα
authority these things I do: The baptism
τὸ Ἰωάννου πόθεν ἦν; ἐξ οὐρανοῦ ἢ
– of John whence was it? from heaven or
ἐξ ἀνθρώπων; οἱ δὲ διελογίζοντο ἐν
from men? And they reasoned among
ἑαυτοῖς λέγοντες· ἐὰν εἴπωμεν· ἐξ οὐρανοῦ,
themselves saying: If we say: From heaven,
ἐρεῖ ἡμῖν· διὰ τί οὖν οὐκ ἐπιστεύσατε
he will say to us: Why then believed ye not
αὐτῷ; **26** ἐὰν δὲ εἴπωμεν· ἐξ ἀνθρώπων,
him? But if we say: From men,
φοβούμεθα τὸν ὄχλον· πάντες γὰρ ὡς
we fear the crowd: for all as
προφήτην ἔχουσιν τὸν Ἰωάννην. **27** καὶ
a prophet have – John. And
ἀποκριθέντες τῷ Ἰησοῦ εἶπαν· οὐκ
answering – Jesus they said: We do
οἴδαμεν. ἔφη αὐτοῖς καὶ αὐτός· οὐδὲ
not know. said to them also He: Neither
ἐγὼ λέγω ὑμῖν ἐν ποίᾳ ἐξουσίᾳ ταῦτα
I tell you by what authority these things
ποιῶ. **28** Τί δὲ ὑμῖν δοκεῖ; ἄνθρωπος
I do. But what to you seems it? A man
εἶχεν τέκνα δύο· προσελθὼν τῷ πρώτῳ
had children two; approaching *to* the first
εἶπεν· τέκνον, ὕπαγε σήμερον ἐργάζου ἐν
he said: Child, go to-day work in
τῷ ἀμπελῶνι. **29** ὁ δὲ ἀποκριθεὶς εἶπεν·
the vineyard. But he answering said:
ἐγώ κύριε, καὶ οὐκ ἀπῆλθεν. **30** προσ-
I [go], lord, and went not. And
ελθὼν δὲ τῷ δευτέρῳ εἶπεν ὡσαύτως.
approaching *to* the second he said similarly.
ὁ δὲ ἀποκριθεὶς εἶπεν· οὐ θέλω, ὕστερον
And he answering said: I will not, later
μεταμεληθεὶς ἀπῆλθεν. **31** τίς ἐκ τῶν δύο
repenting he went. Which of the two
ἐποίησεν τὸ θέλημα τοῦ πατρός; λέγουσιν·
did the will of the father? They say:
ὁ ὕστερος. λέγει αὐτοῖς ὁ Ἰησοῦς· ἀμὴν
The latter. Says to them – Jesus: Truly
λέγω ὑμῖν ὅτι οἱ τελῶναι καὶ αἱ πόρναι
I tell you[,] – The tax-collectors and the harlots
προάγουσιν ὑμᾶς εἰς τὴν βασιλείαν τοῦ
are going before you into the kingdom –
θεοῦ. **32** ἦλθεν γὰρ Ἰωάννης πρὸς ὑμᾶς
of God. For came John to you
ἐν ὁδῷ δικαιοσύνης, καὶ οὐκ ἐπιστεύσατε
in a way of righteousness, and ye believed not
αὐτῷ· οἱ δὲ τελῶναι καὶ αἱ πόρναι
him; but the tax-collectors and the harlots
ἐπίστευσαν αὐτῷ· ὑμεῖς δὲ ἰδόντες οὐδὲ
believed him; but ye seeing not
μετεμελήθητε ὕστερον τοῦ πιστεῦσαι αὐτῷ.
repented later – to believe[d] him.
=so as to believe
33 Ἄλλην παραβολὴν ἀκούσατε. Ἄνθρωπος
Another parable hear ye. *A man*

*** Some such word as 'sign' must be supplied.**

24Jesus replied, "I will
also ask you one question.
If you answer me, I will tell
you by what authority I am
doing these things.
25John's
baptism—where did it
come from? Was it from
heaven, or from men?"
They discussed it among
themselves and said, "If
we say, 'From heaven,' he
will ask, 'Then why didn't
you believe him?'
26But if
we say, 'From men'—we
are afraid of the people, for
they all hold that John was
a prophet."

27So they answered
Jesus, "We don't know."
Then he said, "Neither
will I tell you by what authority I am doing these
things.

The Parable of the Two Sons

28"What do you think?
There was a man who had
two sons. He went to the
first and said, 'Son, go and
work today in the vine-
yard.'

29"'I will not,' he an-
swered, but later he
changed his mind and
went.

30"Then the father went
to the other son and said
the same thing. He an-
swered, 'I will, sir,' but he
did not go.

31"Which of the two did
what his father wanted?"
"The first," they an-
swered.
Jesus said to them, "I tell
you the truth, the tax collectors and the prostitutes
are entering the kingdom of
God ahead of you.
32For
John came to you to show
you the way of righteous-
ness, and you did not be-
lieve him, but the tax collectors and the prostitutes
did. And even after you
saw this, you did not repent
and believe him.

The Parable of the Tenants

33"Listen to another par-
able: There was a landown-

er who PLANTED A VINEYARD
AND PUT A WALL AROUND IT
AND DUG A WINE PRESS IN
IT, AND BUILT A TOWER, and
rented it out to vine-growers, and went on a journey.
34 "And when the harvest
time approached, he sent
his slaves to the vine-growers to receive his produce.
35 "And the vine-growers
took his slaves and beat
one, and killed another,
and stoned a third.
36 "Again he sent another
group of slaves larger than
the first; and they did the
same thing to them.
37 "But afterward he sent
his son to them, saying,
'They will respect my son.'
38 "But when the vine-
growers saw the son, they
said among themselves,
'This is the heir; come, let
us kill him, and seize his
inheritance.'
39 "And they took him,
and threw him out of the
vineyard, and killed him.
40 "Therefore when the
owner of the vineyard
comes, what will he do to
those vine-growers?"
41 They *said to Him, "He
will bring those wretches to
a wretched end, and will
rent out the vineyard to
other vine-growers, who
will pay him the proceeds
at the *proper* seasons."
42 Jesus *said to them,
"Did you never read in the
Scriptures,

'THE STONE WHICH THE BUILDERS REJECTED,
THIS BECAME THE CHIEF CORNER *stone;*
THIS CAME ABOUT FROM THE LORD,
AND IT IS MARVELOUS IN OUR EYES'?

43 "Therefore I say to
you, the kingdom of God
will be taken away from
you, and be given to a na-

ἦν οἰκοδεσπότης ὅστις ἐφύτευσεν ἀμπελῶνα,
there was a housemaster who planted a vineyard,
καὶ φραγμὸν αὐτῷ περιέθηκεν καὶ ὤρυξεν
and ²a hedge ³it ¹put round and dug
ἐν αὐτῷ ληνὸν καὶ ᾠκοδόμησεν πύργον,
in it a winepress and built a tower,
καὶ ἐξέδοτο αὐτὸν γεωργοῖς, καὶ ἀπεδή-
and let it to husbandmen, and departed.
μησεν. **34** ὅτε δὲ ἤγγισεν ὁ καιρὸς τῶν
And when drew near the time of the
καρπῶν, ἀπέστειλεν τοὺς δούλους αὐτοῦ
fruits, he sent the slaves of him
πρὸς τοὺς γεωργοὺς λαβεῖν τοὺς καρποὺς
to the husbandmen to receive the fruits
αὐτοῦ. **35** καὶ λαβόντες οἱ γεωργοὶ
of it. And ³taking ¹the ²husbandmen
τοὺς δούλους αὐτοῦ ὃν μὲν ἔδειραν, ὃν
the slaves of him this one they flogged, that
δὲ ἀπέκτειναν, ὃν δὲ ἐλιθοβόλησαν. **36** πάλιν
one they killed, another they stoned. Again
ἀπέστειλεν ἄλλους δούλους πλείονας τῶν
he sent other slaves more [than] the
πρώτων, καὶ ἐποίησαν αὐτοῖς ὡσαύτως.
first [ones], and they did to them similarly.
37 ὕστερον δὲ ἀπέστειλεν πρὸς αὐτοὺς
But later he sent to them
τὸν υἱὸν αὐτοῦ λέγων· ἐντραπήσονται
the son of him saying: They will reverence
τὸν υἱόν μου. **38** οἱ δὲ γεωργοὶ ἰδόντες
the son of me. But the husbandmen seeing
τὸν υἱὸν εἶπον ἐν ἑαυτοῖς· οὗτός ἐστιν
the son said among themselves: This is
ὁ κληρονόμος· δεῦτε ἀποκτείνωμεν αὐτὸν
the heir; come[,] let us kill him
καὶ σχῶμεν τὴν κληρονομίαν αὐτοῦ·
and let us possess the inheritance of him;
39 καὶ λαβόντες αὐτὸν ἐξέβαλον ἔξω τοῦ
and taking ²him ¹they cast *out* outside the
ἀμπελῶνος καὶ ἀπέκτειναν. **40** ὅταν οὖν
vineyard and killed. When therefore
ἔλθῃ ὁ κύριος τοῦ ἀμπελῶνος, τί ποιήσει
comes the lord of the vineyard, what will he do
τοῖς γεωργοῖς ἐκείνοις; **41** λέγουσιν αὐτῷ·
– husbandmen to those? They say to him:
κακοὺς κακῶς ἀπολέσει αὐτούς, καὶ τὸν
Bad men badly he will destroy them, and the
ἀμπελῶνα ἐκδώσεται ἄλλοις γεωργοῖς,
vineyard he will give out to other husbandmen,
οἵτινες ἀποδώσουσιν αὐτῷ τοὺς καοποὺς
who will render to him the fruits
ἐν τοῖς καιροῖς αὐτῶν. **42** λέγει αὐτοῖς ὁ
in the seasons of them. Says to them –
Ἰησοῦς· οὐδέποτε ἀνέγνωτε ἐν ταῖς
Jesus: Did ye never read in the
γραφαῖς· λίθον ὃν ἀπεδοκίμασαν οἱ
scriptures: A stone which rejected the
οἰκοδομοῦντες, οὗτος ἐγενήθη εἰς κεφαλὴν
building [ones], this became – head
γωνίας· παρὰ κυρίου ἐγένετο αὕτη, καὶ
of [the] corner; from [the] Lord became this, and
ἔστιν θαυμαστὴ ἐν ὀφθαλμοῖς ἡμῶν; **43** διὰ
it is marvellous in [the] eyes of us? There-
τοῦτο λέγω ὑμῖν ὅτι ἀρθήσεται ἀφ' ὑμῶν
fore I tell you[,] – will be taken from you
ἡ βασιλεία τοῦ θεοῦ καὶ δοθήσεται
The kingdom – of God and will be given

er who planted a vineyard.
He put a wall around it, dug
a winepress in it and built a
watchtower. Then he rent-
ed the vineyard to some
farmers and went away on
a journey. 34 When the harvest time approached, he
sent his servants to the tenants to collect his fruit.
35 "The tenants seized his
servants; they beat one,
killed another, and stoned a
third. 36 Then he sent other
servants to them, more
than the first time, and the
tenants treated them the
same way. 37 Last of all, he
sent his son to them. 'They
will respect my son,' he
said.
38 "But when the tenants
saw the son, they said to
each other, 'This is the
heir. Come, let's kill him
and take his inheritance.'
39 So they took him and
threw him out of the vineyard and killed him.
40 "Therefore, when the
owner of the vineyard
comes, what will he do to
those tenants?"
41 "He will bring those
wretches to a wretched
end," they replied, "and
he will rent the vineyard to
other tenants, who will give
him his share of the crop at
harvest time."
42 Jesus said to them,
"Have you never read in
the Scriptures:

" 'The stone the builders rejected
has become the capstone[k];
the Lord has done this,
and it is marvelous in our eyes'[l]?

43 "Therefore I tell you
that the kingdom of God
will be taken away from
you and given to a people

[k]42 Or *cornerstone*
[l]42 Psalm 118:22,23

tion producing the fruit of it.

44"And he who falls on this stone will be broken to pieces; but on whomever it falls, it will scatter him like dust."

45And when the chief priests and the Pharisees heard His parables, they understood that He was speaking about them.

46And when they sought to seize Him, they feared the multitudes, because they held Him to be a prophet.

ἔθνει ποιοῦντι τοὺς καρποὺς αὐτῆς.
to a nation producing the fruits of it.
44 [καὶ ὁ πεσὼν ἐπὶ τὸν λίθον τοῦτον
And the [one] falling on – stone this
συνθλασθήσεται· ἐφ' ὃν δ' ἂν πέσῃ,
will be broken in pieces; but on whomever it falls,
λικμήσει αὐτόν.] 45 Καὶ ἀκούσαντες οἱ
it will crush to powder him. And hearing the
ἀρχιερεῖς καὶ οἱ Φαρισαῖοι τὰς παραβολὰς
chief priests and the Pharisees the parables
αὐτοῦ ἔγνωσαν ὅτι περὶ αὐτῶν λέγει·
of him they knew that concerning them he tells;
46 καὶ ζητοῦντες αὐτὸν κρατῆσαι ἐφοβήθησαν
and seeking him to seize they feared
τοὺς ὄχλους, ἐπεὶ εἰς προφήτην αὐτὸν εἶχον.
the crowds, since for a prophet him they had.

who will produce its fruit.
44He who falls on this stone
will be broken to pieces,
but he on whom it falls will
be crushed."[m]
45When the chief priests
and the Pharisees heard
Jesus' parables, they knew
he was talking about them.
46They looked for a way to
arrest him, but they were
afraid of the crowd because
the people held that he was
a prophet.

Chapter 22

Parable of the Marriage Feast

AND Jesus answered and spoke to them again in parables, saying,

2"The kingdom of heaven may be compared to a king, who gave a wedding feast for his son.

3"And he sent out his slaves to call those who had been invited to the wedding feast, and they were unwilling to come.

4"Again he sent out other slaves saying, 'Tell those who have been invited, "Behold, I have prepared my dinner; my oxen and my fattened livestock are *all* butchered and everything is ready; come to the wedding feast." '

5"But they paid no attention and went their way, one to his own farm, another to his business,

6and the rest seized his slaves and mistreated them and killed them.

7"But the king was enraged and sent his armies, and destroyed those murderers, and set their city on fire.

8"Then he *said to his slaves, 'The wedding is ready, but those who were invited were not worthy.

9'Go therefore to the main highways, and as many as you find *there,* invite to the wedding feast.'

22 Καὶ ἀποκριθεὶς ὁ Ἰησοῦς πάλιν
And answering – Jesus again
εἶπεν ἐν παραβολαῖς αὐτοῖς λέγων·
spoke in parables to them saying:
2 ὡμοιώθη ἡ βασιλεία τῶν οὐρανῶν
Was(is) likened the kingdom of the heavens
ἀνθρώπῳ βασιλεῖ, ὅστις ἐποίησεν γάμους
to *a man* a king, who made a wedding feast
τῷ υἱῷ αὐτοῦ. 3 καὶ ἀπέστειλεν τοὺς
for the son of him. And he sent the
δούλους αὐτοῦ καλέσαι τοὺς κεκλημένους
slaves of him to call the [ones] *having been* invited
εἰς τοὺς γάμους, καὶ οὐκ ἤθελον ἐλθεῖν.
to the feast, and they wished not to come.
4 πάλιν ἀπέστειλεν ἄλλους δούλους λέγων·
Again he sent other slaves saying:
εἴπατε τοῖς κεκλημένοις· ἰδοὺ τὸ
Tell the [ones] *having been* invited: Behold[,] the
ἄριστόν μου ἡτοίμακα, οἱ ταῦροί μου
supper of me I have prepared, the oxen of me
καὶ τὰ σιτιστὰ τεθυμένα, καὶ πάντα
and the fatted beasts having been killed, and all things
ἕτοιμα· δεῦτε εἰς τοὺς γάμους. 5 οἱ δὲ
[are] ready; come to the feast. But they
ἀμελήσαντες ἀπῆλθον, ὃς μὲν εἰς τὸν
not caring went off, one to the(his)
ἴδιον ἀγρόν, ὃς δὲ ἐπὶ τὴν ἐμπορίαν
own field, another on the trading
αὐτοῦ· 6 οἱ δὲ λοιποὶ κρατήσαντες
of him; and the rest seizing
τοὺς δούλους αὐτοῦ ὕβρισαν καὶ ἀπέκτειναν.
the slaves of him insulted and killed.
7 ὁ δὲ βασιλεὺς ὠργίσθη, καὶ πέμψας
So the king became angry, and sending
τὰ στρατεύματα αὐτοῦ ἀπώλεσεν τοὺς
the armies of him destroyed –
φονεῖς ἐκείνους καὶ τὴν πόλιν αὐτῶν
murderers those and the city of them
ἐνέπρησεν. 8 τότε λέγει τοῖς δούλοις
burned. Then he says to the slaves
αὐτοῦ· ὁ μὲν γάμος ἕτοιμός ἐστιν, οἱ δὲ
of him: Indeed the feast ready is, but the [ones]
κεκλημένοι οὐκ ἦσαν ἄξιοι· 9 πορεύεσθε
having been invited were not worthy; go ye
οὖν ἐπὶ τὰς διεξόδους τῶν ὁδῶν, καὶ
therefore onto the partings of the ways, and
ὅσους ἐὰν εὕρητε καλέσατε εἰς τοὺς
as many as ye find call to the

Chapter 22

The Parable of the Wedding Banquet

JESUS spoke to them
again in parables, say-
ing: 2"The kingdom of
heaven is like a king who
prepared a wedding ban-
quet for his son. 3He sent
his servants to those who
had been invited to the banquet to tell them to come,
but they refused to come.
4"Then he sent some
more servants and said,
'Tell those who have been
invited that I have prepared
my dinner: My oxen and
fattened cattle have been
butchered, and everything
is ready. Come to the wedding banquet.'
5"But they paid no atten-
tion and went off—one to
his field, another to his
business. 6The rest seized
his servants, mistreated
them and killed them. 7The
king was enraged. He sent
his army and destroyed
those murderers and
burned their city.
8"Then he said to his servants, 'The wedding ban-
quet is ready, but those I
invited did not deserve to
come. 9Go to the street corners and invite to the banquet anyone you find.' 10So

[m]*44* Some manuscripts do not have verse 44.

10 "And those slaves went
out into the streets, and
gathered together all they
found, both evil and good;
and the wedding hall was
filled with dinner guests.
11 "But when the king
came in to look over the
dinner guests, he saw there
a man not dressed in wed-
ding clothes,
12 and he *said to him,
'Friend, how did you come
in here without wedding
clothes?' And he was
speechless.
13 "Then the king said to
the servants, 'Bind him
hand and foot, and cast him
into the outer darkness; in
that place there shall be
weeping and gnashing of
teeth.'
14 "For many are called,
but few *are* chosen."

Tribute to Caesar

15 Then the Pharisees
went and counseled to-
gether how they might trap
Him in what He said.
16 And they *sent their
disciples to Him, along
with the Herodians, saying,
"Teacher, we know that
You are truthful and teach
the way of God in truth,
and defer to no one; for
You are not partial to any.
17 "Tell us therefore, what
do You think? Is it lawful to
give a poll-tax to Caesar, or
not?"
18 But Jesus perceived
their malice, and said,
"Why are you testing Me,
you hypocrites?
19 "Show Me the coin
used for the poll-tax." And
they brought Him a denarius.
20 And He *said to them,
"Whose likeness and in-
scription is this?"
21 They *said to Him,
"Caesar's." Then He *said

γάμους. 10 καὶ ἐξελθόντες οἱ δοῦλοι
feast. And going forth – slaves
ἐκεῖνοι εἰς τὰς ὁδοὺς συνήγαγον πάντας
those into the ways assembled all
οὓς εὗρον, πονηρούς τε καὶ ἀγαθούς·
whom they found, both bad and good;
καὶ ἐπλήσθη ὁ νυμφὼν ἀνακειμένων.
and was filled the wedding chamber of(with) reclining [ones].
11 εἰσελθὼν δὲ ὁ βασιλεὺς θεάσασθαι
But entering the king to behold
τοὺς ἀνακειμένους εἶδεν ἐκεῖ
the reclining [ones] he saw there
ἄνθρωπον οὐκ ἐνδεδυμένον ἔνδυμα γάμου·
a man not *having been* dressed[in] a dress of wedding;
12 καὶ λέγει αὐτῷ· ἑταῖρε, πῶς
and he says to him: Comrade, how
εἰσῆλθες ὧδε μὴ ἔχων ἔνδυμα γάμου;
enteredst thou here not having a dress of wedding?
ὁ δὲ ἐφιμώθη. 13 τότε ὁ βασιλεὺς
And he was silenced. Then the king
εἶπεν τοῖς διακόνοις· δήσαντες αὐτοῦ
said to the servants: Binding of him
πόδας καὶ χεῖρας ἐκβάλετε αὐτὸν
feet and hands throw out him
εἰς τὸ σκότος τὸ ἐξώτερον· ἐκεῖ ἔσται
into the darkness – outer; there will be
ὁ κλαυθμὸς καὶ ὁ βρυγμὸς τῶν
the wailing and the gnashing of the
ὀδόντων. 14 Πολλοὶ γάρ εἰσιν κλητοί,
teeth. For many are called,
ὀλίγοι δὲ ἐκλεκτοί.
but few chosen.
15 Τότε πορευθέντες οἱ Φαρισαῖοι συμ-
Then going the Pharisees coun-
βούλιον ἔλαβον ὅπως αὐτὸν παγιδεύσωσιν
sel took so as him they might ensnare
ἐν λόγῳ. 16 καὶ ἀποστέλλουσιν αὐτῷ
in a word. And they send to him
τοὺς μαθητὰς αὐτῶν μετὰ τῶν Ἡρω-
the disciples of them with the Hero-
διανῶν λέγοντας· διδάσκαλε, οἴδαμεν
dians saying: Teacher, we know
ὅτι ἀληθὴς εἶ καὶ τὴν ὁδὸν τοῦ
that truthful thou art and the way –
θεοῦ ἐν ἀληθείᾳ διδάσκεις, καὶ οὐ
of God in truth thou teachest, and not
μέλει σοι περὶ οὐδενός, οὐ γὰρ
it concerns *to* thee about no one(anyone), [2]not [1]for
βλέπεις εἰς πρόσωπον ἀνθρώπων·
[3]thou lookest to face of men;
17 εἰπὸν οὖν ἡμῖν, τί σοι δοκεῖ;
tell therefore us, what to thee seems it?
ἔξεστιν δοῦναι κῆνσον Καίσαρι ἢ οὔ;
is it lawful to give tribute to Cæsar or no?
18 γνοὺς δὲ ὁ Ἰησοῦς τὴν πονηρίαν
But knowing – Jesus the wickedness
αὐτῶν εἶπεν· τί με πειράζετε, ὑποκριταί;
of them said: Why me tempt ye, hypocrites?
19 ἐπιδείξατέ μοι τὸ νόμισμα τοῦ κήνσου.
Show me the money of the tribute.
οἱ δὲ προσήνεγκαν αὐτῷ δηνάριον. 20 καὶ
And they brought to him a denarius. And
λέγει αὐτοῖς· τίνος ἡ εἰκὼν αὕτη
he says to them: Of whom – image this
καὶ ἡ ἐπιγραφή; 21 λέγουσιν· Καίσαρος.
and – superscription? They say: Of Cæsar.

the servants went out into
the streets and gathered all
the people they could find,
both good and bad, and the
wedding hall was filled with
guests.
11 "But when the king
came in to see the guests,
he noticed a man there who
was not wearing wedding
clothes. 12 'Friend,' he
asked, 'how did you get in
here without wedding
clothes?' The man was
speechless.
13 "Then the king told the
attendants, 'Tie him hand
and foot, and throw him
outside, into the darkness,
where there will be weep-
ing and gnashing of teeth.'
14 "For many are invited,
but few are chosen."

Paying Taxes to Caesar

15 Then the Pharisees
went out and laid plans to
trap him in his words.
16 They sent their disciples
to him along with the Herodians. "Teacher," they
said, "we know you are a
man of integrity and that
you teach the way of God in
accordance with the truth.
You aren't swayed by men,
because you pay no atten-
tion to who they are. 17 Tell
us then, what is your opinion? Is it right to pay taxes
to Caesar or not?"
18 But Jesus, knowing
their evil intent, said, "You
hypocrites, why are you
trying to trap me? 19 Show
me the coin used for paying
the tax." They brought him
a denarius, 20 and he asked
them, "Whose portrait is
this? And whose inscrip-
tion?"
21 "Caesar's," they re-
plied.
Then he said to them,

to them, "Then render to
Caesar the things that are
Caesar's; and to God the
things that are God's."
22And hearing *this,* they
marveled, and leaving
Him, they went away.

Jesus Answers the Sadducees

23On that day *some* Sad-
ducees (who say there is no
resurrection) came to Him
and questioned Him,
24saying, "Teacher,
Moses said, 'IF A MAN DIES,
HAVING NO CHILDREN, HIS
BROTHER AS NEXT OF KIN
SHALL MARRY HIS WIFE, AND
RAISE UP AN OFFSPRING TO HIS
BROTHER.'
25"Now there were seven
brothers with us; and the
first married and died, and
having no offspring left his
wife to his brother;
26so also the second, and
the third, down to the seventh.
27"And last of all, the
woman died.
28"In the resurrection
therefore whose wife of the
seven shall she be? For
they all had her."
29But Jesus answered and
said to them, "You are mistaken, not understanding
the Scriptures, or the
power of God.
30"For in the resurrection
they neither marry, nor are
given in marriage, but are
like angels in heaven.
31"But regarding the
resurrection of the dead,
have you not read that
which was spoken to you
by God, saying,
32'I AM THE GOD OF ABRA-
HAM, AND THE GOD OF
ISAAC, AND THE GOD OF
JACOB'? He is not the God
of the dead but of the living."
33And when the multi-
tudes heard *this,* they were
astonished at His teaching.
34But when the Pharisees
heard that He had put the

τότε λέγει αὐτοῖς· ἀπόδοτε οὖν τὰ
Then he says to them: Render then the things
Καίσαρος Καίσαρι καὶ τὰ τοῦ θεοῦ
of Cæsar to Cæsar and the things – of God
τῷ θεῷ. **22** καὶ ἀκούσαντες ἐθαύμασαν,
– to God. And hearing they marvelled,
καὶ ἀφέντες αὐτὸν ἀπῆλθαν.
and leaving him went away.
23 Ἐν ἐκείνῃ τῇ ἡμέρᾳ προσῆλθον
On that – day approached
αὐτῷ Σαδδουκαῖοι, λέγοντες μὴ εἶναι
to him Sadducees, saying not to be
ἀνάστασιν, καὶ ἐπηρώτησαν αὐτὸν
a resurrection, and questioned him
24 λέγοντες· διδάσκαλε, Μωϋσῆς εἶπεν·
saying: Teacher, Moses said:
ἐάν τις ἀποθάνῃ μὴ ἔχων τέκνα,
If any man dies not having children,
ἐπιγαμβρεύσει ὁ ἀδελφὸς αὐτοῦ τὴν
shall take to wife after the brother of him the
γυναῖκα αὐτοῦ καὶ ἀναστήσει σπέρμα
wife of him and shall raise up seed
τῷ ἀδελφῷ αὐτοῦ. **25** ἦσαν δὲ παρ'
to the brother of him. Now there were with
ἡμῖν ἑπτὰ ἀδελφοί· καὶ ὁ πρῶτος
us seven brothers; and the first
γήμας ἐτελεύτησεν, καὶ μὴ ἔχων
having married died, and not having
σπέρμα ἀφῆκεν τὴν γυναῖκα αὐτοῦ τῷ
seed left the wife of him to the
ἀδελφῷ αὐτοῦ· **26** ὁμοίως καὶ ὁ δεύτερος
brother of him; likewise also the second
καὶ ὁ τρίτος, ἕως τῶν ἑπτά. **27** ὕστερον
and the third, until the seven. last
δὲ πάντων ἀπέθανεν ἡ γυνή. **28** ἐν τῇ
And of all died the woman. In the
ἀναστάσει οὖν τίνος τῶν ἑπτὰ ἔσται
resurrection then of which of the seven will she be
γυνή; πάντες γὰρ ἔσχον αὐτήν. **29** ἀπο-
wife? for all had her. an-
κριθεὶς δὲ ὁ Ἰησοῦς εἶπεν αὐτοῖς·
swering And – Jesus said to them:
πλανᾶσθε μὴ εἰδότες τὰς γραφὰς μηδὲ
Ye err not knowing the scriptures nor
τὴν δύναμιν τοῦ θεοῦ. **30** ἐν γὰρ τῇ
the power – of God. For in the
ἀναστάσει οὔτε γαμοῦσιν οὔτε γαμίζονται,
resurrection neither they marry nor are given in marriage,
ἀλλ' ὡς ἄγγελοι ἐν τῷ οὐρανῷ εἰσιν.
but as angels in *the* heaven are.
31 περὶ δὲ τῆς ἀναστάσεως τῶν νεκρῶν
But concerning the resurrection of the dead
οὐκ ἀνέγνωτε τὸ ῥηθὲν ὑμῖν ὑπὸ
did ye not read the thing said to you by
τοῦ θεοῦ λέγοντος· **32** ἐγώ εἰμι ὁ θεὸς
– God saying: I am the God
Ἀβραὰμ καὶ ὁ θεὸς Ἰσαὰκ καὶ ὁ θεὸς
of Abraham and the God of Isaac and the God
Ἰακώβ; οὐκ ἔστιν [ὁ] θεὸς νεκρῶν
of Jacob? He is not the God of dead men
ἀλλὰ ζώντων. **33** καὶ ἀκούσαντες οἱ ὄχλοι
but of living [ones]. And hearing the crowds
ἐξεπλήσσοντο ἐπὶ τῇ διδαχῇ αὐτοῦ.
were astounded over(at) the teaching of him.
34 Οἱ δὲ Φαρισαῖοι ἀκούσαντες ὅτι
But the Pharisees hearing that

"Give to Caesar what is
Caesar's, and to God what
is God's."
22When they heard this,
they were amazed. So they
left him and went away.

Marriage at the Resurrection

23That same day the Sad-
ducees, who say there is no
resurrection, came to him
with a question. 24"Teacher," they said, "Moses told
us that if a man dies without
having children, his brother
must marry the widow and
have children for him.
25Now there were seven
brothers among us. The
first one married and died,
and since he had no chil-
dren, he left his wife to his
brother. 26The same thing
happened to the second
and third brother, right on
down to the seventh. 27Fi-
nally, the woman died.
28Now then, at the resur-
rection, whose wife will
she be of the seven, since
all of them were married to
her?"
29Jesus replied, "You are
in error because you do not
know the Scriptures or the
power of God. 30At the resurrection people will neither marry nor be given in
marriage; they will be like
the angels in heaven. 31But
about the resurrection of
the dead—have you not
read what God said to you,
32'I am the God of Abra-
ham, the God of Isaac, and
the God of Jacob'[n]? He is
not the God of the dead but
of the living."
33When the crowds heard
this, they were astonished
at his teaching.

The Greatest Commandment

34Hearing that Jesus had
silenced the Sadducees, the

[n]32 Exodus 3:6

Sadducees to silence, they gathered themselves together.
35And one of them, [q]a lawyer, asked Him *a question,* testing Him,
36"Teacher, which is the great commandment in the Law?"
37And He said to him, " 'YOU SHALL LOVE THE LORD YOUR GOD WITH ALL YOUR HEART, AND WITH ALL YOUR SOUL, AND WITH ALL YOUR MIND.'
38"This is the great and foremost commandment.
39"The second is like it, 'YOU SHALL LOVE YOUR NEIGHBOR AS YOURSELF.'
40"On these two commandments depend the whole Law and the Prophets."
41Now while the Pharisees were gathered together, Jesus asked them a question,
42saying, "What do you think about the Christ, whose son is He?" They *said to Him, "*The son* of David."
43He *said to them, "Then how does David in the Spirit call Him 'Lord,' saying,
44 'THE LORD SAID TO MY LORD,
"SIT AT MY RIGHT HAND,
UNTIL I PUT THINE ENEMIES BENEATH THY FEET" '?
45"If David then calls Him 'Lord,' how is He his son?"
46And no one was able to answer Him a word, nor did anyone dare from that day on to ask Him another question.

ἐφίμωσεν τοὺς Σαδδουκαίους, συνήχθησαν
he silenced the Sadducees, were assembled
ἐπὶ τὸ αὐτό, **35** καὶ ἐπηρώτησεν εἷς
together, and ⁵questioned ¹one
ἐξ αὐτῶν νομικὸς πειράζων αὐτόν· **36** δι-
²of ³them ⁴a lawyer ⁶tempting him: Teach-
δάσκαλε, ποία ἐντολὴ μεγάλη ἐν τῷ
er, what commandment [is] great in the
νόμῳ; **37** ὁ δὲ ἔφη αὐτῷ· ἀγαπήσεις
law? And he said to him: Thou shalt love
κύριον τὸν θεόν σου ἐν ὅλῃ τῇ καρδίᾳ
[the] Lord the God of thee with all the heart
σου καὶ ἐν ὅλῃ τῇ ψυχῇ σου καὶ ἐν
of thee and with all the soul of thee and with
ὅλῃ τῇ διανοίᾳ σου. **38** αὕτη ἐστὶν ἡ
all the understanding of thee. This is the
μεγάλη καὶ πρώτη ἐντολή. **39** δευτέρα
great and first commandment. [The] second
ὁμοία αὐτῇ· ἀγαπήσεις τὸν πλησίον σου
[is] like to it: Thou shalt love the neighbour of thee
ὡς σεαυτόν. **40** ἐν ταύταις ταῖς δυσὶν ἐντολαῖς
as thyself. In(on) these – two commandments
ὅλος ὁ νόμος κρέμαται καὶ οἱ προφῆται.
all the law hangs and the prophets.
41 Συνηγμένων δὲ τῶν Φαρισαίων
And having assembled the Pharisees*
=when the Pharisees were assembled
ἐπηρώτησεν αὐτοὺς ὁ Ἰησοῦς **42** λέγων· τί
questioned them – Jesus saying: What
ὑμῖν δοκεῖ περὶ τοῦ χριστοῦ; τίνος
to you seems it concerning the Christ? of whom
υἱός ἐστιν; λέγουσιν αὐτῷ· τοῦ Δαυίδ.
son is he? They say to him: – Of David.
43 λέγει αὐτοῖς· πῶς οὖν Δαυὶδ ἐν
He says to them: How then David in
πνεύματι καλεῖ αὐτὸν κύριον λέγων·
spirit calls him Lord saying:
44 εἶπεν κύριος τῷ κυρίῳ μου·
Said [the] LORD to the Lord of me:
κάθου ἐκ δεξιῶν μου ἕως ἂν θῶ τοὺς
Sit on [the] right of me until I put the
ἐχθρούς σου ὑποκάτω τῶν ποδῶν σου;
enemies of thee underneath the feet of thee?
45 εἰ οὖν Δαυὶδ καλεῖ αὐτὸν κύριον, πῶς
If then David calls him Lord, how
υἱὸς αὐτοῦ ἐστιν; **46** καὶ οὐδεὶς ἐδύνατο
son of him is he? And no one was able
ἀποκριθῆναι αὐτῷ λόγον οὐδὲ ἐτόλμησέν
to answer him a word nor dared
τις ἀπ' ἐκείνης τῆς ἡμέρας ἐπερωτῆσαι
anyone from that – day *to* question
αὐτὸν οὐκέτι.
him no(any) more.

Pharisees got together.
35One of them, an expert in the law, tested him with this question: 36"Teacher, which is the greatest commandment in the Law?"
37Jesus replied: " 'Love the Lord your God with all your heart and with all your soul and with all your mind.'[o] 38This is the first and greatest commandment. 39And the second is like it: 'Love your neighbor as yourself.'[p] 40All the Law and the Prophets hang on these two commandments."

Whose Son Is the Christ?

41While the Pharisees were gathered together, Jesus asked them, 42"What do you think about the Christ[q]? Whose son is he?"
"The son of David," they replied.
43He said to them, "How is it then that David, speaking by the Spirit, calls him 'Lord'? For he says,

44" 'The Lord said to my Lord:
"Sit at my right hand
until I put your enemies
under your feet." '[r]

45If then David calls him 'Lord,' how can he be his son?" 46No one could say a word in reply, and from that day on no one dared to ask him any more questions.

Chapter 23

Pharisaism Exposed

THEN Jesus spoke to the multitudes and to His disciples,
2saying, "The scribes and the Pharisees have seated themselves in the chair of Moses;
3therefore all that they tell you, do and observe, but do not do according to their deeds; for they say

[q] I.e., an expert in the Mosaic law

23 Τότε ὁ Ἰησοῦς ἐλάλησεν τοῖς ὄχλοις
Then – Jesus spoke to the crowds
καὶ τοῖς μαθηταῖς αὐτοῦ **2** λέγων· ἐπὶ
and to the disciples of him saying: On
τῆς Μωϋσέως καθέδρας ἐκάθισαν οἱ
the of Moses seat sat the
γραμματεῖς καὶ οἱ Φαρισαῖοι. **3** πάντα
scribes and the Pharisees. All things
οὖν ὅσα ἐὰν εἴπωσιν ὑμῖν ποιήσατε
therefore whatever they may tell you do ye
καὶ τηρεῖτε, κατὰ δὲ τὰ ἔργα αὐτῶν
and keep, but according to the works of them

Chapter 23

Seven Woes

THEN Jesus said to the crowds and to his disciples: 2"The teachers of the law and the Pharisees sit in Moses' seat. 3So you must obey them and do everything they tell you. But do not do what they do, for

[o] 37 Deut. 6:5
[p] 39 Lev. 19:18
[q] 42 Or *Messiah*
[r] 44 Psalm 110:1

things, and do not do *them*.
4"And they tie up heavy
loads, and lay them on
men's shoulders; but they
themselves are unwilling to
move them with *so much as*
a finger.
5"But they do all their
deeds to be noticed by men;
for they broaden their
[r]phylacteries, and length-
en the tassels *of their gar-*
ments.
6"And they love the
place of honor at banquets,
and the chief seats in the
synagogues,
7and respectful greetings
in the market places, and
being called by men, Rab-
bi.
8"But do not be called
Rabbi; for One is your
Teacher, and you are all
brothers.
9"And do not call *any-*
one on earth your father;
for One is your Father, He
who is in heaven.
10"And do not be called
leaders; for One is your
Leader, *that is*, Christ.
11"But the greatest
among you shall be your
servant.
12"And whoever exalts
himself shall be humbled;
and whoever humbles him-
self shall be exalted.

Seven Woes

13"But woe to you,
scribes and Pharisees,
hypocrites, because you
shut off the kingdom of
heaven from men; for you
do not enter in yourselves,
nor do you allow those who
are entering to go in.
14["[s]Woe to you, scribes
and Pharisees, hypocrites,
because you devour wid-
ows' houses, even while
for a pretense you make
long prayers; therefore you
shall receive greater condemnation.]
15"Woe to you, scribes
and Pharisees, hypocrites,
because you travel about
on sea and land to make
one proselyte; and when he
becomes one, you make
him twice as much a son of
hell as yourselves.
16"Woe to you, blind

[r]I.e., small boxes containing Scripture texts worn for religious purposes
[s]This verse not found in the earliest mss.

μὴ ποιεῖτε· λέγουσιν γὰρ καὶ οὐ ποιοῦσιν.
do ye not; for they say and do not.
4 δεσμεύουσιν δὲ φορτία βαρέα καὶ
And they bind burdens heavy and
ἐπιτιθέασιν ἐπὶ τοὺς ὤμους τῶν ἀνθρώπων,
put *on* on the shoulders – of men,
αὐτοὶ δὲ τῷ δακτύλῳ αὐτῶν οὐ
but they with the finger of them not
θέλουσιν κινῆσαι αὐτά. **5** πάντα δὲ
are willing to move them. But all
τὰ ἔργα αὐτῶν ποιοῦσιν πρὸς τὸ θεαθῆναι
the works of them they do *for* – to be seen
τοῖς ἀνθρώποις· πλατύνουσιν γὰρ τὰ
– by men; for they broaden the
φυλακτήρια αὐτῶν καὶ μεγαλύνουσιν τὰ
phylacteries of them and enlarge the
κράσπεδα, **6** φιλοῦσιν δὲ τὴν πρωτο-
fringes, and they like the chief
κλισίαν ἐν τοῖς δείπνοις καὶ τὰς πρωτο-
place in the suppers and the chief
καθεδρίας ἐν ταῖς συναγωγαῖς **7** καὶ τοὺς
seats in the synagogues . and the
ἀσπασμοὺς ἐν ταῖς ἀγοραῖς καὶ
greetings in the marketplaces and
καλεῖσθαι ὑπὸ τῶν ἀνθρώπων ῥαββί.
to be called by – men rabbi.
8 ὑμεῖς δὲ μὴ κληθῆτε ῥαββί· εἷς γάρ
But ye be not called rabbi; for one
ἐστιν ὑμῶν ὁ διδάσκαλος, πάντες δὲ ὑμεῖς
is of you the teacher, and all ye
ἀδελφοί ἐστε. **9** καὶ πατέρα μὴ καλέσητε
brothers are. And father call ye not
ὑμῶν ἐπὶ τῆς γῆς· εἷς γάρ ἐστιν
of you on the earth; for one is
ὑμῶν ὁ πατὴρ ὁ οὐράνιος. **10** μηδὲ
of you the Father – heavenly. Neither
κληθῆτε καθηγηταί, ὅτι καθηγητὴς
be ye called leaders, because leader
ὑμῶν ἐστιν εἷς ὁ Χριστός. **11** ὁ δὲ
of you is one the Christ. And the
μείζων ὑμῶν ἔσται ὑμῶν διάκονος.
greater of you shall be of you servant.
12 Ὅστις δὲ ὑψώσει ἑαυτὸν ταπεινωθήσεται,
And [he] who will exalt himself shall be humbled,
καὶ ὅστις ταπεινώσει ἑαυτὸν ὑψωθήσεται.
and [he] who will humble himself shall be exalted.
13 Οὐαὶ δὲ ὑμῖν, γραμματεῖς καὶ Φαρισαῖοι
But woe to you, scribes and Pharisees
ὑποκριταί, ὅτι κλείετε τὴν βασιλείαν
hypocrites, because ye shut the kingdom
τῶν οὐρανῶν ἔμπροσθεν τῶν ἀνθρώπων
of the heavens before – men;
ὑμεῖς γὰρ οὐκ εἰσέρχεσθε, οὐδὲ τοὺς
for ye do not enter, nor the [ones]
εἰσερχομένους ἀφίετε εἰσελθεῖν.‡ **15** Οὐαὶ
entering do ye allow to enter. Woe
ὑμῖν, γραμματεῖς καὶ Φαρισαῖοι ὑποκριταί,
to you, scribes and Pharisees hypocrites,
ὅτι περιάγετε τὴν θάλασσαν καὶ τὴν
because ye go about the sea and the
ξηρὰν ποιῆσαι ἕνα προσήλυτον, καὶ ὅταν
dry [land] to make one proselyte, and when
γένηται, ποιεῖτε αὐτὸν υἱὸν γεέννης διπλό-
he becomes, ye make him a son of gehenna twofold
τερον ὑμῶν. **16** Οὐαὶ ὑμῖν, ὁδηγοὶ τυφλοὶ
more [than] you. Woe to you, leaders blind

they do not practice what
they preach. 4They tie up
heavy loads and put them
on men's shoulders, but
they themselves are not
willing to lift a finger to
move them.
5"Everything they do is
done for men to see: They
make their phylacteries[s]
wide and the tassels on
their garments long; 6they
love the place of honor at
banquets and the most im-
portant seats in the synagogues; 7they love to be
greeted in the marketplaces
and to have men call them
'Rabbi.'
8"But you are not to be
called 'Rabbi,' for you
have only one Master and
you are all brothers. 9And
do not call anyone on earth
'father,' for you have one
Father, and he is in heaven.
10Nor are you to be called
'teacher,' for you have one
Teacher, the Christ.[t]
11The greatest among you
will be your servant. 12For
whoever exalts himself will
be humbled, and whoever
humbles himself will be exalted.
13"Woe to you, teachers
of the law and Pharisees,
you hypocrites! You shut
the kingdom of heaven in
men's faces. You your-
selves do not enter, nor will
you let those enter who are
trying to.[u]
15"Woe to you, teachers
of the law and Pharisees,
you hypocrites! You travel
over land and sea to win a
single convert, and when
he becomes one, you make
him twice as much a son of
hell as you are.
16"Woe to you, blind

[s]5 That is, boxes containing Scripture verses, worn on forehead and arm
[t]10 Or *Messiah*
[u]13 Some manuscripts *to. 14Woe to you, teachers of the law and Pharisees, you hypocrites! You devour widows' houses and for a show make lengthy prayers. Therefore you will be punished more severely.*

guides, who say, 'Whoever swears by the temple, that is nothing; but whoever swears by the gold of the temple, he is obligated.'

17"You fools and blind men; which is more important, the gold, or the temple that sanctified the gold?

18"And, 'Whoever swears by the altar, *that* is nothing, but whoever swears by the offering upon it, he is obligated.'

19"You blind men, which is more important, the offering or the altar that sanctifies the offering?

20"Therefore he who swears, swears *both* by the altar and by everything on it.

21"And he who swears by the temple, swears *both* by the temple and by Him who dwells within it.

22"And he who swears by heaven, swears *both* by the throne of God and by Him who sits upon it.

23"Woe to you, scribes and Pharisees, hypocrites! For you tithe the mint and dill and cummin, and have neglected the weightier provisions of the law: justice and mercy and faithfulness; but these are the things you should have done without neglecting the others.

24"You blind guides, who strain out a gnat and swallow a camel!

25"Woe to you, scribes and Pharisees, hypocrites! For you clean the outside of the cup and of the dish, but inside they are full of robbery and self-indulgence.

26"You blind Pharisee, first clean the inside of the cup and of the dish, so that the outside of it may become clean also.

27"Woe to you, scribes and Pharisees, hypocrites! For you are like white-

οἱ λέγοντες· ὃς ἂν ὀμόσῃ ἐν τῷ ναῷ,
the [ones] saying: Whoever swears by the shrine,
οὐδέν ἐστιν· ὃς δ' ἂν ὀμόσῃ ἐν τῷ χρυσῷ
nothing it is; but whoever swears by the gold
τοῦ ναοῦ, ὀφείλει. 17 μωροὶ καὶ τυφλοί,
of the shrine, he owes. Fools and blind,
τίς γὰρ μείζων ἐστιν, ὁ χρυσὸς ἢ ὁ ναὸς
for which greater is, the gold or the shrine
ὁ ἁγιάσας τὸν χρυσόν; 18 καί· ὃς ἂν
– sanctifying the gold? And: whoever
ὀμόσῃ ἐν τῷ θυσιαστηρίῳ, οὐδέν ἐστιν·
swears by the altar, nothing it is;
ὃς δ' ἂν ὀμόσῃ ἐν τῷ δώρῳ τῷ ἐπάνω
but whoever swears by the gift – upon
αὐτοῦ, ὀφείλει. 19 τυφλοί, τί γὰρ μεῖζον,
it, he owes. Blind, for which [is] greater,
τὸ δῶρον ἢ τὸ θυσιαστήριον τὸ
the gift or the altar –
ἁγιάζον τὸ δῶρον; 20 ὁ οὖν ὀμόσας
sanctifying the gift? Therefore the [one] swearing
ἐν τῷ θυσιαστηρίῳ ὀμνύει ἐν αὐτῷ καὶ
by the altar swears by it and
ἐν πᾶσι τοῖς ἐπάνω αὐτοῦ· 21 καὶ ὁ
by all the things upon it; and the [one]
ὀμόσας ἐν τῷ ναῷ ὀμνύει ἐν αὐτῷ
swearing by the shrine swears by it
καὶ ἐν τῷ κατοικοῦντι αὐτόν· 22 καὶ
and by the [one] inhabiting it; and
ὁ ὀμόσας ἐν τῷ οὐρανῷ ὀμνύει ἐν τῷ
the [one] swearing by *the* heaven swears by the
θρόνῳ τοῦ θεοῦ καὶ ἐν τῷ καθημένῳ
throne – of God and by the [one] sitting
ἐπάνω αὐτοῦ. 23 Οὐαὶ ὑμῖν, γραμματεῖς
upon it. Woe to you, scribes
καὶ Φαρισαῖοι ὑποκριταί, ὅτι ἀποδεκατοῦτε
and Pharisees hypocrites, because ye tithe
τὸ ἡδύοσμον καὶ τὸ ἄνηθον καὶ τὸ
the mint and the dill and the
κύμινον, καὶ ἀφήκατε τὰ βαρύτερα
cummin, and ye [have] left the heavier things
τοῦ νόμου, τὴν κρίσιν καὶ τὸ ἔλεος
of the law, – judgment and – mercy
καὶ τὴν πίστιν· ταῦτα δὲ ἔδει ποιῆσαι
and – faith; but these things it behoved to do
κἀκεῖνα μὴ ἀφεῖναι. 24 ὁδηγοὶ τυφλοί,
and those not to leave. Leaders blind,
οἱ διϋλίζοντες τὸν κώνωπα, τὴν δὲ
the [ones] straining the gnat, but [2]the
κάμηλον καταπίνοντες. 25 Οὐαὶ ὑμῖν,
[3]camel [1]swallowing. Woe to you,
γραμματεῖς καὶ Φαρισαῖοι ὑποκριταί, ὅτι
scribes and Pharisees hypocrites, because
καθαρίζετε τὸ ἔξωθεν τοῦ ποτηρίου καὶ
ye cleanse the outside of the cup and
τῆς παροψίδος, ἔσωθεν δὲ γέμουσιν ἐξ
the dish, but within they are full of
ἁρπαγῆς καὶ ἀκρασίας. 26 Φαρισαῖε τυφλέ,
robbery and intemperance. Pharisee blind,
καθάρισον πρῶτον τὸ ἐντὸς τοῦ ποτηρίου
cleanse thou first the inside of the cup
ἵνα γένηται καὶ τὸ ἐκτὸς αὐτοῦ καθαρόν.
that may be also the outside of it clean.
27 Οὐαὶ ὑμῖν, γραμματεῖς καὶ Φαρισαῖοι
Woe to you, scribes and Pharisees
ὑποκριταί, ὅτι παρομοιάζετε τάφοις κεκονια-
hypocrites, because ye resemble graves *having been*

‡ Ver. 14 omitted by Nestle; *cf.* NIV footnote.

guides! You say, 'If anyone swears by the temple, it means nothing; but if anyone swears by the gold of the temple, he is bound by his oath.' 17You blind fools! Which is greater: the gold, or the temple that makes the gold sacred? 18You also say, 'If anyone swears by the altar, it means nothing; but if anyone swears by the gift on it, he is bound by his oath.' 19You blind men! Which is greater: the gift, or the altar that makes the gift sacred? 20Therefore, he who swears by the altar swears by it and by everything on it. 21And he who swears by the temple swears by it and by the one who dwells in it. 22And he who swears by heaven swears by God's throne and by the one who sits on it.

23"Woe to you, teachers of the law and Pharisees, you hypocrites! You give a tenth of your spices—mint, dill and cummin. But you have neglected the more important matters of the law—justice, mercy and faithfulness. You should have practiced the latter, without neglecting the former. 24You blind guides! You strain out a gnat but swallow a camel.

25"Woe to you, teachers of the law and Pharisees, you hypocrites! You clean the outside of the cup and dish, but inside they are full of greed and self-indulgence. 26Blind Pharisee! First clean the inside of the cup and dish, and then the outside also will be clean.

27"Woe to you, teachers of the law and Pharisees, you hypocrites! You are like whitewashed tombs,

washed tombs which on the
outside appear beautiful,
but inside they are full of
dead men's bones and all
uncleanness.
28“Even so you too out-
wardly appear righteous to
men, but inwardly you are
full of hypocrisy and lawlessness.
29“Woe to you, scribes
and Pharisees, hypocrites!
For you build the tombs of
the prophets and adorn the
monuments of the right-
eous,
30and say, ‘If we had been
living in the days of our fathers, we would not have
been partners with them in
shedding the blood of the
prophets.’
31“Consequently you
bear witness against yourselves, that you are sons of
those who murdered the
prophets.
32“Fill up then the mea-
sure *of the guilt* of your fathers.
33“You serpents, you
brood of vipers, how shall
you escape the sentence of
hell?
34“Therefore, behold, I
am sending you prophets
and wise men and scribes;
some of them you will kill
and crucify, and some of
them you will scourge in
your synagogues, and
persecute from city to city,
35that upon you may fall
the guilt of all the righteous
blood shed on earth, from
the blood of righteous Abel
to the blood of Zechariah,
the son of Berechiah,
whom you murdered be-
tween the temple and the
altar.
36“Truly I say to you, all
these things shall come
upon this generation.

Lament over Jerusalem

37“O Jerusalem, Jerusa-
lem, who kills the prophets
and stones those who are
sent to her! How often I
wanted to gather your chil-

μένοις, οἵτινες ἔξωθεν μὲν φαίνονται
whitewashed, who(which) outwardly indeed appear
ὡραῖοι, ἔσωθεν δὲ γέμουσιν ὀστέων
beautiful, but within they are full of bones
νεκρῶν καὶ πάσης ἀκαθαρσίας. 28 οὕτως
of dead men and of all uncleanness. Thus
καὶ ὑμεῖς ἔξωθεν μὲν φαίνεσθε τοῖς
also ye outwardly indeed appear –
ἀνθρώποις δίκαιοι, ἔσωθεν δέ ἐστε μεστοὶ
to men righteous, but within ye are full
ὑποκρίσεως καὶ ἀνομίας. 29 Οὐαὶ ὑμῖν,
of hypocrisy and of lawlessness. Woe to you
γραμματεῖς καὶ Φαρισαῖοι ὑποκριταί,
scribes and Pharisees hypocrites,
ὅτι οἰκοδομεῖτε τοὺς τάφους τῶν προφητῶν
because ye build the graves of the prophets
καὶ κοσμεῖτε τὰ μνημεῖα τῶν δικαίων,
and adorn the monuments of the righteous,
30 καὶ λέγετε· εἰ ἤμεθα ἐν ταῖς ἡμέραις
and say: If we were in the days
τῶν πατέρων ἡμῶν, οὐκ ἂν ἤμεθα
of the fathers of us, we would not have been
αὐτῶν κοινωνοὶ ἐν τῷ αἵματι τῶν προ-
of them partakers in the blood of the pro-
φητῶν. 31 ὥστε μαρτυρεῖτε ἑαυτοῖς ὅτι
phets. So ye witness to [your]selves that
υἱοί ἐστε τῶν φονευσάντων τοὺς προφήτας.
sons ye are of the [ones] having killed the prophets.
32 καὶ ὑμεῖς πληρώσατε τὸ μέτρον τῶν
And [2]ye [1]fulfil the measure of the
πατέρων ὑμῶν. 33 ὄφεις, γεννήματα ἐχιδνῶν,
fathers of you. Serpents, offspring of vipers,
πῶς φύγητε ἀπὸ τῆς κρίσεως τῆς γεέννης;
how escape ye from the judgment – of gehenna?
34 διὰ τοῦτο ἰδοὺ ἐγὼ ἀποστέλλω πρὸς
Therefore behold I send to
ὑμᾶς προφήτας καὶ σοφοὺς καὶ γραμ-
you prophets and wise men and scribes;
ματεῖς· ἐξ αὐτῶν ἀποκτενεῖτε καὶ
of them ye will kill and
σταυρώσετε, καὶ ἐξ αὐτῶν μαστιγώσετε
will crucify, and of them ye will scourge
ἐν ταῖς συναγωγαῖς ὑμῶν καὶ διώξετε
in the synagogues of you and will persecute
ἀπὸ πόλεως εἰς πόλιν· 35 ὅπως ἔλθῃ
from city to city; so comes
ἐφ' ὑμᾶς πᾶν αἷμα δίκαιον ἐκχυννόμενον
on you all blood righteous being shed
ἐπὶ τῆς γῆς ἀπὸ τοῦ αἵματος Ἅβελ τοῦ
on the earth from the blood of Abel the
δικαίου ἕως τοῦ αἵματος Ζαχαρίου υἱοῦ
righteous until the blood of Zacharias son
Βαραχίου, ὃν ἐφονεύσατε μεταξὺ τοῦ ναοῦ
Barachias, whom ye murdered between the shrine
καὶ τοῦ θυσιαστηρίου. 36 ἀμὴν λέγω
and the altar. Truly I tell
ὑμῖν, ἥξει ταῦτα πάντα ἐπὶ τὴν
you, will come all these things on –
γενεὰν ταύτην. 37 Ἰερουσαλὴμ Ἰερουσαλήμ,
generation this. Jerusalem Jerusalem,
ἡ ἀποκτείνουσα τοὺς προφήτας καὶ
the [one] killing the prophets and
λιθοβολοῦσα τοὺς ἀπεσταλμένους πρὸς αὐτήν,
stoning the [ones] sent to her,
ποσάκις ἠθέλησα ἐπισυναγαγεῖν τὰ τέκνα
how often I wished to gather the children

which look beautiful on the
outside but on the inside
are full of dead men's
bones and everything un-
clean. 28In the same way,
on the outside you appear
to people as righteous but
on the inside you are full of
hypocrisy and wickedness.
29“Woe to you, teachers
of the law and Pharisees,
you hypocrites! You build
tombs for the prophets and
decorate the graves of the
righteous. 30And you say,
‘If we had lived in the days
of our forefathers, we
would not have taken part
with them in shedding the
blood of the prophets.’ 31So
you testify against your-
selves that you are the descendants of those who
murdered the prophets.
32Fill up, then, the measure
of the sin of your forefathers!
33“You snakes! You
brood of vipers! How will
you escape being con-
demned to hell? 34There-
fore I am sending you
prophets and wise men and
teachers. Some of them
you will kill and crucify;
others you will flog in your
synagogues and pursue
from town to town. 35And
so upon you will come all
the righteous blood that has
been shed on earth, from
the blood of righteous Abel
to the blood of Zechariah
son of Berekiah, whom you
murdered between the tem-
ple and the altar. 36I tell you
the truth, all this will come
upon this generation.
37“O Jerusalem, Jerusa-
lem, you who kill the
prophets and stone those
sent to you, how often I
have longed to gather your

dren together, the way a
hen gathers her chicks under her wings, and you
were unwilling.
38"Behold, your house is
being left to you desolate!
39"For I say to you, from
now on you shall not see
Me until you say, 'BLESSED
IS HE WHO COMES IN THE
NAME OF THE LORD!' "

σου, ὃν τρόπον ὄρνις ἐπισυνάγει τὰ
of thee, as a bird gathers the
νοσσία [αὐτῆς] ὑπὸ τὰς πτέρυγας, καὶ
young of her under the(her) wings, and
οὐκ ἠθελήσατε. 38 ἰδοὺ ἀφίεται ὑμῖν ὁ
ye wished not. Behold is left to you the
οἶκος ὑμῶν. 39 λέγω γὰρ ὑμῖν, οὐ μή
house of you. For I tell you, by no means
με ἴδητε ἀπ' ἄρτι ἕως ἂν εἴπητε·
me ye see from now until ye say:
εὐλογημένος ὁ ἐρχόμενος ἐν ὀνόματι
Blessed the [one] coming in [the] name
κυρίου.
of [the] Lord.

children together, as a hen
gathers her chicks under
her wings, but you were not
willing. 38Look, your house
is left to you desolate.
39For I tell you, you will not
see me again until you say,
'Blessed is he who comes
in the name of the Lord.'[v] "

Chapter 24

Signs of Christ's Return

AND Jesus came out
from the temple and
was going away when His
disciples came up to point
out the temple buildings to
Him.
2And He answered and
said to them, "Do you not
see all these things? Truly I
say to you, not one stone
here shall be left upon another, which will not be
torn down."
3And as He was sitting
on the Mount of Olives, the
disciples came to Him privately, saying, "Tell us,
when will these things be,
and what *will be* the sign of
Your coming, and of the
end of the age?"
4And Jesus answered
and said to them, "See to it
that no one misleads you.
5"For many will come in
My name, saying, 'I am the
Christ,' and will mislead
many.
6"And you will be hear-
ing of wars and rumors of
wars; see that you are not
frightened, for *those things*
must take place, but *that* is
not yet the end.
7"For nation will rise
against nation, and king-
dom against kingdom, and
in various places there will
be famines and earth-
quakes.
8"But all these things are
merely the beginning of
birth pangs.
9"Then they will deliver
you to tribulation, and will
kill you, and you will be

24 Καὶ ἐξελθὼν ὁ Ἰησοῦς ἀπὸ τοῦ
And going forth – Jesus from the
ἱεροῦ ἐπορεύετο, καὶ προσῆλθον οἱ μαθηταὶ
temple went, and [4]approached [1]the [2]disciples
αὐτοῦ ἐπιδεῖξαι αὐτῷ τὰς οἰκοδομὰς
[3]of him to show him the buildings
τοῦ ἱεροῦ. 2 ὁ δὲ ἀποκριθεὶς εἶπεν
of the temple. And he answering said
αὐτοῖς· οὐ βλέπετε ταῦτα πάντα; ἀμὴν
to them: See ye not all these things? Truly
λέγω ὑμῖν, οὐ μὴ ἀφεθῇ ὧδε λίθος ἐπὶ
I tell you, by no means will be left here stone on
λίθον ὃς οὐ καταλυθήσεται. 3 Καθημένου
stone which shall not be overthrown. sitting
δὲ αὐτοῦ ἐπὶ τοῦ ὄρους τῶν ἐλαιῶν
and him[a] on the mount of the olives
[a]=And as he sat
προσῆλθον αὐτῷ οἱ μαθηταὶ κατ' ἰδίαν
approached *to* him the disciples privately
λέγοντες· εἰπὲ ἡμῖν, πότε ταῦτα ἔσται,
saying: Tell us, when these things will be,
καὶ τί τὸ σημεῖον τῆς σῆς παρουσίας
and what the sign – of thy presence
καὶ συντελείας τοῦ αἰῶνος; 4 καὶ ἀπο-
and of [the] completion of the age? And answer-
κριθεὶς ὁ Ἰησοῦς εἶπεν αὐτοῖς· βλέπετε
ing – Jesus said to them: See ye
μή τις ὑμᾶς πλανήσῃ. 5 πολλοὶ γὰρ
not(lest) anyone [2]you [1]cause [3]to err. For many
ἐλεύσονται ἐπὶ τῷ ὀνόματί μου λέγοντες·
will come on(in) the name of me saying:
ἐγώ εἰμι ὁ χριστός, καὶ πολλοὺς πλανή-
I am the Christ, and [2]many [1]will cause
σουσιν. 6 μελλήσετε δὲ ἀκούειν πολέ-
[3]to err. But ye will be about to hear [of]
μους καὶ ἀκοὰς πολέμων· ὁρᾶτε μὴ
wars and rumours of wars; see not
θροεῖσθε· δεῖ γὰρ γενέσθαι, ἀλλ'
ye are disturbed; for it behoves to happen, but
οὔπω ἐστὶν τὸ τέλος. 7 ἐγερθήσεται γὰρ
not yet is the end. For will be raised
ἔθνος ἐπὶ ἔθνος καὶ βασιλεία ἐπὶ βασιλείαν,
nation against nation and kingdom against kingdom,
καὶ ἔσονται λιμοὶ καὶ σεισμοὶ
and there will be famines and earthquakes
κατὰ τόπους· 8 πάντα δὲ ταῦτα ἀρχὴ
throughout places; but all these things [are] beginning
ὠδίνων. 9 τότε παραδώσουσιν ὑμᾶς
of birth-pangs. Then they will deliver you
εἰς θλῖψιν καὶ ἀποκτενοῦσιν ὑμᾶς,
to affliction and will kill you,

Chapter 24

Signs of the End of the Age

JESUS left the temple
and was walking away
when his disciples came up
to him to call his attention
to its buildings. 2"Do you
see all these things?" he
asked. "I tell you the truth,
not one stone here will be
left on another; every one
will be thrown down."
3As Jesus was sitting on
the Mount of Olives, the
disciples came to him privately. "Tell us," they
said, "when will this happen, and what will be the
sign of your coming and of
the end of the age?"
4Jesus answered: "Watch
out that no one deceives
you. 5For many will come
in my name, claiming, 'I am
the Christ,[w]' and will deceive many. 6You will hear
of wars and rumors of
wars, but see to it that you
are not alarmed. Such
things must happen, but the
end is still to come. 7Nation
will rise against nation, and
kingdom against kingdom.
There will be famines and
earthquakes in various
places. 8All these are the
beginning of birth pains.
9"Then you will be hand-
ed over to be persecuted
and put to death, and you

[v]39 Psalm 118:26
[w]5 Or *Messiah*; also in verse 23

hated by all nations on account of My name.
10"And at that time many
will fall away and will deliver up one another and
hate one another.
11"And many false
prophets will arise, and will
mislead many.
12"And because lawless-
ness is increased, most
people's love will grow
cold.
13"But the one who en-
dures to the end, he shall be
saved.
14"And this gospel of the
kingdom shall be preached
in the whole world for a
witness to all the nations,
and then the end shall
come.

Perilous Times

15"Therefore when you
see the ABOMINATION OF
DESOLATION which was
spoken of through Daniel
the prophet, standing in the
holy place (let the reader
understand),
16then let those who are in
Judea flee to the moun-
tains;
17let him who is on the
housetop not go down to
get the things out that are in
his house;
18and let him who is in the
field not turn back to get his
cloak.
19"But woe to those who
are with child and to those
who nurse babes in those
days!
20"But pray that your
flight may not be in the winter, or on a Sabbath;
21for then there will be a
great tribulation, such as
has not occurred since the
beginning of the world until
now, nor ever shall.
22"And unless those days
had been cut short, no life
would have been saved; but
for the sake of the elect
those days shall be cut
short.
23"Then if anyone says to
you, 'Behold, here is the

καὶ ἔσεσθε μισούμενοι ὑπὸ πάντων
and ye will be *being* hated by all
τῶν ἐθνῶν διὰ τὸ ὄνομά μου.
the nations because of the name of me.
10 καὶ τότε σκανδαλισθήσονται πολλοὶ καὶ
And then will be offended many and
ἀλλήλους παραδώσουσιν καὶ μισήσουσιν
one another will deliver and they will hate
ἀλλήλους· 11 καὶ πολλοὶ ψευδοπροφῆται
one another; and many false prophets
ἐγερθήσονται καὶ πλανήσουσιν πολλούς·
will be raised and will cause to err many;
12 καὶ διὰ τὸ πληθυνθῆναι τὴν
and because of – to be increased *the*
ἀνομίαν ψυγήσεται ἡ ἀγάπη τῶν
lawlessness will grow cold the love of the
πολλῶν. 13 ὁ δὲ ὑπομείνας εἰς τέλος,
many. But the [one] enduring to [the] end,
οὗτος σωθήσεται. 14 καὶ κηρυχθήσεται
this will be saved. And will be proclaimed
τοῦτο τὸ εὐαγγέλιον τῆς βασιλείας
this – gospel of the kingdom
ἐν ὅλῃ τῇ οἰκουμένῃ εἰς μαρτύριον
in all the inhabited earth for a testimony
πᾶσιν τοῖς ἔθνεσιν, καὶ τότε ἥξει τὸ
to all the nations, and then will come the
τέλος. 15 Ὅταν οὖν ἴδητε τὸ
end. When therefore ye see the
βδέλυγμα τῆς ἐρημώσεως τὸ ῥηθὲν διὰ
abomination – of desolation – spoken through
Δανιὴλ τοῦ προφήτου ἑστὸς ἐν τόπῳ
Daniel the prophet stand in place
ἁγίῳ, ὁ ἀναγινώσκων νοείτω,
holy, the [one] reading let him understand,
16 τότε οἱ ἐν τῇ Ἰουδαίᾳ φευγέτωσαν
then the [ones] in – Judæa let them flee
εἰς τὰ ὄρη, 17 ὁ ἐπὶ τοῦ δώματος μὴ
to the mountains, the [one] on the housetop let him
καταβάτω ἆραι τὰ ἐκ τῆς οἰκίας αὐτοῦ,
not come down to take the things out of the house of him,
18 καὶ ὁ ἐν τῷ ἀγρῷ μὴ ἐπιστρεψάτω
and the [one] in the field let him not turn back
ὀπίσω ἆραι τὸ ἱμάτιον αὐτοῦ. 19 οὐαὶ
behind to take the garment of him. woe
δὲ ταῖς ἐν γαστρὶ ἐχούσαις καὶ ταῖς
And to the women in womb having and to the [ones]
= the pregnant women
θηλαζούσαις ἐν ἐκείναις ταῖς ἡμέραις.
giving suck in those – days.
20 προσεύχεσθε δὲ ἵνα μὴ γένηται ἡ
And pray ye lest happen the
φυγὴ ὑμῶν χειμῶνος μηδὲ σαββάτῳ·
flight of you of(in) winter nor on a sabbath;
21 ἔσται γὰρ τότε θλῖψις μεγάλη, οἵα οὐ
for will be then affliction great, such as not
γέγονεν ἀπ' ἀρχῆς κόσμου ἕως
has happened from [the] beginning of [the] world until
τοῦ νῦν οὐδ' οὐ μὴ γένηται. 22 καὶ
– now neither by no means may happen. And
εἰ μὴ ἐκολοβώθησαν αἱ ἡμέραι ἐκεῖναι,
except were cut short – days those,
οὐκ ἂν ἐσώθη πᾶσα σάρξ· διὰ δὲ τοὺς
not – was saved all flesh; but on account of the
= no flesh would be saved;
ἐκλεκτοὺς κολοβωθήσονται αἱ ἡμέραι ἐκεῖναι.
chosen will be cut short – days those.
23 τότε ἐάν τις ὑμῖν εἴπῃ· ἰδοὺ ὧδε
Then if anyone to you says: Behold here

will be hated by all nations
because of me. 10At that
time many will turn away
from the faith and will betray and hate each other,
11and many false prophets
will appear and deceive
many people. 12Because of
the increase of wickedness,
the love of most will grow
cold, 13but he who stands
firm to the end will be
saved. 14And this gospel of
the kingdom will be
preached in the whole
world as a testimony to all
nations, and then the end
will come.
15"So when you see
standing in the holy place
'the abomination that
causes desolation,'[x] spoken of through the prophet
Daniel—let the reader un-
derstand—16then let those
who are in Judea flee to the
mountains. 17Let no one on
the roof of his house go
down to take anything out
of the house. 18Let no one
in the field go back to get
his cloak. 19How dreadful it
will be in those days for
pregnant women and nurs-
ing mothers! 20Pray that
your flight will not take
place in winter or on the
Sabbath. 21For then there
will be great distress, un-
equaled from the beginning
of the world until now—
and never to be equaled
again. 22If those days had
not been cut short, no one
would survive, but for the
sake of the elect those days
will be shortened. 23At that
time if anyone says to you,
'Look, here is the Christ!'

x *15* Daniel 9:27; 11:31; 12:11

Christ,' or 'There *He is,*'
do not believe *him.*
24"For false Christs and
false prophets will arise
and will show great signs
and wonders, so as to mislead, if possible, even the
elect.
25"Behold, I have told
you in advance.
26"If therefore they say
to you, 'Behold, He is in
the wilderness,' do not go
forth, *or,* 'Behold, He is in
the inner rooms,' do not believe *them.*
27"For just as the light-
ning comes from the east,
and flashes even to the
west, so shall the coming of
the Son of Man be.
28"Wherever the corpse
is, there the vultures will
gather.

The Glorious Return

29"But immediately after
the tribulation of those
days THE SUN WILL BE DARK-
ENED, AND THE MOON WILL
NOT GIVE ITS LIGHT, AND THE
STARS WILL FALL from the
sky, and the powers of the
heavens will be shaken,
30and then the sign of the
Son of Man will appear in
the sky, and then all the
tribes of the earth will
mourn, and they will see
the SON OF MAN COMING ON
THE CLOUDS OF THE SKY with
power and great glory.
31"And He will send forth
His angels with A GREAT
TRUMPET and THEY WILL
GATHER TOGETHER His elect
from the four winds, from
one end of the sky to the
other.

Parable of the Fig Tree

32"Now learn the parable
from the fig tree: when its
branch has already become
tender, and puts forth its
leaves, you know that summer is near;
33even so you too, when

ὁ χριστός, ἤ· ὧδε, μὴ πιστεύσητε·
the Christ, or: Here, do not believe;
24 ἐγερθήσονται γὰρ ψευδόχριστοι καὶ
for will be raised false Christs and
ψευδοπροφῆται, καὶ δώσουσιν σημεῖα μεγάλα
false prophets, and they will give signs great
καὶ τέρατα, ὥστε πλανῆσαι, εἰ δυνατόν,
and marvels, so as to cause to err, if possible,
καὶ τοὺς ἐκλεκτούς. 25 ἰδοὺ προείρηκα
even the chosen. Behold I have before told
ὑμῖν. 26 ἐὰν οὖν εἴπωσιν ὑμῖν· ἰδοὺ
you. If therefore they say to you: Behold
ἐν τῇ ἐρήμῳ ἐστίν, μὴ ἐξέλθητε· ἰδοὺ
in the desert he is, go not ye forth; Behold
ἐν τοῖς ταμιείοις, μὴ πιστεύσητε·
in the private rooms, do not ye believe;
27 ὥσπερ γὰρ ἡ ἀστραπὴ ἐξέρχεται ἀπὸ
for as the lightning comes forth from
ἀνατολῶν καὶ φαίνεται ἕως δυσμῶν,
[the] east and shines unto [the] west,
οὕτως ἔσται ἡ παρουσία τοῦ υἱοῦ
so will be the presence of the Son
τοῦ ἀνθρώπου· 28 ὅπου ἐὰν ᾖ τὸ
– of man; wherever may be the
πτῶμα, ἐκεῖ συναχθήσονται οἱ ἀετοί.
carcase, there will be assembled the eagles.
29 Εὐθέως δὲ μετὰ τὴν θλῖψιν τῶν
And immediately after the affliction –
ἡμερῶν ἐκείνων ὁ ἥλιος σκοτισθήσεται,
days of those the sun will be darkened,
καὶ ἡ σελήνη οὐ δώσει τὸ φέγγος
and the moon will not give the light
αὐτῆς, καὶ οἱ ἀστέρες πεσοῦνται ἀπὸ τοῦ
of her, and the stars will fall from –
οὐρανοῦ, καὶ αἱ δυνάμεις τῶν οὐρανῶν
heaven, and the powers of *the* heavens
σαλευθήσονται. 30 καὶ τότε φανήσεται
will be shaken. And then will appear
τὸ σημεῖον τοῦ υἱοῦ τοῦ ἀνθρώπου ἐν
the sign of the Son – of man in
οὐρανῷ, καὶ τότε κόψονται πᾶσαι αἱ
heaven, and then will bewail all the
φυλαὶ τῆς γῆς καὶ ὄψονται τὸν υἱὸν
tribes of the land and they will see the Son
τοῦ ἀνθρώπου ἐρχόμενον ἐπὶ τῶν
– of man coming on the
νεφελῶν τοῦ οὐρανοῦ μετὰ δυνάμεως καὶ
clouds – of heaven with power and
δόξης πολλῆς· 31 καὶ ἀποστελεῖ τοὺς
glory much; and he will send the
ἀγγέλους αὐτοῦ μετὰ σάλπιγγος μεγάλης,
angels of him with trumpet a great,
καὶ ἐπισυνάξουσιν τοὺς ἐκλεκτοὺς αὐτοῦ
and they will assemble the chosen of him
ἐκ τῶν τεσσάρων ἀνέμων ἀπ᾽ ἄκρων
out of the four winds from [the] extremities
οὐρανῶν ἕως [τῶν] ἄκρων αὐτῶν. 32 Ἀπὸ
of [the] heavens unto the extremities of them. from
δὲ τῆς συκῆς μάθετε τὴν παραβολήν·
Now the fig-tree learn ye the parable:
ὅταν ἤδη ὁ κλάδος αὐτῆς γένηται ἁπαλὸς
When now the branch of it becomes tender
καὶ τὰ φύλλα ἐκφύῃ, γινώσκετε ὅτι
and the leaves it puts forth, ye know that
ἐγγὺς τὸ θέρος· 33 οὕτως καὶ ὑμεῖς
near [is] the summer; so also ye

or, 'There he is!' do not believe it. 24For false Christs
and false prophets will appear and perform great
signs and miracles to de-
ceive even the elect—if
that were possible. 25See, I
have told you ahead of
time.
26"So if anyone tells you,
'There he is, out in the desert,' do not go out; or,
'Here he is, in the inner
rooms,' do not believe it.
27For as lightning that
comes from the east is visible even in the west, so will
be the coming of the Son of
Man. 28Wherever there is a
carcass, there the vultures
will gather.
29"Immediately after the
distress of those days

" 'the sun will be darkened,
and the moon will not give its light;
the stars will fall from the sky,
and the heavenly bodies will be shaken.'[y]

30"At that time the sign of
the Son of Man will appear
in the sky, and all the nations of the earth will
mourn. They will see the
Son of Man coming on the
clouds of the sky, with
power and great glory.
31And he will send his angels with a loud trumpet
call, and they will gather
his elect from the four
winds, from one end of the
heavens to the other.
32"Now learn this lesson
from the fig tree: As soon as
its twigs get tender and its
leaves come out, you know
that summer is near.
33Even so, when you see all

[y]29 Isaiah 13:10; 34:4

you see all these things,
recognize that He is near,
right at the door.
34"Truly I say to you, this
generation will not pass
away until all these things
take place.
35"Heaven and earth will
pass away, but My words
shall not pass away.
36"But of that day and
hour no one knows, not
even the angels of heaven,
nor the Son, but the Father
alone.
37"For the coming of the
Son of Man will be just like
the days of Noah.
38"For as in those days
which were before the
flood they were eating and
drinking, they were marrying and giving in marriage,
until the day that Noah entered the ark,
39and they did not under-
stand until the flood came
and took them all away; so
shall the coming of the Son
of Man be.
40"Then there shall be
two men in the field; one
will be taken, and one will
be left.
41"Two women *will be*
grinding at the mill; one will
be taken, and one will be
left.

Be Ready for His Coming

42"Therefore be on the
alert, for you do not know
which day your Lord is
coming.
43"But be sure of this,
that if the head of the house
had known at what time of
the night the thief was coming, he would have been on
the alert and would not
have allowed his house to
be broken into.
44"For this reason you be
ready too; for the Son of
Man is coming at an hour
when you do not think *He
will.*
45"Who then is the faith-
ful and sensible slave
whom his master put in
charge of his household to

ὅταν ἴδητε πάντα ταῦτα, γινώσκετε ὅτι
when ye see all these things, know that
ἐγγύς ἐστιν ἐπὶ θύραις. **34** ἀμὴν λέγω
near it is on(at) [the] doors. Truly I tell
ὑμῖν ὅτι οὐ μὴ παρέλθῃ ἡ γενεὰ
you that by no means passes away – generation
αὕτη ἕως ἂν πάντα ταῦτα γένηται.
this until all these things happens.
35 ὁ οὐρανὸς καὶ ἡ γῆ παρελεύσεται, οἱ
The heaven and the earth will pass away, ²the
δὲ λόγοι μου οὐ μὴ παρέλθωσιν. **36** Περὶ
¹but words of me by no means may pass away. concerning
δὲ τῆς ἡμέρας ἐκείνης καὶ ὥρας οὐδεὶς
But – day that and hour no one
οἶδεν, οὐδὲ οἱ ἄγγελοι τῶν οὐρανῶν
knows, neither the angels of *the* heavens
οὐδὲ ὁ υἱός, εἰ μὴ ὁ πατὴρ μόνος.
nor the Son, except the Father only.
37 ὥσπερ γὰρ αἱ ἡμέραι τοῦ Νῶε, οὕτως
For as the days – of Noah, so
ἔσται ἡ παρουσία τοῦ υἱοῦ τοῦ ἀνθρώπου.
will be the presence of the Son – of man.
38 ὡς γὰρ ἦσαν ἐν ταῖς ἡμέραις
For as they were in – days
[ἐκείναις] ταῖς πρὸ τοῦ κατακλυσμοῦ
those the [ones] before the flood
τρώγοντες καὶ πίνοντες, γαμοῦντες καὶ
eating and drinking, marrying and
γαμίζοντες, ἄχρι ἧς ἡμέρας εἰσῆλθεν
being given in marriage, until which day entered
Νῶε εἰς τὴν κιβωτόν, **39** καὶ οὐκ ἔγνωσαν
Noah into the ark, and knew not
ἕως ἦλθεν ὁ κατακλυσμὸς καὶ ἦρεν
until came the flood and took
ἅπαντας, οὕτως ἔσται καὶ ἡ παρουσία
all, so will be also the presence
τοῦ υἱοῦ τοῦ ἀνθρώπου **40** τότε ἔσονται
of the Son – of man. Then will be
δύο ἐν τῷ ἀγρῷ, εἷς παραλαμβάνεται
two men in the field, one is taken
καὶ εἷς ἀφίεται· **41** δύο ἀλήθουσαι
and one is left; two women grinding
ἐν τῷ μύλῳ, μία παραλαμβάνεται καὶ
in(at) the mill, one is taken and
μία ἀφίεται. **42** γρηγορεῖτε οὖν, ὅτι
one is left. Watch ye therefore, because
οὐκ οἴδατε ποίᾳ ἡμέρᾳ ὁ κύριος
ye know not on what day the lord
ὑμῶν ἔρχεται. **43** Ἐκεῖνο δὲ γινώσκετε
of you is coming. And that know ye
ὅτι εἰ ᾔδει ὁ οἰκοδεσπότης ποίᾳ
that if knew the housemaster in what
φυλακῇ ὁ κλέπτης ἔρχεται, ἐγρηγόρησεν
watch the thief is coming, he would have
ἂν καὶ οὐκ ἂν εἴασεν διορυχθῆναι
watched and would not have allowed to be dug through
τὴν οἰκίαν αὐτοῦ. **44** διὰ τοῦτο καὶ
the house of him. Therefore also
ὑμεῖς γίνεσθε ἕτοιμοι, ὅτι ᾗ οὐ δοκεῖτε
ye be ready, because ¹in which ³ye think not
ὥρᾳ ὁ υἱὸς τοῦ ἀνθρώπου ἔρχεται. **45** Τίς
²hour the Son – of man comes. Who
ἄρα ἐστὶν ὁ πιστὸς δοῦλος καὶ φρόνιμος
then is the faithful slave and prudent
ὃν κατέστησεν ὁ κύριος ἐπὶ τῆς οἰκετείας
whom appointed the lord over the household

these things, you know that
it[z] is near, right at the
door. 34I tell you the truth,
this generation[a] will certainly not pass away until
all these things have happened. 35Heaven and earth
will pass away, but my
words will never pass
away.

The Day and Hour Unknown

36"No one knows about
that day or hour, not even
the angels in heaven, nor
the Son,[b] but only the Father. 37As it was in the days
of Noah, so it will be at the
coming of the Son of Man.
38For in the days before the
flood, people were eating
and drinking, marrying and
giving in marriage, up to
the day Noah entered the
ark; 39and they knew nothing about what would hap-
pen until the flood came
and took them all away.
That is how it will be at the
coming of the Son of Man.
40Two men will be in the
field; one will be taken and
the other left. 41Two wom-
en will be grinding with a
hand mill; one will be taken
and the other left.
42"Therefore keep
watch, because you do not
know on what day your
Lord will come. 43But un-
derstand this: If the owner
of the house had known at
what time of night the thief
was coming, he would have
kept watch and would not
have let his house be broken into. 44So you also
must be ready, because the
Son of Man will come at an
hour when you do not ex-
pect him.
45"Who then is the faith-
ful and wise servant, whom
the master has put in
charge of the servants in his

[z]33 Or *he*
[a]34 Or *race*
[b]36 Some manuscripts do not have *nor the Son.*

give them their food at the proper time?

46"Blessed is that slave whom his master finds so doing when he comes.

47"Truly I say to you, that he will put him in charge of all his possessions.

48"But if that evil slave says in his heart, 'My master is not coming for a long time,'

49and shall begin to beat his fellow slaves and eat and drink with drunkards;

50the master of that slave will come on a day when he does not expect *him* and at an hour which he does not know,

51and shall cut him in pieces and assign him a place with the hypocrites; weeping shall be there and the gnashing of teeth.

Chapter 25

Parable of Ten Virgins

"THEN the kingdom of heaven will be comparable to ten virgins, who took their lamps, and went out to meet the bridegroom.

2"And five of them were foolish, and five were prudent.

3"For when the foolish took their lamps, they took no oil with them,

4but the prudent took oil in flasks along with their lamps.

5"Now while the bridegroom was delaying, they all got drowsy and *began* to sleep.

6"But at midnight there was a shout, 'Behold, the bridegroom! Come out to meet *him*.'

7"Then all those virgins

αὐτοῦ τοῦ δοῦναι αὐτοῖς τὴν τροφὴν ἐν
of him – to give[d] to them the food in
καιρῷ; 46 μακάριος ὁ δοῦλος ἐκεῖνος ὃν
season? blessed [is] – slave that whom
ἐλθὼν ὁ κύριος αὐτοῦ εὑρήσει οὕτως
coming the lord of him will find so
ποιοῦντα· 47 ἀμὴν λέγω ὑμῖν ὅτι ἐπὶ
doing; truly I tell you that over
πᾶσιν τοῖς ὑπάρχουσιν αὐτοῦ καταστήσει
all the goods of him he will appoint
αὐτόν. 48 ἐὰν δὲ εἴπῃ ὁ κακὸς δοῦλος
him. But if says – wicked slave
ἐκεῖνος ἐν τῇ καρδίᾳ αὐτοῦ· χρονίζει
that in the heart of him: Delays
μου ὁ κύριος, 49 καὶ ἄρξηται τύπτειν
of me the lord, and begins to strike
τοὺς συνδούλους αὐτοῦ, ἐσθίῃ δὲ καὶ
the fellow-slaves of him, and eats and
πίνῃ μετὰ τῶν μεθυόντων, 50 ἥξει ὁ
drinks with the [ones] being drunk, will come the
κύριος τοῦ δούλου ἐκείνου ἐν ἡμέρᾳ ᾗ
lord – slave of that on a day on which
οὐ προσδοκᾷ καὶ ἐν ὥρᾳ ᾗ οὐ
he does not expect and in an hour in which not
γινώσκει, 51 καὶ διχοτομήσει αὐτόν,
he knows, and will cut asunder him,
καὶ τὸ μέρος αὐτοῦ μετὰ τῶν
and the portion of him with the
ὑποκριτῶν θήσει· ἐκεῖ ἔσται ὁ
hypocrites will place; there will be the
κλαυθμὸς καὶ ὁ βρυγμὸς τῶν ὀδόντων.
wailing and the gnashing of the teeth.

25 Τότε ὁμοιωθήσεται ἡ βασιλεία
Then shall be likened the kingdom
τῶν οὐρανῶν δέκα παρθένοις, αἵτινες
of the heavens to ten virgins, who
λαβοῦσαι τὰς λαμπάδας ἑαυτῶν ἐξῆλθον
taking the lamps of them* went forth
εἰς ὑπάντησιν τοῦ νυμφίου. 2 πέντε δὲ
to a meeting of the bridegroom. Now five
ἐξ αὐτῶν ἦσαν μωραὶ καὶ πέντε φρόνιμοι.
of them were foolish and five prudent.
3 αἱ γὰρ μωραὶ λαβοῦσαι τὰς λαμπάδας
For the foolish [ones] taking the lamps
οὐκ ἔλαβον μεθ' ἑαυτῶν ἔλαιον.
did not take with them oil.
4 αἱ δὲ φρόνιμοι ἔλαβον ἔλαιον ἐν
But the prudent [ones] took oil in
τοῖς ἀγγείοις μετὰ τῶν λαμπάδων ἑαυτῶν.
the vessels with the lamps of them.
5 χρονίζοντος δὲ τοῦ νυμφίου ἐνύσταξαν
But delaying the bridegroom[a] slumbered
=while the bridegroom delayed
πᾶσαι καὶ ἐκάθευδον. 6 μέσης δὲ
all and slept. And of(in) [the] middle
νυκτὸς κραυγὴ γέγονεν· ἰδοὺ ὁ
of [the] night a cry there has been: Behold[,] the
νυμφίος, ἐξέρχεσθε εἰς ἀπάντησιν. 7 τότε
bridegroom, go ye forth to a meeting. Then
ἠγέρθησαν πᾶσαι αἱ παρθένοι ἐκεῖναι
were raised all – virgins those

*Here, and in the three following occurrences, as elsewhere, the strict meaning is emphatic or reflexive—'of themselves'; but this cannot be insisted on.

household to give them their food at the proper time? 46It will be good for that servant whose master finds him doing so when he returns. 47I tell you the truth, he will put him in charge of all his possessions. 48But suppose that servant is wicked and says to himself, 'My master is staying away a long time,' 49and he then begins to beat his fellow servants and to eat and drink with drunkards. 50The master of that servant will come on a day when he does not expect him and at an hour he is not aware of. 51He will cut him to pieces and assign him a place with the hypocrites, where there will be weeping and gnashing of teeth.

Chapter 25

The Parable of the Ten Virgins

"AT that time the kingdom of heaven will be like ten virgins who took their lamps and went out to meet the bridegroom. 2Five of them were foolish and five were wise. 3The foolish ones took their lamps but did not take any oil with them. 4The wise, however, took oil in jars along with their lamps. 5The bridegroom was a long time in coming, and they all became drowsy and fell asleep.

6"At midnight the cry rang out: 'Here's the bridegroom! Come out to meet him!'

7"Then all the virgins

rose, and trimmed their
lamps.
8 "And the foolish said to
the prudent, 'Give us some
of your oil, for our lamps
are going out.'
9 "But the prudent an-
swered, saying, 'No, there
will not be enough for us
and you *too;* go instead to
the dealers and buy *some*
for yourselves.'
10 "And while they were
going away to make the
purchase, the bridegroom
came, and those who were
ready went in with him to
the wedding feast; and the
door was shut.
11 "And later the other
virgins also came, saying,
'Lord, lord, open up for
us.'
12 "But he answered and
said, 'Truly I say to you, I
do not know you.'
13 "Be on the alert then,
for you do not know the
day nor the hour.

Parable of the Talents

14 "For *it is* just like a man
about to go on a journey,
who called his own slaves,
and entrusted his posses-
sions to them.
15 "And to one he gave
five talents, to another,
two, and to another, one,
each according to his own
ability; and he went on his
journey.
16 "Immediately the one
who had received the five
talents went and traded
with them, and gained five
more talents.
17 "In the same manner
the one who *had received*
the two *talents* gained two
more.
18 "But he who received
the one *talent* went away
and dug in the ground, and
hid his master's money.
19 "Now after a long time
the master of those slaves
*came and *settled ac-
counts with them.

καὶ ἐκόσμησαν τὰς λαμπάδας ἑαυτῶν.
and trimmed the lamps of them.
8 αἱ δὲ μωραὶ ταῖς φρονίμοις εἶπαν·
So the foolish [ones] to the prudent said:
δότε ἡμῖν ἐκ τοῦ ἐλαίου ὑμῶν, ὅτι
Give us of the oil of you, because
αἱ λαμπάδες ἡμῶν σβέννυνται. 9 ἀπεκρί-
the lamps of us are being quenched. But
θησαν δὲ αἱ φρόνιμοι λέγουσαι· μήποτε
answered the prudent saying: Lest
οὐ μὴ ἀρκέσῃ ἡμῖν καὶ ὑμῖν·
by no means it suffices to us and to you;
πορεύεσθε μᾶλλον πρὸς τοὺς πωλοῦντας
go ye rather to the [ones] selling
καὶ ἀγοράσατε ἑαυταῖς. 10 ἀπερχομένων
and buy for [your]selves. And going =as they
δὲ αὐτῶν ἀγοράσαι ἦλθεν ὁ νυμφίος,
away them[a] to buy came the bridegroom, were going away
καὶ αἱ ἕτοιμοι εἰσῆλθον μετ' αὐτοῦ
and the ready [ones] went in with him
εἰς τοὺς γάμους, καὶ ἐκλείσθη ἡ
to the wedding festivities, and was shut the
θύρα. 11 ὕστερον δὲ ἔρχονται καὶ αἱ
door. Then later come also the
λοιπαὶ παρθένοι λέγουσαι· κύριε κύριε,
remaining virgins saying: Lord[,] Lord,
ἄνοιξον ἡμῖν. 12 ὁ δὲ ἀποκριθεὶς εἶπεν·
open to us. But he answering said:
ἀμὴν λέγω ὑμῖν, οὐκ οἶδα ὑμᾶς.
Truly I say to you, I know not you.
13 Γρηγορεῖτε οὖν, ὅτι οὐκ οἴδατε
Watch ye therefore, because ye know not
τὴν ἡμέραν οὐδὲ τὴν ὥραν. 14 Ὥσπερ
the day nor the hour. as
γὰρ ἄνθρωπος ἀποδημῶν ἐκάλεσεν
For a man going from home called
τοὺς ἰδίους δούλους καὶ παρέδωκεν αὐτοῖς
the(his) own slaves and delivered to them
τὰ ὑπάρχοντα αὐτοῦ, 15 καὶ ᾧ μὲν ἔδωκεν
the goods of him, and to one he gave
πέντε τάλαντα, ᾧ δὲ δύο, ᾧ δὲ
five talents, to another two, to another
ἕν, ἑκάστῳ κατὰ τὴν ἰδίαν δύναμιν,
one, to each according to the(his) own ability,
καὶ ἀπεδήμησεν. 16 εὐθέως πορευθεὶς
and went from home. Immediately going
ὁ τὰ πέντε τάλαντα λαβὼν ἠργάσατο
the [one] the five talents receiving traded
ἐν αὐτοῖς καὶ ἐκέρδησεν ἄλλα
in them and gained other
πέντε· 17 ὡσαύτως ὁ τὰ δύο ἐκέρδησεν
five; similarly the [one] [receiving] the two gained
ἄλλα δύο. 18 ὁ δὲ τὸ ἓν λαβὼν
other two. But the [one] the one receiving
ἀπελθὼν ὤρυξεν γῆν καὶ ἔκρυψεν
going away dug earth and hid
τὸ ἀργύριον τοῦ κυρίου αὐτοῦ.
the silver of the lord of him.
19 μετὰ δὲ πολὺν χρόνον ἔρχεται ὁ
Then after much time comes the
κύριος τῶν δούλων ἐκείνων καὶ συναίρει
lord – slaves of those and takes
λόγον μετ' αὐτῶν. 20 καὶ προσελθὼν
account with them. And approaching

woke up and trimmed their
lamps. 8 The foolish ones
said to the wise, 'Give us
some of your oil; our lamps
are going out.'
9 " 'No,' they replied,
'there may not be enough
for both us and you. In-
stead, go to those who sell
oil and buy some for yourselves.'
10 "But while they were
on their way to buy the oil,
the bridegroom arrived.
The virgins who were
ready went in with him to
the wedding banquet. And
the door was shut.
11 "Later the others also
came. 'Sir! Sir!' they said.
'Open the door for us!'
12 "But he replied, 'I tell
you the truth, I don't know
you.'
13 "Therefore keep
watch, because you do not
know the day or the hour.

The Parable of the Talents

14 "Again, it will be like a
man going on a journey,
who called his servants and
entrusted his property to
them. 15 To one he gave five
talents[c] of money, to another two talents, and to
another one talent, each according to his ability. Then
he went on his journey.
16 The man who had re-
ceived the five talents went
at once and put his money
to work and gained five
more. 17 So also, the one
with the two talents gained
two more. 18 But the man
who had received the one
talent went off, dug a hole
in the ground and hid his
master's money.
19 "After a long time the
master of those servants returned and settled accounts

[c] *15* A talent was worth more than a thousand dollars.

20"And the one who had
received the five talents
came up and brought five
more talents, saying, 'Master, you entrusted five talents to me; see, I have
gained five more talents.'
21"His master said to
him, 'Well done, good and
faithful slave; you were
faithful with a few things, I
will put you in charge of
many things, enter into the
joy of your master.'
22"The one also who *had*
received the two talents
came up and said, 'Master,
you entrusted to me two
talents; see, I have gained
two more talents.'
23"His master said to
him, 'Well done, good and
faithful slave; you were
faithful with a few things, I
will put you in charge of
many things; enter into the
joy of your master.'
24"And the one also who
had received the one talent
came up and said, 'Master,
I knew you to be a hard
man, reaping where you
did not sow, and gathering
where you scattered no
seed.
25'And I was afraid, and
went away and hid your talent in the ground; see, you
have what is yours.'
26"But his master an-
swered and said to him,
'You wicked, lazy slave,
you knew that I reap where
I did not sow, and gather
where I scattered no *seed*.
27'Then you ought to
have put my money in the
bank, and on my arrival I
would have received my
money back with interest.
28'Therefore take away
the talent from him, and
give it to the one who has
the ten talents.'
29"For to everyone who
has shall *more* be given,

ὁ τὰ πέντε τάλαντα λαβὼν προσ-
the [one] the five talents receiving brought
ήνεγκεν ἄλλα πέντε τάλαντα λέγων· κύριε,
other five talents saying: Lord,
πέντε τάλαντά μοι παρέδωκας· ἴδε ἄλλα
five talents to me thou deliveredst; behold other
πέντε τάλαντα ἐκέρδησα. 21 ἔφη αὐτῷ
five talents I gained. Said to him
ὁ κύριος αὐτοῦ· εὖ, δοῦλε ἀγαθὲ καὶ
the lord of him: Well, slave good and
πιστέ, ἐπὶ ὀλίγα ἦς πιστός,
faithful, over a few things thou wast faithful,
ἐπὶ πολλῶν σε καταστήσω· εἴσελθε
over many thee I will set; enter thou
εἰς τὴν χαρὰν τοῦ κυρίου σου. 22 προσ-
into the joy of the lord of thee. Ap-
ελθὼν καὶ ὁ τὰ δύο τάλαντα
proaching also the [one] the two talents
[having received]
εἶπεν· κύριε, δύο τάλαντά μοι
said: Lord, two talents to me
παρέδωκας· ἴδε ἄλλα δύο τάλαντα
thou deliveredst; behold other two talents
ἐκέρδησα. 23 ἔφη αὐτῷ ὁ κύριος αὐτοῦ·
I gained. Said to him the lord of him:
εὖ, δοῦλε ἀγαθὲ καὶ πιστέ, ἐπὶ
Well, slave good and faithful, over
ὀλίγα ἦς πιστός, ἐπὶ πολλῶν
a few things thou wast faithful, over many
σε καταστήσω· εἴσελθε εἰς τὴν
thee I will set; enter thou into the
χαρὰν τοῦ κυρίου σου. 24 προσ-
joy of the lord of thee. ap-
ελθὼν δὲ καὶ ὁ τὸ ἓν τάλαντον
proaching And also the [one] the one talent
εἰληφὼς εἶπεν· κύριε, ἔγνων σε
having received said: Lord, I knew thee
ὅτι σκληρὸς εἶ ἄνθρωπος, θερίζων
that [2]a hard [1]thou art [3]man, reaping
ὅπου οὐκ ἔσπειρας, καὶ συνάγων
where thou didst not sow, and gathering
ὅθεν οὐ διεσκόρπισας· 25 καὶ φοβηθεὶς
whence thou didst not scatter; and fearing
ἀπελθὼν ἔκρυψα τὸ τάλαντόν σου
going away I hid the talent of thee
ἐν τῇ γῇ· ἴδε ἔχεις τὸ σόν.
in the earth; behold thou hast the thine.
26 ἀποκριθεὶς δὲ ὁ κύριος αὐτοῦ εἶπεν
And answering the lord of him said
αὐτῷ· πονηρὲ δοῦλε καὶ ὀκνηρέ,
to him: Evil slave and slothful,
ᾔδεις ὅτι θερίζω ὅπου οὐκ ἔσπειρα,
thou knewest that I reap where I sowed not,
καὶ συνάγω ὅθεν οὐ διεσκόρπισα;
and I gather whence I did not scatter?
27 ἔδει σε οὖν βαλεῖν τὰ ἀργύριά
it behoved thee therefore to put the silver pieces
μου τοῖς τραπεζίταις, καὶ ἐλθὼν ἐγὼ
of me to the bankers, and coming I
ἐκομισάμην ἂν τὸ ἐμὸν σὺν τόκῳ.
would have received the mine with interest.
28 ἄρατε οὖν ἀπ' αὐτοῦ τὸ τάλαντον
Take therefore from him the talent
καὶ δότε τῷ ἔχοντι τὰ δέκα τάλαντα·
and give to the [one] having the ten talents;
29 τῷ γὰρ ἔχοντι παντὶ δοθήσεται καὶ
for to [2]having [1]everyone will be given and

with them. 20The man who
had received the five talents brought the other five.
'Master,' he said, 'you entrusted me with five tal-
ents. See, I have gained
five more.'
21"His master replied,
'Well done, good and faithful servant! You have been
faithful with a few things; I
will put you in charge of
many things. Come and
share your master's happi-
ness!'
22"The man with the two
talents also came. 'Mas-
ter,' he said, 'you entrusted
me with two talents; see, I
have gained two more.'
23"His master replied,
'Well done, good and faithful servant! You have been
faithful with a few things; I
will put you in charge of
many things. Come and
share your master's happi-
ness!'
24"Then the man who had
received the one talent
came. 'Master,' he said, 'I
knew that you are a hard
man, harvesting where you
have not sown and gather-
ing where you have not
scattered seed. 25So I was
afraid and went out and hid
your talent in the ground.
See, here is what belongs to
you.'
26"His master replied,
'You wicked, lazy servant!
So you knew that I harvest
where I have not sown and
gather where I have not
scattered seed? 27Well
then, you should have put
my money on deposit with
the bankers, so that when I
returned I would have re-
ceived it back with interest.
28" 'Take the talent from
him and give it to the one
who has the ten talents.
29For everyone who has
will be given more, and he

and he shall have an abundance; but from the one
who does not have, even
what he does have shall be
taken away.
30"And cast out the
worthless slave into the
outer darkness; in that
place there shall be weeping and gnashing of teeth.

The Judgment

31"But when the Son of
Man comes in His glory,
and all the angels with Him,
then He will sit on His
glorious throne.
32"And all the nations
will be gathered before
Him; and He will separate
them from one another, as
the shepherd separates the
sheep from the goats;
33and He will put the
sheep on His right, and the
goats on the left.
34"Then the King will say
to those on His right,
'Come, you who are
blessed of My Father, in-
herit the kingdom prepared
for you from the foundation
of the world.
35'For I was hungry, and
you gave Me *something* to
eat; I was thirsty, and you
gave Me drink; I was a
stranger, and you invited
Me in;
36naked, and you clothed
Me; I was sick, and you
visited Me; I was in prison,
and you came to Me.'
37"Then the righteous
will answer Him, saying,
'Lord, when did we see
You hungry, and feed You,
or thirsty, and give You
drink?
38'And when did we see
You a stranger, and invite
You in, or naked, and
clothe You?
39'And when did we see
You sick, or in prison, and
come to You?'
40"And the King will an-
swer and say to them,
'Truly I say to you, to the

περισσευθήσεται· τοῦ δὲ μὴ ἔχοντος
he will have abundance; but from the [one] not having

καὶ ὃ ἔχει ἀρθήσεται ἀπ' αὐτοῦ.
even what he has will be taken from him.

30 καὶ τὸν ἀχρεῖον δοῦλον ἐκβάλετε εἰς
And the useless slave cast ye out into

τὸ σκότος τὸ ἐξώτερον· ἐκεῖ ἔσται ὁ
the darkness – outer; there will be the

κλαυθμὸς καὶ ὁ βρυγμὸς τῶν ὀδόντων.
wailing and the gnashing of the teeth.

31 Ὅταν δὲ ἔλθῃ ὁ υἱὸς τοῦ ἀνθρώπου
And when comes the Son – of man

ἐν τῇ δόξῃ αὐτοῦ καὶ πάντες οἱ ἄγγελοι
in the glory of him and all the angels

μετ' αὐτοῦ, τότε καθίσει ἐπὶ θρόνου
with him, then he will sit on a throne

δόξης αὐτοῦ· 32 καὶ συναχθήσονται
of glory of him; and will be assembled

ἔμπροσθεν αὐτοῦ πάντα τὰ ἔθνη, καὶ
before him all the nations, and

ἀφορίσει αὐτοὺς ἀπ' ἀλλήλων, ὥσπερ
he will separate them from one another, as

ὁ ποιμὴν ἀφορίζει τὰ πρόβατα ἀπὸ
the shepherd separates the sheep from

τῶν ἐρίφων, 33 καὶ στήσει τὰ μὲν
the goats, and will set the –

πρόβατα ἐκ δεξιῶν αὐτοῦ, τὰ δὲ ἐρίφια
sheep on [the] right of him, but the goats

ἐξ εὐωνύμων. 34 τότε ἐρεῖ ὁ
on [the] left. Then will say the

βασιλεὺς τοῖς ἐκ δεξιῶν αὐτοῦ·
king to the [ones] on [the] right of him:

δεῦτε οἱ εὐλογημένοι τοῦ πατρός μου,
Come the [ones] blessed of the Father of me,

κληρονομήσατε τὴν ἡτοιμασμένην ὑμῖν
inherit ye the [2]*having been* prepared [3]for you

βασιλείαν ἀπὸ καταβολῆς κόσμου.
[1]kingdom from [the] foundation of [the] world.

35 ἐπείνασα γὰρ καὶ ἐδώκατέ μοι
For I hungered and ye gave me

φαγεῖν, ἐδίψησα καὶ ἐποτίσατέ με,
to eat, I thirsted and ye gave [2]drink [1]me,

ξένος ἤμην καὶ συνηγάγετέ με,
a stranger I was and ye entertained me,

36 γυμνὸς καὶ περιεβάλετέ με, ἠσθένησα
naked and ye clothed me, I ailed

καὶ ἐπεσκέψασθέ με, ἐν φυλακῇ ἤμην
and ye visited me, in prison I was

καὶ ἤλθατε πρός με. 37 τότε ἀποκριθή-
and ye came to me. Then will

σονται αὐτῷ οἱ δίκαιοι λέγοντες· κύριε,
answer him the righteous saying: Lord,

πότε σε εἴδομεν πεινῶντα καὶ ἐθρέψαμεν,
when thee saw we hungering and fed,

ἢ διψῶντα καὶ ἐποτίσαμεν; 38 πότε δέ
or thirsting and gave drink? and when

σε εἴδομεν ξένον καὶ συνηγάγομεν,
thee saw we a stranger and entertained,

ἢ γυμνὸν καὶ περιεβάλομεν; 39 πότε δέ
or naked and clothed? and when

σε εἴδομεν ἀσθενοῦντα ἢ ἐν φυλακῇ καὶ
thee saw we ailing or in prison and

ἤλθομεν πρὸς σέ; 40 καὶ ἀποκριθεὶς ὁ
came to thee? And answering the

βασιλεὺς ἐρεῖ αὐτοῖς· ἀμὴν λέγω
king will say to them: Truly I tell

will have an abundance.
Whoever does not have,
even what he has will be
taken from him. 30And
throw that worthless ser-
vant outside, into the darkness, where there will be
weeping and gnashing of
teeth.'

The Sheep and the Goats

31"When the Son of Man
comes in his glory, and all
the angels with him, he will
sit on his throne in heavenly glory. 32All the nations
will be gathered before
him, and he will separate
the people one from another as a shepherd separates
the sheep from the goats.
33He will put the sheep on
his right and the goats on
his left.
34"Then the King will say
to those on his right,
'Come, you who are
blessed by my Father; take
your inheritance, the kingdom prepared for you since
the creation of the world.
35For I was hungry and you
gave me something to eat, I
was thirsty and you gave
me something to drink, I
was a stranger and you invited me in, 36I needed
clothes and you clothed
me, I was sick and you
looked after me, I was in
prison and you came to visit me.'
37"Then the righteous
will answer him, 'Lord,
when did we see you hun-
gry and feed you, or thirsty
and give you something to
drink? 38When did we see
you a stranger and invite
you in, or needing clothes
and clothe you? 39When did
we see you sick or in prison
and go to visit you?'
40"The King will reply, 'I
tell you the truth, whatever

extent that you did it to one
of these brothers of Mine,
even the least *of them,* you
did it to Me.'
41"Then He will also say
to those on His left, 'Depart from Me, accursed
ones, into the eternal fire
which has been prepared
for the devil and his angels;
42for I was hungry, and
you gave Me *nothing* to eat;
I was thirsty, and you gave
Me nothing to drink;
43I was a stranger, and
you did not invite Me in;
naked, and you did not
clothe Me; sick, and in prison, and you did not visit
Me.'
44"Then they themselves
also will answer, saying,
'Lord, when did we see
You hungry, or thirsty, or a
stranger, or naked, or sick,
or in prison, and did not
take care of You?'
45"Then He will answer
them, saying, 'Truly I say
to you, to the extent that
you did not do it to one of
the least of these, you did
not do it to Me.'
46"And these will go
away into eternal punish-
ment, but the righteous into
eternal life."

ὑμῖν, ἐφ' ὅσον ἐποιήσατε ἑνὶ τούτων
you, inasmuch as ye did to one of these
τῶν ἀδελφῶν μου τῶν ἐλαχίστων, ἐμοὶ
– brothers of me the least, to me
ἐποιήσατε. 41 τότε ἐρεῖ καὶ τοῖς ἐξ
ye did. Then he will say also to the [ones] on
εὐωνύμων· πορεύεσθε ἀπ' ἐμοῦ κατ-
[the] left: Go from me *having been*
ηραμένοι εἰς τὸ πῦρ τὸ αἰώνιον
cursed [ones] into the fire – eternal
τὸ ἡτοιμασμένον τῷ διαβόλῳ καὶ τοῖς
– *having been* prepared for the devil and the
ἀγγέλοις αὐτοῦ. 42 ἐπείνασα γὰρ καὶ
angels of him. For I hungered and
οὐκ ἐδώκατέ μοι φαγεῖν, ἐδίψησα
ye gave not me to eat, I thirsted
καὶ οὐκ ἐποτίσατέ με, 43 ξένος
and ye [1]gave [3]not [4]drink [2]me, a stranger
ἤμην καὶ οὐ συνηγάγετέ με, γυμνὸς
I was and ye entertained not me, naked
καὶ οὐ περιεβάλετέ με, ἀσθενὴς καὶ ἐν
and ye clothed not me, ill and in
φυλακῇ καὶ οὐκ ἐπεσκέψασθέ με. 44 τότε
prison and ye visited not me. Then
ἀποκριθήσονται καὶ αὐτοὶ λέγοντες· κύριε,
will answer also they saying: Lord,
πότε σε εἴδομεν πεινῶντα ἢ διψῶντα ἢ
when thee saw we hungering or thirsting or
ξένον ἢ γυμνὸν ἢ ἀσθενῆ ἢ ἐν φυλακῇ
a stranger or naked or ill or in prison
καὶ οὐ διηκονήσαμέν σοι; 45 τότε
and did not minister to thee? Then
ἀποκριθήσεται αὐτοῖς λέγων· ἀμὴν λέγω
he will answer them saying: Truly I tell
ὑμῖν, ἐφ' ὅσον οὐκ ἐποιήσατε ἑνὶ
you, inasmuch as ye did not to one
τούτων τῶν ἐλαχίστων, οὐδὲ ἐμοὶ
of these – least [ones], neither to me
ἐποιήσατε. 46 καὶ ἀπελεύσονται οὗτοι εἰς
ye did. And will go away these into
κόλασιν αἰώνιον, οἱ δὲ δίκαιοι εἰς
punishment eternal, but the righteous into
ζωὴν αἰώνιον.
life eternal.

you did for one of the least
of these brothers of mine,
you did for me.'
41"Then he will say to
those on his left, 'Depart
from me, you who are
cursed, into the eternal fire
prepared for the devil and
his angels. 42For I was hungry and you gave me noth-
ing to eat, I was thirsty and
you gave me nothing to
drink, 43I was a stranger
and you did not invite me
in, I needed clothes and
you did not clothe me, I
was sick and in prison and
you did not look after me.'
44"They also will answer,
'Lord, when did we see you
hungry or thirsty or a
stranger or needing clothes
or sick or in prison, and did
not help you?'
45"He will reply, 'I tell
you the truth, whatever
you did not do for one of
the least of these, you did
not do for me.'
46"Then they will go
away to eternal punish-
ment, but the righteous to
eternal life."

Chapter 26

The Plot to Kill Jesus

AND it came about that
when Jesus had fin-
ished all these words, He
said to His disciples,
2"You know that after
two days the Passover is
coming, and the Son of
Man is *to be* delivered up
for crucifixion."
3Then the chief priests
and the elders of the people
were gathered together in
the court of the high priest,
named Caiaphas;
4and they plotted to-
gether to seize Jesus by

26 Καὶ ἐγένετο ὅτε ἐτέλεσεν ὁ
And it came to pass when ended –
Ἰησοῦς πάντας τοὺς λόγους τούτους,
Jesus all – words these,
εἶπεν τοῖς μαθηταῖς αὐτοῦ· 2 οἴδατε
he said to the disciples of him: Ye know
ὅτι μετὰ δύο ἡμέρας τὸ πάσχα γίνεται,
that after two days the passover occurs,
καὶ ὁ υἱὸς τοῦ ἀνθρώπου παραδίδοται εἰς
and the Son – of man is delivered –
τὸ σταυρωθῆναι. 3 Τότε συνήχθησαν οἱ
– to be crucified. Then were assembled the
ἀρχιερεῖς καὶ οἱ πρεσβύτεροι τοῦ λαοῦ
chief priests and the elders of the people
εἰς τὴν αὐλὴν τοῦ ἀρχιερέως τοῦ
in the court of the high priest –
λεγομένου Καϊάφα, 4 καὶ συνεβουλεύ-
named Caiaphas, and con-
σαντο ἵνα τὸν Ἰησοῦν δόλῳ κρατή-
sulted that – Jesus by guile they might

Chapter 26

The Plot Against Jesus

WHEN Jesus had fin-
ished saying all these
things, he said to his disciples, 2"As you know, the
Passover is two days away
—and the Son of Man will
be handed over to be crucified."
3Then the chief priests
and the elders of the people
assembled in the palace of
the high priest, whose
name was Caiaphas, 4and
they plotted to arrest Jesus

stealth, and kill *Him*.

5But they were saying, "Not during the festival, lest a riot occur among the people."

The Precious Ointment

6Now when Jesus was in Bethany, at the home of Simon the leper,

7a woman came to Him with an alabaster vial of very costly perfume, and she poured it upon His head as He reclined *at the table*.

8But the disciples were indignant when they saw *this*, and said, "Why this waste?

9"For this *perfume* might have been sold for a high price and *the money* given to the poor."

10But Jesus, aware of this, said to them, "Why do you bother the woman? For she has done a good deed to Me.

11"For the poor you have with you always; but you do not always have Me.

12"For when she poured this perfume upon My body, she did it to prepare Me for burial.

13"Truly I say to you, wherever this gospel is preached in the whole world, what this woman has done shall also be spoken of in memory of her."

Judas' Bargain

14Then one of the twelve, named Judas Iscariot, went to the chief priests,

15and said, "What are you willing to give me to deliver Him up to you?" And they weighed out to him thirty pieces of silver.

16And from then on he *began* looking for a good opportunity to betray Him.

17Now on the first *day* of Unleavened Bread the disciples came to Jesus, saying, "Where do You want us to prepare for You to eat the Passover?"

σωσιν καὶ ἀποκτείνωσιν· 5 ἔλεγον δέ·
seize and might kill; but they said:

μὴ ἐν τῇ ἑορτῇ, ἵνα μὴ θόρυβος
Not at the feast, lest a disturbance

γένηται ἐν τῷ λαῷ.
occurs among the people.

6 Τοῦ δὲ Ἰησοῦ γενομένου ἐν Βηθανίᾳ
– And Jesus being[a] in Bethany
=when Jesus was

ἐν οἰκίᾳ Σίμωνος τοῦ λεπροῦ,
in [the] house of Simon the leper,

7 προσῆλθεν αὐτῷ γυνὴ ἔχουσα ἀλάβαστρον
approached *to* him a woman having an alabaster phial

μύρου βαρυτίμου καὶ κατέχεεν ἐπὶ
of ointment very expensive and poured [it] on

τῆς κεφαλῆς αὐτοῦ ἀνακειμένου. 8 ἰδόντες
the head of him reclining. And see-

δὲ οἱ μαθηταὶ ἠγανάκτησαν λέγοντες·
ing the disciples were angry saying:

εἰς τί ἡ ἀπώλεια αὕτη; 9 ἐδύνατο γὰρ
To what – waste this? for could

τοῦτο πραθῆναι πολλοῦ καὶ δοθῆναι
this *to* be sold of(for) much and *to* be given

πτωχοῖς. 10 γνοὺς δὲ ὁ Ἰησοῦς εἶπεν
to poor. And knowing – Jesus said

αὐτοῖς· τί κόπους παρέχετε τῇ γυναικί;
to them: Why trouble ye the woman?

ἔργον γὰρ καλὸν ἠργάσατο εἰς ἐμέ·
for work a good she wrought to me:

11 πάντοτε γὰρ τοὺς πτωχοὺς ἔχετε μεθ'
for always the poor ye have with

ἑαυτῶν, ἐμὲ δὲ οὐ πάντοτε ἔχετε·
yourselves, but me not always ye have;

12 βαλοῦσα γὰρ αὕτη τὸ μύρον τοῦτο
for [2]putting [1]this woman – [4]ointment [3]this

ἐπὶ τοῦ σώματός μου πρὸς τὸ ἐνταφιάσαι
on the body of me for – to bury

με ἐποίησεν. 13 ἀμὴν λέγω ὑμῖν, ὅπου
me she did. Truly I tell you, wher-

ἐὰν κηρυχθῇ τὸ εὐαγγέλιον τοῦτο ἐν
ever is proclaimed – gospel this in

ὅλῳ τῷ κόσμῳ, λαληθήσεται καὶ ὃ
all the world, will be spoken also what

ἐποίησεν αὕτη εἰς μνημόσυνον αὐτῆς.
did this woman for a memorial of her.

14 Τότε πορευθεὶς εἷς τῶν δώδεκα, ὁ
Then going one of the twelve, the [one]

λεγόμενος Ἰούδας Ἰσκαριώτης, πρὸς
named Judas Iscariot, to

τοὺς ἀρχιερεῖς 15 εἶπεν· τί θέλετε μοι
the chief priests he said: What are ye willing me

δοῦναι, κἀγὼ ὑμῖν παραδώσω αὐτόν;
to give, and I to you will deliver him?

οἱ δὲ ἔστησαν αὐτῷ τριάκοντα ἀργύρια.
And they weighed him thirty pieces of silver.

16 καὶ ἀπὸ τότε ἐζήτει εὐκαιρίαν ἵνα
And from then he sought opportunity that

αὐτὸν παραδῷ.
him he might deliver.

17 Τῇ δὲ πρώτῃ τῶν ἀζύμων
Now on the first [day] – of unleavened bread

προσῆλθον οἱ μαθηταὶ τῷ Ἰησοῦ
approached the disciples – *to* Jesus

λέγοντες· ποῦ θέλεις ἑτοιμάσωμέν
saying: Where willest thou we may prepare

σοι φαγεῖν τὸ πάσχα; 18 ὁ δὲ
for thee to eat the passover? So he

in some sly way and kill him. 5"But not during the Feast," they said, "or there may be a riot among the people."

Jesus Anointed at Bethany

6While Jesus was in Bethany in the home of a man known as Simon the Leper, 7a woman came to him with an alabaster jar of very expensive perfume, which she poured on his head as he was reclining at the table.

8When the disciples saw this, they were indignant. "Why this waste?" they asked. 9"This perfume could have been sold at a high price and the money given to the poor."

10Aware of this, Jesus said to them, "Why are you bothering this woman? She has done a beautiful thing to me. 11The poor you will always have with you, but you will not always have me. 12When she poured this perfume on my body, she did it to prepare me for burial. 13I tell you the truth, wherever this gospel is preached throughout the world, what she has done will also be told, in memory of her."

Judas Agrees to Betray Jesus

14Then one of the Twelve—the one called Judas Iscariot—went to the chief priests 15and asked, "What are you willing to give me if I hand him over to you?" So they counted out for him thirty silver coins. 16From then on Judas watched for an opportunity to hand him over.

The Lord's Supper

17On the first day of the Feast of Unleavened Bread, the disciples came to Jesus and asked, "Where do you want us to make preparations for you to eat the Passover?"

18And He said, "Go into
the city to a certain man,
and say to him, 'The
Teacher says, "My time is
at hand; I *am to* keep the
Passover at your house
with My disciples."' "
19And the disciples did as
Jesus had directed them;
and they prepared the Passover.

The Last Passover

20Now when evening had
come, He was reclining *at
the table* with the twelve
disciples.
21And as they were eat-
ing, He said, "Truly I say
to you that one of you will
betray Me."
22And being deeply
grieved, they each one began to say to Him, "Surely
not I, Lord?"
23And He answered and
said, "He who dipped his
hand with Me in the bowl is
the one who will betray
Me.
24"The Son of Man *is to*
go, just as it is written of
Him; but woe to that man
by whom the Son of Man is
betrayed! It would have
been good for that man if he
had not been born."
25And Judas, who was be-
traying Him, answered and
said, "Surely it is not I,
Rabbi?" He *said to him,
"You have said *it* your-
self."

The Lord's Supper Instituted

26And while they were
eating, Jesus took *some*
bread, and after a blessing,
He broke *it* and gave *it* to
the disciples, and said,
"Take, eat; this is My
body."
27And when He had taken
a cup and given thanks, He
gave *it* to them, saying,
"Drink from it, all of you;
28for this is My blood of
the covenant, which is
poured out for many for
forgiveness of sins.

εἶπεν· ὑπάγετε εἰς τὴν πόλιν πρὸς
said: Go ye into the city to
τὸν δεῖνα καὶ εἴπατε αὐτῷ· ὁ
such a one and say to him: The
διδάσκαλος λέγει· ὁ καιρός μου
teacher says: The time of me
ἐγγύς ἐστιν· πρὸς σὲ ποιῶ τὸ πάσχα
near is; with thee I make the passover
μετὰ τῶν μαθητῶν μου. 19 καὶ ἐποίησαν
with the disciples of me. And did
οἱ μαθηταὶ ὡς συνέταξεν αὐτοῖς ὁ
the disciples as enjoined them –
Ἰησοῦς, καὶ ἡτοίμασαν τὸ πάσχα. 20 Ὀψίας
Jesus, and prepared the passover. evening
δὲ γενομένης ἀνέκειτο μετὰ τῶν δώδεκα
And coming[a] he reclined with the twelve
=when evening came
[μαθητῶν]. 21 καὶ ἐσθιόντων αὐτῶν εἶπεν·
disciples. And eating them[a] he said:
=as they were eating
ἀμὴν λέγω ὑμῖν ὅτι εἷς ἐξ ὑμῶν παρα-
Truly I tell you that one of you will
δώσει με. 22 καὶ λυπούμενοι σφόδρα
betray me. And grieving exceedingly
ἤρξαντο λέγειν αὐτῷ εἷς ἕκαστος·
they began to say to him [2]one [1]each:
μήτι ἐγώ εἰμι, κύριε; 23 ὁ δὲ ἀποκριθεὶς
Not I am, Lord? And he answering
=It is not I,
εἶπεν· ὁ ἐμβάψας μετ' ἐμοῦ τὴν
said: The [one] dipping with me the(his)
χεῖρα ἐν τῷ τρυβλίῳ, οὗτός με παρα-
hand in the dish, this man me will
δώσει. 24 ὁ μὲν υἱὸς τοῦ ἀνθρώπου
betray. Indeed the Son – of man
ὑπάγει καθὼς γέγραπται περὶ αὐτοῦ,
goes as it has been written concerning him,
οὐαὶ δὲ τῷ ἀνθρώπῳ ἐκείνῳ δι'
but woe – man to that through
οὗ ὁ υἱὸς τοῦ ἀνθρώπου παραδίδοται·
whom the Son – of man is betrayed;
καλὸν ἦν αὐτῷ εἰ οὐκ ἐγεννήθη
good were it for him if was not born
ὁ ἄνθρωπος ἐκεῖνος. 25 ἀποκριθεὶς δὲ
– man that. And answering
Ἰούδας ὁ παραδιδοὺς αὐτὸν εἶπεν·
Judas the [one] betraying him said:
μήτι ἐγώ εἰμι, ῥαββί; λέγει αὐτῷ·
Not I am, rabbi? He says to him:
=It is not I,
σὺ εἶπας. 26 Ἐσθιόντων δὲ αὐτῶν
Thou saidst. And eating them[a]
=as they were eating
λαβὼν ὁ Ἰησοῦς ἄρτον καὶ εὐλογήσας
taking – Jesus a loaf and blessing
ἔκλασεν καὶ δοὺς τοῖς μαθηταῖς εἶπεν·
he broke and giving to the disciples said:
λάβετε φάγετε· τοῦτό ἐστιν τὸ σῶμά
Take ye[,] eat ye; this is the body
μου. 27 καὶ λαβὼν ποτήριον καὶ εὐχαρι-
of me. And taking a cup and giving
στήσας ἔδωκεν αὐτοῖς λέγων· πίετε ἐξ
thanks he gave to them saying: Drink ye of
αὐτοῦ πάντες· 28 τοῦτο γάρ ἐστιν τὸ
it all; for this is the
αἷμά μου τῆς διαθήκης τὸ περὶ πολλῶν
blood of me of the covenant the [blood] concerning many
ἐκχυννόμενον εἰς ἄφεσιν ἁμαρτιῶν. 29 λέγω
being shed for forgiveness of sins. I tell

18He replied, "Go into
the city to a certain man
and tell him, 'The Teacher
says: My appointed time is
near. I am going to cele-
brate the Passover with my
disciples at your house.' "
19So the disciples did as
Jesus had directed them
and prepared the Passover.
20When evening came,
Jesus was reclining at the
table with the Twelve.
21And while they were eating, he said, "I tell you the
truth, one of you will betray me."
22They were very sad and
began to say to him one after the other, "Surely not I,
Lord?"
23Jesus replied, "The one
who has dipped his hand
into the bowl with me will
betray me. 24The Son of
Man will go just as it is written about him. But woe to
that man who betrays the
Son of Man! It would be
better for him if he had not
been born."
25Then Judas, the one
who would betray him,
said, "Surely not I, Rab-
bi?"
Jesus answered, "Yes, it
is you."[d]
26While they were eating,
Jesus took bread, gave
thanks and broke it, and
gave it to his disciples, saying, "Take and eat; this is
my body."
27Then he took the cup,
gave thanks and offered it
to them, saying, "Drink
from it, all of you. 28This is
my blood of the[e] covenant,
which is poured out for
many for the forgiveness of

5 Or *"You yourself have said it"*
8 Some manuscripts *the new*

29"But I say to you, I will
not drink of this fruit of the
vine from now on until that
day when I drink it new
with you in My Father's
kingdom."
30And after singing a
hymn, they went out to the
Mount of Olives.
31Then Jesus *said to
them, "You will all fall
away because of Me this
night, for it is written, 'I
WILL STRIKE DOWN THE SHEP-
HERD, AND THE SHEEP OF THE
FLOCK SHALL BE SCATTERED.'
32"But after I have been
raised, I will go before you
to Galilee."
33But Peter answered and
said to Him, "_Even_ though
all may fall away because
of You, I will never fall
away."
34Jesus said to him,
"Truly I say to you that this
very night, before a cock
crows, you shall deny Me
three times."
35Peter *said to Him,
"Even if I have to die with
You, I will not deny You."
All the disciples said the
same thing too.

The Garden of Gethsemane

36Then Jesus *came with
them to a place called Gethsemane, and *said to His
disciples, "Sit here while I
go over there and pray."
37And He took with Him
Peter and the two sons of
Zebedee, and began to be
grieved and distressed.
38Then He *said to them,
"My soul is deeply
grieved, to the point of
death; remain here and
keep watch with Me."
39And He went a little
beyond _them_, and fell on
His face and prayed, say-
ing, "My Father, if it is

δὲ ὑμῖν, οὐ μὴ πίω ἀπ' ἄρτι ἐκ
And you, by no means will I drink from now of
τούτου τοῦ γενήματος τῆς ἀμπέλου ἕως
this – fruit of the vine until
τῆς ἡμέρας ἐκείνης ὅταν αὐτὸ πίνω μεθ'
– day that when it I drink with
ὑμῶν καινὸν ἐν τῇ βασιλείᾳ τοῦ πατρός
you new in the kingdom of the Father
μου.
of me.
30 Καὶ ὑμνήσαντες ἐξῆλθον εἰς τὸ
And having sung a hymn they went forth to the
ὄρος τῶν ἐλαιῶν. 31 Τότε λέγει αὐτοῖς ὁ
mount of the olives. Then says to them –
Ἰησοῦς· πάντες ὑμεῖς σκανδαλισθήσεσθε
Jesus: All ye will be offended
ἐν ἐμοὶ ἐν τῇ νυκτὶ ταύτῃ· γέγραπται
in me to-night; it has been written
γάρ· πατάξω τὸν ποιμένα, καὶ δια-
for: I will strike the shepherd, and will
σκορπισθήσονται τὰ πρόβατα τῆς ποίμνης·
be scattered the sheep of the flock;
32 μετὰ δὲ τὸ ἐγερθῆναί με προάξω
but after the to be raised me[b] I will go before
=I am raised
ὑμᾶς εἰς τὴν Γαλιλαίαν. 33 ἀποκριθεὶς
you to – Galilee. answering
δὲ ὁ Πέτρος εἶπεν αὐτῷ· εἰ πάντες
And – Peter said to him: If all men
σκανδαλισθήσονται ἐν σοί, ἐγὼ οὐδέποτε
shall be offended in thee, I never
σκανδαλισθήσομαι. 34 ἔφη αὐτῷ ὁ Ἰησοῦς·
will be offended. Said to him – Jesus:
ἀμὴν λέγω σοι ὅτι ἐν ταύτῃ τῇ νυκτὶ
Truly I tell thee that to-night
πρὶν ἀλέκτορα φωνῆσαι τρὶς ἀπαρνήσῃ
before a cock to crow[b] three times thou wilt deny
με. 35 λέγει αὐτῷ ὁ Πέτρος· κἂν
me. Says to him – Peter: Even if
δέῃ με σὺν σοὶ ἀποθανεῖν, οὐ μή σε
it behoves me with thee to die, by no means thee
=I must die with thee.
ἀπαρνήσομαι. ὁμοίως καὶ πάντες οἱ
I will deny. Likewise also all the
μαθηταὶ εἶπαν.
disciples said.
36 Τότε ἔρχεται μετ' αὐτῶν ὁ Ἰησοῦς
Then comes with them – Jesus
εἰς χωρίον λεγόμενον Γεθσημανί, καὶ λέγει
to a piece of land called Gethsemane, and says
τοῖς μαθηταῖς· καθίσατε αὐτοῦ ἕως οὗ
to the disciples: Sit ye here until
ἀπελθὼν ἐκεῖ προσεύξωμαι. 37 καὶ παρα-
going away there I may pray. And tak-
λαβὼν τὸν Πέτρον καὶ τοὺς δύο υἱοὺς
ing – Peter and the two sons
Ζεβεδαίου ἤρξατο λυπεῖσθαι καὶ ἀδημονεῖν.
of Zebedee he began to grieve and to be distressed.
38 τότε λέγει αὐτοῖς· περίλυπός ἐστιν
Then he says to them: Deeply grieved is
ἡ ψυχή μου ἕως θανάτου· μείνατε
the soul of me unto death; remain ye
ὧδε καὶ γρηγορεῖτε μετ' ἐμοῦ. 39 καὶ
here and watch ye with me. And
προελθὼν μικρὸν ἔπεσεν ἐπὶ πρόσωπον
going forward a little he fell on [the] face
αὐτοῦ προσευχόμενος καὶ λέγων· πάτερ
of him praying and saying: Father

sins. 29I tell you, I will not
drink of this fruit of the vine
from now on until that day
when I drink it anew with
you in my Father's king-
dom."
30When they had sung a
hymn, they went out to the
Mount of Olives.

Jesus Predicts Peter's Denial

31Then Jesus told them,
"This very night you will
all fall away on account of
me, for it is written:

" 'I will strike the
shepherd,
and the sheep of the
flock will be
scattered.'[f]

32But after I have risen, I
will go ahead of you into
Galilee."
33Peter replied, "Even if
all fall away on account of
you, I never will."
34"I tell you the truth,"
Jesus answered, "this very
night, before the rooster
crows, you will disown me
three times."
35But Peter declared,
"Even if I have to die with
you, I will never disown
you." And all the other disciples said the same.

Gethsemane

36Then Jesus went with
his disciples to a place
called Gethsemane, and he
said to them, "Sit here
while I go over there and
pray." 37He took Peter and
the two sons of Zebedee
along with him, and he began to be sorrowful and
troubled. 38Then he said to
them, "My soul is over-
whelmed with sorrow to
the point of death. Stay
here and keep watch with
me."
39Going a little farther, he
fell with his face to the
ground and prayed, "My

[f]Zech. 13:7

possible, let this cup pass from Me; yet not as I will, but as Thou wilt."
40And He *came to the disciples and *found them sleeping, and *said to Peter, "So, you *men* could not keep watch with Me for one hour?
41"Keep watching and praying, that you may not enter into temptation; the spirit is willing, but the flesh is weak."
42He went away again a second time and prayed, saying, "My Father, if this cannot pass away unless I drink it, Thy will be done."
43And again He came and found them sleeping, for their eyes were heavy.
44And He left them again, and went away and prayed a third time, saying the same thing once more.
45Then He *came to the disciples, and *said to them, "Are you still sleeping and taking your rest? Behold, the hour is at hand and the Son of Man is being betrayed into the hands of sinners.
46"Arise, let us be going; behold, the one who betrays Me is at hand!"

Jesus' Betrayal and Arrest

47And while He was still speaking, behold, Judas, one of the twelve, came up, accompanied by a great multitude with swords and clubs, from the chief priests and elders of the people.
48Now he who was betraying Him gave them a sign, saying, "Whomever I shall kiss, He is the one; seize Him."
49And immediately he went to Jesus and said, "Hail, Rabbi!" and kissed Him.

μου, εἰ δυνατόν ἐστιν, παρελθάτω ἀπ'
of me, if possible it is, let pass from
ἐμοῦ τὸ ποτήριον τοῦτο· πλὴν οὐχ
me – cup this; yet not
ὡς ἐγὼ θέλω ἀλλ' ὡς σύ. **40** καὶ
as I will but as thou. And
ἔρχεται πρὸς τοὺς μαθητὰς καὶ εὑρίσκει
he comes to the disciples and finds
αὐτοὺς καθεύδοντας, καὶ λέγει τῷ Πέτρῳ·
them sleeping, and says – to Peter:
οὕτως οὐκ ἰσχύσατε μίαν ὥραν
So were ye not able one hour
γρηγορῆσαι μετ' ἐμοῦ; **41** γρηγορεῖτε καὶ
to watch with me? Watch ye and
προσεύχεσθε, ἵνα μὴ εἰσέλθητε εἰς
pray, lest ye enter into
πειρασμόν· τὸ μὲν πνεῦμα πρόθυμον,
temptation; indeed the spirit [is] eager,
ἡ δὲ σὰρξ ἀσθενής. **42** πάλιν ἐκ
but the flesh weak. Again –
δευτέρου ἀπελθὼν προσηύξατο λέγων·
second [time] going away he prayed saying:
πάτερ μου, εἰ οὐ δύναται τοῦτο παρελθεῖν
Father of me, if cannot this *to* pass away
ἐὰν μὴ αὐτὸ πίω, γενηθήτω τὸ θέλημά
except it I drink, let be done the will
σου. **43** καὶ ἐλθὼν πάλιν εὗρεν αὐτοὺς
of thee. And coming again he found them
καθεύδοντας, ἦσαν γὰρ αὐτῶν οἱ ὀφθαλμοὶ
sleeping, for were of them the eyes
βεβαρημένοι. **44** καὶ ἀφεὶς αὐτοὺς πάλιν
having been burdened. And leaving them again
ἀπελθὼν προσηύξατο ἐκ τρίτου, τὸν
going away he prayed a third [time], the
αὐτὸν λόγον εἰπὼν πάλιν. **45** τότε ἔρχεται
same word saying again. Then he comes
πρὸς τοὺς μαθητὰς καὶ λέγει αὐτοῖς·
to the disciples and says to them:
καθεύδετε λοιπὸν καὶ ἀναπαύεσθε·
Sleep ye now and rest;
ἰδοὺ ἤγγικεν ἡ ὥρα καὶ ὁ υἱὸς τοῦ
behold has drawn near the hour and the Son –
ἀνθρώπου παραδίδοται εἰς χεῖρας
of man is betrayed into [the] hands
ἁμαρτωλῶν. **46** ἐγείρεσθε, ἄγωμεν· ἰδοὺ
of sinners. Rise ye, let us be going; behold
ἤγγικεν ὁ παραδιδούς με.
has drawn near the [one] betraying me.
47 Καὶ ἔτι αὐτοῦ λαλοῦντος, ἰδοὺ
And still him speaking,[a] behold
[a] = while he was still speaking,
Ἰούδας εἷς τῶν δώδεκα ἦλθεν, καὶ μετ'
Judas one of the twelve came, and with
αὐτοῦ ὄχλος πολὺς μετὰ μαχαιρῶν καὶ
him crowd a much with swords and
ξύλων ἀπὸ τῶν ἀρχιερέων καὶ πρεσβυτέρων
clubs from the chief priests and elders
τοῦ λαοῦ. **48** ὁ δὲ παραδιδοὺς αὐτὸν ἔδωκεν
of the people. Now the [one] betraying him gave
αὐτοῖς σημεῖον λέγων· ὃν ἂν φιλήσω
them a sign saying: Whomever I may kiss
αὐτός ἐστιν· κρατήσατε αὐτόν. **49** καὶ
he it is; seize ye him. And
εὐθέως προσελθὼν τῷ Ἰησοῦ εἶπεν· χαῖρε,
immediately approaching – *to* Jesus he said: Hail,
ῥαββί, καὶ κατεφίλησεν αὐτόν. **50** ὁ
rabbi, and affectionately kissed him. –

Father, if it is possible, may this cup be taken from me. Yet not as I will, but as you will."
40Then he returned to his disciples and found them sleeping. "Could you men not keep watch with me for one hour?" he asked Peter.
41"Watch and pray so that you will not fall into temptation. The spirit is willing, but the body is weak."
42He went away a second time and prayed, "My Father, if it is not possible for this cup to be taken away unless I drink it, may your will be done."
43When he came back, he again found them sleeping, because their eyes were heavy. 44So he left them and went away once more and prayed the third time, saying the same thing.
45Then he returned to the disciples and said to them, "Are you still sleeping and resting? Look, the hour is near, and the Son of Man is betrayed into the hands of sinners. 46Rise, let us go! Here comes my betrayer!"

Jesus Arrested

47While he was still speaking, Judas, one of the Twelve, arrived. With him was a large crowd armed with swords and clubs, sent from the chief priests and the elders of the people.
48Now the betrayer had arranged a signal with them: "The one I kiss is the man; arrest him." 49Going at once to Jesus, Judas said, "Greetings, Rabbi!" and kissed him.

[50]And Jesus said to him, "Friend, *do* what you have come for." Then they came and laid hands on Jesus and seized Him.

[51]And behold, one of those who were with Jesus reached and drew out his sword, and struck the slave of the high priest, and cut off his ear.

[52]Then Jesus *said to him, "Put your sword back into its place; for all those who take up the sword shall perish by the sword.

[53]"Or do you think that I cannot appeal to My Father, and He will at once put at My disposal more than twelve [l]legions of angels?

[54]"How then shall the Scriptures be fulfilled, that it must happen this way?"

[55]At that time Jesus said to the multitudes, "Have you come out with swords and clubs to arrest Me as against a robber? Every day I used to sit in the temple teaching and you did not seize Me.

[56]"But all this has taken place that the Scriptures of the prophets may be fulfilled." Then all the disciples left Him and fled.

Jesus before Caiaphas

[57]And those who had seized Jesus led Him away to Caiaphas, the high priest, where the scribes and the elders were gathered together.

[58]But Peter also was following Him at a distance as far as the courtyard of the high priest, and entered in, and sat down with the officers to see the outcome.

[59]Now the chief priests and the whole Council kept trying to obtain false testimony against Jesus, in or-

[l] A legion equaled 6,000 troops

δὲ Ἰησοῦς εἶπεν αὐτῷ· ἑταῖρε,
But Jesus said to him: Comrade, [do that]
ἐφ' ὃ πάρει. τότε προσελθόντες ἐπέβαλον
on what thou art here. Then approaching they laid *on*
τὰς χεῖρας ἐπὶ τὸν Ἰησοῦν καὶ ἐκράτησαν
the(ir) hands on – Jesus and seized
αὐτόν. 51 καὶ ἰδοὺ εἷς τῶν μετὰ
him. And behold one of the [ones] with
Ἰησοῦ ἐκτείνας τὴν χεῖρα ἀπέσπασεν
Jesus stretching out the(his) hand drew
τὴν μάχαιραν αὐτοῦ, καὶ πατάξας τὸν
the sword of him, and striking the
δοῦλον τοῦ ἀρχιερέως ἀφεῖλεν αὐτοῦ τὸ
slave of the high priest cut off of him the
ὠτίον. 52 τότε λέγει αὐτῷ ὁ Ἰησοῦς·
ear. Then says to him – Jesus:
ἀπόστρεψον τὴν μάχαιράν σου εἰς τὸν
Put back the sword of thee into the
τόπον αὐτῆς· πάντες γὰρ οἱ λαβόντες
place of it; for all the [ones] taking
μάχαιραν ἐν μαχαίρῃ ἀπολοῦνται. 53 ἢ
a sword by a sword will perish. Or
δοκεῖς ὅτι οὐ δύναμαι παρακαλέσαι
thinkest thou that I cannot *to* ask
τὸν πατέρα μου, καὶ παραστήσει μοι
the Father of me, and he will provide me
ἄρτι πλείω δώδεκα λεγιῶνας ἀγγέλων;
now more [than] twelve legions of angels?
54 πῶς οὖν πληρωθῶσιν αἱ γραφαὶ ὅτι
how then may be fulfilled the scriptures that
οὕτως δεῖ γενέσθαι; 55 Ἐν ἐκείνῃ τῇ ὥρᾳ
thus it must be? In that – hour
εἶπεν ὁ Ἰησοῦς τοῖς ὄχλοις· ὡς ἐπὶ
said – Jesus to the crowds: As against
λῃστὴν ἐξήλθατε μετὰ μαχαιρῶν καὶ
a robber came ye forth with swords and
ξύλων συλλαβεῖν με; καθ' ἡμέραν ἐν
clubs to take me? daily in
τῷ ἱερῷ ἐκαθεζόμην διδάσκων, καὶ οὐκ
the temple I sat teaching, and not
ἐκρατήσατέ με. 56 τοῦτο δὲ ὅλον
ye seized me. But this all
γέγονεν ἵνα πληρωθῶσιν αἱ γραφαὶ
has come to pass that may be fulfilled the scriptures
τῶν προφητῶν. Τότε οἱ μαθηταὶ πάντες
of the prophets. Then the disciples all
ἀφέντες αὐτὸν ἔφυγον.
leaving him fled.
57 Οἱ δὲ κρατήσαντες τὸν Ἰησοῦν
But the [ones] having seized – Jesus
ἀπήγαγον πρὸς Καϊάφαν τὸν ἀρχιερέα,
led [him] away to Caiaphas the high priest,
ὅπου οἱ γραμματεῖς καὶ οἱ πρεσβύτεροι
where the scribes and the elders
συνήχθησαν. 58 ὁ δὲ Πέτρος ἠκολούθει
were assembled. – And Peter followed
αὐτῷ [ἀπὸ] μακρόθεν ἕως τῆς αὐλῆς
him from afar up to the court
τοῦ ἀρχιερέως, καὶ εἰσελθὼν ἔσω ἐκάθητο
of the high priest, and entering within sat
μετὰ τῶν ὑπηρετῶν ἰδεῖν τὸ τέλος.
with the attendants to see the end.
59 Οἱ δὲ ἀρχιερεῖς καὶ τὸ συνέδριον
And the chief priests and the council
ὅλον ἐζήτουν ψευδομαρτυρίαν κατὰ τοῦ
whole sought false witness against –

[50]Jesus replied, "Friend, do what you came for."[g] Then the men stepped forward, seized Jesus and arrested him. [51]With that, one of Jesus' companions reached for his sword, drew it out and struck the servant of the high priest, cutting off his ear.

[52]"Put your sword back in its place," Jesus said to him, "for all who draw the sword will die by the sword. [53]Do you think I cannot call on my Father, and he will at once put at my disposal more than twelve legions of angels? [54]But how then would the Scriptures be fulfilled that say it must happen in this way?"

[55]At that time Jesus said to the crowd, "Am I leading a rebellion, that you have come out with swords and clubs to capture me? Every day I sat in the temple courts teaching, and you did not arrest me. [56]But this has all taken place that the writings of the prophets might be fulfilled." Then all the disciples deserted him and fled.

Before the Sanhedrin

[57]Those who had arrested Jesus took him to Caiaphas, the high priest, where the teachers of the law and the elders had assembled. [58]But Peter followed him at a distance, right up to the courtyard of the high priest. He entered and sat down with the guards to see the outcome.

[59]The chief priests and the whole Sanhedrin were looking for false evidence against Jesus so that they

[g]50 Or *"Friend, why have you come?"*

der that they might put Him to death;

60and they did not find *any*, even though many false witnesses came forward. But later on two came forward,

61and said, "This man stated, 'I am able to destroy the temple of God and to rebuild it in three days.'"

62And the high priest stood up and said to Him, "Do You make no answer? What is it that these men are testifying against You?"

63But Jesus kept silent. And the high priest said to Him, "I adjure You by the living God, that You tell us whether You are the Christ, the Son of God."

64Jesus *said to him, "You have said it *yourself*; nevertheless I tell you, hereafter you shall see THE SON OF MAN SITTING AT THE RIGHT HAND OF POWER, and COMING ON THE CLOUDS OF HEAVEN."

65Then the high priest tore his robes, saying, "He has blasphemed! What further need do we have of witnesses? Behold, you have now heard the blasphemy;

66what do you think?" They answered and said, "He is deserving of death!"

67Then they spat in His face and beat Him with their fists; and others slapped Him,

68and said, "Prophesy to us, You Christ; who is the one who hit You?"

Peter's Denials

69Now Peter was sitting outside in the courtyard, and a certain servant-girl came to him and said, "You too were with Jesus the Galilean."

70But he denied *it* before them all, saying, "I do not know what you are talking about."

71And when he had gone out to the gateway, another *servant-girl* saw him and

Ἰησου ὅπως αὐτὸν θανατώσωσιν, 60 καὶ
Jesus so as him they might put to death, and

οὐχ εὗρον πολλῶν προσελθόντων
did not find[,] many approaching
=when many false witnesses approached.

ψευδομαρτύρων. ὕστερον δὲ προσελθόντες
false witnesses•. But later approaching

δύο 61 εἶπαν· οὗτος ἔφη· δύναμαι κατα-
two said: This man said: I can *to* de-

λῦσαι τὸν ναὸν τοῦ θεοῦ καὶ διὰ τριῶν
stroy the shrine – of God and through(after) three

ἡμερῶν οἰκοδομῆσαι. 62 καὶ ἀναστὰς
days *to* build. And standing up

ὁ ἀρχιερεὺς εἶπεν αὐτῷ· οὐδὲν
the high priest said to him: Nothing

ἀποκρίνῃ, τί οὗτοί σου κατα-
answerest thou, what these men thee give

μαρτυροῦσιν; 63 ὁ δὲ Ἰησοῦς ἐσιώπα.
evidence against? – But Jesus remained silent.

καὶ ὁ ἀρχιερεὺς εἶπεν αὐτῷ· ἐξορκίζω
And the high priest said to him: I adjure

σε κατὰ τοῦ θεοῦ τοῦ ζῶντος ἵνα ἡμῖν
thee by – God the living that us

εἴπῃς εἰ σὺ εἶ ὁ χριστὸς ὁ υἱὸς τοῦ
thou tell if thou art the Christ the Son –

θεοῦ. 64 λέγει αὐτῷ ὁ Ἰησοῦς· σὺ εἶπας·
of God. Says to him – Jesus: Thou saidst;

πλὴν λέγω ὑμῖν, ἀπ' ἄρτι ὄψεσθε τὸν
yet I tell you, from now ye will see the

υἱὸν τοῦ ἀνθρώπου καθήμενον ἐκ
Son – of man sitting on [the]

δεξιῶν τῆς δυνάμεως καὶ ἐρχόμενον
right [hand] of the power and coming

ἐπὶ τῶν νεφελῶν τοῦ οὐρανοῦ. 65 τότε
on the clouds – of heaven. Then

ὁ ἀρχιερεὺς διέρρηξεν τὰ ἱμάτια αὐτοῦ
the high priest rent the garments of him

λέγων· ἐβλασφήμησεν· τί ἔτι χρείαν ἔχομεν
saying: He blasphemed; what yet need have we

μαρτύρων; ἴδε νῦν ἠκούσατε τὴν βλασφη-
of witnesses? behold now ye heard the blas-

μίαν· 66 τί ὑμῖν δοκεῖ; οἱ δὲ ἀπο-
phemy; what to you seems it? And they answer-

κριθέντες εἶπαν· ἔνοχος θανάτου ἐστίν.
ing said: Liable of(to) death he is.

67 Τότε ἐνέπτυσαν εἰς τὸ πρόσωπον αὐτοῦ
Then they spat in the face of him

καὶ ἐκολάφισαν αὐτόν, οἱ δὲ
and violently maltreated him, and they

ἐρράπισαν 68 λέγοντες· προφήτευσον ἡμῖν,
slapped [him] saying: Prophesy thou to us,

χριστέ, τίς ἐστιν ὁ παίσας σε;
Christ, who is it the [one] having struck thee?

69 Ὁ δὲ Πέτρος ἐκάθητο ἔξω ἐν
– And Peter sat outside in

τῇ αὐλῇ· καὶ προσῆλθεν αὐτῷ μία
the court; and approached *to* him one

παιδίσκη λέγουσα· καὶ σὺ ἦσθα μετὰ
maidservant saying: Also thou wast with

Ἰησοῦ τοῦ Γαλιλαίου. 70 ὁ δὲ ἠρνήσατο
Jesus the Galilæan. But he denied

ἔμπροσθεν πάντων λέγων· οὐκ οἶδα
before all saying: I know not

τί λέγεις. 71 ἐξελθόντα δὲ εἰς τὸν
what thou sayest. And [4]going out [5]into [6]the

πυλῶνα εἶδεν αὐτὸν ἄλλη καὶ λέγει
[7]porch [2]saw [3]him [1]another and says

could put him to death. 60But they did not find any, though many false witnesses came forward.

Finally two came forward 61and declared, "This fellow said, 'I am able to destroy the temple of God and rebuild it in three days.'"

62Then the high priest stood up and said to Jesus, "Are you not going to answer? What is this testimony that these men are bringing against you?" 63But Jesus remained silent.

The high priest said to him, "I charge you under oath by the living God: Tell us if you are the Christ,[h] the Son of God."

64"Yes, it is as you say," Jesus replied. "But I say to all of you: In the future you will see the Son of Man sitting at the right hand of the Mighty One and coming on the clouds of heaven."

65Then the high priest tore his clothes and said, "He has spoken blasphemy! Why do we need any more witnesses? Look, now you have heard the blasphemy. 66What do you think?"

"He is worthy of death," they answered.

67Then they spit in his face and struck him with their fists. Others slapped him 68and said, "Prophesy to us, Christ. Who hit you?"

Peter Disowns Jesus

69Now Peter was sitting out in the courtyard, and a servant girl came to him. "You also were with Jesus of Galilee," she said.

70But he denied it before them all. "I don't know what you're talking about," he said.

71Then he went out to the gateway, where another girl saw him and said to the

[h]*63* Or *Messiah*; also in verse 68

*said to those who were there, "This man was with Jesus of Nazareth."

72 And again he denied *it* with an oath, "I do not know the man."

73 And a little later the bystanders came up and said to Peter, "Surely you too are *one* of them; for the way you talk gives you away."

74 Then he began to curse and swear, "I do not know the man!" And immediately a cock crowed.

75 And Peter remembered the word which Jesus had said, "Before a cock crows, you will deny Me three times." And he went out and wept bitterly.

τοῖς ἐκεῖ· οὗτος ἦν μετὰ Ἰησοῦ τοῦ
to the [ones] there: This man was with Jesus the
Ναζωραίου. 72 καὶ πάλιν ἠρνήσατο
Nazarene. And again he denied
μετὰ ὅρκου ὅτι οὐκ οἶδα τὸν ἄνθρωπον.
with an oath[,] – I know not the man.
73 μετὰ μικρὸν δὲ προσελθόντες οἱ
And after a little approaching the [ones]
ἑστῶτες εἶπον τῷ Πέτρῳ· ἀληθῶς καὶ
standing said – to Peter: Truly also
σὺ ἐξ αὐτῶν εἶ, καὶ γὰρ ἡ λαλιά σου
thou of them art, for indeed the speech of thee
δῆλόν σε ποιεῖ. 74 τότε ἤρξατο καταθε-
manifest thee makes. Then he began to
ματίζειν καὶ ὀμνύειν ὅτι οὐκ οἶδα τὸν
curse and to swear[,] – I know not the
ἄνθρωπον. καὶ εὐθὺς ἀλέκτωρ ἐφώνησεν
man. And immediately a cock crowed.
75 καὶ ἐμνήσθη ὁ Πέτρος τοῦ ῥήματος
And remembered – Peter the word
Ἰησοῦ εἰρηκότος ὅτι πρὶν ἀλέκτορα
of Jesus having said[,] – Before a cock
φωνῆσαι τρὶς ἀπαρνήσῃ με· καὶ
to crow[b] three times thou wilt deny me; and
ἐξελθὼν ἔξω ἔκλαυσεν πικρῶς.
going forth outside he wept bitterly.

people there, "This fellow was with Jesus of Nazareth."

72 He denied it again, with an oath: "I don't know the man!"

73 After a little while, those standing there went up to Peter and said, "Surely you are one of them, for your accent gives you away."

74 Then he began to call down curses on himself and he swore to them, "I don't know the man!"

Immediately a rooster crowed. 75 Then Peter remembered the word Jesus had spoken: "Before the rooster crows, you will disown me three times." And he went outside and wept bitterly.

Chapter 27

Judas' Remorse

NOW when morning had come, all the chief priests and the elders of the people took counsel against Jesus to put Him to death;

2 and they bound Him, and led Him away, and delivered Him up to Pilate the governor.

3 Then when Judas, who had betrayed Him, saw that He had been condemned, he felt remorse and returned the thirty pieces of silver to the chief priests and elders,

4 saying, "I have sinned by betraying innocent blood." But they said, "What is that to us? See *to that* yourself!"

5 And he threw the pieces of silver into the sanctuary and departed; and he went away and hanged himself.

6 And the chief priests took the pieces of silver and said, "It is not lawful to put them into the temple treasury, since it is the price of blood."

7 And they counseled together and with the money bought the Potter's Field as a burial place for strangers.

27 Πρωΐας δὲ γενομένης συμβούλιον
And early morning coming[a] counsel
= when early morning came
ἔλαβον πάντες οἱ ἀρχιερεῖς καὶ οἱ
took all the chief priests and the
πρεσβύτεροι τοῦ λαοῦ κατὰ τοῦ
elders of the people against –
Ἰησοῦ ὥστε θανατῶσαι αὐτόν· 2 καὶ
Jesus so as to put to death him; and
δήσαντες αὐτὸν ἀπήγαγον καὶ παρ-
having bound him they led away and de-
έδωκαν Πιλάτῳ τῷ ἡγεμόνι. 3 Τότε
livered to Pilate the governor. Then
ἰδὼν Ἰούδας ὁ παραδοὺς αὐτὸν
[6]seeing [1]Judas [2]the [one] [3]having betrayed [4]him
ὅτι κατεκρίθη, μεταμεληθεὶς ἔστρεψεν τὰ
that he was condemned, repenting returned the
τριάκοντα ἀργύρια τοῖς ἀρχιερεῦσιν
thirty pieces of silver to the chief priests
καὶ πρεσβυτέροις 4 λέγων· ἥμαρτον
and elders saying: I sinned
παραδοὺς αἷμα ἀθῷον. οἱ δὲ εἶπαν·
betraying blood innocent. But they said:
τί πρὸς ἡμᾶς; σὺ ὄψῃ. 5 καὶ ῥίψας
What to us? thou shalt see [to it]. And tossing
τὰ ἀργύρια εἰς τὸν ναὸν ἀν-
the pieces of silver into the shrine he
εχώρησεν, καὶ ἀπελθὼν ἀπήγξατο. 6 οἱ
departed, and going away hanged himself. the
δὲ ἀρχιερεῖς λαβόντες τὰ ἀργύρια εἶπαν·
But chief priests taking the pieces of silver said:
οὐκ ἔξεστιν βαλεῖν αὐτὰ εἰς τὸν
It is not lawful to put them into the
κορβανᾶν, ἐπεὶ τιμὴ αἵματός ἐστιν.
treasury, since price of blood it is.
7 συμβούλιον δὲ λαβόντες ἠγόρασαν ἐξ
So counsel taking they bought of(with)
αὐτῶν τὸν ἀγρὸν τοῦ κεραμέως εἰς ταφὴν
them the field of the potter for burial

Chapter 27

Judas Hangs Himself

EARLY in the morning, all the chief priests and the elders of the people came to the decision to put Jesus to death. 2 They bound him, led him away and handed him over to Pilate, the governor.

3 When Judas, who had betrayed him, saw that Jesus was condemned, he was seized with remorse and returned the thirty silver coins to the chief priests and the elders. 4 "I have sinned," he said, "for I have betrayed innocent blood."

"What is that to us?" they replied. "That's your responsibility."

5 So Judas threw the money into the temple and left. Then he went away and hanged himself.

6 The chief priests picked up the coins and said, "It is against the law to put this into the treasury, since it is blood money." 7 So they decided to use the money to buy the potter's field as a burial place for foreigners.

[8]For this reason that
field has been called the
Field of Blood to this day.
[9]Then that which was
spoken through Jeremiah
the prophet was fulfilled,
saying, "AND THEY TOOK
THE THIRTY PIECES OF SILVER,
THE PRICE OF THE ONE WHOSE
PRICE HAD BEEN SET by the
sons of Israel;
[10]AND THEY GAVE THEM
FOR THE POTTER'S FIELD, AS
THE LORD DIRECTED ME."

Jesus before Pilate

[11]Now Jesus stood before
the governor, and the governor questioned Him, saying, "Are You the King of
the Jews?" And Jesus said
to him, "*It is as* you say."
[12]And while He was being
accused by the chief priests
and elders, He made no answer.
[13]Then Pilate *said to
Him, "Do You not hear
how many things they testify against You?"
[14]And He did not answer
him with regard to even a
single charge, so that the
governor was quite
amazed.
[15]Now at *the* feast the
governor was accustomed
to release for the multitude
any one prisoner whom
they wanted.
[16]And they were holding
at that time a notorious
prisoner, called Barabbas.
[17]When therefore they
were gathered together, Pilate said to them, "Whom
do you want me to release
for you? Barabbas, or Jesus
who is called Christ?"
[18]For he knew that be-
cause of envy they had delivered Him up.
[19]And while he was sit-
ting on the judgment seat,
his wife sent to him, saying,
"Have nothing to do with
that righteous Man; for last
night I suffered greatly in a

τοῖς ξένοις. **8** διὸ ἐκλήθη ὁ ἀγρὸς
for the strangers. Wherefore was called – field
ἐκεῖνος ἀγρὸς αἵματος ἕως τῆς σήμερον.
that Field of blood until – to-day.
9 τότε ἐπληρώθη τὸ ῥηθὲν διὰ
Then was fulfilled the [thing] spoken through
Ἰερεμίου τοῦ προφήτου λέγοντος· καὶ
Jeremiah the prophet saying: And
ἔλαβον τὰ τριάκοντα ἀργύρια, τὴν
they took the thirty pieces of silver, the
τιμὴν τοῦ τετιμημένου ὃν ἐτιμήσαντο
price of the [one] *having been* priced whom they priced
ἀπὸ υἱῶν Ἰσραήλ, **10** καὶ ἔδωκαν
from [the] sons of Israel, and gave
αὐτὰ εἰς τὸν ἀγρὸν τοῦ κεραμέως, καθὰ
them for the field of the potter, as
συνέταξέν μοι κύριος. **11** Ὁ δὲ
directed me [the] Lord. – And
Ἰησοῦς ἐστάθη ἔμπροσθεν τοῦ ἡγεμόνος·
Jesus stood before the governor;
καὶ ἐπηρώτησεν αὐτὸν ὁ ἡγεμὼν λέγων·
and questioned him the governor saying:
σὺ εἶ ὁ βασιλεὺς τῶν Ἰουδαίων; ὁ δὲ
Thou art the king of the Jews? – And
Ἰησοῦς ἔφη· σὺ λέγεις. **12** καὶ ἐν
Jesus said: Thou sayest. And in
τῷ κατηγορεῖσθαι αὐτὸν ὑπὸ τῶν
the to be accused him[e] by the
=as he was accused
ἀρχιερέων καὶ πρεσβυτέρων οὐδὲν
chief priests and elders nothing
ἀπεκρίνατο. **13** τότε λέγει αὐτῷ ὁ Πιλᾶτος·
he answered. Then says to him – Pilate:
οὐκ ἀκούεις πόσα σου κατα-
Hearest thou not what things [3]thee [1]they
μαρτυροῦσιν; **14** καὶ οὐκ ἀπεκρίθη αὐτῷ
[2]give evidence against? And he answered not him
πρὸς οὐδὲ ἓν ῥῆμα, ὥστε θαυμάζειν
to not one word, so as to marvel
=so that the governor marvelled
τὸν ἡγεμόνα λίαν. **15** Κατὰ δὲ ἑορτὴν
the governor[b] exceedingly. Now at a feast
εἰώθει ὁ ἡγεμὼν ἀπολύειν ἕνα τῷ ὄχλῳ
was accustomed the governor to release [3]one [1]to the [2]crowd
δέσμιον ὃν ἤθελον. **16** εἶχον δὲ τότε
[4]prisoner whom they wished. And they had then
δέσμιον ἐπίσημον λεγόμενον Βαραββᾶν.
prisoner a notable named Barabbas.
17 συνηγμένων οὖν αὐτῶν εἶπεν αὐτοῖς
Therefore having assembled them[a] said to them
=when they were assembled
ὁ Πιλᾶτος· τίνα θέλετε ἀπολύσω
– Pilate: Whom do ye wish I may release
ὑμῖν, [τὸν] Βαραββᾶν ἢ Ἰησοῦν τὸν
to you, – Barabbas or Jesus –
λεγόμενον χριστόν; **18** ᾔδει γὰρ ὅτι
called Christ? for he knew that
διὰ φθόνον παρέδωκαν αὐτόν. **19** Καθη-
because of envy they delivered him. sit-
μένου δὲ αὐτοῦ ἐπὶ τοῦ βήματος
ting Now him[a] on the tribunal
=Now as he sat
ἀπέστειλεν πρὸς αὐτὸν ἡ γυνὴ αὐτοῦ
sent to him the wife of him
λέγουσα· μηδὲν σοὶ καὶ τῷ δικαίῳ
saying: Nothing to thee and – just man
ἐκείνῳ· πολλὰ γὰρ ἔπαθον σήμερον κατ᾽
to that; for many things I suffered to-day by

[8]That is why it has been
called the Field of Blood to
this day. [9]Then what was
spoken by Jeremiah the
prophet was fulfilled:
"They took the thirty silver
coins, the price set on him
by the people of Israel,
[10]and they used them to
buy the potter's field, as
the Lord commanded
me."[i]

Jesus Before Pilate

[11]Meanwhile Jesus stood
before the governor, and
the governor asked him,
"Are you the king of the
Jews?"
"Yes, it is as you say,"
Jesus replied.
[12]When he was accused
by the chief priests and the
elders, he gave no answer.
[13]Then Pilate asked him,
"Don't you hear the testimony they are bringing
against you?" [14]But Jesus
made no reply, not even to
a single charge—to the
great amazement of the
governor.
[15]Now it was the gover-
nor's custom at the Feast to
release a prisoner chosen
by the crowd. [16]At that
time they had a notorious
prisoner, called Barabbas.
[17]So when the crowd had
gathered, Pilate asked
them, "Which one do you
want me to release to you:
Barabbas, or Jesus who is
called Christ?" [18]For he
knew it was out of envy
that they had handed Jesus
over to him.
[19]While Pilate was sitting
on the judge's seat, his wife
sent him this message:
"Don't have anything to do
with that innocent man, for
I have suffered a great deal

[i]*10* See Zech. 11:12,13; Jer. 19:1-13; 32:6-9.

dream because of Him.”
20 But the chief priests and
the elders persuaded the
multitudes to ask for
Barabbas, and to put Jesus
to death.
21 But the governor an-
swered and said to them,
“Which of the two do you
want me to release for
you?” And they said,
“Barabbas.”
22 Pilate *said to them,
“Then what shall I do with
Jesus who is called
Christ?” They all *said,
“Let Him be crucified!”
23 And he said, “Why,
what evil has He done?”
But they kept shouting all
the more, saying, “Let
Him be crucified!”
24 And when Pilate saw
that he was accomplishing
nothing, but rather that a
riot was starting, he took
water and washed his
hands in front of the multitude, saying, “I am inno-
cent of this Man's blood;
see *to that* yourselves.”
25 And all the people an-
swered and said, “His
blood *be* on us and on our
children!”
26 Then he released
Barabbas for them; but after having Jesus scourged,
he delivered Him to be
crucified.

Jesus Is Mocked

27 Then the soldiers of the
governor took Jesus into
the Praetorium and gath-
ered the whole *Roman* cohort around Him.
28 And they stripped Him,
and put a scarlet robe on
Him.
29 And after weaving a
crown of thorns, they put it
on His head, and a reed in
His right hand; and they
kneeled down before Him
and mocked Him, saying,
“Hail, King of the Jews!”
30 And they spat on Him,
and took the reed and *began* to beat Him on the
head.
31 And after they had

ὄναρ δι' αὐτόν. 20 Οἱ δὲ ἀρχιερεῖς
a dream because of him. But the chief priests
καὶ οἱ πρεσβύτεροι ἔπεισαν τοὺς
and the elders persuaded the
ὄχλους ἵνα αἰτήσωνται τὸν Βαραββᾶν,
crowds that they should ask – Barabbas,
τὸν δὲ Ἰησοῦν ἀπολέσωσιν. 21 ἀπο-
– and Jesus should destroy. So
κριθεὶς δὲ ὁ ἡγεμὼν εἶπεν αὐτοῖς·
answering the governor said to them:
τίνα θέλετε ἀπὸ τῶν δύο ἀπολύσω
Which do ye wish from the two I may release
ὑμῖν; οἱ δὲ εἶπαν· τὸν Βαραββᾶν.
to you? And they said: – Barabbas.
22 λέγει αὐτοῖς ὁ Πιλᾶτος· τί οὖν
Says to them – Pilate: What then
ποιήσω Ἰησοῦν τὸν λεγόμενον χριστόν;
may I do [to] Jesus – called Christ?
λέγουσιν πάντες· σταυρωθήτω. 23 ὁ δὲ
They say all: Let him be crucified. But he
ἔφη· τί γὰρ κακὸν ἐποίησεν; οἱ δὲ
said: Why what evil did he? But they
περισσῶς ἔκραζον λέγοντες· σταυρω-
more cried out saying: Let him be
θήτω. 24 ἰδὼν δὲ ὁ Πιλᾶτος ὅτι οὐδὲν
crucified. And seeing – Pilate that nothing
ὠφελεῖ ἀλλὰ μᾶλλον θόρυβος γίνεται,
is gained but rather an uproar occurs,
λαβὼν ὕδωρ ἀπενίψατο τὰς χεῖρας
taking water he washed the(his) hands
κατέναντι τοῦ ὄχλου λέγων· ἀθῷός
in front of the crowd saying: Innocent
εἰμι ἀπὸ τοῦ αἵματος τούτου· ὑμεῖς
I am from the blood of this man; ye
ὄψεσθε. 25 καὶ ἀποκριθεὶς πᾶς ὁ λαὸς
will see [to it]. And answering all the people
εἶπεν· τὸ αἷμα αὐτοῦ ἐφ' ἡμᾶς καὶ
said: The blood of him on us and
ἐπὶ τὰ τέκνα ἡμῶν. 26 τότε ἀπέλυσεν
on the children of us. Then he released
αὐτοῖς τὸν Βαραββᾶν, τὸν δὲ Ἰησοῦν
to them – Barabbas, – but Jesus
φραγελλώσας παρέδωκεν ἵνα σταυρωθῇ.
having scourged he delivered that he might be crucified.
27 Τότε οἱ στρατιῶται τοῦ ἡγεμόνος
Then the soldiers of the governor
παραλαβόντες τὸν Ἰησοῦν εἰς τὸ πραιτώ-
having taken – Jesus into the præ-
ριον συνήγαγον ἐπ' αὐτὸν ὅλην τὴν
torium assembled against him all the
σπεῖραν. 28 καὶ ἐκδύσαντες αὐτὸν χλαμύδα
band. And stripping him cloak
κοκκίνην περιέθηκαν αὐτῷ, 29 καὶ
a purple they placed round him, and
πλέξαντες στέφανον ἐξ ἀκανθῶν ἐπέθηκαν
having plaited a crown of thorns they placed [it] *on*
ἐπὶ τῆς κεφαλῆς αὐτοῦ καὶ κάλαμον
on the head of him and a reed
ἐν τῇ δεξιᾷ αὐτοῦ, καὶ γονυπετή-
in the right [hand] of him, and bowing
σαντες ἔμπροσθεν αὐτοῦ ἐνέπαιξαν αὐτῷ
the knee in front of him mocked at him
λέγοντες· χαῖρε, βασιλεῦ τῶν Ἰουδαίων,
saying: Hail, king of the Jews,
30 καὶ ἐμπτύσαντες εἰς αὐτὸν ἔλαβον
and spitting at him took

today in a dream because of
him.”
20 But the chief priests and
the elders persuaded the
crowd to ask for Barabbas
and to have Jesus execut-
ed.
21 “Which of the two do
you want me to release to
you?” asked the governor.
“Barabbas,” they an-
swered.
22 “What shall I do, then,
with Jesus who is called
Christ?” Pilate asked.
They all answered, “Cru-
cify him!”
23 “Why? What crime has
he committed?” asked Pi-
late.
But they shouted all the
louder, “Crucify him!”
24 When Pilate saw that he
was getting nowhere, but
that instead an uproar was
starting, he took water and
washed his hands in front
of the crowd. “I am inno-
cent of this man's blood,”
he said. “It is your responsibility!”
25 All the people an-
swered, “Let his blood be
on us and on our children!”
26 Then he released Bar-
abbas to them. But he had
Jesus flogged, and handed
him over to be crucified.

The Soldiers Mock Jesus

27 Then the governor's
soldiers took Jesus into the
Praetorium and gathered
the whole company of sol-
diers around him. 28 They
stripped him and put a scarlet robe on him, 29 and then
twisted together a crown of
thorns and set it on his
head. They put a staff in his
right hand and knelt in front
of him and mocked him.
“Hail, king of the Jews!”
they said. 30 They spit on
him, and took the staff and
struck him on the head
again and again. 31 After
they had mocked him, they

mocked Him, they took
His robe off and put His
garments on Him, and led
Him away to crucify *Him*.
32And as they were com-
ing out, they found a man of
Cyrene named Simon,
whom they pressed into
service to bear His cross.

The Crucifixion

33And when they had
come to a place called Golgotha, which means Place
of a Skull,
34they gave Him wine to
drink mingled with gall; and
after tasting *it*, He was unwilling to drink.
35And when they had
crucified Him, they divided
up His garments among
themselves, casting lots;
36and sitting down, they
began to keep watch over
Him there.
37And they put up above
His head the charge against
Him which read, "THIS IS
JESUS THE KING OF
THE JEWS."
38At that time two rob-
bers *were crucified with
Him, one on the right and
one on the left.
39And those passing by
were hurling abuse at Him,
wagging their heads,
40and saying, "You who
are going to destroy the
temple and rebuild it in
three days, save Yourself!
If You are the Son of God,
come down from the
cross."
41In the same way the
chief priests also, along
with the scribes and elders,
were mocking *Him*, and
saying,
42"He saved others; He
cannot save Himself. He is
the King of Israel; let Him
now come down from the
cross, and we shall believe
in Him.
43"HE TRUSTS IN GOD; LET

τὸν κάλαμον καὶ ἔτυπτον εἰς τὴν κεφαλὴν
the reed and struck at the head
αὐτοῦ. 31 καὶ ὅτε ἐνέπαιξαν αὐτῷ,
of him. And when they mocked at him,
ἐξέδυσαν αὐτὸν τὴν χλαμύδα καὶ ἐνέδυσαν
they took off him the cloak and put on
αὐτὸν τὰ ἱμάτια αὐτοῦ, καὶ ἀπήγαγον
him the garments of him, and led away
αὐτὸν εἰς τὸ σταυρῶσαι. 32 Ἐξερχόμενοι
him – – to crucify. going forth
δὲ εὗρον ἄνθρωπον Κυρηναῖον, ὀνό-
And they found *a man* a Cyrenian, by
ματι Σίμωνα· τοῦτον ἠγγάρευσαν ἵνα
name Simon; this man they impressed that
ἄρῃ τὸν σταυρὸν αὐτοῦ. 33 Καὶ
he should bear the cross of him. And
ἐλθόντες εἰς τόπον λεγόμενον Γολγοθά,
coming to a place called Golgotha,
ὅ ἐστιν κρανίου τόπος λεγόμενος,
which is [3]of a skull [2]A place [1]called,
34 ἔδωκαν αὐτῷ πιεῖν οἶνον μετὰ
they gave him to drink wine with
χολῆς μεμιγμένον· καὶ γευσάμενος οὐκ
gall *having been* mixed; and tasting not
ἠθέλησεν πιεῖν. 35 σταυρώσαντες δὲ
he would *to* drink. And having crucified
αὐτὸν διεμερίσαντο τὰ ἱμάτια αὐτοῦ
him they divided the garments of him
βάλλοντες κλῆρον, 36 καὶ καθήμενοι ἐτήρουν
casting a lot, and sitting they guarded
αὐτὸν ἐκεῖ. 37 καὶ ἐπέθηκαν ἐπάνω
him there. And they placed *on* above
τῆς κεφαλῆς αὐτοῦ τὴν αἰτίαν αὐτοῦ
the head of him the charge of him
γεγραμμένην· ΟΥΤΟΣ ΕΣΤΙΝ ΙΗΣΟΥΣ
having been written: THIS IS JESUS
Ο ΒΑΣΙΛΕΥΣ ΤΩΝ ΙΟΥΔΑΙΩΝ. 38 Τότε
THE KING OF THE JEWS. Then
σταυροῦνται σὺν αὐτῷ δύο λῃσταί,
are crucified with him two robbers,
εἷς ἐκ δεξιῶν καὶ εἷς ἐξ εὐωνύμων.
one on [the] right and one on [the] left.
39 Οἱ δὲ παραπορευόμενοι ἐβλασφήμουν
And the [ones] passing by blasphemed
αὐτὸν κινοῦντες τὰς κεφαλὰς αὐτῶν
him wagging the heads of them
40 καὶ λέγοντες· ὁ καταλύων τὸν ναὸν
and saying: The [one] destroying the shrine
καὶ ἐν τρισὶν ἡμέραις οἰκοδομῶν,
and in three days building [it],
σῶσον σεαυτόν, εἰ υἱὸς εἶ τοῦ θεοῦ,
save thyself, if Son thou art – of God,
καὶ κατάβηθι ἀπὸ τοῦ σταυροῦ. 41 ὁμοίως
and come down from the cross. Likewise
[καὶ] οἱ ἀρχιερεῖς ἐμπαίζοντες μετὰ
also the chief priests mocking with
τῶν γραμματέων καὶ πρεσβυτέρων ἔλεγον
the scribes and elders said:
42 ἄλλους ἔσωσεν, ἑαυτὸν οὐ δύναται
Others he saved, himself he cannot
σῶσαι· βασιλεὺς Ἰσραήλ ἐστιν,
to save; King of Israel he is,
καταβάτω νῦν ἀπὸ τοῦ σταυροῦ καὶ
let him come down now from the cross and
πιστεύσομεν ἐπ᾿ αὐτόν. 43 πέποιθεν
we will believe on him. He has trusted

took off the robe and put
his own clothes on him.
Then they led him away to
crucify him.

The Crucifixion

32As they were going out,
they met a man from Cyre-
ne, named Simon, and they
forced him to carry the
cross. 33They came to a
place called Golgotha
(which means The Place of
the Skull). 34There they offered Jesus wine to drink,
mixed with gall; but after
tasting it, he refused to
drink it. 35When they had
crucified him, they divided
up his clothes by casting
lots.[j] 36And sitting down,
they kept watch over him
there. 37Above his head
they placed the written
charge against him: THIS IS
JESUS, THE KING OF THE
JEWS. 38Two robbers were
crucified with him, one on
his right and one on his left.
39Those who passed by
hurled insults at him, shaking their heads 40and saying, "You who are going to
destroy the temple and
build it in three days, save
yourself! Come down from
the cross, if you are the Son
of God!"
41In the same way the
chief priests, the teachers
of the law and the elders
mocked him. 42"He saved
others," they said, "but he
can't save himself! He's
the King of Israel! Let him
come down now from the
cross, and we will believe
in him. 43He trusts in God.

j35 A few late manuscripts *lots that the word spoken by the prophet might be fulfilled: "They divided my garments among themselves and cast lots for my clothing"* (Psalm 22:18)

HIM DELIVER *Him* now, IF
HE TAKES PLEASURE IN HIM;
for He said, 'I am the Son
of God.' "
44And the robbers also
who had been crucified
with Him were casting the
same insult at Him.
45Now from the [u]sixth
hour darkness fell upon all
the land until the [v]ninth
hour.
46And about the ninth
hour Jesus cried out with a
loud voice, saying, "ELI,
ELI, LAMA SABACHTHANI?"
that is, "MY GOD, MY GOD,
WHY HAST THOU FORSAKEN
ME?"
47And some of those who
were standing there, when
they heard it, *began* saying, "This man is calling for
Elijah."
48And immediately one of
them ran, and taking a
sponge, he filled it with
sour wine, and put it on a
reed, and gave Him a drink.
49But the rest *of them*
said, "Let us see whether
Elijah will come to save
Him."[w]
50And Jesus cried out
again with a loud voice, and
yielded up *His* spirit.
51And behold, the veil of
the temple was torn in two
from top to bottom, and the
earth shook; and the rocks
were split,
52and the tombs were
opened; and many bodies
of the saints who had fallen
asleep were raised;
53and coming out of the
tombs after His resurrec-
tion they entered the holy
city and appeared to many.
54Now the centurion, and
those who were with him
keeping guard over Jesus,
when they saw the earth-
quake and the things that
were happening, became
very frightened and said,
"Truly this was the Son of
God!"
55And many women were

[u]I.e., noon
[v]I.e., 3 p.m.
[w]Some early mss. add: *And another took a spear and pierced His side, and there came out water and blood.* (cf. John 19:34)

ἐπὶ τὸν θεόν, ῥυσάσθω νῦν εἰ θέλει
on – God, let him rescue now if he wants
αὐτόν· εἶπεν γὰρ ὅτι θεοῦ εἰμι υἱός.
him; for he said[,] – of God I am Son.
44 τὸ δ' αὐτὸ καὶ οἱ λῃσταὶ οἱ συσταυρω-
And the same also the robbers – crucified
θέντες σὺν αὐτῷ ὠνείδιζον αὐτόν. 45 Ἀπὸ
with with him reproached him. from
δὲ ἕκτης ὥρας σκότος ἐγένετο ἐπὶ
Now [the] sixth hour darkness occurred over
πᾶσαν τὴν γῆν ἕως ὥρας ἐνάτης.
all the land until hour [the] ninth.
46 περὶ δὲ τὴν ἐνάτην ὥραν ἀνεβόησεν ὁ
And about the ninth hour cried out –
Ἰησους φωνῇ μεγάλῃ λέγων· ἠλὶ ἠλὶ
Jesus voice with a great saying: Eli Eli
λεμὰ σαβαχθάνι; τοῦτ' ἔστιν· θεέ μου
lema sabachthani? this is: God of me[,]
θεέ μου, ἱνατί με ἐγκατέλιπες; 47 τινὲς
God of me, why me didst thou forsake? some
δὲ τῶν ἐκεῖ ἑστηκότων ἀκούσαντες
And of the [ones] there standing hearing
ἔλεγον ὅτι Ἠλίαν φωνεῖ οὗτος.
said[,] – [3]Elias [2]calls [1]this man.
48 καὶ εὐθέως δραμὼν εἷς ἐξ αὐτῶν καὶ
And immediately running one of them and
λαβὼν σπόγγον πλήσας τε ὄξους καὶ
taking a sponge and filling of(with) vinegar and
περιθεὶς καλάμῳ ἐπότιζεν αὐτόν.
putting [it] round a reed gave to drink him.
49 οἱ δὲ λοιποὶ εἶπαν· ἄφες ἴδωμεν
But the rest said: Leave[,] let us see
εἰ ἔρχεται Ἠλίας σώσων αὐτόν. 50 ὁ
if comes Elias saving him. –
δὲ Ἰησοῦς πάλιν κράξας φωνῇ
And Jesus again crying out voice
μεγάλῃ ἀφῆκεν τὸ πνεῦμα. 51 Καὶ
with a great released the(his) spirit. And
ἰδοὺ τὸ καταπέτασμα τοῦ ναοῦ ἐσχίσθη
behold the veil of the shrine was rent
[ἀπ'] ἄνωθεν ἕως κάτω εἰς δύο, καὶ ἡ
from above to below in two, and the
γῆ ἐσείσθη, καὶ αἱ πέτραι ἐσχίσ-
earth was shaken, and the rocks were
θησαν, 52 καὶ τὰ μνημεῖα ἀνεῴχθησαν
rent, and the tombs were opened
καὶ πολλὰ σώματα τῶν κεκοιμημένων
and many bodies of the having fallen asleep
ἁγίων ἠγέρθησαν· 53 καὶ ἐξελθόντες
saints were raised; and coming forth
ἐκ τῶν μνημείων μετὰ τὴν ἔγερσιν
out of the tombs after the rising
αὐτοῦ εἰσῆλθον εἰς τὴν ἁγίαν πόλιν καὶ
of him entered into the holy city and
ἐνεφανίσθησαν πολλοῖς. 54 Ὁ δὲ ἑκατόν-
appeared to many. And the centu-
ταρχος καὶ οἱ μετ' αὐτοῦ τηροῦντες
rion and the [ones] with him guarding
τὸν Ἰησοῦν ἰδόντες τὸν σεισμὸν καὶ
– Jesus seeing the earthquake and
τὰ γινόμενα ἐφοβήθησαν σφόδρα,
the things happening feared exceedingly,
λέγοντες· ἀληθῶς θεοῦ υἱὸς ἦν οὗτος.
saying: Truly [4]of God [3]Son [2]was [1]this man.
55 Ἦσαν δὲ ἐκεῖ γυναῖκες πολλαί
Now there were there women many

Let God rescue him now if
he wants him, for he said, 'I
am the Son of God.' " 44In
the same way the robbers
who were crucified with
him also heaped insults on
him.

The Death of Jesus

45From the sixth hour un-
til the ninth hour darkness
came over all the land.
46About the ninth hour
Jesus cried out in a loud
voice, *"Eloi, Eloi,*[k] *lama
sabachthani?"*—which
means, "My God, my God,
why have you forsaken
me?"[l]
47When some of those
standing there heard this,
they said, "He's calling
Elijah."
48Immediately one of
them ran and got a sponge.
He filled it with wine vinegar, put it on a stick, and
offered it to Jesus to drink.
49The rest said, "Now
leave him alone. Let's see
if Elijah comes to save
him."
50And when Jesus had
cried out again in a loud
voice, he gave up his spirit.
51At that moment the cur-
tain of the temple was torn
in two from top to bottom.
The earth shook and the
rocks split. 52The tombs
broke open and the bodies
of many holy people who
had died were raised to life.
53They came out of the
tombs, and after Jesus' resurrection they went into
the holy city and appeared
to many people.
54When the centurion and
those with him who were
guarding Jesus saw the
earthquake and all that had
happened, they were terrified, and exclaimed,
"Surely he was the Son[m] of
God!"
55Many women were

[k]*46* Some manuscripts *Eli, Eli*
[l]*46* Psalm 22:1
[m]*54* Or *a son*

there looking on from a distance, who had followed Jesus from Galilee, ministering to Him,

56among whom was Mary Magdalene, *along with* Mary the mother of James and Joseph, and the mother of the sons of Zebedee.

Jesus Is Buried

57And when it was evening, there came a rich man from Arimathea, named Joseph, who himself had also become a disciple of Jesus.

58This man went to Pilate and asked for the body of Jesus. Then Pilate ordered *it* to be given over *to him.*

59And Joseph took the body and wrapped it in a clean linen cloth,

60and laid it in his own new tomb, which he had hewn out in the rock; and he rolled a large stone against the entrance of the tomb and went away.

61And Mary Magdalene was there, and the other Mary, sitting opposite the grave.

62Now on the next day, which is *the one* after the preparation, the chief priests and the Pharisees gathered together with Pilate,

63and said, "Sir, we remember that when He was still alive that deceiver said, 'After three days I *am to* rise again.'

64"Therefore, give orders for the grave to be made secure until the third day, lest the disciples come and steal Him away and say to the people, 'He has risen from the dead,' and the last deception will be worse than the first."

65Pilate said to them, "You have a guard; go,

ἀπὸ μακρόθεν θεωροῦσαι, αἵτινες ἠκολού-
from afar beholding, who followed
θησαν τῷ Ἰησοῦ ἀπὸ τῆς Γαλιλαίας
– Jesus from – Galilee
διακονοῦσαι αὐτῷ· 56 ἐν αἷς ἦν
ministering to him; among whom was
Μαρία ἡ Μαγδαληνή, καὶ Μαρία ἡ
Mary the Magdalene, and Mary the
τοῦ Ἰακώβου καὶ Ἰωσὴφ μήτηρ, καὶ ἡ
– of James and of Joseph mother, and the
μήτηρ τῶν υἱῶν Ζεβεδαίου.
mother of the sons of Zebedee.
57 Ὀψίας δὲ γενομένης ἦλθεν ἄνθρωπος
Now evening having come* came man
= when evening had come
πλούσιος ἀπὸ Ἁριμαθαίας, τοὔνομα Ἰωσήφ,
a rich from Arimathæa, the name Joseph,
ὃς καὶ αὐτὸς ἐμαθητεύθη τῷ Ἰησοῦ·
who also himself was discipled – to Jesus;
58 οὗτος προσελθὼν τῷ Πιλάτῳ ᾐτήσατο
this man approaching – *to* Pilate asked
τὸ σῶμα τοῦ Ἰησοῦ. τότε ὁ Πιλᾶτος
the body – of Jesus. Then – Pilate
ἐκέλευσεν ἀποδοθῆναι. 59 καὶ λαβὼν
commanded [it] to be given [him]. And taking
τὸ σῶμα ὁ Ἰωσὴφ ἐνετύλιξεν αὐτὸ [ἐν]
the body – Joseph wrapped it in
σινδόνι καθαρᾷ, 60 καὶ ἔθηκεν αὐτὸ ἐν
sheet a clean, and placed it in
τῷ καινῷ αὐτοῦ μνημείῳ ὃ ἐλατό-
the new of him tomb which he
μησεν ἐν τῇ πέτρᾳ, καὶ προσκυλίσας
hewed in the rock, and having rolled *to*
λίθον μέγαν τῇ θύρᾳ τοῦ μνημείου
stone a great to the door of the tomb
ἀπῆλθεν. 61 Ἦν δὲ ἐκεῖ Μαριὰμ
went away. And there was there Mary
ἡ Μαγδαληνὴ καὶ ἡ ἄλλη Μαρία,
the Magdalene and the other Mary,
καθήμεναι ἀπέναντι τοῦ τάφου. 62 Τῇ
sitting opposite the grave. on the
δὲ ἐπαύριον, ἥτις ἐστὶν μετὰ τὴν παρα-
And morrow, which is after the prepara-
σκευήν, συνήχθησαν οἱ ἀρχιερεῖς
tion, were assembled the chief priests
καὶ οἱ Φαρισαῖοι πρὸς Πιλᾶτον 63 λέ-
and the Pharisees to Pilate say-
γοντες· κύριε, ἐμνήσθημεν ὅτι ἐκεῖνος
ing: Sir, we remembered that that
ὁ πλάνος εἶπεν ἔτι ζῶν· μετὰ τρεῖς
– deceiver said yet living: After three
ἡμέρας ἐγείρομαι. 64 κέλευσον οὖν
days I am raised. Command therefore
ἀσφαλισθῆναι τὸν τάφον ἕως τῆς
to be made fast the grave until the
τρίτης ἡμέρας, μήποτε ἐλθόντες οἱ μαθηταὶ
third day, lest coming the disciples
κλέψωσιν αὐτὸν καὶ εἴπωσιν τῷ λαῷ·
may steal him and may say to the people:
ἠγέρθη ἀπὸ τῶν νεκρῶν, καὶ ἔσται
He was raised from the dead, and will be
ἡ ἐσχάτη πλάνη χείρων τῆς πρώτης.
the last deceit worse [than] the first.
65 ἔφη αὐτοῖς ὁ Πιλᾶτος· ἔχετε κου-
Said to them – Pilate: Ye have a

there, watching from a distance. They had followed
Jesus from Galilee to care
for his needs. 56Among
them were Mary Magda-
lene, Mary the mother of
James and Joses, and the
mother of Zebedee's sons.

The Burial of Jesus

57As evening ap-
proached, there came a
rich man from Arimathea,
named Joseph, who had
himself become a disciple
of Jesus. 58Going to Pilate,
he asked for Jesus' body,
and Pilate ordered that it be
given to him. 59Joseph took
the body, wrapped it in a
clean linen cloth, 60and
placed it in his own new
tomb that he had cut out of
the rock. He rolled a big
stone in front of the en-
trance to the tomb and
went away. 61Mary Magda-
lene and the other Mary
were sitting there opposite
the tomb.

The Guard at the Tomb

62The next day, the one
after Preparation Day, the
chief priests and the Pharisees went to Pilate.
63"Sir," they said, "we remember that while he was
still alive that deceiver
said, 'After three days I
will rise again.' 64So give
the order for the tomb to be
made secure until the third
day. Otherwise, his disciples may come and steal
the body and tell the people
that he has been raised
from the dead. This last deception will be worse than
the first."
65"Take a guard," Pilate
answered. "Go, make the

make it *as* secure as you
know how.''
66 And they went and
made the grave secure, and
along with the guard they
set a seal on the stone.

Chapter 28

Jesus Is Risen!

NOW after the Sabbath,
as it began to dawn
toward the first *day* of the
week, Mary Magdalene
and the other Mary came to
look at the grave.
2 And behold, a severe
earthquake had occurred,
for an angel of the Lord descended from heaven and
came and rolled away the
stone and sat upon it.
3 And his appearance was
like lightning, and his garment as white as snow;
4 and the guards shook
for fear of him, and became
like dead men.
5 And the angel answered
and said to the women,
''Do not be afraid; for I
know that you are looking
for Jesus who has been
crucified.
6 ''He is not here, for He
has risen, just as He said.
Come, see the place where
He was lying.
7 ''And go quickly and
tell His disciples that He
has risen from the dead;
and behold, He is going before you into Galilee, there
you will see Him; behold, I
have told you.''
8 And they departed
quickly from the tomb with
fear and great joy and ran to
report it to His disciples.
9 And behold, Jesus met
them and greeted them.
And they came up and took
hold of His feet and wor-
shiped Him.

στωδίαν· ὑπάγετε ἀσφαλίσασθε ὡς οἴδατε.
guard; go ye make fast as ye know*.
66 οἱ δὲ πορευθέντες ἠσφαλίσαντο τὸν
And they going made fast the
τάφον σφραγίσαντες τὸν λίθον μετὰ τῆς
grave sealing the stone with the
κουστωδίας.
guard.

28 Ὀψὲ δὲ σαββάτων, τῇ ἐπιφωσκούσῃ
But late of [the] sabbaths, at the drawing on
εἰς μίαν σαββάτων, ἦλθεν Μαριὰμ ἡ
toward one of [the] sabbaths, came Mary the
= the first day of the week,
Μαγδαληνὴ καὶ ἡ ἄλλη Μαρία θεωρῆσαι
Magdalene and the other Mary to view
τὸν τάφον. **2** καὶ ἰδοὺ σεισμὸς ἐγένετο
the grave. And behold earthquake occurred
μέγας· ἄγγελος γὰρ κυρίου καταβὰς
a great; for an angel of [the] Lord descending
ἐξ οὐρανοῦ καὶ προσελθὼν ἀπεκύλισεν
out of heaven and approaching rolled away
τὸν λίθον καὶ ἐκάθητο ἐπάνω αὐτοῦ.
the stone and sat upon it.
3 ἦν δὲ ἡ εἰδέα αὐτοῦ ὡς ἀστραπή,
And was the appearance of him as lightning,
καὶ τὸ ἔνδυμα αὐτοῦ λευκὸν ὡς χιών.
and the dress of him white as snow.
4 ἀπὸ δὲ τοῦ φόβου αὐτοῦ ἐσείσθησαν
And from the fear of him were shaken
οἱ τηροῦντες καὶ ἐγενήθησαν ὡς
the [ones] guarding and they became as
νεκροί. **5** ἀποκριθεὶς δὲ ὁ ἄγγελος
dead. And answering the angel
εἶπεν ταῖς γυναιξίν· μὴ φοβεῖσθε ὑμεῖς·
said to the women: Fear not ye;
οἶδα γὰρ ὅτι Ἰησοῦν τὸν ἐσταυρω-
for I know that Jesus the [one] ***having been***
μένον ζητεῖτε· **6** οὐκ ἔστιν ὧδε·
crucified ye seek; he is not here;
ἠγέρθη γὰρ καθὼς εἶπεν· δεῦτε ἴδετε τὸν
for he was raised as he said; come see ye the
τόπον ὅπου ἔκειτο. **7** καὶ ταχὺ πορευθεῖσαι
place where he lay. And quickly going
εἴπατε τοῖς μαθηταῖς αὐτοῦ ὅτι ἠγέρθη
tell the disciples of him that he was raised
ἀπὸ τῶν νεκρῶν, καὶ ἰδοὺ προάγει ὑμᾶς
from the dead, and behold he goes before you
εἰς τὴν Γαλιλαίαν, ἐκεῖ αὐτὸν ὄψεσθε.
to – Galilee, there him ye will see.
ἰδοὺ εἶπον ὑμῖν. **8** καὶ ἀπελθοῦσαι ταχὺ
Behold I told you. And going away quickly
ἀπὸ τοῦ μνημείου μετὰ φόβου καὶ χαρᾶς
from the tomb with fear and joy
μεγάλης ἔδραμον ἀπαγγεῖλαι τοῖς
great they ran to announce to the
μαθηταῖς αὐτοῦ. **9** καὶ ἰδοὺ Ἰησοῦς
disciples of him. And behold Jesus
ὑπήντησεν αὐταῖς λέγων· χαίρετε. αἱ δὲ
met them saying: Hail. And they
προσελθοῦσαι ἐκράτησαν αὐτοῦ τοὺς πόδας
approaching held of him the feet
καὶ προσεκύνησαν αὐτῷ. **10** τότε λέγει
and worshipped him. Then says

*** can. See note on page xviii.**

tomb as secure as you
know how.'' 66 So they
went and made the tomb
secure by putting a seal on
the stone and posting the
guard.

Chapter 28

The Resurrection

AFTER the Sabbath, at
dawn on the first day
of the week, Mary Magda-
lene and the other Mary
went to look at the tomb.
2 There was a violent
earthquake, for an angel of
the Lord came down from
heaven and, going to the
tomb, rolled back the stone
and sat on it. 3 His appearance was like lightning, and
his clothes were white as
snow. 4 The guards were so
afraid of him that they
shook and became like
dead men.
5 The angel said to the
women, ''Do not be afraid,
for I know that you are
looking for Jesus, who was
crucified. 6 He is not here;
he has risen, just as he said.
Come and see the place
where he lay. 7 Then go
quickly and tell his disciples: 'He has risen from the
dead and is going ahead of
you into Galilee. There you
will see him.' Now I have
told you.''
8 So the women hurried
away from the tomb, afraid
yet filled with joy, and ran
to tell his disciples. 9 Suddenly Jesus met them.
''Greetings,'' he said. They
came to him, clasped his
feet and worshiped him.

10Then Jesus *said to
them, "Do not be afraid; go
and take word to My brethren to leave for Galilee, and
there they shall see Me."
11Now while they were
on their way, behold, some
of the guard came into the
city and reported to the
chief priests all that had
happened.
12And when they had as-
sembled with the elders
and counseled together,
they gave a large sum of
money to the soldiers,
13and said, "You are to
say, 'His disciples came by
night and stole Him away
while we were asleep.'
14"And if this should
come to the governor's
ears, we will win him over
and keep you out of trou-
ble."
15And they took the
money and did as they had
been instructed; and this
story was widely spread
among the Jews, *and is* to
this day.

The Great Commission

16But the eleven disciples
proceeded to Galilee, to the
mountain which Jesus had
designated.
17And when they saw
Him, they worshiped *Him*;
but some were doubtful.
18And Jesus came up and
spoke to them, saying, "All
authority has been given to
Me in heaven and on earth.
19"Go therefore and
make disciples of all the nations, baptizing them in the
name of the Father and the
Son and the Holy Spirit,
20teaching them to ob-
serve all that I commanded
you; and lo, I am with you
always, even to the end of
the age."

αὐταῖς ὁ Ἰησοῦς· μὴ φοβεῖσθε· ὑπάγετε
to them – Jesus: Fear ye not; go ye
ἀπαγγείλατε τοῖς ἀδελφοῖς μου ἵνα
announce to the brothers of me that
ἀπέλθωσιν εἰς τὴν Γαλιλαίαν, κἀκεῖ
they may go away into – Galilee, and there
με ὄψονται. 11 Πορευομένων δὲ αὐτῶν
me they will see. And going them[a]
=as they were going
ἰδού τινες τῆς κουστωδίας ἐλθόντες εἰς
behold some of the guard coming into
τὴν πόλιν ἀπήγγειλαν τοῖς ἀρχιερεῦσιν
the city announced to the chief priests
ἅπαντα τὰ γενόμενα. 12 καὶ συν-
all the things having happened. And being
αχθέντες μετὰ τῶν πρεσβυτέρων συμβούλιόν
assembled with the elders [3]counsel
τε λαβόντες ἀργύρια ἱκανὰ ἔδωκαν τοῖς
[1]and [2]taking silver enough gave to the
στρατιώταις, 13 λέγοντες· εἴπατε ὅτι οἱ
soldiers, saying: Say ye that the
μαθηταὶ αὐτοῦ νυκτὸς ἐλθόντες ἔκλεψαν
disciples of him of(by) night coming stole
αὐτὸν ἡμῶν κοιμωμένων. 14 καὶ ἐὰν
him we sleeping.[a] And if
=while we slept.
ἀκουσθῇ τοῦτο ἐπὶ τοῦ ἡγεμόνος,
be heard this before the governor,
ἡμεῖς πείσομεν καὶ ὑμᾶς ἀμερίμνους
we will persuade and you free from anxiety
ποιήσομεν. 15 οἱ δὲ λαβόντες ἀργύρια
we will make. And they taking silver
ἐποίησαν ὡς ἐδιδάχθησαν. Καὶ διεφη-
did as they were taught. And was spread
μίσθη ὁ λόγος οὗτος παρὰ Ἰουδαίοις
about – saying this by Jews
μέχρι τῆς σήμερον [ἡμέρας]. 16 Οἱ δὲ
until to-day. So the
ἕνδεκα μαθηταὶ ἐπορεύθησαν εἰς τὴν
eleven disciples went to –
Γαλιλαίαν, εἰς τὸ ὄρος οὗ ἐτάξατο
Galilee, to the mountain where appointed
αὐτοῖς ὁ Ἰησοῦς, 17 καὶ ἰδόντες αὐτὸν
them – Jesus, and seeing him
προσεκύνησαν, οἱ δὲ ἐδίστασαν. 18 καὶ
they worshipped, but some doubted. And
προσελθὼν ὁ Ἰησοῦς ἐλάλησεν αὐτοῖς
approaching – Jesus talked with them
λέγων· ἐδόθη μοι πᾶσα ἐξουσία ἐν
saying: was given to me All authority in
οὐρανῷ καὶ ἐπὶ [τῆς] γῆς. 19 πορευθέντες
heaven and on the earth. Going
οὖν μαθητεύσατε πάντα τὰ ἔθνη, βαπτίζ-
therefore disciple ye all the nations, baptiz-
οντες αὐτοὺς εἰς τὸ ὄνομα τοῦ πατρὸς
ing them in the name of the Father
καὶ τοῦ υἱοῦ καὶ τοῦ ἁγίου πνεύματος,
and of the Son and of the Holy Spirit,
20 διδάσκοντες αὐτοὺς τηρεῖν πάντα
teaching them to observe all things
ὅσα ἐνετειλάμην ὑμῖν· καὶ ἰδοὺ ἐγὼ
whatever I gave command to you; and behold I
μεθ' ὑμῶν εἰμι πάσας τὰς ἡμέρας ἕως
with you am all the days until
τῆς συντελείας τοῦ αἰῶνος.
the completion of the age.

10Then Jesus said to them,
"Do not be afraid. Go and
tell my brothers to go to
Galilee; there they will see
me."

The Guards' Report

11While the women were
on their way, some of the
guards went into the city
and reported to the chief
priests everything that had
happened. 12When the
chief priests had met with
the elders and devised a
plan, they gave the soldiers
a large sum of money,
13telling them, "You are to
say, 'His disciples came
during the night and stole
him away while we were
asleep.' 14If this report gets
to the governor, we will
satisfy him and keep you
out of trouble." 15So the
soldiers took the money
and did as they were in-
structed. And this story has
been widely circulated
among the Jews to this very
day.

The Great Commission

16Then the eleven disci-
ples went to Galilee, to the
mountain where Jesus had
told them to go. 17When
they saw him, they wor-
shiped him; but some
doubted. 18Then Jesus
came to them and said,
"All authority in heaven
and on earth has been given
to me. 19Therefore go and
make disciples of all na-
tions, baptizing them in[n]
the name of the Father and
of the Son and of the Holy
Spirit, 20and teaching them
to obey everything I have
commanded you. And
surely I am with you al-
ways, to the very end of the
age."

[n]19 Or *into*; see Acts 8:16; 19:5; Romans 6:3; 1 Cor. 1:13; 10:2 and Gal. 3:27.

ΚΑΤΑ ΜΑΡΚΟΝ
According to Mark

Chapter 1

Preaching of John the Baptist

THE beginning of the gospel of Jesus Christ, [a]the Son of God.

2As it is written in Isaiah the prophet,

"BEHOLD, I SEND MY MESSENGER BEFORE YOUR FACE,
WHO WILL PREPARE YOUR WAY;
3 THE VOICE OF ONE CRYING IN THE WILDERNESS,
'MAKE READY THE WAY OF THE LORD,
MAKE HIS PATHS STRAIGHT.'"

4John the Baptist appeared in the wilderness [b]preaching a baptism of repentance for the forgiveness of sins.

5And all the country of Judea was going out to him, and all the people of Jerusalem; and they were being baptized by him in the Jordan River, confessing their sins.

6And John was clothed with camel's hair and *wore* a leather belt around his waist, and his diet was locusts and wild honey.

7And he was preaching, and saying, "After me One is coming who is mightier than I, and I am not fit to stoop down and untie the thong of His sandals.

8"I baptized you [c]with water; but He will baptize you [c]with the Holy Spirit."

The Baptism of Jesus

9And it came about in those days that Jesus came from Nazareth in Galilee, and was baptized by John in the Jordan.

10And immediately coming up out of the water, He saw the heavens opening, and the Spirit like a dove descending upon Him;

11and a voice came out of the heavens: "Thou art My beloved Son, in Thee I am well-pleased."

12And immediately the Spirit *impelled Him *to go* out into the wilderness.

13And He was in the wilderness forty days being tempted by Satan; and He was with the wild beasts, and the angels were minis-

[a] Many mss. do not contain *the Son of God*
[b] Or, *proclaiming*
[c] The Gr. here can be translated *in, with* or *by*

1 Ἀρχὴ τοῦ εὐαγγελίου Ἰησοῦ Χριστοῦ.
[The] beginning of the gospel of Jesus Christ.
2 Καθὼς γέγραπται ἐν τῷ Ἠσαΐᾳ τῷ
As it has been written in – Isaiah the
προφήτῃ· ἰδοὺ ἀποστέλλω τὸν ἄγγελόν μου
prophet: Behold[,] I send the messenger of me
πρὸ προσώπου σου, ὃς κατασκευάσει τὴν ὁδόν
before [the] face of thee, who will prepare the way
σου· **3** φωνὴ βοῶντος ἐν τῇ ἐρήμῳ· ἑτοιμάσατε
of thee; a voice of [one] crying in the desert: Prepare ye
τὴν ὁδὸν κυρίου, εὐθείας ποιεῖτε τὰς τρίβους
the way of [the] Lord, straight make the paths
αὐτοῦ, **4** ἐγένετο Ἰωάννης ὁ βαπτίζων ἐν τῇ
of him, came John the [one] baptizing in the
ἐρήμῳ κηρύσσων βάπτισμα μετανοίας εἰς
desert proclaiming a baptism of repentance for
ἄφεσιν ἁμαρτιῶν. **5** καὶ ἐξεπορεύετο πρὸς
forgiveness of sins. And went out to
αὐτὸν πᾶσα ἡ Ἰουδαία χώρα καὶ οἱ Ἱεροσο-
him all the Judæan country and the Jerusa-
λυμῖται πάντες, καὶ ἐβαπτίζοντο ὑπ' αὐτοῦ
lemites all, and were baptized by him
ἐν τῷ Ἰορδάνῃ ποταμῷ ἐξομολογούμενοι τὰς
in the Jordan river confessing the
ἁμαρτίας αὐτῶν. **6** καὶ ἦν ὁ Ἰωάννης
sins of them. And was – John
ἐνδεδυμένος τρίχας καμήλου καὶ ζώνην
having been clothed [in] hairs of a camel and girdle
δερματίνην περὶ τὴν ὀσφὺν αὐτοῦ, καὶ ἔσθων
a leathern round the loin[s] of him, and eating
ἀκρίδας καὶ μέλι ἄγριον. **7** καὶ ἐκήρυσσεν
locusts and honey wild. And he proclaimed
λέγων· ἔρχεται ὁ ἰσχυρότερός μου ὀπίσω
saying: Comes the [one] stronger of me after
• =than I
[μου], οὗ οὐκ εἰμὶ ἱκανὸς κύψας λῦσαι
me, of whom I am not competent stooping to loosen
τὸν ἱμάντα τῶν ὑποδημάτων αὐτοῦ. **8** ἐγὼ
the thong of the sandals of him. I
ἐβάπτισα ὑμᾶς ὕδατι, αὐτὸς δὲ βαπτίσει ὑμᾶς
baptized you in water, but he will baptize you
πνεύματι ἁγίῳ.
Spirit in [the] Holy.
9 Καὶ ἐγένετο ἐν ἐκείναις ταῖς ἡμέραις
And it came to pass in those – days
ἦλθεν Ἰησοῦς ἀπὸ Ναζαρὲθ τῆς Γαλιλαίας
came Jesus from Nazareth – of Galilee
καὶ ἐβαπτίσθη εἰς τὸν Ἰορδάνην ὑπὸ
and was baptized in the Jordan by
Ἰωάννου. **10** καὶ εὐθὺς ἀναβαίνων ἐκ τοῦ
John. And immediately going up out of the
ὕδατος εἶδεν σχιζομένους τοὺς οὐρανοὺς
water he saw being rent the heavens
καὶ τὸ πνεῦμα ὡς περιστερὰν καταβαῖνον
and the Spirit as a dove coming down
εἰς αὐτόν· **11** καὶ φωνὴ [ἐγένετο] ἐκ τῶν
to him; and a voice there was out of the
οὐρανῶν· σὺ εἶ ὁ υἱός μου ὁ ἀγαπητός,
heavens: Thou art the Son of me the beloved,
ἐν σοὶ εὐδόκησα. **12** Καὶ εὐθὺς τὸ
in thee I was well pleased. And immediately the
πνεῦμα αὐτὸν ἐκβάλλει εἰς τὴν ἔρημον.
Spirit him thrusts forth into the desert.
13 καὶ ἦν ἐν τῇ ἐρήμῳ τεσσεράκοντα
And he was in the desert forty
ἡμέρας πειραζόμενος ὑπὸ τοῦ σατανᾶ, καὶ
days being tempted by – Satan, and
ἦν μετὰ τῶν θηρίων, καὶ οἱ ἄγγελοι
was with the wild beasts, and the angels

Chapter 1

John the Baptist Prepares the Way

THE beginning of the gospel about Jesus Christ, the Son of God.[a]

2It is written in Isaiah the prophet:

"I will send my messenger ahead of you,
who will prepare your way"[b]—
3"a voice of one calling in the desert,
'Prepare the way for the Lord,
make straight paths for him.'"[c]

4And so John came, baptizing in the desert region and preaching a baptism of repentance for the forgiveness of sins. 5The whole Judean countryside and all the people of Jerusalem went out to him. Confessing their sins, they were baptized by him in the Jordan River. 6John wore clothing made of camel's hair, with a leather belt around his waist, and he ate locusts and wild honey.
7And this was his message: "After me will come one more powerful than I, the thongs of whose sandals I am not worthy to stoop down and untie. 8I baptize you with[d] water, but he will baptize you with the Holy Spirit."

The Baptism and Temptation of Jesus

9At that time Jesus came from Nazareth in Galilee and was baptized by John in the Jordan. 10As Jesus was coming up out of the water, he saw heaven being torn open and the Spirit descending on him like a dove. 11And a voice came from heaven: "You are my Son, whom I love; with you I am well pleased."

12At once the Spirit sent him out into the desert,
13and he was in the desert forty days, being tempted by Satan. He was with the wild animals, and angels attended him.

[a]*1* Some manuscripts do not have *the Son of God.*
[b]*2* Mal. 3:1
[c]*3* Isaiah 40:3
[d]*8* Or *in*

tering to Him.

Jesus Preaches in Galilee

14And after John had
been taken into custody,
Jesus came into Galilee,
preaching the gospel of
God,
15and saying, "The time
is fulfilled, and the kingdom of God is at hand; repent and believe in the gospel."
16And as He was going
along by the Sea of Galilee,
He saw Simon and An-
drew, the brother of Si-
mon, casting a net in the
sea; for they were fish-
ermen.
17And Jesus said to them,
"Follow Me, and I will
make you become fishers
of men."
18And they immediately
left the nets and followed
Him.
19And going on a little farther, He saw James the *son*
of Zebedee, and John his
brother, who were also in
the boat mending the nets.
20And immediately He
called them; and they left
their father Zebedee in the
boat with the hired ser-
vants, and went away to
follow Him.
21And they *went into
Capernaum; and immedi-
ately on the Sabbath He entered the synagogue and
began to teach.
22And they were amazed
at His teaching; for He was
teaching them as *one* having authority, and not as
the scribes.
23And just then there was
in their synagogue a man
with an unclean spirit; and
he cried out,
24saying, "What do we
have to do with You, Jesus
[d]of Nazareth? Have You
come to destroy us? I know
who You are—the Holy
One of God!"
25And Jesus rebuked him,

[d] Lit., *the Nazarene*

διηκόνουν αὐτῷ.
ministered to him.

14 Καὶ μετὰ τὸ παραδοθῆναι τὸν
And after the to be delivered –
= after John was delivered

Ἰωάννην ἦλθεν ὁ Ἰησοῦς εἰς τὴν Γαλιλαίαν
John[b] came – Jesus into – Galilee

κηρύσσων τὸ εὐαγγέλιον τοῦ θεοῦ 15 [καὶ
proclaiming the gospel – of God and

λέγων], ὅτι πεπλήρωται ὁ καιρὸς καὶ
saying, – Has been fulfilled the time and

ἤγγικεν ἡ βασιλεία τοῦ θεοῦ· μετανοεῖτε
has drawn near the kingdom – of God; repent ye

καὶ πιστεύετε ἐν τῷ εὐαγγελίῳ. 16 Καὶ
and believe in the gospel. And

παράγων παρὰ τὴν θάλασσαν τῆς Γαλιλαίας
passing along beside the sea – of Galilee

εἶδεν Σίμωνα καὶ Ἀνδρέαν τὸν ἀδελφὸν
he saw Simon and Andrew the brother

Σίμωνος ἀμφιβάλλοντας ἐν τῇ θαλάσσῃ·
of Simon casting [a net] in the sea;

ἦσαν γὰρ ἁλεεῖς. 17 καὶ εἶπεν αὐτοῖς
for they were fishers. And said to them

ὁ Ἰησοῦς· δεῦτε ὀπίσω μου, καὶ ποιήσω
– Jesus: Come after me, and I will make

ὑμᾶς γενέσθαι ἁλεεῖς ἀνθρώπων. 18 καὶ
you to become fishers of men. And

εὐθὺς ἀφέντες τὰ δίκτυα ἠκολούθησαν
immediately leaving the nets they followed

αὐτῷ. 19 Καὶ προβὰς ὀλίγον εἶδεν
him. And going forward a little he saw

Ἰάκωβον τὸν τοῦ Ζεβεδαίου καὶ Ἰωάννην
James the [son] – of Zebedee and John

τὸν ἀδελφὸν αὐτοῦ καὶ αὐτοὺς ἐν τῷ
the brother of him even them in the

πλοίῳ καταρτίζοντας τὰ δίκτυα. 20 καὶ
ship mending the nets. And

εὐθὺς ἐκάλεσεν αὐτούς· καὶ ἀφέντες τὸν
immediately he called them; and leaving the

πατέρα αὐτῶν Ζεβεδαῖον ἐν τῷ πλοίῳ
father of them Zebedee in the ship

μετὰ τῶν μισθωτῶν ἀπῆλθον ὀπίσω αὐτοῦ.
with the hired servants they went after him.

21 Καὶ εἰσπορεύονται εἰς Καφαρναούμ·
And they enter into Capernaum;

καὶ εὐθὺς τοῖς σάββασιν εἰσελθὼν
and immediately on the sabbaths entering

εἰς τὴν συναγωγὴν ἐδίδασκεν. 22 καὶ
into the synagogue he taught. And

ἐξεπλήσσοντο ἐπὶ τῇ διδαχῇ αὐτοῦ· ἦν
they were astounded on(at) the teaching of him; [2]he was

γὰρ διδάσκων αὐτοὺς ὡς ἐξουσίαν ἔχων,
[1]for teaching them as authority having,

καὶ οὐχ ὡς οἱ γραμματεῖς. 23 Καὶ εὐθὺς
and not as the scribes. And immediately

ἦν ἐν τῇ συναγωγῇ αὐτῶν ἄνθρωπος
there was in the synagogue of them a man

ἐν πνεύματι ἀκαθάρτῳ, καὶ ἀνέκραξεν
in spirit an unclean, and he cried out

24 λέγων· τί ἡμῖν καὶ σοί, Ἰησοῦ
saying: What to us and to thee, Jesus

Ναζαρηνέ; ἦλθες ἀπολέσαι ἡμᾶς; οἶδά
Nazarene? camest thou to destroy us? I know

σε τίς εἶ, ὁ ἅγιος τοῦ θεοῦ. 25 καὶ
thee who thou art, the holy [one] – of God. And

ἐπετίμησεν αὐτῷ ὁ Ἰησοῦς [λέγων]·
rebuked him – Jesus saying:

The Calling of the First Disciples

14After John was put in
prison, Jesus went into
Galilee, proclaiming the
good news of God. 15"The
time has come," he said.
"The kingdom of God is
near. Repent and believe
the good news!"
16As Jesus walked beside
the Sea of Galilee, he saw
Simon and his brother An-
drew casting a net into the
lake, for they were fishermen. 17"Come, follow
me," Jesus said, "and I
will make you fishers of
men." 18At once they left
their nets and followed
him.
19When he had gone a lit-
tle farther, he saw James
son of Zebedee and his
brother John in a boat, preparing their nets. 20Without
delay he called them, and
they left their father Zebedee in the boat with the
hired men and followed
him.

Jesus Drives Out an Evil Spirit

21They went to Caperna-
um, and when the Sabbath
came, Jesus went into the
synagogue and began to
teach. 22The people were
amazed at his teaching, because he taught them as
one who had authority, not
as the teachers of the law.
23Just then a man in their
synagogue who was pos-
sessed by an evil[e] spirit
cried out, 24"What do you
want with us, Jesus of Nazareth? Have you come to
destroy us? I know who
you are—the Holy One of
God!"
25"Be quiet!" said Jesus

[e]*23* Greek *unclean*; also in verses 26 and 27

saying, "Be quiet, and
come out of him!"
26And throwing him into
convulsions, the unclean
spirit cried out with a loud
voice, and came out of him.
27And they were all
amazed, so that they debated among themselves, say-
ing, "What is this? A new
teaching with authority! He
commands even the un-
clean spirits, and they obey
Him."
28And immediately the
news about Him went out
everywhere into all the surrounding district of Galilee.

Multitudes Healed

29And immediately after
they had come out of the
synagogue, they came into
the house of Simon and Andrew, with James and
John.
30Now Simon's mother-
in-law was lying sick with a
fever; and immediately
they *spoke to Him about
her.
31And He came to her and
raised her up, taking her by
the hand, and the fever left
her, and she [e]waited on
them.
32And when evening had
come, after the sun had set,
they *began* bringing to Him
all who were ill and those
who were demon-pos-
sessed.
33And the whole city had
gathered at the door.
34And He healed many
who were ill with various
diseases, and cast out
many demons; and He was
not permitting the demons
to speak, because they
[f]knew who He was.
35And in the early morn-
ing, while it was still dark,
He arose and went out and
departed to a lonely place,
and was praying there.
36And Simon and his
companions hunted for
Him;
37and they found Him,
and *said to Him, "Every-
one is looking for You."
38And He *said to them,
"Let us go somewhere else

[e] Or, *served*
[f] Some mss. read: *knew Him to be Christ*

φιμώθητι καὶ ἔξελθε [ἐξ αὐτοῦ]. 26 καὶ
Be quiet and come *out* out of him. And
σπαράξαν αὐτὸν τὸ πνεῦμα τὸ ἀκάθαρτον
throwing him the spirit – unclean
καὶ φωνῆσαν φωνῇ μεγάλῃ ἐξῆλθεν ἐξ
and shouting voice with a great he came *out* out of
αὐτοῦ. 27 καὶ ἐθαμβήθησαν ἅπαντες, ὥστε
him. And were astounded all, so as = so that
συζητεῖν αὐτοὺς λέγοντας· τί ἐστιν τοῦτο;
to debate them[b] saying: What is this? they debated
διδαχὴ καινὴ κατ᾽ ἐξουσίαν· καὶ τοῖς
teaching a new by authority; and the
πνεύμασι τοῖς ἀκαθάρτοις ἐπιτάσσει, καὶ
spirits – unclean he commands, and
ὑπακούουσιν αὐτῷ. 28 καὶ ἐξῆλθεν ἡ
they obey him. And went forth the
ἀκοὴ αὐτοῦ εὐθὺς πανταχοῦ εἰς ὅλην
report of him immediately everywhere into all
τὴν περίχωρον τῆς Γαλιλαίας. 29 Καὶ
the neighbourhood – of Galilee. And
εὐθὺς ἐκ τῆς συναγωγῆς ἐξελθόντες ἦλθον
immediately out of the synagogue going forth they came
εἰς τὴν οἰκίαν Σίμωνος καὶ Ἀνδρέου
into the house of Simon and Andrew
μετὰ Ἰακώβου καὶ Ἰωάννου. 30 ἡ δὲ
with James and John. Now the
πενθερὰ Σίμωνος κατέκειτο πυρέσσουσα,
mother-in-law of Simon was laid [aside] fever-stricken,
καὶ εὐθὺς λέγουσιν αὐτῷ περὶ αὐτῆς.
and immediately they tell him about her.
31 καὶ προσελθὼν ἤγειρεν αὐτὴν κρατήσας
And approaching he raised her holding
τῆς χειρός· καὶ ἀφῆκεν αὐτὴν ὁ πυρετός,
the(her) hand; and left her the fever,
καὶ διηκόνει αὐτοῖς. 32 Ὀψίας δὲ γενο-
and she served them. And evening com- = when evening
μένης, ὅτε ἔδυσεν ὁ ἥλιος, ἔφερον πρὸς
ing,[a] came, when set the sun, they brought to
αὐτὸν πάντας τοὺς κακῶς ἔχοντας καὶ
him all the [ones] ill having and = those who were ill
τοὺς δαιμονιζομένους· 33 καὶ ἦν ὅλη ἡ
the being demon-possessed; and was all the
πόλις ἐπισυνηγμένη πρὸς τὴν θύραν.
city *having been* assembled at the door.
34 καὶ ἐθεράπευσεν πολλοὺς κακῶς ἔχοντας
And he healed many ill having = who were ill
ποικίλαις νόσοις, καὶ δαιμόνια πολλὰ
with various diseases, and demons many
ἐξέβαλεν, καὶ οὐκ ἤφιεν λαλεῖν τὰ δαιμόνια,
he expelled, and did not allow to speak the demons,
ὅτι ᾔδεισαν αὐτόν. 35 Καὶ πρωῒ ἔννυχα
because they knew him. And [3]early [4]in the night
λίαν ἀναστὰς ἐξῆλθεν καὶ ἀπῆλθεν εἰς
[2]very [1]rising up he went out and went away to
ἔρημον τόπον, κἀκεῖ προσηύχετο. 36 καὶ
a desert place, and there prayed. And
κατεδίωξεν αὐτὸν Σίμων καὶ οἱ μετ᾽
hunted down him Simon and the [ones] with
αὐτοῦ, καὶ εὗρον αὐτὸν καὶ λέγουσιν
him, and found him and say
αὐτῷ 37 ὅτι πάντες ζητοῦσίν σε. 38 καὶ
to him[,] – All are seeking thee. And
λέγει αὐτοῖς· ἄγωμεν ἀλλαχοῦ εἰς τὰς
he says to them: Let us go elsewhere into the

sternly. "Come out of
him!" 26The evil spirit
shook the man violently
and came out of him with a
shriek.
27The people were all so
amazed that they asked
each other, "What is this?
A new teaching—and with
authority! He even gives
orders to evil spirits and
they obey him." 28News
about him spread quickly
over the whole region of
Galilee.

Jesus Heals Many

29As soon as they left the
synagogue, they went with
James and John to the
home of Simon and An-
drew. 30Simon's mother-in-
law was in bed with a fever,
and they told Jesus about
her. 31So he went to her,
took her hand and helped
her up. The fever left her
and she began to wait on
them.
32That evening after sun-
set the people brought to
Jesus all the sick and demon-possessed. 33The
whole town gathered at the
door, 34and Jesus healed
many who had various dis-
eases. He also drove out
many demons, but he
would not let the demons
speak because they knew
who he was.

Jesus Prays in a Solitary Place

35Very early in the morn-
ing, while it was still dark,
Jesus got up, left the house
and went off to a solitary
place, where he prayed.
36Simon and his compan-
ions went to look for him,
37and when they found him,
they exclaimed: "Every-
one is looking for you!"
38Jesus replied, "Let us
go somewhere else—to the

to the towns nearby, in order that I may preach there also; for that is what I came out for."

39And He went into their synagogues throughout all Galilee, preaching and casting out the demons.

40And a leper *came to Him, beseeching Him and falling on his knees before Him, and saying to Him, "If You are willing, You can make me clean."

41And moved with compassion, He stretched out His hand, and touched him, and *said to him, "I am willing; be cleansed."

42And immediately the leprosy left him and he was cleansed.

43And He sternly warned him and immediately sent him away,

44and He *said to him, "See that you say nothing to anyone; but go, show yourself to the priest and offer for your cleansing what Moses commanded, for a testimony to them."

45But he went out and began to proclaim it freely and to spread the news about, to such an extent that Jesus could no longer publicly enter a city, but [g]stayed out in unpopulated areas; and they were coming to Him from everywhere.

Chapter 2

The Paralytic Healed

AND when He had come back to Capernaum several days afterward, it was heard that He was at home.

2And many were gathered together, so that there was no longer room, even near the door; and He was speaking the word to them.

3And they *came, bringing to Him a paralytic, carried by four men.

4And being unable to get to Him because of the crowd, they removed the roof above Him; and when they had dug an opening, they let down the pallet on

ἐχομένας κωμοπόλεις,' ἵνα καὶ ἐκεῖ
neighbouring towns, that also there
κηρύξω· εἰς τοῦτο γὰρ ἐξῆλθον. 39 καὶ
I may proclaim; for for this [purpose] I came forth. And
ἦλθεν κηρύσσων εἰς τὰς συναγωγὰς αὐτῶν
he came proclaiming in the synagogues of them
εἰς ὅλην τὴν Γαλιλαίαν καὶ τὰ δαιμόνια
in all – Galilee and the demons
ἐκβάλλων.
expelling.

40 Καὶ ἔρχεται πρὸς αὐτὸν λεπρὸς
And comes to him a leper
παρακαλῶν αὐτὸν καὶ γονυπετῶν λέγων
beseeching him and falling on [his] knees saying
αὐτῷ ὅτι ἐὰν θέλῃς δύνασαί με καθαρίσαι.
to him[,] – If thou art willing thou art able me to cleanse.
41 καὶ σπλαγχνισθεὶς ἐκτείνας τὴν
And being filled with tenderness stretching forth the(his)
χεῖρα αὐτοῦ ἥψατο καὶ λέγει αὐτῷ· θέλω,
hand [2]him [1]he touched and says to him: I am willing,
καθαρίσθητι. 42 καὶ εὐθὺς ἀπῆλθεν ἀπ'
be thou cleansed. And immediately departed from
αὐτοῦ ἡ λέπρα, καὶ ἐκαθαρίσθη. 43 καὶ
him the leprosy, and he was cleansed. And
ἐμβριμησάμενος αὐτῷ εὐθὺς ἐξέβαλεν αὐτόν,
sternly admonishing him immediately he put out him,
44 καὶ λέγει αὐτῷ· ὅρα μηδενὶ μηδὲν
and says to him: See no one no(any)thing
εἴπῃς, ἀλλὰ ὕπαγε σεαυτὸν δεῖξον τῷ
thou tellest, but go thyself show to the
ἱερεῖ καὶ προσένεγκε περὶ τοῦ καθαρισμοῦ σου
priest and offer concerning the cleansing of thee
ἃ προσέταξεν Μωϋσῆς, εἰς μαρτύριον
[the things] which commanded Moses, for a testimony
αὐτοῖς. 45 ὁ δὲ ἐξελθὼν ἤρξατο κηρύσσειν
to them. But he going out began to proclaim
πολλὰ καὶ διαφημίζειν τὸν λόγον, ὥστε
many things and to spread about the matter, so as
= so that
μηκέτι αὐτὸν δύνασθαι φανερῶς εἰς πόλιν
no longer him to be able[b] openly into a city
he was no longer able
εἰσελθεῖν, ἀλλ' ἔξω ἐπ' ἐρήμοις τόποις
to enter, but outside on(in) desert places
ἦν· καὶ ἤρχοντο πρὸς αὐτὸν πάντοθεν.
he was; and they came to him from all directions.

2 Καὶ εἰσελθὼν πάλιν εἰς Καφαρναοὺμ
And entering again into Capernaum
δι' ἡμερῶν ἠκούσθη ὅτι ἐν οἴκῳ ἐστίν.
through days it was heard that at home he is(was).
= after [some] days
2 καὶ συνήχθησαν πολλοί, ὥστε μηκέτι
And were assembled many, so as no longer
χωρεῖν μηδὲ τὰ πρὸς τὴν θύραν, καὶ
to have room not – at the door, and
ἐλάλει αὐτοῖς τὸν λόγον. 3 καὶ ἔρχονται
he spoke to them the word. And they come
φέροντες πρὸς αὐτὸν παραλυτικὸν αἰρόμενον
carrying to him a paralytic being borne
ὑπὸ τεσσάρων. 4 καὶ μὴ δυνάμενοι
by four [men]. And not being able
προσενέγκαι αὐτῷ διὰ τὸν ὄχλον
to bring to him because of the crowd
ἀπεστέγασαν τὴν στέγην ὅπου ἦν, καὶ
they unroofed the roof where he was, and
ἐξορύξαντες χαλῶσι τὸν κράβατον ὅπου ὁ
having opened up they lower the mattress where the

nearby villages—so I can
preach there also. That is
why I have come." 39So he
traveled throughout Galilee, preaching in their synagogues and driving out demons.

A Man With Leprosy

40A man with leprosy[f]
came to him and begged
him on his knees, "If you
are willing, you can make
me clean."
41Filled with compassion,
Jesus reached out his hand
and touched the man. "I
am willing," he said. "Be
clean!" 42Immediately the
leprosy left him and he was
cured.
43Jesus sent him away at
once with a strong warning:
44"See that you don't tell
this to anyone. But go,
show yourself to the priest
and offer the sacrifices that
Moses commanded for
your cleansing, as a testimony to them." 45Instead
he went out and began to
talk freely, spreading the
news. As a result, Jesus
could no longer enter a
town openly but stayed
outside in lonely places.
Yet the people still came to
him from everywhere.

Chapter 2

Jesus Heals a Paralytic

A FEW days later, when
Jesus again entered
Capernaum, the people
heard that he had come
home. 2So many gathered
that there was no room left,
not even outside the door,
and he preached the word
to them. 3Some men came,
bringing to him a paralytic,
carried by four of them.
4Since they could not get
him to Jesus because of the
crowd, they made an opening in the roof above Jesus
and, after digging through
it, lowered the mat the par-

[f]40 The Greek word was used for various diseases affecting the skin—not necessarily leprosy.

which the paralytic was lying.

5And Jesus seeing their faith *said to the paralytic, "My [h]son, your sins are forgiven."

6But there were some of the scribes sitting there and reasoning in their hearts,

7"Why does this man speak that way? He is blaspheming; who can forgive sins but God alone?"

8And immediately Jesus, aware in His spirit that they were reasoning that way within themselves, *said to them, "Why are you reasoning about these things in your hearts?

9"Which is easier, to say to the paralytic, 'Your sins are forgiven'; or to say, 'Arise, and take up your pallet and walk'?

10"But in order that you may know that the Son of Man has authority on earth to forgive sins"—He *said to the paralytic—

11"I say to you, rise, take up your pallet and go home."

12And he rose and immediately took up the pallet and went out in the sight of all; so that they were all amazed and were glorifying God, saying, "We have never seen anything like this."

13And He went out again by the seashore; and all the multitude were coming to Him, and He was teaching them.

Levi (Matthew) Called

14And as He passed by, He saw Levi the *son* of Alphaeus sitting in the tax office, and He *said to him, "Follow Me!" And he rose and followed Him.

15And it came about that He was reclining *at the table* in his house, and many tax-gatherers and sinners

[g] Lit., *was*
[h] Lit., *child*

παραλυτικὸς κατέκειτο. **5** καὶ ἰδὼν ὁ
paralytic was lying. And seeing –

Ἰησοῦς τὴν πίστιν αὐτῶν λέγει τῷ
Jesus the faith of them he says to the

παραλυτικῷ· τέκνον, ἀφίενταί σου αἱ
paralytic: Child, are forgiven of thee the

ἁμαρτίαι. **6** ἦσαν δέ τινες τῶν γραμματέων
sins. Now there were some of the scribes

ἐκεῖ καθήμενοι καὶ διαλογιζόμενοι ἐν ταῖς
there sitting and reasoning in the

καρδίαις αὐτῶν· **7** τί οὗτος οὕτως λαλεῖ;
hearts of them: Why this [man] thus speaks?

βλασφημεῖ· τίς δύναται ἀφιέναι ἁμαρτίας
he blasphemes; who can *to* forgive sins

εἰ μὴ εἷς ὁ θεός; **8** καὶ εὐθὺς ἐπιγνοὺς
except one[,] – God? And immediately knowing

ὁ Ἰησοῦς τῷ πνεύματι αὐτοῦ ὅτι οὕτως
– Jesus in the spirit of him that thus

διαλογίζονται ἐν ἑαυτοῖς, λέγει αὐτοῖς·
they reason among themselves, he says to them:

τί ταῦτα διαλογίζεσθε ἐν ταῖς καρδίαις
Why these things reason ye in the hearts

ὑμῶν; **9** τί ἐστιν εὐκοπώτερον, εἰπεῖν
of you? What is easier, to say

τῷ παραλυτικῷ· ἀφίενταί σου αἱ ἁμαρτίαι,
to the paralytic: are forgiven of thee the sins,

ἢ εἰπεῖν· ἔγειρε καὶ ἆρον τὸν κράβατόν
or to say: Rise and take the mattress

σου καὶ περιπάτει; **10** ἵνα δὲ εἰδῆτε
of thee and walk? But that ye may know

ὅτι ἐξουσίαν ἔχει ὁ υἱὸς τοῦ ἀνθρώπου
that authority has the Son – of man

ἀφιέναι ἁμαρτίας ἐπὶ τῆς γῆς,—λέγει τῷ
to forgive sins on the earth,—he says to the

παραλυτικῷ· **11** σοὶ λέγω, ἔγειρε ἆρον
paralytic: To thee I say, rise[,] take

τὸν κράβατόν σου καὶ ὕπαγε εἰς τὸν
the mattress of thee and go to the

οἶκόν σου. **12** καὶ ἠγέρθη καὶ εὐθὺς
house of thee. And he arose and immediately

ἄρας τὸν κράβατον ἐξῆλθεν ἔμπροσθεν
taking the mattress he went forth before

πάντων, ὥστε ἐξίστασθαι πάντας καὶ
all, so as to be astonished all and
= so that they were all astonished and glorified

δοξάζειν τὸν θεὸν λέγοντας ὅτι οὕτως
to glorify[b] – God saying[,] – Thus

οὐδέποτε εἴδαμεν.
never we saw.

13 Καὶ ἐξῆλθεν πάλιν παρὰ τὴν θάλασσαν·
And he went forth again by the sea;

καὶ πᾶς ὁ ὄχλος ἤρχετο πρὸς αὐτόν,
and all the crowd came to him,

καὶ ἐδίδασκεν αὐτούς. **14** Καὶ παράγων
and he taught them. And passing along

εἶδεν Λευὶν τὸν τοῦ Ἁλφαίου καθήμενον
he saw Levi the [son] – Alphæus sitting

ἐπὶ τὸ τελώνιον, καὶ λέγει αὐτῷ· ἀκολούθει
on(in *or* at) the custom house, and says to him: Follow

μοι. καὶ ἀναστὰς ἠκολούθησεν αὐτῷ.
me. And rising up he followed him.

15 Καὶ γίνεται κατακεῖσθαι αὐτὸν ἐν τῇ
And it comes to pass to recline him[b] in the
= he reclines

οἰκίᾳ αὐτοῦ, καὶ πολλοὶ τελῶναι καὶ
house of him, and many tax-collectors and

alyzed man was lying on. 5When Jesus saw their faith, he said to the paralytic, "Son, your sins are forgiven."

6Now some teachers of the law were sitting there, thinking to themselves, 7"Why does this fellow talk like that? He's blaspheming! Who can forgive sins but God alone?"

8Immediately Jesus knew in his spirit that this was what they were thinking in their hearts, and he said to them, "Why are you thinking these things? 9Which is easier: to say to the paralytic, 'Your sins are forgiven,' or to say, 'Get up, take your mat and walk'? 10But that you may know that the Son of Man has authority on earth to forgive sins . . . ." He said to the paralytic, 11"I tell you, get up, take your mat and go home." 12He got up, took his mat and walked out in full view of them all. This amazed everyone and they praised God, saying, "We have never seen anything like this!"

The Calling of Levi

13Once again Jesus went out beside the lake. A large crowd came to him, and he began to teach them. 14As he walked along, he saw Levi son of Alphaeus sitting at the tax collector's booth. "Follow me," Jesus told him, and Levi got up and followed him.

15While Jesus was having dinner at Levi's house, many tax collectors and

were dining with Jesus and His disciples; for there were many of them, and they were following Him.

16And when the scribes of the Pharisees saw that He was eating with the sinners and tax-gatherers, they *began* saying to His disciples, "Why is He eating and drinking with tax-gatherers and sinners?"

17And hearing this, Jesus *said to them, "*It is* not those who are healthy who need a physician, but those who are sick; I did not come to call the righteous, but sinners."

18And John's disciples and the Pharisees were fasting; and they *came and *said to Him, "Why do John's disciples and the disciples of the Pharisees fast, but Your disciples do not fast?"

19And Jesus said to them, "While the bridegroom is with them, the attendants of the bridegroom do not fast, do they? So long as they have the bridegroom with them, they cannot fast.

20"But the days will come when the bridegroom is taken away from them, and then they will fast in that day.

21"No one sews a patch of unshrunk cloth on an old garment; otherwise the patch pulls away from it, the new from the old, and a worse tear results.

22"And no one puts new wine into old wineskins; otherwise the wine will burst the skins, and the wine is lost, and the skins *as well;* but *one puts* new wine into fresh wineskins."

Question of the Sabbath

23And it came about that

ἁμαρτωλοὶ συνανέκειντο τῷ Ἰησοῦ καὶ
sinners reclined with – Jesus and
τοῖς μαθηταῖς αὐτοῦ· ἦσαν γὰρ πολλοί,
the disciples of him; for there were many,
καὶ ἠκολούθουν αὐτῷ. 16 καὶ οἱ γραμματεῖς
and they followed him. And the scribes
τῶν Φαρισαίων ἰδόντες ὅτι ἐσθίει
of the Pharisees seeing that he eats(ate)
μετὰ τῶν ἁμαρτωλῶν καὶ τελωνῶν ἔλεγον
with – sinners and tax-collectors said
τοῖς μαθηταῖς αὐτοῦ· ὅτι μετὰ τῶν
to the disciples of him: – With –
τελωνῶν καὶ ἁμαρτωλῶν ἐσθίει; 17 καὶ
tax-collectors and sinners does he eat ? And
ἀκούσας ὁ Ἰησοῦς λέγει αὐτοῖς [ὅτι] οὐ
hearing – Jesus says to them[,] – Not
χρείαν ἔχουσιν οἱ ἰσχύοντες ἰατροῦ ἀλλ'
need have the [ones] being strong of a physician but
οἱ κακῶς ἔχοντες· οὐκ ἦλθον καλέσαι
the [ones] ill having; I came not to call
= those who are ill;
δικαίους ἀλλὰ ἁμαρτωλούς. 18 Καὶ ἦσαν
righteous men but sinners. And [7]were
οἱ μαθηταὶ Ἰωάννου καὶ οἱ Φαρισαῖοι
[1]the [2]disciples [3]of John [4]and [5]the [6]Pharisees
νηστεύοντες. καὶ ἔρχονται καὶ λέγουσιν
[8]fasting. And they come and say
αὐτῷ· διὰ τί οἱ μαθηταὶ Ἰωάννου καὶ
to him: Why the disciples of John and
οἱ μαθηταὶ τῶν Φαρισαίων νηστεύουσιν,
the disciples of the Pharisees fast,
οἱ δὲ σοὶ μαθηταὶ οὐ νηστεύουσιν; 19 καὶ
– but thy disciples do not fast ? And
εἶπεν αὐτοῖς ὁ Ἰησοῦς· μὴ δύνανται οἱ
said to them – Jesus: *not* can the
υἱοὶ τοῦ νυμφῶνος, ἐν ᾧ ὁ νυμφίος
sons of the bridechamber, while† the bridegroom
μετ' αὐτῶν ἐστιν, νηστεύειν; ὅσον χρόνον
with them is, *to* fast ? what time
ἔχουσιν τὸν νυμφίον μετ' αὐτῶν, οὐ
they have the bridegroom with them, not
δύνανται νηστεύειν. 20 ἐλεύσονται δὲ ἡμέραι
they can *to* fast. But will come days
ὅταν ἀπαρθῇ ἀπ' αὐτῶν ὁ νυμφίος, καὶ
when taken away from them the bridegroom, and
τότε νηστεύσουσιν ἐν ἐκείνῃ τῇ ἡμέρᾳ.
then they will fast in that – day.
21 Οὐδεὶς ἐπίβλημα ῥάκους ἀγνάφου ἐπιράπτει
No one a patch cloth of unfulled sews
ἐπὶ ἱμάτιον παλαιόν· εἰ δὲ μή, αἴρει
on garment an old; otherwise, [3]takes
τὸ πλήρωμα ἀπ' αὐτοῦ τὸ καινὸν τοῦ
[4]the [5]fulness [6]from [9]itself [1]the [2]new [7]the
παλαιοῦ, καὶ χεῖρον σχίσμα γίνεται. 22 καὶ
[8]old, and a worse rent occurs. And
οὐδεὶς βάλλει οἶνον νέον εἰς ἀσκοὺς παλαιούς·
no one puts wine new into wineskins old;
εἰ δὲ μή, ῥήξει ὁ οἶνος τοὺς ἀσκούς,
otherwise, [3]will burst [1]the [2]wine the wineskins,
καὶ ὁ οἶνος ἀπόλλυται καὶ οἱ ἀσκοί.
and the wine perishes and the wineskins.
[ἀλλὰ οἶνον νέον εἰς ἀσκοὺς καινούς.]
But wine new into wineskins fresh.
23 Καὶ ἐγένετο αὐτὸν ἐν τοῖς σάββασιν
And it came to pass him on the sabbaths
= as he passed on the sabbath

"sinners" were eating with him and his disciples, for there were many who followed him.
16When the teachers of the law who were Pharisees saw him eating with the "sinners" and tax collectors, they asked his disciples: "Why does he eat with tax collectors and 'sinners'?"

17On hearing this, Jesus said to them, "It is not the healthy who need a doctor, but the sick. I have not come to call the righteous, but sinners."

Jesus Questioned About Fasting

18Now John's disciples and the Pharisees were fasting. Some people came and asked Jesus, "How is it that John's disciples and the disciples of the Pharisees are fasting, but yours are not?"

19Jesus answered, "How can the guests of the bridegroom fast while he is with them? They cannot, so long as they have him with them.
20But the time will come when the bridegroom will be taken from them, and on that day they will fast.

21"No one sews a patch of unshrunk cloth on an old garment. If he does, the new piece will pull away from the old, making the tear worse.
22And no one pours new wine into old wineskins. If he does, the wine will burst the skins, and both the wine and the wineskins will be ruined. No, he pours new wine into new wineskins."

Lord of the Sabbath

23One Sabbath Jesus was going through the grain-

He was passing through the grainfields on the Sabbath, and His disciples began to make their way along while picking the heads *of grain*.

24And the Pharisees were saying to Him, "See here, why are they doing what is not lawful on the Sabbath?"

25And He *said to them, "Have you never read what David did when he was in need and became hungry, he and his companions:

26how he entered the house of God in the time of Abiathar *the* high priest, and ate the consecrated bread, which is not lawful for *anyone* to eat except the priests, and he gave *it* also to those who were with him?"

27And He was saying to them, "The Sabbath was made for man, and not man for the Sabbath.

28"Consequently, the Son of Man is Lord even of the Sabbath."

παραπορεύεσθαι διὰ τῶν σπορίμων, καὶ
to pass[b] through the cornfields, and

οἱ μαθηταὶ αὐτοῦ ἤρξαντο ὁδὸν ποιεῖν
the disciples of him began way to make

τίλλοντες τοὺς στάχυας. 24 καὶ οἱ Φαρισαῖοι
plucking the ears of corn. And the Pharisees

ἔλεγον αὐτῷ· ἴδε τί ποιοῦσιν τοῖς σάββασιν
said to him: Behold[,] why do on the sabbaths

ὃ οὐκ ἔξεστιν; 25 καὶ λέγει αὐτοῖς·
what is not lawful? And he says to them:

οὐδέποτε ἀνέγνωτε τί ἐποίησεν Δαυίδ,
never read ye what did David,

ὅτε χρείαν ἔσχεν καὶ ἐπείνασεν αὐτὸς
when need he had and hungered he

καὶ οἱ μετ' αὐτοῦ; 26 [πῶς] εἰσῆλθεν
and the [ones] with him? how he entered

εἰς τὸν οἶκον τοῦ θεοῦ ἐπὶ Ἀβιαθὰρ
into the house – of God on(in the days of) Abiathar

ἀρχιερέως καὶ τοὺς ἄρτους τῆς προθέσεως
high priest and the loaves of the setting forth

ἔφαγεν, οὓς οὐκ ἔξεστιν φαγεῖν εἰ μὴ
ate, which it is not lawful to eat except

τοὺς ἱερεῖς, καὶ ἔδωκεν καὶ τοῖς σὺν
the priests, and gave also to the [ones] with

αὐτῷ οὖσιν; 27 καὶ ἔλεγεν αὐτοῖς·
him being? And he said to them:

τὸ σάββατον διὰ τὸν ἄνθρωπον ἐγένετο,
The sabbath on account of – man was,

καὶ οὐχ ὁ ἄνθρωπος διὰ τὸ σάββατον·
and not – man on account of the sabbath;

28 ὥστε κύριός ἐστιν ὁ υἱὸς τοῦ ἀνθρώπου
so as Lord is the Son – of man

καὶ τοῦ σαββάτου.
also of the sabbath.

fields, and as his disciples walked along, they began to pick some heads of grain. 24The Pharisees said to him, "Look, why are they doing what is unlawful on the Sabbath?"

25He answered, "Have you never read what David did when he and his companions were hungry and in need? 26In the days of Abiathar the high priest, he entered the house of God and ate the consecrated bread, which is lawful only for priests to eat. And he also gave some to his companions."

27Then he said to them, "The Sabbath was made for man, not man for the Sabbath. 28So the Son of Man is Lord even of the Sabbath."

Chapter 3

Jesus Heals on the Sabbath

AND He entered again into a synagogue; and a man was there with a withered hand.

2And they were watching Him *to see* if He would heal him on the Sabbath, in order that they might accuse Him.

3And He *said to the man with the withered hand, "Rise and *come* forward!"

4And He *said to them, "Is it lawful on the Sabbath to do good or to do harm, to save a life or to kill?" But they kept silent.

5And after looking around at them with anger, grieved at their hardness of heart, He *said to the man, "Stretch out your hand." And he stretched it out, and his hand was restored.

6And the Pharisees went out and immediately *began*

3 Καὶ εἰσῆλθεν πάλιν εἰς συναγωγήν.
And he entered again into a synagogue.

καὶ ἦν ἐκεῖ ἄνθρωπος ἐξηραμμένην ἔχων
And there was there a man [4]having been withered [1]having

τὴν χεῖρα· 2 καὶ παρετήρουν αὐτὸν εἰ
[2]the [3]hand; and they watched carefully him if

τοῖς σάββασιν θεραπεύσει αὐτόν, ἵνα
on the sabbaths he will heal him, that

κατηγορήσωσιν αὐτοῦ. 3 καὶ λέγει τῷ
they might accuse him. And he says to the

ἀνθρώπῳ τῷ τὴν χεῖρα ἔχοντι ξηράν·
man – the hand having dry:

ἔγειρε εἰς τὸ μέσον. 4 καὶ λέγει αὐτοῖς·
Rise into the midst. And he says to them:

ἔξεστιν τοῖς σάββασιν ἀγαθὸν ποιῆσαι
Lawful on the sabbaths good to do

ἢ κακοποιῆσαι, ψυχὴν σῶσαι ἢ ἀποκτεῖναι;
or to do evil, life to save or to kill?

οἱ δὲ ἐσιώπων. 5 καὶ περιβλεψάμενος
But they were silent. And looking round

αὐτοὺς μετ' ὀργῆς, συλλυπούμενος ἐπὶ
[on] them with anger, being greatly grieved on(at)

τῇ πωρώσει τῆς καρδίας αὐτῶν, λέγει
the hardness of the heart of them, he says

τῷ ἀνθρώπῳ· ἔκτεινον τὴν χεῖρα. καὶ
to the man: Stretch forth the hand. And

ἐξέτεινεν, καὶ ἀπεκατεστάθη ἡ χεὶρ αὐτοῦ.
he stretched forth, and was restored the hand of him.

6 καὶ ἐξελθόντες οἱ Φαρισαῖοι εὐθὺς μετὰ
And going forth the Pharisees immediately with

Chapter 3

ANOTHER time he went into the synagogue, and a man with a shriveled hand was there. 2Some of them were looking for a reason to accuse Jesus, so they watched him closely to see if he would heal him on the Sabbath. 3Jesus said to the man with the shriveled hand, "Stand up in front of everyone."

4Then Jesus asked them, "Which is lawful on the Sabbath: to do good or to do evil, to save life or to kill?" But they remained silent.

5He looked around at them in anger and, deeply distressed at their stubborn hearts, said to the man, "Stretch out your hand." He stretched it out, and his hand was completely restored. 6Then the Pharisees went out and began to plot

taking counsel with the
Herodians against Him, *as*
to how they might destroy
Him.
7And Jesus withdrew to
the sea with His disciples;
and a great multitude from
Galilee followed; and *also*
from Judea,
8and from Jerusalem,
and from Idumea, and
beyond the Jordan, and the
vicinity of Tyre and Sidon,
a great multitude heard of
all that He was doing and
came to Him.
9And He told His disci-
ples that a boat should
stand ready for Him be-
cause of the multitude, in
order that they might not
crowd Him;
10for He had healed
many, with the result that
all those who had afflic-
tions pressed about Him in
order to touch Him.
11And whenever the un-
clean spirits beheld Him,
they would fall down be-
fore Him and cry out, saying, "You are the Son of
God!"
12And He earnestly
warned them not to make
Him known.

The Twelve Are Chosen

13And He *went up to the
mountain and *summoned
those whom He Himself
wanted, and they came to
Him.
14And He appointed
twelve[i], that they might be
with Him, and that He
might send them out to
preach,
15and to have authority to
cast out the demons.
16And He appointed the
twelve: Simon (to whom
He gave the name Peter),
17and James, the *son* of
Zebedee, and John the
brother of James (to them
He gave the name Boaner-
ges, which means, "Sons
of Thunder");
18and Andrew, and
Philip, and Bartholomew,
and Matthew, and Thomas,
and James the *son* of Alphaeus, and Thaddaeus,

[i]Some early mss. add: *whom He named apostles*

τῶν Ἡρῳδιανῶν συμβούλιον ἐδίδουν κατ᾽
the Herodians counsel gave against
αὐτοῦ, ὅπως αὐτὸν ἀπολέσωσιν.
him, that him they might destroy.
7 Καὶ ὁ Ἰησοῦς μετὰ τῶν μαθητῶν
And – Jesus with the disciples
αὐτοῦ ἀνεχώρησεν πρὸς τὴν θάλασσαν·
of him departed to the sea;
καὶ πολὺ πλῆθος ἀπὸ τῆς Γαλιλαίας
and a much(great) multitude from – Galilee
ἠκολούθησεν· καὶ ἀπὸ τῆς Ἰουδαίας 8 καὶ
followed; and from – Judæa and
ἀπὸ Ἱεροσολύμων καὶ ἀπὸ τῆς Ἰδουμαίας
from Jerusalem and from – Idumæa
καὶ πέραν τοῦ Ἰορδάνου καὶ περὶ Τύρον
and beyond the Jordan and round Tyre
καὶ Σιδῶνα, πλῆθος πολύ, ἀκούοντες ὅσα
and Sidon, multitude a much(great), hearing what things
ποιεῖ, ἦλθον πρὸς αὐτόν. 9 καὶ εἶπεν
he does, came to him. And he told
τοῖς μαθηταῖς αὐτοῦ ἵνα πλοιάριον προσκαρτερῇ
the disciples of him that a boat should remain near
αὐτῷ διὰ τὸν ὄχλον, ἵνα μὴ θλίβωσιν
him because of the crowd, lest they should press upon
αὐτόν· 10 πολλοὺς γὰρ ἐθεράπευσεν, ὥστε
him; for many he healed, so as
ἐπιπίπτειν αὐτῷ ἵνα αὐτοῦ ἅψωνται
to fall upon him that him they might touch
ὅσοι εἶχον μάστιγας. 11 καὶ τὰ πνεύματα
as many as had plagues. And the spirits
τὰ ἀκάθαρτα, ὅταν αὐτὸν ἐθεώρουν, προσέπιπτον
– unclean, when him they saw, fell before
αὐτῷ καὶ ἔκραζον λέγοντα ὅτι σὺ εἶ ὁ
him and cried out saying[,] – Thou art the
υἱὸς τοῦ θεοῦ. 12 καὶ πολλὰ ἐπετίμα
Son – of God. And much he warned
αὐτοῖς ἵνα μὴ αὐτὸν φανερὸν ποιήσωσιν.
them that not him manifest they should make.
13 Καὶ ἀναβαίνει εἰς τὸ ὄρος, καὶ
And he goes up into the mountain, and
προσκαλεῖται οὓς ἤθελεν αὐτός, καὶ
calls to [him] [those] whom wished he, and
ἀπῆλθον πρὸς αὐτόν. 14 καὶ ἐποίησεν δώδεκα
they went to him. And he made twelve
ἵνα ὦσιν μετ᾽ αὐτοῦ, καὶ ἵνα ἀποστέλλῃ
that they might be with him, and that he might send
αὐτοὺς κηρύσσειν 15 καὶ ἔχειν ἐξουσίαν
them to proclaim and to have authority
ἐκβάλλειν τὰ δαιμόνια· 16 καὶ ἐποίησεν
to expel the demons; and he made
τοὺς δώδεκα, καὶ ἐπέθηκεν ὄνομα τῷ
the twelve, and he added a name –
Σίμωνι Πέτρον· 17 καὶ Ἰάκωβον τὸν τοῦ
to Simon[,] Peter; and James the [son] –
Ζεβεδαίου καὶ Ἰωάννην τὸν ἀδελφὸν τοῦ
of Zebedee and John the brother –
Ἰακώβου, καὶ ἐπέθηκεν αὐτοῖς ὄνομα
of James, and he added to them a name[,]
Βοανηργές, ὅ ἐστιν υἱοὶ βροντῆς· 18 καὶ
Boanerges, which is sons of thunder; and
Ἀνδρέαν καὶ Φίλιππον καὶ Βαρθολομαῖον
Andrew and Philip and Bartholomew
καὶ Μαθθαῖον καὶ Θωμᾶν καὶ Ἰάκωβον
and Matthew and Thomas and James
τὸν τοῦ Ἁλφαίου καὶ Θαδδαῖον καὶ
the [son] – of Alphæus and Thaddæus and

with the Herodians how
they might kill Jesus.

Crowds Follow Jesus

7Jesus withdrew with his
disciples to the lake, and a
large crowd from Galilee
followed. 8When they
heard all he was doing,
many people came to him
from Judea, Jerusalem, Idumea, and the regions
across the Jordan and
around Tyre and Sidon.
9Because of the crowd he
told his disciples to have a
small boat ready for him, to
keep the people from
crowding him. 10For he had
healed many, so that those
with diseases were pushing
forward to touch him.
11Whenever the evil[g] spirits saw him, they fell down
before him and cried out,
"You are the Son of God."
12But he gave them strict
orders not to tell who he
was.

The Appointing of the Twelve Apostles

13Jesus went up on a
mountainside and called to
him those he wanted, and
they came to him. 14He appointed twelve—designat-
ing them apostles[h]—that
they might be with him and
that he might send them out
to preach 15and to have authority to drive out de-
mons. 16These are the
twelve he appointed: Si-
mon (to whom he gave the
name Peter); 17James son of
Zebedee and his brother
John (to them he gave the
name Boanerges, which
means Sons of Thunder);
18Andrew, Philip, Bartholomew, Matthew, Thomas,
James son of Alphaeus,
Thaddaeus, Simon the

[g]11 Greek *unclean;* also in verse 30
[h]14 Some manuscripts do not have *designating them apostles.*

and Simon the Zealot;
[19]and Judas Iscariot, who also betrayed Him.
[20]And He *came [j] home, and the multitude *gathered again, to such an extent that they could not even eat a meal.
[21]And when His own [k]people heard *of this,* they went out to take custody of Him; for they were saying, "He has lost His senses."
[22]And the scribes who came down from Jerusalem were saying, "He is possessed by Beelzebul," and "He casts out the demons by the ruler of the demons."
[23]And He called them to Himself and began speaking to them in parables, "How can Satan cast out Satan?
[24]"And if a kingdom is divided against itself, that kingdom cannot stand.
[25]"And if a house is divided against itself, that house will not be able to stand.
[26]"And if Satan has risen up against himself and is divided, he cannot stand, but he is finished!
[27]"But no one can enter the strong man's house and plunder his property unless he first binds the strong man, and then he will plunder his house.
[28]"Truly I say to you, all sins shall be forgiven the sons of men, and whatever blasphemies they utter;
[29]but whoever blasphemes against the Holy Spirit never has forgiveness, but is guilty of an eternal sin"—
[30]because they were saying, "He has an unclean spirit."
[31]And His mother and His brothers *arrived, and standing outside they sent *word* to Him, and called Him.

[j]Lit., *into a house*
[k]Or, *kinsmen*

Σίμωνα τὸν Καναναῖον **19** καὶ Ἰούδαν
Simon the Cananæan and Judas

Ἰσκαριώθ, ὃς καὶ παρέδωκεν αὐτόν.
Iscariot, who indeed betrayed him.

20 Καὶ ἔρχεται εἰς οἶκον· καὶ συνέρχεται
And he comes into a house; and comes together

πάλιν [ὁ] ὄχλος, ὥστε μὴ δύνασθαι
again the crowd, so as not to be able
= so that they were not able

αὐτοὺς μηδὲ ἄρτον φαγεῖν. **21** καὶ ἀκούσαντες
them[b] *not* bread to eat. And hearing

οἱ παρ' αὐτοῦ ἐξῆλθον κρατῆσαι αὐτόν·
the[ones] with him went forth to seize him;
= his relations

ἔλεγον γὰρ ὅτι ἐξέστη. **22** καὶ οἱ
for they said[,] – He is beside himself. And the

γραμματεῖς οἱ ἀπὸ Ἱεροσολύμων καταβάντες
scribes – from Jerusalem coming down

ἔλεγον ὅτι Βεεζεβοὺλ ἔχει, καὶ ὅτι ἐν
said[,] – Beelzebub he has, and[,] – By

τῷ ἄρχοντι τῶν δαιμονίων ἐκβάλλει τὰ
the ruler of the demons he expels the

δαιμόνια. **23** καὶ προσκαλεσάμενος αὐτοὺς
demons. And calling to [him] them

ἐν παραβολαῖς ἔλεγεν αὐτοῖς· πῶς δύναται
in parables he said to them: How can

σατανᾶς σατανᾶν ἐκβάλλειν; **24** καὶ ἐὰν
Satan ²Satan ¹*to* expel? and if

βασιλεία ἐφ' ἑαυτὴν μερισθῇ, οὐ δύναται
a kingdom against itself be divided, cannot

σταθῆναι ἡ βασιλεία ἐκείνη· **25** καὶ ἐὰν
stand – kingdom that; and if

οἰκία ἐφ' ἑαυτὴν μερισθῇ, οὐ δυνήσεται
a house against itself be divided, will not be able

ἡ οἰκία ἐκείνη στῆναι. **26** καὶ εἰ ὁ
– house that to stand. And if –

σατανᾶς ἀνέστη ἐφ' ἑαυτὸν καὶ ἐμερίσθη,
Satan stood up against himself and was divided,

οὐ δύναται στῆναι ἀλλὰ τέλος ἔχει.
he cannot *to* stand but an end has.

27 ἀλλ' οὐ δύναται οὐδεὶς εἰς τὴν οἰκίαν
But cannot no(any)one into the house

τοῦ ἰσχυροῦ εἰσελθὼν τὰ σκεύη αὐτοῦ
of the strong man entering the goods of him

διαρπάσαι, ἐὰν μὴ πρῶτον τὸν ἰσχυρὸν
to plunder, unless first the strong man

δήσῃ, καὶ τότε τὴν οἰκίαν αὐτοῦ διαρπάσει.
he bind, and then the house of him he will plunder.

28 Ἀμὴν λέγω ὑμῖν ὅτι πάντα ἀφεθήσεται
Truly I tell you that all will be forgiven

τοῖς υἱοῖς τῶν ἀνθρώπων τὰ ἁμαρτήματα
to the sons – of men the sins

καὶ αἱ βλασφημίαι, ὅσα ἐὰν βλασφημήσωσιν·
and the blasphemies, whatever they may blaspheme;

29 ὃς δ' ἂν βλασφημήσῃ εἰς τὸ πνεῦμα
but whoever blasphemes against the Spirit

τὸ ἅγιον, οὐκ ἔχει ἄφεσιν εἰς τὸν αἰῶνα,
– Holy, has not forgiveness unto the age,

ἀλλὰ ἔνοχός ἐστιν αἰωνίου ἁμαρτήματος.
but liable is of an eternal sin.

30 ὅτι ἔλεγον· πνεῦμα ἀκάθαρτον ἔχει.
Because they said: spirit an unclean he has.

31 Καὶ ἔρχονται ἡ μήτηρ αὐτοῦ καὶ οἱ
And come the mother of him and the

ἀδελφοὶ αὐτοῦ, καὶ ἔξω στήκοντες ἀπέστειλαν
brothers of him, and outside standing sent

πρὸς αὐτὸν καλοῦντες αὐτόν. **32** καὶ
to him calling him. And

Zealot [19]and Judas Iscariot, who betrayed him.

Jesus and Beelzebub

[20]Then Jesus entered a house, and again a crowd gathered, so that he and his disciples were not even able to eat. [21]When his family heard about this, they went to take charge of him, for they said, "He is out of his mind."

[22]And the teachers of the law who came down from Jerusalem said, "He is possessed by Beelzebub[i]! By the prince of demons he is driving out demons."

[23]So Jesus called them and spoke to them in parables: "How can Satan drive out Satan? [24]If a kingdom is divided against itself, that kingdom cannot stand. [25]If a house is divided against itself, that house cannot stand. [26]And if Satan opposes himself and is divided, he cannot stand; his end has come. [27]In fact, no one can enter a strong man's house and carry off his possessions unless he first ties up the strong man. Then he can rob his house. [28]I tell you the truth, all the sins and blasphemies of men will be forgiven them. [29]But whoever blasphemes against the Holy Spirit will never be forgiven; he is guilty of an eternal sin."

[30]He said this because they were saying, "He has an evil spirit."

Jesus' Mother and Brothers

[31]Then Jesus' mother and brothers arrived. Standing outside, they sent someone in to call him. [32]A crowd

[i]22 Greek *Beezeboul* or *Beelzeboul*

32And a multitude was sitting around Him, and they
*said to Him, "Behold,
Your mother and Your
brothers[l] are outside looking for You."
33And answering them,
He *said, "Who are My
mother and My brothers?"
34And looking about on
those who were sitting
around Him, He *said,
"Behold, My mother and
My brothers!
35"For whoever does the
will of God, he is My brother and sister and mother."

ἐκάθητο περὶ αὐτὸν ὄχλος, καὶ λέγουσιν
sat round him a crowd, and they say
αὐτῷ· ἰδοὺ ἡ μήτηρ σου καὶ οἱ ἀδελφοί
to him: Behold[,] the mother of thee and the brothers
σου καὶ αἱ ἀδελφαί σου ἔξω ζητοῦσίν σε.
of thee and the sisters of thee outside seek thee.
33 καὶ ἀποκριθεὶς αὐτοῖς λέγει· τίς ἐστιν
And answering them he says: Who is
ἡ μήτηρ μου καὶ οἱ ἀδελφοί; 34 καὶ
the mother of me and the brothers ? And
περιβλεψάμενος τοὺς περὶ αὐτὸν κύκλῳ
looking round [at] the [ones] round him in a circle
καθημένους λέγει· ἴδε ἡ μήτηρ μου
sitting he says: Behold[,] the mother of me
καὶ οἱ ἀδελφοί μου. 35 ὃς ἂν ποιήσῃ τὸ
and the brothers of me. Whoever does the
θέλημα τοῦ θεοῦ, οὗτος ἀδελφός μου
will – of God, this one brother of me
καὶ ἀδελφὴ καὶ μήτηρ ἐστίν.
and sister and mother is.

was sitting around him, and
they told him, "Your mother and brothers are outside
looking for you."
33"Who are my mother
and my brothers?" he
asked.
34Then he looked at those
seated in a circle around
him and said, "Here are my
mother and my brothers!
35Whoever does God's will
is my brother and sister and
mother."

Chapter 4

Parable of the Sower and Soils

AND He began to teach
again by the sea. And
such a very great multitude
gathered to Him that He
got into a boat in the sea
and sat down; and the
whole multitude was by the
sea on the land.
2And He was teaching
them many things in para-
bles, and was saying to
them in His teaching,
3"Listen *to this*! Behold,
the sower went out to sow;
4and it came about that
as he was sowing, some
seed fell beside the road,
and the birds came and ate
it up.
5"And other *seed* fell on
the rocky *ground* where it
did not have much soil; and
immediately it sprang up
because it had no depth of
soil.
6"And after the sun had
risen, it was scorched; and
because it had no root, it
withered away.
7"And other *seed* fell
among the thorns, and the
thorns came up and choked
it, and it yielded no crop.
8"And other *seeds* fell
into the good soil and as

4 Καὶ πάλιν ἤρξατο διδάσκειν παρὰ τὴν
And again he began to teach by the
θάλασσαν· καὶ συνάγεται πρὸς αὐτὸν ὄχλος
sea; and is assembled to him crowd
πλεῖστος, ὥστε αὐτὸν εἰς πλοῖον ἐμβάντα
a very large, so as him in a ship embarking
= so that embarking in a ship he sat
καθῆσθαι ἐν τῇ θαλάσσῃ, καὶ πᾶς ὁ
to sit[b] in the sea, and all the
ὄχλος πρὸς τὴν θάλασσαν ἐπὶ τῆς γῆς
crowd toward the sea on the land
ἦσαν. 2 καὶ ἐδίδασκεν αὐτοὺς ἐν παραβολαῖς
were. And he taught them in parables
πολλά, καὶ ἔλεγεν αὐτοῖς ἐν τῇ διδαχῇ
many things, and said to them in the teaching
αὐτοῦ· 3 ἀκούετε. ἰδοὺ ἐξῆλθεν ὁ σπείρων
of him: Hear ye. Behold[,] went out the [one] sowing
σπεῖραι. 4 καὶ ἐγένετο ἐν τῷ σπείρειν
to sow. And it came to pass in the to sow[e]
= as he sowed
ὃ μὲν ἔπεσεν παρὰ τὴν ὁδόν, καὶ ἦλθεν
some fell by the way, and came
τὰ πετεινὰ καὶ κατέφαγεν αὐτό. 5 καὶ
the birds and devoured it. And
ἄλλο ἔπεσεν ἐπὶ τὸ πετρῶδες ὅπου οὐκ
other fell on the rocky place where not
εἶχεν γῆν πολλήν, καὶ εὐθὺς ἐξανέτειλεν
it had earth much, and immediately it sprang up
διὰ τὸ μὴ ἔχειν βάθος γῆς·
on account of the not to have depth of earth;
= because it had no depth of earth;
6 καὶ ὅτε ἀνέτειλεν ὁ ἥλιος ἐκαυματίσθη, καὶ
and when rose the sun it was scorched, and
διὰ τὸ μὴ ἔχειν ῥίζαν ἐξηράνθη. 7 καὶ
on account of the not to have root it was withered. And
= because it had no root
ἄλλο ἔπεσεν εἰς τὰς ἀκάνθας, καὶ ἀνέβησαν
other fell among the thorns, and came up
αἱ ἄκανθαι καὶ συνέπνιξαν αὐτό, καὶ
the thorns and choked it, and
καρπὸν οὐκ ἔδωκεν. 8 καὶ ἄλλα ἔπεσεν
fruit it gave not. And others fell
εἰς τὴν γῆν τὴν καλὴν καὶ ἐδίδου καρπὸν
into the earth – good and gave fruit

Chapter 4

The Parable of the Sower

AGAIN Jesus began to
teach by the lake. The
crowd that gathered around
him was so large that he got
into a boat and sat in it out
on the lake, while all the
people were along the
shore at the water's edge.
2He taught them many
things by parables, and in
his teaching said: 3"Listen!
A farmer went out to sow
his seed. 4As he was scattering the seed, some fell
along the path, and the
birds came and ate it up.
5Some fell on rocky places,
where it did not have much
soil. It sprang up quickly,
because the soil was shal-
low. 6But when the sun
came up, the plants were
scorched, and they with-
ered because they had no
root. 7Other seed fell
among thorns, which grew
up and choked the plants,
so that they did not bear
grain. 8Still other seed fell
on good soil. It came up,

[l]Later mss. add: *and Your sisters*

they grew up and in-
creased, they yielded a
crop and produced thirty,
sixty, and a hundredfold."
9And He was saying,
"He who has ears to hear,
let him hear."
10And as soon as He was
alone, His followers, along
with the twelve, *began* asking Him *about* the para-
bles.
11And He was saying to
them, "To you has been
given the mystery of the
kingdom of God; but those
who are outside get everything in parables,
12in order that WHILE SEE-
ING, THEY MAY SEE AND NOT
PERCEIVE; AND WHILE HEAR-
ING, THEY MAY HEAR AND
NOT UNDERSTAND LEST THEY
RETURN AND BE FORGIVEN."

Explanation

13And He *said to them,
"Do you not understand
this parable? And how will
you understand all the parables?
14"The sower sows the
word.
15"And these are the ones
who are beside the road
where the word is sown;
and when they hear,
immediately Satan comes
and takes away the word
which has been sown in
them.
16"And in a similar way
these are the ones on whom
seed was sown on the
rocky *places,* who, when
they hear the word,
immediately receive it with
joy;
17and they have no *firm*
root in themselves, but are
only temporary; then, when
affliction or persecution
arises because of the word,
immediately they fall away.
18"And others are the
ones on whom seed was
sown among the thorns;
these are the ones who
have heard the word,
19and the worries of the
[m]world, and the deceitfulness of riches, and the desires for other things enter
in and choke the word, and
it becomes unfruitful.
20"And those are the

ἀναβαίνοντα καὶ αὐξανόμενα καὶ ἔφερεν
coming up and growing and bore
εἰς τριάκοντα καὶ ἐν ἑξήκοντα καὶ ἐν
in thirty and in sixty and in
ἑκατόν. **9** καὶ ἔλεγεν· ὃς ἔχει ὦτα
a hundred. And he said: Who has ears
ἀκούειν ἀκουέτω. **10** Καὶ ὅτε ἐγένετο
to hear let him hear. And when he was
κατὰ μόνας, ἠρώτων αὐτὸν οἱ περὶ
alone,† asked him the [ones] round
αὐτὸν σὺν τοῖς δώδεκα τὰς παραβολάς.
him with the twelve the parables.
11 καὶ ἔλεγεν αὐτοῖς· ὑμῖν τὸ μυστήριον
And he said to them: To you the mystery
δέδοται τῆς βασιλείας τοῦ θεοῦ· ἐκείνοις δὲ
has been given of the kingdom – of God; but to those
τοῖς ἔξω ἐν παραβολαῖς τὰ πάντα
the [ones] outside in parables – all things
γίνεται, **12** ἵνα βλέποντες βλέπωσιν καὶ
is(are), that seeing they may see and
μὴ ἴδωσιν, καὶ ἀκούοντες ἀκούωσιν καὶ
not perceive, and hearing they may hear and
μὴ συνιῶσιν, μήποτε ἐπιστρέψωσιν καὶ
not understand, lest they should turn and
ἀφεθῇ αὐτοῖς. **13** καὶ λέγει αὐτοῖς·
it should be forgiven them. And he says to them:
οὐκ οἴδατε τὴν παραβολὴν ταύτην, καὶ πῶς
Know ye not – parable this, and how
πάσας τὰς παραβολὰς γνώσεσθε; **14** ὁ
all the parables will ye know? The [one]
σπείρων τὸν λόγον σπείρει. **15** οὗτοι δέ εἰσιν
sowing ²the ³word ¹sows. And these are
οἱ παρὰ τὴν ὁδόν, ὅπου σπείρεται ὁ
the [ones] by the way, where is sown the
λόγος, καὶ ὅταν ἀκούσωσιν, εὐθὺς ἔρχεται
word, and when they hear, immediately comes
ὁ σατανᾶς καὶ αἴρει τὸν λόγον τὸν
– Satan and takes the word –
ἐσπαρμένον εἰς αὐτούς. **16** καὶ οὗτοί εἰσιν
having been sown in them. And these are
ὁμοίως οἱ ἐπὶ τὰ πετρώδη σπειρόμενοι,
likewise the [ones] on the rocky places being sown,
οἳ ὅταν ἀκούσωσιν τὸν λόγον εὐθὺς
who when they hear the word immediately
μετὰ χαρᾶς λαμβάνουσιν αὐτόν, **17** καὶ
with joy receive it, and
οὐκ ἔχουσιν ῥίζαν ἐν ἑαυτοῖς ἀλλὰ
have not root in themselves but
πρόσκαιροί εἰσιν, εἶτα γενομένης θλίψεως
shortlived are, then happening affliction
= when affliction or persecution happens
ἢ διωγμοῦ διὰ τὸν λόγον εὐθὺς
or persecution[a] on account of the word immediately
σκανδαλίζονται. **18** καὶ ἄλλοι εἰσὶν οἱ εἰς
they are offended. And others are the [ones] among
τὰς ἀκάνθας σπειρόμενοι· οὗτοί εἰσιν οἱ
the thorns being sown; these are the [ones]
τὸν λόγον ἀκούσαντες, **19** καὶ αἱ μέριμναι
the word hearing, and the cares
τοῦ αἰῶνος καὶ ἡ ἀπάτη τοῦ πλούτου
of the age and the deceitfulness – of riches
καὶ αἱ περὶ τὰ λοιπὰ ἐπιθυμίαι
and ¹the ³about ⁴the ⁵other things ²desires
εἰσπορευόμεναι συμπνίγουσιν τὸν λόγον, καὶ
coming in choke the word, and
ἄκαρπος γίνεται. **20** καὶ ἐκεῖνοί εἰσιν
unfruitful it becomes. And those are

grew and produced a crop,
multiplying thirty, sixty, or
even a hundred times."
9Then Jesus said, "He
who has ears to hear, let
him hear."
10When he was alone, the
Twelve and the others
around him asked him
about the parables. 11He
told them, "The secret of
the kingdom of God has
been given to you. But to
those on the outside everything is said in parables 12so
that,

"'they may be ever
seeing but never
perceiving,
and ever hearing but
never
understanding;
otherwise they might
turn and be
forgiven!'[j]"

13Then Jesus said to
them, "Don't you under-
stand this parable? How
then will you understand
any parable? 14The farmer
sows the word. 15Some
people are like seed along
the path, where the word is
sown. As soon as they hear
it, Satan comes and takes
away the word that was
sown in them. 16Others,
like seed sown on rocky
places, hear the word and
at once receive it with joy.
17But since they have no
root, they last only a short
time. When trouble or persecution comes because of
the word, they quickly fall
away. 18Still others, like
seed sown among thorns,
hear the word; 19but the
worries of this life, the deceitfulness of wealth and
the desires for other things
come in and choke the
word, making it unfruitful.
20Others, like seed sown on

[m]Or, *age*

[j]12 Isaiah 6:9,10

ones on whom seed was
sown on the good soil; and
they hear the word and accept it, and bear fruit,
thirty, sixty, and a hun-
dredfold."
21And He was saying to
them, "A lamp is not
brought to be put under a
peck-measure, is it, or under a bed? Is it not *brought*
to be put on the lampstand?
22"For nothing is hidden,
except to be revealed; nor
has *anything* been secret,
but that it should come to
light.
23"If any man has ears to
hear, let him hear."
24And He was saying to
them, "Take care what you
listen to. By your standard
of measure it shall be measured to you; and more
shall be given you besides.
25"For whoever has, to
him shall *more* be given;
and whoever does not
have, even what he has
shall be taken away from
him."

Parable of the Seed

26And He was saying,
"The kingdom of God is
like a man who casts seed
upon the soil;
27and goes to bed at night
and gets up by day, and the
seed sprouts up and
grows—how, he himself
does not know.
28"The soil produces
crops by itself; first the
blade, then the head, then
the mature grain in the
head.
29"But when the crop
permits, he immediately
puts in the sickle, because
the harvest has come."

Parable of the Mustard Seed

30And He said, "How
shall we [n]picture the kingdom of God, or by what
parable shall we present it?
31"*It is* like a mustard
seed, which, when sown
upon the soil, though it is
smaller than all the seeds
that are upon the soil,
32yet when it is sown,
grows up and becomes
larger than all the garden
plants and forms large

[n]Lit., *compare*

οἱ ἐπὶ τὴν γῆν τὴν καλὴν σπαρέντες,
the [ones] on the earth – good sown,
οἵτινες ἀκούουσιν τὸν λόγον καὶ παραδέχονται
who hear the word and welcome [it]
καὶ καρποφοροῦσιν ἐν τριάκοντα καὶ ἐν
and bear fruit in thirty and in
ἑξήκοντα καὶ ἐν ἑκατόν. 21 Καὶ ἔλεγεν
sixty and in a hundred. And he said
αὐτοῖς ὅτι μήτι ἔρχεται ὁ λύχνος ἵνα
to them[,] – *not* Comes the lamp that
ὑπὸ τὸν μόδιον τεθῇ ἢ ὑπὸ τὴν
under the bushel it may be placed or under the
κλίνην; οὐχ ἵνα ἐπὶ τὴν λυχνίαν
couch ? not that on the lampstand
τεθῇ; 22 οὐ γάρ ἐστίν τι κρυπτόν,
it may be placed ? For there is not anything hidden,
ἐὰν μὴ ἵνα φανερωθῇ· οὐδὲ ἐγένετο
except that it may be manifested; nor became
ἀπόκρυφον, ἀλλ' ἵνα ἔλθῃ εἰς φανερόν.
covered, but that it may come into [the] open.
23 εἴ τις ἔχει ὦτα ἀκούειν ἀκουέτω.
If anyone has ears to hear let him hear.
24 Καὶ ἔλεγεν αὐτοῖς· βλέπετε τί
And he said to them: Take heed what
ἀκούετε. ἐν ᾧ μέτρῳ μετρεῖτε
ye hear. With what measure ye measure
μετρηθήσεται ὑμῖν, καὶ προστεθήσεται ὑμῖν.
it will be measured to you, and it will be added to you.
25 ὃς γὰρ ἔχει, δοθήσεται αὐτῷ· καὶ ὃς
For [he] who has, it will be given to him; and who
οὐκ ἔχει, καὶ ὃ ἔχει ἀρθήσεται ἀπ'
has not, even what he has will be taken from
αὐτοῦ. 26 Καὶ ἔλεγεν· οὕτως ἐστὶν ἡ
him. And he said: Thus is the
βασιλεία τοῦ θεοῦ, ὡς ἄνθρωπος βάλῃ
kingdom – of God, as a man might cast
τὸν σπόρον ἐπὶ τῆς γῆς, 27 καὶ καθεύδῃ
the seed on the earth, and might sleep
καὶ ἐγείρηται νύκτα καὶ ἡμέραν, καὶ ὁ
and rise night and day, and the
σπόρος βλαστᾷ καὶ μηκύνηται ὡς οὐκ
seed sprouts and lengthens as not
οἶδεν αὐτός. 28 αὐτομάτη ἡ γῆ καρποφορεῖ,
knows he. Of its own accord the earth bears fruit,
πρῶτον χόρτον, εἶτεν στάχυν, εἶτεν πλήρης
first grass, then an ear, then full
σῖτος ἐν τῷ στάχυϊ. 29 ὅταν δὲ παραδοῖ
corn in the ear. But when permits
ὁ καρπός, εὐθὺς ἀποστέλλει τὸ δρέπανον,
the fruit, immediately he sends(puts) forth the sickle,
ὅτι παρέστηκεν ὁ θερισμός. 30 Καὶ ἔλεγεν·
because has come the harvest. And he said:
πῶς ὁμοιώσωμεν τὴν βασιλείαν τοῦ θεοῦ,
How may we liken the kingdom – of God,
ἢ ἐν τίνι αὐτὴν παραβολῇ θῶμεν; 31 ὡς
or by [1]what [4]it [2]parable [3]may we place ? As
κόκκῳ σινάπεως, ὃς ὅταν σπαρῇ ἐπὶ τῆς
a grain of mustard, which when it is sown on the
γῆς, μικρότερον ὂν πάντων τῶν σπερμάτων
earth, smaller being [than] all the seeds
τῶν ἐπὶ τῆς γῆς, 32 καὶ ὅταν σπαρῇ,
– on the earth, and when it is sown,
ἀναβαίνει καὶ γίνεται μεῖζον πάντων τῶν
comes up and becomes greater [than] all the
λαχάνων, καὶ ποιεῖ κλάδους μεγάλους,
herbs, and makes branches great,

good soil, hear the word,
accept it, and produce a
crop—thirty, sixty or even
a hundred times what was
sown."

A Lamp on a Stand

21He said to them, "Do
you bring in a lamp to put it
under a bowl or a bed? Instead, don't you put it on its
stand? 22For whatever is
hidden is meant to be disclosed, and whatever is
concealed is meant to be
brought out into the open.
23If anyone has ears to
hear, let him hear."
24"Consider carefully
what you hear," he continued. "With the measure
you use, it will be measured
to you—and even more.
25Whoever has will be giv-
en more; whoever does not
have, even what he has will
be taken from him."

The Parable of the Growing Seed

26He also said, "This is
what the kingdom of God is
like. A man scatters seed
on the ground. 27Night and
day, whether he sleeps or
gets up, the seed sprouts
and grows, though he does
not know how. 28All by itself the soil produces grain
—first the stalk, then the
head, then the full kernel in
the head. 29As soon as the
grain is ripe, he puts the
sickle to it, because the
harvest has come."

The Parable of the Mustard Seed

30Again he said, "What
shall we say the kingdom of
God is like, or what parable
shall we use to describe it?
31It is like a mustard seed,
which is the smallest seed
you plant in the ground.
32Yet when planted, it
grows and becomes the
largest of all garden plants,

branches; so that THE BIRDS
OF THE °AIR can NEST UNDER
ITS SHADE."
33And with many such
parables He was speaking
the word to them as they
were able to hear it;
34and He did not speak to
them without a parable; but
He was explaining every-
thing privately to His own
disciples.

Jesus Stills the Sea

35And on that day, when
evening had come, He
*said to them, "Let us go
over to the other side."
36And leaving the multi-
tude, they *took Him along
with them, just as He was,
in the boat; and other boats
were with Him.
37And there *arose a
fierce gale of wind, and the
waves were breaking over
the boat so much that the
boat was already filling up.
38And He Himself was in
the stern, asleep on the
cushion; and they *awoke
Him and *said to Him,
"Teacher, do You not care
that we are perishing?"
39And being aroused, He
rebuked the wind and said
to the sea, "Hush, be
still." And the wind died
down and it became per-
fectly calm.
40And He said to them,
"Why are you so timid?
How is it that you have no
faith?"
41And they became very
much afraid and said to one
another, "Who then is this,
that even the wind and the
sea obey Him?"

Chapter 5

The Gerasene Demoniac

AND they came to th
other side of the sea
into the country of the Ger
asenes.
2And when He had com
out of the boat, immedi
ately a man from the tomb

°Or, *sky*

ὥστε δύνασθαι ὑπὸ τὴν σκιὰν αὐτοῦ τὰ
so as to be able under the shade of it the
= so that the birds of heaven are able to dwell under its shade.
πετεινὰ τοῦ οὐρανοῦ κατασκηνοῦν. 33 Καὶ
birds – of heaven to dwell.[b] And
τοιαύταις παραβολαῖς πολλαῖς ἐλάλει αὐτοῖς
[2]such [3]parables [1]in many he spoke to them
τὸν λόγον, καθὼς ἠδύναντο ἀκούειν·
the word, as they were able to hear;
34 χωρὶς δὲ παραβολῆς οὐκ ἐλάλει αὐτοῖς,
and without a parable he spoke not to them,
κατʼ ἰδίαν δὲ τοῖς ἰδίοις μαθηταῖς ἐπέλυεν
but privately to the(his) own disciples he explained
πάντα.
all things.

35 Καὶ λέγει αὐτοῖς ἐν ἐκείνῃ τῇ
And he says to them on that –
ἡμέρᾳ ὀψίας γενομένης· διέλθωμεν εἰς τὸ
day evening having come[a]: Let us pass over to the
=when evening had come:
πέραν. 36 καὶ ἀφέντες τὸν ὄχλον
other side. And leaving the crowd
παραλαμβάνουσιν αὐτὸν ὡς ἦν ἐν τῷ
they take him as he was in the
πλοίῳ, καὶ ἄλλα πλοῖα ἦν μετʼ αὐτοῦ.
ship, and other ships were with him.
37 καὶ γίνεται λαῖλαψ μεγάλη ἀνέμου,
And occurs storm a great of wind,
καὶ τὰ κύματα ἐπέβαλλεν εἰς τὸ πλοῖον,
and the waves struck into the ship,
ὥστε ἤδη γεμίζεσθαι τὸ πλοῖον. 38 καὶ
so as now to be filled the ship.[b] And
αὐτὸς ἦν ἐν τῇ πρύμνῃ ἐπὶ τὸ
he was in the stern on the
προσκεφάλαιον καθεύδων. καὶ ἐγείρουσιν
pillow sleeping. And they rouse
αὐτὸν καὶ λέγουσιν αὐτῷ· διδάσκαλε, οὐ μέλει
him and say to him: Teacher, matters it not
σοι ὅτι ἀπολλύμεθα; 39 καὶ διεγερθεὶς
to thee that we are perishing? And being roused
ἐπετίμησεν τῷ ἀνέμῳ καὶ εἶπεν τῇ
he rebuked the wind and said to the
θαλάσσῃ· σιώπα, πεφίμωσο. καὶ ἐκόπασεν
sea: Be quiet, be muzzled. And dropped
ὁ ἄνεμος, καὶ ἐγένετο γαλήνη μεγάλη.
the wind, and there was calm a great.
40 καὶ εἶπεν αὐτοῖς· τί δειλοί ἐστε
And he said to them: Why fearful are ye
οὕτως; πῶς οὐκ ἔχετε πίστιν; 41 καὶ
thus? how have ye not faith? And
ἐφοβήθησαν φόβον μέγαν, καὶ ἔλεγον πρὸς
they feared fear a great, and said to
ἀλλήλους· τίς ἄρα οὗτός ἐστιν, ὅτι καὶ
one another: Who then this man is, that both
ὁ ἄνεμος καὶ ἡ θάλασσα ὑπακούει αὐτῷ;
the wind and the sea obeys him?

5 Καὶ ἦλθον εἰς τὸ πέραν τῆς θαλάσσης
And they came to the other side of the sea
εἰς τὴν χώραν τῶν Γερασηνῶν. 2 καὶ
into the country of the Gerasenes. And
ἐξελθόντος αὐτοῦ ἐκ τοῦ πλοίου, [εὐθὺς]
coming *out* him[a] out of the ship, immediately
= as he came *out*
ὑπήντησεν αὐτῷ ἐκ τῶν μνημείων ἄνθρωπος
met him out of the tombs a man

with such big branches that
the birds of the air can
perch in its shade."
33With many similar para-
bles Jesus spoke the word
to them, as much as they
could understand. 34He did
not say anything to them
without using a parable.
But when he was alone
with his own disciples, he
explained everything.

Jesus Calms the Storm

35That day when evening
came, he said to his disciples, "Let us go over to the
other side." 36Leaving the
crowd behind, they took
him along, just as he was, in
the boat. There were also
other boats with him. 37A
furious squall came up, and
the waves broke over the
boat, so that it was nearly
swamped. 38Jesus was in
the stern, sleeping on a
cushion. The disciples
woke him and said to him,
"Teacher, don't you care if
we drown?"
39He got up, rebuked the
wind and said to the waves,
"Quiet! Be still!" Then the
wind died down and it was
completely calm.
40He said to his disciples,
"Why are you so afraid?
Do you still have no faith?"
41They were terrified and
asked each other, "Who is
this? Even the wind and the
waves obey him!"

Chapter 5

The Healing of a Demon-possessed Man

THEY went across the
lake to the region of
the Gerasenes.[k] 2When
Jesus got out of the boat, a
man with an evil[l] spirit
came from the tombs to

[k]1 Some manuscripts *Gadarenes*; other manuscripts *Gergesenes*

[l]2 Greek *unclean*; also in verses 8 and 13

with an unclean spirit met Him,
3and he had his dwelling among the tombs. And no one was able to bind him anymore, even with a chain;
4because he had often been bound with shackles and chains, and the chains had been torn apart by him, and the shackles broken in pieces, and no one was strong enough to subdue him.
5And constantly night and day, among the tombs and in the mountains, he was crying out and gashing himself with stones.
6And seeing Jesus from a distance, he ran up and bowed down before Him;
7and crying out with a loud voice, he *said, "What do I have to do with You, Jesus, Son of the Most High God? I implore You by God, do not torment me!"
8For He had been saying to him, "Come out of the man, you unclean spirit!"
9And He was asking him, "What is your name?" And he *said to Him, "My name is Legion; for we are many."
10And he *began* to entreat Him earnestly not to send them out of the country.
11Now there was a big herd of swine feeding there on the mountain.
12And *the demons* entreated Him, saying, "Send us into the swine so that we may enter them."
13And He gave them permission. And coming out, the unclean spirits entered the swine; and the herd rushed down the steep bank into the sea, about two thousand *of them;* and they were drowned in the sea.
14And their herdsmen ran away and reported it in the city and *out* in the country. And *the people* came to see

ἐν πνεύματι ἀκαθάρτῳ, 3 ὃς τὴν κατοίκησιν
in(with) spirit an unclean, who the(his) dwelling
εἶχεν ἐν τοῖς μνήμασιν, καὶ οὐδὲ ἁλύσει
had among the tombs, and not with a chain
=no one any more
οὐκέτι οὐδεὶς ἐδύνατο αὐτὸν δῆσαι, 4 διὰ
no longer no one was able him to bind, on account of
was able to bind him with a chain, = because
τὸ αὐτὸν πολλάκις πέδαις καὶ ἁλύσεσιν
the him often with fetters and chains
he had often been bound with fetters and chains, and . . .
δεδέσθαι, καὶ διεσπάσθαι ὑπ' αὐτοῦ τὰς
to have been bound, and to be burst by him the
ἁλύσεις καὶ τὰς πέδας συντετρῖφθαι, καὶ
chains and the fetters to have been broken, and
οὐδεὶς ἴσχυεν αὐτὸν δαμάσαι· 5 καὶ
no one was able him to subdue; and
διὰ παντὸς νυκτὸς καὶ ἡμέρας ἐν τοῖς μνήμασιν
always of(by) night and day among the tombs
καὶ ἐν τοῖς ὄρεσιν ἦν κράζων καὶ
and in the mountains he was crying out and
κατακόπτων ἑαυτὸν λίθοις. 6 καὶ ἰδὼν
cutting himself with stones. And seeing
τὸν Ἰησοῦν ἀπὸ μακρόθεν ἔδραμεν καὶ
– Jesus from afar he ran and
προσεκύνησεν αὐτόν, 7 καὶ κράξας φωνῇ
worshipped him, and crying out with a voice
μεγάλῃ λέγει· τί ἐμοὶ καὶ σοί, Ἰησοῦ
great(loud) he says: What to me and to thee, Jesus
υἱὲ τοῦ θεοῦ τοῦ ὑψίστου; ὁρκίζω σε
Son – of God the most high ? I adjure thee
τὸν θεόν, μή με βασανίσῃς. 8 ἔλεγεν
– by God, not me thou mayest torment. he said
γὰρ αὐτῷ· ἔξελθε τὸ πνεῦμα τὸ ἀκάθαρτον
For to him: Come *out* the spirit – unclean
ἐκ τοῦ ἀνθρώπου. 9 καὶ ἐπηρώτα αὐτόν·
out of the man. And he questioned him:
τί ὄνομά σοι; καὶ λέγει αὐτῷ· λεγιὼν
What name to thee?[c] And he says to him: Legion
= What name hast thou ? = My
ὄνομά μοι, ὅτι πολλοί ἐσμεν. 10 καὶ
name to me,[c] because many we are. And
name is Legion,
παρεκάλει αὐτὸν πολλὰ ἵνα μὴ αὐτὰ
he besought him much that not them
ἀποστείλῃ ἔξω τῆς χώρας. 11 ἦν δὲ
he would send outside the country. Now there was
ἐκεῖ πρὸς τῷ ὄρει ἀγέλη χοίρων μεγάλη
there near the mountain herd of pigs a great
βοσκομένη· 12 καὶ παρεκάλεσαν αὐτὸν
feeding; and they besought him
λέγοντες· πέμψον ἡμᾶς εἰς τοὺς χοίρους,
saying: Send us into the pigs,
ἵνα εἰς αὐτοὺς εἰσέλθωμεν. 13 καὶ ἐπέτρεψεν
that into them we may enter. And he allowed
αὐτοῖς. καὶ ἐξελθόντα τὰ πνεύματα τὰ
them. And coming out the spirits –
ἀκάθαρτα εἰσῆλθον εἰς τοὺς χοίρους, καὶ
unclean entered into the pigs, and
ὥρμησεν ἡ ἀγέλη κατὰ τοῦ κρημνοῦ εἰς
rushed the herd down the precipice into
τὴν θάλασσαν, ὡς δισχίλιοι, καὶ ἐπνίγοντο
the sea, about two thousand, and were choked
ἐν τῇ θαλάσσῃ. 14 καὶ οἱ βόσκοντες
in the sea. And the [ones] feeding
αὐτοὺς ἔφυγον καὶ ἀπήγγειλαν εἰς τὴν
them fled and reported in the
πόλιν καὶ εἰς τοὺς ἀγρούς· καὶ ἦλθον
city and in the fields; and they came

meet him. 3This man lived
in the tombs, and no one
could bind him any more,
not even with a chain. 4For
he had often been chained
hand and foot, but he tore
the chains apart and broke
the irons on his feet. No
one was strong enough to
subdue him. 5Night and
day among the tombs and
in the hills he would cry out
and cut himself with
stones.
6When he saw Jesus from
a distance, he ran and fell
on his knees in front of him.
7He shouted at the top of
his voice, "What do you
want with me, Jesus, Son
of the Most High God?
Swear to God that you
won't torture me!" 8For
Jesus had said to him,
"Come out of this man,
you evil spirit!"
9Then Jesus asked him,
"What is your name?"
"My name is Legion," he
replied, "for we are
many." 10And he begged
Jesus again and again not to
send them out of the area.
11A large herd of pigs was
feeding on the nearby hill-
side. 12The demons begged
Jesus, "Send us among the
pigs; allow us to go into
them." 13He gave them
permission, and the evil
spirits came out and went
into the pigs. The herd,
about two thousand in
number, rushed down the
steep bank into the lake and
were drowned.
14Those tending the pigs
ran off and reported this in
the town and countryside,
and the people went out to

what it was that had happened.

15And they *came to Jesus and *observed the man who had been demon-possessed sitting down, clothed and in his right mind, the very man who had had the "legion"; and they became frightened.

16And those who had seen it described to them how it had happened to the demon-possessed man, and *all* about the swine.

17And they began to entreat Him to depart from their region.

18And as He was getting into the boat, the man who had been demon-possessed was entreating Him that he might accompany Him.

19And He did not let him, but He *said to him, "Go home to your people and report to them [p]what great things the Lord has done for you, and *how* He had mercy on you."

20And he went away and began to proclaim in Decapolis what great things Jesus had done for him; and everyone marveled.

Miracles and Healing

21And when Jesus had crossed over again in the boat to the other side, a great multitude gathered about Him; and He stayed by the seashore.

22And one of the synagogue officials named Jairus *came up, and upon seeing Him, *fell at His feet,

23and *entreated Him earnestly, saying, "My little daughter is at the point of death; *please* come and lay Your hands on her, that she may get well and live."

24And He went off with him; and a great multitude was following Him and pressing in on Him.

25And a woman who had had a hemorrhage for twelve years,

26and had endured much at the hands of many physicians, and had spent all that she had and was not helped

[p]Or, *everything that*

ἰδεῖν τί ἐστιν τὸ γεγονός. 15 καὶ
to see what is the thing having happened. And

ἔρχονται πρὸς τὸν Ἰησοῦν, καὶ θεωροῦσιν τὸν
they come to – Jesus, and see the

δαιμονιζόμενον καθήμενον ἱματισμένον καὶ
demon-possessed man sitting *having been* clothed and

σωφρονοῦντα, τὸν ἐσχηκότα τὸν λεγιῶνα,
being in his senses, the man having had the legion,

καὶ ἐφοβήθησαν. 16 καὶ διηγήσαντο αὐτοῖς οἱ
and they were afraid. And related to them the [ones]

ἰδόντες πῶς ἐγένετο τῷ δαιμονιζομένῳ
seeing how it happened to the demon-possessed man

καὶ περὶ τῶν χοίρων. 17 καὶ ἤρξαντο
and about the pigs. And they began

παρακαλεῖν αὐτὸν ἀπελθεῖν ἀπὸ τῶν ὁρίων
to beseech him to depart from the territory

αὐτῶν. 18 καὶ ἐμβαίνοντος αὐτοῦ εἰς τὸ
of them. And embarking him[a] in the
=as he embarked

πλοῖον παρεκάλει αὐτὸν ὁ δαιμονισθεὶς
ship besought him the [one] demon-possessed

ἵνα μετ' αὐτοῦ ᾖ. 19 καὶ οὐκ ἀφῆκεν
that with him he might be. And he permitted not

αὐτόν, ἀλλὰ λέγει αὐτῷ· ὕπαγε εἰς τὸν
him, but says to him: Go to the

οἶκόν σου πρὸς τοὺς σούς, καὶ ἀπάγγειλον
house of thee to the thine, and report
= thy people,

αὐτοῖς ὅσα ὁ κύριός σοι πεποίηκεν καὶ
to them what things the Lord to thee has done and

ἠλέησέν σε. 20 καὶ ἀπῆλθεν καὶ ἤρξατο
pitied thee. And he departed and began

κηρύσσειν ἐν τῇ Δεκαπόλει ὅσα ἐποίησεν
to proclaim in – Decapolis what things did

αὐτῷ ὁ Ἰησοῦς, καὶ πάντες ἐθαύμαζον.
to him – Jesus, and all men marvelled.

21 Καὶ διαπεράσαντος τοῦ Ἰησοῦ ἐν τῷ
And crossing over – Jesus[a] in the
= when Jesus had crossed over

πλοίῳ πάλιν εἰς τὸ πέραν συνήχθη ὄχλος
ship again to the other side was assembled crowd

πολὺς ἐπ' αὐτόν, καὶ ἦν παρὰ τὴν θάλασσαν.
a much(great) to him, and he was by the sea.

22 Καὶ ἔρχεται εἷς τῶν ἀρχισυναγώγων,
And comes one of the synagogue chiefs,

ὀνόματι Ἰάϊρος, καὶ ἰδὼν αὐτὸν πίπτει
by name Jairus, and seeing him falls

πρὸς τοὺς πόδας αὐτοῦ, 23 καὶ παρακαλεῖ
at the feet of him, and beseeches

αὐτὸν πολλὰ λέγων ὅτι τὸ θυγάτριόν μου
him much saying[,] – The daughter of me

ἐσχάτως ἔχει, ἵνα ἐλθὼν ἐπιθῇς
is at the point of death,† that coming thou mayest lay *on*

τὰς χεῖρας αὐτῇ, ἵνα σωθῇ καὶ ζήσῃ.
the(thy) hands on her, that she may be healed and may live.

24 καὶ ἀπῆλθεν μετ' αὐτοῦ. καὶ ἠκολούθει αὐτῷ
And he went with him. And followed him

ὄχλος πολύς, καὶ συνέθλιβον αὐτόν. 25 Καὶ
crowd a much(great), and pressed upon him. And

γυνὴ οὖσα ἐν ῥύσει αἵματος δώδεκα
a woman being in a flow of blood twelve
= having

ἔτη, 26 καὶ πολλὰ παθοῦσα ὑπὸ πολλῶν
years, and many things suffering by many

ἰατρῶν καὶ δαπανήσασα τὰ παρ' αὐτῆς
physicians and having spent *the* with her

πάντα, καὶ μηδὲν ὠφεληθεῖσα ἀλλὰ μᾶλλον
all things, and nothing having been profited but rather

see what had happened.
15When they came to Jesus,
they saw the man who had
been possessed by the le-
gion of demons, sitting
there, dressed and in his
right mind; and they were
afraid. 16Those who had
seen it told the people what
had happened to the de-
mon-possessed man—and
told about the pigs as well.
17Then the people began to
plead with Jesus to leave
their region.
18As Jesus was getting
into the boat, the man who
had been demon-possessed
begged to go with him.
19Jesus did not let him, but
said, "Go home to your
family and tell them how
much the Lord has done for
you, and how he has had
mercy on you." 20So the
man went away and began
to tell in the Decapolis[m]
how much Jesus had done
for him. And all the people
were amazed.

A Dead Girl and a Sick Woman

21When Jesus had again
crossed over by boat to the
other side of the lake, a
large crowd gathered
around him while he was by
the lake. 22Then one of the
synagogue rulers, named
Jairus, came there. Seeing
Jesus, he fell at his feet
23and pleaded earnestly
with him, "My little daughter is dying. Please come
and put your hands on her
so that she will be healed
and live." 24So Jesus went
with him.
A large crowd followed
and pressed around him.
25And a woman was there
who had been subject to
bleeding for twelve years.
26She had suffered a great
deal under the care of many
doctors and had spent all

[m]20 That is, the Ten Cities

at all, but rather had grown
worse,
27after hearing about
Jesus, came up in the
crowd behind *Him,* and
touched His cloak.
28For she thought, "If I
just touch His garments, I
shall get well."
29And immediately the
flow of her blood was dried
up; and she felt in her body
that she was healed of her
affliction.
30And immediately Jesus,
perceiving in Himself that
the power *proceeding* from
Him had gone forth, turned
around in the crowd and
said, "Who touched My
garments?"
31And His disciples said
to Him, "You see the mul-
titude pressing in on You,
and You say, 'Who
touched Me?' "
32And He looked around
to see the woman who had
done this.
33But the woman fearing
and trembling, aware of
what had happened to her,
came and fell down before
Him, and told Him the
whole truth.
34And He said to her,
"Daughter, your faith has
made you well; go in peace,
and be healed of your affliction."
35While He was still
speaking, they *came from
the *house of* the synagogue
official, saying, "Your
daughter has died; why
trouble the Teacher any-
more?"
36But Jesus, overhearing
what was being spoken,
*said to the synagogue offi-
cial, "Do not be afraid *any
longer,* only believe."
37And He allowed no one
to follow with Him, except
Peter and James and John
the brother of James.
38And they *came to the
house of the synagogue official; and He *beheld a
commotion, and *people*
loudly weeping and wail-
ing.
39And entering in, He
*said to them, "Why make
a commotion and weep?

εἰς τὸ χεῖρον ἐλθοῦσα, 27 ἀκούσασα τὰ
to the worse having come, hearing the things
περὶ τοῦ Ἰησοῦ, ἐλθοῦσα ἐν τῷ ὄχλῳ
about – Jesus, coming in the crowd
ὄπισθεν ἥψατο τοῦ ἱματίου αὐτοῦ· 28 ἔλεγεν
behind touched the garment of him; she said[,]
γὰρ ὅτι ἐὰν ἅψωμαι κἂν τῶν ἱματίων
for – If I may touch even the garments
αὐτοῦ, σωθήσομαι. 29 καὶ εὐθὺς ἐξηράνθη
of him, I shall be healed. And immediately was dried up
ἡ πηγὴ τοῦ αἵματος αὐτῆς, καὶ ἔγνω
the fountain of the blood of her, and she knew
τῷ σώματι ὅτι ἴαται ἀπὸ τῆς
in the(her) body that she is(was) cured from the
μάστιγος. 30 καὶ εὐθὺς ὁ Ἰησοῦς ἐπιγνοὺς ἐν
plague. And immediately – Jesus knowing in
ἑαυτῷ τὴν ἐξ αὐτοῦ δύναμιν ἐξελθοῦσαν,
himself [1]the [4]out of [5]him [2]power [3]going forth,
ἐπιστραφεὶς ἐν τῷ ὄχλῳ ἔλεγεν· τίς μου ἥψατο τῶν
turning in the crowd said: Who of me touched the
ἱματίων; 31 καὶ ἔλεγον αὐτῷ οἱ μαθηταὶ
garments? And said to him the disciples
αὐτοῦ· βλέπεις τὸν ὄχλον συνθλίβοντά σε,
of him: Thou seest the crowd pressing upon thee,
καὶ λέγεις· τίς μου ἥψατο; 32 καὶ
and thou sayest: Who me touched? And
περιεβλέπετο ἰδεῖν τὴν τοῦτο ποιήσασαν.
he looked round to see the [one] this having done.
33 ἡ δὲ γυνὴ φοβηθεῖσα καὶ τρέμουσα,
And the woman fearing and trembling,
εἰδυῖα ὃ γέγονεν αὐτῇ, ἦλθεν καὶ προσέ-
knowing what has happened to her, came and fell
πεσεν αὐτῷ καὶ εἶπεν αὐτῷ πᾶσαν τὴν ἀλήθειαν.
before him and told him all the truth.
34 ὁ δὲ εἶπεν αὐτῇ· θυγάτηρ, ἡ πίστις
And he said to her: Daughter, the faith
σου σέσωκέν σε· ὕπαγε εἰς εἰρήνην, καὶ
of thee has healed thee; go in peace, and
ἴσθι ὑγιὴς ἀπὸ τῆς μάστιγός σου. 35 Ἔτι
be whole from the plague of thee. Still
= While
αὐτοῦ λαλοῦντος ἔρχονται ἀπὸ τοῦ
him speaking[a] they come from the
he was still speaking
ἀρχισυναγώγου λέγοντες ὅτι ἡ θυγάτηρ
synagogue chief saying[,] – The daughter
σου ἀπέθανεν· τί ἔτι σκύλλεις τὸν διδάσκαλον;
of thee died; why still troublest thou the teacher?
36 ὁ δὲ Ἰησοῦς παρακούσας τὸν λόγον
– But Jesus overhearing the word
λαλούμενον λέγει τῷ ἀρχισυναγώγῳ· μὴ
being spoken says to the synagogue chief: not
φοβοῦ, μόνον πίστευε. 37 καὶ οὐκ ἀφῆκεν
Fear, only believe. And he allowed not
οὐδένα μετ' αὐτοῦ συνακολουθῆσαι εἰ μὴ
no(any)one with him to accompany except
τὸν Πέτρον καὶ Ἰάκωβον καὶ Ἰωάννην
– Peter and James and John
τὸν ἀδελφὸν Ἰακώβου. 38 καὶ ἔρχονται
the brother of James. And they come
εἰς τὸν οἶκον τοῦ ἀρχισυναγώγου, καὶ
into the house of the synagogue chief, and
θεωρεῖ θόρυβον, καὶ κλαίοντας καὶ
he sees an uproar, and [men] weeping and
ἀλαλάζοντας πολλά, 39 καὶ εἰσελθὼν λέγει
crying aloud much, and entering he says
αὐτοῖς· τί θορυβεῖσθε καὶ κλαίετε; τὸ
to them: Why make ye an uproar and weep? the

she had, yet instead of getting better she grew worse.
27When she heard about
Jesus, she came up behind
him in the crowd and
touched his cloak, 28be-
cause she thought, "If I
just touch his clothes, I will
be healed." 29Immediately
her bleeding stopped and
she felt in her body that she
was freed from her suffering.
30At once Jesus realized
that power had gone out
from him. He turned
around in the crowd and
asked, "Who touched my
clothes?"
31"You see the people
crowding against you," his
disciples answered, "and
yet you can ask, 'Who
touched me?' "
32But Jesus kept looking
around to see who had
done it. 33Then the woman,
knowing what had hap-
pened to her, came and fell
at his feet and, trembling
with fear, told him the
whole truth. 34He said to
her, "Daughter, your faith
has healed you. Go in
peace and be freed from
your suffering."
35While Jesus was still
speaking, some men came
from the house of Jairus,
the synagogue ruler. "Your
daughter is dead," they
said. "Why bother the
teacher any more?"
36Ignoring what they said,
Jesus told the synagogue
ruler, "Don't be afraid; just
believe."
37He did not let anyone
follow him except Peter,
James and John the brother
of James. 38When they
came to the home of the
synagogue ruler, Jesus saw
a commotion, with people
crying and wailing loudly.
39He went in and said to
them, "Why all this com-

The child has not died, but
is asleep.''
40And they *began* laugh-
ing at Him. But putting
them all out, He *took
along the child's father and
mother and His own com-
panions, and *entered *the
room* where the child was.
41And taking the child by
the hand, He *said to her,
''Talitha kum!'' (which
translated means, ''Little
girl, I say to you, arise!'').
42And immediately the
girl rose and *began* to walk;
for she was twelve years
old. And immediately they
were completely astound-
ed.
43And He gave them
strict orders that no one
should know about this;
and He said that *something*
should be given her to eat.

παιδίον οὐκ ἀπέθανεν ἀλλὰ καθεύδει.
child did not die but sleeps.
40 καὶ κατεγέλων αὐτοῦ. αὐτὸς δὲ ἐκβαλὼν
And they ridiculed him. But he putting out
πάντας παραλαμβάνει τὸν πατέρα τοῦ
all takes the father of the
παιδίου καὶ τὴν μητέρα καὶ τοὺς μετ'
child and the mother and the [ones] with
αὐτοῦ, καὶ εἰσπορεύεται ὅπου ἦν τὸ
him, and goes in where was the
παιδίον. 41 καὶ κρατήσας τῆς χειρὸς
child. And taking hold of the hand
τοῦ παιδίου λέγει αὐτῇ· ταλιθὰ κοῦμ, ὅ
of the child he says to her: Talitha koum, which
ἐστιν μεθερμηνευόμενον· τὸ κοράσιον, σοὶ
is being interpreted: – Maid, to thee
λέγω, ἔγειρε. 42 καὶ εὐθὺς ἀνέστη τὸ
I say, arise. And immediately rose up the
κοράσιον καὶ περιεπάτει· ἦν γὰρ
maid and walked; for she was
ἐτῶν δώδεκα. καὶ ἐξέστησαν εὐθὺς
[of the age] of years twelve. And they were astonished immediately
=immediately they were exceedingly astonished.
ἐκστάσει μεγάλῃ. 43 καὶ διεστείλατο
astonishment with a great. And he ordered
αὐτοῖς πολλὰ ἵνα μηδεὶς γνοῖ τοῦτο, καὶ
them much that no one should know this, and
εἶπεν δοθῆναι αὐτῇ φαγεῖν.
told to be given to her to eat.
=[them] to give her [something] to eat.

motion and wailing? The
child is not dead but
asleep.'' 40But they
laughed at him.
After he put them all out,
he took the child's father
and mother and the disci-
ples who were with him,
and went in where the child
was. 41He took her by the
hand and said to her, *''Talitha koum!''* (which means,
''Little girl, I say to you,
get up!''). 42Immediately
the girl stood up and
walked around (she was
twelve years old). At this
they were completely as-
tonished. 43He gave strict
orders not to let anyone
know about this, and told
them to give her something
to eat.

Chapter 6

Teaching at Nazareth

AND He went out from
there, and He *came
into His home town; and
His disciples *followed
Him.
2And when the Sabbath
had come, He began to
teach in the synagogue; and
the many listeners were astonished, saying, ''Where
did this man *get* these
things, and what is *this* wisdom given to Him, and
such miracles as these performed by His hands?
3''Is not this the carpenter, the son of Mary, and
brother of James, and
Joses, and Judas, and Si-
mon? Are not His sisters
here with us?'' And they
took offense at Him.
4And Jesus said to them,
''A prophet is not without
honor except in his home
town and among his *own*
relatives and in his *own*
household.''

6 Καὶ ἐξῆλθεν ἐκεῖθεν, καὶ ἔρχεται εἰς
And he went forth thence, and comes into
τὴν πατρίδα αὐτοῦ, καὶ ἀκολουθοῦσιν
the native place of him, and follow
αὐτῷ οἱ μαθηταὶ αὐτοῦ. 2 καὶ γενομένου
him the disciples of him. And coming
= when
σαββάτου ἤρξατο διδάσκειν ἐν τῇ συναγωγῇ·
a sabbath[a] he began to teach in the synagogue;
a sabbath came
καὶ οἱ πολλοὶ ἀκούοντες ἐξεπλήσσοντο
and the many hearing were astonished
λέγοντες· πόθεν τούτῳ ταῦτα, καὶ τίς ἡ
saying: Whence to this man these things, and what the
σοφία ἡ δοθεῖσα τούτῳ; καὶ αἱ δυνάμεις
wisdom – given to this(him)? And *the* powerful deeds
τοιαῦται διὰ τῶν χειρῶν αὐτοῦ γινόμεναι;
such through the hands of him coming about?
3 οὐχ οὗτός ἐστιν ὁ τέκτων, ὁ υἱὸς
[2]Not [3]this man [1]is the carpenter, the son
τῆς Μαρίας καὶ ἀδελφὸς Ἰακώβου καὶ
– of Mary and brother of James and
Ἰωσῆτος καὶ Ἰούδα καὶ Σίμωνος; καὶ
Joses and Judas and Simon? and
οὐκ εἰσὶν αἱ ἀδελφαὶ αὐτοῦ ὧδε πρὸς
[2]not [1]are the sisters of him here with
ἡμᾶς; καὶ ἐσκανδαλίζοντο ἐν αὐτῷ. 4 καὶ
us? And they were offended in(at) him. And
ἔλεγεν αὐτοῖς ὁ Ἰησοῦς ὅτι οὐκ ἔστιν
said to them – Jesus[,] – [3]not [2]is
προφήτης ἄτιμος εἰ μὴ ἐν τῇ πατρίδι
[1]A prophet unhonoured except in the native place
αὐτοῦ καὶ ἐν τοῖς συγγενεῦσιν αὐτοῦ
of him and among the relatives of him
καὶ ἐν τῇ οἰκίᾳ αὐτοῦ. 5 καὶ οὐκ
and in the house of him. And not

Chapter 6

A Prophet Without Honor

JESUS left there and
went to his hometown,
accompanied by his disci-
ples. 2When the Sabbath
came, he began to teach in
the synagogue, and many
who heard him were
amazed.
''Where did this man get
these things?'' they asked.
''What's this wisdom that
has been given him, that he
even does miracles! 3Isn't
this the carpenter? Isn't
this Mary's son and the
brother of James, Joseph,[n]
Judas and Simon? Aren't
his sisters here with us?''
And they took offense at
him.
4Jesus said to them,
''Only in his hometown,
among his relatives and in
his own house is a prophet
without honor.'' 5He could

[n]3 Greek *Joses*, a variant of *Joseph*

5And He could do no miracle there except that He laid His hands upon a few sick people and healed them.

6And He wondered at their unbelief.

And He was going around the villages teaching.

The Twelve Sent Out

7And He *summoned the twelve and began to send them out in pairs; and He was giving them authority over the unclean spirits;

8and He instructed them that they should take nothing for *their* journey, except a mere staff; no bread, no bag, no money in their belt;

9but *to* wear sandals; and *He added,* "Do not put on two [q]tunics."

10And He said to them, "Wherever you enter a house, stay there until you leave town.

11"And any place that does not receive you or listen to you, as you go out from there, shake off the dust from the soles of your feet for a testimony against them."

12And they went out and preached that *men* should repent.

13And they were casting out many demons and were anointing with oil many sick people and healing them.

John's Fate Recalled

14And King Herod heard *of it,* for His name had become well known; and *people* were saying, "John the Baptist has risen from the dead, and that is why these miraculous powers are at work in Him."

15But others were saying, "He is Elijah." And others were saying, "*He is* a prophet, like one of the prophets *of old.*"

16But when Herod heard *of it,* he kept saying, "John, whom I beheaded, has risen!"

17For Herod himself had sent and had John arrested

[q]Or, *inner garments*

ἐδύνατο ἐκεῖ ποιῆσαι οὐδεμίαν δύναμιν,
he could there *to* do no(any) powerful deed,

εἰ μὴ ὀλίγοις ἀρρώστοις ἐπιθεὶς τὰς
except *on* a few sick [ones] laying on the(his)

χεῖρας ἐθεράπευσεν. 6 καὶ ἐθαύμασεν διὰ
hands he healed. And he marvelled because of

τὴν ἀπιστίαν αὐτῶν.
the unbelief of them.

Καὶ περιῆγεν τὰς κώμας κύκλῳ
And he went round the villages in circuit

διδάσκων. 7 Καὶ προσκαλεῖται τοὺς δώδεκα,
teaching. And he calls to [him] the twelve,

καὶ ἤρξατο αὐτοὺς ἀποστέλλειν δύο δύο,
and began them to send forth two [by] two,

καὶ ἐδίδου αὐτοῖς ἐξουσίαν τῶν πνευμάτων
and gave them authority the spirits

τῶν ἀκαθάρτων, 8 καὶ παρήγγειλεν αὐτοῖς
– of(over) unclean, and charged them

ἵνα μηδὲν αἴρωσιν εἰς ὁδὸν εἰ μὴ ῥάβδον
that nothing they should take in [the] way except a staff

μόνον, μὴ ἄρτον, μὴ πήραν, μὴ εἰς τὴν
only, not bread, not a wallet, not in the

ζώνην χαλκόν, 9 ἀλλὰ ὑποδεδεμένους σανδάλια,
girdle copper [money], but having had tied on sandals,

καὶ μὴ ἐνδύσησθε δύο χιτῶνας. 10 καὶ
and do not put on two tunics. And

ἔλεγεν αὐτοῖς· ὅπου ἐὰν εἰσέλθητε εἰς
he said to them: Wherever ye enter into

οἰκίαν, ἐκεῖ μένετε ἕως ἂν ἐξέλθητε
a house, there remain until ye go out

ἐκεῖθεν. 11 καὶ ὃς ἂν τόπος μὴ δέξηται
thence. And whatever place receives not

ὑμᾶς μηδὲ ἀκούσωσιν ὑμῶν, ἐκπορευόμενοι
you nor they hear you, going out

ἐκεῖθεν ἐκτινάξατε τὸν χοῦν τὸν ὑποκάτω
thence shake off the dust – under

τῶν ποδῶν ὑμῶν εἰς μαρτύριον αὐτοῖς.
the feet of you for a testimony to them.

12 Καὶ ἐξελθόντες ἐκήρυξαν ἵνα μετανοῶσιν,
And going forth they proclaimed that men should repent,

13 καὶ δαιμόνια πολλὰ ἐξέβαλλον, καὶ
and demons many they expelled, and

ἤλειφον ἐλαίῳ πολλοὺς ἀρρώστους καὶ
anointed with oil many sick [ones] and

ἐθεράπευον.
healed.

14 Καὶ ἤκουσεν ὁ βασιλεὺς Ἡρῴδης,
And heard the king Herod,

φανερὸν γὰρ ἐγένετο τὸ ὄνομα αὐτοῦ, καὶ
for manifest became the name of him, and

ἔλεγον ὅτι Ἰωάννης ὁ βαπτίζων ἐγήγερται
they said[,] – John the baptizing [one] has been raised

ἐκ νεκρῶν, καὶ διὰ τοῦτο ἐνεργοῦσιν αἱ
from [the] dead, and therefore operate the

δυνάμεις ἐν αὐτῷ. 15 ἄλλοι δὲ ἔλεγον
powerful deeds in him. But others said[,]

ὅτι Ἠλίας ἐστίν· ἄλλοι δὲ ἔλεγον ὅτι
– Elias it/he is; and [yet] others said[,] –

προφήτης ὡς εἷς τῶν προφητῶν. 16 ἀκούσας δὲ
A prophet as one of the prophets. But hearing

ὁ Ἡρῴδης ἔλεγεν· ὃν ἐγὼ ἀπεκεφάλισα
– Herod said: [2]whom [3]I [4]beheaded

Ἰωάννην, οὗτος ἠγέρθη. 17 Αὐτὸς γὰρ ὁ
[1]John, this was raised. For [2]himself –

Ἡρῴδης ἀποστείλας ἐκράτησεν τὸν Ἰωάννην
[1]Herod sending seized – John

not do any miracles there, except lay his hands on a few sick people and heal them. 6And he was amazed at their lack of faith.

Jesus Sends Out the Twelve

Then Jesus went around teaching from village to village. 7Calling the Twelve to him, he sent them out two by two and gave them authority over evil[o] spirits.

8These were his instructions: "Take nothing for the journey except a staff—no bread, no bag, no money in your belts. 9Wear sandals but not an extra tunic. 10Whenever you enter a house, stay there until you leave that town. 11And if any place will not welcome you or listen to you, shake the dust off your feet when you leave, as a testimony against them."

12They went out and preached that people should repent. 13They drove out many demons and anointed many sick people with oil and healed them.

John the Baptist Beheaded

14King Herod heard about this, for Jesus' name had become well known. Some were saying,[p] "John the Baptist has been raised from the dead, and that is why miraculous powers are at work in him."

15Others said, "He is Elijah."

And still others claimed, "He is a prophet, like one of the prophets of long ago."

16But when Herod heard this, he said, "John, the man I beheaded, has been raised from the dead!"

17For Herod himself had given orders to have John

[o]7 Greek *unclean*

[p]14 Some early manuscripts *He was saying*

and bound in prison on account of Herodias, the wife
of his brother Philip, because he had married her.
18For John had been say-
ing to Herod, "It is not lawful for you to have your
brother's wife."
19And Herodias had a
grudge against him and
wanted to put him to death
and could not *do so;*
20for Herod was afraid of
John, knowing that he was
a righteous and holy man,
and kept him safe. And
when he heard him, he was
very perplexed; but he used
to enjoy listening to him.
21And a strategic day
came when Herod on his
birthday gave a banquet for
his lords and military commanders and the leading
men of Galilee;
22and when the daughter
of Herodias herself came in
and danced, she pleased
Herod and his dinner
guests; and the king said to
the girl, "Ask me for whatever you want and I will
give it to you."
23And he swore to her,
"Whatever you ask of me,
I will give it to you; up to
half of my kingdom."
24And she went out and
said to her mother, "What
shall I ask for?" And she
said, "The head of John the
Baptist."
25And immediately she
came in haste before the
king and asked, saying, "I
want you to give me right
away the head of John the
Baptist on a platter."
26And although the king
was very sorry, *yet* be-
cause of his oaths and because of his dinner guests,
he was unwilling to refuse
her.
27And immediately the
king sent an executioner

καὶ ἔδησεν αὐτὸν ἐν φυλακῇ διὰ Ἡρῳδιάδα
and bound him in prison because of Herodias
τὴν γυναῖκα Φιλίππου τοῦ ἀδελφοῦ αὐτοῦ,
the wife of Philip the brother of him,
ὅτι αὐτὴν ἐγάμησεν· 18 ἔλεγεν γὰρ ὁ
because her he married; for said –
Ἰωάννης τῷ Ἡρῴδῃ ὅτι οὐκ ἔξεστίν
John – to Herod[,] – It is not lawful
σοι ἔχειν τὴν γυναῖκα τοῦ ἀδελφοῦ σου.
for thee to have the wife of the brother of thee.
19 ἡ δὲ Ἡρῳδιὰς ἐνεῖχεν αὐτῷ καὶ
– Now Herodias had a grudge against him and
ἤθελεν αὐτὸν ἀποκτεῖναι, καὶ οὐκ ἠδύνατο·
wished ²him ¹to kill, and could not;
20 ὁ γὰρ Ἡρῴδης ἐφοβεῖτο τὸν Ἰωάννην,
– for Herod feared – John,
εἰδὼς αὐτὸν ἄνδρα δίκαιον καὶ ἅγιον, καὶ
knowing him a man just and holy, and
συνετήρει αὐτόν, καὶ ἀκούσας αὐτοῦ πολλὰ
kept safe him, and hearing him much
= was
ἠπόρει, καὶ ἡδέως αὐτοῦ ἤκουεν. 21 καὶ
was in difficulties, and gladly him heard. And
in great difficulties,
γενομένης ἡμέρας εὐκαίρου ὅτε Ἡρῴδης
coming day a suitable^a when Herod
= when a suitable day came
τοῖς γενεσίοις αὐτοῦ δεῖπνον ἐποίησεν τοῖς
on the birthday festivities of him a supper made for the
μεγιστᾶσιν αὐτοῦ καὶ τοῖς χιλιάρχοις καὶ
courtiers of him and the chiliarchs and
τοῖς πρώτοις τῆς Γαλιλαίας, 22 καὶ
the chief men – of Galilee, and
εἰσελθούσης τῆς θυγατρὸς αὐτῆς τῆς
entering the daughter ²*of* herself –
= when the daughter of Herodias herself entered and danced,
Ἡρῳδιάδος καὶ ὀρχησαμένης, ἤρεσεν τῷ
¹of Herodias and dancing,^a she pleased –
Ἡρῴδῃ καὶ τοῖς συνανακειμένοις. ὁ δὲ
Herod and the [ones] reclining with [him]. And the
βασιλεὺς εἶπεν τῷ κορασίῳ· αἴτησόν με
king said to the girl: Ask me
ὃ ἐὰν θέλῃς, καὶ δώσω σοι· 23 καὶ
whatever thou wishest, and I will give thee; and
ὤμοσεν αὐτῇ ὅτι ὃ ἐὰν αἰτήσῃς δώσω
he swore to her[,] – Whatever thou askest I will give
σοι ἕως ἡμίσους τῆς βασιλείας μου.
thee up to half of the kingdom of me.
24 καὶ ἐξελθοῦσα εἶπεν τῇ μητρὶ αὐτῆς·
And going out she said to the mother of her:
τί αἰτήσωμαι; ἡ δὲ εἶπεν· τὴν κεφαλὴν
What may I ask? And she said: The head
Ἰωάννου τοῦ βαπτίζοντος. 25 καὶ
of John the [one] baptizing. And
εἰσελθοῦσα εὐθὺς μετὰ σπουδῆς πρὸς τὸν
entering immediately with haste to the
βασιλέα ᾐτήσατο λέγουσα· θέλω ἵνα ἐξαυτῆς
king she asked saying: I wish that at once
δῷς μοι ἐπὶ πίνακι τὴν κεφαλὴν Ἰωάννου
thou mayest give me on a dish the head of John
τοῦ βαπτιστοῦ. 26 καὶ περίλυπος γενόμενος
the Baptist. And deeply grieved becoming
ὁ βασιλεὺς διὰ τοὺς ὅρκους καὶ τοὺς
the king because of the oaths and the [ones]
ἀνακειμένους οὐκ ἠθέλησεν ἀθετῆσαι αὐτήν.
reclining did not wish to reject her.
27 καὶ εὐθὺς ἀποστείλας ὁ βασιλεὺς
And immediately ³sending ¹the ²king

arrested, and he had him
bound and put in prison.
He did this because of Herodias, his brother Philip's
wife, whom he had mar-
ried. 18For John had been
saying to Herod, "It is not
lawful for you to have your
brother's wife." 19So He-
rodias nursed a grudge
against John and wanted to
kill him. But she was not
able to, 20because Herod
feared John and protected
him, knowing him to be a
righteous and holy man.
When Herod heard John,
he was greatly puzzled[q];
yet he liked to listen to him.
21Finally the opportune
time came. On his birthday
Herod gave a banquet for
his high officials and military commanders and the
leading men of Galilee.
22When the daughter of Herodias came in and danced,
she pleased Herod and his
dinner guests.
The king said to the girl,
"Ask me for anything you
want, and I'll give it to
you." 23And he promised
her with an oath, "Whatever you ask I will give you,
up to half my kingdom."
24She went out and said to
her mother, "What shall I
ask for?"
"The head of John the
Baptist," she answered.
25At once the girl hurried
in to the king with the request: "I want you to give
me right now the head of
John the Baptist on a platter."
26The king was greatly
distressed, but because of
his oaths and his dinner
guests, he did not want to
refuse her. 27So he immediately sent an executioner

q20 Some early manuscripts *he did many things*

and commanded *him* to
bring *back* his head. And he
went and had him behead-
ed in the prison,
28and brought his head on
a platter, and gave it to the
girl; and the girl gave it to
her mother.
29And when his disciples
heard *about this*, they
came and took away his
body and laid it in a tomb.
30And the apostles *gath-
ered together with Jesus;
and they reported to Him
all that they had done and
taught.
31And He *said to them,
"Come away by your-
selves to a lonely place and
rest a while." (For there
were many *people* coming
and going, and they did not
even have time to eat.)
32And they went away in
the boat to a lonely place by
themselves.

Five Thousand Fed

33And *the people* saw
them going, and many
recognized *them*, and they
ran there together on foot
from all the cities, and got
there ahead of them.
34And when He went
ashore, He saw a great multitude, and He felt compassion for them because they
were like sheep without a
shepherd; and He began to
teach them many things.
35And when it was al-
ready quite late, His disciples came up to Him and
began saying, "The place
is desolate and it is already
quite late;
36send them away so that
they may go into the sur-
rounding countryside and
villages and buy them-
selves something to eat."
37But He answered and
said to them, "You give
them *something* to eat!"
And they *said to Him,

σπεκουλάτορα ἐπέταξεν ἐνέγκαι τὴν κεφαλὴν
an executioner gave order to bring the head
αὐτοῦ. καὶ ἀπελθὼν ἀπεκεφάλισεν αὐτὸν
of him. And going he beheaded him
ἐν τῇ φυλακῇ, 28 καὶ ἤνεγκεν τὴν κεφαλὴν
in the prison, and brought the head
αὐτοῦ ἐπὶ πίνακι καὶ ἔδωκεν αὐτὴν τῷ
of him on a dish and gave it to the
κορασίῳ, καὶ τὸ κοράσιον ἔδωκεν αὐτὴν
girl, and the girl gave it
τῇ μητρὶ αὐτῆς. 29 καὶ ἀκούσαντες οἱ
to the mother of her. And hearing the
μαθηταὶ αὐτοῦ ἦλθαν καὶ ἦραν τὸ πτῶμα
disciples of him went and took the corpse
αὐτοῦ καὶ ἔθηκαν αὐτὸ ἐν μνημείῳ.
of him and put it in a tomb.
30 Καὶ συνάγονται οἱ ἀπόστολοι πρὸς
And assemble the apostles to
τὸν Ἰησοῦν, καὶ ἀπήγγειλαν αὐτῷ πάντα
– Jesus, and reported to him all things
ὅσα ἐποίησαν καὶ ὅσα ἐδίδαξαν. 31 καὶ
which they did and which they taught. And
λέγει αὐτοῖς· δεῦτε ὑμεῖς αὐτοὶ κατ'
he says to them: Come ye [your]selves pri-
ἰδίαν εἰς ἔρημον τόπον καὶ ἀναπαύσασθε ὀλίγον.
vately to a desert place and rest a little.
ἦσαν γὰρ οἱ ἐρχόμενοι καὶ οἱ
For [2]were [3]the [ones] [4]coming [5]and [6]the [ones]
ὑπάγοντες πολλοί, καὶ οὐδὲ φαγεῖν
[7]going [1]many, and not to eat
εὐκαίρουν. 32 καὶ ἀπῆλθον ἐν τῷ πλοίῳ
they had opportunity. And they went away in the ship
εἰς ἔρημον τόπον κατ' ἰδίαν. 33 καὶ
to a desert place privately. And
εἶδον αὐτοὺς ὑπάγοντας καὶ ἐπέγνωσαν
[2]saw [3]them [4]going [5]and [6]knew
πολλοί, καὶ πεζῇ ἀπὸ πασῶν τῶν πόλεων
[1]many, and on foot from all the cities
συνέδραμον ἐκεῖ καὶ προῆλθον αὐτούς.
ran together there and came before them.
34 Καὶ ἐξελθὼν εἶδεν πολὺν ὄχλον, καὶ
And going forth he saw a much(great) crowd, and
ἐσπλαγχνίσθη ἐπ' αὐτοὺς ὅτι ἦσαν ὡς
had compassion on them because they were as
πρόβατα μὴ ἔχοντα ποιμένα, καὶ ἤρξατο
sheep not having a shepherd, and he began
διδάσκειν αὐτοὺς πολλά. 35 Καὶ ἤδη ὥρας
to teach them many things. And now an hour
= it being
πολλῆς γενομένης προσελθόντες αὐτῷ οἱ
much coming[a] approaching *to* him the
late
μαθηταὶ αὐτοῦ ἔλεγον ὅτι ἔρημός ἐστιν
disciples of him said[,] – Desert is
ὁ τόπος καὶ ἤδη ὥρα πολλή· 36 ἀπόλυσον
the place and now hour a much; dismiss
= it is late;
αὐτούς, ἵνα ἀπελθόντες εἰς τοὺς κύκλῳ
them, that going away to the round about
ἀγροὺς καὶ κώμας ἀγοράσωσιν ἑαυτοῖς τί
fields and villages they may buy for themselves what
φάγωσιν. 37 ὁ δὲ ἀποκριθεὶς εἶπεν αὐτοῖς·
they may eat. But he answering said to them:
δότε αὐτοῖς ὑμεῖς φαγεῖν. καὶ λέγουσιν
Give them ye to eat. And they say

with orders to bring John's
head. The man went, be-
headed John in the prison,
28and brought back his
head on a platter. He presented it to the girl, and she
gave it to her mother. 29On
hearing of this, John's disciples came and took his
body and laid it in a tomb.

Jesus Feeds the Five Thousand

30The apostles gathered
around Jesus and reported
to him all they had done
and taught. 31Then, be-
cause so many people were
coming and going that they
did not even have a chance
to eat, he said to them,
"Come with me by your-
selves to a quiet place and
get some rest."
32So they went away by
themselves in a boat to a
solitary place. 33But many
who saw them leaving rec-
ognized them and ran on
foot from all the towns and
got there ahead of them.
34When Jesus landed and
saw a large crowd, he had
compassion on them, be-
cause they were like sheep
without a shepherd. So he
began teaching them many
things.
35By this time it was late
in the day, so his disciples
came to him. "This is a remote place," they said,
"and it's already very late.
36Send the people away so
they can go to the sur-
rounding countryside and
villages and buy them-
selves something to eat."
37But he answered, "You
give them something to
eat."
They said to him, "That

"Shall we go and spend
two hundred [r]denarii on
bread and give them *something* to eat?"
38And He *said to them,
"How many loaves do you
have? Go look!" And when
they found out, they *said,
"Five and two fish."
39And He commanded
them all to recline by
groups on the green grass.
40And they reclined in
companies of hundreds and
of fifties.
41And He took the five
loaves and the two fish, and
looking up toward heaven,
He blessed *the food* and
broke the loaves and He
kept giving *them* to the disciples to set before them;
and He divided up the two
fish among them all.
42And they all ate and
were satisfied.
43And they picked up
twelve full baskets of the
broken pieces, and also of
the fish.
44And there were five
thousand men who ate the
loaves.

Jesus Walks on the Water

45And immediately He
made His disciples get into
the boat and go ahead of
Him to the other side to
Bethsaida, while He Him-
self was sending the multitude away.
46And after bidding them
farewell, He departed to
the mountain to pray.
47And when it was eve-
ning, the boat was in the
midst of the sea, and He
was alone on the land.
48And seeing them strain-
ing at the oars, for the wind
was against them, at about
the fourth watch of the
night, He *came to them,
walking on the sea; and He
intended to pass by them.
49But when they saw Him
walking on the sea, they
supposed that it was a
ghost, and cried out;

[r]The denarius was equivalent to one day's wage

αὐτῷ· ἀπελθόντες ἀγοράσωμεν δηναρίων
to him: Going away may we buy [2]of(for) [4]denarii

διακοσίων ἄρτους, καὶ δώσομεν αὐτοῖς
[3]two hundred [1]loaves, and shall we give them

φαγεῖν; 38 ὁ δὲ λέγει αὐτοῖς· πόσους
to eat ? And he says to them: How many

ἔχετε ἄρτους; ὑπάγετε ἴδετε. καὶ γνόντες
have ye loaves ? Go see. And knowing

λέγουσιν· πέντε, καὶ δύο ἰχθύας. 39 καὶ
they say: Five, and two fishes. And

ἐπέταξεν αὐτοῖς ἀνακλιθῆναι πάντας συμπόσια
he instructed them to recline all companies

συμπόσια ἐπὶ τῷ χλωρῷ χόρτῳ. 40 καὶ
companies on the green grass. And

ἀνέπεσαν πρασιαὶ πρασιαὶ κατὰ ἑκατὸν
they reclined groups groups by a hundred

καὶ κατὰ πεντήκοντα. 41 καὶ λαβὼν τοὺς
and by fifty. And taking the

πέντε ἄρτους καὶ τοὺς δύο ἰχθύας,
five loaves and the two fishes,

ἀναβλέψας εἰς τὸν οὐρανὸν εὐλόγησεν καὶ
looking up to – heaven he blessed and

κατέκλασεν τοὺς ἄρτους καὶ ἐδίδου τοῖς
broke the loaves and gave to the

μαθηταῖς ἵνα παρατιθῶσιν αὐτοῖς, καὶ
disciples that they might set before them, and

τοὺς δύο ἰχθύας ἐμέρισεν πᾶσιν. 42 καὶ
the two fishes he divided to all. And

ἔφαγον πάντες καὶ ἐχορτάσθησαν, 43 καὶ
they ate all and were satisfied, and

ἦραν κλάσματα δώδεκα κοφίνων πληρώματα
they took fragments twelve [2]of baskets [1]fullnesses

καὶ ἀπὸ τῶν ἰχθύων. 44 καὶ ἦσαν οἱ
and from the fishes. And were the

φαγόντες τοὺς ἄρτους πεντακισχίλιοι ἄνδρες.
[ones] eating the loaves five thousand males.

45 Καὶ εὐθὺς ἠνάγκασεν τοὺς μαθητὰς
And immediately he constrained the disciples

αὐτοῦ ἐμβῆναι εἰς τὸ πλοῖον καὶ προάγειν
of him to embark in the ship and to go before

εἰς τὸ πέραν πρὸς Βηθσαϊδάν, ἕως αὐτὸς
to the other side to Bethsaida, until he

ἀπολύει τὸν ὄχλον. 46 καὶ ἀποταξάμενος
dismisses the crowd. And having said farewell

αὐτοῖς ἀπῆλθεν εἰς τὸ ὄρος προσεύξασθαι.
to them he went away to the mountain to pray.

47 καὶ ὀψίας γενομένης ἦν τὸ πλοῖον ἐν
And evening coming on[a] was the ship in
= when evening came on

μέσῳ τῆς θαλάσσης, καὶ αὐτὸς μόνος ἐπὶ
[the] midst of the sea, and he alone on

τῆς γῆς. 48 καὶ ἰδὼν αὐτοὺς βασανιζομένους
the land. And seeing them being distressed

ἐν τῷ ἐλαύνειν, ἦν γὰρ ὁ ἄνεμος ἐναντίος
in the to row, [4]was [1]for [2]the [3]wind contrary
= rowing,

αὐτοῖς, περὶ τετάρτην φυλακὴν τῆς νυκτὸς
to them, about [the] fourth watch of the night

ἔρχεται πρὸς αὐτοὺς περιπατῶν ἐπὶ τῆς
he comes toward them walking on the

θαλάσσης· καὶ ἤθελεν παρελθεῖν αὐτούς.
sea; and wished to go by them.

49 οἱ δὲ ἰδόντες αὐτὸν ἐπὶ τῆς θαλάσσης
But they seeing him on the sea

περιπατοῦντα ἔδοξαν ὅτι φάντασμά ἐστιν,
walking thought that a phantasm it is(was),

would take eight months of
a man's wages[r]! Are we to
go and spend that much on
bread and give it to them to
eat?"
38"How many loaves do
you have?" he asked. "Go
and see."
When they found out,
they said, "Five—and two
fish."
39Then Jesus directed
them to have all the people
sit down in groups on the
green grass. 40So they sat
down in groups of hun-
dreds and fifties. 41Taking
the five loaves and the two
fish and looking up to heav-
en, he gave thanks and
broke the loaves. Then he
gave them to his disciples
to set before the people. He
also divided the two fish
among them all. 42They all
ate and were satisfied,
43and the disciples picked
up twelve basketfuls of
broken pieces of bread and
fish. 44The number of the
men who had eaten was
five thousand.

Jesus Walks on the Water

45Immediately Jesus
made his disciples get into
the boat and go on ahead of
him to Bethsaida, while he
dismissed the crowd. 46Af-
ter leaving them, he went
up on a mountainside to
pray.
47When evening came,
the boat was in the middle
of the lake, and he was
alone on land. 48He saw the
disciples straining at the
oars, because the wind was
against them. About the
fourth watch of the night he
went out to them, walking
on the lake. He was about
to pass by them, 49but
when they saw him walking
on the lake, they thought he
was a ghost. They cried

[r]37 Greek *take two hundred denarii*

50for they all saw Him and were frightened. But immediately He spoke with them and *said to them, "Take courage; it is I, do not be afraid."

51And He got into the boat with them, and the wind stopped; and they were greatly astonished,

52for they had not gained any insight from the *incident of* the loaves, but their heart was hardened.

Healing at Gennesaret

53And when they had crossed over they came to land at Gennesaret, and moored to the shore.

54And when they had come out of the boat, immediately *the people* recognized Him,

55and ran about that whole country and began to carry about on their pallets those who were sick, to the place they heard He was.

56And wherever He entered villages, or cities, or countryside, they were laying the sick in the market places, and entreating Him that they might just touch the fringe of His cloak; and as many as touched it were being cured.

καὶ ἀνέκραξαν· **50** πάντες γὰρ αὐτὸν εἶδαν
and cried out; for all him saw
καὶ ἐταράχθησαν. ὁ δὲ εὐθὺς ἐλάλησεν
and were troubled. But he immediately talked
μετ᾽ αὐτῶν, καὶ λέγει αὐτοῖς· θαρσεῖτε,
with them, and says to them: Be of good cheer,
ἐγώ εἰμι· μὴ φοβεῖσθε. **51** καὶ ἀνέβη
I am; be ye not afraid. And he went up
πρὸς αὐτοὺς εἰς τὸ πλοῖον, καὶ ἐκόπασεν
to them into the ship, and ceased
ὁ ἄνεμος· καὶ λίαν ἐκ περισσοῦ ἐν ἑαυτοῖς
the wind; and very much exceedingly in themselves
ἐξίσταντο· **52** οὐ γὰρ συνῆκαν ἐπὶ
they were astonished ; for they did not understand concerning
τοῖς ἄρτοις ἀλλ᾽ ἦν αὐτῶν ἡ καρδία
the loaves, but was of them the heart
πεπωρωμένη. **53** Καὶ διαπεράσαντες ἐπὶ
having been hardened. And crossing over [2]onto
τὴν γῆν ἦλθον εἰς Γεννησαρὲτ καὶ
[3]the [4]land [1]they came to Gennesaret and
προσωρμίσθησαν. **54** καὶ ἐξελθόντων αὐτῶν
anchored. And coming *out* them[a]
= as they came
ἐκ τοῦ πλοίου εὐθὺς ἐπιγνόντες αὐτὸν
out of the ship immediately knowing him
55 περιέδραμον ὅλην τὴν χώραν ἐκείνην
they ran round all – country that
καὶ ἤρξαντο ἐπὶ τοῖς κραβάτοις τοὺς
and began on the pallets the [ones]
= those
κακῶς ἔχοντας περιφέρειν, ὅπου ἤκουον
ill having to carry round, where they heard
who were ill
ὅτι ἐστίν. **56** καὶ ὅπου ἂν εἰσεπορεύετο
that he is(was). And wherever he entered
εἰς κώμας ἢ εἰς πόλεις ἢ εἰς ἀγρούς,
into villages or into cities or into country,
ἐν ταῖς ἀγοραῖς ἐτίθεσαν τοὺς ἀσθενοῦντας,
in the marketplaces they put the ailing [ones],
καὶ παρεκάλουν αὐτὸν ἵνα κἂν τοῦ
and besought him that if even the
κρασπέδου τοῦ ἱματίου αὐτοῦ ἅψωνται·
fringe of the garment of him they might touch;
καὶ ὅσοι ἂν ἥψαντο αὐτοῦ ἐσῴζοντο.
and as many as touched him were healed.

out, 50because they all saw him and were terrified.

Immediately he spoke to them and said, "Take courage! It is I. Don't be afraid." 51Then he climbed into the boat with them, and the wind died down. They were completely amazed, 52for they had not understood about the loaves; their hearts were hardened.

53When they had crossed over, they landed at Gennesaret and anchored there. 54As soon as they got out of the boat, people recognized Jesus. 55They ran throughout that whole region and carried the sick on mats to wherever they heard he was. 56And wherever he went—into villages, towns or countryside—they placed the sick in the marketplaces. They begged him to let them touch even the edge of his cloak, and all who touched him were healed.

Chapter 7

Followers of Tradition

AND the Pharisees and some of the scribes gathered together around Him when they had come from Jerusalem,

2and had seen that some of His disciples were eating their bread with impure hands, that is, unwashed.

3(For the Pharisees and all the Jews do not eat unless they carefully wash their hands, *thus* observing the traditions of the elders;

4and *when they come* from the market place, they do not eat unless they cleanse themselves; and

7 Καὶ συνάγονται πρὸς αὐτὸν οἱ Φαρισαῖοι
And assemble to him the Pharisees
καί τινες τῶν γραμματέων ἐλθόντες ἀπὸ
and some of the scribes coming from
Ἱεροσολύμων. **2** καὶ ἰδόντες τινὰς τῶν
Jerusalem. And seeing some of the
μαθητῶν αὐτοῦ ὅτι κοιναῖς χερσίν, τοῦτ᾽
disciples of him that with unclean hands, this
ἔστιν ἀνίπτοις, ἐσθίουσιν τοὺς ἄρτους,
is unwashed, they eat bread,
3 — οἱ γὰρ Φαρισαῖοι καὶ πάντες οἱ
— for the Pharisees and all the
Ἰουδαῖοι ἐὰν μὴ πυγμῇ νίψωνται τὰς
Jews unless with [the] fist they wash the
= ? carefully
χεῖρας οὐκ ἐσθίουσιν, κρατοῦντες τὴν
hands eat not, holding the
παράδοσιν τῶν πρεσβυτέρων, **4** καὶ ἀπ᾽
tradition of the elders, and from
ἀγορᾶς ἐὰν μὴ ῥαντίσωνται οὐκ ἐσθίουσιν, καὶ
marketplaces unless they sprinkle they eat not, and

Chapter 7

Clean and Unclean

THE Pharisees and some of the teachers of the law who had come from Jerusalem gathered around Jesus and 2saw some of his disciples eating food with hands that were "unclean," that is, unwashed. 3(The Pharisees and all the Jews do not eat unless they give their hands a ceremonial washing, holding to the tradition of the elders. 4When they come from the marketplace they do not eat unless they wash. And

there are many other things which they have received in order to observe, such as the washing of cups and pitchers and copper pots.)
5And the Pharisees and the scribes *asked Him, "Why do Your disciples not walk according to the tradition of the elders, but eat their bread with impure hands?"
6And He said to them, "Rightly did Isaiah prophesy of you hypocrites, as it is written,

'This people honors Me with their lips,
But their heart is far away from Me.
7 'But in vain do they worship Me,
Teaching as doctrines the precepts of men.'

8"Neglecting the commandment of God, you hold to the tradition of men."
9He was also saying to them, "You nicely set aside the commandment of God in order to keep your tradition.
10"For Moses said, 'Honor your father and your mother'; and, 'He who speaks evil of father or mother, let him be put to death';
11but you say, 'If a man says to *his* father or *his* mother, anything of mine you might have been helped by is Corban (that is to say, [s]given *to God*),'
12you no longer permit him to do anything for *his* father or *his* mother;
13*thus* invalidating the word of God by your tradition which you have handed down; and you do many things such as that."

The Heart of Man

14And after He called the multitude to Him again, He *began* saying to them, "Listen to Me, all of you, and understand:
15there is nothing outside the man which going into him can defile him; but the things which proceed out of

[s]Or, *a gift, an offering*

ἄλλα πολλά ἐστιν ἃ παρέλαβον κρατεῖν,
other things many there are which they received to hold,
βαπτισμοὺς ποτηρίων καὶ ξεστῶν καὶ
washings of cups and of utensils and
χαλκίων, — 5 καὶ ἐπερωτῶσιν αὐτὸν οἱ
of bronze vessels, — and questioned him the
Φαρισαῖοι καὶ οἱ γραμματεῖς· διὰ τί
Pharisees and the scribes: Why
οὐ περιπατοῦσιν οἱ μαθηταί σου κατὰ τὴν
walk not the disciples of thee according to the
παράδοσιν τῶν πρεσβυτέρων, ἀλλὰ κοιναῖς
tradition of the elders, but with unclean
χερσὶν ἐσθίουσιν τὸν ἄρτον; 6 ὁ δὲ εἶπεν
hands eat – bread ? And he said
αὐτοῖς· καλῶς ἐπροφήτευσεν Ἠσαΐας περὶ
to them: Well prophesied Esaias concerning
ὑμῶν τῶν ὑποκριτῶν, ὡς γέγραπται ὅτι
you *the* hypocrites, as it has been written[:] –
οὗτος ὁ λαὸς τοῖς χείλεσίν με τιμᾷ,
This – people with the lips me honours,
ἡ δὲ καρδία αὐτῶν πόρρω ἀπέχει ἀπ'
but the heart of them [2]far [1]is [3]away from
ἐμοῦ· 7 μάτην δὲ σέβονταί με, διδάσκοντες
me; and in vain they worship me, teaching
διδασκαλίας ἐντάλματα ἀνθρώπων. 8 ἀφέντες
teachings [which are] commands of men. Leaving
τὴν ἐντολὴν τοῦ θεοῦ κρατεῖτε τὴν
the commandment – of God ye hold the
παράδοσιν τῶν ἀνθρώπων. 9 καὶ ἔλεγεν
tradition – of men. And he said
αὐτοῖς· καλῶς ἀθετεῖτε τὴν ἐντολὴν τοῦ
to them: Well ye set aside the commandment –
θεοῦ, ἵνα τὴν παράδοσιν ὑμῶν τηρήσητε.
of God, that the tradition of you ye may keep.
10 Μωϋσῆς γὰρ εἶπεν· τίμα τὸν πατέρα σου
For Moses said: Honour the father of thee
καὶ τὴν μητέρα σου, καί· ὁ κακολογῶν
and the mother of thee, and: The [one] speaking evil of
πατέρα ἢ μητέρα θανάτῳ τελευτάτω. 11 ὑμεῖς
father or mother by death let him end(die). ye
δὲ λέγετε· ἐὰν εἴπῃ ἄνθρωπος τῷ πατρὶ
But say: If says a man to the(his) father
ἢ τῇ μητρί· κορβᾶν, ὅ ἐστιν δῶρον,
or to the mother: Korban, which is a gift,
ὃ ἐὰν ἐξ ἐμοῦ ὠφελήθῃς, 12 οὐκέτι ἀφίετε
whatever by me thou mightest profit, no longer ye allow
αὐτὸν οὐδὲν ποιῆσαι τῷ πατρὶ ἢ τῇ
him no(any)thing to do for the father or the
μητρί, 13 ἀκυροῦντες τὸν λόγον τοῦ θεοῦ
mother, annulling the word – of God
τῇ παραδόσει ὑμῶν ᾗ παρεδώκατε· καὶ
by the tradition of you which ye received; and
παρόμοια τοιαῦτα πολλὰ ποιεῖτε. 14 Καὶ
[3]similar things [2]such [1]many ye do. And
προσκαλεσάμενος πάλιν τὸν ὄχλον ἔλεγεν
calling to [him] again the crowd he said
αὐτοῖς· ἀκούσατέ μου πάντες καὶ σύνετε.
to them: Hear ye me all and understand.
15 οὐδέν ἐστιν ἔξωθεν τοῦ ἀνθρώπου
Nothing there is from without – a man
εἰσπορευόμενον εἰς αὐτὸν ὃ δύναται κοινῶσαι
entering into him which can *to* defile
αὐτόν· ἀλλὰ τὰ ἐκ τοῦ ἀνθρώπου ἐκπο-
him; but the things out of – a man coming

they observe many other traditions, such as the washing of cups, pitchers and kettles.[s])
5So the Pharisees and teachers of the law asked Jesus, "Why don't your disciples live according to the tradition of the elders instead of eating their food with 'unclean' hands?"
6He replied, "Isaiah was right when he prophesied about you hypocrites; as it is written:

" 'These people honor me with their lips,
but their hearts are far from me.
7They worship me in vain;
their teachings are but rules taught by men.'[t]

8You have let go of the commands of God and are holding on to the traditions of men."
9And he said to them: "You have a fine way of setting aside the commands of God in order to observe[u] your own traditions! 10For Moses said, 'Honor your father and your mother,'[v] and, 'Anyone who curses his father or mother must be put to death.'[w] 11But you say that if a man says to his father or mother: 'Whatever help you might otherwise have received from me is Corban' (that is, a gift devoted to God),
12then you no longer let him do anything for his father or mother. 13Thus you nullify the word of God by your tradition that you have handed down. And you do many things like that."
14Again Jesus called the crowd to him and said, "Listen to me, everyone, and understand this.
15Nothing outside a man can make him 'unclean' by going into him. Rather, it is what comes out of a man

[s]4 Some early manuscripts *pitchers, kettles and dining couches*
[t]6,7 Isaiah 29:13
[u]9 Some manuscripts *set up*
[v]10 Exodus 20:12; Deut. 5:16
[w]10 Exodus 21:17; Lev. 20:9

the man are what defile the
man.
16["[t]If any man has ears
to hear, let him hear."]
17And when leaving the
multitude, He had entered
the house, His disciples
questioned Him about the
parable.
18And He *said to them,
"Are you so lacking in
understanding also? Do
you not understand that
whatever goes into the man
from outside cannot defile
him;
19because it does not go
into his heart, but into his
stomach, and is elimi-
nated?" (*Thus He* declared
all foods clean.)
20And He was saying,
"That which proceeds out
of the man, that is what
defiles the man.
21"For from within, out
of the heart of men, pro-
ceed the evil thoughts, fornications, thefts, murders,
adulteries,
22deeds of coveting *and*
wickedness, *as well as* deceit, sensuality, envy, slander, pride *and* foolishness.
23"All these evil things
proceed from within and
defile the man."

The Syrophoenician Woman

24And from there He
arose and went away to the
region of Tyre[u]. And when
He had entered a house, He
wanted no one to know *of*
it; yet He could not escape
notice.
25But after hearing of
Him, a woman whose little
daughter had an unclean
spirit, immediately came
and fell at His feet.
26Now the woman was a
[v]Gentile, of the Syrophoenician race. And she kept
asking Him to cast the demon out of her daughter.
27And He was saying to
her, "Let the children be
satisfied first, for it is not
good to take the children's
bread and throw it to the
dogs."

[t] Many mss. do not contain this verse
[u] Some early mss. add: *and Sidon*
[v] Lit., *Greek*

ῥευόμενά ἐστιν τὰ κοινοῦντα τὸν ἄνθρωπον.‡
forth are the [ones] defiling – a man.
17 Καὶ ὅτε εἰσῆλθεν εἰς οἶκον ἀπὸ τοῦ
And when he entered into a house from the
ὄχλου, ἐπηρώτων αὐτὸν οἱ μαθηταὶ αὐτοῦ
crowd, questioned him the disciples of him
τὴν παραβολήν. **18** καὶ λέγει αὐτοῖς·
the parable. And he says to them:
οὕτως καὶ ὑμεῖς ἀσύνετοί ἐστε; οὐ
Thus also ye undiscerning are? do ye not
νοεῖτε ὅτι πᾶν τὸ ἔξωθεν εἰσπορευόμενον
understand that everything from without entering
εἰς τὸν ἄνθρωπον οὐ δύναται αὐτὸν
into – a man cannot him
κοινῶσαι, **19** ὅτι οὐκ εἰσπορεύεται αὐτοῦ
to defile, because it enters not of him
εἰς τὴν καρδίαν ἀλλ' εἰς τὴν κοιλίαν,
into the heart but into the belly,
καὶ εἰς τὸν ἀφεδρῶνα ἐκπορεύεται, καθα-
and into the drain goes out, purg-
ρίζων πάντα τὰ βρώματα; **20** ἔλεγεν δὲ
ing all – foods? And he said[,]
ὅτι τὸ ἐκ τοῦ ἀνθρώπου ἐκπορευόμενον,
– The thing out of – a man coming forth,
ἐκεῖνο κοινοῖ τὸν ἄνθρωπον. **21** ἔσωθεν
that defiles – a man. from within
γὰρ ἐκ τῆς καρδίας τῶν ἀνθρώπων
For out of the heart – of men
οἱ διαλογισμοὶ οἱ κακοὶ ἐκπορεύονται,
– thoughts – evil come forth,
πορνεῖαι, κλοπαί, φόνοι, **22** μοιχεῖαι,
fornications, thefts, murders, adulteries,
πλεονεξίαι, πονηρίαι, δόλος, ἀσέλγεια, ὀφθαλμὸς
greedinesses, iniquities, deceit, lewdness, eye
πονηρός, βλασφημία, ὑπερηφανία, ἀφροσύνη·
an evil, blasphemy, arrogance, foolishness;
23 πάντα ταῦτα τὰ πονηρὰ ἔσωθεν ἐκπορεύεται
all these – evil things from within comes forth
καὶ κοινοῖ τὸν ἄνθρωπον.
and defile – a man.
24 Ἐκεῖθεν δὲ ἀναστὰς ἀπῆλθεν εἰς τὰ ὅρια
And thence rising up he went away into the district
Τύρου. Καὶ εἰσελθὼν εἰς οἰκίαν οὐδένα ἤθελεν
of Tyre. And entering into a house no one he wished
γνῶναι, καὶ οὐκ ἠδυνάσθη λαθεῖν· **25** ἀλλ'
to know, and could not *to* be hidden; but
εὐθὺς ἀκούσασα γυνὴ περὶ αὐτοῦ, ἧς
immediately [2]hearing [1]a woman about him, of whom = whose
εἶχεν τὸ θυγάτριον αὐτῆς πνεῦμα ἀκάθαρτον,
had the daughter of her spirit an unclean,
daughter had
ἐλθοῦσα προσέπεσεν πρὸς τοὺς πόδας αὐτοῦ·
coming fell at the feet of him;
26 ἡ δὲ γυνὴ ἦν Ἑλληνίς, Συροφοινίκισσα
and the woman was a Greek, a Syrophenician
τῷ γένει· καὶ ἠρώτα αὐτὸν ἵνα τὸ
– by race; and she asked him tl the
δαιμόνιον ἐκβάλῃ ἐκ τῆς θυγατρὸς αὐτῆς.
demon he would expel out of the daughter of her.
27 καὶ ἔλεγεν αὐτῇ· ἄφες πρῶτον
And he said to her: Permit first
χορτασθῆναι τὰ τέκνα· οὐ γάρ ἐστιν καλὸν
to be satisfied the children; for it is not good
λαβεῖν τὸν ἄρτον τῶν τέκνων καὶ τοῖς
to take the bread of the children and to the

‡ Verse 16 omitted by Nestle; *cf.* NIV footnote.

that makes him 'un-
clean.'[x]"
17After he had left the
crowd and entered the
house, his disciples asked
him about this parable.
18"Are you so dull?" he
asked. "Don't you see that
nothing that enters a man
from the outside can make
him 'unclean'? 19For it
doesn't go into his heart but
into his stomach, and then
out of his body." (In saying
this, Jesus declared all
foods "clean.")
20He went on: "What
comes out of a man is what
makes him 'unclean.' 21For
from within, out of men's
hearts, come evil thoughts,
sexual immorality, theft,
murder, adultery, 22greed,
malice, deceit, lewdness,
envy, slander, arrogance
and folly. 23All these evils
come from inside and make
a man 'unclean.' "

The Faith of a Syrophoenician Woman

24Jesus left that place and
went to the vicinity of
Tyre.[y] He entered a house
and did not want anyone to
know it; yet he could not
keep his presence secret.
25In fact, as soon as she
heard about him, a woman
whose little daughter was
possessed by an evil[z] spirit
came and fell at his feet.
26The woman was a Greek,
born in Syrian Phoenicia.
She begged Jesus to drive
the demon out of her
daughter.
27"First let the children
eat all they want," he told
her, "for it is not right to
take the children's bread
and toss it to their dogs."

[x] 15 Some early manuscripts *'unclean.' 16If anyone has ears to hear, let him hear.*
[y] 24 Many early manuscripts *Tyre and Sidon*
[z] 25 Greek *unclean*

28But she answered and
*said to Him, "Yes, Lord,
but even the dogs under the
table feed on the children's
crumbs."
29And He said to her,
"Because of this answer go
your way; the demon has
gone out of your daugh-
ter."
30And going back to her
home, she found the child
lying on the bed, the demon
having departed.
31And again He went out
from the region of Tyre,
and came through Sidon to
the Sea of Galilee, within
the region of Decapolis.
32And they *brought to
Him one who was deaf and
spoke with difficulty, and
they *entreated Him to lay
His hand upon him.
33And He took him aside
from the multitude by himself, and put His fingers
into his ears, and after spitting, He touched his tongue
with the saliva;
34and looking up to
heaven with a deep sigh,
He *said to him, "Ephpha-
tha!" that is, "Be
opened!"
35And his ears were
opened, and the impedi-
ment of his tongue was removed, and he *began*
speaking plainly.
36And He gave them or-
ders not to tell anyone; but
the more He ordered them,
the more widely they con-
tinued to proclaim it.
37And they were utterly
astonished, saying, "He
has done all things well; He
makes even the deaf to
hear, and the dumb to
speak."

κυναρίοις βαλεῖν. **28** ἡ δὲ ἀπεκρίθη καὶ
dogs to throw [it]. And she answered and
λέγει αὐτῷ· ναί, κύριε· καὶ τὰ κυνάρια
says to him: Yes, Lord; and yet the dogs
ὑποκάτω τῆς τραπέζης ἐσθίουσιν ἀπὸ τῶν
under the table eat from the
ψιχίων τῶν παιδίων. **29** καὶ εἶπεν αὐτῇ·
crumbs of the children. And he said to her:
διὰ τοῦτον τὸν λόγον ὕπαγε, ἐξελήλυθεν
Because of this – word go, has gone forth
ἐκ τῆς θυγατρός σου τὸ δαιμόνιον. **30** καὶ
out of the daughter of thee the demon. And
ἀπελθοῦσα εἰς τὸν οἶκον αὐτῆς εὗρεν τὸ
going away to the house of her she found the
παιδίον βεβλημένον ἐπὶ τὴν κλίνην καὶ τὸ
child *having been* laid on the couch and the
δαιμόνιον ἐξεληλυθός. **31** Καὶ πάλιν ἐξελθὼν
demon having gone forth. And again going forth
ἐκ τῶν ὁρίων Τύρου ἦλθεν διὰ Σιδῶνος
out of the district of Tyre he came through Sidon
εἰς τὴν θάλασσαν τῆς Γαλιλαίας ἀνὰ
to the sea – of Galilee in the
μέσον τῶν ὁρίων Δεκαπόλεως. **32** Καὶ
midst of the district of Decapolis. And
φέρουσιν αὐτῷ κωφὸν καὶ μογιλάλον, καὶ
they bring to him a man deaf and speaking with difficulty, and
παρακαλοῦσιν αὐτὸν ἵνα ἐπιθῇ αὐτῷ τὴν
they beseech him that he would put *on* on him the(his)
χεῖρα. **33** καὶ ἀπολαβόμενος αὐτὸν ἀπὸ
hand. And taking away him from
τοῦ ὄχλου κατ' ἰδίαν ἔβαλεν τοὺς δακτύλους
the crowd privately he put the fingers
αὐτοῦ εἰς τὰ ὦτα αὐτοῦ καὶ πτύσας
of him into the ears of him and spitting
ἥψατο τῆς γλώσσης αὐτοῦ, **34** καὶ
he touched the tongue of him, and
ἀναβλέψας εἰς τὸν οὐρανὸν ἐστέναξεν,
looking up to – heaven he groaned,
καὶ λέγει αὐτῷ· ἐφφαθά, ὅ ἐστιν διανοίχθητι.
and says to him: Ephphatha, which is Be thou opened.
35 καὶ ἠνοίγησαν αὐτοῦ αἱ ἀκοαί, καὶ
And were opened of him the ears, and
εὐθὺς ἐλύθη ὁ δεσμὸς τῆς γλώσσης αὐτοῦ,
immediately was loosened the bond of the tongue of him,
καὶ ἐλάλει ὀρθῶς. **36** καὶ διεστείλατο
and he spoke correctly. And he ordered
αὐτοῖς ἵνα μηδενὶ λέγωσιν· ὅσον δὲ
them that no one they should tell; but as much as
αὐτοῖς διεστέλλετο, αὐτοὶ μᾶλλον περισσότερον
them he ordered, they more exceedingly
ἐκήρυσσον. **37** καὶ ὑπερπερισσῶς ἐξεπλήσσοντο
proclaimed. And most exceedingly they were astounded
λέγοντες· καλῶς πάντα πεποίηκεν, καὶ
saying: Well all things he has done, both
τοὺς κωφοὺς ποιεῖ ἀκούειν καὶ ἀλάλους
the deaf he makes to hear and dumb
λαλεῖν.
to speak.

28"Yes, Lord," she re-
plied, "but even the dogs
under the table eat the children's crumbs."
29Then he told her, "For
such a reply, you may go;
the demon has left your
daughter."
30She went home and
found her child lying on the
bed, and the demon gone.

The Healing of a Deaf and Mute Man

31Then Jesus left the vi-
cinity of Tyre and went
through Sidon, down to the
Sea of Galilee and into the
region of the Decapolis.[a]
32There some people
brought to him a man who
was deaf and could hardly
talk, and they begged him
to place his hand on the
man.
33After he took him aside,
away from the crowd,
Jesus put his fingers into
the man's ears. Then he
spit and touched the man's
tongue. 34He looked up to
heaven and with a deep
sigh said to him, *"Ephphatha!"* (which means, "Be
opened!"). 35At this, the
man's ears were opened,
his tongue was loosened
and he began to speak
plainly.
36Jesus commanded them
not to tell anyone. But the
more he did so, the more
they kept talking about it.
37People were over-
whelmed with amazement.
"He has done everything
well," they said. "He even
makes the deaf hear and the
mute speak."

Chapter 8

Four Thousand Fed

IN those days again, when there was a great multitude and they had nothing to eat, He called His disciples and *said to them,

8 Ἐν ἐκείναις ταῖς ἡμέραις πάλιν πολλοῦ
In those – days again a much(great)
= there being
ὄχλου ὄντος καὶ μὴ ἐχόντων τί φάγωσιν,
crowd being[a] and not having[a] anything they might eat,
a great crowd
προσκαλεσάμενος τοὺς μαθητὰς λέγει αὐτοῖς·
calling to [him] the disciples he says to them:

Chapter 8

Jesus Feeds the Four Thousand

DURING those days another large crowd gathered. Since they had nothing to eat, Jesus called his disciples to him and

[a]*31* That is, the Ten Cities

2"I feel compassion for
the multitude because they
have remained with Me
now three days, and have
nothing to eat;
3and if I send them away
hungry to their home, they
will faint on the way; and
some of them have come
from a distance."
4And His disciples answered Him, "Where will
anyone be able to *find
enough to* satisfy these
men with bread here in a
desolate place?"
5And He was asking
them, "How many loaves
do you have?" And they
said, "Seven."
6And He *directed the
multitude to sit down on
the ground; and taking the
seven loaves, He gave
thanks and broke them,
and started giving them to
His disciples to serve to
them, and they served
them to the multitude.
7They also had a few
small fish; and after He had
blessed them, He ordered
these to be served as well.
8And they ate and were
satisfied; and they picked
up seven large baskets full
of what was left over of the
broken pieces.
9And about four thousand were *there;* and He
sent them away.
10And immediately He
entered the boat with His
disciples, and came to the
district of Dalmanutha.
11And the Pharisees came
out and began to argue with
Him, seeking from Him a
sign from heaven, to test
Him.
12And sighing deeply in
His spirit, He *said, "Why
does this generation seek
for a sign? Truly I say to
you, no sign shall be given
to this generation."
13And leaving them, He
again embarked and went
away to the other side.
14And they had forgotten
to take bread; and did not
have more than one loaf in
the boat with them.
15And He was giving or-

2 σπλαγχνίζομαι ἐπὶ τὸν ὄχλον, ὅτι ἤδη
I have compassion on the crowd, because now
ἡμέραι τρεῖς προσμένουσίν μοι καὶ οὐκ
days three they remain with me and not
ἔχουσιν τί φάγωσιν· 3 καὶ ἐὰν ἀπολύσω
they have anything they may eat; and if I dismiss
αὐτοὺς νήστεις εἰς οἶκον αὐτῶν, ἐκλυθήσονται
them fasting to house of them, they will faint
ἐν τῇ ὁδῷ· καί τινες αὐτῶν ἀπὸ μακρόθεν
in the way; and some of them from afar
εἰσίν. 4 καὶ ἀπεκρίθησαν αὐτῷ οἱ μαθηταὶ
are. And answered him the disciples
αὐτοῦ ὅτι πόθεν τούτους δυνήσεταί τις
of him[,] – [1]Whence [6]these people [3]will [4]be able [2]anyone
ὧδε χορτάσαι ἄρτων ἐπ' ἐρημίας; 5 καὶ
[8]here [5]to satisfy [7]of(with) loaves [9]on(in) [10]a desert ? And
ἠρώτα αὐτούς· πόσους ἔχετε ἄρτους;
he asked them: How many have ye loaves ?
οἱ δὲ εἶπαν· ἑπτά. 6 καὶ παραγγέλλει τῷ
And they said: Seven. And he commands the
ὄχλῳ ἀναπεσεῖν ἐπὶ τῆς γῆς· καὶ λαβὼν
crowd to recline on the ground; and taking
τοὺς ἑπτὰ ἄρτους εὐχαριστήσας ἔκλασεν
the seven loaves giving thanks he broke
καὶ ἐδίδου τοῖς μαθηταῖς αὐτοῦ ἵνα
and gave to the disciples of him that
παρατιθῶσιν, καὶ παρέθηκαν τῷ ὄχλῳ.
they might serve, and they served the crowd.
7 καὶ εἶχον ἰχθύδια ὀλίγα· καὶ εὐλογήσας
And they had fishes a few; and blessing
αὐτὰ εἶπεν καὶ ταῦτα παρατιθέναι. 8 καὶ
them he told also these to be served. And
ἔφαγον καὶ ἐχορτάσθησαν, καὶ ἦραν
they ate and were satisfied, and took
περισσεύματα κλασμάτων, ἑπτὰ σπυρίδας.
excesses of fragments, seven baskets.
9 ἦσαν δὲ ὡς τετρακισχίλιοι. καὶ ἀπέλυσεν
Now they were about four thousand. And he dismissed
αὐτούς. 10 Καὶ εὐθὺς ἐμβὰς εἰς τὸ
them. And immediately embarking in the
πλοῖον μετὰ τῶν μαθητῶν αὐτοῦ
ship with the disciples of him
ἦλθεν εἰς τὰ μέρη Δαλμανουθά.
he came into the region of Dalmanutha.
11 Καὶ ἐξῆλθον οἱ Φαρισαῖοι καὶ ἤρξαντο
And came forth the Pharisees and began
συζητεῖν αὐτῷ, ζητοῦντες παρ' αὐτοῦ
to debate with him, seeking from him
σημεῖον ἀπὸ τοῦ οὐρανοῦ, πειράζοντες
a sign from – heaven, tempting
αὐτόν. 12 καὶ ἀναστενάξας τῷ πνεύματι
him. And groaning in the spirit
αὐτοῦ λέγει· τί ἡ γενεὰ αὕτη ζητεῖ
of him he says: Why – [3]generation [2]this [1]does [4]seek
σημεῖον; ἀμὴν λέγω ὑμῖν, εἰ δοθήσεται
a sign ? Truly I tell you, if will be given
τῇ γενεᾷ ταύτῃ σημεῖον. 13 καὶ ἀφεὶς
– generation to this a sign. And leaving
αὐτοὺς πάλιν ἐμβὰς ἀπῆλθεν εἰς τὸ
them again embarking he went away to the
πέραν. 14 Καὶ ἐπελάθοντο λαβεῖν ἄρτους,
other side. And they forgot to take loaves,
καὶ εἰ μὴ ἕνα ἄρτον οὐκ εἶχον μεθ'
and except one loaf they had not with
ἑαυτῶν ἐν τῷ πλοίῳ. 15 καὶ διεστέλλετο
them*selves* in the ship. And he charged

said, 2"I have compassion
for these people; they have
already been with me three
days and have nothing to
eat. 3If I send them home
hungry, they will collapse
on the way, because some
of them have come a long
distance."
4His disciples answered,
"But where in this remote
place can anyone get
enough bread to feed
them?"
5"How many loaves do
you have?" Jesus asked.
"Seven," they replied.
6He told the crowd to sit
down on the ground. When
he had taken the seven
loaves and given thanks, he
broke them and gave them
to his disciples to set before
the people, and they did so.
7They had a few small fish
as well; he gave thanks for
them also and told the disciples to distribute them.
8The people ate and were
satisfied. Afterward the
disciples picked up seven
basketfuls of broken pieces
that were left over. 9About
four thousand men were
present. And having sent
them away, 10he got into
the boat with his disciples
and went to the region of
Dalmanutha.
11The Pharisees came and
began to question Jesus. To
test him, they asked him for
a sign from heaven. 12He
sighed deeply and said,
"Why does this generation
ask for a miraculous sign? I
tell you the truth, no sign
will be given to it." 13Then
he left them, got back into
the boat and crossed to the
other side.

*The Yeast of the Pharisees
and Herod*

14The disciples had forgotten to bring bread, except for one loaf they had
with them in the boat.
15"Be careful," Jesus

ders to them, saying,
"Watch out! Beware of the
leaven of the Pharisees and
the leaven of Herod."
16And they *began* to discuss with one another *the*
fact that they had no bread.
17And Jesus, aware of
this, *said to them, "Why
do you discuss *the fact* that
you have no bread? Do you
not yet see or understand?
Do you have a hardened
heart?
18"HAVING EYES, DO YOU
NOT SEE? AND HAVING EARS,
DO YOU NOT HEAR? And do
you not remember,
19when I broke the five
loaves for the five thou-
sand, how many baskets
full of broken pieces you
picked up?" They *said to
Him, "Twelve."
20"And when *I broke* the
seven for the four thou-
sand, how many large bas-
kets full of broken pieces
did you pick up?" And they
*said to Him, "Seven."
21And He was saying to
them, "Do you not yet un-
derstand?"
22And they *came to
Bethsaida. And they
*brought a blind man to
Him, and *entreated Him
to touch him.
23And taking the blind
man by the hand, He
brought him out of the village; and after spitting on
his eyes, and laying His
hands upon him, He asked
him, "Do you see any-
thing?"
24And he looked up and
said, "I see men, for I am
seeing *them* like trees,
walking about."
25Then again He laid His
hands upon his eyes; and he
looked intently and was restored, and *began* to see
everything clearly.
26And He sent him to his
home, saying, "Do not
even enter the village."

Peter's Confession of Christ

27And Jesus went out,
along with His disciples, to
the villages of Caesarea

αὐτοῖς λέγων· ὁρᾶτε, βλέπετε ἀπὸ τῆς
them saying: See, look ye from the
=Beware of
ζύμης τῶν Φαρισαίων καὶ τῆς ζύμης
leaven of the Pharisees and of the leaven
Ἡρῴδου. 16 καὶ διελογίζοντο πρὸς ἀλλήλους
of Herod. And they reasoned with one another
ὅτι ἄρτους οὐκ ἔχουσιν. 17 καὶ γνοὺς
because loaves they have(had) not. And knowing
λέγει αὐτοῖς· τί διαλογίζεσθε ὅτι ἄρτους
he says to them: Why reason ye because loaves
οὐκ ἔχετε; οὔπω νοεῖτε οὐδὲ συνίετε;
ye have not? not yet understand ye nor realize?
πεπωρωμένην ἔχετε τὴν καρδίαν ὑμῶν;
having been hardened have ye the heart of you?
18 ὀφθαλμοὺς ἔχοντες οὐ βλέπετε, καὶ
eyes having see ye not, and
ὦτα ἔχοντες οὐκ ἀκούετε; καὶ
ears having hear ye not? and
οὐ μνημονεύετε, 19 ὅτε τοὺς πέντε ἄρτους
do ye not remember, when the five loaves
ἔκλασα εἰς τοὺς πεντακισχιλίους, πόσους
I broke to the five thousand, how many
κοφίνους κλασμάτων πλήρεις ἤρατε; λέγουσιν
baskets of fragments full ye took? They say
αὐτῷ· δώδεκα. 20 ὅτε τοὺς ἑπτὰ εἰς
to him: Twelve. When the seven to
τοὺς τετρακισχιλίους, πόσων σπυρίδων
the four thousand, [2]of how many [3]baskets
πληρώματα κλασμάτων ἤρατε; καὶ λέγουσιν·
[1]fullnesses [4]of fragments ye took? And they say:
ἑπτά. 21 καὶ ἔλεγεν αὐτοῖς· οὔπω συνίετε;
Seven. And he said to them: Not yet do ye realize?
22 Καὶ ἔρχονται εἰς Βηθσαϊδάν. Καὶ
And they come to Bethsaida. And
φέρουσιν αὐτῷ τυφλόν, καὶ παρακαλοῦσιν
they bring to him a blind man, and beseech
αὐτὸν ἵνα αὐτοῦ ἅψηται. 23 καὶ ἐπιλαβόμενος
him that him he would touch. And laying hold of
τῆς χειρὸς τοῦ τυφλοῦ ἐξήνεγκεν αὐτὸν
the hand of the blind man he led forth him
ἔξω τῆς κώμης, καὶ πτύσας εἰς τὰ
outside the village, and spitting in the
ὄμματα αὐτοῦ, ἐπιθεὶς τὰς χεῖρας αὐτῷ,
eyes of him, putting *on* the hands on him,
ἐπηρώτα αὐτόν· εἴ τι βλέπεις; 24 καὶ
questioned him: If anything thou seest? And
ἀναβλέψας ἔλεγεν· βλέπω τοὺς ἀνθρώπους,
looking up he said: I see – men,
ὅτι ὡς δένδρα ὁρῶ περιπατοῦντας.
that as trees I behold walking.
25 εἶτα πάλιν ἐπέθηκεν τὰς χεῖρας ἐπὶ
Then again he put *on* the hands on
τοὺς ὀφθαλμοὺς αὐτοῦ, καὶ διέβλεψεν καὶ
the eyes of him, and he looked steadily and
ἀπεκατέστη, καὶ ἐνέβλεπεν τηλαυγῶς ἅπαντα.
was restored, and saw clearly all things.
26 καὶ ἀπέστειλεν αὐτὸν εἰς οἶκον αὐτοῦ
And he sent him to house of him
λέγων· μηδὲ εἰς τὴν κώμην εἰσέλθῃς.
saying: Not into the village thou mayest enter.
27 Καὶ ἐξῆλθεν ὁ Ἰησοῦς καὶ οἱ μαθηταὶ
And went forth – Jesus and the disciples
αὐτοῦ εἰς τὰς κώμας Καισαρείας τῆς
of him to the villages of Cæsarea –

warned them. "Watch out
for the yeast of the Pharisees and that of Herod."
16They discussed this
with one another and said,
"It is because we have no
bread."
17Aware of their discus-
sion, Jesus asked them:
"Why are you talking
about having no bread? Do
you still not see or understand? Are your hearts
hardened? 18Do you have
eyes but fail to see, and
ears but fail to hear? And
don't you remember?
19When I broke the five
loaves for the five thou-
sand, how many basketfuls
of pieces did you pick up?"
"Twelve," they replied.
20"And when I broke the
seven loaves for the four
thousand, how many bas-
ketfuls of pieces did you
pick up?"
They answered, "Sev-
en."
21He said to them, "Do
you still not understand?"

The Healing of a Blind Man at Bethsaida

22They came to Bethsai-
da, and some people
brought a blind man and
begged Jesus to touch him.
23He took the blind man by
the hand and led him out-
side the village. When he
had spit on the man's eyes
and put his hands on him,
Jesus asked, "Do you see
anything?"
24He looked up and said,
"I see people; they look
like trees walking around."
25Once more Jesus put his
hands on the man's eyes.
Then his eyes were
opened, his sight was re-
stored, and he saw every-
thing clearly. 26Jesus sent
him home, saying, "Don't
go into the village.[b]"

Peter's Confession of Christ

27Jesus and his disciples
went on to the villages
around Caesarea Philippi.

[b]26 Some manuscripts *Don't go and tell anyone in the village*

Philippi; and on the way He
questioned His disciples,
saying to them, "Who do
people say that I am?"
28And they told Him, say-
ing, "John the Baptist; and
others *say* Elijah; but others, one of the prophets."
29And He *continued* by
questioning them, "But
who do you say that I am?"
Peter *answered and *said
to Him, "Thou art the
Christ."
30And He warned them to
tell no one about Him.
31And He began to teach
them that the Son of Man
must suffer many things
and be rejected by the elders and the chief priests
and the scribes, and be
killed, and after three days
rise again.
32And He was stating the
matter plainly. And Peter
took Him aside and began
to rebuke Him.
33But turning around and
seeing His disciples, He
rebuked Peter, and *said,
"Get behind Me, Satan; for
you are not setting your
mind on [w]God's interests,
but man's."
34And He summoned the
multitude with His disci-
ples, and said to them, "If
anyone wishes to come af-
ter Me, let him deny him-
self, and take up his cross,
and follow Me.
35"For whoever wishes
to save his life shall lose it;
but whoever loses his life
for My sake and the gos-
pel's shall save it.
36"For what does it profit
a man to gain the whole
world, and forfeit his soul?
37"For what shall a man
give in exchange for his
soul?

[w] Lit., *the things of God*

Φιλίππου· καὶ ἐν τῇ ὁδῷ ἐπηρώτα τοὺς
of Philip; and in the way he questioned the
μαθητὰς αὐτοῦ λέγων αὐτοῖς· τίνα με
disciples of him saying to them: Whom me
λέγουσιν οἱ ἄνθρωποι εἶναι; **28** οἱ δὲ
say – men to be ? And they
εἶπαν αὐτῷ λέγοντες ὅτι Ἰωάννην τὸν
told him saying[,] – John the
βαπτιστήν, καὶ ἄλλοι Ἠλίαν, ἄλλοι δὲ
Baptist, and others Elias, but others[,]
ὅτι εἷς τῶν προφητῶν. **29** καὶ αὐτὸς
– one of the prophets. And he
ἐπηρώτα αὐτούς· ὑμεῖς δὲ τίνα με λέγετε
questioned them: But ye whom me say ye
εἶναι; ἀποκριθεὶς ὁ Πέτρος λέγει αὐτῷ·
to be ? Answering – Peter says to him:
σὺ εἶ ὁ χριστός. **30** καὶ ἐπετίμησεν
Thou art the Christ. And he warned
αὐτοῖς ἵνα μηδενὶ λέγωσιν περὶ αὐτοῦ.
them that no one they might tell about him.
31 Καὶ ἤρξατο διδάσκειν αὐτοὺς ὅτι δεῖ
And he began to teach them that it behoves
τὸν υἱὸν τοῦ ἀνθρώπου πολλὰ παθεῖν,
the Son – of man many things to suffer,
καὶ ἀποδοκιμασθῆναι ὑπὸ τῶν πρεσβυτέρων
and to be rejected by the elders
καὶ τῶν ἀρχιερέων καὶ τῶν γραμματέων
and the chief priests and the scribes
καὶ ἀποκτανθῆναι καὶ μετὰ τρεῖς ἡμέρας
and to be killed and after three days
ἀναστῆναι· **32** καὶ παρρησίᾳ τὸν λόγον
to rise again; and openly the word
ἐλάλει. καὶ προσλαβόμενος ὁ Πέτρος
he spoke. And [2]taking [4]aside – [1]Peter
αὐτὸν ἤρξατο ἐπιτιμᾶν αὐτῷ. **33** ὁ δὲ
[3]him began to rebuke him. But he
ἐπιστραφεὶς καὶ ἰδὼν τοὺς μαθητὰς αὐτοῦ
turning round and seeing the disciples of him
ἐπετίμησεν Πέτρῳ καὶ λέγει· ὕπαγε ὀπίσω
rebuked Peter and says: Go behind
μου, σατανᾶ, ὅτι οὐ φρονεῖς τὰ τοῦ
me, Satan, because thou mindest not the things –
θεοῦ ἀλλὰ τὰ τῶν ἀνθρώπων. **34** Καὶ
of God but the things – of men. And
προσκαλεσάμενος τὸν ὄχλον σὺν τοῖς μαθηταῖς
calling to [him] the crowd with the disciples
αὐτοῦ εἶπεν αὐτοῖς· εἴ τις θέλει ὀπίσω
of him he said to them: If anyone wishes after
μου ἐλθεῖν, ἀπαρνησάσθω ἑαυτὸν καὶ ἀράτω
me to come, let him deny himself and take
τὸν σταυρὸν αὐτοῦ, καὶ ἀκολουθείτω μοι.
the cross of him, and let him follow me.
35 ὃς γὰρ ἐὰν θέλῃ τὴν ψυχὴν αὐτοῦ σώ-
For whoever wishes the life of him to
σαι, ἀπολέσει αὐτήν· ὃς δ' ἂν ἀπολέσει
save, will lose it; but whoever will lose
τὴν ψυχὴν αὐτοῦ ἕνεκεν ἐμοῦ καὶ τοῦ
the life of him for the sake of me and the
εὐαγγελίου, σώσει αὐτήν. **36** τί γὰρ ὠφελεῖ
gospel, will save it. For what profits
ἄνθρωπον κερδῆσαι τὸν κόσμον ὅλον καὶ
a man to gain the world whole and
ζημιωθῆναι τὴν ψυχὴν αὐτοῦ; **37** τί γὰρ
to be fined the soul of him ? For what
δοῖ ἄνθρωπος ἀντάλλαγμα τῆς ψυχῆς αὐτοῦ;
might give a man an exchange of the soul of him ?

On the way he asked them,
"Who do people say I
am?"
28They replied, "Some
say John the Baptist; others
say Elijah; and still others,
one of the prophets."
29"But what about you?"
he asked. "Who do you say
I am?"
Peter answered, "You
are the Christ.[c]"
30Jesus warned them not
to tell anyone about him.

Jesus Predicts His Death

31He then began to teach
them that the Son of Man
must suffer many things
and be rejected by the elders, chief priests and
teachers of the law, and
that he must be killed and
after three days rise again.
32He spoke plainly about
this, and Peter took him
aside and began to rebuke
him.
33But when Jesus turned
and looked at his disciples,
he rebuked Peter. "Get behind me, Satan!" he said.
"You do not have in mind
the things of God, but the
things of men."
34Then he called the
crowd to him along with his
disciples and said: "If anyone would come after me,
he must deny himself and
take up his cross and follow
me. 35For whoever wants
to save his life[d] will lose it,
but whoever loses his life
for me and for the gospel
will save it. 36What good is
it for a man to gain the
whole world, yet forfeit his
soul? 37Or what can a man
give in exchange for his
soul? 38If anyone is

[c]29 Or *Messiah*. "The Christ" (Greek) and "the Messiah" (Hebrew) both mean "the Anointed One."
[d]35 The Greek word means either *life* or *soul*; also in verse 36.

38"For whoever is ashamed of Me and My words in this adulterous and sinful generation, the Son of Man will also be ashamed of him when He comes in the glory of His Father with the holy angels."

Chapter 9

The Transfiguration

AND He was saying to them, "Truly I say to you, there are some of those who are standing here who shall not taste death until they see the kingdom of God after it has come with power."

2And six days later, Jesus *took with Him Peter and James and John, and *brought them up to a high mountain by themselves. And He was transfigured before them;

3and His garments became radiant and exceedingly white, as no launderer on earth can whiten them.

4And Elijah appeared to them along with Moses; and they were talking with Jesus.

5And Peter answered and *said to Jesus, "Rabbi, it is good for us to be here; and let us make three tabernacles, one for You, and one for Moses, and one for Elijah."

6For he did not know what to answer; for they became terrified.

7Then a cloud formed, overshadowing them, and a voice came out of the cloud, "This is My beloved Son, listen to Him!"

8And all at once they looked around and saw no one with them anymore, except Jesus alone.

9And as they were coming down from the mountain, He gave them orders

38 ὃς γὰρ ἐὰν ἐπαισχυνθῇ με καὶ
For whoever is ashamed of me and
τοὺς ἐμοὺς λόγους ἐν τῇ γενεᾷ ταύτῃ
– my words in – generation this
τῇ μοιχαλίδι καὶ ἁμαρτωλῷ, καὶ ὁ
– adulterous and sinful, also the
υἱὸς τοῦ ἀνθρώπου ἐπαισχυνθήσεται αὐτόν,
Son – of man will be ashamed *of* him,
ὅταν ἔλθῃ ἐν τῇ δόξῃ τοῦ πατρὸς
when he comes in the glory of the Father
αὐτοῦ μετὰ τῶν ἀγγέλων τῶν ἁγίων.
of him with the angels – holy.

9 καὶ ἔλεγεν αὐτοῖς· ἀμὴν λέγω ὑμῖν
And he said to them: Truly I tell you
ὅτι εἰσίν τινες ὧδε τῶν ἑστηκότων
that there are some here of the [ones] standing
οἵτινες οὐ μὴ γεύσωνται θανάτου ἕως ἂν
who by no means may taste of death until
ἴδωσιν τὴν βασιλείαν τοῦ θεοῦ ἐληλυθυῖαν
they see the kingdom – of God having come
ἐν δυνάμει.
in power.
2 Καὶ μετὰ ἡμέρας ἓξ παραλαμβάνει
And after days six takes
ὁ Ἰησοῦς τὸν Πέτρον καὶ τὸν Ἰάκωβον
– Jesus – Peter and – James
καὶ Ἰωάννην, καὶ ἀναφέρει αὐτοὺς εἰς
and John, and leads up them into
ὄρος ὑψηλὸν κατ' ἰδίαν μόνους. καὶ
mountain a high privately alone. And
μετεμορφώθη ἔμπροσθεν αὐτῶν, **3** καὶ τὰ
he was transfigured before them, and the
ἱμάτια αὐτοῦ ἐγένετο στίλβοντα λευκὰ λίαν,
garments of him became gleaming white exceedingly,
οἷα γναφεὺς ἐπὶ τῆς γῆς οὐ δύναται
such as fuller on the earth cannot
οὕτως λευκᾶναι. **4** καὶ ὤφθη αὐτοῖς Ἠλίας
so *to* whiten. And appeared to them Elias
σὺν Μωϋσεῖ, καὶ ἦσαν συλλαλοῦντες τῷ
with Moses, and they were conversing with –
Ἰησοῦ. **5** καὶ ἀποκριθεὶς ὁ Πέτρος λέγει
Jesus. And answering – Peter says
τῷ Ἰησοῦ· ῥαββί, καλόν ἐστιν ἡμᾶς ὧδε
– to Jesus: Rabbi, good it is us here
εἶναι, καὶ ποιήσωμεν τρεῖς σκηνάς, σοὶ
to be, and let us make three tents, for thee
μίαν καὶ Μωϋσεῖ μίαν καὶ Ἠλίᾳ μίαν.
one and for Moses one and for Elias one.
6 οὐ γὰρ ᾔδει τί ἀποκριθῇ· ἔκφοβοι γὰρ
For he knew not what he answered; for exceedingly afraid
ἐγένοντο. **7** καὶ ἐγένετο νεφέλη ἐπισκιάζουσα
they became. And there came a cloud overshadowing
αὐτοῖς, καὶ ἐγένετο φωνὴ ἐκ τῆς νεφέλης·
them, and there came a voice out of the cloud:
οὗτός ἐστιν ὁ υἱός μου ὁ ἀγαπητός,
This is the Son of me *the* beloved,
ἀκούετε αὐτοῦ. **8** καὶ ἐξάπινα περιβλεψάμενοι
hear ye him. And suddenly looking round
οὐκέτι οὐδένα εἶδον εἰ μὴ τὸν Ἰησοῦν
no longer no(any)one they saw except – Jesus
μόνον μεθ' ἑαυτῶν. **9** Καὶ καταβαινόντων
only with themselves. And coming down
= as they came down
αὐτῶν ἐκ τοῦ ὄρους διεστείλατο αὐτοῖς
them[a] out of the mountain he ordered them

ashamed of me and my
words in this adulterous
and sinful generation, the
Son of Man will be
ashamed of him when he
comes in his Father's glory
with the holy angels."

Chapter 9

AND he said to them, "I
tell you the truth,
some who are standing
here will not taste death before they see the kingdom
of God come with power."

The Transfiguration

2After six days Jesus took
Peter, James and John with
him and led them up a high
mountain, where they were
all alone. There he was
transfigured before them.
3His clothes became daz-
zling white, whiter than
anyone in the world could
bleach them. 4And there
appeared before them Eli-
jah and Moses, who were
talking with Jesus.
5Peter said to Jesus,
"Rabbi, it is good for us to
be here. Let us put up three
shelters—one for you, one
for Moses and one for Elijah." 6(He did not know
what to say, they were so
frightened.)
7Then a cloud appeared
and enveloped them, and a
voice came from the cloud:
"This is my Son, whom I
love. Listen to him!"
8Suddenly, when they
looked around, they no longer saw anyone with them
except Jesus.
9As they were coming
down the mountain, Jesus
gave them orders not to tell

not to relate to anyone
what they had seen, until
the Son of Man should rise
from the dead.
10And they seized upon
that statement, discussing
with one another what rising from the dead might
mean.
11And they asked Him,
saying, "*Why is it* that the
scribes say that Elijah must
come first?"
12And He said to them,
"Elijah does first come and
restore all things. And *yet*
how is it written of the Son
of Man that He should suffer many things and be
treated with contempt?
13"But I say to you, that
Elijah has indeed come,
and they did to him what-
ever they wished, just as it
is written of him."

All Things Possible

14And when they came
back to the disciples, they
saw a large crowd around
them, and *some* scribes arguing with them.
15And immediately, when
the entire crowd saw Him,
they were amazed, and *began* running up to greet
Him.
16And He asked them,
"What are you discussing
with them?"
17And one of the crowd
answered Him, "Teacher,
I brought You my son, possessed with a spirit which
makes him mute;
18and whenever it seizes
him, it dashes him *to the
ground* and he foams *at the
mouth,* and grinds his
teeth, and stiffens out. And
I told Your disciples to cast
it out, and they could not
do it."
19And He *answered
them and *said, "O un-
believing generation, how
long shall I be with you?
How long shall I put up
with you? Bring him to
Me!"
20And they brought the
boy to Him. And when he
saw Him, immediately the
spirit threw him into a con-

ἵνα μηδενὶ ἃ εἶδον διηγήσωνται,
that to no one [the] things which they saw they should relate,

εἰ μὴ ὅταν ὁ υἱὸς τοῦ ἀνθρώπου ἐκ νεκρῶν
except when the Son – of man out of [the] dead

ἀναστῇ. 10 καὶ τὸν λόγον ἐκράτησαν πρὸς
should rise. And the word they held to

ἑαυτοὺς συζητοῦντες τί ἐστιν τὸ ἐκ
themselves debating what is the "out of

νεκρῶν ἀναστῆναι. 11 Καὶ ἐπηρώτων αὐτὸν
[the] dead to rise." And they questioned him

λέγοντες· ὅτι λέγουσιν οἱ γραμματεῖς ὅτι
saying: Why say the scribes that

Ἠλίαν δεῖ ἐλθεῖν πρῶτον; 12 ὁ δὲ ἔφη
Elias it behoves to come first? And he said

αὐτοῖς· Ἠλίας μὲν ἐλθὼν πρῶτον
to them: Elias indeed coming first

ἀποκαθιστάνει πάντα· καὶ πῶς γέγραπται
restores all things; and how has it been written

ἐπὶ τὸν υἱὸν τοῦ ἀνθρώπου, ἵνα πολλὰ
on(concerning) the Son – of man, that many things

πάθῃ καὶ ἐξουδενηθῇ; 13 ἀλλὰ λέγω ὑμῖν
he should suffer and be set at naught? But I tell you

ὅτι καὶ Ἠλίας ἐλήλυθεν, καὶ ἐποίησαν
that indeed Elias has come, and they did

αὐτῷ ὅσα ἤθελον, καθὼς γέγραπται
to him what they wished, as it has been written

ἐπ' αὐτόν.
on(concerning) him.

14 Καὶ ἐλθόντες πρὸς τοὺς μαθητὰς
And coming to the disciples

εἶδον ὄχλον πολὺν περὶ αὐτοὺς καὶ
they saw crowd a much(great) around them and

γραμματεῖς συζητοῦντας πρὸς αὐτούς.
scribes debating with them.

15 καὶ εὐθὺς πᾶς ὁ ὄχλος ἰδόντες αὐτὸν
And immediately all the crowd seeing him

ἐξεθαμβήθησαν, καὶ προστρέχοντες ἠσπάζοντο
were greatly astonished, and running up to greeted

αὐτόν. 16 καὶ ἐπηρώτησεν αὐτούς· τί
him. And he questioned them: What

συζητεῖτε πρὸς αὐτούς; 17 καὶ ἀπεκρίθη
are ye debating with them? And answered

αὐτῷ εἷς ἐκ τοῦ ὄχλου· διδάσκαλε,
him one of the crowd: Teacher,

ἤνεγκα τὸν υἱόν μου πρὸς σέ, ἔχοντα
I brought the son of me to thee, having

πνεῦμα ἄλαλον· 18 καὶ ὅπου ἐὰν αὐτὸν
spirit a dumb; and wherever him

καταλάβῃ, ῥήσσει αὐτόν, καὶ ἀφρίζει καὶ
it seizes, it tears him, and he foams and

τρίζει τοὺς ὀδόντας καὶ ξηραίνεται· καὶ
grinds the(his) teeth and he wastes away; and

εἶπα τοῖς μαθηταῖς σου ἵνα αὐτὸ
I told the disciples of thee that it

ἐκβάλωσιν, καὶ οὐκ ἴσχυσαν. 19 ὁ δὲ
they might expel, and they were not able. And he

ἀποκριθεὶς αὐτοῖς λέγει· ὦ γενεὰ ἄπιστος,
answering them says: O generation unbelieving,

ἕως πότε πρὸς ὑμᾶς ἔσομαι; ἕως πότε
until when with you shall I be? how long
= how long

ἀνέξομαι ὑμῶν; φέρετε αὐτὸν πρός με.
shall I endure you? bring him to me.

20 καὶ ἤνεγκαν αὐτὸν πρὸς αὐτόν. καὶ
And they brought him to him. And

ἰδὼν αὐτὸν τὸ πνεῦμα εὐθὺς συνεσπάραξεν
seeing him the spirit immediately violently threw

anyone what they had seen
until the Son of Man had
risen from the dead. 10They
kept the matter to them-
selves, discussing what
"rising from the dead"
meant.
11And they asked him,
"Why do the teachers of
the law say that Elijah must
come first?"
12Jesus replied, "To be
sure, Elijah does come
first, and restores all
things. Why then is it written that the Son of Man
must suffer much and be rejected? 13But I tell you, Elijah has come, and they
have done to him every-
thing they wished, just as it
is written about him."

The Healing of a Boy With an Evil Spirit

14When they came to the
other disciples, they saw a
large crowd around them
and the teachers of the law
arguing with them. 15As
soon as all the people saw
Jesus, they were over-
whelmed with wonder and
ran to greet him.
16"What are you arguing
with them about?" he
asked.
17A man in the crowd an-
swered, "Teacher, I
brought you my son, who is
possessed by a spirit that
has robbed him of speech.
18Whenever it seizes him, it
throws him to the ground.
He foams at the mouth,
gnashes his teeth and be-
comes rigid. I asked your
disciples to drive out the
spirit, but they could not."
19"O unbelieving genera-
tion," Jesus replied, "how
long shall I stay with you?
How long shall I put up
with you? Bring the boy to
me."
20So they brought him.
When the spirit saw Jesus,
it immediately threw the
boy into a convulsion. He

vulsion, and falling to the
ground, he *began* rolling
about and foaming *at the*
mouth.
21 And He asked his fa-
ther, "How long has this
been happening to him?"
And he said, "From child-
hood.
22 "And it has often
thrown him both into the
fire and into the water to
destroy him. But if You can
do anything, take pity on us
and help us!"
23 And Jesus said to him,
" 'If You can!' All things
are possible to him who believes."
24 Immediately the boy's
father cried out and *began*
saying, "I do believe; help
my unbelief."
25 And when Jesus saw
that a crowd was rapidly
gathering, He rebuked the
unclean spirit, saying to it,
"You deaf and dumb spirit,
I command you, come out
of him and do not enter him
again."
26 And after crying out
and throwing him into terrible convulsions, it came
out; and *the boy* became so
much like a corpse that
most *of them* said, "He is
dead!"
27 But Jesus took him by
the hand and raised him;
and he got up.
28 And when He had come
into *the* house, His disciples *began* questioning
Him privately, "Why could
we not cast it out?"
29 And He said to them,
"This kind cannot come
out by anything but
prayer[x]."

Death and Resurrection Foretold

30 And from there they
went out and *began* to go
through Galilee, and He
was unwilling for anyone to
know *about it*.
31 For He was teaching
His disciples and telling
them, "The Son of Man is
to be [y]delivered into the
hands of men, and they will
kill Him; and when He has
been killed, He will rise
three days later."

αὐτόν, καὶ πεσὼν ἐπὶ τῆς γῆς ἐκυλίετο
him, and falling on the earth he wallowed
ἀφρίζων. 21 καὶ ἐπηρώτησεν τὸν πατέρα
foaming. And he questioned the father
αὐτοῦ· πόσος χρόνος ἐστὶν ὡς τοῦτο
of him: What time is it while this
γέγονεν αὐτῷ; ὁ δὲ εἶπεν· ἐκ παιδιόθεν·
has happened to him ? And he said: From childhood;
22 καὶ πολλάκις καὶ εἰς πῦρ αὐτὸν
and often both into fire him
ἔβαλεν καὶ εἰς ὕδατα ἵνα ἀπολέσῃ αὐτόν· ἀλλ'
it threw and into waters that it may destroy him; but
εἴ τι δύνῃ, βοήθησον ἡμῖν σπλαγχνισθεὶς
if anything thou canst, help us having compassion
ἐφ' ἡμᾶς. 23 ὁ δὲ Ἰησοῦς εἶπεν αὐτῷ· τὸ εἰ
on us. – And Jesus said to him: The "if
δύνῃ, πάντα δυνατὰ τῷ πιστεύοντι.
thou canst," all things possible to the [one] believing.
24 εὐθὺς κράξας ὁ πατὴρ τοῦ παιδίου
Immediately crying out the father of the child
ἔλεγεν· πιστεύω· βοήθει μου τῇ ἀπιστίᾳ.
said: I believe; help thou of me the unbelief.
25 ἰδὼν δὲ ὁ Ἰησοῦς ὅτι ἐπισυντρέχει
And ²seeing – ¹Jesus that is(was) running together
ὄχλος, ἐπετίμησεν τῷ πνεύματι τῷ ἀκαθάρτῳ
a crowd, rebuked the spirit – unclean
λέγων αὐτῷ· τὸ ἄλαλον καὶ κωφὸν
saying to it: – Dumb and deaf
πνεῦμα, ἐγὼ ἐπιτάσσω σοι, ἔξελθε ἐξ
spirit, I command thee, come forth out of
αὐτοῦ καὶ μηκέτι εἰσέλθῃς εἰς αὐτόν.
him and no more mayest thou enter into him.
26 καὶ κράξας καὶ πολλὰ σπαράξας
And crying out and much convulsing [him]
ἐξῆλθεν· καὶ ἐγένετο ὡσεὶ νεκρός, ὥστε
it came out; and he was as dead, so as
τοὺς πολλοὺς λέγειν ὅτι ἀπέθανεν. 27 ὁ
– many to say[b] that he died. –
= many said
δὲ Ἰησοῦς κρατήσας τῆς χειρὸς αὐτοῦ
But Jesus taking hold of the hand of him
ἤγειρεν αὐτόν, καὶ ἀνέστη. 28 καὶ
raised him, and he stood up. And
εἰσελθόντος αὐτοῦ εἰς οἶκον οἱ μαθηταὶ
entering him[a] into a house the disciples
=when he entered
αὐτοῦ κατ' ἰδίαν ἐπηρώτων αὐτόν· ὅτι
of him privately questioned him: Why
ἡμεῖς οὐκ ἠδυνήθημεν ἐκβαλεῖν αὐτό;
we were not able to expel it ?
29 καὶ εἶπεν αὐτοῖς· τοῦτο τὸ γένος ἐν
And he told them: This – kind by
οὐδενὶ δύναται ἐξελθεῖν εἰ μὴ ἐν προσευχῇ.
nothing can to come out except by prayer.
30 Κἀκεῖθεν ἐξελθόντες παρεπορεύοντο διὰ
And thence going forth they passed through
τῆς Γαλιλαίας, καὶ οὐκ ἤθελεν ἵνα
– Galilee, and he wished not that
τις γνοῖ· 31 ἐδίδασκεν γὰρ τοὺς μαθητὰς
anyone should know; for he was teaching the disciples
αὐτοῦ, καὶ ἔλεγεν αὐτοῖς ὅτι ὁ υἱὸς τοῦ
of him, and told them[,] – The Son –
ἀνθρώπου παραδίδοται εἰς χεῖρας ἀνθρώπων,
of man is betrayed into [the] hands of men,
καὶ ἀποκτενοῦσιν αὐτόν, καὶ ἀποκτανθεὶς
and they will kill him, and being killed
μετὰ τρεῖς ἡμέρας ἀναστήσεται. 32 οἱ
after three days he will rise up. they

fell to the ground and rolled
around, foaming at the
mouth.
21 Jesus asked the boy's
father, "How long has he
been like this?"
"From childhood," he
answered. 22 "It has often
thrown him into fire or water to kill him. But if you
can do anything, take pity
on us and help us."
23 " 'If you can'?" said
Jesus. "Everything is possible for him who be-
lieves."
24 Immediately the boy's
father exclaimed, "I do believe; help me overcome
my unbelief!"
25 When Jesus saw that a
crowd was running to the
scene, he rebuked the evil[e]
spirit. "You deaf and mute
spirit," he said, "I com-
mand you, come out of him
and never enter him
again."
26 The spirit shrieked,
convulsed him violently
and came out. The boy
looked so much like a
corpse that many said,
"He's dead." 27 But Jesus
took him by the hand and
lifted him to his feet, and he
stood up.
28 After Jesus had gone in-
doors, his disciples asked
him privately, "Why
couldn't we drive it out?"
29 He replied, "This kind
can come out only by
prayer.[f]"
30 They left that place and
passed through Galilee.
Jesus did not want anyone
to know where they were,
31 because he was teaching
his disciples. He said to
them, "The Son of Man is
going to be betrayed into
the hands of men. They will
kill him, and after three
days he will rise." 32 But

[x] Many mss. add: *and fasting*
[y] Or, *betrayed*

[e] 25 Greek *unclean*
[f] 29 Some manuscripts *prayer and fasting*

32But they did not under-
stand *this* statement, and
they were afraid to ask
Him.
33And they came to
Capernaum; and when He
was in the house, He *began*
to question them, "What
were you discussing on the
way?"
34But they kept silent, for
on the way they had dis-
cussed with one another
which *of them was* the
greatest.
35And sitting down, He
called the twelve and *said
to them, "If anyone wants
to be first, he shall be last of
all, and servant of all."
36And taking a child, He
set him before them, and
taking him in His arms, He
said to them,
37"Whoever receives one
child like this in My name
receives Me; and whoever
receives Me does not re-
ceive Me, but Him who
sent Me."

Dire Warnings

38John said to Him,
"Teacher, we saw some-
one casting out demons in
Your name, and we tried to
hinder him because he was
not following us."
39But Jesus said, "Do not
hinder him, for there is no
one who shall perform a
miracle in My name, and be
able soon afterward to
speak evil of Me.
40"For he who is not
against us is [z]for us.
41"For whoever gives
you a cup of water to drink
because of your name as
followers of Christ, truly I
say to you, he shall not lose
his reward.
42"And whoever causes
one of these little ones who
believe to stumble, it would
be better for him if, with a
heavy millstone hung
around his neck, he had
been cast into the sea.
43"And if your hand
causes you to stumble, cut

[z] Or, *on our side*

δὲ ἠγνόουν τὸ ῥῆμα, καὶ ἐφοβοῦντο
But did not know the word, and feared
αὐτὸν ἐπερωτῆσαι.
him to question.
33 Καὶ ἦλθον εἰς Καφαρναούμ. Καὶ
And they came to Capernaum. And
ἐν τῇ οἰκίᾳ γενόμενος ἐπηρώτα αὐτούς·
in the house being he questioned them:
τί ἐν τῇ ὁδῷ διελογίζεσθε; **34** οἱ δὲ
What in the way were ye debating? And they
ἐσιώπων· πρὸς ἀλλήλους γὰρ διελέχθησαν
were silent; [2]with [3]one another [1]for they debated
ἐν τῇ ὁδῷ τίς μείζων. **35** καὶ καθίσας
in the way who [was] greater. And sitting
ἐφώνησεν τοὺς δώδεκα καὶ λέγει αὐτοῖς·
he called the twelve and says to them:
εἴ τις θέλει πρῶτος εἶναι, ἔσται πάντων
If anyone wishes first to be, he shall be of all
ἔσχατος καὶ πάντων διάκονος. **36** καὶ
last and of all servant. And
λαβὼν παιδίον ἔστησεν αὐτὸ ἐν μέσῳ
taking a child he set it(him) in [the] midst
αὐτῶν, καὶ ἐναγκαλισάμενος αὐτὸ εἶπεν
of them, and folding in [his] arms it he said
αὐτοῖς· **37** ὃς ἂν ἓν τῶν τοιούτων παιδίων
to them: Whoever one – of such children
δέξηται ἐπὶ τῷ ὀνόματί μου, ἐμὲ δέχεται·
receives on(in) the name of me, me receives;
καὶ ὃς ἂν ἐμὲ δέχηται, οὐχ ἐμὲ δέχεται
and whoever me receives, not me receives
ἀλλὰ τὸν ἀποστείλαντά με. **38** Ἔφη αὐτῷ
but the [one] having sent me. Said to him
ὁ Ἰωάννης· διδάσκαλε, εἴδομέν τινα ἐν
– John: Teacher, we saw someone in
τῷ ὀνόματί σου ἐκβάλλοντα δαιμόνια, ὃς
the name of thee expelling demons, who
οὐκ ἀκολουθεῖ ἡμῖν, καὶ ἐκωλύομεν αὐτόν,
does not follow us, and we forbade him,
ὅτι οὐκ ἠκολούθει ἡμῖν. **39** ὁ δὲ Ἰησοῦς
because he was not following us. – But Jesus
εἶπεν· μὴ κωλύετε αὐτόν· οὐδεὶς γάρ
said: Do not forbid him: for no one
ἐστιν ὃς ποιήσει δύναμιν ἐπὶ τῷ ὀνόματί
there is who shall do a mighty work on(in) the name
μου καὶ δυνήσεται ταχὺ κακολογῆσαί με·
of me and will be able quickly to speak evil of me;
40 ὃς γὰρ οὐκ ἔστιν καθ᾽ ἡμῶν, ὑπὲρ
for who is not against us, for
ἡμῶν ἐστιν. **41** Ὃς γὰρ ἂν ποτίσῃ
us is. For whoever [1]gives [3]drink
ὑμᾶς ποτήριον ὕδατος ἐν ὀνόματι, ὅτι
[2]you a cup of water in [the] name, because
Χριστοῦ ἐστε, ἀμὴν λέγω ὑμῖν ὅτι
of Christ ye are, truly I tell you that
οὐ μὴ ἀπολέσῃ τὸν μισθὸν αὐτοῦ. **42** Καὶ
by no means he will lose the reward of him. And
ὃς ἂν σκανδαλίσῃ ἕνα τῶν μικρῶν τούτων
whoever offends one – [3]little [ones] [1]of these
τῶν πιστευόντων, καλόν ἐστιν αὐτῷ μᾶλλον
– [2]believing, good is it for him rather
εἰ περίκειται μύλος ὀνικὸς περὶ τὸν
if be laid *round* a [heavy] millstone round the
τράχηλον αὐτοῦ καὶ βέβληται εἰς τὴν
neck of him and he be thrown into the
θάλασσαν. **43** Καὶ ἐὰν σκανδαλίσῃ σε ἡ
sea. And if offends thee the

they did not understand
what he meant and were
afraid to ask him about it.

Who Is the Greatest?

33They came to Caperna-
um. When he was in the
house, he asked them,
"What were you arguing
about on the road?" 34But
they kept quiet because on
the way they had argued
about who was the great-
est.
35Sitting down, Jesus
called the Twelve and said,
"If anyone wants to be
first, he must be the very
last, and the servant of
all."
36He took a little child
and had him stand among
them. Taking him in his
arms, he said to them,
37"Whoever welcomes one
of these little children in my
name welcomes me; and
whoever welcomes me
does not welcome me but
the one who sent me."

Whoever Is Not Against Us Is for Us

38"Teacher," said John,
"we saw a man driving out
demons in your name and
we told him to stop, be-
cause he was not one of
us."
39"Do not stop him,"
Jesus said. "No one who
does a miracle in my name
can in the next moment say
anything bad about me,
40for whoever is not against
us is for us. 41I tell you the
truth, anyone who gives
you a cup of water in my
name because you belong
to Christ will certainly not
lose his reward.

Causing to Sin

42"And if anyone causes
one of these little ones who
believe in me to sin, it
would be better for him to
be thrown into the sea with
a large millstone tied
around his neck. 43If your
hand causes you to sin, cut

it off; it is better for you to enter life crippled, than having your two hands, to go into hell, into the unquenchable fire,

44[ᵃwhere THEIR WORM DOES NOT DIE, AND THE FIRE IS NOT QUENCHED.]

45"And if your foot causes you to stumble, cut it off; it is better for you to enter life lame, than having your two feet, to be cast into hell,

46[ᵃwhere THEIR WORM DOES NOT DIE, AND THE FIRE IS NOT QUENCHED.]

47"And if your eye causes you to stumble, cast it out; it is better for you to enter the kingdom of God with one eye, than having two eyes, to be cast into hell,

48where THEIR WORM DOES NOT DIE, AND THE FIRE IS NOT QUENCHED.

49"For everyone will be salted with fire.

50"Salt is good; but if the salt becomes unsalty, with what will you make it salty *again*? Have salt in yourselves, and be at peace with one another."

χεὶρ σου, ἀπόκοψον αὐτήν· καλόν ἐστίν
hand of thee, cut off it; good is it

σε κυλλὸν εἰσελθεῖν εἰς τὴν ζωήν, ἢ τὰς
thee maimed to enter into – life, than the

δύο χεῖρας ἔχοντα ἀπελθεῖν εἰς τὴν
two hands having to go away into –

γέενναν, εἰς τὸ πῦρ τὸ ἄσβεστον.‡ **45** καὶ
gehenna, into the fire *the* unquenchable. And

ἐὰν ὁ πούς σου σκανδαλίζῃ σε, ἀπόκοψον
if the foot of thee offends thee, cut off

αὐτόν· καλόν ἐστίν σε εἰσελθεῖν εἰς τὴν
it; good is it thee to enter into –

ζωὴν χωλόν, ἢ τοὺς δύο πόδας ἔχοντα
life lame, than the two feet having

βληθῆναι εἰς τὴν γέενναν.‡ **47** καὶ ἐὰν ὁ
to be cast into – gehenna. And if the

ὀφθαλμός σου σκανδαλίζῃ σε, ἔκβαλε αὐτόν·
eye of thee offends thee, cast out it;

καλόν σέ ἐστιν μονόφθαλμον εἰσελθεῖν εἰς
good thee is it one-eyed to enter into

τὴν βασιλείαν τοῦ θεοῦ, ἢ δύο ὀφθαλμοὺς
the kingdom – of God, than two eyes

ἔχοντα βληθῆναι εἰς τὴν γέενναν, **48** ὅπου
having to be cast into – gehenna, where

ὁ σκώληξ αὐτῶν οὐ τελευτᾷ καὶ τὸ
the worm of them dies not and the

πῦρ οὐ σβέννυται. **49** Πᾶς γὰρ πυρὶ
fire is not quenched. For everyone with fire

ἁλισθήσεται. **50** καλὸν τὸ ἅλας· ἐὰν δὲ
shall be salted. Good [is] – salt; but if

τὸ ἅλας ἄναλον γένηται, ἐν τίνι αὐτὸ
– salt saltless becomes, by what it

ἀρτύσετε; ἔχετε ἐν ἑαυτοῖς ἅλα καὶ
will ye season ? Have in yourselves salt and

εἰρηνεύετε ἐν ἀλλήλοις.
be at peace among one another.

it off. It is better for you to enter life maimed than with two hands to go into hell, where the fire never goes
out.ᵍ 45And if your foot
causes you to sin, cut it off. It is better for you to enter life crippled than to have two feet and be thrown into
hell.ʰ 47And if your eye
causes you to sin, pluck it out. It is better for you to enter the kingdom of God with one eye than to have two eyes and be thrown
into hell, 48where

" 'their worm does not die,
and the fire is not quenched.'ⁱ

49Everyone will be salted with fire.

50"Salt is good, but if it loses its saltiness, how can you make it salty again? Have salt in yourselves, and be at peace with each other."

Chapter 10

Jesus' Teaching about Divorce

AND rising up, He *went from there to the region of Judea, and beyond the Jordan; and crowds *gathered around Him again, and, according to His custom, He once more *began* to teach them.

2And *some* Pharisees came up to Him, testing Him, and *began* to question Him whether it was lawful for a man to divorce a wife.

3And He answered and said to them, "What did Moses command you?"

4And they said, "Moses permitted *a man* TO WRITE A CERTIFICATE OF DIVORCE AND SEND *her* AWAY."

5But Jesus said to them, "Because of your hardness of heart he wrote you this commandment.

6"But from the beginning of creation, *God* MADE

ᵃVv. 44 and 46, which are identical with v. 48, are not found in the best ancient mss.

10 Καὶ ἐκεῖθεν ἀναστὰς ἔρχεται εἰς τὰ
And thence rising up he comes into the

ὅρια τῆς Ἰουδαίας καὶ πέραν τοῦ
territory – of Judæa and beyond the

Ἰορδάνου, καὶ συμπορεύονται πάλιν ὄχλοι
Jordan, and [3]go *with* [1]again [2]crowds

πρὸς αὐτόν, καὶ ὡς εἰώθει πάλιν ἐδίδασκεν
[4]with [5]him, and as he was wont again he taught

αὐτούς. **2** Καὶ προσελθόντες Φαρισαῖοι
them. And [2]approaching [1]Pharisees

ἐπηρώτων αὐτὸν εἰ ἔξεστιν ἀνδρὶ γυναῖκα
questioned him if it is(was) lawful for a man a wife

ἀπολῦσαι, πειράζοντες αὐτόν. **3** ὁ δὲ
to dismiss, testing him. And he

ἀποκριθεὶς εἶπεν αὐτοῖς· **4** τί ὑμῖν ἐνετείλατο
answering said to them: What you ordered

Μωϋσῆς; οἱ δὲ εἶπαν· ἐπέτρεψεν Μωϋσῆς
Moses ? And they said: permitted Moses

βιβλίον ἀποστασίου γράψαι καὶ ἀπολῦσαι.
a roll of divorce to write and to dismiss.

5 ὁ δὲ Ἰησοῦς εἶπεν αὐτοῖς· πρὸς τὴν
– And Jesus said to them: For the

σκληροκαρδίαν ὑμῶν ἔγραψεν ὑμῖν τὴν
hardheartedness of you he wrote to you –

ἐντολὴν ταύτην. **6** ἀπὸ δὲ ἀρχῆς κτίσεως
this commandment. But from [the] beginning of creation

‡ Verse 44 omitted by Nestle; *cf.* NIV footnote.

‡ Verse 46 omitted by Nestle; *cf.* NIV footnote.

Chapter 10

Divorce

JESUS then left that place and went into the region of Judea and across the Jordan. Again crowds of people came to him, and as was his custom, he taught them.

2Some Pharisees came and tested him by asking, "Is it lawful for a man to divorce his wife?"

3"What did Moses command you?" he replied.

4They said, "Moses permitted a man to write a certificate of divorce and send her away."

5"It was because your
hearts were hard that Moses wrote you this law,"
Jesus replied. 6"But at the
beginning of creation God

ᵍ*43* Some manuscripts *out,* *44where / " 'their worm does not die, / and the fire is not quenched.'*
ʰ*45* Some manuscripts *hell,* *46where / " 'their worm does not die, / and the fire is not quenched.'*
ⁱ*48* Isaiah 66:24

THEM MALE AND FEMALE.
7"FOR THIS CAUSE A MAN
SHALL LEAVE HIS FATHER
AND MOTHER,[b]
8AND THE TWO SHALL
BECOME ONE FLESH; conse-
quently they are no longer
two, but one flesh.
9"What therefore God
has joined together, let no
man separate."
10And in the house the
disciples *began* questioning Him about this again.
11And He *said to them,
"Whoever divorces his
wife and marries another
woman commits adultery
against her;
12and if she herself di-
vorces her husband and
marries another man, she is
committing adultery."

Jesus Blesses Little Children

13And they were bringing
children to Him so that He
might touch them; and the
disciples rebuked them.
14But when Jesus saw
this, He was indignant and
said to them, "Permit the
children to come to Me; do
not hinder them; for the
kingdom of God belongs to
such as these.
15"Truly I say to you,
whoever does not receive
the kingdom of God like a
child shall not enter it *at
all*."
16And He took them in
His arms and *began*
blessing them, laying His
hands upon them.

The Rich Young Ruler

17And as He was setting
out on a journey, a man ran
up to Him and knelt before
Him, and *began* asking
Him, "Good Teacher,
what shall I do to inherit
eternal life?"
18And Jesus said to him,
"Why do you call Me
good? No one is good ex-
cept God alone.
19"You know the com-
mandments, 'DO NOT MUR-
DER, DO NOT COMMIT ADUL-
TERY, DO NOT STEAL, DO
NOT BEAR FALSE WITNESS, Do
not defraud, HONOR YOUR
FATHER AND MOTHER.' "
20And he said to Him,
"Teacher, I have kept all

[b] Some mss. add: *and shall cleave to his wife*

ἄρσεν καὶ θῆλυ ἐποίησεν αὐτούς· 7 ἕνεκεν
male and female he made them; for the sake of
τούτου καταλείψει ἄνθρωπος τὸν πατέρα
this shall leave a man the father
αὐτοῦ καὶ τὴν μητέρα, 8 καὶ ἔσονται
of him and the mother, and shall be
οἱ δύο εἰς σάρκα μίαν· ὥστε οὐκέτι
the two – flesh one; so as no longer
εἰσὶν δύο ἀλλὰ μία σάρξ. 9 ὃ οὖν ὁ
are they two but one flesh. What then –
θεὸς συνέζευξεν, ἄνθρωπος μὴ χωριζέτω.
God yoked together, [3]man [2]not [1]let [4]separate.
10 καὶ εἰς τὴν οἰκίαν πάλιν οἱ μαθηταὶ
And in the house again the disciples
περὶ τούτου ἐπηρώτων αὐτόν. 11 καὶ
about this questioned him. And
λέγει αὐτοῖς· ὃς ἂν ἀπολύσῃ τὴν γυναῖκα
he says to them: Whoever dismisses the wife
αὐτοῦ καὶ γαμήσῃ ἄλλην, μοιχᾶται ἐπ'
of him and marries another, commits adultery with
αὐτήν· 12 καὶ ἐὰν αὐτὴ ἀπολύσασα τὸν
her; and if she having dismissed the
ἄνδρα αὐτῆς γαμήσῃ ἄλλον, μοιχᾶται.
husband of her marries another, she commits adultery.
13 Καὶ προσέφερον αὐτῷ παιδία ἵνα
And they brought to him children that
αὐτῶν ἅψηται· οἱ δὲ μαθηταὶ ἐπετίμησαν
them he might touch; but the disciples rebuked
αὐτοῖς. 14 ἰδὼν δὲ ὁ Ἰησοῦς ἠγανάκτησεν
them. But [2]seeing – [1]Jesus was angry
καὶ εἶπεν αὐτοῖς· ἄφετε τὰ παιδία
and said to them: Allow the children
ἔρχεσθαι πρός με, μὴ κωλύετε αὐτά·
to come to me, do not prevent them;
τῶν γὰρ τοιούτων ἐστὶν ἡ βασιλεία τοῦ
– for of such is the kingdom –
θεοῦ. 15 ἀμὴν λέγω ὑμῖν, ὃς ἂν
of God. Truly I tell you, whoever
μὴ δέξηται τὴν βασιλείαν τοῦ θεοῦ ὡς
receives not the kingdom – of God as
παιδίον, οὐ μὴ εἰσέλθῃ εἰς αὐτήν. 16 καὶ
a child, by no means may enter into it. And
ἐναγκαλισάμενος αὐτὰ κατευλόγει τιθεὶς τὰς
folding in [his] arms them he blesses putting the(his)
χεῖρας ἐπ' αὐτά.
hands on them.
17 Καὶ ἐκπορευομένου αὐτοῦ εἰς ὁδὸν
And going forth him• into [the] way
= as he went forth
προσδραμὼν εἷς καὶ γονυπετήσας αὐτὸν
running to one and kneeling to him
ἐπηρώτα αὐτόν· διδάσκαλε ἀγαθέ, τί ποιήσω
questioned him: Teacher good, what may I do
ἵνα ζωὴν αἰώνιον κληρονομήσω; 18 ὁ δὲ
that life eternal I may inherit? – And
Ἰησοῦς εἶπεν αὐτῷ· τί με λέγεις ἀγαθόν;
Jesus said to him: Why me callest thou good?
οὐδεὶς ἀγαθὸς εἰ μὴ εἷς ὁ θεός. 19 τὰς ἐντολὰς
no one good except one – God. The commandments
οἶδας· μὴ φονεύσῃς, μὴ μοιχεύσῃς,
thou knowest: Do not kill, Do not commit adultery,
μὴ κλέψῃς, μὴ ψευδομαρτυρήσῃς, μὴ
Do not steal, Do not bear false witness, Do
ἀποστερήσῃς, τίμα τὸν πατέρα σου καὶ
not defraud, Honour the father of thee and
τὴν μητέρα. 20 ὁ δὲ ἔφη αὐτῷ· διδάσκαλε,
the mother. And he said to him: Teacher,

'made them male and fe-
male.'[j] 7'For this reason a
man will leave his father
and mother and be united
to his wife,[k] 8and the two
will become one flesh.'[l] So
they are no longer two, but
one. 9Therefore what God
has joined together, let man
not separate."
10When they were in the
house again, the disciples
asked Jesus about this.
11He answered, "Anyone
who divorces his wife and
marries another woman
commits adultery against
her. 12And if she divorces
her husband and marries
another man, she commits
adultery."

The Little Children and Jesus

13People were bringing
little children to Jesus to
have him touch them, but
the disciples rebuked them.
14When Jesus saw this, he
was indignant. He said to
them, "Let the little children come to me, and do
not hinder them, for the
kingdom of God belongs to
such as these. 15I tell you
the truth, anyone who will
not receive the kingdom of
God like a little child will
never enter it." 16And he
took the children in his
arms, put his hands on
them and blessed them.

The Rich Young Man

17As Jesus started on his
way, a man ran up to him
and fell on his knees before
him. "Good teacher," he
asked, "what must I do to
inherit eternal life?"
18"Why do you call me
good?" Jesus answered.
"No one is good—except
God alone. 19You know the
commandments: 'Do not
murder, do not commit
adultery, do not steal, do
not give false testimony, do
not defraud, honor your father and mother.'[m]"
20"Teacher," he de-
clared, "all these I have

[j]6 Gen. 1:27
[k]7 Some early manuscripts do not have *and be united to his wife.*
[l]8 Gen. 2:24
[m]19 Exodus 20:12-16; Deut. 5:16-20

these things from my youth
up.''
21And looking at him,
Jesus felt a love for him,
and said to him, ''One thing
you lack: go and sell all you
possess, and give to the
poor, and you shall have
treasure in heaven; and
come, follow Me.''
22But at these words his
face fell, and he went away
grieved, for he was one
who owned much property.
23And Jesus, looking
around, *said to His disciples, ''How hard it will be
for those who are wealthy
to enter the kingdom of
God!''
24And the disciples were
amazed at His words. But
Jesus *answered again and
*said to them, ''Children,
how hard it is [c]to enter the
kingdom of God!
25''It is easier for a camel
to go through the eye of a
needle than for a rich man
to enter the kingdom of
God.''
26And they were even
more astonished and said
to Him, ''Then who can be
saved?''
27Looking upon them,
Jesus *said, ''With men it is
impossible, but not with
God; for all things are possible with God.''
28Peter began to say to
Him, ''Behold, we have
left everything and fol-
lowed You.''
29Jesus said, ''Truly I say
to you, there is no one who
has left house or brothers
or sisters or mother or father or children or farms,
for My sake and for the gospel's sake,
30but that he shall receive
a hundred times as much
now in the present age,
houses and brothers and
sisters and mothers and
children and farms, along

[c] Later mss. insert: *for those who trust in wealth*

ταῦτα πάντα ἐφυλαξάμην ἐκ νεότητός μου.
all these things I observed from youth of me.
21 ὁ δὲ Ἰησοῦς ἐμβλέψας αὐτῷ ἠγάπησεν
– But Jesus looking at him loved
αὐτὸν καὶ εἶπεν αὐτῷ· ἕν σε ὑστερεῖ·
him and said to him: One thing thee is wanting:
ὕπαγε, ὅσα ἔχεις πώλησον καὶ δὸς [τοῖς]
go, what things thou hast sell and give to the
πτωχοῖς, καὶ ἕξεις θησαυρὸν ἐν οὐρανῷ,
poor, and thou wilt have treasure in heaven,
καὶ δεῦρο ἀκολούθει μοι. 22 ὁ δὲ στυγνάσας
and come follow me. But he being sad
ἐπὶ τῷ λόγῳ ἀπῆλθεν λυπούμενος, ἦν
at the word went away grieving, [1]he was
γὰρ ἔχων κτήματα πολλά. 23 Καὶ
[1]for having possessions many. And
περιβλεψάμενος ὁ Ἰησοῦς λέγει τοῖς
looking round – Jesus says to the
μαθηταῖς αὐτοῦ· πῶς δυσκόλως οἱ τὰ
disciples of him: How hardly the [ones] the
χρήματα ἔχοντες εἰς τὴν βασιλείαν τοῦ
riches having into the kingdom –
θεοῦ εἰσελεύσονται. 24 οἱ δὲ μαθηταὶ
of God shall enter. And the disciples
ἐθαμβοῦντο ἐπὶ τοῖς λόγοις αὐτοῦ. ὁ δὲ
were amazed at the words of him. – And
Ἰησοῦς πάλιν ἀποκριθεὶς λέγει αὐτοῖς·
Jesus again answering says to them:
τέκνα, πῶς δύσκολόν ἐστιν εἰς τὴν
Children, how hard it is into the
βασιλείαν τοῦ θεοῦ εἰσελθεῖν· 25 εὐκοπώτερόν
kingdom – of God to enter; easier
ἐστιν κάμηλον διὰ τῆς τρυμαλιᾶς τῆς
it is a camel through the eye –
ῥαφίδος διελθεῖν ἢ πλούσιον εἰς τὴν
of a needle to go *through* than a rich man into the
βασιλείαν τοῦ θεοῦ εἰσελθεῖν. 26 οἱ δὲ
kingdom – of God to enter. But they
περισσῶς ἐξεπλήσσοντο λέγοντες πρὸς
exceedingly were astonished saying to
ἑαυτούς· καὶ τίς δύναται σωθῆναι;
themselves: And who can *to* be saved?
27 ἐμβλέψας αὐτοῖς ὁ Ἰησοῦς λέγει· παρὰ
Looking at them – Jesus says: With
ἀνθρώποις ἀδύνατον, ἀλλ' οὐ παρὰ θεῷ·
men [it is] impossible, but not with God;
πάντα γὰρ δυνατὰ παρὰ τῷ θεῷ. 28 Ἤρξατο
for all things [are] possible with – God. Began
λέγειν ὁ Πέτρος αὐτῷ· ἰδοὺ ἡμεῖς ἀφήκαμεν
to say – Peter to him: Behold [,] we left
πάντα καὶ ἠκολουθήκαμέν σοι. 29 ἔφη ὁ
all things and have followed thee. Said –
Ἰησοῦς· ἀμὴν λέγω ὑμῖν, οὐδείς ἐστιν
Jesus: Truly I tell you, no one there is
ὃς ἀφῆκεν οἰκίαν ἢ ἀδελφοὺς ἢ ἀδελφὰς
who left house or brothers or sisters
ἢ μητέρα ἢ πατέρα ἢ τέκνα ἢ ἀγροὺς
or mother or father or children or fields
ἕνεκεν ἐμοῦ καὶ ἕνεκεν τοῦ εὐαγγελίου,
for the sake of me and for the sake of the gospel,
30 ἐὰν μὴ λάβῃ ἑκατονταπλασίονα νῦν
but he receives a hundredfold now
ἐν τῷ καιρῷ τούτῳ οἰκίας καὶ ἀδελφοὺς
in – time this houses and brothers
καὶ ἀδελφὰς καὶ μητέρας καὶ τέκνα καὶ
and sisters and mothers and children and

kept since I was a boy.''
21Jesus looked at him and
loved him. ''One thing you
lack,'' he said. ''Go, sell
everything you have and
give to the poor, and you
will have treasure in heav-
en. Then come, follow
me.''
22At this the man's face
fell. He went away sad, because he had great wealth.
23Jesus looked around
and said to his disciples,
''How hard it is for the rich
to enter the kingdom of
God!''
24The disciples were
amazed at his words. But
Jesus said again, ''Chil-
dren, how hard it is[n] to enter the kingdom of God! 25It
is easier for a camel to go
through the eye of a needle
than for a rich man to enter
the kingdom of God.''
26The disciples were even
more amazed, and said to
each other, ''Who then can
be saved?''
27Jesus looked at them
and said, ''With man this is
impossible, but not with
God; all things are possible
with God.''
28Peter said to him, ''We
have left everything to follow you!''
29''I tell you the truth,''
Jesus replied, ''no one who
has left home or brothers or
sisters or mother or father
or children or fields for me
and the gospel 30will fail to
receive a hundred times as
much in this present age
(homes, brothers, sisters,
mothers, children and

[n]24 Some manuscripts *is for those who trust in riches*

with persecutions; and in
the age to come, eternal
life.
31"But many *who are*
first, will be last; and the
last, first."

Jesus' Sufferings Foretold

32And they were on the
road, going up to Jerusa-
lem, and Jesus was walking
on ahead of them; and they
were amazed, and those
who followed were fearful.
And again He took the
twelve aside and began to
tell them what was going to
happen to Him,
33*saying,* "Behold, we
are going up to Jerusalem,
and the Son of Man will be
[d]delivered to the chief
priests and the scribes; and
they will condemn Him to
death, and will deliver Him
to the Gentiles.
34"And they will mock
Him and spit upon Him,
and scourge Him, and kill
Him, and three days later
He will rise again."
35And James and John,
the two sons of Zebedee,
*came up to Him, saying to
Him, "Teacher, we want
You to do for us whatever
we ask of You."
36And He said to them,
"What do you want Me to
do for you?"
37And they said to Him,
"Grant that we may sit in
Your glory, one on Your
right, and one on *Your*
left."
38But Jesus said to them,
"You do not know what
you are asking for. Are you
able to drink the cup that I
drink, or to be baptized
with the baptism with
which I am baptized?"
39And they said to Him,
"We are able." And Jesus
said to them, "The cup that
I drink you shall drink; and
you shall be baptized with
the baptism with which I
am baptized.

[d]Or, *betrayed*

ἀγροὺς μετὰ διωγμῶν, καὶ ἐν τῷ αἰῶνι
fields with persecutions, and in the age
τῷ ἐρχομένῳ ζωὴν αἰώνιον. 31 πολλοὶ δὲ
– coming life eternal. And [1]many
ἔσονται πρῶτοι ἔσχατοι καὶ οἱ ἔσχατοι
[3]will be [2]first [4]last and the last
πρῶτοι.
first.
32 Ἦσαν δὲ ἐν τῇ ὁδῷ ἀναβαίνοντες
Now they were in the way going up
εἰς Ἰεροσόλυμα, καὶ ἦν προάγων αὐτοὺς
to Jerusalem, and was going before them
ὁ Ἰησοῦς, καὶ ἐθαμβοῦντο, οἱ δὲ
– Jesus, and they were astonished, and the
ἀκολουθοῦντες ἐφοβοῦντο. καὶ παραλαβὼν
[ones] following were afraid. And taking
πάλιν τοὺς δώδεκα ἤρξατο αὐτοῖς λέγειν
again the twelve he began them to tell
τὰ μέλλοντα αὐτῷ συμβαίνειν, 33 ὅτι ἰδοὺ
the things about to him to happen, – Behold
ἀναβαίνομεν εἰς Ἰεροσόλυμα, καὶ ὁ υἱὸς
we are going up to Jerusalem, and the Son
τοῦ ἀνθρώπου παραδοθήσεται τοῖς
– of man will be betrayed to the
ἀρχιερεῦσιν καὶ τοῖς γραμματεῦσιν, καὶ
chief priests and to the scribes, and
κατακρινοῦσιν αὐτὸν θανάτῳ καὶ παραδώσουσιν
they will condemn him to death and will deliver
αὐτὸν τοῖς ἔθνεσιν 34 καὶ ἐμπαίξουσιν
him to the nations and they will mock
αὐτῷ καὶ ἐμπτύσουσιν αὐτῷ καὶ μαστι-
him and will spit at him and will
γώσουσιν αὐτὸν καὶ ἀποκτενοῦσιν, καὶ
scourge him and will kill, and
μετὰ τρεῖς ἡμέρας ἀναστήσεται.
after three days he will rise again.
35 Καὶ προσπορεύονται αὐτῷ Ἰάκωβος
And approach *to* him James
καὶ Ἰωάννης οἱ [δύο] υἱοὶ Ζεβεδαίου
and John the two sons of Zebedee
λέγοντες αὐτῷ· διδάσκαλε, θέλομεν ἵνα ὃ ἐὰν
saying to him: Teacher, we wish that whatever
αἰτήσωμέν σε ποιήσῃς ἡμῖν. 36 ὁ
we may ask thee thou mayest do for us. he
δὲ εἶπεν αὐτοῖς· τί θέλετέ με ποιήσω
And said to them: What wish ye me I may do
ὑμῖν; 37 οἱ δὲ εἶπαν αὐτῷ· δὸς ἡμῖν
for you? And they said to him: Give us
ἵνα εἷς σου ἐκ δεξιῶν καὶ εἷς ἐξ
that one of thee out of(on) [the] right and one on
= on thy right
ἀριστερῶν καθίσωμεν ἐν τῇ δόξῃ σου.
[thy] left we may sit in the glory of thee.
38 ὁ δὲ Ἰησοῦς εἶπεν αὐτοῖς· οὐκ οἴδατε
– And Jesus said to them: Ye know not
τί αἰτεῖσθε. δύνασθε πιεῖν τὸ ποτήριον
what ye ask. Can ye *to* drink the cup
ὃ ἐγὼ πίνω, ἢ τὸ βάπτισμα ὃ ἐγὼ
which I drink, or the baptism which I
βαπτίζομαι βαπτισθῆναι; 39 οἱ δὲ εἶπαν
am baptized *to* be baptized [with]? And they said
αὐτῷ· δυνάμεθα. ὁ δὲ Ἰησοῦς εἶπεν
to him: We can. – And Jesus said
αὐτοῖς· τὸ ποτήριον ὃ ἐγὼ πίνω πίεσθε,
to them: The cup which I drink shall ye drink,
καὶ τὸ βάπτισμα ὃ ἐγὼ βαπτίζομαι
and the baptism which I am baptized [with]

fields—and with them, persecutions) and in the age to
come, eternal life. 31But
many who are first will be
last, and the last first."

Jesus Again Predicts His Death

32They were on their way
up to Jerusalem, with Jesus
leading the way, and the
disciples were astonished,
while those who followed
were afraid. Again he took
the Twelve aside and told
them what was going to
happen to him. 33"We are
going up to Jerusalem," he
said, "and the Son of Man
will be betrayed to the chief
priests and teachers of the
law. They will condemn
him to death and will hand
him over to the Gentiles,
34who will mock him and
spit on him, flog him and
kill him. Three days later
he will rise."

The Request of James and John

35Then James and John,
the sons of Zebedee, came
to him. "Teacher," they
said, "we want you to do
for us whatever we ask."
36"What do you want me
to do for you?" he asked.
37They replied, "Let one
of us sit at your right and
the other at your left in
your glory."
38"You don't know what
you are asking," Jesus
said. "Can you drink the
cup I drink or be baptized
with the baptism I am baptized with?"
39"We can," they an-
swered.
Jesus said to them, "You
will drink the cup I drink
and be baptized with the
baptism I am baptized

40"But to sit on My right or on *My* left, this is not Mine to give; but it is for those for whom it has been prepared."

41And hearing this, the ten began to feel indignant with James and John.

42And calling them to Himself, Jesus *said to them, "You know that those who are recognized as rulers of the Gentiles lord it over them; and their great men exercise authority over them.

43"But it is not so among you, but whoever wishes to become great among you shall be your servant;

44and whoever wishes to be first among you shall be slave of all.

45"For even the Son of Man did not come to be served, but to serve, and to give His life a ransom for many."

Bartimaeus Receives His Sight

46And they *came to Jericho. And as He was going out from Jericho with His disciples and a great multitude, a blind beggar *named* Bartimaeus, the son of Timaeus, was sitting by the road.

47And when he heard that it was Jesus the Nazarene, he began to cry out and say, "Jesus, Son of David, have mercy on me!"

48And many were sternly telling him to be quiet, but he kept crying out all the more, "Son of David, have mercy on me!"

49And Jesus stopped and said, "Call him *here*." And they *called the blind man, saying to him, "Take courage, arise! He is calling for you."

50And casting aside his cloak, he jumped up, and came to Jesus.

51And answering him, Jesus said, "What do you want Me to do for you?"

βαπτισθήσεσθε· 40 τὸ δὲ καθίσαι ἐκ δεξιῶν
ye shall be baptized; – but to sit on right
μου ἢ ἐξ εὐωνύμων οὐκ ἔστιν ἐμὸν
of me or on [my] left is not mine
δοῦναι, ἀλλ' οἷς ἡτοίμασται. 41 Καὶ
to give, but for whom it has been prepared. And
ἀκούσαντες οἱ δέκα ἤρξαντο ἀγανακτεῖν
[2]hearing [1]the [3]ten began to be incensed
περὶ Ἰακώβου καὶ Ἰωάννου. 42 καὶ
about James and John. And
προσκαλεσάμενος αὐτοὺς ὁ Ἰησοῦς λέγει
[1]calling [3]to [4][him] [2]them – Jesus says
αὐτοῖς· οἴδατε ὅτι οἱ δοκοῦντες ἄρχειν
to them: Ye know that the [ones] thinking to rule
τῶν ἐθνῶν κατακυριεύουσιν αὐτῶν καὶ
the nations lord it over them and
οἱ μεγάλοι αὐτῶν κατεξουσιάζουσιν αὐτῶν.
the great [ones] of them exercise authority over them.
43 οὐχ οὕτως δέ ἐστιν ἐν ὑμῖν· ἀλλ'
[2]not [3]so [1]But is it among you; but
ὃς ἂν θέλῃ μέγας γενέσθαι ἐν ὑμῖν,
whoever wishes great to become among you,
ἔσται ὑμῶν διάκονος, 44 καὶ ὃς ἂν
shall be of you servant, and whoever
θέλῃ ἐν ὑμῖν εἶναι πρῶτος, ἔσται πάντων
wishes among you to be first, shall be of all
δοῦλος· 45 καὶ γὰρ ὁ υἱὸς τοῦ ἀνθρώπου
slave; for even the Son – of man
οὐκ ἦλθεν διακονηθῆναι ἀλλὰ διακονῆσαι
did not come to be served but to serve
καὶ δοῦναι τὴν ψυχὴν αὐτοῦ λύτρον ἀντὶ
and to give the life of him a ransom instead of
πολλῶν.
many.

46 Καὶ ἔρχονται εἰς Ἰεριχώ. Καὶ
And they come to Jericho. And
ἐκπορευομένου αὐτοῦ ἀπὸ Ἰεριχὼ καὶ τῶν
going out him[a] from Jericho and the
= as he was going out
μαθητῶν αὐτοῦ καὶ ὄχλου ἱκανοῦ ὁ υἱὸς
disciples[a] of him and crowd a considerable[a] the son
Τιμαίου Βαρτιμαῖος, τυφλὸς προσαίτης,
of Timæus Bartimæus, a blind beggar,
ἐκάθητο παρὰ τὴν ὁδόν. 47 καὶ ἀκούσας
sat by the way. And hearing
ὅτι Ἰησοῦς ὁ Ναζαρηνός ἐστιν ἤρξατο
that Jesus the Nazarene it is(was) he began
κράζειν καὶ λέγειν· υἱὲ Δαυὶδ Ἰησοῦ,
to cry out and to say: Son of David Jesus,
ἐλέησόν με. 48 καὶ ἐπετίμων αὐτῷ πολλοὶ
pity me. And rebuked him many
ἵνα σιωπήσῃ· ὁ δὲ πολλῷ μᾶλλον ἔκραζεν·
that he should be quiet. But he much more cried out:
υἱὲ Δαυίδ, ἐλέησόν με. 49 καὶ στὰς
Son of David, pity me. And standing
ὁ Ἰησοῦς εἶπεν· φωνήσατε αὐτόν. καὶ
– Jesus said: Call him. And
φωνοῦσιν τὸν τυφλὸν λέγοντες αὐτῷ·
they call the blind man saying to him:
θάρσει, ἔγειρε, φωνεῖ σε. 50 ὁ δὲ
Be of good courage, rise, he calls thee. So he
ἀποβαλὼν τὸ ἱμάτιον αὐτοῦ ἀναπηδήσας ἦλθεν
throwing away the garment of him leaping up came
πρὸς τὸν Ἰησοῦν. 51 καὶ ἀποκριθεὶς αὐτῷ ὁ
to – Jesus. And answering him –
Ἰησοῦς εἶπεν· τί σοι θέλεις ποιήσω;
Jesus said: What for thee wishest thou I may do?

with, 40but to sit at my right
or left is not for me to grant.
These places belong to
those for whom they have
been prepared."
41When the ten heard
about this, they became indignant with James and
John. 42Jesus called them
together and said, "You
know that those who are regarded as rulers of the Gentiles lord it over them, and
their high officials exercise
authority over them. 43Not
so with you. Instead, whoever wants to become great
among you must be your
servant, 44and whoever
wants to be first must be
slave of all. 45For even the
Son of Man did not come to
be served, but to serve, and
to give his life as a ransom
for many."

Blind Bartimaeus Receives His Sight

46Then they came to Jeri-
cho. As Jesus and his disciples, together with a large
crowd, were leaving the
city, a blind man, Barti-
maeus (that is, the Son of
Timaeus), was sitting by
the roadside begging.
47When he heard that it was
Jesus of Nazareth, he be-
gan to shout, "Jesus, Son
of David, have mercy on
me!"
48Many rebuked him and
told him to be quiet, but he
shouted all the more, "Son
of David, have mercy on
me!"
49Jesus stopped and said,
"Call him."
So they called to the blind
man, "Cheer up! On your
feet! He's calling you."
50Throwing his cloak aside,
he jumped to his feet and
came to Jesus.
51"What do you want me
to do for you?" Jesus asked
him.

And the blind man said to
Him, "[e]Rabboni, *I want* to
regain my sight!"
52And Jesus said to him,
"Go your way; your faith
has made you well." And
immediately he regained
his sight and *began* following Him on the road.

ὁ δὲ τυφλὸς εἶπεν αὐτῷ· ραββουνί, ἵνα
And the blind man said to him: Rabboni, that
ἀναβλέψω. 52 καὶ ὁ Ἰησοῦς εἶπεν αὐτῷ·
I may see again. And – Jesus said to him:
ὕπαγε, ἡ πίστις σου σέσωκέν σε. καὶ
Go, the faith of thee has healed thee. And
εὐθὺς ἀνέβλεψεν, καὶ ἠκολούθει αὐτῷ ἐν
immediately he saw again, and followed him in
τῇ ὁδῷ.
the way.

The blind man said,
"Rabbi, I want to see."
52"Go," said Jesus,
"your faith has healed
you." Immediately he re-
ceived his sight and fol-
lowed Jesus along the road.

Chapter 11

The Triumphal Entry

AND as they *ap-
proached Jerusalem,
at Bethphage and Bethany,
near the Mount of Olives,
He *sent two of His disciples,
2and *said to them, "Go
into the village opposite
you, and immediately as
you enter it, you will find a
colt tied *there,* on which no
one yet has ever sat; untie it
and bring it *here.*
3"And if anyone says to
you, 'Why are you doing
this?' you say, 'The Lord
has need of it'; and immediately he will send it back
here."
4And they went away
and found a colt tied at the
door outside in the street;
and they *untied it.
5And some of the by-
standers were saying to
them, "What are you do-
ing, untying the colt?"
6And they spoke to them
just as Jesus had told *them,*
and they gave them permission.
7And they *brought the
colt to Jesus and put their
garments on it; and He sat
upon it.
8And many spread their
garments in the road, and
others *spread* leafy
branches which they had
cut from the fields.
9And those who went be-
fore, and those who fol-
lowed after, were crying
out,
"Hosanna!
BLESSED IS HE WHO
COMES IN THE NAME OF
THE LORD;
10 Blessed *is* the coming
kingdom of our fa-
ther David;
Hosanna in the high-
est!"

11 Καὶ ὅτε ἐγγίζουσιν εἰς Ἰεροσόλυμα
And when they draw near to Jerusalem
εἰς Βηθφαγὴ καὶ Βηθανίαν πρὸς τὸ
to Bethphage and Bethany at the
ὄρος τῶν ἐλαιῶν, ἀποστέλλει δύο τῶν
mount of the olives, he sends two of the
μαθητῶν αὐτοῦ 2 καὶ λέγει αὐτοῖς· ὑπάγετε
disciples of him and tells them: Go ye
εἰς τὴν κώμην τὴν κατέναντι ὑμῶν, καὶ
into the village – opposite you, and
εὐθὺς εἰσπορευόμενοι εἰς αὐτὴν εὑρήσετε
immediately entering into it ye will find
πῶλον δεδεμένον ἐφ' ὃν οὐδεὶς οὔπω
a colt *having been* tied on which [1]no one [2]*not* yet
ἀνθρώπων ἐκάθισεν· λύσατε αὐτὸν καὶ
[3]of men [4]sat; loosen it and
φέρετε. 3 καὶ ἐάν τις ὑμῖν εἴπῃ· τί
bring. And if anyone to you says: Why
ποιεῖτε τοῦτο; εἴπατε· ὁ κύριος αὐτοῦ
do ye this? say: The Lord of it
χρείαν ἔχει, καὶ εὐθὺς αὐτὸν ἀποστέλλει
need has, and immediately it he sends
πάλιν ὧδε. 4 καὶ ἀπῆλθον καὶ εὗρον
again here. And they went and found
πῶλον δεδεμένον πρὸς θύραν ἔξω ἐπὶ
a colt *having been* tied at a door outside on
τοῦ ἀμφόδου, καὶ λύουσιν αὐτόν. 5 καί
the open street, and they loosen it. And
τινες τῶν ἐκεῖ ἑστηκότων ἔλεγον αὐτοῖς·
some of the [ones] there standing said to them:
τί ποιεῖτε λύοντες τὸν πῶλον; 6 οἱ δὲ
What do ye loosening the colt? And they
εἶπαν αὐτοῖς καθὼς εἶπεν ὁ Ἰησοῦς·
said to them as said – Jesus;
καὶ ἀφῆκαν αὐτούς. 7 καὶ φέρουσιν τὸν
and they let go them. And they bring the
πῶλον πρὸς τὸν Ἰησοῦν, καὶ ἐπιβάλλουσιν
colt to – Jesus, and they throw on
αὐτῷ τὰ ἱμάτια αὐτῶν, καὶ ἐκάθισεν
it the garments of them, and he sat
ἐπ' αὐτόν. 8 καὶ πολλοὶ τὰ ἱμάτια αὐτῶν
on it. And many the garments of them
ἔστρωσαν εἰς τὴν ὁδόν, ἄλλοι δὲ στιβάδας,
strewed in the way, and others wisps of twigs,
κόψαντες ἐκ τῶν ἀγρῶν. 9 καὶ οἱ
cutting out of the fields. And the [ones]
προάγοντες καὶ οἱ ἀκολουθοῦντες ἔκραζον·
going before and the [ones] following cried out:
ὡσαννά· εὐλογημένος ὁ ἐρχόμενος ἐν
Hosanna; blessed the [one] coming in
ὀνόματι κυρίου· 10 εὐλογημένη ἡ ἐρχομένη
[the] name of [the] Lord; blessed the coming
βασιλεία τοῦ πατρὸς ἡμῶν Δαυίδ· ὡσαννὰ
kingdom of the father of us David; Hosanna

Chapter 11

The Triumphal Entry

AS they approached Jeru-
salem and came to
Bethphage and Bethany at
the Mount of Olives, Jesus
sent two of his disciples,
2saying to them, "Go to the
village ahead of you, and
just as you enter it, you will
find a colt tied there, which
no one has ever ridden. Untie it and bring it here. 3If
anyone asks you, 'Why are
you doing this?' tell him,
'The Lord needs it and will
send it back here short-
ly.'"
4They went and found a
colt outside in the street,
tied at a doorway. As they
untied it, 5some people
standing there asked,
"What are you doing, untying that colt?" 6They an-
swered as Jesus had told
them to, and the people let
them go. 7When they
brought the colt to Jesus
and threw their cloaks over
it, he sat on it. 8Many people spread their cloaks on
the road, while others
spread branches they had
cut in the fields. 9Those
who went ahead and those
who followed shouted,

"Hosanna![o]"

"Blessed is he who
comes in the name
of the Lord!"[p]

10"Blessed is the coming
kingdom of our
father David!"

"Hosanna in the
highest!"

[e]I.e., My Master

[o]9 A Hebrew expression meaning "Save!" which became an exclamation of praise; also in verse 10
[p]9 Psalm 118:25,26

11And He entered Jerusa-
lem *and came* into the temple; and after looking all
around, He departed for
Bethany with the twelve,
since it was already late.
12And on the next day,
when they had departed
from Bethany, He became
hungry.
13And seeing at a distance
a fig tree in leaf, He went *to*
see if perhaps He would
find anything on it; and
when He came to it, He
found nothing but leaves,
for it was not the season for
figs.
14And He answered and
said to it, "May no one
ever eat fruit from you
again!" And His disciples
were listening.

Jesus Drives Moneychangers from the Temple

15And they *came to
Jerusalem. And He entered
the temple and began to
cast out those who were
buying and selling in the
temple, and overturned the
tables of the moneychang-
ers and the seats of those
who were selling doves;
16and He would not per-
mit anyone to carry goods
through the temple.
17And He *began* to teach
and say to them, "Is it not
written, 'MY HOUSE SHALL
BE CALLED A HOUSE OF
PRAYER FOR ALL THE NA-
TIONS'? But you have made
it a ROBBERS' DEN."
18And the chief priests
and the scribes heard *this*,
and *began* seeking how to
destroy Him; for they were
afraid of Him, for all the
multitude was astonished
at His teaching.
19And whenever evening
came, they would go out of
the city.
20And as they were pass-
ing by in the morning, they
saw the fig tree withered
from the roots *up*.
21And being reminded,
Peter *said to Him, "Rab-
bi, behold, the fig tree
which You cursed has

ἐν τοῖς ὑψίστοις. 11 Καὶ εἰσῆλθεν εἰς
in the highest [places]. And he entered into
Ἱεροσόλυμα εἰς τὸ ἱερόν· καὶ περιβλεψάμενος
Jerusalem into the temple; and looking round at
πάντα, ὀψὲ ἤδη οὔσης τῆς ὥρας, ἐξῆλθεν
all things, [5]late [4]now [3]being [1]the [2]hour,[a] he went forth
εἰς Βηθανίαν μετὰ τῶν δώδεκα.
to Bethany with the twelve.
12 Καὶ τῇ ἐπαύριον ἐξελθόντων αὐτῶν
And on the morrow going forth them[a]
= as they went forth
ἀπὸ Βηθανίας ἐπείνασεν. 13 καὶ ἰδὼν
from Bethany he hungered. And seeing
συκῆν ἀπὸ μακρόθεν ἔχουσαν φύλλα ἦλθεν
a fig-tree from afar having leaves he came
εἰ ἄρα τι εὑρήσει ἐν αὐτῇ, καὶ ἐλθὼν
if perhaps something he will find in it, and coming
ἐπ' αὐτὴν οὐδὲν εὗρεν εἰ μὴ φύλλα·
upon it nothing he found except leaves;
ὁ γὰρ καιρὸς οὐκ ἦν σύκων. 14 καὶ
for the time was not of figs. And
ἀποκριθεὶς εἶπεν αὐτῇ· μηκέτι εἰς τὸν
answering he said to it: No more to the
αἰῶνα ἐκ σοῦ μηδεὶς καρπὸν φάγοι.
age of thee no one fruit may eat.
= May no one eat fruit of thee for ever.
καὶ ἤκουον οἱ μαθηταὶ αὐτοῦ. 15 Καὶ
And [4]heard [1]the [2]disciples [3]of him. And
ἔρχονται εἰς Ἱεροσόλυμα. Καὶ εἰσελθὼν
they come to Jerusalem. And entering
εἰς τὸ ἱερὸν ἤρξατο ἐκβάλλειν τοὺς
into the temple he began to cast out the [ones]
πωλοῦντας καὶ τοὺς ἀγοράζοντας ἐν τῷ
selling and the [ones] buying in the
ἱερῷ, καὶ τὰς τραπέζας τῶν κολλυβιστῶν
temple, and the tables of the moneychangers
καὶ τὰς καθέδρας τῶν πωλούντων τὰς
and the seats of the [ones] selling the
περιστερὰς κατέστρεψεν, 16 καὶ οὐκ ἤφιεν
doves he overturned, and did not permit
ἵνα τις διενέγκῃ σκεῦος διὰ τοῦ
that anyone should carry *through* a vessel through the
ἱεροῦ, 17 καὶ ἐδίδασκεν καὶ ἔλεγεν αὐτοῖς· οὐ
temple, and taught and said to them: Not
γέγραπται ὅτι ὁ οἶκός μου οἶκος προσευχῆς
has it been written that the house of me a house of prayer
κληθήσεται πᾶσιν τοῖς ἔθνεσιν; ὑμεῖς δὲ
shall be called for all the nations? but ye
πεποιήκατε αὐτὸν σπήλαιον λῃστῶν. 18 καὶ
have made it a den of robbers. And
ἤκουσαν οἱ ἀρχιερεῖς καὶ οἱ γραμματεῖς,
[6]heard [1]the [2]chief priests [3]and [4]the [5]scribes,
καὶ ἐζήτουν πῶς αὐτὸν ἀπολέσωσιν·
and they sought how him they might destroy;
ἐφοβοῦντο γὰρ αὐτόν, πᾶς γὰρ ὁ ὄχλος
for they feared him, for all the crowd
ἐξεπλήσσετο ἐπὶ τῇ διδαχῇ αὐτοῦ. 19 Καὶ
was astounded at the teaching of him. And
ὅταν ὀψὲ ἐγένετο, ἐξεπορεύοντο ἔξω τῆς
when late it became, they went forth outside the
πόλεως. 20 Καὶ παραπορευόμενοι πρωῒ
city. And passing along early
εἶδον τὴν συκῆν ἐξηραμμένην ἐκ ῥιζῶν.
they saw the fig-tree *having been* withered from [the] roots.
21 καὶ ἀναμνησθεὶς ὁ Πέτρος λέγει αὐτῷ·
And [2]remembering – [1]Peter says to him:
ῥαββί, ἴδε ἡ συκῆ ἣν κατηράσω
Rabbi, behold[,] the fig-tree which thou cursedst

11Jesus entered Jerusa-
lem and went to the temple.
He looked around at everything, but since it was already late, he went out to
Bethany with the Twelve.

Jesus Clears the Temple

12The next day as they
were leaving Bethany,
Jesus was hungry. 13Seeing
in the distance a fig tree in
leaf, he went to find out if it
had any fruit. When he
reached it, he found nothing but leaves, because it
was not the season for figs.
14Then he said to the tree,
"May no one ever eat fruit
from you again." And his
disciples heard him say it.
15On reaching Jerusalem,
Jesus entered the temple
area and began driving out
those who were buying and
selling there. He over-
turned the tables of the
money changers and the
benches of those selling
doves, 16and would not allow anyone to carry mer-
chandise through the tem-
ple courts. 17And as he
taught them, he said, "Is it
not written:

" 'My house will be
called
a house of prayer for
all nations'[q]?

But you have made it 'a den
of robbers.'[r]"
18The chief priests and
the teachers of the law
heard this and began looking for a way to kill him, for
they feared him, because
the whole crowd was
amazed at his teaching.
19When evening came,
they[s] went out of the city.

The Withered Fig Tree

20In the morning, as they
went along, they saw the fig
tree withered from the
roots. 21Peter remembered
and said to Jesus, "Rabbi,
look! The fig tree you
cursed has withered!"

[q]*17* Isaiah 56:7
[r]*17* Jer. 7:11
[s]*19* Some early manuscripts *he*

withered."
22 And Jesus *answered
saying to them, "Have
faith in God.
23 "Truly I say to you,
whoever says to this mountain, 'Be taken up and cast
into the sea,' and does not
doubt in his heart, but believes that what he says is
going to happen, it shall be
granted him.
24 "Therefore I say to
you, all things for which
you pray and ask, believe
that you have received
them, and they shall be
granted you.
25 "And whenever you
stand praying, forgive, if
you have anything against
anyone; so that your Father
also who is in heaven may
forgive you your transgressions.
26 ["[f]But if you do not
forgive, neither will your
Father who is in heaven
forgive your transgres-
sions."]

Jesus' Authority Questioned

27 And they *came again
to Jerusalem. And as He
was walking in the temple,
the chief priests, and
scribes, and elders *came
to Him,
28 and *began* saying to
Him, "By what authority
are You doing these things,
or who gave You this au-
thority to do these things?"
29 And Jesus said to them,
"I will ask you one ques-
tion, and you answer Me,
and *then* I will tell you by
what authority I do these
things.
30 "Was the baptism of
John from heaven, or from
men? Answer Me."
31 And they *began* reasoning among themselves, saying, "If we say, 'From
heaven,' He will say, 'Then
why did you not believe
him?'
32 "But shall we say,
'From men'?"—they were
afraid of the multitude, for
all considered John to have
been a prophet indeed.
33 And answering Jesus,
they *said, "We do not
know." And Jesus *said to
them, "Neither will I tell
you by what authority I do
these things."

[f]Many mss. do not contain this verse

ἐξήρανται. 22 καὶ ἀποκριθεὶς ὁ Ἰησοῦς λέγει
has been withered. And answering – Jesus says
αὐτοῖς· ἔχετε πίστιν θεοῦ. 23 ἀμὴν λέγω ὑμῖν
to them: Have [the] faith of God. Truly I tell you
ὅτι ὃς ἂν εἴπῃ τῷ ὄρει τούτῳ· ἄρθητι
that whoever says – mountain to this: Be thou taken
καὶ βλήθητι εἰς τὴν θάλασσαν, καὶ μὴ
and be thou cast into the sea, and not
διακριθῇ ἐν τῇ καρδίᾳ αὐτοῦ ἀλλὰ πιστεύῃ
doubts in the heart of him but believes
ὅτι ὃ λαλεῖ γίνεται, ἔσται αὐτῷ. 24 διὰ
that what he says happens, it will be to him.[c] There-
= he will have it.
τοῦτο λέγω ὑμῖν, πάντα ὅσα προσεύχεσθε
fore I tell you, all things which ye pray
καὶ αἰτεῖσθε, πιστεύετε ὅτι ἐλάβετε, καὶ
and ask, believe that ye received, and
ἔσται ὑμῖν. 25 καὶ ὅταν στήκετε
it will be to you.[c] And when ye stand
= ye will have it.
προσευχόμενοι, ἀφίετε εἴ τι ἔχετε κατά
praying, forgive if anything ye have against
τινος, ἵνα καὶ ὁ πατὴρ ὑμῶν ὁ ἐν τοῖς
anyone, that also the Father of you – in the
οὐρανοῖς ἀφῇ ὑμῖν τὰ παραπτώματα ὑμῶν.‡
heavens may forgive you the trespasses of you.
27 Καὶ ἔρχονται πάλιν εἰς Ἱεροσόλυμα.
And they come again to Jerusalem.
καὶ ἐν τῷ ἱερῷ περιπατοῦντος αὐτοῦ
And in the temple walking him[a]
=as he walked
ἔρχονται πρὸς αὐτὸν οἱ ἀρχιερεῖς καὶ οἱ
come to him the chief priests and the
γραμματεῖς καὶ οἱ πρεσβύτεροι, 28 καὶ
scribes and the elders, and
ἔλεγον αὐτῷ· ἐν ποίᾳ ἐξουσίᾳ ταῦτα
said to him: By what authority these things
ποιεῖς; ἢ τίς σοι ἔδωκεν τὴν ἐξουσίαν
doest thou? or who thee gave – authority
ταύτην ἵνα ταῦτα ποιῇς; 29 ὁ δὲ Ἰησοῦς
this that these things thou mayest do? – And Jesus
εἶπεν αὐτοῖς· ἐπερωτήσω ὑμᾶς ἕνα λόγον,
said to them: I will question you one word,
καὶ ἀποκρίθητέ μοι, καὶ ἐρῶ ὑμῖν ἐν
and answer ye me, and I will tell you by
ποίᾳ ἐξουσίᾳ ταῦτα ποιῶ. 30 τὸ βάπτισμα
what authority these things I do. The baptism
τὸ Ἰωάννου ἐξ οὐρανοῦ ἦν ἢ ἐξ ἀνθρώπων;
– of John of heaven was it or of men?
ἀποκρίθητέ μοι. 31 καὶ διελογίζοντο πρὸς
answer ye me. And they debated with
ἑαυτοὺς λέγοντες· ἐὰν εἴπωμεν· ἐξ οὐρανοῦ,
themselves saying: If we say: Of heaven,
ἐρεῖ· διὰ τί οὖν οὐκ ἐπιστεύσατε αὐτῷ;
he will say: Why then did ye not believe him?
32 ἀλλὰ εἴπωμεν· ἐξ ἀνθρώπων;—ἐφοβοῦντο
But may we say: Of men? — they feared
τὸν ὄχλον· ἅπαντες γὰρ εἶχον τὸν Ἰωάννην
the crowd; for all men held – John
ὄντως ὅτι προφήτης ἦν. 33 καὶ
[3]really [1]that [4]a prophet [2]he was. And
ἀποκριθέντες τῷ Ἰησοῦ λέγουσιν· οὐκ
answering – Jesus they say: not
οἴδαμεν. καὶ ὁ Ἰησοῦς λέγει αὐτοῖς·
We know. And – Jesus says to them:
οὐδὲ ἐγὼ λέγω ὑμῖν ἐν ποίᾳ ἐξουσίᾳ
Neither I tell you by what authority

‡ Verse 26 omitted by Nestle; *cf.* NIV footnote.

22 "Have[t] faith in God,"
Jesus answered. 23 "I tell
you the truth, if anyone
says to this mountain, 'Go,
throw yourself into the
sea,' and does not doubt in
his heart but believes that
what he says will happen, it
will be done for him.
24 Therefore I tell you,
whatever you ask for in
prayer, believe that you
have received it, and it will
be yours. 25 And when you
stand praying, if you hold
anything against anyone,
forgive him, so that your
Father in heaven may for-
give you your sins.[u]"

The Authority of Jesus Questioned

27 They arrived again in
Jerusalem, and while Jesus
was walking in the temple
courts, the chief priests,
the teachers of the law and
the elders came to him.
28 "By what authority are
you doing these things?"
they asked. "And who
gave you authority to do
this?"
29 Jesus replied, "I will
ask you one question. An-
swer me, and I will tell you
by what authority I am doing these things. 30 John's
baptism—was it from
heaven, or from men? Tell
me!"
31 They discussed it
among themselves and
said, "If we say, 'From
heaven,' he will ask, 'Then
why didn't you believe
him?' 32 But if we say,
'From men' . . . ." (They
feared the people, for everyone held that John really was a prophet.)
33 So they answered
Jesus, "We don't know."
Jesus said, "Neither will
I tell you by what authority
I am doing these things."

[t]22 Some early manuscripts *If you have*
[u]25 Some manuscripts *sins.* 26 *But if you do not forgive, neither will your Father who is in heaven forgive your sins.*

Chapter 12

Parable of the Vine-growers

AND He began to speak to them in parables: "A man PLANTED A VINEYARD, AND PUT A WALL AROUND IT, AND DUG A VAT UNDER THE WINE PRESS, AND BUILT A TOWER, and rented it out to [g]vine-growers and went on a journey.

2 "And at the *harvest* time he sent a slave to the vine-growers, in order to receive *some* of the produce of the vineyard from the vine-growers.

3 "And they took him, and beat him, and sent him away empty-handed.

4 "And again he sent them another slave, and they wounded him in the head, and treated him shamefully.

5 "And he sent another, and that one they killed; and *so with* many others, beating some, and killing others.

6 "He had one more *to send,* a beloved son; he sent him last *of all* to them, saying, 'They will respect my son.'

7 "But those vine-growers said to one another, 'This is the heir; come, let us kill him, and the inheritance will be ours!'

8 "And they took him, and killed him, and threw him out of the vineyard.

9 "What will the owner of the vineyard do? He will come and destroy the vine-growers, and will give the vineyard to others.

10 "Have you not even read this Scripture:

'THE STONE WHICH THE BUILDERS REJECTED,
THIS BECAME THE CHIEF CORNER *stone;*
11 THIS CAME ABOUT FROM THE LORD,
AND IT IS MARVELOUS IN OUR EYES'?"

12 And they were seeking to seize Him; and *yet* they feared the multitude; for they understood that He spoke the parable against

[g] Or, *tenant farmers,* also vv. 2, 7, 9

ταῦτα ποιῶ. **12** Καὶ ἤρξατο αὐτοῖς ἐν
these things I do. And he began to them in
παραβολαῖς λαλεῖν. ἀμπελῶνα ἄνθρωπος
parables to speak. [3]a vineyard [1]A man
ἐφύτευσεν, καὶ περιέθηκεν φραγμὸν καὶ ὤρυξεν
[2]planted, and put round [it] a hedge and dug
ὑπολήνιον καὶ ᾠκοδόμησεν πύργον, καὶ
a winepress and built a tower, and
ἐξέδοτο αὐτὸν γεωργοῖς, καὶ ἀπεδήμησεν.
let out it to husbandmen, and went away.
2 καὶ ἀπέστειλεν πρὸς τοὺς γεωργοὺς τῷ
And he sent to the husbandmen at the
καιρῷ δοῦλον, ἵνα παρὰ τῶν γεωργῶν
time a slave, that from the husbandmen
λάβῃ ἀπὸ τῶν καρπῶν τοῦ ἀμπελῶνος·
he might receive from(of) the fruits of the vineyard;
3 καὶ λαβόντες αὐτὸν ἔδειραν καὶ ἀπέστειλαν
And taking him they beat and sent away
κενόν. **4** καὶ πάλιν ἀπέστειλεν πρὸς αὐτοὺς
empty. And again he sent to them
ἄλλον δοῦλον· κἀκεῖνον ἐκεφαλαίωσαν καὶ
another slave; and that one they wounded in the head and
ἠτίμασαν. **5** καὶ ἄλλον ἀπέστειλεν· κἀκεῖνον
insulted. And another he sent; and that one
ἀπέκτειναν, καὶ πολλοὺς ἄλλους, οὓς μὲν
they killed, and many others, [2]some
δέροντες, οὓς δὲ ἀποκτέννοντες. **6** ἔτι ἕνα
[1]beating, [2]others [1]killing. Still one
εἶχεν, υἱὸν ἀγαπητόν· ἀπέστειλεν αὐτὸν
he had, a son beloved; he sent him
ἔσχατον πρὸς αὐτοὺς λέγων ὅτι ἐντραπήσονται
last to them saying[,] – They will reverence
τὸν υἱόν μου. **7** ἐκεῖνοι δὲ οἱ γεωργοὶ
the son of me. But those – husbandmen
πρὸς ἑαυτοὺς εἶπαν ὅτι οὗτός ἐστιν ὁ
to themselves said[,] – This is the
κληρονόμος· δεῦτε ἀποκτείνωμεν αὐτόν, καὶ
heir; come[,] let us kill him, and
ἡμῶν ἔσται ἡ κληρονομία. **8** καὶ λαβόντες
of us will be the inheritance. And taking
ἀπέκτειναν αὐτόν, καὶ ἐξέβαλον αὐτὸν
they killed him, and cast *out* him
ἔξω τοῦ ἀμπελῶνος. **9** τί ποιήσει ὁ
outside the vineyard. What will do the
κύριος τοῦ ἀμπελῶνος; ἐλεύσεται καὶ
lord of the vineyard ? he will come and
ἀπολέσει τοὺς γεωργούς, καὶ δώσει τὸν
will destroy the husbandmen, and will give the
ἀμπελῶνα ἄλλοις. **10** οὐδὲ τὴν γραφὴν
vineyard to others. [2]not – [4]scripture
ταύτην ἀνέγνωτε· λίθον ὃν ἀπεδοκίμασαν
[3]this [1]Read ye : A stone which [3]rejected
οἱ οἰκοδομοῦντες, οὗτος ἐγενήθη εἰς κεφαλὴν
[1]the [ones] [2]building, this became for head
γωνίας· **11** παρὰ κυρίου ἐγένετο αὕτη,
of corner; from [the] Lord was this,
καὶ ἔστιν θαυμαστὴ ἐν ὀφθαλμοῖς ἡμῶν;
and it is marvellous in eyes of us ?
12 Καὶ ἐζήτουν αὐτὸν κρατῆσαι, καὶ
And they sought him to seize, and
ἐφοβήθησαν τὸν ὄχλον· ἔγνωσαν γὰρ
feared the crowd; for they knew
ὅτι πρὸς αὐτοὺς τὴν παραβολὴν
that to them the parable

Chapter 12

The Parable of the Tenants

HE then began to speak to them in parables: "A man planted a vineyard. He put a wall around it, dug a pit for the winepress and built a watchtower. Then he rented the vineyard to some farmers and went away on a journey.
2 At harvest time he sent a servant to the tenants to collect from them some of the fruit of the vineyard.
3 But they seized him, beat him and sent him away empty-handed.
4 Then he sent another servant to them; they struck this man on the head and treated him shamefully.
5 He sent still another, and that one they killed. He sent many others; some of them they beat, others they killed.

6 "He had one left to send, a son, whom he loved. He sent him last of all, saying, 'They will respect my son.'

7 "But the tenants said to one another, 'This is the heir. Come, let's kill him, and the inheritance will be ours.'
8 So they took him and killed him, and threw him out of the vineyard.

9 "What then will the owner of the vineyard do? He will come and kill those tenants and give the vineyard to others.
10 Haven't you read this scripture:

" 'The stone the builders rejected
has become the capstone[v];
11 the Lord has done this,
and it is marvelous in our eyes'[w]?"

12 Then they looked for a way to arrest him because they knew he had spoken the parable against them.

[v] 10 Or *cornerstone*
[w] 11 Psalm 118:22,23

them. And *so* they left Him, and went away.

Jesus Answers the Pharisees, Sadducees and Scribes

13And they *sent some of the Pharisees and Herodians to Him, in order to trap Him in a statement.

14And they *came and *said to Him, "Teacher, we know that You are truthful, and defer to no one; for You are not partial to any, but teach the way of God in truth. Is it lawful to pay a poll-tax to Caesar, or not?

15"Shall we pay, or shall we not pay?" But He, knowing their hypocrisy, said to them, "Why are you testing Me? Bring Me a [h]denarius to look at."

16And they brought *one*. And He *said to them, "Whose likeness and inscription is this?" And they said to Him, "Caesar's."

17And Jesus said to them, "Render to Caesar the things that are Caesar's, and to God the things that are God's." And they were amazed at Him.

18And *some* Sadducees (who say that there is no resurrection) *came to Him, and *began* questioning Him, saying,

19"Teacher, Moses wrote for us that IF A MAN'S BROTHER DIES, and leaves behind a wife, AND LEAVES NO CHILD, HIS BROTHER SHOULD TAKE THE WIFE, AND RAISE UP OFFSPRING TO HIS BROTHER.

20"There were seven brothers; and the first took a wife, and died, leaving no offspring.

21"And the second one took her, and died, leaving behind no offspring; and the third likewise;

22and *so* all seven left no offspring. Last of all the woman died also.

23"In the resurrection, [i]when they rise again,

[h] The denarius was equivalent to one day's wage

[i] Most ancient mss. do not contain *when they rise again*

εἶπεν. καὶ ἀφέντες αὐτὸν ἀπῆλθον.
he told. And leaving him they went away.

13 Καὶ ἀποστέλλουσιν πρός αὐτόν τινας τῶν
And they send to him some of the

Φαρισαίων καὶ τῶν Ἡρῳδιανῶν ἵνα αὐτὸν
Pharisees and of the Herodians that him

ἀγρεύσωσιν λόγῳ. 14 καὶ ἐλθόντες
they might catch in a word. And coming

λέγουσιν αὐτῷ· διδάσκαλε, οἴδαμεν ὅτι
they say to him: Teacher, we know that

ἀληθὴς εἶ καὶ οὐ μέλει σοι περὶ
true thou art and it matters not to thee about

οὐδενός· οὐ γὰρ βλέπεις εἰς πρόσωπον
no(any)one; for thou lookest not at [the] face

ἀνθρώπων, ἀλλ' ἐπ' ἀληθείας τὴν ὁδὸν
of men, but on(in) truth the way

τοῦ θεοῦ διδάσκεις· ἔξεστιν δοῦναι κῆνσον
– of God teachest; is it lawful to give tribute

Καίσαρι ἢ οὔ; δῶμεν ἢ μὴ δῶμεν;
to Cæsar or no? may we give or may we not give?

15 ὁ δὲ εἰδὼς αὐτῶν τὴν ὑπόκρισιν εἶπεν
But he knowing of them the hypocrisy said

αὐτοῖς· τί με πειράζετε; φέρετέ μοι
to them: Why me tempt ye? bring me

δηνάριον ἵνα ἴδω. 16 οἱ δὲ ἤνεγκαν. καὶ
a denarius that I may see. And they brought. And

λέγει αὐτοῖς· τίνος ἡ εἰκὼν αὕτη καὶ ἡ
he says to them: Of whom – image this and –

ἐπιγραφή; οἱ δὲ εἶπαν αὐτῷ· Καίσαρος.
superscription? And they tell him: Of Cæsar.

17 ὁ δὲ Ἰησοῦς εἶπεν αὐτοῖς· τὰ Καίσαρος
– So Jesus said to them: The things of Cæsar

ἀπόδοτε Καίσαρι καὶ τὰ τοῦ θεοῦ τῷ
render to Cæsar and the things – of God –

θεῷ. καὶ ἐξεθαύμαζον ἐπ' αὐτῷ.
to God. And they marvelled at him.

18 Καὶ ἔρχονται Σαδδουκαῖοι πρὸς αὐτόν,
And come Sadducees to him,

οἵτινες λέγουσιν ἀνάστασιν μὴ εἶναι, καὶ
who say resurrection not to be, and
= that there is no resurrection,

ἐπηρώτων αὐτὸν λέγοντες· 19 διδάσκαλε,
questioned him saying: Teacher,

Μωϋσῆς ἔγραψεν ἡμῖν ὅτι ἐάν τινος
Moses wrote to us that if of anyone

ἀδελφὸς ἀποθάνῃ καὶ καταλίπῃ γυναῖκα
a brother should die and leave behind a wife

καὶ μὴ ἀφῇ τέκνον, ἵνα λάβῃ ὁ ἀδελφὸς
and leave not a child, – [4]may take [1]the [2]brother

αὐτοῦ τὴν γυναῖκα καὶ ἐξαναστήσῃ σπέρμα
[3]of him the wife and may raise up seed

τῷ ἀδελφῷ αὐτοῦ. 20 ἑπτὰ ἀδελφοὶ ἦσαν·
to the brother of him. Seven brothers there were;

καὶ ὁ πρῶτος ἔλαβεν γυναῖκα, καὶ
and the first took a wife, and

ἀποθνῄσκων οὐκ ἀφῆκεν σπέρμα· 21 καὶ
dying left not seed; and

ὁ δεύτερος ἔλαβεν αὐτήν, καὶ ἀπέθανεν μὴ
the second took her, and died not

καταλιπὼν σπέρμα· καὶ ὁ τρίτος ὡσαύτως·
leaving behind seed; and the third similarly;

22 καὶ οἱ ἑπτὰ οὐκ ἀφῆκαν σπέρμα.
and the seven left not seed.

ἔσχατον πάντων καὶ ἡ γυνὴ ἀπέθανεν.
Last of all also the wife died.

23 ἐν τῇ ἀναστάσει, ὅταν ἀναστῶσιν,
In the resurrection, when they rise again,

But they were afraid of the crowd; so they left him and went away.

Paying Taxes to Caesar

13Later they sent some of the Pharisees and Herodians to Jesus to catch him in his words. 14They came to him and said, "Teacher, we know you are a man of integrity. You aren't swayed by men, because you pay no attention to who they are; but you teach the way of God in accordance with the truth. Is it right to pay taxes to Caesar or not? 15Should we pay or shouldn't we?"

But Jesus knew their hypocrisy. "Why are you trying to trap me?" he asked. "Bring me a denarius and let me look at it." 16They brought the coin, and he asked them, "Whose portrait is this? And whose inscription?"

"Caesar's," they replied.

17Then Jesus said to them, "Give to Caesar what is Caesar's and to God what is God's."

And they were amazed at him.

Marriage at the Resurrection

18Then the Sadducees, who say there is no resurrection, came to him with a question. 19"Teacher," they said, "Moses wrote for us that if a man's brother dies and leaves a wife but no children, the man must marry the widow and have children for his brother. 20Now there were seven brothers. The first one married and died without leaving any children. 21The second one married the widow, but he also died, leaving no child. It was the same with the third. 22In fact, none of the seven left any children. Last of all, the woman died too. 23At the resurrection[x] whose

[x] 23 Some manuscripts *resurrection, when men rise from the dead,*

which one's wife will she
be? For all seven had her as
wife."
24Jesus said to them, "Is
this not the reason you are
mistaken, that you do not
understand the Scriptures,
or the power of God?
25"For when they rise
from the dead, they neither
marry, nor are given in
marriage, but are like angels in heaven.
26"But regarding the fact
that the dead rise again,
have you not read in the
book of Moses, in the *passage about the burning*
bush, how God spoke to
him, saying, 'I AM THE GOD
OF ABRAHAM, AND THE GOD
OF ISAAC, AND THE GOD OF
JACOB'?
27"He is not the God of
the dead, but of the living;
you are greatly mistaken."
28And one of the scribes
came and heard them argu-
ing, and recognizing that
He had answered them
well, asked Him, "What
commandment is the fore-
most of all?"
29Jesus answered, "The
foremost is, 'HEAR, O IS-
RAEL! THE LORD OUR GOD IS
ONE LORD;
30AND YOU SHALL LOVE THE
LORD YOUR GOD WITH ALL
YOUR HEART, AND WITH
ALL YOUR SOUL, AND
WITH ALL YOUR MIND, AND
WITH ALL YOUR STRENGTH.'
31"The second is this,
'YOU SHALL LOVE YOUR
NEIGHBOR AS YOURSELF.'
There is no other com-
mandment greater than
these."
32And the scribe said to
Him, "Right, Teacher,
You have truly stated that
HE IS ONE; AND THERE IS NO
ONE ELSE BESIDES HIM;
33AND TO LOVE HIM WITH
ALL THE HEART AND WITH
ALL THE UNDERSTANDING
AND WITH ALL THE
STRENGTH, AND TO LOVE
ONE'S NEIGHBOR AS HIMSELF,

τίνος αὐτῶν ἔσται γυνή; οἱ γὰρ ἑπτὰ
of which of them will she be wife? for the seven
ἔσχον αὐτὴν γυναῖκα. 24 ἔφη αὐτοῖς ὁ
had her [as] wife. Said to them –
Ἰησοῦς· οὐ διὰ τοῦτο πλανᾶσθε μὴ
Jesus: [3]not [4]therefore [1]Do [2]ye [5]err not
εἰδότες τὰς γραφὰς μηδὲ τὴν δύναμιν
knowing the scriptures nor the power
τοῦ θεοῦ; 25 ὅταν γὰρ ἐκ νεκρῶν
– of God? for when out of [the] dead
ἀναστῶσιν, οὔτε γαμοῦσιν οὔτε γαμίζονται,
they rise again, they neither marry nor are given in marriage,
ἀλλ' εἰσὶν ὡς ἄγγελοι ἐν τοῖς οὐρανοῖς.
but are as angels in the heavens.
26 περὶ δὲ τῶν νεκρῶν ὅτι ἐγείρονται,
But concerning the dead that they are raised,
οὐκ ἀνέγνωτε ἐν τῇ βίβλῳ Μωϋσέως ἐπὶ
did ye not read in the roll of Moses at
τοῦ βάτου πῶς εἶπεν αὐτῷ ὁ θεὸς λέγων·
the bush how said to him – God saying:
ἐγὼ ὁ θεὸς Ἀβραὰμ καὶ θεὸς Ἰσαὰκ
I [am] the God of Abraham and God of Isaac
καὶ θεὸς Ἰακώβ; 27 οὐκ ἔστιν θεὸς
and God of Jacob? he is not God
νεκρῶν ἀλλὰ ζώντων. πολὺ πλανᾶσθε.
of dead [persons] but of living [ones]. Much ye err.
28 Καὶ προσελθὼν εἷς τῶν γραμματέων,
And [4]approaching [1]one [2]of the [3]scribes,
ἀκούσας αὐτῶν συζητούντων, εἰδὼς ὅτι
hearing them debating, knowing that
καλῶς ἀπεκρίθη αὐτοῖς, ἐπηρώτησεν αὐτόν·
well he answered them, questioned him:
ποία ἐστὶν ἐντολὴ πρώτη πάντων;
What is [the] commandment first of all?
29 ἀπεκρίθη ὁ Ἰησοῦς ὅτι πρώτη ἐστίν·
Answered – Jesus[,] – [The] first is:
ἄκουε, Ἰσραήλ, κύριος ὁ θεὸς ἡμῶν κύριος
Hear, Israel, Lord the God of us Lord
= The Lord our God is one Lord,
εἷς ἐστιν, 30 καὶ ἀγαπήσεις κύριον τὸν
one is, and thou shalt love Lord the
θεόν σου ἐξ ὅλης τῆς καρδίας σου καὶ
God of thee from(with) all the heart of thee and
ἐξ ὅλης τῆς ψυχῆς σου καὶ ἐξ ὅλης
with all the soul of thee and with all
τῆς διανοίας σου καὶ ἐξ ὅλης τῆς ἰσχύος
the mind of thee and with all the strength
σου. 31 δευτέρα αὕτη· ἀγαπήσεις τὸν
of thee. [The] second [is] this: Thou shalt love the
πλησίον σου ὡς σεαυτόν. μείζων τούτων
neighbour of thee as thyself. Greater [than] these
ἄλλη ἐντολὴ οὐκ ἔστιν. 32 καὶ εἶπεν
other commandment there is not. And said
αὐτῷ ὁ γραμματεύς· καλῶς, διδάσκαλε, ἐπ'
to him the scribe: Well, teacher, on(in)
ἀληθείας εἶπες ὅτι εἷς ἐστιν καὶ οὐκ
truth thou sayest that one there is and not
ἔστιν ἄλλος πλὴν αὐτοῦ· 33 καὶ τὸ
there is another besides him; and –
ἀγαπᾶν αὐτὸν ἐξ ὅλης τῆς καρδίας καὶ ἐξ
to love him with all the heart and with
ὅλης τῆς συνέσεως καὶ ἐξ ὅλης τῆς
all the understanding and with all the
ἰσχύος, καὶ τὸ ἀγαπᾶν τὸν πλησίον ὡς
strength, and – to love the(one's) neighbour as

wife will she be, since the
seven were married to
her?"
24Jesus replied, "Are you
not in error because you do
not know the Scriptures or
the power of God? 25When
the dead rise, they will neither marry nor be given in
marriage; they will be like
the angels in heaven.
26Now about the dead ris-
ing—have you not read in
the book of Moses, in the
account of the bush, how
God said to him, 'I am the
God of Abraham, the God
of Isaac, and the God of Jacob'[y]? 27He is not the God
of the dead, but of the living. You are badly mistak-
en!"

The Greatest Commandment

28One of the teachers of
the law came and heard
them debating. Noticing
that Jesus had given them a
good answer, he asked
him, "Of all the command-
ments, which is the most
important?"
29"The most important
one," answered Jesus, "is
this: 'Hear, O Israel, the
Lord our God, the Lord is
one.[z] 30Love the Lord
your God with all your
heart and with all your soul
and with all your mind and
with all your strength.'[a]
31The second is this: 'Love
your neighbor as your-
self.'[b] There is no commandment greater than
these."
32"Well said, teacher,"
the man replied. "You are
right in saying that God is
one and there is no other
but him. 33To love him with
all your heart, with all your
understanding and with all
your strength, and to love
your neighbor as yourself is

[y]*26* Exodus 3:6
[z]*29* Or *the Lord our God is one Lord*
[a]*30* Deut. 6:4,5
[b]*31* Lev. 19:18

is much more than all burnt
offerings and sacrifices.''
34And when Jesus saw
that he had answered intel-
ligently, He said to him,
''You are not far from the
kingdom of God.'' And af-
ter that, no one would venture to ask Him any more
questions.
35And Jesus answering
began to say, as He taught
in the temple, ''How *is it
that* the scribes say that the
Christ is the son of David?
36''David himself said in
the Holy Spirit,

'THE LORD SAID TO MY
LORD,
''SIT AT MY RIGHT
HAND,
UNTIL I PUT THINE
ENEMIES BENEATH
THY FEET.'' '

37''David himself calls
Him 'Lord'; and *so* in what
sense is He his son?'' And
the great crowd enjoyed listening to Him.
38And in His teaching He
was saying: ''Beware of the
scribes who like to walk
around in long robes, and
like respectful greetings in
the market places,
39and chief seats in the
synagogues, and places of
honor at banquets,
40who devour widows'
houses, and for appear-
ance's sake offer long
prayers; these will receive
greater condemnation.''

The Widow's Mite

41And He sat down oppo-
site the treasury, and *began* observing how the
multitude were putting
money into the treasury;
and many rich people were
putting in large sums.
42And a poor widow came
and put in two small copper
coins, which amount to a
cent.
43And calling His disci-
ples to Him, He said to
them, ''Truly I say to you,
this poor widow put in

ἑαυτὸν περισσότερόν ἐστιν πάντων τῶν
himself more is [than] all the
ὁλοκαυτωμάτων καὶ θυσιῶν. 34 καὶ ὁ
burnt offerings and sacrifices. And –
Ἰησοῦς, ἰδὼν αὐτὸν ὅτι νουνεχῶς ἀπεκρίθη,
Jesus, seeing him that sensibly he answered,
εἶπεν αὐτῷ· οὐ μακρὰν εἶ ἀπὸ τῆς
said to him: Not far thou art from the
βασιλείας τοῦ θεοῦ. καὶ οὐδεὶς οὐκέτι
kingdom – of God. And no one no(any) more
ἐτόλμα αὐτὸν ἐπερωτῆσαι.
dared him to question.
35 Καὶ ἀποκριθεὶς ὁ Ἰησοῦς ἔλεγεν
And answering – Jesus said
διδάσκων ἐν τῷ ἱερῷ· πῶς λέγουσιν οἱ
teaching in the temple: How say the
γραμματεῖς ὅτι ὁ χριστὸς υἱὸς Δαυίδ
scribes that the Christ son of David
ἐστιν; 36 αὐτὸς Δαυὶδ εἶπεν ἐν τῷ πνεύματι
is? himself David said by the Spirit
τῷ ἁγίῳ· εἶπεν κύριος τῷ κυρίῳ μου·
– Holy: said [the] LORD to the Lord of me:
κάθου ἐκ δεξιῶν μου ἕως ἂν θῶ τοὺς
Sit at [the] right [hand] of me until I put the
ἐχθρούς σου ὑποκάτω τῶν ποδῶν σου.
enemies of thee under the feet of thee.
37 αὐτὸς Δαυὶδ λέγει αὐτὸν κύριον, καὶ
himself David says(calls) him Lord, and
πόθεν αὐτοῦ ἐστιν υἱός;
whence of him is he son ?
Καὶ ὁ πολὺς ὄχλος ἤκουεν αὐτοῦ
And the much crowd heard him
ἡδέως. 38 Καὶ ἐν τῇ διδαχῇ αὐτοῦ
gladly. And in the teaching of him
ἔλεγεν· βλέπετε ἀπὸ τῶν γραμματέων
he said: Beware from(of) the scribes
τῶν θελόντων ἐν στολαῖς περιπατεῖν καὶ
the [ones] wishing in robes to walk about and
ἀσπασμοὺς ἐν ταῖς ἀγοραῖς 39 καὶ
greetings in the marketplaces and
πρωτοκαθεδρίας ἐν ταῖς συναγωγαῖς καὶ
chief seats in the synagogues and
πρωτοκλισίας ἐν τοῖς δείπνοις· 40 οἱ
chief places in the dinners; the [ones]
κατέσθοντες τὰς οἰκίας τῶν χηρῶν καὶ
devouring the houses of the widows and
προφάσει μακρὰ προσευχόμενοι, οὗτοι
under pretence long praying, these
λήμψονται περισσότερον κρίμα. 41 Καὶ
will receive greater condemnation. And
καθίσας κατέναντι τοῦ γαζοφυλακείου ἐθεώρει
sitting opposite the treasury he beheld
πῶς ὁ ὄχλος βάλλει χαλκὸν εἰς τὸ
how the crowd puts copper money into the
γαζοφυλακεῖον· καὶ πολλοὶ πλούσιοι ἔβαλλον
treasury; and many rich men put
πολλά· 42 καὶ ἐλθοῦσα μία χήρα πτωχὴ
much; and coming one widow poor
ἔβαλεν λεπτὰ δύο, ὅ ἐστιν κοδράντης.
put lepta two, which is a quadrans.
43 καὶ προσκαλεσάμενος τοὺς μαθητὰς αὐτοῦ
And calling to [him] the disciples of him
εἶπεν αὐτοῖς· ἀμὴν λέγω ὑμῖν ὅτι
he said to them: Truly I tell you that
ἡ χήρα αὕτη ἡ πτωχὴ πλεῖον πάντων
– [3]widow [1]this – [2]poor [5]more [than] [6]all

more important than all
burnt offerings and sacrifices.''
34When Jesus saw that he
had answered wisely, he
said to him, ''You are not
far from the kingdom of
God.'' And from then on no
one dared ask him any
more questions.

Whose Son Is the Christ?

35While Jesus was teach-
ing in the temple courts, he
asked, ''How is it that the
teachers of the law say that
the Christ[c] is the son of
David? 36David himself,
speaking by the Holy Spirit, declared:

'' 'The Lord said to my
Lord:
''Sit at my right hand
until I put your enemies
under your feet.'' '[d]

37David himself calls him
'Lord.' How then can he be
his son?''
The large crowd listened
to him with delight.
38As he taught, Jesus
said, ''Watch out for the
teachers of the law. They
like to walk around in flowing robes and be greeted in
the marketplaces, 39and
have the most important
seats in the synagogues and
the places of honor at banquets. 40They devour wid-
ows' houses and for a show
make lengthy prayers.
Such men will be punished
most severely.''

The Widow's Offering

41Jesus sat down opposite
the place where the offerings were put and watched
the crowd putting their
money into the temple treasury. Many rich people
threw in large amounts.
42But a poor widow came
and put in two very small
copper coins,[e] worth only
a fraction of a penny.[f]
43Calling his disciples to
him, Jesus said, ''I tell you
the truth, this poor widow

[c]35 Or *Messiah*
[d]36 Psalm 110:1
[e]42 Greek *two lepta*
[f]42 Greek *kodrantes*

more than all the contribu-
tors to the treasury;
44for they all put in out of
their surplus, but she, out
of her poverty, put in all
she owned, all she had to
live on.''

Chapter 13

Things to Come

AND as He was going out
of the temple, one of
His disciples *said to Him,
''Teacher, behold [j] what
wonderful stones and what
wonderful buildings!''
2And Jesus said to him,
''Do you see these great
buildings? Not one stone
shall be left upon another
which will not be torn
down.''
3And as He was sitting
on the Mount of Olives opposite the temple, Peter
and James and John and
Andrew were questioning
Him privately,
4''Tell us, when will
these things be, and what
will be the sign when all
these things are going to be
fulfilled?''
5And Jesus began to say
to them, ''See to it that no
one misleads you.
6''Many will come in My
name, saying, 'I am *He!*'
and will mislead many.
7''And when you hear of
wars and rumors of wars,
do not be frightened; *those
things* must take place; but
that is not yet the end.
8''For nation will arise
against nation, and king-
dom against kingdom; there
will be earthquakes in various places; there will *also*
be famines. These things
are *merely* the beginning of
birth pangs.
9''But be on your guard;
for they will deliver you to
the courts, and you will be
flogged in *the* synagogues,
and you will stand before
governors and kings for My
sake, as a testimony to

[j] Lit., *how great*

ἔβαλεν τῶν βαλλόντων εἰς τὸ γαζοφυλακεῖον·
[4]put the [ones] putting into the treasury;
44 πάντες γὰρ ἐκ τοῦ περισσεύοντος αὐτοῖς
for all out of the abounding to them[c]
= their abundance
ἔβαλον, αὕτη δὲ ἐκ τῆς ὑστερήσεως αὐτῆς
put, but this woman out of the want of her
πάντα ὅσα εἶχεν ἔβαλεν, ὅλον τὸν βίον
[2]all things [3]how many [4]she had [1]put, all the living
αὐτῆς.
of her.

13 Καὶ ἐκπορευομένου αὐτοῦ ἐκ τοῦ
And going forth him[a] out of the
= as he went forth
ἱεροῦ λέγει αὐτῷ εἷς τῶν μαθητῶν αὐτοῦ·
temple says to him one of the disciples of him:
διδάσκαλε, ἴδε ποταποὶ λίθοι καὶ ποταπαὶ
Teacher, behold[,] what great stones and what great
οἰκοδομαί. **2** καὶ ὁ Ἰησοῦς εἶπεν αὐτῷ·
buildings. And – Jesus said to him:
βλέπεις ταύτας τὰς μεγάλας οἰκοδομάς;
Seest thou these – great buildings?
οὐ μὴ ἀφεθῇ λίθος ἐπὶ λίθον ὃς οὐ
by no means be left stone on stone which by no
= there shall by no means be left stone on stone which will not
μὴ καταλυθῇ. **3** Καὶ καθημένου αὐτοῦ
means be overthrown. And sitting him[a]
be overthrown. = as he sat
εἰς τὸ ὄρος τῶν ἐλαιῶν κατέναντι τοῦ
in(on) the mount of the olives opposite the
ἱεροῦ, ἐπηρώτα αὐτὸν κατ᾽ ἰδίαν Πέτρος
temple, questioned him privately Peter
καὶ Ἰάκωβος καὶ Ἰωάννης καὶ Ἀνδρέας·
and James and John and Andrew:
4 εἰπὸν ἡμῖν, πότε ταῦτα ἔσται, καὶ τί
Tell us, when these things will be, and what
τὸ σημεῖον ὅταν μέλλῃ ταῦτα συντελεῖσθαι
the sign when [3]are about [2]these things [4]to be completed
πάντα; **5** ὁ δὲ Ἰησοῦς ἤρξατο λέγειν
[1]all? – And Jesus began to say
αὐτοῖς· βλέπετε μή τις ὑμᾶς πλανήσῃ.
to them: See lest anyone you lead astray.
6 πολλοὶ ἐλεύσονται ἐπὶ τῷ ὀνόματί μου
Many will come on(in) the name of me
λέγοντες ὅτι ἐγώ εἰμι, καὶ πολλοὺς
saying[,] – I am, and many
πλανήσουσιν. **7** ὅταν δὲ ἀκούσητε πολέμους
they will lead astray. But when ye hear [of] wars
καὶ ἀκοὰς πολέμων, μὴ θροεῖσθε· δεῖ
and rumours of wars, be not disturbed; it behoves
γενέσθαι, ἀλλ᾽ οὔπω τὸ τέλος. **8** ἐγερθήσεται
to happen, but not yet the end. will be raised
γὰρ ἔθνος ἐπ᾽ ἔθνος καὶ βασιλεία ἐπὶ
For nation against nation and kingdom against
βασιλείαν. ἔσονται σεισμοὶ κατὰ τόπους,
kingdom. There will be earthquakes in places,
ἔσονται λιμοί· ἀρχὴ ὠδίνων ταῦτα.
there will be famines; beginning of birth-pangs these things [are].
9 Βλέπετε δὲ ὑμεῖς ἑαυτούς· παραδώσουσιν
But see ye yourselves; they will deliver
ὑμᾶς εἰς συνέδρια καὶ εἰς συναγωγὰς
you to councils and in synagogues
δαρήσεσθε καὶ ἐπὶ ἡγεμόνων καὶ βασιλέων
ye will be beaten and before rulers and kings
σταθήσεσθε ἕνεκεν ἐμοῦ, εἰς μαρτύριον
ye will stand for the sake of me, for a testimony

has put more into the treasury than all the others.
44They all gave out of their
wealth; but she, out of her
poverty, put in everything
—all she had to live on.''

Chapter 13

*Signs of the End of the
Age*

AS he was leaving the
temple, one of his dis-
ciples said to him, ''Look,
Teacher! What massive
stones! What magnificent
buildings!''
2''Do you see all these
great buildings?'' replied
Jesus. ''Not one stone here
will be left on another; every one will be thrown
down.''
3As Jesus was sitting on
the Mount of Olives oppo-
site the temple, Peter,
James, John and Andrew
asked him privately, 4''Tell
us, when will these things
happen? And what will be
the sign that they are all
about to be fulfilled?''
5Jesus said to them:
''Watch out that no one deceives you. 6Many will
come in my name, claim-
ing, 'I am he,' and will deceive many. 7When you
hear of wars and rumors of
wars, do not be alarmed.
Such things must happen,
but the end is still to come.
8Nation will rise against nation, and kingdom against
kingdom. There will be
earthquakes in various
places, and famines. These
are the beginning of birth
pains.
9''You must be on your
guard. You will be handed
over to the local councils
and flogged in the syna-
gogues. On account of me
you will stand before governors and kings as wit-

them.
10"And the gospel must first be preached to all the nations.
11"And when they arrest you and deliver you up, do not be anxious beforehand about what you are to say, but say whatever is given you in that hour; for it is not you who speak, but *it is* the Holy Spirit.
12"And brother will deliver brother to death, and a father *his* child; and children will rise up against parents and have them put to death.
13"And you will be hated by all on account of My name, but the one who endures to the end, he shall be saved.
14"But when you see the ABOMINATION OF DESOLATION standing where it should not be (let the reader understand), then let those who are in Judea flee to the mountains.
15"And let him who is on the housetop not go down, or enter in, to get anything out of his house;
16and let him who is in the field not turn back to get his cloak.
17"But woe to those who are with child and to those who nurse babes in those days!
18"But pray that it may not happen in the winter.
19"For those days will be a *time of* tribulation such as has not occurred since the beginning of the creation which God created, until now, and never shall.
20"And unless the Lord had shortened *those* days, no life would have been saved; but for the sake of the elect whom He chose, He shortened the days.
21"And then if anyone says to you, 'Behold, here is the Christ'; or, 'Behold, *He is* there'; do not believe *him;*

αὐτοῖς. 10 καὶ εἰς πάντα τὰ ἔθνη πρῶτον
to them. And to all the nations first
δεῖ κηρυχθῆναι τὸ εὐαγγέλιον. 11 καὶ ὅταν
it behoves to be proclaimed the gospel. And when
= the gospel must be proclaimed.
ἄγωσιν ὑμᾶς παραδιδόντες, μὴ προμεριμνᾶτε
they lead you delivering, be not anxious beforehand
τί λαλήσητε, ἀλλ' ὃ ἐὰν δοθῇ ὑμῖν ἐν
what ye speak, but whatever is given you in
ἐκείνῃ τῇ ὥρᾳ, τοῦτο λαλεῖτε· οὐ γάρ
that – hour. this speak ye; for not
ἐστε ὑμεῖς οἱ λαλοῦντες ἀλλὰ τὸ πνεῦμα
are - ye the [ones] speaking but the Spirit
τὸ ἅγιον. 12 καὶ παραδώσει ἀδελφὸς
– Holy. And [2]will deliver [1]a brother
ἀδελφὸν εἰς θάνατον καὶ πατὴρ τέκνον, καὶ
a brother to death and a father a child, and
ἐπαναστήσονται τέκνα ἐπὶ γονεῖς καὶ
[2]will rise *against* [1]children against parents and
θανατώσουσιν αὐτούς· 13 καὶ ἔσεσθε
will put to death them; and ye will be
μισούμενοι ὑπὸ πάντων διὰ τὸ ὄνομά
being hated by all men on account of the name
μου· ὁ δὲ ὑπομείνας εἰς τέλος, οὗτος
of me; but the [one] enduring to [the] end, this
σωθήσεται. 14 Ὅταν δὲ ἴδητε τὸ βδέλυγμα
will be saved. But when ye see the abomination
τῆς ἐρημώσεως ἑστηκότα ὅπου οὐ δεῖ, ὁ
– of desolation stand where he (it) behoves not, the
ἀναγινώσκων νοείτω, τότε οἱ ἐν τῇ
[one] reading let him understand, then the [ones] in –
Ἰουδαίᾳ φευγέτωσαν εἰς τὰ ὄρη, 15 ὁ ἐπὶ
Judæa let them flee to the mountains, the [one] on
τοῦ δώματος μὴ καταβάτω μηδὲ εἰσελθάτω
the roof let him not come down nor let him enter
τι ἆραι ἐκ τῆς οἰκίας αὐτοῦ, 16 καὶ ὁ
anything to take out of the house of him, and the [one]
εἰς τὸν ἀγρὸν μὴ ἐπιστρεψάτω εἰς τὰ
in the field let him not return to the things
ὀπίσω ἆραι τὸ ἱμάτιον αὐτοῦ. 17 οὐαὶ
behind to take the garment of him. woe
δὲ ταῖς ἐν γαστρὶ ἐχούσαις καὶ ταῖς
But to the women pregnant† and to the
θηλαζούσαις ἐν ἐκείναις ταῖς ἡμέραις.
[ones] giving suck in those – days.
18 προσεύχεσθε δὲ ἵνα μὴ γένηται χειμῶνος·
But pray ye that it may not happen of(in) winter;
19 ἔσονται γὰρ αἱ ἡμέραι ἐκεῖναι θλῖψις, οἵα
for [3]will be – [2]days [1]those [4]affliction, of such a kind
οὐ γέγονεν τοιαύτη ἀπ' ἀρχῆς κτίσεως
[2]has not happened [1]as from [the] beginning of [the] creation
ἣν ἔκτισεν ὁ θεὸς ἕως τοῦ νῦν καὶ οὐ
which created – God until – now and by
μὴ γένηται. 20 καὶ εἰ μὴ ἐκολόβωσεν
no means may be. And unless [2]shortened
κύριος τὰς ἡμέρας, οὐκ ἂν ἐσώθη πᾶσα
[1][the] Lord the days, would not be saved all
= no flesh would be saved;
σάρξ· ἀλλὰ διὰ τοὺς ἐκλεκτοὺς οὓς
flesh; but on account of the chosen whom
ἐξελέξατο ἐκολόβωσεν τὰς ἡμέρας. 21 καὶ
he chose he shortened the days. And
τότε ἐάν τις ὑμῖν εἴπῃ· ἴδε ὧδε ὁ
then if anyone [2]you [1]tells: Behold here [is] the
χριστός, ἴδε ἐκεῖ, μὴ πιστεύετε· 22 ἐγερθή-
Christ, behold there, believe ye not; [6]will be

nesses to them. 10And the
gospel must first be
preached to all nations.
11Whenever you are arrested and brought to trial, do
not worry beforehand
about what to say. Just say
whatever is given you at
the time, for it is not you
speaking, but the Holy
Spirit.
12"Brother will betray
brother to death, and a father his child. Children will
rebel against their parents
and have them put to death.
13All men will hate you because of me, but he who
stands firm to the end will
be saved.
14"When you see 'the
abomination that causes
desolation'[g] standing
where it[h] does not belong
—let the reader under-
stand—then let those who
are in Judea flee to the
mountains. 15Let no one on
the roof of his house go
down or enter the house to
take anything out. 16Let no
one in the field go back to
get his cloak. 17How dreadful it will be in those days
for pregnant women and
nursing mothers! 18Pray
that this will not take place
in winter, 19because those
will be days of distress un-
equaled from the begin-
ning, when God created the
world, until now—and
never to be equaled again.
20If the Lord had not cut
short those days, no one
would survive. But for the
sake of the elect, whom he
has chosen, he has short-
ened them. 21At that time if
anyone says to you, 'Look,
here is the Christ[i]!' or,
'Look, there he is!' do not
believe it. 22For false

[g]*14* Daniel 9:27; 11:31; 12:11
[h]*14* Or *he*; also in verse 29
[i]*21* Or *Messiah*

22for false Christs and
false prophets will arise,
and will show signs and
wonders, in order, if possible, to lead the elect astray.
23"But take heed; behold,
I have told you everything
in advance.

The Return of Christ

24"But in those days, af-
ter that tribulation, THE SUN
WILL BE DARKENED, AND THE
MOON WILL NOT GIVE ITS
LIGHT,
25AND THE STARS WILL BE
FALLING from heaven, and
the powers that are in the
heavens will be shaken.
26"And then they will see
THE SON OF MAN COMING IN
CLOUDS with great power
and glory.
27"And then He will send
forth the angels, and will
gather together His elect
from the four winds, from
the farthest end of the
earth, to the farthest end of
heaven.
28"Now learn the parable
from the fig tree: when its
branch has already become
tender, and puts forth its
leaves, you know that summer is near.
29"Even so, you too,
when you see these things
happening, recognize that
He is near, *right* at the
door.
30"Truly I say to you, this
[k]generation will not pass
away until all these things
take place.
31"Heaven and earth will
pass away, but My words
will not pass away.
32"But of that day or hour
no one knows, not even the
angels in heaven, nor the
Son, but the Father *alone*.
33"Take heed, keep on
the alert; for you do not
know when the *appointed*
time is.
34"*It is* like a man, away
on a journey, *who* upon
leaving his house and putting his slaves in charge,
assigning to each one his
task, also commanded the

[k]Or, *race*

σονται δὲ ψευδόχριστοι καὶ ψευδοπροφῆται
raised [1]and [2]false Christs [3]and [4]false prophets
καὶ ποιήσουσιν σημεῖα καὶ τέρατα πρὸς
and they will do signs and wonders *for*
τὸ ἀποπλανᾶν, εἰ δυνατόν, τοὺς ἐκλεκτούς.
– to lead astray, if possible, the chosen.
23 ὑμεῖς δὲ βλέπετε· προείρηκα ὑμῖν πάντα.
But [2]ye [1]see; [1]I have told [4]before [2]you [3]all things.
24 Ἀλλὰ ἐν ἐκείναις ταῖς ἡμέραις μετὰ
But in those – days after
τὴν θλῖψιν ἐκείνην ὁ ἥλιος σκοτισθήσεται,
– affliction that the sun will be darkened,
καὶ ἡ σελήνη οὐ δώσει τὸ φέγγος αὐτῆς,
and the moon will not give the light of her,
25 καὶ οἱ ἀστέρες ἔσονται ἐκ τοῦ οὐρανοῦ
and the stars [1]will be [3]out of – [4]heaven
πίπτοντες, καὶ αἱ δυνάμεις αἱ ἐν τοῖς
[2]falling, and the powers – in the
οὐρανοῖς σαλευθήσονται. 26 καὶ τότε ὄψονται
heavens will be shaken. And then they will see
τὸν υἱὸν τοῦ ἀνθρώπου ἐρχόμενον ἐν
the Son – of man coming in
νεφέλαις μετὰ δυνάμεως πολλῆς καὶ δόξης.
clouds with power much and glory.
27 καὶ τότε ἀποστελεῖ τοὺς ἀγγέλους καὶ
And then he will send the angels and
ἐπισυνάξει τοὺς ἐκλεκτοὺς [αὐτοῦ] ἐκ τῶν
they will assemble the chosen of him out of the
τεσσάρων ἀνέμων ἀπ' ἄκρου γῆς ἕως
four winds from [the] extremity of earth to
ἄκρου οὐρανοῦ. 28 Ἀπὸ δὲ τῆς συκῆς
[the] extremity of heaven. Now from the fig-tree
μάθετε τὴν παραβολήν· ὅταν ἤδη ὁ
learn the parable; when now the
κλάδος αὐτῆς ἁπαλὸς γένηται καὶ ἐκφύῃ
branch of it tender becomes and puts forth
τὰ φύλλα, γινώσκετε ὅτι ἐγγὺς τὸ θέρος
the leaves, ye know that near the summer
ἐστίν· 29 οὕτως καὶ ὑμεῖς, ὅταν ἴδητε
is; so also ye, when ye see
ταῦτα γινόμενα, γινώσκετε ὅτι ἐγγύς ἐστιν
these things happening, know that near he/it is
ἐπὶ θύραις. 30 ἀμὴν λέγω ὑμῖν ὅτι οὐ
at [the] doors. Truly I tell you that by no
μὴ παρέλθῃ ἡ γενεὰ αὕτη μέχρις οὗ
means passes – generation this until
ταῦτα πάντα γένηται. 31 ὁ οὐρανὸς καὶ
these things all happen. The heaven and
ἡ γῆ παρελεύσονται, οἱ δὲ λόγοι μου
the earth will pass away, but the words of me
οὐ παρελεύσονται. 32 Περὶ δὲ τῆς ἡμέρας
will not pass away. But concerning – day
ἐκείνης ἢ τῆς ὥρας οὐδεὶς οἶδεν, οὐδὲ
that or – hour no one knows, not
οἱ ἄγγελοι ἐν οὐρανῷ οὐδὲ ὁ υἱός, εἰ
the angels in heaven neither the Son, ex-
μὴ ὁ πατήρ. 33 Βλέπετε, ἀγρυπνεῖτε·
cept the Father. Look, be wakeful;
οὐκ οἴδατε γὰρ πότε ὁ καιρός ἐστιν.
for ye know not when the time is.
34 ὡς ἄνθρωπος ἀπόδημος ἀφεὶς τὴν οἰκίαν
As a man away from home leaving the house
αὐτοῦ καὶ δοὺς τοῖς δούλοις αὐτοῦ τὴν
of him and giving to the slaves of him –
ἐξουσίαν, ἑκάστῳ τὸ ἔργον αὐτοῦ, καὶ
authority, to each the work of him, and

Christs and false prophets
will appear and perform
signs and miracles to de-
ceive the elect—if that
were possible. 23So be on
your guard; I have told you
everything ahead of time.
24"But in those days, following that distress,

" 'the sun will be
darkened,
and the moon will not
give its light;
25the stars will fall from
the sky,
and the heavenly
bodies will be
shaken.'[j]

26"At that time men will
see the Son of Man coming
in clouds with great power
and glory. 27And he will
send his angels and gather
his elect from the four
winds, from the ends of the
earth to the ends of the
heavens.
28"Now learn this lesson
from the fig tree: As soon as
its twigs get tender and its
leaves come out, you know
that summer is near.
29Even so, when you see
these things happening,
you know that it is near,
right at the door. 30I tell you
the truth, this generation[k]
will certainly not pass away
until all these things have
happened. 31Heaven and
earth will pass away, but
my words will never pass
away.

The Day and Hour Unknown

32"No one knows about
that day or hour, not even
the angels in heaven, nor
the Son, but only the Fa-
ther. 33Be on guard! Be
alert[l]! You do not know
when that time will come.
34It's like a man going
away: He leaves his house
and puts his servants in
charge, each with his as-
signed task, and tells the

[j]*25* Isaiah 13:10; 34:4
[k]*30* Or *race*
[l]*33* Some manuscripts *alert and pray*

doorkeeper to stay on the
alert.
35"Therefore, be on the
alert—for you do not know
when the master of the
house is coming, whether
in the evening, at midnight,
at cockcrowing, or in the
morning—
36lest he come suddenly
and find you asleep.
37"And what I say to you
I say to all, 'Be on the
alert!' "

τῷ θυρωρῷ ἐνετείλατο ἵνα γρηγορῇ.
the doorkeeper he commanded that he should watch.
35 γρηγορεῖτε οὖν· οὐκ οἴδατε γὰρ πότε
Watch ye therefore; for ye know not when
ὁ κύριος τῆς οἰκίας ἔρχεται, ἢ ὀψὲ ἢ
the lord of the house comes, either late or
μεσονύκτιον ἢ ἀλεκτοροφωνίας ἢ πρωΐ·
at midnight or at cock-crowing or early;
36 μὴ ἐλθὼν ἐξαίφνης εὕρῃ ὑμᾶς καθεύδ-
lest coming suddenly he find you sleep-
οντας. 37 ὃ δὲ ὑμῖν λέγω, πᾶσιν λέγω,
ing. And what to you I say, to all I say,
γρηγορεῖτε.
watch ye.

one at the door [illegible]p
watch.
35"Therefore keep watch
because you do not know
when the owner of the
house will come back—
whether in the evening, or
at midnight, or when the
rooster crows, or at dawn.
36If he comes suddenly, do
not let him find you sleeping. 37What I say to you, I
say to everyone:
'Watch!' "

Chapter 14

Death Plot and Anointing

NOW the Passover and
Unleavened Bread
was two days off; and the
chief priests and the scribes
were seeking how to seize
Him by stealth, and kill
Him;
2for they were saying,
"Not during the festival,
lest there be a riot of the
people."
3And while He was in
Bethany at the home of Simon the leper, and reclining *at the table,* there came
a woman with an alabaster
vial of very costly perfume
of pure nard; *and* she broke
the vial and poured it over
His head.
4But some were indig-
nantly *remarking* to one another, "Why has this per-
fume been wasted?
5"For this perfume
might have been sold for
over three hundred [l] denarii, and *the money* given
to the poor." And they
were scolding her.
6But Jesus said, "Let
her alone; why do you
bother her? She has done a
good deed to Me.
7"For the poor you al-
ways have with you, and
whenever you wish, you
can do them good; but you
do not always have Me.
8"She has done what she
could; she has anointed My
body beforehand for the
burial.

14 Ἦν δὲ τὸ πάσχα καὶ τὰ ἄζυμα
Now it was the Passover and [the feast of] the unleavened bread†
μετὰ δύο ἡμέρας. καὶ ἐζήτουν οἱ ἀρχιερεῖς
after two days. And sought the chief priests
καὶ οἱ γραμματεῖς πῶς αὐτὸν ἐν δόλῳ
and the scribes how [2]him [3]by [4]guile
κρατήσαντες ἀποκτείνωσιν. 2 ἔλεγον γάρ·
[1]seizing they might kill. For they said:
μὴ ἐν τῇ ἑορτῇ, μήποτε ἔσται θόρυβος
Not at the feast, lest there will be a disturbance
τοῦ λαοῦ.
of the people.
3 Καὶ ὄντος αὐτοῦ ἐν Βηθανίᾳ ἐν τῇ
And being him[a] in Bethany in the
= when he was
οἰκίᾳ Σίμωνος τοῦ λεπροῦ, κατακειμένου
house of Simon the leper, reclining
= as he reclined
αὐτοῦ ἦλθεν γυνὴ ἔχουσα ἀλάβαστρον
him[a] came a woman having an alabaster phial
μύρου νάρδου πιστικῆς πολυτελοῦς·
of ointment [2]nard [1]of pure [3]costly;
συντρίψασα τὴν ἀλάβαστρον κατέχεεν αὐτοῦ
breaking the alabaster phial she poured over of him
τῆς κεφαλῆς. 4 ἦσαν δέ τινες ἀγανακτοῦντες
the head. Now there were some being angry
πρὸς ἑαυτούς· εἰς τί ἡ ἀπώλεια αὕτη
with themselves: Why – waste this
τοῦ μύρου γέγονεν; 5 ἠδύνατο γὰρ τοῦτο
of the ointment has occurred? for [3]could [1]this
τὸ μύρον πραθῆναι ἐπάνω δηναρίων
– [2]ointment *to* be sold [for] over denarii
τριακοσίων καὶ δοθῆναι τοῖς πτωχοῖς·
three hundred and *to* be given to the poor;
καὶ ἐνεβριμῶντο αὐτῇ. 6 ὁ δὲ Ἰησοῦς
and they were indignant with her. – But Jesus
εἶπεν· ἄφετε αὐτήν· τί αὐτῇ κόπους
said: Leave her; why [3]to her [2]troubles
παρέχετε; καλὸν ἔργον ἠργάσατο ἐν ἐμοί.
[1]cause ye? a good work she wrought in me.
7 πάντοτε γὰρ τοὺς πτωχοὺς ἔχετε μεθ'
For always the poor ye have with
ἑαυτῶν, καὶ ὅταν θέλητε δύνασθε αὐτοῖς
your*selves,* and whenever ye wish ye can to them
εὖ ποιῆσαι, ἐμὲ δὲ οὐ πάντοτε ἔχετε.
well *to* do, but me not always ye have.
8 ὃ ἔσχεν ἐποίησεν· προέλαβεν μυρίσαι τὸ
What she had she did; she was beforehand to anoint the
σῶμά μου εἰς τὸν ἐνταφιασμόν. 9 ἀμὴν
body of me for the burial. truly

Chapter 14

Jesus Anointed at Bethany

NOW the Passover and
the Feast of Unleav-
ened Bread were only two
days away, and the chief
priests and the teachers of
the law were looking for
some sly way to arrest
Jesus and kill him. 2"But
not during the Feast," they
said, "or the people may
riot."
3While he was in Betha-
ny, reclining at the table in
the home of a man known
as Simon the Leper, a
woman came with an ala-
baster jar of very expensive
perfume, made of pure
nard. She broke the jar and
poured the perfume on his
head.
4Some of those present
were saying indignantly to
one another, "Why this
waste of perfume? 5It could
have been sold for more
than a year's wages[m] and
the money given to the
poor." And they rebuked
her harshly.
6"Leave her alone," said
Jesus. "Why are you both-
ering her? She has done a
beautiful thing to me. 7The
poor you will always have
with you, and you can help
them any time you want.
But you will not always
have me. 8She did what she
could. She poured perfume
on my body beforehand to
prepare for my burial. 9I

[l]The denarius was equivalent to one day's wage

[m]5 Greek *than three hundred denarii*

9"And truly I say to you,
wherever the gospel is
preached in the whole
world, that also which this
woman has done shall be
spoken of in memory of
her."
10And Judas Iscariot,
who was one of the twelve,
went off to the chief
priests, in order to betray
Him to them.
11And they were glad
when they heard _this_, and
promised to give him
money. And he _began_
seeking how to betray Him
at an opportune time.

The Last Passover

12And on the first day of
Unleavened Bread, when
the Passover _lamb_ was being sacrificed, His disciples
*said to Him, "Where do
You want us to go and prepare for You to eat the
Passover?"
13And He *sent two of
His disciples, and *said to
them, "Go into the city,
and a man will meet you
carrying a pitcher of water;
follow him;
14and wherever he enters,
say to the owner of the
house, 'The Teacher says,
"Where is My guest room
in which I may eat the Passover with My disciples?" '
15"And he himself will
show you a large upper
room furnished _and_ ready;
and prepare for us there."
16And the disciples went
out, and came to the city,
and found _it_ just as He had
told them; and they pre-
pared the Passover.
17And when it was eve-
ning He *came with the
twelve.
18And as they were re-
clining _at the table_ and eating, Jesus said, "Truly I
say to you that one of you
will betray Me—one who is
eating with Me."
19They began to be
grieved and to say to Him
one by one, "Surely not
I?"
20And He said to them,
"_It is_ one of the twelve, one
who dips with Me in the

δὲ λέγω ὑμῖν, ὅπου ἐὰν κηρυχθῇ τὸ
And I tell you, wherever is proclaimed the
εὐαγγέλιον εἰς ὅλον τὸν κόσμον, καὶ ὃ
gospel in all the world, also what
ἐποίησεν αὕτη λαληθήσεται εἰς μνημόσυνον
did this woman will be spoken for a memorial
αὐτῆς. 10 Καὶ Ἰούδας Ἰσκαριώθ, ὁ εἷς
of her. And Judas Iscariot, the one
τῶν δώδεκα, ἀπῆλθεν πρὸς τοὺς ἀρχιερεῖς
of the twelve, went to the chief priests
ἵνα αὐτὸν παραδοῖ αὐτοῖς. 11 οἱ δὲ
that him he might betray to them. And they
ἀκούσαντες ἐχάρησαν καὶ ἐπηγγείλαντο αὐτῷ
hearing rejoiced and promised him
ἀργύριον δοῦναι. καὶ ἐζήτει πῶς αὐτὸν
silver to give. And he sought how him
εὐκαίρως παραδοῖ.
opportunely he might betray.
12 Καὶ τῇ πρώτῃ ἡμέρᾳ τῶν ἀζύμων,
And on the first day of unleavened bread,†
ὅτε τὸ πάσχα ἔθυον, λέγουσιν αὐτῷ οἱ
when the passover they sacrificed, say to him the
μαθηταὶ αὐτοῦ· ποῦ θέλεις ἀπελθόντες
disciples of him: Where wishest thou going
ἑτοιμάσωμεν ἵνα φάγῃς τὸ πάσχα; 13 καὶ
we may prepare that thou eatest the passover? And
ἀποστέλλει δύο τῶν μαθητῶν αὐτοῦ καὶ
he sends two of the disciples of him and
λέγει αὐτοῖς· ὑπάγετε εἰς τὴν πόλιν, καὶ
tells them: Go ye into the city, and
ἀπαντήσει ὑμῖν ἄνθρωπος κεράμιον ὕδατος
will meet you a man a pitcher of water
βαστάζων· ἀκολουθήσατε αὐτῷ, 14 καὶ ὅπου
carrying; follow him, and wher-
ἐὰν εἰσέλθῃ εἴπατε τῷ οἰκοδεσπότῃ ὅτι ὁ
ever he enters tell the housemaster[,] – The
διδάσκαλος λέγει· ποῦ ἐστιν τὸ κατάλυμά
teacher says: Where is the guest room
μου, ὅπου τὸ πάσχα μετὰ τῶν μαθητῶν
of me, where the passover with the disciples
μου φάγω; 15 καὶ αὐτὸς ὑμῖν δείξει
of me I may eat? And he you will show
ἀνάγαιον μέγα ἐστρωμένον ἕτοιμον· καὶ
upper room a large _having been_ spread ready; and
ἐκεῖ ἑτοιμάσατε ἡμῖν. 16 καὶ ἐξῆλθον οἱ
there prepare ye for us. And went forth the
μαθηταὶ καὶ ἦλθον εἰς τὴν πόλιν καὶ
disciples and came into the city and
εὗρον καθὼς εἶπεν αὐτοῖς, καὶ ἡτοίμασαν
found as he told them, and they prepared
τὸ πάσχα. 17 Καὶ ὀψίας γενομένης ἔρχεται
the passover. And evening coming[a] he comes
= when evening came
μετὰ τῶν δώδεκα. 18 καὶ ἀνακειμένων
with the twelve. And reclining
= as they reclined and ate
αὐτῶν καὶ ἐσθιόντων ὁ Ἰησοῦς εἶπεν·
them and eating[a] – Jesus said:
ἀμὴν λέγω ὑμῖν ὅτι εἷς ἐξ ὑμῶν παραδώσει
Truly I tell you that one of you will betray
με, ὁ ἐσθίων μετ' ἐμοῦ. 19 ἤρξαντο
me, the [one] eating with me. They began
λυπεῖσθαι καὶ λέγειν αὐτῷ εἷς κατὰ εἷς·
to grieve and to say to him one by one:
μήτι ἐγώ; 20 ὁ δὲ εἶπεν αὐτοῖς· εἷς τῶν
Not I? And he said to them: One of the
δώδεκα, ὁ ἐμβαπτόμενος μετ' ἐμοῦ εἰς
twelve, the [one] dipping with me in

tell you the truth, wherever
the gospel is preached
throughout the world, what
she has done will also be
told, in memory of her."
10Then Judas Iscariot,
one of the Twelve, went to
the chief priests to betray
Jesus to them. 11They were
delighted to hear this and
promised to give him mon-
ey. So he watched for an
opportunity to hand him
over.

The Lord's Supper

12On the first day of the
Feast of Unleavened
Bread, when it was cus-
tomary to sacrifice the
Passover lamb, Jesus' disciples asked him, "Where
do you want us to go and
make preparations for you
to eat the Passover?"
13So he sent two of his
disciples, telling them, "Go
into the city, and a man carrying a jar of water will
meet you. Follow him.
14Say to the owner of the
house he enters, 'The
Teacher asks: Where is my
guest room, where I may
eat the Passover with my
disciples?' 15He will show
you a large upper room,
furnished and ready. Make
preparations for us there."
16The disciples left, went
into the city and found
things just as Jesus had told
them. So they prepared the
Passover.
17When evening came,
Jesus arrived with the
Twelve. 18While they were
reclining at the table eating,
he said, "I tell you the
truth, one of you will betray me—one who is eating
with me."
19They were saddened,
and one by one they said to
him, "Surely not I?"
20"It is one of the
Twelve," he replied, "one
who dips bread into the

bowl.
21"For the Son of Man *is*
to go, just as it is written of
Him; but woe to that man
by whom the Son of Man is
betrayed! *It would have*
been good for that man if he
had not been born."

The Lord's Supper

22And while they were
eating, He took *some*
bread, and after a blessing
He broke *it;* and gave *it* to
them, and said, "Take *it;*
this is My body."
23And when He had taken
a cup, *and* given thanks,
He gave *it* to them; and
they all drank from it.
24And He said to them,
"This is My blood of the
covenant, which is poured
out for many.
25"Truly I say to you, I
shall never again drink of
the fruit of the vine until
that day when I drink it new
in the kingdom of God."
26And after singing a
hymn, they went out to the
Mount of Olives.
27And Jesus *said to
them, "You will all fall
away, because it is written,
'I WILL STRIKE DOWN THE
SHEPHERD, AND THE SHEEP
SHALL BE SCATTERED.'
28"But after I have been
raised, I will go before you
to Galilee."
29But Peter said to Him,
"*Even* though all may fall
away, yet I will not."
30And Jesus *said to him,
"Truly I say to you, that
you yourself this very
night, before a cock crows
twice, shall three times
deny Me."
31But *Peter* kept saying
insistently, "*Even* if I have
to die with You, I will not
deny You!" And they all
were saying the same thing,
too.

Jesus in Gethsemane

32And they *came to a

τὸ [ἐν] τρύβλιον. 21 ὅτι ὁ μὲν υἱὸς τοῦ
the one dish. Because indeed the Son –
ἀνθρώπου ὑπάγει καθὼς γέγραπται περὶ
of man is going as it has been written concerning
αὐτοῦ· οὐαὶ δὲ τῷ ἀνθρώπῳ ἐκείνῳ δι'
him; but woe – man to that through
οὗ ὁ υἱὸς τοῦ ἀνθρώπου παραδίδοται·
whom the Son – of man is betrayed;
καλὸν αὐτῷ εἰ οὐκ ἐγεννήθη ὁ ἄνθρωπος
good for him if was not born – man
ἐκεῖνος. 22 Καὶ ἐσθιόντων αὐτῶν λαβὼν
that. And eating them[a] taking
= as they were eating
ἄρτον εὐλογήσας ἔκλασεν καὶ ἔδωκεν αὐτοῖς
a loaf blessing he broke and gave to them
καὶ εἶπεν· λάβετε· τοῦτό ἐστιν τὸ σῶμά
and said: Take ye; this is the body
μου. 23 καὶ λαβὼν ποτήριον εὐχαριστήσας
of me. And taking a cup giving thanks
ἔδωκεν αὐτοῖς, καὶ ἔπιον ἐξ αὐτοῦ πάντες.
he gave to them, and drank of it all.
24 καὶ εἶπεν αὐτοῖς· τοῦτό ἐστιν τὸ αἷμά
And he said to them: This is the blood
μου τῆς διαθήκης τὸ ἐκχυννόμενον ὑπὲρ
of me of the covenant – being shed for
πολλῶν. 25 ἀμὴν λέγω ὑμῖν ὅτι οὐκέτι
many. Truly I tell you[,] – No more
οὐ μὴ πίω ἐκ τοῦ γενήματος τῆς ἀμπέλου
by no(any) means will I drink of the fruit of the vine
ἕως τῆς ἡμέρας ἐκείνης ὅταν αὐτὸ πίνω
until – day that when it I drink
καινὸν ἐν τῇ βασιλείᾳ τοῦ θεοῦ.
new in the kingdom – of God.
26 Καὶ ὑμνήσαντες ἐξῆλθον εἰς τὸ
And having sung a hymn they went forth to the
ὄρος τῶν ἐλαιῶν. 27 Καὶ λέγει αὐτοῖς ὁ
mount of the olives. And says to them –
Ἰησοῦς ὅτι πάντες σκανδαλισθήσεσθε, ὅτι
Jesus[,] – [2]All [1]ye [3]will [4]be offended, because
γέγραπται· πατάξω τὸν ποιμένα, καὶ τὰ
it has been written: I will strike the shepherd, and the
πρόβατα διασκορπισθήσονται. 28 ἀλλὰ μετὰ
sheep will be scattered. But after
τὸ ἐγερθῆναί με προάξω ὑμᾶς εἰς τὴν
the to be raised me[b] I will go before you to –
= I am raised
Γαλιλαίαν. 29 ὁ δὲ Πέτρος ἔφη αὐτῷ·
Galilee. – And Peter said to him:
εἰ καὶ πάντες σκανδαλισθήσονται, ἀλλ'
If even all men shall be offended, yet
οὐκ ἐγώ. 30 καὶ λέγει αὐτῷ ὁ Ἰησοῦς·
not I. And says to him – Jesus:
ἀμὴν λέγω σοι ὅτι σὺ σήμερον ταύτῃ τῇ
Truly I tell thee[,] – Thou to-day in this –
νυκτὶ πρὶν ἢ δὶς ἀλέκτορα φωνῆσαι τρίς
night before twice a cock to sound[b] thrice
με ἀπαρνήσῃ. 31 ὁ δὲ ἐκπερισσῶς ἐλάλει·
me thou wilt deny. But he more exceedingly said:
ἐὰν δέῃ με συναποθανεῖν σοι, οὐ μή
If it should behove me *to* die with thee, by no means
= I must
σε ἀπαρνήσομαι. ὡσαύτως [δὲ] καὶ πάντες
thee will I deny. And similarly also all
ἔλεγον.
said.
32 Καὶ ἔρχονται εἰς χωρίον οὗ τὸ
And they come to a piece of land of which the

bowl with me. 21The Son of
Man will go just as it is written about him. But woe to
that man who betrays the
Son of Man! It would be
better for him if he had not
been born."
22While they were eating,
Jesus took bread, gave
thanks and broke it, and
gave it to his disciples, saying, "Take it; this is my
body."
23Then he took the cup,
gave thanks and offered it
to them, and they all drank
from it.
24"This is my blood of
the[n] covenant, which is
poured out for many," he
said to them. 25"I tell you
the truth, I will not drink
again of the fruit of the vine
until that day when I drink
it anew in the kingdom of
God."
26When they had sung a
hymn, they went out to the
Mount of Olives.

Jesus Predicts Peter's Denial

27"You will all fall
away," Jesus told them,
"for it is written:

" 'I will strike the
shepherd,
and the sheep will be
scattered.'[o]

28But after I have risen, I
will go ahead of you into
Galilee."
29Peter declared, "Even
if all fall away, I will not."
30"I tell you the truth,"
Jesus answered, "today—
yes, tonight—before the
rooster crows twice[p] you
yourself will disown me
three times."
31But Peter insisted em-
phatically, "Even if I have
to die with you, I will never
disown you." And all the
others said the same.

Gethsemane

32They went to a place

[n]24 Some manuscripts *the new*
[o]27 Zech. 13:7
[p]30 Some early manuscripts do not have *twice*.

place named Gethsemane;
and He *said to His disciples, "Sit here until I have
prayed."
33And He *took with Him
Peter and James and John,
and began to be very dis-
tressed and troubled.
34And He *said to them,
"My soul is deeply grieved
to the point of death; remain here and keep
watch."
35And He went a little
beyond *them,* and fell to
the ground, and *began* to
pray that if it were possible,
the hour might pass Him
by.
36And He was saying,
"Abba! Father! All things
are possible for Thee; remove this cup from Me, yet
not what I will, but what
Thou wilt."
37And He *came and
*found them sleeping, and
*said to Peter, "Simon, are
you asleep? Could you not
keep watch for one hour?
38"Keep watching and
praying, that you may not
come into temptation; the
spirit is willing, but the
flesh is weak."
39And again He went
away and prayed, saying
the same words.
40And again He came and
found them sleeping, for
their eyes were very heavy;
and they did not know what
to answer Him.
41And He *came the third
time, and *said to them,
"Are you still sleeping and
taking your rest? It is
enough; the hour has come;
behold, the Son of Man is
being betrayed into the
hands of sinners.
42"Arise, let us be going;
behold, the one who be-
trays Me is at hand!"

Betrayal and Arrest

43And immediately while
He was still speaking,
Judas, one of the twelve,
*came up, accompanied by
a multitude with swords
and clubs, from the chief

ὄνομα Γεθσημανί, καὶ λέγει τοῖς μαθηταῖς
name [was] Gethsemane, and he says to the disciples
αὐτοῦ· καθίσατε ὧδε ἕως προσεύξωμαι.
of him: Sit ye here while I pray.
33 καὶ παραλαμβάνει τὸν Πέτρον καὶ τὸν
And he takes – Peter and –
Ἰάκωβον καὶ τὸν Ἰωάννην μετ' αὐτοῦ,
James and – John with him,
καὶ ἤρξατο ἐκθαμβεῖσθαι καὶ ἀδημονεῖν,
and began to be greatly astonished and to be distressed,
34 καὶ λέγει αὐτοῖς· περίλυπός ἐστιν ἡ
and says to them: Deeply grieved is the
ψυχή μου ἕως θανάτου· μείνατε ὧδε καὶ
soul of me unto death; remain ye here and
γρηγορεῖτε. 35 καὶ προελθὼν μικρὸν ἔπιπτεν
watch. And going forward a little he fell
ἐπὶ τῆς γῆς, καὶ προσηύχετο ἵνα εἰ
on the ground, and prayed that if
δυνατόν ἐστιν παρέλθῃ ἀπ' αὐτοῦ ἡ ὥρα,
possible it is might pass away from him the hour,
36 καὶ ἔλεγεν· ἀββὰ ὁ πατήρ, πάντα
and said: Abba – Father, all things
δυνατά σοι· παρένεγκε τὸ ποτήριον τοῦτο
[are] possible to thee; remove – cup this
ἀπ' ἐμοῦ· ἀλλ' οὐ τί ἐγὼ θέλω ἀλλὰ
from me; but not what I wish but
τί σύ. 37 καὶ ἔρχεται καὶ εὑρίσκει
what thou. And he comes and finds
αὐτοὺς καθεύδοντας, καὶ λέγει τῷ Πέτρῳ·
them sleeping, and says – to Peter:
Σίμων, καθεύδεις; οὐκ ἴσχυσας μίαν ὥραν
Simon, sleepest thou? couldest thou not one hour
γρηγορῆσαι; 38 γρηγορεῖτε καὶ προσεύχεσθε,
to watch? Watch ye and pray,
ἵνα μὴ ἔλθητε εἰς πειρασμόν· τὸ μὲν
lest ye come into temptation; indeed the
πνεῦμα πρόθυμον, ἡ δὲ σὰρξ ἀσθενής.
spirit [is] eager, but the flesh weak.
39 καὶ πάλιν ἀπελθὼν προσηύξατο τὸν
And again going away he prayed [2]the
αὐτὸν λόγον εἰπών. 40 καὶ πάλιν ἐλθὼν
[3]same [4]word [1]saying. And again coming
εὗρεν αὐτοὺς καθεύδοντας, ἦσαν γὰρ αὐτῶν
he found them sleeping, for were of them
οἱ ὀφθαλμοὶ καταβαρυνόμενοι, καὶ οὐκ
the eyes becoming heavy, and not
ᾔδεισαν τί ἀποκριθῶσιν αὐτῷ. 41 καὶ
they knew what they might answer him. And
ἔρχεται τὸ τρίτον καὶ λέγει αὐτοῖς·
he comes the third [time] and says to them:
καθεύδετε τὸ λοιπὸν καὶ ἀναπαύεσθε·
Sleep ye now† and rest;
ἀπέχει· ἦλθεν ἡ ὥρα, ἰδοὺ παραδίδοται ὁ
it is enough; came the hour, behold is betrayed the
υἱὸς τοῦ ἀνθρώπου εἰς τὰς χεῖρας τῶν
Son – man into the hands –
ἁμαρτωλῶν. 42 ἐγείρεσθε, ἄγωμεν· ἰδοὺ ὁ
of sinners. Rise ye, let us go; behold the
παραδιδούς με ἤγγικεν. 43 Καὶ εὐθὺς ἔτι
[one] betraying me has drawn near. And immediately yet
αὐτοῦ λαλοῦντος παραγίνεται [ὁ] Ἰούδας
him speaking[a] arrives – Judas
= while he was still speaking
εἷς τῶν δώδεκα, καὶ μετ' αὐτοῦ ὄχλος
one of the twelve, and with him a crowd
μετὰ μαχαιρῶν καὶ ξύλων παρὰ τῶν
with swords and clubs from the

called Gethsemane, and
Jesus said to his disciples,
"Sit here while I pray."
33He took Peter, James and
John along with him, and
he began to be deeply distressed and troubled.
34"My soul is over-
whelmed with sorrow to
the point of death," he said
to them. "Stay here and
keep watch."
35Going a little farther, he
fell to the ground and
prayed that if possible the
hour might pass from him.
36"*Abba,*[q] Father," he
said, "everything is possible for you. Take this cup
from me. Yet not what I
will, but what you will."
37Then he returned to his
disciples and found them
sleeping. "Simon," he said
to Peter, "are you asleep?
Could you not keep watch
for one hour? 38Watch and
pray so that you will not fall
into temptation. The spirit
is willing, but the body is
weak."
39Once more he went
away and prayed the same
thing. 40When he came
back, he again found them
sleeping, because their
eyes were heavy. They did
not know what to say to
him.
41Returning the third
time, he said to them, "Are
you still sleeping and resting? Enough! The hour has
come. Look, the Son of
Man is betrayed into the
hands of sinners. 42Rise!
Let us go! Here comes my
betrayer!"

Jesus Arrested

43Just as he was speaking,
Judas, one of the Twelve,
appeared. With him was a
crowd armed with swords
and clubs, sent from the

q36 Aramaic for *Father*

priests and the scribes and the elders.

44 Now he who was betraying Him had given them a signal, saying, "Whomever I shall kiss, He is the one; seize Him, and lead Him away under guard."

45 And after coming, he immediately went to Him, saying, "Rabbi!" and kissed Him.

46 And they laid hands on Him, and seized Him.

47 But a certain one of those who stood by drew his sword, and struck the slave of the high priest, and cut off his ear.

48 And Jesus answered and said to them, "Have you come out with swords and clubs to arrest Me, as against a robber?

49 "Every day I was with you in the temple teaching, and you did not seize Me; but *this has happened* that the Scriptures might be fulfilled."

50 And they all left Him and fled.

51 And a certain young man was following Him, wearing *nothing but* a linen sheet over *his* naked *body;* and they *seized him.

52 But he left the linen sheet behind, and escaped naked.

Jesus before His Accusers

53 And they led Jesus away to the high priest; and all the chief priests and the elders and the scribes *gathered together.

54 And Peter had followed Him at a distance, right into the courtyard of the high priest; and he was sitting with the officers, and warming himself at the fire.

55 Now the chief priests and the whole [m]Council kept trying to obtain testimony against Jesus to put Him to death; and they were not finding any.

56 For many were giving false testimony against Him, and *yet* their testimony was not consistent.

[m] Or, *Sanhedrin*

ἀρχιερέων καὶ τῶν γραμματέων καὶ τῶν
chief priests and the scribes and the
πρεσβυτέρων. **44** δεδώκει δὲ ὁ παραδιδοὺς
elders. 1Now 5had given 2the [one] 3betraying
αὐτὸν σύσσημον αὐτοῖς λέγων· ὃν ἂν
4him 7a signal 6them saying: Whomever
φιλήσω αὐτός ἐστιν· κρατήσατε αὐτὸν καὶ
I may kiss he is; seize ye him and
ἀπάγετε ἀσφαλῶς. **45** καὶ ἐλθὼν εὐθὺς
lead away securely. And coming immediately
προσελθὼν αὐτῷ λέγει· ῥαββί, καὶ
approaching *to* him he says: Rabbi, and
κατεφίλησεν αὐτόν· **46** οἱ δὲ ἐπέβαλαν τὰς
fervently kissed him; and they 1laid 4on 2the(their)
χεῖρας αὐτῷ καὶ ἐκράτησαν αὐτόν. **47** εἷς
3hands him and seized him. 3one
δέ τις τῶν παρεστηκότων σπασάμενος
1But 2a certain of the [ones] standing by drawing
τὴν μάχαιραν ἔπαισεν τὸν δοῦλον τοῦ ἀρχιερέως
the sword struck the slave of the high priest
καὶ ἀφεῖλεν αὐτοῦ τὸ ὠτάριον. **48** καὶ
and cut off of him the ear. And
ἀποκριθεὶς ὁ Ἰησοῦς εἶπεν αὐτοῖς· ὡς
answering – Jesus said to them: As
ἐπὶ λῃστὴν ἐξήλθατε μετὰ μαχαιρῶν καὶ
against a robber came ye forth with swords and
ξύλων συλλαβεῖν με; **49** καθ' ἡμέραν ἤμην
clubs to arrest me? Daily I was
πρὸς ὑμᾶς ἐν τῷ ἱερῷ διδάσκων, καὶ οὐκ
with you in the temple teaching, and not
ἐκρατήσατέ με· ἀλλ' ἵνα πληρωθῶσιν αἱ
ye did seize me; but that may be fulfilled the
γραφαί. **50** καὶ ἀφέντες αὐτὸν ἔφυγον
scriptures. And leaving him they fled
πάντες. **51** Καὶ νεανίσκος τις συνηκολούθει
all. And a certain young man accompanied
αὐτῷ περιβεβλημένος σινδόνα ἐπὶ γυμνοῦ,
him *having been* clothed [in] a nightgown over [his] naked [body],
καὶ κρατοῦσιν αὐτόν· **52** ὁ δὲ καταλιπὼν
and they seize him; and he leaving
τὴν σινδόνα γυμνὸς ἔφυγεν.
the nightgown naked fled.

53 Καὶ ἀπήγαγον τὸν Ἰησοῦν πρὸς τὸν
And they led away – Jesus to the
ἀρχιερέα, καὶ συνέρχονται πάντες οἱ
high priest, and come together all the
ἀρχιερεῖς καὶ οἱ πρεσβύτεροι καὶ οἱ
chief priests and the elders and the
γραμματεῖς. **54** καὶ ὁ Πέτρος ἀπὸ μακρόθεν
scribes. And – Peter from afar
ἠκολούθησεν αὐτῷ ἕως ἔσω εἰς τὴν αὐλὴν
followed him until within *in* the court
τοῦ ἀρχιερέως, καὶ ἦν συγκαθήμενος μετὰ
of the high priest, and was sitting *with* with
τῶν ὑπηρετῶν καὶ θερμαινόμενος πρὸς τὸ
the attendants and warming himself by the
φῶς. **55** Οἱ δὲ ἀρχιερεῖς καὶ ὅλον τὸ
bright fire. Now the chief priests and all the
συνέδριον ἐζήτουν κατὰ τοῦ Ἰησοῦ
council sought against – Jesus
μαρτυρίαν εἰς τὸ θανατῶσαι αὐτόν, καὶ
witness for the to put to death him, and
= so as
οὐχ ηὕρισκον· **56** πολλοὶ γὰρ ἐψευδομαρτύρουν
found not; for many falsely witnessed
κατ' αὐτοῦ, καὶ ἴσαι αἱ μαρτυρίαι οὐκ
against him, and 4identical 1the 2testimonies 3not

chief priests, the teachers of the law, and the elders.

44 Now the betrayer had arranged a signal with them: "The one I kiss is the man; arrest him and lead him away under guard."
45 Going at once to Jesus, Judas said, "Rabbi!" and kissed him. 46 The men seized Jesus and arrested him. 47 Then one of those standing near drew his sword and struck the servant of the high priest, cutting off his ear.

48 "Am I leading a rebellion," said Jesus, "that you have come out with swords and clubs to capture me?
49 Every day I was with you, teaching in the temple courts, and you did not arrest me. But the Scriptures must be fulfilled." 50 Then everyone deserted him and fled.

51 A young man, wearing nothing but a linen garment, was following Jesus. When they seized him, 52 he fled naked, leaving his garment behind.

Before the Sanhedrin

53 They took Jesus to the high priest, and all the chief priests, elders and teachers of the law came together.
54 Peter followed him at a distance, right into the courtyard of the high priest. There he sat with the guards and warmed himself at the fire.

55 The chief priests and the whole Sanhedrin were looking for evidence against Jesus so that they could put him to death, but they did not find any.
56 Many testified falsely against him, but their statements did not agree.

57 And some stood up and
began to give false testimony against Him, saying,
58 "We heard Him say, 'I
will destroy this temple
made with hands, and in
three days I will build another made without
hands.' "
59 And not even in this respect was their testimony
consistent.
60 And the high priest
stood up *and came* forward
and questioned Jesus, saying, "Do You make no an-
swer? What is it that these
men are testifying against
You?"
61 But He kept silent, and
made no answer. Again the
high priest was questioning
Him, and saying to Him,
"Are You the Christ, the
Son of the Blessed *One?*"
62 And Jesus said, "I am;
and you shall see THE SON
OF MAN SITTING AT THE
RIGHT HAND OF POWER, and
COMING WITH THE CLOUDS OF
HEAVEN."
63 And tearing his clothes,
the high priest *said,
"What further need do we
have of witnesses?
64 "You have heard the
blasphemy; how does it
seem to you?" And they all
condemned Him to be de-
serving of death.
65 And some began to spit
at Him, and to blindfold
Him, and to beat Him with
their fists, and to say to
Him, "Prophesy!" And the
officers received Him with
slaps *in the face*.

Peter's Denials

66 And as Peter was below
in the courtyard, one of the
servant-girls of the high
priest *came,
67 and seeing Peter warm-
ing himself, she looked at
him, and *said, "You, too,
were with Jesus the Naza-
rene."
68 But he denied *it*, saying,
"I neither know nor understand what you are talking
about." And he went out
onto the porch.[n]

[n] Later mss. add: *and a cock crowed*

ἦσαν. 57 καί τινες ἀναστάντες ἐψευδομαρτύρουν
[2]were. And some standing up falsely witnessed
κατ' αὐτοῦ λέγοντες 58 ὅτι ἡμεῖς ἠκούσαμεν
against him saying[,] – We heard
αὐτοῦ λέγοντος ὅτι ἐγὼ καταλύσω τὸν
him saying[,] – I will overthrow –
ναὸν τοῦτον τὸν χειροποίητον καὶ διὰ
[2]shrine [1]this – [3]handmade and through(after)
τριῶν ἡμερῶν ἄλλον ἀχειροποίητον οἰκο-
three days another not handmade I will
δομήσω. 59 καὶ οὐδὲ οὕτως ἴση ἦν ἡ
build. And not so identical was the
μαρτυρία αὐτῶν. 60 καὶ ἀναστὰς ὁ
witness of them. And standing up the
ἀρχιερεὺς εἰς μέσον ἐπηρώτησεν τὸν Ἰησοῦν
high priest in [the] midst questioned – Jesus
λέγων· οὐκ ἀποκρίνῃ οὐδὲν τί οὗτοί σου
saying: Answerest thou not no(any)thing what these men [2]thee
καταμαρτυροῦσιν; 61 ὁ δὲ ἐσιώπα καὶ
[1]testify against ? But he was silent and
οὐκ ἀπεκρίνατο οὐδέν. πάλιν ὁ ἀρχιερεὺς
answered not no(any)thing. Again the high priest
ἐπηρώτα αὐτὸν καὶ λέγει αὐτῷ· σὺ εἶ ὁ
questioned him and says to him: Thou art the
χριστὸς ὁ υἱὸς τοῦ εὐλογητοῦ; 62 ὁ δὲ
Christ the Son of the Blessed [one] ? – And
Ἰησοῦς εἶπεν· ἐγώ εἰμι, καὶ ὄψεσθε
Jesus said: I am, and ye will see
τὸν υἱὸν τοῦ ἀνθρώπου ἐκ δεξιῶν καθήμενον
the Son – of man [2]at [the] right [hand] [1]sitting
τῆς δυνάμεως καὶ ἐρχόμενον μετὰ τῶν
of the Power and coming with the
νεφελῶν τοῦ οὐρανοῦ. 63 ὁ δὲ ἀρχιερεὺς
clouds – of heaven. And the high priest
διαρήξας τοὺς χιτῶνας αὐτοῦ λέγει· τί
rending the tunics of him says: What
ἔτι χρείαν ἔχομεν μαρτύρων; 64 ἠκούσατε
more need have we of witnesses ? ye heard
τῆς βλασφημίας· τί ὑμῖν φαίνεται; οἱ δὲ
the blasphemy; what to you appears it ? And they
πάντες κατέκριναν αὐτὸν ἔνοχον εἶναι
all condemned him liable to be
θανάτου. 65 Καὶ ἤρξαντό τινες ἐμπτύειν
of(to) death. And began some to spit at
αὐτῷ καὶ περικαλύπτειν αὐτοῦ τὸ πρόσωπον
him and to cover of him the face
καὶ κολαφίζειν αὐτὸν καὶ λέγειν αὐτῷ·
and to maltreat him and to say to him:
προφήτευσον, καὶ οἱ ὑπηρέται ῥαπίσμασιν
Prophesy, and the attendants with slaps
αὐτὸν ἔλαβον. 66 Καὶ ὄντος τοῦ Πέτρου
[2]him [1]took. And being – Peter[a]
= as Peter was
κάτω ἐν τῇ αὐλῇ ἔρχεται μία τῶν
below in the court comes one of the
παιδισκῶν τοῦ ἀρχιερέως, 67 καὶ ἰδοῦσα
maidservants of the high priest, and seeing
τὸν Πέτρον θερμαινόμενον ἐμβλέψασα αὐτῷ
– Peter warming himself looking at him
λέγει· καὶ σὺ μετὰ τοῦ Ναζαρηνοῦ ἦσθα
says: And [1]thou [3]with [4]the [5]Nazarene [2]wast
τοῦ Ἰησοῦ. 68 ὁ δὲ ἠρνήσατο λέγων· οὔτε
– [6]Jesus. But he denied saying: [2]neither
οἶδα οὔτε ἐπίσταμαι σὺ τί λέγεις. καὶ
[1]I [3]know [4]nor [5]understand [7]thou [6]what [8]sayest. And
ἐξῆλθεν ἔξω εἰς τὸ προαύλιον· 69 καὶ ἡ
he went forth outside into the forecourt; and the

57 Then some stood up
and gave this false testimony against him: 58 "We
heard him say, 'I will destroy this man-made tem-
ple and in three days will
build another, not made by
man.' " 59 Yet even then
their testimony did not
agree.
60 Then the high priest
stood up before them and
asked Jesus, "Are you not
going to answer? What is
this testimony that these
men are bringing against
you?" 61 But Jesus re-
mained silent and gave no
answer.
Again the high priest
asked him, "Are you the
Christ,[r] the Son of the
Blessed One?"
62 "I am," said Jesus.
"And you will see the Son
of Man sitting at the right
hand of the Mighty One and
coming on the clouds of
heaven."
63 The high priest tore his
clothes. "Why do we need
any more witnesses?" he
asked. 64 "You have heard
the blasphemy. What do
you think?"
They all condemned him
as worthy of death. 65 Then
some began to spit at him;
they blindfolded him,
struck him with their fists,
and said, "Prophesy!" And
the guards took him and
beat him.

Peter Disowns Jesus

66 While Peter was below
in the courtyard, one of the
servant girls of the high
priest came by. 67 When she
saw Peter warming himself,
she looked closely at him.
"You also were with that
Nazarene, Jesus," she
said.
68 But he denied it. "I
don't know or understand
what you're talking
about," he said, and went
out into the entryway.[s]

[r] 61 Or *Messiah*
[s] 68 Some early manuscripts *entryway and the rooster crowed*

69And the maid saw him,
and began once more to say
to the bystanders, "This is
one of them!"
70But again he was deny-
ing it. And after a little
while the bystanders were
again saying to Peter,
"Surely you are *one* of
them, for you are a Galilean
too."
71But he began to curse
and swear, "I do not know
this man you are talking
about!"
72And immediately a cock
crowed a second time. And
Peter remembered how
Jesus had made the remark
to him, "Before a cock
crows twice, you will deny
Me three times." And he
began to weep.

Chapter 15

Jesus before Pilate

AND early in the morning
the chief priests with
the elders and scribes, and
the whole [m]Council,
immediately held a consul-
tation; and binding Jesus,
they led Him away, and delivered Him up to Pilate.
2And Pilate questioned
Him, "Are You the King of
the Jews?" And answering
He *said to him, "*It is as*
you say."
3And the chief priests
began to accuse Him
harshly.
4And Pilate was ques-
tioning Him again, saying,
"Do You make no answer?
See how many charges
they bring against You!"
5But Jesus made no fur-
ther answer; so that Pilate
was amazed.
6Now at *the* feast he
used to release for them
any one prisoner whom
they requested.
7And the man named
Barabbas had been impris-
oned with the insurrectionists who had committed
murder in the insurrection.
8And the multitude went
up and began asking him *to*
do as he had been accustomed to do for them.
9And Pilate answered
them, saying, "Do you

[m]Or, *Sanhedrin*

παιδίσκη ἰδοῦσα αὐτὸν ἤρξατο πάλιν λέγειν
maidservant seeing him began again to say
τοῖς παρεστῶσιν ὅτι οὗτος ἐξ αὐτῶν ἐστιν.
to the [ones] standing by[,] – This man of them is.
70 ὁ δὲ πάλιν ἠρνεῖτο. καὶ μετὰ μικρὸν
But he again denied. And after a little
πάλιν οἱ παρεστῶτες ἔλεγον τῷ Πέτρῳ·
again the [ones] standing by said – to Peter:
ἀληθῶς ἐξ αὐτῶν εἶ· καὶ γὰρ Γαλιλαῖος
Truly of them thou art; [3]indeed [1]for [4]a Galilæan
εἶ. 71 ὁ δὲ ἤρξατο ἀναθεματίζειν καὶ
[2]thou art. And he began to curse and
ὀμνύναι ὅτι οὐκ οἶδα τὸν ἄνθρωπον
to swear[,] – I know not – man
τοῦτον ὃν λέγετε. 72 καὶ εὐθὺς ἐκ
this whom ye say. And immediately a
δευτέρου ἀλέκτωρ ἐφώνησεν. καὶ ἀνεμνήσθη
second time a cock crew. And remembered
ὁ Πέτρος τὸ ῥῆμα ὡς εἶπεν αὐτῷ ὁ
– Peter the word as said to him –
Ἰησοῦς ὅτι πρὶν ἀλέκτορα δὶς φωνῆσαι
Jesus[,] – Before a cock twice *to* crow[b]
τρίς με ἀπαρνήσῃ· καὶ ἐπιβαλὼν ἔκλαιεν.
thrice me thou wilt deny; and thinking thereon he wept.

15 Καὶ εὐθὺς πρωῒ συμβούλιον ἑτοιμάσαντες
And immediately early [2]a council [1]preparing
οἱ ἀρχιερεῖς μετὰ τῶν πρεσβυτέρων καὶ
the chief priests with the elders and
γραμματέων καὶ ὅλον τὸ συνέδριον, δήσαντες
scribes and all the council, having bound
τὸν Ἰησοῦν ἀπήνεγκαν καὶ παρέδωκαν
– Jesus led [him] away and delivered [him]
Πιλάτῳ. 2 καὶ ἐπηρώτησεν αὐτὸν ὁ
to Pilate. And questioned him –
Πιλᾶτος· σὺ εἶ ὁ βασιλεὺς τῶν Ἰουδαίων;
Pilate: Thou art the king of the Jews?
ὁ δὲ ἀποκριθεὶς αὐτῷ λέγει· σὺ λέγεις.
And he answering him says: Thou sayest.
3 καὶ κατηγόρουν αὐτοῦ οἱ ἀρχιερεῖς πολλά.
And accused him the chief priests many things.
4 ὁ δὲ Πιλᾶτος πάλιν ἐπηρώτα αὐτόν [λέγων]·
– But Pilate again questioned him saying:
οὐκ ἀποκρίνῃ οὐδέν; ἴδε πόσα
Answerest thou not no(any)thing? Behold how many things
σου κατηγοροῦσιν. 5 ὁ δὲ Ἰησοῦς οὐκ-
thee they accuse. – But Jesus no(any)
ἔτι οὐδὲν ἀπεκρίθη, ὥστε θαυμάζειν
more nothing answered, so as to marvel
= so that Pilate marvelled.
τὸν Πιλᾶτον. 6 Κατὰ δὲ ἑορτὴν ἀπέλυεν
– Pilate[b]. Now at a feast he released
αὐτοῖς ἕνα δέσμιον ὃν παρῃτοῦντο. 7 ἦν δὲ
to them one prisoner whom they begged. Now there was
ὁ λεγόμενος Βαραββᾶς μετὰ τῶν
the [one] named Barabbas with the
στασιαστῶν δεδεμένος, οἵτινες ἐν τῇ στάσει
rebels *having been* bound, who* in the rebellion
φόνον πεποιήκεισαν. 8 καὶ ἀναβὰς ὁ ὄχλος
murder had done. And going up the crowd
ἤρξατο αἰτεῖσθαι καθὼς ἐποίει αὐτοῖς.
began to ask as he used to do for them.
9 ὁ δὲ Πιλᾶτος ἀπεκρίθη αὐτοῖς λέγων·
– But Pilate answered them saying:

* Note the plural.

69When the servant girl
saw him there, she said
again to those standing
around, "This fellow is one
of them." 70Again he de-
nied it.
After a little while, those
standing near said to Peter,
"Surely you are one of
them, for you are a Galilean."
71He began to call down
curses on himself, and he
swore to them, "I don't
know this man you're talking about."
72Immediately the rooster
crowed the second time.[t]
Then Peter remembered
the word Jesus had spoken
to him: "Before the rooster
crows twice[u] you will disown me three times." And
he broke down and wept.

Chapter 15

Jesus Before Pilate

VERY early in the
morning, the chief
priests, with the elders, the
teachers of the law and the
whole Sanhedrin, reached
a decision. They bound
Jesus, led him away and
handed him over to Pilate.
2"Are you the king of the
Jews?" asked Pilate.
"Yes, it is as you say,"
Jesus replied.
3The chief priests ac-
cused him of many things.
4So again Pilate asked him,
"Aren't you going to an-
swer? See how many things
they are accusing you of."
5But Jesus still made no
reply, and Pilate was
amazed.
6Now it was the custom at
the Feast to release a prisoner whom the people re-
quested. 7A man called
Barabbas was in prison
with the insurrectionists
who had committed murder
in the uprising. 8The crowd
came up and asked Pilate to
do for them what he usually
did.
9"Do you want me to re-
lease to you the king of the

[t]72 Some early manuscripts do not have *the second time.*
[u]72 Some early manuscripts do not have *twice.*

want me to release for you
the King of the Jews?"
10For he was aware that
the chief priests had de-
livered Him up because of
envy.
11But the chief priests
stirred up the multitude *to*
ask him to release Barabbas for them instead.
12And answering again,
Pilate was saying to them,
"Then what shall I do with
Him whom you call the
King of the Jews?"
13And they shouted back,
"Crucify Him!"
14But Pilate was saying to
them, "Why, what evil has
He done?" But they shout-
ed all the more, "Crucify
Him!"
15And wishing to satisfy
the multitude, Pilate re-
leased Barabbas for them,
and after having Jesus
scourged, he delivered *Him*
to be crucified.

Jesus Is Mocked

16And the soldiers took
Him away into the palace
(that is, the Praetorium),
and they *called together
the whole *Roman* [o]cohort.
17And they *dressed Him
up in purple, and after
weaving a crown of thorns,
they put it on Him;
18and they began to ac-
claim Him, "Hail, King of
the Jews!"
19And they kept beating
His head with a [p]reed, and
spitting at Him, and kneeling and bowing before
Him.
20And after they had
mocked Him, they took the
purple off Him, and put His
garments on Him. And
they *led Him out to crucify Him.
21And they *pressed into
service a passer-by coming
from the country, Simon of
Cyrene (the father of Alexander and Rufus), to bear
His cross.

The Crucifixion

22And they *brought Him
to the place Golgotha,
which is translated, Place
of a Skull.

[o] Or, *battalion*
[p] Or, *staff* (made of a reed)

θέλετε ἀπολύσω ὑμῖν τὸν βασιλέα τῶν
Do ye wish I may release to you the king of the
Ἰουδαίων; **10** ἐγίνωσκεν γὰρ ὅτι διὰ φθόνον
Jews ? For he knew that on account of envy
παραδεδώκεισαν αὐτὸν οἱ ἀρχιερεῖς. **11** οἱ
had delivered him the chief priests. the
δὲ ἀρχιερεῖς ἀνέσεισαν τὸν ὄχλον ἵνα
But chief priests stirred up the crowd that
μᾶλλον τὸν Βαραββᾶν ἀπολύσῃ αὐτοῖς.
rather – Barabbas he should release to them.
12 ὁ δὲ Πιλᾶτος πάλιν ἀποκριθεὶς ἔλεγεν
– So Pilate again answering said
αὐτοῖς· τί οὖν ποιήσω [ὃν] λέγετε τὸν
to them: What then may I do [to him] whom ye call the
βασιλέα τῶν Ἰουδαίων; **13** οἱ δὲ πάλιν
king of the Jews ? And they again
ἔκραξαν· σταύρωσον αὐτόν. **14** ὁ δὲ
cried out: Crucify him. – But
Πιλᾶτος ἔλεγεν αὐτοῖς· τί γὰρ ἐποίησεν
Pilate said to them: Indeed what [s]did he
κακόν; οἱ δὲ περισσῶς ἔκραξαν· σταύρωσον
[1]evil ? and they more cried out: Crucify
αὐτόν. **15** ὁ δὲ Πιλᾶτος βουλόμενος τῷ
him. – And Pilate resolving the
ὄχλῳ τὸ ἱκανὸν ποιῆσαι ἀπέλυσεν αὐτοῖς
crowd to satisfy† released to them
τὸν Βαραββᾶν, καὶ παρέδωκεν τὸν Ἰησοῦν
– Barabbas, and delivered – Jesus
φραγελλώσας ἵνα σταυρωθῇ.
having scourged [him] that he might be crucified.
16 Οἱ δὲ στρατιῶται ἀπήγαγον αὐτὸν
Then the soldiers led away him
ἔσω τῆς αὐλῆς, ὅ ἐστιν πραιτώριον, καὶ
inside the court, which is prætorium, and
συγκαλοῦσιν ὅλην τὴν σπεῖραν. **17** καὶ
they call together all the cohort. And
ἐνδιδύσκουσιν αὐτὸν πορφύραν καὶ περιτιθέασιν
they put on him a purple [robe] and place round
αὐτῷ πλέξαντες ἀκάνθινον στέφανον· **18** καὶ
him plaiting a thorny crown; and
ἤρξαντο ἀσπάζεσθαι αὐτόν· χαῖρε, βασιλεῦ
they began to salute him: Hail, king
τῶν Ἰουδαίων· **19** καὶ ἔτυπτον αὐτοῦ τὴν
of the Jews; and they struck of him the
κεφαλὴν καλάμῳ καὶ ἐνέπτυον αὐτῷ, καὶ
head with a reed and spat at him, and
τιθέντες τὰ γόνατα προσεκύνουν αὐτῷ.
placing(bending) the(their) knees worshipped him.
20 καὶ ὅτε ἐνέπαιξαν αὐτῷ, ἐξέδυσαν
And when they mocked him, they took off
αὐτὸν τὴν πορφύραν καὶ ἐνέδυσαν αὐτὸν
him the purple [robe] and put on him
τὰ ἱμάτια αὐτοῦ. Καὶ ἐξάγουσιν αὐτὸν
the garments of him. And they lead forth him
ἵνα σταυρώσωσιν αὐτόν. **21** καὶ ἀγγαρεύουσιν
that they might crucify him. And they impress
παράγοντά τινα Σίμωνα Κυρηναῖον ἐρχόμενον
passing by a certain Simon a Cyrenian coming
ἀπ' ἀγροῦ, τὸν πατέρα Ἀλεξάνδρου καὶ
from [the] country, the father of Alexander and
Ῥούφου, ἵνα ἄρῃ τὸν σταυρὸν αὐτοῦ.
of Rufus, that he might bear the cross of him.
22 καὶ φέρουσιν αὐτὸν ἐπὶ τὸν Γολγοθᾶν
And they bring him to the Golgotha
τόπον, ὅ ἐστιν μεθερμηνευόμενος κρανίου
place, which is being interpreted of a skull

Jews?" asked Pilate,
10knowing it was out of
envy that the chief priests
had handed Jesus over to
him. 11But the chief priests
stirred up the crowd to
have Pilate release Barabbas instead.
12"What shall I do, then,
with the one you call the
king of the Jews?" Pilate
asked them.
13"Crucify him!" they
shouted.
14"Why? What crime has
he committed?" asked Pi-
late.
But they shouted all the
louder, "Crucify him!"
15Wanting to satisfy the
crowd, Pilate released Barabbas to them. He had
Jesus flogged, and handed
him over to be crucified.

The Soldiers Mock Jesus

16The soldiers led Jesus
away into the palace (that
is, the Praetorium) and
called together the whole
company of soldiers.
17They put a purple robe on
him, then twisted together
a crown of thorns and set it
on him. 18And they began
to call out to him, "Hail,
king of the Jews!" 19Again
and again they struck him
on the head with a staff and
spit on him. Falling on their
knees, they paid homage to
him. 20And when they had
mocked him, they took off
the purple robe and put his
own clothes on him. Then
they led him out to crucify
him.

The Crucifixion

21A certain man from Cy-
rene, Simon, the father of
Alexander and Rufus, was
passing by on his way in
from the country, and they
forced him to carry the
cross. 22They brought
Jesus to the place called
Golgotha (which means
The Place of the Skull).

23 And they tried to give Him wine mixed with myrrh; but He did not take it.

24 And they *crucified Him, and *divided up His garments among themselves, casting lots for them, *to decide* what each should take.

25 And it was the [q]third hour when they crucified Him.

26 And the inscription of the charge against Him read, "THE KING OF THE JEWS."

27 And they *crucified two robbers with Him, one on His right and one on His left.

28 [[r]And the Scripture was fulfilled which says, "And He was numbered with transgressors."]

29 And those passing by were hurling abuse at Him, wagging their heads, and saying, "Ha! You who *are going to* destroy the temple and rebuild it in three days,

30 save Yourself, and come down from the cross!"

31 In the same way the chief priests also, along with the scribes, were mocking *Him* among themselves and saying, "He saved others; He cannot save Himself.

32 "Let *this* Christ, the King of Israel, now come down from the cross, so that we may see and believe!" And those who were crucified with Him were casting the same insult at Him.

33 And when the [s]sixth hour had come, darkness fell over the whole land until the [t]ninth hour.

34 And at the ninth hour Jesus cried out with a loud voice, "ELOI, ELOI, LAMA SABACHTHANI?" which is translated, "MY GOD, MY GOD, WHY HAST THOU FORSAKEN ME?"

35 And when some of the bystanders heard it, they *began* saying, "Behold, He is calling for Elijah."

36 And someone ran and filled a sponge with sour wine, put it on a reed, and gave Him a drink, saying, "Let us see whether Elijah will come to take Him down."

[q]I.e., 9 a.m.
[r]Many mss. do not contain this verse
[s]I.e., noon
[t]I.e., 3 p.m.

τόπος. 23 καὶ ἐδίδουν αὐτῷ ἐσμυρνισμένον
place. And they gave him [2]*having been* spiced with myrrh
οἶνον· ὃς δὲ οὐκ ἔλαβεν. 24 καὶ σταυροῦσιν
[1]wine; but who(he) received not. And they crucify
αὐτόν, καὶ διαμερίζονται τὰ ἱμάτια αὐτοῦ,
him, and divide the garments of him,
βάλλοντες κλῆρον ἐπ' αὐτὰ τίς τί ἄρῃ.
casting a lot on them [2]one [1]what might take.
25 ἦν δὲ ὥρα τρίτη καὶ ἐσταύρωσαν
Now it was hour third and they crucified
αὐτόν. 26 καὶ ἦν ἡ ἐπιγραφὴ τῆς αἰτίας
him. And was the superscription of the accusation
αὐτοῦ ἐπιγεγραμμένη· Ο ΒΑΣΙΛΕΥΣ ΤΩΝ
of him *having been* written over: THE KING OF THE
ΙΟΥΔΑΙΩΝ. 27 Καὶ σὺν αὐτῷ σταυροῦσιν
JEWS. And with him they crucify
δύο λῃστάς, ἕνα ἐκ δεξιῶν καὶ ἕνα ἐξ
two robbers, one on [the] right and one on
εὐωνύμων αὐτοῦ.‡ 29 Καὶ οἱ παραπορευόμενοι
[the] left of him. And the [ones] passing by
ἐβλασφήμουν αὐτὸν κινοῦντες τὰς κεφαλὰς
blasphemed him wagging the heads
αὐτῶν καὶ λέγοντες· οὐὰ ὁ καταλύων
of them and saying: Ah the [one] overthrowing
τὸν ναὸν καὶ οἰκοδομῶν [ἐν] τρισὶν
the shrine and building in three
ἡμέραις, 30 σῶσον σεαυτὸν καταβὰς ἀπὸ
days, save thyself coming down from
τοῦ σταυροῦ. 31 ὁμοίως καὶ οἱ ἀρχιερεῖς
the cross. Likewise also the chief priests
ἐμπαίζοντες πρὸς ἀλλήλους μετὰ τῶν
mocking to one another with the
γραμματέων ἔλεγον· ἄλλους ἔσωσεν, ἑαυτὸν
scribes said: Others he saved, himself
οὐ δύναται σῶσαι· 32 ὁ χριστὸς ὁ βασιλεὺς
he cannot *to* save; the Christ the king
Ἰσραὴλ καταβάτω νῦν ἀπὸ τοῦ σταυροῦ,
of Israel let come down now from the cross,
ἵνα ἴδωμεν καὶ πιστεύσωμεν. καὶ οἱ
that we may see and believe. And the
συνεσταυρωμένοι σὺν αὐτῷ ὠνείδιζον αὐτόν.
[ones] crucified *with* with him reproached him.
33 Καὶ γενομένης ὥρας ἕκτης σκότος
And becoming hour sixth* darkness
= when it was the sixth hour
ἐγένετο ἐφ' ὅλην τὴν γῆν ἕως ὥρας
came over all the land until [the] hour
ἐνάτης. 34 καὶ τῇ ἐνάτῃ ὥρᾳ ἐβόησεν ὁ
ninth. And at the ninth hour cried –
Ἰησοῦς φωνῇ μεγάλῃ· ἐλωῒ ἐλωῒ λαμὰ
Jesus with a voice great(loud): Eloi[,] Eloi[,] lama
σαβαχθάνι; ὅ ἐστιν μεθερμηνευόμενον· ὁ
sabachthani ? which is being interpreted: The
θεός μου ὁ θεός μου, εἰς τί ἐγκατέλιπές
God of me[,] the God of me, why didst thou forsake
με; 35 καί τινες τῶν παρεστηκότων
me ? And some of the [ones] standing by
ἀκούσαντες ἔλεγον· ἴδε Ἠλίαν φωνεῖ.
hearing said: Behold Elias he calls.
36 δραμὼν δέ τις γεμίσας σπόγγον ὄξους
And running one having filled a sponge of(with) vinegar
περιθεὶς καλάμῳ ἐπότιζεν αὐτόν, λέγων·
placing it round a reed [1]gave [3]to drink [2]him, saying:
ἄφετε ἴδωμεν εἰ ἔρχεται Ἠλίας καθελεῖν
Leave[,] let us see if comes Elias [1]to take [2]down

‡ Verse 28 omitted by Nestle; *cf.* NIV footnote.

23 Then they offered him
wine mixed with myrrh,
but he did not take it. 24 And
they crucified him. Dividing up his clothes, they cast
lots to see what each would
get.
25 It was the third hour
when they crucified him.
26 The written notice of the
charge against him read:
THE KING OF THE JEWS.
27 They crucified two robbers with him, one on his
right and one on his left.[v]
29 Those who passed by
hurled insults at him, shaking their heads and saying,
"So! You who are going to
destroy the temple and
build it in three days,
30 come down from the
cross and save yourself!"
31 In the same way the
chief priests and the teachers of the law mocked him
among themselves. "He
saved others," they said,
"but he can't save himself!
32 Let this Christ,[w] this
King of Israel, come down
now from the cross, that we
may see and believe."
Those crucified with him
also heaped insults on him.

The Death of Jesus

33 At the sixth hour darkness came over the whole
land until the ninth hour.
34 And at the ninth hour
Jesus cried out in a loud
voice, *"Eloi, Eloi, lama
sabachthani?"* — which
means, "My God, my God,
why have you forsaken
me?"[x]
35 When some of those
standing near heard this,
they said, "Listen, he's
calling Elijah."
36 One man ran, filled a
sponge with wine vinegar,
put it on a stick, and offered
it to Jesus to drink. "Now
leave him alone. Let's see
if Elijah comes to take him
down," he said.

[v]27 Some manuscripts *left,* [28]*and the scripture was fulfilled which says, "He was counted with the lawless ones"* (Isaiah 53:12)
[w]32 Or *Messiah*
[x]34 Psalm 22:1

37And Jesus uttered a loud cry, and breathed His last.

38And the veil of the temple was torn in two from top to bottom.

39And when the centurion, who was standing right in front of Him, saw the way He breathed His last, he said, "Truly this man was the Son of God!"

40And there were also *some* women looking on from a distance, among whom *were* Mary Magdalene, and Mary the mother of James the Less and Joses, and Salome.

41And when He was in Galilee, they used to follow Him and minister to Him; and *there were* many other women who had come up with Him to Jerusalem.

Jesus Is Buried

42And when evening had already come, because it was the preparation day, that is, the day before the Sabbath,

43Joseph of Arimathea came, a prominent member of the Council, who himself was waiting for the kingdom of God; and he gathered up courage and went in before Pilate, and asked for the body of Jesus.

44And Pilate wondered if He was dead by this time, and summoning the centurion, he questioned him as to whether He was already dead.

45And ascertaining this from the centurion, he granted the body to Joseph.

46And *Joseph* bought a linen cloth, took Him down, wrapped Him in the linen cloth, and laid Him in a tomb which had been hewn out in the rock; and he rolled a stone against the entrance of the tomb.

47And Mary Magdalene and Mary the *mother* of Joses were looking on *to see* where He was laid.

αὐτόν. **37** ὁ δὲ Ἰησοῦς ἀφεὶς φωνὴν
[3]him. – But Jesus letting go voice
μεγάλην ἐξέπνευσεν. **38** Καὶ τὸ καταπέτασμα
a great(loud) expired. And the veil
τοῦ ναοῦ ἐσχίσθη εἰς δύο ἀπ' ἄνωθεν
of the shrine was rent in two from top
ἕως κάτω. **39** Ἰδὼν δὲ ὁ κεντυρίων ὁ
to bottom. And [3]seeing [1]the [2]centurion –
παρεστηκὼς ἐξ ἐναντίας αὐτοῦ ὅτι οὕτως
[5]standing by [6]opposite [7]him that thus
ἐξέπνευσεν, εἶπεν· ἀληθῶς οὗτος ὁ ἄνθρωπος
he expired, said: Truly this – man
υἱὸς θεοῦ ἦν. **40** Ἦσαν δὲ καὶ γυναῖκες
son of God was. Now there were also women
ἀπὸ μακρόθεν θεωροῦσαι, ἐν αἷς καὶ
from afar beholding, among whom both
Μαρία ἡ Μαγδαληνὴ καὶ Μαρία ἡ
Mary the Magdalene and Mary [1]the
Ἰακώβου τοῦ μικροῦ καὶ Ἰωσῆτος μήτηρ
[5]of James [4]the [3]little [6]and [7]of Joses [2]mother
καὶ Σαλώμη, **41** αἳ ὅτε ἦν ἐν τῇ Γαλιλαίᾳ
and Salome, who when he was in – Galilee
ἠκολούθουν αὐτῷ καὶ διηκόνουν αὐτῷ, καὶ
followed him and served him, and
ἄλλαι πολλαὶ αἱ συναναβᾶσαι αὐτῷ εἰς
others many – having come up with him to
Ἱεροσόλυμα.
Jerusalem.

42 Καὶ ἤδη ὀψίας γενομένης, ἐπεὶ ἦν
And now evening coming,[a] since it was
= when it was evening,
παρασκευή, ὅ ἐστιν προσάββατον, **43** ἐλθὼν
[the] preparation, which is the day before the sabbath, coming
Ἰωσὴφ ὁ ἀπὸ Ἁριμαθαίας, εὐσχήμων
Joseph the [one] from Arimathæa, an honourable
βουλευτής, ὃς καὶ αὐτὸς ἦν προσδεχόμενος
councillor, who also [him]self was expecting
τὴν βασιλείαν τοῦ θεοῦ, τολμήσας εἰσῆλθεν
the kingdom – of God, taking courage went in
πρὸς τὸν Πιλᾶτον καὶ ᾐτήσατο τὸ σῶμα
to – Pilate and asked the body
τοῦ Ἰησοῦ. **44** ὁ δὲ Πιλᾶτος ἐθαύμασεν
– of Jesus. – And Pilate marvelled
εἰ ἤδη τέθνηκεν, καὶ προσκαλεσάμενος τὸν
if already he has died, and calling to [him] the
κεντυρίωνα ἐπηρώτησεν αὐτὸν εἰ πάλαι
centurion questioned him if long ago
ἀπέθανεν· **45** καὶ γνοὺς ἀπὸ τοῦ κεντυρίωνος
he died; and knowing from the centurion
ἐδωρήσατο τὸ πτῶμα τῷ Ἰωσήφ. **46** καὶ
he granted the corpse – to Joseph. And
ἀγοράσας σινδόνα καθελὼν αὐτὸν ἐνείλησεν
having bought a piece of unused linen taking down him he wrapped
τῇ σινδόνι καὶ κατέθηκεν αὐτὸν ἐν μνήματι
with the linen and deposited him in a tomb
ὃ ἦν λελατομημένον ἐκ πέτρας, καὶ
which was *having been* hewn out of rock, and
προσεκύλισεν λίθον ἐπὶ τὴν θύραν τοῦ
rolled a stone against the door of the
μνημείου. **47** ἡ δὲ Μαρία ἡ Μαγδαληνὴ
tomb. – And Mary the Magdalene
καὶ Μαρία ἡ Ἰωσῆτος ἐθεώρουν ποῦ
and Mary the [mother] of Joses beheld where
τέθειται.
he has been laid.

37With a loud cry, Jesus
breathed his last.
38The curtain of the tem-
ple was torn in two from
top to bottom. 39And when
the centurion, who stood
there in front of Jesus,
heard his cry and[y] saw how
he died, he said, "Surely
this man was the Son[z] of
God!"
40Some women were
watching from a distance.
Among them were Mary
Magdalene, Mary the
mother of James the youn-
ger and of Joses, and Salome. 41In Galilee these
women had followed him
and cared for his needs.
Many other women who
had come up with him to
Jerusalem were also there.

The Burial of Jesus

42It was Preparation Day
(that is, the day before the
Sabbath). So as evening approached, 43Joseph of Arimathea, a prominent mem-
ber of the Council, who
was himself waiting for the
kingdom of God, went
boldly to Pilate and asked
for Jesus' body. 44Pilate
was surprised to hear that
he was already dead. Sum-
moning the centurion, he
asked him if Jesus had already died. 45When he
learned from the centurion
that it was so, he gave the
body to Joseph. 46So Jo-
seph bought some linen
cloth, took down the body,
wrapped it in the linen, and
placed it in a tomb cut out
of rock. Then he rolled a
stone against the entrance
of the tomb. 47Mary Mag-
dalene and Mary the moth-
er of Joses saw where he
was laid.

y39 Some manuscripts do not have *heard his cry and*.
z39 Or *a son*

Chapter 16

The Resurrection

AND when the Sabbath
was over, Mary Mag-
dalene, and Mary the
mother of James, and
Salome, bought spices, that
they might come and anoint
Him.
2 And very early on the
first day of the week, they
*came to the tomb when
the sun had risen.
3 And they were saying to
one another, "Who will roll
away the stone for us from
the entrance of the tomb?"
4 And looking up, they
*saw that the stone had
been rolled away, although
it was extremely large.
5 And entering the tomb,
they saw a young man sit-
ting at the right, wearing a
white robe; and they were
amazed.
6 And he *said to them,
"Do not be amazed; you
are looking for Jesus the
Nazarene, who has been
crucified. He has risen; He
is not here; behold, *here is*
the place where they laid
Him.
7 "But go, tell His disciples and Peter, 'He is going
before you into Galilee;
there you will see Him, just
as He said to you.' "
8 And they went out and
fled from the tomb, for
trembling and astonish-
ment had gripped them;
and they said nothing to
anyone, for they were
afraid.
9 [[a]Now after He had ris-
en early on the first day of
the week, He first appeared
to Mary Magdalene, from
whom He had cast out
seven demons.
10 She went and reported
to those who had been with
Him, while they were
mourning and weeping.
11 And when they heard
that He was alive, and had
been seen by her, they
refused to believe it.
12 And after that, He ap-
peared in a different form
to two of them, while they
were walking along on their
way to the country.

[a] Some of the oldest mss. do not contain vv. 9–20

---

16 Καὶ διαγενομένου τοῦ σαββάτου [ἡ]
And passing the sabbath[a] –
= when the sabbath was past
Μαρία ἡ Μαγδαληνὴ καὶ Μαρία ἡ [τοῦ]
Mary the Magdalene and Mary the [mother] –
Ἰακώβου καὶ Σαλώμη ἠγόρασαν ἀρώματα
of James and Salome bought spices
ἵνα ἐλθοῦσαι ἀλείψωσιν αὐτόν. **2** καὶ λίαν
that coming · they might anoint him. And very
πρωῒ [τῇ] μιᾷ τῶν σαββάτων ἔρχονται
early on the first day of the week† they come
ἐπὶ τὸ μνῆμα, ἀνατείλαντος τοῦ ἡλίου.
upon the tomb, rising the sun.[a]
= as the sun rose.
3 καὶ ἔλεγον πρὸς ἑαυτάς· τίς ἀποκυλίσει
And they said to themselves: Who will roll away
ἡμῖν τὸν λίθον ἐκ τῆς θύρας τοῦ μνημείου;
for us the stone out of the door of the tomb ?
4 καὶ ἀναβλέψασαι θεωροῦσιν ὅτι ἀνακεκύλισται
And looking up they behold that has been rolled back
ὁ λίθος· ἦν γὰρ μέγας σφόδρα. **5** καὶ
the stone: for it was great exceedingly. And
εἰσελθοῦσαι εἰς τὸ μνημεῖον εἶδον νεανίσκον
entering into the tomb they saw a young man
καθήμενον ἐν τοῖς δεξιοῖς περιβεβλημένον
sitting on the right *having been* clothed
στολὴν λευκήν, καὶ ἐξεθαμβήθησαν. **6** ὁ δὲ
robe [in] a white, and they were greatly astonished. But he
λέγει αὐταῖς· μὴ ἐκθαμβεῖσθε· Ἰησοῦν
says to them: Be not greatly astonished; Jesus
ζητεῖτε τὸν Ναζαρηνὸν τὸν ἐσταυρωμένον·
ye seek the Nazarene – *having been* crucified;
ἠγέρθη, οὐκ ἔστιν ὧδε· ἴδε ὁ τόπος
he was raised, he is not here; behold[,] the place
ὅπου ἔθηκαν αὐτόν. **7** ἀλλὰ ὑπάγετε εἴπατε
where they put him. But go ye tell
τοῖς μαθηταῖς αὐτοῦ καὶ τῷ Πέτρῳ ὅτι
the disciples of him and – Peter that
προάγει ὑμᾶς εἰς τὴν Γαλιλαίαν· ἐκεῖ
he goes before you to – Galilee; there
αὐτὸν ὄψεσθε, καθὼς εἶπεν ὑμῖν. **8** καὶ
him ye will see, as he told you. And
ἐξελθοῦσαι ἔφυγον ἀπὸ τοῦ μνημείου, εἶχεν
going forth they fled from the tomb, [5]had
γὰρ αὐτὰς τρόμος καὶ ἔκστασις· καὶ
[1]for [6]them [2]trembling [3]and [4]bewilderment; and
οὐδενὶ οὐδὲν εἶπαν· ἐφοβοῦντο γάρ.
no one no(any)thing they told; for they were afraid.
9 Ἀναστὰς δὲ πρωῒ πρώτῃ σαββάτου
And rising early on the first day of the week†
ἐφάνη πρῶτον Μαρίᾳ τῇ Μαγδαληνῇ, παρ'
he appeared first to Mary the Magdalene, from
ἧς ἐκβεβλήκει ἑπτὰ δαιμόνια. **10** ἐκείνη
whom he had expelled seven demons. That [one]
= She
πορευθεῖσα ἀπήγγειλεν τοῖς μετ' αὐτοῦ
going reported to the [ones] with him
= those who had been with him
γενομένοις πενθοῦσι καὶ κλαίουσιν· **11** κἀκεῖνοι
having been mourning and weeping; and those
ἀκούσαντες ὅτι ζῇ καὶ ἐθεάθη ὑπ' αὐτῆς
hearing that he lives and was seen by her
ἠπίστησαν. **12** Μετὰ δὲ ταῦτα δυσὶν ἐξ
disbelieved. And after these things to two of
αὐτῶν περιπατοῦσιν ἐφανερώθη ἐν ἑτέρᾳ
them walking he was manifested in a different
μορφῇ πορευομένοις εἰς ἀγρόν· **13** κἀκεῖνοι
form going into [the] country; and those

Chapter 16

The Resurrection

WHEN the Sabbath
was over, Mary
Magdalene, Mary the
mother of James, and Salome bought spices so that
they might go to anoint
Jesus' body. 2 Very early on
the first day of the week,
just after sunrise, they
were on their way to the
tomb 3 and they asked each
other, "Who will roll the
stone away from the en-
trance of the tomb?"
4 But when they looked
up, they saw that the stone,
which was very large, had
been rolled away. 5 As they
entered the tomb, they saw
a young man dressed in a
white robe sitting on the
right side, and they were
alarmed.
6 "Don't be alarmed," he
said. "You are looking for
Jesus the Nazarene, who
was crucified. He has ris-
en! He is not here. See the
place where they laid him.
7 But go, tell his disciples
and Peter, 'He is going
ahead of you into Galilee.
There you will see him, just
as he told you.' "
8 Trembling and bewil-
dered, the women went out
and fled from the tomb.
They said nothing to any-
one, because they were
afraid.

[The most reliable early manuscripts and other ancient witnesses do not have Mark 16:9–20.]

9 When Jesus rose early
on the first day of the week,
he appeared first to Mary
Magdalene, out of whom
he had driven seven de-
mons. 10 She went and told
those who had been with
him and who were mourn-
ing and weeping. 11 When
they heard that Jesus was
alive and that she had seen
him, they did not believe it.
12 Afterward Jesus ap-
peared in a different form
to two of them while they
were walking in the coun-

13And they went away and reported it to the others, but they did not believe them either.

The Disciples Commissioned

14And afterward He appeared to the eleven themselves as they were reclining *at the table;* and He reproached them for their unbelief and hardness of heart, because they had not believed those who had seen Him after He had risen.

15And He said to them, "Go into all the world and preach the gospel to all creation.

16"He who has believed and has been baptized shall be saved; but he who has disbelieved shall be condemned.

17"And these signs will accompany those who have believed: in My name they will cast out demons, they will speak with new tongues;

18they will pick up serpents, and if they drink any deadly *poison,* it shall not hurt them; they will lay hands on the sick, and they will recover."

19So then, when the Lord Jesus had spoken to them, He was received up into heaven, and sat down at the right hand of God.

20And they went out and preached everywhere, while the Lord worked with them, and confirmed the word by the signs that followed.][v *And they promptly reported all these instructions to Peter and his companions. And after that, Jesus Himself sent out through them from east to west the sacred and imperishable proclamation of eternal salvation.*]

ἀπελθόντες ἀπήγγειλαν τοῖς λοιποῖς· οὐδὲ
going reported to the rest; neither
ἐκείνοις ἐπίστευσαν. **14** Ὕστερον [δὲ]
those they believed. And later
ἀνακειμένοις αὐτοῖς τοῖς ἕνδεκα ἐφανερώθη,
to the reclining them the eleven he was manifested,
= to the eleven as they reclined
καὶ ὠνείδισεν τὴν ἀπιστίαν αὐτῶν καὶ
and reproached the disbelief of them and
σκληροκαρδίαν ὅτι τοῖς θεασαμένοις αὐτὸν
hardness of heart because the [ones] beholding him
ἐγηγερμένον οὐκ ἐπίστευσαν. **15** καὶ εἶπεν
having been raised they did not believe. And he said
αὐτοῖς· πορευθέντες εἰς τὸν κόσμον ἅπαντα
to them: Going into [2]the [3]world [1]all
κηρύξατε τὸ εὐαγγέλιον πάσῃ τῇ κτίσει.
proclaim ye the gospel to all the creation.
16 ὁ πιστεύσας καὶ βαπτισθεὶς σωθήσεται,
The [one] believing and being baptized will be saved,
ὁ δὲ ἀπιστήσας κατακριθήσεται. **17** σημεῖα
but the [one] disbelieving will be condemned. [3]signs
δὲ τοῖς πιστεύσασιν ταῦτα παρακολουθήσει·
[1]And [5]the [ones] [6]believing [2]these [4]will follow:
ἐν τῷ ὀνόματί μου δαιμόνια ἐκβαλοῦσιν,
in the name of me demons they will expel,
γλώσσαις λαλήσουσιν καιναῖς, **18** ὄφεις
[3]tongues [1]they will speak [2]with new, serpents
ἀροῦσιν κἂν θανάσιμόν τι πίωσιν
they will take and if [3]deadly [2]anything [1]they drink
οὐ μὴ αὐτοὺς βλάψῃ, ἐπὶ ἀρρώστους χεῖρας
by no means them it will hurt, on sick [ones] hands
ἐπιθήσουσιν καὶ καλῶς ἕξουσιν. **19** Ὁ μὲν
they will place *on* and well they will have. [1]The [4]therefore
= they will recover.
οὖν κύριος [Ἰησοῦς] μετὰ τὸ λαλῆσαι
[2]Lord [3]Jesus after the to speak
= speaking
αὐτοῖς ἀνελήμφθη εἰς τὸν οὐρανὸν καὶ
to them was taken up into – heaven and
ἐκάθισεν ἐκ δεξιῶν τοῦ θεοῦ. **20** ἐκεῖνοι
sat at [the] right [hand] – of God. those
δὲ ἐξελθόντες ἐκήρυξαν πανταχοῦ, τοῦ
But going forth proclaimed everywhere, the
κυρίου συνεργοῦντος καὶ τὸν λόγον
Lord working with and the word
= while the Lord worked with [them] and confirmed the word
βεβαιοῦντος διὰ τῶν ἐπακολουθούντων
confirming[a] through the accompanying
σημείων.
signs.

try. 13These returned and
reported it to the rest; but
they did not believe them
either.
14Later Jesus appeared to
the Eleven as they were
eating; he rebuked them for
their lack of faith and their
stubborn refusal to believe
those who had seen him after he had risen.
15He said to them, "Go
into all the world and
preach the good news to all
creation. 16Whoever believes and is baptized will
be saved, but whoever
does not believe will be
condemned. 17And these
signs will accompany those
who believe: In my name
they will drive out demons;
they will speak in new
tongues; 18they will pick up
snakes with their hands;
and when they drink deadly
poison, it will not hurt them
at all; they will place their
hands on sick people, and
they will get well."
19After the Lord Jesus
had spoken to them, he was
taken up into heaven and
he sat at the right hand of
God. 20Then the disciples
went out and preached everywhere, and the Lord
worked with them and confirmed his word by the
signs that accompanied it.

[v] A few later mss. and versions contain this paragraph, usually after verse 8; a few have it at the end of chapter.

ΚΑΤΑ ΛΟΥΚΑΝ
According to Luke

Luke

Chapter 1

Introduction

INASMUCH as many have undertaken to compile an account of the things accomplished among us,

2just as those who from the beginning were eyewitnesses and servants of the [a]word have handed them down to us,

3it seemed fitting for me as well, having investigated everything carefully from the beginning, to write *it* out for you in consecutive order, most excellent Theophilus;

4so that you might know the exact truth about the things you have been taught.

Birth of John the Baptist Foretold

5In the days of Herod, king of Judea, there was a certain priest named Zacharias, of the division of [b]Abijah; and he had a wife [c]from the daughters of Aaron, and her name was Elizabeth.

6And they were both righteous in the sight of God, walking blamelessly in all the commandments and requirements of the Lord.

7And they had no child, because Elizabeth was barren, and they were both advanced in years.

8Now it came about, while he was performing his priestly service before God in the *appointed* order of his division,

9according to the custom of the priestly office, he was chosen by lot to enter the temple of the Lord and burn incense.

10And the whole multitude of the people were in prayer outside at the hour of the incense offering.

11And an angel of the Lord appeared to him, standing to the right of the altar of incense.

12And Zacharias was troubled when he saw *him,* and fear gripped him.

13But the angel said to him, "Do not be afraid, Zacharias, for your petition has been heard, and your

[a] I.e., gospel
[b] Gr., *Abia*
[c] I.e., of priestly descent

1 Ἐπειδήπερ πολλοὶ ἐπεχείρησαν ἀνατάξασθαι
Since many took in hand to draw up
διήγησιν περὶ τῶν πεπληροφορημένων
a narrative concerning [1]the [3]having been fully carried out
ἐν ἡμῖν πραγμάτων, **2** καθὼς παρέδοσαν ἡμῖν
[4]among [5]us [2]matters, as delivered to us
οἱ ἀπ' ἀρχῆς αὐτόπται καὶ ὑπηρέται
the [ones] from [the] beginning eyewitnesses and attendants
γενόμενοι τοῦ λόγου, **3** ἔδοξε κἀμοὶ
becoming of the Word, it seemed good to me also
παρηκολουθηκότι ἄνωθεν πᾶσιν ἀκριβῶς
having investigated from their source all things accurately
καθεξῆς σοι γράψαι, κράτιστε Θεόφιλε,
[3]in order [2]to thee [1]to write, most excellent Theophilus,
4 ἵνα ἐπιγνῷς περὶ ὧν
that thou mightest know [4]concerning [5]which
κατηχήθης λόγων τὴν ἀσφάλειαν.
[6]thou wast instructed [3]of [the] things [1]the [2]reliability.
5 Ἐγένετο ἐν ταῖς ἡμέραις
There was in the days
Ἡρῴδου βασιλέως τῆς Ἰουδαίας ἱερεύς
of Herod king – of Judæa [2]priest
τις ὀνόματι Ζαχαρίας ἐξ ἐφημερίας Ἀβιά,
[1]a certain by name Zacharias of [the] course of Abia,
καὶ γυνὴ αὐτῷ ἐκ τῶν θυγατέρων Ἀαρών,
and wife to him[c] of the daughters of Aaron,
=his wife
καὶ τὸ ὄνομα αὐτῆς Ἐλισάβετ. **6** ἦσαν δὲ
and the name of her Elisabeth. And they were
δίκαιοι ἀμφότεροι ἐναντίον τοῦ θεοῦ,
righteous both before – God,
πορευόμενοι ἐν πάσαις ταῖς ἐντολαῖς καὶ
going in all the commandments and
δικαιώμασιν τοῦ κυρίου ἄμεμπτοι. **7** καὶ
ordinances of the Lord blameless. And
οὐκ ἦν αὐτοῖς τέκνον, καθότι ἦν ἡ
there was not to them a child,[c] because [2]was –
=they had no child,
Ἐλισάβετ στεῖρα, καὶ ἀμφότεροι προβεβηκότες
[1]Elisabeth barren, and both *having* advanced
ἐν ταῖς ἡμέραις αὐτῶν ἦσαν. **8** Ἐγένετο
in the days of them were. it came to pass
δὲ ἐν τῷ ἱερατεύειν αὐτὸν ἐν τῇ τάξει
Now in the to serve as priest him[be] in the order
=while he served as priest
τῆς ἐφημερίας αὐτοῦ ἔναντι τοῦ θεοῦ,
of the course of him before – God,
9 κατὰ τὸ ἔθος τῆς ἱερατείας ἔλαχε τοῦ
according to the custom of the priesthood his lot was –
θυμιᾶσαι εἰσελθὼν εἰς τὸν ναὸν τοῦ κυρίου,
to burn incense[d] entering into the shrine of the Lord,
10 καὶ πᾶν τὸ πλῆθος ἦν τοῦ λαοῦ
and all [1]the [2]multitude [5]was [3]of the [4]people
προσευχόμενον ἔξω τῇ ὥρᾳ τοῦ θυμιάματος.
praying outside at the hour – of incense.
11 ὤφθη δὲ αὐτῷ ἄγγελος κυρίου ἑστὼς
And there appeared to him an angel of [the] Lord standing
ἐκ δεξιῶν τοῦ θυσιαστηρίου τοῦ θυμιάματος.
on [the] right of the altar – of incense.
12 καὶ ἐταράχθη Ζαχαρίας ἰδών, καὶ φόβος
And was troubled Zacharias seeing, and fear
ἐπέπεσεν ἐπ' αὐτόν. **13** εἶπεν δὲ πρὸς
fell *on* upon him. But said to
αὐτὸν ὁ ἄγγελος· μὴ φοβοῦ, Ζαχαρία,
him the angel: Fear not, Zacharias,
διότι εἰσηκούσθη ἡ δέησίς σου, καὶ ἡ
because was heard the request of thee, and the

Luke

Chapter 1

Introduction

MANY have undertaken to draw up an account of the things that have been fulfilled[a] among us,
2just as they were handed down to us by those who from the first were eyewitnesses and servants of the word.
3Therefore, since I myself have carefully investigated everything from the beginning, it seemed good also to me to write an orderly account for you, most excellent Theophilus,
4so that you may know the certainty of the things you have been taught.

The Birth of John the Baptist Foretold

5In the time of Herod king of Judea there was a priest named Zechariah, who belonged to the priestly division of Abijah; his wife Elizabeth was also a descendant of Aaron.
6Both of them were upright in the sight of God, observing all the Lord's commandments and regulations blamelessly.
7But they had no children, because Elizabeth was barren; and they were both well along in years.
8Once when Zechariah's division was on duty and he was serving as priest before God,
9he was chosen by lot, according to the custom of the priesthood, to go into the temple of the Lord and burn incense.
10And when the time for the burning of incense came, all the assembled worshipers were praying outside.
11Then an angel of the Lord appeared to him, standing at the right side of the altar of incense.
12When Zechariah saw him, he was startled and was gripped with fear.
13But the angel said to him: "Do not be afraid, Zechariah; your prayer has been heard. Your wife Elizabeth

[a] 1 Or *been surely believed*

wife Elizabeth will bear
you a son, and you will give
him the name John.
14"And you will have joy
and gladness, and many
will rejoice at his birth.
15"For he will be great in
the sight of the Lord, and
he will drink no wine or li-
quor; and he will be filled
with the Holy Spirit, while
yet in his mother's womb.
16"And he will turn back
many of the sons of Israel
to the Lord their God.
17"And it is he who will
go *as a forerunner* before
Him in the spirit and power
of Elijah, TO TURN THE
HEARTS OF THE FATHERS
BACK TO THE CHILDREN, and
the disobedient to the attitude of the righteous; so as
to make ready a people prepared for the Lord."
18And Zacharias said to
the angel, "How shall I
know this *for certain*? For I
am an old man, and my wife
is advanced in years."
19And the angel answered
and said to him, "I am Gabriel, who stands in the
presence of God; and I
have been sent to speak to
you, and to bring you this
good news.
20"And behold, you shall
be silent and unable to
speak until the day when
these things take place, because you did not believe
my words, which shall be
fulfilled in their proper
time."
21And the people were
waiting for Zacharias, and
were wondering at his
delay in the temple.
22But when he came out,
he was unable to speak to
them; and they realized
that he had seen a vision in
the temple; and he kept
making signs to them, and
remained mute.

γυνή σου Ἐλισάβετ γεννήσει υἱόν σοι,
wife of thee Elisabeth will bear a son to thee,
καὶ καλέσεις τὸ ὄνομα αὐτοῦ Ἰωάννην·
and thou shalt call the name of him John;
14 καὶ ἔσται χαρά σοι καὶ ἀγαλλίασις,
and there shall be joy to thee and gladness,[c]
=thou shalt have joy and gladness,
καὶ πολλοὶ ἐπὶ τῇ γενέσει αὐτοῦ χαρή-
and many over the birth of him will
σονται. 15 ἔσται γὰρ μέγας ἐνώπιον
rejoice. For he will be great in the eyes of
κυρίου, καὶ οἶνον καὶ σίκερα οὐ μὴ
[the] Lord, and wine and strong drink by no means
πίῃ, καὶ πνεύματος ἁγίου πλησθήσεται
may he drink, and of(with) Spirit [the] Holy he will be filled
ἔτι ἐκ κοιλίας μητρὸς αὐτοῦ, 16 καὶ
even from [the] womb of [the] mother of him, and
πολλοὺς τῶν υἱῶν Ἰσραὴλ ἐπιστρέψει ἐπὶ κύριον
many of the sons of Israel he will turn to [the] Lord
τὸν θεὸν αὐτῶν· 17 καὶ αὐτὸς προελεύσεται
the God of them; and he will go *before*
ἐνώπιον αὐτοῦ ἐν πνεύματι καὶ δυνάμει
before him in [the] spirit and power
Ἠλίου, ἐπιστρέψαι καρδίας πατέρων ἐπὶ
of Elias, to turn [the] hearts of fathers to
τέκνα καὶ ἀπειθεῖς ἐν φρονήσει
children and disobedient [ones] to [the] understanding
δικαίων, ἑτοιμάσαι κυρίῳ λαὸν κατεσκευασ-
of [the] just, to prepare for [the] Lord a people *having been*
μένον. 18 καὶ εἶπεν Ζαχαρίας πρὸς τὸν ἄγγελον·
prepared. And said Zacharias to the angel:
κατὰ τί γνώσομαι τοῦτο; ἐγὼ γάρ εἰμι
By what shall I know this? for I am
πρεσβύτης καὶ ἡ γυνή μου προβεβηκυῖα
old and the wife of me *having* advanced
ἐν ταῖς ἡμέραις αὐτῆς. 19 καὶ ἀποκριθεὶς
in the days of her. And answering
ὁ ἄγγελος εἶπεν αὐτῷ· ἐγώ εἰμι Γαβριὴλ
the angel said to him: I am Gabriel
ὁ παρεστηκὼς ἐνώπιον τοῦ θεοῦ, καὶ
the [one] standing before – God, and
ἀπεστάλην λαλῆσαι πρὸς σὲ καὶ εὐαγ-
I was sent to speak to thee and to
γελίσασθαι σοι ταῦτα· 20 καὶ ἰδοὺ
announce to thee these things; and behold
ἔσῃ σιωπῶν καὶ μὴ δυνάμενος λαλῆσαι
thou shalt be being silent and not being able to speak
ἄχρι ἧς ἡμέρας γένηται ταῦτα, ἀνθ' ὧν οὐκ
until which day happen*s* these things, because not
=the day when these things happen,
ἐπίστευσας τοῖς λόγοις μου, οἵτινες πληρω-
thou believedst the words of me, which will be
θήσονται εἰς τὸν καιρὸν αὐτῶν. 21 καὶ ἦν
fulfilled in the time of them. And was
ὁ λαὸς προσδοκῶν τὸν Ζαχαρίαν, καὶ
the people expecting – Zacharias, and
ἐθαύμαζον ἐν τῷ χρονίζειν ἐν τῷ ναῷ
they marvelled in(at) the to delay in the shrine
=when he delayed in the shrine.
αὐτόν. 22 ἐξελθὼν δὲ οὐκ ἐδύνατο λαλῆσαι
him.[be] And going out he was not able to speak
αὐτοῖς καὶ ἐπέγνωσαν ὅτι ὀπτασίαν ἑώρακεν
to them, and they knew that a vision he has(had) seen
ἐν τῷ ναῷ· καὶ αὐτὸς ἦν διανεύων
in the shrine; and he was beckoning
αὐτοῖς, καὶ διέμενεν κωφός. 23 καὶ
to them, and remained dumb. And

will bear you a son, and you
are to give him the name
John. 14He will be a joy and
delight to you, and many
will rejoice because of his
birth, 15for he will be great
in the sight of the Lord. He
is never to take wine or other fermented drink, and he
will be filled with the Holy
Spirit even from birth.[b]
16Many of the people of Israel will he bring back to
the Lord their God. 17And
he will go on before the
Lord, in the spirit and power of Elijah, to turn the
hearts of the fathers to their
children and the disobedient to the wisdom of the
righteous—to make ready
a people prepared for the
Lord."
18Zechariah asked the an-
gel, "How can I be sure of
this? I am an old man and
my wife is well along in
years."
19The angel answered, "I
am Gabriel. I stand in the
presence of God, and I
have been sent to speak to
you and to tell you this
good news. 20And now you
will be silent and not able to
speak until the day this
happens, because you did
not believe my words,
which will come true at
their proper time."
21Meanwhile, the people
were waiting for Zechariah
and wondering why he
stayed so long in the temple. 22When he came out,
he could not speak to them.
They realized he had seen a
vision in the temple, for he
kept making signs to them
but remained unable to
speak.

[b]15 Or *from his mother's womb*

23And it came about, when the days of his priestly service were ended, that he went back home.

24And after these days Elizabeth his wife became pregnant; and she kept herself in seclusion for five months, saying,

25"This is the way the Lord has dealt with me in the days when He looked *with favor* upon *me,* to take away my disgrace among men."

Jesus' Birth Foretold

26Now in the sixth month the angel Gabriel was sent from God to a city in Galilee, called Nazareth,

27to a virgin engaged to a man whose name was Joseph, of the descendants of David; and the virgin's name was Mary.

28And coming in, he said to her, "Hail, favored one! The Lord *is* with you."[d]

29But she was greatly troubled at *this* statement, and kept pondering what kind of salutation this might be.

30And the angel said to her, "Do not be afraid, Mary; for you have found favor with God.

31"And behold, you will conceive in your womb, and bear a son, and you shall name Him Jesus.

32"He will be great, and will be called the Son of the Most High; and the Lord God will give Him the throne of His father David;

33and He will reign over the house of Jacob forever; and His kingdom will have no end."

34And Mary said to the angel, "How can this be, since I am a virgin?"

35And the angel answered and said to her, "The Holy Spirit will come upon you, and the power of the Most High will overshadow you; and for that reason the holy

[d] Later mss. add: *you are blessed among women*

ἐγένετο ὡς ἐπλήσθησαν αἱ ἡμέραι τῆς
it came to pass when were fulfilled the days of the
λειτουργίας αὐτοῦ, ἀπῆλθεν εἰς τὸν οἶκον
service of him, he went away to the house
αὐτοῦ. **24** Μετὰ δὲ ταύτας τὰς ἡμέρας
of him. And after these – days
συνέλαβεν Ἐλισάβετ ἡ γυνὴ αὐτοῦ, καὶ
conceived Elisabeth the wife of him, and
περιέκρυβεν ἑαυτὴν μῆνας πέντε, λέγουσα
hid herself months five, saying[,]
25 ὅτι οὕτως μοι πεποίηκεν κύριος ἐν
– Thus to me has done [the] Lord in
ἡμέραις αἷς ἐπεῖδεν ἀφελεῖν ὄνειδός
days in which he looked upon to take away reproach
μου ἐν ἀνθρώποις.
of me among men.
26 Ἐν δὲ τῷ μηνὶ τῷ ἕκτῳ ἀπεστάλη
Now in the month – sixth was sent
ὁ ἄγγελος Γαβριὴλ ἀπὸ τοῦ θεοῦ εἰς
the angel Gabriel from – God to
πόλιν τῆς Γαλιλαίας ᾗ ὄνομα Ναζαρέθ,
a city – of Galilee to which name[e] Nazareth,
= the name of which [was]
27 πρὸς παρθένον ἐμνηστευμένην ἀνδρὶ ᾧ ὄνομα
to a virgin *having been* betrothed to a man to whom name[e]
Ἰωσήφ, ἐξ οἴκου Δαυίδ, καὶ τὸ ὄνομα
Joseph, of [the] house of David, and the name
τῆς παρθένου Μαριάμ. **28** καὶ εἰσελθὼν
of the virgin [was] Mary. And entering
πρὸς αὐτὴν εἶπεν· χαῖρε, κεχαριτωμένη, ὁ
to her he said : Hail, *having been* favoured [one], the
κύριος μετὰ σοῦ. **29** ἡ δὲ ἐπὶ τῷ λόγῳ
Lord [is] with thee. And she at the saying
διεταράχθη, καὶ διελογίζετο ποταπὸς εἴη
was greatly disturbed, and considered of what sort [3]might be
ὁ ἀσπασμὸς οὗτος. **30** καὶ εἶπεν ὁ ἄγγελος
– [2]greeting [1]this. And said the angel
αὐτῇ· μὴ φοβοῦ, Μαριάμ· εὗρες γὰρ
to her : Fear not, Mary : for thou didst find
χάριν παρὰ τῷ θεῷ. **31** καὶ ἰδοὺ συλλήμψῃ
favour with – God. And behold thou wilt conceive
ἐν γαστρὶ καὶ τέξῃ υἱόν, καὶ καλέσεις τὸ
in womb and bear a son, and thou shalt call the
ὄνομα αὐτοῦ Ἰησοῦν. **32** οὗτος ἔσται μέγας
name of him Jesus. This will be great
καὶ υἱὸς ὑψίστου κληθήσεται, καὶ δώσει
and Son of [the] Most High will be called, and will give
αὐτῷ κύριος ὁ θεὸς τὸν θρόνον Δαυὶδ
him [the] Lord – God the throne of David
τοῦ πατρὸς αὐτοῦ, **33** καὶ βασιλεύσει ἐπὶ
the father of him, and he will reign over
τὸν οἶκον Ἰακὼβ εἰς τοὺς αἰῶνας, καὶ
the house of Jacob unto the ages, and
=for ever,
τῆς βασιλείας αὐτοῦ οὐκ ἔσται τέλος.
of the kingdom of him there will not be an end.
34 εἶπεν δὲ Μαριὰμ πρὸς τὸν ἄγγελον·
And said Mary to the angel :
πῶς ἔσται τοῦτο, ἐπεὶ ἄνδρα οὐ γινώσκω;
How will be this, since a man I know not?
35 καὶ ἀποκριθεὶς ὁ ἄγγελος εἶπεν αὐτῇ·
And answering the angel said to her :
πνεῦμα ἅγιον ἐπελεύσεται ἐπὶ σέ, καὶ
[1][The] [3]Spirit [2]Holy will come *upon* upon thee, and
δύναμις ὑψίστου ἐπισκιάσει σοι· διὸ
[the] power of [the] Most High will overshadow thee; wherefore

23When his time of ser-
vice was completed, he returned home. 24After this
his wife Elizabeth became
pregnant and for five
months remained in seclu-
sion. 25"The Lord has done
this for me," she said. "In
these days he has shown
his favor and taken away
my disgrace among the
people."

The Birth of Jesus Foretold

26In the sixth month, God
sent the angel Gabriel to
Nazareth, a town in Gali-
lee, 27to a virgin pledged to
be married to a man named
Joseph, a descendant of
David. The virgin's name
was Mary. 28The angel
went to her and said,
"Greetings, you who are
highly favored! The Lord is
with you."
29Mary was greatly trou-
bled at his words and wondered what kind of greeting
this might be. 30But the angel said to her, "Do not be
afraid, Mary, you have
found favor with God.
31You will be with child and
give birth to a son, and you
are to give him the name
Jesus. 32He will be great
and will be called the Son of
the Most High. The Lord
God will give him the
throne of his father David,
33and he will reign over the
house of Jacob forever; his
kingdom will never end."
34"How will this be,"
Mary asked the angel,
"since I am a virgin?"
35The angel answered,
"The Holy Spirit will come
upon you, and the power of
the Most High will over-
shadow you. So the holy

offspring shall be called the Son of God.
36"And behold, even your relative Elizabeth has also conceived a son in her old age; and she who was called barren is now in her sixth month.
37"For nothing will be impossible with God."
38And Mary said, "Behold, the [e]bondslave of the Lord; be it done to me according to your word." And the angel departed from her.

Mary Visits Elizabeth

39Now at this time Mary arose and went with haste to the hill country, to a city of Judah,
40and entered the house of Zacharias and greeted Elizabeth.
41And it came about that when Elizabeth heard Mary's greeting, the baby leaped in her womb; and Elizabeth was filled with the Holy Spirit.
42And she cried out with a loud voice, and said, "Blessed among women *are* you, and blessed *is* the fruit of your womb!
43"And how has it *happened* to me, that the mother of my Lord should come to me?
44"For behold, when the sound of your greeting reached my ears, the baby leaped in my womb for joy.
45"And blessed *is* she who believed that there would be a fulfillment of what had been spoken to her by the Lord."

The Magnificat

46And Mary said:
"My soul exalts the Lord,
47"And my spirit has rejoiced in God my Savior.
48"For He has had regard for the humble state of His bondslave;
For behold, from this time on all generations will count me blessed.
49"For the Mighty One has done great things for me;

[e] I.e., female slave

καὶ τὸ γεννώμενον ἅγιον κληθήσεται υἱὸς θεοῦ.
also the thing being born holy will be called[,] Son of God.
36 καὶ ἰδοὺ Ἐλισάβετ ἡ συγγενίς σου καὶ
And behold Elisabeth the relative of thee also
αὐτὴ συνείληφεν υἱὸν ἐν γήρει αὐτῆς, καὶ
she conceived a son in old age of her, and
οὗτος μὴν ἕκτος ἐστὶν αὐτῇ τῇ καλουμένῃ
this month sixth is with her the [one] *being* called
στείρᾳ· **37** ὅτι οὐκ ἀδυνατήσει παρὰ τοῦ
barren; because will not be impossible with –
θεοῦ πᾶν ῥῆμα. **38** εἶπεν δὲ Μαριάμ· ἰδοὺ ἡ
God every word. And said Mary: Behold[,] the
δούλη κυρίου· γένοιτό μοι κατὰ
handmaid of [the] Lord; may it be to me according to
τὸ ῥῆμά σου. καὶ ἀπῆλθεν ἀπ' αὐτῆς
the word of thee. And went away from her
ὁ ἄγγελος. **39** Ἀναστᾶσα δὲ Μαριὰμ ἐν
the angel. And rising up Mary in
ταῖς ἡμέραις ταύταις ἐπορεύθη εἰς τὴν
– days these she went to the
ὀρεινὴν μετὰ σπουδῆς εἰς πόλιν Ἰούδα,
mountain country with haste to a city of Juda,
40 καὶ εἰσῆλθεν εἰς τὸν οἶκον Ζαχαρίου
and entered into the house of Zacharias
καὶ ἠσπάσατο τὴν Ἐλισάβετ. **41** καὶ
and greeted – Elisabeth. And
ἐγένετο ὡς ἤκουσεν τὸν ἀσπασμὸν τῆς
it came to pass when [2]heard [3]the [4]greeting –
Μαρίας ἡ Ἐλισάβετ, ἐσκίρτησεν τὸ βρέφος
[5]of Mary – [1]Elisabeth, leaped the babe
ἐν τῇ κοιλίᾳ αὐτῆς, καὶ ἐπλήσθη πνεύματος
in the womb of her, and [2]was filled [3]of(with) [5]Spirit
ἁγίου ἡ Ἐλισάβετ, **42** καὶ ἀνεφώνησεν
[4][the] Holy – [1]Elisabeth, and she called out
κραυγῇ μεγάλῃ καὶ εἶπεν· εὐλογημένη
cry with a great and said: Blessed [art]
σὺ ἐν γυναιξίν, καὶ εὐλογημένος ὁ καρπὸς
thou among women, and blessed [is] the fruit
τῆς κοιλίας σου. **43** καὶ πόθεν μοι τοῦτο
of the womb of thee. And whence to me this
ἵνα ἔλθῃ ἡ μήτηρ τοῦ κυρίου μου πρὸς
that comes the mother of the Lord of me to
ἐμέ; **44** ἰδοὺ γὰρ ὡς ἐγένετο ἡ φωνὴ τοῦ
me? For behold when came the sound of the
ἀσπασμοῦ σου εἰς τὰ ὦτά μου, ἐσκίρτησεν
greeting of thee in the ears of me, leaped
ἐν ἀγαλλιάσει τὸ βρέφος ἐν τῇ κοιλίᾳ
in gladness the babe in the womb
μου. **45** καὶ μακαρία ἡ πιστεύσασα ὅτι
of me. And blessed the [one] believing because
ἔσται τελείωσις τοῖς λελαλημένοις αὐτῇ
there shall be a completion to the things *having been spoken* to her
παρὰ κυρίου. **46** Καὶ εἶπεν Μαριάμ·
from [the] Lord. And said Mary:
Μεγαλύνει ἡ ψυχή μου τὸν κύριον, **47** καὶ
Magnifies the soul of me the Lord, and
ἠγαλλίασεν τὸ πνεῦμά μου ἐπὶ τῷ θεῷ
exulted the spirit of me in – God
τῷ σωτῆρί μου· **48** ὅτι ἐπέβλεψεν ἐπὶ τὴν
the saviour of me; because he looked *on* upon the
ταπείνωσιν τῆς δούλης αὐτοῦ. ἰδοὺ γὰρ
humiliation of the handmaid of him. For behold
ἀπὸ τοῦ νῦν μακαριοῦσίν με πᾶσαι αἱ
from – now [4]will [5]deem [7]blessed [6]me [1]all [2]the
γενεαί· **49** ὅτι ἐποίησέν μοι μεγάλα ὁ
[3]generations; because did to me great things the

one to be born will be called[c] the Son of God.
36Even Elizabeth your relative is going to have a child in her old age, and she who was said to be barren is in her sixth month.
37For nothing is impossible with God."
38"I am the Lord's servant," Mary answered. "May it be to me as you have said." Then the angel left her.

Mary Visits Elizabeth

39At that time Mary got ready and hurried to a town in the hill country of Judea,
40where she entered Zechariah's home and greeted Elizabeth.
41When Elizabeth heard Mary's greeting, the baby leaped in her womb, and Elizabeth was filled with the Holy Spirit.
42In a loud voice she exclaimed: "Blessed are you among women, and blessed is the child you will bear!
43But why am I so favored, that the mother of my Lord should come to me?
44As soon as the sound of your greeting reached my ears, the baby in my womb leaped for joy.
45Blessed is she who has believed that what the Lord has said to her will be accomplished!"

Mary's Song

46And Mary said:
"My soul glorifies the Lord
47 and my spirit rejoices in God my Savior,
48for he has been mindful of the humble state of his servant.
From now on all generations will call me blessed,
49 for the Mighty One has done great things for me—

[c]35 Or *So the child to be born will be called holy,*

And holy is His name.
50 "AND HIS MERCY IS UPON GENERATION AFTER GENERATION
TOWARD THOSE WHO FEAR HIM.
51 "He has done mighty deeds with His arm;
He has scattered *those who were* proud in the thoughts of their heart.
52 "He has brought down rulers from *their* thrones,
And has exalted those who were humble.
53 "HE HAS FILLED THE HUNGRY WITH GOOD THINGS;
And sent away the rich empty-handed.
54 "He has given help to Israel His servant,
In remembrance of His mercy,
55 As He spoke to our fathers,
To Abraham and his offspring forever."
56 And Mary stayed with her about three months, and *then* returned to her home.

John Is Born

57 Now the time had come for Elizabeth to give birth, and she brought forth a son.
58 And her neighbors and her relatives heard that the Lord had displayed His great mercy toward her; and they were rejoicing with her.
59 And it came about that on the eighth day they came to circumcise the child, and they were going to call him Zacharias, after his father.
60 And his mother answered and said, "No indeed; but he shall be called John."
61 And they said to her, "There is no one among your relatives who is called by that name."
62 And they made signs to his father, as to what he wanted him called.
63 And he asked for a tablet, and wrote as follows, "His name is John." And they were all astonished.
64 And at once his mouth was opened and his tongue

δυνατός. καὶ ἅγιον τὸ ὄνομα αὐτοῦ,
Mighty [one]. And holy the name of him,
50 καὶ τὸ ἔλεος αὐτοῦ εἰς γενεὰς καὶ
and the mercy of him to generations and
γενεὰς τοῖς φοβουμένοις αὐτόν. 51 Ἐποίησεν
generations to the [ones] fearing him. He did
κράτος ἐν βραχίονι αὐτοῦ, διεσκόρπισεν
might with [the] arm of him, he scattered
ὑπερηφάνους διανοίᾳ καρδίας αὐτῶν·
haughty [ones] in [the] understanding of [the] heart of them;
52 καθεῖλεν δυνάστας ἀπὸ θρόνων καὶ ὕψω-
he pulled down potentates from thrones and exalt-
σεν ταπεινούς, 53 πεινῶντας ἐνέπλησεν
ed humble [ones], hungering [ones] he filled
ἀγαθῶν καὶ πλουτοῦντας ἐξαπέστειλεν
of(with) good things and rich [ones] he sent away
κενούς. 54 ἀντελάβετο Ἰσραὴλ παιδὸς αὐτοῦ,
empty. He succoured Israel servant of him,
μνησθῆναι ἐλέους, 55 καθὼς ἐλάλησεν
to remember mercy, as he spoke
πρὸς τοὺς πατέρας ἡμῶν, τῷ Ἀβραὰμ
to the fathers of us, – to Abraham
καὶ τῷ σπέρματι αὐτοῦ εἰς τὸν αἰῶνα.
and to the seed of him unto the age.
=for ever.
56 Ἔμεινεν δὲ Μαριὰμ σὺν αὐτῇ ὡς
And remained Mary with her about
μῆνας τρεῖς, καὶ ὑπέστρεψεν εἰς τὸν
months three, and returned to the
οἶκον αὐτῆς.
house of her.
57 Τῇ δὲ Ἐλισάβετ ἐπλήσθη ὁ χρόνος
– Now [4]to Elisabeth [3]was fulfilled [1]the [2]time
τοῦ τεκεῖν αὐτήν, καὶ ἐγέννησεν υἱόν.
– to bear her,[bd] and she brought forth a son.
=that she should bear,
58 καὶ ἤκουσαν οἱ περίοικοι καὶ οἱ
And heard the neighbours and the
συγγενεῖς αὐτῆς ὅτι ἐμεγάλυνεν κύριος τὸ
relatives of her that magnified [the] Lord the
ἔλεος αὐτοῦ μετ' αὐτῆς, καὶ συνέχαιρον
mercy of him with her, and they rejoiced with
αὐτῇ. 59 Καὶ ἐγένετο ἐν τῇ ἡμέρᾳ τῇ
her. And it came to pass on the day –
ὀγδόῃ ἦλθον περιτεμεῖν τὸ παιδίον, καὶ
eighth they came to circumcise the child, and
ἐκάλουν αὐτὸ ἐπὶ τῷ ὀνόματι τοῦ πατρὸς
were calling it(him) by the name of the father
αὐτοῦ Ζαχαρίαν. 60 καὶ ἀποκριθεῖσα ἡ
of him Zacharias. And answering the
μήτηρ αὐτοῦ εἶπεν· οὐχί, ἀλλὰ κληθήσεται
mother of him said: No, but he shall be called
Ἰωάννης. 61 καὶ εἶπαν πρὸς αὐτὴν ὅτι
John. And they said to her[,] –
οὐδείς ἐστιν ἐκ τῆς συγγενείας σου ὃς
No one there is of the kindred of thee who
καλεῖται τῷ ὀνόματι τούτῳ. 62 ἐνένευον
is called – name by this. they nodded
δὲ τῷ πατρὶ αὐτοῦ τὸ τί ἂν θέλοι
And to the father of him – what he might wish
καλεῖσθαι αὐτό. 63 καὶ αἰτήσας πινακίδιον
[2]to be called [1]him. And asking for a tablet
ἔγραψεν λέγων· Ἰωάννης ἐστὶν ὄνομα
he wrote saying: John is name
αὐτοῦ. καὶ ἐθαύμασαν πάντες. 64 ἀνεῴχθη δὲ
of him. And they marvelled all. And was opened
τὸ στόμα αὐτοῦ παραχρῆμα καὶ ἡ
the mouth of him instantly and the

holy is his name.
50 His mercy extends to those who fear him,
from generation to generation.
51 He has performed mighty deeds with his arm;
he has scattered those who are proud in their inmost thoughts.
52 He has brought down rulers from their thrones
but has lifted up the humble.
53 He has filled the hungry with good things
but has sent the rich away empty.
54 He has helped his servant Israel,
remembering to be merciful
55 to Abraham and his descendants forever,
even as he said to our fathers."

56 Mary stayed with Elizabeth for about three months and then returned home.

The Birth of John the Baptist

57 When it was time for
Elizabeth to have her baby,
she gave birth to a son.
58 Her neighbors and relatives heard that the Lord
had shown her great mer-
cy, and they shared her joy.
59 On the eighth day they
came to circumcise the
child, and they were going
to name him after his father
Zechariah, 60 but his mother
spoke up and said, "No!
He is to be called John."
61 They said to her,
"There is no one among
your relatives who has that
name."
62 Then they made signs to
his father, to find out what
he would like to name the
child. 63 He asked for a writing tablet, and to every-
one's astonishment he
wrote, "His name is
John." 64 Immediately his
mouth was opened and his

loosed, and he *began* to speak in praise of God.
65And fear came on all those living around them; and all these matters were being talked about in all the hill country of Judea.
66And all who heard them kept them in mind, saying, "What then will this child *turn out to* be?" For the hand of the Lord was certainly with him.

Zacharias' Prophecy

67And his father Zacharias was filled with the Holy Spirit, and prophesied, saying:
68"Blessed *be* the Lord God of Israel,
For He has visited us and accomplished redemption for His people,
69 And has raised up a horn of salvation for us
In the house of David His servant—
70 As He spoke by the mouth of His holy prophets from of old—
71 Salvation FROM OUR ENEMIES,
And FROM THE HAND OF ALL WHO HATE US;
72 To show mercy toward our fathers,
And to remember His holy covenant,
73 The oath which He swore to Abraham our father,
74 To grant us that we, being delivered from the hand of our enemies,
Might serve Him without fear,
75 In holiness and righteousness before Him all our days.
76"And you, child, will be called the prophet of the Most High;
For you will go on BEFORE THE LORD TO PREPARE HIS WAYS;
77 To give to His people *the* knowledge of salvation
By the forgiveness of their sins,
78 Because of the tender mercy of our God,
With which the Sunrise from on high shall visit us,
79 TO SHINE UPON THOSE WHO SIT IN DARKNESS AND THE SHADOW OF DEATH,

γλῶσσα αὐτοῦ, καὶ ἐλάλει εὐλογῶν τὸν
tongue of him, and he spoke blessing –
θεόν. 65 Καὶ ἐγένετο ἐπὶ πάντας φόβος
God. And [2]came [3]on [4]all [1]fear
τοὺς περιοικοῦντας αὐτούς, καὶ ἐν ὅλῃ τῇ
the [ones] dwelling round them, and in all the
ὀρεινῇ τῆς Ἰουδαίας διελαλεῖτο πάντα
mountain country – of Judæa [4]were talked over [1]all
τὰ ῥήματα ταῦτα, 66 καὶ ἔθεντο πάντες
– [3]facts [2]these, and [4]put [1]all
οἱ ἀκούσαντες ἐν τῇ καρδίᾳ αὐτῶν,
[2]the [ones] [3]hearing in the heart of them,
λέγοντες· τί ἄρα τὸ παιδίον τοῦτο ἔσται;
saying: What then – child this will be?
καὶ γὰρ χεὶρ κυρίου ἦν μετ' αὐτοῦ.
for indeed [the] hand of [the] Lord was with him.
67 Καὶ Ζαχαρίας ὁ πατὴρ αὐτοῦ ἐπλήσθη
And Zacharias the father of him was filled
πνεύματος ἁγίου καὶ ἐπροφήτευσεν λέγων·
of(with) Spirit [the] Holy and prophesied saying:
68 Εὐλογητὸς κύριος ὁ θεὸς τοῦ Ἰσραήλ,
Blessed [be] [the] Lord the God – of Israel,
ὅτι ἐπεσκέψατο καὶ ἐποίησεν λύτρωσιν τῷ
because he visited and wrought redemption for the
λαῷ αὐτοῦ, 69 καὶ ἤγειρεν κέρας σωτηρίας
people of him, and raised a horn of salvation
ἡμῖν ἐν οἴκῳ Δαυὶδ παιδὸς αὐτοῦ, 70 καθὼς
for us in [the] house of David servant of him, as
ἐλάλησεν διὰ στόματος τῶν ἁγίων ἀπ'
he spoke through [the] mouth of the [1]holy [4]from
αἰῶνος προφητῶν αὐτοῦ, 71 σωτηρίαν ἐξ
[5][the] age [2]prophets [3]of him, salvation out of
ἐχθρῶν ἡμῶν καὶ ἐκ χειρὸς πάντων τῶν
[the] enemies of us and out of [the] hand of all the [ones]
μισούντων ἡμᾶς, 72 ποιῆσαι ἔλεος μετὰ
hating us, to perform mercy with
τῶν πατέρων ἡμῶν καὶ μνησθῆναι διαθήκης
the fathers of us and to remember [the] covenant
ἁγίας αὐτοῦ, 73 ὅρκον ὃν ὤμοσεν πρὸς Ἀβραὰμ
holy of him, [the] oath which he swore to Abraham
τὸν πατέρα ἡμῶν, 74 τοῦ δοῦναι ἡμῖν
the father of us, – to give[d] us
ἀφόβως ἐκ χειρὸς ἐχθρῶν ῥυσθέντας
[5]fearlessly [2]out of [3][the] hand [4]of [our] enemies [1]having been delivered
λατρεύειν αὐτῷ 75 ἐν ὁσιότητι καὶ δικαιοσύνῃ
[6]to serve him in holiness and righteousness
ἐνώπιον αὐτοῦ πάσαις ταῖς ἡμέραις ἡμῶν.
before him all the days[e] of us.
76 Καὶ σὺ δέ, παιδίον, προφήτης ὑψίστου
And thou also, child, a prophet of [the] Most High
κληθήσῃ· προπορεύσῃ γὰρ ἐνώπιον κυρίου
wilt be called; for thou wilt go *before* before [the] Lord
ἑτοιμάσαι ὁδοὺς αὐτοῦ, 77 τοῦ δοῦναι
to prepare [the] ways of him, – to give[d]
γνῶσιν σωτηρίας τῷ λαῷ αὐτοῦ ἐν
a knowledge of salvation to the people of him by
ἀφέσει ἁμαρτιῶν αὐτῶν, 78 διὰ σπλάγχνα·
forgiveness of sins of them, because of [the] bowels
ἐλέους θεοῦ ἡμῶν, ἐν οἷς ἐπισκέψεται
of mercy of God of us, whereby will visit
ἡμᾶς ἀνατολὴ ἐξ ὕψους, 79 ἐπιφᾶναι τοῖς
us a [sun]rising from [the] height, to appear [1]to the [ones]
ἐν σκότει καὶ σκιᾷ θανάτου καθημένοις,
[2]in [4]darkness [5]and [6]in a shadow [7]of death [3]sitting,

tongue was loosed, and he began to speak, praising God. 65The neighbors were all filled with awe, and throughout the hill country of Judea people were talking about all these things. 66Everyone who heard this wondered about it, asking, "What then is this child going to be?" For the Lord's hand was with him.

Zechariah's Song

67His father Zechariah was filled with the Holy Spirit and prophesied:
68"Praise be to the Lord, the God of Israel,
because he has come and has redeemed his people.
69He has raised up a horn[d] of salvation for us
in the house of his servant David
70(as he said through his holy prophets of long ago),
71salvation from our enemies
and from the hand of all who hate us—
72to show mercy to our fathers
and to remember his holy covenant,
73 the oath he swore to our father Abraham:
74to rescue us from the hand of our enemies,
and to enable us to serve him without fear
75 in holiness and righteousness before him all our days.
76And you, my child, will be called a prophet of the Most High;
for you will go on before the Lord to prepare the way for him,
77to give his people the knowledge of salvation
through the forgiveness of their sins,
78because of the tender mercy of our God,
by which the rising sun will come to us from heaven
79to shine on those living in darkness
and in the shadow of death,

[d]69 *Horn* here symbolizes strength.

To guide our feet into
the way of peace."
80 And the child continued
to grow, and to become
strong in spirit, and he lived
in the deserts until the day
of his public appearance to
Israel.

Chapter 2

Jesus' Birth in Bethlehem

NOW it came about in
those days that a de-
cree went out from Caesar
Augustus, that a census be
taken of all [f]the inhabited
earth.
2 This was the first cen-
sus taken while [g]Quirinius
was governor of Syria.
3 And all were proceed-
ing to register for the census, everyone to his own
city.
4 And Joseph also went
up from Galilee, from the
city of Nazareth, to Judea,
to the city of David, which
is called Bethlehem, be-
cause he was of the house
and family of David,
5 in order to register,
along with Mary, who was
engaged to him, and was
with child.
6 And it came about that
while they were there, the
days were completed for
her to give birth.
7 And she gave birth to
her first-born son; and she
wrapped Him in cloths, and
laid Him in a manger, be-
cause there was no room
for them in the inn.
8 And in the same region
there were *some* shepherds
staying out in the fields,
and keeping watch over
their flock by night.
9 And an angel of the
Lord suddenly stood be-
fore them, and the glory of
the Lord shone around
them; and they were terribly frightened.
10 And the angel said to
them, "Do not be afraid;
for behold, I bring you

τοῦ κατευθῦναι τοὺς πόδας ἡμῶν εἰς ὁδὸν
– to guide[d] the feet of us into a way
εἰρήνης.
of peace.
80 Τὸ δὲ παιδίον ηὔξανεν καὶ ἐκραταιοῦτο
And the child grew and became strong
πνεύματι, καὶ ἦν ἐν ταῖς ἐρήμοις ἕως
in spirit, and was in the deserts until
ἡμέρας ἀναδείξεως αὐτοῦ πρὸς τὸν Ἰσραήλ.
[the] days of showing of him to – Israel.

2 Ἐγένετο δὲ ἐν ταῖς ἡμέραις ἐκείναις
Now it came to pass in – days those
ἐξῆλθεν δόγμα παρὰ Καίσαρος Αὐγούστου
went out a decree from Cæsar Augustus
ἀπογράφεσθαι πᾶσαν τὴν οἰκουμένην. 2 αὕτη
to be enrolled all the inhabited earth. This
ἀπογραφὴ πρώτη ἐγένετο ἡγεμονεύοντος τῆς
[2]enrolment [1]first was governing –
=when Cyrenius governed Syria.
Συρίας Κυρηνίου. 3 καὶ ἐπορεύοντο πάντες
Syria Cyrenius.[a] And went all
ἀπογράφεσθαι, ἕκαστος εἰς τὴν ἑαυτοῦ
to be enrolled, each man to the of himself
πόλιν. 4 Ἀνέβη δὲ καὶ Ἰωσὴφ ἀπὸ τῆς
city. So went up also Joseph from –
Γαλιλαίας ἐκ πόλεως Ναζαρὲθ εἰς τὴν
Galilee out of a city Nazareth to –
Ἰουδαίαν εἰς πόλιν Δαυὶδ ἥτις καλεῖται Βηθλέεμ,
Judæa to a city of David which is called Bethlehem,
διὰ τὸ εἶναι αὐτὸν ἐξ οἴκου καὶ
because of the to be him[b] *out* of [the] house and
=because he was
πατριᾶς Δαυίδ, 5 ἀπογράψασθαι σὺν Μαριὰμ
family of David, to be enrolled with Mary
τῇ ἐμνηστευμένῃ αὐτῷ, οὔσῃ ἐγκύῳ.
the [one] *having been* betrothed to him, being pregnant.
6 Ἐγένετο δὲ ἐν τῷ εἶναι αὐτοὺς ἐκεῖ
And it came to pass in the to be them[be] there
=while they were
ἐπλήσθησαν αἱ ἡμέραι τοῦ τεκεῖν αὐτήν,
were fulfilled the days – to bear her,[bd]
=for her to bear,
7 καὶ ἔτεκεν τὸν υἱὸν αὐτῆς τὸν πρωτότοκον,
and she bore the son of her the firstborn,
καὶ ἐσπαργάνωσεν αὐτὸν καὶ ἀνέκλινεν
and she swathed him and laid
αὐτὸν ἐν φάτνῃ, διότι οὐκ ἦν αὐτοῖς
him in a manger, because there was not for them
τόπος ἐν τῷ καταλύματι. 8 Καὶ ποιμένες
place in the inn. And shepherds
ἦσαν ἐν τῇ χώρᾳ τῇ αὐτῇ ἀγραυλοῦντες
there were in the country – same living in the fields
καὶ φυλάσσοντες φυλακὰς τῆς νυκτὸς ἐπὶ
and keeping guard of(in) the night over
τὴν ποίμνην αὐτῶν. 9 καὶ ἄγγελος κυρίου
the flock of them. And an angel of [the] Lord
ἐπέστη αὐτοῖς καὶ δόξα κυρίου περιέλαμψεν
came upon them and [the] glory of [the] Lord shone around
αὐτούς, καὶ ἐφοβήθησαν φόβον μέγαν.
them, and they feared fear a great.
=exceedingly.
10 καὶ εἶπεν αὐτοῖς ὁ ἄγγελος· μὴ
And said to them the angel : not
φοβεῖσθε· ἰδοὺ γὰρ εὐαγγελίζομαι ὑμῖν
Fear ye; for behold I announce to you

to guide our feet into the
path of peace."
80 And the child grew and
became strong in spirit; and
he lived in the desert until
he appeared publicly to Israel.

Chapter 2

The Birth of Jesus

IN those days Caesar Au-
gustus issued a decree
that a census should be tak-
en of the entire Roman
world. 2 (This was the first
census that took place
while Quirinius was governor of Syria.) 3 And everyone went to his own town
to register.
4 So Joseph also went up
from the town of Nazareth
in Galilee to Judea, to Bethlehem the town of David,
because he belonged to the
house and line of David.
5 He went there to register
with Mary, who was
pledged to be married to
him and was expecting a
child. 6 While they were
there, the time came for the
baby to be born, 7 and she
gave birth to her firstborn,
a son. She wrapped him in
cloths and placed him in a
manger, because there was
no room for them in the inn.

The Shepherds and the Angels

8 And there were shep-
herds living out in the fields
nearby, keeping watch
over their flocks at night.
9 An angel of the Lord appeared to them, and the
glory of the Lord shone
around them, and they
were terrified. 10 But the angel said to them, "Do not
be afraid. I bring you good

[f]I.e., the Roman empire
[g]Gr., *Kyrenios*

good news of a great joy
which shall be for all the
people;
11for today in the city of
David there has been born
for you a Savior, who is
[h]Christ the Lord.
12"And this *will be* a sign
for you: you will find a baby
wrapped in cloths, and lying in a manger."
13And suddenly there ap-
peared with the angel a
multitude of the heavenly
host praising God, and saying,
14"Glory to God in the
highest,
And on earth peace
among men [i] with
whom He is
pleased."
15And it came about when
the angels had gone away
from them into heaven,
that the shepherds *began*
saying to one another,
"Let us go straight to Bethlehem then, and see this
thing that has happened
which the Lord has made
known to us."
16And they came in haste
and found their way to
Mary and Joseph, and the
baby as He lay in the manger.
17And when they had
seen this, they made
known the statement which
had been told them about
this Child.
18And all who heard it
wondered at the things
which were told them by
the shepherds.
19But Mary treasured up
all these things, pondering
them in her heart.
20And the shepherds went
back, glorifying and praising God for all that they had
heard and seen, just as had
been told them.

Jesus Presented at the Temple

21And when eight days
were completed before His
circumcision, His name
was *then* called Jesus, the
name given by the angel before He was conceived in
the womb.
22And when the days for

[h] I.e., Messiah
[i] Lit., *of good pleasure;* or possibly, *of good will*

χαρὰν μεγάλην, ἥτις ἔσται παντὶ τῷ λαῷ,
joy a great, which will be to all the people,

11 ὅτι ἐτέχθη ὑμῖν σήμερον σωτήρ, ὅς
because was born to you to-day a Saviour, who

ἐστιν χριστὸς κύριος, ἐν πόλει Δαυίδ.
is Christ [the] Lord, in a city of David.

12 καὶ τοῦτο ὑμῖν σημεῖον, εὑρήσετε βρέφος
And this to you a sign, ye will find a babe

ἐσπαργανωμένον καὶ κείμενον ἐν φάτνῃ.
having been swathed and lying in a manger.

13 καὶ ἐξαίφνης ἐγένετο σὺν τῷ ἀγγέλῳ
And suddenly there was with the angel

πλῆθος στρατιᾶς οὐρανίου αἰνούντων τὸν
a multitude army of a heavenly praising –

θεὸν καὶ λεγόντων· 14 δόξα ἐν ὑψίστοις
God and saying : Glory in highest [places]

θεῷ καὶ ἐπὶ γῆς εἰρήνη ἐν ἀνθρώποις
to God and on earth peace among men

εὐδοκίας. 15 Καὶ ἐγένετο ὡς ἀπῆλθον
of goodwill. And it came to pass when went away

ἀπ' αὐτῶν εἰς τὸν οὐρανὸν οἱ ἄγγελοι,
from them to – heaven the angels,

οἱ ποιμένες ἐλάλουν πρὸς ἀλλήλους·
the shepherds said to one another :

διέλθωμεν δὴ ἕως Βηθλέεμ καὶ ἴδωμεν
Let us go then unto Bethlehem and let us see

τὸ ῥῆμα τοῦτο τὸ γεγονὸς ὃ ὁ κύριος
– thing this – having happened which the Lord

ἐγνώρισεν ἡμῖν. 16 καὶ ἦλθαν σπεύσαντες,
made known to us. And they came hastening,

καὶ ἀνεῦραν τήν τε Μαριὰμ καὶ τὸν
and found – both Mary and –

Ἰωσὴφ καὶ τὸ βρέφος κείμενον ἐν τῇ
Joseph and the babe lying in the

φάτνῃ· 17 ἰδόντες δὲ ἐγνώρισαν περὶ τοῦ
manger; and seeing they made known concerning the

ῥήματος τοῦ λαληθέντος αὐτοῖς περὶ τοῦ
word – spoken to them concerning –

παιδίου τούτου. 18 καὶ πάντες οἱ ἀκούσαντες
child this. And all the [ones] hearing

ἐθαύμασαν περὶ τῶν λαληθέντων ὑπὸ τῶν
marvelled concerning the things spoken by the

ποιμένων πρὸς αὐτούς· 19 ἡ δὲ Μαρία
shepherds to them; – but Mary

πάντα συνετήρει τὰ ῥήματα ταῦτα συμβάλλουσα
[2]all [1]kept – [4]things [3]these pondering

ἐν τῇ καρδίᾳ αὐτῆς. 20 καὶ ὑπέστρεψαν
in the heart of her. And returned

οἱ ποιμένες δοξάζοντες καὶ αἰνοῦντες τὸν
the shepherds glorifying and praising –

θεὸν ἐπὶ πᾶσιν οἷς ἤκουσαν καὶ εἶδον
God at all things which they heard and saw

καθὼς ἐλαλήθη πρὸς αὐτούς.
as was spoken to them.

21 Καὶ ὅτε ἐπλήσθησαν ἡμέραι ὀκτὼ
And when were completed days eight

τοῦ περιτεμεῖν αὐτόν, καὶ ἐκλήθη τὸ
– to circumcise him[d], *and* was called the

ὄνομα αὐτοῦ Ἰησοῦς, τὸ κληθὲν ὑπὸ τοῦ
name of him Jesus, the [name] called by the

ἀγγέλου πρὸ τοῦ συλλημφθῆναι αὐτὸν ἐν
angel before the to be conceived him[b] in
=he was conceived

τῇ κοιλίᾳ.
the womb.

22 Καὶ ὅτε ἐπλήσθησαν αἱ ἡμέραι τοῦ
And when were completed the days of the

news of great joy that will
be for all the people. 11To-
day in the town of David a
Savior has been born to
you; he is Christ[c] the Lord.
12This will be a sign to you:
You will find a baby
wrapped in cloths and lying
in a manger."
13Suddenly a great com-
pany of the heavenly host
appeared with the angel,
praising God and saying,
14"Glory to God in the
highest,
and on earth peace to
men on whom his
favor rests."
15When the angels had
left them and gone into
heaven, the shepherds said
to one another, "Let's go
to Bethlehem and see this
thing that has happened,
which the Lord has told us
about."
16So they hurried off and
found Mary and Joseph,
and the baby, who was ly-
ing in the manger. 17When
they had seen him, they
spread the word concern-
ing what had been told
them about this child, 18and
all who heard it were
amazed at what the shep-
herds said to them. 19But
Mary treasured up all these
things and pondered them
in her heart. 20The shep-
herds returned, glorifying
and praising God for all the
things they had heard and
seen, which were just as
they had been told.

Jesus Presented in the Temple

21On the eighth day,
when it was time to circumcise him, he was named
Jesus, the name the angel
had given him before he
had been conceived.
22When the time of their

[c] *11* Or *Messiah*. "The Christ" (Greek) and "the Messiah" (Hebrew) both mean "the Anointed One"; also in verse 26.

their purification according to the law of Moses were completed, they brought Him up to Jerusalem to present Him to the Lord

23(as it is written in the Law of the Lord, "EVERY *first-born* MALE THAT OPENS THE WOMB SHALL BE CALLED HOLY TO THE LORD"),

24and to offer a sacrifice according to what was said in the Law of the Lord, "A PAIR OF TURTLEDOVES, OR TWO YOUNG PIGEONS."

25And behold, there was a man in Jerusalem whose name was Simeon; and this man was righteous and devout, looking for the consolation of Israel; and the Holy Spirit was upon him.

26And it had been revealed to him by the Holy Spirit that he would not see death before he had seen the Lord's Christ.

27And he came in the Spirit into the temple; and when the parents brought in the child Jesus, to carry out for Him the custom of the Law,

28then he took Him into his arms, and blessed God, and said,

29"Now Lord, Thou dost
let Thy bond-servant
depart
In peace, according to
Thy word;
30 For my eyes have
seen Thy salvation,
31 Which Thou hast prepared in the presence
of all peoples,
32 A LIGHT OF REVELATION TO THE GENTILES,
And the glory of Thy
people Israel."

33And His father and mother were amazed at the things which were being said about Him.

34And Simeon blessed them, and said to Mary His mother, "Behold, this *Child* is appointed for the fall and rise of many in Is-

καθαρισμοῦ αὐτῶν κατὰ τὸν νόμον
cleansing of them according to the law

Μωϋσέως, ἀνήγαγον αὐτὸν εἰς Ἱεροσόλυμα
of Moses, they took up him to Jerusalem

παραστῆσαι τῷ κυρίῳ, 23 καθὼς γέγραπται
to present to the Lord, as it has been written

ἐν νόμῳ κυρίου ὅτι πᾶν ἄρσεν διανοῖγον
in [the] law of the Lord[,] – Every male opening

μήτραν ἅγιον τῷ κυρίῳ κληθήσεται, 24 καὶ
a womb holy to the Lord shall be called, and

τοῦ δοῦναι θυσίαν κατὰ τὸ εἰρημένον ἐν
– to give[d] a sacrifice according to the thing said in

τῷ νόμῳ κυρίου, ζεῦγος τρυγόνων ἢ δύο
the law of [the] Lord, a pair of turtledoves or two

νοσσοὺς περιστερῶν. 25 Καὶ ἰδοὺ ἄνθρωπος
nestlings of doves. And behold[,] a man

ἦν ἐν Ἰερουσαλὴμ ᾧ ὄνομα Συμεών, καὶ
was in Jerusalem to whom name[c] Simeon, and
=whose name was

ὁ ἄνθρωπος οὗτος δίκαιος καὶ εὐλαβής,
– man this [was] just and devout,

προσδεχόμενος παράκλησιν τοῦ Ἰσραήλ, καὶ
expecting [the] consolation – of Israel, and

πνεῦμα ἦν ἅγιον ἐπ' αὐτόν· 26 καὶ ἦν
[1][the] [3]Spirit [4]was [2]Holy upon him; and it was

αὐτῷ κεχρηματισμένον ὑπὸ τοῦ πνεύματος
to him *having been* communicated by the Spirit

τοῦ ἁγίου μὴ ἰδεῖν θάνατον πρὶν ἢ ἂν
– Holy not to see death before

ἴδῃ τὸν χριστὸν κυρίου. 27 καὶ ἦλθεν
he should see the Christ of [the] Lord. And he came

ἐν τῷ πνεύματι εἰς τὸ ἱερόν· καὶ ἐν τῷ
by the Spirit into the temple; and in the
=as the(his) parents brought in

εἰσαγαγεῖν τοὺς γονεῖς τὸ παιδίον Ἰησοῦν
to bring in the parents[be] the child Jesus

τοῦ ποιῆσαι αὐτοὺς κατὰ τὸ εἰθισμένον
– to do them[bd] according to the custom
=for them to do

τοῦ νόμου περὶ αὐτοῦ, 28 καὶ αὐτὸς
of the law concerning him, *and* he

ἐδέξατο αὐτὸ εἰς τὰς ἀγκάλας καὶ
received him in the(his) arms and

εὐλόγησεν τὸν θεὸν καὶ εἶπεν· 29 νῦν
blessed – God and said : Now

ἀπολύεις τὸν δοῦλόν σου, δέσποτα, κατὰ
thou releasest the slave of thee, Master, according to

τὸ ῥῆμά σου ἐν εἰρήνῃ· 30 ὅτι εἶδον οἱ
the word of thee in peace; because saw the

ὀφθαλμοί μου τὸ σωτήριόν σου, 31 ὃ
eyes of me the salvation of thee, which

ἡτοίμασας κατὰ πρόσωπον πάντων τῶν
thou didst prepare before [the] face of all the

λαῶν, 32 φῶς εἰς ἀποκάλυψιν ἐθνῶν καὶ
peoples, a light for a revelation of [the] nations and

δόξαν λαοῦ σου Ἰσραήλ. 33 καὶ ἦν
a glory of [the] people of thee Israel. And [7]was(were)

ὁ πατὴρ αὐτοῦ καὶ ἡ μήτηρ θαυμάζοντες
[1]the [2]father [3]of him [4]and [5]the [6]mother [8]marvelling

ἐπὶ τοῖς λαλουμένοις περὶ αὐτοῦ. 34 καὶ
at the things being said concerning him. And

εὐλόγησεν αὐτοὺς Συμεὼν καὶ εἶπεν πρὸς
blessed them Simeon and said to

Μαριὰμ τὴν μητέρα αὐτοῦ· ἰδοὺ οὗτος
Mary the mother of him : Behold[,] this

κεῖται εἰς πτῶσιν καὶ ἀνάστασιν πολλῶν
is set for fall and rising again of many

purification according to
the Law of Moses had been
completed, Joseph and
Mary took him to Jerusa-
lem to present him to the
Lord 23(as it is written
in the Law of the Lord,
"Every firstborn male is
to be consecrated to the
Lord"[f]), 24and to offer a
sacrifice in keeping with
what is said in the Law of
the Lord: "a pair of doves
or two young pigeons."[g]

25Now there was a man in
Jerusalem called Simeon,
who was righteous and de-
vout. He was waiting for
the consolation of Israel
and the Holy Spirit was
upon him. 26It had been revealed to him by the Holy
Spirit that he would not die
before he had seen the
Lord's Christ. 27Moved by
the Spirit, he went into the
temple courts. When the
parents brought in the child
Jesus to do for him what the
custom of the Law re-
quired, 28Simeon took him
in his arms and praised
God, saying:

29"Sovereign Lord, as you
have promised,
you now dismiss[h] your
servant in peace.
30For my eyes have seen
your salvation,
31 which you have
prepared in the sight
of all people,
32a light for revelation to
the Gentiles
and for glory to your
people Israel."

33The child's father and
mother marveled at what
was said about him. 34Then
Simeon blessed them and
said to Mary, his mother:
"This child is destined to
cause the falling and rising
of many in Israel, and to be

[f]23 Exodus 13:2,12
[g]24 Lev. 12:8
[h]29 Or *promised, / now dismiss*

rael, and for a sign to be
opposed—
35 and a sword will pierce
even your own soul—to the
end that thoughts from
many hearts may be re-
vealed.''
36 And there was a proph-
etess, Anna the daughter of
Phanuel, of the tribe of
Asher. She was advanced
in years, having lived with
a husband seven years after
her marriage,
37 and then as a widow to
the age of eighty-four. And
she never left the temple,
serving night and day with
fastings and prayers.
38 And at that very mo-
ment she came up and *be-
gan* giving thanks to God,
and continued to speak of
Him to all those who were
looking for the redemption
of Jerusalem.

Return to Nazareth

39 And when they had per-
formed everything accord-
ing to the Law of the Lord,
they returned to Galilee, to
their own city of Nazareth.
40 And the Child con-
tinued to grow and become
strong, increasing in wisdom; and the grace of God
was upon Him.

Visit to Jerusalem

41 And His parents used to
go to Jerusalem every year
at the Feast of the Pass-
over.
42 And when He became
twelve, they went up *there*
according to the custom of
the Feast;
43 and as they were returning, after spending the full
number of days, the boy
Jesus stayed behind in
Jerusalem. And His par-
ents were unaware of it,
44 but supposed Him to be
in the caravan, and went a
day's journey; and they *began* looking for Him among
their relatives and ac-
quaintances.
45 And when they did not
find Him, they returned to

ἐν τῷ Ἰσραὴλ καὶ εἰς σημεῖον ἀντιλεγ-
in – Israel and for a sign spoken

όμενον — 35 καὶ σοῦ δὲ αὐτῆς τὴν ψυχὴν
against — and [5]of thee [7]also [6][thy]self [3]the [4]soul

διελεύσεται ῥομφαία—, ὅπως ἂν ἀποκαλυφθῶσιν
[2]will go through [1]a sword —, so as – may be revealed

ἐκ πολλῶν καρδιῶν διαλογισμοί. 36 Καὶ
of many hearts [the] thoughts. And

ἦν Ἄννα προφῆτις, θυγάτηρ Φανουήλ, ἐκ
there was Anna a prophetess, a daughter of Phanuel, of

φυλῆς Ἀσήρ· αὕτη προβεβηκυῖα ἐν ἡμέραις
[the] tribe of Asher; this having advanced in days

πολλαῖς, ζήσασα μετὰ ἀνδρὸς ἔτη ἑπτὰ
many, having lived with a husband years seven

ἀπὸ τῆς παρθενίας αὐτῆς, 37 καὶ αὐτὴ
from the virginity of her, and she [was]

χήρα ἕως ἐτῶν ὀγδοήκοντα τεσσάρων, ἣ
a widow until years eighty-four, who

οὐκ ἀφίστατο τοῦ ἱεροῦ νηστείαις καὶ
withdrew not from the temple with fastings and

δεήσεσιν λατρεύουσα νύκτα καὶ ἡμέραν.
petitionings serving night and day.

38 καὶ αὐτῇ τῇ ὥρᾳ ἐπιστᾶσα ἀνθωμολογεῖτο
And at the very hour* coming upon she gave thanks

τῷ θεῷ καὶ ἐλάλει περὶ αὐτοῦ πᾶσιν τοῖς
– to God and spoke about him to all the [ones]

προσδεχομένοις λύτρωσιν Ἰερουσαλήμ. 39 Καὶ
expecting redemption in Jerusalem. And

ὡς ἐτέλεσαν πάντα τὰ κατὰ τὸν νόμον
when they finished all things – according to the law

κυρίου, ἐπέστρεψαν εἰς τὴν Γαλιλαίαν εἰς
of [the] Lord, they returned to – Galilee to

πόλιν ἑαυτῶν Ναζαρέθ.
a city of them*selves* Nazareth.

40 Τὸ δὲ παιδίον ηὔξανεν καὶ ἐκραταιοῦτο
And the child grew and became strong

πληρούμενον σοφίᾳ, καὶ χάρις θεοῦ ἦν ἐπ'
being filled with wisdom, and [the] grace of God was upon

αὐτό.
him.

41 Καὶ ἐπορεύοντο οἱ γονεῖς αὐτοῦ κατ'
And went the parents of him year

ἔτος εἰς Ἰερουσαλὴμ τῇ ἑορτῇ τοῦ πάσχα.
by year† to Jerusalem at the feast of the Passover.

42 Καὶ ὅτε ἐγένετο ἐτῶν δώδεκα, ἀναβαινόντων
And when he became of years twelve, going up
=as they went up

αὐτῶν κατὰ τὸ ἔθος τῆς ἑορτῆς, 43 καὶ
them[a] according to the custom of the feast, and

τελειωσάντων τὰς ἡμέρας, ἐν τῷ ὑποστρέφειν
fulfilling[a] the days, in the to return
=when they returned

αὐτοὺς ὑπέμεινεν Ἰησοῦς ὁ παῖς ἐν
them[be] [4]remained [3]Jesus [1]the [2]boy in

Ἰερουσαλήμ, καὶ οὐκ ἔγνωσαν οἱ γονεῖς
Jerusalem, and [4]knew not [1]the [2]parents

αὐτοῦ. 44 νομίσαντες δὲ αὐτὸν εἶναι ἐν
[3]of him. But supposing him to be in

τῇ συνοδίᾳ ἦλθον ἡμέρας ὁδὸν καὶ ἀνεζήτουν
the company they went of a day a journey and sought

αὐτὸν ἐν τοῖς συγγενεῦσιν καὶ τοῖς
him among the(ir) relatives and the(ir)

γνωστοῖς, 45 καὶ μὴ εὑρόντες ὑπέστρεψαν
acquaintances, and not finding returned

a sign that will be spoken
against, 35 so that the
thoughts of many hearts
will be revealed. And a
sword will pierce your own
soul too.''
36 There was also a prophetess, Anna, the daughter
of Phanuel, of the tribe of
Asher. She was very old;
she had lived with her husband seven years after her
marriage, 37 and then was a
widow until she was eighty-
four.[i] She never left the
temple but worshiped night
and day, fasting and praying. 38 Coming up to them at
that very moment, she gave
thanks to God and spoke
about the child to all who
were looking forward to the
redemption of Jerusalem.
39 When Joseph and Mary
had done everything re-
quired by the Law of the
Lord, they returned to Galilee to their own town of
Nazareth. 40 And the child
grew and became strong;
he was filled with wisdom,
and the grace of God was
upon him.

The Boy Jesus at the Temple

41 Every year his parents
went to Jerusalem for the
Feast of the Passover.
42 When he was twelve
years old, they went up to
the Feast, according to the
custom. 43 After the Feast
was over, while his parents
were returning home, the
boy Jesus stayed behind in
Jerusalem, but they were
unaware of it. 44 Thinking
he was in their company,
they traveled on for a day.
Then they began looking
for him among their rela-
tives and friends. 45 When
they did not find him, they

* Strictly, this construction should mean "the hour itself"; but the context demands "the same hour". See 10. 7, 21; 12. 12; 13. 1, 31; 20. 19; 23. 12; 24. 13. "Luke seems to be the only N.T. writer who affects the construction" (C. F. D. Moule). See also Acts 16. 18; 22. 13. Of course there is not a great difference between "the hour itself", "the very hour", and "the same hour".

[i]37 Or *widow for eighty-four years*

Jerusalem, looking for
Him.
46 And it came about that
after three days they found
Him in the temple, sitting in
the midst of the teachers,
both listening to them, and
asking them questions.
47 And all who heard Him
were amazed at His under-
standing and His answers.
48 And when they saw
Him, they were astonished;
and His mother said to
Him, "Son, why have You
treated us this way? Be-
hold, Your father and I
have been anxiously look-
ing for You."
49 And He said to them,
"Why is it that you were
looking for Me? Did you
not know that I had to be in
My Father's *house?*"
50 And they did not understand the statement which
He had made to them.
51 And He went down
with them, and came to
Nazareth; and He con-
tinued in subjection to
them; and His mother treasured all *these* things in her
heart.
52 And Jesus kept increasing in wisdom and stature,
and in favor with God and
men.

Chapter 3

John the Baptist Preaches

NOW in the fifteenth
year of the reign of
Tiberius Caesar, when
Pontius Pilate was gover-
nor of Judea, and Herod
was tetrarch of Galilee, and
his brother Philip was tetrarch of the region of
Ituraea and Trachonitis,
and Lysanias was tetrarch
of Abilene,
2 in the high priesthood of
Annas and Caiaphas, the
word of God came to John,
the son of Zacharias, in the
wilderness.

εἰς Ἰερουσαλὴμ ἀναζητοῦντες αὐτόν. **46** καὶ
to Jerusalem seeking him. And
ἐγένετο μετὰ ἡμέρας τρεῖς εὗρον αὐτὸν
it came to pass after days three they found him
ἐν τῷ ἱερῷ καθεζόμενον ἐν μέσῳ τῶν
in the temple sitting in [the] midst of the
διδασκάλων καὶ ἀκούοντα αὐτῶν καὶ
teachers both hearing them and
ἐπερωτῶντα αὐτούς· **47** ἐξίσταντο δὲ πάντες
questioning them; and were astonished all
οἱ ἀκούοντες αὐτοῦ ἐπὶ τῇ συνέσει καὶ
the [ones] hearing him at the intelligence and
ταῖς ἀποκρίσεσιν αὐτοῦ. **48** καὶ ἰδόντες
the answers of him. And seeing
αὐτὸν ἐξεπλάγησαν, καὶ εἶπεν πρὸς αὐτὸν
him they were astounded, and said to him
ἡ μήτηρ αὐτοῦ· τέκνον, τί ἐποίησας ἡμῖν
the mother of him: Child, why didst thou to us
οὕτως; ἰδοὺ ὁ πατήρ σου κἀγὼ ὀδυνώμενοι
thus? behold[,] the father of thee and I greatly distressed
ζητοῦμέν σε. **49** καὶ εἶπεν πρὸς αὐτούς·
are seeking thee. And he said to them:
τί ὅτι ἐζητεῖτέ με; οὐκ ᾔδειτε ὅτι ἐν
Why [is it] that ye sought me? did ye not know that in
=I
τοῖς τοῦ πατρός μου δεῖ εἶναί με;
the [affairs] of the Father of me it behoves to be me?
must be about my Father's business?
50 καὶ αὐτοὶ οὐ συνῆκαν τὸ ῥῆμα ὃ
And they did not understand the word which
ἐλάλησεν αὐτοῖς. **51** καὶ κατέβη μετ'
he spoke to them. And he went down with
αὐτῶν καὶ ἦλθεν εἰς Ναζαρέθ, καὶ ἦν
them and came to Nazareth, and was
ὑποτασσόμενος αὐτοῖς. καὶ ἡ μήτηρ
being subject to them. And the mother
αὐτοῦ διετήρει πάντα τὰ ῥήματα ἐν τῇ
of him carefully kept all the matters in the
καρδίᾳ αὐτῆς. **52** Καὶ Ἰησοῦς προέκοπτεν
heart of her. And Jesus progressed
ἐν τῇ σοφίᾳ καὶ ἡλικίᾳ καὶ χάριτι παρὰ
in – wisdom and age and favour before
θεῷ καὶ ἀνθρώποις.
God and men.

3 Ἐν ἔτει δὲ πεντεκαιδεκάτῳ τῆς
Now in [the] year fifteenth of the
ἡγεμονίας Τιβερίου Καίσαρος, ἡγεμονεύοντος
government of Tiberius Cæsar, governing
=while Pontius Pilate
Ποντίου Πιλάτου τῆς Ἰουδαίας, καὶ
Pontius Pilate* – of Judæa, and
was governing
τετρααρχοῦντος τῆς Γαλιλαίας Ἡρῴδου,
ruling as tetrarch – of Galilee Herod,*
=while Herod was ruling as tetrarch of Galilee,
Φιλίππου δὲ τοῦ ἀδελφοῦ αὐτοῦ τετρα-
and Philip the brother of him ruling
αρχοῦντος τῆς Ἰτουραίας καὶ Τραχωνίτιδος
as tetrarch* [1]of the [2]of Ituræa [4]and [5]of Trachonitis
χώρας, καὶ Λυσανίου τῆς Ἀβιληνῆς
[3]country, and Lysanias – of Abilene
τετρααρχοῦντος, **2** ἐπὶ ἀρχιερέως Ἅννα
ruling as tetrarch*, in the time of [the] high priest Anna
καὶ Καϊαφᾶ, ἐγένετο ῥῆμα θεοῦ ἐπὶ Ἰωάννην
and Caiaphas, came a word of God to John
τὸν Ζαχαρίου υἱὸν ἐν τῇ ἐρήμῳ. **3** καὶ
the of Zacharias son in the desert. And

went back to Jerusalem to
look for him. 46 After three
days they found him in the
temple courts, sitting
among the teachers, listening to them and asking
them questions. 47 Every-
one who heard him was
amazed at his understand-
ing and his answers.
48 When his parents saw
him, they were astonished.
His mother said to him,
"Son, why have you treat-
ed us like this? Your father
and I have been anxiously
searching for you."
49 "Why were you search-
ing for me?" he asked.
"Didn't you know I had to
be in my Father's house?"
50 But they did not understand what he was saying to
them.
51 Then he went down to
Nazareth with them and
was obedient to them. But
his mother treasured all
these things in her heart.
52 And Jesus grew in wis-
dom and stature, and in favor with God and men.

Chapter 3

John the Baptist Prepares the Way

IN the fifteenth year of
the reign of Tiberius
Caesar—when Pontius Pi-
late was governor of Judea,
Herod tetrarch of Galilee,
his brother Philip tetrarch
of Iturea and Traconitis,
and Lysanias tetrarch of
Abilene—2 during the high
priesthood of Annas and
Caiaphas, the word of God
came to John son of Zechariah in the desert. 3 He went

3And he came into all the district around the Jordan, preaching a baptism of repentance for the forgiveness of sins;
4as it is written in the book of the words of Isaiah the prophet,

"THE VOICE OF ONE CRYING IN THE WILDERNESS,
'MAKE READY THE WAY OF THE LORD,
MAKE HIS PATHS STRAIGHT.
5 'EVERY RAVINE SHALL BE FILLED UP,
AND EVERY MOUNTAIN AND HILL SHALL BE BROUGHT LOW;
AND THE CROOKED SHALL BECOME STRAIGHT,
AND THE ROUGH ROADS SMOOTH;
6 AND ALL FLESH SHALL SEE THE SALVATION OF GOD.' "

7He therefore *began* saying to the multitudes who were going out to be baptized by him, "You brood of vipers, who warned you to flee from the wrath to come?
8"Therefore bring forth fruits in keeping with repentance, and do not begin to say to yourselves, 'We have Abraham for our father,' for I say to you that God is able from these stones to raise up children to Abraham.
9"And also the axe is already laid at the root of the trees; every tree therefore that does not bear good fruit is cut down and thrown into the fire."
10And the multitudes were questioning him, saying, "Then what shall we do?"
11And he would answer and say to them, "Let the man who has two tunics share with him who has none; and let him who has food do likewise."
12And *some* [j] tax-gatherers also came to be baptized, and they said to him, "Teacher, what shall we do?"
13And he said to them, "Collect no more than what you have been ordered to."
14And *some* [k] soldiers were questioning him, saying, "And *what about* us,

[j] I.e., Collectors of Roman taxes for profit
[k] I.e., men in active military service

ἦλθεν εἰς πᾶσαν τὴν περίχωρον τοῦ
he came into all the neighbourhood of the
Ἰορδάνου κηρύσσων βάπτισμα μετανοίας
Jordan proclaiming a baptism of repentance
εἰς ἄφεσιν ἁμαρτιῶν, 4 ὡς γέγραπται ἐν
for forgiveness of sins, as it has been written in
βίβλῳ λόγων Ἠσαΐου τοῦ προφήτου·
[the] roll of [the] words of Esaias the prophet :
φωνὴ βοῶντος ἐν τῇ ἐρήμῳ· ἑτοιμάσατε
Voice of [one] crying in the desert : Prepare ye
τὴν ὁδὸν κυρίου, εὐθείας ποιεῖτε τὰς
the way of [the] Lord, straight make the
τρίβους αὐτοῦ· 5 πᾶσα φάραγξ πληρωθήσεται
paths of him; every valley shall be filled up
καὶ πᾶν ὄρος καὶ βουνὸς ταπεινωθήσεται,
and every mountain and hill shall be laid low,
καὶ ἔσται τὰ σκολιὰ εἰς εὐθείας καὶ αἱ
and shall be the crooked [places] into straight [ones] and the
τραχεῖαι εἰς ὁδοὺς λείας· 6 καὶ ὄψεται
rough [places] into ways smooth; and [3]shall see
πᾶσα σὰρξ τὸ σωτήριον τοῦ θεοῦ.
[1]all [2]flesh the salvation – of God.
7 Ἔλεγεν οὖν τοῖς ἐκπορευομένοις ὄχλοις
He said therefore to the [2]going out [1]crowds
βαπτισθῆναι ὑπ' αὐτοῦ· γεννήματα ἐχιδνῶν,
to be baptized by him : Offspring of vipers,
τίς ὑπέδειξεν ὑμῖν φυγεῖν ἀπὸ τῆς
who warned you to flee from the
μελλούσης ὀργῆς; 8 ποιήσατε οὖν καρποὺς
coming wrath? Produce therefore fruits
ἀξίους τῆς μετανοίας· καὶ μὴ ἄρξησθε
worthy – of repentance; and do not begin
λέγειν ἐν ἑαυτοῖς· πατέρα ἔχομεν τὸν
to say among yourselves : Father we have –
Ἀβραάμ· λέγω γὰρ ὑμῖν ὅτι δύναται ὁ
Abraham; for I tell you that [2]can –
θεὸς ἐκ τῶν λίθων τούτων ἐγεῖραι τέκνα
[1]God out of – stones these *to* raise children
τῷ Ἀβραάμ. 9 ἤδη δὲ καὶ ἡ ἀξίνη πρὸς
– to Abraham. And [2]already [1]even the axe at
τὴν ῥίζαν τῶν δένδρων κεῖται· πᾶν οὖν
the root of the trees is laid; [2]every [1]therefore
δένδρον μὴ ποιοῦν καρπὸν καλὸν
tree not producing fruit good
ἐκκόπτεται καὶ εἰς πῦρ βάλλεται. 10 Καὶ
is being cut down and into fire is being cast. And
ἐπηρώτων αὐτὸν οἱ ὄχλοι λέγοντες· τί
asked him the crowds saying : What
οὖν ποιήσωμεν; 11 ἀποκριθεὶς δὲ ἔλεγεν
then may we do? And answering he told
αὐτοῖς· ὁ ἔχων δύο χιτῶνας μεταδότω
them : The [one] having two tunics let him impart
τῷ μὴ ἔχοντι, καὶ ὁ ἔχων βρώματα
to the [one] not having, and the [one] having foods
ὁμοίως ποιείτω. 12 ἦλθον δὲ καὶ τελῶναι
likewise let him do. And there came also tax-collectors
βαπτισθῆναι καὶ εἶπαν πρὸς αὐτόν·
to be baptized and they said to him :
διδάσκαλε, τί ποιήσωμεν; 13 ὁ δὲ εἶπεν
Teacher, what may we do? And he said
πρὸς αὐτούς· μηδὲν πλέον παρὰ τὸ
to them : Nothing more besides the [thing]
διατεταγμένον ὑμῖν πράσσετε. 14 ἐπηρώτων δὲ
having been commanded you do ye. And asked
αὐτὸν καὶ στρατευόμενοι λέγοντες· τί
him also men serving in the army saying : What

into all the country around the Jordan, preaching a baptism of repentance for the forgiveness of sins. 4As is written in the book of the words of Isaiah the prophet:

"A voice of one calling in the desert,
'Prepare the way for the Lord,
make straight paths for him.
5Every valley shall be filled in,
every mountain and hill made low.
The crooked roads shall become straight,
the rough ways smooth.
6And all mankind will see God's salvation.' "[j]

7John said to the crowds coming out to be baptized by him, "You brood of vipers! Who warned you to flee from the coming wrath? 8Produce fruit in keeping with repentance. And do not begin to say to yourselves, 'We have Abraham as our father.' For I tell you that out of these stones God can raise up children for Abraham. 9The ax is already at the root of the trees, and every tree that does not produce good fruit will be cut down and thrown into the fire."
10"What should we do then?" the crowd asked.
11John answered, "The man with two tunics should share with him who has none, and the one who has food should do the same."
12Tax collectors also came to be baptized. "Teacher," they asked, "what should we do?"

[j] 6 Isaiah 40:3-5

what shall we do?" And he
said to them, "Do not take
money from anyone by
force, or accuse *anyone*
falsely, and be content with
your wages."
15 Now while the people
were in a state of expectation and all were wondering
in their hearts about John,
as to whether he might be
the Christ,
16 John answered and said
to them all, "As for me, I
baptize you with water; but
One is coming who is
mightier than I, and I am
not fit to untie the thong of
His sandals; He will bap-
tize you with the Holy
Spirit and fire.
17 "And His winnowing
fork is in His hand to
thoroughly clear His
threshing floor, and to
gather the wheat into His
barn; but He will burn up
the chaff with unquench-
able fire."
18 So with many other ex-
hortations also he preached
the gospel to the people.
19 But when Herod the te-
trarch was reproved by him
on account of Herodias, his
brother's wife, and on account of all the wicked
things which Herod had
done,
20 he added this also to
them all, that he locked
John up in prison.

Jesus Is Baptized

21 Now it came about
when all the people were
baptized, that Jesus also
was baptized, and while He
was praying, heaven was
opened,
22 and the Holy Spirit descended upon Him in bodi-
ly form like a dove, and a
voice came out of heaven,
"Thou art My beloved
Son, in Thee I am well-
pleased."

Genealogy of Jesus

23 And when He began
His ministry, Jesus Himself
was about thirty years of

ποιήσωμεν καὶ ἡμεῖς; καὶ εἶπεν αὐτοῖς·
may do also we? And he told them :
μηδένα διασείσητε μηδὲ συκοφαντήσητε,
No one intimidate nor accuse falsely,
καὶ ἀρκεῖσθε τοῖς ὀψωνίοις ὑμῶν.
and be satisfied with the pay of you.
15 Προσδοκῶντος δὲ τοῦ λαοῦ καὶ
Now expecting the people[a] and
=while the people were expecting and all were debating
διαλογιζομένων πάντων ἐν ταῖς καρδίαις
debating all[a] in the hearts
αὐτῶν περὶ τοῦ Ἰωάννου, μήποτε αὐτὸς
of them concerning – John, perhaps he
εἴη ὁ χριστός, **16** ἀπεκρίνατο λέγων πᾶσιν
might be the Christ, [2]answered [3]saying [4]to all
ὁ Ἰωάννης· ἐγὼ μὲν ὕδατι βαπτίζω ὑμᾶς·
– [1]John : I indeed with water baptize you;
ἔρχεται δὲ ὁ ἰσχυρότερός μου, οὗ οὐκ
but there comes the [one] stronger of me, of whom not
=than I,
εἰμὶ ἱκανὸς λῦσαι τὸν ἱμάντα τῶν ὑποδημά-
I am competent to loosen the thong of the san-
των αὐτοῦ· αὐτὸς ὑμᾶς βαπτίσει ἐν
dals of him; he you will baptize with
πνεύματι ἁγίῳ καὶ πυρί· **17** οὗ τὸ πτύον
Spirit [the] Holy and fire; of whom the fan [is]
ἐν τῇ χειρὶ αὐτοῦ διακαθᾶραι τὴν ἅλωνα
in the hand of him thoroughly to cleanse the threshing-floor
αὐτοῦ καὶ συναγαγεῖν τὸν σῖτον εἰς τὴν
of him and to gather the wheat into the
ἀποθήκην αὐτοῦ, τὸ δὲ ἄχυρον κατακαύσει
barn of him, but the chaff he will burn up
πυρὶ ἀσβέστῳ. **18** Πολλὰ μὲν οὖν καὶ
with fire unquenchable. Many things indeed therefore and
ἕτερα παρακαλῶν εὐηγγελίζετο τὸν λαόν·
different exhorting he evangelized the people;
19 ὁ δὲ Ἡρῴδης ὁ τετραάρχης, ἐλεγχόμενος
– but Herod the tetrarch, being reproved
ὑπ' αὐτοῦ περὶ Ἡρῳδιάδος τῆς γυναικὸς
by him concerning Herodias the wife
τοῦ ἀδελφοῦ αὐτοῦ καὶ περὶ πάντων ὧν
of the brother of him and concerning [1]all [3]things [4]which
ἐποίησεν πονηρῶν ὁ Ἡρῴδης, **20** προσέθηκεν
[6]did [2]evil – [5]Herod, added
καὶ τοῦτο ἐπὶ πᾶσιν, κατέκλεισεν τὸν
also this above all, he shut up
Ἰωάννην ἐν φυλακῇ.
John in prison.
21 Ἐγένετο δὲ ἐν τῷ βαπτισθῆναι ἅπαντα
Now it came to pass in the to be baptized all
=when all the people were baptized
τὸν λαὸν καὶ Ἰησοῦ βαπτισθέντος καὶ
the people[be] and Jesus being baptized and
=as Jesus had been baptized and was praying
προσευχομένου ἀνεῳχθῆναι τὸν οὐρανὸν **22** καὶ
praying[a] to be opened the heaven and
=the heaven was opened and the Holy Spirit came down
καταβῆναι τὸ πνεῦμα τὸ ἅγιον σωματικῷ
to come down the Spirit – Holy[b] in a bodily
εἴδει ὡς περιστερὰν ἐπ' αὐτόν, καὶ φωνὴν
form as a dove upon him, and a voice
ἐξ οὐρανοῦ γενέσθαι· σὺ εἶ ὁ υἱός μου
out of heaven to come[b] : Thou art the Son of me
ὁ ἀγαπητός, ἐν σοὶ εὐδόκησα. **23** Καὶ
– beloved, in thee I was well pleased. And
αὐτὸς ἦν Ἰησοῦς ἀρχόμενος ὡσεὶ ἐτῶν
[2]himself [3]was [1]Jesus [4]beginning about years

13 "Don't collect any
more than you are required
to," he told them.
14 Then some soldiers
asked him, "And what
should we do?"
He replied, "Don't extort
money and don't accuse
people falsely—be content
with your pay."
15 The people were wait-
ing expectantly and were
all wondering in their
hearts if John might possibly be the Christ.[k] 16 John
answered them all, "I baptize you with[l] water. But
one more powerful than I
will come, the thongs of
whose sandals I am not
worthy to untie. He will
baptize you with the Holy
Spirit and with fire. 17 His
winnowing fork is in his
hand to clear his threshing
floor and to gather the
wheat into his barn, but he
will burn up the chaff with
unquenchable fire." 18 And
with many other words
John exhorted the people
and preached the good
news to them.
19 But when John rebuked
Herod the tetrarch because
of Herodias, his brother's
wife, and all the other evil
things he had done, 20 Herod added this to them all:
He locked John up in prison.

The Baptism and Genealogy of Jesus

21 When all the people
were being baptized, Jesus
was baptized too. And as
he was praying, heaven
was opened 22 and the Holy
Spirit descended on him in
bodily form like a dove.
And a voice came from
heaven: "You are my Son,
whom I love; with you I am
well pleased."
23 Now Jesus himself was
about thirty years old when
he began his ministry. He

[k] 15 Or *Messiah*
[l] 16 Or *in*

age, being supposedly *the*
son of Joseph, the *son* of
Eli,
24the *son* of Matthat, the
son of Levi, the *son* of Melchi, the *son* of Jannai, the
son of Joseph,
25the *son* of Mattathias,
the *son* of Amos, the *son* of
Nahum, the *son* of Hesli,
the *son* of Naggai,
26the *son* of Maath, the
son of Mattathias, the *son*
of Semein, the *son* of Josech, the *son* of Joda,
27the *son* of Joanan, the
son of Rhesa, the *son* of
Zerubbabel, the *son* of Shealtiel, the *son* of Neri,
28the *son* of Melchi, the
son of Addi, the *son* of
Cosam, the *son* of El-
madam, the *son* of Er,
29the *son* of Joshua, the
son of Eliezer, the *son* of
Jorim, the *son* of Matthat,
the *son* of Levi,
30the *son* of Simeon, the
son of Judah, the *son* of Joseph, the *son* of Jonam, the
son of Eliakim,
31the *son* of Melea, the
son of Menna, the *son* of
Mattatha, the *son* of Nathan, the *son* of David,
32the *son* of Jesse, the *son*
of Obed, the *son* of Boaz,
the *son* of Salmon, the *son*
of Nahshon,
33the *son* of Amminadab,
the *son* of Admin, the *son*
of Ram, the *son* of Hezron,
the *son* of Perez, the *son* of
Judah,
34the *son* of Jacob, the
son of Isaac, the *son* of
Abraham, the *son* of Terah,
the *son* of Nahor,
35the *son* of Serug, the
son of Reu, the *son* of
Peleg, the *son* of Heber, the
son of Shelah,
36the *son* of Cainan, the
son of Arphaxad, the *son* of
Shem, the *son* of Noah, the
son of Lamech,
37the *son* of Methuselah,
the *son* of Enoch, the *son* of
Jared, the *son* of Mahala-
leel, the *son* of Cainan,
38the *son* of Enosh, the
son of Seth, the *son* of
Adam, the *son* of God.

τριάκοντα, ὢν υἱός, ὡς ἐνομίζετο, Ἰωσήφ,
thirty, being son, as was supposed, of Joseph,
τοῦ Ἠλὶ 24 τοῦ Μαθθὰτ τοῦ Λευὶ τοῦ
– of Eli – of Matthat – of Levi –
Μελχὶ τοῦ Ἰανναὶ τοῦ Ἰωσὴφ 25 τοῦ
of Melchi – of Jannai – of Joseph –
Ματταθίου τοῦ Ἀμὼς τοῦ Ναοὺμ τοῦ
of Mattathias – of Amos – of Naum –
Ἑσλὶ τοῦ Ναγγαὶ 26 τοῦ Μάαθ τοῦ
of Hesli – of Naggai – of Maath –
Ματταθίου τοῦ Σεμεΐν τοῦ Ἰωσὴχ τοῦ
of Mattathias – of Semein – of Josech –
Ἰωδὰ 27 τοῦ Ἰωανὰν τοῦ Ῥησὰ τοῦ
of Jodah – of Joanan – of Rhesa –
Ζοροβαβὲλ τοῦ Σαλαθιὴλ τοῦ Νηρὶ 28 τοῦ
of Zorobabel – of Salathiel – of Neri –
Μελχὶ τοῦ Ἀδδὶ τοῦ Κωσὰμ τοῦ
of Melchi – of Addi – of Kosam –
Ἐλμαδὰμ τοῦ Ἢρ 29 τοῦ Ἰησοῦ τοῦ
of Elmadam – of Er – of Jesus –
Ἐλιέζερ τοῦ Ἰωρὶμ τοῦ Μαθθὰτ τοῦ
of Eliezer – of Jorim – of Matthat –
Λευὶ 30 τοῦ Συμεὼν τοῦ Ἰούδα τοῦ
of Levi – of Simeon – of Juda –
Ἰωσὴφ τοῦ Ἰωνὰμ τοῦ Ἐλιακὶμ 31 τοῦ
of Joseph – of Jonam – of Eliakim –
Μελεὰ τοῦ Μεννὰ τοῦ Ματταθὰ τοῦ
of Melea – of Menna – of Mattatha –
Ναθὰμ τοῦ Δαυὶδ 32 τοῦ Ἰεσσαὶ τοῦ
of Natham – of David – of Jesse –
Ἰωβὴδ τοῦ Βόος τοῦ Σάλα τοῦ Ναασσὼν
of Jobed – of Boos – of Sala – of Naasson
33 τοῦ Ἀμιναδὰβ τοῦ Ἀδμὶν τοῦ Ἀρνὶ
– of Aminadab – of Admin – of Arni
τοῦ Ἑσρὼμ τοῦ Φάρες τοῦ Ἰούδα
– of Hesrom – of Phares – of Juda
34 τοῦ Ἰακὼβ τοῦ Ἰσαὰκ τοῦ Ἀβραὰμ
– of Jacob – of Isaac – of Abraham
τοῦ Θάρα τοῦ Ναχὼρ 35 τοῦ Σεροὺχ
– of Thara – of Nachor – of Seruch
τοῦ Ῥαγαὺ τοῦ Φάλεκ τοῦ Ἔβερ τοῦ
– of Rhagau – of Phalek – of Eber –
Σάλα 36 τοῦ Καϊνὰμ τοῦ Ἀρφαξὰδ τοῦ
of Sala – of Cainam – of Arphaxad –
Σὴμ τοῦ Νῶε τοῦ Λάμεχ 37 τοῦ Μαθουσάλα
of Sem – of Noe – of Lamech – of Mathusala
τοῦ Ἑνὼχ τοῦ Ἰάρετ τοῦ Μαλελεὴλ
– of Henoch – of Jaret – of Maleleel
τοῦ Καϊνὰμ 38 τοῦ Ἐνὼς τοῦ Σὴθ τοῦ
– of Cainam – of Enos – of Seth –
Ἀδὰμ τοῦ θεοῦ.
of Adam – of God.

was the son, so it was
thought, of Joseph,
the son of Heli, 24the
son of Matthat,
the son of Levi, the son
of Melki,
the son of Jannai, the
son of Joseph,
25the son of Mattathias,
the son of Amos,
the son of Nahum, the
son of Esli,
the son of Naggai, 26the
son of Maath,
the son of Mattathias,
the son of Semein,
the son of Josech, the
son of Joda,
27the son of Joanan, the
son of Rhesa,
the son of Zerubbabel,
the son of Shealtiel,
the son of Neri, 28the
son of Melki,
the son of Addi, the son
of Cosam,
the son of Elmadam,
the son of Er,
29the son of Joshua, the
son of Eliezer,
the son of Jorim, the
son of Matthat,
the son of Levi, 30the
son of Simeon,
the son of Judah, the
son of Joseph,
the son of Jonam, the
son of Eliakim,
31the son of Melea, the
son of Menna,
the son of Mattatha, the
son of Nathan,
the son of David, 32the
son of Jesse,
the son of Obed, the son
of Boaz,
the son of Salmon,[m] the
son of Nahshon,
33the son of Amminadab,
the son of Ram,[n]
the son of Hezron, the
son of Perez,
the son of Judah, 34the
son of Jacob,
the son of Isaac, the son
of Abraham,
the son of Terah, the
son of Nahor,
35the son of Serug, the
son of Reu,
the son of Peleg, the son
of Eber,
the son of Shelah, 36the
son of Cainan,
the son of Arphaxad,
the son of Shem,
the son of Noah, the son
of Lamech,
37the son of Methuselah,
the son of Enoch,
the son of Jared, the son
of Mahalalel,
the son of Kenan, 38the
son of Enosh,
the son of Seth, the son
of Adam,
the son of God.

Chapter 4

The Temptation of Jesus

AND Jesus, full of the
Holy Spirit, returned
from the Jordan and was
led about by the Spirit in
the wilderness
2for forty days, being
tempted by the devil. And

4 Ἰησοῦς δὲ πλήρης πνεύματος ἁγίου
And Jesus full of [1][the] [3]Spirit [2]Holy
ὑπέστρεψεν ἀπὸ τοῦ Ἰορδάνου, καὶ ἤγετο
returned from the Jordan, and was led
ἐν τῷ πνεύματι ἐν τῇ ἐρήμῳ 2 ἡμέρας
by the Spirit in the desert days
τεσσεράκοντα πειραζόμενος ὑπὸ τοῦ διαβόλου.
forty being tempted by the devil.

[m]*32* Some early manuscripts *Sala*
[n]*33* Some manuscripts *Amminadab, the son of Admin, the son of Arni*; other manuscripts vary widely.

He ate nothing during those days; and when they had ended, He became hungry.
3And the devil said to Him, "If You are the Son of God, tell this stone to become bread."
4And Jesus answered him, "It is written, 'MAN SHALL NOT LIVE ON BREAD ALONE.' "
5And he led Him up and showed Him all the kingdoms of the world in a moment of time.
6And the devil said to Him, "I will give You all this domain and its glory; for it has been handed over to me, and I give it to whomever I wish.
7"Therefore if You worship before me, it shall all be Yours."
8And Jesus answered and said to him, "It is written, 'YOU SHALL WORSHIP THE LORD YOUR GOD AND SERVE HIM ONLY.' "
9And he led Him to Jerusalem and had Him stand on the pinnacle of the temple, and said to Him, "If You are the Son of God, throw Yourself down from here;
10for it is written,

'HE WILL GIVE HIS ANGELS CHARGE CONCERNING YOU TO GUARD YOU,'

11 and,

'ON *their* HANDS THEY WILL BEAR YOU UP,
LEST YOU STRIKE YOUR FOOT AGAINST A STONE.' "

12And Jesus answered and said to him, "It is said, 'YOU SHALL NOT [l]PUT THE LORD YOUR GOD TO THE TEST.' "
13And when the devil had finished every temptation, he departed from Him until an opportune time.

Jesus' Public Ministry

14And Jesus returned to Galilee in the power of the Spirit; and news about Him spread through all the surrounding district.
15And He *began* teaching

[l]Or, *tempt . . . God*

Καὶ οὐκ ἔφαγεν οὐδὲν ἐν ταῖς ἡμέραις
And he ate not no(any)thing in – days
ἐκείναις, καὶ συντελεσθεισῶν αὐτῶν ἐπεί-
those, and being ended them[a] he
=when they were ended
νασεν. 3 εἶπεν δὲ αὐτῷ ὁ διάβολος·
hungered. And said to him the devil :
εἰ υἱὸς εἶ τοῦ θεοῦ, εἰπὲ τῷ λίθῳ
If Son thou art – of God, tell – stone
τούτῳ ἵνα γένηται ἄρτος. 4 καὶ ἀπεκρίθη
this that it become a loaf. And made answer
πρὸς αὐτὸν ὁ Ἰησοῦς· γέγραπται ὅτι
to him – Jesus : It has been written[,] –
οὐκ ἐπ' ἄρτῳ μόνῳ ζήσεται ὁ ἄνθρωπος.
Not on bread only shall live – man.
5 Καὶ ἀναγαγὼν αὐτὸν ἔδειξεν αὐτῷ πάσας
And leading up him he showed him all
τὰς βασιλείας τῆς οἰκουμένης ἐν στιγμῇ
the kingdoms of the inhabited earth in a moment
χρόνου. 6 καὶ εἶπεν αὐτῷ ὁ διάβολος·
of time. And said to him the devil :
σοὶ δώσω τὴν ἐξουσίαν ταύτην ἅπασαν καὶ
To thee I will give – authority this all and
τὴν δόξαν αὐτῶν, ὅτι ἐμοὶ παραδέδοται
the glory of them, because to me it has been delivered
καὶ ᾧ ἐὰν θέλω δίδωμι αὐτήν· 7 σὺ οὖν
and to whomever I wish I give it; [a]thou [1]therefore
ἐὰν προσκυνήσῃς ἐνώπιον ἐμοῦ, ἔσται σοῦ
[a]if worship before me, will be of thee
πᾶσα. 8 καὶ ἀποκριθεὶς ὁ Ἰησοῦς εἶπεν
all. And answering – Jesus said
αὐτῷ· γέγραπται· προσκυνήσεις κύριον τὸν
to him : It has been written: Thou shalt worship [the] Lord the
θεόν σου καὶ αὐτῷ μόνῳ λατρεύσεις.
God of thee and him only shalt thou serve.
9 Ἤγαγεν δὲ αὐτὸν εἰς Ἰερουσαλὴμ καὶ
And he led him to Jerusalem and
ἔστησεν ἐπὶ τὸ πτερύγιον τοῦ ἱεροῦ, καὶ
set on the gable of the temple, and
εἶπεν αὐτῷ· εἰ υἱὸς εἶ τοῦ θεοῦ, βάλε
said to him : If Son thou art – of God, throw
σεαυτὸν ἐντεῦθεν κάτω· 10 γέγραπται γὰρ ὅτι
thyself hence down; for it has been written[,] –
τοῖς ἀγγέλοις αὐτοῦ ἐντελεῖται περὶ
The angels of him he will command concerning
σοῦ τοῦ διαφυλάξαι σε, 11 καὶ ὅτι ἐπὶ
thee – to preserve[d] thee, and – on
χειρῶν ἀροῦσίν σε, μήποτε προσκόψῃς
[their] hands they will bear thee, lest thou dash
πρὸς λίθον τὸν πόδα σου. 12 καὶ
against a stone the foot of thee. And
ἀποκριθεὶς εἶπεν αὐτῷ ὁ Ἰησοῦς ὅτι
answering said to him – Jesus[,] –
εἴρηται· οὐκ ἐκπειράσεις κύριον τὸν
It has been said : Thou shalt not overtempt [the] Lord the
θεόν σου. 13 Καὶ συντελέσας πάντα πειρασμὸν
God of thee. And having finished every temptation
ὁ διάβολος ἀπέστη ἀπ' αὐτοῦ ἄχρι καιροῦ.
the devil went away from him until a season.
14 Καὶ ὑπέστρεψεν ὁ Ἰησοῦς ἐν τῇ
And returned – Jesus in the
δυνάμει τοῦ πνεύματος εἰς τὴν Γαλιλαίαν·
power of the Spirit to – Galilee;
καὶ φήμη ἐξῆλθεν καθ' ὅλης τῆς περιχώρου
and a rumour went forth throughout all the neighbourhood
περὶ αὐτοῦ. 15 καὶ αὐτὸς ἐδίδασκεν ἐν
concerning him. And he taught in

Chapter 4

The Temptation of Jesus

JESUS, full of the Holy Spirit, returned from the Jordan and was led by the Spirit in the desert,
2where for forty days he was tempted by the devil. He ate nothing during those days, and at the end of them he was hungry.
3The devil said to him, "If you are the Son of God, tell this stone to become bread."
4Jesus answered, "It is written: 'Man does not live on bread alone.'[o]"
5The devil led him up to a high place and showed him in an instant all the kingdoms of the world.
6And he said to him, "I will give you all their authority and splendor, for it has been given to me, and I can give it to anyone I want to.
7So if you worship me, it will all be yours."
8Jesus answered, "It is written: 'Worship the Lord your God and serve him only.'[p]"
9The devil led him to Jerusalem and had him stand on the highest point of the temple. "If you are the Son of God," he said, "throw yourself down from here.
10For it is written:

" 'He will command his angels concerning you
to guard you carefully;
11they will lift you up in their hands,
so that you will not strike your foot against a stone.'[q]"

12Jesus answered, "It says: 'Do not put the Lord your God to the test.'[r]"
13When the devil had finished all this tempting, he left him until an opportune time.

Jesus Rejected at Nazareth

14Jesus returned to Galilee in the power of the Spirit, and news about him spread through the whole countryside.
15He taught in

[o]*4* Deut. 8:3
[p]*8* Deut. 6:13
[q]*11* Psalm 91:11,12
[r]*12* Deut. 6:16

in their synagogues and
was praised by all.
16And He came to Nazareth, where He had been brought up; and as was His custom, He entered the synagogue on the Sabbath, and stood up to read.
17And the book of the prophet Isaiah was handed to Him. And He opened the book, and found the place where it was written,
18"THE SPIRIT OF THE
LORD IS UPON ME,
BECAUSE HE ANOINTED
ME TO PREACH THE
GOSPEL TO THE POOR.
HE HAS SENT ME TO
PROCLAIM RELEASE TO
THE CAPTIVES,
AND RECOVERY OF
SIGHT TO THE BLIND,
TO SET FREE THOSE
WHO ARE DOWNTRODDEN,
19 TO PROCLAIM THE FAVORABLE YEAR OF THE
LORD."
20And He closed the book, and gave it back to the attendant, and sat down; and the eyes of all in the synagogue were fixed upon Him.
21And He began to say to them, "Today this Scripture has been fulfilled in your hearing."
22And all were speaking well of Him, and wondering at the gracious words which were falling from His lips; and they were saying, "Is this not Joseph's son?"
23And He said to them, "No doubt you will quote this proverb to Me, 'Physician, heal yourself! Whatever we heard was done at Capernaum, do here in your home town as well.' "
24And He said, "Truly I say to you, no prophet is welcome in his home town.
25"But I say to you in truth, there were many widows in Israel in the days of Elijah, when the sky was shut up for three years and

ταῖς συναγωγαῖς αὐτῶν, δοξαζόμενος ὑπὸ
the synagogues of them, being glorified by
πάντων.
all.
16 Καὶ ἦλθεν εἰς Ναζαρά, οὗ ἦν
And he came to Nazareth, where he was
τεθραμμένος, καὶ εἰσῆλθεν κατὰ τὸ εἰωθὸς
having been brought up, and entered according to the custom =his custom
αὐτῷ ἐν τῇ ἡμέρᾳ τῶν σαββάτων εἰς τὴν
to him[e] on the day of the sabbaths into the
συναγωγήν, καὶ ἀνέστη ἀναγνῶναι. 17 καὶ
synagogue, and stood up to read. And
ἐπεδόθη αὐτῷ βιβλίον τοῦ προφήτου
was handed to him a roll of the prophet
Ἠσαΐου, καὶ ἀνοίξας τὸ βιβλίον εὗρεν
Esaias, and having opened the roll he found
[τὸν] τόπον οὗ ἦν γεγραμμένον· 18 πνεῦμα
the place where it was *having been* written: [The] Spirit
κυρίου ἐπ' ἐμέ, οὗ εἵνεκεν ἔχρισέν με
of [the] Lord [is] upon me, wherefore he anointed me
εὐαγγελίσασθαι πτωχοῖς, ἀπέσταλκέν με
to evangelize [the] poor, he has sent me
κηρῦξαι αἰχμαλώτοις ἄφεσιν καὶ τυφλοῖς
to proclaim to captives release and to blind [ones]
ἀνάβλεψιν, ἀποστεῖλαι τεθραυσμένους ἐν
sight, to send away *having been* crushed [ones] in
ἀφέσει, 19 κηρῦξαι ἐνιαυτὸν κυρίου δεκτόν.
release, to proclaim a year of [the] Lord acceptable.
20 καὶ πτύξας τὸ βιβλίον ἀποδοὺς τῷ
And having closed the roll returning [it] to the
ὑπηρέτῃ ἐκάθισεν· καὶ πάντων οἱ ὀφθαλμοὶ
attendant he sat; and of all the eyes
ἐν τῇ συναγωγῇ ἦσαν ἀτενίζοντες αὐτῷ.
in the synagogue were gazing at him.
21 ἤρξατο δὲ λέγειν πρὸς αὐτοὺς ὅτι
And he began to say to them[,] –
σήμερον πεπλήρωται ἡ γραφὴ αὕτη ἐν
To-day has been fulfilled – scripture this in
τοῖς ὠσὶν ὑμῶν. 22 καὶ πάντες ἐμαρτύρουν
the ears of you. And all bore witness
αὐτῷ καὶ ἐθαύμαζον ἐπὶ τοῖς λόγοις τῆς
to him and marvelled at the words –
χάριτος τοῖς ἐκπορευομένοις ἐκ τοῦ στόματος
of grace – proceeding out of the mouth
αὐτοῦ, καὶ ἔλεγον· οὐχὶ υἱός ἐστιν Ἰωσὴφ
of him, and they said: [2]not [4]son [1]Is [5]of Joseph
οὗτος; 23 καὶ εἶπεν πρὸς αὐτούς· πάντως
[3]this man? And he said to them: To be sure
ἐρεῖτέ μοι τὴν παραβολὴν ταύτην· ἰατρέ,
ye will say to me – parable this: Physician,
θεράπευσον σεαυτόν· ὅσα ἠκούσαμεν γεν-
heal thyself; what things we heard hap-
όμενα εἰς τὴν Καφαρναούμ, ποίησον καὶ
pening in – Capernaum, do also
ὧδε ἐν τῇ πατρίδι σου. 24 εἶπεν δέ·
here in the native place of thee. And he said:
ἀμὴν λέγω ὑμῖν ὅτι οὐδεὶς προφήτης
Truly I tell you that no prophet
δεκτός ἐστιν ἐν τῇ πατρίδι αὐτοῦ. 25 ἐπ'
acceptable is in the native place of him. [2]on(in)
ἀληθείας δὲ λέγω ὑμῖν, πολλαὶ χῆραι ἦσαν
[3]truth [1]But I tell you, many widows were
ἐν ταῖς ἡμέραις Ἠλίου ἐν τῷ Ἰσραήλ,
in the days of Elias in – Israel,
ὅτε ἐκλείσθη ὁ οὐρανὸς ἐπὶ ἔτη τρία καὶ
when was shut up the heaven over years three and

their synagogues, and everyone praised him.
16He went to Nazareth, where he had been brought up, and on the Sabbath day he went into the synagogue, as was his custom. And he stood up to read.
17The scroll of the prophet Isaiah was handed to him. Unrolling it, he found the place where it is written:
18"The Spirit of the Lord
is on me,
because he has
anointed me
to preach good news to
the poor.
He has sent me to
proclaim freedom
for the prisoners
and recovery of sight
for the blind,
to release the oppressed,
19 to proclaim the year of
the Lord's favor."[s]
20Then he rolled up the scroll, gave it back to the attendant and sat down. The eyes of everyone in the synagogue were fastened on him, 21and he began by saying to them, "Today this scripture is fulfilled in your hearing."
22All spoke well of him and were amazed at the gracious words that came from his lips. "Isn't this Joseph's son?" they asked.
23Jesus said to them, "Surely you will quote this proverb to me: 'Physician, heal yourself! Do here in your hometown what we have heard that you did in Capernaum.' "
24"I tell you the truth," he continued, "no prophet is accepted in his hometown. 25I assure you that there were many widows in Israel in Elijah's time, when the sky was shut for three and a half years and

[s]*19* Isaiah 61:1,2

six months, when a great
famine came over all the
land;
26and yet Elijah was sent
to none of them, but only to
Zarephath, *in the land* of
Sidon, to a woman who
was a widow.
27"And there were many
lepers in Israel in the time
of Elisha the prophet; and
none of them was cleansed,
but only Naaman the Syri-
an."
28And all in the syna-
gogue were filled with rage
as they heard these things;
29and they rose up and
cast Him out of the city,
and led Him to the brow of
the hill on which their city
had been built, in order to
throw Him down the cliff.
30But passing through
their midst, He went His
way.
31And He came down to
Capernaum, a city of Galilee. And He was teaching
them on the Sabbath;
32and they were amazed
at His teaching, for His
message was with author-
ity.
33And there was a man in
the synagogue possessed
by the spirit of an unclean
demon, and he cried out
with a loud voice,
34"Ha! What do we have
to do with You, Jesus of
Nazareth? Have You come
to destroy us? I know who
You are—the Holy One of
God!"
35And Jesus rebuked him,
saying, "Be quiet and
come out of him!" And
when the demon had
thrown him down in *their*
midst, he came out of him
without doing him any
harm.
36And amazement came
upon them all, and they *began* discussing with one another saying, "What is this
message? For with author-
ity and power He com-
mands the unclean spirits,
and they come out."
37And the report about
Him was getting out into

μῆνας ἕξ, ὡς ἐγένετο λιμὸς μέγας ἐπὶ
months six, when came famine a great over
πᾶσαν τὴν γῆν, 26 καὶ πρὸς οὐδεμίαν
all the land, and to not one
αὐτῶν ἐπέμφθη Ἠλίας εἰ μὴ εἰς Σάρεπτα
of them was sent Elias except to Sarepta
τῆς Σιδωνίας πρὸς γυναῖκα χήραν. 27 καὶ
– of Sidon to a woman a widow. And
πολλοὶ λεπροὶ ἦσαν ἐν τῷ Ἰσραὴλ ἐπὶ
many lepers were in – Israel during
Ἐλισαίου τοῦ προφήτου, καὶ οὐδεὶς αὐτῶν
Elisæus the prophet, and not one of them
ἐκαθαρίσθη εἰ μὴ Ναιμὰν ὁ Σύρος.
was cleansed except Naaman the Syrian.
28 καὶ ἐπλήσθησαν πάντες θυμοῦ ἐν τῇ
And [2]were filled [1]all of(with) anger in the
συναγωγῇ ἀκούοντες ταῦτα, 29 καὶ ἀναστάντες
synagogue hearing these things, and rising up
ἐξέβαλον αὐτὸν ἔξω τῆς πόλεως, καὶ
they cast *out* him outside the city, and
ἤγαγον αὐτὸν ἕως ὀφρύος τοῦ ὄρους ἐφ᾽
led him to a brow of the hill on
οὗ ἡ πόλις ᾠκοδόμητο αὐτῶν, ὥστε
which the city was built of them, so as
κατακρημνίσαι αὐτόν· 30 αὐτὸς δὲ διελθὼν
to throw down him; but he passing *through*
διὰ μέσου αὐτῶν ἐπορεύετο.
through [the] midst of them went.
31 Καὶ κατῆλθεν εἰς Καφαρναοὺμ πόλιν
And he went down to Capernaum a city
τῆς Γαλιλαίας. καὶ ἦν διδάσκων αὐτοὺς
– of Galilee. And he was teaching them
ἐν τοῖς σάββασιν· 32 καὶ ἐξεπλήσσοντο
on the sabbaths; and they were astounded
ἐπὶ τῇ διδαχῇ αὐτοῦ, ὅτι ἐν ἐξουσίᾳ
at the teaching of him, because with authority
ἦν ὁ λόγος αὐτοῦ. 33 καὶ ἐν τῇ συναγωγῇ
was the word of him. And in the synagogue
ἦν ἄνθρωπος ἔχων πνεῦμα δαιμονίου
there was a man having a spirit [2]demon
ἀκαθάρτου, καὶ ἀνέκραξεν φωνῇ μεγάλῃ·
[1]of an unclean, and he shouted voice with a great :
34 ἔα, τί ἡμῖν καὶ σοί, Ἰησοῦ Ναζαρηνέ;
Ah, what to us and to thee, Jesus Nazarene?
ἦλθες ἀπολέσαι ἡμᾶς; οἶδά σε τίς εἶ,
Camest thou to destroy us? I know thee who thou art,
ὁ ἅγιος τοῦ θεοῦ. 35 καὶ ἐπετίμησεν αὐτῷ
the holy one – of God. And rebuked him
ὁ Ἰησοῦς λέγων· φιμώθητι καὶ ἔξελθε
– Jesus saying : Be muzzled and come out
ἀπ᾽ αὐτοῦ. καὶ ῥίψαν αὐτὸν τὸ δαιμόνιον
from him. And [3]throwing [4]him [1]the [2]demon
εἰς τὸ μέσον ἐξῆλθεν ἀπ᾽ αὐτοῦ μηδὲν
in the midst came out from him nothing
βλάψαν αὐτόν. 36 καὶ ἐγένετο θάμβος
injuring him. And came astonishment
ἐπὶ πάντας, καὶ συνελάλουν πρὸς ἀλλήλους
on all, and they spoke to one another
λέγοντες· τίς ὁ λόγος οὗτος, ὅτι ἐν
saying : What [is] – word this, because with
ἐξουσίᾳ καὶ δυνάμει ἐπιτάσσει τοῖς
authority and power he commands the
ἀκαθάρτοις πνεύμασιν καὶ ἐξέρχονται; 37 καὶ
unclean spirits and they come out? And
ἐξεπορεύετο ἦχος περὶ αὐτοῦ εἰς πάντα
went forth a rumour concerning him into every

there was a severe famine
throughout the land. 26Yet
Elijah was not sent to any
of them, but to a widow in
Zarephath in the region of
Sidon. 27And there were
many in Israel with leprosy[t] in the time of Elisha the
prophet, yet not one of
them was cleansed—only
Naaman the Syrian."
28All the people in the
synagogue were furious
when they heard this.
29They got up, drove him
out of the town, and took
him to the brow of the hill
on which the town was
built, in order to throw him
down the cliff. 30But he
walked right through the
crowd and went on his
way.

Jesus Drives Out an Evil Spirit

31Then he went down to
Capernaum, a town in Galilee, and on the Sabbath began to teach the people.
32They were amazed at his
teaching, because his message had authority.
33In the synagogue there
was a man possessed by a
demon, an evil[u] spirit. He
cried out at the top of his
voice, 34"Ha! What do you
want with us, Jesus of Nazareth? Have you come to
destroy us? I know who
you are—the Holy One of
God!"
35"Be quiet!" Jesus said
sternly. "Come out of
him!" Then the demon
threw the man down before
them all and came out without injuring him.
36All the people were
amazed and said to each
other, "What is this teaching? With authority and
power he gives orders to
evil spirits and they come
out!" 37And the news about

[t]27 The Greek word was used for various diseases affecting the skin—not necessarily leprosy.
[u]33 Greek *unclean*; also in verse 36

every locality in the surrounding district.

Many Are Healed

38And He arose and *left*
the synagogue, and entered
Simon's home. Now Si-
mon's mother-in-law was
suffering from a high fever;
and they made request of
Him on her behalf.
39And standing over her,
He rebuked the fever, and
it left her; and she immediately arose and waited on
them.
40And while the sun was
setting, all who had any
sick with various diseases
brought them to Him; and
laying His hands on every
one of them, He was heal-
ing them.
41And demons also were
coming out of many, crying
out and saying, "You are
the Son of God!" And
rebuking them, He would
not allow them to speak,
because they knew Him to
be the Christ.
42And when day came,
He departed and went to a
lonely place; and the multitudes were searching for
Him, and came to Him, and
tried to keep Him from going away from them.
43But He said to them, "I
must preach the kingdom
of God to the other cities
also, for I was sent for this
purpose."
44And He kept on preach-
ing in the synagogues of
[m]Judea.

τόπον τῆς περιχώρου. **38** Ἀναστὰς δὲ
place of the neighbourhood. And rising up
ἀπὸ τῆς συναγωγῆς εἰσῆλθεν εἰς τὴν
from the synagogue he entered into the
οἰκίαν Σίμωνος. πενθερὰ δὲ τοῦ Σίμωνος
house of Simon. And [the] mother-in-law – of Simon
ἦν συνεχομένη πυρετῷ μεγάλῳ, καὶ
was being seized fever with a great, and
ἠρώτησαν αὐτὸν περὶ αὐτῆς. **39** καὶ
they ask him about her. And
ἐπιστὰς ἐπάνω αὐτῆς ἐπετίμησεν τῷ πυρετῷ,
standing over her he rebuked the fever,
καὶ ἀφῆκεν αὐτήν· παραχρῆμα δὲ ἀναστᾶσα
and it left her; and at once rising up
διηκόνει αὐτοῖς. **40** Δύνοντος δὲ τοῦ
she served them. And setting the
=as the sun was setting
ἡλίου ἅπαντες ὅσοι εἶχον ἀσθενοῦντας
sun[a] all as many as had ailing [ones]
νόσοις ποικίλαις ἤγαγον αὐτοὺς πρὸς αὐτόν·
diseases with various brought them to him;
ὁ δὲ ἑνὶ ἑκάστῳ αὐτῶν τὰς χεῖρας
and he [5]one [4]on each [6]of them [2]the(his) [3]hands
ἐπιτιθεὶς ἐθεράπευεν αὐτούς. **41** ἐξήρχετο
[1]putting *on* healed them. came out
δὲ καὶ δαιμόνια ἀπὸ πολλῶν, κραυγάζοντα
And also demons from many, crying out
καὶ λέγοντα ὅτι σὺ εἶ ὁ υἱὸς τοῦ θεοῦ.
and saying[,] – Thou art the Son – of God.
καὶ ἐπιτιμῶν οὐκ εἴα αὐτὰ λαλεῖν, ὅτι
And rebuking he allowed not them to speak, because
ᾔδεισαν τὸν χριστὸν αὐτὸν εἶναι. **42** Γενομένης
they knew [3]the [4]Christ [1]him [2]to be. coming
=And when
δὲ ἡμέρας ἐξελθὼν ἐπορεύθη εἰς ἔρημον
And day[a] going forth he went to a desert
day came
τόπον· καὶ οἱ ὄχλοι ἐπεζήτουν αὐτόν, καὶ
place; and the crowds sought him, and
ἦλθον ἕως αὐτοῦ, καὶ κατεῖχον αὐτὸν
came up to him, and detained him
τοῦ μὴ πορεύεσθαι ἀπ' αὐτῶν. **43** ὁ δὲ
– not to go[d] from them. And he
=so that he should not go
εἶπεν πρὸς αὐτοὺς ὅτι καὶ ταῖς ἑτέραις
said to them[,] – Also to the other
πόλεσιν εὐαγγελίσασθαί με δεῖ τὴν
cities [3]to preach [2]me [1]it behoves the
βασιλείαν τοῦ θεοῦ, ὅτι ἐπὶ τοῦτο ἀπεστάλην.
kingdom – of God, because on this I was sent.
44 καὶ ἦν κηρύσσων εἰς τὰς συναγωγὰς
And he was proclaiming in the synagogues
τῆς Ἰουδαίας.
– of Judæa.

him spread throughout the
surrounding area.

Jesus Heals Many

38Jesus left the synagogue
and went to the home of Simon. Now Simon's moth-
er-in-law was suffering
from a high fever, and they
asked Jesus to help her.
39So he bent over her and
rebuked the fever, and it
left her. She got up at once
and began to wait on them.
40When the sun was set-
ting, the people brought to
Jesus all who had various
kinds of sickness, and laying his hands on each one,
he healed them. 41More-
over, demons came out of
many people, shouting,
"You are the Son of God!"
But he rebuked them and
would not allow them to
speak, because they knew
he was the Christ.[v]
42At daybreak Jesus went
out to a solitary place. The
people were looking for
him and when they came to
where he was, they tried to
keep him from leaving
them. 43But he said, "I
must preach the good news
of the kingdom of God to
the other towns also, be-
cause that is why I was
sent." 44And he kept on
preaching in the syna-
gogues of Judea.[w]

Chapter 5

The First Disciples

NOW it came about that
while the multitude
were pressing around Him
and listening to the word of
God, He was standing by
the lake of Gennesaret;
2and He saw two boats
lying at the edge of the lake;
but the fishermen had gotten out of them, and were
washing their nets.

5 Ἐγένετο δὲ ἐν τῷ τὸν ὄχλον ἐπικεῖσθαι
Now it came to pass in the the crowd to press upon
=as the crowd pressed upon him and heard
αὐτῷ καὶ ἀκούειν τὸν λόγον τοῦ θεοῦ,
him and to hear[be] the word – of God,
καὶ αὐτὸς ἦν ἑστὼς παρὰ τὴν λίμνην
and he was standing by the lake
Γεννησαρέτ, **2** καὶ εἶδεν δύο πλοιάρια
Gennesaret, and saw two boats
ἑστῶτα παρὰ τὴν λίμνην· οἱ δὲ ἁλεεῖς
standing by the lake; but the fishermen
ἀπ' αὐτῶν ἀποβάντες ἔπλυνον τὰ δίκτυα.
from them having gone away were washing the nets.

Chapter 5

The Calling of the First Disciples

ONE day as Jesus was
standing by the Lake
of Gennesaret,[x] with the
people crowding around
him and listening to the
word of God, 2he saw at the
water's edge two boats, left
there by the fishermen,
who were washing their

[m]I.e., the country of the Jews (including Galilee); some mss. read *Galilee*

[v]*41* Or *Messiah*
[w]*44* Or *the land of the Jews*; some manuscripts *Galilee*
[x]*1* That is, Sea of Galilee

[3]And He got into one of the boats, which was Simon's, and asked him to put out a little way from the land. And He sat down and *began* teaching the multitudes from the boat.

[4]And when He had finished speaking, He said to Simon, "Put out into the deep water and let down your nets for a catch."

[5]And Simon answered and said, "Master, we worked hard all night and caught nothing, but at Your bidding I will let down the nets."

[6]And when they had done this, they enclosed a great quantity of fish; and their nets *began* to break;

[7]and they signaled to their partners in the other boat, for them to come and help them. And they came, and filled both of the boats, so that they began to sink.

[8]But when Simon Peter saw *that,* he fell down at Jesus' feet, saying, "Depart from me, for I am a sinful man, O Lord!"

[9]For amazement had seized him and all his companions because of the catch of fish which they had taken;

[10]and so also James and John, sons of Zebedee, who were partners with Simon. And Jesus said to Simon, "Do not fear, from now on you will be catching men."

[11]And when they had brought their boats to land, they left everything and followed Him.

The Leper and the Paralytic

[12]And it came about that while He was in one of the cities, behold, *there was* a man full of leprosy; and when he saw Jesus, he fell on his face and implored Him, saying, "Lord, if You

3 ἐμβὰς δὲ εἰς ἓν τῶν πλοίων, ὃ ἦν
And embarking in one of the boats, which was
Σίμωνος, ἠρώτησεν αὐτὸν ἀπὸ τῆς γῆς
of Simon, he asked him from the land
ἐπαναγαγεῖν ὀλίγον· καθίσας δὲ ἐκ τοῦ
to put out a little; and sitting [4]out of [5]the
πλοίου ἐδίδασκεν τοὺς ὄχλους. **4** ὡς δὲ
[6]boat [1]he taught [2]the [3]crowds. And when
ἐπαύσατο λαλῶν, εἶπεν πρὸς τὸν Σίμωνα·
he ceased speaking, he said to – Simon :
ἐπανάγαγε εἰς τὸ βάθος, καὶ χαλάσατε
Put out into the deep, and let down
τὰ δίκτυα ὑμῶν εἰς ἄγραν. **5** καὶ
the nets of you for a draught. And
ἀποκριθεὶς Σίμων εἶπεν· ἐπιστάτα, δι'
answering Simon said : Master, through
ὅλης νυκτὸς κοπιάσαντες οὐδὲν ἐλάβομεν·
[the] whole night labouring nothing we took;
ἐπὶ δὲ τῷ ῥήματί σου χαλάσω τὰ δίκτυα.
but at the word of thee I will let down the nets.
6 καὶ τοῦτο ποιήσαντες συνέκλεισαν πλῆθος
And this doing they enclosed multitude
ἰχθύων πολύ· διερρήσσετο δὲ τὰ δίκτυα
of fishes a much; and were being torn the nets
αὐτῶν. **7** καὶ κατένευσαν τοῖς μετόχοις
of them. And they nodded to the(ir) partners
ἐν τῷ ἑτέρῳ πλοίῳ τοῦ ἐλθόντας
in the other boat – coming
=that they should come
συλλαβέσθαι αὐτοῖς· καὶ ἦλθαν, καὶ ἔπλησαν
to help[d] them; and they came, and filled
ἀμφότερα τὰ πλοῖα ὥστε βυθίζεσθαι αὐτά.
both the boats so as to be sinking them.[b]
=so that they were sinking.
8 ἰδὼν δὲ Σίμων Πέτρος προσέπεσεν τοῖς
And seeing Simon Peter fell at the
γόνασιν Ἰησοῦ λέγων· ἔξελθε ἀπ' ἐμοῦ,
knees of Jesus saying : Depart from me,
ὅτι ἀνὴρ ἁμαρτωλός εἰμι, κύριε. **9** θάμβος
because man a sinful I am, Lord. astonishment
γὰρ περιέσχεν αὐτὸν καὶ πάντας τοὺς
For seized him and all the [ones]
σὺν αὐτῷ ἐπὶ τῇ ἄγρᾳ τῶν ἰχθύων ᾗ
with him at the draught of the fishes which
συνέλαβον, **10** ὁμοίως δὲ καὶ Ἰάκωβον καὶ
they took, and likewise both James and
Ἰωάννην υἱοὺς Ζεβεδαίου, οἳ ἦσαν κοινωνοὶ
John sons of Zebedee, who were sharers
τῷ Σίμωνι. καὶ εἶπεν πρὸς τὸν Σίμωνα
– with Simon. And said to – Simon
ὁ Ἰησοῦς· μὴ φοβοῦ· ἀπὸ τοῦ νῦν
– Jesus: Fear thou not; from – now
ἀνθρώπους ἔσῃ ζωγρῶν. **11** καὶ καταγαγόντες
men thou wilt be taking alive. And bringing down
τὰ πλοῖα ἐπὶ τὴν γῆν, ἀφέντες πάντα
the boats onto the land, leaving all things
ἠκολούθησαν αὐτῷ.
they followed him.
12 Καὶ ἐγένετο ἐν τῷ εἶναι αὐτὸν ἐν
And it came to pass in the to be him[be] in
=as he was
μιᾷ τῶν πόλεων καὶ ἰδοὺ ἀνὴρ πλήρης
one of the cities *and* behold[,] a man full
λέπρας· ἰδὼν δὲ τὸν Ἰησοῦν, πεσὼν ἐπὶ
of leprosy; and seeing — Jesus, falling on
πρόσωπον ἐδεήθη αὐτοῦ λέγων· κύριε,
[his] face he begged him saying : Lord,

nets. [3]He got into one of the boats, the one belonging to Simon, and asked him to put out a little from shore. Then he sat down and taught the people from the boat.

[4]When he had finished speaking, he said to Simon, "Put out into deep water, and let down[y] the nets for a catch."

[5]Simon answered, "Master, we've worked hard all night and haven't caught anything. But because you say so, I will let down the nets."

[6]When they had done so, they caught such a large number of fish that their nets began to break. [7]So they signaled their partners in the other boat to come and help them, and they came and filled both boats so full that they began to sink.

[8]When Simon Peter saw this, he fell at Jesus' knees and said, "Go away from me, Lord; I am a sinful man!" [9]For he and all his companions were astonished at the catch of fish they had taken, [10]and so were James and John, the sons of Zebedee, Simon's partners.

Then Jesus said to Simon, "Don't be afraid; from now on you will catch men." [11]So they pulled their boats up on shore, left everything and followed him.

The Man With Leprosy

[12]While Jesus was in one of the towns, a man came along who was covered with leprosy.[z] When he saw Jesus, he fell with his face to the ground and begged him, "Lord, if you

[y]*4* The Greek verb is plural.
[z]*12* The Greek word was used for various diseases affecting the skin—not necessarily leprosy.

are willing, You can make me clean."

13And He stretched out His hand, and touched him, saying, "I am willing; be cleansed." And immediately the leprosy left him.

14And He ordered him to tell no one, "But go and show yourself to the priest, and make an offering for your cleansing, just as Moses commanded, for a testimony to them."

15But the news about Him was spreading even farther, and great multitudes were gathering to hear *Him* and to be healed of their sicknesses.

16But He Himself would *often* slip away to the wilderness and pray.

17And it came about one day that He was teaching; and there were *some* Pharisees and teachers of the law sitting *there,* who had come from every village of Galilee and Judea and *from* Jerusalem; and the power of the Lord was *present* for Him to perform healing.

18And behold, *some* men *were* carrying on a bed a man who was paralyzed; and they were trying to bring him in, and to set him down in front of Him.

19And not finding any *way* to bring him in because of the crowd, they went up on the roof and let him down through the tiles with his stretcher, right in the center, in front of Jesus.

20And seeing their faith, He said, "Friend, your sins are forgiven you."

21And the scribes and the Pharisees began to reason, saying, "Who is this *man* who speaks blasphemies? Who can forgive sins, but God alone?"

22But Jesus, aware of

ἐὰν θέλῃς, δύνασαί με καθαρίσαι. **13** καὶ
if thou willest, thou canst me *to* cleanse. And
ἐκτείνας τὴν χεῖρα ἥψατο αὐτοῦ λέγων·
stretching out the(his) hand he touched him saying :
θέλω, καθαρίσθητι· καὶ εὐθέως ἡ λέπρα
I am willing, be thou cleansed; and immediately the leprosy
ἀπῆλθεν ἀπ' αὐτοῦ. **14** καὶ αὐτὸς παρήγγειλεν
departed from him. And he charged
αὐτῷ μηδενὶ εἰπεῖν, ἀλλὰ ἀπελθὼν δεῖξον
him no one to tell, but going away show
σεαυτὸν τῷ ἱερεῖ, καὶ προσένεγκε περὶ
thyself to the priest, and offer concerning
τοῦ καθαρισμοῦ σου καθὼς προσέταξεν
the cleansing of thee as commanded
Μωϋσῆς, εἰς μαρτύριον αὐτοῖς. **15** διήρχετο
Moses, for a testimony to them. went
δὲ μᾶλλον ὁ λόγος περὶ αὐτοῦ, καὶ
But rather the word concerning him, and
συνήρχοντο ὄχλοι πολλοὶ ἀκούειν καὶ
[3]accompanied [2]crowds [1]many to hear and
θεραπεύεσθαι ἀπὸ τῶν ἀσθενειῶν αὐτῶν·
to be healed from the infirmities of them;
16 αὐτὸς δὲ ἦν ὑποχωρῶν ἐν ταῖς ἐρήμοις
but he was withdrawing in the deserts
καὶ προσευχόμενος.
and praying.

17 Καὶ ἐγένετο ἐν μιᾷ τῶν ἡμερῶν καὶ
And it came to pass on one of the days *and*
αὐτὸς ἦν διδάσκων, καὶ ἦσαν καθήμενοι
he was teaching, and were sitting
Φαρισαῖοι καὶ νομοδιδάσκαλοι οἳ ἦσαν
Pharisees and law-teachers who were
ἐληλυθότες ἐκ πάσης κώμης τῆς Γαλιλαίας
having come out of every village – of Galilee
καὶ Ἰουδαίας καὶ Ἰερουσαλήμ· καὶ δύναμις
and Judæa and Jerusalem; and [the] power
κυρίου ἦν εἰς τὸ ἰᾶσθαι αὐτόν. **18** καὶ
of [the] Lord was [1]in – [3]to cure [2]him. And
ἰδοὺ ἄνδρες φέροντες ἐπὶ κλίνης ἄνθρωπον
behold[,] men bearing on a couch a man
ὃς ἦν παραλελυμένος, καὶ ἐζήτουν αὐτὸν
who was *having been* paralysed, and they sought [2]him
εἰσενεγκεῖν καὶ θεῖναι [αὐτὸν] ἐνώπιον
[1]to carry in and to lay him before
αὐτοῦ. **19** καὶ μὴ εὑρόντες ποίας εἰσ-
him. And not finding how† they
ενέγκωσιν αὐτὸν διὰ τὸν ὄχλον, ἀναβάντες
might carry in him because of the crowd, going up
ἐπὶ τὸ δῶμα διὰ τῶν κεράμων καθῆκαν
onto the roof through the tiles they let down
αὐτὸν σὺν τῷ κλινιδίῳ εἰς τὸ μέσον
him with the couch into the midst
ἔμπροσθεν τοῦ Ἰησοῦ. **20** καὶ ἰδὼν τὴν
in front of – Jesus. And seeing the
πίστιν αὐτῶν εἶπεν· ἄνθρωπε, ἀφέωνταί
faith of them he said : Man, have been forgiven
σοι αἱ ἁμαρτίαι σου. **21** καὶ ἤρξαντο
thee the sins of thee. And began
διαλογίζεσθαι οἱ γραμματεῖς καὶ οἱ Φαρισαῖοι
to reason the scribes and the Pharisees
λέγοντες· τίς ἐστιν οὗτος ὃς λαλεῖ
saying : Who is this man who speaks
βλασφημίας; τίς δύναται ἁμαρτίας ἀφεῖναι
blasphemies? Who can sins *to* forgive
εἰ μὴ μόνος ὁ θεός; **22** ἐπιγνοὺς δὲ ὁ
except only – God? But knowing –

are willing, you can make
me clean."
13Jesus reached out his
hand and touched the man.
"I am willing," he said.
"Be clean!" And immedi-
ately the leprosy left him.
14Then Jesus ordered
him, "Don't tell anyone,
but go, show yourself to the
priest and offer the sacrifices that Moses command-
ed for your cleansing, as a
testimony to them."
15Yet the news about him
spread all the more, so that
crowds of people came to
hear him and to be healed
of their sicknesses. 16But
Jesus often withdrew to
lonely places and prayed.

Jesus Heals a Paralytic

17One day as he was
teaching, Pharisees and
teachers of the law, who
had come from every vil-
lage of Galilee and from Judea and Jerusalem, were
sitting there. And the power of the Lord was present
for him to heal the sick.
18Some men came carrying
a paralytic on a mat and
tried to take him into the
house to lay him before
Jesus. 19When they could
not find a way to do this
because of the crowd, they
went up on the roof and
lowered him on his mat
through the tiles into the
middle of the crowd, right
in front of Jesus.
20When Jesus saw their
faith, he said, "Friend,
your sins are forgiven."
21The Pharisees and the
teachers of the law began
thinking to themselves,
"Who is this fellow who
speaks blasphemy? Who
can forgive sins but God
alone?"
22Jesus knew what they

their reasonings, answered and said to them, "Why are you reasoning in your hearts?

23"Which is easier, to say, 'Your sins have been forgiven you,' or to say, 'Rise and walk'?

24"But in order that you may know that the Son of Man has authority on earth to forgive sins,"—He said to the paralytic—"I say to you, rise, and take up your stretcher and go home."

25And at once he rose up before them, and took up what he had been lying on, and went home, glorifying God.

26And they were all seized with astonishment and *began* glorifying God; and they were filled with fear, saying, "We have seen remarkable things today."

Call of Levi (Matthew)

27And after that He went out, and noticed a [n]tax-gatherer named Levi, sitting in the tax office, and He said to him, "Follow Me."

28And he left everything behind, and rose and *began* to follow Him.

29And Levi gave a big reception for Him in his house; and there was a great crowd of tax-gatherers and other *people* who were reclining *at the table* with them.

30And the Pharisees and their scribes *began* grumbling at His disciples, saying, "Why do you eat and drink with the tax-gatherers and sinners?"

31And Jesus answered and said to them, "*It is* not those who are well who need a physician, but those who are sick.

32"I have not come to call the righteous but sinners to repentance."

33And they said to Him, "The disciples of John often fast and offer prayers;

[n]I.e., Collector of Roman taxes for profit

Ἰησοῦς τοὺς διαλογισμοὺς αὐτῶν, ἀποκριθεὶς
Jesus the reasonings of them, answering
εἶπεν πρὸς αὐτούς· τί διαλογίζεσθε ἐν
said to them : Why reason ye in
ταῖς καρδίαις ὑμῶν; 23 τί ἐστιν εὐκοπώτερον,
the hearts of you? What is easier,
εἰπεῖν· ἀφέωνταί σοι αἱ ἁμαρτίαι σου, ἢ
to say : Have been forgiven thee the sins of thee, or
εἰπεῖν· ἔγειρε καὶ περιπάτει; 24 ἵνα δὲ
to say : Rise and walk ? but that
εἰδῆτε ὅτι ὁ υἱὸς τοῦ ἀνθρώπου ἐξουσίαν
ye may know that the Son – of man authority
ἔχει ἐπὶ τῆς γῆς ἀφιέναι ἁμαρτίας, —
has on the earth to forgive sins, —
εἶπεν τῷ παραλελυμένῳ· σοὶ λέγω, ἔγειρε
he said to the paralysed [one] : To thee I say, rise
καὶ ἄρας τὸ κλινίδιόν σου πορεύου εἰς
and taking the pallet of thee go to
τὸν οἶκόν σου. 25 καὶ παραχρῆμα ἀναστὰς
the house of thee. And at once rising up
ἐνώπιον αὐτῶν, ἄρας ἐφ' ὃ κατέκειτο,
before them, taking [that] on which he was lying,
ἀπῆλθεν εἰς τὸν οἶκον αὐτοῦ δοξάζων τὸν
he went away to the house of him glorifying –
θεόν. 26 καὶ ἔκστασις ἔλαβεν ἅπαντας, καὶ
God. And bewilderment took all, and
ἐδόξαζον τὸν θεόν, καὶ ἐπλήσθησαν φόβου
they glorified – God, and were filled of(with) fear
λέγοντες ὅτι εἴδομεν παράδοξα σήμερον.
saying[,] – We saw wonderful things to-day.
27 Καὶ μετὰ ταῦτα ἐξῆλθεν, καὶ ἐθεάσατο
And after these things he went forth, and saw
τελώνην ὀνόματι Λευὶν καθήμενον ἐπὶ τὸ
a tax-collector by name Levi sitting on(in) the
τελώνιον, καὶ εἶπεν αὐτῷ· ἀκολούθει μοι.
custom house, and said to him : Follow me.
28 καὶ καταλιπὼν πάντα ἀναστὰς ἠκολούθει
And abandoning all things rising up he followed
αὐτῷ. 29 Καὶ ἐποίησεν δοχὴν μεγάλην
him. And [2]made [4]feast [3]a great
Λευὶς αὐτῷ ἐν τῇ οἰκίᾳ αὐτοῦ· καὶ ἦν
[1]Levi for him in the house of him; and there was
ὄχλος πολὺς τελωνῶν καὶ ἄλλων οἳ ἦσαν
crowd a much of tax-collectors and of others who were
μετ' αὐτῶν κατακείμενοι. 30 καὶ ἐγόγγυζον
[2]with [3]them [1]reclining. And grumbled
οἱ Φαρισαῖοι καὶ οἱ γραμματεῖς αὐτῶν
the Pharisees and the scribes of them
πρὸς τοὺς μαθητὰς αὐτοῦ λέγοντες· διὰ
at the disciples of him saying : Why
τί μετὰ τῶν τελωνῶν καὶ ἁμαρτωλῶν
with the tax-collectors and sinners
ἐσθίετε καὶ πίνετε; 31 καὶ ἀποκριθεὶς ὁ
eat ye and drink ye? And answering –
Ἰησοῦς εἶπεν πρὸς αὐτούς· οὐ χρείαν
Jesus said to them : not need
ἔχουσιν οἱ ὑγιαίνοντες ἰατροῦ ἀλλὰ οἱ
have the [ones] being healthy of a physician but the
=those who are ill;
κακῶς ἔχοντες· 32 οὐκ ἐλήλυθα καλέσαι
[ones] ill having; I have not come to call
δικαίους ἀλλὰ ἁμαρτωλοὺς εἰς μετάνοιαν.
righteous persons but sinners to repentance.
33 Οἱ δὲ εἶπαν πρὸς αὐτόν· οἱ μαθηταὶ
And they said to him : The disciples
Ἰωάννου νηστεύουσιν πυκνὰ καὶ δεήσεις
of John fast often and prayers

were thinking and asked,
"Why are you thinking
these things in your hearts?
23Which is easier: to say,
'Your sins are forgiven,' or
to say, 'Get up and walk'?
24But that you may know
that the Son of Man has authority on earth to forgive
sins. . . ." He said to the
paralyzed man, "I tell you,
get up, take your mat and
go home." 25Immediately
he stood up in front of
them, took what he had
been lying on and went
home praising God. 26Everyone was amazed and
gave praise to God. They
were filled with awe and
said, "We have seen remarkable things today."

The Calling of Levi

27After this, Jesus went
out and saw a tax collector
by the name of Levi sitting
at his tax booth. "Follow
me," Jesus said to him,
28and Levi got up, left everything and followed him.
29Then Levi held a great
banquet for Jesus at his
house, and a large crowd of
tax collectors and others
were eating with them.
30But the Pharisees and the
teachers of the law who belonged to their sect complained to his disciples,
"Why do you eat and drink
with tax collectors and 'sinners'?"
31Jesus answered them,
"It is not the healthy who
need a doctor, but the sick.
32I have not come to call
the righteous, but sinners
to repentance."

Jesus Questioned About Fasting

33They said to him,
"John's disciples often fast
and pray, and so do the dis-

the *disciples* of the Pharisees also do the same; but
Yours eat and drink.''
34And Jesus said to them,
''You cannot make the at-
tendants of the bridegroom
fast while the bridegroom is
with them, can you?
35''But *the* days will
come; and when the bride-
groom is taken away from
them, then they will fast in
those days.''
36And He was also telling
them a parable: ''No one
tears a piece from a new
garment and puts it on an
old garment; otherwise he
will both tear the new, and
the piece from the new will
not match the old.
37''And no one puts new
wine into old wineskins;
otherwise the new wine
will burst the skins, and it
will be spilled out, and the
skins will be ruined.
38''But new wine must be
put into fresh wineskins.
39''And no one, after
drinking old *wine* wishes
for new; for he says, 'The
old is good *enough*.' ''

ποιοῦνται, ὁμοίως καὶ οἱ τῶν Φαρισαίων,
make, likewise also those of the Pharisees,

οἱ δὲ σοὶ ἐσθίουσιν καὶ πίνουσιν. 34 ὁ
but those to thee[c] eat and drink. –
=but thine

δὲ Ἰησοῦς εἶπεν πρὸς αὐτούς· μὴ δύνασθε
And Jesus said to them: *not* [1]Can ye

τοὺς υἱοὺς τοῦ νυμφῶνος, ἐν ᾧ ὁ νυμφίος
[3]the [4]sons [5]of the [6]bride-chamber, [8]while [9]the [10]bridegroom

μετ' αὐτῶν ἐστιν, ποιῆσαι νηστεῦσαι;
[11]with [12]them [11]is, [2]*to* make [7]to fast?

35 ἐλεύσονται δὲ ἡμέραι, καὶ ὅταν ἀπαρθῇ
but will come days, and when is taken away

ἀπ' αὐτῶν ὁ νυμφίος, τότε νηστεύσουσιν
from them the bridegroom, then they will fast

ἐν ἐκείναις ταῖς ἡμέραις. 36 Ἔλεγεν δὲ
in those – days. And he told

καὶ παραβολὴν πρὸς αὐτοὺς ὅτι οὐδεὶς
also a parable to them[:] – No one

ἐπίβλημα ἀπὸ ἱματίου καινοῦ σχίσας
[2]a patch [3]from [5]garment [4]a new [1]tearing

ἐπιβάλλει ἐπὶ ἱμάτιον παλαιόν· εἰ δὲ μή γε,
[6]puts [it] [7]on [9]a garment [8]an old; otherwise,

καὶ τὸ καινὸν σχίσει καὶ τῷ παλαιῷ
both the new will tear and [7]with the [8]old

οὐ συμφωνήσει τὸ ἐπίβλημα τὸ ἀπὸ τοῦ
[6]will not agree [1]the [2]patch – [3]from [4]the

καινοῦ. 37 καὶ οὐδεὶς βάλλει οἶνον νέον
[5]new. And no one puts wine new

εἰς ἀσκοὺς παλαιούς· εἰ δὲ μή γε, ῥήξει
into wineskins old; otherwise, [4]will burst

ὁ οἶνος ὁ νέος τοὺς ἀσκούς, καὶ αὐτὸς
[1]the [3]wine – [2]new [5]the [6]wineskins, and it

ἐκχυθήσεται καὶ οἱ ἀσκοὶ ἀπολοῦνται.
will be poured out and the wineskins will perish.

38 ἀλλὰ οἶνον νέον εἰς ἀσκοὺς καινοὺς
But wine new into wineskins new

βλητέον. 39 καὶ οὐδεὶς πιὼν παλαιὸν
one must put. And no one having drunk old

θέλει νέον· λέγει γάρ· ὁ παλαιὸς χρηστός
desires new; for he says: The old good

ἐστιν.
is.

ciples of the Pharisees, but
yours go on eating and
drinking.''
34Jesus answered, ''Can
you make the guests of the
bridegroom fast while he is
with them? 35But the time
will come when the bride-
groom will be taken from
them; in those days they
will fast.''
36He told them this para-
ble: ''No one tears a patch
from a new garment and
sews it on an old one. If he
does, he will have torn the
new garment, and the patch
from the new will not
match the old. 37And no
one pours new wine into
old wineskins. If he does,
the new wine will burst the
skins, the wine will run out
and the wineskins will be
ruined. 38No, new wine
must be poured into new
wineskins. 39And no one after drinking old wine wants
the new, for he says, 'The
old is better.' ''

Chapter 6

Jesus Is Lord of the Sabbath

NOW it came about that
on a *certain* Sabbath
He was passing through
some grainfields; and His
disciples were picking and
eating the heads *of grain*,
rubbing them in their
hands.
2But some of the Phari-
sees said, ''Why do you do
what is not lawful on the
Sabbath?''
3And Jesus answering
them said, ''Have you not
even read what David did
when he was hungry, he
and those who were with
him,
4how he entered the
house of God, and took and
ate the [o]consecrated bread
which is not lawful for any
to eat except the priests

[o]Or, *showbread*, lit., *loaves of presentation*

6 Ἐγένετο δὲ ἐν σαββάτῳ διαπορεύεσθαι
And it came to pass on a sabbath to go through
=he went through

αὐτὸν διὰ σπορίμων, καὶ ἔτιλλον οἱ
him[b] *through* cornfields, and [4]plucked [1]the

μαθηταὶ αὐτοῦ καὶ ἤσθιον τοὺς στάχυας
[2]disciples [3]of him and ate the ears

ψώχοντες ταῖς χερσίν. 2 τινὲς δὲ τῶν
rubbing with the(ir) hands. And some of the

Φαρισαίων εἶπαν· τί ποιεῖτε ὃ οὐκ ἔξεστιν
Pharisees said: Why do ye what is not lawful

τοῖς σάββασιν; 3 καὶ ἀποκριθεὶς πρὸς
on the sabbaths? And replying to

αὐτοὺς εἶπεν ὁ Ἰησοῦς· οὐδὲ τοῦτο ἀνέγνωτε
them said – Jesus: [2]not [3]this [1]read ye

ὃ ἐποίησεν Δαυίδ, ὁπότε ἐπείνασεν αὐτὸς
which did David, when hungered he

καὶ οἱ μετ' αὐτοῦ ὄντες; 4 ὡς εἰσῆλθεν
and the [ones] with him being? how he entered

εἰς τὸν οἶκον τοῦ θεοῦ καὶ τοὺς ἄρτους
into the house – of God and the loaves

τῆς προθέσεως λαβὼν ἔφαγεν καὶ ἔδωκεν
of the setting forth taking he ate and gave

Chapter 6

Lord of the Sabbath

ONE Sabbath Jesus was
going through the
grainfields, and his disciples began to pick some
heads of grain, rub them in
their hands and eat the ker-
nels. 2Some of the Phari-
sees asked, ''Why are you
doing what is unlawful on
the Sabbath?''
3Jesus answered them,
''Have you never read
what David did when he
and his companions were
hungry? 4He entered the
house of God, and taking
the consecrated bread, he
ate what is lawful only for

alone, and gave it to his
companions?"
5And He was saying to
them, "The Son of Man is
Lord of the Sabbath."
6And it came about on
another Sabbath, that He
entered the synagogue and
was teaching; and there
was a man there whose
right hand was withered.
7And the scribes and the
Pharisees were watching
Him closely, *to see* if He
healed on the Sabbath, in
order that they might find
reason to accuse Him.
8But He knew what they
were thinking, and He said
to the man with the withered hand, "Rise and come
forward!" And he rose and
came forward.
9And Jesus said to them,
"I ask you, is it lawful on
the Sabbath to do good, or
to do harm, to save a life, or
to destroy it?"
10And after looking
around at them all, He said
to him, "Stretch out your
hand!" And he did *so;* and
his hand was restored.
11But they themselves
were filled with rage, and
discussed together what
they might do to Jesus.

Choosing the Twelve

12And it was at this time
that He went off to the
mountain to pray, and He
spent the whole night in
prayer to God.
13And when day came,
He called His disciples to
Him; and chose twelve of
them, whom He also
named as apostles:
14Simon, whom He also
named Peter, and Andrew
his brother; and James and
John; and Philip and Bartholomew;
15and Matthew and
Thomas; James *the son* of

τοῖς μετ' αὐτοῦ, οὓς οὐκ ἔξεστιν φαγεῖν
to the [ones] with him, which it is not lawful to eat
εἰ μὴ μόνους τοὺς ἱερεῖς; 5 καὶ ἔλεγεν
except only the priests? And he said
αὐτοῖς· κύριός ἐστιν τοῦ σαββάτου ὁ
to them: Lord is of the sabbath the
υἱὸς τοῦ ἀνθρώπου. 6 Ἐγένετο δὲ ἐν
Son – of man. And it came to pass on
ἑτέρῳ σαββάτῳ εἰσελθεῖν αὐτὸν εἰς τὴν
another sabbath to enter him into the
=he entered into the synagogue and
συναγωγὴν καὶ διδάσκειν· καὶ ἦν ἄνθρωπος
synagogue and to teach[b]; and there was a man
taught;
ἐκεῖ καὶ ἡ χεὶρ αὐτοῦ ἡ δεξιὰ ἦν ξηρά·
there and the [3]hand [4]of him – [1]right was withered;
7 παρετηροῦντο δὲ αὐτὸν οἱ γραμματεῖς
and carefully watched him the scribes
καὶ οἱ Φαρισαῖοι εἰ ἐν τῷ σαββάτῳ
and the Pharisees if on the sabbath
θεραπεύει, ἵνα εὕρωσιν κατηγορεῖν αὐτοῦ.
he heals, that they might find to accuse him.
8 αὐτὸς δὲ ᾔδει τοὺς διαλογισμοὺς αὐτῶν,
But he knew the reasonings of them,
εἶπεν δὲ τῷ ἀνδρὶ τῷ ξηρὰν ἔχοντι τὴν
and said to the man – [2]withered [1]having [3]the
χεῖρα· ἔγειρε καὶ στῆθι εἰς τὸ μέσον·
[4]hand: Rise and stand in the midst;
καὶ ἀναστὰς ἔστη. 9 εἶπεν δὲ ὁ Ἰησοῦς
and rising up he stood. And said – Jesus
πρὸς αὐτούς· ἐπερωτῶ ὑμᾶς εἰ ἔξεστιν
to them: I ask you if it is lawful
τῷ σαββάτῳ ἀγαθοποιῆσαι ἢ κακοποιῆσαι,
on the sabbath to do good or to do evil,
ψυχὴν σῶσαι ἢ ἀπολέσαι; 10 καὶ περι-
life to save or to destroy? And looking
βλεψάμενος πάντας αὐτοὺς εἶπεν αὐτῷ·
round at all them he said to him:
ἔκτεινον τὴν χεῖρά σου. ὁ δὲ ἐποίησεν,
Stretch out the hand of thee. And he did,
καὶ ἀπεκατεστάθη ἡ χεὶρ αὐτοῦ. 11 αὐτοὶ
and was restored the hand of him. they
δὲ ἐπλήσθησαν ἀνοίας, καὶ διελάλουν πρὸς
But were filled of (with) madness, and talked to
ἀλλήλους τί ἂν ποιήσαιεν τῷ Ἰησοῦ.
one another what they might do – to Jesus.
12 Ἐγένετο δὲ ἐν ταῖς ἡμέραις ταύταις
Now it came to pass in – days these
ἐξελθεῖν αὐτὸν εἰς τὸ ὄρος προσεύξασθαι,
to go forth him[b] to the mountain to pray,
=he went forth
καὶ ἦν διανυκτερεύων ἐν τῇ προσευχῇ τοῦ
and was spending the whole night in the prayer –
θεοῦ. 13 καὶ ὅτε ἐγένετο ἡμέρα, προσεφώνησεν
of God. And when it became day, he called to [him]
τοὺς μαθητὰς αὐτοῦ, καὶ ἐκλεξάμενος ἀπ'
the disciples of him, and choosing from
αὐτῶν δώδεκα, οὓς καὶ ἀποστόλους ὠνόμασεν,
them twelve, whom also apostles he named,
14 Σίμωνα, ὃν καὶ ὠνόμασεν Πέτρον, καὶ
Simon, whom also he named Peter, and
Ἀνδρέαν τὸν ἀδελφὸν αὐτοῦ, καὶ Ἰάκωβον
Andrew the brother of him, and James
καὶ Ἰωάννην, καὶ Φίλιππον καὶ Βαρθο-
and John, and Philip and Bartho-
λομαῖον, 15 καὶ Μαθθαῖον καὶ Θωμᾶν,
lomew, and Matthew and Thomas,

priests to eat. And he also
gave some to his companions." 5Then Jesus said to
them, "The Son of Man is
Lord of the Sabbath."
6On another Sabbath he
went into the synagogue
and was teaching, and a
man was there whose right
hand was shriveled. 7The
Pharisees and the teachers
of the law were looking for
a reason to accuse Jesus, so
they watched him closely
to see if he would heal on
the Sabbath. 8But Jesus
knew what they were
thinking and said to the
man with the shriveled
hand, "Get up and stand in
front of everyone." So he
got up and stood there.
9Then Jesus said to them,
"I ask you, which is lawful
on the Sabbath: to do good
or to do evil, to save life or
to destroy it?"
10He looked around at
them all, and then said to
the man, "Stretch out your
hand." He did so, and his
hand was completely restored. 11But they were furious and began to discuss
with one another what they
might do to Jesus.

The Twelve Apostles

12One of those days Jesus
went out to a mountainside
to pray, and spent the night
praying to God. 13When
morning came, he called
his disciples to him and
chose twelve of them,
whom he also designated
apostles: 14Simon (whom
he named Peter), his brother Andrew, James, John,
Philip, Bartholomew,
15Matthew, Thomas,
James son of Alphaeus, Si-

Alphaeus, and Simon who
was called the Zealot;
16Judas *the son* of James,
and Judas Iscariot, who
became a traitor.
17And He descended with
them, and stood on a level
place; and *there was* a great
multitude of His disciples,
and a great throng of people
from all Judea and Jerusalem and the coastal region
of Tyre and Sidon,
18who had come to hear
Him, and to be healed of
their diseases; and those
who were troubled with unclean spirits were being
cured.
19And all the multitude
were trying to touch Him,
for power was coming from
Him and healing *them* all.

The Beatitudes

20And turning His gaze on
His disciples, He *began* to
say, "Blessed *are* you *who
are* poor, for yours is the
kingdom of God.
21"Blessed *are* you who
hunger now, for you shall
be satisfied. Blessed *are*
you who weep now, for you
shall laugh.
22"Blessed are you when
men hate you, and ostra-
cize you, and cast insults at
you, and spurn your name
as evil, for the sake of the
Son of Man.
23"Be glad in that day,
and leap *for joy*, for behold,
your reward is great in
heaven; for in the same way
their fathers used to treat
the prophets.
24"But woe to you who
are rich, for you are receiving your comfort in full.
25"Woe to you who are
well-fed now, for you shall
be hungry. Woe *to you* who
laugh now, for you shall
mourn and weep.
26"Woe *to you* when all

[καὶ] Ἰάκωβον Ἁλφαίου καὶ Σίμωνα τὸν
and James [son] of Alphæus and Simon the [one]
καλούμενον ζηλωτήν, 16 καὶ Ἰούδαν Ἰακώβου,
being called a Zealot, and Judas of James,
καὶ Ἰούδαν Ἰσκαριώθ, ὃς ἐγένετο προδότης,
and Judas Iscariot, who became betrayer,
17 καὶ καταβὰς μετ' αὐτῶν ἔστη ἐπὶ
and coming down with them he stood on
τόπου πεδινοῦ, καὶ ὄχλος πολὺς μαθητῶν
place a level, and crowd a much of disciples
αὐτοῦ, καὶ πλῆθος πολὺ τοῦ λαοῦ ἀπὸ
of him, and multitude a much of the people from
πάσης τῆς Ἰουδαίας καὶ Ἰερουσαλὴμ καὶ
all – Judæa and Jerusalem and
τῆς παραλίου Τύρου καὶ Σιδῶνος, 18 οἳ
the coast country of Tyre and Sidon, who
ἦλθον ἀκοῦσαι αὐτοῦ καὶ ἰαθῆναι ἀπὸ
came to hear him and to be cured from
τῶν νόσων αὐτῶν, καὶ οἱ ἐνοχλούμενοι
the diseases of them, and the [ones] being tormented
ἀπὸ πνευμάτων ἀκαθάρτων ἐθεραπεύοντο.
from spirits unclean were healed.
19 καὶ πᾶς ὁ ὄχλος ἐζήτουν ἅπτεσθαι
And all the crowd sought to touch
αὐτοῦ, ὅτι δύναμις παρ' αὐτοῦ ἐξήρχετο
him, because power from him went forth
καὶ ἰᾶτο πάντας. 20 Καὶ αὐτὸς ἐπάρας
and cured all. And he lifting up
τοὺς ὀφθαλμοὺς αὐτοῦ εἰς τοὺς μαθητὰς
the eyes of him to the disciples
αὐτοῦ ἔλεγεν·
of him said :
Μακάριοι οἱ πτωχοί, ὅτι ὑμετέρα ἐστὶν
Blessed [are] the poor, because yours is
ἡ βασιλεία τοῦ θεοῦ. 21 μακάριοι οἱ
the kingdom – of God. Blessed [are] the [ones]
πεινῶντες νῦν, ὅτι χορτασθήσεσθε. μακάριοι
hungering now, because ye will be satisfied. Blessed [are]
οἱ κλαίοντες νῦν, ὅτι γελάσετε. 22 μακάριοί
the [ones] weeping now, because ye will laugh. Blessed
ἐστε ὅταν μισήσωσιν ὑμᾶς οἱ ἄνθρωποι,
are ye when [2]hate [3]you – [1]men.
καὶ ὅταν ἀφορίσωσιν ὑμᾶς καὶ ὀνειδίσωσιν
and when they separate you and reproach
καὶ ἐκβάλωσιν τὸ ὄνομα ὑμῶν ὡς πονηρὸν
and cast out the name of you as evil
ἕνεκα τοῦ υἱοῦ τοῦ ἀνθρώπου. 23 χάρητε
for the sake of the Son – of man. Rejoice
ἐν ἐκείνῃ τῇ ἡμέρᾳ καὶ σκιρτήσατε·
in that – day and leap for joy;
ἰδοὺ γὰρ ὁ μισθὸς ὑμῶν πολὺς ἐν τῷ
for behold[,] the reward of you much in –
οὐρανῷ· κατὰ τὰ αὐτὰ γὰρ ἐποίουν τοῖς
heaven; for according to the same things [4]did [5]to the
=in the same way
προφήταις οἱ πατέρες αὐτῶν.
[6]prophets [1]the [2]fathers [3]of them.
24 Πλὴν οὐαὶ ὑμῖν τοῖς πλουσίοις, ὅτι
But woe to you the rich [ones], because
ἀπέχετε τὴν παράκλησιν ὑμῶν. 25 οὐαὶ ὑμῖν,
ye have the consolation of you. Woe to you,
οἱ ἐμπεπλησμένοι νῦν, ὅτι πεινάσετε.
the [ones] *having been* filled up now, because ye will hunger.
οὐαί, οἱ γελῶντες νῦν, ὅτι πενθήσετε
Woe, the [ones] laughing now, because ye will mourn
καὶ κλαύσετε. 26 οὐαὶ ὅταν καλῶς ὑμᾶς
and lament. Woe when well [of] you

mon who was called the
Zealot, 16Judas son of
James, and Judas Iscariot,
who became a traitor.

Blessings and Woes

17He went down with
them and stood on a level
place. A large crowd of his
disciples was there and a
great number of people
from all over Judea, from
Jerusalem, and from the
coast of Tyre and Sidon,
18who had come to hear
him and to be healed of
their diseases. Those troubled by evil[a] spirits were
cured, 19and the people all
tried to touch him, because
power was coming from
him and healing them all.
20Looking at his disci
ples, he said:

"Blessed are you who
are poor,
for yours is the
kingdom of God.
21Blessed are you who
hunger now,
for you will be
satisfied.
Blessed are you who
weep now,
for you will laugh.
22Blessed are you when
men hate you,
when they exclude you
and insult you
and reject your name
as evil,
because of the Son of
Man.

23"Rejoice in that day
and leap for joy, because
great is your reward in
heaven. For that is how
their fathers treated the
prophets.

24"But woe to you who
are rich,
for you have already
received your
comfort.
25Woe to you who are well
fed now,
for you will go hungry.
Woe to you who laugh
now,
for you will mourn and
weep.
26Woe to you when all

[a]*18* Greek *unclean*

men speak well of you, for in the same way their fathers used to treat the false prophets.

27"But I say to you who hear, love your enemies, do good to those who hate you,

28bless those who curse you, pray for those who mistreat you.

29"Whoever hits you on the cheek, offer him the other also; and whoever takes away your coat, do not withhold your shirt from him either.

30"Give to everyone who asks of you, and whoever takes away what is yours, do not demand it back.

31"And just as you want people to treat you, treat them in the same way.

32"And if you love those who love you, what credit is *that* to you? For even sinners love those who love them.

33"And if you do good to those who do good to you, what credit is *that* to you? For even sinners do the same.

34"And if you lend to those from whom you expect to receive, what credit is *that* to you? Even sinners lend to sinners, in order to receive back the same *amount*.

35"But love your enemies, and do good, and lend, expecting nothing in return; and your reward will be great, and you will be sons of the Most High; for He Himself is kind to ungrateful and evil *men*.

36"Be merciful, just as your Father is merciful.

37"And do not judge and you will not be judged; and

εἴπωσιν πάντες οἱ ἄνθρωποι· κατὰ τὰ
say all – men; for according to
=in the same way

αὐτὰ γὰρ ἐποίουν τοῖς ψευδοπροφήταις οἱ
the same things did to the false prophets the

πατέρες αὐτῶν. 27 Ἀλλὰ ὑμῖν λέγω
fathers of them. But you I tell

τοῖς ἀκούουσιν· ἀγαπᾶτε τοὺς ἐχθροὺς
the [ones] hearing: Love ye the enemies

ὑμῶν, καλῶς ποιεῖτε τοῖς μισοῦσιν ὑμᾶς,
of you, [2]well [1]do to the [ones] hating you,

28 εὐλογεῖτε τοὺς καταρωμένους ὑμᾶς,
bless the [ones] cursing you,

προσεύχεσθε περὶ τῶν ἐπηρεαζόντων ὑμᾶς.
pray about the [ones] insulting you.

29 τῷ τύπτοντί σε ἐπὶ τὴν σιαγόνα
To the [one] striking thee on the cheek

πάρεχε καὶ τὴν ἄλλην, καὶ ἀπὸ τοῦ
turn also the other, and from the [one]

αἴροντός σου τὸ ἱμάτιον καὶ τὸν χιτῶνα
taking of thee the garment also the tunic

μὴ κωλύσῃς. 30 παντὶ αἰτοῦντί σε δίδου,
do not prevent. To everyone asking thee give,

καὶ ἀπὸ τοῦ αἴροντος τὰ σὰ μὴ ἀπαίτει.
and from the [one] taking thy things do not ask back.

31 καὶ καθὼς θέλετε ἵνα ποιῶσιν ὑμῖν
And as ye wish that may do to you

οἱ ἄνθρωποι, ποιεῖτε αὐτοῖς ὁμοίως. 32 καὶ
– men, do ye to them likewise. And

εἰ ἀγαπᾶτε τοὺς ἀγαπῶντας ὑμᾶς, ποία
if ye love the [ones] loving you, what

ὑμῖν χάρις ἐστίν; καὶ γὰρ οἱ ἁμαρτωλοὶ
to you thanks is there?[c] for even – sinners
=thanks have ye?

τοὺς ἀγαπῶντας αὐτοὺς ἀγαπῶσιν. 33 καὶ
[2]the [ones] [3]loving [4]them [1]love. even

γὰρ ἐὰν ἀγαθοποιῆτε τοὺς ἀγαθοποιοῦντας
For if ye do good to the [ones] doing good to

ὑμᾶς, ποία ὑμῖν χάρις ἐστίν; καὶ οἱ
you, what to you thanks is there?[c] even –
=thanks have ye?

ἁμαρτωλοὶ τὸ αὐτὸ ποιοῦσιν. 34 καὶ ἐὰν
sinners the same thing do. And if

δανείσητε παρ' ὧν ἐλπίζετε λαβεῖν, ποία
ye lend from whom ye hope to receive, what

ὑμῖν χάρις [ἐστίν]; καὶ ἁμαρτωλοὶ
to you thanks is there?[c] even sinners
=thanks have ye?

ἁμαρτωλοῖς δανείζουσιν ἵνα ἀπολάβωσιν τὰ
to sinners lend that they may receive back the

ἴσα. 35 πλὴν ἀγαπᾶτε τοὺς ἐχθροὺς ὑμῶν
equal things. But love ye the enemies of you

καὶ ἀγαθοποιεῖτε καὶ δανείζετε μηδὲν
and do good and lend nothing

ἀπελπίζοντες· καὶ ἔσται ὁ μισθὸς ὑμῶν
despairing; and will be the reward of you
=despairing not at all;

πολύς, καὶ ἔσεσθε υἱοὶ ὑψίστου, ὅτι
much, and ye will be sons of [the] Most High, because

αὐτὸς χρηστός ἐστιν ἐπὶ τοὺς ἀχαρίστους
he kind is to the unthankful

καὶ πονηρούς. 36 Γίνεσθε οἰκτίρμονες,
and evil. Be ye compassionate,

καθὼς ὁ πατὴρ ὑμῶν οἰκτίρμων ἐστίν.
as the Father of you compassionate is.

37 καὶ μὴ κρίνετε, καὶ οὐ μὴ κριθῆτε· καὶ
And do not judge, and by no means ye may be judged; and

men speak well of
you,
for that is how their
fathers treated the
false prophets.

Love for Enemies

27"But I tell you who hear
me: Love your enemies, do
good to those who hate
you, 28bless those who
curse you, pray for those
who mistreat you. 29If
someone strikes you on
one cheek, turn to him the
other also. If someone
takes your cloak, do not
stop him from taking your
tunic. 30Give to everyone
who asks you, and if any-
one takes what belongs to
you, do not demand it
back. 31Do to others as you
would have them do to you.
32"If you love those who
love you, what credit is that
to you? Even 'sinners' love
those who love them.
33And if you do good to
those who are good to you,
what credit is that to you?
Even 'sinners' do that.
34And if you lend to those
from whom you expect re-
payment, what credit is
that to you? Even 'sinners'
lend to 'sinners,' expecting
to be repaid in full. 35But
love your enemies, do good
to them, and lend to them
without expecting to get
anything back. Then your
reward will be great, and
you will be sons of the Most
High, because he is kind to
the ungrateful and wicked.
36Be merciful, just as your
Father is merciful.

Judging Others

37"Do not judge, and you
will not be judged. Do not

do not condemn, and you will not be condemned; pardon, and you will be pardoned.

38 "Give, and it will be given to you; good measure, pressed down, shaken together, running over, they will pour into your lap. For by your standard of measure it will be measured to you in return."

39 And He also spoke a parable to them: "A blind man cannot guide a blind man, can he? Will they not both fall into a pit?

40 "A pupil is not above his teacher; but everyone, after he has been fully trained, will be like his teacher.

41 "And why do you look at the speck that is in your brother's eye, but do not notice the log that is in your own eye?

42 "Or how can you say to your brother, 'Brother, let me take out the speck that is in your eye,' when you yourself do not see the log that is in your own eye? You hypocrite, first take the log out of your own eye, and then you will see clearly to take out the speck that is in your brother's eye.

43 "For there is no good tree which produces bad fruit; nor, on the other hand, a bad tree which produces good fruit.

44 "For each tree is known by its own fruit. For men do not gather figs from thorns, nor do they pick grapes from a briar bush.

45 "The good man out of the good treasure of his heart brings forth what is good; and the evil *man* out of the evil *treasure* brings forth what is evil; for his mouth speaks from that which fills his heart.

μὴ καταδικάζετε, καὶ οὐ μὴ καταδικασθῆτε.
do not condemn, and by no means ye may be condemned.
ἀπολύετε, καὶ ἀπολυθήσεσθε· 38 δίδοτε, καὶ
Forgive, and ye will be forgiven; give, and
δοθήσεται ὑμῖν· μέτρον καλὸν πεπιεσμένον
it will be given to you; measure good *having been* pressed down
σεσαλευμένον ὑπερεκχυννόμενον δώσουσιν εἰς
having been shaken running over they will give into
τὸν κόλπον ὑμῶν· ᾧ γὰρ μέτρῳ μετρεῖτε
the bosom of you; for in what measure ye measure
ἀντιμετρηθήσεται ὑμῖν. 39 Εἶπεν δὲ καὶ
it will be measured in return to you. And he told also
παραβολὴν αὐτοῖς· μήτι δύναται τυφλὸς
a parable to them: *Not* can a blind man
τυφλὸν ὁδηγεῖν; οὐχὶ ἀμφότεροι εἰς βόθυνον
[2]a blind man [1]guide? not both into a ditch
ἐμπεσοῦνται; 40 οὐκ ἔστιν μαθητὴς ὑπὲρ
will fall *in*? [3]not [2]is [1]A disciple above
τὸν διδάσκαλον· κατηρτισμένος δὲ πᾶς
the teacher; [1]but [4]*having been* perfected [2]everyone
ἔσται ὡς ὁ διδάσκαλος αὐτοῦ. 41 Τί δὲ
[3]will be as the teacher of him. And why
βλέπεις τὸ κάρφος τὸ ἐν τῷ ὀφθαλμῷ
seest thou the mote – in the eye
τοῦ ἀδελφοῦ σου, τὴν δὲ δοκὸν τὴν ἐν
of the brother of thee, but the beam – in
τῷ ἰδίῳ ὀφθαλμῷ οὐ κατανοεῖς; 42 πῶς
thine own eye thou considerest not? how
δύνασαι λέγειν τῷ ἀδελφῷ σου· ἀδελφέ,
canst thou *to* say to the brother of thee: Brother,
ἄφες ἐκβάλω τὸ κάρφος τὸ ἐν τῷ
allow I may take out the mote – in the
=allow me to take out
ὀφθαλμῷ σου, αὐτὸς τὴν ἐν τῷ ὀφθαλμῷ
eye of thee, [1][thy]self [4]the [6]in [7]the [8]eye
σου δοκὸν οὐ βλέπων; ὑποκριτά, ἔκβαλε
[9]of thee [5]beam [3]not [2]seeing? hypocrite, take *out*
πρῶτον τὴν δοκὸν ἐκ τοῦ ὀφθαλμοῦ σου,
first the beam out of the eye of thee,
καὶ τότε διαβλέψεις τὸ κάρφος τὸ ἐν τῷ
and then thou wilt see clearly the mote – in the
ὀφθαλμῷ τοῦ ἀδελφοῦ σου ἐκβαλεῖν. 43 Οὐ
eye of the brother of thee to take out. [3]no
γάρ ἐστιν δένδρον καλὸν ποιοῦν καρπὸν
[1]For [2]there is [5]tree [4]good producing fruit
σαπρόν, οὐδὲ πάλιν δένδρον σαπρὸν ποιοῦν
bad, nor again tree a bad producing
καρπὸν καλόν. 44 ἕκαστον γὰρ δένδρον
fruit good. For each tree
ἐκ τοῦ ἰδίου καρποῦ γινώσκεται· οὐ γὰρ
by the(its) own fruit is known; for not
ἐξ ἀκανθῶν συλλέγουσιν σῦκα, οὐδὲ ἐκ
of thorns do they gather figs, nor of
βάτου σταφυλὴν τρυγῶσιν. 45 ὁ ἀγαθὸς
a thorn bush a grape do they pick. The good
ἄνθρωπος ἐκ τοῦ ἀγαθοῦ θησαυροῦ τῆς
man out of the good treasure of the(his)
καρδίας προφέρει τὸ ἀγαθόν, καὶ ὁ
heart brings forth the good, and the
=that which is good,
πονηρὸς ἐκ τοῦ πονηροῦ προφέρει τὸ
evil man out of the evil brings forth the
πονηρόν· ἐκ γὰρ περισσεύματος καρδίας
evil; for out of [the] abundance of [his] heart
=that which is evil;

condemn, and you will not
be condemned. Forgive,
and you will be forgiven.
38 Give, and it will be given
to you. A good measure,
pressed down, shaken to-
gether and running over,
will be poured into your
lap. For with the measure
you use, it will be measured
to you."
39 He also told them this
parable: "Can a blind man
lead a blind man? Will they
not both fall into a pit? 40 A
student is not above his
teacher, but everyone who
is fully trained will be like
his teacher.
41 "Why do you look at
the speck of sawdust in
your brother's eye and pay
no attention to the plank in
your own eye? 42 How can
you say to your brother,
'Brother, let me take the
speck out of your eye,'
when you yourself fail to
see the plank in your own
eye? You hypocrite, first
take the plank out of your
eye, and then you will see
clearly to remove the speck
from your brother's eye.

A Tree and Its Fruit

43 "No good tree bears
bad fruit, nor does a bad
tree bear good fruit. 44 Each
tree is recognized by its
own fruit. People do not
pick figs from thornbushes,
or grapes from briers.
45 The good man brings
good things out of the good
stored up in his heart, and
the evil man brings evil
things out of the evil stored
up in his heart. For out of
the overflow of his heart his
mouth speaks.

Builders and Foundations

46"And why do you call Me, 'Lord, Lord,' and do not do what I say?

47"Everyone who comes to Me, and hears My words, and acts upon them, I will show you whom he is like:

48he is like a man building a house, who dug deep and laid a foundation upon the rock; and when a flood rose, the torrent burst against that house and could not shake it, because it had been well built.

49"But the one who has heard, and has not acted *accordingly*, is like a man who built a house upon the ground without any foundation; and the torrent burst against it and immediately it collapsed, and the ruin of that house was great."

λαλεῖ τὸ στόμα αὐτοῦ. 46 Τί δέ με καλεῖτε·
speaks the mouth of him. And why me call ye :
κύριε κύριε, καὶ οὐ ποιεῖτε ἃ
Lord[,] Lord, and do not [the things] which
λέγω; 47 Πᾶς ὁ ἐρχόμενος πρός με καὶ
I say? Everyone coming to me and
ἀκούων μου τῶν λόγων καὶ ποιῶν αὐτούς,
hearing of me the words and doing them,
ὑποδείξω ὑμῖν τίνι ἐστὶν ὅμοιος. 48 ὅμοιός
I will show you to whom he is like. Like
ἐστιν ἀνθρώπῳ οἰκοδομοῦντι οἰκίαν, ὃς
he is to a man building a house, who
ἔσκαψεν καὶ ἐβάθυνεν καὶ ἔθηκεν θεμέλιον
dug and deepened and laid a foundation
ἐπὶ τὴν πέτραν· πλημμύρης δὲ γενομένης
on the rock; and a flood occurring[a]
=when a flood occurred
προσέρρηξεν ὁ ποταμὸς τῇ οἰκίᾳ ἐκείνῃ,
[3]dashed against [1]the [2]river – house that,
καὶ οὐκ ἴσχυσεν σαλεῦσαι αὐτὴν διὰ
and was not able to shake it because of
τὸ καλῶς οἰκοδομῆσθαι αὐτήν. 49 ὁ δὲ
the well to be built it.[b] But the [one]
=because it was well built.
ἀκούσας καὶ μὴ ποιήσας ὅμοιός ἐστιν
hearing and not doing [2]like [1]is
ἀνθρώπῳ οἰκοδομήσαντι οἰκίαν ἐπὶ τὴν
a man having built a house on the
γῆν χωρὶς θεμελίου, ᾗ προσέρρηξεν ὁ
earth without a foundation, [2]which [5]dashed [1]against [3]the
ποταμός, καὶ εὐθὺς συνέπεσεν, καὶ ἐγένετο
[4]river, and immediately it collapsed, and [5]was
τὸ ῥῆγμα τῆς οἰκίας ἐκείνης μέγα.
[1]the [2]ruin – [4]house [3]of that [6]great.

The Wise and Foolish Builders

46"Why do you call me, 'Lord, Lord,' and do not do what I say? 47I will show you what he is like who comes to me and hears my words and puts them into practice. 48He is like a man building a house, who dug down deep and laid the foundation on rock. When a flood came, the torrent struck that house but could not shake it, because it was well built. 49But the one who hears my words and does not put them into practice is like a man who built a house on the ground without a foundation. The moment the torrent struck that house, it collapsed and its destruction was complete."

Chapter 7

Jesus Heals a Centurion's Servant

WHEN He had completed all His discourse in the hearing of the people, He went to Capernaum.

2And a certain centurion's slave, who was highly regarded by him, was sick and about to die.

3And when he heard about Jesus, he sent some Jewish elders asking Him to come and save the life of his slave.

4And when they had come to Jesus, they earnestly entreated Him, saying, "He is worthy for You to grant this to him;

5for he loves our nation, and it was he who built us our synagogue."

6Now Jesus *started* on His way with them; and when He was already not far from the house, the cen-

7 Ἐπειδὴ ἐπλήρωσεν πάντα τὰ ῥήματα
When he completed all the words
αὐτοῦ εἰς τὰς ἀκοὰς τοῦ λαοῦ, εἰσῆλθεν
of him in the ears of the people, he entered
εἰς Καφαρναούμ. 2 Ἑκατοντάρχου δέ
into Capernaum. Now [2]of [3]a [5]centurion
τινος δοῦλος κακῶς ἔχων ἤμελλεν τελευτᾶν,
[4]certain [1]a slave [7]ill [6]having(being) [12]was about [13]to die,
ὃς ἦν αὐτῷ ἔντιμος. 3 ἀκούσας δὲ περὶ
[8]who [9]was [11]to him [10]dear. And hearing about
τοῦ Ἰησοῦ ἀπέστειλεν πρὸς αὐτὸν πρε-
– Jesus he sent to him eld-
σβυτέρους τῶν Ἰουδαίων, ἐρωτῶν αὐτὸν
ers of the Jews, asking him
ὅπως ἐλθὼν διασώσῃ τὸν δοῦλον αὐτοῦ.
that coming he might recover the slave of him.
4 οἱ δὲ παραγενόμενοι πρὸς τὸν Ἰησοῦν
And they coming to – Jesus
παρεκάλουν αὐτὸν σπουδαίως, λέγοντες ὅτι ἄξιός
besought him earnestly, saying[,] – Worthy
ἐστιν ᾧ παρέξῃ τοῦτο· 5 ἀγαπᾷ γὰρ
he is for whom thou shouldest grant this; for he loves
τὸ ἔθνος ἡμῶν καὶ τὴν συναγωγὴν
the nation of us and the synagogue
αὐτὸς ᾠκοδόμησεν ἡμῖν. 6 ὁ δὲ Ἰησοῦς
he built for us. – And Jesus
ἐπορεύετο σὺν αὐτοῖς. ἤδη δὲ αὐτοῦ οὐ
went with them. And yet him not
=while he was yet
μακρὰν ἀπέχοντος ἀπὸ τῆς οἰκίας, ἔπεμψεν
far being away[a] from the house, sent
not far away

Chapter 7

The Faith of the Centurion

WHEN Jesus had finished saying all this in the hearing of the people, he entered Capernaum.
2There a centurion's servant, whom his master valued highly, was sick and about to die. 3The centurion heard of Jesus and sent some elders of the Jews to him, asking him to come and heal his servant.
4When they came to Jesus, they pleaded earnestly with him, "This man deserves to have you do this, 5because he loves our nation and has built our synagogue." 6So Jesus went with them.

He was not far from the house when the centurion

turion sent friends, saying
to Him, "Lord, do not
trouble Yourself further,
for I am not worthy for You
to come under my roof;
7for this reason I did not
even consider myself
worthy to come to You, but
just say the word, and my
servant will be healed.
8"For I, too, am a man
under authority, with soldiers under me; and I say to
this one, 'Go!' and he goes;
and to another, 'Come!'
and he comes; and to my
slave, 'Do this!' and he
does it."
9Now when Jesus heard
this, He marveled at him,
and turned and said to the
multitude that was following Him, "I say to you, not
even in Israel have I found
such great faith."
10And when those who
had been sent returned to
the house, they found the
slave in good health.
11And it came about soon
afterwards, that He went to
a city called Nain; and His
disciples were going along
with Him, accompanied by
a large multitude.
12Now as He approached
the gate of the city, behold,
a dead man was being car-
ried out, the only son of his
mother, and she was a
widow; and a sizeable
crowd from the city was
with her.
13And when the Lord saw
her, He felt compassion for
her, and said to her, "Do
not weep."
14And He came up and
touched the coffin; and the
bearers came to a halt. And
He said, "Young man, I
say to you, arise!"
15And the dead man sat
up, and began to speak.
And *Jesus* gave him back to
his mother.
16And fear gripped them
all, and they *began* glorifying God, saying, "A great
prophet has arisen among
us!" and, "God has visited

φίλους ὁ ἑκατοντάρχης λέγων αὐτῷ· κύριε,
friends the centurion saying to him : Lord,
μὴ σκύλλου· οὐ γὰρ ἱκανός εἰμι ἵνα ὑπὸ
do not trouble; for not worthy am I that under
τὴν στέγην μου εἰσέλθῃς· 7 διὸ οὐδὲ
the roof of me thou shouldest enter; wherefore not
ἐμαυτὸν ἠξίωσα πρὸς σὲ ἐλθεῖν· ἀλλὰ εἰπὲ
myself I accounted worthy to thee to come; but say
λόγῳ, καὶ ἰαθήτω ὁ παῖς μου. 8 καὶ
in a word, and let be cured the servant of me. [3]also
γὰρ ἐγὼ ἄνθρωπός εἰμι ὑπὸ ἐξουσίαν
[1]For [2]I [5]a man [4]am [7]under [8]authority
τασσόμενος, ἔχων ὑπ' ἐμαυτὸν στρατιώτας,
[6]*being* set, having under myself soldiers,
καὶ λέγω τούτῳ· πορεύθητι, καὶ πορεύεται,
and I tell this one : Go, and he goes,
καὶ ἄλλῳ· ἔρχου, καὶ ἔρχεται, καὶ τῷ
and another : Come, and he comes, and the
δούλῳ μου· ποίησον τοῦτο, καὶ ποιεῖ.
slave of me : Do this, and he does.
9 ἀκούσας δὲ ταῦτα ὁ Ἰησοῦς ἐθαύμασεν
And hearing these [words] – Jesus marvelled at
αὐτόν, καὶ στραφεὶς τῷ ἀκολουθοῦντι αὐτῷ
him, and turning to the [2]following [3]him
ὄχλῳ εἶπεν· λέγω ὑμῖν, οὐδὲ ἐν τῷ
[1]crowd said : I tell you, not in –
Ἰσραὴλ τοσαύτην πίστιν εὗρον. 10 καὶ
Israel such faith I found. And
ὑποστρέψαντες εἰς τὸν οἶκον οἱ πεμφθέντες
returning to the house the [ones] sent
εὗρον τὸν δοῦλον ὑγιαίνοντα. 11 Καὶ
found the slave well. And
ἐγένετο ἐν τῷ ἑξῆς ἐπορεύθη εἰς πόλιν
it came to pass on the next day he went into a city
καλουμένην Ναΐν, καὶ συνεπορεύοντο αὐτῷ
being called Nain, and went with him
οἱ μαθηταὶ αὐτοῦ καὶ ὄχλος πολύς.
the disciples of him and crowd a much.
12 ὡς δὲ ἤγγισεν τῇ πύλῃ τῆς πόλεως, καὶ
And as he drew near to the gate of the city, *and*
ἰδοὺ ἐξεκομίζετο τεθνηκὼς μονογενὴς
behold was being carried out [for burial] having died an only born
υἱὸς τῇ μητρὶ αὐτοῦ, καὶ αὕτη ἦν χήρα,
son to the mother of him, and this was a widow,
καὶ ὄχλος τῆς πόλεως ἱκανὸς ἦν σὺν
and a [2]crowd [3]of the [4]city [1]considerable was with
αὐτῇ. 13 καὶ ἰδὼν αὐτὴν ὁ κύριος
her. And seeing her the Lord
ἐσπλαγχνίσθη ἐπ' αὐτῇ καὶ εἶπεν αὐτῇ·
felt compassion over her and said to her :
μὴ κλαῖε. 14 καὶ προσελθὼν ἥψατο τῆς
Do not weep. And approaching he touched the
σοροῦ, οἱ δὲ βαστάζοντες ἔστησαν, καὶ
bier, and the [ones] bearing stood, and
εἶπεν· νεανίσκε, σοὶ λέγω, ἐγέρθητι. 15 καὶ
he said : Young man, to thee I say, Arise. And
ἀνεκάθισεν ὁ νεκρὸς καὶ ἤρξατο λαλεῖν,
sat up the dead man and began to speak,
καὶ ἔδωκεν αὐτὸν τῇ μητρὶ αὐτοῦ.
and he gave him to the mother of him.
16 ἔλαβεν δὲ φόβος πάντας, καὶ ἐδόξαζον
And [2]took [1]fear [3]all, and they glorified
τὸν θεὸν λέγοντες ὅτι προφήτης μέγας
– God saying[,] – prophet A great
ἠγέρθη ἐν ἡμῖν, καὶ ὅτι ἐπεσκέψατο ὁ
was raised among us, and[,] – [2]visited –

sent friends to say to him:
"Lord, don't trouble yourself, for I do not deserve to
have you come under my
roof. 7That is why I did not
even consider myself wor-
thy to come to you. But say
the word, and my servant
will be healed. 8For I myself am a man under authority, with soldiers under me.
I tell this one, 'Go,' and he
goes; and that one, 'Come,'
and he comes. I say to my
servant, 'Do this,' and he
does it."
9When Jesus heard this,
he was amazed at him, and
turning to the crowd fol-
lowing him, he said, "I tell
you, I have not found such
great faith even in Israel."
10Then the men who had
been sent returned to the
house and found the ser-
vant well.

Jesus Raises a Widow's Son

11Soon afterward, Jesus
went to a town called Nain,
and his disciples and a large
crowd went along with
him. 12As he approached
the town gate, a dead person was being carried out
—the only son of his mother, and she was a widow.
And a large crowd from the
town was with her. 13When
the Lord saw her, his heart
went out to her and he said,
"Don't cry."
14Then he went up and
touched the coffin, and
those carrying it stood still.
He said, "Young man, I
say to you, get up!" 15The
dead man sat up and began
to talk, and Jesus gave him
back to his mother.
16They were all filled with
awe and praised God. "A
great prophet has appeared
among us," they said.

His people!''
17And this report concerning Him went out all over Judea, and in all the surrounding district.

A Deputation from John

18And the disciples of John reported to him about all these things.
19And summoning two of his disciples, John sent them to the Lord, saying, "Are You the Expected One, or do we look for someone else?" "
20And when the men had come to Him, they said, "John the Baptist has sent us to You, saying, 'Are You the Expected One, or do we look for someone else?' "
21At that very time He cured many *people* of diseases and afflictions and evil spirits; and He granted sight to many *who were* blind.
22And He answered and said to them, "Go and report to John what you have seen and heard: *the* BLIND RECEIVE SIGHT, *the* lame walk, *the* lepers are cleansed, and *the* deaf hear, *the* dead are raised up, *the* POOR HAVE THE GOSPEL PREACHED TO THEM.
23"And blessed is he who keeps from stumbling over Me."
24And when the messengers of John had left, He began to speak to the multitudes about John, "What did you go out into the wilderness to look at? A reed shaken by the wind?
25"But what did you go out to see? A man dressed in soft clothing? Behold, those who are splendidly clothed and live in luxury are *found* in royal palaces.
26"But what did you go out to see? A prophet? Yes, I say to you, and one who is more than a prophet.
27"This is the one about whom it is written,

θεὸς τὸν λαὸν αὐτοῦ. 17 καὶ ἐξῆλθεν ὁ
¹God the people of him. And went forth –
λόγος οὗτος ἐν ὅλῃ τῇ Ἰουδαίᾳ περὶ
word this in all – Judæa ³concerning
αὐτοῦ καὶ πάσῃ τῇ περιχώρῳ.
⁴him ¹and ²all ³the ⁴neighbourhood.
18 Καὶ ἀπήγγειλαν Ἰωάννῃ οἱ μαθηταὶ
And reported to John the disciples
αὐτοῦ περὶ πάντων τούτων. καὶ
of him about all these things. And
προσκαλεσάμενος δύο τινὰς τῶν μαθητῶν
calling to [him] ²two ¹a certain of the disciples
αὐτοῦ ὁ Ἰωάννης 19 ἔπεμψεν πρὸς τὸν
of him – John sent to the
κύριον λέγων· σὺ εἶ ὁ ἐρχόμενος, ἢ ἄλλον
Lord saying : Thou art the coming [one], or another
προσδοκῶμεν; 20 παραγενόμενοι δὲ πρὸς
may we expect? And coming to
αὐτὸν οἱ ἄνδρες εἶπαν· Ἰωάννης ὁ βαπτιστὴς
him the men said : John the Baptist
ἀπέστειλεν ἡμᾶς πρὸς σὲ λέγων· σὺ εἶ ὁ
sent us to thee saying : Thou art the
ἐρχόμενος, ἢ ἄλλον προσδοκῶμεν; 21 ἐν
coming [one], or another may we expect? In
ἐκείνῃ τῇ ὥρᾳ ἐθεράπευσεν πολλοὺς ἀπὸ
that – hour he healed many from(of)
νόσων καὶ μαστίγων καὶ πνευμάτων πονηρῶν,
diseases and plagues and spirits evil,
καὶ τυφλοῖς πολλοῖς ἐχαρίσατο βλέπειν.
and blind persons to many he gave to see.
22 καὶ ἀποκριθεὶς εἶπεν αὐτοῖς· πορευθέντες
And answering he said to them : Going
ἀπαγγείλατε Ἰωάννῃ ἃ εἴδετε καὶ
report to John [the things] which ye saw and
ἠκούσατε· τυφλοὶ ἀναβλέπουσιν, χωλοὶ
heard: blind men see again, lame men
περιπατοῦσιν, λεπροὶ καθαρίζονται, καὶ κωφοὶ
walk, lepers are being cleansed, and deaf men
ἀκούουσιν, νεκροὶ ἐγείρονται, πτωχοὶ
hear, dead men are raised, poor people
εὐαγγελίζονται· 23 καὶ μακάριός ἐστιν ὃς ἐὰν
are evangelized; and blessed is whoever
μὴ σκανδαλισθῇ ἐν ἐμοί. 24 Ἀπελθόντων δὲ
is not offended in me. And going away =as the
τῶν ἀγγέλων Ἰωάννου ἤρξατο λέγειν πρὸς
the messengers of John[a] he began to say to
messengers of John went away
τοὺς ὄχλους περὶ Ἰωάννου· τί ἐξήλθατε
the crowds concerning John : What went ye forth
εἰς τὴν ἔρημον θεάσασθαι; κάλαμον ὑπὸ
into the desert to see? a reed by
ἀνέμου σαλευόμενον; 25 ἀλλὰ τί ἐξήλθατε
wind being shaken? But what went ye forth
ἰδεῖν; ἄνθρωπον ἐν μαλακοῖς ἱματίοις
to see? a man in soft garments
ἠμφιεσμένον; ἰδοὺ οἱ ἐν ἱματισμῷ ἐνδόξῳ
having been clothed? behold[,] the [ones] ¹in ³raiment ²splendid
καὶ τρυφῇ ὑπάρχοντες ἐν τοῖς βασιλείοις
⁴and ⁶in luxury ⁵being ⁸in – ⁹royal palaces
εἰσίν. 26 ἀλλὰ τί ἐξήλθατε ἰδεῖν; προφήτην;
⁷are. But what went ye forth to see? a prophet?
ναὶ λέγω ὑμῖν, καὶ περισσότερον προφήτου.
yes I tell you, and more [than] a prophet.
27 οὗτός ἐστιν περὶ οὗ γέγραπται· ἰδοὺ
This is he concerning whom it has been written : Behold

"God has come to help his people." 17This news about
Jesus spread throughout Judea[b] and the surrounding country.

Jesus and John the Baptist

18John's disciples told him about all these things.
Calling two of them, 19he
sent them to the Lord to ask, "Are you the one who was to come, or should we expect someone else?"
20When the men came to Jesus, they said, "John the Baptist sent us to you to ask, 'Are you the one who was to come, or should we expect someone else?' "
21At that very time Jesus cured many who had diseases, sicknesses and evil spirits, and gave sight to many who were blind. 22So
he replied to the messengers, "Go back and report to John what you have seen and heard: The blind receive sight, the lame walk, those who have leprosy[c] are cured, the deaf hear, the dead are raised, and the good news is preached to the poor. 23Blessed is the
man who does not fall away on account of me."
24After John's messengers left, Jesus began to speak to the crowd about John: "What did you go out into the desert to see? A reed swayed by the wind?
25If not, what did you go out to see? A man dressed in fine clothes? No, those who wear expensive clothes and indulge in luxury are in palaces. 26But
what did you go out to see? A prophet? Yes, I tell you, and more than a prophet.
27This is the one about whom it is written:

[b]17 Or *the land of the Jews*
[c]22 The Greek word was used for various diseases affecting the skin—not necessarily leprosy.

'BEHOLD, I SEND MY
MESSENGER BEFORE
YOUR FACE,
WHO WILL PREPARE
YOUR WAY BEFORE
YOU.'
28"I say to you, among
those born of women, there
is no one greater than John;
yet he who is least in the
kingdom of God is greater
than he."
29And when all the people
and the [p]tax-gatherers
heard *this,* they acknowledged God's justice, having
been baptized with the
baptism of John.
30But the Pharisees and
the [q]lawyers rejected
God's purpose for them-
selves, not having been
baptized by John.
31"To what then shall I
compare the men of this
generation, and what are
they like?
32"They are like children
who sit in the market place
and call to one another; and
they say, 'We played the
flute for you, and you did
not dance; we sang a dirge,
and you did not weep.'
33"For John the Baptist
has come eating no bread
and drinking no wine; and
you say, 'He has a demon!'
34"The Son of Man has
come eating and drinking;
and you say, 'Behold, a
gluttonous man, and a
drunkard, a friend of tax-
gatherers and sinners!'
35"Yet wisdom is vin-
dicated by all her chil-
dren."
36Now one of the Phari-
sees was requesting Him to
dine with him. And He en-
tered the Pharisee's house,
and reclined *at the table.*
37And behold, there was a
woman in the city who was
a sinner; and when she
learned that He was reclining *at the table* in the Pharisee's house, she brought an
alabaster vial of perfume,
38and standing behind
Him at His feet, weeping,
she began to wet His feet
with her tears, and kept

[p]I.e., Collectors of Roman taxes for profit
[q]I.e., experts in the Mosaic law

ἀποστέλλω τὸν ἄγγελόν μου πρὸ προσώπου
I send the messenger of me before [the] face
σου, ὃς κατασκευάσει τὴν ὁδόν σου
of thee, who will prepare the way of thee
ἔμπροσθέν σου. 28 λέγω ὑμῖν, μείζων
before thee. I tell you, [6]greater
ἐν γεννητοῖς γυναικῶν Ἰωάννου οὐδείς
[1]among [2][those] born [3]of women [[7]than] [8]John [4]no one
ἐστιν· ὁ δὲ μικρότερος ἐν τῇ βασιλείᾳ τοῦ
[5]is; but the less in the kingdom –
θεοῦ μείζων αὐτοῦ ἐστιν. 29 καὶ πᾶς ὁ
of God greater [than] he is. And all the
λαὸς ἀκούσας καὶ οἱ τελῶναι ἐδικαίωσαν
people hearing and the tax-collectors justified
τὸν θεόν, βαπτισθέντες τὸ βάπτισμα
– God, being baptized [with] the baptism
Ἰωάννου· 30 οἱ δὲ Φαρισαῖοι καὶ οἱ
of John; but the Pharisees and the
νομικοὶ τὴν βουλὴν τοῦ θεοῦ ἠθέτησαν εἰς
lawyers [4]the [5]counsel – [6]of God [1]rejected [2]for
ἑαυτούς, μὴ βαπτισθέντες ὑπ' αὐτοῦ. 31 Τίνι
[3]themselves, not being baptized by him. To what
οὖν ὁμοιώσω τοὺς ἀνθρώπους τῆς γενεᾶς
then may I liken the men – generation
ταύτης, καὶ τίνι εἰσὶν ὅμοιοι; 32 ὅμοιοί εἰσιν
of this, and to what are they like? Like are they
παιδίοις τοῖς ἐν ἀγορᾷ καθημένοις καὶ
to children – in a marketplace sitting and
προσφωνοῦσιν ἀλλήλοις ἃ λέγει· ηὐλήσαμεν
calling to one another who says : We piped
ὑμῖν καὶ οὐκ ὠρχήσασθε· ἐθρηνήσαμεν καὶ
to you and ye did not dance; we mourned and
οὐκ ἐκλαύσατε. 33 ἐλήλυθεν γὰρ Ἰωάννης
ye did not weep. For has come John
ὁ βαπτιστὴς μὴ ἐσθίων ἄρτον μήτε πίνων
the Baptist not eating bread nor drinking
οἶνον, καὶ λέγετε· δαιμόνιον ἔχει.
wine, and ye say : A demon he has.
34 ἐλήλυθεν ὁ υἱὸς τοῦ ἀνθρώπου ἐσθίων
Has come the Son – of man eating
καὶ πίνων, καὶ λέγετε· ἰδοὺ ἄνθρωπος
and drinking, and ye say : Behold[,] a man
φάγος καὶ οἰνοπότης, φίλος τελωνῶν καὶ
a glutton and a winebibber, a friend of tax-collectors and
ἁμαρτωλῶν. 35 καὶ ἐδικαιώθη ἡ σοφία
of sinners. And was(is) justified – wisdom
ἀπὸ πάντων τῶν τέκνων αὐτῆς.
from(by) all the children of her.
36 Ἠρώτα δέ τις αὐτὸν τῶν Φαρισαίων
And [4]asked [1]a certain one [5]him [2]of the [3]Pharisees
ἵνα φάγῃ μετ' αὐτοῦ· καὶ εἰσελθὼν εἰς
that he would eat with him; and entering into
τὸν οἶκον τοῦ Φαρισαίου κατεκλίθη. 37 καὶ
the house of the Pharisee he reclined. And[,]
ἰδοὺ γυνὴ ἥτις ἦν ἐν τῇ πόλει ἁμαρτωλός,
behold[,] a woman who was in the city a sinner,
καὶ ἐπιγνοῦσα ὅτι κατάκειται ἐν τῇ
and knowing that he reclines in the
οἰκίᾳ τοῦ Φαρισαίου, κομίσασα ἀλάβαστρον
house of the Pharisee, bringing an alabaster box
μύρου 38 καὶ στᾶσα ὀπίσω παρὰ τοὺς
of ointment and standing behind at the
πόδας αὐτοῦ κλαίουσα, τοῖς δάκρυσιν
feet of him weeping, with the(her) tears
ἤρξατο βρέχειν τοὺς πόδας αὐτοῦ, καὶ
began to wet the feet of him, and

" 'I will send my
messenger ahead of
you,
who will prepare your
way before you.' [d]

28I tell you, among those
born of women there is no
one greater than John; yet
the one who is least in the
kingdom of God is greater
than he."
29(All the people, even
the tax collectors, when
they heard Jesus' words,
acknowledged that God's
way was right, because
they had been baptized by
John. 30But the Pharisees
and experts in the law rejected God's purpose for
themselves, because they
had not been baptized by
John.)
31"To what, then, can I
compare the people of this
generation? What are they
like? 32They are like children sitting in the marketplace and calling out to
each other:

" 'We played the flute
for you,
and you did not dance;
we sang a dirge,
and you did not cry.'

33For John the Baptist
came neither eating bread
nor drinking wine, and you
say, 'He has a demon.'
34The Son of Man came
eating and drinking, and
you say, 'Here is a glutton
and a drunkard, a friend of
tax collectors and "sin-
ners." ' 35But wisdom is
proved right by all her children."

Jesus Anointed by a Sinful Woman

36Now one of the Phari-
sees invited Jesus to have
dinner with him, so he went
to the Pharisee's house and
reclined at the table.
37When a woman who had
lived a sinful life in that
town learned that Jesus
was eating at the Pharisee's
house, she brought an alabaster jar of perfume, 38and
as she stood behind him at
his feet weeping, she began
to wet his feet with her

[d]27 Mal. 3:1

wiping them with the hair
of her head, and kissing His
feet, and anointing them
with the perfume.
39Now when the Pharisee
who had invited Him saw
this, he said to himself, "If
this man were a prophet He
would know who and what
sort of person this woman
is who is touching Him,
that she is a sinner."

Parable of Two Debtors

40And Jesus answered
and said to him, "Simon, I
have something to say to
you." And he replied,
"Say it, Teacher."
41"A certain moneylend-
er had two debtors: one
owed five hundred [f]de-
narii, and the other fifty.
42"When they were un-
able to repay, he graciously
forgave them both. Which
of them therefore will love
him more?"
43Simon answered and
said, "I suppose the one
whom he forgave more."
And He said to him, "You
have judged correctly."
44And turning toward the
woman, He said to Simon,
"Do you see this woman? I
entered your house; you
gave Me no water for My
feet, but she has wet My
feet with her tears, and
wiped them with her hair.
45"You gave Me no kiss;
but she, since the time I
came in, has not ceased to
kiss My feet.
46"You did not anoint My
head with oil, but she
anointed My feet with perfume.
47"For this reason I say
to you, her sins, which are
many, have been forgiven,
for she loved much; but he
who is forgiven little, loves
little."
48And He said to her,
"Your sins have been for-
given."
49And those who were re-
clining *at the table* with
Him began to say to them-

[f]The denarius was equivalent to one day's wage

ταῖς θριξὶν τῆς κεφαλῆς αὐτῆς ἐξέμασσεν,
with the hairs of the head of her wiped off,
καὶ κατεφίλει τοὺς πόδας αὐτοῦ καὶ
and fervently kissed the feet of him and
ἤλειφεν τῷ μύρῳ. 39 ἰδὼν δὲ ὁ Φαρισαῖος
anointed with the ointment. But [5]seeing [1]the [2]Pharisee
ὁ καλέσας αὐτὸν εἶπεν ἐν ἑαυτῷ λέγων·
– [3]having invited [4]him spoke within himself saying :
οὗτος εἰ ἦν [ὁ] προφήτης, ἐγίνωσκεν ἂν
This man if he was the prophet, would have known
τίς καὶ ποταπὴ ἡ γυνὴ ἥτις ἅπτεται
who and what sort the woman who is touching
αὐτοῦ, ὅτι ἁμαρτωλός ἐστιν. 40 καὶ
him, because a sinner she is. And
ἀποκριθεὶς ὁ Ἰησοῦς εἶπεν πρὸς αὐτόν·
answering – Jesus said to him :
Σίμων, ἔχω σοί τι εἰπεῖν. ὁ δέ· διδάσκαλε,
Simon, I have to thee something to say. And he : Teacher,
εἰπέ, φησίν. 41 δύο χρεοφειλέται ἦσαν
say, says. Two debtors were
=A certain creditor had two debtors;
δανειστῇ τινι· ὁ εἷς ὤφειλεν δηνάρια
creditor to a certain;[c] the one owed denarii
πεντακόσια, ὁ δὲ ἕτερος πεντήκοντα. 42 μὴ
five hundred, and the other fifty. Not
=As they had no[thing]
ἐχόντων αὐτῶν ἀποδοῦναι ἀμφοτέροις
having them[a] to repay [2]both
ἐχαρίσατο. τίς οὖν αὐτῶν πλεῖον ἀγαπήσει
[1]he freely forgave. Who then of them more will love
αὐτόν; 43 ἀποκριθεὶς Σίμων εἶπεν·
him? Answering Simon said :
ὑπολαμβάνω ὅτι ᾧ τὸ πλεῖον ἐχαρίσατο.
I suppose[,] – to whom the more he freely forgave.
ὁ δὲ εἶπεν αὐτῷ· ὀρθῶς ἔκρινας. 44 καὶ
And he said to him : Rightly thou didst judge. And
στραφεὶς πρὸς τὴν γυναῖκα τῷ Σίμωνι
turning to the woman – to Simon
ἔφη· βλέπεις ταύτην τὴν γυναῖκα; εἰσῆλθόν
he said : Seest thou this – woman? I entered
σου εἰς τὴν οἰκίαν, ὕδωρ μοι ἐπὶ πόδας
of thee into the house, water to me on(for) [my] feet
οὐκ ἔδωκας· αὕτη δὲ τοῖς δάκρυσιν
thou gavest not; but this woman with the(her) tears
ἔβρεξέν μου τοὺς πόδας καὶ ταῖς θριξὶν
wet of me the feet and with the hairs
αὐτῆς ἐξέμαξεν. 45 φίλημά μοι οὐκ ἔδωκας·
of her wiped off. A kiss to me thou gavest not;
αὕτη δὲ ἀφ' ἧς εἰσῆλθον οὐ διέλειπεν
but this woman from [the time] which I entered ceased not
καταφιλοῦσά μου τοὺς πόδας. 46 ἐλαίῳ
fervently kissing of me the feet. With oil
τὴν κεφαλήν μου οὐκ ἤλειψας· αὕτη δὲ
the head of me thou didst not anoint; but this woman
μύρῳ ἤλειψεν τοὺς πόδας μου. 47 οὗ
with ointment anointed the feet of me. Of which
=Wherefore
χάριν λέγω σοι, ἀφέωνται αἱ ἁμαρτίαι
for the sake *of* I tell thee, [5]have been forgiven [1]the [2]sins
αὐτῆς αἱ πολλαί, ὅτι ἠγάπησεν πολύ·
[4]of her – [3]many, because she loved much;
ᾧ δὲ ὀλίγον ἀφίεται, ὀλίγον ἀγαπᾷ.
but to whom little is forgiven, little he loves.
48 εἶπεν δὲ αὐτῇ· ἀφέωνταί σου αἱ
And he said to her : Have been forgiven of thee the
ἁμαρτίαι. 49 καὶ ἤρξαντο οἱ συνανακείμενοι
sins. And began the [ones] reclining with [him]

tears. Then she wiped them
with her hair, kissed them
and poured perfume on
them.
39When the Pharisee who
had invited him saw this, he
said to himself, "If this
man were a prophet, he
would know who is touch-
ing him and what kind of
woman she is—that she is a
sinner."
40Jesus answered him,
"Simon, I have something
to tell you."
"Tell me, teacher," he
said.
41"Two men owed money
to a certain moneylender.
One owed him five hundred
denarii,[e] and the other fifty. 42Neither of them had
the money to pay him back,
so he canceled the debts of
both. Now which of them
will love him more?"
43Simon replied, "I sup-
pose the one who had the
bigger debt canceled."
"You have judged cor-
rectly," Jesus said.
44Then he turned toward
the woman and said to Si-
mon, "Do you see this
woman? I came into your
house. You did not give me
any water for my feet, but
she wet my feet with her
tears and wiped them with
her hair. 45You did not give
me a kiss, but this woman,
from the time I entered, has
not stopped kissing my
feet. 46You did not put oil
on my head, but she has
poured perfume on my
feet. 47Therefore, I tell you,
her many sins have been
forgiven—for she loved
much. But he who has been
forgiven little loves little."
48Then Jesus said to her,
"Your sins are forgiven."
49The other guests began
to say among themselves,

[e]*41* A denarius was a coin worth about a day's wages.

selves, "Who is this *man* who even forgives sins?"

50 And He said to the woman, "Your faith has saved you; go in peace."

λέγειν ἐν ἑαυτοῖς· τίς οὗτός ἐστιν, ὃς καὶ
to say among themselves : Who this is, who even
ἁμαρτίας ἀφίησιν; 50 εἶπεν δὲ πρὸς τὴν
sins forgives? But he said to the
γυναῖκα· ἡ πίστις σου σέσωκέν σε·
woman : The faith of thee has saved thee;
πορεύου εἰς εἰρήνην.
go in peace.

"Who is this who even forgives sins?"

50 Jesus said to the woman, "Your faith has saved you; go in peace."

Chapter 8

Ministering Women

AND it came about soon afterwards, that He *began* going about from one city and village to another, proclaiming and preaching the kingdom of God; and the twelve were with Him,

2 and *also* some women who had been healed of evil spirits and sicknesses: Mary who was called Magdalene, from whom seven demons had gone out,

3 and Joanna the wife of Chuza, Herod's steward, and Susanna, and many others who were contributing to their support out of their private means.

Parable of the Sower

4 And when a great multitude were coming together, and those from the various cities were journeying to Him, He spoke by way of a parable:

5 "The sower went out to sow his seed; and as he sowed, some fell beside the road; and it was trampled under foot, and the birds of the air ate it up.

6 "And other *seed* fell on rocky *soil*, and as soon as it grew up, it withered away, because it had no moisture.

7 "And other *seed* fell among the thorns; and the thorns grew up with it, and choked it out.

8 "And other *seed* fell into the good soil, and grew up, and produced a crop a hundred times as great." As He said these things, He would call out, "He who has ears to hear, let him hear."

8 Καὶ ἐγένετο ἐν τῷ καθεξῆς καὶ αὐτὸς
And it came to pass afterwards *and* he
διώδευεν κατὰ πόλιν καὶ κώμην κηρύσσων
journeyed through every† city and village proclaiming
καὶ εὐαγγελιζόμενος τὴν βασιλείαν τοῦ
and preaching the kingdom –
θεοῦ, καὶ οἱ δώδεκα σὺν αὐτῷ, 2 καὶ
of God, and the twelve with him, and
γυναῖκές τινες αἳ ἦσαν τεθεραπευμέναι ἀπὸ
women certain who were having been healed from
πνευμάτων πονηρῶν καὶ ἀσθενειῶν, Μαρία
spirits evil and infirmities, Mary
ἡ καλουμένη Μαγδαληνή, ἀφ' ἧς δαιμόνια
– *being* called Magdalene, from whom demons
ἑπτὰ ἐξεληλύθει, 3 καὶ Ἰωάννα γυνὴ Χουζᾶ
seven had gone out, and Joanna wife of Chuza
ἐπιτρόπου Ἡρῴδου καὶ Σουσάννα καὶ
steward of Herod and Susanna and
ἕτεραι πολλαί, αἵτινες διηκόνουν αὐτοῖς
others many, who ministered to them
ἐκ τῶν ὑπαρχόντων αὐταῖς.
out of the possessions to them.[c]

4 Συνιόντος δὲ ὄχλου πολλοῦ καὶ τῶν
And coming together crowd a much and the [ones]
=when a great crowd came together and people in each city
κατὰ πόλιν ἐπιπορευομένων πρὸς αὐτὸν
in each city† resorting[a] to him
resorted
εἶπεν διὰ παραβολῆς· 5 ἐξῆλθεν ὁ σπείρων
he said by a parable : Went forth the [one] sowing
τοῦ σπεῖραι τὸν σπόρον αὐτοῦ. καὶ ἐν τῷ
– to sow[d] the seed of him. And in the
σπείρειν αὐτὸν ὃ μὲν ἔπεσεν παρὰ τὴν
to sow him[be] this fell by the
=as he sowed
ὁδὸν καὶ κατεπατήθη, καὶ τὰ πετεινὰ τοῦ
way and was trodden down, and the birds of the
οὐρανοῦ κατέφαγεν αὐτό. 6 καὶ ἕτερον
heaven(air) devoured it. And other [seed]
κατέπεσεν ἐπὶ τὴν πέτραν, καὶ φυὲν
fell on the rock, and grown
ἐξηράνθη διὰ τὸ μὴ ἔχειν ἰκμάδα.
it was withered because of the not to have moisture.
=because it had no moisture.
7 καὶ ἕτερον ἔπεσεν ἐν μέσῳ τῶν ἀκανθῶν, καὶ
And other fell in [the] midst of the thorns, and
συμφυεῖσαι αἱ ἄκανθαι ἀπέπνιξαν αὐτό.
growing up with [it] the thorns choked it.
8 καὶ ἕτερον ἔπεσεν εἰς τὴν γῆν τὴν
And other fell in the soil –
ἀγαθὴν καὶ φυὲν ἐποίησεν καρπὸν
good and grown it produced fruit
ἑκατονταπλασίονα. ταῦτα λέγων ἐφώνει· ὁ
a hundredfold. These things saying he called: The [one]
ἔχων ὦτα ἀκούειν ἀκουέτω. 9 Ἐπηρώτων δὲ
having ears to hear let him hear. And questioned

Chapter 8

The Parable of the Sower

AFTER this, Jesus traveled about from one town and village to another, proclaiming the good news of the kingdom of God. The Twelve were with him, 2 and also some women who had been cured of evil spirits and diseases: Mary (called Magdalene) from whom seven demons had come out; 3 Joanna the wife of Cuza, the manager of Herod's household; Susanna; and many others. These women were helping to support them out of their own means.

4 While a large crowd was gathering and people were coming to Jesus from town after town, he told this parable: 5 "A farmer went out to sow his seed. As he was scattering the seed, some fell along the path; it was trampled on, and the birds of the air ate it up. 6 Some fell on rock, and when it came up, the plants withered because they had no moisture. 7 Other seed fell among thorns, which grew up with it and choked the plants. 8 Still other seed fell on good soil. It came up and yielded a crop, a hundred times more than was sown."

When he said this, he called out, "He who has ears to hear, let him hear."

9And His disciples *be-
gan questioning Him as to
what this parable might be.
10And He said, "To you it
has been granted to know
the mysteries of the kingdom of God, but to the rest
it is in parables, in order
that SEEING THEY MAY NOT
SEE, AND HEARING THEY MAY
NOT UNDERSTAND.
11"Now the parable is
this: the seed is the word of
God.
12"And those beside the
road are those who have
heard; then the devil comes
and takes away the word
from their heart, so that
they may not believe and
be saved.
13"And those on the
rocky *soil are* those who,
when they hear, receive the
word with joy; and these
have no *firm* root; they believe for a while, and in
time of temptation fall
away.
14"And the *seed* which
fell among the thorns, these
are the ones who have
heard, and as they go on
their way they are choked
with worries and riches and
pleasures of *this* life, and
bring no fruit to maturity.
15"And the *seed* in the
good soil, these are the
ones who have heard
the word in an honest and
good heart, and hold it fast,
and bear fruit with perseverance.

Parable of the Lamp

16"Now no one after
lighting a lamp covers it
over with a container, or
puts it under a bed; but he
puts it on a lampstand, in
order that those who come
in may see the light.
17"For nothing is hidden
that shall not become evident, nor *anything* secret
that shall not be known and
come to light.
18"Therefore take care
how you listen; for who-
ever has, to him shall *more*
be given; and whoever does
not have, even what he
thinks he has shall be taken
away from him."
19And His mother and
brothers came to Him, and

αὐτὸν οἱ μαθηταὶ αὐτοῦ τίς αὕτη εἴη ἡ
him the disciples of him what [1]this [2]might be –
παραβολή. **10** ὁ δὲ εἶπεν· ὑμῖν δέδοται
[3]parable. And he said : To you it has been given
γνῶναι τὰ μυστήρια τῆς βασιλείας τοῦ
to know the mysteries of the kingdom –
θεοῦ, τοῖς δὲ λοιποῖς ἐν παραβολαῖς, ἵνα
of God, but to the rest in parables, that
βλέποντες μὴ βλέπωσιν καὶ ἀκούοντες μὴ
seeing they may not see and hearing not
συνιῶσιν. **11** ἔστιν δὲ αὕτη ἡ παραβολή.
they may understand. [4]is [1]Now [2]this – [3]parable.
ὁ σπόρος ἐστὶν ὁ λόγος τοῦ θεοῦ.
The seed is the word – of God.
12 οἱ δὲ παρὰ τὴν ὁδόν εἰσιν οἱ ἀκούσαντες,
And the [ones] by the way are the [ones] hearing,
εἶτα ἔρχεται ὁ διάβολος καὶ αἴρει τὸν
then comes the devil and takes the
λόγον ἀπὸ τῆς καρδίας αὐτῶν, ἵνα μὴ
word from the heart of them, lest
πιστεύσαντες σωθῶσιν. **13** οἱ δὲ ἐπὶ τῆς
believing they may be saved. And the [ones] on the
πέτρας οἳ ὅταν ἀκούσωσιν μετὰ χαρᾶς
rock who when they hear with joy
δέχονται τὸν λόγον· καὶ οὗτοι ῥίζαν
receive the word; and these root
οὐκ ἔχουσιν, οἳ πρὸς καιρὸν πιστεύουσιν
have not, who for a time believe
καὶ ἐν καιρῷ πειρασμοῦ ἀφίστανται. **14** τὸ
and in time of trial withdraw. the [one]
δὲ εἰς τὰς ἀκάνθας πεσόν, οὗτοί εἰσιν
And in the thorns falling, these are
οἱ ἀκούσαντες, καὶ ὑπὸ μεριμνῶν καὶ
the [ones] hearing, [1]and [4]by [5]cares [6]and
πλούτου καὶ ἡδονῶν τοῦ βίου πορευόμενοι
[7]riches [8]and [9]pleasures – [10]of life [2]going
συμπνίγονται καὶ οὐ τελεσφοροῦσιν. **15** τὸ
[3]are choked and do not bear [fruit] to maturity. the [one]
δὲ ἐν τῇ καλῇ γῇ, οὗτοί εἰσιν οἵτινες ἐν
And in the good soil, these are [those] who in
καρδίᾳ καλῇ καὶ ἀγαθῇ ἀκούσαντες τὸν
heart a worthy and good hearing the
λόγον κατέχουσιν καὶ καρποφοροῦσιν ἐν
word hold fast and bear fruit in
ὑπομονῇ. **16** Οὐδεὶς δὲ λύχνον ἅψας
patience. Now no one a lamp having lit
καλύπτει αὐτὸν σκεύει ἢ ὑποκάτω κλίνης
hides it with a vessel or underneath a couch
τίθησιν, ἀλλ' ἐπὶ λυχνίας τίθησιν, ἵνα οἱ
puts, but on a lampstand puts, that the
εἰσπορευόμενοι βλέπωσιν τὸ φῶς. **17** οὐ
[ones] coming in may see the light. not
γάρ ἐστιν κρυπτὸν ὃ οὐ φανερὸν
For [anything] is hidden which [3]not [4]manifest
γενήσεται, οὐδὲ ἀπόκρυφον ὃ οὐ μὴ
[1]will [2]become, nor secret which by no means
γνωσθῇ καὶ εἰς φανερὸν ἔλθῃ. **18** βλέπετε
will be known and to [be] manifest come. See
οὖν πῶς ἀκούετε· ὃς ἂν γὰρ ἔχῃ,
therefore how ye hear; for whoever has,
δοθήσεται αὐτῷ· καὶ ὃς ἂν μὴ ἔχῃ,
it will be given to him; and whoever has not,
καὶ ὃ δοκεῖ ἔχειν ἀρθήσεται ἀπ' αὐτοῦ.
even what he seems to have will be taken from him.
19 Παρεγένετο δὲ πρὸς αὐτὸν ἡ μήτηρ
And came to him the mother

9His disciples asked him
what this parable meant.
10He said, "The knowledge
of the secrets of the kingdom of God has been given
to you, but to others I
speak in parables, so that,

" 'though seeing, they
may not see;
though hearing, they
may not
understand.'[f]

11"This is the meaning of
the parable: The seed is the
word of God. 12Those along
the path are the ones who
hear, and then the devil
comes and takes away the
word from their hearts, so
that they may not believe
and be saved. 13Those on
the rock are the ones who
receive the word with joy
when they hear it, but they
have no root. They believe
for a while, but in the time
of testing they fall away.
14The seed that fell among
thorns stands for those who
hear, but as they go on their
way they are choked by
life's worries, riches and
pleasures, and they do not
mature. 15But the seed on
good soil stands for those
with a noble and good
heart, who hear the word,
retain it, and by persevering produce a crop.

A Lamp on a Stand

16"No one lights a lamp
and hides it in a jar or puts it
under a bed. Instead, he
puts it on a stand, so that
those who come in can see
the light. 17For there is
nothing hidden that will not
be disclosed, and nothing
concealed that will not be
known or brought out into
the open. 18Therefore consider carefully how you listen. Whoever has will be
given more; whoever does
not have, even what he
thinks he has will be taken
from him."

Jesus' Mother and
Brothers

19Now Jesus' mother and
brothers came to see him,

[f]10 Isaiah 6:9

they were unable to get to
Him because of the crowd.
20And it was reported to
Him, "Your mother and
Your brothers are standing
outside, wishing to see
You."
21But He answered and
said to them, "My mother
and My brothers are these
who hear the word of God
and do it."

Jesus Stills the Sea

22Now it came about on
one of *those* days, that He
and His disciples got into a
boat, and He said to them,
"Let us go over to the other
side of the lake." And they
launched out.
23But as they were sailing
along He fell asleep; and a
fierce gale of wind de-
scended upon the lake, and
they *began* to be swamped
and to be in danger.
24And they came to Him
and woke Him up, saying,
"Master, Master, we are
perishing!" And being
aroused, He rebuked the
wind and the surging
waves, and they stopped,
and it became calm.
25And He said to them,
"Where is your faith?"
And they were fearful and
amazed, saying to one an-
other, "Who then is this,
that He commands even
the winds and the water,
and they obey Him?"

The Demoniac Cured

26And they sailed to the
country of the Gerasenes,
which is opposite Galilee.
27And when He had come
out onto the land, He was
met by a certain man from
the city who was possessed
with demons; and who had
not put on any clothing for
a long time, and was not living in a house, but in the
tombs.
28And seeing Jesus, he
cried out and fell before
Him, and said in a loud
voice, "What do I have to
do with You, Jesus, Son of
the Most High God? I beg

καὶ οἱ ἀδελφοὶ αὐτοῦ, καὶ οὐκ ἠδύναντο
and the brothers of him, and were not able
συντυχεῖν αὐτῷ διὰ τὸν ὄχλον. 20 ἀπηγγέλη δὲ
to come up with him be- cause of the crowd. And it was reported
αὐτῷ· ἡ μήτηρ σου καὶ οἱ ἀδελφοί σου
to him : The mother of thee and the brothers of thee
ἑστήκασιν ἔξω ἰδεῖν θέλοντές σε. 21 ὁ δὲ
are standing outside [2]to see [1]wishing thee. But he
ἀποκριθεὶς εἶπεν πρὸς αὐτούς· μήτηρ μου
answering said to them : Mother of me
καὶ ἀδελφοί μου οὗτοί εἰσιν οἱ τὸν λόγον
and brothers of me [2]these [1]are [3]the [ones] [7]the [8]word
τοῦ θεοῦ ἀκούοντες καὶ ποιοῦντες.
– [9]of God [4]hearing [5]and [6]doing.
22 Ἐγένετο δὲ ἐν μιᾷ τῶν ἡμερῶν καὶ
And it came to pass on one of the days *and*
αὐτὸς ἐνέβη εἰς πλοῖον καὶ οἱ μαθηταὶ
he embarked in a boat and the disciples
αὐτοῦ, καὶ εἶπεν πρὸς αὐτούς· διέλθωμεν
of him, and he said to them; Let us go over
εἰς τὸ πέραν τῆς λίμνης· καὶ ἀνήχθησαν.
to the other side of the lake; and they put to sea.
23 πλεόντων δὲ αὐτῶν ἀφύπνωσεν. καὶ
And sailing them[e] he fell asleep. And
=as they sailed
κατέβη λαῖλαψ ἀνέμου εἰς τὴν λίμνην, καὶ
came down a storm of wind to the lake, and
συνεπληροῦντο καὶ ἐκινδύνευον. 24 προσ-
they were filling up and were in danger. ap-
ελθόντες δὲ διήγειραν αὐτὸν λέγοντες·
proaching And they awoke him saying :
ἐπιστάτα ἐπιστάτα, ἀπολλύμεθα. ὁ δὲ
Master[,] Master, we are perishing. But he
διεγερθεὶς ἐπετίμησεν τῷ ἀνέμῳ καὶ τῷ
being awakened rebuked the wind and the
κλύδωνι τοῦ ὕδατος· καὶ ἐπαύσαντο, καὶ ἐγένετο
roughness of the water; and they ceased, and there was
γαλήνη. 25 εἶπεν δὲ αὐτοῖς· ποῦ ἡ πίστις ὑμῶν;
a calm. Then he said to them: Where the faith of you?
φοβηθέντες δὲ ἐθαύμασαν, λέγοντες πρὸς
And fearing they marvelled, saying to
ἀλλήλους· τίς ἄρα οὗτός ἐστιν, ὅτι καὶ
one another : Who then [2]this man [1]is, that [3]even
τοῖς ἀνέμοις ἐπιτάσσει καὶ τῷ ὕδατι, καὶ
[5]the [4]winds [1]he commands and the water, and
ὑπακούουσιν αὐτῷ; 26 Καὶ κατέπλευσαν εἰς
they obey him? And they sailed down to
τὴν χώραν τῶν Γερασηνῶν, ἥτις ἐστὶν
the country of the Gerasenes, which is
ἀντιπέρα τῆς Γαλιλαίας. 27 ἐξελθόντι δὲ
opposite – Galilee. And going out
=as he went out
αὐτῷ ἐπὶ τὴν γῆν ὑπήντησεν ἀνήρ τις
him[e] onto the land met [him] man a certain
ἔκ τῆς πόλεως ἔχων δαιμόνια, καὶ χρόνῳ
out of the city having demons, and [2]time
ἱκανῷ οὐκ ἐνεδύσατο ἱμάτιον, καὶ ἐν οἰκίᾳ
[1]for a con- siderable put not on a garment, and in a house
οὐκ ἔμενεν ἀλλ' ἐν τοῖς μνήμασιν. 28 ἰδὼν
remained not but among the tombs. seeing
δὲ τὸν Ἰησοῦν ἀνακράξας προσέπεσεν αὐτῷ
And – Jesus crying out he fell prostrate before him
καὶ φωνῇ μεγάλῃ εἶπεν· τί ἐμοὶ καὶ σοί,
and voice in a great(loud) said : What to me and to thee,
Ἰησοῦ υἱὲ τοῦ θεοῦ τοῦ ὑψίστου; δέομαί
Jesus Son – of God – most high? I beg

but they were not able to
get near him because of the
crowd. 20Someone told
him, "Your mother and
brothers are standing outside, wanting to see you."
21He replied, "My moth-
er and brothers are those
who hear God's word and
put it into practice."

Jesus Calms the Storm

22One day Jesus said to
his disciples, "Let's go
over to the other side of the
lake." So they got into a
boat and set out. 23As they
sailed, he fell asleep. A
squall came down on the
lake, so that the boat was
being swamped, and they
were in great danger.
24The disciples went and
woke him, saying, "Mas-
ter, Master, we're going to
drown!"
He got up and rebuked
the wind and the raging waters; the storm subsided,
and all was calm. 25"Where
is your faith?" he asked his
disciples.
In fear and amazement
they asked one another,
"Who is this? He com-
mands even the winds and
the water, and they obey
him."

The Healing of a Demon-possessed Man

26They sailed to the re-
gion of the Gerasenes,[g]
which is across the lake
from Galilee. 27When Jesus
stepped ashore, he was met
by a demon-possessed man
from the town. For a long
time this man had not worn
clothes or lived in a house,
but had lived in the tombs.
28When he saw Jesus, he
cried out and fell at his feet,
shouting at the top of his
voice, "What do you want
with me, Jesus, Son of the
Most High God? I beg you,

[g]26 Some manuscripts *Gadarenes*; other manuscripts *Gergesenes*; also in verse 37

You, do not torment me."
29For He had been com-
manding the unclean spirit
to come out of the man. For
it had seized him many
times; and he was bound
with chains and shackles
and kept under guard; and
yet he would burst his fetters and be driven by the
demon into the desert.
30And Jesus asked him,
"What is your name?" And
he said, "Legion"; for
many demons had entered
him.
31And they were entreat-
ing Him not to command
them to depart into the
abyss.
32Now there was a herd of
many swine feeding there
on the mountain; and *the*
demons entreated Him to
permit them to enter the
swine. And He gave them
permission.
33And the demons came
out from the man and en-
tered the swine; and the
herd rushed down the steep
bank into the lake, and
were drowned.
34And when the herds-
men saw what had hap-
pened, they ran away and
reported it in the city and
out in the country.
35And *the people* went
out to see what had hap-
pened; and they came to
Jesus, and found the man
from whom the demons
had gone out, sitting down
at the feet of Jesus, clothed
and in his right mind; and
they became frightened.
36And those who had
seen it reported to them
how the man who was de-
mon-possessed had been
made well.
37And all the people of the
country of the Gerasenes
and the surrounding district
asked Him to depart from
them; for they were gripped
with great fear; and He got
into a boat, and returned.

σου, μή με βασανίσῃς. 29 παρήγγελλεν
of thee, do not me torment. he charged
γὰρ τῷ πνεύματι τῷ ἀκαθάρτῳ ἐξελθεῖν
For the spirit – unclean to come out
ἀπὸ τοῦ ἀνθρώπου. πολλοῖς γὰρ χρόνοις
from the man. For many times
συνηρπάκει αὐτόν, καὶ ἐδεσμεύετο ἁλύσεσιν
it had seized him, and he was bound with chains
καὶ πέδαις φυλασσόμενος, καὶ διαρήσσων
and fetters being guarded, and tearing asunder
τὰ δεσμὰ ἠλαύνετο ἀπὸ τοῦ δαιμονίου εἰς
the bonds he was driven from(by) the demon into
τὰς ἐρήμους. 30 ἐπηρώτησεν δὲ αὐτὸν ὁ
the deserts. And questioned him . –
Ἰησοῦς· τί σοι ὄνομά ἐστιν; ὁ δὲ εἶπεν·
Jesus : What to thee name is?[c] And he said :
λεγιών, ὅτι εἰσῆλθεν δαιμόνια πολλὰ εἰς
Legion, because 3entered 2demons 1many into
αὐτόν. 31 καὶ παρεκάλουν αὐτὸν ἵνα μὴ
him. And they besought him that not
ἐπιτάξῃ αὐτοῖς εἰς τὴν ἄβυσσον ἀπελθεῖν.
he would order them into the abyss to go away.
32 ἦν δὲ ἐκεῖ ἀγέλη χοίρων ἱκανῶν
Now there was there a herd pigs of many
βοσκομένη ἐν τῷ ὄρει· καὶ παρεκάλεσαν
feeding in the mountain; and they besought
αὐτὸν ἵνα ἐπιτρέψῃ αὐτοῖς εἰς ἐκείνους
him that he would allow them into those
εἰσελθεῖν· καὶ ἐπέτρεψεν αὐτοῖς. 33 ἐξελθόντα
to enter; and he allowed them. 4coming out
δὲ τὰ δαιμόνια ἀπὸ τοῦ ἀνθρώπου εἰσῆλθον
1So 2the 3demons from the man entered
εἰς τοὺς χοίρους, καὶ ὥρμησεν ἡ ἀγέλη
into the pigs, and rushed the herd
κατὰ τοῦ κρημνοῦ εἰς τὴν λίμνην καὶ
down the precipice into the lake and
ἀπεπνίγη. 34 ἰδόντες δὲ οἱ βόσκοντες
was choked. And 3seeing 1the [ones] 2feeding
τὸ γεγονὸς ἔφυγον καὶ ἀπήγγειλαν εἰς
4the thing 5having happened fled and reported in
=what had happened
τὴν πόλιν καὶ εἰς τοὺς ἀγρούς. 35 ἐξῆλθον
the city and in the farms. they went out
δὲ ἰδεῖν τὸ γεγονός, καὶ ἦλθον πρὸς τὸν
And to see the thing having happened, and came to –
=what had happened,
Ἰησοῦν, καὶ εὗρον καθήμενον τὸν ἄνθρωπον
Jesus, and found sitting the man
ἀφ' οὗ τὰ δαιμόνια ἐξῆλθεν ἱματισμένον
from whom the demons went out *having been* clothed
καὶ σωφρονοῦντα παρὰ τοὺς πόδας τοῦ
and being in his senses by the feet –
Ἰησοῦ, καὶ ἐφοβήθησαν. 36 ἀπήγγειλαν δὲ
of Jesus, and they were afraid. And 3reported
αὐτοῖς οἱ ἰδόντες πῶς ἐσώθη ὁ δαιμο-
4to them 1the [ones] 2seeing 5how 8was healed 6the 7demon-
νισθείς. 37 καὶ ἠρώτησεν αὐτὸν ἅπαν τὸ
possessed. And asked him all the
πλῆθος τῆς περιχώρου τῶν Γερασηνῶν
multitude of the neighbourhood of the Gerasenes
ἀπελθεῖν ἀπ' αὐτῶν, ὅτι φόβῳ μεγάλῳ
to go away from them, because fear with a great
συνείχοντο· αὐτὸς δὲ ἐμβὰς εἰς πλοῖον
they were seized; so he embarking in a boat

don't torture me!" 29For
Jesus had commanded the
evil[h] spirit to come out of
the man. Many times it had
seized him, and though he
was chained hand and foot
and kept under guard, he
had broken his chains and
had been driven by the demon into solitary places.
30Jesus asked him,
"What is your name?"
"Legion," he replied, be-
cause many demons had
gone into him. 31And they
begged him repeatedly not
to order them to go into the
Abyss.
32A large herd of pigs was
feeding there on the hill-
side. The demons begged
Jesus to let them go into
them, and he gave them
permission. 33When the demons came out of the man,
they went into the pigs, and
the herd rushed down the
steep bank into the lake and
was drowned.
34When those tending the
pigs saw what had hap-
pened, they ran off and reported this in the town and
countryside, 35and the people went out to see what
had happened. When they
came to Jesus, they found
the man from whom the de-
mons had gone out, sitting
at Jesus' feet, dressed and
in his right mind; and they
were afraid. 36Those who
had seen it told the people
how the demon-possessed
man had been cured.
37Then all the people of the
region of the Gerasenes
asked Jesus to leave them,
because they were over-
come with fear. So he got
into the boat and left.

h29 Greek *unclean*

38But the man from whom
the demons had gone out
was begging Him that he
might accompany Him; but
He sent him away, saying,
39"Return to your house
and describe what great
things God has done for
you." And he went away,
proclaiming throughout the
whole city what great
things Jesus had done for
him.

Miracles of Healing

40And as Jesus returned,
the multitude welcomed
Him, for they had all been
waiting for Him.
41And behold, there came
a man named Jairus, and he
was an official of the synagogue; and he fell at Jesus'
feet, and *began* to entreat
Him to come to his house;
42for he had an only
daughter, about twelve
years old, and she was dying. But as He went, the
multitudes were pressing
against Him.
43And a woman who had
a hemorrhage for twelve
years, [s]and could not be
healed by anyone,
44came up behind Him,
and touched the fringe of
His cloak; and immediately
her hemorrhage stopped.
45And Jesus said, "Who
is the one who touched
Me?" And while they were
all denying it, Peter said,
"Master, the multitudes
are crowding and pressing
upon You."
46But Jesus said, "Some-
one did touch Me, for I was
aware that power had gone
out of Me."
47And when the woman
saw that she had not es-
caped notice, she came
trembling and fell down before Him, and declared in
the presence of all the
people the reason why she
had touched Him, and how

[s] Some mss. add *who had spent all her living upon physicians*

ὑπέστρεψεν. 38 ἐδεῖτο δὲ αὐτοῦ ὁ ἀνὴρ
returned. And begged of him the man
ἀφ' οὗ ἐξεληλύθει τὰ δαιμόνια εἶναι σὺν
from whom had gone out the demons to be with
αὐτῷ· ἀπέλυσεν δὲ αὐτὸν λέγων· 39 ὑπόστρεφε
him; but he dismissed him saying : Return
εἰς τὸν οἶκόν σου, καὶ διηγοῦ ὅσα σοι
to the house of thee, and relate what [3]to thee things
ἐποίησεν ὁ θεός. καὶ ἀπῆλθεν καθ' ὅλην
[2]did – [1]God. And he went away throughout all
τὴν πόλιν κηρύσσων ὅσα ἐποίησεν αὐτῷ
the city proclaiming what things [2]did [3]to him
ὁ Ἰησοῦς.
– [1]Jesus.
40 Ἐν δὲ τῷ ὑποστρέφειν τὸν Ἰησοῦν
Now in the to return – Jesus[be]
=when Jesus returned
ἀπεδέξατο αὐτὸν ὁ ὄχλος· ἦσαν γὰρ
welcomed him the crowd; for they were
πάντες προσδοκῶντες αὐτόν. 41 καὶ ἰδοὺ
all expecting him. And behold
ἦλθεν ἀνὴρ ᾧ ὄνομα Ἰάϊρος, καὶ οὗτος
came a man to whom name Jairus,[c] and this man
ἄρχων τῆς συναγωγῆς ὑπῆρχεν· καὶ πεσὼν
a ruler of the synagogue was; and falling
παρὰ τοὺς πόδας Ἰησοῦ παρεκάλει αὐτὸν
at the feet of Jesus he besought him
εἰσελθεῖν εἰς τὸν οἶκον αὐτοῦ, 42 ὅτι
to enter into the house of him, because
θυγάτηρ μονογενὴς ἦν αὐτῷ ὡς ἐτῶν
daughter an only born was to him[c] about of years
=he had an only daughter
δώδεκα καὶ αὐτὴ ἀπέθνῃσκεν. Ἐν δὲ τῷ
twelve and this(she) was dying. Now in the
=as he went
ὑπάγειν αὐτὸν οἱ ὄχλοι συνέπνιγον αὐτόν.
to go him[be] the crowds pressed upon him.
43 καὶ γυνὴ οὖσα ἐν ῥύσει αἵματος ἀπὸ
And a woman being in a flow of blood from
=having
ἐτῶν δώδεκα, ἥτις οὐκ ἴσχυσεν ἀπ'
years twelve, who was not able from
οὐδενὸς θεραπευθῆναι, 44 προσελθοῦσα ὄπισθεν
no(any)one to be healed, approaching behind
ἥψατο τοῦ κρασπέδου τοῦ ἱματίου αὐτοῦ,
touched the fringe of the garment of him,
καὶ παραχρῆμα ἔστη ἡ ῥύσις τοῦ αἵματος
and at once stood the flow of the blood
αὐτῆς. 45 καὶ εἶπεν ὁ Ἰησοῦς· τίς ὁ
of her. And said – Jesus : Who the
ἁψάμενός μου; ἀρνουμένων δὲ πάντων
[one] touching me? And denying all[a]
=when all denied
εἶπεν ὁ Πέτρος· ἐπιστάτα, οἱ ὄχλοι
said – Peter : Master, the crowds
συνέχουσίν σε καὶ ἀποθλίβουσιν. 46 ὁ δὲ
press upon thee and jostle. – But
Ἰησοῦς εἶπεν· ἥψατό μού τις· ἐγὼ γὰρ
Jesus said : Touched me someone; for I
ἔγνων δύναμιν ἐξεληλυθυῖαν ἀπ' ἐμοῦ.
knew power having gone forth from me.
47 ἰδοῦσα δὲ ἡ γυνὴ ὅτι οὐκ ἔλαθεν,
And [3]seeing [1]the [2]woman that she was not hidden,
τρέμουσα ἦλθεν καὶ προσπεσοῦσα αὐτῷ δι'
trembling came and prostrating before him [6]for
ἣν αἰτίαν ἥψατο αὐτοῦ ἀπήγγειλεν ἐνώπιον
[7]what [8]cause [9]she touched [10]him [1]declared [2]before

38The man from whom
the demons had gone out
begged to go with him, but
Jesus sent him away, say-
ing, 39"Return home and
tell how much God has
done for you." So the man
went away and told all over
town how much Jesus had
done for him.

A Dead Girl and a Sick Woman

40Now when Jesus re-
turned, a crowd welcomed
him, for they were all expecting him. 41Then a man
named Jairus, a ruler of the
synagogue, came and fell at
Jesus' feet, pleading with
him to come to his house
42because his only daugh-
ter, a girl of about twelve,
was dying.
As Jesus was on his way,
the crowds almost crushed
him. 43And a woman was
there who had been subject
to bleeding for twelve
years,[i] but no one could
heal her. 44She came up behind him and touched the
edge of his cloak, and immediately her bleeding
stopped.
45"Who touched me?"
Jesus asked.
When they all denied it,
Peter said, "Master, the
people are crowding and
pressing against you."
46But Jesus said, "Some-
one touched me; I know
that power has gone out
from me."
47Then the woman, see-
ing that she could not go
unnoticed, came trembling
and fell at his feet. In the
presence of all the people,
she told why she had
touched him and how she

[i]43 Many manuscripts *years, and she had spent all she had on doctors*

she had been immediately
healed.
48And He said to her,
"Daughter, your faith has
made you well; go in
peace."
49While He was still
speaking, someone *came
from *the house of* the synagogue official, saying,
"Your daughter has died;
do not trouble the Teacher
anymore."
50But when Jesus heard
this, He answered him,
"Do not be afraid *any
longer;* only believe, and
she shall be made well."
51And when He had come
to the house, He did not allow anyone to enter with
Him, except Peter and
John and James, and the
girl's father and mother.
52Now they were all
weeping and lamenting for
her; but He said, "Stop
weeping, for she has not
died, but is asleep."
53And they *began* laugh-
ing at Him, knowing that
she had died.
54He, however, took her
by the hand and called, saying, "Child, arise!"
55And her spirit returned,
and she rose immediately;
and He gave orders for
something to be given her
to eat.
56And her parents were
amazed; but He instructed
them to tell no one what
had happened.

παντὸς τοῦ λαοῦ, καὶ ὡς ἰάθη παραχρῆμα.
[3]all [4]the [5]people, and how she was cured at once.
48 ὁ δὲ εἶπεν αὐτῇ· θυγάτηρ, ἡ πίστις
And he said to her: Daughter, the faith
σου σέσωκέν σε· πορεύου εἰς εἰρήνην.
of thee has healed thee; go in peace.
49 Ἔτι αὐτοῦ λαλοῦντος ἔρχεταί τις παρὰ
Yet him speaking[a] comes someone from
=While he was yet speaking
τοῦ ἀρχισυναγώγου λέγων ὅτι τέθνηκεν
the synagogue ruler saying[,] – Has died
ἡ θυγάτηρ σου· μηκέτι σκύλλε τὸν
the daughter of thee; no more trouble the
διδάσκαλον. **50** ὁ δὲ Ἰησοῦς ἀκούσας
teacher. – But Jesus hearing
ἀπεκρίθη αὐτῷ· μὴ φοβοῦ· μόνον πίστευσον,
answered him: Fear thou not; only believe,
καὶ σωθήσεται. **51** ἐλθὼν δὲ εἰς τὴν
and she will be healed. And coming into the
οἰκίαν οὐκ ἀφῆκεν εἰσελθεῖν τινα σὺν
house he allowed not to enter anyone with
αὐτῷ εἰ μὴ Πέτρον καὶ Ἰωάννην καὶ
him except Peter and John and
Ἰάκωβον καὶ τὸν πατέρα τῆς παιδὸς καὶ
James and the father of the maid and
τὴν μητέρα. **52** ἔκλαιον δὲ πάντες καὶ
the mother. And were weeping all and
ἐκόπτοντο αὐτήν. ὁ δὲ εἶπεν· μὴ κλαίετε·
bewailing her. But he said: Weep ye not;
οὐκ ἀπέθανεν ἀλλὰ καθεύδει. **53** καὶ
she did not die but sleeps. And
κατεγέλων αὐτοῦ, εἰδότες ὅτι ἀπέθανεν.
they ridiculed him, knowing that she died.
54 αὐτὸς δὲ κρατήσας τῆς χειρὸς αὐτῆς
But he holding the hand of her
ἐφώνησεν λέγων· ἡ παῖς, ἔγειρε. **55** καὶ
called saying: – Maid, arise. And
ἐπέστρεψεν τὸ πνεῦμα αὐτῆς, καὶ ἀνέστη
returned the spirit of her, and she rose up
παραχρῆμα, καὶ διέταξεν αὐτῇ δοθῆναι
at once, and he commanded [2]to her [1]to be given
φαγεῖν. **56** καὶ ἐξέστησαν οἱ γονεῖς
to eat. And were amazed the parents
αὐτῆς· ὁ δὲ παρήγγειλεν αὐτοῖς μηδενὶ
of her; but he enjoined them [2]no one
εἰπεῖν τὸ γεγονός.
[1]to tell the thing having happened.
=what had happened.

had been instantly healed.
48Then he said to her,
"Daughter, your faith has
healed you. Go in peace."
49While Jesus was still
speaking, someone came
from the house of Jairus,
the synagogue ruler. "Your
daughter is dead," he said.
"Don't bother the teacher
any more."
50Hearing this, Jesus said
to Jairus, "Don't be afraid;
just believe, and she will be
healed."
51When he arrived at the
house of Jairus, he did not
let anyone go in with him
except Peter, John and
James, and the child's father and mother. 52Mean-
while, all the people were
wailing and mourning for
her. "Stop wailing," Jesus
said. "She is not dead but
asleep."
53They laughed at him,
knowing that she was dead.
54But he took her by the
hand and said, "My child,
get up!" 55Her spirit re-
turned, and at once she
stood up. Then Jesus told
them to give her something
to eat. 56Her parents were
astonished, but he ordered
them not to tell anyone
what had happened.

Chapter 9

Ministry of the Twelve

AND He called the
twelve together, and
gave them power and au-
thority over all the demons,
and to heal diseases.
2And He sent them out
to proclaim the kingdom of
God, and to perform heal-
ing.
3And He said to them,
"Take nothing for *your*
journey, neither a staff, nor
a bag, nor bread, nor
money; and do not *even*
have two tunics apiece.

9 Συγκαλεσάμενος δὲ τοὺς δώδεκα ἔδωκεν
And having called together the twelve he gave
αὐτοῖς δύναμιν καὶ ἐξουσίαν ἐπὶ πάντα τὰ
them power and authority over all the
δαιμόνια καὶ νόσους θεραπεύειν· **2** καὶ
demons and diseases to heal; and
ἀπέστειλεν αὐτοὺς κηρύσσειν τὴν βασιλείαν
sent them to proclaim the kingdom
τοῦ θεοῦ καὶ ἰᾶσθαι, **3** καὶ εἶπεν πρὸς
– of God and to cure, and said to
αὐτούς· μηδὲν αἴρετε εἰς τὴν ὁδόν, μήτε
them: Nothing take ye for the way, neither
ῥάβδον μήτε πήραν μήτε ἄρτον μήτε
staff nor wallet nor bread nor
ἀργύριον μήτε ἀνὰ δύο χιτῶνας ἔχειν.
silver nor each two tunics to have.

Chapter 9

Jesus Sends Out the Twelve

WHEN Jesus had
called the Twelve to-
gether, he gave them power
and authority to drive out
all demons and to cure diseases, 2and he sent them
out to preach the kingdom
of God and to heal the sick.
3He told them: "Take nothing for the journey—no
staff, no bag, no bread, no
money, no extra tunic.

4"And whatever house you enter, stay there, and take your leave from there.
5"And as for those who do not receive you, as you go out from that city, shake off the dust from your feet as a testimony against them."
6And departing, they *began* going about among the villages, preaching the gospel, and healing everywhere.
7Now Herod the tetrarch heard of all that was happening; and he was greatly perplexed, because it was said by some that John had risen from the dead,
8and by some that Elijah had appeared, and by others, that one of the prophets of old had risen again.
9And Herod said, "I myself had John beheaded; but who is this man about whom I hear such things?" And he kept trying to see Him.
10And when the apostles returned, they gave an account to Him of all that they had done. And taking them with Him, He withdrew by Himself to a city called Bethsaida.
11But the multitudes were aware of this and followed Him; and welcoming them, He *began* speaking to them about the kingdom of God and curing those who had need of healing.

Five Thousand Fed

12And the day began to decline, and the twelve came and said to Him, "Send the multitude away, that they may go into the surrounding villages and countryside and find lodging and get something to eat; for here we are in a desolate place."
13But He said to them, "You give them *something* to eat!" And they said, "We have no more than five loaves and two fish,

4 καὶ εἰς ἣν ἂν οἰκίαν εἰσέλθητε, ἐκεῖ
And into whatever house ye may enter, there
μένετε καὶ ἐκεῖθεν ἐξέρχεσθε. **5** καὶ
remain and thence go forth. And
ὅσοι ἂν μὴ δέχωνται ὑμᾶς, ἐξερχόμενοι
as many as may not receive you, going forth
ἀπὸ τῆς πόλεως ἐκείνης τὸν κονιορτὸν
from – city that the dust
ἀπὸ τῶν ποδῶν ὑμῶν ἀποτινάσσετε εἰς
from the feet of you shake off for
μαρτύριον ἐπ' αὐτούς. **6** ἐξερχόμενοι δὲ
a testimony against them. And going forth
διήρχοντο κατὰ τὰς κώμας εὐαγγελιζόμενοι
they went *through* throughout the villages evangelizing
καὶ θεραπεύοντες πανταχοῦ. **7** Ἤκουσεν
and healing everywhere. [5]heard
δὲ Ἡρῴδης ὁ τετραάρχης τὰ γινόμενα
[1]And [3]Herod [2]the [4]tetrarch the things happening
πάντα, καὶ διηπόρει διὰ τὸ λέγεσθαι
all, and was in perplexity because of the to be said =because it was said
ὑπό τινων ὅτι Ἰωάννης ἠγέρθη ἐκ νεκρῶν,
by some that John was raised from [the] dead,
8 ὑπό τινων δὲ ὅτι Ἠλίας ἐφάνη, ἄλλων
and by some that Elias appeared, [2]others
δὲ ὅτι προφήτης τις τῶν ἀρχαίων ἀνέστη.
[1]but that prophet a certain of the ancients rose again.
9 εἶπεν δὲ [ὁ] Ἡρῴδης· Ἰωάννην ἐγὼ
But said – Herod: John I
ἀπεκεφάλισα· τίς δέ ἐστιν οὗτος περὶ οὗ
beheaded; but who is this about whom
ἀκούω τοιαῦτα; καὶ ἐζήτει ἰδεῖν αὐτόν.
I hear such things? And he sought to see him.
10 Καὶ ὑποστρέψαντες οἱ ἀπόστολοι
And having returned the apostles
διηγήσαντο αὐτῷ ὅσα ἐποίησαν. Καὶ
narrated to him what things they did. And
παραλαβὼν αὐτοὺς ὑπεχώρησεν κατ' ἰδίαν
taking them he departed privately
εἰς πόλιν καλουμένην Βηθσαϊδά. **11** οἱ δὲ
to a city *being* called Bethsaida. But the
ὄχλοι γνόντες ἠκολούθησαν αὐτῷ· καὶ
crowds knowing followed him; and
ἀποδεξάμενος αὐτοὺς ἐλάλει αὐτοῖς περὶ
welcoming them he spoke to them about
τῆς βασιλείας τοῦ θεοῦ, καὶ τοὺς χρείαν
the kingdom – of God, and the [ones] [2]need
ἔχοντας θεραπείας ἰᾶτο. **12** Ἡ δὲ ἡμέρα
[1]having of healing he cured. But the day
ἤρξατο κλίνειν· προσελθόντες δὲ οἱ δώδεκα
began to decline; and approaching the twelve
εἶπαν αὐτῷ· ἀπόλυσον τὸν ὄχλον, ἵνα
said to him: Dismiss the crowd, that
πορευθέντες εἰς τὰς κύκλῳ κώμας καὶ
going to [1]the [2]around [3]villages [5]and
ἀγροὺς καταλύσωσιν καὶ εὕρωσιν ἐπισιτισμόν,
[4]farms they may lodge and may find provisions,
ὅτι ὧδε ἐν ἐρήμῳ τόπῳ ἐσμέν. **13** εἶπεν
because here in a desert place we are. he said
δὲ πρὸς αὐτούς· δότε αὐτοῖς φαγεῖν
And to them: [1]Give [3]them [4]to eat
ὑμεῖς. οἱ δὲ εἶπαν· οὐκ εἰσὶν ἡμῖν
[2]ye. But they said: There are not to us[c] =We have not
πλεῖον ἢ ἄρτοι πέντε καὶ ἰχθύες δύο, εἰ
more than loaves five and fishes two, un-

4Whatever house you enter, stay there until you leave that town. 5If people do not welcome you, shake the dust off your feet when you leave their town, as a testimony against them." 6So they set out and went from village to village, preaching the gospel and healing people everywhere.
7Now Herod the tetrarch heard about all that was going on. And he was perplexed, because some were saying that John had been raised from the dead, 8others that Elijah had appeared, and still others that one of the prophets of long ago had come back to life. 9But Herod said, "I beheaded John. Who, then, is this I hear such things about?" And he tried to see him.

Jesus Feeds the Five Thousand

10When the apostles returned, they reported to Jesus what they had done. Then he took them with him and they withdrew by themselves to a town called Bethsaida, 11but the crowds learned about it and followed him. He welcomed them and spoke to them about the kingdom of God, and healed those who needed healing.
12Late in the afternoon the Twelve came to him and said, "Send the crowd away so they can go to the surrounding villages and countryside and find food and lodging, because we are in a remote place here."
13He replied, "You give them something to eat."
They answered, "We have only five loaves of bread and two fish—unless

unless perhaps we go and
buy food for all these
people."
14(For there were about
five thousand men.) And
He said to His disciples,
"Have them recline *to eat*
in groups of about fifty
each."
15And they did so, and
had them all recline.
16And He took the five
loaves and the two fish, and
looking up to heaven, He
blessed them, and broke
them, and kept giving *them*
to the disciples to set before the multitude.
17And they all ate and
were satisfied; and the broken pieces which they had
left over were picked up,
twelve baskets *full.*
18And it came about that
while He was praying
alone, the disciples were
with Him, and He ques-
tioned them, saying, "Who
do the multitudes say that I
am?"
19And they answered and
said, "John the Baptist,
and others *say* Elijah; but
others, that one of the
prophets of old has risen
again."
20And He said to them,
"But who do you say that I
am?" And Peter answered
and said, "The Christ of
God."
21But He warned them,
and instructed *them* not to
tell this to anyone,
22saying, "The Son of
Man must suffer many
things, and be rejected by
the elders and chief priests
and scribes, and be killed,
and be raised up on the
third day."
23And He was saying to
them all, "If anyone wishes
to come after Me, let him
deny himself, and take up
his cross daily, and follow
Me.

μήτι πορευθέντες ἡμεῖς ἀγοράσωμεν εἰς
less going we may buy for
πάντα τὸν λαὸν τοῦτον βρώματα. 14 ἦσαν
all – people this foods. there were
γὰρ ὡσεὶ ἄνδρες πεντακισχίλιοι. εἶπεν δὲ
For about men five thousand. And he said
πρὸς τοὺς μαθητὰς αὐτοῦ· κατακλίνατε
to the disciples of him : [1]Make [3]to recline
αὐτοὺς κλισίας ὡσεὶ ἀνὰ πεντήκοντα.
[2]them [in] groups [1]about [2]each [3]fifty.
15 καὶ ἐποίησαν οὕτως καὶ κατέκλιναν
And they did so and made to recline
ἅπαντας. 16 λαβὼν δὲ τοὺς πέντε ἄρτους
all. And taking the five loaves
καὶ τοὺς δύο ἰχθύας, ἀναβλέψας εἰς τὸν
and the two fishes, looking up to –
οὐρανὸν εὐλόγησεν αὐτοὺς καὶ κατέκλασεν,
heaven he blessed them and broke,
καὶ ἐδίδου τοῖς μαθηταῖς παραθεῖναι τῷ
and gave to the disciples to set before the
ὄχλῳ. 17 καὶ ἔφαγον καὶ ἐχορτάσθησαν
crowd. And they ate and were satisfied
πάντες· καὶ ἤρθη τὸ περισσεῦσαν αὐτοῖς
all; and were taken the excess to them
κλασμάτων κόφινοι δώδεκα.
of fragments baskets twelve.
18 Καὶ ἐγένετο ἐν τῷ εἶναι αὐτὸν
And it came to pass in the to be him[be]
=as he was
προσευχόμενον κατὰ μόνας συνῆσαν αὐτῷ
praying alone were with him
οἱ μαθηταί, καὶ ἐπηρώτησεν αὐτοὺς λέγων·
the disciples, and he questioned them saying :
τίνα με οἱ ὄχλοι λέγουσιν εἶναι; 19 οἱ δὲ
Whom me the crowds say to be? And they
=Whom do the crowds say that I am?
ἀποκριθέντες εἶπαν· Ἰωάννην τὸν βαπτιστήν,
answering said : John the Baptist,
ἄλλοι δὲ Ἠλίαν, ἄλλοι δὲ ὅτι προφήτης
but others Elias, and others that prophet
τις τῶν ἀρχαίων ἀνέστη. 20 εἶπεν δὲ
a certain of the ancients rose again. And he said
αὐτοῖς· ὑμεῖς δὲ τίνα με λέγετε εἶναι;
to them : But ye whom me say to be?
=whom say ye that I am?
Πέτρος δὲ ἀποκριθεὶς εἶπεν· τὸν χριστὸν
And Peter answering said: The Christ
τοῦ θεοῦ. 21 ὁ δὲ ἐπιτιμήσας αὐτοῖς
— of God. But he warning [2]them
παρήγγειλεν μηδενὶ λέγειν τοῦτο, 22 εἰπὼν
[1]charged [4]no one [3]to tell [5]this, saying
ὅτι δεῖ τὸν υἱὸν τοῦ ἀνθρώπου πολλὰ
that it behoves the Son – of man many things
παθεῖν καὶ ἀποδοκιμασθῆναι ἀπὸ τῶν
to suffer and to be rejected from(by) the
πρεσβυτέρων καὶ ἀρχιερέων καὶ γραμματέων
elders and chief priests and scribes
καὶ ἀποκτανθῆναι καὶ τῇ τρίτῃ ἡμέρᾳ
and to be killed and on the third day
ἐγερθῆναι. 23 Ἔλεγεν δὲ πρὸς πάντας·
to be raised. And he said to all :
εἴ τις θέλει ὀπίσω μου ἔρχεσθαι, ἀρνησάσθω
If anyone wishes after me to come, let him deny
ἑαυτὸν καὶ ἀράτω τὸν σταυρὸν
himself and take the cross
αὐτοῦ καθ' ἡμέραν, καὶ ἀκολουθείτω μοι.
of him daily, and let him follow me.

we go and buy food for all
this crowd." 14(About five
thousand men were there.)
But he said to his disci-
ples, "Have them sit down
in groups of about fifty
each." 15The disciples did
so, and everybody sat
down. 16Taking the five
loaves and the two fish and
looking up to heaven, he
gave thanks and broke
them. Then he gave them to
the disciples to set before
the people. 17They all ate
and were satisfied, and the
disciples picked up twelve
basketfuls of broken pieces
that were left over.

Peter's Confession of Christ

18Once when Jesus was
praying in private and his
disciples were with him, he
asked them, "Who do the
crowds say I am?"
19They replied, "Some
say John the Baptist; others
say Elijah; and still others,
that one of the prophets of
long ago has come back to
life."
20"But what about you?"
he asked. "Who do you say
I am?"
Peter answered, "The
Christ[j] of God."
21Jesus strictly warned
them not to tell this to anyone. 22And he said, "The
Son of Man must suffer
many things and be rejected by the elders, chief
priests and teachers of the
law, and he must be killed
and on the third day be
raised to life."
23Then he said to them all:
"If anyone would come af-
ter me, he must deny him-
self and take up his cross
daily and follow me. 24For

j20 Or *Messiah*

24"For whoever wishes
to save his life shall lose it,
but whoever loses his life
for My sake, he is the one
who will save it.
25"For what is a man
profited if he gains the
whole world, and loses or
forfeits himself?
26"For whoever is
ashamed of Me and My
words, of him will the Son
of Man be ashamed when
He comes in His glory, and
the glory of the Father and
of the holy angels.
27"But I say to you truthfully, there are some of
those standing here who
shall not taste death until
they see the kingdom of
God."

The Transfiguration

28And some eight days af-
ter these sayings, it came
about that He took along
Peter and John and James,
and went up to the moun-
tain to pray.
29And while He was pray-
ing, the appearance of His
face became different, and
His clothing *became* white
and gleaming.
30And behold, two men
were talking with Him; and
they were Moses and Eli-
jah,
31who, appearing in
glory, were speaking of His
departure which He was
about to accomplish at
Jerusalem.
32Now Peter and his com-
panions had been over-
come with sleep; but when
they were fully awake, they
saw His glory and the two
men standing with Him.
33And it came about, as
these were parting from
Him, Peter said to Jesus,
"Master, it is good for us to
be here; and let us make
three tabernacles: one for

24 ὃς γὰρ ἐὰν θέλῃ τὴν ψυχὴν αὐτοῦ
For whoever wishes the life of him
σῶσαι, ἀπολέσει αὐτήν· ὃς δ' ἂν ἀπολέσῃ
to save, he will lose it; but whoever loses
τὴν ψυχὴν αὐτοῦ ἕνεκεν ἐμοῦ, οὗτος
the life of him for the sake of me, this [one]
σώσει αὐτήν. **25** τί γὰρ ὠφελεῖται
will save it. For what is profited
ἄνθρωπος κερδήσας τὸν κόσμον ὅλον ἑαυτὸν
a man gaining the world whole [3]himself
δὲ ἀπολέσας ἢ ζημιωθείς; **26** ὃς γὰρ ἂν
[1]but [2]losing or suffering loss? For whoever
ἐπαισχυνθῇ με καὶ τοὺς ἐμοὺς λόγους,
is ashamed of me and – my words,
τοῦτον ὁ υἱὸς τοῦ ἀνθρώπου ἐπαι-
this [one] the Son – of man will be
σχυνθήσεται, ὅταν ἔλθῃ ἐν τῇ δόξῃ
ashamed of, when he comes in the glory
αὐτοῦ καὶ τοῦ πατρὸς καὶ τῶν ἁγίων
of him and of the Father and of the holy
ἀγγέλων. **27** λέγω δὲ ὑμῖν ἀληθῶς,
angels. But I tell you truly,
εἰσίν τινες τῶν αὐτοῦ ἑστηκότων οἳ
there are some of the [ones] here standing who
οὐ μὴ γεύσωνται θανάτου ἕως ἂν ἴδωσιν
by no means may taste of death until they see
τὴν βασιλείαν τοῦ θεοῦ.
the kingdom – of God.
28 Ἐγένετο δὲ μετὰ τοὺς λόγους τούτους
And it came to pass [4]after – [6]sayings [5]these
ὡσεὶ ἡμέραι ὀκτώ, καὶ παραλαβὼν Πέτρον
[1]about [3]days [2]eight, *and* taking Peter
καὶ Ἰωάννην καὶ Ἰάκωβον ἀνέβη εἰς τὸ
and John and James he went up into the
ὄρος προσεύξασθαι. **29** καὶ ἐγένετο ἐν τῷ
mountain to pray. And [9]became in the
=[1]as [2]he [3]prayed
προσεύχεσθαι αὐτὸν τὸ εἶδος τοῦ προσώπου
to pray him[be] [4]the [5]appearance [6]of the [7]face
αὐτοῦ ἕτερον καὶ ὁ ἱματισμὸς αὐτοῦ
[8]of him [10]different and the raiment of him
λευκὸς ἐξαστράπτων. **30** καὶ ἰδοὺ ἄνδρες
[2]white [1]gleaming. And[,] behold[,] men
δύο συνελάλουν αὐτῷ, οἵτινες ἦσαν Μωϋσῆς
two conversed with him, who were Moses
καὶ Ἠλίας, **31** οἳ ὀφθέντες ἐν δόξῃ ἔλεγον
and Elias, who appearing in glory spoke of
τὴν ἔξοδον αὐτοῦ, ἣν ἤμελλεν πληροῦν
the exodus of him, which he was about to accomplish
ἐν Ἰερουσαλήμ. **32** ὁ δὲ Πέτρος καὶ οἱ
in Jerusalem. – But Peter and the [ones]
σὺν αὐτῷ ἦσαν βεβαρημένοι ὕπνῳ· δια-
with him were *having been* burdened with sleep; [2]wak-
γρηγορήσαντες δὲ εἶδαν τὴν δόξαν αὐτοῦ
ing thoroughly [1]but they saw the glory of him
καὶ τοὺς δύο ἄνδρας τοὺς συνεστῶτας
and the two men – standing with
αὐτῷ. **33** καὶ ἐγένετο ἐν τῷ διαχωρίζεσθαι
him. And it came to pass in the to part
=when they parted
αὐτοὺς ἀπ' αὐτοῦ εἶπεν ὁ Πέτρος πρὸς
them[be] from him said – Peter to
τὸν Ἰησοῦν· ἐπιστάτα, καλόν ἐστιν ἡμᾶς
– Jesus: Master, good it is [for] us
ὧδε εἶναι, καὶ ποιήσωμεν σκηνὰς τρεῖς,
here to be, and let us make tents three,

whoever wants to save his
life will lose it, but whoever
loses his life for me will
save it. 25What good is it for
a man to gain the whole
world, and yet lose or forfeit his very self? 26If anyone is ashamed of me and
my words, the Son of Man
will be ashamed of him
when he comes in his glory
and in the glory of the Father and of the holy angels.
27I tell you the truth, some
who are standing here will
not taste death before they
see the kingdom of God."

The Transfiguration

28About eight days after
Jesus said this, he took Peter, John and James with
him and went up onto a
mountain to pray. 29As he
was praying, the appear-
ance of his face changed,
and his clothes became as
bright as a flash of lightning. 30Two men, Moses
and Elijah, 31appeared in
glorious splendor, talking
with Jesus. They spoke
about his departure, which
he was about to bring to fulfillment at Jerusalem. 32Pe-
ter and his companions
were very sleepy, but when
they became fully awake,
they saw his glory and the
two men standing with him.
33As the men were leaving
Jesus, Peter said to him,
"Master, it is good for us to
be here. Let us put up three
shelters—one for you, one

You, and one for Moses,
and one for Elijah"—not
realizing what he was saying.
34And while he was say-
ing this, a cloud formed and
began to overshadow
them; and they were afraid
as they entered the cloud.
35And a voice came out of
the cloud, saying, "This is
My Son, *My* Chosen One;
listen to Him!"
36And when the voice had
spoken, Jesus was found
alone. And they kept silent,
and reported to no one in
those days any of the things
which they had seen.
37And it came about on
the next day, that when
they had come down from
the mountain, a great multitude met Him.
38And behold, a man from
the multitude shouted out,
saying, "Teacher, I beg
You to look at my son, for
he is my only *boy,*
39and behold, a spirit
seizes him, and he suddenly screams, and it throws
him into a convulsion with
foaming *at the mouth,* and
as it mauls him, it scarcely
leaves him.
40"And I begged Your
disciples to cast it out, and
they could not."
41And Jesus answered
and said, "O unbelieving
and perverted generation,
how long shall I be with
you, and put up with you?
Bring your son here."
42And while he was still
approaching, the demon
dashed him *to the ground,*
and threw him into a con-
vulsion. But Jesus rebuked
the unclean spirit, and
healed the boy, and gave
him back to his father.
43And they were all

μίαν σοὶ καὶ μίαν Μωϋσεῖ καὶ μίαν
one for thee and one for Moses and one
Ἠλίᾳ, μὴ εἰδὼς ὃ λέγει. 34 ταῦτα δὲ
for Elias, not knowing what he says. And these things
αὐτοῦ λέγοντος ἐγένετο νεφέλη καὶ
him saying[a] came a cloud and
=while he said these things
ἐπεσκίαζεν αὐτούς· ἐφοβήθησαν δὲ ἐν τῷ
overshadowed them; and they feared in the
=as they entered
εἰσελθεῖν αὐτοὺς εἰς τὴν νεφέλην. 35 καὶ
to enter them[be] into the cloud. And
φωνὴ ἐγένετο ἐκ τῆς νεφέλης λέγουσα·
a voice came out of the cloud saying:
οὗτός ἐστιν ὁ υἱός μου ὁ ἐκλελεγμένος,
This is the Son of me – *having been* chosen,
αὐτοῦ ἀκούετε, 36 καὶ ἐν τῷ γενέσθαι
him hear ye, and in the to become
=when the voice came
τὴν φωνὴν εὑρέθη Ἰησοῦς μόνος. καὶ
the voice[be] was found Jesus alone. And
αὐτοὶ ἐσίγησαν καὶ οὐδενὶ ἀπήγγειλαν ἐν ἐκείναις
they were silent and to no one reported in those
ταῖς ἡμέραις οὐδὲν ὧν ἑώρακαν.
– days no(any) thing of [the things] which they have (had) seen.
37 Ἐγένετο δὲ τῇ ἑξῆς ἡμέρᾳ κατελ-
And it came to pass on the following day coming
θόντων αὐτῶν ἀπὸ τοῦ ὄρους συνήντησεν
down them[a] from the mountain met
=as they came down
αὐτῷ ὄχλος πολύς. 38 καὶ ἰδοὺ ἀνὴρ
him crowd a much. And[,] behold[,] a man
ἀπὸ τοῦ ὄχλου ἐβόησεν λέγων· διδάσκαλε,
from the crowd called aloud saying: Teacher,
δέομαί σου ἐπιβλέψαι ἐπὶ τὸν υἱόν μου,
I beg of thee to look *at* at the son of me,
ὅτι μονογενής μοί ἐστιν, 39 καὶ ἰδοὺ
because only born to me he is, and[,] behold[,]
πνεῦμα λαμβάνει αὐτόν, καὶ ἐξαίφνης
a spirit takes him, and suddenly
κράζει καὶ σπαράσσει αὐτὸν μετὰ ἀφροῦ,
cries out and throws him with foam,
καὶ μόλις ἀποχωρεῖ ἀπ' αὐτοῦ συντρῖβον
and scarcely departs from him bruising
αὐτόν· 40 καὶ ἐδεήθην τῶν μαθητῶν σου
him; and I begged of the disciples of thee
ἵνα ἐκβάλωσιν αὐτό, καὶ οὐκ ἠδυνήθησαν.
that they would expel it, and they were not able.
41 ἀποκριθεὶς δὲ ὁ Ἰησοῦς εἶπεν· ὦ
And answering – Jesus said: O
γενεὰ ἄπιστος καὶ διεστραμμένη, ἕως πότε
generation unbelieving and *having been* perverted, until when
ἔσομαι πρὸς ὑμᾶς καὶ ἀνέξομαι ὑμῶν;
shall I be with you and endure you?
προσάγαγε ὧδε τὸν υἱόν σου. 42 ἔτι
Bring here the son of thee. yet
δὲ προσερχομένου αὐτοῦ ἔρρηξεν αὐτὸν τὸ
But approaching him[a] tore him the
=But while he was yet approaching
δαιμόνιον καὶ συνεσπάραξεν· ἐπετίμησεν δὲ
demon and threw violently; but [2]rebuked
ὁ Ἰησοῦς τῷ πνεύματι τῷ ἀκαθάρτῳ, καὶ
– [1]Jesus [3]the [5]spirit – [4]unclean, and
ἰάσατο τὸν παῖδα καὶ ἀπέδωκεν αὐτὸν τῷ
cured the boy and restored him to the
πατρὶ αὐτοῦ. 43 ἐξεπλήσσοντο δὲ πάντες
father of him. And were astounded all

for Moses and one for Elijah." (He did not know
what he was saying.)
34While he was speaking,
a cloud appeared and en-
veloped them, and they
were afraid as they entered
the cloud. 35A voice came
from the cloud, saying,
"This is my Son, whom I
have chosen; listen to
him." 36When the voice
had spoken, they found
that Jesus was alone. The
disciples kept this to themselves, and told no one at
that time what they had
seen.

The Healing of a Boy With an Evil Spirit

37The next day, when
they came down from the
mountain, a large crowd
met him. 38A man in the
crowd called out, "Teach-
er, I beg you to look at my
son, for he is my only child.
39A spirit seizes him and he
suddenly screams; it
throws him into convul-
sions so that he foams at
the mouth. It scarcely ever
leaves him and is destroying him. 40I begged your
disciples to drive it out, but
they could not."
41"O unbelieving and per-
verse generation," Jesus
replied, "how long shall I
stay with you and put up
with you? Bring your son
here."
42Even while the boy was
coming, the demon threw
him to the ground in a convulsion. But Jesus rebuked
the evil[k] spirit, healed the
boy and gave him back to
his father. 43And they were

[k]42 Greek *unclean*

amazed at the greatness of God.

But while everyone was marveling at all that He was doing, He said to His disciples,

44“Let these words sink into your ears; for the Son of Man is going to be delivered into the hands of men.”

45But they did not understand this statement, and it was concealed from them so that they might not perceive it; and they were afraid to ask Him about this statement.

The Test of Greatness

46And an argument arose among them as to which of them might be the greatest.

47But Jesus, knowing what they were thinking in their heart, took a child and stood him by His side,

48and said to them, “Whoever receives this child in My name receives Me; and whoever receives Me receives Him who sent Me; for he who is least among you, this is the one who is great.”

49And John answered and said, “Master, we saw someone casting out demons in Your name; and we tried to hinder him because he does not follow along with us.”

50But Jesus said to him, “Do not hinder *him;* for he who is not against you is for you.”

51And it came about, when the days were approaching for His ascension, that He resolutely set His face to go to Jerusalem;

52and He sent messengers on ahead of Him. And they went, and entered a village of the Samaritans, to make arrangements for Him.

53And they did not re-

ἐπὶ τῇ μεγαλειότητι τοῦ θεοῦ.
at the majesty – of God.

Πάντων δὲ θαυμαζόντων ἐπὶ πᾶσιν οἷς
And all marvelling[a] at all things which
=while all marvelled

ἐποίει εἶπεν πρὸς τοὺς μαθητὰς αὐτοῦ·
he did he said to the disciples of him :

44 θέσθε ὑμεῖς εἰς τὰ ὦτα ὑμῶν τοὺς
Lay ye in the ears of you –

λόγους τούτους· ὁ γὰρ υἱὸς τοῦ ἀνθρώπου
sayings these; for the Son – of man

μέλλει παραδίδοσθαι εἰς χεῖρας ἀνθρώπων.
is about to be betrayed into [the] hands of men.

45 οἱ δὲ ἠγνόουν τὸ ῥῆμα τοῦτο, καὶ ἦν
But they knew not – word this, and it was

παρακεκαλυμμένον ἀπ᾽ αὐτῶν ἵνα μὴ
having been veiled from them lest

αἴσθωνται αὐτό, καὶ ἐφοβοῦντο ἐρωτῆσαι
they should perceive it, and they feared to ask

αὐτὸν περὶ τοῦ ῥήματος τούτου. 46 Εἰσῆλθεν
him about – word this. entered

δὲ διαλογισμὸς ἐν αὐτοῖς, τὸ τίς ἂν εἴη
And a debate among them, – who might be
=a debate arose

μείζων αὐτῶν. 47 ὁ δὲ Ἰησοῦς εἰδὼς τὸν
greater(est) of them. – And Jesus knowing the

διαλογισμὸν τῆς καρδίας αὐτῶν, ἐπιλαβόμενος
debate of the heart of them, taking

παιδίον ἔστησεν αὐτὸ παρ᾽ ἑαυτῷ, 48 καὶ
a child stood it(him) beside himself, and

εἶπεν αὐτοῖς· ὃς ἐὰν δέξηται τοῦτο τὸ
said to them : Whoever receives this –

παιδίον ἐπὶ τῷ ὀνόματί μου, ἐμὲ δέχεται·
child on(in) the name of me, me receives;

καὶ ὃς ἂν ἐμὲ δέξηται, δέχεται τὸν
and whoever me receives, receives the [one]

ἀποστείλαντά με· ὁ γὰρ μικρότερος ἐν
having sent me; for [1]the [one] [3]lesser [4]among

πᾶσιν ὑμῖν ὑπάρχων, οὗτός ἐστιν μέγας.
[6]all [5]you [2]being, this [one] is great.

49 Ἀποκριθεὶς δὲ ὁ Ἰωάννης εἶπεν· ἐπιστάτα,
And answering – John said : Master,

εἴδομέν τινα ἐν τῷ ὀνόματί σου ἐκβάλλοντα
we saw someone in the name of thee expelling

δαιμόνια, καὶ ἐκωλύομεν αὐτόν, ὅτι
demons, and we prevented him, because

οὐκ ἀκολουθεῖ μεθ᾽ ἡμῶν. 50 εἶπεν δὲ πρὸς
he does not follow with us. And said to

αὐτὸν Ἰησοῦς· μὴ κωλύετε· ὃς γὰρ οὐκ
him Jesus: Do not prevent; for [he] who not

ἔστιν καθ᾽ ὑμῶν, ὑπὲρ ὑμῶν ἐστιν.
is against you, for you is.

51 Ἐγένετο δὲ ἐν τῷ συμπληροῦσθαι
And it came to pass in the to be fulfilled

τὰς ἡμέρας τῆς ἀναλήμψεως αὐτοῦ καὶ
the days of the assumption of him[be] *and*
=as the days of his assumption were fulfilled

αὐτὸς τὸ πρόσωπον ἐστήρισεν τοῦ
he the(his) face set –

πορεύεσθαι εἰς Ἰερουσαλήμ, 52 καὶ ἀπέστειλεν
to go[d] to Jerusalem, and sent

ἀγγέλους πρὸ προσώπου αὐτοῦ. καὶ
messengers before face of him. And

πορευθέντες εἰσῆλθον εἰς κώμην Σαμαριτῶν,
going they entered into a village of Samaritans,

ὥστε ἑτοιμάσαι αὐτῷ· 53 καὶ οὐκ ἐδέξαντο
so as to prepare for him; and they did not receive

all amazed at the greatness of God.

While everyone was marveling at all that Jesus did, he said to his disciples,
44“Listen carefully to what I am about to tell you: The Son of Man is going to be betrayed into the hands of men.”
45But they did not understand what this meant. It was hidden from them, so that they did not grasp it, and they were afraid to ask him about it.

Who Will Be the Greatest?

46An argument started among the disciples as to which of them would be the greatest.
47Jesus, knowing their thoughts, took a little child and had him stand beside him.
48Then he said to them, “Whoever welcomes this little child in my name welcomes me; and whoever welcomes me welcomes the one who sent me. For he who is least among you all—he is the greatest.”

49“Master,” said John, “we saw a man driving out demons in your name and we tried to stop him, because he is not one of us.”

50“Do not stop him,” Jesus said, “for whoever is not against you is for you.”

Samaritan Opposition

51As the time approached for him to be taken up to heaven, Jesus resolutely set out for Jerusalem.
52And he sent messengers on ahead, who went into a Samaritan village to get things ready for him;
53but the people there did not

ceive Him, because He was journeying with His face toward Jerusalem.
54And when His disciples James and John saw *this,*
they said, "Lord, do You want us to command fire to come down from heaven and consume them?"
55But He turned and rebuked them, [and said, "You do not know what kind of spirit you are of;
56for the Son of Man did not come to destroy men's lives, but to save them."] And they went on to another village.

Exacting Discipleship

57And as they were going along the road, someone said to Him, "I will follow You wherever You go."
58And Jesus said to him, "The foxes have holes, and the birds of the air *have* nests, but the Son of Man has nowhere to lay His head."
59And He said to another, "Follow Me." But he said, "[l]Permit me first to go and bury my father."
60But He said to him, "Allow the dead to bury their own dead; but as for you, go and proclaim everywhere the kingdom of God."
61And another also said, "I will follow You, Lord; but first permit me to say good-bye to those at home."
62But Jesus said to him, "No one, after putting his hand to the plow and looking back, is fit for the kingdom of God."

Chapter 10

The Seventy Sent Out

NOW after this the Lord appointed seventy others, and sent them two and two ahead of Him to every city and place where He Himself was going to come.
2And He was saying to them, "The harvest is plentiful, but the laborers are

[l]Some mss. add *Lord*

αὐτόν, ὅτι τὸ πρόσωπον αὐτοῦ ἦν
him, because the face of him was
πορευόμενον εἰς Ἰερουσαλήμ. 54 ἰδόντες
going to Jerusalem. [6]seeing
δὲ οἱ μαθηταὶ Ἰάκωβος καὶ Ἰωάννης
And [1]the [2]disciples [3]James [4]and [5]John
εἶπαν· κύριε, θέλεις εἴπωμεν πῦρ κατα-
[7]said : Lord, wilt thou we may tell fire to come
βῆναι ἀπὸ τοῦ οὐρανοῦ καὶ ἀναλῶσαι
down from – heaven and to destroy
αὐτούς; 55 στραφεὶς δὲ ἐπετίμησεν αὐτοῖς.
them? But turning he rebuked them.
56 καὶ ἐπορεύθησαν εἰς ἑτέραν κώμην.
And they went to another village.
57 Καὶ πορευομένων αὐτῶν ἐν τῇ ὁδῷ
And going them[a] in the way
=as they went
εἶπέν τις πρὸς αὐτόν· ἀκολουθήσω σοι
said one to him : I will follow thee
ὅπου ἐὰν ἀπέρχῃ. 58 καὶ εἶπεν αὐτῷ ὁ
wherever thou goest. And said to him –
Ἰησοῦς· αἱ ἀλώπεκες φωλεοὺς ἔχουσιν καὶ
Jesus : The foxes holes have and
τὰ πετεινὰ τοῦ οὐρανοῦ κατασκηνώσεις, ὁ
the birds – of heaven nests, [2]the
δὲ υἱὸς τοῦ ἀνθρώπου οὐκ ἔχει ποῦ τὴν
[1]but Son – of man has not where the(his)
κεφαλὴν κλίνῃ. 59 Εἶπεν δὲ πρὸς ἕτερον·
head he may lay. And he said to another :
ἀκολούθει μοι. ὁ δὲ εἶπεν· ἐπίτρεψόν μοι
Follow me. But he said : Allow me
πρῶτον ἀπελθόντι θάψαι τὸν πατέρα μου.
first going to bury the father of me.
60 εἶπεν δὲ αὐτῷ· ἄφες τοὺς νεκροὺς
But he said to him : Leave the dead
θάψαι τοὺς ἑαυτῶν νεκρούς, σὺ δὲ ἀπελθὼν
to bury the of themselves dead, but thou going
=their own dead,
διάγγελλε τὴν βασιλείαν τοῦ θεοῦ. 61 Εἶπεν
announce the kingdom – of God. said
δὲ καὶ ἕτερος· ἀκολουθήσω σοι, κύριε·
And also another : I will follow thee, Lord;
πρῶτον δὲ ἐπίτρεψόν μοι ἀποτάξασθαι τοῖς
but first allow me to say farewell to the [ones]
εἰς τὸν οἶκόν μου. 62 εἶπεν δὲ [πρὸς
in the house of me. But said to
αὐτὸν] ὁ Ἰησοῦς· οὐδεὶς ἐπιβαλὼν τὴν
him – Jesus : No one putting *on* the(his)
χεῖρα ἐπ' ἄροτρον καὶ βλέπων εἰς τὰ
hand on a plough and looking at the things
ὀπίσω εὔθετός ἐστιν τῇ βασιλείᾳ τοῦ θεοῦ.
behind fit is for the kingdom – of God.

10 Μετὰ δὲ ταῦτα ἀνέδειξεν ὁ κύριος
Now after these things appointed the Lord
ἑτέρους ἑβδομήκοντα [δύο], καὶ ἀπέστειλεν
others seventy-two, and sent
αὐτοὺς ἀνὰ δύο πρὸ προσώπου αὐτοῦ εἰς
them two by two† before face of him into
πᾶσαν πόλιν καὶ τόπον οὗ ἤμελλεν αὐτὸς
every city and place where [2]was about [1]he
ἔρχεσθαι. 2 ἔλεγεν δὲ πρὸς αὐτούς· ὁ
to come. And he said to them : the
μὲν θερισμὸς πολύς, οἱ δὲ ἐργάται ὀλίγοι·
Indeed harvest much, but the workmen few;

welcome him, because he was heading for Jerusalem.
54When the disciples James and John saw this, they asked, "Lord, do you want us to call fire down from heaven to destroy them[l]?"
55But Jesus turned and rebuked them, 56and[m] they went to another village.

The Cost of Following Jesus

57As they were walking along the road, a man said to him, "I will follow you wherever you go."
58Jesus replied, "Foxes have holes and birds of the air have nests, but the Son of Man has no place to lay his head."
59He said to another man, "Follow me."
But the man replied, "Lord, first let me go and bury my father."
60Jesus said to him, "Let the dead bury their own dead, but you go and proclaim the kingdom of God."
61Still another said, "I will follow you, Lord; but first let me go back and say good-by to my family."
62Jesus replied, "No one who puts his hand to the plow and looks back is fit for service in the kingdom of God."

Chapter 10

Jesus Sends Out the Seventy-two

AFTER this the Lord appointed seventy-two[n] others and sent them two by two ahead of him to every town and place where he was about to go. 2He told them, "The harvest is plentiful, but the workers

[l]54 Some manuscripts *them, even as Elijah did*
[m]55,56 Some manuscripts *them. And he said, "You do not know what kind of spirit you are of, for the Son of Man did not come to destroy men's lives, but to save them." 56And*
[n]1 Some manuscripts *seventy;* also in verse 17

few; therefore beseech the
Lord of the harvest to send
out laborers into His harvest.
3"Go your ways; behold,
I send you out as lambs in
the midst of wolves.
4"Carry no purse, no
bag, no shoes; and greet no
one on the way.
5"And whatever house
you enter, first say, 'Peace
be to this house.'
6"And if a man of peace
is there, your peace will
rest upon him; but if not, it
will return to you.
7"And stay in that
house, eating and drinking
what they give you; for the
laborer is worthy of his
wages. Do not keep moving
from house to house.
8"And whatever city
you enter, and they receive
you, eat what is set before
you;
9and heal those in it who
are sick, and say to them,
'The kingdom of God has
come near to you.'
10"But whatever city you
enter and they do not receive you, go out into its
streets and say,
11'Even the dust of your
city which clings to our
feet, we wipe off *in protest*
against you; yet be sure of
this, that the kingdom of
God has come near.'
12"I say to you, it will be
more tolerable in that day
for Sodom, than for that
city.
13"Woe to you, Chorazin! Woe to you, Bethsaida! For if the miracles
had been performed in
Tyre and Sidon which occurred in you, they would
have repented long ago, sitting in sackcloth and ashes.

δεήθητε οὖν τοῦ κυρίου τοῦ θερισμοῦ
beg ye therefore of the Lord of the harvest
ὅπως ἐργάτας ἐκβάλῃ εἰς τὸν θερισμὸν
that workmen he would thrust forth into the harvest
αὐτοῦ. 3 ὑπάγετε· ἰδοὺ ἀποστέλλω ὑμᾶς
of him. Go ye; behold I send you
ὡς ἄρνας ἐν μέσῳ λύκων. 4 μὴ βαστάζετε
as lambs in [the] midst of wolves. Do not carry
βαλλάντιον, μὴ πήραν, μὴ ὑποδήματα· καὶ
a purse, nor a wallet, nor sandals; and
μηδένα κατὰ τὴν ὁδὸν ἀσπάσησθε. 5 εἰς
no one by the way greet. [2]into
ἣν δ' ἂν εἰσέλθητε οἰκίαν, πρῶτον λέγετε·
[1]And [3]whatever [5]ye enter [4]house, first say:
εἰρήνη τῷ οἴκῳ τούτῳ. 6 καὶ ἐὰν ἐκεῖ
Peace – house to this. And if there
ᾖ υἱὸς εἰρήνης, ἐπαναπαήσεται ἐπ' αὐτὸν
there is a son of peace, shall rest on it(?him)
ἡ εἰρήνη ὑμῶν· εἰ δὲ μή γε, ἐφ' ὑμᾶς
the peace of you; otherwise, on you
ἀνακάμψει. 7 ἐν αὐτῇ δὲ τῇ οἰκίᾳ μένετε,
it shall return. [3]in [4]same [1]And [5]the house* remain,
ἐσθοντες καὶ πίνοντες τὰ παρ' αὐτῶν·
eating and drinking the things with them;
ἄξιος γὰρ ὁ ἐργάτης τοῦ μισθοῦ αὐτοῦ.
for worthy [is] the workman of the pay of him.
μὴ μεταβαίνετε ἐξ οἰκίας εἰς οἰκίαν.
Do not remove from house to house.
8 καὶ εἰς ἣν ἂν πόλιν εἰσέρχησθε καὶ
And into whatever city ye enter and
δέχωνται ὑμᾶς, ἐσθίετε τὰ παρατιθέμενα
they receive you, eat the things being set before
ὑμῖν, 9 καὶ θεραπεύετε τοὺς ἐν αὐτῇ
you, and heal the [2]in [3]it
ἀσθενεῖς, καὶ λέγετε αὐτοῖς· ἤγγικεν ἐφ'
[1]sick, and tell them: Has drawn near on(to)
ὑμᾶς ἡ βασιλεία τοῦ θεοῦ. 10 εἰς ἣν δ'
you the kingdom – of God. And into what-
ἂν πόλιν εἰσέλθητε καὶ μὴ δέχωνται ὑμᾶς,
ever city ye enter and they do not receive you,
ἐξελθόντες εἰς τὰς πλατείας αὐτῆς εἴπατε·
going forth into the streets of it say:
11 καὶ τὸν κονιορτὸν τὸν κολληθέντα ἡμῖν
Even the dust – adhering to us
=the dust of your city adhering to us, on our feet,
ἐκ τῆς πόλεως ὑμῶν εἰς τοὺς πόδας
of the city of you on the(our) feet
ἀπομασσόμεθα ὑμῖν· πλὴν τοῦτο γινώσκετε,
we shake off to you; nevertheless this know ye,
ὅτι ἤγγικεν ἡ βασιλεία τοῦ θεοῦ. 12 λέγω
that has drawn near the kingdom – of God. I tell
ὑμῖν ὅτι Σοδόμοις ἐν τῇ ἡμέρᾳ ἐκείνῃ
you that for Sodom in – day that
ἀνεκτότερον ἔσται ἢ τῇ πόλει ἐκείνῃ.
more endurable it will be than – city for that.
13 Οὐαί σοι, Χοραζίν, οὐαί σοι, Βηθσαϊδά·
Woe to thee, Chorazin, woe to thee, Bethsaida;
ὅτι εἰ ἐν Τύρῳ καὶ Σιδῶνι ἐγενήθησαν αἱ
because if in Tyre and Sidon happened the
δυνάμεις αἱ γενόμεναι ἐν ὑμῖν, πάλαι ἂν ἐν
powerful deeds – happening in you, long ago – in
σάκκῳ καὶ σποδῷ καθήμενοι μετενόησαν.
sackcloth and ashes sitting they would have repented.

* Luke here, and in 2. 38; 10. 21; 12. 12; 13. 31; 24. 13, as well as in Acts 16. 18; 22. 13, ignores the strict idiomatic construction of αὐτός when in apposition. The words here should mean "in the house itself" but obviously do mean "in the same house". So elsewhere. See note on Luke 2. 38.

are few. Ask the Lord of
the harvest, therefore, to
send out workers into his
harvest field. 3Go! I am
sending you out like lambs
among wolves. 4Do not
take a purse or bag or sandals; and do not greet anyone on the road.
5"When you enter a
house, first say, 'Peace to
this house.' 6If a man of
peace is there, your peace
will rest on him; if not, it
will return to you. 7Stay in
that house, eating and
drinking whatever they
give you, for the worker deserves his wages. Do not
move around from house to
house.
8"When you enter a town
and are welcomed, eat
what is set before you.
9Heal the sick who are
there and tell them, 'The
kingdom of God is near
you.' 10But when you enter
a town and are not welcomed, go into its streets
and say, 11'Even the dust of
your town that sticks to our
feet we wipe off against
you. Yet be sure of this:
The kingdom of God is
near.' 12I tell you, it will be
more bearable on that day
for Sodom than for that
town.
13"Woe to you, Korazin!
Woe to you, Bethsaida!
For if the miracles that
were performed in you had
been performed in Tyre
and Sidon, they would
have repented long ago, sitting in sackcloth and ashes.

14"But it will be more tolerable for Tyre and Sidon in the judgment, than for you.

15"And you, Capernaum, will not be exalted to heaven, will you? You will be brought down to Hades!

16"The one who listens to you listens to Me, and the one who rejects you rejects Me; and he who rejects Me rejects the One who sent Me."

The Happy Results

17And the seventy returned with joy, saying, "Lord, even the demons are subject to us in Your name."

18And He said to them, "I was watching Satan fall from heaven like lightning.

19"Behold, I have given you authority to tread upon serpents and scorpions, and over all the power of the enemy, and nothing shall injure you.

20"Nevertheless do not rejoice in this, that the spirits are subject to you, but rejoice that your names are recorded in heaven."

21At that very time He rejoiced greatly in the Holy Spirit, and said, "I praise Thee, O Father, Lord of heaven and earth, that Thou didst hide these things from *the* wise and intelligent and didst reveal them to babes. Yes, Father, for thus it was well-pleasing in Thy sight.

22"All things have been handed over to Me by My Father, and no one knows who the Son is except the Father, and who the Father is except the Son, and anyone to whom the Son wills to reveal *Him*."

23And turning to the disciples, He said privately, "Blessed *are* the eyes which see the things you see,

24for I say to you, that

14 πλὴν Τύρῳ καὶ Σιδῶνι ἀνεκτότερον
Nevertheless for Tyre and Sidon more endurable
ἔσται ἐν τῇ κρίσει ἢ ὑμῖν. 15 καὶ σύ,
it will be in the judgment than for you. And thou,
Καφαρναούμ, μὴ ἕως οὐρανοῦ ὑψωθήσῃ;
Capernaum, not to heaven wast thou lifted?
ἕως τοῦ ᾅδου καταβήσῃ. 16 Ὁ ἀκούων
to – hades thou shalt come down. The [one] hearing
ὑμῶν ἐμοῦ ἀκούει, καὶ ὁ ἀθετῶν ὑμᾶς
you me hears, and the [one] rejecting you
ἐμὲ ἀθετεῖ· ὁ δὲ ἐμὲ ἀθετῶν ἀθετεῖ τὸν
me rejects; and the [one] me rejecting rejects the [one]
ἀποστείλαντά με. 17 Ὑπέστρεψαν δὲ οἱ
having sent me. And returned the
ἑβδομήκοντα [δύο] μετὰ χαρᾶς λέγοντες·
seventy-two with joy saying :
κύριε, καὶ τὰ δαιμόνια ὑποτάσσεται ἡμῖν
Lord, even the demons submits to us
ἐν τῷ ὀνόματί σου. 18 εἶπεν δὲ αὐτοῖς·
in the name of thee. And he said to them :
ἐθεώρουν τὸν σατανᾶν ὡς ἀστραπὴν ἐκ
I beheld – Satan as lightning out of
τοῦ οὐρανοῦ πεσόντα. 19 ἰδοὺ δέδωκα
– heaven fall. Behold I have given
ὑμῖν τὴν ἐξουσίαν τοῦ πατεῖν ἐπάνω
you the authority – to tread[d] on
ὄφεων καὶ σκορπίων, καὶ ἐπὶ πᾶσαν τὴν
serpents and scorpions, and on all the
δύναμιν τοῦ ἐχθροῦ, καὶ οὐδὲν ὑμᾶς οὐ μὴ
power of the enemy, and nothing you by no(any) means
ἀδικήσει. 20 πλὴν ἐν τούτῳ μὴ χαίρετε
shall hurt. Nevertheless in this rejoice not
ὅτι τὰ πνεύματα ὑμῖν ὑποτάσσεται, χαίρετε
that the spirits to you submits, [2]rejoice
δὲ ὅτι τὰ ὀνόματα ὑμῶν ἐγγέγραπται ἐν
[1]but that the names of you have been enrolled in
τοῖς οὐρανοῖς. 21 Ἐν αὐτῇ τῇ ὥρᾳ
the heavens. In [2]same [1]the hour
ἠγαλλιάσατο τῷ πνεύματι τῷ ἁγίῳ καὶ
he exulted in(?by) the Spirit – Holy and
εἶπεν· ἐξομολογοῦμαί σοι, πάτερ, κύριε
said: I praise thee, Father, Lord
τοῦ οὐρανοῦ καὶ τῆς γῆς, ὅτι ἀπέκρυψας
– of heaven and – of earth, because thou didst hide
ταῦτα ἀπὸ σοφῶν καὶ συνετῶν, καὶ
these things from wise and intelligent [ones], and
ἀπεκάλυψας αὐτὰ νηπίοις· ναί, ὁ πατήρ,
didst reveal them to infants; yes – Father,
ὅτι οὕτως εὐδοκία ἐγένετο ἔμπροσθέν σου.
because thus good pleasure it was before thee.
22 πάντα μοι παρεδόθη ὑπὸ τοῦ πατρός
All things to me were delivered by the Father
μου, καὶ οὐδεὶς γινώσκει τίς ἐστιν ὁ
of me, and no one knows who is the
υἱὸς εἰ μὴ ὁ πατήρ, καὶ τίς ἐστιν ὁ πατὴρ
Son except the Father, and who is the Father
εἰ μὴ ὁ υἱὸς καὶ ᾧ ἐὰν βούληται
except the Son and [he] to whomever wills
ὁ υἱὸς ἀποκαλύψαι. 23 Καὶ στραφεὶς
the Son to reveal [him]. And turning
πρὸς τοὺς μαθητὰς κατ᾽ ἰδίαν εἶπεν·
to the disciples privately he said :
μακάριοι οἱ ὀφθαλμοὶ οἱ βλέποντες ἃ
Blessed the eyes – seeing the things which
βλέπετε. 24 λέγω γὰρ ὑμῖν ὅτι πολλοὶ
ye see. For I tell you that many

14But it will be more bearable for Tyre and Sidon at the judgment than for you.
15And you, Capernaum, will you be lifted up to the skies? No, you will go down to the depths.[o]
16"He who listens to you listens to me; he who rejects you rejects me; but he who rejects me rejects him who sent me."
17The seventy-two returned with joy and said, "Lord, even the demons submit to us in your name."
18He replied, "I saw Satan fall like lightning from
heaven. 19I have given you
authority to trample on snakes and scorpions and to overcome all the power of the enemy; nothing will
harm you. 20However, do
not rejoice that the spirits submit to you, but rejoice that your names are written in heaven."
21At that time Jesus, full of joy through the Holy Spirit, said, "I praise you, Father, Lord of heaven and earth, because you have hidden these things from the wise and learned, and revealed them to little children. Yes, Father, for this was your good pleasure.
22"All things have been committed to me by my Father. No one knows who the Son is except the Father, and no one knows who the Father is except the Son and those to whom the Son chooses to reveal him."
23Then he turned to his disciples and said privately, "Blessed are the eyes that see what you see.
24For I tell you that many

[o]15 Greek *Hades*

many prophets and kings wished to see the things which you see, and did not see *them*, and to hear the things which you hear, and did not hear *them*."

25And behold, a certain lawyer stood up and put Him to the test, saying, "Teacher, what shall I do to inherit eternal life?"

26And He said to him, "What is written in the Law? How does it read to you?"

27And he answered and said, "YOU SHALL LOVE THE LORD YOUR GOD WITH ALL YOUR HEART, AND WITH ALL YOUR SOUL, AND WITH ALL YOUR STRENGTH, AND WITH ALL YOUR MIND, AND YOUR NEIGHBOR AS YOURSELF."

28And He said to him, "You have answered correctly; DO THIS, AND YOU WILL LIVE."

29But wishing to justify himself, he said to Jesus, "And who is my neighbor?"

The Good Samaritan

30Jesus replied and said, "A certain man was going down from Jerusalem to Jericho; and he fell among robbers, and they stripped him and beat him, and went off leaving him half dead.

31"And by chance a certain priest was going down on that road, and when he saw him, he passed by on the other side.

32"And likewise a Levite also, when he came to the place and saw him, passed by on the other side.

33"But a certain Samaritan, who was on a journey, came upon him; and when he saw him, he felt compassion,

34and came to him, and bandaged up his wounds, pouring oil and wine on *them;* and he put him on his own beast, and brought him to an inn, and took care of him.

35"And on the next day he took out two [a]denarii and gave them to the innkeeper and said, 'Take care

[a]The denarius was equivalent to one day's wage

προφῆται καὶ βασιλεῖς ἠθέλησαν ἰδεῖν ἃ
prophets and kings desired to see the things which
ὑμεῖς βλέπετε καὶ οὐκ εἶδαν, καὶ ἀκοῦσαι
ye see and did not see, and to hear
ἃ ἀκούετε καὶ οὐκ ἤκουσαν.
the things which ye hear and did not hear.
25 Καὶ ἰδοὺ νομικός τις ἀνέστη
And[,] behold[,] lawyer a certain stood up
ἐκπειράζων αὐτὸν λέγων· διδάσκαλε, τί
tempting him saying : Teacher, what
ποιήσας ζωὴν αἰώνιον κληρονομήσω; 26 ὁ
doing ⁵life ⁴eternal ²I ¹may ³inherit? he
δὲ εἶπεν πρὸς αὐτόν· ἐν τῷ νόμῳ τί
And said to him : In the law what
γέγραπται; πῶς ἀναγινώσκεις; 27 ὁ δὲ
has been written? how readest thou? And he
ἀποκριθεὶς εἶπεν· ἀγαπήσεις κύριον τὸν
answering said : Thou shalt love [the] Lord the
θεόν σου ἐξ ὅλης τῆς καρδίας σου καὶ
God of thee from all the heart of thee and
ἐν ὅλῃ τῇ ψυχῇ σου καὶ ἐν ὅλῃ τῇ
with all the soul of thee and with all the
ἰσχύϊ σου καὶ ἐν ὅλῃ τῇ διανοίᾳ σου,
strength of thee and with all the mind of thee,
καὶ τὸν πλησίον σου ὡς σεαυτόν. 28 εἶπεν
and the neighbour of thee as thyself. he said
δὲ αὐτῷ· ὀρθῶς ἀπεκρίθης· τοῦτο ποίει
And to him : Rightly thou didst answer; this do
καὶ ζήσῃ. 29 ὁ δὲ θέλων δικαιῶσαι ἑαυτὸν
and thou shalt live. But he wishing to justify himself
εἶπεν πρὸς τὸν Ἰησοῦν· καὶ τίς ἐστίν
said to – Jesus : And who is
μου πλησίον; 30 ὑπολαβὼν ὁ Ἰησοῦς
of me neighbour? Taking [him] up – Jesus
εἶπεν· ἄνθρωπός τις κατέβαινεν ἀπὸ
said : A certain man was going down from
Ἰερουσαλὴμ εἰς Ἰεριχώ, καὶ λῃσταῖς
Jerusalem to Jericho, and ²robbers
περιέπεσεν, οἳ καὶ ἐκδύσαντες αὐτὸν καὶ
¹fell in with, who both stripping him and
πληγὰς ἐπιθέντες ἀπῆλθον ἀφέντες ἡμιθανῆ.
²blows ¹laying ³on ⁴[him] went away leaving [him] half dead.
31 κατὰ συγκυρίαν δὲ ἱερεύς τις κατέβαινεν
And by a coincidence a certain priest was going down
ἐν τῇ ὁδῷ ἐκείνῃ, καὶ ἰδὼν αὐτὸν
in – way that, and seeing him
ἀντιπαρῆλθεν. 32 ὁμοίως δὲ καὶ Λευίτης
passed by opposite. And likewise also a Levite
κατὰ τὸν τόπον ἐλθὼν καὶ ἰδὼν
upon the place coming and seeing
ἀντιπαρῆλθεν. 33 Σαμαρίτης δέ τις ὁδεύων
passed by opposite. And a certain Samaritan journeying
ἦλθεν κατ' αὐτὸν καὶ ἰδὼν ἐσπλαγχνίσθη,
came upon him and seeing was filled with pity,
34 καὶ προσελθὼν κατέδησεν τὰ τραύματα
and approaching bound up the wounds
αὐτοῦ ἐπιχέων ἔλαιον καὶ οἶνον, ἐπιβιβάσας
of him pouring on oil and wine, ²placing
δὲ αὐτὸν ἐπὶ τὸ ἴδιον κτῆνος ἤγαγεν
¹and him on the(his) own beast brought
αὐτὸν εἰς πανδοχεῖον καὶ ἐπεμελήθη αὐτοῦ.
him to an inn and cared for him.
35 καὶ ἐπὶ τὴν αὔριον ἐκβαλὼν δύο
And on the morrow taking out two
δηνάρια ἔδωκεν τῷ πανδοχεῖ καὶ εἶπεν·
denarii he gave to the innkeeper and said:

prophets and kings wanted to see what you see but did not see it, and to hear what you hear but did not hear it."

The Parable of the Good Samaritan

25On one occasion an expert in the law stood up to test Jesus. "Teacher," he asked, "what must I do to inherit eternal life?"

26"What is written in the Law?" he replied. "How do you read it?"

27He answered: " 'Love the Lord your God with all your heart and with all your soul and with all your strength and with all your mind'[p]; and, 'Love your neighbor as yourself.'[q]"

28"You have answered correctly," Jesus replied. "Do this and you will live."

29But he wanted to justify himself, so he asked Jesus, "And who is my neighbor?"

30In reply Jesus said: "A
man was going down from
Jerusalem to Jericho, when
he fell into the hands of robbers. They stripped him of
his clothes, beat him and
went away, leaving him
half dead. 31A priest happened to be going down the
same road, and when he
saw the man, he passed by
on the other side. 32So too,
a Levite, when he came to
the place and saw him,
passed by on the other side.
33But a Samaritan, as he
traveled, came where the
man was; and when he saw
him, he took pity on him.
34He went to him and ban-
daged his wounds, pouring
on oil and wine. Then he
put the man on his own
donkey, took him to an inn
and took care of him. 35The
next day he took out two
silver coins[r] and gave
them to the innkeeper.
'Look after him,' he said,

[p]27 Deut. 6:5
[q]27 Lev. 19:18
[r]35 Greek *two denarii*

of him; and whatever more you spend, when I return, I will repay you.'

36"Which of these three do you think proved to be a neighbor to the man who fell into the robbers' *hands?*"

37And he said, "The one who showed mercy toward him." And Jesus said to him, "Go and do the same."

Martha and Mary

38Now as they were traveling along, He entered a certain village; and a woman named Martha welcomed Him into her home.

39And she had a sister called Mary, who moreover was listening to the Lord's word, seated at His feet.

40But Martha was distracted with all her preparations; and she came up *to Him,* and said, "Lord, do You not care that my sister has left me to do all the serving alone? Then tell her to help me."

41But the Lord answered and said to her, "Martha, Martha, you are worried and bothered about so many things;

42but *only* a few things are necessary, really *only* one, for Mary has chosen the good part, which shall not be taken away from her."

ἐπιμελήθητι αὐτοῦ, καὶ ὅ τι ἂν προσδα-
Care thou for him, and whatever thou spendest
πανήσῃς ἐγὼ ἐν τῷ ἐπανέρχεσθαί με
in addition I in the to return me[be]
=when I return
ἀποδώσω σοι. 36 τίς τούτων τῶν τριῶν πλησίον
will repay thee. Who of these – three [4]neighbour
δοκεῖ σοι γεγονέναι τοῦ ἐμπεσόντος
[1]seems it [2]to thee [3]to have become of the [one] falling *into*
εἰς τοὺς λῃστάς; 37 ὁ δὲ εἶπεν· ὁ ποιήσας
among the robbers? And he said: The [one] doing
τὸ ἔλεος μετ' αὐτοῦ. εἶπεν δὲ αὐτῷ ὁ
the mercy with him. And said to him
Ἰησοῦς· πορεύου καὶ σὺ ποίει ὁμοίως.
Jesus: Go and thou do likewise.
38 Ἐν δὲ τῷ πορεύεσθαι αὐτοὺς αὐτὸς
And in the to go them[be] he
=as they went
εἰσῆλθεν εἰς κώμην τινά· γυνὴ δέ τις
entered into a certain village; and a certain woman
ὀνόματι Μάρθα ὑπεδέξατο αὐτὸν εἰς τὴν
by name Martha received him into the
οἰκίαν. 39 καὶ τῇδε ἦν ἀδελφὴ καλουμένη
house. And to this was a sister[c] *being* called
=she had a sister
Μαριάμ, ἣ καὶ παρακαθεσθεῖσα πρὸς τοὺς
Mary, who also sitting beside at the
πόδας τοῦ κυρίου ἤκουεν τὸν λόγον αὐτοῦ.
feet of the Lord heard the word of him.
40 ἡ δὲ Μάρθα περιεσπᾶτο περὶ πολλὴν
– But Martha was distracted about much
διακονίαν· ἐπιστᾶσα δὲ εἶπεν· κύριε, οὐ
serving; and coming upon [him] she said: Lord, not
μέλει σοι ὅτι ἡ ἀδελφή μου μόνην με
matters it to thee that the sister of me [3]alone [2]me
κατέλειπεν διακονεῖν; εἰπὸν οὖν αὐτῇ ἵνα
[1]left to serve? tell therefore her that
μοι συναντιλάβηται. 41 ἀποκριθεὶς δὲ εἶπεν
[2]me [1]she may help. And answering said
αὐτῇ ὁ κύριος· Μάρθα Μάρθα, μεριμνᾷς
to her the Lord: Martha[,] Martha, thou art anxious
καὶ θορυβάζῃ περὶ πολλά, 42 ὀλίγων δέ
and disturbed about many things, but of few things
ἐστιν χρεία ἢ ἑνός· Μαριὰμ γὰρ τὴν
there is need or of one; for Mary the
ἀγαθὴν μερίδα ἐξελέξατο, ἥτις οὐκ
good part chose, which not
ἀφαιρεθήσεται αὐτῆς.
shall be taken from her.

'and when I return, I will
reimburse you for any ex-
tra expense you may have.'
36"Which of these three
do you think was a neigh-
bor to the man who fell into
the hands of robbers?"
37The expert in the law replied, "The one who had
mercy on him."
Jesus told him, "Go and
do likewise."

At the Home of Martha and Mary

38As Jesus and his disci-
ples were on their way, he
came to a village where a
woman named Martha
opened her home to him.
39She had a sister called
Mary, who sat at the
Lord's feet listening to
what he said. 40But Martha
was distracted by all the
preparations that had to be
made. She came to him and
asked, "Lord, don't you
care that my sister has left
me to do the work by my-
self? Tell her to help me!"
41"Martha, Martha," the
Lord answered, "you are
worried and upset about
many things, 42but only one
thing is needed.[s] Mary has
chosen what is better, and
it will not be taken away
from her."

Chapter 11

Instruction about Prayer

AND it came about that while He was praying in a certain place, after He had finished, one of His disciples said to Him, "Lord, teach us to pray just as John also taught his disciples."

2And He said to them, "When you pray, say:
'[v]Father, hallowed be

11 Καὶ ἐγένετο ἐν τῷ εἶναι αὐτὸν ἐν
And it came to pass in the to be him[be] in
=when he was
τόπῳ τινὶ προσευχόμενον, ὡς ἐπαύσατο,
a certain place praying, as he ceased,
εἶπέν τις τῶν μαθητῶν αὐτοῦ πρὸς
said a certain one of the disciples of him to
αὐτόν· κύριε, δίδαξον ἡμᾶς προσεύχεσθαι,
him: Lord, teach us to pray,
καθὼς καὶ Ἰωάννης ἐδίδαξεν τοὺς μαθητὰς
even as also John taught the disciples
αὐτοῦ. 2 εἶπεν δὲ αὐτοῖς· ὅταν
of him. And he said to them: When
προσεύχησθε, λέγετε· Πάτερ, ἁγιασθήτω τὸ
ye pray, say: Father, let be hallowed the

Chapter 11

Jesus' Teaching on Prayer

ONE day Jesus was
praying in a certain
place. When he finished,
one of his disciples said to
him, "Lord, teach us to
pray, just as John taught his
disciples."
2He said to them, "When
you pray, say:

"'Father,[t]
hallowed be your name,

[s]42 Some manuscripts *but few things are needed—or only one*
[t]2 Some manuscripts *Our Father in heaven*

Thy name.
Thy kingdom come.
3 'Give us each day our
daily bread.
4 'And forgive us our
sins,
For we ourselves also
forgive everyone
who is indebted to
us.
And lead us not into
temptation.' "
5And He said to them,
"Suppose one of you shall
have a friend, and shall go
to him at midnight, and say
to him, 'Friend, lend me
three loaves;
6for a friend of mine has
come to me from a journey,
and I have nothing to set
before him';
7and from inside he shall
answer and say, 'Do not
bother me; the door has already been shut and my
children and I are in bed; I
cannot get up and give you
anything.'
8"I tell you, even though
he will not get up and give
him *anything* because he is
his friend, yet because of
his persistence he will get
up and give him as much as
he needs.
9"And I say to you, ask,
and it shall be given to you;
seek, and you shall find;
knock, and it shall be
opened to you.
10"For everyone who
asks, receives; and he who
seeks, finds; and to him
who knocks, it shall be
opened.
11"Now suppose one of
you fathers is asked by his
son for a fish; he will not
give him a snake instead of
a fish, will he?
12"Or *if* he is asked for an
egg, he will not give him a
scorpion, will he?
13"If you then, being evil,
know how to give good
gifts to your children, how
much more shall *your* heavenly Father give the Holy
Spirit to those who ask
Him?"

Pharisees' Blasphemy

14And He was casting out
a demon, and it was dumb;
and it came about that
when the demon had gone

ᵛSome mss. insert phrases from Matt. 6:9–13 to make the two passages closely similar

ὄνομά σου· ἐλθάτω ἡ βασιλεία σου·
name of thee; let come the kingdom of thee;
3 τὸν ἄρτον ἡμῶν τὸν ἐπιούσιον δίδου
the bread of us – belonging to the morrow give
ἡμῖν τὸ καθ' ἡμέραν· **4** καὶ ἄφες ἡμῖν τὰς
us each day†; and forgive us the
ἁμαρτίας ἡμῶν, καὶ γὰρ αὐτοὶ ἀφίομεν
sins of us, for indeed [our]selves we forgive
παντὶ ὀφείλοντι ἡμῖν· καὶ μὴ εἰσενέγκῃς
everyone owing to us; and lead not
ἡμᾶς εἰς πειρασμόν. **5** Καὶ εἶπεν πρὸς
us into temptation. And he said to
αὐτούς· τίς ἐξ ὑμῶν ἕξει φίλον, καὶ
them: Who of you shall have a friend, and
πορεύσεται πρὸς αὐτὸν μεσονυκτίου καὶ
will come to him at midnight and
εἴπῃ αὐτῷ· φίλε, χρῆσόν μοι τρεῖς ἄρτους,
say to him: Friend, lend me three loaves,
6 ἐπειδὴ φίλος μου παρεγένετο ἐξ ὁδοῦ
since a friend of me arrived off a journey
πρός με καὶ οὐκ ἔχω ὃ παραθήσω αὐτῷ·
to me and I have not what I may set before him;
7 κἀκεῖνος ἔσωθεν ἀποκριθεὶς εἴπῃ· μή
and that one within answering may say: Not
μοι κόπους πάρεχε· ἤδη ἡ θύρα κέκλεισται,
me troubles cause; now the door has been shut,
καὶ τὰ παιδία μου μετ' ἐμοῦ εἰς τὴν
and the children of me with me in the
κοίτην εἰσίν· οὐ δύναμαι ἀναστὰς δοῦναί
bed are; I cannot rising up *to* give
σοι. **8** λέγω ὑμῖν, εἰ καὶ οὐ δώσει
thee. I tell you, if even he will not give
αὐτῷ ἀναστὰς διὰ τὸ εἶναι φίλον αὐτοῦ,
him rising up on account of the to be friend of him,
=because he is his friend,
διά γε τὴν ἀναίδειαν αὐτοῦ ἐγερθεὶς
yet on account of the importunity of him rising
δώσει αὐτῷ ὅσων χρῄζει. **9** Κἀγὼ ὑμῖν
he will give him as many as he needs. And I ²you
λέγω, αἰτεῖτε, καὶ δοθήσεται ὑμῖν· ζητεῖτε,
¹tell, ask, and it will be given you; seek,
καὶ εὑρήσετε· κρούετε, καὶ ἀνοιγήσεται
and ye will find; knock, and it will be opened
ὑμῖν. **10** πᾶς γὰρ ὁ αἰτῶν λαμβάνει, καὶ
to you. For everyone asking receives, and
ὁ ζητῶν εὑρίσκει, καὶ τῷ κρούοντι
the [one] seeking finds, and to the [one] knocking
ἀνοιγήσεται. **11** τίνα δὲ ἐξ ὑμῶν τὸν
it will be opened. And ¹what ⁴of ⁵you –
πατέρα αἰτήσει ὁ υἱὸς ἰχθύν, μὴ
²father ³[is there] ⁶[of whom] ⁹will ask ⁷the ⁸son ¹⁰a fish, *not*
ἀντὶ ἰχθύος ὄφιν αὐτῷ ἐπιδώσει; **12** ἢ
instead of a fish ³a serpent ²to him ¹will hand? or
καὶ αἰτήσει ᾠόν, ἐπιδώσει αὐτῷ σκορπίον;
even he will ask an egg, will hand to him a scorpion?
13 εἰ οὖν ὑμεῖς πονηροὶ ὑπάρχοντες οἴδατε δόματα
If therefore ye ²evil ¹being know gifts
ἀγαθὰ διδόναι τοῖς τέκνοις ὑμῶν, πόσῳ
good to give to the children of you, how much
μᾶλλον ὁ πατὴρ ὁ ἐξ οὐρανοῦ δώσει
more the Father – of heaven will give
πνεῦμα ἅγιον τοῖς αἰτοῦσιν αὐτόν.
Spirit [the] Holy to the [ones] asking him.
14 Καὶ ἦν ἐκβάλλων δαιμόνιον, καὶ αὐτὸ
And he was expelling a demon, and it
ἦν κωφόν· ἐγένετο δὲ τοῦ δαιμονίου
was dumb; and it came to pass the demon
=as the demon went out

your kingdom come.ᵘ
3Give us each day our
daily bread.
4Forgive us our sins,
for we also forgive
everyone who sins
against us.ᵛ
And lead us not into
temptation.ʷ' "
5Then he said to them,
"Suppose one of you has a
friend, and he goes to him
at midnight and says,
'Friend, lend me three
loaves of bread, 6because a
friend of mine on a journey
has come to me, and I have
nothing to set before him.'
7"Then the one inside an-
swers, 'Don't bother me.
The door is already locked,
and my children are with
me in bed. I can't get up
and give you anything.' 8I
tell you, though he will not
get up and give him the
bread because he is his
friend, yet because of the
man's boldnessˣ he will get
up and give him as much as
he needs.
9"So I say to you: Ask
and it will be given to you;
seek and you will find;
knock and the door will be
opened to you. 10For ev-
eryone who asks receives;
he who seeks finds; and to
him who knocks, the door
will be opened.
11"Which of you fathers,
if your son asks forʸ a fish,
will give him a snake in-
stead? 12Or if he asks for an
egg, will give him a scorpion? 13If you then, though
you are evil, know how to
give good gifts to your children, how much more will
your Father in heaven give
the Holy Spirit to those
who ask him!"

Jesus and Beelzebub

14Jesus was driving out a
demon that was mute.
When the demon left, the

ᵘ2 Some manuscripts *come. May your will be done on earth as it is in heaven.*
ᵛ4 Greek *everyone who is indebted to us*
ʷ4 Some manuscripts *temptation but deliver us from the evil one*
ˣ8 Or *persistence*
ʸ11 Some manuscripts *for bread, will give him a stone; or if he asks for*

out, the dumb man spoke;
and the multitudes mar-
veled.
15But some of them said,
"He casts out demons by
Beelzebul, the ruler of the
demons."
16And others, to test
Him, were demanding of
Him a sign from heaven.
17But He knew their
thoughts, and said to them,
"Any kingdom divided
against itself is laid waste;
and a house *divided* against
itself falls.
18"And if Satan also is divided against himself, how
shall his kingdom stand?
For you say that I cast out
demons by Beelzebul.
19"And if I by Beelzebul
cast out demons, by whom
do your sons cast them out?
Consequently they shall be
your judges.
20"But if I cast out de-
mons by the finger of God,
then the kingdom of God
has come upon you.
21"When a strong *man,*
fully armed, guards his own
homestead, his possessions
are undisturbed;
22but when someone
stronger than he attacks
him and overpowers him,
he takes away from him all
his armor on which he had
relied, and distributes his
plunder.
23"He who is not with Me
is against Me; and he who
does not gather with Me,
scatters.
24"When the unclean
spirit goes out of a man, it
passes through waterless
places seeking rest, and not
finding any, it says, 'I will
return to my house from
which I came.'
25"And when it comes, it
finds it swept and put in order.
26"Then it goes and takes
along seven other spirits
more evil than itself, and

ἐξελθόντος ἐλάλησεν ὁ κωφός· καὶ
going out[a] spoke the dumb man; and
ἐθαύμασαν οἱ ὄχλοι· **15** τινὲς δὲ ἐξ
marvelled the crowds; but some of
αὐτῶν εἶπαν· ἐν Βεεζεβοὺλ τῷ ἄρχοντι
them said : By Beelzebub the chief
τῶν δαιμονίων ἐκβάλλει τὰ δαιμόνια·
of the demons he expels the demons;
16 ἕτεροι δὲ πειράζοντες σημεῖον ἐξ οὐρανοῦ
and others tempting a sign out of heaven
ἐζήτουν παρ' αὐτοῦ. **17** αὐτὸς δὲ εἰδὼς
sought from him. But he knowing
αὐτῶν τὰ διανοήματα εἶπεν αὐτοῖς· πᾶσα
of them the thoughts said to them : Every
βασιλεία ἐφ' ἑαυτὴν διαμερισθεῖσα ἐρημοῦται,
kingdom against itself divided is made desolate,
καὶ οἶκος ἐπὶ οἶκον πίπτει. **18** εἰ δὲ
and a house against a house falls. And if
καὶ ὁ σατανᾶς ἐφ' ἑαυτὸν διεμερίσθη,
also – Satan against himself was divided,
πῶς σταθήσεται ἡ βασιλεία αὐτοῦ; ὅτι
how will stand the kingdom of him? because
λέγετε ἐν Βεεζεβοὺλ ἐκβάλλειν με τὰ
ye say by Beelzebub to expel me[b] the
=[that] by Beelzebub I expel
δαιμόνια. **19** εἰ δὲ ἐγὼ ἐν Βεεζεβοὺλ
demons. But if I by Beelzebub
ἐκβάλλω τὰ δαιμόνια, οἱ υἱοὶ ὑμῶν ἐν
expel the demons, the sons of you by
τίνι ἐκβάλλουσιν; διὰ τοῦτο αὐτοὶ ὑμῶν
what do they expel? therefore they of you
κριταὶ ἔσονται. **20** εἰ δὲ ἐν δακτύλῳ
judges shall be. But if by [the] finger
θεοῦ [ἐγὼ] ἐκβάλλω τὰ δαιμόνια, ἄρα
of God I expel the demons, then
ἔφθασεν ἐφ' ὑμᾶς ἡ βασιλεία τοῦ θεοῦ.
came upon you the kingdom – of God.
21 ὅταν ὁ ἰσχυρὸς καθωπλισμένος φυλάσσῃ
When the strong man *having been* well armed guards
τὴν ἑαυτοῦ αὐλήν, ἐν εἰρήνῃ ἐστὶν τὰ
the of him*self* palace, in peace is(are) the
ὑπάρχοντα αὐτοῦ· **22** ἐπὰν δὲ ἰσχυρότερος
goods of him; but when a stronger
αὐτοῦ ἐπελθὼν νικήσῃ αὐτόν, τὴν πανοπλίαν
[than] him coming upon overcomes him, the armour
αὐτοῦ αἴρει, ἐφ' ᾗ ἐπεποίθει, καὶ τὰ
of him he takes, on which he had relied, and the
σκῦλα αὐτοῦ διαδίδωσιν. **23** Ὁ μὴ ὢν
arms of him distributes. The [one] not being
μετ' ἐμοῦ κατ' ἐμοῦ ἐστιν, καὶ ὁ μὴ
with me against me is, and the [one] not
συνάγων μετ' ἐμοῦ σκορπίζει. **24** Ὅταν
gathering with me scatters. When
τὸ ἀκάθαρτον πνεῦμα ἐξέλθῃ ἀπὸ τοῦ
the unclean spirit goes out from the
ἀνθρώπου, διέρχεται δι' ἀνύδρων τόπων
man, he goes *through* through dry places
ζητοῦν ἀνάπαυσιν, καὶ μὴ εὑρίσκον λέγει·
seeking rest, and not finding says :
ὑποστρέψω εἰς τὸν οἶκόν μου ὅθεν ἐξῆλθον·
I will return to the house of me whence I came out;
25 καὶ ἐλθὸν εὑρίσκει σεσαρωμένον καὶ
and coming he finds [it] *having been* swept and
κεκοσμημένον. **26** τότε πορεύεται καὶ
having been furnished. Then he goes and
παραλαμβάνει ἕτερα πνεύματα πονηρότερα
takes other spirits more wicked

man who had been mute
spoke, and the crowd was
amazed. 15But some of
them said, "By Beelze-
bub,[z] the prince of de-
mons, he is driving out demons." 16Others tested
him by asking for a sign
from heaven.
17Jesus knew their
thoughts and said to them:
"Any kingdom divided
against itself will be ruined,
and a house divided against
itself will fall. 18If Satan is
divided against himself,
how can his kingdom
stand? I say this because
you claim that I drive out
demons by Beelzebub.
19Now if I drive out de-
mons by Beelzebub, by
whom do your followers
drive them out? So then,
they will be your judges.
20But if I drive out demons
by the finger of God, then
the kingdom of God has
come to you.
21"When a strong man,
fully armed, guards his own
house, his possessions are
safe. 22But when someone
stronger attacks and overpowers him, he takes away
the armor in which the man
trusted and divides up the
spoils.
23"He who is not with me
is against me, and he who
does not gather with me,
scatters.
24"When an evil[a] spirit
comes out of a man, it goes
through arid places seeking
rest and does not find it.
Then it says, 'I will return
to the house I left.' 25When
it arrives, it finds the house
swept clean and put in order. 26Then it goes and
takes seven other spirits
more wicked than itself,

[z] *15* Greek *Beezeboul* or *Beelzeboul*; also in verses 18 and 19
[a] *24* Greek *unclean*

they go in and live there; and the last state of that man becomes worse than the first."

27And it came about while He said these things, one of the women in the crowd raised her voice, and said to Him, "Blessed is the womb that bore You, and the breasts at which You nursed."

28But He said, "On the contrary, blessed are those who hear the word of God, and observe it."

The Sign of Jonah

29And as the crowds were increasing, He began to say, "This generation is a wicked generation; it seeks for a sign, and *yet* no sign shall be given to it but the sign of Jonah.

30"For just as Jonah became a sign to the Ninevites, so shall the Son of Man be to this generation.

31"The Queen of the South shall rise up with the men of this generation at the judgment and condemn them, because she came from the ends of the earth to hear the wisdom of Solomon; and behold, something greater than Solomon is here.

32"The men of Nineveh shall stand up with this generation at the judgment and condemn it, because they repented at the preaching of Jonah; and behold, something greater than Jonah is here.

33"No one, after lighting a lamp, puts it away in a cellar, nor under a peck-measure, but on the lampstand, in order that those who enter may see the light.

34"The lamp of your body is your eye; when your eye is clear, your whole body also is full of light; but when it is bad, your body also is full of darkness.

ἑαυτοῦ ἑπτά, καὶ εἰσελθόντα κατοικεῖ
[than] himself seven, and entering he dwells
ἐκεῖ· καὶ γίνεται τὰ ἔσχατα τοῦ ἀνθρώπου
there; and becomes the last things – man
ἐκείνου χείρονα τῶν πρώτων. 27 Ἐγένετο
of that worse [than] the first. it came to pass
δὲ ἐν τῷ λέγειν αὐτὸν ταῦτα ἐπάρασά τις
And in the to say him[be] these things [6]lifting up [1]a certain
=as he said
φωνὴν γυνὴ ἐκ τοῦ ὄχλου εἶπεν αὐτῷ·
[7][her] [8]voice [2]woman [3]of [4]the [5]crowd said to him:
μακαρία ἡ κοιλία ἡ βαστάσασά σε καὶ
Blessed the womb – having borne thee and
μαστοὶ οὓς ἐθήλασας. 28 αὐτὸς δὲ εἶπεν·
[the] breasts which thou didst suck. But he said:
μενοῦν μακάριοι οἱ ἀκούοντες τὸν λόγον
Nay rather blessed the [ones] hearing the word
τοῦ θεοῦ καὶ φυλάσσοντες.
– of God and keeping.

29 Τῶν δὲ ὄχλων ἐπαθροιζομένων ἤρξατο
And the crowds pressing upon[a] he began
=as the crowds pressed upon [him]
λέγειν· ἡ γενεὰ αὕτη γενεὰ πονηρά ἐστιν·
to say: – [2]generation [1]This [3]generation [4]an evil [5]is;
σημεῖον ζητεῖ, καὶ σημεῖον οὐ δοθήσεται
a sign it seeks, and a sign will not be given
αὐτῇ εἰ μὴ τὸ σημεῖον Ἰωνᾶ. 30 καθὼς
to it except the sign of Jonas. even as
γὰρ ἐγένετο [ὁ] Ἰωνᾶς τοῖς Νινευίταις
For [2]became – [1]Jonas [4]to the [5]Ninevites
σημεῖον, οὕτως ἔσται καὶ ὁ υἱὸς τοῦ
[3]a sign, so will be also the Son –
ἀνθρώπου τῇ γενεᾷ ταύτῃ. 31 βασίλισσα
of man – generation to this. [The] queen
νότου ἐγερθήσεται ἐν τῇ κρίσει μετὰ τῶν
of [the] south will be raised in the judgment with the
ἀνδρῶν τῆς γενεᾶς ταύτης καὶ κατακρινεῖ
men – generation of this and will condemn
αὐτούς· ὅτι ἦλθεν ἐκ τῶν περάτων τῆς
them; because she came from the extremities of the
γῆς ἀκοῦσαι τὴν σοφίαν Σολομῶνος, καὶ
earth to hear the wisdom of Solomon, and
ἰδοὺ πλεῖον Σολομῶνος ὧδε. 32 ἄνδρες
behold a greater [than] Solomon [is] here. *Men*
Νινευῖται ἀναστήσονται ἐν τῇ κρίσει μετὰ
Ninevites will rise up in the judgment with
τῆς γενεᾶς ταύτης καὶ κατακρινοῦσιν αὐτήν·
– generation this and will condemn it;
ὅτι μετενόησαν εἰς τὸ κήρυγμα Ἰωνᾶ, καὶ
because they repented at the proclamation of Jonas, and
ἰδοὺ πλεῖον Ἰωνᾶ ὧδε. 33 Οὐδεὶς λύχνον
behold a greater [than] Jonas [is] here. No one [2]a lamp
ἅψας εἰς κρύπτην τίθησιν οὐδὲ ὑπὸ τὸν
[1]having lit [4]in [5]secret [3]places [it] nor under the
μόδιον, ἀλλ' ἐπὶ τὴν λυχνίαν, ἵνα οἱ
bushel, but on the lampstand, that the
εἰσπορευόμενοι τὸ φέγγος βλέπωσιν. 34 ὁ
ones] entering the light may see. The
λύχνος τοῦ σώματός ἐστιν ὁ ὀφθαλμός σου.
lamp of the body is the eye of thee.
ὅταν ὁ ὀφθαλμός σου ἁπλοῦς ᾖ, καὶ
When the eye of thee single is, also
ὅλον τὸ σῶμά σου φωτεινόν ἐστιν· ἐπὰν
all the body of thee bright is; [2]when
δὲ πονηρὸς ᾖ, καὶ τὸ σῶμά σου σκοτεινόν.
[1]but evil it is, also the body of thee [is] dark.

and they go in and live there. And the final condition of that man is worse than the first."

27As Jesus was saying these things, a woman in the crowd called out, "Blessed is the mother who gave you birth and nursed you."

28He replied, "Blessed rather are those who hear the word of God and obey it."

The Sign of Jonah

29As the crowds increased, Jesus said, "This is a wicked generation. It asks for a miraculous sign, but none will be given it except the sign of Jonah.
30For as Jonah was a sign to the Ninevites, so also will the Son of Man be to this generation.
31The Queen of the South will rise at the judgment with the men of this generation and condemn them; for she came from the ends of the earth to listen to Solomon's wisdom, and now one[b] greater than Solomon is here.
32The men of Nineveh will stand up at the judgment with this generation and condemn it; for they repented at the preaching of Jonah, and now one greater than Jonah is here.

The Lamp of the Body

33"No one lights a lamp and puts it in a place where it will be hidden, or under a bowl. Instead he puts it on its stand, so that those who come in may see the light.
34Your eye is the lamp of your body. When your eyes are good, your whole body also is full of light. But when they are bad, your body also is full of

[b]31 Or *something*; also in verse 32

35"Then watch out that the light in you may not be darkness.
36"If therefore your whole body is full of light, with no dark part in it, it shall be wholly illumined, as when the lamp illumines you with its rays."

Woes upon the Pharisees

37Now when He had spoken, a Pharisee *asked Him to have lunch with him; and He went in, and reclined *at the table*.
38And when the Pharisee saw it, he was surprised that He had not first ceremonially washed before the meal.
39But the Lord said to him, "Now you Pharisees clean the outside of the cup and of the platter; but inside of you, you are full of robbery and wickedness.
40"You foolish ones, did not He who made the outside make the inside also?
41"But give that which is within as charity, and then all things are clean for you.
42"But woe to you Pharisees! For you pay tithe of mint and rue and every *kind of* garden herb, and *yet* disregard justice and the love of God; but these are the things you should have done without neglecting the others.
43"Woe to you Pharisees! For you love the front seats in the synagogues, and the respectful greetings in the market places.
44"Woe to you! For you are like concealed tombs, and the people who walk over *them* are unaware *of it*."
45And one of the [w]lawyers *said to Him in reply, "Teacher, when You say this, You insult us too."
46But He said, "Woe to you lawyers as well! For you weigh men down with burdens hard to bear, while you yourselves will not

[w] I.e., experts in the Mosaic law

35 σκόπει οὖν μὴ τὸ φῶς τὸ ἐν σοὶ
Watch therefore lest the light – in thee
σκότος ἐστίν. **36** εἰ οὖν τὸ σῶμά σου
darkness is. If therefore [1]the [3]body [4]of thee
ὅλον φωτεινόν, μὴ ἔχον μέρος τι σκοτεινόν,
[2]whole [is] bright, not having [2]part [1]any dark,
ἔσται φωτεινὸν ὅλον ὡς ὅταν ὁ λύχνος
[2]will be [3]bright [1]all as when the lamp
τῇ ἀστραπῇ φωτίζῃ σε.
with the(its) shining enlightens thee.
37 Ἐν δὲ τῷ λαλῆσαι ἐρωτᾷ αὐτὸν
Now in the to speak[e] asks him
=as [he] spoke
Φαρισαῖος ὅπως ἀριστήσῃ παρ' αὐτῷ·
a Pharisee that he would dine with him;
εἰσελθὼν δὲ ἀνέπεσεν. **38** ὁ δὲ Φαρισαῖος
and entering he reclined. But the Pharisee
ἰδὼν ἐθαύμασεν ὅτι οὐ πρῶτον ἐβαπτίσθη
seeing marvelled that not first he washed
πρὸ τοῦ ἀρίστου. **39** εἶπεν δὲ ὁ κύριος
before the dinner. But said the Lord
πρὸς αὐτόν· νῦν ὑμεῖς οἱ Φαρισαῖοι τὸ
to him: Now ye – Pharisees the
ἔξωθεν τοῦ ποτηρίου καὶ τοῦ πίνακος
outside of the cup and of the dish
καθαρίζετε, τὸ δὲ ἔσωθεν ὑμῶν γέμει
cleanse, but the inside of you is full
ἁρπαγῆς καὶ πονηρίας. **40** ἄφρονες, οὐχ
of robbery and wickedness. Foolish men, not
ὁ ποιήσας τὸ ἔξωθεν καὶ τὸ ἔσωθεν
the [one] making the outside also the inside
ἐποίησεν; **41** πλὴν τὰ ἐνόντα δότε
made? Nevertheless the things being within give
ἐλεημοσύνην, καὶ ἰδοὺ πάντα καθαρὰ ὑμῖν
alms, and behold all things clean to you
ἐστιν. **42** ἀλλὰ οὐαὶ ὑμῖν τοῖς Φαρισαίοις,
is(are). But woe to you – Pharisees,
ὅτι ἀποδεκατοῦτε τὸ ἡδύοσμον καὶ τὸ
because ye tithe the mint and the
πήγανον καὶ πᾶν λάχανον, καὶ παρέρχεσθε
rue and every herb, and pass by
τὴν κρίσιν καὶ τὴν ἀγάπην τοῦ θεοῦ·
the judgment and the love – of God;
ταῦτα δὲ ἔδει ποιῆσαι κἀκεῖνα μὴ
but these things it behoved to do and those not
παρεῖναι. **43** οὐαὶ ὑμῖν τοῖς Φαρισαίοις,
to pass by. Woe to you – Pharisees,
ὅτι ἀγαπᾶτε τὴν πρωτοκαθεδρίαν ἐν ταῖς
because ye love the chief seat in the
συναγωγαῖς καὶ τοὺς ἀσπασμοὺς ἐν ταῖς
synagogues and the greetings in the
ἀγοραῖς. **44** οὐαὶ ὑμῖν, ὅτι ἐστὲ ὡς τὰ
marketplaces. Woe to you, because ye are as the
μνημεῖα τὰ ἄδηλα, καὶ οἱ ἄνθρωποι οἱ
tombs – unseen, and the men –
περιπατοῦντες ἐπάνω οὐκ οἴδασιν.
walking over do not know.
45 Ἀποκριθεὶς δέ τις τῶν νομικῶν λέγει
And answering one of the lawyers says
αὐτῷ· διδάσκαλε, ταῦτα λέγων καὶ ἡμᾶς
to him: Teacher, these things saying also us
ὑβρίζεις. **46** ὁ δὲ εἶπεν· καὶ ὑμῖν τοῖς
thou insultest. And he said: Also to you –
νομικοῖς οὐαί, ὅτι φορτίζετε τοὺς ἀνθρώπους
lawyers woe, because ye burden – men
φορτία δυσβάστακτα, καὶ αὐτοὶ ἑνὶ τῶν
[with] burdens difficult to carry, and [your]selves with one of the

darkness. 35See to it, then, that the light within you is not darkness. 36Therefore, if your whole body is full of light, and no part of it dark, it will be completely lighted, as when the light of a lamp shines on you."

Six Woes

37When Jesus had finished speaking, a Pharisee invited him to eat with him; so he went in and reclined at the table. 38But the Pharisee, noticing that Jesus did not first wash before the meal, was surprised.
39Then the Lord said to him, "Now then, you Pharisees clean the outside of the cup and dish, but inside you are full of greed and wickedness. 40You foolish people! Did not the one who made the outside make the inside also? 41But give what is inside ⌊the dish,[c] to the poor, and everything will be clean for you.
42"Woe to you Pharisees, because you give God a tenth of your mint, rue and all other kinds of garden herbs, but you neglect justice and the love of God. You should have practiced the latter without leaving the former undone.
43"Woe to you Pharisees, because you love the most important seats in the synagogues and greetings in the marketplaces.
44"Woe to you, because you are like unmarked graves, which men walk over without knowing it."
45One of the experts in the law answered him, "Teacher, when you say these things, you insult us also."
46Jesus replied, "And you experts in the law, woe to you, because you load people down with burdens they can hardly carry, and you yourselves will not lift

[c] 41 Or *what you have*

even touch the burdens
with one of your fingers.
47"Woe to you! For you
build the tombs of the
prophets, and *it was* your
fathers *who* killed them.
48"Consequently, you
are witnesses and approve
the deeds of your fathers;
because it was they who
killed them, and you build
their tombs.
49"For this reason also
the wisdom of God said, 'I
will send to them prophets
and apostles, and *some* of
them they will kill and
some they will persecute,
50in order that the blood
of all the prophets, shed
since the foundation of the
world, may be charged
against this generation,
51from the blood of Abel
to the blood of Zechariah,
who perished between the
altar and the house *of God;*
yes, I tell you, it shall be
charged against this gen-
eration.'
52"Woe to you lawyers!
For you have taken away
the key of knowledge; you
did not enter in yourselves,
and those who were enter-
ing in you hindered."
53And when He left there,
the scribes and the Pharisees began to be very hostile and to question Him
closely on many subjects,
54plotting against Him, to
catch *Him* in something He
might say.

δακτύλων ὑμῶν οὐ προσψαύετε τοῖς φορτίοις.
fingers of you ye do not touch the burdens.

47 οὐαὶ ὑμῖν, ὅτι οἰκοδομεῖτε τὰ μνημεῖα
Woe to you, because ye build the tombs

τῶν προφητῶν, οἱ δὲ πατέρες ὑμῶν
of the prophets, and the fathers of you

ἀπέκτειναν αὐτούς. 48 ἄρα μάρτυρές ἐστε
killed them. Therefore witnesses ye are

καὶ συνευδοκεῖτε τοῖς ἔργοις τῶν πατέρων
and ye entirely approve the works of the fathers

ὑμῶν, ὅτι αὐτοὶ μὲν ἀπέκτειναν αὐτούς,
of you, because they on one hand killed them,

ὑμεῖς δὲ οἰκοδομεῖτε. 49 διὰ τοῦτο καὶ
ye on the other hand build. Therefore also

ἡ σοφία τοῦ θεοῦ εἶπεν· ἀποστελῶ εἰς
the Wisdom – of God said: I will send to

αὐτοὺς προφήτας καὶ ἀποστόλους, καὶ ἐξ
them prophets and apostles, and of

αὐτῶν ἀποκτενοῦσιν καὶ διώξουσιν, 50 ἵνα
them they will kill and persecute, that

ἐκζητηθῇ τὸ αἷμα πάντων τῶν προφητῶν
11may be required 1the 2blood 3of all 4the 5prophets

τὸ ἐκκεχυμένον ἀπὸ καταβολῆς κόσμου
– 6*having been* shed 7from 8[the] 9foundation 10of [the] world

ἀπὸ τῆς γενεᾶς ταύτης, 51 ἀπὸ αἵματος
11from – generation this, from [the] blood

*Ἄβελ ἕως αἵματος Ζαχαρίου τοῦ
of Abel to [the] blood of Zacharias –

ἀπολομένου μεταξὺ τοῦ θυσιαστηρίου καὶ
destroyed between the altar and

τοῦ οἴκου· ναὶ λέγω ὑμῖν, ἐκζητηθήσεται
the house; yes I tell you, it will be required

ἀπὸ τῆς γενεᾶς ταύτης. 52 οὐαὶ ὑμῖν τοῖς
from – generation this. Woe to you –

νομικοῖς, ὅτι ἤρατε τὴν κλεῖδα τῆς
lawyers, because ye took the key –

γνώσεως· αὐτοὶ οὐκ εἰσήλθατε καὶ τοὺς
of knowledge; [your]selves ye did not enter and the

εἰσερχομένους ἐκωλύσατε. 53 Κἀκεῖθεν ἐξελ-
[ones] entering ye prevented. And thence going
=as he went forth thence

θόντος αὐτοῦ ἤρξαντο οἱ γραμματεῖς καὶ
forth him* began the scribes and

οἱ Φαρισαῖοι δεινῶς ἐνέχειν καὶ ἀποστοματίζειν
the Pharisees 2terribly 1to be 3angry and to 1draw 3out

αὐτὸν περὶ πλειόνων, 54 ἐνεδρεύοντες
2him concerning a great number of things, lying in wait for

αὐτὸν θηρεῦσαί τι ἐκ τοῦ στόματος αὐτοῦ.
him to catch something out of the mouth of him.

one finger to help them.
47"Woe to you, because
you build tombs for the
prophets, and it was your
forefathers who killed
them. 48So you testify that
you approve of what your
forefathers did; they killed
the prophets, and you build
their tombs. 49Because of
this, God in his wisdom
said, 'I will send them
prophets and apostles,
some of whom they will kill
and others they will persecute.' 50Therefore this generation will be held responsible for the blood of all the
prophets that has been
shed since the beginning of
the world, 51from the blood
of Abel to the blood of
Zechariah, who was killed
between the altar and the
sanctuary. Yes, I tell you,
this generation will be held
responsible for it all.
52"Woe to you experts in
the law, because you have
taken away the key to
knowledge. You your-
selves have not entered,
and you have hindered
those who were entering."
53When Jesus left there,
the Pharisees and the
teachers of the law began to
oppose him fiercely and to
besiege him with questions,
54waiting to catch him in
something he might say.

Chapter 12

God Knows and Cares

UNDER these circum-
stances, after so
many thousands of the multitude had gathered to-
gether that they were stepping on one another, He began saying to His disciples
first *of all,* "Beware of the
leaven of the Pharisees,
which is hypocrisy.
2"But there is nothing
covered up that will not be
revealed, and hidden that
will not be known.

12 Ἐν οἷς ἐπισυναχθεισῶν τῶν μυριάδων
In which things being assembled the thousands
=Meanwhile as the thousands of the crowd were assembled,

τοῦ ὄχλου, ὥστε καταπατεῖν ἀλλήλους,
of the crowd,* so as to tread on one another,

ἤρξατο λέγειν πρὸς τοὺς μαθητὰς αὐτοῦ
he began to say to the disciples of him

πρῶτον· προσέχετε ἑαυτοῖς ἀπὸ τῆς ζύμης,
first: Take heed to yourselves from the leaven,

ἥτις ἐστὶν ὑπόκρισις, τῶν Φαρισαίων.
which is hypocrisy, of the Pharisees.

2 οὐδὲν δὲ συγκεκαλυμμένον ἐστὶν ὃ οὐκ
And 2nothing 3*having been* completely covered 1there is which not

ἀποκαλυφθήσεται, καὶ κρυπτὸν ὃ οὐ γνωσθήσεται.
will be uncovered, and hidden which will not be known.

Chapter 12

Warnings and Encouragements

MEANWHILE, when a
crowd of many thou-
sands had gathered, so that
they were trampling on one
another, Jesus began to
speak first to his disciples,
saying: "Be on your guard
against the yeast of the
Pharisees, which is hypocrisy. 2There is nothing concealed that will not be disclosed, or hidden that will
not be made known. 3What

3"Accordingly, whatever you have said in the dark shall be heard in the light, and what you have whispered in the inner rooms shall be proclaimed upon the housetops.

4"And I say to you, My friends, do not be afraid of those who kill the body, and after that have no more that they can do.

5"But I will warn you whom to fear: fear the One who after He has killed has authority to cast into hell; yes, I tell you, fear Him!

6"Are not five sparrows sold for two cents? And *yet* not one of them is forgotten before God.

7"Indeed, the very hairs of your head are all numbered. Do not fear; you are of more value than many sparrows.

8"And I say to you, everyone who confesses Me before men, the Son of Man shall confess him also before the angels of God;

9but he who denies Me before men shall be denied before the angels of God.

10"And everyone who will speak a word against the Son of Man, it shall be forgiven him; but he who blasphemes against the Holy Spirit, it shall not be forgiven him.

11"And when they bring you before the synagogues and the rulers and the authorities, do not become anxious about how or what you should speak in your defense, or what you should say;

12for the Holy Spirit will teach you in that very hour what you ought to say."

Covetousness Denounced

13And someone in the crowd said to Him, "Teacher, tell my brother to divide the *family* inheritance with me."

3 ἀνθ' ὧν ὅσα ἐν τῇ σκοτίᾳ εἴπατε ἐν
Therefore what things in the darkness ye said in
τῷ φωτὶ ἀκουσθήσεται, καὶ ὃ πρὸς τὸ
the light will be heard, and what to the
οὖς ἐλαλήσατε ἐν τοῖς ταμιείοις κηρυχθήσεται
ear ye spoke in the private rooms will be proclaimed
ἐπὶ τῶν δωμάτων. **4** Λέγω δὲ ὑμῖν τοῖς
on the roofs. And I say to you the
φίλοις μου, μὴ φοβηθῆτε ἀπὸ τῶν
friends of me, do not be afraid from(of) the [ones]
ἀποκτεννόντων τὸ σῶμα καὶ μετὰ ταῦτα
killing the body and after these things
μὴ ἐχόντων περισσότερόν τι ποιῆσαι.
no· having anything more to do.
5 ὑποδείξω δὲ ὑμῖν τίνα φοβηθῆτε·
But I will warn you whom ye may fear :
φοβήθητε τὸν μετὰ τὸ ἀποκτεῖναι ἔχοντα
[1]fear [2]the [one] [5]after *the* [6]*to* kill(killing) [3]having
ἐξουσίαν ἐμβαλεῖν εἰς τὴν γέενναν. ναί
[4]authority [7]to cast *in* into – gehenna. Yes[,]
λέγω ὑμῖν, τοῦτον φοβήθητε. **6** οὐχὶ
I say to you, this one fear ye. Not
πέντε στρουθία πωλοῦνται ἀσσαρίων δύο;
five sparrows are sold of(for) farthings two?
καὶ ἓν ἐξ αὐτῶν οὐκ ἔστιν ἐπιλελησμένον
and one of them is not *having been* forgotten
ἐνώπιον τοῦ θεοῦ. **7** ἀλλὰ καὶ αἱ τρίχες
before – God. But even the hairs
τῆς κεφαλῆς ὑμῶν πᾶσαι ἠρίθμηνται.
of the head of you all have been numbered.
μὴ φοβεῖσθε· πολλῶν στρουθίων διαφέρετε.
Fear ye not; from many sparrows ye differ.
8 λέγω δὲ ὑμῖν, πᾶς ὃς ἂν ὁμολογήσῃ
But I tell you, everyone whoever confesses
ἐν ἐμοὶ ἔμπροσθεν τῶν ἀνθρώπων, καὶ ὁ
– me before – men, also the
υἱὸς τοῦ ἀνθρώπου ὁμολογήσει ἐν αὐτῷ
Son – of man will confess – him
ἔμπροσθεν τῶν ἀγγέλων τοῦ θεοῦ· **9** ὁ δὲ
before the angels – of God; and the
ἀρνησάμενός με ἐνώπιον τῶν ἀνθρώπων
[one] denying me before – men
ἀπαρνηθήσεται ἐνώπιον τῶν ἀγγέλων τοῦ
will be denied before the angels –
θεοῦ. **10** καὶ πᾶς ὃς ἐρεῖ λόγον εἰς τὸν
of God. And everyone who shall say a word against the
υἱὸν τοῦ ἀνθρώπου, ἀφεθήσεται αὐτῷ· τῷ
Son – of man, it will be forgiven him; [2]the [one]
δὲ εἰς τὸ ἅγιον πνεῦμα βλασφημήσαντι
[1]but against the Holy Spirit blaspheming
οὐκ ἀφεθήσεται. **11** ὅταν δὲ εἰσφέρωσιν
will not be forgiven. And when they bring in
ὑμᾶς ἐπὶ τὰς συναγωγὰς καὶ τὰς ἀρχὰς
you before – synagogues and – rulers
καὶ τὰς ἐξουσίας, μὴ μεριμνήσητε πῶς ἢ
and – authorities, do not be anxious how or
τί ἀπολογήσησθε ἢ τί εἴπητε· **12** τὸ γὰρ
what ye may answer or what ye may say; for the
ἅγιον πνεῦμα διδάξει ὑμᾶς ἐν αὐτῇ τῇ
Holy Spirit will teach you in [2]same [1]the
ὥρᾳ ἃ δεῖ εἰπεῖν. **13** Εἶπεν δέ τις
hour what things it behoves [you] to say. And said someone
ἐκ τοῦ ὄχλου αὐτῷ· διδάσκαλε, εἰπὲ τῷ
out of the crowd to him : Teacher, tell the
ἀδελφῷ μου μερίσασθαι μετ' ἐμοῦ τὴν
brother of me to divide with me the

you have said in the dark
will be heard in the day-
light, and what you have
whispered in the ear in the
inner rooms will be pro-
claimed from the roofs.
4"I tell you, my friends,
do not be afraid of those
who kill the body and after
that can do no more. 5But I
will show you whom you
should fear: Fear him who,
after the killing of the body,
has power to throw you
into hell. Yes, I tell you,
fear him. 6Are not five
sparrows sold for two pen-
nies[d]? Yet not one of them
is forgotten by God. 7In-
deed, the very hairs of your
head are all numbered.
Don't be afraid; you are
worth more than many
sparrows.
8"I tell you, whoever ac-
knowledges me before
men, the Son of Man will
also acknowledge him be-
fore the angels of God. 9But
he who disowns me before
men will be disowned be-
fore the angels of God.
10And everyone who
speaks a word against the
Son of Man will be forgiv-
en, but anyone who blas-
phemes against the Holy
Spirit will not be forgiven.
11"When you are brought
before synagogues, rulers
and authorities, do not
worry about how you will
defend yourselves or what
you will say, 12for the Holy
Spirit will teach you at that
time what you should say."

The Parable of the Rich Fool

13Someone in the crowd
said to him, "Teacher, tell
my brother to divide the inheritance with me."

[d]6 Greek *two assaria*

14But He said to him,
"Man, who appointed Me a
judge or arbiter over you?"
15And He said to them,
"Beware, and be on your
guard against every form of
greed; for not *even* when
one has an abundance does
his life consist of his
possessions."
16And He told them a par-
able, saying, "The land of a
certain rich man was very
productive.
17"And he began reason-
ing to himself, saying,
'What shall I do, since I
have no place to store my
crops?'
18"And he said, 'This is
what I will do: I will tear
down my barns and build
larger ones, and there I will
store all my grain and my
goods.
19'And I will say to my
soul, "Soul, you have
many goods laid up for
many years *to come;* take
your ease, eat, drink *and* be
merry." '
20"But God said to him,
'You fool! This *very* night
your soul is required of
you; and *now* who will own
what you have prepared?'
21"So is the man who lays
up treasure for himself, and
is not rich toward God."
22And He said to His dis-
ciples, "For this reason I
say to you, do not be anxious for *your* life, *as to* what
you shall eat; nor for your
body, *as to* what you shall
put on.
23"For life is more than
food, and the body than
clothing.
24"Consider the ravens,
for they neither sow nor
reap; and they have no
storeroom nor barn; and
yet God feeds them; how
much more valuable you
are than the birds!
25"And which of you by
being anxious can add a
single [x]cubit to his [y]life's
span?

[x] I.e., One cubit equals approx. 18 in.
[y] Or, *height*

κληρονομίαν. **14** ὁ δὲ εἶπεν αὐτῷ· ἄνθρωπε,
inheritance But he said to him: Man,
τίς με κατέστησεν κριτὴν ἢ μεριστὴν ἐφ'
who me appointed a judge or a divider over
ὑμᾶς; **15** εἶπεν δὲ πρὸς αὐτούς· ὁρᾶτε
you? And he said to them: Beware
καὶ φυλάσσεσθε ἀπὸ πάσης πλεονεξίας,
and guard from(against) all covetousness,
ὅτι οὐκ ἐν τῷ περισσεύειν τινὶ ἡ ζωὴ
because [5]not [6]in [7]the [8]to abound [9]to anyone [1]the [2]life
αὐτοῦ ἐστιν ἐκ τῶν ὑπαρχόντων αὐτῷ.
[3]of him [4]is [10]of the things existing to him.[c]
=[11]his [12]possessions.

16 Εἶπεν δὲ παραβολὴν πρὸς αὐτοὺς λέγων·
And he told a parable to them saying:
ἀνθρώπου τινὸς πλουσίου εὐφόρησεν ἡ
[3]of a certain [5]man [4]rich [6]bore well [1]The
χώρα. **17** καὶ διελογίζετο ἐν ἑαυτῷ λέγων·
[2]land. And he reasoned in himself saying:
τί ποιήσω, ὅτι οὐκ ἔχω ποῦ συνάξω τοὺς
What may I do, because I have not where I may gather the
καρπούς μου; **18** καὶ εἶπεν· τοῦτο ποιήσω·
fruits of me? And he said: This will I do:
καθελῶ μου τὰς ἀποθήκας καὶ μείζονας
I will pull down of me the barns and larger ones
οἰκοδομήσω, καὶ συνάξω ἐκεῖ πάντα τὸν
I will build, and I will gather there all the
σῖτον καὶ τὰ ἀγαθά μου, **19** καὶ ἐρῶ τῇ
wheat and the goods of me, and I will say to the
ψυχῇ μου· ψυχή, ἔχεις πολλὰ ἀγαθὰ
soul of me: Soul, thou hast many goods
κείμενα εἰς ἔτη πολλά· ἀναπαύου, φάγε,
laid [up] for years many; take rest, eat,
πίε, εὐφραίνου. **20** εἶπεν δὲ αὐτῷ ὁ
drink, be glad. But said to him –
θεός· ἄφρων, ταύτῃ τῇ νυκτὶ τὴν ψυχήν
God: Foolish man, in this – night the soul
σου ἀπαιτοῦσιν ἀπὸ σοῦ· ἃ δὲ
of thee they demand from thee; then [the] things which
ἡτοίμασας, τίνι ἔσται; **21** οὕτως ὁ
thou preparedst, to whom will they be?[c] So the [one]
=whose will they be?
θησαυρίζων αὑτῷ καὶ μὴ εἰς θεὸν πλουτῶν.
treasuring to himself and not toward God being rich.
22 Εἶπεν δὲ πρὸς τοὺς μαθητὰς [αὐτοῦ]· διὰ τοῦτο
And he said to the disciples of him: Therefore
λέγω ὑμῖν· μὴ μεριμνᾶτε τῇ ψυχῇ τί
I tell you: Do not be anxious for the life what
φάγητε, μηδὲ τῷ σώματι [ὑμῶν] τί
ye may eat, nor for the body of you what
ἐνδύσησθε. **23** ἡ γὰρ ψυχὴ πλεῖόν ἐστιν
ye may put on. For the life more is
τῆς τροφῆς καὶ τὸ σῶμα τοῦ ἐνδύματος.
[than] the food and the body [than] the clothing.
24 κατανοήσατε τοὺς κόρακας, ὅτι οὔτε
Consider ye the ravens, that neither
σπείρουσιν οὔτε θερίζουσιν, οἷς οὐκ ἔστιν
they sow nor reap, to which is not[c]
=which have not
ταμιεῖον οὐδὲ ἀποθήκη, καὶ ὁ θεὸς τρέφει
storehouse nor barn, and – God feeds
αὐτούς· πόσῳ μᾶλλον ὑμεῖς διαφέρετε τῶν
them; by how much rather ye differ from the
πετεινῶν. **25** τίς δὲ ἐξ ὑμῶν μεριμνῶν
birds. And who of you being anxious
δύναται ἐπὶ τὴν ἡλικίαν αὐτοῦ προσθεῖναι
can on the stature of him *to* add

14Jesus replied, "Man,
who appointed me a judge
or an arbiter between
you?" 15Then he said to
them, "Watch out! Be on
your guard against all kinds
of greed; a man's life does
not consist in the abun-
dance of his possessions."
16And he told them this
parable: "The ground of a
certain rich man produced
a good crop. 17He thought
to himself, 'What shall I
do? I have no place to store
my crops.'
18"Then he said, 'This is
what I'll do. I will tear
down my barns and build
bigger ones, and there I will
store all my grain and my
goods. 19And I'll say to myself, "You have plenty of
good things laid up for
many years. Take life easy;
eat, drink and be merry." '
20"But God said to him,
'You fool! This very night
your life will be demanded
from you. Then who will
get what you have prepared
for yourself?'
21"This is how it will be
with anyone who stores up
things for himself but is not
rich toward God."

Do Not Worry

22Then Jesus said to his
disciples: "Therefore I tell
you, do not worry about
your life, what you will eat;
or about your body, what
you will wear. 23Life is
more than food, and the
body more than clothes.
24Consider the ravens:
They do not sow or reap,
they have no storeroom or
barn; yet God feeds them.
And how much more valu-
able you are than birds!
25Who of you by worrying
can add a single hour to his

26"If then you cannot do even a very little thing, why are you anxious about other matters?
27"Consider the lilies, how they grow; they neither toil nor spin; but I tell you, even Solomon in all his glory did not clothe himself like one of these.
28"But if God so arrays the grass in the field, which is *alive* today and tomorrow is thrown into the furnace, how much more *will He clothe* you, O men of little faith!
29"And do not seek what you shall eat, and what you shall drink, and do not keep worrying.
30"For all these things the nations of the world eagerly seek; but your Father knows that you need these things.
31"But seek for His kingdom, and these things shall be added to you.
32"Do not be afraid, little flock, for your Father has chosen gladly to give you the kingdom.
33"Sell your possessions and give to charity; make yourselves purses which do not wear out, an unfailing treasure in heaven, where no thief comes near, nor moth destroys.
34"For where your treasure is, there will your heart be also.

Be in Readiness

35"Be dressed in readiness, and *keep* your lamps alight.
36"And be like men who are waiting for their master when he returns from the wedding feast, so that they may immediately open *the door* to him when he comes and knocks.
37"Blessed are those slaves whom the master shall find on the alert when he comes; truly I say to you, that he will gird himself *to serve*, and have them recline *at the table*, and will come up and wait on them.

πῆχυν; 26 εἰ οὖν οὐδὲ ἐλάχιστον δύνασθε,
a cubit? If therefore not [the] least ye can,
τί περὶ τῶν λοιπῶν μεριμνᾶτε; 27 κατα-
why concerning the other things are ye anxious? Con-
νοήσατε τὰ κρίνα, πῶς οὔτε νήθει οὔτε
sider ye the lilies, how neither they spin nor
ὑφαίνει· λέγω δὲ ὑμῖν, οὐδὲ Σολομὼν ἐν
weave; but I tell you, not Solomon in
πάσῃ τῇ δόξῃ αὐτοῦ περιεβάλετο ὡς ἓν
all the glory of him was arrayed as one
τούτων. 28 εἰ δὲ ἐν ἀγρῷ τὸν χόρτον
of these. [1]And [2]if [9]in [10]a field [6]the [7]grass
ὄντα σήμερον καὶ αὔριον εἰς κλίβανον
[8]being [11]to-day [12]and [13]tomorrow [15]into [16]an oven
βαλλόμενον ὁ θεὸς οὕτως ἀμφιάζει, πόσῳ
[14]being thrown – [3]God [4]so [5]clothes, by how much
μᾶλλον ὑμᾶς, ὀλιγόπιστοι. 29 καὶ ὑμεῖς
rather you, little-faiths. And ye
μὴ ζητεῖτε τί φάγητε καὶ τί πίητε, καὶ
do not seek what ye may eat and what ye may drink, and
μὴ μετεωρίζεσθε· 30 ταῦτα γὰρ πάντα τὰ
do not be in suspense; for these things all the
ἔθνη τοῦ κόσμου ἐπιζητοῦσιν· ὑμῶν δὲ
nations of the world seek after; but of you
ὁ πατὴρ οἶδεν ὅτι χρῄζετε τούτων·
the Father knows that ye have need of them;
31 πλὴν ζητεῖτε τὴν βασιλείαν αὐτοῦ, καὶ
but seek ye the kingdom of him, and
ταῦτα προστεθήσεται ὑμῖν. 32 Μὴ φοβοῦ,
these things will be added to you. Fear not,
τὸ μικρὸν ποίμνιον· ὅτι εὐδόκησεν ὁ
– little flock; because was well pleased the
πατὴρ ὑμῶν δοῦναι ὑμῖν τὴν βασιλείαν.
Father of you to give you the kingdom.
33 Πωλήσατε τὰ ὑπάρχοντα ὑμῶν καὶ
Sell the possessions of you and
δότε ἐλεημοσύνην· ποιήσατε ἑαυτοῖς βαλ-
give alms; make for yourselves
λάντια μὴ παλαιούμενα, θησαυρὸν ἀνέκλειπτον
purses not becoming old, a treasure unfailing
ἐν τοῖς οὐρανοῖς, ὅπου κλέπτης οὐκ
in the heavens, where a thief not
ἐγγίζει οὐδὲ σὴς διαφθείρει· 34 ὅπου γάρ
comes near nor moth corrupts; for where
ἐστιν ὁ θησαυρὸς ὑμῶν, ἐκεῖ καὶ ἡ
is the treasure of you, there also the
καρδία ὑμῶν ἔσται. 35 Ἔστωσαν ὑμῶν αἱ
heart of you will be. Let be of you the
ὀσφύες περιεζωσμέναι καὶ οἱ λύχνοι
loins *having been* girded and the lamps
καιόμενοι· 36 καὶ ὑμεῖς ὅμοιοι ἀνθρώποις
burning; and ye like men
προσδεχομένοις τὸν κύριον ἑαυτῶν, πότε
awaiting the lord of them*selves*, when
ἀναλύσῃ ἐκ τῶν γάμων, ἵνα ἐλθόντος
he returns from the wedding festivities, that coming*
καὶ κρούσαντος εὐθέως ἀνοίξωσιν αὐτῷ.
and knocking* immediately they may open to him.
37 μακάριοι οἱ δοῦλοι ἐκεῖνοι, οὓς ἐλθὼν
Blessed – slaves those, whom coming
ὁ κύριος εὑρήσει γρηγοροῦντας· ἀμὴν λέγω
the lord will find watching; truly I tell
ὑμῖν ὅτι περιζώσεται καὶ ἀνακλινεῖ αὐτοὺς
you that he will gird himself and [1]make [3]to recline [2]them
καὶ παρελθὼν διακονήσει αὐτοῖς. 38 κἂν
and coming up to will serve them. And if

life[e]? 26Since you cannot do this very little thing, why do you worry about the rest?
27"Consider how the lilies grow. They do not labor or spin. Yet I tell you, not even Solomon in all his splendor was dressed like one of these. 28If that is how God clothes the grass of the field, which is here today, and tomorrow is thrown into the fire, how much more will he clothe you, O you of little faith! 29And do not set your heart on what you will eat or drink; do not worry about it. 30For the pagan world runs after all such things, and your Father knows that you need them. 31But seek his kingdom, and these things will be given to you as well.
32"Do not be afraid, little flock, for your Father has been pleased to give you the kingdom. 33Sell your possessions and give to the poor. Provide purses for yourselves that will not wear out, a treasure in heaven that will not be exhausted, where no thief comes near and no moth destroys. 34For where your treasure is, there your heart will be also.

Watchfulness

35"Be dressed ready for service and keep your lamps burning, 36like men waiting for their master to return from a wedding banquet, so that when he comes and knocks they can immediately open the door for him. 37It will be good for those servants whose master finds them watching when he comes. I tell you the truth, he will dress himself to serve, will have them recline at the table and will come and wait on

[e]25 Or *single cubit to his height*

38“Whether he comes in
the [z]second watch, or even
in the [a]third, and finds
them so, blessed are those
slaves.
39“And be sure of this,
that if the head of the house
had known at what hour the
thief was coming, he would
not have allowed his house
to be broken into.
40“You too, be ready; for
the Son of Man is coming at
an hour that you do not expect.”
41And Peter said, “Lord,
are You addressing this
parable to us, or to everyone *else* as well?”
42And the Lord said,
“Who then is the faithful
and sensible steward,
whom his master will put in
charge of his servants, to
give them their rations at
the proper time?
43“Blessed is that slave
whom his master finds so
doing when he comes.
44“Truly I say to you,
that he will put him in
charge of all his posses-
sions.
45“But if that slave says
in his heart, ‘My master
will be a long time in coming,’ and begins to beat the
slaves, *both* men and
women, and to eat and
drink and get drunk;
46the master of that slave
will come on a day when he
does not expect *him*, and at
an hour he does not know,
and will cut him in pieces,
and assign him a place with
the unbelievers.
47“And that slave who
knew his master's will and
did not get ready or act in
accord with his will, shall
receive many lashes,
48but the one who did not
know *it*, and committed
deeds worthy of a flogging,
will receive but few. And
from everyone who has
been given much shall
much be required; and to

[z]I.e., 9 p.m. to midnight
[a]I.e., midnight to 3 a.m.

ἐν τῇ δευτέρᾳ κἂν ἐν τῇ τρίτῃ φυλακῇ
in the second and if in the third watch
ἔλθῃ καὶ εὕρῃ οὕτως, μακάριοί εἰσιν
he comes and finds so, blessed are
ἐκεῖνοι. **39** τοῦτο δὲ γινώσκετε, ὅτι εἰ
those [slaves]. But this know ye, that if
ᾔδει ὁ οἰκοδεσπότης ποίᾳ ὥρᾳ ὁ κλέπτης
knew the house-master in what hour the thief
ἔρχεται, οὐκ ἂν ἀφῆκεν διορυχθῆναι τὸν
comes, he would not have allowed to be dug through the
οἶκον αὐτοῦ. **40** καὶ ὑμεῖς γίνεσθε ἕτοιμοι,
house of him. And [2]ye [1]be prepared,
ὅτι ᾗ ὥρᾳ οὐ δοκεῖτε ὁ υἱὸς τοῦ
because in what hour ye think not the Son –
ἀνθρώπου ἔρχεται. **41** Εἶπεν δὲ ὁ Πέτρος·
of man comes. And said – Peter :
κύριε, πρὸς ἡμᾶς τὴν παραβολὴν ταύτην
Lord, to us – parable this
λέγεις ἢ καὶ πρὸς πάντας; **42** καὶ εἶπεν
sayest thou or also to all? And said
ὁ κύριος· τίς ἄρα ἐστὶν ὁ πιστὸς
the Lord : Who then is the faithful
οἰκονόμος ὁ φρόνιμος, ὃν καταστήσει ὁ
steward the prudent, whom will appoint the
κύριος ἐπὶ τῆς θεραπείας αὐτοῦ τοῦ
lord over the household attendants of him –
διδόναι ἐν καιρῷ [τὸ] σιτομέτριον;
to give[d] in season the portion of food?
43 μακάριος ὁ δοῦλος ἐκεῖνος, ὃν ἐλθὼν
Blessed – slave that, whom coming
ὁ κύριος αὐτοῦ εὑρήσει ποιοῦντα οὕτως.
the lord of him will find doing so.
44 ἀληθῶς λέγω ὑμῖν ὅτι ἐπὶ πᾶσιν τοῖς
Truly I tell you that over all the
ὑπάρχουσιν αὐτοῦ καταστήσει αὐτόν. **45** ἐὰν
possessions of him he will appoint him. if
δὲ εἴπῃ ὁ δοῦλος ἐκεῖνος ἐν τῇ καρδίᾳ
But says – slave that in the heart
αὐτοῦ· χρονίζει ὁ κύριός μου ἔρχεσθαι,
of him : Delays the lord of me to come,
καὶ ἄρξηται τύπτειν τοὺς παῖδας καὶ τὰς
and begins to strike the menservants and the
παιδίσκας, ἐσθίειν τε καὶ πίνειν καὶ
maidservants, [2]to eat [1]both and to drink and
μεθύσκεσθαι, **46** ἥξει ὁ κύριος τοῦ δούλου
to become drunk, will come the lord – slave
ἐκείνου ἐν ἡμέρᾳ ᾗ οὐ προσδοκᾷ καὶ ἐν
of that in a day in which he does not expect and in
ὥρᾳ ᾗ οὐ γινώσκει, καὶ διχοτομήσει
an hour *in* which he knows not, and will cut asunder
αὐτόν, καὶ τὸ μέρος αὐτοῦ μετὰ τῶν
him, and the portion of him with the
ἀπίστων θήσει. **47** ἐκεῖνος δὲ ὁ δοῦλος
unbelievers will place. But that – slave
ὁ γνοὺς τὸ θέλημα τοῦ κυρίου αὐτοῦ
– having known the will of the lord of him
καὶ μὴ ἑτοιμάσας ἢ ποιήσας πρὸς τὸ θέλημα
and not having prepared or done according to the will
αὐτοῦ δαρήσεται πολλάς· **48** ὁ δὲ
of him will be beaten [with] many [stripes]; but the [one]
μὴ γνούς, ποιήσας δὲ ἄξια πληγῶν,
not having known, but having done things worthy of stripes,
δαρήσεται ὀλίγας. παντὶ δὲ ᾧ
will be beaten [with] few [stripes]. But to everyone to whom
ἐδόθη πολύ, πολὺ ζητηθήσεται παρ᾽ αὐτοῦ, καὶ
was given much, much will be demanded from him, and

them. 38It will be good for
those servants whose mas-
ter finds them ready, even
if he comes in the second or
third watch of the night.
39But understand this: If
the owner of the house had
known at what hour the
thief was coming, he would
not have let his house be
broken into. 40You also
must be ready, because the
Son of Man will come at an
hour when you do not ex-
pect him.”
41Peter asked, “Lord, are
you telling this parable to
us, or to everyone?”
42The Lord answered,
“Who then is the faithful
and wise manager, whom
the master puts in charge of
his servants to give them
their food allowance at the
proper time? 43It will be
good for that servant whom
the master finds doing so
when he returns. 44I tell
you the truth, he will put
him in charge of all his possessions. 45But suppose the
servant says to himself,
‘My master is taking a long
time in coming,’ and he
then begins to beat the
menservants and maidser-
vants and to eat and drink
and get drunk. 46The mas-
ter of that servant will
come on a day when he
does not expect him and at
an hour he is not aware of.
He will cut him to pieces
and assign him a place with
the unbelievers.
47“That servant who
knows his master's will and
does not get ready or does
not do what his master
wants will be beaten with
many blows. 48But the one
who does not know and
does things deserving punishment will be beaten with
few blows. From everyone
who has been given much,
much will be demanded;

whom they entrusted
much, of him they will ask
all the more.

Christ Divides Men

49"I have come to cast
fire upon the earth; and
how I wish it were already
kindled!
50"But I have a baptism
to undergo, and how dis-
tressed I am until it is accomplished!
51"Do you suppose that I
came to grant peace on
earth? I tell you, no, but
rather division;
52for from now on five
members in one household
will be divided, three
against two, and two
against three.
53"They will be divided,
father against son, and son
against father; mother
against daughter, and
daughter against mother;
mother-in-law against
daughter-in-law, and
daughter-in-law against
mother-in-law."
54And He was also saying
to the multitudes, "When
you see a cloud rising in the
west, immediately you say,
'A shower is coming,' and
so it turns out.
55"And when *you see* a
south wind blowing, you
say, 'It will be a hot day,'
and it turns out *that way*.
56"You hypocrites! You
know how to analyze the
appearance of the earth and
the sky, but why do you not
analyze this present time?
57"And why do you not
even on your own initiative
judge what is right?
58"For while you are go-
ing with your opponent to
appear before the magis-
trate, on *your* way *there*
make an effort to settle
with him, in order that he
may not drag you before
the judge, and the judge
turn you over to the constable, and the constable
throw you into prison.
59"I say to you, you shall
not get out of there until
you have paid the very last
cent."

Chapter 13

Call to Repent

NOW on the same occa-
sion there were some
present who reported to
Him about the Galileans,

ᾧ παρέθεντο πολύ, περισσότερον αἰτήσουσιν
with whom was deposited much, more exceedingly they will ask
αὐτόν. **49** Πῦρ ἦλθον βαλεῖν ἐπὶ τὴν γῆν,
him. Fire I came to cast on the earth,
καὶ τί θέλω εἰ ἤδη ἀνήφθη. **50** βάπτισμα
and what will I if already it was kindled. ³a baptism
δὲ ἔχω βαπτισθῆναι, καὶ πῶς συνέχομαι
¹And ²I have to be baptized [with], and how am I pressed
ἕως ὅτου τελεσθῇ. **51** δοκεῖτε ὅτι εἰρήνην
until it is accomplished. Think ye that peace
παρεγενόμην δοῦναι ἐν τῇ γῇ; οὐχί, λέγω
I came to give in the earth? No, I tell
ὑμῖν, ἀλλ' ἢ διαμερισμόν. **52** ἔσονται γὰρ
you, but rather division. For there will be
ἀπὸ τοῦ νῦν πέντε ἐν ἑνὶ οἴκῳ διαμεμε-
from – now five in one house *having been*
ρισμένοι, τρεῖς ἐπὶ δυσὶν καὶ δύο ἐπὶ
divided, three against two and two against
τρισὶν **53** διαμερισθήσονται, πατὴρ ἐπὶ υἱῷ
three will be divided, father against son
καὶ υἱὸς ἐπὶ πατρί, μήτηρ ἐπὶ θυγατέρα
and son against father, mother against daughter
καὶ θυγάτηρ ἐπὶ τὴν μητέρα, πενθερὰ
and daughter against the mother, mother-in-law
ἐπὶ τὴν νύμφην αὐτῆς καὶ νύμφη ἐπὶ
against the daughter-in-law of her and daughter-in-law against
τὴν πενθεράν. **54** Ἔλεγεν δὲ καὶ τοῖς
the mother-in-law. And he said also to the
ὄχλοις· ὅταν ἴδητε νεφέλην ἀνατέλλουσαν
crowds: When ye see a cloud rising
ἐπὶ δυσμῶν, εὐθέως λέγετε ὅτι ὄμβρος
over [the] west, immediately ye say that a storm
ἔρχεται, καὶ γίνεται οὕτως· **55** καὶ ὅταν
is coming, and it becomes so; and when
νότον πνέοντα, λέγετε ὅτι καύσων ἔσται,
a south wind blowing, ye say that heat there will be,
καὶ γίνεται. **56** ὑποκριταί, τὸ πρόσωπον
and it becomes. Hypocrites, the face
τῆς γῆς καὶ τοῦ οὐρανοῦ οἴδατε δοκιμάζειν,
of the earth and of the heaven ye know* to discern,
τὸν καιρὸν δὲ τοῦτον πῶς οὐ δοκιμάζετε;
– ³time ¹but ²this how do ye not discern?
57 Τί δὲ καὶ ἀφ' ἑαυτῶν οὐ κρίνετε
And why even from yourselves do ye not judge
τὸ δίκαιον; **58** ὡς γὰρ ὑπάγεις μετὰ τοῦ
the righteous thing? For as thou goest with the
ἀντιδίκου σου ἐπ' ἄρχοντα, ἐν τῇ ὁδῷ
adversary of thee to a ruler, in the way
δὸς ἐργασίαν ἀπηλλάχθαι ἀπ' αὐτοῦ, μήποτε
give(take) pains to be rid from(of) him, lest
κατασύρῃ σε πρὸς τὸν κριτήν, καὶ ὁ
he drag thee to the judge, and the
κριτής σε παραδώσει τῷ πράκτορι, καὶ ὁ
judge thee will deliver to the usher, and the
πράκτωρ σε βαλεῖ εἰς φυλακήν. **59** λέγω
usher thee will cast into prison. I tell
σοι, οὐ μὴ ἐξέλθῃς ἐκεῖθεν ἕως
thee, by no means mayest thou come out thence until
καὶ τὸ ἔσχατον λεπτὸν ἀποδῷς.
even the last lepton thou payest.

13 Παρῆσαν δέ τινες ἐν αὐτῷ τῷ
And there were present some at ²same ¹the
καιρῷ ἀπαγγέλλοντες αὐτῷ περὶ τῶν
time reporting to him about the

* can, as Mat. 16. 3.

and from the one who has
been entrusted with much,
much more will be asked.

Not Peace but Division

49"I have come to bring
fire on the earth, and how I
wish it were already kin-
dled! 50But I have a bap-
tism to undergo, and how
distressed I am until it is
completed! 51Do you think
I came to bring peace on
earth? No, I tell you, but
division. 52From now on
there will be five in one
family divided against each
other, three against two
and two against three.
53They will be divided, father against son and son
against father, mother
against daughter and
daughter against mother,
mother-in-law against
daughter-in-law and daughter-in-law against mother-
in-law."

Interpreting the Times

54He said to the crowd:
"When you see a cloud rising in the west, immediately you say, 'It's going to
rain,' and it does. 55And
when the south wind
blows, you say, 'It's going
to be hot,' and it is. 56Hyp-
ocrites! You know how to
interpret the appearance of
the earth and the sky. How
is it that you don't know
how to interpret this present time?
57"Why don't you judge
for yourselves what is
right? 58As you are going
with your adversary to the
magistrate, try hard to be
reconciled to him on the
way, or he may drag you off
to the judge, and the judge
turn you over to the officer,
and the officer throw you
into prison. 59I tell you, you
will not get out until you
have paid the last pen-
ny.[f]"

Chapter 13

Repent or Perish

NOW there were some
present at that time
who told Jesus about the

[f]59 Greek *lepton*

whose blood Pilate had
mingled with their sacri-
fices.
2 And He answered and
said to them, "Do you suppose that these Galileans
were *greater* sinners than
all *other* Galileans, because
they suffered this *fate?*
3 "I tell you, no, but, unless you repent, you will all
likewise perish.
4 "Or do you suppose
that those eighteen on
whom the tower in Siloam
fell and killed them, were
worse culprits than all the
men who live in Jerusalem?
5 "I tell you, no, but unless you repent, you will all
likewise perish."
6 And He *began* telling
this parable: "A certain
man had a fig tree which
had been planted in his
vineyard; and he came
looking for fruit on it, and
did not find any.
7 "And he said to the
vineyard-keeper, 'Behold,
for three years I have come
looking for fruit on this fig
tree without finding any.
Cut it down! Why does it
even use up the ground?'
8 "And he answered and
said to him, 'Let it alone,
sir, for this year too, until I
dig around it and put in fer-
tilizer;
9 and if it bears fruit next
year, *fine;* but if not, cut it
down.' "

Healing on the Sabbath

10 And He was teaching in
one of the synagogues on
the Sabbath.
11 And behold, there was a
woman who for eighteen
years had had a sickness
caused by a spirit; and she
was bent double, and could
not straighten up at all.
12 And when Jesus saw
her, He called her over and
said to her, "Woman, you
are freed from your sick-
ness."

Γαλιλαίων ὧν τὸ αἷμα Πιλᾶτος ἔμιξεν
Galilæans of whom the blood Pilate mixed
μετὰ τῶν θυσιῶν αὐτῶν. **2** καὶ ἀποκριθεὶς
with the sacrifices of them. And answering
εἶπεν αὐτοῖς· δοκεῖτε ὅτι οἱ Γαλιλαῖοι
he said to them : Think ye that – Galilæans
οὗτοι ἁμαρτωλοὶ παρὰ πάντας τοὺς Γαλι-
these sinners above all the Gali-
λαίους ἐγένοντο, ὅτι ταῦτα πεπόνθασιν;
læans were, because these things they have suffered?
3 οὐχί, λέγω ὑμῖν, ἀλλ' ἐὰν μὴ μετανοῆτε,
No, I tell you, but unless ye repent,
πάντες ὁμοίως ἀπολεῖσθε. **4** ἢ ἐκεῖνοι οἱ
all likewise ye will perish. Or those –
δεκαοκτὼ ἐφ' οὓς ἔπεσεν ὁ πύργος ἐν
eighteen on whom fell the tower in
τῷ Σιλωὰμ καὶ ἀπέκτεινεν αὐτούς, δοκεῖτε
– Siloam and killed them, think ye
ὅτι αὐτοὶ ὀφειλέται ἐγένοντο παρὰ πάντας
that they debtors were above all
τοὺς ἀνθρώπους τοὺς κατοικοῦντας Ἰερου-
the men – dwelling in Jeru-
σαλήμ; **5** οὐχί, λέγω ὑμῖν, ἀλλ' ἐὰν μὴ
salem? No, I tell you, but unless
μετανοήσητε, πάντες ὡσαύτως ἀπολεῖσθε.
ye repent, all similarly ye will perish.
6 Ἔλεγεν δὲ ταύτην τὴν παραβολήν. συκῆν
And he told this – parable. [2]A fig-tree
εἶχέν τις πεφυτευμένην ἐν τῷ ἀμπελῶνι
[3]had [1]a certain man *having been* planted in the vineyard
αὐτοῦ, καὶ ἦλθεν ζητῶν καρπὸν ἐν αὐτῇ
of him, and came seeking fruit in it
καὶ οὐχ εὗρεν. **7** εἶπεν δὲ πρὸς τὸν
and found not. And he said to the
ἀμπελουργόν· ἰδοὺ τρία ἔτη ἀφ' οὗ
vinedresser : Behold[,] three years [it is] since
ἔρχομαι ζητῶν καρπὸν ἐν τῇ συκῇ ταύτῃ
I come seeking fruit in – fig-tree this
καὶ οὐχ εὑρίσκω· ἔκκοψον αὐτήν· ἱνατί
and find not; cut down it; why
καὶ τὴν γῆν καταργεῖ; **8** ὁ δὲ ἀποκριθεὶς
even the ground it spoils? But he answering
λέγει αὐτῷ· κύριε, ἄφες αὐτὴν καὶ τοῦτο
says to him : Lord, leave it also this
τὸ ἔτος, ἕως ὅτου σκάψω περὶ αὐτὴν καὶ
– year, until I may dig round it and
βάλω κόπρια, **9** κἂν μὲν ποιήσῃ καρπὸν
may throw dung, and if indeed it makes fruit
εἰς τὸ μέλλον· εἰ δὲ μή γε, ἐκκόψεις
in the future; otherwise, thou shalt cut down
αὐτήν.
it.

10 Ἦν δὲ διδάσκων ἐν μιᾷ τῶν συναγωγῶν
And he was teaching in one of the synagogues
ἐν τοῖς σάββασιν. **11** καὶ ἰδοὺ γυνὴ
on the sabbaths. And[,] behold[,] a woman
πνεῦμα ἔχουσα ἀσθενείας ἔτη δεκαοκτώ,
[2]a spirit [1]having of infirmity years eighteen,
καὶ ἦν συγκύπτουσα καὶ μὴ δυναμένη
and was bending double and not being able
ἀνακῦψαι εἰς τὸ παντελές. **12** ἰδὼν δὲ
to become erect entirely.† And seeing
αὐτὴν ὁ Ἰησοῦς προσεφώνησεν καὶ εἶπεν
her – Jesus called to [him] and said
αὐτῇ· γύναι, ἀπολέλυσαι τῆς ἀσθενείας
to her : Woman, thou hast been loosed from the infirmity

Galileans whose blood Pi-
late had mixed with their
sacrifices. 2 Jesus an-
swered, "Do you think that
these Galileans were worse
sinners than all the other
Galileans because they suffered this way? 3 I tell you,
no! But unless you repent,
you too will all perish. 4 Or
those eighteen who died
when the tower in Siloam
fell on them—do you think
they were more guilty than
all the others living in Jerusalem? 5 I tell you, no! But
unless you repent, you too
will all perish."
6 Then he told this para-
ble: "A man had a fig tree,
planted in his vineyard, and
he went to look for fruit on
it, but did not find any. 7 So
he said to the man who took
care of the vineyard, 'For
three years now I've been
coming to look for fruit on
this fig tree and haven't
found any. Cut it down!
Why should it use up the
soil?'
8 " 'Sir,' the man replied,
'leave it alone for one more
year, and I'll dig around it
and fertilize it. 9 If it bears
fruit next year, fine! If not,
then cut it down.' "

A Crippled Woman Healed on the Sabbath

10 On a Sabbath Jesus was
teaching in one of the synagogues, 11 and a woman was
there who had been crip-
pled by a spirit for eighteen
years. She was bent over
and could not straighten up
at all. 12 When Jesus saw
her, he called her forward
and said to her, "Woman,
you are set free from your

13And He laid His hands upon her; and immediately she was made erect again, and *began* glorifying God.
14And the synagogue official, indignant because Jesus had healed on the Sabbath, *began* saying to the multitude in response, "There are six days in which work should be done; therefore come during them and get healed, and not on the Sabbath day."
15But the Lord answered him and said, "You hypocrites, does not each of you on the Sabbath untie his ox or his donkey from the stall, and lead him away to water *him?*
16"And this woman, a daughter of Abraham as she is, whom Satan has bound for eighteen long years, should she not have been released from this bond on the Sabbath day?"
17And as He said this, all His opponents were being humiliated; and the entire multitude was rejoicing over all the glorious things being done by Him.

Parables of Mustard Seed and Leaven

18Therefore He was saying, "What is the kingdom of God like, and to what shall I compare it?
19"It is like a mustard seed, which a man took and threw into his own garden; and it grew and became a tree; and THE BIRDS OF THE AIR NESTED IN ITS BRANCHES."
20And again He said, "To what shall I compare the kingdom of God?
21"It is like leaven, which a woman took and hid in three pecks of meal, until it was all leavened."

Teaching in the Villages

22And He was passing through from one city and village to another, teaching, and proceeding on His way to Jerusalem.
23And someone said to

σου, 13 καὶ ἐπέθηκεν αὐτῇ τὰς χεῖρας·
of thee, and he put on her the(his) hands;
καὶ παραχρῆμα ἀνωρθώθη, καὶ ἐδόξαζεν
and at once she was straightened, and glorified
τὸν θεόν. 14 ἀποκριθεὶς δὲ ὁ ἀρχι-
– God. But answering the syn-
συνάγωγος, ἀγανακτῶν ὅτι τῷ σαββάτῳ
agogue ruler, being angry that [3]on the [4]sabbath
ἐθεράπευσεν ὁ Ἰησοῦς, ἔλεγεν τῷ ὄχλῳ
[2]healed – [1]Jesus, said to the crowd[,]
ὅτι ἓξ ἡμέραι εἰσὶν ἐν αἷς δεῖ ἐργάζεσθαι·
– six days there are on which it behoves to work;
ἐν αὐταῖς οὖν ἐρχόμενοι θεραπεύεσθε καὶ
on them therefore coming be ye healed and
μὴ τῇ ἡμέρᾳ τοῦ σαββάτου. 15 ἀπεκρίθη δὲ
not on the day of the sabbath. But answered
αὐτῷ ὁ κύριος καὶ εἶπεν· ὑποκριταί,
him the Lord and said: Hypocrites,
ἕκαστος ὑμῶν τῷ σαββάτῳ οὐ λύει τὸν
each one of you on the sabbath does he not loosen the
βοῦν αὐτοῦ ἢ τὸν ὄνον ἀπὸ τῆς φάτνης
ox of him or the ass from the manger
καὶ ἀπαγαγὼν ποτίζει; 16 ταύτην δὲ
and leading [it] away give drink? And this woman
θυγατέρα Ἀβραὰμ οὖσαν, ἣν ἔδησεν ὁ
a daughter of Abraham being, whom bound –
σατανᾶς ἰδοὺ δέκα καὶ ὀκτὼ ἔτη, οὐκ ἔδει
Satan behold ten and eight years, behoved it not
λυθῆναι ἀπὸ τοῦ δεσμοῦ τούτου τῇ
to be loosened from – bond this on the
ἡμέρᾳ τοῦ σαββάτου; 17 καὶ ταῦτα λέγοντος
day of the sabbath? And these things saying
=when he said these things
αὐτοῦ κατῃσχύνοντο πάντες οἱ ἀντικείμενοι
him[a] were put to shame all the [ones] opposing
αὐτῷ, καὶ πᾶς ὁ ὄχλος ἔχαιρεν ἐπὶ
him, and all the crowd rejoiced over
πᾶσιν τοῖς ἐνδόξοις τοῖς γινομένοις ὑπ'
all the glorious things – happening by
αὐτοῦ. 18 Ἔλεγεν οὖν· τίνι ὁμοία ἐστὶν ἡ
him. He said therefore: To what like is the
βασιλεία τοῦ θεοῦ, καὶ τίνι ὁμοιώσω
kingdom – of God, and to what may I liken
αὐτήν; 19 ὁμοία ἐστὶν κόκκῳ σινάπεως, ὃν
it? Like it is to a grain of mustard, which
λαβὼν ἄνθρωπος ἔβαλεν εἰς κῆπον ἑαυτοῦ,
[2]taking [1]a man cast into a garden of him*self*,
καὶ ηὔξησεν καὶ ἐγένετο εἰς δένδρον, καὶ
and it grew and became into a tree, and
τὰ πετεινὰ τοῦ οὐρανοῦ κατεσκήνωσεν
the birds of the heaven(air) lodged
ἐν τοῖς κλάδοις αὐτοῦ. 20 Καὶ πάλιν
in the branches of it. And again
εἶπεν· τίνι ὁμοιώσω τὴν βασιλείαν τοῦ
he said: To what may I liken the kingdom –
θεοῦ; 21 ὁμοία ἐστὶν ζύμῃ, ἣν λαβοῦσα
of God? Like it is to leaven, which [2]taking
γυνὴ ἔκρυψεν εἰς ἀλεύρου σάτα τρία,
[1]a woman hid in of meal measures three,
ἕως οὗ ἐζυμώθη ὅλον.
until was leavened all.
22 Καὶ διεπορεύετο κατὰ πόλεις καὶ
And he journeyed *through* throughout cities and
κώμας διδάσκων καὶ πορείαν ποιούμενος
villages teaching and journey making
εἰς Ἱεροσόλυμα. 23 Εἶπεν δέ τις αὐτῷ·
to Jerusalem. And said someone to him:

infirmity." 13Then he put his hands on her, and immediately she straightened up and praised God.
14Indignant because Jesus had healed on the Sabbath, the synagogue ruler said to the people, "There are six days for work. So come and be healed on those days, not on the Sabbath."
15The Lord answered him, "You hypocrites! Doesn't each of you on the Sabbath untie his ox or donkey from the stall and lead it out to give it water? 16Then should not this woman, a daughter of Abraham, whom Satan has kept bound for eighteen long years, be set free on the Sabbath day from what bound her?"
17When he said this, all his opponents were humiliated, but the people were delighted with all the wonderful things he was doing.

The Parables of the Mustard Seed and the Yeast

18Then Jesus asked, "What is the kingdom of God like? What shall I compare it to? 19It is like a mustard seed, which a man took and planted in his garden. It grew and became a tree, and the birds of the air perched in its branches."
20Again he asked, "What shall I compare the kingdom of God to? 21It is like yeast that a woman took and mixed into a large amount[g] of flour until it worked all through the dough."

The Narrow Door

22Then Jesus went through the towns and villages, teaching as he made his way to Jerusalem. 23Someone asked him,

[g]*21* Greek *three satas* (probably about 1/2 bushel or 22 liters)

Him, "Lord, are there *just* a few who are being saved?" And He said to them,

24"Strive to enter by the narrow door; for many, I tell you, will seek to enter and will not be able.

25"Once the head of the house gets up and shuts the door, and you begin to stand outside and knock on the door, saying, 'Lord, open up to us!' then He will answer and say to you, 'I do not know where you are from.'

26"Then you will begin to say, 'We ate and drank in Your presence, and You taught in our streets';

27and He will say, 'I tell you, I do not know where you are from; DEPART FROM ME, ALL YOU EVILDOERS.'

28"There will be weeping and gnashing of teeth there when you see Abraham and Isaac and Jacob and all the prophets in the kingdom of God, but yourselves being cast out.

29"And they will come from east and west, and from north and south, and will recline *at the table* in the kingdom of God.

30"And behold, *some* are last who will be first and *some* are first who will be last."

31Just at that time some Pharisees came up, saying to Him, "Go away and depart from here, for Herod wants to kill You."

32And He said to them, "Go and tell that fox, 'Behold, I cast out demons and perform cures today and tomorrow, and the third *day* I reach My goal.'

33"Nevertheless I must journey on today and tomorrow and the next *day;* for it cannot be that a prophet should perish outside of Jerusalem.

34"O Jerusalem, Jerusa-

κύριε, εἰ ὀλίγοι οἱ σῳζόμενοι; ὁ δὲ εἶπεν
Lord, if few the [ones] being saved? And he said
πρὸς αὐτούς· **24** ἀγωνίζεσθε εἰσελθεῖν διὰ
to them: Struggle to enter through
τῆς στενῆς θύρας, ὅτι πολλοί, λέγω ὑμῖν,
the strait door, because many, I tell you,
ζητήσουσιν εἰσελθεῖν καὶ οὐκ ἰσχύσουσιν.
will seek to enter and will not be able.
25 ἀφ' οὗ ἂν ἐγερθῇ ὁ οἰκοδεσπότης καὶ
From [the time] when is risen the house-master and
ἀποκλείσῃ τὴν θύραν, καὶ ἄρξησθε ἔξω
he shuts the door, and ye begin outside
ἑστάναι καὶ κρούειν τὴν θύραν λέγοντες·
to stand and to knock the door saying:
κύριε, ἄνοιξον ἡμῖν, καὶ ἀποκριθεὶς ἐρεῖ
Lord, open to us, and answering he will say
ὑμῖν· οὐκ οἶδα ὑμᾶς πόθεν ἐστέ. **26** τότε
to you: I know not you whence ye are. Then
ἄρξεσθε λέγειν· ἐφάγομεν ἐνώπιόν σου καὶ
ye will begin to say: We ate before thee and
ἐπίομεν, καὶ ἐν ταῖς πλατείαις ἡμῶν
drank, and in the streets of us
ἐδίδαξας· **27** καὶ ἐρεῖ λέγων ὑμῖν· οὐκ
thou didst teach; and he will say telling you: not
οἶδα πόθεν ἐστέ· ἀποστητε ἀπ' ἐμοῦ
I know whence ye are; stand away from me
πάντες ἐργάται ἀδικίας. **28** ἐκεῖ ἔσται ὁ
all workers of unrighteousness. There will be the
κλαυθμὸς καὶ ὁ βρυγμὸς τῶν ὀδόντων,
weeping and the gnashing of the teeth,
ὅταν ὄψησθε Ἀβραὰμ καὶ Ἰσαὰκ καὶ
when ye see Abraham and Isaac and
Ἰακὼβ καὶ πάντας τοὺς προφήτας ἐν τῇ
Jacob and all the prophets in the
βασιλείᾳ τοῦ θεοῦ, ὑμᾶς δὲ ἐκβαλλομένους
kingdom – of God, but you being thrust *out*
ἔξω. **29** καὶ ἥξουσιν ἀπὸ ἀνατολῶν καὶ
outside. And they will come from east and
δυσμῶν καὶ ἀπὸ βορρᾶ καὶ νότου, καὶ
west and from north and south, and
ἀνακλιθήσονται ἐν τῇ βασιλείᾳ τοῦ θεοῦ.
will recline in the kingdom – of God.
30 καὶ ἰδοὺ εἰσὶν ἔσχατοι οἳ ἔσονται
And behold there are last [ones] who will be
πρῶτοι, καὶ εἰσὶν πρῶτοι οἳ ἔσονται
first, and there are first [ones] who will be
ἔσχατοι. **31** Ἐν αὐτῇ τῇ ὥρᾳ προσῆλθάν
last. In [2]same [1]the hour approached
τινες Φαρισαῖοι λέγοντες αὐτῷ· ἔξελθε καὶ
some Pharisees saying to him: Depart and
πορεύου ἐντεῦθεν, ὅτι Ἡρῴδης θέλει σε
go hence, because Herod wishes thee
ἀποκτεῖναι. **32** καὶ εἶπεν αὐτοῖς· πορευθέντες
to kill. And he said to them: Going
εἴπατε τῇ ἀλώπεκι ταύτῃ· ἰδοὺ ἐκβάλλω
tell – fox this: Behold I expel
δαιμόνια καὶ ἰάσεις ἀποτελῶ σήμερον καὶ
demons and [2]cures [1]accomplish to-day and
αὔριον, καὶ τῇ τρίτῃ τελειοῦμαι. **33** πλὴν
to-morrow, and on the third [day] I am perfected. Nevertheless
δεῖ με σήμερον καὶ αὔριον καὶ τῇ ἐχομένῃ
it behoves me to-day and to-morrow and on the following [day]
πορεύεσθαι, ὅτι οὐκ ἐνδέχεται προφήτην
to journey, because it is not possible a prophet
ἀπολέσθαι ἔξω Ἰερουσαλήμ. **34** Ἰερουσαλὴμ
to perish outside Jerusalem. Jerusalem[,]

"Lord, are only a few people going to be saved?"
He said to them, 24"Make
every effort to enter
through the narrow door,
because many, I tell you,
will try to enter and will not
be able to. 25Once the owner of the house gets up and
closes the door, you will
stand outside knocking and
pleading, 'Sir, open the
door for us.'
"But he will answer, 'I
don't know you or where
you come from.'
26"Then you will say,
'We ate and drank with
you, and you taught in our
streets.'
27"But he will reply, 'I
don't know you or where
you come from. Away from
me, all you evildoers!'
28"There will be weeping
there, and gnashing of
teeth, when you see Abra-
ham, Isaac and Jacob and
all the prophets in the kingdom of God, but you your-
selves thrown out. 29People
will come from east and
west and north and south,
and will take their places at
the feast in the kingdom of
God. 30Indeed there are
those who are last who will
be first, and first who will
be last."

Jesus' Sorrow for Jerusalem

31At that time some Phar-
isees came to Jesus and
said to him, "Leave this
place and go somewhere
else. Herod wants to kill
you."
32He replied, "Go tell
that fox, 'I will drive out
demons and heal people to-
day and tomorrow, and on
the third day I will reach
my goal.' 33In any case, I
must keep going today and
tomorrow and the next day
—for surely no prophet can
die outside Jerusalem!
34"O Jerusalem, Jerusa-

lem, *the city* that kills the
prophets and stones those
sent to her! How often I
wanted to gather your children together, just as a hen
gathers her brood under
her wings, and you would
not *have it!*
35“Behold, your house is
left to you *desolate;* and I
say to you, you shall not
see Me until *the time* comes
when you say, ‘BLESSED IS
HE WHO COMES IN THE NAME
OF THE LORD!’ ”

Chapter 14

Jesus Heals on the Sabbath

AND it came about when
He went into the
house of one of the leaders
of the Pharisees on *the* Sabbath to eat bread, that they
were watching Him close-
ly.
2And there, in front of
Him was a certain man suffering from dropsy.
3And Jesus answered
and spoke to the lawyers
and Pharisees, saying, “Is
it lawful to heal on the Sabbath, or not?”
4But they kept silent.
And He took hold of him,
and healed him, and sent
him away.
5And He said to them,
“Which one of you shall
have a son or an ox fall into
a well, and will not immediately pull him out on a Sabbath day?”
6And they could make
no reply to this.

Parable of the Guests

7And He *began* speaking
a parable to the invited
guests when He noticed
how they had been picking
out the places of honor *at
the table;* saying to them,
8“When you are invited
by someone to a wedding
feast, do not take the place
of honor, lest someone
more distinguished than
you may have been invited
by him,
9and he who invited you
both shall come and say to
you, ‘Give place to this
man,’ and then in disgrace
you proceed to occupy the
last place.

Ἰερουσαλήμ, ἡ ἀποκτείνουσα τοὺς προφήτας
Jerusalem, the [one] killing the prophets
καὶ λιθοβολοῦσα τοὺς ἀπεσταλμένους πρὸς
and stoning the [ones] *having been* sent to
αὐτήν, ποσάκις ἠθέλησα ἐπισυνάξαι τὰ
her, how often I wished to gather the
τέκνα σου ὃν τρόπον ὄρνις τὴν ἑαυτῆς
children of thee as † a bird the of herself
νοσσιὰν ὑπὸ τὰς πτέρυγας, καὶ οὐκ
brood under the(her) wings, and not
ἠθελήσατε. 35 ἰδοὺ ἀφίεται ὑμῖν ὁ οἶκος
ye wished. Behold is left to you the house
ὑμῶν. λέγω [δὲ] ὑμῖν, οὐ μὴ ἴδητέ με
of you. And I tell you, by no means ye may see me
ἕως ἥξει ὅτε εἴπητε· εὐλογημένος ὁ
until shall come [the time] when ye say: Blessed the
ἐρχόμενος ἐν ὀνόματι κυρίου.
[one] coming in [the] name of [the] Lord.

14 Καὶ ἐγένετο ἐν τῷ ἐλθεῖν αὐτὸν εἰς
And it came to pass in the to go him[be] into
=as he went
οἶκόν τινος τῶν ἀρχόντων τῶν Φαρισαίων
a house of one of the leaders of the Pharisees
σαββάτῳ φαγεῖν ἄρτον, καὶ αὐτοὶ ἦσαν
on a sabbath to eat bread, *and* they were
παρατηρούμενοι αὐτόν. 2 καὶ ἰδοὺ ἄνθρωπός
carefully watching him. And[,] behold[,] man
τις ἦν ὑδρωπικὸς ἔμπροσθεν αὐτοῦ. 3 καὶ
a certain was dropsical before him. And
ἀποκριθεὶς ὁ Ἰησοῦς εἶπεν πρὸς τοὺς
answering – Jesus spoke to the
νομικοὺς καὶ Φαρισαίους λέγων· ἔξεστιν
lawyers and Pharisees saying: Is it lawful
τῷ σαββάτῳ θεραπεῦσαι ἢ οὔ; 4 οἱ δὲ
on the sabbath to heal or not? And they
ἡσύχασαν. καὶ ἐπιλαβόμενος ἰάσατο αὐτὸν
were silent. And taking he cured him
καὶ ἀπέλυσεν. 5 καὶ πρὸς αὐτοὺς εἶπεν·
and dismissed. And to them he said:
τίνος ὑμῶν υἱὸς ἢ βοῦς εἰς φρέαρ πεσεῖται,
Of whom of you a son or an ox into a pit shall fall,
καὶ οὐκ εὐθέως ἀνασπάσει αὐτὸν ἐν
and not immediately he will pull up it on
ἡμέρᾳ τοῦ σαββάτου; 6 καὶ οὐκ ἴσχυσαν
a day of the sabbath? And they were not able
ἀνταποκριθῆναι πρὸς ταῦτα. 7 Ἔλεγεν δὲ
to reply against these things. And he said
πρὸς τοὺς κεκλημένους παραβολήν, ἐπέχων
to the [ones] *having been* invited a parable, noting
πῶς τὰς πρωτοκλισίας ἐξελέγοντο, λέγων
how [2]the [3]chief seats [1]they were choosing, saying
πρὸς αὐτούς· 8 ὅταν κληθῇς ὑπό τινος εἰς
to them: When thou art invited by anyone to
γάμους, μὴ κατακλιθῇς εἰς τὴν πρωτοκλισίαν,
wedding festivities, do not recline in the chief seat,
μήποτε ἐντιμότερός σου ᾖ κεκλημένος ὑπ᾽
lest a more honourable [than] thou be *having been* invited by
αὐτοῦ, 9 καὶ ἐλθὼν ὁ σὲ καὶ αὐτὸν καλέσας
him, and coming [1]the [one] [3]thee [4]and [5]him [2]inviting
ἐρεῖ σοι· δὸς τούτῳ τόπον, καὶ τότε
will say to thee: Give this man place, and then
ἄρξῃ μετὰ αἰσχύνης τὸν ἔσχατον τόπον
thou wilt begin with shame the last place

lem, you who kill the
prophets and stone those
sent to you, how often I
have longed to gather your
children together, as a hen
gathers her chicks under
her wings, but you were not
willing! 35Look, your house
is left to you desolate. I tell
you, you will not see me
again until you say,
‘Blessed is he who comes
in the name of the Lord.’[h] ”

Chapter 14

Jesus at a Pharisee's House

ONE Sabbath, when
Jesus went to eat in
the house of a prominent
Pharisee, he was being
carefully watched. 2There
in front of him was a man
suffering from dropsy.
3Jesus asked the Pharisees
and experts in the law, “Is
it lawful to heal on the Sabbath or not?” 4But they remained silent. So taking
hold of the man, he healed
him and sent him away.
5Then he asked them, “If
one of you has a son[i] or an
ox that falls into a well on
the Sabbath day, will you
not immediately pull him
out?” 6And they had noth-
ing to say.
7When he noticed how
the guests picked the
places of honor at the table,
he told them this parable:
8“When someone invites
you to a wedding feast, do
not take the place of honor,
for a person more distin-
guished than you may have
been invited. 9If so, the
host who invited both of
you will come and say to
you, ‘Give this man your
seat.’ Then, humiliated,
you will have to take the
least important place. 10But

[h]35 Psalm 118:26
[i]5 Some manuscripts *donkey*

10“But when you are invited, go and recline at the last place, so that when the one who has invited you comes, he may say to you, ‘Friend, move up higher’; then you will have honor in the sight of all who are at the table with you.

11“For everyone who exalts himself shall be humbled, and he who humbles himself shall be exalted.”

12And He also went on to say to the one who had invited Him, “When you give a luncheon or a dinner, do not invite your friends or your brothers or your relatives or rich neighbors, lest they also invite you in return, and repayment come to you.

13“But when you give a reception, invite *the* poor, *the* crippled, *the* lame, *the* blind,

14and you will be blessed, since they do not have *the means* to repay you; for you will be repaid at the resurrection of the righteous.”

15And when one of those who were reclining *at the table* with Him heard this, he said to Him, “Blessed is everyone who shall eat bread in the kingdom of God!”

Parable of the Dinner

16But He said to him, “A certain man was giving a big dinner, and he invited many;

17and at the dinner hour he sent his slave to say to those who had been invited, ‘Come; for everything is ready now.’

18“But they all alike began to make excuses. The first one said to him, ‘I have bought a piece of land and I need to go out and look at it; please consider me excused.’

19“And another one said, ‘I have bought five yoke of oxen, and I am going to try them out; please consider me excused.’

20“And another one said, ‘I have married a wife, and

κατέχειν. 10 ἀλλ’ ὅταν κληθῇς, πορευθεὶς
to take. But when thou art invited, going

ἀνάπεσε εἰς τὸν ἔσχατον τόπον, ἵνα ὅταν ἔλθῃ
recline in the last place, that when [4]comes

ὁ κεκληκώς σε ἐρεῖ σοι· φίλε,
[1]the [one] [2]having invited [3]thee he will say to thee : Friend,

προσανάβηθι ἀνώτερον· τότε ἔσται σοι δόξα
go up higher; then there will be to thee[c] glory

ἐνώπιον πάντων τῶν συνανακειμένων σοι.
before all the [ones] reclining with thee.

11 ὅτι πᾶς ὁ ὑψῶν ἑαυτὸν ταπεινωθήσεται,
Because everyone exalting himself will be humbled,

καὶ ὁ ταπεινῶν ἑαυτὸν ὑψωθήσεται.
and the [one] humbling himself will be exalted.

12 Ἔλεγεν δὲ καὶ τῷ κεκληκότι αὐτόν·
And he said also to the [one] having invited him :

ὅταν ποιῇς ἄριστον ἢ δεῖπνον, μὴ φώνει
When thou makest a dinner or a supper, do not call

τοὺς φίλους σου μηδὲ τοὺς ἀδελφούς
the friends of thee nor the brothers

σου μηδὲ τοὺς συγγενεῖς σου μηδὲ
of thee nor the relatives of thee nor

γείτονας πλουσίους, μήποτε καὶ αὐτοὶ
neighbours rich, lest also they

ἀντικαλέσωσίν σε καὶ γένηται ἀνταπόδομά
[1]invite [3]in [4]return [2]thee and it becomes a recompence

σοι. 13 ἀλλ’ ὅταν δοχὴν ποιῇς, κάλει
to thee. But when a party thou makest, invite

πτωχούς, ἀναπήρους, χωλούς, τυφλούς·
poor [persons], maimed, lame, blind;

14 καὶ μακάριος ἔσῃ, ὅτι οὐκ ἔχουσιν
and blessed thou shalt be, because they have not

ἀνταποδοῦναί σοι· ἀνταποδοθήσεται γάρ σοι
to recompense thee; for it will be recompensed to thee

ἐν τῇ ἀναστάσει τῶν δικαίων. 15 Ἀκούσας
in the resurrection of the just. [2]hearing

δέ τις τῶν συνανακειμένων ταῦτα εἶπεν
[1]And [4]one [5]of the [ones] [6]reclining with [3]these things said

αὐτῷ· μακάριος ὅστις φάγεται ἄρτον ἐν
to him : Blessed [is he] who shall eat bread in

τῇ βασιλείᾳ τοῦ θεοῦ. 16 ὁ δὲ εἶπεν
the kingdom – of God. And he said

αὐτῷ· ἄνθρωπός τις ἐποίει δεῖπνον μέγα,
to him : A certain man made supper a great,

καὶ ἐκάλεσεν πολλούς, 17 καὶ ἀπέστειλεν
and invited many, and sent

τὸν δοῦλον αὐτοῦ τῇ ὥρᾳ τοῦ δείπνου
the slave of him at the hour of the supper

εἰπεῖν τοῖς κεκλημένοις· ἔρχεσθε, ὅτι ἤδη
to say to the [ones] having been invited : Come, because [2]now

ἕτοιμά ἐστιν. 18 καὶ ἤρξαντο ἀπὸ μιᾶς
[3]prepared [1]it is. And they began from one [mind]

πάντες παραιτεῖσθαι. ὁ πρῶτος εἶπεν
all to beg off. The first said

αὐτῷ· ἀγρὸν ἠγόρασα, καὶ ἔχω ἀνάγκην
to him : [2]A farm [1]I bought, and I am obliged†

ἐξελθὼν ἰδεῖν αὐτόν· ἐρωτῶ σε, ἔχε με
going out to see it; I ask thee, have me

παρῃτημένον. 19 καὶ ἕτερος εἶπεν· ζεύγη
begged off. And another said : [3]Yoke

βοῶν ἠγόρασα πέντε, καὶ πορεύομαι
[4]of oxen [1]I bought [2]five, and I am going

δοκιμάσαι αὐτά· ἐρωτῶ σε, ἔχε με
to prove them; I ask thee, have me

παρῃτημένον. 20 καὶ ἕτερος εἶπεν· γυναῖκα
begged off. And another said : [2]A wife

when you are invited, take
the lowest place, so that
when your host comes, he
will say to you, ‘Friend,
move up to a better place.’
Then you will be honored
in the presence of all your
fellow guests. 11For everyone who exalts himself will
be humbled, and he who
humbles himself will be exalted.”
12Then Jesus said to his
host, “When you give a
luncheon or dinner, do not
invite your friends, your
brothers or relatives, or
your rich neighbors; if you
do, they may invite you
back and so you will be repaid. 13But when you give a
banquet, invite the poor,
the crippled, the lame, the
blind, 14and you will be
blessed. Although they
cannot repay you, you will
be repaid at the resurrection of the righteous.”

The Parable of the Great Banquet

15When one of those at
the table with him heard
this, he said to Jesus,
“Blessed is the man who
will eat at the feast in the
kingdom of God.”
16Jesus replied: “A cer-
tain man was preparing a
great banquet and invited
many guests. 17At the time
of the banquet he sent his
servant to tell those who
had been invited, ‘Come,
for everything is now
ready.’
18“But they all alike be-
gan to make excuses. The
first said, ‘I have just
bought a field, and I must
go and see it. Please excuse
me.’
19“Another said, ‘I have
just bought five yoke of
oxen, and I’m on my way to
try them out. Please excuse
me.’
20“Still another said, ‘I

for that reason I cannot
come.'
21"And the slave came
back and reported this to
his master. Then the head
of the household became
angry and said to his slave,
'Go out at once into the
streets and lanes of the city
and bring in here the poor
and crippled and blind and
lame.'
22"And the slave said,
'Master, what you com-
manded has been done, and
still there is room.'
23"And the master said to
the slave, 'Go out into the
highways and along the
hedges, and compel *them*
to come in, that my house
may be filled.
24'For I tell you, none of
those men who were in-
vited shall taste of my dinner.' "

Discipleship Tested

25Now great multitudes
were going along with Him;
and He turned and said to
them,
26"If anyone comes to
Me, and does not [b]hate his
own father and mother and
wife and children and
brothers and sisters, yes,
and even his own life, he
cannot be My disciple.
27"Whoever does not car-
ry his own cross and come
after Me cannot be My disciple.
28"For which one of you,
when he wants to build a
tower, does not first sit
down and calculate the
cost, to see if he has enough
to complete it?
29"Otherwise, when he
has laid a foundation, and is
not able to finish, all who
observe it begin to ridicule
him,
30saying, 'This man began
to build and was not able to
finish.'
31"Or what king, when he
sets out to meet another

ἔγημα, καὶ διὰ τοῦτο οὐ δύναμαι ἐλθεῖν.
[1]I married, and therefore I cannot *to* come.
21 καὶ παραγενόμενος ὁ δοῦλος ἀπήγγειλεν
And coming up the slave reported
τῷ κυρίῳ αὐτοῦ ταῦτα. τότε ὀργισθεὶς ὁ
to the lord of him these things. Then being angry the
οἰκοδεσπότης εἶπεν τῷ δούλῳ αὐτοῦ· ἔξελθε
house-master told the slave of him : Go out
ταχέως εἰς τὰς πλατείας καὶ ῥύμας τῆς
quickly into the streets and lanes of the
πόλεως, καὶ τοὺς πτωχοὺς καὶ ἀναπήρους
city, and the poor and maimed
καὶ τυφλοὺς καὶ χωλοὺς εἰσάγαγε ὧδε.
and blind and lame bring in here.
22 καὶ εἶπεν ὁ δοῦλος· κύριε, γέγονεν ὃ
And said the slave : Lord, has happened what
ἐπέταξας, καὶ ἔτι τόπος ἐστίν. 23 καὶ
thou didst command, and yet room there is. And
εἶπεν ὁ κύριος πρὸς τὸν δοῦλον· ἔξελθε εἰς
said the lord to the slave : Go out into
τὰς ὁδοὺς καὶ φραγμοὺς καὶ ἀνάγκασον
the ways and hedges and compel
εἰσελθεῖν, ἵνα γεμισθῇ μου ὁ οἶκος·
to come in, that may be filled of me the house ;
24 λέγω γὰρ ὑμῖν ὅτι οὐδεὶς τῶν ἀνδρῶν
for I tell you that not one – men
ἐκείνων τῶν κεκλημένων γεύσεταί μου
of those – having been invited shall taste of me
τοῦ δείπνου.
the supper.
25 Συνεπορεύοντο δὲ αὐτῷ ὄχλοι πολλοί,
And came together to him crowds many,
καὶ στραφεὶς εἶπεν πρὸς αὐτούς· 26 εἴ τις
and turning he said to them : If anyone
ἔρχεται πρός με καὶ οὐ μισεῖ τὸν πατέρα
comes to me and hates not the father
αὐτοῦ καὶ τὴν μητέρα καὶ τὴν γυναῖκα
of him and the mother and the wife
καὶ τὰ τέκνα καὶ τοὺς ἀδελφοὺς καὶ τὰς
and the children and the brothers and the
ἀδελφάς, ἔτι τε καὶ τὴν ψυχὴν ἑαυτοῦ,
sisters, and besides also the life of himself,
οὐ δύναται εἶναί μου μαθητής. 27 ὅστις
he cannot *to* be of me a disciple. Who
οὐ βαστάζει τὸν σταυρὸν ἑαυτοῦ καὶ
bears not the cross of himself and
ἔρχεται ὀπίσω μου, οὐ δύναται εἶναί μου
comes after me, he cannot *to* be of me
μαθητής. 28 Τίς γὰρ ἐξ ὑμῶν θέλων
a disciple. For who of you wishing
πύργον οἰκοδομῆσαι οὐχὶ πρῶτον καθίσας
a tower to build not first sitting
ψηφίζει τὴν δαπάνην, εἰ ἔχει εἰς ἀπαρ-
counts the cost, if he has for com-
τισμόν; 29 ἵνα μή ποτε θέντος αὐτοῦ
pletion? Lest when laying him[a]
=he has laid
θεμέλιον καὶ μὴ ἰσχύοντος ἐκτελέσαι πάντες
a foundation and not being able[a] to finish all
οἱ θεωροῦντες ἄρξωνται αὐτῷ ἐμπαίζειν
the [ones] seeing begin him to mock
30 λέγοντες ὅτι οὗτος ὁ ἄνθρωπος ἤρξατο
saying[,] – This – man began
οἰκοδομεῖν καὶ οὐκ ἴσχυσεν ἐκτελέσαι.
to build and was not able to finish.
31 Ἢ τίς βασιλεὺς πορευόμενος ἑτέρῳ βασιλεῖ
Or what king [1]going [5]another [6]king

just got married, so I can't
come.'
21"The servant came
back and reported this to
his master. Then the owner
of the house became angry
and ordered his servant,
'Go out quickly into the
streets and alleys of the
town and bring in the poor,
the crippled, the blind and
the lame.'
22" 'Sir,' the servant
said, 'what you ordered has
been done, but there is still
room.'
23"Then the master told
his servant, 'Go out to the
roads and country lanes
and make them come in, so
that my house will be full.
24I tell you, not one of those
men who were invited will
get a taste of my ban-
quet.' "

The Cost of Being a Disciple

25Large crowds were
traveling with Jesus, and
turning to them he said:
26"If anyone comes to me
and does not hate his father
and mother, his wife and
children, his brothers and
sisters—yes, even his own
life—he cannot be my dis-
ciple. 27And anyone who
does not carry his cross and
follow me cannot be my
disciple.
28"Suppose one of you
wants to build a tower. Will
he not first sit down and es-
timate the cost to see if he
has enough money to com-
plete it? 29For if he lays the
foundation and is not able
to finish it, everyone who
sees it will ridicule him,
30saying, 'This fellow began to build and was not
able to finish.'
31"Or suppose a king is
about to go to war against

[b]I.e., by comparison of his love for Me

king in battle, will not first
sit down and take counsel
whether he is strong
enough with ten thousand
men to encounter the one
coming against him with
twenty thousand?
32"Or else, while the
other is still far away, he
sends a delegation and asks
terms of peace.
33"So therefore, no one
of you can be My disciple
who does not give up all his
own possessions.
34"Therefore, salt is
good; but if even salt has
become tasteless, with
what will it be seasoned?
35"It is useless either for
the soil or for the manure
pile; it is thrown out. He
who has ears to hear, let
him hear."

Chapter 15

The Lost Sheep

NOW all the tax-gather-
ers and the sinners
were coming near Him to
listen to Him.
2And both the Pharisees
and the scribes *began* to
grumble, saying, "This
man receives sinners and
eats with them."
3And He told them this
parable, saying,
4"What man among you,
if he has a hundred sheep
and has lost one of them,
does not leave the ninety-
nine in the open pasture,
and go after the one which
is lost, until he finds it?
5"And when he has
found it, he lays it on his
shoulders, rejoicing.
6"And when he comes
home, he calls together his
friends and his neighbors,
saying to them, 'Rejoice
with me, for I have found
my sheep which was lost!'
7"I tell you that in the
same way, there will be
more joy in heaven over
one sinner who repents,
than over ninety-nine right-

συμβαλεῖν εἰς πόλεμον οὐχὶ καθίσας πρῶτον
[2]to attack [3]in [4]war not sitting first
βουλεύσεται εἰ δυνατός ἐστιν ἐν δέκα
will deliberate if able he is with ten
χιλιάσιν ὑπαντῆσαι τῷ μετὰ εἴκοσι χιλιάδων
thousands to meet [1]the [one] [5]with [6]twenty [7]thousands
ἐρχομένῳ ἐπ' αὐτόν; 32 εἰ δὲ μή γε, ἔτι
[2]coming [3]upon [4]him? Otherwise, yet =while
αὐτοῦ πόρρω ὄντος πρεσβείαν ἀποστείλας
him afar being[a] a delegation sending
he is yet at a distance
ἐρωτᾷ τὰ πρὸς εἰρήνην. 33 οὕτως οὖν
he asks the things for peace. So therefore
πᾶς ἐξ ὑμῶν ὃς οὐκ ἀποτάσσεται πᾶσιν
everyone of you who does not say farewell to all
τοῖς ἑαυτοῦ ὑπάρχουσιν οὐ δύναται εἶναί
[1]the [3]of himself [2]possessions cannot *to* be
μου μαθητής. 34 Καλὸν οὖν τὸ ἅλας·
of me a disciple. Good therefore the salt;
ἐὰν δὲ καὶ τὸ ἅλας μωρανθῇ, ἐν τίνι
but if even the salt becomes useless, with what
ἀρτυθήσεται; 35 οὔτε εἰς γῆν οὔτε εἰς
will it be seasoned? neither for soil nor for
κοπρίαν εὔθετόν ἐστιν· ἔξω βάλλουσιν
manure suitable is it; outside they cast
αὐτό. ὁ ἔχων ὦτα ἀκούειν ἀκουέτω.
it The [one] having ears to hear let him hear.

15 Ἦσαν δὲ αὐτῷ ἐγγίζοντες πάντες
Now there were to him drawing near all
οἱ τελῶναι καὶ οἱ ἁμαρτωλοὶ ἀκούειν
the tax-collectors and the sinners to hear
αὐτοῦ. 2 καὶ διεγόγγυζον οἵ τε Φαρισαῖοι
him. And greatly murmured both the Pharisees
καὶ οἱ γραμματεῖς λέγοντες ὅτι οὗτος
and the scribes saying[,] – This man
ἁμαρτωλοὺς προσδέχεται καὶ συνεσθίει αὐ-
sinners receives and eats with them.
τοῖς. 3 εἶπεν δὲ πρὸς αὐτοὺς τὴν παρα-
And he spoke to them – para-
βολὴν ταύτην λέγων· 4 τίς ἄνθρωπος ἐξ
ble this saying: What man of
ὑμῶν ἔχων ἑκατὸν πρόβατα καὶ ἀπολέσας
you having a hundred sheep and losing
ἐξ αὐτῶν ἓν οὐ καταλείπει τὰ ἐνενήκοντα
of them one does not leave the ninety-
ἐννέα ἐν τῇ ἐρήμῳ καὶ πορεύεται ἐπὶ
nine in the desert and goes after
τὸ ἀπολωλὸς ἕως εὕρῃ αὐτό; 5 καὶ
the [one] having been lost until he finds it? and
εὑρὼν ἐπιτίθησιν ἐπὶ τοὺς ὤμους αὐτοῦ
finding places *on* [it] on the shoulders of him
χαίρων, 6 καὶ ἐλθὼν εἰς τὸν οἶκον
rejoicing, and coming into the house
συγκαλεῖ τοὺς φίλους καὶ τοὺς γείτονας,
he calls together the friends and the neighbours,
λέγων αὐτοῖς· συγχάρητέ μοι, ὅτι εὗρον
saying to them: Rejoice with me, because I found
τὸ πρόβατόν μου τὸ ἀπολωλός. 7 λέγω
the sheep of me – having been lost. I tell
ὑμῖν ὅτι οὕτως χαρὰ ἐν τῷ οὐρανῷ
you that thus joy in – heaven
ἔσται ἐπὶ ἑνὶ ἁμαρτωλῷ μετανοοῦντι ἢ
will be over one sinner repenting than
ἐπὶ ἐνενήκοντα ἐννέα δικαίοις οἵτινες οὐ
over ninety-nine just men who no

another king. Will he not
first sit down and consider
whether he is able with ten
thousand men to oppose
the one coming against him
with twenty thousand? 32If
he is not able, he will send a
delegation while the other
is still a long way off and
will ask for terms of peace.
33In the same way, any of
you who does not give up
everything he has cannot
be my disciple.
34"Salt is good, but if it
loses its saltiness, how can
it be made salty again? 35It
is fit neither for the soil nor
for the manure pile; it is
thrown out.
"He who has ears to
hear, let him hear."

Chapter 15

The Parable of the Lost Sheep

NOW the tax collectors
and "sinners" were
all gathering around to hear
him. 2But the Pharisees and
the teachers of the law mut-
tered, "This man wel-
comes sinners and eats
with them."
3Then Jesus told them
this parable: 4"Suppose
one of you has a hundred
sheep and loses one of
them. Does he not leave the
ninety-nine in the open
country and go after the
lost sheep until he finds it?
5And when he finds it, he
joyfully puts it on his shoulders 6and goes home. Then
he calls his friends and
neighbors together and
says, 'Rejoice with me; I
have found my lost sheep.'
7I tell you that in the same
way there will be more rejoicing in heaven over one
sinner who repents than
over ninety-nine righteous

eous persons who need no repentance.

The Lost Coin

8"Or what woman, if she has ten silver coins and loses one coin, does not light a lamp and sweep the house and search carefully until she finds it?

9"And when she has found it, she calls together her friends and neighbors, saying, 'Rejoice with me, for I have found the coin which I had lost!'

10"In the same way, I tell you, there is joy in the presence of the angels of God over one sinner who repents."

The Prodigal Son

11And He said, "A certain man had two sons;

12and the younger of them said to his father, 'Father, give me the share of the estate that falls to me.' And he divided his wealth between them.

13"And not many days later, the younger son gathered everything together and went on a journey into a distant country, and there he squandered his estate with loose living.

14"Now when he had spent everything, a severe famine occurred in that country, and he began to be in need.

15"And he went and attached himself to one of the citizens of that country, and he sent him into his fields to feed swine.

16"And he was longing to fill his stomach with the pods that the swine were eating, and no one was giving *anything* to him.

17"But when he came to his senses, he said, 'How many of my father's hired men have more than enough bread, but I am dying here with hunger!

18'I will get up and go to my father, and will say to him, "Father, I have sinned against heaven, and in your sight;

19I am no longer worthy to be called your son; make

χρείαν ἔχουσιν μετανοίας. 8 Ἢ τίς γυνὴ
need have of repentance. Or what woman
δραχμὰς ἔχουσα δέκα, ἐὰν ἀπολέσῃ
[2]drachmae [1]having [3]ten, if she loses
δραχμὴν μίαν, οὐχὶ ἅπτει λύχνον καὶ
drachma one, does not light a lamp and
σαροῖ τὴν οἰκίαν καὶ ζητεῖ ἐπιμελῶς
sweep the house and seek carefully
ἕως οὗ εὕρῃ; 9 καὶ εὑροῦσα συγκαλεῖ
until she finds? and finding she calls together
τὰς φίλας καὶ γείτονας λέγουσα· συγχάρητέ
the friends and neighbours saying: Rejoice with
μοι, ὅτι εὗρον τὴν δραχμὴν ἣν ἀπώλεσα.
me, because I found the drachma which I lost.
10 οὕτως, λέγω ὑμῖν, γίνεται χαρὰ ἐνώπιον
So, I tell you, there is joy before
τῶν ἀγγέλων τοῦ θεοῦ ἐπὶ ἑνὶ ἁμαρτωλῷ
the angels – of God over one sinner
μετανοοῦντι. 11 Εἶπεν δέ· ἄνθρωπός τις
repenting. And he said: A certain man
εἶχεν δύο υἱούς. 12 καὶ εἶπεν ὁ νεώτερος
had two sons. And said the younger
αὐτῶν τῷ πατρί· πάτερ, δός μοι τὸ
of them to the father: Father, give me the
ἐπιβάλλον μέρος τῆς οὐσίας. ὁ δὲ διεῖλες
falling upon share of the property. And he divided
=share of the property falling to [me].
αὐτοῖς τὸν βίον. 13 καὶ μετ' οὐ πολλὰς
to them the living. And after not many
ἡμέρας συναγαγὼν πάντα ὁ νεώτερος υἱὸς
days having gathered all things the younger son
ἀπεδήμησεν εἰς χώραν μακράν, καὶ ἐκεῖ
departed to country a far, and there
διεσκόρπισεν τὴν οὐσίαν αὐτοῦ ζῶν ἀσώτως.
scattered the property of him living prodigally.
14 δαπανήσαντος δὲ αὐτοῦ πάντα ἐγένετο
But having spent him[a] all things there came
=when he had spent
λιμὸς ἰσχυρὰ κατὰ τὴν χώραν ἐκείνην,
famine a severe throughout – country that,
καὶ αὐτὸς ἤρξατο ὑστερεῖσθαι. 15 καὶ
and he began to be in want. And
πορευθεὶς ἐκολλήθη ἑνὶ τῶν πολιτῶν τῆς
going he was joined to one of the citizens –
χώρας ἐκείνης, καὶ ἔπεμψεν αὐτὸν εἰς
country of that, and he sent him into
τοὺς ἀγροὺς αὐτοῦ βόσκειν χοίρους· 16 καὶ
the fields of him to feed pigs; and
ἐπεθύμει γεμίσαι τὴν κοιλίαν αὐτοῦ ἐκ
he longed to fill the stomach of him out of(with)
τῶν κερατίων ὧν ἤσθιον οἱ χοῖροι, καὶ
the husks which [3]ate [1]the [2]pigs, and
οὐδεὶς ἐδίδου αὐτῷ. 17 εἰς ἑαυτὸν δὲ
no one gave to him. [3]to [4]himself [1]But
ἐλθὼν ἔφη· πόσοι μίσθιοι τοῦ πατρός μου
[2]coming he said: How many hired servants of the father of me
περισσεύονται ἄρτων, ἐγὼ δὲ λιμῷ ὧδε
abound of loaves, but I with famine here
=have abundance of bread,
ἀπόλλυμαι. 18 ἀναστὰς πορεύσομαι πρὸς
am perishing. Rising up I will go to
τὸν πατέρα μου καὶ ἐρῶ αὐτῷ· πάτερ,
the father of me and I will say to him: Father,
ἥμαρτον εἰς τὸν οὐρανὸν καὶ ἐνώπιόν σου,
I sinned against – heaven and before thee,
19 οὐκέτι εἰμὶ ἄξιος κληθῆναι υἱός σου·
no longer am I worthy to be called a son of thee;

persons who do not need to repent.

The Parable of the Lost Coin

8"Or suppose a woman
has ten silver coins[j] and
loses one. Does she not
light a lamp, sweep the
house and search carefully
until she finds it? 9And
when she finds it, she calls
her friends and neighbors
together and says, 'Rejoice
with me; I have found my
lost coin.' 10In the same
way, I tell you, there is rejoicing in the presence of
the angels of God over one
sinner who repents."

The Parable of the Lost Son

11Jesus continued:
"There was a man who had
two sons. 12The younger
one said to his father, 'Father, give me my share of
the estate.' So he divided
his property between them.
13"Not long after that,
the younger son got together all he had, set off for a
distant country and there
squandered his wealth in
wild living. 14After he had
spent everything, there was
a severe famine in that
whole country, and he began to be in need. 15So he
went and hired himself out
to a citizen of that country,
who sent him to his fields to
feed pigs. 16He longed to
fill his stomach with the
pods that the pigs were eating, but no one gave him
anything.
17"When he came to his
senses, he said, 'How
many of my father's hired
men have food to spare,
and here I am starving to
death! 18I will set out and
go back to my father and
say to him: Father, I have
sinned against heaven and
against you. 19I am no longer worthy to be called

j8 Greek *ten drachmas*, each worth about a day's wages

me as one of your hired
men." '
20 "And he got up and
came to his father. But
while he was still a long
way off, his father saw him,
and felt compassion *for
him,* and ran and embraced
him, and kissed him.
21 "And the son said to
him, 'Father, I have sinned
against heaven and in your
sight; I am no longer
worthy to be called your
son.'
22 "But the father said to
his slaves, 'Quickly bring
out the best robe and put it
on him, and put a ring on
his hand and sandals on his
feet;
23 and bring the fattened
calf, kill it, and let us eat
and be merry;
24 for this son of mine was
dead, and has come to life
again; he was lost, and has
been found.' And they be-
gan to be merry.
25 "Now his older son was
in the field, and when he
came and approached the
house, he heard music and
dancing.
26 "And he summoned
one of the servants and *began* inquiring what these
things might be.
27 "And he said to him,
'Your brother has come,
and your father has killed
the fattened calf, because
he has received him back
safe and sound.'
28 "But he became angry,
and was not willing to go in;
and his father came out and
began entreating him.
29 "But he answered and
said to his father, 'Look!
For so many years I have
been serving you, and I
have never neglected a
command of yours; and *yet*
you have never given me a
kid, that I might be merry
with my friends;
30 but when this son of
yours came, who has de-
voured your wealth with

ποίησόν με ὡς ἕνα τῶν μισθίων σου.
make me as one of the hired servants of thee.
20 καὶ ἀναστὰς ἦλθεν πρὸς τὸν πατέρα
And rising up he came to the father
ἑαυτοῦ. ἔτι δὲ αὐτοῦ μακρὰν ἀπέχοντος
of him*self*. But yet him afar being away[a]
=while he was yet far away
εἶδεν αὐτὸν ὁ πατὴρ αὐτοῦ καὶ ἐσπλαγχνίσθη,
saw him the father of him and was moved with pity,
καὶ δραμὼν ἐπέπεσεν ἐπὶ τὸν τράχηλον
and running fell *on* on the neck
αὐτοῦ καὶ κατεφίλησεν αὐτόν. 21 εἶπεν δὲ
of him and fervently kissed him. And said
ὁ υἱὸς αὐτῷ· πάτερ, ἥμαρτον εἰς τὸν
the son to him: Father, I sinned against –
οὐρανὸν καὶ ἐνώπιόν σου, οὐκέτι εἰμὶ
heaven and before thee, no longer am I
ἄξιος κληθῆναι υἱός σου. 22 εἶπεν δὲ
worthy to be called a son of thee. But said
ὁ πατὴρ πρὸς τοὺς δούλους αὐτοῦ· ταχὺ
the father to the slaves of him: Quickly
ἐξενέγκατε στολὴν τὴν πρώτην καὶ ἐνδύσατε
bring ye out a robe the first and clothe
αὐτόν, καὶ δότε δακτύλιον εἰς τὴν χεῖρα
him, and give(put) a ring to the hand
αὐτοῦ καὶ ὑποδήματα εἰς τοὺς πόδας,
of him and sandals to the feet,
23 καὶ φέρετε τὸν μόσχον τὸν σιτευτόν,
and bring the calf – fattened,
θύσατε, καὶ φαγόντες εὐφρανθῶμεν, 24 ὅτι
kill, and eating let us be merry, because
οὗτος ὁ υἱός μου νεκρὸς ἦν καὶ ἀνέζησεν,
this – son of me dead was and lived again,
ἦν ἀπολωλὼς καὶ εὑρέθη. καὶ ἤρξαντο
was *having been* lost and was found. And they began
εὐφραίνεσθαι. 25 ἦν δὲ ὁ υἱὸς αὐτοῦ
to be merry. But was the son of him
ὁ πρεσβύτερος ἐν ἀγρῷ· καὶ ὡς ἐρχόμενος
– older in a field; and as coming
ἤγγισεν τῇ οἰκίᾳ, ἤκουσεν συμφωνίας καὶ
he drew near to the house, he heard music and
χορῶν, 26 καὶ προσκαλεσάμενος ἕνα τῶν
dances, and calling to [him] one of the
παίδων ἐπυνθάνετο τί ἂν εἴη ταῦτα.
lads he inquired what might be these things.
27 ὁ δὲ εἶπεν αὐτῷ ὅτι ὁ ἀδελφός σου
And he said to him[,] – The brother of thee
ἥκει, καὶ ἔθυσεν ὁ πατήρ σου τὸν μόσχον τὸν
has come, and [4]killed [1]the [2]father [3]of thee [5]the [7]calf –
σιτευτόν, ὅτι ὑγιαίνοντα αὐτὸν ἀπέλαβεν.
[6]fattened, because [5]being in health [3]him [1]he [2]received [4]back.
28 ὠργίσθη δὲ καὶ οὐκ ἤθελεν εἰσελθεῖν·
But he was angry and did not wish to enter;
ὁ δὲ πατὴρ αὐτοῦ ἐξελθὼν παρεκάλει
so the father of him coming out besought
αὐτόν. 29 ὁ δὲ ἀποκριθεὶς εἶπεν τῷ
him. But he answering said to the
πατρί· ἰδοὺ τοσαῦτα ἔτη δουλεύω σοι καὶ
father: Behold[,] so many years I serve thee and
οὐδέποτε ἐντολήν σου παρῆλθον, καὶ ἐμοὶ
never a command of thee I transgressed, and to me
οὐδέποτε ἔδωκας ἔριφον ἵνα μετὰ τῶν
never thou gavest a goat that with the
φίλων μου εὐφρανθῶ· 30 ὅτε δὲ ὁ υἱός
friends of me I might be merry; but when – [2]son
σου οὗτος ὁ καταφαγών σου τὸν βίον
[3]of thee [1]this – having devoured of thee the living

your son; make me like one
of your hired men.' 20 So he
got up and went to his father.
"But while he was still a
long way off, his father saw
him and was filled with
compassion for him; he ran
to his son, threw his arms
around him and kissed him.
21 "The son said to him,
'Father, I have sinned
against heaven and against
you. I am no longer worthy
to be called your son.[k]'
22 "But the father said to
his servants, 'Quick! Bring
the best robe and put it on
him. Put a ring on his finger
and sandals on his feet.
23 Bring the fattened calf
and kill it. Let's have a
feast and celebrate. 24 For
this son of mine was dead
and is alive again: he was
lost and is found.' So they
began to celebrate.
25 "Meanwhile, the older
son was in the field. When
he came near the house, he
heard music and dancing.
26 So he called one of the
servants and asked him
what was going on. 27 'Your
brother has come,' he re-
plied, 'and your father has
killed the fattened calf because he has him back safe
and sound.'
28 "The older brother be-
came angry and refused to
go in. So his father went out
and pleaded with him.
29 But he answered his father, 'Look! All these years
I've been slaving for you
and never disobeyed your
orders. Yet you never gave
me even a young goat so I
could celebrate with my
friends. 30 But when this
son of yours who has
squandered your property

[k]21 Some early manuscripts *son. Make me like one of your hired men.*

harlots, you killed the fattened calf for him.'
31"And he said to him,
'*My* child, you have always
been with me, and all that is
mine is yours.
32'But we had to be merry
and rejoice, for this brother
of yours was dead and *has
begun* to live, and *was* lost
and has been found.'"

Chapter 16

The Unrighteous Steward

NOW He was also say-
ing to the disciples,
"There was a certain rich
man who had a steward,
and this *steward* was reported to him as squander-
ing his possessions.
2"And he called him and
said to him, 'What is this I
hear about you? Give an account of your stewardship,
for you can no longer be
steward.'
3"And the steward said
to himself, 'What shall I do,
since my master is taking
the stewardship away from
me? I am not strong enough
to dig; I am ashamed to beg.
4'I know what I shall do,
so that when I am removed
from the stewardship, they
will receive me into their
homes.'
5"And he summoned
each one of his master's
debtors, and he *began* saying to the first, 'How much
do you owe my master?'
6"And he said, 'A hun-
dred measures of oil.' And
he said to him, 'Take your
bill, and sit down quickly
and write fifty.'
7"Then he said to an-
other, 'And how much do
you owe?' And he said, 'A
hundred measures of
wheat.' He *said to him,
'Take your bill, and write
eighty.'
8"And his master
praised the unrighteous
steward because he had
acted shrewdly; for the
sons of this age are more

μετὰ πορνῶν ἦλθεν, ἔθυσας αὐτῷ τὸν
with harlots came, thou killedst for him the
σιτευτὸν μόσχον. 31 ὁ δὲ εἶπεν αὐτῷ·
fattened calf. And he said to him:
τέκνον, σὺ πάντοτε μετ' ἐμοῦ εἶ, καὶ
Child, thou always with me art, and
πάντα τὰ ἐμὰ σά ἐστιν· 32 εὐφρανθῆναι
[1]all [3]things – [2]my [5]thine [4]is(are); [3]to be merry
δὲ καὶ χαρῆναι ἔδει, ὅτι ὁ ἀδελφός
[1]And [4]and [5]to rejoice [2]it behoved [us], because – [2]brother
σου οὗτος νεκρὸς ἦν καὶ ἔζησεν, καὶ ἀπο-
[3]of thee [1]this [5]dead [4]was and came to life, and having
λωλὼς καὶ εὑρέθη.
been lost also was found.

16 Ἔλεγεν δὲ καὶ πρὸς τοὺς μαθητάς·
And he said also to the disciples:
ἄνθρωπός τις ἦν πλούσιος ὃς εἶχεν
[3]A certain [4]man [1]there was [2]rich who had
οἰκονόμον, καὶ οὗτος διεβλήθη αὐτῷ ὡς
a steward, and this was complained of to him as
διασκορπίζων τὰ ὑπάρχοντα αὐτοῦ. 2 καὶ
wasting the possessions of him. And
φωνήσας αὐτὸν εἶπεν αὐτῷ· τί τοῦτο
calling him he said to him: What [is] this
ἀκούω περὶ σοῦ; ἀπόδος τὸν λόγον τῆς
I hear about thee? render the account of the
οἰκονομίας σου· οὐ γὰρ δύνῃ ἔτι οἰκονομεῖν.
stewardship of thee; for thou canst not longer *to* be steward.
3 εἶπεν δὲ ἐν ἑαυτῷ ὁ οἰκονόμος· τί
And said in himself the steward: What
ποιήσω, ὅτι ὁ κύριός μου ἀφαιρεῖται τὴν
may I do, because the lord of me takes away the
οἰκονομίαν ἀπ' ἐμοῦ; σκάπτειν οὐκ ἰσχύω,
stewardship from me? to dig I am not able,
ἐπαιτεῖν αἰσχύνομαι. 4 ἔγνων τί ποιήσω,
to beg I am ashamed. I knew(know) what I may do,
ἵνα ὅταν μετασταθῶ ἐκ τῆς οἰκονομίας
that when I am removed out of the stewardship
δέξωνταί με εἰς τοὺς οἴκους ἑαυτῶν.
they may receive me into the houses of them*selves*.
5 καὶ προσκαλεσάμενος ἕνα ἕκαστον τῶν
And calling to [him] [2]one [1]each of the
χρεοφειλετῶν τοῦ κυρίου ἑαυτοῦ ἔλεγεν τῷ
debtors of the lord of him*self* he said to the
πρώτῳ· πόσον ὀφείλεις τῷ κυρίῳ μου;
first: How much owest thou to the lord of me?
6 ὁ δὲ εἶπεν· ἑκατὸν βάτους ἐλαίου. ὁ δὲ
And he said: A hundred baths of oil. And he
εἶπεν αὐτῷ· δέξαι σου τὰ γράμματα καὶ
told him: Take of thee the letters(bill) and
καθίσας ταχέως γράψον πεντήκοντα. 7 ἔπειτα
sitting quickly write fifty. Then
ἑτέρῳ εἶπεν· σὺ δὲ πόσον ὀφείλεις; ὁ δὲ
to another he said: [4]thou [1]And [2]how much [3]owest? And he
εἶπεν· ἑκατὸν κόρους σίτου. λέγει αὐτῷ·
said: A hundred cors of wheat. He tells him:
δέξαι σου τὰ γράμματα καὶ γράψον
Take of thee the bill and write
ὀγδοήκοντα. 8 καὶ ἐπῄνεσεν ὁ κύριος τὸν
eighty. And [3]praised [1]the [2]lord the
οἰκονόμον τῆς ἀδικίας ὅτι φρονίμως
steward – of unrighteousness because prudently
ἐποίησεν· ὅτι οἱ υἱοὶ τοῦ αἰῶνος τούτου
he acted; because the sons – age of this

with prostitutes comes
home, you kill the fattened
calf for him!'
31"'My son,' the father
said, 'you are always with
me, and everything I have
is yours. 32But we had to
celebrate and be glad, because this brother of yours
was dead and is alive again;
he was lost and is found.'"

Chapter 16

The Parable of the Shrewd Manager

JESUS told his disciples:
"There was a rich man
whose manager was ac-
cused of wasting his pos-
sessions. 2So he called him
in and asked him, 'What is
this I hear about you? Give
an account of your manage-
ment, because you cannot
be manager any longer.'
3"The manager said to
himself, 'What shall I do
now? My master is taking
away my job. I'm not
strong enough to dig, and
I'm ashamed to beg— 4I
know what I'll do so that,
when I lose my job here,
people will welcome me
into their houses.'
5"So he called in each
one of his master's debtors.
He asked the first, 'How
much do you owe my mas-
ter?'
6"'Eight hundred gal-
lons[l] of olive oil,' he replied.
"The manager told him,
'Take your bill, sit down
quickly, and make it four
hundred.'
7"Then he asked the sec-
ond, 'And how much do
you owe?'
"'A thousand bushels[m]
of wheat,' he replied.
"He told him, 'Take your
bill and make it eight hundred.'
8"The master commend-
ed the dishonest manager
because he had acted
shrewdly. For the people of

[l]6 Greek *one hundred batous* (probably about 3 kiloliters)
[m]7 Greek *one hundred korous* (probably about 35 kiloliters)

shrewd in relation to their own kind than the sons of light.

9"And I say to you, make friends for yourselves by means of the [c]mammon of unrighteousness; that when it fails, they may receive you into the eternal dwellings.

10"He who is faithful in a very little thing is faithful also in much; and he who is unrighteous in a very little thing is unrighteous also in much.

11"If therefore you have not been faithful in the *use of* unrighteous mammon, who will entrust the true *riches* to you?

12"And if you have not been faithful in *the use of* that which is another's, who will give you that which is your own?

13"No servant can serve two masters; for either he will hate the one, and love the other, or else he will hold to one, and despise the other. You cannot serve God and mammon."

14Now the Pharisees, who were lovers of money, were listening to all these things, and they were scoffing at Him.

15And He said to them, "You are those who justify yourselves in the sight of men, but God knows your hearts; for that which is highly esteemed among men is detestable in the sight of God.

16"The Law and the Prophets *were proclaimed* until John; since then the gospel of the kingdom of God is preached, and everyone is forcing his way into it.

17"But it is easier for heaven and earth to pass away than for one stroke of a letter of the Law to fail.

18"Everyone who divorces his wife and marries another commits adultery; and he who marries one

[c] Or, *riches*

φρονιμώτεροι ὑπὲρ τοὺς υἱοὺς τοῦ φωτὸς
more prudent than the sons of the light
εἰς τὴν γενεὰν τὴν ἑαυτῶν εἰσιν. 9 Καὶ
in the generation – of them*selves* are. And
ἐγὼ ὑμῖν λέγω, ἑαυτοῖς ποιήσατε φίλους
I [2]you [1]tell, To yourselves make friends
ἐκ τοῦ μαμωνᾶ τῆς ἀδικίας, ἵνα ὅταν
by the mammon – of unrighteousness, that when
ἐκλίπῃ δέξωνται ὑμᾶς εἰς τὰς αἰωνίους
it fails they may receive you into the eternal
σκηνάς. 10 ὁ πιστὸς ἐν ἐλαχίστῳ καὶ ἐν
tabernacles. The man faithful in least also in
πολλῷ πιστός ἐστιν, καὶ ὁ ἐν ἐλαχίστῳ
much faithful is, and the man in least
ἄδικος καὶ ἐν πολλῷ ἄδικός ἐστιν. 11 εἰ
unrighteous also in much unrighteous is. If
οὖν ἐν τῷ ἀδίκῳ μαμωνᾷ πιστοὶ οὐκ
therefore in the unrighteous mammon faithful not
ἐγένεσθε, τὸ ἀληθινὸν τίς ὑμῖν πιστεύσει;
ye were, the true who to you will entrust ?
12 καὶ εἰ ἐν τῷ ἀλλοτρίῳ πιστοὶ οὐκ
And if in the thing belonging to another faithful not
ἐγένεσθε, τὸ ἡμέτερον τίς δώσει ὑμῖν;
ye were, the ours who will give you?
=that which is ours
13 Οὐδεὶς οἰκέτης δύναται δυσὶ κυρίοις
No household slave can two lords
δουλεύειν· ἢ γὰρ τὸν ἕνα μισήσει καὶ τὸν
to serve; for either the one he will hate and the
ἕτερον ἀγαπήσει, ἢ ἑνὸς ἀνθέξεται καὶ
other he will love, or one he will hold fast to and
τοῦ ἑτέρου καταφρονήσει. οὐ δύνασθε
the other he will despise. Ye cannot
θεῷ δουλεύειν καὶ μαμωνᾷ. 14 Ἤκουον
God *to* serve and mammon. [6]heard
δὲ ταῦτα πάντα οἱ Φαρισαῖοι φιλάργυροι
[1]Now [8]these things [7]all [2]the [3]Pharisees [5]moneylovers
ὑπάρχοντες, καὶ ἐξεμυκτήριζον αὐτόν. 15 καὶ
[4]being, and they scoffed at him. And
εἶπεν αὐτοῖς· ὑμεῖς ἐστε οἱ δικαιοῦντες
he said to them : Ye are the [ones] justifying
ἑαυτοὺς ἐνώπιον τῶν ἀνθρώπων, ὁ δὲ
yourselves before – men, – but
θεὸς γινώσκει τὰς καρδίας ὑμῶν· ὅτι τὸ
God knows the hearts of you; because the thing
ἐν ἀνθρώποις ὑψηλὸν βδέλυγμα ἐνώπιον
[2]among [3]men [1]lofty [is] an abomination before
τοῦ θεοῦ. 16 Ὁ νόμος καὶ οἱ προφῆται
– God. The law and the prophets
μέχρι Ἰωάννου· ἀπὸ τότε ἡ βασιλεία τοῦ
[were] until John; from then the kingdom –
θεοῦ εὐαγγελίζεται καὶ πᾶς εἰς αὐτὴν
of God is being preached and everyone into it
βιάζεται. 17 εὐκοπώτερον δέ ἐστιν τὸν οὐρανὸν
is pressing. But easier it is the heaven
καὶ τὴν γῆν παρελθεῖν ἢ τοῦ νόμου μίαν
and the earth to pass away than of the law one
κεραίαν πεσεῖν. 18 Πᾶς ὁ ἀπολύων τὴν
little horn* to fall. Everyone dismissing the
γυναῖκα αὐτοῦ καὶ γαμῶν ἑτέραν μοιχεύει,
wife of him and marrying another commits adultery,
καὶ ὁ ἀπολελυμένην ἀπὸ
and [1]the [one] [3]a woman having been dismissed [4]from

* The little projection which distinguishes some Hebrew letters from those otherwise similar.

this world are more shrewd in dealing with their own kind than are the people of the light. 9I tell you, use worldly wealth to gain friends for yourselves, so that when it is gone, you will be welcomed into eternal dwellings.

10"Whoever can be trusted with very little can also be trusted with much, and whoever is dishonest with very little will also be dishonest with much. 11So if you have not been trustworthy in handling worldly wealth, who will trust you with true riches? 12And if you have not been trustworthy with someone else's property, who will give you property of your own?

13"No servant can serve two masters. Either he will hate the one and love the other, or he will be devoted to the one and despise the other. You cannot serve both God and Money."

14The Pharisees, who loved money, heard all this and were sneering at Jesus. 15He said to them, "You are the ones who justify yourselves in the eyes of men, but God knows your hearts. What is highly valued among men is detestable in God's sight.

Additional Teachings

16"The Law and the Prophets were proclaimed until John. Since that time, the good news of the kingdom of God is being preached, and everyone is forcing his way into it. 17It is easier for heaven and earth to disappear than for the least stroke of a pen to drop out of the Law.

18"Anyone who divorces his wife and marries another woman commits adultery, and the man who marries a divorced woman commits adultery.

who is divorced from a husband commits adultery.

The Rich Man and Lazarus

19"Now there was a cer-
tain rich man, and he
habitually dressed in purple
and fine linen, gaily living
in splendor every day.
20"And a certain poor
man named Lazarus was
laid at his gate, covered
with sores,
21and longing to be fed
with the *crumbs* which
were falling from the rich
man's table; besides, even
the dogs were coming and
licking his sores.
22"Now it came about
that the poor man died and
he was carried away by the
angels to Abraham's bo-
som; and the rich man also
died and was buried.
23"And in Hades he lifted
up his eyes, being in torment, and *saw Abraham
far away, and Lazarus in
his bosom.
24"And he cried out and
said, 'Father Abraham,
have mercy on me, and
send Lazarus, that he may
dip the tip of his finger in
water and cool off my
tongue; for I am in agony in
this flame.'
25"But Abraham said,
'Child, remember that during your life you received
your good things, and likewise Lazarus bad things;
but now he is being com-
forted here, and you are in
agony.
26'And besides all this,
between us and you there is
a great chasm fixed, in order that those who wish to
come over from here to you
may not be able, and *that*
none may cross over from
there to us.'
27"And he said, 'Then I
beg you, Father, that you
send him to my father's
house—
28for I have five broth-
ers—that he may warn
them, lest they also come

ἀνδρὸς γαμῶν μοιχεύει. 19 Ἄνθρωπος δέ
[3]a husband [2]marrying [1]commits adultery. Now a certain
τις ἦν πλούσιος, καὶ ἐνεδιδύσκετο πορφύραν
man was rich, and used to put on a purple robe
καὶ βύσσον εὐφραινόμενος καθ' ἡμέραν
and fine linen being merry every day†
λαμπρῶς. **20** πτωχὸς δέ τις ὀνόματι
splendidly. And a certain poor man by name
Λάζαρος ἐβέβλητο πρὸς τὸν πυλῶνα αὐτοῦ
Lazarus had been placed at the gate of him
εἱλκωμένος **21** καὶ ἐπιθυμῶν χορτασθῆναι
being covered with sores and desiring to be satisfied
ἀπὸ τῶν πιπτόντων ἀπὸ τῆς τραπέζης
from the things falling from the table
τοῦ πλουσίου· ἀλλὰ καὶ οἱ κύνες ἐρχόμενοι
of the rich man; but even the dogs coming
ἐπέλειχον τὰ ἕλκη αὐτοῦ. **22** ἐγένετο δὲ
licked the sores of him. And it came to pass
ἀποθανεῖν τὸν πτωχὸν καὶ ἀπενεχθῆναι
to die the poor man and to be carried away
=that the poor man died and he was carried away
αὐτὸν ὑπὸ τῶν ἀγγέλων εἰς τὸν κόλπον
him[b] by the angels into the bosom
Ἀβραάμ· ἀπέθανεν δὲ καὶ ὁ πλούσιος καὶ
of Abraham; and died also the rich man and
ἐτάφη. **23** καὶ ἐν τῷ ᾅδῃ ἐπάρας τοὺς
was buried. And in – hades lifting up the
ὀφθαλμοὺς αὐτοῦ, ὑπάρχων ἐν βασάνοις,
eyes of him, being in torments,
ὁρᾷ Ἀβραὰμ ἀπὸ μακρόθεν καὶ Λάζαρον
he sees Abraham from afar and Lazarus
ἐν τοῖς κόλποις αὐτοῦ. **24** καὶ αὐτὸς
in the bosoms of him. And he
φωνήσας εἶπεν· πάτερ Ἀβραάμ, ἐλέησόν
calling said: Father Abraham, pity
με καὶ πέμψον Λάζαρον ἵνα βάψῃ τὸ
me and send Lazarus that he may dip the
ἄκρον τοῦ δακτύλου αὐτοῦ ὕδατος καὶ
tip of the finger of him of(in) water and
καταψύξῃ τὴν γλῶσσάν μου, ὅτι ὀδυνῶμαι
may cool the tongue of me, because I am suffering
ἐν τῇ φλογὶ ταύτῃ. **25** εἶπεν δὲ Ἀβραάμ·
in – flame this. But said Abraham :
τέκνον, μνήσθητι ὅτι ἀπέλαβες τὰ ἀγαθά
Child, remember that thou didst receive the good things
σου ἐν τῇ ζωῇ σου, καὶ Λάζαρος ὁμοίως
of thee in the life of thee, and Lazarus likewise
τὰ κακά· νῦν δὲ ὧδε παρακαλεῖται, σὺ δὲ
the bad; but now here he is comforted, but thou
ὀδυνᾶσαι. **26** καὶ ἐν πᾶσι τούτοις μεταξὺ
art suffering. And among all these things between
ἡμῶν καὶ ὑμῶν χάσμα μέγα ἐστήρικται,
us and you chasm a great has been firmly fixed,
ὅπως οἱ θέλοντες διαβῆναι ἔνθεν πρὸς
so that the [ones] wishing to pass hence to
ὑμᾶς μὴ δύνωνται, μηδὲ ἐκεῖθεν πρὸς
you cannot, neither thence to
ἡμᾶς διαπερῶσιν. **27** εἶπεν δέ· ἐρωτῶ
us may they cross over. And he said : I ask
σε οὖν, πάτερ, ἵνα πέμψῃς αὐτὸν εἰς
thee therefore, father, that thou mayest send him to
τὸν οἶκον τοῦ πατρός μου· **28** ἔχω γὰρ
the house of the father of me; for I have
πέντε ἀδελφούς· ὅπως διαμαρτύρηται αὐτοῖς,
five brothers; so that he may witness to them,
ἵνα μὴ καὶ αὐτοὶ ἔλθωσιν εἰς τὸν τόπον
lest also they come to – place

The Rich Man and Lazarus

19"There was a rich man
who was dressed in purple
and fine linen and lived in
luxury every day. 20At his
gate was laid a beggar
named Lazarus, covered
with sores 21and longing to
eat what fell from the rich
man's table. Even the dogs
came and licked his sores.
22"The time came when
the beggar died and the angels carried him to Abra-
ham's side. The rich man
also died and was buried.
23In hell,[n] where he was in
torment, he looked up and
saw Abraham far away,
with Lazarus by his side.
24So he called to him, 'Father Abraham, have pity on
me and send Lazarus to dip
the tip of his finger in water
and cool my tongue, be-
cause I am in agony in this
fire.'
25"But Abraham replied,
'Son, remember that in
your lifetime you received
your good things, while
Lazarus received bad
things, but now he is comforted here and you are in
agony. 26And besides all
this, between us and you a
great chasm has been fixed,
so that those who want to
go from here to you cannot,
nor can anyone cross over
from there to us.'
27"He answered, 'Then I
beg you, father, send Lazarus to my father's house,
28for I have five brothers.
Let him warn them, so that
they will not also come to

[n]23 Greek *Hades*

to this place of torment.'

29"But Abraham *said, 'They have Moses and the Prophets; let them hear them.'

30"But he said, 'No, Father Abraham, but if someone goes to them from the dead, they will repent!'

31"But he said to him, 'If they do not listen to Moses and the Prophets, neither will they be persuaded if someone rises from the dead.'"

τοῦτον τῆς βασάνου. 29 λέγει δὲ Ἀβραάμ·
this – of torment. But says Abraham :

ἔχουσι Μωϋσέα καὶ τοὺς προφήτας·
They have Moses and the prophets;

ἀκουσάτωσαν αὐτῶν. 30 ὁ δὲ εἶπεν·
let them hear them. But he said :

οὐχί, πάτερ Ἀβραάμ, ἀλλ' ἐάν τις ἀπὸ
No, father Abraham, but if someone from

νεκρῶν πορευθῇ πρὸς αὐτούς, μετανοήσουσιν.
[the] dead should go to them, they will repent.

31 εἶπεν δὲ αὐτῷ· εἰ Μωϋσέως καὶ τῶν
But he said to him : If Moses and the

προφητῶν οὐκ ἀκούουσιν, οὐδὲ ἐάν τις
prophets they do not hear, neither if someone

ἐκ νεκρῶν ἀναστῇ πεισθήσονται.
out of [the] dead should rise again will they be persuaded.

this place of torment.'

29"Abraham replied, 'They have Moses and the Prophets; let them listen to them.'

30" 'No, father Abraham,' he said, 'but if someone from the dead goes to them, they will repent.'

31"He said to him, 'If they do not listen to Moses and the Prophets, they will not be convinced even if someone rises from the dead.' "

Chapter 17

Instructions

AND He said to His disciples, "It is inevitable that stumbling blocks should come, but woe to him through whom they come!

2"It would be better for him if a millstone were hung around his neck and he were thrown into the sea, than that he should cause one of these little ones to stumble.

3"Be on your guard! If your brother sins, rebuke him; and if he repents, forgive him.

4"And if he sins against you seven times a day, and returns to you seven times, saying, 'I repent,' forgive him."

5And the apostles said to the Lord, "Increase our faith!"

6And the Lord said, "If you had faith like a mustard seed, you would say to this mulberry tree, 'Be uprooted and be planted in the sea'; and it would obey you.

7"But which of you, having a slave plowing or tending sheep, will say to him when he has come in from the field, 'Come immediately and sit down to eat'?

8"But will he not say to him, 'Prepare something for me to eat, and *properly* clothe yourself and serve me until I have eaten and drunk; and afterward you will eat and drink'?

9"He does not thank the

17 Εἶπεν δὲ πρὸς τοὺς μαθητὰς αὐτοῦ·
And he said to the disciples of him :

ἀνένδεκτόν ἐστιν τοῦ τὰ σκάνδαλα μὴ ἐλθεῖν,
Impossible it is – the offences not to come,[d]

οὐαὶ δὲ δι' οὗ ἔρχεται· 2 λυσιτελεῖ
but woe [to him] through whom they come; it profits

αὐτῷ εἰ λίθος μυλικὸς περίκειται περὶ
him if a millstone is put *round* round

τὸν τράχηλον αὐτοῦ καὶ ἔρριπται εἰς τὴν
the neck of him and he has been thrown into the

θάλασσαν, ἢ ἵνα σκανδαλίσῃ τῶν μικρῶν
sea, than that he should offend – [3]little ones

τούτων ἕνα. 3 προσέχετε ἑαυτοῖς. ἐὰν
[2]of these [1]one. Take heed to yourselves. If

ἁμάρτῃ ὁ ἀδελφός σου, ἐπιτίμησον αὐτῷ,
sins the brother of thee, rebuke him,

καὶ ἐὰν μετανοήσῃ, ἄφες αὐτῷ. 4 καὶ
and if he repents, forgive him. And

ἐὰν ἑπτάκις τῆς ἡμέρας ἁμαρτήσῃ εἰς σὲ
if seven times of(in) the day he sins against thee

καὶ ἑπτάκις ἐπιστρέψῃ πρὸς σὲ λέγων·
and seven times turns to thee saying :

μετανοῶ, ἀφήσεις αὐτῷ. 5 Καὶ εἶπαν οἱ
I repent, thou shalt forgive him. And said the

ἀπόστολοι τῷ κυρίῳ· πρόσθες ἡμῖν πίστιν.
apostles to the Lord : Add to us faith.

6 εἶπεν δὲ ὁ κύριος· εἰ ἔχετε πίστιν ὡς
And said the Lord : If ye have faith as

κόκκον σινάπεως, ἐλέγετε ἂν τῇ συκαμίνῳ
a grain of mustard, ye would have said – sycamine-tree

ταύτῃ· ἐκριζώθητι καὶ φυτεύθητι ἐν τῇ
to this : Be thou uprooted and be thou planted in the

θαλάσσῃ· καὶ ὑπήκουσεν ἂν ὑμῖν. 7 Τίς
sea; and it would have obeyed you. who

δὲ ἐξ ὑμῶν δοῦλον ἔχων ἀροτριῶντα ἢ
But of you [2]a slave [1]having ploughing or

ποιμαίνοντα, ὃς εἰσελθόντι ἐκ τοῦ ἀγροῦ
herding, who on [his] coming in• out of the farm

ἐρεῖ αὐτῷ· εὐθέως παρελθὼν ἀνάπεσε,
will say to him : Immediately coming up recline,

8 ἀλλ' οὐχὶ ἐρεῖ αὐτῷ· ἑτοίμασον τί
but will not say to him : Prepare something

δειπνήσω, καὶ περιζωσάμενος διακόνει μοι
I may dine, and having girded thyself serve me

ἕως φάγω καὶ πίω, καὶ μετὰ ταῦτα
until I eat and drink, and after these things

φάγεσαι καὶ πίεσαι σύ; 9 μὴ ἔχει χάριν
eat and drink thou? *Not* he has thanks

Chapter 17

Sin, Faith, Duty

JESUS said to his disci-
ples: "Things that cause
people to sin are bound to
come, but woe to that person through whom they
come. 2It would be better
for him to be thrown into
the sea with a millstone tied
around his neck than for
him to cause one of these
little ones to sin. 3So watch
yourselves.
"If your brother sins, rebuke him, and if he repents,
forgive him. 4If he sins
against you seven times in a
day, and seven times
comes back to you and
says, 'I repent,' forgive
him."
5The apostles said to the
Lord, "Increase our
faith!"
6He replied, "If you have
faith as small as a mustard
seed, you can say to this
mulberry tree, 'Be uprooted and planted in the sea,'
and it will obey you.
7"Suppose one of you
had a servant plowing or
looking after the sheep.
Would he say to the servant
when he comes in from the
field, 'Come along now and
sit down to eat'? 8Would he
not rather say, 'Prepare my
supper, get yourself ready
and wait on me while I eat
and drink; after that you
may eat and drink'?
9Would he thank the ser-

slave because he did the
things which were com-
manded, does he?
10"So you too, when you
do all the things which are
commanded you, say, 'We
are unworthy slaves; we
have done *only* that which
we ought to have done.' "

Ten Lepers Cleansed

11And it came about while
He was on the way to
Jerusalem, that He was
passing between Samaria
and Galilee.
12And as He entered a
certain village, ten leprous
men who stood at a dis-
tance met Him;
13and they raised their
voices, saying, "Jesus,
Master, have mercy on
us!"
14And when He saw
them, He said to them,
"Go and show yourselves
to the priests." And it came
about that as they were going, they were cleansed.
15Now one of them, when
he saw that he had been
healed, turned back, glorifying God with a loud
voice,
16and he fell on his face at
His feet, giving thanks to
Him. And he was a Samari-
tan.
17And Jesus answered
and said, "Were there not
ten cleansed? But the
nine—where are they?
18"Was no one found
who turned back to give
glory to God, except this
foreigner?"
19And He said to him,
"Rise, and go your way;
your faith [d]has made you
well."
20Now having been ques-
tioned by the Pharisees as
to when the kingdom of
God was coming, He an-
swered them and said,
"The kingdom of God is
not coming with signs to be
observed;
21nor will they say,
'Look, here *it is!*' or,
'There *it is!*' For behold,
the kingdom of God is in
your midst."

Second Coming Foretold

22And He said to the dis-

[d] Or, *has saved you*

τῷ δούλῳ ὅτι ἐποίησεν τὰ διαταχθέντα;
to the slave because he did the things commanded?
10 οὕτως καὶ ὑμεῖς, ὅταν ποιήσητε πάντα
So also ye, when ye do all
τὰ διαταχθέντα ὑμῖν, λέγετε ὅτι δοῦλοι
the things commanded you, say[,] – Slaves
ἀχρεῖοί ἐσμεν, ὃ ὠφείλομεν ποιῆσαι
unprofitable we are, what we ought to do
πεποιήκαμεν.
we have done.
11 Καὶ ἐγένετο ἐν τῷ πορεύεσθαι εἰς
And it came to pass in the to go[e] to
=as [he] went
Ἰερουσαλήμ, καὶ αὐτὸς διήρχετο διὰ μέσον
Jerusalem, *and* he passed through [the]
through midst
Σαμαρείας καὶ Γαλιλαίας. 12 καὶ εἰσερχομένου
of Samaria and Galilee. And entering
=as he entered
αὐτοῦ εἴς τινα κώμην ἀπήντησαν δέκα
him[a] into a certain village met [him] ten
λεπροὶ ἄνδρες, οἳ ἔστησαν πόρρωθεν, 13 καὶ
leprous men, who stood afar off, and
αὐτοὶ ἦραν φωνὴν λέγοντες· Ἰησοῦ
they lifted voice saying : Jesus
ἐπιστάτα, ἐλέησον ἡμᾶς. 14 καὶ ἰδὼν εἶπεν
Master, pity us. And seeing he said
αὐτοῖς· πορευθέντες ἐπιδείξατε ἑαυτοὺς τοῖς
to them : Going show yourselves to the
ἱερεῦσιν. καὶ ἐγένετο ἐν τῷ ὑπάγειν
priests. And it came to pass in the to go
= as they went
αὐτοὺς ἐκαθαρίσθησαν. 15 εἷς δὲ ἐξ
them[be] they were cleansed. But one of
αὐτῶν, ἰδὼν ὅτι ἰάθη, ὑπέστρεψεν μετὰ
them, seeing that he was cured, returned with
φωνῆς μεγάλης δοξάζων τὸν θεόν, 16 καὶ
voice a great glorifying – God, and
ἔπεσεν ἐπὶ πρόσωπον παρὰ τοὺς πόδας
fell on [his] face at the feet
αὐτοῦ εὐχαριστῶν αὐτῷ· καὶ αὐτὸς ἦν
of him thanking him; and he was
Σαμαρίτης. 17 ἀποκριθεὶς δὲ ὁ Ἰησοῦς
a Samaritan. And answering – Jesus
εἶπεν· οὐχ οἱ δέκα ἐκαθαρίσθησαν; οἱ [δὲ]
said : Not the ten were cleansed? but the
ἐννέα ποῦ; 18 οὐχ εὑρέθησαν ὑποστρέψαντες
nine where? were there not found returning
δοῦναι δόξαν τῷ θεῷ εἰ μὴ ὁ ἀλλογενὴς
to give glory – to God only – stranger
οὗτος; 19 καὶ εἶπεν αὐτῷ· ἀναστὰς πορεύου·
this ? And he said to him : Rising up go;
ἡ πίστις σου σέσωκέν σε.
the faith of thee has healed thee.
20 Ἐπερωτηθεὶς δὲ ὑπὸ τῶν Φαρισαίων
And being questioned by the Pharisees
πότε ἔρχεται ἡ βασιλεία τοῦ θεοῦ,
when comes the kingdom – of God,
ἀπεκρίθη αὐτοῖς καὶ εἶπεν· οὐκ ἔρχεται
he answered them and said : Comes not
ἡ βασιλεία τοῦ θεοῦ μετὰ παρατηρήσεως,
the kingdom – of God with observation,
21 οὐδὲ ἐροῦσιν· ἰδοὺ ὧδε ἤ· ἐκεῖ· ἰδοὺ
nor will they say : Behold[,] here or: there; [3]behold
γὰρ ἡ βασιλεία τοῦ θεοῦ ἐντὸς ὑμῶν
[1]for the kingdom – of God within you
ἐστιν. 22 Εἶπεν δὲ πρὸς τοὺς μαθητάς·
is. And he said to the disciples :

vant because he did what
he was told to do? 10So you
also, when you have done
everything you were told to
do, should say, 'We are unworthy servants; we have
only done our duty.' "

Ten Healed of Leprosy

11Now on his way to Jeru-
salem, Jesus traveled along
the border between Samar-
ia and Galilee. 12As he was
going into a village, ten
men who had leprosy[o] met
him. They stood at a dis-
tance 13and called out in a
loud voice, "Jesus, Mas-
ter, have pity on us!"
14When he saw them, he
said, "Go, show your-
selves to the priests." And
as they went, they were
cleansed.
15One of them, when he
saw he was healed, came
back, praising God in a
loud voice. 16He threw
himself at Jesus' feet and
thanked him—and he was a
Samaritan.
17Jesus asked, "Were not
all ten cleansed? Where are
the other nine? 18Was no
one found to return and
give praise to God except
this foreigner?" 19Then he
said to him, "Rise and go;
your faith has made you
well."

The Coming of the Kingdom of God

20Once, having been
asked by the Pharisees
when the kingdom of God
would come, Jesus replied,
"The kingdom of God does
not come with your careful
observation, 21nor will people say, 'Here it is,' or
'There it is,' because the
kingdom of God is within[p]
you."
22Then he said to his dis-

[o]*12* The Greek word was used for various diseases affecting the skin—not necessarily leprosy.
[p]*21* Or *among*

ciples, "The days shall come when you will long to see one of the days of the Son of Man, and you will not see it.

23"And they will say to you, 'Look there! Look here!' Do not go away, and do not run after *them*.

24"For just as the lightning, when it flashes out of one part of the sky, shines to the other part of the sky, so will the Son of Man be in His day.

25"But first He must suffer many things and be rejected by this generation.

26"And just as it happened in the days of Noah, so it shall be also in the days of the Son of Man:

27they were eating, they were drinking, they were marrying, they were being given in marriage, until the day that Noah entered the ark, and the flood came and destroyed them all.

28"It was the same as happened in the days of Lot: they were eating, they were drinking, they were buying, they were selling, they were planting, they were building;

29but on the day that Lot went out from Sodom it rained fire and brimstone from heaven and destroyed them all.

30"It will be just the same on the day that the Son of Man is revealed.

31"On that day, let not the one who is on the housetop and whose goods are in the house go down to take them away; and likewise let not the one who is in the field turn back.

32"Remember Lot's wife.

33"Whoever seeks to keep his life shall lose it, and whoever loses *his life* shall preserve it.

34"I tell you, on that night there will be two men in one bed; one will be taken, and the other will be left.

ἐλεύσονται ἡμέραι ὅτε ἐπιθυμήσετε μίαν
Will come days when ye will long one
τῶν ἡμερῶν τοῦ υἱοῦ τοῦ ἀνθρώπου ἰδεῖν
of the days of the Son – of man to see
καὶ οὐκ ὄψεσθε. 23 καὶ ἐροῦσιν ὑμῖν·
and will not see. And they will say to you :
ἰδοὺ ἐκεῖ, ἰδοὺ ὧδε· μὴ ἀπέλθητε μηδὲ
Behold there, behold here; do not go away nor
διώξητε. 24 ὥσπερ γὰρ ἡ ἀστραπὴ
follow. For as the lightning
ἀστράπτουσα ἐκ τῆς ὑπὸ τὸν οὐρανὸν
flashing out of the [one part] under – heaven
εἰς τὴν ὑπ' οὐρανὸν λάμπει, οὕτως ἔσται
to the [other part] under heaven shines, so will be
ὁ υἱὸς τοῦ ἀνθρώπου ἐν τῇ ἡμέρᾳ αὐτοῦ.
the Son – of man in the day of him.
25 πρῶτον δὲ δεῖ αὐτὸν πολλὰ παθεῖν καὶ
But first it behoves him many things to suffer and
ἀποδοκιμασθῆναι ἀπὸ τῆς γενεᾶς ταύτης.
to be rejected from – generation this.
26 καὶ καθὼς ἐγένετο ἐν ταῖς ἡμέραις
And as it was in the days
Νῶε, οὕτως ἔσται καὶ ἐν ταῖς ἡμέραις
of Noah, so it will be also in the days
τοῦ υἱοῦ τοῦ ἀνθρώπου· 27 ἤσθιον, ἔπινον,
of the Son – of man; they were eating, drinking,
ἐγάμουν, ἐγαμίζοντο, ἄχρι ἧς ἡμέρας
marrying, giving in marriage, until which day
= the day when
εἰσῆλθεν Νῶε εἰς τὴν κιβωτόν, καὶ
entered Noah into the ark, and
ἦλθεν ὁ κατακλυσμὸς καὶ ἀπώλεσεν πάντας.
came the flood and destroyed all.
28 ὁμοίως καθὼς ἐγένετο ἐν ταῖς ἡμέραις
Likewise as it was in the days
Λώτ· ἤσθιον, ἔπινον, ἠγόραζον, ἐπώλουν,
of Lot; they were eating, drinking, buying, selling,
ἐφύτευον, ᾠκοδόμουν· 29 ᾗ δὲ ἡμέρᾳ ἐξῆλθεν
planting, building; but on which day went forth
Λὼτ ἀπὸ Σοδόμων, ἔβρεξεν πῦρ καὶ
Lot from Sodom, it rained fire and
θεῖον ἀπ' οὐρανοῦ καὶ ἀπώλεσεν πάντας.
brimstone from heaven and destroyed all.
30 κατὰ τὰ αὐτὰ ἔσται ᾗ ἡμέρᾳ ὁ υἱὸς
According to the same things it will be in which day the Son
= In the same way = on the day when
τοῦ ἀνθρώπου ἀποκαλύπτεται. 31 ἐν ἐκείνῃ
– of man is revealed. In that
τῇ ἡμέρᾳ ὃς ἔσται ἐπὶ τοῦ δώματος καὶ
– day who will be on the roof and
τὰ σκεύη αὐτοῦ ἐν τῇ οἰκίᾳ, μὴ καταβάτω
the goods of him in the house, let him not come down
ἆραι αὐτά, καὶ ὁ ἐν ἀγρῷ ὁμοίως μὴ
to take them, and the [one] in a field likewise not
ἐπιστρεψάτω εἰς τὰ ὀπίσω. 32 μνημονεύετε
let him turn back to the things behind. Remember
τῆς γυναικὸς Λώτ. 33 ὃς ἐὰν ζητήσῃ
the wife of Lot. Whoever seeks
τὴν ψυχὴν αὐτοῦ περιποιήσασθαι, ἀπολέσει
the life of him to preserve, he will lose
αὐτήν, καὶ ὃς ἂν ἀπολέσει, ζῳογονήσει
it, and whoever will lose, will preserve
αὐτήν. 34 λέγω ὑμῖν, ταύτῃ τῇ νυκτὶ
it. I tell you, in this – night
ἔσονται δύο ἐπὶ κλίνης μιᾶς, ὁ εἷς
there will be two men on couch one, the one
παραλημφθήσεται καὶ ὁ ἕτερος ἀφεθήσεται·
will be taken and the other will be left;

ciples, "The time is coming
when you will long to see
one of the days of the Son
of Man, but you will not see
it. 23Men will tell you,
'There he is!' or 'Here he
is!' Do not go running off
after them. 24For the Son of
Man in his day[q] will be like
the lightning, which flashes
and lights up the sky from
one end to the other. 25But
first he must suffer many
things and be rejected by
this generation.

26"Just as it was in the
days of Noah, so also will it
be in the days of the Son of
Man. 27People were eating,
drinking, marrying and being given in marriage up to
the day Noah entered the
ark. Then the flood came
and destroyed them all.

28"It was the same in the
days of Lot. People were
eating and drinking, buying
and selling, planting and
building. 29But the day Lot
left Sodom, fire and sulfur
rained down from heaven
and destroyed them all.

30"It will be just like this
on the day the Son of Man
is revealed. 31On that day
no one who is on the roof of
his house, with his goods
inside, should go down to
get them. Likewise, no one
in the field should go back
for anything. 32Remember
Lot's wife! 33Whoever tries
to keep his life will lose it,
and whoever loses his life
will preserve it. 34I tell you,
on that night two people
will be in one bed; one will
be taken and the other left.

[q]24 Some manuscripts do not have *in his day.*

35"There will be two women grinding at the same place; one will be taken, and the other will be left.
36[" [e]Two men will be in the field; one will be taken and the other will be left."]
37And answering they *said to Him, "Where, Lord?" And He said to them, "Where the body *is*, there also will the vultures be gathered."

Chapter 18

Parables on Prayer

NOW He was telling them a parable to show that at all times they ought to pray and not to lose heart,
2saying, "There was in a certain city a judge who did not fear God, and did not respect man.
3"And there was a widow in that city, and she kept coming to him, saying, 'Give me legal protection from my opponent.'
4"And for a while he was unwilling; but afterward he said to himself, 'Even though I do not fear God nor respect man,
5yet because this widow bothers me, I will give her legal protection, lest by continually coming she wear me out.' "
6And the Lord said, "Hear what the unrighteous judge *said;
7now shall not God bring about justice for His elect, who cry to Him day and night, and will He delay long over them?
8"I tell you that He will bring about justice for them speedily. However, when the Son of Man comes, will He find faith on the earth?"

The Pharisee and the Publican

9And He also told this parable to certain ones who trusted in themselves that they were righteous, and viewed others with contempt:

[e] Many mss. do not contain this verse

---

35 ἔσονται δύο ἀλήθουσαι ἐπὶ τὸ αὐτό, ἡ
there will be two women grinding together,† the
μία παραλημφθήσεται ἡ δὲ ἑτέρα ἀφεθήσεται.‡
one will be taken but the other will be left.
37 καὶ ἀποκριθέντες λέγουσιν αὐτῷ· ποῦ,
And answering they say to him: Where,
κύριε; ὁ δὲ εἶπεν αὐτοῖς· ὅπου τὸ σῶμα,
Lord? And he said to them: Where the body,
ἐκεῖ καὶ οἱ ἀετοὶ ἐπισυναχθήσονται.
there also the eagles will be gathered together.

18 Ἔλεγεν δὲ παραβολὴν αὐτοῖς πρὸς
And he told [2]a parable [1]them to =that
τὸ δεῖν πάντοτε προσεύχεσθαι αὐτοὺς καὶ
the [1]to behove [3]always [4]to pray [2]them and
they must always pray and not faint,
μὴ ἐγκακεῖν, **2** λέγων· κριτής τις ἦν ἐν
not to faint, saying: [3]judge [2]a certain [1]There was [4]in
τινι πόλει τὸν θεὸν μὴ φοβούμενος καὶ
[5]a certain [6]city – [3]God [1]not [2]fearing and
ἄνθρωπον μὴ ἐντρεπόμενος. **3** χήρα δὲ ἦν
[3]man [1]not [2]regarding. And [2]a widow [1]there was
ἐν τῇ πόλει ἐκείνῃ, καὶ ἤρχετο πρὸς
in – city that, and she came to
αὐτὸν λέγουσα· ἐκδίκησόν με ἀπὸ τοῦ
him saying: Vindicate me from the
ἀντιδίκου μου. **4** καὶ οὐκ ἤθελεν ἐπὶ
opponent of me. And he would not for
χρόνον· μετὰ ταῦτα δὲ εἶπεν ἐν ἑαυτῷ·
a time; but after these things he said in himself:
εἰ καὶ τὸν θεὸν οὐ φοβοῦμαι οὐδὲ ἄνθρωπον
If indeed – God I fear not nor man
ἐντρέπομαι, **5** διά γε τὸ παρέχειν
regard, at least because of – to cause
=because this widow causes me trouble
μοι κόπον τὴν χήραν ταύτην ἐκδικήσω αὐτήν,
me trouble – widow this[b] I will vindicate her,
ἵνα μὴ εἰς τέλος ἐρχομένη ὑπωπιάζῃ με.
lest in [the] end coming she exhausts me.
6 Εἶπεν δὲ ὁ κύριος· ἀκούσατε τί ὁ κριτὴς
And said the Lord: Hear ye what the judge
τῆς ἀδικίας λέγει· **7** ὁ δὲ θεὸς οὐ μὴ
– of unrighteousness says; – and God by no means
ποιήσῃ τὴν ἐκδίκησιν τῶν ἐκλεκτῶν
will he make the vindication of the chosen [ones]
αὐτοῦ τῶν βοώντων αὐτῷ ἡμέρας καὶ
of him – crying to him day and
νυκτός, καὶ μακροθυμεῖ ἐπ' αὐτοῖς; **8** λέγω
night, and be patient over them? I tell
ὑμῖν ὅτι ποιήσει τὴν ἐκδίκησιν αὐτῶν
you that he will make the vindication of them
ἐν τάχει. πλὴν ὁ υἱὸς τοῦ ἀνθρώπου ἐλθὼν
quickly. Nevertheless the Son – of man coming
ἆρα εὑρήσει τὴν πίστιν ἐπὶ τῆς γῆς;
then will he find the faith on the earth?
9 Εἶπεν δὲ καὶ πρός τινας τοὺς
And he said also to some the [ones]
πεποιθότας ἐφ' ἑαυτοῖς ὅτι εἰσὶν
relying on themselves that they are
δίκαιοι καὶ ἐξουθενοῦντας τοὺς λοιποὺς
righteous and despising the rest
τὴν παραβολὴν ταύτην. **10** Ἄνθρωποι δύο
– parable this. Men two

‡ Verse 36 omitted by Nestle; *cf.* NIV footnote.

35Two women will be grinding grain together; one will be taken and the other left.[r]"
37"Where, Lord?" they asked.
He replied, "Where there is a dead body, there the vultures will gather."

Chapter 18

The Parable of the Persistent Widow

THEN Jesus told his disciples a parable to show them that they should always pray and not give up. 2He said: "In a certain town there was a judge who neither feared God nor cared about men. 3And there was a widow in that town who kept coming to him with the plea, 'Grant me justice against my adversary.'
4"For some time he refused. But finally he said to himself, 'Even though I don't fear God or care about men, 5yet because this widow keeps bothering me, I will see that she gets justice, so that she won't eventually wear me out with her coming!' "
6And the Lord said, "Listen to what the unjust judge says. 7And will not God bring about justice for his chosen ones, who cry out to him day and night? Will he keep putting them off? 8I tell you, he will see that they get justice, and quickly. However, when the Son of Man comes, will he find faith on the earth?"

The Parable of the Pharisee and the Tax Collector

9To some who were confident of their own righteousness and looked down on everybody else, Jesus told this parable: 10"Two

[r]35 Some manuscripts *left.* [36]*Two men will be in the field; one will be taken and the other left.*

10“Two men went up into the temple to pray, one a Pharisee, and the other a tax-gatherer.

11“The Pharisee stood and was praying thus to himself, ‘God, I thank Thee that I am not like other people: swindlers, unjust, adulterers, or even like this tax-gatherer.

12‘I fast twice a week; I pay tithes of all that I get.’

13“But the tax-gatherer, standing some distance away, was even unwilling but was beating his breast, saying, ‘God, be merciful to me, the sinner!’

14“I tell you, this man went down to his house justified rather than the other; for everyone who exalts himself shall be humbled, but he who humbles himself shall be exalted.”

15And they were bringing even their babies to Him so that He might touch them, but when the disciples saw it, they *began* rebuking them.

16But Jesus called for them, saying, “Permit the children to come to Me, and do not hinder them, for the kingdom of God belongs to such as these.

17“Truly I say to you, whoever does not receive the kingdom of God like a child shall not enter it *at all*.”

The Rich Young Ruler

18And a certain ruler questioned Him, saying, “Good Teacher, what shall I do to inherit eternal life?”

19And Jesus said to him, “Why do you call Me good? No one is good except God alone.

20“You know the commandments, ‘Do not commit adultery, Do not murder, Do not steal, Do not bear false witness, Honor

ἀνέβησαν εἰς τὸ ἱερὸν προσεύξασθαι, ὁ εἷς
went up to the temple to pray, the one

Φαρισαῖος καὶ ὁ ἕτερος τελώνης. 11 ὁ
a Pharisee and the other a tax-collector. The

Φαρισαῖος σταθεὶς ταῦτα πρὸς ἑαυτὸν
Pharisee standing these things to himself

προσηύχετο· ὁ θεός, εὐχαριστῶ σοι ὅτι
prayed : – God, I thank thee that

οὐκ εἰμὶ ὥσπερ οἱ λοιποὶ τῶν ἀνθρώπων,
I am not as the rest – of men,

ἅρπαγες, ἄδικοι, μοιχοί, ἢ καὶ ὡς οὗτος
rapacious, unjust, adulterers, or even as this

ὁ τελώνης· 12 νηστεύω δὶς τοῦ σαββάτου,
– tax-collector; I fast twice of(in) the week,

ἀποδεκατεύω πάντα ὅσα κτῶμαι. 13 ὁ δὲ
I tithe all things how many I get. But the

τελώνης μακρόθεν ἑστὼς οὐκ ἤθελεν οὐδὲ
tax-collector far off standing would not *not* even

τοὺς ὀφθαλμοὺς ἐπᾶραι εἰς τὸν οὐρανόν,
the(his) eyes *to* lift up to – heaven,

ἀλλ᾽ ἔτυπτεν τὸ στῆθος αὐτοῦ λέγων· ὁ
but smote the breast of him saying : –

θεός, ἱλάσθητί μοι τῷ ἁμαρτωλῷ. 14 λέγω
God, be propitious to me the sinner. I tell

ὑμῖν, κατέβη οὗτος δεδικαιωμένος εἰς τὸν
you, went down this man having been justified to the

οἶκον αὐτοῦ παρ᾽ ἐκεῖνον· ὅτι πᾶς ὁ
house of him [rather] than that one; because everyone

ὑψῶν ἑαυτὸν ταπεινωθήσεται, ὁ δὲ ταπεινῶν
exalting himself will be humbled, and the [one] humbling

ἑαυτὸν ὑψωθήσεται.
himself will be exalted.

15 Προσέφερον δὲ αὐτῷ καὶ τὰ βρέφη
And they brought to him also the babes

ἵνα αὐτῶν ἅπτηται· ἰδόντες δὲ οἱ μαθηταὶ
that them he might touch; but [3]seeing [1]the [2]disciples

ἐπετίμων αὐτοῖς. 16 ὁ δὲ Ἰησοῦς
rebuked them. – But Jesus

προσεκαλέσατο αὐτὰ λέγων· ἄφετε τὰ
called to [him] them* saying : Allow the

παιδία ἔρχεσθαι πρός με καὶ μὴ κωλύετε
children to come to me and do not prevent

αὐτά· τῶν γὰρ τοιούτων ἐστὶν ἡ βασιλεία
them; – for of such is the kingdom

τοῦ θεοῦ. 17 ἀμὴν λέγω ὑμῖν, ὃς ἂν
– of God. Truly I tell you, whoever

μὴ δέξηται τὴν βασιλείαν τοῦ θεοῦ ὡς
does not receive the kingdom – of God as

παιδίον, οὐ μὴ εἰσέλθῃ εἰς αὐτήν.
a child, by no means enters into it.

18 Καί ἐπηρώτησέν τις αὐτὸν ἄρχων
And [3]questioned [1]a certain [4]him [2]ruler

λέγων· διδάσκαλε ἀγαθέ, τί ποιήσας ζωὴν
saying : Teacher good, what doing life

αἰώνιον κληρονομήσω; 19 εἶπεν δὲ αὐτῷ
eternal may I inherit? And said to him

ὁ Ἰησοῦς· τί με λέγεις ἀγαθόν; οὐδεὶς
– Jesus : Why me sayest thou good? no one

ἀγαθὸς εἰ μὴ εἷς [ὁ] θεός. 20 τὰς ἐντολὰς
[is] good except one[,] – God. The commandments

οἶδας· μὴ μοιχεύσῃς, μὴ φονεύσῃς,
thou knowest : Do not commit adultery, Do not kill,

μὴ κλέψῃς, μὴ ψευδομαρτυρήσῃς, τίμα
Do not steal, Do not bear false witness, Honour

* That is, “the babes” (τὰ βρέφη in ver. 15).

men went up to the temple to pray, one a Pharisee and the other a tax collector. 11The Pharisee stood up and prayed about[s] himself: ‘God, I thank you that I am not like other men—robbers, evildoers, adulterers—or even like this tax collector. 12I fast twice a week and give a tenth of all I get.’

13“But the tax collector stood at a distance. He would not even look up to heaven, but beat his breast and said, ‘God, have mercy on me, a sinner.’

14“I tell you that this man, rather than the other, went home justified before God. For everyone who exalts himself will be humbled, and he who humbles himself will be exalted.”

The Little Children and Jesus

15People were also bringing babies to Jesus to have him touch them. When the disciples saw this, they rebuked them. 16But Jesus called the children to him and said, “Let the little children come to me, and do not hinder them, for the kingdom of God belongs to such as these. 17I tell you the truth, anyone who will not receive the kingdom of God like a little child will never enter it.”

The Rich Ruler

18A certain ruler asked him, “Good teacher, what must I do to inherit eternal life?”

19“Why do you call me good?” Jesus answered. “No one is good—except God alone. 20You know the commandments: ‘Do not commit adultery, do not murder, do not steal, do not give false testimony, honor

s 11 Or *to*

YOUR FATHER AND MOTHER.' "

21And he said, "All these things I have kept from *my* youth."

22And when Jesus heard *this,* He said to him, "One thing you still lack; sell all that you possess, and distribute it to the poor, and you shall have treasure in heaven; and come, follow Me."

23But when he had heard these things, he became very sad; for he was extremely rich.

24And Jesus looked at him and said, "How hard it is for those who are wealthy to enter the kingdom of God!

25"For it is easier for a camel to go through the eye of a needle, than for a rich man to enter the kingdom of God."

26And they who heard it said, "Then who can be saved?"

27But He said, "The things impossible with men are possible with God."

28And Peter said, "Behold, we have left our own *homes,* and followed You."

29And He said to them, "Truly I say to you, there is no one who has left house or wife or brothers or parents or children, for the sake of the kingdom of God,

30who shall not receive many times as much at this time and in the age to come, eternal life."

31And He took the twelve aside and said to them, "Behold, we are going up to Jerusalem, and all things which are written through the prophets about the Son of Man will be accomplished.

32"For He will be delivered to the Gentiles, and will be mocked and mistreated and spit upon,

33and after they have scourged Him, they will kill Him; and the third day He

τὸν πατέρα σου καὶ τὴν μητέρα. 21 ὁ δὲ
the father of thee and the mother. And he
εἶπεν· ταῦτα πάντα ἐφύλαξα ἐκ νεότητος.
said: All these things I kept from youth.
22 ἀκούσας δὲ ὁ Ἰησοῦς εἶπεν αὐτῷ· ἔτι
But hearing – Jesus said to him: Yet
ἕν σοι λείπει· πάντα ὅσα ἔχεις
one thing to thee is lacking; all things how many thou hast
πώλησον καὶ διάδος πτωχοῖς, καὶ ἕξεις
sell and distribute to poor people, and thou wilt have
θησαυρὸν ἐν [τοῖς] οὐρανοῖς, καὶ δεῦρο
treasure in – heavens, and come
ἀκολούθει μοι. 23 ὁ δὲ ἀκούσας ταῦτα
follow me. But he hearing these things
περίλυπος ἐγενήθη, ἦν γὰρ πλούσιος σφόδρα.
very grieved became, for he was rich exceedingly.
24 ἰδὼν δὲ αὐτὸν ὁ Ἰησοῦς εἶπεν· πῶς
And seeing him – Jesus said: How
δυσκόλως οἱ τὰ χρήματα ἔχοντες εἰς τὴν
hardly [1]the [ones] – [3]property [2]having into the
βασιλείαν τοῦ θεοῦ εἰσπορεύονται· 25 εὐκο-
kingdom – of God go *in*; [2]easi-
πώτερον γάρ ἐστιν κάμηλον διὰ τρήματος
er [1]for it is [for] a camel through [the] eye
βελόνης εἰσελθεῖν ἢ πλούσιον εἰς τὴν
of a needle to enter than a rich man into the
βασιλείαν τοῦ θεοῦ εἰσελθεῖν. 26 εἶπαν
kingdom – of God to enter. said
δὲ οἱ ἀκούσαντες· καὶ τίς δύναται
And the [ones] hearing: And who can
σωθῆναι; 27 ὁ δὲ εἶπεν· τὰ ἀδύνατα παρὰ
to be saved? And he said: The things impossible with
ἀνθρώποις δυνατὰ παρὰ τῷ θεῷ ἐστιν.
men possible with – God is(are).
28 Εἶπεν δὲ ὁ Πέτρος· ἰδοὺ ἡμεῖς ἀφέντες
And said – Peter: Behold[,] we leaving
τὰ ἴδια ἠκολουθήσαμέν σοι. 29 ὁ δὲ
our own things followed thee. And he
εἶπεν αὐτοῖς· ἀμὴν λέγω ὑμῖν ὅτι οὐδείς
said to them: Truly I tell you that no one
ἐστιν ὃς ἀφῆκεν οἰκίαν ἢ γυναῖκα ἢ
there is who left house or wife or
ἀδελφοὺς ἢ γονεῖς ἢ τέκνα εἵνεκεν τῆς
brothers or parents or children for the sake of the
βασιλείας τοῦ θεοῦ, 30 ὃς οὐχὶ μὴ λάβῃ
kingdom – of God, who by no means receives
πολλαπλασίονα ἐν τῷ καιρῷ τούτῳ καὶ ἐν
many times over in – time this and in
τῷ αἰῶνι τῷ ἐρχομένῳ ζωὴν αἰώνιον.
the age – coming life eternal.
31 Παραλαβὼν δὲ τοὺς δώδεκα εἶπεν πρὸς
And taking the twelve he said to
αὐτούς· ἰδοὺ ἀναβαίνομεν εἰς Ἰερουσαλήμ,
them: Behold we are going up to Jerusalem,
καὶ τελεσθήσεται πάντα τὰ γεγραμ-
and will be accomplished all things – having been
μένα διὰ τῶν προφητῶν τῷ υἱῷ τοῦ
written through the prophets to the Son –
ἀνθρώπου· 32 παραδοθήσεται γὰρ τοῖς ἔθνεσιν
of man; for he will be delivered to the nations
καὶ ἐμπαιχθήσεται καὶ ὑβρισθήσεται καὶ
and will be mocked and *will be* insulted and
ἐμπτυσθήσεται, 33 καὶ μαστιγώσαντες
will be spit at, and having scourged
ἀποκτενοῦσιν αὐτόν, καὶ τῇ ἡμέρᾳ τῇ
they will kill him, and on the day –

your father and mother.'[t] "
21"All these I have kept
since I was a boy," he said.
22When Jesus heard this,
he said to him, "You still
lack one thing. Sell everything you have and give to
the poor, and you will have
treasure in heaven. Then
come, follow me."
23When he heard this, he
became very sad, because
he was a man of great
wealth. 24Jesus looked at
him and said, "How hard it
is for the rich to enter the
kingdom of God! 25Indeed,
it is easier for a camel to go
through the eye of a needle
than for a rich man to enter
the kingdom of God."
26Those who heard this
asked, "Who then can be
saved?"
27Jesus replied, "What is
impossible with men is possible with God."
28Peter said to him, "We
have left all we had to follow you!"
29"I tell you the truth,"
Jesus said to them, "no one
who has left home or wife
or brothers or parents or
children for the sake of the
kingdom of God 30will fail
to receive many times as
much in this age and, in the
age to come, eternal life."

Jesus Again Predicts His Death

31Jesus took the Twelve
aside and told them, "We
are going up to Jerusalem,
and everything that is written by the prophets about
the Son of Man will be fulfilled. 32He will be handed
over to the Gentiles. They
will mock him, insult him,
spit on him, flog him and

[t]20 Exodus 20:12-16; Deut. 5:16-20

will rise again.''
34And they understood
none of these things, and
this saying was hidden
from them, and they did not
comprehend the things that
were said.

Bartimaeus Receives Sight

35And it came about that
as He was approaching
Jericho, a certain blind man
was sitting by the road,
begging.
36Now hearing a multi-
tude going by, he *began* to
inquire what this might be.
37And they told him that
Jesus of Nazareth was
passing by.
38And he called out, say-
ing, ''Jesus, Son of David,
have mercy on me!''
39And those who led the
way were sternly telling
him to be quiet; but he kept
crying out all the more,
''Son of David, have mercy
on me!''
40And Jesus stopped and
commanded that he be
brought to Him; and when
he had come near, He questioned him,
41''What do you want Me
to do for you?'' And he
said, ''Lord, *I want* to regain my sight!''
42And Jesus said to him,
''Receive your sight; your
faith has made you well.''
43And immediately he re-
gained his sight, and *began*
following Him, glorifying
God; and when all the
people saw it, they gave
praise to God.

τρίτῃ ἀναστήσεται. **34** καὶ αὐτοὶ οὐδὲν
third he will rise again. And they none
τούτων συνῆκαν, καὶ ἦν τὸ ῥῆμα τοῦτο
of these things understood, and [3]was – [2]utterance [1]this
κεκρυμμένον ἀπ᾽ αὐτῶν, καὶ οὐκ ἐγίνωσκον
[4]*having been* hidden from them, and they knew not
τὰ λεγόμενα.
the things being said.
35 Ἐγένετο δὲ ἐν τῷ ἐγγίζειν αὐτὸν εἰς
And it came to pass in the to draw near him[bc] to
=as he drew near
Ἰεριχὼ τυφλός τις ἐκάθητο παρὰ τὴν ὁδὸν
Jericho a certain blind man sat by the way
ἐπαιτῶν. **36** ἀκούσας δὲ ὄχλου διαπορευομένου
begging. And hearing a crowd passing through
ἐπυνθάνετο τί εἴη τοῦτο. **37** ἀπήγγειλαν
he inquired what [2]might be [1]this. And they re-
δὲ αὐτῷ ὅτι Ἰησοῦς ὁ Ναζωραῖος
ported to him[,] – Jesus the Nazarene
παρέρχεται. **38** καὶ ἐβόησεν λέγων· Ἰησοῦ
is passing by. And he cried saying: Jesus
υἱὲ Δαυίδ, ἐλέησόν με. **39** καὶ οἱ
son of David, pity me. And the [ones]
προάγοντες ἐπετίμων αὐτῷ ἵνα σιγήσῃ·
going before rebuked him that he should be quiet;
αὐτὸς δὲ πολλῷ μᾶλλον ἔκραζεν· υἱὲ
but he by much more cried out : Son
Δαυίδ, ἐλέησόν με. **40** σταθεὶς δὲ ὁ
of David, pity me. And standing –
Ἰησοῦς ἐκέλευσεν αὐτὸν ἀχθῆναι πρὸς
Jesus commanded him to be brought to
αὐτόν. ἐγγίσαντος δὲ αὐτοῦ ἐπηρώτησεν
him. And drawing near him[a] he questioned
=as he drew near
αὐτόν· **41** τί σοι θέλεις ποιήσω; ὁ δὲ
him : What for thee wishest thou I may do? And he
εἶπεν· κύριε, ἵνα ἀναβλέψω. **42** καὶ ὁ Ἰησοῦς
said : Lord, that I may see again. And – Jesus
εἶπεν αὐτῷ· ἀνάβλεψον· ἡ πίστις σου
said to him : See again; the faith of thee
σέσωκέν σε. **43** καὶ παραχρῆμα ἀνέβλεψεν,
has healed thee. And at once he saw again,
καὶ ἠκολούθει αὐτῷ δοξάζων τὸν θεόν.
and followed him glorifying – God.
καὶ πᾶς ὁ λαὸς ἰδὼν ἔδωκεν αἶνον τῷ
And all the people seeing gave praise –
θεῷ.
to God.

kill him. 33On the third day
he will rise again.''
34The disciples did not
understand any of this. Its
meaning was hidden from
them, and they did not
know what he was talking
about.

A Blind Beggar Receives His Sight

35As Jesus approached
Jericho, a blind man was
sitting by the roadside begging. 36When he heard the
crowd going by, he asked
what was happening.
37They told him, ''Jesus of
Nazareth is passing by.''
38He called out, ''Jesus,
Son of David, have mercy
on me!''
39Those who led the way
rebuked him and told him
to be quiet, but he shouted
all the more, ''Son of David, have mercy on me!''
40Jesus stopped and or-
dered the man to be
brought to him. When he
came near, Jesus asked
him, 41''What do you want
me to do for you?''
''Lord, I want to see,'' he
replied.
42Jesus said to him, ''Receive your sight; your faith
has healed you.'' 43Imme-
diately he received his sight
and followed Jesus, praising God. When all the people saw it, they also praised
God.

Chapter 19

Zaccheus Converted

AND He entered and was
passing through Jeri-
cho.
2And behold, there was a
man called by the name of
Zaccheus; and he was a
chief tax-gatherer, and he
was rich.
3And he was trying to
see who Jesus was, and he
was unable because of the
crowd, for he was small in
stature.
4And he ran on ahead
and climbed up into a syca-
more tree in order to see
Him, for He was about to
pass through that way.

19 Καὶ εἰσελθὼν διήρχετο τὴν Ἰεριχώ.
And having entered he passed through – Jericho.
2 Καὶ ἰδοὺ ἀνὴρ ὀνόματι καλούμενος
And behold[,] a man by name *being* called
Ζακχαῖος, καὶ αὐτὸς ἦν ἀρχιτελώνης, καὶ
Zacchæus, and he was a chief tax-collector, and
αὐτὸς πλούσιος· **3** καὶ ἐζήτει ἰδεῖν τὸν
he [was] rich; and he sought to see –
Ἰησοῦν τίς ἐστιν, καὶ οὐκ ἠδύνατο ἀπὸ
Jesus who he is(was), and was not able from
τοῦ ὄχλου, ὅτι τῇ ἡλικίᾳ μικρὸς ἦν.
the crowd, because – [3]in stature [2]little [1]he was.
4 καὶ προδραμὼν εἰς τὸ ἔμπροσθεν ἀνέβη
And having run forward to the front he went up
ἐπὶ συκομορέαν, ἵνα ἴδῃ αὐτόν, ὅτι
onto a sycamore-tree, that he might see him, because
ἐκείνης ἤμελλεν διέρχεσθαι. **5** καὶ ὡς
[3]that [way] [1]he was about [2]to pass along. And as

Chapter 19

Zacchaeus the Tax Collector

JESUS entered Jericho
and was passing
through. 2A man was there
by the name of Zacchaeus;
he was a chief tax collector
and was wealthy. 3He
wanted to see who Jesus
was, but being a short man
he could not, because of
the crowd. 4So he ran
ahead and climbed a syca-
more-fig tree to see him,
since Jesus was coming
that way.

5And when Jesus came
to the place, He looked up
and said to him, "Zac-
cheus, hurry and come
down, for today I must stay
at your house."
6And he hurried and
came down, and received
Him gladly.
7And when they saw it,
they all *began* to grumble,
saying, "He has gone to be
the guest of a man who is a
sinner."
8And Zaccheus stopped
and said to the Lord, "Behold, Lord, half of my
possessions I will give to
the poor, and if I have defrauded anyone of any-
thing, I will give back four
times as much."
9And Jesus said to him,
"Today salvation has come
to this house, because he,
too, is a son of Abraham.
10"For the Son of Man
has come to seek and to
save that which was lost."

Parable of Money Usage

11And while they were listening to these things, He
went on to tell a parable,
because He was near
Jerusalem, and they sup-
posed that the kingdom of
God was going to appear
immediately.
12He said therefore, "A
certain nobleman went to a
distant country to receive a
kingdom for himself, and
then return.
13"And he called ten of
his slaves, and gave them
ten [f]minas, and said to
them, 'Do business *with*
this until I come *back*.'
14"But his citizens hated
him, and sent a delegation
after him, saying, 'We do
not want this man to reign
over us.'
15"And it came about that

ἦλθεν ἐπὶ τὸν τόπον, ἀναβλέψας ὁ Ἰησοῦς
he came upon the place, looking up – Jesus
εἶπεν πρὸς αὐτόν· Ζακχαῖε, σπεύσας
said to him : Zacchæus, making haste
κατάβηθι· σήμερον γὰρ ἐν τῷ οἴκῳ σου
come down; for to-day in the house of thee
δεῖ με μεῖναι. 6 καὶ σπεύσας κατέβη,
it behoves me to remain. And making haste he came down,
καὶ ὑπεδέξατο αὐτὸν χαίρων. 7 καὶ
and welcomed him rejoicing. And
ἰδόντες πάντες διεγόγγυζον λέγοντες ὅτι
seeing all murmured saying[,] –
παρὰ ἁμαρτωλῷ ἀνδρὶ εἰσῆλθεν καταλῦσαι.
With a sinful man he entered to lodge.
8 σταθεὶς δὲ Ζακχαῖος εἶπεν πρὸς τὸν
And standing Zacchæus said to the
κύριον· ἰδοὺ τὰ ἡμίση μου τῶν ὑπαρχόντων,
Lord : Behold[,] the half of me of the possessions,
κύριε, τοῖς πτωχοῖς δίδωμι, καὶ εἴ τινός
Lord, to the poor I give, and if anyone
τι ἐσυκοφάντησα, ἀποδίδωμι τετραπλοῦν.
anything I accused falsely, I restore fourfold.
9 εἶπεν δὲ πρὸς αὐτὸν ὁ Ἰησοῦς ὅτι
And said to him – Jesus[,] –
σήμερον σωτηρία τῷ οἴκῳ τούτῳ ἐγένετο,
To-day salvation – house to this came,
καθότι καὶ αὐτὸς υἱὸς Ἀβραάμ [ἐστιν]·
because even he a son of Abraham is;
10 ἦλθεν γὰρ ὁ υἱὸς τοῦ ἀνθρώπου ζητῆσαι
for came the Son – of man to seek
καὶ σῶσαι τὸ ἀπολωλός.
and to save the thing having been lost.
11 Ἀκουόντων δὲ αὐτῶν ταῦτα προσθεὶς
And hearing them[a] these things adding
=as they heard
εἶπεν παραβολήν, διὰ τὸ ἐγγὺς εἶναι
he told a parable, because of the near to be
=because he was near to Jerusalem and they thought
Ἰερουσαλὴμ αὐτὸν καὶ δοκεῖν αὐτοὺς ὅτι
Jerusalem him and to think them[b] that
παραχρῆμα μέλλει ἡ βασιλεία τοῦ θεοῦ
at once is(was) about the kingdom – of God
ἀναφαίνεσθαι· 12 εἶπεν οὖν· ἄνθρωπός τις
to appear; he said therefore : A certain man
εὐγενὴς ἐπορεύθη εἰς χώραν μακρὰν λαβεῖν
well born went to country a far to receive
ἑαυτῷ βασιλείαν καὶ ὑποστρέψαι. 13 καλέσας
for himself a kingdom and to return. having called
δὲ δέκα δούλους ἑαυτοῦ ἔδωκεν αὐτοῖς
And ten slaves of him*self* he gave them
δέκα μνᾶς, καὶ εἶπεν πρὸς αὐτούς·
ten minas, and said to them :
πραγματεύσασθε ἐν ᾧ ἔρχομαι. 14 οἱ δὲ
Trade ye while I am coming.* But the
πολῖται αὐτοῦ ἐμίσουν αὐτόν, καὶ ἀπέστειλαν
citizens of him hated him, and sent
πρεσβείαν ὀπίσω αὐτοῦ λέγοντες· οὐ θέλομεν
a delegation after him saying : We do not wish
τοῦτον βασιλεῦσαι ἐφ' ἡμᾶς. 15 καὶ
this man to reign over us. And
ἐγένετο ἐν τῷ ἐπανελθεῖν αὐτὸν λαβόντα
it came to pass in the to return him[be] having received
=when he returned

5When Jesus reached the
spot, he looked up and said
to him, "Zacchaeus, come
down immediately. I must
stay at your house today."
6So he came down at once
and welcomed him gladly.
7All the people saw this
and began to mutter, "He
has gone to be the guest of a
'sinner.' "
8But Zacchaeus stood up
and said to the Lord,
"Look, Lord! Here and
now I give half of my possessions to the poor, and if
I have cheated anybody out
of anything, I will pay back
four times the amount."
9Jesus said to him, "To-
day salvation has come to
this house, because this
man, too, is a son of Abraham. 10For the Son of Man
came to seek and to save
what was lost."

The Parable of the Ten Minas

11While they were listen-
ing to this, he went on to
tell them a parable, be-
cause he was near Jerusa-
lem and the people thought
that the kingdom of God
was going to appear at
once. 12He said: "A man of
noble birth went to a distant country to have him-
self appointed king and
then to return. 13So he
called ten of his servants
and gave them ten minas.[u]
'Put this money to work,'
he said, 'until I come back.'
14"But his subjects hated
him and sent a delegation
after him to say, 'We don't
want this man to be our
king.'
15"He was made king,

[f] A mina is equal to about 100 days' wages or nearly $20

*That is, "again." The present of this verb often has a futurist significance; *cf.* John 14. 3.

[u] *13* A mina was about three months' wages.

when he returned, after receiving the kingdom, he ordered that these slaves, to whom he had given the money, be called to him in order that he might know what business they had done.

16"And the first appeared, saying, 'Master, your mina has made ten minas more.'

17"And he said to him, 'Well done, good slave, because you have been faithful in a very little thing, be in authority over ten cities.'

18"And the second came, saying, 'Your mina, master, has made five minas.'

19"And he said to him also, 'And you are to be over five cities.'

20"And another came, saying, 'Master, behold your mina, which I kept put away in a handkerchief;

21for I was afraid of you, because you are an exacting man; you take up what you did not lay down, and reap what you did not sow.'

22"He *said to him, 'By your own words I will judge you, you worthless slave. Did you know that I am an exacting man, taking up what I did not lay down, and reaping what I did not sow?

23'Then why did you not put the money in the bank, and having come, I would have collected it with interest?'

24"And he said to the bystanders, 'Take the mina away from him, and give it to the one who has the ten minas.'

25"And they said to him, 'Master, he has ten minas *already*.'

26"I tell you, that to everyone who has shall *more* be given, but from the one who does not have, even what he does have shall be taken away.

27"But these enemies of mine, who did not want me to reign over them, bring them here and slay them in my presence."

Triumphal Entry

28And after He had said these things, He was going

τὴν βασιλείαν καὶ εἶπεν φωνηθῆναι αὐτῷ
the kingdom *and* he said to be called to him

τοὺς δούλους τούτους οἷς δεδώκει τὸ
– slaves these to whom he had given the

ἀργύριον, ἵνα γνοῖ τίς τί
money, that he might know [2]anyone [1]what

διεπραγματεύσατο. 16 παρεγένετο δὲ ὁ πρῶτος
gained by trading. And came the first

λέγων· κύριε, ἡ μνᾶ σου δέκα προσηργάσατο
saying : Lord, the mina of thee [2]ten [1]gained

μνᾶς. 17 καὶ εἶπεν αὐτῷ· εὖ γε, ἀγαθὲ δοῦλε,
[3]minas. And he said to him : Well, good slave,

ὅτι ἐν ἐλαχίστῳ πιστὸς ἐγένου, ἴσθι
because in a least thing faithful thou wast, be thou

ἐξουσίαν ἔχων ἐπάνω δέκα πόλεων. 18 καὶ
[2]authority [1]having over ten cities. And

ἦλθεν ὁ δεύτερος λέγων· ἡ μνᾶ σου,
came the second saying: The mina of thee,

κύριε, ἐποίησεν πέντε μνᾶς. 19 εἶπεν δὲ
lord, made five minas. And he said

καὶ τούτῳ· καὶ σὺ ἐπάνω γίνου πέντε
also to this one : And [2]thou [3]over [1]be five

πόλεων. 20 καὶ ὁ ἕτερος ἦλθεν λέγων·
cities. And the other came saying :

κύριε, ἰδοὺ ἡ μνᾶ σου, ἣν εἶχον
Lord, behold[,] the mina of thee, which I had

ἀποκειμένην ἐν σουδαρίῳ· 21 ἐφοβούμην γάρ
being put away in a napkin; for I feared

σε, ὅτι ἄνθρωπος αὐστηρὸς εἶ, αἴρεις ὃ
thee, because man an exacting thou art, thou takest what

οὐκ ἔθηκας, καὶ θερίζεις ὃ οὐκ ἔσπειρας.
thou didst not lay, and thou reapest what thou didst not sow.

22 λέγει αὐτῷ· ἐκ τοῦ στόματός σου
He says to him : Out of the mouth of thee

κρινῶ σε, πονηρὲ δοῦλε. ᾔδεις ὅτι ἐγὼ
I will judge thee, wicked slave. Knewest thou that I

ἄνθρωπος αὐστηρός εἰμι, αἴρων ὃ οὐκ
man an exacting am, taking what not

ἔθηκα, καὶ θερίζων ὃ οὐκ ἔσπειρα; 23 καὶ
I laid, and reaping what I sowed not ? And

διὰ τί οὐκ ἔδωκάς μου τὸ ἀργύριον ἐπὶ
why didst thou not give of me the money on

τράπεζαν; κἀγὼ ἐλθὼν σὺν τόκῳ ἂν
a table?* And I coming with interest –

αὐτὸ ἔπραξα. 24 καὶ τοῖς παρεστῶσιν
it would have exacted. And to the [ones] standing by

εἶπεν· ἄρατε ἀπ' αὐτοῦ τὴν μνᾶν καὶ
he said : Take from him the mina and

δότε τῷ τὰς δέκα μνᾶς ἔχοντι. 25 καὶ
give [1]to the [one] [3]the [4]ten [5]minas [2]having. And

εἶπαν αὐτῷ· κύριε, ἔχει δέκα μνᾶς.
they said to him : Lord, he has ten minas.

26 λέγω ὑμῖν ὅτι παντὶ τῷ ἔχοντι
I tell you that to everyone having

δοθήσεται, ἀπὸ δὲ τοῦ μὴ ἔχοντος καὶ
it will be given, and from the [one] not having even

ὃ ἔχει ἀρθήσεται. 27 πλὴν τοὺς ἐχθρούς
what he has will be taken. Nevertheless – enemies

μου τούτους τοὺς μὴ θελήσαντάς με
of me these the [ones] not wishing me

βασιλεῦσαι ἐπ' αὐτοὺς ἀγάγετε ὧδε καὶ
to reign over them bring ye here and

κατασφάξατε αὐτοὺς ἔμπροσθέν μου.
slay them before me.

28 Καὶ εἰπὼν ταῦτα ἐπορεύετο ἔμπροσθεν
And having said these things he went in front

* That is, a moneychanger's or banker's table.

however, and returned home. Then he sent for the servants to whom he had given the money, in order to find out what they had gained with it.

16"The first one came and said, 'Sir, your mina has earned ten more.'

17" 'Well done, my good servant!' his master replied. 'Because you have been trustworthy in a very small matter, take charge of ten cities.'

18"The second came and said, 'Sir, your mina has earned five more.'

19"His master answered, 'You take charge of five cities.'

20"Then another servant came and said, 'Sir, here is your mina; I have kept it laid away in a piece of cloth. 21I was afraid of you, because you are a hard man. You take out what you did not put in and reap what you did not sow.'

22"His master replied, 'I will judge you by your own words, you wicked servant! You knew, did you, that I am a hard man, taking out what I did not put in, and reaping what I did not sow? 23Why then didn't you put my money on deposit, so that when I came back, I could have collected it with interest?'

24"Then he said to those standing by, 'Take his mina away from him and give it to the one who has ten minas.'

25" 'Sir,' they said, 'he already has ten!'

26"He replied, 'I tell you that to everyone who has, more will be given, but as for the one who has nothing, even what he has will be taken away. 27But those enemies of mine who did not want me to be king over them—bring them here and kill them in front of me.' "

The Triumphal Entry

28After Jesus had said this, he went on ahead, go-

on ahead, ascending to
Jerusalem.
29And it came about that
when He approached Beth-
phage and Bethany, near
the mount that is called
Olivet, He sent two of the
disciples,
30saying, "Go into the village opposite *you*, in which
as you enter you will find a
colt tied, on which no one
yet has ever sat; untie it,
and bring it *here*.
31"And if anyone asks
you, 'Why are you untying
it?' thus shall you speak,
'The Lord has need of it.' "
32And those who were
sent went away and found
it just as He had told them.
33And as they were unty-
ing the colt, its owners said
to them, "Why are you un-
tying the colt?"
34And they said, "The
Lord has need of it."
35And they brought it to
Jesus, and they threw their
garments on the colt, and
put Jesus *on it*.
36And as He was going,
they were spreading their
garments in the road.
37And as He was now ap-
proaching, near the descent
of the Mount of Olives, the
whole multitude of the disciples began to praise God
joyfully with a loud voice
for all the miracles which
they had seen,
38saying,
"BLESSED IS THE King
WHO COMES IN THE
NAME OF THE LORD;
Peace in heaven and
glory in the highest!"
39And some of the Phari-
sees in the multitude said to
Him, "Teacher, rebuke
Your disciples."
40And He answered and
said, "I tell you, if these
become silent, the stones

ἀναβαίνων εἰς Ἱεροσόλυμα. **29** Καὶ ἐγένετο
going up to Jerusalem. And it came to pass
ὡς ἤγγισεν εἰς Βηθφαγὴ καὶ Βηθανίαν
as he drew near to Bethphage and Bethany
πρὸς τὸ ὄρος τὸ καλούμενον ἐλαιών,
toward the mount – *being* called of olives,
ἀπέστειλεν δύο τῶν μαθητῶν λέγων·
he sent two of the disciples saying :
30 ὑπάγετε εἰς τὴν κατέναντι κώμην, ἐν ᾗ
Go ye into the opposite village, in which
εἰσπορευόμενοι εὑρήσετε πῶλον δεδεμένον,
entering ye will find a colt *having been* tied,
ἐφ' ὃν οὐδεὶς πώποτε ἀνθρώπων ἐκάθισεν,
on which no one ever yet of men sat,
καὶ λύσαντες αὐτὸν ἀγάγετε. **31** καὶ ἐάν
and loosening it bring. And if
τις ὑμᾶς ἐρωτᾷ· διὰ τί λύετε; οὕτως
anyone you asks : Why loosen ye? thus
ἐρεῖτε· ὅτι ὁ κύριος αὐτοῦ χρείαν ἔχει.
shall ye say : Because the Lord of it need has.
32 ἀπελθόντες δὲ οἱ ἀπεσταλμένοι εὗρον
And going the [ones] *having been* sent found
καθὼς εἶπεν αὐτοῖς. **33** λυόντων δὲ
as he told them. And loosening
=as they were
αὐτῶν τὸν πῶλον εἶπαν οἱ κύριοι αὐτοῦ
them[a] the colt said the owners of it
loosening
πρὸς αὐτούς· τί λύετε τὸν πῶλον; **34** οἱ
to them : Why loosen ye the colt? [2]they
δὲ εἶπαν· ὅτι ὁ κύριος αὐτοῦ χρείαν ἔχει.
[1]And said : Because the Lord of it need has.
35 καὶ ἤγαγον αὐτὸν πρὸς τὸν Ἰησοῦν,
And they led it to – Jesus,
καὶ ἐπιρίψαντες αὐτῶν τὰ ἱμάτια ἐπὶ τὸν
and throwing *on* of them the garments on the
πῶλον ἐπεβίβασαν τὸν Ἰησοῦν. **36** πορευ-
colt they put on [it] – Jesus. And
ομένου δὲ αὐτοῦ ὑπεστρώννυον τὰ ἱμάτια
going him[a] they strewed the garments
=as he went
ἑαυτῶν ἐν τῇ ὁδῷ. **37** ἐγγίζοντος δὲ
of them*selves* in the way. And drawing near
=as he drew near
αὐτοῦ ἤδη πρὸς τῇ καταβάσει τοῦ ὄρους
him[a] now to the descent of the mount
τῶν ἐλαιῶν ἤρξαντο ἅπαν τὸ πλῆθος τῶν
of the olives began all the multitude of the
μαθητῶν χαίροντες αἰνεῖν τὸν θεὸν φωνῇ
disciples rejoicing to praise – God voice
μεγάλῃ περὶ πασῶν ὧν εἶδον δυνάμεων,
with a great about [1]all [3]which [4]they saw [2][the] powerful deeds,
38 λέγοντες· εὐλογημένος ὁ ἐρχόμενος, ὁ
saying : Blessed the coming [one], the
βασιλεὺς ἐν ὀνόματι κυρίου· ἐν οὐρανῷ
king in [the] name of [the] Lord; in heaven
εἰρήνη καὶ δόξα ἐν ὑψίστοις. **39** καί
peace and glory in highest places. And
τινες τῶν Φαρισαίων ἀπὸ τοῦ ὄχλου
some of the Pharisees from the crowd
εἶπαν πρὸς αὐτόν· διδάσκαλε, ἐπιτίμησον
said to him : Teacher, rebuke
τοῖς μαθηταῖς σου. **40** καὶ ἀποκριθεὶς
the disciples of thee. And answering
εἶπεν· λέγω ὑμῖν, ἐὰν οὗτοι σιωπήσουσιν,
he said : I tell you, if these shall(should) be silent,

ing up to Jerusalem. 29As
he approached Bethphage
and Bethany at the hill
called the Mount of Olives,
he sent two of his disciples,
saying to them, 30"Go to
the village ahead of you,
and as you enter it, you will
find a colt tied there, which
no one has ever ridden. Untie it and bring it here. 31If
anyone asks you, 'Why are
you untying it?' tell him,
'The Lord needs it.' "
32Those who were sent
ahead went and found it
just as he had told them.
33As they were untying the
colt, its owners asked
them, "Why are you unty-
ing the colt?"
34They replied, "The
Lord needs it."
35They brought it to
Jesus, threw their cloaks
on the colt and put Jesus on
it. 36As he went along, people spread their cloaks on
the road.
37When he came near the
place where the road goes
down the Mount of Olives,
the whole crowd of disci-
ples began joyfully to
praise God in loud voices
for all the miracles they had
seen:

38"Blessed is the king who
comes in the name
of the Lord!"[v]

"Peace in heaven and
glory in the
highest!"

39Some of the Pharisees
in the crowd said to Jesus,
"Teacher, rebuke your disciples!"
40"I tell you," he replied,
"if they keep quiet, the

[v]38 Psalm 118:26

will cry out!"

41And when He approached, He saw the city and wept over it,

42saying, "If you had known in this day, even you, the things which make for peace! But now they have been hidden from your eyes.

43"For the days shall come upon you when your enemies will throw up a bank before you, and surround you, and hem you in on every side,

44and will level you to the ground and your children within you, and they will not leave in you one stone upon another, because you did not recognize the time of your visitation."

Traders Driven from the Temple

45And He entered the temple and began to cast out those who were selling,

46saying to them, "It is written, 'AND MY HOUSE SHALL BE A HOUSE OF PRAYER,' but you have made it a ROBBERS' DEN."

47And He was teaching daily in the temple; but the chief priests and the scribes and the leading men among the people were trying to destroy Him,

48and they could not find anything that they might do, for all the people were hanging upon His words.

οἱ λίθοι κράξουσιν. **41** Καὶ ὡς ἤγγισεν,
the stones will cry out. And as he drew near,
ἰδὼν τὴν πόλιν ἔκλαυσεν ἐπ' αὐτήν,
seeing the city he wept over it,
42 λέγων ὅτι εἰ ἔγνως ἐν τῇ ἡμέρᾳ
saying[,] – If thou knewest in – day
ταύτῃ καὶ σὺ τὰ πρὸς εἰρήνην· νῦν δὲ
this even thou the things for peace; but now
ἐκρύβη ἀπὸ ὀφθαλμῶν σου. **43** ὅτι ἥξουσιν
they were hidden from eyes of thee. Because will come
ἡμέραι ἐπὶ σὲ καὶ παρεμβαλοῦσιν οἱ
days upon thee and [4]will raise up [1]the
ἐχθροί σου χάρακά σοι καὶ περικυκλώσουσίν
[2]enemies [3]of thee [5]a rampart to thee and will surround
σε καὶ συνέξουσίν σε πάντοθεν, **44** καὶ
thee and will press thee on all sides, and
ἐδαφιοῦσίν σε καὶ τὰ τέκνα σου ἐν σοί,
dash to the ground thee and the children of thee in thee,
καὶ οὐκ ἀφήσουσιν λίθον ἐπὶ λίθον ἐν σοί,
and will not leave stone upon stone in thee,
ἀνθ' ὧν οὐκ ἔγνως τὸν καιρὸν τῆς
because† thou knewest not the time of the
ἐπισκοπῆς σου. **45** Καὶ εἰσελθὼν εἰς τὸ
visitation of thee. And entering into the
ἱερὸν ἤρξατο ἐκβάλλειν τοὺς πωλοῦντας,
temple he began to expel the [ones] selling,
46 λέγων αὐτοῖς· γέγραπται· καὶ ἔσται ὁ
telling them : It has been written : And shall be the
οἶκός μου οἶκος προσευχῆς· ὑμεῖς δὲ
house of me a house of prayer; but ye
αὐτὸν ἐποιήσατε σπήλαιον λῃστῶν.
it made a den of robbers.
47 Καὶ ἦν διδάσκων τὸ καθ' ἡμέραν ἐν
And he was teaching daily† in
τῷ ἱερῷ· οἱ δὲ ἀρχιερεῖς καὶ οἱ
the temple; but the chief priests and the
γραμματεῖς ἐζήτουν αὐτὸν ἀπολέσαι καὶ οἱ
scribes [6]sought [8]him [7]to destroy [1]and [2]the
πρῶτοι τοῦ λαοῦ, **48** καὶ οὐχ εὕρισκον
[3]chief men [4]of the [5]people, and did not find
τὸ τί ποιήσωσιν· ὁ λαὸς γὰρ ἅπας
– what they might do; [3]the [4]people [1]for [2]all
ἐξεκρέματο αὐτοῦ ἀκούων.
hung upon him hearing.

stones will cry out."
41As he approached Jeru-
salem and saw the city, he
wept over it 42and said, "If
you, even you, had only
known on this day what
would bring you peace—
but now it is hidden from
your eyes. 43The days will
come upon you when your
enemies will build an em-
bankment against you and
encircle you and hem you
in on every side. 44They
will dash you to the ground,
you and the children within
your walls. They will not
leave one stone on another,
because you did not recognize the time of God's coming to you."

Jesus at the Temple

45Then he entered the
temple area and began driving out those who were selling. 46"It is written," he
said to them, " 'My house
will be a house of prayer'[w];
but you have made it 'a den
of robbers.'[x]"
47Every day he was
teaching at the temple. But
the chief priests, the teachers of the law and the leaders among the people were
trying to kill him. 48Yet
they could not find any way
to do it, because all the people hung on his words.

Chapter 20

Jesus' Authority Questioned

AND it came about on one of the days while He was teaching the people in the temple and preaching the gospel, that the chief priests and the scribes with the elders confronted *Him,*

2and they spoke, saying to Him, "Tell us by what authority You are doing these things, or who is the one who gave You this authority?"

3And He answered and said to them, "I shall also ask you a question, and you tell Me:

4"Was the baptism of John from heaven or from men?"

20 Καὶ ἐγένετο ἐν μιᾷ τῶν ἡμερῶν
And it came to pass on one of the days
διδάσκοντος αὐτοῦ τὸν λαὸν ἐν τῷ ἱερῷ
teaching him[a] the people in the temple
=as he was teaching
καὶ εὐαγγελιζομένου ἐπέστησαν οἱ ἀρχιερεῖς
and preaching good news[a] came upon [him] the chief priests
καὶ οἱ γραμματεῖς σὺν τοῖς πρεσβυτέροις,
and the scribes with the elders,
2 καὶ εἶπαν λέγοντες πρὸς αὐτόν· εἰπὸν
and spoke, saying to him : Tell
ἡμῖν ἐν ποίᾳ ἐξουσίᾳ ταῦτα ποιεῖς, ἢ τίς
us by what authority these things thou doest, or who
ἐστιν ὁ δούς σοι τὴν ἐξουσίαν ταύτην;
is the [one] having given thee – authority this?
3 ἀποκριθεὶς δὲ εἶπεν πρὸς αὐτούς·
And answering he said to them :
ἐρωτήσω ὑμᾶς κἀγὼ λόγον, καὶ εἴπατέ
Will ask you I also a word, and tell ye
μοι· **4** τὸ βάπτισμα Ἰωάννου ἐξ οὐρανοῦ
me : The baptism of John from heaven

Chapter 20

The Authority of Jesus Questioned

ONE day as he was
teaching the people in
the temple courts and
preaching the gospel, the
chief priests and the teachers of the law, together
with the elders, came up to
him. 2"Tell us by what authority you are doing these
things," they said. "Who
gave you this authority?"
3He replied, "I will also
ask you a question. Tell
me, 4John's baptism—was
it from heaven, or from
men?"

[w]*46* Isaiah 56:7
[x]*46* Jer. 7:11

5And they reasoned among themselves, saying, "If we say, 'From heaven,' He will say, 'Why did you not believe him?'

6"But if we say, 'From men,' all the people will stone us to death, for they are convinced that John was a prophet."

7And they answered that they did not know where *it came* from.

8And Jesus said to them, "Neither will I tell you by what authority I do these things."

Parable of the Vine-growers

9And He began to tell the people this parable: "A man planted a vineyard and rented it out to vine-growers, and went on a journey for a long time.

10"And at the *harvest* time he sent a slave to the vine-growers, in order that they might give him *some* of the produce of the vineyard; but the vine-growers beat him and sent him away empty-handed.

11"And he proceeded to send another slave; and they beat him also and treated him shamefully, and sent him away empty-handed.

12"And he proceeded to send a third; and this one also they wounded and cast out.

13"And the owner of the vineyard said, 'What shall I do? I will send my beloved son; perhaps they will respect him.'

14"But when the vine-growers saw him, they reasoned with one another, saying, 'This is the heir; let us kill him that the inheritance may be ours.'

15"And they threw him out of the vineyard and killed him. What, therefore, will the owner of the vineyard do to them?

16"He will come and destroy these vine-growers and will give the vineyard to others." And when they

ἦν ἢ ἐξ ἀνθρώπων; 5 οἱ δὲ συνελογίσαντο
was it or from men? And they debated

πρὸς ἑαυτοὺς λέγοντες ὅτι ἐὰν εἴπωμεν·
with themselves saying[,] – If we say :

ἐξ οὐρανοῦ, ἐρεῖ· διὰ τί οὐκ ἐπιστεύσατε
From heaven, he will say: Why did ye not believe

αὐτῷ; 6 ἐὰν δὲ εἴπωμεν· ἐξ ἀνθρώπων, ὁ
him? And if we say : From men, the

λαὸς ἅπας καταλιθάσει ἡμᾶς· πεπεισμένος
people all will stone us; for having been per-

γάρ ἐστιν Ἰωάννην προφήτην εἶναι. 7 καὶ
suaded it is* John a prophet to be. And

ἀπεκρίθησαν μὴ εἰδέναι πόθεν. 8 καὶ ὁ
they answered not to know whence. And –

Ἰησοῦς εἶπεν αὐτοῖς· οὐδὲ ἐγὼ λέγω
Jesus said to them : Neither I tell

ὑμῖν ἐν ποίᾳ ἐξουσίᾳ ταῦτα ποιῶ. 9 Ἤρξατο
you by what authority these things I do. he began

δὲ πρὸς τὸν λαὸν λέγειν τὴν παραβολὴν
And to the people to tell – parable

ταύτην. ἄνθρωπος ἐφύτευσεν ἀμπελῶνα,
this. A man planted a vineyard,

καὶ ἐξέδοτο αὐτὸν γεωργοῖς, καὶ ἀπεδή-
and let out it to husbandmen, and went

μησεν χρόνους ἱκανούς. 10 καὶ καιρῷ
away periods for considerable. And in time
=a long time.

ἀπέστειλεν πρὸς τοὺς γεωργοὺς δοῦλον,
he sent to the husbandmen a slave,

ἵνα ἀπὸ τοῦ καρποῦ τοῦ ἀμπελῶνος
that from the fruit of the vineyard

δώσουσιν αὐτῷ· οἱ δὲ γεωργοὶ ἐξαπέστειλαν
they will give him; but the husbandmen [2]sent [4]away out

αὐτὸν δείραντες κενόν. 11 καὶ προσέθετο
[3]him [1]beating [5]empty. And he added

ἕτερον πέμψαι δοῦλον· οἱ δὲ κἀκεῖνον
[2]another [1]to send slave; but they that one also
=he sent another slave in addition;

δείραντες καὶ ἀτιμάσαντες ἐξαπέστειλαν
beating and insulting sent away out

κενόν. 12 καὶ προσέθετο τρίτον πέμψαι·
empty. And he added a third to send;

οἱ δὲ καὶ τοῦτον τραυματίσαντες ἐξέβαλον.
but they also this one wounding threw out.

13 εἶπεν δὲ ὁ κύριος τοῦ ἀμπελῶνος· τί
And said the owner of the vineyard : What

ποιήσω; πέμψω τὸν υἱόν μου τὸν ἀγαπητόν·
may I do? I will send the son of me – beloved;

ἴσως τοῦτον ἐντραπήσονται. 14 ἰδόντες δὲ
perhaps this one they will regard. But seeing

αὐτὸν οἱ γεωργοὶ διελογίζοντο πρὸς
him the husbandmen debated with

ἀλλήλους λέγοντες· οὗτός ἐστιν ὁ κληρονόμος·
one another saying : This is the heir;

ἀποκτείνωμεν αὐτόν, ἵνα ἡμῶν γένηται
let us kill him, that of us may become

ἡ κληρονομία. 15 καὶ ἐκβαλόντες αὐτὸν
the inheritance. And throwing out him

ἔξω τοῦ ἀμπελῶνος ἀπέκτειναν. τί οὖν
outside the vineyard they killed. What therefore

ποιήσει αὐτοῖς ὁ κύριος τοῦ ἀμπελῶνος;
will do to them the owner of the vineyard?

16 ἐλεύσεται καὶ ἀπολέσει τοὺς γεωργοὺς
he will come and *will* destroy – husbandmen

τούτους, καὶ δώσει τὸν ἀμπελῶνα ἄλλοις.
these, and will give the vineyard to others.

* That is, the people (a collective singular) have been (=are) persuaded.

5They discussed it among
themselves and said, "If
we say, 'From heaven,' he
will ask, 'Why didn't you
believe him?' 6But if we
say, 'From men,' all the
people will stone us, be-
cause they are persuaded
that John was a prophet."
7So they answered, "We
don't know where it was
from."
8Jesus said, "Neither will
I tell you by what authority
I am doing these things."

The Parable of the Tenants

9He went on to tell the
people this parable: "A
man planted a vineyard,
rented it to some farmers
and went away for a long
time. 10At harvest time he
sent a servant to the tenants so they would give him
some of the fruit of the
vineyard. But the tenants
beat him and sent him away
empty-handed. 11He sent
another servant, but that
one also they beat and
treated shamefully and sent
away empty-handed. 12He
sent still a third, and they
wounded him and threw
him out.
13"Then the owner of the
vineyard said, 'What shall I
do? I will send my son,
whom I love; perhaps they
will respect him.'
14"But when the tenants
saw him, they talked the
matter over. 'This is the
heir,' they said. 'Let's kill
him, and the inheritance
will be ours.' 15So they
threw him out of the vineyard and killed him.
"What then will the own-
er of the vineyard do to
them? 16He will come and
kill those tenants and give
the vineyard to others."
When the people heard

heard it, they said, "May it
never be!"
17 But He looked at them
and said, "What then is this
that is written,
'THE STONE WHICH THE
BUILDERS REJECTED,
THIS BECAME THE CHIEF
CORNER *stone*'?
18 "Everyone who falls on
that stone will be broken to
pieces; but on whomever it
falls, it will scatter him like
dust."

Tribute to Caesar

19 And the scribes and the
chief priests tried to lay
hands on Him that very
hour, and they feared the
people; for they understood
that He spoke this parable
against them.
20 And they watched Him,
and sent spies who pre-
tended to be righteous, in
order that they might catch
Him in some statement, so
as to deliver Him up to the
rule and the authority of the
governor.
21 And they questioned
Him, saying, "Teacher, we
know that You speak and
teach correctly, and You
are not partial to any, but
teach the way of God in
truth.
22 "Is it lawful for us to
pay taxes to Caesar, or
not?"
23 But He detected their
trickery and said to them,
24 "Show Me a [g] denarius.
Whose likeness and in-
scription does it have?"
And they said, "Caesar's."
25 And He said to them,
"Then render to Caesar the
things that are Caesar's,
and to God the things that
are God's."
26 And they were unable
to catch Him in a saying in
the presence of the people;
and marveling at His an-
swer, they became silent.

Is There a Resurrection?

27 Now there came to Him
some of the Sadducees
(who say that there is no
resurrection),

[g] The denarius was equivalent to one day's wage

ἀκούσαντες δὲ εἶπαν· μὴ γένοιτο. **17** ὁ δὲ
And hearing they said : May it not be. And he
ἐμβλέψας αὐτοῖς εἶπεν· τί οὖν ἐστιν τὸ
looking at them said : What therefore is –
γεγραμμένον τοῦτο· λίθον ὃν ἀπεδοκίμασαν
having been written this : [The] stone which [3]rejected
οἱ οἰκοδομοῦντες, οὗτος ἐγενήθη εἰς κεφαλὴν
[1]the [ones] [2]building, this came to be for [the] head
γωνίας; **18** πᾶς ὁ πεσὼν ἐπ' ἐκεῖνον τὸν
of [the] corner? Everyone falling on that –
λίθον συνθλασθήσεται· ἐφ' ὃν δ' ἂν πέσῃ,
stone will be broken in pieces; but on whomever it falls,
λικμήσει αὐτόν. **19** Καὶ ἐζήτησαν οἱ
it will crush to powder him. And sought the
γραμματεῖς καὶ οἱ ἀρχιερεῖς ἐπιβαλεῖν ἐπ'
scribes and the chief priests to lay *on* on
αὐτὸν τὰς χεῖρας ἐν αὐτῇ τῇ ὥρᾳ, καὶ
him the(ir) hands in [2]same [1]the hour, and
ἐφοβήθησαν τὸν λαόν· ἔγνωσαν γὰρ ὅτι
feared the people; for they knew that
πρὸς αὐτοὺς εἶπεν τὴν παραβολὴν ταύτην.
at them he told – parable this.
20 Καὶ παρατηρήσαντες ἀπέστειλαν ἐγκαθέτους
And watching carefully they sent spies
ὑποκρινομένους ἑαυτοὺς δικαίους εἶναι, ἵνα
pretending themselves righteous to be, that
ἐπιλάβωνται αὐτοῦ λόγου, ὥστε παραδοῦναι
they might seize of him a word, so as to deliver
αὐτὸν τῇ ἀρχῇ καὶ τῇ ἐξουσίᾳ τοῦ
him to the rule and to the authority of the
ἡγεμόνος. **21** καὶ ἐπηρώτησαν αὐτὸν
governor. And they questioned him
λέγοντες· διδάσκαλε, οἴδαμεν ὅτι ὀρθῶς
saying : Teacher, we know that [4]rightly
λέγεις καὶ διδάσκεις καὶ οὐ λαμβάνεις
[1]thou speakest [2]and [3]teachest and receivest not
=regardest not persons,
πρόσωπον, ἀλλ' ἐπ' ἀληθείας τὴν ὁδὸν τοῦ
a face, but on [the basis of] truth the way –
θεοῦ διδάσκεις· **22** ἔξεστιν ἡμᾶς Καίσαρι
of God teachest; is it lawful for us to Cæsar
φόρον δοῦναι ἢ οὔ; **23** κατανοήσας δὲ
tribute to give or not? And perceiving
αὐτῶν τὴν πανουργίαν εἶπεν πρὸς αὐτούς·
of them the cleverness he said to them :
24 δείξατέ μοι δηνάριον· τίνος ἔχει εἰκόνα
Show me a denarius; of whom has it an image
καὶ ἐπιγραφήν; οἱ δὲ εἶπαν· Καίσαρος.
and superscription? And they said : Of Cæsar.
25 ὁ δὲ εἶπεν πρὸς αὐτούς· τοίνυν ἀπόδοτε
And he said to them : So render
τὰ Καίσαρος Καίσαρι καὶ τὰ τοῦ θεοῦ
the things of Cæsar to Cæsar and the things – of God
τῷ θεῷ. **26** καὶ οὐκ ἴσχυσαν ἐπιλαβέσθαι
– to God. And they were not able to seize
αὐτοῦ ῥήματος ἐναντίον τοῦ λαοῦ, καὶ
of him a word in the presence of the people, and
θαυμάσαντες ἐπὶ τῇ ἀποκρίσει αὐτοῦ
marvelling at the answer of him
ἐσίγησαν.
they were silent.
27 Προσελθόντες δέ τινες τῶν Σαδ-
And [4]approaching [1]some [2]of the [3]Sad-
δουκαίων, οἱ ἀντιλέγοντες ἀνάστασιν μὴ
ducees, the [ones] saying in opposition* a resurrection not

*That is, to the Pharisees and to the generally held opinion.

this, they said, "May this
never be!"
17 Jesus looked directly at
them and asked, "Then
what is the meaning of that
which is written:

" 'The stone the builders
rejected
has become the
capstone'[y] [z]?

18 Everyone who falls on
that stone will be broken to
pieces, but he on whom it
falls will be crushed."
19 The teachers of the law
and the chief priests looked
for a way to arrest him immediately, because they
knew he had spoken this
parable against them. But
they were afraid of the people.

Paying Taxes to Caesar

20 Keeping a close watch
on him, they sent spies,
who pretended to be hon-
est. They hoped to catch
Jesus in something he said
so that they might hand him
over to the power and au-
thority of the governor.
21 So the spies questioned
him: "Teacher, we know
that you speak and teach
what is right, and that you
do not show partiality but
teach the way of God in accordance with the truth.
22 Is it right for us to pay
taxes to Caesar or not?"
23 He saw through their
duplicity and said to them,
24 "Show me a denarius.
Whose portrait and inscription are on it?"
25 "Caesar's," they re-
plied.
He said to them, "Then
give to Caesar what is Caesar's, and to God what is
God's."
26 They were unable to
trap him in what he had said
there in public. And astonished by his answer, they
became silent.

The Resurrection and Marriage

27 Some of the Sadducees,
who say there is no resurrection, came to Jesus with

[y] 17 Or *cornerstone*
[z] 17 Psalm 118:22

28and they questioned
Him, saying, "Teacher,
Moses wrote for us that IF A
MAN'S BROTHER DIES, having
a wife, AND HE IS CHILDLESS,
HIS BROTHER SHOULD TAKE
THE WIFE AND RAISE UP OFF-
SPRING TO HIS BROTHER.
29"Now there were seven
brothers; and the first took
a wife, and died childless;
30and the second
31and the third took her;
and in the same way all
seven died, leaving no children.
32"Finally the woman
died also.
33"In the resurrection
therefore, which one's wife
will she be? For all seven
had her as wife."
34And Jesus said to them,
"The sons of this age marry
and are given in marriage,
35but those who are con-
sidered worthy to attain to
that age and the resurrection from the dead, neither
marry, nor are given in
marriage;
36for neither can they die
anymore, for they are like
angels, and are sons of
God, being sons of the
resurrection.
37"But that the dead are
raised, even Moses
showed, in the *passage*
about the burning bush,
where he calls the Lord THE
GOD OF ABRAHAM, AND THE
GOD OF ISAAC, AND THE GOD
OF JACOB.
38"Now He is not the
God of the dead, but of the
living; for all live to Him."
39And some of the scribes
answered and said "Teach-
er, You have spoken
well."
40For they did not have
courage to question Him
any longer about anything.
41And He said to them,
"How *is it that* they say
[h]the Christ is David's son?
42"For David himself
says in the book of Psalms,

[h]I.e., the Messiah

εἶναι, ἐπηρώτησαν αὐτὸν **28** λέγοντες·
to be, they questioned him saying :
διδάσκαλε, Μωϋσῆς ἔγραψεν ἡμῖν, ἐάν
Teacher, Moses wrote to us, If
τινος ἀδελφὸς ἀποθάνῃ ἔχων γυναῖκα, καὶ
of anyone a brother dies having a wife, and
οὗτος ἄτεκνος ᾖ, ἵνα λάβῃ ὁ ἀδελφὸς
this man childless is, that [4]should take [1]the [2]brother
αὐτοῦ τὴν γυναῖκα καὶ ἐξαναστήσῃ σπέρμα
[3]of him [5]the [6]wife and raise up seed
τῷ ἀδελφῷ αὐτοῦ. **29** ἑπτὰ οὖν ἀδελφοὶ
to the brother of him. Seven therefore brothers
ἦσαν· καὶ ὁ πρῶτος λαβὼν γυναῖκα
there were; and the first having taken a wife
ἀπέθανεν ἄτεκνος· **30** καὶ ὁ δεύτερος **31** καὶ
died childless; and the second and
ὁ τρίτος ἔλαβεν αὐτήν, ὡσαύτως δὲ καὶ
the third took her, and similarly also
οἱ ἑπτὰ οὐ κατέλιπον τέκνα καὶ ἀπέθανον.
the seven did not leave children and died.
32 ὕστερον καὶ ἡ γυνὴ ἀπέθανεν. **33** ἡ
Lastly also the woman died. The
γυνὴ οὖν ἐν τῇ ἀναστάσει τίνος αὐτῶν
woman therefore in the resurrection of which of them
γίνεται γυνή; οἱ γὰρ ἑπτὰ ἔσχον αὐτὴν
becomes she wife? for the seven had her
γυναῖκα. **34** καὶ εἶπεν αὐτοῖς ὁ Ἰησοῦς·
[as] wife. And said to them – Jesus :
οἱ υἱοὶ τοῦ αἰῶνος τούτου γαμοῦσιν καὶ
The sons – age of this marry and
γαμίσκονται, **35** οἱ δὲ καταξιωθέντες τοῦ
are given in marriage, but the [ones] counted worthy –
αἰῶνος ἐκείνου τυχεῖν καὶ τῆς ἀναστάσεως
[3]age [2]*of* that [1]to obtain and *of* the resurrection
τῆς ἐκ νεκρῶν οὔτε γαμοῦσιν οὔτε
– out of [the] dead neither marry nor
γαμίζονται· **36** οὐδὲ γὰρ ἀποθανεῖν ἔτι
are given in marriage; for not even *to* die more
δύνανται, ἰσάγγελοι γάρ εἰσιν, καὶ υἱοί
can they, for equal to angels they are, and [2]sons
εἰσιν θεοῦ τῆς ἀναστάσεως υἱοὶ ὄντες.
[1]they are [3]of God [6]of the [7]resurrection [5]sons [4]being.
37 ὅτι δὲ ἐγείρονται οἱ νεκροί, καὶ
But that are raised the dead, even
Μωϋσῆς ἐμήνυσεν ἐπὶ τῆς βάτου, ὡς
Moses pointed out at the bush, as
λέγει κύριον τὸν θεὸν Ἀβραὰμ καὶ θεὸν
he calls [the] Lord the God of Abraham and God
Ἰσαὰκ καὶ θεὸν Ἰακώβ· **38** θεὸς δὲ οὐκ
of Isaac and God of Jacob; but God not
ἔστιν νεκρῶν ἀλλὰ ζώντων· πάντες γὰρ
he is of dead persons but of living; for all
αὐτῷ ζῶσιν. **39** ἀποκριθέντες δέ τινες
to him live. And answering some
τῶν γραμματέων εἶπαν· διδάσκαλε, καλῶς
of the scribes said : Teacher, well
εἶπας. **40** οὐκέτι γὰρ ἐτόλμων ἐπερωτᾶν
thou sayest. For no more dared they *to* question
αὐτὸν οὐδέν.
him no(any)thing.

41 Εἶπεν δὲ πρὸς αὐτούς· πῶς λέγουσιν
And he said to them : How say they
τὸν χριστὸν εἶναι Δαυὶδ υἱόν; **42** αὐτὸς
the Christ to be of David son? himself
γὰρ Δαυὶδ λέγει ἐν βίβλῳ ψαλμῶν·
For David says in [the] roll of psalms :

a question. 28"Teacher,"
they said, "Moses wrote
for us that if a man's brother dies and leaves a wife but
no children, the man must
marry the widow and have
children for his brother.
29Now there were seven
brothers. The first one married a woman and died
childless. 30The second
31and then the third married
her, and in the same way
the seven died, leaving no
children. 32Finally, the
woman died too. 33Now
then, at the resurrection
whose wife will she be,
since the seven were mar-
ried to her?"
34Jesus replied, "The
people of this age marry
and are given in marriage.
35But those who are considered worthy of taking part
in that age and in the resurrection from the dead will
neither marry nor be given
in marriage, 36and they can
no longer die; for they are
like the angels. They are
God's children, since they
are children of the resurrection. 37But in the ac-
count of the bush, even
Moses showed that the
dead rise, for he calls the
Lord 'the God of Abraham,
and the God of Isaac, and
the God of Jacob.'[a] 38He is
not the God of the dead, but
of the living, for to him all
are alive."
39Some of the teachers of
the law responded, "Well
said, teacher!" 40And no
one dared to ask him any
more questions.

Whose Son Is the Christ?

41Then Jesus said to
them, "How is it that they
say the Christ[b] is the Son
of David? 42David himself
declares in the Book of

[a]*37* Exodus 3:6
[b]*41* Or *Messiah*

'THE LORD SAID TO MY
LORD,
"SIT AT MY RIGHT
HAND,
43 UNTIL I MAKE THINE
ENEMIES A FOOTSTOOL
FOR THY FEET." '
44"David therefore calls
Him 'Lord,' and how is He
his son?"
45And while all the people
were listening, He said to
the disciples,
46"Beware of the scribes,
who like to walk around in
long robes, and love re-
spectful greetings in the
market places, and chief
seats in the synagogues,
and places of honor at banquets,
47who devour widows'
houses, and for appear-
ance's sake offer long
prayers; these will receive
greater condemnation."

εἶπεν κύριος τῷ κυρίῳ μου· κάθου ἐκ
Said [the] LORD to the Lord of me: Sit thou at
δεξιῶν μου 43 ἕως ἂν θῶ τοὺς ἐχθρούς σου
[the] right of me until I put the enemies of thee
ὑποπόδιον τῶν ποδῶν σου. 44 Δαυὶδ
a footstool of the feet of thee. David
οὖν αὐτὸν κύριον καλεῖ, καὶ πῶς αὐτοῦ
therefore him Lord calls, and how of him
υἱός ἐστιν;
son is he?
45 Ἀκούοντος δὲ παντὸς τοῦ λαοῦ εἶπεν
And hearing all the people* he said
=as all the people heard
τοῖς μαθηταῖς· 46 προσέχετε ἀπὸ τῶν
to the disciples: Beware from(of) the
γραμματέων τῶν θελόντων περιπατεῖν ἐν
scribes – wishing to walk about in
στολαῖς καὶ φιλούντων ἀσπασμοὺς ἐν ταῖς
robes and liking greetings in the
ἀγοραῖς καὶ πρωτοκαθεδρίας ἐν ταῖς
marketplaces and chief seats in the
συναγωγαῖς καὶ πρωτοκλισίας ἐν τοῖς
synagogues and chief couches in the
δείπνοις, 47 οἳ κατεσθίουσιν τὰς οἰκίας
suppers, who devour the houses
τῶν χηρῶν καὶ προφάσει μακρὰ προσεύχονται·
of the widows and under pretence long pray;
οὗτοι λήμψονται περισσότερον κρίμα.
these will receive severer judgment.

Psalms:
" 'The Lord said to my
Lord:
"Sit at my right hand
43until I make your
enemies
a footstool for your
feet." '[c]
44David calls him 'Lord.'
How then can he be his
son?"
45While all the people
were listening, Jesus said
to his disciples, 46"Beware
of the teachers of the law.
They like to walk around in
flowing robes and love to
be greeted in the market-
places and have the most
important seats in the synagogues and the places of
honor at banquets. 47They
devour widows' houses
and for a show make
lengthy prayers. Such men
will be punished most se-
verely."

Chapter 21

The Widow's Gift

AND He looked up and
saw the rich putting
their gifts into the treasury.
2And He saw a certain
poor widow putting in two
small copper coins.
3And He said, "Truly I
say to you, this poor widow
put in more than all *of
them;*
4for they all out of their
surplus put into the offering; but she out of her poverty put in all that she had
to live on."
5And while some were
talking about the temple,
that it was adorned with
beautiful stones and votive
gifts, He said,
6"*As for* these things
which you are looking at,
the days will come in which
there will not be left one
stone upon another which
will not be torn down."
7And they questioned
Him, saying, "Teacher,
when therefore will these
things be? And what *will be*
the sign when these things

21 Ἀναβλέψας δὲ εἶδεν τοὺς βάλλοντας
And looking up he saw [1]the [3]putting
εἰς τὸ γαζοφυλακεῖον τὰ δῶρα αὐτῶν
[4]into [5]the [6]treasury [7]the [8]gifts [9]of them
πλουσίους. 2 εἶδεν δέ τινα χήραν πενιχρὰν
[2]rich [ones]. And he saw a certain widow poor
βάλλουσαν ἐκεῖ λεπτὰ δύο, 3 καὶ εἶπεν·
putting there lepta two, and he said:
ἀληθῶς λέγω ὑμῖν ὅτι ἡ χήρα αὕτη ἡ
Truly I tell you that – [3]widow [1]this –
πτωχὴ πλεῖον πάντων ἔβαλεν· 4 πάντες
[2]poor more [than] all put; [2]all
γὰρ οὗτοι ἐκ τοῦ περισσεύοντος αὐτοῖς
[1]for these out of the abounding to them*
=their abundance
ἔβαλον εἰς τὰ δῶρα, αὕτη δὲ ἐκ τοῦ
put into the gifts, but this woman out of the
ὑστερήματος αὐτῆς πάντα τὸν βίον ὃν
want of her [2]all [3]the [4]living [5]which
εἶχεν ἔβαλεν.
[6]she had [1]put.
5 Καί τινων λεγόντων περὶ τοῦ ἱεροῦ, ὅτι
And some speaking* about the temple, that
=as some spoke
λίθοις καλοῖς καὶ ἀναθήμασιν κεκόσμηται,
with stones beautiful and gifts it has(had) been adorned,
εἶπεν· 6 ταῦτα ἃ θεωρεῖτε, ἐλεύσονται
he said: These things which ye behold, will come
ἡμέραι ἐν αἷς οὐκ ἀφεθήσεται λίθος ἐπὶ
days in which there will not be left stone on
λίθῳ ὃς οὐ καταλυθήσεται. 7 ἐπηρώτησαν δὲ
stone which will not be overthrown. And they questioned
αὐτὸν λέγοντες· διδάσκαλε, πότε οὖν
him saying: Teacher, when therefore
ταῦτα ἔσται; καὶ τί τὸ σημεῖον ὅταν
these things will be? And what [will be] the sign when

Chapter 21

The Widow's Offering

AS he looked up, Jesus
saw the rich putting
their gifts into the temple
treasury. 2He also saw a
poor widow put in two very
small copper coins.[d] 3"I
tell you the truth," he said,
"this poor widow has put in
more than all the others.
4All these people gave their
gifts out of their wealth; but
she out of her poverty put
in all she had to live on."

Signs of the End of the Age

5Some of his disciples
were remarking about how
the temple was adorned
with beautiful stones and
with gifts dedicated to God.
But Jesus said, 6"As for
what you see here, the time
will come when not one
stone will be left on another; every one of them will
be thrown down."
7"Teacher," they asked,
"when will these things
happen? And what will be
the sign that they are about

[c]43 Psalm 110:1
[d]2 Greek *two lepta*

are about to take place?"
8And He said, "See to it
that you be not misled; for
many will come in My
name, saying, 'I am *He*,'
and, 'The time is at hand';
do not go after them.
9"And when you hear of
wars and disturbances, do
not be terrified; for these
things must take place first,
but the end *does* not *follow*
immediately."

Things to Come

10Then He continued by
saying to them, "Nation
will rise against nation, and
kingdom against kingdom,
11and there will be great
earthquakes, and in various
places plagues and famines;
and there will be terrors
and great signs from
heaven.
12"But before all these
things, they will lay their
hands on you and will
persecute you, delivering
you to the synagogues and
prisons, bringing you be-
fore kings and governors
for My name's sake.
13"It will lead to an op-
portunity for your testi-
mony.
14"So make up your
minds not to prepare
beforehand to defend yourselves;
15for I will give you utterance and wisdom which
none of your opponents
will be able to resist or refute.
16"But you will be de-
livered up even by parents
and brothers and relatives
and friends, and they will
put *some* of you to death,
17and you will be hated by
all on account of My name.
18"Yet not a hair of your
head will perish.
19"By your endurance
you will gain your lives.
20"But when you see
Jerusalem surrounded by
armies, then recognize that
her desolation is at hand.
21"Then let those who are
in Judea flee to the mountains, and let those who are

μέλλῃ ταῦτα γίνεσθαι; **8** ὁ δὲ εἶπεν·
[2]are about [1]these things [3]to happen? And he said :

βλέπετε μὴ πλανηθῆτε· πολλοὶ γὰρ
Beware lest ye be led astray; for many

ἐλεύσονται ἐπὶ τῷ ὀνόματί μου λέγοντες·
will come on(in) the name of me saying :

ἐγώ εἰμι, καί· ὁ καιρὸς ἤγγικεν· μὴ
I am, and : The time has drawn near; not

πορευθῆτε ὀπίσω αὐτῶν. **9** ὅταν δὲ
go ye after them. And when

ἀκούσητε πολέμους καὶ ἀκαταστασίας, μὴ
ye hear [of] wars and commotions, not

πτοηθῆτε· δεῖ γὰρ ταῦτα γενέσθαι
be ye scared; for it behoves these things to happen

πρῶτον, ἀλλ' οὐκ εὐθέως τὸ τέλος. **10** Τότε
first, but not immediately the end. Then

ἔλεγεν αὐτοῖς· ἐγερθήσεται ἔθνος ἐπ' ἔθνος
he said to them : Will be raised nation against nation

καὶ βασιλεία ἐπὶ βασιλείαν, **11** σεισμοί τε
and kingdom against kingdom, and earthquakes

μεγάλοι καὶ κατὰ τόπους λοιμοὶ καὶ λιμοὶ
great and from place to place† pestilences and famines

ἔσονται, φόβητρά τε καὶ ἀπ' οὐρανοῦ
there will be, and terrors and [3]from [4]heaven

σημεῖα μεγάλα ἔσται. **12** πρὸ δὲ τούτων
[2]signs [1]great there will be. But before these things

πάντων ἐπιβαλοῦσιν ἐφ' ὑμᾶς τὰς χεῖρας
all they will lay *on* on you the hands

αὐτῶν καὶ διώξουσιν, παραδιδόντες εἰς τὰς
of them and will persecute, delivering to the

συναγωγὰς καὶ φυλακάς, ἀπαγομένους ἐπὶ
synagogues and prisons, being led away on(before)

βασιλεῖς καὶ ἡγεμόνας ἕνεκεν τοῦ ὀνόματός
kings and governors for the sake of the name

μου· **13** ἀποβήσεται ὑμῖν εἰς μαρτύριον.
of me; it will turn out to you for a testimony.

14 θέτε οὖν ἐν ταῖς καρδίαις ὑμῶν μὴ
Put therefore in the hearts of you not

προμελετᾶν ἀπολογηθῆναι· **15** ἐγὼ γὰρ
to practise beforehand to defend [yourselves]; for I

δώσω ὑμῖν στόμα καὶ σοφίαν, ᾗ οὐ
will give you a mouth and wisdom, which not

δυνήσονται ἀντιστῆναι ἢ ἀντειπεῖν ἅπαντες οἱ
will be able to withstand or to contradict all the

ἀντικείμενοι ὑμῖν. **16** παραδοθήσεσθε δὲ καὶ
[ones] opposing you. And ye will be betrayed also

ὑπὸ γονέων καὶ ἀδελφῶν καὶ συγγενῶν
by parents and brothers and relatives

καὶ φίλων, καὶ θανατώσουσιν ἐξ ὑμῶν,
and friends, and they will put to death [some] of you,

17 καὶ ἔσεσθε μισούμενοι ὑπὸ πάντων διὰ
and ye will be *being* hated by all men because of

τὸ ὄνομά μου. **18** καὶ θρὶξ ἐκ τῆς
the name of me. And a hair of the

κεφαλῆς ὑμῶν οὐ μὴ ἀπόληται· **19** ἐν τῇ
head of you by no means will perish; in the

ὑπομονῇ ὑμῶν κτήσεσθε τὰς ψυχὰς ὑμῶν.
endurance of you ye will gain the souls of you.

20 Ὅταν δὲ ἴδητε κυκλουμένην ὑπὸ
But when ye see [2]being surrounded [3]by

στρατοπέδων Ἰερουσαλήμ, τότε γνῶτε ὅτι
[4]camps [1]Jerusalem, then know ye that

ἤγγικεν ἡ ἐρήμωσις αὐτῆς. **21** τότε οἱ ἐν
has drawn near the desolation of it. Then the [ones] in

τῇ Ἰουδαίᾳ φευγέτωσαν εἰς τὰ ὄρη, καὶ
– Judæa let them flee to the mountains, and

to take place?"
8He replied: "Watch out
that you are not deceived.
For many will come in my
name, claiming, 'I am he,'
and, 'The time is near.' Do
not follow them. 9When
you hear of wars and revo-
lutions, do not be frightened. These things must
happen first, but the end
will not come right away."
10Then he said to them:
"Nation will rise against
nation, and kingdom
against kingdom. 11There
will be great earthquakes,
famines and pestilences in
various places, and fearful
events and great signs from
heaven.
12"But before all this,
they will lay hands on you
and persecute you. They
will deliver you to syna-
gogues and prisons, and
you will be brought before
kings and governors, and
all on account of my name.
13This will result in your
being witnesses to them.
14But make up your mind
not to worry beforehand
how you will defend your-
selves. 15For I will give you
words and wisdom that
none of your adversaries
will be able to resist or contradict. 16You will be betrayed even by parents,
brothers, relatives and
friends, and they will put
some of you to death. 17All
men will hate you because
of me. 18But not a hair of
your head will perish. 19By
standing firm you will gain
life.
20"When you see Jerusa-
lem being surrounded by
armies, you will know that
its desolation is near.
21Then let those who are in
Judea flee to the moun-
tains, let those in the city

in the midst of the city depart, and let not those who
are in the country enter the
city;
22because these are days
of vengeance, in order that
all things which are written
may be fulfilled.
23"Woe to those who are
with child and to those who
nurse babes in those days;
for there will be great distress upon the land, and
wrath to this people,
24and they will fall by the
edge of the sword, and will
be led captive into all the
nations; and Jerusalem will
be trampled under foot by
the Gentiles until the times
of the Gentiles be fulfilled.

The Return of Christ

25"And there will be signs
in sun and moon and stars,
and upon the earth dismay
among nations, in perplexity at the roaring of the sea
and the waves,
26men fainting from fear
and the expectation of the
things which are coming
upon the world; for the
powers of the heavens will
be shaken.
27"And then they will see
THE SON OF MAN COMING IN
A CLOUD with power and
great glory.
28"But when these things
begin to take place,
straighten up and lift up
your heads, because your
redemption is drawing
near."
29And He told them a par-
able: "Behold the fig tree
and all the trees;
30as soon as they put forth
leaves, you see it and know
for yourselves that summer
is now near.
31"Even so you, too,
when you see these things
happening, recognize that
the kingdom of God is near.
32"Truly I say to you, this
generation will not pass
away until all things take
place.
33"Heaven and earth will
pass away, but My words
will not pass away.

οἱ ἐν μέσῳ αὐτῆς ἐκχωρείτωσαν, καὶ
the [ones] in [the] midst of it let them depart out, and
οἱ ἐν ταῖς χώραις μὴ εἰσερχέσθωσαν εἰς
the [ones] in the districts let them not enter into
αὐτήν, 22 ὅτι ἡμέραι ἐκδικήσεως αὗταί
it, because days of vengeance these
εἰσιν τοῦ πλησθῆναι πάντα τὰ γεγραμμένα.
are – to be fulfilled[d] all the things having been written.
23 οὐαὶ ταῖς ἐν γαστρὶ ἐχούσαις καὶ ταῖς
Woe to the pregnant women† and to the
θηλαζούσαις ἐν ἐκείναις ταῖς ἡμέραις·
[ones] giving suck in those – days;
ἔσται γὰρ ἀνάγκη μεγάλη ἐπὶ τῆς γῆς
for there will be distress great on the land
καὶ ὀργὴ τῷ λαῷ τούτῳ, 24 καὶ πεσοῦνται
and wrath – people to this, and they will fall
στόματι μαχαίρης καὶ αἰχμαλωτισθή-
by [the] mouth(edge) of [the] sword and will be led
σονται εἰς τὰ ἔθνη πάντα, καὶ Ἰερουσαλὴμ
captive to the nations all, and Jerusalem
ἔσται πατουμένη ὑπὸ ἐθνῶν, ἄχρι οὗ
will be *being* trodden down by nations, until
πληρωθῶσιν καιροὶ ἐθνῶν. 25 Καὶ ἔσονται
are accomplished [the] times of [the] nations. And there will be
σημεῖα ἐν ἡλίῳ καὶ σελήνῃ καὶ ἄστροις,
signs in sun and moon and stars,
καὶ ἐπὶ τῆς γῆς συνοχὴ ἐθνῶν ἐν ἀπορίᾳ
and on the earth anxiety of nations in perplexity
ἤχους θαλάσσης καὶ σάλου, 26 ἀποψυχόντων
of [the] sound of [the] sea and surf, fainting
=while men faint
ἀνθρώπων ἀπὸ φόβου καὶ προσδοκίας τῶν
men[a] from fear and expectation of the
ἐπερχομένων τῇ οἰκουμένῃ· αἱ γὰρ δυνάμεις
things coming on the inhabited earth; for the powers
τῶν οὐρανῶν σαλευθήσονται. 27 καὶ τότε
of the heavens will be shaken. And then
ὄψονται τὸν υἱὸν τοῦ ἀνθρώπου ἐρχόμενον
they will see the Son – of man coming
ἐν νεφέλῃ μετὰ δυνάμεως καὶ δόξης
in a cloud with power and glory
πολλῆς. 28 ἀρχομένων δὲ τούτων γίνεσθαι
much(great). And beginning these things[a] to happen
=when these things begin
ἀνακύψατε καὶ ἐπάρατε τὰς κεφαλὰς ὑμῶν,
stand erect and lift up the heads of you,
διότι ἐγγίζει ἡ ἀπολύτρωσις ὑμῶν. 29 Καὶ
because draws near the redemption of you. And
εἶπεν παραβολὴν αὐτοῖς· ἴδετε τὴν συκῆν
he told [2]a parable [1]them : Ye see the fig-tree
καὶ πάντα τὰ δένδρα· 30 ὅταν προβάλωσιν
and all the trees; when [a]they burst into leaf
ἤδη, βλέποντες ἀφ' ἑαυτῶν γινώσκετε ὅτι
now, seeing from(of) yourselves ye know that
ἤδη ἐγγὺς τὸ θέρος ἐστίν· 31 οὕτως καὶ
now near the summer is; so also
ὑμεῖς, ὅταν ἴδητε ταῦτα γινόμενα,
ye, when ye see these things happening,
γινώσκετε ὅτι ἐγγύς ἐστιν ἡ βασιλεία
know that near is the kingdom
τοῦ θεοῦ. 32 ἀμὴν λέγω ὑμῖν ὅτι οὐ μὴ
– of God. Truly I tell you that by no means
παρέλθῃ ἡ γενεὰ αὕτη ἕως ἂν πάντα
will pass away – generation this until all things
γένηται. 33 ὁ οὐρανὸς καὶ ἡ γῆ παρ-
happens. The heaven and the earth will
ελεύσονται, οἱ δὲ λόγοι μου οὐ μὴ παρελεύ-
pass away, but the words of me by no means will pass

get out, and let those in the
country not enter the city.
22For this is the time of
punishment in fulfillment of
all that has been written.
23How dreadful it will be in
those days for pregnant
women and nursing moth-
ers! There will be great distress in the land and wrath
against this people. 24They
will fall by the sword and
will be taken as prisoners to
all the nations. Jerusalem
will be trampled on by the
Gentiles until the times of
the Gentiles are fulfilled.
25"There will be signs in
the sun, moon and stars.
On the earth, nations will
be in anguish and perplexity at the roaring and tossing
of the sea. 26Men will faint
from terror, apprehensive
of what is coming on the
world, for the heavenly
bodies will be shaken. 27At
that time they will see the
Son of Man coming in a
cloud with power and great
glory. 28When these things
begin to take place, stand
up and lift up your heads,
because your redemption is
drawing near."
29He told them this para-
ble: "Look at the fig tree
and all the trees. 30When
they sprout leaves, you can
see for yourselves and
know that summer is near.
31Even so, when you see
these things happening,
you know that the kingdom
of God is near.
32"I tell you the truth,
this generation[e] will certainly not pass away until
all these things have happened. 33Heaven and earth
will pass away, but my
words will never pass
away.

[e]32 Or *race*

34"Be on guard, that your
hearts may not be weighted
down with dissipation and
drunkenness and the wor-
ries of life, and that day
come on you suddenly like
a trap;
35for it will come upon all
those who dwell on the face
of all the earth.
36"But keep on the alert
at all times, praying in order that you may have
strength to escape all these
things that are about to take
place, and to stand before
the Son of Man."
37Now during the day He
was teaching in the temple,
but at evening He would go
out and spend the night on
the mount that is called
Olivet.
38And all the people
would get up early in the
morning *to come* to Him in
the temple to listen to Him.

σονται. 34 Προσέχετε δὲ ἑαυτοῖς μήποτε
away. And take heed to yourselves lest
βαρηθῶσιν ὑμῶν αἱ καρδίαι ἐν κραιπάλῃ
become burdened of you the hearts with surfeiting
καὶ μέθῃ καὶ μερίμναις βιωτικαῖς, καὶ
and deep drinking and anxieties of life,† and
ἐπιστῇ ἐφ' ὑμᾶς αἰφνίδιος ἡ ἡμέρα ἐκείνη
come *on* on you suddenly – day that
35 ὡς παγίς· ἐπεισελεύσεται γὰρ ἐπὶ πάντας
as a snare; for it will come in *on* on all
τοὺς καθημένους ἐπὶ πρόσωπον πάσης τῆς
the [ones] sitting on [the] face of all the
γῆς. 36 ἀγρυπνεῖτε δὲ ἐν παντὶ καιρῷ
earth. But be ye watchful at every time
δεόμενοι ἵνα κατισχύσητε ἐκφυγεῖν ταῦτα
begging that ye may be able to escape these things
πάντα τὰ μέλλοντα γίνεσθαι, καὶ σταθῆναι
all – being about to happen, and to stand
ἔμπροσθεν τοῦ υἱοῦ τοῦ ἀνθρώπου.
before the Son – of man.
37 Ἦν δὲ τὰς ἡμέρας ἐν τῷ ἱερῷ
Now he was [in] the days in the temple
διδάσκων, τὰς δὲ νύκτας ἐξερχόμενος
teaching, and [in] the nights going forth
ηὐλίζετο εἰς τὸ ὄρος τὸ καλούμενον
he lodged in the mountain – *being* called
ἐλαιών. 38 καὶ πᾶς ὁ λαὸς ὤρθριζεν
of olives. And all the people came in the morning
πρὸς αὐτὸν ἐν τῷ ἱερῷ ἀκούειν αὐτοῦ.
to him in the temple to hear him.

34"Be careful, or your
hearts will be weighed
down with dissipation,
drunkenness and the anxi-
eties of life, and that day
will close on you unexpect-
edly like a trap. 35For it will
come upon all those who
live on the face of the whole
earth. 36Be always on the
watch, and pray that you
may be able to escape all
that is about to happen, and
that you may be able to
stand before the Son of
Man."
37Each day Jesus was
teaching at the temple, and
each evening he went out to
spend the night on the hill
called the Mount of Olives,
38and all the people came
early in the morning to hear
him at the temple.

Chapter 22

Preparing the Passover

NOW the Feast of Un-
leavened Bread,
which is called the Pass-
over, was approaching.
2And the chief priests
and the scribes were seeking how they might put Him
to death; for they were
afraid of the people.
3And Satan entered into
Judas who was called Is-
cariot, belonging to the
number of the twelve.
4And he went away and
discussed with the chief
priests and officers how he
might betray Him to them.
5And they were glad,
and agreed to give him
money.
6And he consented, and
began seeking a good opportunity to betray Him to
them apart from the multitude.
7Then came the *first* day
of Unleavened Bread on
which the Passover *lamb*
had to be sacrificed.
8And He sent Peter and
John, saying, "Go and prepare the Passover for us,
that we may eat it."
9And they said to Him,
"Where do You want us to
prepare it?"

22 Ἤγγιζεν δὲ ἡ ἑορτὴ τῶν ἀζύμων ἡ
Now drew near the feast of unleavened bread –
λεγομένη πάσχα. 2 καὶ ἐζήτουν οἱ ἀρχιερεῖς
being called Passover. And [6]sought [1]the [2]chief priests
καὶ οἱ γραμματεῖς τὸ πῶς ἀνέλωσιν
[3]and [4]the [5]scribes – how they might destroy
αὐτόν· ἐφοβοῦντο γὰρ τὸν λαόν. 3 Εἰσῆλθεν δὲ
him; for they feared the people. And entered
σατανᾶς εἰς Ἰούδαν τὸν καλούμενον
Satan into Judas – *being* called
Ἰσκαριώτην, ὄντα ἐκ τοῦ ἀριθμοῦ τῶν
Iscariot, being of the number of the
δώδεκα· 4 καὶ ἀπελθὼν συνελάλησεν τοῖς
twelve; and going he conversed with the
ἀρχιερεῦσιν καὶ στρατηγοῖς τὸ πῶς αὐτοῖς
chief priests and captains – how to them
παραδῷ αὐτόν. 5 καὶ ἐχάρησαν, καὶ
he might betray him. And they rejoiced, and
συνέθεντο αὐτῷ ἀργύριον δοῦναι. 6 καὶ
they agreed [2]him [3]money [1]to give. And
ἐξωμολόγησεν, καὶ ἐζήτει εὐκαιρίαν τοῦ
he fully consented, and sought opportunity –
παραδοῦναι αὐτὸν ἄτερ ὄχλου αὐτοῖς.
to betray[d] him apart from a crowd to them.
7 Ἦλθεν δὲ ἡ ἡμέρα τῶν ἀζύμων, ᾗ
And came the day of unleavened bread, on which
ἔδει θύεσθαι τὸ πάσχα· 8 καὶ ἀπέστειλεν
it behoved to kill the passover [lamb]; and he sent
Πέτρον καὶ Ἰωάννην εἰπών· πορευθέντες
Peter and John saying: Going
ἑτοιμάσατε ἡμῖν τὸ πάσχα, ἵνα φάγωμεν. 9 οἱ
prepare ye for us the passover, that we may eat. they
δὲ εἶπαν αὐτῷ· ποῦ θέλεις ἑτοιμάσωμεν;
And said to him: Where wishest thou [that] we may prepare?

Chapter 22

Judas Agrees to Betray Jesus

NOW the Feast of Un-
leavened Bread,
called the Passover, was
approaching, 2and the chief
priests and the teachers of
the law were looking for
some way to get rid of
Jesus, for they were afraid
of the people. 3Then Satan
entered Judas, called Iscariot, one of the Twelve.
4And Judas went to the
chief priests and the officers of the temple guard
and discussed with them
how he might betray Jesus.
5They were delighted and
agreed to give him money.
6He consented, and
watched for an opportunity
to hand Jesus over to them
when no crowd was pre-
sent.

The Last Supper

7Then came the day of
Unleavened Bread on
which the Passover lamb
had to be sacrificed. 8Jesus
sent Peter and John, say-
ing, "Go and make prepa-
rations for us to eat the
Passover."
9"Where do you want us
to prepare for it?" they
asked.

10 And He said to them,
"Behold, when you have
entered the city, a man will
meet you carrying a pitcher
of water; follow him into
the house that he enters.
11 "And you shall say to
the owner of the house,
'The Teacher says to you,
"Where is the guest room
in which I may eat the Passover with My disciples?"'
12 "And he will show you
a large, furnished, upper
room; prepare it there."
13 And they departed and
found *everything* just as He
had told them; and they
prepared the Passover.

The Lord's Supper

14 And when the hour had
come He reclined *at the table,* and the apostles with
Him.
15 And He said to them, "I
have earnestly desired to
eat this Passover with you
before I suffer;
16 for I say to you, I shall
never again eat it until it is
fulfilled in the kingdom of
God."
17 And when He had taken
a cup *and* given thanks, He
said, "Take this and share
it among yourselves;
18 for I say to you, I will
not drink of the fruit of the
vine from now on until the
kingdom of God comes."
19 And when He had taken
some bread *and* given
thanks, He broke *it,* and
gave *it* to them, saying,
"This is My body [i]which is
given for you; do this in
remembrance of Me."
20 And in the same way *He
took* the cup after they had
eaten, saying, "This cup
which is poured out for you
is the new covenant in My
blood.
21 "But behold, the hand
of the one betraying Me is

[i] Some ancient mss. do not contain the remainder of v. 19 nor any of v. 20

10 ὁ δὲ εἶπεν αὐτοῖς· ἰδοὺ εἰσελθόντων
And he told them: Behold[,] entering
=as ye enter
ὑμῶν εἰς τὴν πόλιν συναντήσει ὑμῖν
you[a] into the city will meet you
ἄνθρωπος κεράμιον ὕδατος βαστάζων·
a man a pitcher of water bearing;
ἀκολουθήσατε αὐτῷ εἰς τὴν οἰκίαν εἰς ἣν
follow him into the house into which
εἰσπορεύεται· 11 καὶ ἐρεῖτε τῷ οἰκοδεσπότῃ
he enters; and ye will say to the *house*-master
τῆς οἰκίας· λέγει σοι ὁ διδάσκαλος·
of the house: Says to thee the teacher:
ποῦ ἐστιν τὸ κατάλυμα ὅπου τὸ πάσχα
Where is the guest room where the passover
μετὰ τῶν μαθητῶν μου φάγω; 12 κἀκεῖνος
with the disciples of me I may eat? And that man
ὑμῖν δείξει ἀνάγαιον μέγα ἐστρωμένον·
you will show upper room a large *having been* spread;*
ἐκεῖ ἑτοιμάσατε. 13 ἀπελθόντες δὲ εὗρον
there prepare ye. And going they found
καθὼς εἰρήκει αὐτοῖς, καὶ ἡτοίμασαν τὸ
as he had told them, and they prepared the
πάσχα. 14 Καὶ ὅτε ἐγένετο ἡ ὥρα,
passover. And when came the hour,
ἀνέπεσεν, καὶ οἱ ἀπόστολοι σὺν αὐτῷ.
he reclined, and the apostles with him.
15 καὶ εἶπεν πρὸς αὐτούς· ἐπιθυμίᾳ
And he said to them: With desire
ἐπεθύμησα τοῦτο τὸ πάσχα φαγεῖν μεθ'
I desired this - passover to eat with
ὑμῶν πρὸ τοῦ με παθεῖν· 16 λέγω γὰρ
you before the me to suffer;[b] for I tell
=I suffer;
ὑμῖν ὅτι οὐκέτι οὐ μὴ φάγω αὐτὸ
you that no more by no(any) means I eat it
ἕως ὅτου πληρωθῇ ἐν τῇ βασιλείᾳ τοῦ θεοῦ.
until it is fulfilled in the kingdom - of God.
17 καὶ δεξάμενος ποτήριον εὐχαριστήσας
And taking a cup having given thanks
εἶπεν· λάβετε τοῦτο καὶ διαμερίσατε εἰς
he said: Take this and divide among
ἑαυτούς· 18 λέγω γὰρ ὑμῖν, οὐ μὴ πίω
yourselves; for I tell you, by no means I drink
ἀπὸ τοῦ νῦν ἀπὸ τοῦ γενήματος τῆς
from - now [on] from the produce of the
ἀμπέλου ἕως οὗ ἡ βασιλεία τοῦ θεοῦ
vine until the kingdom - of God
ἔλθῃ. 19 καὶ λαβὼν ἄρτον εὐχαριστήσας
comes. And taking a loaf having given thanks
ἔκλασεν καὶ ἔδωκεν αὐτοῖς λέγων· τοῦτό
he broke and gave to them saying: This
ἐστιν τὸ σῶμά μου [τὸ ὑπὲρ ὑμῶν
is the body of me - for you
διδόμενον· τοῦτο ποιεῖτε εἰς τὴν ἐμὴν
being given; this do ye for - my
ἀνάμνησιν. 20 καὶ τὸ ποτήριον ὡσαύτως
memorial. And the cup similarly
μετὰ τὸ δειπνῆσαι, λέγων· τοῦτο τὸ
after the to sup, saying: This -
ποτήριον ἡ καινὴ διαθήκη ἐν τῷ αἵματί
cup [is] the new covenant in the blood
μου, τὸ ὑπὲρ ὑμῶν ἐκχυννόμενον.] 21 πλὴν
of me, - for you being shed. However
ἰδοὺ ἡ χεὶρ τοῦ παραδιδόντος με μετ'
behold[,] the hand of the [one] betraying me with

* That is, with carpets, and the dining couches supplied with cushions.

10 He replied, "As you enter the city, a man carrying
a jar of water will meet you.
Follow him to the house
that he enters, 11 and say to
the owner of the house,
'The Teacher asks: Where
is the guest room, where I
may eat the Passover with
my disciples?' 12 He will
show you a large upper
room, all furnished. Make
preparations there."
13 They left and found
things just as Jesus had told
them. So they prepared the
Passover.
14 When the hour came,
Jesus and his apostles reclined at the table. 15 And
he said to them, "I have eagerly desired to eat this
Passover with you before I
suffer. 16 For I tell you, I
will not eat it again until it
finds fulfillment in the kingdom of God."
17 After taking the cup, he
gave thanks and said,
"Take this and divide it
among you. 18 For I tell you
I will not drink again of the
fruit of the vine until the
kingdom of God comes."
19 And he took bread,
gave thanks and broke it,
and gave it to them, saying,
"This is my body given for
you; do this in remem-
brance of me."
20 In the same way, after
the supper he took the cup,
saying, "This cup is the
new covenant in my blood,
which is poured out for
you. 21 But the hand of him
who is going to betray me is

with Me on the table.
22"For indeed, the Son of Man is going as it has been determined; but woe to that man by whom He is betrayed!"
23And they began to discuss among themselves which one of them it might be who was going to do this thing.

Who Is Greatest

24And there arose also a dispute among them *as to* which one of them was regarded to be greatest.
25And He said to them, "The kings of the Gentiles lord it over them; and those who have authority over them are called 'Benefactors.'
26"But not so with you, but let him who is the greatest among you become as the youngest, and the leader as the servant.
27"For who is greater, the one who reclines *at the table,* or the one who serves? Is it not the one who reclines *at the table*? But I am among you as the one who serves.
28"And you are those who have stood by Me in My trials;
29and just as My Father has granted Me a kingdom, I grant you
30that you may eat and drink at My table in My kingdom, and you will sit on thrones judging the twelve tribes of Israel.
31"Simon, Simon, behold, Satan has demanded *permission* to sift you like wheat;
32but I have prayed for you, that your faith may not fail; and you, when once you have turned again, strengthen your brothers."
33And he said to Him, "Lord, with You I am ready to go both to prison and to death!"
34And He said, "I say to you, Peter, the cock will not crow today until you have denied three times that you know Me."

ἐμοῦ ἐπὶ τῆς τραπέζης. 22 ὅτι ὁ υἱὸς μὲν
me on the table. Because [2]the [3]Son [1]indeed
τοῦ ἀνθρώπου κατὰ τὸ ὡρισμένον
– of man according to the [thing] having been determined
πορεύεται, πλὴν οὐαὶ τῷ ἀνθρώπῳ ἐκείνῳ
goes, nevertheless woe – man to that
δι' οὗ παραδίδοται. 23 καὶ αὐτοὶ ἤρξαντο
through whom he is betrayed. And they began
συζητεῖν πρὸς ἑαυτοὺς τὸ τίς ἄρα εἴη
to debate with themselves – who then it might be
ἐξ αὐτῶν ὁ τοῦτο μέλλων πράσσειν.
of them the [one] [2]this [1]being about [3]to do.
24 Ἐγένετο δὲ καὶ φιλονεικία ἐν αὐτοῖς,
And there was also a rivalry among them,
τὸ τίς αὐτῶν δοκεῖ εἶναι μείζων. 25 ὁ δὲ
– who of them seems to be greater. So he
εἶπεν αὐτοῖς· οἱ βασιλεῖς τῶν ἐθνῶν
said to them: The kings of the nations
κυριεύουσιν αὐτῶν, καὶ οἱ ἐξουσιάζοντες
lord it over them, and the [ones] having authority over
αὐτῶν εὐεργέται καλοῦνται. 26 ὑμεῖς δὲ
them benefactors are called. But ye
οὐχ οὕτως, ἀλλ' ὁ μείζων ἐν ὑμῖν
not so, but the greater among you
γινέσθω ὡς ὁ νεώτερος, καὶ ὁ ἡγούμενος
let him become as the younger, and the [one] governing
ὡς ὁ διακονῶν. 27 τίς γὰρ μείζων, ὁ
as the [one] serving. For who [is] greater, the
ἀνακείμενος ἢ ὁ διακονῶν; οὐχὶ ὁ
[one] reclining or the [one] serving? not the
ἀνακείμενος; ἐγὼ δὲ ἐν μέσῳ ὑμῶν εἰμι
[one] reclining? But I in [the] midst of you am
ὡς ὁ διακονῶν. 28 ὑμεῖς δέ ἐστε οἱ
as the [one] serving. But ye are the [ones]
διαμεμενηκότες μετ' ἐμοῦ ἐν τοῖς πειρα-
having remained throughout with me in the tempta-
σμοῖς μου· 29 κἀγὼ διατίθεμαι ὑμῖν καθὼς
tions of me; and I appoint to you as
διέθετό μοι ὁ πατήρ μου βασιλείαν,
appointed to me the Father of me a kingdom,
30 ἵνα ἔσθητε καὶ πίνητε ἐπὶ τῆς τραπέζης
that ye may eat and drink at the table
μου ἐν τῇ βασιλείᾳ μου, καὶ καθήσεσθε
of me in the kingdom of me, and ye will sit
ἐπὶ θρόνων τὰς δώδεκα φυλὰς κρίνοντες
on thrones [2]the [3]twelve [4]tribes [1]judging
τοῦ Ἰσραήλ. 31 Σίμων Σίμων, ἰδοὺ ὁ
– of Israel. Simon[,] Simon, behold[,] –
σατανᾶς ἐξῃτήσατο ὑμᾶς τοῦ σινιάσαι ὡς
Satan begged earnestly for you – to sift[d] as
τὸν σῖτον· 32 ἐγὼ δὲ ἐδεήθην περὶ σοῦ
the wheat; but I requested concerning thee
ἵνα μὴ ἐκλίπῃ ἡ πίστις σου· καὶ σύ
that might not fail the faith of thee; and thou
ποτε ἐπιστρέψας στήρισον τοὺς ἀδελφούς
when having turned support the brothers
σου. 33 ὁ δὲ εἶπεν αὐτῷ· κύριε, μετὰ
of thee. And he said to him: Lord, with
σοῦ ἕτοιμός εἰμι καὶ εἰς φυλακὴν καὶ εἰς
thee prepared I am both to prison and to
θάνατον πορεύεσθαι. 34 ὁ δὲ εἶπεν· λέγω
death to go. But he said: I tell
σοι, Πέτρε, οὐ φωνήσει σήμερον ἀλέκτωρ
thee, Peter, will not sound to-day a cock
ἕως τρίς με ἀπαρνήσῃ μὴ εἰδέναι. 35 Καὶ
until thrice me thou wilt deny not to know. And

with mine on the table.
22The Son of Man will go as
it has been decreed, but
woe to that man who be-
trays him." 23They began
to question among them-
selves which of them it
might be who would do
this.
24Also a dispute arose
among them as to which of
them was considered to be
greatest. 25Jesus said to
them, "The kings of the
Gentiles lord it over them;
and those who exercise authority over them call
themselves Benefactors.
26But you are not to be like
that. Instead, the greatest
among you should be like
the youngest, and the one
who rules like the one who
serves. 27For who is greater, the one who is at the
table or the one who
serves? Is it not the one
who is at the table? But I
am among you as one who
serves. 28You are those
who have stood by me in
my trials. 29And I confer on
you a kingdom, just as my
Father conferred one on
me, 30so that you may eat
and drink at my table in my
kingdom and sit on
thrones, judging the twelve
tribes of Israel.
31"Simon, Simon, Satan
has asked to sift you[f] as
wheat. 32But I have prayed
for you, Simon, that your
faith may not fail. And
when you have turned
back, strengthen your
brothers."
33But he replied, "Lord, I
am ready to go with you to
prison and to death."
34Jesus answered, "I tell
you, Peter, before the
rooster crows today, you
will deny three times that
you know me."

f31 The Greek is plural.

35 And He said to them, "When I sent you out without purse and bag and sandals, you did not lack anything, did you?" And they said, "*No,* nothing."

36 And He said to them, "But now, let him who has a purse take it along, likewise also a bag, and let him who has no sword sell his robe and buy one.

37 "For I tell you, that this which is written must be fulfilled in Me, 'AND HE WAS NUMBERED WITH TRANSGRESSORS'; for that which refers to Me has *its* fulfillment."

38 And they said, "Lord, look, here are two swords." And He said to them, "It is enough."

The Garden of Gethsemane

39 And He came out and proceeded as was His custom to the Mount of Olives; and the disciples also followed Him.

40 And when He arrived at the place, He said to them, "Pray that you may not enter into temptation."

41 And He withdrew from them about a stone's throw, and He knelt down and *began* to pray,

42 saying, "Father, if Thou art willing, remove this cup from Me; yet not My will, but Thine be done."

43 Now an angel from heaven appeared to Him, strengthening Him.

44 And being in agony He was praying very fervently; and His sweat became like drops of blood, falling down upon the ground.

45 And when He rose from prayer, He came to the disciples and found them sleeping from sorrow,

46 and said to them, "Why are you sleeping? Rise and pray that you may not enter into temptation."

Jesus Betrayed by Judas

47 While He was still speaking, behold, a multitude *came,* and the one called Judas, one of the

εἶπεν αὐτοῖς· ὅτε ἀπέστειλα ὑμᾶς ἄτερ
he said to them: When I sent you without

βαλλαντίου καὶ πήρας καὶ ὑποδημάτων, μή
a purse and a wallet and sandals, not

τινος ὑστερήσατε; οἱ δὲ εἶπαν· οὐθενός.
of anything were ye short? And they said: Of nothing.

36 εἶπεν δὲ αὐτοῖς· ἀλλὰ νῦν ὁ ἔχων
And he said to them: But now the [one] having

βαλλάντιον ἀράτω, ὁμοίως καὶ πήραν, καὶ
a purse let him take [it], likewise also a wallet, and

ὁ μὴ ἔχων πωλησάτω τὸ ἱμάτιον αὐτοῦ
the [one] not having let him sell the garment of him

καὶ ἀγορασάτω μάχαιραν. 37 λέγω γὰρ
and let him buy a sword. For I tell

ὑμῖν ὅτι τοῦτο τὸ γεγραμμένον δεῖ
you that this – having been written it behoves

τελεσθῆναι ἐν ἐμοί, τό· καὶ μετὰ ἀνόμων
to be finished in me, – And with lawless men

ἐλογίσθη· καὶ γὰρ τὸ περὶ ἐμοῦ τέλος
he was reckoned; for indeed the thing concerning me an end

ἔχει. 38 οἱ δὲ εἶπαν· κύριε, ἰδοὺ μάχαιραι
has. And they said: Lord, behold[,] swords

ὧδε δύο. ὁ δὲ εἶπεν αὐτοῖς· ἱκανόν ἐστιν.
here two. And he said to them: Enough it is.

39 Καὶ ἐξελθὼν ἐπορεύθη κατὰ τὸ ἔθος
And going forth he went according to the(his) habit

εἰς τὸ ὄρος τῶν ἐλαιῶν· ἠκολούθησαν δὲ
to the mountain of the olives; and [4]followed

αὐτῷ καὶ οἱ μαθηταί. 40 γενόμενος δὲ
[5]him [3]also [1]the [2]disciples. And coming

ἐπὶ τοῦ τόπου εἶπεν αὐτοῖς· προσεύχεσθε
upon the place he said to them: Pray ye

μὴ εἰσελθεῖν εἰς πειρασμόν. 41 καὶ αὐτὸς
not to enter into temptation. And he

ἀπεσπάσθη ἀπ' αὐτῶν ὡσεὶ λίθου βολήν,
was withdrawn from them about of a stone a throw,

καὶ θεὶς τὰ γόνατα προσηύχετο 42 λέγων·
and placing the knees he prayed saying:

πάτερ, εἰ βούλει παρένεγκε τοῦτο τὸ
Father, if thou wilt take away this –

ποτήριον ἀπ' ἐμοῦ· πλὴν μὴ τὸ θέλημά
cup from me; nevertheless not the will

μου ἀλλὰ τὸ σὸν γινέσθω. 43 [ὤφθη δὲ
of me but – thine let be. And appeared

αὐτῷ ἄγγελος ἀπ' οὐρανοῦ ἐνισχύων αὐτόν.
to him an angel from heaven strengthening him.

44 καὶ γενόμενος ἐν ἀγωνίᾳ ἐκτενέστερον
And becoming in an agony more earnestly

προσηύχετο· καὶ ἐγένετο ὁ ἱδρὼς αὐτοῦ
he prayed; and became the sweat of him

ὡσεὶ θρόμβοι αἵματος καταβαίνοντες ἐπὶ
as drops of blood falling down onto

τὴν γῆν.] 45 καὶ ἀναστὰς ἀπὸ τῆς
the earth. And rising up from the

προσευχῆς, ἐλθὼν πρὸς τοὺς μαθητὰς
prayer, coming to the disciples

εὗρεν κοιμωμένους αὐτοὺς ἀπὸ τῆς λύπης,
he found [2]sleeping [1]them from the grief,

46 καὶ εἶπεν αὐτοῖς· τί καθεύδετε;
and said to them: Why sleep ye?

ἀναστάντες προσεύχεσθε, ἵνα μὴ εἰσέλθητε
rising up pray ye, lest ye enter

εἰς πειρασμόν. 47 Ἔτι αὐτοῦ λαλοῦντος
into temptation. Yet him speaking[a]
=While he was yet speaking

ἰδοὺ ὄχλος, καὶ ὁ λεγόμενος Ἰούδας εἷς
behold[,] a crowd, and the [one] *being* named Judas one

35 Then Jesus asked them, "When I sent you without purse, bag or sandals, did you lack anything?"

"Nothing," they answered.

36 He said to them, "But now if you have a purse, take it, and also a bag; and if you don't have a sword, sell your cloak and buy one. 37 It is written: 'And he was numbered with the transgressors'[g]; and I tell you that this must be fulfilled in me. Yes, what is written about me is reaching its fulfillment."

38 The disciples said, "See, Lord, here are two swords."

"That is enough," he replied.

Jesus Prays on the Mount of Olives

39 Jesus went out as usual to the Mount of Olives, and his disciples followed him. 40 On reaching the place, he said to them, "Pray that you will not fall into temptation." 41 He withdrew about a stone's throw beyond them, knelt down and prayed, 42 "Father, if you are willing, take this cup from me; yet not my will, but yours be done." 43 An angel from heaven appeared to him and strengthened him. 44 And being in anguish, he prayed more earnestly, and his sweat was like drops of blood falling to the ground.[h]

45 When he rose from prayer and went back to the disciples, he found them asleep, exhausted from sorrow. 46 "Why are you sleeping?" he asked them. "Get up and pray so that you will not fall into temptation."

Jesus Arrested

47 While he was still speaking a crowd came up, and the man who was called Judas, one of the

[g] *37* Isaiah 53:12
[h] *44* Some early manuscripts do not have verses 43 and 44.

twelve, was preceding them; and he approached Jesus to kiss Him.

48But Jesus said to him, "Judas, are you betraying the Son of Man with a kiss?"

49And when those who were around Him saw what was going to happen, they said, "Lord, shall we strike with the sword?"

50And a certain one of them struck the slave of the high priest and cut off his right ear.

51But Jesus answered and said, "Stop! No more of this." And He touched his ear and healed him.

52And Jesus said to the chief priests and officers of the temple and elders who had come against Him, "Have you come out with swords and clubs as against a robber?

53"While I was with you daily in the temple, you did not lay hands on Me; but this hour and the power of darkness are yours."

Jesus' Arrest

54And having arrested Him, they led Him *away,* and brought Him to the house of the high priest; but Peter was following at a distance.

55And after they had kindled a fire in the middle of the courtyard and had sat down together, Peter was sitting among them.

56And a certain servant-girl, seeing him as he sat in the firelight, and looking intently at him, said, "This man was with Him too."

57But he denied *it,* saying, "Woman, I do not know Him."

58And a little later, another saw him and said, "You are *one* of them too!" But Peter said, "Man, I am not!"

59And after about an hour had passed, another man

τῶν δώδεκα προήρχετο αὐτούς, καὶ ἤγγισεν
of the twelve came before them, and drew near
τῷ Ἰησοῦ φιλῆσαι αὐτόν. 48 Ἰησοῦς δὲ
– to Jesus to kiss him. But Jesus
εἶπεν αὐτῷ· Ἰούδα, φιλήματι τὸν υἱὸν
said to him: Judas, with a kiss the Son
τοῦ ἀνθρώπου παραδίδως; 49 ἰδόντες δὲ
– of man betrayest thou? And [4]seeing
οἱ περὶ αὐτὸν τὸ ἐσόμενον εἶπαν· κύριε,
[1]the [ones] [2]round [3]him the thing going to be said: Lord,
εἰ πατάξομεν ἐν μαχαίρῃ; 50 καὶ ἐπάταξεν
if we shall strike with a sword? And [4]struck
εἷς τις ἐξ αὐτῶν τοῦ ἀρχιερέως τὸν
[1]a certain one [2]of [3]them [7]of the [8]high priest [5]the
δοῦλον καὶ ἀφεῖλεν τὸ οὖς αὐτοῦ τὸ
[6]slave and cut off [1]the [3]ear [4]of him –
δεξιόν. 51 ἀποκριθεὶς δὲ ὁ Ἰησοῦς εἶπεν·
[2]right. And answering – Jesus said:
ἐᾶτε ἕως τούτου· καὶ ἁψάμενος τοῦ
Permit ye until this; and touching the
ὠτίου ἰάσατο αὐτόν. 52 Εἶπεν δὲ Ἰησοῦς
ear he cured him. And said Jesus
πρὸς τοὺς παραγενομένους ἐπ' αὐτὸν
to [1]the [9]coming [10]upon [11]him
ἀρχιερεῖς καὶ στρατηγοὺς τοῦ ἱεροῦ καὶ
[2]chief priests [3]and [4]captains [5]of the [6]temple [7]and
πρεσβυτέρους· ὡς ἐπὶ λῃστὴν ἐξήλθατε
[8]elders: As against a robber came ye out
μετὰ μαχαιρῶν καὶ ξύλων; 53 καθ' ἡμέραν
with swords and clubs? daily
ὄντος μου μεθ' ὑμῶν ἐν τῷ ἱερῷ οὐκ
being me[a] with you in the temple not
=while I was
ἐξετείνατε τὰς χεῖρας ἐπ' ἐμέ· ἀλλ' αὕτη
ye stretched out the(your) hands against me; but this
ἐστὶν ὑμῶν ἡ ὥρα καὶ ἡ ἐξουσία τοῦ
is of you the hour and the authority of the
σκότους.
darkness.

54 Συλλαβόντες δὲ αὐτὸν ἤγαγον καὶ
And having arrested him they led and
εἰσήγαγον εἰς τὴν οἰκίαν τοῦ ἀρχιερέως·
brought *in* into the house of the high priest;
ὁ δὲ Πέτρος ἠκολούθει μακρόθεν. 55 περι-
– and Peter followed afar off. light-
αψάντων δὲ πῦρ ἐν μέσῳ τῆς αὐλῆς καὶ
ing And a fire in [the] centre of the court and
=when they had lit a fire . . . and had sat down together
συγκαθισάντων ἐκάθητο ὁ Πέτρος μέσος
sitting down together[a] sat – Peter among
αὐτῶν. 56 ἰδοῦσα δὲ αὐτὸν παιδίσκη τις
them. And [2]seeing [3]him [1]a certain maidservant
καθήμενον πρὸς τὸ φῶς καὶ ἀτενίσασα
sitting near the light and gazing at
αὐτῷ εἶπεν· καὶ οὗτος σὺν αὐτῷ ἦν. 57 ὁ
him said: And this man with him was. he
δὲ ἠρνήσατο λέγων· οὐκ οἶδα αὐτόν,
But denied saying: I know not him,
γύναι. 58 καὶ μετὰ βραχὺ ἕτερος ἰδὼν
woman. And after a short while another seeing
αὐτὸν ἔφη· καὶ σὺ ἐξ αὐτῶν εἶ. ὁ
him said: And thou of them art. –
δὲ Πέτρος ἔφη· ἄνθρωπε, οὐκ εἰμί.
But Peter said: Man, I am not.
59 καὶ διαστάσης ὡσεὶ ὥρας μιᾶς ἄλλος
And intervening about hour one[a] [2]other man
=when about an hour had intervened

Twelve, was leading them. He approached Jesus to kiss him, 48but Jesus asked him, "Judas, are you betraying the Son of Man with a kiss?"

49When Jesus' followers saw what was going to happen, they said, "Lord, should we strike with our swords?" 50And one of them struck the servant of the high priest, cutting off his right ear.

51But Jesus answered, "No more of this!" And he touched the man's ear and healed him.

52Then Jesus said to the chief priests, the officers of the temple guard, and the elders, who had come for him, "Am I leading a rebellion, that you have come with swords and clubs? 53Every day I was with you in the temple courts, and you did not lay a hand on me. But this is your hour—when darkness reigns."

Peter Disowns Jesus

54Then seizing him, they led him away and took him into the house of the high priest. Peter followed at a distance. 55But when they had kindled a fire in the middle of the courtyard and had sat down together, Peter sat down with them. 56A servant girl saw him seated there in the firelight. She looked closely at him and said, "This man was with him."

57But he denied it. "Woman, I don't know him," he said.

58A little later someone else saw him and said, "You also are one of them."

"Man, I am not!" Peter replied.

59About an hour later another asserted, "Certainly

began to insist, saying,
"Certainly this man also
was with Him, for he is a
Galilean too."
60But Peter said, "Man, I
do not know what you are
talking about." And
immediately, while he was
still speaking, a cock
crowed.
61And the Lord turned
and looked at Peter. And
Peter remembered the
word of the Lord, how He
had told him, "Before a
cock crows today, you will
deny Me three times."
62And he went out and
wept bitterly.
63And the men who were
holding Jesus in custody
were mocking Him, and
beating Him,
64and they blindfolded
Him and were asking Him,
saying, "Prophesy, who is
the one who hit You?"
65And they were saying
many other things against
Him, blaspheming.

Jesus before the Sanhedrin

66And when it was day,
the [j]Council of elders of
the people assembled, both
chief priests and scribes,
and they led Him away to
their council *chamber,* saying,
67"If You are the Christ,
tell us." But He said to
them, "If I tell you, you
will not believe;
68and if I ask a question,
you will not answer.
69"But from now on THE
SON OF MAN WILL BE SEATED
AT THE RIGHT HAND of the
power OF GOD."
70And they all said, "Are
You the Son of God,
then?" And He said to
them, "Yes, I am."
71And they said, "What
further need do we have of
testimony? For we have
heard it ourselves from His
own mouth."

τις διϊσχυρίζετο λέγων· ἐπ᾽ ἀληθείας καὶ
[1]a certain emphatically asserted saying : Of a truth also
οὗτος μετ᾽ αὐτοῦ ἦν, καὶ γὰρ Γαλιλαῖός
this man with him was, for indeed a Galilæan
ἐστιν. 60 εἶπεν δὲ ὁ Πέτρος· ἄνθρωπε,
he is. But said – Peter : Man,
οὐκ οἶδα ὃ λέγεις. καὶ παραχρῆμα ἔτι
I know not what thou sayest. And at once yet
λαλοῦντος αὐτοῦ ἐφώνησεν ἀλέκτωρ. 61 καὶ
speaking him[a] sounded a cock. And
=while he was yet speaking
στραφεὶς ὁ κύριος ἐνέβλεψεν τῷ Πέτρῳ,
turning the Lord looked at – Peter,
καὶ ὑπεμνήσθη ὁ Πέτρος τοῦ λόγου τοῦ
and remembered – Peter the word of the
κυρίου, ὡς εἶπεν αὐτῷ ὅτι πρὶν ἀλέκτορα
Lord, as he told him that before a cock
φωνῆσαι σήμερον ἀπαρνήσῃ με τρίς. 62 καὶ
to sound[b] to-day thou wilt deny me thrice. And
ἐξελθὼν ἔξω ἔκλαυσεν πικρῶς. 63 Καὶ οἱ
going *out* outside he wept bitterly. And the
ἄνδρες οἱ συνέχοντες αὐτὸν ἐνέπαιζον αὐτῷ
men – having in charge him* mocked him
δέροντες, 64 καὶ περικαλύψαντες αὐτὸν
beating, and covering over him
ἐπηρώτων λέγοντες· προφήτευσον, τίς ἐστιν
questioned saying : Prophesy, who is
ὁ παίσας σε; 65 καὶ ἕτερα πολλὰ
the [one] playing thee? And other things many
βλασφημοῦντες ἔλεγον εἰς αὐτόν.
blaspheming they said against him.
66 Καὶ ὡς ἐγένετο ἡμέρα, συνήχθη τὸ
And when came day, was assembled the
πρεσβυτέριον τοῦ λαοῦ, ἀρχιερεῖς τε καὶ
body of elders of the people, both chief priests and
γραμματεῖς, καὶ ἀπήγαγον αὐτὸν εἰς τὸ
scribes, and led away him to the
συνέδριον αὐτῶν, 67 λέγοντες· εἰ σὺ εἶ ὁ
council of them, saying : If thou art the
χριστός, εἰπὸν ἡμῖν. εἶπεν δὲ αὐτοῖς·
Christ, tell us. And he said to them :
ἐὰν ὑμῖν εἴπω, οὐ μὴ πιστεύσητε· 68 ἐὰν
If you I tell, by no means will ye believe; [2]if
δὲ ἐρωτήσω, οὐ μὴ ἀποκριθῆτε. 69 ἀπὸ
[1]and I question, by no means will ye answer. [2]from
τοῦ νῦν δὲ ἔσται ὁ υἱὸς τοῦ ἀνθρώπου
– [3]now [1]But [7]will be [4]the [5]Son – [6]of man
καθήμενος ἐκ δεξιῶν τῆς δυνάμεως τοῦ
[8]sitting at [the] right of the power –
θεοῦ. 70 εἶπαν δὲ πάντες· σὺ οὖν εἶ ὁ
of God. And they said all : Thou therefore art the
υἱὸς τοῦ θεοῦ; ὁ δὲ πρὸς αὐτοὺς ἔφη·
Son – of God? And he to them said :
ὑμεῖς λέγετε ὅτι ἐγώ εἰμι. 71 οἱ δὲ
Ye say that I am. And they
εἶπαν· τί ἔτι ἔχομεν μαρτυρίας χρείαν;
said : Why yet have we of witness need ?
αὐτοὶ γὰρ ἠκούσαμεν ἀπὸ τοῦ στόματος
for [our]selves we heard from the mouth
αὐτοῦ.
of him.

this fellow was with him,
for he is a Galilean."
60Peter replied, "Man, I
don't know what you're
talking about!" Just as he
was speaking, the rooster
crowed. 61The Lord turned
and looked straight at Peter. Then Peter remem-
bered the word the Lord
had spoken to him: "Be-
fore the rooster crows to-
day, you will disown me
three times." 62And he
went outside and wept bitterly.

The Soldiers Mock Jesus

63The men who were
guarding Jesus began
mocking and beating him.
64They blindfolded him and
demanded, "Prophesy!
Who hit you?" 65And they
said many other insulting
things to him.

Jesus Before Pilate and Herod

66At daybreak the council
of the elders of the people,
both the chief priests and
teachers of the law, met together, and Jesus was led
before them. 67"If you are
the Christ,[i]" they said,
"tell us."
Jesus answered, "If I tell
you, you will not believe
me, 68and if I asked you,
you would not answer.
69But from now on, the Son
of Man will be seated at the
right hand of the mighty
God."
70They all asked, "Are
you then the Son of God?"
He replied, "You are
right in saying I am."
71Then they said, "Why
do we need any more testimony? We have heard it
from his own lips."

[j] Or, *Sanhedrin*

* That is, Jesus (as some texts have it).

[i]67 Or *Messiah*

Chapter 23

Jesus before Pilate

THEN the whole body of them arose and brought Him before Pilate.
2And they began to accuse Him, saying, "We found this man misleading our nation and forbidding to pay taxes to Caesar, and saying that He Himself is Christ, a King."
3And Pilate asked Him, saying, "Are You the King of the Jews?" And He answered him and said, "*It is as* you say."
4And Pilate said to the chief priests and the multitudes, "I find no guilt in this man."
5But they kept on insisting, saying, "He stirs up the people, teaching all over Judea, starting from Galilee, even as far as this place."
6But when Pilate heard it, he asked whether the man was a Galilean.
7And when he learned that He belonged to Herod's jurisdiction, he sent Him to Herod, who himself also was in Jerusalem at that time.

Jesus before Herod

8Now Herod was very glad when he saw Jesus; for he had wanted to see Him for a long time, because he had been hearing about Him and was hoping to see some sign performed by Him.
9And he questioned Him at some length; but He answered him nothing.
10And the chief priests and the scribes were standing there, accusing Him vehemently.
11And Herod with his soldiers, after treating Him with contempt and mocking Him, dressed Him in a gorgeous robe and sent Him back to Pilate.

23 Καὶ ἀναστὰν ἅπαν τὸ πλῆθος αὐτῶν
And rising up all the multitude of them
ἤγαγον αὐτὸν ἐπὶ τὸν Πιλᾶτον. **2** ἤρξαντο
led him before – Pilate. they began
δὲ κατηγορεῖν αὐτοῦ λέγοντες· τοῦτον
And to accuse him saying : This man
εὕραμεν διαστρέφοντα τὸ ἔθνος ἡμῶν καὶ
we found perverting the nation of us and
κωλύοντα φόρους Καίσαρι διδόναι, καὶ
forbidding tribute to Cæsar to give, and
λέγοντα ἑαυτὸν χριστὸν βασιλέα εἶναι.
saying himself Christ a king to be.
3 ὁ δὲ Πιλᾶτος ἠρώτησεν αὐτὸν λέγων·
– And Pilate questioned him saying :
σὺ εἶ ὁ βασιλεὺς τῶν Ἰουδαίων; ὁ δὲ
Thou art the king of the Jews? And he
ἀποκριθεὶς αὐτῷ ἔφη· σὺ λέγεις. **4** ὁ δὲ
answering him said : Thou sayest. – And
Πιλᾶτος εἶπεν πρὸς τοὺς ἀρχιερεῖς καὶ
Pilate said to the chief priests and
τοὺς ὄχλους· οὐδὲν εὑρίσκω αἴτιον ἐν
the crowds : [3]No [1]I find [2]crime in
τῷ ἀνθρώπῳ τούτῳ. **5** οἱ δὲ ἐπίσχυον λέγοντες
– man this. But they insisted saying[,]
ὅτι ἀνασείει τὸν λαόν, διδάσκων καθ'
– He excites the people, teaching throughout
ὅλης τῆς Ἰουδαίας, καὶ ἀρξάμενος ἀπὸ
all – Judæa, even beginning from
τῆς Γαλιλαίας ἕως ὧδε. **6** Πιλᾶτος δὲ
– Galilee to here. And Pilate
ἀκούσας ἐπηρώτησεν εἰ ὁ ἄνθρωπος
hearing questioned if the man
Γαλιλαῖός ἐστιν, **7** καὶ ἐπιγνοὺς ὅτι ἐκ
a Galilæan is(was), and perceiving that of
τῆς ἐξουσίας Ἡρῴδου ἐστίν, ἀνέπεμψεν
the authority of Herod he is(was), he sent up
αὐτὸν πρὸς Ἡρῴδην, ὄντα καὶ αὐτὸν ἐν
him to Herod, being also him(he) in
Ἰεροσολύμοις ἐν ταύταις ταῖς ἡμέραις.
Jerusalem in these – days.
8 ὁ δὲ Ἡρῴδης ἰδὼν τὸν Ἰησοῦν ἐχάρη
– And Herod seeing – Jesus rejoiced
λίαν· ἦν γὰρ ἐξ ἱκανῶν χρόνων θέλων
greatly; for he was of a long times wishing
ἰδεῖν αὐτὸν διὰ τὸ ἀκούειν περὶ αὐτοῦ,
to see him because of the to hear[b] about him,
=because he had heard
καὶ ἤλπιζέν τι σημεῖον ἰδεῖν ὑπ' αὐτοῦ
and he hoped some sign to see by him
γινόμενον. **9** ἐπηρώτα δὲ αὐτὸν ἐν λόγοις
brought about. And he questioned him in words
ἱκανοῖς· αὐτὸς δὲ οὐδὲν ἀπεκρίνατο αὐτῷ.
many; but he nothing answered him.
10 εἱστήκεισαν δὲ οἱ ἀρχιερεῖς καὶ οἱ
And stood the chief priests and the
γραμματεῖς εὐτόνως κατηγοροῦντες αὐτοῦ.
scribes vehemently accusing him.
11 ἐξουθενήσας δὲ αὐτὸν ὁ Ἡρῴδης σὺν
And despising him – Herod with
τοῖς στρατεύμασιν αὐτοῦ καὶ ἐμπαίξας,
the soldiery of him and mocking,
περιβαλὼν ἐσθῆτα λαμπρὰν ἀνέπεμψεν αὐτὸν
throwing round clothing splendid sent back him
τῷ Πιλάτῳ. **12** ἐγένοντο δὲ φίλοι ὅ τε
– to Pilate. And became friends – both

Chapter 23

THEN the whole assembly rose and led him
off to Pilate. 2And they be-
gan to accuse him, saying, "We have found this man subverting our nation. He opposes payment of taxes to Caesar and claims to be Christ,[j] a king."
3So Pilate asked Jesus, "Are you the king of the Jews?"
"Yes, it is as you say," Jesus replied.
4Then Pilate announced to the chief priests and the crowd, "I find no basis for a charge against this man."
5But they insisted, "He stirs up the people all over Judea[k] by his teaching. He started in Galilee and has come all the way here."
6On hearing this, Pilate asked if the man was a Galilean.
7When he learned that
Jesus was under Herod's jurisdiction, he sent him to Herod, who was also in Jerusalem at that time.
8When Herod saw Jesus, he was greatly pleased, because for a long time he had been wanting to see him. From what he had heard about him, he hoped to see him perform some miracle.
9He plied him with many questions, but Jesus gave him no answer.
10The chief priests and the teachers of the law were standing there, vehemently accusing him.
11Then Herod and his soldiers ridiculed and mocked him. Dressing him in an elegant robe, they sent him back to Pilate.

[j]2 Or *Messiah*; also in verses 35 and 39
[k]5 Or *over the land of the Jews*

12Now Herod and Pilate
became friends with one
another that very day; for
before they had been at enmity with each other.

Pilate Seeks Jesus' Release

13And Pilate summoned
the chief priests and the rulers and the people,
14and said to them, "You
brought this man to me as
one who incites the people
to rebellion, and behold,
having examined Him be-
fore you, I have found no
guilt in this man regarding
the charges which you
make against Him.
15"No, nor has Herod,
for he sent Him back to us;
and behold, nothing de-
serving death has been
done by Him.
16"I will therefore punish
Him and release Him."
17[[k]Now he was obliged
to release to them at the
feast one prisoner.]
18But they cried out all together, saying, "Away
with this man, and release
for us Barabbas!"
19(He was one who had
been thrown into prison for
a certain insurrection made
in the city, and for murder.)
20And Pilate, wanting to
release Jesus, addressed
them again,
21but they kept on calling
out, saying, "Crucify,
crucify Him!"
22And he said to them the
third time, "Why, what
evil has this man done? I
have found in Him no guilt
demanding death; I will
therefore punish Him and
release Him."
23But they were insistent,
with loud voices asking
that He be crucified. And
their voices *began* to prevail.
24And Pilate pronounced
sentence that their demand
should be granted.
25And he released the
man they were asking for
who had been thrown into
prison for insurrection and
murder, but he delivered
Jesus to their will.

[k]Many mss. do not contain this verse

Ἡρῴδης καὶ ὁ Πιλᾶτος ἐν αὐτῇ τῇ
Herod and – Pilate on [2]same [1]the

ἡμέρᾳ μετ' ἀλλήλων· προϋπῆρχον γὰρ ἐν
day with each other; for they were previously in

ἔχθρᾳ ὄντες πρὸς αὐτούς. 13 Πιλᾶτος δὲ
enmity being with themselves. And Pilate

συγκαλεσάμενος τοὺς ἀρχιερεῖς καὶ τοὺς
calling together the chief priests and the

ἄρχοντας καὶ τὸν λαὸν 14 εἶπεν πρὸς
leaders and the people said to

αὐτούς· προσηνέγκατέ μοι τὸν ἄνθρωπον
them: Ye brought to me – man

τοῦτον ὡς ἀποστρέφοντα τὸν λαόν, καὶ
this as perverting the people, and

ἰδοὺ ἐγὼ ἐνώπιον ὑμῶν ἀνακρίνας οὐθὲν
behold I [2]before [3]you [1]examining [8]*nothing*

εὗρον ἐν τῷ ἀνθρώπῳ τούτῳ αἴτιον ὧν
[4]found [7]in – [6]man [5]this [9]crime of the [things] which

κατηγορεῖτε κατ' αὐτοῦ. 15 ἀλλ' οὐδὲ
ye bring accusation against him. And neither

Ἡρῴδης· ἀνέπεμψεν γὰρ αὐτὸν πρὸς ἡμᾶς·
Herod; for he sent back him to us;

καὶ ἰδοὺ οὐδὲν ἄξιον θανάτου ἐστὶν
and behold nothing worthy of death is

πεπραγμένον αὐτῷ· 16 παιδεύσας οὖν αὐτὸν
having been done by him; chastising therefore him

ἀπολύσω.‡ 18 ἀνέκραγον δὲ παμπληθεὶ
I will release. But they shouted with the whole multitude

λέγοντες· αἶρε τοῦτον, ἀπόλυσον δὲ ἡμῖν
saying: Take this man, and release to us

τὸν Βαραββᾶν· 19 ὅστις ἦν διὰ στάσιν
– Barabbas; who was because of [2]insurrection

τινὰ γενομένην ἐν τῇ πόλει καὶ φόνον
[1]some happening in the city and murder

βληθεὶς ἐν τῇ φυλακῇ. 20 πάλιν δὲ
thrown in the prison. But again

ὁ Πιλᾶτος προσεφώνησεν αὐτοῖς, θέλων
– Pilate called to them, wishing

ἀπολῦσαι τὸν Ἰησοῦν. 21 οἱ δὲ ἐπεφώνουν
to release – Jesus. But they shouted

λέγοντες· σταύρου σταύρου αὐτόν. 22 ὁ δὲ
saying: Crucify[,] crucify thou him. But he

τρίτον εἶπεν πρὸς αὐτούς· τί γὰρ κακὸν
a third time said to them: But what evil

ἐποίησεν οὗτος; οὐδὲν αἴτιον θανάτου
did this man? no*thing* cause of death

εὗρον ἐν αὐτῷ· παιδεύσας οὖν αὐτὸν
I found in him; chastising therefore him

ἀπολύσω. 23 οἱ δὲ ἐπέκειντο φωναῖς
I will release. But they insisted voices

μεγάλαις αἰτούμενοι αὐτὸν σταυρωθῆναι,
with great asking him to be crucified,

καὶ κατίσχυον αἱ φωναὶ αὐτῶν. 24 καὶ
and prevailed the voices of them. And

Πιλᾶτος ἐπέκρινεν γενέσθαι τὸ αἴτημα
Pilate decided to be [carried out] the request

αὐτῶν· 25 ἀπέλυσεν δὲ τὸν διὰ στάσιν
of them; and he released the [one] because of insurrection

καὶ φόνον βεβλημένον εἰς φυλακήν, ὃν
and murder having been thrown into prison, whom

ᾐτοῦντο, τὸν δὲ Ἰησοῦν παρέδωκεν τῷ
they asked, – but Jesus he delivered to the

θελήματι αὐτῶν.
will of them.

‡ Ver. 17 omitted by Nestle; *cf.* NIV footnote.

12That day Herod and Pi-
late became friends—be-
fore this they had been enemies.
13Pilate called together
the chief priests, the rulers
and the people, 14and said
to them, "You brought me
this man as one who was
inciting the people to rebellion. I have examined him
in your presence and have
found no basis for your
charges against him. 15Nei-
ther has Herod, for he sent
him back to us; as you can
see, he has done nothing to
deserve death. 16There-
fore, I will punish him and
then release him.[l]"
18With one voice they
cried out, "Away with this
man! Release Barabbas to
us!" 19(Barabbas had been
thrown into prison for an
insurrection in the city, and
for murder.)
20Wanting to release
Jesus, Pilate appealed to
them again. 21But they kept
shouting, "Crucify him!
Crucify him!"
22For the third time he
spoke to them: "Why?
What crime has this man
committed? I have found in
him no grounds for the
death penalty. Therefore I
will have him punished and
then release him."
23But with loud shouts
they insistently demanded
that he be crucified, and
their shouts prevailed. 24So
Pilate decided to grant their
demand. 25He released the
man who had been thrown
into prison for insurrection
and murder, the one they
asked for, and surrendered
Jesus to their will.

[l]*16 Some manuscripts him." 17Now he was obliged to release one man to them at the Feast.*

Simon Bears the Cross
26 And when they led Him
away, they laid hold of one
Simon of Cyrene, coming
in from the country, and
placed on him the cross to
carry behind Jesus.
27 And there were follow-
ing Him a great multitude
of the people, and of
women who were mourn-
ing and lamenting Him.
28 But Jesus turning to
them said, "Daughters of
Jerusalem, stop weeping
for Me, but weep for yourselves and for your chil-
dren.
29 "For behold, the days
are coming when they will
say, 'Blessed are the barren, and the wombs that
never bore, and the breasts
that never nursed.'
30 "Then they will begin
TO SAY TO THE MOUNTAINS,
'FALL ON US,' AND TO THE
HILLS, 'COVER US.'
31 "For if they do these
things in the green tree,
what will happen in the
dry?"
32 And two others also,
who were criminals, were
being led away to be put to
death with Him.

The Crucifixion
33 And when they came to
the place called The Skull,
there they crucified Him
and the criminals, one on
the right and the other on
the left.
34 But Jesus was saying,
"Father, forgive them; for
they do not know what they
are doing." And they cast
lots, dividing up His garments among themselves.
35 And the people stood
by, looking on. And even
the rulers were sneering at
Him, saying, "He saved
others; let Him save Him-
self if this is the Christ of
God, His Chosen One."
36 And the soldiers also
mocked Him, coming up to
Him, offering Him sour
wine,

26 Καὶ ὡς ἀπήγαγον αὐτόν, ἐπιλαβόμενοι
And as they led away him, seizing
Σίμωνά τινα Κυρηναῖον ἐρχόμενον ἀπ'
Simon a certain Cyrenian coming from
ἀγροῦ ἐπέθηκαν αὐτῷ τὸν σταυρὸν φέρειν
[the] country they placed on him the cross to carry
ὄπισθεν τοῦ Ἰησοῦ. **27** Ἠκολούθει δὲ
behind – Jesus. And followed
αὐτῷ πολὺ πλῆθος τοῦ λαοῦ καὶ γυναικῶν
him a much multitude of the people and of women
αἳ ἐκόπτοντο καὶ ἐθρήνουν αὐτόν. **28** στρα-
who mourned and lamented him. turn
φεὶς δὲ πρὸς αὐτὰς Ἰησοῦς εἶπεν·
ing And to them Jesus said:
θυγατέρες Ἰερουσαλήμ, μὴ κλαίετε ἐπ'
Daughters of Jerusalem, do not weep over
ἐμέ· πλὴν ἐφ' ἑαυτὰς κλαίετε καὶ ἐπὶ
me; but over yourselves weep and over
τὰ τέκνα ὑμῶν, **29** ὅτι ἰδοὺ ἔρχονται
the children of you, because behold come
ἡμέραι ἐν αἷς ἐροῦσιν· μακάριαι αἱ
days in which they will say: Blessed the
στεῖραι, καὶ αἱ κοιλίαι αἳ οὐκ ἐγέννησαν,
barren, and the wombs which bare not,
καὶ μαστοὶ οἳ οὐκ ἔθρεψαν. **30** τότε
and breasts which gave not suck. Then
ἄρξονται λέγειν τοῖς ὄρεσιν· πέσατε ἐφ'
they will begin to say to the mountains: Fall on
ἡμᾶς, καὶ τοῖς βουνοῖς· καλύψατε ἡμᾶς·
us, and to the hills: Cover us;
31 ὅτι εἰ ἐν ὑγρῷ ξύλῳ ταῦτα ποιοῦσιν,
because if in ²full of sap ¹a tree these things they do,
ἐν τῷ ξηρῷ τί γένηται; **32** Ἤγοντο δὲ
in the dry what may happen? And were led
καὶ ἕτεροι κακοῦργοι δύο σὺν αὐτῷ
also others* criminals two with him
ἀναιρεθῆναι. **33** Καὶ ὅτε ἦλθον ἐπὶ τὸν
to be killed. And when they came upon the
τόπον τὸν καλούμενον Κρανίον, ἐκεῖ ἐσταύ-
place – *being* called Skull, there they
ρωσαν αὐτὸν καὶ τοὺς κακούργους, ὃν μὲν
crucified him and the criminals, one†
ἐκ δεξιῶν ὃν δὲ ἐξ ἀριστερῶν. **34** [ὁ δὲ
on [the] right and one† on [the] left. – And
Ἰησοῦς ἔλεγεν· πάτερ, ἄφες αὐτοῖς· οὐ
Jesus said: Father, forgive them; ³not
γὰρ οἴδασιν τί ποιοῦσιν.] διαμεριζόμενοι
¹for ²they know what they are doing. dividing
δὲ τὰ ἱμάτια αὐτοῦ ἔβαλον κλήρους.
And the garments of him they cast lots.
35 καὶ εἱστήκει ὁ λαὸς θεωρῶν. ἐξεμυκ-
And stood the people beholding. scoff-
τήριζον δὲ καὶ οἱ ἄρχοντες λέγοντες·
ed And also the rulers saying:
ἄλλους ἔσωσεν, σωσάτω ἑαυτόν, εἰ οὗτός
Others he saved, let him save himself, if this man
ἐστιν ὁ χριστὸς τοῦ θεοῦ ὁ ἐκλεκτός.
is the Christ – of God the chosen [one].
36 ἐνέπαιξαν δὲ αὐτῷ καὶ οἱ στρατιῶται
And mocked him also the soldiers
προσερχόμενοι, ὄξος προσφέροντες αὐτῷ
approaching, vinegar offering *to* him

* Luke uses ἕτεροι here with strict accuracy = "different." Jesus was not himself a criminal. Note punctuation of A.V. *Cf.* Acts 28. 1.

The Crucifixion
26 As they led him away,
they seized Simon from
Cyrene, who was on his
way in from the country,
and put the cross on him
and made him carry it be-
hind Jesus. 27 A large number of people followed him,
including women who
mourned and wailed for
him. 28 Jesus turned and
said to them, "Daughters
of Jerusalem, do not weep
for me; weep for your-
selves and for your chil-
dren. 29 For the time will
come when you will say,
'Blessed are the barren
women, the wombs that
never bore and the breasts
that never nursed!' 30 Then
" 'they will say to the
mountains, "Fall on
us!"
and to the hills,
"Cover us!" '[m]
31 For if men do these things
when the tree is green,
what will happen when it is
dry?"
32 Two other men, both
criminals, were also led out
with him to be executed.
33 When they came to the
place called the Skull, there
they crucified him, along
with the criminals—one on
his right, the other on his
left. 34 Jesus said, "Father,
forgive them, for they do
not know what they are doing."[n] And they divided up
his clothes by casting lots.
35 The people stood
watching, and the rulers
even sneered at him. They
said, "He saved others; let
him save himself if he is the
Christ of God, the Chosen
One."
36 The soldiers also came
up and mocked him. They
offered him wine vinegar

[m] *30* Hosea 10:8
[n] *34* Some early manuscripts do not have this sentence.

37 and saying, "If You are
the King of the Jews, save
Yourself!"
38 Now there was also an
inscription above Him,
"THIS IS THE KING OF
THE JEWS."
39 And one of the crimi-
nals who were hanged
there was hurling abuse at
Him, saying, "Are You not
the Christ? Save Yourself
and us!"
40 But the other answered,
and rebuking him said,
"Do you not even fear
God, since you are under
the same sentence of con-
demnation?
41 "And we indeed justly,
for we are receiving what
we deserve for our deeds;
but this man has done nothing wrong."
42 And he was saying,
"Jesus, remember me
when You come in Your
kingdom!"
43 And He said to him,
"Truly I say to you, today
you shall be with Me in
Paradise."
44 And it was now about
[l]the sixth hour, and darkness fell over the whole
land until [m]the ninth hour,
45 the sun being obscured;
and the veil of the temple
was torn in two.
46 And Jesus, crying out
with a loud voice, said,
"Father, INTO THY HANDS I
COMMIT MY SPIRIT." And
having said this, He
breathed His last.
47 Now when the centu-
rion saw what had hap-
pened, he *began* praising
God, saying, "Certainly
this man was innocent."
48 And all the multitudes
who came together for this
spectacle, when they ob-
served what had happened,
began to return, beating
their breasts.
49 And all His acquaint-
ances and the women who
accompanied Him from
Galilee, were standing at a
distance, seeing these
things.

Jesus Is Buried

50 And behold, a man
named Joseph, who was a

[l]I.e., 12 noon
[m]I.e., 3 p.m.

37 καὶ λέγοντες· εἰ σὺ εἶ ὁ βασιλεὺς
and saying: If thou art the king
τῶν Ἰουδαίων, σῶσον σεαυτόν. **38** ἦν δὲ
of the Jews, save thyself. And there was
καὶ ἐπιγραφὴ ἐπ' αὐτῷ· Ο ΒΑΣΙΛΕΥΣ
also a superscription over him: THE KING
ΤΩΝ ΙΟΥΔΑΙΩΝ ΟΥΤΟΣ. **39** Εἷς δὲ
OF THE JEWS THIS. And one
τῶν κρεμασθέντων κακούργων ἐβλασφήμει
of the hanged criminals blasphemed
αὐτόν· οὐχὶ σὺ εἶ ὁ χριστός; σῶσον
him: Not thou art the Christ? save
σεαυτὸν καὶ ἡμᾶς **40** ἀποκριθεὶς δὲ ὁ
thyself and us. But answering the
ἕτερος ἐπιτιμῶν αὐτῷ ἔφη· οὐδὲ φοβῇ σὺ
other rebuking him said: Not fearest thou
τὸν θεόν, ὅτι ἐν τῷ αὐτῷ κρίματι εἶ;
– God, because in the same judgment thou art?
41 καὶ ἡμεῖς μὲν δικαίως, ἄξια γὰρ ὧν
And we indeed justly, for things worthy of what
ἐπράξαμεν ἀπολαμβάνομεν· οὗτος δὲ οὐδὲν
we did we receive back; but this man nothing
ἄτοπον ἔπραξεν. **42** καὶ ἔλεγεν Ἰησοῦ,
amiss did. And he said: Jesus,
μνήσθητί μου ὅταν ἔλθῃς εἰς τὴν βασιλείαν
remember me when thou comest into the kingdom
σου. **43** καὶ εἶπεν αὐτῷ· ἀμήν σοι λέγω,
of thee. And he said to him. Truly thee I tell,
σήμερον μετ' ἐμοῦ ἔσῃ ἐν τῷ παραδείσῳ.
to-day with me thou wilt be in the paradise.
44 Καὶ ἦν ἤδη ὡσεὶ ὥρα ἕκτη καὶ
And it was now about hour sixth and
σκότος ἐγένετο ἐφ' ὅλην τὴν γῆν ἕως
darkness came over all the land until
ὥρας ἐνάτης **45** τοῦ ἡλίου ἐκλιπόντος·
hour ninth the sun failing;[a]
=as the sun failed;
ἐσχίσθη δὲ τὸ καταπέτασμα τοῦ ναοῦ
and was torn the veil of the shrine
μέσον. **46** καὶ φωνήσας φωνῇ μεγάλῃ ὁ
in the middle. And crying voice with a great –
Ἰησοῦς εἶπεν· πάτερ, εἰς χεῖράς σου
Jesus said: Father, into hands of thee
παρατίθεμαι τὸ πνεῦμά μου. τοῦτο δὲ
I commit the spirit of me. And this
εἰπὼν ἐξέπνευσεν. **47** ἰδὼν δὲ ὁ ἑκατον-
saying he expired. And [3]seeing [1]the [2]cen-
τάρχης τὸ γενόμενον ἐδόξαζεν τὸν θεὸν
turion the thing happening glorified – God
λέγων· ὄντως ὁ ἄνθρωπος οὗτος δίκαιος
saying: Really – man this righteous
ἦν. **48** καὶ πάντες οἱ συμπαραγενόμενοι
was. And all [1]the [3]arriving together
ὄχλοι ἐπὶ τὴν θεωρίαν ταύτην, θεωρήσαντες τὰ
[2]crowds at – sight this, beholding the things
γενόμενα, τύπτοντες τὰ στήθη ὑπέστρεφον.
happening, smiting the(ir) breasts returned.
49 εἱστήκεισαν δὲ πάντες οἱ γνωστοὶ αὐτῷ
And [5]stood [1]all [2]the [ones] [3]known [4]to him
ἀπὸ μακρόθεν, καὶ γυναῖκες αἱ συνακο-
[6]afar off, and women the [ones] accom-
λουθοῦσαι αὐτῷ ἀπὸ τῆς Γαλιλαίας, ὁρῶσαι
panying him from – Galilee, seeing
ταῦτα.
these things.
50 Καὶ ἰδοὺ ἀνὴρ ὀνόματι Ἰωσὴφ
And behold[,] a man by name Joseph

37 and said, "If you are the
king of the Jews, save yourself."
38 There was a written notice above him, which read:
THIS IS THE KING OF THE
JEWS.
39 One of the criminals
who hung there hurled in-
sults at him: "Aren't you
the Christ? Save yourself
and us!"
40 But the other criminal
rebuked him. "Don't you
fear God," he said, "since
you are under the same
sentence? 41 We are pun-
ished justly, for we are getting what our deeds de-
serve. But this man has
done nothing wrong."
42 Then he said, "Jesus,
remember me when you
come into your king-
dom.[o]"
43 Jesus answered him, "I
tell you the truth, today
you will be with me in paradise."

Jesus' Death

44 It was now about the
sixth hour, and darkness
came over the whole land
until the ninth hour, 45 for
the sun stopped shining.
And the curtain of the temple was torn in two. 46 Jesus
called out with a loud
voice, "Father, into your
hands I commit my spirit."
When he had said this, he
breathed his last.
47 The centurion, seeing
what had happened,
praised God and said,
"Surely this was a right-
eous man." 48 When all the
people who had gathered to
witness this sight saw what
took place, they beat their
breasts and went away.
49 But all those who knew
him, including the women
who had followed him from
Galilee, stood at a distance,
watching these things.

Jesus' Burial

50 Now there was a man
named Joseph, a member

[o]42 Some manuscripts *come with your kingly power*

member of the Council, a
good and righteous man
51(he had not consented
to their plan and action), *a*
man from Arimathea, a city
of the Jews, who was waiting for the kingdom of God;
52this man went to Pilate
and asked for the body of
Jesus.
53And he took it down
and wrapped it in a linen
cloth, and laid Him in a
tomb cut into the rock,
where no one had ever lain.
54And it was the prepara-
tion day, and the Sabbath
was about to begin.
55Now the women who
had come with Him out of
Galilee followed after, and
saw the tomb and how His
body was laid.
56And they returned and
prepared spices and per-
fumes.
And on the Sabbath they
rested according to the
commandment.

Chapter 24

The Resurrection

BUT on the first day of
the week, at early
dawn, they came to the
tomb, bringing the spices
which they had prepared.
2And they found the
stone rolled away from the
tomb,
3but when they entered,
they did not find the body
of the Lord Jesus.
4And it happened that
while they were perplexed
about this, behold, two
men suddenly stood near
them in dazzling apparel;
5and as *the women* were
terrified and bowed their
faces to the ground, *the*
men said to them, "Why do
you seek the living One
among the dead?
6"He is not here, but He
has risen. Remember how
He spoke to you while He
was still in Galilee,
7saying that the Son of
Man must be delivered into
the hands of sinful men,

βουλευτὴς ὑπάρχων, ἀνὴρ ἀγαθὸς καὶ
a councillor being, a man good and
δίκαιος, — **51** οὗτος οὐκ ἦν συγκατατεθειμένος
righteous, — this man was not agreeing with
τῇ βουλῇ καὶ τῇ πράξει αὐτῶν, — ἀπὸ
the counsel and the action of them, — from
Ἁριμαθαίας πόλεως τῶν Ἰουδαίων, ὃς
Arimathæa a city of the Jews, who
προσεδέχετο τὴν βασιλείαν τοῦ θεοῦ,
was awaiting the kingdom – of God,
52 οὗτος προσελθὼν τῷ Πιλάτῳ ᾐτήσατο
this man approaching – *to* Pilate asked
τὸ σῶμα τοῦ Ἰησοῦ, **53** καὶ καθελὼν
the body – of Jesus, and taking down
ἐνετύλιξεν αὐτὸ σινδόνι, καὶ ἔθηκεν αὐτὸν
wrapped it in linen, and placed him
ἐν μνήματι λαξευτῷ, οὗ οὐκ ἦν οὐδεὶς
in tomb a hewn, where was not no(any)one
οὔπω κείμενος. **54** καὶ ἡμέρα ἦν παρασκευῆς,
not yet laid. And day it was of preparation,
καὶ σάββατον ἐπέφωσκεν. **55** Κατακολουθήσασαι
and a sabbath was coming on. [4]following after
δὲ αἱ γυναῖκες, αἵτινες ἦσαν συνεληλυθυῖαι
[1]And [2]the [3]women, who were [1]having come *with*
ἐκ τῆς Γαλιλαίας αὐτῷ, ἐθεάσαντο τὸ
[3]out of – [4]Galilee [2]with him, beheld the
μνημεῖον καὶ ὡς ἐτέθη τὸ σῶμα αὐτοῦ,
tomb and how was placed the body of him,
56 ὑποστρέψασαι δὲ ἡτοίμασαν ἀρώματα καὶ
and returning prepared spices and
μύρα.
ointment.
Καὶ τὸ μὲν σάββατον ἡσύχασαν κατὰ
And [on] the [2]indeed [1]sabbath they rested according to
τὴν ἐντολήν. **24** τῇ δὲ μιᾷ τῶν σαββάτων
the commandment. But on the one of the week
ὄρθρου βαθέως ἐπὶ τὸ μνῆμα ἦλθον φέρουσαι
while still very early† upon the tomb they came carrying
ἃ ἡτοίμασαν ἀρώματα. **2** εὗρον δὲ τὸν
[2]which [3]they prepared [1]spices. And they found the
λίθον ἀποκεκυλισμένον ἀπὸ τοῦ μνημείου,
stone *having been* rolled away from the tomb,
3 εἰσελθοῦσαι δὲ οὐχ εὗρον τὸ σῶμα
and entering they found not the body
τοῦ κυρίου Ἰησοῦ. **4** καὶ ἐγένετο ἐν τῷ
of the Lord Jesus. And it was in the
=as they were perplexed
ἀπορεῖσθαι αὐτὰς περὶ τούτου καὶ ἰδοὺ
to be perplexed them[be] about this *and* behold[,]
ἄνδρες δύο ἐπέστησαν αὐταῖς ἐν ἐσθῆτι
men two stood by them in clothing
ἀστραπτούσῃ· **5** ἐμφόβων δὲ γενομένων
shining; and terrified becoming
=as they became terrified and bent their faces
αὐτῶν καὶ κλινουσῶν τὰ πρόσωπα εἰς τὴν
them and bending the(ir) faces[*] to the
γῆν, εἶπαν πρὸς αὐτάς· τί ζητεῖτε τὸν
earth, they said to them: Why seek ye the
ζῶντα μετὰ τῶν νεκρῶν; **6** [οὐκ ἔστιν
living [one] with the dead [ones]? He is not
ὧδε, ἀλλὰ ἠγέρθη.] μνήσθητε ὡς ἐλάλησεν
here, but was raised. Remember how he spoke
ὑμῖν ἔτι ὢν ἐν τῇ Γαλιλαίᾳ, **7** λέγων
to you yet being in – Galilee, saying[,]
τὸν υἱὸν τοῦ ἀνθρώπου ὅτι δεῖ παραδο-
The Son – of man – it behoves to be de-
θῆναι εἰς χεῖρας ἀνθρώπων ἁμαρτωλῶν καὶ
livered into hands men of sinful and

of the Council, a good and
upright man, 51who had not
consented to their decision
and action. He came from
the Judean town of Arima-
thea and he was waiting for
the kingdom of God. 52Go-
ing to Pilate, he asked for
Jesus' body. 53Then he
took it down, wrapped it in
linen cloth and placed it in a
tomb cut in the rock, one in
which no one had yet been
laid. 54It was Preparation
Day, and the Sabbath was
about to begin.
55The women who had
come with Jesus from Galilee followed Joseph and
saw the tomb and how his
body was laid in it. 56Then
they went home and pre-
pared spices and perfumes.
But they rested on the Sabbath in obedience to the
commandment.

Chapter 24

The Resurrection

ON the first day of the
week, very early in
the morning, the women
took the spices they had
prepared and went to the
tomb. 2They found the
stone rolled away from the
tomb, 3but when they en-
tered, they did not find the
body of the Lord Jesus.
4While they were wonder-
ing about this, suddenly
two men in clothes that
gleamed like lightning
stood beside them. 5In their
fright the women bowed
down with their faces to the
ground, but the men said to
them, "Why do you look
for the living among the
dead? 6He is not here; he
has risen! Remember how
he told you, while he was
still with you in Galilee:
7'The Son of Man must be
delivered into the hands of

and be crucified, and the
third day rise again.''
8And they remembered
His words,
9and returned from the
tomb and reported all these
things to the eleven and to
all the rest.
10Now they were Mary
Magdalene and Joanna and
Mary the *mother* of James;
also the other women with
them were telling these
things to the apostles.
11And these words ap-
peared to them as non-
sense, and they would not
believe them.
12[[n]But Peter arose and
ran to the tomb; stooping
and looking in, he *saw the
linen wrappings only; and
he went away to his home,
marveling at that which had
happened.]

The Road to Emmaus

13And behold, two of
them were going that very
day to a village named Emmaus, which was [o]about
seven miles from Jerusa-
lem.
14And they were convers-
ing with each other about
all these things which had
taken place.
15And it came about that
while they were conversing
and discussing, Jesus Himself approached, and *began*
traveling with them.
16But their eyes were prevented from recognizing
Him.
17And He said to them,
''What are these words that
you are exchanging with
one another as you are
walking?'' And they stood
still, looking sad.
18And one of them,
named Cleopas, answered
and said to Him, ''Are You
the only one visiting
Jerusalem and unaware of
the things which have happened here in these days?''
19And He said to them,
''What things?'' And they
said to Him, ''The things
about Jesus the Nazarene,
who was a prophet mighty
in deed and word in the
sight of God and all the
people,
20and how the chief
priests and our rulers delivered Him up to the sen-

[n]Some ancient mss. do not contain v. 12
[o]I.e., 60 stadia, one stadion was about 600 feet

σταυρωθῆναι καὶ τῇ τρίτῃ ἡμέρᾳ ἀναστῆναι.
to be crucified and on the third day to rise again.
8 καὶ ἐμνήσθησαν τῶν ῥημάτων αὐτοῦ,
And they remembered the words of him,
9 καὶ ὑποστρέψασαι ἀπὸ τοῦ μνημείου
and returning from the tomb
ἀπήγγειλαν ταῦτα πάντα τοῖς ἕνδεκα καὶ
reported these things all to the eleven and
πᾶσιν τοῖς λοιποῖς. 10 ἦσαν δὲ ἡ
to all the rest. Now they were the
Μαγδαληνὴ Μαρία καὶ Ἰωάννα καὶ Μαρία
Magdalene Mary and Joanna and Mary
ἡ Ἰακώβου· καὶ αἱ λοιπαὶ* σὺν αὐταῖς*
the [mother] of James; and the rest with them
ἔλεγον πρὸς τοὺς ἀποστόλους ταῦτα. 11 καὶ
told to the apostles these things. And
ἐφάνησαν ἐνώπιον αὐτῶν ὡσεὶ λῆρος
seemed before them as folly
τὰ ῥήματα ταῦτα, καὶ ἠπίστουν αὐταῖς.* ‡
– words these, and they disbelieved them.
13 Καὶ ἰδοὺ δύο ἐξ αὐτῶν ἐν αὐτῇ τῇ
And behold[,] two of them on same the
ἡμέρᾳ ἦσαν πορευόμενοι εἰς κώμην ἀπέχουσαν
day were journeying to a village being distant
σταδίους ἑξήκοντα ἀπὸ Ἰερουσαλήμ, ᾗ
furlongs sixty from Jerusalem, to which
ὄνομα Ἐμμαοῦς, 14 καὶ αὐτοὶ ὡμίλουν
name Emmaus, and they talked
πρὸς ἀλλήλους περὶ πάντων τῶν συμβεβηκότων
to each other about all – [2]having occurred
τούτων. 15 καὶ ἐγένετο ἐν τῷ ὁμιλεῖν
[1]these things. And it came to pass in the to talk
αὐτοὺς καὶ συζητεῖν, καὶ αὐτὸς Ἰησοῦς
them and to discuss[be], *and* [him]self Jesus
=as they talked and discussed,
ἐγγίσας συνεπορεύετο αὐτοῖς· 16 οἱ δὲ
drawing near journeyed with them; but the
ὀφθαλμοὶ αὐτῶν ἐκρατοῦντο τοῦ μὴ
eyes of them were held – not
ἐπιγνῶναι αὐτόν. 17 εἶπεν δὲ πρὸς αὐτούς·
to recognize[d] him. And he said to them:
τίνες οἱ λόγοι οὗτοι οὓς ἀντιβάλλετε
What – words these which ye exchange
πρὸς ἀλλήλους περιπατοῦντες; καὶ ἐστάθησαν
with each other walking? And they stood
σκυθρωποί. 18 ἀποκριθεὶς δὲ εἷς ὀνόματι
sad-faced. And answering one by name
Κλεοπᾶς εἶπεν πρὸς αὐτόν· σὺ μόνος
Cleopas said to him: Thou only
παροικεῖς Ἰερουσαλὴμ καὶ οὐκ ἔγνως τὰ
a stranger in Jerusalem and knewest not the things
γενόμενα ἐν αὐτῇ ἐν ταῖς ἡμέραις ταύταις;
happening in it in – days these?
19 καὶ εἶπεν αὐτοῖς· ποῖα; οἱ δὲ εἶπαν
And he said to them: What things? And they said
αὐτῷ· τὰ περὶ Ἰησοῦ τοῦ Ναζαρηνοῦ, ὃς
to him: The things about Jesus the Nazarene, who
ἐγένετο ἀνὴρ προφήτης δυνατὸς ἐν ἔργῳ
was a *man* prophet powerful in work
καὶ λόγῳ ἐναντίον τοῦ θεοῦ καὶ παντὸς
and word before – God and all
τοῦ λαοῦ, 20 ὅπως τε παρέδωκαν αὐτὸν οἱ
the people, how both [7]delivered [8]him [1]the
ἀρχιερεῖς καὶ οἱ ἄρχοντες ἡμῶν εἰς
[2]chief priests [3]and [4]the [5]rulers [6]of us to

*** Note the feminines.**
‡ Verse 12 omitted by Nestle.

sinful men, be crucified and
on the third day be raised
again.' '' 8Then they re-
membered his words.
9When they came back
from the tomb, they told all
these things to the Eleven
and to all the others. 10It
was Mary Magdalene, Jo-
anna, Mary the mother of
James, and the others with
them who told this to the
apostles. 11But they did not
believe the women, be-
cause their words seemed
to them like nonsense.
12Peter, however, got up
and ran to the tomb. Bending over, he saw the strips
of linen lying by them-
selves, and he went away,
wondering to himself what
had happened.

On the Road to Emmaus

13Now that same day two
of them were going to a village called Emmaus, about
seven miles[p] from Jerusalem. 14They were talking
with each other about ev-
erything that had hap-
pened. 15As they talked and
discussed these things with
each other, Jesus himself
came up and walked along
with them; 16but they were
kept from recognizing him.
17He asked them, ''What
are you discussing together
as you walk along?''
They stood still, their
faces downcast. 18One of
them, named Cleopas,
asked him, ''Are you only a
visitor to Jerusalem and do
not know the things that
have happened there in
these days?''
19''What things?'' he
asked.
''About Jesus of Naza-
reth,'' they replied. ''He
was a prophet, powerful in
word and deed before God
and all the people. 20The
chief priests and our rulers
handed him over to be sen-

[p]13 Greek *sixty stadia* (about 11 kilometers)

tence of death, and crucified Him.
21"But we were hoping
that it was He who was going to redeem Israel. In-
deed, besides all this, it is
the third day since these
things happened.
22"But also some women
among us amazed us.
When they were at the
tomb early in the morning,
23and did not find His
body, they came, saying
that they had also seen a
vision of angels, who said
that He was alive.
24"And some of those
who were with us went to
the tomb and found it just
exactly as the women also
had said; but Him they did
not see."
25And He said to them,
"O foolish men and slow of
heart to believe in all that
the prophets have spoken!
26"Was it not necessary
for the Christ to suffer
these things and to enter
into His glory?"
27And beginning with
Moses and with all the
prophets, He explained to
them the things concerning
Himself in all the Scrip-
tures.
28And they approached
the village where they were
going, and He acted as
though He would go far-
ther.
29And they urged Him,
saying, "Stay with us, for it
is *getting* toward evening,
and the day is now nearly
over." And He went in to
stay with them.
30And it came about that
when He had reclined *at
the table* with them, He
took the bread and blessed
it, and breaking *it*, He *began* giving *it* to them.
31And their eyes were
opened and they recog-
nized Him; and He van-
ished from their sight.
32And they said to one another, "Were not our

κρίμα θανάτου καὶ ἐσταύρωσαν αὐτόν.
[the] judgment of death and crucified him.
21 ἡμεῖς δὲ ἠλπίζομεν ὅτι αὐτός ἐστιν
But we were hoping that he it is(was)
ὁ μέλλων λυτροῦσθαι τὸν Ἰσραήλ· ἀλλά
the [one] being about to redeem – Israel; but
γε καὶ σὺν πᾶσιν τούτοις τρίτην ταύτην
– also with all these things third this
=this is the third day
ἡμέραν ἄγει ἀφ' οὗ ταῦτα ἐγένετο.
day it leads since these things happened.
22 ἀλλὰ καὶ γυναῖκές τινες ἐξ ἡμῶν
But also [2]women [1]some of us
ἐξέστησαν ἡμᾶς, γενόμεναι ὀρθριναὶ ἐπὶ τὸ
astonished us, being early at the
μνημεῖον, 23 καὶ μὴ εὑροῦσαι τὸ σῶμα
tomb, and not finding the body
αὐτοῦ ἦλθον λέγουσαι καὶ ὀπτασίαν ἀγγέλων
of him came saying also a vision of angels
ἑωρακέναι, οἳ λέγουσιν αὐτὸν ζῆν. 24 καὶ
to have seen, who say him to live. And
=that he lives.
ἀπῆλθόν τινες τῶν σὺν ἡμῖν ἐπὶ τὸ
[5]went [1]some [2]of the [ones] [3]with [4]us to the
μνημεῖον, καὶ εὗρον οὕτως καθὼς καὶ αἱ
tomb, and found so as indeed the
γυναῖκες εἶπον, αὐτὸν δὲ οὐκ εἶδον.
women said, but him they saw not.
25 καὶ αὐτὸς εἶπεν πρὸς αὐτούς· ὦ
And he said to them : O
ἀνόητοι καὶ βραδεῖς τῇ καρδίᾳ τοῦ πιστεύειν
foolish [ones] and slow – in heart – to believe[d]
ἐπὶ πᾶσιν οἷς ἐλάλησαν οἱ προφῆται·
on(in) all things which spoke the prophets :
26 οὐχὶ ταῦτα ἔδει παθεῖν τὸν χριστὸν καὶ
[2]not [6]these things [1]behoved it [5]to suffer [3]the [4]Christ and
εἰσελθεῖν εἰς τὴν δόξαν αὐτοῦ; 27 καὶ
to enter into the glory of him? And
ἀρξάμενος ἀπὸ Μωϋσέως καὶ ἀπὸ πάντων
beginning from Moses and from all
τῶν προφητῶν διηρμήνευσεν αὐτοῖς ἐν
the prophets he explained to them in
πάσαις ταῖς γραφαῖς τὰ περὶ ἑαυτοῦ.
all the scriptures the things concerning himself.
28 Καὶ ἤγγισαν εἰς τὴν κώμην οὗ
And they drew near to the village whither
ἐπορεύοντο, καὶ αὐτὸς προσεποιήσατο
they were journeying, and he pretended
πορρώτερον πορεύεσθαι. 29 καὶ παρε-
farther to journey. And they
βιάσαντο αὐτὸν λέγοντες· μεῖνον μεθ'
urged him saying : Remain with
ἡμῶν, ὅτι πρὸς ἑσπέραν ἐστὶν καὶ κέκλικεν
us, because toward evening it is and has declined
ἤδη ἡ ἡμέρα. καὶ εἰσῆλθεν τοῦ μεῖναι
now the day. And he went in – to remain[d]
σὺν αὐτοῖς. 30 καὶ ἐγένετο ἐν τῷ
with them. And it came to pass in the
=as he reclined
κατακλιθῆναι αὐτὸν μετ' αὐτῶν λαβὼν τὸν
to recline him[be] with them taking the
ἄρτον εὐλόγησεν καὶ κλάσας ἐπεδίδου
loaf he blessed and having broken he handed
αὐτοῖς· 31 αὐτῶν δὲ διηνοίχθησαν οἱ
to them; and of them were opened up the
ὀφθαλμοί, καὶ ἐπέγνωσαν αὐτόν· καὶ αὐτὸς
eyes, and they recognized him; and he
ἄφαντος ἐγένετο ἀπ' αὐτῶν. 32 καὶ
invisible became from them. And

tenced to death, and they
crucified him; 21but we had
hoped that he was the one
who was going to redeem
Israel. And what is more, it
is the third day since all this
took place. 22In addition,
some of our women
amazed us. They went to
the tomb early this morning
23but didn't find his body.
They came and told us that
they had seen a vision of
angels, who said he was
alive. 24Then some of our
companions went to the
tomb and found it just as
the women had said, but
him they did not see."
25He said to them, "How
foolish you are, and how
slow of heart to believe all
that the prophets have spoken! 26Did not the Christ[q]
have to suffer these things
and then enter his glory?"
27And beginning with Mo-
ses and all the Prophets, he
explained to them what
was said in all the Scriptures concerning himself.
28As they approached the
village to which they were
going, Jesus acted as if he
were going farther. 29But
they urged him strongly,
"Stay with us, for it is nearly evening; the day is almost over." So he went in
to stay with them.
30When he was at the ta-
ble with them, he took
bread, gave thanks, broke
it and began to give it to
them. 31Then their eyes
were opened and they rec-
ognized him, and he disappeared from their sight.
32They asked each other,

[q]26 Or *Messiah*; also in verse 46

hearts burning within us
while He was speaking to
us on the road, while He
was explaining the Scrip-
tures to us?"
33And they arose that
very hour and returned to
Jerusalem, and found gathered together the eleven
and those who were with
them,
34saying, "The Lord has
really risen, and has ap-
peared to Simon."
35And they *began* to re-
late their experiences on
the road and how He was
recognized by them in the
breaking of the bread.

Other Appearances

36And while they were
telling these things, He
Himself stood in their
midst.[p]
37But they were startled
and frightened and thought
that they were seeing a
spirit.
38And He said to them,
"Why are you troubled,
and why do doubts arise in
your hearts?
39"See My hands and My
feet, that it is I Myself;
touch Me and see, for a
spirit does not have flesh
and bones as you see that I
have."
40[[q]And when He had
said this, He showed them
His hands and His feet.]
41And while they still
could not believe *it* for joy
and were marveling, He
said to them, "Have you
anything here to eat?"
42And they gave Him a
piece of a broiled fish;
43and He took it and ate *it*
before them.
44Now He said to them,
"These are My words
which I spoke to you while
I was still with you, that all
things which are written
about Me in the Law of
Moses and the Prophets
and the Psalms must be fulfilled."
45Then He opened their
minds to understand the
Scriptures,
46and He said to them,
"Thus it is written, that the
Christ should suffer and

[p] Some ancient mss. insert *And He says to them, "Peace be to you."*
[q] Many mss. do not contain this verse

εἶπαν πρὸς ἀλλήλους· οὐχὶ ἡ καρδία
they said to each other : Not the heart
ἡμῶν καιομένη ἦν ἐν ἡμῖν, ὡς ἐλάλει
of us burning was in us, as he spoke
ἡμῖν ἐν τῇ ὁδῷ, ὡς διήνοιγεν ἡμῖν τὰς
to us in the way, as he opened up to us the
γραφάς; 33 Καὶ ἀναστάντες αὐτῇ τῇ ὥρᾳ
scriptures? And rising up [2]same [1]in the hour
ὑπέστρεψαν εἰς Ἰερουσαλήμ, καὶ εὗρον
they returned to Jerusalem, and found
ἠθροισμένους τοὺς ἕνδεκα καὶ τοὺς σὺν
having been collected the eleven and the [ones] with
αὐτοῖς, 34 λέγοντας ὅτι ὄντως ἠγέρθη ὁ
them, saying[,] – Really was raised the
κύριος καὶ ὤφθη Σίμωνι. 35 καὶ αὐτοὶ ἐξηγοῦντο
Lord and appeared to Simon. And they related
τὰ ἐν τῇ ὁδῷ καὶ ὡς ἐγνώσθη
the things in the way and how he was known
αὐτοῖς ἐν τῇ κλάσει τοῦ ἄρτου. 36 Ταῦτα
by them in the breaking of the loaf. these things
δὲ αὐτῶν λαλούντων αὐτὸς ἔστη ἐν
And them saying[a] he stood in
=as they said these things
μέσῳ αὐτῶν. 37 πτοηθέντες δὲ καὶ
[the] midst of them. But scared and
ἔμφοβοι γενόμενοι ἐδόκουν πνεῦμα θεωρεῖν.
terrified becoming they thought a spirit to behold.
38 καὶ εἶπεν αὐτοῖς· τί τεταραγμένοι ἐστέ,
And he said to them : Why *having been* troubled are ye,
καὶ διὰ τί διαλογισμοὶ ἀναβαίνουσιν ἐν
and why thoughts come up in
τῇ καρδίᾳ ὑμῶν; 39 ἴδετε τὰς χεῖράς
the heart of you? See the hands
μου καὶ τοὺς πόδας μου, ὅτι ἐγώ εἰμι
of me and the feet of me, that I am
αὐτός· ψηλαφήσατέ με καὶ ἴδετε, ὅτι
[my]self; feel me and see, because
πνεῦμα σάρκα καὶ ὀστέα οὐκ ἔχει καθὼς
a spirit flesh and bones has not as
ἐμὲ θεωρεῖτε ἔχοντα. ‡ 41 ἔτι δὲ ἀπιστούντων
me ye behold having. And yet disbelieving
=while they yet disbelieved
αὐτῶν ἀπὸ τῆς χαρᾶς καὶ θαυμαζόντων,
them[a] from the joy and marvelling[a],
εἶπεν αὐτοῖς· ἔχετέ τι βρώσιμον ἐνθάδε;
he said to them : Have ye any food here?
42 οἱ δὲ ἐπέδωκαν αὐτῷ ἰχθύος ὀπτοῦ
And they handed to him [3]fish [2]of a broiled
μέρος· 43 καὶ λαβὼν ἐνώπιον αὐτῶν ἔφαγεν.
[1]part; and taking before them he ate.
44 Εἶπεν δὲ πρὸς αὐτούς· οὗτοι οἱ λόγοι
And he said to them : These – words
μου οὓς ἐλάλησα πρὸς ὑμᾶς ἔτι ὢν σὺν
of me which I spoke to you yet being with
ὑμῖν, ὅτι δεῖ πληρωθῆναι πάντα τὰ
you, that it behoves to be fulfilled all the things
γεγραμμένα ἐν τῷ νόμῳ Μωϋσέως καὶ
having been written in the law of Moses and
τοῖς προφήταις καὶ ψαλμοῖς περὶ ἐμοῦ.
the prophets and psalms concerning me.
45 τότε διήνοιξεν αὐτῶν τὸν νοῦν τοῦ
Then he opened up of them the mind –
συνιέναι τὰς γραφάς· 46 καὶ εἶπεν αὐτοῖς
to understand[d] the scriptures; and said to them[,]
ὅτι οὕτως γέγραπται παθεῖν τὸν χριστὸν
– Thus it has been written [3]to suffer [1]the [2]Christ

‡ Verse 40 omitted by Nestle.

"Were not our hearts burning within us while he
talked with us on the road
and opened the Scriptures
to us?"
33They got up and re-
turned at once to Jerusa-
lem. There they found the
Eleven and those with
them, assembled together
34and saying, "It is true!
The Lord has risen and has
appeared to Simon."
35Then the two told what
had happened on the way,
and how Jesus was recog-
nized by them when he
broke the bread.

Jesus Appears to the Disciples

36While they were still
talking about this, Jesus
himself stood among them
and said to them, "Peace
be with you."
37They were startled and
frightened, thinking they
saw a ghost. 38He said to
them, "Why are you trou-
bled, and why do doubts
rise in your minds? 39Look
at my hands and my feet. It
is I myself! Touch me and
see; a ghost does not have
flesh and bones, as you see
I have."
40When he had said this,
he showed them his hands
and feet. 41And while they
still did not believe it because of joy and amaze-
ment, he asked them, "Do
you have anything here to
eat?" 42They gave him a
piece of broiled fish, 43and
he took it and ate it in their
presence.
44He said to them, "This
is what I told you while I
was still with you: Everything must be fulfilled that
is written about me in the
Law of Moses, the Proph-
ets and the Psalms."
45Then he opened their
minds so they could understand the Scriptures. 46He
told them, "This is what is
written: The Christ will suf-

rise again from the dead the third day;

47and that repentance for forgiveness of sins should be proclaimed in His name to all the nations, beginning from Jerusalem.

48"You are witnesses of these things.

49"And behold, I am sending forth the promise of My Father upon you; but you are to stay in the city until you are clothed with power from on high."

The Ascension

50And He led them out as far as Bethany, and He lifted up His hands and blessed them.

51And it came about that while He was blessing them, He parted from them.[r]

52And they[s] returned to Jerusalem with great joy,

53and were continually in the temple, praising God.

καὶ ἀναστῆναι ἐκ νεκρῶν τῇ τρίτῃ ἡμέρᾳ,
and to rise again out of [the] dead on the third day,

47 καὶ κηρυχθῆναι ἐπὶ τῷ ὀνόματι αὐτοῦ
and to be proclaimed on(in) the name of him

μετάνοιαν εἰς ἄφεσιν ἁμαρτιῶν εἰς πάντα
repentance unto forgiveness of sins to all

τὰ ἔθνη, — ἀρξάμενοι ἀπὸ Ἰερουσαλήμ.
the nations, — beginning from Jerusalem.

48 ὑμεῖς μάρτυρες τούτων. **49** καὶ ἰδοὺ
Ye [are] witnesses of these things. And behold

ἐγὼ ἐξαποστέλλω τὴν ἐπαγγελίαν τοῦ
I send forth the promise of the

πατρός μου ἐφ' ὑμᾶς· ὑμεῖς δὲ καθίσατε
Father of me on you; but ye sit

ἐν τῇ πόλει ἕως οὗ ἐνδύσησθε ἐξ ὕψους
in the city until [1]ye are clothed[with][3]out of [4]height

δύναμιν.
[2]power.

50 Ἐξήγαγεν δὲ αὐτοὺς ἕως πρὸς
And he led out them until toward

Βηθανίαν, καὶ ἐπάρας τὰς χεῖρας αὐτοῦ
Bethany, and lifting up the hands of him

εὐλόγησεν αὐτούς. **51** καὶ ἐγένετο ἐν τῷ
he blessed them. And it came to pass in the

εὐλογεῖν αὐτὸν αὐτοὺς διέστη ἀπ' αὐτῶν.
to bless him[be] them he withdrew from them.
=while he blessed

52 καὶ αὐτοὶ ὑπέστρεψαν εἰς Ἰερουσαλὴμ
And they returned to Jerusalem

μετὰ χαρᾶς μεγάλης, **53** καὶ ἦσαν διὰ παντὸς
with joy great, and were continually

ἐν τῷ ἱερῷ εὐλογοῦντες τὸν θεόν.
in the temple blessing – God.

fer and rise from the dead
on the third day, 47and repentance and forgiveness
of sins will be preached in
his name to all nations, beginning at Jerusalem.
48You are witnesses of
these things. 49I am going
to send you what my Fa-
ther has promised; but stay
in the city until you have
been clothed with power
from on high."

The Ascension

50When he had led them
out to the vicinity of Bethany, he lifted up his hands
and blessed them. 51While
he was blessing them, he
left them and was taken up
into heaven. 52Then they
worshiped him and re-
turned to Jerusalem with
great joy. 53And they
stayed continually at the
temple, praising God.

[r] Some mss. add *and was carried up into heaven*

[s] Some mss. insert *worshiped Him, and*

John

Chapter 1

The Deity of Jesus Christ

IN the beginning was the Word, and the Word was with God, and the Word was God.

2He was in the beginning with God.

3All things came into being by Him, and apart from Him nothing came into being that has come into being.

4In Him was life, and the life was the light of men.

5And the light shines in the darkness, and the darkness did not [a]comprehend it.

The Witness of John

6There [b]came a man, sent from God, whose name was John.

7He came for a witness, that he might bear witness of the light, that all might believe through him.

8He was not the light, but *came* that he might bear witness of the light.

9There was the true light [c]which, coming into the world, enlightens every man.

10He was in the world, and the world was made through Him, and the world did not know Him.

11He came to His [d]own, and those who were His own did not receive Him.

12But as many as received Him, to them He gave the right to become children of God, *even* to those who believe in His name,

13who were born not of blood, nor of the will of the flesh, nor of the will of man, but of God.

The Word Made Flesh

14And the Word became flesh, and dwelt among us, and we beheld His glory, glory as of the only begotten from the Father, full of grace and truth.

15John *bore witness of Him, and cried out, saying, "This was He of whom I said, 'He who comes after

[a] Or, *overpower*
[b] Or, *came into being*
[c] Or, *which enlightens every man coming into the world*
[d] Or, *own things, possessions, domain*

ΚΑΤΑ ΙΩΑΝΝΗΝ

According to John

1 Ἐν ἀρχῇ ἦν ὁ λόγος, καὶ ὁ λόγος
In [the] beginning was the Word, and the Word
ἦν πρὸς τὸν θεόν, καὶ θεὸς ἦν ὁ λόγος.
was with – God, and God was the Word.*
2 οὗτος ἦν ἐν ἀρχῇ πρὸς τὸν θεόν.
This one was in [the] beginning with – God.
3 πάντα δι' αὐτοῦ ἐγένετο, καὶ χωρὶς
All things through him became, and without
αὐτοῦ ἐγένετο οὐδὲ ἕν ὃ γέγονεν. **4** ἐν
him became not one thing which has become. In
αὐτῷ ζωὴ ἦν, καὶ ἡ ζωὴ ἦν τὸ φῶς
him life was, and the life was the light
τῶν ἀνθρώπων· **5** καὶ τὸ φῶς ἐν τῇ
– of men; and the light in the
σκοτίᾳ φαίνει, καὶ ἡ σκοτία αὐτὸ οὐ
darkness shines, and the darkness it not
κατέλαβεν. **6** Ἐγένετο ἄνθρωπος, ἀπεσταλμένος
overtook. There was a man, *having been* sent
παρὰ θεοῦ, ὄνομα αὐτῷ Ἰωάννης· **7** οὗτος
from God, name to him[c] John; this man
ἦλθεν εἰς μαρτυρίαν, ἵνα μαρτυρήσῃ περὶ
came for witness, that he might witness concerning
τοῦ φωτός, ἵνα πάντες πιστεύσωσιν δι'
the light, that all men might believe through
αὐτοῦ. **8** οὐκ ἦν ἐκεῖνος τὸ φῶς, ἀλλ' ἵνα
him. He was not that – light, but that
μαρτυρήσῃ περὶ τοῦ φωτός. **9** Ἦν τὸ φῶς
he might witness concerning the light. It was the light
τὸ ἀληθινόν, ὃ φωτίζει πάντα ἄνθρωπον,
– true, which enlightens every man,
ἐρχόμενον εἰς τὸν κόσμον. **10** ἐν τῷ
coming into the world. In the
κόσμῳ ἦν, καὶ ὁ κόσμος δι' αὐτοῦ
world he was, and the world through him
ἐγένετο, καὶ ὁ κόσμος αὐτὸν οὐκ ἔγνω.
became, and the world him knew not.
11 εἰς τὰ ἴδια ἦλθεν, καὶ οἱ ἴδιοι αὐτὸν
To his own things he came, and his own people him
οὐ παρέλαβον. **12** ὅσοι δὲ ἔλαβον αὐτόν,
received not. But as many as received him,
ἔδωκεν αὐτοῖς ἐξουσίαν τέκνα θεοῦ γεν-
he gave to them right children of God to be-
έσθαι, τοῖς πιστεύουσιν εἰς τὸ ὄνομα αὐτοῦ,
come, to the [ones] believing in the name of him,
13 οἳ οὐκ ἐξ αἱμάτων οὐδὲ ἐκ θελήματος
who not of bloods nor of [the] will
σαρκὸς οὐδὲ ἐκ θελήματος ἀνδρὸς ἀλλ'
of [the] flesh nor of [the] will of a man but
ἐκ θεοῦ ἐγεννήθησαν. **14** Καὶ ὁ λόγος
of God were born. And the Word
σὰρξ ἐγένετο καὶ ἐσκήνωσεν ἐν ἡμῖν,
flesh became and tabernacled among us,
καὶ ἐθεασάμεθα τὴν δόξαν αὐτοῦ, δόξαν
and we beheld the glory of him, glory
ὡς μονογενοῦς παρὰ πατρός, πλήρης χάριτος
as of an only begotten from a father, full of grace
καὶ ἀληθείας. **15** Ἰωάννης μαρτυρεῖ περὶ
and of truth. John witnesses concerning
αὐτοῦ καὶ κέκραγεν λέγων· οὗτος ἦν ὃν
him and has cried out saying : This man was he whom
εἶπον· ὁ ὀπίσω μου ἐρχόμενος ἔμπροσθέν
I said : The [one] after me coming before

*** But note that the subject has the article and the predicate has it not; hence translate—"the Word was God."**

John

Chapter 1

The Word Became Flesh

IN the beginning was the Word, and the Word was with God, and the Word was God. 2He was with God in the beginning.

3Through him all things were made; without him nothing was made that has been made. 4In him was life, and that life was the light of men. 5The light shines in the darkness, but the darkness has not understood[a] it.

6There came a man who was sent from God; his name was John. 7He came as a witness to testify concerning that light, so that through him all men might believe. 8He himself was not the light; he came only as a witness to the light. 9The true light that gives light to every man was coming into the world.[b]

10He was in the world, and though the world was made through him, the world did not recognize him. 11He came to that which was his own, but his own did not receive him. 12Yet to all who received him, to those who believed in his name, he gave the right to become children of God— 13children born not of natural descent,[c] nor of human decision or a husband's will, but born of God.

14The Word became flesh and made his dwelling among us. We have seen his glory, the glory of the One and Only,[d] who came from the Father, full of grace and truth.

15John testifies concerning him. He cries out, saying, "This was he of whom I said, 'He who comes after

[a]5 Or *darkness, and the darkness has not overcome*
[b]9 Or *This was the true light that gives light to every man who comes into the world*
[c]13 Greek *of bloods*
[d]14,18 Or *the Only Begotten*

me has a higher rank than I,
for He existed before
me.' "
16For of His fulness we
have all received, and
grace upon grace.
17For the Law was given
through Moses; grace and
truth were realized through
Jesus Christ.
18No man has seen God at
any time; the only begotten
[e]God, who is in the bosom
of the Father, He has ex-
plained *Him*.

The Testimony of John

19And this is the witness
of John, when the Jews
sent to him priests and Levites from Jerusalem to ask
him, "Who are you?"
20And he confessed, and
did not deny, and he con-
fessed, "I am not the
Christ."
21And they asked him,
"What then? Are you Eli-
jah?" And he *said, "I am
not." "Are you the
Prophet?" And he an-
swered, "No."
22They said then to him,
"Who are you, so that we
may give an answer to
those who sent us? What do
you say about yourself?"
23He said, "I am A VOICE
OF ONE CRYING IN THE WIL-
DERNESS, 'MAKE STRAIGHT
THE WAY OF THE LORD,' as
Isaiah the prophet said."
24Now they had been sent
from the Pharisees.
25And they asked him,
and said to him, "Why then
are you baptizing, if you
are not the Christ, nor Elijah, nor the Prophet?"
26John answered them
saying, "I baptize [f]in
water, *but* among you
stands One whom you do
not know.
27"*It is* He who comes after me, the thong of whose
sandal I am not worthy to
untie."
28These things took place
in Bethany beyond the Jordan, where John was bap-
tizing.
29The next day he *saw

[e] Some later mss. read *Son*
[f] The Gr. here can be translated *in, with* or *by*

μου γέγονεν, ὅτι πρῶτός μου ἦν. 16 ὅτι
me has become, because first of me he was. Because
ἐκ τοῦ πληρώματος αὐτοῦ ἡμεῖς πάντες
of the fulness of him we all
ἐλάβομεν, καὶ χάριν ἀντὶ χάριτος· 17 ὅτι
received, and grace instead of grace; because
ὁ νόμος διὰ Μωϋσέως ἐδόθη, ἡ χάρις καὶ
the law through Moses was given, the grace and
ἡ ἀλήθεια διὰ Ἰησοῦ Χριστοῦ ἐγένετο.
the truth through Jesus Christ became.
18 Θεὸν οὐδεὶς ἑώρακεν πώποτε· μονογενὴς
God no man has seen *never*; [the] only begotten
θεὸς ὁ ὢν εἰς τὸν κόλπον τοῦ πατρός,
God the [one] being in the bosom of the Father,
ἐκεῖνος ἐξηγήσατο.
that one declared [?him].
19 Καὶ αὕτη ἐστὶν ἡ μαρτυρία τοῦ
And this is the witness –
Ἰωάννου, ὅτε ἀπέστειλαν πρὸς αὐτὸν οἱ
of John, when 3sent 4to 5him 1the
Ἰουδαῖοι ἐξ Ἱεροσολύμων ἱερεῖς καὶ Λευίτας
2Jews 9from 10Jerusalem 6priests 7and 8Levites
ἵνα ἐρωτήσωσιν αὐτόν· σὺ τίς εἶ; 20 καὶ
that they might ask him : Thou who art? And
ὡμολόγησεν καὶ οὐκ ἠρνήσατο, καὶ
he confessed and denied not, and
ὡμολόγησεν ὅτι ἐγὼ οὐκ εἰμὶ ὁ χριστός.
he confessed[,] – I am not the Christ.
21 καὶ ἠρώτησαν αὐτόν· τί οὖν; Ἠλίας εἶ
And they asked him: · What then? Elias art
σύ; καὶ λέγει· οὐκ εἰμί. ὁ προφήτης εἶ σύ;
thou? And he says : I am not. The prophet art thou?
καὶ ἀπεκρίθη· οὔ. 22 εἶπαν οὖν αὐτῷ·
And he answered : No. They said therefore to him :
τίς εἶ; ἵνα ἀπόκρισιν δῶμεν τοῖς
Who art thou? that an answer we may give to the [ones]
πέμψασιν ἡμᾶς· τί λέγεις περὶ σεαυτοῦ;
having sent us; What sayest thou concerning thyself?
23 ἔφη· ἐγὼ φωνὴ βοῶντος ἐν τῇ ἐρήμῳ·
He said : I [am] a voice of [one] crying in the desert :
εὐθύνατε τὴν ὁδὸν κυρίου, καθὼς εἶπεν
Make straight the way of [the] Lord, as said
Ἠσαΐας ὁ προφήτης. 24 Καὶ ἀπεσταλμένοι
Esaias the prophet. And [the ones] *having been* sent
ἦσαν ἐκ τῶν Φαρισαίων. 25 καὶ ἠρώτησαν
were of the Pharisees. And they asked
αὐτὸν καὶ εἶπαν αὐτῷ· τι οὖν βαπτίζεις
him and said to him: Why then baptizest thou
εἰ σὺ οὐκ εἶ ὁ χριστὸς οὐδὲ Ἠλίας
if thou art not the Christ nor Elias
οὐδὲ ὁ προφήτης; 26 ἀπεκρίθη αὐτοῖς ὁ
nor the prophet? Answered them –
Ἰωάννης λέγων· ἐγὼ βαπτίζω ἐν ὕδατι·
John saying : I baptize in water;
μέσος ὑμῶν στήκει ὃν ὑμεῖς οὐκ οἴδατε,
among you stands [one] whom ye know not,
27 ὁ ὀπίσω μου ἐρχόμενος, οὗ οὐκ εἰμὶ
the [one] after me coming, of whom am not
ἐγὼ ἄξιος ἵνα λύσω αὐτοῦ τὸν ἱμάντα
I worthy that I should loosen of him the thong
τοῦ ὑποδήματος. 28 Ταῦτα ἐν Βηθανίᾳ
of the sandal. These things in Bethany
ἐγένετο πέραν τοῦ Ἰορδάνου, ὅπου ἦν ὁ
happened beyond the Jordan, where was –
Ἰωάννης βαπτίζων. 29 Τῇ ἐπαύριον βλέπει
John baptizing. On the morrow he sees

me has surpassed me be-
cause he was before me.' "
16From the fullness of his
grace we have all received
one blessing after another.
17For the law was given
through Moses; grace and
truth came through Jesus
Christ. 18No one has ever
seen God, but God the One
and Only,[d] [e]who is at the
Father's side, has made
him known.

John the Baptist Denies Being the Christ

19Now this was John's
testimony when the Jews of
Jerusalem sent priests and
Levites to ask him who he
was. 20He did not fail to
confess, but confessed
freely, "I am not the
Christ.[f]"
21They asked him, "Then
who are you? Are you Eli-
jah?"
He said, "I am not."
"Are you the Prophet?"
He answered, "No."
22Finally they said, "Who
are you? Give us an answer
to take back to those who
sent us. What do you say
about yourself?"
23John replied in the
words of Isaiah the prophet, "I am the voice of one
calling in the desert, 'Make
straight the way for the
Lord.' "[g]
24Now some Pharisees
who had been sent 25ques-
tioned him, "Why then do
you baptize if you are not
the Christ, nor Elijah, nor
the Prophet?"
26"I baptize with[h] wa-
ter," John replied, "but
among you stands one you
do not know. 27He is the
one who comes after me,
the thongs of whose san-
dals I am not worthy to untie."
28This all happened at
Bethany on the other side
of the Jordan, where John
was baptizing.

Jesus the Lamb of God

29The next day John saw

[e] 18 Some manuscripts *but the only* (or *only begotten*) *Son*
[f] 20 Or *Messiah.* "The Christ" (Greek) and "the Messiah" (Hebrew) both mean "the Anointed One"; also in verse 25.
[g] 23 Isaiah 40:3
[h] 26 Or *in*; also in verses 31 and 33

Jesus coming to him, and
*said, "Behold, the Lamb
of God who takes away the
sin of the world!
30"This is He on behalf of
whom I said, 'After me
comes a Man who has a
higher rank than I, for He
existed before me.'
31"And I did not recog-
nize Him, but in order that
He might be manifested to
Israel, I came baptizing [g]in
water."
32And John bore witness
saying, "I have beheld the
Spirit descending as a dove
out of heaven, and He re-
mained upon Him.
33"And I did not recog-
nize Him, but He who sent
me to baptize [g]in water
said to me, 'He upon whom
you see the Spirit descending and remaining upon
Him, this is the one who
baptizes in the Holy Spirit.'
34"And I have seen, and
have borne witness that
this is the Son of God."

Jesus' Public Ministry, First Converts

35Again the next day John
was standing with two of
his disciples,
36and he looked upon
Jesus as He walked, and
*said, "Behold, the Lamb
of God!"
37And the two disciples
heard him speak, and they
followed Jesus.
38And Jesus turned, and
beheld them following, and
*said to them, "What do
you seek?" And they said
to Him, "Rabbi (which
translated means Teacher),
where are You staying?"
39He *said to them,
"Come, and you will see."
They came therefore and

[g] The Gr. here can be translated *in*, *with* or *by*

τὸν Ἰησοῦν ἐρχόμενον πρὸς αὐτόν, καὶ
– Jesus coming toward him, and
λέγει· ἴδε ὁ ἀμνὸς τοῦ θεοῦ ὁ αἴρων
says : Behold[,] the Lamb – of God – taking
τὴν ἁμαρτίαν τοῦ κόσμου. **30** οὗτός ἐστιν
the sin of the world. This is he
ὑπὲρ οὗ ἐγὼ εἶπον· ὀπίσω μου ἔρχεται
as to whom I said : After me comes
ἀνὴρ ὃς ἔμπροσθέν μου γέγονεν, ὅτι
a man who before me has become, because
πρῶτός μου ἦν. **31** κἀγὼ οὐκ ᾔδειν
first of me he was. And I knew not
αὐτόν, ἀλλ' ἵνα φανερωθῇ τῷ Ἰσραήλ,
him, but that he might be manifested – to Israel,
διὰ τοῦτο ἦλθον ἐγὼ ἐν ὕδατι βαπτίζων.
therefore came I in water baptizing.
32 Καὶ ἐμαρτύρησεν Ἰωάννης λέγων ὅτι
And witnessed John saying[,] –
τεθέαμαι τὸ πνεῦμα καταβαῖνον ὡς
I have beheld the Spirit coming down as
περιστερὰν ἐξ οὐρανοῦ, καὶ ἔμεινεν ἐπ'
a dove out of heaven, and he remained on
αὐτόν. **33** κἀγὼ οὐκ ᾔδειν αὐτόν, ἀλλ'
him. And I knew not him, but
ὁ πέμψας με βαπτίζειν ἐν ὕδατι, ἐκεῖνός
the [one] having sent me to baptize in water, that [one].
μοι εἶπεν· ἐφ' ὃν ἂν ἴδῃς τὸ πνεῦμα
to me said: On whomever thou seest the Spirit
καταβαῖνον καὶ μένον ἐπ' αὐτόν, οὗτός
coming down and remaining on him, this
ἐστιν ὁ βαπτίζων ἐν πνεύματι ἁγίῳ.
is the [one] baptizing in Spirit Holy.
34 κἀγὼ ἑώρακα, καὶ μεμαρτύρηκα ὅτι
And I have seen, and have witnessed that
οὗτός ἐστιν ὁ υἱὸς τοῦ θεοῦ.
this [one] is the Son – of God.
35 Τῇ ἐπαύριον πάλιν εἱστήκει ὁ Ἰωάννης
On the morrow again stood – John
καὶ ἐκ τῶν μαθητῶν αὐτοῦ δύο, **36** καὶ
and of the disciples of him two, and
ἐμβλέψας τῷ Ἰησοῦ περιπατοῦντι λέγει·
looking at – Jesus walking he says:
ἴδε ὁ ἀμνὸς τοῦ θεοῦ. **37** καὶ ἤκουσαν
Behold[,] the Lamb – of God. And [4]heard
οἱ δύο μαθηταὶ αὐτοῦ λαλοῦντος καὶ
[1]the [2]two [3]disciples [5]him [6]speaking and
ἠκολούθησαν τῷ Ἰησοῦ. **38** στραφεὶς δὲ
they followed – Jesus. And [2]turning
ὁ Ἰησοῦς καὶ θεασάμενος αὐτοὺς ἀκολουθοῦντας
– [1]Jesus and beholding them following
λέγει αὐτοῖς· τί ζητεῖτε; οἱ δὲ εἶπαν
says to them : What seek ye? And they said
αὐτῷ· ῥαββί (ὃ λέγεται μεθερμηνευόμενον
to him : Rabbi (which is called being translated
διδάσκαλε), ποῦ μένεις; **39** λέγει αὐτοῖς·
Teacher), where remainest thou? He says to them :
ἔρχεσθε καὶ ὄψεσθε. ἦλθαν οὖν καὶ εἶδαν
Come and ye will see. They went therefore and saw
ποῦ μένει, καὶ παρ' αὐτῷ ἔμειναν τὴν
where he remains(ed), and with him remained –
ἡμέραν ἐκείνην· ὥρα ἦν ὡς δεκάτη.
day that; hour was about tenth.
40 Ἦν Ἀνδρέας ὁ ἀδελφὸς Σίμωνος Πέτρου
It was Andrew the brother of Simon Peter
εἷς ἐκ τῶν δύο τῶν ἀκουσάντων παρὰ
one of the two – hearing from

Jesus coming toward him
and said, "Look, the Lamb
of God, who takes away the
sin of the world! 30This is
the one I meant when I
said, 'A man who comes after me has surpassed me
because he was before me.'
31I myself did not know
him, but the reason I came
baptizing with water was
that he might be revealed to
Israel."
32Then John gave this testimony: "I saw the Spirit
come down from heaven as
a dove and remain on him.
33I would not have known
him, except that the one
who sent me to baptize
with water told me, 'The
man on whom you see the
Spirit come down and re-
main is he who will baptize
with the Holy Spirit.' 34I
have seen and I testify that
this is the Son of God."

Jesus' First Disciples

35The next day John was
there again with two of his
disciples. 36When he saw
Jesus passing by, he said,
"Look, the Lamb of God!"
37When the two disciples
heard him say this, they followed Jesus. 38Turning
around, Jesus saw them
following and asked,
"What do you want?"
They said, "Rabbi"
(which means Teacher),
"where are you staying?"
39"Come," he replied,
"and you will see."
So they went and saw

saw where He was staying;
and they stayed with Him
that day, for it was about
the [h]tenth hour.
40One of the two who
heard John *speak,* and followed Him, was Andrew,
Simon Peter's brother.
41He *found first his own
brother Simon, and *said to
him, "We have found the
Messiah" (which trans-
lated means Christ).
42He brought him to
Jesus. Jesus looked at him,
and said, "You are Simon
the son of John; you shall
be called Cephas" (which
is translated Peter).
43The next day He pur-
posed to go forth into Galilee, and He *found Philip.
And Jesus *said to him,
"Follow Me."
44Now Philip was from
Bethsaida, of the city of
Andrew and Peter.
45Philip *found Nathana-
el and *said to him, "We
have found Him of whom
Moses in the Law and *also*
the Prophets wrote, Jesus
of Nazareth, the son of Joseph."
46And Nathanael *said to
him, "Can any good thing
come out of Nazareth?"
Philip *said to him, "Come
and see."
47Jesus saw Nathanael
coming to Him, and *said
of him, "Behold, an Israelite indeed, in whom is no
guile!"
48Nathanael *said to
Him, "How do You know
me?" Jesus answered and
said to him, "Before Philip
called you, when you were
under the fig tree, I saw
you."
49Nathanael answered
Him, "Rabbi, You are the
Son of God; You are the
King of Israel."
50Jesus answered and
said to him, "Because I
said to you that I saw you
under the fig tree, do you
believe? You shall see
greater things than these."
51And He *said to him,
"Truly, truly, I say to you,
you shall see the heavens

[h]Perhaps 10 a.m. (Roman time)

Ἰωάννου καὶ ἀκολουθησάντων αὐτῷ·
John and following him;
41 εὑρίσκει οὗτος πρῶτον τὸν ἀδελφὸν τὸν
[3]finds [1]this one [2]first [4]the(his) [6]brother –
ἴδιον Σίμωνα καὶ λέγει αὐτῷ· εὑρήκαμεν
[5]own Simon and tells him : We have found
τὸν Μεσσίαν (ὅ ἐστιν μεθερμηνευόμενον
the Messiah (which is being translated
χριστός). 42 ἤγαγεν αὐτὸν πρὸς τὸν
Christ). He led him to –
Ἰησοῦν. ἐμβλέψας αὐτῷ ὁ Ἰησοῦς εἶπεν·
Jesus. Looking at him – Jesus said :
σὺ εἶ Σίμων ὁ υἱὸς Ἰωάννου, σὺ κληθήσῃ
Thou art Simon the son of John, thou shalt be called
Κηφᾶς (ὃ ἑρμηνεύεται Πέτρος). 43 Τῇ
Cephas (which is translated Peter). On the
ἐπαύριον ἠθέλησεν ἐξελθεῖν εἰς τὴν Γαλιλαίαν,
morrow he wished to go forth into – Galilee,
καὶ εὑρίσκει Φίλιππον. καὶ λέγει αὐτῷ ὁ
and finds Philip. And says to him –
Ἰησοῦς· ἀκολούθει μοι. 44 ἦν δὲ ὁ
Jesus : Follow me. Now was –
Φίλιππος ἀπὸ Βηθσαϊδά, ἐκ τῆς πόλεως
Philip from Bethsaida, of the city
Ἀνδρέου καὶ Πέτρου. 45 εὑρίσκει Φίλιππος
of Andrew and of Peter. [2]Finds [1]Philip
τὸν Ναθαναὴλ καὶ λέγει αὐτῷ· ὃν ἔγραψεν
– [3]Nathanael and tells him : [He] whom wrote
Μωϋσῆς ἐν τῷ νόμῳ καὶ οἱ προφῆται
Moses in the law and the prophets
εὑρήκαμεν, Ἰησοῦν υἱὸν τοῦ Ἰωσὴφ τὸν
we have found, Jesus son – of Joseph –
ἀπὸ Ναζαρέθ. 46 καὶ εἶπεν αὐτῷ
from Nazareth. And said to him
Ναθαναήλ· ἐκ Ναζαρὲθ δύναταί τι ἀγαθὸν
Nathanael : Out of Nazareth can anything good
εἶναι; λέγει αὐτῷ ὁ Φίλιππος· ἔρχου καὶ
to be? Says to him – Philip : Come and
ἴδε. 47 εἶδεν Ἰησοῦς τὸν Ναθαναὴλ
see. [2]Saw [1]Jesus – [3]Nathanael
ἐρχόμενον πρὸς αὐτὸν καὶ λέγει περὶ
coming toward him and says concerning
αὐτοῦ· ἴδε ἀληθῶς Ἰσραηλίτης, ἐν ᾧ
him: Behold[,] truly an Israelite, in whom
δόλος οὐκ ἔστιν. 48 λέγει αὐτῷ Ναθαναήλ·
guile is not. Says to him Nathanael :
πόθεν με γινώσκεις; ἀπεκρίθη Ἰησοῦς καὶ
Whence me knowest thou? Answered Jesus and
εἶπεν αὐτῷ· πρὸ τοῦ σε Φίλιππον φωνῆσαι
said to him : Before *the* thee Philip to call[b]
=Philip called thee
ὄντα ὑπὸ τὴν συκῆν εἶδόν σε. 49 ἀπεκρίθη
being under the fig-tree I saw thee. Answered
αὐτῷ Ναθαναήλ· ῥαββί, σὺ εἶ ὁ υἱὸς τοῦ
him Nathanael : Rabbi, thou art the Son –
θεοῦ, σὺ βασιλεὺς εἶ τοῦ Ἰσραήλ.
of God, thou king art – of Israel.
50 ἀπεκρίθη Ἰησοῦς καὶ εἶπεν αὐτῷ·
Answered Jesus and said to him :
ὅτι εἶπόν σοι ὅτι εἶδόν σε ὑποκάτω τῆς
Because I told thee that I saw thee underneath the
συκῆς, πιστεύεις; μείζω τούτων ὄψῃ.
fig-tree, believest thou? greater [than] these things thou shalt see.
51 καὶ λέγει αὐτῷ· ἀμὴν ἀμὴν λέγω
And he says to him : Truly truly I tell
ὑμῖν, ὄψεσθε τὸν οὐρανὸν ἀνεῳγότα καὶ
you, ye shall see the heaven *having been* opened and

where he was staying, and
spent that day with him. It
was about the tenth hour.
40Andrew, Simon Peter's
brother, was one of the two
who heard what John had
said and who had followed
Jesus. 41The first thing Andrew did was to find his
brother Simon and tell him,
"We have found the Messi-
ah" (that is, the Christ).
42And he brought him to
Jesus.
Jesus looked at him and
said, "You are Simon son
of John. You will be called
Cephas" (which, when
translated, is Peter[i]).

Jesus Calls Philip and Nathanael

43The next day Jesus de-
cided to leave for Galilee.
Finding Philip, he said to
him, "Follow me."
44Philip, like Andrew and
Peter, was from the town of
Bethsaida. 45Philip found
Nathanael and told him,
"We have found the one
Moses wrote about in the
Law, and about whom the
prophets also wrote—
Jesus of Nazareth, the son
of Joseph."
46"Nazareth! Can any-
thing good come from
there?" Nathanael asked.
"Come and see," said
Philip.
47When Jesus saw Na-
thanael approaching, he
said of him, "Here is a true
Israelite, in whom there is
nothing false."
48"How do you know
me?" Nathanael asked.
Jesus answered, "I saw
you while you were still under the fig tree before Philip
called you."
49Then Nathanael de-
clared, "Rabbi, you are the
Son of God; you are the
King of Israel."
50Jesus said, "You be-
lieve[j] because I told you I
saw you under the fig tree.
You shall see greater things
than that." 51He then added, "I tell you[k] the truth,
you[k] shall see heaven

[i]*42* Both *Cephas* (Aramaic) and *Peter* (Greek) mean *rock.*
[j]*50* Or *Do you believe . . . ?*
[k]*51* The Greek is plural.

opened, and the angels of
God ascending and de-
scending on the Son of
Man."

Chapter 2

Miracle at Cana

AND on the third day
there was a wedding
in Cana of Galilee, and the
mother of Jesus was there;
2and Jesus also was in-
vited, and His disciples, to
the wedding.
3And when the wine
gave out, the mother of
Jesus *said to Him, "They
have no wine."
4And Jesus *said to her,
"Woman, what do I have
to do with you? My hour
has not yet come."
5His mother *said to the
servants, "Whatever He
says to you, do it."
6Now there were six
stone waterpots set there
for the Jewish custom of
purification, containing
twenty or thirty gallons
each.
7Jesus *said to them,
"Fill the waterpots with
water." And they filled
them up to the brim.
8And He *said to them,
"Draw *some* out now, and
take it to the [i] headwait-
er." And they took it *to
him*.
9And when the head-
waiter tasted the water
which had become wine,
and did not know where it
came from (but the ser-
vants who had drawn the
water knew), the headwait-
er *called the bridegroom,
10and *said to him,
"Every man serves the
good wine first, and when
men have drunk freely,
then that which is poorer;
you have kept the good
wine until now."
11This beginning of *His*
signs Jesus did in Cana of
Galilee, and manifested His
glory, and His disciples believed in Him.
12After this He went
down to Capernaum, He

[i] Or, *steward*

τοὺς ἀγγέλους τοῦ θεοῦ ἀναβαίνοντας καὶ
the angels – of God going up and
καταβαίνοντας ἐπὶ τὸν υἱὸν τοῦ ἀνθρώπου.
coming down on the Son – of man.

2 Καὶ τῇ ἡμέρᾳ τῇ τρίτῃ γάμος ἐγένετο
And on the day – third a wedding there was
ἐν Κανὰ τῆς Γαλιλαίας, καὶ ἦν ἡ μήτηρ
in Cana – of Galilee, and was the mother
τοῦ Ἰησοῦ ἐκεῖ· 2 ἐκλήθη δὲ καὶ ὁ
– of Jesus there; and was invited both –
Ἰησοῦς καὶ οἱ μαθηταὶ αὐτοῦ εἰς τὸν
Jesus and the disciples of him to the
γάμον. 3 καὶ ὑστερήσαντος οἴνου λέγει ἡ
wedding. And lacking wine[a] says the
=when wine was lacking
μήτηρ τοῦ Ἰησοῦ πρὸς αὐτόν· οἶνον
mother – of Jesus to him : Wine
οὐκ ἔχουσιν. 4 καὶ λέγει αὐτῇ ὁ Ἰησοῦς·
they have not. And says to her – Jesus :
τί ἐμοὶ καὶ σοί, γύναι; οὔπω ἥκει ἡ
What to me and to thee, woman? not yet is come the
ὥρα μου. 5 λέγει ἡ μήτηρ αὐτοῦ τοῖς
hour of me. Says the mother of him to the
διακόνοις· ὅ τι ἂν λέγῃ ὑμῖν, ποιήσατε.
servants: Whatever he tells you, do ye.
6 ἦσαν δὲ ἐκεῖ λίθιναι ὑδρίαι ἓξ κατὰ
Now there were there stone water-pots six according to
τὸν καθαρισμὸν τῶν Ἰουδαίων κείμεναι,
the purifying of the Jews lying,
χωροῦσαι ἀνὰ μετρητὰς δύο ἢ τρεῖς.
containing each† measures two or three.
7 λέγει αὐτοῖς ὁ Ἰησοῦς· γεμίσατε τὰς
Tells them – Jesus : Fill ye the
ὑδρίας ὕδατος. καὶ ἐγέμισαν αὐτὰς ἕως
water-pots of(with) water. And they filled them up to
ἄνω. 8 καὶ λέγει αὐτοῖς· ἀντλήσατε νῦν
[the] top. And he tells them : Draw now
καὶ φέρετε τῷ ἀρχιτρικλίνῳ. οἱ δὲ
and carry to the master of the feast. And they
ἤνεγκαν. 9 ὡς δὲ ἐγεύσατο ὁ ἀρχιτρίκλινος
carried. But when tasted the master of the feast
τὸ ὕδωρ οἶνον γεγενημένον, καὶ οὐκ ᾔδει
the water [2]wine [1]having become, and did not know
πόθεν ἐστίν, οἱ δὲ διάκονοι ᾔδεισαν οἱ
whence it is(was), but the servants knew the [ones]
ἠντληκότες τὸ ὕδωρ, φωνεῖ τὸν νυμφίον
having drawn the water, [3]calls [4]the [5]bridegroom
ὁ ἀρχιτρίκλινος 10 καὶ λέγει αὐτῷ· πᾶς
[1]the [2]master of the feast and says to him : Every
ἄνθρωπος πρῶτον τὸν καλὸν οἶνον τίθησιν,
man first the good wine sets forth,
καὶ ὅταν μεθυσθῶσιν τὸν ἐλάσσω· σὺ
and when they become drunk the worse; thou
τετήρηκας τὸν καλὸν οἶνον ἕως ἄρτι.
hast kept the good wine until now.
11 Ταύτην ἐποίησεν ἀρχὴν τῶν σημείων ὁ
[1]This [5]did [2]beginning [3]of the [4]signs –
Ἰησοῦς ἐν Κανὰ τῆς Γαλιλαίας καὶ
Jesus in Cana – of Galilee and
ἐφανέρωσεν τὴν δόξαν αὐτοῦ, καὶ ἐπίστευσαν
manifested the glory of him, and believed
εἰς αὐτὸν οἱ μαθηταὶ αὐτοῦ.
in him the disciples of him.
12 Μετὰ τοῦτο κατέβη εἰς Καφαρναοὺμ
After this went down to Capernaum

open, and the angels of God
ascending and descending
on the Son of Man."

Chapter 2

Jesus Changes Water to Wine

ON the third day a wed-
ding took place at
Cana in Galilee. Jesus'
mother was there, 2and
Jesus and his disciples had
also been invited to the
wedding. 3When the wine
was gone, Jesus' mother
said to him, "They have no
more wine."
4"Dear woman, why do
you involve me?" Jesus replied. "My time has not yet
come."
5His mother said to the
servants, "Do whatever he
tells you."
6Nearby stood six stone
water jars, the kind used by
the Jews for ceremonial
washing, each holding from
twenty to thirty gallons.[l]
7Jesus said to the ser-
vants, "Fill the jars with
water"; so they filled them
to the brim.
8Then he told them,
"Now draw some out and
take it to the master of the
banquet."
They did so, 9and the
master of the banquet tasted the water that had been
turned into wine. He did
not realize where it had
come from, though the servants who had drawn the
water knew. Then he called
the bridegroom aside 10and
said, "Everyone brings out
the choice wine first and
then the cheaper wine after
the guests have had too
much to drink; but you
have saved the best till
now."
11This, the first of his miraculous signs, Jesus performed in Cana of Galilee.
He thus revealed his glory,
and his disciples put their
faith in him.

Jesus Clears the Temple

12After this he went down
to Capernaum with his

[l]6 Greek *two to three metretes* (probably about 75 to 115 liters)

and His mother, and *His*
brothers, and His disciples;
and there they stayed a few
days.

First Passover—Cleansing the Temple

13And the Passover of the
Jews was at hand, and
Jesus went up to Jerusa-
lem.
14And He found in the
temple those who were
selling oxen and sheep and
doves, and the money-
changers seated.
15And He made a scourge
of cords, and drove *them*
all out of the temple, with
the sheep and the oxen; and
He poured out the coins of
the moneychangers, and
overturned their tables;
16and to those who were
selling the doves He said,
"Take these things away;
stop making My Father's
house a house of merchan-
dise."
17His disciples remem-
bered that it was written,
"ZEAL FOR THY HOUSE WILL
CONSUME ME."
18The Jews therefore an-
swered and said to Him,
"What sign do You show to
us, seeing that You do
these things?"
19Jesus answered and
said to them, "Destroy this
temple, and in three days I
will raise it up."
20The Jews therefore
said, "It took forty-six
years to build this temple,
and will You raise it up in
three days?"
21But He was speaking of
the temple of His body.
22When therefore He was
raised from the dead, His
disciples remembered that
He said this; and they believed the Scripture, and
the word which Jesus had
spoken.
23Now when He was in
Jerusalem at the Passover,
during the feast, many believed in His name, behold-

αὐτὸς καὶ ἡ μήτηρ αὐτοῦ καὶ
he and the mother of him and
οἱ ἀδελφοὶ καὶ οἱ μαθηταὶ αὐτοῦ, καὶ
the brothers and the disciples of him, and
ἐκεῖ ἔμειναν οὐ πολλὰς ἡμέρας.
there remained not many days.
13 Καὶ ἐγγὺς ἦν τὸ πάσχα τῶν Ἰουδαίων,
And near was the Passover of the Jews,
καὶ ἀνέβη εἰς Ἱεροσόλυμα ὁ Ἰησοῦς.
and went up to Jerusalem – Jesus.
14 καὶ εὗρεν ἐν τῷ ἱερῷ τοὺς πωλοῦντας
And he found in the temple the [ones] selling
βόας καὶ πρόβατα καὶ περιστερὰς καὶ τοὺς
oxen and sheep and doves and the
κερματιστὰς καθημένους, 15 καὶ ποιήσας
coindealers sitting, and having made
φραγέλλιον ἐκ σχοινίων πάντας ἐξέβαλεν
a lash out of ropes [2]all [1]he expelled
ἐκ τοῦ ἱεροῦ, τά τε πρόβατα καὶ τοὺς
out of the temple, both the sheep and the
βόας, καὶ τῶν κολλυβιστῶν ἐξέχεεν τὰ
oxen, and [4]of the [5]moneychangers [1]poured out [2]the
κέρματα καὶ τὰς τραπέζας ἀνέτρεψεν,
[3]coins [6]and [8]the [9]tables [7]overturned,
16 καὶ τοῖς τὰς περιστερὰς πωλοῦσιν
and [2]to the [ones] [4]the [5]doves [3]selling
εἶπεν· ἄρατε ταῦτα ἐντεῦθεν, μὴ ποιεῖτε
[1]said : Take these things hence, do not make
τὸν οἶκον τοῦ πατρός μου οἶκον ἐμπορίου.
the house of the Father of me a house of merchandise.
17 ἐμνήσθησαν οἱ μαθηταὶ αὐτοῦ ὅτι
Remembered the disciples of him that
γεγραμμένον ἐστίν· ὁ ζῆλος τοῦ οἴκου
having been written it is : The zeal of the house
σου καταφάγεταί με. 18 ἀπεκρίθησαν οὖν
of thee will consume me. Answered therefore
οἱ Ἰουδαῖοι καὶ εἶπαν αὐτῷ· τί σημεῖον
the Jews and said to him: What sign
δεικνύεις ἡμῖν, ὅτι ταῦτα ποιεῖς;
showest thou to us, because these things thou doest?
19 ἀπεκρίθη Ἰησοῦς καὶ εἶπεν αὐτοῖς· λύσατε τὸν
Answered Jesus and said to them: Destroy –
ναὸν τοῦτον, καὶ ἐν τρισὶν ἡμέραις ἐγερῶ αὐτόν.
shrine this, and in three days I will raise it.
20 εἶπαν οὖν οἱ Ἰουδαῖοι· τεσσεράκοντα
Said therefore the Jews : In forty
καὶ ἓξ ἔτεσιν οἰκοδομήθη ὁ ναὸς οὗτος,
and six years was built – shrine this,
καὶ σὺ ἐν τρισὶν ἡμέραις ἐγερεῖς αὐτόν;
and thou in three days wilt raise it?
21 ἐκεῖνος δὲ ἔλεγεν περὶ τοῦ ναοῦ τοῦ
But that [one]* spoke about the shrine of the
σώματος αὐτοῦ. 22 ὅτε οὖν ἠγέρθη ἐκ
body of him. When therefore he was raised from
νεκρῶν, ἐμνήσθησαν οἱ μαθηταὶ αὐτοῦ
[the] dead, remembered the disciples of him
ὅτι τοῦτο ἔλεγεν, καὶ ἐπίστευσαν τῇ
that this he said, and they believed the
γραφῇ καὶ τῷ λόγῳ ὃν εἶπεν ὁ Ἰησοῦς.
scripture and the word which said – Jesus.
23 Ὡς δὲ ἦν ἐν τοῖς Ἱεροσολύμοις ἐν
And when he was in – Jerusalem at
τῷ πάσχα ἐν τῇ ἑορτῇ, πολλοὶ ἐπίστευσαν
the Passover at the feast, many believed
εἰς τὸ ὄνομα αὐτοῦ, θεωροῦντες αὐτοῦ τὰ
in the name of him, beholding of him the

* John repeatedly uses the demonstrative adjective ἐκεῖνος in the sense of "he," referring to Christ.

mother and brothers and
his disciples. There they
stayed for a few days.
13When it was almost
time for the Jewish Pass-
over, Jesus went up to Jerusalem. 14In the temple
courts he found men selling
cattle, sheep and doves,
and others sitting at tables
exchanging money. 15So he
made a whip out of cords,
and drove all from the temple area, both sheep and
cattle; he scattered the
coins of the money chang-
ers and overturned their tables. 16To those who sold
doves he said, "Get these
out of here! How dare you
turn my Father's house
into a market!"
17His disciples remem-
bered that it is written:
"Zeal for your house will
consume me."[m]
18Then the Jews demand-
ed of him, "What miracu-
lous sign can you show us
to prove your authority to
do all this?"
19Jesus answered them,
"Destroy this temple, and I
will raise it again in three
days."
20The Jews replied, "It
has taken forty-six years to
build this temple, and you
are going to raise it in three
days?" 21But the temple he
had spoken of was his
body. 22After he was raised
from the dead, his disciples
recalled what he had said.
Then they believed the
Scripture and the words
that Jesus had spoken.
23Now while he was in Je-
rusalem at the Passover
Feast, many people saw

m17 Psalm 69:9

ing His signs which He was doing.
[24]But Jesus, on His part, was not entrusting Himself to them, for He knew all men,
[25]and because He did not need anyone to bear witness concerning man for He Himself knew what was in man.

Chapter 3

The New Birth

NOW there was a man of the Pharisees, named Nicodemus, a ruler of the Jews;
[2]this man came to Him by night, and said to Him, "Rabbi, we know that You have come from God *as* a teacher; for no one can do these signs that You do unless God is with him."
[3]Jesus answered and said to him, "Truly, truly, I say to you, unless one is born again, he cannot see the kingdom of God."
[4]Nicodemus *said to Him, "How can a man be born when he is old? He cannot enter a second time into his mother's womb and be born, can he?"
[5]Jesus answered, "Truly, truly, I say to you, unless one is born of water and the Spirit, he cannot enter into the kingdom of God.
[6]"That which is born of the flesh is flesh, and that which is born of the Spirit is spirit.
[7]"Do not marvel that I said to you, 'You must be born again.'
[8]"The wind blows where it wishes and you hear the sound of it, but do not know where it comes from and where it is going; so is everyone who is born of the Spirit."
[9]Nicodemus answered and said to Him, "How can these things be?"

σημεῖα ἃ ἐποίει· **24** αὐτὸς δὲ Ἰησοῦς
signs which he was doing; ¹but ³[him]self, ²Jesus
οὐκ ἐπίστευεν αὐτὸν αὐτοῖς διὰ τὸ αὐτὸν
did not commit himself to them because of the him
=because he knew
γινώσκειν πάντας, **25** καὶ ὅτι οὐ χρείαν εἶχεν
to know[b] all men, and because no need he had
ἵνα τις μαρτυρήσῃ περὶ τοῦ ἀνθρώπου·
that anyone should witness concerning – man;
αὐτὸς γὰρ ἐγίνωσκεν τί ἦν ἐν τῷ ἀνθρώπῳ.
for he knew what was in – man.
3 Ἦν δὲ ἄνθρωπος ἐκ τῶν Φαρισαίων,
Now there was a man of the Pharisees,
Νικόδημος ὄνομα αὐτῷ, ἄρχων τῶν
Nicodemus name to him[c], a ruler of the
=his name,
Ἰουδαίων· **2** οὗτος ἦλθεν πρὸς αὐτὸν νυκτὸς
Jews; this man came to him of(by) night
καὶ εἶπεν αὐτῷ· ῥαββί, οἴδαμεν ὅτι ἀπὸ
and said to him: Rabbi, we know that from
θεοῦ ἐλήλυθας διδάσκαλος· οὐδεὶς γὰρ
God thou hast come a teacher; for no one
δύναται ταῦτα τὰ σημεῖα ποιεῖν ἃ σὺ
can these – signs *to* do which thou
ποιεῖς, ἐὰν μὴ ᾖ ὁ θεὸς μετ' αὐτοῦ.
doest, except ²is – ¹God with him.
3 ἀπεκρίθη Ἰησοῦς καὶ εἶπεν αὐτῷ· ἀμὴν
Answered Jesus and said to him: Truly
ἀμὴν λέγω σοι, ἐὰν μή τις γεννηθῇ
truly I tell thee, except anyone is born
ἄνωθεν, οὐ δύναται ἰδεῖν τὴν βασιλείαν
from above, he cannot *to* see the kingdom
τοῦ θεοῦ. **4** λέγει πρὸς αὐτὸν ὁ Νικόδημος·
– of God. Says to him – Nicodemus:
πῶς δύναται ἄνθρωπος γεννηθῆναι γέρων ὤν;
How can a man *to* be born old being?
μὴ δύναται εἰς τὴν κοιλίαν τῆς μητρὸς
not can he into the womb of the mother
αὐτοῦ δεύτερον εἰσελθεῖν καὶ γεννηθῆναι;
of him secondly *to* enter and *to* be born?
5 ἀπεκρίθη Ἰησοῦς· ἀμὴν ἀμὴν λέγω σοι,
Answered Jesus: Truly truly I tell thee,
ἐὰν μή τις γεννηθῇ ἐξ ὕδατος καὶ
except anyone is born of water and
πνεύματος, οὐ δύναται εἰσελθεῖν εἰς τὴν
spirit, he cannot *to* enter into the
βασιλείαν τοῦ θεοῦ. **6** τὸ γεγεννημένον ἐκ
kingdom – of God. The thing *having been* born of
τῆς σαρκὸς σάρξ ἐστιν, καὶ τὸ γεγεννημένον
the flesh flesh is, and the thing *having been* born
ἐκ τοῦ πνεύματος πνεῦμά ἐστιν. **7** μὴ
of the Spirit spirit is. not
θαυμάσῃς ὅτι εἶπόν σοι· δεῖ ὑμᾶς
Marvel because I told thee: It behoves you
γεννηθῆναι ἄνωθεν. **8** τὸ πνεῦμα ὅπου θέλει
to be born from above. The spirit(?wind) where it wishes
πνεῖ, καὶ τὴν φωνὴν αὐτοῦ ἀκούεις, ἀλλ'
blows, and the sound of it thou hearest, but
οὐκ οἶδας πόθεν ἔρχεται καὶ ποῦ ὑπάγει·
thou knowest not whence it comes and whither it goes;
οὕτως ἐστὶν πᾶς ὁ γεγεννημένος ἐκ τοῦ
so is everyone *having been* born of the
πνεύματος. **9** ἀπεκρίθη Νικόδημος καὶ
Spirit. Answered Nicodemus and
εἶπεν αὐτῷ· πῶς δύναται ταῦτα γενέσθαι;
said to him: How can these things *to* come about?

the miraculous signs he was doing and believed in his name.[n] [24]But Jesus would not entrust himself to them, for he knew all men. [25]He did not need man's testimony about man, for he knew what was in a man.

Chapter 3

Jesus Teaches Nicodemus

NOW there was a man of the Pharisees named Nicodemus, a member of the Jewish ruling council. [2]He came to Jesus at night and said, "Rabbi, we know you are a teacher who has come from God. For no one could perform the miraculous signs you are doing if God were not with him."
[3]In reply Jesus declared, "I tell you the truth, no one can see the kingdom of God unless he is born again.[o]"
[4]"How can a man be born when he is old?" Nicodemus asked. "Surely he cannot enter a second time into his mother's womb to be born!"
[5]Jesus answered, "I tell you the truth, no one can enter the kingdom of God unless he is born of water and the Spirit. [6]Flesh gives birth to flesh, but the Spirit[p] gives birth to spirit. [7]You should not be surprised at my saying, 'You[q] must be born again.' [8]The wind blows wherever it pleases. You hear its sound, but you cannot tell where it comes from or where it is going. So it is with everyone born of the Spirit."
[9]"How can this be?" Nicodemus asked.

[n]23 Or *and believed in him*
[o]3 Or *born from above*; also in verse 7
[p]6 Or *but spirit*
[q]7 The Greek is plural.

10Jesus answered and
said to him, "Are you the
teacher of Israel, and do
not understand these
things?
11"Truly, truly, I say to
you, we speak that which
we know, and bear witness
of that which we have seen;
and you do not receive our
witness.
12"If I told you earthly
things and you do not be-
lieve, how shall you believe
if I tell you heavenly
things?
13"And no one has as-
cended into heaven, but He
who descended from
heaven, *even* the Son of
Man.
14"And as Moses lifted
up the serpent in the wilderness, even so must the
Son of Man be lifted up;
15that whoever [j] believes
may in Him have eternal
life.
16"For God so loved the
world, that He gave His
only begotten Son, that
whoever believes in Him
should not perish, but have
eternal life.
17"For God did not send
the Son into the world to
judge the world, but that
the world should be saved
through Him.
18"He who believes in
Him is not judged; he who
does not believe has been
judged already, because he
has not believed in the
name of the only begotten
Son of God.
19"And this is the judg-
ment, that the light is come
into the world, and men
loved the darkness rather
than the light; for their
deeds were evil.
20"For everyone who
does evil hates the light,
and does not come to the
light, lest his deeds should
be exposed.
21"But he who practices
the truth comes to the light,
that his deeds may be mani-

[j] Some mss. read *believes in Him may have eternal life*

10 ἀπεκρίθη Ἰησοῦς καὶ εἶπεν αὐτῷ· σὺ
Answered Jesus and said to him : Thou
εἶ ὁ διδάσκαλος τοῦ Ἰσραὴλ καὶ ταῦτα
art the teacher – of Israel and these things
οὐ γινώσκεις; **11** ἀμὴν ἀμὴν λέγω σοι ὅτι
knowest not? Truly truly I tell thee[,] –
ὃ οἴδαμεν λαλοῦμεν καὶ ὃ ἑωράκαμεν
What we know we speak and what we have seen
μαρτυροῦμεν, καὶ τὴν μαρτυρίαν ἡμῶν
we witness, and the witness of us
οὐ λαμβάνετε. **12** εἰ τὰ ἐπίγεια εἶπον
ye receive not. If the earthly things I told
ὑμῖν καὶ οὐ πιστεύετε, πῶς ἐὰν εἴπω
you and ye believe not, how if I tell
ὑμῖν τὰ ἐπουράνια πιστεύσετε; **13** καὶ
you the heavenly things will ye believe? And
οὐδεὶς ἀναβέβηκεν εἰς τὸν οὐρανὸν εἰ μὴ
no man has gone up into – heaven except
ὁ ἐκ τοῦ οὐρανοῦ καταβάς, ὁ υἱὸς
the [one] out of – heaven having come down, the Son
τοῦ ἀνθρώπου. **14** Καὶ καθὼς Μωϋσῆς ὕψωσεν
– of man. And as Moses lifted up
τὸν ὄφιν ἐν τῇ ἐρήμῳ, οὕτως ὑψωθῆναι
the serpent in the desert, so to be lifted up
δεῖ τὸν υἱὸν τοῦ ἀνθρώπου, **15** ἵνα πᾶς ὁ
it behoves the Son – of man, that everyone
πιστεύων ἐν αὐτῷ ἔχῃ ζωὴν αἰώνιον.
believing in him may have life eternal.
16 οὕτως γὰρ ἠγάπησεν ὁ θεὸς τὸν
For thus [2]loved – [1]God the
κόσμον, ὥστε τὸν υἱὸν τὸν μονογενῆ
world, so as the Son the only begotten
ἔδωκεν, ἵνα πᾶς ὁ πιστεύων εἰς αὐτὸν
he gave, that everyone believing in him
μὴ ἀπόληται ἀλλ' ἔχῃ ζωὴν αἰώνιον.
may not perish but may have life eternal.
17 οὐ γὰρ ἀπέστειλεν ὁ θεὸς τὸν υἱὸν
For [3]not [2]sent – [1]God the Son
εἰς τὸν κόσμον ἵνα κρίνῃ τὸν κόσμον,
into the world that he might judge the world,
ἀλλ' ἵνα σωθῇ ὁ κόσμος δι' αὐτοῦ.
but that [3]might be saved [1]the [2]world through him.
18 ὁ πιστεύων εἰς αὐτὸν οὐ κρίνεται·
The [one] believing in him is not judged;
ὁ μὴ πιστεύων ἤδη κέκριται, ὅτι
the[one]not believing already has been judged, because
μὴ πεπίστευκεν εἰς τὸ ὄνομα τοῦ μονογενοῦς
he has not believed in the name of the only begotten
υἱοῦ τοῦ θεοῦ. **19** αὕτη δέ ἐστιν ἡ
Son – of God. And this is the
κρίσις, ὅτι τὸ φῶς ἐλήλυθεν εἰς τὸν
judgment, that the light has come into the
κόσμον καὶ ἠγάπησαν οἱ ἄνθρωποι μᾶλλον
world and [2]loved – [1]men [5]rather
τὸ σκότος ἢ τὸ φῶς· ἦν γὰρ αὐτῶν
[3]the [4]darkness [6]than the light; for was(were) of them
πονηρὰ τὰ ἔργα. **20** πᾶς γὰρ ὁ φαῦλα
evil the works. For everyone evil things
πράσσων μισεῖ τὸ φῶς καὶ οὐκ ἔρχεται
doing hates the light and does not come
πρὸς τὸ φῶς, ἵνα μὴ ἐλεγχθῇ τὰ ἔργα
to the light, lest is(are) reproved the works
αὐτοῦ· **21** ὁ δὲ ποιῶν τὴν ἀλήθειαν ἔρχεται
of him; but the [one] doing the truth comes
πρὸς τὸ φῶς, ἵνα φανερωθῇ αὐτοῦ τὰ
to the light, that may be manifested of him the

10"You are Israel's teacher," said Jesus, "and do
you not understand these
things? 11I tell you the
truth, we speak of what we
know, and we testify to
what we have seen, but still
you people do not accept
our testimony. 12I have
spoken to you of earthly
things and you do not be-
lieve; how then will you believe if I speak of heavenly
things? 13No one has ever
gone into heaven except
the one who came from
heaven—the Son of Man.[r]
14Just as Moses lifted up
the snake in the desert, so
the Son of Man must be lifted up, 15that everyone who
believes in him may have
eternal life.[s]
16"For God so loved the
world that he gave his one
and only Son,[t] that whoever believes in him shall not
perish but have eternal life.
17For God did not send his
Son into the world to condemn the world, but to save
the world through him.
18Whoever believes in him
is not condemned, but
whoever does not believe
stands condemned already
because he has not be-
lieved in the name of God's
one and only Son.[u] 19This
is the verdict: Light has
come into the world, but
men loved darkness instead
of light because their deeds
were evil. 20Everyone who
does evil hates the light,
and will not come into the
light for fear that his deeds
will be exposed. 21But whoever lives by the truth
comes into the light, so that
it may be seen plainly that

[r] 13 Some manuscripts *Man, who is in heaven*
[s] 15 Or *believes may have eternal life in him*
[t] 16 Or *his only begotten Son*
[u] 18 Or *God's only begotten Son*

fested as having been
wrought in God."

John's Last Testimony

22After these things Jesus
and His disciples came into
the land of Judea, and there
He was spending time with
them and baptizing.
23And John also was bap-
tizing in Aenon near Salim,
because there was much
water there; and they were
coming and were being
baptized.
24For John had not yet
been thrown into prison.
25There arose therefore a
discussion on the part of
John's disciples with a Jew
about purification.
26And they came to John
and said to him, "Rabbi,
He who was with you
beyond the Jordan, to
whom you have borne wit-
ness, behold, He is baptizing, and all are coming to
Him."
27John answered and
said, "A man can receive
nothing, unless it has been
given him from heaven.
28"You yourselves bear
me witness, that I said, 'I
am not the Christ,' but, 'I
have been sent before
Him.'
29"He who has the bride
is the bridegroom; but the
friend of the bridegroom,
who stands and hears him,
rejoices greatly because of
the bridegroom's voice.
And so this joy of mine has
been made full.
30"He must increase, but
I must decrease.
31"He who comes from
above is above all, he who
is of the earth is from the
earth and speaks of the
earth. He who comes from
heaven is above all.
32"What He has seen and
heard, of that He bears witness; and no man receives
His witness.
33"He who has received

ἔργα ὅτι ἐν θεῷ ἐστιν εἰργασμένα.
works that in God they are *having been* wrought.
22 Μετὰ ταῦτα ἦλθεν ὁ Ἰησοῦς καὶ οἱ
After these things came – Jesus and the
μαθηταὶ αὐτοῦ εἰς τὴν Ἰουδαίαν γῆν, καὶ
disciples of him into *the* Judæa*n* *land,* and
ἐκεῖ διέτριβεν μετ' αὐτῶν καὶ ἐβάπτιζεν.
there continued with them and baptized.
23 ἦν δὲ καὶ Ἰωάννης βαπτίζων ἐν
And was also John baptizing in
Αἰνὼν ἐγγὺς τοῦ Σαλίμ, ὅτι ὕδατα
Ainon near – Salim, because waters
πολλὰ ἦν ἐκεῖ, καὶ παρεγίνοντο καὶ
many was(were) there, and they came and
ἐβαπτίζοντο· 24 οὔπω γὰρ ἦν βεβλημένος
were baptized; for [3]not yet [2]was [4]*having been* cast
εἰς τὴν φυλακὴν Ἰωάννης. 25 Ἐγένετο
[5]into [6]the [7]prison [1]John. There was
οὖν ζήτησις ἐκ τῶν μαθητῶν Ἰωάννου
therefore a questioning of the disciples of John
μετὰ Ἰουδαίου περὶ καθαρισμοῦ. 26 καὶ
with a Jew about purifying. And
ἦλθον πρὸς τὸν Ἰωάννην καὶ εἶπαν αὐτῷ·
they came to – John and said to him :
ῥαββί, ὃς ἦν μετὰ σοῦ πέραν τοῦ
Rabbi, [he] who was with thee beyond the
Ἰορδάνου, ᾧ σὺ μεμαρτύρηκας, ἴδε
Jordan, to whom thou hast borne witness, behold[,]
οὗτος βαπτίζει καὶ πάντες ἔρχονται πρὸς
this man baptizes and all men are coming to
αὐτόν. 27 ἀπεκρίθη Ἰωάννης καὶ εἶπεν·
him. Answered John and said :
οὐ δύναται ἄνθρωπος λαμβάνειν οὐδὲν ἐὰν μὴ
Cannot a man *to* receive no(any)thing unless
ᾖ δεδομένον αὐτῷ ἐκ τοῦ οὐρανοῦ.
it is *having been* given to him out of – heaven.
28 αὐτοὶ ὑμεῖς μοι μαρτυρεῖτε ὅτι εἶπον·
[Your]selves ye to me bear witness that I said :
οὐκ εἰμὶ ἐγὼ ὁ χριστός, ἀλλ' ὅτι
[3]not [2]am [1]I the Christ, but that
ἀπεσταλμένος εἰμὶ ἔμπροσθεν ἐκείνου. 29 ὁ
having been sent I am before that one.* The [one]
ἔχων τὴν νύμφην νυμφίος ἐστίν· ὁ δὲ
having the bride a bridegroom is; but the
φίλος τοῦ νυμφίου, ὁ ἑστηκὼς καὶ ἀκούων
friend of the bridegroom, – standing and hearing
αὐτοῦ, χαρᾷ χαίρει διὰ τὴν φωνὴν τοῦ
him, with joy rejoices because of the voice of the
νυμφίου. αὕτη οὖν ἡ χαρὰ ἡ ἐμὴ
bridegroom. [2]This [1]therefore – [4]joy – [3]my
πεπλήρωται. 30 ἐκεῖνον δεῖ αὐξάνειν, ἐμὲ
has been fulfilled. That one it behoves to increase, [2]me
δὲ ἐλαττοῦσθαι. 31 Ὁ ἄνωθεν ἐρχόμενος
[1]but to decrease. The [one] from above coming
ἐπάνω πάντων ἐστίν· ὁ ὢν ἐκ τῆς γῆς
over all is; the [one] being of the earth
ἐκ τῆς γῆς ἐστιν καὶ ἐκ τῆς γῆς λαλεῖ.
of the earth is and of the earth speaks.
ὁ ἐκ τοῦ οὐρανοῦ ἐρχόμενος ἐπάνω
The [one] of – heaven coming over
πάντων ἐστίν· 32 ὃ ἑώρακεν καὶ ἤκουσεν,
all is; what he has seen and heard,
τοῦτο μαρτυρεῖ, καὶ τὴν μαρτυρίαν αὐτοῦ
this he witnesses [to], and the witness of him
οὐδεὶς λαμβάνει. 33 ὁ λαβὼν αὐτοῦ τὴν
no man receives. The [one] receiving of him the

* See note to 2. 21.

what he has done has been
done through God."[v]

John the Baptist's
Testimony About Jesus

22After this, Jesus and his
disciples went out into the
Judean countryside, where
he spent some time with
them, and baptized. 23Now
John also was baptizing at
Aenon near Salim, because
there was plenty of water,
and people were constantly
coming to be baptized.
24(This was before John
was put in prison.) 25An argument developed between
some of John's disciples
and a certain Jew[w] over the
matter of ceremonial washing. 26They came to John
and said to him, "Rabbi,
that man who was with you
on the other side of the Jordan—the one you testified
about—well, he is baptiz-
ing, and everyone is going
to him."
27To this John replied,
"A man can receive only
what is given him from
heaven. 28You yourselves
can testify that I said, 'I am
not the Christ[x] but am sent
ahead of him.' 29The bride
belongs to the bridegroom.
The friend who attends the
bridegroom waits and lis-
tens for him, and is full of
joy when he hears the
bridegroom's voice. That
joy is mine, and it is now
complete. 30He must be-
come greater; I must be-
come less.
31"The one who comes
from above is above all; the
one who is from the earth
belongs to the earth, and
speaks as one from the
earth. The one who comes
from heaven is above all.
32He testifies to what he
has seen and heard, but no
one accepts his testimony.
33The man who has accept-

[v]*21* Some interpreters end the quotation after verse 15.
[w]*25* Some manuscripts *and certain Jews*
[x]*28* Or *Messiah*

His witness has set his seal to *this,* that God is true.
34 "For He whom God has sent speaks the words of God; for He gives the Spirit without measure.
35 "The Father loves the Son, and has given all things into His hand.
36 "He who believes in the Son has eternal life; but he who does not obey the Son shall not see life, but the wrath of God abides on him."

Chapter 4

Jesus Goes to Galilee

WHEN therefore the Lord knew that the Pharisees had heard that Jesus was making and baptizing more disciples than John
2(although Jesus Himself was not baptizing, but His disciples were),
3He left Judea, and departed again into Galilee.
4And He had to pass through Samaria.
5So He *came to a city of Samaria, called Sychar, near the parcel of ground that Jacob gave to his son Joseph;
6and Jacob's well was there. Jesus therefore, being wearied from His journey, was sitting thus by the well. It was about [k]the sixth hour.

The Woman of Samaria

7There *came a woman of Samaria to draw water. Jesus *said to her, "Give Me a drink."
8For His disciples had gone away into the city to buy food.
9The Samaritan woman therefore *said to Him, "How is it that You, being a Jew, ask me for a drink since I am a Samaritan woman?" (For Jews have no dealings with Samaritans.)
10Jesus answered and said to her, "If you knew

[k]Perhaps 6 p.m. (Roman time)

μαρτυρίαν ἐσφράγισεν ὅτι ὁ θεὸς ἀληθής
witness sealed that – God true
ἐστιν. **34** ὃν γὰρ ἀπέστειλεν ὁ θεὸς τὰ
is. For [he] whom [2]sent – [1]God the
ῥήματα τοῦ θεοῦ λαλεῖ· οὐ γὰρ ἐκ
words – of God speaks; for not by
μέτρου δίδωσιν τὸ πνεῦμα. **35** ὁ πατὴρ
measure he gives the Spirit. The Father
ἀγαπᾷ τὸν υἱόν, καὶ πάντα δέδωκεν ἐν
loves the Son, and all things has given in[to]
τῇ χειρὶ αὐτοῦ. **36** ὁ πιστεύων εἰς τὸν
the hand of him. The [one] believing in the
υἱὸν ἔχει ζωὴν αἰώνιον· ὁ δὲ ἀπειθῶν
Son has life eternal; but the [one] disobeying
τῷ υἱῷ οὐκ ὄψεται ζωήν, ἀλλ' ἡ ὀργὴ
the Son will not see life, but the wrath
τοῦ θεοῦ μένει ἐπ' αὐτόν.
– of God remains on him.

4 Ὡς οὖν ἔγνω ὁ κύριος ὅτι ἤκουσαν
[2]When [1]therefore [5]knew [3]the [4]Lord [6]that [9]heard
οἱ Φαρισαῖοι ὅτι Ἰησοῦς πλείονας μαθητὰς
[7]the [8]Pharisees that Jesus more disciples
ποιεῖ καὶ βαπτίζει ἢ Ἰωάννης, — **2** καίτοι γε
makes and baptizes than John, — though
Ἰησοῦς αὐτὸς οὐκ ἐβάπτιζεν ἀλλ' οἱ
Jesus [him]self baptized not but the
μαθηταὶ αὐτοῦ, — **3** ἀφῆκεν τὴν Ἰουδαίαν
disciples of him, — he left – Judæa
καὶ ἀπῆλθεν πάλιν εἰς τὴν Γαλιλαίαν.
and went away again into – Galilee.
4 Ἔδει δὲ αὐτὸν διέρχεσθαι διὰ τῆς
And it behoved him to pass through *through* –
Σαμαρείας. **5** ἔρχεται οὖν εἰς πόλιν τῆς
Samaria. He comes therefore to a city –
Σαμαρείας λεγομένην Σύχαρ, πλησίον τοῦ
of Samaria *being* called Sychar, near the
χωρίου ὃ ἔδωκεν Ἰακὼβ [τῷ] Ἰωσὴφ
piece of land which [2]gave [1]Jacob – to Joseph
τῷ υἱῷ αὐτοῦ· **6** ἦν δὲ ἐκεῖ πηγὴ τοῦ
the son of him; and was there a fountain –
Ἰακώβ. ὁ οὖν Ἰησοῦς κεκοπιακὼς ἐκ
of Jacob. – Therefore Jesus having become wearied from
τῆς ὁδοιπορίας ἐκαθέζετο οὕτως ἐπὶ τῇ
the journey sat thus at the
πηγῇ· ὥρα ἦν ὡς ἕκτη. **7** ἔρχεται γυνὴ
fountain; [the] hour was about sixth. Comes a woman
ἐκ τῆς Σαμαρείας ἀντλῆσαι ὕδωρ. λέγει
of – Samaria to draw water. Says
αὐτῇ ὁ Ἰησοῦς· δός μοι πεῖν. **8** οἱ γὰρ
to her – Jesus : Give me to drink. For the
μαθηταὶ αὐτοῦ ἀπεληλύθεισαν εἰς τὴν
disciples of him had gone away into the
πόλιν, ἵνα τροφὰς ἀγοράσωσιν. **9** λέγει
city, that foods they might buy. Says
οὖν αὐτῷ ἡ γυνὴ ἡ Σαμαρῖτις· πῶς
therefore to him the woman – Samaritan : How
σὺ Ἰουδαῖος ὢν παρ' ἐμοῦ πεῖν
thou [2]a Jew [1]being [5]from [6]me [4]to drink
αἰτεῖς γυναικὸς Σαμαρίτιδος οὔσης;
[3]askest [9]woman [8]a Samaritan [7]being?
[οὐ γὰρ συγχρῶνται Ἰουδαῖοι Σαμαρίταις.]
[1]For [4]not [3]associate [2]Jews [5]with Samaritans.
10 ἀπεκρίθη Ἰησοῦς καὶ εἶπεν αὐτῇ· εἰ ᾔδεις
Answered Jesus and said to her : If thou knewest

ed it has certified that God is truthful. 34For the one whom God has sent speaks the words of God, for God[y] gives the Spirit without limit. 35The Father loves the Son and has placed everything in his hands. 36Whoever believes in the Son has eternal life, but whoever rejects the Son will not see life, for God's wrath remains on him."[z]

Chapter 4

Jesus Talks With a Samaritan Woman

THE Pharisees heard that Jesus was gaining and baptizing more disciples than John, 2although in fact it was not Jesus who baptized, but his disciples.
3When the Lord learned of this, he left Judea and went back once more to Galilee.
4Now he had to go through Samaria. 5So he came to a town in Samaria called Sychar, near the plot of ground Jacob had given to his son Joseph. 6Jacob's well was there, and Jesus, tired as he was from the journey, sat down by the well. It was about the sixth hour.
7When a Samaritan woman came to draw water, Jesus said to her, "Will you give me a drink?" 8(His disciples had gone into the town to buy food.)
9The Samaritan woman said to him, "You are a Jew and I am a Samaritan woman. How can you ask me for a drink?" (For Jews do not associate with Samaritans.[a])
10Jesus answered her, "If you knew the gift of God

[y]*34* Greek *he*
[z]*36* Some interpreters end the quotation after verse 30.
[a]*9* Or *do not use dishes Samaritans have used*

the gift of God, and who it
is who says to you, 'Give
Me a drink,' you would
have asked Him, and He
would have given you liv-
ing water."
11She *said to Him, "Sir,
You have nothing to draw
with and the well is deep;
where then do You get that
living water?
12"You are not greater
than our father Jacob, are
You, who gave us the well,
and drank of it himself, and
his sons, and his cattle?"
13Jesus answered and
said to her, "Everyone
who drinks of this water
shall thirst again;
14but whoever drinks of
the water that I shall give
him shall never thirst; but
the water that I shall give
him shall become in him a
well of water springing up
to eternal life."
15The woman *said to
Him, "Sir, give me this
water, so I will not be
thirsty, nor come all the
way here to draw."
16He *said to her, "Go,
call your husband, and
come here."
17The woman answered
and said, "I have no hus-
band." Jesus *said to her,
"You have well said, 'I
have no husband';
18for you have had five
husbands, and the one
whom you now have is not
your husband; this you
have said truly."
19The woman *said to
Him, "Sir, I perceive that
You are a prophet.
20"Our fathers worshiped
in this mountain, and you
people say that in Jerusalem is the place where men
ought to worship."
21Jesus *said to her,
"Woman, believe Me, an
hour is coming when
neither in this mountain,
nor in Jerusalem, shall you

τὴν δωρεὰν τοῦ θεοῦ, καὶ τίς ἐστιν ὁ
the gift – of God, and who is the [one]
λέγων σοι· δός μοι πεῖν, σὺ ἂν ᾔτησας
saying to thee: Give me to drink, thou wouldest have asked
αὐτὸν καὶ ἔδωκεν ἂν σοι ὕδωρ ζῶν.
him and he would have given thee water living.
11 λέγει αὐτῷ· κύριε, οὔτε ἄντλημα ἔχεις
She says to him: Sir, no pail thou hast
καὶ τὸ φρέαρ ἐστὶν βαθύ· πόθεν οὖν
and the well is deep; whence then
ἔχεις τὸ ὕδωρ τὸ ζῶν; 12 μὴ σὺ μείζων
hast thou the water – living? *not* thou greater
εἶ τοῦ πατρὸς ἡμῶν Ἰακώβ, ὃς ἔδωκεν
art [than] the father of us Jacob, who gave
ἡμῖν τὸ φρέαρ, καὶ αὐτὸς ἐξ αὐτοῦ
us the well, and [him]self of it
ἔπιεν καὶ οἱ υἱοὶ αὐτοῦ καὶ τὰ θρέμματα
drank and the sons of him and the cattle
αὐτοῦ; 13 ἀπεκρίθη Ἰησοῦς καὶ εἶπεν αὐτῇ·
of him? Answered Jesus and said to her:
πᾶς ὁ πίνων ἐκ τοῦ ὕδατος τούτου
Everyone drinking of – water this
διψήσει πάλιν· 14 ὃς δ' ἂν πίῃ ἐκ τοῦ
will thirst again; but whoever drinks of the
ὕδατος οὗ ἐγὼ δώσω αὐτῷ, οὐ μὴ
water which I will give him, by no means
διψήσει εἰς τὸν αἰῶνα, ἀλλὰ τὸ ὕδωρ ὃ
will thirst unto the age, but the water which
δώσω αὐτῷ γενήσεται ἐν αὐτῷ πηγὴ
I will give him will become in him a fountain
ὕδατος ἁλλομένου εἰς ζωὴν αἰώνιον. 15 λέγει
of water springing to life eternal. Says
πρὸς αὐτὸν ἡ γυνή· κύριε, δός μοι
to him the woman: Sir, give me
τοῦτο τὸ ὕδωρ, ἵνα μὴ διψῶ μηδὲ
this – water, that I thirst not nor
διέρχωμαι ἐνθάδε ἀντλεῖν. 16 λέγει αὐτῇ·
come through hither to draw. He says to her:
ὕπαγε φώνησον τὸν ἄνδρα σου καὶ ἐλθὲ
Go call the husband of thee and come
ἐνθάδε. 17 ἀπεκρίθη ἡ γυνὴ καὶ εἶπεν·
hither. Answered the woman and said:
οὐκ ἔχω ἄνδρα. λέγει αὐτῇ ὁ Ἰησοῦς·
I have not a husband. Says to her – Jesus:
καλῶς εἶπες ὅτι ἄνδρα οὐκ ἔχω· 18 πέντε
Well sayest thou[,] – A husband I have not; [2]five
γὰρ ἄνδρας ἔσχες, καὶ νῦν ὃν ἔχεις
[1]for husbands thou hadst, and now [he] whom thou hast
οὐκ ἔστιν σου ἀνήρ· τοῦτο ἀληθὲς εἴρηκας.
is not of thee husband; this truly thou hast said.
19 λέγει αὐτῷ ἡ γυνή· κύριε, θεωρῶ
Says to him the woman: Sir, I perceive
ὅτι προφήτης εἶ σύ. 20 οἱ πατέρες
that a prophet art thou. The fathers
ἡμῶν ἐν τῷ ὄρει τούτῳ προσεκύνησαν·
of us in – mountain this worshipped;
καὶ ὑμεῖς λέγετε ὅτι ἐν Ἱεροσολύμοις
and ye say that in Jerusalem
ἐστὶν ὁ τόπος ὅπου προσκυνεῖν δεῖ.
is the place where to worship it behoves.
21 λέγει αὐτῇ ὁ Ἰησοῦς· πίστευέ μοι,
Says to her – Jesus: Believe me,
γύναι, ὅτι ἔρχεται ὥρα ὅτε οὔτε ἐν
woman, that is coming an hour when neither in
τῷ ὄρει τούτῳ οὔτε ἐν Ἱεροσολύμοις
– mountain this nor in Jerusalem

and who it is that asks you
for a drink, you would have
asked him and he would
have given you living wa-
ter."
11"Sir," the woman said,
"you have nothing to draw
with and the well is deep.
Where can you get this living water? 12Are you greater than our father Jacob,
who gave us the well and
drank from it himself, as
did also his sons and his
flocks and herds?"
13Jesus answered, "Ev-
eryone who drinks this water will be thirsty again,
14but whoever drinks the
water I give him will never
thirst. Indeed, the water I
give him will become in him
a spring of water welling up
to eternal life."
15The woman said to him,
"Sir, give me this water so
that I won't get thirsty and
have to keep coming here
to draw water."
16He told her, "Go, call
your husband and come
back."
17"I have no husband,"
she replied.
Jesus said to her, "You
are right when you say you
have no husband. 18The
fact is, you have had five
husbands, and the man you
now have is not your hus-
band. What you have just
said is quite true."
19"Sir," the woman said,
"I can see that you are a
prophet. 20Our fathers worshiped on this mountain,
but you Jews claim that the
place where we must wor-
ship is in Jerusalem."
21Jesus declared, "Be-
lieve me, woman, a time is
coming when you will wor-
ship the Father neither on

worship the Father.
22"You worship that which you do not know; we worship that which we know, for salvation is from the Jews.
23"But an hour is coming, and now is, when the true worshipers shall worship the Father in spirit and truth; for such people the Father seeks to be His worshipers.
24"God is spirit, and those who worship Him must worship in spirit and truth."
25The woman *said to Him, "I know that Messiah is coming (He who is called Christ); when that One comes, He will declare all things to us."
26Jesus *said to her, "I who speak to you am *He*."
27And at this point His disciples came, and they marveled that He had been speaking with a woman; yet no one said, "What do You seek?" or, "Why do You speak with her?"
28So the woman left her waterpot, and went into the city, and *said to the men
29"Come, see a man who told me all the things that I *have* done; this is not the Christ, is it?"
30They went out of the city, and were coming to Him.
31In the meanwhile the disciples were requesting Him, saying, "Rabbi, eat."
32But He said to them, "I have food to eat that you do not know about."
33The disciples therefore were saying to one another, "No one brought Him *anything* to eat, did he?"
34Jesus *said to them, "My food is to do the will of Him who sent Me, and to accomplish His work.
35"Do you not say,

προσκυνήσετε τῷ πατρί. 22 ὑμεῖς προσκυ-
will ye worship the Father. Ye wor-
νεῖτε ὃ οὐκ οἴδατε, ἡμεῖς προσκυνοῦμεν ὃ
ship what ye know not, we worship what
οἴδαμεν, ὅτι ἡ σωτηρία ἐκ τῶν Ἰουδαίων
we know, because – salvation of the Jews
ἐστίν· 23 ἀλλὰ ἔρχεται ὥρα καὶ νῦν
is; but is coming an hour and now
ἐστιν, ὅτε οἱ ἀληθινοὶ προσκυνηταὶ προσκυνή-
is, when the true worshippers will
σουσιν τῷ πατρὶ ἐν πνεύματι καὶ ἀληθείᾳ·
worship the Father in spirit and truth;
καὶ γὰρ ὁ πατὴρ τοιούτους ζητεῖ τοὺς
for indeed the Father ²such ¹seeks the [ones]
προσκυνοῦντας αὐτόν· 24 πνεῦμα ὁ θεός,
worshipping him; God [is] spirit,*
καὶ τοὺς προσκυνοῦντας ἐν πνεύματι καὶ
and ²the [ones] ³worshipping ⁵in ⁶spirit ⁷and
ἀληθείᾳ δεῖ προσκυνεῖν. 25 λέγει αὐτῷ
⁸truth ¹it behoves ⁴to worship. Says to him
ἡ γυνή· οἶδα ὅτι Μεσσίας ἔρχεται, ὁ
the woman : I know that Messiah is coming, the [one]
λεγόμενος χριστός· ὅταν ἔλθῃ ἐκεῖνος,
being called Christ; when comes that one,
ἀναγγελεῖ ἡμῖν ἅπαντα. 26 λέγει αὐτῇ
he will announce to us all things. Says to her
ὁ Ἰησοῦς· ἐγώ εἰμι, ὁ λαλῶν σοι.
– Jesus : I am, the [one] speaking to thee.
27 Καὶ ἐπὶ τούτῳ ἦλθαν οἱ μαθηταὶ
And on this came the disciples
αὐτοῦ, καὶ ἐθαύμαζον ὅτι μετὰ γυναικὸς
of him, and marvelled that with a woman
ἐλάλει· οὐδεὶς μέντοι εἶπεν· τί ζητεῖς
he was speaking; no one however said : What seekest thou
ἢ τί λαλεῖς μετ' αὐτῆς; 28 ἀφῆκεν οὖν
or why speakest thou with her? ⁴Left ³therefore
τὴν ὑδρίαν αὐτῆς ἡ γυνὴ καὶ ἀπῆλθεν
⁵the ⁶waterpot ⁷of her ¹the ²woman and went away
εἰς τὴν πόλιν, καὶ λέγει τοῖς ἀνθρώποις·
into the city, and says to the men :
29 δεῦτε ἴδετε ἄνθρωπον ὃς εἶπέν μοι
Come see a man who told me
πάντα ἃ ἐποίησα· μήτι οὗτός ἐστιν ὁ
all things which I did; *not* this is the
χριστός; 30 ἐξῆλθον ἐκ τῆς πόλεως καὶ
Christ? They went forth out of the city and
ἤρχοντο πρὸς αὐτόν. 31 Ἐν τῷ μεταξὺ
came to him. In the meantime
ἠρώτων αὐτὸν οἱ μαθηταὶ λέγοντες· ῥαββί,
asked him the disciples saying : Rabbi,
φάγε. 32 ὁ δὲ εἶπεν αὐτοῖς· ἐγὼ βρῶσιν
eat. But he said to them : I food
ἔχω φαγεῖν ἣν ὑμεῖς οὐκ οἴδατε. 33 ἔλεγον
have to eat which ye do not know. Said
οὖν οἱ μαθηταὶ πρὸς ἀλλήλους· μή τις
therefore the disciples to one another : *Not* anyone
ἤνεγκεν αὐτῷ φαγεῖν; 34 λέγει αὐτοῖς ὁ
brought him to eat? Says to them –
Ἰησοῦς· ἐμὸν βρῶμά ἐστιν ἵνα ποιῶ τὸ
Jesus : My food is that I may do the
θέλημα τοῦ πέμψαντός με καὶ τελειώσω
will of the [one] having sent me and may finish
αὐτοῦ τὸ ἔργον. 35 οὐχ ὑμεῖς λέγετε ὅτι
of him the work. ³Not ²ye ¹say that

* See note on 1. 1.

this mountain nor in Jerusalem. 22You Samaritans worship what you do not know; we worship what we do know, for salvation is from the Jews. 23Yet a time is coming and has now come when the true worshipers will worship the Father in spirit and truth, for they are the kind of worshipers the Father seeks.
24God is spirit, and his worshipers must worship in spirit and in truth."
25The woman said, "I know that Messiah" (called Christ) "is coming. When he comes, he will explain everything to us."
26Then Jesus declared, "I who speak to you am he."

The Disciples Rejoin Jesus

27Just then his disciples returned and were surprised to find him talking with a woman. But no one asked, "What do you want?" or "Why are you talking with her?"
28Then, leaving her water jar, the woman went back to the town and said to the people, 29"Come, see a man who told me everything I ever did. Could this be the Christ[b]?" 30They came out of the town and made their way toward him.
31Meanwhile his disciples urged him, "Rabbi, eat something."
32But he said to them, "I have food to eat that you know nothing about."
33Then his disciples said to each other, "Could someone have brought him food?"
34"My food," said Jesus, "is to do the will of him who sent me and to finish his work. 35Do you not say,

[b]29 Or *Messiah*

'There are yet four months,
and *then* comes the har-
vest'? Behold, I say to you,
lift up your eyes, and look
on the fields, that they are
white for harvest.
36"Already he who reaps
is receiving wages, and is
gathering fruit for life eternal; that he who sows and
he who reaps may rejoice
together.
37"For in this *case* the
saying is true, 'One sows,
and another reaps.'
38"I sent you to reap that
for which you have not labored; others have labored,
and you have entered into
their labor."

The Samaritans

39And from that city
many of the Samaritans believed in Him because of
the word of the woman who
testified, "He told me all
the things that I *have*
done."
40So when the Samaritans
came to Him, they were
asking Him to stay with
them; and He stayed there
two days.
41And many more be-
lieved because of His word;
42and they were saying to
the woman, "It is no longer
because of what you said
that we believe, for we
have heard for ourselves
and know that this One is
indeed the Savior of the
world."
43And after the two days
He went forth from there
into Galilee.
44For Jesus Himself testified that a prophet has no
honor in his own country.
45So when He came to
Galilee, the Galileans received Him, having seen all
the things that He did in
Jerusalem at the feast; for
they themselves also went
to the feast.

Healing a Nobleman's Son

46He came therefore
again to Cana of Galilee

ἔτι τετράμηνός ἐστιν καὶ ὁ θερισμὸς
yet four months it is and the harvest
ἔρχεται; ἰδοὺ λέγω ὑμῖν, ἐπάρατε τοὺς
comes? Behold I tell you, lift up the
ὀφθαλμοὺς ὑμῶν καὶ θεάσασθε τὰς χώρας,
eyes of you and behold the fields,
ὅτι λευκαί εἰσιν πρὸς θερισμόν. ἤδη
because white they are to harvest. Already
36 ὁ θερίζων μισθὸν λαμβάνει καὶ συνάγει
the [one] reaping wages receives and gathers
καρπὸν εἰς ζωὴν αἰώνιον, ἵνα ὁ σπείρων
fruit to life eternal, that [1]the [one] [2]sowing
ὁμοῦ χαίρῃ καὶ ὁ θερίζων. 37 ἐν γὰρ
[7]together [6]may rejoice [3]and [4]the [one] [5]reaping. For in
τούτῳ ὁ λόγος ἐστὶν ἀληθινὸς ὅτι ἄλλος
this the word is true that another(one)
ἐστὶν ὁ σπείρων καὶ ἄλλος ὁ θερίζων.
is the [one] sowing and another the [one] reaping.
38 ἐγὼ ἀπέστειλα ὑμᾶς θερίζειν ὃ οὐχ
I sent you to reap what not
ὑμεῖς κεκοπιάκατε· ἄλλοι κεκοπιάκασιν, καὶ
ye have laboured; others have laboured, and
ὑμεῖς εἰς τὸν κόπον αὐτῶν εἰσεληλύθατε.
ye into the labour of them have entered.
39 Ἐκ δὲ τῆς πόλεως ἐκείνης πολλοὶ
And out of – city that many
ἐπίστευσαν εἰς αὐτὸν τῶν Σαμαριτῶν διὰ
believed in him of the Samaritans because of
τὸν λόγον τῆς γυναικὸς μαρτυρούσης ὅτι
the word of the woman witnessing[,] –
εἶπέν μοι πάντα ἃ ἐποίησα. 40 ὡς
He told me all things which I did. When
οὖν ἦλθον πρὸς αὐτὸν οἱ Σαμαρῖται,
therefore came to him the Samaritans,
ἠρώτων αὐτὸν μεῖναι παρ' αὐτοῖς· καὶ
they asked him to remain with them; and
ἔμεινεν ἐκεῖ δύο ἡμέρας. 41 καὶ πολλῷ
he remained there two days. And [2]more
πλείους ἐπίστευσαν διὰ τὸν λόγον αὐτοῦ,
[1]many believed because of the word of him,
42 τῇ τε γυναικὶ ἔλεγον ὅτι οὐκέτι διὰ
and to the woman they said[,] – No longer because of
τὴν σὴν λαλιὰν πιστεύομεν· αὐτοὶ γὰρ
– thy talk we believe; for [our]selves
ἀκηκόαμεν, καὶ οἴδαμεν ὅτι οὗτός ἐστιν
we have heard, and we know that this man is
ἀληθῶς ὁ σωτὴρ τοῦ κόσμου.
truly the Saviour of the world.
43 Μετὰ δὲ τὰς δύο ἡμέρας ἐξῆλθεν
And after the two days he went forth
ἐκεῖθεν εἰς τὴν Γαλιλαίαν. 44 αὐτὸς γὰρ
thence into – Galilee. For [2][him]self
Ἰησοῦς ἐμαρτύρησεν ὅτι προφήτης ἐν
[1]Jesus witnessed that a prophet in
τῇ ἰδίᾳ πατρίδι τιμὴν οὐκ ἔχει. 45 ὅτε
the(his) own native place honour has not. When
οὖν ἦλθεν εἰς τὴν Γαλιλαίαν, ἐδέξαντο
therefore he came into – Galilee, received
αὐτὸν οἱ Γαλιλαῖοι, πάντα ἑωρακότες
him the Galilæans, all things having seen
ὅσα ἐποίησεν ἐν Ἱεροσολύμοις ἐν τῇ
which he did in Jerusalem at the
ἑορτῇ· καὶ αὐτοὶ γὰρ ἦλθον εἰς τὴν
feast; [3]also [2]they [1]for went to the
ἑορτήν. 46 Ἦλθεν οὖν πάλιν εἰς τὴν
feast. He came therefore again to –

'Four months more and
then the harvest'? I tell
you, open your eyes and
look at the fields! They are
ripe for harvest. 36Even
now the reaper draws his
wages, even now he har-
vests the crop for eternal
life, so that the sower and
the reaper may be glad together. 37Thus the saying
'One sows and another
reaps' is true. 38I sent you
to reap what you have not
worked for. Others have
done the hard work, and
you have reaped the bene-
fits of their labor."

Many Samaritans Believe

39Many of the Samaritans
from that town believed in
him because of the wom-
an's testimony, "He told
me everything I ever did."
40So when the Samaritans
came to him, they urged
him to stay with them, and
he stayed two days. 41And
because of his words many
more became believers.
42They said to the wom-
an, "We no longer believe
just because of what you
said; now we have heard
for ourselves, and we know
that this man really is the
Savior of the world."

Jesus Heals the Official's Son

43After the two days he
left for Galilee. 44(Now
Jesus himself had pointed
out that a prophet has no
honor in his own country.)
45When he arrived in Galilee, the Galileans wel-
comed him. They had seen
all that he had done in Jerusalem at the Passover
Feast, for they also had
been there.
46Once more he visited
Cana in Galilee, where he

where He had made the
water wine. And there was
a certain royal official,
whose son was sick at
Capernaum.
47When he heard that
Jesus had come out of
Judea into Galilee, he went
to Him, and was requesting
Him to come down and
heal his son; for he was at
the point of death.
48Jesus therefore said to
him, "Unless you *people*
see signs and wonders, you
simply will not believe."
49The royal official *said
to Him, "Sir, come down
before my child dies."
50Jesus *said to him, "Go
your way; your son lives."
The man believed the word
that Jesus spoke to him,
and he started off.
51And as he was now go-
ing down, *his* slaves met
him, saying that his son
was living.
52So he inquired of them
the hour when he began to
get better. They said therefore to him, "Yesterday at
the [l]seventh hour the fever
left him."
53So the father knew that
it was at that hour in which
Jesus said to him, "Your
son lives"; and he himself
believed, and his whole
household.
54This is again a second
sign that Jesus performed,
when He had come out of
Judea into Galilee.

Κανὰ τῆς Γαλιλαίας, ὅπου ἐποίησεν τὸ
Cana – of Galilee, where he made the
ὕδωρ οἶνον. καὶ ἦν τις βασιλικὸς
water wine. And there was a certain courtier
οὗ ὁ υἱὸς ἠσθένει ἐν Καφαρναούμ· 47 οὗτος
of whom the son ailed in Capernaum; this man
ἀκούσας ὅτι Ἰησοῦς ἥκει ἐκ τῆς Ἰουδαίας
hearing that Jesus comes(came) out of – Judæa
εἰς τὴν Γαλιλαίαν, ἀπῆλθεν πρὸς αὐτὸν καὶ
into – Galilee, went to him and
ἠρώτα ἵνα καταβῇ καὶ ἰάσηται αὐτοῦ
asked that he would come down and would cure of him
τὸν υἱόν· ἤμελλεν γὰρ ἀποθνήσκειν. 48 εἶπεν
the son; for he was about to die. Said
οὖν ὁ Ἰησοῦς πρὸς αὐτόν· ἐὰν μὴ σημεῖα
therefore – Jesus to him: Except signs
καὶ τέρατα ἴδητε, οὐ μὴ πιστεύσητε.
and prodigies ye see, by no means ye believe.
49 λέγει πρὸς αὐτὸν ὁ βασιλικός· κύριε,
Says to him the courtier: Sir,
κατάβηθι πρὶν ἀποθανεῖν τὸ παιδίον μου.
come down before to die the child[b] of me.
50 λέγει αὐτῷ ὁ Ἰησοῦς· πορεύου, ὁ
Tells him – Jesus: Go, the
υἱός σου ζῇ. ἐπίστευσεν ὁ ἄνθρωπος τῷ
son of thee lives. [3]Believed [1]the [2]man [4]the
λόγῳ ὃν εἶπεν αὐτῷ ὁ Ἰησοῦς, καὶ
[5]word [6]which [8]said [9]to him – [7]Jesus, and
ἐπορεύετο. 51 ἤδη δὲ αὐτοῦ καταβαίνοντος
went. And already him going down[a]
=while he was going down
οἱ δοῦλοι ὑπήντησαν αὐτῷ λέγοντες ὅτι
the slaves met him saying that
ὁ παῖς αὐτοῦ ζῇ. 52 ἐπύθετο οὖν τὴν
the boy of him lives. He inquired therefore the
ὥραν παρ' αὐτῶν ἐν ᾗ κομψότερον ἔσχεν·
hour from them in which better he had;
=he got better;
εἶπαν οὖν αὐτῷ ὅτι ἐχθὲς ὥραν ἑβδόμην
they said therefore to him[,] – Yesterday [at] hour seventh
ἀφῆκεν αὐτὸν ὁ πυρετός. 53 ἔγνω οὖν
left him the fever. Knew therefore
ὁ πατὴρ ὅτι ἐκείνῃ τῇ ὥρᾳ ἐν ᾗ εἶπεν
the father that in that – hour in which told
αὐτῷ ὁ Ἰησοῦς· ὁ υἱός σου ζῇ· καὶ
him – Jesus: The son of thee lives; and
ἐπίστευσεν αὐτὸς καὶ ἡ οἰκία αὐτοῦ ὅλη.
believed he and the household of him whole.
54 Τοῦτο [δὲ] πάλιν δεύτερον σημεῖον
And this again a second sign
ἐποίησεν ὁ Ἰησοῦς ἐλθὼν ἐκ τῆς Ἰουδαίας
did – Jesus having come out of – Judæa
εἰς τὴν Γαλιλαίαν.
into – Galilee.

had turned the water into
wine. And there was a certain royal official whose
son lay sick at Capernaum.
47When this man heard that
Jesus had arrived in Galilee
from Judea, he went to him
and begged him to come
and heal his son, who was
close to death.
48"Unless you people see
miraculous signs and won-
ders," Jesus told him,
"you will never believe."
49The royal official said,
"Sir, come down before
my child dies."
50Jesus replied, "You
may go. Your son will
live."
The man took Jesus at his
word and departed.
51While he was still on the
way, his servants met him
with the news that his boy
was living. 52When he in-
quired as to the time when
his son got better, they said
to him, "The fever left him
yesterday at the seventh
hour."
53Then the father realized
that this was the exact time
at which Jesus had said to
him, "Your son will live."
So he and all his household
believed.
54This was the second mi-
raculous sign that Jesus
performed, having come
from Judea to Galilee.

Chapter 5

The Healing at Bethesda

AFTER these things
there was [m]a feast of
the Jews, and Jesus went
up to Jerusalem.
2Now there is in Jerusa-
lem by the sheep *gate* a
pool, which is called in He-

5 Μετὰ ταῦτα ἦν ἑορτὴ τῶν Ἰουδαίων,
After these things there was a feast of the Jews,
καὶ ἀνέβη Ἰησοῦς εἰς Ἱεροσόλυμα. 2 ἔστιν
and went up Jesus to Jerusalem. there is
δὲ ἐν τοῖς Ἱεροσολύμοις ἐπὶ τῇ προβατικῇ
Now in – Jerusalem at the sheepgate
κολυμβήθρα, ἡ ἐπιλεγομένη Ἑβραϊστὶ
a pool, the [one] *being* called in Hebrew

Chapter 5

The Healing at the Pool

SOME time later, Jesus
went up to Jerusalem
for a feast of the Jews.
2Now there is in Jerusalem
near the Sheep Gate a pool,
which in Aramaic is called

[l] Perhaps 7 p.m. (Roman time)
[m] Many mss. read *the feast*, i.e., the Passover

brew Bethesda, having five
porticoes.
3In these lay a multitude
of those who were sick,
blind, lame, and withered,
[[n]waiting for the moving of
the waters;
4for an angel of the Lord
went down at certain sea-
sons into the pool, and
stirred up the water; whoever then first, after the
stirring up of the water,
stepped in was made well
from whatever disease with
which he was afflicted.]
5And a certain man was
there, who had been thirty-
eight years in his sickness.
6When Jesus saw him ly-
ing there, and knew that he
had already been a long
time *in that condition,* He
*said to him, "Do you wish
to get well?"
7The sick man answered
Him, "Sir, I have no man
to put me into the pool
when the water is stirred
up, but while I am coming,
another steps down before
me."
8Jesus *said to him,
"Arise, take up your pallet,
and walk."
9And immediately the
man became well, and took
up his pallet and *began* to
walk.
Now it was the Sabbath
on that day.
10Therefore the Jews
were saying to him who
was cured, "It is the Sabbath, and it is not permissible for you to carry your
pallet."
11But he answered them,
"He who made me well
was the one who said to
me, 'Take up your pallet
and walk.'"
12They asked him, "Who
is the man who said to you,
'Take up *your pallet,* and
walk'?"
13But he who was healed
did not know who it was;
for Jesus had slipped away
while there was a crowd in
that place.
14Afterward Jesus *found
him in the temple, and said
to him, "Behold, you have
become well; do not sin
anymore, so that nothing
worse may befall you."
15The man went away,
and told the Jews that it
was Jesus who had made
him well.

[n]Many mss. do not contain the remainder of v. 3 nor v. 4

Βηθζαθά, πέντε στοὰς ἔχουσα. 3 ἐν
Bethzatha, five porches having. In
ταύταις κατέκειτο πλῆθος τῶν ἀσθενούντων,
these lay a multitude of the ailing [ones],
τυφλῶν, χωλῶν, ξηρῶν. ‡ 5 ἦν δέ τις
blind, lame, withered. And there was a
ἄνθρωπος ἐκεῖ τριάκοντα καὶ ὀκτὼ ἔτη
certain man there thirty-eight years
ἔχων ἐν τῇ ἀσθενείᾳ αὐτοῦ· 6 τοῦτον
having in the ailment of him; [3]this man
ἰδὼν ὁ Ἰησοῦς κατακείμενον, καὶ γνοὺς
[2]seeing – [1]Jesus [4]lying, and knowing
ὅτι πολὺν ἤδη χρόνον ἔχει, λέγει αὐτῷ·
that [3]much [2]already [4]time [1]he has, says to him:
θέλεις ὑγιὴς γενέσθαι; 7 ἀπεκρίθη αὐτῷ
Wishest thou whole to become? Answered him
ὁ ἀσθενῶν· κύριε, ἄνθρωπον οὐκ ἔχω,
the ailing [one]: Sir, a man I have not,
ἵνα ὅταν ταραχθῇ τὸ ὕδωρ βάλῃ με εἰς
that when is troubled the water he may put me into
τὴν κολυμβήθραν· ἐν ᾧ δὲ ἔρχομαι ἐγώ,
the pool; but while am coming I,
ἄλλος πρὸ ἐμοῦ καταβαίνει. 8 λέγει αὐτῷ
another before me goes down. Says to him
ὁ Ἰησοῦς· ἔγειρε ἆρον τὸν κράβατόν
– Jesus: Rise[,] take the mattress
σου καὶ περιπάτει. 9 καὶ εὐθέως ἐγένετο
of thee and walk. And immediately became
ὑγιὴς ὁ ἄνθρωπος, καὶ ἦρεν τὸν κράβατον
whole the man, and took the mattress
αὐτοῦ καὶ περιεπάτει. Ἦν δὲ σάββατον
of him and walked. And it was a sabbath
ἐν ἐκείνῃ τῇ ἡμέρᾳ. 10 ἔλεγον οὖν οἱ
on that – day. Said therefore the
Ἰουδαῖοι τῷ τεθεραπευμένῳ· σάββατόν ἐστιν,
Jews to the [one] having been healed: A sabbath it is,
καὶ οὐκ ἔξεστίν σοι ἆραι τὸν κράβατον.
and it is not lawful for thee to take the mattress.
11 ὃς δὲ ἀπεκρίθη αὐτοῖς· ὁ ποιήσας
But who(he) answered them: The [one] making
με ὑγιῆ, ἐκεῖνός μοι εἶπεν· ἆρον τὸν
me whole, that one me told: Take the
κράβατόν σου καὶ περιπάτει. 12 ἠρώτησαν
mattress of thee and walk. They asked
αὐτόν· τίς ἐστιν ὁ ἄνθρωπος ὁ εἰπών
him: Who is the man – telling
σοι· ἆρον καὶ περιπάτει; 13 ὁ δὲ ἰαθεὶς
thee: Take and walk? But the [one] cured
οὐκ ᾔδει τίς ἐστιν· ὁ γὰρ Ἰησοῦς
did not know who it is(was); – for Jesus
ἐξένευσεν ὄχλου ὄντος ἐν τῷ τόπῳ.
withdrew a crowd being[a] in the place.
[a]=as there was a crowd
14 μετὰ ταῦτα εὑρίσκει αὐτὸν ὁ Ἰησοῦς
After these things finds him – Jesus
ἐν τῷ ἱερῷ καὶ εἶπεν αὐτῷ· ἴδε ὑγιὴς
in the temple and said to him: Behold[,] whole
γέγονας· μηκέτι ἁμάρτανε, ἵνα μὴ χεῖρόν
thou hast become; no longer sin, lest [2]worse
σοί τι γένηται. 15 ἀπῆλθεν ὁ ἄνθρωπος
[4]to thee [1]something [3]happens. Went away the man
καὶ εἶπεν τοῖς Ἰουδαίοις ὅτι Ἰησοῦς
and told the Jews that Jesus
ἐστιν ὁ ποιήσας αὐτὸν ὑγιῆ. 16 καὶ διὰ
it is(was) the [one] having made him whole. And there-

‡ End of ver. 3 and ver. 4 omitted by Nestle; *cf.* NIV footnote.

Bethesda[c] and which is
surrounded by five covered
colonnades. 3Here a great
number of disabled people
used to lie—the blind, the
lame, the paralyzed.[d] 5One
who was there had been an
invalid for thirty-eight
years. 6When Jesus saw
him lying there and learned
that he had been in this condition for a long time, he
asked him, "Do you want
to get well?"
7"Sir," the invalid re-
plied, "I have no one to
help me into the pool when
the water is stirred. While I
am trying to get in, someone else goes down ahead
of me."
8Then Jesus said to him,
"Get up! Pick up your mat
and walk." 9At once the
man was cured; he picked
up his mat and walked.
The day on which this
took place was a Sabbath,
10and so the Jews said to
the man who had been
healed, "It is the Sabbath;
the law forbids you to carry
your mat."
11But he replied, "The
man who made me well
said to me, 'Pick up your
mat and walk.'"
12So they asked him,
"Who is this fellow who
told you to pick it up and
walk?"
13The man who was
healed had no idea who it
was, for Jesus had slipped
away into the crowd that
was there.
14Later Jesus found him
at the temple and said to
him, "See, you are well
again. Stop sinning or
something worse may hap-
pen to you." 15The man
went away and told the
Jews that it was Jesus who
had made him well.

[c]2 Some manuscripts *Bethzatha;* other manuscripts *Bethsaida*
[d]3 Some less important manuscripts *paralyzed—and they waited for the moving of the waters. 4From time to time an angel of the Lord would come down and stir up the waters. The first one into the pool after each such disturbance would be cured of whatever disease he had.*

[16]And for this reason the Jews were persecuting Jesus, because He was doing these things on the Sabbath.

[17]But He answered them, "My Father is working until now, and I Myself am working."

Jesus' Equality with God

[18]For this cause therefore the Jews were seeking all the more to kill Him, because He not only was breaking the Sabbath, but also was calling God His own Father, making Himself equal with God.

[19]Jesus therefore answered and was saying to them, "Truly, truly, I say to you, the Son can do nothing of Himself, unless *it is* something He sees the Father doing; for whatever *the Father* does, these things the Son also does in like manner.

[20]"For the Father loves the Son, and shows Him all things that He Himself is doing; and greater works than these will He show Him, that you may marvel.

[21]"For just as the Father raises the dead and gives them life, even so the Son also gives life to whom He wishes.

[22]"For not even the Father judges anyone, but He has given all judgment to the Son,

[23]in order that all may honor the Son, even as they honor the Father. He who does not honor the Son does not honor the Father who sent Him.

[24]"Truly, truly, I say to you, he who hears My word, and believes Him who sent Me, has eternal life, and does not come into judgment, but has passed out of death into life.

τοῦτο ἐδίωκον οἱ Ἰουδαῖοι τὸν Ἰησοῦν,
fore [3]persecuted [1]the [2]Jews – [4]Jesus,
ὅτι ταῦτα ἐποίει ἐν σαββάτῳ. 17 ὁ δὲ
because these things he did on a sabbath. But he
ἀπεκρίνατο αὐτοῖς· ὁ πατήρ μου ἕως
answered them : The Father of me until
ἄρτι ἐργάζεται, κἀγὼ ἐργάζομαι· 18 διὰ
now works, and I work; because of
τοῦτο οὖν μᾶλλον ἐζήτουν αὐτὸν οἱ
this therefore [4]the more [3]sought [6]him [1]the
Ἰουδαῖοι ἀποκτεῖναι, ὅτι οὐ μόνον ἔλυεν
[2]Jews [5]to kill, because not only he broke
τὸ σάββατον, ἀλλὰ καὶ πατέρα ἴδιον
the sabbath, but also Father [his] own
ἔλεγεν τὸν θεόν, ἴσον ἑαυτὸν ποιῶν τῷ
said – God [to be], equal himself making –
θεῷ. 19 Ἀπεκρίνατο οὖν ὁ Ἰησοῦς καὶ
to God. Answered therefore – Jesus and
ἔλεγεν αὐτοῖς· ἀμὴν ἀμὴν λέγω· ὑμῖν,
said to them : Truly truly I say to you,
οὐ δύναται ὁ υἱὸς ποιεῖν ἀφ' ἑαυτοῦ
cannot the Son *to* do from himself
οὐδέν, ἂν μή τι βλέπῃ τὸν πατέρα
no(any)thing, except what he sees the Father
ποιοῦντα· ἃ γὰρ ἂν ἐκεῖνος ποιῇ, ταῦτα
doing; for whatever things that one does, these
καὶ ὁ υἱὸς ὁμοίως ποιεῖ. 20 ὁ γὰρ
also the Son likewise does. For the
πατὴρ φιλεῖ τὸν υἱὸν καὶ πάντα δείκνυσιν
Father loves the Son and all things shows
αὐτῷ ἃ αὐτὸς ποιεῖ, καὶ μείζονα τούτων
him which he does, and [1]greater [3][than] [4]these
δείξει αὐτῷ ἔργα, ἵνα ὑμεῖς θαυμάζητε.
[5]he will show [6]him [2]works, that ye may marvel.
21 ὥσπερ γὰρ ὁ πατὴρ ἐγείρει τοὺς
For as the Father raises the
νεκροὺς καὶ ζωοποιεῖ, οὕτως καὶ ὁ υἱὸς
dead and quickens, so also the Son
οὓς θέλει ζωοποιεῖ. 22 οὐδὲ γὰρ ὁ
whom he wills quickens. For not the
πατὴρ κρίνει οὐδένα, ἀλλὰ τὴν κρίσιν
Father judges no(any) one, but – judgment
πᾶσαν δέδωκεν τῷ υἱῷ, 23 ἵνα πάντες
all he has given to the Son, that all men
τιμῶσι τὸν υἱὸν καθὼς τιμῶσι τὸν πατέρα.
may honour the Son as they honour the Father.
ὁ μὴ τιμῶν τὸν υἱὸν οὐ τιμᾷ τὸν πατέρα
The [one] not honouring the Son honours not the Father
τὸν πέμψαντα αὐτόν. 24 Ἀμὴν ἀμὴν
– having sent him. Truly truly
λέγω ὑμῖν ὅτι ὁ τὸν λόγον μου ἀκούων
I say to you[,] – The [one] the word of me hearing
καὶ πιστεύων τῷ πέμψαντί με ἔχει
and believing the [one] having sent me has
ζωὴν αἰώνιον, καὶ εἰς κρίσιν οὐκ ἔρχεται
life eternal, and into judgment comes not
ἀλλὰ μεταβέβηκεν ἐκ τοῦ θανάτου εἰς
but has passed over out of – death into
τὴν ζωήν. 25 ἀμὴν ἀμὴν λέγω ὑμῖν ὅτι
– life. Truly truly I say to you[,] –
ἔρχεται ὥρα καὶ νῦν ἐστιν ὅτε οἱ νεκροὶ
Comes an hour and now is when the dead
ἀκούσουσιν τῆς φωνῆς τοῦ υἱοῦ τοῦ
will hear the voice of the Son –
θεοῦ καὶ οἱ ἀκούσαντες ζήσουσιν. 26 ὥσπερ
of God and the [ones] hearing will live. as

Life Through the Son

[16]So, because Jesus was doing these things on the Sabbath, the Jews persecuted him. [17]Jesus said to them, "My Father is always at his work to this very day, and I, too, am working." [18]For this reason the Jews tried all the harder to kill him; not only was he breaking the Sabbath, but he was even calling God his own Father, making himself equal with God.

[19]Jesus gave them this answer: "I tell you the truth, the Son can do nothing by himself; he can do only what he sees his Father doing, because whatever the Father does the Son also does. [20]For the Father loves the Son and shows him all he does. Yes, to your amazement he will show him even greater things than these. [21]For just as the Father raises the dead and gives them life, even so the Son gives life to whom he is pleased to give it. [22]Moreover, the Father judges no one, but has entrusted all judgment to the Son, [23]that all may honor the Son just as they honor the Father. He who does not honor the Son does not honor the Father, who sent him.

[24]"I tell you the truth, whoever hears my word and believes him who sent me has eternal life and will not be condemned; he has crossed over from death to

Two Resurrections

25"Truly, truly, I say to you, an hour is coming and now is, when the dead shall hear the voice of the Son of God; and those who hear shall live.

26"For just as the Father has life in Himself, even so He gave to the Son also to have life in Himself;

27and He gave Him authority to execute judgment, because He is *the* Son of Man.

28"Do not marvel at this; for an hour is coming, in which all who are in the tombs shall hear His voice,

29and shall come forth; those who did the good *deeds* to a resurrection of life, those who committed the evil *deeds* to a resurrection of judgment.

30"I can do nothing on My own initiative. As I hear, I judge; and My judgment is just, because I do not seek My own will, but the will of Him who sent Me.

31"If I *alone* bear witness of Myself, My testimony is not true.

32"There is another who bears witness of Me, and I know that the testimony which He bears of Me is true.

Witness of John

33"You have sent to John, and he has borne witness to the truth.

34"But the witness which I receive is not from man, but I say these things that you may be saved.

35"He was the lamp that was burning and was shining and you were willing to rejoice for a while in his light.

Witness of Works

36"But the witness which I have is greater than *that of* John; for the works which the Father has given Me to accomplish, the very works that I do, bear witness of Me, that the Father has sent Me.

Witness of the Father

37"And the Father who sent Me, He has borne witness of Me. You have neither heard His voice at any time, nor seen His form.

γὰρ ὁ πατὴρ ἔχει ζωὴν ἐν ἑαυτῷ, οὕτως
For the Father has life in himself, so
καὶ τῷ υἱῷ ἔδωκεν ζωὴν ἔχειν ἐν ἑαυτῷ.
also to the Son he gave life to have in himself.
27 καὶ ἐξουσίαν ἔδωκεν αὐτῷ κρίσιν ποιεῖν,
And authority he gave him judgment to do,
ὅτι υἱὸς ἀνθρώπου ἐστίν. 28 μὴ θαυμάζετε
because son of man* he is. Marvel not [at]
τοῦτο, ὅτι ἔρχεται ὥρα ἐν ᾗ πάντες οἱ
this, because comes an hour in which all the [ones]
ἐν τοῖς μνημείοις ἀκούσουσιν τῆς φωνῆς
in the tombs will hear the voice
αὐτοῦ 29 καὶ ἐκπορεύσονται οἱ τὰ ἀγαθὰ
of him and will come forth the [ones] the good things
ποιήσαντες εἰς ἀνάστασιν ζωῆς, οἱ τὰ
having done to a resurrection of life, the [ones] the
φαῦλα πράξαντες εἰς ἀνάστασιν κρίσεως.
evil things having done to a resurrection of judgment.
30 Οὐ δύναμαι ἐγὼ ποιεῖν ἀπ' ἐμαυτοῦ
Cannot I *to* do from myself
οὐδέν· καθὼς ἀκούω κρίνω, καὶ ἡ κρίσις
no(any)thing; as I hear I judge, and – judgment
ἡ ἐμὴ δικαία ἐστίν, ὅτι οὐ ζητῶ τὸ
– my just is, because I seek not –
θέλημα τὸ ἐμὸν ἀλλὰ τὸ θέλημα τοῦ
will – my but the will of the [one]
πέμψαντός με. 31 Ἐὰν ἐγὼ μαρτυρῶ
having sent me. If I witness
περὶ ἐμαυτοῦ, ἡ μαρτυρία μου οὐκ ἔστιν
concerning myself, the witness of me is not
ἀληθής· 32 ἄλλος ἐστὶν ὁ μαρτυρῶν περὶ
true; another there is the [one] witnessing concerning
ἐμοῦ, καὶ οἶδα ὅτι ἀληθής ἐστιν ἡ
me, and I know that true is the
μαρτυρία ἣν μαρτυρεῖ περὶ ἐμοῦ. 33 ὑμεῖς
witness which he witnesses concerning me. Ye
ἀπεστάλκατε πρὸς Ἰωάννην, καὶ μεμαρ-
have sent to John, and he has
τύρηκεν τῇ ἀληθείᾳ· 34 ἐγὼ δὲ οὐ παρὰ
witnessed to the truth; but I not from
ἀνθρώπου τὴν μαρτυρίαν λαμβάνω, ἀλλὰ
man the witness receive, but
ταῦτα λέγω ἵνα ὑμεῖς σωθῆτε. 35 ἐκεῖνος
these things I say that ye may be saved. That man
ἦν ὁ λύχνος ὁ καιόμενος καὶ φαίνων,
was the lamp – burning and shining,
ὑμεῖς δὲ ἠθελήσατε ἀγαλλιαθῆναι πρὸς
and ye were willing to exult for
ὥραν ἐν τῷ φωτὶ αὐτοῦ. 36 Ἐγὼ δὲ
an hour in the light of him. But I
ἔχω τὴν μαρτυρίαν μείζω τοῦ Ἰωάννου·
have the witness greater [than] – of John;
τὰ γὰρ ἔργα ἃ δέδωκέν μοι ὁ πατὴρ ἵνα
for the works which has given me the Father that
τελειώσω αὐτά, αὐτὰ τὰ ἔργα ἃ ποιῶ,
I may finish them, [3][them]selves [1]the [2]works which I do,
μαρτυρεῖ περὶ ἐμοῦ ὅτι ὁ πατήρ με
witness*es* concerning me that the Father me
ἀπέσταλκεν. 37 καὶ ὁ πέμψας με πατήρ,
has sent. And [1]the [3]having sent [4]me [2]Father,
ἐκεῖνος μεμαρτύρηκεν περὶ ἐμοῦ. οὔτε
that [one] has witnessed concerning me. Neither
φωνὴν αὐτοῦ πώποτε ἀκηκόατε οὔτε εἶδος
voice of him *never* ye have heard nor form

* Note the absence of the definite article here. See also Rev. 1. 13 and 14. 14.

life. 25I tell you the truth, a
time is coming and has now
come when the dead will
hear the voice of the Son of
God and those who hear
will live. 26For as the Father has life in himself, so
he has granted the Son to
have life in himself. 27And
he has given him authority
to judge because he is the
Son of Man.

28"Do not be amazed at
this, for a time is coming
when all who are in their
graves will hear his voice
29and come out—those
who have done good will
rise to live, and those who
have done evil will rise to
be condemned. 30By my-
self I can do nothing; I
judge only as I hear, and
my judgment is just, for I
seek not to please myself
but him who sent me.

Testimonies About Jesus

31"If I testify about my-
self, my testimony is not
valid. 32There is another
who testifies in my favor,
and I know that his testimony about me is valid.

33"You have sent to John
and he has testified to the
truth. 34Not that I accept
human testimony; but I
mention it that you may be
saved. 35John was a lamp
that burned and gave light,
and you chose for a time to
enjoy his light.

36"I have testimony
weightier than that of John.
For the very work that the
Father has given me to finish, and which I am doing,
testifies that the Father has
sent me. 37And the Father
who sent me has himself
testified concerning me.
You have never heard his
voice nor seen his form,

38 "And you do not have His word abiding in you, for you do not believe Him whom He sent.

Witness of the Scripture

39 "[o]You search the Scriptures, because you think that in them you have eternal life; and it is these that bear witness of Me;

40 and you are unwilling to come to Me, that you may have life.

41 "I do not receive glory from men;

42 but I know you, that you do not have the love of God in yourselves.

43 "I have come in My Father's name, and you do not receive Me; if another shall come in his own name, you will receive him.

44 "How can you believe, when you receive glory from one another, and you do not seek the glory that is from the *one and* only God?

45 "Do not think that I will accuse you before the Father; the one who accuses you is Moses, in whom you have set your hope.

46 "For if you believed Moses, you would believe Me; for he wrote of Me.

47 "But if you do not believe his writings, how will you believe My words?"

αὐτοῦ ἑωράκατε, 38 καὶ τὸν λόγον αὐτοῦ
of him ye have seen, and the word of him

οὐκ ἔχετε ἐν ὑμῖν μένοντα, ὅτι ὃν
ye have not in you remaining, because [he] whom

ἀπέστειλεν ἐκεῖνος, τούτῳ ὑμεῖς οὐ πιστεύετε.
[2]sent [1]that [one], this [one] ye do not believe.

39 ἐρευνᾶτε τὰς γραφάς, ὅτι ὑμεῖς δοκεῖτε
Ye search the scriptures, because ye think

ἐν αὐταῖς ζωὴν αἰώνιον ἔχειν· καὶ ἐκεῖναί
in them life eternal to have; and those

εἰσιν αἱ μαρτυροῦσαι περὶ ἐμοῦ· 40 καὶ
are the [ones] witnessing concerning me; and

οὐ θέλετε ἐλθεῖν πρός με ἵνα ζωὴν
ye wish not to come to me that life

ἔχητε. 41 Δόξαν παρὰ ἀνθρώπων οὐ
ye may have. Glory from men not

λαμβάνω, 42 ἀλλὰ ἔγνωκα ὑμᾶς ὅτι τὴν
I receive, but I have known you that the

ἀγάπην τοῦ θεοῦ οὐκ ἔχετε ἐν ἑαυτοῖς.
love – of God ye have not in your*selves*.

43 ἐγὼ ἐλήλυθα ἐν τῷ ὀνόματι τοῦ πατρός
I have come in the name of the Father

μου, καὶ οὐ λαμβάνετέ με· ἐὰν ἄλλος
of me, and ye receive not me; if another

ἔλθῃ ἐν τῷ ὀνόματι τῷ ἰδίῳ, ἐκεῖνον
comes in – name the(his) own, that [one]

λήμψεσθε. 44 πῶς δύνασθε ὑμεῖς πιστεῦσαι,
ye will receive. How can ye *to* believe,

δόξαν παρὰ ἀλλήλων λαμβάνοντες, καὶ
glory from one another receiving, and

τὴν δόξαν τὴν παρὰ τοῦ μόνου θεοῦ
the glory – from the only God

οὐ ζητεῖτε; 45 μὴ δοκεῖτε ὅτι ἐγὼ κατηγορήσω
ye seek not? Do not think that I will accuse

ὑμῶν πρὸς τὸν πατέρα· ἔστιν ὁ κατηγορῶν
you to the Father; there is the [one] accusing

ὑμῶν Μωϋσῆς, εἰς ὃν ὑμεῖς ἠλπίκατε. 46 εἰ
you[,] Moses, in whom ye have hoped. if

γὰρ ἐπιστεύετε Μωϋσεῖ, ἐπιστεύετε ἂν
For ye believed Moses, ye would have believed

ἐμοί· περὶ γὰρ ἐμοῦ ἐκεῖνος ἔγραψεν.
me; for concerning me that [one] wrote.

47 εἰ δὲ τοῖς ἐκείνου γράμμασιν οὐ
But [1]if [4]the [6]of that [one] [5]letters [3]not

πιστεύετε, πῶς τοῖς ἐμοῖς ῥήμασιν
[2]ye believe, how – my words

πιστεύσετε;
will ye believe?

38 nor does his word dwell in you, for you do not believe the one he sent. 39 You diligently study[e] the Scriptures because you think that by them you possess eternal life. These are the Scriptures that testify about me, 40 yet you refuse to come to me to have life.

41 "I do not accept praise from men, 42 but I know you. I know that you do not have the love of God in your hearts. 43 I have come in my Father's name, and you do not accept me; but if someone else comes in his own name, you will accept him. 44 How can you believe if you accept praise from one another, yet make no effort to obtain the praise that comes from the only God[f]?

45 "But do not think I will accuse you before the Father. Your accuser is Moses, on whom your hopes are set. 46 If you believed Moses, you would believe me, for he wrote about me. 47 But since you do not believe what he wrote, how are you going to believe what I say?"

Chapter 6

Five Thousand Fed

AFTER these things Jesus went away to the other side of the Sea of Galilee (or Tiberias).

2 And a great multitude was following Him, because they were seeing the signs which He was performing on those who were sick.

3 And Jesus went up on the mountain, and there He sat with His disciples.

4 Now the Passover, the feast of the Jews, was at hand.

5 Jesus therefore lifting

[o]Or, (a command) *Search the Scriptures!*

6 Μετὰ ταῦτα ἀπῆλθεν ὁ Ἰησοῦς πέραν
After these things went away – Jesus across

τῆς θαλάσσης τῆς Γαλιλαίας τῆς Τιβεριάδος.
the sea – of Galilee[,] – of Tiberias.

2 ἠκολούθει δὲ αὐτῷ ὄχλος πολύς, ὅτι
And followed him crowd a much, because

ἑώρων τὰ σημεῖα ἃ ἐποίει ἐπὶ τῶν
they saw the signs which he did on the

ἀσθενούντων. 3 ἀνῆλθεν δὲ εἰς τὸ ὄρος
ailing [ones]. And went up to the mountain

Ἰησοῦς, καὶ ἐκεῖ ἐκάθητο μετὰ τῶν
Jesus, and there sat with the

μαθητῶν αὐτοῦ. 4 ἦν δὲ ἐγγὺς τὸ πάσχα,
disciples of him. And was near the Passover,

ἡ ἑορτὴ τῶν Ἰουδαίων. 5 ἐπάρας οὖν
the feast of the Jews. Lifting up therefore

Chapter 6

Jesus Feeds the Five Thousand

SOME time after this, Jesus crossed to the far shore of the Sea of Galilee (that is, the Sea of Tiberias), 2 and a great crowd of people followed him because they saw the miraculous signs he had performed on the sick. 3 Then Jesus went up on a mountainside and sat down with his disciples. 4 The Jewish Passover Feast was near.

5 When Jesus looked up

[e]39 Or *Study diligently* (the imperative)

[f]44 Some early manuscripts *the Only One*

up His eyes, and seeing that a great multitude was coming to Him, *said to Philip, "Where are we to buy bread, that these may eat?"

6And this He was saying to test him; for He Himself knew what He was intending to do.

7Philip answered Him, "Two hundred [p]denarii worth of bread is not sufficient for them, for everyone to receive a little."

8One of His disciples, Andrew, Simon Peter's brother, *said to Him,

9"There is a lad here who has five barley loaves and two fish, but what are these for so many people?"

10Jesus said, "Have the people sit down." Now there was much grass in the place. So the men sat down, in number about five thousand.

11Jesus therefore took the loaves; and having given thanks, He distributed to those who were seated; likewise also of the fish as much as they wanted.

12And when they were filled, He *said to His disciples, "Gather up the leftover fragments that nothing may be lost."

13And so they gathered them up, and filled twelve baskets with fragments from the five barley loaves, which were left over by those who had eaten.

14When therefore the people saw the sign which He had performed, they said, "This is of a truth the Prophet who is to come into the world."

Jesus Walks on the Water

15Jesus therefore perceiving that they were intending to come and take Him by force, to make Him king, withdrew again to the mountain by Himself alone.

[p]The denarius was equivalent to one day's wage

τοὺς ὀφθαλμοὺς ὁ Ἰησοῦς καὶ θεασάμενος
the(his) eyes – Jesus and beholding

ὅτι πολὺς ὄχλος ἔρχεται πρὸς αὐτόν,
that a much crowd is(was) coming toward him,

λέγει πρὸς Φίλιππον· πόθεν ἀγοράσωμεν
he says to Philip : Whence may we buy

ἄρτους ἵνα φάγωσιν οὗτοι; 6 τοῦτο δὲ
loaves that may eat these? And this

ἔλεγεν πειράζων αὐτόν· αὐτὸς γὰρ ᾔδει
he said testing him; for he knew

τί ἔμελλεν ποιεῖν. 7 ἀπεκρίθη αὐτῷ ὁ
what he was about to do. Answered him –

Φίλιππος· διακοσίων δηναρίων ἄρτοι οὐκ
Philip : [3]Of two hundred [2]denarii [1]loaves not

ἀρκοῦσιν αὐτοῖς, ἵνα ἕκαστος βραχύ τι
are enough for them, that each a little

λάβῃ. 8 λέγει αὐτῷ εἷς ἐκ τῶν μαθητῶν
may take. Says to him one of the disciples

αὐτοῦ, Ἀνδρέας ὁ ἀδελφὸς Σίμωνος
of him, Andrew the brother of Simon

Πέτρου· 9 ἔστιν παιδάριον ὧδε ὃς ἔχει
Peter : There is a lad here who has

πέντε ἄρτους κριθίνους καὶ δύο ὀψάρια·
five loaves barley and two fishes;

ἀλλὰ ταῦτα τί ἐστιν εἰς τοσούτους;
but [3]these [1]what [2]is(are) among so many?

10 εἶπεν ὁ Ἰησοῦς· ποιήσατε τοὺς ἀνθρώπους
Said – Jesus : Make the men*

ἀναπεσεῖν. ἦν δὲ χόρτος πολὺς ἐν τῷ
to recline. Now there was grass much in the

τόπῳ. ἀνέπεσαν οὖν οἱ ἄνδρες τὸν ἀριθμὸν
place. Reclined therefore the men the number

ὡς πεντακισχίλιοι. 11 ἔλαβεν οὖν τοὺς
about five thousand. Took therefore the

ἄρτους ὁ Ἰησοῦς καὶ εὐχαριστήσας
loaves – Jesus and having given thanks

διέδωκεν τοῖς ἀνακειμένοις, ὁμοίως καὶ
distributed to the [ones] lying down, likewise also

ἐκ τῶν ὀψαρίων ὅσον ἤθελον. 12 ὡς δὲ
of the fishes as much as they wished. Now when

ἐνεπλήσθησαν, λέγει τοῖς μαθηταῖς αὐτοῦ·
they were filled, he tells the disciples of him:

συναγάγετε τὰ περισσεύσαντα κλάσματα, ἵνα
Gather ye the left over fragments, that

μή τι ἀπόληται. 13 συνήγαγον οὖν, καὶ
not anything is lost. They gathered therefore, and

ἐγέμισαν δώδεκα κοφίνους κλασμάτων ἐκ
filled twelve baskets of fragments of

τῶν πέντε ἄρτων τῶν κριθίνων ἃ ἐπερίσσευσαν
the five loaves – barley which were left over

τοῖς βεβρωκόσιν. 14 Οἱ οὖν ἄνθρωποι
to the [ones] having eaten. Therefore the men*

ἰδόντες ὃ ἐποίησεν σημεῖον ἔλεγον ὅτι
seeing [1]what [3]he did [2]sign said[,] –

οὗτός ἐστιν ἀληθῶς ὁ προφήτης ὁ
This is truly the prophet –

ἐρχόμενος εἰς τὸν κόσμον. 15 Ἰησοῦς
coming into the world. Jesus

οὖν γνοὺς ὅτι μέλλουσιν ἔρχεσθαι καὶ
therefore knowing that they are(were) about to come and

ἁρπάζειν αὐτὸν ἵνα ποιήσωσιν βασιλέα,
seize him that they might make a king,

ἀνεχώρησεν πάλιν εἰς τὸ ὄρος αὐτὸς
departed again to the mountain [him]self

* That is, people. Compare ἄνδρες in ver. 10.

and saw a great crowd coming toward him, he said to
Philip, "Where shall we
buy bread for these people
to eat?" 6He asked this
only to test him, for he already had in mind what he
was going to do.
7Philip answered him,
"Eight months' wages[g]
would not buy enough
bread for each one to have
a bite!"
8Another of his disciples,
Andrew, Simon Peter's
brother, spoke up, 9"Here
is a boy with five small barley loaves and two small
fish, but how far will they
go among so many?"
10Jesus said, "Have the
people sit down." There
was plenty of grass in that
place, and the men sat
down, about five thousand
of them. 11Jesus then took
the loaves, gave thanks,
and distributed to those
who were seated as much
as they wanted. He did the
same with the fish.
12When they had all had
enough to eat, he said to his
disciples, "Gather the
pieces that are left over.
Let nothing be wasted."
13So they gathered them
and filled twelve baskets
with the pieces of the five
barley loaves left over by
those who had eaten.
14After the people saw
the miraculous sign that
Jesus did, they began to
say, "Surely this is the
Prophet who is to come
into the world." 15Jesus,
knowing that they intended
to come and make him king
by force, withdrew again to
a mountain by himself.

[g]7 Greek *two hundred denarii*

16Now when evening
came, His disciples went
down to the sea,
17and after getting into a
boat, they *started to* cross
the sea to Capernaum. And
it had already become
dark, and Jesus had not yet
come to them.
18And the sea *began* to be
stirred up because a strong
wind was blowing.
19When therefore they
had rowed about three or
four miles, they *beheld
Jesus walking on the sea
and drawing near to the
boat; and they were frightened.
20But He *said to them,
"It is I; do not be afraid."
21They were willing
therefore to receive Him
into the boat; and immediately the boat was at the
land to which they were going.
22The next day the multi-
tude that stood on the other
side of the sea saw that
there was no other small
boat there, except one, and
that Jesus had not entered
with His disciples into the
boat, but *that* His disciples
had gone away alone.
23There came other small
boats from Tiberias near to
the place where they ate
the bread after the Lord
had given thanks.
24When the multitude
therefore saw that Jesus
was not there, nor His disciples, they themselves got
into the small boats, and
came to Capernaum, seek-
ing Jesus.
25And when they found
Him on the other side of the
sea, they said to Him,
"Rabbi, when did You get
here?"

Words to the People

26Jesus answered them
and said, "Truly, truly, I
say to you, you seek Me,
not because you saw

μόνος. 16 Ὡς δὲ ὀψία ἐγένετο, κατέβησαν
alone. And when evening came, went down

οἱ μαθηταὶ αὐτοῦ ἐπὶ τὴν θάλασσαν,
the disciples of him to the sea,

17 καὶ ἐμβάντες εἰς πλοῖον ἤρχοντο πέραν
and embarking in a boat came across

τῆς θαλάσσης εἰς Καφαρναούμ. καὶ
the sea to Capernaum. And

σκοτία ἤδη ἐγεγόνει καὶ οὔπω ἐληλύθει
darkness now had come and not yet had come

πρὸς αὐτοὺς ὁ Ἰησοῦς, 18 ἥ τε θάλασσα
to them – Jesus, and the sea

ἀνέμου μεγάλου πνέοντος διηγείρετο.
wind a great blowing[a] was roused.
=as a great wind blew

19 ἐληλακότες οὖν ὡς σταδίους εἴκοσι
Having rowed therefore about furlongs twenty-

πέντε ἢ τριάκοντα θεωροῦσιν τὸν Ἰησοῦν
five or thirty they behold – Jesus

περιπατοῦντα ἐπὶ τῆς θαλάσσης καὶ ἐγγὺς
walking on the sea and near

τοῦ πλοίου γινόμενον, καὶ ἐφοβήθησαν.
the boat becoming, and they feared.

20 ὁ δὲ λέγει αὐτοῖς· ἐγώ εἰμι· μὴ
But he says to them : I am; not

φοβεῖσθε. 21 ἤθελον οὖν λαβεῖν αὐτὸν εἰς
fear ye. They wished therefore to take him into

τὸ πλοῖον, καὶ εὐθέως ἐγένετο τὸ πλοῖον
the boat, and immediately was the boat

ἐπὶ τῆς γῆς εἰς ἣν ὑπῆγον.
at the land to which they were going.

22 Τῇ ἐπαύριον ὁ ὄχλος ὁ ἑστηκὼς
On the morrow the crowd – standing

πέραν τῆς θαλάσσης εἶδον ὅτι πλοιάριον
across the sea saw that boat

ἄλλο οὐκ ἦν ἐκεῖ εἰ μὴ ἕν, καὶ ὅτι
other was not there except one, and that

οὐ συνεισῆλθεν τοῖς μαθηταῖς αὐτοῦ ὁ
[2]did not come *in* with [3]the [4]disciples [5]of him –

Ἰησοῦς εἰς τὸ πλοῖον ἀλλὰ μόνοι οἱ
[1]Jesus in the boat but alone the

μαθηταὶ αὐτοῦ ἀπῆλθον· 23 ἄλλα ἦλθεν
disciples of him went away; [1]other [3]came

πλοιάρια ἐκ Τιβεριάδος ἐγγὺς τοῦ τόπου
[2]boats from Tiberias near the place

ὅπου ἔφαγον τὸν ἄρτον εὐχαριστήσαντος
where they ate the bread having given thanks

τοῦ κυρίου. 24 ὅτε οὖν εἶδεν ὁ ὄχλος
the Lord.[a] When therefore saw the crowd
=when the Lord had given thanks.

ὅτι Ἰησοῦς οὐκ ἔστιν ἐκεῖ οὐδὲ οἱ
that Jesus is(was) not there nor the

μαθηταὶ αὐτοῦ, ἐνέβησαν αὐτοὶ εἰς τὰ
disciples of him, embarked they in the

πλοιάρια καὶ ἦλθον εἰς Καφαρναοὺμ
boats and came to Capernaum

ζητοῦντες τὸν Ἰησοῦν. 25 καὶ εὑρόντες
seeking – Jesus. And finding

αὐτὸν πέραν τῆς θαλάσσης εἶπον αὐτῷ·
him across the sea they said to him :

ῥαββί, πότε ὧδε γέγονας; 26 ἀπεκρίθη
Rabbi, when here hast thou come? Answered

αὐτοῖς ὁ Ἰησοῦς καὶ εἶπεν· ἀμὴν ἀμὴν
them – Jesus and said: Truly truly

λέγω ὑμῖν, ζητεῖτέ με οὐχ ὅτι εἴδετε
I say to you, ye seek me not because ye saw

Jesus Walks on the Water

16When evening came,
his disciples went down to
the lake, 17where they got
into a boat and set off
across the lake for Capernaum. By now it was dark,
and Jesus had not yet
joined them. 18A strong
wind was blowing and the
waters grew rough. 19When
they had rowed three or
three and a half miles,[h]
they saw Jesus approach-
ing the boat, walking on the
water; and they were terrified. 20But he said to them,
"It is I; don't be afraid."
21Then they were willing to
take him into the boat, and
immediately the boat
reached the shore where
they were heading.
22The next day the crowd
that had stayed on the opposite shore of the lake realized that only one boat
had been there, and that
Jesus had not entered it
with his disciples, but that
they had gone away alone.
23Then some boats from Tiberias landed near the
place where the people had
eaten the bread after the
Lord had given thanks.
24Once the crowd realized
that neither Jesus nor his
disciples were there, they
got into the boats and went
to Capernaum in search of
Jesus.

Jesus the Bread of Life

25When they found him
on the other side of the
lake, they asked him,
"Rabbi, when did you get
here?"
26Jesus answered, "I tell
you the truth, you are looking for me, not because you

[h]19 Greek *rowed twenty-five or thirty stadia* (about 5 or 6 kilometers)

signs, but because you ate of the loaves, and were filled.

27"Do not work for the food which perishes, but for the food which endures to eternal life, which the Son of Man shall give to you, for on Him the Father, *even* God, has set His seal."

28They said therefore to Him, "What shall we do, that we may work the works of God?"

29Jesus answered and said to them, "This is the work of God, that you believe in Him whom He has sent."

30They said therefore to Him, "What then do You do for a sign, that we may see, and believe You? What work do You perform?

31"Our fathers ate the manna in the wilderness; as it is written, 'HE GAVE THEM BREAD OUT OF HEAVEN TO EAT.'"

32Jesus therefore said to them, "Truly, truly, I say to you, it is not Moses who has given you the bread out of heaven, but it is My Father who gives you the true bread out of heaven.

33"For the bread of God is [a]that which comes down out of heaven, and gives life to the world."

34They said therefore to Him, "Lord, evermore give us this bread."

35Jesus said to them, "I am the bread of life; he who comes to Me shall not hunger, and he who believes in Me shall never thirst.

36"But I said to you, that you have seen Me, and yet do not believe.

37"All that the Father gives Me shall come to Me, and the one who comes to Me I will certainly not cast out.

38"For I have come down

[a]Or, *He who comes*

σημεῖα, ἀλλ' ὅτι ἐφάγετε ἐκ τῶν ἄρτων
signs, but because ye ate of the loaves
καὶ ἐχορτάσθητε. 27 ἐργάζεσθε μὴ τὴν
and were satisfied. Work not [for] the
βρῶσιν τὴν ἀπολλυμένην, ἀλλὰ τὴν βρῶσιν
food – perishing, but [for] the food
τὴν μένουσαν εἰς ζωὴν αἰώνιον, ἣν ὁ
– remaining to life eternal, which the
υἱὸς τοῦ ἀνθρώπου ὑμῖν δώσει· τοῦτον γὰρ
Son – of man you will give; for this [one]
ὁ πατὴρ ἐσφράγισεν ὁ θεός. 28 εἶπον
[2]the [3]Father [4]sealed – [1]God. They said
οὖν πρὸς αὐτόν· τί ποιῶμεν ἵνα ἐργαζ-
therefore to him: What may we do that we may
ώμεθα τὰ ἔργα τοῦ θεοῦ; 29 ἀπεκρίθη
work the works – of God? Answered
Ἰησοῦς καὶ εἶπεν αὐτοῖς· τοῦτό ἐστιν τὸ
Jesus and said to them: This is the
ἔργον τοῦ θεοῦ, ἵνα πιστεύητε εἰς ὃν
work – of God, that ye believe in [him] whom
ἀπέστειλεν ἐκεῖνος. 30 εἶπον οὖν αὐτῷ·
sent that [one]. They said therefore to him:
τί οὖν ποιεῖς σὺ σημεῖον, ἵνα ἴδωμεν
[1]What [2]then [3]doest [4]thou [5]sign, that we may see
καὶ πιστεύσωμέν σοι; τί ἐργάζῃ; 31 οἱ
and believe thee? what workest thou? The
πατέρες ἡμῶν τὸ μάννα ἔφαγον ἐν τῇ
fathers of us the manna ate in the
ἐρήμῳ, καθώς ἐστιν γεγραμμένον· ἄρτον
desert, as it is *having been* written: Bread
ἐκ τοῦ οὐρανοῦ ἔδωκεν αὐτοῖς φαγεῖν.
out of – heaven he gave them to eat.
32 Εἶπεν οὖν αὐτοῖς ὁ Ἰησοῦς· ἀμὴν
Said therefore to them – Jesus: Truly
ἀμὴν λέγω ὑμῖν, οὐ Μωϋσῆς δέδωκεν
truly I say to you, not Moses has given
ὑμῖν τὸν ἄρτον ἐκ τοῦ οὐρανοῦ, ἀλλ' ὁ
you the bread out of – heaven, but the
πατήρ μου δίδωσιν ὑμῖν τὸν ἄρτον ἐκ
Father of me gives you [1]the [3]bread [4]out of
τοῦ οὐρανοῦ τὸν ἀληθινόν· 33 ὁ γὰρ ἄρτος
– [5]heaven *the* [2]true; for the bread
τοῦ θεοῦ ἐστιν ὁ καταβαίνων ἐκ τοῦ
– of God is the [one] coming down out of –
οὐρανοῦ καὶ ζωὴν διδοὺς τῷ κόσμῳ.
heaven and life giving to the world.
34 εἶπον οὖν πρὸς αὐτόν· κύριε, πάντοτε
They said therefore to him: Lord, always
δὸς ἡμῖν τὸν ἄρτον τοῦτον. 35 εἶπεν
give us – bread this. Said
αὐτοῖς ὁ Ἰησοῦς· ἐγώ εἰμι ὁ ἄρτος τῆς
to them – Jesus: I am the bread –
ζωῆς· ὁ ἐρχόμενος πρὸς ἐμὲ οὐ μὴ
of life; the [one] coming to me by no means
πεινάσῃ, καὶ ὁ πιστεύων εἰς ἐμὲ οὐ μὴ
hungers, and the [one] believing in me by no means
διψήσει πώποτε. 36 Ἀλλ' εἶπον ὑμῖν ὅτι
will thirst *never*. But I told you that
καὶ ἑωράκατέ [με] καὶ οὐ πιστεύετε.
both ye have seen me and do not believe.
37 πᾶν ὃ δίδωσίν μοι ὁ πατὴρ πρὸς
All which gives to me the Father to
ἐμὲ ἥξει, καὶ τὸν ἐρχόμενον πρός με
me will come, and the [one] coming to me
οὐ μὴ ἐκβάλω ἔξω, 38 ὅτι καταβέβηκα
by no means I will cast *out* outside, because I have come down

saw miraculous signs but because you ate the loaves and had your fill. 27Do not work for food that spoils, but for food that endures to eternal life, which the Son of Man will give you. On him God the Father has placed his seal of approval."

28Then they asked him, "What must we do to do the works God requires?"

29Jesus answered, "The work of God is this: to believe in the one he has sent."

30So they asked him, "What miraculous sign then will you give that we may see it and believe you? What will you do? 31Our forefathers ate the manna in the desert; as it is written: 'He gave them bread from heaven to eat.'[i]"

32Jesus said to them, "I tell you the truth, it is not Moses who has given you the bread from heaven, but it is my Father who gives you the true bread from heaven. 33For the bread of God is he who comes down from heaven and gives life to the world."

34"Sir," they said, "from now on give us this bread."

35Then Jesus declared, "I am the bread of life. He who comes to me will never go hungry, and he who believes in me will never be thirsty. 36But as I told you, you have seen me and still you do not believe. 37All that the Father gives me will come to me, and whoever comes to me I will never drive away. 38For I have come down from

[i]*31* Exodus 16:4; Neh. 9:15; Psalm 78:24,25

from heaven, not to do My
own will, but the will of
Him who sent Me.
39 "And this is the will of
Him who sent Me, that of
all that He has given Me I
lose nothing, but raise it up
on the last day.
40 "For this is the will of
My Father, that everyone
who beholds the Son and
believes in Him, may have
eternal life; and I Myself
will raise him up on the last
day."

Words to the Jews

41 The Jews therefore
were grumbling about Him,
because He said, "I am the
bread that came down out
of heaven."
42 And they were saying,
"Is not this Jesus, the son
of Joseph, whose father
and mother we know? How
does He now say, 'I have
come down out of
heaven'?"
43 Jesus answered and
said to them, "Do not
grumble among your-
selves.
44 "No one can come to
Me, unless the Father who
sent Me draws him; and I
will raise him up on the last
day.
45 "It is written in the
prophets, 'AND THEY SHALL
ALL BE TAUGHT OF GOD.'
Everyone who has heard
and learned from the Fa-
ther, comes to Me.
46 "Not that any man has
seen the Father, except the
One who is from God; He
has seen the Father.
47 "Truly, truly, I say to
you, he who believes has
eternal life.
48 "I am the bread of life.
49 "Your fathers ate the
manna in the wilderness,
and they died.
50 "This is the bread
which comes down out of
heaven, so that one may eat

ἀπὸ τοῦ οὐρανοῦ οὐχ ἵνα ποιῶ τὸ θέλημα
from – heaven not that I may do *the* [2]will
τὸ ἐμὸν ἀλλὰ τὸ θέλημα τοῦ πέμψαντός
– [1]my but the will of the [one] having sent
με. 39 τοῦτο δέ ἐστιν τὸ θέλημα τοῦ
me. And this is the will of the [one]
πέμψαντός με, ἵνα πᾶν ὃ δέδωκέν μοι
having sent me, that all which he has given me
μὴ ἀπολέσω ἐξ αὐτοῦ, ἀλλὰ ἀναστήσω
I shall not lose of it, but shall raise up
αὐτὸ ἐν τῇ ἐσχάτῃ ἡμέρᾳ. 40 τοῦτο
it in the last day. this
γάρ ἐστιν τὸ θέλημα τοῦ πατρός μου,
For is the will of the Father of me,
ἵνα πᾶς ὁ θεωρῶν τὸν υἱὸν καὶ πιστεύων
that everyone beholding the Son and believing
εἰς αὐτὸν ἔχῃ ζωὴν αἰώνιον, καὶ ἀναστήσω
in him may have life eternal, and will raise up
αὐτὸν ἐγὼ ἐν τῇ ἐσχάτῃ ἡμέρᾳ. 41 Ἐγόγ-
him I in the last day. Mur-
γυζον οὖν οἱ Ἰουδαῖοι περὶ αὐτοῦ ὅτι
mured therefore the Jews about him because
εἶπεν· ἐγώ εἰμι ὁ ἄρτος ὁ καταβὰς ἐκ
he said: I am the bread – having come down out
τοῦ οὐρανοῦ, 42 καὶ ἔλεγον· οὐχ οὗτός
– of heaven, and they said: Not this man
ἐστιν Ἰησοῦς ὁ υἱὸς Ἰωσήφ, οὗ ἡμεῖς
is Jesus the son of Joseph, of whom we
οἴδαμεν τὸν πατέρα καὶ τὴν μητέρα;
know the father and the mother?
πῶς νῦν λέγει ὅτι ἐκ τοῦ οὐρανοῦ
how now says he[,] – Out of – heaven
καταβέβηκα; 43 ἀπεκρίθη Ἰησοῦς καὶ εἶπεν
I have come down? Answered Jesus and said
αὐτοῖς· μὴ γογγύζετε μετ' ἀλλήλων.
to them: Do not murmur with one another.
44 Οὐδεὶς δύναται ἐλθεῖν πρός με ἐὰν μὴ
No one can *to* come to me unless
ὁ πατὴρ ὁ πέμψας με ἑλκύσῃ αὐτόν,
the Father the [one] having sent me should draw him,
κἀγὼ ἀναστήσω αὐτὸν ἐν τῇ ἐσχάτῃ
and I will raise up him in the last
ἡμέρᾳ. 45 ἔστιν γεγραμμένον ἐν τοῖς
day. It is *having been* written in the
προφήταις· καὶ ἔσονται πάντες διδακτοὶ
prophets: And they shall be all taught
θεοῦ· πᾶς ὁ ἀκούσας παρὰ τοῦ πατρὸς
of God; everyone hearing from the Father
καὶ μαθὼν ἔρχεται πρὸς ἐμέ. 46 οὐχ
and learning comes to me. Not
ὅτι τὸν πατέρα ἑώρακέν τις, εἰ μὴ ὁ
that [2]the [4]Father [3]has seen [1]anyone, except the [one]
ὢν παρὰ τοῦ θεοῦ, οὗτος ἑώρακεν τὸν
being from – God, this [one] has seen the
πατέρα. 47 ἀμὴν ἀμὴν λέγω ὑμῖν, ὁ
Father. Truly truly I say to you, the
πιστεύων ἔχει ζωὴν αἰώνιον. 48 Ἐγώ
[one] believing has life eternal. I
εἰμι ὁ ἄρτος τῆς ζωῆς. 49 οἱ πατέρες
am the bread – of life. The fathers
ὑμῶν ἔφαγον ἐν τῇ ἐρήμῳ τὸ μάννα καὶ
of you ate in the desert the manna and
ἀπέθανον· 50 οὗτός ἐστιν ὁ ἄρτος ὁ ἐκ
died; this is the bread – out of
τοῦ οὐρανοῦ καταβαίνων, ἵνα τις ἐξ
– heaven coming down, that anyone of

heaven not to do my will
but to do the will of him
who sent me. 39 And this is
the will of him who sent
me, that I shall lose none of
all that he has given me, but
raise them up at the last
day. 40 For my Father's will
is that everyone who looks
to the Son and believes in
him shall have eternal life,
and I will raise him up at
the last day."
41 At this the Jews began
to grumble about him be-
cause he said, "I am the
bread that came down from
heaven." 42 They said, "Is
this not Jesus, the son of
Joseph, whose father and
mother we know? How can
he now say, 'I came down
from heaven'?"
43 "Stop grumbling among
yourselves," Jesus an-
swered. 44 "No one can
come to me unless the Fa-
ther who sent me draws
him, and I will raise him up
at the last day. 45 It is written in the Prophets: 'They
will all be taught by God.'[j]
Everyone who listens to
the Father and learns from
him comes to me. 46 No one
has seen the Father except
the one who is from God;
only he has seen the Fa-
ther. 47 I tell you the truth,
he who believes has ever-
lasting life. 48 I am the bread
of life. 49 Your forefathers
ate the manna in the desert,
yet they died. 50 But here is
the bread that comes down
from heaven, which a man
may eat and not die. 51 I am

[j]45 Isaiah 54:13

of it and not die.
51"I am the living bread
that came down out of
heaven; if anyone eats of
this bread, he shall live forever; and the bread also
which I shall give for the
life of the world is My
flesh."
52The Jews therefore *be-
gan* to argue with one another, saying, "How can
this man give us *His* flesh to
eat?"
53Jesus therefore said to
them, "Truly, truly, I say
to you, unless you eat the
flesh of the Son of Man and
drink His blood, you have
no life in yourselves.
54"He who eats My flesh
and drinks My blood has
eternal life, and I will raise
him up on the last day.
55"For My flesh is true
food, and My blood is true
drink.
56"He who eats My flesh
and drinks My blood abides
in Me, and I in him.
57"As the living Father
sent Me, and I live because
of the Father, so he who
eats Me, he also shall live
because of Me.
58"This is the bread
which came down out of
heaven; not as the fathers
ate, and died, he who eats
this bread shall live forever."

Words to the Disciples

59These things He said in
the synagogue, as He
taught in Capernaum.
60Many therefore of His
disciples, when they heard
this said, "This is a difficult
statement; who can listen
to it?"
61But Jesus, conscious
that His disciples grumbled
at this, said to them, "Does
this cause you to stumble?

αὐτοῦ φάγῃ καὶ μὴ ἀποθάνῃ. **51** ἐγώ
it may eat and may not die. I
εἰμι ὁ ἄρτος ὁ ζῶν ὁ ἐκ τοῦ οὐρανοῦ
am the bread – living the [one] out of – heaven
καταβάς· ἐάν τις φάγῃ ἐκ τούτου τοῦ
having come down; if anyone eats of this –
ἄρτου, ζήσει εἰς τὸν αἰῶνα· καὶ ὁ ἄρτος
bread, he will live to the age; 2indeed 3the 4bread
δὲ ὃν ἐγὼ δώσω ἡ σάρξ μού ἐστιν
1and which I will give the flesh of me is
ὑπὲρ τῆς τοῦ κόσμου ζωῆς. **52** Ἐμάχοντο
for 1the 3of the 4world 2life. Fought
οὖν πρὸς ἀλλήλους οἱ Ἰουδαῖοι λέγοντες·
therefore with one another the Jews saying:
πῶς δύναται οὗτος ἡμῖν δοῦναι τὴν
How can this man us *to* give the(his)
σάρκα φαγεῖν; **53** εἶπεν οὖν αὐτοῖς ὁ
flesh to eat? Said therefore to them –
Ἰησοῦς· ἀμὴν ἀμὴν λέγω ὑμῖν, ἐὰν μὴ
Jesus: Truly truly I say to you, unless
φάγητε τὴν σάρκα τοῦ υἱοῦ τοῦ ἀνθρώπου
ye eat the flesh of the Son – of man
καὶ πίητε αὐτοῦ τὸ αἷμα, οὐκ ἔχετε
and drink of him the blood, ye have not
ζωὴν ἐν ἑαυτοῖς. **54** ὁ τρώγων μου τὴν
life in yourselves. The [one] eating of me the
σάρκα καὶ πίνων μου τὸ αἷμα ἔχει ζωὴν
flesh and drinking of me the blood has life
αἰώνιον, κἀγὼ ἀναστήσω αὐτὸν τῇ ἐσχάτῃ
eternal, and I will raise up him in the last
ἡμέρᾳ. **55** ἡ γὰρ σάρξ μου ἀληθής
day. For the flesh of me 2true
ἐστιν βρῶσις, καὶ τὸ αἷμά μου ἀληθής
1is 3food, and the blood of me 2true
ἐστιν πόσις. **56** ὁ τρώγων μου τὴν
1is 3drink. The [one] eating of me the
σάρκα καὶ πίνων μου τὸ αἷμα ἐν ἐμοὶ
flesh and drinking of me the blood in me
μένει κἀγὼ ἐν αὐτῷ. **57** καθὼς ἀπέστειλέν
remains and I in him. As sent
με ὁ ζῶν πατὴρ κἀγὼ ζῶ διὰ τὸν
me the living Father and I live because of the
πατέρα, καὶ ὁ τρώγων με κἀκεῖνος
Father, also the [one] eating me even that one
ζήσει δι' ἐμέ. **58** οὗτός ἐστιν ὁ ἄρτος ὁ
will live because of me. This is the bread –
ἐξ οὐρανοῦ καταβάς, οὐ καθὼς ἔφαγον
out of heaven having come down, not as ate
οἱ πατέρες καὶ ἀπέθανον· ὁ τρώγων
the fathers and died; the [one] eating
τοῦτον τὸν ἄρτον ζήσει εἰς τὸν αἰῶνα.
this – bread will live unto the age.
59 Ταῦτα εἶπεν ἐν συναγωγῇ διδάσκων ἐν
These things he said in a synagogue teaching in
Καφαρναούμ. **60** Πολλοὶ οὖν ἀκούσαντες
Capernaum. 2Many 1therefore 7hearing
ἐκ τῶν μαθητῶν αὐτοῦ εἶπαν· σκληρός
3of 4the 5disciples 6of him said: Hard
ἐστιν ὁ λόγος οὗτος· τίς δύναται αὐτοῦ
is – word this; who can it
ἀκούειν; **61** εἰδὼς δὲ ὁ Ἰησοῦς ἐν ἑαυτῷ
to hear? But knowing – Jesus in himself
ὅτι γογγύζουσιν περὶ τούτου οἱ μαθηταὶ
that 4are murmuring 5about 6this 1the 2disciples
αὐτοῦ, εἶπεν αὐτοῖς· τοῦτο ὑμᾶς σκανδαλίζει;
3of him, said to them: This you offends?

the living bread that came
down from heaven. If any-
one eats of this bread, he
will live forever. This bread
is my flesh, which I will
give for the life of the
world."
52Then the Jews began to
argue sharply among them-
selves, "How can this man
give us his flesh to eat?"
53Jesus said to them, "I
tell you the truth, unless
you eat the flesh of the Son
of Man and drink his blood,
you have no life in you.
54Whoever eats my flesh
and drinks my blood has
eternal life, and I will raise
him up at the last day. 55For
my flesh is real food and my
blood is real drink. 56Who-
ever eats my flesh and
drinks my blood remains in
me, and I in him. 57Just as
the living Father sent me
and I live because of the
Father, so the one who
feeds on me will live be-
cause of me. 58This is the
bread that came down from
heaven. Your forefathers
ate manna and died, but he
who feeds on this bread will
live forever." 59He said
this while teaching in the
synagogue in Capernaum.

Many Disciples Desert Jesus

60On hearing it, many of
his disciples said, "This is a
hard teaching. Who can accept it?"
61Aware that his disciples
were grumbling about this,
Jesus said to them, "Does
this offend you? 62What if

62"*What* then if you
should behold the Son of
Man ascending where He
was before?
63"It is the Spirit who
gives life; the flesh profits
nothing; the words that I
have spoken to you are
spirit and are life.
64"But there are some of
you who do not believe."
For Jesus knew from the
beginning who they were
who did not believe, and
who it was that would be-
tray Him.
65And He was saying,
"For this reason I have
said to you, that no one can
come to Me, unless it has
been granted him from the
Father."

Peter's Confession of Faith

66As a result of this many
of His disciples withdrew,
and were not walking with
Him anymore.
67Jesus said therefore to
the twelve, "You do not
want to go away also, do
you?"
68Simon Peter answered
Him, "Lord, to whom shall
we go? You have words of
eternal life.
69"And we have believed
and have come to know
that You are the Holy One
of God."
70Jesus answered them,
"Did I Myself not choose
you, the twelve, and *yet*
one of you is a devil?"
71Now He meant Judas
the son of Simon Iscariot,
for he, one of the twelve,
was going to betray Him.

62 ἐὰν οὖν θεωρῆτε τὸν υἱὸν τοῦ ἀνθρώπου
If then ye behold the Son – of man
ἀναβαίνοντα ὅπου ἦν τὸ πρότερον; **63** τὸ
ascending where he was at first? † The
πνεῦμά ἐστιν τὸ ζωοποιοῦν, ἡ σὰρξ οὐκ
spirit is the [thing] quickening, the flesh not
ὠφελεῖ οὐδέν· τὰ ῥήματα ἃ ἐγὼ λελάληκα
profits no(any)thing; the words which I have spoken
ὑμῖν πνεῦμά ἐστιν καὶ ζωή ἐστιν. **64** ἀλλ'
to you spirit is(are) and life is(are). But
εἰσὶν ἐξ ὑμῶν τινες οἳ οὐ πιστεύουσιν. ᾔδει
there are of you some who do not believe. knew
γὰρ ἐξ ἀρχῆς ὁ Ἰησοῦς τίνες εἰσὶν
For from [the] beginning – Jesus who are(were)
οἱ μὴ πιστεύοντες καὶ τίς ἐστιν ὁ
the [ones] not believing and who is(was) the
παραδώσων αὐτόν. **65** καὶ ἔλεγεν·
[one] betraying him. And he said :
διὰ τοῦτο εἴρηκα ὑμῖν ὅτι οὐδεὶς δύναται
Therefore I have told you that no one can
ἐλθεῖν πρός με ἐὰν μὴ ᾖ δεδομένον
to come to me unless it is *having been* given
αὐτῷ ἐκ τοῦ πατρός.
to him of the Father.
66 Ἐκ τούτου πολλοὶ τῶν μαθητῶν
From this many of the disciples
αὐτοῦ ἀπῆλθον εἰς τὰ ὀπίσω καὶ οὐκέτι
of him went away back† and no longer
μετ' αὐτοῦ περιεπάτουν. **67** εἶπεν οὖν ὁ
with him walked. Said therefore –
Ἰησοῦς τοῖς δώδεκα· μὴ καὶ ὑμεῖς
Jesus to the twelve : *Not* also ye
θέλετε ὑπάγειν; **68** ἀπεκρίθη αὐτῷ Σίμων
wish to go? Answered him Simon
Πέτρος· κύριε, πρὸς τίνα ἀπελευσόμεθα;
Peter : Lord, to whom shall we go away?
ῥήματα ζωῆς αἰωνίου ἔχεις· **69** καὶ ἡμεῖς
words of life eternal thou hast; and we
πεπιστεύκαμεν καὶ ἐγνώκαμεν ὅτι σὺ εἶ
have believed and have known that thou art
ὁ ἅγιος τοῦ θεοῦ. **70** ἀπεκρίθη αὐτοῖς ὁ
the holy one – of God. Answered them –
Ἰησοῦς· οὐκ ἐγὼ ὑμᾶς τοὺς δώδεκα
Jesus : [3]Not [2]I [4]you [5]the [6]twelve
ἐξελεξάμην; καὶ ἐξ ὑμῶν εἷς διάβολός
[1]chose? and of you one a devil
ἐστιν. **71** ἔλεγεν δὲ τὸν Ἰούδαν Σίμωνος
is. Now he spoke [of] – Judas [son] of Simon
Ἰσκαριώτου· οὗτος γὰρ ἔμελλεν παραδιδόναι
Iscariot; for this one was about to betray
αὐτόν, εἷς ἐκ τῶν δώδεκα.
him, one of the twelve.

you see the Son of Man ascend to where he was be-
fore! 63The Spirit gives life;
the flesh counts for nothing. The words I have spoken to you are spirit[k] and
they are life. 64Yet there
are some of you who do not
believe." For Jesus had
known from the beginning
which of them did not be-
lieve and who would betray
him. 65He went on to say,
"This is why I told you that
no one can come to me un-
less the Father has enabled
him."
66From this time many of
his disciples turned back
and no longer followed
him.
67"You do not want to
leave too, do you?" Jesus
asked the Twelve.
68Simon Peter answered
him, "Lord, to whom shall
we go? You have the words
of eternal life. 69We believe
and know that you are the
Holy One of God."
70Then Jesus replied,
"Have I not chosen you,
the Twelve? Yet one of you
is a devil!" 71(He meant Judas, the son of Simon Iscariot, who, though one of the
Twelve, was later to betray
him.)

Chapter 7

Jesus Teaches at the Feast

AND after these things
Jesus was walking in
Galilee; for He was unwilling to walk in Judea, be-
cause the Jews were seek-
ing to kill Him.
2Now the feast of the
Jews, the Feast of Booths,
was at hand.
3His brothers therefore
said to Him, "Depart from

7 Καὶ μετὰ ταῦτα περιεπάτει ὁ Ἰησοῦς
And after these things walked – Jesus
ἐν τῇ Γαλιλαίᾳ· οὐ γὰρ ἤθελεν ἐν τῇ
in – Galilee; for he did not wish in –
Ἰουδαίᾳ περιπατεῖν, ὅτι ἐζήτουν αὐτὸν οἱ
Judæa to walk, because [3]were seeking [5]him [1]the
Ἰουδαῖοι ἀποκτεῖναι. **2** ἦν δὲ ἐγγὺς ἡ
[2]Jews [4]to kill. Now was near the
ἑορτὴ τῶν Ἰουδαίων ἡ σκηνοπηγία. **3** εἶπον
feast of the Jews the Tabernacles. Said
οὖν πρὸς αὐτὸν οἱ ἀδελφοὶ αὐτοῦ·
therefore to him the brothers of him :

Chapter 7

Jesus Goes to the Feast of Tabernacles

AFTER this, Jesus went
around in Galilee,
purposely staying away
from Judea because the
Jews there were waiting to
take his life. 2But when the
Jewish Feast of Taberna-
cles was near, 3Jesus'
brothers said to him, "You

[k]63 Or *Spirit*

here, and go into Judea,
that Your disciples also
may behold Your works
which You are doing.
4"For no one does any-
thing in secret, when he
himself seeks to be *known*
publicly. If You do these
things, show Yourself to
the world."
5For not even His broth-
ers were believing in Him.
6Jesus therefore *said to
them, "My time is not yet
at hand, but your time is
always opportune.
7"The world cannot hate
you; but it hates Me be-
cause I testify of it, that its
deeds are evil.
8"Go up to the feast
yourselves; I do not go up
to this feast because My
time has not yet fully
come."
9And having said these
things to them, He stayed
in Galilee.
10But when His brothers
had gone up to the feast,
then He Himself also went
up, not publicly, but as it
were, in secret.
11The Jews therefore
were seeking Him at the
feast, and were saying,
"Where is He?"
12And there was much
grumbling among the multitudes concerning Him;
some were saying, "He is a
good man"; others were
saying, "No, on the con-
trary, He leads the multitude astray."
13Yet no one was speak-
ing openly of Him for fear
of the Jews.
14But when it was now
the midst of the feast Jesus
went up into the temple,
and *began to* teach.
15The Jews therefore
were marveling, saying,
"How has this man
become learned, having
never been educated?"
16Jesus therefore an-
swered them, and said,

μετάβηθι ἐντεῦθεν καὶ ὕπαγε εἰς τὴν Ἰουδαίαν,
Depart hence and go into – Judæa,
ἵνα καὶ οἱ μαθηταί σου θεωρήσουσιν τὰ
that also the disciples of thee will behold the
ἔργα σου ἃ ποιεῖς· 4 οὐδεὶς γάρ τι ἐν
works of thee which thou doest; for no one anything in
κρυπτῷ ποιεῖ καὶ ζητεῖ αὐτὸς ἐν παρρησίᾳ
secret does and seeks [him]self in [the] open
εἶναι. εἰ ταῦτα ποιεῖς, φανέρωσον σεαυτὸν
to be. If these things thou doest, manifest thyself
τῷ κόσμῳ. 5 οὐδὲ γὰρ οἱ ἀδελφοὶ
to the world. For not the brothers
αὐτοῦ ἐπίστευον εἰς αὐτόν. 6 λέγει οὖν
of him believed in him. Says therefore
αὐτοῖς ὁ Ἰησοῦς· ὁ καιρὸς ὁ ἐμὸς
to them – Jesus: *The* [2]time – [1]my
οὔπω πάρεστιν, ὁ δὲ καιρὸς ὁ ὑμέτερος
not yet is arrived, but *the* [2]time – [1]your
πάντοτέ ἐστιν ἕτοιμος. 7 οὐ δύναται ὁ
always is ready. Cannot the
κόσμος μισεῖν ὑμᾶς, ἐμὲ δὲ μισεῖ, ὅτι
world *to* hate you, but me it hates, because
ἐγὼ μαρτυρῶ περὶ αὐτοῦ ὅτι τὰ ἔργα
I witness about it that the works
αὐτοῦ πονηρά ἐστιν. 8 ὑμεῖς ἀνάβητε εἰς
of it evil is(are). [2]Ye [1]go [3]up to
τὴν ἑορτήν· ἐγὼ οὐκ ἀναβαίνω εἰς τὴν
the feast; I am not going up to –
ἑορτὴν ταύτην, ὅτι ὁ ἐμὸς καιρὸς οὔπω
feast this, because *the* my time not yet
πεπλήρωται. 9 ταῦτα δὲ εἰπὼν αὐτοῖς
has been fulfilled. And these things saying to them
ἔμεινεν ἐν τῇ Γαλιλαίᾳ. 10 Ὡς δὲ
he remained in – Galilee. But when
ἀνέβησαν οἱ ἀδελφοὶ αὐτοῦ εἰς τὴν ἑορτήν,
went up the brothers of him to the feast,
τότε καὶ αὐτὸς ἀνέβη, οὐ φανερῶς ἀλλὰ
then also he went up, not manifestly but
ὡς ἐν κρυπτῷ. 11 οἱ οὖν Ἰουδαῖοι
as in secret. Therefore the Jews
ἐζήτουν αὐτὸν ἐν τῇ ἑορτῇ καὶ ἔλεγον·
sought him at the feast and said:
ποῦ ἐστιν ἐκεῖνος; 12 καὶ γογγυσμὸς περὶ
Where is that man? And [3]murmuring [4]about
αὐτοῦ ἦν πολὺς ἐν τοῖς ὄχλοις· οἱ μὲν
[5]him [1]there was [2]much in the crowds; some
ἔλεγον ὅτι ἀγαθός ἐστιν· ἄλλοι [δὲ]
said[,] – A good man he is; but others
ἔλεγον· οὔ, ἀλλὰ πλανᾷ τὸν ὄχλον.
said: No, but he deceives the crowd.
13 οὐδεὶς μέντοι παρρησίᾳ ἐλάλει περὶ
No one however openly spoke about
αὐτοῦ διὰ τὸν φόβον τῶν Ἰουδαίων.
him because of the fear of the Jews.
14 Ἤδη δὲ τῆς ἑορτῆς μεσούσης ἀνέβη
But now the feast being in [its] middle[a] went up
[a] = in the middle of the feast
Ἰησοῦς εἰς τὸ ἱερὸν καὶ ἐδίδασκεν.
Jesus to the temple and taught.
15 ἐθαύμαζον οὖν οἱ Ἰουδαῖοι λέγοντες·
Marvelled therefore the Jews saying:
πῶς οὗτος γράμματα οἶδεν μὴ μεμαθηκώς;
How this man letters knows not having learned?
16 ἀπεκρίθη οὖν αὐτοῖς Ἰησοῦς καὶ εἶπεν·
Answered therefore them Jesus and said:

ought to leave here and go
to Judea, so that your disciples may see the miracles
you do. 4No one who wants
to become a public figure
acts in secret. Since you
are doing these things,
show yourself to the
world." 5For even his own
brothers did not believe in
him.
6Therefore Jesus told
them, "The right time for
me has not yet come; for
you any time is right. 7The
world cannot hate you, but
it hates me because I testify
that what it does is evil.
8You go to the Feast. I am
not yet[l] going up to this
Feast, because for me the
right time has not yet
come." 9Having said this,
he stayed in Galilee.
10However, after his
brothers had left for the
Feast, he went also, not
publicly, but in secret.
11Now at the Feast the
Jews were watching for
him and asking, "Where is
that man?"
12Among the crowds
there was widespread whispering about him. Some
said, "He is a good man."
Others replied, "No, he
deceives the people."
13But no one would say
anything publicly about
him for fear of the Jews.

Jesus Teaches at the Feast

14Not until halfway
through the Feast did Jesus
go up to the temple courts
and begin to teach. 15The
Jews were amazed and
asked, "How did this man
get such learning without
having studied?"
16Jesus answered, "My

[l]8 Some early manuscripts do not have *yet*.

"My teaching is not Mine,
but His who sent Me.
17 "If any man is willing to
do His will, he shall know
of the teaching, whether it
is of God, or *whether* I
speak from Myself.
18 "He who speaks from
himself seeks his own
glory; but He who is seeking the glory of the one who
sent Him, He is true, and
there is no unrighteousness
in Him.
19 "Did not Moses give
you the Law, and *yet* none
of you carries out the Law?
Why do you seek to kill
Me?"
20 The multitude an-
swered, "You have a de-
mon! Who seeks to kill
You?"
21 Jesus answered and
said to them, "I did one
deed, and you all marvel.
22 "On this account
Moses has given you cir-
cumcision (not because it is
from Moses, but from the
fathers), and on *the* Sabbath you circumcise a man.
23 "If a man receives circumcision on *the* Sabbath
that the Law of Moses may
not be broken, are you angry with Me because I
made an entire man well on
the Sabbath?
24 "Do not judge accord-
ing to appearance, but
judge with righteous judgment."
25 Therefore some of the
people of Jerusalem were
saying, "Is this not the man
whom they are seeking to
kill?
26 "And look, He is
speaking publicly, and they
are saying nothing to Him.
The rulers do not really
know that this is the Christ,
do they?
27 "However, we know
where this man is from; but
whenever the Christ may
come, no one knows where
He is from."
28 Jesus therefore cried
out in the temple, teaching

ἡ ἐμὴ διδαχὴ οὐκ ἔστιν ἐμὴ ἀλλὰ τοῦ
The my teaching is not mine but of the
πέμψαντός με· 17 ἐάν τις θέλῃ τὸ θέλημα
[one] having sent me; if anyone wishes the will
αὐτοῦ ποιεῖν, γνώσεται περὶ τῆς διδαχῆς,
of him to do, he will know concerning the teaching,
πότερον ἐκ τοῦ θεοῦ ἐστιν ἢ ἐγὼ ἀπ'
whether of – God it is or I from
ἐμαυτοῦ λαλῶ. 18 ὁ ἀφ' ἑαυτοῦ λαλῶν
myself speak. The [one] from himself speaking
τὴν δόξαν τὴν ἰδίαν ζητεῖ· ὁ δὲ ζητῶν
his own glory seeks; but the [one] seeking
τὴν δόξαν τοῦ πέμψαντος αὐτόν, οὗτος
the glory of the [one] having sent him, this man
ἀληθής ἐστιν καὶ ἀδικία ἐν αὐτῷ οὐκ
true is and unrighteousness in him not
ἔστιν. 19 οὐ Μωϋσῆς ἔδωκεν ὑμῖν τὸν
is. Not Moses gave you the
νόμον; καὶ οὐδεὶς ἐξ ὑμῶν ποιεῖ τὸν
law? and no one of you does the
νόμον. τί με ζητεῖτε ἀποκτεῖναι;
law. Why me seek ye to kill?
20 ἀπεκρίθη ὁ ὄχλος· δαιμόνιον ἔχεις·
Answered the crowd: A demon thou hast;
τίς σε ζητεῖ ἀποκτεῖναι; 21 ἀπεκρίθη
who thee seeks to kill? Answered
Ἰησοῦς καὶ εἶπεν αὐτοῖς· ἓν ἔργον ἐποίησα
Jesus and said to them: One work I did
καὶ πάντες θαυμάζετε. 22 διὰ τοῦτο
and all ye marvel. Because of this
Μωϋσῆς δέδωκεν ὑμῖν τὴν περιτομήν, —
Moses has given you – circumcision, —
οὐχ ὅτι ἐκ τοῦ Μωϋσέως ἐστὶν ἀλλ' ἐκ
not that of – Moses it is but of
τῶν πατέρων, — καὶ ἐν σαββάτῳ
the fathers, — and on a sabbath
περιτέμνετε ἄνθρωπον 23 εἰ περιτομὴν
ye circumcise a man. If [3]circumcision
λαμβάνει [ὁ] ἄνθρωπος ἐν σαββάτῳ ἵνα
[2]receives – [1]a man on a sabbath that
μὴ λυθῇ ὁ νόμος Μωϋσέως, ἐμοὶ χολᾶτε,
is not broken the law of Moses, with me are ye angry
ὅτι ὅλον ἄνθρωπον ὑγιῆ ἐποίησα ἐν
because a whole man healthy I made on
σαββάτῳ; 24 μὴ κρίνετε κατ' ὄψιν, ἀλλὰ
a sabbath? Judge not according to face, but
τὴν δικαίαν κρίσιν κρίνατε. 25 Ἔλεγον
– righteous judgment judge. Said
οὖν τινες ἐκ τῶν Ἱεροσολυμιτῶν· οὐχ
therefore some of the Jerusalemites: [2]Not
οὗτός ἐστιν ὃν ζητοῦσιν ἀποκτεῖναι; 26 καὶ
[3]this man [1]is it whom they are seeking to kill? and
ἴδε παρρησίᾳ λαλεῖ, καὶ οὐδὲν αὐτῷ
behold openly he speaks, and nothing to him
λέγουσιν. μήποτε ἀληθῶς ἔγνωσαν οἱ
they say. Perhaps indeed knew the
ἄρχοντες ὅτι οὗτός ἐστιν ὁ χριστός;
rulers that this is the Christ? *
27 ἀλλὰ τοῦτον οἴδαμεν πόθεν ἐστίν· ὁ δὲ
But this man we know whence he is; but [2]the
χριστὸς ὅταν ἔρχηται, οὐδεὶς γινώσκει
[3]Christ [1]when comes, no one knows
πόθεν ἐστίν. 28 ἔκραξεν οὖν ἐν τῷ ἱερῷ
whence he is. [3]Cried out [2]therefore [4]in [5]the [6]temple

* As this question is introduced by μήποτε, a negative answer is expected; see page xiii, and note ver. 31 below.

teaching is not my own. It
comes from him who sent
me. 17 If anyone chooses to
do God's will, he will find
out whether my teaching
comes from God or wheth-
er I speak on my own. 18 He
who speaks on his own
does so to gain honor for
himself, but he who works
for the honor of the one
who sent him is a man of
truth; there is nothing false
about him. 19 Has not Mo-
ses given you the law? Yet
not one of you keeps the
law. Why are you trying to
kill me?"
20 "You are demon-pos-
sessed," the crowd an-
swered. "Who is trying to
kill you?"
21 Jesus said to them, "I
did one miracle, and you
are all astonished. 22 Yet,
because Moses gave you
circumcision (though actually it did not come from
Moses, but from the patriarchs), you circumcise a
child on the Sabbath.
23 Now if a child can be circumcised on the Sabbath
so that the law of Moses
may not be broken, why
are you angry with me for
healing the whole man on
the Sabbath? 24 Stop judging by mere appearances,
and make a right judg-
ment."

Is Jesus the Christ?

25 At that point some of
the people of Jerusalem began to ask, "Isn't this the
man they are trying to kill?
26 Here he is, speaking publicly, and they are not saying a word to him. Have the
authorities really concluded that he is the Christ[m]?
27 But we know where this
man is from; when the
Christ comes, no one will
know where he is from."
28 Then Jesus, still teaching in the temple courts,

[m]26 Or *Messiah*; also in verses 27, 31, 41 and 42

and saying, "You both know Me and know where I am from; and I have not come of Myself, but He who sent Me is true, whom you do not know.

29"I know Him; because I am from Him, and He sent Me."

30They were seeking therefore to seize Him; and no man laid his hand on Him, because His hour had not yet come.

31But many of the multitude believed in Him; and they were saying, "When the Christ shall come, He will not perform more signs than those which this man has, will He?"

32The Pharisees heard the multitude muttering these things about Him; and the chief priests and the Pharisees sent officers to seize Him.

33Jesus therefore said, "For a little while longer I am with you, then I go to Him who sent Me.

34"You shall seek Me, and shall not find Me; and where I am, you cannot come."

35The Jews therefore said to one another, "Where does this man intend to go that we shall not find Him? He is not intending to go to the Dispersion among the Greeks, and teach the Greeks, is He?

36"What is this statement that He said, 'You will seek Me, and will not find Me; and where I am, you cannot come'?"

37Now on the last day, the great *day* of the feast, Jesus stood and cried out, saying, "If any man is thirsty, let him come to Me and drink.

38"He who believes in Me, as the Scripture said, 'From his innermost being

διδάσκων ὁ Ἰησοῦς καὶ λέγων· κἀμὲ
[7]teaching – [1]Jesus [8]and [9]saying : Both me

οἴδατε καὶ οἴδατε πόθεν εἰμί· καὶ ἀπ'
ye know and ye know whence I am; and from

ἐμαυτοῦ οὐκ ἐλήλυθα, ἀλλ' ἔστιν ἀληθινὸς
myself I have not come, but he is true

ὁ πέμψας με, ὃν ὑμεῖς οὐκ οἴδατε·
the [one] having sent me, whom ye know not;

29 ἐγὼ οἶδα αὐτόν, ὅτι παρ' αὐτοῦ εἰμι
I know him, because [2]from [3]him [1]I am

κἀκεῖνός με ἀπέστειλεν. 30 Ἐζήτουν οὖν
[4]and that one [6]me [5]sent. They sought therefore

αὐτὸν πιάσαι, καὶ οὐδεὶς ἐπέβαλεν ἐπ'
him to arrest, and no one laid *on* on

αὐτὸν τὴν χεῖρα, ὅτι οὔπω ἐληλύθει ἡ
him the hand, because not yet had come the

ὥρα αὐτοῦ. 31 Ἐκ τοῦ ὄχλου δὲ πολλοὶ
hour of him. [3]of [4]the [5]crowd [1]But [2]many

ἐπίστευσαν εἰς αὐτόν, καὶ ἔλεγον· ὁ
believed in him, and said : [2]The

χριστὸς ὅταν ἔλθῃ, μὴ πλείονα σημεῖα
[3]Christ [1]when [4]comes, *not* more signs

ποιήσει ὧν οὗτος ἐποίησεν; 32 ἤκουσαν
will he do [than] which this man did? [3]Heard

οἱ Φαρισαῖοι τοῦ ὄχλου γογγύζοντος περὶ
[1]the [2]Pharisees [4]the [5]crowd [6]murmuring [8]about

αὐτοῦ ταῦτα, καὶ ἀπέστειλαν οἱ ἀρχιερεῖς
[9]him [7]these things, and [6]sent [1]the [2]chief priests

καὶ οἱ Φαρισαῖοι ὑπηρέτας ἵνα πιάσωσιν
[3]and [4]the [5]Pharisees [7]attendants that they might arrest

αὐτόν. 33 εἶπεν οὖν ὁ Ἰησοῦς· ἔτι
him. Said therefore – Jesus : Yet

χρόνον μικρὸν μεθ' ὑμῶν εἰμι καὶ ὑπάγω
time a little with you I am and I go

πρὸς τὸν πέμψαντά με. 34 ζητήσετέ με
to the [one] having sent me. Ye will seek me

καὶ οὐχ εὑρήσετε, καὶ ὅπου εἰμὶ ἐγὼ
and will not find, and where am I

ὑμεῖς οὐ δύνασθε ἐλθεῖν. 35 εἶπον οὖν
ye cannot *to* come. Said therefore

οἱ Ἰουδαῖοι πρὸς ἑαυτούς· ποῦ οὗτος
the Jews to themselves : Where this man

μέλλει πορεύεσθαι, ὅτι ἡμεῖς οὐχ εὑρήσομεν
is about to go, that we will not find

αὐτόν; μὴ εἰς τὴν διασπορὰν τῶν Ἑλλήνων
him? *not* to the dispersion of the Greeks

μέλλει πορεύεσθαι καὶ διδάσκειν τοὺς
is he about to go and to teach the

Ἕλληνας; 36 τίς ἐστιν ὁ λόγος οὗτος
Greeks? What is – word this

ὃν εἶπεν· ζητήσετέ με καὶ οὐχ εὑρήσετε,
which he said : Ye will seek me and will not find,

καὶ ὅπου εἰμὶ ἐγὼ ὑμεῖς οὐ δύνασθε
and where am I ye cannot

ἐλθεῖν;
to come?

37 Ἐν δὲ τῇ ἐσχάτῃ ἡμέρᾳ τῇ μεγάλῃ
Now in the last day the great [day]

τῆς ἑορτῆς εἱστήκει ὁ Ἰησοῦς καὶ ἔκραξεν
of the feast stood – Jesus and cried out

λέγων· ἐάν τις διψᾷ, ἐρχέσθω πρός με
saying : If anyone thirsts, let him come to me

καὶ πινέτω. 38 ὁ πιστεύων εἰς ἐμέ,
and drink. The [one] believing in me,

καθὼς εἶπεν ἡ γραφή, ποταμοὶ ἐκ τῆς
as said the scripture, [1]rivers [5]out of [6]the

cried out, "Yes, you know me, and you know where I am from. I am not here on my own, but he who sent me is true. You do not know him, 29but I know him because I am from him and he sent me."

30At this they tried to seize him, but no one laid a hand on him, because his time had not yet come.
31Still, many in the crowd put their faith in him. They said, "When the Christ comes, will he do more miraculous signs than this man?"

32The Pharisees heard the crowd whispering such things about him. Then the chief priests and the Pharisees sent temple guards to arrest him.

33Jesus said, "I am with you for only a short time, and then I go to the one who sent me. 34You will look for me, but you will not find me; and where I am, you cannot come."

35The Jews said to one another, "Where does this man intend to go that we cannot find him? Will he go where our people live scattered among the Greeks, and teach the Greeks?
36What did he mean when he said, 'You will look for me, but you will not find me,' and 'Where I am, you cannot come'?"

37On the last and greatest day of the Feast, Jesus stood and said in a loud voice, "If anyone is thirsty, let him come to me and drink. 38Whoever believes in me, as[n] the Scripture has said, streams of

[n]37,38 Or / *If anyone is thirsty, let him come to me. / And let him drink,* [38]*who believes in me. / As*

shall flow rivers of living
water.' "
39But this He spoke of the
Spirit, whom those who believed in Him were to re-
ceive; for the Spirit was not
yet *given,* because Jesus
was not yet glorified.

Division of People over Jesus

40*Some* of the multitude
therefore, when they heard
these words, were saying,
"This certainly is the
Prophet."
41Others were saying,
"This is the Christ." Still
others were saying, "Surely the Christ is not going to
come from Galilee, is He?
42"Has not the Scripture
said that the Christ comes
from the offspring of Da-
vid, and from Bethlehem,
the village where David
was?"
43So there arose a divi-
sion in the multitude be-
cause of Him.
44And some of them
wanted to seize Him, but
no one laid hands on Him.
45The officers therefore
came to the chief priests
and Pharisees, and they
said to them, "Why did you
not bring Him?"
46The officers answered,
"Never did a man speak
the way this man speaks."
47The Pharisees therefore
answered them, "You have
not also been led astray,
have you?
48"No one of the rulers or
Pharisees has believed in
Him, has he?
49"But this multitude
which does not know the
Law is accursed."
50Nicodemus *said to
them (he who came to Him
before, being one of them),
51"Our Law does not
judge a man, unless it first
hears from him and knows
what he is doing, does it?"
52They answered and said
to him, "You are not also
from Galilee, are you?
Search, and see that no

κοιλίας αὐτοῦ ῥεύσουσιν ὕδατος ζῶντος.
[7]belly [8]of him [4]will flow [5]water [6]of living.

39 τοῦτο δὲ εἶπεν περὶ τοῦ πνεύματος
But this he said concerning the Spirit

οὗ ἔμελλον λαμβάνειν οἱ πιστεύσαντες
whom were about to receive the [ones] believing

εἰς αὐτόν· οὔπω γὰρ ἦν πνεῦμα, ὅτι
in him; for not yet was [?the] Spirit, because

Ἰησοῦς οὐδέπω ἐδοξάσθη. **40** Ἐκ τοῦ
Jesus not yet was glorified. [Some] of the

ὄχλου οὖν ἀκούσαντες τῶν λόγων τούτων
crowd therefore hearing – words these

ἔλεγον [ὅτι]· οὗτός ἐστιν ἀληθῶς ὁ
said – : This man is truly the

προφήτης· **41** ἄλλοι ἔλεγον· οὗτός ἐστιν ὁ
prophet; Others said : This man is the

χριστός· οἱ δὲ ἔλεγον· μὴ γὰρ ἐκ τῆς
Christ; But others† said : *Not* then out of –

Γαλιλαίας ὁ χριστὸς ἔρχεται; **42** οὐχ ἡ
Galilee the Christ comes? not the

γραφὴ εἶπεν ὅτι ἐκ τοῦ σπέρματος Δαυίδ,
scripture said that of the seed of David,

καὶ ἀπὸ Βηθλέεμ τῆς κώμης ὅπου ἦν
and from Bethlehem the village where was

Δαυίδ, ἔρχεται ὁ χριστός; **43** σχίσμα
David, comes the Christ? A division

οὖν ἐγένετο ἐν τῷ ὄχλῳ δι' αὐτόν·
therefore became in the crowd because of him;

44 τινὲς δὲ ἤθελον ἐξ αὐτῶν πιάσαι αὐτόν,
and [1]some [4]wished [2]of [3]them to arrest him,

ἀλλ' οὐδεὶς ἐπέβαλεν ἐπ' αὐτὸν τὰς χεῖρας.
but no one laid *on* on him the(his) hands.

45 Ἦλθον οὖν οἱ ὑπηρέται πρὸς τοὺς
Came therefore the attendants to the

ἀρχιερεῖς καὶ Φαρισαίους, καὶ εἶπον αὐτοῖς
chief priests and Pharisees, and [2]said [3]to them

ἐκεῖνοι· διὰ τί οὐκ ἠγάγετε αὐτόν;
[1]those: Why did ye not bring him?

46 ἀπεκρίθησαν οἱ ὑπηρέται· οὐδέποτε
Answered the attendants : Never

ἐλάλησεν οὕτως ἄνθρωπος, ὡς οὗτος λαλεῖ
spoke so a man, as [1]this [3]speaks

ὁ ἄνθρωπος. **47** ἀπεκρίθησαν οὖν αὐτοῖς
– [2]man. Answered therefore them

οἱ Φαρισαῖοι· μὴ καὶ ὑμεῖς πεπλάνησθε;
the Pharisees : *Not* also ye have been deceived?

48 μή τις ἐκ τῶν ἀρχόντων ἐπίστευσεν
not anyone of the rulers believed

εἰς αὐτὸν ἢ ἐκ τῶν Φαρισαίων; **49** ἀλλὰ
in him or of the Pharisees? But

ὁ ὄχλος οὗτος ὁ μὴ γινώσκων τὸν
– crowd this – not knowing the

νόμον ἐπάρατοί εἰσιν. **50** λέγει Νικόδημος
law cursed are. Says Nicodemus

πρὸς αὐτούς, ὁ ἐλθὼν πρὸς αὐτὸν πρότερον,
to them, the [one] having come to him firstly,

εἷς ὢν ἐξ αὐτῶν· **51** μὴ ὁ νόμος ἡμῶν
[2]one [1]being of them : *Not* the law of us

κρίνει τὸν ἄνθρωπον ἐὰν μὴ ἀκούσῃ
judges the man unless it hears

πρῶτον παρ' αὐτοῦ καὶ γνῷ τί ποιεῖ;
first from him and knows what he does?

52 ἀπεκρίθησαν καὶ εἶπαν αὐτῷ· μὴ καὶ
They answered and said to him : *Not* also

σὺ ἐκ τῆς Γαλιλαίας εἶ; ἐρεύνησον καὶ
thou of – Galilee art? search and

living water will flow from
within him." 39By this he
meant the Spirit, whom
those who believed in him
were later to receive. Up to
that time the Spirit had not
been given, since Jesus had
not yet been glorified.
40On hearing his words,
some of the people said,
"Surely this man is the
Prophet."
41Others said, "He is the
Christ."
Still others asked, "How
can the Christ come from
Galilee? 42Does not the
Scripture say that the
Christ will come from Da-
vid's family[o] and from
Bethlehem, the town where
David lived?" 43Thus the
people were divided be-
cause of Jesus. 44Some
wanted to seize him, but no
one laid a hand on him.

Unbelief of the Jewish Leaders

45Finally the temple
guards went back to the
chief priests and Pharisees,
who asked them, "Why
didn't you bring him in?"
46"No one ever spoke the
way this man does," the
guards declared.
47"You mean he has de-
ceived you also?" the Pharisees retorted. 48"Has any
of the rulers or of the Pharisees believed in him? 49No!
But this mob that knows
nothing of the law—there
is a curse on them."
50Nicodemus, who had
gone to Jesus earlier and
who was one of their own
number, asked, 51"Does
our law condemn anyone
without first hearing him to
find out what he is doing?"
52They replied, "Are you
from Galilee, too? Look

[o]42 Greek *seed*

prophet arises out of Galilee."

53[[r]And everyone went to his home.

Chapter 8

The Adulterous Woman

BUT Jesus went to the Mount of Olives.

2And early in the morning He came again into the temple, and all the people were coming to Him; and He sat down and *began* to teach them.

3And the scribes and the Pharisees *brought a woman caught in adultery, and having set her in the midst,

4they *said to Him, "Teacher, this woman has been caught in adultery, in the very act.

5"Now in the Law Moses commanded us to stone such women; what then do You say?"

6And they were saying this, testing Him, in order that they might have grounds for accusing Him. But Jesus stooped down, and with His finger wrote on the ground.

7But when they persisted in asking Him, He straightened up, and said to them, "He who is without sin among you, let him *be the* first to throw a stone at her."

8And again He stooped down, and wrote on the ground.

9And when they heard it, they *began* to go out one by one, beginning with the older ones, and He was left alone, and the woman, where she was, in the midst.

10And straightening up, Jesus said to her, "Woman, where are they? Did no one condemn you?"

11And she said, "No one, Lord." And Jesus said, "Neither do I condemn you; go your way. From now on sin no more."]

Jesus Is the Light of the World

12Again therefore Jesus spoke to them, saying, "I am the light of the world; he who follows Me shall not walk in the darkness, but

[r]John 7:53–8:11 is not found in most of the old mss.

ἴδε ὅτι ἐκ τῆς Γαλιλαίας προφήτης οὐκ
see that out of – Galilee a prophet not

ἐγείρεται.
is raised.

53 Καὶ ἐπορεύθησαν ἕκαστος εἰς τὸν οἶκον
And they went each one to the house

αὐτοῦ, 8 Ἰησοῦς δὲ ἐπορεύθη εἰς τὸ
of him, but Jesus went to the

Ὄρος τῶν Ἐλαιῶν. 2 Ὄρθρου δὲ πάλιν
Mount of the Olives. And at dawn again

παρεγένετο εἰς τὸ ἱερόν [, καὶ πᾶς ὁ
he arrived in the temple, and all the

λαὸς ἤρχετο πρὸς αὐτόν, καὶ καθίσας
people came to him, and sitting

ἐδίδασκεν αὐτούς]. 3 Ἄγουσιν δὲ οἱ
he taught them. And lead the

γραμματεῖς καὶ οἱ Φαρισαῖοι γυναῖκα ἐπὶ
scribes and the Pharisees a woman in

μοιχείᾳ κατειλημμένην, καὶ στήσαντες αὐτὴν
adultery *having been* caught, and standing her

ἐν μέσῳ 4 λέγουσιν αὐτῷ Διδάσκαλε,
in [the] midst they say to him[,] Teacher,

αὕτη ἡ γυνὴ κατείληπται ἐπ' αὐτοφώρῳ
this – woman has been caught in the act

μοιχευομένη· 5 ἐν δὲ τῷ νόμῳ [ἡμῖν]
committing adultery; now in the law to us[e]

Μωυσῆς ἐνετείλατο τὰς τοιαύτας λιθάζειν·
Moses enjoined – [2]such [1]to stone;

σὺ οὖν τί λέγεις; 6 [τοῦτο δὲ ἔλεγον
thou therefore what sayest thou? But this they said

πειράζοντες αὐτόν, ἵνα ἔχωσιν κατηγορεῖν
tempting him, that they might have to accuse

αὐτοῦ.] ὁ δὲ Ἰησοῦς κάτω κύψας τῷ
him. – But Jesus down stooping with the

δακτύλῳ κατέγραφεν εἰς τὴν γῆν. 7 ὡς δὲ
finger wrote in the earth. But as

ἐπέμενον ἐρωτῶντες [αὐτόν], ἀνέκυψεν καὶ
they remained questioning him, he stood erect and

εἶπεν [αὐτοῖς] Ὁ ἀναμάρτητος ὑμῶν
said to them[,] The [one] sinless of you

πρῶτος ἐπ' αὐτὴν βαλέτω λίθον. 8 καὶ
first on her let him cast a stone. And

πάλιν κατακύψας ἔγραφεν εἰς τὴν γῆν.
again stooping down he wrote in the earth.

9 οἱ δὲ ἀκούσαντες ἐξήρχοντο εἷς καθ'
And they hearing went out one by

εἷς ἀρξάμενοι ἀπὸ τῶν πρεσβυτέρων, καὶ
one beginning from the older ones, and

κατελείφθη μόνος, καὶ ἡ γυνὴ ἐν μέσῳ
he was left alone, and the woman in [the] midst

οὖσα. 10 ἀνακύψας δὲ ὁ Ἰησοῦς εἶπεν
being. And standing erect – Jesus said

αὐτῇ Γύναι, ποῦ εἰσιν; οὐδείς σε κατέκρινεν;
to her[,] Woman, where are they? no one thee condemned?

11 ἡ δὲ εἶπεν Οὐδείς, κύριε. εἶπεν δὲ
And she said[,] No one, sir. So said

ὁ Ἰησοῦς Οὐδὲ ἐγώ σε κατακρίνω·
– Jesus[,] Neither I thee condemn;

πορεύου, ἀπὸ τοῦ νῦν μηκέτι ἁμάρτανε.
go, from – now no longer sin.

12 Πάλιν οὖν αὐτοῖς ἐλάλησεν ὁ Ἰησοῦς
Again therefore to them spoke – Jesus

λέγων· ἐγώ εἰμι τὸ φῶς τοῦ κόσμου·
saying: I am the light of the world;

ὁ ἀκολουθῶν μοι οὐ μὴ περιπατήσῃ ἐν
the [one] following me by no means will walk in

into it, and you will find
that a prophet[p] does not
come out of Galilee."

[The earliest and most reliable manuscripts and other ancient witnesses do not have John 7:53–8:11.]

53Then each went to his
own home.

Chapter 8

BUT Jesus went to the
Mount of Olives. 2At
dawn he appeared again in
the temple courts, where
all the people gathered
around him, and he sat
down to teach them. 3The
teachers of the law and the
Pharisees brought in a
woman caught in adultery.
They made her stand be-
fore the group 4and said to
Jesus, "Teacher, this woman was caught in the act of
adultery. 5In the Law Mo-
ses commanded us to stone
such women. Now what do
you say?" 6They were us-
ing this question as a trap,
in order to have a basis for
accusing him.
But Jesus bent down and
started to write on the
ground with his finger.
7When they kept on ques-
tioning him, he straight-
ened up and said to them,
"If any one of you is without sin, let him be the first
to throw a stone at her."
8Again he stooped down
and wrote on the ground.
9At this, those who heard
began to go away one at a
time, the older ones first,
until only Jesus was left,
with the woman still standing there. 10Jesus straightened up and asked her,
"Woman, where are they?
Has no one condemned
you?"
11"No one, sir," she said.
"Then neither do I con-
demn you," Jesus de-
clared. "Go now and leave
your life of sin."

The Validity of Jesus' Testimony

12When Jesus spoke again
to the people, he said, "I
am the light of the world.
Whoever follows me will
never walk in darkness, but

[p]52 Two early manuscripts *the Prophet*

shall have the light of life."
13The Pharisees therefore
said to Him, "You are
bearing witness of Your-
self; Your witness is not
true."
14Jesus answered and
said to them, "Even if I
bear witness of Myself, My
witness is true; for I know
where I came from, and
where I am going; but you
do not know where I come
from, or where I am going.
15"You people judge ac-
cording to the flesh; I am
not judging anyone.
16"But even if I do judge,
My judgment is true; for I
am not alone *in it*, but I and
[s]He who sent Me.
17"Even in your law it has
been written, that the testimony of two men is true.
18"I am He who bears
witness of Myself, and the
Father who sent Me bears
witness of Me."
19And so they were say-
ing to Him, "Where is
Your Father?" Jesus an-
swered, "You know
neither Me, nor My Father;
if you knew Me, you would
know My Father also."
20These words He spoke
in the treasury, as He
taught in the temple; and no
one seized Him, because
His hour had not yet come.
21He said therefore again
to them, "I go away, and
you shall seek Me, and
shall die in your sin; where
I am going, you cannot
come."
22Therefore the Jews
were saying, "Surely He
will not kill Himself, will
He, since He says, 'Where
I am going, you cannot
come'?"
23And He was saying to
them, "You are from
below, I am from above;

τῇ σκοτίᾳ, ἀλλ' ἕξει τὸ φῶς τῆς ζωῆς.
the darkness, but will have the light – of life.
13 εἶπον οὖν αὐτῷ οἱ Φαρισαῖοι· σὺ περὶ
Said therefore to him the Pharisees; Thou concerning
σεαυτοῦ μαρτυρεῖς· ἡ μαρτυρία σου οὐκ
thyself witnessest; the witness of thee not
ἔστιν ἀληθής. **14** ἀπεκρίθη Ἰησοῦς καὶ
is true. Answered Jesus and
εἶπεν αὐτοῖς· κἂν ἐγὼ μαρτυρῶ περὶ
said to them: Even if I witness concerning
ἐμαυτοῦ, ἀληθής ἐστιν ἡ μαρτυρία μου,
myself, true is the witness of me,
ὅτι οἶδα πόθεν ἦλθον καὶ ποῦ ὑπάγω·
because I know whence I came and where I go;
ὑμεῖς δὲ οὐκ οἴδατε πόθεν ἔρχομαι ἢ
but ye know not whence I come or
ποῦ ὑπάγω. **15** ὑμεῖς κατὰ τὴν σάρκα
where I go. Ye according to the flesh
κρίνετε, ἐγὼ οὐ κρίνω οὐδένα. **16** καὶ
judge, I judge not no(any)one. [2]even
ἐὰν κρίνω δὲ ἐγώ, ἡ κρίσις ἡ ἐμὴ
[3]if [5]judge [1]But [4]I, *the* [2]judgment – [1]my
ἀληθινή ἐστιν, ὅτι μόνος οὐκ εἰμί, ἀλλ'
true is, because alone I am not, but
ἐγὼ καὶ ὁ πέμψας με. **17** καὶ ἐν τῷ
I and the [one] having sent me. [2]even [3]in *the*
νόμῳ δὲ τῷ ὑμετέρῳ γέγραπται ὅτι δύο
[5]law [1]And – [4]your it has been written that of two
ἀνθρώπων ἡ μαρτυρία ἀληθής ἐστιν.
men the witness true is.
18 ἐγώ εἰμι ὁ μαρτυρῶν περὶ ἐμαυτοῦ,
I am the [one] witnessing concerning myself,
καὶ μαρτυρεῖ περὶ ἐμοῦ ὁ πέμψας με
and witnesses concerning me [1]the [3]having sent [4]me
πατήρ. **19** ἔλεγον οὖν αὐτῷ· ποῦ ἐστιν ὁ
[2]Father. They said therefore to him: Where is the
πατήρ σου; ἀπεκρίθη Ἰησοῦς· οὔτε ἐμὲ
Father of thee? Answered Jesus: Neither me
οἴδατε οὔτε τὸν πατέρα μου· εἰ ἐμὲ
ye know nor the Father of me; if me
ᾔδειτε, καὶ τὸν πατέρα μου ἂν ᾔδειτε.
ye knew, also the Father of me ye would have known.
20 Ταῦτα τὰ ῥήματα ἐλάλησεν ἐν τῷ
These – words he spoke in the
γαζοφυλακείῳ διδάσκων ἐν τῷ ἱερῷ· καὶ
treasury teaching in the temple; and
οὐδεὶς ἐπίασεν αὐτόν, ὅτι οὔπω ἐληλύθει
no one seized him, because not yet had come
ἡ ὥρα αὐτοῦ.
the hour of him.
21 Εἶπεν οὖν πάλιν αὐτοῖς· ἐγὼ ὑπάγω
He said therefore again to them: I go
καὶ ζητήσετέ με, καὶ ἐν τῇ ἁμαρτίᾳ
and ye will seek me, and in the sin
ὑμῶν ἀποθανεῖσθε· ὅπου ἐγὼ ὑπάγω ὑμεῖς
of you ye will die; where I go ye
οὐ δύνασθε ἐλθεῖν. **22** ἔλεγον οὖν οἱ
cannot *to* come. Said therefore the
Ἰουδαῖοι· μήτι ἀποκτενεῖ ἑαυτόν, ὅτι
Jews: *Not* will he kill himself, because
λέγει· ὅπου ἐγὼ ὑπάγω ὑμεῖς οὐ δύνασθε
he says: Where I go ye cannot
ἐλθεῖν; **23** καὶ ἔλεγεν αὐτοῖς· ὑμεῖς ἐκ
to come? And he said to them: Ye of
τῶν κάτω ἐστέ, ἐγὼ ἐκ τῶν ἄνω εἰμί·
the things below are, I of the things above am;

will have the light of life."
13The Pharisees chal-
lenged him, "Here you are,
appearing as your own witness; your testimony is not
valid."
14Jesus answered, "Even
if I testify on my own behalf, my testimony is valid,
for I know where I came
from and where I am going.
But you have no idea where
I come from or where I am
going. 15You judge by hu-
man standards; I pass judgment on no one. 16But if I
do judge, my decisions are
right, because I am not
alone. I stand with the Father, who sent me. 17In
your own Law it is written
that the testimony of two
men is valid. 18I am one
who testifies for myself; my
other witness is the Father,
who sent me."
19Then they asked him,
"Where is your father?"
"You do not know me or
my Father," Jesus replied.
"If you knew me, you
would know my Father
also." 20He spoke these
words while teaching in the
temple area near the place
where the offerings were
put. Yet no one seized him,
because his time had not
yet come.
21Once more Jesus said to
them, "I am going away,
and you will look for me,
and you will die in your sin.
Where I go, you cannot
come."
22This made the Jews ask,
"Will he kill himself? Is
that why he says, 'Where I
go, you cannot come'?"
23But he continued, "You
are from below; I am from
above. You are of this

[s]Many ancient mss. read *the Father who sent Me*

you are of this world, I am
not of this world.
24"I said therefore to
you, that you shall die in
your sins; for unless you
believe that I am *He*, you
shall die in your sins."
25And so they were say-
ing to Him, "Who are
You?" Jesus said to them,
"What have I been saying
to you *from* the beginning?
26"I have many things to
speak and to judge con-
cerning you, but He who
sent Me is true; and the
things which I heard from
Him, these I speak to the
world."
27They did not realize
that He had been speaking
to them about the Father.
28Jesus therefore said,
"When you lift up the Son
of Man, then you will know
that I am *He*, and I do nothing on My own initiative,
but I speak these things as
the Father taught Me.
29"And He who sent Me
is with Me; He has not left
Me alone, for I always do
the things that are pleasing
to Him."
30As He spoke these
things, many came to be-
lieve in Him.

The Truth Shall Make You Free

31Jesus therefore was
saying to those Jews who
had believed Him, "If you
abide in My word, *then* you
are truly disciples of Mine;
32and you shall know the
truth, and the truth shall
make you free."
33They answered Him,
"We are Abraham's off-
spring, and have never yet
been enslaved to anyone;
how is it that You say, 'You
shall become free'?"
34Jesus answered them,
"Truly, truly, I say to you,
everyone who commits sin
is the slave of sin.
35"And the slave does not
remain in the house for-

ὑμεῖς ἐκ τούτου τοῦ κόσμου ἐστέ, ἐγὼ
ye of this – world are, I
οὐκ εἰμὶ ἐκ τοῦ κόσμου τούτου. 24 εἶπον
am not of – world this. I said
οὖν ὑμῖν ὅτι ἀποθανεῖσθε ἐν ταῖς ἁμαρτίαις
therefore to you that ye will die in the sins
ὑμῶν· ἐὰν γὰρ μὴ πιστεύσητε ὅτι ἐγώ
of you; for if ye believe not that I
εἰμι, ἀποθανεῖσθε ἐν ταῖς ἁμαρτίαις ὑμῶν.
am, ye will die in the sins of you.
25 ἔλεγον οὖν αὐτῷ· σὺ τίς εἶ; εἶπεν
They said therefore to him: [2]Thou [1]who [3]art? Said
αὐτοῖς ὁ Ἰησοῦς· τὴν ἀρχὴν ὅ τι καὶ
to them – Jesus: [5]at all † [1]Why [2]indeed
λαλῶ ὑμῖν; 26 πολλὰ ἔχω περὶ ὑμῶν
[3]speak I [4]to you? Many things I have about you
λαλεῖν καὶ κρίνειν· ἀλλ' ὁ πέμψας με
to speak and to judge; but the [one] having sent me
ἀληθής ἐστιν, κἀγὼ ἃ ἤκουσα παρ'
true is, and I what I heard from
αὐτοῦ, ταῦτα λαλῶ εἰς τὸν κόσμον.
him, these things I speak in the world.
27 οὐκ ἔγνωσαν ὅτι τὸν πατέρα αὐτοῖς
They did not know that [2]the [3]Father [4]to them
ἔλεγεν. 28 εἶπεν οὖν ὁ Ἰησοῦς· ὅταν
[1]he spoke [of]. Said therefore – Jesus: When
ὑψώσητε τὸν υἱὸν τοῦ ἀνθρώπου, τότε
ye lift up the Son – of man, then
γνώσεσθε ὅτι ἐγώ εἰμι, καὶ ἀπ' ἐμαυτοῦ
ye will know that I am, and from myself
ποιῶ οὐδέν, ἀλλὰ καθὼς ἐδίδαξέν με ὁ
I do nothing, but as taught me the
πατήρ, ταῦτα λαλῶ. 29 καὶ ὁ πέμψας
Father, these things I speak. And the [one] having sent
με μετ' ἐμοῦ ἐστιν· οὐκ ἀφῆκέν με
me with me is; he did not leave me
μόνον, ὅτι ἐγὼ τὰ ἀρεστὰ αὐτῷ ποιῶ
alone, because I the things pleasing to him do
πάντοτε.
always.
30 Ταῦτα αὐτοῦ λαλοῦντος πολλοὶ ἐπίσ-
These things him saying* many be-
=As he said these things
τευσαν εἰς αὐτόν. 31 ἔλεγεν οὖν ὁ Ἰησοῦς
lieved in him. Said therefore – Jesus
πρὸς τοὺς πεπιστευκότας αὐτῷ Ἰουδαίους·
to [1]the [3]having believed [4]him [2]Jews:
ἐὰν ὑμεῖς μείνητε ἐν τῷ λόγῳ τῷ ἐμῷ,
If ye continue in *the* [2]word – [1]my,
ἀληθῶς μαθηταί μού ἐστε, 32 καὶ γνώσεσθε
truly disciples of me ye are, and ye will know
τὴν ἀλήθειαν, καὶ ἡ ἀλήθεια ἐλευθερώσει
the truth, and the truth will free
ὑμᾶς. 33 ἀπεκρίθησαν πρὸς αὐτόν· σπέρμα
you. They answered *to* him: Seed
Ἀβραάμ ἐσμεν, καὶ οὐδενὶ δεδουλεύκαμεν
of Abraham we are, and to no one have we been enslaved
πώποτε· πῶς σὺ λέγεις ὅτι ἐλεύθεροι
never; how thou sayest that free
γενήσεσθε; 34 ἀπεκρίθη αὐτοῖς ὁ Ἰησοῦς·
ye will become? Answered them – Jesus:
ἀμὴν ἀμὴν λέγω ὑμῖν ὅτι πᾶς ὁ ποιῶν
Truly truly I tell you that everyone doing
τὴν ἁμαρτίαν δοῦλός ἐστιν τῆς ἁμαρτίας.
– sin a slave is – of sin.
35 ὁ δὲ δοῦλος οὐ μένει ἐν τῇ οἰκίᾳ
But the slave does not remain in the house

world; I am not of this
world. 24I told you that you
would die in your sins; if
you do not believe that I am
⌊the one I claim to be⌋,[q] you
will indeed die in your
sins."
25"Who are you?" they
asked.
"Just what I have been
claiming all along," Jesus
replied. 26"I have much to
say in judgment of you. But
he who sent me is reliable,
and what I have heard from
him I tell the world."
27They did not under-
stand that he was telling
them about his Father. 28So
Jesus said, "When you
have lifted up the Son of
Man, then you will know
that I am ⌊the one I claim to
be⌋ and that I do nothing on
my own but speak just what
the Father has taught me.
29The one who sent me is
with me; he has not left me
alone, for I always do what
pleases him." 30Even as he
spoke, many put their faith
in him.

The Children of Abraham

31To the Jews who had
believed him, Jesus said,
"If you hold to my teach-
ing, you are really my disciples. 32Then you will know
the truth, and the truth will
set you free."
33They answered him,
"We are Abraham's de-
scendants[r] and have never
been slaves of anyone.
How can you say that we
shall be set free?"
34Jesus replied, "I tell
you the truth, everyone
who sins is a slave to sin.
35Now a slave has no per-
manent place in the family,

q24 Or *I am he*; also in verse 28
r33 Greek *seed*; also in verse 37

ever; the son does remain forever.
36"If therefore the Son shall make you free, you shall be free indeed.
37"I know that you are Abraham's offspring; yet you seek to kill Me, because My word has no place in you.
38"I speak the things which I have seen with *My* Father; therefore you also do the things which you heard from *your* father."
39They answered and said to Him, "Abraham is our father." Jesus *said to them, "If you are Abraham's children, do the deeds of Abraham.
40"But as it is, you are seeking to kill Me, a man who has told you the truth, which I heard from God; this Abraham did not do.
41"You are doing the deeds of your father." They said to Him, "We were not born of fornication; we have one Father, *even* God."
42Jesus said to them, "If God were your Father, you would love Me; for I proceeded forth and have come from God, for I have not even come on My own initiative, but He sent Me.
43"Why do you not understand what I am saying? *It is* because you cannot hear My word.
44"You are of *your* father the devil, and you want to do the desires of your father. He was a murderer from the beginning, and does not stand in the truth, because there is no truth in him. Whenever he speaks a lie, he speaks from his own *nature;* for he is a liar, and the father of lies.
45"But because I speak the truth, you do not believe Me.

εἰς τὸν αἰῶνα· ὁ υἱὸς μένει εἰς τὸν
unto the age; the son remains unto the
αἰῶνα. **36** ἐὰν οὖν ὁ υἱὸς ὑμᾶς ἐλευθερώσῃ,
age. If therefore the Son you frees,
ὄντως ἐλεύθεροι ἔσεσθε. **37** Οἶδα ὅτι
really free ye will be. I know that
σπέρμα Ἀβραάμ ἐστε· ἀλλὰ ζητεῖτέ με
seed of Abraham ye are; but ye seek me
ἀποκτεῖναι, ὅτι ὁ λόγος ὁ ἐμὸς οὐ χωρεῖ
to kill, because *the* [2]word – [1]my finds no room
ἐν ὑμῖν. **38** ἃ ἐγὼ ἑώρακα παρὰ τῷ
in you. What I have seen with the
πατρὶ λαλῶ· καὶ ὑμεῖς οὖν ἃ ἠκού-
Father I speak; and ye therefore what ye
σατε παρὰ τοῦ πατρὸς ποιεῖτε. **39** ἀπεκρί-
heard from the father ye do. They
θησαν καὶ εἶπαν αὐτῷ· ὁ πατὴρ ἡμῶν Ἀβραάμ
answered and said to him: The father of us Abraham
ἐστιν. λέγει αὐτοῖς ὁ Ἰησοῦς· εἰ τέκνα
is. Says to them – Jesus: If children
τοῦ Ἀβραάμ ἐστε, τὰ ἔργα τοῦ Ἀβραὰμ
– of Abraham ye are, the works – of Abraham
ποιεῖτε· **40** νῦν δὲ ζητεῖτέ με ἀποκτεῖναι,
ye do; but now ye seek me to kill,
ἄνθρωπον ὃς τὴν ἀλήθειαν ὑμῖν λελάληκα,
a man who the truth to you has spoken,
ἣν ἤκουσα παρὰ τοῦ θεοῦ· τοῦτο Ἀβραὰμ
which I heard from – God; this Abraham
οὐκ ἐποίησεν. **41** ὑμεῖς ποιεῖτε τὰ ἔργα
did not. Ye do the works
τοῦ πατρὸς ὑμῶν. εἶπαν αὐτῷ· ἡμεῖς ἐκ
of the father of you. They said to him: We of
πορνείας οὐκ ἐγεννήθημεν, ἕνα πατέρα
fornication were not born, one father
ἔχομεν τὸν θεόν. **42** εἶπεν αὐτοῖς ὁ
we have[,] – God. Said to them –
Ἰησοῦς· εἰ ὁ θεὸς πατὴρ ὑμῶν ἦν,
Jesus: If – God father of you was,
ἠγαπᾶτε ἂν ἐμέ· ἐγὼ γὰρ ἐκ τοῦ θεοῦ
ye would have loved me; for I of – God
ἐξῆλθον καὶ ἥκω· οὐδὲ γὰρ ἀπ' ἐμαυτοῦ
came forth and have come; for not from myself
ἐλήλυθα, ἀλλ' ἐκεῖνός με ἀπέστειλεν. **43** διὰ τί
I have come, but that one me sent. Why
τὴν λαλιὰν τὴν ἐμὴν οὐ γινώσκετε;
the [2]speech – [1]my know ye not?
ὅτι οὐ δύνασθε ἀκούειν τὸν λόγον τὸν
because ye cannot *to* hear *the* [2]word –
ἐμόν. **44** ὑμεῖς ἐκ τοῦ πατρὸς τοῦ
[1]my. Ye of the father *of* the
διαβόλου ἐστὲ καὶ τὰς ἐπιθυμίας τοῦ
devil are and the desires of the
πατρὸς ὑμῶν θέλετε ποιεῖν. ἐκεῖνος
father of you ye wish to do. That one
ἀνθρωποκτόνος ἦν ἀπ' ἀρχῆς, καὶ ἐν
a murderer was from [the] beginning, and in
τῇ ἀληθείᾳ οὐκ ἔστηκεν, ὅτι οὐκ ἔστιν
the truth stood not, because not is
ἀλήθεια ἐν αὐτῷ. ὅταν λαλῇ τὸ ψεῦδος,
truth in him. When he speaks the lie,
ἐκ τῶν ἰδίων λαλεῖ, ὅτι ψεύστης ἐστὶν
out of his own things he speaks, because a liar he is
καὶ ὁ πατὴρ αὐτοῦ. **45** ἐγὼ δὲ ὅτι τὴν
and the father of it. But [2]I [1]because [4]the
ἀλήθειαν λέγω, οὐ πιστεύετέ μοι. **46** τίς
[5]truth [3]say, ye do not believe me. Who

but a son belongs to it forever. 36So if the Son sets you free, you will be free indeed. 37I know you are Abraham's descendants. Yet you are ready to kill me, because you have no room for my word. 38I am telling you what I have seen in the Father's presence, and you do what you have heard from your father.[s]"
39"Abraham is our father," they answered.
"If you were Abraham's children," said Jesus, "then you would[t] do the things Abraham did. 40As it is, you are determined to kill me, a man who has told you the truth that I heard from God. Abraham did not do such things. 41You are doing the things your own father does."
"We are not illegitimate children," they protested. "The only Father we have is God himself."

The Children of the Devil

42Jesus said to them, "If God were your Father, you would love me, for I came from God and now am here. I have not come on my own; but he sent me. 43Why is my language not clear to you? Because you are unable to hear what I say. 44You belong to your father, the devil, and you want to carry out your father's desire. He was a murderer from the beginning, not holding to the truth, for there is no truth in him. When he lies, he speaks his native language, for he is a liar and the father of lies. 45Yet because I tell the truth, you do not be-

[s]38 Or *presence. Therefore do what you have heard from the Father.*
[t]39 Some early manuscripts *"If you are Abraham's children," said Jesus, "then*

46"Which one of you convicts Me of sin? If I speak truth, why do you not believe Me?

47"He who is of God hears the words of God; for this reason you do not hear *them,* because you are not of God."

48The Jews answered and said to Him, "Do we not say rightly that You are a Samaritan and have a demon?"

49Jesus answered, "I do not have a demon; but I honor My Father, and you dishonor Me.

50"But I do not seek My glory; there is One who seeks and judges.

51"Truly, truly, I say to you, if anyone keeps My word he shall never see death."

52The Jews said to Him, "Now we know that You have a demon. Abraham died, and the prophets *also;* and You say, 'If anyone keeps My word, he shall never taste of death.'

53"Surely You are not greater than our father Abraham, who died? The prophets died too; whom do You make Yourself out *to be?*"

54Jesus answered, "If I glorify Myself, My glory is nothing; it is My Father who glorifies Me, of whom you say, 'He is our God';

55and you have not come to know Him, but I know Him; and if I say that I do not know Him, I shall be a liar like you, but I do know Him, and keep His word.

56"Your father Abraham rejoiced to see My day, and he saw *it* and was glad."

57The Jews therefore said

ἐξ ὑμῶν ἐλέγχει με περὶ ἁμαρτίας; εἰ
of you reproves me concerning sin? If
ἀλήθειαν λέγω, διὰ τί ὑμεῖς οὐ πιστεύετέ
truth I say, why [2]ye [1]do not believe
μοι; **47** ὁ ὢν ἐκ τοῦ θεοῦ τὰ ῥήματα
me? The [one] being of – God the words
τοῦ θεοῦ ἀκούει· διὰ τοῦτο ὑμεῖς οὐκ
– of God hears; therefore ye not
ἀκούετε, ὅτι ἐκ τοῦ θεοῦ οὐκ ἐστέ.
hear, because of – God ye are not.
48 Ἀπεκρίθησαν οἱ Ἰουδαῖοι καὶ εἶπαν
Answered the Jews and said
αὐτῷ· οὐ καλῶς λέγομεν ἡμεῖς ὅτι
to him : [3]Not [4]well [1]say [2]we [5]that
Σαμαρίτης εἶ σὺ καὶ δαιμόνιον ἔχεις;
[6]a Samaritan [7]art [8]thou [9]and [11]a demon [10]hast?
49 ἀπεκρίθη Ἰησοῦς· ἐγὼ δαιμόνιον οὐκ
Answered Jesus : I a demon not
ἔχω, ἀλλὰ τιμῶ τὸν πατέρα μου, καὶ
have, but I honour the Father of me, and
ὑμεῖς ἀτιμάζετέ με. **50** ἐγὼ δὲ οὐ ζητῶ
ye dishonour me. But I seek not
τὴν δόξαν μου· ἔστιν ὁ ζητῶν καὶ
the glory of me; there is the [one] seeking and
κρίνων. **51** ἀμὴν ἀμὴν λέγω ὑμῖν, ἐάν
judging. Truly truly I tell you, if
τις τὸν ἐμὸν λόγον τηρήσῃ, θάνατον
anyone – my word keeps, death
οὐ μὴ θεωρήσῃ εἰς τὸν αἰῶνα. **52** εἶπαν
by no means will he behold unto the age. Said
αὐτῷ οἱ Ἰουδαῖοι· νῦν ἐγνώκαμεν ὅτι
to him the Jews : Now we have known that
δαιμόνιον ἔχεις. Ἀβραὰμ ἀπέθανεν καὶ οἱ
a demon thou hast. Abraham died and the
προφῆται, καὶ σὺ λέγεις· ἐάν τις τὸν
prophets, and thou sayest : If anyone the
λόγον μου τηρήσῃ, οὐ μὴ γεύσηται
word of me keeps, by no means will he taste
θανάτου εἰς τὸν αἰῶνα. **53** μὴ σὺ μείζων
of death unto the age. *Not* thou greater
εἶ τοῦ πατρὸς ἡμῶν Ἀβραάμ, ὅστις
art [than] the father of us Abraham, who
ἀπέθανεν; καὶ οἱ προφῆται ἀπέθανον· τίνα
died? and the prophets died; whom
σεαυτὸν ποιεῖς; **54** ἀπεκρίθη Ἰησοῦς· ἐὰν
thyself makest thou? Answered Jesus : If
ἐγὼ δοξάσω ἐμαυτόν, ἡ δόξα μου οὐδέν
I glorify myself, the glory of me nothing
ἐστιν· ἔστιν ὁ πατήρ μου ὁ δοξάζων με,
is; [4]is [1]the [2]Father [3]of me the [one] glorifying me,
ὃν ὑμεῖς λέγετε ὅτι θεὸς ἡμῶν ἐστιν,
whom ye say[,] – God of us he is,
55 καὶ οὐκ ἐγνώκατε αὐτόν, ἐγὼ δὲ
and ye have not known him, but I
οἶδα αὐτόν. κἂν εἴπω ὅτι οὐκ οἶδα
know him. Even if I say that I know not
αὐτόν, ἔσομαι ὅμοιος ὑμῖν ψεύστης· ἀλλὰ
him, I shall be like you a liar; but
οἶδα αὐτὸν καὶ τὸν λόγον αὐτοῦ τηρῶ.
I know him and the word of him I keep.
56 Ἀβραὰμ ὁ πατὴρ ὑμῶν ἠγαλλιάσατο
Abraham the father of you was glad
ἵνα ἴδῃ τὴν ἡμέραν τὴν ἐμήν, καὶ εἶδεν
that he should see *the* [2]day – [1]my, and he saw
καὶ ἐχάρη. **57** εἶπαν οὖν οἱ Ἰουδαῖοι
and rejoiced. Said therefore the Jews

lieve me! 46Can any of you
prove me guilty of sin? If I
am telling the truth, why
don't you believe me? 47He
who belongs to God hears
what God says. The reason
you do not hear is that you
do not belong to God."

The Claims of Jesus About Himself

48The Jews answered
him, "Aren't we right in
saying that you are a Sa-
maritan and demon-pos-
sessed?"
49"I am not possessed by
a demon," said Jesus, "but
I honor my Father and you
dishonor me. 50I am not
seeking glory for myself;
but there is one who seeks
it, and he is the judge. 51I
tell you the truth, if anyone
keeps my word, he will
never see death."
52At this the Jews ex-
claimed, "Now we know
that you are demon-pos-
sessed! Abraham died and
so did the prophets, yet you
say that if anyone keeps
your word, he will never
taste death. 53Are you
greater than our father
Abraham? He died, and so
did the prophets. Who do
you think you are?"
54Jesus replied, "If I glorify myself, my glory
means nothing. My Father,
whom you claim as your
God, is the one who glorifies me. 55Though you do
not know him, I know him.
If I said I did not, I would
be a liar like you, but I do
know him and keep his
word. 56Your father Abra-
ham rejoiced at the thought
of seeing my day; he saw it
and was glad."
57"You are not yet fifty

to Him, "You are not yet fifty years old, and have You seen Abraham?"
58Jesus said to them, "Truly, truly, I say to you, before Abraham was born, I am."
59Therefore they picked up stones to throw at Him; but Jesus hid Himself, and went out of the temple.

πρὸς αὐτόν· πεντήκοντα ἔτη οὔπω ἔχεις
to him : Fifty years not yet thou hast
καὶ Ἀβραὰμ ἑώρακας; **58** εἶπεν αὐτοῖς
and Abraham hast thou seen? Said to them
Ἰησοῦς· ἀμὴν ἀμὴν λέγω ὑμῖν, πρὶν
Jesus: Truly truly I tell you, before
Ἀβραὰμ γενέσθαι ἐγὼ εἰμί. **59** ἦραν
Abraham to become[b] =became I am. They took
οὖν λίθους ἵνα βάλωσιν ἐπ' αὐτόν·
therefore stones that they might cast on him;
Ἰησοῦς δὲ ἐκρύβη καὶ ἐξῆλθεν ἐκ τοῦ
but Jesus was hidden and went forth out of the
ἱεροῦ.
temple.

years old," the Jews said to him, "and you have seen Abraham!"
58"I tell you the truth," Jesus answered, "before Abraham was born, I am!"
59At this, they picked up stones to stone him, but Jesus hid himself, slipping away from the temple grounds.

Chapter 9

Healing the Man Born Blind

AND as He passed by, He saw a man blind from birth.
2And His disciples asked Him, saying, "Rabbi, who sinned, this man or his parents, that he should be born blind?"
3Jesus answered, "*It was* neither *that* this man sinned, nor his parents; but *it was* in order that the works of God might be displayed in him.
4"We must work the works of Him who sent Me, as long as it is day; night is coming, when no man can work.
5"While I am in the world, I am the light of the world."
6When He had said this, He spat on the ground, and made clay of the spittle, and applied the clay to his eyes,
7and said to him, "Go, wash in the pool of Siloam" (which is translated, Sent). And so he went away and washed, and came *back* seeing.
8The neighbors therefore, and those who previously saw him as a beggar, were saying, "Is not this the one who used to sit and beg?"
9Others were saying, "This is he," *still* others were saying, "No, but he is like him." He kept saying, "I am the one."
10Therefore they were saying to him, "How then were your eyes opened?"

9 Καὶ παράγων εἶδεν ἄνθρωπον τυφλὸν
And passing along he saw a man blind
ἐκ γενετῆς. **2** καὶ ἠρώτησαν αὐτὸν οἱ
from birth. And asked him the
μαθηταὶ αὐτοῦ λέγοντες· ῥαββί, τίς ἥμαρτεν,
disciples of him saying : Rabbi, who sinned,
οὗτος ἢ οἱ γονεῖς αὐτοῦ, ἵνα τυφλὸς
this man or the parents of him, that blind
γεννηθῇ; **3** ἀπεκρίθη Ἰησοῦς· οὔτε οὗτος
he was born? Answered Jesus : Neither this man
ἥμαρτεν οὔτε οἱ γονεῖς αὐτοῦ, ἀλλ' ἵνα
sinned nor the parents of him, but that
φανερωθῇ τὰ ἔργα τοῦ θεοῦ ἐν αὐτῷ.
might be manifested the works – of God in him.
4 ἡμᾶς δεῖ ἐργάζεσθαι τὰ ἔργα τοῦ
Us it behoves to work the works of the
πέμψαντός με ἕως ἡμέρα ἐστίν· ἔρχεται
[one] having sent me while day it is; comes
νὺξ ὅτε οὐδεὶς δύναται ἐργάζεσθαι. **5** ὅταν
night when no one can *to* work. When
ἐν τῷ κόσμῳ ὦ, φῶς εἰμι τοῦ κόσμου.
in the world I am, light I am of the world.
6 ταῦτα εἰπὼν ἔπτυσεν χαμαὶ καὶ ἐποίησεν
These things having said he spat on the ground and made
πηλὸν ἐκ τοῦ πτύσματος, καὶ ἐπέθηκεν
clay out of the spittle, and [1]put *on*
αὐτοῦ τὸν πηλὸν ἐπὶ τοὺς ὀφθαλμούς,
[7]of him [2]the [3]clay [4]on [5]the [6]eyes,
7 καὶ εἶπεν αὐτῷ· ὕπαγε νίψαι εἰς τὴν
and said to him : Go wash in the
κολυμβήθραν τοῦ Σιλωάμ (ὃ ἑρμηνεύεται
pool – of Siloam (which is translated
ἀπεσταλμένος). ἀπῆλθεν οὖν καὶ ἐνίψατο,
having been sent). He went therefore and washed,
καὶ ἦλθεν βλέπων. **8** Οἱ οὖν γείτονες
and came seeing. Therefore the neighbours
καὶ οἱ θεωροῦντες αὐτὸν τὸ πρότερον,
and the [ones] beholding him formerly, †
ὅτι προσαίτης ἦν, ἔλεγον· οὐχ οὗτός
that a beggar he was, said : [2]Not [3]this man
ἐστιν ὁ καθήμενος καὶ προσαιτῶν; **9** ἄλλοι
[1]is the [one] sitting and begging? Some
ἔλεγον ὅτι οὗτός ἐστιν· ἄλλοι ἔλεγον·
said[,] – This is he; others said :
οὐχί, ἀλλὰ ὅμοιος αὐτῷ ἐστιν. ἐκεῖνος
No, but like *to* him he is. That [one]
ἔλεγεν ὅτι ἐγώ εἰμι. **10** ἔλεγον οὖν
said[,] – I am. They said therefore
αὐτῷ· πῶς [οὖν] ἠνεῴχθησάν σου οἱ
to him : How then were opened of thee the

Chapter 9

Jesus Heals a Man Born Blind

AS he went along, he saw a man blind from birth. 2His disciples asked him, "Rabbi, who sinned, this man or his parents, that he was born blind?"
3"Neither this man nor his parents sinned," said Jesus, "but this happened so that the work of God might be displayed in his life. 4As long as it is day, we must do the work of him who sent me. Night is coming, when no one can work. 5While I am in the world, I am the light of the world."
6Having said this, he spit on the ground, made some mud with the saliva, and put it on the man's eyes. 7"Go," he told him, "wash in the Pool of Siloam" (this word means Sent). So the man went and washed, and came home seeing.
8His neighbors and those who had formerly seen him begging asked, "Isn't this the same man who used to sit and beg?" 9Some claimed that he was.
Others said, "No, he only looks like him."
But he himself insisted, "I am the man."
10"How then were your eyes opened?" they demanded.

11He answered, "The man who is called Jesus made clay, and anointed my eyes, and said to me, 'Go to Siloam, and wash'; so I went away and washed, and I received sight."

12And they said to him, "Where is He?" He *said, "I do not know."

Controversy over the Man

13They *brought to the Pharisees him who was formerly blind.

14Now it was a Sabbath on the day when Jesus made the clay, and opened his eyes.

15Again, therefore, the Pharisees also were asking him how he received his sight. And he said to them, "He applied clay to my eyes, and I washed, and I see."

16Therefore some of the Pharisees were saying, "This man is not from God, because He does not keep the Sabbath." But others were saying, "How can a man who is a sinner perform such signs?" And there was a division among them.

17They *said therefore to the blind man again, "What do you say about Him, since He opened your eyes?" And he said, "He is a prophet."

18The Jews therefore did not believe *it* of him, that he had been blind, and had received sight, until they called the parents of the very one who had received his sight,

19and questioned them, saying, "Is this your son, who you say was born blind? Then how does he now see?"

20His parents answered them and said, "We know that this is our son, and that he was born blind;

21but how he now sees,

ὀφθαλμοί; **11** ἀπεκρίθη ἐκεῖνος· ὁ ἄνθρωπος
eyes? Answered that [one] : The man
ὁ λεγόμενος Ἰησοῦς πηλὸν ἐποίησεν καὶ
– *being* named Jesus clay made and
ἐπέχρισέν μου τοὺς ὀφθαλμοὺς καὶ εἶπέν
anointed of me the eyes and told
μοι ὅτι ὕπαγε εἰς τὸν Σιλωὰμ καὶ
me[,] – Go to – Siloam and
νίψαι· ἀπελθὼν οὖν καὶ νιψάμενος ἀνέβλεψα.
wash; going therefore and washing I saw.
12 καὶ εἶπαν αὐτῷ· ποῦ ἐστιν ἐκεῖνος;
And they said to him : Where is that [one]?
λέγει· οὐκ οἶδα. **13** Ἄγουσιν αὐτὸν
He says: I do not know. They lead him
πρὸς τοὺς Φαρισαίους, τόν ποτε τυφλόν.
to the Pharisees, the at one time blind.
14 ἦν δὲ σάββατον ἐν ᾗ ἡμέρᾳ τὸν
Now it was a sabbath on which day [3]the
πηλὸν ἐποίησεν ὁ Ἰησοῦς καὶ ἀνέῳξεν
[4]clay [2]made – [1]Jesus and opened
αὐτοῦ τοὺς ὀφθαλμούς. **15** πάλιν οὖν
of him the eyes. Again therefore
ἠρώτων αὐτὸν καὶ οἱ Φαρισαῖοι πῶς
[4]asked [5]him [2]also [1]the [3]Pharisees how
ἀνέβλεψεν. ὁ δὲ εἶπεν αὐτοῖς· πηλὸν
he saw. And he said to them : Clay
ἐπέθηκέν μου ἐπὶ τοὺς ὀφθαλμούς, καὶ
he put *on* [4]of me [1]on [2]the [3]eyes, and
ἐνιψάμην, καὶ βλέπω. **16** ἔλεγον οὖν ἐκ
I washed, and I see. Said therefore of
τῶν Φαρισαίων τινές· οὐκ ἔστιν οὗτος
the Pharisees some : [4]not [3]is [1]This
παρὰ θεοῦ ὁ ἄνθρωπος, ὅτι τὸ σάββατον
[5]from [6]God – [2]man, because the sabbath
οὐ τηρεῖ. ἄλλοι [δὲ] ἔλεγον· πῶς δύναται
he keeps not. But others said : How can
ἄνθρωπος ἁμαρτωλὸς τοιαῦτα σημεῖα ποιεῖν;
man a sinful such signs *to* do?
καὶ σχίσμα ἦν ἐν αὐτοῖς. **17** λέγουσιν
And a division there was among them. They say
οὖν τῷ τυφλῷ πάλιν· τί σὺ λέγεις
therefore to the blind man again : What thou sayest
περὶ αὐτοῦ, ὅτι ἠνέῳξέν σου τοὺς
about him, because he opened of thee the
ὀφθαλμούς; ὁ δὲ εἶπεν ὅτι προφήτης ἐστίν.
eyes? And he said[,] – A prophet he is.
18 οὐκ ἐπίστευσαν οὖν οἱ Ἰουδαῖοι περὶ
Did not believe therefore the Jews about
αὐτοῦ ὅτι ἦν τυφλὸς καὶ ἀνέβλεψεν,
him that he was blind and saw,
ἕως ὅτου ἐφώνησαν τοὺς γονεῖς αὐτοῦ
until they called the parents of him
τοῦ ἀναβλέψαντος **19** καὶ ἠρώτησαν αὐτοὺς
of the [one] having seen and asked them
λέγοντες· οὗτός ἐστιν ὁ υἱὸς ὑμῶν, ὃν
saying : This is the son of you, whom
ὑμεῖς λέγετε ὅτι τυφλὸς ἐγεννήθη; πῶς
ye say that blind he was born? how
οὖν βλέπει ἄρτι; **20** ἀπεκρίθησαν οὖν οἱ
then sees he now? Answered therefore the
γονεῖς αὐτοῦ καὶ εἶπαν· οἴδαμεν ὅτι
parents of him and said : We know that
οὗτός ἐστιν ὁ υἱὸς ἡμῶν καὶ ὅτι τυφλὸς
this is the son of us and that blind
ἐγεννήθη· **21** πῶς δὲ νῦν βλέπει οὐκ
he was born; but how now he sees not

11He replied, "The man they call Jesus made some mud and put it on my eyes. He told me to go to Siloam and wash. So I went and washed, and then I could see."

12"Where is this man?" they asked him.

"I don't know," he said.

The Pharisees Investigate the Healing

13They brought to the Pharisees the man who had been blind. 14Now the day on which Jesus had made the mud and opened the man's eyes was a Sabbath. 15Therefore the Pharisees also asked him how he had received his sight. "He put mud on my eyes," the man replied, "and I washed, and now I see."

16Some of the Pharisees said, "This man is not from God, for he does not keep the Sabbath."

But others asked, "How can a sinner do such miraculous signs?" So they were divided.

17Finally they turned again to the blind man, "What have you to say about him? It was your eyes he opened."

The man replied, "He is a prophet."

18The Jews still did not believe that he had been blind and had received his sight until they sent for the man's parents. 19"Is this your son?" they asked. "Is this the one you say was born blind? How is it that now he can see?"

20"We know he is our son," the parents answered, "and we know he was born blind. 21But how

we do not know; or who
opened his eyes, we do not
know. Ask him; he is of
age, he shall speak for himself.''
22His parents said this because they were afraid of
the Jews; for the Jews had
already agreed, that if anyone should confess Him to
be Christ, he should be put
out of the synagogue.
23For this reason his parents said, ''He is of age; ask
him.''
24So a second time they
called the man who had
been blind, and said to him,
''Give glory to God; we
know that this man is a sinner.''
25He therefore answered,
''Whether He is a sinner, I
do not know; one thing I do
know, that, whereas I was
blind, now I see.''
26They said therefore to
him, ''What did He do to
you? How did He open
your eyes?''
27He answered them, ''I
told you already, and you
did not listen; why do you
want to hear *it* again? You
do not want to become His
disciples too, do you?''
28And they reviled him,
and said, ''You are His disciple, but we are disciples
of Moses.
29''We know that God has
spoken to Moses; but as for
this man, we do not know
where He is from.''
30The man answered and
said to them, ''Well, here is
an amazing thing, that you
do not know where He is
from, and *yet* He opened
my eyes.
31''We know that God
does not hear sinners; but if
anyone is God-fearing, and
does His will, He hears
him.
32''Since the beginning of
time it has never been
heard that anyone opened
the eyes of a person born
blind.

οἴδαμεν, ἢ τίς ἤνοιξεν αὐτοῦ τοὺς ὀφθαλμοὺς
we know, or who opened of him the eyes
ἡμεῖς οὐκ οἴδαμεν· αὐτὸν ἐρωτήσατε,
we know not; him ask ye,
ἡλικίαν ἔχει, αὐτὸς περὶ ἑαυτοῦ λαλήσει.
age he has, he about himself will speak.
22 ταῦτα εἶπαν οἱ γονεῖς αὐτοῦ ὅτι ἐφο-
These things said the parents of him because they
βοῦντο τοὺς Ἰουδαίους· ἤδη γὰρ συνετέθειντο
feared the Jews; for already had agreed
οἱ Ἰουδαῖοι ἵνα ἐάν τις αὐτὸν ὁμολογήσῃ
the Jews that if anyone him should acknowledge
χριστόν, ἀποσυνάγωγος γένηται.
[to be] Christ, put away from [the] synagogue he would be.
23 διὰ τοῦτο οἱ γονεῖς αὐτοῦ εἶπαν ὅτι
Therefore the parents of him said[,] –
ἡλικίαν ἔχει, αὐτὸν ἐπερωτήσατε. **24** Ἐφώνησαν
Age he has, him question ye. They called
οὖν τὸν ἄνθρωπον ἐκ δευτέρου ὃς ἦν
therefore the man a second time who was
τυφλός, καὶ εἶπαν αὐτῷ· δὸς δόξαν τῷ
blind, and said to him: Give glory –
θεῷ· ἡμεῖς οἴδαμεν ὅτι οὗτος ὁ ἄνθρωπος
to God; we know that this – man
ἁμαρτωλός ἐστιν. **25** ἀπεκρίθη οὖν ἐκεῖνος·
sinful is. Answered therefore that [one]:
εἰ ἁμαρτωλός ἐστιν οὐκ οἶδα· ἓν οἶδα,
If sinful he is I know not; one thing I know,
ὅτι τυφλὸς ὢν ἄρτι βλέπω. **26** εἶπαν
that blind being now I see. They said
οὖν αὐτῷ· τί ἐποίησέν σοι; πῶς ἤνοιξέν
therefore to him: What did he to thee? how opened he
σου τοὺς ὀφθαλμούς; **27** ἀπεκρίθη αὐτοῖς·
of thee the eyes? He answered them:
εἶπον ὑμῖν ἤδη καὶ οὐκ ἠκούσατε· τί
I told you already and ye heard not; why
πάλιν θέλετε ἀκούειν; μὴ καὶ ὑμεῖς
again wish ye to hear? *not* also ye
θέλετε αὐτοῦ μαθηταὶ γενέσθαι; **28** καὶ
wish of him disciples to become? And
ἐλοιδόρησαν αὐτὸν καὶ εἶπαν· σὺ μαθητὴς
they reviled him and said: Thou a disciple
εἶ ἐκείνου, ἡμεῖς δὲ τοῦ Μωϋσέως ἐσμὲν
art of that man, but we – of Moses are
μαθηταί· **29** ἡμεῖς οἴδαμεν ὅτι Μωϋσεῖ
disciples; we know that by Moses
λελάληκεν ὁ θεός, τοῦτον δὲ οὐκ οἴδαμεν
has spoken – God, but this man we know not
πόθεν ἐστίν. **30** ἀπεκρίθη ὁ ἄνθρωπος
whence he is. Answered the man
καὶ εἶπεν αὐτοῖς· ἐν τούτῳ γὰρ τὸ
and said to them: In this then the
θαυμαστόν ἐστιν, ὅτι ὑμεῖς οὐκ οἴδατε
marvellous thing is, that ye do not know
πόθεν ἐστίν, καὶ ἤνοιξέν μου τοὺς
whence he is, and he opened of me the
ὀφθαλμούς. **31** οἴδαμεν ὅτι ὁ θεὸς
eyes. We know that – God
ἁμαρτωλῶν οὐκ ἀκούει, ἀλλ' ἐάν τις
sinful men does not hear, but if anyone
θεοσεβὴς ᾖ καὶ τὸ θέλημα αὐτοῦ ποιῇ,
godfearing is and the will of him does,
τούτου ἀκούει. **32** ἐκ τοῦ αἰῶνος οὐκ
this man he hears. From the age not
ἠκούσθη ὅτι ἠνέῳξέν τις ὀφθαλμοὺς τυφλοῦ
it was heard that ²opened ¹anyone eyes of a blind man

he can see now, or who
opened his eyes, we don't
know. Ask him. He is of
age; he will speak for himself.'' 22His parents said
this because they were
afraid of the Jews, for already the Jews had decided
that anyone who acknowl-
edged that Jesus was the
Christ[u] would be put out of
the synagogue. 23That was
why his parents said, ''He
is of age; ask him.''
24A second time they
summoned the man who
had been blind. ''Give glory to God,[v]'' they said.
''We know this man is a
sinner.''
25He replied, ''Whether
he is a sinner or not, I don't
know. One thing I do
know. I was blind but now I
see!''
26Then they asked him,
''What did he do to you?
How did he open your
eyes?''
27He answered, ''I have
told you already and you
did not listen. Why do you
want to hear it again? Do
you want to become his disciples, too?''
28Then they hurled insults
at him and said, ''You are
this fellow's disciple! We
are disciples of Moses!
29We know that God spoke
to Moses, but as for this fellow, we don't even know
where he comes from.''
30The man answered,
''Now that is remarkable!
You don't know where he
comes from, yet he opened
my eyes. 31We know that
God does not listen to sinners. He listens to the godly man who does his will.
32Nobody has ever heard of
opening the eyes of a man
born blind. 33If this man

[u]22 Or *Messiah*
[v]24 A solemn charge to tell the truth (see Joshua 7:19)

33 "If this man were not
from God, He could do
nothing."
34 They answered and said
to him, "You were born entirely in sins, and are you
teaching us?" And they put
him out.

Jesus Affirms His Deity

35 Jesus heard that they
had put him out; and finding him, He said, "Do you
believe in the Son of
Man?"
36 He answered and said,
"And who is He, Lord,
that I may believe in Him?"
37 Jesus said to him, "You
have both seen Him, and
He is the one who is talking
with you."
38 And he said, "Lord, I
believe." And he wor-
shiped Him.
39 And Jesus said, "For
judgment I came into this
world, that those who do
not see may see; and that
those who see may become
blind."
40 Those of the Pharisees
who were with Him heard
these things, and said to
Him, "We are not blind
too, are we?"
41 Jesus said to them, "If
you were blind, you would
have no sin; but since you
say, 'We see,' your sin remains.

γεγεννημένου· 33 εἰ μὴ ἦν οὗτος παρὰ
having been born; if [3]not [2]was [1]this man from

θεοῦ, οὐκ ἠδύνατο ποιεῖν οὐδέν. 34 ἀπεκρίθησαν
God, he could not *to* do no(any)thing. They answered

καὶ εἶπαν αὐτῷ· ἐν ἁμαρτίαις σὺ ἐγεννήθης
and said to him: In sins thou wast born

ὅλος, καὶ σὺ διδάσκεις ἡμᾶς; καὶ ἐξέβαλον
wholly, and thou teachest us? and they cast *out*

αὐτὸν ἔξω. 35 Ἤκουσεν Ἰησοῦς ὅτι
him outside. Heard Jesus that

ἐξέβαλον αὐτὸν ἔξω, καὶ εὑρὼν αὐτὸν
they cast *out* him outside, and finding him

εἶπεν· σὺ πιστεύεις εἰς τὸν υἱὸν τοῦ
said: Thou believest in the Son –

ἀνθρώπου; 36 ἀπεκρίθη ἐκεῖνος καὶ εἶπεν·
of man? Answered that [one] and said:

καὶ τίς ἐστιν, κύριε, ἵνα πιστεύσω εἰς
And who is he, sir, that I may believe in

αὐτόν; 37 εἶπεν αὐτῷ ὁ Ἰησοῦς· καὶ
him? Said to him – Jesus: Both

ἑώρακας αὐτὸν καὶ ὁ λαλῶν μετὰ σοῦ
thou hast seen him and the [one] speaking with thee

ἐκεῖνός ἐστιν. 38 ὁ δὲ ἔφη· πιστεύω, κύριε·
that [one] is. And he said: I believe, sir;

καὶ προσεκύνησεν αὐτῷ. 39 καὶ εἶπεν ὁ
and he worshipped him. And said –

Ἰησοῦς· εἰς κρίμα ἐγὼ εἰς τὸν κόσμον
Jesus: For judgment I into – world

τοῦτον ἦλθον, ἵνα οἱ μὴ βλέποντες
this came, that the [ones] not seeing

βλέπωσιν καὶ οἱ βλέποντες τυφλοὶ γένωνται.
may see and the [ones] seeing blind may become.

40 Ἤκουσαν ἐκ τῶν Φαρισαίων ταῦτα
[8]heard [1][Some] [2]of [3]the [4]Pharisees [9]these things

οἱ μετ' αὐτοῦ ὄντες, καὶ εἶπαν αὐτῷ·
– [6]with [7]him [5]being, and they said to him:

μὴ καὶ ἡμεῖς τυφλοί ἐσμεν; 41 εἶπεν
Not also we blind are? Said

αὐτοῖς ὁ Ἰησοῦς· εἰ τυφλοὶ ἦτε, οὐκ
to them – Jesus: If blind ye were, not

ἂν εἴχετε ἁμαρτίαν· νῦν δὲ λέγετε ὅτι
ye would have had sin; but now ye say[,] –

βλέπομεν· ἡ ἁμαρτία ὑμῶν μένει.
We see; the sin of you remains.

were not from God, he
could do nothing."
34 To this they replied,
"You were steeped in sin at
birth; how dare you lecture
us!" And they threw him
out.

Spiritual Blindness

35 Jesus heard that they
had thrown him out, and
when he found him, he
said, "Do you believe in
the Son of Man?"
36 "Who is he, sir?" the
man asked. "Tell me so
that I may believe in him."
37 Jesus said, "You have
now seen him; in fact, he is
the one speaking with
you."
38 Then the man said,
"Lord, I believe," and he
worshiped him.
39 Jesus said, "For judg-
ment I have come into this
world, so that the blind will
see and those who see will
become blind."
40 Some Pharisees who
were with him heard him
say this and asked, "What?
Are we blind too?"
41 Jesus said, "If you were
blind, you would not be
guilty of sin; but now that
you claim you can see,
your guilt remains.

Chapter 10

Parable of the Good Shepherd

"TRULY, truly, I say
to you, he who
does not enter by the door
into the fold of the sheep,
but climbs up some other
way, he is a thief and a robber.
2 "But he who enters by
the door is a shepherd of
the sheep.
3 "To him the doorkeep-
er opens, and the sheep
hear his voice, and he calls
his own sheep by name,
and leads them out.
4 "When he puts forth all

10 Ἀμὴν ἀμὴν λέγω ὑμῖν, ὁ μὴ
Truly truly I say to you, the [one] not

εἰσερχόμενος διὰ τῆς θύρας εἰς τὴν
entering through the door into the

αὐλὴν τῶν προβάτων ἀλλὰ ἀναβαίνων
fold of the sheep but going up

ἀλλαχόθεν, ἐκεῖνος κλέπτης ἐστὶν καὶ
by another way, that [one] a thief is and

λῃστής· 2 ὁ δὲ εἰσερχόμενος διὰ τῆς
a robber; but the [one] entering through the

θύρας ποιμήν ἐστιν τῶν προβάτων. 3 τούτῳ
door shepherd is of the sheep. To this [one]

ὁ θυρωρὸς ἀνοίγει, καὶ τὰ πρόβατα τῆς
the doorkeeper opens, and the sheep the

φωνῆς αὐτοῦ ἀκούει, καὶ τὰ ἴδια πρόβατα
voice of him hears, and the(his) own sheep

φωνεῖ κατ' ὄνομα καὶ ἐξάγει αὐτά.
he calls by name and leads out them.

4 ὅταν τὰ ἴδια πάντα ἐκβάλῃ, ἔμπροσθεν
When the(his) own all he puts forth, in front of

Chapter 10

The Shepherd and His Flock

"I TELL you the
truth, the man who
does not enter the sheep
pen by the gate, but climbs
in by some other way, is a
thief and a robber. 2 The
man who enters by the gate
is the shepherd of his
sheep. 3 The watchman
opens the gate for him, and
the sheep listen to his
voice. He calls his own
sheep by name and leads
them out. 4 When he has

his own, he goes before them, and the sheep follow him because they know his voice.
5"And a stranger they simply will not follow, but will flee from him, because they do not know the voice of strangers."
6This figure of speech Jesus spoke to them, but they did not understand what those things were which He had been saying to them.
7Jesus therefore said to them again, "Truly, truly, I say to you, I am the door of the sheep.
8"All who came before Me are thieves and robbers, but the sheep did not hear them.
9"I am the door; if anyone enters through Me, he shall be saved, and shall go in and out, and find pasture.
10"The thief comes only to steal, and kill, and destroy; I came that they might have life, and might have *it* abundantly.
11"I am the good shepherd; the good shepherd lays down His life for the sheep.
12"He who is a hireling, and not a shepherd, who is not the owner of the sheep, beholds the wolf coming, and leaves the sheep, and flees, and the wolf snatches them, and scatters *them*.
13"*He flees* because he is a hireling, and is not concerned about the sheep.
14"I am the good shepherd; and I know My own, and My own know Me,
15even as the Father knows Me and I know the Father; and I lay down My life for the sheep.
16"And I have other sheep, which are not of this

αὐτῶν πορεύεται, καὶ τὰ πρόβατα αὐτῷ
them he goes, and the sheep him

ἀκολουθεῖ, ὅτι οἴδασιν τὴν φωνὴν αὐτοῦ·
follows, because they know the voice of him;

5 ἀλλοτρίῳ δὲ οὐ μὴ ἀκολουθήσουσιν,
but a stranger by no means will they follow,

ἀλλὰ φεύξονται ἀπ' αὐτοῦ, ὅτι οὐκ
but will flee from him, because not

οἴδασιν τῶν ἀλλοτρίων τὴν φωνήν.
they know of the strangers the voice.

6 Ταύτην τὴν παροιμίαν εἶπεν αὐτοῖς ὁ
This – allegory told them –

Ἰησοῦς· ἐκεῖνοι δὲ οὐκ ἔγνωσαν τίνα
Jesus; but those men knew not what things

ἦν ἃ ἐλάλει αὐτοῖς. **7** Εἶπεν οὖν πάλιν
they were which he spoke to them. Said therefore again

ὁ Ἰησοῦς· ἀμὴν ἀμὴν λέγω ὑμῖν ὅτι
– Jesus: Truly truly I say to you that

ἐγώ εἰμι ἡ θύρα τῶν προβάτων. **8** πάντες
I am the door of the sheep. All

ὅσοι ἦλθον πρὸ ἐμοῦ κλέπται εἰσὶν καὶ
who came before me thieves are and

λῃσταί· ἀλλ' οὐκ ἤκουσαν αὐτῶν τὰ
robbers; but did not hear them the

πρόβατα. **9** ἐγώ εἰμι ἡ θύρα· δι' ἐμοῦ
sheep. I am the door; through me

ἐάν τις εἰσέλθῃ, σωθήσεται, καὶ εἰσελεύ-
if anyone enters, he will be saved, and will go

σεται καὶ ἐξελεύσεται καὶ νομὴν εὑρήσει.
in and *will* go out and pasture *will* find.

10 ὁ κλέπτης οὐκ ἔρχεται εἰ μὴ ἵνα
The thief comes not except that

κλέψῃ καὶ θύσῃ καὶ ἀπολέσῃ· ἐγὼ ἦλθον
he may steal and kill and destroy; I came

ἵνα ζωὴν ἔχωσιν καὶ περισσὸν ἔχωσιν.
that life they may have and abundantly *they* may have.

11 Ἐγώ εἰμι ὁ ποιμὴν ὁ καλός. ὁ
I am the shepherd – good. The

ποιμὴν ὁ καλὸς τὴν ψυχὴν αὐτοῦ τίθησιν
shepherd – good the life of him lays down

ὑπὲρ τῶν προβάτων· **12** ὁ μισθωτὸς καὶ
for the sheep; the hireling and

οὐκ ὢν ποιμήν, οὗ οὐκ ἔστιν τὰ πρόβατα
not being a shepherd, of whom is(are) not the sheep

ἴδια, θεωρεῖ τὸν λύκον ἐρχόμενον καὶ
[his] own, beholds the wolf coming and

ἀφίησιν τὰ πρόβατα καὶ φεύγει, — καὶ
leaves the sheep and flees, — and

ὁ λύκος ἁρπάζει αὐτὰ καὶ σκορπίζει· —
the wolf seizes them and scatters; —

13 ὅτι μισθωτός ἐστιν καὶ οὐ μέλει
because a hireling he is and it matters not

αὐτῷ περὶ τῶν προβάτων. **14** ἐγώ εἰμι
to him about the sheep. I am

ὁ ποιμὴν ὁ καλός, καὶ γινώσκω τὰ
the shepherd – good, and I know –

ἐμὰ καὶ γινώσκουσί με τὰ ἐμά, **15** καθὼς
mine and [2]know [3]me – [1]mine, as

γινώσκει με ὁ πατὴρ κἀγὼ γινώσκω τὸν
[3]knows [4]me [1]the [2]Father and I know the

πατέρα, καὶ τὴν ψυχήν μου τίθημι ὑπὲρ
Father, and the life of me I lay down for

τῶν προβάτων. **16** καὶ ἄλλα πρόβατα
the sheep. And other sheep

ἔχω ἃ οὐκ ἔστιν ἐκ τῆς αὐλῆς ταύτης·
I have which is(are) not of – fold this;

brought out all his own, he goes on ahead of them, and his sheep follow him because they know his voice. 5But they will never follow a stranger; in fact, they will run away from him because they do not recognize a stranger's voice." 6Jesus used this figure of speech, but they did not understand what he was telling them.
7Therefore Jesus said again, "I tell you the truth, I am the gate for the sheep. 8All who ever came before me were thieves and robbers, but the sheep did not listen to them. 9I am the gate; whoever enters through me will be saved.[w] He will come in and go out, and find pasture. 10The thief comes only to steal and kill and destroy; I have come that they may have life, and have it to the full.
11"I am the good shepherd. The good shepherd lays down his life for the sheep. 12The hired hand is not the shepherd who owns the sheep. So when he sees the wolf coming, he abandons the sheep and runs away. Then the wolf attacks the flock and scatters it. 13The man runs away because he is a hired hand and cares nothing for the sheep.
14"I am the good shepherd; I know my sheep and my sheep know me— 15just as the Father knows me and I know the Father—and I lay down my life for the sheep. 16I have other sheep that are not of this

w9 Or *kept safe*

fold; I must bring them also, and they shall hear My voice; and they shall become one flock *with* one shepherd.

17"For this reason the Father loves Me, because I lay down My life that I may take it again.

18"No one [t]has taken it away from Me, but I lay it down on My own initiative. I have authority to lay it down, and I have authority to take it up again. This commandment I received from My Father."

19There arose a division again among the Jews because of these words.

20And many of them were saying, "He has a demon and is insane. Why do you listen to Him?"

21Others were saying, "These are not the sayings of one demon-possessed. A demon cannot open the eyes of the blind, can he?"

Jesus Asserts His Deity

22At that time the Feast of the Dedication took place at Jerusalem;

23it was winter, and Jesus was walking in the temple in the portico of Solomon.

24The Jews therefore gathered around Him, and were saying to Him, "How long will You keep us in suspense? If You are the Christ, tell us plainly."

25Jesus answered them, "I told you, and you do not believe; the works that I do in My Father's name, these bear witness of Me.

26"But you do not believe, because you are not of My sheep.

27"My sheep hear My voice, and I know them, and they follow Me;

28and I give eternal life to them, and they shall never

[t]Many Gr. mss. read *takes*

κἀκεῖνα δεῖ με ἀγαγεῖν, καὶ τῆς φωνῆς
those also it behoves me to bring, and the voice
μου ἀκούσουσιν, καὶ γενήσεται μία ποίμνη,
of me they will hear, and there will become one flock,
εἷς ποιμήν. **17** διὰ τοῦτό με ὁ πατὴρ
one shepherd. Therefore me the Father
ἀγαπᾷ ὅτι ἐγὼ τίθημι τὴν ψυχήν μου,
loves because I lay down the life of me,
ἵνα πάλιν λάβω αὐτήν. **18** οὐδεὶς ἦρεν
that again I may take it. No one took
αὐτὴν ἀπ' ἐμοῦ, ἀλλ' ἐγὼ τίθημι αὐτὴν
it from me, but I lay down it
ἀπ' ἐμαυτοῦ. ἐξουσίαν ἔχω θεῖναι αὐτήν,
from myself. Authority I have to lay down it,
καὶ ἐξουσίαν ἔχω πάλιν λαβεῖν αὐτήν·
and authority I have again to take it;
ταύτην τὴν ἐντολὴν ἔλαβον παρὰ τοῦ
this – commandment I received from the
πατρός μου. **19** Σχίσμα πάλιν ἐγένετο ἐν
Father of me. A division again there was among
τοῖς Ἰουδαίοις διὰ τοὺς λόγους τούτους.
the Jews because of – words these.
20 ἔλεγον δὲ πολλοὶ ἐξ αὐτῶν· δαιμόνιον
And said many of them: A demon
ἔχει καὶ μαίνεται· τί αὐτοῦ ἀκούετε;
he has and raves; why him hear ye?
21 ἄλλοι ἔλεγον· ταῦτα τὰ ῥήματα οὐκ
Others said: These – words not
ἔστιν δαιμονιζομένου· μὴ δαιμόνιον δύναται
is(are) of one demon-possessed; *not* a demon can
τυφλῶν ὀφθαλμοὺς ἀνοῖξαι;
of blind men eyes *to* open?
22 Ἐγένετο τότε τὰ ἐγκαίνια ἐν τοῖς
There was then the Dedication in –
Ἱεροσολύμοις· χειμὼν ἦν· **23** καὶ περιεπάτει
Jerusalem; winter it was; and walked
ὁ Ἰησοῦς ἐν τῷ ἱερῷ ἐν τῇ στοᾷ τοῦ
– Jesus in the temple in the porch –
Σολομῶνος. **24** ἐκύκλωσαν οὖν αὐτὸν οἱ
of Solomon. Surrounded therefore him the
Ἰουδαῖοι καὶ ἔλεγον αὐτῷ· ἕως πότε
Jews and said to him: Until when
τὴν ψυχὴν ἡμῶν αἴρεις; εἰ σὺ εἶ
the life(soul) of us holdest thou * ? if thou art
ὁ χριστός, εἰπὸν ἡμῖν παρρησίᾳ. **25** ἀπεκρίθη
the Christ, tell us plainly. Answered
αὐτοῖς ὁ Ἰησοῦς· εἶπον ὑμῖν, καὶ
them – Jesus: I told you, and
οὐ πιστεύετε· τὰ ἔργα ἃ ἐγὼ ποιῶ ἐν τῷ
ye do not believe; the works which I do in the
ὀνόματι τοῦ πατρός μου, ταῦτα μαρτυρεῖ
name of the Father of me, these witnesses
περὶ ἐμοῦ· **26** ἀλλὰ ὑμεῖς οὐ πιστεύετε,
concerning me; but ye do not believe,
ὅτι οὐκ ἐστὲ ἐκ τῶν προβάτων τῶν
because ye are not of *the* [l]sheep –
ἐμῶν. **27** τὰ πρόβατα τὰ ἐμὰ τῆς φωνῆς
[l]my. *the* sheep – My the voice
μου ἀκούουσιν, κἀγὼ γινώσκω αὐτά, καὶ
of me hear, and I know them, and
ἀκολουθοῦσίν μοι, **28** κἀγὼ δίδωμι αὐτοῖς
they follow me, and I give to them
ζωὴν αἰώνιον, καὶ οὐ μὴ ἀπόλωνται εἰς
life eternal, and by no means they perish unto

* That is, in suspense.

sheep pen. I must bring them also. They too will listen to my voice, and there shall be one flock and one shepherd. 17The reason my Father loves me is that I lay down my life—only to take it up again. 18No one takes it from me, but I lay it down of my own accord. I have authority to lay it down and authority to take it up again. This command I received from my Father."

19At these words the Jews were again divided. 20Many of them said, "He is demon-possessed and raving mad. Why listen to him?"

21But others said, "These are not the sayings of a man possessed by a demon. Can a demon open the eyes of the blind?"

The Unbelief of the Jews

22Then came the Feast of Dedication[x] at Jerusalem. It was winter, 23and Jesus was in the temple area walking in Solomon's Colonnade. 24The Jews gathered around him, saying, "How long will you keep us in suspense? If you are the Christ,[y] tell us plainly."

25Jesus answered, "I did tell you, but you do not believe. The miracles I do in my Father's name speak for me, 26but you do not believe because you are not my sheep. 27My sheep listen to my voice; I know them, and they follow me. 28I give them eternal life, and they shall never perish;

[x]*22* That is, Hanukkah
[y]*24* Or *Messiah*

perish; and no one shall
snatch them out of My
hand.
29"[u]My Father, who has
given *them* to Me, is
greater than all; and no one
is able to snatch *them* out of
the Father's hand.
30"I and the Father are
one."
31The Jews took up
stones again to stone Him.
32Jesus answered them,
"I showed you many good
works from the Father; for
which of them are you stoning Me?"
33The Jews answered
Him, "For a good work we
do not stone You, but for
blasphemy; and because
You, being a man, make
Yourself out *to be* God."
34Jesus answered them,
"Has it not been written in
your Law, 'I SAID, YOU ARE
GODS'?
35"If he called them gods,
to whom the word of God
came (and the Scripture
cannot be broken),
36do you say of Him,
whom the Father sanctified
and sent into the world,
'You are blaspheming,' because I said, 'I am the Son
of God'?
37"If I do not do the
works of My Father, do not
believe Me;
38but if I do them, though
you do not believe Me, believe the works, that you
may know and understand
that the Father is in Me,
and I in the Father."
39Therefore they were
seeking again to seize Him,
and He eluded their grasp.
40And He went away
again beyond the Jordan to
the place where John was
first baptizing, and He was
staying there.
41And many came to Him

τὸν αἰῶνα, καὶ οὐχ ἁρπάσει τις αὐτὰ
the age, and [2]shall not seize [1]anyone them
ἐκ τῆς χειρός μου. **29** ὁ πατήρ μου ὃ
out of the hand of me. The Father of me who
δέδωκέν μοι πάντων μεῖζόν ἐστιν, καὶ
has given to me [than] all greater is, and
οὐδεὶς δύναται ἁρπάζειν ἐκ τῆς χειρὸς
no one can *to* seize out of the hand
τοῦ πατρός. **30** ἐγὼ καὶ ὁ πατὴρ ἕν
of the Father. I and the Father one
ἐσμεν. **31** Ἐβάστασαν πάλιν λίθους οἱ
we are. Lifted again stones the
Ἰουδαῖοι ἵνα λιθάσωσιν αὐτόν. **32** ἀπ-
Jews that they might stone him. An-
εκρίθη αὐτοῖς ὁ Ἰησοῦς· πολλὰ ἔργα
swered them – Jesus : Many [3]works
ἔδειξα ὑμῖν καλὰ ἐκ τοῦ πατρός· διὰ
[1]I showed [4]you [2]good of the Father; because of
ποῖον αὐτῶν ἔργον ἐμὲ λιθάζετε;
which [2]of them [1]work [4]me [3]stone ye?
33 ἀπεκρίθησαν αὐτῷ οἱ Ἰουδαῖοι· περὶ
Answered him the Jews : Concerning
καλοῦ ἔργου οὐ λιθάζομέν σε ἀλλὰ περὶ
a good work we do not stone thee but concerning
βλασφημίας, καὶ ὅτι σὺ ἄνθρωπος ὢν
blasphemy, and because thou a man being
ποιεῖς σεαυτὸν θεόν. **34** ἀπεκρίθη αὐτοῖς
makest thyself God. Answered them
ὁ Ἰησοῦς· οὐκ ἔστιν γεγραμμένον ἐν τῷ
– Jesus : Is it not *having been* written in the
νόμῳ ὑμῶν ὅτι ἐγὼ εἶπα· θεοί ἐστε;
law of you[,] – I said : Gods ye are?
35 εἰ ἐκείνους εἶπεν θεοὺς πρὸς οὓς ὁ
[1]if [3]those [2]he called [4]gods with whom the
λόγος τοῦ θεοῦ ἐγένετο, καὶ οὐ δύναται
word – of God was, and cannot
λυθῆναι ἡ γραφή, **36** ὃν ὁ πατὴρ
to be broken the scripture, [5][him] whom [1]the [2]Father
ἡγίασεν καὶ ἀπέστειλεν εἰς τὸν κόσμον
[3]sanctified [7]and [8]sent [9]into [10]the [11]world
ὑμεῖς λέγετε ὅτι βλασφημεῖς, ὅτι εἶπον·
[6]ye [4]tell[,] – Thou blasphemest, because I said :
υἱὸς τοῦ θεοῦ εἰμι; **37** εἰ οὐ ποιῶ τὰ ἔργα
Son – of God I am? If I do not the works
τοῦ πατρός μου, μὴ πιστεύετέ μοι· **38** εἰ δὲ
of the Father of me, do not believe me; but if
ποιῶ, κἂν ἐμοὶ μὴ πιστεύητε, τοῖς ἔργοις
I do, even if me ye do not believe, the works
πιστεύετε, ἵνα γνῶτε καὶ γινώσκητε
believe, that ye may know• and continue to know•
ὅτι ἐν ἐμοὶ ὁ πατὴρ κἀγὼ ἐν τῷ πατρί.
that in me the Father [is] and I in the Father.
39 Ἐζήτουν οὖν αὐτὸν πάλιν πιάσαι· καὶ
They sought therefore him again to arrest; and
ἐξῆλθεν ἐκ τῆς χειρὸς αὐτῶν.
he went forth out of the hand of them.
40 Καὶ ἀπῆλθεν πάλιν πέραν τοῦ
And he went away again across the
Ἰορδάνου εἰς τὸν τόπον ὅπου ἦν Ἰωάννης
Jordan to the place where was John
τὸ πρῶτον βαπτίζων, καὶ ἔμενεν ἐκεῖ.
at first baptizing, and remained there.
41 καὶ πολλοὶ ἦλθον πρὸς αὐτὸν καὶ
And many came to him and

no one can snatch them out
of my hand. 29My Father,
who has given them to me,
is greater than all[z]; no one
can snatch them out of my
Father's hand. 30I and the
Father are one."
31Again the Jews picked
up stones to stone him,
32but Jesus said to them, "I
have shown you many
great miracles from the Father. For which of these do
you stone me?"
33"We are not stoning
you for any of these," replied the Jews, "but for
blasphemy, because you, a
mere man, claim to be
God."
34Jesus answered them,
"Is it not written in your
Law, 'I have said you are
gods'[a]? 35If he called them
'gods,' to whom the word
of God came—and the
Scripture cannot be broken
—36what about the one
whom the Father set apart
as his very own and sent
into the world? Why then
do you accuse me of blas-
phemy because I said, 'I
am God's Son'? 37Do not
believe me unless I do what
my Father does. 38But if I
do it, even though you do
not believe me, believe the
miracles, that you may
know and understand that
the Father is in me, and I in
the Father." 39Again they
tried to seize him, but he
escaped their grasp.
40Then Jesus went back
across the Jordan to the
place where John had been
baptizing in the early days.
Here he stayed 41and many
people came to him. They

[u] Some early mss. read *What My Father has given Me is greater than all*

• Different tenses (aorist and present) of the same verb.

[z] 29 Many early manuscripts *What my Father has given me is greater than all*
[a] 34 Psalm 82:6

and were saying, "While John performed no sign, yet everything John said about this man was true."
42And many believed in Him there.

Chapter 11

The Death and Resurrection of Lazarus

NOW a certain man was sick, Lazarus of Bethany, the village of Mary and her sister Martha.
2And it was the Mary who anointed the Lord with ointment, and wiped His feet with her hair, whose brother Lazarus was sick.
3The sisters therefore sent to Him, saying, "Lord, behold, he whom You love is sick."
4But when Jesus heard it, He said, "This sickness is not unto death, but for the glory of God, that the Son of God may be glorified by it."
5Now Jesus loved Martha, and her sister, and Lazarus.
6When therefore He heard that he was sick, He stayed then two days *longer* in the place where He was.
7Then after this He *said to the disciples, "Let us go to Judea again."
8The disciples *said to Him, "Rabbi, the Jews were just now seeking to stone You, and are You going there again?"
9Jesus answered, "Are there not twelve hours in the day? If anyone walks in the day, he does not stumble, because he sees the light of this world.
10"But if anyone walks in the night, he stumbles, because the light is not in him."
11This He said, and after that He *said to them, "Our friend Lazarus has

ἔλεγον ὅτι Ἰωάννης μὲν σημεῖον ἐποίησεν
said[,] – John indeed sign did
οὐδέν, πάντα δὲ ὅσα εἶπεν Ἰωάννης περὶ
none, but all things how many said John about
τούτου ἀληθῆ ἦν. **42** καὶ πολλοὶ ἐπίστευσαν
this man true was(were). And many believed
εἰς αὐτὸν ἐκεῖ.
in him there.

11 Ἦν δέ τις ἀσθενῶν, Λάζαρος ἀπὸ
Now there was a certain [man] ailing, Lazarus from
Βηθανίας, ἐκ τῆς κώμης Μαρίας καὶ
Bethany, of the village of Mary and
Μάρθας τῆς ἀδελφῆς αὐτῆς. **2** ἦν δὲ
Martha the sister of her. And it was
Μαριὰμ ἡ ἀλείψασα τὸν κύριον μύρῳ
Mary the [one] anointing the Lord with ointment
καὶ ἐκμάξασα τοὺς πόδας αὐτοῦ ταῖς
and wiping off the feet of him with the
θριξὶν αὐτῆς, ἧς ὁ ἀδελφὸς Λάζαρος
hairs of her, of whom the brother Lazarus
ἠσθένει. **3** ἀπέστειλαν οὖν αἱ ἀδελφαὶ
ailed. Sent therefore the sisters
πρὸς αὐτὸν λέγουσαι· κύριε, ἴδε ὃν
to him saying: Lord, behold[,] [he] whom
φιλεῖς ἀσθενεῖ. **4** ἀκούσας δὲ ὁ Ἰησοῦς
thou lovest ails. And hearing – Jesus
εἶπεν· αὕτη ἡ ἀσθένεια οὐκ ἔστιν πρὸς
said: This – ailment is not to
θάνατον ἀλλ' ὑπὲρ τῆς δόξης τοῦ θεοῦ,
death but for the glory – of God,
ἵνα δοξασθῇ ὁ υἱὸς τοῦ θεοῦ δι' αὐτῆς.
that may be glorified the Son – of God through it.
5 ἠγάπα δὲ ὁ Ἰησοῦς τὴν Μάρθαν καὶ
Now [2]loved – [1]Jesus – Martha and
τὴν ἀδελφὴν αὐτῆς καὶ τὸν Λάζαρον.
the sister of her and – Lazarus.
6 ὡς οὖν ἤκουσεν ὅτι ἀσθενεῖ, τότε μὲν
When therefore he heard that he ails(ed), then –
ἔμεινεν ἐν ᾧ ἦν τόπῳ δύο ἡμέρας·
he remained [1]in [2]which [4]he was [3]place two days;
7 ἔπειτα μετὰ τοῦτο λέγει τοῖς μαθηταῖς·
then after this he says to the disciples:
ἄγωμεν εἰς τὴν Ἰουδαίαν πάλιν. **8** λέγουσιν
Let us go into – Judæa again. Say
αὐτῷ οἱ μαθηταί· ῥαββί, νῦν ἐζήτουν
to him the disciples: Rabbi, [4]now [3]were [5]seeking
σε λιθάσαι οἱ Ἰουδαῖοι, καὶ πάλιν ὑπάγεις
[7]thee [6]to stone [1]the [2]Jews, and again goest thou
ἐκεῖ; **9** ἀπεκρίθη Ἰησοῦς· οὐχὶ δώδεκα
there? Answered Jesus: Not twelve
ὧραί εἰσιν τῆς ἡμέρας; ἐάν τις περιπατῇ
hours are there of the day? if anyone walks
ἐν τῇ ἡμέρᾳ, οὐ προσκόπτει, ὅτι τὸ φῶς
in the day, he does not stumble, because the light
τοῦ κόσμου τούτου βλέπει· **10** ἐὰν δέ
– world of this he sees; but if
τις περιπατῇ ἐν τῇ νυκτί, προσκόπτει,
anyone walks in the night, he stumbles,
ὅτι τὸ φῶς οὐκ ἔστιν ἐν αὐτῷ. **11** ταῦτα
because the light is not in him. These things
εἶπεν, καὶ μετὰ τοῦτο λέγει αὐτοῖς·
he said, and after this he says to them:
Λάζαρος ὁ φίλος ἡμῶν κεκοίμηται· ἀλλὰ
Lazarus the friend of us has fallen asleep; but

said, "Though John never performed a miraculous sign, all that John said about this man was true."
42And in that place many believed in Jesus.

Chapter 11

The Death of Lazarus

NOW a man named Lazarus was sick. He was from Bethany, the village of Mary and her sister Martha. 2This Mary, whose brother Lazarus now lay sick, was the same one who poured perfume on the Lord and wiped his feet with her hair. 3So the sisters sent word to Jesus, "Lord, the one you love is sick."
4When he heard this, Jesus said, "This sickness will not end in death. No, it is for God's glory so that God's Son may be glorified through it." 5Jesus loved Martha and her sister and Lazarus. 6Yet when he heard that Lazarus was sick, he stayed where he was two more days.
7Then he said to his disciples, "Let us go back to Judea."
8"But Rabbi," they said, "a short while ago the Jews tried to stone you, and yet you are going back there?"
9Jesus answered, "Are there not twelve hours of daylight? A man who walks by day will not stumble, for he sees by this world's light. 10It is when he walks by night that he stumbles, for he has no light."
11After he had said this, he went on to tell them, "Our friend Lazarus has

fallen asleep; but I go, that I
may awaken him out of
sleep."
12 The disciples therefore
said to Him, "Lord, if he
has fallen asleep, he will
recover."
13 Now Jesus had spoken
of his death, but they
thought that He was speaking of literal sleep.
14 Then Jesus therefore
said to them plainly,
"Lazarus is dead,
15 and I am glad for your
sakes that I was not there,
so that you may believe;
but let us go to him."
16 Thomas therefore, who
is called Didymus, said to
his fellow disciples, "Let
us also go, that we may die
with Him."
17 So when Jesus came,
He found that he had al-
ready been in the tomb four
days.
18 Now Bethany was near
Jerusalem, about two miles
off;
19 and many of the Jews
had come to Martha and
Mary, to console them concerning *their* brother.
20 Martha therefore, when
she heard that Jesus was
coming, went to meet Him;
but Mary still sat in the
house.
21 Martha therefore said to
Jesus, "Lord, if You had
been here, my brother
would not have died.
22 "Even now I know that
whatever You ask of God,
God will give You."
23 Jesus *said to her,
"Your brother shall rise
again."
24 Martha *said to Him, "I
know that he will rise again
in the resurrection on the
last day."
25 Jesus said to her, "I am
the resurrection and the
life; he who believes in Me
shall live even if he dies,
26 and everyone who lives
and believes in Me shall
never die. Do you believe

πορεύομαι ἵνα ἐξυπνίσω αὐτόν. 12 εἶπαν
I am going that I may awaken him. Said

οὖν οἱ μαθηταὶ αὐτῷ· κύριε, εἰ κεκοίμηται,
there- fore the disciples to him: Lord, if he has fallen asleep,

σωθήσεται. 13 εἰρήκει δὲ ὁ Ἰησοῦς περὶ
he will be healed. Now had spoken – Jesus concerning

τοῦ θανάτου αὐτοῦ· ἐκεῖνοι δὲ ἔδοξαν ὅτι
the death of him; but those men thought that

περὶ τῆς κοιμήσεως τοῦ ὕπνου λέγει.
concerning the sleep – of slumber he says.

14 τότε οὖν εἶπεν αὐτοῖς ὁ Ἰησοῦς
Then therefore told them – Jesus

παρρησίᾳ· Λάζαρος ἀπέθανεν, 15 καὶ χαίρω
plainly: Lazarus died, and I rejoice

δι' ὑμᾶς, ἵνα πιστεύσητε, ὅτι οὐκ ἤμην
because of you, that ye may believe, that I was not

ἐκεῖ· ἀλλὰ ἄγωμεν πρὸς αὐτόν. 16 εἶπεν
there; but let us go to him. Said

οὖν Θωμᾶς ὁ λεγόμενος Δίδυμος τοῖς
therefore Thomas – *being* called Twin to the(his)

συμμαθηταῖς· ἄγωμεν καὶ ἡμεῖς ἵνα
fellow-disciples: Let go also we(us) that

ἀποθάνωμεν μετ' αὐτοῦ. 17 Ἐλθὼν οὖν
we may die with him. Coming therefore

ὁ Ἰησοῦς εὗρεν αὐτὸν τέσσαρας ἤδη
– Jesus found him [2]four [1]already

ἡμέρας ἔχοντα ἐν τῷ μνημείῳ. 18 ἦν δὲ
[3]days having(being) in the tomb. Now was

Βηθανία ἐγγὺς τῶν Ἱεροσολύμων ὡς ἀπὸ
Bethany near – Jerusalem about [3]away

σταδίων δεκαπέντε. 19 πολλοὶ δὲ ἐκ τῶν
[2]furlongs [1]fifteen. And many of the

Ἰουδαίων ἐληλύθεισαν πρὸς τὴν Μάρθαν
Jews had come to – Martha

καὶ Μαριάμ, ἵνα παραμυθήσωνται αὐτὰς
and Mary, that they might console them

περὶ τοῦ ἀδελφοῦ. 20 ἡ οὖν Μάρθα ὡς
concerning the(ir) brother. – Therefore Martha when

ἤκουσεν ὅτι Ἰησοῦς ἔρχεται, ὑπήντησεν
she heard that Jesus is(was) coming, met

αὐτῷ· Μαριὰμ δὲ ἐν τῷ οἴκῳ ἐκαθέζετο.
him; but Mary in the house sat.

21 εἶπεν οὖν ἡ Μάρθα πρὸς Ἰησοῦν·
Said therefore – Martha to Jesus:

κύριε, εἰ ἦς ὧδε, οὐκ ἂν ἀπέθανεν ὁ
Lord, if thou wast here, would not have died the

ἀδελφός μου. 22 καὶ νῦν οἶδα ὅτι ὅσα ἂν
brother of me. And now I know that whatever things

αἰτήσῃ τὸν θεὸν δώσει σοι ὁ θεός.
thou askest – God [3]will give [3]thee – [1]God.

23 λέγει αὐτῇ ὁ Ἰησοῦς· ἀναστήσεται ὁ
Says to her – Jesus: Will rise again the

ἀδελφός σου. 24 λέγει αὐτῷ ἡ Μάρθα·
brother of thee. Says to him – Martha:

οἶδα ὅτι ἀναστήσεται ἐν τῇ ἀναστάσει
I know that he will rise again in the resurrection

ἐν τῇ ἐσχάτῃ ἡμέρᾳ. 25 εἶπεν αὐτῇ ὁ
in the last day. Said to her –

Ἰησοῦς· ἐγώ εἰμι ἡ ἀνάστασις καὶ ἡ
Jesus: I am the resurrection and the

ζωή· ὁ πιστεύων εἰς ἐμὲ κἂν ἀποθάνῃ
life; the [one] believing in me even if he should die

ζήσεται, 26 καὶ πᾶς ὁ ζῶν καὶ πιστεύων
will live, and everyone living and believing

εἰς ἐμὲ οὐ μὴ ἀποθάνῃ εἰς τὸν αἰῶνα·
in me by no means dies unto the age:

fallen asleep; but I am going
there to wake him up."
12 His disciples replied,
"Lord, if he sleeps, he will
get better." 13 Jesus had
been speaking of his death,
but his disciples thought he
meant natural sleep.
14 So then he told them
plainly, "Lazarus is dead,
15 and for your sake I am
glad I was not there, so that
you may believe. But let us
go to him."
16 Then Thomas (called
Didymus) said to the rest of
the disciples, "Let us also
go, that we may die with
him."

Jesus Comforts the Sisters

17 On his arrival, Jesus
found that Lazarus had already been in the tomb for
four days. 18 Bethany was
less than two miles[b] from
Jerusalem, 19 and many
Jews had come to Martha
and Mary to comfort them
in the loss of their brother.
20 When Martha heard that
Jesus was coming, she
went out to meet him, but
Mary stayed at home.
21 "Lord," Martha said to
Jesus, "if you had been
here, my brother would not
have died. 22 But I know
that even now God will give
you whatever you ask."
23 Jesus said to her,
"Your brother will rise
again."
24 Martha answered, "I
know he will rise again in
the resurrection at the last
day."
25 Jesus said to her, "I am
the resurrection and the
life. He who believes in me
will live, even though he
dies; 26 and whoever lives
and believes in me will never die. Do you believe
this?"

[b]18 Greek *fifteen stadia* (about 3 kilometers)

this?"
27 She *said to Him, "Yes, Lord; I have believed that You are the Christ, the Son of God, *even* He who comes into the world."
28 And when she had said this, she went away, and called Mary her sister, saying secretly, "The Teacher is here, and is calling for you."
29 And when she heard it, she *arose quickly, and was coming to Him.
30 Now Jesus had not yet come into the village, but was still in the place where Martha met Him.
31 The Jews then who were with her in the house, and consoling her, when they saw that Mary rose up quickly and went out, followed her, supposing that she was going to the tomb to weep there.
32 Therefore, when Mary came where Jesus was, she saw Him, and fell at His feet, saying to Him, "Lord, if You had been here, my brother would not have died."
33 When Jesus therefore saw her weeping, and the Jews who came with her, *also* weeping, He was deeply moved in spirit, and was troubled,
34 and said, "Where have you laid him?" They *said to Him, "Lord, come and see."
35 Jesus wept.
36 And so the Jews were saying, "Behold how He loved him!"
37 But some of them said, "Could not this man, who opened the eyes of him who was blind, have kept this man also from dying?"
38 Jesus therefore again being deeply moved within, *came to the tomb. Now it was a cave, and a stone was

πιστεύεις τοῦτο; **27** λέγει αὐτῷ· ναί, κύριε·
believest thou this? She says to him : Yes, Lord;
ἐγὼ πεπίστευκα ὅτι σὺ εἶ ὁ χριστὸς ὁ
I have believed that thou art the Christ the
υἱὸς τοῦ θεοῦ ὁ εἰς τὸν κόσμον ἐρχόμενος.
Son – of God [1]the [3]into [4]the [5]world [2][one] coming.
28 καὶ τοῦτο εἰποῦσα ἀπῆλθεν καὶ ἐφώνησεν
And this saying she went away and called
Μαριὰμ τὴν ἀδελφὴν αὐτῆς λάθρα εἰποῦσα·
Mary the sister of her secretly saying :
ὁ διδάσκαλος πάρεστιν καὶ φωνεῖ σε.
The Teacher is here and calls thee.
29 ἐκείνη δὲ ὡς ἤκουσεν, ἐγείρεται ταχὺ
And that [one] when she heard, *rose quickly
καὶ ἤρχετο πρὸς αὐτόν· **30** οὔπω δὲ
and came to him; now not yet
ἐληλύθει ὁ Ἰησοῦς εἰς τὴν κώμην, ἀλλ'
had come – Jesus into the village, but
ἦν ἔτι ἐν τῷ τόπῳ ὅπου ὑπήντησεν
was still in the place where met
αὐτῷ ἡ Μάρθα. **31** οἱ οὖν Ἰουδαῖοι
him – Martha. Therefore the Jews
οἱ ὄντες μετ' αὐτῆς ἐν τῇ οἰκίᾳ καὶ
the [ones] being with her in the house and
παραμυθούμενοι αὐτήν, ἰδόντες τὴν Μαριὰμ
consoling her, seeing – Mary
ὅτι ταχέως ἀνέστη καὶ ἐξῆλθεν,
that quickly she rose up and went out,
ἠκολούθησαν αὐτῇ, δόξαντες ὅτι ὑπάγει
followed her, thinking[,] – She is going
εἰς τὸ μνημεῖον ἵνα κλαύσῃ ἐκεῖ. **32** ἡ
to the tomb that she may weep there. –
οὖν Μαριὰμ ὡς ἦλθεν ὅπου ἦν Ἰησοῦς,
Therefore Mary when she came where was Jesus,
ἰδοῦσα αὐτὸν ἔπεσεν αὐτοῦ πρὸς τοὺς
seeing him fell of him at the
πόδας, λέγουσα αὐτῷ· κύριε, εἰ ἦς ὧδε,
feet, saying to him : Lord, if thou wast here,
οὐκ ἄν μου ἀπέθανεν ὁ ἀδελφός.
[4]would not [3]of me [5]have died [1]the [2]brother.
33 Ἰησοῦς οὖν ὡς εἶδεν αὐτὴν κλαίουσαν
Jesus therefore when he saw her weeping
καὶ τοὺς συνελθόντας αὐτῇ Ἰουδαίους
and [1]the [3]coming with [4]her [2]Jews
κλαίοντας, ἐνεβριμήσατο τῷ πνεύματι καὶ
weeping, groaned in the(his) spirit and
ἐτάραξεν ἑαυτόν, **34** καὶ εἶπεν· ποῦ
troubled himself, and said : Where
τεθείκατε αὐτόν; λέγουσιν αὐτῷ· κύριε,
have ye put him? They say to him : Lord,
ἔρχου καὶ ἴδε. **35** ἐδάκρυσεν ὁ Ἰησοῦς.
come and see. Shed tears – Jesus.
36 ἔλεγον οὖν οἱ Ἰουδαῖοι· ἴδε πῶς
Said therefore the Jews : See how
ἐφίλει αὐτόν. **37** τινὲς δὲ ἐξ αὐτῶν
he loved him. But some of them
εἶπαν· οὐκ ἐδύνατο οὗτος ὁ ἀνοίξας
said : Could not this man the [one] opening
τοὺς ὀφθαλμοὺς τοῦ τυφλοῦ ποιῆσαι ἵνα
the eyes of the blind man *to* cause that
καὶ οὗτος μὴ ἀποθάνῃ; **38** Ἰησοῦς οὖν
even this man should not die ? Jesus therefore
πάλιν ἐμβριμώμενος ἐν ἑαυτῷ ἔρχεται
again groaning in himself comes
εἰς τὸ μνημεῖον· ἦν δὲ σπήλαιον, καὶ
to the tomb; now it was a cave, and

27 "Yes, Lord," she told
him, "I believe that you are
the Christ,[c] the Son of
God, who was to come into
the world."
28 And after she had said
this, she went back and
called her sister Mary
aside. "The Teacher is
here," she said, "and is
asking for you." 29 When
Mary heard this, she got up
quickly and went to him.
30 Now Jesus had not yet
entered the village, but was
still at the place where Martha had met him. 31 When
the Jews who had been
with Mary in the house,
comforting her, noticed
how quickly she got up and
went out, they followed
her, supposing she was going to the tomb to mourn
there.
32 When Mary reached the
place where Jesus was and
saw him, she fell at his feet
and said, "Lord, if you had
been here, my brother
would not have died."
33 When Jesus saw her
weeping, and the Jews who
had come along with her
also weeping, he was deeply moved in spirit and troubled. 34 "Where have you
laid him?" he asked.
"Come and see, Lord,"
they replied.
35 Jesus wept.
36 Then the Jews said,
"See how he loved him!"
37 But some of them said,
"Could not he who opened
the eyes of the blind man
have kept this man from
dying?"

Jesus Raises Lazarus From the Dead

38 Jesus, once more deep-
ly moved, came to the
tomb. It was a cave with a
stone laid across the en-

[c]27 Or *Messiah*

lying against it.
39Jesus *said, "Remove
the stone." Martha, the sister of the deceased, *said to
Him, "Lord, by this time
there will be a stench, for
he has been *dead* four
days."
40Jesus *said to her, "Did
I not say to you, if you believe, you will see the glory
of God?"
41And so they removed
the stone. And Jesus raised
His eyes, and said, "Fa-
ther, I thank Thee that
Thou heardest Me.
42"And I knew that Thou
hearest Me always; but because of the people standing around I said it, that
they may believe that Thou
didst send Me."
43And when He had said
these things, He cried out
with a loud voice, "Laza-
rus, come forth."
44He who had died came
forth, bound hand and foot
with wrappings; and his
face was wrapped around
with a cloth. Jesus *said to
them, "Unbind him, and
let him go."
45Many therefore of the
Jews, who had come to
Mary and beheld what He
had done, believed in Him.
46But some of them went
away to the Pharisees, and
told them the things which
Jesus had done.

Conspiracy to Kill Jesus

47Therefore the chief
priests and the Pharisees
convened a council, and
were saying, "What are we
doing? For this man is performing many signs.
48"If we let Him *go on*
like this, all men will believe in Him, and the Ro-
mans will come and take
away both our place and
our nation."
49But a certain one of
them, Caiaphas, who was
high priest that year, said to

λίθος ἐπέκειτο ἐπ' αὐτῷ. **39** λέγει ὁ
a stone was lying *on* on it. Says –
Ἰησοῦς· ἄρατε τὸν λίθον. λέγει αὐτῷ
Jesus : Lift ye the stone. Says to him
ἡ ἀδελφὴ τοῦ τετελευτηκότος Μάρθα·
the sister of the [one] having died Martha :
κύριε, ἤδη ὄζει· τεταρταῖος γάρ ἐστιν.
Lord, now he smells; for fourth [day] it is.
40 λέγει αὐτῇ ὁ Ἰησοῦς· οὐκ εἶπόν
Says to her – Jesus : Not I told
σοι ὅτι ἐὰν πιστεύσῃς ὄψῃ τὴν δόξαν
thee that if thou believest thou wilt see the glory
τοῦ θεοῦ; **41** ἦραν οὖν τὸν λίθον. ὁ
– of God? They lifted therefore the stone. –
δὲ Ἰησοῦς ἦρεν τοὺς ὀφθαλμοὺς ἄνω
And Jesus lifted the(his) eyes up
καὶ εἶπεν· πάτερ, εὐχαριστῶ σοι ὅτι
and said : Father, I thank thee that
ἤκουσάς μου. **42** ἐγὼ δὲ ᾔδειν ὅτι
thou didst hear me. And I knew that
πάντοτέ μου ἀκούεις· ἀλλὰ διὰ τὸν
always me thou hearest; but because of the
ὄχλον τὸν περιεστῶτα εἶπον, ἵνα
crowd – standing round I said, that
πιστεύσωσιν ὅτι σύ με ἀπέστειλας.
they may believe that thou me didst send.
43 καὶ ταῦτα εἰπὼν φωνῇ μεγάλῃ
And these things saying voice with a great
ἐκραύγασεν· Λάζαρε, δεῦρο ἔξω. **44** ἐξῆλθεν
he cried out : Lazarus, come out. Came out
ὁ τεθνηκὼς δεδεμένος τοὺς πόδας καὶ
the [one] having died *having been* bound the feet and
τὰς χεῖρας κειρίαις, καὶ ἡ ὄψις αὐτοῦ
the hands with bandages, and the face of him
σουδαρίῳ περιεδέδετο. λέγει αὐτοῖς ὁ
with a napkin had been bound round. Says to them –
Ἰησοῦς· λύσατε αὐτὸν καὶ ἄφετε αὐτὸν ὑπάγειν.
Jesus : Loosen him and let him *to* go.
45 Πολλοὶ οὖν ἐκ τῶν Ἰουδαίων, οἱ
Many therefore of the Jews, the [ones]
ἐλθόντες πρὸς τὴν Μαριὰμ καὶ θεασάμενοι
having come to – Mary and having beheld
ὃ ἐποίησεν, ἐπίστευσαν εἰς αὐτόν· **46** τινὲς δὲ
what he did, believed in him; but some
ἐξ αὐτῶν ἀπῆλθον πρὸς τοὺς Φαρισαίους
of them went away to the Pharisees
καὶ εἶπαν αὐτοῖς ἃ ἐποίησεν Ἰησοῦς.
and told them what things did Jesus.
47 συνήγαγον οὖν οἱ ἀρχιερεῖς καὶ οἱ
Assembled therefore the chief priests and the
Φαρισαῖοι συνέδριον, καὶ ἔλεγον· τί
Pharisees a council, and said : What
ποιοῦμεν, ὅτι οὗτος ὁ ἄνθρωπος πολλὰ
are we doing, because this – man [2]many
ποιεῖ σημεῖα; **48** ἐὰν ἀφῶμεν αὐτὸν οὕτως,
[1]does [3]signs? If we leave him thus,
πάντες πιστεύσουσιν εἰς αὐτόν, καὶ
all men will believe in him, and
ἐλεύσονται οἱ Ῥωμαῖοι καὶ ἀροῦσιν ἡμῶν
will come the Romans and will take of us
καὶ τὸν τόπον καὶ τὸ ἔθνος. **49** εἷς
both the place and the nation. [2]one
δέ τις ἐξ αὐτῶν Καϊάφας, ἀρχιερεὺς
[1]But [2]a certain of them[,] Caiaphas, high priest
ὢν τοῦ ἐνιαυτοῦ ἐκείνου, εἶπεν αὐτοῖς·
being – year of that, said to them :

trance. 39"Take away the
stone," he said.
"But, Lord," said Mar-
tha, the sister of the dead
man, "by this time there is
a bad odor, for he has been
there four days."
40Then Jesus said, "Did I
not tell you that if you believed, you would see the
glory of God?"
41So they took away the
stone. Then Jesus looked
up and said, "Father, I
thank you that you have
heard me. 42I knew that
you always hear me, but I
said this for the benefit of
the people standing here,
that they may believe that
you sent me."
43When he had said this,
Jesus called in a loud voice,
"Lazarus, come out!"
44The dead man came out,
his hands and feet wrapped
with strips of linen, and a
cloth around his face.
Jesus said to them, "Take
off the grave clothes and let
him go."

The Plot to Kill Jesus

45Therefore many of the
Jews who had come to visit
Mary, and had seen what
Jesus did, put their faith in
him. 46But some of them
went to the Pharisees and
told them what Jesus had
done. 47Then the chief
priests and the Pharisees
called a meeting of the Sanhedrin.
"What are we accom-
plishing?" they asked.
"Here is this man performing many miraculous signs.
48If we let him go on like
this, everyone will believe
in him, and then the Ro-
mans will come and take
away both our place[d] and
our nation."
49Then one of them,
named Caiaphas, who was
high priest that year, spoke

[d]48 Or *temple*

them, "You know nothing at all,

[50]nor do you take into account that it is expedient for you that one man should die for the people, and that the whole nation should not perish."

[51]Now this he did not say on his own initiative; but being high priest that year, he prophesied that Jesus was going to die for the nation,

[52]and not for the nation only, but that He might also gather together into one the children of God who are scattered abroad.

[53]So from that day on they planned together to kill Him.

[54]Jesus therefore no longer continued to walk publicly among the Jews, but went away from there to the country near the wilderness, into a city called Ephraim; and there He stayed with the disciples.

[55]Now the Passover of the Jews was at hand, and many went up to Jerusalem out of the country before the Passover, to purify themselves.

[56]Therefore they were seeking for Jesus, and were saying to one another, as they stood in the temple, "What do you think; that He will not come to the feast at all?"

[57]Now the chief priests and the Pharisees had given orders that if anyone knew where He was, he should report it, that they might seize Him.

Chapter 12

Mary Anoints Jesus

JESUS, therefore, six days before the Passover, came to Bethany where Lazarus was, whom Jesus had raised from the dead.

[2]So they made Him a supper there, and Martha was serving; but Lazarus was one of those reclining *at the table* with Him.

ὑμεῖς οὐκ οἴδατε οὐδέν, 50 οὐδὲ λογίζεσθε
Ye know not no(any)thing, nor reckon

ὅτι συμφέρει ὑμῖν ἵνα εἷς ἄνθρωπος
that it is expedient for us that one man

ἀποθάνῃ ὑπὲρ τοῦ λαοῦ καὶ μὴ ὅλον
should die for the people and not all

τὸ ἔθνος ἀπόληται. 51 τοῦτο δὲ ἀφ'
the nation perish. But this from

ἑαυτοῦ οὐκ εἶπεν, ἀλλὰ ἀρχιερεὺς ὢν
himself he said not, but high priest being

τοῦ ἐνιαυτοῦ ἐκείνου ἐπροφήτευσεν ὅτι
– year of that he prophesied that

ἔμελλεν Ἰησοῦς ἀποθνήσκειν ὑπὲρ τοῦ
was about Jesus to die for the

ἔθνους, 52 καὶ οὐχ ὑπὲρ τοῦ ἔθνους
nation, and not for the nation

μόνον, ἀλλ' ἵνα καὶ τὰ τέκνα τοῦ θεοῦ
only, but that also the children – of God

τὰ διεσκορπισμένα συναγάγῃ εἰς ἕν.
– *having been* scattered he might gather into one.

53 ἀπ' ἐκείνης οὖν τῆς ἡμέρας ἐβουλεύσαντο
From [1]that [3]therefore – [2]day they took counsel

ἵνα ἀποκτείνωσιν αὐτόν. 54 Ὁ οὖν
that they might kill him. – Therefore

Ἰησοῦς οὐκέτι παρρησίᾳ περιεπάτει ἐν
Jesus no longer openly walked among

τοῖς Ἰουδαίοις, ἀλλὰ ἀπῆλθεν ἐκεῖθεν εἰς
the Jews, but went away thence into

τὴν χώραν ἐγγὺς τῆς ἐρήμου, εἰς Ἐφραὶμ
the country near the desert, to [3]Ephraim

λεγομένην πόλιν, κἀκεῖ ἔμεινεν μετὰ τῶν
[2]*being* called [1]a city, and there remained with the

μαθητῶν.
disciples.

55 Ἦν δὲ ἐγγὺς τὸ πάσχα τῶν
Now was near the Passover of the

Ἰουδαίων, καὶ ἀνέβησαν πολλοὶ εἰς
Jews, and went up many to

Ἱεροσόλυμα ἐκ τῆς χώρας πρὸ τοῦ
Jerusalem out of the country before the

πάσχα, ἵνα ἁγνίσωσιν ἑαυτούς.
Passover, that they might purify themselves.

56 ἐζήτουν οὖν τὸν Ἰησοῦν καὶ ἔλεγον
They sought therefore – Jesus and said

μετ' ἀλλήλων ἐν τῷ ἱερῷ ἑστηκότες·
with one another in the temple standing :

τί δοκεῖ ὑμῖν; ὅτι οὐ μὴ ἔλθῃ εἰς
What seems it to you? that by no means he comes to

τὴν ἑορτήν; 57 δεδώκεισαν δὲ οἱ ἀρχιερεῖς
the feast? Now had given the chief priests

καὶ οἱ Φαρισαῖοι ἐντολὰς ἵνα ἐάν τις
and the Pharisees commands that if anyone

γνῷ ποῦ ἐστιν μηνύσῃ, ὅπως πιάσωσιν
knew where he is (was) he should inform, so as they might arrest

αὐτόν. 12 Ὁ οὖν Ἰησοῦς πρὸ ἓξ ἡμερῶν
him. – Therefore Jesus [3]before [1]six [2]days

τοῦ πάσχα ἦλθεν εἰς Βηθανίαν, ὅπου
the Passover came to Bethany, where

ἦν Λάζαρος, ὃν ἤγειρεν ἐκ νεκρῶν
was Lazarus, whom [2]raised [3]out of [the] [4]dead

Ἰησοῦς. 2 ἐποίησαν οὖν αὐτῷ δεῖπνον ἐκεῖ,
[1]Jesus. They made therefore for him a supper there,

καὶ ἡ Μάρθα διηκόνει, ὁ δὲ Λάζαρος εἷς
and – Martha served, – but Lazarus one

ἦν ἐκ τῶν ἀνακειμένων σὺν αὐτῷ· 3 ἡ
was of the [ones] reclining with him; –

up, "You know nothing at all! [50]You do not realize that it is better for you that one man die for the people than that the whole nation perish."

[51]He did not say this on his own, but as high priest that year he prophesied that Jesus would die for the Jewish nation, [52]and not only for that nation but also for the scattered children of God, to bring them together and make them one. [53]So from that day on they plotted to take his life.

[54]Therefore Jesus no longer moved about publicly among the Jews. Instead he withdrew to a region near the desert, to a village called Ephraim, where he stayed with his disciples.

[55]When it was almost time for the Jewish Passover, many went up from the country to Jerusalem for their ceremonial cleansing before the Passover. [56]They kept looking for Jesus, and as they stood in the temple area they asked one another, "What do you think? Isn't he coming to the Feast at all?" [57]But the chief priests and Pharisees had given orders that if anyone found out where Jesus was, he should report it so that they might arrest him.

Chapter 12

Jesus Anointed at Bethany

SIX days before the Passover, Jesus arrived at Bethany, where Lazarus lived, whom Jesus had raised from the dead. [2]Here a dinner was given in Jesus' honor. Martha served, while Lazarus was among those reclining at the table with him. [3]Then

3Mary therefore took a pound of very costly perfume of pure nard, and anointed the feet of Jesus, and wiped His feet with her hair; and the house was filled with the fragrance of the perfume.

4But Judas Iscariot, one of His disciples, who was intending to betray Him, *said,

5"Why was this perfume not sold for [v]three hundred denarii, and given to poor *people*?"

6Now he said this, not because he was concerned about the poor, but because he was a thief, and as he had the money box, he used to pilfer what was put into it.

7Jesus therefore said, "Let her alone, in order that she may keep [w]it for the day of My burial.

8"For the poor you always have with you, but you do not always have Me."

9The great multitude therefore of the Jews learned that He was there; and they came, not for Jesus' sake only, but that they might also see Lazarus, whom He raised from the dead.

10But the chief priests took counsel that they might put Lazarus to death also;

11because on account of him many of the Jews were going away, and were believing in Jesus.

Jesus Enters Jerusalem

12On the next day the great multitude who had come to the feast, when they heard that Jesus was coming to Jerusalem,

13took the branches of the palm trees, and went out to meet Him, and *began* to cry out, "Hosanna! BLESSED IS HE WHO COMES IN THE NAME OF THE LORD,

[v] Equivalent to 11 months' wages
[w] I.e., The custom of anointing for burial

οὖν Μαριὰμ λαβοῦσα λίτραν μύρου
therefore Mary taking a pound [3]ointment
νάρδου πιστικῆς πολυτίμου ἤλειψεν τοὺς
[4]of spikenard [1]of pure [2]costly anointed the
πόδας τοῦ Ἰησοῦ καὶ ἐξέμαξεν ταῖς
feet – of Jesus and wiped off with the
θριξὶν αὐτῆς τοὺς πόδας αὐτοῦ· ἡ δὲ
hairs of her the feet of him; and the
οἰκία ἐπληρώθη ἐκ τῆς ὀσμῆς τοῦ
house was filled of(with) the odour of the
μύρου. **4** λέγει δὲ Ἰούδας ὁ Ἰσκαριώτης
ointment. And says Judas the Iscariot
εἷς τῶν μαθητῶν αὐτοῦ, ὁ μέλλων
one of the disciples of him, the [one] being about
αὐτὸν παραδιδόναι· **5** διὰ τί τοῦτο τὸ
him to betray : Why this –
μύρον οὐκ ἐπράθη τριακοσίων δηναρίων
ointment not was sold of(for) three hundred denarii
καὶ ἐδόθη πτωχοῖς; **6** εἶπεν δὲ τοῦτο
and given to [the] poor? But he said this
οὐχ ὅτι περὶ τῶν πτωχῶν ἔμελεν αὐτῷ,
not because about the poor it mattered to him,
ἀλλ' ὅτι κλέπτης ἦν καὶ τὸ γλωσσόκομον
but because a thief he was and [2]the [3]bag
ἔχων τὰ βαλλόμενα ἐβάσταζεν.
[1]having [5]the things [6]being put [in] [4]carried. *
7 εἶπεν οὖν ὁ Ἰησοῦς· ἄφες αὐτήν,
Said therefore – Jesus : Leave her,
ἵνα εἰς τὴν ἡμέραν τοῦ ἐνταφιασμοῦ
that to the day of the burial
μου τηρήσῃ αὐτό· **8** τοὺς πτωχοὺς γὰρ
of me she may keep it; [2]the [3]poor [1]for
πάντοτε ἔχετε μεθ' ἑαυτῶν, ἐμὲ δὲ
always ye have with your*selves*, but me
οὐ πάντοτε ἔχετε. **9** Ἔγνω οὖν ὁ ὄχλος
not always ye have. Knew therefore the crowd
πολὺς ἐκ τῶν Ἰουδαίων ὅτι ἐκεῖ ἐστιν,
great of the Jews that there he is(was),
καὶ ἦλθον οὐ διὰ τὸν Ἰησοῦν μόνον,
and they came not because of – Jesus only,
ἀλλ' ἵνα καὶ τὸν Λάζαρον ἴδωσιν ὃν
but that also – Lazarus they might see whom
ἤγειρεν ἐκ νεκρῶν. **10** ἐβουλεύσαντο δὲ
he raised out of [the] dead. But took counsel
οἱ ἀρχιερεῖς ἵνα καὶ τὸν Λάζαρον
the chief priests that also – Lazarus
ἀποκτείνωσιν, **11** ὅτι πολλοὶ δι' αὐτὸν
they might kill, because [1]many [4]because of [5]him
ὑπῆγον τῶν Ἰουδαίων καὶ ἐπίστευον εἰς
[6]went [2]of the [3]Jews and believed in
τὸν Ἰησοῦν.
– Jesus.

12 Τῇ ἐπαύριον ὁ ὄχλος πολὺς ὁ
On the morrow the crowd much –
ἐλθὼν εἰς τὴν ἑορτήν, ἀκούσαντες ὅτι
coming to the feast, hearing that
ἔρχεται Ἰησοῦς εἰς Ἱεροσόλυμα, **13** ἔλαβον
is(was) coming Jesus to Jerusalem, took
τὰ βαΐα τῶν φοινίκων καὶ ἐξῆλθον εἰς
the branches of the palm-trees and went out to
ὑπάντησιν αὐτῷ, καὶ ἐκραύγαζον· ὡσαννά,
a meeting with him, and cried out : Hosanna,
εὐλογημένος ὁ ἐρχόμενος ἐν ὀνόματι
being blessed the [one] coming in [the] name

* This may mean "stole"; *cf.* our euphemism for "steal"—to "lift" a thing.

Mary took about a pint[e] of
pure nard, an expensive
perfume; she poured it on
Jesus' feet and wiped his
feet with her hair. And the
house was filled with the
fragrance of the perfume.
4But one of his disciples,
Judas Iscariot, who was
later to betray him, objected, 5"Why wasn't this perfume sold and the money
given to the poor? It was
worth a year's wages.[f]"
6He did not say this be-
cause he cared about the
poor but because he was a
thief; as keeper of the money bag, he used to help himself to what was put into it.
7"Leave her alone,"
Jesus replied. "It was intended that she should
save this perfume for the
day of my burial. 8You will
always have the poor
among you, but you will
not always have me."
9Meanwhile a large
crowd of Jews found out
that Jesus was there and
came, not only because of
him but also to see Laza-
rus, whom he had raised
from the dead. 10So the
chief priests made plans to
kill Lazarus as well, 11for
on account of him many of
the Jews were going over to
Jesus and putting their faith
in him.

The Triumphal Entry

12The next day the great
crowd that had come for
the Feast heard that Jesus
was on his way to Jerusa-
lem. 13They took palm
branches and went out to
meet him, shouting,

"Hosanna![g]"

"Blessed is he who
comes in the name
of the Lord!"[h]

[e] *3* Greek *a litra* (probably about 0.5 liter)
[f] *5* Greek *three hundred denarii*
[g] *13* A Hebrew expression meaning "Save!" which became an exclamation of praise
[h] *13* Psalm 118:25, 26

even the King of Israel.''
14 And Jesus, finding a
young donkey, sat on it; as
it is written,
15 ''FEAR NOT, DAUGHTER
OF ZION; BEHOLD, YOUR
KING IS COMING, SEATED ON
A DONKEY'S COLT.''
16 These things His disciples did not understand at
the first; but when Jesus
was glorified, then they
remembered that these
things were written of Him,
and that they had done
these things to Him.
17 And so the multitude
who were with Him when
He called Lazarus out of
the tomb, and raised him
from the dead, were bear-
ing Him witness.
18 For this cause also the
multitude went and met
Him, because they heard
that He had performed this
sign.
19 The Pharisees therefore
said to one another, ''You
see that you are not doing
any good; look, the world
has gone after Him.''

Greeks Seek Jesus

20 Now there were certain
Greeks among those who
were going up to worship at
the feast;
21 these therefore came to
Philip, who was from Bethsaida of Galilee, and *began
to* ask him, saying, ''Sir,
we wish to see Jesus.''
22 Philip *came and *told
Andrew; Andrew and
Philip *came, and they
*told Jesus.
23 And Jesus *answered
them, saying, ''The hour
has come for the Son of
Man to be glorified.
24 ''Truly, truly, I say to
you, unless a grain of wheat
falls into the earth and dies,
it remains by itself alone;
but if it dies, it bears much
fruit.
25 ''He who loves his life

κυρίου, καὶ ὁ βασιλεὺς τοῦ Ἰσραήλ.
of [the] Lord, even the king – of Israel.
14 εὑρὼν δὲ ὁ Ἰησοῦς ὀνάριον ἐκάθισεν
And ²having found – ¹Jesus a young ass sat
ἐπ' αὐτό, καθώς ἐστιν γεγραμμένον·
on it, as it is *having been* written :
15 μὴ φοβοῦ, θυγάτηρ Σιών· ἰδοὺ ὁ
Fear not, daughter of Sion : behold[,] the
βασιλεύς σου ἔρχεται, καθήμενος ἐπὶ
king of thee comes, sitting on
πῶλον ὄνου. **16** ταῦτα οὐκ ἔγνωσαν
a foal of an ass. These things knew not
αὐτοῦ οἱ μαθηταὶ τὸ πρῶτον, ἀλλ' ὅτε
of him the disciples at first, but when
ἐδοξάσθη Ἰησοῦς, τότε ἐμνήσθησαν ὅτι
was glorified Jesus, then they remembered that
ταῦτα ἦν ἐπ' αὐτῷ γεγραμμένα καὶ
these things were on him *having been* written and
ταῦτα ἐποίησαν αὐτῷ. **17** ἐμαρτύρει οὖν
these things they did to him. Witnessed therefore
ὁ ὄχλος ὁ ὢν μετ' αὐτοῦ ὅτε τὸν
the crowd – being with him when –
Λάζαρον ἐφώνησεν ἐκ τοῦ μνημείου καὶ
Lazarus he called out of the tomb and
ἤγειρεν αὐτὸν ἐκ νεκρῶν. **18** διὰ τοῦτο
raised him out of [the] dead. Therefore
καὶ ὑπήντησεν αὐτῷ ὁ ὄχλος, ὅτι
also met him the crowd, because
ἤκουσαν τοῦτο αὐτὸν πεποιηκέναι τὸ
¹they heard ⁴this ²him ³to have done[b] –
σημεῖον. **19** οἱ οὖν Φαρισαῖοι εἶπαν
⁵sign. Therefore the Pharisees said
πρὸς ἑαυτούς· θεωρεῖτε ὅτι οὐκ ὠφελεῖτε
to themselves : Behold ye that ye profit not
οὐδέν· ἴδε ὁ κόσμος ὀπίσω αὐτοῦ ἀπῆλθεν.
no(any)thing; see[,] the world after him went(is gone).
20 Ἦσαν δὲ Ἕλληνές τινες ἐκ τῶν
Now there were ²Greeks ¹some of the
ἀναβαινόντων ἵνα προσκυνήσωσιν ἐν τῇ
[ones] going up that they might worship at the
ἑορτῇ· **21** οὗτοι οὖν προσῆλθον Φιλίππῳ
feast; these therefore approached *to* Philip
τῷ ἀπὸ Βηθσαϊδὰ τῆς Γαλιλαίας, καὶ
the [one] from Bethsaida – of Galilee, and
ἠρώτων αὐτὸν λέγοντες· κύριε, θέλομεν
asked him saying : Sir, we wish
τὸν Ἰησοῦν ἰδεῖν. **22** ἔρχεται ὁ Φίλιππος
– Jesus to see. Comes – Philip
καὶ λέγει τῷ Ἀνδρέᾳ· ἔρχεται Ἀνδρέας
and tells – Andrew; comes Andrew
καὶ Φίλιππος καὶ λέγουσιν τῷ Ἰησοῦ.
and Philip and tell – Jesus.
23 ὁ δὲ Ἰησοῦς ἀποκρίνεται αὐτοῖς λέγων·
– And Jesus answers them saying:
ἐλήλυθεν ἡ ὥρα ἵνα δοξασθῇ ὁ υἱὸς τοῦ
Has come the hour that is glorified the Son –
ἀνθρώπου. **24** ἀμὴν ἀμὴν λέγω ὑμῖν,
of man. Truly truly I say to you,
ἐὰν μὴ ὁ κόκκος τοῦ σίτου πεσὼν εἰς
unless the grain – of wheat falling into
τὴν γῆν ἀποθάνῃ, αὐτὸς μόνος μένει·
the ground dies, it alone remains;
ἐὰν δὲ ἀποθάνῃ, πολὺν καρπὸν φέρει.
but if it dies, much fruit it bears.
25 ὁ φιλῶν τὴν ψυχὴν αὐτοῦ ἀπολλύει
The [one] loving the life of him loses

''Blessed is the King of
Israel!''
14 Jesus found a young donkey and sat upon it, as it is
written,
15 ''Do not be afraid, O
Daughter of Zion;
see, your king is
coming,
seated on a donkey's
colt.''[i]
16 At first his disciples did
not understand all this.
Only after Jesus was glorified did they realize that
these things had been written about him and that they
had done these things to
him.
17 Now the crowd that
was with him when he
called Lazarus from the
tomb and raised him from
the dead continued to
spread the word. 18 Many
people, because they had
heard that he had given this
miraculous sign, went out
to meet him. 19 So the Pharisees said to one another,
''See, this is getting us nowhere. Look how the
whole world has gone after
him!''

Jesus Predicts His Death

20 Now there were some
Greeks among those who
went up to worship at the
Feast. 21 They came to Philip, who was from Bethsai-
da in Galilee, with a re-
quest. ''Sir,'' they said,
''we would like to see
Jesus.'' 22 Philip went to tell
Andrew; Andrew and Phil-
ip in turn told Jesus.
23 Jesus replied, ''The
hour has come for the Son
of Man to be glorified. 24 I
tell you the truth, unless a
kernel of wheat falls to the
ground and dies, it remains
only a single seed. But if it
dies, it produces many
seeds. 25 The man who
loves his life will lose it,

[i] *15* Zech. 9:9

loses it; and he who hates
his life in this world shall
keep it to life eternal.
26“If anyone serves Me,
let him follow Me; and
where I am, there shall My
servant also be; if anyone
serves Me, the Father will
honor him.

Jesus Foretells His Death

27“Now My soul has
become troubled; and what
shall I say, ‘Father, save
Me from this hour’? But for
this purpose I came to this
hour.
28“Father, glorify Thy
name.” There came there-
fore a voice out of heaven:
“I have both glorified it,
and will glorify it again.”
29The multitude there-
fore, who stood by and
heard it, were saying that it
had thundered; others were
saying, “An angel has
spoken to Him.”
30Jesus answered and
said, “This voice has not
come for My sake, but for
your sakes.
31“Now judgment is upon
this world; now the ruler of
this world shall be cast out.
32“And I, if I be lifted up
from the earth, will draw all
men to Myself.”
33But He was saying this
to indicate the kind of death
by which He was to die.
34The multitude therefore
answered Him, “We have
heard out of the Law that
the Christ is to remain forever; and how can You say,
‘The Son of Man must be
lifted up’? Who is this Son
of Man?”
35Jesus therefore said to
them, “For a little while
longer the light is among
you. Walk while you have
the light, that darkness may
not overtake you; he who
walks in the darkness does
not know where he goes.

αὐτήν, καὶ ὁ μισῶν τὴν ψυχὴν αὐτοῦ
it, and the [one] hating the life of him
ἐν τῷ κόσμῳ τούτῳ εἰς ζωὴν αἰώνιον
in – world this unto life eternal
φυλάξει αὐτήν. **26** ἐάν ἐμοί τις διακονῇ,
will keep it. If me anyone serves,
ἐμοὶ ἀκολουθείτω, καὶ ὅπου εἰμὶ ἐγώ,
me let him follow, and where am I,
ἐκεῖ καὶ ὁ διάκονος ὁ ἐμὸς ἔσται·
there also *the* ²servant – ¹my will be;
ἐάν τις ἐμοὶ διακονῇ, τιμήσει αὐτὸν
if anyone me serves, will honour him
ὁ πατήρ. **27** νῦν ἡ ψυχή μου τετάρακται,
the Father. Now the soul of me has been troubled,
καὶ τί εἴπω; πάτερ, σῶσόν με ἐκ
and what may I say? Father, save me out of
τῆς ὥρας ταύτης. ἀλλὰ διὰ τοῦτο ἦλθον
– hour this. But therefore I came
εἰς τὴν ὥραν ταύτην. **28** πάτερ, δόξασόν
to – hour this. Father, glorify
σου τὸ ὄνομα. ἦλθεν οὖν φωνὴ ἐκ
of thee the name. Came therefore a voice out of
τοῦ οὐρανοῦ· καὶ ἐδόξασα καὶ πάλιν
– heaven: Both I glorified and again
δοξάσω. **29** ὁ οὖν ὄχλος ὁ ἑστὼς καὶ
I will glorify. Therefore the crowd – standing and
ἀκούσας ἔλεγεν βροντὴν γεγονέναι· ἄλλοι
hearing said thunder to have happened; others
ἔλεγον· ἄγγελος αὐτῷ λελάληκεν.
said: An angel to him has spoken.
30 ἀπεκρίθη Ἰησοῦς καὶ εἶπεν· οὐ δι’ ἐμὲ
Answered Jesus and said: Not because of me
ἡ φωνὴ αὕτη γέγονεν ἀλλὰ δι’ ὑμᾶς.
– voice this has happened but because of you.
31 νῦν κρίσις ἐστὶν τοῦ κόσμου τούτου·
Now judgment is – world of this;
νῦν ὁ ἄρχων τοῦ κόσμου τούτου
now the ruler – world of this
ἐκβληθήσεται ἔξω· **32** κἀγὼ ἐὰν ὑψωθῶ
shall be cast *out* outside; and I if I am lifted up
ἐκ τῆς γῆς, πάντας ἑλκύσω πρὸς
out of the earth, all men will draw to
ἐμαυτόν. **33** τοῦτο δὲ ἔλεγεν σημαίνων
myself. And this he said signifying
ποίῳ θανάτῳ ἤμελλεν ἀποθνήσκειν.
by what kind of death he was about to die.
34 ἀπεκρίθη οὖν αὐτῷ ὁ ὄχλος· ἡμεῖς
Answered therefore him the crowd: We
ἠκούσαμεν ἐκ τοῦ νόμου ὅτι ὁ χριστὸς
heard out of the law that the Christ
μένει εἰς τὸν αἰῶνα, καὶ πῶς λέγεις
remains unto the age, and how sayest
σὺ ὅτι δεῖ ὑψωθῆναι τὸν υἱὸν τοῦ
thou that it behoves to be lifted up the Son –
ἀνθρώπου; τίς ἐστιν οὗτος ὁ υἱὸς τοῦ
of man? who is this – Son –
ἀνθρώπου; **35** εἶπεν οὖν αὐτοῖς ὁ Ἰησοῦς·
of man? Said therefore to them – Jesus:
ἔτι μικρὸν χρόνον τὸ φῶς ἐν ὑμῖν
Yet a little time the light among you
ἐστιν. περιπατεῖτε ὡς τὸ φῶς ἔχετε,
is. Walk while the light ye have,
ἵνα μὴ σκοτία ὑμᾶς καταλάβῃ· καὶ
lest darkness you overtakes; and
ὁ περιπατῶν ἐν τῇ σκοτίᾳ οὐκ οἶδεν
the [one] walking in the darkness knows not

while the man who hates
his life in this world will
keep it for eternal life.
26Whoever serves me must
follow me; and where I am,
my servant also will be. My
Father will honor the one
who serves me.
27“Now my heart is trou-
bled, and what shall I say?
‘Father, save me from this
hour’? No, it was for this
very reason I came to this
hour. 28Father, glorify your
name!”
Then a voice came from
heaven, “I have glorified
it, and will glorify it again.”
29The crowd that was there
and heard it said it had
thundered; others said an
angel had spoken to him.
30Jesus said, “This voice
was for your benefit, not
mine. 31Now is the time for
judgment on this world;
now the prince of this
world will be driven out.
32But I, when I am lifted up
from the earth, will draw all
men to myself.” 33He said
this to show the kind of
death he was going to die.
34The crowd spoke up,
“We have heard from the
Law that the Christ[j] will
remain forever, so how can
you say, ‘The Son of Man
must be lifted up’? Who is
this ‘Son of Man’?”
35Then Jesus told them,
“You are going to have the
light just a little while longer. Walk while you have
the light, before darkness
overtakes you. The man
who walks in the dark does
not know where he is go-

j34 Or *Messiah*

36"While you have the
light, believe in the light, in
order that you may become
sons of light."
These things Jesus
spoke, and He departed
and hid Himself from them.
37But though He had per-
formed so many signs be-
fore them, *yet* they were
not believing in Him;
38that the word of Isaiah
the prophet might be ful-
filled, which he spoke,
"LORD, WHO HAS BELIEVED
OUR REPORT? AND TO WHOM
HAS THE ARM OF THE LORD
BEEN REVEALED?"
39For this cause they
could not believe, for
Isaiah said again,
40"HE HAS BLINDED THEIR
EYES, AND HE HARDENED
THEIR HEART; LEST THEY SEE
WITH THEIR EYES, AND PER-
CEIVE WITH THEIR HEART,
AND BE CONVERTED, AND I
HEAL THEM."
41These things Isaiah
said, because he saw His
glory, and he spoke of Him.
42Nevertheless many
even of the rulers believed
in Him, but because of the
Pharisees they were not
confessing *Him,* lest they
should be put out of the
synagogue;
43for they loved the ap-
proval of men rather than
the approval of God.
44And Jesus cried out and
said, "He who believes in
Me does not believe in Me,
but in Him who sent Me.
45"And he who beholds
Me beholds the One who
sent Me.
46"I have come *as* light
into the world, that everyone who believes in Me
may not remain in dark-
ness.
47"And if anyone hears
My sayings, and does not
keep them, I do not judge
him; for I did not come to

ποῦ ὑπάγει. **36** ὡς τὸ φῶς ἔχετε,
where he is going. While the light ye have,
πιστεύετε εἰς τὸ φῶς, ἵνα υἱοὶ φωτὸς
believe in the light, that sons of light
γένησθε.
ye may become.
Ταῦτα ἐλάλησεν Ἰησοῦς, καὶ ἀπελθὼν
These things spoke Jesus, and going away
ἐκρύβη ἀπ' αὐτῶν. **37** Τοσαῦτα δὲ αὐτοῦ
was hidden from them. But so many him
σημεῖα πεποιηκότος ἔμπροσθεν αὐτῶν οὐκ
signs having done[a] before them not
=But while he did so many signs
ἐπίστευον εἰς αὐτόν, **38** ἵνα ὁ λόγος
they believed in him, that the word
Ἠσαΐου τοῦ προφήτου πληρωθῇ ὃν
of Esaias the prophet might be fulfilled which
εἶπεν· κύριε, τίς ἐπίστευσεν τῇ ἀκοῇ
he said: Lord, who believed the report
ἡμῶν; καὶ ὁ βραχίων κυρίου τίνι
of us? and the arm of [the] Lord to whom
ἀπεκαλύφθη; **39** διὰ τοῦτο οὐκ ἠδύναντο
was it revealed? Therefore they could not
πιστεύειν, ὅτι πάλιν εἶπεν Ἠσαΐας·
to believe, because again said Esaias:
40 τετύφλωκεν αὐτῶν τοὺς ὀφθαλμοὺς καὶ
He has blinded of them the eyes and
ἐπώρωσεν αὐτῶν τὴν καρδίαν, ἵνα
hardened of them the heart, that
μὴ ἴδωσιν τοῖς ὀφθαλμοῖς καὶ νοήσωσιν
they might not see with the eyes and understand
τῇ καρδίᾳ καὶ στραφῶσιν, καὶ ἰάσομαι
with the heart and might turn, and I will cure
αὐτούς. **41** ταῦτα εἶπεν Ἠσαΐας ὅτι
them. These things said Esaias because
εἶδεν τὴν δόξαν αὐτοῦ, καὶ ἐλάλησεν
he saw the glory of him, and spoke
περὶ αὐτοῦ. **42** ὅμως μέντοι καὶ ἐκ
about him. Nevertheless however even of
τῶν ἀρχόντων πολλοὶ ἐπίστευσαν εἰς αὐτόν,
the rulers many believed in him,
ἀλλὰ διὰ τοὺς Φαρισαίους οὐχ ὡμολόγουν,
but because of the Pharisees did not confess,
ἵνα μὴ ἀποσυνάγωγοι γένωνται·
lest put out of [the] synagogue they should become;
43 ἠγάπησαν γὰρ τὴν δόξαν τῶν ἀνθρώπων
for they loved the glory – of men
μᾶλλον ἤπερ τὴν δόξαν τοῦ θεοῦ.
more than the glory – of God.
44 Ἰησοῦς δὲ ἔκραξεν καὶ εἶπεν· ὁ
But Jesus cried out and said: The
πιστεύων εἰς ἐμὲ οὐ πιστεύει εἰς ἐμὲ
[one] believing in me believes not in me
ἀλλὰ εἰς τὸν πέμψαντά με, **45** καὶ ὁ
but in the [one] having sent me, and the
θεωρῶν ἐμὲ θεωρεῖ τὸν πέμψαντά με.
[one] beholding me beholds the [one] having sent me.
46 ἐγὼ φῶς εἰς τὸν κόσμον ἐλήλυθα,
I a light into the world have come,
ἵνα πᾶς ὁ πιστεύων εἰς ἐμὲ ἐν τῇ
that everyone believing in me in the
σκοτίᾳ μὴ μείνῃ. **47** καὶ ἐάν τίς μου
darkness may not remain. And if anyone of me
ἀκούσῃ τῶν ῥημάτων καὶ μὴ φυλάξῃ,
hears the words and keeps not,
ἐγὼ οὐ κρίνω αὐτόν· οὐ γὰρ ἦλθον
I do not judge him; for I came not

ing. 36Put your trust in the
light while you have it, so
that you may become sons
of light." When he had finished speaking, Jesus left
and hid himself from them.

The Jews Continue in Their Unbelief

37Even after Jesus had
done all these miraculous
signs in their presence,
they still would not believe
in him. 38This was to fulfill
the word of Isaiah the
prophet:

"Lord, who has believed
our message
and to whom has the
arm of the Lord
been revealed?"[k]

39For this reason they
could not believe, because,
as Isaiah says elsewhere:

40"He has blinded their
eyes
and deadened their
hearts,
so they can neither see
with their eyes,
nor understand with
their hearts,
nor turn—and I would
heal them."[l]

41Isaiah said this because
he saw Jesus' glory and
spoke about him.
42Yet at the same time
many even among the lead-
ers believed in him. But because of the Pharisees they
would not confess their
faith for fear they would be
put out of the synagogue;
43for they loved praise from
men more than praise from
God.
44Then Jesus cried out,
"When a man believes in
me, he does not believe in
me only, but in the one who
sent me. 45When he looks
at me, he sees the one who
sent me. 46I have come into
the world as a light, so that
no one who believes in me
should stay in darkness.
47"As for the person who
hears my words but does
not keep them, I do not
judge him. For I did not

[k] *38* Isaiah 53:1
[l] *40* Isaiah 6:10

judge the world, but to save the world.

48"He who rejects Me, and does not receive My sayings, has one who judges him; the word I spoke is what will judge him at the last day.

49"For I did not speak on My own initiative, but the Father Himself who sent Me has given Me commandment, what to say, and what to speak.

50"And I know that His commandment is eternal life; therefore the things I speak, I speak just as the Father has told Me."

Chapter 13

The Lord's Supper

NOW before the Feast of the Passover, Jesus knowing that His hour had come that He should depart out of this world to the Father, having loved His own who were in the world, He loved them to the end.

2And during supper, the devil having already put into the heart of Judas Iscariot, *the son* of Simon, to betray Him,

3*Jesus,* knowing that the Father had given all things into His hands, and that He had come forth from God, and was going back to God,

4*rose from supper, and *laid aside His garments; and taking a towel, He girded Himself about.

Jesus Washes the Disciples' Feet

5Then He *poured water into the basin, and began to wash the disciples' feet, and to wipe them with the towel with which He was girded.

6And so He *came to Simon Peter. He *said to Him, "Lord, do You wash my feet?"

ἵνα κρίνω τὸν κόσμον, ἀλλ' ἵνα σώσω
that I might judge the world, but that I might save
τὸν κόσμον. **48** ὁ ἀθετῶν ἐμὲ καὶ μὴ
the world. The [one] rejecting me and not
λαμβάνων τὰ ῥήματά μου ἔχει τὸν
receiving the words of me has the
κρίνοντα αὐτόν· ὁ λόγος ὃν ἐλάλησα,
[one] judging him; the word which I spoke,
ἐκεῖνος κρινεῖ αὐτὸν ἐν τῇ ἐσχάτῃ ἡμέρᾳ.
that will judge him in the last day.
49 ὅτι ἐγὼ ἐξ ἐμαυτοῦ οὐκ ἐλάλησα,
Because I of myself did not speak,
ἀλλ' ὁ πέμψας με πατὴρ αὐτός μοι
but [1]the [3]having sent [4]me [2]Father [5]he [7]me
ἐντολὴν δέδωκεν τί εἴπω καὶ τί
[8]commandment [6]has given what I may say and what
λαλήσω. **50** καὶ οἶδα ὅτι ἡ ἐντολὴ
I may speak. And I know that the commandment
αὐτοῦ ζωὴ αἰώνιός ἐστιν. ἃ οὖν ἐγὼ
of him life eternal is. What things therefore I
λαλῶ, καθὼς εἴρηκέν μοι ὁ πατήρ,
speak, as has said to me the Father,
οὕτως λαλῶ.
so I speak.

13 Πρὸ δὲ τῆς ἑορτῆς τοῦ πάσχα
Now before the feast of the Passover
εἰδὼς ὁ Ἰησοῦς ὅτι ἦλθεν αὐτοῦ ἡ
[2]knowing – [1]Jesus that came of him the
ὥρα ἵνα μεταβῇ ἐκ τοῦ κόσμου τούτου
hour that he should remove out of – world this
πρὸς τὸν πατέρα, ἀγαπήσας τοὺς ἰδίους
to the Father, loving the(his) own
τοὺς ἐν τῷ κόσμῳ, εἰς τέλος ἠγάπησεν
– in the world, to [the] end he loved
αὐτούς. **2** καὶ δείπνου γινομένου, τοῦ
them. And supper taking place,[a] the
=during supper,
διαβόλου ἤδη βεβληκότος εἰς τὴν καρδίαν
devil now having put[a] into the heart
=as the devil had now put
ἵνα παραδοῖ αὐτὸν Ἰούδας Σίμωνος
that [4]should betray [5]him [1]Judas [2][son] of Simon
Ἰσκαριώτης, **3** εἰδὼς ὅτι πάντα ἔδωκεν
[3]Iscariot, knowing* that all things gave
αὐτῷ ὁ πατὴρ εἰς τὰς χεῖρας, καὶ
him the Father into the(his) hands, and
ὅτι ἀπὸ θεοῦ ἐξῆλθεν καὶ πρὸς τὸν
that from God he came forth and to –
θεὸν ὑπάγει, **4** ἐγείρεται ἐκ τοῦ δείπνου
God goes, he rises out of(from) the supper
καὶ τίθησιν τὰ ἱμάτια, καὶ λαβὼν
and places [aside] the(his) garments, and taking
λέντιον διέζωσεν ἑαυτόν· **5** εἶτα βάλλει
a towel he girded himself; then he puts
ὕδωρ εἰς τὸν νιπτῆρα, καὶ ἤρξατο νίπτειν
water into the basin, and began to wash
τοὺς πόδας τῶν μαθητῶν καὶ ἐκμάσσειν
the feet of the disciples and to wipe off
τῷ λεντίῳ ᾧ ἦν διεζωσμένος.
with the towel with which he was *having been* girded.
6 ἔρχεται οὖν πρὸς Σίμωνα Πέτρον·
He comes therefore to Simon Peter;
λέγει αὐτῷ· κύριε, σύ μου νίπτεις τοὺς
he says to him: Lord, thou of me washest the

* Repeated from ver. 1; the subject is therefore again "Jesus".

come to judge the world, but to save it. 48There is a judge for the one who rejects me and does not accept my words; that very word which I spoke will condemn him at the last day. 49For I did not speak of my own accord, but the Father who sent me commanded me what to say and how to say it. 50I know that his command leads to eternal life. So whatever I say is just what the Father has told me to say."

Chapter 13

Jesus Washes His Disciples' Feet

IT was just before the Passover Feast. Jesus knew that the time had come for him to leave this world and go to the Father. Having loved his own who were in the world, he now showed them the full extent of his love.[m]

2The evening meal was being served, and the devil had already prompted Judas Iscariot, son of Simon, to betray Jesus. 3Jesus knew that the Father had put all things under his power, and that he had come from God and was returning to God; 4so he got up from the meal, took off his outer clothing, and wrapped a towel around his waist. 5After that, he poured water into a basin and began to wash his disciples' feet, drying them with the towel that was wrapped around him.

6He came to Simon Peter, who said to him, "Lord, are you going to wash my feet?"

[m]1 Or *he loved them to the last*

7Jesus answered and
said to him, "What I do you
do not realize now, but
you shall understand hereafter."
8Peter *said to Him,
"Never shall You wash my
feet!" Jesus answered him,
"If I do not wash you, you
have no part with Me."
9Simon Peter *said to
Him, "Lord, not my feet
only, but also my hands
and my head."
10Jesus *said to him, "He
who has bathed needs only
to wash his feet, but is completely clean; and you are
clean, but not all *of you*."
11For He knew the one
who was betraying Him;
for this reason He said,
"Not all of you are clean."
12And so when He had
washed their feet, and tak-
en His garments, and re-
clined *at the table* again,
He said to them, "Do you
know what I have done to
you?
13"You call Me Teacher
and Lord; and you are
right, for *so* I am.
14"If I then, the Lord and
the Teacher, washed your
feet, you also ought to
wash one another's feet.
15"For I gave you an ex-
ample that you also should
do as I did to you.
16"Truly, truly, I say to
you, a slave is not greater
than his master; neither *is*
one who is sent greater
than the one who sent him.
17"If you know these
things, you are blessed if
you do them.
18"I do not speak of all of
you. I know the ones I have
chosen; but *it is* that the
Scripture may be fulfilled,
'HE WHO EATS MY BREAD

πόδας; 7 ἀπεκρίθη Ἰησοῦς καὶ εἶπεν αὐτῷ·
feet? Answered Jesus and said to him :
ὃ ἐγὼ ποιῶ σὺ οὐκ οἶδας ἄρτι,
What I am doing thou knowest not yet,
γνώσῃ δὲ μετὰ ταῦτα. 8 λέγει αὐτῷ
but thou wilt know after these things. Says to him
Πέτρος· οὐ μὴ νίψῃς μου τοὺς πόδας
Peter : By no means shalt thou wash of me the feet
εἰς τὸν αἰῶνα. ἀπεκρίθη Ἰησοῦς αὐτῷ·
unto the age. ²Answered ¹Jesus ³him :
ἐὰν μὴ νίψω σε, οὐκ ἔχεις μέρος μετ'
Unless I wash thee, thou hast no part with
ἐμοῦ. 9 λέγει αὐτῷ Σίμων Πέτρος·
me. Says to him Simon Peter :
κύριε, μὴ τοὺς πόδας μου μόνον ἀλλὰ
Lord, not the feet of me only but
καὶ τὰς χεῖρας καὶ τὴν κεφαλήν. 10 λέγει
also the hands and the head. Says
αὐτῷ Ἰησοῦς· ὁ λελουμένος οὐκ ἔχει
to him Jesus : The [one] having been bathed has not
χρείαν [εἰ μὴ τοὺς πόδας] νίψασθαι,
need except the feet to wash,
ἀλλ' ἔστιν καθαρὸς ὅλος· καὶ ὑμεῖς
but is clean wholly; and ye
καθαροί ἐστε, ἀλλ' οὐχὶ πάντες. 11 ᾔδει
clean are, but not all. he knew
γὰρ τὸν παραδιδόντα αὐτόν· διὰ τοῦτο
For the [one] betraying him; therefore
εἶπεν ὅτι οὐχὶ πάντες καθαροί ἐστε.
he said[,] – Not all clean ye are.
12 Ὅτε οὖν ἔνιψεν τοὺς πόδας αὐτῶν
When therefore he washed the feet of them
καὶ ἔλαβεν τὰ ἱμάτια αὐτοῦ καὶ ἀνέπεσεν
and took the garments of him and reclined
πάλιν, εἶπεν αὐτοῖς· γινώσκετε τί πε-
again, he said to them : Do ye know what I
ποίηκα ὑμῖν; 13 ὑμεῖς φωνεῖτέ με· ὁ
have done to you? Ye call me : The
διδάσκαλος καὶ ὁ κύριος, καὶ καλῶς
Teacher and the Lord, and well
λέγετε· εἰμὶ γάρ. 14 εἰ οὖν ἐγὼ ἔνιψα
ye say; for I am. If therefore I washed
ὑμῶν τοὺς πόδας ὁ κύριος καὶ ὁ
of you the feet the Lord and the
διδάσκαλος, καὶ ὑμεῖς ὀφείλετε ἀλλήλων
Teacher, also ye ought of one another
νίπτειν τοὺς πόδας· 15 ὑπόδειγμα γὰρ
to wash the feet; for an example
ἔδωκα ὑμῖν ἵνα καθὼς ἐγὼ ἐποίησα
I gave you that as I did
ὑμῖν καὶ ὑμεῖς ποιῆτε. 16 ἀμὴν ἀμὴν
to you also ye may do. Truly truly
λέγω ὑμῖν, οὐκ ἔστιν δοῦλος μείζων
I tell you, is not a slave greater [than]
τοῦ κυρίου αὐτοῦ, οὐδὲ ἀπόστολος μείζων
the lord of him, nor a sent one greater [than]
τοῦ πέμψαντος αὐτόν. 17 εἰ ταῦτα
the [one] sending him. If these things
οἴδατε, μακάριοί ἐστε ἐὰν ποιῆτε αὐτά.
ye know, blessed are ye if ye do them.
18 Οὐ περὶ πάντων ὑμῶν λέγω· ἐγὼ
Not concerning ²all ¹you I speak; I
οἶδα τίνας ἐξελεξάμην· ἀλλ' ἵνα ἡ
know whom I chose; but that the
γραφὴ πληρωθῇ· ὁ τρώγων μου τὸν
scripture may be fulfilled : The [one] eating of me the

7Jesus replied, "You do
not realize now what I am
doing, but later you will understand."
8"No," said Peter, "you
shall never wash my feet."
Jesus answered, "Unless
I wash you, you have no
part with me."
9"Then, Lord," Simon
Peter replied, "not just my
feet but my hands and my
head as well!"
10Jesus answered, "A
person who has had a bath
needs only to wash his feet;
his whole body is clean.
And you are clean, though
not every one of you."
11For he knew who was go-
ing to betray him, and that
was why he said not every
one was clean.
12When he had finished
washing their feet, he put
on his clothes and returned
to his place. "Do you un-
derstand what I have done
for you?" he asked them.
13"You call me 'Teacher'
and 'Lord,' and rightly so,
for that is what I am. 14Now
that I, your Lord and
Teacher, have washed your
feet, you also should wash
one another's feet. 15I have
set you an example that
you should do as I have
done for you. 16I tell you
the truth, no servant is
greater than his master, nor
is a messenger greater than
the one who sent him.
17Now that you know these
things, you will be blessed
if you do them.

Jesus Predicts His Betrayal

18"I am not referring to
all of you; I know those I
have chosen. But this is to
fulfill the scripture: 'He
who shares my bread has

HAS LIFTED UP HIS HEEL AGAINST ME.'
19"From now on I am telling you before *it* comes to pass, so that when it does occur, you may believe that I am *He*.
20"Truly, truly, I say to you, he who receives whomever I send receives Me; and he who receives Me receives Him who sent Me."

Jesus Predicts His Betrayal

21When Jesus had said this, He became troubled in spirit, and testified, and said, "Truly, truly, I say to you, that one of you will betray Me."
22The disciples *began* looking at one another, at a loss *to know* of which one He was speaking.
23There was reclining on Jesus' breast one of His disciples, whom Jesus loved.
24Simon Peter therefore *gestured to him, and *said to him, "Tell *us* who it is of whom He is speaking."
25He, leaning back thus on Jesus' breast, *said to Him, "Lord, who is it?"
26Jesus therefore *answered, "That is the one for whom I shall dip the morsel and give it to him." So when He had dipped the morsel, He *took and *gave it to Judas, *the son* of Simon Iscariot.
27And after the morsel, Satan then entered into him. Jesus therefore *said to him, "What you do, do quickly."
28Now no one of those reclining *at the table* knew for what purpose He had said this to him.
29For some were supposing, because Judas had the money box, that Jesus was saying to him, "Buy the things we have need of for the feast"; or else, that he should give something to the poor.
30And so after receiving

ἄρτον ἐπῆρεν ἐπ' ἐμὲ τὴν πτέρναν αὐτοῦ.
bread lifted up against me the heel of him.
19 ἀπ' ἄρτι λέγω ὑμῖν πρὸ τοῦ γενέσθαι,
From now I tell you before the to happen, =it happens,
ἵνα πιστεύητε ὅταν γένηται ὅτι ἐγώ
that ye may believe when it happens that I
εἰμι. 20 ἀμὴν ἀμὴν λέγω ὑμῖν, ὁ
am. Truly truly I say to you, the
λαμβάνων ἄν τινα πέμψω ἐμὲ λαμβάνει,
[one] receiving whomever I may send me receives,
ὁ δὲ ἐμὲ λαμβάνων λαμβάνει τὸν
and the [one] me receiving receives the [one]
πέμψαντά με. 21 ταῦτα εἰπὼν Ἰησοῦς
having sent me. These things saying Jesus
ἐταράχθη τῷ πνεύματι καὶ ἐμαρτύρησεν
was troubled in the(his) spirit and witnessed
καὶ εἶπεν· ἀμὴν ἀμὴν λέγω ὑμῖν ὅτι
and said: Truly truly I tell you that
εἷς ἐξ ὑμῶν παραδώσει με. 22 ἔβλεπον
one of you will betray me. Looked
εἰς ἀλλήλους οἱ μαθηταὶ ἀπορούμενοι περὶ
at one another the disciples being perplexed about
τίνος λέγει. 23 ἦν ἀνακείμενος εἷς ἐκ
whom he speaks. Was reclining one of
τῶν μαθητῶν αὐτοῦ ἐν τῷ κόλπῳ τοῦ
the disciples of him in the bosom –
Ἰησοῦ, ὃν ἠγάπα ὁ Ἰησοῦς· 24 νεύει
of Jesus, whom [2]loved – [1]Jesus; nods
οὖν τούτῳ Σίμων Πέτρος καὶ λέγει
therefore to this one Simon Peter and says
αὐτῷ· εἰπὲ τίς ἐστιν περὶ οὗ λέγει.
to him: Say who it is about whom he speaks.
25 ἀναπεσὼν ἐκεῖνος οὕτως ἐπὶ τὸ
Falling back that one thus on the
στῆθος τοῦ Ἰησοῦ λέγει αὐτῷ· κύριε,
breast – of Jesus he says to him: Lord,
τίς ἐστιν; 26 ἀποκρίνεται οὖν ὁ Ἰησοῦς·
who is it? Answers therefore – Jesus:
ἐκεῖνός ἐστιν ᾧ ἐγὼ βάψω τὸ ψωμίον
That one it is to whom I shall dip the morsel
καὶ δώσω αὐτῷ. βάψας οὖν [τὸ]
and shall give him. Dipping therefore the
ψωμίον λαμβάνει καὶ δίδωσιν Ἰούδᾳ
morsel he takes and gives to Judas
Σίμωνος Ἰσκαριώτου. 27 καὶ μετὰ τὸ
[son] of Simon Iscariot. And after the
ψωμίον τότε εἰσῆλθεν εἰς ἐκεῖνον ὁ
morsel then entered into that one –
σατανᾶς. λέγει οὖν αὐτῷ Ἰησοῦς· ὃ
Satan. Says therefore to him Jesus: What
ποιεῖς ποίησον τάχιον. 28 τοῦτο [δὲ]
thou doest do quickly. But this
οὐδεὶς ἔγνω τῶν ἀνακειμένων πρὸς τί
no one knew of the [ones] reclining for what
εἶπεν αὐτῷ· 29 τινὲς γὰρ ἐδόκουν, ἐπεὶ
he told him; for some thought, since
τὸ γλωσσόκομον εἶχεν Ἰούδας, ὅτι λέγει
[3]the [4]bag [2]had [1]Judas, that tells
αὐτῷ Ἰησοῦς· ἀγόρασον ὧν χρείαν
him Jesus: Buy [the] things of which need
ἔχομεν εἰς τὴν ἑορτήν, ἢ τοῖς πτωχοῖς
we have for the feast, or to the poor
ἵνα τι δῷ. 30 λαβὼν οὖν τὸ
that something he should give. Having taken therefore the

lifted up his heel against
me.'[n]
19"I am telling you now
before it happens, so that
when it does happen you
will believe that I am He.
20I tell you the truth, whoever accepts anyone I send
accepts me; and whoever
accepts me accepts the one
who sent me."
21After he had said this,
Jesus was troubled in spirit
and testified, "I tell you the
truth, one of you is going to
betray me."
22His disciples stared at
one another, at a loss to
know which of them he
meant. 23One of them, the
disciple whom Jesus loved,
was reclining next to him.
24Simon Peter motioned to
this disciple and said, "Ask
him which one he means."
25Leaning back against
Jesus, he asked him,
"Lord, who is it?"
26Jesus answered, "It is
the one to whom I will give
this piece of bread when I
have dipped it in the dish."
Then, dipping the piece of
bread, he gave it to Judas
Iscariot, son of Simon.
27As soon as Judas took the
bread, Satan entered into
him.
"What you are about to
do, do quickly," Jesus told
him, 28but no one at the
meal understood why Jesus
said this to him. 29Since Judas had charge of the money, some thought Jesus was
telling him to buy what was
needed for the Feast, or to
give something to the poor.
30As soon as Judas had tak-

[n]18 Psalm 41:9

the morsel he went out immediately; and it was night.
31When therefore he had gone out, Jesus *said, "Now is the Son of Man glorified, and God is glorified in Him;
32if God is glorified in Him, God will also glorify Him in Himself, and will glorify Him immediately.
33"Little children, I am with you a little while longer. You shall seek Me; and as I said to the Jews, I now say to you also, 'Where I am going, you cannot come.'
34"A new commandment I give to you, that you love one another, even as I have loved you, that you also love one another.
35"By this all men will know that you are My disciples, if you have love for one another."
36Simon Peter *said to Him, "Lord, where are You going?" Jesus answered, "Where I go, you cannot follow Me now; but you shall follow later."
37Peter *said to Him, "Lord, why can I not follow You right now? I will lay down my life for You."
38Jesus *answered, "Will you lay down your life for Me? Truly, truly, I say to you, a cock shall not crow, until you deny Me three times.

Chapter 14

Jesus Comforts His Disciples

"LET not your heart be troubled; [x]believe in God, believe also in Me.
2"In My Father's house are many dwelling places; if it were not so, I would have told you; for I go to prepare a place for you.
3"And if I go and pre-

[x]Or, *you believe in God*

ψωμίον ἐκεῖνος ἐξῆλθεν εὐθύς· ἦν δὲ
morsel that one went out immediately; and it was
νύξ.
night.
31 Ὅτε οὖν ἐξῆλθεν, λέγει Ἰησοῦς·
When therefore he went out, says Jesus :
νῦν ἐδοξάσθη ὁ υἱὸς τοῦ ἀνθρώπου,
Now was(is) glorified the Son – of man,
καὶ ὁ θεὸς ἐδοξάσθη ἐν αὐτῷ· 32 εἰ
and – God was(is) glorified in him; if
ὁ θεὸς ἐδοξάσθη ἐν αὐτῷ, καὶ ὁ θεὸς
– God was(is) glorified in him, both – God
δοξάσει αὐτὸν ἐν αὐτῷ, καὶ εὐθὺς
will glorify him in him, and immediately
δοξάσει αὐτόν. 33 τεκνία, ἔτι μικρὸν
will glorify him. Children, yet a little while
μεθ᾽ ὑμῶν εἰμι· ζητήσετέ με, καὶ καθὼς
with you I am; ye will seek me, and as
εἶπον τοῖς Ἰουδαίοις ὅτι ὅπου ἐγὼ
I said to the Jews that where I
ὑπάγω ὑμεῖς οὐ δύνασθε ἐλθεῖν, καὶ
go ye cannot *to* come, also
ὑμῖν λέγω ἄρτι. 34 Ἐντολὴν καινὴν
to you I say now. commandment A new
δίδωμι ὑμῖν, ἵνα ἀγαπᾶτε ἀλλήλους,
I give you, that ye love one another,
καθὼς ἠγάπησα ὑμᾶς ἵνα καὶ ὑμεῖς
as I loved you that also ye
ἀγαπᾶτε ἀλλήλους. 35 ἐν τούτῳ γνώσονται
love one another. By this will know
πάντες ὅτι ἐμοὶ μαθηταί ἐστε, ἐὰν
all men that to me° disciples ye are, if
ἀγάπην ἔχητε ἐν ἀλλήλοις. 36 Λέγει
love ye have among one another. Says
αὐτῷ Σίμων Πέτρος· κύριε, ποῦ ὑπάγεις;
to him Simon Peter : Lord, where goest thou?
ἀπεκρίθη Ἰησοῦς· ὅπου ὑπάγω οὐ δύνασαί
Answered Jesus : Where I go thou canst not
μοι νῦν ἀκολουθῆσαι, ἀκολουθήσεις δὲ
me now *to* follow, but thou wilt follow
ὕστερον. 37 λέγει αὐτῷ [ὁ] Πέτρος·
later. Says to him – Peter :
κύριε, διὰ τί οὐ δύναμαί σοι ἀκολουθῆσαι
Lord, why can I not thee *to* follow
ἄρτι; τὴν ψυχήν μου ὑπὲρ σοῦ θήσω.
yet? the life of me for thee I will lay down.
38 ἀποκρίνεται Ἰησοῦς· τὴν ψυχήν σου
Answers Jesus : The life of thee
ὑπὲρ ἐμοῦ θήσεις; ἀμὴν ἀμὴν λέγω
for me wilt thou lay down? truly truly I tell
σοι, οὐ μὴ ἀλέκτωρ φωνήσῃ ἕως οὗ
thee, by no means a cock crows until
ἀρνήσῃ με τρίς. 14 Μὴ ταρασσέσθω
thou deniest me thrice. Let not be troubled
ὑμῶν ἡ καρδία· πιστεύετε εἰς τὸν θεόν, καὶ
of you the heart; believe in – God, also
εἰς ἐμὲ πιστεύετε. 2 ἐν τῇ οἰκίᾳ τοῦ
in me believe. In the house of the
πατρός μου μοναὶ πολλαί εἰσιν· εἰ δὲ μή,
Father of me abodes many there are; otherwise,
εἶπον ἂν ὑμῖν· ὅτι πορεύομαι ἑτοιμάσαι
I would have told you; because I go to prepare
τόπον ὑμῖν· 3 καὶ ἐὰν πορευθῶ καὶ
a place for you; and if I go and

en the bread, he went out. And it was night.

Jesus Predicts Peter's Denial

31When he was gone, Jesus said, "Now is the Son of Man glorified and God is glorified in him. 32If God is glorified in him,[o] God will glorify the Son in himself, and will glorify him at once.
33"My children, I will be with you only a little longer. You will look for me, and just as I told the Jews, so I tell you now: Where I am going, you cannot come.
34"A new command I give you: Love one another. As I have loved you, so you must love one another. 35By this all men will know that you are my disciples, if you love one another."
36Simon Peter asked him, "Lord, where are you going?"
Jesus replied, "Where I am going, you cannot follow now, but you will follow later."
37Peter asked, "Lord, why can't I follow you now? I will lay down my life for you."
38Then Jesus answered, "Will you really lay down your life for me? I tell you the truth, before the rooster crows, you will disown me three times!

Chapter 14

Jesus Comforts His Disciples

"DO not let your hearts be troubled. Trust in God[p]; trust also in me. 2In my Father's house are many rooms; if it were not so, I would have told you. I am going there to prepare a place for you. 3And if I go and prepare a

[o]*32* Many early manuscripts do not have *If God is glorified in him.*
[p]*1* Or *You trust in God*

pare a place for you, I will
come again, and receive
you to Myself; that where I
am, *there* you may be also.
4 "[y]And you know the
way where I am going."
5Thomas *said to Him,
"Lord, we do not know
where You are going, how
do we know the way?"
6Jesus *said to him, "I
am the way, and the truth,
and the life; no one comes
to the Father, but through
Me.

Oneness with the Father

7"If you had known Me,
you would have known My
Father also; from now on
you know Him, and have
seen Him."
8Philip *said to Him,
"Lord, show us the Father,
and it is enough for us."
9Jesus *said to him,
"Have I been so long with
you, and *yet* you have not
come to know Me, Philip?
He who has seen Me has
seen the Father; how do
you say, 'Show us the Father'?
10"Do you not believe
that I am in the Father, and
the Father is in Me? The
words that I say to you I do
not speak on My own initiative,
but the Father abiding
in Me does His works.
11"Believe Me that I am
in the Father, and the Father
in Me; otherwise believe
on account of the
works themselves.
12"Truly, truly, I say to
you, he who believes in
Me, the works that I do
shall he do also; and greater
works than these shall he
do; because I go to the Father.
13"And whatever you ask
in My name, that will I do,
that the Father may be
glorified in the Son.
14"If you ask Me anything
in My name, I will do
it.

[y] Many ancient authorities read *And where I go you know, and the way you know*

ἑτοιμάσω τόπον ὑμῖν, πάλιν ἔρχομαι καὶ
prepare a place for you, again I come and
παραλήμψομαι ὑμᾶς πρὸς ἐμαυτόν, ἵνα
will receive you to myself, that
ὅπου εἰμὶ ἐγὼ καὶ ὑμεῖς ἦτε. **4** Καὶ
where am I also ye may be. And
ὅπου ἐγὼ ὑπάγω οἴδατε τὴν ὁδόν.
where I go ye know the way.
5 λέγει αὐτῷ Θωμᾶς· κύριε, οὐκ οἴδαμεν
Says to him Thomas: Lord, we know not
ποῦ ὑπάγεις· πῶς οἴδαμεν τὴν ὁδόν;
where thou goest; how do we know the way?
6 λέγει αὐτῷ Ἰησοῦς· ἐγώ εἰμι ἡ ὁδὸς
Says to him Jesus: I am the way
καὶ ἡ ἀλήθεια καὶ ἡ ζωή· οὐδεὶς ἔρχεται
and the truth and the life; no one comes
πρὸς τὸν πατέρα εἰ μὴ δι' ἐμοῦ. **7** εἰ
to the Father except through me. If
ἐγνώκειτέ με, καὶ τὸν πατέρα μου
ye had known me, also the Father of me
ἂν ᾔδειτε. ἀπ' ἄρτι γινώσκετε αὐτὸν
ye would have known. From now ye know him
καὶ ἑωράκατε. **8** Λέγει αὐτῷ Φίλιππος·
and have seen. Says to him Philip:
κύριε, δεῖξον ἡμῖν τὸν πατέρα, καὶ
Lord, show us the Father, and
ἀρκεῖ ἡμῖν. **9** λέγει αὐτῷ ὁ Ἰησοῦς·
it suffices for us. Says to him – Jesus:
τοσοῦτον χρόνον μεθ' ὑμῶν εἰμι καὶ
So long time with you I am and
οὐκ ἔγνωκάς με, Φίλιππε; ὁ ἑωρακὼς
thou hast not known me, Philip? The [one] having seen
ἐμὲ ἑώρακεν τὸν πατέρα· πῶς σὺ λέγεις·
me has seen the Father; how thou sayest:
δεῖξον ἡμῖν τὸν πατέρα; **10** οὐ πιστεύεις
Show us the Father? believest thou not
ὅτι ἐγὼ ἐν τῷ πατρὶ καὶ ὁ πατὴρ
that I in the Father and the Father
ἐν ἐμοί ἐστιν; τὰ ῥήματα ἃ ἐγὼ λέγω
in me is? the words which I say
ὑμῖν ἀπ' ἐμαυτοῦ οὐ λαλῶ· ὁ δὲ πατὴρ
to you from myself I speak not; but the Father
ἐν ἐμοὶ μένων ποιεῖ τὰ ἔργα αὐτοῦ.
in me remaining does the works of him.
11 πιστεύετέ μοι ὅτι ἐγὼ ἐν τῷ πατρὶ
Believe ye me that I in the Father
καὶ ὁ πατὴρ ἐν ἐμοί· εἰ δὲ μή, διὰ
and the Father in me; otherwise, because of
τὰ ἔργα αὐτὰ πιστεύετε. **12** ἀμὴν ἀμὴν
the works [them]selves believe ye. Truly truly
λέγω ὑμῖν, ὁ πιστεύων εἰς ἐμὲ τὰ
I tell you, the [one] believing in me the
ἔργα ἃ ἐγὼ ποιῶ κἀκεῖνος ποιήσει,
works which I do that one also will do,
καὶ μείζονα τούτων ποιήσει, ὅτι ἐγὼ
and greater [than] these he will do, because I
πρὸς τὸν πατέρα πορεύομαι· **13** καὶ ὅ τι
to the Father am going; and what-
ἂν αἰτήσητε ἐν τῷ ὀνόματί μου, τοῦτο
ever ye ask in the name of me, this
ποιήσω, ἵνα δοξασθῇ ὁ πατὴρ ἐν τῷ
I will do, that may be glorified the Father in the
υἱῷ. **14** ἐάν τι αἰτήσητέ με ἐν τῷ
Son. If anything ye ask me in the
ὀνόματί μου, ἐγὼ ποιήσω. **15** Ἐὰν
name of me, I will do. If

place for you, I will come
back and take you to be
with me that you also may
be where I am. 4You know
the way to the place where
I am going."

Jesus the Way to the Father

5Thomas said to him,
"Lord, we don't know
where you are going, so
how can we know the
way?"
6Jesus answered, "I am
the way and the truth and
the life. No one comes to
the Father except through
me. 7If you really knew me,
you would know[q] my Father
as well. From now on,
you do know him and have
seen him."
8Philip said, "Lord, show
us the Father and that will
be enough for us."
9Jesus answered: "Don't
you know me, Philip, even
after I have been among
you such a long time? Anyone
who has seen me has
seen the Father. How can
you say, 'Show us the Father'?
10Don't you believe
that I am in the Father, and
that the Father is in me?
The words I say to you are
not just my own. Rather, it
is the Father, living in me,
who is doing his work.
11Believe me when I say
that I am in the Father and
the Father is in me; or at
least believe on the evidence
of the miracles themselves.
12I tell you the
truth, anyone who has faith
in me will do what I have
been doing. He will do even
greater things than these,
because I am going to the
Father. 13And I will do
whatever you ask in my
name, so that the Son may
bring glory to the Father.
14You may ask me for anything
in my name, and I will
do it.

[q] 7 Some early manuscripts *If you really have known me, you will know*

15"If you love Me, you will keep My commandments.

Role of the Spirit

16"And I will ask the Father, and He will give you another Helper, that He may be with you forever;

17*that is* the Spirit of truth, whom the world cannot receive, because it does not behold Him or know Him, *but* you know Him because He abides with you, and will be in you.

18"I will not leave you as orphans; I will come to you.

19"After a little while the world will behold Me no more; but you *will* behold Me; because I live, you shall live also.

20"In that day you shall know that I am in My Father, and you in Me, and I in you.

21"He who has My commandments and keeps them, he it is who loves Me; and he who loves Me shall be loved by My Father, and I will love him, and will disclose Myself to him."

22Judas (not Iscariot) *said to Him, "Lord, what then has happened that You are going to disclose Yourself to us, and not to the world?"

23Jesus answered and said to him, "If anyone loves Me, he will keep My word; and My Father will love him, and We will come to him, and make Our abode with him.

24"He who does not love Me does not keep My words; and the word which you hear is not Mine, but the Father's who sent Me.

25"These things I have

ἀγαπᾶτέ με, τὰς ἐντολὰς τὰς ἐμὰς
ye love me, *the* [2]commandments – [1]my
τηρήσετε. 16 κἀγὼ ἐρωτήσω τὸν πατέρα
ye will keep. And I will request the Father
καὶ ἄλλον παράκλητον δώσει ὑμῖν, ἵνα
and another Comforter he will give you, that
ᾖ μεθ' ὑμῶν εἰς τὸν αἰῶνα, 17 τὸ
he may be with you unto the age, the
πνεῦμα τῆς ἀληθείας, ὃ ὁ κόσμος
Spirit – of truth, which* the world
οὐ δύναται λαβεῖν, ὅτι οὐ θεωρεῖ αὐτὸ
cannot *to* receive, because it beholds not it*
οὐδὲ γινώσκει· ὑμεῖς γινώσκετε αὐτό,
nor knows; ye know it,*
ὅτι παρ' ὑμῖν μένει καὶ ἐν ὑμῖν ἔσται.
because with you he remains and in you will be.
18 Οὐκ ἀφήσω ὑμᾶς ὀρφανούς, ἔρχομαι
I will not leave you orphans, I am coming
πρὸς ὑμᾶς. 19 ἔτι μικρὸν καὶ ὁ κόσμος
to you. Yet a little and the world
με οὐκέτι θεωρεῖ, ὑμεῖς δὲ θεωρεῖτέ
me no longer beholds, but ye behold
με, ὅτι ἐγὼ ζῶ καὶ ὑμεῖς ζήσετε.
me, because I live also ye will live.
20 ἐν ἐκείνῃ τῇ ἡμέρᾳ γνώσεσθε ὑμεῖς
In that – day will know ye
ὅτι ἐγὼ ἐν τῷ πατρί μου καὶ ὑμεῖς
that I in the Father of me and ye
ἐν ἐμοὶ κἀγὼ ἐν ὑμῖν. 21 Ὁ ἔχων
in me and I in you. The [one] having
τὰς ἐντολάς μου καὶ τηρῶν αὐτάς,
the commandments of me and keeping them,
ἐκεῖνός ἐστιν ὁ ἀγαπῶν με· ὁ δὲ ἀγαπῶν
that is the [one] loving me; and the [one] loving
με ἀγαπηθήσεται ὑπὸ τοῦ πατρός μου,
me will be loved by the Father of me,
κἀγὼ ἀγαπήσω αὐτὸν καὶ ἐμφανίσω αὐτῷ
and I will love him and will manifest to him
ἐμαυτόν. 22 λέγει αὐτῷ Ἰούδας, οὐχ
myself. Says to him Judas, not
ὁ Ἰσκαριώτης· κύριε, καὶ τί γέγονεν
the Iscariot: Lord, and what has happened
ὅτι ἡμῖν μέλλεις ἐμφανίζειν σεαυτὸν καὶ
that to us thou art about to manifest thyself and
οὐχὶ τῷ κόσμῳ; 23 ἀπεκρίθη Ἰησοῦς
not to the world? Answered Jesus
καὶ εἶπεν αὐτῷ· ἐάν τις ἀγαπᾷ με,
and said to him: If anyone loves me,
τὸν λόγον μου τηρήσει, καὶ ὁ πατήρ
the word of me he will keep, and the Father
μου ἀγαπήσει αὐτόν, καὶ πρὸς αὐτὸν
of me will love him, and to him
ἐλευσόμεθα καὶ μονὴν παρ' αὐτῷ
we will come and abode with him
ποιησόμεθα. 24 ὁ μὴ ἀγαπῶν με τοὺς
we will make. The [one] not loving me the
λόγους μου οὐ τηρεῖ· καὶ ὁ λόγος ὃν
words of me keeps not; and the word which
ἀκούετε οὐκ ἔστιν ἐμὸς ἀλλὰ τοῦ
ye hear is not mine but [1]of the
πέμψαντός με πατρός. 25 Ταῦτα λελάληκα
[3]having sent [4]me [2]Father. These things I have spoken

* The gender of these pronouns agrees, of course, with the antecedent πνεῦμα (neuter); and this has been kept though the personal Spirit of God is meant. Elsewhere, masculine pronouns are in fact used.

Jesus Promises the Holy Spirit

15"If you love me, you
will obey what I command.
16And I will ask the Father,
and he will give you another
Counselor to be with you
forever— 17the Spirit of
truth. The world cannot accept
him, because it neither
sees him nor knows him.
But you know him, for he
lives with you and will be[r]
in you. 18I will not leave
you as orphans; I will come
to you. 19Before long, the
world will not see me anymore,
but you will see me.
Because I live, you also
will live. 20On that day you
will realize that I am in my
Father, and you are in me,
and I am in you. 21Whoever
has my commands and
obeys them, he is the one
who loves me. He who
loves me will be loved by
my Father, and I too will
love him and show myself
to him."

22Then Judas (not Judas
Iscariot) said, "But, Lord,
why do you intend to show
yourself to us and not to the
world?"

23Jesus replied, "If anyone
loves me, he will obey
my teaching. My Father
will love him, and we will
come to him and make our
home with him. 24He who
does not love me will not
obey my teaching. These
words you hear are not my
own; they belong to the Father
who sent me.

25"All this I have spoken

r17 Some early manuscripts *and is*

spoken to you, while abiding with you.
26"But the Helper, the Holy Spirit, whom the Father will send in My name, He will teach you all things, and bring to your remembrance all that I said to you.
27"Peace I leave with you; My peace I give to you; not as the world gives, do I give to you. Let not your heart be troubled, nor let it be fearful.
28"You heard that I said to you, 'I go away, and I will come to you.' If you loved Me, you would have rejoiced, because I go to the Father; for the Father is greater than I.
29"And now I have told you before it comes to pass, that when it comes to pass, you may believe.
30"I will not speak much more with you, for the ruler of the world is coming, and he has nothing in Me;
31but that the world may know that I love the Father, and as the Father gave Me commandment, even so I do. Arise, let us go from here.

Chapter 15

Jesus Is the Vine—Followers Are Branches

"I am the true vine, and My Father is the vinedresser.
2"Every branch in Me that does not bear fruit, He takes away; and every *branch* that bears fruit, He [z]prunes it, that it may bear more fruit.
3"You are already clean because of the word which I have spoken to you.
4"Abide in Me, and I in you. As the branch cannot bear fruit of itself, unless it abides in the vine, so neither *can* you, unless you abide in Me.

[z] Lit., *cleanses*

ὑμῖν παρ' ὑμῖν μένων· **26** ὁ δὲ παρά-
to you with you remaining; but the Com-
κλητος, τὸ πνεῦμα τὸ ἅγιον ὃ πέμψει ὁ
forter, the Spirit – Holy which will send the
πατὴρ ἐν τῷ ὀνόματί μου, ἐκεῖνος ὑμᾶς
Father in the name of me, that one you
διδάξει πάντα καὶ ὑπομνήσει ὑμᾶς πάντα
will teach all things and remind you [of] all things
ἃ εἶπον ὑμῖν ἐγώ. **27** Εἰρήνην ἀφίημι
which [2]told [3]you [1]I. Peace I leave
ὑμῖν, εἰρήνην τὴν ἐμὴν δίδωμι ὑμῖν·
to you, [2]peace – [1]my I give you;
οὐ καθὼς ὁ κόσμος δίδωσιν ἐγὼ δίδωμι
not as the world gives I give
ὑμῖν. μὴ ταρασσέσθω ὑμῶν ἡ καρδία
you. Let not be troubled of you the heart
μηδὲ δειλιάτω. **28** ἠκούσατε ὅτι ἐγὼ
nor let it be fearful. Ye heard that I
εἶπον ὑμῖν· ὑπάγω καὶ ἔρχομαι πρὸς
told you : I go and come to
ὑμᾶς. εἰ ἠγαπᾶτέ με, ἐχάρητε ἂν ὅτι
you. If ye loved me, ye would have rejoiced that
πορεύομαι πρὸς τὸν πατέρα, ὅτι ὁ πατὴρ
I am going to the Father, because the Father
μείζων μού ἐστιν. **29** καὶ νῦν εἴρηκα
greater [than] me(I) is. And now I have told
ὑμῖν πρὶν γενέσθαι, ἵνα ὅταν γένηται
you before to happen, that when it happens
=it happens,
πιστεύσητε. **30** οὐκέτι πολλὰ λαλήσω μεθ'
ye may believe. No longer many things I will speak with
ὑμῶν, ἔρχεται γὰρ ὁ τοῦ κόσμου ἄρχων·
you, for [5]is coming [1]the [3]of the [4]world [2]ruler;
καὶ ἐν ἐμοὶ οὐκ ἔχει οὐδέν, **31** ἀλλ'
and in me he has not no(any)thing, but
ἵνα γνῷ ὁ κόσμος ὅτι ἀγαπῶ τὸν
that may know the world that I love the
πατέρα, καὶ καθὼς ἐνετείλατό μοι ὁ
Father, and as commanded me the
πατήρ, οὕτως ποιῶ. Ἐγείρεσθε, ἄγωμεν
Father, so I do. Rise, let us go
ἐντεῦθεν.
hence.

15 Ἐγώ εἰμι ἡ ἄμπελος ἡ ἀληθινή,
I am the vine – true,
καὶ ὁ πατήρ μου ὁ γεωργός ἐστιν.
and the Father of me the husbandman is.
2 πᾶν κλῆμα ἐν ἐμοὶ μὴ φέρον καρπόν,
Every branch in me not bearing fruit,
αἴρει αὐτό, καὶ πᾶν τὸ καρπὸν φέρον,
he takes it, and every [branch] the fruit bearing,
καθαίρει αὐτὸ ἵνα καρπὸν πλείονα φέρῃ.
he prunes it that fruit more it may bear.
3 ἤδη ὑμεῖς καθαροί ἐστε διὰ τὸν λόγον
Now ye clean are because of the word
ὃν λελάληκα ὑμῖν· **4** μείνατε ἐν ἐμοί,
which I have spoken to you; remain in me,
κἀγὼ ἐν ὑμῖν. καθὼς τὸ κλῆμα
and I in you. As the branch
οὐ δύναται καρπὸν φέρειν ἀφ' ἑαυτοῦ ἐὰν μὴ
cannot fruit *to* bear from itself unless
μένῃ ἐν τῇ ἀμπέλῳ, οὕτως οὐδὲ ὑμεῖς
it remains in the vine, so not ye
ἐὰν μὴ ἐν ἐμοὶ μένητε. **5** ἐγώ εἰμι
unless in me ye remain. I am

while still with you. 26But the Counselor, the Holy Spirit, whom the Father will send in my name, will teach you all things and will remind you of everything I have said to you. 27Peace I leave with you; my peace I give you. I do not give to you as the world gives. Do not let your hearts be troubled and do not be afraid.
28"You heard me say, 'I am going away and I am coming back to you.' If you loved me, you would be glad that I am going to the Father, for the Father is greater than I. 29I have told you now before it happens, so that when it does happen you will believe. 30I will not speak with you much longer, for the prince of this world is coming. He has no hold on me, 31but the world must learn that I love the Father and that I do exactly what my Father has commanded me.
"Come now; let us leave.

Chapter 15

The Vine and the Branches

"I AM the true vine, and my Father is the gardener. 2He cuts off every branch in me that bears no fruit, while every branch that does bear fruit he prunes[s] so that it will be even more fruitful. 3You are already clean because of the word I have spoken to you. 4Remain in me, and I will remain in you. No branch can bear fruit by itself; it must remain in the vine. Neither can you bear fruit unless you remain in me.

[s]2 The Greek for *prunes* also means *cleans*.

[5]"I am the vine, you are the branches; he who abides in Me, and I in him, he bears much fruit; for apart from Me you can do nothing.

[6]"If anyone does not abide in Me, he is thrown away as a branch, and dries up; and they gather them, and cast them into the fire, and they are burned.

[7]"If you abide in Me, and My words abide in you, ask whatever you wish, and it shall be done for you.

[8]"By this is My Father glorified, that you bear much fruit, and *so* prove to be My disciples.

[9]"Just as the Father has loved Me, I have also loved you; abide in My love.

[10]"If you keep My commandments, you will abide in My love; just as I have kept My Father's commandments, and abide in His love.

[11]"These things I have spoken to you, that My joy may be in you, and *that* your joy may be made full.

Disciples' Relation to Each Other

[12]"This is My commandment, that you love one another, just as I have loved you.

[13]"Greater love has no one than this, that one lay down his life for his friends.

[14]"You are My friends, if you do what I command you.

[15]"No longer do I call you slaves, for the slave does not know what his master is doing; but I have called you friends, for all things that I have heard from My Father I have made known to you.

[16]"You did not choose Me, but I chose you, and appointed you, that you should go and bear fruit,

ἡ ἄμπελος, ὑμεῖς τὰ κλήματα. ὁ μένων
the vine, ye the branches. The [one] remaining

ἐν ἐμοὶ κἀγὼ ἐν αὐτῷ, οὗτος φέρει
in me and I in him, this one bears

καρπὸν πολύν, ὅτι χωρὶς ἐμοῦ οὐ δύνασθε
fruit much, because apart from me ye cannot

ποιεῖν οὐδέν. 6 ἐὰν μή τις μένῃ ἐν
to do no(any)thing. Unless anyone remains in

ἐμοί, ἐβλήθη ἔξω ὡς τὸ κλῆμα καὶ
me, he was(is) cast outside as the branch and

ἐξηράνθη, καὶ συνάγουσιν αὐτὰ καὶ εἰς
was(is) dried, and they gather them and into

τὸ πῦρ βάλλουσιν, καὶ καίεται. 7 ἐὰν
the fire they cast, and they are burned. If

μείνητε ἐν ἐμοὶ καὶ τὰ ῥήματά μου
ye remain in me and the words of me

ἐν ὑμῖν μείνῃ, ὃ ἐὰν θέλητε αἰτήσασθε,
in you remain*s*, whatever ye wish ask,

καὶ γενήσεται ὑμῖν. 8 ἐν τούτῳ ἐδοξάσθη
and it shall happen to you. By this was glorified

ὁ πατήρ μου, ἵνα καρπὸν πολὺν φέρητε
the Father of me, that fruit much ye bear

καὶ γενήσεσθε ἐμοὶ μαθηταί. 9 καθὼς
and ye will be to me° disciples. As

ἠγάπησέν με ὁ πατήρ, κἀγὼ ὑμᾶς
loved me the Father, I also you

ἠγάπησα· μείνατε ἐν τῇ ἀγάπῃ τῇ ἐμῇ.
loved; remain ye in *the* [2]love – [1]my.

10 ἐὰν τὰς ἐντολάς μου τηρήσητε, μενεῖτε
If the commandments of me ye keep, ye will remain

ἐν τῇ ἀγάπῃ μου, καθὼς ἐγὼ τοῦ πατρός
in the love of me, as I of the Father

μου τὰς ἐντολὰς τετήρηκα καὶ μένω
of me the commandments have kept and remain

αὐτοῦ ἐν τῇ ἀγάπῃ. 11 Ταῦτα λελάληκα
of him in the love. These things I have spoken

ὑμῖν ἵνα ἡ χαρὰ ἡ ἐμὴ ἐν ὑμῖν ᾖ
to you that *the* [2]joy – [1]my in you may be

καὶ ἡ χαρὰ ὑμῶν πληρωθῇ. 12 αὕτη
and the joy of you may be filled. This

ἐστὶν ἡ ἐντολὴ ἡ ἐμή, ἵνα ἀγαπᾶτε
is *the* [2]commandment – [1]my, that ye love

ἀλλήλους καθὼς ἠγάπησα ὑμᾶς. 13 μείζονα
one another as I loved you. [1]Greater

ταύτης ἀγάπην οὐδεὶς ἔχει, ἵνα τις
[[3]than] [4]this [2]love no one has, that anyone

τὴν ψυχὴν αὐτοῦ θῇ ὑπὲρ τῶν φίλων
the life of him should lay down for the friends

αὐτοῦ. 14 ὑμεῖς φίλοι μού ἐστε, ἐὰν
of him. Ye friends of me are, if

ποιῆτε ὃ ἐγὼ ἐντέλλομαι ὑμῖν. 15 οὐκέτι
ye do what I command you. No longer

λέγω ὑμᾶς δούλους, ὅτι ὁ δοῦλος οὐκ οἶδεν
I call you slaves, because the slave knows not

τί ποιεῖ αὐτοῦ ὁ κύριος· ὑμᾶς δὲ
what does of him the lord; but you

εἴρηκα φίλους, ὅτι πάντα ἃ ἤκουσα
I have called friends, because all things which I heard

παρὰ τοῦ πατρός μου ἐγνώρισα ὑμῖν.
from the Father of me I made known to you.

16 οὐχ ὑμεῖς με ἐξελέξασθε, ἀλλ' ἐγὼ
Not ye me chose, but I

ἐξελεξάμην ὑμᾶς, καὶ ἔθηκα ὑμᾶς ἵνα
chose you, and appointed you that

ὑμεῖς ὑπάγητε καὶ καρπὸν φέρητε καὶ
ye should go and fruit should bear and

[5]"I am the vine; you are
the branches. If a man remains in me and I in him, he
will bear much fruit; apart
from me you can do noth-
ing. [6]If anyone does not remain in me, he is like a
branch that is thrown away
and withers; such branches
are picked up, thrown into
the fire and burned. [7]If you
remain in me and my words
remain in you, ask whatever you wish, and it will be
given you. [8]This is to my
Father's glory, that you
bear much fruit, showing
yourselves to be my disciples.

[9]"As the Father has
loved me, so have I loved
you. Now remain in my
love. [10]If you obey my
commands, you will remain
in my love, just as I have
obeyed my Father's com-
mands and remain in his
love. [11]I have told you this
so that my joy may be in
you and that your joy may
be complete. [12]My com-
mand is this: Love each
other as I have loved you.
[13]Greater love has no one
than this, that he lay down
his life for his friends.
[14]You are my friends if you
do what I command. [15]I no
longer call you servants,
because a servant does not
know his master's busi-
ness. Instead, I have called
you friends, for everything
that I learned from my Father I have made known to
you. [16]You did not choose
me, but I chose you and appointed you to go and bear

and *that* your fruit should remain, that whatever you ask of the Father in My name, He may give to you.

17"This I command you, that you love one another.

Disciples' Relation to the World

18"If the world hates you, you know that it has hated Me before *it hated* you.

19"If you were of the world, the world would love its own; but because you are not of the world, but I chose you out of the world, therefore the world hates you.

20"Remember the word that I said to you, 'A slave is not greater than his master.' If they persecuted Me, they will also persecute you; if they kept My word, they will keep yours also.

21"But all these things they will do to you for My name's sake, because they do not know the One who sent Me.

22"If I had not come and spoken to them, they would not have sin, but now they have no excuse for their sin.

23"He who hates Me hates My Father also.

24"If I had not done among them the works which no one else did, they would not have sin; but now they have both seen and hated Me and My Father as well.

25"But *they have done this* in order that the word may be fulfilled that is written in their Law, 'THEY HATED ME WITHOUT A CAUSE.'

26"When the Helper comes, whom I will send to you from the Father, *that is* the Spirit of truth, who proceeds from the Father, He will bear witness of Me,

27and you *will* bear witness also, because you have been with Me from the beginning.

ὁ καρπὸς ὑμῶν μένῃ, ἵνα ὅ τι ἂν
the fruit of you should remain, that whatever
αἰτήσητε τὸν πατέρα ἐν τῷ ὀνόματί
ye may ask the Father in the name
μου δῷ ὑμῖν. **17** ταῦτα ἐντέλλομαι ὑμῖν,
of me he may give you. These things I command you,
ἵνα ἀγαπᾶτε ἀλλήλους. **18** Εἰ ὁ κόσμος
that ye love one another. If the world
ὑμᾶς μισεῖ, γινώσκετε ὅτι ἐμὲ πρῶτον
you hates, ye know that me before
ὑμῶν μεμίσηκεν. **19** εἰ ἐκ τοῦ κόσμου ἦτε,
you it has hated. If of the world ye were,
ὁ κόσμος ἂν τὸ ἴδιον ἐφίλει· ὅτι δὲ
the world [1]would [3]the(its) [4]own [2]have loved; but because
ἐκ τοῦ κόσμου οὐκ ἐστέ, ἀλλ' ἐγὼ
of the world ye are not, but I
ἐξελεξάμην ὑμᾶς ἐκ τοῦ κόσμου, διὰ τοῦτο
chose you out of the world, therefore
μισεῖ ὑμᾶς ὁ κόσμος. **20** μνημονεύετε
hates you the world. Remember ye
τοῦ λόγου οὗ ἐγὼ εἶπον ὑμῖν· οὐκ
the word which I said to you: Not
ἔστιν δοῦλος μείζων τοῦ κυρίου αὐτοῦ.
is a slave greater [than] the lord of him.
εἰ ἐμὲ ἐδίωξαν, καὶ ὑμᾶς διώξουσιν·
If me they persecuted, also you they will persecute;
εἰ τὸν λόγον μου ἐτήρησαν, καὶ τὸν
if the word of me they kept, also –
ὑμέτερον τηρήσουσιν. **21** ἀλλὰ ταῦτα πάντα
yours they will keep. But these things all
ποιήσουσιν εἰς ὑμᾶς διὰ τὸ ὄνομά μου,
they will do to you because of the name of me,
ὅτι οὐκ οἴδασιν τὸν πέμψαντά με.
because they know not the [one] having sent me.
22 εἰ μὴ ἦλθον καὶ ἐλάλησα αὐτοῖς, ἁμαρτίαν
Unless I came and spoke to them, sin
οὐκ εἴχοσαν· νῦν δὲ πρόφασιν οὐκ ἔχουσιν
they had not had; but now cloak they have not
περὶ τῆς ἁμαρτίας αὐτῶν. **23** ὁ ἐμὲ
concerning the sin of them. The [one] me
μισῶν καὶ τὸν πατέρα μου μισεῖ. **24** εἰ
hating also the Father of me hates. If
τὰ ἔργα μὴ ἐποίησα ἐν αὐτοῖς ἃ οὐδεὶς
the works I did not among them which no man
ἄλλος ἐποίησεν, ἁμαρτίαν οὐκ εἴχοσαν·
other did, sin they had not had;
νῦν δὲ καὶ ἑωράκασιν καὶ μεμισήκασιν
but now both they have seen and have hated
καὶ ἐμὲ καὶ τὸν πατέρα μου. **25** ἀλλ'
both me and the Father of me. But
ἵνα πληρωθῇ ὁ λόγος ὁ ἐν τῷ νόμῳ
that may be fulfilled the word – in the law
αὐτῶν γεγραμμένος ὅτι Ἐμίσησάν με
of them *having been* written[,] – They hated me
δωρεάν. **26** Ὅταν ἔλθῃ ὁ παράκλητος
freely. When comes the Comforter
ὃν ἐγὼ πέμψω ὑμῖν παρὰ τοῦ πατρός,
whom I will send to you from the Father,
τὸ πνεῦμα τῆς ἀληθείας ὃ παρὰ τοῦ
the Spirit – of truth which from the
πατρὸς ἐκπορεύεται, ἐκεῖνος μαρτυρήσει
Father proceeds, that one will witness
περὶ ἐμοῦ· **27** καὶ ὑμεῖς δὲ μαρτυρεῖτε,
concerning me; [3]also [2]ye [1]and witness,
ὅτι ἀπ' ἀρχῆς μετ' ἐμοῦ ἐστε.
because from [the] beginning with me ye are.

fruit—fruit that will last. Then the Father will give you whatever you ask in my name. 17This is my command: Love each other.

The World Hates the Disciples

18"If the world hates you, keep in mind that it hated me first. 19If you belonged to the world, it would love you as its own. As it is, you do not belong to the world, but I have chosen you out of the world. That is why the world hates you. 20Remember the words I spoke to you: 'No servant is greater than his master.'[t] If they persecuted me, they will persecute you also. If they obeyed my teaching, they will obey yours also. 21They will treat you this way because of my name, for they do not know the One who sent me. 22If I had not come and spoken to them, they would not be guilty of sin. Now, however, they have no excuse for their sin. 23He who hates me hates my Father as well. 24If I had not done among them what no one else did, they would not be guilty of sin. But now they have seen these miracles, and yet they have hated both me and my Father. 25But this is to fulfill what is written in their Law: 'They hated me without reason.'[u]

26"When the Counselor comes, whom I will send to you from the Father, the Spirit of truth who goes out from the Father, he will testify about me. 27And you also must testify, for you have been with me from the beginning.

t20 John 13:16
u25 Psalms 35:19; 69:4

Chapter 16

Jesus' Warning

"THESE things I have spoken to you, that you may be kept from stumbling.

2"They will make you outcasts from the synagogue, but an hour is coming for everyone who kills you to think that he is offering service to God.

3"And these things they will do, because they have not known the Father, or Me.

4"But these things I have spoken to you, that when their hour comes, you may remember that I told you of them. And these things I did not say to you at the beginning, because I was with you.

The Holy Spirit Promised

5"But now I am going to Him who sent Me; and none of you asks Me, 'Where are You going?'

6"But because I have said these things to you, sorrow has filled your heart.

7"But I tell you the truth, it is to your advantage that I go away; for if I do not go away, the Helper shall not come to you; but if I go, I will send Him to you.

8"And He, when He comes, will convict the world concerning sin, and righteousness, and judgment;

9concerning sin, because they do not believe in Me;

10and concerning righteousness, because I go to the Father, and you no longer behold Me;

11and concerning judgment, because the ruler of this world has been judged.

12"I have many more things to say to you, but you cannot bear *them* now.

13"But when He, the Spirit of truth, comes, He will guide you into all the truth; for He will not speak on His own initiative, but whatever He hears, He will speak; and He will disclose to you what is to come.

14"He shall glorify Me;

16 Ταῦτα λελάληκα ὑμῖν ἵνα μὴ
These things I have spoken to you that not

σκανδαλισθῆτε. **2** ἀποσυναγώγους ποιή-
ye be offended. Put away from [the] synagogue they

σουσιν ὑμᾶς· ἀλλ' ἔρχεται ὥρα ἵνα πᾶς ὁ
will make you; but comes an hour that everyone

ἀποκτείνας ὑμᾶς δόξῃ λατρείαν προσφέρειν
killing you thinks service to offer

τῷ θεῷ. **3** καὶ ταῦτα ποιήσουσιν ὅτι
– to God. And these things they will do because

οὐκ ἔγνωσαν τὸν πατέρα οὐδὲ ἐμέ.
they knew not the Father nor me.

4 ἀλλὰ ταῦτα λελάληκα ὑμῖν ἵνα ὅταν
But these things I have spoken to you that when

ἔλθῃ ἡ ὥρα αὐτῶν μνημονεύητε αὐτῶν,
comes the hour of them ye may remember them,

ὅτι ἐγὼ εἶπον ὑμῖν. Ταῦτα δὲ ὑμῖν
that I told you. And these things to you

ἐξ ἀρχῆς οὐκ εἶπον, ὅτι μεθ' ὑμῶν
from [the] beginning I said not, because with you

ἤμην. **5** νῦν δὲ ὑπάγω πρὸς τὸν πέμψαντά
I was. But now I am going to the [one] having sent

με, καὶ οὐδεὶς ἐξ ὑμῶν ἐρωτᾷ με·
me, and not one of you asks me:

ποῦ ὑπάγεις; **6** ἀλλ' ὅτι ταῦτα λελάληκα
Where goest thou? but because these things I have spoken

ὑμῖν, ἡ λύπη πεπλήρωκεν ὑμῶν τὴν
to you, – grief has filled of you the

καρδίαν. **7** ἀλλ' ἐγὼ τὴν ἀλήθειαν λέγω
heart. But I the truth tell

ὑμῖν, συμφέρει ὑμῖν ἵνα ἐγὼ ἀπέλθω.
you, it is expedient for you that I should go away.

ἐὰν γὰρ μὴ ἀπέλθω, ὁ παράκλητος
For if I go not away, the Comforter

οὐ μὴ ἔλθῃ πρὸς ὑμᾶς· ἐὰν δὲ πορευθῶ,
by no means comes to you; but if I go,

πέμψω αὐτὸν πρὸς ὑμᾶς. **8** καὶ ἐλθὼν
I will send him to you. And coming

ἐκεῖνος ἐλέγξει τὸν κόσμον περὶ ἁμαρτίας
that one will reprove the world concerning sin

καὶ περὶ δικαιοσύνης καὶ περὶ κρίσεως·
and concerning righteousness and concerning judgment;

9 περὶ ἁμαρτίας μέν, ὅτι οὐ πιστεύουσιν
concerning sin, – because they believe not

εἰς ἐμέ· **10** περὶ δικαιοσύνης δέ, ὅτι
in me; concerning righteousness, – because

πρὸς τὸν πατέρα ὑπάγω καὶ οὐκέτι
to the Father I am going and no longer

θεωρεῖτέ με· **11** περὶ δὲ κρίσεως, ὅτι
ye behold me; concerning – judgment, because

ὁ ἄρχων τοῦ κόσμου τούτου κέκριται.
the ruler – world of this has been judged.

12 Ἔτι πολλὰ ἔχω ὑμῖν λέγειν, ἀλλ'
Yet many things I have you to tell, but

οὐ δύνασθε βαστάζειν ἄρτι· **13** ὅταν δὲ
ye cannot *to* bear now; but when

ἔλθῃ ἐκεῖνος, τὸ πνεῦμα τῆς ἀληθείας,
comes that one, the Spirit – of truth,

ὁδηγήσει ὑμᾶς εἰς τὴν ἀλήθειαν πᾶσαν·
he will guide you into the truth all;

οὐ γὰρ λαλήσει ἀφ' ἑαυτοῦ, ἀλλ' ὅσα
for not will he speak from himself, but what things

ἀκούει λαλήσει, καὶ τὰ ἐρχόμενα
he hears he will speak, and the coming things

ἀναγγελεῖ ὑμῖν. **14** ἐκεῖνος ἐμὲ δοξάσει,
he will announce to you. That one me will glorify,

Chapter 16

"ALL this I have told you so that you will not go astray. 2They will put you out of the synagogue; in fact, a time is coming when anyone who kills you will think he is offering a service to God. 3They will do such things because they have not known the Father or me. 4I have told you this, so that when the time comes you will remember that I warned you. I did not tell you this at first because I was with you.

The Work of the Holy Spirit

5"Now I am going to him who sent me, yet none of you asks me, 'Where are you going?' 6Because I have said these things, you are filled with grief. 7But I tell you the truth: It is for your good that I am going away. Unless I go away, the Counselor will not come to you; but if I go, I will send him to you. 8When he comes, he will convict the world of guilt[v] in regard to sin and righteousness and judgment: 9in regard to sin, because men do not believe in me; 10in regard to righteousness, because I am going to the Father, where you can see me no longer; 11and in regard to judgment, because the prince of this world now stands condemned.

12"I have much more to say to you, more than you can now bear. 13But when he, the Spirit of truth, comes, he will guide you into all truth. He will not speak on his own; he will speak only what he hears, and he will tell you what is

v8 Or *will expose the guilt of the world*

for He shall take of Mine,
and shall disclose *it* to you.
15"All things that the Father has are Mine; there-
fore I said, that He takes of
Mine, and will disclose *it* to
you.

Jesus' Death and Resurrection Foretold

16"A little while, and you
will no longer behold Me;
and again a little while, and
you will see Me."
17*Some* of His disciples
therefore said to one an-
other, "What is this thing
He is telling us, 'A little
while, and you will not behold Me; and again a little
while, and you will see
Me'; and, 'because I go to
the Father'?"
18And so they were say-
ing, "What is this that He
says, 'A little while'? We
do not know what He is
talking about."
19Jesus knew that they
wished to question Him,
and He said to them, "Are
you deliberating together
about this, that I said, 'A
little while, and you will not
behold Me, and again a little while, and you will see
Me'?
20"Truly, truly, I say to
you, that you will weep and
lament, but the world will
rejoice; you will be sorrowful, but your sorrow will be
turned to joy.
21"Whenever a woman is
in travail she has sorrow,
because her hour has come;
but when she gives birth to
the child, she remembers
the anguish no more, for
joy that a child has been
born into the world.
22"Therefore you too
now have sorrow; but I will
see you again, and your
heart will rejoice, and no
one takes your joy away
from you.

Prayer Promises

23"And in that day you
will ask Me no question.
Truly, truly, I say to you, if
you shall ask the Father for
anything, He will give it to
you in My name.

ὅτι ἐκ τοῦ ἐμοῦ λήμψεται καὶ ἀναγγελεῖ
because of the of me * he will receive and will announce
ὑμῖν. 15 πάντα ὅσα ἔχει ὁ πατὴρ ἐμά
to you. All things which has the Father mine
ἐστιν· διὰ τοῦτο εἶπον ὅτι ἐκ τοῦ ἐμοῦ
is(are); therefore I said that of the of me *
λαμβάνει καὶ ἀναγγελεῖ ὑμῖν. 16 Μικρὸν
he receives and will announce to you. A little while
καὶ οὐκέτι θεωρεῖτέ με, καὶ πάλιν
and no longer ye behold me, and again
μικρὸν καὶ ὄψεσθέ με. 17 εἶπαν οὖν
a little while and ye will see me. Said therefore
ἐκ τῶν μαθητῶν αὐτοῦ πρὸς ἀλλήλους·
[some] of the disciples of him to one another:
τί ἐστιν τοῦτο ὃ λέγει ἡμῖν· μικρὸν
What is this which he tells us: A little while
καὶ οὐ θεωρεῖτέ με, καὶ πάλιν μικρὸν
and ye behold not me, and again a little while
καὶ ὄψεσθέ με; καί· ὅτι ὑπάγω
and ye will see me? and: Because I am going
πρὸς τὸν πατέρα; 18 ἔλεγον οὖν· τοῦτο
to the Father? They said therefore: [3]This
τί ἐστιν ὃ λέγει τὸ μικρόν; οὐκ οἴδαμεν
[1]what [2]is which he says[,] the "little while"? We do not know
τί λαλεῖ. 19 ἔγνω Ἰησοῦς ὅτι ἤθελον
what he speaks. Knew Jesus that they wished
αὐτὸν ἐρωτᾶν, καὶ εἶπεν αὐτοῖς· περὶ
him to question, and said to them: Concerning
τούτου ζητεῖτε μετ' ἀλλήλων ὅτι εἶπον·
this seek ye with one another because I said:
μικρὸν καὶ οὐ θεωρεῖτέ με, καὶ πάλιν
A little while and ye behold not me, and again
μικρὸν καὶ ὄψεσθέ με; 20 ἀμὴν ἀμὴν
a little while and ye will see me? Truly truly
λέγω ὑμῖν ὅτι κλαύσετε καὶ θρηνήσετε
I tell you that will weep and will lament
ὑμεῖς, ὁ δὲ κόσμος χαρήσεται· ὑμεῖς
ye, and the world will rejoice; ye
λυπηθήσεσθε, ἀλλ' ἡ λύπη ὑμῶν εἰς
will be grieved, but the grief of you into
χαρὰν γενήσεται. 21 ἡ γυνὴ ὅταν τίκτῃ
joy will become. The woman when she gives birth
λύπην ἔχει, ὅτι ἦλθεν ἡ ὥρα αὐτῆς·
grief has, because came the hour of her;
ὅταν δὲ γεννήσῃ τὸ παιδίον, οὐκέτι
but when she brings forth the child, no longer
μνημονεύει τῆς θλίψεως διὰ τὴν χαρὰν
she remembers the distress because of the joy
ὅτι ἐγεννήθη ἄνθρωπος εἰς τὸν κόσμον.
that was born a man into the world.
22 καὶ ὑμεῖς οὖν νῦν μὲν λύπην ἔχετε·
And ye therefore now indeed grief have;
πάλιν δὲ ὄψομαι ὑμᾶς, καὶ χαρήσεται
but again I will see you, and [4]will rejoice
ὑμῶν ἡ καρδία, καὶ τὴν χαρὰν ὑμῶν
[3]of you [1]the [2]heart, and the joy of you
οὐδεὶς αἴρει ἀφ' ὑμῶν. 23 καὶ ἐν ἐκείνῃ τῇ
no one takes from you. And in that –
ἡμέρᾳ ἐμὲ οὐκ ἐρωτήσετε οὐδέν.
day me ye will not question no(any)thing.
ἀμὴν ἀμὴν λέγω ὑμῖν, ἄν τι αἰτήσητε
Truly truly I tell you, whatever ye ask
τὸν πατέρα δώσει ὑμῖν ἐν τῷ ὀνόματί
the Father he will give you in the name

* Understand "that which is mine".

yet to come. 14He will bring
glory to me by taking from
what is mine and making it
known to you. 15All that
belongs to the Father is
mine. That is why I said the
Spirit will take from what is
mine and make it known to
you.
16"In a little while you
will see me no more, and
then after a little while you
will see me."

The Disciples' Grief Will Turn to Joy

17Some of his disciples
said to one another, "What
does he mean by saying, 'In
a little while you will see
me no more, and then after
a little while you will see
me,' and 'Because I am going to the Father'?" 18They
kept asking, "What does
he mean by 'a little while'?
We don't understand what
he is saying."
19Jesus saw that they
wanted to ask him about
this, so he said to them,
"Are you asking one an-
other what I meant when I
said, 'In a little while you
will see me no more, and
then after a little while you
will see me'? 20I tell you the
truth, you will weep and
mourn while the world re-
joices. You will grieve, but
your grief will turn to joy.
21A woman giving birth to a
child has pain because her
time has come; but when
her baby is born she forgets
the anguish because of her
joy that a child is born into
the world. 22So with you:
Now is your time of grief,
but I will see you again and
you will rejoice, and no one
will take away your joy.
23In that day you will no
longer ask me anything. I
tell you the truth, my Father will give you whatever
you ask in my name. 24Un-

24"Until now you have asked for nothing in My name; ask, and you will receive, that your joy may be made full.

25"These things I have spoken to you in figurative language; an hour is coming when I will speak no more to you in figurative language, but will tell you plainly of the Father.

26"In that day you will ask in My name, and I do not say to you that I will request the Father on your behalf;

27for the Father Himself loves you, because you have loved Me, and have believed that I came forth from the Father.

28"I came forth from the Father, and have come into the world; I am leaving the world again, and going to the Father."

29His disciples *said, "Lo, now You are speaking plainly, and are not using a figure of speech.

30"Now we know that You know all things, and have no need for anyone to question You; by this we believe that You came from God."

31Jesus answered them, "Do you now believe?

32"Behold, an hour is coming, and has *already* come, for you to be scattered, each to his own *home,* and to leave Me alone; and *yet* I am not alone, because the Father is with Me.

33"These things I have spoken to you, that in Me you may have peace. In the world you have tribulation, but take courage; I have overcome the world."

μου. 24 ἕως ἄρτι οὐκ ᾐτήσατε οὐδὲν
of me. Until now ye asked not no(any)thing
ἐν τῷ ὀνόματί μου· αἰτεῖτε, καὶ λήμψεσθε,
in the name of me; ask, and ye will receive,
ἵνα ἡ χαρὰ ὑμῶν ᾖ πεπληρωμένη.
that the joy of you may be *having been* filled.
25 Ταῦτα ἐν παροιμίαις λελάληκα ὑμῖν·
These things in allegories I have spoken to you;
ἔρχεται ὥρα ὅτε οὐκέτι ἐν παροιμίαις
comes an hour when no longer in allegories
λαλήσω ὑμῖν, ἀλλὰ παρρησίᾳ περὶ τοῦ
I will speak to you, but plainly concerning the
πατρὸς ἀπαγγελῶ ὑμῖν. 26 ἐν ἐκείνῃ τῇ
Father will declare to you. In that –
ἡμέρᾳ ἐν τῷ ὀνόματί μου αἰτήσεσθε,
day in the name of me ye will ask,
καὶ οὐ λέγω ὑμῖν ὅτι ἐγὼ ἐρωτήσω
and I tell not you that I will request
τὸν πατέρα περὶ ὑμῶν· 27 αὐτὸς γὰρ
the Father concerning you; for [him]self
ὁ πατὴρ φιλεῖ ὑμᾶς, ὅτι ὑμεῖς ἐμὲ
the Father loves you, because ye me
πεφιλήκατε καὶ πεπιστεύκατε ὅτι ἐγὼ
have loved and have believed that I
παρὰ τοῦ θεοῦ ἐξῆλθον. 28 ἐξῆλθον
from – God came forth. I came forth
ἐκ τοῦ πατρὸς καὶ ἐλήλυθα εἰς τὸν
out of the Father and have come into the
κόσμον· πάλιν ἀφίημι τὸν κόσμον καὶ
world; again I leave the world and
πορεύομαι πρὸς τὸν πατέρα. 29 Λέγουσιν
go to the Father. Say
οἱ μαθηταὶ αὐτοῦ· ἴδε νῦν ἐν παρρησίᾳ
the disciples of him: Behold[,] now in plainness
λαλεῖς, καὶ παροιμίαν οὐδεμίαν λέγεις.
thou speakest, and [2]allegory [1]no thou sayest.
30 νῦν οἴδαμεν ὅτι οἶδας πάντα καὶ
Now we know that thou knowest all things and
οὐ χρείαν ἔχεις ἵνα τίς σε ἐρωτᾷ· ἐν
no need hast that anyone thee should question; by
τούτῳ πιστεύομεν ὅτι ἀπὸ θεοῦ ἐξῆλθες.
this we believe that from God thou camest forth.
31 ἀπεκρίθη αὐτοῖς Ἰησοῦς· ἄρτι πιστεύετε;
Answered them Jesus: Now believe ye?
32 ἰδοὺ ἔρχεται ὥρα καὶ ἐλήλυθεν ἵνα
behold[,] comes an hour and has come that
σκορπισθῆτε ἕκαστος εἰς τὰ ἴδια κἀμὲ
ye are scattered each one to the(his) own and me
μόνον ἀφῆτε· καὶ οὐκ εἰμὶ μόνος, ὅτι
alone ye leave; and I am not alone, because
ὁ πατὴρ μετ' ἐμοῦ ἐστιν. 33 ταῦτα
the Father with me is. These things
λελάληκα ὑμῖν ἵνα ἐν ἐμοὶ εἰρήνην
I have spoken to you that in me peace
ἔχητε. ἐν τῷ κόσμῳ θλῖψιν ἔχετε·
ye may have. In the world distress ye have;
ἀλλὰ θαρσεῖτε, ἐγὼ νενίκηκα τὸν κόσμον.
but cheer ye up, I have overcome the world.

til now you have not asked
for anything in my name.
Ask and you will receive,
and your joy will be complete.

25"Though I have been
speaking figuratively, a
time is coming when I will
no longer use this kind of
language but will tell you
plainly about my Father.
26In that day you will ask in
my name. I am not saying
that I will ask the Father on
your behalf. 27No, the Father
himself loves you because
you have loved me
and have believed that I
came from God. 28I came
from the Father and entered
the world; now I am
leaving the world and going
back to the Father."

29Then Jesus' disciples
said, "Now you are speaking
clearly and without figures
of speech. 30Now we
can see that you know all
things and that you do not
even need to have anyone
ask you questions. This
makes us believe that you
came from God."

31"You believe at last!"[w]
Jesus answered. 32"But a
time is coming, and has
come, when you will be
scattered, each to his own
home. You will leave me all
alone. Yet I am not alone,
for my Father is with me.

33"I have told you these
things, so that in me you
may have peace. In this
world you will have trouble.
But take heart! I have
overcome the world."

Chapter 17

The High Priestly Prayer

THESE things Jesus spoke; and lifting up His eyes to heaven, He said, "Father, the hour has come; glorify Thy Son, that

17 Ταῦτα ἐλάλησεν Ἰησοῦς, καὶ ἐπάρας
These things spoke Jesus, and lifting up
τοὺς ὀφθαλμοὺς αὐτοῦ εἰς τὸν οὐρανὸν
the eyes of him to – heaven
εἶπεν· πάτερ, ἐλήλυθεν ἡ ὥρα· δόξασόν
said: Father, has come the hour; glorify

Chapter 17

Jesus Prays for Himself

AFTER Jesus said this, he looked toward heaven and prayed:

"Father, the time has come. Glorify your

[w]*31* Or *"Do you now believe?"*

the Son may glorify Thee,
2 even as Thou gavest
Him authority over all
mankind, that to all whom
Thou hast given Him, He
may give eternal life.
3 "And this is eternal life,
that they may know Thee,
the only true God, and
Jesus Christ whom Thou
hast sent.
4 "I glorified Thee on the
earth, having accomplished
the work which Thou hast
given Me to do.
5 "And now, glorify
Thou Me together with
Thyself, Father, with the
glory which I had with
Thee before the world was.
6 "I manifested Thy
name to the men whom
Thou gavest Me out of the
world; Thine they were,
and Thou gavest them to
Me, and they have kept
Thy word.
7 "Now they have come
to know that everything
Thou hast given Me is from
Thee;
8 for the words which
Thou gavest Me I have giv-
en to them; and they re-
ceived *them*, and truly understood that I came forth
from Thee, and they be-
lieved that Thou didst send
Me.
9 "I ask on their behalf; I
do not ask on behalf of the
world, but of those whom
Thou hast given Me; for
they are Thine;
10 and all things that are
Mine are Thine, and Thine
are Mine; and I have been
glorified in them.
11 "And I am no more in
the world; and *yet* they
themselves are in the
world, and I come to Thee.
Holy Father, keep them in
Thy name, *the name* which
Thou hast given Me, that
they may be one, even as
We *are*.
12 "While I was with
them, I was keeping them
in Thy name which Thou
hast given Me; and I guard-

σου τὸν υἱόν, ἵνα ὁ υἱὸς δοξάσῃ σέ,
of thee the Son, that the Son may glorify thee,

2 καθὼς ἔδωκας αὐτῷ ἐξουσίαν πάσης
as thou gavest him authority of(over) all

σαρκός, ἵνα πᾶν ὃ δέδωκας αὐτῷ δώσῃ
flesh, that all which thou hast given him he may give

αὐτοῖς ζωὴν αἰώνιον. 3 αὕτη δέ ἐστιν
to them life eternal. And this is

ἡ αἰώνιος ζωή, ἵνα γινώσκωσιν σὲ τὸν
– eternal life, that they may know thee the

μόνον ἀληθινὸν θεὸν καὶ ὃν ἀπέστειλας
only true God and [he] whom thou didst send

Ἰησοῦν Χριστόν. 4 ἐγώ σε ἐδόξασα
Jesus Christ. I thee glorified

ἐπὶ τῆς γῆς, τὸ ἔργον τελειώσας ὃ
on the earth, the work finishing which

δέδωκάς μοι ἵνα ποιήσω· 5 καὶ νῦν
thou hast given to me that I should do; and now

δόξασόν με σύ, πάτερ, παρὰ σεαυτῷ
glorify me thou, Father, with thyself

τῇ δόξῃ ᾗ εἶχον πρὸ τοῦ τὸν κόσμον
with the glory which I had before *the* the world
=before the world was

εἶναι παρὰ σοί. 6 Ἐφανέρωσά σου τὸ
to be[b] with thee. I manifested of thee the

ὄνομα τοῖς ἀνθρώποις οὓς ἔδωκάς μοι
name to the men whom thou gavest to me

ἐκ τοῦ κόσμου. σοὶ ἦσαν κἀμοὶ αὐτοὺς
out of the world. To thee[c] they were and to me them
=Thine

ἔδωκας, καὶ τὸν λόγον σου τετήρηκαν.
thou gavest, and the word of thee they have kept.

7 νῦν ἔγνωκαν ὅτι πάντα ὅσα δέδωκάς
Now they have known that all things as many as thou hast given

μοι παρὰ σοῦ εἰσιν· 8 ὅτι τὰ ῥήματα
to me from thee are; because the words

ἃ ἔδωκάς μοι δέδωκα αὐτοῖς, καὶ αὐτοὶ
which thou gavest to me I have given to them, and they

ἔλαβον, καὶ ἔγνωσαν ἀληθῶς ὅτι παρὰ
received, and knew truly that from

σοῦ ἐξῆλθον, καὶ ἐπίστευσαν ὅτι σύ
thee I came forth, and they believed that thou

με ἀπέστειλας. 9 ἐγὼ περὶ αὐτῶν ἐρωτῶ·
me didst send. I concerning them make request;

οὐ περὶ τοῦ κόσμου ἐρωτῶ, ἀλλὰ περὶ
not concerning the world do I make request, but concerning

ὧν δέδωκάς μοι, ὅτι σοί εἰσιν,
[those] whom thou hast given to me, because to thee[c] they are,
=thine

10 καὶ τὰ ἐμὰ πάντα σά ἐστιν καὶ
and [2]*the* [3]my things [1]all [5]thine [4]is(are) and

τὰ σὰ ἐμά, καὶ δεδόξασμαι ἐν αὐτοῖς.
the thy things mine, and I have been glorified in them.

11 καὶ οὐκέτι εἰμὶ ἐν τῷ κόσμῳ, καὶ
And no longer am I in the world, and

αὐτοὶ ἐν τῷ κόσμῳ εἰσίν, κἀγὼ πρὸς
they in the world are, and I to

σὲ ἔρχομαι. πάτερ ἅγιε, τήρησον αὐτοὺς
thee come. Father holy, keep them

ἐν τῷ ὀνόματί σου ᾧ δέδωκάς μοι,
in the name of thee which thou hast given to me,

ἵνα ὦσιν ἓν καθὼς ἡμεῖς. 12 ὅτε ἤμην
that they may be one as we. When I was

μετ' αὐτῶν, ἐγὼ ἐτήρουν αὐτοὺς ἐν
with them, I kept them in

τῷ ὀνόματί σου ᾧ δέδωκάς μοι, καὶ
the name of thee which thou hast given to me, and

Son, that your Son may
glorify you. 2 For you
granted him authority
over all people that he
might give eternal life to
all those you have given
him. 3 Now this is eter-
nal life: that they may
know you, the only true
God, and Jesus Christ,
whom you have sent. 4 I
have brought you glory
on earth by completing
the work you gave me
to do. 5 And now, Fa-
ther, glorify me in your
presence with the glory
I had with you before
the world began.

Jesus Prays for His Disciples

6 "I have revealed
you[x] to those whom
you gave me out of the
world. They were
yours; you gave them to
me and they have
obeyed your word.
7 Now they know that
everything you have
given me comes from
you. 8 For I gave them
the words you gave me
and they accepted
them. They knew with
certainty that I came
from you, and they be-
lieved that you sent me.
9 I pray for them. I am
not praying for the
world, but for those you
have given me, for they
are yours. 10 All I have is
yours, and all you have
is mine. And glory has
come to me through
them. 11 I will remain in
the world no longer, but
they are still in the
world, and I am coming
to you. Holy Father,
protect them by the
power of your name—
the name you gave me
—so that they may be
one as we are one.
12 While I was with
them, I protected them
and kept them safe by

[x]6 Greek *your name*; also in verse 26

ed them, and not one of
them perished but the son
of perdition, that the Scripture might be fulfilled.

The Disciples in the World

13"But now I come to
Thee; and these things I
speak in the world, that
they may have My joy
made full in themselves.
14"I have given them Thy
word; and the world has
hated them, because they
are not of the world, even
as I am not of the world.
15"I do not ask Thee to
take them out of the world,
but to keep them from the
evil *one*.
16"They are not of the
world, even as I am not of
the world.
17"Sanctify them in the
truth; Thy word is truth.
18"As Thou didst send
Me into the world, I also
have sent them into the
world.
19"And for their sakes I
sanctify Myself, that they
themselves also may be
sanctified in truth.
20"I do not ask in behalf
of these alone, but for those
also who believe in Me
through their word;
21that they may all be one;
even as Thou, Father, *art*
in Me, and I in Thee, that
they also may be in Us,
that the world may believe
that Thou didst send Me.

Their Future Glory

22"And the glory which
Thou hast given Me I have
given to them; that they
may be one, just as We are
one;
23I in them, and Thou in
Me, that they may be per-
fected in unity, that the
world may know that Thou
didst send Me, and didst
love them, even as Thou
didst love Me.
24"Father, I desire that
they also, whom Thou hast
given Me, be with Me

ἐφύλαξα, καὶ οὐδεὶς ἐξ αὐτῶν ἀπώλετο
I guarded, and not one of them perished
εἰ μὴ ὁ υἱὸς τῆς ἀπωλείας, ἵνα ἡ
except the son – perdition, that the
γραφὴ πληρωθῇ. **13** νῦν δὲ πρὸς σὲ
scripture might be fulfilled. But now to thee
ἔρχομαι, καὶ ταῦτα λαλῶ ἐν τῷ κόσμῳ
I come, and these things I speak in the world
ἵνα ἔχωσιν τὴν χαρὰν τὴν ἐμὴν
that they may have *the* ²joy – ¹my
πεπληρωμένην ἐν ἑαυτοῖς. **14** ἐγὼ δέδωκα
having been fulfilled in themselves. I have given
αὐτοῖς τὸν λόγον σου, καὶ ὁ κόσμος
to them the word of thee, and the world
ἐμίσησεν αὐτούς, ὅτι οὐκ εἰσὶν ἐκ τοῦ
hated them, because they are not of the
κόσμου καθὼς ἐγὼ οὐκ εἰμὶ ἐκ τοῦ
world as I am not of the
κόσμου. **15** οὐκ ἐρωτῶ ἵνα ἄρῃς αὐτοὺς
world. I do not request that thou shouldest take them
ἐκ τοῦ κόσμου, ἀλλ' ἵνα τηρήσῃς αὐτοὺς
out of the world, but that thou shouldest keep them
ἐκ τοῦ πονηροῦ. **16** ἐκ τοῦ κόσμου
out of the evil [?one]. Of the world
οὐκ εἰσὶν καθὼς ἐγὼ οὐκ εἰμὶ ἐκ τοῦ
they are not as I am not of the
κόσμου. **17** ἁγίασον αὐτοὺς ἐν τῇ
world. Sanctify them in(?by) the
ἀληθείᾳ· ὁ λόγος ὁ σὸς ἀλήθειά ἐστιν.
truth; *the* ²word – ¹thy truth is.
18 καθὼς ἐμὲ ἀπέστειλας εἰς τὸν κόσμον,
As me thou didst send into the world,
κἀγὼ ἀπέστειλα αὐτοὺς εἰς τὸν κόσμον·
I also sent them into the world;
19 καὶ ὑπὲρ αὐτῶν [ἐγὼ] ἁγιάζω ἐμαυτόν,
and on behalf of them I sanctify myself,
ἵνα ὦσιν καὶ αὐτοὶ ἡγιασμένοι ἐν ἀληθείᾳ.
that ³may be ²also ¹they *having been* sanctified in truth.
20 Οὐ περὶ τούτων δὲ ἐρωτῶ μόνον,
²Not ³concerning ⁴these ¹but I make request only,
ἀλλὰ καὶ περὶ τῶν πιστευόντων διὰ
but also concerning the [ones] believing through
τοῦ λόγου αὐτῶν εἰς ἐμέ, **21** ἵνα πάντες
the word of them in me, that all
ἓν ὦσιν, καθὼς σύ, πατήρ, ἐν ἐμοὶ
one may be, as thou, Father, in me
κἀγὼ ἐν σοί, ἵνα καὶ αὐτοὶ ἐν ἡμῖν
and I in thee, that also they in us
ὦσιν, ἵνα ὁ κόσμος πιστεύῃ ὅτι σύ
may be, that the world may believe that thou
με ἀπέστειλας. **22** κἀγὼ τὴν δόξαν ἣν
me didst send. And I the glory which
δέδωκάς μοι δέδωκα αὐτοῖς, ἵνα ὦσιν
thou hast given to me have given to them, that they may be
ἓν καθὼς ἡμεῖς ἕν· **23** ἐγὼ ἐν αὐτοῖς
one as we [are] one; I in them
καὶ σὺ ἐν ἐμοί, ἵνα ὦσιν τετελειωμένοι
and thou in me, that they may be *having been* perfected
εἰς ἕν, ἵνα γινώσκῃ ὁ κόσμος ὅτι σύ
in one, that may know the world that thou
με ἀπέστειλας καὶ ἠγάπησας αὐτοὺς
me didst send and didst love them
καθὼς ἐμὲ ἠγάπησας. **24** Πατήρ, ὃ
as me thou didst love. Father, what
δέδωκάς μοι, θέλω ἵνα ὅπου εἰμὶ ἐγὼ
thou hast given to me, I wish that where am I

that name you gave me.
None has been lost ex-
cept the one doomed to
destruction so that
Scripture would be ful-
filled.
13"I am coming to you
now, but I say these
things while I am still in
the world, so that they
may have the full mea-
sure of my joy within
them. 14I have given
them your word and the
world has hated them,
for they are not of the
world any more than I
am of the world. 15My
prayer is not that you
take them out of the
world but that you pro-
tect them from the evil
one. 16They are not of
the world, even as I am
not of it. 17Sanctify[y]
them by the truth; your
word is truth. 18As you
sent me into the world, I
have sent them into the
world. 19For them I
sanctify myself, that
they too may be truly
sanctified.

Jesus Prays for All Believers

20"My prayer is not
for them alone. I pray
also for those who will
believe in me through
their message, 21that all
of them may be one, Fa-
ther, just as you are in
me and I am in you.
May they also be in us
so that the world may
believe that you have
sent me. 22I have given
them the glory that you
gave me, that they may
be one as we are one: 23I
in them and you in me.
May they be brought to
complete unity to let the
world know that you
sent me and have loved
them even as you have
loved me.
24"Father, I want
those you have given
me to be with me where

[y]17 Greek *hagiazo (set apart for sacred use* or *make holy)*; also in verse 19

where I am, in order that
they may behold My glory,
which Thou hast given Me;
for Thou didst love Me before the foundation of the
world.
25"O righteous Father, although the world has not
known Thee, yet I have
known Thee; and these
have known that Thou
didst send Me;
26and I have made Thy
name known to them, and
will make it known; that the
love wherewith Thou didst
love Me may be in them,
and I in them."

Chapter 18

Judas Betrays Jesus

WHEN Jesus had
spoken these words,
He went forth with His disciples over the ravine of the
Kidron, where there was a
garden, into which He
Himself entered, and His
disciples.
2Now Judas also, who
was betraying Him, knew
the place; for Jesus had
often met there with His
disciples.
3Judas then, having re-
ceived the *Roman* cohort,
and officers from the chief
priests and the Pharisees,
*came there with lanterns
and torches and weapons.
4Jesus therefore, know-
ing all the things that were
coming upon Him, went
forth, and *said to them,
"Whom do you seek?"
5They answered Him,
"Jesus the Nazarene." He
*said to them, "I am *He*."
And Judas also who was
betraying Him, was stand-
ing with them.
6When therefore He said
to them, "I am *He*," they
drew back, and fell to the
ground.
7Again therefore He
asked them, "Whom do
you seek?" And they said,
"Jesus the Nazarene."
8Jesus answered, "I told
you that I am *He*; if therefore you seek Me, let these
go their way,"

κἀκεῖνοι ὦσιν μετ' ἐμοῦ, ἵνα θεωρῶσιν
those also may be with me, that they may behold
τὴν δόξαν τὴν ἐμήν, ἣν δέδωκάς μοι
the [2]glory – [1]my, which thou hast given to me
ὅτι ἠγάπησάς με πρὸ καταβολῆς κόσμου.
because thou didst love me before [the] foundation of [the] world.
25 πατὴρ δίκαιε, καὶ ὁ κόσμος σε
Father righteous, indeed the world thee
οὐκ ἔγνω, ἐγὼ δέ σε ἔγνων, καὶ οὗτοι
knew not, but I thee knew, and these
ἔγνωσαν ὅτι σύ με ἀπέστειλας· 26 καὶ
knew that thou me didst send; and
ἐγνώρισα αὐτοῖς τὸ ὄνομά σου καὶ
I made known to them the name of thee and
γνωρίσω, ἵνα ἡ ἀγάπη ἣν ἠγάπησάς
will make known, that the love [with] which thou lovedst
με ἐν αὐτοῖς ᾖ κἀγὼ ἐν αὐτοῖς.
me in them may be and I in them.

18 Ταῦτα εἰπὼν Ἰησοῦς ἐξῆλθεν σὺν
These things having said Jesus went forth with
τοῖς μαθηταῖς αὐτοῦ πέραν τοῦ χειμάρρου
the disciples of him across the torrent
τοῦ Κεδρὼν, ὅπου ἦν κῆπος, εἰς ὃν
– Kedron, where there was a garden, into which
εἰσῆλθεν αὐτὸς καὶ οἱ μαθηταὶ αὐτοῦ.
entered he and the disciples of him.
2 ᾔδει δὲ καὶ Ἰούδας ὁ παραδιδοὺς
[1]Now [7]knew [3]also [2]Judas [4]the [one] [5]betraying
αὐτὸν τὸν τόπον, ὅτι πολλάκις συνήχθη
[6]him [8]the [9]place, because often assembled
Ἰησοῦς ἐκεῖ μετὰ τῶν μαθητῶν αὐτου.
Jesus there with the disciples of him.
3 ὁ οὖν Ἰούδας λαβὼν τὴν σπεῖραν
– Therefore Judas taking the band
καὶ ἐκ τῶν ἀρχιερέων καὶ [ἐκ] τῶν
and [2]from [3]the [4]chief priests [5]and [6]from [7]the
Φαρισαίων ὑπηρέτας ἔρχεται ἐκεῖ μετὰ
[8]Pharisees [1]attendants comes there with
φανῶν καὶ λαμπάδων καὶ ὅπλων. 4 Ἰησοῦς
lanterns and lamps and weapons. Jesus
οὖν εἰδὼς πάντα τὰ ἐρχόμενα ἐπ' αὐτὸν
therefore knowing all the things coming on him
ἐξῆλθεν καὶ λέγει αὐτοῖς· τίνα ζητεῖτε;
went forth and says to them: Whom seek ye?
5 ἀπεκρίθησαν αὐτῷ· Ἰησοῦν τὸν
They answered him: Jesus the
Ναζωραῖον. λέγει αὐτοῖς· ἐγώ εἰμι.
Nazarene. He tells them: I am.
εἱστήκει δὲ καὶ Ἰούδας ὁ παραδιδοὺς
Now stood also Judas the [one] betraying
αὐτὸν μετ' αὐτῶν. 6 ὡς οὖν εἶπεν
him with them. When therefore he told
αὐτοῖς· ἐγώ εἰμι, ἀπῆλθαν εἰς τὰ ὀπίσω
them: I am, they went away back †
καὶ ἔπεσαν χαμαί. 7 πάλιν οὖν
and fell on the ground. Again therefore
ἐπηρώτησεν αὐτούς· τίνα ζητεῖτε; οἱ δὲ
he questioned them: Whom seek ye? And they
εἶπαν· Ἰησοῦν τὸν Ναζωραῖον. 8 ἀπεκρίθη
said: Jesus the Nazarene. Answered
Ἰησοῦς· εἶπον ὑμῖν ὅτι ἐγώ εἰμι· εἰ
Jesus: I told you that I am; if
οὖν ἐμὲ ζητεῖτε, ἄφετε τούτους ὑπάγειν·
therefore me ye seek, allow these to go;

I am, and to see my glo-
ry, the glory you have
given me because you
loved me before the cre-
ation of the world.
25"Righteous Father,
though the world does
not know you, I know
you, and they know that
you have sent me. 26I
have made you known
to them, and will con-
tinue to make you
known in order that the
love you have for me
may be in them and that
I myself may be in
them."

Chapter 18

Jesus Arrested

WHEN he had finished
praying, Jesus left
with his disciples and
crossed the Kidron Valley.
On the other side there was
an olive grove, and he and
his disciples went into it.
2Now Judas, who be-
trayed him, knew the
place, because Jesus had
often met there with his disciples. 3So Judas came to
the grove, guiding a detachment of soldiers and some
officials from the chief
priests and Pharisees. They
were carrying torches, lanterns and weapons.
4Jesus, knowing all that
was going to happen to
him, went out and asked
them, "Who is it you
want?"
5"Jesus of Nazareth,"
they replied.
"I am he," Jesus said.
(And Judas the traitor was
standing there with them.)
6When Jesus said, "I am
he," they drew back and
fell to the ground.
7Again he asked them,
"Who is it you want?"
And they said, "Jesus of
Nazareth."
8"I told you that I am
he," Jesus answered. "If
you are looking for me,
then let these men go."

9that the word might be
fulfilled which He spoke,
"Of those whom Thou hast
given Me I lost not one."
10Simon Peter therefore
having a sword, drew it,
and struck the high priest's
slave, and cut off his right
ear; and the slave's name
was Malchus.
11Jesus therefore said to
Peter, "Put the sword into
the sheath; the cup which
the Father has given Me,
shall I not drink it?"

Jesus before the Priests

12So the *Roman* cohort
and the commander, and
the officers of the Jews, arrested Jesus and bound
Him,
13and led Him to Annas
first; for he was father-in-
law of Caiaphas, who was
high priest that year.
14Now Caiaphas was the
one who had advised the
Jews that it was expedient
for one man to die on behalf
of the people.
15And Simon Peter was
following Jesus, and *so was*
another disciple. Now that
disciple was known to the
high priest, and entered
with Jesus into the court of
the high priest,
16but Peter was standing
at the door outside. So the
other disciple, who was
known to the high priest,
went out and spoke to the
doorkeeper, and brought in
Peter.
17The slave-girl therefore
who kept the door *said to
Peter, "You are not also
one of this man's disciples,
are you?" He *said, "I am
not."
18Now the slaves and the
officers were standing
there, having made a charcoal fire, for it was cold and
they were warming them-
selves; and Peter also was

9 ἵνα πληρωθῇ ὁ λόγος ὃν εἶπεν, ὅτι
that might be fulfilled the word which he said, –

οὓς δέδωκάς μοι, οὐκ ἀπώλεσα ἐξ
[Those] whom thou hast given to me, I lost not of

αὐτῶν οὐδένα. 10 Σίμων οὖν Πέτρος
them no(any)one. [1]Simon [3]therefore [2]Peter

ἔχων μάχαιραν εἵλκυσεν αὐτὴν καὶ ἔπαισεν
having a sword drew it and smote

τὸν τοῦ ἀρχιερέως δοῦλον καὶ ἀπέκοψεν
[1]the [3]of the [4]high priest [2]slave and cut off

αὐτοῦ τὸ ὠτάριον τὸ δεξιόν· ἦν δὲ
of him the [2]ear – [1]right; and was

ὄνομα τῷ δούλῳ Μάλχος. 11 εἶπεν οὖν
name to the slave° Malchus. Said therefore

ὁ Ἰησοῦς τῷ Πέτρῳ· βάλε τὴν μάχαιραν
– Jesus – to Peter: Put the sword

εἰς τὴν θήκην· τὸ ποτήριον ὃ δέδωκέν
into the sheath; the cup which has given

μοι ὁ πατήρ, οὐ μὴ πίω αὐτό;
to me the Father, by no means shall I drink it?

12 Ἡ οὖν σπεῖρα καὶ ὁ χιλίαρχος
Therefore the band and the chiliarch

καὶ οἱ ὑπηρέται τῶν Ἰουδαίων συνέλαβον
and the attendants of the Jews took

τὸν Ἰησοῦν καὶ ἔδησαν αὐτόν, 13 καὶ
– Jesus and bound him, and

ἤγαγον πρὸς Ἄνναν πρῶτον· ἦν γὰρ
led to Annas first; for he was

πενθερὸς τοῦ Καϊαφᾶ, ὃς ἦν ἀρχιερεὺς
father-in-law – of Caiaphas, who was high priest

τοῦ ἐνιαυτοῦ ἐκείνου· 14 ἦν δὲ Καϊαφᾶς
– year of that; now it was Caiaphas

ὁ συμβουλεύσας τοῖς Ἰουδαίοις ὅτι
the [one] having advised the Jews that

συμφέρει ἕνα ἄνθρωπον ἀποθανεῖν ὑπὲρ
it is(was) expedient one man to die on behalf of

τοῦ λαοῦ. 15 Ἠκολούθει δὲ τῷ Ἰησοῦ
the people. And followed – Jesus

Σίμων Πέτρος καὶ ἄλλος μαθητής. ὁ δὲ
Simon Peter and another disciple. – And

μαθητὴς ἐκεῖνος ἦν γνωστὸς τῷ ἀρχιερεῖ,
disciple that was known to the high priest,

καὶ συνεισῆλθεν τῷ Ἰησοῦ εἰς τὴν αὐλὴν
and entered with – Jesus into the court

τοῦ ἀρχιερέως, 16 ὁ δὲ Πέτρος εἱστήκει
of the high priest, – but Peter stood

πρὸς τῇ θύρᾳ ἔξω. ἐξῆλθεν οὖν ὁ
at the door outside. Went out therefore the

μαθητὴς ὁ ἄλλος ὁ γνωστὸς τοῦ ἀρχιερέως
[2]disciple – [1]other – known of(to) the high priest

καὶ εἶπεν τῇ θυρωρῷ, καὶ εἰσήγαγεν
and told the portress, and brought in

τὸν Πέτρον. 17 λέγει οὖν τῷ Πέτρῳ ἡ
– Peter. Says therefore – to Peter the

παιδίσκη ἡ θυρωρός· μὴ καὶ σὺ ἐκ
maidservant the portress : *Not* also thou of

τῶν μαθητῶν εἶ τοῦ ἀνθρώπου τούτου;
the disciples art – man of this?

λέγει ἐκεῖνος· οὐκ εἰμί. 18 εἱστήκεισαν δὲ
Says that one : I am not. And stood

οἱ δοῦλοι καὶ οἱ ὑπηρέται ἀνθρακιὰν
the slaves and the attendants a fire

πεποιηκότες, ὅτι ψῦχος ἦν, καὶ
having made, because cold it was, and

ἐθερμαίνοντο· ἦν δὲ καὶ ὁ Πέτρος μετ'
were warming themselves; and was also – Peter with

9This happened so that the
words he had spoken
would be fulfilled: "I have
not lost one of those you
gave me."[z]
10Then Simon Peter, who
had a sword, drew it and
struck the high priest's servant, cutting off his right
ear. (The servant's name
was Malchus.)
11Jesus commanded Pe-
ter, "Put your sword away!
Shall I not drink the cup the
Father has given me?"

Jesus Taken to Annas

12Then the detachment of
soldiers with its commander and the Jewish officials
arrested Jesus. They bound
him 13and brought him first
to Annas, who was the fa-
ther-in-law of Caiaphas,
the high priest that year.
14Caiaphas was the one
who had advised the Jews
that it would be good if one
man died for the people.

Peter's First Denial

15Simon Peter and anoth-
er disciple were following
Jesus. Because this disciple
was known to the high
priest, he went with Jesus
into the high priest's courtyard, 16but Peter had to
wait outside at the door.
The other disciple, who
was known to the high
priest, came back, spoke to
the girl on duty there and
brought Peter in.
17"You are not one of his
disciples, are you?" the girl
at the door asked Peter.
He replied, "I am not."
18It was cold, and the servants and officials stood
around a fire they had made
to keep warm. Peter also

[z]9 John 6:39

with them, standing and
warming himself.
19The high priest there-
fore questioned Jesus
about His disciples, and
about His teaching.
20Jesus answered him, "I
have spoken openly to the
world; I always taught in
synagogues, and in the
temple, where all the Jews
come together; and I spoke
nothing in secret.
21"Why do you question
Me? Question those who
have heard what I spoke to
them; behold, these know
what I said."
22And when He had said
this, one of the officers
standing by gave Jesus a
blow, saying, "Is that the
way You answer the high
priest?"
23Jesus answered him,
"If I have spoken wrongly,
bear witness of the wrong;
but if rightly, why do you
strike Me?"
24Annas therefore sent
Him bound to Caiaphas the
high priest.

Peter's Denial of Jesus

25Now Simon Peter was
standing and warming him-
self. They said therefore to
him, "You are not also *one*
of His disciples, are you?"
He denied *it,* and said, "I
am not."
26One of the slaves of the
high priest, being a relative
of the one whose ear Peter
cut off, *said, "Did I not
see you in the garden with
Him?"
27Peter therefore denied *it*
again; and immediately a
cock crowed.

Jesus before Pilate

28They *led Jesus there-
fore from Caiaphas into the
[a]Praetorium, and it was
early; and they themselves
did not enter into the Praetorium in order that they
might not be defiled, but
might eat the Passover.
29Pilate therefore went
out to them, and *said,
"What accusation do you
bring against this Man?"
30They answered and said
to him, "If this Man were
not an evildoer, we would
not have delivered Him up
to you."
31Pilate therefore said to

[a]I.e., governor's official residence

αὐτῶν ἑστὼς καὶ θερμαινόμενος. 19 Ὁ
them standing and warming himself. – [1]The
οὖν ἀρχιερεὺς ἠρώτησεν τὸν Ἰησοῦν
[3]therefore [2]high priest questioned – Jesus
περὶ τῶν μαθητῶν αὐτοῦ καὶ περὶ τῆς
about the disciples of him and about the
διδαχῆς αὐτοῦ. 20 ἀπεκρίθη αὐτῷ Ἰησοῦς·
teaching of him. Answered him Jesus:
ἐγὼ παρρησίᾳ λελάληκα τῷ κόσμῳ· ἐγὼ
I with plainness have spoken to the world; I
πάντοτε ἐδίδαξα ἐν συναγωγῇ καὶ ἐν
always taught in a synagogue and in
τῷ ἱερῷ, ὅπου πάντες οἱ Ἰουδαῖοι
the temple, where all the Jews
συνέρχονται, καὶ ἐν κρυπτῷ ἐλάλησα
come together, and in secret I spoke
οὐδέν. 21 τί με ἐρωτᾷς; ἐρώτησον
nothing. Why me questionest thou? question
τοὺς ἀκηκοότας τί ἐλάλησα αὐτοῖς· ἴδε
the [ones] having heard what I spoke to them; behold[,]
οὗτοι οἴδασιν ἃ εἶπον ἐγώ. 22 ταῦτα
these know what things said I. These things
δὲ αὐτοῦ εἰπόντος εἷς παρεστηκὼς τῶν
and him saying[a] one standing by of the
=And as he said this
ὑπηρετῶν ἔδωκεν ῥάπισμα τῷ Ἰησοῦ
attendants gave a blow – to Jesus
εἰπών· οὕτως ἀποκρίνῃ τῷ ἀρχιερεῖ;
saying: Thus answerest thou the high priest?
23 ἀπεκρίθη αὐτῷ Ἰησοῦς· εἰ κακῶς
Answered him Jesus: If ill
ἐλάλησα, μαρτύρησον περὶ τοῦ κακοῦ·
I spoke, witness concerning the evil;
εἰ δὲ καλῶς, τί με δέρεις; 24 ἀπέστειλεν
but if well, why me beatest thou? [3]Sent
οὖν αὐτὸν ὁ Ἅννας δεδεμένον πρὸς
[2]therefore [4]him – [1]Annas *having been* bound to
Καϊαφᾶν τὸν ἀρχιερέα. 25 Ἦν δὲ Σίμων
Caiaphas the high priest. Now was Simon
Πέτρος ἑστὼς καὶ θερμαινόμενος. εἶπον
Peter standing and warming himself. They said
οὖν αὐτῷ· μὴ καὶ σὺ ἐκ τῶν μαθητῶν
therefore to him: *Not* also thou of the disciples
αὐτοῦ εἶ; ἠρνήσατο ἐκεῖνος καὶ εἶπεν·
of him art? Denied that one and said:
οὐκ εἰμί. 26 λέγει εἷς ἐκ τῶν δούλων τοῦ
I am not. Says one of the slaves of the
ἀρχιερέως, συγγενὴς ὢν οὗ ἀπέκοψεν
high priest, [2]a relative [1]being [3][of him] of whom [5]cut off
Πέτρος τὸ ὠτίον· οὐκ ἐγώ σε εἶδον
[4]Peter [6]the [7]ear: [3]Not [2]I [4]thee [1]saw
ἐν τῷ κήπῳ μετ᾽ αὐτοῦ; 27 πάλιν οὖν
in the garden with him? Again therefore
ἠρνήσατο Πέτρος, καὶ εὐθέως ἀλέκτωρ
denied Peter, and immediately a cock
ἐφώνησεν.
sounded(crew).

28 Ἄγουσιν οὖν τὸν Ἰησοῦν ἀπὸ τοῦ
They lead therefore – Jesus from –
Καϊάφα εἰς τὸ πραιτώριον· ἦν δὲ πρωΐ·
Caiaphas to the prætorium; and it was early;
καὶ αὐτοὶ οὐκ εἰσῆλθον εἰς τὸ πραιτώριον,
and they entered not into the prætorium,
ἵνα μὴ μιανθῶσιν ἀλλὰ φάγωσιν τὸ
lest they should be defiled but might eat the
πάσχα. 29 ἐξῆλθεν οὖν ὁ Πιλᾶτος ἔξω
passover. Went forth therefore – Pilate outside

was standing with them,
warming himself.

The High Priest Questions Jesus

19Meanwhile, the high
priest questioned Jesus
about his disciples and his
teaching.
20"I have spoken openly
to the world," Jesus re-
plied. "I always taught in
synagogues or at the tem-
ple, where all the Jews
come together. I said nothing in secret. 21Why question me? Ask those who
heard me. Surely they
know what I said."
22When Jesus said this,
one of the officials nearby
struck him in the face. "Is
this the way you answer the
high priest?" he demanded.
23"If I said something
wrong," Jesus replied,
"testify as to what is
wrong. But if I spoke the
truth, why did you strike
me?" 24Then Annas sent
him, still bound, to Caiaphas the high priest.[a]

Peter's Second and Third Denials

25As Simon Peter stood
warming himself, he was
asked, "You are not one of
his disciples, are you?"
He denied it, saying, "I
am not."
26One of the high priest's
servants, a relative of the
man whose ear Peter had
cut off, challenged him,
"Didn't I see you with him
in the olive grove?"
27Again Peter denied it, and
at that moment a rooster
began to crow.

Jesus Before Pilate

28Then the Jews led Jesus
from Caiaphas to the pal-
ace of the Roman gover-
nor. By now it was early
morning, and to avoid ceremonial uncleanness the
Jews did not enter the palace; they wanted to be able
to eat the Passover. 29So
Pilate came out to them and
asked, "What charges are
you bringing against this
man?"
30"If he were not a criminal," they replied, "we
would not have handed him
over to you."
31Pilate said, "Take him

[a]24 Or *(Now Annas had sent him, still bound, to Caiaphas the high priest.)*

them, "Take Him yourselves, and judge Him according to your law." The Jews said to him, "We are not permitted to put anyone to death,"

32 that the word of Jesus might be fulfilled, which He spoke, signifying by what kind of death He was about to die.

33 Pilate therefore entered again into the [a]Praetorium, and summoned Jesus, and said to Him, "Are You the King of the Jews?"

34 Jesus answered, "Are you saying this on your own initiative, or did others tell you about Me?"

35 Pilate answered, "I am not a Jew, am I? Your own nation and the chief priests delivered You up to me; what have You done?"

36 Jesus answered, "My kingdom is not of this world. If My kingdom were of this world, then My servants would be fighting, that I might not be delivered up to the Jews; but as it is, My kingdom is not [b]of this realm."

37 Pilate therefore said to Him, "So You are a king?" Jesus answered, "You say *correctly* that I am a king. For this I have been born, and for this I have come into the world, to bear witness to the truth. Everyone who is of the truth hears My voice."

38 Pilate *said to Him, "What is truth?"

πρὸς αὐτοὺς καὶ φησίν· τίνα κατηγορίαν
to them and says: What accusation
φέρετε τοῦ ἀνθρώπου τούτου; 30 ἀπεκρίθησαν
bring ye – man of this? They answered
καὶ εἶπαν αὐτῷ· εἰ μὴ ἦν
and said to him: Unless was
οὗτος κακὸν ποιῶν, οὐκ ἄν σοι
this man evil doing, [2]would [3]not [7]to thee
παρεδώκαμεν αὐτόν. 31 εἶπεν οὖν αὐτοῖς
[1]we [4]have [5]delivered [6]him. Said therefore to them
ὁ Πιλᾶτος· λάβετε αὐτὸν ὑμεῖς, καὶ
– Pilate: Take him ye, and
κατὰ τὸν νόμον ὑμῶν κρίνατε αὐτόν.
according to the law of you judge ye him.
εἶπον αὐτῷ οἱ Ἰουδαῖοι· ἡμῖν οὐκ ἔξεστιν
Said to him the Jews: For us it is not lawful
ἀποκτεῖναι οὐδένα· 32 ἵνα ὁ λόγος τοῦ
to kill no(any)one; that the word –
Ἰησοῦ πληρωθῇ ὃν εἶπεν σημαίνων ποίῳ
of Jesus might be fulfilled which he said signifying by what
θανάτῳ ἤμελλεν ἀποθνῄσκειν. 33 Εἰσῆλθεν
death he was about to die. Entered
οὖν πάλιν εἰς τὸ πραιτώριον ὁ Πιλᾶτος
therefore again into the prætorium – Pilate
καὶ ἐφώνησεν τὸν Ἰησοῦν καὶ εἶπεν
and called – Jesus and said
αὐτῷ· σὺ εἶ ὁ βασιλεὺς τῶν Ἰουδαίων;
to him: Thou art the king of the Jews?
34 ἀπεκρίθη Ἰησοῦς· ἀφ' ἑαυτοῦ σὺ τοῦτο
Answered Jesus: From [thy]self [2]thou [3]this
λέγεις, ἢ ἄλλοι εἶπόν σοι περὶ ἐμοῦ;
[1]sayest, or others told thee about me?
35 ἀπεκρίθη ὁ Πιλᾶτος· μήτι ἐγὼ
Answered – Pilate: *not* I
Ἰουδαῖός εἰμι; τὸ ἔθνος τὸ σὸν καὶ
a Jew am? *the* [2]nation – [1]thy and
οἱ ἀρχιερεῖς παρέδωκάν σε ἐμοί· τί
the chief priests delivered thee to me; what
ἐποίησας; 36 ἀπεκρίθη Ἰησοῦς· ἡ βασιλεία
didst thou? Answered Jesus: *The* [2]kingdom
ἡ ἐμὴ οὐκ ἔστιν ἐκ τοῦ κόσμου τούτου·
– [1]my is not of – world this;
εἰ ἐκ τοῦ κόσμου τούτου ἦν ἡ βασιλεία
if of – world this was *the* [2]kingdom
ἡ ἐμή, οἱ ὑπηρέται ἂν οἱ ἐμοὶ ἠγωνίζοντο,
– [1]my, *the* [2]attendants [3]would – [1]my [4]have struggled,
ἵνα μὴ παραδοθῶ τοῖς Ἰουδαίοις· νῦν
that I should not be delivered to the Jews; [2]now
δὲ ἡ βασιλεία ἡ ἐμὴ οὐκ ἔστιν ἐντεῦθεν.
[1]but *the* [2]kingdom – [1]my is not hence.
37 εἶπεν οὖν αὐτῷ ὁ Πιλᾶτος· οὐκοῦν
Said therefore to him – Pilate: Not really
βασιλεὺς εἶ σύ; ἀπεκρίθη [ὁ] Ἰησοῦς·
a king art thou? Answered – Jesus:
σὺ λέγεις ὅτι βασιλεύς εἰμι. ἐγὼ εἰς
Thou sayest that a king I am. I for
τοῦτο γεγέννημαι καὶ εἰς τοῦτο ἐλήλυθα
this have been born and for this I have come
εἰς τὸν κόσμον, ἵνα μαρτυρήσω τῇ
into the world, that I might witness to the
ἀληθείᾳ· πᾶς ὁ ὢν ἐκ τῆς ἀληθείας
truth; everyone being of the truth
ἀκούει μου τῆς φωνῆς. 38 λέγει αὐτῷ
hears of me the voice. Says to him
ὁ Πιλᾶτος· τί ἐστιν ἀλήθεια; Καὶ
– Pilate: What is truth? And

yourselves and judge him by your own law."

"But we have no right to execute anyone," the Jews objected. 32 This happened so that the words Jesus had spoken indicating the kind of death he was going to die would be fulfilled.

33 Pilate then went back inside the palace, summoned Jesus and asked him, "Are you the king of the Jews?"

34 "Is that your own idea," Jesus asked, "or did others talk to you about me?"

35 "Am I a Jew?" Pilate replied. "It was your people and your chief priests who handed you over to me. What is it you have done?"

36 Jesus said, "My kingdom is not of this world. If it were, my servants would fight to prevent my arrest by the Jews. But now my kingdom is from another place."

37 "You are a king, then!" said Pilate.

Jesus answered, "You are right in saying I am a king. In fact, for this reason I was born, and for this I came into the world, to testify to the truth. Everyone on the side of truth listens to me."

38 "What is truth?" Pilate asked. With this he went

[b] Lit., *from here*

And when he had said this, he went out again to the Jews, and *said to them, "I find no guilt in Him.

39"But you have a custom, that I should release someone for you at the Passover; do you wish then that I release for you the King of the Jews?"

40Therefore they cried out again, saying, "Not this Man, but Barabbas." Now Barabbas was a robber.

Chapter 19

The Crown of Thorns

THEN Pilate therefore took Jesus, and scourged Him.

2And the soldiers wove a crown of thorns and put it on His head, and arrayed Him in a purple robe;

3and they *began* to come up to Him, and say, "Hail, King of the Jews!" and to give Him blows *in the face*.

4And Pilate came out again, and *said to them, "Behold, I am bringing Him out to you, that you may know that I find no guilt in Him."

5Jesus therefore came out, wearing the crown of thorns and the purple robe. And *Pilate* *said to them, "Behold, the Man!"

6When therefore the chief priests and the officers saw Him, they cried out, saying, "Crucify, crucify!" Pilate *said to them, "Take Him yourselves, and crucify Him, for I find no guilt in Him."

7The Jews answered him, "We have a law, and by that law He ought to die because He made Himself out *to be* the Son of God."

8When Pilate therefore heard this statement, he was the more afraid;

τοῦτο εἰπὼν πάλιν ἐξῆλθεν πρὸς τοὺς
this having said again he went forth to the
Ἰουδαίους, καὶ λέγει αὐτοῖς· ἐγὼ οὐδεμίαν
Jews, and tells them : [1]I [3]no
εὑρίσκω ἐν αὐτῷ αἰτίαν. 39 ἔστιν δὲ
[2]find [5]in [6]him [4]crime. But there is
συνήθεια ὑμῖν ἵνα ἕνα ἀπολύσω ὑμῖν
a custom to you[e] that one I should release to you
ἐν τῷ πάσχα· βούλεσθε οὖν ἀπολύσω
at the Passover; will ye therefore [that] I release
ὑμῖν τὸν βασιλέα τῶν Ἰουδαίων; 40 ἐκραύ-
to you the king of the Jews? They cried
γασαν οὖν πάλιν λέγοντες· μὴ τοῦτον,
out therefore again saying : Not this man,
ἀλλὰ τὸν Βαραββᾶν. ἦν δὲ ὁ Βαραββᾶς
but – Barabbas [1]But [3]was – [2]Barabbas
λῃστής. 19 Τότε οὖν ἔλαβεν ὁ Πιλᾶτος
[4]a robber. Then therefore [2]took – [1]Pilate
τὸν Ἰησοῦν καὶ ἐμαστίγωσεν. 2 καὶ οἱ
– [3]Jesus and scourged [him]. And the
στρατιῶται πλέξαντες στέφανον ἐξ ἀκανθῶν
soldiers having plaited a wreath out of thorns
ἐπέθηκαν αὐτοῦ τῇ κεφαλῇ, καὶ ἱμάτιον
put [it] on of him the head, and [4]garment
πορφυροῦν περιέβαλον αὐτόν, 3 καὶ ἤρχοντο
[3]a purple [1]threw round [2]him, and came
πρὸς αὐτὸν καὶ ἔλεγον· χαῖρε ὁ βασιλεὺς
to him and said : Hail[,] – king
τῶν Ἰουδαίων· καὶ ἐδίδοσαν αὐτῷ
of the Jews; and they gave him
ῥαπίσματα. 4 Καὶ ἐξῆλθεν πάλιν ἔξω
blows. And went forth again outside
ὁ Πιλᾶτος καὶ λέγει αὐτοῖς· ἴδε ἄγω
– Pilate and says to them : Behold [1]I bring
ὑμῖν αὐτὸν ἔξω, ἵνα γνῶτε ὅτι οὐδεμίαν
[4]to you [2]him [3]out, that ye may know that no
αἰτίαν εὑρίσκω ἐν αὐτῷ. 5 ἐξῆλθεν
crime I find in him. Came forth
οὖν ὁ Ἰησοῦς ἔξω, φορῶν τὸν ἀκάνθινον
therefore – Jesus outside, wearing the thorny
στέφανον καὶ τὸ πορφυροῦν ἱμάτιον. καὶ
wreath and the purple garment. And
λέγει αὐτοῖς· ἰδοὺ ὁ ἄνθρωπος. 6 ὅτε
he says to them : Behold[,] the man. When
οὖν εἶδον αὐτὸν οἱ ἀρχιερεῖς καὶ οἱ
therefore saw him the chief priests and the
ὑπηρέται, ἐκραύγασαν λέγοντες· σταύρωσον
attendants, they shouted saying : Crucify[,]
σταύρωσον. λέγει αὐτοῖς ὁ Πιλᾶτος·
crucify. Says to them – Pilate :
λάβετε αὐτὸν ὑμεῖς καὶ σταυρώσατε·
[1]Take [3]him [2]ye and crucify;
ἐγὼ γὰρ οὐχ εὑρίσκω ἐν αὐτῷ αἰτίαν.
for I find not in him crime.
7 ἀπεκρίθησαν αὐτῷ οἱ Ἰουδαῖοι· ἡμεῖς
Answered him the Jews : We
νόμον ἔχομεν, καὶ κατὰ τὸν νόμον
a law have, and according to the law
ὀφείλει ἀποθανεῖν, ὅτι υἱὸν θεοῦ ἑαυτὸν
he ought to die, because Son of God himself
ἐποίησεν. 8 Ὅτε οὖν ἤκουσεν ὁ Πιλᾶτος
he made. When therefore heard – Pilate
τοῦτον τὸν λόγον, μᾶλλον ἐφοβήθη, 9 καὶ
this – word, more he was afraid, and

out again to the Jews and said, "I find no basis for a charge against him. 39But it is your custom for me to release to you one prisoner at the time of the Passover. Do you want me to release 'the king of the Jews'?"

40They shouted back, "No, not him! Give us Barabbas!" Now Barabbas had taken part in a rebellion.

Chapter 19

Jesus Sentenced to be Crucified

THEN Pilate took Jesus and had him flogged. 2The soldiers twisted together a crown of thorns and put it on his head. They clothed him in a purple robe 3and went up to him again and again, saying, "Hail, king of the Jews!" And they struck him in the face.

4Once more Pilate came out and said to the Jews, "Look, I am bringing him out to you to let you know that I find no basis for a charge against him." 5When Jesus came out wearing the crown of thorns and the purple robe, Pilate said to them, "Here is the man!"

6As soon as the chief priests and their officials saw him, they shouted, "Crucify! Crucify!"

But Pilate answered, "You take him and crucify him. As for me, I find no basis for a charge against him."

7The Jews insisted, "We have a law, and according to that law he must die, because he claimed to be the Son of God."

8When Pilate heard this, he was even more afraid,

9 and he entered into the [c]Praetorium again, and *said to Jesus, "Where are You from?" But Jesus gave him no answer.
10 Pilate therefore *said to Him, "You do not speak to me? Do You not know that I have authority to release You, and I have authority to crucify You?"
11 Jesus answered, "You would have no authority over Me, unless it had been given you from above; for this reason he who delivered Me up to you has *the* greater sin."
12 As a result of this Pilate made efforts to release Him, but the Jews cried out, saying, "If you release this Man, you are no friend of Caesar; everyone who makes himself out *to be* a king opposes Caesar."
13 When Pilate therefore heard these words, he brought Jesus out, and sat down on the judgment seat at a place called The Pavement, but in Hebrew, Gabbatha.
14 Now it was the day of preparation for the Passover; it was about the [d]sixth hour. And he *said to the Jews, "Behold, your King!"
15 They therefore cried out, "Away with *Him,* away with *Him,* crucify Him!" Pilate *said to them, "Shall I crucify your King?" The chief priests answered, "We have no king but Caesar."

The Crucifixion

16 So he then delivered Him to them to be crucified.
17 They took Jesus therefore, and He went out, bearing His own cross, to the place called the Place of a Skull, which is called in Hebrew, Golgotha.
18 There they crucified Him, and with Him two other men, one on either side, and Jesus in between.

εἰσῆλθεν εἰς τὸ πραιτώριον πάλιν καὶ
entered into the prætorium again and
λέγει τῷ Ἰησοῦ· πόθεν εἶ σύ; ὁ δὲ
says – to Jesus : Whence art thou? – But
Ἰησοῦς ἀπόκρισιν οὐκ ἔδωκεν αὐτῷ.
Jesus answer did not give him.
10 λέγει οὖν αὐτῷ ὁ Πιλᾶτος· ἐμοὶ
Says therefore to him – Pilate : To me
οὐ λαλεῖς; οὐκ οἶδας ὅτι ἐξουσίαν ἔχω
speakest thou not? knowest thou not that authority I have
ἀπολῦσαί σε καὶ ἐξουσίαν ἔχω σταυρῶσαί
to release thee and authority I have to crucify
σε; 11 ἀπεκρίθη Ἰησοῦς· οὐκ εἶχες
thee? Answered Jesus : Thou hadst not
ἐξουσίαν κατ᾽ ἐμοῦ οὐδεμίαν εἰ μὴ ἦν
^{2}authority ^{3}against ^{4}me ^{1}no(any) unless it was
δεδομένον σοι ἄνωθεν· διὰ τοῦτο ὁ
having been given thee from above; therefore the [one]
παραδούς μέ σοι μείζονα ἁμαρτίαν ἔχει.
having delivered me to thee a greater sin has.
12 ἐκ τούτου ὁ Πιλᾶτος ἐζήτει ἀπολῦσαι
From this – Pilate sought to release
αὐτόν· οἱ δὲ Ἰουδαῖοι ἐκραύγασαν λέγοντες·
him; but the Jews shouted saying :
ἐὰν τοῦτον ἀπολύσῃς, οὐκ εἶ φίλος τοῦ
If this man thou releasest, thou art not a friend –
Καίσαρος· πᾶς ὁ βασιλέα ἑαυτὸν ποιῶν
of Cæsar; everyone a king himself making
ἀντιλέγει τῷ Καίσαρι. 13 Ὁ οὖν Πιλᾶτος
speaks against – Cæsar. – Therefore Pilate
ἀκούσας τῶν λόγων τούτων ἤγαγεν ἔξω
hearing – words these brought outside
τὸν Ἰησοῦν, καὶ ἐκάθισεν ἐπὶ βήματος
– Jesus, and sat on a tribunal
εἰς τόπον λεγόμενον Λιθόστρωτον, Ἑβραϊστὶ δὲ
in a place *being* called Pavement, but in Hebrew
Γαββαθά. 14 ἦν δὲ παρασκευὴ τοῦ
Gabbatha. Now it was preparation of the
πάσχα, ὥρα ἦν ὡς ἕκτη· καὶ λέγει
Passover, hour it was about sixth; and he says
τοῖς Ἰουδαίοις· ἴδε ὁ βασιλεὺς ὑμῶν.
to the Jews; Behold[,] the king of you.
15 ἐκραύγασαν οὖν ἐκεῖνοι· ἆρον ἆρον,
Shouted therefore those : Take[,] take,
σταύρωσον αὐτόν. λέγει αὐτοῖς ὁ Πιλᾶτος·
crucify him. Says to them – Pilate :
τὸν βασιλέα ὑμῶν σταυρώσω; ἀπεκρίθησαν
The king of you shall I crucify? Answered
οἱ ἀρχιερεῖς· οὐκ ἔχομεν βασιλέα εἰ
the chief priests : We have not a king ex-
μὴ Καίσαρα. 16 τότε οὖν παρέδωκεν
cept Cæsar. Then therefore he delivered
αὐτὸν αὐτοῖς ἵνα σταυρωθῇ.
him to them that he should be crucified.
Παρέλαβον οὖν τὸν Ἰησοῦν· 17 καὶ
They took therefore – Jesus; and
βαστάζων ἑαυτῷ τὸν σταυρὸν ἐξῆλθεν
carrying ^{3}to himself [c] ^{1}the ^{2}cross he went forth
εἰς τὸν λεγόμενον κρανίου τόπον, ὃ
to ^{1}the ^{3}*being* called ^{4}of a skull ^{2}place, which
λέγεται Ἑβραϊστὶ Γολγοθά, 18 ὅπου αὐτὸν
is called in Hebrew Golgotha, where him
ἐσταύρωσαν, καὶ μετ᾽ αὐτοῦ ἄλλους δύο
they crucified, and with him others two
ἐντεῦθεν καὶ ἐντεῦθεν, μέσον δὲ τὸν
on this side and on that, † and in the middle –

9 and he went back inside
the palace. "Where do you
come from?" he asked
Jesus, but Jesus gave him
no answer. 10 "Do you re-
fuse to speak to me?" Pi-
late said. "Don't you realize I have power either to
free you or to crucify
you?"
11 Jesus answered, "You
would have no power over
me if it were not given to
you from above. Therefore
the one who handed me
over to you is guilty of a
greater sin."
12 From then on, Pilate
tried to set Jesus free, but
the Jews kept shouting, "If
you let this man go, you are
no friend of Caesar. Any-
one who claims to be a king
opposes Caesar."
13 When Pilate heard this,
he brought Jesus out and
sat down on the judge's
seat at a place known as the
Stone Pavement (which in
Aramaic is Gabbatha). 14 It
was the day of Preparation
of Passover Week, about
the sixth hour.
"Here is your king," Pi-
late said to the Jews.
15 But they shouted,
"Take him away! Take him
away! Crucify him!"
"Shall I crucify your
king?" Pilate asked.
"We have no king but
Caesar," the chief priests
answered.
16 Finally Pilate handed
him over to them to be crucified.

The Crucifixion

So the soldiers took
charge of Jesus. 17 Carrying
his own cross, he went out
to the place of the Skull
(which in Aramaic is called
Golgotha). 18 Here they crucified him, and with him
two others—one on each
side and Jesus in the middle.

[c] I.e., governor's official residence
[d] Perhaps 6 a.m. (Roman time)

19And Pilate wrote an in-
scription also, and put it on
the cross. And it was written, "JESUS THE NAZA-
RENE, THE KING OF
THE JEWS."
20Therefore this inscrip-
tion many of the Jews read,
for the place where Jesus
was crucified was near the
city; and it was written in
Hebrew, Latin, *and* in
Greek.
21And so the chief priests
of the Jews were saying to
Pilate, "Do not write, 'The
King of the Jews'; but that
He said, 'I am King of the
Jews.' "
22Pilate answered, "What
I have written I have written."
23The soldiers therefore,
when they had crucified
Jesus, took His outer garments and made four parts,
a part to every soldier and
also the [c]tunic; now the tunic was seamless, woven in
one piece.
24They said therefore to
one another, "Let us not
tear it, but cast lots for it, *to*
decide whose it shall be";
that the Scripture might be
fulfilled, "THEY DIVIDED
MY OUTER GARMENTS AMONG
THEM, AND FOR MY CLOTH-
ING THEY CAST LOTS."
25Therefore the soldiers
did these things. But there
were standing by the cross
of Jesus His mother, and
His mother's sister, Mary
the *wife* of Clopas, and
Mary Magdalene.
26When Jesus therefore
saw His mother, and the
disciple whom He loved
standing nearby, He *said
to His mother, "Woman,
behold, your son!"
27Then He *said to the
disciple, "Behold, your
mother!" And from that

'Ἰησοῦν. **19** ἔγραψεν δὲ καὶ τίτλον ὁ
Jesus. And wrote also a title –
Πιλᾶτος καὶ ἔθηκεν ἐπὶ τοῦ σταυροῦ·
Pilate and put [it] on the cross;
ἦν δὲ γεγραμμένον· ΙΗΣΟΥΣ Ο
and it was ***having been*** written : JESUS THE
ΝΑΖΩΡΑΙΟΣ Ο ΒΑΣΙΛΕΥΣ ΤΩΝ
NAZARENE THE KING OF THE
ΙΟΥΔΑΙΩΝ. **20** τοῦτον οὖν τὸν τίτλον
JEWS. [1]This [3]therefore – [2]title
πολλοὶ ἀνέγνωσαν τῶν Ἰουδαίων, ὅτι
[1]many [4]read [2]of the [3]Jews, because
ἐγγὺς ἦν ὁ τόπος τῆς πόλεως ὅπου
[7]near [6]was [1]the [2]place [8]the [9]city [3]where
ἐσταυρώθη ὁ Ἰησοῦς· καὶ ἦν γεγραμμένον
[5]was crucified – [4]Jesus; and it was ***having been*** written
Ἑβραϊστί, Ῥωμαϊστί, Ἑλληνιστί. **21** ἔλεγον
in Hebrew, in Latin, in Greek. Said
οὖν τῷ Πιλάτῳ οἱ ἀρχιερεῖς τῶν Ἰουδαίων·
therefore – to Pilate the chief priests of the Jews :
μὴ γράφε· ὁ βασιλεὺς τῶν Ἰουδαίων,
Write not : The king of the Jews,
ἀλλ' ὅτι ἐκεῖνος εἶπεν· βασιλεύς εἰμι
but that that man said : King I am
τῶν Ἰουδαίων. **22** ἀπεκρίθη ὁ Πιλᾶτος·
of the Jews. Answered – Pilate :
ὃ γέγραφα, γέγραφα. **23** Οἱ οὖν
What I have written, I have written. Therefore the
στρατιῶται, ὅτε ἐσταύρωσαν τὸν Ἰησοῦν,
soldiers. when they crucified – Jesus,
ἔλαβον τὰ ἱμάτια αὐτοῦ καὶ ἐποίησαν
took the garments of him and made
τέσσερα μέρη, ἑκάστῳ στρατιώτῃ μέρος,
four parts, to each soldier a part,
καὶ τὸν χιτῶνα. ἦν δὲ ὁ χιτὼν ἄρραφος,
and the tunic. Now was the tunic seamless,
ἐκ τῶν ἄνωθεν ὑφαντὸς δι' ὅλου. **24** εἶπαν
from the top woven throughout. They said
οὖν πρὸς ἀλλήλους· μὴ σχίσωμεν αὐτόν,
therefore to one another : Let us not tear it,
ἀλλὰ λάχωμεν περὶ αὐτοῦ τίνος ἔσται·
but let us cast lots about it of whom it shall be;
ἵνα ἡ γραφὴ πληρωθῇ· διεμερίσαντο τὰ
that the scripture might be fulfilled : They parted the
ἱμάτιά μου ἑαυτοῖς καὶ ἐπὶ τὸν ἱματισμόν
garments of me to themselves and over the raiment
μου ἔβαλον κλῆρον. Οἱ μὲν οὖν στρατιῶται
of me they cast a lot. [2]The –* [3]therefore [4]soldiers
ταῦτα ἐποίησαν. **25** εἱστήκεισαν δὲ παρὰ
[1]these things did. [2]there stood [1]But by
τῷ σταυρῷ τοῦ Ἰησοῦ ἡ μήτηρ αὐτοῦ
the cross – of Jesus the mother of him
καὶ ἡ ἀδελφὴ τῆς μητρὸς αὐτοῦ, Μαρία
and the sister of the mother of him, Mary
ἡ τοῦ Κλωπᾶ καὶ Μαρία ἡ Μαγδαληνή.
the [?wife] – of Clopas and Mary the Magdalene.
26 Ἰησοῦς οὖν ἰδὼν τὴν μητέρα καὶ
Jesus therefore seeing the(his) mother and
τὸν μαθητὴν παρεστῶτα ὃν ἠγάπα, λέγει
the disciple standing by whom he loved, says
τῇ μητρί· γύναι, ἴδε ὁ υἱός σου.
to the(his) mother : Woman, behold[,] the son of thee.
27 εἶτα λέγει τῷ μαθητῇ· ἴδε ἡ μήτηρ
Then he says to the disciple : Behold[,] the mother

19Pilate had a notice prepared and fastened to the
cross. It read: JESUS OF NAZ-
ARETH, THE KING OF THE
JEWS. 20Many of the Jews
read this sign, for the place
where Jesus was crucified
was near the city, and the
sign was written in Aramaic, Latin and Greek. 21The
chief priests of the Jews
protested to Pilate, "Do
not write 'The King of the
Jews,' but that this man
claimed to be king of the
Jews."
22Pilate answered, "What
I have written, I have written."
23When the soldiers cru-
cified Jesus, they took his
clothes, dividing them into
four shares, one for each of
them, with the undergar-
ment remaining. This gar-
ment was seamless, woven
in one piece from top to
bottom.
24"Let's not tear it," they
said to one another. "Let's
decide by lot who will get
it."
This happened that the
scripture might be fulfilled
which said,

"They divided my
garments among
them
and cast lots for my
clothing."[b]

So this is what the soldiers
did.
25Near the cross of Jesus
stood his mother, his mother's sister, Mary the wife of
Clopas, and Mary Magda-
lene. 26When Jesus saw his
mother there, and the disciple whom he loved stand-
ing nearby, he said to his
mother, "Dear woman,
here is your son," 27and to
the disciple, "Here is your
mother." From that time

[c] Gr., *khiton*, the garment worn next to the skin

* μέν is scarcely translatable. But note the δέ in ver. 25 : John contrasts two groups—the soldiers and the women.

[b] *24* Psalm 22:18

hour the disciple took her
into his own *household*.
28After this, Jesus, knowing that all things had already been accomplished,
in order that the Scripture
might be fulfilled, *said, "I
am thirsty."
29A jar full of sour wine
was standing there; so they
put a sponge full of the sour
wine upon *a branch of* hyssop, and brought it up to
His mouth.
30When Jesus therefore
had received the sour wine,
He said, "It is finished!"
And He bowed His head,
and gave up His spirit.

Care of the Body of Jesus

31The Jews therefore, be-
cause it was the day of
preparation, so that the
bodies should not remain
on the cross on the Sabbath
(for that Sabbath was a high
day), asked Pilate that their
legs might be broken, and
that they might be taken
away.
32The soldiers therefore
came, and broke the legs of
the first man, and of the
other man who was cruci-
fied with Him;
33but coming to Jesus,
when they saw that He was
already dead, they did not
break His legs;
34but one of the soldiers
pierced His side with a
spear, and immediately
there came out blood and
water.
35And he who has seen
has borne witness, and his
witness is true; and he
knows that he is telling the
truth, so that you also may
believe.
36For these things came
to pass, that the Scripture
might be fulfilled, "NOT A
BONE OF HIM SHALL BE BRO-
KEN."
37And again another
Scripture says, "THEY
SHALL LOOK ON HIM WHOM
THEY PIERCED."
38And after these things
Joseph of Arimathea, being

σου. καὶ ἀπ' ἐκείνης τῆς ὥρας ἔλαβεν
of thee. And from that – hour took
ὁ μαθητὴς αὐτὴν εἰς τὰ ἴδια. 28 Μετὰ
the disciple her to his own [home]. † After
τοῦτο εἰδὼς ὁ Ἰησοῦς ὅτι ἤδη πάντα
this knowing – Jesus that now all things
τετέλεσται, ἵνα τελειωθῇ ἡ γραφή, λέγει·
have been finished, that might be fulfilled the scripture, says:
διψῶ. 29 σκεῦος ἔκειτο ὄξους μεστόν·
I thirst. A vessel was set of vinegar full;
σπόγγον οὖν μεστὸν τοῦ ὄξους ὑσσώπῳ
[2]a sponge therefore [4]full [5]of the [6]vinegar [8]a hyssop §
περιθέντες προσήνεγκαν αὐτοῦ τῷ στόματι.
[1]putting [7]round they brought [it] to of him the mouth.
30 ὅτε οὖν ἔλαβεν τὸ ὄξος [ὁ] Ἰησοῦς
When therefore took the vinegar – Jesus
εἶπεν· τετέλεσται, καὶ κλίνας τὴν κεφαλὴν
he said: It has been finished, and inclining the(his) head
παρέδωκεν τὸ πνεῦμα.
delivered up the(his) spirit.
31 Οἱ οὖν Ἰουδαῖοι, ἐπεὶ παρασκευὴ
The [2]therefore [1]Jews, since preparation
ἦν, ἵνα μὴ μείνῃ ἐπὶ τοῦ σταυροῦ τὰ
it was, that might not remain on the cross the
σώματα ἐν τῷ σαββάτῳ, ἦν γὰρ μεγάλη
bodies on the sabbath, for was great
ἡ ἡμέρα ἐκείνου τοῦ σαββάτου, ἠρώτησαν
the day of that – sabbath, they asked
τὸν Πιλᾶτον ἵνα κατεαγῶσιν αὐτῶν τὰ
– Pilate that might be broken of them the
σκέλη καὶ ἀρθῶσιν. 32 ἦλθον οὖν οἱ
legs and they might be taken. Came therefore the
στρατιῶται, καὶ τοῦ μὲν πρώτου κατέαξαν
soldiers, and of the –* first broke
τὰ σκέλη καὶ τοῦ ἄλλου τοῦ
the legs and of the other –
συσταυρωθέντος αὐτῷ· 33 ἐπὶ δὲ τὸν
crucified with him; [3]on [1]but –
Ἰησοῦν ἐλθόντες, ὡς εἶδον ἤδη αὐτὸν
[4]Jesus [2]coming, when they saw already him
τεθνηκότα, οὐ κατέαξαν αὐτοῦ τὰ σκέλη,
to have died, they did not break of him the legs,
34 ἀλλ' εἷς τῶν στρατιωτῶν λόγχῃ αὐτοῦ
but one of the soldiers with a lance of him
τὴν πλευρὰν ἔνυξεν, καὶ ἐξῆλθεν εὐθὺς αἷμα
the side pricked, and there came out imme-diately blood
καὶ ὕδωρ. 35 καὶ ὁ ἑωρακὼς μεμαρτύρηκεν,
and water. And the [one] having seen has witnessed,
καὶ ἀληθινὴ αὐτοῦ ἐστιν ἡ μαρτυρία,
and true of him is the witness,
καὶ ἐκεῖνος οἶδεν ὅτι ἀληθῆ λέγει, ἵνα
and that one knows that truly he says, that
καὶ ὑμεῖς πιστεύητε. 36 ἐγένετο γὰρ
also ye may believe. For happened
ταῦτα ἵνα ἡ γραφὴ πληρωθῇ· ὀστοῦν
these things that the scripture might be fulfilled: A bone
οὐ συντριβήσεται αὐτοῦ. 37 καὶ πάλιν
shall not be broken of him. And again
ἑτέρα γραφὴ λέγει· ὄψονται εἰς ὃν
another scripture says: They shall look at [him] whom
ἐξεκέντησαν. 38 Μετὰ δὲ ταῦτα ἠρώτησεν
they pierced. Now after these things [14]asked
τὸν Πιλᾶτον Ἰωσὴφ ἀπὸ Ἀριμαθαίας,
– [15]Pilate [1]Joseph [2]from [3]Arimathæa,

§ It has been suggested that ὑσσώπῳ is a graphic error for ὑσσῷ (*pilum*), pike; but *cf.* Mat. 27. 48.

* See note on 19. 24. Here see ver. 33—two actions contrasted.

on, this disciple took her
into his home.

The Death of Jesus

28Later, knowing that all
was now completed, and so
that the Scripture would be
fulfilled, Jesus said, "I am
thirsty." 29A jar of wine
vinegar was there, so they
soaked a sponge in it, put
the sponge on a stalk of the
hyssop plant, and lifted it to
Jesus' lips. 30When he had
received the drink, Jesus
said, "It is finished." With
that, he bowed his head and
gave up his spirit.
31Now it was the day of
Preparation, and the next
day was to be a special Sabbath. Because the Jews did
not want the bodies left on
the crosses during the Sabbath, they asked Pilate to
have the legs broken and
the bodies taken down.
32The soldiers therefore
came and broke the legs of
the first man who had been
crucified with Jesus, and
then those of the other.
33But when they came to
Jesus and found that he was
already dead, they did not
break his legs. 34Instead,
one of the soldiers pierced
Jesus' side with a spear,
bringing a sudden flow of
blood and water. 35The
man who saw it has given
testimony, and his testimony is true. He knows that
he tells the truth, and he
testifies so that you also
may believe. 36These
things happened so that the
scripture would be fulfilled:
"Not one of his bones will
be broken,"[c] 37and, as another scripture says,
"They will look on the one
they have pierced."[d]

The Burial of Jesus

38Later, Joseph of Arima-
thea asked Pilate for the

[c]*36* Exodus 12:46; Num. 9:12; Psalm 34:20
[d]*37* Zech. 12:10

a disciple of Jesus, but a secret *one,* for fear of the
Jews, asked Pilate that he
might take away the body
of Jesus; and Pilate granted
permission. He came therefore, and took away His
body.
39And Nicodemus came
also, who had first come to
Him by night; bringing a
mixture of myrrh and
aloes, about a hundred
pounds *weight.*
40And so they took the
body of Jesus, and bound it
in linen wrappings with the
spices, as is the burial custom of the Jews.
41Now in the place where
He was crucified there was
a garden; and in the garden
a new tomb, in which no
one had yet been laid.
42Therefore on account of
the Jewish day of preparation, because the tomb was
nearby, they laid Jesus
there.

ὢν μαθητὴς [τοῦ] Ἰησοῦ κεκρυμμένος
[4]being [5]a disciple – [6]of Jesus [8]*having been* hidden
δὲ διὰ τὸν φόβον τῶν Ἰουδαίων, ἵνα
[7]but [9]because of [10]the [11]fear [12]of the [13]Jews, that
ἄρῃ τὸ σῶμα τοῦ Ἰησοῦ· καὶ
he might take the body – of Jesus; and
ἐπέτρεψεν ὁ Πιλᾶτος. ἦλθεν οὖν καὶ ἦρεν
allowed – Pilate. He came therefore and took
τὸ σῶμα αὐτοῦ. 39 ἦλθεν δὲ καὶ Νικόδημος,
the body of him. And came also Nicodemus,
ὁ ἐλθὼν πρὸς αὐτὸν νυκτὸς τὸ πρῶτον,
the [one] having come to him of (by) night at first,†
φέρων μίγμα σμύρνης καὶ ἀλόης ὡς
bearing a mixture of myrrh and aloes about
λίτρας ἑκατόν. 40 ἔλαβον οὖν τὸ σῶμα
pounds a hundred. They took therefore the body
τοῦ Ἰησοῦ καὶ ἔδησαν αὐτὸ ὀθονίοις
– of Jesus and bound it in sheets
μετὰ τῶν ἀρωμάτων, καθὼς ἔθος ἐστὶν
with the spices, as custom is
τοῖς Ἰουδαίοις ἐνταφιάζειν. 41 ἦν δὲ
with the Jews to bury. Now there was
ἐν τῷ τόπῳ ὅπου ἐσταυρώθη κῆπος,
in the place where he was crucified a garden,
καὶ ἐν τῷ κήπῳ μνημεῖον καινόν, ἐν
and in the garden tomb a new, in
ᾧ οὐδέπω οὐδεὶς ἦν τεθειμένος· 42 ἐκεῖ
which never yet no(any) one was *having been* put; there
οὖν διὰ τὴν παρασκευὴν τῶν Ἰουδαίων,
therefore because of the preparation of the Jews,
ὅτι ἐγγὺς ἦν τὸ μνημεῖον, ἔθηκαν τὸν
because near was the tomb, they put –
Ἰησοῦν.
Jesus.

body of Jesus. Now Joseph
was a disciple of Jesus, but
secretly because he feared
the Jews. With Pilate's
permission, he came and
took the body away. 39He
was accompanied by Nic-
odemus, the man who
earlier had visited Jesus at
night. Nicodemus brought
a mixture of myrrh and
aloes, about seventy-five
pounds.[e] 40Taking Jesus'
body, the two of them
wrapped it, with the spices,
in strips of linen. This was
in accordance with Jewish
burial customs. 41At the
place where Jesus was crucified, there was a garden,
and in the garden a new
tomb, in which no one had
ever been laid. 42Because it
was the Jewish day of Preparation and since the tomb
was nearby, they laid Jesus
there.

Chapter 20

The Empty Tomb

NOW on the first *day* of
the week Mary Mag-
dalene *came early to the
tomb, while it *was still
dark, and *saw the stone
already taken away from
the tomb.
2And so she *ran and
*came to Simon Peter, and
to the other disciple whom
Jesus loved, and *said to
them, "They have taken
away the Lord out of the
tomb, and we do not know
where they have laid
Him."
3Peter therefore went
forth, and the other disciple, and they were going to
the tomb.
4And the two were run-
ning together; and the other
disciple ran ahead faster
than Peter, and came to the
tomb first;
5and stooping and look-

20 Τῇ δὲ μιᾷ τῶν σαββάτων Μαρία
Now on the one(first) [day] of the week Mary
ἡ Μαγδαληνὴ ἔρχεται πρωῒ σκοτίας ἔτι
the Magdalene comes early darkness yet =while it was yet dark
οὔσης εἰς τὸ μνημεῖον, καὶ βλέπει τὸν
being[a] to the tomb, and sees the
λίθον ἠρμένον ἐκ τοῦ μνημείου.
stone having been taken out of the tomb.
2 τρέχει οὖν καὶ ἔρχεται πρὸς Σίμωνα
She runs therefore and comes to Simon
Πέτρον καὶ πρὸς τὸν ἄλλον μαθητὴν ὃν
Peter and to the other disciple whom
ἐφίλει ὁ Ἰησοῦς, καὶ λέγει αὐτοῖς· ἦραν
[2]loved — [1]Jesus, and says to them: They took
τὸν κύριον ἐκ τοῦ μνημείου, καὶ οὐκ οἴδαμεν
the Lord out of the tomb, and we do not know
ποῦ ἔθηκαν αὐτόν. 3 Ἐξῆλθεν οὖν ὁ
where they put him. Went forth therefore –
Πέτρος καὶ ὁ ἄλλος μαθητής, καὶ ἤρχοντο
Peter and the other disciple, and came
εἰς τὸ μνημεῖον. 4 ἔτρεχον δὲ οἱ δύο
to the tomb. And ran the two
ὁμοῦ· καὶ ὁ ἄλλος μαθητὴς προέδραμεν
together; and the other disciple ran before
τάχιον τοῦ Πέτρου καὶ ἦλθεν πρῶτος
more quickly [than] – Peter and came first
εἰς τὸ μνημεῖον, 5 καὶ παρακύψας βλέπει
to the tomb, and stooping sees

Chapter 20

The Empty Tomb

EARLY on the first day
of the week, while it
was still dark, Mary Mag-
dalene went to the tomb
and saw that the stone had
been removed from the en-
trance. 2So she came run-
ning to Simon Peter and the
other disciple, the one
Jesus loved, and said,
"They have taken the Lord
out of the tomb, and we
don't know where they
have put him!"
3So Peter and the other
disciple started for the
tomb. 4Both were running,
but the other disciple out-
ran Peter and reached the
tomb first. 5He bent over
and looked in at the strips

[e]39 Greek *a hundred litrai* (about 34 kilograms)

ing in, he *saw the linen wrappings lying *there;* but he did not go in.

6 Simon Peter therefore also *came, following him, and entered the tomb; and he *beheld the linen wrappings lying *there,*

7 and the face-cloth, which had been on His head, not lying with the linen wrappings, but rolled up in a place by itself.

8 So the other disciple who had first come to the tomb entered then also, and he saw and believed.

9 For as yet they did not understand the Scripture, that He must rise again from the dead.

10 So the disciples went away again to their own homes.

11 But Mary was standing outside the tomb weeping; and so, as she wept, she stooped and looked into the tomb;

12 and she *beheld two angels in white sitting, one at the head, and one at the feet, where the body of Jesus had been lying.

13 And they *said to her, "Woman, why are you weeping?" She *said to them, "Because they have taken away my Lord, and I do not know where they have laid Him."

14 When she had said this, she turned around, and *beheld Jesus standing *there,* and did not know that it was Jesus.

15 Jesus *said to her, "Woman, why are you weeping? Whom are you seeking?" Supposing Him to be the gardener, she *said to Him, "Sir, if you have carried Him away, tell me where you have laid Him, and I will take Him away."

16 Jesus *said to her, "Mary!" She *turned and *said to Him in Hebrew, "Rabboni!" (which means, Teacher).

17 Jesus *said to her,

κείμενα τὰ ὀθόνια, οὐ μέντοι εἰσῆλθεν.
lying the sheets, not however he entered.
6 ἔρχεται οὖν καὶ Σίμων Πέτρος ἀκο-
Comes therefore also Simon Peter follow-
λουθῶν αὐτῷ, καὶ εἰσῆλθεν εἰς τὸ
ing him, and entered into the
μνημεῖον· καὶ θεωρεῖ τὰ ὀθόνια κείμενα,
tomb; and he beholds the sheets lying,
7 καὶ τὸ σουδάριον, ὃ ἦν ἐπὶ τῆς
and the kerchief, which was on the
κεφαλῆς αὐτοῦ, οὐ μετὰ τῶν ὀθονίων
head of him, not with the sheets
κείμενον ἀλλὰ χωρὶς ἐντετυλιγμένον εἰς
lying but apart having been wrapped up in
ἕνα τόπον. 8 τότε οὖν εἰσῆλθεν καὶ
one place. Then therefore entered also
ὁ ἄλλος μαθητὴς ὁ ἐλθὼν πρῶτος εἰς
the other disciple – having come first to
τὸ μνημεῖον, καὶ εἶδεν καὶ ἐπίστευσεν·
the tomb, and he saw and believed;
9 οὐδέπω γὰρ ᾔδεισαν τὴν γραφήν, ὅτι
for not yet they knew the scripture, that
δεῖ αὐτὸν ἐκ νεκρῶν ἀναστῆναι.
it behoves him from [the] dead to rise again.
10 ἀπῆλθον οὖν πάλιν πρὸς αὐτοὺς οἱ
Went away therefore again to themselves* the
μαθηταί. 11 Μαρία δὲ εἱστήκει πρὸς
disciples. But Mary stood at
τῷ μνημείῳ ἔξω κλαίουσα. ὡς οὖν
the tomb outside weeping. As therefore
ἔκλαιεν, παρέκυψεν εἰς τὸ μνημεῖον,
she was weeping, she stooped into the tomb,
12 καὶ θεωρεῖ δύο ἀγγέλους ἐν λευκοῖς
and beholds two angels in white
καθεζομένους, ἕνα πρὸς τῇ κεφαλῇ καὶ
sitting, one at the head and
ἕνα πρὸς τοῖς ποσίν, ὅπου ἔκειτο τὸ
one at the feet, where lay the
σῶμα τοῦ Ἰησοῦ. 13 καὶ λέγουσιν αὐτῇ
body – of Jesus. And say to her
ἐκεῖνοι· γύναι, τί κλαίεις; λέγει αὐτοῖς
those: Woman, why weepest thou? She says to them[,]
ὅτι ἦραν τὸν κύριόν μου, καὶ οὐκ οἶδα
– They took the Lord of me, and I know not
ποῦ ἔθηκαν αὐτόν. 14 ταῦτα εἰποῦσα
where they put him. These things saying
ἐστράφη εἰς τὰ ὀπίσω, καὶ θεωρεῖ τὸν
she turned back,† and beholds –
Ἰησοῦν ἑστῶτα, καὶ οὐκ ᾔδει ὅτι Ἰησοῦς
Jesus standing, and knew not that Jesus
ἐστιν. 15 λέγει αὐτῇ Ἰησοῦς· γύναι,
it is(was). Says to her Jesus: Woman,
τί κλαίεις; τίνα ζητεῖς; ἐκείνη δοκοῦσα
why weepest thou? whom seekest thou? That one thinking
ὅτι ὁ κηπουρός ἐστιν, λέγει αὐτῷ· κύριε,
that the gardener it is(was), says to him: Sir,
εἰ σὺ ἐβάστασας αὐτόν, εἰπέ μοι ποῦ
if thou didst carry him, tell me where
ἔθηκας αὐτόν, κἀγὼ αὐτὸν ἀρῶ. 16 λέγει
thou didst put him, and I him will take. Says
αὐτῇ Ἰησοῦς· Μαριάμ. στραφεῖσα ἐκείνη
to her Jesus: Mary. Turning that one
λέγει αὐτῷ Ἑβραϊστί· ῥαββουνί (ὃ λέγεται
says to him in Hebrew: Rabboni (which is said
διδάσκαλε). 17 λέγει αὐτῇ Ἰησοῦς· μή
Teacher). Says to her Jesus: Not

* That is, to their own home; *cf.* 19. 27.

of linen lying there but did
not go in. 6 Then Simon Peter, who was behind him,
arrived and went into the
tomb. He saw the strips of
linen lying there, 7 as well as
the burial cloth that had
been around Jesus' head.
The cloth was folded up by
itself, separate from the lin-
en. 8 Finally the other disciple, who had reached the
tomb first, also went in-
side. He saw and believed.
9 (They still did not understand from Scripture that
Jesus had to rise from the
dead.)

Jesus Appears to Mary Magdalene

10 Then the disciples went
back to their homes, 11 but
Mary stood outside the
tomb crying. As she wept,
she bent over to look into
the tomb 12 and saw two angels in white, seated where
Jesus' body had been, one
at the head and the other at
the foot.
13 They asked her,
"Woman, why are you cry-
ing?"

"They have taken my
Lord away," she said,
"and I don't know where
they have put him." 14 At
this, she turned around and
saw Jesus standing there,
but she did not realize that
it was Jesus.
15 "Woman," he said,
"why are you crying? Who
is it you are looking for?"

Thinking he was the gar-
dener, she said, "Sir, if you
have carried him away, tell
me where you have put
him, and I will get him."
16 Jesus said to her,
"Mary."

She turned toward him
and cried out in Aramaic,
"Rabboni!" (which means
Teacher).
17 Jesus said, "Do not

"Stop clinging to Me, for I
have not yet ascended to
the Father; but go to My
brethren, and say to them,
'I ascend to My Father and
your Father, and My God
and your God.' "
18 Mary Magdalene
*came, announcing to the
disciples, "I have seen the
Lord," and *that* He had
said these things to her.

Jesus among His Disciples

19 When therefore it was
evening, on that day, the
first *day* of the week, and
when the doors were shut
where the disciples were,
for fear of the Jews, Jesus
came and stood in their
midst, and *said to them,
"Peace *be* with you."
20 And when He had said
this, He showed them both
His hands and His side.
The disciples therefore rejoiced when they saw the
Lord.
21 Jesus therefore said to
them again, "Peace *be* with
you; as the Father has sent
Me, I also send you."
22 And when He had said
this, He breathed on them,
and *said to them, "Re-
ceive the Holy Spirit.
23 "If you forgive the sins
of any, *their sins* have been
forgiven them; if you retain
the *sins* of any, they have
been retained."
24 But Thomas, one of the
twelve, called Didymus,
was not with them when
Jesus came.
25 The other disciples
therefore were saying to
him, "We have seen the
Lord!" But he said to
them, "Unless I shall see in
His hands the imprint of the
nails, and put my finger
into the place of the nails,
and put my hand into His
side, I will not believe."

μου ἅπτου, οὔπω γὰρ ἀναβέβηκα πρὸς
me touch, for not yet have I ascended to
τὸν πατέρα· πορεύου δὲ πρὸς τοὺς
the Father; but go thou to the
ἀδελφούς μου καὶ εἰπὲ αὐτοῖς· ἀναβαίνω
brothers of me and tell them: I ascend
πρὸς τὸν πατέρα μου καὶ πατέρα ὑμῶν
to the Father of me and Father of you
καὶ θεόν μου καὶ θεὸν ὑμῶν. 18 ἔρχεται
and God of me and God of you. Comes
Μαριὰμ ἡ Μαγδαληνὴ ἀγγέλλουσα τοῖς
Mary the Magdalene announcing to the
μαθηταῖς ὅτι ἑώρακα τὸν κύριον, καὶ
disciples[,] – I have seen the Lord, and
ταῦτα εἶπεν αὐτῇ.
these things he said to her.
19 Οὔσης οὖν ὀψίας τῇ ἡμέρᾳ ἐκείνῃ
Being therefore early evening[a] – day on that
=Therefore when it was early evening
τῇ μιᾷ σαββάτων, καὶ τῶν θυρῶν
the one(first) of the week, and the doors
κεκλεισμένων ὅπου ἦσαν οἱ μαθηταὶ διὰ
having been shut[a] where were the disciples because of
τὸν φόβον τῶν Ἰουδαίων, ἦλθεν ὁ Ἰησοῦς
the fear of the Jews, came – Jesus
καὶ ἔστη εἰς τὸ μέσον, καὶ λέγει αὐτοῖς·
and stood in the midst, and says to them:
εἰρήνη ὑμῖν. 20 καὶ τοῦτο εἰπὼν ἔδειξεν
Peace to you. And this saying he showed
καὶ τὰς χεῖρας καὶ τὴν πλευρὰν αὐτοῖς.
both the(his) hands and the(his) side to them.
ἐχάρησαν οὖν οἱ μαθηταὶ ἰδόντες τὸν
Rejoiced therefore the disciples seeing the
κύριον. 21 εἶπεν οὖν αὐτοῖς [ὁ Ἰησοῦς]
Lord. Said therefore to them – Jesus
πάλιν· εἰρήνη ὑμῖν· καθὼς ἀπέσταλκέν
again: Peace to you; as has sent
με ὁ πατήρ, κἀγὼ πέμπω ὑμᾶς. 22 καὶ
me the Father, I also send you. And
τοῦτο εἰπὼν ἐνεφύσησεν καὶ λέγει αὐτοῖς·
this saying he breathed in and says to them:
λάβετε πνεῦμα ἅγιον. 23 ἄν τινων
Receive ye Spirit Holy. Of whomever
ἀφῆτε τὰς ἁμαρτίας, ἀφέωνται αὐτοῖς·
ye forgive the sins, they have been forgiven to them;
ἄν τινων κρατῆτε, κεκράτηνται.
of whomever ye hold, they have been held.
24 Θωμᾶς δὲ εἷς ἐκ τῶν δώδεκα,
But Thomas one of the twelve,
ὁ λεγόμενος Δίδυμος, οὐκ ἦν μετ' αὐτῶν
– *being* called Twin, was not with them
ὅτε ἦλθεν Ἰησοῦς. 25 ἔλεγον οὖν αὐτῷ
when came Jesus. Said therefore to him
οἱ ἄλλοι μαθηταί· ἑωράκαμεν τὸν κύριον.
the other disciples: We have seen the Lord.
ὁ δὲ εἶπεν αὐτοῖς· ἐὰν μὴ ἴδω ἐν
But he said to them: Unless I see in
ταῖς χερσὶν αὐτοῦ τὸν τύπον τῶν ἥλων
the hands of him the mark of the nails
καὶ βάλω τὸν δάκτυλόν μου εἰς τὸν
and put the finger of me into the
τόπον τῶν ἥλων καὶ βάλω μου τὴν
place of the nails and put of me the
χεῖρα εἰς τὴν πλευρὰν αὐτοῦ, οὐ μὴ
hand into the side of him, by no means

hold on to me, for I have
not yet returned to the Father. Go instead to my
brothers and tell them, 'I
am returning to my Father
and your Father, to my
God and your God.' "
18 Mary Magdalene went
to the disciples with the
news: "I have seen the
Lord!" And she told them
that he had said these
things to her.

Jesus Appears to His Disciples

19 On the evening of that
first day of the week, when
the disciples were together,
with the doors locked for
fear of the Jews, Jesus
came and stood among
them and said, "Peace be
with you!" 20 After he said
this, he showed them his
hands and side. The disciples were overjoyed when
they saw the Lord.
21 Again Jesus said,
"Peace be with you! As the
Father has sent me, I am
sending you." 22 And with
that he breathed on them
and said, "Receive the
Holy Spirit. 23 If you forgive
anyone his sins, they are
forgiven; if you do not forgive them, they are not forgiven."

Jesus Appears to Thomas

24 Now Thomas (called
Didymus), one of the
Twelve, was not with the
disciples when Jesus came.
25 So the other disciples told
him, "We have seen the
Lord!"
But he said to them, "Un-
less I see the nail marks in
his hands and put my finger
where the nails were, and
put my hand into his side, I
will not believe it."

26And after eight days
again His disciples were inside, and Thomas with
them. Jesus *came, the
doors having been shut,
and stood in their midst,
and said, "Peace *be* with
you."
27Then He *said to Thom-
as, "Reach here your fin-
ger, and see My hands; and
reach here your hand, and
put it into My side; and be
not unbelieving, but believing."
28Thomas answered and
said to Him, "My Lord and
my God!"
29Jesus *said to him,
"Because you have seen
Me, have you believed?
Blessed *are* they who did
not see, and *yet* believed."

Why This Gospel Was Written

30Many other signs there-
fore Jesus also performed
in the presence of the disciples, which are not written
in this book;
31but these have been
written that you may be-
lieve that Jesus is the
Christ, the Son of God; and
that believing you may
have life in His name.

Chapter 21

Jesus Appears at the Sea of Galilee

AFTER these things
Jesus manifested Him-
self again to the disci-
ples at the Sea of Tiberias,
and He manifested *Himself*
in this way.
2There were together Si-
mon Peter, and Thomas
called Didymus, and Na-
thanael of Cana in Galilee,
and the *sons* of Zebedee,
and two others of His disciples.
3Simon Peter *said to
them, "I am going fish-
ing." They *said to him,
"We will also come with
you." They went out, and
got into the boat; and that

πιστεύσω. 26 Καὶ μεθ' ἡμέρας ὀκτὼ
will I believe. And after days eight
πάλιν ἦσαν ἔσω οἱ μαθηταὶ αὐτοῦ, καὶ
again were within the disciples of him, and
Θωμᾶς μετ' αὐτῶν. ἔρχεται ὁ Ἰησοῦς
Thomas with them. Comes – Jesus
τῶν θυρῶν κεκλεισμένων, καὶ ἔστη εἰς
the doors having been shut[a], and stood in
τὸ μέσον καὶ εἶπεν· εἰρήνη ὑμῖν. 27 εἶτα
the midst and said: Peace to you. Then
λέγει τῷ Θωμᾷ· φέρε τὸν δάκτυλόν
he says – to Thomas: Bring the finger
σου ὧδε καὶ ἴδε τὰς χεῖράς μου, καὶ
of thee here and see the hands of me, and
φέρε τὴν χεῖρά σου καὶ βάλε εἰς τὴν
bring the hand of thee and put into the
πλευράν μου, καὶ μὴ γίνου ἄπιστος
side of me, and be not faithless
ἀλλὰ πιστός. 28 ἀπεκρίθη Θωμᾶς καὶ
but faithful. Answered Thomas and
εἶπεν αὐτῷ· ὁ κύριός μου καὶ ὁ θεός
said to him: The Lord of me and the God
μου. 29 λέγει αὐτῷ ὁ Ἰησοῦς· ὅτι
of me. Says to him – Jesus: Because
ἑώρακάς με, πεπίστευκας; μακάριοι οἱ
thou hast seen me, hast thou believed? blessed the [ones]
μὴ ἰδόντες καὶ πιστεύσαντες.
not seeing and§ believing.
30 Πολλὰ μὲν οὖν καὶ ἄλλα σημεῖα
Many –* therefore and other signs
ἐποίησεν ὁ Ἰησοῦς ἐνώπιον τῶν μαθητῶν,
did – Jesus before the disciples,
ἃ οὐκ ἔστιν γεγραμμένα ἐν τῷ βιβλίῳ
which is(are) not *having been* written in – roll
τούτῳ· 31 ταῦτα δὲ γέγραπται ἵνα
this; but these* has(ve) been written that
πιστεύητε ὅτι Ἰησοῦς ἐστιν ὁ χριστὸς ὁ
ye may believe that Jesus is the Christ the
υἱὸς τοῦ θεοῦ, καὶ ἵνα πιστεύοντες ζωὴν
Son – of God, and that believing life
ἔχητε ἐν τῷ ὀνόματι αὐτοῦ.
ye may have in the name of him.

21 Μετὰ ταῦτα ἐφανέρωσεν ἑαυτὸν πάλιν
After these things manifested himself again
Ἰησοῦς τοῖς μαθηταῖς ἐπὶ τῆς θαλάσσης
Jesus to the disciples on the sea
τῆς Τιβεριάδος· ἐφανέρωσεν δὲ οὕτως.
– of Tiberias; and he manifested [himself] thus.
2 ἦσαν ὁμοῦ Σίμων Πέτρος καὶ Θωμᾶς
There were together Simon Peter and Thomas
ὁ λεγόμενος Δίδυμος καὶ Ναθαναὴλ ὁ
– *being* called Twin and Nathanael –
ἀπὸ Κανὰ τῆς Γαλιλαίας καὶ οἱ τοῦ
from Cana – of Galilee and the [sons] –
Ζεβεδαίου καὶ ἄλλοι ἐκ τῶν μαθητῶν
of Zebedee and others of the disciples
αὐτοῦ δύο. 3 λέγει αὐτοῖς Σίμων Πέτρος·
of him two. Says to them Simon Peter:
ὑπάγω ἁλιεύειν. λέγουσιν αὐτῷ· ἐρχόμεθα
I am going to fish. They say to him: Are coming
καὶ ἡμεῖς σὺν σοί. ἐξῆλθον καὶ ἐνέβησαν
also we with thee. They went forth and embarked
εἰς τὸ πλοῖον, καὶ ἐν ἐκείνῃ τῇ νυκτὶ
in the boat, and in that – night

* See note on 19. 24 and 32.
§ καί sometimes = and yet; see 5. 40; 8. 55; 9. 30; 16. 32; 17. 11.

26A week later his disci-
ples were in the house
again, and Thomas was
with them. Though the
doors were locked, Jesus
came and stood among
them and said, "Peace be
with you!" 27Then he said
to Thomas, "Put your fin-
ger here; see my hands.
Reach out your hand and
put it into my side. Stop
doubting and believe."
28Thomas said to him,
"My Lord and my God!"
29Then Jesus told him,
"Because you have seen
me, you have believed;
blessed are those who have
not seen and yet have be-
lieved."
30Jesus did many other
miraculous signs in the
presence of his disciples,
which are not recorded in
this book. 31But these are
written that you may[f] believe that Jesus is the
Christ, the Son of God, and
that by believing you may
have life in his name.

Chapter 21

Jesus and the Miraculous Catch of Fish

AFTERWARD Jesus ap-
peared again to his
disciples, by the Sea of Tiberias.[g] It happened this
way: 2Simon Peter, Thom-
as (called Didymus), Na-
thanael from Cana in Galilee, the sons of Zebedee,
and two other disciples
were together. 3"I'm going
out to fish," Simon Peter
told them, and they said,
"We'll go with you." So
they went out and got into
the boat, but that night they

f31 Some manuscripts *may continue to*
g1 That is, Sea of Galilee

night they caught nothing.
4But when the day was
now breaking, Jesus stood
on the beach; yet the disciples did not know that it
was Jesus.
5Jesus therefore *said to
them, "Children, you do
not have any fish, do you?"
They answered Him,
"No."
6And He said to them,
"Cast the net on the right-
hand side of the boat, and
you will find *a catch.*"
They cast therefore, and
then they were not able to
haul it in because of the
great number of fish.
7That disciple therefore
whom Jesus loved *said to
Peter, "It is the Lord."
And so when Simon Peter
heard that it was the Lord,
he put his outer garment on
(for he was stripped *for
work*), and threw himself
into the sea.
8But the other disciples
came in the little boat, for
they were not far from the
land, but about one hun-
dred yards away, dragging
the net *full* of fish.
9And so when they got
out upon the land, they
*saw a charcoal fire *al-
ready* laid, and fish placed
on it, and bread.
10Jesus *said to them,
"Bring some of the fish
which you have now
caught."
11Simon Peter went up,
and drew the net to land,
full of large fish, a hundred
and fifty-three; and al-
though there were so
many, the net was not torn.

Jesus Provides

12Jesus *said to them,
"Come *and* have break-
fast." None of the disciples
ventured to question Him,
"Who are You?" knowing
that it was the Lord.
13Jesus *came and *took
the bread, and *gave them,
and the fish likewise.
14This is now the third
time that Jesus was mani-
fested to the disciples, after
He was raised from the

ἐπίασαν οὐδέν. **4** πρωΐας δὲ ἤδη γινομένης
they caught nothing. Early morning but now becoming[a]
=But when it became early morning
ἔστη Ἰησοῦς εἰς τὸν αἰγιαλόν· οὐ μέντοι
stood Jesus in(on) the shore; not however
ᾔδεισαν οἱ μαθηταὶ ὅτι Ἰησοῦς ἐστιν.
knew the disciples that Jesus it is(was).
5 λέγει οὖν αὐτοῖς Ἰησοῦς· παιδία, μή
Says therefore to them Jesus: Children, *not*
τι προσφάγιον ἔχετε; ἀπεκρίθησαν αὐτῷ·
any fish have ye? They answered him:
οὔ. **6** ὁ δὲ εἶπεν αὐτοῖς· βάλετε εἰς τὰ
No. So he said to them: Cast in the
δεξιὰ μέρη τοῦ πλοίου τὸ δίκτυον, καὶ
right parts of the boat the net, and
εὑρήσετε. ἔβαλον οὖν, καὶ οὐκέτι αὐτὸ
ye will find. They cast therefore, and [1]no longer [4]it
ἑλκύσαι ἴσχυον ἀπὸ τοῦ πλήθους τῶν
[3]to drag [2]were they able from the multitude of the
ἰχθύων. **7** λέγει οὖν ὁ μαθητὴς ἐκεῖνος
fishes. Says therefore – disciple that
ὃν ἠγάπα ὁ Ἰησοῦς τῷ Πέτρῳ· ὁ κύριός
whom [2]loved – [1]Jesus – to Peter: The Lord
ἐστιν. Σίμων οὖν Πέτρος, ἀκούσας ὅτι
it is. [2]Simon [1]therefore [3]Peter, hearing that
ὁ κύριός ἐστιν, τὸν ἐπενδύτην διεζώσατο,
the Lord it is(was), [2][with]the [3]coat [1]girded himself,
ἦν γὰρ γυμνός, καὶ ἔβαλεν ἑαυτὸν εἰς
for he was naked, and threw himself into
τὴν θάλασσαν· **8** οἱ δὲ ἄλλοι μαθηταὶ
the sea; but the other disciples
τῷ πλοιαρίῳ ἦλθον, οὐ γὰρ ἦσαν μακρὰν
in the little boat came, for not they were far
ἀπὸ τῆς γῆς ἀλλὰ ὡς ἀπὸ πηχῶν
from the land but about from cubits
διακοσίων, σύροντες τὸ δίκτυον τῶν ἰχθύων.
two hundred dragging the net of the fishes.
9 ὡς οὖν ἀπέβησαν εἰς τὴν γῆν, βλέπουσιν
When therefore they disembarked onto the land, they see
ἀνθρακιὰν κειμένην καὶ ὀψάριον ἐπικείμενον
a coal fire lying and a fish lying on
καὶ ἄρτον. **10** λέγει αὐτοῖς ὁ Ἰησοῦς·
and bread. Says to them – Jesus:
ἐνέγκατε ἀπὸ τῶν ὀψαρίων ὧν ἐπιάσατε
Bring from the fishes which ye caught
νῦν. **11** ἀνέβη Σίμων Πέτρος καὶ εἵλκυσεν
now. Went up Simon Peter and dragged
τὸ δίκτυον εἰς τὴν γῆν μεστὸν ἰχθύων
the net to the land full fishes
μεγάλων ἑκατὸν πεντήκοντα τριῶν· καὶ
of great a hundred fifty three; and
τοσούτων ὄντων οὐκ ἐσχίσθη τὸ δίκτυον.
so many being[a] was not torn the net.
12 λέγει αὐτοῖς ὁ Ἰησοῦς· δεῦτε ἀριστήσατε.
Says to them – Jesus: Come breakfast ye.
οὐδεὶς ἐτόλμα τῶν μαθητῶν ἐξετάσαι
No one dared of the disciples to question
αὐτόν· σὺ τίς εἶ; εἰδότες ὅτι ὁ κύριός
him: Thou who art? knowing that the Lord
ἐστιν. **13** ἔρχεται Ἰησοῦς καὶ λαμβάνει
it is(was). Comes Jesus and takes
τὸν ἄρτον καὶ δίδωσιν αὐτοῖς, καὶ τὸ
the bread and gives to them, and the
ὀψάριον ὁμοίως. **14** τοῦτο ἤδη τρίτον
fish likewise. This [was] now [the] third [time] [that]
ἐφανερώθη Ἰησοῦς τοῖς μαθηταῖς ἐγερθεὶς
[2]was manifested [1]Jesus to the disciples raised

caught nothing.
4Early in the morning,
Jesus stood on the shore,
but the disciples did not realize that it was Jesus.
5He called out to them,
"Friends, haven't you any
fish?"
"No," they answered.
6He said, "Throw your
net on the right side of the
boat and you will find
some." When they did,
they were unable to haul
the net in because of the
large number of fish.
7Then the disciple whom
Jesus loved said to Peter,
"It is the Lord!" As soon
as Simon Peter heard him
say, "It is the Lord," he
wrapped his outer garment
around him (for he had tak-
en it off) and jumped into
the water. 8The other disciples followed in the boat,
towing the net full of fish,
for they were not far from
shore, about a hundred
yards.[h] 9When they landed, they saw a fire of burning coals there with fish on
it, and some bread.
10Jesus said to them,
"Bring some of the fish you
have just caught."
11Simon Peter climbed
aboard and dragged the net
ashore. It was full of large
fish, 153, but even with so
many the net was not torn.
12Jesus said to them,
"Come and have break-
fast." None of the disciples
dared ask him, "Who are
you?" They knew it was
the Lord. 13Jesus came,
took the bread and gave it
to them, and did the same
with the fish. 14This was
now the third time Jesus
appeared to his disciples after he was raised from the
dead.

[h]8 Greek *about two hundred cubits* (about 90 meters)

dead.

The Love Motivation

15So when they had fin-
ished breakfast, Jesus *said
to Simon Peter, "Simon,
son of John, do you love
Me more than these?" He
*said to Him, "Yes, Lord;
You know that I love
You." He *said to him,
"Tend My lambs."
16He *said to him again a
second time, "Simon, *son*
of John, do you love Me?"
He *said to Him, "Yes,
Lord; You know that I love
You." He *said to him,
"Shepherd My sheep."
17He *said to him the
third time, "Simon, *son* of
John, do you love Me?"
Peter was grieved because
He said to him the third
time, "Do you love Me?"
And he said to Him,
"Lord, You know all
things; You know that I
love You." Jesus *said to
him, "Tend My sheep.

Our Times Are in His Hand

18"Truly, truly, I say to
you, when you were youn-
ger, you used to gird yourself, and walk wherever
you wished; but when you
grow old, you will stretch
out your hands, and some-
one else will gird you, and
bring you where you do not
wish to *go*."
19Now this He said, signifying by what kind of death
he would glorify God. And
when He had spoken this,
He *said to him, "Follow
Me!"
20Peter, turning around,
*saw the disciple whom
Jesus loved following
them; the one who also had
leaned back on His breast
at the supper, and said,
"Lord, who is the one who
betrays You?"
21Peter therefore seeing
him *said to Jesus, "Lord,
and what about this man?"
22Jesus *said to him, "If I
want him to remain until I
come, what *is that* to you?
You follow Me!"
23This saying therefore
went out among the breth-
ren that that disciple would

ἐκ νεκρῶν.
from [the] dead.
15 Ὅτε οὖν ἠρίστησαν, λέγει τῷ
When therefore they breakfasted, says –
Σίμωνι Πέτρῳ ὁ Ἰησοῦς· Σίμων Ἰωάννου,
to Simon Peter – Jesus: Simon [son] of John,
ἀγαπᾷς με πλέον τούτων; λέγει αὐτῷ·
lovest thou me more [than] these? He says to him:
ναί, κύριε, σὺ οἶδας ὅτι φιλῶ σε. λέγει
Yes, Lord, thou knowest that I love thee. He says
αὐτῷ· βόσκε τὰ ἀρνία μου. 16 λέγει
to him: Feed the lambs of me. He says
αὐτῷ πάλιν δεύτερον· Σίμων Ἰωάννου,
to him again secondly: Simon [son] of John,
ἀγαπᾷς με; λέγει αὐτῷ· ναί, κύριε,
lovest thou me? He says to him: Yes, Lord,
σὺ οἶδας ὅτι φιλῶ σε. λέγει αὐτῷ·
thou knowest that I love thee. He says to him:
ποίμαινε τὰ προβάτιά μου. 17 λέγει
Shepherd the little sheep of me. He says
αὐτῷ τὸ τρίτον· Σίμων Ἰωάννου, φιλεῖς
to him the third [time]: Simon [son] of John, lovest thou
με; ἐλυπήθη ὁ Πέτρος ὅτι εἶπεν αὐτῷ
me? Was grieved – Peter that he said to him
τὸ τρίτον· φιλεῖς με; καὶ εἶπεν αὐτῷ·
the third [time]: Lovest thou me? and said to him:
κύριε, πάντα σὺ οἶδας, σὺ γινώσκεις
Lord, all things thou knowest, thou knowest
ὅτι φιλῶ σε· λέγει αὐτῷ Ἰησοῦς· βόσκε
that I love thee; says to him Jesus: Feed
τὰ προβάτιά μου. 18 ἀμὴν ἀμὴν λέγω
the little sheep of me. Truly truly I tell
σοι, ὅτε ἦς νεώτερος, ἐζώννυες σεαυτὸν
thee, when thou wast younger, thou girdedst thyself
καὶ περιεπάτεις ὅπου ἤθελες· ὅταν δὲ
and walkedst where thou wishedst; but when
γηράσῃς, ἐκτενεῖς τὰς χεῖράς σου, καὶ
thou growest old, thou wilt stretch out the hands of thee, and
ἄλλος ζώσει σε καὶ οἴσει ὅπου οὐ θέλεις.
another will gird thee and will carry where thou wishest not.
19 τοῦτο δὲ εἶπεν σημαίνων ποίῳ θανάτῳ
And this he said signifying by what death
δοξάσει τὸν θεόν. καὶ τοῦτο εἰπὼν λέγει
he will glorify – God. And this saying he tells
αὐτῷ· ἀκολούθει μοι. 20 ἐπιστραφεὶς ὁ
him: Follow me. Turning –
Πέτρος βλέπει τὸν μαθητὴν ὃν ἠγάπα ὁ
Peter sees the disciple whom [2]loved –
Ἰησοῦς ἀκολουθοῦντα, ὃς καὶ ἀνέπεσεν
[1]Jesus following, who also leaned
ἐν τῷ δείπνῳ ἐπὶ τὸ στῆθος αὐτοῦ καὶ
at the supper on the breast of him and
εἶπεν· κύριε, τίς ἐστιν ὁ παραδιδούς σε;
said: Lord, who is the[one] betraying thee?
21 τοῦτον οὖν ἰδὼν ὁ Πέτρος λέγει τῷ
[4]This one [2]therefore [3]seeing – [1]Peter says –
Ἰησοῦ· κύριε, οὗτος δὲ τί; 22 λέγει
to Jesus: Lord, and this one what? Says
αὐτῷ ὁ Ἰησοῦς· ἐὰν αὐτὸν θέλω μένειν
to him – Jesus: If him I wish to remain
ἕως ἔρχομαι, τί πρὸς σέ; σύ μοι
until I come, what to thee? [2]thou [3]me
ἀκολούθει. 23 ἐξῆλθεν οὖν οὗτος ὁ λόγος
[1]follow. Went forth therefore this – word
εἰς τοὺς ἀδελφοὺς ὅτι ὁ μαθητὴς ἐκεῖνος
to the brothers that – disciple that

Jesus Reinstates Peter

15When they had finished
eating, Jesus said to Simon
Peter, "Simon son of John,
do you truly love me more
than these?"
"Yes, Lord," he said,
"you know that I love
you."
Jesus said, "Feed my
lambs."
16Again Jesus said, "Si-
mon son of John, do you
truly love me?"
He answered, "Yes,
Lord, you know that I love
you."
Jesus said, "Take care of
my sheep."
17The third time he said to
him, "Simon son of John,
do you love me?"
Peter was hurt because
Jesus asked him the third
time, "Do you love me?"
He said, "Lord, you know
all things; you know that I
love you."
Jesus said, "Feed my
sheep. 18I tell you the truth,
when you were younger
you dressed yourself and
went where you wanted;
but when you are old you
will stretch out your hands,
and someone else will dress
you and lead you where
you do not want to go."
19Jesus said this to indicate
the kind of death by which
Peter would glorify God.
Then he said to him, "Follow me!"
20Peter turned and saw
that the disciple whom
Jesus loved was following
them. (This was the one
who had leaned back
against Jesus at the supper
and had said, "Lord, who
is going to betray you?")
21When Peter saw him, he
asked, "Lord, what about
him?"
22Jesus answered, "If I
want him to remain alive
until I return, what is that
to you? You must follow
me." 23Because of this, the
rumor spread among the
brothers that this disciple

not die; yet Jesus did not say to him that he would not die, but *only,* "If I want him to remain until I come, what *is that* to you?"

24 This is the disciple who bears witness of these things, and wrote these things; and we know that his witness is true.

25 And there are also many other things which Jesus did, which if they *were written in detail, I suppose that even the world itself *would not contain the books which *were written.

οὐκ ἀποθνήσκει· οὐκ εἶπεν δὲ αὐτῷ ὁ
does not die; but said not to him –

Ἰησοῦς ὅτι οὐκ ἀποθνήσκει, ἀλλ'· ἐὰν
Jesus that he does not die, but : If

αὐτὸν θέλω μένειν ἕως ἔρχομαι, τί πρὸς
him I wish to remain until I come, what to

σέ;
thee?

24 Οὗτός ἐστιν ὁ μαθητὴς ὁ μαρτυρῶν
This is the disciple – witnessing

περὶ τούτων καὶ ὁ γράψας ταῦτα,
concerning these things and – having written these things,

καὶ οἴδαμεν ὅτι ἀληθὴς αὐτοῦ ἡ μαρτυρία
and we know that true of him the witness

ἐστίν. 25 Ἔστιν δὲ καὶ ἄλλα πολλὰ ἃ
is. And there are also other things many which

ἐποίησεν ὁ Ἰησοῦς, ἅτινα ἐὰν γράφηται
did – Jesus, which if they were written

καθ' ἕν, οὐδ' αὐτὸν οἶμαι τὸν κόσμον
singly,† [5]not [4][it]self [1]I think [2]the [3]world

χωρήσειν τὰ γραφόμενα βιβλία.
[6]to contain [7]the [8]being written [9]rolls.

would not die. But Jesus did not say that he would not die; he only said, "If I want him to remain alive until I return, what is that to you?"

24 This is the disciple who testifies to these things and who wrote them down. We know that his testimony is true.

25 Jesus did many other things as well. If every one of them were written down, I suppose that even the whole world would not have room for the books that would be written.

ΠΡΑΞΕΙΣ ΑΠΟΣΤΟΛΩΝ

Acts of Apostles

Acts

Chapter 1

Introduction

THE first account I composed, Theophilus, about all that Jesus began to do and teach,

2until the day when He was taken up, after He had by the Holy Spirit given orders to the apostles whom He had chosen.

3To these He also presented Himself alive, after His suffering, by many convincing proofs, appearing to them over *a period of* forty days, and speaking of the things concerning the kingdom of God.

4And gathering them together, He commanded them not to leave Jerusalem, but to wait for what the Father had promised, "Which," *He said,* "you heard of from Me;

5for John baptized with water, but you shall be baptized with the Holy Spirit not many days from now."

6And so when they had come together, they were asking Him, saying, "Lord, is it at this time You are restoring the kingdom to Israel?"

7He said to them, "It is not for you to know times or epochs which the Father has fixed by His own authority;

8but you shall receive power when the Holy Spirit has come upon you; and you shall be My witnesses both in Jerusalem, and in all Judea and Samaria, and even to the remotest part of the earth."

The Ascension

9And after He had said these things, He was lifted up while they were looking on, and a cloud received Him out of their sight.

10And as they were gazing intently into the sky while He was departing, behold, two men in white clothing stood beside them;

1 Τὸν μὲν πρῶτον λόγον ἐποιησάμην
The – first account I made

περὶ πάντων, ὦ Θεόφιλε, ὧν ἤρξατο
concerning all things, O Theophilus, which began

ὁ Ἰησοῦς ποιεῖν τε καὶ διδάσκειν,
– Jesus both to do and to teach,

2 ἄχρι ἧς ἡμέρας ἐντειλάμενος τοῖς
until which day [2]having given injunctions [6]to the
=the day on which

ἀποστόλοις διὰ πνεύματος ἁγίου οὓς
[7]apostles [3]through [5]Spirit [4]Holy [8]whom

ἐξελέξατο ἀνελήμφθη· **3** οἷς καὶ παρέστησεν
[9]he chose [1]he was taken up; to whom also he presented

ἑαυτὸν ζῶντα μετὰ τὸ παθεῖν αὐτὸν ἐν
himself living after the to suffer him[b] by
=he suffered

πολλοῖς τεκμηρίοις, δι' ἡμερῶν τεσσεράκοντα
many infallible proofs, through days forty

ὀπτανόμενος αὐτοῖς καὶ λέγων τὰ περὶ
being seen by them and speaking the things concerning

τῆς βασιλείας τοῦ θεοῦ· **4** καὶ συναλιζόμενος
the kingdom – of God; and meeting with [them]

παρήγγειλεν αὐτοῖς ἀπὸ Ἱεροσολύμων μὴ
he charged them from Jerusalem not

χωρίζεσθαι, ἀλλὰ περιμένειν τὴν ἐπαγγελίαν
to depart, but to await the promise

τοῦ πατρὸς ἣν ἠκούσατέ μου· **5** ὅτι
of the Father which ye heard of me: because

Ἰωάννης μὲν ἐβάπτισεν ὕδατι, ὑμεῖς δὲ
John indeed baptized in water, but ye

ἐν πνεύματι βαπτισθήσεσθε ἁγίῳ οὐ μετὰ
in [2]Spirit [3]will be baptized [1]Holy not after

πολλὰς ταύτας ἡμέρας. **6** Οἱ μὲν οὖν
many *these* days. [2]the [ones] [1]So then

συνελθόντες ἠρώτων αὐτὸν λέγοντες· κύριε,
[3]coming together questioned him saying: Lord,

εἰ ἐν τῷ χρόνῳ τούτῳ ἀποκαθιστάνεις
if at this time restorest thou

τὴν βασιλείαν τῷ Ἰσραήλ; **7** εἶπεν πρὸς
the kingdom – to Israel? He said to

αὐτούς· οὐχ ὑμῶν ἐστιν γνῶναι χρόνους
them: Not of you it is to know times

ἢ καιροὺς οὓς ὁ πατὴρ ἔθετο ἐν τῇ
or seasons which the Father placed in the(his)

ἰδίᾳ ἐξουσίᾳ, **8** ἀλλὰ λήμψεσθε δύναμιν
own authority, but ye will receive power

ἐπελθόντος τοῦ ἁγίου πνεύματος ἐφ' ὑμᾶς,
coming *upon* the Holy Spirit[a] upon you,
=when the Holy Spirit comes

καὶ ἔσεσθέ μου μάρτυρες ἔν τε Ἰερουσαλὴμ
and ye will be of me witnesses both in Jerusalem

καὶ ἐν πάσῃ τῇ Ἰουδαίᾳ καὶ Σαμαρείᾳ
and in all – Judæa and Samaria

καὶ ἕως ἐσχάτου τῆς γῆς. **9** καὶ ταῦτα
and unto [the] extremity of the earth. And these things

εἰπὼν βλεπόντων αὐτῶν ἐπήρθη, καὶ
saying looking them[a] he was taken up, and
=as they looked

νεφέλη ὑπέλαβεν αὐτὸν ἀπὸ τῶν ὀφθαλμῶν
a cloud received him from the eyes

αὐτῶν. **10** καὶ ὡς ἀτενίζοντες ἦσαν εἰς
of them. And as gazing they were to

τὸν οὐρανὸν πορευομένου αὐτοῦ, καὶ ἰδοὺ
– heaven going him,[a] – behold[,]
=as he went,

ἄνδρες δύο παρειστήκεισαν αὐτοῖς ἐν ἐσθήσεσι
men two stood by them in garments

Acts

Chapter 1

Jesus Taken Up Into Heaven

IN my former book, The-
ophilus, I wrote about
all that Jesus began to do
and to teach 2until the day
he was taken up to heaven,
after giving instructions
through the Holy Spirit to
the apostles he had chosen.
3After his suffering, he
showed himself to these
men and gave many con-
vincing proofs that he was
alive. He appeared to them
over a period of forty days
and spoke about the king-
dom of God. 4On one occa-
sion, while he was eating
with them, he gave them
this command: "Do not
leave Jerusalem, but wait
for the gift my Father
promised, which you have
heard me speak about. 5For
John baptized with[a] water,
but in a few days you will
be baptized with the Holy
Spirit."

6So when they met to-
gether, they asked him,
"Lord, are you at this time
going to restore the kingdom to Israel?"

7He said to them: "It is
not for you to know the
times or dates the Father
has set by his own authority. 8But you will receive
power when the Holy Spirit
comes on you; and you will
be my witnesses in Jerusalem, and in all Judea and
Samaria, and to the ends of
the earth."

9After he said this, he was
taken up before their very
eyes, and a cloud hid him
from their sight.

10They were looking in-
tently up into the sky as he
was going, when suddenly
two men dressed in white
stood beside them. 11"Men

[a]5 Or *in*

11and they also said,
"Men of Galilee, why do
you stand looking into the
sky? This Jesus, who has
been taken up from you
into heaven, will come in
just the same way as you
have watched Him go into
heaven."

The Upper Room

12Then they returned to
Jerusalem from the mount
called Olivet, which is near
Jerusalem, a Sabbath day's
journey away.
13And when they had en-
tered, they went up to the
upper room, where they
were staying; that is, Peter
and John and James and
Andrew, Philip and Thom-
as, Bartholomew and Mat-
thew, James *the son* of Alphaeus, and Simon the
Zealot, and Judas *the son*
of James.
14These all with one mind
were continually devoting
themselves to prayer, along
with *the* women, and Mary
the mother of Jesus, and
with His brothers.
15And at this time Peter
stood up in the midst of the
brethren (a gathering of
about one hundred and
twenty persons was there
together), and said,
16"Brethren, the Scrip-
ture had to be fulfilled,
which the Holy Spirit foretold by the mouth of David
concerning Judas, who
became a guide to those
who arrested Jesus.
17"For he was counted
among us, and received his
portion in this ministry."
18(Now this man acquired
a field with the price of his
wickedness; and falling
headlong, he burst open in
the middle and all his bowels gushed out.

λευκαῖς, **11** οἳ καὶ εἶπαν· ἄνδρες Γαλιλαῖοι,
white, who also said: *Men* Galilæans,

τί ἑστήκατε βλέποντες εἰς τὸν οὐρανόν;
why stand ye looking to – heaven?

οὗτος ὁ Ἰησοῦς ὁ ἀναλημφθεὶς
This – Jesus the [one] having been taken up

ἀφ' ὑμῶν εἰς τὸν οὐρανὸν οὕτως ἐλεύσεται
from you to – heaven thus will come

ὃν τρόπον ἐθεάσασθε αὐτὸν πορευόμενον
in the way† ye beheld him going

εἰς τὸν οὐρανόν. **12** Τότε ὑπέστρεψαν
to – heaven. Then they returned

εἰς Ἰερουσαλὴμ ἀπὸ ὄρους τοῦ καλου-
to Jerusalem from [the] mount the [one] *being*

μένου ἐλαιῶνος, ὅ ἐστιν ἐγγὺς Ἰερουσαλὴμ
called of [the] olive grove, which is near Jerusalem

σαββάτου ἔχον ὁδόν. **13** καὶ ὅτε εἰσῆλθον,
of a sabbath having a way. And when they entered,
=a sabbath's journey off.

εἰς τὸ ὑπερῷον ἀνέβησαν οὗ ἦσαν
into the upper room they went up where they were

καταμένοντες, ὅ τε Πέτρος καὶ Ἰωάννης
waiting, – both Peter and John

καὶ Ἰάκωβος καὶ Ἀνδρέας, Φίλιππος καὶ
and James and Andrew, Philip and

Θωμᾶς, Βαρθολομαῖος καὶ Μαθθαῖος,
Thomas, Bartholomew and Matthew,

Ἰάκωβος Ἁλφαίου καὶ Σίμων ὁ ζηλωτὴς
James [son] of Alphæus and Simon the zealot

καὶ Ἰούδας Ἰακώβου. **14** οὗτοι πάντες
and Judas [brother] of James. These all

ἦσαν προσκαρτεροῦντες ὁμοθυμαδὸν τῇ
were continuing steadfastly with one mind –

προσευχῇ σὺν γυναιξὶν καὶ Μαριὰμ τῇ
in prayer with [the] women and Mary the

μητρὶ [τοῦ] Ἰησοῦ καὶ σὺν τοῖς ἀδελφοῖς
mother – of Jesus and with the brothers

αὐτοῦ.
of him.

15 Καὶ ἐν ταῖς ἡμέραις ταύταις ἀναστὰς
And in these days standing up

Πέτρος ἐν μέσῳ τῶν ἀδελφῶν εἶπεν·
Peter in [the] midst of the brothers said:

ἦν τε ὄχλος ὀνομάτων ἐπὶ τὸ αὐτὸ
[6]was [1]and [2][the] [3]crowd [4]of names [5]together

ὡσεὶ ἑκατὸν εἴκοσι· **16** ἄνδρες ἀδελφοί,
about a hundred twenty: *Men* brothers,

ἔδει πληρωθῆναι τὴν γραφὴν ἣν
it behoved to be fulfilled the scripture which

προεῖπεν τὸ πνεῦμα τὸ ἅγιον διὰ στόματος
spoke before the Spirit – Holy through [the] mouth

Δαυὶδ περὶ Ἰούδα τοῦ γενομένου ὁδηγοῦ
of David concerning Judas the [one] having become guide

τοῖς συλλαβοῦσιν Ἰησοῦν, **17** ὅτι κατ-
to the [ones] taking Jesus, because *having*

ηριθμημένος ἦν ἐν ἡμῖν καὶ ἔλαχεν τὸν
been numbered he was among us and obtained the

κλῆρον τῆς διακονίας ταύτης. **18** οὗτος μὲν οὖν
portion of this ministry. This one therefore

ἐκτήσατο χωρίον ἐκ μισθοῦ τῆς
bought a field out of [the] reward –

ἀδικίας, καὶ πρηνὴς γενόμενος ἐλάκησεν
of unrighteousness, and swollen up having become he burst asunder

μέσος, καὶ ἐξεχύθη πάντα τὰ σπλάγχνα
in the middle, and were poured out all the bowels

of Galilee," they said,
"why do you stand here
looking into the sky? This
same Jesus, who has been
taken from you into heav-
en, will come back in the
same way you have seen
him go into heaven."

Matthias Chosen to Replace Judas

12Then they returned to
Jerusalem from the hill
called the Mount of Olives,
a Sabbath day's walk[b]
from the city. 13When they
arrived, they went upstairs
to the room where they
were staying. Those pre-
sent were Peter, John,
James and Andrew; Philip
and Thomas, Bartholomew
and Matthew; James son of
Alphaeus and Simon the
Zealot, and Judas son of
James. 14They all joined together constantly in prayer,
along with the women and
Mary the mother of Jesus,
and with his brothers.
15In those days Peter
stood up among the believers[c] (a group numbering
about a hundred and twen-
ty) 16and said, "Brothers,
the Scripture had to be fulfilled which the Holy Spirit
spoke long ago through the
mouth of David concerning
Judas, who served as guide
for those who arrested
Jesus—17he was one of our
number and shared in this
ministry."
18(With the reward he got
for his wickedness, Judas
bought a field; there he fell
headlong, his body burst
open and all his intestines

[b] *12* That is, about 3/4 mile (about 1,100 meters)
[c] *15* Greek *brothers*

19And it became known
to all who were living in
Jerusalem; so that in their
own language that field was
called Hakeldama, that is,
Field of Blood.)
20"For it is written in the
book of Psalms,
'LET HIS HOMESTEAD BE
MADE DESOLATE,
AND LET NO MAN
DWELL IN IT';
and,
'HIS OFFICE LET AN-
OTHER MAN TAKE.'
21"It is therefore neces-
sary that of the men who
have accompanied us all
the time that the Lord Jesus
went in and out among us—
22beginning with the
baptism of John, until the
day that He was taken up
from us—one of these
should become a witness
with us of His resurrec-
tion."
23And they put forward
two men, Joseph called
Barsabbas (who was also
called Justus), and
Matthias.
24And they prayed, and
said, "Thou, Lord, who
knowest the hearts of all
men, show which one of
these two Thou hast cho-
sen
25to occupy this ministry
and apostleship from which
Judas turned aside to go to
his own place."
26And they drew lots for
them, and the lot fell to
Matthias; and he was num-
bered with the eleven apostles.

αὐτοῦ· **19** καὶ γνωστὸν ἐγένετο πᾶσι τοῖς
of him; and known it became to all the
κατοικοῦσιν Ἰερουσαλήμ, ὥστε κληθῆναι
[ones] inhabiting Jerusalem, so as to be called
τὸ χωρίον ἐκεῖνο τῇ ἰδίᾳ διαλέκτῳ αὐτῶν
that field in their own language
Ἀκελδαμάχ, τοῦτ' ἔστιν χωρίον
Aceldamach, this is Field
αἵματος. **20** γέγραπται γὰρ ἐν βίβλῳ
of blood. For it has been written in [the] roll
ψαλμῶν· γενηθήτω ἡ ἔπαυλις αὐτοῦ ἔρημος
of Psalms: Let become the estate of him deserted
καὶ μὴ ἔστω ὁ κατοικῶν ἐν αὐτῇ, καί·
and let not be the [one] dwelling in it, and:
τὴν ἐπισκοπὴν αὐτοῦ λαβέτω ἕτερος.
The office of him let take another.
21 δεῖ οὖν τῶν συνελθόντων ἡμῖν ἀνδρῶν
It behoves* therefore [1]of the [3]accompanying [4]us [2]men
ἐν παντὶ χρόνῳ ᾧ εἰσῆλθεν καὶ
in all [the] time in which went in and
ἐξῆλθεν ἐφ' ἡμᾶς ὁ κύριος Ἰησοῦς,
went out among us the Lord Jesus,
22 ἀρξάμενος ἀπὸ τοῦ βαπτίσματος
beginning from the baptism
Ἰωάννου ἕως τῆς ἡμέρας ἧς ἀνελήμφθη
of John until the day when he was taken up
ἀφ' ἡμῶν, μάρτυρα τῆς ἀναστάσεως
from us, [4]a witness* [7]of the [8]resurrection
αὐτοῦ σὺν ἡμῖν γενέσθαι ἕνα τούτων.
[9]of him [5]with [6]us [3]to become [1]one* [2]of these.
23 Καὶ ἔστησαν δύο, Ἰωσὴφ τὸν καλού-
And they set two, Joseph the [one] *being*
μενον Βαρσαββᾶν, ὃς ἐπεκλήθη Ἰοῦστος,
called Barsabbas, who was surnamed Justus,
καὶ Μαθθίαν. **24** καὶ προσευξάμενοι εἶπαν·
and Matthias. And praying they said:
σὺ κύριε καρδιογνῶστα πάντων, ἀνάδειξον
Thou Lord Heart-knower of all men, show
ὃν ἐξελέξω ἐκ τούτων τῶν δύο ἕνα
whom thou didst choose of these – two one
25 λαβεῖν τὸν τόπον τῆς διακονίας ταύτης
to take the place of this ministry
καὶ ἀποστολῆς, ἀφ' ἧς παρέβη Ἰούδας
and apostleship, from which fell Judas
πορευθῆναι εἰς τὸν τόπον τὸν ἴδιον.
to go to the(his) place – own.
26 καὶ ἔδωκαν κλήρους αὐτοῖς, καὶ ἔπεσεν
And they gave lots for them, and fell
ὁ κλῆρος ἐπὶ Μαθθίαν, καὶ συγκατεψηφίσθη
the lot on Matthias, and he was reckoned along *with*
μετὰ τῶν ἕνδεκα ἀποστόλων.
with the eleven apostles.

spilled out. 19Everyone in
Jerusalem heard about this,
so they called that field in
their language Akeldama,
that is, Field of Blood.)
20"For," said Peter, "it is
written in the book of
Psalms,
" 'May his place be
deserted;
let there be no one to
dwell in it,'[d]
and,
" 'May another take his
place of
leadership.'[e]
21Therefore it is necessary
to choose one of the men
who have been with us the
whole time the Lord Jesus
went in and out among us,
22beginning from John's
baptism to the time when
Jesus was taken up from
us. For one of these must
become a witness with us
of his resurrection."
23So they proposed two
men: Joseph called Barsabbas (also known as Justus)
and Matthias. 24Then they
prayed, "Lord, you know
everyone's heart. Show us
which of these two you
have chosen 25to take over
this apostolic ministry,
which Judas left to go
where he belongs." 26Then
they cast lots, and the lot
fell to Matthias; so he was
added to the eleven apos-
tles.

Chapter 2

The Day of Pentecost

AND when the day of
Pentecost had come,
they were all together in
one place.
2And suddenly there
came from heaven a noise
like a violent, rushing

2 Καὶ ἐν τῷ συμπληροῦσθαι τὴν ἡμέραν
And in the to be completed the day
=when the day of Pentecost was completed
τῆς πεντηκοστῆς ἦσαν πάντες ὁμοῦ ἐπὶ
– of Pentecost[e] they were all *together* to-
τὸ αὐτό· **2** καὶ ἐγένετο ἄφνω ἐκ τοῦ
gether;† and there was suddenly out of –
οὐρανοῦ ἦχος ὥσπερ φερομένης πνοῆς
heaven a sound as [5]being borne [1]of [2]a [4]wind

Chapter 2

The Holy Spirit Comes at Pentecost

WHEN the day of Pen-
tecost came, they
were all together in one
place. 2Suddenly a sound
like the blowing of a violent

* The object (according to the Greek construction) of the verb δεῖ is ἕνα, with μάρτυρα as its complement after γενέσθαι.

[d]20 Psalm 69:25
[e]20 Psalm 109:8

wind, and it filled the whole
house where they were sitting.
3And there appeared to
them tongues as of fire distributing themselves, and
they rested on each one of
them.
4And they were all filled
with the Holy Spirit and began to speak with other
tongues, as the Spirit was
giving them utterance.
5Now there were Jews
living in Jerusalem, devout
men, from every nation under heaven.
6And when this sound
occurred, the multitude
came together, and were
bewildered, because they
were each one hearing
them speak in his own language.
7And they were amazed
and marveled, saying,
"Why, are not all these
who are speaking Gali-
leans?
8"And how is it that we
each hear *them* in our own
language to which we were
born?
9"Parthians and Medes
and Elamites, and residents
of Mesopotamia, Judea and
Cappadocia, Pontus and
Asia,
10Phrygia and Pamphylia,
Egypt and the districts of
Libya around Cyrene, and
visitors from Rome, both
Jews and [a]proselytes,
11Cretans and Arabs—we
hear them in our *own*
tongues speaking of the
mighty deeds of God."
12And they all continued
in amazement and great
perplexity, saying to one
another, "What does this
mean?"
13But others were mock-
ing and saying, "They are
full of sweet wine."

Peter's Sermon

14But Peter, taking his
stand with the eleven,
raised his voice and de-

[a]I.e., Gentile converts to Judaism

βιαίας καὶ ἐπλήρωσεν ὅλον τὸν οἶκον
[3]violent and it filled all the house

οὗ ἦσαν καθήμενοι, 3 καὶ ὤφθησαν αὐτοῖς
where they were sitting, and there appeared to them

διαμεριζόμεναι γλῶσσαι ὡσεὶ πυρός, καὶ
being distributed tongues as of fire, and

ἐκάθισεν ἐφʼ ἕνα ἕκαστον αὐτῶν, 4 καὶ
it sat on [2]one [1]each of them, and

ἐπλήσθησαν πάντες πνεύματος ἁγίου, καὶ
they were filled all of(with) Spirit Holy, and

ἤρξαντο λαλεῖν ἑτέραις γλώσσαις καθὼς
began to speak in other tongues as

τὸ πνεῦμα ἐδίδου ἀποφθέγγεσθαι αὐτοῖς.
the Spirit gave [2]to speak out [1]them.

5 Ἦσαν δὲ εἰς Ἰερουσαλὴμ κατοικοῦντες
Now there were in Jerusalem dwelling

Ἰουδαῖοι, ἄνδρες εὐλαβεῖς ἀπὸ παντὸς ἔθνους
Jews, men devout from every nation

τῶν ὑπὸ τὸν οὐρανόν· 6 γενομένης
of the [ones] under – heaven; happening

δὲ τῆς φωνῆς ταύτης συνῆλθεν τὸ πλῆθος
and this sound[a] came together the multitude
[a]=when this sound happened

καὶ συνεχύθη, ὅτι ἤκουον εἷς ἕκαστος
and were confounded, because they heard [4]one [3]each

τῇ ἰδίᾳ διαλέκτῳ λαλούντων αὐτῶν.
[5]in his own language [2]speaking [1]them.

7 ἐξίσταντο δὲ καὶ ἐθαύμαζον λέγοντες·
And they were amazed and marvelled saying:

οὐχὶ ἰδοὺ πάντες οὗτοί εἰσιν οἱ λαλοῦντες
[3]not [1]behold [4]all [5]these [2]are [6]the [ones] [7]speaking

Γαλιλαῖοι; 8 καὶ πῶς ἡμεῖς ἀκούομεν
[8]Galilæans? and how [2]we [1]hear

ἕκαστος τῇ ἰδίᾳ διαλέκτῳ ἡμῶν ἐν ᾗ
[3]each [5]in his own language [4]of us in which

ἐγεννήθημεν, 9 Πάρθοι καὶ Μῆδοι καὶ
we were born, Parthians and Medes and

Ἐλαμῖται, καὶ οἱ κατοικοῦντες τὴν
Elamites, and the [ones] inhabiting –

Μεσοποταμίαν, Ἰουδαίαν τε καὶ Καππα-
Mesopotamia, both Judæa and Cappa-

δοκίαν, Πόντον καὶ τὴν Ἀσίαν, 10 Φρυγίαν
docia, Pontus and – Asia, Phrygia

τε καὶ Παμφυλίαν, Αἴγυπτον καὶ τὰ
both and Pamphylia, Egypt and the

μέρη τῆς Λιβύης τῆς κατὰ Κυρήνην,
regions – of Libya – over against Cyrene,

καὶ οἱ ἐπιδημοῦντες Ῥωμαῖοι, 11 Ἰουδαῖοί
and the temporarily residing Romans, [2]Jews

τε καὶ προσήλυτοι, Κρῆτες καὶ Ἄραβες,
[1]both and proselytes, Cretans and Arabians,

ἀκούομεν λαλούντων αὐτῶν ταῖς ἡμετέραις
we hear [2]speaking [1]them in *the* our

γλώσσαις τὰ μεγαλεῖα τοῦ θεοῦ;
tongues the great deeds – of God?

12 ἐξίσταντο δὲ πάντες καὶ διηποροῦντο,
And were amazed all and were troubled,

ἄλλος πρὸς ἄλλον λέγοντες· τί θέλει
other to other saying: What wishes

τοῦτο εἶναι; 13 ἕτεροι δὲ διαχλευάζοντες
this to be? But others mocking

ἔλεγον ὅτι γλεύκους μεμεστωμένοι εἰσίν.
said[,] – Of(with) sweet wine *having been* filled they are.

14 Σταθεὶς δὲ ὁ Πέτρος σὺν τοῖς ἕνδεκα
But standing – Peter with the eleven

ἐπῆρεν τὴν φωνὴν αὐτοῦ καὶ ἀπεφθέγξατο
lifted up the voice of him and spoke out

wind came from heaven
and filled the whole house
where they were sitting.
3They saw what seemed to
be tongues of fire that separated and came to rest on
each of them. 4All of them
were filled with the Holy
Spirit and began to speak in
other tongues[f] as the Spirit
enabled them.
5Now there were staying
in Jerusalem God-fearing
Jews from every nation under heaven. 6When they
heard this sound, a crowd
came together in bewilderment, because each one
heard them speaking in his
own language. 7Utterly
amazed, they asked: "Are
not all these men who are
speaking Galileans? 8Then
how is it that each of us
hears them in his own na-
tive language? 9Parthians,
Medes and Elamites; resi-
dents of Mesopotamia, Ju-
dea and Cappadocia, Pon-
tus and Asia, 10Phrygia and
Pamphylia, Egypt and the
parts of Libya near Cyrene;
visitors from Rome 11(both
Jews and converts to Judaism); Cretans and Arabs—
we hear them declaring the
wonders of God in our own
tongues!" 12Amazed and
perplexed, they asked one
another, "What does this
mean?"
13Some, however, made
fun of them and said,
"They have had too much
wine.[g]"

Peter Addresses the Crowd

14Then Peter stood up
with the Eleven, raised his
voice and addressed the

[f]4 Or *languages*; also in verse 11
[g]13 Or *sweet wine*

clared to them: "Men of Judea, and all you who live in Jerusalem, let this be known to you, and give heed to my words.
15"For these men are not drunk, as you suppose, for it is *only* the [b]third hour of the day;
16but this is what was spoken of through the prophet Joel:
17 'AND IT SHALL BE IN THE LAST DAYS,' God says,
'THAT I WILL POUR FORTH OF MY SPIRIT UPON ALL MANKIND;
AND YOUR SONS AND YOUR DAUGHTERS SHALL PROPHESY,
AND YOUR YOUNG MEN SHALL SEE VISIONS,
AND YOUR OLD MEN SHALL DREAM DREAMS;
18 EVEN UPON MY BONDSLAVES, BOTH MEN AND WOMEN,
I WILL IN THOSE DAYS POUR FORTH OF MY SPIRIT
And they shall prophesy.
19 'AND I WILL GRANT WONDERS IN THE SKY ABOVE,
AND SIGNS ON THE EARTH BENEATH,
BLOOD, AND FIRE, AND VAPOR OF SMOKE.
20 'THE SUN SHALL BE TURNED INTO DARKNESS,
AND THE MOON INTO BLOOD,
BEFORE THE GREAT AND GLORIOUS DAY OF THE LORD SHALL COME.
21 'AND IT SHALL BE, THAT EVERYONE WHO CALLS ON THE NAME OF THE LORD SHALL BE SAVED.'
22"Men of Israel, listen to these words: Jesus the Nazarene, a man attested to you by God with miracles and wonders and signs which God performed through Him in your midst, just as you yourselves know—
23this *Man*, delivered up by the predetermined plan and foreknowledge of God, you nailed to a cross by the

[b]I.e., 9 a.m.

αὐτοῖς·
to them :
Ἄνδρες Ἰουδαῖοι καὶ οἱ κατοικοῦντες
Men Jews and the [ones] inhabiting
Ἰερουσαλὴμ πάντες, τοῦτο ὑμῖν γνωστὸν
Jerusalem all, this to you known
ἔστω, καὶ ἐνωτίσασθε τὰ ῥήματά μου.
let be, and give ear to the words of me.
15 οὐ γὰρ ὡς ὑμεῖς ὑπολαμβάνετε οὗτοι
For not as ye imagine these men
μεθύουσιν, ἔστιν γὰρ ὥρα τρίτη τῆς
are drunk, for it is hour third of the
ἡμέρας, 16 ἀλλὰ τοῦτό ἐστιν τὸ εἰρημένον
day, but this is the thing having been spoken
διὰ τοῦ προφήτου Ἰωήλ· 17 καὶ ἔσται
through the prophet Joel : And it shall be
ἐν ταῖς ἐσχάταις ἡμέραις, λέγει ὁ θεός,
in the last days, says – God,
ἐκχεῶ ἀπὸ τοῦ πνεύματός μου ἐπὶ
I will pour out from the Spirit of me on
πᾶσαν σάρκα, καὶ προφητεύσουσιν οἱ υἱοὶ
all flesh, and will prophesy the sons
ὑμῶν καὶ αἱ θυγατέρες ὑμῶν, καὶ οἱ
of you and the daughters of you, and the
νεανίσκοι ὑμῶν ὁράσεις ὄψονται, καὶ οἱ
young men of you visions will see, and the
πρεσβύτεροι ὑμῶν ἐνυπνίοις ἐνυπνιασθήσονται·
old men of you dreams will dream;
18 καί γε ἐπὶ τοὺς δούλους μου καὶ ἐπὶ
and – on the male slaves of me and on
τὰς δούλας μου ἐν ταῖς ἡμέραις ἐκείναις
the female slaves of me in those days
ἐκχεῶ ἀπὸ τοῦ πνεύματός μου, καὶ
I will pour out from the Spirit of me, and
προφητεύσουσιν. 19 καὶ δώσω τέρατα ἐν
they will prophesy. And I will give wonders in
τῷ οὐρανῷ ἄνω καὶ σημεῖα ἐπὶ τῆς
the heaven above and signs on the
γῆς κάτω, αἷμα καὶ πῦρ καὶ ἀτμίδα
earth below, blood and fire and vapour
καπνοῦ. 20 ὁ ἥλιος μεταστραφήσεται εἰς
of smoke. The sun will be turned into
σκότος καὶ ἡ σελήνη εἰς αἷμα, πρὶν
darkness and the moon into blood, before
ἐλθεῖν ἡμέραν κυρίου τὴν μεγάλην καὶ
[7]to come(comes) [5]day [6]of [the] Lord [1]the [2]great [3]and
ἐπιφανῆ. 21 καὶ ἔσται πᾶς ὃς ἐὰν
[4]notable.[b] And it will be everyone whoever
ἐπικαλέσηται τὸ ὄνομα κυρίου σωθήσεται.
invokes the name of [the] Lord will be saved.
22 Ἄνδρες Ἰσραηλῖται, ἀκούσατε τοὺς
Men Israelites, hear ye –
λόγους τούτους· Ἰησοῦν τὸν Ναζωραῖον,
words these: Jesus the Nazarene,
ἄνδρα ἀποδεδειγμένον ἀπὸ τοῦ θεοῦ εἰς
a man *having been* approved from – God among
ὑμᾶς δυνάμεσι καὶ τέρασι καὶ σημείοις,
you by powerful deeds and wonders and signs,
οἷς ἐποίησεν δι' αὐτοῦ ὁ θεὸς ἐν μέσῳ
which did through him – God in [the] midst
ὑμῶν, καθὼς αὐτοὶ οἴδατε, 23 τοῦτον
of you, as [your]selves ye know, this man
τῇ ὡρισμένῃ βουλῇ καὶ προγνώσει τοῦ
[2]by the [3]*having been* fixed [4]counsel [5]and [6]foreknowledge –
θεοῦ ἔκδοτον διὰ χειρὸς ἀνόμων
[7]of God [1]given up [9]through [10][the] hand [11]of lawless men

crowd: "Fellow Jews and all of you who live in Jerusalem, let me explain this to you; listen carefully to what I say. 15These men are not drunk, as you suppose. It's only nine in the morning! 16No, this is what was spoken by the prophet Joel:
17" 'In the last days, God says,
I will pour out my Spirit on all people.
Your sons and daughters will prophesy,
your young men will see visions,
your old men will dream dreams.
18Even on my servants, both men and women,
I will pour out my Spirit in those days,
and they will prophesy.
19I will show wonders in the heaven above
and signs on the earth below,
blood and fire and billows of smoke.
20The sun will be turned to darkness
and the moon to blood
before the coming of the great and glorious day of the Lord.
21And everyone who calls on the name of the Lord will be saved.'[h]
22"Men of Israel, listen to this: Jesus of Nazareth was a man accredited by God to you by miracles, wonders and signs, which God did among you through him, as you yourselves know. 23This man was handed over to you by God's set purpose and foreknowledge; and you, with the help of wicked men,[i] put him to death by nailing him

[h]*21* Joel 2:28-32
[i]*23* Or *of those not having the law* (that is, Gentiles)

hands of godless men and put *Him* to death.
24"And God raised Him up again, putting an end to the agony of death, since it was impossible for Him to be held in its power.
25"For David says of Him,
'I WAS ALWAYS BEHOLDING THE LORD IN MY PRESENCE;
FOR HE IS AT MY RIGHT HAND, THAT I MAY NOT BE SHAKEN.
26 'THEREFORE MY HEART WAS GLAD AND MY TONGUE EXULTED;
MOREOVER MY FLESH ALSO WILL ABIDE IN HOPE;
27 BECAUSE THOU WILT NOT ABANDON MY SOUL TO HADES,
NOR ALLOW THY HOLY ONE TO UNDERGO DECAY.
28 'THOU HAST MADE KNOWN TO ME THE WAYS OF LIFE;
THOU WILT MAKE ME FULL OF GLADNESS WITH THY PRESENCE.'
29"Brethren, I may confidently say to you regarding the patriarch David that he both died and was buried, and his tomb is with us to this day.
30"And so, because he was a prophet, and knew that GOD HAD SWORN TO HIM WITH AN OATH TO SEAT *one* OF HIS DESCENDANTS UPON HIS THRONE,
31he looked ahead and spoke of the resurrection of [c]the Christ, that HE WAS NEITHER ABANDONED TO HADES, NOR DID His flesh SUFFER DECAY.
32"This Jesus God raised up again, to which we are all witnesses.
33"Therefore having been exalted to the right hand of God, and having received from the Father the promise of the Holy Spirit, He has poured forth this which you both see and hear.
34"For it was not David

[c]I.e., the Messiah

προσπήξαντες ἀνείλατε, 24 ὃν ὁ θεὸς
[8]fastening* [12]ye killed, whom – God
ἀνέστησεν λύσας τὰς ὠδῖνας τοῦ θανάτου,
raised up loosening the pangs – of death,
καθότι οὐκ ἦν δυνατὸν κρατεῖσθαι αὐτὸν
because it was not possible [2]to be held [1]him
ὑπ' αὐτοῦ. 25 Δαυὶδ γὰρ λέγει εἰς
by it. For David says [as] to
αὐτόν· προορώμην τὸν κύριον ἐνώπιόν
him: I foresaw the Lord before
μου διὰ παντός, ὅτι ἐκ δεξιῶν μού
me always, because on right of me
ἐστιν, ἵνα μὴ σαλευθῶ. 26 διὰ τοῦτο
he is, lest I be moved. Therefore
ηὐφράνθη μου ἡ καρδία καὶ ἠγαλλιάσατο
was glad of me the heart and exulted
ἡ γλῶσσά μου, ἔτι δὲ καὶ ἡ σάρξ
the tongue of me, and now also the flesh
μου κατασκηνώσει ἐπ' ἐλπίδι, 27 ὅτι οὐκ
of me will dwell on(in) hope, because not
ἐγκαταλείψεις τὴν ψυχήν μου εἰς ᾅδην
thou wilt abandon the soul of me in hades
οὐδὲ δώσεις τὸν ὅσιόν σου ἰδεῖν
nor wilt thou give the holy one of thee to see
διαφθοράν. 28 ἐγνώρισάς μοι ὁδοὺς ζωῆς,
corruption. Thou madest known to me ways of life,
πληρώσεις με εὐφροσύνης μετὰ τοῦ προσώ-
thou wilt fill me of(with) gladness with the pres-
που σου. 29 Ἄνδρες ἀδελφοί, ἐξὸν εἰπεῖν
ence of thee. *Men* brothers, it is permitted to speak
μετὰ παρρησίας πρὸς ὑμᾶς περὶ τοῦ
with plainness to you concerning the
πατριάρχου Δαυίδ, ὅτι καὶ ἐτελεύτησεν
patriarch David, that both he died
καὶ ἐτάφη, καὶ τὸ μνῆμα αὐτοῦ ἔστιν
and was buried, and the tomb of him is
ἐν ἡμῖν ἄχρι τῆς ἡμέρας ταύτης.
among us until this day.
30 προφήτης οὖν ὑπάρχων καὶ εἰδὼς ὅτι
A prophet therefore being and knowing that
ὅρκῳ ὤμοσεν αὐτῷ ὁ θεὸς ἐκ καρποῦ
with an oath swore to him – God of [the] fruit
τῆς ὀσφύος αὐτοῦ καθίσαι ἐπὶ τὸν θρόνον
of the loin[s] of him to sit on the throne
αὐτοῦ, 31 προϊδὼν ἐλάλησεν περὶ τῆς
of him, foreseeing he spoke concerning the
ἀναστάσεως τοῦ Χριστοῦ, ὅτι οὔτε
resurrection of the Christ, that neither
ἐγκατελείφθη εἰς ᾅδην οὔτε ἡ σὰρξ
he was abandoned in hades nor the flesh
αὐτοῦ εἶδεν διαφθοράν. 32 τοῦτον τὸν
of him saw corruption. This –
Ἰησοῦν ἀνέστησεν ὁ θεός, οὗ πάντες
Jesus [2]raised up – [1]God, of which all
ἡμεῖς ἐσμεν μάρτυρες· 33 τῇ δεξιᾷ οὖν
we are witnesses; to the right [hand] therefore
τοῦ θεοῦ ὑψωθεὶς τήν τε ἐπαγγελίαν
– of God having been exalted [6]the [1]and [7]promise
τοῦ πνεύματος τοῦ ἁγίου λαβὼν παρὰ
[8]of the [10]Spirit – [9]Holy [2]receiving [3]from
τοῦ πατρὸς ἐξέχεεν τοῦτο ὃ ὑμεῖς καὶ
[4]the [5]Father he poured out this which ye both
βλέπετε καὶ ἀκούετε. 34 οὐ γὰρ Δαυὶδ
see and hear. For not David

* That is, to a tree; see ch. 5. 30.

to the cross. 24But God
raised him from the dead,
freeing him from the agony
of death, because it was impossible for death to keep
its hold on him. 25David
said about him:

"'I saw the Lord always
before me.
Because he is at my
right hand,
I will not be shaken.
26Therefore my heart is
glad and my tongue
rejoices;
my body also will live
in hope,
27because you will not
abandon me to the
grave,
nor will you let your
Holy One see
decay.
28You have made known
to me the paths of
life;
you will fill me with joy
in your presence.'[j]

29"Brothers, I can tell
you confidently that the patriarch David died and was
buried, and his tomb is here
to this day. 30But he was a
prophet and knew that God
had promised him on oath
that he would place one of
his descendants on his
throne. 31Seeing what was
ahead, he spoke of the resurrection of the Christ,[k]
that he was not abandoned
to the grave, nor did his
body see decay. 32God has
raised this Jesus to life, and
we are all witnesses of the
fact. 33Exalted to the right
hand of God, he has re-
ceived from the Father the
promised Holy Spirit and
has poured out what you
now see and hear. 34For
David did not ascend to

[j]*28* Psalm 16:8-11
[k]*31* Or *Messiah*. "The Christ" (Greek) and "the Messiah" (Hebrew) both mean "the Anointed One"; also in verse 36.

who ascended into heaven,
but he himself says:
'THE LORD SAID TO MY
LORD,
"SIT AT MY RIGHT
HAND,
35 UNTIL I MAKE THINE
ENEMIES A FOOTSTOOL
FOR THY FEET." '
36"Therefore let all the
house of Israel know for
certain that God has made
Him both Lord and
Christ—this Jesus whom
you crucified."

The Ingathering

37Now when they heard
this, they were pierced to
the heart, and said to Peter
and the rest of the apostles,
"Brethren, what shall we
do?"
38And Peter *said* to them,
"Repent, and let each of
you be baptized in the
name of Jesus Christ for the
forgiveness of your sins;
and you shall receive the
gift of the Holy Spirit.
39"For the promise is for
you and your children, and
for all who are far off, as
many as the Lord our God
shall call to Himself."
40And with many other
words he solemnly testified
and kept on exhorting
them, saying, "Be saved
from this perverse generation!"
41So then, those who had
received his word were
baptized; and there were
added that day about three
thousand [d]souls.
42And they were continu-
ally devoting themselves to
the apostles' teaching and
to fellowship, to the breaking of bread and to prayer.
43And everyone kept feel-
ing a sense of awe; and
many wonders and signs
were taking place through
the apostles[e].
44And all those who had
believed [f]were together,
and had all things in common;
45and they *began* selling
their property and posses-

ἀνέβη εἰς τοὺς οὐρανούς, λέγει δὲ αὐτός·
ascended to the heavens, but says he:
εἶπεν κύριος τῷ κυρίῳ μου· κάθου ἐκ
Said [the] LORD to the Lord of me: Sit at
δεξιῶν μου, 35 ἕως ἂν θῶ τοὺς ἐχθρούς
right of me, until I put the enemies
σου ὑποπόδιον τῶν ποδῶν σου. 36 ἀσφαλῶς
of thee a footstool of the feet of thee. Assuredly
οὖν γινωσκέτω πᾶς οἶκος Ἰσραὴλ ὅτι
therefore [1]let [6]know [2]all [3][the] [4]house [5]of Israel that
καὶ κύριον αὐτὸν καὶ χριστὸν ἐποίησεν
[4]both [5]Lord [3]him [6]and [7]Christ [2]made
ὁ θεός, τοῦτον τὸν Ἰησοῦν ὃν ὑμεῖς
– [1]God, this – Jesus whom ye
ἐσταυρώσατε. 37 Ἀκούσαντες δὲ κατενύγ-
crucified. And hearing they were
ησαν τὴν καρδίαν, εἶπόν τε πρὸς τὸν
stung [in] the heart, and said to –
Πέτρον καὶ τοὺς λοιποὺς ἀποστόλους·
Peter and the remaining apostles:
τί ποιήσωμεν, ἄνδρες ἀδελφοί; 38 Πέτρος
What may we do, *men* brothers? Peter
δὲ πρὸς αὐτούς· μετανοήσατε, καὶ
And to them: Repent ye, and
βαπτισθήτω ἕκαστος ὑμῶν ἐπὶ τῷ ὀνόματι
let be baptized each of you on the name
Ἰησοῦ Χριστοῦ εἰς ἄφεσιν τῶν
of Jesus Christ [with a view] to forgiveness of the
ἁμαρτιῶν ὑμῶν, καὶ λήμψεσθε τὴν δωρεὰν
sins of you, and ye will receive the gift
τοῦ ἁγίου πνεύματος. 39 ὑμῖν γάρ ἐστιν
of the Holy Spirit. For to you is
ἡ ἐπαγγελία καὶ τοῖς τέκνοις ὑμῶν καὶ
the promise and to the children of you and
πᾶσιν τοῖς εἰς μακράν, ὅσους ἂν
to all the [ones] far away, as many as
προσκαλέσηται κύριος ὁ θεὸς ἡμῶν.
may call to [him] [the] Lord the God of us.
40 ἑτέροις τε λόγοις πλείοσιν διεμαρτύρατο,
And with other words many he solemnly witnessed,
καὶ παρεκάλει αὐτοὺς λέγων· σώθητε
and exhorted them saying: Be ye saved
ἀπὸ τῆς γενεᾶς τῆς σκολιᾶς ταύτης. 41 οἱ
from – [3]generation – [2]perverse [1]this. The [ones]
μὲν οὖν ἀποδεξάμενοι τὸν λόγον αὐτοῦ
– therefore welcoming the word of him
ἐβαπτίσθησαν, καὶ προσετέθησαν ἐν
were baptized, and there were added in
τῇ ἡμέρᾳ ἐκείνῃ ψυχαὶ ὡσεὶ τρισχίλιαι·
that day souls about three thousand;
42 ἦσαν δὲ προσκαρτεροῦντες τῇ διδαχῇ
and they were continuing steadfastly in the teaching
τῶν ἀποστόλων καὶ τῇ κοινωνίᾳ, τῇ
of the apostles and in the fellowship, in the
κλάσει τοῦ ἄρτου καὶ ταῖς προσευχαῖς.
breaking of the loaf and in the prayers.
43 Ἐγίνετο δὲ πάσῃ ψυχῇ φόβος· πολλὰ δὲ
And came to every soul fear; and many
τέρατα καὶ σημεῖα διὰ τῶν ἀποστόλων
wonders and signs through the apostles
ἐγίνετο. 44 πάντες δὲ οἱ πιστεύσαντες
happened. And all the believing [ones]
ἐπὶ τὸ αὐτὸ εἶχον ἅπαντα κοινά, 45 καὶ
together had all things common, and
τὰ κτήματα καὶ τὰς ὑπάρξεις ἐπίπρασκον
the properties and the possessions they sold

heaven, and yet he said,
" 'The Lord said to my
Lord:
"Sit at my right hand
35until I make your
enemies
a footstool for your
feet." '[l]
36"Therefore let all Israel
be assured of this: God has
made this Jesus, whom you
crucified, both Lord and
Christ."
37When the people heard
this, they were cut to the
heart and said to Peter and
the other apostles, "Brothers, what shall we do?"
38Peter replied, "Repent
and be baptized, every one
of you, in the name of Jesus
Christ for the forgiveness
of your sins. And you will
receive the gift of the Holy
Spirit. 39The promise is for
you and your children and
for all who are far off—for
all whom the Lord our God
will call."
40With many other words
he warned them; and he
pleaded with them, "Save
yourselves from this cor-
rupt generation." 41Those
who accepted his message
were baptized, and about
three thousand were added
to their number that day.

The Fellowship of the Believers

42They devoted them-
selves to the apostles'
teaching and to the fellowship, to the breaking of
bread and to prayer. 43Ev-
eryone was filled with awe,
and many wonders and mi-
raculous signs were done
by the apostles. 44All the
believers were together and
had everything in common.
45Selling their possessions

[d]I.e., persons
[e]Some ancient mss. add *in Jerusalem; and great fear was upon all*
[f]Some ancient mss. do not contain *were*

[l]*35* Psalm 110:1

sions, and were sharing them with all, as anyone might have need.
46And day by day continuing with one mind in the temple, and breaking bread from house to house, they were taking their meals together with gladness and sincerity of heart,
47praising God, and having favor with all the people. And the Lord was adding to their number day by day those who were being saved.

Chapter 3

Healing the Lame Beggar

NOW Peter and John were going up to the temple at the [g]ninth *hour*, the hour of prayer.
2And a certain man who had been lame from his mother's womb was being carried along, whom they used to set down every day at the gate of the temple which is called Beautiful, in order to beg [h]alms of those who were entering the temple.
3And when he saw Peter and John about to go into the temple, he *began* asking to receive alms.
4And Peter, along with John, fixed his gaze upon him and said, "Look at us!"
5And he *began* to give them his attention, expecting to receive something from them.
6But Peter said, "I do not possess silver and gold, but what I do have I give to you: In the name of Jesus Christ the Nazarene—walk!"
7And seizing him by the right hand, he raised him up; and immediately his feet and his ankles were strengthened.
8And with a leap, he stood upright and *began* to walk; and he entered the temple with them, walking and leaping and praising

[g] I.e., 3 p.m.
[h] Or, *a gift of charity*

καὶ διεμέριζον αὐτὰ πᾶσιν, καθότι ἄν
and distributed them to all, according as
τις χρείαν εἶχεν. **46** καθ' ἡμέραν τε
anyone need had. And from day to day†
προσκαρτεροῦντες ὁμοθυμαδὸν ἐν τῷ ἱερῷ,
continuing steadfastly with one mind in the temple,
κλῶντές τε κατ' οἶκον ἄρτον, μετε-
and [1]breaking [3]from house to house† [2]bread, they
λάμβανον τροφῆς ἐν ἀγαλλιάσει καὶ
shared food in gladness and
ἀφελότητι καρδίας, **47** αἰνοῦντες τὸν θεὸν
simplicity of heart, praising – God
καὶ ἔχοντες χάριν πρὸς ὅλον τὸν λαόν.
and having favour with all the people.
ὁ δὲ κύριος προσετίθει τοὺς σῳζομένους
And the Lord added the [ones] being saved
καθ' ἡμέραν ἐπὶ τὸ αὐτό.
from day to day† together.†

3 Πέτρος δὲ καὶ Ἰωάννης ἀνέβαινον
Now Peter and John were going up
εἰς τὸ ἱερὸν ἐπὶ τὴν ὥραν τῆς προσευχῆς
to the temple at the hour of the prayer
τὴν ἐνάτην. **2** καί τις ἀνὴρ χωλὸς ἐκ
the ninth. And a certain man [2]lame [3]from
κοιλίας μητρὸς αὐτοῦ ὑπάρχων ἐβαστάζετο,
[4][the] womb [5]of [the] mother [6]of him [1]being was being carried,
ὃν ἐτίθουν καθ' ἡμέραν πρὸς τὴν θύραν
whom they used to put from day to day† at the door
τοῦ ἱεροῦ τὴν λεγομένην ὡραίαν τοῦ
of the temple – *being* called Beautiful –
αἰτεῖν ἐλεημοσύνην παρὰ τῶν εἰσπορευομέ-
to ask[d] alms from the [ones] enter-
νων εἰς τὸ ἱερόν· **3** ὃς ἰδὼν Πέτρον καὶ
ing into the temple; who seeing Peter and
Ἰωάννην μέλλοντας εἰσιέναι εἰς τὸ ἱερὸν
John being about to go *in* into the temple
ἠρώτα ἐλεημοσύνην λαβεῖν. **4** ἀτενίσας δὲ
asked alms to receive. And [2]gazing
Πέτρος εἰς αὐτὸν σὺν τῷ Ἰωάννῃ εἶπεν·
[1]Peter at him with – John said:
βλέψον εἰς ἡμᾶς. **5** ὁ δὲ ἐπεῖχεν αὐτοῖς
Look at us. And he paid heed to them
προσδοκῶν τι παρ' αὐτῶν λαβεῖν. **6** εἶπεν
expecting something from them to receive. said
δὲ Πέτρος· ἀργύριον καὶ χρυσίον οὐχ
And Peter: Silver and gold not
ὑπάρχει μοι· ὃ δὲ ἔχω, τοῦτό σοι δίδωμι·
is to me[c]; but what I have, this to thee I give;
=I have not;
ἐν τῷ ὀνόματι Ἰησοῦ Χριστοῦ τοῦ
in the name of Jesus Christ the
Ναζωραίου περιπάτει. **7** καὶ πιάσας αὐτὸν τῆς
Nazarene walk. And seizing him of(by)
δεξιᾶς χειρὸς ἤγειρεν αὐτόν· παραχρῆμα
the right hand he raised him; [2]at once
δὲ ἐστερεώθησαν αἱ βάσεις αὐτοῦ καὶ τὰ
[1]and were made firm the feet of him and the
σφυδρά, **8** καὶ ἐξαλλόμενος ἔστη, καὶ
ankle-bones, and leaping up he stood, and
περιεπάτει, καὶ εἰσῆλθεν σὺν αὐτοῖς εἰς
walked, and entered with them into
τὸ ἱερὸν περιπατῶν καὶ ἁλλόμενος καὶ
the temple walking and leaping and

and goods, they gave to anyone as he had need.
46Every day they continued to meet together in the temple courts. They broke bread in their homes and ate together with glad and sincere hearts, 47praising God and enjoying the favor of all the people. And the Lord added to their number daily those who were being saved.

Chapter 3

Peter Heals the Crippled Beggar

ONE day Peter and John were going up to the temple at the time of prayer —at three in the afternoon.
2Now a man crippled from birth was being carried to the temple gate called Beautiful, where he was put every day to beg from those going into the temple courts. 3When he saw Peter and John about to enter, he asked them for money. 4Peter looked straight at him, as did John. Then Peter said, "Look at us!" 5So the man gave them his attention, expecting to get something from them.
6Then Peter said, "Silver or gold I do not have, but what I have I give you. In the name of Jesus Christ of Nazareth, walk." 7Taking him by the right hand, he helped him up, and instantly the man's feet and ankles became strong. 8He jumped to his feet and began to walk. Then he went with them into the temple courts, walking and jump-

God.
9And all the people saw him walking and praising God;
10and they were taking note of him as being the one who used to sit at the Beautiful Gate of the temple to *beg* alms, and they were filled with wonder and amazement at what had happened to him.

Peter's Second Sermon

11And while he was clinging to Peter and John, all the people ran together to them at the so-called portico of Solomon, full of amazement.
12But when Peter saw *this*, he replied to the people, "Men of Israel, why do you marvel at this, or why do you gaze at us, as if by our own power or piety we had made him walk?
13"The God of Abraham, Isaac, and Jacob, the God of our fathers, has glorified His servant Jesus, *the one* whom you delivered up, and disowned in the presence of Pilate, when he had decided to release Him.
14"But you disowned the Holy and Righteous One, and asked for a murderer to be granted to you,
15but put to death the Prince of life, *the one* whom God raised from the dead, *a fact* to which we are witnesses.
16"And on the basis of faith in His name, *it is* the name of Jesus which has strengthened this man whom you see and know; and the faith which *comes* through Him has given him this perfect health in the presence of you all.
17"And now, brethren, I know that you acted in ignorance, just as your rulers

αἰνῶν τὸν θεόν. **9** καὶ εἶδεν πᾶς ὁ
praising – God. And [4]saw [1]all [2]the
λαὸς αὐτὸν περιπατοῦντα καὶ αἰνοῦντα
[3]people him walking and praising
τὸν θεόν· **10** ἐπεγίνωσκον δὲ αὐτόν, ὅτι
– God; and they recognized him, that
οὗτος ἦν ὁ πρὸς τὴν ἐλεημοσύνην
this was the [one] for – alms
καθήμενος ἐπὶ τῇ ὡραίᾳ πύλῃ τοῦ ἱεροῦ,
sitting at the Beautiful gate of the temple,
καὶ ἐπλήσθησαν θάμβους καὶ ἐκστάσεως
and they were filled of(with) amazement and bewilderment
ἐπὶ τῷ συμβεβηκότι αὐτῷ. **11** Κρατοῦντος δὲ
at the thing having happened to him. And holding =as he held
αὐτοῦ τὸν Πέτρον καὶ τὸν Ἰωάννην
him[a] – Peter and – John
συνέδραμεν πᾶς ὁ λαὸς πρὸς αὐτοὺς
ran together all the people to them
ἐπὶ τῇ στοᾷ τῇ καλουμένῃ Σολομῶντος
at the porch – *being* called of Solomon
ἔκθαμβοι. **12** ἰδὼν δὲ ὁ Πέτρος ἀπεκρίνατο
greatly amazed. And [2]seeing – [1]Peter answered
πρὸς τὸν λαόν· ἄνδρες Ἰσραηλῖται, τί
to the people: *Men* Israelites, why
θαυμάζετε ἐπὶ τούτῳ, ἢ ἡμῖν τί ἀτενίζετε
marvel ye at this man, or at us why gaze ye
ὡς ἰδίᾳ δυνάμει ἢ εὐσεβείᾳ πεποιηκόσιν
as by [our] own power or piety having made
τοῦ περιπατεῖν αὐτόν; **13** ὁ θεὸς Ἀβραὰμ
– to walk[d] him? The God of Abraham
καὶ Ἰσαὰκ καὶ Ἰακώβ, ὁ θεὸς τῶν
and Isaac and Jacob, the God of the
πατέρων ἡμῶν, ἐδόξασεν τὸν παῖδα αὐτοῦ
fathers of us, glorified the servant of him
Ἰησοῦν, ὃν ὑμεῖς μὲν παρεδώκατε καὶ
Jesus, whom ye – delivered and
ἠρνήσασθε κατὰ πρόσωπον Πιλάτου,
denied in [the] presence of Pilate,
κρίναντος ἐκείνου ἀπολύειν· **14** ὑμεῖς δὲ
having decided that one[a] to release [him]; but ye
=when he had decided
τὸν ἅγιον καὶ δίκαιον ἠρνήσασθε, καὶ
the holy and just one denied, and
ᾐτήσασθε ἄνδρα φονέα χαρισθῆναι ὑμῖν,
asked *a man* a murderer to be granted you,
15 τὸν δὲ ἀρχηγὸν τῆς ζωῆς ἀπεκτείνατε,
and the Author – of life ye killed,
ὃν ὁ θεὸς ἤγειρεν ἐκ νεκρῶν, οὗ ἡμεῖς
whom – God raised from [the] dead, of which we
μάρτυρές ἐσμεν. **16** καὶ ἐπὶ τῇ πίστει
witnesses are. And on the faith
τοῦ ὀνόματος αὐτοῦ τοῦτον, ὃν θεωρεῖτε
of(in) the name* of him [5]this man, [6]whom [7]ye behold
καὶ οἴδατε, ἐστερέωσεν τὸ ὄνομα αὐτοῦ,
[8]and [9]know, [4]made firm [1]the [2]name [3]of him,
καὶ ἡ πίστις ἡ δι' αὐτοῦ ἔδωκεν αὐτῷ
and the faith – through him gave him
τὴν ὁλοκληρίαν ταύτην ἀπέναντι πάντων
this soundness before all
ὑμῶν. **17** καὶ νῦν, ἀδελφοί, οἶδα ὅτι
you. And now, brothers, I know that
κατὰ ἄγνοιαν ἐπράξατε, ὥσπερ καὶ οἱ
by way of ignorance ye acted, as also the

* Objective genitive; *cf.* "the fear of God" = the fear which has God for its object; and see Gal. 2. 20, etc.

ing, and praising God. 9When all the people saw him walking and praising God, 10they recognized him as the same man who used to sit begging at the temple gate called Beautiful, and they were filled with wonder and amazement at what had happened to him.

Peter Speaks to the Onlookers

11While the beggar held on to Peter and John, all the people were astonished and came running to them in the place called Solomon's Colonnade. 12When Peter saw this, he said to them: "Men of Israel, why does this surprise you? Why do you stare at us as if by our own power or godliness we had made this man walk? 13The God of Abraham, Isaac and Jacob, the God of our fathers, has glorified his servant Jesus. You handed him over to be killed, and you disowned him before Pilate, though he had decided to let him go. 14You disowned the Holy and Righteous One and asked that a murderer be released to you. 15You killed the author of life, but God raised him from the dead. We are witnesses of this. 16By faith in the name of Jesus, this man whom you see and know was made strong. It is Jesus' name and the faith that comes through him that has given this complete healing to him, as you can all see.
17"Now, brothers, I know that you acted in ignorance, as did your lead-

did also.
18"But the things which
God announced before-
hand by the mouth of all the
prophets, that His Christ
should suffer, He has thus
fulfilled.
19"Repent therefore and
return, that your sins may
be wiped away, in order
that times of refreshing
may come from the pres-
ence of the Lord;
20and that He may send
Jesus, the Christ appointed
for you,
21whom heaven must re-
ceive until *the* period of
restoration of all things
about which God spoke by
the mouth of His holy
prophets from ancient
time.
22"Moses said, 'THE
LORD GOD SHALL RAISE UP
FOR YOU A PROPHET LIKE ME
FROM YOUR BRETHREN; TO
HIM YOU SHALL GIVE HEED in
everything He says to you.
23'And it shall be that
every soul that does not
heed that prophet shall be
utterly destroyed from
among the people.'
24"And likewise, all the
prophets who have spoken,
from Samuel and *his*
successors onward, also
announced these days.
25"It is you who are the
sons of the prophets, and of
the covenant which God
made with your fathers,
saying to Abraham, 'AND
IN YOUR SEED ALL THE FAMI-
LIES OF THE EARTH SHALL BE
BLESSED.'
26"For you first, God
raised up His Servant, and
sent Him to bless you by
turning every one *of you*
from your wicked ways."

Chapter 4

Peter and John Arrested

AND as they were speak-
ing to the people, the
priests and the captain of
the temple *guard*, and the

ἄρχοντες ὑμῶν· 18 ὁ δὲ θεὸς ἃ
rulers of you; – but God the things which
προκατήγγειλεν διὰ στόματος πάντων
he foreannounced through [the] mouth of all
τῶν προφητῶν, παθεῖν τὸν χριστὸν αὐτοῦ,
the prophets, to suffer the Christ of him[b],
=that his Christ was to suffer,
ἐπλήρωσεν οὕτως. 19 μετανοήσατε οὖν
fulfilled thus. Repent ye therefore
καὶ ἐπιστρέψατε πρὸς τὸ ἐξαλειφθῆναι
and turn for the to be wiped away
=that your sins may be wiped away,
ὑμῶν τὰς ἁμαρτίας, 20 ὅπως ἂν ἔλθωσιν
of you the sins, so as may come
καιροὶ ἀναψύξεως ἀπὸ προσώπου τοῦ
times of refreshing from [the] presence of the
κυρίου καὶ ἀποστείλῃ τὸν προκεχειρισμένον
Lord and he may send [1]the [3]*having been* foreappointed
ὑμῖν χριστὸν Ἰησοῦν, 21 ὃν δεῖ οὐρανὸν
[4]for you [2]Christ [5]Jesus, whom it behoves heaven
μὲν δέξασθαι ἄχρι χρόνων ἀποκαταστάσεως
– to receive until [the] times of restitution
πάντων ὧν ἐλάλησεν ὁ θεὸς διὰ στόματος
of all things which [2]spoke – [1]God [3]through [4][the] mouth
τῶν ἁγίων ἀπ' αἰῶνος αὐτοῦ προφητῶν.
[5]of the [6]holy [9]from [10][the] age [8]of him [7]prophets.
22 Μωϋσῆς μὲν εἶπεν ὅτι προφήτην ὑμῖν
Moses indeed said[,] – [4]A prophet [5]for you
ἀναστήσει κύριος ὁ θεὸς ἐκ τῶν ἀδελφῶν
[3]will raise up [1](the) Lord – [2]God of the brothers
ὑμῶν ὡς ἐμέ· αὐτοῦ ἀκούσεσθε κατὰ
of you as me; him shall ye hear according to
πάντα ὅσα ἂν λαλήσῃ πρὸς ὑμᾶς.
all things whatever he may speak to you.
23 ἔσται δὲ πᾶσα ψυχὴ ἥτις ἐὰν μὴ ἀκούσῃ
And it shall be every soul whoever hears not
τοῦ προφήτου ἐκείνου ἐξολεθρευθήσεται
that prophet will be utterly destroyed
ἐκ τοῦ λαοῦ. 24 καὶ πάντες δὲ οἱ
out of the people. [2]also [3]all [1]And the
προφῆται ἀπὸ Σαμουὴλ καὶ τῶν καθεξῆς
prophets from Samuel and the [ones] in order
ὅσοι ἐλάλησαν καὶ κατήγγειλαν τὰς ἡμέρας
as many as spoke also announced – days
ταύτας. 25 ὑμεῖς ἐστε οἱ υἱοὶ τῶν
these. Ye are the sons of the
προφητῶν καὶ τῆς διαθήκης ἧς ὁ θεὸς
prophets and of the covenant which – God
διέθετο πρὸς τοὺς πατέρας ὑμῶν, λέγων
made with the fathers of us, saying
πρὸς Ἀβραάμ· καὶ ἐν τῷ σπέρματί
to Abraham: And in the seed
σου ἐνευλογηθήσονται πᾶσαι αἱ πατριαὶ
of thee shall be blessed all the families
τῆς γῆς. 26 ὑμῖν πρῶτον ἀναστήσας ὁ
of the earth. To you first [2]having raised up –
θεὸς τὸν παῖδα αὐτοῦ ἀπέστειλεν αὐτὸν
[1]God the servant of him sent him
εὐλογοῦντα ὑμᾶς ἐν τῷ ἀποστρέφειν
blessing you in the to turn away
=in turning away
ἕκαστον ἀπὸ τῶν πονηριῶν ὑμῶν.
each one from the iniquities of you.
4 Λαλούντων δὲ αὐτῶν πρὸς τὸν λαόν,
And speaking them[a] to the people,
=while they were speaking
ἐπέστησαν αὐτοῖς οἱ ἱερεῖς καὶ ὁ στρατηγὸς
came upon them the priests and the commandant

ers. 18But this is how God
fulfilled what he had foretold through all the prophets, saying that his Christ[m]
would suffer. 19Repent,
then, and turn to God, so
that your sins may be
wiped out, that times of refreshing may come from
the Lord, 20and that he may
send the Christ, who has
been appointed for you—
even Jesus. 21He must re-
main in heaven until the
time comes for God to re-
store everything, as he
promised long ago through
his holy prophets. 22For
Moses said, 'The Lord
your God will raise up for
you a prophet like me from
among your own people;
you must listen to every-
thing he tells you. 23Any-
one who does not listen to
him will be completely cut
off from among his peo-
ple.'[n]
24"Indeed, all the proph-
ets from Samuel on, as
many as have spoken, have
foretold these days. 25And
you are heirs of the prophets and of the covenant
God made with your fa-
thers. He said to Abraham,
'Through your offspring all
peoples on earth will be
blessed.'[o] 26When God
raised up his servant, he
sent him first to you to
bless you by turning each
of you from your wicked
ways."

Chapter 4

Peter and John Before the Sanhedrin

THE priests and the cap-
tain of the temple
guard and the Sadducees

[m]18 Or *Messiah*; also in verse 20
[n]23 Deut. 18:15,18,19
[o]25 Gen. 22:18; 26:4

Sadducees, came upon
them,
2being greatly disturbed
because they were teaching
the people and proclaiming
in Jesus the resurrection
from the dead.
3And they laid hands on
them, and put them in jail
until the next day, for it was
already evening.
4But many of those who
had heard the message be-
lieved; and the number of
the men came to be about
five thousand.
5And it came about on
the next day, that their rulers and elders and scribes
were gathered together in
Jerusalem;
6and Annas the high
priest *was there*, and Caiaphas and John and Alexan-
der, and all who were of
high-priestly descent.
7And when they had
placed them in the center,
they *began to* inquire, "By
what power, or in what
name, have you done
this?"
8Then Peter, filled with
the Holy Spirit, said to
them, "Rulers and elders
of the people,
9if we are on trial today
for a benefit done to a sick
man, as to how this man
has been made well,
10let it be known to all of
you, and to all the people of
Israel, that by the name of
Jesus Christ the Nazarene,
whom you crucified, whom
God raised from the dead—
by this *name* this man
stands here before you in
good health.
11"He is the STONE WHICH
WAS REJECTED by you, THE
BUILDERS, *but* WHICH
BECAME THE VERY CORNER
stone.
12"And there is salvation
in no one else; for there is
no other name under

τοῦ ἱεροῦ καὶ οἱ Σαδδουκαῖοι, 2 διαπονούμενοι
of the temple and the Sadducees, being greatly troubled
διὰ τὸ διδάσκειν αὐτοὺς τὸν λαὸν καὶ
because of the to teach them[b] the people and
=because they taught . . . announced
καταγγέλλειν ἐν τῷ Ἰησοῦ τὴν ἀνάστασιν
to announce[b] by – Jesus the resurrection
τὴν ἐκ νεκρῶν, 3 καὶ ἐπέβαλον αὐτοῖς
– from [the] dead, and laid on them
τὰς χεῖρας καὶ ἔθεντο εἰς τήρησιν εἰς
the(ir) hands and put in guard till
τὴν αὔριον· ἦν γὰρ ἑσπέρα ἤδη. 4 πολλοὶ
the morrow; for it was evening now. many
δὲ τῶν ἀκουσάντων τὸν λόγον ἐπίστευσαν,
But of the [ones] hearing the word believed,
καὶ ἐγενήθη ἀριθμὸς τῶν ἀνδρῶν ὡς
and became [the] number of the men about
χιλιάδες πέντε.
thousands five.

5 Ἐγένετο δὲ ἐπὶ τὴν αὔριον
Now it came to pass on the morrow
συναχθῆναι αὐτῶν τοὺς ἄρχοντας καὶ τοὺς
to be assembled of them the rulers and the
πρεσβυτέρους καὶ τοὺς γραμματεῖς ἐν
elders and the scribes in
Ἰερουσαλήμ, 6 καὶ Ἅννας ὁ ἀρχιερεὺς
Jerusalem, and Annas* the high priest
καὶ Καϊαφᾶς καὶ Ἰωάννης καὶ Ἀλέξανδρος
and Caiaphas and John and Alexander
καὶ ὅσοι ἦσαν ἐκ γένους ἀρχιερατικοῦ,
and as many as were of [the] race high-priestly,
7 καὶ στήσαντες αὐτοὺς ἐν τῷ μέσῳ
and having stood them in the midst
ἐπυνθάνοντο· ἐν ποίᾳ δυνάμει ἢ ἐν ποίῳ
inquired: By what power or in what
ὀνόματι ἐποιήσατε τοῦτο ὑμεῖς; 8 τότε
name did this ye? Then
Πέτρος πλησθεὶς πνεύματος ἁγίου εἶπεν
Peter filled of(with) [the] Spirit Holy said
πρὸς αὐτούς· ἄρχοντες τοῦ λαοῦ καὶ
to them: Rulers of the people and
πρεσβύτεροι, 9 εἰ ἡμεῖς σήμερον ἀνα-
elders, if we to-day are be-
κρινόμεθα ἐπὶ εὐεργεσίᾳ ἀνθρώπου ἀσθενοῦς,
ing examined on a good deed man of an infirm,
=[done to] an infirm man,
ἐν τίνι οὗτος σέσωσται, 10 γνωστὸν ἔστω
by what this man has been healed, known let it be
πᾶσιν ὑμῖν καὶ παντὶ τῷ λαῷ Ἰσραήλ,
to all you and to all the people of Israel,
ὅτι ἐν τῷ ὀνόματι Ἰησοῦ Χριστοῦ τοῦ
that in the name of Jesus Christ the
Ναζωραίου, ὃν ὑμεῖς ἐσταυρώσατε, ὃν ὁ
Nazarene, whom ye crucified, whom –
θεὸς ἤγειρεν ἐκ νεκρῶν, ἐν τούτῳ οὗτος
God raised from [the] dead, in this [name] this man
παρέστηκεν ἐνώπιον ὑμῶν ὑγιής. 11 οὗτός
stands before you whole. This
ἐστιν ὁ λίθος ὁ ἐξουθενηθεὶς ὑφ' ὑμῶν
is the stone – despised by you
τῶν οἰκοδόμων, ὁ γενόμενος εἰς κεφαλὴν
the [ones] building, the [one] become *to* head
γωνίας. 12 καὶ οὐκ ἔστιν ἐν ἄλλῳ οὐδενὶ
of [the] corner. And there is not ¹in ³other ²no(any)
ἡ σωτηρία· οὐδὲ γὰρ ὄνομά ἐστιν ἕτερον
the salvation: for neither ³name ¹is there ²other

* The rough breathing in the Greek is ignored in the transliteration of some familiar proper names.

came up to Peter and John
while they were speaking
to the people. 2They were
greatly disturbed because
the apostles were teaching
the people and proclaiming
in Jesus the resurrection of
the dead. 3They seized Peter and John, and because it
was evening, they put them
in jail until the next day.
4But many who heard the
message believed, and the
number of men grew to
about five thousand.
5The next day the rulers,
elders and teachers of the
law met in Jerusalem. 6An-
nas the high priest was
there, and so were Caia-
phas, John, Alexander and
the other men of the high
priest's family. 7They had
Peter and John brought before them and began to
question them: "By what
power or what name did
you do this?"
8Then Peter, filled with
the Holy Spirit, said to
them: "Rulers and elders of
the people! 9If we are being
called to account today for
an act of kindness shown to
a cripple and are asked how
he was healed, 10then know
this, you and all the people
of Israel: It is by the name
of Jesus Christ of Naza-
reth, whom you crucified
but whom God raised from
the dead, that this man
stands before you healed.
11He is

" 'the stone you builders
rejected,
which has become the
capstone.'[p] [q]

12Salvation is found in no
one else, for there is no other name under heaven giv-

[p]*11* Or *cornerstone*
[q]*11* Psalm 118:22

heaven that has been given among men, by which we must be saved."

Threat and Release

13Now as they observed the confidence of Peter and John, and understood that they were uneducated and untrained men, they were marveling, and *began* to recognize them as having been with Jesus.

14And seeing the man who had been healed standing with them, they had nothing to say in reply.

15But when they had ordered them to go aside out of the Council, they *began* to confer with one another,

16saying, "What shall we do with these men? For the fact that a noteworthy miracle has taken place through them is apparent to all who live in Jerusalem, and we cannot deny it.

17"But in order that it may not spread any further among the people, let us warn them to speak no more to any man in this name."

18And when they had summoned them, they commanded them not to speak or teach at all in the name of Jesus.

19But Peter and John answered and said to them, "Whether it is right in the sight of God to give heed to you rather than to God, you be the judge;

20for we cannot stop speaking what we have seen and heard."

21And when they had threatened them further, they let them go (finding no basis on which they might punish them) on account of the people, because they were all glorifying God for what had happened;

22for the man was more than forty years old on whom this miracle of healing had been performed.

ὑπὸ τὸν οὐρανὸν τὸ δεδομένον ἐν
under – heaven – having been given among

ἀνθρώποις ἐν ᾧ δεῖ σωθῆναι ἡμᾶς.
men by which it behoves [2]to be saved [1]us.

13 Θεωροῦντες δὲ τὴν τοῦ Πέτρου
And beholding the – of Peter

παρρησίαν καὶ Ἰωάννου, καὶ καταλαβόμενοι
boldness and of John, and perceiving

ὅτι ἄνθρωποι ἀγράμματοί εἰσιν καὶ
that men unlettered they are(were) and

ἰδιῶται, ἐθαύμαζον, ἐπεγίνωσκόν τε αὐτοὺς
laymen, they marvelled, and recognized them

ὅτι σὺν τῷ Ἰησοῦ ἦσαν, **14** τόν τε
that with – Jesus they were(had been), [3]the [1]and

ἄνθρωπον βλέποντες σὺν αὐτοῖς ἑστῶτα τὸν
[4]man [2]seeing [7]with [8]them [6]standing –

τεθεραπευμένον, οὐδὲν εἶχον ἀντειπεῖν.
[5]having been healed, nothing they had to say against.

15 κελεύσαντες δὲ αὐτοὺς ἔξω τοῦ συνεδρίου
So having commanded them outside the council

ἀπελθεῖν, συνέβαλλον πρὸς ἀλλήλους
to go, they discussed *with* with one another

16 λέγοντες· τί ποιήσωμεν τοῖς ἀνθρώποις
saying: What may we do – men

τούτοις; ὅτι μὲν γὰρ γνωστὸν σημεῖον
to these? for that indeed a notable sign

γέγονεν δι' αὐτῶν, πᾶσιν τοῖς κατοικοῦσιν
has happened through them, to all the [ones] inhabiting

Ἰερουσαλὴμ φανερόν, καὶ οὐ δυνάμεθα
Jerusalem [is] manifest, and we cannot

ἀρνεῖσθαι· **17** ἀλλ' ἵνα μὴ ἐπὶ πλεῖον
to deny [it]; but [1]lest [3]more†

διανεμηθῇ εἰς τὸν λαόν, ἀπειλησώμεθα
[2]it is spread abroad [4]to the people, let us threaten

αὐτοῖς μηκέτι λαλεῖν ἐπὶ τῷ ὀνόματι
them no longer to speak on – name

τούτῳ μηδενὶ ἀνθρώπων. **18** καὶ καλέσαντες
this to no(any)one of men. And calling

αὐτοὺς παρήγγειλαν καθόλου μὴ φθέγγεσθαι
them they charged at all not to utter

μηδὲ διδάσκειν ἐπὶ τῷ ὀνόματι τοῦ
nor to teach on the name –

Ἰησοῦ. **19** ὁ δὲ Πέτρος καὶ Ἰωάννης
of Jesus. – But Peter and John

ἀποκριθέντες εἶπον πρὸς αὐτούς· εἰ
answering said to them: If

δίκαιόν ἐστιν ἐνώπιον τοῦ θεοῦ, ὑμῶν
right it is before – God, you

ἀκούειν μᾶλλον ἢ τοῦ θεοῦ, κρίνατε·
to hear rather than – God, decide ye;

20 οὐ δυνάμεθα γὰρ ἡμεῖς ἃ εἴδαμεν
for cannot we [the] things which we saw

καὶ ἠκούσαμεν μὴ λαλεῖν. **21** οἱ δὲ
and heard not *to* speak. And they

προσαπειλησάμενοι ἀπέλυσαν αὐτούς, μηδὲν
having added threats released them, nothing

εὑρίσκοντες τὸ πῶς κολάσωνται αὐτούς,
finding – how they might punish them,

διὰ τὸν λαόν, ὅτι πάντες ἐδόξαζον τὸν
because of the people, because all men glorified –

θεὸν ἐπὶ τῷ γεγονότι· **22** ἐτῶν γὰρ
God on the thing having happened; for of years

ἦν πλειόνων τεσσεράκοντα ὁ ἄνθρωπος
was more [than] forty the man

ἐφ' ὃν γεγόνει τὸ σημεῖον τοῦτο τῆς
on whom had happened this sign –

en to men by which we must be saved."

13When they saw the courage of Peter and John and realized that they were unschooled, ordinary men, they were astonished and they took note that these men had been with Jesus. 14But since they could see the man who had been healed standing there with them, there was nothing they could say. 15So they ordered them to withdraw from the Sanhedrin and then conferred together. 16"What are we going to do with these men?" they asked. "Everybody living in Jerusalem knows they have done an outstanding miracle, and we cannot deny it. 17But to stop this thing from spreading any further among the people, we must warn these men to speak no longer to anyone in this name."

18Then they called them in again and commanded them not to speak or teach at all in the name of Jesus. 19But Peter and John replied, "Judge for yourselves whether it is right in God's sight to obey you rather than God. 20For we cannot help speaking about what we have seen and heard."

21After further threats they let them go. They could not decide how to punish them, because all the people were praising God for what had happened. 22For the man who was miraculously healed was over forty years old.

23And when they had been released, they went to their own *companions,* and reported all that the chief priests and the elders had said to them.

24And when they heard *this,* they lifted their voices to God with one accord and said, "O Lord, it is Thou who DIDST MAKE THE HEAVEN AND THE EARTH AND THE SEA, AND ALL THAT IS IN THEM,

25who by the Holy Spirit, *through* the mouth of our father David Thy servant, didst say,

'WHY DID THE [i]GENTILES RAGE,
AND THE PEOPLES DEVISE FUTILE THINGS?

26 'THE KINGS OF THE EARTH TOOK THEIR STAND,
AND THE RULERS WERE GATHERED TOGETHER
AGAINST THE LORD, AND AGAINST HIS CHRIST.'

27"For truly in this city there were gathered together against Thy holy servant Jesus, whom Thou didst anoint, both Herod and Pontius Pilate, along with the Gentiles and the peoples of Israel,

28to do whatever Thy hand and Thy purpose predestined to occur.

29"And now, Lord, take note of their threats, and grant that Thy bond-servants may speak Thy word with all confidence,

30while Thou dost extend Thy hand to heal, and signs and wonders take place through the name of Thy holy servant Jesus."

31And when they had prayed, the place where they had gathered together was shaken, and they were all filled with the Holy Spirit, and *began* to speak the word of God with boldness.

Sharing among Believers

32And the congregation of those who believed were of

[i]Or, *nations*

ἰάσεως. **23** Ἀπολυθέντες δὲ ἦλθον πρὸς
of cure. And being released they went to

τοὺς ἰδίους καὶ ἀπήγγειλαν ὅσα πρὸς
the(ir) own [people] and reported what things to

αὐτοὺς οἱ ἀρχιερεῖς καὶ οἱ πρεσβύτεροι
them the chief priests and the elders

εἶπαν. **24** οἱ δὲ ἀκούσαντες ὁμοθυμαδὸν
said. And they having heard with one mind

ἦραν φωνὴν πρὸς τὸν θεὸν καὶ εἶπαν·
lifted voice to – God and said:

δέσποτα, σὺ ὁ ποιήσας τὸν οὐρανὸν καὶ
Master, thou the [one] having made the heaven and

τὴν γῆν καὶ τὴν θάλασσαν καὶ πάντα
the earth and the sea and all things

τὰ ἐν αὐτοῖς, **25** ὁ τοῦ πατρὸς ἡμῶν
– in them, [1]the [one] [8]the [9]father [10]of us

διὰ πνεύματος ἁγίου στόματος Δαυὶδ
[3]through [5][the] Spirit [4]Holy [6][by] mouth [7]of David

παιδός σου εἰπών· ἱνατί ἐφρύαξαν ἔθνη
[11]servant [12]of thee [2]saying:* Why raged nations

καὶ λαοὶ ἐμελέτησαν κενά; **26** παρέστησαν
and peoples devised vain things? came

οἱ βασιλεῖς τῆς γῆς καὶ οἱ ἄρχοντες
the kings of the earth and the rulers

συνήχθησαν ἐπὶ τὸ αὐτὸ κατὰ τοῦ κυρίου
assembled together against the Lord

καὶ κατὰ τοῦ χριστοῦ αὐτοῦ.
and against the Christ of him.

27 συνήχθησαν γὰρ ἐπ' ἀληθείας ἐν τῇ
For assembled in truth in –

πόλει ταύτῃ ἐπὶ τὸν ἅγιον παῖδά σου
city this against the holy servant of thee

Ἰησοῦν, ὃν ἔχρισας, Ἡρῴδης τε καὶ
Jesus, whom thou didst anoint, both Herod and

Πόντιος Πιλᾶτος σὺν ἔθνεσιν καὶ λαοῖς
Pontius Pilate with nations and peoples

Ἰσραήλ, **28** ποιῆσαι ὅσα ἡ χείρ σου καὶ
of Israel, to do what things the hand of thee and

ἡ βουλὴ προώρισεν γενέσθαι. **29** καὶ τὰ
the counsel foreordained to happen. And –

νῦν, κύριε, ἔπιδε ἐπὶ τὰς ἀπειλὰς αὐτῶν,
now, Lord, look *on* on the threatenings of them,

καὶ δὸς τοῖς δούλοις σου μετὰ παρρησίας
and give to the slaves of thee with [2]boldness

πάσης λαλεῖν τὸν λόγον σου, **30** ἐν τῷ
[1]all to speak the word of thee, by the

τὴν χεῖρα ἐκτείνειν σε εἰς ἴασιν καὶ
the hand to stretch forth thee[b] for cure and
=by stretching forth thy hand

σημεῖα καὶ τέρατα γίνεσθαι διὰ τοῦ
signs and wonders to happen through the

ὀνόματος τοῦ ἁγίου παιδός σου Ἰησοῦ.
name of the holy servant of thee Jesus.

31 καὶ δεηθέντων αὐτῶν ἐσαλεύθη ὁ τόπος
And requesting them[a] was shaken the place
=as they were making request

ἐν ᾧ ἦσαν συνηγμένοι, καὶ ἐπλήσθησαν
in which they were *having been* assembled, and they were filled

ἅπαντες τοῦ ἁγίου πνεύματος, καὶ ἐλάλουν
all of(with) the Holy Spirit, and spoke

τὸν λόγον τοῦ θεοῦ μετὰ παρρησίας.
the word – of God with boldness.

32 Τοῦ δὲ πλήθους τῶν πιστευσάντων
[1]Now [2]of [7]the [8]multitude [9]of the [ones] [10]having believed

* It is recognized that there is a primitive error in the text in the first half of ver. 25; it is impossible to construe it as it stands. See ch. 1. 16.

The Believers' Prayer

23On their release, Peter
and John went back to their
own people and reported
all that the chief priests and
elders had said to them.
24When they heard this,
they raised their voices together in prayer to God.
"Sovereign Lord," they
said, "you made the heaven and the earth and the
sea, and everything in
them. 25You spoke by the
Holy Spirit through the
mouth of your servant, our
father David:

" 'Why do the nations rage
and the peoples plot in vain?
26The kings of the earth take their stand
and the rulers gather together
against the Lord
and against his Anointed One.[r]' [s]

27Indeed Herod and Pontius Pilate met together
with the Gentiles and the
people[t] of Israel in this city
to conspire against your
holy servant Jesus, whom
you anointed. 28They did
what your power and will
had decided beforehand
should happen. 29Now,
Lord, consider their threats
and enable your servants to
speak your word with great
boldness. 30Stretch out
your hand to heal and perform miraculous signs and
wonders through the name
of your holy servant
Jesus."

31After they prayed, the
place where they were
meeting was shaken. And
they were all filled with the
Holy Spirit and spoke the
word of God boldly.

The Believers Share Their Possessions

32All the believers were
one in heart and mind. No

[r]26 That is, Christ or Messiah
[s]26 Psalm 2:1,2
[t]27 The Greek is plural.

one heart and soul; and not one *of them* claimed that anything belonging to him was his own; but all things were common property to them.

33And with great power the apostles were giving witness to the resurrection of the Lord Jesus, and abundant grace was upon them all.

34For there was not a needy person among them, for all who were owners of land or houses would sell them and bring the proceeds of the sales,

35and lay them at the apostles' feet; and they would be distributed to each, as any had need.

36And Joseph, a Levite of Cyprian birth, who was also called Barnabas by the apostles (which translated means, Son of Encouragement),

37and who owned a tract of land, sold it and brought the money and laid it at the apostles' feet.

ἦν καρδία καὶ ψυχὴ μία, καὶ οὐδὲ
[11]was [3][the] [2]heart [4]and [5]soul [12]one, and [1]not

εἷς τι τῶν ὑπαρχόντων αὐτῷ ἔλεγεν
[2]one [4]any-thing [6]of the [8]possessions [belonging] [7]to him[c] [3]said

ἴδιον εἶναι, ἀλλ' ἦν αὐτοῖς πάντα κοινά.
[9][his] own [5]to be, but were to them[c] all things common.

33 καὶ δυνάμει μεγάλῃ ἀπεδίδουν τὸ
And [1]with [3]power [2]great [6]gave [7]the

μαρτύριον οἱ ἀπόστολοι τοῦ κυρίου Ἰησοῦ
[8]testimony [4]the [5]apostles [11]of the [12]Lord [13]Jesus

τῆς ἀναστάσεως, χάρις τε μεγάλη ἦν
[9]of the [10]resurrection, and [2]grace [1]great was

ἐπὶ πάντας αὐτούς. 34 οὐδὲ γὰρ ἐνδεής
upon all them. [1]For [2]neither [5]needy

τις ἦν ἐν αὐτοῖς· ὅσοι γὰρ κτήτορες
[4]anyone [3]was among them; for as many as owners

χωρίων ἢ οἰκιῶν ὑπῆρχον, πωλοῦντες
of lands or of houses were, selling

ἔφερον τὰς τιμὰς τῶν πιπρασκομένων
brought the prices of the things being sold

35 καὶ ἐτίθουν παρὰ τοὺς πόδας τῶν
and placed at the feet of the

ἀποστόλων· διεδίδοτο δὲ ἑκάστῳ καθότι ἄν
apostles; and it was distributed to each according as

τις χρείαν εἶχεν. 36 Ἰωσὴφ δὲ ὁ
anyone need had. And Joseph the [one]

ἐπικληθεὶς Βαρναβᾶς ἀπὸ τῶν ἀποστόλων,
surnamed Barnabas from(by) the apostles,

ὅ ἐστιν μεθερμηνευόμενον υἱὸς παρακλήσεως,
which is being translated Son of consolation,

Λευίτης, Κύπριος τῷ γένει, 37 ὑπάρχοντος
a Levite, a Cypriote – by race, being

αὐτῷ ἀγροῦ, πωλήσας ἤνεγκεν τὸ χρῆμα
to him[c] a field,[a] having sold [it] brought the proceeds
=as he had a field,

καὶ ἔθηκεν πρὸς τοὺς πόδας τῶν ἀποστόλων.
and placed at the feet of the apostles.

one claimed that any of his
possessions was his own,
but they shared everything
they had. 33With great power the apostles continued to
testify to the resurrection
of the Lord Jesus, and
much grace was upon them
all. 34There were no needy
persons among them. For
from time to time those
who owned lands or houses
sold them, brought the
money from the sales 35and
put it at the apostles' feet,
and it was distributed to
anyone as he had need.
36Joseph, a Levite from
Cyprus, whom the apostles
called Barnabas (which
means Son of Encourage-
ment), 37sold a field he
owned and brought the
money and put it at the
apostles' feet.

Chapter 5

Fate of Ananias and Sapphira

BUT a certain man named Ananias, with his wife Sapphira, sold a piece of property,

2and kept back *some* of the price for himself, with his wife's full knowledge, and bringing a portion of it, he laid it at the apostles' feet.

3But Peter said, "Ananias, why has Satan filled your heart to lie to the Holy Spirit, and to keep back *some* of the price of the land?

4"While it remained *unsold,* did it not remain your own? And after it was sold, was it not under your control? Why is it that you have conceived this deed in

5 Ἀνὴρ δέ τις Ἁνανίας ὀνόματι σὺν
And a certain man Ananias* by name with

Σαπφίρῃ τῇ γυναικὶ αὐτοῦ ἐπώλησεν
Sapphira the wife of him sold

κτῆμα, 2 καὶ ἐνοσφίσατο ἀπὸ τῆς τιμῆς,
a property, and appropriated from the price,

συνειδυίης καὶ τῆς γυναικός, καὶ ἐνέγκας
aware of [it] also the(his) wife,[a] and bringing
=his wife also being aware of it,

μέρος τι παρὰ τοὺς πόδας τῶν ἀποστόλων
a certain part at the feet of the apostles

ἔθηκεν. 3 εἶπεν δὲ ὁ Πέτρος· Ἁνανία,
placed [it]. But said – Peter : Ananias,

διὰ τί ἐπλήρωσεν ὁ σατανᾶς τὴν καρδίαν
why filled – Satan the heart

σου, ψεύσασθαί σε τὸ πνεῦμα τὸ ἅγιον
of thee, to deceive thee[b] the Spirit – Holy
=that thou shouldest deceive

καὶ νοσφίσασθαι ἀπὸ τῆς τιμῆς τοῦ
and to appropriate from the price of the

χωρίου; 4 οὐχὶ μένον σοὶ ἔμενεν καὶ
land? Not remaining to thee it remained and

πραθὲν ἐν τῇ σῇ ἐξουσίᾳ ὑπῆρχεν; τί ὅτι
sold in – thy authority it was? Why

ἔθου ἐν τῇ καρδίᾳ σου τὸ πρᾶγμα
was put in the heart of thee – action

* See note to 4. 6.

Chapter 5

Ananias and Sapphira

NOW a man named An-
anias, together with
his wife Sapphira, also sold
a piece of property. 2With
his wife's full knowledge he
kept back part of the money for himself, but brought
the rest and put it at the
apostles' feet.
3Then Peter said, "Ana-
nias, how is it that Satan
has so filled your heart that
you have lied to the Holy
Spirit and have kept for
yourself some of the money
you received for the land?
4Didn't it belong to you before it was sold? And after
it was sold, wasn't the
money at your disposal?
What made you think of doing such a thing? You have

your heart? You have not lied to men, but to God."

5And as he heard these words, Ananias fell down and breathed his last; and great fear came upon all who heard of it.

6And the young men arose and covered him up, and after carrying him out, they buried him.

7Now there elapsed an interval of about three hours, and his wife came in, not knowing what had happened.

8And Peter responded to her, "Tell me whether you sold the land for such and such a price?" And she said, "Yes, that was the price."

9Then Peter *said* to her, "Why is it that you have agreed together to put the Spirit of the Lord to the test? Behold, the feet of those who have buried your husband are at the door, and they shall carry you out *as well*."

10And she fell immediately at his feet, and breathed her last; and the young men came in and found her dead, and they carried her out and buried her beside her husband.

11And great fear came upon the whole church, and upon all who heard of these things.

12And at the hands of the apostles many signs and wonders were taking place among the people; and they were all with one accord in Solomon's portico.

13But none of the rest dared to associate with them; however, the people held them in high esteem.

14And all the more believers in the Lord, multitudes of men and women, were constantly added to *their number*;

15to such an extent that they even carried the sick out into the streets, and laid them on cots and pallets, so

τοῦτο; οὐκ ἐψεύσω ἀνθρώποις ἀλλὰ
this? thou didst not lie to men but

τῷ θεῷ. 5 ἀκούων δὲ ὁ Ἁνανίας
– to God. And hearing – Ananias

τοὺς λόγους τούτους πεσὼν ἐξέψυξεν· καὶ
these words falling expired; and

ἐγένετο φόβος μέγας ἐπὶ πάντας τοὺς
came fear great on all the [ones]

ἀκούοντας. 6 ἀναστάντες δὲ οἱ νεώτεροι
hearing. And rising up the young men

συνέστειλαν αὐτὸν καὶ ἐξενέγκαντες ἔθαψαν.
wrapped him and carrying out buried [him].

7 Ἐγένετο δὲ ὡς ὡρῶν τριῶν διάστημα
1And there was 3of about 5hours 4three 2an interval

καὶ ἡ γυνὴ αὐτοῦ μὴ εἰδυῖα τὸ γεγονὸς
and the wife of him not knowing the thing having happened

εἰσῆλθεν. 8 ἀπεκρίθη δὲ πρὸς αὐτὴν
entered. And answered *to* her

Πέτρος· εἰπέ μοι, εἰ τοσούτου τὸ χωρίον
Peter: Tell me, if of(for) so much the land

ἀπέδοσθε; ἡ δὲ εἶπεν· ναί, τοσούτου.
ye sold? And she said: Yes, of(for) so much.

9 ὁ δὲ Πέτρος πρὸς αὐτήν· τί ὅτι
– And Peter to her: Why

συνεφωνήθη ὑμῖν πειράσαι τὸ πνεῦμα
was it agreed with you to tempt the Spirit

κυρίου; ἰδοὺ οἱ πόδες τῶν θαψάντων τὸν
of [the] Lord? behold[,] the feet of the [ones] having buried the

ἄνδρα σου ἐπὶ τῇ θύρᾳ καὶ ἐξοίσουσίν
husband of thee at the door and they will carry out

σε. 10 ἔπεσεν δὲ παραχρῆμα πρὸς τοὺς
thee. And she fell at once at the

πόδας αὐτοῦ καὶ ἐξέψυξεν· εἰσελθόντες δὲ
feet of him and expired; and entering

οἱ νεανίσκοι εὗρον αὐτὴν νεκράν, καὶ
the young men found her dead, and

ἐξενέγκαντες ἔθαψαν πρὸς τὸν ἄνδρα
carrying out buried [her] beside the husband

αὐτῆς. 11 Καὶ ἐγένετο φόβος μέγας
of her. And came fear great

ἐφ' ὅλην τὴν ἐκκλησίαν καὶ ἐπὶ πάντας
on all the church and on all

τοὺς ἀκούοντας ταῦτα.
the [ones] hearing these things.

12 Διὰ δὲ τῶν χειρῶν τῶν ἀποστόλων
And through the hands of the apostles

ἐγίνετο σημεῖα καὶ τέρατα πολλὰ ἐν
5happened 2signs 3and 4wonders 1many among

τῷ λαῷ· καὶ ἦσαν ὁμοθυμαδὸν πάντες
the people; and were with one mind all

ἐν τῇ στοᾷ Σολομῶντος· 13 τῶν δὲ
in the porch of Solomon; and of the

λοιπῶν οὐδεὶς ἐτόλμα κολλᾶσθαι αὐτοῖς,
rest no one dared to be joined to them,

ἀλλ' ἐμεγάλυνεν αὐτοὺς ὁ λαός· 14 μᾶλλον
but magnified them the people; 2more

δὲ προσετίθεντο πιστεύοντες τῷ κυρίῳ,
1and were added believing [ones] to the Lord,

πλήθη ἀνδρῶν τε καὶ γυναικῶν· 15 ὥστε
multitudes both of men and of women; so as

καὶ εἰς τὰς πλατείας ἐκφέρειν τοὺς
even into the streets to bring out =they brought out the

ἀσθενεῖς καὶ τιθέναι ἐπὶ κλιναρίων καὶ
ailing and to place on pallets and

not lied to men but to God."

5When Ananias heard this, he fell down and died. And great fear seized all who heard what had happened. 6Then the young men came forward, wrapped up his body, and carried him out and buried him.

7About three hours later his wife came in, not knowing what had happened. 8Peter asked her, "Tell me, is this the price you and Ananias got for the land?"

"Yes," she said, "that is the price."

9Peter said to her, "How could you agree to test the Spirit of the Lord? Look! The feet of the men who buried your husband are at the door, and they will carry you out also."

10At that moment she fell down at his feet and died. Then the young men came in and, finding her dead, carried her out and buried her beside her husband. 11Great fear seized the whole church and all who heard about these events.

The Apostles Heal Many

12The apostles performed many miraculous signs and wonders among the people. And all the believers used to meet together in Solomon's Colonnade. 13No one else dared join them, even though they were highly regarded by the people. 14Nevertheless, more and more men and women believed in the Lord and were added to their number. 15As a result, people brought the sick into the streets and laid them on beds and mats so that at

that when Peter came by, at
least his shadow might fall
on any one of them.
16And also the people
from the cities in the vicinity of Jerusalem were com-
ing together, bringing
people who were sick [j] or
afflicted with unclean
spirits; and they were all
being healed.

Imprisonment and Release

17But the high priest rose
up, along with all his associates (that is the sect of the
Sadducees), and they were
filled with jealousy;
18and they laid hands on
the apostles, and put them
in a public jail.
19But an angel of the Lord
during the night opened the
gates of the prison, and taking them out he said,
20"Go your way, stand
and speak to the people in
the temple the whole mes-
sage of this Life."
21And upon hearing *this,*
they entered into the temple about daybreak, and
began to teach. Now when
the high priest and his associates had come, they
called the Council together,
even all the Senate of the
sons of Israel, and sent *orders* to the prison house for
them to be brought.
22But the officers who
came did not find them in
the prison; and they re-
turned, and reported back,
23saying, "We found the
prison house locked quite
securely and the guards
standing at the doors; but
when we had opened up,
we found no one inside."
24Now when the captain
of the temple *guard* and the
chief priests heard these
words, they were greatly
perplexed about them as to
what would come of this.
25But someone came and
reported to them, "Behold,
the men whom you put in

κραβάτων, ἵνα ἐρχομένου Πέτρου κἂν ἡ σκιὰ
mattresses, that [5]coming [4]of Peter [1]if even [2]the [3]shadow
ἐπισκιάσῃ τινὶ αὐτῶν. 16 συνήρχετο δὲ
might overshadow some one of them. And came together
καὶ τὸ πλῆθος τῶν πέριξ πόλεων
also the multitude of the [2]round about [1]cities
Ἰερουσαλήμ, φέροντες ἀσθενεῖς καὶ
Jerusalem, carrying ailing [ones] and
ὀχλουμένους ὑπὸ πνευμάτων ἀκαθάρτων,
being tormented by spirits unclean,
οἵτινες ἐθεραπεύοντο ἅπαντες.
who were healed all.
17 Ἀναστὰς δὲ ὁ ἀρχιερεὺς καὶ πάντες
And rising up the high priest and all
οἱ σὺν αὐτῷ, ἡ οὖσα αἵρεσις τῶν
the[ones] with him, the existing sect of the
Σαδδουκαίων, ἐπλήσθησαν ζήλου 18 καὶ
Sadducees, were filled of(with) jealousy and
ἐπέβαλον τὰς χεῖρας ἐπὶ τοὺς ἀποστόλους
laid *on* the(ir) hands on the apostles
καὶ ἔθεντο αὐτοὺς ἐν τηρήσει δημοσίᾳ.
and put them in custody publicly.
19 Ἄγγελος δὲ κυρίου διὰ νυκτὸς
But an angel of [the] Lord through(during) [the] night
ἤνοιξε τὰς θύρας τῆς φυλακῆς ἐξαγαγών τε
opened the doors of the prison and leading out
αὐτοὺς εἶπεν· 20 πορεύεσθε καὶ σταθέντες
them said : Go ye and standing
λαλεῖτε ἐν τῷ ἱερῷ τῷ λαῷ πάντα
speak in the temple to the people all
τὰ ῥήματα τῆς ζωῆς ταύτης.
the words of this life.
21 ἀκούσαντες δὲ εἰσῆλθον ὑπὸ τὸν ὄρθρον
And having heard they entered about the dawn
εἰς τὸ ἱερὸν καὶ ἐδίδασκον. Παραγενόμενος δὲ
into the temple and taught. And having come
ὁ ἀρχιερεὺς καὶ οἱ σὺν αὐτῷ
the high priest and the [ones] with him
συνεκάλεσαν τὸ συνέδριον καὶ πᾶσαν τὴν
called together the council and all the
γερουσίαν τῶν υἱῶν Ἰσραήλ, καὶ ἀπέστειλαν
senate of the sons of Israel, and sent
εἰς τὸ δεσμωτήριον ἀχθῆναι αὐτούς.
to the jail to be brought them.[b]
22 οἱ δὲ παραγενόμενοι ὑπηρέται οὐχ εὗρον
[1]But [2]the [4]having come [3]attendants found not
αὐτοὺς ἐν τῇ φυλακῇ· ἀναστρέψαντες δὲ
them in the prison; and having returned
ἀπήγγειλαν 23 λέγοντες ὅτι τὸ δεσμωτήριον
they reported saying[,] – The jail
εὕρομεν κεκλεισμένον ἐν πάσῃ ἀσφαλείᾳ
we found *having been* shut in all security
καὶ τοὺς φύλακας ἑστῶτας ἐπὶ τῶν
and the guards standing at the
θυρῶν, ἀνοίξαντες δὲ ἔσω οὐδένα εὕρομεν.
doors, but having opened [3]inside [2]no one [1]we found.
24 ὡς δὲ ἤκουσαν τοὺς λόγους τούτους
And as [9]heard [10]these [11]words
ὅ τε στρατηγὸς τοῦ ἱεροῦ καὶ οἱ ἀρχιερεῖς,
[2]the [1]both [3]commandant [4]of the [5]temple [6]and [7]the [8]chief priests,
διηπόρουν περὶ αὐτῶν τί ἂν γένοιτο
they were in doubt about them what [2]might become
τοῦτο. 25 παραγενόμενος δέ τις ἀπήγγειλεν
[1]this thing. And having come someone reported
αὐτοῖς ὅτι ἰδοὺ οἱ ἄνδρες, οὓς
to them[,] – Behold[,] the men, whom

least Peter's shadow might
fall on some of them as he
passed by. 16Crowds gath-
ered also from the towns
around Jerusalem, bringing
their sick and those tor-
mented by evil [u] spirits,
and all of them were
healed.

The Apostles Persecuted

17Then the high priest and
all his associates, who were
members of the party of the
Sadducees, were filled with
jealousy. 18They arrested
the apostles and put them
in the public jail. 19But during the night an angel of the
Lord opened the doors of
the jail and brought them
out. 20"Go, stand in the
temple courts," he said,
"and tell the people the full
message of this new life."
21At daybreak they en-
tered the temple courts, as
they had been told, and began to teach the people.
When the high priest and
his associates arrived, they
called together the Sanhedrin—the full assembly of
the elders of Israel—and
sent to the jail for the apostles. 22But on arriving at the
jail, the officers did not find
them there. So they went
back and reported, 23"We
found the jail securely
locked, with the guards
standing at the doors; but
when we opened them, we
found no one inside." 24On
hearing this report, the captain of the temple guard and
the chief priests were puzzled, wondering what
would come of this.
25Then someone came
and said, "Look! The men
you put in jail are standing

[j] Lit., *and*

[u] *16* Greek *unclean*

prison are standing in the
temple and teaching the
people!"
26Then the captain went
along with the officers and
proceeded to bring them
back without violence (for
they were afraid of the
people, lest they should be
stoned).
27And when they had
brought them, they stood
them before the Council.
And the high priest ques-
tioned them,
28saying, "We gave you
strict orders not to con-
tinue teaching in this name,
and behold, you have filled
Jerusalem with your teaching, and intend to bring this
man's blood upon us."
29But Peter and the apos-
tles answered and said,
"We must obey God rather
than men.
30"The God of our fathers
raised up Jesus, whom you
had put to death by hanging
Him on a cross.
31"He is the one whom
God exalted to His right
hand as a Prince and a Savior, to grant repentance to
Israel, and forgiveness of
sins.
32"And we are wit-
nesses[k] of these things;
and *so is* the Holy Spirit,
whom God has given to
those who obey Him."

Gamaliel's Counsel

33But when they heard
this, they were cut to the
quick and were intending to
slay them.
34But a certain Pharisee
named Gamaliel, a teacher
of the Law, respected by all
the people, stood up in the
Council and gave orders to
put the men outside for a
short time.
35And he said to them,
"Men of Israel, take care
what you propose to do

ἔθεσθε ἐν τῇ φυλακῇ, εἰσὶν ἐν τῷ ἱερῷ
ye put in the prison, are in the temple
ἑστῶτες καὶ διδάσκοντες τὸν λαόν.
standing and teaching the people.
26 Τότε ἀπελθὼν ὁ στρατηγὸς σὺν τοῖς
Then going the commandant with the
ὑπηρέταις ἦγεν αὐτούς, οὐ μετὰ βίας,
attendants brought them, not with force,
ἐφοβοῦντο γὰρ τὸν λαόν, μὴ λιθασθῶσιν·
for they feared the people, lest they should be stoned;
27 ἀγαγόντες δὲ αὐτοὺς ἔστησαν ἐν τῷ
and bringing them they stood in the
συνεδρίῳ. καὶ ἐπηρώτησεν αὐτοὺς ὁ
council. And questioned them the
ἀρχιερεὺς 28 λέγων· παραγγελίᾳ παρηγ-
high priest saying : With charge we
=We strictly
γείλαμεν ὑμῖν μὴ διδάσκειν ἐπὶ
charged you not to teach on(in)
τῷ ὀνόματι τούτῳ, καὶ ἰδοὺ πεπληρώκατε
this name, and behold ye have filled
τὴν Ἰερουσαλὴμ τῆς διδαχῆς ὑμῶν, καὶ
– Jerusalem of(with) the teaching of you and
βούλεσθε ἐπαγαγεῖν ἐφ᾽ ἡμᾶς τὸ αἷμα
intend to bring *on* on us the blood
τοῦ ἀνθρώπου τούτου. 29 ἀποκριθεὶς δὲ
of this man. And answering
Πέτρος καὶ οἱ ἀπόστολοι εἶπαν· πειθαρχεῖν
Peter and the apostles said : [2]to obey
δεῖ θεῷ μᾶλλον ἢ ἀνθρώποις. 30 ὁ
[1]It behoves God rather than men. The
θεὸς τῶν πατέρων ἡμῶν ἤγειρεν Ἰησοῦν,
God of the fathers of us raised Jesus,
ὃν ὑμεῖς διεχειρίσασθε κρεμάσαντες ἐπὶ
whom ye killed hanging on
ξύλου· 31 τοῦτον ὁ θεὸς ἀρχηγὸν καὶ
a tree; this man – God a Ruler and
σωτῆρα ὕψωσεν τῇ δεξιᾷ αὐτοῦ τοῦ
a Saviour exalted to the right [hand] of him –
δοῦναι μετάνοιαν τῷ Ἰσραὴλ καὶ ἄφεσιν
to give[d] repentance – to Israel and forgiveness
ἁμαρτιῶν. 32 καὶ ἡμεῖς ἐσμεν μάρτυρες
of sins. And we are witnesses
τῶν ῥημάτων τούτων, καὶ τὸ πνεῦμα
of these words(things), and the Spirit
τὸ ἅγιον ὃ ἔδωκεν ὁ θεὸς τοῖς
– Holy which [2]gave – [1]God to the
πειθαρχοῦσιν αὐτῷ. 33 οἱ δὲ ἀκούσαντες
[ones] obeying him. And the [ones] hearing
διεπρίοντο καὶ ἐβούλοντο ἀνελεῖν αὐτούς.
were cut* and intended to kill them.
34 Ἀναστὰς δέ τις ἐν τῷ συνεδρίῳ
[1]But [4]standing up [2]a certain [5]in [6]the [7]council
Φαρισαῖος ὀνόματι Γαμαλιήλ, νομοδιδάσκαλος
[3]Pharisee by name Gamaliel, a teacher of the law
τίμιος παντὶ τῷ λαῷ, ἐκέλευσεν ἔξω
honoured by all the people, commanded [4]outside
βραχὺ τοὺς ἀνθρώπους ποιῆσαι, 35 εἶπέν
[5]a little [2]the [3]men [1]to make(put), [2]said
τε πρὸς αὐτούς· ἄνδρες Ἰσραηλῖται,
[1]and to them : *Men* Israelites,
προσέχετε ἑαυτοῖς ἐπὶ τοῖς ἀνθρώποις τούτοις
take heed to yourselves [4]on(to) [5]these [6]men

* That is, to the heart; *cf.* 7. 54.

in the temple courts teaching the people." 26At that,
the captain went with his
officers and brought the
apostles. They did not use
force, because they feared
that the people would stone
them.
27Having brought the
apostles, they made them
appear before the Sanhe-
drin to be questioned by the
high priest. 28"We gave
you strict orders not to
teach in this name," he
said. "Yet you have filled
Jerusalem with your teaching and are determined to
make us guilty of this man's
blood."
29Peter and the other
apostles replied: "We must
obey God rather than men!
30The God of our fathers
raised Jesus from the dead
—whom you had killed by
hanging him on a tree.
31God exalted him to his
own right hand as Prince
and Savior that he might
give repentance and for-
giveness of sins to Israel.
32We are witnesses of these
things, and so is the Holy
Spirit, whom God has giv-
en to those who obey him."
33When they heard this,
they were furious and
wanted to put them to
death. 34But a Pharisee
named Gamaliel, a teacher
of the law, who was hon-
ored by all the people,
stood up in the Sanhedrin
and ordered that the men
be put outside for a little
while. 35Then he addressed
them: "Men of Israel, consider carefully what you in-

with these men.
36"For some time ago
Theudas rose up, claiming
to be somebody; and a
group of about four hun-
dred men joined up with
him. And he was slain; and
all who followed him were
dispersed and came to
nothing.
37"After this man Judas
of Galilee rose up in the
days of the census, and
drew away *some* people after him, he too perished,
and all those who followed
him were scattered.
38"And so in the present
case, I say to you, stay
away from these men and
let them alone, for if this
plan or action should be of
men, it will be overthrown;
39but if it is of God, you
will not be able to over-
throw them; or else you
may even be found fighting
against God."
40And they took his ad-
vice; and after calling the
apostles in, they flogged
them and ordered them to
speak no more in the name
of Jesus, and *then* released
them.
41So they went on their
way from the presence of
the Council, rejoicing that
they had been considered
worthy to suffer shame for
His name.
42And every day, in the
temple and from house to
house, they kept right on
teaching and preaching
Jesus *as* the Christ.

τί μέλλετε πράσσειν. **36** πρὸ γὰρ
[1]what [2]ye intend [3]to do. For before

τούτων τῶν ἡμερῶν ἀνέστη Θευδᾶς, λέγων
these – days stood up Theudas, saying

εἶναί τινα ἑαυτόν, ᾧ προσεκλίθη ἀνδρῶν
to be someone himself, [1]to whom [6]were attached [3]of men

ἀριθμὸς ὡς τετρακοσίων· ὃς ἀνῃρέθη, καὶ
[2]a number [4]about [5]four hundreds; who was killed, and

πάντες ὅσοι ἐπείθοντο αὐτῷ διελύθησαν
all as many as obeyed him were dispersed

καὶ ἐγένοντο εἰς οὐδέν. **37** μετὰ τοῦτον
and came to nothing. After this

ἀνέστη Ἰούδας ὁ Γαλιλαῖος ἐν ταῖς
stood up Judas the Galilæan in the

ἡμέραις τῆς ἀπογραφῆς καὶ ἀπέστησεν
days of the enrolment and drew away

λαὸν ὀπίσω αὐτοῦ· κἀκεῖνος ἀπώλετο,
people after him; and that man perished,

καὶ πάντες ὅσοι ἐπείθοντο αὐτῷ
and all as many as obeyed him

διεσκορπίσθησαν. **38** καὶ τὰ νῦν λέγω
were scattered. And – now I say

ὑμῖν, ἀπόστητε ἀπὸ τῶν ἀνθρώπων τούτων
to you, stand away from these men

καὶ ἄφετε αὐτούς· ὅτι ἐὰν ᾖ ἐξ ἀνθρώπων
and leave them; because if be of men

ἡ βουλὴ αὕτη ἢ τὸ ἔργον τοῦτο,
this counsel or this work,

καταλυθήσεται· **39** εἰ δὲ ἐκ θεοῦ ἐστιν,
it will be destroyed; but if of God it is,

οὐ δυνήσεσθε καταλῦσαι αὐτούς, μήποτε
ye will not be able to destroy them, lest

καὶ θεομάχοι εὑρεθῆτε. ἐπείσθησαν δὲ
even fighters against God ye be found. And they obeyed

αὐτῷ, **40** καὶ προσκαλεσάμενοι τοὺς
him, and having called to [them] the

ἀποστόλους δείραντες παρήγγειλαν μὴ
apostles beating charged not

λαλεῖν ἐπὶ τῷ ὀνόματι τοῦ Ἰησοῦ καὶ
to speak on(in) the name – of Jesus and

ἀπέλυσαν. **41** Οἱ μὲν οὖν ἐπορεύοντο
released [them]. They – therefore went

χαίροντες ἀπὸ προσώπου τοῦ συνεδρίου,
rejoicing from [the] presence of the council,

ὅτι κατηξιώθησαν ὑπὲρ τοῦ ὀνόματος
because they were deemed worthy on behalf of the name

ἀτιμασθῆναι· **42** πᾶσάν τε ἡμέραν ἐν τῷ
to be dishonoured; and every day in the

ἱερῷ καὶ κατ' οἶκον οὐκ ἐπαύοντο
temple and from house to house† they ceased not

διδάσκοντες καὶ εὐαγγελιζόμενοι τὸν χριστὸν
teaching and preaching the Christ

Ἰησοῦν.
Jesus.

tend to do to these men.
36Some time ago Theudas
appeared, claiming to be
somebody, and about four
hundred men rallied to him.
He was killed, all his followers were dispersed, and
it all came to nothing. 37Af-
ter him, Judas the Galilean
appeared in the days of the
census and led a band of
people in revolt. He too
was killed, and all his followers were scattered.
38Therefore, in the present
case I advise you: Leave
these men alone! Let them
go! For if their purpose or
activity is of human origin,
it will fail. 39But if it is from
God, you will not be able to
stop these men; you will
only find yourselves fighting against God."
40His speech persuaded
them. They called the apostles in and had them
flogged. Then they ordered
them not to speak in the
name of Jesus, and let them
go.
41The apostles left the
Sanhedrin, rejoicing be-
cause they had been counted worthy of suffering disgrace for the Name. 42Day
after day, in the temple
courts and from house to
house, they never stopped
teaching and proclaiming
the good news that Jesus is
the Christ.[v]

Chapter 6

Choosing of the Seven

NOW at this time while
the disciples were in-
creasing *in number*, a complaint arose on the part of
the [l]Hellenistic *Jews*
against the *native* He-
brews, because their wid-
ows were being overlooked
in the daily serving *of food*.

[l]I.e., non-Palestinian Jews who normally spoke Greek

6 Ἐν δὲ ταῖς ἡμέραις ταύταις
Now in these days

πληθυνόντων τῶν μαθητῶν ἐγένετο
being multiplied the disciples[a] there was
=as the disciples were multiplied

γογγυσμὸς τῶν Ἑλληνιστῶν πρὸς τοὺς
a murmuring of the Hellenists against the

Ἑβραίους, ὅτι παρεθεωροῦντο ἐν τῇ
Hebrews, because [4]were overlooked [5]in [6]the

διακονίᾳ τῇ καθημερινῇ αἱ χῆραι αὐτῶν.
[8]service – [7]daily [1]the [2]widows [3]of them.

Chapter 6

The Choosing of the Seven

IN those days when the
number of disciples was
increasing, the Grecian
Jews among them com-
plained against the Hebraic
Jews because their widows
were being overlooked in
the daily distribution of

[v]42 Or *Messiah*

2And the twelve sum-
moned the congregation of
the disciples and said, "It is
not desirable for us to neglect the word of God in order to serve tables.
3"But select from among
you, brethren, seven men
of good reputation, full of
the Spirit and of wisdom,
whom we may put in
charge of this task.
4"But we will devote
ourselves to prayer, and to
the ministry of the word."
5And the statement
found approval with the
whole congregation; and
they chose Stephen, a man
full of faith and of the Holy
Spirit, and Philip, Prochorus, Nicanor, Timon, Par-
menas and Nicolas, a
[m]proselyte from Antioch.
6And these they brought
before the apostles; and after praying, they laid their
hands on them.
7And the word of God
kept on spreading; and the
number of the disciples
continued to increase
greatly in Jerusalem, and a
great many of the priests
were becoming obedient to
the faith.
8And Stephen, full of
grace and power, was per-
forming great wonders and
signs among the people.
9But some men from
what was called the Syna-
gogue of the Freedmen, *including* both Cyrenians and
Alexandrians, and some
from Cilicia and Asia, rose
up and argued with Ste-
phen.
10And *yet* they were un-
able to cope with the wisdom and the Spirit with
which he was speaking.
11Then they secretly in-
duced men to say, "We
have heard him speak blasphemous words against
Moses and *against* God."
12And they stirred up the

[m]I.e., a Gentile convert to Judaism

2 προσκαλεσάμενοι δὲ οἱ δώδεκα τὸ
[4]having called to [them] [1]And [2]the [3]twelve the
πλῆθος τῶν μαθητῶν εἶπαν· οὐκ ἀρεστόν
multitude of the disciples said : not pleasing
ἐστιν ἡμᾶς καταλείψαντας τὸν λόγον τοῦ
It is us leaving the word –
θεοῦ διακονεῖν τραπέζαις. **3** ἐπισκέψασθε
of God to serve tables. look ye out
δέ, ἀδελφοί, ἄνδρας ἐξ ὑμῶν μαρτυρουμένους
But, brothers, [2]men [3]of [4]you [5]being witnessed to
ἑπτὰ πλήρεις πνεύματος καὶ σοφίας, οὓς
[1]seven [as] full of Spirit and of wisdom, whom
καταστήσομεν ἐπὶ τῆς χρείας ταύτης·
we will appoint over this office;
4 ἡμεῖς δὲ τῇ προσευχῇ καὶ τῇ διακονίᾳ
but we to the prayer and to the service
τοῦ λόγου προσκαρτερήσομεν. **5** καὶ ἤρεσεν
of the word will keep. And [3]pleased
ὁ λόγος ἐνώπιον παντὸς τοῦ πλήθους,
[1]the [2]word before all the multitude,
καὶ ἐξελέξαντο Στέφανον, ἄνδρα πλήρη
and they chose Stephen, a man full
πίστεως καὶ πνεύματος ἁγίου, καὶ Φίλιππον
of faith and Spirit of Holy, and Philip
καὶ Πρόχορον καὶ Νικάνορα καὶ Τίμωνα
and Prochorus and Nicanor and Timon
καὶ Παρμενᾶν καὶ Νικόλαον προσήλυτον
and Parmenas and Nicolaus a proselyte
Ἀντιοχέα, **6** οὓς ἔστησαν ἐνώπιον τῶν
of Antioch, whom they set before the
ἀποστόλων, καὶ προσευξάμενοι ἐπέθηκαν
apostles, and having prayed they placed on
αὐτοῖς τὰς χεῖρας.
them the(ir) hands.
7 Καὶ ὁ λόγος τοῦ θεοῦ ηὔξανεν, καὶ
And the word – of God grew, and
ἐπληθύνετο ὁ ἀριθμὸς τῶν μαθητῶν ἐν
was multiplied the number of the disciples in
Ἰερουσαλὴμ σφόδρα, πολύς τε ὄχλος τῶν
Jerusalem greatly, and a much(great) crowd of the
ἱερέων ὑπήκουον τῇ πίστει.
priests obeyed the faith.
8 Στέφανος δὲ πλήρης χάριτος καὶ
And Stephen full of grace and
δυνάμεως ἐποίει τέρατα καὶ σημεῖα μεγάλα
of power did wonders and signs great
ἐν τῷ λαῷ. **9** ἀνέστησαν δέ τινες τῶν
among the people. But rose up some of the [ones]
ἐκ τῆς συναγωγῆς τῆς λεγομένης
of the synagogue – *being* called
Λιβερτίνων καὶ Κυρηναίων καὶ Ἀλεξ-
of Freedmen and of Cyrenians and of
ανδρέων καὶ τῶν ἀπὸ Κιλικίας καὶ
Alexandrians and of the [ones] from Cilicia and
Ἀσίας συζητοῦντες τῷ Στεφάνῳ, **10** καὶ
Asia discussing – with Stephen, and
οὐκ ἴσχυον ἀντιστῆναι τῇ σοφίᾳ καὶ
were not able to withstand the wisdom and
τῷ πνεύματι ᾧ ἐλάλει. **11** τότε ὑπέβαλον
the spirit with which he spoke. Then they suborned
ἄνδρας λέγοντας ὅτι ἀκηκόαμεν αὐτοῦ
men saying[,] – We have heard him
λαλοῦντος ῥήματα βλάσφημα εἰς Μωϋσῆν
speaking words blasphemous against Moses
καὶ τὸν θεόν· **12** συνεκίνησάν τε τὸν
and – God; and they stirred up the

food. 2So the Twelve gathered all the disciples together and said, "It would
not be right for us to neglect
the ministry of the word of
God in order to wait on tables. 3Brothers, choose
seven men from among you
who are known to be full of
the Spirit and wisdom. We
will turn this responsibility
over to them 4and will give
our attention to prayer and
the ministry of the word."
5This proposal pleased
the whole group. They
chose Stephen, a man full
of faith and of the Holy
Spirit; also Philip, Proco-
rus, Nicanor, Timon, Par-
menas, and Nicolas from
Antioch, a convert to Judaism. 6They presented these
men to the apostles, who
prayed and laid their hands
on them.
7So the word of God
spread. The number of disciples in Jerusalem in-
creased rapidly, and a large
number of priests became
obedient to the faith.

Stephen Seized

8Now Stephen, a man full
of God's grace and power,
did great wonders and mi-
raculous signs among the
people. 9Opposition arose,
however, from members of
the Synagogue of the
Freedmen (as it was called)
—Jews of Cyrene and Al-
exandria as well as the
provinces of Cilicia and
Asia. These men began to
argue with Stephen, 10but
they could not stand up
against his wisdom or the
Spirit by whom he spoke.
11Then they secretly per-
suaded some men to say,
"We have heard Stephen
speak words of blasphemy
against Moses and against
God."
12So they stirred up the

people, the elders and the scribes, and they came upon him and dragged him away, and brought him before the Council.

13And they put forward false witnesses who said, "This man incessantly speaks against this holy place, and the Law;

14for we have heard him say that this Nazarene, Jesus, will destroy this place and alter the customs which Moses handed down to us."

15And fixing their gaze on him, all who were sitting in the Council saw his face like the face of an angel.

λαὸν καὶ τοὺς πρεσβυτέρους καὶ τοὺς
people and the elders and the

γραμματεῖς, καὶ ἐπιστάντες συνήρπασαν
scribes, and coming on they seized

αὐτὸν καὶ ἤγαγον εἰς τὸ συνέδριον,
him and led to the council,

13 ἔστησάν τε μάρτυρας ψευδεῖς λέγοντας·
and stood witnesses false saying :

ὁ ἄνθρωπος οὗτος οὐ παύεται λαλῶν
This man ceases not speaking

ῥήματα κατὰ τοῦ τόπου τοῦ ἁγίου [τούτου]
words against – [3]place – [2]holy [1]this

καὶ τοῦ νόμου· 14 ἀκηκόαμεν γὰρ αὐτοῦ
and the law; for we have heard him

λέγοντος ὅτι Ἰησοῦς ὁ Ναζωραῖος οὗτος
saying that [2]Jesus [3]the [4]Nazarene [1]this

καταλύσει τὸν τόπον τοῦτον καὶ ἀλλάξει
will destroy this place and will change

τὰ ἔθη ἃ παρέδωκεν ἡμῖν Μωϋσῆς.
the customs which delivered to us Moses.

15 καὶ ἀτενίσαντες εἰς αὐτὸν πάντες οἱ
And gazing at him all the

καθεζόμενοι ἐν τῷ συνεδρίῳ εἶδον τὸ
[ones] sitting in the council saw the

πρόσωπον αὐτοῦ ὡσεὶ πρόσωπον ἀγγέλου.
face of him as a face of an angel.

people and the elders and the teachers of the law. They seized Stephen and brought him before the Sanhedrin. 13They produced false witnesses, who testified, "This fellow never stops speaking against this holy place and against the law. 14For we have heard him say that this Jesus of Nazareth will destroy this place and change the customs Moses handed down to us."

15All who were sitting in the Sanhedrin looked intently at Stephen, and they saw that his face was like the face of an angel.

Chapter 7

Stephen's Defense

AND the high priest said, "Are these things so?"

2And he said, "Hear me, brethren and fathers! The God of glory appeared to our father Abraham when he was in Mesopotamia, before he lived in Haran,

3and said to him, 'DEPART FROM YOUR COUNTRY AND YOUR RELATIVES, AND COME INTO THE LAND THAT I WILL SHOW YOU.'

4"Then he departed from the land of the Chaldeans, and settled in Haran. And from there, after his father died, *God* removed him into this country in which you are now living.

5"And He gave him no inheritance in it, not even a foot of ground; and *yet*, even when he had no child, He promised that HE WOULD GIVE IT TO HIM AS A POSSESSION, AND TO HIS OFFSPRING AFTER HIM.

7 Εἶπεν δὲ ὁ ἀρχιερεύς· εἰ ταῦτα
And said the high priest : If these things

οὕτως ἔχει; 2 ὁ δὲ ἔφη·
thus have(are)? And he said:

Ἄνδρες ἀδελφοὶ καὶ πατέρες, ἀκούσατε.
Men brothers and fathers, hear ye.

Ὁ θεὸς τῆς δόξης ὤφθη τῷ πατρὶ
The God – of glory appeared to the father

ἡμῶν Ἀβραὰμ ὄντι ἐν τῇ Μεσοποταμίᾳ
of us Abraham being in – Mesopotamia

πρὶν ἢ κατοικῆσαι αὐτὸν ἐν Χαρράν,
before to dwell him[b] in Charran,
=he dwelt

3 καὶ εἶπεν πρὸς αὐτόν· ἔξελθε ἐκ τῆς
and said to him : Go forth out of the

γῆς σου καὶ τῆς συγγενείας σου, καὶ
land of thee and the kindred of thee, and

δεῦρο εἰς τὴν γῆν ἣν ἂν σοι δείξω.
come into the land whichever to thee I may show.

4 τότε ἐξελθὼν ἐκ γῆς Χαλδαίων
Then going forth out of [the] land of [the] Chaldæans

κατῴκησεν ἐν Χαρράν. κἀκεῖθεν μετὰ
he dwelt in Charran. And thence after

τὸ ἀποθανεῖν τὸν πατέρα αὐτοῦ μετῴκισεν
the to die the father of him[b] [God] removed
=his father died

αὐτὸν εἰς τὴν γῆν ταύτην εἰς ἣν ὑμεῖς
him into this land in which ye

νῦν κατοικεῖτε, 5 καὶ οὐκ ἔδωκεν αὐτῷ
now dwell, and gave not to him

κληρονομίαν ἐν αὐτῇ οὐδὲ βῆμα ποδός,
an inheritance in it nor a foot's space,

καὶ ἐπηγγείλατο δοῦναι αὐτῷ εἰς
and promised to give him for

κατάσχεσιν αὐτὴν καὶ τῷ σπέρματι αὐτοῦ
a possession it and to the seed of him

μετ' αὐτόν, οὐκ ὄντος αὐτῷ τέκνου.
after him, not being to him[c] a child.[a]
=while he had no child.

Chapter 7

Stephen's Speech to the Sanhedrin

THEN the high priest asked him, "Are these charges true?"

2To this he replied: "Brothers and fathers, listen to me! The God of glory appeared to our father Abraham while he was still in Mesopotamia, before he lived in Haran. 3'Leave your country and your people,' God said, 'and go to the land I will show you.'[w]

4"So he left the land of the Chaldeans and settled in Haran. After the death of his father, God sent him to this land where you are now living. 5He gave him no inheritance here, not even a foot of ground. But God promised him that he and his descendants after him would possess the land, even though at that time Abraham had no

[w]*3* Gen. 12:1

6 "But God spoke to this effect, that his OFFSPRING WOULD BE ALIENS IN A FOREIGN LAND, AND THAT THEY WOULD BE ENSLAVED AND MISTREATED FOR FOUR HUNDRED YEARS.

7 " 'AND WHATEVER NATION TO WHICH THEY SHALL BE IN BONDAGE I MYSELF WILL JUDGE,' said God, 'AND AFTER THAT THEY WILL COME OUT AND [n]SERVE ME IN THIS PLACE.'

8 "And He gave him the covenant of circumcision; and so *Abraham* became the father of Isaac, and circumcised him on the eighth day; and Isaac *became the father of* Jacob, and Jacob *of* the twelve patriarchs.

9 "And the patriarchs became jealous of Joseph and sold him into Egypt. And *yet* God was with him,

10 and rescued him from all his afflictions, and granted him favor and wisdom in the sight of Pharaoh, king of Egypt; and he made him governor over Egypt and all his household.

11 "Now a famine came over all Egypt and Canaan, and great affliction *with it;* and our fathers could find no food.

12 "But when Jacob heard that there was grain in Egypt, he sent our fathers *there* the first time.

13 "And on the second *visit* Joseph made himself known to his brothers, and Joseph's family was disclosed to Pharaoh.

14 "And Joseph sent *word* and invited Jacob his father and all his relatives to come to him, seventy-five persons *in all.*

15 "And Jacob went down to Egypt and *there* passed away, he and our fathers.

[n]Or, *worship*

6 ἐλάλησεν δὲ οὕτως ὁ θεός, ὅτι ἔσται
And spoke thus – God, that will be
τὸ σπέρμα αὐτοῦ πάροικον ἐν γῇ ἀλλοτρίᾳ,
the seed of him a sojourner in a land belonging to others,
καὶ δουλώσουσιν αὐτὸ καὶ κακώσουσιν
and they will enslave it and will ill-treat
ἔτη τετρακόσια· 7 καὶ τὸ ἔθνος ᾧ ἐὰν
years four hundred; and the nation whichever
δουλεύσουσιν κρινῶ ἐγώ, ὁ θεὸς εἶπεν,
they will serve will judge I, – God said,
καὶ μετὰ ταῦτα ἐξελεύσονται καὶ
and after these things they will come forth and
λατρεύσουσίν μοι ἐν τῷ τόπῳ τούτῳ.
will worship me in this place.
8 καὶ ἔδωκεν αὐτῷ διαθήκην περιτομῆς·
And he gave him a covenant of circumcision;
καὶ οὕτως ἐγέννησεν τὸν Ἰσαὰκ καὶ
and thus he begat – Isaac and
περιέτεμεν αὐτὸν τῇ ἡμέρᾳ τῇ ὀγδόῃ,
circumcised him on the day – eighth,
καὶ Ἰσαὰκ τὸν Ἰακώβ, καὶ Ἰακὼβ
and Isaac [begat] – Jacob, and Jacob [begat]
τοὺς δώδεκα πατριάρχας. 9 Καὶ οἱ
the twelve patriarchs. And the
πατριάρχαι ζηλώσαντες τὸν Ἰωσὴφ
patriarchs becoming jealous – [2]Joseph
ἀπέδοντο εἰς Αἴγυπτον· καὶ ἦν ὁ θεὸς
[1]sold into Egypt; and was – God
μετ᾽ αὐτοῦ, 10 καὶ ἐξείλατο αὐτὸν ἐκ
with him, and rescued him out of
πασῶν τῶν θλίψεων αὐτοῦ, καὶ ἔδωκεν
all the afflictions of him, and gave
αὐτῷ χάριν καὶ σοφίαν ἐναντίον Φαραὼ
him favour and wisdom before Pharaoh
βασιλέως Αἰγύπτου, καὶ κατέστησεν αὐτὸν
king of Egypt, and he appointed him
ἡγούμενον ἐπ᾽ Αἴγυπτον καὶ ὅλον τὸν
governor over Egypt and all the
οἶκον αὐτοῦ. 11 ἦλθεν δὲ λιμὸς ἐφ᾽
household of him. But came a famine over
ὅλην τὴν Αἴγυπτον καὶ Χανάαν καὶ
all – Egypt and Canaan and
θλῖψις μεγάλη, καὶ οὐχ ηὕρισκον
affliction great, and found not
χορτάσματα οἱ πατέρες ἡμῶν. 12 ἀκούσας
sustenance the fathers of us. [3]having heard
δὲ Ἰακὼβ ὄντα σιτία εἰς Αἴγυπτον
[1]But [2]Jacob [5]being [4]corn in Egypt
ἐξαπέστειλεν τοὺς πατέρας ἡμῶν πρῶτον·
sent forth the fathers of us first;
13 καὶ ἐν τῷ δευτέρῳ ἐγνωρίσθη Ἰωσὴφ
and at the second [time] was made known Joseph
τοῖς ἀδελφοῖς αὐτοῦ, καὶ φανερὸν ἐγένετο τῷ
to the brothers of him, and [5]manifest [4]became –
Φαραὼ τὸ γένος Ἰωσήφ. 14 ἀποστείλας δὲ
[6]to Pharaoh [1]the [2]race [3]of Joseph. And sending
Ἰωσὴφ μετεκαλέσατο Ἰακὼβ τὸν πατέρα
Joseph called Jacob the father
αὐτοῦ καὶ πᾶσαν τὴν συγγένειαν ἐν
of him and all the(his) kindred in
ψυχαῖς ἑβδομήκοντα πέντε. 15 καὶ κατέβη
souls seventy-five. And went down
Ἰακὼβ εἰς Αἴγυπτον, καὶ ἐτελεύτησεν
Jacob to Egypt, and died
αὐτὸς καὶ οἱ πατέρες ἡμῶν, 16 καὶ
he and the fathers of us, and

child. 6God spoke to him in this way: 'Your descendants will be strangers in a country not their own, and they will be enslaved and mistreated four hundred years. 7But I will punish the nation they serve as slaves,' God said, 'and afterward they will come out of that country and worship me in this place.'[x] 8Then he gave Abraham the covenant of circumcision. And Abraham became the father of Isaac and circumcised him eight days after his birth. Later Isaac became the father of Jacob, and Jacob became the father of the twelve patriarchs.

9 "Because the patriarchs were jealous of Joseph, they sold him as a slave into Egypt. But God was with him 10and rescued him from all his troubles. He gave Joseph wisdom and enabled him to gain the goodwill of Pharaoh king of Egypt; so he made him ruler over Egypt and all his palace.

11 "Then a famine struck all Egypt and Canaan, bringing great suffering, and our fathers could not find food. 12When Jacob heard that there was grain in Egypt, he sent our fathers on their first visit. 13On their second visit, Joseph told his brothers who he was, and Pharaoh learned about Joseph's family. 14After this, Joseph sent for his father Jacob and his whole family, seventy-five in all. 15Then Jacob went down to Egypt, where he and our fathers

[x]7 Gen. 15:13,14

16"And *from there* they were removed to Shechem, and laid in the tomb which Abraham had purchased for a sum of money from the sons of Hamor in Shechem.

17"But as the time of the promise was approaching which God had assured to Abraham, the people increased and multiplied in Egypt,

18until THERE AROSE ANOTHER KING OVER EGYPT WHO KNEW NOTHING ABOUT JOSEPH.

19"It was he who took shrewd advantage of our race, and mistreated our fathers so that they would expose their infants and they would not survive.

20"And it was at this time that Moses was born; and he was lovely in the sight of God; and he was nurtured three months in his father's home.

21"And after he had been exposed, Pharaoh's daughter took him away, and nurtured him as her own son.

22"And Moses was educated in all the learning of the Egyptians, and he was a man of power in words and deeds.

23"But when he was approaching the age of forty, it entered his mind to visit his brethren, the sons of Israel.

24"And when he saw one *of them* being treated unjustly, he defended him and took vengeance for the oppressed by striking down the Egyptian.

25"And he supposed that his brethren understood that God was granting them deliverance through him; but they did not understand.

26"And on the following day he appeared to them as they were fighting together, and he tried to reconcile them in peace, saying, 'Men, you are brethren, why do you injure one another?'

μετετέθησαν εἰς Συχὲμ καὶ ἐτέθησαν ἐν
were transferred to Sychem and were put in
τῷ μνήματι ᾧ ὠνήσατο Ἀβραὰμ τιμῆς
the tomb which [2]bought [1]Abraham of(for) a price
ἀργυρίου παρὰ τῶν υἱῶν Ἐμμὼρ ἐν
of silver from the sons of Emmor in
Συχέμ. 17 Καθὼς δὲ ἤγγιζεν ὁ χρόνος
Sychem. And as drew near the time
τῆς ἐπαγγελίας ἧς ὡμολόγησεν ὁ θεὸς
of the promise which [2]declared – [1]God
τῷ Ἀβραάμ, ηὔξησεν ὁ λαὸς καὶ
to Abraham, [3]grew [1]the [2]people and
ἐπληθύνθη ἐν Αἰγύπτῳ, 18 ἄχρι οὗ ἀνέστη
were multiplied in Egypt, until [3]rose up
βασιλεὺς ἕτερος ἐπ' Αἴγυπτον, ὃς οὐκ ᾔδει
[2]king [1]another over Egypt, who did not know
τὸν Ἰωσήφ. 19 οὗτος κατασοφισάμενος
– Joseph. This man dealing craftily with
τὸ γένος ἡμῶν ἐκάκωσεν τοὺς πατέρας
the race of us ill-treated the fathers
τοῦ ποιεῖν τὰ βρέφη ἔκθετα αὐτῶν
– to make[d] [1]the [2]babes [4]exposed [3]of them
εἰς τὸ μὴ ζῳογονεῖσθαι. 20 Ἐν ᾧ
to the not to be preserved alive. At which
=so that they should not be . . .
καιρῷ ἐγεννήθη Μωϋσῆς, καὶ ἦν ἀστεῖος
time was born Moses, and was fair
τῷ θεῷ· ὃς ἀνετράφη μῆνας τρεῖς ἐν
– to God; who was reared months three in
τῷ οἴκῳ τοῦ πατρός· 21 ἐκτεθέντος δὲ
the house of the(his) father; being exposed and
=and when he was exposed
αὐτοῦ ἀνείλατο αὐτὸν ἡ θυγάτηρ Φαραὼ
him[a] took up him the daughter of Pharaoh
καὶ ἀνεθρέψατο αὐτὸν ἑαυτῇ εἰς υἱόν.
and reared him to herself for a son.
=as her own son.
22 καὶ ἐπαιδεύθη Μωϋσῆς πάσῃ σοφίᾳ
And was trained Moses in all [the] wisdom
Αἰγυπτίων, ἦν δὲ δυνατὸς ἐν λόγοις
of [the] Egyptians, and was powerful in words
καὶ ἔργοις αὐτοῦ. 23 Ὡς δὲ ἐπληροῦτο
and works of him. But when [3]was fulfilled
αὐτῷ τεσσερακονταέτης χρόνος, ἀνέβη ἐπὶ
[4]to him [2]of forty years [1]a time, it came up upon
τὴν καρδίαν αὐτοῦ ἐπισκέψασθαι τοὺς
the heart of him to visit the
ἀδελφοὺς αὐτοῦ τοὺς υἱοὺς Ἰσραήλ. 24 καὶ
brothers of him the sons of Israel. And
ἰδών τινα ἀδικούμενον ἠμύνατο, καὶ
seeing one being injured he defended [him], and
ἐποίησεν ἐκδίκησιν τῷ καταπονουμένῳ
he wrought vengeance for the [one] getting the worse
πατάξας τὸν Αἰγύπτιον. 25 ἐνόμιζεν δὲ
striking the Egyptian. Now he supposed
συνιέναι τοὺς ἀδελφοὺς ὅτι ὁ θεὸς διὰ
to understand the(his) brothers[b] that – God through
=that his brothers would understand
χειρὸς αὐτοῦ δίδωσιν σωτηρίαν αὐτοῖς·
hand of him would give salvation to them;
οἱ δὲ οὐ συνῆκαν. 26 τῇ τε ἐπιούσῃ
but they understood not. And on the coming
ἡμέρᾳ ὤφθη αὐτοῖς μαχομένοις, καὶ
day he appeared to them fighting, and
συνήλλασσεν αὐτοὺς εἰς εἰρήνην εἰπών·
attempted to reconcile them in peace saying:
ἄνδρες, ἀδελφοί ἐστε· ἱνατί ἀδικεῖτε
Men, brothers ye are; why injure ye

died. 16Their bodies were
brought back to Shechem
and placed in the tomb that
Abraham had bought from
the sons of Hamor at She-
chem for a certain sum of
money.
17"As the time drew near
for God to fulfill his promise to Abraham, the num-
ber of our people in Egypt
greatly increased. 18Then
another king, who knew
nothing about Joseph, be-
came ruler of Egypt. 19He
dealt treacherously with
our people and oppressed
our forefathers by forcing
them to throw out their
newborn babies so that
they would die.
20"At that time Moses
was born, and he was no
ordinary child.[y] For three
months he was cared for in
his father's house. 21When
he was placed outside,
Pharaoh's daughter took
him and brought him up as
her own son. 22Moses was
educated in all the wisdom
of the Egyptians and was
powerful in speech and action.
23"When Moses was for-
ty years old, he decided to
visit his fellow Israelites.
24He saw one of them being
mistreated by an Egyptian,
so he went to his defense
and avenged him by killing
the Egyptian. 25Moses
thought that his own people
would realize that God was
using him to rescue them,
but they did not. 26The next
day Moses came upon two
Israelites who were fighting. He tried to reconcile
them by saying, 'Men, you
are brothers; why do you
want to hurt each other?'

[y]20 Or *was fair in the sight of God*

27"But the one who was
injuring his neighbor
pushed him away, saying,
'WHO MADE YOU A RULER
AND JUDGE OVER US?
28'YOU DO NOT MEAN TO
KILL ME AS YOU KILLED THE
EGYPTIAN YESTERDAY, DO
YOU?'
29"And at this remark
MOSES FLED, AND BECAME AN
ALIEN IN THE LAND OF MIDI-
AN, where he became the
father of two sons.
30"And after forty years
had passed, AN ANGEL AP-
PEARED TO HIM IN THE WIL-
DERNESS OF MOUNT Sinai, IN
THE FLAME OF A BURNING
THORN BUSH.
31"And when Moses saw
it, he *began* to marvel at the
sight; and as he approached
to look *more* closely, there
came the voice of the Lord:
32'I AM THE GOD OF YOUR
FATHERS, THE GOD OF ABRA-
HAM AND ISAAC AND JACOB.'
And Moses shook with fear
and would not venture to
look.
33"BUT THE LORD SAID TO
HIM, 'TAKE OFF THE SANDALS
FROM YOUR FEET, FOR THE
PLACE ON WHICH YOU ARE
STANDING IS HOLY GROUND.
34'I HAVE CERTAINLY SEEN
THE OPPRESSION OF MY
PEOPLE IN EGYPT, AND HAVE
HEARD THEIR GROANS, AND I
HAVE COME DOWN TO DE-
LIVER THEM; COME NOW, AND
I WILL SEND YOU TO EGYPT.'
35"This Moses whom
they disowned, saying,
'WHO MADE YOU A RULER
AND A JUDGE?' is the one
whom God sent *to be* both a
ruler and a deliverer with
the help of the angel who
appeared to him in the
thorn bush.
36"This man led them
out, performing wonders
and signs in the land of
Egypt and in the Red Sea
and in the wilderness for
forty years.
37"This is the Moses who

ἀλλήλους; **27** ὁ δὲ ἀδικῶν τὸν πλησίον
each other? But the [one] injuring the(his) neighbour

ἀπώσατο αὐτὸν εἰπών· τίς σε κατέστησεν
thrust away him saying: Who thee appointed

ἄρχοντα καὶ δικαστὴν ἐφ' ἡμῶν; **28** μὴ
a ruler and a judge over us? *not*

ἀνελεῖν με σὺ θέλεις ὃν τρόπον ἀνεῖλες
to kill me thou wishest in the same way as† thou killedst

ἐχθὲς τὸν Αἰγύπτιον; **29** ἔφυγεν δὲ
yesterday the Egyptian? So fled

Μωϋσῆς ἐν τῷ λόγῳ τούτῳ, καὶ ἐγένετο
Moses at this word, and became

πάροικος ἐν γῇ Μαδιάμ, οὗ ἐγέννησεν
a sojourner in [the] land Midian, where he begat

υἱοὺς δύο. **30** Καὶ πληρωθέντων ἐτῶν
sons two. And being fulfilled years
=when forty years were fulfilled

τεσσεράκοντα ὤφθη αὐτῷ ἐν τῇ ἐρήμῳ
forty[a] appeared to him in the desert

τοῦ ὄρους Σινὰ ἄγγελος ἐν φλογὶ πυρὸς
of the mount Sinai an angel in a flame of fire

βάτου. **31** ὁ δὲ Μωϋσῆς ἰδὼν ἐθαύμαζεν
of a thorn bush. – And Moses seeing marvelled at

τὸ ὅραμα· προσερχομένου δὲ αὐτοῦ κατα-
the vision; and approaching him[a] to take
=as he approached

νοῆσαι ἐγένετο φωνὴ κυρίου· **32** ἐγὼ ὁ
notice there was a voice of [the] Lord: I the

θεὸς τῶν πατέρων σου, ὁ θεὸς Ἀβραὰμ
God of the fathers of thee, the God of Abraham

καὶ Ἰσαὰκ καὶ Ἰακώβ. ἔντρομος δὲ
and of Isaac and of Jacob. But trembling

γενόμενος Μωϋσῆς οὐκ ἐτόλμα κατανοῆσαι.
becoming Moses dared not *to* take notice.

33 εἶπεν δὲ αὐτῷ ὁ κύριος· λῦσον τὸ
And said to him the Lord: Loosen the

ὑπόδημα τῶν ποδῶν σου· ὁ γὰρ τόπος
sandal of the feet of thee; for the place

ἐφ' ᾧ ἕστηκας γῆ ἁγία ἐστίν. **34** ἰδὼν
on which thou standest ground holy is. Seeing

εἶδον τὴν κάκωσιν τοῦ λαοῦ μου τοῦ
I saw the ill-treatment of the people of me –

ἐν Αἰγύπτῳ, καὶ τοῦ στεναγμοῦ αὐτοῦ
in Egypt, and the groan of it

ἤκουσα, καὶ κατέβην ἐξελέσθαι αὐτούς·
I heard, and I came down to rescue them;

καὶ νῦν δεῦρο ἀποστείλω σε εἰς Αἴγυπτον.
and now come I will send thee to Egypt.

35 Τοῦτον τὸν Μωϋσῆν, ὃν ἠρνήσαντο
This – Moses, whom they denied

εἰπόντες· τίς σε κατέστησεν ἄρχοντα καὶ
saying: Who thee appointed a ruler and

δικαστήν; τοῦτον ὁ θεὸς καὶ ἄρχοντα
a judge? this man – God both a ruler

καὶ λυτρωτὴν ἀπέσταλκεν σὺν χειρὶ
and a redeemer has sent with [the] hand

ἀγγέλου τοῦ ὀφθέντος αὐτῷ ἐν τῇ βάτῳ.
of [the] angel – appearing to him in the bush.

36 οὗτος ἐξήγαγεν αὐτοὺς ποιήσας τέρατα
This man led forth them doing wonders

καὶ σημεῖα ἐν γῇ Αἰγύπτῳ καὶ ἐν
and signs in [the] land Egypt and in

ἐρυθρᾷ θαλάσσῃ καὶ ἐν τῇ ἐρήμῳ ἔτη
[the] Red Sea and in the desert years

τεσσεράκοντα. **37** οὗτός ἐστιν ὁ Μωϋσῆς
forty. This is the Moses

27"But the man who was
mistreating the other
pushed Moses aside and
said, 'Who made you ruler
and judge over us? 28Do
you want to kill me as you
killed the Egyptian yesterday?'[z] 29When Moses
heard this, he fled to Midian, where he settled as a
foreigner and had two sons.
30"After forty years had
passed, an angel appeared
to Moses in the flames of a
burning bush in the desert
near Mount Sinai. 31When
he saw this, he was amazed
at the sight. As he went
over to look more closely,
he heard the Lord's voice:
32'I am the God of your fathers, the God of Abraham,
Isaac and Jacob.'[a] Moses
trembled with fear and did
not dare to look.
33"Then the Lord said to
him, 'Take off your san-
dals; the place where you
are standing is holy ground.
34I have indeed seen the oppression of my people in
Egypt. I have heard their
groaning and have come
down to set them free. Now
come, I will send you back
to Egypt.'[b]
35"This is the same Mo-
ses whom they had rejected
with the words, 'Who made
you ruler and judge?' He
was sent to be their ruler
and deliverer by God him-
self, through the angel who
appeared to him in the
bush. 36He led them out of
Egypt and did wonders and
miraculous signs in Egypt,
at the Red Sea[c] and for forty years in the desert.
37"This is that Moses

[z] *28* Exodus 2:14
[a] *32* Exodus 3:6
[b] *34* Exodus 3:5,7,8,10
[c] *36* That is, Sea of Reeds

said to the sons of Israel,
'God shall raise up for
you a prophet like me from
your brethren.'
38"This is the one who
was in the congregation in
the wilderness together
with the angel who was
speaking to him on Mount
Sinai, and *who was* with
our fathers; and he re-
ceived living oracles to
pass on to you.
39"And our fathers were
unwilling to be obedient to
him, but repudiated him
and in their hearts turned
back to Egypt,
40saying to Aaron,
'Make for us gods who
will go before us; for this
Moses who led us out of
the land of Egypt—we do
not know what happened
to him.'
41"And at that time they
made a calf and brought a
sacrifice to the idol, and
were rejoicing in the works
of their hands.
42"But God turned away
and delivered them up to
serve the host of heaven; as
it is written in the book of
the prophets, 'It was not
to Me that you offered
victims and sacrifices
forty years in the wilderness, was it, O house of
Israel?
43'You also took along
the tabernacle of Mo-
loch and the star of the
god Rompha, the images
which you made to wor-
ship them. I also will remove you beyond Bab-
ylon.'
44"Our fathers had the
tabernacle of testimony in
the wilderness, just as He
who spoke to Moses directed *him* to make it according
to the pattern which he had
seen.
45"And having received it
in their turn, our fathers
brought it in with Joshua
upon dispossessing the nations whom God drove out

ὁ εἴπας τοῖς υἱοῖς Ἰσραήλ· προφήτην
– saying to the sons of Israel : A prophet

ὑμῖν ἀναστήσει ὁ θεὸς ἐκ τῶν ἀδελφῶν
for you will raise up – God of the brothers

ὑμῶν ὡς ἐμέ. 38 οὗτός ἐστιν ὁ γενόμενος
of you as me. This is the [one] having been

ἐν τῇ ἐκκλησίᾳ ἐν τῇ ἐρήμῳ μετὰ τοῦ
in the church in the desert with the

ἀγγέλου τοῦ λαλοῦντος αὐτῷ ἐν τῷ
angel – speaking to him in the

ὄρει Σινᾶ καὶ τῶν πατέρων ἡμῶν, ὃς
mount Sinai and [with] the fathers of us, who

ἐδέξατο λόγια ζῶντα δοῦναι ὑμῖν, 39 ᾧ
received oracles living to give to you, [1]to whom

οὐκ ἠθέλησαν ὑπήκοοι γενέσθαι οἱ πατέρες
[8]wished [6]not [5]obedient [7]to become [2]the [3]fathers

ἡμῶν, ἀλλὰ ἀπώσαντο καὶ ἐστράφησαν
[4]of us, but thrust away and turned

ἐν ταῖς καρδίαις αὐτῶν εἰς Αἴγυπτον,
in the hearts of them to Egypt,

40 εἰπόντες τῷ Ἀαρών· ποίησον ἡμῖν
saying – to Aaron : Make for us

θεοὺς οἳ προπορεύσονται ἡμῶν· ὁ γὰρ
gods which will go before us; – for

Μωϋσῆς οὗτος, ὃς ἐξήγαγεν ἡμᾶς ἐκ
this Moses, who led forth us out of

γῆς Αἰγύπτου, οὐκ οἴδαμεν τί ἐγένετο
[the] land Egypt, we know not what happened

αὐτῷ. 41 καὶ ἐμοσχοποίησαν ἐν
to him. And they made [a model of] a calf in

ταῖς ἡμέραις ἐκείναις καὶ ἀνήγαγον θυσίαν τῷ
those days and brought up a sacrifice to the

εἰδώλῳ, καὶ εὐφραίνοντο ἐν τοῖς ἔργοις
idol, and made merry in the works

τῶν χειρῶν αὐτῶν. 42 ἔστρεψεν δὲ ὁ
of the hands of them. And [2]turned –

θεὸς καὶ παρέδωκεν αὐτοὺς λατρεύειν
[1]God and delivered them to worship

τῇ στρατιᾷ τοῦ οὐρανοῦ, καθὼς γέγραπται
the host – of heaven, as it has been written

ἐν βίβλῳ τῶν προφητῶν· μὴ σφάγια
in [the] roll of the prophets : *Not* victims

καὶ θυσίας προσηνέγκατέ μοι ἔτη
and sacrifices ye offered to me years

τεσσεράκοντα ἐν τῇ ἐρήμῳ, οἶκος Ἰσραήλ,
forty in the desert, [O] house of Israel,

43 καὶ ἀνελάβετε τὴν σκηνὴν τοῦ Μόλοχ
and ye took up the tent – of Moloch

καὶ τὸ ἄστρον τοῦ θεοῦ Ῥομφά, τοὺς
and the star of the god Rompha, the

τύπους οὓς ἐποιήσατε προσκυνεῖν αὐτοῖς;
models which ye made to worship them?

καὶ μετοικιῶ ὑμᾶς ἐπέκεινα Βαβυλῶνος.
and I will deport you beyond Babylon.

44 Ἡ σκηνὴ τοῦ μαρτυρίου ἦν τοῖς
The tent – of witness was to the
=Our fathers had the tent of witness

πατράσιν ἡμῶν ἐν τῇ ἐρήμῳ, καθὼς
fathers of us° in the desert, as

διετάξατο ὁ λαλῶν τῷ Μωϋσῇ ποιῆσαι
commanded the [one] speaking – to Moses to make

αὐτὴν κατὰ τὸν τύπον ὃν ἑωράκει·
it according to the model which he had seen;

45 ἣν καὶ εἰσήγαγον διαδεξάμενοι οἱ
which also [4]brought in [5]having received [1]the

πατέρες ἡμῶν μετὰ Ἰησοῦ ἐν τῇ κατα-
[2]fathers [3]of us with Jesus in the pos-

who told the Israelites,
'God will send you a prophet like me from your own
people.'[d] 38He was in the
assembly in the desert,
with the angel who spoke to
him on Mount Sinai, and
with our fathers; and he received living words to pass
on to us.
39"But our fathers re-
fused to obey him. Instead,
they rejected him and in
their hearts turned back to
Egypt. 40They told Aaron,
'Make us gods who will go
before us. As for this fellow
Moses who led us out of
Egypt—we don't know
what has happened to
him!'[e] 41That was the time
they made an idol in the
form of a calf. They
brought sacrifices to it and
held a celebration in honor
of what their hands had
made. 42But God turned
away and gave them over
to the worship of the heavenly bodies. This agrees
with what is written in the
book of the prophets:

" 'Did you bring me
sacrifices and
offerings
forty years in the
desert, O house of
Israel?
43You have lifted up the
shrine of Molech
and the star of your
god Rephan,
the idols you made to
worship.
Therefore I will send you
into exile'[f] beyond
Babylon.

44"Our forefathers had
the tabernacle of the Testimony with them in the desert. It had been made as
God directed Moses, ac-
cording to the pattern he
had seen. 45Having re-
ceived the tabernacle, our
fathers under Joshua
brought it with them when
they took the land from the
nations God drove out be-
fore them. It remained in

d37 Deut. 18:15
e40 Exodus 32:1
f43 Amos 5:25-27

before our fathers, until the
time of David.
46"And *David* found fa-
vor in God's sight, and
asked that he might find a
dwelling place for the [o]God
of Jacob.
47"But it was Solomon
who built a house for Him.
48"However, the Most
High does not dwell in
houses made by *human*
hands; as the prophet says:
49 'HEAVEN IS MY
THRONE,
AND EARTH IS THE
FOOTSTOOL OF MY
FEET;
WHAT KIND OF HOUSE
WILL YOU BUILD FOR
ME?' says the Lord;
'OR WHAT PLACE IS
THERE FOR MY
REPOSE?
50 'WAS IT NOT MY HAND
WHICH MADE ALL
THESE THINGS?'
51"You men who are
stiff-necked and uncircumcised in heart and ears are
always resisting the Holy
Spirit; you are doing just as
your fathers did.
52"Which one of the
prophets did your fathers
not persecute? And they
killed those who had previously announced the com-
ing of the Righteous One,
whose betrayers and mur-
derers you have now
become;
53you who received the
law as ordained by angels,
and *yet* did not keep it."

Stephen Put to Death

54Now when they heard
this, they were cut to the
quick, and they *began*
gnashing their teeth at him.
55But being full of the
Holy Spirit, he gazed in-
tently into heaven and saw
the glory of God, and Jesus
standing at the right hand of
God;
56and he said, "Behold, I
see the heavens opened up
and the Son of Man stand-
ing at the right hand of
God."
57But they cried out with
a loud voice, and covered
their ears, and they rushed
upon him with one impulse.
58And when they had

[o] The earliest mss. read *house* instead of *God;* the Septuagint reads *God*

σχέσει τῶν ἐθνῶν, ὧν ἐξῶσεν ὁ θεὸς
session of the nations, whom put out - God
ἀπὸ προσώπου τῶν πατέρων ἡμῶν, ἕως
from [the] face of the fathers of us, until
τῶν ἡμερῶν Δαυίδ· **46** ὃς εὗρεν χάριν
the days of David; who found favour
ἐνώπιον τοῦ θεοῦ καὶ ᾐτήσατο εὑρεῖν
before – God and asked to find
σκήνωμα τῷ οἴκῳ Ἰακώβ. **47** Σολομὼν δὲ
a tent for the house of Jacob. But Solomon
οἰκοδόμησεν αὐτῷ οἶκον. **48** ἀλλ'
built for him a house. But
οὐχ ὁ ὕψιστος ἐν χειροποιήτοις κατοικεῖ·
[4]not [1]the [2]Most High [5]in [6][places] made by hand [3]dwells;
καθὼς ὁ προφήτης λέγει· **49** ὁ οὐρανός
as the prophet says: The heaven
μοι θρόνος, ἡ δὲ γῆ ὑποπόδιον τῶν
to me a throne, and the earth a footstool of the
ποδῶν μου· ποῖον οἶκον οἰκοδομήσετέ μοι,
feet of me; what house will ye build for me,
λέγει κύριος, ἢ τίς τόπος τῆς καταπαύσεώς
says [the] Lord, or what place of the rest
μου; **50** οὐχὶ ἡ χείρ μου ἐποίησεν ταῦτα
of me? not the hand of me made these things
πάντα; **51** Σκληροτράχηλοι καὶ ἀπερίτμητοι
all? Hard-necked and uncircumcised
καρδίαις καὶ τοῖς ὠσίν, ὑμεῖς ἀεὶ τῷ
in hearts and – ears, ye always the
πνεύματι τῷ ἁγίῳ ἀντιπίπτετε, ὡς οἱ
Spirit – Holy oppose, as the
πατέρες ὑμῶν καὶ ὑμεῖς. **52** τίνα τῶν
fathers of you also ye. Which of the
προφητῶν οὐκ ἐδίωξαν οἱ πατέρες ὑμῶν;
prophets persecuted not the fathers of you?
καὶ ἀπέκτειναν τοὺς προκαταγγείλαντας
and they killed the [ones] announcing beforehand
περὶ τῆς ἐλεύσεως τοῦ δικαίου, οὗ
concerning the coming of the righteous one, of whom
νῦν ὑμεῖς προδόται καὶ φονεῖς ἐγένεσθε,
now ye betrayers and murderers became,
53 οἵτινες ἐλάβετε τὸν νόμον εἰς διαταγὰς
who received the law in(by) dispositions
ἀγγέλων, καὶ οὐκ ἐφυλάξατε.
of angels, and did not keep [it].
54 Ἀκούοντες δὲ ταῦτα διεπρίοντο ταῖς
And hearing these things they were cut to the
καρδίαις αὐτῶν καὶ ἔβρυχον τοὺς ὀδόντας
hearts of them and gnashed the teeth
ἐπ' αὐτόν. **55** ὑπάρχων δὲ πλήρης
at him. But being full
πνεύματος ἁγίου ἀτενίσας εἰς τὸν οὐρανὸν
of [the] Spirit Holy gazing into – heaven
εἶδεν δόξαν θεοῦ καὶ Ἰησοῦν ἑστῶτα ἐκ
he saw [the] glory of God and Jesus standing at
δεξιῶν τοῦ θεοῦ, **56** καὶ εἶπεν· ἰδοὺ
[the] right [hand] – of God, and said: Behold
θεωρῶ τοὺς οὐρανοὺς διηνοιγμένους καὶ
I see the heavens *having been* opened up and
τὸν υἱὸν τοῦ ἀνθρώπου ἐκ δεξιῶν ἑστῶτα
the Son – of man at [the] right [hand] standing
τοῦ θεοῦ. **57** κράξαντες δὲ φωνῇ μεγάλῃ
– of God. And crying out voice with a great
συνέσχον τὰ ὦτα αὐτῶν, καὶ ὥρμησαν
they closed the ears of them, and rushed
ὁμοθυμαδὸν ἐπ' αὐτόν, **58** καὶ ἐκβαλόντες
with one mind on him, and casting *out*

the land until the time of
David, 46who enjoyed
God's favor and asked that
he might provide a dwelling
place for the God of Ja-
cob.[g] 47But it was Solomon
who built the house for
him.
48"However, the Most
High does not live in
houses made by men. As
the prophet says:
49" 'Heaven is my throne,
and the earth is my
footstool.
What kind of house will
you build for me?
says the Lord.
Or where will my
resting place be?
50Has not my hand made
all these things?'[h]
51"You stiff-necked peo-
ple, with uncircumcised
hearts and ears! You are
just like your fathers: You
always resist the Holy Spirit! 52Was there ever a
prophet your fathers did
not persecute? They even
killed those who predicted
the coming of the Right-
eous One. And now you
have betrayed and mur-
dered him— 53you who
have received the law that
was put into effect through
angels but have not obeyed
it."

The Stoning of Stephen

54When they heard this,
they were furious and
gnashed their teeth at him.
55But Stephen, full of the
Holy Spirit, looked up to
heaven and saw the glory of
God, and Jesus standing at
the right hand of God.
56"Look," he said, "I see
heaven open and the Son of
Man standing at the right
hand of God."
57At this they covered

[g] *46* Some early manuscripts *the house of Jacob*

[h] *50* Isaiah 66:1,2

driven him out of the city, they *began* stoning *him,* and the witnesses laid aside their robes at the feet of a young man named Saul.
59And they went on stoning Stephen as he called upon *the Lord* and said, "Lord Jesus, receive my spirit!"
60And falling on his knees, he cried out with a loud voice, "Lord, do not hold this sin against them!" And having said this, he fell asleep.

Chapter 8

Saul Persecutes the Church

AND Saul was in hearty agreement with putting him to death.
And on that day a great persecution arose against the church in Jerusalem; and they were all scattered throughout the regions of Judea and Samaria, except the apostles.
2And *some* devout men buried Stephen, and made loud lamentation over him.
3But Saul *began* ravaging the church, entering house after house; and dragging off men and women, he would put them in prison.

Philip in Samaria

4Therefore, those who had been scattered went about preaching the word.
5And Philip went down to the city of Samaria and *began* proclaiming Christ to them.
6And the multitudes with one accord were giving attention to what was said by Philip, as they heard and saw the signs which he was performing.
7For *in the case of* many who had unclean spirits, they were coming out *of them* shouting with a loud voice; and many who had been paralyzed and lame were healed.
8And there was much re-

ἔξω τῆς πόλεως ἐλιθοβόλουν. καὶ οἱ
outside the city they stoned [him]. And the
μάρτυρες ἀπέθεντο τὰ ἱμάτια αὐτῶν παρὰ
witnesses put off the garments of them at
τοὺς πόδας νεανίου καλουμένου Σαύλου.
the feet of a young man *being* called Saul.
59 καὶ ἐλιθοβόλουν τὸν Στέφανον, ἐπικαλ-
And they stoned – Stephen, invok-
ούμενον καὶ λέγοντα· κύριε Ἰησοῦ, δέξαι
ing [God] and saying: Lord Jesus, receive
τὸ πνεῦμά μου. 60 θεὶς δὲ τὰ γόνατα
the spirit of me. And placing the knees
=kneeling down
ἔκραξεν φωνῇ μεγάλῃ· κύριε, μὴ στήσῃς
he cried voice with a great: Lord, place not
αὐτοῖς ταύτην τὴν ἁμαρτίαν. καὶ τοῦτο
to them this – sin. And [2]this
εἰπὼν ἐκοιμήθη. 8 Σαῦλος δὲ ἦν συνευδοκῶν
[1]saying he fell asleep. And Saul was consenting
τῇ ἀναιρέσει αὐτοῦ.
to the killing of him.
Ἐγένετο δὲ ἐν ἐκείνῃ τῇ ἡμέρᾳ
And there was in that – day
διωγμὸς μέγας ἐπὶ τὴν ἐκκλησίαν τὴν
persecution a great on(against) the church –
ἐν Ἱεροσολύμοις· πάντες [δὲ] διεσπάρησαν
in Jerusalem; and all were scattered
κατὰ τὰς χώρας τῆς Ἰουδαίας καὶ
throughout the countries – of Judæa and
Σαμαρείας πλὴν τῶν ἀποστόλων.
Samaria except the apostles.
2 συνεκόμισαν δὲ τὸν Στέφανον ἄνδρες
And [3]recovered – [4]Stephen [2]men
εὐλαβεῖς καὶ ἐποίησαν κοπετὸν μέγαν
[1]devout and made lamentation great
ἐπ' αὐτῷ. 3 Σαῦλος δὲ ἐλυμαίνετο τὴν
over him. But Saul ravaged the
ἐκκλησίαν κατὰ τοὺς οἴκους εἰσπορευόμενος,
church house by house† entering,
σύρων τε ἄνδρας καὶ γυναῖκας παρεδίδου
dragging both men and women delivered
εἰς φυλακήν.
to prison.
4 Οἱ μὲν οὖν διασπαρέντες διῆλθον
The [ones] –* therefore being scattered passed through
εὐαγγελιζόμενοι τὸν λόγον. 5 Φίλιππος δὲ
preaching the word. But Philip
κατελθὼν εἰς τὴν πόλιν τῆς
going down to the city –
Σαμαρείας ἐκήρυσσεν αὐτοῖς τὸν Χριστόν.
of Samaria proclaimed to them the Christ.
6 προσεῖχον δὲ οἱ ὄχλοι τοῖς
And gave heed the crowds to the things
λεγομένοις ὑπὸ τοῦ Φιλίππου ὁμοθυμαδὸν
being said by – Philip with one mind
ἐν τῷ ἀκούειν αὐτοὺς καὶ βλέπειν τὰ
in the to hear them and to see[be] the
=as they heard and saw
σημεῖα ἃ ἐποίει. 7 πολλοὶ γὰρ τῶν
signs which he was doing. For many of the
ἐχόντων πνεύματα ἀκάθαρτα βοῶντα φωνῇ
[ones] having spirits unclean crying [2]voice
μεγάλῃ ἐξήρχοντο· πολλοὶ δὲ παραλελυμένοι
[1]with a great came out; and many *having been* paralysed
καὶ χωλοὶ ἐθεραπεύθησαν· 8 ἐγένετο δὲ
and lame were healed; and there was

* See note on John 19. 24.

their ears and, yelling at the top of their voices, they all rushed at him, 58dragged him out of the city and began to stone him. Meanwhile, the witnesses laid their clothes at the feet of a young man named Saul.
59While they were stoning him, Stephen prayed, "Lord Jesus, receive my spirit." 60Then he fell on his knees and cried out, "Lord, do not hold this sin against them." When he had said this, he fell asleep.

Chapter 8

AND Saul was there, giving approval to his death.

The Church Persecuted and Scattered

On that day a great persecution broke out against the church at Jerusalem, and all except the apostles were scattered throughout Judea and Samaria. 2Godly men buried Stephen and mourned deeply for him. 3But Saul began to destroy the church. Going from house to house, he dragged off men and women and put them in prison.

Philip in Samaria

4Those who had been scattered preached the word wherever they went. 5Philip went down to a city in Samaria and proclaimed the Christ[i] there. 6When the crowds heard Philip and saw the miraculous signs he did, they all paid close attention to what he said. 7With shrieks, evil[j] spirits came out of many, and many paralytics and cripples were healed. 8So

[i]5 Or *Messiah*
[j]7 Greek *unclean*

joicing in that city.

9Now there was a certain man named Simon, who formerly was practicing magic in the city, and astonishing the people of Samaria, claiming to be someone great;

10and they all, from smallest to greatest, were giving attention to him, saying, "This man is what is called the Great Power of God."

11And they were giving him attention because he had for a long time astonished them with his magic arts.

12But when they believed Philip preaching the good news about the kingdom of God and the name of Jesus Christ, they were being baptized, men and women alike.

13And even Simon himself believed; and after being baptized, he continued on with Philip; and as he observed signs and great miracles taking place, he was constantly amazed.

14Now when the apostles in Jerusalem heard that Samaria had received the word of God, they sent them Peter and John,

15who came down and prayed for them, that they might receive the Holy Spirit.

16For He had not yet fallen upon any of them; they had simply been baptized in the name of the Lord Jesus.

17Then they *began* laying their hands on them, and they were receiving the Holy Spirit.

18Now when Simon saw that the Spirit was bestowed through the laying on of the apostles' hands, he offered them money,

19saying, "Give this authority to me as well, so that everyone on whom I lay my hands may receive

πολλὴ χαρὰ ἐν τῇ πόλει ἐκείνῃ. 9 Ἀνὴρ δέ τις
much joy in that city. And a certain man

ὀνόματι Σίμων προϋπῆρχεν ἐν τῇ
by name Simon was previously in the

πόλει μαγεύων καὶ ἐξιστάνων τὸ
city practising sorcery and astonishing the

ἔθνος τῆς Σαμαρείας, λέγων εἶναί τινα
nation – of Samaria, saying [2]to be [3]someone

ἑαυτὸν μέγαν, 10 ᾧ προσεῖχον πάντες
[1]himself [4]great, to whom gave heed all

ἀπὸ μικροῦ ἕως μεγάλου λέγοντες· οὗτός
from small to great saying : This man

ἐστιν ἡ δύναμις τοῦ θεοῦ ἡ καλουμένη
is the power – of God – *being* called

μεγάλη. 11 προσεῖχον δὲ αὐτῷ διὰ τὸ
great. And they gave heed to him because of the

ἱκανῷ χρόνῳ ταῖς μαγείαις ἐξεστακέναι
for a considerable time by the sorceries to have astonished
=because for a considerable time he had astonished them by his sorceries.

αὐτούς. 12 ὅτε δὲ ἐπίστευσαν τῷ Φιλίππῳ
them. But when they believed – Philip

εὐαγγελιζομένῳ περὶ τῆς βασιλείας τοῦ
preaching about the kingdom –

θεοῦ καὶ τοῦ ὀνόματος Ἰησοῦ Χριστοῦ,
of God and the name of Jesus Christ,

ἐβαπτίζοντο ἄνδρες τε καὶ γυναῖκες.
they were baptized both men and women.

13 ὁ δὲ Σίμων καὶ αὐτὸς ἐπίστευσεν,
– And Simon also [him]self believed,

καὶ βαπτισθεὶς ἦν προσκαρτερῶν τῷ
and having been baptized was attaching himself –

Φιλίππῳ, θεωρῶν τε σημεῖα καὶ δυνάμεις
to Philip, and beholding signs and powerful deeds

μεγάλας γινομένας ἐξίστατο. 14 Ἀκούσαντες
great happening he was amazed. [6]hearing

δὲ οἱ ἐν Ἱεροσολύμοις ἀπόστολοι ὅτι
[1]And [2]the [4]in [5]Jerusalem [3]apostles that

δέδεκται ἡ Σαμάρεια τὸν λόγον τοῦ
[2]has received – [1]Samaria the word –

θεοῦ, ἀπέστειλαν πρὸς αὐτοὺς Πέτρον
of God, they sent to them Peter

καὶ Ἰωάννην, 15 οἵτινες καταβάντες
and John, who going down

προσηύξαντο περὶ αὐτῶν ὅπως λάβωσιν
prayed concerning them so as they might receive

πνεῦμα ἅγιον· 16 οὐδέπω γὰρ ἦν ἐπ'
Spirit Holy; for [2]not yet [1]he was [4]on

οὐδενὶ αὐτῶν ἐπιπεπτωκός, μόνον δὲ
[5]no(any)one [6]of them [3]having fallen *on*, but only

βεβαπτισμένοι ὑπῆρχον εἰς τὸ ὄνομα τοῦ
having been baptized they were in the name of the

κυρίου Ἰησοῦ. 17 τότε ἐπετίθεσαν τὰς
Lord Jesus. Then they laid *on* the(ir)

χεῖρας ἐπ' αὐτούς, καὶ ἐλάμβανον πνεῦμα
hands on them, and they received [2]Spirit

ἅγιον. 18 ἰδὼν δὲ ὁ Σίμων ὅτι διὰ
[1]Holy. And [2]seeing – [1]Simon that through

τῆς ἐπιθέσεως τῶν χειρῶν τῶν ἀποστόλων
the laying on of the hands of the apostles

δίδοται τὸ πνεῦμα, προσήνεγκεν αὐτοῖς
is(was) given the Spirit, he offered them

χρήματα λέγων· 19 δότε κἀμοὶ τὴν
money saying : Give me also –

ἐξουσίαν ταύτην ἵνα ᾧ ἐὰν ἐπιθῶ τὰς
authority this that whomever I lay on the(my)

there was great joy in that
city.

Simon the Sorcerer

9Now for some time a
man named Simon had
practiced sorcery in the
city and amazed all the people of Samaria. He boasted
that he was someone great,
10and all the people, both
high and low, gave him
their attention and ex-
claimed, "This man is the
divine power known as the
Great Power." 11They fol-
lowed him because he had
amazed them for a long
time with his magic. 12But
when they believed Philip
as he preached the good
news of the kingdom of
God and the name of Jesus
Christ, they were baptized,
both men and women. 13Si-
mon himself believed and
was baptized. And he fol-
lowed Philip everywhere,
astonished by the great
signs and miracles he saw.
14When the apostles in Jerusalem heard that Samaria
had accepted the word of
God, they sent Peter and
John to them. 15When they
arrived, they prayed for
them that they might re-
ceive the Holy Spirit, 16be-
cause the Holy Spirit had
not yet come upon any of
them; they had simply been
baptized into[k] the name of
the Lord Jesus. 17Then Peter and John placed their
hands on them, and they received the Holy Spirit.
18When Simon saw that
the Spirit was given at the
laying on of the apostles'
hands, he offered them
money 19and said, "Give
me also this ability so that
everyone on whom I lay my
hands may receive the
Holy Spirit."

[k]16 Or *in*

the Holy Spirit.''
20But Peter said to him,
''May your silver perish
with you, because you
thought you could obtain
the gift of God with money!
21''You have no part or
portion in this matter, for
your heart is not right before God.
22''Therefore repent of
this wickedness of yours,
and pray the Lord that if
possible, the intention of
your heart may be forgiven
you.
23''For I see that you are
in the gall of bitterness and
in the bondage of iniquity.''
24But Simon answered
and said, ''Pray to the Lord
for me yourselves, so that
nothing of what you have
said may come upon me.''

An Ethiopian Receives Christ

25And so, when they had
solemnly testified and
spoken the word of the
Lord, they started back to
Jerusalem, and were
preaching the gospel to
many villages of the
Samaritans.
26But an angel of the Lord
spoke to Philip saying,
''Arise and go south to the
road that descends from
Jerusalem to Gaza.'' (This
is a desert *road*.)
27And he arose and went;
and behold, there was an
Ethiopian eunuch, a court
official of Candace, queen
of the Ethiopians, who was
in charge of all her treasure;
and he had come to Jerusalem to worship.
28And he was returning
and sitting in his chariot,
and was reading the
prophet Isaiah.
29And the Spirit said to
Philip, ''Go up and join this

χεῖρας λαμβάνῃ πνεῦμα ἅγιον. 20 Πέτρος δὲ
hands he may receive Spirit Holy. But Peter

εἶπεν πρὸς αὐτόν· τὸ ἀργύριόν σου
said to him: The silver of thee

σὺν σοὶ εἴη εἰς ἀπώλειαν, ὅτι τὴν δωρεὰν
with thee may it be into perdition, because the gift

τοῦ θεοῦ ἐνόμισας διὰ χρημάτων κτᾶσθαι.
– of God thou didst suppose through money to get.

21 οὐκ ἔστιν σοι μερὶς οὐδὲ κλῆρος
There is not to thee° part nor lot
=Thou hast no

ἐν τῷ λόγῳ τούτῳ· ἡ γὰρ καρδία σου
in this matter; for the heart of thee

οὐκ ἔστιν εὐθεῖα ἔναντι τοῦ θεοῦ.
is not right before – God.

22 μετανόησον οὖν ἀπὸ τῆς κακίας σου
Repent thou therefore from – [2]wickedness [3]of thee

ταύτης, καὶ δεήθητι τοῦ κυρίου εἰ ἄρα
[1]this, and petition the Lord if perhaps

ἀφεθήσεταί σοι ἡ ἐπίνοια τῆς καρδίας
will be forgiven thee the thought of the heart

σου· 23 εἰς γὰρ χολὴν πικρίας καὶ
of thee; for in gall of bitterness and

σύνδεσμον ἀδικίας ὁρῶ σε ὄντα.
bond of unrighteousness I see thee being.

24 ἀποκριθεὶς δὲ ὁ Σίμων εἶπεν· δεήθητε
And answering – Simon said: Petition

ὑμεῖς ὑπὲρ ἐμοῦ πρὸς τὸν κύριον, ὅπως
ye for me to the Lord, so as

μηδὲν ἐπέλθῃ ἐπ' ἐμὲ ὧν εἰρήκατε.
[1]not one [4]may come *on* [5]on [6]me [2]of the things which [3]ye have spoken.

25 Οἱ μὲν οὖν διαμαρτυράμενοι καὶ λαλή-
They – therefore having solemnly witnessed and having

σαντες τὸν λόγον τοῦ κυρίου ὑπέστρεφον
spoken the word of the Lord returned

εἰς Ἱεροσόλυμα, πολλάς τε κώμας τῶν
to Jerusalem, and [2]many [3]villages [4]of the

Σαμαριτῶν εὐηγγελίζοντο.
[5]Samaritans [1]evangelized.

26 Ἄγγελος δὲ κυρίου ἐλάλησεν πρὸς
But an angel of [the] Lord spoke to

Φίλιππον λέγων· ἀνάστηθι καὶ πορεύου
Philip saying: Rise up and go

κατὰ μεσημβρίαν ἐπὶ τὴν ὁδὸν τὴν
along south on the way –

καταβαίνουσαν ἀπὸ Ἰερουσαλὴμ εἰς Γάζαν·
going down from Jerusalem to Gaza;

αὕτη ἐστὶν ἔρημος. 27 καὶ ἀναστὰς
this is desert. And rising up

ἐπορεύθη. καὶ ἰδοὺ ἀνὴρ Αἰθίοψ εὐνοῦχος
he went. And behold[,] *a man* Ethiopian a eunuch

δυνάστης Κανδάκης βασιλίσσης Αἰθιόπων,
a courtier of Candace queen of [the] Ethiopians,

ὃς ἦν ἐπὶ πάσης τῆς γάζης αὐτῆς,
who was over all the treasure of her,

[ὃς] ἐληλύθει προσκυνήσων εἰς Ἰερουσαλήμ,
who had come worshipping in Jerusalem,

28 ἦν δὲ ὑποστρέφων καὶ καθήμενος ἐπὶ
and was returning and sitting on

τοῦ ἅρματος αὐτοῦ καὶ ἀνεγίνωσκεν τὸν
the chariot of him and was reading the

προφήτην Ἠσαΐαν. 29 εἶπεν δὲ τὸ πνεῦμα
prophet Esaias. And said the Spirit

τῷ Φιλίππῳ· πρόσελθε καὶ κολλήθητι
– to Philip: Approach and keep company with

20Peter answered: ''May
your money perish with
you, because you thought
you could buy the gift of
God with money! 21You
have no part or share in this
ministry, because your
heart is not right before
God. 22Repent of this wickedness and pray to the
Lord. Perhaps he will forgive you for having such a
thought in your heart. 23For
I see that you are full of bitterness and captive to sin.''
24Then Simon answered,
''Pray to the Lord for me so
that nothing you have said
may happen to me.''
25When they had testified
and proclaimed the word of
the Lord, Peter and John
returned to Jerusalem,
preaching the gospel in
many Samaritan villages.

Philip and the Ethiopian

26Now an angel of the
Lord said to Philip, ''Go
south to the road—the desert road—that goes down
from Jerusalem to Gaza.''
27So he started out, and on
his way he met an Ethiopian[l] eunuch, an important
official in charge of all the
treasury of Candace, queen
of the Ethiopians. This man
had gone to Jerusalem to
worship, 28and on his way
home was sitting in his
chariot reading the book of
Isaiah the prophet. 29The
Spirit told Philip, ''Go to

[l]27 That is, from the upper Nile region

chariot."
30And when Philip had run up, he heard him reading Isaiah the prophet, and said, "Do you understand what you are reading?"
31And he said, "Well, how could I, unless someone guides me?" And he invited Philip to come up and sit with him.
32Now the passage of Scripture which he was reading was this:

"HE WAS LED AS A SHEEP
TO SLAUGHTER;
AND AS A LAMB BEFORE
ITS SHEARER IS SILENT,
SO HE DOES NOT OPEN
HIS MOUTH.
33"IN HUMILIATION HIS
JUDGMENT WAS TAKEN
AWAY;
WHO SHALL RELATE
HIS GENERATION?
FOR HIS LIFE IS REMOVED FROM THE
EARTH."

34And the eunuch answered Philip and said, "Please *tell me*, of whom does the prophet say this? Of himself, or of someone else?"
35And Philip opened his mouth, and beginning from this Scripture he preached Jesus to him.
36And as they went along the road they came to some water; and the eunuch *said, "Look! Water! What prevents me from being baptized?"
37[pAnd Philip said, "If you believe with all your heart, you may." And he answered and said, "I believe that Jesus Christ is the Son of God."]
38And he ordered the chariot to stop; and they both went down into the water, Philip as well as the eunuch; and he baptized him.
39And when they came up out of the water, the Spirit of the Lord snatched Philip away; and the eunuch saw him no more, but went on his way rejoicing.
40But Philip found himself at Azotus; and as he passed

τῷ ἅρματι τούτῳ. **30** προσδραμὼν δὲ
this chariot. And running up
ὁ Φίλιππος ἤκουσεν αὐτοῦ ἀναγινώσκοντος
– Philip heard him reading
Ἠσαΐαν τὸν προφήτην, καὶ εἶπεν· ἆρά γε
Esaias the prophet, and said : Then
γινώσκεις ἃ ἀναγινώσκεις; **31** ὁ δὲ
knowest thou what things thou art reading? And he
εἶπεν· πῶς γὰρ ἂν δυναίμην ἐὰν μή
said : How indeed should I be able unless
τις ὁδηγήσει με; παρεκάλεσέν τε τὸν
someone shall guide me? And he besought –
Φίλιππον ἀναβάντα καθίσαι σὺν αὐτῷ.
Philip coming up to sit with him.
32 ἡ δὲ περιοχὴ τῆς γραφῆς ἣν ἀνεγίνω-
Now the passage of the scripture which he was
σκεν ἦν αὕτη· ὡς πρόβατον ἐπὶ σφαγὴν
reading was this : As a sheep to slaughter
ἤχθη, καὶ ὡς ἀμνὸς ἐναντίον τοῦ κείροντος
he was led, and as a lamb before the [one] shearing
αὐτὸν ἄφωνος, οὕτως οὐκ ἀνοίγει τὸ
it [is] dumb, so he opens not the
στόμα αὐτοῦ. **33** Ἐν τῇ ταπεινώσει
mouth of him. In the humiliation
ἡ κρίσις αὐτοῦ ἤρθη· τὴν γενεὰν αὐτοῦ
the judgment of him was taken away; the generation of him
τίς διηγήσεται; ὅτι αἴρεται ἀπὸ τῆς
who will relate? because is taken from the
γῆς ἡ ζωὴ αὐτοῦ. **34** ἀποκριθεὶς δὲ ὁ
earth the life of him. And answering the
εὐνοῦχος τῷ Φιλίππῳ εἶπεν· δέομαί σου,
eunuch – to Philip said : I ask thee,
περὶ τίνος ὁ προφήτης λέγει τοῦτο;
about whom the prophet says this?
περὶ ἑαυτοῦ ἢ περὶ ἑτέρου τινός;
about himself or about other someone?
35 ἀνοίξας δὲ ὁ Φίλιππος τὸ στόμα
And opening – Philip the mouth
αὐτοῦ καὶ ἀρξάμενος ἀπὸ τῆς γραφῆς ταύτης
of him and beginning from this scripture
εὐηγγελίσατο αὐτῷ τὸν Ἰησοῦν.
preached to him – Jesus.
36 ὡς δὲ ἐπορεύοντο κατὰ τὴν ὁδόν,
And as they were going along the way,
ἦλθον ἐπί τι ὕδωρ, καί φησιν ὁ εὐνοῦχος·
they came upon certain water, and says the eunuch :
ἰδοὺ ὕδωρ· τί κωλύει με βαπτισθῆναι;‡
Behold[,] water; what prevents me to be baptized?
38 καὶ ἐκέλευσεν στῆναι τὸ ἅρμα, καὶ
And he commanded to stand the chariot, and
κατέβησαν ἀμφότεροι εἰς τὸ ὕδωρ, ὅ
went down both into the water, –
τε Φίλιππος καὶ ὁ εὐνοῦχος, καὶ ἐβάπτισεν
both Philip and the eunuch, and he baptized
αὐτόν. **39** ὅτε δὲ ἀνέβησαν ἐκ τοῦ ὕδατος,
him. And when they came up out of the water,
πνεῦμα κυρίου ἥρπασεν τὸν Φίλιππον,
[the] Spirit of [the] Lord seized – Philip,
καὶ οὐκ εἶδεν αὐτὸν οὐκέτι ὁ εὐνοῦχος,
and saw not him no(any) more the eunuch,
ἐπορεύετο γὰρ τὴν ὁδὸν αὐτοῦ χαίρων.
for he went the way of him rejoicing.
40 Φίλιππος δὲ εὑρέθη εἰς Ἄζωτον, καὶ
But Philip was found in Azotus, and

that chariot and stay near it."
30Then Philip ran up to the chariot and heard the man reading Isaiah the prophet. "Do you understand what you are reading?" Philip asked.
31"How can I," he said, "unless someone explains it to me?" So he invited Philip to come up and sit with him.
32The eunuch was reading this passage of Scripture:

"He was led like a sheep
to the slaughter,
and as a lamb before
the shearer is silent,
so he did not open his
mouth.
33In his humiliation he was
deprived of justice.
Who can speak of his
descendants?
For his life was taken
from the earth."[m]

34The eunuch asked Philip, "Tell me, please, who is the prophet talking about, himself or someone else?"
35Then Philip began with that very passage of Scripture and told him the good news about Jesus.
36As they traveled along the road, they came to some water and the eunuch said, "Look, here is water. Why shouldn't I be baptized?"[n] 38And he gave orders to stop the chariot. Then both Philip and the eunuch went down into the water and Philip baptized him. 39When they came up out of the water, the Spirit of the Lord suddenly took Philip away, and the eunuch did not see him again, but went on his way rejoicing. 40Philip, however, appeared at Azotus and trav-

p Many mss. do not contain this verse

‡ Verse 37 omitted by Nestle; *cf.* NIV footnote.

m*33* Isaiah 53:7,8
n*36* Some late manuscripts *baptized?" 37Philip said, "If you believe with all your heart, you may." The eunuch answered, "I believe that Jesus Christ is the Son of God."*

through he kept preaching
the gospel to all the cities,
until he came to Caesarea.

Chapter 9

The Conversion of Saul

NOW Saul, still breath-
ing threats and mur-
der against the disciples of
the Lord, went to the high
priest,
2and asked for letters
from him to the synagogues
at Damascus, so that if he
found any belonging to the
Way, both men and
women, he might bring
them bound to Jerusalem.
3And it came about that
as he journeyed, he was approaching Damascus, and
suddenly a light from
heaven flashed around him;
4and he fell to the
ground, and heard a voice
saying to him, "Saul, Saul,
why are you persecuting
Me?"
5And he said, "Who art
Thou, Lord?" And He
said, "I am Jesus whom
you are persecuting,
6but rise, and enter the
city, and it shall be told you
what you must do."
7And the men who trav-
eled with him stood
speechless, hearing the
voice, but seeing no one.
8And Saul got up from
the ground, and though his
eyes were open, he could
see nothing; and leading
him by the hand, they
brought him into Damas-
cus.
9And he was three days
without sight, and neither
ate nor drank.
10Now there was a certain
disciple at Damascus,
named Ananias; and the
Lord said to him in a vision,
"Ananias." And he said,
"Behold, *here am* I,
Lord."
11And the Lord *said* to
him, "Arise and go to the

διερχόμενος εὐηγγελίζετο τὰς πόλεις πάσας
passing through he evangelized the cities all
ἕως τοῦ ἐλθεῖν αὐτὸν εἰς Καισάρειαν.
until the to come him[b] to Cæsarea.
=he came

9 Ὁ δὲ Σαῦλος ἔτι ἐμπνέων ἀπειλῆς
– But Saul still breathing threatening
καὶ φόνου εἰς τοὺς μαθητὰς τοῦ κυρίου,
and murder against the disciples of the Lord,
προσελθὼν τῷ ἀρχιερεῖ 2 ᾐτήσατο παρ'
approaching *to* the high priest asked from
αὐτοῦ ἐπιστολὰς εἰς Δαμασκὸν πρὸς τὰς
him letters to Damascus for the
συναγωγάς, ὅπως ἐάν τινας εὕρῃ τῆς
synagogues, so as if [2]any [1]he found [4]of the
ὁδοῦ ὄντας, ἄνδρας τε καὶ γυναῖκας, δεδεμένους
[5]way [3]being, both men and women, [2]*having been* bound
ἀγάγῃ εἰς Ἰερουσαλήμ. 3 Ἐν
[1]he might bring [them] to Jerusalem. in
δὲ τῷ πορεύεσθαι ἐγένετο αὐτὸν ἐγγίζειν
Now the to go[e] it came to pass him to draw near[b]
=as he went =he drew near
τῇ Δαμασκῷ, ἐξαίφνης τε αὐτὸν περιήστ-
– to Damascus, and suddenly [5]him [4]shone
ραψεν φῶς ἐκ τοῦ οὐρανοῦ, 4 καὶ πεσὼν
round [1]a light [2]out of – [3]heaven, and falling
ἐπὶ τὴν γῆν ἤκουσεν φωνὴν λέγουσαν
on the earth he heard a voice saying
αὐτῷ· Σαοὺλ Σαούλ, τί με διώκεις;
to him: Saul[,] Saul, why me persecutest thou?
5 εἶπεν δέ· τίς εἶ, κύριε; ὁ δέ· ἐγώ
And he said: Who art thou, Lord? And he [said]: I
εἰμι Ἰησοῦς ὃν σὺ διώκεις· 6 ἀλλὰ
am Jesus whom thou persecutest; but
ἀνάστηθι καὶ εἴσελθε εἰς τὴν πόλιν,
rise thou up, and enter into the city,
καὶ λαληθήσεταί σοι ὅ τί σε δεῖ ποιεῖν.
and it shall be told thee what thee it behoves to do.
7 οἱ δὲ ἄνδρες οἱ συνοδεύοντες αὐτῷ
Now the men – journeying with him
εἱστήκεισαν ἐνεοί, ἀκούοντες μὲν τῆς
stood speechless, hearing indeed the
φωνῆς, μηδένα δὲ θεωροῦντες. 8 ἠγέρθη δὲ
sound, but no man beholding. And was raised
Σαῦλος ἀπὸ τῆς γῆς, ἀνεῳγμένων δὲ
Saul from the ground, and having been opened
=when his eyes were opened
τῶν ὀφθαλμῶν αὐτοῦ οὐδὲν ἔβλεπεν·
the eyes of him[a] nothing he saw;
χειραγωγοῦντες δὲ αὐτὸν εἰσήγαγον εἰς
and leading by the hand him they brought *in* into
Δαμασκόν. 9 καὶ ἦν ἡμέρας τρεῖς μὴ
Damascus. And he was days three not
βλέπων, καὶ οὐκ ἔφαγεν οὐδὲ ἔπιεν.
seeing, and ate not nor drank.
10 Ἦν δέ τις μαθητὴς ἐν Δαμασκῷ
Now there was a certain disciple in Damascus
ὀνόματι Ἁνανίας, καὶ εἶπεν πρὸς αὐτὸν
by name Ananias, and said to him
ἐν ὁράματι ὁ κύριος· Ἁνανία. ὁ δὲ
in a vision the Lord: Ananias. And he
εἶπεν· ἰδοὺ ἐγώ, κύριε. 11 ὁ δὲ κύριος
said: Behold[,] I, Lord. And the Lord
πρὸς αὐτόν· ἀναστὰς πορεύθητι ἐπὶ τὴν
[said] to him: Rising up go thou to the

eled about, preaching the
gospel in all the towns until
he reached Caesarea.

Chapter 9

Saul's Conversion

MEANWHILE, Saul
was still breathing
out murderous threats
against the Lord's disci-
ples. He went to the high
priest 2and asked him for
letters to the synagogues in
Damascus, so that if he
found any there who be-
longed to the Way, whether
men or women, he might
take them as prisoners to
Jerusalem. 3As he neared
Damascus on his journey,
suddenly a light from heav-
en flashed around him. 4He
fell to the ground and heard
a voice say to him, "Saul,
Saul, why do you persecute
me?"
5"Who are you, Lord?"
Saul asked.
"I am Jesus, whom you
are persecuting," he re-
plied. 6"Now get up and go
into the city, and you will
be told what you must do."
7The men traveling with
Saul stood there speech-
less; they heard the sound
but did not see anyone.
8Saul got up from the
ground, but when he
opened his eyes he could
see nothing. So they led
him by the hand into Da-
mascus. 9For three days he
was blind, and did not eat
or drink anything.
10In Damascus there was
a disciple named Ananias.
The Lord called to him in a
vision, "Ananias!"
"Yes, Lord," he an-
swered.
11The Lord told him, "Go
to the house of Judas on

street called Straight, and inquire at the house of Judas for a man from Tarsus named Saul, for behold, he is praying,

12and he has seen [q]in a vision a man named Ananias come in and lay his hands on him, so that he might regain his sight."

13But Ananias answered, "Lord, I have heard from many about this man, how much harm he did to Thy saints at Jerusalem;

14and here he has authority from the chief priests to bind all who call upon Thy name."

15But the Lord said to him, "Go, for he is a chosen [r]instrument of Mine, to bear My name before the Gentiles and kings and the sons of Israel;

16for I will show him how much he must suffer for My name's sake."

17And Ananias departed and entered the house, and after laying his hands on him said, "Brother Saul, the Lord Jesus, who appeared to you on the road by which you were coming, has sent me so that you may regain your sight, and be filled with the Holy Spirit."

18And immediately there fell from his eyes something like scales, and he regained his sight, and he arose and was baptized;

19and he took food and was strengthened.

Saul Begins to Preach Christ

Now for several days he was with the disciples who were at Damascus,

20and immediately he *began* to proclaim Jesus in the synagogues, saying, "He is the Son of God."

21And all those hearing him continued to be amazed, and were saying, "Is this not he who in Jerusalem destroyed those who called on this name,

[q]Some mss. do not contain *in a vision*
[r]Or, *vessel*

ῥύμην τὴν καλουμένην εὐθεῖαν καὶ ζήτησον
street – *being* called Straight and seek

ἐν οἰκίᾳ Ἰούδα Σαῦλον ὀνόματι Ταρσέα·
in [the] house of Judas [3]Saul [2]by name [1]a Tarsian;

ἰδοὺ γὰρ προσεύχεται, **12** καὶ εἶδεν ἄνδρα
for behold he is praying, and saw [3]a man

[ἐν ὁράματι] Ἁνανίαν ὀνόματι εἰσελθόντα
[1]in [2]a vision Ananias by name coming in

καὶ ἐπιθέντα αὐτῷ χεῖρας, ὅπως ἀναβλέψῃ.
and putting on him hands, so as he may see again.

13 ἀπεκρίθη δὲ Ἁνανίας· κύριε, ἤκουσα
And answered Ananias : Lord, I heard

ἀπὸ πολλῶν περὶ τοῦ ἀνδρὸς τούτου,
from many about this man,

ὅσα κακὰ τοῖς ἁγίοις σου ἐποίησεν
how many evil things to the saints of thee he did

ἐν Ἰερουσαλήμ· **14** καὶ ὧδε ἔχει ἐξουσίαν
in Jerusalem; and here he has authority

παρὰ τῶν ἀρχιερέων δῆσαι πάντας τοὺς
from the chief priests to bind all the

ἐπικαλουμένους τὸ ὄνομά σου. **15** εἶπεν
[ones] invoking the name of thee. said

δὲ πρὸς αὐτὸν ὁ κύριος· πορεύου, ὅτι
But to him the Lord : Go thou, because

σκεῦος ἐκλογῆς ἐστίν μοι οὗτος τοῦ
[3]a vessel [4]of choice [2]is [5]to me [1]this man –

βαστάσαι τὸ ὄνομά μου ἐνώπιον [τῶν]
to bear[d] the name of me [2]before [3]the

ἐθνῶν τε καὶ βασιλέων υἱῶν τε Ἰσραήλ·
[4]nations [1]both [5]and [6]kings [8]sons [7]and [9]of Israel;

16 ἐγὼ γὰρ ὑποδείξω αὐτῷ ὅσα δεῖ
for I will show him how many things it behoves

αὐτὸν ὑπὲρ τοῦ ὀνόματός μου παθεῖν.
him on behalf of the name of me to suffer.

17 Ἀπῆλθεν δὲ Ἁνανίας καὶ εἰσῆλθεν
And went away Ananias and entered

εἰς τὴν οἰκίαν, καὶ ἐπιθεὶς ἐπ' αὐτὸν
into the house, and putting *on* on him

τὰς χεῖρας εἶπεν· Σαοὺλ ἀδελφέ, ὁ
the(his) hands said : Saul brother, the

κύριος ἀπέσταλκέν με, Ἰησοῦς ὁ ὀφθείς σοι
Lord has sent me, Jesus the [one] appearing to thee

ἐν τῇ ὁδῷ ᾗ ἤρχου, ὅπως ἀναβλέψῃς
in the way which thou camest, so as thou mayest see again

καὶ πλησθῇς πνεύματος ἁγίου. **18** καὶ
and be filled of(with) Spirit Holy. And

εὐθέως ἀπέπεσαν αὐτοῦ ἀπὸ τῶν ὀφθαλμῶν
immediately fell away of him from the eyes

ὡς λεπίδες, ἀνέβλεψέν τε, καὶ ἀναστὰς
as scales, and he saw again, and rising up

ἐβαπτίσθη, **19** καὶ λαβὼν τροφὴν ἐνίσχυσεν.
was baptized, and taking food was strengthened.

Ἐγένετο δὲ μετὰ τῶν ἐν Δαμασκῷ
Now he was with the in Damascus

μαθητῶν ἡμέρας τινάς, **20** καὶ εὐθέως
disciples days some, and immediately

ἐν ταῖς συναγωγαῖς ἐκήρυσσεν τὸν Ἰησοῦν,
in the synagogues he proclaimed – Jesus,

ὅτι οὗτός ἐστιν ὁ υἱὸς τοῦ θεοῦ.
that this one is the Son – of God.

21 ἐξίσταντο δὲ πάντες οἱ ἀκούοντες καὶ
And were amazed all the [ones] hearing and

ἔλεγον· οὐχ οὗτός ἐστιν ὁ πορθήσας
said : Not this man is the [one] having destroyed

εἰς Ἰερουσαλὴμ τοὺς ἐπικαλουμένους
in Jerusalem the [ones] invoking

Straight Street and ask for a man from Tarsus named Saul, for he is praying. 12In a vision he has seen a man named Ananias come and place his hands on him to restore his sight."

13"Lord," Ananias answered, "I have heard many reports about this man and all the harm he has done to your saints in Jerusalem. 14And he has come here with authority from the chief priests to arrest all who call on your name."

15But the Lord said to Ananias, "Go! This man is my chosen instrument to carry my name before the Gentiles and their kings and before the people of Israel. 16I will show him how much he must suffer for my name."

17Then Ananias went to the house and entered it. Placing his hands on Saul, he said, "Brother Saul, the Lord—Jesus, who appeared to you on the road as you were coming here—has sent me so that you may see again and be filled with the Holy Spirit." 18Immediately, something like scales fell from Saul's eyes, and he could see again. He got up and was baptized, 19and after taking some food, he regained his strength.

Saul in Damascus and Jerusalem

Saul spent several days with the disciples in Damascus. 20At once he began to preach in the synagogues that Jesus is the Son of God. 21All those who heard him were astonished and asked, "Isn't he the man who raised havoc in Jerusalem among those who call on this name? And hasn't

and *who* had come here for
the purpose of bringing
them bound before the
chief priests?"
22But Saul kept increas-
ing in strength and con-
founding the Jews who
lived at Damascus by proving that this *Jesus* is the
Christ.
23And when many days
had elapsed, the Jews plotted together to do away
with him,
24but their plot became
known to Saul. And they
were also watching the
gates day and night so that
they might put him to
death;
25but his disciples took
him by night, and let him
down through *an opening*
in the wall, lowering him in
a large basket.
26And when he had come
to Jerusalem, he was trying
to associate with the disciples; and they were all
afraid of him, not believing
that he was a disciple.
27But Barnabas took hold
of him and brought him to
the apostles and described
to them how he had seen
the Lord on the road, and
that He had talked to him,
and how at Damascus he
had spoken out boldly in
the name of Jesus.
28And he was with them
moving about freely in
Jerusalem, speaking out
boldly in the name of the
Lord.
29And he was talking and
arguing with the Hellenistic
Jews; but they were at-
tempting to put him to
death.
30But when the brethren
learned *of it,* they brought
him down to Caesarea and
sent him away to Tarsus.
31So the church through-
out all Judea and Galilee
and Samaria enjoyed
peace, being built up; and,

τὸ ὄνομα τοῦτο, καὶ ὧδε εἰς τοῦτο ἐληλύθει,
this name, and here for this he had come,
ἵνα δεδεμένους αὐτοὺς ἀγάγῃ ἐπὶ τοὺς
that *having been* bound them he might bring before the
ἀρχιερεῖς; 22 Σαῦλος δὲ μᾶλλον ἐνε-
chief priests? But Saul more was filled
δυναμοῦτο καὶ συνέχυννεν Ἰουδαίους τοὺς κατ-
with power and confounded Jews the [ones]
οικοῦντας ἐν Δαμασκῷ, συμβιβάζων ὅτι οὗτός
dwelling in Damascus, proving that this one
ἐστιν ὁ χριστός. 23 Ὡς δὲ ἐπληροῦντο
is the Christ. And when were fulfilled
ἡμέραι ἱκαναί, 24 συνεβουλεύσαντο
days considerable(many), consulted together
οἱ Ἰουδαῖοι ἀνελεῖν αὐτόν· ἐγνώσθη δὲ
the Jews to kill him; but was known
τῷ Σαύλῳ ἡ ἐπιβουλὴ αὐτῶν. παρετη-
– to Saul the plot of them. And they
ροῦντο δὲ καὶ τὰς πύλας ἡμέρας τε καὶ
carefully watched also the gates both by day and
νυκτὸς ὅπως αὐτὸν ἀνέλωσιν· 25 λαβόντες δὲ
by night so as him they might destroy; but [4]taking
οἱ μαθηταὶ αὐτοῦ νυκτὸς διὰ τοῦ
[1]the [2]disciples [3]of him by night through the
τείχους καθῆκαν αὐτὸν χαλάσαντες ἐν
wall let down him lowering in
σπυρίδι. 26 Παραγενόμενος δὲ εἰς
a basket. And arriving at
Ἰερουσαλὴμ ἐπείραζεν κολλᾶσθαι τοῖς
Jerusalem he tried to be joined to the
μαθηταῖς· καὶ πάντες ἐφοβοῦντο αὐτόν,
disciples; and all feared him,
μὴ πιστεύοντες ὅτι ἐστὶν μαθητής.
not believing that he is(was) a disciple.
27 Βαρναβᾶς δὲ ἐπιλαβόμενος αὐτὸν ἤγαγεν
But Barnabas taking hold of him led
πρὸς τοὺς ἀποστόλους, καὶ διηγήσατο
to the apostles, and narrated
αὐτοῖς πῶς ἐν τῇ ὁδῷ εἶδεν τὸν κύριον
to them how in the way he saw the Lord
καὶ ὅτι ἐλάλησεν αὐτῷ, καὶ πῶς ἐν
and that he spoke to him, and how in
Δαμασκῷ ἐπαρρησιάσατο ἐν τῷ ὀνόματι
Damascus he spoke boldly in the name
Ἰησοῦ. 28 καὶ ἦν μετ' αὐτῶν εἰσπορευόμενος
of Jesus. And he was with them going in
καὶ ἐκπορευόμενος εἰς Ἰερουσαλήμ,
and going out in Jerusalem,
παρρησιαζόμενος ἐν τῷ ὀνόματι τοῦ
speaking boldly in the name of the
κυρίου, 29 ἐλάλει τε καὶ συνεζήτει πρὸς
Lord, [2]spoke [1]both [3]and [4]discussed with
τοὺς Ἑλληνιστάς· οἱ δὲ ἐπεχείρουν ἀνελεῖν
the Hellenists; and they attempted to kill
αὐτόν. 30 ἐπιγνόντες δὲ οἱ ἀδελφοὶ
him. But [3]knowing [1]the [2]brothers
κατήγαγον αὐτὸν εἰς Καισάρειαν καὶ
brought down him to Cæsarea and
ἐξαπέστειλαν αὐτὸν εἰς Ταρσόν.
sent forth him to Tarsus.
31 Ἡ μὲν οὖν ἐκκλησία καθ' ὅλης
[2]The – [1]therefore [3]church throughout all
τῆς Ἰουδαίας καὶ Γαλιλαίας καὶ Σαμαρείας
– Judæa and Galilee and Samaria
εἶχεν εἰρήνην οἰκοδομουμένη καὶ πορευομένη
had peace being built and going

he come here to take them
as prisoners to the chief
priests?" 22Yet Saul grew
more and more powerful
and baffled the Jews living
in Damascus by proving
that Jesus is the Christ.[o]
23After many days had
gone by, the Jews con-
spired to kill him, 24but
Saul learned of their plan.
Day and night they kept
close watch on the city
gates in order to kill him.
25But his followers took
him by night and lowered
him in a basket through an
opening in the wall.
26When he came to Jeru-
salem, he tried to join the
disciples, but they were all
afraid of him, not believing
that he really was a disciple. 27But Barnabas took
him and brought him to the
apostles. He told them how
Saul on his journey had
seen the Lord and that the
Lord had spoken to him,
and how in Damascus he
had preached fearlessly in
the name of Jesus. 28So
Saul stayed with them and
moved about freely in Jerusalem, speaking boldly in
the name of the Lord. 29He
talked and debated with the
Grecian Jews, but they
tried to kill him. 30When
the brothers learned of this,
they took him down to
Caesarea and sent him off
to Tarsus.
31Then the church
throughout Judea, Galilee
and Samaria enjoyed a time
of peace. It was strengthened; and encouraged by

[o]22 Or *Messiah*

going on in the fear of the
Lord and in the comfort of
the Holy Spirit, it con-
tinued to increase.

Peter's Ministry

32Now it came about that
as Peter was traveling
through all *those parts,* he
came down also to the
saints who lived at Lydda.
33And there he found a
certain man named
Aeneas, who had been bed-
ridden eight years, for he
was paralyzed.
34And Peter said to him,
"Aeneas, Jesus Christ
heals you; arise, and make
your bed." And immedi-
ately he arose.
35And all who lived at
Lydda and Sharon saw
him, and they turned to the
Lord.
36Now in Joppa there was
a certain disciple named
Tabitha (which translated
in Greek is called Dorcas);
this woman was abounding
with deeds of kindness and
charity, which she continually did.
37And it came about at
that time that she fell sick
and died; and when they
had washed her body, they
laid it in an upper room.
38And since Lydda was
near Joppa, the disciples,
having heard that Peter was
there, sent two men to him,
entreating him, "Do not
delay to come to us."
39And Peter arose and
went with them. And when
he had come, they brought
him into the upper room;
and all the widows stood
beside him weeping, and
showing all the [s]tunics and
garments that Dorcas used
to make while she was with
them.
40But Peter sent them all
out and knelt down and
prayed, and turning to the
body, he said, "Tabitha,

τῷ φόβῳ τοῦ κυρίου, καὶ τῇ παρακλήσει
in the fear of the Lord, and in the comfort
τοῦ ἁγίου πνεύματος ἐπληθύνετο.
of the Holy Spirit was multiplied.
32 Ἐγένετο δὲ Πέτρον διερχόμενον διὰ
Now it came to pass Peter passing *through* through
πάντων κατελθεῖν καὶ πρὸς τοὺς ἁγίους
all [quarters] to come down[b] also to the saints
τοὺς κατοικοῦντας Λύδδα. 33 εὗρεν δὲ
– inhabiting Lydda. And he found
ἐκεῖ ἄνθρωπόν τινα ὀνόματι Αἰνέαν ἐξ
there a certain man by name Aeneas of
ἐτῶν ὀκτὼ κατακείμενον ἐπὶ κραβάτου,
years eight lying on a mattress,
ὃς ἦν παραλελυμένος. 34 καὶ εἶπεν αὐτῷ
who was *having been* paralysed. And said to him
ὁ Πέτρος· Αἰνέα, ἰᾶταί σε Ἰησοῦς Χριστός·
– Peter: Aeneas, cures thee Jesus Christ;
ἀνάστηθι καὶ στρῶσον σεαυτῷ. καὶ
rise up and gird thyself. And
εὐθέως ἀνέστη. 35 καὶ εἶδαν αὐτὸν
immediately he rose up. And saw him
πάντες οἱ κατοικοῦντες Λύδδα καὶ τὸν
all the [ones] inhabiting Lydda and –
Σαρῶνα, οἵτινες ἐπέστρεψαν ἐπὶ τὸν κύριον.
Saron, who turned to the Lord.
Ἐν Ἰόππῃ δέ τις ἦν μαθήτρια ὀνόματι
[2]in [3]Joppa [1]Now [5]a certain [4]was [6]disciple by name
Ταβιθά, 36 ἣ διερμηνευομένη λέγεται
Tabitha, who being translated is called
Δορκάς· αὕτη ἦν πλήρης ἔργων ἀγαθῶν
Dorcas; this woman was full works of good
καὶ ἐλεημοσυνῶν ὧν ἐποίει. 37 ἐγένετο δὲ
and of alms which she did. And it happened
ἐν ταῖς ἡμέραις ἐκείναις ἀσθενήσασαν
in those days ailing
αὐτὴν ἀποθανεῖν· λούσαντες δὲ ἔθηκαν
she to die[b]; and having washed they put [her]
=being ill she died;
ἐν ὑπερῴῳ. 38 ἐγγὺς δὲ οὔσης Λύδδας
in an upper room. Now [3]near [2]being [1]Lydda[a]
τῇ Ἰόππῃ οἱ μαθηταὶ ἀκούσαντες ὅτι
– to Joppa the disciples having heard that
Πέτρος ἐστὶν ἐν αὐτῇ ἀπέστειλαν δύο
Peter is(was) in it sent two
ἄνδρας πρὸς αὐτὸν παρακαλοῦντες· μὴ
men to him beseeching: [2]not
ὀκνήσῃς διελθεῖν ἕως ἡμῶν. 39 ἀναστὰς δὲ
[1]hesitate to come to us. And rising up
Πέτρος συνῆλθεν αὐτοῖς· ὃν παραγενόμενον
Peter went with them; whom arriving
ἀνήγαγον εἰς τὸ ὑπερῷον, καὶ παρέστησαν
they led up into the upper room, and stood by
αὐτῷ πᾶσαι αἱ χῆραι κλαίουσαι καὶ
him all the widows weeping and
ἐπιδεικνύμεναι χιτῶνας καὶ ἱμάτια, ὅσα
showing tunics and garments, which
ἐποίει μετ' αὐτῶν οὖσα ἡ Δορκάς.
[2]made [4]with [5]them [3]being – [1]Dorcas.
40 ἐκβαλὼν δὲ ἔξω πάντας ὁ Πέτρος
And [2]putting *out* [4]outside [3]all – [1]Peter
καὶ θεὶς τὰ γόνατα προσηύξατο, καὶ
and placing the knees he prayed, and
=kneeling down
ἐπιστρέψας πρὸς τὸ σῶμα εἶπεν· Ταβιθά,
turning to the body said: Tabitha,

the Holy Spirit, it grew in
numbers, living in the fear
of the Lord.

Aeneas and Dorcas

32As Peter traveled about
the country, he went to visit the saints in Lydda.
33There he found a man
named Aeneas, a paralytic
who had been bedridden
for eight years. 34"Aene-
as," Peter said to him,
"Jesus Christ heals you.
Get up and take care of
your mat." Immediately
Aeneas got up. 35All those
who lived in Lydda and
Sharon saw him and turned
to the Lord.
36In Joppa there was a
disciple named Tabitha
(which, when translated, is
Dorcas[p]), who was always
doing good and helping the
poor. 37About that time she
became sick and died, and
her body was washed and
placed in an upstairs room.
38Lydda was near Joppa; so
when the disciples heard
that Peter was in Lydda,
they sent two men to him
and urged him, "Please
come at once!"
39Peter went with them,
and when he arrived he was
taken upstairs to the room.
All the widows stood
around him, crying and
showing him the robes and
other clothing that Dorcas
had made while she was
still with them.
40Peter sent them all out
of the room; then he got
down on his knees and
prayed. Turning toward the
dead woman, he said,

[s] Or, *inner garments*

[p]36 Both *Tabitha* (Aramaic) and *Dorcas* (Greek) mean *gazelle.*

arise." And she opened her
eyes, and when she saw Peter, she sat up.
41And he gave her his
hand and raised her up; and
calling the saints and widows, he presented her
alive.
42And it became known
all over Joppa, and many
believed in the Lord.
43And it came about that
he stayed many days in
Joppa with a certain tan-
ner, Simon.

ἀνάστηθι. ἡ δὲ ἤνοιξεν τοὺς ὀφθαλμοὺς
rise up. And she opened the eyes
αὐτῆς, καὶ ἰδοῦσα τὸν Πέτρον ἀνεκάθισεν.
of her, and seeing – Peter sat up.
41 δοὺς δὲ αὐτῇ χεῖρα ἀνέστησεν αὐτήν·
And giving her a hand he raised up her;
φωνήσας δὲ τοὺς ἁγίους καὶ τὰς χήρας
and calling the saints and the widows
παρέστησεν αὐτὴν ζῶσαν. **42** γνωστὸν δὲ
he presented her living. And known
ἐγένετο καθ' ὅλης τῆς Ἰόππης, καὶ
it became throughout all – Joppa, and
ἐπίστευσαν πολλοὶ ἐπὶ τὸν κύριον.
believed many on the Lord.
43 Ἐγένετο δὲ ἡμέρας ἱκανὰς μεῖναι ἐν
And it came to pass days several to remain in
=he remained many days
Ἰόππῃ παρά τινι Σίμωνι βυρσεῖ.
Joppa with one Simon a tanner.

"Tabitha, get up." She
opened her eyes, and see-
ing Peter she sat up. 41He
took her by the hand and
helped her to her feet. Then
he called the believers and
the widows and presented
her to them alive. 42This
became known all over
Joppa, and many people
believed in the Lord. 43Pe-
ter stayed in Joppa for
some time with a tanner
named Simon.

Chapter 10

Cornelius' Vision

NOW *there was* a cer-
tain man at Caesarea
named Cornelius, a centu-
rion of what was called the
Italian [t] cohort,
2a devout man, and one
who feared God with all his
household, and gave many
[u]alms to the *Jewish* people,
and prayed to God continually.
3About the [v]ninth hour
of the day he clearly saw in
a vision an angel of God
who had *just* come in to
him, and said to him, "Cornelius!"
4And fixing his gaze
upon him and being much
alarmed, he said, "What is
it, Lord?" And he said to
him, "Your prayers and
[w]alms have ascended as a
memorial before God.
5"And now dispatch
some men to Joppa, and
send for a man *named* Simon, who is also called Peter;
6he is staying with a certain tanner *named* Simon,
whose house is by the
sea."
7And when the angel
who was speaking to him
had departed, he sum-
moned two of his servants
and a devout soldier of
those who were in constant
attendance upon him,
8and after he had ex-
plained everything to them,

10 Ἀνὴρ δέ τις ἐν Καισαρείᾳ ὀνόματι
Now a certain man in Cæsarea by name
Κορνήλιος, ἑκατοντάρχης ἐκ σπείρης τῆς
Cornelius, a centurion of a cohort –
καλουμένης Ἰταλικῆς, **2** εὐσεβὴς καὶ
being called Italian, devout and
φοβούμενος τὸν θεὸν σὺν παντὶ τῷ οἴκῳ
fearing – God with all the household
αὐτοῦ, ποιῶν ἐλεημοσύνας πολλὰς τῷ
of him, doing alms many to the
λαῷ καὶ δεόμενος τοῦ θεοῦ διὰ παντός,
people and petitioning – God continually,
3 εἶδεν ἐν ὁράματι φανερῶς, ὡσεὶ περὶ
saw in a vision clearly, as it were around
ὥραν ἐνάτην τῆς ἡμέρας, ἄγγελον τοῦ
hour ninth of the day, an angel –
θεοῦ εἰσελθόντα πρὸς αὐτὸν καὶ εἰπόντα
of God entering to him and saying
αὐτῷ· Κορνήλιε. **4** ὁ δὲ ἀτενίσας αὐτῷ
to him: Cornelius. And he gazing at him
καὶ ἔμφοβος γενόμενος εἶπεν· τί ἐστιν,
and terrified becoming said: What is it,
κύριε; εἶπεν δὲ αὐτῷ· αἱ προσευχαί
lord? And he said to him: The prayers
σου καὶ αἱ ἐλεημοσύναι σου ἀνέβησαν
of thee and the alms of thee went up
εἰς μνημόσυνον ἔμπροσθεν τοῦ θεοῦ. **5** καὶ
for a memorial before – God. And
νῦν πέμψον ἄνδρας εἰς Ἰόππην καὶ
now send men to Joppa and
μετάπεμψαι Σίμωνά τινα ὃς ἐπικαλεῖται
[summon [2]Simon [1]one who is surnamed
Πέτρος· **6** οὗτος ξενίζεται παρά τινι
Peter; this man is lodged with one
Σίμωνι βυρσεῖ, ᾧ ἐστιν οἰκία παρὰ
Simon a tanner, to whom is a house[c] by
=who has a house
θάλασσαν. **7** ὡς δὲ ἀπῆλθεν ὁ ἄγγελος ὁ
[the] sea. And as went away the angel –
λαλῶν αὐτῷ, φωνήσας δύο τῶν οἰκετῶν
speaking to him, calling two of the household slaves
καὶ στρατιώτην εὐσεβῆ τῶν προσκαρτερούν-
and soldier a devout of the [ones] waiting
των αὐτῷ, **8** καὶ ἐξηγησάμενος ἅπαντα
on him, and explaining all things

Chapter 10

Cornelius Calls for Peter

AT Caesarea there was a
man named Corneli-
us, a centurion in what was
known as the Italian Regiment. 2He and all his family
were devout and God-fear-
ing; he gave generously to
those in need and prayed to
God regularly. 3One day at
about three in the after-
noon he had a vision. He
distinctly saw an angel of
God, who came to him and
said, "Cornelius!"
4Cornelius stared at him
in fear. "What is it, Lord?"
he asked.
The angel answered,
"Your prayers and gifts to
the poor have come up as a
memorial offering before
God. 5Now send men to
Joppa to bring back a man
named Simon who is called
Peter. 6He is staying with
Simon the tanner, whose
house is by the sea."
7When the angel who
spoke to him had gone,
Cornelius called two of his
servants and a devout soldier who was one of his attendants. 8He told them ev-

[t] Or, *battalion*
[u] Or, *gifts of charity*
[v] I.e., 3 p.m.
[w] Or, *deeds of charity*

he sent them to Joppa.

9And on the next day, as they were on their way, and approaching the city, Peter went up on the housetop about the [x]sixth hour to pray.

10And he became hungry, and was desiring to eat; but while they were making preparations, he fell into a trance;

11and he *beheld the sky opened up, and a certain [y]object like a great sheet coming down, lowered by four corners to the ground,

12and there were in it all *kinds of* four-footed animals and [z]crawling creatures of the earth and birds of the air.

13And a voice came to him, "Arise, Peter, kill and eat!"

14But Peter said, "By no means, Lord, for I have never eaten anything unholy and unclean."

15And again a voice *came* to him a second time, "What God has cleansed, no *longer* consider unholy."

16And this happened three times; and immediately the object was taken up into the sky.

17Now while Peter was greatly perplexed in mind as to what the vision which he had seen might be, behold, the men who had been sent by Cornelius, having asked directions for Simon's house, appeared at the gate;

18and calling out, they were asking whether Simon, who was also called Peter, was staying there.

19And while Peter was reflecting on the vision, the Spirit said to him, "Behold, three men are looking for you.

20"But arise, go downstairs, and accompany them without misgivings; for I have sent them Myself."

[x] I.e., noon
[y] Or, *vessel*
[z] Or possibly, *reptiles*

αὐτοῖς ἀπέστειλεν αὐτοὺς εἰς τὴν Ἰόππην.
to them sent them to – Joppa.
9 Τῇ δὲ ἐπαύριον ὁδοιπορούντων ἐκείνων
And on the morrow journeying those
καὶ τῇ πόλει ἐγγιζόντων ἀνέβη Πέτρος
and to the city drawing near[a] went up Peter
=as they journeyed and drew near to the city
ἐπὶ τὸ δῶμα προσεύξασθαι περὶ ὥραν
onto the roof to pray about hour
ἕκτην. 10 ἐγένετο δὲ πρόσπεινος καὶ
sixth. And he became hungry and
ἤθελεν γεύσασθαι· παρασκευαζόντων δὲ
wished to taste(eat); and preparing
=while they prepared
αὐτῶν ἐγένετο ἐπ' αὐτὸν ἔκστασις, 11 καὶ
them[a] there came on him an ecstasy, and
θεωρεῖ τὸν οὐρανὸν ἀνεῳγμένον καὶ
he beholds the heaven having been opened and
καταβαῖνον σκεῦός τι ὡς ὀθόνην μεγάλην,
coming down a certain vessel like sheet a great,
τέσσαρσιν ἀρχαῖς καθιέμενον ἐπὶ τῆς γῆς,
by four corners being let down onto the earth,
12 ἐν ᾧ ὑπῆρχεν πάντα τὰ τετράποδα
in which were all the quadrupeds
καὶ ἑρπετὰ τῆς γῆς καὶ πετεινὰ τοῦ
and reptiles of the earth and birds of the
οὐρανοῦ. 13 καὶ ἐγένετο φωνὴ πρὸς
heaven(air). And there came a voice to
αὐτόν· ἀναστάς, Πέτρε, θῦσον καὶ φάγε.
him : Rise up, Peter, slay and eat.
14 ὁ δὲ Πέτρος εἶπεν· μηδαμῶς, κύριε,
– But Peter said : Not at all, Lord,
ὅτι οὐδέποτε ἔφαγον πᾶν κοινὸν καὶ
because never did I eat every(any)thing common and
ἀκάθαρτον. 15 καὶ φωνὴ πάλιν ἐκ δευτέρου
unclean. And a voice again a second [time]
πρὸς αὐτόν· ἃ ὁ θεὸς ἐκαθάρισεν σὺ
[came] to him : What things – God cleansed [3]thou
μὴ κοίνου. 16 τοῦτο δὲ ἐγένετο ἐπὶ
[2]not [1]treat [4]as [5]unclean. And this occurred on
τρίς, καὶ εὐθὺς ἀνελήμφθη τὸ σκεῦος
three [occasions], and immediately was taken up the vessel
εἰς τὸν οὐρανόν. 17 Ὡς δὲ ἐν ἑαυτῷ
into – heaven. Now as in himself
διηπόρει ὁ Πέτρος τί ἂν εἴη τὸ ὅραμα
was doubting – Peter what might be the vision
ὃ εἶδεν, ἰδοὺ οἱ ἄνδρες οἱ ἀπεσταλμένοι
which he saw, behold[,] the men – *having been* sent
ὑπὸ τοῦ Κορνηλίου διερωτήσαντες τὴν
by – Cornelius asking for the
οἰκίαν τοῦ Σίμωνος ἐπέστησαν ἐπὶ τὸν
house – of Simon stood *at* at the
πυλῶνα, 18 καὶ φωνήσαντες ἐπυνθάνοντο
porch, and calling inquired
εἰ Σίμων ὁ ἐπικαλούμενος Πέτρος ἐνθάδε
if Simon – *being* surnamed Peter here
ξενίζεται. 19 Τοῦ δὲ Πέτρου διενθυμουμένου
is lodged. – And Peter pondering[a]
=while Peter pondered
περὶ τοῦ ὁράματος εἶπεν τὸ πνεῦμα·
about the vision [3]said [1]the [2]Spirit :
ἰδοὺ ἄνδρες δύο ζητοῦντές σε· 20 ἀλλὰ
Behold[,] men two seeking thee; but
ἀναστὰς κατάβηθι, καὶ πορεύου σὺν αὐτοῖς
rising up go down, and go with them
μηδὲν διακρινόμενος, ὅτι ἐγὼ ἀπέσταλκα
nothing doubting, because I have sent

erything that had happened
and sent them to Joppa.

Peter's Vision

9About noon the follow-
ing day as they were on
their journey and ap-
proaching the city, Peter
went up on the roof to pray.
10He became hungry and
wanted something to eat,
and while the meal was being prepared, he fell into a
trance. 11He saw heaven
opened and something like
a large sheet being let down
to earth by its four corners.
12It contained all kinds of
four-footed animals, as
well as reptiles of the earth
and birds of the air. 13Then
a voice told him, "Get up,
Peter. Kill and eat."
14"Surely not, Lord!"
Peter replied. "I have never eaten anything impure or
unclean."
15The voice spoke to him
a second time, "Do not call
anything impure that God
has made clean."
16This happened three
times, and immediately the
sheet was taken back to
heaven.
17While Peter was won-
dering about the meaning
of the vision, the men sent
by Cornelius found out
where Simon's house was
and stopped at the gate.
18They called out, asking if
Simon who was known as
Peter was staying there.
19While Peter was still
thinking about the vision,
the Spirit said to him, "Simon, three[q] men are looking for you. 20So get up and
go downstairs. Do not hesi-
tate to go with them, for I
have sent them."

[q]19 One early manuscript *two*; other manuscripts do not have the number.

21 And Peter went down to
the men and said, "Behold,
I am the one you are looking for; what is the reason
for which you have come?"
22 And they said, "Cor-
nelius, a centurion, a righteous and God-fearing man
well spoken of by the entire
nation of the Jews, was *divinely* directed by a holy
angel to send for you *to
come* to his house and hear
a message from you."
23 And so he invited them
in and gave them lodging.

Peter at Caesarea

And on the next day he
arose and went away with
them, and some of the
brethren from Joppa ac-
companied him.
24 And on the following
day he entered Caesarea.
Now Cornelius was waiting
for them, and had called together his relatives and
close friends.
25 And when it came about
that Peter entered, Cornelius met him, and fell at his
feet and worshiped *him*.
26 But Peter raised him up,
saying, "Stand up; I too am
just a man."
27 And as he talked with
him, he entered, and found
many people assembled.
28 And he said to them,
"You yourselves know
how unlawful it is for a man
who is a Jew to associate
with a foreigner or to visit
him; and *yet* God has
shown me that I should not
call any man unholy or unclean.
29 "That is why I came
without even raising any
objection when I was sent
for. And so I ask for what
reason you have sent for
me."
30 And Cornelius said,
"Four days ago to this
hour, I was praying in my
house during the [a]ninth

[a] I.e., 3 to 4 p.m.

αὐτούς. **21** καταβὰς δὲ Πέτρος πρὸς
them. And going down Peter to
τοὺς ἄνδρας εἶπεν· ἰδοὺ ἐγώ εἰμι ὃν
the men said: Behold[,] I am [he] whom
ζητεῖτε· τίς ἡ αἰτία δι' ἣν πάρεστε;
ye seek; what [is] the cause for which ye are here?
22 οἱ δὲ εἶπαν· Κορνήλιος ἑκατοντάρχης,
And they said: Cornelius a centurion,
ἀνὴρ δίκαιος καὶ φοβούμενος τὸν θεόν,
a man just and fearing – God,
μαρτυρούμενός τε ὑπὸ ὅλου τοῦ ἔθνους
and being witnessed to by all the nation
τῶν Ἰουδαίων, ἐχρηματίσθη ὑπὸ ἀγγέλου
of the Jews, was warned by angel
ἁγίου μεταπέμψασθαί σε εἰς τὸν οἶκον
a holy to summon thee to the house
αὐτοῦ καὶ ἀκοῦσαι ῥήματα παρὰ σοῦ.
of him and to hear words from thee.
23 εἰσκαλεσάμενος οὖν αὐτοὺς ἐξένισεν.
Calling in therefore them he lodged.
Τῇ δὲ ἐπαύριον ἀναστὰς ἐξῆλθεν σὺν
And on the morrow rising up he went forth with
αὐτοῖς, καί τινες τῶν ἀδελφῶν τῶν
them, and some of the brothers –
ἀπὸ Ἰόππης συνῆλθον αὐτῷ. **24** τῇ δὲ
from Joppa accompanied him. And on the
ἐπαύριον εἰσῆλθεν εἰς τὴν Καισάρειαν·
morrow he entered into – Cæsarea;
ὁ δὲ Κορνήλιος ἦν προσδοκῶν αὐτούς,
– and Cornelius was awaiting them,
συγκαλεσάμενος τοὺς συγγενεῖς αὐτοῦ καὶ
having called together the relatives of him and
τοὺς ἀναγκαίους φίλους. **25** Ὡς δὲ
the intimate friends. Now when
ἐγένετο τοῦ εἰσελθεῖν τὸν Πέτρον,
it came to pass the to enter – Peter,[b]
= Now it came to pass when Peter entered,
συναντήσας αὐτῷ ὁ Κορνήλιος πεσὼν
[2]meeting [3]him – [1]Cornelius falling
ἐπὶ τοὺς πόδας προσεκύνησεν. **26** ὁ δὲ
at the(his) feet worshipped. – But
Πέτρος ἤγειρεν αὐτὸν λέγων· ἀνάστηθι·
Peter raised him saying: Stand up;
καὶ ἐγὼ αὐτὸς ἄνθρωπός εἰμι. **27** καὶ
also I [my]self a man am. And
συνομιλῶν αὐτῷ εἰσῆλθεν, καὶ εὑρίσκει
talking with him he entered, and finds
συνεληλυθότας πολλούς, **28** ἔφη τε πρὸς
having come together many, and said to
αὐτούς· ὑμεῖς ἐπίστασθε ὡς ἀθέμιτόν ἐστιν
them: Ye understand how unlawful it is
ἀνδρὶ Ἰουδαίῳ κολλᾶσθαι ἢ προσέρχεσθαι
for *a man* a Jew to adhere or to approach
ἀλλοφύλῳ· κἀμοὶ ὁ θεὸς ἔδειξεν μηδένα
a foreigner; and to me – God showed [2]not any
κοινὸν ἢ ἀκάθαρτον λέγειν ἄνθρωπον·
[4]common [5]or [6]unclean [1]to call [3]man;
29 διὸ καὶ ἀναντιρρήτως ἦλθον μετα-
wherefore indeed [3]unquestioningly [2]I came [1]being
πεμφθείς. πυνθάνομαι οὖν, τίνι λόγῳ
summoned. I inquire therefore, for what reason
μετεπέμψασθέ με; **30** καὶ ὁ Κορνήλιος
ye summoned me? And – Cornelius
ἔφη· ἀπὸ τετάρτης ἡμέρας μέχρι ταύτης τῆς
said: From fourth day until this –
= Four days ago
ὥρας ἤμην τὴν ἐνάτην προσευχόμενος
hour I was [at] the ninth praying

21 Peter went down and
said to the men, "I'm the
one you're looking for.
Why have you come?"
22 The men replied, "We
have come from Cornelius
the centurion. He is a righteous and God-fearing man,
who is respected by all the
Jewish people. A holy an-
gel told him to have you
come to his house so that
he could hear what you
have to say." 23 Then Peter
invited the men into the
house to be his guests.

Peter at Cornelius' House

The next day Peter start-
ed out with them, and some
of the brothers from Joppa
went along. 24 The following day he arrived in Caesarea. Cornelius was expecting them and had called together his relatives and
close friends. 25 As Peter
entered the house, Cornelius met him and fell at his
feet in reverence. 26 But Peter made him get up.
"Stand up," he said, "I am
only a man myself."
27 Talking with him, Peter
went inside and found a
large gathering of people.
28 He said to them: "You
are well aware that it is
against our law for a Jew to
associate with a Gentile or
visit him. But God has
shown me that I should not
call any man impure or unclean. 29 So when I was sent
for, I came without raising
any objection. May I ask
why you sent for me?"
30 Cornelius answered:
"Four days ago I was in my
house praying at this hour,
at three in the afternoon.

hour; and behold, a man stood before me in shining garments,

31 and he *said, 'Cornelius, your prayer has been heard and your alms have been remembered before God.

32 'Send therefore to Joppa and invite Simon, who is also called Peter, to come to you; he is staying at the house of Simon *the* tanner by the sea.'

33 "And so I sent to you immediately, and you have been kind enough to come. Now then, we are all here present before God to hear all that you have been commanded by the Lord."

Gentiles Hear Good News

34 And opening his mouth, Peter said:

"I most certainly understand *now* that God is not one to show partiality,

35 but in every nation the man who fears Him and does what is right, is welcome to Him.

36 "The word which He sent to the sons of Israel, preaching peace through Jesus Christ (He is Lord of all)—

37 you yourselves know the thing which took place throughout all Judea, starting from Galilee, after the baptism which John proclaimed.

38 "*You know of* Jesus of Nazareth, how God anointed Him with the Holy Spirit and with power, and *how* He went about doing good, and healing all who were oppressed by the devil; for God was with Him.

39 "And we are witnesses of all the things He did both in the land of the Jews and in Jerusalem. And they also put Him to death by hanging Him on a cross.

40 "God raised Him up on the third day, and granted

ἐν τῷ οἴκῳ μου, καὶ ἰδοὺ ἀνὴρ ἔστη
in the house of me, and behold[,] a man stood
ἐνώπιόν μου ἐν ἐσθῆτι λαμπρᾷ, 31 καὶ
before me in clothing bright, and
φησίν· Κορνήλιε, εἰσηκούσθη σου ἡ
says: Cornelius, was heard of thee the
προσευχὴ καὶ αἱ ἐλεημοσύναι σου ἐμνήσθησαν
prayer and the alms of thee were remembered
ἐνώπιον τοῦ θεοῦ. 32 πέμψον οὖν εἰς
before – God. Send thou therefore to
Ἰόππην καὶ μετακάλεσαι Σίμωνα ὃς ἐπι-
Joppa and send for Simon who is
καλεῖται Πέτρος· οὗτος ξενίζεται ἐν οἰκίᾳ
surnamed Peter; this man is lodged in [the] house
Σίμωνος βυρσέως παρὰ θάλασσαν. 33 ἐξαυτῆς
of Simon a tanner by [the] sea. At once
οὖν ἔπεμψα πρὸς σέ, σύ τε καλῶς
therefore I sent to thee, and thou well
ἐποίησας παραγενόμενος. νῦν οὖν πάντες
didst arriving. Now therefore all
ἡμεῖς ἐνώπιον τοῦ θεοῦ πάρεσμεν ἀκοῦσαι
we before – God are present to hear
πάντα τὰ προστεταγμένα σοι ὑπὸ τοῦ
all the things having been commanded thee by the
κυρίου. 34 Ἀνοίξας δὲ Πέτρος τὸ στόμα
Lord. And opening Peter the(his) mouth
εἶπεν· ἐπ' ἀληθείας καταλαμβάνομαι ὅτι
said: On(in) truth I perceive that
οὐκ ἔστιν προσωπολήμπτης ὁ θεός, 35 ἀλλ'
[3]not [2]is [4]a respecter of persons – [1]God, but
ἐν παντὶ ἔθνει ὁ φοβούμενος αὐτὸν καὶ
in every nation the [one] fearing him and
ἐργαζόμενος δικαιοσύνην δεκτὸς αὐτῷ ἐστιν·
working righteousness acceptable to him is;
36 τὸν λόγον ὃν ἀπέστειλεν τοῖς υἱοῖς
the word which he sent to the sons
Ἰσραὴλ εὐαγγελιζόμενος εἰρήνην διὰ Ἰησοῦ
of Israel preaching peace through Jesus
Χριστοῦ· οὗτός ἐστιν πάντων κύριος.
Christ: this one is of all Lord.
37 ὑμεῖς οἴδατε τὸ γενόμενον ῥῆμα καθ'
Ye know the having become thing throughout
=that which took place
ὅλης τῆς Ἰουδαίας, ἀρξάμενος ἀπὸ τῆς
all – Judæa, beginning from –
Γαλιλαίας μετὰ τὸ βάπτισμα ὃ ἐκήρυξεν
Galilee after the baptism which [2]proclaimed
Ἰωάννης, 38 Ἰησοῦν τὸν ἀπὸ Ναζαρέθ,
[1]John, Jesus the one from Nazareth,
ὡς ἔχρισεν αὐτὸν ὁ θεὸς πνεύματι ἁγίῳ
how anointed him – God with Spirit Holy
καὶ δυνάμει, ὃς διῆλθεν εὐεργετῶν καὶ
and power, who went about doing good and
ἰώμενος πάντας τοὺς καταδυναστευομένους
curing all the [ones] being oppressed
ὑπὸ τοῦ διαβόλου, ὅτι ὁ θεὸς ἦν μετ'
by the devil, because – God was with
αὐτοῦ· 39 καὶ ἡμεῖς μάρτυρες πάντων
him; and we [are] witnesses of all things
ὧν ἐποίησεν ἔν τε τῇ χώρᾳ τῶν Ἰουδαίων
which he did both in the country of the Jews
καὶ Ἰερουσαλήμ· ὃν καὶ ἀνεῖλαν
and Jerusalem; whom indeed they killed
κρεμάσαντες ἐπὶ ξύλου. 40 τοῦτον ὁ
hanging on a tree. This one –
θεὸς ἤγειρεν ἐν τῇ τρίτῃ ἡμέρᾳ καὶ
God raised on the third day and

Suddenly a man in shining
clothes stood before me
31 and said, 'Cornelius, God
has heard your prayer and
remembered your gifts to
the poor. 32 Send to Joppa
for Simon who is called Peter.
He is a guest in the
home of Simon the tanner,
who lives by the sea.' 33 So I
sent for you immediately,
and it was good of you to
come. Now we are all here
in the presence of God to
listen to everything the
Lord has commanded you
to tell us."

34 Then Peter began to
speak: "I now realize how
true it is that God does not
show favoritism 35 but accepts
men from every nation
who fear him and do
what is right. 36 You know
the message God sent to
the people of Israel, telling
the good news of peace
through Jesus Christ, who
is Lord of all. 37 You know
what has happened
throughout Judea, beginning
in Galilee after the
baptism that John preached
—38 how God anointed
Jesus of Nazareth with the
Holy Spirit and power, and
how he went around doing
good and healing all who
were under the power of
the devil, because God was
with him.

39 "We are witnesses of
everything he did in the
country of the Jews and in
Jerusalem. They killed him
by hanging him on a tree,
40 but God raised him from
the dead on the third day

that He should become visible,
41not to all the people, but
to witnesses who were chosen beforehand by God,
that is, to us, who ate and
drank with Him after He
arose from the dead.
42"And He ordered us to
preach to the people, and
solemnly to testify that this
is the One who has been appointed by God as Judge of
the living and the dead.
43"Of Him all the proph-
ets bear witness that
through His name every-
one who believes in Him
receives forgiveness of
sins."
44While Peter was still
speaking these words, the
Holy Spirit fell upon all
those who were listening to
the message.
45And all the circumcised
believers who had come
with Peter were amazed,
because the gift of the Holy
Spirit had been poured out
upon the Gentiles also.
46For they were hearing
them speaking with
tongues and exalting God.
Then Peter answered,
47"Surely no one can
refuse the water for these
to be baptized who have received the Holy Spirit just
as we *did,* can he?"
48And he ordered them to
be baptized in the name of
Jesus Christ. Then they
asked him to stay on for a
few days.

ἔδωκεν αὐτὸν ἐμφανῆ γενέσθαι, 41 οὐ
gave him visible to become, not
παντὶ τῷ λαῷ, ἀλλὰ μάρτυσιν τοῖς
to all the people, but to witnesses –
προκεχειροτονημένοις ὑπὸ τοῦ θεοῦ, ἡμῖν,
having been previously appointed by – God, to us,
οἵτινες συνεφάγομεν καὶ συνεπίομεν αὐτῷ
who ate with and drank with him
μετὰ τὸ ἀναστῆναι αὐτὸν ἐκ νεκρῶν·
after the to rise again him[b] out of [the] dead;
=he rose again
42 καὶ παρήγγειλεν ἡμῖν κηρῦξαι τῷ λαῷ
and he commanded us to proclaim to the people
καὶ διαμαρτύρασθαι ὅτι οὗτός ἐστιν ὁ
and solemnly to witness that this man is the [one]
ὡρισμένος ὑπὸ τοῦ θεοῦ κριτὴς ζώντων
having been designated by – God judge of living
καὶ νεκρῶν. 43 τούτῳ πάντες οἱ προφῆται
and of dead. To this man all the prophets
μαρτυροῦσιν, ἄφεσιν ἁμαρτιῶν λαβεῖν διὰ
witness, 6forgiveness 7of sins 5to receive 8through
τοῦ ὀνόματος αὐτοῦ πάντα τὸν πιστεύοντα
9the 10name 11of him 1everyone 2believing
εἰς αὐτόν. 44 Ἔτι λαλοῦντος τοῦ Πέτρου
3in 4him. Yet speaking – Peter[a]
=While Peter was still speaking
τὰ ῥήματα ταῦτα ἐπέπεσεν τὸ πνεῦμα
these words 4fell *on* 1the 3Spirit
τὸ ἅγιον ἐπὶ πάντας τοὺς ἀκούοντας
– 2Holy on all the [ones] hearing
τὸν λόγον. 45 καὶ ἐξέστησαν οἱ ἐκ
the discourse. And 5were amazed 1the 3of [the]
περιτομῆς πιστοὶ ὅσοι συνῆλθαν τῷ Πέτρῳ,
4circumcision 2faithful as many as accompanied – Peter,
ὅτι καὶ ἐπὶ τὰ ἔθνη ἡ δωρεὰ τοῦ ἁγίου
because also on the nations the gift of the Holy
πνεύματος ἐκκέχυται· 46 ἤκουον γὰρ
Spirit has been poured out; for they heard
αὐτῶν λαλούντων γλώσσαις καὶ μεγαλυνόν-
them speaking in tongues and magnify-
των τὸν θεόν. τότε ἀπεκρίθη Πέτρος·
ing – God. Then answered Peter:
47 μήτι τὸ ὕδωρ δύναται κωλῦσαί τις
Not 4the 5water 1can 3*to* forbid 2anyone
τοῦ μὴ βαπτισθῆναι τούτους, οἵτινες τὸ
– 7not 8to be baptized[d] 6these, who the
πνεῦμα τὸ ἅγιον ἔλαβον ὡς καὶ ἡμεῖς;
Spirit – Holy received as also we?
48 προσέταξεν δὲ αὐτοὺς ἐν τῷ ὀνόματι
And he commanded them in the name
Ἰησοῦ Χριστοῦ βαπτισθῆναι. τότε ἠρώτησαν
of Jesus Christ to be baptized. Then they asked
αὐτὸν ἐπιμεῖναι ἡμέρας τινάς.
him to remain days some.

and caused him to be seen.
41He was not seen by all the
people, but by witnesses
whom God had already
chosen—by us who ate and
drank with him after he
rose from the dead. 42He
commanded us to preach to
the people and to testify
that he is the one whom
God appointed as judge of
the living and the dead.
43All the prophets testify
about him that everyone
who believes in him re-
ceives forgiveness of sins
through his name."
44While Peter was still
speaking these words, the
Holy Spirit came on all who
heard the message. 45The
circumcised believers who
had come with Peter were
astonished that the gift of
the Holy Spirit had been
poured out even on the
Gentiles. 46For they heard
them speaking in tongues[r]
and praising God.
Then Peter said, 47"Can
anyone keep these people
from being baptized with
water? They have received
the Holy Spirit just as we
have." 48So he ordered that
they be baptized in the
name of Jesus Christ. Then
they asked Peter to stay
with them for a few days.

Chapter 11

Peter Reports at Jerusalem

NOW the apostles and
the brethren who
were throughout Judea
heard that the Gentiles also
had received the word of
God.
2And when Peter came
up to Jerusalem, those who

11 Ἤκουσαν δὲ οἱ ἀπόστολοι καὶ οἱ
Now heard the apostles and the
ἀδελφοὶ οἱ ὄντες κατὰ τὴν Ἰουδαίαν
brothers – being throughout – Judæa
ὅτι καὶ τὰ ἔθνη ἐδέξαντο τὸν λόγον
that also the nations received the word
τοῦ θεοῦ. 2 Ὅτε δὲ ἀνέβη Πέτρος εἰς
– of God. And when went up Peter to
Ἰερουσαλήμ, διεκρίνοντο πρὸς αὐτὸν οἱ
Jerusalem, disputed with him the [ones]

Chapter 11

Peter Explains His Actions

THE apostles and the
brothers throughout
Judea heard that the Gen-
tiles also had received the
word of God. 2So when Pe-
ter went up to Jerusalem,

r46 Or *other languages*

were circumcised took issue with him,

3saying, "You went to uncircumcised men and ate with them."

4But Peter began *speaking* and *proceeded* to explain to them in orderly sequence, saying,

5"I was in the city of Joppa praying; and in a trance I saw a vision, a certain object coming down like a great sheet lowered by four corners from the sky; and it came right down to me,

6and when I had fixed my gaze upon it and was observing it I saw the four-footed animals of the earth and the wild beasts and the [b]crawling creatures and the birds of the air.

7"And I also heard a voice saying to me, 'Arise, Peter; kill and eat.'

8"But I said, 'By no means, Lord, for nothing unholy or unclean has ever entered my mouth.'

9"But a voice from heaven answered a second time, 'What God has cleansed, no longer consider unholy.'

10"And this happened three times, and everything was drawn back up into the sky.

11"And behold, at that moment three men appeared before the house in which we were *staying*, having been sent to me from Caesarea.

12"And the Spirit told me to go with them without misgivings. And these six brethren also went with me, and we entered the man's house.

13"And he reported to us how he had seen the angel standing in his house, and saying, 'Send to Joppa, and have Simon, who is also called Peter, brought here;

14and he shall speak words to you by which you will be saved, you and all your household.'

ἐκ περιτομῆς 3 λέγοντες ὅτι εἰσῆλθες
of [the] circumcision saying[.] – Thou enteredst

πρὸς ἄνδρας ἀκροβυστίαν ἔχοντας καὶ
to men uncircumcision having and

συνέφαγες αὐτοῖς. 4 ἀρξάμενος δὲ Πέτρος
didst eat with them. And beginning Peter

ἐξετίθετο αὐτοῖς καθεξῆς λέγων· 5 ἐγὼ
explained to them in order saying: I

ἤμην ἐν πόλει Ἰόππῃ προσευχόμενος, καὶ
was in [the] city Joppa praying, and

εἶδον ἐν ἐκστάσει ὅραμα, καταβαῖνον
I saw in an ecstasy a vision, coming down

σκεῦός τι ὡς ὀθόνην μεγάλην τέσσαρσιν
a certain vessel as sheet a great by four

ἀρχαῖς καθιεμένην ἐκ τοῦ οὐρανοῦ, καὶ
corners having been let down out of – heaven, and

ἦλθεν ἄχρι ἐμοῦ· 6 εἰς ἣν ἀτενίσας
it came up to me; into which gazing

κατενόουν, καὶ εἶδον τὰ τετράποδα τῆς
I perceived, and I saw the quadrupeds of the

γῆς καὶ τὰ θηρία καὶ τὰ ἑρπετὰ καὶ τὰ
earth and the wild beasts and the reptiles and the

πετεινὰ τοῦ οὐρανοῦ. 7 ἤκουσα δὲ καὶ
birds of the heaven(air). And I heard also

φωνῆς λεγούσης μοι· ἀναστάς, Πέτρε,
a voice saying to me: Rise up, Peter,

θῦσον καὶ φάγε. 8 εἶπον δέ· μηδαμῶς,
slay and eat. And I said : Not at all,

κύριε, ὅτι κοινὸν ἢ ἀκάθαρτον οὐδέποτε
Lord, because a common or unclean thing never

εἰσῆλθεν εἰς τὸ στόμα μου. 9 ἀπεκρίθη δὲ
entered into the mouth of me. And answered

ἐκ δευτέρου φωνὴ ἐκ τοῦ οὐρανοῦ·
a second [time] a voice out of – heaven:

ἃ ὁ θεὸς ἐκαθάρισεν σὺ μὴ κοίνου.
What things – God cleansed thou regard not common.

10 τοῦτο δὲ ἐγένετο ἐπὶ τρίς, καὶ
And this happened on three [occasions], and

ἀνεσπάσθη πάλιν ἅπαντα εἰς τὸν οὐρανόν.
was pulled up again all things to – heaven.

11 καὶ ἰδοὺ ἐξαυτῆς τρεῖς ἄνδρες ἐπέστησαν
And behold at once three men stood *at*

ἐπὶ τὴν οἰκίαν ἐν ᾗ ἦμεν, ἀπεσταλμένοι
at the house in which I was, having been sent

ἀπὸ Καισαρείας πρός με. 12 εἶπεν δὲ
from Cæsarea to me. And [3]told

τὸ πνεῦμά μοι συνελθεῖν αὐτοῖς μηδὲν
[1]the [2]Spirit [4]me to go with them nothing

διακρίναντα. ἦλθον δὲ σὺν ἐμοὶ καὶ
doubting. And came with me also

οἱ ἓξ ἀδελφοὶ οὗτοι, καὶ εἰσήλθομεν εἰς
– six brothers these, and we entered into

τὸν οἶκον τοῦ ἀνδρός. 13 ἀπήγγειλεν δὲ
the house of the man. And he reported

ἡμῖν πῶς εἶδεν τὸν ἄγγελον ἐν τῷ
to us how he saw the angel in the

οἴκῳ αὐτοῦ σταθέντα καὶ εἰπόντα·
house of him standing and saying:

ἀπόστειλον εἰς Ἰόππην καὶ μετάπεμψαι
Send to Joppa and summon

Σίμωνα τὸν ἐπικαλούμενον Πέτρον, 14 ὃς
Simon – *being* surnamed Peter, who

λαλήσει ῥήματα πρὸς σὲ ἐν οἷς σωθήσῃ
will speak words to thee by which mayest be saved

σὺ καὶ πᾶς ὁ οἶκός σου. 15 ἐν δὲ
thou and all the household of thee. And in

the circumcised believers
criticized him 3and said,
"You went into the house
of uncircumcised men and
ate with them."
4Peter began and ex-
plained everything to them
precisely as it had hap-
pened: 5"I was in the city of
Joppa praying, and in a
trance I saw a vision. I saw
something like a large sheet
being let down from heaven
by its four corners, and it
came down to where I was.
6I looked into it and saw
four-footed animals of the
earth, wild beasts, reptiles,
and birds of the air. 7Then I
heard a voice telling me,
'Get up, Peter. Kill and
eat.'
8"I replied, 'Surely not,
Lord! Nothing impure or
unclean has ever entered
my mouth.'
9"The voice spoke from
heaven a second time, 'Do
not call anything impure
that God has made clean.'
10This happened three
times, and then it was all
pulled up to heaven again.
11"Right then three men
who had been sent to me
from Caesarea stopped at
the house where I was staying. 12The Spirit told me to
have no hesitation about
going with them. These six
brothers also went with
me, and we entered the
man's house. 13He told us
how he had seen an angel
appear in his house and
say, 'Send to Joppa for Simon who is called Peter.
14He will bring you a message through which you
and all your household will
be saved.'

[b] Or possibly, *reptiles*

15"And as I began to
speak, the Holy Spirit fell
upon them, just as *He did*
upon us at the beginning.
16"And I remembered the
word of the Lord, how He
used to say, 'John baptized
with water, but you shall be
baptized with the Holy
Spirit.'
17"If God therefore gave
to them the same gift as *He*
gave to us also after believing in the Lord Jesus
Christ, who was I that I
could stand in God's
way?"
18And when they heard
this, they quieted down,
and glorified God, saying,
"Well then, God has
granted to the Gentiles also
the repentance *that leads*
to life."

The Church at Antioch

19So then those who were
scattered because of the
persecution that arose in
connection with Stephen
made their way to Phoe-
nicia and Cyprus and Antioch, speaking the word to
no one except to Jews
alone.
20But there were some of
them, men of Cyprus and
Cyrene, who came to Anti-
och and *began* speaking to
the [c]Greeks also, preaching the Lord Jesus.
21And the hand of the
Lord was with them, and a
large number who believed
turned to the Lord.
22And the news about
them reached the ears of
the church at Jerusalem,
and they sent Barnabas off
to Antioch.
23Then when he had come
and witnessed the grace of
God, he rejoiced and *began*
to encourage them all with
resolute heart to remain
true to the Lord;
24for he was a good man,
and full of the Holy Spirit
and of faith. And consider-

[c] Some mss. read *Greek-speaking Jews*

τῷ ἄρξασθαί με λαλεῖν ἐπέπεσεν τὸ
the to begin me[be] to speak [4]fell *on* [1]the
=as I began
πνεῦμα τὸ ἅγιον ἐπ' αὐτοὺς ὥσπερ καὶ
[3]Spirit – [2]Holy on them as also
ἐφ' ἡμᾶς ἐν ἀρχῇ. 16 ἐμνήσθην δὲ τοῦ
on us at [the] beginning. And I remembered the
ῥήματος τοῦ κυρίου, ὡς ἔλεγεν· Ἰωάννης
word of the Lord, how he said: John
μὲν ἐβάπτισεν ὕδατι, ὑμεῖς δὲ βαπτισθήσεσθε
indeed baptized with water, but ye will be baptized
ἐν πνεύματι ἁγίῳ. 17 εἰ οὖν τὴν ἴσην
in Spirit Holy. If therefore [4]the [5]equal
δωρεὰν ἔδωκεν αὐτοῖς ὁ θεὸς ὡς καὶ
[6]gift [2]gave [3]them – [1]God as also
ἡμῖν, πιστεύσασιν ἐπὶ τὸν κύριον Ἰησοῦν
to us, having believed on the Lord Jesus
Χριστόν, ἐγὼ τίς ἤμην δυνατὸς κωλῦσαι
Christ, [2]I [1]who [3]was [to be] able to hinder
τὸν θεόν; 18 ἀκούσαντες δὲ ταῦτα ἡσύχασαν,
– God? And hearing these things they kept silence
καὶ ἐδόξασαν τὸν θεὸν λέγοντες· ἄρα καὶ
and glorified – God saying: Then also
τοῖς ἔθνεσιν ὁ θεὸς τὴν μετάνοιαν εἰς
to the nations – God – repentance to
ζωὴν ἔδωκεν.
life gave.
19 Οἱ μὲν οὖν διασπαρέντες ἀπὸ τῆς
The [ones] – therefore being scattered from the
θλίψεως τῆς γενομένης ἐπὶ Στεφάνῳ
affliction – occurring over Stephen
διῆλθον ἕως Φοινίκης καὶ Κύπρου καὶ
passed through to Phœnicia and Cyprus and
Ἀντιοχείας, μηδενὶ λαλοῦντες τὸν λόγον
Antioch, to no one speaking the word
εἰ μὴ μόνον Ἰουδαίοις. 20 Ἦσαν δέ
except only to Jews. But [4]were
τινες ἐξ αὐτῶν ἄνδρες Κύπριοι καὶ
[1]some [2]of [3]them *men* Cypriotes and
Κυρηναῖοι, οἵτινες ἐλθόντες εἰς Ἀντιόχειαν
Cyrenians, who coming to Antioch
ἐλάλουν καὶ πρὸς τοὺς Ἕλληνας,
spoke also to the Greeks,
εὐαγγελιζόμενοι τὸν κύριον Ἰησοῦν. 21 καὶ ἦν
preaching the Lord Jesus. And was
χεὶρ κυρίου μετ' αὐτῶν, πολύς τε
[the] hand of [the] Lord with them, and a much(great)
ἀριθμὸς ὁ πιστεύσας ἐπέστρεψεν ἐπὶ τὸν
number – believing turned to the
κύριον. 22 Ἠκούσθη δὲ ὁ λόγος εἰς
Lord. And was heard the account in
τὰ ὦτα τῆς ἐκκλησίας τῆς οὔσης ἐν
the ears of the church – being in
Ἰερουσαλὴμ περὶ αὐτῶν, καὶ ἐξαπέστειλαν
Jerusalem about them, and they sent out
Βαρναβᾶν ἕως Ἀντιοχείας· 23 ὃς παραγεν-
Barnabas to Antioch; who arriv-
όμενος καὶ ἰδὼν τὴν χάριν τὴν τοῦ
ing and seeing the grace – –
θεοῦ ἐχάρη, καὶ παρεκάλει πάντας τῇ
of God rejoiced, and exhorted all –
προθέσει τῆς καρδίας προσμένειν τῷ
with purpose – of heart to remain with the
κυρίῳ, 24 ὅτι ἦν ἀνὴρ ἀγαθὸς καὶ
Lord, because he was man a good and
πλήρης πνεύματος ἁγίου καὶ πίστεως.
full of [the] Spirit Holy and of faith.

15"As I began to speak,
the Holy Spirit came on
them as he had come on us
at the beginning. 16Then I
remembered what the Lord
had said: 'John baptized
with[s] water, but you will
be baptized with the Holy
Spirit.' 17So if God gave
them the same gift as he
gave us, who believed in
the Lord Jesus Christ, who
was I to think that I could
oppose God?"
18When they heard this,
they had no further objec-
tions and praised God, saying, "So then, God has
granted even the Gentiles
repentance unto life."

The Church in Antioch

19Now those who had
been scattered by the persecution in connection with
Stephen traveled as far as
Phoenicia, Cyprus and An-
tioch, telling the message
only to Jews. 20Some of
them, however, men from
Cyprus and Cyrene, went
to Antioch and began to
speak to Greeks also, telling them the good news
about the Lord Jesus.
21The Lord's hand was
with them, and a great
number of people believed
and turned to the Lord.
22News of this reached
the ears of the church at Jerusalem, and they sent Barnabas to Antioch. 23When
he arrived and saw the evidence of the grace of God,
he was glad and encour-
aged them all to remain true
to the Lord with all their
hearts. 24He was a good
man, full of the Holy Spirit
and faith, and a great num-

[s] 16 Or *in*

able numbers were brought
to the Lord.
25And he left for Tarsus to
look for Saul;
26and when he had found
him, he brought him to Antioch.
And it came about
that for an entire year they
met with the church, and
taught considerable numbers;
and the disciples were
first called Christians in
Antioch.
27Now at this time some
prophets came down from
Jerusalem to Antioch.
28And one of them named
Agabus stood up and *began*
to indicate by the Spirit that
there would certainly be a
great famine all over the
world. And this took place
in the *reign* of Claudius.
29And in the proportion
that any of the disciples had
means, each of them determined
to send *a contribution*
for the relief of the
brethren living in Judea.
30And this they did, sending
it in charge of Barnabas
and Saul to the elders.

καὶ προσετέθη ὄχλος ἱκανὸς τῷ κυρίῳ.
And was added a crowd considerable to the Lord.
25 ἐξῆλθεν δὲ εἰς Ταρσὸν ἀναζητῆσαι
And he went forth to Tarsus to seek
Σαῦλον, 26 καὶ εὑρὼν ἤγαγεν εἰς Ἀντιόχειαν.
Saul, and finding brought to Antioch.
ἐγένετο δὲ αὐτοῖς καὶ ἐνιαυτὸν ὅλον
And it happened to them also year a whole
συναχθῆναι ἐν τῇ ἐκκλησίᾳ καὶ διδάξαι
to be assembled in the church and to teach
ὄχλον ἱκανόν, χρηματίσαι τε πρώτως ἐν
a crowd considerable, and to call firstly in
Ἀντιοχείᾳ τοὺς μαθητὰς Χριστιανούς.
Antioch the disciples Christians.
27 Ἐν ταύταις δὲ ταῖς ἡμέραις κατῆλθον
And in these – days came down
ἀπὸ Ἱεροσολύμων προφῆται εἰς Ἀντιόχειαν·
from Jerusalem prophets to Antioch;
28 ἀναστὰς δὲ εἷς ἐξ αὐτῶν ὀνόματι
and rising up one of them by name
Ἅγαβος ἐσήμαινεν διὰ τοῦ πνεύματος
Agabus signified through the Spirit
λιμὸν μεγάλην μέλλειν ἔσεσθαι ἐφ᾽ ὅλην τὴν
famine a great to be about to be over all the
οἰκουμένην· ἥτις ἐγένετο ἐπὶ Κλαυδίου.
inhabited earth; which happened in the time of Claudius.
29 τῶν δὲ μαθητῶν καθὼς εὐπορεῖτό
So 3of the 4disciples 1as 6was prosperous
τις, ὥρισαν ἕκαστος αὐτῶν εἰς διακονίαν
5anyone, they determined each of them for ministration
πέμψαι τοῖς κατοικοῦσιν ἐν τῇ Ἰουδαίᾳ
to send 1to the 3dwelling 4in – 5Judæa
ἀδελφοῖς· 30 ὃ καὶ ἐποίησαν ἀποστείλαντες
2brothers; which indeed they did sending
πρὸς τοὺς πρεσβυτέρους διὰ χειρὸς
to the elders through [the] hand
Βαρναβᾶ καὶ Σαύλου.
of Barnabas and of Saul.

ber of people were brought
to the Lord.
25Then Barnabas went to
Tarsus to look for Saul,
26and when he found him,
he brought him to Antioch.
So for a whole year Barnabas
and Saul met with the
church and taught great
numbers of people. The
disciples were called Christians
first at Antioch.
27During this time some
prophets came down from
Jerusalem to Antioch.
28One of them, named Agabus,
stood up and through
the Spirit predicted that a
severe famine would
spread over the entire Roman
world. (This happened
during the reign of Claudius.)
29The disciples, each
according to his ability, decided
to provide help for
the brothers living in Judea.
30This they did, sending
their gift to the elders by
Barnabas and Saul.

Chapter 12

Peter's Arrest and Deliverance

NOW about that time
Herod the king laid
hands on some who belonged
to the church, in order
to mistreat them.
2And he had James the
brother of John put to death
with a sword.
3And when he saw that it
pleased the Jews, he proceeded
to arrest Peter also.
Now it was during the days
of Unleavened Bread.
4And when he had seized
him, he put him in prison,
delivering him to four
squads of soldiers to guard
him, intending after the
Passover to bring him out
before the people.
5So Peter was kept in the
prison, but prayer for him

12 Κατ᾽ ἐκεῖνον δὲ τὸν καιρὸν ἐπέβαλεν
Now at that – time laid on
Ἡρῴδης ὁ βασιλεὺς τὰς χεῖρας κακῶσαί
Herod the king the(his) hands to ill-treat
τινας τῶν ἀπὸ τῆς ἐκκλησίας. 2 ἀνεῖλεν δὲ
some of the [ones] from the church. And he killed
Ἰάκωβον τὸν ἀδελφὸν Ἰωάννου μαχαίρῃ.
James the brother of John with a sword.
3 ἰδὼν δὲ ὅτι ἀρεστόν ἐστιν τοῖς Ἰουδαίοις
And seeing that pleasing it is(was) to the Jews
προσέθετο συλλαβεῖν καὶ Πέτρον, ἦσαν δὲ
he added to arrest also Peter, and they were
ἡμέραι τῶν ἀζύμων, 4 ὃν καὶ πιάσας
days – of unleavened bread, whom also seizing
ἔθετο εἰς φυλακήν, παραδοὺς τέσσαρσιν
he put in prison, delivering to four
τετραδίοις στρατιωτῶν φυλάσσειν αὐτόν,
quaternions of soldiers to guard him,
βουλόμενος μετὰ τὸ πάσχα ἀναγαγεῖν
intending after the Passover to bring up
αὐτὸν τῷ λαῷ. 5 ὁ μὲν οὖν Πέτρος
him to the people. – –* therefore Peter
ἐτηρεῖτο ἐν τῇ φυλακῇ· προσευχὴ δὲ ἦν
was kept in the prison; but prayer was

* μέν and δέ are in contrast : " on one hand . . ."—" on the other . . ."

Chapter 12

Peter's Miraculous Escape From Prison

IT was about this time
that King Herod arrested
some who belonged to
the church, intending to
persecute them. 2He had
James, the brother of John,
put to death with the
sword. 3When he saw that
this pleased the Jews, he
proceeded to seize Peter
also. This happened during
the Feast of Unleavened
Bread. 4After arresting
him, he put him in prison,
handing him over to be
guarded by four squads of
four soldiers each. Herod
intended to bring him out
for public trial after the
Passover.
5So Peter was kept in
prison, but the church was

was being made fervently
by the church to God.
6And on the very night
when Herod was about to
bring him forward, Peter
was sleeping between two
soldiers, bound with two
chains; and guards in front
of the door were watching
over the prison.
7And behold, an angel of
the Lord suddenly ap-
peared, and a light shone in
the cell; and he struck Peter's side and roused him,
saying, "Get up quickly."
And his chains fell off his
hands.
8And the angel said to
him, "Gird yourself and
put on your sandals." And
he did so. And he *said to
him, "Wrap your cloak
around you and follow
me."
9And he went out and
continued to follow, and he
did not know that what was
being done by the angel
was real, but thought he
was seeing a vision.
10And when they had
passed the first and second
guard, they came to the
iron gate that leads into the
city, which opened for
them by itself; and they
went out and went along
one street; and immediately
the angel departed from
him.
11And when Peter came
to himself, he said, "Now I
know for sure that the Lord
has sent forth His angel and
rescued me from the hand
of Herod and from all that
the Jewish people were expecting."
12And when he realized
this, he went to the house
of Mary, the mother of
John who was also called
Mark, where many were
gathered together and were
praying.

ἐκτενῶς γινομένη ὑπὸ τῆς ἐκκλησίας πρὸς
earnestly being made by the church to
τὸν θεὸν περὶ αὐτοῦ. **6** Ὅτε δὲ ἤμελλεν
– God concerning him. And when [2]was about
προαγαγεῖν αὐτὸν ὁ Ἡρῴδης, τῇ νυκτὶ
[3]to bring forward [4]him – [1]Herod, – [2]night
ἐκείνῃ ἦν ὁ Πέτρος κοιμώμενος μεταξὺ
[1]in that was – Peter sleeping between
δύο στρατιωτῶν δεδεμένος ἁλύσεσιν δυσίν,
two soldiers having been bound with chains two,
φύλακές τε πρὸ τῆς θύρας ἐτήρουν τὴν
and guards before the door were keeping the
φυλακήν. **7** καὶ ἰδοὺ ἄγγελος κυρίου
prison. And behold[,] an angel of [the] Lord
ἐπέστη, καὶ φῶς ἔλαμψεν ἐν τῷ οἰκήματι·
came upon, and a light shone in the building;
πατάξας δὲ τὴν πλευρὰν τοῦ Πέτρου
and striking the side – of Peter
ἤγειρεν αὐτὸν λέγων· ἀνάστα ἐν τάχει.
he raised him saying: Rise up in haste.
καὶ ἐξέπεσαν αὐτοῦ αἱ ἁλύσεις ἐκ τῶν
And fell *off* of him the chains off the(his)
χειρῶν. **8** εἶπεν δὲ ὁ ἄγγελος πρὸς
hands. And said the angel to
αὐτόν· ζῶσαι καὶ ὑπόδησαι τὰ σανδάλιά
him: Gird thyself and put on the sandals
σου. ἐποίησεν δὲ οὕτως. καὶ λέγει
of thee. And he did so. And he tells
αὐτῷ· περιβαλοῦ τὸ ἱμάτιόν σου καὶ
him: Cast round the garment of thee and
ἀκολούθει μοι. **9** καὶ ἐξελθὼν ἠκολούθει,
follow me. And going forth he followed,
καὶ οὐκ ᾔδει ὅτι ἀληθές ἐστιν τὸ
and knew not that [3]true [2]is(was) [1]the thing
γινόμενον διὰ τοῦ ἀγγέλου, ἐδόκει δὲ
happening through the angel, but he thought
ὅραμα βλέπειν. **10** διελθόντες δὲ πρώτην
a vision to see. And going through [the] first
φυλακὴν καὶ δευτέραν ἦλθαν ἐπὶ τὴν
prison and [the] second they came on the
πύλην τὴν σιδηρᾶν τὴν φέρουσαν εἰς τὴν
gate – iron – leading to the
πόλιν, ἥτις αὐτομάτη ἠνοίγη αὐτοῖς, καὶ
city, which of itself was opened to them, and
ἐξελθόντες προῆλθον ῥύμην μίαν, καὶ
going out they went forward street one, and
εὐθέως ἀπέστη ὁ ἄγγελος ἀπ' αὐτοῦ.
immediately departed the angel from him.
11 καὶ ὁ Πέτρος ἐν ἑαυτῷ γενόμενος
And – Peter in himself having become
εἶπεν· νῦν οἶδα ἀληθῶς ὅτι ἐξαπέστειλεν
said: Now I know truly that sent forth
ὁ κύριος τὸν ἄγγελον αὐτοῦ καὶ ἐξείλατό
the Lord the angel of him and delivered
με ἐκ χειρὸς Ἡρῴδου καὶ πάσης τῆς
me out of [the] hand of Herod and of all the
προσδοκίας τοῦ λαοῦ τῶν Ἰουδαίων.
expectation of the people of the Jews.
12 συνιδών τε ἦλθεν ἐπὶ τὴν οἰκίαν τῆς
And realizing he came on the house –
Μαρίας τῆς μητρὸς Ἰωάννου τοῦ
of Mary the mother of John –
ἐπικαλουμένου Μάρκου, οὗ ἦσαν ἱκανοὶ
being surnamed Mark, where were many
συνηθροισμένοι καὶ προσευχόμενοι. **13** κρού-
having been assembled and praying. And

earnestly praying to God
for him.
6The night before Herod
was to bring him to trial,
Peter was sleeping between
two soldiers, bound with
two chains, and sentries
stood guard at the en-
trance. 7Suddenly an angel
of the Lord appeared and a
light shone in the cell. He
struck Peter on the side and
woke him up. "Quick, get
up!" he said, and the
chains fell off Peter's
wrists.
8Then the angel said to
him, "Put on your clothes
and sandals." And Peter
did so. "Wrap your cloak
around you and follow
me," the angel told him.
9Peter followed him out of
the prison, but he had no
idea that what the angel
was doing was really hap-
pening; he thought he was
seeing a vision. 10They
passed the first and second
guards and came to the iron
gate leading to the city. It
opened for them by itself,
and they went through it.
When they had walked the
length of one street, suddenly the angel left him.
11Then Peter came to
himself and said, "Now I
know without a doubt that
the Lord sent his angel and
rescued me from Herod's
clutches and from every-
thing the Jewish people
were anticipating."
12When this had dawned
on him, he went to the
house of Mary the mother
of John, also called Mark,
where many people had
gathered and were praying.

13And when he knocked at the door of the gate, a servant-girl named Rhoda came to answer.

14And when she recognized Peter's voice, because of her joy she did not open the gate, but ran in and announced that Peter was standing in front of the gate.

15And they said to her, "You are out of your mind!" But she kept insisting that it was so. And they kept saying, "It is his angel."

16But Peter continued knocking; and when they had opened *the door*, they saw him and were amazed.

17But motioning to them with his hand to be silent, he described to them how the Lord had led him out of the prison. And he said, "Report these things to James and the brethren." And he departed and went to another place.

18Now when day came, there was no small disturbance among the soldiers *as to* what could have become of Peter.

19And when Herod had searched for him and had not found him, he examined the guards and ordered that they be led away *to execution*. And he went down from Judea to Caesarea and was spending time there.

Death of Herod

20Now he was very angry with the people of Tyre and Sidon; and with one accord they came to him, and having won over Blastus the king's chamberlain, they were asking for peace, because their country was fed by the king's country.

21And on an appointed day Herod, having put on his royal apparel, took his seat on the rostrum and *began* delivering an address to them.

22And the people kept crying out, "The voice of a

σαντος δὲ αὐτοῦ τὴν θύραν τοῦ πυλῶνος
knocking him[a] the door of the porch
=as he knocked

προσῆλθεν παιδίσκη ὑπακοῦσαι ὀνόματι
approached a maidservant to listen by name

Ῥόδη, 14 καὶ ἐπιγνοῦσα τὴν φωνὴν τοῦ
Rhoda, and recognizing the voice –

Πέτρου ἀπὸ τῆς χαρᾶς οὐκ ἤνοιξεν τὸν
of Peter from – joy she did not open the

πυλῶνα, εἰσδραμοῦσα δὲ ἀπήγγειλεν ἑστάναι
porch, but running in announced [a]to stand

τὸν Πέτρον πρὸ τοῦ πυλῶνος. 15 οἱ δὲ
– [a]Peter before the porch. But they

πρὸς αὐτὴν εἶπαν· μαίνῃ. ἡ δὲ διϊσχυρίζετο
to her said: Thou ravest. But she emphatically asserted

οὕτως ἔχειν. οἱ δὲ ἔλεγον· ὁ ἄγγελός
so to have(be). So they said: The angel

ἐστιν αὐτοῦ. 16 ὁ δὲ Πέτρος ἐπέμενεν
it is of him. – But Peter continued

κρούων· ἀνοίξαντες δὲ εἶδαν αὐτὸν καὶ
knocking; and having opened they saw him and

ἐξέστησαν. 17 κατασείσας δὲ αὐτοῖς τῇ
were amazed. And beckoning to them with the

χειρὶ σιγᾶν διηγήσατο αὐτοῖς πῶς ὁ
hand to be quiet he related to them how the

κύριος αὐτὸν ἐξήγαγεν ἐκ τῆς φυλακῆς,
Lord him led *out* out of the prison,

εἶπέν τε· ἀπαγγείλατε Ἰακώβῳ καὶ τοῖς
and said: Report to James and to the

ἀδελφοῖς ταῦτα. καὶ ἐξελθὼν ἐπορεύθη εἰς
brothers these things. And going out he went to

ἕτερον τόπον. 18 Γενομένης δὲ ἡμέρας ἦν
another place. And becoming day[a] there was
=when it became day

τάραχος οὐκ ὀλίγος ἐν τοῖς στρατιώταις,
disturbance not a little among the soldiers,

τί ἄρα ὁ Πέτρος ἐγένετο. 19 Ἡρῴδης δὲ
what then – [of] Peter became. And Herod

ἐπιζητήσας αὐτὸν καὶ μὴ εὑρών,
searching for him and not finding,

ἀνακρίνας τοὺς φύλακας ἐκέλευσεν ἀπ-
examining the guards commanded to

αχθῆναι, καὶ κατελθὼν ἀπὸ τῆς Ἰουδαίας
be led away,* and going down from – Judæa

εἰς Καισάρειαν διέτριβεν. 20 Ἦν δὲ
to Cæsarea stayed. Now he was

θυμομαχῶν Τυρίοις καὶ Σιδωνίοις·
being furiously angry with Tyrians and Sidonians;

ὁμοθυμαδὸν δὲ παρῆσαν πρὸς αὐτόν, καὶ
and with one mind they came to him, and

πείσαντες Βλάστον τὸν ἐπὶ τοῦ κοιτῶνος
having persuaded Blastus the one over the bedchamber

τοῦ βασιλέως ᾐτοῦντο εἰρήνην, διὰ τὸ
of the king they asked peace, because the

τρέφεσθαι αὐτῶν τὴν χώραν ἀπὸ τῆς
to be fed of them the country[b] from the
=their country was fed

βασιλικῆς. 21 τακτῇ δὲ ἡμέρᾳ ὁ Ἡρῴδης
royal. And on an appointed day – Herod

ἐνδυσάμενος ἐσθῆτα βασιλικὴν καθίσας ἐπὶ
having been arrayed with clothing regal sitting on

τοῦ βήματος ἐδημηγόρει πρὸς αὐτούς·
the tribunal made a public speech to them;

22 ὁ δὲ δῆμος ἐπεφώνει· θεοῦ φωνὴ
and the mob cried out: Of a god a voice

* That is, to execution.

13Peter knocked at the outer entrance, and a servant girl named Rhoda came to answer the door. 14When she recognized Peter's voice, she was so overjoyed she ran back without opening it and exclaimed, "Peter is at the door!"

15"You're out of your mind," they told her. When she kept insisting that it was so, they said, "It must be his angel."

16But Peter kept on knocking, and when they opened the door and saw him, they were astonished. 17Peter motioned with his hand for them to be quiet and described how the Lord had brought him out of prison. "Tell James and the brothers about this," he said, and then he left for another place.

18In the morning, there was no small commotion among the soldiers as to what had become of Peter. 19After Herod had a thorough search made for him and did not find him, he cross-examined the guards and ordered that they be executed.

Herod's Death

Then Herod went from Judea to Caesarea and stayed there a while. 20He had been quarreling with the people of Tyre and Sidon; they now joined together and sought an audience with him. Having secured the support of Blastus, a trusted personal servant of the king, they asked for peace, because they depended on the king's country for their food supply.

21On the appointed day Herod, wearing his royal robes, sat on his throne and delivered a public address to the people. 22They shouted, "This is the voice

god and not of a man!''
23And immediately an an-
gel of the Lord struck him
because he did not give
God the glory, and he was
eaten by worms and died.
24But the word of the
Lord continued to grow
and to be multiplied.
25And Barnabas and Saul
returned from Jerusalem
when they had fulfilled
their mission, taking along
with *them* John, who was
also called Mark.

καὶ οὐκ ἀνθρώπου. 23 παραχρῆμα δὲ
and not of a man. And at once
ἐπάταξεν αὐτὸν ἄγγελος κυρίου ἀνθ' ὧν
smote him an angel of [the] Lord because
οὐκ ἔδωκεν τὴν δόξαν τῷ θεῷ, καὶ
he gave not the glory – to God, and
γενόμενος σκωληκόβρωτος ἐξέψυξεν.
becoming eaten by worms he expired.
24 Ὁ δὲ λόγος τοῦ κυρίου ηὔξανεν
But the word of the Lord grew
καὶ ἐπληθύνετο. 25 Βαρναβᾶς δὲ καὶ
and increased. And Barnabas and
Σαῦλος ὑπέστρεψαν ἐξ Ἰερουσαλήμ,
Saul returned out of Jerusalem,
πληρώσαντες τὴν διακονίαν, συμπαρα-
having completed the ministration, taking
λαβόντες Ἰωάννην τὸν ἐπικληθέντα Μᾶρκον.
with [them] John – surnamed Mark.

of a god, not of a man.''
23Immediately, because
Herod did not give praise to
God, an angel of the Lord
struck him down, and he
was eaten by worms and
died.
24But the word of God
continued to increase and
spread.
25When Barnabas and
Saul had finished their mission, they returned from[r]
Jerusalem, taking with
them John, also called
Mark.

Chapter 13

First Missionary Journey

NOW there were at An-
tioch, in the church
that was *there*, prophets
and teachers: Barnabas,
and Simeon who was called
Niger, and Lucius of Cy-
rene, and Manaen who had
been brought up with Her-
od the tetrarch, and Saul.
2And while they were
ministering to the Lord and
fasting, the Holy Spirit
said, "Set apart for Me
Barnabas and Saul for the
work to which I have called
them."
3Then, when they had
fasted and prayed and laid
their hands on them, they
sent them away.
4So, being sent out by
the Holy Spirit, they went
down to Seleucia and from
there they sailed to Cyprus.
5And when they reached
Salamis, they *began* to proclaim the word of God in
the synagogues of the Jews;
and they also had John as
their helper.
6And when they had
gone through the whole island as far as Paphos, they
found a certain magician, a
Jewish false prophet whose
name was Bar-Jesus,
7who was with the pro-
consul, Sergius Paulus, a

13 Ἦσαν δὲ ἐν Ἀντιοχείᾳ κατὰ τὴν
Now there were in Antioch among the
οὖσαν ἐκκλησίαν προφῆται καὶ διδάσκαλοι
existing church prophets and teachers
ὅ τε Βαρναβᾶς καὶ Συμεὼν ὁ καλούμενος
– both Barnabas and Simeon – *being* called
Νίγερ, καὶ Λούκιος ὁ Κυρηναῖος, Μαναήν τε
Niger, and Lucius the Cyrenian, and Manaen
Ἡρῴδου τοῦ τετραάρχου σύντροφος
[2]of Herod [3]the [4]tetrarch [1]foster brother
καὶ Σαῦλος. 2 Λειτουργούντων δὲ αὐτῶν
and Saul. And ministering them[a]
=as they ministered
τῷ κυρίῳ καὶ νηστευόντων εἶπεν τὸ
to the Lord and fasting[a] said the
πνεῦμα τὸ ἅγιον· ἀφορίσατε δή μοι
Spirit – Holy: [2]Separate ye [1]so then [3]to me
τὸν Βαρναβᾶν καὶ Σαῦλον εἰς τὸ ἔργον
– Barnabas and Saul for the work
ὃ προσκέκλημαι αὐτούς· 3 τότε νηστεύ-
[to] which I have called them; then having
σαντες καὶ προσευξάμενοι καὶ ἐπιθέντες
fasted and *having* prayed and [1]laying [4]on
τὰς χεῖρας αὐτοῖς ἀπέλυσαν.
[2]the(ir) [3]hands [5]them they dismissed [them].
4 Αὐτοὶ μὲν οὖν ἐκπεμφθέντες ὑπὸ τοῦ
They – therefore sent out by the
ἁγίου πνεύματος κατῆλθον εἰς Σελεύκειαν,
Holy Spirit went down to Seleucia,
ἐκεῖθέν τε ἀπέπλευσαν εἰς Κύπρον, 5 καὶ
and thence sailed away to Cyprus, and
γενόμενοι ἐν Σαλαμῖνι κατήγγελλον τὸν
being in Salamis they announced the
λόγον τοῦ θεοῦ ἐν ταῖς συναγωγαῖς τῶν
word – of God in the synagogues of the
Ἰουδαίων· εἶχον δὲ καὶ Ἰωάννην ὑπηρέτην.
Jews; and they had also John [as] attendant.
6 Διελθόντες δὲ ὅλην τὴν νῆσον ἄχρι
And passing through all the island unto
Πάφου εὗρον ἄνδρα τινὰ μάγον ψευδο-
Paphos they found a certain man a sorcerer a [2]false
προφήτην Ἰουδαῖον, ᾧ ὄνομα Βαριησοῦς,
[3]prophet [1]Jewish, to whom name[c] Barjesus,
=whose name was
7 ὃς ἦν σὺν τῷ ἀνθυπάτῳ Σεργίῳ
who was with the proconsul Sergius

Chapter 13

Barnabas and Saul Sent Off

IN the church at Antioch
there were prophets and
teachers: Barnabas, Sime-
on called Niger, Lucius of
Cyrene, Manaen (who had
been brought up with Her-
od the tetrarch) and Saul.
2While they were worship-
ing the Lord and fasting,
the Holy Spirit said, "Set
apart for me Barnabas and
Saul for the work to which I
have called them." 3So after they had fasted and
prayed, they placed their
hands on them and sent
them off.

On Cyprus

4The two of them, sent on
their way by the Holy Spirit, went down to Seleucia
and sailed from there to Cyprus. 5When they arrived at
Salamis, they proclaimed
the word of God in the Jewish synagogues. John was
with them as their helper.
6They traveled through
the whole island until they
came to Paphos. There
they met a Jewish sorcerer
and false prophet named
Bar-Jesus, 7who was an attendant of the proconsul,

[r]25 Some manuscripts *to*

man of intelligence. This
man summoned Barnabas
and Saul and sought to hear
the word of God.
8But Elymas the magi-
cian (for thus his name is
translated) was opposing
them, seeking to turn the
proconsul away from the
faith.
9But Saul, who was also
known as Paul, filled with
the Holy Spirit, fixed his
gaze upon him,
10and said, "You who are
full of all deceit and fraud,
you son of the devil, you
enemy of all righteousness,
will you not cease to make
crooked the straight ways
of the Lord?
11"And now, behold, the
hand of the Lord is upon
you, and you will be blind
and not see the sun for a
time." And immediately a
mist and a darkness fell
upon him, and he went
about seeking those who
would lead him by the
hand.
12Then the proconsul be-
lieved when he saw what
had happened, being
amazed at the teaching of
the Lord.
13Now Paul and his com-
panions put out to sea from
Paphos and came to Perga
in Pamphylia; and John left
them and returned to
Jerusalem.
14But going on from Per-
ga, they arrived at Pisidian
Antioch, and on the Sab-
bath day they went into the
synagogue and sat down.
15And after the reading of
the Law and the Prophets
the synagogue officials sent
to them, saying, "Breth-
ren, if you have any word
of exhortation for the
people, say it."
16And Paul stood up, and

Παύλῳ, ἀνδρὶ συνετῷ. οὗτος προσ-
Paulus, man an intelligent. This man calling
καλεσάμενος Βαρναβᾶν καὶ Σαῦλον ἐπεζήτησεν
to [him] Barnabas and Saul sought
ἀκοῦσαι τὸν λόγον τοῦ θεοῦ· **8** ἀνθίστατο δὲ
to hear the word – of God; but opposed
αὐτοῖς Ἐλύμας ὁ μάγος, οὕτως γὰρ
them Elymas the sorcerer, for so
μεθερμηνεύεται τὸ ὄνομα αὐτοῦ, ζητῶν
is translated the name of him, seeking
διαστρέψαι τὸν ἀνθύπατον ἀπὸ τῆς
to divert the proconsul from the
πίστεως. **9** Σαῦλος δέ, ὁ καὶ Παῦλος,
faith. But Saul, the [one] also Paul,
πλησθεὶς πνεύματος ἁγίου ἀτενίσας εἰς
filled of(with) Spirit Holy gazing at
αὐτὸν εἶπεν· **10** ὦ πλήρης παντὸς δόλου
him said: O full of all deceit
καὶ πάσης ῥᾳδιουργίας, υἱὲ διαβόλου,
and of all fraud, son of [the] devil,
ἐχθρὲ πάσης δικαιοσύνης, οὐ παύσῃ
enemy of all righteousness, wilt thou not cease
διαστρέφων τὰς ὁδοὺς τοῦ κυρίου τὰς
perverting the ways of the Lord –
εὐθείας; **11** καὶ νῦν ἰδοὺ χεὶρ κυρίου
right? And now behold[,] [the] hand of [the] Lord
ἐπὶ σέ, καὶ ἔσῃ τυφλὸς μὴ βλέπων
[is] on thee, and thou wilt be blind not seeing
τὸν ἥλιον ἄχρι καιροῦ. παραχρῆμα δὲ
the sun until [such] a time. And at once
ἔπεσεν ἐπ' αὐτὸν ἀχλὺς καὶ σκότος, καὶ
fell on him a mist and darkness, and
περιάγων ἐζήτει χειραγωγούς. **12** τότε
going about he sought leaders by the hand. Then
ἰδὼν ὁ ἀνθύπατος τὸ γεγονὸς
[3]seeing [1]the [2]proconsul the thing having occurred
ἐπίστευσεν, ἐκπλησσόμενος ἐπὶ τῇ διδαχῇ
believed, being astounded at the teaching
τοῦ κυρίου.
of the Lord.
13 Ἀναχθέντες δὲ ἀπὸ τῆς Πάφου οἱ
And setting sail from – Paphos the ones
περὶ Παῦλον ἦλθον εἰς Πέργην τῆς
around(with) Paul came to Perga –
Παμφυλίας· Ἰωάννης δὲ ἀποχωρήσας ἀπ'
of Pamphylia; and John departing from
αὐτῶν ὑπέστρεψεν εἰς Ἱεροσόλυμα.
them returned to Jerusalem.
14 Αὐτοὶ δὲ διελθόντες ἀπὸ τῆς Πέργης
And they going through from – Perga
παρεγένοντο εἰς Ἀντιόχειαν τὴν Πισιδίαν,
arrived in Antioch the Pisidian,
καὶ ἐλθόντες εἰς τὴν συναγωγὴν τῇ
and going into the synagogue on the
ἡμέρᾳ τῶν σαββάτων ἐκάθισαν. **15** μετὰ δὲ
day of the sabbaths sat down. And after
τὴν ἀνάγνωσιν τοῦ νόμου καὶ τῶν
the reading of the law and of the
προφητῶν ἀπέστειλαν οἱ ἀρχισυνάγωγοι
prophets sent the synagogue rulers
πρὸς αὐτοὺς λέγοντες· ἄνδρες ἀδελφοί,
to them saying: *Men* brothers,
εἴ τίς ἐστιν ἐν ὑμῖν λόγος παρακλήσεως
[1]if [5]any [2]there is [3]among [4]you [6]word of exhortation
πρὸς τὸν λαόν, λέγετε. **16** ἀναστὰς δὲ
to the people, say ye. And [1]rising up

Sergius Paulus. The pro-
consul, an intelligent man,
sent for Barnabas and Saul
because he wanted to hear
the word of God. 8But Elymas the sorcerer (for that is
what his name means) op-
posed them and tried to
turn the proconsul from the
faith. 9Then Saul, who was
also called Paul, filled with
the Holy Spirit, looked
straight at Elymas and said,
10"You are a child of the
devil and an enemy of ev-
erything that is right! You
are full of all kinds of deceit
and trickery. Will you never stop perverting the right
ways of the Lord? 11Now
the hand of the Lord is
against you. You are going
to be blind, and for a time
you will be unable to see
the light of the sun."
Immediately mist and
darkness came over him,
and he groped about, seeking someone to lead him by
the hand. 12When the pro-
consul saw what had hap-
pened, he believed, for he
was amazed at the teaching
about the Lord.

In Pisidian Antioch

13From Paphos, Paul and
his companions sailed to
Perga in Pamphylia, where
John left them to return to
Jerusalem. 14From Perga
they went on to Pisidian
Antioch. On the Sabbath
they entered the synagogue
and sat down. 15After the
reading from the Law and
the Prophets, the syna-
gogue rulers sent word to
them, saying, "Brothers, if
you have a message of en-
couragement for the peo-
ple, please speak."
16Standing up, Paul mo-

motioning with his hand, he
said,
"Men of Israel, and you
who fear God, listen:
17"The God of this people
Israel chose our fathers,
and made the people great
during their stay in the land
of Egypt, and with an
uplifted arm He led them
out from it.
18"And for a period of
about forty years He put up
with them in the wilder-
ness.
19"And when He had de-
stroyed seven nations in
the land of Canaan, He distributed their land as an inheritance—*all of which*
took about four hundred
and fifty years.
20"And after these things
He gave *them* judges until
Samuel the prophet.
21"And then they asked
for a king, and God gave
them Saul the son of Kish,
a man of the tribe of Benjamin, for forty years.
22"And after He had re-
moved him, He raised up
David to be their king, concerning whom He also tes-
tified and said, 'I HAVE
FOUND DAVID the son of
Jesse, A MAN AFTER MY
HEART, who will do all My
will.'
23"From the offspring of
this man, according to
promise, God has brought
to Israel a Savior, Jesus,
24after John had pro-
claimed before His coming
a baptism of repentance to
all the people of Israel.
25"And while John was
completing his course, he
kept saying, 'What do you
suppose that I am? I am not
He. But behold, one is
coming after me the san-
dals of whose feet I am not
worthy to untie.'
26"Brethren, sons of
Abraham's family, and
those among you who fear

Παῦλος καὶ κατασείσας τῇ χειρὶ εἶπεν·
[1]Paul [2]and [3]beckoning [4]with the(his) [5]hand said:
ἄνδρες Ἰσραηλῖται καὶ οἱ φοβούμενοι τὸν
Men Israelites and the [ones] fearing –
θεόν, ἀκούσατε. 17 ὁ θεὸς τοῦ λαοῦ
God, hear ye. The God – people
τούτου Ἰσραὴλ ἐξελέξατο τοὺς πατέρας
of this Israel chose the fathers
ἡμῶν, καὶ τὸν λαὸν ὕψωσεν ἐν τῇ
of us, and [2]the [3]people [1]exalted in the
παροικίᾳ ἐν γῇ Αἰγύπτου, καὶ μετὰ
sojourn in [the] land of Egypt, and with
βραχίονος ὑψηλοῦ ἐξήγαγεν αὐτοὺς ἐξ
arm a high he led forth them out of
αὐτῆς, 18 καὶ ὡς τεσσερακονταέτη χρόνον
it, and about forty years time
ἐτροποφόρησεν αὐτοὺς ἐν τῇ ἐρήμῳ, 19 καὶ
endured them in the desert, and
καθελὼν ἔθνη ἑπτὰ ἐν γῇ Χανάαν
having destroyed nations seven in [the] land Canaan
κατεκληρονόμησεν τὴν γῆν αὐτῶν 20 ὡς
gave as an inheritance the land of them about
ἔτεσιν τετρακοσίοις καὶ πεντήκοντα. καὶ
years four hundred*s* and fifty. And
μετὰ ταῦτα ἔδωκεν κριτὰς ἕως Σαμουὴλ
after these things he gave judges until Samuel
προφήτου. 21 κἀκεῖθεν ᾐτήσαντο βασιλέα,
a prophet. And thence they asked a king,
καὶ ἔδωκεν αὐτοῖς ὁ θεὸς τὸν Σαοὺλ
and gave them – God – Saul
υἱὸν Κίς, ἄνδρα ἐκ φυλῆς Βενιαμίν,
son of Cis, a man of [the] tribe of Benjamin,
ἔτη τεσσεράκοντα· 22 καὶ μεταστήσας
years forty; and removing
αὐτὸν ἤγειρεν τὸν Δαυὶδ αὐτοῖς εἰς
him he raised – David to them for
βασιλέα, ᾧ καὶ εἶπεν μαρτυρήσας·
a king, to whom also he said giving witness:
εὗρον Δαυὶδ τὸν τοῦ Ἰεσσαί, ἄνδρα
I found David the [son] – of Jesse, a man
κατὰ τὴν καρδίαν μου, ὃς ποιήσει πάντα
according to the heart of me, who will do all
τὰ θελήματά μου. 23 τούτου ὁ θεὸς
the wishes of me. [4]Of this man – [5]God
ἀπὸ τοῦ σπέρματος κατ' ἐπαγγελίαν
[1]from [2]the [3]seed according to promise
ἤγαγεν τῷ Ἰσραὴλ σωτῆρα Ἰησοῦν,
brought – to Israel a Saviour Jesus,
24 προκηρύξαντος Ἰωάννου πρὸ προσώπου
previously proclaiming John[a] before *face*
=when John had previously proclaimed
τῆς εἰσόδου αὐτοῦ βάπτισμα μετανοίας
of the entrance of him a baptism of repentance
παντὶ τῷ λαῷ Ἰσραήλ. 25 ὡς δὲ
to all the people of Israel. Now as
ἐπλήρου Ἰωάννης τὸν δρόμον, ἔλεγεν·
completed John the(his) course, he said:
τί ἐμὲ ὑπονοεῖτε εἶναι; οὐκ εἰμὶ ἐγώ·
What me suppose ye to be? [3]Not [2]am [1]I;
ἀλλ' ἰδοὺ ἔρχεται μετ' ἐμὲ οὗ οὐκ εἰμὶ
but behold he comes after me of whom I am not
ἄξιος τὸ ὑπόδημα τῶν ποδῶν λῦσαι.
worthy the sandal of the feet to loosen.
26 Ἄνδρες ἀδελφοί, υἱοὶ γένους Ἀβραὰμ
Men brothers, sons of [the] race of Abraham
καὶ οἱ ἐν ὑμῖν φοβούμενοι τὸν θεόν,
and the [ones] among you fearing – God,

tioned with his hand and
said: "Men of Israel and
you Gentiles who worship
God, listen to me! 17The
God of the people of Israel
chose our fathers; he made
the people prosper during
their stay in Egypt, with
mighty power he led them
out of that country, 18he endured their conduct[u] for
about forty years in the
desert, 19he overthrew sev-
en nations in Canaan and
gave their land to his people as their inheritance.
20All this took about 450
years.
"After this, God gave
them judges until the time
of Samuel the prophet.
21Then the people asked for
a king, and he gave them
Saul son of Kish, of the
tribe of Benjamin, who
ruled forty years. 22After
removing Saul, he made
David their king. He testified concerning him: 'I
have found David son of
Jesse a man after my own
heart; he will do everything
I want him to do.'
23"From this man's de-
scendants God has brought
to Israel the Savior Jesus,
as he promised. 24Before
the coming of Jesus, John
preached repentance and
baptism to all the people of
Israel. 25As John was
completing his work, he
said: 'Who do you think I
am? I am not that one. No,
but he is coming after me,
whose sandals I am not
worthy to untie.'
26"Brothers, children of
Abraham, and you God-
fearing Gentiles, it is to us

[u]18 Some manuscripts *and cared for them*

God, to us the word of this salvation is sent out.
27"For those who live in Jerusalem, and their rulers, recognizing neither Him nor the utterances of the prophets which are read every Sabbath, fulfilled *these* by condemning *Him*.
28"And though they found no ground for *putting Him to* death, they asked Pilate that He be executed.
29"And when they had carried out all that was written concerning Him, they took Him down from the cross and laid Him in a tomb.
30"But God raised Him from the dead;
31and for many days He appeared to those who came up with Him from Galilee to Jerusalem, the very ones who are now His witnesses to the people.
32"And we preach to you the good news of the promise made to the fathers,
33that God has fulfilled this *promise* to our children in that He raised up Jesus, as it is also written in the second Psalm, 'THOU ART MY SON; TODAY I HAVE BEGOTTEN THEE.'
34"*And as for the fact* that He raised Him up from the dead, no more to return to decay, He has spoken in this way: 'I WILL GIVE YOU THE HOLY *and* SURE *blessings* OF DAVID.'
35"Therefore He also says in another *Psalm*, 'THOU WILT NOT ALLOW THY HOLY ONE TO UNDERGO DECAY.'
36"For David, after he had served the purpose of God in his own generation, fell asleep, and was laid among his fathers, and underwent decay;
37but He whom God raised did not undergo decay.
38"Therefore let it be known to you, brethren, that through Him forgive-

ἡμῖν ὁ λόγος τῆς σωτηρίας ταύτης
to us the word of this salvation
ἐξαπεστάλη. 27 οἱ γὰρ κατοικοῦντες ἐν
was sent forth. For the [ones] dwelling in
Ἰερουσαλὴμ καὶ οἱ ἄρχοντες αὐτῶν τοῦτον
Jerusalem and the rulers of them [2]this man
ἀγνοήσαντες καὶ τὰς φωνὰς τῶν προφητῶν τὰς
[1]not knowing and the voices of the prophets –
κατὰ πᾶν σάββατον ἀναγινωσκομένας
[2]throughout(on) [3]every [4]sabbath [1]being read
κρίναντες ἐπλήρωσαν, 28 καὶ μηδεμίαν
judging they fulfilled, and no
αἰτίαν θανάτου εὑρόντες ᾐτήσαντο Πιλᾶτον
cause of death finding they asked Pilate
ἀναιρεθῆναι αὐτόν· 29 ὡς δὲ ἐτέλεσαν πάντα
to be destroyed him; and when they finished all
τὰ περὶ αὐτοῦ γεγραμμένα, καθελόντες
the things concerning him having been written, taking down
ἀπὸ τοῦ ξύλου ἔθηκαν εἰς μνημεῖον.
from the tree they laid in a tomb.
30 ὁ δὲ θεὸς ἤγειρεν αὐτὸν ἐκ νεκρῶν·
– But God raised him out of [the] dead;
31 ὃς ὤφθη ἐπὶ ἡμέρας πλείους τοῖς
who appeared over days many to the [ones]
συναναβᾶσιν αὐτῷ ἀπὸ τῆς Γαλιλαίας εἰς
having come up with him from – Galilee to
Ἰερουσαλήμ, οἵτινες [νῦν] εἰσιν μάρτυρες
Jerusalem, who now are witnesses
αὐτοῦ πρὸς τὸν λαόν. 32 καὶ ἡμεῖς
of him to the people. And we
ὑμᾶς εὐαγγελιζόμεθα τὴν πρὸς τοὺς
[to] you preach [1]the [4]to [5]the
πατέρας ἐπαγγελίαν γενομένην, 33 ὅτι
[6]fathers [2]promise [3]having come, that
ταύτην ὁ θεὸς ἐκπεπλήρωκεν τοῖς τέκνοις
this [promise] – God has fulfilled [2]*to* the [3]children
ἡμῖν ἀναστήσας Ἰησοῦν, ὡς καὶ ἐν τῷ
[1]to us raising up Jesus, as also in the
ψαλμῷ γέγραπται τῷ δευτέρῳ· υἱός μου
[2]psalm [3]it has been written – [1]second: Son of me
εἶ σύ, ἐγὼ σήμερον γεγέννηκά σε. 34 ὅτι δὲ
art thou, I to-day have begotten thee. And that
ἀνέστησεν αὐτὸν ἐκ νεκρῶν μηκέτι
he raised up him out of [the] dead no more
μέλλοντα ὑποστρέφειν εἰς διαφθοράν, οὕτως
being about to return to corruption, thus
εἴρηκεν ὅτι δώσω ὑμῖν τὰ ὅσια Δαυὶδ τὰ
he has said[,] – I will give you the [2]holy things [3]of David *the*
πιστά. 35 διότι καὶ ἐν ἑτέρῳ λέγει·
[1]faithful. Wherefore also in another [psalm] he says:
οὐ δώσεις τὸν ὅσιόν σου ἰδεῖν διαφθοράν.
Thou wilt not give the holy one of thee to see corruption.
36 Δαυὶδ μὲν γὰρ ἰδίᾳ γενεᾷ ὑπηρετήσας
For David indeed [his] own generation having served
τῇ τοῦ θεοῦ βουλῇ ἐκοιμήθη καὶ προσετέθη
by the – of God counsel fell asleep and was added
πρὸς τοὺς πατέρας αὐτοῦ καὶ εἶδεν
to the fathers of him and saw
διαφθοράν· 37 ὃν δὲ ὁ θεὸς ἤγειρεν,
corruption; but [he] whom – God raised,
οὐκ εἶδεν διαφθοράν. 38 γνωστὸν οὖν
did not see corruption. Known therefore
ἔστω ὑμῖν, ἄνδρες ἀδελφοί, ὅτι διὰ
let it be to you, *men* brothers, that through

that this message of salvation has been sent. 27The
people of Jerusalem and
their rulers did not recognize Jesus, yet in condemning him they fulfilled the
words of the prophets that
are read every Sabbath.
28Though they found no
proper ground for a death
sentence, they asked Pilate
to have him executed.
29When they had carried
out all that was written
about him, they took him
down from the tree and laid
him in a tomb. 30But God
raised him from the dead,
31and for many days he was
seen by those who had
traveled with him from Galilee to Jerusalem. They are
now his witnesses to our
people.
32"We tell you the good
news: What God promised
our fathers 33he has fulfilled
for us, their children, by
raising up Jesus. As it is
written in the second
Psalm:

"'You are my Son;
today I have become
your Father.'[v] [w]

34The fact that God raised
him from the dead, never to
decay, is stated in these
words:

"'I will give you the
holy and sure
blessings promised
to David.'[x]

35So it is stated elsewhere:

"'You will not let your
Holy One see
decay.'[y]

36"For when David had
served God's purpose in
his own generation, he fell
asleep; he was buried with
his fathers and his body de-
cayed. 37But the one whom
God raised from the dead
did not see decay.
38"Therefore, my broth-
ers, I want you to know
that through Jesus the for-

v33 Or *have begotten you*
w33 Psalm 2:7
x34 Isaiah 55:3
y35 Psalm 16:10

ness of sins is proclaimed
to you,
39and through Him every-
one who believes is freed
from all things, from which
you could not be freed
through the Law of Moses.
40"Take heed therefore,
so that the thing spoken of
in the Prophets may not
come upon *you*:
41 'BEHOLD, YOU SCOFF-
ERS, AND MARVEL,
AND PERISH;
FOR I AM ACCOMPLISH-
ING A WORK IN YOUR
DAYS,
A WORK WHICH YOU
WILL NEVER BELIEVE,
THOUGH SOMEONE
SHOULD DESCRIBE IT
TO YOU.' "
42And as Paul and Bar-
nabas were going out, the
people kept begging that
these things might be
spoken to them the next
Sabbath.
43Now when *the meeting
of* the synagogue had broken up, many of the Jews
and of the God-fearing
proselytes followed Paul
and Barnabas, who, speak-
ing to them, were urging
them to continue in the
grace of God.

Paul Turns to the Gentiles

44And the next Sabbath
nearly the whole city as-
sembled to hear the word of
God.
45But when the Jews saw
the crowds, they were
filled with jealousy, and *began* contradicting the
things spoken by Paul, and
were blaspheming.
46And Paul and Barnabas
spoke out boldly and said,
"It was necessary that the
word of God should be
spoken to you first; since
you repudiate it, and judge
yourselves unworthy of
eternal life, behold, we are
turning to the Gentiles.
47"For thus the Lord has
commanded us,
'I HAVE PLACED YOU AS
A LIGHT FOR THE GEN-
TILES,
THAT YOU SHOULD
BRING SALVATION TO
THE END OF THE
EARTH.' "
48And when the Gentiles
heard this, they *began* rejoicing and glorifying the
word of the Lord; and as

τούτου ὑμῖν ἄφεσις ἁμαρτιῶν καταγγέλ-
this man to you forgiveness of sins is an-
λεται, καὶ ἀπὸ πάντων ὧν οὐκ ἠδυνήθητε
nounced, and from all things from which ye could not
ἐν νόμῳ Μωϋσέως δικαιωθῆναι, **39** ἐν
by [the] law of Moses *to* be justified, by
τούτῳ πᾶς ὁ πιστεύων δικαιοῦται. **40** βλέπετε
this man everyone believing is justified. Look ye
οὖν μὴ ἐπέλθῃ τὸ εἰρημένον
therefore lest come on [you] the thing having been said
ἐν τοῖς προφήταις· **41** ἴδετε, οἱ κατα-
in the prophets: See, the des-
φρονηταί, καὶ θαυμάσατε καὶ ἀφανίσθητε,
pisers, and marvel ye and perish,
ὅτι ἔργον ἐργάζομαι ἐγὼ ἐν ταῖς ἡμέραις
because a work work I in the days
ὑμῶν, ἔργον ὃ οὐ μὴ πιστεύσητε ἐάν
of you, a work which by no means ye believe if
τις ἐκδιηγῆται ὑμῖν. **42** Ἐξιόντων δὲ
anyone declares to you. And going out
=as they went out
αὐτῶν παρεκάλουν εἰς τὸ μεταξὺ σάββατον
them[a] they besought in the intervening sabbath(week)
λαληθῆναι αὐτοῖς τὰ ῥήματα ταῦτα.
to be spoken to them these words.
43 λυθείσης δὲ τῆς συναγωγῆς ἠκολούθησαν
And being broken up the assembly[a] [8]followed
=when the assembly was broken up
πολλοὶ τῶν Ἰουδαίων καὶ τῶν σεβομένων
[1]many [2]of the [3]Jews [4]and [5]of the [6]worshipping
προσηλύτων τῷ Παύλῳ καὶ τῷ Βαρναβᾷ,
[7]proselytes – [9]Paul and – Barnabas,
οἵτινες προσλαλοῦντες αὐτοῖς ἔπειθον αὐτοὺς
who speaking to them persuaded them
προσμένειν τῇ χάριτι τοῦ θεοῦ. **44** Τῷ δὲ
to continue in the grace – of God. And on the
ἐρχομένῳ σαββάτῳ σχεδὸν πᾶσα ἡ
coming sabbath almost all the
πόλις συνήχθη ἀκοῦσαι τὸν λόγον τοῦ
city was assembled to hear the word –
θεοῦ. **45** ἰδόντες δὲ οἱ Ἰουδαῖοι τοὺς
of God. But [3]seeing [1]the [2]Jews the
ὄχλους ἐπλήσθησαν ζήλου, καὶ ἀντέλεγον
crowds were filled of(with) jealousy, and contradicted
τοῖς ὑπὸ Παύλου λαλουμένοις βλασφημοῦντες.
the things by Paul being spoken blaspheming.
46 παρρησιασάμενοί τε ὁ Παῦλος καὶ ὁ
And speaking boldly – Paul and –
Βαρναβᾶς εἶπαν· ὑμῖν ἦν ἀναγκαῖον πρῶτον
Barnabas said: To you it was necessary firstly
λαληθῆναι τὸν λόγον τοῦ θεοῦ· ἐπειδὴ
to be spoken the word – of God; since
ἀπωθεῖσθε αὐτὸν καὶ οὐκ ἀξίους κρίνετε
ye put away it and not worthy judge
ἑαυτοὺς τῆς αἰωνίου ζωῆς, ἰδοὺ στρεφόμεθα
yourselves of the eternal life, behold we turn
εἰς τὰ ἔθνη. **47** οὕτως γὰρ ἐντέταλται
to the nations. For thus has commanded
ἡμῖν ὁ κύριος· τέθεικά σε εἰς φῶς
us the Lord: I have set thee for a light
ἐθνῶν τοῦ εἶναί σε εἰς σωτηρίαν ἕως
of nations – to be thee[b] for salvation to
ἐσχάτου τῆς γῆς. **48** ἀκούοντα δὲ τὰ ἔθνη
[the] end of the earth. And [3]hearing [1]the [2]nations
ἔχαιρον καὶ ἐδόξαζον τὸν λόγον τοῦ κυρίου, καὶ
rejoiced and glorified the word of the Lord, and

giveness of sins is pro-
claimed to you. 39Through
him everyone who believes
is justified from everything
you could not be justified
from by the law of Moses.
40Take care that what the
prophets have said does
not happen to you:

41" 'Look, you scoffers,
wonder and perish,
for I am going to do
something in your
days
that you would never
believe,
even if someone told
you.'[z]"

42As Paul and Barnabas
were leaving the syna-
gogue, the people invited
them to speak further about
these things on the next
Sabbath. 43When the con-
gregation was dismissed,
many of the Jews and de-
vout converts to Judaism
followed Paul and Barna-
bas, who talked with them
and urged them to continue
in the grace of God.
44On the next Sabbath al-
most the whole city gath-
ered to hear the word of the
Lord. 45When the Jews saw
the crowds, they were
filled with jealousy and
talked abusively against
what Paul was saying.
46Then Paul and Barna-
bas answered them boldly:
"We had to speak the word
of God to you first. Since
you reject it and do not consider yourselves worthy of
eternal life, we now turn to
the Gentiles. 47For this is
what the Lord has com-
manded us:

" 'I have made you[a] a
light for the
Gentiles,
that you[a] may bring
salvation to the ends
of the earth.'[b]"

48When the Gentiles
heard this, they were glad
and honored the word of

[z]*41* Hab. 1:5
[a]*47* The Greek is singular.
[b]*47* Isaiah 49:6

many as had been appointed to eternal life believed.

49And the word of the Lord was being spread through the whole region.

50But the Jews aroused the devout women of prominence and the leading men of the city, and instigated a persecution against Paul and Barnabas, and drove them out of their district.

51But they shook off the dust of their feet *in protest* against them and went to Iconium.

52And the disciples were continually filled with joy and with the Holy Spirit.

ἐπίστευσαν ὅσοι ἦσαν τεταγμένοι εἰς
[7]believed [1]as many as [2]were [3]*having been* disposed [4]to
ζωὴν αἰώνιον· **49** διεφέρετο δὲ ὁ λόγος τοῦ
[6]life [5]eternal; and was carried *through* the word of the
κυρίου δι' ὅλης τῆς χώρας. **50** οἱ δὲ
Lord through all the country. But the
Ἰουδαῖοι παρώτρυναν τὰς σεβομένας γυναῖκας
Jews urged on the [2]worshipping [3]women
τὰς εὐσχήμονας καὶ τοὺς πρώτους τῆς
– [1]honourable and the chief men of the
πόλεως, καὶ ἐπήγειραν διωγμὸν ἐπὶ τὸν
city, and raised up persecution against –
Παῦλον καὶ Βαρναβᾶν, καὶ ἐξέβαλον αὐτοὺς
Paul and Barnabas, and expelled them
ἀπὸ τῶν ὁρίων αὐτῶν. **51** οἱ δὲ ἐκτιναξάμενοι
from the borders of them. But they shaking off
τὸν κονιορτὸν τῶν ποδῶν ἐπ' αὐτοὺς ἦλθον
the dust of the(ir) feet on them came
εἰς Ἰκόνιον, **52** οἵ τε μαθηταὶ ἐπλη-
to Iconium, and the disciples were
ροῦντο χαρᾶς καὶ πνεύματος ἁγίου.
filled of(with) joy and of(with) Spirit Holy.

the Lord; and all who were
appointed for eternal life
believed.
49The word of the Lord
spread through the whole
region. 50But the Jews in-
cited the God-fearing wom-
en of high standing and the
leading men of the city.
They stirred up persecution
against Paul and Barnabas,
and expelled them from
their region. 51So they
shook the dust from their
feet in protest against them
and went to Iconium.
52And the disciples were
filled with joy and with the
Holy Spirit.

Chapter 14

Acceptance and Opposition

AND it came about that in Iconium they entered the synagogue of the Jews together, and spoke in such a manner that a great multitude believed, both of Jews and of Greeks.

2But the Jews who disbelieved stirred up the minds of the Gentiles, and embittered them against the brethren.

3Therefore they spent a long time *there* speaking boldly *with reliance* upon the Lord, who was bearing witness to the word of His grace, granting that signs and wonders be done by their hands.

4But the multitude of the city was divided; and some sided with the Jews, and some with the apostles.

5And when an attempt was made by both the Gentiles and the Jews with their rulers, to mistreat and to stone them,

6they became aware of it and fled to the cities of Lycaonia, Lystra and Derbe, and the surrounding region;

7and there they continued to preach the gospel.

8And at Lystra there was sitting a certain man, with-

14 Ἐγένετο δὲ ἐν Ἰκονίῳ κατὰ τὸ αὐτὸ
Now it happened in Iconium [2]together†
εἰσελθεῖν αὐτοὺς εἰς τὴν συναγωγὴν
[1]to enter them[b] into the synagogue
=they entered
τῶν Ἰουδαίων καὶ λαλῆσαι οὕτως ὥστε
of the Jews and to speak[b] so as
πιστεῦσαι Ἰουδαίων τε καὶ Ἑλλήνων
to believe both of Jews and of Greeks
πολὺ πλῆθος. **2** οἱ δὲ ἀπειθήσαντες
a much(great) multitude. But the disobeying
Ἰουδαῖοι ἐπήγειραν καὶ ἐκάκωσαν τὰς
Jews excited and embittered the
ψυχὰς τῶν ἐθνῶν κατὰ τῶν ἀδελφῶν.
minds of the nations against the brothers.
3 ἱκανὸν μὲν οὖν χρόνον διέτριψαν
A considerable – [2]therefore [1]time they continued
παρρησιαζόμενοι ἐπὶ τῷ κυρίῳ τῷ μαρ-
speaking boldly on the Lord – wit-
τυροῦντι ἐπὶ τῷ λόγῳ τῆς χάριτος αὐτοῦ,
nessing to the word of the grace of him,
διδόντι σημεῖα καὶ τέρατα γίνεσθαι διὰ
giving signs and wonders to happen through
τῶν χειρῶν αὐτῶν. **4** ἐσχίσθη δὲ τὸ
the hands of them. But was divided the
πλῆθος τῆς πόλεως, καὶ οἱ μὲν ἦσαν
multitude of the city, and some were
σὺν τοῖς Ἰουδαίοις, οἱ δὲ σὺν τοῖς
with the Jews, but others with the
ἀποστόλοις. **5** ὡς δὲ ἐγένετο ὁρμὴ τῶν
apostles. And when there was a rush [2]of the
ἐθνῶν τε καὶ Ἰουδαίων σὺν τοῖς ἄρχουσιν
[3]nations [1]both [4]and of Jews with the rulers
αὐτῶν ὑβρίσαι καὶ λιθοβολῆσαι αὐτούς,
of them to insult and to stone them,
6 συνιδόντες κατέφυγον εἰς τὰς πόλεις
perceiving they escaped to the cities
τῆς Λυκαονίας Λύστραν καὶ Δέρβην καὶ
– of Lycaonia Lystra and Derbe and
τὴν περίχωρον· **7** κἀκεῖ εὐαγγελιζόμενοι
the neighbourhood; and there evangelizing
ἦσαν. **8** Καί τις ἀνὴρ ἀδύνατος ἐν
they were. And a certain man impotent in

Chapter 14

In Iconium

AT Iconium Paul and
Barnabas went as
usual into the Jewish synagogue. There they spoke so
effectively that a great
number of Jews and Gen-
tiles believed. 2But the
Jews who refused to be-
lieve stirred up the Gentiles
and poisoned their minds
against the brothers. 3So
Paul and Barnabas spent
considerable time there,
speaking boldly for the
Lord, who confirmed the
message of his grace by en-
abling them to do miracu-
lous signs and wonders.
4The people of the city
were divided; some sided
with the Jews, others with
the apostles. 5There was a
plot afoot among the Gen-
tiles and Jews, together
with their leaders, to mistreat them and stone them.
6But they found out about it
and fled to the Lycaonian
cities of Lystra and Derbe
and to the surrounding
country, 7where they con-
tinued to preach the good
news.

In Lystra and Derbe

8In Lystra there sat a man
crippled in his feet, who

out strength in his feet, lame from his mother's womb, who had never walked.

9 This man was listening to Paul as he spoke, who, when he had fixed his gaze upon him, and had seen that he had faith to be made well,

10 said with a loud voice, "Stand upright on your feet." And he leaped up and *began* to walk.

11 And when the multitudes saw what Paul had done, they raised their voice, saying in the Lycaonian language, "The gods have become like men and have come down to us."

12 And they *began* calling Barnabas, Zeus, and Paul, Hermes, because he was the chief speaker.

13 And the priest of Zeus, whose *temple* was just outside the city, brought oxen and garlands to the gates, and wanted to offer sacrifice with the crowds.

14 But when the apostles, Barnabas and Paul, heard of it, they tore their robes and rushed out into the crowd, crying out

15 and saying, "Men, why are you doing these things? We are also men of the same nature as you, and preach the gospel to you in order that you should turn from these [d]vain things to a living God, WHO MADE THE HEAVEN AND THE EARTH AND THE SEA, AND ALL THAT IS IN THEM.

16 "And in the generations gone by He permitted all the nations to go their own ways;

17 and yet He did not leave Himself without witness, in that He did good and gave you rains from heaven and fruitful seasons, satisfying your hearts with food and gladness."

[d]I.e., idols

Λύστροις τοῖς ποσὶν ἐκάθητο, χωλὸς ἐκ
Lystra in the feet sat, lame from

κοιλίας μητρὸς αὐτοῦ ὃς οὐδέποτε
[the] womb of [the] mother of him who never

περιεπάτησεν. 9 οὗτος ἤκουεν τοῦ Παύλου
walked. This man heard – Paul

λαλοῦντος· ὃς ἀτενίσας αὐτῷ καὶ ἰδὼν
speaking; who gazing at him and seeing

ὅτι ἔχει πίστιν τοῦ σωθῆναι, 10 εἶπεν
that he has(had) faith – to be healed,[d] said

μεγάλῃ φωνῇ· Ἀνάστηθι ἐπὶ τοὺς πόδας
with a great(loud) voice: Stand up on the feet

σου ὀρθός. καὶ ἥλατο καὶ περιεπάτει.
of thee erect. And he leaped up and walked.

11 οἵ τε ὄχλοι ἰδόντες ὃ ἐποίησεν Παῦλος
And the crowds seeing what did Paul

ἐπῆραν τὴν φωνὴν αὐτῶν Λυκαονιστὶ
lifted up the voice of them in Lycaonian

λέγοντες· οἱ θεοὶ ὁμοιωθέντες ἀνθρώποις
saying: The gods made like men

κατέβησαν πρὸς ἡμᾶς, 12 ἐκάλουν τε τὸν
came down to us, and they called –

Βαρναβᾶν Δία, τὸν δὲ Παῦλον Ἑρμῆν,
Barnabas Zeus, – and Paul Hermes,

ἐπειδὴ αὐτὸς ἦν ὁ ἡγούμενος τοῦ λόγου.
since he was the leader of the discourse.

13 ὅ τε ἱερεὺς τοῦ Διὸς τοῦ ὄντος πρὸ
And the priest – of Zeus – being before

τῆς πόλεως, ταύρους καὶ στέμματα ἐπὶ
the city, bulls and garlands to

τοὺς πυλῶνας ἐνέγκας, σὺν τοῖς ὄχλοις
the gates bringing, with the crowds

ἤθελεν θύειν. 14 ἀκούσαντες δὲ οἱ
wished to sacrifice. But [6]hearing [1]the

ἀπόστολοι Βαρναβᾶς καὶ Παῦλος, διαρ-
[2]apostles [3]Barnabas [4]and [5]Paul, rend-

ρήξαντες τὰ ἱμάτια ἑαυτῶν ἐξεπήδησαν εἰς
ing the garments of them*selves* rushed out into

τὸν ὄχλον, κράζοντες 15 καὶ λέγοντες·
the crowd, crying out and saying:

ἄνδρες, τί ταῦτα ποιεῖτε; καὶ ἡμεῖς
Men, why these things do ye? [2]also [1]we

ὁμοιοπαθεῖς ἐσμεν ὑμῖν ἄνθρωποι, εὐαγ-
[5]of like nature [3]are [6]to you [4]men, preach-

γελιζόμενοι ὑμᾶς ἀπὸ τούτων τῶν ματαίων
ing [to] you from these – vanities

ἐπιστρέφειν ἐπὶ θεὸν ζῶντα, ὃς ἐποίησεν
to turn to God a living, who made

τὸν οὐρανὸν καὶ τὴν γῆν καὶ τὴν
the heaven and the earth and the

θάλασσαν καὶ πάντα τὰ ἐν αὐτοῖς· 16 ὃς
sea and all the things in them; who

ἐν ταῖς παρῳχημέναις γενεαῖς εἴασεν πάντα
in the having passed generations allowed all

τὰ ἔθνη πορεύεσθαι ταῖς ὁδοῖς αὐτῶν·
the nations to go in the ways of them;

17 καίτοι οὐκ ἀμάρτυρον αὐτὸν ἀφῆκεν
and yet [2]not [4]unwitnessed [3]himself [1]left

ἀγαθουργῶν, οὐρανόθεν ὑμῖν ὑετοὺς διδοὺς
doing good, [4]from heaven [2]us [3]rain [1]giving

καὶ καιροὺς καρποφόρους, ἐμπιπλῶν τροφῆς
and times fruit-bearing, filling of(with) food

καὶ εὐφροσύνης τὰς καρδίας ὑμῶν. 18 καὶ
and of(with) gladness the hearts of us. And

was lame from birth and
had never walked. 9 He listened to Paul as he was
speaking. Paul looked di-
rectly at him, saw that he
had faith to be healed 10 and
called out, "Stand up on
your feet!" At that, the
man jumped up and began
to walk.

11 When the crowd saw
what Paul had done, they
shouted in the Lycaonian
language, "The gods have
come down to us in human
form!" 12 Barnabas they
called Zeus, and Paul they
called Hermes because he
was the chief speaker.
13 The priest of Zeus, whose
temple was just outside the
city, brought bulls and
wreaths to the city gates
because he and the crowd
wanted to offer sacrifices
to them.

14 But when the apostles
Barnabas and Paul heard of
this, they tore their clothes
and rushed out into the
crowd, shouting: 15 "Men,
why are you doing this? We
too are only men, human
like you. We are bringing
you good news, telling you
to turn from these worth-
less things to the living
God, who made heaven
and earth and sea and ev-
erything in them. 16 In the
past, he let all nations go
their own way. 17 Yet he has
not left himself without testimony: He has shown
kindness by giving you rain
from heaven and crops in
their seasons; he provides
you with plenty of food and
fills your hearts with joy."

18And *even* saying these
things, they with difficulty
restrained the crowds from
offering sacrifice to them.
19But Jews came from
Antioch and Iconium, and
having won over the multitudes, they stoned Paul and
dragged him out of the city,
supposing him to be dead.
20But while the disciples
stood around him, he arose
and entered the city. And
the next day he went away
with Barnabas to Derbe.
21And after they had
preached the gospel to that
city and had made many
disciples, they returned to
Lystra and to Iconium and
to Antioch,
22strengthening the souls
of the disciples, encouraging them to continue in the
faith, and *saying*,
"Through many tribula-
tions we must enter the
kingdom of God."
23And when they had ap-
pointed elders for them in
every church, having
prayed with fasting, they
commended them to the
Lord in whom they had be-
lieved.
24And they passed
through Pisidia and came
into Pamphylia.
25And when they had
spoken the word in Perga,
they went down to Attalia;
26and from there they
sailed to Antioch, from
which they had been com-
mended to the grace of God
for the work that they had
accomplished.
27And when they had ar-
rived and gathered the
church together, they *be-*
gan to report all things that
God had done with them
and how He had opened a
door of faith to the Gen-
tiles.
28And they spent a long
time with the disciples.

ταῦτα λέγοντες μόλις κατέπαυσαν τοὺς
these things saying scarcely they restrained the
ὄχλους τοῦ μὴ θύειν αὐτοῖς. **19** Ἐπῆλθαν
crowds – not to sacrifice[d] to them. [6]came upon [the scene]
δὲ ἀπὸ Ἀντιοχείας καὶ Ἰκονίου Ἰουδαῖοι,
And [2]from [3]Antioch [4]and [5]Iconium [1]Jews,
καὶ πείσαντες τοὺς ὄχλους καὶ λιθάσαντες
and persuading the crowds and stoning
τὸν Παῦλον ἔσυρον ἔξω τῆς πόλεως,
– Paul dragged outside the city,
νομίζοντες αὐτὸν τεθνηκέναι. **20** κυκλω-
supposing him to have died. But sur-
σάντων δὲ τῶν μαθητῶν αὐτὸν ἀναστὰς
rounding the disciples[a] him rising up
=as the disciples surrounded
εἰσῆλθεν εἰς τὴν πόλιν. Καὶ τῇ ἐπαύριον
he entered into the city. And on the morrow
ἐξῆλθεν σὺν τῷ Βαρναβᾷ εἰς Δέρβην.
he went forth with – Barnabas to Derbe.
21 εὐαγγελιζόμενοί τε τὴν πόλιν ἐκείνην
And evangelizing that city
καὶ μαθητεύσαντες ἱκανοὺς ὑπέστρεψαν εἰς
and having made disciples many they returned to
τὴν Λύστραν καὶ εἰς Ἰκόνιον καὶ [εἰς]
– Lystra and to Iconium and to
Ἀντιόχειαν, **22** ἐπιστηρίζοντες τὰς ψυχὰς
Antioch, confirming the minds
τῶν μαθητῶν, παρακαλοῦντες ἐμμένειν τῇ
of the disciples, exhorting to continue in the
πίστει, καὶ ὅτι διὰ πολλῶν θλίψεων
faith, and that through many afflictions
δεῖ ἡμᾶς εἰσελθεῖν εἰς τὴν βασιλείαν τοῦ
it behoves us to enter into the kingdom –
θεοῦ. **23** χειροτονήσαντες δὲ αὐτοῖς κατ᾽
of God. And having appointed for them in
ἐκκλησίαν πρεσβυτέρους, προσευξάμενοι
every church elders, praying
μετὰ νηστειῶν παρέθεντο αὐτοὺς τῷ κυρίῳ
with fastings they committed them to the Lord
εἰς ὃν πεπιστεύκεισαν. **24** καὶ διελθόντες
in whom they had believed. And passing through
τὴν Πισιδίαν ἦλθον εἰς τὴν Παμφυλίαν,
– Pisidia they came to – Pamphylia,
25 καὶ λαλήσαντες εἰς τὴν Πέργην τὸν
and speaking in – Perga the
λόγον κατέβησαν εἰς Ἀττάλειαν, κἀκεῖθεν
word they came down to Attalia, and thence
ἀπέπλευσαν εἰς Ἀντιόχειαν, **26** ὅθεν ἦσαν
sailed away to Antioch, whence they were
παραδεδομένοι τῇ χάριτι τοῦ θεοῦ εἰς
having been commended to the grace – of God for
τὸ ἔργον ὃ ἐπλήρωσαν. **27** Παραγεν-
the work which they accomplished. And having
όμενοι δὲ καὶ συναγαγόντες τὴν ἐκκλησίαν,
arrived and assembling the church,
ἀνήγγελλον ὅσα ἐποίησεν ὁ θεὸς μετ᾽
they reported what things did – God with
αὐτῶν, καὶ ὅτι ἤνοιξεν τοῖς ἔθνεσιν
them, and that he opened to the nations
θύραν πίστεως. **28** διέτριβον δὲ χρόνον
a door of faith. And they continued time
οὐκ ὀλίγον σὺν τοῖς μαθηταῖς.
not a little with the disciples.

18Even with these words,
they had difficulty keeping
the crowd from sacrificing
to them.
19Then some Jews came
from Antioch and Iconium
and won the crowd over.
They stoned Paul and
dragged him outside the
city, thinking he was dead.
20But after the disciples had
gathered around him, he
got up and went back into
the city. The next day he
and Barnabas left for Derbe.

The Return to Antioch in Syria

21They preached the good
news in that city and won a
large number of disciples.
Then they returned to Lystra, Iconium and Antioch,
22strengthening the disciples and encouraging them
to remain true to the faith.
"We must go through
many hardships to enter
the kingdom of God," they
said. 23Paul and Barnabas
appointed elders[c] for them
in each church and, with
prayer and fasting, committed them to the Lord, in
whom they had put their
trust. 24After going through
Pisidia, they came into
Pamphylia, 25and when
they had preached the
word in Perga, they went
down to Attalia.
26From Attalia they sailed
back to Antioch, where
they had been committed
to the grace of God for the
work they had now com-
pleted. 27On arriving there,
they gathered the church
together and reported all
that God had done through
them and how he had
opened the door of faith to
the Gentiles. 28And they
stayed there a long time
with the disciples.

[c]23 Or *Barnabas ordained elders*; or *Barnabas had elders elected*

Chapter 15

The Council at Jerusalem

AND some men came
down from Judea and
began teaching the brethren, "Unless you are cir-
cumcised according to the
custom of Moses, you can-
not be saved."
2And when Paul and
Barnabas had great dissension and debate with them,
the brethren determined
that Paul and Barnabas and
certain others of them
should go up to Jerusalem
to the apostles and elders
concerning this issue.
3Therefore, being sent
on their way by the church,
they were passing through
both Phoenicia and Sa-
maria, describing in detail
the conversion of the Gentiles, and were bringing
great joy to all the brethren.
4And when they arrived
at Jerusalem, they were received by the church and
the apostles and the elders,
and they reported all that
God had done with them.
5But certain ones of the
sect of the Pharisees who
had believed, stood up,
saying, "It is necessary to
circumcise them, and to direct them to observe the
Law of Moses."
6And the apostles and
the elders came together to
look into this matter.
7And after there had
been much debate, Peter
stood up and said to them,
"Brethren, you know that
in the early days God made
a choice among you, that
by my mouth the Gentiles
should hear the word of the
gospel and believe.
8"And God, who knows
the heart, bore witness to

15 *Καί τινες κατελθόντες ἀπὸ τῆς*
And some going down from –
Ἰουδαίας ἐδίδασκον τοὺς ἀδελφοὺς ὅτι
Judæa taught the brothers[,] –
ἐὰν μὴ περιτμηθῆτε τῷ ἔθει τῷ Μωϋσέως,
Unless ye are circumcised by the custom – of Moses,
οὐ δύνασθε σωθῆναι. **2** *γενομένης δὲ*
ye cannot *to* be saved. And taking place
στάσεως καὶ ζητήσεως οὐκ ὀλίγης τῷ
discord and questioning not a little[a] –
=when there took place not a little . . .
Παύλῳ καὶ τῷ Βαρναβᾷ πρὸς αὐτούς,
by Paul and – Barnabas with them,
ἔταξαν ἀναβαίνειν Παῦλον καὶ Βαρναβᾶν
they assigned to go up Paul and Barnabas
καί τινας ἄλλους ἐξ αὐτῶν πρὸς τοὺς
and some others of them to the
ἀποστόλους καὶ πρεσβυτέρους εἰς Ἰερουσαλὴμ
apostles and elders in Jerusalem
περὶ τοῦ ζητήματος τούτου. **3** *Οἱ μὲν*
about this question. They –
οὖν προπεμφθέντες ὑπὸ τῆς ἐκκλησίας
therefore being set forward by the church
διήρχοντο τήν τε Φοινίκην καὶ Σαμάρειαν
passed through – both Phœnicia and Samaria
ἐκδιηγούμενοι τὴν ἐπιστροφὴν τῶν ἐθνῶν,
telling in detail the conversion of the nations,
καὶ ἐποίουν χαρὰν μεγάλην πᾶσιν τοῖς
and caused joy great to all the
ἀδελφοῖς. **4** *παραγενόμενοι δὲ εἰς Ἰεροσόλυμα*
brothers. And having arrived in Jerusalem
παρεδέχθησαν ἀπὸ τῆς ἐκκλησίας καὶ τῶν
they were welcomed from the church and the
ἀποστόλων καὶ τῶν πρεσβυτέρων, ἀνήγ-
apostles and the elders, and
γειλάν τε ὅσα ὁ θεὸς ἐποίησεν μετ'
reported what things – God did with
αὐτῶν. **5** *Ἐξανέστησαν δέ τινες τῶν*
them. But stood forth some of the [ones]
ἀπὸ τῆς αἱρέσεως τῶν Φαρισαίων
from the sect of the Pharisees
πεπιστευκότες, λέγοντες ὅτι δεῖ περιτέμνειν
having believed, saying[,] – It behoves to circumcise
αὐτοὺς παραγγέλλειν τε τηρεῖν τὸν νόμον
them and to charge to keep the law
Μωϋσέως.
of Moses.
6 *Συνήχθησάν τε οἱ ἀπόστολοι καὶ οἱ*
And were assembled the apostles and the
πρεσβύτεροι ἰδεῖν περὶ τοῦ λόγου τούτου.
elders to see about this matter.
7 *Πολλῆς δὲ ζητήσεως γενομένης ἀναστὰς*
And much questioning having taken place[a] rising up
=When much questioning had . . .
Πέτρος εἶπεν πρὸς αὐτούς· ἄνδρες ἀδελφοί,
Peter said to them: *Men* brothers,
ὑμεῖς ἐπίστασθε ὅτι ἀφ' ἡμερῶν ἀρχαίων
ye understand that from days olden
ἐν ὑμῖν ἐξελέξατο ὁ θεὸς διὰ τοῦ στόματός
[3]among [4]you [2]chose – [1]God through the mouth
μου ἀκοῦσαι τὰ ἔθνη τὸν λόγον τοῦ
of me [3]to hear [1]the [2]nations the word of the
εὐαγγελίου καὶ πιστεῦσαι. **8** *καὶ ὁ*
gospel and to believe. And [2]the
καρδιογνώστης θεὸς ἐμαρτύρησεν αὐτοῖς
[3]Heart-knower [1]God witnessed to them

Chapter 15

The Council at Jerusalem

SOME men came down
from Judea to Antioch
and were teaching the
brothers: "Unless you are
circumcised, according to
the custom taught by Mo-
ses, you cannot be saved."
2This brought Paul and
Barnabas into sharp dis-
pute and debate with them.
So Paul and Barnabas were
appointed, along with some
other believers, to go up to
Jerusalem to see the apostles and elders about this
question. 3The church sent
them on their way, and as
they traveled through
Phoenicia and Samaria,
they told how the Gentiles
had been converted. This
news made all the brothers
very glad. 4When they
came to Jerusalem, they
were welcomed by the
church and the apostles
and elders, to whom they
reported everything God
had done through them.
5Then some of the believ-
ers who belonged to the
party of the Pharisees
stood up and said, "The
Gentiles must be circum-
cised and required to obey
the law of Moses."
6The apostles and elders
met to consider this question. 7After much discus-
sion, Peter got up and addressed them: "Brothers,
you know that some time
ago God made a choice
among you that the Gen-
tiles might hear from my
lips the message of the gospel and believe. 8God, who
knows the heart, showed

them, giving them the Holy
Spirit, just as He also did to
us;
9and He made no distinc-
tion between us and them,
cleansing their hearts by
faith.
10"Now therefore why do
you put God to the test by
placing upon the neck of
the disciples a yoke which
neither our fathers nor we
have been able to bear?
11"But we believe that we
are saved through the grace
of the Lord Jesus, in the
same way as they also
are."
12And all the multitude
kept silent, and they were
listening to Barnabas and
Paul as they were relating
what signs and wonders
God had done through
them among the Gentiles.

James' Judgment

13And after they had
stopped speaking, James
answered, saying, "Breth-
ren, listen to me.
14"Simeon has related
how God first concerned
Himself about taking from
among the Gentiles a
people for His name.
15"And with this the
words of the Prophets
agree, just as it is written,
16 'AFTER THESE THINGS I
WILL RETURN,
AND I WILL REBUILD
THE TABERNACLE OF
DAVID WHICH HAS
FALLEN,
AND I WILL REBUILD ITS
RUINS,
AND I WILL RESTORE IT,
17 IN ORDER THAT THE
REST OF MANKIND MAY
SEEK THE LORD,
AND ALL THE GENTILES
WHO ARE CALLED BY
MY NAME,'
18 SAYS THE LORD, WHO
MAKES THESE THINGS
KNOWN FROM OF OLD.
19"Therefore it is my
judgment that we do not
trouble those who are turn-
ing to God from among the
Gentiles,
20but that we write to

δοὺς τὸ πνεῦμα τὸ ἅγιον καθὼς καὶ
giving the Spirit – Holy as also
ἡμῖν, 9 καὶ οὐθὲν διέκρινεν μεταξὺ ἡμῶν
to us, and nothing distinguished between [2]us
τε καὶ αὐτῶν, τῇ πίστει καθαρίσας τὰς
[1]both and them, – by faith cleansing the
καρδίας αὐτῶν. 10 νῦν οὖν τί πειράζετε
hearts of them. Now therefore why test ye
τὸν θεόν, ἐπιθεῖναι ζυγὸν ἐπὶ τὸν
– God, to put *on* a yoke on the
τράχηλον τῶν μαθητῶν, ὃν οὔτε οἱ
neck of the disciples, which neither the
πατέρες ἡμῶν οὔτε ἡμεῖς ἰσχύσαμεν
fathers of us nor we were able
βαστάσαι; 11 ἀλλὰ διὰ τῆς χάριτος τοῦ
to bear? but through the grace of the
κυρίου Ἰησοῦ πιστεύομεν σωθῆναι καθ'
Lord Jesus we believe to be saved in
ὃν τρόπον κἀκεῖνοι. 12 Ἐσίγησεν δὲ
the same way as† those also. And was silent
πᾶν τὸ πλῆθος, καὶ ἤκουον Βαρναβᾶ
all the multitude, and heard Barnabas
καὶ Παύλου ἐξηγουμένων ὅσα ἐποίησεν
and Paul relating [1]what [6]did
ὁ θεὸς σημεῖα καὶ τέρατα ἐν τοῖς
– [5]God [2]signs [3]and [4]wonders among the
ἔθνεσιν δι' αὐτῶν. 13 Μετὰ δὲ τὸ σιγῆσαι
nations through them. And after the to keep silence =they kept silence
αὐτοὺς ἀπεκρίθη Ἰάκωβος λέγων· 14 ἄνδρες
them[b] answered James saying: *Men*
ἀδελφοί, ἀκούσατέ μου. Συμεὼν ἐξηγήσατο
brothers, hear ye me. Simeon declared
καθὼς πρῶτον ὁ θεὸς ἐπεσκέψατο λαβεῖν ἐξ
even as firstly – God visited to take out of
ἐθνῶν λαὸν τῷ ὀνόματι αὐτοῦ. 15 καὶ
[the] nations a people for the name of him. And
τούτῳ συμφωνοῦσιν οἱ λόγοι τῶν προφητῶν,
to this agree the words of the prophets,
καθὼς γέγραπται· 16 μετὰ ταῦτα
even as it has been written: After these things
ἀναστρέψω καὶ ἀνοικοδομήσω τὴν σκηνὴν
I will return and I will rebuild the tent
Δαυὶδ τὴν πεπτωκυῖαν, καὶ τὰ κατεστραμ-
of David – having fallen, and the things having been
μένα αὐτῆς ἀνοικοδομήσω καὶ ἀνορθώσω
overturned =its ruins of it I will rebuild and I will rear again
αὐτήν, 17 ὅπως ἂν ἐκζητήσωσιν οἱ
it, so as – [4]may seek [1]the
κατάλοιποι τῶν ἀνθρώπων τὸν κύριον,
[2]rest – [3]of men [5]the [6]Lord,
καὶ πάντα τὰ ἔθνη ἐφ' οὓς ἐπικέκληται
even all the nations on whom has been invoked
τὸ ὄνομά μου ἐπ' αὐτούς, λέγει κύριος
the name of me *on them,* says [the] Lord
ποιῶν ταῦτα 18 γνωστὰ ἀπ' αἰῶνος.
doing these things known from [the] age.
19 διὸ ἐγὼ κρίνω μὴ παρενοχλεῖν τοῖς
Wherefore I decide not to trouble the [ones]
ἀπὸ τῶν ἐθνῶν ἐπιστρέφουσιν ἐπὶ τὸν
from the nations turning to –
θεόν, 20 ἀλλὰ ἐπιστεῖλαι αὐτοῖς τοῦ
God, but to write word to them –

that he accepted them by
giving the Holy Spirit to
them, just as he did to us.
9He made no distinction
between us and them, for
he purified their hearts by
faith. 10Now then, why do
you try to test God by putting on the necks of the disciples a yoke that neither
we nor our fathers have
been able to bear? 11No!
We believe it is through the
grace of our Lord Jesus
that we are saved, just as
they are."
12The whole assembly be-
came silent as they listened
to Barnabas and Paul telling about the miraculous
signs and wonders God had
done among the Gentiles
through them. 13When they
finished, James spoke up:
"Brothers, listen to me.
14Simon[d] has described to
us how God at first showed
his concern by taking from
the Gentiles a people for
himself. 15The words of the
prophets are in agreement
with this, as it is written:

16" 'After this I will return
and rebuild David's
fallen tent.
Its ruins I will rebuild,
and I will restore it,
17that the remnant of men
may seek the Lord,
and all the Gentiles
who bear my name,
says the Lord, who does
these things'[e]
18 that have been known
for ages.[f]

19"It is my judgment,
therefore, that we should
not make it difficult for the
Gentiles who are turning to
God. 20Instead we should
write to them, telling them

[d]*14* Greek *Simeon,* a variant of *Simon;* that is, Peter
[e]*17* Amos 9:11,12
[f]*17,18* Some manuscripts *things'— / [18]known to the Lord for ages is his work*

them that they abstain from things contaminated by idols and from fornication and from what is strangled and from blood.
21"For Moses from ancient generations has in every city those who preach him, since he is read in the synagogues every Sabbath."
22Then it seemed good to the apostles and the elders, with the whole church, to choose men from among them to send to Antioch with Paul and Barnabas—Judas called Barsabbas, and Silas, leading men among the brethren,
23and they sent this letter by them,
"The apostles and the brethren who are elders, to the brethren in Antioch and Syria and Cilicia who are from the Gentiles, greetings.
24"Since we have heard that some of our number to whom we gave no instruction have disturbed you with *their* words, unsettling your souls,
25 it seemed good to us, having become of one mind, to select men to send to you with our beloved Barnabas and Paul,
26 men who have risked their lives for the name of our Lord Jesus Christ.
27"Therefore we have sent Judas and Silas, who themselves will also report the same things by word *of mouth*.
28"For it seemed good to the Holy Spirit and to us to lay upon you no greater burden than these essentials:
29 that you abstain from things sacrificed to idols and from blood and from things strangled and from fornication; if you keep yourselves free from such

ἀπέχεσθαι τῶν ἀλισγημάτων τῶν εἰδώλων
to abstain from[d] the pollutions – of idols

καὶ τῆς πορνείας καὶ πνικτοῦ καὶ τοῦ
and – fornication and a thing strangled and –

αἵματος. **21** Μωϋσῆς γὰρ ἐκ γενεῶν
blood. For [1]Moses [2]from [4]generations

ἀρχαίων κατὰ πόλιν τοὺς κηρύσσοντας
[3]ancient [6]in every city [7]the [ones] [8]proclaiming

αὐτὸν ἔχει ἐν ταῖς συναγωγαῖς κατὰ
[9]him [5]has [11]in [12]the [13]synagogues [14]on

πᾶν σάββατον ἀναγινωσκόμενος. **22** Τότε
[15]every [16]sabbath [10]being read. Then

ἔδοξε τοῖς ἀποστόλοις καὶ τοῖς πρεσ-
it seemed [good] to the apostles and to the el-

βυτέροις σὺν ὅλῃ τῇ ἐκκλησίᾳ ἐκλεξαμένους
ders with all the church chosen

ἄνδρας ἐξ αὐτῶν πέμψαι εἰς Ἀντιόχειαν
men of them to send to Antioch

σὺν τῷ Παύλῳ καὶ Βαρναβᾷ, Ἰούδαν
with – Paul and Barnabas, Judas

τὸν καλούμενον Βαρσαββᾶν καὶ Σιλᾶν,
– *being* called Barsabbas and Silas,

ἄνδρας ἡγουμένους ἐν τοῖς ἀδελφοῖς,
men leading among the brothers,

23 γράψαντες διὰ χειρὸς αὐτῶν· Οἱ
writing through [the] hand of them: The

ἀπόστολοι καὶ οἱ πρεσβύτεροι ἀδελφοὶ
apostles and the elder brothers

τοῖς κατὰ τὴν Ἀντιόχειαν καὶ Συρίαν
[1]to the [5]throughout – [6]Antioch [7]and [8]Syria

καὶ Κιλικίαν ἀδελφοῖς τοῖς ἐξ ἐθνῶν
[9]and [10]Cilicia [2]brothers – [3]of [the] [4]nations

χαίρειν. **24** Ἐπειδὴ ἠκούσαμεν ὅτι τινὲς
[11]greeting. Since we heard that some

ἐξ ἡμῶν ἐτάραξαν ὑμᾶς λόγοις ἀνασκευάζ-
of us troubled you with words unsettl-

οντες τὰς ψυχὰς ὑμῶν, οἷς οὐ διεστειλάμεθα,
ing the minds of you, to whom we did not give commission,

25 ἔδοξεν ἡμῖν γενομένοις ὁμοθυμαδόν,
it seemed [good] to us becoming of one mind,

ἐκλεξαμένους ἄνδρας πέμψαι πρὸς ὑμᾶς
chosen men to send to you

σὺν τοῖς ἀγαπητοῖς ἡμῶν Βαρναβᾷ καὶ
with the beloved of us Barnabas and

Παύλῳ, **26** ἀνθρώποις παραδεδωκόσι τὰς
Paul, men having given up the

ψυχὰς αὐτῶν ὑπὲρ τοῦ ὀνόματος τοῦ
lives of them on behalf of the name of the

κυρίου ἡμῶν Ἰησοῦ Χριστοῦ. **27** ἀπεστάλ-
Lord of us Jesus Christ. We have

καμεν οὖν Ἰούδαν καὶ Σιλᾶν, καὶ αὐτοὺς
sent therefore Judas and Silas, and they

διὰ λόγου ἀπαγγέλλοντας τὰ αὐτά.
through (by) speech announcing the same things.

28 ἔδοξεν γὰρ τῷ πνεύματι τῷ ἁγίῳ
For it seemed [good] to the Spirit – Holy

καὶ ἡμῖν μηδὲν πλέον ἐπιτίθεσθαι ὑμῖν
and to us [3]*nothing* [5]more [1]to be put on [2]you

βάρος πλὴν τούτων τῶν ἐπάναγκες,
[4]burden than these – necessary things,

29 ἀπέχεσθαι εἰδωλοθύτων καὶ αἵματος καὶ
to abstain from idol sacrifices and blood and

πνικτῶν καὶ πορνείας· ἐξ ὧν διατηροῦντες
things strangled and fornication; from which keeping

to abstain from food polluted by idols, from sexual immorality, from the meat of strangled animals and from blood. 21For Moses has been preached in every city from the earliest times and is read in the synagogues on every Sabbath."

The Council's Letter to Gentile Believers

22Then the apostles and elders, with the whole church, decided to choose some of their own men and send them to Antioch with Paul and Barnabas. They chose Judas (called Barsabbas) and Silas, two men who were leaders among the brothers. 23With them they sent the following letter:

The apostles and elders, your brothers,

To the Gentile believers in Antioch, Syria and Cilicia:

Greetings.

24We have heard that some went out from us without our authorization and disturbed you, troubling your minds by what they said. 25So we all agreed to choose some men and send them to you with our dear friends Barnabas and Paul— 26men who have risked their lives for the name of our Lord Jesus Christ. 27Therefore we are sending Judas and Silas to confirm by word of mouth what we are writing. 28It seemed good to the Holy Spirit and to us not to burden you with anything beyond the following requirements: 29You are to abstain from food sacrificed to idols, from blood, from the meat of strangled animals and from sexual immorality.

things, you will do
well. Farewell."
30So, when they were
sent away, they went down
to Antioch; and having
gathered the congregation
together, they delivered the
letter.
31And when they had
read it, they rejoiced because of its encourage-
ment.
32And Judas and Silas,
also being prophets them-
selves, encouraged and
strengthened the brethren
with a lengthy message.
33And after they had
spent time *there*, they were
sent away from the breth-
ren in peace to those who
had sent them out.
34[[e]But it seemed good to
Silas to remain there.]
35But Paul and Barnabas
stayed in Antioch, teaching
and preaching, with many
others also, the word of the
Lord.

Second Missionary Journey

36And after some days
Paul said to Barnabas,
"Let us return and visit the
brethren in every city in
which we proclaimed the
word of the Lord, *and see*
how they are."
37And Barnabas was de-
sirous of taking John,
called Mark, along with
them also.
38But Paul kept insisting
that they should not take
him along who had desert-
ed them in Pamphylia and
had not gone with them to
the work.
39And there arose such a
sharp disagreement that
they separated from one
another, and Barnabas
took Mark with him and
sailed away to Cyprus.
40But Paul chose Silas
and departed, being com-
mitted by the brethren to
the grace of the Lord.
41And he was traveling
through Syria and Cili-
cia, strengthening the
churches.

[e] Many mss. do not contain this verse

ἑαυτοὺς εὖ πράξετε. Ἔρρωσθε.
yourselves well ye will do. Farewell.

30 Οἱ μὲν οὖν ἀπολυθέντες κατῆλθον εἰς
They – therefore being dismissed went down to

Ἀντιόχειαν, καὶ συναγαγόντες τὸ πλῆθος
Antioch, and assembling the multitude

ἐπέδωκαν τὴν ἐπιστολήν. 31 ἀναγνόντες δὲ
handed in the letter. And having read

ἐχάρησαν ἐπὶ τῇ παρακλήσει. 32 Ἰούδας τε
they rejoiced at the exhortation. And Judas

καὶ Σιλᾶς, καὶ αὐτοὶ προφῆται ὄντες,
and Silas, also [them]selves prophets being,

διὰ λόγου πολλοῦ παρεκάλεσαν τοὺς
through (by) speech much exhorted the

ἀδελφοὺς καὶ ἐπεστήριξαν· 33 ποιήσαντες δὲ
brothers and confirmed; and having continued

χρόνον ἀπελύθησαν μετ' εἰρήνης ἀπὸ
a time they were dismissed with peace from

τῶν ἀδελφῶν πρὸς τοὺς ἀποστείλαντας
the brothers to the [ones] having sent

αὐτούς. ‡ 35 Παῦλος δὲ καὶ Βαρναβᾶς
them. But Paul and Barnabas

διέτριβον ἐν Ἀντιοχείᾳ, διδάσκοντες καὶ
stayed in Antioch, teaching and

εὐαγγελιζόμενοι μετὰ καὶ ἑτέρων πολλῶν
preaching [1]with [4]also [3]others [2]many

τὸν λόγον τοῦ κυρίου.
the word of the Lord.

36 Μετὰ δέ τινας ἡμέρας εἶπεν πρὸς
Now after some days [2]said [3]to

Βαρναβᾶν Παῦλος· ἐπιστρέψαντες δὴ
[4]Barnabas [1]Paul: Returning then

ἐπισκεψώμεθα τοὺς ἀδελφοὺς κατὰ πόλιν
let us visit the brothers throughout [2]city

πᾶσαν ἐν αἷς κατηγγείλαμεν τὸν λόγον
[1]every in which we announced the word

τοῦ κυρίου, πῶς ἔχουσιν. 37 Βαρναβᾶς
of the Lord, how they have(are). Barnabas

δὲ ἐβούλετο συμπαραλαβεῖν καὶ τὸν
And wished to take with [them] also –

Ἰωάννην τὸν καλούμενον Μᾶρκον· 38 Παῦλος
John – *being* called Mark; [2]Paul

δὲ ἠξίου, τὸν ἀποστάντα ἀπ' αὐτῶν
[1]but [3]thought fit, – [7]withdrawing [8]from [9]them

ἀπὸ Παμφυλίας καὶ μὴ συνελθόντα αὐτοῖς
[10]from [11]Pamphylia [12]and [13]not [14]going with [15]them

εἰς τὸ ἔργον, μὴ συμπαραλαμβάνειν τοῦτον.
[16]to [17]the [18]work, [4]not [5]to take with [them] [6]this one.

39 ἐγένετο δὲ παροξυσμός, ὥστε ἀποχωρισ-
And there was sharp feeling, so as to separ-

θῆναι αὐτοὺς ἀπ' ἀλλήλων, τόν τε
ate them from each other, – and

Βαρναβᾶν παραλαβόντα τὸν Μᾶρκον
Barnabas taking – Mark

ἐκπλεῦσαι εἰς Κύπρον. 40 Παῦλος δὲ
to sail away to Cyprus. But Paul

ἐπιλεξάμενος Σιλᾶν ἐξῆλθεν, παραδοθεὶς
having chosen Silas went forth, being commended

τῇ χάριτι τοῦ κυρίου ὑπὸ τῶν
to the grace of the Lord by the

ἀδελφῶν· 41 διήρχετο δὲ τὴν Συρίαν
brothers; and he went through – Syria

καὶ Κιλικίαν ἐπιστηρίζων τὰς ἐκκλησίας.
and Cilicia confirming the churches.

‡ Verse 34 omitted by Nestle; *cf.* NIV

You will do well to
avoid these things.
Farewell.
30The men were sent off
and went down to Antioch,
where they gathered the
church together and delivered the letter. 31The people read it and were glad for
its encouraging message.
32Judas and Silas, who
themselves were prophets,
said much to encourage
and strengthen the broth-
ers. 33After spending some
time there, they were sent
off by the brothers with the
blessing of peace to return
to those who had sent
them.[g] 35But Paul and Barnabas remained in Antioch,
where they and many oth-
ers taught and preached the
word of the Lord.

Disagreement Between Paul and Barnabas

36Some time later Paul
said to Barnabas, "Let us
go back and visit the brothers in all the towns where
we preached the word of
the Lord and see how they
are doing." 37Barnabas
wanted to take John, also
called Mark, with them,
38but Paul did not think it
wise to take him, because
he had deserted them in
Pamphylia and had not
continued with them in the
work. 39They had such a
sharp disagreement that
they parted company. Bar-
nabas took Mark and sailed
for Cyprus, 40but Paul
chose Silas and left, commended by the brothers to
the grace of the Lord. 41He
went through Syria and Cilicia, strengthening the
churches.

[g] 33 Some manuscripts *them,* [34]*but Silas decided to remain there*

Chapter 16

The Macedonian Vision

AND he came also to
Derbe and to Lystra.
And behold, a certain disciple was there, named Tim-
othy, the son of a Jewish
woman who was a believer,
but his father was a Greek,
2and he was well spoken
of by the brethren who
were in Lystra and Iconi-
um.
3Paul wanted this man to
go with him; and he took
him and circumcised him
because of the Jews who
were in those parts, for
they all knew that his father
was a Greek.
4Now while they were
passing through the cities,
they were delivering the
decrees, which had been
decided upon by the apos-
tles and elders who were in
Jerusalem, for them to observe.
5So the churches were
being strengthened in the
faith, and were increasing
in number daily.
6And they passed
through the Phrygian and
Galatian region, having
been forbidden by the Holy
Spirit to speak the word in
Asia;
7and when they had
come to Mysia, they were
trying to go into Bithynia,
and the Spirit of Jesus did
not permit them;
8and passing by Mysia,
they came down to Troas.
9And a vision appeared
to Paul in the night: a certain man of Macedonia was
standing and appealing to
him, and saying, "Come
over to Macedonia and
help us."
10And when he had seen
the vision, immediately we
sought to go into Mace-
donia, concluding that God
had called us to preach the

16 Κατήντησεν δὲ καὶ εἰς Δέρβην καὶ
And he came down also to Derbe and
εἰς Λύστραν. καὶ ἰδοὺ μαθητής τις ἦν
to Lystra. And behold[,] a certain disciple was
ἐκεῖ ὀνόματι Τιμόθεος, υἱὸς γυναικὸς
there by name Timothy, son [3]woman
Ἰουδαίας πιστῆς πατρὸς δὲ Ἕλληνος,
[2]Jewish [1]of a faithful [4]but [6]father [5]of a Greek,
2 ὃς ἐμαρτυρεῖτο ὑπὸ τῶν ἐν Λύστροις
who was witnessed to by [1]the [3]in [4]Lystra
καὶ Ἰκονίῳ ἀδελφῶν. **3** τοῦτον ἠθέλησεν
[5]and [6]Iconium [2]brothers. [3]This one [2]wished
ὁ Παῦλος σὺν αὐτῷ ἐξελθεῖν, καὶ λαβὼν
– [1]Paul with him to go forth, and taking
περιέτεμεν αὐτὸν διὰ τοὺς Ἰουδαίους τοὺς
circumcised him on account of the Jews –
ὄντας ἐν τοῖς τόποις ἐκείνοις· ᾔδεισαν
being in those places; [2]they knew
γὰρ ἅπαντες ὅτι Ἕλλην ὁ πατὴρ αὐτοῦ
[1]for all that a Greek the father of him
ὑπῆρχεν. **4** Ὡς δὲ διεπορεύοντο τὰς
was. Now as they went through the
πόλεις, παρεδίδοσαν αὐτοῖς φυλάσσειν τὰ
cities, they delivered to them* to keep the
δόγματα τὰ κεκριμένα ὑπὸ τῶν ἀποστόλων
decrees – having been decided [on] by the apostles
καὶ πρεσβυτέρων τῶν ἐν Ἰεροσολύμοις.
and elders – in Jerusalem.
5 Αἱ μὲν οὖν ἐκκλησίαι ἐστερεοῦντο
[2]The – [1]therefore [3]churches were strengthened
τῇ πίστει καὶ ἐπερίσσευον τῷ ἀριθμῷ
in the faith and increased – in number
καθ' ἡμέραν.
daily.
6 Διῆλθον δὲ τὴν Φρυγίαν καὶ Γαλατικὴν
And they went through the Phrygian and Galatian
χώραν, κωλυθέντες ὑπὸ τοῦ ἁγίου
country, being prevented by the Holy
πνεύματος λαλῆσαι τὸν λόγον ἐν τῇ
Spirit to speak =from speaking the word in –
Ἀσίᾳ· **7** ἐλθόντες δὲ κατὰ τὴν Μυσίαν
Asia; but coming against – Mysia
ἐπείραζον εἰς τὴν Βιθυνίαν πορευθῆναι,
they attempted into – Bithynia to go,
καὶ οὐκ εἴασεν αὐτοὺς τὸ πνεῦμα Ἰησοῦ·
and [4]not [5]allowed [6]them [1]the [2]Spirit [3]of Jesus;
8 παρελθόντες δὲ τὴν Μυσίαν κατέβησαν
so passing by – Mysia they came down
εἰς Τρῳάδα. **9** καὶ ὅραμα διὰ νυκτὸς
to Troas. And a vision through (during) [the] night
τῷ Παύλῳ ὤφθη, ἀνήρ Μακεδών τις
– to Paul appeared, a *man* Macedonian certain
ἦν ἑστὼς καὶ παρακαλῶν αὐτὸν καὶ
was standing and beseeching him and
λέγων· διαβὰς εἰς Μακεδονίαν βοήθησον
saying: Crossing into Macedonia help
ἡμῖν. **10** ὡς δὲ τὸ ὅραμα εἶδεν, εὐθέως
us. So when the vision he saw, immediately
ἐζητήσαμεν ἐξελθεῖν εἰς Μακεδονίαν,
we sought to go forth to Macedonia,
συμβιβάζοντες ὅτι προσκέκληται ἡμᾶς ὁ
concluding that [2]has(had) called [3]us –

* Note the gender: *πόλις* is feminine.

Chapter 16

Timothy Joins Paul and Silas

HE came to Derbe and
then to Lystra, where
a disciple named Timothy
lived, whose mother was a
Jewess and a believer, but
whose father was a Greek.
2The brothers at Lystra and
Iconium spoke well of him.
3Paul wanted to take him
along on the journey, so he
circumcised him because of
the Jews who lived in that
area, for they all knew that
his father was a Greek. 4As
they traveled from town to
town, they delivered the
decisions reached by the
apostles and elders in Jerusalem for the people to
obey. 5So the churches
were strengthened in the
faith and grew daily in numbers.

Paul's Vision of the Man of Macedonia

6Paul and his companions
traveled throughout the region of Phrygia and Gala-
tia, having been kept by the
Holy Spirit from preaching
the word in the province of
Asia. 7When they came to
the border of Mysia, they
tried to enter Bithynia, but
the Spirit of Jesus would
not allow them to. 8So they
passed by Mysia and went
down to Troas. 9During the
night Paul had a vision of a
man of Macedonia standing
and begging him, "Come
over to Macedonia and
help us." 10After Paul had
seen the vision, we got
ready at once to leave for
Macedonia, concluding
that God had called us to

gospel to them.

11Therefore putting out to sea from Troas, we ran a straight course to Samothrace, and on the day following to Neapolis;

12and from there to Philippi, which is a leading city of the district of Macedonia, a *Roman* colony; and we were staying in this city for some days.

13And on the Sabbath day we went outside the gate to a riverside, where we were supposing that there would be a place of prayer; and we sat down and began speaking to the women who had assembled.

First Convert in Europe

14And a certain woman named Lydia, from the city of Thyatira, a seller of purple fabrics, a worshiper of God, was listening; and the Lord opened her heart to respond to the things spoken by Paul.

15And when she and her household had been baptized, she urged us, saying, "If you have judged me to be faithful to the Lord, come into my house and stay." And she prevailed upon us.

16And it happened that as we were going to the place of prayer, a certain slave-girl having a spirit of divination met us, who was bringing her masters much profit by fortunetelling.

17Following after Paul and us, she kept crying out, saying, "These men are bond-servants of the Most High God, who are proclaiming to you the way of salvation."

18And she continued doing this for many days. But Paul was greatly annoyed, and turned and said to the spirit, "I command you in the name of Jesus Christ to come out of her!" And it came out at that very moment.

θεὸς εὐαγγελίσασθαι αὐτούς.
[1]God to evangelize them.
11 Ἀναχθέντες δὲ ἀπὸ Τρῳάδος εὐθυδρο-
And setting sail from Troas we ran a
μήσαμεν εἰς Σαμοθρᾴκην, τῇ δὲ ἐπιούσῃ
straight course to Samothracia, and on the next day
εἰς Νέαν πόλιν, 12 κἀκεῖθεν εἰς Φιλίππους,
to Neapolis, and thence to Philippi,
ἥτις ἐστὶν πρώτη τῆς μερίδος Μακεδονίας
which is [1][the] [2]first [4]of the [5]part [6]of Macedonia
πόλις, κολωνία. Ἦμεν δὲ ἐν ταύτῃ τῇ
[3]city, a colony. And we were in this –
πόλει διατρίβοντες ἡμέρας τινάς. 13 τῇ τε
city staying days some. And on the
ἡμέρᾳ τῶν σαββάτων ἐξήλθομεν ἔξω τῆς
day of the sabbath*s* we went forth outside the
πύλης παρὰ ποταμὸν οὗ ἐνομίζομεν
gate by a river where we supposed
προσευχὴν εἶναι, καὶ καθίσαντες ἐλαλοῦμεν
a place of prayer to be, and sitting we spoke
ταῖς συνελθούσαις γυναιξίν. 14 καί τις
to the [2]coming together [1]women. And a certain
γυνὴ ὀνόματι Λυδία, πορφυρόπωλις
woman by name Lydia, a dealer in purple-dyed [garments]
πόλεως Θυατίρων, σεβομένη τὸν θεόν,
of [the] city of Thyatira, worshipping – God,
ἤκουεν, ἧς ὁ κύριος διήνοιξεν τὴν καρδίαν
heard, of whom the Lord opened up the heart
προσέχειν τοῖς λαλουμένοις ὑπὸ Παύλου.
to take heed to the things being spoken by Paul.
15 ὡς δὲ ἐβαπτίσθη καὶ ὁ οἶκος αὐτῆς,
And when she was baptized and the household of her,
παρεκάλεσεν λέγουσα· εἰ κεκρίκατέ με
she besought saying: If ye have decided me
πιστὴν τῷ κυρίῳ εἶναι, εἰσελθόντες εἰς
faithful to the Lord to be, entering into
τὸν οἶκόν μου μένετε· καὶ παρεβιάσατο
the house of me remain; and she urged
ἡμᾶς. 16 Ἐγένετο δὲ πορευομένων ἡμῶν
us. And it happened going us[a]
=as we went
εἰς τὴν προσευχήν, παιδίσκην τινὰ ἔχουσαν
to the place of prayer, a certain maid having
πνεῦμα πύθωνα ὑπαντῆσαι ἡμῖν, ἥτις
a spirit of a python to meet us, who
ἐργασίαν πολλὴν παρεῖχεν τοῖς κυρίοις
[3]gain [2]much [1]brought to the masters
αὐτῆς μαντευομένη. 17 αὕτη κατακολουθοῦσα
of her practising soothsaying. This one following after
τῷ Παύλῳ καὶ ἡμῖν ἔκραζεν λέγουσα·
– Paul and us cried out saying:
οὗτοι οἱ ἄνθρωποι δοῦλοι τοῦ θεοῦ τοῦ
These – men slaves of the God –
ὑψίστου εἰσίν, οἵτινες καταγγέλλουσιν ὑμῖν
most high are, who announce to you
ὁδὸν σωτηρίας. 18 τοῦτο δὲ ἐποίει ἐπὶ
a way of salvation. And this she did over
πολλὰς ἡμέρας. διαπονηθεὶς δὲ Παῦλος
many days. But becoming greatly troubled Paul
καὶ ἐπιστρέψας τῷ πνεύματι εἶπεν· παραγ-
and turning [2]to the [3]spirit [1]he said: I
γέλλω σοι ἐν ὀνόματι Ἰησοῦ Χριστοῦ
charge thee in [the] name of Jesus Christ
ἐξελθεῖν ἀπ' αὐτῆς· καὶ ἐξῆλθεν αὐτῇ
to come out from her; and it came out in the

preach the gospel to them.

Lydia's Conversion in Philippi

11From Troas we put out
to sea and sailed straight
for Samothrace, and the
next day on to Neapolis.
12From there we traveled to
Philippi, a Roman colony
and the leading city of that
district of Macedonia. And
we stayed there several
days.
13On the Sabbath we
went outside the city gate
to the river, where we expected
to find a place of
prayer. We sat down and
began to speak to the women
who had gathered there.
14One of those listening
was a woman named Lydia,
a dealer in purple cloth
from the city of Thyatira,
who was a worshiper of
God. The Lord opened her
heart to respond to Paul's
message. 15When she and
the members of her household
were baptized, she invited
us to her home. "If
you consider me a believer
in the Lord," she said,
"come and stay at my
house." And she persuaded
us.

Paul and Silas in Prison

16Once when we were going
to the place of prayer,
we were met by a slave girl
who had a spirit by which
she predicted the future.
She earned a great deal of
money for her owners by
fortune-telling. 17This girl
followed Paul and the rest
of us, shouting, "These
men are servants of the
Most High God, who are
telling you the way to be
saved." 18She kept this up
for many days. Finally Paul
became so troubled that he
turned around and said to
the spirit, "In the name of
Jesus Christ I command
you to come out of her!" At
that moment the spirit left
her.

19But when her masters
saw that their hope of profit
was gone, they seized Paul
and Silas and dragged them
into the market place be-
fore the authorities,
20and when they had
brought them to the chief
magistrates, they said,
"These men are throwing
our city into confusion, being Jews,
21and are proclaiming
customs which it is not lawful for us to accept or to
observe, being Romans."

Paul and Silas Imprisoned

22And the crowd rose up
together against them, and
the chief magistrates tore
their robes off them, and
proceeded to order *them* to
be beaten with rods.
23And when they had in-
flicted many blows upon
them, they threw them into
prison, commanding the
jailer to guard them securely;
24and he, having received
such a command, threw
them into the inner prison,
and fastened their feet in
the stocks.
25But about midnight Paul
and Silas were praying and
singing hymns of praise to
God, and the prisoners
were listening to them;
26and suddenly there
came a great earthquake,
so that the foundations of
the prison house were
shaken; and immediately
all the doors were opened,
and everyone's chains
were unfastened.
27And when the jailer had
been roused out of sleep
and had seen the prison
doors opened, he drew his
sword and was about to kill
himself, supposing that the
prisoners had escaped.
28But Paul cried out with
a loud voice, saying, "Do
yourself no harm, for we
are all here!"
29And he called for lights

τῇ ὥρᾳ. 19 Ἰδόντες δὲ οἱ κύριοι αὐτῆς
same hour.* And [4]seeing [1]the [2]masters [3]of her
ὅτι ἐξῆλθεν ἡ ἐλπὶς τῆς ἐργασίας αὐτῶν,
[5]that [11]went out [6]the [7]hope [8]of the [9]gain [10]of them,
ἐπιλαβόμενοι τὸν Παῦλον καὶ τὸν Σιλᾶν
having seized – Paul and – Silas
εἵλκυσαν εἰς τὴν ἀγορὰν ἐπὶ τοὺς ἄρχοντας,
dragged to the marketplace before the rulers,
20 καὶ προσαγαγόντες αὐτοὺς τοῖς στρατηγοῖς
and [1]bringing [3]to [2]them the prætors
εἶπαν· οὗτοι οἱ ἄνθρωποι ἐκταράσσουσιν
said: These – men are greatly troubling
ἡμῶν τὴν πόλιν, Ἰουδαῖοι ὑπάρχοντες,
of us the city, [2]Jews [1]being,
21 καὶ καταγγέλλουσιν ἔθη ἃ οὐκ ἔξεστιν
and they announce customs which it is not lawful
ἡμῖν παραδέχεσθαι οὐδὲ ποιεῖν Ῥωμαίοις
for us to receive nor to do [2]Romans
οὖσιν. 22 καὶ συνεπέστη ὁ ὄχλος κατ'
[1]being. And rose up together the crowd against
αὐτῶν, καὶ οἱ στρατηγοὶ περιρήξαντες
them, and the prætors tearing off
αὐτῶν τὰ ἱμάτια ἐκέλευον ῥαβδίζειν,
of them the garments commanded to flog,
23 πολλάς δὲ ἐπιθέντες αὐτοῖς πληγὰς
and [3]many [1]laying on [2]them [4]stripes
ἔβαλον εἰς φυλακήν, παραγγείλαντες τῷ
threw into prison, charging the
δεσμοφύλακι ἀσφαλῶς τηρεῖν αὐτούς· 24 ὃς
jailer securely to keep them; who
παραγγελίαν τοιαύτην λαβὼν ἔβαλεν αὐτοὺς
[3]a charge [2]such [1]having received threw them
εἰς τὴν ἐσωτέραν φυλακὴν καὶ τοὺς
into the inner prison and [2]the
πόδας ἠσφαλίσατο αὐτῶν εἰς τὸ ξύλον.
[3]feet [1]secured [4]of them in the stocks.
25 Κατὰ δὲ τὸ μεσονύκτιον Παῦλος καὶ
And about – midnight Paul and
Σιλᾶς προσευχόμενοι ὕμνουν τὸν θεόν,
Silas praying [1]praised [2]in a hymn – [3]God,
ἐπηκροῶντο δὲ αὐτῶν οἱ δέσμιοι· 26 ἄφνω δὲ
and [3]listened to [4]them [1]the [2]prisoners; and suddenly
σεισμὸς ἐγένετο μέγας, ὥστε σαλευ-
[3]earthquake [1]there was [2]a great, so as to be
θῆναι τὰ θεμέλια τοῦ δεσμωτηρίου·
shaken the foundations of the jail;
ἠνεῴχθησαν δὲ παραχρῆμα αἱ θύραι πᾶσαι,
and [5]were opened [1]at once [3]the [4]doors [2]all,
καὶ πάντων τὰ δεσμὰ ἀνέθη. 27 ἔξυπνος δὲ
and [3]of all [1]the [2]bonds were loosened. And [4]awake
γενόμενος ὁ δεσμοφύλαξ καὶ ἰδὼν
[5]having become [1]the [2]jailer and seeing
ἀνεῳγμένας τὰς θύρας τῆς φυλακῆς,
having been opened the doors of the prison,
σπασάμενος τὴν μάχαιραν ἤμελλεν ἑαυτὸν
having drawn the sword was about himself
ἀναιρεῖν, νομίζων ἐκπεφευγέναι τοὺς
to kill, supposing to have escaped the
δεσμίους. 28 ἐφώνησεν δὲ Παῦλος μεγάλῃ
prisoners. But called Paul with a great(loud)
φωνῇ λέγων· μηδὲν πράξῃς σεαυτῷ κακόν,
voice saying: [1]No*thing* [3]do [4]thyself [2]harm,
ἅπαντες γάρ ἐσμεν ἐνθάδε. 29 αἰτήσας
for [2]all [1]we are [3]here. asking

* See Luke 2. 38.

19When the owners of the
slave girl realized that their
hope of making money was
gone, they seized Paul and
Silas and dragged them into
the marketplace to face the
authorities. 20They brought
them before the magis-
trates and said, "These
men are Jews, and are
throwing our city into an
uproar 21by advocating
customs unlawful for us
Romans to accept or prac-
tice."
22The crowd joined in the
attack against Paul and Silas, and the magistrates ordered them to be stripped
and beaten. 23After they
had been severely flogged,
they were thrown into prison, and the jailer was commanded to guard them
carefully. 24Upon receiving
such orders, he put them in
the inner cell and fastened
their feet in the stocks.
25About midnight Paul
and Silas were praying and
singing hymns to God, and
the other prisoners were
listening to them. 26Sud-
denly there was such a violent earthquake that the
foundations of the prison
were shaken. At once all
the prison doors flew open,
and everybody's chains
came loose. 27The jailer
woke up, and when he saw
the prison doors open, he
drew his sword and was
about to kill himself be-
cause he thought the prisoners had escaped. 28But
Paul shouted, "Don't harm
yourself! We are all here!"
29The jailer called for

and rushed in and, trembling with fear, he fell down before Paul and Silas,
30and after he brought them out, he said, "Sirs, what must I do to be saved?"

The Jailer Converted

31And they said, "Believe in the Lord Jesus, and you shall be saved, you and your household."
32And they spoke the word of the Lord to him together with all who were in his house.
33And he took them that *very* hour of the night and washed their wounds, and immediately he was baptized, he and all his *household*.
34And he brought them into his house and set food before them, and rejoiced greatly, having believed in God with his whole household.
35Now when day came, the chief magistrates sent their policemen, saying, "Release those men."
36And the jailer reported these words to Paul, *saying*, "The chief magistrates have sent to release you. Now therefore, come out and go in peace."
37But Paul said to them, "They have beaten us in public without trial, men who are Romans, and have thrown us into prison; and now are they sending us away secretly? No indeed! But let them come themselves and bring us out."
38And the policemen reported these words to the chief magistrates. And they were afraid when they heard that they were Romans,
39and they came and appealed to them, and when they had brought them out, they kept begging them to

δὲ φῶτα εἰσεπήδησεν, καὶ ἔντρομος
And lights he rushed in, and trembling

γενόμενος προσέπεσεν τῷ Παύλῳ καὶ
becoming he fell before – Paul and

Σιλᾷ, 30 καὶ προαγαγὼν αὐτοὺς ἔξω ἔφη·
Silas, and [1]leading [3]forward [2]them outside said:

κύριοι, τί με δεῖ ποιεῖν ἵνα σωθῶ;
Sirs, what [2]me [1]behoves it to do that I may be saved?

31 οἱ δὲ εἶπαν· πίστευσον ἐπὶ τὸν κύριον
And they said: Believe on the Lord

Ἰησοῦν, καὶ σωθήσῃ σὺ καὶ ὁ οἶκός
Jesus, and shalt be saved thou and the household

σου. 32 καὶ ἐλάλησαν αὐτῷ τὸν λόγον
of thee. And they spoke to him the word

τοῦ θεοῦ σὺν πᾶσιν τοῖς ἐν τῇ οἰκίᾳ
– of God with all the [ones] in the house

αὐτοῦ. 33 καὶ παραλαβὼν αὐτοὺς ἐν
of him. And taking them in

ἐκείνῃ τῇ ὥρᾳ τῆς νυκτὸς ἔλουσεν ἀπὸ
that – hour of the night he washed *from*

τῶν πληγῶν, καὶ ἐβαπτίσθη αὐτὸς καὶ
the stripes, and was baptized he and

οἱ αὐτοῦ ἅπαντες παραχρῆμα, 34 ἀναγαγών
the of him all at once, [2]bringing up
=all his

τε αὐτοὺς εἰς τὸν οἶκον παρέθηκεν
[1]and them to the house he set before [them]

τράπεζαν, καὶ ἠγαλλιάσατο πανοικεὶ πεπι-
a table, and exulted with all the household having

στευκὼς τῷ θεῷ. 35 Ἡμέρας δὲ γενομένης
believed – God. And day coming[a]
=when day came

ἀπέστειλαν οἱ στρατηγοὶ τοὺς ῥαβδούχους
[3]sent [1]the [2]prætors the tipstaffs

λέγοντες· ἀπόλυσον τοὺς ἀνθρώπους
saying: Release – men

ἐκείνους. 36 ἀπήγγειλεν δὲ ὁ δεσμοφύλαξ
those. And announced the jailer

τοὺς λόγους τούτους πρὸς τὸν Παῦλον,
these words to – Paul,

ὅτι ἀπέσταλκαν οἱ στρατηγοὶ ἵνα ἀπολυθῆτε.
– [3]have sent [1]The [2]prætors that ye may be released.

νῦν οὖν ἐξελθόντες πορεύεσθε ἐν εἰρήνῃ.
Now therefore going forth proceed in peace.

37 ὁ δὲ Παῦλος ἔφη πρὸς αὐτούς·
– But Paul said to them:

δείραντες ἡμᾶς δημοσίᾳ ἀκατακρίτους,
Having beaten us publicly uncondemned,

ἀνθρώπους Ῥωμαίους ὑπάρχοντας, ἔβαλαν
men [2]Romans [1]being, they threw [us]

εἰς φυλακήν· καὶ νῦν λάθρᾳ ἡμᾶς ἐκβάλ-
into prison; and now secretly us they

λουσιν; οὐ γάρ, ἀλλὰ ἐλθόντες αὐτοὶ
expel? No indeed, but coming [them]selves

ἡμᾶς ἐξαγαγέτωσαν. 38 ἀπήγγειλαν δὲ τοῖς
us let them bring out. And [3]reported [4]to the

στρατηγοῖς οἱ ῥαβδοῦχοι τὰ ῥήματα ταῦτα.
[5]prætors [1]the [2]tipstaffs these words.

ἐφοβήθησαν δὲ ἀκούσαντες ὅτι Ῥωμαῖοί
And they were afraid hearing that Romans

εἰσιν, 39 καὶ ἐλθόντες παρεκάλεσαν
they are(were), and coming besought

αὐτούς, καὶ ἐξαγαγόντες ἠρώτων ἀπελθεῖν
them, and bringing out asked to go away

lights, rushed in and fell
trembling before Paul and
Silas. 30He then brought
them out and asked, "Sirs,
what must I do to be
saved?"
31They replied, "Believe
in the Lord Jesus, and you
will be saved—you and
your household." 32Then
they spoke the word of the
Lord to him and to all the
others in his house. 33At
that hour of the night the
jailer took them and
washed their wounds; then
immediately he and all his
family were baptized.
34The jailer brought them
into his house and set a
meal before them; he was
filled with joy because he
had come to believe in God
—he and his whole family.
35When it was daylight,
the magistrates sent their
officers to the jailer with
the order: "Release those
men." 36The jailer told
Paul, "The magistrates
have ordered that you and
Silas be released. Now you
can leave. Go in peace."
37But Paul said to the officers: "They beat us publicly without a trial, even
though we are Roman citizens, and threw us into
prison. And now do they
want to get rid of us quietly? No! Let them come
themselves and escort us
out."
38The officers reported
this to the magistrates, and
when they heard that Paul
and Silas were Roman citizens, they were alarmed.
39They came to appease
them and escorted them
from the prison, requesting

leave the city.

40And they went out of the prison and entered *the house of* Lydia, and when they saw the brethren, they encouraged them and departed.

ἀπὸ τῆς πόλεως. **40** ἐξελθόντες δὲ ἀπὸ
from the city. And going out from
τῆς φυλακῆς εἰσῆλθον πρὸς τὴν Λυδίαν,
the prison they entered to [the house of] – Lydia,
καὶ ἰδόντες παρεκάλεσαν τοὺς ἀδελφοὺς
and seeing they exhorted the brothers
καὶ ἐξῆλθαν.
and went forth.

them to leave the city. 40Af-
ter Paul and Silas came out
of the prison, they went to
Lydia's house, where they
met with the brothers and
encouraged them. Then
they left.

Chapter 17

Paul at Thessalonica

NOW when they had traveled through Amphipolis and Apollonia, they came to Thessalonica, where there was a synagogue of the Jews.

2And according to Paul's custom, he went to them, and for three Sabbaths reasoned with them from the Scriptures,

3explaining and giving evidence that the Christ had to suffer and rise again from the dead, and *saying,* "This Jesus whom I am proclaiming to you is the Christ."

4And some of them were persuaded and joined Paul and Silas, along with a great multitude of the God-fearing Greeks and a number of the leading women.

5But the Jews, becoming jealous and taking along some wicked men from the market place, formed a mob and set the city in an uproar; and coming upon the house of Jason, they were seeking to bring them out to the people.

6And when they did not find them, they *began* dragging Jason and some brethren before the city authorities, shouting, "These men who have upset [f]the world have come here also;

7and Jason has welcomed them, and they all act contrary to the decrees of Caesar, saying that there is another king, Jesus."

8And they stirred up the crowd and the city authori-

[f]Lit., *the inhabited earth*

17 Διοδεύσαντες δὲ τὴν Ἀμφίπολιν καὶ
And travelling through – Amphipolis and
τὴν Ἀπολλωνίαν ἦλθον εἰς Θεσσαλονίκην,
– Apollonia they came to Thessalonica,
ὅπου ἦν συναγωγὴ τῶν Ἰουδαίων. **2** κατὰ
where was a synagogue of the Jews. according to
δὲ τὸ εἰωθὸς τῷ Παύλῳ εἰσῆλθεν πρὸς
And the custom – with Paul° he entered to
αὐτούς, καὶ ἐπὶ σάββατα τρία διελέξατο
them, and on sabbaths three lectured
αὐτοῖς ἀπὸ τῶν γραφῶν, **3** διανοίγων
to them from the scriptures, opening up
καὶ παρατιθέμενος ὅτι τὸν χριστὸν ἔδει
and setting before [them] that [2]the [3]Christ [1]it behoved
παθεῖν καὶ ἀναστῆναι ἐκ νεκρῶν, καὶ
to suffer and to rise again out of [the] dead, and
ὅτι οὗτός ἐστιν ὁ χριστός, ὁ Ἰησοῦς,
that this is(was) the Christ, – Jesus,
ὃν ἐγὼ καταγγέλλω ὑμῖν. **4** καί τινες
whom I announce to you. And some
ἐξ αὐτῶν ἐπείσθησαν καὶ προσεκληρώθησαν
of them were persuaded and threw in their lot
τῷ Παύλῳ καὶ τῷ Σιλᾷ, τῶν τε
– with Paul and – Silas, both of the
σεβομένων Ἑλλήνων πλῆθος πολύ, γυναικῶν τε
worshipping Greeks [2]multitude [1]a much (great), and of [2]women
τῶν πρώτων οὐκ ὀλίγαι. **5** Ζηλώσαντες δὲ
[1]the [3]chief not a few. But becoming jealous
οἱ Ἰουδαῖοι καὶ προσλαβόμενοι τῶν
the Jews and taking aside of the
ἀγοραίων ἄνδρας τινὰς πονηροὺς καὶ
loungers in the marketplace men some wicked and
ὀχλοποιήσαντες ἐθορύβουν τὴν πόλιν, καὶ
having gathered a crowd disturbed the city, and
ἐπιστάντες τῇ οἰκίᾳ Ἰάσονος ἐζήτουν
coming on the house of Jason sought
αὐτοὺς προαγαγεῖν εἰς τὸν δῆμον· **6** μὴ
them to bring forward to the mob; [2]not
εὑρόντες δὲ αὐτοὺς ἔσυρον Ἰάσονα καί
[3]finding [1]but them they dragged Jason and
τινας ἀδελφοὺς ἐπὶ τοὺς πολιτάρχας,
some brothers to the politarchs,
βοῶντες ὅτι οἱ τὴν οἰκουμένην ἀναστατώ-
crying[,] – [2]the [ones] [4]the [5]inhabited earth [3]having turned
σαντες οὗτοι καὶ ἐνθάδε πάρεισιν, **7** οὓς
upside down [1]these men also here have arrived, whom
ὑποδέδεκται Ἰάσων· καὶ οὗτοι πάντες
[2]has received [1]Jason; and these all
ἀπέναντι τῶν δογμάτων Καίσαρος
[2]contrary to [3]the [4]decrees [5]of Cæsar
πράσσουσιν, βασιλέα ἕτερον λέγοντες εἶναι
[1]act, [4]king [3]another [1]saying [2]to be
Ἰησοῦν. **8** ἐτάραξαν δὲ τὸν ὄχλον καὶ
[5]Jesus. And they troubled the crowd and

Chapter 17

In Thessalonica

WHEN they had passed
through Amphipolis
and Apollonia, they came
to Thessalonica, where
there was a Jewish syna-
gogue. 2As his custom was,
Paul went into the syna-
gogue, and on three Sab-
bath days he reasoned with
them from the Scriptures,
3explaining and proving
that the Christ[h] had to suffer and rise from the dead.
"This Jesus I am proclaiming to you is the Christ,[h]"
he said. 4Some of the Jews
were persuaded and joined
Paul and Silas, as did a
large number of God-fear-
ing Greeks and not a few
prominent women.
5But the Jews were jeal-
ous; so they rounded up
some bad characters from
the marketplace, formed a
mob and started a riot in the
city. They rushed to Ja-
son's house in search of
Paul and Silas in order to
bring them out to the
crowd.[i] 6But when they
did not find them, they
dragged Jason and some
other brothers before the
city officials, shouting:
"These men who have
caused trouble all over the
world have now come here,
7and Jason has welcomed
them into his house. They
are all defying Caesar's decrees, saying that there is
another king, one called
Jesus." 8When they heard
this, the crowd and the city

[h]3 Or *Messiah*
[i]5 Or *the assembly of the people*

ties who heard these
things.
9And when they had re-
ceived a pledge from Jason
and the others, they
released them.

Paul at Berea

10And the brethren
immediately sent Paul and
Silas away by night to
Berea; and when they ar-
rived, they went into the
synagogue of the Jews.
11Now these were more
noble-minded than those in
Thessalonica, for they received the word with great
eagerness, examining the
Scriptures daily, *to see*
whether these things were
so.
12Many of them therefore
believed, along with a number of prominent Greek
women and men.
13But when the Jews of
Thessalonica found out
that the word of God had
been proclaimed by Paul in
Berea also, they came
there likewise, agitating
and stirring up the crowds.
14And then immediately
the brethren sent Paul out
to go as far as the sea; and
Silas and Timothy re-
mained there.
15Now those who con-
ducted Paul brought him as
far as Athens; and receiving a command for Silas
and Timothy to come to
him as soon as possible,
they departed.

Paul at Athens

16Now while Paul was
waiting for them at Athens,
his spirit was being pro-
voked within him as he was
beholding the city full of
idols.
17So he was reasoning in
the synagogue with the
Jews and the God-fearing

τοὺς πολιτάρχας ἀκούοντας ταῦτα, **9** καὶ
the politarchs hearing these things, and
λαβόντες τὸ ἱκανὸν παρὰ τοῦ Ἰάσονος
taking the surety from – Jason
καὶ τῶν λοιπῶν ἀπέλυσαν αὐτούς. **10** Οἱ δὲ
and the rest released them. And the
ἀδελφοὶ εὐθέως διὰ νυκτὸς ἐξέπεμψαν
brothers immediately through (during) [the] night sent forth
τόν τε Παῦλον καὶ τὸν Σιλᾶν εἰς Βέροιαν,
– both Paul and – Silas to Berœa,
οἵτινες παραγενόμενοι εἰς τὴν συναγωγὴν
who having arrived [2]into [3]the synagogue
τῶν Ἰουδαίων ἀπῄεσαν· **11** οὗτοι δὲ ἦσαν
[4]of the [5]Jews [1]went; and these were
εὐγενέστεροι τῶν ἐν Θεσσαλονίκῃ, οἵτινες
more noble [than] the [ones] in Thessalonica, who
ἐδέξαντο τὸν λόγον μετὰ πάσης προθυμίας,
received the word with all eagerness,
[τὸ] καθ' ἡμέραν ἀνακρίνοντες τὰς γραφὰς
– daily examining the scriptures
εἰ ἔχοι ταῦτα οὕτως. **12** πολλοὶ μὲν
if [2]have(are) [1]these things [3]so. Many –
οὖν ἐξ αὐτῶν ἐπίστευσαν, καὶ τῶν
therefore of them believed, and of the
Ἑλληνίδων γυναικῶν τῶν εὐσχημόνων καὶ
[2]Greek [3]women – [1]honourable and
ἀνδρῶν οὐκ ὀλίγοι. **13** Ὡς δὲ ἔγνωσαν
of men not a few. But when [6]knew
οἱ ἀπὸ τῆς Θεσσαλονίκης Ἰουδαῖοι ὅτι
[1]the [3]from – [4]Thessalonica [2]Jews that
καὶ ἐν τῇ Βεροίᾳ κατηγγέλη ὑπὸ τοῦ
also in – Berœa was announced by –
Παύλου ὁ λόγος τοῦ θεοῦ, ἦλθον κἀκεῖ
Paul the word – of God, they came there also
σαλεύοντες καὶ ταράσσοντες τοὺς ὄχλους.
shaking and troubling the crowds.
14 εὐθέως δὲ τότε τὸν Παῦλον ἐξαπέστειλαν
So immediately then – [4]Paul [3]sent away
οἱ ἀδελφοὶ πορεύεσθαι ἕως ἐπὶ τὴν
[1]the [2]brothers to go as far as to the
θάλασσαν· ὑπέμεινάν τε ὅ τε Σιλᾶς καὶ
sea; [1]but [6]remained – [2]both [3]Silas [4]and
ὁ Τιμόθεος ἐκεῖ. **15** οἱ δὲ καθιστάνοντες
– [5]Timothy [7]there. And the [ones] conducting
τὸν Παῦλον ἤγαγον ἕως Ἀθηνῶν, καὶ
– Paul brought [him] as far as Athens, and
λαβόντες ἐντολὴν πρὸς τὸν Σιλᾶν καὶ τὸν
receiving a command to – Silas and –
Τιμόθεον ἵνα ὡς τάχιστα ἔλθωσιν πρὸς
Timothy that as quickly [as possible] they should come to
αὐτὸν ἐξῄεσαν.
him they departed.
16 Ἐν δὲ ταῖς Ἀθήναις ἐκδεχομένου
And in – Athens awaiting
=while Paul awaited them,
αὐτοὺς τοῦ Παύλου, παρωξύνετο τὸ πνεῦμα
them – Paul,[a] [4]was provoked [1]the [2]spirit
αὐτοῦ ἐν αὐτῷ θεωροῦντος κατείδωλον
[3]of him in him beholding [4]full of images
οὖσαν τὴν πόλιν. **17** διελέγετο μὲν οὖν
[5]being [1]the [2]city. He addressed –* therefore
ἐν τῇ συναγωγῇ τοῖς Ἰουδαίοις καὶ
in the synagogue the Jews and

* See note on ch. 12. 5.

officials were thrown into
turmoil. 9Then they made
Jason and the others post
bond and let them go.

In Berea

10As soon as it was night,
the brothers sent Paul and
Silas away to Berea. On arriving there, they went to
the Jewish synagogue.
11Now the Bereans were of
more noble character than
the Thessalonians, for they
received the message with
great eagerness and exam-
ined the Scriptures every
day to see if what Paul said
was true. 12Many of the
Jews believed, as did also a
number of prominent
Greek women and many
Greek men.
13When the Jews in Thes-
salonica learned that Paul
was preaching the word of
God at Berea, they went
there too, agitating the
crowds and stirring them
up. 14The brothers immediately sent Paul to the coast,
but Silas and Timothy
stayed at Berea. 15The men
who escorted Paul brought
him to Athens and then left
with instructions for Silas
and Timothy to join him as
soon as possible.

In Athens

16While Paul was waiting
for them in Athens, he was
greatly distressed to see
that the city was full of
idols. 17So he reasoned in
the synagogue with the
Jews and the God-fearing

Gentiles, and in the market place every day with those who happened to be present.

18And also some of the Epicurean and Stoic philosophers were conversing with him. And some were saying, "What would this idle babbler wish to say?" Others, "He seems to be a proclaimer of strange deities,"—because he was preaching Jesus and the resurrection.

19And they took him and brought him to the Areopagus, saying, "May we know what this new teaching is which you are proclaiming?

20"For you are bringing some strange things to our ears; we want to know therefore what these things mean."

21(Now all the Athenians and the strangers visiting there used to spend their time in nothing other than telling or hearing something new.)

Sermon on Mars Hill

22And Paul stood in the midst of the Areopagus and said, "Men of Athens, I observe that you are very religious in all respects.

23"For while I was passing through and examining the objects of your worship, I also found an altar with this inscription, 'TO AN UNKNOWN GOD.' What therefore you worship in ignorance, this I proclaim to you.

24"The God who made the world and all things in it, since He is Lord of heaven and earth, does not dwell in temples made with hands;

25neither is He served by human hands, as though He needed anything, since He Himself gives to all life and breath and all things;

26and He made from [g]one, every nation of mankind to live on all the face of the earth, having determined *their* appointed

[g] Some later mss. read *one blood*

τοῖς σεβομένοις καὶ ἐν τῇ ἀγορᾷ κατὰ
the [ones] worshipping and in the marketplace –
πᾶσαν ἡμέραν πρὸς τοὺς παρατυγχάνοντας.
every day to the [ones] chancing to be [there].
18 τινὲς δὲ καὶ τῶν Ἐπικουρείων καὶ
But some also of the Epicurean and
Στωϊκῶν φιλοσόφων συνέβαλλον αὐτῷ, καί
Stoic philosophers fell in with him, and
τινες ἔλεγον· τί ἂν θέλοι ὁ σπερμολόγος
some said: What may wish – [2]ignorant plagiarist
οὗτος λέγειν; οἱ δέ· ξένων δαιμονίων
[1]this to say? And others [said]: Of foreign demons
δοκεῖ καταγγελεὺς εἶναι· ὅτι τὸν Ἰησοῦν
he seems an announcer to be; because – Jesus
καὶ τὴν ἀνάστασιν εὐηγγελίζετο. **19** ἐπιλα-
and the resurrection he preached. taking
βόμενοι δὲ αὐτοῦ ἐπὶ τὸν Ἄρειον πάγον
hold And of him to the Areopagus
ἤγαγον, λέγοντες· δυνάμεθα γνῶναι τίς
they led [him], saying: Can we *to* know what
ἡ καινὴ αὕτη ἡ ὑπὸ σοῦ λαλουμένη
[1]this [2]new – [5]by [6]thee [4]being spoken
διδαχή; **20** ξενίζοντα γάρ τινα εἰσφέρεις
[3]teaching [is]? for [2]startling things [1]some thou bringest *in*
εἰς τὰς ἀκοὰς ἡμῶν· βουλόμεθα οὖν
to the ears of us; we are minded therefore
γνῶναι τίνα θέλει ταῦτα εἶναι. **21** Ἀθηναῖοι
to know what wish*es* these things to be. [2]Athenians
δὲ πάντες καὶ οἱ ἐπιδημοῦντες ξένοι εἰς
Now [1]all [3]and [4]the [6]dwelling [5]strangers [8]for
οὐδὲν ἕτερον ηὐκαίρουν ἢ λέγειν τι ἢ
[9]nothing [10]different [7]have leisure either to say something or
ἀκούειν τι καινότερον. **22** Σταθεὶς δὲ
to hear something newer. And standing
Παῦλος ἐν μέσῳ τοῦ Ἀρείου πάγου
[5]Paul [1]in [2][the] midst [3]of the [4]Areopagus
ἔφη· ἄνδρες Ἀθηναῖοι, κατὰ πάντα ὡς
said: *Men* Athenians, in everything how
δεισιδαιμονεστέρους ὑμᾶς θεωρῶ. **23** διερχόμενος
very religious [2]you [1]I behold. passing along
γὰρ καὶ ἀναθεωρῶν τὰ σεβάσματα ὑμῶν
For and looking up at the objects of worship of you
εὗρον καὶ βωμὸν ἐν ᾧ ἐπεγέγραπτο·
I found also an altar in which had been inscribed:
ΑΓΝΩΣΤΩ ΘΕΩ. ὃ οὖν ἀγνοοῦντες
TO AN UNKNOWN GOD. What therefore being ignorant
εὐσεβεῖτε, τοῦτο ἐγὼ καταγγέλλω ὑμῖν.
ye reverence, this I announce to you.
24 ὁ θεὸς ὁ ποιήσας τὸν κόσμον καὶ
The God the [one] having made the world and
πάντα τὰ ἐν αὐτῷ, οὗτος οὐρανοῦ καὶ
all the things in it, this one [3]of heaven [4]and
γῆς ὑπάρχων κύριος οὐκ ἐν χειροποιήτοις
[5]of earth [1]being [2]lord [2]not [3]in [4]hand-made
ναοῖς κατοικεῖ, **25** οὐδὲ ὑπὸ χειρῶν
[5]shrines [1]dwells, nor [2]by [4]hands
ἀνθρωπίνων θεραπεύεται προσδεόμενός
[3]human [1]is served having need
τινος, αὐτὸς διδοὺς πᾶσι ζωὴν καὶ πνοὴν
of anything, he giving to all life and breath
καὶ τὰ πάντα· **26** ἐποίησέν τε ἐξ ἑνὸς
and – all things; and he made of one
πᾶν ἔθνος ἀνθρώπων κατοικεῖν ἐπὶ παντὸς
every nation of men to dwell on all
προσώπου τῆς γῆς, ὁρίσας προστεταγμένους
[the] face of the earth, fixing *having been* appointed

Greeks, as well as in the
marketplace day by day
with those who happened
to be there. 18A group of
Epicurean and Stoic philosophers began to dispute
with him. Some of them
asked, "What is this bab-
bler trying to say?" Others
remarked, "He seems to be
advocating foreign gods."
They said this because Paul
was preaching the good
news about Jesus and the
resurrection. 19Then they
took him and brought him
to a meeting of the Areopagus, where they said to
him, "May we know what
this new teaching is that
you are presenting? 20You
are bringing some strange
ideas to our ears, and we
want to know what they
mean." 21(All the Atheni-
ans and the foreigners who
lived there spent their time
doing nothing but talking
about and listening to the
latest ideas.)

22Paul then stood up in
the meeting of the Areopagus and said: "Men of Athens! I see that in every way
you are very religious.
23For as I walked around
and looked carefully at
your objects of worship, I
even found an altar with
this inscription: TO AN UN-
KNOWN GOD. Now what you
worship as something un-
known I am going to pro-
claim to you.

24"The God who made
the world and everything in
it is the Lord of heaven and
earth and does not live in
temples built by hands.
25And he is not served by
human hands, as if he needed anything, because he
himself gives all men life
and breath and everything
else. 26From one man he
made every nation of men,
that they should inhabit the
whole earth; and he determined the times set for

times, and the boundaries
of their habitation,
27that they should seek
God, if perhaps they might
grope for Him and find
Him, though He is not far
from each one of us;
28for in Him we live and
move and exist, as even
some of your own poets
have said, 'For we also are
His offspring.'
29"Being then the off-
spring of God, we ought not
to think that the Divine Nature is like gold or silver or
stone, an image formed by
the art and thought of man.
30"Therefore having
overlooked the times of ignorance, God is now de-
claring to men that all
everywhere should repent,
31because He has fixed a
day in which He will judge
the world in righteousness
through a Man whom He
has appointed, having furnished proof to all men by
raising Him from the
dead."
32Now when they heard
of the resurrection of the
dead, some *began* to sneer,
but others said, "We shall
hear you again concerning
this."
33So Paul went out of
their midst.
34But some men joined
him and believed, among
whom also were Dionysius
the Areopagite and a
woman named Damaris
and others with them.

καιροὺς καὶ τὰς ὁροθεσίας τῆς κατοικίας
seasons and the boundaries of the dwelling
αὐτῶν, 27 ζητεῖν τὸν θεόν, εἰ ἄρα γε
of them, to seek – God, if perchance
ψηλαφήσειαν αὐτὸν καὶ εὕροιεν, καὶ γε
they might feel after him and might find, though
οὐ μακρὰν ἀπὸ ἑνὸς ἑκάστου ἡμῶν
[2]not [3]far [4]from [5]one [6]each [7]of us
ὑπάρχοντα. 28 ἐν αὐτῷ γὰρ ζῶμεν καὶ
[1]being. [2]in [3]him [1]For we live and
κινούμεθα καὶ ἐσμέν, ὡς καί τινες τῶν
move and are, as indeed some of the
καθ' ὑμᾶς ποιητῶν εἰρήκασιν· τοῦ γὰρ
[2]among [3]you [1]poets have said: [3]of him [1]For
καὶ γένος ἐσμέν. 29 γένος οὖν ὑπάρχοντες
[2]also [5]offspring [4]we are. Offspring therefore being
τοῦ θεοῦ οὐκ ὀφείλομεν νομίζειν, χρυσῷ
– of God we ought not to suppose, [5]*to* gold
ἢ ἀργύρῳ ἢ λίθῳ, χαράγματι τέχνης
[6]or [7]*to* silver [8]or [9]*to* stone, [10]*to* an engraved work [11]of art
καὶ ἐνθυμήσεως ἀνθρώπου, τὸ θεῖον εἶναι
[12]and [13]of meditation [14]of man, [1]the [2]divine nature [3]to be
ὅμοιον. 30 τοὺς μὲν οὖν χρόνους τῆς
[4]like. [5]The [1]so [2]then [6]times –
ἀγνοίας ὑπεριδὼν ὁ θεὸς τὰ νῦν
[7]of ignorance [4]having overlooked – [3]God – now
ἀπαγγέλλει τοῖς ἀνθρώποις πάντας πανταχοῦ
declares – to men all men everywhere
μετανοεῖν, 31 καθότι ἔστησεν ἡμέραν ἐν
to repent, because he set a day in
ᾗ μέλλει κρίνειν τὴν οἰκουμένην ἐν
which he is about to judge the inhabited earth in
δικαιοσύνῃ, ἐν ἀνδρὶ ᾧ ὥρισεν, πίστιν
righteousness, by a man whom he designated, [2]a guarantee
παρασχὼν πᾶσιν ἀναστήσας αὐτὸν ἐκ
[1]offering to all having raised up him out of
νεκρῶν. 32 ἀκούσαντες δὲ ἀνάστασιν
[the] dead. And hearing [of] a resurrection
νεκρῶν, οἱ μὲν ἐχλεύαζον, οἱ δὲ εἶπαν·
of dead persons, some scoffed, others said:
ἀκουσόμεθά σου περὶ τούτου καὶ πάλιν.
We will hear thee concerning this also **again.**
33 οὕτως ὁ Παῦλος ἐξῆλθεν ἐκ μέσου
Thus – Paul went forth from [the] midst
αὐτῶν. 34 τινὲς δὲ ἄνδρες κολληθέντες
of them. But some men adhering
αὐτῷ ἐπίστευσαν, ἐν οἷς καὶ Διονύσιος
to him believed, among whom both Dionysius
ὁ Ἀρεοπαγίτης καὶ γυνὴ ὀνόματι Δάμαρις
the Areopagite and a woman by name Damaris
καὶ ἕτεροι σὺν αὐτοῖς.
and others with them.

them and the exact places
where they should live.
27God did this so that men
would seek him and per-
haps reach out for him and
find him, though he is not
far from each one of us.
28'For in him we live and
move and have our being.'
As some of your own poets
have said, 'We are his offspring.'
29"Therefore since we
are God's offspring, we
should not think that the divine being is like gold or silver or stone—an image
made by man's design and
skill. 30In the past God
overlooked such igno-
rance, but now he com-
mands all people every-
where to repent. 31For he
has set a day when he will
judge the world with justice
by the man he has appointed. He has given proof of
this to all men by raising
him from the dead."
32When they heard about
the resurrection of the
dead, some of them
sneered, but others said,
"We want to hear you
again on this subject." 33At
that, Paul left the Council.
34A few men became fol-
lowers of Paul and be-
lieved. Among them was
Dionysius, a member of the
Areopagus, also a woman
named Damaris, and a
number of others.

Chapter 18

Paul at Corinth

AFTER these things he
left Athens and went
to Corinth.
2And he found a certain
Jew named Aquila, a native
of Pontus, having recently
come from Italy with his
wife Priscilla, because

18 Μετὰ ταῦτα χωρισθεὶς ἐκ τῶν
After these things departing out of –
Ἀθηνῶν ἦλθεν εἰς Κόρινθον. 2 καὶ
Athens he came to Corinth. And
εὑρών τινα Ἰουδαῖον ὀνόματι Ἀκύλαν,
finding a certain Jew by name Aquila,
Ποντικὸν τῷ γένει, προσφάτως ἐληλυθότα
belonging to Pontus – by race, recently having come
ἀπὸ τῆς Ἰταλίας, καὶ Πρίσκιλλαν γυναῖκα
from – Italy, and Priscilla wife

Chapter 18

In Corinth

AFTER this, Paul left
Athens and went to
Corinth. 2There he met a
Jew named Aquila, a native
of Pontus, who had recently come from Italy with his
wife Priscilla, because

Claudius had commanded
all the Jews to leave Rome.
He came to them,
3and because he was of
the same trade, he stayed
with them and they were
working; for by trade they
were tent-makers.
4And he was reasoning
in the synagogue every
Sabbath and trying to persuade Jews and Greeks.
5But when Silas and
Timothy came down from
Macedonia, Paul *began* devoting himself completely
to the word, solemnly testifying to the Jews that Jesus
was the Christ.
6And when they resisted
and blasphemed, he shook
out his garments and said to
them, "Your blood *be*
upon your own heads! I am
clean. From now on I shall
go to the Gentiles."
7And he departed from
there and went to the house
of a certain man named
Titius Justus, a worshiper
of God, whose house was
next to the synagogue.
8And Crispus, the leader
of the synagogue, believed
in the Lord with all his
household, and many of the
Corinthians when they
heard were believing and
being baptized.
9And the Lord said to
Paul in the night by a vision, "Do not be afraid *any
longer*, but go on speaking
and do not be silent;
10for I am with you, and
no man will attack you in
order to harm you, for I
have many people in this
city."
11And he settled *there* a
year and six months, teaching the word of God among
them.
12But while Gallio was

αὐτοῦ, διὰ τὸ διατεταχέναι Κλαύδιον
of him, because of the to have commanded Claudius[b]
=because Claudius had commanded
χωρίζεσθαι πάντας τοὺς Ἰουδαίους ἀπὸ
to depart all the Jews from
τῆς Ῥώμης, προσῆλθεν αὐτοῖς, 3 καὶ
– Rome, he came to them, and
διὰ τὸ ὁμότεχνον εἶναι ἔμενεν παρ᾽
because of the of the same trade to be[b] he remained with
=because [he] was of the same trade
αὐτοῖς, καὶ ἠργάζοντο· ἦσαν γὰρ σκηνοποιοὶ
them, and they wrought; for they were tentmakers
τῇ τέχνῃ. 4 διελέγετο δὲ ἐν τῇ συναγωγῇ
– by trade. And he lectured in the synagogue
κατὰ πᾶν σάββατον, ἔπειθέν τε Ἰουδαίους
on every sabbath, he persuaded both Jews
καὶ Ἕλληνας. 5 Ὡς δὲ κατῆλθον ἀπὸ
and Greeks. And when came down from
τῆς Μακεδονίας ὅ τε Σιλᾶς καὶ ὁ
– Macedonia – both Silas and –
Τιμόθεος, συνείχετο τῷ λόγῳ ὁ Παῦλος,
Timothy, was pressed by the word – Paul,
διαμαρτυρόμενος τοῖς Ἰουδαίοις εἶναι τὸν
solemnly witnessing to the Jews to be the
=that Jesus was the Christ.
χριστὸν Ἰησοῦν. 6 ἀντιτασσομένων δὲ αὐτῶν
Christ Jesus. But resisting them
=when they resisted and blasphemed
καὶ βλασφημούντων ἐκτιναξάμενος τὰ ἱμάτια
and blaspheming[a] shaking off the(his) garments
εἶπεν πρὸς αὐτούς· τὸ αἷμα ὑμῶν ἐπὶ
he said to them: The blood of you on
τὴν κεφαλὴν ὑμῶν· καθαρὸς ἐγὼ ἀπὸ
the head of you; clean I from
τοῦ νῦν εἰς τὰ ἔθνη πορεύσομαι. 7 καὶ
– now to the nations will go. And
μεταβὰς ἐκεῖθεν ἦλθεν εἰς οἰκίαν τινὸς
removing thence he went into [the] house of one
ὀνόματι Τιτίου Ἰούστου σεβομένου τὸν
by name Titius Justus worshipping –
θεόν, οὗ ἡ οἰκία ἦν συνομοροῦσα τῇ
God, of whom the house was being next door to the
συναγωγῇ. 8 Κρίσπος δὲ ὁ ἀρχισυνάγωγος
synagogue. Now Crispus the synagogue ruler
ἐπίστευσεν τῷ κυρίῳ σὺν ὅλῳ τῷ οἴκῳ
believed the Lord with all the household
αὐτοῦ, καὶ πολλοὶ τῶν Κορινθίων ἀκούοντες
of him, and many of the Corinthians hearing
ἐπίστευον καὶ ἐβαπτίζοντο. 9 Εἶπεν δὲ
believed and were baptized. And said
ὁ κύριος ἐν νυκτὶ δι᾽ ὁράματος τῷ
the Lord in [the] night through a vision –
Παύλῳ· μὴ φοβοῦ, ἀλλὰ λάλει καὶ
to Paul: Do not fear, but speak and
μὴ σιωπήσῃς, 10 διότι ἐγώ εἰμι μετὰ σοῦ
keep not silence, because I am with thee
καὶ οὐδεὶς ἐπιθήσεταί σοι τοῦ κακῶσαί
and no one shall set on thee – to illtreat[d]
σε, διότι λαός ἐστί μοι πολὺς ἐν
thee, because people is to me much[e] in
=I have a great people
τῇ πόλει ταύτῃ. 11 Ἐκάθισεν δὲ ἐνιαυτὸν
this city. And he sat a year
καὶ μῆνας ἓξ διδάσκων ἐν αὐτοῖς τὸν
and months six teaching among them the
λόγον τοῦ θεοῦ. 12 Γαλλίωνος δὲ
word – of God. And Gallio
=when Gallio

Claudius had ordered all
the Jews to leave Rome.
Paul went to see them, 3and
because he was a tentmak-
er as they were, he stayed
and worked with them.
4Every Sabbath he rea-
soned in the synagogue,
trying to persuade Jews
and Greeks.
5When Silas and Timothy
came from Macedonia,
Paul devoted himself exclusively to preaching, testifying to the Jews that Jesus
was the Christ.[j] 6But when
the Jews opposed Paul and
became abusive, he shook
out his clothes in protest
and said to them, "Your
blood be on your own
heads! I am clear of my responsibility. From now on
I will go to the Gentiles."
7Then Paul left the syna-
gogue and went next door
to the house of Titius Justus, a worshiper of God.
8Crispus, the synagogue
ruler, and his entire household believed in the Lord;
and many of the Corinthi-
ans who heard him be-
lieved and were baptized.
9One night the Lord
spoke to Paul in a vision:
"Do not be afraid; keep on
speaking, do not be silent.
10For I am with you, and no
one is going to attack and
harm you, because I have
many people in this city."
11So Paul stayed for a year
and a half, teaching them
the word of God.
12While Gallio was pro-

[j] Or *Messiah;* also in verse 28

proconsul of Achaia, the
Jews with one accord rose
up against Paul and brought
him before the judgment
seat,
13 saying, "This man per-
suades men to worship God
contrary to the law."
14 But when Paul was
about to open his mouth,
Gallio said to the Jews, "If
it were a matter of wrong or
of vicious crime, O Jews, it
would be reasonable for me
to put up with you;
15 but if there are ques-
tions about words and
names and your own law,
look after it yourselves; I
am unwilling to be a judge
of these matters."
16 And he drove them
away from the judgment
seat.
17 And they all took hold
of Sosthenes, the leader of
the synagogue, and *began*
beating him in front of the
judgment seat. And Gallio
was not concerned about
any of these things.
18 And Paul, having re-
mained many days longer,
took leave of the brethren
and put out to sea for Syria,
and with him were Priscilla
and Aquila. In Cenchrea he
had his hair cut, for he was
keeping a vow.
19 And they came to Ephe-
sus, and he left them there.
Now he himself entered the
synagogue and reasoned
with the Jews.
20 And when they asked
him to stay for a longer
time, he did not consent,
21 but taking leave of them
and saying, "I will return to
you again if God wills," he
set sail from Ephesus.
22 And when he had land-
ed at Caesarea, he went up
and greeted the church,

ἀνθυπάτου ὄντος τῆς Ἀχαΐας κατεπέστησαν
proconsul being[a] – of Achaia [4]set on
was proconsul

ὁμοθυμαδὸν οἱ Ἰουδαῖοι τῷ Παύλῳ καὶ
[3]with one mind [1]the [2]Jews – Paul and

ἤγαγον αὐτὸν ἐπὶ τὸ βῆμα, 13 λέγοντες
brought him to the tribunal, saying[,]

ὅτι παρὰ τὸν νόμον ἀναπείθει οὗτος
– [6][differently] from [7]the [8]law [2]urges [1]This man

τοὺς ἀνθρώπους σέβεσθαι τὸν θεόν.
– [3]men [4]to worship – [5]God.

14 μέλλοντος δὲ τοῦ Παύλου ἀνοίγειν τὸ
And being about – Paul[a] to open the(his)
=when Paul was about

στόμα εἶπεν ὁ Γαλλίων πρὸς τοὺς
mouth said – Gallio to the

Ἰουδαίους· εἰ μὲν ἦν ἀδίκημά τι
Jews: If indeed it was crime some

ἢ ῥᾳδιούργημα πονηρόν, ὦ Ἰουδαῖοι,
or villainy evil, O Jews,

κατὰ λόγον ἂν ἀνεσχόμην ὑμῶν· 15 εἰ δὲ ζητή-
rightly I would endure you; but if ques-

ματά ἐστιν περὶ λόγου καὶ ὀνομάτων καὶ
tions it is concerning a word and names and

νόμου τοῦ καθ' ὑμᾶς, ὄψεσθε αὐτοί·
law the according to you, ye will see [your]selves;
=your law,

κριτὴς ἐγὼ τούτων οὐ βούλομαι εἶναι.
a judge [1]I [4]of these things [2]do not intend [3]to be.

16 καὶ ἀπήλασεν αὐτοὺς ἀπὸ τοῦ βήματος.
And he drove away them from the tribunal.

17 ἐπιλαβόμενοι δὲ πάντες Σωσθένην τὸν
But [2]seizing [1]all Sosthenes the

ἀρχισυνάγωγον ἔτυπτον ἔμπροσθεν τοῦ
synagogue ruler they struck [him] in front of the

βήματος· καὶ οὐδὲν τούτων τῷ Γαλλίωνι
tribunal; and not one of these things – [2]to Gallio

ἔμελεν. 18 Ὁ δὲ Παῦλος ἔτι προσμείνας
[1]mattered. – But Paul yet having remained

ἡμέρας ἱκανάς, τοῖς ἀδελφοῖς ἀποταξάμενος
days many, to the brothers bidding farewell

ἐξέπλει εἰς τὴν Συρίαν, καὶ σὺν αὐτῷ
he sailed away to – Syria, and with him

Πρίσκιλλα καὶ Ἀκύλας, κειράμενος ἐν
Priscilla and Aquila, having shorn in

Κεγχρεαῖς τὴν κεφαλήν· εἶχεν γὰρ εὐχήν.
Cenchrea the(his) head; for he had a vow.

19 κατήντησαν δὲ εἰς Ἔφεσον, κἀκείνους
And they came down to Ephesus, and those

κατέλιπεν αὐτοῦ, αὐτὸς δὲ εἰσελθὼν εἰς
he left there, but he entering into

τὴν συναγωγὴν διελέξατο τοῖς Ἰουδαίοις.
the synagogue lectured to the Jews.

20 ἐρωτώντων δὲ αὐτῶν ἐπὶ πλείονα
And asking them[a] over a more(longer)
=as they asked

χρόνον μεῖναι οὐκ ἐπένευσεν, 21 ἀλλὰ
time to remain he consented not, but

ἀποταξάμενος καὶ εἰπών· πάλιν ἀνακάμψω
bidding farewell and saying: Again I will return

πρὸς ὑμᾶς τοῦ θεοῦ θέλοντος, ἀνήχθη
to you – God willing,[a] he set sail
=if God wills,

ἀπὸ τῆς Ἐφέσου, 22 καὶ κατελθὼν εἰς
from – Ephesus, and coming down to

Καισάρειαν, ἀναβὰς καὶ ἀσπασάμενος τὴν
Cæsarea, going up and greeting the

consul of Achaia, the Jews
made a united attack on
Paul and brought him into
court. 13 "This man," they
charged, "is persuading the
people to worship God in
ways contrary to the law."
14 Just as Paul was about
to speak, Gallio said to the
Jews, "If you Jews were
making a complaint about
some misdemeanor or seri-
ous crime, it would be reasonable for me to listen to
you. 15 But since it involves
questions about words and
names and your own law—
settle the matter your-
selves. I will not be a judge
of such things." 16 So he
had them ejected from the
court. 17 Then they all
turned on Sosthenes the
synagogue ruler and beat
him in front of the court.
But Gallio showed no con-
cern whatever.

Priscilla, Aquila and Apollos

18 Paul stayed on in Cor-
inth for some time. Then he
left the brothers and sailed
for Syria, accompanied by
Priscilla and Aquila. Before
he sailed, he had his hair
cut off at Cenchrea because
of a vow he had taken.
19 They arrived at Ephesus,
where Paul left Priscilla
and Aquila. He himself
went into the synagogue
and reasoned with the
Jews. 20 When they asked
him to spend more time
with them, he declined.
21 But as he left, he promised, "I will come back if it
is God's will." Then he set
sail from Ephesus. 22 When
he landed at Caesarea, he
went up and greeted the

and went down to Antioch.

Third Missionary Journey

23And having spent some
time *there,* he departed
and passed successively
through the Galatian region
and Phrygia, strengthening
all the disciples.
24Now a certain Jew
named Apollos, an Alexan-
drian by birth, an eloquent
man, came to Ephesus; and
he was mighty in the Scriptures.
25This man had been in-
structed in the way of the
Lord; and being fervent in
spirit, he was speaking and
teaching accurately the
things concerning Jesus,
being acquainted only with
the baptism of John;
26and he began to speak
out boldly in the syna-
gogue. But when Priscilla
and Aquila heard him, they
took him aside and ex-
plained to him the way of
God more accurately.
27And when he wanted to
go across to Achaia, the
brethren encouraged him
and wrote to the disciples
to welcome him; and when
he had arrived, he helped
greatly those who had be-
lieved through grace;
28for he powerfully refuted the Jews in public,
demonstrating by the
Scriptures that Jesus was
the Christ.

ἐκκλησίαν, κατέβη εἰς Ἀντιόχειαν, 23 καὶ
church, he went down to Antioch, and
ποιήσας χρόνον τινὰ ἐξῆλθεν, διερχόμενος
having spent time some he went forth, passing through
καθεξῆς τὴν Γαλατικὴν χώραν καὶ Φρυγίαν,
in order the Galatian country and Phrygia,
στηρίζων πάντας τοὺς μαθητάς.
confirming all the disciples.
24 Ἰουδαῖος δέ τις Ἀπολλῶς ὀνόματι,
And a certain Jew Apollos by name,
Ἀλεξανδρεὺς τῷ γένει, ἀνὴρ λόγιος,
an Alexandrian – by race, a man eloquent,
κατήντησεν εἰς Ἔφεσον, δυνατὸς ὢν ἐν
came to Ephesus, powerful being in
ταῖς γραφαῖς. 25 οὗτος ἦν κατηχημένος
the scriptures. This man was orally instructed [in]
τὴν ὁδὸν τοῦ κυρίου, καὶ ζέων τῷ
the way of the Lord, and burning –
πνεύματι ἐλάλει καὶ ἐδίδασκεν ἀκριβῶς
in spirit he spoke and taught accurately
τὰ περὶ τοῦ Ἰησοῦ, ἐπιστάμενος
the things concerning – Jesus, understanding
μόνον τὸ βάπτισμα Ἰωάννου· 26 οὗτός τε
only the baptism of John; and this man
ἤρξατο παρρησιάζεσθαι ἐν τῇ συναγωγῇ.
began to speak boldly in the synagogue.
ἀκούσαντες δὲ αὐτοῦ Πρίσκιλλα καὶ
And hearing him Priscilla and
Ἀκύλας προσελάβοντο αὐτὸν καὶ ἀκριβέστε-
Aquila took him and more accurate-
ρον αὐτῷ ἐξέθεντο τὴν ὁδὸν τοῦ θεοῦ.
ly to him explained the way – of God.
27 βουλομένου δὲ αὐτοῦ διελθεῖν εἰς τὴν
And intending him[a] to go through into –
=when he intended
Ἀχαΐαν, προτρεψάμενοι οἱ ἀδελφοὶ ἔγραψαν
Achaia, being encouraged the brothers wrote
τοῖς μαθηταῖς ἀποδέξασθαι αὐτόν· ὃς
to the disciples to welcome him; who
παραγενόμενος συνεβάλετο πολὺ τοῖς
arriving contributed much to the [ones]
πεπιστευκόσιν διὰ τῆς χάριτος· 28 εὐτόνως
having believed through – grace; [2]vehemently
γὰρ τοῖς Ἰουδαίοις διακατηλέγχετο δημοσίᾳ
[1]for [4]the [5]Jews [3]he confuted publicly
ἐπιδεικνὺς διὰ τῶν γραφῶν εἶναι τὸν
proving through the scriptures [2]to be [3]the
χριστὸν Ἰησοῦν.
[4]Christ [1]Jesus.

church and then went down
to Antioch.
23After spending some
time in Antioch, Paul set
out from there and traveled
from place to place
throughout the region of
Galatia and Phrygia,
strengthening all the disciples.
24Meanwhile a Jew
named Apollos, a native of
Alexandria, came to Ephe-
sus. He was a learned man,
with a thorough knowledge
of the Scriptures. 25He had
been instructed in the way
of the Lord, and he spoke
with great fervor[k] and
taught about Jesus accu-
rately, though he knew
only the baptism of John.
26He began to speak boldly
in the synagogue. When
Priscilla and Aquila heard
him, they invited him to
their home and explained
to him the way of God more
adequately.
27When Apollos wanted
to go to Achaia, the brothers encouraged him and
wrote to the disciples there
to welcome him. On arriv-
ing, he was a great help to
those who by grace had believed. 28For he vigorously
refuted the Jews in public
debate, proving from the
Scriptures that Jesus was
the Christ.

Chapter 19

Paul at Ephesus

AND it came about that
while Apollos was at
Corinth, Paul having
passed through the upper
country came to Ephesus
and found some disciples,
2and he said to them,
"Did you receive the Holy
Spirit when you believed?"
And they *said* to him, "No,
we have not even heard
whether there is a Holy
Spirit."
3And he said, "Into what

19 Ἐγένετο δὲ ἐν τῷ τὸν Ἀπολλῶ
Now it came to pass in the – Apollos
=while Apollos was
εἶναι ἐν Κορίνθῳ Παῦλον διελθόντα τὰ
to be[be] in Corinth Paul having passed through the
ἀνωτερικὰ μέρη ἐλθεῖν εἰς Ἔφεσον καὶ
higher parts to come[b] to Ephesus and
εὑρεῖν τινας μαθητάς, 2 εἶπέν τε πρὸς
to find[b] some disciples, and said to
αὐτούς· εἰ πνεῦμα ἅγιον ἐλάβετε πιστεύσαν-
them: If Spirit Holy ye received believ-
τες; οἱ δὲ πρὸς αὐτόν· ἀλλ' οὐδ' εἰ
ing? And they [said] to him: But [2]not [3]if
πνεῦμα ἅγιον ἔστιν ἠκούσαμεν. 3 εἶπέν τε·
[6]Spirit [5]Holy [4]there is [1]we heard. And he said:

Chapter 19

Paul in Ephesus

WHILE Apollos was at
Corinth, Paul took
the road through the interi-
or and arrived at Ephesus.
There he found some disciples 2and asked them, "Did
you receive the Holy Spirit
when[l] you believed?"
They answered, "No, we
have not even heard that
there is a Holy Spirit."
3So Paul asked, "Then

[k]25 Or *with fervor in the Spirit*
[l]2 Or *after*

then were you baptized?" And they said, "Into John's baptism."

4And Paul said, "John baptized with the baptism of repentance, telling the people to believe in Him who was coming after him, that is, in Jesus."

5And when they heard this, they were baptized in the name of the Lord Jesus.

6And when Paul had laid his hands upon them, the Holy Spirit came on them, and they *began* speaking with tongues and prophesying.

7And there were in all about twelve men.

8And he entered the synagogue and continued speaking out boldly for three months, reasoning and persuading *them* about the kingdom of God.

9But when some were becoming hardened and disobedient, speaking evil of the Way before the multitude, he withdrew from them and took away the disciples, reasoning daily in the school of Tyrannus.

10And this took place for two years, so that all who lived in Asia heard the word of the Lord, both Jews and Greeks.

Miracles at Ephesus

11And God was performing extraordinary miracles by the hands of Paul,

12so that handkerchiefs or aprons were even carried from his body to the sick, and the diseases left them and the evil spirits went out.

13But also some of the Jewish exorcists, who went from place to place, attempted to name over those who had the evil

εἰς τί οὖν ἐβαπτίσθητε; οἱ δὲ εἶπαν·
To what therefore were ye baptized? And they said:
εἰς τὸ Ἰωάννου βάπτισμα. 4 εἶπεν δὲ
To the of John baptism. And said
Παῦλος· Ἰωάννης ἐβάπτισεν βάπτισμα μετα-
Paul: John baptized [with] a baptism of repent-
νοίας, τῷ λαῷ λέγων εἰς τὸν ἐρχόμενον
ance, [2]to the [3]people [1]saying [8]in [7]the [one] [6]coming
μετ' αὐτὸν ἵνα πιστεύσωσιν, τοῦτ' ἔστιν
[9]after [10]him [4]that [5]they should believe, this is
εἰς τὸν Ἰησοῦν. 5 ἀκούσαντες δὲ ἐβαπτίσ-
in – Jesus. And hearing they were
θησαν εἰς τὸ ὄνομα τοῦ κυρίου Ἰησοῦ.
baptized in the name of the Lord Jesus.
6 καὶ ἐπιθέντος αὐτοῖς τοῦ Παύλου χεῖρας
And laying on them – Paul hands[a]
=as Paul laid [his] hands on them
ἦλθε τὸ πνεῦμα τὸ ἅγιον ἐπ' αὐτούς,
came the Spirit – Holy on them,
ἐλάλουν τε γλώσσαις καὶ ἐπροφήτευον.
and they spoke in tongues and prophesied.
7 ἦσαν δὲ οἱ πάντες ἄνδρες ὡσεὶ δώδεκα.
And [4]were [2]the [1]all [3]men about twelve.
8 Εἰσελθὼν δὲ εἰς τὴν συναγωγὴν
And entering into the synagogue
ἐπαρρησιάζετο ἐπὶ μῆνας τρεῖς διαλεγόμενος
he spoke boldly over months three lecturing
καὶ πείθων περὶ τῆς βασιλείας τοῦ θεοῦ.
and persuading concerning the kingdom – of God.
9 ὡς δέ τινες ἐσκληρύνοντο καὶ ἠπείθουν
But as some were hardened and disobeyed
κακολογοῦντες τὴν ὁδὸν ἐνώπιον τοῦ
speaking ill [of] the way before the
πλήθους, ἀποστὰς ἀπ' αὐτῶν ἀφώρισεν
multitude, withdrawing from them he separated
τοὺς μαθητάς, καθ' ἡμέραν διαλεγόμενος
the disciples, daily lecturing
ἐν τῇ σχολῇ Τυράννου. 10 τοῦτο δὲ
in the school of Tyrannus. And this
ἐγένετο ἐπὶ ἔτη δύο, ὥστε πάντας τοὺς
happened over years two, so as all the
=so that all who inhabited
κατοικοῦντας τὴν Ἀσίαν ἀκοῦσαι τὸν
[ones] inhabiting – Asia to hear[b] the
Asia heard
λόγον τοῦ κυρίου, Ἰουδαιους τε καὶ
word of the Lord, [2]Jews [1]both and
Ἕλληνας. 11 Δυνάμεις τε οὐ τὰς τυχούσας
Greeks. And powerful deeds not the ordinary
ὁ θεὸς ἐποίει διὰ τῶν χειρῶν Παύλου,
– God did through the hands of Paul,
12 ὥστε καὶ ἐπὶ τοὺς ἀσθενοῦντας
so as even onto the [ones] ailing
=so that there were even brought away from his skin hand-
ἀποφέρεσθαι ἀπὸ τοῦ χρωτὸς αὐτοῦ
to be brought away from the skin of him
kerchiefs or aprons onto those who ailed and the diseases were rid
σουδάρια ἢ σιμικίνθια καὶ ἀπαλλάσσεσθαι
handkerchiefs or aprons and to be rid
from them, and the evil spirits went out.
ἀπ' αὐτῶν τὰς νόσους, τά τε πνεύματα
from them the diseases, and the spirits
τὰ πονηρὰ ἐκπορεύεσθαι. 13 Ἐπεχείρησαν δέ
evil to go out. But [7]attempted
τινες καὶ τῶν περιερχομένων Ἰουδαίων
[1]some [2]also [3]of the [4]strolling [5]Jews
ἐξορκιστῶν ὀνομάζειν ἐπὶ τοὺς ἔχοντας
[6]exorcists to name over the [ones] having

what baptism did you receive?"

"John's baptism," they replied.

4Paul said, "John's baptism was a baptism of repentance. He told the people to believe in the one coming after him, that is, in Jesus." 5On hearing this, they were baptized into[m] the name of the Lord Jesus. 6When Paul placed his hands on them, the Holy Spirit came on them, and they spoke in tongues[n] and prophesied. 7There were about twelve men in all.

8Paul entered the synagogue and spoke boldly there for three months, arguing persuasively about the kingdom of God. 9But some of them became obstinate; they refused to believe and publicly maligned the Way. So Paul left them. He took the disciples with him and had discussions daily in the lecture hall of Tyrannus. 10This went on for two years, so that all the Jews and Greeks who lived in the province of Asia heard the word of the Lord.

11God did extraordinary miracles through Paul, 12so that even handkerchiefs and aprons that had touched him were taken to the sick, and their illnesses were cured and the evil spirits left them.

13Some Jews who went around driving out evil spirits tried to invoke the name of the Lord Jesus over those who were de-

m5 Or *in*
n6 Or *other languages*

spirits the name of the Lord
Jesus, saying, "I adjure
you by Jesus whom Paul
preaches."
14And seven sons of one
Sceva, a Jewish chief
priest, were doing this.
15And the evil spirit an-
swered and said to them, "I
recognize Jesus, and I
know about Paul, but who
are you?"
16And the man, in whom
was the evil spirit, leaped
on them and subdued all of
them and overpowered
them, so that they fled out
of that house naked and
wounded.
17And this became known
to all, both Jews and
Greeks, who lived in Ephesus; and fear fell upon them
all and the name of the
Lord Jesus was being mag-
nified.
18Many also of those who
had believed kept coming,
confessing and disclosing
their practices.
19And many of those who
practiced magic brought
their books together and
began burning them in the
sight of all; and they counted up the price of them and
found it fifty thousand
pieces of silver.
20So the word of the Lord
was growing mightily and
prevailing.
21Now after these things
were finished, Paul pur-
posed in the spirit to go to
Jerusalem after he had
passed through Macedonia
and Achaia, saying, "After
I have been there, I must
also see Rome."
22And having sent into
Macedonia two of those

τὰ πνεύματα τὰ πονηρὰ τὸ ὄνομα τοῦ
the spirits – evil the name of the
κυρίου Ἰησοῦ λέγοντες· ὁρκίζω ὑμᾶς τὸν
Lord Jesus saying: I exorcise you [by] –
Ἰησοῦν ὃν Παῦλος κηρύσσει. **14** ἦσαν δέ
Jesus whom Paul proclaims. And there were
τινος Σκευᾶ Ἰουδαίου ἀρχιερέως ἑπτὰ
2of one 4Sceva 5a Jewish 6chief priest 1seven
υἱοὶ τοῦτο ποιοῦντες. **15** ἀποκριθὲν δὲ
3sons 8this 7doing. And answering
τὸ πνεῦμα τὸ πονηρὸν εἶπεν αὐτοῖς·
the spirit – evil said to them:
τὸν [μὲν] Ἰησοῦν γινώσκω καὶ τὸν
– 2indeed 1Jesus I know and –
Παῦλον ἐπίσταμαι· ὑμεῖς δὲ τίνες ἐστέ;
Paul I understand; but ye who are?
16 καὶ ἐφαλόμενος ὁ ἄνθρωπος ἐπ' αὐτούς,
And 9leaping *on* 1the 2man 10on 11them,
ἐν ᾧ ἦν τὸ πνεῦμα τὸ πονηρόν,
3in 4whom 5was 6the 8spirit – 7evil,
κατακυριεύσας ἀμφοτέρων ἴσχυσεν κατ'
overmastering both was strong against
αὐτῶν, ὥστε γυμνοὺς καὶ τετραυματισμένους
them, so as naked and *having been* wounded
=so that they escaped out of that house naked and wounded.
ἐκφυγεῖν ἐκ τοῦ οἴκου ἐκείνου. **17** τοῦτο
to escape out of that house. this
δὲ ἐγένετο γνωστὸν πᾶσιν Ἰουδαίοις τε
And became known to all 2Jews 1both
καὶ Ἕλλησιν τοῖς κατοικοῦσιν τὴν Ἔφεσον,
and Greeks – inhabiting – Ephesus,
καὶ ἐπέπεσεν φόβος ἐπὶ πάντας αὐτούς,
and 2fell *on* 1fear 3on 5all 4them,
καὶ ἐμεγαλύνετο τὸ ὄνομα τοῦ κυρίου
and was magnified the name of the Lord
Ἰησοῦ· **18** πολλοί τε τῶν πεπιστευκότων
Jesus; and many of the [ones] having believed
ἤρχοντο ἐξομολογούμενοι καὶ ἀναγγέλλοντες
came confessing and telling
τὰς πράξεις αὐτῶν. **19** ἱκανοὶ δὲ τῶν τὰ
the doings of them. And a consider-able number of the [ones] the
περίεργα πραξάντων συνενέγκαντες τὰς βίβλους
curious things doing bringing together the rolls
κατέκαιον ἐνώπιον πάντων· καὶ συνεψήφισαν
burnt before all; and they reckoned up
τὰς τιμὰς αὐτῶν καὶ εὗρον ἀργυρίου μυριάδας
the prices of them and found [pieces] 3of silver 2thousand
πέντε. **20** Οὕτως κατὰ κράτος τοῦ κυρίου
1five. Thus by might 3of the 4Lord
ὁ λόγος ηὔξανεν καὶ ἴσχυεν.
1the 2word increased and was strong.
21 Ὡς δὲ ἐπληρώθη ταῦτα, ἔθετο ὁ
And when were fulfilled these things, purposed –
Παῦλος ἐν τῷ πνεύματι διελθὼν τὴν
Paul in the(his) spirit passing through –
Μακεδονίαν καὶ Ἀχαΐαν πορεύεσθαι εἰς
Macedonia and Achaia to go to
Ἱεροσόλυμα, εἰπὼν ὅτι μετὰ τὸ γενέσθαι
Jerusalem, saying[,] – After the to become =After I am
με ἐκεῖ δεῖ με καὶ Ῥώμην ἰδεῖν.
me[b] there it behoves me 2also 3Rome 1to see.
22 ἀποστείλας δὲ εἰς Μακεδονίαν δύο
And sending into Macedonia two

mon-possessed. They
would say, "In the name of
Jesus, whom Paul
preaches, I command you
to come out." 14Seven sons
of Sceva, a Jewish chief
priest, were doing this.
15⌊One day⌋ the evil spirit
answered them, "Jesus I
know, and I know about
Paul, but who are you?"
16Then the man who had
the evil spirit jumped on
them and overpowered
them all. He gave them
such a beating that they ran
out of the house naked and
bleeding.
17When this became
known to the Jews and
Greeks living in Ephesus,
they were all seized with
fear, and the name of the
Lord Jesus was held in high
honor. 18Many of those
who believed now came
and openly confessed their
evil deeds. 19A number
who had practiced sorcery
brought their scrolls to-
gether and burned them
publicly. When they calcu-
lated the value of the
scrolls, the total came to
fifty thousand drachmas.[o]
20In this way the word of
the Lord spread widely and
grew in power.
21After all this had hap-
pened, Paul decided to go
to Jerusalem, passing
through Macedonia and
Achaia. "After I have been
there," he said, "I must
visit Rome also." 22He sent
two of his helpers, Timothy

[o]19 A drachma was a silver coin worth about a day's wages.

who ministered to him,
Timothy and Erastus, he
himself stayed in Asia for a
while.
23And about that time
there arose no small disturbance concerning the Way.
24For a certain man
named Demetrius, a silversmith, who made silver
shrines of Artemis, was
bringing no little business
to the craftsmen;
25these he gathered to-
gether with the workmen of
similar *trades,* and said,
"Men, you know that our
prosperity depends upon
this business.
26"And you see and hear
that not only in Ephesus,
but in almost all of Asia,
this Paul has persuaded and
turned away a considerable
number of people, saying
that gods made with hands
are no gods *at all.*
27"And not only is there
danger that this trade of
ours fall into disrepute, but
also that the temple of the
great goddess Artemis be
regarded as worthless and
that she whom all of Asia
and the world worship
should even be dethroned
from her magnificence."
28And when they heard
this and were filled with
rage, they *began* crying
out, saying, "Great is Artemis of the Ephesians!"
29And the city was filled
with the confusion, and
they rushed with one ac-
cord into the theater, dragging along Gaius and Aristarchus, Paul's traveling
companions from Mace-
donia.
30And when Paul wanted
to go into the assembly, the
disciples would not let him.
31And also some of the
[h]Asiarchs who were

[h]I.e., political or religious officials of the province of Asia

τῶν διακονούντων αὐτῷ, Τιμόθεον καὶ
of the [ones] ministering to him, Timothy and

Ἔραστον, αὐτὸς ἐπέσχεν χρόνον εἰς τὴν
Erastus, he delayed a time in –

Ἀσίαν. 23 Ἐγένετο δὲ κατὰ τὸν καιρὸν
Asia. Now there was about – time

ἐκεῖνον τάραχος οὐκ ὀλίγος περὶ τῆς
that [3]trouble [1]no [2]little concerning the

ὁδοῦ. 24 Δημήτριος γάρ τις ὀνόματι,
way. For [2]Demetrius [1]one by name,

ἀργυροκόπος, ποιῶν ναοὺς ἀργυροῦς
a silversmith, making shrines silver

Ἀρτέμιδος παρείχετο τοῖς τεχνίταις οὐκ
of Artemis provided the artisans no

ὀλίγην ἐργασίαν, 25 οὓς συναθροίσας καὶ
little trade, [2]whom [1]assembling also

τοὺς περὶ τὰ τοιαῦτα ἐργάτας εἶπεν·
[1]the [3]about(in) – [4]such things [2]workmen said:

ἄνδρες, ἐπίστασθε ὅτι ἐκ ταύτης τῆς
Men, ye understand that from this –

ἐργασίας ἡ εὐπορία ἡμῖν ἐστιν, 26 καὶ
trade the gain to us is,[c] and
=we have [our] gain,

θεωρεῖτε καὶ ἀκούετε ὅτι οὐ μόνον
ye behold and hear that [7]not [8]only

Ἐφέσου ἀλλὰ σχεδὸν πάσης τῆς Ἀσίας
[9]of Ephesus [10]but [11]almost [12]of all – [13]Asia

ὁ Παῦλος οὗτος πείσας μετέστησεν ἱκανὸν
– [2]Paul [1]this [3]having persuaded [4]perverted [5]a considerable

ὄχλον, λέγων ὅτι οὐκ εἰσὶν θεοὶ οἱ διὰ
[6]crowd, saying that they are not gods [1]the [ones] [3]through

χειρῶν γινόμενοι. 27 οὐ μόνον δὲ τοῦτο
[4]hands [2]coming into being. [2]not [3]only [1]Now [4]this

κινδυνεύει ἡμῖν τὸ μέρος εἰς ἀπελεγμὸν
[6]is in danger to us the share[c] [8]into [9]disrepute
=[5]our share

ἐλθεῖν, ἀλλὰ καὶ τὸ τῆς μεγάλης θεᾶς
[7]to come, but also [1]the [3]of the [4]great [5]goddess

Ἀρτέμιδος ἱερὸν εἰς οὐθὲν λογισθῆναι,
[6]Artemis [2]temple [8]for(as) [9]nothing [7]to be reckoned,

μέλλειν τε καὶ καθαιρεῖσθαι τῆς μεγα-
[3]to be about [1]and [2]also [4]to be diminished the great-

λειότητος αὐτῆς, ἣν ὅλη ἡ Ἀσία καὶ
ness of her, whom all – Asia and

ἡ οἰκουμένη σέβεται. 28 ἀκούσαντες δὲ
the inhabited earth worships. And hearing

καὶ γενόμενοι πλήρεις θυμοῦ ἔκραζον
and becoming full of anger they cried out

λέγοντες· μεγάλη ἡ Ἄρτεμις Ἐφεσίων.
saying: Great [is] – Artemis of [the] Ephesians.

29 καὶ ἐπλήσθη ἡ πόλις τῆς συγχύσεως,
And was filled the city of(with) the confusion,

ὥρμησάν τε ὁμοθυμαδὸν εἰς τὸ θέατρον,
and they rushed with one mind into the theatre,

συναρπάσαντες Γάϊον καὶ Ἀρίσταρχον
keeping a firm grip on Gaius and Aristarchus[,]

Μακεδόνας, συνεκδήμους Παύλου. 30 Παύλου
Macedonians, travelling companions of Paul. Paul

δὲ βουλομένου εἰσελθεῖν εἰς τὸν δῆμον
And intending[a] to enter into the mob
=as Paul intended

οὐκ εἴων αὐτὸν οἱ μαθηταί· 31 τινὲς
[5]not [6]allowed [4]him [1]the [2]disciples; some

δὲ καὶ τῶν Ἀσιαρχῶν, ὄντες αὐτῷ
and also of the Asiarchs, being to him

and Erastus, to Macedonia,
while he stayed in the province of Asia a little longer.

The Riot in Ephesus

23About that time there
arose a great disturbance
about the Way. 24A silversmith named Demetrius,
who made silver shrines of
Artemis, brought in no little business for the craftsmen. 25He called them to-
gether, along with the
workmen in related trades,
and said: "Men, you know
we receive a good income
from this business. 26And
you see and hear how this
fellow Paul has convinced
and led astray large num-
bers of people here in Ephesus and in practically the
whole province of Asia. He
says that man-made gods
are no gods at all. 27There is
danger not only that our
trade will lose its good
name, but also that the temple of the great goddess Artemis will be discredited,
and the goddess herself,
who is worshiped through-
out the province of Asia
and the world, will be
robbed of her divine majesty."
28When they heard this,
they were furious and be-
gan shouting: "Great is Artemis of the Ephesians!"
29Soon the whole city was
in an uproar. The people
seized Gaius and Aristar-
chus, Paul's traveling companions from Macedonia,
and rushed as one man into
the theater. 30Paul wanted
to appear before the crowd,
but the disciples would not
let him. 31Even some of the
officials of the province,

friends of his sent to him
and repeatedly urged him
not to venture into the theater.
32So then, some were
shouting one thing and
some another, for the as-
sembly was in confusion,
and the majority did not
know for what cause they
had come together.
33And some of the crowd
concluded *it was* Alexander, since the Jews had put
him forward; and having
motioned with his hand,
Alexander was intending to
make a defense to the as-
sembly.
34But when they recog-
nized that he was a Jew, a
single outcry arose from
them all as they shouted for
about two hours, "Great is
Artemis of the Ephesians!"
35And after quieting the
multitude, the town clerk
*said, "Men of Ephesus,
what man is there after all
who does not know that the
city of the Ephesians is
guardian of the temple of
the great Artemis, and of
the *image* which fell down
from heaven?
36"Since then these are
undeniable facts, you ought
to keep calm and to do
nothing rash.
37"For you have brought
these men *here* who are
neither robbers of temples
nor blasphemers of our
goddess.
38"So then, if Demetrius
and the craftsmen who are
with him have a complaint
against any man, the courts
are in session and proconsuls are *available*; let them
bring charges against one
another.
39"But if you want any-
thing beyond this, it shall
be settled in the lawful assembly.
40"For indeed we are in
danger of being accused of
a riot in connection with to-
day's affair, since there is
no *real* cause *for it*; and in
this connection we shall be
unable to account for this
disorderly gathering."

φίλοι, πέμψαντες πρὸς αὐτὸν παρεκάλουν
friends, sending to him besought

μὴ δοῦναι ἑαυτὸν εἰς τὸ θέατρον. 32 ἄλλοι
not to give himself in the theatre. Others

μὲν οὖν ἄλλο τι ἔκραζον· ἦν γὰρ
indeed therefore [2]different [1]something cried out; for [3]was

ἡ ἐκκλησία συγκεχυμένη, καὶ οἱ πλείους
[1]the [2]assembly *having been* confounded, and the majority

οὐκ ᾔδεισαν τίνος ἕνεκα συνεληλύθεισαν.
knew not [2]of what [1]on account they had come together.

33 ἐκ δὲ τοῦ ὄχλου συνεβίβασαν Ἀλέξανδρον,
But [some] of the crowd instructed Alexander,

προβαλόντων αὐτὸν τῶν Ἰουδαίων· ὁ δὲ
putting forward him the Jews[a]; – and
=as the Jews put him forward;

Ἀλέξανδρος κατασείσας τὴν χεῖρα ἤθελεν
Alexander waving the(his) hand wished

ἀπολογεῖσθαι τῷ δήμῳ. 34 ἐπιγνόντες δὲ
to defend himself to the mob. But knowing

ὅτι Ἰουδαῖός ἐστιν, φωνὴ ἐγένετο μία
that a Jew he is(was), [3]voice [1]there was [2]one

ἐκ πάντων, ὡς ἐπὶ ὥρας δύο κράζοντες·
from all, about over hours two crying out:

μεγάλη ἡ Ἄρτεμις Ἐφεσίων. 35 κατα-
Great [is] – Artemis of [the] Ephesians. [4]having

στείλας δὲ ὁ γραμματεὺς τὸν ὄχλον
quietened [1]And [2]the [3]town clerk the crowd

φησίν· ἄνδρες Ἐφέσιοι, τίς γάρ ἐστιν
says: *Men* Ephesians, who indeed is there

ἀνθρώπων ὃς οὐ γινώσκει τὴν Ἐφεσίων
of men who does not know [1]the [3]of [the] Ephesians

πόλιν νεωκόρον οὖσαν τῆς μεγάλης
[2]city [5]temple warden [4]being of the great

Ἀρτέμιδος καὶ τοῦ διοπετοῦς; 36 ἀναντιρ-
Artemis and of the [image] fallen from the sky? undeni-

ρήτων οὖν ὄντων τούτων δέον ἐστὶν
able therefore being these things[a] necessary it is
=as these things are undeniable

ὑμᾶς κατεσταλμένους ὑπάρχειν καὶ μηδὲν
you [2]*having been* quietened [1]to be and [2]nothing

προπετὲς πράσσειν. 37 ἠγάγετε γὰρ τοὺς
[3]rash [1]to do. For ye brought –

ἄνδρας τούτους οὔτε ἱεροσύλους οὔτε
men these neither temple robbers nor

βλασφημοῦντας τὴν θεὸν ἡμῶν. 38 εἰ
blaspheming the goddess of you. If

μὲν οὖν Δημήτριος καὶ οἱ σὺν αὐτῷ
indeed therefore Demetrius and [1]the [3]with [4]him

τεχνῖται ἔχουσι πρός τινα λόγον, ἀγοραῖοι
[2]artisans have against anyone an account, assizes

ἄγονται καὶ ἀνθύπατοί εἰσιν, ἐγκαλείτωσαν
are being(held) and proconsuls there are, let them bring a charge against

ἀλλήλοις. 39 εἰ δέ τι περαιτέρω ἐπιζητεῖτε,
one another. But if [2]anything [3]further [1]ye seek,

ἐν τῇ ἐννόμῳ ἐκκλησίᾳ ἐπιλυθήσεται.
in the lawful assembly it will be settled.

40 καὶ γὰρ κινδυνεύομεν ἐγκαλεῖσθαι
For indeed we are in danger to be charged with

στάσεως περὶ τῆς σήμερον, μηδενὸς
insurrection concerning to-day, no*thing*

αἰτίου ὑπάρχοντος, περὶ οὗ οὐ δυνησόμεθα
cause being[a], concerning which we shall *not* be able
=there being no cause,

ἀποδοῦναι λόγον περὶ τῆς συστροφῆς
to give account concerning – [2]crowding together

friends of Paul, sent him a
message begging him not to
venture into the theater.
32The assembly was in
confusion: Some were
shouting one thing, some
another. Most of the people
did not even know why
they were there. 33The
Jews pushed Alexander to
the front, and some of the
crowd shouted instructions
to him. He motioned for silence in order to make a defense before the people.
34But when they realized he
was a Jew, they all shouted
in unison for about two
hours: "Great is Artemis of
the Ephesians!"
35The city clerk quieted
the crowd and said: "Men
of Ephesus, doesn't all the
world know that the city of
Ephesus is the guardian of
the temple of the great Artemis and of her image,
which fell from heaven?
36Therefore, since these
facts are undeniable, you
ought to be quiet and not do
anything rash. 37You have
brought these men here,
though they have neither
robbed temples nor blas-
phemed our goddess. 38If,
then, Demetrius and his fellow craftsmen have a griev-
ance against anybody, the
courts are open and there
are proconsuls. They can
press charges. 39If there is
anything further you want
to bring up, it must be settled in a legal assembly.
40As it is, we are in danger
of being charged with riot-
ing because of today's
events. In that case we
would not be able to ac-
count for this commotion,
since there is no reason for

41And after saying this he
dismissed the assembly.

Chapter 20

Paul in Macedonia and Greece

AND after the uproar had
ceased, Paul sent for
the disciples and when he
had exhorted them and tak-
en his leave of them, he departed to go to Macedonia.
2And when he had gone
through those districts and
had given them much ex-
hortation, he came to
Greece.
3And *there* he spent
three months, and when a
plot was formed against
him by the Jews as he was
about to set sail for Syria,
he determined to return
through Macedonia.
4And he was accom-
panied by Sopater of
Berea, *the son* of Pyrrhus;
and by Aristarchus and
Secundus of the Thessalo-
nians; and Gaius of Derbe,
and Timothy; and Tychicus
and Trophimus of Asia.
5But these had gone on
ahead and were waiting for
us at Troas.
6And we sailed from
Philippi after the days of
Unleavened Bread, and
came to them at Troas
within five days; and there
we stayed seven days.
7And on the first day of
the week, when we were
gathered together to break
bread, Paul *began* talking
to them, intending to de-
part the next day, and he
prolonged his message until
midnight.
8And there were many
lamps in the upper room
where we were gathered together.
9And there was a certain
young man named Euty-
chus sitting on the window
sill, sinking into a deep
sleep; and as Paul kept on

ταύτης. **41** καὶ ταῦτα εἰπὼν ἀπέλυσεν τὴν
[1]this. And these things saying he dismissed the

ἐκκλησίαν.
assembly.

20 Μετὰ δὲ τὸ παύσασθαι τὸν θόρυβον
And after the to cease the uproar[b]
=after the uproar ceased

μεταπεμψάμενος ὁ Παῦλος τοὺς μαθητὰς
[2]summoning – [1]Paul [5]the [6]disciples

καὶ παρακαλέσας, ἀσπασάμενος ἐξῆλθεν
[3]and [4]exhorting, taking leave he went forth

πορεύεσθαι εἰς Μακεδονίαν. **2** διελθὼν δὲ
to go to Macedonia. And having gone through

τὰ μέρη ἐκεῖνα καὶ παρακαλέσας αὐτοὺς
those parts and having exhorted them

λόγῳ πολλῷ ἦλθεν εἰς τὴν Ἑλλάδα,
[1]with [3]speech [2]much he came into – Greece,

3 ποιήσας τε μῆνας τρεῖς, γενομένης
and spending months three, there being

ἐπιβουλῆς αὐτῷ ὑπὸ τῶν Ἰουδαίων
a plot[a] [against] him by the Jews

μέλλοντι ἀνάγεσθαι εἰς τὴν Συρίαν, ἐγένετο
being about to set sail to(for) – Syria, he was
=as he was about

γνώμης τοῦ ὑποστρέφειν διὰ Μακεδονίας.
of a mind – to return[d] through Macedonia.

4 συνείπετο δὲ αὐτῷ Σώπατρος Πύρρου
And there accompanied him Sopater [son] of Pyrrhus

Βεροιαῖος, Θεσσαλονικέων δὲ Ἀρίσταρχος
a Berœan, and of Thessalonians Aristarchus

καὶ Σέκουνδος, καὶ Γάϊος Δερβαῖος καὶ
and Secundus, and Gaius a Derbæan and

Τιμόθεος, Ἀσιανοὶ δὲ Τύχικος καὶ
Timothy, and Asians Tychicus and

Τρόφιμος. **5** οὗτοι δὲ προελθόντες ἔμενον
Trophimus. And these men going forward awaited

ἡμᾶς ἐν Τρῳάδι· **6** ἡμεῖς δὲ ἐξεπλεύσαμεν
us in Troas; and we sailed away

μετὰ τὰς ἡμέρας τῶν ἀζύμων ἀπὸ
after the days – of unleavened bread from

Φιλίππων, καὶ ἤλθομεν πρὸς αὐτοὺς εἰς
Philippi, and came to them in

τὴν Τρῳάδα ἄχρι ἡμερῶν πέντε, ὅπου
– Troas until days five, where

διετρίψαμεν ἡμέρας ἑπτά. **7** Ἐν δὲ τῇ
we stayed days seven. And on the

μιᾷ τῶν σαββάτων συνηγμένων ἡμῶν
one(first) of the [day] sabbaths(week) having been assembled us[a]
=as we were assembled

κλάσαι ἄρτον ὁ Παῦλος διελέγετο αὐτοῖς,
to break bread – Paul lectured to them,

μέλλων ἐξιέναι τῇ ἐπαύριον, παρέτεινέν τε
being about to depart on the morrow, and continued

τὸν λόγον μέχρι μεσονυκτίου. **8** ἦσαν δὲ
the speech until midnight. Now there were

λαμπάδες ἱκαναὶ ἐν τῷ ὑπερῴῳ οὗ
lamps a considerable number of in the upper room where

ἦμεν συνηγμένοι. **9** καθεζόμενος δέ τις
we were *having been* assembled. And sitting a certain

νεανίας ὀνόματι Εὔτυχος ἐπὶ τῆς θυρίδος,
young man by name Eutychus on the window sill,

καταφερόμενος ὕπνῳ βαθεῖ, διαλεγομένου
being overborne sleep by a deep, lecturing

it." 41After he had said
this, he dismissed the assembly.

Chapter 20

Through Macedonia and Greece

WHEN the uproar had
ended, Paul sent for
the disciples and, after encouraging them, said good-
by and set out for Macedonia. 2He traveled through
that area, speaking many
words of encouragement to
the people, and finally arrived in Greece, 3where he
stayed three months. Be-
cause the Jews made a plot
against him just as he was
about to sail for Syria, he
decided to go back through
Macedonia. 4He was ac-
companied by Sopater son
of Pyrrhus from Berea, Aristarchus and Secundus
from Thessalonica, Gaius
from Derbe, Timothy also,
and Tychicus and Trophi-
mus from the province of
Asia. 5These men went on
ahead and waited for us at
Troas. 6But we sailed from
Philippi after the Feast of
Unleavened Bread, and
five days later joined the
others at Troas, where we
stayed seven days.

Eutychus Raised From the Dead at Troas

7On the first day of the
week we came together to
break bread. Paul spoke to
the people and, because he
intended to leave the next
day, kept on talking until
midnight. 8There were
many lamps in the upstairs
room where we were meet-
ing. 9Seated in a window
was a young man named
Eutychus, who was sinking
into a deep sleep as Paul
talked on and on. When he

talking, he was overcome
by sleep and fell down from
the third floor, and was
picked up dead.
10But Paul went down
and fell upon him and after
embracing him, he said,
"Do not be troubled, for
his life is in him."
11And when he had gone
back up, and had broken
the bread and eaten, he
talked with them a long
while, until daybreak, and
so departed.
12And they took away the
boy alive, and were greatly
comforted.

Troas to Miletus

13But we, going ahead to
the ship, set sail for Assos,
intending from there to
take Paul on board; for thus
he had arranged it, intending himself to go by land.
14And when he met us at
Assos, we took him on
board and came to Mity-
lene.
15And sailing from there,
we arrived the following
day opposite Chios; and the
next day we crossed over
to Samos; and the day following we came to Miletus.
16For Paul had decided to
sail past Ephesus in order
that he might not have to
spend time in Asia; for he
was hurrying to be in
Jerusalem, if possible, on
the day of Pentecost.

Farewell to Ephesus

17And from Miletus he
sent to Ephesus and called
to him the elders of the
church.
18And when they had
come to him, he said to
them,
"You yourselves know,
from the first day that I set

τοῦ Παύλου ἐπὶ πλεῖον, κατενεχθεὶς ἀπὸ
– Paul* for a longer time, having been overborne from
=while Paul lectured

τοῦ ὕπνου ἔπεσεν ἀπὸ τοῦ τριστέγου
the sleep he fell from the third floor*

κάτω καὶ ἤρθη νεκρός. 10 καταβὰς δὲ
down and was taken up dead. But going down

ὁ Παῦλος ἐπέπεσεν αὐτῷ καὶ συμπεριλαβὼν
– Paul fell on him and closely embracing [him]

εἶπεν· μὴ θορυβεῖσθε· ἡ γὰρ ψυχὴ αὐτοῦ
said: Be ye not terrified; for the life of him

ἐν αὐτῷ ἐστιν. 11 ἀναβὰς δὲ καὶ κλάσας
in him is. And going up and breaking

τὸν ἄρτον καὶ γευσάμενος, ἐφ' ἱκανόν τε
the bread and tasting, and over a considerable [time]

ὁμιλήσας ἄχρι αὐγῆς, οὕτως ἐξῆλθεν.
conversing until light [of day], thus he went forth.

12 ἤγαγον δὲ τὸν παῖδα ζῶντα, καὶ
And they brought the lad living, and

παρεκλήθησαν οὐ μετρίως. 13 Ἡμεῖς δὲ
were comforted not moderately. And we

προελθόντες ἐπὶ τὸ πλοῖον ἀνήχθημεν
going before onto the ship set sail

ἐπὶ τὴν Ἄσσον, ἐκεῖθεν μέλλοντες ἀνα-
to(for) – Assos, thence intending to

λαμβάνειν τὸν Παῦλον· οὕτως γὰρ
take up – Paul; for thus

διατεταγμένος ἦν, μέλλων αὐτὸς πεζεύειν.
having been arranged it was, [2]intending [1]he to go afoot.

14 ὡς δὲ συνέβαλλεν ἡμῖν εἰς τὴν Ἄσσον,
Now when he met with us in – Assos,

ἀναλαβόντες αὐτὸν ἤλθομεν εἰς Μιτυλήνην·
taking up him we came to Mitylene;

15 κἀκεῖθεν ἀποπλεύσαντες τῇ ἐπιούσῃ
and thence sailing away on the next [day]

κατηντήσαμεν ἄντικρυς Χίου, τῇ δὲ ἑτέρᾳ
we arrived off Chios, and on the other(next)

παρεβάλομεν εἰς Σάμον, τῇ δὲ ἐχομένῃ
we crossed over to Samos, and on the next

ἤλθομεν εἰς Μίλητον. 16 κεκρίκει γὰρ ὁ
we came to Miletus. For had decided –

Παῦλος παραπλεῦσαι τὴν Ἔφεσον, ὅπως
Paul to sail past – Ephesus, so as

μὴ γένηται αὐτῷ χρονοτριβῆσαι ἐν τῇ
not be to him to spend time in –
=so that he should not . . .

Ἀσίᾳ· ἔσπευδεν γάρ, εἰ δυνατὸν εἴη
Asia; for he hasted, if possible it might be

αὐτῷ, τὴν ἡμέραν τῆς πεντηκοστῆς
to him, the day – of Pentecost

γενέσθαι εἰς Ἱεροσόλυμα.
to be in Jerusalem.

17 Ἀπὸ δὲ τῆς Μιλήτου πέμψας εἰς
And from – Miletus sending to

Ἔφεσον μετεκαλέσατο τοὺς πρεσβυτέρους
Ephesus he summoned the elders

τῆς ἐκκλησίας. 18 ὡς δὲ παρεγένοντο
of the church. And when they came

πρὸς αὐτόν, εἶπεν αὐτοῖς· ὑμεῖς ἐπίστασθε,
to him, he said to them: Ye understand,

ἀπὸ πρώτης ἡμέρας ἀφ' ἧς ἐπέβην εἰς
from [the] first day from which I set foot *on* in

* Souter remarks that it is uncertain whether the ground floor was counted or not in the enunciation; "if so, we should have to translate 'the second floor'."

was sound asleep, he fell to
the ground from the third
story and was picked up
dead. 10Paul went down,
threw himself on the young
man and put his arms
around him. "Don't be
alarmed," he said. "He's
alive!" 11Then he went upstairs again and broke
bread and ate. After talking
until daylight, he left. 12The
people took the young man
home alive and were greatly comforted.

Paul's Farewell to the Ephesian Elders

13We went on ahead to
the ship and sailed for Assos, where we were going
to take Paul aboard. He had
made this arrangement be-
cause he was going there on
foot. 14When he met us at
Assos, we took him aboard
and went on to Mitylene.
15The next day we set sail
from there and arrived off
Kios. The day after that we
crossed over to Samos, and
on the following day ar-
rived at Miletus. 16Paul had
decided to sail past Ephesus to avoid spending time
in the province of Asia, for
he was in a hurry to reach
Jerusalem, if possible, by
the day of Pentecost.
17From Miletus, Paul sent
to Ephesus for the elders of
the church. 18When they
arrived, he said to them:
"You know how I lived the
whole time I was with you,

foot in Asia, how I was with
you the whole time,
19 serving the Lord with
all humility and with tears
and with trials which came
upon me through the plots
of the Jews;
20 how I did not shrink
from declaring to you anything that was profitable,
and teaching you publicly
and from house to house,
21 solemnly testifying to
both Jews and Greeks of repentance toward God and
faith in our Lord Jesus
Christ.
22 "And now, behold,
bound in spirit, I am on my
way to Jerusalem, not
knowing what will happen
to me there,
23 except that the Holy
Spirit solemnly testifies to
me in every city, saying
that bonds and afflictions
await me.
24 "But I do not consider
my life of any account as
dear to myself, in order that
I may finish my course, and
the ministry which I re-
ceived from the Lord
Jesus, to testify solemnly
of the gospel of the grace of
God.
25 "And now, behold, I
know that all of you, among
whom I went about preach-
ing the kingdom, will see
my face no more.
26 "Therefore I testify to
you this day, that I am innocent of the blood of all
men.
27 "For I did not shrink
from declaring to you the
whole purpose of God.
28 "Be on guard for your-
selves and for all the flock,
among which the Holy
Spirit has made you over-
seers, to shepherd the
church of God which He
purchased with His own
blood.

τὴν Ἀσίαν, πῶς μεθ' ὑμῶν τὸν πάντα
– Asia, how with you the whole

χρόνον ἐγενόμην, 19 δουλεύων τῷ κυρίῳ
time I was, serving the Lord

μετὰ πάσης ταπεινοφροσύνης καὶ δακρύων
with all humility and tears

καὶ πειρασμῶν τῶν συμβάντων μοι ἐν
and trials – happening to me by

ταῖς ἐπιβουλαῖς τῶν Ἰουδαίων, 20 ὡς
the plots of the Jews, as

οὐδὲν ὑπεστειλάμην τῶν συμφερόντων τοῦ
[2]nothing [1]I kept back of the things beneficial –

μὴ ἀναγγεῖλαι ὑμῖν καὶ διδάξαι ὑμᾶς
not to declare[d] to you and to teach[d] you

δημοσίᾳ καὶ κατ' οἴκους, 21 διαμαρτυρόμενος
publicly and from house to house,† solemnly witnessing

Ἰουδαίοις τε καὶ Ἕλλησιν τὴν εἰς θεὸν
[2]to Jews [1]both and to Greeks – toward God

μετάνοιαν καὶ πίστιν εἰς τὸν κύριον
repentance and faith toward(?in) the Lord

ἡμῶν Ἰησοῦν. 22 καὶ νῦν ἰδοὺ δεδεμένος
of us Jesus. And now behold having been bound

ἐγὼ τῷ πνεύματι πορεύομαι εἰς Ἰερου-
I by the Spirit am going to Jeru-

σαλήμ, τὰ ἐν αὐτῇ συναντήσοντα ἐμοὶ
salem, [3]the things [6]in [7]it [4]going to meet [5]me

μὴ εἰδώς, 23 πλὴν ὅτι τὸ πνεῦμα τὸ
[1]not [2]knowing, except that the Spirit –

ἅγιον κατὰ πόλιν διαμαρτύρεταί μοι λέγον
Holy in every city† solemnly witnesses to me saying

ὅτι δεσμὰ καὶ θλίψεις με μένουσιν.
that bonds and afflictions me await.

24 ἀλλ' οὐδενὸς λόγου ποιοῦμαι τὴν ψυχὴν
But [4]of no*thing* [5]account [1]I make [2]the(my) [3]life

τιμίαν ἐμαυτῷ ὡς τελειώσω τὸν δρόμον
precious to myself so as I may finish the course

μου καὶ τὴν διακονίαν ἣν ἔλαβον παρὰ
of me and the ministry which I received from

τοῦ κυρίου Ἰησοῦ, διαμαρτύρασθαι τὸ
the Lord Jesus, to witness solemnly the

εὐαγγέλιον τῆς χάριτος τοῦ θεοῦ. 25 καὶ
gospel of the grace – of God. And

νῦν ἰδοὺ ἐγὼ οἶδα ὅτι οὐκέτι ὄψεσθε
now behold I know that [4]no more [3]will see

τὸ πρόσωπόν μου ὑμεῖς πάντες ἐν οἷς
[5]the [6]face [7]of me [1]ye [2]all among whom

διῆλθον κηρύσσων τὴν βασιλείαν. 26 διότι
I went about proclaiming the kingdom. Wherefore

μαρτύρομαι ὑμῖν ἐν τῇ σήμερον ἡμέρᾳ
I witness to you on this day

ὅτι καθαρός εἰμι ἀπὸ τοῦ αἵματος πάντων·
that clean I am from the blood of all men;

27 οὐ γὰρ ὑπεστειλάμην τοῦ μὴ ἀναγγεῖλαι
for I kept not back – not to declare[d]

πᾶσαν τὴν βουλὴν τοῦ θεοῦ ὑμῖν.
all the counsel – of God to you.

28 προσέχετε ἑαυτοῖς καὶ παντὶ τῷ
Take heed to yourselves and to all the

ποιμνίῳ, ἐν ᾧ ὑμᾶς τὸ πνεῦμα τὸ
flock, in which [5]you [1]the [3]Spirit –

ἅγιον ἔθετο ἐπισκόπους, ποιμαίνειν τὴν
[2]Holy [4]placed overseers, to shepherd the

ἐκκλησίαν τοῦ θεοῦ, ἣν περιεποιήσατο
church – of God, which he acquired

διὰ τοῦ αἵματος τοῦ ἰδίου.* 29 ἐγὼ
through the blood of the(his) own.* I

*** This = his own blood *or* the blood of his own [?Son].**

from the first day I came
into the province of Asia.
19 I served the Lord with
great humility and with
tears, although I was se-
verely tested by the plots of
the Jews. 20 You know that
I have not hesitated to
preach anything that would
be helpful to you but have
taught you publicly and
from house to house. 21 I
have declared to both Jews
and Greeks that they must
turn to God in repentance
and have faith in our Lord
Jesus.
22 "And now, compelled
by the Spirit, I am going to
Jerusalem, not knowing
what will happen to me
there. 23 I only know that in
every city the Holy Spirit
warns me that prison and
hardships are facing me.
24 However, I consider my
life worth nothing to me, if
only I may finish the race
and complete the task the
Lord Jesus has given me—
the task of testifying to the
gospel of God's grace.
25 "Now I know that none
of you among whom I have
gone about preaching the
kingdom will ever see me
again. 26 Therefore, I declare to you today that I am
innocent of the blood of all
men. 27 For I have not hesitated to proclaim to you the
whole will of God. 28 Keep
watch over yourselves and
all the flock of which the
Holy Spirit has made you
overseers.[p] Be shepherds
of the church of God,[q]
which he bought with his
own blood. 29 I know that

[p] 28 Traditionally *bishops*
[q] 28 Many manuscripts *of the Lord*

29"I know that after my departure savage wolves will come in among you, not sparing the flock;

30and from among your own selves men will arise, speaking perverse things, to draw away the disciples after them.

31"Therefore be on the alert, remembering that night and day for a period of three years I did not cease to admonish each one with tears.

32"And now I commend you to God and to the word of His grace, which is able to build *you* up and to give *you* the inheritance among all those who are sanctified.

33"I have coveted no one's silver or gold or clothes.

34"You yourselves know that these hands ministered to my *own* needs and to the men who were with me.

35"In everything I showed you that by working hard in this manner you must help the weak and remember the words of the Lord Jesus, that He Himself said, 'It is more blessed to give than to receive.' "

36And when he had said these things, he knelt down and prayed with them all.

37And they *began* to weep aloud and embraced Paul, and repeatedly kissed him,

38grieving especially over the word which he had spoken, that they should see his face no more. And they were accompanying him to the ship.

Chapter 21

Paul Sails from Miletus

AND when it came about that we had parted from them and had set sail, we ran a straight course to Cos and the next day to

οἶδα ὅτι εἰσελεύσονται μετὰ τὴν ἄφιξίν
know that [7]will come in [1]after [2]the [3]departure

μου λύκοι βαρεῖς εἰς ὑμᾶς μὴ φειδόμενοι
[4]of me [6]wolves [5]grievous [8]*in*to you not sparing

τοῦ ποιμνίου, 30 καὶ ἐξ ὑμῶν αὐτῶν
the flock, and of you [your]selves

ἀναστήσονται ἄνδρες λαλοῦντες διεστραμμένα
will rise up men speaking *having been* perverted things

τοῦ ἀποσπᾶν τοὺς μαθητὰς ὀπίσω ἑαυτῶν.
– to drag away[d] the disciples after themselves.

31 διὸ γρηγορεῖτε, μνημονεύοντες ὅτι
Wherefore watch ye, remembering that

τριετίαν νύκτα καὶ ἡμέραν οὐκ ἐπαυσάμην
for three years night and day I ceased not

μετὰ δακρύων νουθετῶν ἕνα ἕκαστον.
with tears admonishing [2]one [1]each.

32 καὶ τὰ νῦν παρατίθεμαι ὑμᾶς τῷ
And – now I commend you to the

κυρίῳ καὶ τῷ λόγῳ τῆς χάριτος αὐτοῦ
Lord and to the word of the grace of him

τῷ δυναμένῳ οἰκοδομῆσαι καὶ δοῦναι τὴν
– being able to build and to give the

κληρονομίαν ἐν τοῖς ἡγιασμένοις πᾶσιν.
inheritance among [2]the [ones] [3]having been sanctified [1]all.

33 ἀργυρίου ἢ χρυσίου ἢ ἱματισμοῦ οὐδενὸς
Silver or gold or raiment of no one

ἐπεθύμησα· 34 αὐτοὶ γινώσκετε ὅτι ταῖς
I coveted; [your]selves ye know that [4]to the

χρείαις μου καὶ τοῖς οὖσιν μετ' ἐμοῦ
[5]needs [6]of me [7]and [8]to the [ones] [9]being [10]with [11]me

ὑπηρέτησαν αἱ χεῖρες αὗται. 35 πάντα
[3]ministered [1]these [2]hands. All things

ὑπέδειξα ὑμῖν, ὅτι οὕτως κοπιῶντας δεῖ
I showed you, that thus labouring it behoves

ἀντιλαμβάνεσθαι τῶν ἀσθενούντων, μνημονεύειν
to succour the ailing [ones], [2]to remember

τε τῶν λόγων τοῦ κυρίου Ἰησοῦ, ὅτι
[1]and the words of the Lord Jesus, that

αὐτὸς εἶπεν· μακάριόν ἐστιν μᾶλλον διδόναι
he said: Blessed it is rather to give

ἢ λαμβάνειν. 36 καὶ ταῦτα εἰπών,
than to receive. And [2]these things [1]having said,

θεὶς τὰ γόνατα αὐτοῦ σὺν πᾶσιν αὐτοῖς
placing the knees of him with [2]all [1]them
=kneeling down

προσηύξατο. 37 ἱκανὸς δὲ κλαυθμὸς ἐγένετο
he prayed. And [2]considerable [3]weeping [1]there was

πάντων, καὶ ἐπιπεσόντες ἐπὶ τὸν τράχηλον
of all, and falling *on* on the neck

τοῦ Παύλου κατεφίλουν αὐτόν, 38 ὀδυνώ-
– of Paul they kissed fervently him, suffer-

μενοι μάλιστα ἐπὶ τῷ λόγῳ ᾧ εἰρήκει,
ing most over the word which he had said,

ὅτι οὐκέτι μέλλουσιν τὸ πρόσωπον αὐτοῦ
that no more they are(were) the face of him

θεωρεῖν. προέπεμπον δὲ αὐτὸν εἰς τὸ
to behold. And they escorted him to the

πλοῖον.
ship.

21 Ὡς δὲ ἐγένετο ἀναχθῆναι ἡμᾶς
Now when it came to pass to set sail we

ἀποσπασθέντας ἀπ' αὐτῶν, εὐθυδρομήσαντες
having been withdrawn from them, taking a straight course

ἤλθομεν εἰς τὴν Κῶ, τῇ δὲ ἑξῆς εἰς
we came to – Cos, and on the next [day] to

after I leave, savage wolves
will come in among you and
will not spare the flock.
30Even from your own
number men will arise and
distort the truth in order to
draw away disciples after
them. 31So be on your
guard! Remember that for
three years I never stopped
warning each of you night
and day with tears.
32"Now I commit you to
God and to the word of his
grace, which can build you
up and give you an inheritance among all those who
are sanctified. 33I have not
coveted anyone's silver or
gold or clothing. 34You
yourselves know that these
hands of mine have sup-
plied my own needs and the
needs of my companions.
35In everything I did, I
showed you that by this
kind of hard work we must
help the weak, remember-
ing the words the Lord
Jesus himself said: 'It is
more blessed to give than
to receive.' "
36When he had said this,
he knelt down with all of
them and prayed. 37They
all wept as they embraced
him and kissed him. 38What
grieved them most was his
statement that they would
never see his face again.
Then they accompanied
him to the ship.

Chapter 21

On to Jerusalem

AFTER we had torn ourselves away from them, we put out to sea and sailed straight to Cos. The

Rhodes, and from there
to Patara;
2 and having found a ship
crossing over to Phoenicia,
we went aboard and set
sail.
3 And when we had come
in sight of Cyprus, leaving
it on the left, we kept sailing to Syria and landed at
Tyre; for there the ship was
to unload its cargo.
4 And after looking up the
disciples, we stayed there
seven days; and they kept
telling Paul through the
Spirit not to set foot in
Jerusalem.
5 And when it came about
that our days there were
ended, we departed and
started on our journey,
while they all, with wives
and children, escorted us
until *we were* out of the
city. And after kneeling
down on the beach and
praying, we said farewell to
one another.
6 Then we went on board
the ship, and they returned
home again.
7 And when we had fin-
ished the voyage from
Tyre, we arrived at Ptolemais; and after greeting the
brethren, we stayed with
them for a day.
8 And on the next day we
departed and came to Caesarea; and entering the
house of Philip the evangelist, who was one of the
seven, we stayed with him.
9 Now this man had four
virgin daughters who were
prophetesses.
10 And as we were staying
there for some days, a certain prophet named Agabus
came down from Judea.
11 And coming to us, he
took Paul's belt and bound

τὴν Ῥόδον κἀκεῖθεν εἰς Πάταρα· **2** καὶ
– Rhodes and thence to Patara; and
εὑρόντες πλοῖον διαπερῶν εἰς Φοινίκην,
having found a ship crossing over to Phœnice,
ἐπιβάντες ἀνήχθημεν. **3** ἀναφάναντες δὲ
embarking we set sail. And sighting
τὴν Κύπρον καὶ καταλιπόντες αὐτὴν
– Cyprus and leaving it
εὐώνυμον ἐπλέομεν εἰς Συρίαν, καὶ κατήλ-
on the left we sailed to Syria, and came
θομεν εἰς Τύρον· ἐκεῖσε γὰρ τὸ πλοῖον
down to Tyre; for there the ship
ἦν ἀποφορτιζόμενον τὸν γόμον. **4** ἀνευρ-
was unloading the cargo. find-
όντες δὲ τοὺς μαθητὰς ἐπεμείναμεν αὐτοῦ
ing And the disciples we remained there
ἡμέρας ἑπτά· οἵτινες τῷ Παύλῳ ἔλεγον
days seven; who – [2]Paul [1]told
διὰ τοῦ πνεύματος μὴ ἐπιβαίνειν εἰς
through the Spirit not to go up to
Ἱεροσόλυμα. **5** ὅτε δὲ ἐγένετο ἐξαρτίσαι
Jerusalem. But when it came to pass to accomplish
=we accomplished
ἡμᾶς τὰς ἡμέρας, ἐξελθόντες ἐπορευόμεθα
us[b] the days, going forth we journeyed
προπεμπόντων ἡμᾶς πάντων σὺν γυναιξὶ
[3]escorting [3]us [1]all[a] with women
καὶ τέκνοις ἕως ἔξω τῆς πόλεως, καὶ
and children as far as outside the city, and
θέντες τὰ γόνατα ἐπὶ τὸν αἰγιαλὸν
placing the knees on the shore
=kneeling
προσευξάμενοι **6** ἀπησπασάμεθα ἀλλήλους,
praying we gave parting greetings to one another,
καὶ ἐνέβημεν εἰς τὸ πλοῖον, ἐκεῖνοι δὲ
and embarked in the ship, and those
ὑπέστρεψαν εἰς τὰ ἴδια. **7** Ἡμεῖς δὲ
returned to [1]the(ir) [3]things [2]own. But we
=home.
τὸν πλοῦν διανύσαντες ἀπὸ Τύρου κατηντή-
[2]the [3]voyage [1]finishing from Tyre ar-
σαμεν εἰς Πτολεμαΐδα, καὶ ἀσπασάμενοι
rived at Ptolemais, and greeting
τοὺς ἀδελφοὺς ἐμείναμεν ἡμέραν μίαν
the brothers we remained day one
παρ' αὐτοῖς. **8** τῇ δὲ ἐπαύριον ἐξελθόντες
with them. And on the morrow going forth
ἤλθομεν εἰς Καισάρειαν, καὶ εἰσελθόντες
we came to Cæsarea, and entering
εἰς τὸν οἶκον Φιλίππου τοῦ εὐαγγελιστοῦ
into the house of Philip the evangelist
ὄντος ἐκ τῶν ἑπτά, ἐμείναμεν παρ'
being of the seven, we remained with
αὐτῷ. **9** τούτῳ δὲ ἦσαν θυγατέρες
him. Now to this man were daughters
=this man had four daughters
τέσσαρες παρθένοι προφητεύουσαι. **10** Ἐπιμεν-
four[c] virgins prophesying. remain-
όντων δὲ ἡμέρας πλείους κατῆλθέν τις
ing[a] And days more(many) [5]came down [1]a certain
ἀπὸ τῆς Ἰουδαίας προφήτης ὀνόματι
[6]from – [7]Judæa [2]prophet [3]by name
Ἅγαβος, **11** καὶ ἐλθὼν πρὸς ἡμᾶς καὶ
[4]Agabus, and coming to us and
ἄρας τὴν ζώνην τοῦ Παύλου, δήσας
taking the girdle – of Paul, having bound

next day we went to
Rhodes and from there to
Patara. 2 We found a ship
crossing over to Phoenicia,
went on board and set sail.
3 After sighting Cyprus and
passing to the south of it,
we sailed on to Syria. We
landed at Tyre, where our
ship was to unload its cargo. 4 Finding the disciples
there, we stayed with them
seven days. Through the
Spirit they urged Paul not
to go on to Jerusalem. 5 But
when our time was up, we
left and continued on our
way. All the disciples and
their wives and children accompanied us out of the
city, and there on the beach
we knelt to pray. 6 After
saying good-by to each other, we went aboard the
ship, and they returned
home.
7 We continued our voy-
age from Tyre and landed
at Ptolemais, where we
greeted the brothers and
stayed with them for a day.
8 Leaving the next day, we
reached Caesarea and
stayed at the house of Philip the evangelist, one of the
Seven. 9 He had four un-
married daughters who
prophesied.
10 After we had been there
a number of days, a prophet named Agabus came
down from Judea. 11 Com-
ing over to us, he took
Paul's belt, tied his own

his own feet and hands, and
said, "This is what the
Holy Spirit says: 'In this
way the Jews at Jerusalem
will bind the man who owns
this belt and deliver him
into the hands of the Gentiles.' "
12And when we had heard
this, we as well as the local
residents *began* begging
him not to go up to Jerusalem.
13Then Paul answered,
"What are you doing,
weeping and breaking my
heart? For I am ready not
only to be bound, but even
to die at Jerusalem for the
name of the Lord Jesus."
14And since he would not
be persuaded, we fell si-
lent, remarking, "The will
of the Lord be done!"

Paul at Jerusalem

15And after these days we
got ready and started on
our way up to Jerusalem.
16And *some* of the disciples from Caesarea also
came with us, taking us to
Mnason of Cyprus, a disciple of long standing with
whom we were to lodge.
17And when we had come
to Jerusalem, the brethren
received us gladly.
18And now the following
day Paul went in with us to
James, and all the elders
were present.
19And after he had greet-
ed them, he *began* to relate
one by one the things which
God had done among the
Gentiles through his ministry.
20And when they heard it
they *began* glorifying God;
and they said to him, "You
see, brother, how many
thousands there are among
the Jews of those who have

ἑαυτοῦ τοὺς πόδας καὶ τὰς χεῖρας εἶπεν·
of himself the feet and the hands said:

τάδε λέγει τὸ πνεῦμα τὸ ἅγιον· τὸν
These things says the Spirit – Holy: [7]The

ἄνδρα οὗ ἐστιν ἡ ζώνη αὕτη οὕτως
[8]man [9]of whom [10]is [11]this [12]girdle [1]thus

δήσουσιν ἐν Ἰερουσαλὴμ οἱ Ἰουδαῖοι καὶ
[4]will bind [5]in [6]Jerusalem [2]the [3]Jews and

παραδώσουσιν εἰς χεῖρας ἐθνῶν. 12 ὡς
will deliver into [the] hands of [the] nations. when

δὲ ἠκούσαμεν ταῦτα, παρεκαλοῦμεν ἡμεῖς
And we heard these things, [6]besought [5]we

τε καὶ οἱ ἐντόπιοι τοῦ μὴ ἀναβαίνειν
[1]both [2]and [3]the [4]residents – [8]not [9]to go up[d]

αὐτὸν εἰς Ἰερουσαλήμ. 13 τότε ἀπεκρίθη
[7]him to Jerusalem. Then answered

ὁ Παῦλος τί ποιεῖτε κλαίοντες καὶ
– Paul: What are ye doing weeping and

συνθρύπτοντές μου τὴν καρδίαν; ἐγὼ γὰρ
weakening of me the heart? For I

οὐ μόνον δεθῆναι ἀλλὰ καὶ ἀποθανεῖν
not only to be bound but also to die

εἰς Ἰερουσαλὴμ ἑτοίμως ἔχω ὑπὲρ τοῦ
in Jerusalem readily have on behalf of the
=am ready

ὀνόματος τοῦ κυρίου Ἰησοῦ. 14 μὴ
name of the Lord Jesus. Not

πειθομένου δὲ αὐτοῦ ἡσυχάσαμεν εἰπόντες·
being persuaded and him[a] we kept silence having said:
=And when he was not persuaded

τοῦ κυρίου τὸ θέλημα γινέσθω.
[4]Of the [5]Lord [2]the [3]will [1]let [6]be [done].

15 Μετὰ δὲ τὰς ἡμέρας ταύτας
And after these days

ἐπισκευασάμενοι ἀνεβαίνομεν εἰς Ἰεροσόλυμα·
having made ready we went up to Jerusalem;

16 συνῆλθον δὲ καὶ τῶν μαθητῶν ἀπὸ
and went *with* also [some] of the disciples from

Καισαρείας σὺν ἡμῖν, ἄγοντες παρ' ᾧ
Cæsarea with us, bringing [one] with whom

ξενισθῶμεν Μνάσωνί τινι Κυπρίῳ,
we might be lodged Mnason a certain Cypriote,

ἀρχαίῳ μαθητῇ. 17 Γενομένων δὲ ἡμῶν εἰς
an ancient (early) disciple. And being us[a] in
= when we were

Ἰεροσόλυμα ἀσμένως ἀπεδέξαντο ἡμᾶς οἱ
Jerusalem [5]joyfully [3]received [4]us [1]the

ἀδελφοί. 18 τῇ δὲ ἐπιούσῃ εἰσῄει ὁ
[2]brothers. And on the next day went in –

Παῦλος σὺν ἡμῖν πρὸς Ἰάκωβον, πάντες
Paul with us to James, [2]all

τε παρεγένοντο οἱ πρεσβύτεροι. 19 καὶ
[1]and [5]came [3]the [4]elders. And

ἀσπασάμενος αὐτοὺς ἐξηγεῖτο καθ' ἓν
having greeted them he related according to one
=singly

ἕκαστον ὧν ἐποίησεν ὁ θεὸς ἐν τοῖς
each of [the things] which did – God among the

ἔθνεσιν διὰ τῆς διακονίας αὐτοῦ. 20 οἱ
nations through the ministry of him. they

δὲ ἀκούσαντες ἐδόξαζον τὸν θεόν, εἶπάν τε
And hearing glorified – God, and said

αὐτῷ· θεωρεῖς, ἀδελφέ, πόσαι μυριάδες
to him: Thou beholdest, brother, how many *ten* thousands

εἰσὶν ἐν τοῖς Ἰουδαίοις τῶν πεπιστευκότων,
there are among the Jews – having believed,

hands and feet with it and
said, "The Holy Spirit
says, 'In this way the Jews
of Jerusalem will bind the
owner of this belt and will
hand him over to the Gen-
tiles.' "
12When we heard this, we
and the people there pleaded with Paul not to go up to
Jerusalem. 13Then Paul answered, "Why are you
weeping and breaking my
heart? I am ready not only
to be bound, but also to die
in Jerusalem for the name
of the Lord Jesus." 14When
he would not be dissuaded,
we gave up and said, "The
Lord's will be done."
15After this, we got ready
and went up to Jerusalem.
16Some of the disciples
from Caesarea accompa-
nied us and brought us to
the home of Mnason,
where we were to stay. He
was a man from Cyprus and
one of the early disciples.

Paul's Arrival at Jerusalem

17When we arrived at Je-
rusalem, the brothers re-
ceived us warmly. 18The
next day Paul and the rest
of us went to see James,
and all the elders were present. 19Paul greeted them
and reported in detail what
God had done among the
Gentiles through his ministry.
20When they heard this,
they praised God. Then
they said to Paul: "You
see, brother, how many
thousands of Jews have be-

believed, and they are all
zealous for the Law;
21and they have been told
about you, that you are
teaching all the Jews who
are among the Gentiles to
forsake Moses, telling them
not to circumcise their children nor to walk according
to the customs.
22"What, then, is *to be*
done? They will certainly
hear that you have come.
23"Therefore do this that
we tell you. We have four
men who are under a vow;
24take them and purify
yourself along with them,
and pay their expenses in
order that they may shave
their heads; and all will
know that there is nothing
to the things which they
have been told about you,
but that you yourself also
walk orderly, keeping the
Law.
25"But concerning the
Gentiles who have be-
lieved, we wrote, having
decided that they should
abstain from meat sacri-
ficed to idols and from
blood and from what is
strangled and from fornication."
26Then Paul took the
men, and the next day,
purifying himself along
with them, went into the
temple, giving notice of the
completion of the days of
purification, until the sacrifice was offered for each
one of them.

Paul Seized in the Temple

27And when the seven
days were almost over, the
Jews from Asia, upon see-
ing him in the temple, *be-*
gan to stir up all the multitude and laid hands on him,
28crying out, "Men of Is-
rael, come to our aid! This
is the man who preaches to
all men everywhere against

καὶ πάντες ζηλωταὶ τοῦ νόμου ὑπάρχουσιν·
and all zealots of the law are;

21 κατηχήθησαν δὲ περὶ σοῦ ὅτι ἀποστα-
and they were informed about thee that [8]apo-

σίαν διδάσκεις ἀπὸ Μωϋσέως τοὺς κατὰ
stasy [1]thou teachest [9]from [10]Moses [3]the [5]throughout

τὰ ἔθνη πάντας Ἰουδαίους, λέγων μὴ
[6]the [7]nations [2]all [4]Jews, [1]telling [3]not

περιτέμνειν αὐτοὺς τὰ τέκνα μηδὲ τοῖς
[4]to circumcise [2]them the children nor in the

ἔθεσιν περιπατεῖν. 22 τί οὖν ἐστιν;
customs to walk. What therefore is it?

πάντως ἀκούσονται ὅτι ἐλήλυθας. 23 τοῦτο
At all events they will hear that thou hast come. This

οὖν ποίησον ὅ σοι λέγομεν· εἰσὶν ἡμῖν
therefore do thou which thee we tell: There are to us[c]
=We have

ἄνδρες τέσσαρες εὐχὴν ἔχοντες ἐφ' ἑαυτῶν·
men four a vow having on themselves;

24 τούτους παραλαβὼν ἁγνίσθητι σὺν αὐτοῖς,
these taking be thou purified with them,

καὶ δαπάνησον ἐπ' αὐτοῖς ἵνα ξυρήσονται
and spend on them that they will shave

τὴν κεφαλήν, καὶ γνώσονται πάντες ὅτι
the head, and will know all men that

ὧν κατήχηνται περὶ σοῦ οὐδέν
[3][of the things] of which [4]they have been informed [5]about [6]thee [2]nothing

ἐστιν, ἀλλὰ στοιχεῖς καὶ αὐτὸς φυλάσσων τὸν
[1]there is, but thou walkest also [thy]self keeping the

νόμον. 25 περὶ δὲ τῶν πεπιστευκότων
law. And concerning [1]the [3]having believed

ἐθνῶν ἡμεῖς ἐπεστείλαμεν κρίναντες φυλάσ-
[2]nations we joined in writing [1]judging [3]to keep

σεσθαι αὐτοὺς τό τε εἰδωλόθυτον καὶ
themselves [2]them [4][from] [6]the [5]both idol sacrifice and

αἷμα καὶ πνικτὸν καὶ πορνείαν. 26 τότε
blood and a thing strangled and fornication. Then

ὁ Παῦλος παραλαβὼν τοὺς ἄνδρας τῇ
– Paul taking the men on the

ἐχομένῃ ἡμέρᾳ σὺν αὐτοῖς ἁγνισθεὶς εἰσῄει
next day with them having been purified went in

εἰς τὸ ἱερόν, διαγγέλλων τὴν ἐκπλήρωσιν
to the temple, announcing the completion

τῶν ἡμερῶν τοῦ ἁγνισμοῦ, ἕως οὗ
of the days of the purification, until

προσηνέχθη ὑπὲρ ἑνὸς ἑκάστου αὐτῶν ἡ
should be offered on behalf of [2]one [1]each of them the

προσφορά.
offering.

27 Ὡς δὲ ἔμελλον αἱ ἑπτὰ ἡμέραι
Now when were about the seven days

συντελεῖσθαι, οἱ ἀπὸ τῆς Ἀσίας Ἰουδαῖοι
to be fulfilled, [1]the [3]from – [4]Asia [2]Jews

θεασάμενοι αὐτὸν ἐν τῷ ἱερῷ συνέχεον
seeing him in the temple stirred up

πάντα τὸν ὄχλον, καὶ ἐπέβαλαν ἐπ'
all the crowd, and laid *on* on

αὐτὸν τὰς χεῖρας, 28 κράζοντες· ἄνδρες
him the(ir) hands, crying out: *Men*

Ἰσραηλῖται, βοηθεῖτε· οὗτός ἐστιν ὁ
Israelites, help: this is the

ἄνθρωπος ὁ κατὰ τοῦ λαοῦ καὶ τοῦ
man [1]the [one] [5]against [6]the [7]people [8]and [9]the

νόμου καὶ τοῦ τόπου τούτου πάντας
[10]law [11]and [12]this [13]place [3]all men

lieved, and all of them are
zealous for the law. 21They
have been informed that
you teach all the Jews who
live among the Gentiles to
turn away from Moses, telling them not to circumcise
their children or live according to our customs.
22What shall we do? They
will certainly hear that you
have come, 23so do what
we tell you. There are four
men with us who have
made a vow. 24Take these
men, join in their purification rites and pay their expenses, so that they can
have their heads shaved.
Then everybody will know
there is no truth in these reports about you, but that
you yourself are living in
obedience to the law. 25As
for the Gentile believers,
we have written to them
our decision that they
should abstain from food
sacrificed to idols, from
blood, from the meat of
strangled animals and from
sexual immorality."
26The next day Paul took
the men and purified him-
self along with them. Then
he went to the temple to
give notice of the date
when the days of purification would end and the offering would be made for
each of them.

Paul Arrested

27When the seven days
were nearly over, some
Jews from the province of
Asia saw Paul at the tem-
ple. They stirred up the
whole crowd and seized
him, 28shouting, "Men of
Israel, help us! This is the
man who teaches all men
everywhere against our

our people, and the Law, and this place; and besides he has even brought Greeks into the temple and has defiled this holy place."

29 For they had previously seen Trophimus the Ephesian in the city with him, and they supposed that Paul had brought him into the temple.

30 And all the city was aroused, and the people rushed together; and taking hold of Paul, they dragged him out of the temple; and immediately the doors were shut.

31 And while they were seeking to kill him, a report came up to the [i] commander of the *Roman* cohort that all Jerusalem was in confusion.

32 And at once he took along *some* soldiers and centurions, and ran down to them; and when they saw the commander and the soldiers, they stopped beating Paul.

33 Then the commander came up and took hold of him, and ordered him to be bound with two chains; and he *began* asking who he was and what he had done.

34 But among the crowd some were shouting one thing *and* some another, and when he could not find out the facts on account of the uproar, he ordered him to be brought into the barracks.

35 And when he got to the stairs, it so happened that he was carried by the soldiers because of the violence of the mob;

36 for the multitude of the people kept following behind, crying out, "Away with him!"

37 And as Paul was about to be brought into the barracks, he said to the commander, "May I say something to you?" And he

[i] I.e., chiliarch, in command of one thousand troops

πανταχῇ διδάσκων, ἔτι τε καὶ Ἕλληνας
[4]everywhere [3]teaching, and even also Greeks

εἰσήγαγεν εἰς τὸ ἱερὸν καὶ κεκοίνωκεν
brought *in* into the temple and has profaned

τὸν ἅγιον τόπον τοῦτον. 29 ἦσαν γὰρ
– [2]holy [3]place [1]this. For they were

προεωρακότες Τρόφιμον τὸν Ἐφέσιον ἐν
having previously seen Trophimus the Ephesian in

τῇ πόλει σὺν αὐτῷ, ὃν ἐνόμιζον ὅτι
the city with him, whom they supposed that

εἰς τὸ ἱερὸν εἰσήγαγεν ὁ Παῦλος. 30 ἐκινήθη
[3]into [4]the [5]temple [2]brought *in* – [1]Paul. [5]was moved

τε ἡ πόλις ὅλη καὶ ἐγένετο συνδρομὴ
[1]And [2]the [4]city [3]whole and there was a running together

τοῦ λαοῦ, καὶ ἐπιλαβόμενοι τοῦ Παύλου
of the people, and laying hold – of Paul

εἷλκον αὐτὸν ἔξω τοῦ ἱεροῦ, καὶ εὐθέως
they dragged him outside the temple, and immediately

ἐκλείσθησαν αἱ θύραι. 31 Ζητούντων τε
were shut the doors. And [while they were] seeking[a]

αὐτὸν ἀποκτεῖναι ἀνέβη φάσις τῷ
[2]him [1]to kill [4]came up [3]information to the

χιλιάρχῳ τῆς σπείρης ὅτι ὅλη συγχύννεται
chiliarch of the cohort that [1]all [3]is(was) in confusion

Ἰερουσαλήμ· 32 ὃς ἐξαυτῆς παραλαβὼν
[2]Jerusalem; who at once taking

στρατιώτας καὶ ἑκατοντάρχας
soldiers and centurions

κατέδραμεν ἐπ᾽ αὐτούς· οἱ δὲ ἰδόντες
ran down on them; and they seeing

τὸν χιλίαρχον καὶ τοὺς στρατιώτας
the chiliarch and the soldiers

ἐπαύσαντο τύπτοντες τὸν Παῦλον. 33 τότε
ceased beating – Paul. Then

ἐγγίσας ὁ χιλίαρχος ἐπελάβετο αὐτοῦ
drawing near the chiliarch laid hold of him

καὶ ἐκέλευσεν δεθῆναι ἁλύσεσι δυσί, καὶ
and commanded to be bound chains with two, and

ἐπυνθάνετο τίς εἴη καὶ τί ἐστιν πεποιηκώς.
inquired who he might be and what he is having done.

34 ἄλλοι δὲ ἄλλο τι ἐπεφώνουν ἐν τῷ
And [1]others [7]different [6]something [5]called out [2]among [3]the

ὄχλῳ· μὴ δυναμένου δὲ αὐτοῦ γνῶναι
[4]crowd; and not being able him[a] to know
=as he was not able

τὸ ἀσφαλὲς διὰ τὸν θόρυβον, ἐκέλευσεν
the certain thing because of the uproar, he commanded

ἄγεσθαι αὐτὸν εἰς τὴν παρεμβολήν. 35 ὅτε
to be brought him into the fort. when

δὲ ἐγένετο ἐπὶ τοὺς ἀναβαθμούς, συνέβη
And he was on the steps, it happened

βαστάζεσθαι αὐτὸν ὑπὸ τῶν στρατιωτῶν
to be carried him[b] by he soldiers
=he was carried

διὰ τὴν βίαν τοῦ ὄχλου· 36 ἠκολούθει
because of the violence of the crowd; [5]followed

γὰρ τὸ πλῆθος τοῦ λαοῦ κράζοντες·
[1]for [2]the [3]multitude [4]of the [5]people crying out:

αἶρε αὐτόν. 37 Μέλλων τε εἰσάγεσθαι
Take away him. And being about to be brought *in*

εἰς τὴν παρεμβολὴν ὁ Παῦλος λέγει τῷ
into the fort – Paul says to the

χιλιάρχῳ· εἰ ἔξεστίν μοι εἰπεῖν τι πρὸς
chiliarch: If it is lawful for me to say something to

people and our law and this
place. And besides, he has
brought Greeks into the
temple area and defiled this
holy place." 29 (They had
previously seen Trophimus
the Ephesian in the city
with Paul and assumed that
Paul had brought him into
the temple area.)

30 The whole city was
aroused, and the people
came running from all directions.
Seizing Paul, they
dragged him from the temple,
and immediately the
gates were shut. 31 While
they were trying to kill him,
news reached the commander
of the Roman
troops that the whole city
of Jerusalem was in an uproar.
32 He at once took
some officers and soldiers
and ran down to the crowd.
When the rioters saw the
commander and his soldiers,
they stopped beating
Paul.

33 The commander came
up and arrested him and ordered
him to be bound with
two chains. Then he asked
who he was and what he
had done. 34 Some in the
crowd shouted one thing
and some another, and
since the commander could
not get at the truth because
of the uproar, he ordered
that Paul be taken into the
barracks. 35 When Paul
reached the steps, the violence
of the mob was so
great he had to be carried
by the soldiers. 36 The
crowd that followed kept
shouting, "Away with
him!"

Paul Speaks to the Crowd

37 As the soldiers were
about to take Paul into the
barracks, he asked the
commander, "May I say
something to you?"

*said, "Do you know Greek?

[38]"Then you are not the Egyptian who some time ago stirred up a revolt and led the four thousand men of the Assassins out into the wilderness?"

[39]But Paul said, "I am a Jew of Tarsus in Cilicia, a citizen of no insignificant city; and I beg you, allow me to speak to the people."

[40]And when he had given him permission, Paul, standing on the stairs, motioned to the people with his hand; and when there was a great hush, he spoke to them in the Hebrew dialect, saying,

σέ; ὁ δὲ ἔφη· Ἑλληνιστὶ γινώσκεις;
thee? And he said: in Greek Knowest thou [to speak]?*

38 οὐκ ἄρα σὺ εἶ ὁ Αἰγύπτιος ὁ πρὸ
[2]Not [4]then [3]thou [1]art the Egyptian the [one] before

τούτων τῶν ἡμερῶν ἀναστατώσας καὶ
these – days unsettling and

ἐξαγαγὼν εἰς τὴν ἔρημον τοὺς τετρα-
leading out into the desert the four

κισχιλίους ἄνδρας τῶν σικαρίων; 39 εἶπεν
thousand men of the Sicarii? said

δὲ ὁ Παῦλος· ἐγὼ ἄνθρωπος μέν εἰμι
And – Paul: I *a man* indeed am

Ἰουδαῖος, Ταρσεύς, τῆς Κιλικίας οὐκ
a Jew, a Tarsian, – of Cilicia not

ἀσήμου πόλεως πολίτης· δέομαι δέ σου,
of a mean city a citizen; and I beg of thee,

ἐπίτρεψόν μοι λαλῆσαι πρὸς τὸν λαόν.
permit me to speak to the people.

40 ἐπιτρέψαντος δὲ αὐτοῦ ὁ Παῦλος ἑστὼς
And permitting him[a] – Paul standing
=when he gave permission

ἐπὶ τῶν ἀναβαθμῶν κατέσεισεν τῇ χειρὶ
on the steps beckoned with the (his) hand

τῷ λαῷ· πολλῆς δὲ σιγῆς γενομένης
to the people; and much silence becoming[a]
=when there was great silence

προσεφώνησεν τῇ Ἑβραΐδι διαλέκτῳ λέγων·
he addressed in the Hebrew language saying:

"Do you speak Greek?"
he replied. [38]"Aren't you
the Egyptian who started a
revolt and led four thou-
sand terrorists out into the
desert some time ago?"
[39]Paul answered, "I am a
Jew, from Tarsus in Cilicia,
a citizen of no ordinary
city. Please let me speak to
the people."
[40]Having received the
commander's permission,
Paul stood on the steps and
motioned to the crowd.
When they were all silent,
he said to them in Arama-
ic[r]: [1]"Brothers and fathers, listen now to my defense."
[2]When they heard him
speak to them in Aramaic,
they became very quiet.
Then Paul said: [3]"I am a
Jew, born in Tarsus of Cilicia, but brought up in this
city. Under Gamaliel I was
thoroughly trained in the
law of our fathers and was
just as zealous for God as
any of you are today. [4]I
persecuted the followers of
this Way to their death, arresting both men and wom-
en and throwing them into
prison, [5]as also the high
priest and all the Council
can testify. I even obtained
letters from them to their
brothers in Damascus, and

Chapter 22

Paul's Defense before the Jews

"BRETHREN and fathers, hear my defense which I now *offer* to you."

[2]And when they heard that he was addressing them in the Hebrew dialect, they became even more quiet; and he *said,

[3]"I am a Jew, born in Tarsus of Cilicia, but brought up in this city, educated under Gamaliel, strictly according to the law of our fathers, being zealous for God, just as you all are today.

[4]"And I persecuted this Way to the death, binding and putting both men and women into prisons,

[5]as also the high priest and all the Council of the elders can testify. From them I also received letters to the brethren, and started off for Damascus in order

22 Ἄνδρες ἀδελφοὶ καὶ πατέρες, ἀκούσατέ
Men brothers and fathers, hear ye

μου τῆς πρὸς ὑμᾶς νυνὶ ἀπολογίας.
[5]of me [1]the [3]to [6]you [4]now [2]defence.

— 2 ἀκούσαντες δὲ ὅτι τῇ Ἑβραΐδι
(And hearing that in the Hebrew

διαλέκτῳ προσεφώνει αὐτοῖς μᾶλλον
language he addressed them more

παρέσχον ἡσυχίαν. καὶ φησίν· — 3 ἐγώ εἰμι
they showed quietness. And he says:) I am

ἀνὴρ Ἰουδαῖος, γεγεννημένος ἐν Ταρσῷ
a man a Jew, having been born in Tarsus

τῆς Κιλικίας, ἀνατεθραμμένος δὲ ἐν τῇ
– of Cilicia, and having been brought up in –

πόλει ταύτῃ, παρὰ τοὺς πόδας Γαμαλιὴλ
city this, at the feet of Gamaliel

πεπαιδευμένος κατὰ ἀκρίβειαν τοῦ πατρῴου
having been trained according to [the] exactness of the ancestral

νόμου, ζηλωτὴς ὑπάρχων τοῦ θεοῦ καθὼς
law a zealot being – of God even as

πάντες ὑμεῖς ἐστε σήμερον· 4 ὃς ταύτην
all ye are to-day; who this

τὴν ὁδὸν ἐδίωξα ἄχρι θανάτου, δεσμεύων
– way persecuted as far as to death, binding

καὶ παραδιδοὺς εἰς φυλακὰς ἄνδρας τε
and delivering to prisons both men

καὶ γυναῖκας. 5 ὡς καὶ ὁ ἀρχιερεὺς
and women. As even the high priest

μαρτυρεῖ μοι καὶ πᾶν τὸ πρεσβυτέριον·
witnesses to me and all the senate;

παρ' ὧν καὶ ἐπιστολὰς δεξάμενος πρὸς
from whom also letters having received to

τοὺς ἀδελφοὺς εἰς Δαμασκὸν ἐπορευόμην,
the brothers in Damascus I journeyed,

* See note on page xviii.

r40 Or possibly *Hebrew*; also in 22:2

to bring even those who
were there to Jerusalem as
prisoners to be punished.
6"And it came about that
as I was on my way, ap-
proaching Damascus about
noontime, a very bright
light suddenly flashed from
heaven all around me,
7and I fell to the ground
and heard a voice saying to
me, 'Saul, Saul, why are
you persecuting Me?'
8"And I answered, 'Who
art Thou, Lord?' And He
said to me, 'I am Jesus the
Nazarene, whom you are
persecuting.'
9"And those who were
with me beheld the light, to
be sure, but did not understand the voice of the One
who was speaking to me.
10"And I said, 'What
shall I do, Lord?' And the
Lord said to me, 'Arise and
go on into Damascus; and
there you will be told of all
that has been appointed for
you to do.'
11"But since I could not
see because of the bright-
ness of that light, I was led
by the hand by those who
were with me, and came
into Damascus.
12"And a certain
Ananias, a man who was
devout by the standard of
the Law, *and* well spoken
of by all the Jews who lived
there,
13came to me, and stand-
ing near said to me, 'Brother Saul, receive your sight!'
And at that very time I
looked up at him.
14"And he said, 'The God
of our fathers has ap-
pointed you to know His
will, and to see the Righteous One, and to hear an
utterance from His mouth.
15'For you will be a wit-
ness for Him to all men of
what you have seen and
heard.
16'And now why do you
delay? Arise, and be bap-
tized, and wash away your

ἄξων καὶ τοὺς ἐκεῖσε ὄντας δεδεμένους
leading also the [ones] [2]there [1]being *having been* bound
εἰς Ἰερουσαλὴμ ἵνα τιμωρηθῶσιν.
to Jerusalem that they might be punished.
6 Ἐγένετο δέ μοι πορευομένῳ καὶ ἐγγίζοντι
Now it happened to me journeying and drawing near
τῇ Δαμασκῷ περὶ μεσημβρίαν ἐξαίφνης ἐκ
– to Damascus about midday suddenly out of
τοῦ οὐρανοῦ περιαστράψαι φῶς ἱκανὸν
– heaven [4]to shine *round* [1]a [3]light [2]considerable
περὶ ἐμέ, 7 ἔπεσά τε εἰς τὸ ἔδαφος
round me, and I fell to the ground
καὶ ἤκουσα φωνῆς λεγούσης μοι· Σαοὺλ
and heard a voice saying to me: Saul[,]
Σαούλ, τί με διώκεις; 8 ἐγὼ δὲ ἀπεκρίθην·
Saul, why me persecutest thou? And I answered:
τίς εἶ, κύριε; εἶπέν τε πρός ἐμέ· ἐγώ
Who art thou, Lord? And he said to me: I
εἰμι Ἰησοῦς ὁ Ναζωραῖος, ὃν σὺ διώκεις.
am Jesus the Nazarene, whom thou persecutest.
9 οἱ δὲ σὺν ἐμοὶ ὄντες τὸ μὲν φῶς
Now [1]the [ones] [3]with [4]me [2]being [7]the [6]indeed [8]light
ἐθεάσαντο, τὴν δὲ φωνὴν οὐκ ἤκουσαν
[5]beheld, but the voice they heard not
τοῦ λαλοῦντός μοι. 10 εἶπον δέ· τί
of the [one] speaking to me. And I said: What
ποιήσω, κύριε; ὁ δὲ κύριος εἶπεν πρός
may I do, Lord? And the Lord said to
με· ἀναστὰς πορεύου εἰς Δαμασκόν, κἀκεῖ σοι
me: Rising up go into Damascus, and there to thee
λαληθήσεται περὶ πάντων ὧν τέτακταί
it will be told concerning all things which has(ve) been arranged
σοι ποιῆσαι. 11 ὡς δὲ οὐκ ἐνέβλεπον
for thee to do. And as I saw not
ἀπὸ τῆς δόξης τοῦ φωτὸς ἐκείνου,
from the glory of that light,
χειραγωγούμενος ὑπὸ τῶν συνόντων μοι
being led by the hand by the [ones] being with me
ἦλθον εἰς Δαμασκόν. 12 Ἁνανίας δέ τις,
I went into Damascus. And a certain Ananias,
ἀνὴρ εὐλαβὴς κατὰ τὸν νόμον, μαρτυρού-
a man devout according to the law, being witnessed
μενος ὑπὸ πάντων τῶν κατοικούντων
[to] by all [1]the [3]dwelling [4][there]
Ἰουδαίων, 13 ἐλθὼν πρὸς ἐμὲ καὶ ἐπιστὰς
[2]Jews, coming to me and standing by
εἶπέν μοι· Σαοὺλ ἀδελφέ, ἀνάβλεψον.
said to me: Saul brother, look up.
κἀγὼ αὐτῇ τῇ ὥρᾳ ἀνέβλεψα εἰς αὐτόν.
And I in that hour* looked up at him.
14 ὁ δὲ εἶπεν· ὁ θεὸς τῶν πατέρων
And he said: The God of the fathers
ἡμῶν προεχειρίσατό σε γνῶναι τὸ θέλημα
of us previously appointed thee to know the will
αὐτοῦ καὶ ἰδεῖν τὸν δίκαιον καὶ ἀκοῦσαι
of him and to see the Just One and to hear
φωνὴν ἐκ τοῦ στόματος αὐτοῦ, 15 ὅτι
a voice out of the mouth of him, because
ἔσῃ μάρτυς αὐτῷ πρὸς πάντας ἀνθρώπους
thou wilt be a witness to him[c] to all men
ὧν ἑώρακας καὶ ἤκουσας. 16 καὶ νῦν
of things which thou hast seen and didst hear. And now
τί μέλλεις; ἀναστὰς βάπτισαι καὶ ἀπόλου-
what intendest thou? Rising up be baptized and wash

* See Luke 2. 38.

went there to bring these
people as prisoners to Jerusalem to be punished.
6"About noon as I came
near Damascus, suddenly a
bright light from heaven
flashed around me. 7I fell to
the ground and heard a
voice say to me, 'Saul!
Saul! Why do you perse-
cute me?'
8" 'Who are you, Lord?' I
asked.
" 'I am Jesus of Naza-
reth, whom you are perse-
cuting,' he replied. 9My
companions saw the light,
but they did not understand
the voice of him who was
speaking to me.
10" 'What shall I do,
Lord?' I asked.
" 'Get up,' the Lord said,
'and go into Damascus.
There you will be told all
that you have been as-
signed to do.' 11My com-
panions led me by the hand
into Damascus, because
the brilliance of the light
had blinded me.
12"A man named Ananias
came to see me. He was a
devout observer of the law
and highly respected by all
the Jews living there. 13He
stood beside me and said,
'Brother Saul, receive your
sight!' And at that very moment I was able to see him.
14"Then he said: 'The
God of our fathers has chosen you to know his will
and to see the Righteous
One and to hear words
from his mouth. 15You will
be his witness to all men of
what you have seen and
heard. 16And now what are
you waiting for? Get up, be
baptized and wash your

sins, calling on His name.'
17"And it came about when I returned to Jerusalem and was praying in the temple, that I fell into a trance,
18and I saw Him saying to me, 'Make haste, and get out of Jerusalem quickly, because they will not accept your testimony about Me.'
19"And I said, 'Lord, they themselves understand that in one synagogue after another I used to imprison and beat those who believed in Thee.
20'And when the blood of Thy witness Stephen was being shed, I also was standing by approving, and watching out for the cloaks of those who were slaying him.'
21"And He said to me, 'Go! For I will send you far away to the Gentiles.' "
22And they listened to him up to this statement, and *then* they raised their voices and said, "Away with such a fellow from the earth, for he should not be allowed to live!"
23And as they were crying out and throwing off their cloaks and tossing dust into the air,
24the [j]commander ordered him to be brought into the barracks, stating that he should be examined by scourging so that he might find out the reason why they were shouting against him that way.
25And when they stretched him out with thongs, Paul said to the centurion who was standing by, "Is it lawful for you to scourge a man who is a Roman and uncondemned?"
26And when the centurion heard *this,* he went to the commander and told him,

[j] I.e., chiliarch, in command of one thousand troops

σαι τὰς ἁμαρτίας σου, ἐπικαλεσάμενος τὸ
away the sins of thee, invoking the
ὄνομα αὐτοῦ. **17** Ἐγένετο δέ μοι ὑποστρέ-
name of him. And it happened to me having
ψαντι εἰς Ἰερουσαλὴμ καὶ προσευχομένου
returned to Jerusalem and praying
=as I was praying
μου ἐν τῷ ἱερῷ γενέσθαι με ἐν ἐκστάσει,
me[a] in the temple to become me[b] in an ecstasy,
=I became
18 καὶ ἰδεῖν αὐτὸν λέγοντά μοι· σπεῦσον
and to see[b] him saying to me; Haste
=I saw
καὶ ἔξελθε ἐν τάχει ἐξ Ἰερουσαλήμ,
and go forth quickly out of Jerusalem,
διότι οὐ παραδέξονταί σου μαρτυρίαν
because they will not receive of thee witness
περὶ ἐμοῦ. **19** κἀγὼ εἶπον· κύριε, αὐτοὶ
concerning me. And I said: Lord, they
ἐπίστανται ὅτι ἐγὼ ἤμην φυλακίζων καὶ
understand that I was imprisoning and
δέρων κατὰ τὰς συναγωγὰς τοὺς πιστεύον-
beating throughout the synagogues the [ones] believ-
τας ἐπὶ σέ· **20** καὶ ὅτε ἐξεχύννετο τὸ αἷμα
ing on thee; and when was being shed the blood
Στεφάνου τοῦ μάρτυρός σου, καὶ αὐτὸς
of Stephen the witness of thee, even [my]self
ἤμην ἐφεστὼς καὶ συνευδοκῶν καὶ
I was standing by and consenting and
φυλάσσων τὰ ἱμάτια τῶν ἀναιρούντων
keeping the garments of the [ones] killing
αὐτόν. **21** καὶ εἶπεν πρός με· πορεύου,
him. And he said to me: Go,
ὅτι ἐγὼ εἰς ἔθνη μακρὰν ἐξαποστελῶ σε.
because I to nations afar will send forth thee.
22 Ἤκουον δὲ αὐτοῦ ἄχρι τούτου τοῦ
And they heard him as far as to this –
λόγου, καὶ ἐπῆραν τὴν φωνὴν αὐτῶν
word, and lifted up the voice of them
λέγοντες· αἶρε ἀπὸ τῆς γῆς τὸν τοιοῦτον·
saying: Take from the earth such a man;
οὐ γὰρ καθῆκεν αὐτὸν ζῆν. **23** κραυγαζόν-
for not it is fitting him to live. And shout-
των τε αὐτῶν καὶ ῥιπτούντων τὰ ἱμάτια
ing them and tearing[a] the(ir) garments
=as they shouted and tore . . .
καὶ κονιορτὸν βαλλόντων εἰς τὸν ἀέρα,
and [2]dust [1]throwing[a] in the air,
=threw dust
24 ἐκέλευσεν ὁ χιλίαρχος εἰσάγεσθαι αὐτὸν
commanded the chiliarch to be brought *in* him
εἰς τὴν παρεμβολήν, εἴπας μάστιξιν
into the fort, bidding [3]with scourges
ἀνετάζεσθαι αὐτόν, ἵνα ἐπιγνῷ δι' ἣν
[2]to be examined [1]him, that he might fully know for what
αἰτίαν οὕτως ἐπεφώνουν αὐτῷ. **25** ὡς δὲ
crime thus they were calling against him. But as
προέτειναν αὐτὸν τοῖς ἱμᾶσιν, εἶπεν πρὸς
they stretched forward him with the thongs, [2]said [3]to
τὸν ἑστῶτα ἑκατόνταρχον ὁ Παῦλος· εἰ
[4]the [5]standing [by] [6]centurion – [1]Paul: [1]If
ἄνθρωπον Ῥωμαῖον καὶ ἀκατάκριτον ἔξεστιν
a man [6]a Roman [8]and [7]uncondemned [2]it is lawful
ὑμῖν μαστίζειν; **26** ἀκούσας δὲ ὁ ἑκατον-
[3]for you [4]to scourge? And [3]hearing [1]the [2]cen-
τάρχης προσελθὼν τῷ χιλιάρχῳ ἀπήγγειλεν
turion approaching *to* the chiliarch reported

sins away, calling on his name.'
17"When I returned to Jerusalem and was praying at the temple, I fell into a trance 18and saw the Lord speaking. 'Quick!' he said to me. 'Leave Jerusalem immediately, because they will not accept your testimony about me.'
19" 'Lord,' I replied, 'these men know that I went from one synagogue to another to imprison and beat those who believe in you. 20And when the blood of your martyr[s] Stephen was shed, I stood there giving my approval and guarding the clothes of those who were killing him.'
21"Then the Lord said to me, 'Go; I will send you far away to the Gentiles.' "

Paul the Roman Citizen

22The crowd listened to Paul until he said this. Then they raised their voices and shouted, "Rid the earth of him! He's not fit to live!"
23As they were shouting and throwing off their cloaks and flinging dust into the air, 24the commander ordered Paul to be taken into the barracks. He directed that he be flogged and questioned in order to find out why the people were shouting at him like this. 25As they stretched him out to flog him, Paul said to the centurion standing there, "Is it legal for you to flog a Roman citizen who hasn't even been found guilty?"
26When the centurion heard this, he went to the commander and reported

[s] 20 Or *witness*

saying, "What are you about to do? For this man is a Roman."
27And the commander came and said to him, "Tell me, are you a Roman?" And he said, "Yes."
28And the commander answered, "I acquired this citizenship with a large sum of money." And Paul said, "But I was actually born *a citizen*."
29Therefore those who were about to examine him immediately let go of him; and the commander also was afraid when he found out that he was a Roman, and because he had put him in chains.
30But on the next day, wishing to know for certain why he had been accused by the Jews, he released him and ordered the chief priests and all the Council to assemble, and brought Paul down and set him before them.

Chapter 23

Paul before the Council

AND Paul, looking intently at the Council, said, "Brethren, I have lived my life with a perfectly good conscience before God up to this day."
2And the high priest Ananias commanded those standing beside him to strike him on the mouth.
3Then Paul said to him, "God is going to strike you, you whitewashed wall! And do you sit to try me according to the Law, and in violation of the Law order me to be struck?"
4But the bystanders said, "Do you revile God's high priest?"
5And Paul said, "I was not aware, brethren, that he was high priest; for it is written, 'YOU SHALL NOT SPEAK EVIL OF A RULER OF YOUR PEOPLE.' "
6But perceiving that one part were Sadducees and

λέγων· τί μέλλεις ποιεῖν; ὁ γὰρ ἄνθρωπος
saying: What art thou about to do? – for [2]man

οὗτος Ῥωμαῖός ἐστιν. 27 προσελθὼν δὲ
[1]this [4]a Roman [3]is. And approaching

ὁ χιλίαρχος εἶπεν αὐτῷ· λέγε μοι, σὺ
the chiliarch said to him: Tell me, thou

Ῥωμαῖος εἶ; ὁ δὲ ἔφη· ναί. 28 ἀπεκρίθη
a Roman art? And he said: Yes. answered

δὲ ὁ χιλίαρχος· ἐγὼ πολλοῦ κεφαλαίου
And the chiliarch: [1]I [5]of(for) much(great) [6]sum [of money]

τὴν πολιτείαν ταύτην ἐκτησάμην. ὁ δὲ
[3]this [4]citizenship [2]acquired. – So

Παῦλος ἔφη· ἐγὼ δὲ καὶ γεγέννημαι.
Paul said: But I indeed have been born.

29 εὐθέως οὖν ἀπέστησαν ἀπ' αὐτοῦ οἱ
Immediately therefore [5]stood away [6]from [7]him [1]the [ones]

μέλλοντες αὐτὸν ἀνετάζειν· καὶ ὁ χιλίαρχος
[2]being about [4]him [3]to examine; [4]also [2]the [3]chiliarch

δὲ ἐφοβήθη ἐπιγνοὺς ὅτι Ῥωμαῖός ἐστιν
[1]and [5]feared fully knowing that a Roman he is(was)

καὶ ὅτι αὐτὸν ἦν δεδεκώς.
and that [3]him [1]he was [2]having bound.

30 Τῇ δὲ ἐπαύριον βουλόμενος γνῶναι τὸ
And on the morrow being minded to know the

ἀσφαλές, τὸ τί κατηγορεῖται ὑπὸ τῶν
certain thing, – why he was accused by the

Ἰουδαίων, ἔλυσεν αὐτόν, καὶ ἐκέλευσεν
Jews, he released him, and commanded

συνελθεῖν τοὺς ἀρχιερεῖς καὶ πᾶν τὸ
to come together the chief priests and all the

συνέδριον, καὶ καταγαγὼν τὸν Παῦλον
council, and having brought down – Paul

ἔστησεν εἰς αὐτούς. 23 ἀτενίσας δὲ
set [him] among them. And [2]gazing

ὁ Παῦλος τῷ συνεδρίῳ εἶπεν· ἄνδρες
– [1]Paul at the council said: *Men*

ἀδελφοί, ἐγὼ πάσῃ συνειδήσει ἀγαθῇ
brothers, I in all conscience good

πεπολίτευμαι τῷ θεῷ ἄχρι ταύτης τῆς
have lived – to God until this –

ἡμέρας. 2 ὁ δὲ ἀρχιερεὺς Ἁνανίας
day. And the high priest Ananias

ἐπέταξεν τοῖς παρεστῶσιν αὐτῷ τύπτειν
gave order to the [ones] standing by him to strike

αὐτοῦ τὸ στόμα. 3 τότε ὁ Παῦλος πρὸς
of him the mouth. Then – Paul to

αὐτὸν εἶπεν· τύπτειν σε μέλλει ὁ θεός,
him said: [3]To strike [4]thee [2]is about – [1]God,

τοῖχε κεκονιαμένε· καὶ σὺ κάθῃ κρίνων
wall *having been* whitened; and thou sittest judging

με κατὰ τὸν νόμον, καὶ παρανομῶν
me according to the law, and contravening law

κελεύεις με τύπτεσθαι; 4 οἱ δὲ παρεστῶτες
commandest me to be struck? And the [ones] standing by

εἶπαν· τὸν ἀρχιερέα τοῦ θεοῦ λοιδορεῖς;
said: The high priest – of God revilest thou?

5 ἔφη τε ὁ Παῦλος· οὐκ ᾔδειν, ἀδελφοί,
And said – Paul: I did not know, brothers,

ὅτι ἐστὶν ἀρχιερεύς· γέγραπται γὰρ ὅτι
that he is high priest; for it has been written[,] –

ἄρχοντα τοῦ λαοῦ σου οὐκ ἐρεῖς κακῶς.
A ruler of the people of thee thou shalt not speak evilly.

6 γνοὺς δὲ ὁ Παῦλος ὅτι τὸ ἓν μέρος
And knowing – Paul that the one part

it. "What are you going to do?" he asked. "This man is a Roman citizen."
27The commander went to Paul and asked, "Tell me, are you a Roman citizen?"
"Yes, I am," he answered.
28Then the commander said, "I had to pay a big price for my citizenship."
"But I was born a citizen," Paul replied.
29Those who were about to question him withdrew immediately. The commander himself was alarmed when he realized that he had put Paul, a Roman citizen, in chains.

Before the Sanhedrin

30The next day, since the commander wanted to find out exactly why Paul was being accused by the Jews, he released him and ordered the chief priests and all the Sanhedrin to assemble. Then he brought Paul and had him stand before them.

Chapter 23

PAUL looked straight at the Sanhedrin and said, "My brothers, I have fulfilled my duty to God in all good conscience to this day." 2At this the high priest Ananias ordered those standing near Paul to strike him on the mouth.
3Then Paul said to him, "God will strike you, you whitewashed wall! You sit there to judge me according to the law, yet you yourself violate the law by commanding that I be struck!"
4Those who were standing near Paul said, "You dare to insult God's high priest?"
5Paul replied, "Brothers, I did not realize that he was the high priest; for it is written: 'Do not speak evil about the ruler of your people.'[r]"
6Then Paul, knowing that some of them were Saddu-

[r]5 Exodus 22:28

the other Pharisees, Paul
began crying out in the
Council, "Brethren, I am a
Pharisee, a son of Phari-
sees; I am on trial for the
hope and resurrection of
the dead!"
7And as he said this,
there arose a dissension between the Pharisees and
Sadducees; and the assem-
bly was divided.
8For the Sadducees say
that there is no resurrection, nor an angel, nor a
spirit; but the Pharisees acknowledge them all.
9And there arose a great
uproar; and some of the
scribes of the Pharisaic
party stood up and *began*
to argue heatedly, saying,
"We find nothing wrong
with this man; suppose a
spirit or an angel has
spoken to him?"
10And as a great dissen-
sion was developing, the
[k]commander was afraid
Paul would be torn to
pieces by them and ordered
the troops to go down and
take him away from them
by force, and bring him into
the barracks.
11But on the night
immediately following, the
Lord stood at his side and
said, "Take courage; for as
you have solemnly wit-
nessed to My cause at
Jerusalem, so you must
witness at Rome also."

A Conspiracy to Kill Paul

12And when it was day,
the Jews formed a con-
spiracy and bound them-
selves under an oath, saying that they would neither
eat nor drink until they had
killed Paul.
13And there were more
than forty who formed this
plot.
14And they came to the
chief priests and the elders,
and said, "We have bound
ourselves under a solemn

[k]I.e., chiliarch, in command of one thousand troops

ἐστὶν Σαδδουκαίων τὸ δὲ ἕτερον Φαρισαίων
is(was) of Sadducees but the other of Pharisees
ἔκραζεν ἐν τῷ συνεδρίῳ· ἄνδρες ἀδελφοί,
cried out in the council: *Men* brothers,
ἐγὼ Φαρισαῖός εἰμι, υἱὸς Φαρισαίων· περὶ
I a Pharisee am, a son of Pharisees; concerning
ἐλπίδος καὶ ἀναστάσεως νεκρῶν κρίνομαι.
hope and resurrection of dead ones I am being judged.
7 τοῦτο δὲ αὐτοῦ λαλοῦντος ἐγένετο
And this him saying[a] there was
=as he said this
στάσις τῶν Φαρισαίων καὶ Σαδδουκαίων,
a discord of the Pharisees and Sadducees,
καὶ ἐσχίσθη τὸ πλῆθος. 8 Σαδδουκαῖοι
and was divided the multitude. Sadducees
γὰρ λέγουσιν μὴ εἶναι ἀνάστασιν μήτε
For say not to be a resurrection nor
ἄγγελον μήτε πνεῦμα, Φαρισαῖοι δὲ
angel nor spirit, but Pharisees
ὁμολογοῦσιν τὰ ἀμφότερα. 9 ἐγένετο δὲ
confess – both. And there was
κραυγὴ μεγάλη, καὶ ἀναστάντες τινὲς
cry a great, and rising up some
τῶν γραμματέων τοῦ μέρους τῶν Φαρισαίων
of the scribes of the part of the Pharisees
διεμάχοντο λέγοντες· οὐδὲν κακὸν εὑρίσκομεν
strove saying: Nothing evil we find
ἐν τῷ ἀνθρώπῳ τούτῳ· εἰ δὲ πνεῦμα
in this man; and if [1]a spirit
ἐλάλησεν αὐτῷ ἢ ἄγγελος —. 10 Πολλῆς δὲ
[4]spoke [5]to him [2]or [3]an angel —. And much
γινομένης στάσεως φοβηθεὶς ὁ χιλίαρχος
arising discord[a] [3]fearing [1]the [2]chiliarch
=when much discord arose
μὴ διασπασθῇ ὁ Παῦλος ὑπ' αὐτῶν,
[4]lest [6]should be torn asunder – [5]Paul by them,
ἐκέλευσεν τὸ στράτευμα καταβὰν ἁρπάσαι
commanded the soldiery coming down to seize
αὐτὸν ἐκ μέσου αὐτῶν ἄγειν τε εἰς
him out of [the] midst of them and to bring [him] into
τὴν παρεμβολήν. 11 Τῇ δὲ ἐπιούσῃ
the fort. And in the following
νυκτὶ ἐπιστὰς αὐτῷ ὁ κύριος εἶπεν·
night [3]coming *on* [4]to him [1]the [2]Lord said:
θάρσει· ὡς γὰρ διεμαρτύρω τὰ περὶ
Be of good courage; for as thou didst solemnly witness the concerning things
ἐμοῦ εἰς Ἰερουσαλήμ, οὕτω σε δεῖ καὶ
me in Jerusalem, so thee it behoves also
εἰς Ῥώμην μαρτυρῆσαι. 12 Γενομένης δὲ
in Rome to witness. And becoming
ἡμέρας ποιήσαντες συστροφὴν οἱ Ἰουδαῖοι
day[a] [3]making [4]a conspiracy [1]the [2]Jews
=when it became day
ἀνεθεμάτισαν ἑαυτούς, λέγοντες μήτε φαγεῖν
cursed themselves, saying neither to eat
μήτε πεῖν ἕως οὗ ἀποκτείνωσιν τὸν
nor to drink until they should kill –
Παῦλον. 13 ἦσαν δὲ πλείους τεσσεράκοντα
Paul. And there were more [than] forty
οἱ ταύτην τὴν συνωμοσίαν ποιησάμενοι·
the [ones] this – plot making;
14 οἵτινες προσελθόντες τοῖς ἀρχιερεῦσιν
who approaching *to* the chief priests
καὶ τοῖς πρεσβυτέροις εἶπαν· ἀναθέματι
and *to* the elders said: With a curse

cees and the others Pharisees, called out in the Sanhedrin, "My brothers, I am
a Pharisee, the son of a
Pharisee. I stand on trial
because of my hope in the
resurrection of the dead."
7When he said this, a dispute broke out between the
Pharisees and the Saddu-
cees, and the assembly was
divided. 8(The Sadducees
say that there is no resurrection, and that there are
neither angels nor spirits,
but the Pharisees acknowledge them all.)
9There was a great up-
roar, and some of the
teachers of the law who
were Pharisees stood up
and argued vigorously.
"We find nothing wrong
with this man," they said.
"What if a spirit or an angel
has spoken to him?" 10The
dispute became so violent
that the commander was
afraid Paul would be torn to
pieces by them. He ordered
the troops to go down and
take him away from them
by force and bring him into
the barracks.
11The following night the
Lord stood near Paul and
said, "Take courage! As
you have testified about me
in Jerusalem, so you must
also testify in Rome."

The Plot to Kill Paul

12The next morning the
Jews formed a conspiracy
and bound themselves with
an oath not to eat or drink
until they had killed Paul.
13More than forty men
were involved in this plot.
14They went to the chief
priests and elders and said,
"We have taken a solemn
oath not to eat anything un-

oath to taste nothing until we have killed Paul.

15"Now, therefore, you and the Council notify the commander to bring him down to you, as though you were going to determine his case by a more thorough investigation; and we for our part are ready to slay him before he comes near *the place*."

16But the son of Paul's sister heard of their ambush, and he came and entered the barracks and told Paul.

17And Paul called one of the centurions to him and said, "Lead this young man to the commander, for he has something to report to him."

18So he took him and led him to the commander and *said, "Paul the prisoner called me to him and asked me to lead this young man to you since he has something to tell you."

19And the commander took him by the hand and stepping aside, *began* to inquire of him privately, "What is it that you have to report to me?"

20And he said, "The Jews have agreed to ask you to bring Paul down tomorrow to the Council, as though they were going to inquire somewhat more thoroughly about him.

21"So do not listen to them, for more than forty of them are lying in wait for him who have bound themselves under a curse not to eat or drink until they slay him; and now they are ready and waiting for the promise from you."

22Therefore the com-

ἀνεθεματίσαμεν ἑαυτοὺς μηδενὸς γεύσασθαι
we cursed ourselves *of* nothing to taste

ἕως οὗ ἀποκτείνωμεν τὸν Παῦλον. 15 νῦν
until we may kill – Paul. Now

οὖν ὑμεῖς ἐμφανίσατε τῷ χιλιάρχῳ σὺν
therefore [2]ye [1]inform the chiliarch with

τῷ συνεδρίῳ ὅπως καταγάγῃ αὐτὸν εἰς
the council so as he may bring down him to

ὑμᾶς ὡς μέλλοντας διαγινώσκειν ἀκριβέστε-
you as intending to ascertain *exactly* more accurate-

ρον τὰ περὶ αὐτοῦ· ἡμεῖς δὲ πρὸ τοῦ
ly the things concerning him; and we before –

ἐγγίσαι αὐτὸν ἕτοιμοί ἐσμεν τοῦ ἀνελεῖν
to draw near him[b] ready are – to kill[c]
=he draws near

αὐτόν. 16 Ἀκούσας δὲ ὁ υἱὸς τῆς ἀδελφῆς
him. And [6]hearing [1]the [2]son [3]of the [4]sister

Παύλου τὴν ἐνέδραν, παραγενόμενος καὶ
[5]of Paul the treachery, coming and

εἰσελθὼν εἰς τὴν παρεμβολὴν ἀπήγγειλεν
entering into the fort reported

τῷ Παύλῳ. 17 προσκαλεσάμενος δὲ ὁ
– to Paul. And [2]calling to [him] –

Παῦλος ἕνα τῶν ἑκατονταρχῶν ἔφη· τὸν
[1]Paul one of the centurions said: –

νεανίαν τοῦτον ἄπαγε πρὸς τὸν χιλίαρχον,
[3]youth [2]this [1]Bring up to the chiliarch,

ἔχει γὰρ ἀπαγγεῖλαί τι αὐτῷ. 18 ὁ
for [1]he has [3]to report [2]something [4]to him. He

μὲν οὖν παραλαβὼν αὐτὸν ἤγαγεν πρὸς
– therefore taking [2]him [1]brought to

τὸν χιλίαρχον καὶ φησίν· ὁ δέσμιος
the chiliarch and says: The prisoner

Παῦλος προσκαλεσάμενός με ἠρώτησεν
Paul calling to [him] me asked

τοῦτον τὸν νεανίσκον ἀγαγεῖν πρὸς σέ,
[2]this – [3]young man [1]to bring to thee,

ἔχοντά τι λαλῆσαί σοι. 19 ἐπιλαβόμενος
having something to tell thee. [3]laying hold

δὲ τῆς χειρὸς αὐτοῦ ὁ χιλίαρχος καὶ
And [4]of the [5]hand [6]of him [1]the [2]chiliarch and

ἀναχωρήσας κατ' ἰδίαν ἐπυνθάνετο· τί
retiring [2]privately [1]inquired: What

ἐστιν ὃ ἔχεις ἀπαγγεῖλαί μοι; 20 εἶπεν
is it which thou hast to report to me? he said[,]

δὲ ὅτι οἱ Ἰουδαῖοι συνέθεντο τοῦ ἐρωτῆσαί
And – The Jews agreed – to ask[d]

σε ὅπως αὔριον τὸν Παῦλον καταγάγῃς
thee so as to-morrow – [2]Paul [1]thou shouldest bring down

εἰς τὸ συνέδριον ὡς μέλλον τι ἀκριβέστερον
to the council as intending something more accurately

πυνθάνεσθαι περὶ αὐτοῦ. 21 σὺ οὖν μὴ
to inquire concerning him. Thou therefore not

πεισθῇς αὐτοῖς· ἐνεδρεύουσιν γὰρ αὐτὸν
be persuaded by them; for there lie in wait for him

ἐξ αὐτῶν ἄνδρες πλείους τεσσεράκοντα,
of them [4]men [1]more [2][than] [3]forty,

οἵτινες ἀνεθεμάτισαν ἑαυτοὺς μήτε φαγεῖν
who cursed themselves neither to eat

μήτε πεῖν ἕως οὗ ἀνέλωσιν αὐτόν, καὶ νῦν
nor to drink until they kill him, and now

εἰσιν ἕτοιμοι προσδεχόμενοι τὴν ἀπὸ σοῦ
they are ready awaiting [1]the [3]from [4]thee

ἐπαγγελίαν. 22 ὁ μὲν οὖν χιλίαρχος
[2]promise. the – Therefore chiliarch

til we have killed Paul. 15Now then, you and the Sanhedrin petition the commander to bring him before you on the pretext of wanting more accurate information about his case. We are ready to kill him before he gets here."

16But when the son of Paul's sister heard of this plot, he went into the barracks and told Paul.

17Then Paul called one of the centurions and said, "Take this young man to the commander; he has something to tell him." 18So he took him to the commander.

The centurion said, "Paul, the prisoner, sent for me and asked me to bring this young man to you because he has something to tell you."

19The commander took the young man by the hand, drew him aside and asked, "What is it you want to tell me?"

20He said: "The Jews have agreed to ask you to bring Paul before the Sanhedrin tomorrow on the pretext of wanting more accurate information about him. 21Don't give in to them, because more than forty of them are waiting in ambush for him. They have taken an oath not to eat or drink until they have killed him. They are ready now, waiting for your consent to their request."

22The commander dis-

mander let the young man
go, instructing him, "Tell
no one that you have noti-
fied me of these things."

Paul Moved to Caesarea

23And he called to him
two of the centurions, and
said, "Get two hundred
soldiers ready by [l]the third
hour of the night to proceed
to Caesarea, with seventy
horsemen and two hundred
spearmen."
24*They were* also to provide mounts to put Paul on
and bring him safely to
Felix the governor.
25And he wrote a letter
having this form:
26"Claudius Lysias, to
the most excellent
governor Felix,
greetings.
27"When this man was
arrested by the Jews
and was about to be
slain by them, I
came upon them
with the troops and
rescued him, having
learned that he was
a Roman.
28"And wanting to as-
certain the charge
for which they were
accusing him, I
brought him down to
their Council;
29 and I found him to
be accused over
questions about
their Law, but under
no accusation de-
serving death or im-
prisonment.
30"And when I was in-
formed that there
would be a plot
against the man, I
sent him to you at
once, also instruct-
ing his accusers to
bring charges
against him before
you."
31So the soldiers, in
accordance with their or-
ders, took Paul and brought
him by night to Antipatris.
32But the next day, leav-
ing the horsemen to go on
with him, they returned to
the barracks.
33And when these had
come to Caesarea and de-

[l] I.e., 9 p.m.

ἀπέλυσε τὸν νεανίσκον, παραγγείλας μηδενὶ
dismissed the young man, charging [him] to no one

ἐκλαλῆσαι ὅτι ταῦτα ἐνεφάνισας πρὸς ἐμέ.
to divulge that these things thou reportedst to me.

23 Καὶ προσκαλεσάμενός τινας δύο τῶν
And calling to [him] a certain two of the

ἑκατονταρχῶν εἶπεν· ἑτοιμάσατε στρατιώτας
centurions he said: Prepare ye soldiers

διακοσίους ὅπως πορευθῶσιν ἕως Καισαρείας,
two hundred so as they may go as far as Cæsarea,

καὶ ἱππεῖς ἑβδομήκοντα καὶ δεξιολάβους
and horsemen seventy and spearmen

διακοσίους, ἀπὸ τρίτης ὥρας τῆς νυκτός,
two hundred, from third hour of the night,

24 κτήνη τε παραστῆσαι, ἵνα ἐπιβιβάσαντες
and beasts to stand by, that putting on

τὸν Παῦλον διασώσωσι πρὸς Φήλικα τὸν
– Paul they may bring [him] safely to Felix the

ἡγεμόνα, 25 γράψας ἐπιστολὴν ἔχουσαν
governor, writing a letter having

τὸν τύπον τοῦτον· 26 Κλαύδιος Λυσίας τῷ
this pattern: Claudius Lysias to the

κρατίστῳ ἡγεμόνι Φήλικι χαίρειν. 27 Τὸν
most excellent governor Felix greeting. –

ἄνδρα τοῦτον συλλημφθέντα ὑπὸ τῶν
man This having been arrested by the

Ἰουδαίων καὶ μέλλοντα ἀναιρεῖσθαι ὑπ'
Jews and being about to be killed by

αὐτῶν ἐπιστὰς σὺν τῷ στρατεύματι
them coming on [the scene] with the soldiery

ἐξειλάμην, μαθὼν ὅτι Ῥωμαῖός ἐστιν·
I rescued, having learned that a Roman he is;

28 βουλόμενός τε ἐπιγνῶναι τὴν αἰτίαν
and being minded to know fully the cause

δι' ἣν ἐνεκάλουν αὐτῷ, κατήγαγον εἰς
on account of which they were accusing him, I brought [him] down to

τὸ συνέδριον αὐτῶν· 29 ὃν εὗρον ἐγκαλούμενον
the council of them; whom I found being accused

περὶ ζητημάτων τοῦ νόμου αὐτῶν, μηδὲν
about questions of the law of them, [3]*nothing*

δὲ ἄξιον θανάτου ἢ δεσμῶν ἔχοντα
[1]but [5]worthy [6]of death [7]or [8]of bonds [2]having

ἔγκλημα. 30 μηνυθείσης δέ μοι ἐπιβουλῆς
[4]charge. And being revealed to me a plot[a]
=when it was revealed to me that there was a plot

εἰς τὸν ἄνδρα ἔσεσθαι, ἐξαυτῆς ἔπεμψα
against the man to be, at once I sent

πρὸς σέ, παραγγείλας καὶ τοῖς κατηγόροις
to thee, commanding also the accusers

λέγειν πρὸς αὐτὸν ἐπὶ σοῦ. 31 Οἱ μὲν
to say to him before thee. the –

οὖν στρατιῶται κατὰ τὸ διατεταγμένον
Therefore soldiers according to the thing *having been* appointed

αὐτοῖς ἀναλαβόντες τὸν Παῦλον ἤγαγον
them taking up – Paul brought

διὰ νυκτὸς εἰς τὴν Ἀντιπατρίδα· 32 τῇ δὲ
through (during) [the] night to – Antipatris; and on the

ἐπαύριον ἐάσαντες τοὺς ἱππεῖς ἀπέρχεσθαι
morrow allowing the horsemen to depart

σὺν αὐτῷ, ὑπέστρεψαν εἰς τὴν παρεμβολήν·
with him, they returned to the fort;

33 οἵτινες εἰσελθόντες εἰς τὴν Καισάρειαν
who entering into – Cæsarea

missed the young man and
cautioned him, "Don't tell
anyone that you have re-
ported this to me."

Paul Transferred to Caesarea

23Then he called two of
his centurions and ordered
them, "Get ready a detachment of two hundred sol-
diers, seventy horsemen
and two hundred spear-
men[u] to go to Caesarea at
nine tonight. 24Provide
mounts for Paul so that he
may be taken safely to
Governor Felix."
25He wrote a letter as follows:

26Claudius Lysias,

To His Excellency,
Governor Felix:

Greetings.

27This man was seized
by the Jews and they
were about to kill him,
but I came with my
troops and rescued him,
for I had learned that he
is a Roman citizen. 28I
wanted to know why
they were accusing him,
so I brought him to their
Sanhedrin. 29I found
that the accusation had
to do with questions
about their law, but
there was no charge
against him that de-
served death or impris-
onment. 30When I was
informed of a plot to be
carried out against the
man, I sent him to you
at once. I also ordered
his accusers to present
to you their case against
him.

31So the soldiers, carry-
ing out their orders, took
Paul with them during the
night and brought him as
far as Antipatris. 32The
next day they let the cavalry go on with him, while
they returned to the bar-
racks. 33When the cavalry
arrived in Caesarea, they

[u] *23* The meaning of the Greek for this word is uncertain.

livered the letter to the governor, they also presented
Paul to him.
34 And when he had read
it, he asked from what
province he was; and when
he learned that he was from
Cilicia,
35 he said, "I will give you
a hearing after your accusers arrive also," giving orders for him to be kept in
Herod's [m]Praetorium.

Chapter 24

Paul before Felix

24 AND after five days the
high priest Ananias
came down with some el-
ders, with a certain attor-
ney *named* Tertullus; and
they brought charges to the
governor against Paul.
2 And after *Paul* had been
summoned, Tertullus be-
gan to accuse him, saying
to the governor,
"Since we have through
you attained much peace,
and since by your provi-
dence reforms are being
carried out for this nation,
3 we acknowledge *this* in
every way and every-
where, most excellent
Felix, with all thankful-
ness.
4 "But, that I may not
weary you any further, I
beg you to grant us, by your
kindness, a brief hearing.
5 "For we have found
this man a real pest and a
fellow who stirs up dissension among all the Jews
throughout [n]the world, and
a ringleader of the sect of
the Nazarenes.
6 "And he even tried to
desecrate the temple; and
then we arrested him.
[[o]And we wanted to judge
him according to our own
Law.
7 "But Lysias the com-
mander came along, and
with much violence took
him out of our hands,
8 ordering his accusers to
come before you.] And by
examining him yourself
concerning all these mat-
ters, you will be able to ascertain the things of which
we accuse him."
9 And the Jews also
joined in the attack, asserting that these things were
so.

[m] I.e., governor's official residence
[n] Lit., *the inhabited earth*
[o] Many mss. do not contain the remainder of v. 6, v. 7, nor the first part of v. 8

καὶ ἀναδόντες τὴν ἐπιστολὴν τῷ ἡγεμόνι,
and handing over the letter to the governor,
παρέστησαν καὶ τὸν Παῦλον αὐτῷ.
presented also – Paul to him.
34 ἀναγνοὺς δὲ καὶ ἐπερωτήσας ἐκ ποίας
And having read and asking of what
ἐπαρχείας ἐστίν, καὶ πυθόμενος ὅτι ἀπὸ
province he is(was), and learning[,] – From
Κιλικίας, 35 διακούσομαί σου, ἔφη, ὅταν
Cilicia, I will hear thee, he said, when
καὶ οἱ κατήγοροί σου παραγένωνται·
also the accusers of thee arrive;
κελεύσας ἐν τῷ πραιτωρίῳ τοῦ Ἡρῴδου
commanding in the prætorium – of Herod
=that he be kept in Herod's prætorium.
φυλάσσεσθαι αὐτόν.
to be kept him.

24 Μετὰ δὲ πέντε ἡμέρας κατέβη ὁ
And after five days came down the
ἀρχιερεὺς Ἁνανίας μετὰ πρεσβυτέρων τινῶν
high priest Ananias with elders some
καὶ ῥήτορος Τερτύλλου τινός, οἵτινες
and an orator Tertullus one, who
ἐνεφάνισαν τῷ ἡγεμόνι κατὰ τοῦ Παύλου.
informed the governor against – Paul.
2 κληθέντος δὲ [αὐτοῦ] ἤρξατο κατηγορεῖν
And being called him[a] [2]began [3]to accuse
=when he was called
ὁ Τέρτυλλος λέγων· πολλῆς εἰρήνης
– [1]Tertullus saying: Much peace
τυγχάνοντες διὰ σοῦ καὶ διορθωμάτων
obtaining through thee and reforms
γινομένων τῷ ἔθνει τούτῳ διὰ τῆς σῆς
coming to this nation through – thy
προνοίας, 3 πάντῃ τε καὶ πανταχοῦ
forethought, both in everything and everywhere
ἀποδεχόμεθα, κράτιστε Φῆλιξ, μετὰ πάσης
we welcome, most excellent Felix, with all
εὐχαριστίας. 4 ἵνα δὲ μὴ ἐπὶ πλεῖόν
thankfulness. But that [3]not [4]more
σε ἐγκόπτω, παρακαλῶ ἀκοῦσαί σε ἡμῶν
[2]thee [1]I hinder, I beseech [2]to hear [1]thee us
συντόμως τῇ σῇ ἐπιεικείᾳ. 5 εὑρόντες γὰρ
briefly – in thy forbearance. For having found
τὸν ἄνδρα τοῦτον λοιμὸν καὶ κινοῦντα
this man pestilent and moving
στάσεις πᾶσιν τοῖς Ἰουδαίοις τοῖς κατὰ
seditions [among] all the Jews – throughout
τὴν οἰκουμένην πρωτοστάτην τε τῆς τῶν
the inhabited [earth] and a ringleader of the [2]of the
Ναζωραίων αἱρέσεως, 6 ὃς καὶ τὸ ἱερὸν
[3]Nazarenes [1]sect, who also [3]the [4]temple
ἐπείρασεν βεβηλῶσαι, ὃν καὶ ἐκρατήσαμεν,
[1]attempted [2]to profane, whom also we laid hold of,‡
8 παρ' οὗ δυνήσῃ αὐτὸς ἀνακρίνας
from whom thou wilt be able [thy]self [2]having examined
περὶ πάντων τούτων ἐπιγνῶναι ὧν ἡμεῖς
[3]concerning [4]all [5]these things [1]to know fully of which we
κατηγοροῦμεν αὐτοῦ. 9 συνεπέθεντο δὲ
accuse him. And [4]joined in
καὶ οἱ Ἰουδαῖοι φάσκοντες ταῦτα οὕτως
[3]also [1]the [2]Jews alleging these things thus

‡ Verse 7 omitted by Nestle; *cf.* NIV footnote.

delivered the letter to the
governor and handed Paul
over to him. 34 The governor read the letter and
asked what province he
was from. Learning that he
was from Cilicia, 35 he said,
"I will hear your case when
your accusers get here."
Then he ordered that Paul
be kept under guard in Herod's palace.

Chapter 24

The Trial Before Felix

FIVE days later the high
priest Ananias went
down to Caesarea with
some of the elders and a
lawyer named Tertullus,
and they brought their
charges against Paul before
the governor. 2 When Paul
was called in, Tertullus
presented his case before
Felix: "We have enjoyed a
long period of peace under
you, and your foresight has
brought about reforms in
this nation. 3 Everywhere
and in every way, most excellent Felix, we acknowledge this with profound
gratitude. 4 But in order not
to weary you further, I
would request that you be
kind enough to hear us
briefly.
5 "We have found this
man to be a troublemaker,
stirring up riots among the
Jews all over the world. He
is a ringleader of the Nazarene sect 6 and even tried to
desecrate the temple; so we
seized him. 8 By[v] examining him yourself you will be
able to learn the truth about
all these charges we are
bringing against him."
9 The Jews joined in the
accusation, asserting that
these things were true.

[v] 6-8 Some manuscripts *him and wanted to judge him according to our law. 7 But the commander, Lysias, came and with the use of much force snatched him from our hands 8 and ordered his accusers to come before you. By*

10And when the governor
had nodded for him to
speak, Paul responded:
"Knowing that for many
years you have been a
judge to this nation, I
cheerfully make my de-
fense,
11since you can take note
of the fact that no more
than twelve days ago I went
up to Jerusalem to worship.
12"And neither in the
temple, nor in the syna-
gogues, nor in the city *itself*
did they find me carrying
on a discussion with any-
one or causing a riot.
13"Nor can they prove to
you *the charges* of which
they now accuse me.
14"But this I admit to
you, that according to the
Way which they call a sect I
do serve the God of our fathers, believing everything
that is in accordance with
the Law, and that is written
in the Prophets;
15having a hope in God,
which these men cherish
themselves, that there shall
certainly be a resurrection
of both the righteous and
the wicked.
16"In view of this, I also
do my best to maintain always a blameless con-
science *both* before God
and before men.
17"Now after several
years I came to bring [p] alms
to my nation and to present
offerings;
18in which they found me
occupied in the temple,
having been purified, without *any* crowd or uproar.
But *there were* certain Jews
from Asia—
19who ought to have been
present before you, and to
make accusation, if they
should have anything
against me.
20"Or else let these men

[p] Or, *gifts to charity*

ἔχειν. 10 Ἀπεκρίθη τε ὁ Παῦλος,
to have(be). And answered – Paul,

νεύσαντος αὐτῷ τοῦ ἡγεμόνος λέγειν· ἐκ
[3]having beckoned [4]to him [1]the [2]governor[a] to speak: [4]of (for)

πολλῶν ἐτῶν ὄντα σε κριτὴν τῷ ἔθνει τούτῳ
[5]many [6]years [3]being (to be) [2]thee [7]a judge [8]to [9]this [10]nation

ἐπιστάμενος εὐθύμως τὰ περὶ
[1]understanding [12]cheerfully [13][as to] [14]the things [15]concerning

ἐμαυτοῦ ἀπολογοῦμαι, 11 δυναμένου σου
[16]myself [11]I defend myself, being able thee[a] =as thou art able

ἐπιγνῶναι ὅτι οὐ πλείους εἰσίν μοι ἡμέραι
to know fully that [3]not [4]more [1]there are [2]to me [5][than] [7]days

δώδεκα ἀφ' ἧς ἀνέβην προσκυνήσων εἰς
[6]twelve from =since which I went up worshipping in

Ἰερουσαλήμ. 12 καὶ οὔτε ἐν τῷ ἱερῷ
Jerusalem. And neither in the temple

εὗρόν με πρός τινα διαλεγόμενον ἢ
they found me [2]with [3]anyone [1]discoursing or

ἐπίστασιν ποιοῦντα ὄχλου, οὔτε ἐν ταῖς
[2]collection [1]making of a crowd, neither in the

συναγωγαῖς οὔτε κατὰ τὴν πόλιν, 13 οὐδὲ
synagogues nor throughout the city, nor

παραστῆσαι δύνανταί σοι περὶ ὧν νυνὶ
[2]to prove [1]are they able to thee con- cerning [the] things of which now

κατηγοροῦσίν μου. 14 ὁμολογῶ δὲ τοῦτό
they accuse me. But I confess this

σοι, ὅτι κατὰ τὴν ὁδὸν ἣν λέγουσιν
to thee, that according to the way which they say(call)

αἵρεσιν οὕτως λατρεύω τῷ πατρῴῳ θεῷ,
a sect thus I worship the ancestral God,

πιστεύων πᾶσι τοῖς κατὰ τὸν νόμον καὶ
believing all the things according to the law and

τοῖς ἐν τοῖς προφήταις γεγραμμένοις,
the things in the prophets *having been* written,

15 ἐλπίδα ἔχων εἰς τὸν θεόν, ἣν καὶ
hope having toward – God, which [3]also

αὐτοὶ οὗτοι προσδέχονται, ἀνάστασιν μέλ-
[2][them]selves [1]these expect, a resurrection to be

λειν ἔσεσθαι δικαίων τε καὶ ἀδίκων.
about to be both of just and of unjust.

16 ἐν τούτῳ καὶ αὐτὸς ἀσκῶ ἀπρόσκοπον
By this also [2][my]self [1]I exercise [4]a blameless

συνείδησιν ἔχειν πρὸς τὸν θεὸν καὶ τοὺς
[5]conscience [3]to have toward – God and –

ἀνθρώπους διὰ παντός. 17 δι' ἐτῶν δὲ
men always. And after years

πλειόνων ἐλεημοσύνας ποιήσων εἰς τὸ
many [2]alms [1]making(bringing) [3]to [4]the

ἔθνος μου παρεγενόμην καὶ προσφοράς,
[5]nation [6]of me [9]I arrived [7]and [8]offerings,

18 ἐν αἷς εὗρόν με ἡγνισμένον ἐν τῷ
among which they found me *having been* purified in the

ἱερῷ, οὐ μετὰ ὄχλου οὐδὲ μετὰ θορύβου,
temple, not with a crowd nor with uproar,

19 τινὲς δὲ ἀπὸ τῆς Ἀσίας Ἰουδαῖοι,
but some [2]from – [3]Asia [1]Jews,

οὓς ἔδει ἐπὶ σοῦ παρεῖναι καὶ κατηγορεῖν
whom it be- hoved before thee to be present and to accuse

εἴ τι ἔχοιεν πρὸς ἐμέ. 20 ἢ αὐτοὶ
if anything they have against me. Or [2][them]selves

10When the governor mo-
tioned for him to speak,
Paul replied: "I know that
for a number of years you
have been a judge over this
nation; so I gladly make my
defense. 11You can easily
verify that no more than
twelve days ago I went up
to Jerusalem to worship.
12My accusers did not find
me arguing with anyone at
the temple, or stirring up a
crowd in the synagogues or
anywhere else in the city.
13And they cannot prove to
you the charges they are
now making against me.
14However, I admit that I
worship the God of our fathers as a follower of the
Way, which they call a
sect. I believe everything
that agrees with the Law
and that is written in the
Prophets, 15and I have the
same hope in God as these
men, that there will be a
resurrection of both the
righteous and the wicked.
16So I strive always to keep
my conscience clear before
God and man.
17"After an absence of
several years, I came to Jerusalem to bring my people
gifts for the poor and to present offerings. 18I was ceremonially clean when they
found me in the temple
courts doing this. There
was no crowd with me, nor
was I involved in any disturbance. 19But there are
some Jews from the prov-
ince of Asia, who ought to
be here before you and
bring charges if they have
anything against me. 20Or
these who are here should

themselves tell what misdeed they found when I stood before the Council,

21other than for this one statement which I shouted out while standing among them, 'For the resurrection of the dead I am on trial before you today.' "

22But Felix, having a more exact knowledge about the Way, put them off, saying, "When Lysias the [q]commander comes down, I will decide your case."

23And he gave orders to the centurion for him to be kept in custody and *yet* have *some* freedom, and not to prevent any of his friends from ministering to him.

24But some days later, Felix arrived with Drusilla, his wife who was a Jewess, and sent for Paul, and heard him *speak* about faith in Christ Jesus.

25And as he was discussing righteousness, self-control and the judgment to come, Felix became frightened and said, "Go away for the present, and when I find time, I will summon you."

26At the same time too, he was hoping that money would be given him by Paul; therefore he also used to send for him quite often and converse with him.

27But after two years had passed, Felix was succeeded by Porcius Festus; and wishing to do the Jews a favor, Felix left Paul imprisoned.

Chapter 25

Paul before Festus

FESTUS therefore, having arrived in the province, three days later went up to Jerusalem from Caesarea.

[q]I.e., chiliarch, in command of one thousand troops

οὗτοι εἰπάτωσαν τί εὗρον ἀδίκημα στάντος
[2]these [1]let [4]say [1]what [3]they found [2]misdeed standing

μου ἐπὶ τοῦ συνεδρίου, 21 ἢ περὶ μιᾶς
me[a] before the council, unless concerning [2]one
=while I stood

ταύτης φωνῆς ἧς ἐκέκραξα ἐν αὐτοῖς
[1]this voice which I have cried out [2]among [3]them

ἑστὼς ὅτι περὶ ἀναστάσεως νεκρῶν ἐγὼ
[1]standing[,] – Concerning a resurrection of dead persons I

κρίνομαι σήμερον ἐφ' ὑμῶν. 22 'Ανεβάλετο
am being judged to-day before you. [2]postponed

δὲ αὐτοὺς ὁ Φῆλιξ, ἀκριβέστερον εἰδὼς
And [3]them – [1]Felix, more exactly knowing

τὰ περὶ τῆς ὁδοῦ, εἴπας· ὅταν Λυσίας ὁ
the things concerning the way, saying: When Lysias the

χιλίαρχος καταβῇ, διαγνώσομαι τὰ καθ'
chiliarch comes down, I will determine the things as to

ὑμᾶς· 23 διαταξάμενος τῷ ἑκατοντάρχῃ
you; commanding the centurion

τηρεῖσθαι αὐτὸν ἔχειν τε ἄνεσιν καὶ
to keep him and to have indulgence and

μηδένα κωλύειν τῶν ἰδίων αὐτοῦ ὑπηρετεῖν
[2]no one [1]to forbid of his own [people] to attend

αὐτῷ. 24 Μετὰ δὲ ἡμέρας τινὰς παραγενό-
him. And after days some [2]arriv-

μενος ὁ Φῆλιξ σὺν Δρουσίλλῃ τῇ ἰδίᾳ
ing – [1]Felix with Drusilla the(his) own

γυναικὶ οὔσῃ Ἰουδαίᾳ μετεπέμψατο τὸν
wife being a Jewess he sent for –

Παῦλον, καὶ ἤκουσεν αὐτοῦ περὶ τῆς
Paul, and heard him about [1]the(?his)

εἰς Χριστὸν Ἰησοῦν πίστεως. 25 διαλεγομέ-
[3]in [4]Christ [5]Jesus [2]faith. discours-
=And as he discoursed

νου δὲ αὐτοῦ περὶ δικαιοσύνης καὶ
ing And him[a] concerning righteousness and

ἐγκρατείας καὶ τοῦ κρίματος τοῦ μέλλοντος
self-control and the [2]judgment – [1]coming

ἔμφοβος γενόμενος ὁ Φῆλιξ ἀπεκρίθη·
afraid becoming – Felix answered:

τὸ νῦν ἔχον πορεύου, καιρὸν δὲ μεταλαβὼν
For the present† go thou, but [2]time [1]taking [3]later

μετακαλέσομαί σε· 26 ἅμα καὶ ἐλπίζων
I will send for thee; at the same time also hoping

ὅτι χρήματα δοθήσεται αὐτῷ ὑπὸ τοῦ
that money will be given him by –

Παύλου· διὸ καὶ πυκνότερον αὐτὸν
Paul: wherefore also more frequently him

μεταπεμπόμενος ὡμίλει αὐτῷ. 27 Διετίας δὲ
sending for he conversed with him. And two years

πληρωθείσης ἔλαβεν διάδοχον ὁ Φῆλιξ
being completed[a] [2]received [3]a successor – [1]Felix

Πόρκιον Φῆστον· θέλων τε χάριτα κατα-
Porcius Festus; and wishing a favour to

θέσθαι τοῖς Ἰουδαίοις ὁ Φῆλιξ κατέλιπε
show to the Jews – Felix left

τὸν Παῦλον δεδεμένον.
– Paul *having been* bound.

25 Φῆστος οὖν ἐπιβὰς τῇ ἐπαρχείῳ
Festus therefore having entered the province

μετὰ τρεῖς ἡμέρας ἀνέβη εἰς Ἱεροσόλυμα
after three days went up to Jerusalem

state what crime they
found in me when I stood
before the Sanhedrin—
21unless it was this one
thing I shouted as I stood in
their presence: 'It is concerning the resurrection of
the dead that I am on trial
before you today.' "
22Then Felix, who was
well acquainted with the
Way, adjourned the pro-
ceedings. "When Lysias
the commander comes,"
he said, "I will decide your
case." 23He ordered the
centurion to keep Paul under guard but to give him
some freedom and permit
his friends to take care of
his needs.
24Several days later Felix
came with his wife Drusilla, who was a Jewess. He
sent for Paul and listened to
him as he spoke about faith
in Christ Jesus. 25As Paul
discoursed on righteous-
ness, self-control and the
judgment to come, Felix
was afraid and said,
"That's enough for now!
You may leave. When I
find it convenient, I will
send for you." 26At the
same time he was hoping
that Paul would offer him a
bribe, so he sent for him
frequently and talked with
him.
27When two years had
passed, Felix was succeeded by Porcius Festus, but
because Felix wanted to
grant a favor to the Jews,
he left Paul in prison.

Chapter 25

The Trial Before Festus

THREE days after arriving in the province,
Festus went up from Caes-
area to Jerusalem, 2where

2And the chief priests and the leading men of the Jews brought charges against Paul; and they were urging him,

3requesting a concession against Paul, that he might have him brought to Jerusalem (*at the same time,* setting an ambush to kill him on the way).

4Festus then answered that Paul was being kept in custody at Caesarea and that he himself was about to leave shortly.

5"Therefore," he *said, "let the influential men among you go there with me, and if there is anything wrong about the man, let them prosecute him."

6And after he had spent not more than eight or ten days among them, he went down to Caesarea; and on the next day he took his seat on the tribunal and ordered Paul to be brought.

7And after he had arrived, the Jews who had come down from Jerusalem stood around him, bringing many and serious charges against him which they could not prove;

8while Paul said in his own defense, "I have committed no offense either against the Law of the Jews or against the temple or against Caesar."

9But Festus, wishing to do the Jews a favor, answered Paul and said, "Are you willing to go up to Jerusalem and stand trial before me on these *charges?*"

10But Paul said, "I am standing before Caesar's tribunal, where I ought to be tried. I have done no wrong to *the* Jews, as you also very well know.

11"If then I am a wrongdoer, and have committed anything worthy of death, I do not refuse to die; but if

ἐν ὑμῖν, φησίν, δυνατοὶ συγκαταβάντες,
[4]among [5]you, [6]he says, [3]able men going down with [me],

ἀπὸ Καισαρείας, **2** ἐνεφάνισάν τε αὐτῷ
from Cæsarea, and [8]informed [9]him

οἱ ἀρχιερεῖς καὶ οἱ πρῶτοι τῶν Ἰουδαίων
[1]the [2]chief priests [3]and [4]the [5]chiefs [6]of the [7]Jews

κατὰ τοῦ Παύλου, καὶ παρεκάλουν αὐτὸν
against – Paul, and they besought him

3 αἰτούμενοι χάριν κατ᾽ αὐτοῦ, ὅπως μετα-
asking a favour against him, so as he might

πέμψηται αὐτὸν εἰς Ἰερουσαλήμ, ἐνέδραν
summon him to Jerusalem, a plot

ποιοῦντες ἀνελεῖν αὐτὸν κατὰ τὴν ὁδόν.
making to kill him by the way.

4 ὁ μὲν οὖν Φῆστος ἀπεκρίθη τηρεῖσθαι
– – Therefore Festus answered [2]to be kept

τὸν Παῦλον εἰς Καισάρειαν, ἑαυτὸν δὲ
– [1]Paul in Cæsarea, and [2]himself

μέλλειν ἐν τάχει ἐκπορεύεσθαι· **5** οἱ οὖν
[1]to intend shortly to go forth; [2]the [1]therefore

εἴ τι ἔστιν ἐν τῷ ἀνδρὶ ἄτοπον,
if anything there is in the man amiss,

κατηγορείτωσαν αὐτοῦ. **6** Διατρίψας δὲ ἐν
let them accuse him. And having stayed among

αὐτοῖς ἡμέρας οὐ πλείους ὀκτὼ ἢ δέκα,
them days not more [than] eight or ten,

καταβὰς εἰς Καισάρειαν, τῇ ἐπαύριον
going down to Cæsarea, on the morrow

καθίσας ἐπὶ τοῦ βήματος ἐκέλευσεν τὸν
sitting on the tribunal he commanded –

Παῦλον ἀχθῆναι. **7** παραγενομένου δὲ
Paul to be brought. And arriving
=when he arrived

αὐτοῦ περιέστησαν αὐτὸν οἱ ἀπὸ Ἱεροσο-
him[a] [6]stood round [7]him [1]the [4]from [5]Jeru-

λύμων καταβεβηκότες Ἰουδαῖοι, πολλὰ καὶ
salem [3]having come down [2]Jews, many and

βαρέα αἰτιώματα καταφέροντες, ἃ οὐκ
heavy charges bringing against [him], which not

ἴσχυον ἀποδεῖξαι, **8** τοῦ Παύλου ἀπολογου-
they were able to prove, – Paul defending him-

μένου ὅτι οὔτε εἰς τὸν νόμον τῶν
self[,][a] – Neither against the law of the
=while Paul defended himself,

Ἰουδαίων οὔτε εἰς τὸ ἱερὸν οὔτε εἰς
Jews nor against the temple nor against

Καίσαρά τι ἥμαρτον. **9** ὁ Φῆστος δέ,
Cæsar anything I sinned. – But Festus,

θέλων τοῖς Ἰουδαίοις χάριν καταθέσθαι,
wishing the Jews a favour to show,

ἀποκριθεὶς τῷ Παύλῳ εἶπεν· θέλεις εἰς
answering – Paul said: Dost thou wish [2]to

Ἱεροσόλυμα ἀναβὰς ἐκεῖ περὶ τούτων
[3]Jerusalem [1]going up [4]there [8]concerning [9]these things

κριθῆναι ἐπ᾽ ἐμοῦ; **10** εἶπεν δὲ ὁ Παῦλος·
[5]to be judged [6]before [7]me? And said – Paul:

ἑστὼς ἐπὶ τοῦ βήματος Καίσαρός εἰμι,
Standing before the tribunal of Cæsar I am,

οὗ με δεῖ κρίνεσθαι. Ἰουδαίους οὐδὲν
where me it behoves to be judged. Jews nothing

ἠδίκηκα, ὡς καὶ σὺ κάλλιον ἐπιγινώσκεις.
I have wronged, as indeed thou very well knowest.

11 εἰ μὲν οὖν ἀδικῶ καὶ ἄξιον θανάτου
If – therefore I do wrong and worthy of death

πέπραχά τι, οὐ παραιτοῦμαι τὸ ἀποθανεῖν·
I have done anything, I do not refuse *the* to die;

the chief priests and Jewish leaders appeared before him and presented the charges against Paul. 3They urgently requested Festus, as a favor to them, to have Paul transferred to Jerusalem, for they were preparing an ambush to kill him along the way. 4Festus answered, "Paul is being held at Caesarea, and I myself am going there soon. 5Let some of your leaders come with me and press charges against the man there, if he has done anything wrong."

6After spending eight or ten days with them, he went down to Caesarea, and the next day he convened the court and ordered that Paul be brought before him. 7When Paul appeared, the Jews who had come down from Jerusalem stood around him, bringing many serious charges against him, which they could not prove.

8Then Paul made his defense: "I have done nothing wrong against the law of the Jews or against the temple or against Caesar."

9Festus, wishing to do the Jews a favor, said to Paul, "Are you willing to go up to Jerusalem and stand trial before me there on these charges?"

10Paul answered: "I am now standing before Caesar's court, where I ought to be tried. I have not done any wrong to the Jews, as you yourself know very well. 11If, however, I am guilty of doing anything deserving death, I do not refuse to die. But if the none of those things is *true* of which these men accuse me, no one can hand me over to them. I appeal to Caesar.''

12Then when Festus had conferred with his council, he answered, ''You have appealed to Caesar, to Caesar you shall go.''

13Now when several days had elapsed, King Agrippa and Bernice arrived at Caesarea, and paid their respects to Festus.

14And while they were spending many days there, Festus laid Paul's case before the king, saying, ''There is a certain man left a prisoner by Felix;

15and when I was at Jerusalem, the chief priests and the elders of the Jews brought charges against him, asking for a sentence of condemnation upon him.

16''And I answered them that it is not the custom of the Romans to hand over any man before the accused meets his accusers face to face, and has an opportunity to make his defense against the charges.

17''And so after they had assembled here, I made no delay, but on the next day took my seat on the tribunal, and ordered the man to be brought.

18''And when the accusers stood up, they *began* bringing charges against him not of such crimes as I was expecting;

19but they *simply* had some points of disagreement with him about their own religion and about a certain dead man, Jesus, whom Paul asserted to be alive.

20''And being at a loss how to investigate such matters, I asked whether he was willing to go to

εἰ δὲ οὐδέν ἐστιν ὧν οὗτοι κατηγοροῦσίν
but if not one there is of [the things] which these accuse

μου, οὐδείς με δύναται αὐτοῖς χαρίσασθαι·
me, no one [3]me [1]can [4]to them [2]*to* grant;

Καίσαρα ἐπικαλοῦμαι. 12 τότε ὁ Φῆστος
[2]Cæsar [1]I appeal to. Then – Festus

συλλαλήσας μετὰ τοῦ συμβουλίου ἀπεκρίθη·
having talked *with* with the council answered:

Καίσαρα ἐπικέκλησαι, ἐπὶ Καίσαρα πορεύσῃ.
[2]Cæsar [1]thou hast appealed to, before Cæsar thou shalt go.

13 Ἡμερῶν δὲ διαγενομένων τινῶν
And days passing some[a]
=when some days had passed

Ἀγρίππας ὁ βασιλεὺς καὶ Βερνίκη
Agrippa the king and Bernice

κατήντησαν εἰς Καισάρειαν ἀσπασάμενοι
arrived at Cæsarea greeting

τὸν Φῆστον. 14 ὡς δὲ πλείους ἡμέρας
– Festus. And as more days

διέτριβον ἐκεῖ, ὁ Φῆστος τῷ βασιλεῖ
they stayed there, – Festus [2]to the [3]king

ἀνέθετο τὰ κατὰ τὸν Παῦλον λέγων·
[1]set forth the matters regarding – Paul saying:

ἀνήρ τίς ἐστιν καταλελειμμένος ὑπὸ
A certain man there is having been left behind by

Φήλικος δέσμιος, 15 περὶ οὗ γενομένου
Felix prisoner, about whom being
=when I was

μου εἰς Ἱεροσόλυμα ἐνεφάνισαν οἱ ἀρχιερεῖς
me[a] in Jerusalem [8]informed [1]the [2]chief priests

καὶ οἱ πρεσβύτεροι τῶν Ἰουδαίων,
[3]and [4]the [5]elders [6]of the [7]Jews,

αἰτούμενοι κατ' αὐτοῦ καταδίκην· 16 πρὸς
asking against him sentence; to

οὓς ἀπεκρίθην ὅτι οὐκ ἔστιν ἔθος Ῥωμαίοις
whom I answered that it is not a custom with Romans

χαρίζεσθαί τινα ἄνθρωπον πρὶν ἢ ὁ
to grant any man before the

κατηγορούμενος κατὰ πρόσωπον ἔχοι τοὺς
[one] being accused face to face† should have the

κατηγόρους τόπον τε ἀπολογίας λάβοι
accusers [3]place* [1]and [4]of defence [2]receive

περὶ τοῦ ἐγκλήματος. 17 συνελθόντων
concerning the charge. Coming together[a]

οὖν ἐνθάδε ἀναβολὴν μηδεμίαν ποιησάμενος
therefore thither [3]delay [2]no [1]making

τῇ ἑξῆς καθίσας ἐπὶ τοῦ βήματος ἐκέλευσα
on the next [day] sitting on the tribunal I commanded

ἀχθῆναι τὸν ἄνδρα· 18 περὶ οὗ σταθέντες
to be brought the man; concerning whom standing

οἱ κατήγοροι οὐδεμίαν αἰτίαν ἔφερον ὧν
the accusers [2]no [3]charge [1]brought [4]of [6]things [7]which

ἐγὼ ὑπενόουν πονηρῶν, 19 ζητήματα δέ
[8]I [9]suspected [5]evil, but [2]questions

τινα περὶ τῆς ἰδίας δεισιδαιμονίας εἶχον
[3]certain [4]about [5]the(ir) own [6]religion [1]they had

πρὸς αὐτὸν καὶ περί τινος Ἰησοῦ
with him and about one Jesus

τεθνηκότος, ὃν ἔφασκεν ὁ Παῦλος ζῆν.
having died, whom [2]asserted – [1]Paul to live.

20 ἀπορούμενος δὲ ἐγὼ τὴν περὶ τούτων
And [2]being perplexed at [1]I [3]the [5]about [6]these things

ζήτησιν ἔλεγον εἰ βούλοιτο πορεύεσθαι εἰς
[4]debate said if he wished to go to

* That is, opportunity.

charges brought against me
by these Jews are not true,
no one has the right to hand
me over to them. I appeal
to Caesar!''
12After Festus had con-
ferred with his council, he
declared: ''You have ap-
pealed to Caesar. To Cae-
sar you will go!''

Festus Consults King Agrippa

13A few days later King
Agrippa and Bernice ar-
rived at Caesarea to pay
their respects to Festus.
14Since they were spending
many days there, Festus
discussed Paul's case with
the king. He said: ''There is
a man here whom Felix left
as a prisoner. 15When I
went to Jerusalem, the
chief priests and elders of
the Jews brought charges
against him and asked that
he be condemned.
16''I told them that it is
not the Roman custom to
hand over any man before
he has faced his accusers
and has had an opportunity
to defend himself against
their charges. 17When they
came here with me, I did
not delay the case, but convened the court the next
day and ordered the man to
be brought in. 18When his
accusers got up to speak,
they did not charge him
with any of the crimes I had
expected. 19Instead, they
had some points of dispute
with him about their own
religion and about a dead
man named Jesus who Paul
claimed was alive. 20I was
at a loss how to investigate
such matters; so I asked if
he would be willing to go to

Jerusalem and there stand trial on these matters.

21"But when Paul appealed to be held in custody for [r]the Emperor's decision, I ordered him to be kept in custody until I send him to Caesar."

22And Agrippa *said* to Festus, "I also would like to hear the man myself." "Tomorrow," he *said, "you shall hear him."

Paul before Agrippa

23And so, on the next day when Agrippa had come together with Bernice, amid great pomp, and had entered the auditorium [s]accompanied by the commanders and the prominent men of the city, at the command of Festus, Paul was brought in.

24And Festus *said, "King Agrippa, and all you gentlemen here present with us, you behold this man about whom all the people of the Jews appealed to me, both at Jerusalem and here, loudly declaring that he ought not to live any longer.

25"But I found that he had committed nothing worthy of death; and since he himself appealed to the Emperor, I decided to send him.

26"Yet I have nothing definite about him to write to my lord. Therefore I have brought him before you *all* and especially before you, King Agrippa, so that after the investigation has taken place, I may have something to write.

27"For it seems absurd to me in sending a prisoner, not to indicate also the charges against him."

Ἱεροσόλυμα κἀκεῖ κρίνεσθαι περὶ τούτων.
Jerusalem and there to be judged about these things.

21 τοῦ δὲ Παύλου ἐπικαλεσαμένου τηρηθῆναι
– But Paul having appealed[a] to be kept
=when Paul appealed

αὐτὸν εἰς τὴν τοῦ Σεβαστοῦ διάγνωσιν,
him to the – [2]of Augustus [1]decision,

ἐκέλευσα τηρεῖσθαι αὐτὸν ἕως οὗ ἀναπέμψω
I commanded to be kept him until I may send up

αὐτὸν πρὸς Καίσαρα. 22 Ἀγρίππας δὲ
him to Cæsar. And Agrippa

πρὸς τὸν Φῆστον· ἐβουλόμην καὶ αὐτὸς
[said] to – Festus: I was minded also [my]self

τοῦ ἀνθρώπου ἀκοῦσαι. αὔριον, φησίν,
the man to hear. Tomorrow, he says,

ἀκούσῃ αὐτοῦ. 23 Τῇ οὖν ἐπαύριον
thou shalt hear him. [2]On the [1]therefore [3]morrow

ἐλθόντος τοῦ Ἀγρίππα καὶ τῆς Βερνίκης
coming – Agrippa and – Bernice[a]
=when Agrippa and Bernice came

μετὰ πολλῆς φαντασίας καὶ εἰσελθόντων
with much display and entering[a]

εἰς τὸ ἀκροατήριον σύν τε χιλιάρχοις
into the place of audience with both chiliarchs

καὶ ἀνδράσιν τοῖς κατ' ἐξοχὴν τῆς πόλεως,
and [3]men [1]the [2]chief † of the city,

καὶ κελεύσαντος τοῦ Φήστου ἤχθη ὁ
and having commanded – Festus[a] [2]was brought –
=when Festus commanded

Παῦλος. 24 καί φησιν ὁ Φῆστος· Ἀγρίππα
[1]Paul. And says – Festus: Agrippa

βασιλεῦ καὶ πάντες οἱ συμπαρόντες ἡμῖν
king and all the [2]present together with [3]us

ἄνδρες, θεωρεῖτε τοῦτον περὶ οὗ ἅπαν τὸ
[1]men, ye behold this man about whom all the

πλῆθος τῶν Ἰουδαίων ἐνέτυχόν μοι ἔν τε
multitude of the Jews petitioned me [2]in [1]both

Ἱεροσολύμοις καὶ ἐνθάδε, βοῶντες μὴ
Jerusalem and here, crying not

δεῖν αὐτὸν ζῆν μηκέτι. 25 ἐγὼ δὲ κατε-
ought him to live *no* longer. But I dis-
=that he ought not to live any longer.

λαβόμην μηδὲν ἄξιον αὐτὸν θανάτου
covered [3]nothing [4]worthy [1]him [5]of death

πεπραχέναι, αὐτοῦ δὲ τούτου ἐπικαλεσαμένου
[2]to have done, but [him]self this man appealing to[a]
=when he himself appealed to

τὸν Σεβαστὸν ἔκρινα πέμπειν. 26 περὶ
– Augustus I decided to send. Concerning

οὗ ἀσφαλές τι γράψαι τῷ κυρίῳ οὐκ
whom [4]certain [3]anything [5]to write [6]to the [7]lord [2]not

ἔχω· διὸ προήγαγον αὐτὸν ἐφ' ὑμῶν καὶ
[1]I have; wherefore I brought forth him before you and

μάλιστα ἐπὶ σοῦ, βασιλεῦ Ἀγρίππα, ὅπως
most of all before thee, king Agrippa, so as
=when

τῆς ἀνακρίσεως γενομένης σχῶ τί γράψω·
the examination being[a] I may have what I may write;
there has been an examination

27 ἄλογον γάρ μοι δοκεῖ πέμποντα δέσμιον
for [3]unreasonable [2]to me [1]it seems sending a prisoner

μὴ καὶ τὰς κατ' αὐτοῦ αἰτίας σημᾶναι.
not also [3]the [4]against [5]him [2]charges [1]to signify.

Jerusalem and stand trial
there on these charges.
21When Paul made his ap-
peal to be held over for the
Emperor's decision, I or-
dered him held until I could
send him to Caesar."
22Then Agrippa said to
Festus, "I would like to
hear this man myself."
He replied, "Tomorrow
you will hear him."

Paul Before Agrippa

23The next day Agrippa
and Bernice came with
great pomp and entered the
audience room with the
high ranking officers and
the leading men of the city.
At the command of Festus,
Paul was brought in. 24Fes-
tus said: "King Agrippa,
and all who are present
with us, you see this man!
The whole Jewish commu-
nity has petitioned me
about him in Jerusalem and
here in Caesarea, shouting
that he ought not to live any
longer. 25I found he had
done nothing deserving of
death, but because he made
his appeal to the Emperor I
decided to send him to
Rome. 26But I have nothing
definite to write to His Majesty about him. Therefore I
have brought him before all
of you, and especially before you, King Agrippa, so
that as a result of this investigation I may have some-
thing to write. 27For I think
it is unreasonable to send
on a prisoner without spec-
ifying the charges against
him."

Chapter 26

Paul's Defense before Agrippa

AND Agrippa said to Paul, "You are permitted to speak for your-

26 Ἀγρίππας δὲ πρὸς τὸν Παῦλον ἔφη·
And Agrippa to – Paul said:

ἐπιτρέπεταί σοι ὑπὲρ σεαυτοῦ λέγειν.
It is permitted to thee on behalf of thyself to speak.

Chapter 26

THEN Agrippa said to Paul, "You have permission to speak for yourself."

[r] Lit., *the Augustus'* (in this case Nero)
[s] Lit., *and with*

self." Then Paul stretched
out his hand and *proceeded*
to make his defense:
2 "In regard to all the
things of which I am
accused by the Jews, I consider myself fortunate,
King Agrippa, that I am
about to make my defense
before you today;
3 especially because you
are an expert in all customs
and questions among *the*
Jews; therefore I beg you to
listen to me patiently.
4 "So then, all Jews
know my manner of life
from my youth up, which
from the beginning was
spent among my *own* na-
tion and at Jerusalem;
5 since they have known
about me for a long time
previously, if they are willing to testify, that I lived *as*
a Pharisee according to the
strictest sect of our religion.
6 "And now I am stand-
ing trial for the hope of the
promise made by God to
our fathers;
7 *the promise* to which
our twelve tribes hope to
attain, as they earnestly
serve *God* night and day.
And for this hope, O King,
I am being accused by
Jews.
8 "Why is it considered
incredible among you
people if God does raise the
dead?
9 "So then, I thought to
myself that I had to do
many things hostile to the
name of Jesus of Nazareth.
10 "And this is just what I
did in Jerusalem; not only
did I lock up many of the
saints in prisons, having received authority from the
chief priests, but also when
they were being put to
death I cast my vote against
them.
11 "And as I punished
them often in all the synagogues, I tried to force
them to blaspheme; and being furiously enraged at
them, I kept pursuing them

τότε ὁ Παῦλος ἐκτείνας τὴν χεῖρα
Then – Paul stretching out the(his) hand

ἀπελογεῖτο· **2** Περὶ πάντων ὧν ἐγκαλοῦμαι
defended himself: Concerning all things of which I am being accused

ὑπὸ Ἰουδαίων, βασιλεῦ Ἀγρίππα, ἥγημαι
by Jews, king Agrippa, I consider

ἐμαυτὸν μακάριον ἐπὶ σοῦ μέλλων σήμερον
myself happy [3]before [4]thee [1]being about [5]to-day

ἀπολογεῖσθαι, **3** μάλιστα γνώστην ὄντα σε
[2]to defend myself, most of all [3]an expert [2]being [1]thee

πάντων τῶν κατὰ Ἰουδαίους ἐθῶν τε
[5]of all [6]the [8]among [9]Jews [7]customs [4]both

καὶ ζητημάτων· διὸ δέομαι μακροθύμως
[10]and [11]questions; wherefore I beg patiently

ἀκοῦσαί μου. **4** Τὴν μὲν οὖν βίωσίν
to hear me. [3]the [1]So [2]then [4]manner of life

μου ἐκ νεότητος τὴν ἀπ' ἀρχῆς γενομένην
of me from youth – [2]from [4]beginning [1]having been [3][the]

ἐν τῷ ἔθνει μου ἐν τε Ἱεροσολύμοις
in the nation of me [2]in [1]and Jerusalem

ἴσασι πάντες Ἰουδαῖοι, **5** προγινώσκοντές
know all Jews, previously knowing

με ἄνωθεν, ἐὰν θέλωσι μαρτυρεῖν, ὅτι
me from the first, if they are willing to testify, that

κατὰ τὴν ἀκριβεστάτην αἵρεσιν τῆς
according to the most exact sect –

ἡμετέρας θρησκείας ἔζησα Φαρισαῖος. **6** καὶ
of our religion I lived a Pharisee. And

νῦν ἐπ' ἐλπίδι τῆς εἰς τοὺς πατέρας
now on(in) hope of the [5]to [6]the [7]fathers

ἡμῶν ἐπαγγελίας γενομένης ὑπὸ τοῦ θεοῦ
[8]of us [1]promise [2]having been [made] [3]by – [4]God

ἕστηκα κρινόμενος, **7** εἰς ἣν τὸ δωδεκά-
I stand being judged, to which the twelve

φυλον ἡμῶν ἐν ἐκτενείᾳ νύκτα καὶ
tribes of us with earnestness night and

ἡμέραν λατρεῦον ἐλπίζει καταντῆσαι· περὶ
day worshipping hopes to arrive; concerning

ἧς ἐλπίδος ἐγκαλοῦμαι ὑπὸ Ἰουδαίων,
which hope I am accused by Jews,

βασιλεῦ. **8** τί ἄπιστον κρίνεται παρ'
[O] king. Why incredible is it judged by

ὑμῖν εἰ ὁ θεὸς νεκροὺς ἐγείρει; **9** ἐγὼ
you if – God [2]dead persons [1]raises? [3]I

μὲν οὖν ἔδοξα ἐμαυτῷ πρὸς τὸ ὄνομα
[1]indeed [2]then [4]thought [5]to myself [10]to [11]the [12]name

Ἰησοῦ τοῦ Ναζωραίου δεῖν πολλὰ ἐναντία
[13]of Jesus [14]the [15]Nazarene [6]ought [8]many things [9]contrary

πρᾶξαι· **10** ὃ καὶ ἐποίησα ἐν Ἱεροσολύμοις,
[7]to do; which indeed I did in Jerusalem,

καὶ πολλούς τε τῶν ἁγίων ἐγὼ ἐν
and many – of the saints [1]I [3]in

φυλακαῖς κατέκλεισα τὴν παρὰ τῶν
[4]prisons [2]shut up [6]the [8]from [9]the

ἀρχιερέων ἐξουσίαν λαβών, ἀναιρουμένων τε
[10]chief priests [7]authority [5]having received, being killed and
=and when they were killed

αὐτῶν κατήνεγκα ψῆφον, **11** καὶ κατὰ
them* I cast a vote, and throughout

πάσας τὰς συναγωγὰς πολλάκις τιμωρῶν
all the synagogues often punishing

αὐτοὺς ἠνάγκαζον βλασφημεῖν, περισσῶς τε
them I compelled [them] to blaspheme, and excessively

ἐμμαινόμενος αὐτοῖς ἐδίωκον ἕως καὶ εἰς
raging against them I persecuted as far as even to

So Paul motioned with his
hand and began his de-
fense: 2 "King Agrippa, I
consider myself fortunate
to stand before you today
as I make my defense
against all the accusations
of the Jews, 3 and especially
so because you are well acquainted with all the Jewish
customs and controversies.
Therefore, I beg you to listen to me patiently.
4 "The Jews all know the
way I have lived ever since
I was a child, from the beginning of my life in my
own country, and also in
Jerusalem. 5 They have
known me for a long time
and can testify, if they are
willing, that according to
the strictest sect of our religion, I lived as a Pharisee.
6 And now it is because of
my hope in what God has
promised our fathers that I
am on trial today. 7 This is
the promise our twelve
tribes are hoping to see fulfilled as they earnestly
serve God day and night. O
king, it is because of this
hope that the Jews are accusing me. 8 Why should
any of you consider it incredible that God raises the
dead?
9 "I too was convinced
that I ought to do all that
was possible to oppose the
name of Jesus of Nazareth.
10 And that is just what I did
in Jerusalem. On the au-
thority of the chief priests I
put many of the saints in
prison, and when they were
put to death, I cast my vote
against them. 11 Many a
time I went from one synagogue to another to have
them punished, and I tried
to force them to blas-
pheme. In my obsession
against them, I even went

even to foreign cities.

[12]"While thus engaged as I was journeying to Damascus with the authority and commission of the chief priests,

[13]at midday, O King, I saw on the way a light from heaven, brighter than the sun, shining all around me and those who were journeying with me.

[14]"And when we had all fallen to the ground, I heard a voice saying to me in the Hebrew dialect, 'Saul, Saul, why are you persecuting Me? It is hard for you to kick against the goads.'

[15]"And I said, 'Who art Thou, Lord?' And the Lord said, 'I am Jesus whom you are persecuting.

[16]'But arise, and stand on your feet; for this purpose I have appeared to you, to appoint you a minister and a witness not only to the things which you have seen, but also to the things in which I will appear to you;

[17]delivering you from the *Jewish* people and from the Gentiles, to whom I am sending you,

[18]to open their eyes so that they may turn from darkness to light and from the dominion of Satan to God, in order that they may receive forgiveness of sins and an inheritance among those who have been sanctified by faith in Me.'

[19]"Consequently, King Agrippa, I did not prove disobedient to the heavenly vision,

[20]but *kept* declaring both to those of Damascus first, and *also* at Jerusalem and *then* throughout all the region of Judea, and *even* to the Gentiles, that they should repent and turn to God, performing deeds appropriate to repentance.

[21]"For this reason *some* Jews seized me in the tem-

τὰς ἔξω πόλεις. **12** Ἐν οἷς πορευόμενος
the outside cities. In which journeying

εἰς τὴν Δαμασκὸν μετ' ἐξουσίας καὶ
to – Damascus with authority and

ἐπιτροπῆς τῆς τῶν ἀρχιερέων, **13** ἡμέρας
power to decide – of the chief priests, at [2]day

μέσης κατὰ τὴν ὁδὸν εἶδον, βασιλεῦ,
[1]mid along the way I saw, [O] king,

οὐρανόθεν ὑπὲρ τὴν λαμπρότητα τοῦ ἡλίου
[2]from heaven [3]above [4]the [5]brightness [6]of the [7]sun

περιλάμψαν με φῶς καὶ τοὺς σὺν ἐμοὶ
[8]shining round [9]me [1]a light [10]and [11]the [ones] [13]with [14]me

πορευομένους· **14** πάντων τε καταπεσόντων
[12]journeying; and all having fallen down
=when we had all fallen

ἡμῶν εἰς τὴν γῆν ἤκουσα φωνὴν λέγουσαν
us[a] to the earth I heard a voice saying

πρός με τῇ Ἑβραΐδι διαλέκτῳ· Σαοὺλ
to me in the Hebrew language: Saul[,]

Σαοὺλ, τί με διώκεις; σκληρόν σοι
Saul, why me persecutest thou? hard for thee

πρὸς κέντρα λακτίζειν. **15** ἐγὼ δὲ εἶπα·
against goads to kick. And I said:

τίς εἶ, κύριε; ὁ δὲ κύριος εἶπεν· ἐγώ
Who art thou, Lord? And the Lord said: I

εἰμι Ἰησοῦς ὃν σὺ διώκεις. **16** ἀλλὰ
am Jesus whom thou persecutest. But

ἀνάστηθι καὶ στῆθι ἐπὶ τοὺς πόδας σου·
rise thou up and stand on the feet of thee;

εἰς τοῦτο γὰρ ὤφθην σοι, προχειρίσασθαί
[2]for [3]this [purpose] [1]for I appeared to thee, to appoint

σε ὑπηρέτην καὶ μάρτυρα ὧν τε
thee an attendant and a witness [2]of the things which [1]both

εἶδές με ὧν τε ὀφθήσομαί σοι,
[3]thou sawest [4]me [6]of the things which [5]and I will appear to thee,

17 ἐξαιρούμενός σε ἐκ τοῦ λαοῦ καὶ ἐκ
delivering thee from the people and from

τῶν ἐθνῶν, εἰς οὓς ἐγὼ ἀποστέλλω σε,
the nations, to whom I send thee,

18 ἀνοῖξαι ὀφθαλμοὺς αὐτῶν, τοῦ ἐπιστρέψαι
to open eyes of them, – to turn[b]

ἀπὸ σκότους εἰς φῶς καὶ τῆς ἐξουσίας
from darkness to light and [from] the authority

τοῦ σατανᾶ ἐπὶ τὸν θεόν, τοῦ λαβεῖν
– of Satan to – God, – to receive
=that they may receive

αὐτοὺς ἄφεσιν ἁμαρτιῶν καὶ κλῆρον ἐν
them[bd] forgiveness of sins and a lot among

τοῖς ἡγιασμένοις πίστει τῇ εἰς ἐμέ.
the [ones] *having been* sanctified by faith – in me.

19 Ὅθεν, βασιλεῦ Ἀγρίππα, οὐκ ἐγενόμην
Whence, king Agrippa, I was not

ἀπειθὴς τῇ οὐρανίῳ ὀπτασίᾳ, **20** ἀλλὰ
disobedient to the heavenly vision, but

τοῖς ἐν Δαμασκῷ πρῶτόν τε καὶ
to the [ones] in Damascus first*ly* and also

Ἱεροσολύμοις, πᾶσάν τε τὴν χώραν τῆς
[in] Jerusalem, and all the country –

Ἰουδαίας καὶ τοῖς ἔθνεσιν ἀπήγγελλον
of Judæa and to the nations I announced

μετανοεῖν καὶ ἐπιστρέφειν ἐπὶ τὸν θεόν,
to repent and to turn to – God,

ἄξια τῆς μετανοίας ἔργα πράσσοντας.
[3]worthy [4]of the [5]repentance [2]works [1]doing.

21 ἕνεκα τούτων με Ἰουδαῖοι συλλαβόμενοι
On account of these things [3]me [1]Jews [2]having seized

to foreign cities to persecute them.

[12]"On one of these journeys I was going to Damascus with the authority and commission of the chief priests. [13]About noon, O king, as I was on the road, I saw a light from heaven, brighter than the sun, blazing around me and my companions. [14]We all fell to the ground, and I heard a voice saying to me in Aramaic,[w] 'Saul, Saul, why do you persecute me? It is hard for you to kick against the goads.'

[15]"Then I asked, 'Who are you, Lord?'

"'I am Jesus, whom you are persecuting,' the Lord replied. [16]'Now get up and stand on your feet. I have appeared to you to appoint you as a servant and as a witness of what you have seen of me and what I will show you. [17]I will rescue you from your own people and from the Gentiles. I am sending you to them [18]to open their eyes and turn them from darkness to light, and from the power of Satan to God, so that they may receive forgiveness of sins and a place among those who are sanctified by faith in me.'

[19]"So then, King Agrippa, I was not disobedient to the vision from heaven. [20]First to those in Damascus, then to those in Jerusalem and in all Judea, and to the Gentiles also, I preached that they should repent and turn to God and prove their repentance by their deeds. [21]That is why the Jews seized me in the

[w]14 Or *Hebrew*

ple and tried to put me to
death.
22"And so, having ob-
tained help from God, I
stand to this day testifying
both to small and great,
stating nothing but what
the Prophets and Moses
said was going to take
place;
23that the Christ was to
suffer, *and* that by reason
of *His* resurrection from
the dead He should be the
first to proclaim light both
to the *Jewish* people and to
the Gentiles."
24And while *Paul* was
saying this in his defense,
Festus *said in a loud
voice, "Paul, you are out of
your mind! *Your* great
learning is driving you
mad."
25But Paul *said, "I am
not out of my mind, most
excellent Festus, but I utter
words of sober truth.
26"For the king knows
about these matters, and I
speak to him also with confidence, since I am per-
suaded that none of these
things escape his notice; for
this has not been done in a
corner.
27"King Agrippa, do you
believe the Prophets? I
know that you do."
28And Agrippa *replied* to
Paul, "In a short time you
will persuade me to
become a Christian."
29And Paul *said,* "I
would to God, that whether
in a short or long time, not
only you, but also all who
hear me this day, might
become such as I am, ex-
cept for these chains."
30And the king arose and
the governor and Bernice,
and those who were sitting
with them,
31and when they had
drawn aside, they *began*
talking to one another, saying, "This man is not doing

ἐν τῷ ἱερῷ ἐπειρῶντο διαχειρίσασθαι.
in the temple tried to kill [me].

22 ἐπικουρίας οὖν τυχὼν τῆς ἀπὸ τοῦ
Succour therefore having obtained – from –

θεοῦ ἄχρι τῆς ἡμέρας ταύτης ἕστηκα
God until this day I stand

μαρτυρόμενος μικρῷ τε καὶ μεγάλῳ, οὐδὲν
witnessing [2]to small [1]both and to great, [2]nothing

ἐκτὸς λέγων ὧν τε οἱ προφῆται
[3]apart from [1]saying [4]the things which [5]both [6]the [7]prophets

ἐλάλησαν μελλόντων γίνεσθαι καὶ Μωϋσῆς,
[10]said [11]being about [12]to happen [8]and [9]Moses,

23 εἰ παθητὸς ὁ χριστός, εἰ πρῶτος
if subject to suffering the Christ, if first

ἐξ ἀναστάσεως νεκρῶν φῶς μέλλει
by a resurrection of dead persons [3]a light [1]he is about

καταγγέλλειν τῷ τε λαῷ καὶ τοῖς ἔθνεσιν.
[2]to announce [5]to the [4]both people and to the nations.

24 Ταῦτα δὲ αὐτοῦ ἀπολογουμένου ὁ Φῆστος
And these things him defending himself[a] – Festus
=as he defended himself with these things

μεγάλῃ τῇ φωνῇ φησιν· μαίνῃ, Παῦλε·
[3]great [1]with the(his) [2]voice says: Thou ravest, Paul:

τὰ πολλά σε γράμματα εἰς μανίαν
[1]the [2]many [5]thee [3]letters [6]to [7]madness

περιτρέπει. 25 ὁ δὲ Παῦλος· οὐ μαίνομαι,
[4]turn[s]. – But Paul: I do not rave,

φησίν, κράτιστε Φῆστε, ἀλλὰ ἀληθείας
he says, most excellent Festus, but [3]of truth

καὶ σωφροσύνης ῥήματα ἀποφθέγγομαι.
[4]and [5]of good sense [2]words [1]speak forth.

26 ἐπίσταται γὰρ περὶ τούτων ὁ βασιλεύς,
For [3]understands [4]about [5]these things [1]the [2]king,

πρὸς ὃν καὶ παρρησιαζόμενος λαλῶ·
to whom indeed being bold of speech I speak;

λανθάνειν γὰρ αὐτὸν τούτων οὐ πείθομαι
for [4]to be hidden [from] [5]him [3]of these things *not* [1]I am persuaded

οὐθέν· οὐ γάρ ἐστιν ἐν γωνίᾳ πεπραγμένον
[2]nothing; for [3]not [2]is [5]in [6]a corner [4]having been done

τοῦτο. 27 πιστεύεις, βασιλεῦ Ἀγρίππα,
[1]this. Believest thou, king Agrippa,

τοῖς προφήταις; οἶδα ὅτι πιστεύεις. 28 ὁ
the prophets? I know that thou believest. –

δὲ Ἀγρίππας πρὸς τὸν Παῦλον· ἐν
And Agrippa [said] to – Paul: In

ὀλίγῳ με πείθεις Χριστιανὸν ποιῆσαι.
a little [2]me [1]thou persuadest [4]a Christian [3]to make(act).

29 ὁ δὲ Παῦλος· εὐξαίμην ἂν τῷ θεῷ
– And Paul [said]: I would pray – God

καὶ ἐν ὀλίγῳ καὶ ἐν μεγάλῳ οὐ μόνον
both in a little and in great not only

σὲ ἀλλὰ καὶ πάντας τοὺς ἀκούοντάς
thee but also all the [ones] hearing

μου σήμερον γενέσθαι τοιούτους ὁποῖος
me to-day [2]to become [1]such of what kind

καὶ ἐγώ εἰμι, παρεκτὸς τῶν δεσμῶν
indeed I am, except – bonds

τούτων. 30 Ἀνέστη τε ὁ βασιλεὺς καὶ
these. Rose up both the king and

ὁ ἡγεμὼν ἥ τε Βερνίκη καὶ οἱ συγ-
the governor – and Bernice and the [ones] sit-

καθήμενοι αὐτοῖς, 31 καὶ ἀναχωρήσαντες
ting with them, and having left

ἐλάλουν πρὸς ἀλλήλους λέγοντες ὅτι οὐδὲν
spoke to one another saying [,] – [4]nothing

temple courts and tried to
kill me. 22But I have had
God's help to this very day,
and so I stand here and testify to small and great alike.
I am saying nothing beyond
what the prophets and Mo-
ses said would happen—
23that the Christ[x] would
suffer and, as the first to
rise from the dead, would
proclaim light to his own
people and to the Gen-
tiles."
24At this point Festus in-
terrupted Paul's defense.
"You are out of your mind,
Paul!" he shouted. "Your
great learning is driving
you insane."
25"I am not insane, most
excellent Festus," Paul replied. "What I am saying is
true and reasonable. 26The
king is familiar with these
things, and I can speak
freely to him. I am con-
vinced that none of this has
escaped his notice, because
it was not done in a corner.
27King Agrippa, do you believe the prophets? I know
you do."
28Then Agrippa said to
Paul, "Do you think that in
such a short time you can
persuade me to be a Christian?"
29Paul replied, "Short
time or long—I pray God
that not only you but all
who are listening to me to-
day may become what I
am, except for these
chains."
30The king rose, and with
him the governor and Ber-
nice and those sitting with
them. 31They left the room,
and while talking with one
another, they said, "This

x23 Or *Messiah*

anything worthy of death or imprisonment."
32And Agrippa said to Festus, "This man might have been set free if he had not appealed to Caesar."

Chapter 27

Paul Is Sent to Rome

AND when it was decided that we should sail for Italy, they proceeded to deliver Paul and some other prisoners to a centurion of the Augustan ' cohort named Julius.
2And embarking in an Adramyttian ship, which was about to sail to the regions along the coast of Asia, we put out to sea, accompanied by Aristarchus, a Macedonian of Thessalonica.
3And the next day we put in at Sidon; and Julius treated Paul with consideration and allowed him to go to his friends and receive care.
4And from there we put out to sea and sailed under the shelter of Cyprus because the winds were contrary.
5And when we had sailed through the sea along the coast of Cilicia and Pamphylia, we landed at Myra in Lycia.
6And there the centurion found an Alexandrian ship sailing for Italy, and he put us aboard it.
7And when we had sailed slowly for a good many days, and with difficulty had arrived off Cnidus, since the wind did not permit us *to go* farther, we sailed under the shelter of Crete, off Salmone;
8and with difficulty sailing past it we came to a certain place called Fair Havens, near which was the city of Lasea.
9And when considerable

' Or, *battalion*

θανάτου ἢ δεσμῶν ἄξιον πράσσει ὁ
[6]of death [7]or [8]of bonds [5]worthy [3]does –
ἄνθρωπος οὗτος. 32 Ἀγρίππας δὲ τῷ
[2]man [1]This. And Agrippa –
Φήστῳ ἔφη· ἀπολελύσθαι ἐδύνατο
to Festus said: [3]*to* have been released [2]was able(could)
ὁ ἄνθρωπος οὗτος εἰ μὴ ἐπεκέκλητο Καίσαρα.
[1]This man if he had not appealed to Cæsar.

27 Ὡς δὲ ἐκρίθη τοῦ ἀποπλεῖν ἡμᾶς
And when it was decided – to sail us[bd]
=that we should sail
εἰς τὴν Ἰταλίαν, παρεδίδουν τόν τε
to – Italy, they delivered – both
Παῦλον καί τινας ἑτέρους δεσμώτας
Paul and some other prisoners
ἑκατοντάρχῃ ὀνόματι Ἰουλίῳ σπείρης
to a centurion by name Julius of a cohort
Σεβαστῆς. 2 ἐπιβάντες δὲ πλοίῳ Ἀδρα-
Augustan. And embarking in a ship belonging to
μυττηνῷ μέλλοντι πλεῖν εἰς τοὺς κατὰ
Adramyttium being about to sail [1]for [3]the [4]along [the coast of]
τὴν Ἀσίαν τόπους ἀνήχθημεν, ὄντος σὺν
– [5]Asia [2]places we set sail, being with
ἡμῖν Ἀριστάρχου Μακεδόνος Θεσσαλονικέως·
us Aristarchus a Macedonian[a] of Thessalonica;
3 τῇ τε ἑτέρᾳ κατήχθημεν εἰς Σιδῶνα,
and on the next [day] we were brought to land at Sidon,
φιλανθρώπως τε ὁ Ἰούλιος τῷ Παύλῳ
and [3]kindly – [1]Julius – [5]Paul
χρησάμενος ἐπέτρεψεν πρὸς τοὺς φίλους
[2]treating [him] [4]allowed [7]to [8]the [9]friends
πορευθέντι ἐπιμελείας τυχεῖν. 4 κἀκεῖθεν
[6]going [11]attention [10]to obtain. And thence
ἀναχθέντες ὑπεπλεύσαμεν τὴν Κύπρον διὰ
putting to sea we sailed close to – Cyprus because of
τὸ τοὺς ἀνέμους εἶναι ἐναντίους, 5 τό τε
– the winds to be(being) contrary, and [1]the
πέλαγος τὸ κατὰ τὴν Κιλικίαν καὶ
[2]sea – [4]against – [5]Cilicia [6]and
Παμφυλίαν διαπλεύσαντες κατήλθαμεν εἰς
[7]Pamphylia [1]sailing over we came down to
Μύρα τῆς Λυκίας. 6 Κἀκεῖ εὑρὼν ὁ
Myra – of Lycia. And there [3]having found [1]the
ἑκατοντάρχης πλοῖον Ἀλεξανδρῖνον πλέον
[2]centurion ship an Alexandrian sailing
εἰς τὴν Ἰταλίαν ἐνεβίβασεν ἡμᾶς εἰς
to – Italy he embarked us in
αὐτό. 7 ἐν ἱκαναῖς δὲ ἡμέραις βραδυπλο-
it. And in a number of days sailing
οῦντες καὶ μόλις γενόμενοι κατὰ τὴν
slowly and hardly coming against –
Κνίδον, μὴ προσεῶντος ἡμᾶς τοῦ ἀνέμου,
Cnidus, not allowing us the wind,[a]
=as the wind did not allow us,
ὑπεπλεύσαμεν τὴν Κρήτην κατὰ Σαλμώνην,
we sailed close to – Crete against Salmone,
8 μόλις τε παραλεγόμενοι αὐτὴν ἤλθομεν
and hardly sailing along it we came
εἰς τόπον τινὰ καλούμενον Καλοὺς λιμένας,
to place a certain *being* called Fair Havens,
ᾧ ἐγγὺς ἦν πόλις Λασαία. 9 Ἱκανοῦ δὲ
[2]to which [1]near was a city Lasæa. And much
=when

man is not doing anything that deserves death or imprisonment."
32Agrippa said to Festus, "This man could have been set free if he had not appealed to Caesar."

Chapter 27

Paul Sails for Rome

WHEN it was decided that we would sail for Italy, Paul and some other prisoners were handed over to a centurion named Julius, who belonged to the Imperial Regiment. 2We boarded a ship from Adramyttium about to sail for ports along the coast of the province of Asia, and we put out to sea. Aristarchus, a Macedonian from Thessalonica, was with us.
3The next day we landed at Sidon; and Julius, in kindness to Paul, allowed him to go to his friends so they might provide for his needs. 4From there we put out to sea again and passed to the lee of Cyprus because the winds were against us. 5When we had sailed across the open sea off the coast of Cilicia and Pamphylia, we landed at Myra in Lycia. 6There the centurion found an Alexandrian ship sailing for Italy and put us on board. 7We made slow headway for many days and had difficulty arriving off Cnidus. When the wind did not allow us to hold our course, we sailed to the lee of Crete, opposite Salmone. 8We moved along the coast with difficulty and came to a place called Fair Havens, near the town of Lasea.
9Much time had been

time had passed and the
voyage was now danger-
ous, since even the [u]fast
was already over, Paul *be-*
gan to admonish them,
10and said to them,
"Men, I perceive that the
voyage will certainly be *at-*
tended with damage and
great loss, not only of the
cargo and the ship, but also
of our lives."
11But the centurion was
more persuaded by the pi-
lot and the captain of the
ship, than by what was being said by Paul.
12And because the harbor
was not suitable for wintering, the majority reached a
decision to put out to sea
from there, if somehow
they could reach Phoenix,
a harbor of Crete, facing
southwest and northwest,
and spend the winter *there.*
13And when a moderate
south wind came up, sup-
posing that they had gained
their purpose, they
weighed anchor and *began*
sailing along Crete, close
inshore.

Shipwreck

14But before very long
there rushed down from the
land a violent wind, called
[v]Euraquilo;
15and when the ship was
caught *in it,* and could not
face the wind, we gave way
to it, and let ourselves be
driven along.
16And running under the
shelter of a small island
called Clauda, we were
scarcely able to get the
ship's boat under control.
17And after they had
hoisted it up, they used
supporting cables in undergirding the ship; and fearing
that they might run
aground on *the shallows* of
Syrtis, they let down the
sea anchor, and so let

χρόνου διαγενομένου καὶ ὄντος ἤδη
time having passed[a] and being now
much time had passed =as the voyage

ἐπισφαλοῦς τοῦ πλοὸς διὰ τὸ καὶ τὴν
dangerous the voyage[a] on account of – also the
was now dangerous =because also the fast had now

νηστείαν ἤδη παρεληλυθέναι, παρῄνει ὁ
fast now to have gone by, [2]advised –
gone by,

Παῦλος 10 λέγων αὐτοῖς· ἄνδρες, θεωρῶ
[1]Paul saying to them: Men, I see

ὅτι μετὰ ὕβρεως καὶ πολλῆς ζημίας οὐ
that with injury and much loss not

μόνον τοῦ φορτίου καὶ τοῦ πλοίου ἀλλὰ
only of the cargo and of the ship but

καὶ τῶν ψυχῶν ἡμῶν μέλλειν ἔσεσθαι
also of the lives of us [3]to be about [4]to be
=will be

τὸν πλοῦν. 11 ὁ δὲ ἑκατοντάρχης τῷ
[1]the [2]voyage. But the centurion [2]the

κυβερνήτῃ καὶ τῷ ναυκλήρῳ μᾶλλον
[3]steersman [4]and [5]the [6]shipmaster [7]rather

ἐπείθετο ἢ τοῖς ὑπὸ Παύλου λεγομένοις.
[1]was persuaded by [8]than [9]the [11]by [12]Paul [10]things said.

12 ἀνευθέτου δὲ τοῦ λιμένος ὑπάρχοντος
But unsuitable the port being[a]
=as the port was unsuitable

πρὸς παραχειμασίαν οἱ πλείονες ἔθεντο
for wintering the majority placed
=decided

βουλὴν ἀναχθῆναι ἐκεῖθεν, εἴ πως δύναιντο
counsel to set sail thence, if some-how they might be able

καταντήσαντες εἰς Φοίνικα παραχειμάσαι,
having arrived at Phœnix to pass the winter,

λιμένα τῆς Κρήτης βλέποντα κατὰ λίβα
a port – of Crete looking toward south-west

καὶ κατὰ χῶρον. 13 Ὑποπνεύσαντος δὲ
and toward north-west. And blowing gently
=when a south wind

νότου δόξαντες τῆς προθέσεως κεκρατηκέναι,
a south wind[a] thinking [2]the(ir) [3]purpose [1]to have obtained,
blew gently

ἄραντες ἆσσον παρελέγοντο τὴν Κρήτην.
raising [3]close in- [1]they coasted by – [2]Crete.
[anchor] shore

14 μετ' οὐ πολὺ δὲ ἔβαλεν κατ' αὐτῆς
And after not much there beat down it

ἄνεμος τυφωνικὸς ὁ καλούμενος εὐρακύλων·
wind a tempestuous – *being* called Euraquilo;

15 συναρπασθέντος δὲ τοῦ πλοίου καὶ μὴ
and [3]being seized [1]the [2]ship[a] and not

δυναμένου ἀντοφθαλμεῖν τῷ ἀνέμῳ ἐπιδόντες
being able[a] to beat up against the wind giving way

ἐφερόμεθα. 16 νησίον δέ τι ὑποδραμόντες
we were borne. And [3]islet [2]a certain [1]running under the lee of

καλούμενον Κλαῦδα ἰσχύσαμεν μόλις
being called Clauda we were able hardly

περικρατεῖς γενέσθαι τῆς σκάφης, 17 ἣν
control to get of the boat, which

ἄραντες βοηθείαις ἐχρῶντο, ὑποζωννύντες
taking [2]helps [1]they used, undergirding

τὸ πλοῖον· φοβούμενοί τε μὴ εἰς τὴν
the ship; and fearing lest into –

Σύρτιν ἐκπέσωσιν, χαλάσαντες τὸ σκεῦος,
Syrtis they might fall off,* lowering the tackle,

lost, and sailing had al-
ready become dangerous
because by now it was after
the Fast.[y] So Paul warned
them, 10"Men, I can see
that our voyage is going to
be disastrous and bring
great loss to ship and cargo,
and to our own lives also."
11But the centurion, in-
stead of listening to what
Paul said, followed the advice of the pilot and of the
owner of the ship. 12Since
the harbor was unsuitable
to winter in, the majority
decided that we should sail
on, hoping to reach Phoe-
nix and winter there. This
was a harbor in Crete, facing both southwest and
northwest.

The Storm

13When a gentle south
wind began to blow, they
thought they had obtained
what they wanted; so they
weighed anchor and sailed
along the shore of Crete.
14Before very long, a wind
of hurricane force, called
the "northeaster," swept
down from the island.
15The ship was caught by
the storm and could not
head into the wind; so we
gave way to it and were
driven along. 16As we
passed to the lee of a small
island called Cauda, we
were hardly able to make
the lifeboat secure. 17When
the men had hoisted it
aboard, they passed ropes
under the ship itself to hold
it together. Fearing that
they would run aground on
the sandbars of Syrtis, they
lowered the sea anchor and

[u]I.e., Day of Atonement in September or October
[v]I.e., a northeaster

* This is the classical Greek word for a ship being driven out of her course on to shoals, rocks, etc. (Page). See also vers 26 and 29.

[y]9 That is, the Day of Atonement (Yom Kippur)

themselves be driven along.

18The next day as we were being violently storm-tossed, they began to jettison the cargo;

19and on the third day they threw the ship's tackle overboard with their own hands.

20And since neither sun nor stars appeared for many days, and no small storm was assailing *us,* from then on all hope of our being saved was gradually abandoned.

21And when they had gone a long time without food, then Paul stood up in their midst and said, "Men, you ought to have followed my advice and not to have set sail from Crete, and incurred this damage and loss.

22"And *yet* now I urge you to keep up your courage, for there shall be no loss of life among you, but *only* of the ship.

23"For this very night an angel of the God to whom I belong and whom I serve stood before me,

24saying, 'Do not be afraid, Paul; you must stand before Caesar; and behold, God has granted you all those who are sailing with you.'

25"Therefore, keep up your courage, men, for I believe God, that it will turn out exactly as I have been told.

26"But we must run aground on a certain island."

27But when the fourteenth night had come, as we were being driven about in the Adriatic Sea, about midnight the sailors *began* to surmise that they were approaching some land.

28And they took soundings, and found *it to be* twenty fathoms; and a little

οὕτως ἐφέροντο. **18** σφοδρῶς δὲ χειμαζ-
thus they were borne. But exceedingly being in
=as we were exceedingly in . . .
ομένων ἡμῶν τῇ ἑξῆς ἐκβολὴν ἐποιοῦντο,
the grip of a storm us[a] on the next [day] a jettisoning they made,
19 καὶ τῇ τρίτῃ αὐτόχειρες τὴν σκευὴν
and on the third [day] with their own hands the tackle
τοῦ πλοίου ἔρριψαν. **20** μήτε δὲ ἡλίου
of the ship they threw [out]. And neither sun
=when neither . . .
μήτε ἄστρων ἐπιφαινόντων ἐπὶ πλείονας
nor stars appearing[a] over many
appeared
ἡμέρας, χειμῶνός τε οὐκ ὀλίγου ἐπικειμένου,
days, and stormy weather no little pressing hard,[a]
λοιπὸν περιῃρεῖτο ἐλπὶς πᾶσα τοῦ σῴζεσθαι
now was taken away [2]hope [1]all – to be saved
=that we might
ἡμᾶς. **21** Πολλῆς τε ἀσιτίας ὑπαρχούσης
us.[bd] And much abstinence being[a]
be saved. =when there was long abstinence
τότε σταθεὶς ὁ Παῦλος ἐν μέσῳ αὐτῶν εἶπεν·
then [2]standing – [1]Paul in [the] midst of them said:
ἔδει μέν, ὦ ἄνδρες, πειθαρχήσαντάς
It behoved [you], – O men, obeying
μοι μὴ ἀνάγεσθαι ἀπὸ τῆς Κρήτης
me not to set sail from – Crete
κερδῆσαί τε τὴν ὕβριν ταύτην καὶ τὴν
and to come by – injury this and –
ζημίαν. **22** καὶ τὰ νῦν παραινῶ ὑμᾶς
loss. And – now I advise you
εὐθυμεῖν· ἀποβολὴ γὰρ ψυχῆς οὐδεμία
to be of good cheer; for [3]throwing away [4]of life [2]no
ἔσται ἐξ ὑμῶν πλὴν τοῦ πλοίου.
[1]there will be of you but of the ship.
23 παρέστη γάρ μοι ταύτῃ τῇ νυκτὶ
For there stood by me *in* this – night
τοῦ θεοῦ οὗ εἰμι, ᾧ καὶ λατρεύω,
– [2]of God [3]of whom [4]I am, [5]whom [6]also [7]I serve,
ἄγγελος **24** λέγων· μὴ φοβοῦ, Παῦλε·
[1]an angel saying: Fear not, Paul;
Καίσαρί σε δεῖ παραστῆναι, καὶ ἰδοὺ
[4]Cæsar [2]thee [1]it behoves [3]to stand before, and behold
κεχάρισταί σοι ὁ θεὸς πάντας τοὺς
[2]has given [3]thee – [1]God all the [ones]
πλέοντας μετὰ σοῦ. **25** διὸ εὐθυμεῖτε,
sailing with thee. Wherefore be ye of good cheer,
ἄνδρες· πιστεύω γὰρ τῷ θεῷ ὅτι οὕτως
men; for I believe – God that thus
ἔσται καθ' ὃν τρόπον λελάληταί μοι.
it will be in the way in which† it has been spoken to me.
26 εἰς νῆσον δέ τινα δεῖ ἡμᾶς ἐκπεσεῖν.
[6]Onto [7]island [1]but [5]a certain [2]it behoves [3]us [4]to fall off.
27 Ὡς δὲ τεσσαρεσκαιδεκάτη νὺξ ἐγένετο
Now when [the] fourteenth night came
διαφερομένων ἡμῶν ἐν τῷ Ἀδρίᾳ, κατὰ
being carried about us[a] in the Adria, about
=while we were being carried about
μέσον τῆς νυκτὸς ὑπενόουν οἱ ναῦται
[the] middle of the night [3]supposed [1]the [2]sailors
προσάγειν τινὰ αὐτοῖς χώραν. **28** καὶ
[4]to approach [6]some [5]to them [7]country. And
βολίσαντες εὗρον ὀργυιὰς εἴκοσι, βραχὺ δὲ
sounding they found fathoms twenty, and [2]a little

let the ship be driven along.
18We took such a violent
battering from the storm
that the next day they began to throw the cargo
overboard. 19On the third
day, they threw the ship's
tackle overboard with their
own hands. 20When neither
sun nor stars appeared for
many days and the storm
continued raging, we finally gave up all hope of being
saved.
21After the men had gone
a long time without food,
Paul stood up before them
and said: "Men, you
should have taken my ad-
vice not to sail from Crete;
then you would have
spared yourselves this
damage and loss. 22But
now I urge you to keep up
your courage, because not
one of you will be lost; only
the ship will be destroyed.
23Last night an angel of the
God whose I am and whom
I serve stood beside me
24and said, 'Do not be
afraid, Paul. You must
stand trial before Caesar;
and God has graciously giv-
en you the lives of all who
sail with you.' 25So keep up
your courage, men, for I
have faith in God that it will
happen just as he told me.
26Nevertheless, we must
run aground on some is-
land."

The Shipwreck

27On the fourteenth night
we were still being driven
across the Adriatic[z] Sea,
when about midnight the
sailors sensed they were
approaching land. 28They
took soundings and found
that the water was a hun-
dred and twenty feet[a]
deep. A short time later

[z]27 In ancient times the name referred to an area extending well south of Italy.

[a]28 Greek *twenty orguias* (about 37 meters)

farther on they took an-
other sounding and found *it*
to be fifteen fathoms.
29And fearing that we
might run aground some-
where on the rocks, they
cast four anchors from the
stern and wished for day-
break.
30And as the sailors were
trying to escape from the
ship, and had let down the
ship's boat into the sea, on
the pretense of intending to
lay out anchors from the
bow,
31Paul said to the centu-
rion and to the soldiers,
"Unless these men remain
in the ship, you yourselves
cannot be saved."
32Then the soldiers cut
away the ropes of the *ship's*
boat, and let it fall away.
33And until the day was
about to dawn, Paul was
encouraging them all to
take some food, saying,
"Today is the fourteenth
day that you have been
constantly watching and
going without eating, having taken nothing.
34"Therefore I encourage
you to take some food, for
this is for your preserva-
tion; for not a hair from the
head of any of you shall
perish."
35And having said this, he
took bread and gave thanks
to God in the presence of
all; and he broke it and began to eat.
36And all of them were
encouraged, and they
themselves also took food.
37And all of us in the ship
were two hundred and sev-
enty-six persons.
38And when they had eat-
en enough, they *began* to
lighten the ship by throwing out the wheat into the
sea.
39And when day came,
they could not recognize
the land; but they did ob-

διαστήσαντες καὶ πάλιν βολίσαντες εὗρον
[1]having moved also again sounding they found

ὀργυιὰς δεκαπέντε· 29 φοβούμενοί τε μή
fathoms fifteen; and fearing lest

που κατὰ τραχεῖς τόπους ἐκπέσωμεν,
[2]somewhere [3]against [4]rough [5]places [1]we might fall off,

ἔκ πρύμνης ῥίψαντες ἀγκύρας τέσσαρας
out of [the] stern throwing anchors four

ηὔχοντο ἡμέραν γενέσθαι. 30 Τῶν δὲ
they prayed day to become. And the

ναυτῶν ζητούντων φυγεῖν ἐκ τοῦ πλοίου
sailors seeking* to flee out of the ship
=when the sailors sought

καὶ χαλασάντων τὴν σκάφην εἰς τὴν
and lowering* the boat into the
=lowered

θάλασσαν προφάσει ὡς ἐκ πρῴρης ἀγκύρας
sea under pretence as [4]out of [5][the] prow [3]anchors

μελλόντων ἐκτείνειν, 31 εἶπεν ὁ Παῦλος
[1]intending [2]to cast *out*, said – Paul

τῷ ἑκατοντάρχῃ καὶ τοῖς στρατιώταις·
to the centurion and to the soldiers:

ἐὰν μὴ οὗτοι μείνωσιν ἐν τῷ πλοίῳ,
Unless these remain in the ship,

ὑμεῖς σωθῆναι οὐ δύνασθε. 32 τότε
ye [2]*to* be saved [1]cannot. Then

ἀπέκοψαν οἱ στρατιῶται τὰ σχοινία τῆς
cut away the soldiers the ropes of the

σκάφης καὶ εἴασαν αὐτὴν ἐκπεσεῖν.
boat and let it *to* fall off.

33 Ἄχρι δὲ οὗ ἡμέρα ἤμελλεν γίνεσθαι,
And until day was about to come,

παρεκάλει ὁ Παῦλος ἅπαντας μεταλαβεῖν
besought – Paul all to partake

τροφῆς λέγων· τεσσαρεσκαιδεκάτην σήμερον
of food saying: [2][the] fourteenth [1]To-day [is]

ἡμέραν προσδοκῶντες ἄσιτοι διατελεῖτε,
[3]day [5]waiting [6]without food [4]ye continued,

μηθὲν προσλαβόμενοι. 34 διὸ παρακαλῶ
nothing taking. Wherefore I beseech

ὑμᾶς μεταλαβεῖν τροφῆς· τοῦτο γὰρ πρὸς
you to partake of food; for this to

τῆς ὑμετέρας σωτηρίας ὑπάρχει· οὐδενὸς
– your salvation is; [2]of no one

γὰρ ὑμῶν θρὶξ ἀπὸ τῆς κεφαλῆς ἀπολεῖται.
[1]for of you a hair from the head shall perish.

35 εἴπας δὲ ταῦτα καὶ λαβὼν ἄρτον
And saying these things and taking bread

εὐχαρίστησεν τῷ θεῷ ἐνώπιον πάντων
he gave thanks – to God before all

καὶ κλάσας ἤρξατο ἐσθίειν. 36 εὔθυμοι δὲ
and breaking began to eat. And [4]in good spirits

γενόμενοι πάντες καὶ αὐτοὶ προσελάβοντο
[3]becoming [1]all [2]also they took

τροφῆς. 37 ἤμεθα δὲ αἱ πᾶσαι ψυχαὶ
food. Now we were [2]the [1]all souls

ἐν τῷ πλοίῳ διακόσιαι ἑβδομήκοντα ἕξ.
in the ship two hundred*s* [and] seventy six.

38 κορεσθέντες δὲ τροφῆς ἐκούφιζον τὸ
And having been satisfied of(with) food they lightened the

πλοῖον ἐκβαλλόμενοι τὸν σῖτον εἰς τὴν
ship throwing out the wheat into the

θάλασσαν. 39 Ὅτε δὲ ἡμέρα ἐγένετο,
sea. And when day came,

τὴν γῆν οὐκ ἐπεγίνωσκον, κόλπον δέ
[3]the [2]land [1]they did not recognize, but [2]bay

they took soundings again
and found it was ninety
feet[b] deep. 29Fearing that
we would be dashed
against the rocks, they
dropped four anchors from
the stern and prayed for
daylight. 30In an attempt to
escape from the ship, the
sailors let the lifeboat down
into the sea, pretending
they were going to lower
some anchors from the
bow. 31Then Paul said to
the centurion and the soldiers, "Unless these men
stay with the ship, you cannot be saved." 32So the soldiers cut the ropes that held
the lifeboat and let it fall
away.
33Just before dawn Paul
urged them all to eat. "For
the last fourteen days," he
said, "you have been in
constant suspense and
have gone without food—
you haven't eaten any-
thing. 34Now I urge you to
take some food. You need
it to survive. Not one of
you will lose a single hair
from his head." 35After he
said this, he took some
bread and gave thanks to
God in front of them all.
Then he broke it and began
to eat. 36They were all encouraged and ate some
food themselves. 37Alto-
gether there were 276 of us
on board. 38When they had
eaten as much as they
wanted, they lightened the
ship by throwing the grain
into the sea.
39When daylight came,
they did not recognize the
land, but they saw a bay

[b]28 Greek *fifteen orguias* (about 27 meters)

serve a certain bay with a beach, and they resolved to [w]drive the ship onto it if they could.

40And casting off the anchors, they left them in the sea while at the same time they were loosening the ropes of the rudders, and hoisting the foresail to the wind, they were heading for the beach.

41But striking a reef where two seas met, they ran the vessel aground; and the prow stuck fast and remained immovable, but the stern *began* to be broken up by the force *of the waves*.

42And the soldiers' plan was to kill the prisoners, that none *of them* should swim away and escape;

43but the centurion, wanting to bring Paul safely through, kept them from their intention, and commanded that those who could swim should jump overboard first and get to land,

44and the rest *should follow*, some on planks, and others on various things from the ship. And thus it happened that they all were brought safely to land.

τινα κατενόουν ἔχοντα αἰγιαλόν, εἰς ὃν
[2]a certain [1]they noticed having a shore, into which

ἐβουλεύοντο εἰ δύναιντο ἐξῶσαι τὸ πλοῖον.
they were minded if they were able to drive the ship.

40 καὶ τὰς ἀγκύρας περιελόντες εἴων
And [2]the [3]anchors [1]having cast off they left [them]

εἰς τὴν θάλασσαν, ἅμα ἀνέντες τὰς
in the sea, at the same time loosening the

ζευκτηρίας τῶν πηδαλίων, καὶ ἐπάραντες
fastenings of the rudders, and raising

τὸν ἀρτέμωνα τῇ πνεούσῃ κατεῖχον εἰς
the foresail to the breeze they held [the ship] to

τὸν αἰγιαλόν. **41** περιπεσόντες δὲ εἰς
the shore. And coming upon *to*

τόπον διθάλασσον ἐπέκειλαν τὴν ναῦν,
a place between two seas they drove the vessel,

καὶ ἡ μὲν πρῷρα ἐρείσασα ἔμεινεν
and [2]the [1]while prow having run aground remained

ἀσάλευτος, ἡ δὲ πρύμνα ἐλύετο ὑπὸ
immovable, [2]the [1]yet stern was broken by

τῆς βίας. **42** Τῶν δὲ στρατιωτῶν βουλὴ
the force.* Now [2]of the [3]soldiers [1][the] mind

ἐγένετο ἵνα τοὺς δεσμώτας ἀποκτείνωσιν,
was that [2]the [3]prisoners [1]they should kill,

μή τις ἐκκολυμβήσας διαφύγῃ· **43** ὁ δὲ
lest anyone swimming out should escape; but the

ἑκατοντάρχης βουλόμενος διασῶσαι τὸν
centurion being minded to save –

Παῦλον ἐκώλυσεν αὐτοὺς τοῦ βουλήματος,
Paul forbade them the(ir) intention,

ἐκέλευσέν τε τοὺς δυναμένους κολυμβᾶν
and commanded the [ones] being able to swim

ἀπορίψαντας πρώτους ἐπὶ τὴν γῆν
casting [themselves] overboard first onto the land

ἐξιέναι, **44** καὶ τοὺς λοιποὺς οὓς μὲν ἐπὶ
to go out, and the rest some on

σανίσιν, οὓς δὲ ἐπί τινων τῶν ἀπὸ τοῦ
planks, others on some of the things from the

πλοίου. καὶ οὕτως ἐγένετο πάντας
ship. And thus it came to pass all

διασωθῆναι ἐπὶ τὴν γῆν.
to be saved on the land.

with a sandy beach, where they decided to run the ship aground if they could.

40Cutting loose the anchors, they left them in the sea and at the same time untied the ropes that held the rudders. Then they hoisted the foresail to the wind and made for the beach. 41But the ship struck a sandbar and ran aground. The bow stuck fast and would not move, and the stern was broken to pieces by the pounding of the surf.

42The soldiers planned to kill the prisoners to prevent any of them from swimming away and escaping. 43But the centurion wanted to spare Paul's life and kept them from carrying out their plan. He ordered those who could swim to jump overboard first and get to land. 44The rest were to get there on planks or on pieces of the ship. In this way everyone reached land in safety.

Chapter 28

Safe at Malta

AND when they had been brought safely through, then we found out that the island was called Malta.

2And the natives showed us extraordinary kindness; for because of the rain that had set in and because of the cold, they kindled a fire and received us all.

3But when Paul had gathered a bundle of sticks and laid them on the fire, a viper came out because of the heat, and fastened on his hand.

4And when the natives

28 Καὶ διασωθέντες τότε ἐπέγνωμεν ὅτι
And having been saved then we found out that

Μελίτη ἡ νῆσος καλεῖται. **2** οἵ τε
Melita the island is(was) called. And the

βάρβαροι παρεῖχον οὐ τὴν τυχοῦσαν
foreigners [1]showed [3]not [4]the [5]ordinary

φιλανθρωπίαν ἡμῖν· ἅψαντες γὰρ πυρὰν
[6]kindness [2]us; for having lit a fire

προσελάβοντο πάντας ἡμᾶς διὰ τὸν ὑετὸν
they welcomed [2]all [1]us because of the rain

τὸν ἐφεστῶτα καὶ διὰ τὸ ψῦχος. **3** συστρέ-
– coming on and because of the cold. col-

ψαντος δὲ τοῦ Παύλου φρυγάνων τι
lecting And – Paul[a] [2]of sticks [1]a
=when Paul collected

πλῆθος καὶ ἐπιθέντος ἐπὶ τὴν πυράν,
[3]quantity and putting *on*[a] on the fire,
=put them

ἔχιδνα ἀπὸ τῆς θέρμης ἐξελθοῦσα καθῆψεν
a snake from the heat coming out fastened on

τῆς χειρὸς αὐτοῦ. **4** ὡς δὲ εἶδον οἱ
the hand of him. And when [2]saw [1]the

Chapter 28

Ashore on Malta

ONCE safely on shore, we found out that the island was called Malta. 2The islanders showed us unusual kindness. They built a fire and welcomed us all because it was raining and cold. 3Paul gathered a pile of brushwood and, as he put it on the fire, a viper, driven out by the heat, fastened itself on his hand. 4When the islanders saw

[w] Some ancient mss. read *bring the ship safely ashore*

* That is, of the waves, as indeed some MSS have.

saw the creature hanging
from his hand, they *began*
saying to one another,
"Undoubtedly this man is a
murderer, and though he
has been saved from the
sea, justice has not allowed
him to live."
5However he shook the
creature off into the fire
and suffered no harm.
6But they were expect-
ing that he was about to
swell up or suddenly fall
down dead. But after they
had waited a long time and
had seen nothing unusual
happen to him, they
changed their minds and
began to say that he was a
god.
7Now in the neighbor-
hood of that place were
lands belonging to the leading man of the island,
named Publius, who wel-
comed us and entertained
us courteously three days.
8And it came about that
the father of Publius was lying *in bed* afflicted with
recurrent fever and dysentery; and Paul went in *to*
see him and after he had
prayed, he laid his hands on
him and healed him.
9And after this had hap-
pened, the rest of the
people on the island who
had diseases were coming
to him and getting cured.
10And they also honored
us with many marks of re-
spect; and when we were
setting sail, they supplied
us with all we needed.

Paul Arrives at Rome

11And at the end of three
months we set sail on an
Alexandrian ship which
had wintered at the island,
and which had the Twin
Brothers for its figurehead.
12And after we put in at
Syracuse, we stayed there
for three days.
13And from there we
sailed around and arrived
at Rhegium, and a day later

βάρβαροι κρεμάμενον τὸ θηρίον ἐκ τῆς
[2]foreigners [6]hanging [4]the [5]beast from the

χειρὸς αὐτοῦ, πρὸς ἀλλήλους ἔλεγον·
hand of him, to one another they said:

πάντως φονεύς ἐστιν ὁ ἄνθρωπος οὗτος,
To be sure [4]a murderer [3]is [1]this man,

ὃν διασωθέντα ἐκ τῆς θαλάσσης ἡ δίκη
whom having been saved out of the sea – justice

ζῆν οὐκ εἴασεν. **5** ὁ μὲν οὖν ἀποτινάξας
[2]to live [1]did not allow. He – then shaking off

τὸ θηρίον εἰς τὸ πῦρ ἔπαθεν οὐδὲν
the beast into the fire suffered no

κακόν· **6** οἱ δὲ προσεδόκων αὐτὸν μέλλειν
harm; but they expected him to be about

πίμπρασθαι ἢ καταπίπτειν ἄφνω νεκρόν.
to swell or to fall down suddenly dead.

ἐπὶ πολὺ δὲ αὐτῶν προσδοκώντων καὶ
But over much [time] they expecting and
=while they expected and beheld

θεωρούντων μηδὲν ἄτοπον εἰς αὐτὸν
beholding[a] nothing amiss [2]to [3]him

γινόμενον, μεταβαλόμενοι ἔλεγον αὐτὸν εἶναι
[1]happening, changing their minds they said him to be

θεόν. **7** Ἐν δὲ τοῖς περὶ τὸν τόπον
a god. Now in the [parts] about – place

ἐκεῖνον ὑπῆρχεν χωρία τῷ πρώτῳ τῆς
that were lands to the chief man[c] of the
=the chief man . . . had lands

νήσου ὀνόματι Ποπλίῳ, ὃς ἀναδεξάμενος
island by name Publius, who welcoming

ἡμᾶς ἡμέρας τρεῖς φιλοφρόνως ἐξένισεν.
us [4]days [3]three [2]friendlily [1]lodged [us].

8 ἐγένετο δὲ τὸν πατέρα τοῦ Ποπλίου
Now it happened the father – of Publius

πυρετοῖς καὶ δυσεντερίῳ συνεχόμενον
[3]feverish attacks [4]and [5]dysentery [2]suffering from

κατακεῖσθαι, πρὸς ὃν ὁ Παῦλος εἰσελθὼν
[1]to be lying down, to whom – Paul entering

καὶ προσευξάμενος, ἐπιθεὶς τὰς χεῖρας
and praying, [1]putting [4]on [2]the(his) [3]hands

αὐτῷ ἰάσατο αὐτόν. **9** τούτου δὲ γενομένου
[5]him cured him. And this happening[a]
=when this happened

καὶ οἱ λοιποὶ οἱ ἐν τῇ νήσῳ ἔχοντες
[3]also [1]the [2]rest – in the island having

ἀσθενείας προσήρχοντο καὶ ἐθεραπεύοντο,
ailments came up and were healed,

10 οἳ καὶ πολλαῖς τιμαῖς ἐτίμησαν ἡμᾶς
who also with many honours honoured us

καὶ ἀναγομένοις ἐπέθεντο τὰ πρὸς τὰς
and on our putting to sea placed on [us] the things for the(our)

χρείας.
needs.

11 Μετὰ δὲ τρεῖς μῆνας ἀνήχθημεν ἐν
And after three months we embarked in

πλοίῳ παρακεχειμακότι ἐν τῇ νήσῳ,
a ship having passed the winter in the island,

Ἀλεξανδρίνῳ, παρασήμῳ Διοσκούροις. **12** καὶ
an Alexandrian, with a sign Dioscuri. And

καταχθέντες εἰς Συρακούσας ἐπεμείναμεν
being brought to land to(at) Syracuse we remained

ἡμέρας τρεῖς, **13** ὅθεν περιελθόντες κατην-
days three, whence tacking we ar-

τήσαμεν εἰς Ῥήγιον. καὶ μετὰ μίαν
rived at Rhegium. And after one

the snake hanging from his
hand, they said to each other, "This man must be a
murderer; for though he escaped from the sea, Justice
has not allowed him to
live." 5But Paul shook the
snake off into the fire and
suffered no ill effects. 6The
people expected him to
swell up or suddenly fall
dead, but after waiting a
long time and seeing nothing unusual happen to him,
they changed their minds
and said he was a god.
7There was an estate
nearby that belonged to
Publius, the chief official of
the island. He welcomed us
to his home and for three
days entertained us hospi-
tably. 8His father was sick
in bed, suffering from fever
and dysentery. Paul went
in to see him and, after
prayer, placed his hands on
him and healed him. 9When
this had happened, the rest
of the sick on the island
came and were cured.
10They honored us in many
ways and when we were
ready to sail, they fur-
nished us with the supplies
we needed.

Arrival at Rome

11After three months we
put out to sea in a ship that
had wintered in the island.
It was an Alexandrian ship
with the figurehead of the
twin gods Castor and Pol-
lux. 12We put in at Syra-
cuse and stayed there three
days. 13From there we set
sail and arrived at Rhegi-

a south wind sprang up, and on the second day we came to Puteoli.

[14]There we found *some* brethren, and were invited to stay with them for seven days; and thus we came to Rome.

[15]And the brethren, when they heard about us, came from there as far as the Market of Appius and Three Inns to meet us; and when Paul saw them, he thanked God and took courage.

[16]And when we entered Rome, Paul was allowed to stay by himself, with the soldier who was guarding him.

[17]And it happened that after three days he called together those who were the leading men of the Jews, and when they had come together, he *began* saying to them, "Brethren, though I had done nothing against our people, or the customs of our fathers, yet I was delivered prisoner from Jerusalem into the hands of the Romans.

[18]"And when they had examined me, they were willing to release me because there was no ground for putting me to death.

[19]"But when the Jews objected, I was forced to appeal to Caesar; not that I had any accusation against my nation.

[20]"For this reason therefore, I requested to see you and to speak with you, for I am wearing this chain for the sake of the hope of Israel."

[21]And they said to him, "We have neither received letters from Judea concern-

ἡμέραν ἐπιγενομένου νότου δευτεραῖοι
day coming on a south wind[a] on the second day
=as a south wind came on

ἤλθομεν εἰς Ποτιόλους, **14** οὗ εὑρόντες
we came to Puteoli, where having found

ἀδελφοὺς παρεκλήθημεν παρ' αὐτοῖς ἐπιμεῖναι
brothers we were besought with them to remain

ἡμέρας ἑπτά· καὶ οὕτως εἰς τὴν Ῥώμην
days seven; and thus to – Rome

ἤλθαμεν. **15** κἀκεῖθεν οἱ ἀδελφοὶ ἀκούσαντες
we went. And thence the brothers having heard

τὰ περὶ ἡμῶν ἦλθαν εἰς ἀπάντησιν ἡμῖν
the things con-cerning us came to a meeting with us

ἄχρι Ἀππίου φόρου καὶ Τριῶν ταβερνῶν,
as far as Appii Forum and Three Taverns,

οὓς ἰδὼν ὁ Παῦλος εὐχαριστήσας τῷ
whom seeing – Paul thanking –

θεῷ ἔλαβε θάρσος. **16** Ὅτε δὲ εἰσήλθομεν
God he took courage. And when we entered

εἰς Ῥώμην, ἐπετράπη τῷ Παύλῳ μένειν
into Rome, he* permitted – Paul to remain

καθ' ἑαυτὸν σὺν τῷ φυλάσσοντι αὐτὸν
by himself with [1]the [3]guarding [4]him

στρατιώτῃ.
[2]soldier.

17 Ἐγένετο δὲ μετὰ ἡμέρας τρεῖς
And it came to pass after days three

συγκαλέσασθαι αὐτὸν τοὺς ὄντας τῶν
to call together him[b] the [ones] being of the
=he called together

Ἰουδαίων πρώτους· συνελθόντων δὲ αὐτῶν
Jews first(chief); and coming together them[a]
=and when they came together

ἔλεγεν πρὸς αὐτούς· ἐγώ, ἄνδρες ἀδελφοί,
he said to them: I, *men* brothers,

οὐδὲν ἐναντίον ποιήσας τῷ λαῷ ἢ τοῖς
[2]nothing [3]contrary [1]having done to the people or to the

ἔθεσι τοῖς πατρῴοις, δέσμιος ἐξ Ἱεροσο-
customs – ancestral, a prisoner from Jeru-

λύμων παρεδόθην εἰς τὰς χεῖρας τῶν
salem I was delivered into the hands of the

Ῥωμαίων, **18** οἵτινες ἀνακρίναντές με ἐβούλοντο
Romans, who having examined me were minded

ἀπολῦσαι διὰ τὸ μηδεμίαν αἰτίαν θανάτου
to release on account of – no cause of death

ὑπάρχειν ἐν ἐμοί· **19** ἀντιλεγόντων δὲ
to be in me; but speaking against [this]
=when the Jews spoke

τῶν Ἰουδαίων ἠναγκάσθην ἐπικαλέσασθαι
the Jews[a] I was compelled to appeal to
against this

Καίσαρα, οὐχ ὡς τοῦ ἔθνους μου ἔχων
Cæsar, not as [4]the [5]nation [6]of me [1]having

τι κατηγορεῖν. **20** διὰ ταύτην οὖν τὴν
[2]anything [3]to accuse. [1]On account of [2]this [4]therefore –

αἰτίαν παρεκάλεσα ὑμᾶς ἰδεῖν καὶ προσ-
[3]cause I called you to see and to

λαλῆσαι· εἵνεκεν γὰρ τῆς ἐλπίδος τοῦ
speak to; for for the sake of the hope –

Ἰσραὴλ τὴν ἅλυσιν ταύτην περίκειμαι.
of Israel [2]this [3]chain [1]I have round [me].

21 οἱ δὲ πρὸς αὐτὸν εἶπαν· ἡμεῖς οὔτε
And they to him said: We neither

γράμματα περὶ σοῦ ἐδεξάμεθα ἀπὸ τῆς
[2]letters [3]about [4]thee [1]received from –

* That is, the officer to whom Paul was handed over by the centurion Julius.

um. The next day the south wind came up, and on the following day we reached Puteoli. [14]There we found some brothers who invited us to spend a week with them. And so we came to Rome. [15]The brothers there had heard that we were coming, and they traveled as far as the Forum of Appius and the Three Taverns to meet us. At the sight of these men Paul thanked God and was encouraged. [16]When we got to Rome, Paul was allowed to live by himself, with a soldier to guard him.

Paul Preaches at Rome Under Guard

[17]Three days later he called together the leaders of the Jews. When they had assembled, Paul said to them: "My brothers, although I have done nothing against our people or against the customs of our ancestors, I was arrested in Jerusalem and handed over to the Romans. [18]They examined me and wanted to release me, because I was not guilty of any crime deserving death. [19]But when the Jews objected, I was compelled to appeal to Caesar—not that I had any charge to bring against my own people. [20]For this reason I have asked to see you and talk with you. It is because of the hope of Israel that I am bound with this chain."

[21]They replied, "We have not received any letters from Judea concerning

ing you, nor have any of the
brethren come here and reported or spoken anything
bad about you.
22"But we desire to hear
from you what your views
are; for concerning this
sect, it is known to us that it
is spoken against every-
where."
23And when they had set
a day for him, they came to
him at his lodging in large
numbers; and he was ex-
plaining to them by sol-
emnly testifying about the
kingdom of God, and trying
to persuade them concern-
ing Jesus, from both the
Law of Moses and from the
Prophets, from morning
until evening.
24And some were being
persuaded by the things
spoken, but others would
not believe.
25And when they did not
agree with one another,
they *began* leaving after
Paul had spoken one *part-*
ing word, "The Holy Spirit
rightly spoke through
Isaiah the prophet to your
fathers,
26saying,
'GO TO THIS PEOPLE AND SAY,
"YOU WILL KEEP ON HEARING, BUT WILL NOT UNDERSTAND;
AND YOU WILL KEEP ON SEEING, BUT WILL NOT PERCEIVE;
27 FOR THE HEART OF THIS PEOPLE HAS BECOME DULL,
AND WITH THEIR EARS THEY SCARCELY HEAR,
AND THEY HAVE CLOSED THEIR EYES;
LEST THEY SHOULD SEE WITH THEIR EYES,
AND HEAR WITH THEIR EARS,
AND UNDERSTAND WITH THEIR HEART AND RETURN,
AND I SHOULD HEAL THEM." '
28"Let it be known to you
therefore, that this salvation of God has been sent to
the Gentiles; they will also
listen."
29[[x]And when he had
spoken these words, the
Jews departed, having a
great dispute among them-
selves.]
30And he stayed two full
years in his own rented
quarters, and was welcom-

Ἰουδαίας, οὔτε παραγενόμενός τις τῶν
Judæa, nor arriving anyone of the

ἀδελφῶν ἀπήγγειλεν ἢ ἐλάλησέν τι περὶ
brothers told or spoke anything [2]about

σοῦ πονηρόν. 22 ἀξιοῦμεν δὲ παρὰ σοῦ
[3]thee [1]evil. But we think fit from thee

ἀκοῦσαι ἃ φρονεῖς· περὶ μὲν γὰρ τῆς
to hear what things thou thinkest; [3]concerning [2]indeed [1]for –

αἱρέσεως ταύτης γνωστὸν ἡμῖν ἐστιν ὅτι
[5]sect [4]this [7]known [8]to us [6]it is that

πανταχοῦ ἀντιλέγεται. 23 Ταξάμενοι δὲ
everywhere it is spoken against. And arranging

αὐτῷ ἡμέραν ἦλθον πρὸς αὐτὸν εἰς τὴν
with him a day [2]came [3]to [4]him [5]in [6]the(his)

ξενίαν πλείονες, οἷς ἐξετίθετο διαμαρτυρ-
[7]lodging [1]more, to whom he set forth solemnly

όμενος τὴν βασιλείαν τοῦ θεοῦ, πείθων
witnessing the kingdom – of God, [2]persuading

τε αὐτοὺς περὶ τοῦ Ἰησοῦ ἀπό τε τοῦ
[1]and them concerning – Jesus from both the

νόμου Μωϋσέως καὶ τῶν προφητῶν, ἀπὸ
law of Moses and the prophets, from

πρωῒ ἕως ἑσπέρας. 24 καὶ οἱ μὲν
morning until evening. And some

ἐπείθοντο τοῖς λεγομένοις, 25 οἱ δὲ
were persuaded by the things being said, others

ἠπίστουν· ἀσύμφωνοι δὲ ὄντες πρὸς ἀλλή-
disbelieved; and [2]disagreed [1]being with one an-

λους ἀπελύοντο, εἰπόντος τοῦ Παύλου
other they were dismissed, having said – Paul[a]
=after Paul had said

ῥῆμα ἕν, ὅτι καλῶς τὸ πνεῦμα τὸ ἅγιον
word one, – Well the Spirit – Holy

ἐλάλησεν διὰ Ἠσαΐου τοῦ προφήτου πρὸς
spoke through Esaias the prophet to

τοὺς πατέρας ὑμῶν 26 λέγων· πορεύθητι
the fathers of you saying: Go thou

πρὸς τὸν λαὸν τοῦτον καὶ εἰπόν· ἀκοῇ
to this people and say: In hearing

ἀκούσετε καὶ οὐ μὴ συνῆτε, καὶ βλέποντες
ye will hear and by no means understand, and looking

βλέψετε καὶ οὐ μὴ ἴδητε· 27 ἐπαχύνθη
ye will look and by no means see; [2]was thickened

γὰρ ἡ καρδία τοῦ λαοῦ τούτου, καὶ
[1]for the heart of this people, and

τοῖς ὠσὶν βαρέως ἤκουσαν, καὶ τοὺς
with the(ir) ears heavily they heard, and the

ὀφθαλμοὺς αὐτῶν ἐκάμμυσαν· μήποτε ἴδωσιν
eyes of them they closed; lest at any time they see

τοῖς ὀφθαλμοῖς καὶ τοῖς ὠσὶν ἀκούσωσιν
with the eyes and with the ears hear

καὶ τῇ καρδίᾳ συνῶσιν καὶ ἐπιστρέψωσιν,
and with the heart understand and turn,

καὶ ἰάσομαι αὐτούς. 28 γνωστὸν οὖν
and I shall cure them. Known therefore

ἔστω ὑμῖν ὅτι τοῖς ἔθνεσιν ἀπεστάλη
let it be to you that to the nations was sent

τοῦτο τὸ σωτήριον τοῦ θεοῦ· αὐτοὶ καὶ
this – salvation – of God; and they

ἀκούσονται.‡
will hear.

30 Ἐνέμεινεν δὲ διετίαν ὅλην ἐν ἰδίῳ
And he remained a whole two years in [his] own

μισθώματι, καὶ ἀπεδέχετο πάντας τοὺς
hired apartment, and welcomed all the

you, and none of the brothers who have come from
there has reported or said
anything bad about you.
22But we want to hear what
your views are, for we
know that people every-
where are talking against
this sect."
23They arranged to meet
Paul on a certain day, and
came in even larger num-
bers to the place where he
was staying. From morning
till evening he explained
and declared to them the
kingdom of God and tried
to convince them about
Jesus from the Law of Mo-
ses and from the Prophets.
24Some were convinced by
what he said, but others
would not believe. 25They
disagreed among them-
selves and began to leave
after Paul had made this final statement: "The Holy
Spirit spoke the truth to
your forefathers when he
said through Isaiah the
prophet:

26" 'Go to this people and say,
"You will be ever hearing but never understanding;
you will be ever seeing but never perceiving."
27For this people's heart has become calloused;
they hardly hear with their ears,
and they have closed their eyes.
Otherwise they might see with their eyes,
hear with their ears,
understand with their hearts
and turn, and I would heal them.'[c]
28"Therefore I want you
to know that God's salva-
tion has been sent to the
Gentiles, and they will listen!"[d]
30For two whole years
Paul stayed there in his
own rented house and wel-

[x] Many mss. do not contain this verse

‡ Verse 29 omitted by Nestle; *cf.* NIV footnote.

[c]27 Isaiah 6:9,10
[d]28 Some manuscripts *listen!"*
29*After he said this, the Jews left, arguing vigorously among themselves.*

ing all who came to him,
[31]preaching the kingdom
of God, and teaching con-
cerning the Lord Jesus
Christ with all openness,
unhindered.

εἰσπορευομένους πρὸς αὐτόν, 31 κηρύσσων
[ones] coming in to him, proclaiming
τὴν βασιλείαν τοῦ θεοῦ καὶ διδάσκων
the kingdom – of God and teaching
τὰ περὶ τοῦ κυρίου Ἰησοῦ Χριστοῦ
the things concerning the Lord Jesus Christ
μετὰ πάσης παρρησίας ἀκωλύτως.
with all boldness unhinderedly.

comed all who came to see
him. [31]Boldly and without
hindrance he preached the
kingdom of God and taught
about the Lord Jesus
Christ.

Chapter 1

The Gospel Exalted

PAUL, a bond-servant of Christ Jesus, called *as* an apostle, set apart for the gospel of God,

2 which He promised beforehand through His prophets in the holy Scriptures,

3 concerning His Son, who was born of a descendant of David according to the flesh,

4 who was declared the Son of God with power [a] by the resurrection from the dead, according to the spirit of holiness, Jesus Christ our Lord,

5 through whom we have received grace and apostleship to bring about *the* obedience of faith among all the Gentiles, for His name's sake,

6 among whom you also are the called of Jesus Christ;

7 to all who are beloved of God in Rome, called *as* saints: Grace to you and peace from God our Father and the Lord Jesus Christ.

8 First, I thank my God through Jesus Christ for you all, because your faith is being proclaimed throughout the whole world.

9 For God, whom I serve in my spirit in the *preaching of the* gospel of His Son, is my witness *as to* how unceasingly I make mention of you,

10 always in my prayers making request, if perhaps now at last by the will of God I may succeed in coming to you.

11 For I long to see you in order that I may impart some spiritual gift to you, that you may be established;

12 that is, that I may be encouraged together with you *while* among you, each of us by the other's faith, both yours and mine.

[a] Or, *as a result of*

---

1 Παῦλος δοῦλος Χριστοῦ Ἰησοῦ, κλητὸς
Paul a slave of Christ Jesus, called
ἀπόστολος ἀφωρισμένος εἰς εὐαγγέλιον
an apostle *having been* separated to [the] gospel
θεοῦ, **2** ὃ προεπηγγείλατο διὰ τῶν
of God, which he promised beforehand through the
προφητῶν αὐτοῦ ἐν γραφαῖς ἁγίαις **3** περὶ
prophets of him in writings holy concerning
τοῦ υἱοῦ αὐτοῦ τοῦ γενομένου ἐκ
the Son of him – come of
σπέρματος Δαυὶδ κατὰ σάρκα, **4** τοῦ
[the] seed of David according to [the] flesh, –
ὁρισθέντος υἱοῦ θεοῦ ἐν δυνάμει
designated Son of God in power
κατὰ πνεῦμα ἁγιωσύνης ἐξ ἀναστάσεως
according to [the] Spirit of holiness by a resurrection
νεκρῶν, Ἰησοῦ Χριστοῦ τοῦ κυρίου ἡμῶν,
of dead persons, Jesus Christ the Lord of us,
5 δι' οὗ ἐλάβομεν χάριν καὶ ἀποστολὴν
through whom we received grace and apostleship
εἰς ὑπακοὴν πίστεως ἐν πᾶσιν τοῖς
for obedience of faith among all the
ἔθνεσιν ὑπὲρ τοῦ ὀνόματος αὐτοῦ, **6** ἐν
nations on behalf of the name of him, among
οἷς ἐστε καὶ ὑμεῖς κλητοὶ Ἰησοῦ Χριστοῦ,
whom are also ye called of Jesus Christ,
7 πᾶσιν τοῖς οὖσιν ἐν Ῥώμῃ ἀγαπητοῖς
to all the [ones] being in Rome beloved
θεοῦ, κλητοῖς ἁγίοις· χάρις ὑμῖν καὶ
of God, called holy: Grace to you and
εἰρήνη ἀπὸ θεοῦ πατρὸς ἡμῶν καὶ κυρίου
peace from God [the] Father of us and Lord
Ἰησοῦ Χριστοῦ.
Jesus Christ.
8 Πρῶτον μὲν εὐχαριστῶ τῷ θεῷ μου
Firstly – I thank the God of me
διὰ Ἰησοῦ Χριστοῦ περὶ πάντων ὑμῶν,
through Jesus Christ concerning all you,
ὅτι ἡ πίστις ὑμῶν καταγγέλλεται ἐν
because the faith of you is being announced in
ὅλῳ τῷ κόσμῳ. **9** μάρτυς γάρ μού
all the world. For witness of me
ἐστιν ὁ θεός, ᾧ λατρεύω ἐν τῷ πνεύματί
is – God, whom I serve in the spirit
μου ἐν τῷ εὐαγγελίῳ τοῦ υἱοῦ αὐτοῦ,
of me in the gospel of the Son of him,
ὡς ἀδιαλείπτως μνείαν ὑμῶν ποιοῦμαι
how unceasingly mention of you I make
10 πάντοτε ἐπὶ τῶν προσευχῶν μου,
always on(in) the prayers of me,
δεόμενος εἴ πως ἤδη ποτὲ εὐοδω-
requesting if somehow now at some time I shall have
θήσομαι ἐν τῷ θελήματι τοῦ θεοῦ ἐλθεῖν
a happy journey in the will – of God to come
πρὸς ὑμᾶς. **11** ἐπιποθῶ γὰρ ἰδεῖν ὑμᾶς,
unto you. For I long to see you,
ἵνα τι μεταδῶ χάρισμα ὑμῖν πνευματικὸν
that [3]some [1]I may impart [4]gift [5]to you [3]spiritual
εἰς τὸ στηριχθῆναι ὑμᾶς, **12** τοῦτο δέ
for the to be established you,[b] and this
=that ye may be established,
ἐστιν συμπαρακληθῆναι ἐν ὑμῖν διὰ τῆς
is to be encouraged *with* among you through [1]the
ἐν ἀλλήλοις πίστεως ὑμῶν τε καὶ ἐμοῦ.
[3]in [4]one another [2]faith [5]of you [5]both [7]and [8]of me.

Chapter 1

PAUL, a servant of
Christ Jesus, called to
be an apostle and set apart
for the gospel of God—
2 the gospel he promised beforehand through his
prophets in the Holy Scriptures 3 regarding his Son,
who as to his human nature
was a descendant of David,
4 and who through the Spirit[a] of holiness was declared
with power to be the Son of
God[b] by his resurrection
from the dead: Jesus Christ
our Lord. 5 Through him
and for his name's sake, we
received grace and apostleship to call people from
among all the Gentiles to
the obedience that comes
from faith. 6 And you also
are among those who are
called to belong to Jesus
Christ.

7 To all in Rome who are
loved by God and called to
be saints:

Grace and peace to you
from God our Father and
from the Lord Jesus Christ.

Paul's Longing to Visit Rome

8 First, I thank my God
through Jesus Christ for all
of you, because your faith
is being reported all over
the world. 9 God, whom I
serve with my whole heart
in preaching the gospel of
his Son, is my witness how
constantly I remember you
10 in my prayers at all times;
and I pray that now at last
by God's will the way may
be opened for me to come
to you.
11 I long to see you so that
I may impart to you some
spiritual gift to make you
strong— 12 that is, that you
and I may be mutually en-
couraged by each other's

[a]4 Or *who as to his spirit*
[b]4 Or *was appointed to be the Son of God with power*

13And I do not want you to be unaware, brethren, that often I have planned to come to you (and have been prevented thus far) in order that I might obtain some fruit among you also, even as among the rest of the Gentiles.

14I am [b]under obligation both to Greeks and to barbarians, both to the wise and to the foolish.

15Thus, for my part, I am eager to preach the gospel to you also who are in Rome.

16For I am not ashamed of the gospel, for it is the power of God for salvation to everyone who believes, to the Jew first and also to the Greek.

17For in it *the* righteousness of God is revealed from faith to faith; as it is written, "BUT THE RIGHTEOUS *man* SHALL LIVE BY FAITH."

Unbelief and Its Consequences

18For the wrath of God is revealed from heaven against all ungodliness and unrighteousness of men, who suppress the truth in unrighteousness,

19because that which is known about God is evident within them; for God made it evident to them.

20For since the creation of the world His invisible attributes, His eternal power and divine nature, have been clearly seen, being understood through what has been made, so that they are without excuse.

21For even though they knew God, they did not [c]honor Him as God, or give thanks; but they became futile in their speculations, and their foolish heart was darkened.

22Professing to be wise, they became fools,

23and exchanged the glory of the incorruptible God for an image in the form of corruptible man and of birds and four-footed animals and [d]crawling creatures.

[b] Lit., *debtor*
[c] Lit., *glorify*
[d] Or possibly, *reptiles*

13 οὐ θέλω δὲ ὑμᾶς ἀγνοεῖν, ἀδελφοί,
[2]not [3]I wish [1]But you to be ignorant, brothers,

ὅτι πολλάκις προεθέμην ἐλθεῖν πρὸς ὑμᾶς,
that often I purposed to come unto you,

καὶ ἐκωλύθην ἄχρι τοῦ δεῦρο, ἵνα τινὰ
and was hindered until the present, that some

καρπὸν σχῶ καὶ ἐν ὑμῖν καθὼς καὶ
fruit I may have also among you as indeed

ἐν τοῖς λοιποῖς ἔθνεσιν. 14 Ἕλλησίν
among the remaining nations. [2]to Greeks

τε καὶ βαρβάροις, σοφοῖς τε καὶ ἀνοήτοις
[1]Both [3]and [4]to foreigners, [6]to wise men [5]both [7]and [8]to foolish

ὀφειλέτης εἰμί· 15 οὕτως τὸ κατ᾽ ἐμὲ
[10]a debtor [9]I am; so as far as in me lies†

πρόθυμον καὶ ὑμῖν τοῖς ἐν Ῥώμῃ
[I am] eager [2]also [3]to you [4]*the* [*ones*] [5]in [6]Rome

εὐαγγελίσασθαι. 16 οὐ γὰρ ἐπαισχύνομαι
[1]to preach. For I am not ashamed of

τὸ εὐαγγέλιον· δύναμις γὰρ θεοῦ ἐστιν
the gospel; [2]power [1]for of God it is

εἰς σωτηρίαν παντὶ τῷ πιστεύοντι, Ἰουδαίῳ
to salvation to everyone believing, [2]to Jew

τε πρῶτον καὶ Ἕλληνι. 17 δικαιοσύνη
[1]both firstly and to Greek. a righteousness

γὰρ θεοῦ ἐν αὐτῷ ἀποκαλύπτεται ἐκ
For of God in it is revealed from

πίστεως εἰς πίστιν, καθὼς γέγραπται·
faith to faith, as it has been written:

ὁ δὲ δίκαιος ἐκ πίστεως ζήσεται.
Now the just man by faith will live.

18 Ἀποκαλύπτεται γὰρ ὀργὴ θεοῦ ἀπ᾽
For [4]is revealed [1][the] [2]wrath [3]of God from

οὐρανοῦ ἐπὶ πᾶσαν ἀσέβειαν καὶ ἀδικίαν
heaven against all impiety and unrighteousness

ἀνθρώπων τῶν τὴν ἀλήθειαν ἐν ἀδικίᾳ
of men – [2]the [3]truth [4]in [5]unrighteousness

κατεχόντων, 19 διότι τὸ γνωστὸν τοῦ θεοῦ
[1]holding fast, because the thing known – of God

φανερόν ἐστιν ἐν αὐτοῖς· ὁ θεὸς γὰρ αὐτοῖς
manifest is among them; – for God to them

ἐφανέρωσεν. 20 τὰ γὰρ ἀόρατα αὐτοῦ
manifested [it]. For the invisible things of him

ἀπὸ κτίσεως κόσμου τοῖς ποιήμασιν
[2]from [3][the] [4]creation [5]of [the] world [7]by the [8]things made

νοούμενα καθορᾶται, ἥ τε
[6]being understood [1]is(are) clearly seen, [10]the [9]both

ἀΐδιος αὐτοῦ δύναμις καὶ θειότης, εἰς
[11]everlasting [15]of him [12]power [13]and [14]divinity, for

τὸ εἶναι αὐτοὺς ἀναπολογήτους, 21 διότι
the to be them[b] without excuse, because
=so that they are

γνόντες τὸν θεὸν οὐχ ὡς θεὸν ἐδόξασαν
knowing – God [2]not [3]as [4]God [1]they glorified [him]

ἢ ηὐχαρίστησαν, ἀλλὰ ἐματαιώθησαν ἐν
[5]or [6]thanked [him], but became vain in

τοῖς διαλογισμοῖς αὐτῶν, καὶ ἐσκοτίσθη
the reasonings of them, and [5]was darkened

ἡ ἀσύνετος αὐτῶν καρδία. 22 φάσκοντες
[1]the [2]undiscerning [4]of them [3]heart. Asserting

εἶναι σοφοὶ ἐμωράνθησαν, 23 καὶ ἤλλαξαν
to be wise they became foolish, and changed

τὴν δόξαν τοῦ ἀφθάρτου θεοῦ ἐν ὁμοιώματι
the glory of the incorruptible God in[to] a likeness

εἰκόνος φθαρτοῦ ἀνθρώπου καὶ πετεινῶν
of an image of corruptible man and birds

καὶ τετραπόδων καὶ ἑρπετῶν· 24 διὸ
and quadrupeds and reptiles; wherefore

faith. 13I do not want you to be unaware, brothers, that I planned many times to come to you (but have been prevented from doing so until now) in order that I might have a harvest among you, just as I have had among the other Gentiles.

14I am obligated both to Greeks and non-Greeks, both to the wise and the foolish. 15That is why I am so eager to preach the gospel also to you who are at Rome.

16I am not ashamed of the gospel, because it is the power of God for the salvation of everyone who believes: first for the Jew, then for the Gentile. 17For in the gospel a righteousness from God is revealed, a righteousness that is by faith from first to last,[c] just as it is written: "The righteous will live by faith."[d]

God's Wrath Against Mankind

18The wrath of God is being revealed from heaven against all the godlessness and wickedness of men who suppress the truth by their wickedness, 19since what may be known about God is plain to them, because God has made it plain to them. 20For since the creation of the world God's invisible qualities—his eternal power and divine nature—have been clearly seen, being understood from what has been made, so that men are without excuse.

21For although they knew God, they neither glorified him as God nor gave thanks to him, but their thinking became futile and their foolish hearts were darkened. 22Although they claimed to be wise, they became fools 23and exchanged the glory of the immortal God for images made to look like mortal man and birds and animals and reptiles.

[c] 17 Or *is from faith to faith*
[d] 17 Hab. 2:4

24Therefore God gave them over in the lusts of their hearts to impurity, that their bodies might be dishonored among them.

25For they exchanged the truth of God for a lie, and worshiped and served the creature rather than the Creator, who is blessed forever. Amen.

26For this reason God gave them over to degrading passions; for their women exchanged the natural function for that which is unnatural,

27and in the same way also the men abandoned the natural function of the woman and burned in their desire toward one another, men with men committing indecent acts and receiving in their own persons the due penalty of their error.

28And just as they did not see fit to acknowledge God any longer, God gave them over to a depraved mind, to do those things which are not proper,

29being filled with all unrighteousness, wickedness, greed, evil; full of envy, murder, strife, deceit, malice; *they are* gossips,

30slanderers, haters of God, insolent, arrogant, boastful, inventors of evil, disobedient to parents,

31without understanding, untrustworthy, unloving, unmerciful;

32and, although they know the ordinance of God, that those who practice such things are worthy of death, they not only do the same, but also give hearty approval to those who practice them.

παρέδωκεν αὐτοὺς ὁ θεὸς ἐν ταῖς
[2]gave up [3]them – [1]God in the
ἐπιθυμίαις τῶν καρδιῶν αὐτῶν εἰς ἀκαθαρ-
desires of the hearts of them to unclean-
σίαν τοῦ ἀτιμάζεσθαι τὰ σώματα αὐτῶν
ness – to be dishonoured[d] the bodies of them
ἐν αὐτοῖς. 25 Οἵτινες μετήλλαξαν τὴν
among them[selves]. Who changed the
ἀλήθειαν τοῦ θεοῦ ἐν τῷ ψεύδει, καὶ
truth – of God in[to] the lie, and
ἐσεβάσθησαν καὶ ἐλάτρευσαν τῇ κτίσει
worshipped and served the creature
παρὰ τὸν κτίσαντα, ὅς ἐστιν εὐλογητὸς
rather than the [one] having created, who is blessed
εἰς τοὺς αἰῶνας· ἀμήν. 26 Διὰ τοῦτο
unto the ages: Amen. Therefore
παρέδωκεν αὐτοὺς ὁ θεὸς εἰς πάθη
[2]gave up [3]them – [1]God to passions
ἀτιμίας· αἵ τε γὰρ θήλειαι αὐτῶν
of dishonour; [2]the [3]even [1]for females of them
μετήλλαξαν τὴν φυσικὴν χρῆσιν εἰς τὴν
changed the natural use to the [use]
παρὰ φύσιν, 27 ὁμοίως τε καὶ οἱ ἄρσενες
against nature, [2]likewise [1]and also the males
ἀφέντες τὴν φυσικὴν χρῆσιν τῆς θηλείας
leaving the natural use of the female
ἐξεκαύθησαν ἐν τῇ ὀρέξει αὐτῶν εἰς
burned in the desire of them toward
ἀλλήλους, ἄρσενες ἐν ἄρσεσιν τὴν
one another, males among males [2]the
ἀσχημοσύνην κατεργαζόμενοι καὶ τὴν
[3]unseemliness [1]working and [4]the
ἀντιμισθίαν ἣν ἔδει τῆς πλάνης αὐτῶν
[5]requital [9]which [10]behoved [6]of the [7]error [8]of them
ἐν ἑαυτοῖς ἀπολαμβάνοντες. 28 Καὶ
[2]in [3]themselves [1]receiving back. And
καθὼς οὐκ ἐδοκίμασαν τὸν θεὸν ἔχειν
as they thought not fit – God to have
ἐν ἐπιγνώσει, παρέδωκεν αὐτοὺς ὁ θεὸς
in knowledge, [2]gave up [3]them – [1]God
εἰς ἀδόκιμον νοῦν, ποιεῖν τὰ μὴ καθήκοντα,
to a reprobate mind, to do the things not *being* proper,
29 πεπληρωμένους πάσῃ ἀδικίᾳ πονηρίᾳ
having been filled with all unrighteousness wickedness
πλεονεξίᾳ κακίᾳ, μεστοὺς φθόνου φόνου
covetousness evil, full of envy *of* murder
ἔριδος δόλου κακοηθείας, ψιθυριστάς,
of strife *of* guile *of* malignity, whisperers,*
30 καταλάλους, θεοστυγεῖς, ὑβριστάς, ὑπερ-
railers, God-haters, insolent, arro-
ηφάνους, ἀλαζόνας, ἐφευρετὰς κακῶν,
gant, boasters, inventors of evil things,
γονεῦσιν ἀπειθεῖς, 31 ἀσυνέτους, ἀσυνθέτους,
to parents disobedient, undiscerning, faithless,
ἀστόργους, ἀνελεήμονας· 32 οἵτινες τὸ
without natural affection, unmerciful; who [2]the
δικαίωμα τοῦ θεοῦ ἐπιγνόντες, ὅτι οἱ
[3]ordinance – [4]of God [1]knowing, that the
τὰ τοιαῦτα πράσσοντες ἄξιοι θανάτου
the [2]such things [1][ones] practising worthy of death
εἰσίν, οὐ μόνον αὐτὰ ποιοῦσιν, ἀλλὰ
are, not only them do, but
καὶ συνευδοκοῦσιν τοῖς πράσσουσιν.
also consent to the [ones] practising.

* "In a bad sense" (Abbott-Smith).

24Therefore God gave them over in the sinful desires of their hearts to sexu-
al impurity for the degrading of their bodies with one
another. 25They exchanged
the truth of God for a lie,
and worshiped and served
created things rather than
the Creator—who is forev-
er praised. Amen.
26Because of this, God
gave them over to shameful
lusts. Even their women
exchanged natural rela-
tions for unnatural ones.
27In the same way the men
also abandoned natural relations with women and
were inflamed with lust for
one another. Men commit-
ted indecent acts with other
men, and received in themselves the due penalty for
their perversion.
28Furthermore, since
they did not think it worth-
while to retain the knowledge of God, he gave them
over to a depraved mind, to
do what ought not to be
done. 29They have become
filled with every kind of
wickedness, evil, greed and
depravity. They are full of
envy, murder, strife, deceit
and malice. They are gos-
sips, 30slanderers, God-
haters, insolent, arrogant
and boastful; they invent
ways of doing evil; they disobey their parents; 31they
are senseless, faithless,
heartless, ruthless. 32Al-
though they know God's
righteous decree that those
who do such things deserve
death, they not only continue to do these very things
but also approve of those
who practice them.

Chapter 2

The Impartiality of God

THEREFORE you are without excuse, every man *of you* who passes judgment, for in that you judge another, you condemn yourself; for you who judge practice the same things.

2And we know that the judgment of God rightly falls upon those who practice such things.

3And do you suppose this, O man, when you pass judgment upon those who practice such things and do the same *yourself*, that you will escape the judgment of God?

4Or do you think lightly of the riches of His kindness and forbearance and patience, not knowing that the kindness of God leads you to repentance?

5But because of your stubbornness and unrepentant heart you are storing up wrath for yourself in the day of wrath and revelation of the righteous judgment of God,

6who WILL RENDER TO EVERY MAN ACCORDING TO HIS DEEDS:

7to those who by perseverance in doing good seek for glory and honor and immortality, eternal life;

8but to those who are selfishly ambitious and do not obey the truth, but obey unrighteousness, wrath and indignation.

9*There will be* tribulation and distress for every soul of man who does evil, of the Jew first and also of the Greek,

10but glory and honor and peace to every man who does good, to the Jew first and also to the Greek.

11For there is no partiality with God.

12For all who have sinned without the Law will also

2 Διὸ ἀναπολόγητος εἶ, ὦ ἄνθρωπε
Wherefore inexcusable thou art, O man

πᾶς ὁ κρίνων· ἐν ᾧ γὰρ κρίνεις τὸν
everyone judging; 2in 3what 1for thou judgest the

ἕτερον, σεαυτὸν κατακρίνεις· τὰ γὰρ αὐτὰ
other, thyself thou condemnest; for the same things

πράσσεις ὁ κρίνων. **2** οἴδαμεν δὲ ὅτι τὸ
thou practisest the [one] judging. But we know that the

κρίμα τοῦ θεοῦ ἐστιν κατὰ ἀλήθειαν ἐπὶ
judgment – of God is according to truth on

τοὺς τὰ τοιαῦτα πράσσοντας. **3** λογίζῃ
the *the* 2such things 1[ones] practising. reckonest thou

δὲ τοῦτο, ὦ ἄνθρωπε ὁ κρίνων τοὺς
And this, O man the [one] judging the [ones]

τὰ τοιαῦτα πράσσοντας καὶ ποιῶν αὐτά,
the such things practising and doing them,

ὅτι σὺ ἐκφεύξῃ τὸ κρίμα τοῦ θεοῦ;
that thou wilt escape the judgment – of God?

4 ἢ τοῦ πλούτου τῆς χρηστότητος αὐτοῦ
or the riches of the kindness of him

καὶ τῆς ἀνοχῆς καὶ τῆς μακροθυμίας
and the forbearance and the longsuffering

καταφρονεῖς, ἀγνοῶν ὅτι τὸ χρηστὸν τοῦ
despisest thou, not knowing that the kindness –

θεοῦ εἰς μετάνοιάν σε ἄγει; **5** κατὰ δὲ
of God to repentance thee leads? but according to

τὴν σκληρότητά σου καὶ ἀμετανόητον
the hardness of thee and impenitent

καρδίαν θησαυρίζεις σεαυτῷ ὀργὴν ἐν
heart treasurest for thyself wrath in

ἡμέρᾳ ὀργῆς καὶ ἀποκαλύψεως δικαιοκρισίας
a day of wrath and *of* revelation of a righteous judgment

τοῦ θεοῦ, **6** ὃς ἀποδώσει ἑκάστῳ κατὰ τὰ
– of God, who will requite to each man according to the

ἔργα αὐτοῦ· **7** τοῖς μὲν καθ' ὑπομονὴν
works of him: to the [ones] on one hand 2by 3endurance

ἔργου ἀγαθοῦ δόξαν καὶ τιμὴν καὶ
5work 4of(in) good 6glory 7and 8honour 9and

ἀφθαρσίαν ζητοῦσιν ζωὴν αἰώνιον·
10incorruption 1seeking 12life 11eternal;

8 τοῖς δὲ ἐξ ἐριθείας καὶ ἀπειθοῦσι τῇ
to the [ones] on the other of self-seeking and disobeying the

ἀληθείᾳ πειθομένοις δὲ τῇ ἀδικίᾳ, ὀργὴ
truth 2obeying 1but – unrighteousness, wrath

καὶ θυμός. **9** θλῖψις καὶ στενοχωρία ἐπὶ
and anger. Affliction and anguish on

πᾶσαν ψυχὴν ἀνθρώπου τοῦ κατεργαζομένου
every soul of man – working

τὸ κακόν, Ἰουδαίου τε πρῶτον καὶ
the evil, both of Jew firstly and

Ἕλληνος· **10** δόξα δὲ καὶ τιμὴ καὶ
of Greek; but glory and honour and

εἰρήνη παντὶ τῷ ἐργαζομένῳ τὸ ἀγαθόν,
peace to everyone working the good,

Ἰουδαίῳ τε πρῶτον καὶ Ἕλληνι. **11** οὐ
both to Jew firstly and to Greek. not

γάρ ἐστιν προσωπολημψία παρὰ τῷ θεῷ.
For is respect of persons with – God.

12 Ὅσοι γὰρ ἀνόμως ἥμαρτον, ἀνόμως
For as many as without law sinned, without law

Chapter 2

God's Righteous Judgment

YOU, therefore, have no excuse, you who pass judgment on someone else, for at whatever point you judge the other, you are condemning yourself, because you who pass judgment do the same things. 2Now we know that God's judgment against those who do such things is based on truth. 3So when you, a mere man, pass judgment on them and yet do the same things, do you think you will escape God's judgment? 4Or do you show contempt for the riches of his kindness, tolerance and patience, not realizing that God's kindness leads you toward repentance?

5But because of your stubbornness and your unrepentant heart, you are storing up wrath against yourself for the day of God's wrath, when his righteous judgment will be revealed. 6God "will give to each person according to what he has done."[e] 7To those who by persistence in doing good seek glory, honor and immortality, he will give eternal life. 8But for those who are self-seeking and who reject the truth and follow evil, there will be wrath and anger. 9There will be trouble and distress for every human being who does evil: first for the Jew, then for the Gentile; 10but glory, honor and peace for everyone who does good: first for the Jew, then for the Gentile. 11For God does not show favoritism.

12All who sin apart from the law will also perish

[e]6 Psalm 62:12; Prov. 24:12

perish without the Law; and all who have sinned under the Law will be judged by the Law;

13for not the hearers of the Law are just before God, but the doers of the Law will be justified.

14For when Gentiles who do not have the Law do instinctively the things of the Law, these, not having the Law, are a law to themselves,

15in that they show the work of the Law written in their hearts, their conscience bearing witness, and their thoughts alternately accusing or else defending them,

16on the day when, according to my gospel, God will judge the secrets of men through Christ Jesus.

The Jew Is Condemned by the Law

17But if you bear the name "Jew," and rely upon the Law, and boast in God,

18and know *His* will, and approve the things that are essential, being instructed out of the Law,

19and are confident that you yourself are a guide to the blind, a light to those who are in darkness,

20a corrector of the foolish, a teacher of the immature, having in the Law the embodiment of knowledge and of the truth,

21you, therefore, who teach another, do you not teach yourself? You who preach that one should not steal, do you steal?

22You who say that one should not commit adultery, do you commit adultery? You who abhor idols, do you rob temples?

23You who boast in the Law, through your breaking the Law, do you dishonor God?

24For "THE NAME OF GOD IS BLASPHEMED AMONG THE GENTILES BECAUSE OF YOU,"

καὶ ἀπολοῦνται· καὶ ὅσοι ἐν νόμῳ
also will perish; and as many as in (under) law
ἥμαρτον, διὰ νόμου κριθήσονται· 13 οὐ
sinned, through law will be judged; [2]not
γὰρ οἱ ἀκροαταὶ νόμου δίκαιοι παρὰ
[1]for the hearers of law [are] just with
[τῷ] θεῷ, ἀλλ' οἱ ποιηταὶ νόμου
– God, but the doers of law
δικαιωθήσονται. 14 ὅταν γὰρ ἔθνη τὰ
will be justified. For whenever nations –
μὴ νόμον ἔχοντα φύσει τὰ τοῦ νόμου
[1]not [3]law [2]having by nature the things of the law
ποιῶσιν, οὗτοι νόμον μὴ ἔχοντες ἑαυτοῖς
do, these [3]law [1]not [2]having to themselves
εἰσιν νόμος· 15 οἵτινες ἐνδείκνυνται τὸ
are a law; who show the
ἔργον τοῦ νόμου γραπτὸν ἐν ταῖς καρδίαις
work of the law written in the hearts
αὐτῶν, συμμαρτυρούσης αὐτῶν τῆς συνει-
of them, witnessing with of them the con-
=while their conscience witnesses with and their
δήσεως καὶ μεταξὺ ἀλλήλων τῶν λογισμῶν
science and between one another the thoughts
thoughts among themselves accuse or even excuse,
κατηγορούντων ἢ καὶ ἀπολογουμένων, 16 ἐν
accusing or even excusing,[a] in
ᾗ ἡμέρᾳ κρίνει ὁ θεὸς τὰ κρυπτὰ τῶν
what day judges – God the hidden things –
ἀνθρώπων κατὰ τὸ εὐαγγέλιόν μου διὰ
of men according to the gospel of me through
Χριστοῦ Ἰησοῦ. 17 Εἰ δὲ σὺ Ἰουδαῖος
Christ Jesus. But if thou [2]a Jew
ἐπονομάζῃ καὶ ἐπαναπαύῃ νόμῳ καὶ
[1]art named and restest on law and
καυχᾶσαι ἐν θεῷ 18 καὶ γινώσκεις τὸ
boastest in God and knowest the
θέλημα καὶ δοκιμάζεις τὰ διαφέροντα
will and approvest the things excelling
κατηχούμενος ἐκ τοῦ νόμου, 19 πέποιθάς τε
being instructed out of the law, and having persuaded
σεαυτὸν ὁδηγὸν εἶναι τυφλῶν, φῶς
thyself a guide to be of blind [persons], a light
τῶν ἐν σκότει, 20 παιδευτὴν ἀφρόνων,
of the [ones] in darkness, an instructor of foolish [persons],
διδάσκαλον νηπίων, ἔχοντα τὴν μόρφωσιν
a teacher of infants, having the form
τῆς γνώσεως καὶ τῆς ἀληθείας ἐν τῷ
– of knowledge and of the truth in the
νόμῳ· 21 ὁ οὖν διδάσκων ἕτερον σεαυτὸν
law: the [one] therefore teaching another thyself
οὐ διδάσκεις; ὁ κηρύσσων μὴ κλέπτειν
teachest thou not? the [one] proclaiming not to steal
κλέπτεις; 22 ὁ λέγων μὴ μοιχεύειν
stealest thou? the [one] saying not to commit adultery
μοιχεύεις; ὁ βδελυσσόμενος τὰ εἴδωλα
dost thou commit adultery? the [one] detesting the idols
ἱεροσυλεῖς; 23 ὃς ἐν νόμῳ καυχᾶσαι, διὰ
dost thou rob temples? who in law boastest, through
τῆς παραβάσεως τοῦ νόμου τὸν θεὸν
– transgression of the law – [2]God
ἀτιμάζεις; 24 τὸ γὰρ ὄνομα τοῦ θεοῦ
[1]dishonourest thou? for the name – of God
δι' ὑμᾶς βλασφημεῖται ἐν τοῖς ἔθνεσιν,
because of you is blasphemed among the nations,

apart from the law, and all who sin under the law will be judged by the law. 13For it is not those who hear the law who are righteous in God's sight, but it is those who obey the law who will be declared righteous. 14(Indeed, when Gentiles, who do not have the law, do by nature things required by the law, they are a law for themselves, even though they do not have the law, 15since they show that the requirements of the law are written on their hearts, their consciences also bearing witness, and their thoughts now accusing, now even defending them.) 16This will take place on the day when God will judge men's secrets through Jesus Christ, as my gospel declares.

The Jews and the Law

17Now you, if you call yourself a Jew; if you rely on the law and brag about your relationship to God; 18if you know his will and approve of what is superior because you are instructed by the law; 19if you are convinced that you are a guide for the blind, a light for those who are in the dark, 20an instructor of the foolish, a teacher of infants, because you have in the law the embodiment of knowledge and truth— 21you, then, who teach others, do you not teach yourself? You who preach against stealing, do you steal? 22You who say that people should not commit adultery, do you commit adultery? You who abhor idols, do you rob temples? 23You who brag about the law, do you dishonor God by breaking the law? 24As it is written: "God's name is blasphemed among the Gentiles because of you."[f]

f24 Isaiah 52:5; Ezek. 36:22

just as it is written.
25For indeed circumci-
sion is of value, if you practice the Law; but if you are
a transgressor of the Law,
your circumcision has
become uncircumcision.
26If therefore the uncir-
cumcised man keeps the requirements of the Law, will
not his uncircumcision be
regarded as circumcision?
27And will not he who is
physically uncircumcised,
if he keeps the Law, will he
not judge you who though
having the letter *of the Law*
and circumcision are a
transgressor of the Law?
28For he is not a Jew who
is one outwardly; neither is
circumcision that which is
outward in the flesh.
29But he is a Jew who is
one inwardly; and circum-
cision is that which is of the
heart, by the Spirit, not by
the letter; and his praise is
not from men, but from
God.

Chapter 3

All the World Guilty

THEN what advantage
has the Jew? Or what
is the benefit of circumcision?
2Great in every respect.
First of all, that they were
entrusted with the oracles
of God.
3What then? If some did
not believe, their unbelief
will not nullify the faithfulness of God, will it?
4May it never be!
Rather, let God be found
true, though every man *be
found* a liar, as it is written,

"THAT THOU MIGHTEST
BE JUSTIFIED IN THY
WORDS,
AND MIGHTEST PREVAIL
WHEN THOU ART
JUDGED."

5But if our unrighteous-
ness demonstrates the
righteousness of God, what
shall we say? The God who
inflicts wrath is not unrighteous, is He? (I am speaking
in human terms.)
6May it never be! For
otherwise how will God
judge the world?
7But if through my lie the
truth of God abounded to

καθὼς γέγραπται. **25** περιτομὴ μὲν γὰρ
as it has been written. circumcision indeed For
ὠφελεῖ ἐὰν νόμον πράσσῃς· ἐὰν δὲ
profits if law thou practisest; but if
παραβάτης νόμου ᾖς, ἡ περιτομή σου
a transgressor of law thou art, the circumcision of thee
ἀκροβυστία γέγονεν. **26** ἐὰν οὖν ἡ ἀκρο-
uncircumcision has become. If therefore the uncir-
βυστία τὰ δικαιώματα τοῦ νόμου φυλάσσῃ,
cumcision the ordinances of the law keeps,
οὐχ ἡ ἀκροβυστία αὐτοῦ εἰς περιτομὴν
not the uncircumcision of him for circumcision
λογισθήσεται; **27** καὶ κρινεῖ ἡ ἐκ φύσεως
will be reckoned? and 8will judge 1the 3by 4nature
ἀκροβυστία τὸν νόμον τελοῦσα σὲ τὸν
2uncircumcision 6the 7law 5keeping 9thee 10the
διὰ γράμματος καὶ περιτομῆς παραβάτην
13through 14letter 15and 16circumcision 11transgressor
νόμου. **28** οὐ γὰρ ὁ ἐν τῷ φανερῷ
12of law. For 2not 3the 5in 6the 7open
Ἰουδαῖός ἐστιν, οὐδὲ ἡ ἐν τῷ φανερῷ
4Jew 1he is, nor 1the 3in 4the 5open
ἐν σαρκὶ περιτομή· **29** ἀλλ' ὁ ἐν τῷ
6in 7flesh 2circumcision; but 1the 3in 4the
κρυπτῷ Ἰουδαῖος, καὶ περιτομὴ καρδίας
5secret 2Jew [is], and circumcision [is] of heart
ἐν πνεύματι οὐ γράμματι, οὗ ὁ ἔπαινος
in spirit not letter, of whom the praise [is]
οὐκ ἐξ ἀνθρώπων ἀλλ' ἐκ τοῦ θεοῦ.
not from men but from – God.
3 Τί οὖν τὸ περισσὸν τοῦ Ἰουδαίου,
What therefore the advantage of the Jew,
ἢ τίς ἡ ὠφέλεια τῆς περιτομῆς; **2** πολὺ
or what the profit – of circumcision? Much
κατὰ πάντα τρόπον. πρῶτον μὲν [γὰρ]
by every way. 3Firstly 2indeed 1for
ὅτι ἐπιστεύθησαν τὰ λόγια τοῦ θεοῦ.
because they were entrusted [with] the oracles – of God.
3 τί γάρ; εἰ ἠπίστησάν τινες, μὴ ἡ
For what? If 2disbelieved 1some, *not* the
ἀπιστία αὐτῶν τὴν πίστιν τοῦ θεοῦ
unbelief of them the faith – of God
καταργήσει; **4** μὴ γένοιτο· γινέσθω δὲ
will destroy? May it not be; but let be
ὁ θεὸς ἀληθής, πᾶς δὲ ἄνθρωπος ψεύστης,
– God true, and every man a liar,
καθάπερ γέγραπται· ὅπως ἂν δικαιωθῇς
as it has been written: So as – thou mayest be justified
ἐν τοῖς λόγοις σου καὶ νικήσεις ἐν
in the sayings of thee and wilt overcome in
τῷ κρίνεσθαί σε. **5** εἰ δὲ ἡ ἀδικία
the to be judged thee.[be] =when thou art judged. Now if the unrighteousness
ἡμῶν θεοῦ δικαιοσύνην συνίστησιν, τί
of us 3of God 2a righteousness 1commends, what
ἐροῦμεν; μὴ ἄδικος ὁ θεὸς ὁ ἐπιφέρων
shall we say? *not* unrighteous – God the [one] inflicting
τὴν ὀργήν; κατὰ ἄνθρωπον λέγω. **6** μὴ
– wrath? according to man I say. not
γένοιτο· ἐπεὶ πῶς κρινεῖ ὁ θεὸς τὸν
May it be; otherwise how will judge – God the
κόσμον; **7** εἰ δὲ ἡ ἀλήθεια τοῦ θεοῦ
world? But if the truth – of God

25Circumcision has value
if you observe the law, but
if you break the law, you
have become as though you
had not been circumcised.
26If those who are not circumcised keep the law's requirements, will they not
be regarded as though they
were circumcised? 27The
one who is not circumcised
physically and yet obeys
the law will condemn you
who, even though you have
the[g] written code and circumcision, are a lawbreaker.
28A man is not a Jew if he
is only one outwardly, nor
is circumcision merely outward and physical. 29No, a
man is a Jew if he is one
inwardly; and circumcision
is circumcision of the
heart, by the Spirit, not by
the written code. Such a
man's praise is not from
men, but from God.

Chapter 3

God's Faithfulness

WHAT advantage,
then, is there in be-
ing a Jew, or what value is
there in circumcision?
2Much in every way! First
of all, they have been entrusted with the very words
of God.
3What if some did not
have faith? Will their lack
of faith nullify God's faithfulness? 4Not at all! Let
God be true, and every man
a liar. As it is written:

"So that you may be
proved right when
you speak
and prevail when you
judge."[h]

5But if our unrighteous-
ness brings out God's righteousness more clearly,
what shall we say? That
God is unjust in bringing his
wrath on us? (I am using a
human argument.) 6Cer-
tainly not! If that were so,
how could God judge the
world? 7Someone might ar-
gue, "If my falsehood en-

[g]27 Or *who, by means of a*
[h]4 Psalm 51:4

His glory, why am I also
still being judged as a sinner?
8And why not *say* (as we
are slanderously reported
and as some affirm that we
say), "Let us do evil that
good may come"? Their
condemnation is just.
9What then? Are we bet-
ter than they? Not at all; for
we have already charged
that both Jews and Greeks
are all under sin;
10as it is written,

"THERE IS NONE RIGHTEOUS, NOT EVEN ONE;
11 THERE IS NONE WHO UNDERSTANDS,
THERE IS NONE WHO SEEKS FOR GOD;
12 ALL HAVE TURNED ASIDE, TOGETHER THEY HAVE BECOME USELESS;
THERE IS NONE WHO DOES GOOD,
THERE IS NOT EVEN ONE."
13"THEIR THROAT IS AN OPEN GRAVE,
WITH THEIR TONGUES THEY KEEP DECEIVING,"
"THE POISON OF ASPS IS UNDER THEIR LIPS";
14"WHOSE MOUTH IS FULL OF CURSING AND BITTERNESS";
15"THEIR FEET ARE SWIFT TO SHED BLOOD,
16 DESTRUCTION AND MISERY ARE IN THEIR PATHS,
17 AND THE PATH OF PEACE HAVE THEY NOT KNOWN."
18"THERE IS NO FEAR OF GOD BEFORE THEIR EYES."

19Now we know that whatever the Law says, it speaks to those who are under the Law, that every mouth may be closed, and all the world may become accountable to God;
20because by the works of the Law no flesh will be justified in His sight; for through the Law *comes* the knowledge of sin.

Justification by Faith

21But now apart from the Law *the* righteousness of God has been manifested, being witnessed by the

ἐν τῷ ἐμῷ ψεύσματι ἐπερίσσευσεν εἰς
by – my lie abounded to
τὴν δόξαν αὐτοῦ, τί ἔτι κἀγὼ ὡς
the glory of him, why still I also as
ἁμαρτωλὸς κρίνομαι; 8 καὶ μὴ καθὼς
a sinner am judged? and not as
βλασφημούμεθα καὶ καθώς φασίν τινες
we are blasphemed and as [2]say [1]some
ἡμᾶς λέγειν ὅτι ποιήσωμεν τὰ κακὰ
us to say[,] – Let us do – evil things
=that we say,
ἵνα ἔλθῃ τὰ ἀγαθά; ὧν τὸ κρίμα
that may come – good things? of whom the judgment
ἔνδικόν ἐστιν. 9 Τί οὖν; προεχόμεθα;
just is. What therefore? Do we excel?
οὐ πάντως· προῃτιασάμεθα γὰρ Ἰουδαίους
not at all; for we previously accused [2]Jews
τε καὶ Ἕλληνας πάντας ὑφ' ἁμαρτίαν
[1]both and Greeks all under sin
εἶναι, 10 καθὼς γέγραπται ὅτι οὐκ ἔστιν
to be, as it has been written[,] – There is not
δίκαιος οὐδὲ εἷς, οὐκ ἔστιν ὁ
a righteous man not one, there is not the [one]
συνίων, 11 οὐκ ἔστιν ὁ ἐκζητῶν τὸν θεόν·
under-standing, there is not the [one] seeking – God;
12 πάντες ἐξέκλιναν, ἅμα ἠχρεώθησαν·
all turned away, together became unprofitable;
οὐκ ἔστιν ὁ ποιῶν χρηστότητα, οὐκ
there is not the [one] doing kindness, not
ἔστιν ἕως ἑνός. 13 τάφος ἀνεῳγμένος
there is so much as one. A grave *having been* opened
ὁ λάρυγξ αὐτῶν, ταῖς γλώσσαις αὐτῶν
the throat of them, with the tongues of them
ἐδολιοῦσαν, ἰὸς ἀσπίδων ὑπὸ τὰ χείλη
they acted deceitfully, poison of asps under the lips
αὐτῶν· 14 ὧν τὸ στόμα ἀρᾶς καὶ πικρίας
of them; of whom the mouth [2]of cursing [3]and [4]bitterness
γέμει· 15 ὀξεῖς οἱ πόδες αὐτῶν ἐκχέαι
[1]is full; swift the feet of them to shed
αἷμα, 16 σύντριμμα καὶ ταλαιπωρία ἐν
blood, ruin and misery in
ταῖς ὁδοῖς αὐτῶν, 17 καὶ ὁδὸν εἰρήνης
the ways of them, and a way of peace
οὐκ ἔγνωσαν. 18 οὐκ ἔστιν φόβος θεοῦ
they knew not. There is not fear of God
ἀπέναντι τῶν ὀφθαλμῶν αὐτῶν. 19 οἴδαμεν
before the eyes of them. we know
δὲ ὅτι ὅσα ὁ νόμος λέγει τοῖς ἐν τῷ
But that whatever things the law says to the [ones] in the
νόμῳ λαλεῖ, ἵνα πᾶν στόμα φραγῇ καὶ
law it speaks, in order that every mouth may be stopped and
ὑπόδικος γένηται πᾶς ὁ κόσμος τῷ
[5]under judgment [4]may become [1]all [2]the [3]world –
θεῷ· 20 διότι ἐξ ἔργων νόμου οὐ
to God; because by works of law not
δικαιωθήσεται πᾶσα σὰρξ ἐνώπιον αὐτοῦ·
will be justified all flesh* before him;
διὰ γὰρ νόμου ἐπίγνωσις ἁμαρτίας.
for through law [is] full knowledge of sin.
21 Νυνὶ δὲ χωρὶς νόμου δικαιοσύνη
But now without law a righteousness
θεοῦ πεφανέρωται, μαρτυρουμένη ὑπὸ τοῦ
of God has been manifested, being witnessed by the

* That is, no flesh will be justified . . .

hances God's truthfulness
and so increases his glory,
why am I still condemned
as a sinner?" 8Why not say
—as we are being slander-
ously reported as saying
and as some claim that we
say—"Let us do evil that
good may result"? Their
condemnation is deserved.

No One Is Righteous

9What shall we conclude
then? Are we any better[i]?
Not at all! We have already
made the charge that Jews
and Gentiles alike are all
under sin. 10As it is written:

"There is no one righteous, not even one;
11 there is no one who understands,
no one who seeks God.
12All have turned away,
they have together become worthless;
there is no one who does good,
not even one."[j]
13"Their throats are open graves;
their tongues practice deceit."[k]
"The poison of vipers is on their lips."[l]
14 "Their mouths are full of cursing and bitterness."[m]
15"Their feet are swift to shed blood;
16 ruin and misery mark their ways,
17and the way of peace they do not know."[n]
18 "There is no fear of God before their eyes."[o]

19Now we know that
whatever the law says, it
says to those who are under
the law, so that every
mouth may be silenced and
the whole world held ac-
countable to God. 20There-
fore no one will be declared
righteous in his sight by observing the law; rather,
men, so also the result of
through the law we become
conscious of sin.

Righteousness Through Faith

21But now a righteous-
ness from God, apart from
law, has been made known,

[i]9 Or *worse*
[j]12 Psalms 14:1-3; 53:1-3; Eccles. 7:20
[k]13 Psalm 5:9
[l]13 Psalm 140:3
[m]14 Psalm 10:7
[n]17 Isaiah 59:7,8
[o]18 Psalm 36:1

Law and the Prophets,
22even *the* righteousness
of God through faith in
Jesus Christ for all those
who believe; for there is no
distinction;
23for all have sinned and
fall short of the glory of
God,
24being justified as a gift
by His grace through the
redemption which is in
Christ Jesus;
25whom God displayed
publicly as a propitiation in
His blood through faith.
This was to demonstrate
His righteousness, because
in the forbearance of God
He passed over the sins
previously committed;
26for the demonstration, *I
say,* of His righteousness at
the present time, that He
might be just and the justifi-
er of the one who has faith
in Jesus.
27Where then is boasting?
It is excluded. By what
kind of law? Of works? No,
but by a law of faith.
28For we maintain that a
man is justified by faith
apart from works of the
Law.
29Or is God *the God* of
Jews only? Is He not *the
God* of Gentiles also? Yes,
of Gentiles also,
30since indeed God who
will justify the circumcised
by faith and the uncircumcised through faith is one.
31Do we then nullify the
Law through faith? May it
never be! On the contrary,
we establish the Law.

Chapter 4

Justification by Faith Evidenced in Old Testament

WHAT then shall we
say that Abraham,
our forefather according to
the flesh, has found?
2For if Abraham was jus-
tified by works, he has
something to boast about;
but not before God.
3For what does the
Scripture say? "AND ABRA-
HAM BELIEVED GOD, AND IT
WAS RECKONED TO HIM AS

νόμου καὶ τῶν προφητῶν, 22 δικαιοσύνη
law and the prophets, [2]a righteousness

δὲ θεοῦ διὰ πίστεως [Ἰησοῦ] Χριστοῦ,
[1]and of God through faith of(in) Jesus Christ,

εἰς πάντας τοὺς πιστεύοντας· οὐ γάρ
to all the [ones] believing; for not

ἐστιν διαστολή· 23 πάντες γὰρ ἥμαρτον
there is difference; for all sinned

καὶ ὑστεροῦνται τῆς δόξης τοῦ θεοῦ,
and come short of the glory – of God,

24 δικαιούμενοι δωρεὰν τῇ αὐτοῦ χάριτι
being justified freely by the of him grace

διὰ τῆς ἀπολυτρώσεως τῆς ἐν Χριστῷ
through the redemption – in Christ

Ἰησοῦ· 25 ὃν προέθετο ὁ θεὸς ἱλαστήριον
Jesus; whom set forth – God a propitiation

διὰ πίστεως ἐν τῷ αὐτοῦ αἵματι, εἰς
through faith by the of him blood, for

ἔνδειξιν τῆς δικαιοσύνης αὐτοῦ διὰ τὴν
a showing forth of the righteousness of him because of the

πάρεσιν τῶν προγεγονότων ἁμαρτημάτων
passing by of the [2]having previously occurred [1]sins

26 ἐν τῇ ἀνοχῇ τοῦ θεοῦ, πρὸς τὴν
in the forbearance – of God, for the

ἔνδειξιν τῆς δικαιοσύνης αὐτοῦ ἐν τῷ
showing forth of the righteousness of him in the

νῦν καιρῷ, εἰς τὸ εἶναι αὐτὸν δίκαιον
present time, for the to be him[b] just
=that he should be

καὶ δικαιοῦντα τὸν ἐκ πίστεως Ἰησοῦ.
and justifying the [one] of faith of(in) Jesus.

27 Ποῦ οὖν ἡ καύχησις; ἐξεκλείσθη. διὰ
Where therefore the boasting? It was shut out. Through

ποίου νόμου; τῶν ἔργων; οὐχί, ἀλλὰ
what law? – of works? no, but

διὰ νόμου πίστεως. 28 λογιζόμεθα γὰρ
through a law of faith. For we reckon

δικαιοῦσθαι πίστει ἄνθρωπον χωρὶς ἔργων
[2]to be justified [3]by faith [1]a man without works

νόμου. 29 ἢ Ἰουδαίων ὁ θεὸς μόνον;
of law. Or of Jews [is he] the God only?

οὐχὶ καὶ ἐθνῶν; ναὶ καὶ ἐθνῶν, 30 εἴπερ
not also of nations? Yes[,] also of nations, since [there is]

εἷς ὁ θεὸς ὃς δικαιώσει περιτομὴν ἐκ
one – God who will justify circumcision by

πίστεως καὶ ἀκροβυστίαν διὰ τῆς πίστεως.
faith and uncircumcision through the faith.

31 νόμον οὖν καταργοῦμεν διὰ τῆς
[3]Law [2]therefore [1]do we destroy through the

πίστεως; μὴ γένοιτο, ἀλλὰ νόμον ἱστάνομεν.
faith? May it not be, but [2]law [1]we establish.

4 Τί οὖν ἐροῦμεν εὑρηκέναι Ἀβραὰμ
What therefore shall we say to have found Abraham

τὸν προπάτορα ἡμῶν κατὰ σάρκα; 2 εἰ
the forefather of us according to flesh? if

γὰρ Ἀβραὰμ ἐξ ἔργων ἐδικαιώθη, ἔχει
For Abraham by works was justified, he has

καύχημα· ἀλλ' οὐ πρὸς θεόν. 3 τί γὰρ
a boast; but not with God. For what

ἡ γραφὴ λέγει; ἐπίστευσεν δὲ Ἀβραὰμ
the scripture says? And [2]believed [1]Abraham

τῷ θεῷ, καὶ ἐλογίσθη αὐτῷ εἰς
– God, and it was reckoned to him for

to which the Law and the
Prophets testify. 22This
righteousness from God
comes through faith in
Jesus Christ to all who believe. There is no difference, 23for all have sinned
and fall short of the glory of
God, 24and are justified
freely by his grace through
the redemption that came
by Christ Jesus. 25God presented him as a sacrifice of
atonement,[p] through faith
in his blood. He did this to
demonstrate his justice, because in his forbearance he
had left the sins committed
beforehand unpunished—
26he did it to demonstrate
his justice at the present
time, so as to be just and
the one who justifies those
who have faith in Jesus.
27Where, then, is boast-
ing? It is excluded. On what
principle? On that of ob-
serving the law? No, but on
that of faith. 28For we
maintain that a man is justified by faith apart from observing the law. 29Is God
the God of Jews only? Is he
not the God of Gentiles
too? Yes, of Gentiles too,
30since there is only one
God, who will justify the
circumcised by faith and
the uncircumcised through
that same faith. 31Do we,
then, nullify the law by this
faith? Not at all! Rather, we
uphold the law.

Chapter 4

Abraham Justified by Faith

WHAT then shall we
say that Abraham,
our forefather, discovered
in this matter? 2If, in fact,
Abraham was justified by
works, he had something to
boast about—but not be-
fore God. 3What does the
Scripture say? "Abraham
believed God, and it was
credited to him as right-
eousness."[q]

[p]25 Or *as the one who would turn aside his wrath, taking away sin*
[q]3 Gen. 15:6; also in verse 22

RIGHTEOUSNESS."

4Now to the one who works, his wage is not reckoned as a favor, but as what is due.

5But to the one who does not work, but believes in Him who justifies the ungodly, his faith is reckoned as righteousness,

6just as David also speaks of the blessing upon the man to whom God reckons righteousness apart from works:

7"BLESSED ARE THOSE WHOSE LAWLESS DEEDS HAVE BEEN FORGIVEN,
AND WHOSE SINS HAVE BEEN COVERED.

8"BLESSED IS THE MAN WHOSE SIN THE LORD WILL NOT TAKE INTO ACCOUNT."

9Is this blessing then upon the circumcised, or upon the uncircumcised also? For we say, "FAITH WAS RECKONED TO ABRAHAM AS RIGHTEOUSNESS."

10How then was it reckoned? While he was circumcised, or uncircumcised? Not while circumcised, but while uncircumcised;

11and he received the sign of circumcision, a seal of the righteousness of the faith which he had while uncircumcised, that he might be the father of all who believe without being circumcised, that righteousness might be reckoned to them,

12and the father of circumcision to those who not only are of the circumcision, but who also follow in the steps of the faith of our father Abraham which he had while uncircumcised.

13For the promise to Abraham or to his descendants that he would be heir of the world was not through the Law, but through the righteousness of faith.

14For if those who are of the Law are heirs, faith is

δικαιοσύνην. 4 τῷ δὲ ἐργαζομένῳ ὁ
righteousness. Now to the [one] working the
μισθὸς οὐ λογίζεται κατὰ χάριν ἀλλὰ
reward is not reckoned according to grace but
κατὰ ὀφείλημα· 5 τῷ δὲ μὴ ἐργαζομένῳ,
according to debt; but to the [one] not working,
πιστεύοντι δὲ ἐπὶ τὸν δικαιοῦντα τὸν
but believing on the [one] justifying the
ἀσεβῆ, λογίζεται ἡ πίστις αὐτοῦ εἰς
impious man, is reckoned the faith of him for
δικαιοσύνην, 6 καθάπερ καὶ Δαυὶδ λέγει
righteousness, even as also David says
τὸν μακαρισμὸν τοῦ ἀνθρώπου ᾧ ὁ
the blessedness of the man to whom –
θεὸς λογίζεται δικαιοσύνην χωρὶς ἔργων·
God reckons righteousness without works :
7 μακάριοι ὧν ἀφέθησαν αἱ ἀνομίαι
Blessed [are they] of whom were forgiven the lawlessnesses
καὶ ὧν ἐπεκαλύφθησαν αἱ ἁμαρτίαι·
and of whom were covered over the sins;
8 μακάριος ἀνὴρ οὗ οὐ μὴ λογίσηται
blessed [is] a man of whom by no means [2]may reckon
κύριος ἁμαρτίαν 9 ὁ μακαρισμὸς οὖν
[1][the] Lord sin. – [2]blessedness [3]then
οὗτος ἐπὶ τὴν περιτομὴν ἢ καὶ ἐπὶ
[1]This on the circumcision or also on
τὴν ἀκροβυστίαν; λέγομεν γάρ· ἐλογίσθη
the uncircumcision? for we say : [3]was reckoned
τῷ Ἀβραὰμ ἡ πίστις εἰς δικαιοσύνην.
– [4]to Abraham [1]The(his) [2]faith for righteousness.
10 πῶς οὖν ἐλογίσθη; ἐν περιτομῇ ὄντι
How then was it reckoned? in circumcision being
ἢ ἐν ἀκροβυστίᾳ; οὐκ ἐν περιτομῇ ἀλλ'
or in uncircumcision? not in circumcision but
ἐν ἀκροβυστίᾳ· 11 καὶ σημεῖον ἔλαβεν
in uncircumcision; and [2]a sign [1]he received
περιτομῆς σφραγῖδα τῆς δικαιοσύνης τῆς
of circumcision a seal of the righteousness of the
πίστεως τῆς ἐν τῇ ἀκροβυστίᾳ, εἰς
faith – [while] in – uncircumcision, for =so
τὸ εἶναι αὐτὸν πατέρα πάντων τῶν
the to be him[b] a father of all the
that he should be
πιστευόντων δι' ἀκροβυστίας, εἰς τὸ
[ones] believing through uncircumcision, for the =that right-
λογισθῆναι αὐτοῖς [τὴν] δικαιοσύνην, 12 καὶ
to be reckoned to them – righteousness,[b] and
eousness should be reckoned to them,
πατέρα περιτομῆς τοῖς οὐκ ἐκ περιτομῆς
a father of circumcision to the [ones] not of circumcision
μόνον ἀλλὰ καὶ τοῖς στοιχοῦσιν τοῖς
only but also to the [ones] walking in the
ἴχνεσιν τῆς ἐν ἀκροβυστίᾳ πίστεως τοῦ
steps [1]of the [7]in [8]uncircumcision [2]faith [3]of the
πατρὸς ἡμῶν Ἀβραάμ. 13 Οὐ γὰρ διὰ
[4]father [5]of us [6]Abraham. For not through
νόμου ἡ ἐπαγγελία τῷ Ἀβραὰμ ἢ τῷ
law the promise – to Abraham or to the
σπέρματι αὐτοῦ, τὸ κληρονόμον αὐτὸν
seed of him, the heir him
=that he should be heir
εἶναι κόσμου, ἀλλὰ διὰ δικαιοσύνης πίστεως.
to be[b] of [the] world, but through a righteousness of faith.
14 εἰ γὰρ οἱ ἐκ νόμου κληρονόμοι,
For if [1]the [3][are] [4]of [5]law [2]heirs,

4Now when a man works,
his wages are not credited
to him as a gift, but as an
obligation. 5However, to
the man who does not work
but trusts God who justifies
the wicked, his faith is
credited as righteousness.
6David says the same thing
when he speaks of the
blessedness of the man to
whom God credits right-
eousness apart from works:

7"Blessed are they
whose transgressions
are forgiven,
whose sins are
covered.
8Blessed is the man
whose sin the Lord will
never count against
him."[r]

9Is this blessedness only
for the circumcised, or also
for the uncircumcised? We
have been saying that
Abraham's faith was cred-
ited to him as righteous-
ness. 10Under what circumstances was it credited?
Was it after he was circumcised, or before? It was not
after, but before! 11And he
received the sign of circumcision, a seal of the righteousness that he had by
faith while he was still uncircumcised. So then, he is
the father of all who believe
but have not been circum-
cised, in order that righteousness might be credited
to them. 12And he is also
the father of the circum-
cised who not only are circumcised but who also
walk in the footsteps of the
faith that our father Abraham had before he was circumcised.
13It was not through law
that Abraham and his off-
spring received the promise
that he would be heir of the
world, but through the
righteousness that comes
by faith. 14For if those who
live by law are heirs, faith

r8 Psalm 32:1,2

made void and the promise is nullified;

15for the Law brings about wrath, but where there is no law, neither is there violation.

16For this reason *it is* by faith, that *it might be* in accordance with grace, in order that the promise may be certain to all the descendants, not only to those who are of the Law, but also to those who are of the faith of Abraham, who is the father of us all,

17(as it is written, "A FATHER OF MANY NATIONS HAVE I MADE YOU") in the sight of Him whom he believed, *even* God, who gives life to the dead and calls into being that which does not exist.

18In hope against hope he believed, in order that he might become a father of many nations, according to that which had been spoken, "SO SHALL YOUR DESCENDANTS BE."

19And without becoming weak in faith he contemplated his own body, now as good as dead since he was about a hundred years old, and the deadness of Sarah's womb;

20yet, with respect to the promise of God, he did not waver in unbelief, but grew strong in faith, giving glory to God,

21and being fully assured that what He had promised, He was able also to perform.

22Therefore also IT WAS RECKONED TO HIM AS RIGHTEOUSNESS.

23Now not for his sake only was it written, that it was reckoned to him,

24but for our sake also, to whom it will be reckoned, as those who believe in Him who raised Jesus our Lord from the dead,

κεκένωται ἡ πίστις καὶ κατήργηται
[2]has been emptied – [1]faith and [3]has been destroyed

ἡ ἐπαγγελία· **15** ὁ γὰρ νόμος ὀργὴν
[1]the [2]promise; for the law [2]wrath

κατεργάζεται· οὗ δὲ οὐκ ἔστιν νόμος,
[1]works; and where there is not law,

οὐδὲ παράβασις. **16** Διὰ τοῦτο ἐκ πίστεως,
neither [is there] transgression. Therefore [it is] of faith,

ἵνα κατὰ χάριν, εἰς τὸ εἶναι βεβαίαν
in order that [it may be] according to grace, for the to be firm
=so that the promise shall be firm

τὴν ἐπαγγελίαν παντὶ τῷ σπέρματι, οὐ
the promise[b] to all the seed, not

τῷ ἐκ τοῦ νόμου μόνον ἀλλὰ καὶ τῷ
to the [seed] of the law only but also to the [seed]

ἐκ πίστεως Ἀβραάμ, ὅς ἐστιν πατὴρ
of [the] faith of Abraham, who is father

πάντων ἡμῶν, **17** καθὼς γέγραπται ὅτι
of all us, as it has been written[,] –

πατέρα πολλῶν ἐθνῶν τέθεικά σε,
A father of many nations I have appointed thee,

κατέναντι οὗ ἐπίστευσεν θεοῦ τοῦ ζωο-
before [2]whom [3]he believed [1]God the [one] quick-

ποιοῦντος τοὺς νεκροὺς καὶ καλοῦντος
ening the dead [ones] and calling

τὰ μὴ ὄντα ὡς ὄντα· **18** ὃς παρ' ἐλπίδα
the things not being as being; who beyond hope

ἐπ' ἐλπίδι ἐπίστευσεν, εἰς τὸ γενέσθαι
on hope believed, for the to become
=so that he should become

αὐτὸν πατέρα πολλῶν ἐθνῶν κατὰ τὸ
him[b] a father of many nations according to the thing

εἰρημένον· οὕτως ἔσται τὸ σπέρμα σου·
having been said : So shall be the seed of thee;

19 καὶ μὴ ἀσθενήσας τῇ πίστει κατενόησεν
and not weakening – in faith he considered

τὸ ἑαυτοῦ σῶμα νενεκρωμένον, ἑκατονταέτης
[1]the [3]of himself [2]body to have died, a hundred years

που ὑπάρχων, καὶ τὴν νέκρωσιν τῆς
about being, and the death of the

μήτρας Σάρρας· **20** εἰς δὲ τὴν ἐπαγγελίαν
womb of Sarah; but [2]against [3]the [4]promise

τοῦ θεοῦ οὐ διεκρίθη τῇ ἀπιστίᾳ, ἀλλὰ
– [5]of God [1]he did not decide – [6]by unbelief, but

ἐνεδυναμώθη τῇ πίστει, δοὺς δόξαν τῷ
was empowered – by faith, giving glory –

θεῷ **21** καὶ πληροφορηθεὶς ὅτι ὃ ἐπήγγελται
to God and being fully persuaded that what he has promised

δυνατός ἐστιν καὶ ποιῆσαι. **22** διὸ [καὶ]
able he is also to do. Wherefore also

ἐλογίσθη αὐτῷ εἰς δικαιοσύνην. **23** Οὐκ
it was reckoned to him for righteousness. not

ἐγράφη δὲ δι' αὐτὸν μόνον ὅτι ἐλογίσθη
it was written Now because of him only that it was reckoned

αὐτῷ, **24** ἀλλὰ καὶ δι' ἡμᾶς, οἷς μέλλει
to him, but also because of us, to whom it is about

λογίζεσθαι, τοῖς πιστεύουσιν ἐπὶ τὸν
to be reckoned, to the [ones] believing on the [one]

ἐγείραντα Ἰησοῦν τὸν κύριον ἡμῶν ἐκ
having raised Jesus the Lord of us out of

has no value and the promise is worthless, 15because law brings wrath. And where there is no law there is no transgression.

16Therefore, the promise comes by faith, so that it may be by grace and may be guaranteed to all Abraham's offspring—not only to those who are of the law but also to those who are of the faith of Abraham. He is the father of us all. 17As it is written: "I have made you a father of many nations."[s] He is our father in the sight of God, in whom he believed—the God who gives life to the dead and calls things that are not as though they were.

18Against all hope, Abraham in hope believed and so became the father of many nations, just as it had been said to him, "So shall your offspring be."[t] 19Without weakening in his faith, he faced the fact that his body was as good as dead—since he was about a hundred years old—and that Sarah's womb was also dead. 20Yet he did not waver through unbelief regarding the promise of God, but was strengthened in his faith and gave glory to God, 21being fully persuaded that God had power to do what he had promised. 22This is why "it was credited to him as righteousness." 23The words "it was credited to him" were written not for him alone, 24but also for us, to whom God will credit righteousness—for us who believe in him who raised Jesus our Lord from the

[s] *17* Gen. 17:5
[t] *18* Gen. 15:5

25 *He* who was delivered up because of our transgressions, and was raised because of our justification.

νεκρῶν, 25 ὃς παρεδόθη διὰ τὰ παραπ-
[the] dead, who was delivered because of the of-
τώματα ἡμῶν καὶ ἠγέρθη διὰ τὴν
fences of us and was raised because of the
δικαίωσιν ἡμῶν.
justification of us.

dead. 25 He was delivered over to death for our sins and was raised to life for our justification.

Chapter 5

Results of Justification

THEREFORE having been justified by faith, we have peace with God through our Lord Jesus Christ,
2 through whom also we have obtained our introduction by faith into this grace in which we stand; and we exult in hope of the glory of God.
3 And not only this, but we also exult in our tribulations, knowing that tribulation brings about perseverance;
4 and perseverance, proven character; and proven character, hope;
5 and hope does not disappoint, because the love of God has been poured out within our hearts through the Holy Spirit who was given to us.
6 For while we were still helpless, at the right time Christ died for the ungodly.
7 For one will hardly die for a righteous man; though perhaps for the good man someone would dare even to die.
8 But God demonstrates His own love toward us, in that while we were yet sinners, Christ died for us.
9 Much more then, having now been justified by His blood, we shall be saved from the wrath *of God* through Him.
10 For if while we were enemies, we were reconciled to God through the death of His Son, much more, having been reconciled, we shall be saved by His life.
11 And not only this, but

5 Δικαιωθέντες οὖν ἐκ πίστεως εἰρήνην
Having been justified therefore by faith peace
ἔχομεν πρὸς τὸν θεὸν διὰ τοῦ κυρίου
we have with – God through the Lord
ἡμῶν Ἰησοῦ Χριστοῦ, 2 δι' οὗ καὶ τὴν
of us Jesus Christ, through whom also the
προσαγωγὴν ἐσχήκαμεν [τῇ πίστει] εἰς
access we have had – by faith into
τὴν χάριν ταύτην ἐν ᾗ ἑστήκαμεν, καὶ
this grace in which we stand, and
καυχώμεθα ἐπ' ἐλπίδι τῆς δόξης τοῦ
boast on hope of the glory –
θεοῦ. 3 οὐ μόνον δέ, ἀλλὰ καὶ καυχώμεθα
of God. And not only [so], but also we boast
ἐν ταῖς θλίψεσιν, εἰδότες ὅτι ἡ θλῖψις
in – afflictions, knowing that – affliction
ὑπομονὴν κατεργάζεται, 4 ἡ δὲ ὑπομονὴ
patience works, – and patience
δοκιμήν, ἡ δὲ δοκιμὴ ἐλπίδα· 5 ἡ δὲ
proof, – and proof hope; – and
ἐλπὶς οὐ καταισχύνει, ὅτι ἡ ἀγάπη
hope does not put to shame, because the love
τοῦ θεοῦ ἐκκέχυται ἐν ταῖς καρδίαις
– of God has been poured out in the hearts
ἡμῶν διὰ πνεύματος ἁγίου τοῦ δοθέντος
of us through Spirit Holy – given
ἡμῖν· 6 εἴ γε Χριστὸς ὄντων ἡμῶν
to us; indeed [7]Christ [2]being [1]us
=when we were weak
ἀσθενῶν ἔτι κατὰ καιρὸν ὑπὲρ ἀσεβῶν
[4]weak[a] [3]yet [5]according to [6]time [9]on behalf of [10]impious ones
ἀπέθανεν. 7 μόλις γὰρ ὑπὲρ δικαίου
[8]died. For hardly on behalf of a just man
τις ἀποθανεῖται· ὑπὲρ γὰρ τοῦ ἀγαθοῦ
anyone will die; for on behalf of the good man
τάχα τις καὶ τολμᾷ ἀποθανεῖν· 8 συνίστησιν
perhaps someone even dares to die; [2]commends
δὲ τὴν ἑαυτοῦ ἀγάπην εἰς ἡμᾶς ὁ θεὸς
but [3]the [5]of himself [4]love [6]to [7]us – [1]God
ὅτι ἔτι ἁμαρτωλῶν ὄντων ἡμῶν Χριστὸς
that yet sinners being us[a] Christ
=while we were yet sinners
ὑπὲρ ἡμῶν ἀπέθανεν. 9 πολλῷ οὖν μᾶλλον
on behalf of us died. By much therefore rather
δικαιωθέντες νῦν ἐν τῷ αἵματι αὐτοῦ
having been justified now by the blood of him
σωθησόμεθα δι' αὐτοῦ ἀπὸ τῆς ὀργῆς.
we shall be saved through him from the wrath.
10 εἰ γὰρ ἐχθροὶ ὄντες κατηλλάγημεν
For if enemies being we were reconciled
τῷ θεῷ διὰ τοῦ θανάτου τοῦ υἱοῦ αὐτοῦ,
– to God through the death of the Son of him,
πολλῷ μᾶλλον καταλλαγέντες σωθησόμεθα
by much rather having been reconciled we shall be saved
ἐν τῇ ζωῇ αὐτοῦ· 11 οὐ μόνον δέ, ἀλλὰ
by the life of him; and not only [so], but

Chapter 5

Peace and Joy

THEREFORE, since we have been justified through faith, we[u] have peace with God through our Lord Jesus Christ, 2 through whom we have gained access by faith into this grace in which we now stand. And we[u] rejoice in the hope of the glory of God. 3 Not only so, but we[u] also rejoice in our sufferings, because we know that suffering produces perseverance; 4 perseverance, character; and character, hope. 5 And hope does not disappoint us, because God has poured out his love into our hearts by the Holy Spirit, whom he has given us.

6 You see, at just the right time, when we were still powerless, Christ died for the ungodly. 7 Very rarely will anyone die for a righteous man, though for a good man someone might possibly dare to die. 8 But God demonstrates his own love for us in this: While we were still sinners, Christ died for us.

9 Since we have now been justified by his blood, how much more shall we be saved from God's wrath through him! 10 For if, when we were God's enemies, we were reconciled to him through the death of his Son, how much more, having been reconciled, shall we be saved through his life! 11 Not only is this so,

[u] *1,2,3* Or *let us*

we also exult in God
through our Lord Jesus
Christ, through whom we
have now received the
reconciliation.
12 Therefore, just as
through one man sin en-
tered into the world, and
death through sin, and so
death spread to all men, because all sinned—
13 for until the Law sin
was in the world; but sin is
not imputed when there is
no law.
14 Nevertheless death
reigned from Adam until
Moses, even over those
who had not sinned in the
likeness of the offense of
Adam, who is a [e]type of
Him who was to come.
15 But the free gift is not
like the transgression. For
if by the transgression of
the one the many died,
much more did the grace of
God and the gift by the
grace of the one Man, Jesus
Christ, abound to the
many.
16 And the gift is not like
that which came through
the one who sinned; for on
the one hand the judgment
arose from one *transgres-*
sion resulting in condemnation, but on the other hand
the free gift *arose* from
many transgressions resulting in justification.
17 For if by the transgression of the one, death
reigned through the one,
much more those who re-
ceive the abundance of
grace and of the gift of
righteousness will reign in
life through the One, Jesus
Christ.
18 So then as through one
transgression there re-
sulted condemnation to all

καὶ καυχώμενοι ἐν τῷ θεῷ διὰ τοῦ
also boasting in – God through the
κυρίου ἡμῶν Ἰησοῦ [Χριστοῦ], δι' οὗ
Lord of us Jesus Christ, through whom
νῦν τὴν καταλλαγὴν ἐλάβομεν.
now the reconciliation we received.
12 Διὰ τοῦτο ὥσπερ δι' ἑνὸς ἀνθρώπου
Therefore as through one man
ἡ ἁμαρτία εἰς τὸν κόσμον εἰσῆλθεν,
– sin into the world entered,
καὶ διὰ τῆς ἁμαρτίας ὁ θάνατος, καὶ
and through – sin – death, [2]also
οὕτως εἰς πάντας ἀνθρώπους ὁ θάνατος
[1]so to all men – death
διῆλθεν, ἐφ' ᾧ πάντες ἥμαρτον· 13 ἄχρι
passed, inasmuch as all sinned; until
γὰρ νόμου ἁμαρτία ἦν ἐν κόσμῳ, ἁμαρτία
for law sin was in [the] world, sin
δὲ οὐκ ἐλλογεῖται μὴ ὄντος νόμου·
but is not reckoned not being law[a];
=when there is no law;
14 ἀλλὰ ἐβασίλευσεν ὁ θάνατος ἀπὸ Ἀδὰμ
but [2]reigned – [1]death from Adam
μέχρι Μωϋσέως καὶ ἐπὶ τοὺς μὴ
until Moses even over the [ones] not
ἁμαρτήσαντας ἐπὶ τῷ ὁμοιώματι τῆς
sinning on the likeness of the
παραβάσεως Ἀδάμ, ὅς ἐστιν τύπος τοῦ
transgression of Adam, who is a type of the
μέλλοντος. 15 Ἀλλ' οὐχ ὡς τὸ παράπτωμα,
[one] coming. But not as the offence,
οὕτως [καὶ] τὸ χάρισμα· εἰ γὰρ τῷ
so also the free gift; for if [1]by the
τοῦ ἑνὸς παραπτώματι οἱ πολλοὶ
[3]of the [4]one [man] [2]offence the many
ἀπέθανον, πολλῷ μᾶλλον ἡ χάρις τοῦ θεοῦ
died, by much rather the grace – of God
καὶ ἡ δωρεὰ ἐν χάριτι τῇ τοῦ ἑνὸς
and the gift in grace – of the one
ἀνθρώπου Ἰησοῦ Χριστοῦ εἰς τοὺς πολλοὺς
man Jesus Christ to the many
ἐπερίσσευσεν. 16 καὶ οὐχ ὡς δι' ἑνὸς
abounded. And not as through one [man]
ἁμαρτήσαντος τὸ δώρημα· τὸ μὲν γὰρ
sinning the gift; [3]the [2]on one hand [1]for
κρίμα ἐξ ἑνὸς εἰς κατάκριμα, τὸ δὲ
judgment [is] of one [offence] to condemnation, on the other the
χάρισμα ἐκ πολλῶν παραπτωμάτων εἰς
free gift [is] of many offences to
δικαίωμα. 17 εἰ γὰρ τῷ τοῦ ἑνὸς
justification. For if [1]by the [3]of the [4]one [man]
παραπτώματι ὁ θάνατος ἐβασίλευσεν διὰ
[2]offence – death reigned through
τοῦ ἑνός, πολλῷ μᾶλλον οἱ τὴν περισσείαν
the one [man], by much rather [1]the [ones] [3]the [4]abundance
τῆς χάριτος καὶ τῆς δωρεᾶς τῆς
[5]of the [6]grace [7]and [8]of the [9]gift –
δικαιοσύνης λαμβάνοντες ἐν ζωῇ βασιλεύ-
[10]of righteousness [2]receiving [12]in [13]life [11]will
σουσιν διὰ τοῦ ἑνὸς Ἰησοῦ Χριστοῦ.
reign through the one [man] Jesus Christ.
18 Ἄρα οὖν ὡς δι' ἑνὸς παραπτώματος
So therefore as through one offence
εἰς πάντας ἀνθρώπους εἰς κατάκριμα,
to all men to condemnation,

but we also rejoice in God
through our Lord Jesus
Christ, through whom we
have now received recon-
ciliation.

Death Through Adam,
Life Through Christ

12 Therefore, just as sin
entered the world through
one man, and death
through sin, and in this way
death came to all men, because all sinned— 13 for before the law was given, sin
was in the world. But sin is
not taken into account
when there is no law.
14 Nevertheless, death
reigned from the time of
Adam to the time of Moses,
even over those who did
not sin by breaking a command, as did Adam, who
was a pattern of the one to
come.
15 But the gift is not like
the trespass. For if the
many died by the trespass
of the one man, how much
more did God's grace and
the gift that came by the
grace of the one man, Jesus
Christ, overflow to the
many! 16 Again, the gift of
God is not like the result of
the one man's sin: The
judgment followed one sin
and brought condemna-
tion, but the gift followed
many trespasses and
brought justification. 17 For
if, by the trespass of the
one man, death reigned
through that one man, how
much more will those who
receive God's abundant
provision of grace and of
the gift of righteousness
reign in life through the one
man, Jesus Christ.
18 Consequently, just as
the result of one trespass
was condemnation for all

[e] Or, *foreshadowing*

men, even so through one
act of righteousness there
resulted justification of life
to all men.
19For as through the one
man's disobedience the
many were made sinners,
even so through the obedience of the One the many
will be made righteous.
20And the Law came in
that the transgression
might increase; but where
sin increased, grace
abounded all the more,
21that, as sin reigned in
death, even so grace might
reign through righteous-
ness to eternal life through
Jesus Christ our Lord.

οὕτως καὶ δι' ἑνὸς δικαιώματος εἰς
so also through one righteous act to

πάντας ἀνθρώπους εἰς δικαίωσιν ζωῆς·
all men to justification of life;

19 ὥσπερ γὰρ διὰ τῆς παρακοῆς τοῦ
for as through the disobedience of the

ἑνὸς ἀνθρώπου ἁμαρτωλοὶ κατεστάθησαν
one man [4]sinners [3]were constituted

οἱ πολλοί, οὕτως καὶ διὰ τῆς ὑπακοῆς
[1]the [2]many, so also through the obedience

τοῦ ἑνὸς δίκαιοι κατασταθήσονται οἱ
of the one [man] [4]righteous [3]will be constituted [1]the

πολλοί. **20** νόμος δὲ παρεισῆλθεν ἵνα
[2]many. But law entered in order that

πλεονάσῃ τὸ παράπτωμα· οὗ δὲ ἐπλεόνασεν
might abound the offence; but where abounded

ἡ ἁμαρτία, ὑπερεπερίσσευσεν ἡ χάρις,
– sin, more abounded – grace,

21 ἵνα ὥσπερ ἐβασίλευσεν ἡ ἁμαρτία ἐν
in order that as reigned – sin by

τῷ θανάτῳ, οὕτως καὶ ἡ χάρις βασιλεύσῃ
– death, so also – grace might reign

διὰ δικαιοσύνης εἰς ζωὴν αἰώνιον διὰ
through righteousness to life eternal through

Ἰησοῦ Χριστοῦ τοῦ κυρίου ἡμῶν.
Jesus Christ the Lord of us.

one act of righteousness
was justification that brings
life for all men. 19For just as
through the disobedience
of the one man the many
were made sinners, so also
through the obedience of
the one man the many will
be made righteous.
20The law was added so
that the trespass might increase. But where sin in-
creased, grace increased all
the more, 21so that, just as
sin reigned in death, so also
grace might reign through
righteousness to bring eternal life through Jesus
Christ our Lord.

Chapter 6

Believers Are Dead to Sin, Alive to God

WHAT shall we say
then? Are we to con-
tinue in sin that grace might
increase?
2May it never be! How
shall we who died to sin still
live in it?
3Or do you not know that
all of us who have been
baptized into Christ Jesus
have been baptized into
His death?
4Therefore we have been
buried with Him through
baptism into death, in order
that as Christ was raised
from the dead through the
glory of the Father, so we
too might walk in newness
of life.
5For if we have become
united with *Him* in the likeness of His death, certainly
we shall be also *in the likeness* of His resurrection,
6knowing this, that our
old self was crucified with
Him, that our body of sin
might be done away with,
that we should no longer be
slaves to sin;
7for he who has died is
freed from sin.

6 Τί οὖν ἐροῦμεν; ἐπιμένωμεν τῇ
What therefore shall we say? May we continue –

ἁμαρτίᾳ, ἵνα ἡ χάρις πλεονάσῃ; **2** μὴ
in sin, in order that – grace may abound? not

γένοιτο. οἵτινες ἀπεθάνομεν τῇ ἁμαρτίᾳ,
May it be. Who *we* died – to sin,

πῶς ἔτι ζήσομεν ἐν αὐτῇ; **3** ἢ ἀγνοεῖτε
how yet shall we live in it? or are ye ignorant

ὅτι ὅσοι ἐβαπτίσθημεν εἰς Χριστὸν
that as many as *we* were baptized into Christ

Ἰησοῦν, εἰς τὸν θάνατον αὐτοῦ ἐβαπτίσ-
Jesus, into the death of him we were

θημεν; **4** συνετάφημεν οὖν αὐτῷ διὰ τοῦ
baptized? [2]We were buried with [1]there fore him through –

βαπτίσματος εἰς τὸν θάνατον, ἵνα ὥσπερ
baptism into – death, in order that as

ἠγέρθη Χριστὸς ἐκ νεκρῶν διὰ τῆς
was raised Christ from [the] dead through the

δόξης τοῦ πατρός, οὕτως καὶ ἡμεῖς ἐν
glory of the Father, so also we in

καινότητι ζωῆς περιπατήσωμεν. **5** εἰ γὰρ
newness of life might walk. For if

σύμφυτοι γεγόναμεν τῷ ὁμοιώματι τοῦ
united with we have become in the likeness of the

θανάτου αὐτοῦ, ἀλλὰ καὶ τῆς ἀναστάσεως
death of him, but(so) also of the(his) resurrection

ἐσόμεθα· **6** τοῦτο γινώσκοντες, ὅτι ὁ
we shall be; this knowing, that the

παλαιὸς ἡμῶν ἄνθρωπος συνεσταυρώθη, ἵνα
[1]old [3]of us [2]man was crucified with [him], in order that

καταργηθῇ τὸ σῶμα τῆς ἁμαρτίας, τοῦ
might be destroyed the body – of sin, –

μηκέτι δουλεύειν ἡμᾶς τῇ ἁμαρτίᾳ· **7** ὁ
no longer to serve us[bd] – sin; [2]the (one)
=that we should no longer serve

γὰρ ἀποθανὼν δεδικαίωται ἀπὸ τῆς
[1]for having died has been justified from –

Chapter 6

Dead to Sin, Alive in Christ

WHAT shall we say,
then? Shall we go on
sinning so that grace may
increase? 2By no means!
We died to sin; how can we
live in it any longer? 3Or
don't you know that all of
us who were baptized into
Christ Jesus were baptized
into his death? 4We were
therefore buried with him
through baptism into death
in order that, just as Christ
was raised from the dead
through the glory of the Father, we too may live a new
life.
5If we have been united
with him like this in his
death, we will certainly
also be united with him in
his resurrection. 6For we
know that our old self was
crucified with him so that
the body of sin might be
done away with,[v] that we
should no longer be slaves
to sin— 7because anyone
who has died has been
freed from sin.

[v]6 Or *be rendered powerless*

8 Now if we have died with Christ, we believe that we shall also live with Him,

9 knowing that Christ, having been raised from the dead, is never to die again; death no longer is master over Him.

10 For the death that He died, He died to sin, once for all; but the life that He lives, He lives to God.

11 Even so consider yourselves to be dead to sin, but alive to God in Christ Jesus.

12 Therefore do not let sin reign in your mortal body that you should obey its lusts,

13 and do not go on presenting the members of your body to sin *as* instruments of unrighteousness; but present yourselves to God as those alive from the dead, and your members *as* instruments of righteousness to God.

14 For sin shall not be master over you, for you are not under law, but under grace.

15 What then? Shall we sin because we are not under law but under grace? May it never be!

16 Do you not know that when you present yourselves to someone *as* slaves for obedience, you are slaves of the one whom you obey, either of sin resulting in death, or of obedience resulting in righteousness?

17 But thanks be to God that though you were slaves of sin, you became obedient from the heart to that form of teaching to which you were committed,

18 and having been freed from sin, you became slaves of righteousness.

19 I am speaking in human terms because of the weakness of your flesh. For just as you presented your members *as* slaves to impurity and to lawlessness,

ἁμαρτίας. **8** εἰ δὲ ἀπεθάνομεν σὺν Χριστῷ,
sin. But if we died with Christ
πιστεύομεν ὅτι καὶ συζήσομεν αὐτῷ,
we believe that also we shall live with him,
9 εἰδότες ὅτι Χριστὸς ἐγερθεὶς ἐκ νεκρῶν
knowing that Christ having been raised from [the] dead
οὐκέτι ἀποθνήσκει, θάνατος αὐτοῦ οὐκέτι
no more dies, death [3]*of* him [1]no more
κυριεύει. **10** ὃ γὰρ ἀπέθανεν, τῇ ἁμαρτίᾳ
[2]lords it over. For in that† he died, – to sin
ἀπέθανεν ἐφάπαξ· ὃ δὲ ζῇ, ζῇ τῷ θεῷ.
he died once; but in that† he lives, he lives – to God.
11 οὕτως καὶ ὑμεῖς λογίζεσθε ἑαυτοὺς
So also [2]ye [1]reckon yourselves
εἶναι νεκροὺς μὲν τῇ ἁμαρτίᾳ ζῶντας
to be dead indeed – to sin [2]living
δὲ τῷ θεῷ ἐν Χριστῷ Ἰησοῦ. **12** μὴ
[1]but – to God in Christ Jesus. [3]not
οὖν βασιλευέτω ἡ ἁμαρτία ἐν τῷ θνητῷ
[1]Therefore [2]let [5]reign – [4]sin [6]in [7]the [8]mortal
ὑμῶν σώματι εἰς τὸ ὑπακούειν ταῖς
[10]of you [9]body for the to obey the
=to obey its lusts,
ἐπιθυμίαις αὐτοῦ, **13** μηδὲ παριστάνετε τὰ
lusts of it, neither present ye the
μέλη ὑμῶν ὅπλα ἀδικίας τῇ ἁμαρτίᾳ,
members of you weapons of unrighteousness – to sin,
ἀλλὰ παραστήσατε ἑαυτοὺς τῷ θεῷ ὡσεὶ
but present ye yourselves – to God as
ἐκ νεκρῶν ζῶντας καὶ τὰ μέλη ὑμῶν
from [the] dead living and the members of you
ὅπλα δικαιοσύνης τῷ θεῷ, **14** ἁμαρτία
weapons of righteousness – to God, [2]sin
γὰρ ὑμῶν οὐ κυριεύσει· οὐ γάρ ἐστε
[1]for [4]*of* you [3]shall not lord it over; for ye are not
ὑπὸ νόμον ἀλλὰ ὑπὸ χάριν. **15** Τί οὖν;
under law but under grace. What therefore?
ἁμαρτήσωμεν, ὅτι οὐκ ἐσμὲν ὑπὸ νόμον
may we sin, because we are not under law
ἀλλὰ ὑπὸ χάριν; μὴ γένοιτο. **16** οὐκ
but under grace? May it not be. not
οἴδατε ὅτι ᾧ παριστάνετε ἑαυτοὺς δούλους
Know ye that to whom ye present yourselves slaves
εἰς ὑπακοήν, δοῦλοί ἐστε ᾧ ὑπακούετε,
for obedience, slaves ye are whom ye obey,
ἤτοι ἁμαρτίας εἰς θάνατον ἢ ὑπακοῆς
whether of sin to death or of obedience
εἰς δικαιοσύνην; **17** χάρις δὲ τῷ θεῷ
to righteousness? But thanks – to God
ὅτι ἦτε δοῦλοι τῆς ἁμαρτίας, ὑπηκούσατε
that ye were slaves – of sin, [2]ye obeyed
δὲ ἐκ καρδίας εἰς ὃν παρεδόθητε τύπον
[1]but out of [the] heart [3]to [4]which [5]ye were delivered [1]a form
διδαχῆς, **18** ἐλευθερωθέντες δὲ ἀπὸ τῆς
[2]of teaching, and having been freed from –
ἁμαρτίας ἐδουλώθητε τῇ δικαιοσύνῃ.
sin ye were enslaved – to righteousness.
19 ἀνθρώπινον λέγω διὰ τὴν ἀσθένειαν
Humanly I say because of the weakness
τῆς σαρκὸς ὑμῶν. ὥσπερ γὰρ παρεστήσατε
of the flesh of you. For as ye presented
τὰ μέλη ὑμῶν δοῦλα τῇ ἀκαθαρσίᾳ καὶ
the members of you slaves – to uncleanness and

8 Now if we died with
Christ, we believe that we
will also live with him. 9 For
we know that since Christ
was raised from the dead,
he cannot die again; death
no longer has mastery over
him. 10 The death he died,
he died to sin once for all;
but the life he lives, he lives
to God.
11 In the same way, count
yourselves dead to sin but
alive to God in Christ
Jesus. 12 Therefore do not
let sin reign in your mortal
body so that you obey its
evil desires. 13 Do not offer
the parts of your body to
sin, as instruments of wickedness,
but rather offer
yourselves to God, as those
who have been brought
from death to life; and offer
the parts of your body to
him as instruments of righteousness.
14 For sin shall
not be your master, because
you are not under
law, but under grace.

Slaves to Righteousness

15 What then? Shall we sin
because we are not under
law but under grace? By no
means! 16 Don't you know
that when you offer yourselves
to someone to obey
him as slaves, you are
slaves to the one whom you
obey—whether you are
slaves to sin, which leads to
death, or to obedience,
which leads to righteousness?
17 But thanks be to
God that, though you used
to be slaves to sin, you
wholeheartedly obeyed the
form of teaching to which
you were entrusted. 18 You
have been set free from sin
and have become slaves to
righteousness.
19 I put this in human
terms because you are
weak in your natural
selves. Just as you used to
offer the parts of your body
in slavery to impurity and

resulting in *further* lawlessness, so now present your
members *as* slaves to righteousness, resulting in sanctification.
20For when you were
slaves of sin, you were free
in regard to righteousness.
21Therefore what benefit
were you then deriving
from the things of which
you are now ashamed? For
the outcome of those things
is death.
22But now having been
freed from sin and enslaved
to God, you derive your
benefit, resulting in sanctification, and the outcome,
eternal life.
23For the wages of sin is
death, but the free gift of
God is eternal life in Christ
Jesus our Lord.

τῇ ἀνομίᾳ εἰς τὴν ἀνομίαν, οὕτως νῦν
– to iniquity unto – iniquity, so now
παραστήσατε τὰ μέλη ὑμῶν δοῦλα τῇ
present ye the members of you slaves –
δικαιοσύνῃ εἰς ἁγιασμόν. **20** ὅτε γὰρ
to righteousness unto sanctification. For when
δοῦλοι ἦτε τῆς ἁμαρτίας, ἐλεύθεροι ἦτε
slaves ye were – of sin, free ye were
τῇ δικαιοσύνῃ. **21** τίνα οὖν καρπὸν εἴχετε
– to righteousness. What [2]therefore [1]fruit had ye
τότε; ἐφ' οἷς νῦν ἐπαισχύνεσθε· τὸ γὰρ
then? Over which things now ye are ashamed; for the
τέλος ἐκείνων θάνατος. **22** νυνὶ δὲ ἐλευ-
end of those things [is] death. But now having
θερωθέντες ἀπὸ τῆς ἁμαρτίας δουλωθέντες
been freed from – sin [2]having been enslaved
δὲ τῷ θεῷ, ἔχετε τὸν καρπὸν ὑμῶν εἰς
[1]and – to God, ye have the fruit of you to
ἁγιασμόν, τὸ δὲ τέλος ζωὴν αἰώνιον.
sanctification, and the end life eternal.
23 τὰ γὰρ ὀψώνια τῆς ἁμαρτίας θάνατος,
For the wages – of sin [is] death,
τὸ δὲ χάρισμα τοῦ θεοῦ ζωὴ αἰώνιος
but the free gift – of God life eternal
ἐν Χριστῷ Ἰησοῦ τῷ κυρίῳ ἡμῶν.
in Christ Jesus the Lord of us.

to ever-increasing wickedness, so now offer them in
slavery to righteousness
leading to holiness. 20When
you were slaves to sin, you
were free from the control
of righteousness. 21What
benefit did you reap at that
time from the things you
are now ashamed of? Those
things result in death! 22But
now that you have been set
free from sin and have become slaves to God, the
benefit you reap leads to
holiness, and the result is
eternal life. 23For the wages
of sin is death, but the gift
of God is eternal life in[w]
Christ Jesus our Lord.

Chapter 7

Believers United to Christ

OR do you not know,
brethren (for I am
speaking to those who
know the law), that the law
has jurisdiction over a person as long as he lives?
2For the married woman
is bound by law to her husband while he is living; but
if her husband dies, she is
released from the law concerning the husband.
3So then if, while her
husband is living, she is
joined to another man, she
shall be called an adulteress; but if her husband dies,
she is free from the law, so
that she is not an adulteress, though she is joined to
another man.
4Therefore, my breth-
ren, you also were made to
die to the Law through the
body of Christ, that you
might be joined to another,
to Him who was raised
from the dead, that we
might bear fruit for God.
5For while we were in
the flesh, the sinful passions, which were *aroused*

7 Ἢ ἀγνοεῖτε, ἀδελφοί, γινώσκουσιν γὰρ
Or are ye ignorant, brothers, for to [ones] knowing
νόμον λαλῶ, ὅτι ὁ νόμος κυριεύει τοῦ
law I speak, that the law lords it over the
ἀνθρώπου ἐφ' ὅσον χρόνον ζῇ; **2** ἡ γὰρ
man over such time [as] he lives? For the
ὕπανδρος γυνὴ τῷ ζῶντι ἀνδρὶ δέδεται
[2]married [1]woman to the living husband has been bound
νόμῳ· ἐὰν δὲ ἀποθάνῃ ὁ ἀνήρ, κατήργηται
by law; but if dies the husband, she has been discharged
ἀπὸ τοῦ νόμου τοῦ ἀνδρός. **3** ἄρα οὖν
from the law of the husband. Therefore
ζῶντος τοῦ ἀνδρὸς μοιχαλὶς χρηματίσει
living the husband[a] an adulteress she will be called
= while the husband lives
ἐὰν γένηται ἀνδρὶ ἑτέρῳ· ἐὰν δὲ ἀποθάνῃ
if she becomes [2]husband [1]to a different; but if dies
ὁ ἀνήρ, ἐλευθέρα ἐστὶν ἀπὸ τοῦ νόμου,
the husband, free she is from the law,
τοῦ μὴ εἶναι αὐτὴν μοιχαλίδα γενομένην
– not to be her[d] an adulteress having become
= so that she is not
ἀνδρὶ ἑτέρῳ. **4** ὥστε, ἀδελφοί μου, καὶ
[2]husband [1]to a different. So, brothers of me, also
ὑμεῖς ἐθανατώθητε τῷ νόμῳ διὰ τοῦ
ye were put to death to the law through the
σώματος τοῦ Χριστοῦ, εἰς τὸ γενέσθαι
body – of Christ, for *the* to become
= that ye might belong
ὑμᾶς ἑτέρῳ, τῷ ἐκ νεκρῶν ἐγερθέντι,
you[b] to a different, to the [one] from [the] dead having been raised,
ἵνα καρποφορήσωμεν τῷ θεῷ. **5** ὅτε
in order that we may bear fruit – to God. when
γὰρ ἦμεν ἐν τῇ σαρκί, τὰ παθήματα
For we were in the flesh, the passions

Chapter 7

An Illustration From Marriage

DO you not know,
brothers—for I am
speaking to men who know
the law—that the law has
authority over a man only
as long as he lives? 2For example, by law a married
woman is bound to her husband as long as he is alive,
but if her husband dies, she
is released from the law of
marriage. 3So then, if she
marries another man while
her husband is still alive,
she is called an adulteress.
But if her husband dies, she
is released from that law
and is not an adulteress,
even though she marries
another man.
4So, my brothers, you
also died to the law through
the body of Christ, that you
might belong to another, to
him who was raised from
the dead, in order that we
might bear fruit to God.
5For when we were con-
trolled by the sinful na-
ture,[x] the sinful passions

[w]23 Or *through*
[x]5 Or *the flesh*; also in verse 25

by the Law, were at work in the members of our body to bear fruit for death.

6But now we have been released from the Law, having died to that by which we were bound, so that we serve in newness of the [f]Spirit and not in oldness of the letter.

7What shall we say then? Is the Law sin? May it never be! On the contrary, I would not have come to know sin except through the Law; for I would not have known about coveting if the Law had not said, "YOU SHALL NOT COVET."

8But sin, taking opportunity through the commandment, produced in me coveting of every kind; for apart from the Law sin *is* dead.

9And I was once alive apart from the Law; but when the commandment came, sin became alive, and I died;

10and this commandment, which was to result in life, proved to result in death for me;

11for sin, taking opportunity through the commandment, deceived me, and through it killed me.

12So then, the Law is holy, and the commandment is holy and righteous and good.

13Therefore did that which is good become *a cause of* death for me? May it never be! Rather it was sin, in order that it might be shown to be sin by effecting my death through that which is good, that through the commandment sin might become utterly sinful.

The Conflict of Two Natures

14For we know that the Law is spiritual; but I am of flesh, sold into bondage to sin.

15For that which I am doing, I do not understand; for I am not practicing what

τῶν ἁμαρτιῶν τὰ διὰ τοῦ νόμου ἐνηργεῖτο
– of sins – through the law operated
ἐν τοῖς μέλεσιν ἡμῶν εἰς τὸ καρποφορῆσαι
in the members of us *for the* to bear fruit
τῷ θανάτῳ· **6** νυνὶ δὲ κατηργήθημεν ἀπὸ
– to death; but now we were discharged from
τοῦ νόμου, ἀποθανόντες ἐν ᾧ κατειχόμεθα,
the law, having died [to that] in which we were held fast,
ὥστε δουλεύειν [ἡμᾶς] ἐν καινότητι
so as to serve us[b] in newness
πνεύματος καὶ οὐ παλαιότητι γράμματος.
of spirit and not [in] oldness of letter.
7 Τί οὖν ἐροῦμεν; ὁ νόμος ἁμαρτία;
What therefore shall we say? the law sin?
μὴ γένοιτο· ἀλλὰ τὴν ἁμαρτίαν οὐκ
May it not be; yet – sin not
ἔγνων εἰ μὴ διὰ νόμου· τήν τε γὰρ
I knew except through law; – [2]also [1]for
ἐπιθυμίαν οὐκ ᾔδειν εἰ μὴ ὁ νόμος
lust I knew not except the law
ἔλεγεν· οὐκ ἐπιθυμήσεις· **8** ἀφορμὴν δὲ
said : Thou shalt not lust; but [3]occasion
λαβοῦσα ἡ ἁμαρτία διὰ τῆς ἐντολῆς
[2]taking – [1]sin through the commandment
κατειργάσατο ἐν ἐμοὶ πᾶσαν ἐπιθυμίαν·
wrought in me every lust;
χωρὶς γὰρ νόμου ἁμαρτία νεκρά. **9** ἐγὼ
for without law sin [is] dead. I
δὲ ἔζων χωρὶς νόμου ποτέ· ἐλθούσης δὲ
And was living without law then; but coming =when the
τῆς ἐντολῆς ἡ ἁμαρτία ἀνέζησεν, **10** ἐγὼ
the commandment[a] – sin revived, [2]I
commandment came
δὲ ἀπέθανον, καὶ εὑρέθη μοι ἡ ἐντολὴ
[1]and died, and [6]was found [7]to me [1]the [2]commandment
ἡ εἰς ζωήν, αὕτη εἰς θάνατον· **11** ἡ γὰρ
– [3]for [4]life, [5]this to death; – for
ἁμαρτία ἀφορμὴν λαβοῦσα διὰ τῆς
sin [2]occasion [1]taking through the
ἐντολῆς ἐξηπάτησέν με καὶ δι' αὐτῆς
commandment deceived me and through it
ἀπέκτεινεν. **12** ὥστε ὁ μὲν νόμος ἅγιος,
killed [me]. So the – law [is] holy,
καὶ ἡ ἐντολὴ ἁγία καὶ δικαία καὶ ἀγαθή.
and the commandment holy and just and good.
13 Τὸ οὖν ἀγαθὸν ἐμοὶ ἐγένετο θάνατος;
[2]The [1]therefore good to me became death?
μὴ γένοιτο· ἀλλὰ ἡ ἁμαρτία, ἵνα φανῇ
May it not be; yet – sin, in order that it might appear
ἁμαρτία, διὰ τοῦ ἀγαθοῦ μοι κατεργαζομένη
sin, through the good [3]to me [1]working
θάνατον, ἵνα γένηται καθ' ὑπερβολὴν
[2]death, in order that [5]might become [6]excessively†
ἁμαρτωλὸς ἡ ἁμαρτία διὰ τῆς ἐντολῆς.
[7]sinful – [1]sin [2]through [3]the [4]commandment.
14 οἴδαμεν γὰρ ὅτι ὁ νόμος πνευματικός
For we know that the law spiritual
ἐστιν· ἐγὼ δὲ σάρκινός εἰμι, πεπραμένος
is; but I fleshy am, *having been* sold
ὑπὸ τὴν ἁμαρτίαν. **15** ὃ γὰρ κατεργάζομαι
under – sin. For what I work
οὐ γινώσκω· οὐ γὰρ ὃ θέλω τοῦτο
I know not; for not what I wish this

aroused by the law were at
work in our bodies, so that
we bore fruit for death.
6But now, by dying to what
once bound us, we have
been released from the law
so that we serve in the new
way of the Spirit, and not in
the old way of the written
code.

Struggling With Sin

7What shall we say, then?
Is the law sin? Certainly
not! Indeed I would not
have known what sin was
except through the law.
For I would not have
known what coveting really
was if the law had not said,
"Do not covet."[y] 8But sin,
seizing the opportunity afforded
by the commandment,
produced in me every
kind of covetous desire.
For apart from law,
sin is dead. 9Once I was
alive apart from law; but
when the commandment
came, sin sprang to life and
I died. 10I found that the
very commandment that
was intended to bring life
actually brought death.
11For sin, seizing the opportunity
afforded by the
commandment, deceived
me, and through the commandment
put me to death.
12So then, the law is holy,
and the commandment is
holy, righteous and good.
13Did that which is good,
then, become death to me?
By no means! But in order
that sin might be recognized
as sin, it produced
death in me through what
was good, so that through
the commandment sin
might become utterly sinful.
14We know that the law is
spiritual; but I am unspiritual,
sold as a slave to sin.
15I do not understand what
I do. For what I want to do

[y]7 Exodus 20:17; Deut. 5:21

I *would* like to *do,* but I am
doing the very thing I hate.
16But if I do the very thing
I do not wish *to do,* I agree
with the Law, *confessing*
that it is good.
17So now, no longer am I
the one doing it, but sin
which indwells me.
18For I know that nothing
good dwells in me, that is,
in my flesh; for the wishing
is present in me, but the doing of the good *is* not.
19For the good that I
wish; I do not do; but
I practice the very evil that
I do not wish.
20But if I am doing the
very thing I do not wish, I
am no longer the one doing
it, but sin which dwells in
me.
21I find then the principle
that evil is present in me,
the one who wishes to do
good.
22For I joyfully concur
with the law of God in the
inner man,
23but I see a different law
in the members of my
body, waging war against
the law of my mind, and
making me a prisoner of the
law of sin which is in my
members.
24Wretched man that I
am! Who will set me free
from the body of this
death?
25Thanks be to God
through Jesus Christ our
Lord! So then, on the one
hand I myself with my mind
am serving the law of God,
but on the other, with my
flesh the law of sin.

Chapter 8

Deliverance from Bondage

THERE is therefore now
no condemnation for
those who are in Christ
Jesus.
2For the law of the Spirit
of life in Christ Jesus has
set [g]you free from the law

[g] Some ancient mss. read *me*

πράσσω, ἀλλ' ὃ μισῶ τοῦτο ποιῶ. 16 εἰ
I practise, but what I hate this I do. if
δὲ ὃ οὐ θέλω τοῦτο ποιῶ, σύμφημι
But what I wish not this I do, I agree with
τῷ νόμῳ ὅτι καλός. 17 νυνὶ δὲ οὐκέτι
the law that [it is] good. But now no longer
ἐγὼ κατεργάζομαι αὐτὸ ἀλλὰ ἡ ἐνοικοῦσα
I work it but [1]the [3]*in*dwelling
ἐν ἐμοὶ ἁμαρτία. 18 οἶδα γὰρ ὅτι οὐκ
[4]in [5]me [2]sin. For I know that not
οἰκεῖ ἐν ἐμοί, τοῦτ' ἔστιν ἐν τῇ σαρκί
dwells in me, this is in the flesh
μου, ἀγαθόν· τὸ γὰρ θέλειν παράκειταί
of me, [that which is] good; – for to wish is present
μοι, τὸ δὲ κατεργάζεσθαι τὸ καλὸν
to me, – but [2]to work [3]the [4]good
οὔ· 19 οὐ γὰρ ὃ θέλω ποιῶ ἀγαθόν,
[1]not; for not what [2]I wish [3]I do [1]good,
ἀλλὰ ὃ οὐ θέλω κακὸν τοῦτο πράσσω.
but what [2]I wish not [1]evil this I practise.
20 εἰ δὲ ὃ οὐ θέλω ἐγὼ τοῦτο ποιῶ,
But if what [2]wish not [1]I this I do,
οὐκέτι ἐγὼ κατεργάζομαι αὐτὸ ἀλλὰ ἡ
no longer I work it but [1]the
οἰκοῦσα ἐν ἐμοὶ ἁμαρτία. 21 εὑρίσκω
[3]dwelling [4]in [5]me [2]sin. I find
ἄρα τὸν νόμον τῷ θέλοντι ἐμοὶ ποιεῖν
then the law [2]the [one] [3]wishing [1]to me to do
τὸ καλόν, ὅτι ἐμοὶ τὸ κακὸν παράκειται·
the good, that to me the evil is present;
22 συνήδομαι γὰρ τῷ νόμῳ τοῦ θεοῦ κατὰ
for I delight in the law – of God according to
τὸν ἔσω ἄνθρωπον, 23 βλέπω δὲ ἕτερον
the inner man, but I see a different
νόμον ἐν τοῖς μέλεσίν μου ἀντιστρατευόμενον
law in the members of me warring against
τῷ νόμῳ τοῦ νοός μου καὶ αἰχμαλωτίζοντά
the law of the mind of me and taking captive
με ἐν τῷ νόμῳ τῆς ἁμαρτίας τῷ ὄντι
me by the law – of sin the [one] being
ἐν τοῖς μέλεσίν μου. 24 Ταλαίπωρος
in the members of me. [1]Wretched
ἐγὼ ἄνθρωπος· τίς με ῥύσεται ἐκ τοῦ
[3]I [2]man; who me will deliver from the
σώματος τοῦ θανάτου τούτου; 25 χάρις
body of this death? Thanks
τῷ θεῷ διὰ Ἰησοῦ Χριστοῦ τοῦ κυρίου
– to God through Jesus Christ the Lord
ἡμῶν. Ἄρα οὖν αὐτὸς ἐγὼ τῷ μὲν
of us. So then [2][my]self [1]I [4]with the [3]on one hand
νοῒ δουλεύω νόμῳ θεοῦ, τῇ δὲ σαρκὶ
[5]mind serve [the] law of God, on the other with the flesh
νόμῳ ἁμαρτίας. 8 οὐδὲν ἄρα νῦν κατάκριμα
[the] law of sin. [4]No [1]then [2][there is] [3]now [5]condemnation
τοῖς ἐν Χριστῷ Ἰησοῦ. 2 ὁ γὰρ νόμος τοῦ
to the [ones] in Christ Jesus. For the law of the
πνεύματος τῆς ζωῆς ἐν Χριστῷ Ἰησοῦ
spirit – of life in Christ Jesus
ἠλευθέρωσέν σε ἀπὸ τοῦ νόμου τῆς
freed thee from the law –

I do not do, but what I hate
I do. 16And if I do what I do
not want to do, I agree that
the law is good. 17As it is, it
is no longer I myself who
do it, but it is sin living in
me. 18I know that nothing
good lives in me, that is, in
my sinful nature.[z] For I
have the desire to do what
is good, but I cannot carry
it out. 19For what I do is not
the good I want to do; no,
the evil I do not want to
do—this I keep on doing.
20Now if I do what I do not
want to do, it is no longer I
who do it, but it is sin living
in me that does it.
21So I find this law at
work: When I want to do
good, evil is right there
with me. 22For in my inner
being I delight in God's
law; 23but I see another law
at work in the members of
my body, waging war
against the law of my mind
and making me a prisoner
of the law of sin at work
within my members.
24What a wretched man I
am! Who will rescue me
from this body of death?
25Thanks be to God—
through Jesus Christ our
Lord!
So then, I myself in my
mind am a slave to God's
law, but in the sinful nature
a slave to the law of sin.

Chapter 8

Life Through the Spirit

THEREFORE, there is
now no condemnation
for those who are in Christ
Jesus,[a] 2because through
Christ Jesus the law of the
Spirit of life set me free

[z] *18* Or *my flesh*

[a] *1* Some later manuscripts *Jesus, who do not live according to the sinful nature but according to the Spirit.*

of sin and of death.

3For what the Law could not do, weak as it was through the flesh, God *did:* sending His own Son in the likeness of sinful flesh and *as an offering* for sin, He condemned sin in the flesh,

4in order that the requirement of the Law might be fulfilled in us, who do not walk according to the flesh, but according to the Spirit.

5For those who are according to the flesh set their minds on the things of the flesh, but those who are according to the Spirit, the things of the Spirit.

6For the mind set on the flesh is death, but the mind set on the Spirit is life and peace,

7because the mind set on the flesh is hostile toward God; for it does not subject itself to the law of God, for it is not even able *to do so*;

8and those who are in the flesh cannot please God.

9However, you are not in the flesh but in the Spirit, if indeed the Spirit of God dwells in you. But if anyone does not have the Spirit of Christ, he does not belong to Him.

10And if Christ is in you, though the body is dead because of sin, yet the spirit is alive because of righteousness.

11But if the Spirit of Him who raised Jesus from the dead dwells in you, He who raised Christ Jesus from the dead will also give life to your mortal bodies [h]through His Spirit who indwells you.

12So then, brethren, we are under obligation, not to

[h] Some ancient mss. read *because of*

ἁμαρτίας καὶ τοῦ θανάτου. 3 τὸ γὰρ
of sin and – of death. For the
ἀδύνατον τοῦ νόμου, ἐν ᾧ ἠσθένει διὰ
impossible thing of the law, in which it was weak through
τῆς σαρκός, ὁ θεὸς τὸν ἑαυτοῦ υἱὸν
the flesh, – 1God 3the 6of himself 4Son
πέμψας ἐν ὁμοιώματι σαρκὸς ἁμαρτίας
2sending in likeness of flesh of sin
καὶ περὶ ἁμαρτίας κατέκρινεν τὴν ἁμαρτίαν
and concerning sin condemned – sin
ἐν τῇ σαρκί, 4 ἵνα τὸ δικαίωμα τοῦ
in the flesh, in order that the ordinance of the
νόμου πληρωθῇ ἐν ἡμῖν τοῖς μὴ κατὰ
law may be fulfilled in us the [ones] not according to
σάρκα περιπατοῦσιν ἀλλὰ κατὰ πνεῦμα.
flesh walking but according to spirit.
5 οἱ γὰρ κατὰ σάρκα ὄντες τὰ τῆς
For the [ones] according to flesh being the things of the
σαρκὸς φρονοῦσιν, οἱ δὲ κατὰ πνεῦμα
flesh mind, but the [ones] according to spirit
τὰ τοῦ πνεύματος. 6 τὸ γὰρ φρόνημα
the things of the Spirit. For the mind
τῆς σαρκὸς θάνατος, τὸ δὲ φρόνημα
of the flesh [is] death, but the mind
τοῦ πνεύματος ζωὴ καὶ εἰρήνη. 7 διότι
of the Spirit life and peace. Wherefore
τὸ φρόνημα τῆς σαρκὸς ἔχθρα εἰς θεόν·
the mind of the flesh [is] enmity against God;
τῷ γὰρ νόμῳ τοῦ θεοῦ οὐχ ὑποτάσσεται,
for to the law – of God it is not subject,
οὐδὲ γὰρ δύναται· 8 οἱ δὲ ἐν σαρκὶ
neither indeed can it; and the [ones] 2in 3flesh
ὄντες θεῷ ἀρέσαι οὐ δύνανται. 9 ὑμεῖς
1being 6God 5to please 4cannot. ye
δὲ οὐκ ἐστὲ ἐν σαρκὶ ἀλλὰ ἐν πνεύματι,
But are not in flesh but in Spirit,
εἴπερ πνεῦμα θεοῦ οἰκεῖ ἐν ὑμῖν. εἰ
since [the] Spirit of God dwells in you. if
δέ τις πνεῦμα Χριστοῦ οὐκ ἔχει, οὗτος
But anyone [the] Spirit of Christ has not, this one
οὐκ ἔστιν αὐτοῦ. 10 εἰ δὲ Χριστὸς
is not of him. But if Christ
ἐν ὑμῖν, τὸ μὲν σῶμα νεκρὸν διὰ
[is] in you, 2the 1on one hand 3body [is] dead because of
ἁμαρτίαν, τὸ δὲ πνεῦμα ζωὴ διὰ
sin, 2the 1on the other 3spirit [is] life because of
δικαιοσύνην. 11 εἰ δὲ τὸ πνεῦμα τοῦ
righteousness. But if the Spirit of the [one]
ἐγείραντος τὸν Ἰησοῦν ἐκ νεκρῶν οἰκεῖ ἐν
having raised – Jesus from [the] dead dwells in
ὑμῖν, ὁ ἐγείρας ἐκ νεκρῶν Χριστὸν
you, the [one] having raised from [the] dead Christ
Ἰησοῦν ζωοποιήσει καὶ τὰ θνητὰ σώματα
Jesus will quicken also the mortal bodies
ὑμῶν διὰ τοῦ ἐνοικοῦντος αὐτοῦ πνεύματος
of you through the 3*in*dwelling 2of him 1Spirit
ἐν ὑμῖν.
4in 5you.
12 Ἄρα οὖν, ἀδελφοί, ὀφειλέται ἐσμέν,
So then, brothers, debtors we are,

from the law of sin and
death. 3For what the law
was powerless to do in that
it was weakened by the sinful nature,[b] God did by
sending his own Son in the
likeness of sinful man to be
a sin offering.[c] And so he
condemned sin in sinful
man,[d] 4in order that the
righteous requirements of
the law might be fully met
in us, who do not live according to the sinful nature
but according to the Spirit.
5Those who live accord-
ing to the sinful nature have
their minds set on what that
nature desires; but those
who live in accordance
with the Spirit have their
minds set on what the Spirit
desires. 6The mind of sinful
man[e] is death, but the mind
controlled by the Spirit is
life and peace; 7the sinful
mind[f] is hostile to God. It
does not submit to God's
law, nor can it do so.
8Those controlled by the
sinful nature cannot please
God.
9You, however, are con-
trolled not by the sinful nature but by the Spirit, if the
Spirit of God lives in you.
And if anyone does not
have the Spirit of Christ, he
does not belong to Christ.
10But if Christ is in you,
your body is dead because
of sin, yet your spirit is
alive because of righteousness. 11And if the Spirit of
him who raised Jesus from
the dead is living in you, he
who raised Christ from the
dead will also give life to
your mortal bodies through
his Spirit, who lives in you.
12Therefore, brothers, we
have an obligation—but it

[b]3 Or *the flesh*; also in verses 4, 5, 8, 9, 12 and 13
[c]3 Or *man, for sin*
[d]3 Or *in the flesh*
[e]6 Or *mind set on the flesh*
[f]7 Or *the mind set on the flesh*

the flesh, to live according
to the flesh—
13for if you are living according to the flesh, you
must die; but if by the Spirit
you are putting to death the
deeds of the body, you will
live.
14For all who are being
led by the Spirit of God,
these are sons of God.
15For you have not re-
ceived a spirit of slavery
leading to fear again, but
you have received a spirit
of adoption as sons by
which we cry out, "Abba!
Father!"
16The Spirit Himself
bears witness with our
spirit that we are children
of God,
17and if children, heirs
also, heirs of God and fellow heirs with Christ, if indeed we suffer with *Him* in
order that we may also be
glorified with *Him*.
18For I consider that the
sufferings of this present
time are not worthy to be
compared with the glory
that is to be revealed to us.
19For the anxious longing
of the creation waits eagerly for the revealing of the
sons of God.
20For the creation was
subjected to futility, not of
its own will, but because of
Him who subjected it, [i] in
hope
21that the creation itself
also will be set free from its
slavery to corruption into
the freedom of the glory of
the children of God.
22For we know that the
whole creation groans and
suffers the pains of childbirth together until now.
23And not only this, but
also we ourselves, having
the first fruits of the Spirit,
even we ourselves groan
within ourselves, waiting
eagerly for *our* adoption as
sons, the redemption of our
body.
24For in hope we have
been saved, but hope that is

[i]Some ancient mss. read *in hope; because the creation*

οὐ τῇ σαρκὶ τοῦ κατὰ σάρκα ζῆν. 13 εἰ
not to the flesh – according to flesh to live[d]. if
γὰρ κατὰ σάρκα ζῆτε, μέλλετε ἀποθνῄσκειν·
For according to flesh ye live, ye are about to die:
εἰ δὲ πνεύματι τὰς πράξεις τοῦ σώματος
but if by [the] Spirit the practices of the body
θανατοῦτε, ζήσεσθε. 14 ὅσοι γὰρ πνεύματι
ye put to death, ye will live. For as many as by [the] Spirit
θεοῦ ἄγονται, οὗτοι υἱοί εἰσιν θεοῦ.
of God are led, these sons are of God.
15 οὐ γὰρ ἐλάβετε πνεῦμα δουλείας πάλιν
For ye received not a spirit of slavery again
εἰς φόβον, ἀλλὰ ἐλάβετε πνεῦμα υἱοθεσίας,
for fear, but ye received a spirit of adoption,
ἐν ᾧ κράζομεν· ἀββὰ ὁ πατήρ. 16 αὐτὸ
by which we cry: Abba – Father. [3]it(him)self
τὸ πνεῦμα συμμαρτυρεῖ τῷ πνεύματι ἡμῶν
[1]The [2]Spirit witnesses with the spirit of us
ὅτι ἐσμὲν τέκνα θεοῦ. 17 εἰ δὲ τέκνα,
that we are children of God. And if children,
καὶ κληρονόμοι· κληρονόμοι μὲν θεοῦ,
also heirs; heirs on one hand of God,
συγκληρονόμοι δὲ Χριστοῦ, εἴπερ συμπάσ-
joint heirs on the other of Christ, since we suffer
χομεν ἵνα καὶ συνδοξασθῶμεν. 18 Λογίζομαι
with[him] in order that also we may be glorified with [him]. I reckon
γὰρ ὅτι οὐκ ἄξια τὰ παθήματα τοῦ
For that [6][are] [7]not [8]worthy [1]the [2]sufferings [3]of the
νῦν καιροῦ πρὸς τὴν μέλλουσαν δόξαν
[4]now [5]time [to (present) be compared] with the coming glory
ἀποκαλυφθῆναι εἰς ἡμᾶς. 19 ἡ γὰρ
to be revealed to us. For the
ἀποκαραδοκία τῆς κτίσεως τὴν ἀποκάλυψιν
anxious watching of the creation [2]the [3]revelation
τῶν υἱῶν τοῦ θεοῦ ἀπεκδέχεται. 20 τῇ
[4]of the [5]sons – [6]of God [1]is eagerly expecting. –
γὰρ ματαιότητι ἡ κτίσις ὑπετάγη, οὐχ
For to vanity the creation was subjected, not
ἑκοῦσα, ἀλλὰ διὰ τὸν ὑποτάξαντα, ἐφ'
willing[ly], but because of the [one] subjecting, in
ἐλπίδι 21 διότι καὶ αὐτὴ ἡ κτίσις
hope because even itself the creation
ἐλευθερωθήσεται ἀπὸ τῆς δουλείας τῆς
will be freed from the slavery –
φθορᾶς εἰς τὴν ἐλευθερίαν τῆς δόξης
of corruption to the freedom of the glory
τῶν τέκνων τοῦ θεοῦ. 22 οἴδαμεν γὰρ
of the children – of God. For we know
ὅτι πᾶσα ἡ κτίσις συστενάζει καὶ
that all the creation groans together and
συνωδίνει ἄχρι τοῦ νῦν· 23 οὐ μόνον δέ,
travails together until – now; and not only [so],
ἀλλὰ καὶ αὐτοὶ τὴν ἀπαρχὴν τοῦ πνεύματος
but also [our]selves [2]the [3]firstfruit [4]of the [5]Spirit
ἔχοντες [ἡμεῖς] καὶ αὐτοὶ ἐν ἑαυτοῖς
[1]having we also [our]selves in ourselves
στενάζομεν υἱοθεσίαν ἀπεκδεχόμενοι, τὴν
groan adoption eagerly expecting, the
ἀπολύτρωσιν τοῦ σώματος ἡμῶν. 24 τῇ
redemption of the body of us. –
γὰρ ἐλπίδι ἐσώθημεν· ἐλπὶς δὲ βλεπομένη
For by hope we were saved; but hope being seen

is not to the sinful nature,
to live according to it. 13For
if you live according to the
sinful nature, you will die;
but if by the Spirit you put
to death the misdeeds of
the body, you will live,
14because those who are
led by the Spirit of God are
sons of God. 15For you did
not receive a spirit that
makes you a slave again to
fear, but you received the
Spirit of sonship.[g] And by
him we cry, "*Abba*,[h] Father." 16The Spirit himself
testifies with our spirit that
we are God's children.
17Now if we are children,
then we are heirs—heirs of
God and co-heirs with
Christ, if indeed we share
in his sufferings in order
that we may also share in
his glory.

Future Glory

18I consider that our present sufferings are not
worth comparing with the
glory that will be revealed
in us. 19The creation waits
in eager expectation for the
sons of God to be revealed.
20For the creation was subjected to frustration, not by
its own choice, but by the
will of the one who subjected it, in hope 21that[i] the
creation itself will be liber-
ated from its bondage to decay and brought into the
glorious freedom of the
children of God.
22We know that the whole
creation has been groaning
as in the pains of childbirth
right up to the present time.
23Not only so, but we ourselves, who have the firstfruits of the Spirit, groan inwardly as we wait eagerly
for our adoption as sons,
the redemption of our bodies. 24For in this hope we
were saved. But hope that

[g]15 Or *adoption*
[h]15 Aramaic for *Father*
[i]20,21 Or *subjected it in hope.* [21]*For*

seen is not hope; for [j] why
does one also hope for what
he sees?
25But if we hope for what
we do not see, with perseverance we wait eagerly for
it.

Our Victory in Christ

26And in the same way
the Spirit also helps our
weakness; for we do not
know how to pray as we
should, but the Spirit Himself intercedes for *us* with
groanings too deep for
words;
27and He who searches
the hearts knows what the
mind of the Spirit is, because He intercedes for the
saints according to *the will
of* God.
28And we know that
[k]God causes all things to
work together for good
to those who love God, to
those who are called ac-
cording to *His* purpose.
29For whom He fore-
knew, He also predestined
to become conformed to
the image of His Son, that
He might be the first-born
among many brethren;
30and whom He predes-
tined, these He also called;
and whom He called, these
He also justified; and
whom He justified, these
He also glorified.
31What then shall we say
to these things? If God *is*
for us, who *is* against us?
32He who did not spare
His own Son, but delivered
Him up for us all, how will
He not also with Him freely
give us all things?
33Who will bring a charge
against God's elect? God is
the one who justifies;
34who is the one who con-
demns? Christ Jesus is He
who died, yes, rather who
was [l]raised, who is at the
right hand of God, who also
intercedes for us.
35Who shall separate us
from the love of [m]Christ?
Shall tribulation, or distress, or persecution, or

[j] Some ancient mss. read *who hopes for what he sees?*
[k] Some ancient mss. read *all things work together for good*
[l] Some ancient mss. read *raised from the dead*
[m] Some ancient mss. read *God*

οὐκ ἔστιν ἐλπίς· ὃ γὰρ βλέπει τις,
is not hope; for what sees anyone,
τί καὶ ἐλπίζει; 25 εἰ δὲ ὃ οὐ βλέπομεν
why also he hopes? but if what we do not see
ἐλπίζομεν, δι' ὑπομονῆς ἀπεκδεχόμεθα.
we hope [for], through patience we eagerly expect.
26 ὡσαύτως δὲ καὶ τὸ πνεῦμα συναντιλαμ-
And similarly also the Spirit takes
βάνεται τῇ ἀσθενείᾳ ἡμῶν· τὸ γὰρ τί
share in the weakness of us; – for what
προσευξώμεθα καθὸ δεῖ οὐκ οἴδαμεν, ἀλλὰ
we may pray as it behoves we know not, but
αὐτὸ τὸ πνεῦμα ὑπερεντυγχάνει στεναγμοῖς
it(him)self the Spirit supplicates on [our] behalf with groanings
ἀλαλήτοις· 27 ὁ δὲ ἐρευνῶν τὰς καρδίας
unutterable; and the [one] searching the hearts
οἶδεν τί τὸ φρόνημα τοῦ πνεύματος,
knows what [is] the mind of the Spirit,
ὅτι κατὰ θεὸν ἐντυγχάνει ὑπὲρ ἁγίων.
be-cause according to God he supplicates on behalf of saints.
28 οἴδαμεν δὲ ὅτι τοῖς ἀγαπῶσιν τὸν
And we know that to the [ones] loving –
θεὸν πάντα συνεργεῖ [ὁ θεὸς] εἰς ἀγαθόν,
God [3]all things [2]works together – [1]God for good,
τοῖς κατὰ πρόθεσιν κλητοῖς οὖσιν. 29 ὅτι
to the [ones] [3]according to [4]purpose [2]called [1]being. Because
οὓς προέγνω, καὶ προώρισεν συμμόρφους
whom he foreknew, also he foreordained conformed to
τῆς εἰκόνος τοῦ υἱοῦ αὐτοῦ, εἰς τὸ
of the image of the Son of him, for *the* =that he should be
εἶναι αὐτὸν πρωτότοκον ἐν πολλοῖς
to be him[b] firstborn among many
ἀδελφοῖς· 30 οὓς δὲ προώρισεν, τούτους
brothers; but whom he foreordained, these
καὶ ἐκάλεσεν· καὶ οὓς ἐκάλεσεν, τούτους
also he called; and whom he called, these
καὶ ἐδικαίωσεν· οὓς δὲ ἐδικαίωσεν, τούτους
also he justified; but whom he justified, these
καὶ ἐδόξασεν. 31 Τί οὖν ἐροῦμεν πρὸς
also he glorified. What therefore shall we say to
ταῦτα; εἰ ὁ θεὸς ὑπὲρ ἡμῶν, τίς καθ'
these things? If – God on behalf of us, who against
ἡμῶν; ὅς γε τοῦ ἰδίου υἱοῦ οὐκ ἐφείσατο,
us? Who indeed the(his) own Son spared not,
32 ἀλλὰ ὑπὲρ ἡμῶν πάντων παρέδωκεν
but on behalf of us all delivered
αὐτόν, πῶς οὐχὶ καὶ σὺν αὐτῷ τὰ πάντα
him, how not also with him – all things
ἡμῖν χαρίσεται; 33 τίς ἐγκαλέσει κατὰ
to us will he freely give? Who will bring a charge *against* against
ἐκλεκτῶν θεοῦ; θεὸς ὁ δικαιῶν· 34 τίς
chosen ones of God? God [is] the [one] justifying; who
ὁ κατακρινῶν; Χριστὸς Ἰησοῦς ὁ ἀποθανών,
the [one] condemning? Christ Jesus [is] the [one] having died,
μᾶλλον δὲ ἐγερθείς, ὅς ἐστιν ἐν δεξιᾷ
but rather having been raised, who is at [the] right [hand]
τοῦ θεοῦ, ὃς καὶ ἐντυγχάνει ὑπὲρ ἡμῶν.
– of God, who also supplicates on behalf of us.
35 τίς ἡμᾶς χωρίσει ἀπὸ τῆς ἀγάπης
Who us will separate from the love
τοῦ Χριστοῦ; θλῖψις ἢ στενοχωρία ἢ
– of Christ? affliction or distress or

is seen is no hope at all.
Who hopes for what he al-
ready has? 25But if we hope
for what we do not yet
have, we wait for it patiently.
26In the same way, the
Spirit helps us in our weakness. We do not know what
we ought to pray for, but
the Spirit himself inter-
cedes for us with groans
that words cannot express.
27And he who searches our
hearts knows the mind of
the Spirit, because the
Spirit intercedes for the
saints in accordance with
God's will.

More Than Conquerors

28And we know that in all
things God works for the
good of those who love
him,[j] who[k] have been
called according to his purpose. 29For those God foreknew he also predestined
to be conformed to the likeness of his Son, that he
might be the firstborn
among many brothers.
30And those he predes-
tined, he also called; those
he called, he also justified;
those he justified, he also
glorified.
31What, then, shall we
say in response to this? If
God is for us, who can be
against us? 32He who did
not spare his own Son, but
gave him up for us all—
how will he not also, along
with him, graciously give
us all things? 33Who will
bring any charge against
those whom God has cho-
sen? It is God who justifies.
34Who is he that con-
demns? Christ Jesus, who
died—more than that, who
was raised to life—is at the
right hand of God and is
also interceding for us.
35Who shall separate us
from the love of Christ?
Shall trouble or hardship or
persecution or famine or

[j]28 Some manuscripts *And we know that all things work together for good to those who love God*
[k]28 Or *works together with those who love him to bring about what is good—with those who*

famine, or nakedness, or peril, or sword?
36Just as it is written,
"FOR THY SAKE WE ARE BEING PUT TO DEATH ALL DAY LONG;
WE WERE CONSIDERED AS SHEEP TO BE SLAUGHTERED."
37But in all these things we overwhelmingly conquer through Him who loved us.
38For I am convinced that neither death, nor life, nor angels, nor principalities, nor things present, nor things to come, nor powers,
39nor height, nor depth, nor any other created thing, shall be able to separate us from the love of God, which is in Christ Jesus our Lord.

Chapter 9

Solicitude for Israel

I am telling the truth in Christ, I am not lying, my conscience bearing me witness in the Holy Spirit,
2that I have great sorrow and unceasing grief in my heart.
3For I could wish that I myself were accursed, *separated* from Christ for the sake of my brethren, my kinsmen according to the flesh,
4who are Israelites, to whom belongs the adoption as sons and the glory and the covenants and the giving of the Law and the *temple* service and the promises,
5whose are the fathers, and from whom is the Christ according to the flesh, who is over all, God blessed forever. Amen.
6But *it is* not as though the word of God has failed. For they are not all Israel who are *descended* from Israel;
7neither are they all children because they are Abraham's descendants, but: "THROUGH ISAAC YOUR DESCENDANTS WILL BE NAMED."
8That is, it is not the children of the flesh who are

διωγμὸς ἢ λιμὸς ἢ γυμνότης ἢ κίνδυνος
persecution or famine or nakedness or peril
ἢ μάχαιρα; 36 καθὼς γέγραπται ὅτι ἕνεκεν
or sword? As it has been written[,] – For the sake
σοῦ θανατούμεθα ὅλην τὴν ἡμέραν,
of thee we are being put to death all the day,
ἐλογίσθημεν ὡς πρόβατα σφαγῆς. 37 ἀλλ'
we were reckoned as sheep of(for) slaughter. But
ἐν τούτοις πᾶσιν ὑπερνικῶμεν διὰ τοῦ
in these things all we overconquer through the
ἀγαπήσαντος ἡμᾶς. 38 πέπεισμαι γὰρ
[one] having loved us. For I have been persuaded
ὅτι οὔτε θάνατος οὔτε ζωὴ οὔτε ἄγγελοι
that not death nor life nor angels
οὔτε ἀρχαὶ οὔτε ἐνεστῶτα οὔτε μέλλοντα
nor rulers nor things present nor things coming
οὔτε δυνάμεις 39 οὔτε ὕψωμα οὔτε βάθος
nor powers nor height nor depth
οὔτε τις κτίσις ἑτέρα δυνήσεται ἡμᾶς
nor any creature other will be able us
χωρίσαι ἀπὸ τῆς ἀγάπης τοῦ θεοῦ τῆς
to separate from the love – of God –
ἐν Χριστῷ Ἰησοῦ τῷ κυρίῳ ἡμῶν.
in Christ Jesus the Lord of us.

9 Ἀλήθειαν λέγω ἐν Χριστῷ, οὐ
Truth I say in Christ, not
ψεύδομαι, συμμαρτυρούσης μοι τῆς
I lie, witnessing with me the
συνειδήσεώς μου ἐν πνεύματι ἁγίῳ, 2 ὅτι
conscience[a] of me in [the] Spirit Holy, that
λύπη μοί ἐστιν μεγάλη καὶ ἀδιάλειπτος
grief to me is great and incessant
=I have great grief and . . .
ὀδύνη τῇ καρδίᾳ μου. 3 ηὐχόμην γὰρ
pain[c] in the heart of me. For I was praying
ἀνάθεμα εἶναι αὐτὸς ἐγὼ ἀπὸ τοῦ Χριστοῦ
[4]a curse [3]to be [2][my]self [1]I from – Christ
ὑπὲρ τῶν ἀδελφῶν μου τῶν συγγενῶν
on behalf of the brothers of me the kinsmen
μου κατὰ σάρκα, 4 οἵτινές εἰσιν Ἰσραη-
of me according to flesh, who are Israel-
λῖται, ὧν ἡ υἱοθεσία καὶ ἡ δόξα καὶ
ites, of whom the adoption and the glory and
αἱ διαθῆκαι καὶ ἡ νομοθεσία καὶ ἡ
the covenants and the giving of [the] law and the
λατρεία καὶ αἱ ἐπαγγελίαι, 5 ὧν οἱ
service and the promises, of whom the
πατέρες, καὶ ἐξ ὧν ὁ Χριστὸς τὸ κατὰ
fathers, and from whom the Christ – according to
σάρκα· ὁ ὢν ἐπὶ πάντων θεὸς εὐλογητὸς
flesh; the [one] being over all God blessed
εἰς τοὺς αἰῶνας, ἀμήν. 6 Οὐχ οἷον δὲ
unto the ages, amen. Not of course
ὅτι ἐκπέπτωκεν ὁ λόγος τοῦ θεοῦ. οὐ
that has failed the word – of God. not
γὰρ πάντες οἱ ἐξ Ἰσραήλ, οὗτοι Ἰσραήλ·
For all the [ones] of Israel, these [are of] Israel;
7 οὐδ' ὅτι εἰσὶν σπέρμα Ἀβραάμ, πάντες
neither because they are seed of Abraham, [are they] all
τέκνα, ἀλλ'· ἐν Ἰσαὰκ κληθήσεταί σοι
children, but: In Isaac will be called to thee
σπέρμα. 8 τοῦτ' ἔστιν, οὐ τὰ τέκνα τῆς
seed.[c] This is, not the children of the
=thy seed.

nakedness or danger or sword? 36As it is written:

"For your sake we face death all day long;
we are considered as sheep to be slaughtered."[l]

37No, in all these things we are more than conquerors through him who loved us.
38For I am convinced that neither death nor life, neither angels nor demons,[m] neither the present nor the future, nor any powers,
39neither height nor depth, nor anything else in all creation, will be able to separate us from the love of God that is in Christ Jesus our Lord.

Chapter 9

God's Sovereign Choice

I SPEAK the truth in Christ—I am not lying, my conscience confirms it in the Holy Spirit— 2I have great sorrow and unceasing anguish in my heart. 3For I could wish that I myself were cursed and cut off from Christ for the sake of my brothers, those of my own race, 4the people of Israel. Theirs is the adoption as sons; theirs the divine glory, the covenants, the receiving of the law, the temple worship and the promises. 5Theirs are the patriarchs, and from them is traced the human ancestry of Christ, who is God over all, forever praised![n] Amen.
6It is not as though God's word had failed. For not all who are descended from Israel are Israel. 7Nor because they are his descendants are they all Abraham's children. On the contrary, "It is through Isaac that your offspring will be reckoned."[o] 8In other words, it is not the natural children

[l]36 Psalm 44:22
[m]38 *Or nor heavenly rulers*
[n]5 *Or Christ, who is over all. God be forever praised! Or Christ. God who is over all be forever praised!*
[o]7 Gen. 21:12

children of God, but the
children of the promise are
regarded as descendants.
9For this is a word of
promise: "At this time I
will come, and Sarah
shall have a son."
10And not only this, but
there was Rebekah also,
when she had conceived
twins by one man, our father Isaac;
11for though *the twins*
were not yet born, and had
not done anything good or
bad, in order that God's
purpose according to *His*
choice might stand, not because of works, but be-
cause of Him who calls,
12it was said to her, "The
older will serve the
younger."
13Just as it is written,
"Jacob I loved, but Esau I
hated."
14What shall we say then?
There is no injustice with
God, is there? May it never
be!
15For He says to Moses,
"I will have mercy on
whom I have mercy, and I
will have compassion on
whom I have compassion."
16So then it *does* not *depend* on the man who wills
or the man who runs, but
on God who has mercy.
17For the Scripture says
to Pharaoh, "For this very
purpose I raised you up, to
demonstrate My power in
you, and that My name
might be proclaimed
throughout the whole
earth."
18So then He has mercy
on whom He desires, and
He hardens whom He de-
sires.
19You will say to me then,
"Why does He still find
fault? For who resists His
will?"
20On the contrary, who
are you, O man, who an-
swers back to God? The
thing molded will not say to
the molder, "Why did you
make me like this," will it?

σαρκὸς ταῦτα τέκνα τοῦ θεοῦ, ἀλλὰ
flesh these children of God, but
τὰ τέκνα τῆς ἐπαγγελίας λογίζεται εἰς
the children of the promise is(are) reckoned for
σπέρμα. 9 ἐπαγγελίας γὰρ ὁ λόγος οὗτος·
a seed. For [5]of promise [3]the [4]word [1]this [2][is]:
κατὰ τὸν καιρὸν τοῦτον ἐλεύσομαι καὶ
According to this time I will come and
ἔσται τῇ Σάρρᾳ υἱός. 10 οὐ μόνον δέ,
will be – to Sara a son.[c] And not only [so],
=Sarah will have a son.
ἀλλὰ καὶ Ῥεβεκκὰ ἐξ ἑνὸς κοίτην ἔχουσα,
but also Rebecca [2]from [3]one [1]conceiving,†
Ἰσαὰκ τοῦ πατρὸς ἡμῶν· 11 μήπω γὰρ
Isaac the father of us; for not yet
γεννηθέντων μηδὲ πραξάντων τι ἀγαθὸν
being born[a] nor practising[a] anything good
ἢ φαῦλον, ἵνα ἡ κατ' ἐκλογὴν πρόθεσις
or bad, in order that [1]the [4]according to [5]choice [2]purpose
τοῦ θεοῦ μένῃ, 12 οὐκ ἐξ ἔργων ἀλλ'
– [3]of God might remain, not of works but
ἐκ τοῦ καλοῦντος, ἐρρέθη αὐτῇ ὅτι ὁ
of the [one] calling, it was said to her[,] – The
μείζων δουλεύσει τῷ ἐλάσσονι· 13 καθάπερ
greater will serve the lesser; even as
γέγραπται· τὸν Ἰακὼβ ἠγάπησα, τὸν δὲ
it has been written: – Jacob I loved, – but
Ἠσαῦ ἐμίσησα.
Esau I hated.
14 Τί οὖν ἐροῦμεν; μὴ ἀδικία παρὰ
What therefore shall we say? *not* unrighteousness with
τῷ θεῷ; μὴ γένοιτο. 15 τῷ Μωϋσεῖ
– God? May it not be. – [2]to Moses
γὰρ λέγει· ἐλεήσω ὃν ἂν ἐλεῶ, καὶ
[1]For he says: I will have mercy on whomever I have mercy, and
οἰκτιρήσω ὃν ἂν οἰκτίρω. 16 ἄρα οὖν
I will pity whomever I pity. So therefore [it is]
οὐ τοῦ θέλοντος οὐδὲ τοῦ τρέχοντος,
not of the [one] wishing nor of the [one] running,
ἀλλὰ τοῦ ἐλεῶντος θεοῦ. 17 λέγει γὰρ
but of the [one] having mercy God. For says
ἡ γραφὴ τῷ Φαραὼ ὅτι εἰς αὐτὸ τοῦτο
the scripture – to Pharaoh[,] – For this very thing
ἐξήγειρά σε, ὅπως ἐνδείξωμαι ἐν σοὶ
I raised up thee, so as I may show forth in thee
τὴν δύναμίν μου, καὶ ὅπως διαγγελῇ τὸ
the power of me, and so as might be published abroad the
ὄνομά μου ἐν πάσῃ τῇ γῇ. 18 ἄρα οὖν
name of me in all the earth. So therefore
ὃν θέλει ἐλεεῖ, ὃν δὲ θέλει σκληρύνει.
whom he wishes he has mercy, but whom he wishes he hardens.
19 Ἐρεῖς μοι οὖν· τί ἔτι μέμφεται;
Thou wilt say to me therefore: Why still finds he fault?
τῷ γὰρ βουλήματι αὐτοῦ τίς ἀνθέστηκεν;
for [3]the [4]counsel [5]of him [1]who [2]resisted?
20 ὦ ἄνθρωπε, μενοῦν γε σὺ τίς εἶ ὁ
O man, nay rather [3]thou [1]who [2]art the
ἀνταποκρινόμενος τῷ θεῷ; μὴ ἐρεῖ τὸ
[one] replying against – God? *not* [3]Will say [1]the
πλάσμα τῷ πλάσαντι· τί με ἐποίησας
[2]thing formed to the [one] having formed: Why [2]me [1]madest thou

who are God's children,
but it is the children of the
promise who are regarded
as Abraham's offspring.
9For this was how the
promise was stated: "At
the appointed time I will return, and Sarah will have a
son."[p]
10Not only that, but Re-
bekah's children had one
and the same father, our father Isaac. 11Yet, before
the twins were born or had
done anything good or bad
—in order that God's pur-
pose in election might
stand: 12not by works but
by him who calls—she was
told, "The older will serve
the younger."[q] 13Just as it
is written: "Jacob I loved,
but Esau I hated."[r]
14What then shall we say?
Is God unjust? Not at all!
15For he says to Moses,

"I will have mercy on
whom I have mercy,
and I will have
compassion on
whom I have
compassion."[s]

16It does not, therefore, depend on man's desire or effort, but on God's mercy.
17For the Scripture says to
Pharaoh: "I raised you up
for this very purpose, that I
might display my power in
you and that my name
might be proclaimed in all
the earth."[t] 18Therefore
God has mercy on whom he
wants to have mercy, and
he hardens whom he wants
to harden.
19One of you will say to
me: "Then why does God
still blame us? For who resists his will?" 20But who
are you, O man, to talk
back to God? "Shall what
is formed say to him who
formed it, 'Why did you
make me like this?' "[u]

[p]9 Gen. 18:10,14
[q]12 Gen. 25:23
[r]13 Mal. 1:2,3
[s]15 Exodus 33:19
[t]17 Exodus 9:16
[u]20 Isaiah 29:16; 45:9

21Or does not the potter have a right over the clay, to make from the same lump one vessel for honorable use, and another for common use?
22What if God, although willing to demonstrate His wrath and to make His power known, endured with much patience vessels of wrath prepared for destruction?
23And *He did so* in order that He might make known the riches of His glory upon vessels of mercy, which He prepared beforehand for glory,
24*even* us, whom He also called, not from among Jews only, but also from among Gentiles.
25As He says also in Hosea,
"I WILL CALL THOSE WHO WERE NOT MY PEOPLE, 'MY PEOPLE,'
AND HER WHO WAS NOT BELOVED, 'BELOVED.'"
26"AND IT SHALL BE THAT IN THE PLACE WHERE IT WAS SAID TO THEM, 'YOU ARE NOT MY PEOPLE,'
THERE THEY SHALL BE CALLED SONS OF THE LIVING GOD."
27And Isaiah cries out concerning Israel, "THOUGH THE NUMBER OF THE SONS OF ISRAEL BE AS THE SAND OF THE SEA, IT IS THE REMNANT THAT WILL BE SAVED;
28FOR THE LORD WILL EXECUTE HIS WORD UPON THE EARTH, THOROUGHLY AND QUICKLY."
29And just as Isaiah foretold,
"EXCEPT THE LORD OF SABAOTH HAD LEFT TO US A POSTERITY,
WE WOULD HAVE BECOME AS SODOM, AND WOULD HAVE RESEMBLED GOMORRAH."
30What shall we say then? That Gentiles, who did not pursue righteousness, attained righteousness, even the righteousness which is by faith;
31but Israel, pursuing a law of righteousness, did not arrive at *that* law.
32Why? Because *they did* not *pursue it* by faith, but as though *it were* by works. They stumbled over the stumbling stone,

οὕτως; 21 ἢ οὐκ ἔχει ἐξουσίαν ὁ κεραμεὺς
thus? or has not [2]authority [1]the [3]potter
τοῦ πηλοῦ ἐκ τοῦ αὐτοῦ φυράματος
of the clay out of the same lump
ποιῆσαι ὃ μὲν εἰς τιμὴν σκεῦος, ὃ δὲ
to make [1]this [3]to [4]honour [2]vessel, that
εἰς ἀτιμίαν; 22 εἰ δὲ θέλων ὁ θεὸς
to dishonour? But if wishing – God
ἐνδείξασθαι τὴν ὀργὴν καὶ γνωρίσαι τὸ
to show forth the(his) wrath and to make known the
δυνατὸν αὐτοῦ ἤνεγκεν ἐν πολλῇ μακρο-
ability of him bore in much long-
θυμίᾳ σκεύη ὀργῆς κατηρτισμένα εἰς
suffering vessels of wrath *having been* fitted for
ἀπώλειαν, 23 καὶ ἵνα γνωρίσῃ τὸν πλοῦτον
destruction, and in order that he might make known the riches
τῆς δόξης αὐτοῦ ἐπὶ σκεύη ἐλέους, ἃ
of the glory of him on vessels of mercy, which
προητοίμασεν εἰς δόξαν, 24 οὓς καὶ
he previously prepared for glory, whom also
ἐκάλεσεν ἡμᾶς οὐ μόνον ἐξ Ἰουδαίων
he called[,] us not only of Jews
ἀλλὰ καὶ ἐξ ἐθνῶν; 25 ὡς καὶ ἐν τῷ
but also of nations? As also in –
Ὡσηὲ λέγει· καλέσω τὸν οὐ λαόν μου
Osee he says: I will call the [2]not [1]people of me
λαόν μου καὶ τὴν οὐκ ἠγαπημένην
a people of me and the not having been loved
ἠγαπημένην· 26 καὶ ἔσται ἐν τῷ τόπῳ
having been loved; and it shall be in the place
οὗ ἐρρέθη [αὐτοῖς]· οὐ λαός μου ὑμεῖς,
where it was said to them: not a people of me ye [are],
ἐκεῖ κληθήσονται υἱοὶ θεοῦ ζῶντος.
there they will be called sons [2]God [1]of a living.
27 Ἠσαΐας δὲ κράζει ὑπὲρ τοῦ Ἰσραήλ·
But Esaias cries on behalf of – Israel:
ἐὰν ᾖ ὁ ἀριθμὸς τῶν υἱῶν Ἰσραὴλ
If be the number of the sons of Israel
ὡς ἡ ἄμμος τῆς θαλάσσης, τὸ ὑπόλειμμα
as the sand of the sea, the remnant
σωθήσεται· 28 λόγον γὰρ συντελῶν καὶ
will be saved; for [6]an account [1]accomplishing [2]and
συντέμνων ποιήσει κύριος ἐπὶ τῆς γῆς.
[3]cutting short [5]will make [4][the] Lord on the earth.
29 καὶ καθὼς προείρηκεν Ἠσαΐας· εἰ μὴ
And as [2]has previously said [1]Esaias: Except
κύριος σαβαὼθ ἐγκατέλιπεν ἡμῖν σπέρμα,
[the] Lord of hosts left to us a seed,
ὡς Σόδομα ἂν ἐγενήθημεν καὶ ὡς Γόμορρα
as Sodom we would have become and as Gomorra
ἂν ὡμοιώθημεν.
we would have been likened.
30 Τί οὖν ἐροῦμεν; ὅτι ἔθνη τὰ μὴ
What therefore shall we say? that nations – not
διώκοντα δικαιοσύνην κατέλαβεν δικαιοσύνην,
pursuing righteousness apprehended righteousness,
δικαιοσύνην δὲ τὴν ἐκ πίστεως· 31 Ἰσραὴλ
but a righteousness – of faith; [2]Israel
δὲ διώκων νόμον δικαιοσύνης εἰς νόμον
[1]but pursuing a law of righteousness [2]to(at) [3]a law
οὐκ ἔφθασεν. 32 διὰ τί; ὅτι οὐκ ἐκ
[1]did not arrive. Why? Because not of
πίστεως ἀλλ' ὡς ἐξ ἔργων· προσέκοψαν
faith but as of works; they stumbled
τῷ λίθῳ τοῦ προσκόμματος, 33 καθὼς
at the stone – of stumbling, as

21Does not the potter have the right to make out of the same lump of clay some pottery for noble purposes and some for common use?
22What if God, choosing to show his wrath and make his power known, bore with great patience the objects of his wrath—prepared for destruction?
23What if he did this to make the riches of his glory known to the objects of his mercy, whom he prepared in advance for glory—
24even us, whom he also called, not only from the Jews but also from the Gen-
tiles? 25As he says in Ho-
sea:

"I will call them 'my people' who are not my people;
and I will call her 'my loved one' who is not my loved one,"[v]

26and,
"It will happen that in the very place where it was said to them,
'You are not my people,'
they will be called 'sons of the living God.'"[w]

27Isaiah cries out concerning Israel:
"Though the number of the Israelites be like the sand by the sea,
only the remnant will be saved.
28For the Lord will carry out
his sentence on earth with speed and finality."[x]
29It is just as Isaiah said previously:

"Unless the Lord Almighty
had left us descendants,
we would have become like Sodom,
we would have been like Gomorrah."[y]

Israel's Unbelief

30What then shall we say? That the Gentiles, who did not pursue righteousness, have obtained it, a righteousness that is by faith;
31but Israel, who pursued a law of righteousness, has
not attained it. 32Why not?
Because they pursued it not by faith but as if it were by works. They stumbled over the "stumbling

[v]25 Hosea 2:23
[w]26 Hosea 1:10
[x]28 Isaiah 10:22,23
[y]29 Isaiah 1:9

33just as it is written,
"BEHOLD, I LAY IN ZION
A STONE OF STUMBLING AND A ROCK OF
OFFENSE,
AND HE WHO BELIEVES
IN HIM WILL NOT BE
DISAPPOINTED."

Chapter 10

The Word of Faith Brings Salvation

BRETHREN, my
heart's desire and my
prayer to God for them is
for *their* salvation.
2For I bear them witness
that they have a zeal for
God, but not in accordance
with knowledge.
3For not knowing about
God's righteousness, and
seeking to establish their
own, they did not subject
themselves to the righteousness of God.
4For Christ is the end of
the law for righteousness to
everyone who believes.
5For Moses writes that
the man who practices the
righteousness which is
based on law shall live by
that righteousness.
6But the righteousness
based on faith speaks thus,
"DO NOT SAY IN YOUR
HEART, 'WHO WILL ASCEND
INTO HEAVEN?' (that is, to
bring Christ down),
7or 'WHO WILL DESCEND
INTO THE ABYSS?' (that is, to
bring Christ up from the
dead)."
8But what does it say?
"THE WORD IS NEAR YOU, IN
YOUR MOUTH AND IN YOUR
HEART"—that is, the word
of faith which we are
preaching,
9that if you confess with
your mouth Jesus *as* Lord,
and believe in your heart
that God raised Him from
the dead, you shall be
saved;
10for with the heart man
believes, resulting in righteousness, and with the
mouth he confesses, resulting in salvation.
11For the Scripture says,
"WHOEVER BELIEVES IN HIM

γέγραπται· ἰδοὺ τίθημι ἐν Σιὼν λίθον
it has been written: Behold I place in Sion a stone
προσκόμματος καὶ πέτραν σκανδάλου, καὶ
of stumbling and a rock of offence, and
ὁ πιστεύων ἐπ' αὐτῷ οὐ καταισχυνθήσεται.
the [one] believing on him will not be put to shame.

10 Ἀδελφοί, ἡ μὲν εὐδοκία τῆς ἐμῆς
Brothers, the – good pleasure – of my
καρδίας καὶ ἡ δέησις πρὸς τὸν θεὸν
heart and the request to – God
ὑπὲρ αὐτῶν εἰς σωτηρίαν. 2 μαρτυρῶ
on behalf of them [is] for salvation. I witness
γὰρ αὐτοῖς ὅτι ζῆλον θεοῦ ἔχουσιν, ἀλλ'
For to them that a zeal of God they have, but
οὐ κατ' ἐπίγνωσιν· 3 ἀγνοοῦντες γὰρ τὴν
not according to knowledge; for not knowing the
τοῦ θεοῦ δικαιοσύνην, καὶ τὴν ἰδίαν
– ²of God ¹righteousness, and the(ir) own
ζητοῦντες στῆσαι, τῇ δικαιοσύνῃ τοῦ θεοῦ
seeking to establish, to the righteousness – of God
οὐχ ὑπετάγησαν. 4 τέλος γὰρ νόμου
they did not submit. For end of law
Χριστὸς εἰς δικαιοσύνην παντὶ τῷ
Christ [is] for righteousness to everyone
πιστεύοντι. 5 Μωϋσῆς γὰρ γράφει ὅτι
believing. For Moses writes[,] –
τὴν δικαιοσύνην τὴν ἐκ νόμου ὁ ποιήσας
⁴the ⁵righteousness – ⁶of ⁷law ¹The ³doing
ἄνθρωπος ζήσεται ἐν αὐτῇ. 6 ἡ δὲ
²man will live by it. But the
ἐκ πίστεως δικαιοσύνη οὕτως λέγει· μὴ
²of ³faith ¹righteousness thus says: not
εἴπῃς ἐν τῇ καρδίᾳ σου· τίς ἀναβήσεται
Say in the heart of thee: Who will ascend
εἰς τὸν οὐρανόν; τοῦτ' ἔστιν Χριστὸν
into – heaven? this is Christ
καταγαγεῖν· 7 ἤ· τίς καταβήσεται εἰς
to bring down; or: Who will descend into
τὴν ἄβυσσον; τοῦτ' ἔστιν Χριστὸν ἐκ
the abyss? this is Christ from
νεκρῶν ἀναγαγεῖν. 8 ἀλλὰ τί λέγει;
[the] dead to bring up. But what says it?
ἐγγύς σου τὸ ῥῆμά ἐστιν, ἐν τῷ στόματί
Near thee the word is, in the mouth
σου καὶ ἐν τῇ καρδίᾳ σου· τοῦτ' ἔστιν
of thee and in the heart of thee; this is
τὸ ῥῆμα τῆς πίστεως ὃ κηρύσσομεν.
the word – of faith which we proclaim.
9 ὅτι ἐὰν ὁμολογήσῃς ἐν τῷ στόματί
Because if thou confessest with the mouth
σου κύριον Ἰησοῦν, καὶ πιστεύσῃς ἐν
of thee Lord Jesus, and believest in
τῇ καρδίᾳ σου ὅτι ὁ θεὸς αὐτὸν ἤγειρεν
the heart of thee that – God him raised
ἐκ νεκρῶν, σωθήσῃ· 10 καρδίᾳ γὰρ
from [the] dead, thou wilt be saved; for with heart
πιστεύεται εἰς δικαιοσύνην, στόματι δὲ
[one] believes to righteousness, and with mouth
ὁμολογεῖται εἰς σωτηρίαν. 11 λέγει γὰρ
[one] confesses to salvation. For says
ἡ γραφή· πᾶς ὁ πιστεύων ἐπ' αὐτῷ
the scripture: Everyone believing on him

stone." 33As it is written:
"See, I lay in Zion a
stone that causes
men to stumble
and a rock that makes
them fall,
and the one who trusts in
him will never be
put to shame."[z]

Chapter 10

BROTHERS, my
heart's desire and
prayer to God for the Israelites is that they may be
saved. 2For I can testify
about them that they are
zealous for God, but their
zeal is not based on knowledge. 3Since they did not
know the righteousness
that comes from God and
sought to establish their
own, they did not submit to
God's righteousness.
4Christ is the end of the law
so that there may be righteousness for everyone who
believes.
5Moses describes in this
way the righteousness that
is by the law: "The man
who does these things will
live by them."[a] 6But the
righteousness that is by
faith says: "Do not say in
your heart, 'Who will ascend into heaven?'[b]" (that
is, to bring Christ down)
7"or 'Who will descend
into the deep?'[c]" (that is,
to bring Christ up from the
dead). 8But what does it
say? "The word is near
you; it is in your mouth and
in your heart,"[d] that is, the
word of faith we are proclaiming: 9That if you confess with your mouth,
"Jesus is Lord," and believe in your heart that God
raised him from the dead,
you will be saved. 10For it
is with your heart that you
believe and are justified,
and it is with your mouth
that you confess and are
saved. 11As the Scripture
says, "Anyone who trusts

[z]33 Isaiah 8:14; 28:16
[a]5 Lev. 18:5
[b]6 Deut. 30:12
[c]7 Deut. 30:13
[d]8 Deut. 30:14

WILL NOT BE DISAPPOINTED.''
12For there is no distinction between Jew and
Greek; for the same *Lord* is
Lord of all, abounding in
riches for all who call upon
Him;
13for "WHOEVER WILL
CALL UPON THE NAME OF THE
LORD WILL BE SAVED."
14How then shall they call
upon Him in whom they
have not believed? And
how shall they believe in
Him whom they have not
heard? And how shall they
hear without a preacher?
15And how shall they
preach unless they are
sent? Just as it is written,
"HOW BEAUTIFUL ARE THE
FEET OF THOSE WHO BRING
GLAD TIDINGS OF GOOD
THINGS!"
16However, they did not
all heed the glad tidings; for
Isaiah says, "LORD, WHO
HAS BELIEVED OUR REPORT?"
17So faith *comes* from
hearing, and hearing by the
word of Christ.
18But I say, surely they
have never heard, have
they? Indeed they have;
"THEIR VOICE HAS GONE
OUT INTO ALL THE
EARTH,
AND THEIR WORDS TO
THE ENDS OF THE
WORLD."
19But I say, surely Israel
did not know, did they? At
the first Moses says,
"I WILL MAKE YOU JEAL-
OUS BY THAT WHICH IS
NOT A NATION,
BY A NATION WITHOUT
UNDERSTANDING WILL
I ANGER YOU."
20And Isaiah is very bold
and says,
"I WAS FOUND BY THOSE
WHO SOUGHT ME NOT,
I BECAME MANIFEST TO
THOSE WHO DID NOT
ASK FOR ME."
21But as for Israel He
says, "ALL THE DAY LONG I
HAVE STRETCHED OUT MY
HANDS TO A DISOBEDIENT
AND OBSTINATE PEOPLE."

οὐ καταισχυνθήσεται. **12** οὐ γάρ ἐστιν
will not be put to shame. For there is no

διαστολὴ Ἰουδαίου τε καὶ Ἕλληνος. ὁ
difference [2]of Jew [1]both [3]and [4]of Greek.* the

γὰρ αὐτὸς κύριος πάντων, πλουτῶν εἰς
For same Lord of all, is rich to

πάντας τοὺς ἐπικαλουμένους αὐτόν· **13** πᾶς
all the [ones] calling on him; [2]everyone

γὰρ ὃς ἂν ἐπικαλέσηται τὸ ὄνομα κυρίου
[1]for whoever calls on the name of [the] Lord

σωθήσεται. **14** Πῶς οὖν ἐπικαλέσωνται εἰς
will be saved. How therefore may they call on in [one]

ὃν οὐκ ἐπίστευσαν; πῶς δὲ πιστεύσωσιν
whom they believed not? And how may they believe

οὗ οὐκ ἤκουσαν; πῶς δὲ ἀκούσωσιν
of whom they heard not? And how may they hear

χωρὶς κηρύσσοντος; **15** πῶς δὲ κηρύξωσιν
without [one] heralding? And how may they herald

ἐὰν μὴ ἀποσταλῶσιν; καθάπερ γέγραπται·
if they are not sent? As it has been written:

ὡς ὡραῖοι οἱ πόδες τῶν εὐαγγελιζομένων
How beautiful the feet of the [ones] announcing *good*

ἀγαθά. **16** ἀλλ' οὐ πάντες ὑπήκουσαν τῷ
good things. But not all obeyed the

εὐαγγελίῳ. Ἠσαΐας γὰρ λέγει· κύριε,
gospel. For Esaias says: Lord,

τίς ἐπίστευσεν τῇ ἀκοῇ ἡμῶν; **17** ἄρα
who believed the hearing of us? Then

ἡ πίστις ἐξ ἀκοῆς, ἡ δὲ ἀκοὴ διὰ
– faith [is] from hearing, and the hearing through

ῥήματος Χριστοῦ. **18** ἀλλὰ λέγω, μὴ
a word of Christ. But I say, *not*

οὐκ ἤκουσαν; μενοῦν γε· εἰς πᾶσαν
did they not hear? Nay rather: To all

τὴν γῆν ἐξῆλθεν ὁ φθόγγος αὐτῶν,
the earth went out the utterance of them,

καὶ εἰς τὰ πέρατα τῆς οἰκουμένης τὰ
and to the ends of the inhabited earth the

ῥήματα αὐτῶν. **19** ἀλλὰ λέγω, μὴ Ἰσραὴλ
words of them. But I say, *not* Israel

οὐκ ἔγνω; πρῶτος Μωϋσῆς λέγει· ἐγὼ
did not know? First Moses says: I

παραζηλώσω ὑμᾶς ἐπ' οὐκ ἔθνει, ἐπ'
will provoke to jealousy you on(by) not a nation, on(by)

ἔθνει ἀσυνέτῳ παροργιῶ ὑμᾶς. **20** Ἠσαΐας
a nation unintelligent I will anger you. Esaias

δὲ ἀποτολμᾷ καὶ λέγει· εὑρέθην τοῖς
But is quite bold and says: I was found by the [ones]

ἐμὲ μὴ ζητοῦσιν, ἐμφανὴς ἐγενόμην τοῖς
[3]me [1]not [2]seeking, manifest I became to the [ones]

ἐμὲ μὴ ἐπερωτῶσιν. **21** πρὸς δὲ τὸν
[3]me [1]not [2]inquiring [for]. But to –

Ἰσραὴλ λέγει· ὅλην τὴν ἡμέραν ἐξεπέτασα
Israel he says: All the day I stretched out

τὰς χεῖράς μου πρὸς λαὸν ἀπειθοῦντα
the hands of me to a people disobeying

καὶ ἀντιλέγοντα.
and contradicting.

* That is, between these two classes.

in him will never be put to
shame."[e] 12For there is no
difference between Jew
and Gentile—the same
Lord is Lord of all and richly blesses all who call on
him, 13for, "Everyone who
calls on the name of the
Lord will be saved."[f]
14How, then, can they
call on the one they have
not believed in? And how
can they believe in the one
of whom they have not
heard? And how can they
hear without someone
preaching to them? 15And
how can they preach unless
they are sent? As it is written, "How beautiful are the
feet of those who bring
good news!"[g]
16But not all the Israelites
accepted the good news.
For Isaiah says, "Lord,
who has believed our mes-
sage?"[h] 17Consequently,
faith comes from hearing
the message, and the mes-
sage is heard through the
word of Christ. 18But I ask:
Did they not hear? Of
course they did:

"Their voice has gone
out into all the
earth,
their words to the ends
of the world."[i]

19Again I ask: Did Israel
not understand? First, Moses says,

"I will make you
envious by those
who are not a
nation;
I will make you angry
by a nation that has
no
understanding."[j]

20And Isaiah boldly says,

"I was found by those
who did not seek
me;
I revealed myself to
those who did not
ask for me."[k]

21But concerning Israel he
says,

"All day long I have
held out my hands
to a disobedient and
obstinate people."[l]

[e] *11* Isaiah 28:16
[f] *13* Joel 2:32
[g] *15* Isaiah 52:7
[h] *16* Isaiah 53:1
[i] *18* Psalm 19:4
[j] *19* Deut. 32:21
[k] *20* Isaiah 65:1
[l] *21* Isaiah 65:2

Chapter 11

Israel Is Not Cast Away

I say then, God has not rejected His people, has He? May it never be! For I too am an Israelite, a descendant of Abraham, of the tribe of Benjamin.

2God has not rejected His people whom He foreknew. Or do you not know what the Scripture says in *the passage about* Elijah, how he pleads with God against Israel?

3"Lord, THEY HAVE KILLED THY PROPHETS, THEY HAVE TORN DOWN THINE ALTARS, AND I ALONE AM LEFT, AND THEY ARE SEEKING MY LIFE."

4But what is the divine response to him? "I HAVE KEPT for Myself SEVEN THOUSAND MEN WHO HAVE NOT BOWED THE KNEE TO BAAL."

5In the same way then, there has also come to be at the present time a remnant according to *God's* gracious choice.

6But if it is by grace, it is no longer on the basis of works, otherwise grace is no longer grace.

7What then? That which Israel is seeking for, it has not obtained, but those who were chosen obtained it, and the rest were hardened;

8just as it is written,

"GOD GAVE THEM A SPIRIT OF STUPOR,
EYES TO SEE NOT AND EARS TO HEAR NOT,
DOWN TO THIS VERY DAY."

9And David says,

"LET THEIR TABLE BECOME A SNARE AND A TRAP,
AND A STUMBLING BLOCK AND A RETRIBUTION TO THEM.

10"LET THEIR EYES BE DARKENED TO SEE NOT,
AND BEND THEIR BACKS FOREVER."

11I say then, they did not stumble so as to fall, did they? May it never be! But by their transgression salvation *has come* to the Gentiles, to make them jealous.

11 Λέγω οὖν, μὴ ἀπώσατο ὁ θεὸς
I say therefore, ²did *not* put away – ¹God
τὸν λαὸν αὐτοῦ; μὴ γένοιτο· καὶ γὰρ
the people of him? May it not be; for even
ἐγὼ Ἰσραηλίτης εἰμί, ἐκ σπέρματος
I an Israelite am, of [the] seed
Ἀβραάμ, φυλῆς Βενιαμίν. **2** οὐκ ἀπώσατο
of Abraham, of [the] tribe of Benjamin. did not put away
ὁ θεὸς τὸν λαὸν αὐτοῦ ὃν προέγνω.
– God the people of him whom he foreknew.
ἢ οὐκ οἴδατε ἐν Ἠλίᾳ τί λέγει ἡ
Or know ye not in Elias what says the
γραφή, ὡς ἐντυγχάνει τῷ θεῷ κατὰ τοῦ
scripture, how he supplicates – God against –
Ἰσραήλ; **3** κύριε, τοὺς προφήτας σου
Israel? Lord, the prophets of thee
ἀπέκτειναν, τὰ θυσιαστήριά σου κατέσκαψαν,
they killed, the altars of thee they dug down,
κἀγὼ ὑπελείφθην μόνος καὶ ζητοῦσιν τὴν
and I was left behind alone and they seek the
ψυχήν μου. **4** ἀλλὰ τί λέγει αὐτῷ ὁ
life of me. But what says to him the
χρηματισμός; κατέλιπον ἐμαυτῷ ἑπτακισ-
[divine] response? I reserved to myself seven
χιλίους ἄνδρας, οἵτινες οὐκ ἔκαμψαν γόνυ
thousand*s* men, who bowed not knee
τῇ Βάαλ. **5** οὕτως οὖν καὶ ἐν τῷ νῦν
– to Baal. So therefore also in the present
καιρῷ λεῖμμα κατ' ἐκλογὴν χάριτος
time a remnant according to a choice of grace
γέγονεν· **6** εἰ δὲ χάριτι, οὐκέτι ἐξ ἔργων,
has become; and if by grace, no more of works,
ἐπεὶ ἡ χάρις οὐκέτι γίνεται χάρις. **7** Τί
since – grace no more becomes grace. What
οὖν; ὃ ἐπιζητεῖ Ἰσραήλ, τοῦτο οὐκ
therefore? What ²seeks after ¹Israel, this not
ἐπέτυχεν, ἡ δὲ ἐκλογὴ ἐπέτυχεν· οἱ δὲ
he obtained, but the choice obtained [it]; and the
λοιποὶ ἐπωρώθησαν, **8** καθάπερ γέγραπται·
rest were hardened, as it has been written:
ἔδωκεν αὐτοῖς ὁ θεὸς πνεῦμα κατανύξεως,
Gave to them – God a spirit of torpor,
ὀφθαλμοὺς τοῦ μὴ βλέπειν καὶ ὦτα
eyes – not to see[d] and ears
τοῦ μὴ ἀκούειν, ἕως τῆς σήμερον ἡμέρας
– not to hear,[d] until the present† day.
9 καὶ Δαυὶδ λέγει· γενηθήτω ἡ τράπεζα
And David says: Let become the table
αὐτῶν εἰς παγίδα καὶ εἰς θήραν καὶ
of them for a snare and for a net and
εἰς σκάνδαλον καὶ εἰς ἀνταπόδομα αὐτοῖς,
for an offence and for a recompence to them,
10 σκοτισθήτωσαν οἱ ὀφθαλμοὶ αὐτῶν τοῦ
let be darkened the eyes of them –
μὴ βλέπειν, καὶ τὸν νῶτον αὐτῶν διὰ
not to see,[d] and the back of them al-
παντὸς σύγκαμψον.
ways bending.

11 Λέγω οὖν, μὴ ἔπταισαν ἵνα πέσωσιν;
I say therefore, did they *not* stumble in order that they might fall?
μὴ γένοιτο· ἀλλὰ τῷ αὐτῶν παραπτώματι
May it not be; but by the ²of them ¹trespass
ἡ σωτηρία τοῖς ἔθνεσιν, εἰς τὸ παραζηλῶσαι
– salvation [came] to the nations, *for the* to provoke to jealousy

Chapter 11

The Remnant of Israel

I ASK then: Did God reject his people? By no means! I am an Israelite myself, a descendant of Abraham, from the tribe of Benjamin. 2God did not reject his people, whom he foreknew. Don't you know what the Scripture says in the passage about Elijah—how he appealed to God against Israel: 3"Lord, they have killed your prophets and torn down your altars; I am the only one left, and they are trying to kill me"[m]? 4And what was God's answer to him? "I have reserved for myself seven thousand who have not bowed the knee to Baal."[n] 5So too, at the present time there is a remnant chosen by grace. 6And if by grace, then it is no longer by works; if it were, grace would no longer be grace.[o]

7What then? What Israel sought so earnestly it did not obtain, but the elect did. The others were hardened, 8as it is written:

"God gave them a spirit of stupor,
eyes so that they could not see
and ears so that they could not hear,
to this very day."[p]

9And David says:

"May their table become a snare and a trap,
a stumbling block and a retribution for them.
10May their eyes be darkened so they cannot see,
and their backs be bent forever."[q]

Ingrafted Branches

11Again I ask: Did they stumble so as to fall beyond recovery? Not at all! Rather, because of their transgression, salvation has come to the Gentiles to make Israel envious. 12But

m3 1 Kings 19:10,14
n4 1 Kings 19:18
o6 Some manuscripts *by grace. But if by works, then it is no longer grace; if it were, work would no longer be work.*
p8 Deut. 29:4; Isaiah 29:10
q10 Psalm 69:22,23

12 Now if their transgression be riches for the world
and their failure be riches
for the Gentiles, how much
more will their fulfillment
be!
13 But I am speaking to
you who are Gentiles. Inasmuch then as I am an apostle of Gentiles, I magnify
my ministry,
14 if somehow I might
move to jealousy my fellow
countrymen and save some
of them.
15 For if their rejection be
the reconciliation of the
world, what will *their* acceptance be but life from
the dead?
16 And if the first piece *of
dough* be holy, the lump is
also; and if the root be holy,
the branches are too.
17 But if some of the
branches were broken off,
and you, being a wild olive,
were grafted in among
them and became partaker
with them of the rich root of
the olive tree,
18 do not be arrogant
toward the branches; but if
you are arrogant, *remem-
ber that* it is not you who
supports the root, but the
root *supports* you.
19 You will say then,
"Branches were broken off
so that I might be grafted
in."
20 Quite right, they were
broken off for their un-
belief, but you stand by
your faith. Do not be conceited, but fear;
21 for if God did not spare
the natural branches,
neither will He spare you.
22 Behold then the kind-
ness and severity of God; to
those who fell, severity,
but to you, God's kindness,
if you continue in His kindness; otherwise you also
will be cut off.
23 And they also, if they
do not continue in their unbelief, will be grafted in; for

αὐτούς. **12** εἰ δὲ τὸ παράπτωμα αὐτῶν
them. But if the trespass of them
πλοῦτος κόσμου καὶ τὸ ἥττημα αὐτῶν
[is] [the] riches of [the] world and the defect of them
πλοῦτος ἐθνῶν, πόσῳ μᾶλλον τὸ πλήρωμα
[is] [the] riches of [the] nations, by how much more the fulness
αὐτῶν. **13** Ὑμῖν δὲ λέγω τοῖς ἔθνεσιν.
of them. But to you [3]I say[,] [1]the [2]nations.
ἐφ᾽ ὅσον μὲν οὖν εἰμι ἐγὼ ἐθνῶν ἀπόστο-
Forasmuch as indeed therefore [2]am [1]I [4]of nations [3]an apos-
λος, τὴν διακονίαν μου δοξάζω, **14** εἴ πως
tle, the ministry of me I glorify, if somehow
παραζηλώσω μου τὴν σάρκα καὶ σώσω
I may provoke to jealousy of me the flesh and may save
τινὰς ἐξ αὐτῶν. **15** εἰ γὰρ ἡ ἀποβολὴ
some of them. For if the casting away
αὐτῶν καταλλαγὴ κόσμου, τίς ἡ πρόσλημψις
of them [is] [the] reconciliation of [the] world, what the reception
εἰ μὴ ζωὴ ἐκ νεκρῶν; **16** εἰ δὲ ἡ
if not life from [the] dead? And if the
ἀπαρχὴ ἁγία, καὶ τὸ φύραμα· καὶ εἰ
firstfruit [is] holy, also the lump; and if
ἡ ῥίζα ἁγία, καὶ οἱ κλάδοι. **17** Εἰ δέ
the root [is] holy, also the branches. But if
τινες τῶν κλάδων ἐξεκλάσθησαν, σὺ δὲ
some of the branches were broken off, and thou
ἀγριέλαιος ὢν ἐνεκεντρίσθης ἐν αὐτοῖς
[2]a wild olive [1]being wast grafted in among them
καὶ συγκοινωνὸς τῆς ῥίζης τῆς πιότητος
and [2]a partaker [3]of the [4]root* [5]of the [6]fatness
τῆς ἐλαίας ἐγένου, **18** μὴ κατακαυχῶ
[7]of the [8]olive-tree [1]didst become, boast not against
τῶν κλάδων· εἰ δὲ κατακαυχᾶσαι, οὐ
of the branches; but if thou boastest, not
σὺ τὴν ῥίζαν βαστάζεις ἀλλὰ ἡ ῥίζα σέ.
thou the root bearest but the root thee.
19 ἐρεῖς οὖν· ἐξεκλάσθησαν κλάδοι ἵνα
Thou wilt say therefore: [2]Were broken off [1]branches in order that
ἐγὼ ἐγκεντρισθῶ. **20** καλῶς· τῇ ἀπιστίᾳ
I might be grafted in. Well: – for unbelief
ἐξεκλάσθησαν, σὺ δὲ τῇ πίστει ἕστηκας.
they were broken off, and thou – by faith standest.
μὴ ὑψηλὰ φρόνει, ἀλλὰ φοβοῦ· **21** εἰ
[2]Not [3]high things [1]mind, but fear; [2]if
γὰρ ὁ θεὸς τῶν κατὰ φύσιν κλάδων
[1]for – [3]God [5]the [7]according to [8]nature [6]branches
οὐκ ἐφείσατο, οὐδὲ σοῦ φείσεται. **22** ἴδε
[4]spared not, neither thee will he spare. See
οὖν χρηστότητα καὶ ἀποτομίαν θεοῦ· ἐπὶ
therefore [the] kindness and [the] severity of God: [2]on
μὲν τοὺς πεσόντας ἀποτομία, ἐπὶ δὲ
[1]on one hand the [ones] having fallen severity, [2]on [1]on the other
σὲ χρηστότης θεοῦ, ἐὰν ἐπιμένῃς τῇ
thee [the] kindness of God, if thou continuest in the (his)
χρηστότητι, ἐπεὶ καὶ σὺ ἐκκοπήσῃ.
kindness, since also thou wilt be cut off.
23 κἀκεῖνοι δέ, ἐὰν μὴ ἐπιμένωσιν τῇ
And those also, if they continue not –
ἀπιστίᾳ, ἐγκεντρισθήσονται· δυνατὸς γάρ
in unbelief, will be grafted in; for [3]able

* Some MSS insert *καί* (and) here; as it is, the two nouns in the genitive must be in apposition; *cf.* Col. 1. 18, 2. 2; John 8. 44.

if their transgression means
riches for the world, and
their loss means riches for
the Gentiles, how much
greater riches will their fullness bring!
13 I am talking to you Gentiles. Inasmuch as I am the
apostle to the Gentiles, I
make much of my ministry
14 in the hope that I may
somehow arouse my own
people to envy and save
some of them. 15 For if their
rejection is the reconciliation of the world, what will
their acceptance be but life
from the dead? 16 If the part
of the dough offered as
firstfruits is holy, then the
whole batch is holy; if the
root is holy, so are the
branches.
17 If some of the branches
have been broken off, and
you, though a wild olive
shoot, have been grafted in
among the others and now
share in the nourishing sap
from the olive root, 18 do
not boast over those
branches. If you do, con-
sider this: You do not support the root, but the root
supports you. 19 You will
say then, "Branches were
broken off so that I could
be grafted in." 20 Granted.
But they were broken off
because of unbelief, and
you stand by faith. Do not
be arrogant, but be afraid.
21 For if God did not spare
the natural branches, he
will not spare you either.
22 Consider therefore the
kindness and sternness of
God: sternness to those
who fell, but kindness to
you, provided that you
continue in his kindness.
Otherwise, you also will be
cut off. 23 And if they do not
persist in unbelief, they will

God is able to graft them in
again.
24For if you were cut off
from what is by nature a
wild olive tree, and were
grafted contrary to nature
into a cultivated olive tree,
how much more shall these
who are the natural
branches be grafted into
their own olive tree?
25For I do not want you,
brethren, to be uninformed
of this mystery, lest you be
wise in your own estima-
tion, that a partial hardening has happened to Israel
until the fulness of the Gentiles has come in;
26and thus all Israel will
be saved; just as it is written,
"THE DELIVERER WILL
COME FROM ZION,
HE WILL REMOVE UN-
GODLINESS FROM
JACOB."
27"AND THIS IS MY COV-
ENANT WITH THEM,
WHEN I TAKE AWAY
THEIR SINS."
28From the standpoint of
the gospel they are enemies
for your sake, but from the
standpoint of *God's* choice
they are beloved for the
sake of the fathers;
29for the gifts and the calling of God are irrevocable.
30For just as you once
were disobedient to God,
but now have been shown
mercy because of their disobedience,
31so these also now have
been disobedient, in order
that because of the mercy
shown to you they also may
now be shown mercy.
32For God has shut up all
in disobedience that He
might show mercy to all.
33Oh, the depth of the
riches both of the wisdom
and knowledge of God!
How unsearchable are His
judgments and unfathoma-
ble His ways!
34For WHO HAS KNOWN
THE MIND OF THE LORD, OR

ἔστιν ὁ θεὸς πάλιν ἐγκεντρίσαι αὐτούς.
[2]is – [1]God [7]again [4]to graft [6]in [5]them.
24 εἰ γὰρ σὺ ἐκ τῆς κατὰ φύσιν ἐξεκόπης
For if thou [2]out of [3]the [5]according to [6]nature [1]wast cut *out*
ἀγριελαίου καὶ παρὰ φύσιν ἐνεκεντρίσθης
[4]wild olive and against nature wast grafted *in*
εἰς καλλιέλαιον, πόσῳ μᾶλλον οὗτοι οἱ
into a cultivated olive, by how much more these the [ones]
κατὰ φύσιν ἐγκεντρισθήσονται τῇ ἰδίᾳ
according to nature will be grafted in the(ir) own
ἐλαίᾳ. 25 Οὐ γὰρ θέλω ὑμᾶς ἀγνοεῖν,
olive-tree. For I wish not you to be ignorant,
ἀδελφοί, τὸ μυστήριον τοῦτο, ἵνα μὴ
brothers, [of] this mystery, lest
ἦτε ἐν ἑαυτοῖς φρόνιμοι, ὅτι πώρωσις
ye be in yourselves wise, that hardness
ἀπὸ μέρους τῷ Ἰσραὴλ γέγονεν ἄχρι οὗ
from(in) part – to Israel has happened until
τὸ πλήρωμα τῶν ἐθνῶν εἰσέλθῃ, 26 καὶ
the fulness of the nations comes in, and
οὕτως πᾶς Ἰσραὴλ σωθήσεται, καθὼς
so all Israel will be saved, as
γέγραπται· ἥξει ἐκ Σιὼν ὁ ῥυόμενος,
it has been written: [3]will come [4]out of [5]Sion [1]The [one] [2]delivering,
ἀποστρέψει ἀσεβείας ἀπὸ Ἰακώβ. 27 καὶ
he will turn away impiety from Jacob. And
αὕτη αὐτοῖς ἡ παρ' ἐμοῦ διαθήκη, ὅταν
this [is] [5]with them [1]the [3]from [4]me [2]covenant, when
ἀφέλωμαι τὰς ἁμαρτίας αὐτῶν. 28 κατὰ
I take away the sins of them. [2]According to
μὲν τὸ εὐαγγέλιον ἐχθροὶ δι' ὑμᾶς,
[1]on one hand the gospel enemies because of you,
κατὰ δὲ τὴν ἐκλογὴν ἀγαπητοὶ διὰ
[2]according to [1]on the other the choice beloved because of
τοὺς πατέρας· 29 ἀμεταμέλητα γὰρ τὰ
the fathers; for unrepented the
χαρίσματα καὶ ἡ κλῆσις τοῦ θεοῦ.
free gifts and the calling – of God.
30 ὥσπερ γὰρ ὑμεῖς ποτε ἠπειθήσατε
For as ye then disobeyed
τῷ θεῷ, νῦν δὲ ἠλεήθητε τῇ τούτων
– God, but now ye obtained mercy [1]by the [3]of these
ἀπειθείᾳ, 31 οὕτως καὶ οὗτοι νῦν ἠπείθησαν
[2]disobedience, so also these now disobeyed
τῷ ὑμετέρῳ ἐλέει ἵνα καὶ αὐτοὶ νῦν
– [2]by your [3]mercy [1]in order that also they now
ἐλεηθῶσιν. 32 συνέκλεισεν γὰρ ὁ θεὸς
may obtain mercy. For [2]shut up – [1]God
τοὺς πάντας εἰς ἀπείθειαν ἵνα τοὺς
– all in disobedience in order that –
πάντας ἐλεήσῃ.
to all he may show mercy.
33 Ὦ βάθος πλούτου καὶ σοφίας καὶ
O [the] depth of [the] riches and of [the] wisdom and
γνώσεως θεοῦ· ὡς ἀνεξερεύνητα τὰ κρίματα
of [the] knowledge of God; how inscrutable the judgments
αὐτοῦ καὶ ἀνεξιχνίαστοι αἱ ὁδοὶ αὐτοῦ.
of him and unsearchable the ways of him.
34 τίς γὰρ ἔγνω νοῦν κυρίου; ἢ τίς
.For who knew [the] mind of [the] Lord? or who

be grafted in, for God is
able to graft them in again.
24After all, if you were cut
out of an olive tree that is
wild by nature, and con-
trary to nature were grafted
into a cultivated olive tree,
how much more readily
will these, the natural
branches, be grafted into
their own olive tree!

All Israel Will Be Saved

25I do not want you to be
ignorant of this mystery,
brothers, so that you may
not be conceited: Israel has
experienced a hardening in
part until the full number of
the Gentiles has come in.
26And so all Israel will be
saved, as it is written:[s]

"The deliverer will come
from Zion;
he will turn
godlessness away
from Jacob.
27And this is[r] my
covenant with them
when I take away their
sins."[s]

28As far as the gospel is
concerned, they are ene-
mies on your account; but
as far as election is concerned, they are loved on
account of the patriarchs,
29for God's gifts and his call
are irrevocable. 30Just as
you who were at one time
disobedient to God have
now received mercy as a
result of their disobedi-
ence, 31so they too have
now become disobedient in
order that they too may
now[t] receive mercy as a
result of God's mercy to
you. 32For God has bound
all men over to disobedi-
ence so that he may have
mercy on them all.

Doxology

33Oh, the depth of the
riches of the wisdom
and[u] knowledge of
God!
How unsearchable his
judgments,
and his paths beyond
tracing out!
34"Who has known the
mind of the Lord?
Or who has been his
counselor?"[v]
35"Who has ever given to
God,

[r]*27* Or *will be*
[s]*27* Isaiah 59:20,21; 27:9; Jer. 31:33,34
[t]*31* Some manuscripts do not have *now*.
[u]*33* Or *riches and the wisdom and the*
[v]*34* Isaiah 40:13

WHO BECAME HIS COUNSEL-
OR?
35Or WHO HAS FIRST GIVEN
TO HIM THAT IT MIGHT BE
PAID BACK TO HIM AGAIN?
36For from Him and
through Him and to Him
are all things. To Him *be*
the glory forever. Amen.

σύμβουλος αὐτοῦ ἐγένετο; **35** ἢ τίς
counsellor of him became? or who

προέδωκεν αὐτῷ, καὶ ἀνταποδοθήσεται
previously gave to him, and it will be repaid

αὐτῷ; **36** ὅτι ἐξ αὐτοῦ καὶ δι' αὐτοῦ
to him? Because of him and through him

καὶ εἰς αὐτὸν τὰ πάντα· αὐτῷ ἡ δόξα
and to him – all things; to him the glory

εἰς τοὺς αἰῶνας· ἀμήν.
unto the ages: Amen.

that God should repay
him?"[w]
36For from him and
through him and to
him are all things.
To him be the glory
forever! Amen.

Chapter 12

Dedicated Service

I urge you therefore,
brethren, by the mercies
of God, to present your
bodies a living and holy
sacrifice, acceptable to
God, *which is* your spiritual
service of worship.
2And do not be con-
formed to this world, but be
transformed by the renew-
ing of your mind, that you
may prove what the will of
God is, that which is good
and acceptable and perfect.
3For through the grace
given to me I say to every
man among you not to
think more highly of him-
self than he ought to think;
but to think so as to have
sound judgment, as God
has allotted to each a measure of faith.
4For just as we have
many members in one body
and all the members do not
have the same function,
5so we, who are many,
are one body in Christ, and
individually members one
of another.
6And since we have gifts
that differ according to the
grace given to us, *let each
exercise them accordingly:*
if prophecy, according to
the proportion of his faith;
7if service, in his serving;
or he who teaches, in his
teaching;
8or he who exhorts, in
his exhortation; he who
gives, with [n]liberality; he
who leads, with diligence;

12 Παρακαλῶ οὖν ὑμᾶς, ἀδελφοί, διὰ
I beseech therefore you, brothers, through

τῶν οἰκτιρμῶν τοῦ θεοῦ, παραστῆσαι τὰ
the compassions – of God, to present the

σώματα ὑμῶν θυσίαν ζῶσαν ἁγίαν τῷ
bodies of you sacrifice a living holy –

θεῷ εὐάρεστον, τὴν λογικὴν λατρείαν
[2]to God [1]well-pleasing, the reasonable service

ὑμῶν· **2** καὶ μὴ συσχηματίζεσθε τῷ αἰῶνι
of you; and be ye not conformed – age

τούτῳ, ἀλλὰ μεταμορφοῦσθε τῇ ἀνακαινώσει
to this, but be ye transformed by the renewing

τοῦ νοός, εἰς τὸ δοκιμάζειν ὑμᾶς τί τὸ
of the mind, *for the* to prove you[b] what the
=so that ye may prove

θέλημα τοῦ θεοῦ, τὸ ἀγαθὸν καὶ εὐάρεστον
will – of God, the good and well-pleasing

καὶ τέλειον.
and perfect.

3 Λέγω γὰρ διὰ τῆς χάριτος τῆς
For I say through the grace –

δοθείσης μοι παντὶ τῷ ὄντι ἐν ὑμῖν,
given to me to everyone being among you,

μὴ ὑπερφρονεῖν παρ' ὃ δεῖ φρονεῖν,
not to have high thoughts beyond what it behoves to think,

ἀλλὰ φρονεῖν εἰς τὸ σωφρονεῖν, ἑκάστῳ
but to think *to the* to be sober-minded, [4]to each

ὡς ὁ θεὸς ἐμέρισεν μέτρον πίστεως.
[1]as – [2]God [3]divided a measure of faith.

4 καθάπερ γὰρ ἐν ἑνὶ σώματι πολλὰ
For as in one body many

μέλη ἔχομεν, τὰ δὲ μέλη πάντα οὐ τὴν
members we have, but [2]the [3]members [1]all [5]not [6]the

αὐτὴν ἔχει πρᾶξιν, **5** οὕτως οἱ πολλοὶ
[7]same [4]has(ve) [8]action, so the many

ἓν σῶμά ἐσμεν ἐν Χριστῷ, τὸ δὲ καθ'
one body we are in Christ, – and each

εἷς ἀλλήλων μέλη. **6** ἔχοντες δὲ χαρίσματα
one [2]of one another [1]members. And having gifts

κατὰ τὴν χάριν τὴν δοθεῖσαν ἡμῖν διάφορα,
[2]according to [3]the [4]grace – [5]given [6]to us [1]differing,

εἴτε προφητείαν, κατὰ τὴν ἀναλογίαν τῆς
whether prophecy, according to the proportion of the

πίστεως· **7** εἴτε διακονίαν, ἐν τῇ διακονίᾳ·
faith; or ministry, in the ministry;

εἴτε ὁ διδάσκων, ἐν τῇ διδασκαλίᾳ·
or the [one] teaching, in the teaching;

8 εἴτε ὁ παρακαλῶν, ἐν τῇ παρακλήσει·
or the [one] exhorting, in the exhortation;

ὁ μεταδιδοὺς ἐν ἁπλότητι, ὁ προϊστάμενος
the [one] sharing in simplicity, the [one] taking the lead

Chapter 12

Living Sacrifices

THEREFORE, I urge
you, brothers, in view
of God's mercy, to offer
your bodies as living sacrifices, holy and pleasing to
God—this is your spiritu-
al[x] act of worship. 2Do not
conform any longer to the
pattern of this world, but be
transformed by the renew-
ing of your mind. Then you
will be able to test and approve what God's will is—
his good, pleasing and perfect will.
3For by the grace given
me I say to every one of
you: Do not think of yourself more highly than you
ought, but rather think of
yourself with sober judg-
ment, in accordance with
the measure of faith God
has given you. 4Just as each
of us has one body with
many members, and these
members do not all have
the same function, 5so in
Christ we who are many
form one body, and each
member belongs to all the
others. 6We have different
gifts, according to the grace
given us. If a man's gift is
prophesying, let him use it
in proportion to his[y] faith.
7If it is serving, let him
serve; if it is teaching, let
him teach; 8if it is encouraging, let him encourage; if it
is contributing to the needs
of others, let him give generously; if it is leadership,
let him govern diligently; if

[n]Or, *simplicity*

[w]*35* Job 41:11
[x]*1* Or *reasonable*
[y]*6* Or *in agreement with the*

he who shows mercy, with cheerfulness.

9Let love be without hypocrisy. Abhor what is evil; cling to what is good.

10Be devoted to one another in brotherly love; give preference to one another in honor;

11not lagging behind in diligence, fervent in spirit, serving the Lord;

12rejoicing in hope, persevering in tribulation, devoted to prayer,

13contributing to the needs of the saints, practicing hospitality.

14Bless those who persecute [a]you; bless and curse not.

15Rejoice with those who rejoice, and weep with those who weep.

16Be of the same mind toward one another; do not be haughty in mind, but associate with the lowly. Do not be wise in your own estimation.

17Never pay back evil for evil to anyone. Respect what is right in the sight of all men.

18If possible, so far as it depends on you, be at peace with all men.

19Never take your own revenge, beloved, but leave room for the wrath *of God,* for it is written, "VENGEANCE IS MINE, I WILL REPAY," says the Lord.

20"BUT IF YOUR ENEMY IS HUNGRY, FEED HIM, AND IF HE IS THIRSTY, GIVE HIM A DRINK; FOR IN SO DOING YOU WILL HEAP BURNING COALS UPON HIS HEAD."

21Do not be overcome by evil, but overcome evil with good.

Chapter 13

Be Subject to Government

LET every person be in subjection to the governing authorities. For there is no authority except from God, and those which

[a] Some ancient mss. do not contain *you*

ἐν σπουδῇ, ὁ ἐλεῶν ἐν ἱλαρότητι. 9 ἡ
in diligence, the [one] showing mercy in cheerfulness. –

ἀγάπη ἀνυπόκριτος. ἀποστυγοῦντες τὸ
[Let] love [be] unassumed. Shrinking from the

πονηρόν, κολλώμενοι τῷ ἀγαθῷ· 10 τῇ
evil, cleaving to the good; –

φιλαδελφίᾳ εἰς ἀλλήλους φιλόστοργοι, τῇ
in brotherly love to one another loving warmly, –

τιμῇ ἀλλήλους προηγούμενοι, 11 τῇ σπουδῇ
in honour one another preferring, – in zeal

μὴ ὀκνηροί, τῷ πνεύματι ζέοντες, τῷ
not slothful, – in spirit burning, the

κυρίῳ δουλεύοντες, 12 τῇ ἐλπίδι χαίροντες,
Lord serving, – in hope rejoicing,

τῇ θλίψει ὑπομένοντες, τῇ προσευχῇ
– in affliction showing endurance, – in prayer

προσκαρτεροῦντες, 13 ταῖς χρείαις τῶν
steadfastly continuing, to the needs of the

ἁγίων κοινωνοῦντες, τὴν φιλοξενίαν
saints imparting, – hospitality

διώκοντες. 14 εὐλογεῖτε τοὺς διώκοντας,
pursuing. Bless ye the [ones] persecuting,

εὐλογεῖτε καὶ μὴ καταρᾶσθε. 15 χαίρειν
bless and do not curse. To rejoice

μετὰ χαιρόντων, κλαίειν μετὰ κλαιόντων.
with rejoicing [ones], to weep with weeping [ones].

16 τὸ αὐτὸ εἰς ἀλλήλους φρονοῦντες· μὴ
The same thing toward one another minding; not

τὰ ὑψηλὰ φρονοῦντες ἀλλὰ τοῖς ταπεινοῖς
[2]the [3]high things [1]minding but to the humble

συναπαγόμενοι. μὴ γίνεσθε φρόνιμοι παρ'
condescending. Become not wise with

ἑαυτοῖς. 17 μηδενὶ κακὸν ἀντὶ κακοῦ
yourselves. To no one evil instead of evil

ἀποδιδόντες· προνοούμενοι καλὰ ἐνώπιον
returning; providing for good things before

πάντων ἀνθρώπων· 18 εἰ δυνατόν, τὸ ἐξ
all men; if possible, as far as it

ὑμῶν, μετὰ πάντων ἀνθρώπων εἰρηνεύοντες·
rests with you,† with all men seeking peace;

19 μὴ ἑαυτοὺς ἐκδικοῦντες, ἀγαπητοί, ἀλλὰ
not [2]yourselves [1]avenging, beloved, but

δότε τόπον τῇ ὀργῇ· γέγραπται γάρ·
give place – to wrath; for it has been written:

ἐμοὶ ἐκδίκησις, ἐγὼ ἀνταποδώσω, λέγει
To me vengeance,[c] =Vengeance is mine, I will repay, says

κύριος. 20 ἀλλὰ ἐὰν πεινᾷ ὁ ἐχθρός
[the] Lord. But if hungers the enemy

σου, ψώμιζε αὐτόν· ἐὰν διψᾷ, πότιζε
of thee, feed him; if he thirsts, give [2]drink

αὐτόν· τοῦτο γὰρ ποιῶν ἄνθρακας πυρὸς
[1]him; for this doing coals of fire

σωρεύσεις ἐπὶ τὴν κεφαλὴν αὐτοῦ. 21 μὴ
thou wilt heap on the head of him. not

νικῶ ὑπὸ τοῦ κακοῦ, ἀλλὰ νίκα
Be conquered by the evil, but conquer

ἐν τῷ ἀγαθῷ τὸ κακόν. 13 Πᾶσα
[3]by [4]the [5]good [1]the [2]evil. [2]Every

ψυχὴ ἐξουσίαις ὑπερεχούσαις ὑποτασσέσθω.
[3]soul [7]authorities [6]to superior [1]let [4]be [5]subject.

οὐ γὰρ ἔστιν ἐξουσία εἰ μὴ
For there is no authority except

ὑπὸ θεοῦ, αἱ δὲ οὖσαι ὑπὸ θεοῦ
by God, and the existing [ones] by God

it is showing mercy, let him
do it cheerfully.

Love

9Love must be sincere.
Hate what is evil; cling to
what is good. 10Be devoted
to one another in brotherly
love. Honor one another
above yourselves. 11Never
be lacking in zeal, but keep
your spiritual fervor, serving the Lord. 12Be joyful in
hope, patient in affliction,
faithful in prayer. 13Share
with God's people who are
in need. Practice hospitality.

14Bless those who perse-
cute you; bless and do not
curse. 15Rejoice with those
who rejoice; mourn with
those who mourn. 16Live in
harmony with one another.
Do not be proud, but be
willing to associate with
people of low position.[z]
Do not be conceited.

17Do not repay anyone
evil for evil. Be careful to
do what is right in the eyes
of everybody. 18If it is possible, as far as it depends on
you, live at peace with everyone. 19Do not take re-
venge, my friends, but
leave room for God's
wrath, for it is written: "It
is mine to avenge; I will repay,"[a] says the Lord. 20On
the contrary:

"If your enemy is
hungry, feed him;
if he is thirsty, give him
something to drink.
In doing this, you will
heap burning coals
on his head."[b]

21Do not be overcome by
evil, but overcome evil
with good.

Chapter 13

Submission to the Authorities

EVERYONE must submit himself to the governing authorities, for there is no authority except that which God has established.

[z]16 Or *willing to do menial work*
[a]19 Deut. 32:35
[b]20 Prov. 25:21,22

exist are established by God.

2 Therefore he who resists authority has opposed the ordinance of God; and they who have opposed will receive condemnation upon themselves.

3 For rulers are not a cause of fear for good behavior, but for evil. Do you want to have no fear of authority? Do what is good, and you will have praise from the same;

4 for it is a minister of God to you for good. But if you do what is evil, be afraid; for it does not bear the sword for nothing; for it is a minister of God, an avenger who brings wrath upon the one who practices evil.

5 Wherefore it is necessary to be in subjection, not only because of wrath, but also for conscience' sake.

6 For because of this you also pay taxes, for *rulers* are servants of God, devoting themselves to this very thing.

7 Render to all what is due them: tax to whom tax *is due;* custom to whom custom; fear to whom fear; honor to whom honor.

8 Owe nothing to anyone except to love one another; for he who loves his neighbor has fulfilled *the* law.

9 For this, "YOU SHALL NOT COMMIT ADULTERY, YOU SHALL NOT MURDER, YOU SHALL NOT STEAL, YOU SHALL NOT COVET," and if there is any other commandment, it is summed up in this saying, "YOU SHALL LOVE YOUR NEIGHBOR AS YOURSELF."

10 Love does no wrong to a neighbor; love therefore is the fulfillment of *the* law.

τεταγμέναι εἰσίν. 2 ὥστε ὁ ἀντιτασσόμενος
having been ordained are. So the [one] resisting

τῇ ἐξουσίᾳ τῇ τοῦ θεοῦ διαταγῇ ἀνθέστη-
the authority [2]the – [4]of God [3]ordinance [1]has op-

κεν· οἱ δὲ ἀνθεστηκότες ἑαυτοῖς κρίμα
posed; and the [ones] having opposed to themselves judgment

λήμψονται. 3 οἱ γὰρ ἄρχοντες οὐκ εἰσὶν
will receive. For the rulers are not

φόβος τῷ ἀγαθῷ ἔργῳ ἀλλὰ τῷ κακῷ.
a fear to the good work but to the evil.

θέλεις δὲ μὴ φοβεῖσθαι τὴν ἐξουσίαν;
And wishest thou not to fear the authority?

τὸ ἀγαθὸν ποίει, καὶ ἕξεις ἔπαινον ἐξ
[2]the [3]good [1]do, and thou wilt have praise from

αὐτῆς· 4 θεοῦ γὰρ διάκονός ἐστιν σοὶ
it; for of God a minister he is to thee

εἰς τὸ ἀγαθόν. ἐὰν δὲ τὸ κακὸν ποιῇς,
for the good. But if the evil thou doest,

φοβοῦ· οὐ γὰρ εἰκῇ τὴν μάχαιραν φορεῖ·
fear; for not in vain the sword he bears;

θεοῦ γὰρ διάκονός ἐστιν ἔκδικος εἰς
for of God a minister he is an avenger for

ὀργὴν τῷ τὸ κακὸν πράσσοντι. 5 διὸ
wrath to the [one] [2]the [3]evil [1]practising. Wherefore

ἀνάγκη ὑποτάσσεσθαι, οὐ μόνον διὰ τὴν
it is necessary to be subject, not only because of –

ὀργὴν ἀλλὰ καὶ διὰ τὴν συνείδησιν.
wrath but also because of – conscience.

6 διὰ τοῦτο γὰρ καὶ φόρους τελεῖτε·
For therefore also taxes pay ye;

λειτουργοὶ γὰρ θεοῦ εἰσιν εἰς αὐτὸ τοῦτο
for ministers of God they are for this very thing

προσκαρτεροῦντες. 7 ἀπόδοτε πᾶσιν τὰς
attending constantly. Render to all men the

ὀφειλάς, τῷ τὸν φόρον τὸν φόρον,
dues, to the [one] the tax the tax,*

τῷ τὸ τέλος τὸ τέλος, τῷ τὸν φόβον
to the [one] the tribute the tribute, to the [one] *the* fear

τὸν φόβον, τῷ τὴν τιμὴν τὴν τιμήν.
the fear, to the [one] *the* honour *the* honour.

8 Μηδενὶ μηδὲν ὀφείλετε, εἰ μὴ τὸ
To no one no(any)thing owe ye, except –

ἀλλήλους ἀγαπᾶν· ὁ γὰρ ἀγαπῶν τὸν
one another to love; for the [one] loving the

ἕτερον νόμον πεπλήρωκεν. 9 τὸ γὰρ
other law has fulfilled. – For

οὐ μοιχεύσεις, οὐ φονεύσεις, οὐ κλέψεις,
Thou shalt not commit adultery, Thou shalt not kill, Thou shalt not steal,

οὐκ ἐπιθυμήσεις, καὶ εἴ τις ἑτέρα ἐντολή,
Thou shalt not covet, and if any [there is] other commandment,

ἐν τῷ λόγῳ τούτῳ ἀνακεφαλαιοῦται, [ἐν
[2]in [3]this [4]word [1]it is summed up, in

τῷ]· ἀγαπήσεις τὸν πλησίον σου ὡς
– : Thou shalt love the neighbour of thee as

σεαυτόν. 10 ἡ ἀγάπη τῷ πλησίον κακὸν
thyself. – Love [3]to the (one's) [4]neighbour [2]evil

οὐκ ἐργάζεται· πλήρωμα οὖν νόμου ἡ
[1]works not; [3][is] [4]fulfilment [1]therefore [5]of law –

* The phrase between the commas is elliptical; understand—to the [one demanding] the tax [render] the tax. So of the following phrases.

The authorities that exist have been established by God. 2 Consequently, he who rebels against the authority is rebelling against what God has instituted, and those who do so will bring judgment on themselves. 3 For rulers hold no terror for those who do right, but for those who do wrong. Do you want to be free from fear of the one in authority? Then do what is right and he will commend you. 4 For he is God's servant to do you good. But if you do wrong, be afraid, for he does not bear the sword for nothing. He is God's servant, an agent of wrath to bring punishment on the wrongdoer. 5 Therefore, it is necessary to submit to the authorities, not only because of possible punishment but also because of conscience.

6 This is also why you pay taxes, for the authorities are God's servants, who give their full time to governing. 7 Give everyone what you owe him: If you owe taxes, pay taxes; if revenue, then revenue; if respect, then respect; if honor, then honor.

Love, for the Day Is Near

8 Let no debt remain outstanding, except the continuing debt to love one another, for he who loves his fellowman has fulfilled the law. 9 The commandments, "Do not commit adultery," "Do not murder," "Do not steal," "Do not covet,"[c] and whatever other commandment there may be, are summed up in this one rule: "Love your neighbor as yourself."[d] 10 Love does no harm to its neighbor. Therefore love is the fulfillment of the law.

c9 Exodus 20:13-15,17; Deut. 5:17-19,21
d9 Lev. 19:18

11 And this *do,* knowing
the time, that it is already
the hour for you to awaken
from sleep; for now [p] salvation is nearer to us than
when we believed.
12 The night is almost
gone, and the day is at
hand. Let us therefore lay
aside the deeds of darkness
and put on the armor of
light.
13 Let us behave properly
as in the day, not in carousing and drunkenness, not in
sexual promiscuity and
sensuality, not in strife and
jealousy.
14 But put on the Lord
Jesus Christ, and make no
provision for the flesh in regard to *its* lusts.

Chapter 14

Principles of Conscience

NOW accept the one
who is weak in faith,
but not for *the purpose of*
passing judgment on his
opinions.
2 One man has faith that
he may eat all things, but he
who is weak eats vegeta-
bles *only.*
3 Let not him who eats regard with contempt him
who does not eat, and let
not him who does not eat
judge him who eats, for
God has accepted him.
4 Who are you to judge
the servant of another? To
his own master he stands or
falls; and stand he will, for
the Lord is able to make
him stand.
5 One man regards one
day above another, another
regards every day *alike.*
Let each man be fully convinced in his own mind.
6 He who observes the
day, observes it for the
Lord, and he who eats,
does so for the Lord, for he
gives thanks to God; and he
who eats not, for the Lord

[p] Or, *our salvation is nearer than when*

ἀγάπη. 11 Καὶ τοῦτο εἰδότες τὸν καιρόν,
[2]love. And this[,] knowing the time,

ὅτι ὥρα ἤδη ὑμᾶς ἐξ ὕπνου ἐγερθῆναι·
that hour now you out of sleep to be raised;[b]
=it is now an hour for you to be raised out of sleep;

νῦν γὰρ ἐγγύτερον ἡμῶν ἡ σωτηρία
for now nearer [is] of us the salvation

ἢ ὅτε ἐπιστεύσαμεν. 12 ἡ νὺξ προέκοψεν,
than when we believed. The night advanced,

ἡ δὲ ἡμέρα ἤγγικεν. ἀποθώμεθα οὖν
and the day has drawn near. Let us cast off therefore

τὰ ἔργα τοῦ σκότους, ἐνδυσώμεθα δὲ
the works of the darkness, and let us put on

τὰ ὅπλα τοῦ φωτός. 13 ὡς ἐν ἡμέρᾳ
the weapons of the light. As in [the] day

εὐσχημόνως περιπατήσωμεν, μὴ κώμοις καὶ
becomingly let us walk, not in revellings and

μέθαις, μὴ κοίταις καὶ ἀσελγείαις, μὴ
in drunken bouts, not in beds* and excesses, not

ἔριδι καὶ ζήλῳ· 14 ἀλλὰ ἐνδύσασθε τὸν
in strife and *in* jealousy; but put ye on the

κύριον Ἰησοῦν Χριστόν, καὶ τῆς σαρκὸς
Lord Jesus Christ, and of the flesh

πρόνοιαν μὴ ποιεῖσθε εἰς ἐπιθυμίας.
forethought make not for [its] lusts.

14 Τὸν δὲ ἀσθενοῦντα τῇ πίστει
Now the [one] being weak in the faith

προσλαμβάνεσθε, μὴ εἰς διακρίσεις διαλογισ-
receive ye, not to judgments of

μῶν. 2 ὃς μὲν πιστεύει φαγεῖν πάντα,
thoughts. One man† indeed believes to eat all things,

ὁ δὲ ἀσθενῶν λάχανα ἐσθίει. 3 ὁ ἐσθίων
but the [one] being weak herbs eats. [3]The [one] [4]eating

τὸν μὴ ἐσθίοντα μὴ ἐξουθενείτω, ὁ δὲ
[6]the [one] [7]not [8]eating [2]not [1]let [5]despise, and [3]the [one]

μὴ ἐσθίων τὸν ἐσθίοντα μὴ κρινέτω,
[4]not [5]eating [7]the [one] [8]eating [2]not [1]let [6]judge,

ὁ θεὸς· γὰρ αὐτὸν προσελάβετο. 4 σὺ
– for God him received. [3]Thou

τίς εἶ ὁ κρίνων ἀλλότριον οἰκέτην; τῷ
[1]who [2]art [4]the [one] [5]judging [7]belonging to another [6]a *household* servant? to the(his)

ἰδίῳ κυρίῳ στήκει ἢ πίπτει· σταθήσεται
own lord he stands or falls; [2]he will stand

δέ, δυνατεῖ γὰρ ὁ κύριος στῆσαι αὐτόν.
[1]but, for is able the Lord to stand him.

5 ὃς μὲν [γὰρ] κρίνει ἡμέραν παρ'
one man† indeed judges a day above

ἡμέραν, ὃς δὲ κρίνει πᾶσαν ἡμέραν·
a day, another† judges every day;

ἕκαστος ἐν τῷ ἰδίῳ νοῒ πληροφορείσθω.
each man in the(his) own mind let him be fully persuaded.

6 ὁ φρονῶν τὴν ἡμέραν κυρίῳ φρονεῖ.
The [one] minding the day to [the] Lord he minds [it].

καὶ ὁ ἐσθίων κυρίῳ ἐσθίει, εὐχαριστεῖ γὰρ
And the [one] eating to [the] Lord he eats, for he gives thanks

τῷ θεῷ· καὶ ὁ μὴ ἐσθίων κυρίῳ
– to God; and the [one] not eating to [the] Lord

* That is, illicit sexual intercourse.

11 And do this, under-
standing the present time.
The hour has come for you
to wake up from your slumber, because our salvation
is nearer now than when we
first believed. 12 The night is
nearly over; the day is almost here. So let us put
aside the deeds of darkness
and put on the armor of
light. 13 Let us behave de-
cently, as in the daytime,
not in orgies and drunkenness, not in sexual immo-
rality and debauchery, not
in dissension and jealousy.
14 Rather, clothe yourselves
with the Lord Jesus Christ,
and do not think about how
to gratify the desires of the
sinful nature.[e]

Chapter 14

The Weak and the Strong

ACCEPT him whose faith
is weak, without pass-
ing judgment on disputable
matters. 2 One man's faith
allows him to eat every-
thing, but another man,
whose faith is weak, eats
only vegetables. 3 The man
who eats everything must
not look down on him who
does not, and the man who
does not eat everything
must not condemn the man
who does, for God has ac-
cepted him. 4 Who are you
to judge someone else's
servant? To his own master
he stands or falls. And he
will stand, for the Lord is
able to make him stand.
5 One man considers one
day more sacred than an-
other; another man considers every day alike. Each
one should be fully con-
vinced in his own mind.
6 He who regards one day as
special, does so to the
Lord. He who eats meat,
eats to the Lord, for he
gives thanks to God; and he
who abstains, does so to

[e] 14 Or *the flesh*

he does not eat, and gives thanks to God.
7For not one of us lives for himself, and not one dies for himself;
8for if we live, we live for the Lord, or if we die, we die for the Lord; therefore whether we live or die, we are the Lord's.
9For to this end Christ died and lived *again,* that He might be Lord both of the dead and of the living.
10But you, why do you judge your brother? Or you again, why do you regard your brother with contempt? For we shall all stand before the judgment seat of God.
11For it is written,
"AS I LIVE, SAYS THE LORD, EVERY KNEE SHALL BOW TO ME,
AND EVERY TONGUE SHALL GIVE PRAISE TO GOD."
12So then each one of us shall give account of himself to God.
13Therefore let us not judge one another anymore, but rather determine this—not to put an obstacle or a stumbling block in a brother's way.
14I know and am convinced in the Lord Jesus that nothing is unclean in itself; but to him who thinks anything to be unclean, to him it is unclean.
15For if because of food your brother is hurt, you are no longer walking according to love. Do not destroy with your food him for whom Christ died.
16Therefore do not let what is for you a good thing be spoken of as evil;
17for the kingdom of God is not eating and drinking, but righteousness and peace and joy in the Holy Spirit.
18For he who in this *way* serves Christ is acceptable

οὐκ ἐσθίει, καὶ εὐχαριστεῖ τῷ θεῷ.
he eats not, and gives thanks – to God.
7 οὐδεὶς γὰρ ἡμῶν ἑαυτῷ ζῇ, καὶ οὐδεὶς
For no one of us to himself lives, and no one
ἑαυτῷ ἀποθνήσκει· 8 ἐάν τε γὰρ ζῶμεν,
to himself dies; for whether we live,
τῷ κυρίῳ ζῶμεν, ἐάν τε ἀποθνήσκωμεν,
to the Lord we live, or if we die,
τῷ κυρίῳ ἀποθνήσκομεν. ἐάν τε οὖν
to the Lord we die. Whether therefore
ζῶμεν ἐάν τε ἀποθνήσκωμεν, τοῦ κυρίου
we live or if we die, of the Lord
ἐσμέν. 9 εἰς τοῦτο γὰρ Χριστὸς ἀπέθανεν
we are. for this For Christ died
καὶ ἔζησεν, ἵνα καὶ νεκρῶν καὶ ζώντων
and lived [again], in order that both of dead and of living [ones]
κυριεύσῃ. 10 σὺ δὲ τί κρίνεις τὸν ἀδελφόν
he might be Lord. [3]thou And [1]why [2]judgest the brother
σου; ἢ καὶ σὺ τί ἐξουθενεῖς τὸν ἀδελφόν
of thee? or [2]indeed [4]thou [1]why [3]despisest the brother
σου; πάντες γὰρ παραστησόμεθα τῷ
of thee? for all we shall stand before the
βήματι τοῦ θεοῦ. 11 γέγραπται γάρ·
tribunal – of God. For it has been written:
ζῶ ἐγώ, λέγει κύριος, ὅτι ἐμοὶ κάμψει
Live I, says [the] Lord, that to me will bend
πᾶν γόνυ, καὶ πᾶσα γλῶσσα ἐξομολογήσεται
every knee, and every tongue will confess
τῷ θεῷ. 12 ἄρα [οὖν] ἕκαστος ἡμῶν
– to God. So therefore each one of us
περὶ ἑαυτοῦ λόγον δώσει [τῷ θεῷ].
concerning himself account will give – to God.
13 Μηκέτι οὖν ἀλλήλους κρίνωμεν· ἀλλὰ
No longer therefore one another let us judge; but
τοῦτο κρίνατε μᾶλλον, τὸ μὴ τιθέναι
this judge ye rather, – not to put
πρόσκομμα τῷ ἀδελφῷ ἢ σκάνδαλον.
a stumbling-block to the brother or an offence.
14 οἶδα καὶ πέπεισμαι ἐν κυρίῳ Ἰησοῦ
I know and have been persuaded by [the] Lord Jesus
ὅτι οὐδὲν κοινὸν δι' ἑαυτοῦ· εἰ μὴ
that nothing [is] common through itself; except
τῷ λογιζομένῳ τι κοινὸν εἶναι, ἐκείνῳ
to the [one] reckoning anything common to be, to that man [it is]
κοινόν. 15 εἰ γὰρ διὰ βρῶμα ὁ ἀδελφός
common. For if because of food the brother
σου λυπεῖται, οὐκέτι κατὰ ἀγάπην
of thee is grieved, no longer according to love
περιπατεῖς. μὴ τῷ βρώματί σου ἐκεῖνον
thou walkest. [2]Not [3]by the [4]food [5]of thee [6]that man
ἀπόλλυε, ὑπὲρ οὗ Χριστὸς ἀπέθανεν.
[1]destroy, on behalf of whom Christ died.
16 μὴ βλασφημείσθω οὖν ὑμῶν τὸ ἀγαθόν.
Let not be blasphemed therefore of you the good.
17 οὐ γάρ ἐστιν ἡ βασιλεία τοῦ θεοῦ
For not is the kingdom – of God
βρῶσις καὶ πόσις, ἀλλὰ δικαιοσύνη καὶ
eating and drinking, but righteousness and
εἰρήνη καὶ χαρὰ ἐν πνεύματι ἁγίῳ·
peace and joy in [the] Spirit Holy;
18 ὁ γὰρ ἐν τούτῳ δουλεύων τῷ Χριστῷ
for the [one] in this serving – Christ

the Lord and gives thanks
to God. 7For none of us
lives to himself alone and
none of us dies to himself
alone. 8If we live, we live to
the Lord; and if we die, we
die to the Lord. So, whether we live or die, we belong
to the Lord.
9For this very reason,
Christ died and returned to
life so that he might be the
Lord of both the dead and
the living. 10You, then,
why do you judge your
brother? Or why do you
look down on your broth-
er? For we will all stand before God's judgment seat.
11It is written:

"'As surely as I live,'
says the Lord,
'every knee will bow
before me;
every tongue will
confess to God.'"[f]

12So then, each of us will
give an account of himself
to God.
13Therefore let us stop
passing judgment on one
another. Instead, make up
your mind not to put any
stumbling block or obstacle
in your brother's way. 14As
one who is in the Lord
Jesus, I am fully convinced
that no food[g] is unclean in
itself. But if anyone regards
something as unclean, then
for him it is unclean. 15If
your brother is distressed
because of what you eat,
you are no longer acting in
love. Do not by your eating
destroy your brother for
whom Christ died. 16Do not
allow what you consider
good to be spoken of as
evil. 17For the kingdom of
God is not a matter of eating and drinking, but of
righteousness, peace and
joy in the Holy Spirit, 18be-
cause anyone who serves

[f]11 Isaiah 45:23
[g]14 Or *that nothing*

to God and approved by
men.
19So then [q]let us pursue
the things which make for
peace and the building up
of one another.
20Do not tear down the
work of God for the sake of
food. All things indeed are
clean, but they are evil for
the man who eats and gives
offense.
21It is good not to eat
meat or to drink wine, or *to*
do anything by which your
brother stumbles.
22The faith which you
have, have as your own
conviction before God.
Happy is he who does not
condemn himself in what
he approves.
23But he who doubts is
condemned if he eats, be-
cause *his eating is* not from
faith; and whatever is not
from faith is sin.

εὐάρεστος τῷ θεῷ καὶ δόκιμος τοῖς
[is] well-pleasing – to God and approved –
ἀνθρώποις. **19** ἄρα οὖν τὰ τῆς εἰρήνης
by men. So therefore the things – of peace
διώκωμεν καὶ τὰ τῆς οἰκοδομῆς τῆς
let us pursue and the things – of building [up] –
εἰς ἀλλήλους. **20** μὴ ἕνεκεν βρώματος
for one another. Not for the sake of food
κατάλυε τὸ ἔργον τοῦ θεοῦ. πάντα
undo thou the work – of God. All things
μὲν καθαρά, ἀλλὰ κακὸν τῷ ἀνθρώπῳ
indeed [are] clean, but evil to the man
τῷ διὰ προσκόμματος ἐσθίοντι. **21** καλὸν
– [2]through [3]a stumbling-block [1]eating. Good [it is]
τὸ μὴ φαγεῖν κρέα μηδὲ πιεῖν οἶνον
– not to eat flesh nor to drink wine
μηδὲ ἐν ᾧ ὁ ἀδελφός σου προσκόπτει.
nor [anything] by which the brother of thee stumbles.
22 σὺ πίστιν ἣν ἔχεις κατὰ σεαυτὸν
[3]Thou [1]faith [2]which [4]hast [6]by [7]thyself
ἔχε ἐνώπιον τοῦ θεοῦ. μακάριος ὁ
[5]have before – God. Blessed the [one]
μὴ κρίνων ἑαυτὸν ἐν ᾧ δοκιμάζει·
not judging himself in what he approves;
23 ὁ δὲ διακρινόμενος ἐὰν φάγῃ κατα-
but the [one] doubting if he eats has been
κέκριται, ὅτι οὐκ ἐκ πίστεως· πᾶν
condemned, because not of faith; [2]all
δὲ ὃ οὐκ ἐκ πίστεως ἁμαρτία ἐστίν.
[1]and which [is] not of faith sin is.

Christ in this way is pleasing to God and approved by
men.
19Let us therefore make
every effort to do what
leads to peace and to mutual edification. 20Do not destroy the work of God for
the sake of food. All food is
clean, but it is wrong for a
man to eat anything that
causes someone else to
stumble. 21It is better not to
eat meat or drink wine or to
do anything else that will
cause your brother to fall.
22So whatever you be-
lieve about these things
keep between yourself and
God. Blessed is the man
who does not condemn
himself by what he ap-
proves. 23But the man who
has doubts is condemned if
he eats, because his eating
is not from faith; and everything that does not come
from faith is sin.

Chapter 15

Self-denial on Behalf of Others

NOW we who are strong
ought to bear the
weaknesses of those with-
out strength and not *just*
please ourselves.
2Let each of us please his
neighbor for his good, to
his edification.
3For even Christ did not
please Himself; but as it is
written, "THE REPROACHES
OF THOSE WHO REPROACHED
THEE FELL UPON ME."
4For whatever was writ-
ten in earlier times was
written for our instruction,
that through perseverance
and the encouragement of
the Scriptures we might
have hope.
5Now may the God who
gives perseverance and encouragement grant you to
be of the same mind with
one another according to
Christ Jesus;
6that with one accord
you may with one voice

15 Ὀφείλομεν δὲ ἡμεῖς οἱ δυνατοὶ τὰ
[5]Ought [1]so [2]we [3]the [4]strong [7]the
ἀσθενήματα τῶν ἀδυνάτων βαστάζειν, καὶ
[8]weaknesses [9]of the [10]not strong [6]to bear, and
μὴ ἑαυτοῖς ἀρέσκειν. **2** ἕκαστος ἡμῶν
not [our]selves to please. Each one of us
τῷ πλησίον ἀρεσκέτω εἰς τὸ ἀγαθὸν
the(his) neighbour let him please for – good
πρὸς οἰκοδομήν· **3** καὶ γὰρ ὁ Χριστὸς
to building [up]; for even – Christ
οὐχ ἑαυτῷ ἤρεσεν· ἀλλὰ καθὼς γέ-
[2]not [3]himself [1]pleased; but as it has
γραπται· οἱ ὀνειδισμοὶ τῶν ὀνειδιζόντων
been written: The reproaches of the [ones] reproaching
σε ἐπέπεσαν ἐπ' ἐμέ. **4** ὅσα γὰρ
thee fell *on* on me. For whatever things
προεγράφη, εἰς τὴν ἡμετέραν διδασκαλίαν
were previously written, for – our teaching
ἐγράφη, ἵνα διὰ τῆς ὑπομονῆς καὶ
were written, in order that through – patience and
διὰ τῆς παρακλήσεως τῶν γραφῶν τὴν
through the comfort of the writings –
ἐλπίδα ἔχωμεν. **5** ὁ δὲ θεὸς τῆς ὑπομονῆς
hope we may have. And the God – of patience
καὶ τῆς παρακλήσεως δῴη ὑμῖν τὸ
and – of comfort give to you [2]the
αὐτὸ φρονεῖν ἐν ἀλλήλοις κατὰ Χριστὸν
[3]same thing [1]to mind among one another according to Christ
Ἰησοῦν, **6** ἵνα ὁμοθυμαδὸν ἐν ἑνὶ στόματι
Jesus, in order that with one accord with one mouth

Chapter 15

WE who are strong
ought to bear with
the failings of the weak and
not to please ourselves.
2Each of us should please
his neighbor for his good,
to build him up. 3For even
Christ did not please himself but, as it is written:
"The insults of those who
insult you have fallen on
me."[h] 4For everything that
was written in the past was
written to teach us, so that
through endurance and the
encouragement of the
Scriptures we might have
hope.
5May the God who gives
endurance and encourage-
ment give you a spirit of
unity among yourselves as
you follow Christ Jesus,
6so that with one heart and
mouth you may glorify the

[q] Many ancient mss. read *we pursue*

[h] 3 Psalm 69:9

glorify the God and Father
of our Lord Jesus Christ.
7Wherefore, accept one
another, just as Christ also
accepted us to the glory of
God.
8For I say that Christ has
become a servant to the cir-
cumcision on behalf of the
truth of God to confirm the
promises *given* to the fa-
thers,
9and for the Gentiles to
glorify God for His mercy;
as it is written,
"THEREFORE I WILL GIVE
PRAISE TO THEE
AMONG THE GEN-
TILES,
AND I WILL SING TO
THY NAME."
10And again he says,
"REJOICE, O GENTILES,
WITH HIS PEOPLE."
11And again,
"PRAISE THE LORD ALL
YOU GENTILES,
AND LET ALL THE PEO-
PLES PRAISE HIM."
12And again Isaiah says,
"THERE SHALL COME THE
ROOT OF JESSE,
AND HE WHO ARISES TO
RULE OVER THE GEN-
TILES,
IN HIM SHALL THE
GENTILES HOPE."
13Now may the God of
hope fill you with all joy
and peace in believing, that
you may abound in hope by
the power of the Holy
Spirit.
14And concerning you,
my brethren, I myself also
am convinced that you
yourselves are full of goodness, filled with all knowledge, and able also to admonish one another.
15But I have written very
boldly to you on some
points, so as to remind you
again, because of the grace
that was given me from
God,
16to be a minister of

δοξάζητε τὸν θεὸν καὶ πατέρα τοῦ
ye may glorify the God and Father of the
κυρίου ἡμῶν Ἰησοῦ Χριστοῦ.
Lord of us Jesus Christ.
7 Διὸ προσλαμβάνεσθε ἀλλήλους, καθὼς
Wherefore receive ye one another, as
καὶ ὁ Χριστὸς προσελάβετο ἡμᾶς εἰς
also – Christ received us to
δόξαν τοῦ θεοῦ. 8 λέγω γὰρ Χριστὸν
[the] glory – of God. For I say Christ
διάκονον γεγενῆσθαι περιτομῆς ὑπὲρ
a minister to have become of [the] circumcision on behalf of
ἀληθείας θεοῦ, εἰς τὸ βεβαιῶσαι τὰς
[the] truth of God, – – to confirm the
ἐπαγγελίας τῶν πατέρων, 9 τὰ δὲ ἔθνη
promises of the fathers, and [1]the [2]nations
ὑπὲρ ἐλέους δοξάσαι τὸν θεόν, καθὼς
[5]on behalf of [6]mercy [3]to glorify – [4]God, as
γέγραπται· διὰ τοῦτο ἐξομολογήσομαί σοι
it has been written: Therefore I will confess to thee
ἐν ἔθνεσιν καὶ τῷ ὀνόματί σου ψαλῶ.
among nations and to the name of thee I will sing praise.
10 καὶ πάλιν λέγει· εὐφράνθητε, ἔθνη,
And again he says: Be glad, nations,
μετὰ τοῦ λαοῦ αὐτοῦ. 11 καὶ πάλιν·
with the people of him. And again:
αἰνεῖτε, πάντα τὰ ἔθνη, τὸν κύριον,
Praise, all the nations, the Lord,
καὶ ἐπαινεσάτωσαν αὐτὸν πάντες οἱ λαοί.
and let praise him all the peoples.
12 καὶ πάλιν Ἠσαΐας λέγει· ἔσται
And again Esaias says: There shall be
ἡ ῥίζα τοῦ Ἰεσσαί, καὶ ὁ ἀνιστάμενος
the root – of Jesse, and the [one] rising up
ἄρχειν ἐθνῶν· ἐπ᾽ αὐτῷ ἔθνη ἐλπιοῦσιν.
to rule nations; on him nations will hope.
13 Ὁ δὲ θεὸς τῆς ἐλπίδος πληρῶσαι
Now the God – of hope fill
ὑμᾶς πάσης χαρᾶς καὶ εἰρήνης ἐν τῷ
you of(with) all joy and peace in –
πιστεύειν, εἰς τὸ περισσεύειν ὑμᾶς ἐν
to believe (believing), for – to abound you[b] in
τῇ ἐλπίδι ἐν δυνάμει πνεύματος ἁγίου.
– hope by [the] power of [the] Spirit Holy.
14 Πέπεισμαι δέ, ἀδελφοί μου, καὶ
But I have been persuaded, brothers of me, even
αὐτὸς ἐγὼ περὶ ὑμῶν, ὅτι καὶ αὐτοί
[2][my]self [1]I concerning you, that also [your]selves
μεστοί ἐστε ἀγαθωσύνης, πεπληρωμένοι
full ye are of goodness, having been filled
πάσης τῆς γνώσεως, δυνάμενοι καὶ
of(with) all – knowledge, being able also
ἀλλήλους νουθετεῖν. 15 τολμηροτέρως δὲ
one another to admonish. And more daringly
ἔγραψα ὑμῖν ἀπὸ μέρους, ὡς ἐπαναμιμνή-
I wrote to you in part, as remind-
σκων ὑμᾶς διὰ τὴν χάριν τὴν δοθεῖσάν
ing you by the grace – given
μοι ἀπὸ τοῦ θεοῦ 16 εἰς τὸ εἶναί με
to me from – God *for the* to be me[b]
=that I should be

God and Father of our Lord
Jesus Christ.
7Accept one another,
then, just as Christ accepted you, in order to bring
praise to God. 8For I tell
you that Christ has become
a servant of the Jews[i] on
behalf of God's truth, to
confirm the promises made
to the patriarchs 9so that
the Gentiles may glorify
God for his mercy, as it is
written:
"Therefore I will praise
you among the
Gentiles;
I will sing hymns to
your name."[j]
10Again, it says,
"Rejoice, O Gentiles,
with his people."[k]
11And again,
"Praise the Lord, all you
Gentiles,
and sing praises to him,
all you peoples."[l]
12And again, Isaiah says,
"The Root of Jesse will
spring up,
one who will arise to
rule over the
nations;
the Gentiles will hope in
him."[m]
13May the God of hope fill
you with all joy and peace
as you trust in him, so that
you may overflow with
hope by the power of the
Holy Spirit.

Paul the Minister to the Gentiles

14I myself am convinced,
my brothers, that you yourselves are full of goodness,
complete in knowledge and
competent to instruct one
another. 15I have written
you quite boldly on some
points, as if to remind you
of them again, because of
the grace God gave me 16to
be a minister of Christ

[i]8 Greek *circumcision*
[j]9 2 Samuel 22:50; Psalm 18:49
[k]10 Deut. 32:43
[l]11 Psalm 117:1
[m]12 Isaiah 11:10

Christ Jesus to the Gentiles, ministering as a priest the gospel of God, that *my* offering of the Gentiles might become acceptable, sanctified by the Holy Spirit.

17Therefore in Christ Jesus I have found reason for boasting in things pertaining to God.

18For I will not presume to speak of anything except what Christ has accomplished through me, resulting in the obedience of the Gentiles by word and deed,

19in the power of signs and wonders, in the power of the Spirit; so that from Jerusalem and round about as far as Illyricum I have fully preached the gospel of Christ.

20And thus I aspired to preach the gospel, not where Christ was *already* named, that I might not build upon another man's foundation;

21but as it is written,

"THEY WHO HAD NO NEWS OF HIM SHALL SEE,
AND THEY WHO HAVE NOT HEARD SHALL UNDERSTAND."

22For this reason I have often been hindered from coming to you;

23but now, with no further place for me in these regions, and since I have had for many years a longing to come to you

24whenever I go to Spain—for I hope to see you in passing, and to be helped on my way there by you, when I have first enjoyed your company for a while—

25but now, I am going to Jerusalem serving the saints.

26For Macedonia and Achaia have been pleased to make a contribution for

λειτουργὸν Χριστοῦ Ἰησοῦ εἰς τὰ ἔθνη,
a minister of Christ Jesus to the nations,
ἱερουργοῦντα τὸ εὐαγγέλιον τοῦ θεοῦ,
sacrificing the gospel – of God,
ἵνα γένηται ἡ προσφορὰ τῶν ἐθνῶν
in order that [5]may be [1]the [2]offering [3]of the [4]nations
εὐπρόσδεκτος, ἡγιασμένη ἐν πνεύματι
acceptable, having been sanctified by [the] Spirit
ἁγίῳ. 17 ἔχω οὖν τὴν καύχησιν ἐν
Holy. I have therefore the boasting in
Χριστῷ Ἰησοῦ τὰ πρὸς τὸν θεόν· 18 οὐ
Christ Jesus the things with* – God; [4]not
γὰρ τολμήσω τι λαλεῖν ὧν οὐ
[1]for [2]I [3]will [6]dare [7]anything [8]to speak of [the] things which [5]not
κατειργάσατο Χριστὸς δι' ἐμοῦ εἰς ὑπακοὴν
[3]did [4]work [5]out [1]Christ through me for obedience
ἐθνῶν, λόγῳ καὶ ἔργῳ, 19 ἐν δυνάμει
of [the] nations, in word and work, by power
σημείων καὶ τεράτων, ἐν δυνάμει πνεύματος·
of signs and wonders, by power of [the] Spirit;
ὥστε με ἀπὸ Ἰερουσαλὴμ καὶ κύκλῳ
so as me from Jerusalem and around
=I should fulfil the gospel . . . from . . . Illyricum.
μέχρι τοῦ Ἰλλυρικοῦ πεπληρωκέναι τὸ
unto – Illyricum to have fulfilled[b] the
εὐαγγέλιον τοῦ Χριστοῦ. 20 οὕτως δὲ
gospel – of Christ. And so
φιλοτιμούμενον εὐαγγελίζεσθαι οὐχ ὅπου
eagerly striving to evangelize not where
ὠνομάσθη Χριστός, ἵνα μὴ ἐπ' ἀλλότριον
[2]was named [1]Christ, in order that not on [3]belonging to another
θεμέλιον οἰκοδομῶ, 21 ἀλλὰ καθὼς
[1]a foundation I should build, but as
γέγραπται· ὄψονται οἷς οὐκ ἀνηγγέλη
it has been written: They shall see to whom it was not announced
περὶ αὐτοῦ, καὶ οἳ οὐκ ἀκηκόασιν
concerning him, and [those] who have not heard
συνήσουσιν. 22 διὸ καὶ ἐνεκοπτόμην τὰ
will understand. Wherefore also I was hindered –
πολλὰ τοῦ ἐλθεῖν πρὸς ὑμᾶς· 23 νυνὶ
many(much) – to come[d] to you; [2]now
δὲ μηκέτι τόπον ἔχων ἐν τοῖς κλίμασι
[1]but no longer [2]place [1]having in – [2]regions
τούτοις, ἐπιποθίαν δὲ ἔχων τοῦ ἐλθεῖν
[1]these, and [2]a desire [1]having – to come[d]
πρὸς ὑμᾶς ἀπὸ ἱκανῶν ἐτῶν, 24 ὡς ἂν
to you from several years, whenever
πορεύωμαι εἰς τὴν Σπανίαν· ἐλπίζω γὰρ
I journey to – Spain; for I hope
διαπορευόμενος θεάσασθαι ὑμᾶς καὶ ὑφ'
journeying through to behold you and by
ὑμῶν προπεμφθῆναι ἐκεῖ, ἐὰν ὑμῶν πρῶτον
you to be set forward there, if of(with) you firstly
ἀπὸ μέρους ἐμπλησθῶ, 25 — νυνὶ δὲ
in part I may be filled, — but now
πορεύομαι εἰς Ἰερουσαλὴμ διακονῶν τοῖς
I am going to Jerusalem ministering to the
ἁγίοις. 26 ηὐδόκησαν γὰρ Μακεδονία καὶ
saints. For thought it good Macedonia and
Ἀχαΐα κοινωνίαν τινὰ ποιήσασθαι εἰς
Achaia [3]contribution [2]some [1]to make for

* That is, the things that have to do with . . .

Jesus to the Gentiles with
the priestly duty of pro-
claiming the gospel of God,
so that the Gentiles might
become an offering acceptable to God, sanctified by
the Holy Spirit.
17Therefore I glory in
Christ Jesus in my service
to God. 18I will not venture
to speak of anything except
what Christ has accom-
plished through me in leading the Gentiles to obey
God by what I have said
and done— 19by the power
of signs and miracles,
through the power of the
Spirit. So from Jerusalem
all the way around to Illyricum, I have fully pro-
claimed the gospel of
Christ. 20It has always been
my ambition to preach the
gospel where Christ was
not known, so that I would
not be building on someone
else's foundation. 21Rath-
er, as it is written:

"Those who were not told about him will see,
and those who have not heard will understand."[n]

22This is why I have often
been hindered from coming
to you.

Paul's Plan to Visit Rome

23But now that there is no
more place for me to work
in these regions, and since I
have been longing for many
years to see you, 24I plan to
do so when I go to Spain. I
hope to visit you while
passing through and to
have you assist me on my
journey there, after I have
enjoyed your company for
a while. 25Now, however, I
am on my way to Jerusalem
in the service of the saints
there. 26For Macedonia
and Achaia were pleased to
make a contribution for the

[n]21 Isaiah 52:15

the poor among the saints in Jerusalem.

27 Yes, they were pleased *to do so,* and they are indebted to them. For if the Gentiles have shared in their spiritual things, they are indebted to minister to them also in material things.

28 Therefore, when I have finished this, and have put my seal on this fruit of theirs, I will go on by way of you to Spain.

29 And I know that when I come to you, I will come in the fulness of the blessing of Christ.

30 Now I urge you, brethren, by our Lord Jesus Christ and by the love of the Spirit, to strive together with me in your prayers to God for me,

31 that I may be delivered from those who are disobedient in Judea, and *that* my service for Jerusalem may prove acceptable to the saints;

32 so that I may come to you in joy by the will of God and find *refreshing* rest in your company.

33 Now the God of peace be with you all. Amen.

τοὺς πτωχοὺς τῶν ἁγίων τῶν ἐν Ἰερου-
the poor of the saints – in Jeru-
σαλήμ. **27** ηὐδόκησαν γάρ, καὶ ὀφειλέται
salem. For they thought it good, and debtors
εἰσὶν αὐτῶν· εἰ γὰρ τοῖς πνευματικοῖς
they are of them; for if in the spiritual things
αὐτῶν ἐκοινώνησαν τὰ ἔθνη, ὀφείλουσιν
of them [3]shared [1]the [2]nations, they ought
καὶ ἐν τοῖς σαρκικοῖς λειτουργῆσαι αὐτοῖς.
also in the fleshly things to minister to them.
28 τοῦτο οὖν ἐπιτελέσας, καὶ σφραγισάμενος
This therefore having completed, and having sealed
αὐτοῖς τὸν καρπὸν τοῦτον, **29** ἀπελεύσομαι
to them this fruit, I will go away
δι' ὑμῶν εἰς Σπανίαν· οἶδα δὲ ὅτι
through you to Spain; and I know that
ἐρχόμενος πρὸς ὑμᾶς ἐν πληρώματι
coming to you in [the] fulness
εὐλογίας Χριστοῦ ἐλεύσομαι. **30** Παρακαλῶ
of [the] blessing of Christ I will come. I beseech
δὲ ὑμᾶς, [ἀδελφοί], διὰ τοῦ κυρίου
Now you, brothers, through the Lord
ἡμῶν Ἰησοῦ Χριστοῦ καὶ διὰ τῆς ἀγάπης
of us Jesus Christ and through the love
τοῦ πνεύματος, συναγωνίσασθαί μοι ἐν
of the Spirit, to strive with me in
ταῖς προσευχαῖς ὑπὲρ ἐμοῦ πρὸς τὸν
the prayers on behalf of me to –
θεόν, **31** ἵνα ῥυσθῶ ἀπὸ τῶν ἀπειθούντων
God, in order that I may be delivered from the [ones] disobeying
ἐν τῇ Ἰουδαίᾳ καὶ ἡ διακονία μου
in – Judæa and the ministry of me
ἡ εἰς Ἰερουσαλὴμ εὐπρόσδεκτος τοῖς
– to Jerusalem [2]acceptable [3]to the
ἁγίοις γένηται, **32** ἵνα ἐν χαρᾷ ἐλθὼν
[4]saints [1]may be, in order that in joy coming
πρὸς ὑμᾶς διὰ θελήματος θεοῦ συνανα-
to you through [the] will of God I may
παύσωμαι ὑμῖν. **33** ὁ δὲ θεὸς τῆς
rest with you. And the God –
εἰρήνης μετὰ πάντων ὑμῶν· ἀμήν.
of peace [be] with all you: Amen.

poor among the saints in
Jerusalem. 27 They were
pleased to do it, and indeed they owe it to them. For if the Gentiles have shared in the Jews' spiritual blessings, they owe it to the Jews to share with them their material blessings.
28 So after I have completed this task and have made sure that they have received this fruit, I will go to Spain and visit you on the
way. 29 I know that when I come to you, I will come in the full measure of the blessing of Christ.

30 I urge you, brothers, by our Lord Jesus Christ and by the love of the Spirit, to join me in my struggle by praying to God for me.
31 Pray that I may be rescued from the unbelievers in Judea and that my service in Jerusalem may be acceptable to the saints
there, 32 so that by God's will I may come to you with joy and together with you
be refreshed. 33 The God of peace be with you all. Amen.

Chapter 16

Greetings and Love Expressed

I commend to you our sister Phoebe, who is a servant of the church which is at Cenchrea;

2 that you receive her in the Lord in a manner worthy of the saints, and that you help her in whatever matter she may have need of you; for she herself has also been a helper of many, and of myself as well.

3 Greet Prisca and Aquila, my fellow workers in Christ Jesus,

16 Συνίστημι δὲ ὑμῖν Φοίβην τὴν
Now I commend to you Phœbe the
ἀδελφὴν ἡμῶν, οὖσαν [καὶ] διάκονον τῆς
sister of us, being also a minister of the
ἐκκλησίας τῆς ἐν Κεγχρεαῖς, **2** ἵνα
church – in Cenchrea, in order that
αὐτὴν προσδέξησθε ἐν κυρίῳ ἀξίως τῶν
[2]her [1]ye may receive in [the] Lord worthily of the
ἁγίων, καὶ παραστῆτε αὐτῇ ἐν ᾧ ἂν
saints, and may stand by her in [1]whatever
ὑμῶν χρῄζῃ πράγματι· καὶ γὰρ αὐτὴ
[4]of you [3]she may have need [2]thing; for indeed she
προστάτις πολλῶν ἐγενήθη καὶ ἐμοῦ αὐτοῦ.
a protectress of many became and of myself.
3 Ἀσπάσασθε Πρίσκαν καὶ Ἀκύλαν τοὺς
Greet ye Prisca and Aquila the
συνεργούς μου ἐν Χριστῷ Ἰησοῦ, **4** οἵτινες
fellow-workers of me in Christ Jesus, who

Chapter 16

Personal Greetings

I COMMEND to you our sister Phoebe, a servant[o] of the church in Cenchrea.
2 I ask you to receive her in the Lord in a way worthy of the saints and to give her any help she may need from you, for she has been a great help to many people, including me.

3 Greet Priscilla[p] and Aquila, my fellow workers in Christ Jesus.
4 They

[o] 1 Or *deaconess*
[p] 3 Greek *Prisca*, a variant of *Priscilla*

4who for my life risked
their own necks, to whom
not only do I give thanks,
but also all the churches of
the Gentiles;
5also *greet* the church
that is in their house. Greet
Epaenetus, my beloved,
who is the first convert to
Christ from Asia.
6Greet Mary, who has
worked hard for you.
7Greet Andronicus and
Junias, my kinsmen, and
my fellow prisoners, who
are outstanding among the
apostles, who also were in
Christ before me.
8Greet Ampliatus, my
beloved in the Lord.
9Greet Urbanus, our fel-
low worker in Christ, and
Stachys my beloved.
10Greet Apelles, the ap-
proved in Christ. Greet
those who are of the *household* of Aristobulus.
11Greet Herodion, my
kinsman. Greet those of the
household of Narcissus,
who are in the Lord.
12Greet Tryphaena and
Tryphosa, workers in the
Lord. Greet Persis the beloved, who has worked
hard in the Lord.
13Greet Rufus, a choice
man in the Lord, also his
mother and mine.
14Greet Asyncritus, Phle-
gon, Hermes, Patrobas,
Hermas and the brethren
with them.
15Greet Philologus and
Julia, Nereus and his sister,
and Olympas, and all the
saints who are with them.
16Greet one another with
a holy kiss. All the
churches of Christ greet
you.

ὑπὲρ τῆς ψυχῆς μου τὸν ἑαυτῶν τράχηλον
on behalf of the life of me [2]the [4]of themselves [3]neck
ὑπέθηκαν, οἷς οὐκ ἐγὼ μόνος εὐχαριστῶ
[1]risked, to whom not I only give thanks
ἀλλὰ καὶ πᾶσαι αἱ ἐκκλησίαι τῶν ἐθνῶν,
but also all the churches of the nations,
5 καὶ τὴν κατ᾽ οἶκον αὐτῶν ἐκκλησίαν.
and [1]the [3]in [4]house [5]of them [2]church.
ἀσπάσασθε Ἐπαίνετον τὸν ἀγαπητόν μου,
Greet Epænetus the beloved of me,
ὅς ἐστιν ἀπαρχὴ τῆς Ἀσίας εἰς Χριστόν.
who is firstfruit – of Asia for Christ.
6 ἀσπάσασθε Μαρίαν, ἥτις πολλὰ ἐκοπίασεν
Greet Mary, who many things (much) laboured
εἰς ὑμᾶς. 7 ἀσπάσασθε Ἀνδρόνικον καὶ
for you. Greet Andronicus and
Ἰουνιᾶν τοὺς συγγενεῖς μου καὶ συναιχμα-
Junius the kinsmen of me and fellow-
λώτους μου, οἵτινές εἰσιν ἐπίσημοι ἐν
captives of me, who are notable among
τοῖς ἀποστόλοις, οἳ καὶ πρὸ ἐμοῦ γέγοναν
the apostles, who indeed before me have been
ἐν Χριστῷ. 8 ἀσπάσασθε Ἀμπλιᾶτον τὸν
in Christ. Greet Ampliatus the
ἀγαπητόν μου ἐν κυρίῳ. 9 ἀσπάσασθε
beloved of me in [the] Lord. Greet
Οὐρβανὸν τὸν συνεργὸν ἡμῶν ἐν Χριστῷ
Urbanus the fellow-worker of us in Christ
καὶ Στάχυν τὸν ἀγαπητόν μου. 10 ἀσπάσ-
and Stachys the beloved of me. Greet
ασθε Ἀπελλῆν τὸν δόκιμον ἐν Χριστῷ.
Apelles the approved in Christ.
ἀσπάσασθε τοὺς ἐκ τῶν Ἀριστοβούλου.
Greet the [ones] of the [family] of Aristobulus.
11 ἀσπάσασθε Ἡρῳδίωνα τὸν συγγενῆ μου.
Greet Herodion the kinsman of me.
ἀσπάσασθε τοὺς ἐκ τῶν Ναρκίσσου τοὺς
Greet the [ones] of the [family] of Narcissus –
ὄντας ἐν κυρίῳ. 12 ἀσπάσασθε Τρύφαιναν
being in [the] Lord. Greet Tryphæna
καὶ Τρυφῶσαν τὰς κοπιώσας ἐν κυρίῳ.
and Tryphosa the [ones] labouring in [the] Lord.
ἀσπάσασθε Περσίδα τὴν ἀγαπητήν, ἥτις
Greet Persis the beloved, who
πολλὰ ἐκοπίασεν ἐν κυρίῳ. 13 ἀσπάσασθε
many things (much) laboured in [the] Lord. Greet
Ῥοῦφον τὸν ἐκλεκτὸν ἐν κυρίῳ καὶ
Rufus the chosen in [the] Lord and
τὴν μητέρα αὐτοῦ καὶ ἐμοῦ. 14 ἀσπάσασθε
the mother of him and of me. Greet
Ἀσύγκριτον, Φλέγοντα, Ἑρμῆν, Πατροβᾶν,
Asyncritus, Phlegon, Hermes, Patrobas,
Ἑρμᾶν, καὶ τοὺς σὺν αὐτοῖς ἀδελφούς.
Hermas, and the [2]with [3]them [1]brothers.
15 ἀσπάσασθε Φιλόλογον καὶ Ἰουλίαν,
Greet Philologus and Julia,
Νηρέα καὶ τὴν ἀδελφὴν αὐτοῦ, καὶ
Nereus and the sister of him, and
Ὀλυμπᾶν, καὶ τοὺς σὺν αὐτοῖς πάντας
Olympas, and [2]the [4]with [5]them [1]all
ἁγίους. 16 ἀσπάσασθε ἀλλήλους ἐν φιλήματι
[3]saints. Greet one another with kiss
ἁγίῳ. ἀσπάζονται ὑμᾶς αἱ ἐκκλησίαι
a holy. [5]greet [6]you [2]the [3]churches

risked their lives for
me. Not only I but all
the churches of the
Gentiles are grateful to
them.
5Greet also the church
that meets at their
house.
Greet my dear friend
Epenetus, who was the
first convert to Christ
in the province of Asia.
6Greet Mary, who
worked very hard for
you.
7Greet Andronicus and
Junias, my relatives
who have been in pris-
on with me. They are
outstanding among the
apostles, and they were
in Christ before I was.
8Greet Ampliatus, whom
I love in the Lord.
9Greet Urbanus, our fel-
low worker in Christ,
and my dear friend Sta-
chys.
10Greet Apelles, tested
and approved in Christ.
Greet those who belong
to the household of
Aristobulus.
11Greet Herodion, my rel-
ative.
Greet those in the house-
hold of Narcissus who
are in the Lord.
12Greet Tryphena and
Tryphosa, those wom-
en who work hard in
the Lord.
Greet my dear friend
Persis, another woman
who has worked very
hard in the Lord.
13Greet Rufus, chosen in
the Lord, and his moth-
er, who has been a
mother to me, too.
14Greet Asyncritus, Phle-
gon, Hermes, Patro-
bas, Hermas and the
brothers with them.
15Greet Philologus, Julia,
Nereus and his sister,
and Olympas and all
the saints with them.
16Greet one another with a
holy kiss.
All the churches of
Christ send greetings.

17Now I urge you, brethren, keep your eye on those who cause dissensions and hindrances contrary to the teaching which you learned, and turn away from them.
18For such men are slaves, not of our Lord Christ but of their own appetites; and by their smooth and flattering speech they deceive the hearts of the unsuspecting.
19For the report of your obedience has reached to all; therefore I am rejoicing over you, but I want you to be wise in what is good, and innocent in what is evil.
20And the God of peace will soon crush Satan under your feet.
The grace of our Lord Jesus be with you.
21Timothy my fellow worker greets you, and *so do* Lucius and Jason and Sosipater, my kinsmen.
22I, Tertius, who write this letter, greet you in the Lord.
23Gaius, host to me and to the whole church, greets you. Erastus, the city treasurer greets you, and Quartus, the brother.
24[[r]The grace of our Lord Jesus Christ be with you all. Amen.]
25Now to Him who is able to establish you according to my gospel and the preaching of Jesus Christ, according to the revelation of the mystery which has been kept secret for long ages past,
26but now is manifested, and by the Scriptures of the prophets, according to the

[r]Many mss. do not contain this verse

πᾶσαι τοῦ Χριστοῦ.
[1]All – [4]of Christ.

17 Παρακαλῶ δὲ ὑμᾶς, ἀδελφοί, σκοπεῖν
Now I beseech you, brothers, to watch
τοὺς τὰς διχοστασίας καὶ τὰ σκάνδαλα
[1]the [ones] [3]the [4]divisions [5]and [6]the [7]offences
παρὰ τὴν διδαχὴν ἣν ὑμεῖς ἐμάθετε
[8]beside [9]the [10]teaching [11]which [12]ye [13]learned
ποιοῦντας, καὶ ἐκκλίνετε ἀπ' αὐτῶν· 18 οἱ
[2]making, and turn away from them; –
γὰρ τοιοῦτοι τῷ κυρίῳ ἡμῶν Χριστῷ
for such men [3]the [4]Lord [5]of us [2]Christ
οὐ δουλεύουσιν ἀλλὰ τῇ ἑαυτῶν κοιλίᾳ,
[1]serve not but the of themselves belly,
καὶ διὰ τῆς χρηστολογίας καὶ εὐλογίας
and through – fair speech and flattering speech
ἐξαπατῶσιν τὰς καρδίας τῶν ἀκάκων.
deceive the hearts of the guileless.
19 ἡ γὰρ ὑμῶν ὑπακοὴ εἰς πάντας
[2]the [1]For [4]of you [3]obedience [6]to [7]all men
ἀφίκετο· ἐφ' ὑμῖν οὖν χαίρω, θέλω
[5]came; over you therefore I rejoice, [2]I wish
δὲ ὑμᾶς σοφοὺς εἶναι εἰς τὸ ἀγαθόν,
[1]and you wise to be to the good,
ἀκεραίους δὲ εἰς τὸ κακόν. 20 ὁ δὲ
but simple to the evil. And the
θεὸς τῆς εἰρήνης συντρίψει τὸν σατανᾶν
God – of peace will crush – Satan
ὑπὸ τοὺς πόδας ὑμῶν ἐν τάχει.
under the feet of you soon.
Ἡ χάρις τοῦ κυρίου ἡμῶν Ἰησοῦ
The grace of the Lord of us Jesus [be]
μεθ' ὑμῶν.
with you.

21 Ἀσπάζεται ὑμᾶς Τιμόθεος ὁ συνεργός
[5]greets [6]you [1]Timothy [2]the [3]fellow-worker
μου, καὶ Λούκιος καὶ Ἰάσων καὶ
[4]of me, and Lucius and Jason and
Σωσίπατρος οἱ συγγενεῖς μου. 22 ἀσπάζ-
Sosipater the kinsmen of me. [7]greet
ομαι ὑμᾶς ἐγὼ Τέρτιος ὁ γράψας τὴν
[8]you [1]I [2]Tertius [3]the [one] [4]writing [5]the
ἐπιστολὴν ἐν κυρίῳ. 23 ἀσπάζεται ὑμᾶς
[6]epistle in [the] Lord. [9]greets [10]you
Γάϊος ὁ ξένος μου καὶ ὅλης τῆς
[1]Gaius [2]the [3]host [4]of me [5]and [6]of all [7]the
ἐκκλησίας. ἀσπάζεται ὑμᾶς Ἔραστος ὁ
[8]church. [6]greets [7]you [1]Erastus [2]the
οἰκονόμος τῆς πόλεως καὶ Κούαρτος ὁ
[3]treasurer [4]of the [5]city and Quartus the (?his)
ἀδελφός.‡
brother.

25 Τῷ δὲ δυναμένῳ ὑμᾶς στηρίξαι κατὰ
Now to the [one] *being* able [2]you [1]to establish according to
τὸ εὐαγγέλιόν μου καὶ τὸ κήρυγμα
the gospel of me and the proclamation
Ἰησοῦ Χριστοῦ, κατὰ ἀποκάλυψιν μυστηρίου
of Jesus Christ, according to [the] revelation of [the] mystery
χρόνοις αἰωνίοις σεσιγημένου, 26 φανερω-
[2]in times [3]eternal [1]having been kept silent, [2]mani-
θέντος δὲ νῦν διά τε γραφῶν προφητικῶν
fested [1]but now and through writings prophetic

‡ Verse 24 omitted by Nestle; *cf.* NIV footnote.

17I urge you, brothers, to watch out for those who cause divisions and put obstacles in your way that are contrary to the teaching you have learned. Keep away from them.
18For such people are not serving our Lord Christ, but their own appetites. By smooth talk and flattery they deceive the minds of naive people.
19Everyone has heard about your obedience, so I am full of joy over you; but I want you to be wise about what is good, and innocent about what is evil.
20The God of peace will soon crush Satan under your feet.
The grace of our Lord Jesus be with you.
21Timothy, my fellow worker, sends his greetings to you, as do Lucius, Jason and Sosipater, my relatives.
22I, Tertius, who wrote down this letter, greet you in the Lord.
23Gaius, whose hospitality I and the whole church here enjoy, sends you his greetings.
Erastus, who is the city's director of public works, and our brother Quartus send you their greetings.[q]
25Now to him who is able to establish you by my gospel and the proclamation of Jesus Christ, according to the revelation of the mystery hidden for long ages past,
26but now revealed and made known through

[q]23 Some manuscripts *their greetings.* 24*May the grace of our Lord Jesus Christ be with all of you. Amen.*

commandment of the eternal God, has been made known to all the nations, *leading* to obedience of faith;
27to the only wise God, through Jesus Christ, be the glory forever. Amen.

κατ' ἐπιταγὴν τοῦ αἰωνίου θεοῦ εἰς
accord-ing to [the] command of the eternal God [6]for

ὑπακοὴν πίστεως εἰς πάντα τὰ ἔθνη
[7]obedience [8]of faith [2]to [3]all [4]the [5]nations

γνωρισθέντος, 27 μόνῳ σοφῷ θεῷ, διὰ
[1]made known, [2]only [3]wise [1]to God, through

Ἰησοῦ Χριστοῦ, ᾧ ἡ δόξα εἰς τοὺς
Jesus Christ, to whom (him)[c] the glory unto the

αἰῶνας τῶν αἰώνων· ἀμήν.
ages of the ages: Amen.

the prophetic writings by the command of the eternal God, so that all nations might believe and obey him
—27to the only wise God be glory forever through Jesus Christ! Amen.

ΠΡΟΣ ΚΟΡΙΝΘΙΟΥΣ Α
To Corinthians 1

1 Corinthians

Chapter 1

Appeal to Unity

PAUL, called *as* an apostle of Jesus Christ by
the will of God, and Sos-
thenes our brother,
2to the church of God
which is at Corinth, to
those who have been sanc-
tified in Christ Jesus, saints
by calling, with all who in
every place call upon the
name of our Lord Jesus
Christ, their *Lord* and ours:
3Grace to you and peace
from God our Father and
the Lord Jesus Christ.
4I thank [a]my God al-
ways concerning you, for
the grace of God which was
given you in Christ Jesus,
5that in everything you
were enriched in Him, in all
speech and all knowledge,
6even as the testimony
concerning Christ was confirmed in you,
7so that you are not lacking in any gift, awaiting eagerly the revelation of our
Lord Jesus Christ,
8who shall also confirm
you to the end, blameless in
the day of our Lord Jesus
Christ.
9God is faithful, through
whom you were called into
fellowship with His Son,
Jesus Christ our Lord.
10Now I exhort you,
brethren, by the name of
our Lord Jesus Christ, that
you all agree, and there be
no divisions among you,
but you be made complete
in the same mind and in the
same judgment.
11For I have been in-

[a] Some ancient mss. do not contain *my*

1 Παῦλος κλητὸς ἀπόστολος Χριστοῦ
Paul a called apostle of Christ

Ἰησοῦ διὰ θελήματος θεοῦ καὶ Σωσθένης
Jesus through [the] will of God and Sosthenes

ὁ ἀδελφὸς **2** τῇ ἐκκλησίᾳ τοῦ θεοῦ
the(?his) brother to the church – of God

τῇ οὔσῃ ἐν Κορίνθῳ, ἡγιασμένοις ἐν
– existing in Corinth, to [ones] having been sanctified in

Χριστῷ Ἰησοῦ, κλητοῖς ἁγίοις, σὺν πᾶσιν
Christ Jesus, called saints, with all

τοῖς ἐπικαλουμένοις τὸ ὄνομα τοῦ κυρίου
the [ones] calling on the name of the Lord

ἡμῶν Ἰησοῦ Χριστοῦ ἐν παντὶ τόπῳ,
of us Jesus Christ in every place,

αὐτῶν καὶ ἡμῶν· **3** χάρις ὑμῖν καὶ
of them and of us: Grace to you and

εἰρήνη ἀπὸ θεοῦ πατρὸς ἡμῶν καὶ κυρίου
peace from God Father of us and Lord

Ἰησοῦ Χριστοῦ.
Jesus Christ.

4 Εὐχαριστῶ τῷ θεῷ πάντοτε περὶ
I gave thanks – to God always concerning

ὑμῶν ἐπὶ τῇ χάριτι τοῦ θεοῦ τῇ δοθείσῃ
you on the grace – of God – given

ὑμῖν ἐν Χριστῷ Ἰησοῦ, **5** ὅτι ἐν παντὶ
to you in Christ Jesus, because in everything

ἐπλουτίσθητε ἐν αὐτῷ, ἐν παντὶ λόγῳ
ye were enriched in him, in all speech

καὶ πάσῃ γνώσει, **6** καθὼς τὸ μαρτύριον
and all knowledge, as the testimony

τοῦ Χριστοῦ ἐβεβαιώθη ἐν ὑμῖν, **7** ὥστε
– of Christ was confirmed in you, so as

ὑμᾶς μὴ ὑστερεῖσθαι ἐν μηδενὶ χαρίσματι,
you not to be wanting[b] in no(any) gift,

ἀπεκδεχομένους τὴν ἀποκάλυψιν τοῦ κυρίου
awaiting the revelation of the Lord

ἡμῶν Ἰησοῦ Χριστοῦ· **8** ὃς καὶ βεβαιώσει
of us Jesus Christ; who also will confirm

ὑμᾶς ἕως τέλους ἀνεγκλήτους ἐν τῇ
you till [the] end blameless in the

ἡμέρᾳ τοῦ κυρίου ἡμῶν Ἰησοῦ [Χριστοῦ].
day of the Lord of us Jesus Christ.

9 πιστὸς ὁ θεός, δι' οὗ ἐκλήθητε εἰς
Faithful [is] – God, through whom ye were called to

κοινωνίαν τοῦ υἱοῦ αὐτοῦ Ἰησοῦ Χριστοῦ
[the] fellowship of the Son of him Jesus Christ

τοῦ κυρίου ἡμῶν.
the Lord of us.

10 Παρακαλῶ δὲ ὑμᾶς, ἀδελφοί, διὰ
Now I beseech you, brothers, through

τοῦ ὀνόματος τοῦ κυρίου ἡμῶν Ἰησοῦ
the name of the Lord of us Jesus

Χριστοῦ, ἵνα τὸ αὐτὸ λέγητε πάντες,
Christ, *in order* that the same thing ye say all,

καὶ μὴ ᾖ ἐν ὑμῖν σχίσματα, ἦτε δὲ
and not be among you divisions, but ye may be

κατηρτισμένοι ἐν τῷ αὐτῷ νοῒ καὶ
having been joined together in the same mind and

ἐν τῇ αὐτῇ γνώμῃ. **11** ἐδηλώθη γάρ μοι
in the same opinion. For it was shown to me

1 Corinthians

Chapter 1

PAUL, called to be an
apostle of Christ Jesus
by the will of God, and our
brother Sosthenes,

2To the church of God in
Corinth, to those sanctified
in Christ Jesus and called to
be holy, together with all
those everywhere who call
on the name of our Lord
Jesus Christ—their Lord
and ours:

3Grace and peace to you
from God our Father and
the Lord Jesus Christ.

Thanksgiving

4I always thank God for
you because of his grace
given you in Christ Jesus.
5For in him you have been
enriched in every way—in
all your speaking and in all
your knowledge— 6be-
cause our testimony about
Christ was confirmed in
you. 7Therefore you do not
lack any spiritual gift as
you eagerly wait for our
Lord Jesus Christ to be revealed. 8He will keep you
strong to the end, so that
you will be blameless on
the day of our Lord Jesus
Christ. 9God, who has
called you into fellowship
with his Son Jesus Christ
our Lord, is faithful.

Divisions in the Church

10I appeal to you, broth-
ers, in the name of our Lord
Jesus Christ, that all of you
agree with one another so
that there may be no divisions among you and that
you may be perfectly united in mind and thought.
11My brothers, some from

formed concerning you, my
brethren, by Chloe's
people, that there are quarrels among you.
12 Now I mean this, that
each one of you is saying,
"I am of Paul," and "I of
Apollos," and "I of Ce-
phas," and "I of Christ."
13 Has Christ been di-
vided? Paul was not crucified for you, was he? Or
were you baptized in the
name of Paul?
14 [b]I thank God that I baptized none of you except
Crispus and Gaius,
15 that no man should say
you were baptized in my
name.
16 Now I did baptize also
the household of Stepha-
nas; beyond that, I do not
know whether I baptized
any other.
17 For Christ did not send
me to baptize, but to
preach the gospel, not in
cleverness of speech, that
the cross of Christ should
not be made void.

The Wisdom of God

18 For the word of the
cross is to those who are
perishing foolishness, but
to us who are being saved it
is the power of God.
19 For it is written,
"I WILL DESTROY THE
WISDOM OF THE WISE,
AND THE CLEVERNESS
OF THE CLEVER I WILL
SET ASIDE."
20 Where is the wise man?
Where is the scribe? Where
is the debater of this age?
Has not God made foolish
the wisdom of the world?
21 For since in the wisdom
of God the world through
its wisdom did not *come to*
know God, God was well-
pleased through the fool-
ishness of the message
preached to save those who
believe.
22 For indeed Jews ask for
signs, and Greeks search
for wisdom;
23 but we preach [c]Christ
crucified, to Jews a stum-

[b] Some ancient mss. read *I give thanks that*
[c] I.e., Messiah

περὶ ὑμῶν, ἀδελφοί μου, ὑπὸ τῶν
concerning you, brothers of me, by the [ones]

Χλόης, ὅτι ἔριδες ἐν ὑμῖν εἰσιν. **12** λέγω
of Chloe, that strifes among you there are. I say

δὲ τοῦτο, ὅτι ἕκαστος ὑμῶν λέγει· ἐγὼ
Now this, because each of you says: I

μέν εἰμι Παύλου, ἐγὼ δὲ Ἀπολλῶ,
indeed am of Paul, but I of Apollos,

ἐγὼ δὲ Κηφᾶ, ἐγὼ δὲ Χριστοῦ.
but I of Cephas, but I of Christ.

13 μεμέρισται ὁ Χριστός; μὴ Παῦλος
Has been divided – Christ? *Not* Paul

ἐσταυρώθη ὑπὲρ ὑμῶν, ἢ εἰς τὸ ὄνομα
was crucified on behalf of you, or in the name

Παύλου ἐβαπτίσθητε; **14** εὐχαριστῶ ὅτι
of Paul were ye baptized? I give thanks that

οὐδένα ὑμῶν ἐβάπτισα εἰ μὴ Κρίσπον
not one of you I baptized except Crispus

καὶ Γάϊον· **15** ἵνα μή τις εἴπῃ ὅτι
and Gaius; lest anyone should say that

εἰς τὸ ἐμὸν ὄνομα ἐβαπτίσθητε. **16** ἐβάπτισα δὲ
in – my name ye were baptized. But I baptized

καὶ τὸν Στεφανᾶ οἶκον· λοιπὸν οὐκ οἶδα
also the of Stephanas household; for the rest I know not

εἴ τινα ἄλλον ἐβάπτισα. **17** οὐ
if any other I baptized. 5not

γὰρ ἀπέστειλέν με Χριστὸς βαπτίζειν
1For 3sent 4me 2Christ to baptize

ἀλλὰ εὐαγγελίζεσθαι, οὐκ ἐν σοφίᾳ λόγου,
but to evangelize, not in wisdom of speech,

ἵνα μὴ κενωθῇ ὁ σταυρὸς τοῦ Χριστοῦ.
lest 4be made vain 1the 2cross – 3of Christ.

18 Ὁ λόγος γὰρ ὁ τοῦ σταυροῦ τοῖς
For the word – of the cross 2to the [ones]

μὲν ἀπολλυμένοις μωρία ἐστίν, τοῖς
1on one hand 3perishing 5folly 4is, 3*to* the [ones]

δὲ σῳζομένοις ἡμῖν δύναμις θεοῦ ἐστιν.
1on the other 4being saved 2to us 6[the] 7power 8of God 5it is.

19 γέγραπται γάρ· ἀπολῶ τὴν σοφίαν
For it has been written: I will destroy the wisdom

τῶν σοφῶν, καὶ τὴν σύνεσιν τῶν συνετῶν
of the wise ones, and the understanding of the prudent

ἀθετήσω. **20** ποῦ σοφός; ποῦ γραμματεύς;
I will set aside. Where [is the] wise man? where [is the] scribe?

ποῦ συζητητὴς τοῦ αἰῶνος τούτου; οὐχὶ
where [is the] disputant of this age? 2Not

ἐμώρανεν ὁ θεὸς τὴν σοφίαν τοῦ κόσμου;
1made 8foolish – 2God 4the 5wisdom 6of the 7world?

21 ἐπειδὴ γὰρ ἐν τῇ σοφίᾳ τοῦ θεοῦ
for since in the wisdom – of God

οὐκ ἔγνω ὁ κόσμος διὰ τῆς σοφίας
6knew 7not 1the 2world 3through 4the(its) 5wisdom

τὸν θεόν, εὐδόκησεν ὁ θεὸς διὰ τῆς
– 8God, 2thought well – 1God through the

μωρίας τοῦ κηρύγματος σῶσαι τοὺς
folly of the proclamation to save the

πιστεύοντας. **22** ἐπειδὴ καὶ Ἰουδαῖοι σημεῖα
[ones] believing. Seeing that both Jews 2signs

αἰτοῦσιν καὶ Ἕλληνες σοφίαν ζητοῦσιν,
1ask and Greeks 2wisdom 1seek,

23 ἡμεῖς δὲ κηρύσσομεν Χριστὸν ἐσταυρωμένον,
2we 1yet proclaim Christ *having been* crucified,

Chloe's household have informed me that there are
quarrels among you.
12 What I mean is this: One
of you says, "I follow
Paul"; another, "I follow
Apollos"; another, "I follow Cephas[a]"; still another, "I follow Christ."
13 Is Christ divided? Was
Paul crucified for you?
Were you baptized into[b]
the name of Paul?
14 I am
thankful that I did not baptize any of you except Crispus and Gaius,
15 so no one
can say that you were baptized into my name.
16 (Yes,
I also baptized the household of Stephanas; beyond
that, I don't remember if I
baptized anyone else.)
17 For Christ did not send
me to baptize, but to
preach the gospel—not
with words of human wis-
dom, lest the cross of
Christ be emptied of its
power.

Christ the Wisdom and Power of God

18 For the message of the
cross is foolishness to
those who are perishing,
but to us who are being
saved it is the power of
God.
19 For it is written:

"I will destroy the
wisdom of the wise;
the intelligence of the
intelligent I will
frustrate."[c]

20 Where is the wise man?
Where is the scholar?
Where is the philosopher of
this age? Has not God made
foolish the wisdom of the
world?
21 For since in the
wisdom of God the world
through its wisdom did not
know him, God was
pleased through the fool-
ishness of what was
preached to save those who
believe.
22 Jews demand mi-
raculous signs and Greeks
look for wisdom,
23 but we
preach Christ crucified: a
stumbling block to Jews

[a] *12* That is, Peter
[b] *13* Or *in*; also in verse 15
[c] *19* Isaiah 29:14

bling block, and to Gentiles foolishness,
24but to those who are the called, both Jews and Greeks, Christ the power of God and the wisdom of God.
25Because the foolishness of God is wiser than men, and the weakness of God is stronger than men.
26For consider your calling, brethren, that there were not many wise according to the flesh, not many mighty, not many noble;
27but God has chosen the foolish things of the world to shame the wise, and God has chosen the weak things of the world to shame the things which are strong,
28and the base things of the world and the despised, God has chosen, the things that are not, that He might nullify the things that are,
29that no man should boast before God.
30But by His doing you are in Christ Jesus, who became to us wisdom from God, and righteousness and sanctification, and redemption,
31that, just as it is written, "LET HIM WHO BOASTS, BOAST IN THE LORD."

Chapter 2

Paul's Reliance upon the Spirit

AND when I came to you, brethren, I did not come with superiority of speech or of wisdom, proclaiming to you the [d]testimony of God.
2For I determined to know nothing among you except Jesus Christ, and Him crucified.
3And I was with you in weakness and in fear and in

[d]Some ancient mss. read *mystery*

Ἰουδαίοις μὲν σκάνδαλον, ἔθνεσιν δὲ
to Jews on one hand an offence, to nations on the other

μωρίαν, 24 αὐτοῖς δὲ τοῖς κλητοῖς,
folly, but to them the called ones,

Ἰουδαίοις τε καὶ Ἕλλησιν, Χριστὸν θεοῦ
²to Jews ¹both and to Greeks, Christ of God

δύναμιν καὶ θεοῦ σοφίαν. 25 ὅτι τὸ
power and of God wisdom. Because the

μωρὸν τοῦ θεοῦ σοφώτερον τῶν ἀνθρώπων
foolish thing – of God wiser [than] – men

ἐστίν, καὶ τὸ ἀσθενὲς τοῦ θεοῦ ἰσχυρότερον
is, and the weak thing – of God stronger [than]

τῶν ἀνθρώπων. 26 Βλέπετε γὰρ τὴν
– men. For ye see the

κλῆσιν ὑμῶν, ἀδελφοί, ὅτι οὐ πολλοὶ
calling of you, brothers, that not many

σοφοὶ κατὰ σάρκα, οὐ πολλοὶ δυνατοί,
wise men according to flesh, not many powerful,

οὐ πολλοὶ εὐγενεῖς· 27 ἀλλὰ τὰ μωρὰ
not many well born; but the foolish things

τοῦ κόσμου ἐξελέξατο ὁ θεὸς ἵνα καται-
of the world ²chose – ¹God in order that he might

σχύνῃ τοὺς σοφούς, καὶ τὰ ἀσθενῆ τοῦ
shame the wise men, and the weak things of the

κόσμου ἐξελέξατο ὁ θεὸς ἵνα καταισχύνῃ
world ²chose – ¹God in order that he might shame

τὰ ἰσχυρά, 28 καὶ τὰ ἀγενῆ τοῦ κόσμου
the strong things, and the base things of the world

καὶ τὰ ἐξουθενημένα ἐξελέξατο ὁ θεός,
and the things being despised ²chose – ¹God,

τὰ μὴ ὄντα, ἵνα τὰ ὄντα καταργήσῃ,
the things not being, in order that ²the things ³being ¹he might abolish,

29 ὅπως μὴ καυχήσηται πᾶσα σὰρξ
so as not might boast all flesh*

ἐνώπιον τοῦ θεοῦ. 30 ἐξ αὐτοῦ δὲ ὑμεῖς
before – God. And of him ye

ἐστε ἐν Χριστῷ Ἰησοῦ, ὃς ἐγενήθη
are in Christ Jesus, who became

σοφία ἡμῖν ἀπὸ θεοῦ, δικαιοσύνη τε
wisdom to us from God, ²righteousness ¹both

καὶ ἁγιασμὸς καὶ ἀπολύτρωσις, 31 ἵνα καθὼς
and sanctification and redemption, in order that as

γέγραπται· ὁ καυχώμενος ἐν κυρίῳ καυχάσθω.
it has been written: The [one] boasting ²in ³[the] Lord ¹let him boast.

2 Κἀγὼ ἐλθὼν πρὸς ὑμᾶς, ἀδελφοί,
And I coming to you, brothers,

ἦλθον οὐ καθ' ὑπεροχὴν λόγου ἢ σοφίας
came not according to excellence of speech or of wisdom

καταγγέλλων ὑμῖν τὸ μαρτύριον τοῦ θεοῦ.
announcing to you the testimony – of God.

2 οὐ γὰρ ἔκρινά τι εἰδέναι ἐν ὑμῖν
For I decided not anything to know among you

εἰ μὴ Ἰησοῦν Χριστὸν καὶ τοῦτον
except Jesus Christ and this one

ἐσταυρωμένον. 3 κἀγὼ ἐν ἀσθενείᾳ καὶ
having been crucified. And I in weakness and

* That is, so that no flesh might boast. *Cf.* Mat. 24. 22.

and foolishness to Gentiles, 24but to those whom God has called, both Jews and Greeks, Christ the power of God and the wisdom of God. 25For the foolishness of God is wiser than man's wisdom, and the weakness of God is stronger than man's strength.
26Brothers, think of what you were when you were called. Not many of you were wise by human standards; not many were influential; not many were of noble birth. 27But God chose the foolish things of the world to shame the wise; God chose the weak things of the world to shame the strong. 28He chose the lowly things of this world and the despised things—and the things that are not—to nullify the things that are, 29so that no one may boast before him. 30It is because of him that you are in Christ Jesus, who has become for us wisdom from God—that is, our righteousness, holiness and redemption. 31Therefore, as it is written: "Let him who boasts boast in the Lord."[d]

Chapter 2

WHEN I came to you, brothers, I did not come with eloquence or superior wisdom as I proclaimed to you the testimony about God.[e] 2For I resolved to know nothing while I was with you except Jesus Christ and him crucified. 3I came to you in weakness and fear, and

[d]31 Jer. 9:24
[e]1 Some manuscripts *as I proclaimed to you God's mystery*

much trembling.
4And my message and
my preaching were not in
persuasive words of wis-
dom, but in demonstration
of the Spirit and of power,
5that your faith should
not rest on the wisdom of
men, but on the power of
God.
6Yet we do speak wis-
dom among those who are
mature; a wisdom, how-
ever, not of this age, nor of
the rulers of this age, who
are passing away;
7but we speak God's
wisdom in a mystery, the
hidden *wisdom,* which God
predestined before the ages
to our glory;
8*the wisdom* which none
of the rulers of this age has
understood; for if they had
understood it, they would
not have crucified the Lord
of glory;
9but just as it is written,
"THINGS WHICH EYE HAS
NOT SEEN AND EAR HAS
NOT HEARD,
AND *which* HAVE NOT
ENTERED THE HEART
OF MAN,
ALL THAT GOD HAS
PREPARED FOR THOSE
WHO LOVE HIM."
10[e]For to us God re-
vealed *them* through the
Spirit; for the Spirit
searches all things, even
the depths of God.
11For who among men
knows the *thoughts* of a
man except the spirit of the
man, which is in him? Even
so the *thoughts* of God no
one knows except the
Spirit of God.
12Now we have received,
not the spirit of the world,
but the Spirit who is from
God, that we might know
the things freely given to us
by God,
13which things we also
speak, not in words taught

ἐν φόβῳ καὶ ἐν τρόμῳ πολλῷ ἐγενόμην
in fear and in trembling much was

πρὸς ὑμᾶς, 4 καὶ ὁ λόγος μου καὶ τὸ
with you, and the speech of me and the

κήρυγμά μου οὐκ ἐν πειθοῖς σοφίας
proclamation of me not in [1]persuasive [3]of wisdom

λόγοις, ἀλλ' ἐν ἀποδείξει πνεύματος καὶ
[2]words, but in demonstration of spirit and

δυνάμεως, 5 ἵνα ἡ πίστις ὑμῶν μὴ ᾖ
of power, in order that the faith of you may not be

ἐν σοφίᾳ ἀνθρώπων ἀλλ' ἐν δυνάμει
in [the] wisdom of men but in [the] power

θεοῦ.
of God.

6 Σοφίαν δὲ λαλοῦμεν ἐν τοῖς τελείοις,
But [2]wisdom [1]we speak among the perfect ones,

σοφίαν δὲ οὐ τοῦ αἰῶνος τούτου οὐδὲ
yet wisdom not of this age neither

τῶν ἀρχόντων τοῦ αἰῶνος τούτου τῶν
of the leaders of this age of the [ones]

καταργουμένων· 7 ἀλλὰ λαλοῦμεν θεοῦ
being brought to naught; but we speak [2]of God

σοφίαν ἐν μυστηρίῳ, τὴν ἀποκεκρυμμένην,
[1]a wisdom in mystery, – having been hidden,

ἣν προώρισεν ὁ θεὸς πρὸ τῶν αἰώνων
which [2]foreordained – [1]God before the ages

εἰς δόξαν ἡμῶν· 8 ἣν οὐδεὶς τῶν ἀρχόντων
for glory of us; which not one of the leaders

τοῦ αἰῶνος τούτου ἔγνωκεν· εἰ γὰρ
of this age has known; for if

ἔγνωσαν, οὐκ ἂν τὸν κύριον τῆς δόξης
they knew, not – the Lord – of glory

ἐσταύρωσαν· 9 ἀλλὰ καθὼς γέγραπται· ἃ
they would have crucified;* but as it has been written: Things which

ὀφθαλμὸς οὐκ εἶδεν καὶ οὖς οὐκ ἤκουσεν
eye saw not and ear heard not

καὶ ἐπὶ καρδίαν ἀνθρώπου οὐκ ἀνέβη,
and on heart of man came not up,

ὅσα ἡτοίμασεν ὁ θεὸς τοῖς ἀγαπῶσιν
how many [2]prepared – [1]God for the [ones] loving

αὐτόν. 10 ἡμῖν γὰρ ἀπεκάλυψεν ὁ θεὸς
him. [1]For [4]to us [3]revealed – [2]God

διὰ τοῦ πνεύματος· τὸ γὰρ πνεῦμα πάντα
through the Spirit; for the Spirit all things

ἐρευνᾷ, καὶ τὰ βάθη τοῦ θεοῦ. 11 τίς
searches, even the deep things – of God. [2]who

γὰρ οἶδεν ἀνθρώπων τὰ τοῦ ἀνθρώπου
[1]For [4]knows [3]of men the things – of a man

εἰ μὴ τὸ πνεῦμα τοῦ ἀνθρώπου τὸ
except the spirit – of a man –

ἐν αὐτῷ; οὕτως καὶ τὰ τοῦ θεοῦ οὐδεὶς
in him? so also the things – of God no one

ἔγνωκεν εἰ μὴ τὸ πνεῦμα τοῦ θεοῦ.
has known except the Spirit – of God.

12 ἡμεῖς δὲ οὐ τὸ πνεῦμα τοῦ κόσμου
And we not the spirit of the world

ἐλάβομεν ἀλλὰ τὸ πνεῦμα τὸ ἐκ τοῦ θεοῦ,
received but the Spirit – from – God,

ἵνα εἰδῶμεν τὰ ὑπὸ τοῦ θεοῦ
in order that we may know the things by – God

χαρισθέντα ἡμῖν· 13 ἃ καὶ λαλοῦμεν οὐκ
freely given to us; which things also we speak not

with much trembling. 4My
message and my preaching
were not with wise and persuasive words, but with a
demonstration of the Spirit's power, 5so that your
faith might not rest on
men's wisdom, but on
God's power.

Wisdom From the Spirit

6We do, however, speak
a message of wisdom
among the mature, but not
the wisdom of this age or of
the rulers of this age, who
are coming to nothing.
7No, we speak of God's secret wisdom, a wisdom that
has been hidden and that
God destined for our glory
before time began. 8None
of the rulers of this age understood it, for if they had,
they would not have crucified the Lord of glory.
9However, as it is written:

"No eye has seen,
no ear has heard,
no mind has conceived
what God has prepared
for those who love
him"[f]—

10but God has revealed it to
us by his Spirit.
The Spirit searches all
things, even the deep
things of God. 11For who
among men knows the
thoughts of a man except
the man's spirit within him?
In the same way no one
knows the thoughts of God
except the Spirit of God.
12We have not received the
spirit of the world but the
Spirit who is from God,
that we may understand
what God has freely given
us. 13This is what we
speak, not in words taught

[e] Some ancient mss. use *But*

* This rendering is demanded by the preceding ἄν.

[f]9 Isaiah 64:4

by human wisdom, but in those taught by the Spirit, combining spiritual *thoughts* with spiritual *words*.
14 But a natural man does not accept the things of the Spirit of God; for they are foolishness to him, and he cannot understand them, because they are spiritually appraised.
15 But he who is spiritual appraises all things, yet he himself is appraised by no man.
16 For WHO HAS KNOWN THE MIND OF THE LORD, THAT HE SHOULD INSTRUCT HIM? But we have the mind of Christ.

ἐν διδακτοῖς ἀνθρωπίνης σοφίας λόγοις,
in [2]taught [3]of human [4]wisdom [1]words,
ἀλλ' ἐν διδακτοῖς πνεύματος, πνευματικοῖς
but in [words] taught of [the] Spirit, [3]with spiritual things
πνευματικὰ συγκρίνοντες. **14** ψυχικὸς δὲ
[2]spiritual things [1]comparing. But a natural
ἄνθρωπος οὐ δέχεται τὰ τοῦ πνεύματος
man receives not the things of the Spirit
τοῦ θεοῦ· μωρία γὰρ αὐτῷ ἐστιν, καὶ
– of God; for folly to him they are, and
οὐ δύναται γνῶναι, ὅτι πνευματικῶς
he cannot *to* know, because [2]spiritually
ἀνακρίνεται. **15** ὁ δὲ πνευματικὸς ἀνακρίνει
[1]they are [3]discerned. But the spiritual man [2]discerns
μὲν πάντα, αὐτὸς δὲ ὑπ' οὐδενὸς
[1]on one hand all things, [2]he [1]on the other [4]by [5]no one
ἀνακρίνεται. **16** τίς γὰρ ἔγνω νοῦν
[3]is discerned. For who knew [the] mind
κυρίου, ὃς συμβιβάσει αὐτόν; ἡμεῖς δὲ
of [the] Lord, who will instruct him? But we
νοῦν Χριστοῦ ἔχομεν.
[the] mind of Christ have.

us by human wisdom but in words taught by the Spirit, expressing spiritual truths in spiritual words.[g] 14 The man without the Spirit does not accept the things that come from the Spirit of God, for they are foolishness to him, and he cannot understand them, because they are spiritually discerned. 15 The spiritual man makes judgments about all things, but he himself is not subject to any man's judgment:

16 "For who has known the mind of the Lord
that he may instruct him?"[h]

But we have the mind of Christ.

Chapter 3

Foundations for Living

AND I, brethren, could not speak to you as to spiritual men, but as to men of flesh, as to babes in Christ.
2 I gave you milk to drink, not solid food; for you were not yet able *to receive it*. Indeed, even now you are not yet able,
3 for you are still fleshly. For since there is jealousy and strife among you, are you not fleshly, and are you not walking like mere men?
4 For when one says, "I am of Paul," and another, "I am of Apollos," are you not *mere* men?
5 What then is Apollos? And what is Paul? Servants through whom you believed, even as the Lord gave *opportunity* to each one.
6 I planted, Apollos watered, but God was causing the growth.
7 So then neither the one who plants nor the one who waters is anything, but God who causes the growth.
8 Now he who plants and he who waters are one; but each will receive his own reward according to his own labor.
9 For we are God's fellow workers; you are God's field, God's building.
10 According to the grace

3 Κἀγώ, ἀδελφοί, οὐκ ἠδυνήθην λαλῆσαι
And I, brothers, was not able to speak
ὑμῖν ὡς πνευματικοῖς ἀλλ' ὡς σαρκίνοις,
to you as to spiritual men but as to fleshy,
ὡς νηπίοις ἐν Χριστῷ. **2** γάλα ὑμᾶς
as to infants in Christ. [3]Milk [2]you
ἐπότισα, οὐ βρῶμα· οὔπω γὰρ ἐδύνασθε.
[1]I gave [4]to drink, not food; for ye were not then able.
ἀλλ' οὐδὲ [ἔτι] νῦν δύνασθε, **3** ἔτι γὰρ
But neither yet now are ye able, for still
σαρκικοί ἐστε. ὅπου γὰρ ἐν ὑμῖν ζῆλος
fleshly ye are. For whereas among you [there is] jealousy
καὶ ἔρις, οὐχὶ σαρκικοί ἐστε καὶ κατὰ
and strife, [2]not [3]fleshly [1]are ye [4]and [6]according to
ἄνθρωπον περιπατεῖτε; **4** ὅταν γὰρ λέγῃ
[7]man [5]walk? For whenever says
τις· ἐγὼ μέν εἰμι Παύλου, ἕτερος δέ·
anyone: I – am of Paul, and another:
ἐγὼ Ἀπολλῶ, οὐκ ἄνθρωποί ἐστε; **5** Τί
I of Apollos, [2]not [3]men [1]are ye? What
οὖν ἐστιν Ἀπολλῶς; τί δέ ἐστιν Παῦλος;
therefore is Apollos? and what is Paul?
διάκονοι δι' ὧν ἐπιστεύσατε, καὶ ἑκάστῳ
Ministers through whom ye believed, even [2]to each one
ὡς ὁ κύριος ἔδωκεν. **6** ἐγὼ ἐφύτευσα,
[1]as the Lord gave. I planted,
Ἀπολλῶς ἐπότισεν, ἀλλὰ ὁ θεὸς ηὔξανεν·
Apollos watered, but – God made to grow;
7 ὥστε οὔτε ὁ φυτεύων ἐστίν τι οὔτε
so as neither the [one] planting is anything nor
ὁ ποτίζων, ἀλλ' ὁ αὐξάνων θεός. **8** ὁ
the [one] watering, but [2]the [one] [3]making to grow [1]God. [2]The [one]
φυτεύων δὲ καὶ ὁ ποτίζων ἕν εἰσιν,
[3]planting [1]so and the [one] watering one* are,
ἕκαστος δὲ τὸν ἴδιον μισθὸν λήμψεται
and each one the(his) own reward will receive

* Notice the neuter gender, though "thing" cannot very well be expressed; *cf.* John 10. 30.

Chapter 3

On Divisions in the Church

BROTHERS, I could not address you as spiritual but as worldly—mere infants in Christ. 2 I gave you milk, not solid food, for you were not yet ready for it. Indeed, you are still not ready. 3 You are still worldly. For since there is jealousy and quarreling among you, are you not worldly? Are you not acting like mere men? 4 For when one says, "I follow Paul," and another, "I follow Apollos," are you not mere men?
5 What, after all, is Apollos? And what is Paul? Only servants, through whom you came to believe—as the Lord has assigned to each his task. 6 I planted the seed, Apollos watered it, but God made it grow. 7 So neither he who plants nor he who waters is anything, but only God, who makes things grow. 8 The man who plants and the man who waters have one purpose, and each will be rewarded according to his own labor. 9 For we are God's fellow workers; you are God's field, God's building.
10 By the grace God has

[g] *13* Or *Spirit, interpreting spiritual truths to spiritual men*
[h] *16* Isaiah 40:13

of God which was given to
me, as a wise master builder I laid a foundation, and
another is building upon it.
But let each man be careful
how he builds upon it.
11For no man can lay a
foundation other than the
one which is laid, which is
Jesus Christ.
12Now if any man builds
upon the foundation with
gold, silver, precious
stones, wood, hay, straw,
13each man's work will
become evident; for the
day will show it, because it
is *to be* revealed with fire;
and the fire itself will test
the quality of each man's
work.
14If any man's work
which he has built upon it
remains, he shall receive a
reward.
15If any man's work is
burned up, he shall suffer
loss; but he himself shall be
saved, yet so as through
fire.
16Do you not know that
you are a temple of God,
and *that* the Spirit of God
dwells in you?
17If any man destroys the
temple of God, God will destroy him, for the temple of
God is holy, and that is
what you are.
18Let no man deceive
himself. If any man among
you thinks that he is wise in
this age, let him become
foolish that he may become
wise.
19For the wisdom of this
world is foolishness before
God. For it is written, "*He*
is THE ONE WHO CATCHES
THE WISE IN THEIR CRAFTI-
NESS";
20and again, "THE LORD
KNOWS THE REASONINGS of
the wise, THAT THEY ARE
USELESS."
21So then let no one boast

κατὰ τὸν ἴδιον κόπον. **9** θεοῦ γάρ ἐσμεν
according to his own labour. For of God we are

συνεργοί· θεοῦ γεώργιον, θεοῦ οἰκοδομή
fellow-workers; [2]of God [3]a tillage, [5]of God [4]a building

ἐστε. **10** Κατὰ τὴν χάριν τοῦ θεοῦ τὴν
[1]ye are. According to the grace – of God –

δοθεῖσάν μοι ὡς σοφὸς ἀρχιτέκτων
given to me as a wise master builder

θεμέλιον ἔθηκα, ἄλλος δὲ ἐποικοδομεῖ.
a foundation I laid, but another builds on [it].

ἕκαστος δὲ βλεπέτω πῶς ἐποικοδομεῖ.
But each one let him look how he builds on [it].

11 θεμέλιον γὰρ ἄλλον οὐδεὶς δύναται θεῖναι
For foundation other no one is able to lay

παρὰ τὸν κείμενον, ὅς ἐστιν Ἰησοῦς
beside the [one] being laid, who is Jesus

Χριστός. **12** εἰ δέ τις ἐποικοδομεῖ ἐπὶ
Christ. Now if anyone builds *on* on

τὸν θεμέλιον χρυσίον, ἀργύριον, λίθους
the foundation gold, silver, stones

τιμίους, ξύλα, χόρτον, καλάμην, **13** ἑκάστου
precious, woods, hay, stubble, of each one

τὸ ἔργον φανερὸν γενήσεται· ἡ γὰρ ἡμέρα
the work manifest will become; for the day

δηλώσει, ὅτι ἐν πυρὶ ἀποκαλύπτεται,
will declare [it], because by fire it is revealed,

καὶ ἑκάστου τὸ ἔργον ὁποῖόν ἐστιν
and [3]of each one [1]the [2]work [8]of what sort [9]it is

τὸ πῦρ αὐτὸ δοκιμάσει. **14** εἴ τινος
[4]the [5]fire [7]it [6]will prove. If of anyone

τὸ ἔργον μενεῖ ὃ ἐποικοδόμησεν, μισθὸν
the work remains which he built *on*, a reward

λήμψεται· **15** εἴ τινος τὸ ἔργον κατακαήσεται,
he will receive; if of anyone the work will be consumed,

ζημιωθήσεται, αὐτὸς δὲ σωθήσεται,
he will suffer loss, but he will be saved,

οὕτως δὲ ὡς διὰ πυρός. **16** Οὐκ οἴδατε
yet so as through fire. Know ye not

ὅτι ναὸς θεοῦ ἐστε καὶ τὸ πνεῦμα τοῦ
that a shrine of God ye are and the Spirit –

θεοῦ ἐν ὑμῖν οἰκεῖ; **17** εἴ τις τὸν ναὸν
of God in you dwells? If anyone the shrine

τοῦ θεοῦ φθείρει, φθερεῖ τοῦτον ὁ θεός·
– of God defiles, [2]will defile [3]this man – [1]God;

ὁ γὰρ ναὸς τοῦ θεοῦ ἅγιός ἐστιν, οἵτινές
for the shrine – of God holy is, who(which)

ἐστε ὑμεῖς.
are ye.

18 Μηδεὶς ἑαυτὸν ἐξαπατάτω· εἴ τις
No one himself let deceive; if anyone

δοκεῖ σοφὸς εἶναι ἐν ὑμῖν ἐν τῷ αἰῶνι
thinks wise to be among you in – age

τούτῳ, μωρὸς γενέσθω, ἵνα γένηται
this, foolish let him become, in order that he may become

σοφός. **19** ἡ γὰρ σοφία τοῦ κόσμου
wise. For the wisdom – world

τούτου μωρία παρὰ τῷ θεῷ ἐστιν.
of this folly with – God is.

γέγραπται γάρ· ὁ δρασσόμενος τοὺς σοφοὺς
For it has been written: The [one] grasping the wise

ἐν τῇ πανουργίᾳ αὐτῶν· **20** καὶ πάλιν·
in the craftiness of them; and again:

κύριος γινώσκει τοὺς διαλογισμοὺς τῶν
[The] Lord knows the reasonings of the

σοφῶν, ὅτι εἰσὶν μάταιοι. **21** ὥστε μηδεὶς
wise, that they are vain. So as no one

given me, I laid a foundation as an expert builder,
and someone else is building on it. But each one
should be careful how he
builds. 11For no one can lay
any foundation other than
the one already laid, which
is Jesus Christ. 12If any
man builds on this foundation using gold, silver, costly stones, wood, hay or
straw, 13his work will be
shown for what it is, be-
cause the Day will bring it
to light. It will be revealed
with fire, and the fire will
test the quality of each
man's work. 14If what he
has built survives, he will
receive his reward. 15If it is
burned up, he will suffer
loss; he himself will be
saved, but only as one escaping through the flames.
16Don't you know that
you yourselves are God's
temple and that God's Spirit lives in you? 17If anyone
destroys God's temple,
God will destroy him; for
God's temple is sacred, and
you are that temple.
18Do not deceive your-
selves. If any one of you
thinks he is wise by the
standards of this age, he
should become a "fool" so
that he may become wise.
19For the wisdom of this
world is foolishness in
God's sight. As it is written: "He catches the wise
in their craftiness"[i]; 20and
again, "The Lord knows
that the thoughts of the
wise are futile."[j] 21So
then, no more boasting

[i]19 Job 5:13
[j]20 Psalm 94:11

in men. For all things belong to you,
[22]whether Paul or Apollos
or Cephas or the world or
life or death or things
present or things to come;
all things belong to you,
[23]and you belong to
Christ; and Christ belongs
to God.

Chapter 4

Servants of Christ

LET a man regard us in
this manner, as ser-
vants of Christ, and stewards of the mysteries of
God.
[2]In this case, moreover,
it is required of stewards
that one be found trust-
worthy.
[3]But to me it is a very
small thing that I should be
examined by you, or by *any*
human court; in fact, I do
not even examine myself.
[4]For I am conscious of
nothing against myself, yet
I am not by this acquitted;
but the one who examines
me is the Lord.
[5]Therefore do not go on
passing judgment before
[f]the time, *but wait* until the
Lord comes who will both
bring to light the things hidden in the darkness and disclose the motives of *men's*
hearts; and then each
man's praise will come to
him from God.
[6]Now these things,
brethren, I have figuratively applied to myself and
Apollos for your sakes,
that in us you might learn
not to exceed what is written, in order that no one of
you might become arrogant
in behalf of one against the
other.
[7]For who regards you as
superior? And what do you
have that you did not re-
ceive? But if you did re-
ceive it, why do you boast
as if you had not received
it?
[8]You are already filled,
you have already become
rich, you have become
kings without us; and *I*
would indeed that you had
become kings so that we
also might reign with you.

καυχάσθω ἐν ἀνθρώποις· πάντα γάρ ὑμῶν
let boast in men; for all things of you
ἐστιν, 22 εἴτε Παῦλος εἴτε Ἀπολλῶς
is(are), whether Paul or Apollos
εἴτε Κηφᾶς, εἴτε κόσμος εἴτε ζωὴ εἴτε
or Cephas, or [the] world or life or
θάνατος, εἴτε ἐνεστῶτα εἴτε μέλλοντα,
death, or things present or things coming,
πάντα ὑμῶν, 23 ὑμεῖς δὲ Χριστοῦ, Χριστὸς δὲ
all things of you, and ye of Christ, and Christ
θεοῦ. 4 Οὕτως ἡμᾶς λογιζέσθω ἄνθρωπος ὡς
of God. So [4]us [1]let [3]reckon [2]a man as
ὑπηρέτας Χριστοῦ καὶ οἰκονόμους μυστηρίων
attendants of Christ and stewards of mysteries
θεοῦ. 2 ὧδε λοιπὸν ζητεῖται ἐν τοῖς
of God. Here for the rest it is sought among –
οἰκονόμοις ἵνα πιστός τις εὑρεθῇ. 3 ἐμοὶ
stewards *in order that* [3]faithful [1]*any*one [2]be found. to me
δὲ εἰς ἐλάχιστόν ἐστιν ἵνα ὑφ' ὑμῶν
And for a very little thing it is *in order* that by you
ἀνακριθῶ ἢ ὑπὸ ἀνθρωπίνης ἡμέρας· ἀλλ'
I am judged or by a human day;* but
οὐδὲ ἐμαυτὸν ἀνακρίνω· 4 οὐδὲν γὰρ
not myself I judge; for nothing
ἐμαυτῷ σύνοιδα, ἀλλ' οὐκ ἐν τούτῳ
against myself I know, but not by this
δεδικαίωμαι· ὁ δὲ ἀνακρίνων με κύριός
have I been justified; but the [one] judging me [the] Lord
ἐστιν. 5 ὥστε μὴ πρὸ καιροῦ τι κρίνετε,
is. So as not before time anything judge ye,
ἕως ἂν ἔλθῃ ὁ κύριος, ὃς καὶ φωτίσει
until comes the Lord, who both will shed light on
τὰ κρυπτὰ τοῦ σκότους καὶ φανερώσει
the hidden things of the darkness and will manifest
τὰς βουλὰς τῶν καρδιῶν· καὶ τότε ὁ
the counsels of the hearts; and then the
ἔπαινος γενήσεται ἑκάστῳ ἀπὸ τοῦ θεοῦ.
praise will be to each one[c] from – God.
6 Ταῦτα δέ, ἀδελφοί, μετεσχημάτισα εἰς
Now these things, brothers, I adapted to
ἐμαυτὸν καὶ Ἀπολλῶν δι' ὑμᾶς, ἵνα
myself and Apollos because of you, in order that
ἐν ἡμῖν μάθητε τὸ μὴ ὑπὲρ ἃ
among us ye may learn – not [to think] above what things
γέγραπται, ἵνα μὴ εἷς ὑπὲρ τοῦ ἑνὸς
has(ve) been written, lest [2]one [3]on behalf of [4]the [5]one
φυσιοῦσθε κατὰ τοῦ ἑτέρου. 7 τίς γάρ σε
[1]ye are puffed up against the other. For who thee
διακρίνει; τί δὲ ἔχεις ὃ οὐκ ἔλαβες;
distinguishes? and what hast thou which thou didst not receive?
εἰ δὲ καὶ ἔλαβες, τί καυχᾶσαι ὡς μὴ
and if indeed thou didst receive, why boastest thou as not
λαβών; 8 ἤδη κεκορεσμένοι ἐστέ· ἤδη
receiving? Now *having been* glutted ye are; now
ἐπλουτήσατε· χωρὶς ἡμῶν ἐβασιλεύσατε· καὶ
ye became rich; without us ye reigned; and
ὄφελόν γε ἐβασιλεύσατε, ἵνα
[3]an advantage [2]really [1][it is] [that] ye reigned, in order that
καὶ ἡμεῖς ὑμῖν συμβασιλεύσωμεν. 9 δοκῶ
also we [2]you [1]might reign with. I think

about men! All things are
yours, [22]whether Paul or
Apollos or Cephas[k] or the
world or life or death or the
present or the future—all
are yours, [23]and you are of
Christ, and Christ is of
God.

Chapter 4

Apostles of Christ

SO then, men ought to
regard us as servants
of Christ and as those entrusted with the secret
things of God. [2]Now it is
required that those who
have been given a trust
must prove faithful. [3]I care
very little if I am judged by
you or by any human court;
indeed, I do not even judge
myself. [4]My conscience is
clear, but that does not
make me innocent. It is the
Lord who judges me.
[5]Therefore judge nothing
before the appointed time;
wait till the Lord comes.
He will bring to light what
is hidden in darkness and
will expose the motives of
men's hearts. At that time
each will receive his praise
from God.
[6]Now, brothers, I have
applied these things to myself and Apollos for your
benefit, so that you may
learn from us the meaning
of the saying, "Do not go
beyond what is written."
Then you will not take
pride in one man over
against another. [7]For who
makes you different from
anyone else? What do you
have that you did not re-
ceive? And if you did re-
ceive it, why do you boast
as though you did not?
[8]Already you have all you
want! Already you have become rich! You have be-
come kings—and that
without us! How I wish that
you really had become
kings so that we might be
kings with you! [9]For it

[f]I.e., the appointed time of judgment

* ? of judgment.

[k]22 That is, Peter

9For, I think, God has
exhibited us apostles last of
all, as men condemned to
death; because we have
become a spectacle to the
world, both to angels and to
men.
10We are fools for
Christ's sake, but you are
prudent in Christ; we are
weak, but you are strong;
you are distinguished, but
we are without honor.
11To this present hour we
are both hungry and
thirsty, and are poorly
clothed, and are roughly
treated, and are homeless;
12and we toil, working
with our own hands; when
we are reviled, we bless;
when we are persecuted,
we endure;
13when we are slandered,
we try to conciliate; we
have become as the scum
of the world, the dregs of all
things, *even* until now.
14I do not write these
things to shame you, but to
admonish you as my be-
loved children.
15For if you were to have
countless tutors in Christ,
yet *you would* not *have*
many fathers; for in Christ
Jesus I became your father
through the gospel.
16I exhort you therefore,
be imitators of me.
17For this reason I have
sent to you Timothy, who
is my beloved and faithful
child in the Lord, and he
will remind you of my ways
which are in Christ, just as I
teach everywhere in every
church.
18Now some have be-
come arrogant, as though I
were not coming to you.
19But I will come to you
soon, if the Lord wills, and
I shall find out, not the
words of those who are arrogant, but their power.
20For the kingdom of God

γάρ, ὁ θεὸς ἡμᾶς τοὺς ἀποστόλους
For, – God us the apostles
ἐσχάτους ἀπέδειξεν ὡς ἐπιθανατίους, ὅτι
last showed forth as doomed to death, because
θέατρον ἐγενήθημεν τῷ κόσμῳ καὶ ἀγγέλοις
a spectacle we became to the world both to angels
καὶ ἀνθρώποις. 10 ἡμεῖς μωροὶ διὰ
and to men. We [are] fools because of
Χριστόν, ὑμεῖς δὲ φρόνιμοι ἐν Χριστῷ·
Christ, but ye [are] prudent in Christ;
ἡμεῖς ἀσθενεῖς, ὑμεῖς δὲ ἰσχυροί· ὑμεῖς
we [are] weak, but ye [are] strong; ye [are]
ἔνδοξοι, ἡμεῖς δὲ ἄτιμοι. 11 ἄχρι τῆς
held in honour, but we [are] unhonoured. Until the
ἄρτι ὥρας καὶ πεινῶμεν καὶ διψῶμεν
present hour [2]both [1]we [3]hunger and thirst
καὶ γυμνιτεύομεν καὶ κολαφιζόμεθα καὶ
and are naked and are buffeted and
ἀστατοῦμεν 12 καὶ κοπιῶμεν ἐργαζόμενοι
are unsettled and labour working
ταῖς ἰδίαις χερσίν· λοιδορούμενοι εὐλο-
with the(our) own hands; being reviled we
γοῦμεν, διωκόμενοι ἀνεχόμεθα, 13 δυσφημού-
bless, being persecuted we endure, being de-
μενοι παρακαλοῦμεν· ὡς περικαθάρματα τοῦ
famed we beseech; as refuse of the
κόσμου ἐγενήθημεν, πάντων περίψημα ἕως
world we became, [2]of all things [1]offscouring until
ἄρτι.
now.

14 Οὐκ ἐντρέπων ὑμᾶς γράφω ταῦτα,
Not shaming you I write these things,
ἀλλ' ὡς τέκνα μου ἀγαπητὰ νουθετῶν.
but as children of me beloved admonishing.
15 ἐὰν γὰρ μυρίους παιδαγωγοὺς ἔχητε
For if ten thousand trainers ye have
ἐν Χριστῷ, ἀλλ' οὐ πολλοὺς πατέρας·
in Christ, yet not many fathers;
ἐν γὰρ Χριστῷ Ἰησοῦ διὰ τοῦ εὐαγγελίου
for in Christ Jesus through the gospel
ἐγὼ ὑμᾶς ἐγέννησα. 16 παρακαλῶ οὖν
I [2]you [1]begat. I beseech therefore
ὑμᾶς, μιμηταί μου γίνεσθε. 17 Διὰ τοῦτο
you, imitators of me become ye. Because of this
αὐτὸ ἔπεμψα ὑμῖν Τιμόθεον, ὅς ἐστίν
very thing I sent to you Timothy, who is
μου τέκνον ἀγαπητὸν καὶ πιστὸν ἐν
of me a child beloved and faithful in
κυρίῳ, ὃς ὑμᾶς ἀναμνήσει τὰς ὁδούς
[the] Lord, who [2]you [1]will remind [of] the ways
μου τὰς ἐν Χριστῷ [Ἰησοῦ], καθὼς
of me – in Christ Jesus, as
πανταχοῦ ἐν πάσῃ ἐκκλησίᾳ διδάσκω.
everywhere in every church I teach.
18 ὡς μὴ ἐρχομένου δέ μου πρὸς ὑμᾶς
When not coming now me[a] to you
=Now when I did not come
ἐφυσιώθησάν τινες· 19 ἐλεύσομαι δὲ ταχέως
[2]were puffed up [1]some; but I will come shortly
πρὸς ὑμᾶς, ἐὰν ὁ κύριος θελήσῃ, καὶ
to you, if the Lord wills, and
γνώσομαι οὐ τὸν λόγον τῶν πεφυσιωμένων
I will know not the speech of the [ones] having been puffed up
ἀλλὰ τὴν δύναμιν· 20 οὐ γὰρ ἐν λόγῳ
but the power; for [4][is] [5]not [6]in [7]speech

seems to me that God has
put us apostles on display
at the end of the proces-
sion, like men condemned
to die in the arena. We have
been made a spectacle to
the whole universe, to angels as well as to men. 10We
are fools for Christ, but you
are so wise in Christ! We
are weak, but you are
strong! You are honored,
we are dishonored! 11To
this very hour we go hun-
gry and thirsty, we are in
rags, we are brutally treated, we are homeless. 12We
work hard with our own
hands. When we are
cursed, we bless; when we
are persecuted, we endure
it; 13when we are slan-
dered, we answer kindly.
Up to this moment we have
become the scum of the
earth, the refuse of the
world.
14I am not writing this to
shame you, but to warn
you, as my dear children.
15Even though you have
ten thousand guardians in
Christ, you do not have
many fathers, for in Christ
Jesus I became your father
through the gospel.
16Therefore I urge you to
imitate me. 17For this reason I am sending to you
Timothy, my son whom I
love, who is faithful in the
Lord. He will remind you
of my way of life in Christ
Jesus, which agrees with
what I teach everywhere in
every church.
18Some of you have be-
come arrogant, as if I were
not coming to you. 19But I
will come to you very soon,
if the Lord is willing, and
then I will find out not only
how these arrogant people
are talking, but what power
they have. 20For the kingdom of God is not a matter

does not consist in words,
but in power.
21What do you desire?
Shall I come to you with a
rod or with love and a spirit
of gentleness?

Chapter 5

Immorality Rebuked

IT is actually reported
that there is immorality
among you, and immorality
of such a kind as does not
exist even among the Gen-
tiles, that someone has his
father's wife.
2And you have become
arrogant, and have not
mourned instead, in order
that the one who had done
this deed might be removed
from your midst.
3For I, on my part,
though absent in body but
present in spirit, have already judged him who has
so committed this, as
though I were present.
4In the name of our Lord
Jesus, when you are assembled, and I with you in
spirit, with the power of
our Lord Jesus,
5*I have decided* to de-
liver such a one to Satan for
the destruction of his flesh,
that his spirit may be saved
in the day of the Lord
[g]Jesus.
6Your boasting is not
good. Do you not know
that a little leaven leavens
the whole lump *of dough*?
7Clean out the old leav-
en, that you may be a new
lump, just as you are *in fact*
unleavened. For Christ our
Passover also has been sacrificed.
8Let us therefore cele-
brate the feast, not with old
leaven, nor with the leaven
of malice and wickedness,
but with the unleavened
bread of sincerity and
truth.
9I wrote you in my letter
not to associate with im-
moral people;
10I *did* not at all *mean*
with the immoral people of
this world, or with the covetous and swindlers, or

[g] Some ancient mss. do not contain *Jesus*

ἡ βασιλεία τοῦ θεοῦ, ἀλλ' ἐν δυνάμει.
1the 2kingdom – 3of God, but in power.
21 τί θέλετε; ἐν ῥάβδῳ ἔλθω πρὸς ὑμᾶς,
What will ye? with a rod I come to you,
ἢ ἐν ἀγάπῃ πνεύματί τε πραΰτητος;
or in love and a spirit of meekness?

5 Ὅλως ἀκούεται ἐν ὑμῖν πορνεία,
Actually is heard among you fornication,
καὶ τοιαύτη πορνεία ἥτις οὐδὲ ἐν τοῖς
and such fornication which [is] not among the
ἔθνεσιν, ὥστε γυναῖκά τινα τοῦ πατρὸς
nations, so as 3wife 1one 4of the 5father
ἔχειν. **2** καὶ ὑμεῖς πεφυσιωμένοι ἐστέ,
2to have.[b] And ye *having been* puffed up are,
καὶ οὐχὶ μᾶλλον ἐπενθήσατε, ἵνα ἀρθῇ
and not rather mourned, *in order* that 5might be removed
ἐκ μέσου ὑμῶν ὁ τὸ ἔργον τοῦτο πράξας;
6from 8midst 9of you 1the 3this 4deed 2having done? 7[the] [one]
3 ἐγὼ μὲν γάρ, ἀπὼν τῷ σώματι,
For I indeed, being absent in the body,
παρὼν δὲ τῷ πνεύματι, ἤδη κέκρικα
but being present in the spirit, already have judged
ὡς παρὼν τὸν οὕτως τοῦτο κατεργα-
as being present 1the [one] 3thus 4this thing 2having
σάμενον **4** ἐν τῷ ὀνόματι τοῦ κυρίου
wrought in the name of the Lord
Ἰησοῦ συναχθέντων ὑμῶν καὶ τοῦ ἐμοῦ
Jesus being assembled you and – my
=when you are assembled . . .
πνεύματος σὺν τῇ δυνάμει τοῦ κυρίου
spirit[a] with the power of the Lord
ἡμῶν Ἰησοῦ **5** παραδοῦναι τὸν τοιοῦτον
of us Jesus to deliver such a person
τῷ σατανᾷ εἰς ὄλεθρον τῆς σαρκός,
– to Satan for destruction of the flesh,
ἵνα τὸ πνεῦμα σωθῇ ἐν τῇ ἡμέρᾳ τοῦ
in order that the spirit may be saved in the day of the
κυρίου. **6** Οὐ καλὸν τὸ καύχημα ὑμῶν.
Lord. Not good [is] the boast of you.
οὐκ οἴδατε ὅτι μικρὰ ζύμη ὅλον τὸ
Know ye not that a little leaven all the
φύραμα ζυμοῖ; **7** ἐκκαθάρατε τὴν παλαιὰν
lump leavens? Purge out the old
ζύμην, ἵνα ἦτε νέον φύραμα, καθώς
leaven, in order that ye may be a new lump, as
ἐστε ἄζυμοι. καὶ γὰρ τὸ πάσχα ἡμῶν
ye are unleavened. For indeed the passover of us
ἐτύθη Χριστός. **8** ὥστε ἑορτάζωμεν μὴ
was sacrificed[,] Christ. So as let us keep feast not
ἐν ζύμῃ παλαιᾷ μηδὲ ἐν ζύμῃ κακίας
with leaven old nor with leaven of malice
καὶ πονηρίας, ἀλλ' ἐν ἀζύμοις εἰλικρινείας
and *of* evil, but with unleavened [loaves] of sincerity
καὶ ἀληθείας. **9** Ἔγραψα ὑμῖν ἐν τῇ
and *of* truth. I wrote to you in the
ἐπιστολῇ μὴ συναναμίγνυσθαι πόρνοις,
epistle not to associate intimately *with* with fornicators,
10 οὐ πάντως τοῖς πόρνοις τοῦ κόσμου
not altogether with the fornicators – world
τούτου ἢ τοῖς πλεονέκταις καὶ ἅρπαξιν
of this or with the covetous and rapacious

of talk but of power.
21What do you prefer? Shall
I come to you with a whip,
or in love and with a gentle
spirit?

Chapter 5

Expel the Immoral Brother!

IT is actually reported
that there is sexual im-
morality among you, and of
a kind that does not occur
even among pagans: A man
has his father's wife. 2And
you are proud! Shouldn't
you rather have been filled
with grief and have put out
of your fellowship the man
who did this? 3Even though
I am not physically pre-
sent, I am with you in spirit. And I have already
passed judgment on the one
who did this, just as if I
were present. 4When you
are assembled in the name
of our Lord Jesus and I am
with you in spirit, and the
power of our Lord Jesus is
present, 5hand this man
over to Satan, so that the
sinful nature[f] may be destroyed and his spirit saved
on the day of the Lord.
6Your boasting is not
good. Don't you know that
a little yeast works through
the whole batch of dough?
7Get rid of the old yeast
that you may be a new
batch without yeast—as
you really are. For Christ,
our Passover lamb, has
been sacrificed. 8Therefore
let us keep the Festival, not
with the old yeast, the
yeast of malice and wickedness, but with the bread without yeast, the bread of sincerity and truth.
9I have written you in my
letter not to associate with
sexually immoral people—
10not at all meaning the
people of this world who
are immoral, or the greedy
and swindlers, or idolaters.

[f]5 Or *that his body*; or *that the flesh*

with idolaters; for then you would have to go out of the world.

11But actually, I wrote to you not to associate with any so-called brother if he should be an immoral person, or covetous, or an idolater, or a reviler, or a drunkard, or a swindler—not even to eat with such a one.

12For what have I to do with judging outsiders? Do you not judge those who are within *the church*?

13But those who are outside, God judges. REMOVE THE WICKED MAN FROM AMONG YOURSELVES.

Chapter 6

Lawsuits Discouraged

DOES any one of you, when he has a case against his neighbor, dare to go to law before the unrighteous, and not before the saints?

2Or do you not know that the saints will judge the world? And if the world is judged by you, are you not competent *to constitute* the smallest law courts?

3Do you not know that we shall judge angels? How much more, matters of this life?

4If then you have law courts dealing with matters of this life, do you appoint them as judges who are of no account in the church?

5I say *this* to your shame. *Is it* so, *that* there is not among you one wise man who will be able to decide between his brethren,

6but brother goes to law with brother, and that before unbelievers?

7Actually, then, it is already a defeat for you, that you have lawsuits with one another. Why not rather be wronged? Why not rather be defrauded?

8On the contrary, you yourselves wrong and defraud, and that *your* brethren.

9Or do you not know that the unrighteous shall not inherit the kingdom of God? Do not be deceived;

ἢ εἰδωλολάτραις, ἐπεὶ ὠφείλετε ἄρα ἐκ
or idolaters, since ye ought then out of

τοῦ κόσμου ἐξελθεῖν. **11** νῦν δὲ ἔγραψα
the world to go *out*. But now I wrote

ὑμῖν μὴ συναναμίγνυσθαι ἐάν τις ἀδελφὸς
to you not to associate intimately with if anyone a brother

ὀνομαζόμενος ᾖ πόρνος ἢ πλεονέκτης ἢ
being named is a fornicator or a covetous man or

εἰδωλολάτρης ἢ λοίδορος ἢ μέθυσος ἢ
an idolater or a railer or a drunkard or

ἅρπαξ, τῷ τοιούτῳ μηδὲ συνεσθίειν. **12** τί
a rapacious man, with such a man not to eat *with*. what

γάρ μοι τοὺς ἔξω κρίνειν; οὐχὶ τοὺς
For [is it] to me ²the ones ³without ¹to judge? ⁵Not ⁴the ones

ἔσω ὑμεῖς κρίνετε; **13** τοὺς δὲ ἔξω
⁶within ²ye ¹judge? But the ones without

ὁ θεὸς κρινεῖ. ἐξάρατε τὸν πονηρὸν ἐξ
– God will judge. Remove the evil man out of

ὑμῶν αὐτῶν.
yourselves.

6 Τολμᾷ τις ὑμῶν πρᾶγμα ἔχων πρὸς
Dares anyone of you ²a matter ¹having against

τὸν ἕτερον κρίνεσθαι ἐπὶ τῶν ἀδίκων,
the(an) other to be judged before the unjust,

καὶ οὐχὶ ἐπὶ τῶν ἁγίων; **2** ἢ οὐκ οἴδατε
and not before the saints? or know ye not

ὅτι οἱ ἅγιοι τὸν κόσμον κρινοῦσιν; καὶ
that the saints the world will judge? and

εἰ ἐν ὑμῖν κρίνεται ὁ κόσμος, ἀνάξιοί
if ⁴by ⁵you ³is judged ¹the ²world, ³unworthy

ἐστε κριτηρίων ἐλαχίστων;
¹are ye ⁴judgments? ²of very little?

3 οὐκ οἴδατε
Know ye not

ὅτι ἀγγέλους κρινοῦμεν, μήτι γε βιωτικά;
that angels we will judge, not to speak of things of this life?

4 βιωτικὰ μὲν οὖν κριτήρια ἐὰν ἔχητε,
⁶Of this life ⁴indeed ³therefore ⁵judgments ¹if ²ye have,

τοὺς ἐξουθενημένους ἐν τῇ ἐκκλησίᾳ,
the ones *being* despised in the church,

τούτους καθίζετε; **5** πρὸς ἐντροπὴν ὑμῖν
these sit ye? For shame to you

λέγω. οὕτως οὐκ ἔνι ἐν ὑμῖν οὐδεὶς
I say. Thus there is no room among you [for] *no* one

σοφός, ὃς δυνήσεται διακρῖναι ἀνὰ μέσον
wise man, who will be able to discern in your midst

τοῦ ἀδελφοῦ αὐτοῦ; **6** ἀλλὰ ἀδελφὸς μετὰ
the brother of him? But brother with

ἀδελφοῦ κρίνεται, καὶ τοῦτο ἐπὶ ἀπίστων;
brother is judged, and this before unbelievers?

7 ἤδη μὲν οὖν ὅλως ἥττημα ὑμῖν ἐστιν
Now indeed therefore ²altogether ³a failure ⁴with you ¹there is

ὅτι κρίματα ἔχετε μεθ' ἑαυτῶν. διὰ τί
⁵that ⁷lawsuits ⁶ye have with yourselves. Why

οὐχὶ μᾶλλον ἀδικεῖσθε; διὰ τί οὐχὶ
not rather be wronged? Why not

μᾶλλον ἀποστερεῖσθε; **8** ἀλλὰ ὑμεῖς ἀδικεῖτε
rather be deprived? But ye do wrong

καὶ ἀποστερεῖτε, καὶ τοῦτο ἀδελφούς.
and deprive, and this brothers.

9 ἢ οὐκ οἴδατε ὅτι ἄδικοι θεοῦ βασιλείαν
Or know ye not that unrighteous men ³of God ²[the] kingdom

οὐ κληρονομήσουσιν; μὴ πλανᾶσθε· οὔτε
¹will not inherit? Be not led astray; not

In that case you would have to leave this world.
11But now I am writing you that you must not associate with anyone who calls himself a brother but is sexually immoral or greedy, an idolater or a slanderer, a drunkard or a swindler. With such a man do not even eat.

12What business is it of mine to judge those outside the church? Are you not to judge those inside? 13God will judge those outside. "Expel the wicked man from among you."[m]

Chapter 6

Lawsuits Among Believers

IF any of you has a dispute with another, dare he take it before the ungodly for judgment instead of before the saints? 2Do you not know that the saints will judge the world? And if you are to judge the world, are you not competent to judge trivial cases? 3Do you not know that we will judge angels? How much more the things of this life! 4Therefore, if you have disputes about such matters, appoint as judges even men of little account in the church![n] 5I say this to shame you. Is it possible that there is nobody among you wise enough to judge a dispute between believers? 6But instead, one brother goes to law against another—and this in front of unbelievers!

7The very fact that you have lawsuits among you means you have been completely defeated already. Why not rather be wronged? Why not rather be cheated? 8Instead, you yourselves cheat and do wrong, and you do this to your brothers.

9Do you not know that the wicked will not inherit the kingdom of God? Do

[m] 13 Deut. 17:7; 19:19; 21:21; 22:21,24; 24:7
[n] 4 Or *matters, do you appoint as judges men of little account in the church?*

neither fornicators, nor idolaters, nor adulterers, nor [h]effeminate, nor homosexuals,
10nor thieves, nor *the* covetous, nor drunkards, nor revilers, nor swindlers, shall inherit the kingdom of God.
11And such were some of you; but you were washed, but you were sanctified, but you were justified in the name of the Lord Jesus Christ, and in the Spirit of our God.

The Body Is the Lord's

12All things are lawful for me, but not all things are profitable. All things are lawful for me, but I will not be mastered by anything.
13Food is for the stomach, and the stomach is for food; but God will do away with both of them. Yet the body is not for immorality, but for the Lord; and the Lord is for the body.
14Now God has not only raised the Lord, but will also raise us up through His power.
15Do you not know that your bodies are members of Christ? Shall I then take away the members of Christ and make them members of a harlot? May it never be!
16Or do you not know that the one who joins himself to a harlot is one body *with her*? For He says, "THE TWO WILL BECOME ONE FLESH."
17But the one who joins himself to the Lord is one spirit *with Him*.
18Flee immorality. Every *other* sin that a man commits is outside the body, but the immoral man sins against his own body.
19Or do you not know that your body is a temple of the Holy Spirit who is in you,

πόρνοι οὔτε εἰδωλολάτραι οὔτε μοιχοὶ
fornicators nor idolaters nor adulterers
οὔτε μαλακοὶ οὔτε ἀρσενοκοῖται 10 οὔτε
nor voluptuous persons nor sodomites nor
κλέπται οὔτε πλεονέκται, οὐ μέθυσοι,
thieves nor covetous persons, not drunkards,
οὐ λοίδοροι, οὐχ ἅρπαγες βασιλείαν θεοῦ
not revilers, not rapacious persons [2][the] kingdom [3]of God
κληρονομήσουσιν. 11 καὶ ταῦτά τινες ἦτε·
[1]will inherit. And these things [2]some [of you] [1]*ye* were;
ἀλλὰ ἀπελούσασθε, ἀλλὰ ἡγιάσθητε, ἀλλὰ
but ye were washed, but ye were sanctified, but
ἐδικαιώθητε ἐν τῷ ὀνόματι τοῦ κυρίου
ye were justified in the name of the Lord
Ἰησοῦ Χριστοῦ καὶ ἐν τῷ πνεύματι
Jesus Christ and by the Spirit
τοῦ θεοῦ ἡμῶν.
of the God of us.
12 Πάντα μοι ἔξεστιν, ἀλλ' οὐ πάντα
All things to me [are] lawful, but not all things
συμφέρει. πάντα μοι ἔξεστιν, ἀλλ' οὐκ
expedient. All things to me [are] lawful, but not
ἐγὼ ἐξουσιασθήσομαι ὑπό τινος. 13 τὰ
I will be ruled by anyone. –
βρώματα τῇ κοιλίᾳ, καὶ ἡ κοιλία τοῖς
Foods for the belly, and the belly –
βρώμασιν· ὁ δὲ θεὸς καὶ ταύτην καὶ
for foods; – but God both this and
ταῦτα καταργήσει. τὸ δὲ σῶμα οὐ τῇ
these will destroy. But the body [is] not –
πορνείᾳ ἀλλὰ τῷ κυρίῳ, καὶ ὁ κύριος
for fornication but for the Lord, and the Lord
τῷ σώματι· 14 ὁ δὲ θεὸς καὶ τὸν κύριον
for the body; – and God both the Lord
ἤγειρεν καὶ ἡμᾶς ἐξεγερεῖ διὰ τῆς
raised and us will raise up through the
δυνάμεως αὐτοῦ. 15 οὐκ οἴδατε ὅτι τὰ
power of him. Know ye not that the
σώματα ὑμῶν μέλη Χριστοῦ ἐστιν; ἄρας
bodies of you members of Christ (is)are? Taking
οὖν τὰ μέλη τοῦ Χριστοῦ ποιήσω πόρνης
there-fore the members – of Christ shall I make [them] [3]of a harlot
μέλη; μὴ γένοιτο. 16 ἢ οὐκ οἴδατε ὅτι
[1]members? May it not be. Or know ye not that
ὁ κολλώμενος τῇ πόρνῃ ἓν σῶμά ἐστιν;
the [one] *being* joined – to a harlot one body is?
ἔσονται γάρ, φησίν, οἱ δύο εἰς σάρκα
For [4]will be, [3]he says, [1]the [2]two [5]into [7]flesh
μίαν. 17 ὁ δὲ κολλώμενος τῷ κυρίῳ
[6]one. But the [one] *being* joined to the Lord
ἓν πνεῦμά ἐστιν. 18 φεύγετε τὴν πορνείαν.
one spirit is. Flee ye – fornication.
πᾶν ἁμάρτημα ὃ ἐὰν ποιήσῃ ἄνθρωπος
Every sin whichever [2]may do [1]a man
ἐκτὸς τοῦ σώματός ἐστιν· ὁ δὲ πορνεύων
outside the body is; but the [one] committing fornication
εἰς τὸ ἴδιον σῶμα ἁμαρτάνει. 19
against the(his) own body sins. Or
οὐκ οἴδατε ὅτι τὸ σῶμα ὑμῶν ναὸς
know ye not that the body of you [2]a shrine
τοῦ ἐν ὑμῖν ἁγίου πνεύματός ἐστιν,
[3]of the [6]in [7]you [4]Holy [5]Spirit [1]is,

not be deceived: Neither
the sexually immoral nor
idolaters nor adulterers nor
male prostitutes nor homo-
sexual offenders 10nor
thieves nor the greedy nor
drunkards nor slanderers
nor swindlers will inherit
the kingdom of God. 11And
that is what some of you
were. But you were
washed, you were sancti-
fied, you were justified in
the name of the Lord Jesus
Christ and by the Spirit of
our God.

Sexual Immorality

12"Everything is permis-
sible for me"—but not ev-
erything is beneficial. "Everything is permissible for
me"—but I will not be
mastered by anything.
13"Food for the stomach
and the stomach for food"
—but God will destroy
them both. The body is not
meant for sexual immorality, but for the Lord, and the
Lord for the body. 14By his
power God raised the Lord
from the dead, and he will
raise us also. 15Do you not
know that your bodies are
members of Christ himself?
Shall I then take the members of Christ and unite
them with a prostitute?
Never! 16Do you not know
that he who unites himself
with a prostitute is one with
her in body? For it is said,
"The two will become one
flesh."[o] 17But he who
unites himself with the
Lord is one with him in
spirit.
18Flee from sexual immo-
rality. All other sins a man
commits are outside his
body, but he who sins sexually sins against his own
body. 19Do you not know
that your body is a temple
of the Holy Spirit, who is in

[h] I.e., effeminate by perversion

[o] *16* Gen. 2:24

whom you have from God,
and that you are not your
own?
20For you have been
bought with a price: therefore glorify God in your
body.

Chapter 7

Advice on Marriage

NOW concerning the
things about which
you wrote, it is good for a
man not to touch a woman.
2But because of im-
moralities, let each man
have his own wife, and let
each woman have her own
husband.
3Let the husband fulfill
his duty to his wife, and
likewise also the wife to her
husband.
4The wife does not have
authority over her own
body, but the husband
does; and likewise also the
husband does not have au-
thority over his own body,
but the wife *does*.
5Stop depriving one an-
other, except by agreement
for a time that you may
devote yourselves to
prayer, and come together
again lest Satan tempt you
because of your lack of
self-control.
6But this I say by way of
concession, not of com-
mand.
7[i]Yet I wish that all men
were even as I myself am.
However, each man has his
own gift from God, one in
this manner, and another in
that.
8But I say to the unmar-
ried and to widows that it is
good for them if they re-
main even as I.
9But if they do not have
self-control, let them
marry; for it is better to
marry than to burn.
10But to the married I give
instructions, not I, but the
Lord, that the wife should
not leave her husband
11(but if she does leave,

[i]Some ancient mss. read *For*

οὗ ἔχετε ἀπὸ θεοῦ, καὶ οὐκ ἐστὲ ἑαυτῶν;
which ye have from God, and ye are not of yourselves?
20 ἠγοράσθητε γὰρ τιμῆς· δοξάσατε δὴ
For ye were bought of(with) a price; glorify ye then
τὸν θεὸν ἐν τῷ σώματι ὑμῶν.
– God in the body of you.

7 Περὶ δὲ ὧν ἐγράψατε, καλὸν ἀνθρώπῳ
Now about things of which ye wrote, [it is] good for a man
γυναικὸς μὴ ἅπτεσθαι· 2 διὰ δὲ τὰς
[3]a woman* [1]not [2]to touch; but because of the
πορνείας ἕκαστος τὴν ἑαυτοῦ γυναῖκα
fornications each man [2]the [4]of himself [3]wife
ἐχέτω, καὶ ἑκάστη τὸν ἴδιον ἄνδρα
[1]let him have, and each woman the(her) own husband
ἐχέτω. 3 τῇ γυναικὶ ὁ ἀνὴρ τὴν ὀφειλὴν
let her have. To the wife [2]the [3]husband [4]the [5]debt
ἀποδιδότω, ὁμοίως δὲ καὶ ἡ γυνὴ τῷ
[1]let *him* pay, and likewise also the wife to the
ἀνδρί. 4 ἡ γυνὴ τοῦ ἰδίου σώματος
husband. The wife of the(her) own body
οὐκ ἐξουσιάζει ἀλλὰ ὁ ἀνήρ· ὁμοίως
has not authority but the husband; [2]likewise
δὲ καὶ ὁ ἀνὴρ τοῦ ἰδίου σώματος οὐκ
[1]and also the husband of the(his) own body not
ἐξουσιάζει ἀλλὰ ἡ γυνή. 5 μὴ ἀποστερεῖτε
has authority but the wife. Deprive not ye
ἀλλήλους, εἰ μήτι ἂν ἐκ συμφώνου πρὸς
each other, unless by agreement for
καιρὸν ἵνα σχολάσητε τῇ προσευχῇ καὶ
a time in order that ye may have leisure – for prayer and
πάλιν ἐπὶ τὸ αὐτὸ ἦτε, ἵνα μὴ πειράζῃ
[3]again [2]together [1]*ye* may be, lest [2]tempt
ὑμᾶς ὁ σατανᾶς διὰ τὴν ἀκρασίαν [ὑμῶν].
[3]you – [1]Satan because of the want of self-control of you.
6 τοῦτο δὲ λέγω κατὰ συγγνώμην, οὐ
Now this I say by allowance, not
κατ' ἐπιταγήν. 7 θέλω δὲ πάντας
by command. And I wish all
ἀνθρώπους εἶναι ὡς καὶ ἐμαυτόν· ἀλλὰ
men to be as even myself; but
ἕκαστος ἴδιον ἔχει χάρισμα ἐκ θεοῦ,
each man [2][his] own [1]has gift of God,
ὁ μὲν οὕτως, ὁ δὲ οὕτως.
one thus, another thus.
8 Λέγω δὲ τοῖς ἀγάμοις καὶ ταῖς χήραις,
Now I say to the unmarried men and to the widows,
καλὸν αὐτοῖς ἐὰν μείνωσιν ὡς κἀγώ· 9 εἰ δὲ
[it is] good for them if they remain as I also; but if
οὐκ ἐγκρατεύονται, γαμησάτωσαν· κρεῖττον
they do not exercise self-control, let them marry; better
γάρ ἐστιν γαμεῖν ἢ πυροῦσθαι. 10 τοῖς
for it is to marry than to burn. to the [ones]
δὲ γεγαμηκόσιν παραγγέλλω, οὐκ ἐγὼ
But having married I enjoin, not I
ἀλλὰ ὁ κύριος, γυναῖκα ἀπὸ ἀνδρὸς μὴ
but the Lord, a woman from [her] husband not
χωρισθῆναι, 11 — ἐὰν δὲ καὶ χωρισθῇ,
to be separated,[b] but if indeed she is separated,

* As the same Greek word γυνή means "wife" or "(?married) woman" it is not always easy to differentiate in translating. So also the one Greek word ἀνήρ means "man" or "husband"

you, whom you have re-
ceived from God? You are
not your own; 20you were
bought at a price. There-
fore honor God with your
body.

Chapter 7

Marriage

NOW for the matters
you wrote about: It is
good for a man not to marry.[p] 2But since there is so
much immorality, each
man should have his own
wife, and each woman her
own husband. 3The hus-
band should fulfill his marital duty to his wife, and
likewise the wife to her
husband. 4The wife's body
does not belong to her
alone but also to her husband. In the same way, the
husband's body does not
belong to him alone but
also to his wife. 5Do not deprive each other except by
mutual consent and for a
time, so that you may de-
vote yourselves to prayer.
Then come together again
so that Satan will not tempt
you because of your lack of
self-control. 6I say this as a
concession, not as a com-
mand. 7I wish that all men
were as I am. But each man
has his own gift from God;
one has this gift, another
has that.
8Now to the unmarried
and the widows I say: It is
good for them to stay un-
married, as I am. 9But if
they cannot control them-
selves, they should marry,
for it is better to marry than
to burn with passion.
10To the married I give
this command (not I, but
the Lord): A wife must not
separate from her husband.
11But if she does, she must

[p]1 Or "*It is good for a man not to have sexual relations with a woman.*"

let her remain unmarried,
or else be reconciled to her
husband), and that the husband should not send his
wife away.
12 But to the rest I say, not
the Lord, that if any brother has a wife who is an unbeliever, and she consents
to live with him, let him not
send her away.
13 And a woman who has
an unbelieving husband,
and he consents to live with
her, let her not send her
husband away.
14 For the unbelieving
husband is sanctified
through his wife, and the
unbelieving wife is sanctified through her believing
husband; for otherwise
your children are unclean,
but now they are holy.
15 Yet if the unbelieving
one leaves, let him leave;
the brother or the sister is
not under bondage in such
cases, but God has called
[j]us to peace.
16 For how do you know,
O wife, whether you will
save your husband? Or
how do you know, O hus-
band, whether you will
save your wife?
17 Only, as the Lord has
assigned to each one, as
God has called each, in this
manner let him walk. And
thus I direct in all the
churches.
18 Was any man called *already* circumcised? Let
him not become uncircum-
cised. Has anyone been
called in uncircumcision?
Let him not be circum-
cised.
19 Circumcision is noth-
ing, and uncircumcision is
nothing, but *what matters
is* the keeping of the commandments of God.
20 Let each man remain in
that condition in which he
was called.
21 Were you called while a
slave? Do not worry about
it; but if you are able also to
become free, rather do
that.

[j] Some ancient mss. read *you*

μενέτω ἄγαμος ἢ τῷ ἀνδρὶ καταλλαγήτω,
let her remain unmarried or to the(her) husband be reconciled,

— καὶ ἄνδρα γυναῖκα μὴ ἀφιέναι. **12** Τοῖς
and a husband [his] wife not to leave.[b] to the

δὲ λοιποῖς λέγω ἐγώ, οὐχ ὁ κύριος·
And rest say I, not the Lord:

εἴ τις ἀδελφὸς γυναῖκα ἔχει ἄπιστον, καὶ
If any brother [2]a wife [1]has unbelieving, and

αὕτη συνευδοκεῖ οἰκεῖν μετ' αὐτοῦ, μὴ
this one consents to dwell with him, not

ἀφιέτω αὐτήν· **13** καὶ γυνὴ ἥτις ἔχει
let him leave her; and a woman who has

ἄνδρα ἄπιστον, καὶ οὗτος συνευδοκεῖ οἰκεῖν
a husband unbelieving, and this one consents to dwell

μετ' αὐτῆς, μὴ ἀφιέτω τὸν ἄνδρα.
with her, let her not leave the(her) husband.

14 ἡγίασται γὰρ ὁ ἀνὴρ ὁ ἄπιστος ἐν
For [4]has been sanctified [1]the [3]husband – [2]unbelieving by

τῇ γυναικί, καὶ ἡγίασται ἡ γυνὴ ἡ
the wife, and [4]has been sanctified [1]the [3]wife –

ἄπιστος ἐν τῷ ἀδελφῷ· ἐπεὶ ἄρα τὰ
[2]unbelieving by the brother; since then the

τέκνα ὑμῶν ἀκάθαρτά ἐστιν, νῦν δὲ
children of you [2]unclean [1]is(are), but now

ἅγιά ἐστιν. **15** εἰ δὲ ὁ ἄπιστος χωρίζ-
[2]holy [1]they are. But if the unbelieving one separates

εται, χωριζέσθω· οὐ δεδούλωται ὁ
him/herself, let him/her be separated; [6]has not been enslaved [1]the

ἀδελφὸς ἢ ἡ ἀδελφὴ ἐν τοῖς τοιούτοις·
[2]brother [3]or [4]the [5]sister in such matters;

ἐν δὲ εἰρήνῃ κέκληκεν ὑμᾶς ὁ θεός.
but [4]in [5]peace [2]has called [3]you – [1]God.

16 τί γὰρ οἶδας, γύναι, εἰ τὸν ἄνδρα
For what knowest thou, wife, if the(thy) husband

σώσεις; ἢ τί οἶδας, ἄνερ, εἰ τὴν
thou wilt save? or what knowest thou, husband, if the(thy)

γυναῖκα σώσεις; **17** Εἰ μὴ ἑκάστῳ ὡς
wife thou wilt save? Only [5]to each [1]as

μεμέρικεν ὁ κύριος, ἕκαστον ὡς κέκληκεν
[4]has divided [2]the [3]Lord, [4]each [1]as [3]has called

ὁ θεός, οὕτως περιπατείτω. καὶ οὕτως
– [2]God, so let him walk. And so

ἐν ταῖς ἐκκλησίαις πάσαις διατάσσομαι.
[2]in [4]the [5]churches [3]all [1]I command.

18 περιτετμημένος τις ἐκλήθη; μὴ
[4]Having been circumcised [2]anyone [1]was [3]called? not

ἐπισπάσθω· ἐν ἀκροβυστίᾳ κέκληταί τις;
let him be uncircumcised; in uncircumcision has been called anyone?

μὴ περιτεμνέσθω. **19** ἡ περιτομὴ οὐδέν
let him not be circumcised. – Circumcision nothing

ἐστιν, καὶ ἡ ἀκροβυστία οὐδέν ἐστιν,
is, and – uncircumcision nothing is,

ἀλλὰ τήρησις ἐντολῶν θεοῦ. **20** ἕκαστος
but [the] keeping of commandments of God. Each one

ἐν τῇ κλήσει ᾗ ἐκλήθη, ἐν ταύτῃ
in the calling in which he was called, in this

μενέτω. **21** δοῦλος ἐκλήθης; μή σοι
let him remain. A slave wast thou called? not to thee

μελέτω· ἀλλ' εἰ καὶ δύνασαι ἐλεύθερος
let it matter; but if indeed thou art able [2]free

γενέσθαι, μᾶλλον χρῆσαι. **22** ὁ γὰρ ἐν
[1]to become, [2]rather [1]use [it]. For [1]the [one] [4]in

remain unmarried or else
be reconciled to her hus-
band. And a husband must
not divorce his wife.
12 To the rest I say this (I,
not the Lord): If any brother has a wife who is not a
believer and she is willing
to live with him, he must
not divorce her. 13 And if a
woman has a husband who
is not a believer and he is
willing to live with her, she
must not divorce him.
14 For the unbelieving husband has been sanctified
through his wife, and the
unbelieving wife has been
sanctified through her believing husband. Otherwise
your children would be unclean, but as it is, they are
holy.
15 But if the unbeliever
leaves, let him do so. A believing man or woman is
not bound in such circum-
stances; God has called us
to live in peace. 16 How do
you know, wife, whether
you will save your hus-
band? Or, how do you
know, husband, whether
you will save your wife?
17 Nevertheless, each one
should retain the place in
life that the Lord assigned
to him and to which God
has called him. This is the
rule I lay down in all the
churches. 18 Was a man already circumcised when he
was called? He should not
become uncircumcised.
Was a man uncircumcised
when he was called? He
should not be circumcised.
19 Circumcision is nothing
and uncircumcision is nothing. Keeping God's com-
mands is what counts.
20 Each one should remain
in the situation which he
was in when God called
him. 21 Were you a slave
when you were called?
Don't let it trouble you—
although if you can gain
your freedom, do so. 22 For

22For he who was called in the Lord while a slave, is the Lord's freedman; likewise he who was called while free, is Christ's slave.

23You were bought with a price; do not become slaves of men.

24Brethren, let each man remain with God in that *condition* in which he was called.

25Now concerning virgins I have no command of the Lord, but I give an opinion as one who by the mercy of the Lord is trustworthy.

26I think then that this is good in view of the present distress, that it is good for a man to remain as he is.

27Are you bound to a wife? Do not seek to be released. Are you released from a wife? Do not seek a wife.

28But if you should marry, you have not sinned; and if a virgin should marry, she has not sinned. Yet such will have trouble in this life, and I am trying to spare you.

29But this I say, brethren, the time has been shortened, so that from now on those who have wives should be as though they had none;

30and those who weep, as though they did not weep; and those who rejoice, as though they did not rejoice; and those who buy, as though they did not possess;

31and those who use the world, as though they did not make full use of it; for the form of this world is passing away.

32But I want you to be free from concern. One who is unmarried is concerned about the things of the Lord, how he may please the Lord;

33but one who is married is concerned about the

κυρίῳ κληθεὶς δοῦλος ἀπελεύθερος κυρίου
[5][the] Lord [2]called [3]a slave [7]a freed man [8]of [the] Lord
ἐστίν· ὁμοίως ὁ ἐλεύθερος κληθεὶς δοῦλός
[6]is; likewise [1]the [one] [3]a free man [2]called [5]a slave
ἐστιν Χριστοῦ. 23 τιμῆς ἠγοράσθητε· μὴ
[4]is [6]of Christ. Of(with) a price ye were bought; not
γίνεσθε δοῦλοι ἀνθρώπων. 24 ἕκαστος ἐν
become ye slaves of men. Each one in
ᾧ ἐκλήθη, ἀδελφοί, ἐν τούτῳ μενέτω
what [state] he was called, brothers, in this let him remain
παρὰ θεῷ.
with God.

25 Περὶ δὲ τῶν παρθένων ἐπιταγὴν
Now about the virgins a command
κυρίου οὐκ ἔχω, γνώμην δὲ δίδωμι ὡς
of [the] Lord I have not, but an opinion I give as
ἠλεημένος ὑπὸ κυρίου πιστὸς εἶναι.
having had mercy by [the] Lord faithful to be.
26 Νομίζω οὖν τοῦτο καλὸν ὑπάρχειν
I suppose therefore this good to be
διὰ τὴν ἐνεστῶσαν ἀνάγκην, ὅτι καλὸν
because of the present necessity, that [it is] good
ἀνθρώπῳ τὸ οὕτως εἶναι. 27 δέδεσαι
for a man – so to be. Hast thou been bound
γυναικί; μὴ ζήτει λύσιν· λέλυσαι ἀπὸ
to a woman? do not seek release; hast thou been released from
γυναικός; μὴ ζήτει γυναῖκα. 28 ἐὰν
a woman? do not seek a woman. if
δὲ καὶ γαμήσῃς, οὐχ ἥμαρτες, καὶ ἐὰν
But indeed thou marriest, thou sinnedst not, and if
γήμῃ ἡ παρθένος, οὐχ ἥμαρτεν· θλῖψιν
[3]marries [1]the [2]virgin, she sinned not; [3]affliction
δὲ τῇ σαρκὶ ἕξουσιν οἱ τοιοῦτοι, ἐγὼ
but [4]in the [5]flesh [2]will have – [1]such, [2]I
δὲ ὑμῶν φείδομαι. 29 Τοῦτο δέ φημι,
[1]and [4]you [3]am sparing. But this I say,
ἀδελφοί, ὁ καιρὸς συνεσταλμένος ἐστίν·
brothers, the time *having been* shortened is;
τὸ λοιπὸν ἵνα καὶ οἱ ἔχοντες γυναῖκας
for the rest in order that both the [ones] having wives
ὡς μὴ ἔχοντες ὦσιν, 30 καὶ οἱ κλαίοντες
as not having may be, and the [ones] weeping
ὡς μὴ κλαίοντες, καὶ οἱ χαίροντες ὡς
as not weeping, and the [ones] rejoicing as
μὴ χαίροντες, καὶ οἱ ἀγοράζοντες ὡς
not rejoicing, and the [ones] buying as
μὴ κατέχοντες, 31 καὶ οἱ χρώμενοι τὸν
not holding, and the [ones] using the
κόσμον ὡς μὴ καταχρώμενοι· παράγει
world as not abusing [it]; [4]is passing away
γὰρ τὸ σχῆμα τοῦ κόσμου τούτου.
for [1]the [2]fashion [3]of this world.
32 Θέλω δὲ ὑμᾶς ἀμερίμνους εἶναι. ὁ
But I wish you without care to be. The
ἄγαμος μεριμνᾷ τὰ τοῦ κυρίου, 33 πῶς
unmarried man cares for the things of the Lord, how
ἀρέσῃ τῷ κυρίῳ· ὁ δὲ γαμήσας μεριμνᾷ
he may please the Lord; but the [one] having married cares for

he who was a slave when he
was called by the Lord is
the Lord's freedman; similarly, he who was a free
man when he was called is
Christ's slave. 23You were
bought at a price; do not become slaves of men.
24Brothers, each man, as
responsible to God, should
remain in the situation God
called him to.
25Now about virgins: I
have no command from the
Lord, but I give a judgment
as one who by the Lord's
mercy is trustworthy. 26Be-
cause of the present crisis,
I think that it is good for
you to remain as you are.
27Are you married? Do not
seek a divorce. Are you unmarried? Do not look for a
wife. 28But if you do marry,
you have not sinned; and if
a virgin marries, she has
not sinned. But those who
marry will face many troubles in this life, and I want
to spare you this.
29What I mean, brothers,
is that the time is short.
From now on those who
have wives should live as if
they had none; 30those who
mourn, as if they did not;
those who are happy, as if
they were not; those who
buy something, as if it were
not theirs to keep; 31those
who use the things of the
world, as if not engrossed
in them. For this world in
its present form is passing
away.
32I would like you to be
free from concern. An un-
married man is concerned
about the Lord's affairs—
how he can please the
Lord. 33But a married man
is concerned about the af-

things of the world, how he may please his [k] wife,
34and *his interests* are divided. And the woman who is unmarried, and the virgin, is concerned about the things of the Lord, that she may be holy both in body and spirit; but one who is married is concerned about the things of the world, how she may please her husband.
35And this I say for your own benefit; not to put a restraint upon you, but to promote what is seemly, and *to secure* undistracted devotion to the Lord.
36But if any man thinks that he is acting unbecomingly toward his virgin *daughter,* if she should be of full age, and if it must be so, let him do what he wishes, he does not sin; let her marry.
37But he who stands firm in his heart, being under no constraint, but has authority over his own will, and has decided this in his own heart, to keep his own virgin *daughter,* he will do well.
38So then both he who gives his own virgin *daughter* in marriage does well, and he who does not give her in marriage will do better.
39A wife is bound as long as her husband lives; but if her husband is dead, she is free to be married to whom she wishes, only in the Lord.
40But in my opinion she is happier if she remains as she is; and I think that I also have the Spirit of God.

Chapter 8

Take Care with Your Liberty

NOW concerning things sacrificed to idols, we

[k] Some mss. read *wife. And there is a difference also between the wife and the virgin. One who is unmarried is concerned . . .*

τὰ τοῦ κόσμου, πῶς ἀρέσῃ τῇ γυναικί,
the things of the world, how he may please the(his) wife,

34 καὶ μεμέρισται. καὶ ἡ γυνὴ ἡ ἄγαμος
and has been divided. And the [2]woman – [1]unmarried

καὶ ἡ παρθένος μεριμνᾷ τὰ τοῦ κυρίου,
and the virgin cares for the things of the Lord,

ἵνα ᾖ ἁγία καὶ τῷ σώματι καὶ τῷ
in order that she may be holy both in the body and in the

πνεύματι· ἡ δὲ γαμήσασα μεριμνᾷ τὰ
spirit; but the [one] having married cares for the things

τοῦ κόσμου, πῶς ἀρέσῃ τῷ ἀνδρί.
of the world, how she may please the(her) husband.

35 τοῦτο δὲ πρὸς τὸ ὑμῶν αὐτῶν σύμφορον
And [2]this [3]for [4]the [6]of yourselves [5]advantage

λέγω, οὐχ ἵνα βρόχον ὑμῖν ἐπιβάλω,
[1]I say, not in order that [3]a restraint [2]you [1]I may put on,

ἀλλὰ πρὸς τὸ εὔσχημον καὶ εὐπάρεδρον
but for the thing comely and waiting on

τῷ κυρίῳ ἀπερισπάστως. 36 Εἰ δέ τις
the Lord undistractedly. But if anyone

ἀσχημονεῖν ἐπὶ τὴν παρθένον αὐτοῦ
[2]to behave dishonourably [3]toward [4]the [5]virgin [6]of him

νομίζει, ἐὰν ᾖ ὑπέρακμος, καὶ οὕτως
[1]thinks, if he/she is past the bloom of youth, and so

ὀφείλει γίνεσθαι, ὃ θέλει ποιείτω· οὐχ
ought to be, what he wishes let him do; not

ἁμαρτάνει· γαμείτωσαν. 37 ὃς δὲ ἕστηκεν
he sins; let them marry. But [he] who stands

ἐν τῇ καρδίᾳ αὐτοῦ ἑδραῖος, μὴ
in the heart of him firm, not

ἔχων ἀνάγκην, ἐξουσίαν δὲ ἔχει περὶ
having necessity, but authority has concerning

τοῦ ἰδίου θελήματος, καὶ τοῦτο κέκρικεν
the(his) own will, and this has decided

ἐν τῇ ἰδίᾳ καρδίᾳ, τηρεῖν τὴν ἑαυτοῦ
in the(his) own heart, to keep the of himself

παρθένον, καλῶς ποιήσει. 38 ὥστε καὶ
virgin, [2]well [1]he will do. So as both

ὁ γαμίζων τὴν ἑαυτοῦ παρθένον καλῶς
the [one] marrying the of himself virgin [2]well

ποιεῖ, καὶ ὁ μὴ γαμίζων κρεῖσσον ποιήσει.
[1]does, and the [one] not marrying [2]better [1]will do.

39 Γυνὴ δέδεται ἐφ᾽ ὅσον χρόνον ζῇ
A wife has been bound for so long a time as lives

ὁ ἀνὴρ αὐτῆς· ἐὰν δὲ κοιμηθῇ ὁ ἀνήρ,
the husband of her; but if sleeps the husband,

ἐλευθέρα ἐστὶν ᾧ θέλει γαμηθῆναι, μόνον
[2]free [1]she is [4]to whom [5]she wishes [3]to be married, only

ἐν κυρίῳ. 40 μακαριωτέρα δέ ἐστιν
in [the] Lord. But happier she is

ἐὰν οὕτως μείνῃ, κατὰ τὴν ἐμὴν γνώμην·
if so she remains, according to – my opinion;

δοκῶ δὲ κἀγὼ πνεῦμα θεοῦ ἔχειν.
and I think I also [the] Spirit of God *to* have.

8 Περὶ δὲ τῶν εἰδωλοθύτων, οἴδαμεν
Now about *the* idolatrous sacrifices, we know

fairs of this world—how he can please his wife— 34and his interests are divided. An unmarried woman or virgin is concerned about the Lord's affairs: Her aim is to be devoted to the Lord in both body and spirit. But a married woman is concerned about the affairs of this world—how she can please her husband. 35I am saying this for your own good, not to restrict you, but that you may live in a right way in undivided devotion to the Lord.
36If anyone thinks he is acting improperly toward the virgin he is engaged to, and if she is getting along in years and he feels he ought to marry, he should do as he wants. He is not sinning. They should get married.
37But the man who has settled the matter in his own mind, who is under no compulsion but has control over his own will, and who has made up his mind not to marry the virgin—this man also does the right thing.
38So then, he who marries the virgin does right, but he who does not marry her does even better. [q]
39A woman is bound to her husband as long as he lives. But if her husband dies, she is free to marry anyone she wishes, but he must belong to the Lord.
40In my judgment, she is happier if she stays as she is—and I think that I too have the Spirit of God.

Chapter 8

Food Sacrificed to Idols

NOW about food sacrificed to idols: We

[q] 36-38 Or *36If anyone thinks he is not treating his daughter properly, and if she is getting along in years, and he feels she ought to marry, he should do as he wants. He is not sinning. He should let her get married. 37But the man who has settled the matter in his own mind, who is under no compulsion but has control over his own will, and who has made up his mind to keep the virgin unmarried—this man also does the right thing. 38So then, he who gives his virgin in marriage does right, but he who does not give her in marriage does even better.*

know that we all have
knowledge. Knowledge
makes arrogant, but love
edifies.
2If anyone supposes that
he knows anything, he has
not yet known as he ought
to know;
3but if anyone loves
God, he is known by Him.
4Therefore concerning
the eating of things sacrificed to idols, we know that
[l]there is no such thing as
an idol in the world, and
that there is no God but
one.
5For even if there are so-
called gods whether in
heaven or on earth, as indeed there are many gods
and many lords,
6yet for us there is *but*
one God, the Father, from
whom are all things, and we
exist for Him; and one
Lord, Jesus Christ, by
whom are all things, and we
exist through Him.
7However not all men
have this knowledge; but
some, being accustomed to
the idol until now, eat *food*
as if it were sacrificed to an
idol; and their conscience
being weak is defiled.
8But food will not com-
mend us to God; we are
neither the worse if we do
not eat, nor the better if we
do eat.
9But take care lest this
liberty of yours somehow
become a stumbling block
to the weak.
10For if someone sees
you, who have knowledge,
dining in an idol's temple,
will not his conscience, if
he is weak, be strengthened
to eat things sacrificed to
idols?
11For through your
knowledge he who is weak
is ruined, the brother for
whose sake Christ died.
12And thus, by sinning
against the brethren and
wounding their conscience
when it is weak, you sin

ὅτι πάντες γνῶσιν ἔχομεν. ἡ γνῶσις
that 2all 4knowledge 1we 3have. – Knowledge

φυσιοῖ, ἡ δὲ ἀγάπη οἰκοδομεῖ· εἴ τις
puffs up, – but love builds up; if anyone

δοκεῖ ἐγνωκέναι τι, 2 οὔπω ἔγνω καθὼς
thinks to have known anything, not yet he knew as

δεῖ γνῶναι· 3 εἰ δέ τις ἀγαπᾷ τὸν
it behoves [him] to know; but if anyone loves –

θεόν, οὗτος ἔγνωσται ὑπ' αὐτοῦ. 4 Περὶ
God, this one has been known by him. About

τῆς βρώσεως οὖν τῶν εἰδωλοθύτων
the eating therefore – of idolatrous sacrifices

οἴδαμεν ὅτι οὐδὲν εἴδωλον ἐν κόσμῳ,
we know that [there is] no idol in [the] world,

καὶ ὅτι οὐδεὶς θεὸς εἰ μὴ εἷς. 5 καὶ
and that [there is] no God except one. even

γὰρ εἴπερ εἰσὶν λεγόμενοι θεοὶ εἴτε ἐν
For if there are *being* called gods either in

οὐρανῷ εἴτε ἐπὶ γῆς, ὥσπερ εἰσὶν θεοὶ
heaven or on earth, even as there are gods

πολλοὶ καὶ κύριοι πολλοί, 6 ἀλλ' ἡμῖν
many and lords many, yet to us

εἷς θεὸς ὁ πατήρ, ἐξ οὗ τὰ πάντα καὶ
[there is] one God the Father, of whom – [are] all things and

ἡμεῖς εἰς αὐτόν, καὶ εἷς κύριος Ἰησοῦς
we in him, and one Lord Jesus

Χριστός, δι' οὗ τὰ πάντα καὶ ἡμεῖς
Christ, through whom – [are] all things and we

δι' αὐτοῦ. 7 Ἀλλ' οὐκ ἐν πᾶσιν ἡ
through him. But [there is] not in all men the (this)

γνῶσις· τινὲς δὲ τῇ συνηθείᾳ ἕως ἄρτι
knowledge; and some by *the* habit until now

τοῦ εἰδώλου ὡς εἰδωλόθυτον ἐσθίουσιν,
3of the 2idol 4as 5an idolatrous sacrifice 1eat,

καὶ ἡ συνείδησις αὐτῶν ἀσθενὴς οὖσα
and the conscience of them 2weak 1being

μολύνεται. 8 βρῶμα δὲ ἡμᾶς οὐ παραστήσει
is defiled. But food 2us 1will not commend

τῷ θεῷ· οὔτε ἐὰν μὴ φάγωμεν ὑστερούμεθα,
– to God; neither if we eat not are we behind,

οὔτε ἐὰν φάγωμεν περισσεύομεν. 9 βλέπετε
nor if we eat do we excel. look ye

δὲ μή πως ἡ ἐξουσία ὑμῶν αὕτη
But lest somehow *the* 2authority 3of you 1this

πρόσκομμα γένηται τοῖς ἀσθενέσιν. 10 ἐὰν
a stumbling-block becomes to the weak ones. if

γάρ τις ἴδῃ σὲ τὸν ἔχοντα γνῶσιν ἐν
For anyone sees thee the [one] having knowledge 8in

εἰδωλείῳ κατακείμενον, οὐχὶ ἡ συνείδησις
9an idol's temple 1sitting, 2not 3the 4conscience

αὐτοῦ ἀσθενοῦς ὄντος οἰκοδομηθήσεται εἰς
5of him 7weak 6[he] being 1will 8be emboldened –

τὸ τὰ εἰδωλόθυτα ἐσθίειν; 11 ἀπόλλυται
– 10the 11idolatrous sacrifices 9to eat? 3is destroyed

γὰρ ὁ ἀσθενῶν ἐν τῇ σῇ γνώσει, ὁ
For 1the [one] 2being weak by – thy knowledge, the

ἀδελφὸς δι' ὃν Χριστὸς ἀπέθανεν. 12 οὕτως
brother because of whom Christ died. so

δὲ ἁμαρτάνοντες εἰς τοὺς ἀδελφοὺς καὶ
And sinning against the brothers and

τύπτοντες αὐτῶν τὴν συνείδησιν ἀσθενοῦσαν
wounding of them the conscience being weak

know that we all possess
knowledge.[r] Knowledge
puffs up, but love builds
up. 2The man who thinks
he knows something does
not yet know as he ought to
know. 3But the man who
loves God is known by
God.
4So then, about eating
food sacrificed to idols: We
know that an idol is nothing
at all in the world and that
there is no God but one.
5For even if there are so-
called gods, whether in
heaven or on earth (as indeed there are many
"gods" and many
"lords"), 6yet for us there
is but one God, the Father,
from whom all things came
and for whom we live; and
there is but one Lord, Jesus
Christ, through whom all
things came and through
whom we live.
7But not everyone knows
this. Some people are still
so accustomed to idols that
when they eat such food
they think of it as having
been sacrificed to an idol,
and since their conscience
is weak, it is defiled. 8But
food does not bring us near
to God; we are no worse if
we do not eat, and no better
if we do.
9Be careful, however,
that the exercise of your
freedom does not become a
stumbling block to the
weak. 10For if anyone with
a weak conscience sees
you who have this knowl-
edge eating in an idol's temple, won't he be embold-
ened to eat what has been
sacrificed to idols? 11So this
weak brother, for whom
Christ died, is destroyed by
your knowledge. 12When
you sin against your brothers in this way and wound
their weak conscience, you
sin against Christ. 13There-

[l] I.e., has no real existence

[r] 1 Or *"We all possess knowledge,"* *as you say*

against Christ.
13Therefore, if food
causes my brother to stumble, I will never eat meat
again, that I might not
cause my brother to stum-
ble.

Chapter 9

Paul's Use of Liberty

AM I not free? Am I not
an apostle? Have I not
seen Jesus our Lord? Are
you not my work in the
Lord?
2If to others I am not an
apostle, at least I am to
you; for you are the seal of
my apostleship in the Lord.
3My defense to those
who examine me is this:
4Do we not have a right
to eat and drink?
5Do we not have a right
to take along a believing
wife, even as the rest of the
apostles, and the brothers
of the Lord, and Cephas?
6Or do only Barnabas
and I not have a right to
refrain from working?
7Who at any time serves
as a soldier at his own expense? Who plants a vine-
yard, and does not eat the
fruit of it? Or who tends a
flock and does not use the
milk of the flock?
8I am not speaking these
things according to human
judgment, am I? Or does
not the Law also say these
things?
9For it is written in the
Law of Moses, "YOU
SHALL NOT MUZZLE THE OX
WHILE HE IS THRESHING."
God is not concerned about
oxen, is He?
10Or is He speaking alto-
gether for our sake? Yes,
for our sake it was written,
because the plowman
ought to plow in hope, and
the thresher *to thresh* in
hope of sharing *the crops*.
11If we sowed spiritual
things in you, is it too much
if we should reap material

εἰς Χριστὸν ἁμαρτάνετε. **13** διόπερ εἰ
[2]against [3]Christ [1]ye sin. Wherefore if
βρῶμα σκανδαλίζει τὸν ἀδελφόν μου, οὐ
food offends the brother of me, by no
μὴ φάγω κρέα εἰς τὸν αἰῶνα, ἵνα μὴ
means I eat flesh unto the age, lest
τὸν ἀδελφόν μου σκανδαλίσω.
[2]the [3]brother [4]of me [1]I offend.

9 Οὐκ εἰμὶ ἐλεύθερος; οὐκ εἰμὶ ἀπόστολος;
Am I not free? am I not an apostle?
οὐχὶ Ἰησοῦν τὸν κύριον ἡμῶν ἑόρακα;
not Jesus the Lord of us I have seen?
οὐ τὸ ἔργον μου ὑμεῖς ἐστε ἐν κυρίῳ;
not the work of me ye are in [the] Lord?
2 εἰ ἄλλοις οὐκ εἰμὶ ἀπόστολος, ἀλλά
If to others I am not an apostle, yet
γε ὑμῖν εἰμι· ἡ γὰρ σφραγίς μου τῆς
indeed to you I am; for the seal [3]of me [1]of the
ἀποστολῆς ὑμεῖς ἐστε ἐν κυρίῳ. **3** Ἡ
[2]apostleship ye are in [the] Lord. –
ἐμὴ ἀπολογία τοῖς ἐμὲ ἀνακρίνουσίν ἐστιν
My defence to the [ones] [2]me [1]examining is
αὕτη. **4** μὴ οὐκ ἔχομεν ἐξουσίαν φαγεῖν
this. *not* Have we not authority to eat
καὶ πεῖν; **5** μὴ οὐκ ἔχομεν ἐξουσίαν
and to drink? *not* have we not authority
ἀδελφὴν γυναῖκα περιάγειν, ὡς καὶ οἱ
a sister a wife to lead about, as also the
λοιποὶ ἀπόστολοι καὶ οἱ ἀδελφοὶ τοῦ
remaining apostles and the brothers of the
κυρίου καὶ Κηφᾶς; **6** ἢ μόνος ἐγὼ καὶ
Lord and Cephas? or only I and
Βαρναβᾶς οὐκ ἔχομεν ἐξουσίαν μὴ
Barnabas have we not authority not
ἐργάζεσθαι; **7** Τίς στρατεύεται ἰδίοις
to work? Who soldiers at [his] own
ὀψωνίοις ποτέ; τίς φυτεύει ἀμπελῶνα καὶ
wages at any time? who plants a vineyard and
τὸν καρπὸν αὐτοῦ οὐκ ἐσθίει; ἢ τίς
the fruit of it eats not? or who
ποιμαίνει ποίμνην καὶ ἐκ τοῦ γάλακτος
shepherds a flock and of the milk
τῆς ποίμνης οὐκ ἐσθίει; **8** μὴ κατὰ
of the flock eats not? *Not* according to
ἄνθρωπον ταῦτα λαλῶ, ἢ καὶ ὁ νόμος
man these things I speak, or also the law
ταῦτα οὐ λέγει; **9** ἐν γὰρ τῷ Μωϋσέως
these things says not? for in the of Moses
νόμῳ γέγραπται· οὐ κημώσεις βοῦν
law it has been written: Thou shalt not muzzle an ox
ἀλοῶντα. μὴ τῶν βοῶν μέλει τῷ θεῷ;
threshing. *not* – of oxen matters it – to God?
10 ἢ δι' ἡμᾶς πάντως λέγει; δι' ἡμᾶς
or because of us altogether he says? because of us
γὰρ ἐγράφη, ὅτι ὀφείλει ἐπ' ἐλπίδι
for it was written, because [3]ought [4]on(in) [5]hope
ὁ ἀροτριῶν ἀροτριᾶν, καὶ ὁ ἀλοῶν ἐπ'
[1]the [one] [2]ploughing [6]to plough, and the [one] threshing on(in)
ἐλπίδι τοῦ μετέχειν. **11** εἰ ἡμεῖς ὑμῖν
hope of the to partake. =of partaking. If we to you
τὰ πνευματικὰ ἐσπείραμεν, μέγα εἰ ἡμεῖς
– spiritual things sowed, [is it] a great thing if we

fore, if what I eat causes
my brother to fall into sin, I
will never eat meat again,
so that I will not cause him
to fall.

Chapter 9

The Rights of an Apostle

AM I not free? Am I not
an apostle? Have I not
seen Jesus our Lord? Are
you not the result of my
work in the Lord? 2Even
though I may not be an
apostle to others, surely I
am to you! For you are the
seal of my apostleship in
the Lord.
3This is my defense to
those who sit in judgment
on me. 4Don't we have the
right to food and drink?
5Don't we have the right to
take a believing wife along
with us, as do the other
apostles and the Lord's
brothers and Cephas[s]? 6Or
is it only I and Barnabas
who must work for a living?
7Who serves as a soldier
at his own expense? Who
plants a vineyard and does
not eat of its grapes? Who
tends a flock and does not
drink of the milk? 8Do I say
this merely from a human
point of view? Doesn't the
Law say the same thing?
9For it is written in the Law
of Moses: "Do not muzzle
an ox while it is treading
out the grain."[t] Is it about
oxen that God is con-
cerned? 10Surely he says
this for us, doesn't he? Yes,
this was written for us, because when the plowman
plows and the thresher
threshes, they ought to do
so in the hope of sharing in
the harvest. 11If we have
sown spiritual seed among

[s]5 That is, Peter
[t]9 Deut. 25:4

things from you?
12 If others share the right
over you, do we not more?
Nevertheless, we did not
use this right, but we endure all things, that we may
cause no hindrance to the
gospel of Christ.
13 Do you not know that
those who perform sacred
services eat the *food* of the
temple, *and* those who attend regularly to the altar
have their share with the altar?
14 So also the Lord directed those who proclaim the
gospel to get their living
from the gospel.
15 But I have used none of
these things. And I am not
writing these things that it
may be done so in my case;
for it would be better for me
to die than have any man
make my boast an empty
one.
16 For if I preach the gospel, I have nothing to boast
of, for I am under compulsion; for woe is me if I do
not preach the gospel.
17 For if I do this voluntarily, I have a reward; but
if against my will, I have a
stewardship entrusted to
me.
18 What then is my re-
ward? That, when I preach
the gospel, I may offer the
gospel without charge, so
as not to make full use of
my right in the gospel.
19 For though I am free
from all *men*, I have made
myself a slave to all, that I
might win the more.
20 And to the Jews I
became as a Jew, that I
might win Jews; to those
who are under the Law, as
under the Law, though not
being myself under the
Law, that I might win those
who are under the Law;

ὑμῶν τὰ σαρκικὰ θερίσομεν; **12** εἰ ἄλλοι
of you – fleshly things shall reap? If others

τῆς ὑμῶν ἐξουσίας μετέχουσιν, οὐ
[2]of the [4]of you [3]authority [1]have a share *of*, not

μᾶλλον ἡμεῖς; ἀλλ᾽ οὐκ ἐχρησάμεθα
rather we? But we did not use

τῇ ἐξουσίᾳ ταύτῃ, ἀλλὰ πάντα στέγομεν
this authority, but [2]all things [1]we put up with

ἵνα μή τινα ἐγκοπὴν δῶμεν τῷ εὐαγγελίῳ
lest [3]anyone [2]an obstacle [1]we should give to the gospel

τοῦ Χριστοῦ. **13** Οὐκ οἴδατε ὅτι οἱ
– of Christ. Know ye not that the [ones]

τὰ ἱερὰ ἐργαζόμενοι τὰ ἐκ τοῦ ἱεροῦ
– [2]sacred things [1]working [at] [4]the things [5]of [6]the [7]temple

ἐσθίουσιν, οἱ τῷ θυσιαστηρίῳ παρεδρεύοντες
[3]eat, the [ones] [2]the [3]altar [1]attending [on]

τῷ θυσιαστηρίῳ συμμερίζονται; **14** οὕτως
[5]the [6]altar [4]partake with? So

καὶ ὁ κύριος διέταξεν τοῖς τὸ εὐαγγέλιον
also the Lord ordained the [ones] [2]the [3]gospel

καταγγέλλουσιν ἐκ τοῦ εὐαγγελίου ζῆν.
[1]announcing [5]of [6]the [7]gospel [4]to live.

15 ἐγὼ δὲ οὐ κέχρημαι οὐδενὶ τούτων.
But I have not used *not* one of these things.

Οὐκ ἔγραψα δὲ ταῦτα ἵνα οὕτως γένηται
And I did not write these things in order that so it might be

ἐν ἐμοί· καλὸν γάρ μοι μᾶλλον ἀποθανεῖν
in me; for good [it is] to me rather to die

ἤ — τὸ καύχημά μου οὐδεὶς κενώσει.
than — the boast of me no man shall empty.

16 ἐὰν γὰρ εὐαγγελίζωμαι, οὐκ ἔστιν
For if I preach good news, there is not =I have no boast;

μοι καύχημα· ἀνάγκη γάρ μοι ἐπίκειται·
to me boast;[c] for necessity [2]me [1]is laid on;

οὐαὶ γάρ μοί ἐστιν ἐὰν μὴ εὐαγγελίσωμαι.
for woe [2]to me [1]is if I do not preach good tidings.

17 εἰ γὰρ ἑκὼν τοῦτο πράσσω, μισθὸν
For if willingly [2]this [1]I do, [3]a reward

ἔχω· εἰ δὲ ἄκων, οἰκονομίαν πεπίστευμαι.
[1]I have; but if unwillingly, [2]a stewardship [1]I have been entrusted [with].

18 τίς οὖν μού ἐστιν ὁ μισθός; ἵνα
What therefore [4]of me [1]is [2]the [3]reward? *in order* that

εὐαγγελιζόμενος ἀδάπανον θήσω τὸ
preaching good tidings [4]without charge [1]I may place [2]the

εὐαγγέλιον, εἰς τὸ μὴ καταχρήσασθαι
[3]good tidings, so as† not to use to the full

τῇ ἐξουσίᾳ μου ἐν τῷ εὐαγγελίῳ.
the authority of me in the good tidings.

19 Ἐλεύθερος γὰρ ὢν ἐκ πάντων πᾶσιν
For [2]free [1]being of all men [3]to all men

ἐμαυτὸν ἐδούλωσα, ἵνα τοὺς πλείονας
[4]myself [1]I enslaved, in order that the more

κερδήσω· **20** καὶ ἐγενόμην τοῖς Ἰουδαίοις
I might gain; and I became to the Jews

ὡς Ἰουδαῖος, ἵνα Ἰουδαίους κερδήσω·
as a Jew, in order that Jews I might gain;

τοῖς ὑπὸ νόμον ὡς ὑπὸ νόμον, μὴ ὢν
to the ones under law as under law, not being

αὐτὸς ὑπὸ νόμον, ἵνα τοὺς ὑπὸ νόμον
[my]self under law, in order that the ones under law

you, is it too much if we
reap a material harvest
from you? 12 If others have
this right of support from
you, shouldn't we have it
all the more?
But we did not use this
right. On the contrary, we
put up with anything rather
than hinder the gospel of
Christ. 13 Don't you know
that those who work in the
temple get their food from
the temple, and those who
serve at the altar share in
what is offered on the altar?
14 In the same way, the
Lord has commanded that
those who preach the gos-
pel should receive their living from the gospel.
15 But I have not used any
of these rights. And I am
not writing this in the hope
that you will do such things
for me. I would rather die
than have anyone deprive
me of this boast. 16 Yet
when I preach the gospel, I
cannot boast, for I am compelled to preach. Woe to
me if I do not preach the
gospel! 17 If I preach voluntarily, I have a reward; if
not voluntarily, I am simply discharging the trust
committed to me. 18 What
then is my reward? Just
this: that in preaching the
gospel I may offer it free of
charge, and so not make
use of my rights in preaching it.
19 Though I am free and
belong to no man, I make
myself a slave to everyone,
to win as many as possible.
20 To the Jews I became like
a Jew, to win the Jews. To
those under the law I be-
came like one under the law
(though I myself am not under the law), so as to win
those under the law. 21 To

21to those who are with-
out law, as without law,
though not being without
the law of God but under
the law of Christ, that I
might win those who are
without law.
22To the weak I became
weak, that I might win the
weak; I have become all
things to all men, that I may
by all means save some.
23And I do all things for
the sake of the gospel, that
I may become a fellow partaker of it.
24Do you not know that
those who run in a race all
run, but *only* one receives
the prize? Run in such a
way that you may win.
25And everyone who
competes in the games ex-
ercises self-control in all
things. They then *do it* to
receive a perishable
wreath, but we an imper-
ishable.
26Therefore I run in such
a way, as not without aim; I
box in such a way, as not
beating the air;
27but I buffet my body
and make it my slave, lest
possibly, after I have
preached to others, I my-
self should be disqualified.

κερδήσω· 21 τοῖς ἀνόμοις ὡς ἄνομος,
I might gain; to the ones without law as without law,
μὴ ὢν ἄνομος θεοῦ ἀλλ' ἔννομος Χριστοῦ,
not being without [the] law of God but under [the] law of Christ,
ἵνα κερδάνω τοὺς ἀνόμους· 22 ἐγενόμην
in order that I may gain the ones without law; I became
τοῖς ἀσθενέσιν ἀσθενής, ἵνα τοὺς ἀσθενεῖς
[2]to the [3]weak [1]weak, in order that the weak
κερδήσω· τοῖς πᾶσιν γέγονα πάντα, ἵνα
I might gain; – to all men I have become all things, in order that
πάντως τινὰς σώσω. 23 πάντα δὲ ποιῶ
in any case [2]some [1]I might save. But all things I do
διὰ τὸ εὐαγγέλιον, ἵνα συγκοινωνὸς αὐτοῦ
because of the good tidings, in order that [2]a joint partaker [3]of it
γένωμαι. 24 Οὐκ οἴδατε ὅτι οἱ ἐν
[1]I may become. Know ye not that the [ones] [2]in
σταδίῳ τρέχοντες πάντες μὲν τρέχουσιν,
[3]a racecourse [1]running all indeed run,
εἷς δὲ λαμβάνει τὸ βραβεῖον; οὕτως
but one receives the prize? So
τρέχετε ἵνα καταλάβητε. 25 πᾶς δὲ ὁ
run in order that ye may obtain. And everyone
ἀγωνιζόμενος πάντα ἐγκρατεύεται, ἐκεῖνοι
struggling [in] all things exercises self-control, those
μὲν οὖν ἵνα φθαρτὸν στέφανον λάβωσιν,
indeed therefore in order that [2]a corruptible [3]crown [1]they may receive,
ἡμεῖς δὲ ἄφθαρτον. 26 ἐγὼ τοίνυν οὕτως
but we an incorruptible. I accordingly so
τρέχω ὡς οὐκ ἀδήλως, οὕτως πυκτεύω
run as not unclearly, so I box
ὡς οὐκ ἀέρα δέρων· 27 ἀλλὰ ὑπωπιάζω
as not [2]air [1]beating; but I treat severely
μου τὸ σῶμα καὶ δουλαγωγῶ, μή πως
of me the body and lead [it] as a slave, lest
ἄλλοις κηρύξας αὐτὸς ἀδόκιμος γένωμαι.
to others having proclaimed [2][my]self [5]disapproved [1]I [3]may [4]become.

those not having the law I
became like one not having
the law (though I am not
free from God's law but am
under Christ's law), so as
to win those not having the
law. 22To the weak I be-
came weak, to win the
weak. I have become all
things to all men so that by
all possible means I might
save some. 23I do all this for
the sake of the gospel, that
I may share in its blessings.
24Do you not know that in
a race all the runners run,
but only one gets the prize?
Run in such a way as to get
the prize. 25Everyone who
competes in the games goes
into strict training. They do
it to get a crown that will
not last; but we do it to get a
crown that will last forever.
26Therefore I do not run
like a man running aimless-
ly; I do not fight like a man
beating the air. 27No, I beat
my body and make it my
slave so that after I have
preached to others, I my-
self will not be disqualified
for the prize.

Chapter 10

Avoid Israel's Mistakes

FOR I do not want you to
be unaware, brethren,
that our fathers were all under the cloud, and all
passed through the sea;
2and all [m]were baptized
into Moses in the cloud and
in the sea;
3and all ate the same
spiritual food;
4and all drank the same
spiritual drink, for they
were drinking from a spiritual rock which followed
them; and the rock was
Christ.
5Nevertheless, with
most of them God was not
well-pleased; for they were
laid low in the wilderness.

[m] Some ancient mss. read *received baptism*

10 Οὐ θέλω γὰρ ὑμᾶς ἀγνοεῖν, ἀδελφοί,
For I wish not you to be ignorant, brothers,
ὅτι οἱ πατέρες ἡμῶν πάντες ὑπὸ τὴν
that the fathers of us all under the
νεφέλην ἦσαν καὶ πάντες διὰ τῆς θαλάσσης
cloud were and all through the sea
διῆλθον, 2 καὶ πάντες εἰς τὸν Μωϋσῆν
passed *through*, and all [2]to – [3]Moses
ἐβαπτίσαντο ἐν τῇ νεφέλῃ καὶ ἐν τῇ
[1]were baptized in the cloud and in the
θαλάσσῃ, 3 καὶ πάντες τὸ αὐτὸ πνευματικὸν
sea, and all [2]the [3]same [4]spiritual
βρῶμα ἔφαγον, 4 καὶ πάντες τὸ αὐτὸ
[5]food [1]ate, and all [2]the [3]same
πνευματικὸν ἔπιον πόμα· ἔπινον γὰρ ἐκ
[4]spiritual [1]drank [5]drink; for they drank of
πνευματικῆς ἀκολουθούσης πέτρας, ἡ πέτρα
a spiritual [2]following [1]rock, [2]the [3]rock
δὲ ἦν ὁ Χριστός. 5 Ἀλλ' οὐκ ἐν τοῖς
[1]and was *the* Christ. But [7]not [1]in(with) [2]the
πλείοσιν αὐτῶν εὐδόκησεν ὁ θεός·
[3]majority [4]of them [6]was [8]well [9]pleased – [5]God;
κατεστρώθησαν γὰρ ἐν τῇ ἐρήμῳ.
for they were scattered in the desert.

Chapter 10

Warnings From Israel's History

FOR I do not want you to
be ignorant of the fact,
brothers, that our forefathers were all under the
cloud and that they all
passed through the sea.
2They were all baptized
into Moses in the cloud and
in the sea. 3They all ate the
same spiritual food 4and
drank the same spiritual
drink; for they drank from
the spiritual rock that accompanied them, and that
rock was Christ. 5Never-
theless, God was not
pleased with most of them;
their bodies were scattered
over the desert.

6 Now these things happened as examples for us, that we should not crave evil things, as they also craved.

7 And do not be idolaters, as some of them were; as it is written, "THE PEOPLE SAT DOWN TO EAT AND DRINK, AND STOOD UP TO PLAY."

8 Nor let us act immorally, as some of them did, and twenty-three thousand fell in one day.

9 Nor let us try the Lord, as some of them did, and were destroyed by the serpents.

10 Nor grumble, as some of them did, and were destroyed by the destroyer.

11 Now these things happened to them as an example, and they were written for our instruction, upon whom the ends of the ages have come.

12 Therefore let him who thinks he stands take heed lest he fall.

13 No temptation has overtaken you but such as is common to man; and God is faithful, who will not allow you to be tempted beyond what you are able, but with the temptation will provide the way of escape also, that you may be able to endure it.

14 Therefore, my beloved, flee from idolatry.

15 I speak as to wise men; you judge what I say.

16 Is not the cup of blessing which we bless a sharing in the blood of Christ? Is not the bread which we break a sharing in the body of Christ?

17 Since there is one bread, we who are many

6 ταῦτα δὲ τύποι ἡμῶν ἐγενήθησαν, εἰς
Now these things types of us were, for

τὸ μὴ εἶναι ἡμᾶς ἐπιθυμητὰς κακῶν,
the not to be us[b] longers after evil things,
=so that we should not be . . .

καθὼς κἀκεῖνοι ἐπεθύμησαν. 7 μηδὲ
as those indeed longed. Neither

εἰδωλολάτραι γίνεσθε, καθώς τινες αὐτῶν·
idolaters be ye, as some of them;

ὥσπερ γέγραπται· ἐκάθισεν ὁ λαὸς φαγεῖν
as it has been written: Sat the people to eat

καὶ πεῖν, καὶ ἀνέστησαν παίζειν. 8 μηδὲ
and to drink, and stood up to play. Neither

πορνεύωμεν, καθώς τινες αὐτῶν ἐπόρνευσαν
let us commit fornication, as some of them committed fornication

καὶ ἔπεσαν μιᾷ ἡμέρᾳ εἴκοσι τρεῖς
and fell in one day twenty-three

χιλιάδες. 9 μηδὲ ἐκπειράζωμεν τὸν κύριον,
thousands. Neither let us overtempt the Lord,

καθώς τινες αὐτῶν ἐπείρασαν καὶ ὑπὸ
as some of them tempted and by

τῶν ὄφεων ἀπώλλυντο. 10 μηδὲ γογγύζετε,
the serpents were destroyed. Neither murmur ye,

καθάπερ τινὲς αὐτῶν ἐγόγγυσαν, καὶ
even as some of them murmured, and

ἀπώλοντο ὑπὸ τοῦ ὀλεθρευτοῦ. 11 ταῦτα δὲ
were destroyed by the destroyer. Now these things

τυπικῶς συνέβαινεν ἐκείνοις, ἐγράφη δὲ
[3]typically [1]happened [2]to those men, and was(were) written

πρὸς νουθεσίαν ἡμῶν, εἰς οὓς τὰ
for admonition of us, to whom the

τέλη τῶν αἰώνων κατήντηκεν. 12 Ὥστε
ends of the ages has(ve) arrived. So as

ὁ δοκῶν ἑστάναι βλεπέτω μὴ πέσῃ.
the [one] thinking to stand let him look lest he falls.

13 πειρασμὸς ὑμᾶς οὐκ εἴληφεν εἰ μὴ
Temptation you has not taken except

ἀνθρώπινος· πιστὸς δὲ ὁ θεός, ὃς οὐκ
[what is] human; but faithful [is] – God, who not

ἐάσει ὑμᾶς πειρασθῆναι ὑπὲρ ὃ δύνασθε,
will allow you to be tempted beyond what you are able [to bear],

ἀλλὰ ποιήσει σὺν τῷ πειρασμῷ καὶ τὴν
but will make with the temptation also the

ἔκβασιν τοῦ δύνασθαι ὑπενεγκεῖν.
way out – to be able to endure.[d]
=so that ye may be able . . .

14 Διόπερ, ἀγαπητοί μου, φεύγετε ἀπὸ
Wherefore, beloved of me, flee ye from

τῆς εἰδωλολατρίας. 15 ὡς φρονίμοις λέγω·
– idolatry. [2]As [3]to prudent men [1]I say;

κρίνατε ὑμεῖς ὅ φημι. 16 Τὸ ποτήριον
judge ye what I say. The cup

τῆς εὐλογίας ὃ εὐλογοῦμεν, οὐχὶ κοινωνία
– of blessing which we bless, [2]not [3]a communion

ἐστὶν τοῦ αἵματος τοῦ Χριστοῦ; τὸν
[1]is it of the blood – of Christ? the

ἄρτον ὃν κλῶμεν, οὐχὶ κοινωνία τοῦ
bread which we break, [2]not [3]a communion [4]of the

σώματος τοῦ Χριστοῦ ἐστιν; 17 ὅτι εἷς
[5]body – [6]of Christ [1]is it? Because [4]one

ἄρτος, ἓν σῶμα οἱ πολλοί ἐσμεν· οἱ γὰρ
[5]bread, [6]one [7]body [2]the [3]many [1]we are; – for

6 Now these things occurred as examples[u] to keep us from setting our hearts on evil things as they did. 7 Do not be idolaters, as some of them were; as it is written: "The people sat down to eat and drink and got up to indulge in pagan revelry."[v] 8 We should not commit sexual immorality, as some of them did—and in one day twenty-three thousand of them died. 9 We should not test the Lord, as some of them did—and were killed by snakes. 10 And do not grumble, as some of them did—and were killed by the destroying angel.

11 These things happened to them as examples and were written down as warnings for us, on whom the fulfillment of the ages has come. 12 So, if you think you are standing firm, be careful that you don't fall! 13 No temptation has seized you except what is common to man. And God is faithful; he will not let you be tempted beyond what you can bear. But when you are tempted, he will also provide a way out so that you can stand up under it.

Idol Feasts and the Lord's Supper

14 Therefore, my dear friends, flee from idolatry. 15 I speak to sensible people; judge for yourselves what I say. 16 Is not the cup of thanksgiving for which we give thanks a participation in the blood of Christ? And is not the bread that we break a participation in the body of Christ? 17 Because there is one loaf, we, who are many, are one

[u]6 Or *types*; also in verse 11
[v]7 Exodus 32:6

are one body; for we all partake of the one bread.
18Look at the nation Is-
rael; are not those who eat
the sacrifices sharers in the
altar?
19What do I mean then?
That a thing sacrificed to
idols is anything, or that an
idol is anything?
20*No,* but *I say* that the
things which the Gentiles
sacrifice, they sacrifice to
demons, and not to God;
and I do not want you to
become sharers in demons.
21You cannot drink the
cup of the Lord and the cup
of demons; you cannot partake of the table of the Lord
and the table of demons.
22Or do we provoke the
Lord to jealousy? We are
not stronger than He, are
we?
23All things are lawful,
but not all things are profitable. All things are lawful,
but not all things edify.
24Let no one seek his own
good, but that of his neighbor.
25Eat anything that is sold
in the meat market, without
asking questions for con-
science' sake;
26FOR THE EARTH IS THE
LORD'S, AND ALL IT CON-
TAINS.
27If one of the unbelievers
invites you, and you wish
to go, eat anything that is
set before you, without
asking questions for con-
science' sake.
28But if anyone should
say to you, "This is meat
sacrificed to idols," do not
eat *it,* for the sake of the
one who informed *you,* and
for conscience' sake;
29I mean not your own
conscience, but the other
man's; for why is my freedom judged by another's
conscience?
30If I partake with thank-

πάντες ἐκ τοῦ ἑνὸς ἄρτου μετέχομεν.
all of the one bread we partake.
18 βλέπετε τὸν Ἰσραὴλ κατὰ σάρκα·
See ye – Israel according to [the] flesh;
οὐχ οἱ ἐσθίοντες τὰς θυσίας κοινωνοὶ
2not 3the [ones] 4eating 5the 6sacrifices 7sharers
τοῦ θυσιαστηρίου εἰσίν; **19** τί οὖν φημι;
8of the 9altar 1are? What therefore do I say?
ὅτι εἰδωλόθυτόν τί ἐστιν; ἢ ὅτι εἴδωλόν
that an idolatrous sacrifice 2anything 1is? or that an idol
τί ἐστιν; **20** ἀλλ' ὅτι ἃ θύουσιν,
2anything 1is? but that [the] things which they sacrifice,
δαιμονίοις και οὐ θεῷ θύουσιν· οὐ θέλω
to demons and not to God they sacrifice; 3not 2I wish
δὲ ὑμᾶς κοινωνοὺς τῶν δαιμονίων γίνεσθαι.
1and you sharers of the demons to become.
21 οὐ δύνασθε ποτήριον κυρίου πίνειν
Ye cannot 2a cup 3of [the] Lord 1*to* drink
καὶ ποτήριον δαιμονίων· οὐ δύνασθε
and a cup of demons; ye cannot
τραπέζης κυρίου μετέχειν καὶ τραπέζης
2of a table 3of [the] Lord 1*to* partake and of a table
δαιμονίων. **22** ἢ παραζηλοῦμεν τὸν κύριον;
of demons. Or do we make jealous the Lord?
μὴ ἰσχυρότεροι αὐτοῦ ἐσμεν;
Not 2stronger [than] 3he 1are we?
23 Πάντα ἔξεστιν, ἀλλ' οὐ πάντα
All things [are] lawful, but not all things
συμφέρει· πάντα ἔξεστιν, ἀλλ' οὐ πάντα
are] expedient; all things [are] lawful, but not all things
οἰκοδομεῖ. **24** μηδεὶς τὸ ἑαυτοῦ ζητείτω
edifies(fy). No one the thing of himself let him seek
ἀλλὰ τὸ τοῦ ἑτέρου. **25** Πᾶν τὸ ἐν
but the thing of the other. Everything 2in
μακέλλῳ πωλούμενον ἐσθίετε μηδὲν
3a meat market 1*being* sold eat ye 2nothing
ἀνακρίνοντες διὰ τὴν συνείδησιν· **26** τοῦ
1examining because of – conscience; 2of the
κυρίου γὰρ ἡ γῆ καὶ τὸ πλήρωμα
3Lord 1for the earth and the fulness
αὐτῆς. **27** εἴ τις καλεῖ ὑμᾶς τῶν ἀπίστων
of it. If anyone invites you of the unbelievers
καὶ θέλετε πορεύεσθαι, πᾶν τὸ παρατι-
and ye wish to go, 2everything 3*being* set
θέμενον ὑμῖν ἐσθίετε μηδὲν ἀνακρίνοντες
before 4you 1eat 6nothing 5examining
διὰ τὴν συνείδησιν. **28** ἐὰν δέ τις ὑμῖν
because of – conscience. But if anyone 2to you
εἴπῃ· τοῦτο ἱερόθυτόν ἐστιν, μὴ ἐσθίετε
1says: This 2slain in sacrifice 1is, do not eat
δι' ἐκεῖνον τὸν μηνύσαντα καὶ τὴν
because of that man the [one] pointing out and –
συνείδησιν· **29** συνείδησιν δὲ λέγω οὐχὶ
conscience: 3conscience 1but 2I say not
τὴν ἑαυτοῦ ἀλλὰ τὴν τοῦ ἑτέρου. ἱνατί
the one of himself but the one of the other.* why
γὰρ ἡ ἐλευθερία μου κρίνεται ὑπὸ ἄλλης
For the freedom of me is judged by 2of another
συνειδήσεως; **30** εἰ ἐγὼ χάριτι μετέχω,
1conscience? If I by grace partake,

* That is, not the conscience of the person invited, to whom the apostle's words are addressed, but the conscience of the person "pointing out."

body, for we all partake of
the one loaf.
18Consider the people of
Israel: Do not those who
eat the sacrifices participate in the altar? 19Do I
mean then that a sacrifice
offered to an idol is anything, or that an idol is anything? 20No, but the sacrifices of pagans are offered
to demons, not to God, and
I do not want you to be par-
ticipants with demons.
21You cannot drink the cup
of the Lord and the cup of
demons too; you cannot
have a part in both the
Lord's table and the table
of demons. 22Are we trying
to arouse the Lord's jealousy? Are we stronger than
he?

The Believer's Freedom

23"Everything is permis-
sible"—but not everything
is beneficial. "Everything
is permissible"—but not
everything is constructive.
24Nobody should seek his
own good, but the good of
others.
25Eat anything sold in the
meat market without rais-
ing questions of con-
science, 26for, "The earth
is the Lord's, and every-
thing in it."[w]
27If some unbeliever in-
vites you to a meal and you
want to go, eat whatever is
put before you without
raising questions of con-
science. 28But if anyone
says to you, "This has been
offered in sacrifice," then
do not eat it, both for the
sake of the man who told
you and for conscience'
sake[x]—29the other man's
conscience, I mean, not
yours. For why should my
freedom be judged by an-
other's conscience? 30If I
take part in the meal with

w26 Psalm 24:1
x28 Some manuscripts *conscience' sake, for "the earth is the Lord's and everything in it"*

fulness, why am I slandered concerning that for which I give thanks?
31Whether, then, you eat or drink or whatever you do, do all to the glory of God.
32Give no offense either to Jews or to Greeks or to the church of God;
33just as I also please all men in all things, not seeking my own profit, but the *profit* of the many, that they may be saved.

Chapter 11

Christian Order

BE imitators of me, just as I also am of Christ.
2Now I praise you because you remember me in everything, and hold firmly to the traditions, just as I delivered them to you.
3But I want you to understand that Christ is the head of every man, and the man is the head of a woman, and God is the head of Christ.
4Every man who has *something* on his head while praying or prophesying, disgraces his head.
5But every woman who has her head uncovered while praying or prophesying, disgraces her head; for she is one and the same with her whose head is shaved.
6For if a woman does not cover her head, let her also have her hair cut off; but if it is disgraceful for a woman to have her hair cut off or her head shaved, let her cover her head.
7For a man ought not to have his head covered, since he is the image and glory of God; but the woman is the glory of man.
8For man does not originate from woman, but woman from man;
9for indeed man was not

τί βλασφημοῦμαι ὑπὲρ οὗ ἐγὼ εὐχαριστῶ;
why am I evil spoken of | because of | what | I | give thanks [for]?

31 Εἴτε οὖν ἐσθίετε εἴτε πίνετε εἴτε
Whether therefore ye eat or *ye* drink or

τι ποιεῖτε, πάντα εἰς δόξαν θεοῦ ποιεῖτε.
what[ever] ye do, all things to [the] glory of God do *ye*.

32 ἀπρόσκοποι καὶ Ἰουδαίοις γίνεσθε καὶ
[2]Without offence [3]both [4]to Jews [1]be ye [5]and

Ἕλλησιν καὶ τῇ ἐκκλησίᾳ τοῦ θεοῦ,
[6]to Greeks and to the church – of God,

33 καθὼς κἀγὼ πάντα πᾶσιν ἀρέσκω,
as I also [in] all things all men please,

μὴ ζητῶν τὸ ἐμαυτοῦ σύμφορον ἀλλὰ
not seeking the of myself advantage but

τὸ τῶν πολλῶν, ἵνα σωθῶσιν. 11 μιμηταί
the (that) of the many, in order that they may be saved. Imitators

μου γίνεσθε, καθὼς κἀγὼ Χριστοῦ.
of me be ye, as I also [am] of Christ.

2 Ἐπαινῶ δὲ ὑμᾶς ὅτι πάντα μου
But I praise you because [2]all things [3]of me

μέμνησθε καὶ καθὼς παρέδωκα ὑμῖν τὰς
[1]ye have remembered and [4]as [5]I delivered [6]to you [2]the

παραδόσεις κατέχετε. 3 Θέλω δὲ ὑμᾶς
[3]traditions [1]ye hold fast. But I wish you

εἰδέναι ὅτι παντὸς ἀνδρὸς ἡ κεφαλὴ ὁ
to know that [5]of every [6]man [3]the [4]head –

Χριστός ἐστιν, κεφαλὴ δὲ γυναικὸς ὁ
[1]Christ [2]is, and [the] head of a woman the

ἀνήρ, κεφαλὴ δὲ τοῦ Χριστοῦ ὁ θεός.
man, and [the] head – of Christ – God.

4 πᾶς ἀνὴρ προσευχόμενος ἢ προφητεύων
Every man praying or prophesying

κατὰ κεφαλῆς ἔχων καταισχύνει τὴν
[3]down over [4][his] head [1]having [2][anything] shames the

κεφαλὴν αὐτοῦ. 5 πᾶσα δὲ γυνὴ προσ-
head of him. But every woman pray-

ευχομένη ἢ προφητεύουσα ἀκατακαλύπτῳ
ing or prophesying [3]unveiled

τῇ κεφαλῇ καταισχύνει τὴν κεφαλὴν αὐτῆς·
[1]with the(her) [2]head shames the head of her;

ἓν γάρ ἐστιν καὶ τὸ αὐτὸ τῇ ἐξυρημένῃ.
for [2]one [1]it is and the same thing with the woman having been shaved.

6 εἰ γὰρ οὐ κατακαλύπτεται γυνή, καὶ
For if [2]is not veiled [1]a woman, also

κειράσθω· εἰ δὲ αἰσχρὸν γυναικὶ τὸ
let her be shorn; but if shameful for a woman –

κείρασθαι ἢ ξυρᾶσθαι, κατακαλυπτέσθω.
to be shorn or *to be* shaved, let her be veiled.

7 ἀνὴρ μὲν γὰρ οὐκ ὀφείλει κατα-
For a man indeed ought not to be

καλύπτεσθαι τὴν κεφαλήν, εἰκὼν καὶ δόξα
veiled the head,[b] [2][the] image [3]and [4]glory

θεοῦ ὑπάρχων· ἡ γυνὴ δὲ δόξα ἀνδρός
[5]of God [1]being; but the woman [2][the] glory [3]of a man

ἐστιν. 8 οὐ γάρ ἐστιν ἀνὴρ ἐκ γυναικός,
[1]is. For [3]not [2]is [1]man of woman,

ἀλλὰ γυνὴ ἐξ ἀνδρός· 9 καὶ γὰρ οὐκ
but woman of man; for indeed [3]not

thankfulness, why am I denounced because of something I thank God for?
31So whether you eat or drink or whatever you do, do it all for the glory of God. 32Do not cause anyone to stumble, whether Jews, Greeks or the church of God— 33even as I try to please everybody in every way. For I am not seeking my own good but the good of many, so that they may be saved. 1Follow my example, as I follow the example of Christ.

Propriety in Worship

2I praise you for remembering me in everything and for holding to the teachings,[y] just as I passed them on to you.
3Now I want you to realize that the head of every man is Christ, and the head of the woman is man, and the head of Christ is God. 4Every man who prays or prophesies with his head covered dishonors his head. 5And every woman who prays or prophesies with her head uncovered dishonors her head—it is just as though her head were shaved. 6If a woman does not cover her head, she should have her hair cut off; and if it is a disgrace for a woman to have her hair cut or shaved off, she should cover her head. 7A man ought not to cover his head,[z] since he is the image and glory of God; but the woman is the glory of man. 8For man did not come from woman, but woman from man; 9neither was man created for wom-

[y]2 Or *traditions*
[z]4-7 Or 4*Every man who prays or prophesies with long hair dishonors his head. 5And every woman who prays or prophesies with no covering of hair on her head dishonors her head—she is just like one of the "shorn women." 6If a woman has no covering, let her be for now with short hair, but since it is a disgrace for a woman to have her hair shorn or shaved, she should grow it again. 7A man ought not to have long hair*

created for the woman's
sake, but woman for the
man's sake.
10Therefore the woman
ought to have *a symbol of*
authority on her head, because of the angels.
11However, in the Lord,
neither is woman indepen-
dent of man, nor is man independent of woman.
12For as the woman origi-
nates from the man, so also
the man *has his birth*
through the woman; and all
things originate from God.
13Judge for yourselves: is
it proper for a woman to
pray to God *with head* uncovered?
14Does not even nature itself teach you that if a man
has long hair, it is a dishon-
or to him,
15but if a woman has long
hair, it is a glory to her? For
her hair is given to her for a
covering.
16But if one is inclined to
be contentious, we have no
other practice, nor have the
churches of God.
17But in giving this in-
struction, I do not praise
you, because you come to-
gether not for the better but
for the worse.
18For, in the first place,
when you come together as
a church, I hear that divisions exist among you; and
in part, I believe it.
19For there must also be
factions among you, in order that those who are approved may have become
evident among you.
20Therefore when you
meet together, it is not to
eat the Lord's Supper,
21for in your eating each
one takes his own supper
first; and one is hungry and

ἐκτίσθη ἀνὴρ διὰ τὴν γυναῖκα, ἀλλὰ
[2]was [4]created [1]man because of the woman, but
γυνὴ διὰ τὸν ἄνδρα. **10** διὰ τοῦτο
woman because of the man. Therefore
ὀφείλει ἡ γυνὴ ἐξουσίαν ἔχειν ἐπὶ τῆς
ought the woman authority to have on the
κεφαλῆς διὰ τοὺς ἀγγέλους. **11** πλὴν
head because of the angels. Nevertheless
οὔτε γυνὴ χωρὶς ἀνδρὸς οὔτε ἀνὴρ χωρὶς
neither woman without man nor man without
γυναικὸς ἐν κυρίῳ· **12** ὥσπερ γὰρ ἡ
woman in [the] Lord; for as the
γυνὴ ἐκ τοῦ ἀνδρός, οὕτως καὶ ὁ ἀνὴρ
woman of the man, so also the man
διὰ τῆς γυναικός· τὰ δὲ πάντα ἐκ τοῦ
through the woman; – but all things of –
θεοῦ. **13** Ἐν ὑμῖν αὐτοῖς κρίνατε· πρέπον
God. Among you [your]selves judge: [2]fitting
ἐστὶν γυναῖκα ἀκατακάλυπτον τῷ θεῷ
[1]is it [3][for] [4]a woman [7]unveiled – [6]to God
προσεύχεσθαι; **14** οὐδὲ ἡ φύσις αὐτὴ
[5]to pray? Not – nature [her]self
διδάσκει ὑμᾶς ὅτι ἀνὴρ μὲν ἐὰν κομᾷ,
teaches you that a man indeed if he wears his hair long,
ἀτιμία αὐτῷ ἐστιν, **15** γυνὴ δὲ ἐὰν
[2]a dishonour [3]to him [1]it is, but a woman if
κομᾷ, δόξα αὐτῇ ἐστιν; ὅτι ἡ κόμη
she wears her hair long, [2]a glory [3]to her [1]it is? because the long hair
ἀντὶ περιβολαίου δέδοται αὐτῇ. **16** Εἰ
instead of a veil has been given to her. if
δέ τις δοκεῖ φιλόνεικος εἶναι, ἡμεῖς
But anyone thinks [2]contentious [1]to be, we
τοιαύτην συνήθειαν οὐκ ἔχομεν, οὐδὲ αἱ
[2]such [3]a custom [1]have not, neither the
ἐκκλησίαι τοῦ θεοῦ.
churches – of God.
17 Τοῦτο δὲ παραγγέλλων οὐκ ἐπαινῶ
But this charging I do not praise
ὅτι οὐκ εἰς τὸ κρεῖσσον ἀλλὰ εἰς τὸ
because not for the better but for the
ἧσσον συνέρχεσθε. **18** πρῶτον μὲν γὰρ
worse ye come together. For firstly indeed
συνερχομένων ὑμῶν ἐν ἐκκλησίᾳ ἀκούω
coming together you[a] in church I hear
=when ye come together
σχίσματα ἐν ὑμῖν ὑπάρχειν, καὶ μέρος
divisions among you to be, and [2]part
τι πιστεύω. **19** δεῖ γὰρ καὶ αἱρέσεις
[1]some I believe. For it behoves indeed sects
ἐν ὑμῖν εἶναι, ἵνα [καὶ] οἱ δόκιμοι
among you to be, in order that also the approved ones
φανεροὶ γένωνται ἐν ὑμῖν. **20** Συν-
manifest may become among you. Coming
ερχομένων οὖν ὑμῶν ἐπὶ τὸ αὐτὸ οὐκ
together therefore you[a] together not
=When therefore ye come
ἔστιν κυριακὸν δεῖπνον φαγεῖν· **21** ἕκαστος
it is of the Lord* a supper to eat; [2]each one
γὰρ τὸ ἴδιον δεῖπνον προλαμβάνει ἐν
[1]for the(his) own supper takes before in
τῷ φαγεῖν, καὶ ὃς μὲν πεινᾷ, ὃς δὲ
– to eat(eating), and one† hungers, another†

* Note that κυριακός is an adjective, for which no exact English equivalent is available. Only other occurrence in N.T., Rev. 1. 10.

an, but woman for man.
10For this reason, and because of the angels, the
woman ought to have a sign
of authority on her head.
11In the Lord, however,
woman is not independent
of man, nor is man independent of woman. 12For as
woman came from man, so
also man is born of woman.
But everything comes from
God. 13Judge for your-
selves: Is it proper for a
woman to pray to God with
her head uncovered?
14Does not the very nature
of things teach you that if a
man has long hair, it is a
disgrace to him, 15but that
if a woman has long hair, it
is her glory? For long hair is
given to her as a covering.
16If anyone wants to be
contentious about this, we
have no other practice—
nor do the churches of
God.

The Lord's Supper

17In the following direc-
tives I have no praise for
you, for your meetings do
more harm than good. 18In
the first place, I hear that
when you come together as
a church, there are divi-
sions among you, and to
some extent I believe it.
19No doubt there have to be
differences among you to
show which of you have
God's approval. 20When
you come together, it is not
the Lord's Supper you eat,
21for as you eat, each of
you goes ahead without
waiting for anybody else.
One remains hungry, an-

another is drunk.
22What! Do you not have
houses in which to eat and
drink? Or do you despise
the church of God, and
shame those who have
nothing? What shall I say to
you? Shall I praise you? In
this I will not praise you.

The Lord's Supper

23For I received from the
Lord that which I also delivered to you, that the
Lord Jesus in the night in
which He was betrayed
took bread;
24and when He had given
thanks, He broke it, and
said, "This is My body,
which [n]is for you; do this in
remembrance of Me."
25In the same way *He
took* the cup also, after supper, saying, "This cup is
the new covenant in My
blood; do this, as often as
you drink *it,* in remem-
brance of Me."
26For as often as you eat
this bread and drink the
cup, you proclaim the
Lord's death until He
comes.
27Therefore whoever eats
the bread or drinks the cup
of the Lord in an unworthy
manner, shall be guilty of
the body and the blood of
the Lord.
28But let a man examine
himself, and so let him eat
of the bread and drink of
the cup.
29For he who eats and
drinks, eats and drinks
judgment to himself, if he
does not judge the body
rightly.
30For this reason many
among you are weak and
sick, and a number sleep.
31But if we judged our-
selves rightly, we should
not be judged.
32But when we are
judged, we are disciplined
by the Lord in order that
we may not be condemned

[n] Some ancient mss. read *is broken*

μεθύει. 22 μὴ γὰρ οἰκίας οὐκ ἔχετε
is drunken. *Not* indeed [2]houses [1]have ye not
εἰς τὸ ἐσθίειν καὶ πίνειν; ἢ τῆς ἐκκλησίας
– – to eat and to drink? or the church
τοῦ θεοῦ καταφρονεῖτε, καὶ καταισχύνετε
– of God despise ye, and shame
τοὺς μὴ ἔχοντας; τί εἴπω ὑμῖν; ἐπαινέσω
the [ones] not having? What may I say to you? shall I praise
ὑμᾶς; ἐν τούτῳ οὐκ ἐπαινῶ. 23 Ἐγὼ
you? In this I praise not. I
γὰρ παρέλαβον ἀπὸ τοῦ κυρίου, ὃ καὶ
For received from the Lord, what also
παρέδωκα ὑμῖν, ὅτι ὁ κύριος Ἰησοῦς
I delivered to you, that the Lord Jesus
ἐν τῇ νυκτὶ ᾗ παρεδίδοτο ἔλαβεν ἄρτον
in the night in which he was betrayed took bread
24 καὶ εὐχαριστήσας ἔκλασεν καὶ εἶπεν·
and having given thanks broke and said:
τοῦτό μού ἐστιν τὸ σῶμα τὸ ὑπὲρ
This of me is the body – on behalf of
ὑμῶν· τοῦτο ποιεῖτε εἰς τὴν ἐμὴν
you; this do ye for – my
ἀνάμνησιν. 25 ὡσαύτως καὶ τὸ ποτήριον
remembrance. Similarly also the cup
μετὰ τὸ δειπνῆσαι, λέγων· τοῦτο τὸ
after the to sup, saying: This –
ποτήριον ἡ καινὴ διαθήκη ἐστὶν ἐν τῷ
cup [2]the [3]new [4]covenant [1]is in –
ἐμῷ αἵματι· τοῦτο ποιεῖτε, ὁσάκις ἐὰν
my blood; this do ye, as often as
πίνητε, εἰς τὴν ἐμὴν ἀνάμνησιν. 26 ὁσάκις
ye drink, for – my remembrance. as often
γὰρ ἐὰν ἐσθίητε τὸν ἄρτον τοῦτον καὶ
For as ye eat this bread and
τὸ ποτήριον πίνητε, τὸν θάνατον τοῦ
[2]the [3]cup [1]drink, the death of the
κυρίου καταγγέλλετε, ἄχρι οὗ ἔλθῃ.
Lord ye declare, until he comes.
27 Ὥστε ὃς ἂν ἐσθίῃ τὸν ἄρτον ἢ
So as whoever eats the bread or
πίνῃ τὸ ποτήριον τοῦ κυρίου ἀναξίως,
drinks the cup of the Lord unworthily,
ἔνοχος ἔσται τοῦ σώματος καὶ τοῦ
guilty will be of the body and of the
αἵματος τοῦ κυρίου. 28 δοκιμαζέτω δὲ
blood of the Lord. But [1]let [3]prove
ἄνθρωπος ἑαυτόν, καὶ οὕτως ἐκ τοῦ
[2]a man [4]himself, and so of the
ἄρτου ἐσθιέτω καὶ ἐκ τοῦ ποτηρίου
bread let him eat and of the cup
πινέτω· 29 ὁ γὰρ ἐσθίων καὶ πίνων
let him drink; for the [one] eating and drinking
κρίμα ἑαυτῷ ἐσθίει καὶ πίνει μὴ διακρίνων
[4]judgment [5]to himself [1]eats [2]and [3]drinks not discerning
τὸ σῶμα. 30 διὰ τοῦτο ἐν ὑμῖν πολλοὶ
the body. Therefore among you many
ἀσθενεῖς καὶ ἄρρωστοι καὶ κοιμῶνται
[are] weak and feeble and [2]sleep
ἱκανοί. 31 εἰ δὲ ἑαυτοὺς διεκρίνομεν,
[1]a number. But if ourselves we discerned,
οὐκ ἂν ἐκρινόμεθα· 32 κρινόμενοι δὲ ὑπὸ
we should not be judged; but being judged by
τοῦ κυρίου παιδευόμεθα, ἵνα μὴ σὺν
the Lord we are chastened, lest with

other gets drunk. 22Don't
you have homes to eat and
drink in? Or do you despise
the church of God and hu-
miliate those who have
nothing? What shall I say to
you? Shall I praise you for
this? Certainly not!
23For I received from the
Lord what I also passed on
to you: The Lord Jesus, on
the night he was betrayed,
took bread, 24and when he
had given thanks, he broke
it and said, "This is my
body, which is for you; do
this in remembrance of
me." 25In the same way, after supper he took the cup,
saying, "This cup is the
new covenant in my blood;
do this, whenever you
drink it, in remembrance of
me." 26For whenever you
eat this bread and drink this
cup, you proclaim the
Lord's death until he
comes.
27Therefore, whoever
eats the bread or drinks the
cup of the Lord in an un-
worthy manner will be
guilty of sinning against the
body and blood of the
Lord. 28A man ought to examine himself before he
eats of the bread and drinks
of the cup. 29For anyone
who eats and drinks with-
out recognizing the body of
the Lord eats and drinks
judgment on himself.
30That is why many among
you are weak and sick, and
a number of you have fallen
asleep. 31But if we judged
ourselves, we would not
come under judgment.
32When we are judged by
the Lord, we are being disciplined so that we will not

along with the world.
33So then, my brethren,
when you come together to
eat, wait for one another.
34If anyone is hungry, let
him eat at home, so that
you may not come together
for judgment. And the re-
maining matters I shall arrange when I come.

Chapter 12

The Use of Spiritual Gifts

NOW concerning spiri-
tual *gifts*, brethren, I
do not want you to be un-
aware.
2You know that when
you were pagans, *you were*
led astray to the dumb
idols, however you were
led.
3Therefore I make
known to you, that no one
speaking by the Spirit of
God says, "Jesus is ac-
cursed"; and no one can
say, "Jesus is Lord," ex-
cept by the Holy Spirit.
4Now there are varieties
of gifts, but the same Spirit.
5And there are varieties
of ministries, and the same
Lord.
6And there are varieties
of effects, but the same
God who works all things in
all *persons*.
7But to each one is given
the manifestation of the
Spirit for the common
good.
8For to one is given the
word of wisdom through
the Spirit, and to another
the word of knowledge ac-
cording to the same Spirit;
9to another faith by the
same Spirit, and to another
gifts of healing by the one
Spirit,
10and to another the ef-
fecting of miracles, and to
another prophecy, and to
another the distinguishing
of spirits, to another *various* kinds of tongues, and
to another the interpretation of tongues.
11But one and the same
Spirit works all these
things, distributing to each

τῷ κόσμῳ κατακριθῶμεν. 33 Ὥστε,
the world we are condemned. So as,
ἀδελφοί μου, συνερχόμενοι εἰς τὸ φαγεῖν
brothers of me, coming together *for* *the* to eat
ἀλλήλους ἐκδέχεσθε. 34 εἴ τις πεινᾷ,
one another await ye. If anyone hungers,
ἐν οἴκῳ ἐσθιέτω, ἵνα μὴ εἰς κρίμα
at home let him eat, lest to judgment
συνέρχησθε. τὰ δὲ λοιπὰ ὡς ἂν ἔλθω
ye come together. And the remaining matters whenever I come
διατάξομαι.
I will arrange.

12 Περὶ δὲ τῶν πνευματικῶν, ἀδελφοί,
Now about the spiritual matters, brothers,
οὐ θέλω ὑμᾶς ἀγνοεῖν. **2** Οἴδατε ὅτι
I do not wish you to be ignorant. Ye know that
ὅτε ἔθνη ἦτε πρὸς τὰ εἴδωλα τὰ ἄφωνα
when [3]nations [1]ye were [4]to [5]the [7]idols – [6]voiceless
ὡς ἂν ἤγεσθε ἀπαγόμενοι. **3** διὸ γνωρίζω
[8]however [2]ye were led [9][ye were] [10]being led away.* Wherefore I make known
ὑμῖν ὅτι οὐδεὶς ἐν πνεύματι θεοῦ λαλῶν
to you that no one [2]by [3][the] Spirit [4]of God [1]speaking
λέγει· ΑΝΑΘΕΜΑ ΙΗΣΟΥΣ, καὶ οὐδεὶς
says: A CURSE [IS] JESUS, and no one
δύναται εἰπεῖν· ΚΥΡΙΟΣ ΙΗΣΟΥΣ, εἰ μὴ
can *to* say: LORD JESUS, except
ἐν πνεύματι ἁγίῳ.
by [the] [2]Spirit [1]Holy.
4 Διαιρέσεις δὲ χαρισμάτων εἰσίν, τὸ δὲ αὐτὸ
Now differences of gifts there are, but the same
πνεῦμα· **5** καὶ διαιρέσεις διακονιῶν εἰσιν, καὶ
Spirit; and differences of ministries there are, and
ὁ αὐτὸς κύριος· **6** καὶ διαιρέσεις ἐνεργημάτων
the same Lord; and differences of operations
εἰσίν, ὁ δὲ αὐτὸς θεὸς ὁ ἐνεργῶν τὰ
there are, but the same God – operating –
πάντα ἐν πᾶσιν. **7** ἑκάστῳ δὲ δίδοται
all things in all. But to each one is given
ἡ φανέρωσις τοῦ πνεύματος πρὸς τὸ
the manifestation of the Spirit to *the*
συμφέρον. **8** ᾧ μὲν γὰρ διὰ τοῦ πνεύματος
profit*ing*. For to one through the Spirit
δίδοται λόγος σοφίας, ἄλλῳ δὲ λόγος
is given a word of wisdom, and to another a word
γνώσεως κατὰ τὸ αὐτὸ πνεῦμα, **9** ἑτέρῳ
of knowledge according to the same Spirit, to another
πίστις ἐν τῷ αὐτῷ πνεύματι, ἄλλῳ δὲ
faith by the same Spirit, and to another
χαρίσματα ἰαμάτων ἐν τῷ ἑνὶ πνεύματι,
gifts of cures by the one Spirit,
10 ἄλλῳ δὲ ἐνεργήματα δυνάμεων, ἄλλῳ
and to another operations of powers, to another
[δὲ] προφητεία, ἄλλῳ δὲ διακρίσεις πνευ-
and prophecy, and to another discernings of
μάτων, ἑτέρῳ γένη γλωσσῶν, ἄλλῳ δὲ
spirits, to another kinds of tongues, and to another
ἑρμηνεία γλωσσῶν· **11** πάντα δὲ ταῦτα
interpretation of tongues: and [8]all [9]these things
ἐνεργεῖ τὸ ἓν καὶ τὸ αὐτὸ πνεῦμα,
[7]operates [1]the [2]one [3]and [4]the [5]same [6]Spirit,

* It is thought that there is a scribal error in this verse; see commentaries on the Greek text. We have been guided by G. G. Findlay, *The Expositor's Greek Testament*.

be condemned with the
world.
33So then, my brothers,
when you come together to
eat, wait for each other. 34If
anyone is hungry, he
should eat at home, so that
when you meet together it
may not result in judgment.
And when I come I will
give further directions.

Chapter 12

Spiritual Gifts

NOW about spiritual
gifts, brothers, I do
not want you to be igno-
rant. 2You know that when
you were pagans, somehow
or other you were influ-
enced and led astray to
mute idols. 3Therefore I tell
you that no one who is
speaking by the Spirit of
God says, "Jesus be
cursed," and no one can
say, "Jesus is Lord," ex-
cept by the Holy Spirit.
4There are different kinds
of gifts, but the same Spirit.
5There are different kinds
of service, but the same
Lord. 6There are different
kinds of working, but the
same God works all of them
in all men.
7Now to each one the
manifestation of the Spirit
is given for the common
good. 8To one there is giv-
en through the Spirit the
message of wisdom, to an-
other the message of
knowledge by means of the
same Spirit, 9to another
faith by the same Spirit, to
another gifts of healing by
that one Spirit, 10to another
miraculous powers, to an-
other prophecy, to another
distinguishing between
spirits, to another speaking
in different kinds of
tongues,[a] and to still another the interpretation of
tongues.[a] 11All these are
the work of one and the
same Spirit, and he gives

[a]10 Or *languages*; also in verse 28

one individually just as He wills.

12For even as the body is one and *yet* has many members, and all the members of the body, though they are many, are one body, so also is Christ.

13For by one Spirit we were all baptized into one body, whether Jews or Greeks, whether slaves or free, and we were all made to drink of one Spirit.

14For the body is not one member, but many.

15If the foot should say, "Because I am not a hand, I am not *a part* of the body," it is not for this reason any the less *a part* of the body.

16And if the ear should say, "Because I am not an eye, I am not *a part* of the body," it is not for this reason any the less *a part* of the body.

17If the whole body were an eye, where would the hearing be? If the whole were hearing, where would the sense of smell be?

18But now God has placed the members, each one of them, in the body, just as He desired.

19And if they were all one member, where would the body be?

20But now there are many members, but one body.

21And the eye cannot say to the hand, "I have no need of you"; or again the head to the feet, "I have no need of you."

22On the contrary, it is much truer that the members of the body which seem to be weaker are necessary;

23and those *members* of the body, which we deem less honorable, on these we bestow more abundant honor, and our unseemly *members come to* have more abundant seemliness,

διαιροῦν ἰδίᾳ ἑκάστῳ καθὼς βούλεται.
distributing [2]separately† [1]to each one as he purposes.
12 Καθάπερ γὰρ τὸ σῶμα ἕν ἐστιν
For as the body [2]one [1]is
καὶ μέλη πολλὰ ἔχει, πάντα δὲ τὰ
and [3]members [2]many [1]has, but all the
μέλη τοῦ σώματος πολλὰ ὄντα ἕν ἐστιν
members of the body [2]many [1]being [4]one [3]is(are)
σῶμα, οὕτως καὶ ὁ Χριστός· 13 καὶ γὰρ
body, so also *the* Christ; for indeed
ἐν ἑνὶ πνεύματι ἡμεῖς πάντες εἰς ἓν
[4]by [5]one [6]Spirit [1]we [2]all [7]into [8]one
σῶμα ἐβαπτίσθημεν, εἴτε Ἰουδαῖοι εἴτε
[9]body [3]were baptized, whether Jews or
Ἕλληνες, εἴτε δοῦλοι εἴτε ἐλεύθεροι, καὶ
Greeks, whether slaves or free, and
πάντες ἓν πνεῦμα ἐποτίσθημεν. 14 καὶ
all one Spirit *we* were given to drink. indeed
γὰρ τὸ σῶμα οὐκ ἔστιν ἓν μέλος ἀλλὰ
For the body is not one member but
πολλά. 15 ἐὰν εἴπῃ ὁ πούς· ὅτι οὐκ
many. If [3]says [1]the [2]foot: Because not
εἰμὶ χείρ, οὐκ εἰμὶ ἐκ τοῦ σώματος,
I am a hand, I am not of the body,
οὐ παρὰ τοῦτο οὐκ ἔστιν ἐκ τοῦ σώματος.
not for this it is not of the body.
16 καὶ ἐὰν εἴπῃ τὸ οὖς· ὅτι οὐκ εἰμὶ
And if says the ear: Because I am not
ὀφθαλμός, οὐκ εἰμὶ ἐκ τοῦ σώματος,
an eye, I am not of the body,
οὐ παρὰ τοῦτο οὐκ ἔστιν ἐκ τοῦ σώματος.
not for this it is not of the body.
17 εἰ ὅλον τὸ σῶμα ὀφθαλμός, ποῦ
If all the body [was] an eye, where
ἡ ἀκοή; εἰ ὅλον ἀκοή, ποῦ ἡ ὄσφρησις;
[would be] the hearing? if all hearing, where the smelling?
18 νῦν δὲ ὁ θεὸς ἔθετο τὰ μέλη, ἓν
But now – God set the members, [2]one
ἕκαστον αὐτῶν ἐν τῷ σώματι καθὼς
[1]each of them in the body as
ἠθέλησεν. 19 εἰ δὲ ἦν τὰ πάντα ἓν
he wished. And if [2]was – [1]all one
μέλος, ποῦ τὸ σῶμα; 20 νῦν δὲ πολλὰ
member, where the body? But now many
μὲν μέλη, ἓν δὲ σῶμα. 21 οὐ δύναται
[2]indeed [1]members, but one body. [3]cannot
δὲ ὁ ὀφθαλμὸς εἰπεῖν τῇ χειρί· χρείαν
And [1]the[2] eye *to* say to the hand: Need
σου οὐκ ἔχω, ἢ πάλιν ἡ κεφαλὴ τοῖς
of thee I have not, or again the head to the
ποσίν· χρείαν ὑμῶν οὐκ ἔχω· 22 ἀλλὰ
feet: Need of you I have not; but
πολλῷ μᾶλλον τὰ δοκοῦντα μέλη τοῦ
by much more [1]the [5]seeming [2]members [3]of the
σώματος ἀσθενέστερα ὑπάρχειν ἀναγκαῖά ἐστιν,
[4]body [7]weaker [6]to be [9]necessary [8]is(are),
23 καὶ ἃ δοκοῦμεν ἀτιμότερα εἶναι
and [1][members] [4]which [5]we think [7]less honourable [6]to be
τοῦ σώματος, τούτοις τιμὴν περισσοτέραν
[2]of the [3]body, to these honour more abundant
περιτίθεμεν, καὶ τὰ ἀσχήμονα ἡμῶν
we put round, and the uncomely [members] of us
εὐσχημοσύνην περισσοτέραν ἔχει, 24 τὰ δὲ
[3]comeliness [2]more abundant [1]has(ve), but th-

them to each one, just as he
determines.

One Body, Many Parts

12The body is a unit,
though it is made up of
many parts; and though all
its parts are many, they
form one body. So it is with
Christ. 13For we were all
baptized by[b] one Spirit
into one body—whether
Jews or Greeks, slave or
free—and we were all giv-
en the one Spirit to drink.
14Now the body is not
made up of one part but of
many. 15If the foot should
say, "Because I am not a
hand, I do not belong to the
body," it would not for that
reason cease to be part of
the body. 16And if the ear
should say, "Because I am
not an eye, I do not belong
to the body," it would not
for that reason cease to be
part of the body. 17If the
whole body were an eye,
where would the sense of
hearing be? If the whole
body were an ear, where
would the sense of smell
be? 18But in fact God has
arranged the parts in the
body, every one of them,
just as he wanted them to
be. 19If they were all one
part, where would the body
be? 20As it is, there are
many parts, but one body.
21The eye cannot say to
the hand, "I don't need
you!" And the head cannot
say to the feet, "I don't
need you!" 22On the con-
trary, those parts of the
body that seem to be weaker are indispensable, 23and
the parts that we think are
less honorable we treat
with special honor. And the
parts that are unpresent-
able are treated with special modesty, 24while our

[b]13 Or *with*; or *in*

24 whereas our seemly *members* have no need *of it*. But God has *so* composed the body, giving more abundant honor to that *member* which lacked,
25 that there should be no division in the body, but *that* the members should have the same care for one another.
26 And if one member suffers, all the members suffer with it; if *one* member is honored, all the members rejoice with it.
27 Now you are Christ's body, and individually members of it.
28 And God has appointed in the church, first apostles, second prophets, third teachers, then miracles, then gifts of healings, helps, administrations, *various* kinds of tongues.
29 All are not apostles, are they? All are not prophets, are they? All are not teachers, are they? All are not *workers of* miracles, are they?
30 All do not have gifts of healings, do they? All do not speak with tongues, do they? All do not interpret, do they?
31 But earnestly desire the greater gifts.
And I show you a still more excellent way.

Chapter 13

The Excellence of Love

IF I speak with the tongues of men and of angels, but do not have love, I have become a noisy gong or a clanging cymbal.
2 And if I have *the gift of* prophecy, and know all mysteries and all knowledge; and if I have all faith, so as to remove mountains, but do not have love, I am nothing.
3 And if I give all my possessions to feed *the poor*, and if I deliver my body [a]to be burned, but do not have love, it profits me nothing.

[a] Some ancient mss. read *that I may boast*

εὐσχήμονα ἡμῶν οὐ χρείαν ἔχει. ἀλλὰ ὁ
comely [members] of us [2]no [3]need [1]has(ve). But –
θεὸς συνεκέρασεν τὸ σῶμα, τῷ ὑστερουμένῳ
God blended together the body, [4]to the [member] [5]lacking
περισσοτέραν δοὺς τιμήν, 25 ἵνα μὴ ᾖ
[2]more abundant [1]giving [3]honour, lest there be
σχίσμα ἐν τῷ σώματι, ἀλλὰ τὸ αὐτὸ
division in the body, but [4]the [5]same
ὑπὲρ ἀλλήλων μεριμνῶσιν τὰ μέλη.
[6]on behalf of [7]one another [3]should care [1]the [2]members.
26 καὶ εἴτε πάσχει ἓν μέλος, συμπάσχει
And whether [3]suffers [1]one [2]member, [7]suffers with [it]
πάντα τὰ μέλη· εἴτε δοξάζεται μέλος,
[4]all [5]the [6]members; or [2]is glorified [1]a member,
συγχαίρει πάντα τὰ μέλη. 27 ὑμεῖς
[6]rejoices with [it] [3]all [4]the [5]members. ye
δέ ἐστε σῶμα Χριστοῦ καὶ μέλη ἐκ
And are a body of Christ and members in
μέρους. 28 Καὶ οὓς μὲν ἔθετο ὁ θεὸς
part. And [3]some† [2]placed – [1]God
ἐν τῇ ἐκκλησίᾳ πρῶτον ἀποστόλους, δεύτερον
in the church firstly apostles, secondly
προφήτας, τρίτον διδασκάλους, ἔπειτα
prophets, thirdly teachers, then
δυνάμεις, ἔπειτα χαρίσματα ἰαμάτων,
powers, then gifts of cures,
ἀντιλήμψεις, κυβερνήσεις, γένη γλωσσῶν.
helps, governings, kinds of tongues.
29 μὴ πάντες ἀπόστολοι; μὴ πάντες
Not all [are] apostles? *not* all
προφῆται; μὴ πάντες διδάσκαλοι; μὴ
prophets; *not* all teachers? *not*
πάντες δυνάμεις; 30 μὴ πάντες χαρίσματα
all powers? *not* all [2]gifts
ἔχουσιν ἰαμάτων; μὴ πάντες γλώσσαις
[1]have of cures? *not* all [2]with tongues
λαλοῦσιν; μὴ πάντες διερμηνεύουσιν;
[1]speak? *not* all interpret?
31 ζηλοῦτε δὲ τὰ χαρίσματα τὰ μείζονα.
but desire ye eagerly the [2]gifts – [1]greater.
Καὶ ἔτι καθʼ ὑπερβολὴν ὁδὸν ὑμῖν
And yet [4]according to [5]excellence [3]a way [2]to you
δείκνυμι. 13 Ἐὰν ταῖς γλώσσαις τῶν ἀνθρώπων
[1]I show. If in the tongues – of men
λαλῶ καὶ τῶν ἀγγέλων, ἀγάπην δὲ
I speak and – of angels, but love
μὴ ἔχω, γέγονα χαλκὸς ἠχῶν ἢ
I have not, I have become [2]brass [1]sounding or
κύμβαλον ἀλαλάζον. 2 καὶ ἐὰν ἔχω
cymbal a tinkling. And if I have
προφητείαν καὶ εἰδῶ τὰ μυστήρια πάντα
prophecy and know [2]the [3]mysteries [1]all
καὶ πᾶσαν τὴν γνῶσιν, κἂν ἔχω πᾶσαν
and all – knowledge, and if I have all
τὴν πίστιν ὥστε ὄρη μεθιστάναι, ἀγάπην
– faith so as mountains to remove, [2]love
δὲ μὴ ἔχω, οὐθέν εἰμι. 3 κἂν ψωμίσω
[1]but I have not, nothing I am. And if I dole out
πάντα τὰ ὑπάρχοντά μου, καὶ ἐὰν παραδῶ
all the goods of me, and if I deliver
τὸ σῶμά μου ἵνα καυθήσομαι, ἀγάπην
the body of me in order that I shall be burned, [2]love
δὲ μὴ ἔχω, οὐδὲν ὠφελοῦμαι. 4 Ἡ
[1]but I have not, nothing I am profited. –

presentable parts need no special treatment. But God has combined the members of the body and has given greater honor to the parts that lacked it, 25 so that there should be no division in the body, but that its parts should have equal concern for each other. 26 If one part suffers, every part suffers with it; if one part is honored, every part rejoices with it.
27 Now you are the body of Christ, and each one of you is a part of it. 28 And in the church God has appointed first of all apostles, second prophets, third teachers, then workers of miracles, also those having gifts of healing, those able to help others, those with gifts of administration, and those speaking in different kinds of tongues. 29 Are all apostles? Are all prophets? Are all teachers? Do all work miracles? 30 Do all have gifts of healing? Do all speak in tongues[c]? Do all interpret? 31 But eagerly desire[d] the greater gifts.

Love

And now I will show you the most excellent way.

Chapter 13

IF I speak in the tongues[e] of men and of angels, but have not love, I am only a resounding gong or a clanging cymbal. 2 If I have the gift of prophecy and can fathom all mysteries and all knowledge, and if I have a faith that can move mountains, but have not love, I am nothing. 3 If I give all I possess to the poor and surrender my body to the flames,[f] but have not love, I gain nothing.

[c] 30 Or *other languages*
[d] 31 Or *But you are eagerly desiring*
[e] 1 Or *languages*
[f] 3 Some early manuscripts *body that I may boast*

4Love is patient, love is
kind, *and* is not jealous;
love does not brag *and* is
not arrogant,
5does not act unbecom-
ingly; it does not seek its
own, is not provoked, does
not take into account a
wrong *suffered*,
6does not rejoice in un-
righteousness, but rejoices
with the truth;
7bears all things, be-
lieves all things, hopes all
things, endures all things.
8Love never fails; but if
there are gifts of prophecy,
they will be done away; if
there are tongues, they will
cease; if *there is* knowledge, it will be done away.
9For we know in part,
and we prophesy in part;
10but when the perfect
comes, the partial will be
done away.
11When I was a child, I
used to speak as a child,
think as a child, reason as a
child; when I became a
man, I did away with child-
ish things.
12For now we see in a mirror dimly, but then face to
face; now I know in part,
but then I shall know fully
just as I also have been fully known.
13But now abide faith,
hope, love, these three; but
the greatest of these is love.

Chapter 14

Prophecy a Superior Gift

PURSUE love, yet de-
sire earnestly spiritual
gifts, but especially that
you may prophesy.
2For one who speaks in a
tongue does not speak to
men, but to God; for no one
understands, but in *his*
spirit he speaks mysteries.
3But one who prophesies
speaks to men for edification and exhortation and
consolation.
4One who speaks in a
tongue edifies himself; but
one who prophesies edifies

ἀγάπη μακροθυμεῖ, χρηστεύεται ἡ ἀγάπη,
Love suffers long, is kind – love,
οὐ ζηλοῖ, ἡ ἀγάπη οὐ περπερεύεται,
is not jealous, – love does not vaunt itself,
οὐ φυσιοῦται, 5 οὐκ ἀσχημονεῖ, οὐ ζητεῖ
is not puffed up, does not act unbecomingly, does not seek
τὰ ἑαυτῆς, οὐ παροξύνεται, οὐ λογίζεται
the things of her(it)self, is not provoked, does not reckon
τὸ κακόν, 6 οὐ χαίρει ἐπὶ τῇ ἀδικίᾳ,
the evil, rejoices not over the wrong,
συγχαίρει δὲ τῇ ἀληθείᾳ· 7 πάντα στέγει,
but rejoices with the truth; all things covers,
πάντα πιστεύει, πάντα ἐλπίζει, πάντα
all things believes, all things hopes, all things
ὑπομένει. 8 Ἡ ἀγάπη οὐδέποτε πίπτει·
endures. – Love never falls;
εἴτε δὲ προφητεῖαι, καταργηθήσονται· εἴτε
but whether prophecies, they will be abolished; or
γλῶσσαι, παύσονται· εἴτε γνῶσις, κατ-
tongues, they will cease; or knowledge, it will
αργηθήσεται. 9 ἐκ μέρους γὰρ γινώσκομεν
be abolished. For in part we know
καὶ ἐκ μέρους προφητεύομεν· 10 ὅταν
and in part we prophesy; [2]when
δὲ ἔλθῃ τὸ τέλειον, τὸ ἐκ μέρους
[1]but [5]comes [3]the [4]perfect thing, the thing in part
καταργηθήσεται. 11 ὅτε ἤμην νήπιος,
will be abolished. When I was an infant,
ἐλάλουν ὡς νήπιος, ἐφρόνουν ὡς νήπιος,
I spoke as an infant, I thought as an infant,
ἐλογιζόμην ὡς νήπιος· ὅτε γέγονα ἀνήρ,
I reckoned as an infant; when I have become a man,
κατήργηκα τὰ τοῦ νηπίου. 12 βλέπομεν
I have abolished the things of the infant. we see
γὰρ ἄρτι δι' ἐσόπτρου ἐν αἰνίγματι,
For yet through a mirror in a riddle,
τότε δὲ πρόσωπον πρὸς πρόσωπον· ἄρτι
but then face to face; yet
γινώσκω ἐκ μέρους, τότε δὲ ἐπιγνώσομαι
I know in part, but then I shall fully know
καθὼς καὶ ἐπεγνώσθην. 13 νυνὶ δὲ μένει
as also I was fully known. But now remains
πίστις, ἐλπίς, ἀγάπη, τὰ τρία ταῦτα·
faith, hope, love, these three;
μείζων δὲ τούτων ἡ ἀγάπη.
and [the] greater of these [is] – love.

14 Διώκετε τὴν ἀγάπην, ζηλοῦτε δὲ
Pursue ye – love, but desire eagerly
τὰ πνευματικά, μᾶλλον δὲ ἵνα προφητεύητε.
the spiritual [gifts], and rather in order that ye may prophesy.
2 ὁ γὰρ λαλῶν γλώσσῃ οὐκ ἀνθρώποις
For the [one] speaking in a tongue [2]not to men
λαλεῖ ἀλλὰ θεῷ· οὐδεὶς γὰρ ἀκούει,
[1]speaks but to God; for no one hears,
πνεύματι δὲ λαλεῖ μυστήρια· 3 ὁ δὲ
but in spirit he speaks mysteries; but the [one]
προφητεύων ἀνθρώποις λαλεῖ οἰκοδομὴν καὶ
prophesying to men speaks edification and
παράκλησιν καὶ παραμυθίαν. 4 ὁ λαλῶν
encouragement and consolation. The [one] speaking
γλώσσῃ ἑαυτὸν οἰκοδομεῖ· ὁ δὲ προφητεύων
in a tongue himself edifies; but the [one] prophesying

4Love is patient, love is
kind. It does not envy, it
does not boast, it is not
proud. 5It is not rude, it is
not self-seeking, it is not
easily angered, it keeps no
record of wrongs. 6Love
does not delight in evil but
rejoices with the truth. 7It
always protects, always
trusts, always hopes, al-
ways perseveres.
8Love never fails. But
where there are prophe-
cies, they will cease; where
there are tongues, they will
be stilled; where there is
knowledge, it will pass
away. 9For we know in part
and we prophesy in part,
10but when perfection
comes, the imperfect disap-
pears. 11When I was a
child, I talked like a child, I
thought like a child, I reasoned like a child. When I
became a man, I put child-
ish ways behind me. 12Now
we see but a poor reflection
as in a mirror; then we shall
see face to face. Now I
know in part; then I shall
know fully, even as I am
fully known.
13And now these three re-
main: faith, hope and love.
But the greatest of these is
love.

Chapter 14

Gifts of Prophecy and Tongues

FOLLOW the way of
love and eagerly desire
spiritual gifts, especially
the gift of prophecy. 2For
anyone who speaks in a
tongue[g] does not speak to
men but to God. Indeed, no
one understands him; he ut-
ters mysteries with his spirit.[h] 3But everyone who
prophesies speaks to men
for their strengthening, encouragement and comfort.
4He who speaks in a tongue
edifies himself, but he who
prophesies edifies the

[g]2 Or *another language*; also in verses 4, 13, 14, 19, 26 and 27
[h]2 Or *by the Spirit*

the church.
5Now I wish that you all
spoke in tongues, but *even*
more that you would
prophesy; and greater is
one who prophesies than
one who speaks in tongues,
unless he interprets, so that
the church may receive edi-
fying.
6But now, brethren, if I
come to you speaking in
tongues, what shall I profit
you, unless I speak to you
either by way of revelation
or of knowledge or of
prophecy or of teaching?
7Yet *even* lifeless things,
either flute or harp, in producing a sound, if they do
not produce a distinction in
the tones, how will it be
known what is played on
the flute or on the harp?
8For if the bugle pro-
duces an indistinct sound,
who will prepare himself
for battle?
9So also you, unless you
utter by the tongue speech
that is clear, how will it be
known what is spoken? For
you will be speaking into
the air.
10There are, perhaps, a
great many kinds of lan-
guages in the world, and no
kind is without meaning.
11If then I do not know
the meaning of the lan-
guage, I shall be to the one
who speaks a barbarian,
and the one who speaks
will be a barbarian to me.
12So also you, since you
are zealous of spiritual
gifts, seek to abound for
the edification of the
church.
13Therefore let one who
speaks in a tongue pray that
he may interpret.
14For if I pray in a tongue,
my spirit prays, but my
mind is unfruitful.
15What is *the outcome*
then? I shall pray with the

ἐκκλησίαν οἰκοδομεῖ. **5** θέλω δὲ πάντας
a church edifies. Now I wish all

ὑμᾶς λαλεῖν γλώσσαις, μᾶλλον δὲ ἵνα
you to speak in tongues, but rather *in order* that

προφητεύητε· μείζων δὲ ὁ προφητεύων ἢ
ye may prophesy; and greater the [one] prophesying than

ὁ λαλῶν γλώσσαις, ἐκτὸς εἰ μὴ διερμηνεύῃ,
the [one] speaking in tongues, *except* unless he interprets,

ἵνα ἡ ἐκκλησία οἰκοδομὴν λάβῃ. **6** νῦν δέ,
in order that the church edification may receive. But now,

ἀδελφοί, ἐὰν ἔλθω πρὸς ὑμᾶς γλώσσαις
brothers, if I come to you in tongues

λαλῶν, τί ὑμᾶς ὠφελήσω, ἐὰν μὴ ὑμῖν
speaking, what [2]you [1]shall I profit, except [3]to you

λαλήσω ἢ ἐν ἀποκαλύψει ἢ ἐν γνώσει
[1]I speak either in a revelation or in knowledge

ἢ ἐν προφητείᾳ ἢ διδαχῇ; **7** ὅμως τὰ
or in prophecy or *in* teaching? Yet –

ἄψυχα φωνὴν διδόντα, εἴτε αὐλὸς εἴτε
lifeless things [2]a sound [1]giving, whether pipe or

κιθάρα, ἐὰν διαστολὴν τοῖς φθόγγοις μὴ
harp, if [3]a distinction [4]in the [5]sounds [2]not

δῷ, πῶς γνωσθήσεται τὸ αὐλούμενον ἢ
[1]they give, how will it be known the thing being piped or

τὸ κιθαριζόμενον; **8** καὶ γὰρ ἐὰν ἄδηλον
the thing being harped? For indeed if [3]an uncertain

σάλπιγξ φωνὴν δῷ, τίς παρασκευάσεται
[1]a trumpet [4]sound [2]gives, who will prepare himself

εἰς πόλεμον; **9** οὕτως καὶ ὑμεῖς διὰ
for war? so also [1]ye [6]through

τῆς γλώσσης ἐὰν μὴ εὔσημον λόγον
[7]the [8]tongue [2]unless [4]a clear [5]word

δῶτε, πῶς γνωσθήσεται τὸ λαλούμενον;
[3]give, how will it be known the thing being said?

ἔσεσθε γὰρ εἰς ἀέρα λαλοῦντες. **10** τοσαῦτα
for [1]ye will be [3]into [4]air [2]speaking. [2]So many

εἰ τύχοι γένη φωνῶν εἰσιν ἐν κόσμῳ,
[3]it may be† [4]kinds [5]of sounds [1]there are in [the] world,

καὶ οὐδὲν ἄφωνον· **11** ἐὰν οὖν μὴ εἰδῶ
and not one [is] voiceless; if therefore I know not

τὴν δύναμιν τῆς φωνῆς, ἔσομαι τῷ
the power of the sound, I shall be to the

λαλοῦντι βάρβαρος καὶ ὁ λαλῶν ἐν ἐμοὶ
[one] speaking a foreigner and the [one] speaking in(to) me

βάρβαρος. **12** οὕτως καὶ ὑμεῖς, ἐπεὶ
a foreigner. So also ye, since

ζηλωταί ἐστε πνευμάτων, πρὸς τὴν
zealots ye are of spirit[ual thing]s, [2]to [3]the

οἰκοδομὴν τῆς ἐκκλησίας ζητεῖτε ἵνα περισ-
[4]edification [5]of the [6]church [1]seek ye in order that ye may

σεύητε. **13** Διὸ ὁ λαλῶν γλώσσῃ προσευχ-
abound. Wherefore the [one] speaking in a tongue let him

έσθω ἵνα διερμηνεύῃ. **14** ἐὰν γὰρ προσεύχωμαι
pray *in order* that he may interpret. For if I pray

γλώσσῃ, τὸ πνεῦμά μου προσεύχεται,
in a tongue, the spirit of me prays,

ὁ δὲ νοῦς μου ἄκαρπός ἐστιν. **15** τί
but the mind of me unfruitful is. What

οὖν ἐστιν; προσεύξομαι τῷ πνεύματι,
therefore is it? I will pray with the spirit,

church. 5I would like every
one of you to speak in
tongues,[i] but I would rather have you prophesy. He
who prophesies is greater
than one who speaks in
tongues,[i] unless he interprets, so that the church
may be edified.
6Now, brothers, if I come
to you and speak in
tongues, what good will I
be to you, unless I bring
you some revelation or
knowledge or prophecy or
word of instruction? 7Even
in the case of lifeless things
that make sounds, such as
the flute or harp, how will
anyone know what tune is
being played unless there is
a distinction in the notes?
8Again, if the trumpet does
not sound a clear call, who
will get ready for battle?
9So it is with you. Unless
you speak intelligible
words with your tongue,
how will anyone know
what you are saying? You
will just be speaking into
the air. 10Undoubtedly
there are all sorts of languages in the world, yet
none of them is without
meaning. 11If then I do not
grasp the meaning of what
someone is saying, I am a
foreigner to the speaker,
and he is a foreigner to me.
12So it is with you. Since
you are eager to have spiritual gifts, try to excel in
gifts that build up the
church.
13For this reason anyone
who speaks in a tongue
should pray that he may interpret what he says. 14For
if I pray in a tongue, my
spirit prays, but my mind is
unfruitful. 15So what shall I
do? I will pray with my spir-

[i]5 Or *other languages*; also in verses 6, 18, 22, 23 and 39

spirit and I shall pray with
the mind also; I shall sing
with the spirit and I shall
sing with the mind also.
16 Otherwise if you bless
in the spirit *only*, how will
the one who fills the place
of the ungifted say the
"Amen" at your giving of
thanks, since he does not
know what you are saying?
17 For you are giving
thanks well enough, but the
other man is not edified.
18 I thank God, I speak in
tongues more than you all;
19 however, in the church
I desire to speak five words
with my mind, that I may
instruct others also, rather
than ten thousand words in
a tongue.

Instruction for the Church

20 Brethren, do not be
children in your thinking;
yet in evil be babes, but in
your thinking be mature.
21 In the Law it is written,
"BY MEN OF STRANGE
TONGUES AND BY THE LIPS OF
STRANGERS I WILL SPEAK TO
THIS PEOPLE, AND EVEN SO
THEY WILL NOT LISTEN TO
ME," says the Lord.
22 So then tongues are for
a sign, not to those who believe, but to unbelievers;
but prophecy *is for a sign*,
not to unbelievers, but to
those who believe.
23 If therefore the whole
church should assemble together and all speak in
tongues, and ungifted men
or unbelievers enter, will
they not say that you are
mad?
24 But if all prophesy, and
an unbeliever or an ungifted man enters, he is con-
victed by all, he is called to
account by all;
25 the secrets of his heart
are disclosed; and so he will
fall on his face and worship
God, declaring that God is
certainly among you.
26 What is *the outcome*

προσεύξομαι δὲ καὶ τῷ νοΐ· ψαλῶ τῷ
[2]I will pray [1]and [3]also with the mind; I will sing with the

πνεύματι, ψαλῶ δὲ καὶ τῷ νοΐ. **16** ἐπεὶ
spirit,. [2]I will sing [1]and [3]also with the mind. Otherwise

ἐὰν εὐλογῇς [ἐν] πνεύματι, ὁ ἀναπληρῶν
if thou blessest in spirit, the [one] occupying

τὸν τόπον τοῦ ἰδιώτου πῶς ἐρεῖ τὸ
the place of the uninstructed how will he say the

ἀμὴν ἐπὶ τῇ σῇ εὐχαριστίᾳ; ἐπειδὴ τί
"amen" at – thy giving thanks? Since what

λέγεις οὐκ οἶδεν· **17** σὺ μὲν γὰρ καλῶς
thou sayest he knows not; [2]thou [3]indeed [1]for [5]well

εὐχαριστεῖς, ἀλλ' ὁ ἕτερος οὐκ οἰκοδομεῖται.
[4]givest thanks, but the other is not edified.

18 εὐχαριστῶ τῷ θεῷ, πάντων ὑμῶν μᾶλ-
I give thanks – to God, [6]all [4]you [3]more

λον γλώσσαις λαλῶ· **19** ἀλλὰ ἐν ἐκκλησίᾳ
than [2]in tongues [1]I speak; but in a church

θέλω πέντε λόγους τῷ νοΐ μου λαλῆσαι,
[1]I wish [3]five [4]words [5]with the [6]mind [7]of me [2]to speak,

ἵνα καὶ ἄλλους κατηχήσω, ἢ μυρίους
in order that also others I may instruct, than ten thousands

λόγους ἐν γλώσσῃ. **20** Ἀδελφοί, μὴ
words in a tongue. Brothers, [2]not

παιδία γίνεσθε ταῖς φρεσίν, ἀλλὰ τῇ
[3]children [1]be ye in the(your) minds, but –

κακίᾳ νηπιάζετε, ταῖς δὲ φρεσὶν τέλειοι
in malice be ye infantlike, and in the(your) minds mature

γίνεσθε. **21** ἐν τῷ νόμῳ γέγραπται ὅτι
be ye. In the law it has been written that

ἐν ἑτερογλώσσοις καὶ ἐν χείλεσιν ἑτέρων
in other tongues and in lips of others

λαλήσω τῷ λαῷ τούτῳ, καὶ οὐδ' οὕτως
I will speak to this people, and not so

εἰσακούσονταί μου, λέγει κύριος. **22** ὥστε
will they hear me, says [the] Lord. So as

αἱ γλῶσσαι εἰς σημεῖόν εἰσιν οὐ τοῖς
the tongues [2]for [3]a sign [1]are not to the

πιστεύουσιν ἀλλὰ τοῖς ἀπίστοις, ἡ δὲ
[ones] believing but to the unbelievers, and *the*

προφητεία οὐ τοῖς ἀπίστοις ἀλλὰ τοῖς
prophecy [is] not to the unbelievers but to the

πιστεύουσιν. **23** Ἐὰν οὖν συνέλθῃ ἡ
[ones] believing. If therefore [4]comes *together* [1]the

ἐκκλησία ὅλη ἐπὶ τὸ αὐτὸ καὶ πάντες
[3]church [2]whole together and all

λαλῶσιν γλώσσαις, εἰσέλθωσιν δὲ ἰδιῶται
speak in tongues, and [4]enter [1]uninstructed

ἢ ἄπιστοι, οὐκ ἐροῦσιν ὅτι μαίνεσθε;
[2]or [3]unbelievers, will they not say that ye rave?

24 ἐὰν δὲ πάντες προφητεύωσιν, εἰσέλθῃ δέ
but if all prophesy, and [5]enters

τις ἄπιστος ἢ ἰδιώτης, ἐλέγχεται ὑπὸ
[1]some [2]unbeliever [3]or [4]uninstructed, he is convicted by

πάντων, ἀνακρίνεται ὑπὸ πάντων, **25** τὰ
all, he is judged by all, the

κρυπτὰ τῆς καρδίας αὐτοῦ φανερὰ γίνεται,
hidden things of the heart of him [2]manifest [1]becomes,

καὶ οὕτως πεσὼν ἐπὶ πρόσωπον προσκυνή-
and so falling on [his] face he will wor-

σει τῷ θεῷ, ἀπαγγέλλων ὅτι ὄντως
ship – God, declaring that really

ὁ θεὸς ἐν ὑμῖν ἐστιν. **26** Τί οὖν ἐστιν,
– God [2]among [3]you [1]is. What therefore is it,

it, but I will also pray with
my mind; I will sing with
my spirit, but I will also
sing with my mind. 16 If you
are praising God with your
spirit, how can one who
finds himself among those
who do not understand[j]
say "Amen" to your
thanksgiving, since he does
not know what you are saying? 17 You may be giving
thanks well enough, but the
other man is not edified.
18 I thank God that I speak
in tongues more than all of
you. 19 But in the church I
would rather speak five intelligible words to instruct
others than ten thousand
words in a tongue.
20 Brothers, stop thinking
like children. In regard to
evil be infants, but in your
thinking be adults. 21 In the
Law it is written:

"Through men of
strange tongues
and through the lips of
foreigners
I will speak to this
people,
but even then they will
not listen to me,"[k]

says the Lord.
22 Tongues, then, are a
sign, not for believers but
for unbelievers; prophecy,
however, is for believers,
not for unbelievers. 23 So if
the whole church comes together and everyone
speaks in tongues, and
some who do not under-
stand[l] or some unbelievers
come in, will they not say
that you are out of your
mind? 24 But if an unbeliever or someone who does
not understand[m] comes in
while everybody is prophesying, he will be convinced
by all that he is a sinner and
will be judged by all, 25 and
the secrets of his heart will
be laid bare. So he will fall
down and worship God, ex-
claiming, "God is really
among you!"

Orderly Worship

26 What then shall we say,

[j]16 Or *among the inquirers*
[k]21 Isaiah 28:11,12
[l]23 Or *some inquirers*
[m]24 Or *or some inquirer*

then, brethren? When you assemble, each one has a psalm, has a teaching, has a revelation, has a tongue, has an interpretation. Let all things be done for edification.

27If anyone speaks in a tongue, *it should be* by two or at the most three, and *each* in turn, and let one interpret;

28but if there is no interpreter, let him keep silent in the church; and let him speak to himself and to God.

29And let two or three prophets speak, and let the others pass judgment.

30But if a revelation is made to another who is seated, let the first keep silent.

31For you can all prophesy one by one, so that all may learn and all may be exhorted;

32and the spirits of prophets are subject to prophets;

33for God is not *a God* of confusion but of peace, as in all the churches of the saints.

34Let the women keep silent in the churches; for they are not permitted to speak, but let them subject themselves, just as the Law also says.

35And if they desire to learn anything, let them ask their own husbands at home; for it is improper for a woman to speak in church.

36Was it from you that the word of God *first* went forth? Or has it come to you only?

37If anyone thinks he is a prophet or spiritual, let him recognize that the things which I write to you are the Lord's commandment.

38But if anyone [p]does not recognize *this*, he is not recognized.

39Therefore, my brethren, desire earnestly to prophesy, and do not forbid to speak in tongues.

40But let all things be done properly and in an orderly manner.

ἀδελφοί; ὅταν συνέρχησθε, ἕκαστος ψαλμὸν
brothers? whenever ye come together, each one a psalm

ἔχει, διδαχὴν ἔχει, ἀποκάλυψιν ἔχει, γλῶσ-
has, a teaching he has, a revelation he has, a

σαν ἔχει, ἑρμηνείαν ἔχει· πάντα πρὸς
tongue he has, an interpretation he has; [2]all things [4]for

οἰκοδομὴν γινέσθω. 27 εἴτε γλώσσῃ τις
[5]edification [1]let [3]be. If in a tongue anyone

λαλεῖ, κατὰ δύο ἢ τὸ πλεῖστον τρεῖς,
speaks, by two or the most three,

καὶ ἀνὰ μέρος, 28 καὶ εἷς διερμηνευέτω·
and in turn,† and [2]one [1]let [3]interpret;

ἐὰν δὲ μὴ ᾖ διερμηνευτής, σιγάτω ἐν
but if there is not an interpreter, let him be silent in

ἐκκλησίᾳ, ἑαυτῷ δὲ λαλείτω καὶ τῷ
church, and to himself let him speak and –

θεῷ. 29 προφῆται δὲ δύο ἢ τρεῖς λαλεί-
to God. And prophets two or three let them

τωσαν, καὶ οἱ ἄλλοι διακρινέτωσαν·
speak, and the others let discern;

30 ἐὰν δὲ ἄλλῳ ἀποκαλυφθῇ καθημένῳ, ὁ
but if [1]to another [3][something] [4]is revealed [2]sitting, the

πρῶτος σιγάτω. 31 δύνασθε γὰρ καθ'
first let be silent. For ye can [3]sin-

ἕνα πάντες προφητεύειν, ἵνα πάντες
gly† [1]all [2]*to* prophesy, in order that all

μανθάνωσιν καὶ πάντες παρακαλῶνται.
may learn and all may be encouraged.

32 καὶ πνεύματα προφητῶν προφήταις
And [the] spirits of prophets to prophets

ὑποτάσσεται· 33 οὐ γάρ ἐστιν ἀκαταστασίας
is(are) subject; for [2]not [3]is [4]of tumult

ὁ θεὸς ἀλλὰ εἰρήνης. Ὡς ἐν πάσαις
– [1]God but of peace. As in all

ταῖς ἐκκλησίαις τῶν ἁγίων, 34 αἱ γυναῖκες
the churches of the saints, [2]the [3]women

ἐν ταῖς ἐκκλησίαις σιγάτωσαν· οὐ γὰρ
[5]in [6]the [7]churches [1]let [4]be silent; [3]not [1]for

ἐπιτρέπεται αὐταῖς λαλεῖν, ἀλλὰ ὑποτασ-
[2]it is [4]permitted to them to speak, but let them

σέσθωσαν, καθὼς καὶ ὁ νόμος λέγει.
be subject, as also the law says.

35 εἰ δέ τι μαθεῖν θέλουσιν, ἐν οἴκῳ
But if [3]anything [2]to learn [1]they wish, [5]at home

τοὺς ἰδίους ἄνδρας ἐπερωτάτωσαν· αἰσχρὸν
[2]the(ir) [3]own [4]husbands [1]let them question; [3]a shame

γάρ ἐστιν γυναικὶ λαλεῖν ἐν ἐκκλησίᾳ.
[1]for [2]it is for a woman to speak in a church.

36 ἢ ἀφ' ὑμῶν ὁ λόγος τοῦ θεοῦ ἐξῆλθεν,
Or from you [2]the [3]word – [4]of God [1]went forth,

ἢ εἰς ὑμᾶς μόνους κατήντησεν; 37 Εἴ
or to you only did it reach? If

τις δοκεῖ προφήτης εἶναι ἢ πνευματικός,
anyone thinks [2]a prophet [1]to be or a spiritual man,

ἐπιγινωσκέτω ἃ γράφω ὑμῖν ὅτι
let him clearly know [the] things which I write to you that

κυρίου ἐστὶν ἐντολή· 38 εἰ δέ τις
of [the] Lord they are a commandment; but if anyone

ἀγνοεῖ, ἀγνοεῖται. 39 Ὥστε, ἀδελφοί
is ignorant, let him be ignorant. So as, brothers

μου, ζηλοῦτε τὸ προφητεύειν, καὶ τὸ
of me, be ye eager – to prophesy, and –

λαλεῖν μὴ κωλύετε γλώσσαις· 40 πάντα
[2]to speak [1]forbid not in tongues; [2]all things

δὲ εὐσχημόνως καὶ κατὰ τάξιν γινέσθω.
and [4]becomingly [5]and [6]according to [7]order [1]let [3]be done.

brothers? When you come together, everyone has a hymn, or a word of instruction, a revelation, a tongue or an interpretation. All of these must be done for the strengthening of the church. 27If anyone speaks in a tongue, two—or at the most three—should speak, one at a time, and someone must interpret. 28If there is no interpreter, the speaker should keep quiet in the church and speak to himself and God.

29Two or three prophets should speak, and the others should weigh carefully what is said. 30And if a revelation comes to someone who is sitting down, the first speaker should stop. 31For you can all prophesy in turn so that everyone may be instructed and encouraged. 32The spirits of prophets are subject to the control of prophets. 33For God is not a God of disorder but of peace.

As in all the congregations of the saints, 34women should remain silent in the churches. They are not allowed to speak, but must be in submission, as the Law says. 35If they want to inquire about something, they should ask their own husbands at home; for it is disgraceful for a woman to speak in the church.

36Did the word of God originate with you? Or are you the only people it has reached? 37If anybody thinks he is a prophet or spiritually gifted, let him acknowledge that what I am writing to you is the Lord's command. 38If he ignores this, he himself will be ignored.[n]

39Therefore, my brothers, be eager to prophesy, and do not forbid speaking in tongues. 40But everything should be done in a fitting and orderly way.

[p] Some ancient mss. read *is ignorant, let him be ignorant*

[n]38 Some manuscripts *If he is ignorant of this, let him be ignorant*

Chapter 15

The Fact of Christ's Resurrection

NOW I make known to
you, brethren, the
gospel which I preached to
you, which also you re-
ceived, in which also you
stand,
2by which also you are
saved, if you hold fast the
word which I preached to
you, unless you believed in
vain.
3For I delivered to you
as of first importance what
I also received, that Christ
died for our sins according
to the Scriptures,
4and that He was buried,
and that He was raised on
the third day according to
the Scriptures,
5and that He appeared to
Cephas, then to the twelve.
6After that He appeared
to more than five hundred
brethren at one time, most
of whom remain until now,
but some have fallen
asleep;
7then He appeared to
James, then to all the apostles;
8and last of all, as it were
to one untimely born, He
appeared to me also.
9For I am the least of the
apostles, who am not fit to
be called an apostle, be-
cause I persecuted the
church of God.
10But by the grace of God
I am what I am, and His
grace toward me did not
prove vain; but I labored
even more than all of them,
yet not I, but the grace of
God with me.
11Whether then *it was* I or
they, so we preach and so
you believed.
12Now if Christ is
preached, that He has been
raised from the dead, how
do some among you say
that there is no resurrection
of the dead?
13But if there is no resurrection of the dead, not
even Christ has been
raised;
14and if Christ has not

15 Γνωρίζω δὲ ὑμῖν, ἀδελφοί, τὸ
Now I make known to you, brothers, the
εὐαγγέλιον ὃ εὐηγγελισάμην ὑμῖν, ὃ καὶ
good tidings which I preached to you, which also
παρελάβετε, ἐν ᾧ καὶ ἑστήκατε, 2 δι'
ye received, in which also ye stand, through
οὗ καὶ σῴζεσθε, τίνι λόγῳ εὐηγγελισάμην
which also ye are saved, [3]to what [4]word [5]I preached
ὑμῖν εἰ κατέχετε, ἐκτὸς εἰ μὴ εἰκῇ
[6]to you [1]if [2]ye hold fast, *except* unless in vain
ἐπιστεύσατε. 3 παρέδωκα γὰρ ὑμῖν ἐν
ye believed. For I delivered to you among
πρώτοις, ὃ καὶ παρέλαβον, ὅτι Χριστὸς
[the] first things, what also I received, that Christ
ἀπέθανεν ὑπὲρ τῶν ἁμαρτιῶν ἡμῶν κατὰ
died on behalf of the sins of us according to
τὰς γραφάς, 4 καὶ ὅτι ἐτάφη, καὶ ὅτι
the scriptures, and that he was buried, and that
ἐγήγερται τῇ ἡμέρᾳ τῇ τρίτῃ κατὰ
he has been raised on the [2]day – [1]third according to
τὰς γραφάς, 5 καὶ ὅτι ὤφθη Κηφᾷ,
the scriptures, and that he was seen by Cephas,
εἶτα τοῖς δώδεκα· 6 ἔπειτα ὤφθη ἐπάνω
then by the twelve; afterward he was seen [2]over
πεντακοσίοις ἀδελφοῖς ἐφάπαξ, ἐξ ὧν οἱ
[1]by [3]five hundreds brothers at one time, of whom the
πλείονες μένουσιν ἕως ἄρτι, τινὲς δὲ
majority remain until now, though some
ἐκοιμήθησαν· 7 ἔπειτα ὤφθη Ἰακώβῳ, εἶτα
fell asleep; afterward he was seen by James, then
τοῖς ἀποστόλοις πᾶσιν· 8 ἔσχατον δὲ
by the apostles all; and lastly
πάντων ὡσπερεὶ τῷ ἐκτρώματι ὤφθη
of all even as if to the(an) abortion he was seen
κἀμοί. 9 Ἐγὼ γάρ εἰμι ὁ ἐλάχιστος
by me also. For I am the least
τῶν ἀποστόλων, ὃς οὐκ εἰμὶ ἱκανὸς
of the apostles, who am not sufficient
καλεῖσθαι ἀπόστολος, διότι ἐδίωξα τὴν
to be called an apostle, because I persecuted the
ἐκκλησίαν τοῦ θεοῦ· 10 χάριτι δὲ θεοῦ
church – of God; but by [the] grace of God
εἰμι ὅ εἰμι, καὶ ἡ χάρις αὐτοῦ ἡ εἰς
I am what I am, and the grace of him – to
ἐμὲ οὐ κενὴ ἐγενήθη, ἀλλὰ περισσότερον
me not empty was, but [2]more abundantly [than]
αὐτῶν πάντων ἐκοπίασα, οὐκ ἐγὼ δὲ
[3]them [4]all [1]I laboured, [2]not [3]I [1]yet
ἀλλὰ ἡ χάρις τοῦ θεοῦ σὺν ἐμοί. 11 εἴτε
but the grace – of God with me. Whether
οὖν ἐγὼ εἴτε ἐκεῖνοι, οὕτως κηρύσσομεν
therefore I or those, so we proclaim
καὶ οὕτως ἐπιστεύσατε.
and so ye believed.
12 Εἰ δὲ Χριστὸς κηρύσσεται ὅτι ἐκ
But if Christ is proclaimed that from
νεκρῶν ἐγήγερται, πῶς λέγουσιν ἐν ὑμῖν
[the] dead he has been raised, how say [2]among [3]you
τινες ὅτι ἀνάστασις νεκρῶν οὐκ ἔστιν;
[1]some that a resurrection of dead persons there is not?
13 εἰ δὲ ἀνάστασις νεκρῶν οὐκ ἔστιν,
Now if a resurrection of dead persons there is not,
οὐδὲ Χριστὸς ἐγήγερται· 14 εἰ δὲ Χριστὸς
neither Christ has been raised; and if Christ

Chapter 15

The Resurrection of Christ

NOW, brothers, I want
to remind you of the
gospel I preached to you,
which you received and on
which you have taken your
stand. 2By this gospel you
are saved, if you hold firmly to the word I preached to
you. Otherwise, you have
believed in vain.
3For what I received I
passed on to you as of first
importance[o]: that Christ
died for our sins according
to the Scriptures, 4that he
was buried, that he was
raised on the third day according to the Scriptures,
5and that he appeared to
Peter,[p] and then to the
Twelve. 6After that, he appeared to more than five
hundred of the brothers at
the same time, most of
whom are still living,
though some have fallen
asleep. 7Then he appeared
to James, then to all the
apostles, 8and last of all he
appeared to me also, as to
one abnormally born.
9For I am the least of the
apostles and do not even
deserve to be called an
apostle, because I perse-
cuted the church of God.
10But by the grace of God I
am what I am, and his grace
to me was not without ef-
fect. No, I worked harder
than all of them—yet not I,
but the grace of God that
was with me. 11Whether,
then, it was I or they, this is
what we preach, and this is
what you believed.

The Resurrection of the Dead

12But if it is preached that
Christ has been raised from
the dead, how can some of
you say that there is no resurrection of the dead? 13If
there is no resurrection of
the dead, then not even
Christ has been raised.
14And if Christ has not been

[o]3 *Or you at the first*
[p]5 Greek *Cephas*

been raised, then our preaching is vain, your faith also is vain.

15 Moreover we are even found *to be* false witnesses of God, because we witnessed against God that He raised [q]Christ, whom He did not raise, if in fact the dead are not raised.

16 For if the dead are not raised, not even Christ has been raised;

17 and if Christ has not been raised, your faith is worthless; you are still in your sins.

18 Then those also who have fallen asleep in Christ have perished.

19 If we have hoped in Christ in this life only, we are of all men most to be pitied.

The Order of Resurrection

20 But now Christ has been raised from the dead, the first fruits of those who are asleep.

21 For since by a man *came* death, by a man also *came* the resurrection of the dead.

22 For as in Adam all die, so also in Christ all shall be made alive.

23 But each in his own order: Christ the first fruits, after that those who are Christ's at His coming,

24 then *comes* the end, when He delivers up the kingdom to the God and Father, when He has abolished all rule and all authority and power.

25 For He must reign until He has put all His enemies under His feet.

26 The last enemy that will be abolished is death.

27 For HE HAS PUT ALL THINGS IN SUBJECTION UNDER HIS FEET. But when He says, "All things are put in subjection," it is evident

[q]I.e., the Messiah

οὐκ ἐγήγερται, κενὸν ἄρα τὸ κήρυγμα
has not been raised, empty then the proclamation

ἡμῶν, κενὴ καὶ ἡ πίστις ὑμῶν· 15 εὑρισκ-
of us, empty also the faith of you; [2]we are

όμεθα δὲ καὶ ψευδομάρτυρες τοῦ θεοῦ,
found [1]and also false witnesses – of God,

ὅτι ἐμαρτυρήσαμεν κατὰ τοῦ θεοῦ ὅτι
because we witnessed as to – God that

ἤγειρεν τὸν Χριστόν, ὃν οὐκ ἤγειρεν
he raised – Christ, whom he raised not

εἴπερ ἄρα νεκροὶ οὐκ ἐγείρονται. 16 εἰ
if then dead persons are not raised. if

γὰρ νεκροὶ οὐκ ἐγείρονται, οὐδὲ Χριστὸς
For dead persons are not raised, neither Christ

ἐγήγερται· 17 εἰ δὲ Χριστὸς οὐκ ἐγήγερται,
has been raised; and if Christ has not been raised,

ματαία ἡ πίστις ὑμῶν [ἐστιν], ἔτι ἐστὲ
[4]useless [1]the [2]faith [3]of you [4]is, [2]still [1]ye are

ἐν ταῖς ἁμαρτίαις ὑμῶν. 18 ἄρα καὶ οἱ
in the sins of you. Then also the [ones]

κοιμηθέντες ἐν Χριστῷ ἀπώλοντο. 19 εἰ
having fallen asleep in Christ perished. If

ἐν τῇ ζωῇ ταύτῃ ἐν Χριστῷ ἠλπικότες
in this life [3]in [4]Christ [2]having hoped

ἐσμὲν μόνον, ἐλεεινότεροι πάντων ἀνθρώπων
[1]we are [5]only, more pitiful [than] all men

ἐσμέν. 20 Νυνὶ δὲ Χριστὸς ἐγήγερται
we are. But now Christ has been raised

ἐκ νεκρῶν, ἀπαρχὴ τῶν κεκοιμημένων.
from [the] dead, firstfruit of the [ones] having fallen asleep.

21 ἐπειδὴ γὰρ δι' ἀνθρώπου θάνατος, καὶ
For since through a man death [came], also

δι' ἀνθρώπου ἀνάστασις νεκρῶν. 22 ὥσπερ
through a man a resurrection of dead persons [came]. as

γὰρ ἐν τῷ Ἀδὰμ πάντες ἀποθνήσκουσιν,
For in – Adam all die,

οὕτως καὶ ἐν τῷ Χριστῷ πάντες ζωοποιη-
so also in – Christ all will be

θήσονται. 23 Ἕκαστος δὲ ἐν τῷ ἰδίῳ
made alive. But each one in the(his) own

τάγματι· ἀπαρχὴ Χριστός, ἔπειτα οἱ τοῦ
order: [the] firstfruit Christ, afterward the [ones] –

Χριστοῦ ἐν τῇ παρουσίᾳ αὐτοῦ, 24 εἶτα
of Christ in the presence of him, then

τὸ τέλος, ὅταν παραδιδοῖ τὴν βασιλείαν
the end, when*ever* he delivers the kingdom

τῷ θεῷ καὶ πατρί, ὅταν καταργήσῃ
– to God even [the] Father, when*ever* he abolishes

πᾶσαν ἀρχὴν καὶ πᾶσαν ἐξουσίαν καὶ
all rule and all authority and

δύναμιν. 25 δεῖ γὰρ αὐτὸν βασιλεύειν
power. For it behoves him to reign

ἄχρι οὗ θῇ πάντας τοὺς ἐχθροὺς ὑπὸ
until he puts all the(his) enemies under

τοὺς πόδας αὐτοῦ. 26 ἔσχατος ἐχθρὸς
the feet of him. [The] last enemy

καταργεῖται ὁ θάνατος· πάντα γὰρ ὑπέταξεν
is abolished – death; for all things he subjected

ὑπὸ τοὺς πόδας αὐτοῦ. 27 ὅταν δὲ
under the feet of him. But when*ever*

εἴπῃ ὅτι πάντα ὑποτέτακται, δῆλον ὅτι
he says that all things have been subjected, [it is] clear that

raised, our preaching is
useless and so is your faith.
15 More than that, we are
then found to be false witnesses about God, for we
have testified about God
that he raised Christ from
the dead. But he did not
raise him if in fact the dead
are not raised. 16 For if the
dead are not raised, then
Christ has not been raised
either. 17 And if Christ has
not been raised, your faith
is futile; you are still in your
sins. 18 Then those also who
have fallen asleep in Christ
are lost. 19 If only for this
life we have hope in Christ,
we are to be pitied more
than all men.
20 But Christ has indeed
been raised from the dead,
the firstfruits of those who
have fallen asleep. 21 For
since death came through a
man, the resurrection of
the dead comes also
through a man. 22 For as in
Adam all die, so in Christ
all will be made alive. 23 But
each in his own turn:
Christ, the firstfruits; then,
when he comes, those who
belong to him. 24 Then the
end will come, when he
hands over the kingdom to
God the Father after he has
destroyed all dominion, authority and power. 25 For he
must reign until he has put
all his enemies under his
feet. 26 The last enemy to be
destroyed is death. 27 For
he "has put everything under his feet."[q] Now when
it says that "everything"
has been put under him, it
is clear that this does not

[q]27 Psalm 8:6

that He is excepted who
put all things in subjection
to Him.
28And when all things are
subjected to Him, then the
Son Himself also will be
subjected to the One who
subjected all things to Him,
that God may be all in all.
29Otherwise, what will
those do who are baptized
for the dead? If the dead are
not raised at all, why then
are they baptized for them?
30Why are we also in danger
every hour?
31I protest, brethren, by
the boasting in you, which I
have in Christ Jesus our
Lord, I die daily.
32If from human motives I
fought with wild beasts at
Ephesus, what does it
profit me? If the dead are
not raised, LET US EAT AND
DRINK, FOR TOMORROW WE
DIE.
33Do not be deceived:
"Bad company corrupts
good morals."
34Become sober-minded
as you ought, and stop sinning;
for some have no
knowledge of God. I speak
this to your shame.
35But someone will say,
"How are the dead raised?
And with what kind of body
do they come?"
36You fool! That which
you sow does not come to
life unless it dies;
37and that which you
sow, you do not sow the
body which is to be, but a
bare grain, perhaps of
wheat or of something else.
38But God gives it a body
just as He wished, and to
each of the seeds a body of
its own.
39All flesh is not the same
flesh, but there is one *flesh*
of men, and another
flesh of beasts, and another
flesh of birds, and
another of fish.

ἐκτὸς τοῦ ὑποτάξαντος αὐτῷ τὰ πάντα.
[it is] apart from [one] the having subjected to him – all things.

28 ὅταν δὲ ὑποταγῇ αὐτῷ τὰ πάντα,
But when*ever* is(are) subjected to him – all things,

τότε καὶ αὐτὸς ὁ υἱὸς ὑποταγήσεται
then also [3][him]self [1]the [2]Son will be subjected

τῷ ὑποτάξαντι αὐτῷ τὰ πάντα, ἵνα
to the [one] having subjected to him – all things, in order that

ᾖ ὁ θεὸς πάντα ἐν πᾶσιν. 29 Ἐπεὶ
[2]may be – [1]God all things in all. Otherwise

τί ποιήσουσιν οἱ βαπτιζόμενοι ὑπὲρ τῶν
what will they do the [ones] being baptized on behalf of the

νεκρῶν; εἰ ὅλως νεκροὶ οὐκ ἐγείρονται,
dead? if actually dead persons are not raised,

τί καὶ βαπτίζονται ὑπὲρ αὐτῶν; 30 τί
why indeed are they baptized on behalf of them? why

καὶ ἡμεῖς κινδυνεύομεν πᾶσαν ὥραν;
also [2]we [1]are [3]in danger every hour?

31 καθ' ἡμέραν ἀποθνῄσκω, νὴ τὴν
Daily I die, by –

ὑμετέραν καύχησιν, ἀδελφοί, ἣν ἔχω ἐν
your boasting, brothers, which I have in

Χριστῷ Ἰησοῦ τῷ κυρίῳ ἡμῶν. 32 εἰ
Christ Jesus the Lord of us. If

κατὰ ἄνθρωπον ἐθηριομάχησα ἐν Ἐφέσῳ,
according to man I fought with wild beasts in Ephesus,

τί μοι τὸ ὄφελος; εἰ νεκροὶ οὐκ ἐγείρονται,
what to me the profit?[c] =what profit have I? If dead persons are not raised,

φάγωμεν καὶ πίωμεν, αὔριον γὰρ ἀποθνή-
let us eat and *let us* drink, for to-morrow we

σκομεν. 33 μὴ πλανᾶσθε· φθείρουσιν ἤθη
die. Be ye not led astray: [3]Corrupt [5]customs

χρηστὰ ὁμιλίαι κακαί. 34 ἐκνήψατε δικαίως
[4]good [2]associations [1]bad. Become ye sober righteously

καὶ μὴ ἁμαρτάνετε· ἀγνωσίαν γὰρ θεοῦ
and do not sin; for [3]ignorance [4]of God

τινες ἔχουσιν· πρὸς ἐντροπὴν ὑμῖν λαλῶ.
[1]some [2]have: [3]for [4]shame [2]to you [1]I speak.

35 Ἀλλὰ ἐρεῖ τις· πῶς ἐγείρονται οἱ
But [2]will say [1]someone: How are raised the

νεκροί; ποίῳ δὲ σώματι ἔρχονται; 36 ἄφρων,
dead? and with what sort [of] body do they come? Foolish man,

σὺ ὃ σπείρεις, οὐ ζωοποιεῖται ἐὰν μὴ
[2]thou [1]what sowest, is not made alive unless

ἀποθάνῃ· 37 καὶ ὃ σπείρεις, οὐ τὸ σῶμα
it dies; and what thou sowest, not the body

τὸ γενησόμενον σπείρεις, ἀλλὰ γυμνὸν
– going to become thou sowest, but a naked

κόκκον εἰ τύχοι σίτου ἤ τινος τῶν
grain it may be† of wheat or some one of the

λοιπῶν· 38 ὁ δὲ θεὸς δίδωσιν αὐτῷ
rest; – but God gives to it

σῶμα καθὼς ἠθέλησεν, καὶ ἑκάστῳ τῶν
a body as he wished, and to each of the

σπερμάτων ἴδιον σῶμα. 39 οὐ πᾶσα
seeds [its] own body. [3][is] not [1]All

σὰρξ ἡ αὐτὴ σάρξ, ἀλλὰ ἄλλη μὲν
[2]flesh the same flesh, but other(one) indeed

ἀνθρώπων, ἄλλη δὲ σὰρξ κτηνῶν, ἄλλη δὲ
of men, and another flesh of animals, and another

σὰρξ πτηνῶν, ἄλλη δὲ ἰχθύων. 40 καὶ
flesh of birds, and another of fishes. And [there

include God himself, who
put everything under
Christ. 28When he has done
this, then the Son himself
will be made subject to him
who put everything under
him, so that God may be all
in all.
29Now if there is no resurrection,
what will those do
who are baptized for the
dead? If the dead are not
raised at all, why are people
baptized for them?
30And as for us, why do we
endanger ourselves every
hour? 31I die every day—I
mean that, brothers—just
as surely as I glory over
you in Christ Jesus our
Lord. 32If I fought wild
beasts in Ephesus for merely
human reasons, what
have I gained? If the dead
are not raised,

"Let us eat and drink,
for tomorrow we
die."[r]

33Do not be misled: "Bad
company corrupts good
character." 34Come back
to your senses as you
ought, and stop sinning; for
there are some who are ignorant
of God—I say this
to your shame.

The Resurrection Body

35But someone may ask,
"How are the dead raised?
With what kind of body will
they come?" 36How foolish!
What you sow does not
come to life unless it dies.
37When you sow, you do
not plant the body that will
be, but just a seed, perhaps
of wheat or of something
else. 38But God gives it a
body as he has determined,
and to each kind of seed he
gives its own body. 39All
flesh is not the same: Men
have one kind of flesh, animals
have another, birds
another and fish another.

[r]32 Isaiah 22:13

40 There are also heavenly bodies and earthly bodies, but the glory of the heavenly is one, and the *glory* of the earthly is another.

41 There is one glory of the sun, and another glory of the moon, and another glory of the stars; for star differs from star in glory.

42 So also is the resurrection of the dead. It is sown a perishable *body*, it is raised an imperishable *body*;

43 it is sown in dishonor, it is raised in glory; it is sown in weakness, it is raised in power;

44 it is sown a natural body, it is raised a spiritual body. If there is a natural body, there is also a spiritual *body*.

45 So also it is written, "The first MAN, Adam, BECAME A LIVING SOUL." The last Adam *became* a life-giving spirit.

46 However, the spiritual is not first, but the natural; then the spiritual.

47 The first man is from the earth, earthy; the second man is from heaven.

48 As is the earthy, so also are those who are earthy; and as is the heavenly, so also are those who are heavenly.

49 And just as we have borne the image of the earthy, [r]we shall also bear the image of the heavenly.

The Mystery of Resurrection

50 Now I say this, brethren, that flesh and blood cannot inherit the kingdom of God; nor does the perishable inherit the imperishable.

51 Behold, I tell you a mystery; we shall not all sleep, but we shall all be changed,

52 in a moment, in the twinkling of an eye, at the last trumpet; for the trumpet will sound, and the dead will be raised imper-

[r]Some ancient mss. read *let us also*

σώματα ἐπουράνια, καὶ σώματα ἐπίγεια·
are] bodies heavenly, and bodies earthly;

ἀλλὰ ἑτέρα μὲν ἡ τῶν ἐπουρανίων δόξα,
but [7]other (one) [5][is] [6]indeed [1]the [3]of the [4]heavenly [bodies] [2]glory,

ἑτέρα δὲ ἡ τῶν ἐπιγείων. 41 ἄλλη
and other the [glory] of the earthly [bodies]. Other(one)

δόξα ἡλίου, καὶ ἄλλη δόξα σελήνης,
glory of [the] sun, and another glory of [the] moon,

καὶ ἄλλη δόξα ἀστέρων· ἀστὴρ γὰρ
and another glory of [the] stars; for star

ἀστέρος διαφέρει ἐν δόξῃ. 42 οὕτως καὶ
from star differs in glory. So also

ἡ ἀνάστασις τῶν νεκρῶν. σπείρεται ἐν
the resurrection of the dead. It is sown in

φθορᾷ, ἐγείρεται ἐν ἀφθαρσίᾳ· 43 σπείρεται
corruption, it is raised in incorruption; it is sown

ἐν ἀτιμίᾳ, ἐγείρεται ἐν δόξῃ· σπείρεται
in dishonour, it is raised in glory; it is sown

ἐν ἀσθενείᾳ, ἐγείρεται ἐν δυνάμει· 44 σπείρ-
in weakness, it is raised in power; it is

εται σῶμα ψυχικόν, ἐγείρεται σῶμα
sown body a natural, it is raised body

πνευματικόν Εἰ ἔστιν σῶμα ψυχικόν,
a spiritual. If there is body a natural,

ἔστιν καὶ πνευματικόν. 45 οὕτως καὶ
there is also a spiritual [body]. So also

γέγραπται· ἐγένετο ὁ πρῶτος ἄνθρωπος
it has been written: [5]became [1]The [2]first [3]man

Ἀδὰμ εἰς ψυχὴν ζῶσαν· ὁ ἔσχατος
[4]Adam – soul a living; the last

Ἀδὰμ εἰς πνεῦμα ζῳοποιοῦν. 46 ἀλλ'
Adam – spirit a life-giving. But

οὐ πρῶτον τὸ πνευματικὸν ἀλλὰ τὸ
not firstly the spiritual [body] but the

ψυχικόν, ἔπειτα τὸ πνευματικόν. 47 ὁ
natural, afterward the spiritual. The

πρῶτος ἄνθρωπος ἐκ γῆς χοϊκός, ὁ
first man [was] out of earth earthy, the

δεύτερος ἄνθρωπος ἐξ οὐρανοῦ. 48 οἷος ὁ
second man [is] out of heaven. Such the

χοϊκός, τοιοῦτοι καὶ οἱ χοϊκοί, καὶ οἷος
earthy man, such also the earthy ones, and such

ὁ ἐπουράνιος, τοιοῦτοι καὶ οἱ ἐπουράνιοι·
the heavenly man, such also the heavenly ones;

49 καὶ καθὼς ἐφορέσαμεν τὴν εἰκόνα τοῦ
and as we bore the image of the

χοϊκοῦ, φορέσομεν καὶ τὴν εἰκόνα τοῦ
earthy man, we shall bear also the image of the

ἐπουρανίου. 50 Τοῦτο δέ φημι, ἀδελφοί,
heavenly man. And this I say, brothers,

ὅτι σὰρξ καὶ αἷμα βασιλείαν θεοῦ κληρο-
that flesh and blood [3][the] kingdom [4]of God [2]*to*

νομῆσαι οὐ δύναται, οὐδὲ ἡ φθορὰ τὴν
inherit [1]cannot, neither – [1]corruption –

ἀφθαρσίαν κληρονομεῖ. 51 ἰδοὺ μυστήριον
[3]incorruption [2]inherits. Behold[,] a mystery

ὑμῖν λέγω· πάντες οὐ κοιμηθησόμεθα,
to you I tell: all We shall not fall asleep,

πάντες δὲ ἀλλαγησόμεθα, 52 ἐν ἀτόμῳ,
but all . we shall be changed, in a moment,

ἐν ῥιπῇ ὀφθαλμοῦ, ἐν τῇ ἐσχάτῃ σάλπιγγι·
in a glance of an eye, at the last trumpet;

σαλπίσει γάρ, καὶ οἱ νεκροὶ ἐγερθήσονται
for a trumpet will sound, and the dead will be raised

40 There are also heavenly
bodies and there are earthly bodies; but the splendor
of the heavenly bodies is
one kind, and the splendor
of the earthly bodies is another. 41 The sun has one
kind of splendor, the moon
another and the stars an-
other; and star differs from
star in splendor.
42 So will it be with the
resurrection of the dead.
The body that is sown is
perishable, it is raised imperishable; 43 it is sown in
dishonor, it is raised in glory; it is sown in weakness,
it is raised in power; 44 it is
sown a natural body, it is
raised a spiritual body.
If there is a natural body,
there is also a spiritual
body. 45 So it is written:
"The first man Adam be-
came a living being"[s]; the
last Adam, a life-giving
spirit. 46 The spiritual did
not come first, but the natural, and after that the spiritual. 47 The first man was of
the dust of the earth, the
second man from heaven.
48 As was the earthly man,
so are those who are of the
earth; and as is the man
from heaven, so also are
those who are of heaven.
49 And just as we have
borne the likeness of the
earthly man, so shall we[t]
bear the likeness of the man
from heaven.
50 I declare to you, brothers, that flesh and blood
cannot inherit the kingdom
of God, nor does the per-
ishable inherit the imperishable. 51 Listen, I tell you
a mystery: We will not all
sleep, but we will all be
changed—52 in a flash, in
the twinkling of an eye, at
the last trumpet. For the
trumpet will sound, the
dead will be raised imper-

[s]*45* Gen. 2:7
[t]*49* Some early manuscripts *so let us*

ishable, and we shall be
changed.
53For this perishable must
put on the imperishable,
and this mortal must put on
immortality.
54But when this perish-
able will have put on the
imperishable, and this mortal will have put on immortality, then will come about
the saying that is written,
"DEATH IS SWALLOWED UP
in victory.
55"O DEATH, WHERE IS
YOUR VICTORY? O DEATH,
WHERE IS YOUR STING?"
56The sting of death is sin,
and the power of sin is the
law;
57but thanks be to God,
who gives us the victory
through our Lord Jesus
Christ.
58Therefore, my beloved
brethren, be steadfast, immovable, always abound-
ing in the work of the Lord,
knowing that your toil is
not *in* vain in the Lord.

ἄφθαρτοι, καὶ ἡμεῖς ἀλλαγησόμεθα. 53 Δεῖ
incorruptible, and we shall be changed. it behoves

γὰρ τὸ φθαρτὸν τοῦτο ἐνδύσασθαι
For – corruptible this to put on

ἀφθαρσίαν καὶ τὸ θνητὸν τοῦτο ἐνδύσασθαι
incorruption and – mortal this to put on

ἀθανασίαν. 54 ὅταν δὲ τὸ φθαρτὸν τοῦτο
immortality. And when*ever* this [that is] corruptible

ἐνδύσηται ἀφθαρσίαν καὶ τὸ θνητὸν τοῦτο
shall put on incorruption and this [that is] mortal

ἐνδύσηται ἀθανασίαν, τότε γενήσεται ὁ
shall put on immortality, then will be the

λόγος ὁ γεγραμμένος· κατεπόθη ὁ θάνατος
word – having been [2]was written: swallowed up – [1]Death

εἰς νῖκος. 55 ποῦ σου, θάνατε, τὸ νῖκος;
in victory. Where of thee, [O] death, the victory?

ποῦ σου, θάνατε, τὸ κέντρον; 56 τὸ δὲ
where of thee, [O] death, the sting? Now the

κέντρον τοῦ θανάτου ἡ ἁμαρτία, ἡ δὲ
sting – of death – [is] sin, and the

δύναμις τῆς ἁμαρτίας ὁ νόμος· 57 τῷ
power – of sin [is] the law; –

δὲ θεῷ χάρις τῷ διδόντι ἡμῖν τὸ νῖκος
but to God thanks the [one] giving to us the victory

διὰ τοῦ κυρίου ἡμῶν Ἰησοῦ Χριστοῦ.
through the Lord of us Jesus Christ.

58 Ὥστε, ἀδελφοί μου ἀγαπητοί, ἑδραῖοι
So as, brothers of me beloved, firm

γίνεσθε, ἀμετακίνητοι, περισσεύοντες ἐν τῷ
be ye, unmovable, abounding in the

ἔργῳ τοῦ κυρίου πάντοτε, εἰδότες ὅτι
work of the Lord always, knowing that

ὁ κόπος ὑμῶν οὐκ ἔστιν κενὸς ἐν κυρίῳ.
the labour of you is not empty in [the] Lord.

ishable, and we will be
changed. 53For the perishable must clothe itself with
the imperishable, and the
mortal with immortality.
54When the perishable has
been clothed with the im-
perishable, and the mortal
with immortality, then the
saying that is written will
come true: "Death has
been swallowed up in vic-
tory."[u]
55"Where, O death, is
your victory?
Where, O death, is
your sting?"[v]
56The sting of death is sin,
and the power of sin is the
law. 57But thanks be to
God! He gives us the victory through our Lord Jesus
Christ.
58Therefore, my dear
brothers, stand firm. Let
nothing move you. Always
give yourselves fully to the
work of the Lord, because
you know that your labor in
the Lord is not in vain.

Chapter 16

Instructions and Greetings

NOW concerning the
collection for the
saints, as I directed the
churches of Galatia, so do
you also.
2On the first day of every
week let each one of you
put aside and save, as he
may prosper, that no col-
lections be made when I
come.
3And when I arrive,
whomever you may ap-
prove, I shall send them
with letters to carry your
gift to Jerusalem;
4and if it is fitting for me
to go also, they will go with
me.
5But I shall come to you
after I go through Mace-
donia, for I am going
through Macedonia;

16 Περὶ δὲ τῆς λογείας τῆς εἰς τοὺς
Now about the collection – for the

ἁγίους, ὥσπερ διέταξα ταῖς ἐκκλησίαις
saints, as I charged the churches

τῆς Γαλατίας, οὕτως καὶ ὑμεῖς ποιήσατε.
– of Galatia, so also [2]ye [1]do.

2 κατὰ μίαν σαββάτου ἕκαστος ὑμῶν
Every one of a week each of you
=On the first day of every week

παρ' ἑαυτῷ τιθέτω θησαυρίζων ὅ τι ἐὰν
by himself let him put storing up whatever

εὐοδῶται, ἵνα μὴ ὅταν ἔλθω τότε λογεῖαι
he is prospered, lest when*ever* I come then [2]collections

γίνωνται. 3 ὅταν δὲ παραγένωμαι, οὓς
[1]there are. And when*ever* I arrive, whom-

ἐὰν δοκιμάσητε, δι' ἐπιστολῶν τούτους
ever ye approve, through epistles these

πέμψω ἀπενεγκεῖν τὴν χάριν ὑμῶν εἰς
I will send to carry the grace(gift) of you to

Ἰερουσαλήμ· 4 ἐὰν δὲ ἄξιον ᾖ τοῦ κἀμὲ
Jerusalem; and if [2]fitting [1]it is – me also

πορεύεσθαι, σὺν ἐμοὶ πορεύσονται.
to go,[d] with me they shall go.

5 Ἐλεύσομαι δὲ πρὸς ὑμᾶς ὅταν Μακε-
And I will come to you when*ever* [2]Mace-

δονίαν διέλθω· Μακεδονίαν γὰρ διέρχομαι,
donia [1]I pass through; for [2]Macedonia [1]I am passing through,*

* "Futuristic present"; *cf.* John 14. 3 and ch. 15. 32.

Chapter 16

The Collection for God's People

NOW about the collec-
tion for God's people:
Do what I told the Galatian
churches to do. 2On the
first day of every week,
each one of you should set
aside a sum of money in
keeping with his income,
saving it up, so that when I
come no collections will
have to be made. 3Then,
when I arrive, I will give
letters of introduction to
the men you approve and
send them with your gift to
Jerusalem. 4If it seems ad-
visable for me to go also,
they will accompany me.

Personal Requests

5After I go through Mace-
donia, I will come to you—
for I will be going through

[u]*54* Isaiah 25:8
[v]*55* Hosea 13:14

6and perhaps I shall stay
with you, or even spend the
winter, that you may send
me on my way wherever I
may go.
7For I do not wish to see
you now *just* in passing; for
I hope to remain with you
for some time, if the Lord
permits.
8But I shall remain in
Ephesus until Pentecost;
9for a wide door for ef-
fective *service* has opened
to me, and there are many
adversaries.
10Now if Timothy comes,
see that he is with you without cause to be afraid; for
he is doing the Lord's
work, as I also am.
11Let no one therefore despise him. But send him on
his way in peace, so that he
may come to me; for I ex-
pect him with the brethren.
12But concerning Apollos
our brother, I encouraged
him greatly to come to you
with the brethren; and it
was not at all *his* desire to
come now, but he will
come when he has opportu-
nity.
13Be on the alert, stand
firm in the faith, act like
men, be strong.
14Let all that you do be
done in love.
15Now I urge you, breth-
ren (you know the house-
hold of Stephanas, that
they were the first fruits of
Achaia, and that they have
devoted themselves for
ministry to the saints),
16that you also be in subjection to such men and to
everyone who helps in the
work and labors.
17And I rejoice over the
coming of Stephanas and
Fortunatus and Achaicus;
because they have supplied
what was lacking on your
part.
18For they have refreshed

6 πρὸς ὑμᾶς δὲ τυχὸν καταμενῶ ἢ
7with 8you 1and 2possibly 3I will remain 4or
καὶ παραχειμάσω, ἵνα ὑμεῖς με προπέμ-
5even 6spend the winter, in order that 2ye 1me may set
ψητε οὗ ἐὰν πορεύωμαι. **7** οὐ θέλω γὰρ
forward wherever I may go. For I do not wish
ὑμᾶς ἄρτι ἐν παρόδῳ ἰδεῖν· ἐλπίζω γὰρ
2you 3yet 4in 5passage 1to see; for I am hoping
χρόνον τινὰ ἐπιμεῖναι πρὸς ὑμᾶς, ἐὰν
3time 2some 1to remain with you, if
ὁ κύριος ἐπιτρέψῃ. **8** ἐπιμενῶ δὲ ἐν
the Lord permits. But I will remain in
Ἐφέσῳ ἕως τῆς πεντηκοστῆς· **9** θύρα
Ephesus until – Pentecost; 5door
γάρ μοι ἀνέῳγεν μεγάλη καὶ ἐνεργής,
1for 7to me 6opened 2a great 3and 4effective,
καὶ ἀντικείμενοι πολλοί. **10** Ἐὰν δὲ
and [there are] 2opposing 1many. Now if
ἔλθῃ Τιμόθεος, βλέπετε ἵνα ἀφόβως
2comes 1Timothy, see *in order* that fearlessly
γένηται πρὸς ὑμᾶς· τὸ γὰρ ἔργον κυρίου
he is with you; for the work of [the] Lord
ἐργάζεται ὡς κἀγώ· **11** μή τις οὖν αὐτὸν
he works as I also; 3not 5any-one 4therefore 2him
ἐξουθενήσῃ. προπέμψατε δὲ αὐτὸν ἐν
1despise. But set ye forward him in
εἰρήνῃ, ἵνα ἔλθῃ πρός με· ἐκδέχομαι γὰρ
peace, in order that he may come to me; for I am awaiting
αὐτὸν μετὰ τῶν ἀδελφῶν. **12** Περὶ δὲ
him with the brothers. Now about
Ἀπολλῶ τοῦ ἀδελφοῦ, πολλὰ παρεκάλεσα
2Apollos *the* 1brother, 3much 1I besought
αὐτὸν ἵνα ἔλθῃ πρὸς ὑμᾶς μετὰ τῶν
2him *in order* that he would come to you with the
ἀδελφῶν· καὶ πάντως οὐκ ἦν θέλημα
brothers; and altogether it was not [his] will
ἵνα νῦν ἔλθῃ, ἐλεύσεται δὲ ὅταν εὐκαιρήσῃ.
in order that 2now 1he should come, but he will come whenever he has opportunity.
13 Γρηγορεῖτε, στήκετε ἐν τῇ πίστει,
Watch ye, stand in the faith,
ἀνδρίζεσθε, κραταιοῦσθε. **14** πάντα ὑμῶν
play the man, be strong. 2All things 3of you
ἐν ἀγάπῃ γινέσθω.
4in 5love 1let be.
15 Παρακαλῶ δὲ ὑμᾶς, ἀδελφοί· οἴδατε
Now I beseech you, brothers: Know ye
τὴν οἰκίαν Στεφανᾶ, ὅτι ἐστὶν ἀπαρχὴ
the household of Stephanas, that it is firstfruit
τῆς Ἀχαΐας καὶ εἰς διακονίαν τοῖς
– of Achaia and to ministry to the
ἁγίοις ἔταξαν ἑαυτούς· **16** ἵνα καὶ ὑμεῖς
saints they appointed themselves; in order that also ye
ὑποτάσσησθε τοῖς τοιούτοις καὶ παντὶ τῷ
may submit – to such ones and to everyone
συνεργοῦντι καὶ κοπιῶντι. **17** χαίρω δὲ
working with [?me] and labouring. Now I rejoice
ἐπὶ τῇ παρουσίᾳ Στεφανᾶ καὶ Φορτουνάτου
at the presence of Stephanas and of Fortunatus
καὶ Ἀχαϊκοῦ, ὅτι τὸ ὑμέτερον ὑστέρημα
and of Achaicus, that – 3your 4lack
οὗτοι ἀνεπλήρωσαν· **18** ἀνέπαυσαν γὰρ τὸ
1these 2supplied; for they refreshed –

Macedonia. 6Perhaps I will
stay with you awhile, or
even spend the winter, so
that you can help me on my
journey, wherever I go. 7I
do not want to see you now
and make only a passing
visit; I hope to spend some
time with you, if the Lord
permits. 8But I will stay on
at Ephesus until Pentecost,
9because a great door for
effective work has opened
to me, and there are many
who oppose me.
10If Timothy comes, see
to it that he has nothing to
fear while he is with you,
for he is carrying on the
work of the Lord, just as I
am. 11No one, then, should
refuse to accept him. Send
him on his way in peace so
that he may return to me. I
am expecting him along
with the brothers.
12Now about our brother
Apollos: I strongly urged
him to go to you with the
brothers. He was quite unwilling to go now, but he
will go when he has the opportunity.
13Be on your guard; stand
firm in the faith; be men of
courage; be strong. 14Do
everything in love.
15You know that the
household of Stephanas
were the first converts in
Achaia, and they have de-
voted themselves to the
service of the saints. I urge
you, brothers, 16to submit
to such as these and to everyone who joins in the
work, and labors at it. 17I
was glad when Stephanas,
Fortunatus and Achaicus
arrived, because they have
supplied what was lacking
from you. 18For they re-

my spirit and yours. Therefore acknowledge such
men.
19The churches of Asia
greet you. Aquila and Prisca greet you heartily in the
Lord, with the church that
is in their house.
20All the brethren greet
you. Greet one another
with a holy kiss.
21The greeting is in my
own hand—Paul.
22If anyone does not love
the Lord, let him be ac-
cursed. Maranatha.
23The grace of the Lord
Jesus be with you.
24My love be with you all
in Christ Jesus. Amen.

ἐμὸν πνεῦμα καὶ τὸ ὑμῶν. ἐπιγινώσκετε
my spirit and – of you(yours). Recognize ye
οὖν τοὺς τοιούτους.
therefore – such ones.
19 Ἀσπάζονται ὑμᾶς αἱ ἐκκλησίαι τῆς
[4]Greet [5]you [1]the [2]churches –
Ἀσίας. ἀσπάζεται ὑμᾶς ἐν κυρίῳ πολλὰ
[3]of Asia. [4]Greets [5]you [7]in [8][the] Lord [6]much
Ἀκύλας καὶ Πρῖσκα σὺν τῇ κατ' οἶκον
[1]Aquila [2]and [3]Prisca [9]with [10]the [12]in [the] house
αὐτῶν ἐκκλησίᾳ. 20 ἀσπάζονται ὑμᾶς οἱ
[13]of them [11]church. [4]Greet [5]you [2]the
ἀδελφοὶ πάντες. Ἀσπάσασθε ἀλλήλους ἐν
[3]brothers [1]all. Greet ye one another with
φιλήματι ἁγίῳ. 21 Ὁ ἀσπασμὸς τῇ
kiss a holy. [1]The [2]greeting –
ἐμῇ χειρὶ Παύλου. 22 εἴ τις οὐ φιλεῖ
[4]with my [5]hand [3]of Paul. If anyone loves not
τὸν κύριον, ἤτω ἀνάθεμα. μαράνα θά.
the Lord, let him be a curse. Marana tha.
23 ἡ χάρις τοῦ κυρίου Ἰησοῦ μεθ' ὑμῶν.
The grace of the Lord Jesus [be] with you.
24 ἡ ἀγάπη μου μετὰ πάντων ὑμῶν ἐν
The love of me [be] with [2]all [1]you in
Χριστῷ Ἰησοῦ.
Christ Jesus.

freshed my spirit and yours
also. Such men deserve
recognition.

Final Greetings

19The churches in the
province of Asia send you
greetings. Aquila and Priscilla[w] greet you warmly in
the Lord, and so does the
church that meets at their
house. 20All the brothers
here send you greetings.
Greet one another with a
holy kiss.
21I, Paul, write this greeting in my own hand.
22If anyone does not love
the Lord—a curse be on
him. Come, O Lord[x]!
23The grace of the Lord
Jesus be with you.
24My love to all of you in
Christ Jesus. Amen.[y]

[w] *19* Greek *Prisca*, a variant of *Priscilla*
[x] *22* In Aramaic the expression *Come, O Lord* is *Marana tha*.
[y] *24* Some manuscripts do not have *Amen*.

ΠΡΟΣ ΚΟΡΙΝΘΙΟΥΣ Β
To Corinthians 2

2 Corinthians

Chapter 1

Introduction

PAUL, an apostle of
Christ Jesus by the will
of God, and Timothy *our*
brother, to the church of
God which is at Corinth
with all the saints who are
throughout Achaia:
2Grace to you and peace
from God our Father and
the Lord Jesus Christ.
3Blessed *be* the God and
Father of our Lord Jesus
Christ, the Father of mercies and God of all comfort;
4who comforts us in all
our affliction so that we
may be able to comfort
those who are in any affliction with the comfort with
which we ourselves are
comforted by God.
5For just as the suffer-
ings of Christ are ours in
abundance, so also our
comfort is abundant
through Christ.
6But if we are afflicted, it
is for your comfort and salvation; or if we are com-
forted, it is for your comfort, which is effective in
the patient enduring of the
same sufferings which we
also suffer;
7and our hope for you is
firmly grounded, knowing
that as you are sharers of
our sufferings, so also you
are *sharers* of our comfort.
8For we do not want you
to be unaware, brethren, of
our affliction which came
to us in Asia, that we were
burdened excessively,
beyond our strength, so
that we despaired even of
life;
9indeed, we had the sen-
tence of death within our-

1 Παῦλος ἀπόστολος Χριστοῦ Ἰησοῦ
Paul an apostle of Christ Jesus

διὰ θελήματος θεοῦ καὶ Τιμόθεος ὁ
through [the] will of God and Timothy the

ἀδελφὸς τῇ ἐκκλησίᾳ τοῦ θεοῦ τῇ οὔσῃ
brother to the church – of God – being

ἐν Κορίνθῳ σὺν τοῖς ἁγίοις πᾶσιν τοῖς
in Corinth with [2]the [3]saints [1]all –

οὖσιν ἐν ὅλῃ τῇ Ἀχαΐᾳ· **2** χάρις ὑμῖν καὶ
being in all – Achaia: Grace to you and

εἰρήνη ἀπὸ θεοῦ πατρὸς ἡμῶν καὶ κυρίου
peace from God [the] Father of us and [the] Lord

Ἰησοῦ Χριστοῦ.
Jesus Christ.

3 Εὐλογητὸς ὁ θεὸς καὶ πατὴρ τοῦ
Blessed [be] the God and Father of the

κυρίου ἡμῶν Ἰησοῦ Χριστοῦ, ὁ πατὴρ
Lord of us Jesus Christ, the Father

τῶν οἰκτιρμῶν καὶ θεὸς πάσης παρακλήσ-
– of compassions and God of all com-

εως, **4** ὁ παρακαλῶν ἡμᾶς ἐπὶ πάσῃ
fort, the [one] comforting us on(in) all

τῇ θλίψει ἡμῶν, εἰς τὸ δύνασθαι ἡμᾶς
the affliction of us, [with a view] to – to be able us[b]
=our being able

παρακαλεῖν τοὺς ἐν πάσῃ θλίψει διὰ
to comfort the ones in every affliction through

τῆς παρακλήσεως ἧς παρακαλούμεθα αὐτοὶ
the comfort of(with) which we are comforted [our-]selves

ὑπὸ τοῦ θεοῦ. **5** ὅτι καθὼς περισσεύει τὰ
by – God. Because as abounds the

παθήματα τοῦ Χριστοῦ εἰς ἡμᾶς, οὕτως
sufferings – of Christ in us, so

διὰ τοῦ Χριστοῦ περισσεύει καὶ ἡ παρά-
through – Christ abounds also the com-

κλησις ἡμῶν. **6** εἴτε δὲ θλιβόμεθα, ὑπὲρ
fort of us. Now whether we are afflicted, on behalf of

τῆς ὑμῶν παρακλήσεως καὶ σωτηρίας· εἴτε
the [4]of you [1]comfort [2]and [3]salvation; or

παρακαλούμεθα, ὑπὲρ τῆς ὑμῶν παρακλή-
we are comforted, on behalf of the [2]of you [1]com-

σεως τῆς ἐνεργουμένης ἐν ὑπομονῇ τῶν
fort – operating in endurance of the

αὐτῶν παθημάτων ὧν καὶ ἡμεῖς πάσχομεν,
same sufferings which also we suffer,

7 καὶ ἡ ἐλπὶς ἡμῶν βεβαία ὑπὲρ ὑμῶν
and the hope of us [is] firm on behalf of you

εἰδότες ὅτι ὡς κοινωνοί ἐστε τῶν παθημά-
knowing that as partakers ye are of the suffer-

των, οὕτως καὶ τῆς παρακλήσεως. **8** Οὐ
ings, so also of the comfort. not

γὰρ θέλομεν ὑμᾶς ἀγνοεῖν, ἀδελφοί, ὑπὲρ
For we wish you to be ignorant, brothers, as to

τῆς θλίψεως ἡμῶν τῆς γενομένης ἐν
the affliction of us – having been in

τῇ Ἀσίᾳ, ὅτι καθ' ὑπερβολὴν ὑπὲρ
– Asia, that excessively† beyond

δύναμιν ἐβαρήθημεν, ὥστε ἐξαπορηθῆναι
power we were burdened, so as to despair
=so that we despaired even

ἡμᾶς καὶ τοῦ ζῆν· **9** ἀλλὰ αὐτοὶ ἐν
us[b] even – to live; but [our]selves in
of life;

ἑαυτοῖς τὸ ἀπόκριμα τοῦ θανάτου ἐσχήκα-
ourselves the sentence – of death we have

Chapter 1

PAUL, an apostle of
Christ Jesus by the will
of God, and Timothy our
brother,

To the church of God in
Corinth, together with all
the saints throughout
Achaia:

2Grace and peace to you
from God our Father and
the Lord Jesus Christ.

The God of All Comfort

3Praise be to the God and
Father of our Lord Jesus
Christ, the Father of compassion and the God of all
comfort, 4who comforts us
in all our troubles, so that
we can comfort those in
any trouble with the com-
fort we ourselves have received from God. 5For just
as the sufferings of Christ
flow over into our lives, so
also through Christ our
comfort overflows. 6If we
are distressed, it is for your
comfort and salvation; if
we are comforted, it is for
your comfort, which pro-
duces in you patient endurance of the same sufferings
we suffer. 7And our hope
for you is firm, because we
know that just as you share
in our sufferings, so also
you share in our comfort.
8We do not want you to
be uninformed, brothers,
about the hardships we suffered in the province of
Asia. We were under great
pressure, far beyond our
ability to endure, so that we
despaired even of life. 9In-
deed, in our hearts we felt

selves in order that we should not trust in ourselves, but in God who raises the dead;

10who delivered us from so great a *peril of* death, and will deliver *us,* He on whom we have set our hope. And He will yet deliver us,

11you also joining in helping us through your prayers, that thanks may be given by many persons on our behalf for the favor bestowed upon us through *the prayers of* many.

Paul's Integrity

12For our proud confidence is this, the testimony of our conscience, that in holiness and godly sincerity, not in fleshly wisdom but in the grace of God, we have conducted ourselves in the world, and especially toward you.

13For we write nothing else to you than what you read and understand, and I hope you will understand until the end;

14just as you also partially did understand us, that we are your reason to be proud as you also are ours, in the day of our Lord Jesus.

15And in this confidence I intended at first to come to you, that you might twice receive a blessing;

16that is, to pass your way into Macedonia, and again from Macedonia to come to you, and by you to be helped on my journey to Judea.

17Therefore, I was not vacillating when I intended to do this, was I? Or that which I purpose, do I purpose according to the flesh, that with me there should

μεν, ἵνα μὴ πεποιθότες ὦμεν ἐφ' ἑαυτοῖς
had, in order that [2]not [3]having trusted [1]we might be on ourselves

ἀλλ' ἐπὶ τῷ θεῷ τῷ ἐγείροντι τοὺς
but on – God the [one] raising the

νεκρούς· 10 ὃς ἐκ τηλικούτου θανάτου
dead; who out of so great a death

ἐρρύσατο ἡμᾶς καὶ ῥύσεται, εἰς ὃν
delivered us and will deliver, in whom

ἠλπίκαμεν [ὅτι] καὶ ἔτι ῥύσεται, 11 συν-
we have hoped that indeed yet he will deliver, co-

υπουργούντων καὶ ὑμῶν ὑπὲρ ἡμῶν τῇ
operating also you[a] on behalf of us –
=while ye also coöperate

δεήσει, ἵνα ἐκ πολλῶν προσώπων τὸ
in petition, in order that [4]by [5]many [6]persons [7][for] [8]the

εἰς ἡμᾶς χάρισμα διὰ πολλῶν εὐχαριστηθῇ
[10]to [11]us [9]gift [12]through [13]many [1]thanks may be given

ὑπὲρ ἡμῶν.
[2]on behalf of [3]us.

12 Ἡ γὰρ καύχησις ἡμῶν αὕτη ἐστίν,
For the boasting of us [2]this [1]is,

τὸ μαρτύριον τῆς συνειδήσεως ἡμῶν, ὅτι
the testimony of the conscience of us, because

ἐν ἁγιότητι καὶ εἰλικρινείᾳ τοῦ θεοῦ,
in sanctity and sincerity – of God,

οὐκ ἐν σοφίᾳ σαρκικῇ ἀλλ' ἐν χάριτι
not in wisdom fleshly but in [the] grace

θεοῦ, ἀνεστράφημεν ἐν τῷ κόσμῳ, περισ-
of God, we behaved in the world, [2]more

σοτέρως δὲ πρὸς ὑμᾶς. 13 οὐ γὰρ ἄλλα
[3]especially [1]and with you. [2]Not [1]for [4]other things

γράφομεν ὑμῖν ἀλλ' ἢ ἃ ἀναγινώσκετε
[3]we write to you *other* than what ye read

ἢ καὶ ἐπιγινώσκετε, ἐλπίζω δὲ ὅτι
or even perceive, and I hope that

ἕως τέλους ἐπιγνώσεσθε, 14 καθὼς καὶ
to [the] end ye will perceive, as also

ἐπέγνωτε ἡμᾶς ἀπὸ μέρους, ὅτι καύχημα
ye perceived us from(in) part, because [3]boast

ὑμῶν ἐσμεν καθάπερ καὶ ὑμεῖς ἡμῶν
[3]of you [1]we are even as also ye of us

ἐν τῇ ἡμέρᾳ τοῦ κυρίου ἡμῶν Ἰησοῦ.
in the day of the Lord of us Jesus.

15 Καὶ ταύτῃ τῇ πεποιθήσει ἐβουλόμην
And in this – persuasion I determined

πρότερον πρὸς ὑμᾶς ἐλθεῖν ἵνα δευτέραν
formerly to you to come in order that a second

χάριν σχῆτε, 16 καὶ δι' ὑμῶν διελθεῖν
grace ye might have, and through you to pass *through*

εἰς Μακεδονίαν, καὶ πάλιν ἀπὸ Μακεδονίας
into Macedonia, and again from Macedonia

ἐλθεῖν πρὸς ὑμᾶς καὶ ὑφ' ὑμῶν
to come to you and by you

προπεμφθῆναι εἰς τὴν Ἰουδαίαν. 17 τοῦτο
to be set forward to – Judæa. This

οὖν βουλόμενος μήτι ἄρα τῇ ἐλαφρίᾳ
therefore determining *not* [3]then – [2]fickleness

ἐχρησάμην; ἢ ἃ βουλεύομαι κατὰ σάρκα
[1]did I use? or [the] things which I determine according to [the] flesh

βουλεύομαι, ἵνα ᾖ παρ' ἐμοὶ τὸ ναὶ
do I determine, in order that there may be with me the Yes

the sentence of death. But
this happened that we
might not rely on ourselves
but on God, who raises the
dead. 10He has delivered us
from such a deadly peril,
and he will deliver us. On
him we have set our hope
that he will continue to deliver us, 11as you help us by
your prayers. Then many
will give thanks on our[a] behalf for the gracious favor
granted us in answer to the
prayers of many.

Paul's Change of Plans

12Now this is our boast:
Our conscience testifies
that we have conducted
ourselves in the world, and
especially in our relations
with you, in the holiness
and sincerity that are from
God. We have done so not
according to worldly wis-
dom but according to
God's grace. 13For we do
not write you anything you
cannot read or understand.
And I hope that, 14as you
have understood us in part,
you will come to under-
stand fully that you can
boast of us just as we will
boast of you in the day of
the Lord Jesus.
15Because I was confi-
dent of this, I planned to
visit you first so that you
might benefit twice. 16I
planned to visit you on my
way to Macedonia and to
come back to you from
Macedonia, and then to
have you send me on my
way to Judea. 17When I
planned this, did I do it
lightly? Or do I make my
plans in a worldly manner
so that in the same breath I

[a]*11* Many manuscripts *your*

be yes, yes and no, no *at the same time*?

18But as God is faithful, our word to you is not yes and no.

19For the Son of God, Christ Jesus, who was preached among you by us—by me and Silvanus and Timothy—was not yes and no, but is yes in Him.

20For as many as may be the promises of God, in Him they are yes; wherefore also by Him is our Amen to the glory of God through us.

21Now He who establishes us with you in Christ and anointed us is God,

22who also sealed us and gave *us* the Spirit in our hearts as a pledge.

23But I call God as witness to my soul, that to spare you I came no more to Corinth.

24Not that we lord it over your faith, but are workers with you for your joy; for in your faith you are standing firm.

Chapter 2

Reaffirm Your Love

BUT I determined this for my own sake, that I would not come to you in sorrow again.

2For if I cause you sorrow, who then makes me glad but the one whom I made sorrowful?

3And this is the very thing I wrote you, lest, when I came, I should have sorrow from those who ought to make me rejoice; having confidence in you all, that my joy would be *the joy* of you all.

4For out of much affliction and anguish of heart I wrote to you with many tears; not that you should be made sorrowful, but that you might know the love which I have especially for

ναὶ καὶ τὸ οὒ οὔ; **18** πιστὸς δὲ ὁ
yes and the No no? But faithful [is] –
θεὸς ὅτι ὁ λόγος ἡμῶν ὁ πρὸς ὑμᾶς
God that the word of us – to you
οὐκ ἔστιν ναὶ καὶ οὔ. **19** ὁ τοῦ θεοῦ
is not yes and no. [3]the – [4]of God
γὰρ υἱὸς Χριστὸς Ἰησοῦς ὁ ἐν ὑμῖν
[1]For [2]Son Christ Jesus [1]the [3]among [4]you [one]
δι᾽ ἡμῶν κηρυχθείς, δι᾽ ἐμοῦ καὶ Σιλουανοῦ
[5]through [6]us [2]proclaimed, through me and Silvanus
καὶ Τιμοθέου, οὐκ ἐγένετο ναὶ καὶ οὔ,
and Timothy, was not yes and no,
ἀλλὰ ναὶ ἐν αὐτῷ γέγονεν. **20** ὅσαι γὰρ
but [2]Yes [3]in [4]him [1]has been. For as many
ἐπαγγελίαι θεοῦ, ἐν αὐτῷ τὸ ναί· διὸ
[as are] promises of God, in him [is] the Yes; wherefore
καὶ δι᾽ αὐτοῦ τὸ ἀμὴν τῷ θεῷ πρὸς
also through him the Amen – [3]to God [1]unto
δόξαν δι᾽ ἡμῶν. **21** ὁ δὲ βεβαιῶν ἡμᾶς
[2]glory through us. But the [one] making firm us
σὺν ὑμῖν εἰς Χριστὸν καὶ χρίσας ἡμᾶς
with you in Christ and having anointed us [is]
θεός, **22** ὁ καὶ σφραγισάμενος ἡμᾶς καὶ
God, the [one] both having sealed us and
δοὺς τὸν ἀρραβῶνα τοῦ πνεύματος ἐν
having given the earnest of the Spirit in
ταῖς καρδίαις ἡμῶν.
the hearts of us.
23 Ἐγὼ δὲ μάρτυρα τὸν θεὸν ἐπικαλοῦμαι
Now [4]I [7][as] witness – [6]God [5]invoke
ἐπὶ τὴν ἐμὴν ψυχήν, ὅτι φειδόμενος
[1]on – [2]my [3]life, that sparing
ὑμῶν οὐκέτι ἦλθον εἰς Κόρινθον. **24** οὐχ ὅτι
you [2]no more [1]I came to Corinth. Not that
κυριεύομεν ὑμῶν τῆς πίστεως, ἀλλὰ συνεργοί
we rule over [3]of you [1]the [2]faith, but [2]fellow-workers
ἐσμεν τῆς χαρᾶς ὑμῶν· τῇ γὰρ πίστει
[1]we are of the joy of you; – for by faith
ἑστήκατε. **2** ἔκρινα δὲ ἐμαυτῷ τοῦτο, τὸ μὴ
ye stand. But I decided in myself this, – not
πάλιν ἐν λύπῃ πρὸς ὑμᾶς ἐλθεῖν. **2** εἰ
again [4]in [5]grief [2]to [3]you [1]to come. if
γὰρ ἐγὼ λυπῶ ὑμᾶς, καὶ τίς ὁ εὐφραίνων
For I grieve you, then who the [one] making glad
με εἰ μὴ ὁ λυπούμενος ἐξ ἐμοῦ; **3** καὶ
me except the [one] being grieved by me? And
ἔγραψα τοῦτο αὐτὸ ἵνα μὴ ἐλθὼν λύπην
I wrote this very thing lest coming grief
σχῶ ἀφ᾽ ὧν ἔδει με χαίρειν, πεποιθὼς
I should have from [those] whom it behoved me to rejoice, having confidence
ἐπὶ πάντας ὑμᾶς ὅτι ἡ ἐμὴ χαρὰ πάντων
in [2]all [1]you that – my joy [3]all
ὑμῶν ἐστιν. **4** ἐκ γὰρ πολλῆς θλίψεως
[2]of you [1]is. For out of much affliction
καὶ συνοχῆς καρδίας ἔγραψα ὑμῖν διὰ
and anxiety of heart I wrote to you through
πολλῶν δακρύων, οὐχ ἵνα λυπηθῆτε, ἀλλὰ
many tears, not in order that ye should be grieved, but
τὴν ἀγάπην ἵνα γνῶτε ἣν ἔχω περισ-
[2]the [4]love [1]in order that [2]ye should know [5]which I have more

say, "Yes, yes" and "No, no"?
18But as surely as God is
faithful, our message to
you is not "Yes" and
"No." 19For the Son of
God, Jesus Christ, who
was preached among you
by me and Silas[b] and Timothy,
was not "Yes" and
"No," but in him it has always
been "Yes." 20For no
matter how many promises
God has made, they are
"Yes" in Christ. And so
through him the "Amen" is
spoken by us to the glory of
God. 21Now it is God who
makes both us and you
stand firm in Christ. He
anointed us, 22set his seal
of ownership on us, and put
his Spirit in our hearts as a
deposit, guaranteeing what
is to come.
23I call God as my witness
that it was in order to spare
you that I did not return to
Corinth. 24Not that we lord
it over your faith, but we
work with you for your joy,
because it is by faith you
stand firm.

1So I made up
my mind that I would not
make another painful visit
to you. 2For if I grieve you,
who is left to make me glad
but you whom I have
grieved? 3I wrote as I did so
that when I came I should
not be distressed by those
who ought to make me rejoice.
I had confidence in
all of you, that you would
all share my joy. 4For I
wrote you out of great distress
and anguish of heart
and with many tears, not to

[b]19 Greek *Silvanus*, a variant of *Silas*

you.
5But if any has caused
sorrow, he has caused sorrow not to me, but in some
degree—in order not to say
too much—to all of you.
6Sufficient for such a one
is this punishment which
was *inflicted by* the majority,
7so that on the contrary
you should rather forgive
and comfort *him*, lest
somehow such a one be
overwhelmed by excessive
sorrow.
8Wherefore I urge you to
reaffirm *your* love for him.
9For to this end also I
wrote that I might put you
to the test, whether you are
obedient in all things.
10But whom you forgive
anything, I *forgive* also; for
indeed what I have for-
given, if I have forgiven
anything, *I did it* for your
sakes in the presence of
Christ,
11in order that no advan-
tage be taken of us by Satan; for we are not ignorant
of his schemes.
12Now when I came to
Troas for the gospel of
Christ and when a door was
opened for me in the Lord,
13I had no rest for my
spirit, not finding Titus
my brother; but taking my
leave of them, I went on to
Macedonia.
14But thanks be to God,
who always leads us in His
triumph in Christ, and
manifests through us the
sweet aroma of the knowl-
edge of Him in every place.
15For we are a fragrance
of Christ to God among
those who are being saved
and among those who are
perishing;
16to the one an aroma
from death to death, to the
other an aroma from life to
life. And who is adequate
for these things?
17For we are not like
many, [a]peddling the word

σοτέρως εἰς ὑμᾶς. **5** Εἰ δέ τις λελύπηκεν,
abundantly to you. But if anyone has grieved,

οὐκ ἐμὲ λελύπηκεν, ἀλλὰ ἀπὸ μέρους,
not me he has grieved, but from(in) part,

ἵνα μὴ ἐπιβαρῶ, πάντας ὑμᾶς. **6** ἱκανὸν
lest I am burdensome, [2]all [1]you. Enough

τῷ τοιούτῳ ἡ ἐπιτιμία αὕτη ἡ ὑπὸ
for such a one this punishment – by

τῶν πλειόνων, **7** ὥστε τοὐναντίον μᾶλλον
the majority, so as on the contrary rather

ὑμᾶς χαρίσασθαι καὶ παρακαλέσαι, μή πως
you to forgive and to comfort,[b] lest
=ye should rather forgive and comfort,

τῇ περισσοτέρᾳ λύπῃ καταποθῇ ὁ τοιοῦτος.
[3]by *the* [4]more abundant [5]grief [2]should be swallowed up [1]such a one.

8 διὸ παρακαλῶ ὑμᾶς κυρῶσαι εἰς αὐτὸν
Wherefore I beseech you to confirm to him

ἀγάπην· **9** εἰς τοῦτο γὰρ καὶ ἔγραψα,
[your] love; [2]to [3]this [end] [1]for indeed I wrote,

ἵνα γνῶ τὴν δοκιμὴν ὑμῶν, εἰ εἰς πάντα
in order that I might know the proof of you, if in all things

ὑπήκοοί ἐστε. **10** ᾧ δέ τι χαρίζεσθε,
obedient ye are. Now *to* whom anything ye forgive,

κἀγώ· καὶ γὰρ ἐγὼ ὃ κεχάρισμαι, εἴ
I also; for indeed [2]I [1]what [3]have forgiven, if

τι κεχάρισμαι, δι' ὑμᾶς ἐν προσώπῳ
[2]anything [1]I have forgiven, [it is] on account of you in [the] person

Χριστοῦ, **11** ἵνα μὴ πλεονεκτηθῶμεν ὑπὸ
of Christ, lest we are taken advantage of by

τοῦ σατανᾶ· οὐ γὰρ αὐτοῦ τὰ νοήματα
– Satan; for [3]not [7]of him [5]the [6]designs

ἀγνοοῦμεν. **12** Ἐλθὼν δὲ εἰς τὴν Τρῳάδα εἰς
[1]we [2]are [4]ignorant [of]. But coming to – Troas in

τὸ εὐαγγέλιον τοῦ Χριστοῦ, καὶ θύρας
the gospel – of Christ, and a door

μοι ἀνεῳγμένης ἐν κυρίῳ, **13** οὐκ ἔσχηκα
to me having been opened[a] by [the] Lord, I *have* had no

ἄνεσιν τῷ πνεύματί μου τῷ μὴ εὑρεῖν
rest to the spirit of me in the not to find
=when I did not find . . .

με Τίτον τὸν ἀδελφόν μου, ἀλλὰ ἀποτα-
me[be] Titus the brother of me, but saying

ξάμενος αὐτοῖς ἐξῆλθον εἰς Μακεδονίαν.
farewell to them I went forth into Macedonia.

14 Τῷ δὲ θεῷ χάρις τῷ πάντοτε
– But [2]to God [1]thanks the [one] always

θριαμβεύοντι ἡμᾶς ἐν τῷ Χριστῷ καὶ
leading in triumph us in – Christ and

τὴν ὀσμὴν τῆς γνώσεως αὐτοῦ φανεροῦντι
[4]the [5]odour [6]of the [7]knowledge [8]of him [1]manifesting

δι' ἡμῶν ἐν παντὶ τόπῳ· **15** ὅτι Χριστοῦ
[2]through [3]us in every place; because of Christ

εὐωδία ἐσμὲν τῷ θεῷ ἐν τοῖς σῳζομένοις
a sweet smell we are – to God in the [ones] being saved

καὶ ἐν τοῖς ἀπολλυμένοις, **16** οἷς μὲν
and in the [ones] perishing, to the [latter]†

ὀσμὴ ἐκ θανάτου εἰς θάνατον, οἷς δὲ
an odour out of death unto death, to the [former]†

ὀσμὴ ἐκ ζωῆς εἰς ζωήν. καὶ πρὸς
an odour out of life unto life. And for

ταῦτα τίς ἱκανός; **17** οὐ γάρ ἐσμεν
these things who [is] competent? For we are not

ὡς οἱ πολλοὶ καπηλεύοντες τὸν λόγον
as the many hawking the word

grieve you but to let you
know the depth of my love
for you.

Forgiveness for the Sinner

5If anyone has caused
grief, he has not so much
grieved me as he has
grieved all of you, to some
extent—not to put it too severely. 6The punishment
inflicted on him by the majority is sufficient for him.
7Now instead, you ought to
forgive and comfort him, so
that he will not be over-
whelmed by excessive sor-
row. 8I urge you, therefore,
to reaffirm your love for
him. 9The reason I wrote
you was to see if you would
stand the test and be obedient in everything. 10If you
forgive anyone, I also forgive him. And what I have
forgiven—if there was anything to forgive—I have
forgiven in the sight of
Christ for your sake, 11in
order that Satan might not
outwit us. For we are not
unaware of his schemes.

Ministers of the New Covenant

12Now when I went to
Troas to preach the gospel
of Christ and found that the
Lord had opened a door for
me, 13I still had no peace of
mind, because I did not find
my brother Titus there. So
I said good-by to them and
went on to Macedonia.
14But thanks be to God,
who always leads us in triumphal procession in
Christ and through us
spreads everywhere the
fragrance of the knowledge
of him. 15For we are to God
the aroma of Christ among
those who are being saved
and those who are perish-
ing. 16To the one we are the
smell of death; to the other,
the fragrance of life. And
who is equal to such a task?
17Unlike so many, we do
not peddle the word of God

[a] Or, *corrupting*

of God, but as from sincerity, but as from God, we
speak in Christ in the sight
of God.

Chapter 3

Ministers of a New Covenant

ARE we beginning to
commend ourselves
again? Or do we need, as
some, letters of commen-
dation to you or from you?
2You are our letter, written in our hearts, known
and read by all men;
3being manifested that
you are a letter of Christ,
cared for by us, written not
with ink, but with the Spirit
of the living God, not on
tablets of stone, but on tablets of human hearts.
4And such confidence
we have through Christ
toward God.
5Not that we are ade-
quate in ourselves to consider anything as *coming*
from ourselves, but our
adequacy is from God,
6who also made us ade-
quate *as* servants of a new
covenant, not of the letter,
but of the Spirit; for the letter kills, but the Spirit gives
life.
7But if the ministry of
death, in letters engraved
on stones, came with glory,
so that the sons of Israel
could not look intently at
the face of Moses because
of the glory of his face, fading *as* it was,
8how shall the ministry
of the Spirit fail to be even
more with glory?
9For if the ministry of
condemnation has glory,
much more does the minis-
try of righteousness
abound in glory.
10For indeed what had

τοῦ θεοῦ, ἀλλ' ὡς ἐξ εἰλικρινείας, ἀλλ'
– of God, but as of sincerity, but

ὡς ἐκ θεοῦ κατέναντι θεοῦ ἐν Χριστῷ
as of God before God in Christ

λαλοῦμεν.
we speak.

3 Ἀρχόμεθα πάλιν ἑαυτοὺς συνιστάνειν;
Do we begin again ourselves to commend?

ἢ μὴ χρῄζομεν ὥς τινες συστατικῶν
or *not* need we as some commendatory

ἐπιστολῶν πρὸς ὑμᾶς ἢ ἐξ ὑμῶν; 2 ἡ
epistles to you or from you? The

ἐπιστολὴ ἡμῶν ὑμεῖς ἐστε, ἐγγεγραμμένη
epistle of us ye are, *having been* inscribed

ἐν ταῖς καρδίαις ἡμῶν, γινωσκομένη καὶ
in the hearts of us, *being* known and

ἀναγινωσκομένη ὑπὸ πάντων ἀνθρώπων,
being read by all men,

3 φανερούμενοι ὅτι ἐστὲ ἐπιστολὴ Χριστοῦ
being manifested that ye are an epistle of Christ

διακονηθεῖσα ὑφ' ἡμῶν, ἐγγεγραμμένη οὐ
ministered by us, *having been* inscribed not

μέλανι ἀλλὰ πνεύματι θεοῦ ζῶντος, οὐκ
by ink but by [the] Spirit of [2]God [1]a living, not

ἐν πλαξὶν λιθίναις ἀλλ' ἐν πλαξὶν καρδίαις
in [2]tablets [1]stony but in tablets [which are] [2]hearts

σαρκίναις.
[1]fleshy.

4 Πεποίθησιν δὲ τοιαύτην ἔχομεν διὰ
[2]confidence [1]And [3]such we have through

τοῦ Χριστοῦ πρὸς τὸν θεόν. 5 οὐχ
– Christ toward – God. Not

ὅτι ἀφ' ἑαυτῶν ἱκανοί ἐσμεν λογίσασθαί
that [3]from [4]ourselves [2]competent [1]we are to reckon

τι ὡς ἐξ ἑαυτῶν, ἀλλ' ἡ ἱκανότης
any-thing as of ourselves, but the competence

ἡμῶν ἐκ τοῦ θεοῦ, 6 ὃς καὶ ἱκάνωσεν
of us [is] of – God, who also made competent

ἡμᾶς διακόνους καινῆς διαθήκης, οὐ
us [as] ministers of a new covenant, not

γράμματος ἀλλὰ πνεύματος· τὸ γὰρ γράμμα
of letter but of spirit; for the letter

ἀποκτείνει, τὸ δὲ πνεῦμα ζωοποιεῖ. 7 Εἰ
kills, but the spirit makes alive. if

δὲ ἡ διακονία τοῦ θανάτου ἐν γράμμασιν
Now the ministry – of death in letters

ἐντετυπωμένη λίθοις ἐγενήθη ἐν δόξῃ,
having been engraved in stones was in glory,

ὥστε μὴ δύνασθαι ἀτενίσαι τοὺς υἱοὺς
so as not to be able to gaze the sons
=so that the sons of Israel were not able to gaze

Ἰσραὴλ εἰς τὸ πρόσωπον Μωϋσέως διὰ
of Israel[b] at the face of Moses on account of

τὴν δόξαν τοῦ προσώπου αὐτοῦ τὴν
the glory of the face of him –

καταργουμένην, 8 πῶς οὐχὶ μᾶλλον ἡ
being done away, how [2]not [3]rather [4]the

διακονία τοῦ πνεύματος ἔσται ἐν δόξῃ;
[5]ministry [6]of the [7]Spirit [1]will [8]be in glory?

9 εἰ γὰρ ἡ διακονία τῆς κατακρίσεως
For if the ministry – of condemnation

δόξα, πολλῷ μᾶλλον περισσεύει ἡ διακονία
[was] glory, by much rather [4]abounds [1]the [2]ministry

τῆς δικαιοσύνης δόξῃ. 10 καὶ γὰρ οὐ
– [3]of righteousness in glory. For indeed [2]not

for profit. On the contrary,
in Christ we speak before
God with sincerity, like
men sent from God.

Chapter 3

ARE we beginning to
commend ourselves
again? Or do we need, like
some people, letters of rec-
ommendation to you or
from you? 2You yourselves
are our letter, written on
our hearts, known and read
by everybody. 3You show
that you are a letter from
Christ, the result of our
ministry, written not with
ink but with the Spirit of the
living God, not on tablets of
stone but on tablets of human hearts.
4Such confidence as this
is ours through Christ before God. 5Not that we are
competent in ourselves to
claim anything for our-
selves, but our competence
comes from God. 6He has
made us competent as min-
isters of a new covenant—
not of the letter but of the
Spirit; for the letter kills,
but the Spirit gives life.

The Glory of the New Covenant

7Now if the ministry that
brought death, which was
engraved in letters on
stone, came with glory, so
that the Israelites could not
look steadily at the face of
Moses because of its glory,
fading though it was, 8will
not the ministry of the Spirit be even more glorious?
9If the ministry that condemns men is glorious,
how much more glorious is
the ministry that brings
righteousness! 10For what
was glorious has no glory

glory in this case has no glory on account of the glory that surpasses *it*.

11For if that which fades away *was* with glory, much more that which remains *is* in glory.

12Having therefore such a hope, we use great boldness in *our* speech,

13and *are* not as Moses, *who* used to put a veil over his face that the sons of Israel might not look intently at the end of what was fading away.

14But their minds were hardened; for until this very day at the reading of the old covenant the same veil remains unlifted, because it is removed in Christ.

15But to this day whenever Moses is read, a veil lies over their heart;

16but whenever a man turns to the Lord, the veil is taken away.

17Now the Lord is the Spirit; and where the Spirit of the Lord is, *there* is liberty.

18But we all, with unveiled face beholding as in a mirror the glory of the Lord, are being transformed into the same image from glory to glory, just as from the Lord, the Spirit.

δεδόξασται τὸ δεδοξασμένον ἐν τούτῳ
[4]has been glorified [1]the [thing] [2]having been glorified in this

τῷ μέρει εἵνεκεν τῆς ὑπερβαλλούσης δόξης.
– respect for the sake of the excelling glory.

11 εἰ γὰρ τὸ καταργούμενον διὰ δόξης,
For if the [thing] being done away [was] through glory,

πολλῷ μᾶλλον τὸ μένον ἐν δόξῃ.
by much more the [thing] remaining [is] in glory.

12 Ἔχοντες οὖν τοιαύτην ἐλπίδα πολλῇ
Having therefore such hope [2]much

παρρησίᾳ χρώμεθα, 13 καὶ οὐ καθάπερ
[3]boldness [1]we use, and not as

Μωϋσῆς ἐτίθει κάλυμμα ἐπὶ τὸ πρόσωπον
Moses put a veil on the face

αὐτοῦ, πρὸς τὸ μὴ ἀτενίσαι τοὺς υἱοὺς
of him, for *the* [4]not [5]to gaze [1]the [2]sons

Ἰσραὴλ εἰς τὸ τέλος τοῦ καταργουμένου.
[3]of Israel[b] at the end of the [thing] being done away.

14 ἀλλὰ ἐπωρώθη τὰ νοήματα αὐτῶν.
But were hardened the thoughts of them.

ἄχρι γὰρ τῆς σήμερον ἡμέρας τὸ αὐτὸ
For until the present day the same

κάλυμμα ἐπὶ τῇ ἀναγνώσει τῆς παλαιᾶς
veil [2]on(at) [3]the [4]reading [5]of the [6]old

διαθήκης μένει, μὴ ἀνακαλυπτόμενον ὅτι
[7]covenant [1]remains, not being unveiled* that

ἐν Χριστῷ καταργεῖται. 15 ἀλλ' ἕως
in Christ it is being done away. But until

σήμερον ἡνίκα ἂν ἀναγινώσκηται Μωϋσῆς
to-day whenever [2]is being read [1]Moses

κάλυμμα ἐπὶ τὴν καρδίαν αὐτῶν κεῖται·
a veil [2]on [3]the [4]heart [5]of them [1]lies;

16 ἡνίκα δὲ ἐὰν ἐπιστρέψῃ πρὸς κύριον,
but whenever it§ turns to [the] Lord,

περιαιρεῖται τὸ κάλυμμα. 17 ὁ δὲ κύριος
[3]is taken away [1]the [2]veil. Now the Lord

τὸ πνεῦμά ἐστιν· οὗ δὲ τὸ πνεῦμα
[2]the [3]Spirit [1]is; and where the Spirit

κυρίου, ἐλευθερία. 18 ἡμεῖς δὲ πάντες
of [the] Lord [is], [there is] freedom. But we all

ἀνακεκαλυμμένῳ προσώπῳ τὴν δόξαν
[2]*having been* unveiled [1]with face [2]the [3]glory

κυρίου κατοπτριζόμενοι τὴν αὐτὴν εἰκόνα
[4]of [the] Lord [1]beholding in a mirror [6]the [7]same [8]image

μεταμορφούμεθα ἀπὸ δόξης εἰς δόξαν,
[5]are being changed [into] from glory to glory,

καθάπερ ἀπὸ κυρίου πνεύματος.
even as from [the] Lord Spirit.

now in comparison with the
surpassing glory. 11And if
what was fading away
came with glory, how much
greater is the glory of that
which lasts!
12Therefore, since we
have such a hope, we are
very bold. 13We are not like
Moses, who would put a
veil over his face to keep
the Israelites from gazing at
it while the radiance was
fading away. 14But their
minds were made dull, for
to this day the same veil remains when the old cove-
nant is read. It has not been
removed, because only in
Christ is it taken away.
15Even to this day when
Moses is read, a veil covers
their hearts. 16But whenever anyone turns to the
Lord, the veil is taken
away. 17Now the Lord is
the Spirit, and where the
Spirit of the Lord is, there
is freedom. 18And we, who
with unveiled faces all reflect[c] the Lord's glory, are
being transformed into his
likeness with ever-increasing glory, which comes
from the Lord, who is the
Spirit.

Chapter 4

Paul's Apostolic Ministry

THEREFORE, since we have this ministry, as we received mercy, we do not lose heart,

2but we have renounced the things hidden because of shame, not walking in craftiness or adulterating the word of God, but by the manifestation of truth com-

4 Διὰ τοῦτο, ἔχοντες τὴν διακονίαν
Therefore, having – ministry

ταύτην, καθὼς ἠλεήθημεν, οὐκ ἐγκακοῦμεν,
this, as we obtained mercy, we faint not,

2 ἀλλὰ ἀπειπάμεθα τὰ κρυπτὰ τῆς αἰσχύνης,
but we have renounced the hidden things – of shame,

μὴ περιπατοῦντες ἐν πανουργίᾳ μηδὲ
not walking in craftiness nor

δολοῦντες τὸν λόγον τοῦ θεοῦ, ἀλλὰ
adulterating the word – of God, but

τῇ φανερώσει τῆς ἀληθείας συνιστάνοντες
by the manifestation of the truth commending

Chapter 4

Treasures in Jars of Clay

THEREFORE, since
through God's mercy
we have this ministry, we
do not lose heart. 2Rather,
we have renounced secret
and shameful ways; we do
not use deception, nor do
we distort the word of God.
On the contrary, by setting
forth the truth plainly we

* That is, revealed (Conybeare and Howson). § ? their heart.

c18 Or *contemplate*

mending ourselves to every
man's conscience in the
sight of God.
3And even if our gospel
is veiled, it is veiled to
those who are perishing,
4in whose case the god of
this world has blinded the
minds of the unbelieving,
that they might not see the
light of the gospel of
the glory of Christ, who
is the image of God.
5For we do not preach
ourselves but Christ Jesus
as Lord, and ourselves as
your bond-servants for
Jesus' sake.
6For God, who said,
"Light shall shine out of
darkness," is the One who
has shone in our hearts to
give the light of the knowledge of the glory of God in
the face of Christ.
7But we have this trea-
sure in earthen vessels,
that the surpassing greatness of the power may be of
God and not from our-
selves;
8*we are* afflicted in every
way, but not crushed; perplexed, but not despairing;
9persecuted, but not for-
saken; struck down, but
not destroyed;
10always carrying about
in the body the dying of
Jesus, that the life of Jesus
also may be manifested in
our body.
11For we who live are
constantly being delivered
over to death for Jesus'
sake, that the life of Jesus
also may be manifested in
our mortal flesh.
12So death works in us,
but life in you.
13But having the same

ἑαυτοὺς πρὸς πᾶσαν συνείδησιν ἀνθρώπων
ourselves to every conscience of men
ἐνώπιον τοῦ θεοῦ. 3 εἰ δὲ καὶ ἔστιν
before – God. But if indeed [4]is
κεκαλυμμένον τὸ εὐαγγέλιον ἡμῶν, ἐν
[5]*having been* hidden [1]the [2]gospel [3]of us, in
τοῖς ἀπολλυμένοις ἐστὶν κεκαλυμμένον, 4 ἐν
the [ones] perishing it is *having been* hidden, in
οἷς ὁ θεὸς τοῦ αἰῶνος τούτου ἐτύφλωσεν
whom the god of this age blinded
τὰ νοήματα τῶν ἀπίστων εἰς τὸ μὴ
the thoughts of the [ones] unbelieving [with a view] to *the* not
=so that the enlightenment . . . should not shine forth,
αὐγάσαι τὸν φωτισμὸν τοῦ εὐαγγελίου
to shine forth the enlightenment of the gospel
τῆς δόξης τοῦ Χριστοῦ, ὅς ἐστιν εἰκὼν
of the glory – of Christ, who is [the] image
τοῦ θεοῦ. 5 Οὐ γὰρ ἑαυτοὺς κηρύσσομεν
– of God. For [2]not [3]ourselves [1]we proclaim
ἀλλὰ Χριστὸν Ἰησοῦν κύριον, ἑαυτοὺς δὲ
but Christ Jesus [as] Lord, and ourselves
δούλους ὑμῶν διὰ Ἰησοῦν. 6 ὅτι ὁ
slaves of you on account of Jesus. Because –
θεὸς ὁ εἰπών· ἐκ σκότους φῶς λάμψει,
God the [one] saying: Out of darkness light shall shine,
ὃς ἔλαμψεν ἐν ταῖς καρδίαις ἡμῶν πρὸς
[is] [he] who shone in the hearts of us for
φωτισμὸν τῆς γνώσεως τῆς δόξης τοῦ
enlightenment of the knowledge of the glory –
θεοῦ ἐν προσώπῳ Χριστοῦ.
of God in [the] face of Christ.
7 Ἔχομεν δὲ τὸν θησαυρὸν τοῦτον ἐν
And we have this treasure in
ὀστρακίνοις σκεύεσιν, ἵνα ἡ ὑπερβολὴ
earthenware vessels, in order that the excellence
τῆς δυνάμεως ᾖ τοῦ θεοῦ καὶ μὴ ἐξ
of the power may be – of God and not of
ἡμῶν· 8 ἐν παντὶ θλιβόμενοι ἀλλ' οὐ
us; in every [way] *being* afflicted but not
στενοχωρούμενοι, ἀπορούμενοι ἀλλ' οὐκ
being restrained, *being* in difficulties but not
ἐξαπορούμενοι, 9 διωκόμενοι ἀλλ' οὐκ
despairing, *being* persecuted but not
ἐγκαταλειπόμενοι, καταβαλλόμενοι ἀλλ' οὐκ
being deserted, *being* cast down but not
ἀπολλύμενοι, 10 πάντοτε τὴν νέκρωσιν τοῦ
perishing, always [5]the [6]dying –
Ἰησοῦ ἐν τῷ σώματι περιφέροντες, ἵνα
[7]of Jesus [2]in [3]the [4]body [1]bearing about, in order that
καὶ ἡ ζωὴ τοῦ Ἰησοῦ ἐν τῷ σώματι
also the life – of Jesus in the body
ἡμῶν φανερωθῇ. 11 ἀεὶ γὰρ ἡμεῖς οἱ
of us might be manifested. For always we the
ζῶντες εἰς θάνατον παραδιδόμεθα διὰ
[ones] living to death are being delivered on account of
Ἰησοῦν, ἵνα καὶ ἡ ζωὴ τοῦ Ἰησοῦ
Jesus, in order that also the life – of Jesus
φανερωθῇ ἐν τῇ θνητῇ σαρκὶ ἡμῶν.
might be manifested in the mortal flesh of us.
12 ὥστε ὁ θάνατος ἐν ἡμῖν ἐνεργεῖται,
So as – death in us operates,
ἡ δὲ ζωὴ ἐν ὑμῖν. 13 ἔχοντες δὲ τὸ
– but life in you. And having the

commend ourselves to ev-
ery man's conscience in the
sight of God. 3And even if
our gospel is veiled, it is
veiled to those who are perishing. 4The god of this age
has blinded the minds of
unbelievers, so that they
cannot see the light of the
gospel of the glory of
Christ, who is the image of
God. 5For we do not preach
ourselves, but Jesus Christ
as Lord, and ourselves as
your servants for Jesus'
sake. 6For God, who said,
"Let light shine out of
darkness,"[d] made his light
shine in our hearts to give
us the light of the knowledge of the glory of God in
the face of Christ.
7But we have this trea-
sure in jars of clay to show
that this all-surpassing
power is from God and not
from us. 8We are hard
pressed on every side, but
not crushed; perplexed, but
not in despair; 9persecuted,
but not abandoned; struck
down, but not destroyed.
10We always carry around
in our body the death of
Jesus, so that the life of
Jesus may also be revealed
in our body. 11For we who
are alive are always being
given over to death for
Jesus' sake, so that his life
may be revealed in our
mortal body. 12So then,
death is at work in us, but
life is at work in you.
13It is written: "I be-

spirit of faith, according to
what is written, "I BE-
LIEVED, THEREFORE I
SPOKE," we also believe,
therefore also we speak;
14knowing that He who
raised the Lord Jesus will
raise us also with Jesus and
will present us with you.
15For all things *are* for
your sakes, that the grace
which is spreading to more
and more people may cause
the giving of thanks to
abound to the glory of God.
16Therefore we do not
lose heart, but though our
outer man is decaying, yet
our inner man is being
renewed day by day.
17For momentary, light
affliction is producing for
us an eternal weight of
glory far beyond all com-
parison,
18while we look not at the
things which are seen, but
at the things which are not
seen; for the things which
are seen are temporal, but
the things which are not
seen are eternal.

Chapter 5

The Temporal and Eternal

FOR we know that if the
earthly tent which is
our house is torn down, we
have a building from God, a
house not made with
hands, eternal in the heavens.
2For indeed in this *house*
we groan, longing to be
clothed with our dwelling
from heaven;
3inasmuch as we, having
put it on, shall not be found
naked.
4For indeed while we are
in this tent, we groan, being
burdened, because we do
not want to be unclothed,
but to be clothed, in order
that what is mortal may be
swallowed up by life.
5Now He who prepared

αὐτὸ πνεῦμα τῆς πίστεως, κατὰ τὸ
same spirit – of faith, according to the thing

γεγραμμένον· ἐπίστευσα, διὸ ἐλάλησα, καὶ
having been written: I believed, therefore I spoke, both

ἡμεῖς πιστεύομεν, διὸ καὶ λαλοῦμεν, **14** εἰδότες
we believe, and therefore we speak, knowing

ὅτι ὁ ἐγείρας τὸν κύριον Ἰησοῦν καὶ
that the [one] having raised the Lord Jesus [3]also

ἡμᾶς σὺν Ἰησοῦ ἐγερεῖ καὶ παραστήσει
[2]us [4]with [5]Jesus [1]will raise and will present [us]

σὺν ὑμῖν. **15** τὰ γὰρ πάντα δι' ὑμᾶς,
with you. – For all things [are] on account of you,

ἵνα ἡ χάρις πλεονάσασα διὰ τῶν πλειόνων
in order that – grace increased through the majority

τὴν εὐχαριστίαν περισσεύσῃ εἰς τὴν δόξαν
[2]the [3]thanksgiving [1]may cause to abound to the glory

τοῦ θεοῦ. **16** Διὸ οὐκ ἐγκακοῦμεν, ἀλλ'
– of God. Wherefore we faint not, but

εἰ καὶ ὁ ἔξω ἡμῶν ἄνθρωπος διαφθείρεται,
if indeed the outward [2]of us [1]man is being disabled,

ἀλλ' ὁ ἔσω ἡμῶν ἀνακαινοῦται ἡμέρᾳ
yet the inward [man] of us is being renewed day

καὶ ἡμέρᾳ. **17** τὸ γὰρ παραυτίκα ἐλαφρὸν
and(by) day. For the present lightness

τῆς θλίψεως καθ' ὑπερβολὴν εἰς ὑπερβολὴν
of the affliction [3]excessively [4]to [5]excess

αἰώνιον βάρος δόξης κατεργάζεται ἡμῖν,
[6]an eternal [7]weight [8]of glory [1]works [2]for us,

18 μὴ σκοπούντων ἡμῶν τὰ βλεπόμενα
not considering us[a] the things *being* seen
=while we do not consider

ἀλλὰ τὰ μὴ βλεπόμενα· τὰ γὰρ βλεπόμενα
but the things not *being* seen; for the things *being* seen

πρόσκαιρα, τὰ δὲ μὴ βλεπόμενα αἰώνια.
[are] temporary, but the things not *being* seen [are] eternal.

5 Οἴδαμεν γὰρ ὅτι ἐὰν ἡ ἐπίγειος
For we know that if the earthly

ἡμῶν οἰκία τοῦ σκήνους καταλυθῇ,
[4]of us [1]house [2]of the [3]tabernacle is destroyed,

οἰκοδομὴν ἐκ θεοῦ ἔχομεν, οἰκίαν ἀχειρο-
a building of God we have, a house not made

ποίητον αἰώνιον ἐν τοῖς οὐρανοῖς. **2** καὶ
by hands eternal in *the* heavens. indeed

γὰρ ἐν τούτῳ στενάζομεν, τὸ οἰκητήριον
For in this* we groan, [3]the [4]dwelling-place

ἡμῶν τὸ ἐξ οὐρανοῦ ἐπενδύσασθαι ἐπιπο-
[5]of us – [6]out of [7]heaven [2]to put on [1]greatly

θοῦντες, **3** εἴ γε καὶ ἐνδυσάμενοι οὐ
desiring, if indeed being clothed not

γυμνοὶ εὑρεθησόμεθα. **4** καὶ γὰρ οἱ
naked we shall be found. For indeed [3]the [ones]

ὄντες ἐν τῷ σκήνει στενάζομεν βαρούμενοι,
[2]being [4]in [5]the [6]tabernacle [1]we groan being burdened,

ἐφ' ᾧ οὐ θέλομεν ἐκδύσασθαι ἀλλ'
inasmuch as we do not wish to put off but

ἐπενδύσασθαι, ἵνα καταποθῇ τὸ θνητὸν
to put on, in order that [3]may be swallowed up [1]the [2]mortal

ὑπὸ τῆς ζωῆς. **5** ὁ δὲ κατεργασάμενος
by *the* life. Now the [one] having wrought

* Neuter, going back to σκῆνος in the preceding verse.

lieved; therefore I have
spoken."[e] With that same
spirit of faith we also believe and therefore speak,
14because we know that the
one who raised the Lord
Jesus from the dead will
also raise us with Jesus and
present us with you in his
presence. 15All this is for
your benefit, so that the
grace that is reaching more
and more people may cause
thanksgiving to overflow to
the glory of God.
16Therefore we do not
lose heart. Though out-
wardly we are wasting
away, yet inwardly we are
being renewed day by day.
17For our light and momentary troubles are achieving
for us an eternal glory that
far outweighs them all. 18So
we fix our eyes not on what
is seen, but on what is unseen. For what is seen is
temporary, but what is unseen is eternal.

Chapter 5

Our Heavenly Dwelling

NOW we know that if
the earthly tent we
live in is destroyed, we
have a building from God,
an eternal house in heaven,
not built by human hands.
2Meanwhile we groan,
longing to be clothed with
our heavenly dwelling, 3be-
cause when we are clothed,
we will not be found naked.
4For while we are in this
tent, we groan and are burdened, because we do not
wish to be unclothed but to
be clothed with our heav-
enly dwelling, so that what
is mortal may be swallowed
up by life. 5Now it is God

[e]13 Psalm 116:10

us for this very purpose is
God, who gave to us the
Spirit as a pledge.
6Therefore, being al-
ways of good courage, and
knowing that while we are
at home in the body we are
absent from the Lord—
7for we walk by faith, not
by sight—
8we are of good courage,
I say, and prefer rather to
be absent from the body
and to be at home with the
Lord.
9Therefore also we have
as our ambition, whether at
home or absent, to be
pleasing to Him.
10For we must all appear
before the judgment seat of
Christ, that each one may
be recompensed for his
deeds in the body, according to what he has done,
whether good or bad.
11Therefore knowing the
fear of the Lord, we per-
suade men, but we are
made manifest to God; and
I hope that we are made
manifest also in your consciences.
12We are not again com-
mending ourselves to you
but *are* giving you an occasion to be proud of us, that
you may have *an answer*
for those who take pride in
appearance, and not in
heart.
13For if we are beside ourselves, it is for God; if we
are of sound mind, it is for
you.
14For the love of Christ
controls us, having con-
cluded this, that one died
for all, therefore all died;
15and He died for all, that
they who live should no

ἡμᾶς εἰς αὐτὸ τοῦτο θεός, ὁ δοὺς
us for this very thing [is] God, the [one] having given

ἡμῖν τὸν ἀρραβῶνα τοῦ πνεύματος. 6 Θαρ-
to us the earnest of the Spirit. Being

ροῦντες οὖν πάντοτε καὶ εἰδότες ὅτι
of good cheer therefore always and knowing that

ἐνδημοῦντες ἐν τῷ σώματι ἐκδημοῦμεν
being at home in the body we are away from home

ἀπὸ τοῦ κυρίου· 7 διὰ πίστεως γὰρ
from the Lord; [2]through [3]faith [1]for

περιπατοῦμεν, οὐ διὰ εἴδους· 8 θαρροῦμεν
we walk, not through appearance; we are of good cheer

δὲ καὶ εὐδοκοῦμεν μᾶλλον ἐκδημῆσαι ἐκ
then and think it good rather to go away from home out of

τοῦ σώματος καὶ ἐνδημῆσαι πρὸς τὸν
the body and to come home to the

κύριον. 9 διὸ καὶ φιλοτιμούμεθα, εἴτε
Lord. Wherefore also we are ambitious, whether

ἐνδημοῦντες εἴτε ἐκδημοῦντες, εὐάρεστοι
being at home or being away from home, wellpleasing

αὐτῷ εἶναι. 10 τοὺς γὰρ πάντας ἡμᾶς
to him to be. – For [3]all [2]us

φανερωθῆναι δεῖ ἔμπροσθεν τοῦ βήματος
[4]to be manifested [1]it behoves before the tribunal

τοῦ Χριστοῦ, ἵνα κομίσηται ἕκαστος τὰ
– of Christ, in order that [2]may receive [1]each one the things

διὰ τοῦ σώματος πρὸς ἃ ἔπραξεν, εἴτε
through the body according to what things he practised, either

ἀγαθὸν εἴτε φαῦλον.
good or worthless.

11 Εἰδότες οὖν τὸν φόβον τοῦ κυρίου
Knowing therefore the fear of the Lord

ἀνθρώπους πείθομεν, θεῷ δὲ πεφανερώμεθα·
[2]men [1]we persuade, and to God we have been made manifest;

ἐλπίζω δὲ καὶ ἐν ταῖς συνειδήσεσιν
and I hope also in the consciences

ὑμῶν πεφανερῶσθαι. 12 οὐ πάλιν ἑαυτοὺς
of you to have been made manifest. Not again [2]ourselves

συνιστάνομεν ὑμῖν, ἀλλὰ ἀφορμὴν διδόντες
[1]we commend to you, but [3]an occasion [1]giving

ὑμῖν καυχήματος ὑπὲρ ἡμῶν, ἵνα ἔχητε
[2]to you of a boast on behalf of us, in order that ye may have [it]

πρὸς τοὺς ἐν προσώπῳ καυχωμένους καὶ
in reference to the [ones] [2]in [3]face [1]boasting and

μὴ ἐν καρδίᾳ. 13 εἴτε γὰρ ἐξέστημεν,
not in heart. For whether we are mad,

θεῷ· εἴτε σωφρονοῦμεν, ὑμῖν. 14 ἡ γὰρ
[it is] to God; or we are in our senses, [it is] for you. For the

ἀγάπη τοῦ Χριστοῦ συνέχει ἡμᾶς, κρίναντας
love – of Christ constrains us, judging

τοῦτο, ὅτι εἷς ὑπὲρ πάντων ἀπέθανεν·
this, that one on behalf of all men died;

ἄρα οἱ πάντες ἀπέθανον· 15 καὶ ὑπὲρ
then the all died; and [2]on behalf of

πάντων ἀπέθανεν ἵνα οἱ ζῶντες μηκέτι
[3]all [1]he died in order that the [ones] living no more

who has made us for this
very purpose and has given
us the Spirit as a deposit,
guaranteeing what is to
come.
6Therefore we are always
confident and know that as
long as we are at home in
the body we are away from
the Lord. 7We live by faith,
not by sight. 8We are confident, I say, and would prefer to be away from the
body and at home with the
Lord. 9So we make it our
goal to please him, whether
we are at home in the body
or away from it. 10For we
must all appear before the
judgment seat of Christ,
that each one may receive
what is due him for the
things done while in the
body, whether good or bad.

The Ministry of Reconciliation

11Since, then, we know
what it is to fear the Lord,
we try to persuade men.
What we are is plain to
God, and I hope it is also
plain to your conscience.
12We are not trying to commend ourselves to you
again, but are giving you an
opportunity to take pride in
us, so that you can answer
those who take pride in
what is seen rather than in
what is in the heart. 13If we
are out of our mind, it is for
the sake of God; if we are in
our right mind, it is for you.
14For Christ's love compels
us, because we are con-
vinced that one died for all,
and therefore all died.
15And he died for all, that
those who live should no

longer live for themselves, but for Him who died and rose again on their behalf.
16 Therefore from now on we recognize no man according to the flesh; even though we have known Christ according to the flesh, yet now we know *Him thus* no longer.
17 Therefore if any man is in Christ, *he is* a new creature; the old things passed away; behold, new things have come.
18 Now all *these* things are from God, who reconciled us to Himself through Christ, and gave us the ministry of reconciliation,
19 namely, that God was in Christ reconciling the world to Himself, not counting their trespasses against them, and He has committed to us the word of reconciliation.
20 Therefore, we are ambassadors for Christ, as though God were entreating through us; we beg you on behalf of Christ, be reconciled to God.
21 He made Him who knew no sin *to be* sin on our behalf, that we might become the righteousness of God in Him.

ἑαυτοῖς ζῶσιν ἀλλὰ τῷ ὑπὲρ αὐτῶν
to themselves may live but to the [one] on behalf of them

ἀποθανόντι καὶ ἐγερθέντι. **16** Ὥστε ἡμεῖς
having died and having been raised. So as [3]we

ἀπὸ τοῦ νῦν οὐδένα οἴδαμεν κατὰ σάρκα·
[1]from – [2]now [5]no man [4]know according to flesh;

εἰ καὶ ἐγνώκαμεν κατὰ σάρκα Χριστόν,
if indeed [1]we have known [3]according to [4]flesh [2]Christ,

ἀλλὰ νῦν οὐκέτι γινώσκομεν. **17** ὥστε
yet now no more we know [him]. So as

εἴ τις ἐν Χριστῷ, καινὴ κτίσις· τὰ
if anyone [is] in Christ, [he is] a new creation; the

ἀρχαῖα παρῆλθεν, ἰδοὺ γέγονεν καινά.
old things passed away, behold they have become new.

18 τὰ δὲ πάντα ἐκ τοῦ θεοῦ τοῦ καταλ-
– And all things [are] of – God the [one] having

λάξαντος ἡμᾶς ἑαυτῷ διὰ Χριστοῦ καὶ
reconciled us to himself through Christ and

δόντος ἡμῖν τὴν διακονίαν τῆς καταλλαγῆς,
having given to us the ministry – of reconciliation,

19 ὡς ὅτι θεὸς ἦν ἐν Χριστῷ κόσμον
as that God was in Christ [2][the] world

καταλλάσσων ἑαυτῷ, μὴ λογιζόμενος αὐτοῖς
[1]reconciling to himself, not reckoning to them

τὰ παραπτώματα αὐτῶν, καὶ θέμενος
the trespasses of them, and placing

ἐν ἡμῖν τὸν λόγον τῆς καταλλαγῆς.
in us the word – of reconciliation.

20 Ὑπὲρ Χριστοῦ οὖν πρεσβεύομεν ὡς
On behalf of Christ therefore we are ambassadors as

τοῦ θεοῦ παρακαλοῦντος δι' ἡμῶν· δεόμεθα
– God beseeching[a] through us; we beg

ὑπὲρ Χριστοῦ, καταλλάγητε τῷ θεῷ.
on behalf of Christ, Be ye reconciled – to God.

21 τὸν μὴ γνόντα ἁμαρτίαν ὑπὲρ ἡμῶν
[3]The [one] [3]not [4]knowing [5]sin [7]on behalf of [8]us

ἁμαρτίαν ἐποίησεν, ἵνα ἡμεῖς γενώμεθα
[6]sin [1]he made, in order that we might become

δικαιοσύνη θεοῦ ἐν αὐτῷ.
[the] righteousness of God in him.

longer live for themselves but for him who died for them and was raised again.
16 So from now on we regard no one from a worldly point of view. Though we once regarded Christ in this way, we do so no longer.
17 Therefore, if anyone is in Christ, he is a new creation; the old has gone, the new has come! 18 All this is from God, who reconciled us to himself through Christ and gave us the ministry of reconciliation: 19 that God was reconciling the world to himself in Christ, not counting men's sins against them. And he has committed to us the message of reconciliation. 20 We are therefore Christ's ambassadors, as though God were making his appeal through us. We implore you on Christ's behalf: Be reconciled to God. 21 God made him who had no sin to be sin[f] for us, so that in him we might become the righteousness of God.

Chapter 6

Their Ministry Commended

AND working together *with Him,* we also urge you not to receive the grace of God in vain—
2 for He says,
"AT THE ACCEPTABLE TIME I LISTENED TO YOU,
AND ON THE DAY OF SALVATION I HELPED YOU";
behold, now is "THE ACCEPTABLE TIME," behold, now is "THE DAY OF SALVATION"—
3 giving no cause for offense in anything, in order that the ministry be not discredited,
4 but in everything commending ourselves as servants of God, in much endurance, in afflictions, in hardships, in distresses,

6 Συνεργοῦντες δὲ καὶ παρακαλοῦμεν μὴ
And working together also we beseech [2]not

εἰς κενὸν τὴν χάριν τοῦ θεοῦ δέξασθαι
[7]to no purpose [4]the [5]grace – [6]of God [3]to receive

ὑμᾶς· **2** λέγει γάρ· καιρῷ δεκτῷ ἐπήκουσά
[1]you; for he says: In a time acceptable I heard

σου καὶ ἐν ἡμέρᾳ σωτηρίας ἐβοήθησά
thee and in a day of salvation I helped

σοι· ἰδοὺ νῦν καιρὸς εὐπρόσδεκτος, ἰδοὺ
thee; behold now a time acceptable, behold

νῦν ἡμέρα σωτηρίας· **3** — μηδεμίαν ἐν
now a day of salvation; [2]no [4]in

μηδενὶ διδόντες προσκοπήν, ἵνα μὴ
[5]no(any)thing [1]giving [3]cause of stumbling, lest

μωμηθῇ ἡ διακονία, **4** ἀλλ' ἐν παντὶ
[3]be blamed [1]the [2]ministry, but in everything

συνιστάνοντες ἑαυτοὺς ὡς θεοῦ διάκονοι,
commending ourselves as [2]of God [1]ministers,

ἐν ὑπομονῇ πολλῇ, ἐν θλίψεσιν, ἐν
in [2]endurance [1]much, in afflictions, in

ἀνάγκαις, ἐν στενοχωρίαις, ἐν πληγαῖς,
necessities, in straits, in stripes,

Chapter 6

AS God's fellow workers we urge you not to receive God's grace in vain.
2 For he says,

"In the time of my favor
I heard you,
and in the day of
salvation I helped
you."[g]

I tell you, now is the time of God's favor, now is the day of salvation.

Paul's Hardships

3 We put no stumbling block in anyone's path, so that our ministry will not be discredited. 4 Rather, as servants of God we commend ourselves in every way: in great endurance; in troubles, hardships and dis-

f21 Or *be a sin offering*
g2 Isaiah 49:8

5in beatings, in imprisonments, in tumults, in labors, in sleeplessness, in hunger,
6in purity, in knowledge, in patience, in kindness, in the Holy Spirit, in genuine love,
7in the word of truth, in the power of God; by the weapons of righteousness for the right hand and the left,
8by glory and dishonor, by evil report and good report; *regarded* as deceivers and yet true;
9as unknown yet well-known, as dying yet behold, we live; as punished yet not put to death,
10as sorrowful yet always rejoicing, as poor yet making many rich, as having nothing yet possessing all things.
11Our mouth has spoken freely to you, O Corinthians, our heart is opened wide.
12You are not restrained by us, but you are restrained in your own affections.
13Now in a like exchange—I speak as to children—open wide *to us* also.
14Do not be bound together with unbelievers; for what partnership have righteousness and lawlessness, or what fellowship has light with darkness?
15Or what harmony has Christ with Belial, or what has a believer in common with an unbeliever?
16Or what agreement has the temple of God with idols? For we are the temple of the living God; just as God said,

"I WILL DWELL IN THEM AND WALK AMONG THEM;
AND I WILL BE THEIR GOD, AND THEY SHALL BE MY PEOPLE.

5 ἐν φυλακαῖς, ἐν ἀκαταστασίαις, ἐν κόποις,
in prisons, in commotions, in labours,
ἐν ἀγρυπνίαις, ἐν νηστείαις, **6** ἐν ἁγνότητι,
in watchings, in fastings, in purity,
ἐν γνώσει, ἐν μακροθυμίᾳ, ἐν χρηστότητι,
in knowledge, in long-suffering, in kindness,
ἐν πνεύματι ἁγίῳ, ἐν ἀγάπῃ ἀνυποκρίτῳ,
in spirit a holy, in love unfeigned,
7 ἐν λόγῳ ἀληθείας, ἐν δυνάμει θεοῦ·
in a word of truth, in power of God;
διὰ τῶν ὅπλων τῆς δικαιοσύνης τῶν
through the weapons – of righteousness of the
δεξιῶν καὶ ἀριστερῶν, **8** διὰ δόξης καὶ
right [hand] and of left, through glory and
ἀτιμίας, διὰ δυσφημίας καὶ εὐφημίας·
dishonour, through ill report and good report;
ὡς πλάνοι καὶ ἀληθεῖς, **9** ὡς ἀγνοούμενοι
as deceivers and* true men, as being unknown
καὶ ἐπιγινωσκόμενοι, ὡς ἀποθνῄσκοντες καὶ
and* being well known, as dying and
ἰδοὺ ζῶμεν, ὡς παιδευόμενοι καὶ μὴ
behold we live, as being chastened and not
θανατούμενοι, **10** ὡς λυπούμενοι ἀεὶ δὲ
being put to death, as being grieved [2]always [1]but
χαίροντες, ὡς πτωχοὶ πολλοὺς δὲ πλουτίζ-
rejoicing, as poor [3]many [1]but [2]en-
οντες, ὡς μηδὲν ἔχοντες καὶ πάντα
riching, as [2]nothing [1]having [3]and* [5]all things
κατέχοντες.
[4]possessing.

11 Τὸ στόμα ἡμῶν ἀνέῳγεν πρὸς ὑμᾶς,
The mouth of us has opened to you,
Κορίνθιοι, ἡ καρδία ἡμῶν πεπλάτυνται·
Corinthians, the heart of us has been enlarged;
12 οὐ στενοχωρεῖσθε ἐν ἡμῖν, στενοχωρεῖσθε
ye are not restrained in us, [2]ye are restrained
δὲ ἐν τοῖς σπλάγχνοις ὑμῶν· **13** τὴν δὲ
[1]but in the bowels of you; but [for] the
αὐτὴν ἀντιμισθίαν, ὡς τέκνοις λέγω,
same recompence, as to children I say,
πλατύνθητε καὶ ὑμεῖς.
be enlarged also ye.

14 Μὴ γίνεσθε ἑτεροζυγοῦντες ἀπίστοις·
Do not ye become unequally yoked [with] unbelievers;
τίς γὰρ μετοχὴ δικαιοσύνῃ καὶ ἀνομίᾳ,
for what share righteousness[c] and lawlessness,[c]
=have righteousness and lawlessness,
ἢ τίς κοινωνία φωτὶ πρὸς σκότος; **15** τίς
or what fellowship light[c] with darkness? what
=has light
δὲ συμφώνησις Χριστοῦ πρὸς Βελιάρ,
and agreement of Christ with Beliar,
ἢ τίς μερὶς πιστῷ μετὰ ἀπίστου; **16** τίς
or what part a believer[c] with an unbeliever? what
=has a believer
δὲ συγκατάθεσις ναῷ θεοῦ μετὰ εἰδώλων;
and union a shrine[c] of God with idols?
=has a shrine
ἡμεῖς γὰρ ναὸς θεοῦ ἐσμεν ζῶντος·
For [1]we [3]a shrine [5]God [2]are [4]of a living;
καθὼς εἶπεν ὁ θεὸς ὅτι ἐνοικήσω ἐν
as said – God[,] – I will dwell among
αὐτοῖς καὶ ἐμπεριπατήσω, καὶ ἔσομαι
them and *I* will walk among [them], and I will be
αὐτῶν θεός, καὶ αὐτοὶ ἔσονταί μου λαός.
of them God, and they shall be of me a people.

* Evidently = and yet, as in some other places; *cf.* John 20. 29.

tresses; 5in beatings, imprisonments and riots; in
hard work, sleepless nights
and hunger; 6in purity, understanding, patience and
kindness; in the Holy Spirit
and in sincere love; 7in
truthful speech and in the
power of God; with weap-
ons of righteousness in the
right hand and in the left;
8through glory and dishon-
or, bad report and good report; genuine, yet regarded
as impostors; 9known, yet
regarded as unknown; dy-
ing, and yet we live on;
beaten, and yet not killed;
10sorrowful, yet always rejoicing; poor, yet making
many rich; having nothing,
and yet possessing every-
thing.
11We have spoken freely
to you, Corinthians, and
opened wide our hearts to
you. 12We are not with-
holding our affection from
you, but you are withhold-
ing yours from us. 13As a
fair exchange—I speak as
to my children—open wide
your hearts also.

Do Not Be Yoked With Unbelievers

14Do not be yoked togeth-
er with unbelievers. For
what do righteousness and
wickedness have in com-
mon? Or what fellowship
can light have with dark-
ness? 15What harmony is
there between Christ and
Belial[h]? What does a believer have in common with
an unbeliever? 16What
agreement is there between
the temple of God and
idols? For we are the temple of the living God. As
God has said: "I will live
with them and walk among
them, and I will be their
God, and they will be my
people."[i]

[h]*15* Greek *Beliar*, a variant of *Belial*

[i]*16* Lev. 26:12; Jer. 32:38; Ezek. 37:27

17 "Therefore, COME OUT
FROM THEIR MIDST AND
BE SEPARATE," says
the Lord.
"AND DO NOT TOUCH
WHAT IS UNCLEAN;
And I will welcome
you.
18 "And I will be a father
to you,
And you shall be sons
and daughters to
Me,"
Says the Lord Almighty.

Chapter 7

Paul Reveals His Heart

THEREFORE, having
these promises, beloved,
let us cleanse ourselves
from all defilement
of flesh and spirit, perfecting
holiness in the fear of
God.
2 Make room for us *in
your hearts;* we wronged
no one, we corrupted no
one, we took advantage of
no one.
3 I do not speak to condemn
you; for I have said
before that you are in our
hearts to die together and
to live together.
4 Great is my confidence
in you, great is my boasting
on your behalf; I am filled
with comfort. I am overflowing
with joy in all our
affliction.
5 For even when we came
into Macedonia our flesh
had no rest, but we were
afflicted on every side: conflicts
without, fears within.
6 But God, who comforts
the depressed, comforted
us by the coming of Titus;
7 and not only by his
coming, but also by the
comfort with which he was
comforted in you, as he reported
to us your longing,
your mourning, your zeal
for me; so that I rejoiced
even more.
8 For though I caused
you sorrow by my letter, I
do not regret it; though I did
regret it—*for* I see that that

17 διὸ ἐξέλθατε ἐκ μέσου αὐτῶν καὶ
Wherefore come ye out from [the] midst of them and
ἀφορίσθητε, λέγει κύριος, καὶ ἀκαθάρτου
be ye separated, says [the] Lord, and an unclean thing
μὴ ἅπτεσθε· **18** κἀγὼ εἰσδέξομαι ὑμᾶς, καὶ
do not touch; and I will welcome in you, and
ἔσομαι ὑμῖν εἰς πατέρα, καὶ ὑμεῖς ἔσεσθέ
I will be to you *for* a father, and ye shall be
μοι εἰς υἱοὺς καὶ θυγατέρας, λέγει κύριος
to me *for* sons and daughters, says [the] Lord
παντοκράτωρ. **7** ταύτας οὖν ἔχοντες τὰς ἐπ-
[the] Almighty. [3]These [2]therefore [1]having – [4]pro-
αγγελίας, ἀγαπητοί, καθαρίσωμεν ἑαυτοὺς ἀπὸ
mises, beloved, let us cleanse ourselves from
παντὸς μολυσμοῦ σαρκὸς καὶ πνεύματος,
all pollution of flesh and of spirit,
ἐπιτελοῦντες ἁγιωσύνην ἐν φόβῳ θεοῦ.
perfecting holiness in [the] fear of God.
2 Χωρήσατε ἡμᾶς· οὐδένα ἠδικήσαμεν,
Make room for us; no one we wronged,
οὐδένα ἐφθείραμεν, οὐδένα ἐπλεονεκτήσαμεν.
no one we injured, no one we defrauded.
3 πρὸς κατάκρισιν οὐ λέγω· προείρηκα
For condemnation I say not; [2]I have previously said
γὰρ ὅτι ἐν ταῖς καρδίαις ἡμῶν ἐστε
[1]for that in the hearts of us ye are
εἰς τὸ συναποθανεῖν καὶ συζῆν. **4** πολλή
***for* – to die with [you] and to live with [you]. Much**
μοι παρρησία πρὸς ὑμᾶς, πολλή μοι
to me[c] boldness toward you, much to me[c]
=I have much =I have much
καύχησις ὑπὲρ ὑμῶν· πεπλήρωμαι τῇ
boasting on behalf of you; I have been filled –
παρακλήσει, ὑπερπερισσεύομαι τῇ χαρᾷ ἐπὶ
with comfort, I overflow – with joy on(in)
πάσῃ τῇ θλίψει ἡμῶν. **5** Καὶ γὰρ
all the affliction of us. For indeed
ἐλθόντων ἡμῶν εἰς Μακεδονίαν οὐδεμίαν
coming us[a] into Macedonia [5]no
=when we came
ἔσχηκεν ἄνεσιν ἡ σὰρξ ἡμῶν, ἀλλ' ἐν
[4]*has* had [6]rest [1]the [2]flesh [3]of us, but in
παντὶ θλιβόμενοι· ἔξωθεν μάχαι, ἔσωθεν
every way being afflicted; without [were] fightings, within
φόβοι. **6** ἀλλ' ὁ παρακαλῶν τοὺς ταπεινοὺς
[were] fears. But [2]the [one] [3]comforting [4]the [5]humble
παρεκάλεσεν ἡμᾶς ὁ θεὸς ἐν τῇ παρουσίᾳ
[6]comforted [7]us – [1]God by the presence
Τίτου· **7** οὐ μόνον δὲ ἐν τῇ παρουσίᾳ
of Titus; and not only by the presence
αὐτοῦ, ἀλλὰ καὶ ἐν τῇ παρακλήσει ᾗ
of him, but also by the comfort with which
παρεκλήθη ἐφ' ὑμῖν, ἀναγγέλλων ἡμῖν
he was comforted over you, reporting to us
τὴν ὑμῶν ἐπιπόθησιν, τὸν ὑμῶν ὀδυρμόν,
[1]the [3]of you [2]eager longing, [1]the [3]of you [2]mourning,
τὸν ὑμῶν ζῆλον ὑπὲρ ἐμοῦ, ὥστε με
[1]the [3]of you [2]zeal on behalf of me, so as me
μᾶλλον χαρῆναι. **8** Ὅτι εἰ καὶ ἐλύπησα
more to rejoice.[b] Because if indeed I grieved
=so that I rejoiced more.
ὑμᾶς ἐν τῇ ἐπιστολῇ, οὐ μεταμέλομαι·
you by the epistle, I do not regret;
εἰ καὶ μετεμελόμην, βλέπω ὅτι ἡ ἐπιστολὴ
if indeed I regretted, I see that – epistle

17 "Therefore come out
from them
and be separate,
says the Lord.
Touch no unclean thing,
and I will receive
you."[j]
18 "I will be a Father to
you,
and you will be my
sons and daughters,
says the Lord
Almighty."[k]

Chapter 7

SINCE we have these
promises, dear friends,
let us purify ourselves from
everything that contaminates
body and spirit, perfecting
holiness out of reverence
for God.

Paul's Joy

2 Make room for us in
your hearts. We have
wronged no one, we have
corrupted no one, we have
exploited no one. 3 I do not
say this to condemn you; I
have said before that you
have such a place in our
hearts that we would live or
die with you. 4 I have great
confidence in you; I take
great pride in you. I am
greatly encouraged; in all
our troubles my joy knows
no bounds.
5 For when we came into
Macedonia, this body of
ours had no rest, but we
were harassed at every turn
—conflicts on the outside,
fears within. 6 But God,
who comforts the downcast,
comforted us by the
coming of Titus, 7 and not
only by his coming but also
by the comfort you had given
him. He told us about
your longing for me, your
deep sorrow, your ardent
concern for me, so that my
joy was greater than ever.
8 Even if I caused you sorrow
by my letter, I do not
regret it. Though I did re-

[j] 17 Isaiah 52:11; Ezek. 20:34,41
[k] 18 2 Samuel 7:14; 7:8

letter caused you sorrow,
though only for a while—
9I now rejoice, not that
you were made sorrowful,
but that you were made
sorrowful to *the point of* repentance; for you were
made sorrowful according
to *the will of* God, in order
that you might not suffer
loss in anything through us.
10For the sorrow that is
according to *the will of* God
produces a repentance
without regret, *leading* to
salvation; but the sorrow of
the world produces death.
11For behold what ear-
nestness this very thing,
this godly sorrow, has produced in you: what vindication of yourselves, what indignation, what fear, what
longing, what zeal, what
avenging of wrong! In
everything you demon-
strated yourselves to be innocent in the matter.
12So although I wrote to
you *it was* not for the sake
of the offender, nor for the
sake of the one offended,
but that your earnestness
on our behalf might be
made known to you in the
sight of God.
13For this reason we have
been comforted.
And besides our comfort,
we rejoiced even much
more for the joy of Titus,
because his spirit has been
refreshed by you all.
14For if in anything I have
boasted to him about you, I
was not put to shame; but
as we spoke all things to
you in truth, so also our
boasting before Titus
proved to be *the* truth.
15And his affection
abounds all the more
toward you, as he remem-
bers the obedience of you
all, how you received him
with fear and trembling.
16I rejoice that in everything I have confidence in
you.

ἐκείνη εἰ καὶ πρὸς ὥραν ἐλύπησεν ὑμᾶς,
that if indeed for an hour it grieved you,
9 νῦν χαίρω, οὐχ ὅτι ἐλυπήθητε, ἀλλ'
now I rejoice, not that ye were grieved, but
ὅτι ἐλυπήθητε εἰς μετάνοιαν· ἐλυπήθητε
that ye were grieved to repentance; [2]ye were grieved
γὰρ κατὰ θεόν, ἵνα ἐν μηδενὶ ζημιωθῆτε
[1]for according to God, in order that in nothing ye might suffer loss
ἐξ ἡμῶν. 10 ἡ γὰρ κατὰ θεὸν λύπη
by us. For [1]the [3]according to [4]God [2]grief
μετάνοιαν εἰς σωτηρίαν ἀμεταμέλητον
[7]repentance [8]to [9]salvation [6]unregrettable
ἐργάζεται· ἡ δὲ τοῦ κόσμου λύπη θάνατον
[5]works; but [1]the [3]of the [4]world [2]grief [6]death
κατεργάζεται. 11 ἰδοὺ γὰρ αὐτὸ τοῦτο
[5]works out. For behold this very thing[,]
τὸ κατὰ θεὸν λυπηθῆναι πόσην κατειργά-
– [2]according to [3]God [1]to be grieved[,] [1]what [3]it worked
σατο ὑμῖν σπουδήν, ἀλλὰ ἀπολογίαν, ἀλλὰ
out [4]in you [2]earnestness, but [what] defence, but
ἀγανάκτησιν, ἀλλὰ φόβον, ἀλλὰ ἐπιπόθησιν,
vexation, but fear, but eager desire,
ἀλλὰ ζῆλον, ἀλλὰ ἐκδίκησιν. ἐν παντὶ
but zeal, but vengeance. In everything
συνεστήσατε ἑαυτοὺς ἁγνοὺς εἶναι τῷ
ye commended yourselves pure to be in the
πράγματι. 12 ἄρα εἰ καὶ ἔγραψα ὑμῖν,
affair. Then if indeed I wrote to you,
οὐχ ἕνεκεν τοῦ ἀδικήσαντος οὐδὲ ἕνεκεν
not for the sake of the [one] having done wrong nor for the sake of
τοῦ ἀδικηθέντος, ἀλλ' ἕνεκεν τοῦ φανερω-
the [one] having been wronged, but for the sake of – to be mani-
θῆναι τὴν σπουδὴν ὑμῶν τὴν ὑπὲρ ἡμῶν
fested the earnestness[bd] of you – on behalf of us
πρὸς ὑμᾶς ἐνώπιον τοῦ θεοῦ. 13 διὰ
toward you before – God. There-
τοῦτο παρακεκλήμεθα. Ἐπὶ δὲ τῇ
fore we have been comforted. But as to the
παρακλήσει ἡμῶν περισσοτέρως μᾶλλον
comfort of us abundantly more
ἐχάρημεν ἐπὶ τῇ χαρᾷ Τίτου, ὅτι ἀναπέ-
we rejoiced over the joy of Titus, because has been
παυται τὸ πνεῦμα αὐτοῦ ἀπὸ πάντων
rested the spirit of him from(by) all
ὑμῶν· 14 ὅτι εἴ τι αὐτῷ ὑπὲρ ὑμῶν
you; because if [2]anything [3]to him [4]on behalf of [5]you
κεκαύχημαι, οὐ κατῃσχύνθην, ἀλλ' ὡς
[1]I have boasted, I was not shamed, but as
πάντα ἐν ἀληθείᾳ ἐλαλήσαμεν ὑμῖν, οὕτως
[2]all things [3]in [4]truth [1]we spoke [5]to you, so
καὶ ἡ καύχησις ἡμῶν ἐπὶ Τίτου ἀλήθεια
also the boasting of us over Titus [2]truth
ἐγενήθη. 15 καὶ τὰ σπλάγχνα αὐτοῦ
[1]became. And the bowels of him
περισσοτέρως εἰς ὑμᾶς ἐστιν ἀναμιμνῃσκομέ-
[2]abundantly [3]toward [4]you [1]is(are) [he] remember-
νου τὴν πάντων ὑμῶν ὑπακοήν, ὡς μετὰ
ing[a] [1]the [3]of all [4]you [2]obedience, as with
φόβου καὶ τρόμου ἐδέξασθε αὐτόν.
fear and trembling ye received him.
16 χαίρω ὅτι ἐν παντὶ θαρρῶ ἐν ὑμῖν.
I rejoice that in everything I am confident in you.

gret it—I see that my letter
hurt you, but only for a little while— 9yet now I am
happy, not because you
were made sorry, but be-
cause your sorrow led you
to repentance. For you became sorrowful as God in-
tended and so were not
harmed in any way by us.
10Godly sorrow brings re-
pentance that leads to salvation and leaves no regret,
but worldly sorrow brings
death. 11See what this godly sorrow has produced in
you: what earnestness,
what eagerness to clear
yourselves, what indigna-
tion, what alarm, what
longing, what concern,
what readiness to see justice done. At every point
you have proved your-
selves to be innocent in this
matter. 12So even though I
wrote to you, it was not on
account of the one who did
the wrong or of the injured
party, but rather that before God you could see for
yourselves how devoted to
us you are. 13By all this we
are encouraged.
In addition to our own encouragement, we were es-
pecially delighted to see
how happy Titus was, be-
cause his spirit has been refreshed by all of you. 14I
had boasted to him about
you, and you have not em-
barrassed me. But just as
everything we said to you
was true, so our boasting
about you to Titus has
proved to be true as well.
15And his affection for you
is all the greater when he
remembers that you were
all obedient, receiving him
with fear and trembling. 16I
am glad I can have com-
plete confidence in you.

Chapter 8

Great Generosity

NOW, brethren, we
wish to make known
to you the grace of God
which has been given in the
churches of Macedonia,
2that in a great ordeal of
affliction their abundance
of joy and their deep poverty overflowed in the
wealth of their liberality.
3For I testify that ac-
cording to their ability, and
beyond their ability *they*
gave of their own accord,
4begging us with much
entreaty for the favor of
participation in the support
of the saints,
5and *this,* not as we had
expected, but they first
gave themselves to the
Lord and to us by the will
of God.
6Consequently we urged
Titus that as he had previously made a beginning, so
he would also complete in
you this gracious work as
well.
7But just as you abound
in everything, in faith and
utterance and knowledge
and in all earnestness and
in the [b]love we inspired in
you, *see* that you abound in
this gracious work also.
8I am not speaking *this*
as a command, but as proving through the earnestness
of others the sincerity of
your love also.
9For you know the grace
of our Lord Jesus Christ,
that though He was rich,
yet for your sake He
became poor, that you
through His poverty might
become rich.
10And I give *my* opinion
in this matter, for this is to
your advantage, who were
the first to begin a year ago
not only to do *this,* but also
to desire *to do it.*
11But now finish doing it

[b] Lit., *love from us in you;* some ancient mss. read *your love for us*

8 Γνωρίζομεν δὲ ὑμῖν, ἀδελφοί, τὴν
Now we make known to you, brothers, the
χάριν τοῦ θεοῦ τὴν δεδομένην ἐν ταῖς
grace – of God – *having been* given among the
ἐκκλησίαις τῆς Μακεδονίας, 2 ὅτι ἐν πολλῇ
churches – of Macedonia, that in much
δοκιμῇ θλίψεως ἡ περισσεία τῆς χαρᾶς
proving of affliction the abundance of the joy
αὐτῶν καὶ ἡ κατὰ βάθους πτωχεία
of them and [1]the [3]according to [4]depth [2]poverty
=their extreme poverty
αὐτῶν ἐπερίσσευσεν εἰς τὸ πλοῦτος τῆς
of them abounded to the riches of the
ἁπλότητος αὐτῶν· 3 ὅτι κατὰ δύναμιν,
liberality of them; that according to [their] power,
μαρτυρῶ, καὶ παρὰ δύναμιν, αὐθαίρετοι
I witness, and beyond [their] power, of their own accord
4 μετὰ πολλῆς παρακλήσεως δεόμενοι ἡμῶν
with much beseeching requesting of us
τὴν χάριν καὶ τὴν κοινωνίαν τῆς διακονίας
the grace and the fellowship of the ministry
τῆς εἰς τοὺς ἁγίους, 5 καὶ οὐ καθὼς
– to the saints, and not as
ἠλπίσαμεν, ἀλλὰ ἑαυτοὺς ἔδωκαν πρῶτον
we hoped, but themselves gave first*ly*
τῷ κυρίῳ καὶ ἡμῖν διὰ θελήματος θεοῦ,
to the Lord and to us through [the] will of God,
6 εἰς τὸ παρακαλέσαι ἡμᾶς Τίτον, ἵνα
for – to beseech us[b] Titus, in order that
=that we should beseech
καθὼς προενήρξατο οὕτως καὶ ἐπιτελέσῃ
as previously he began so also he should complete
εἰς ὑμᾶς καὶ τὴν χάριν ταύτην. 7 ἀλλ'
in you also this grace. But
ὥσπερ ἐν παντὶ περισσεύετε, πίστει καὶ
as in everything ye abound, in faith and
λόγῳ καὶ γνώσει καὶ πάσῃ σπουδῇ
in word and in knowledge and in all diligence
καὶ τῇ ἐξ ἡμῶν ἐν ὑμῖν ἀγάπῃ, ἵνα
and – [2]from [3]us [4]in(to) [5]you [1]in love, [see] that
καὶ ἐν ταύτῃ τῇ χάριτι περισσεύητε.
[5]also [2]in [3]this – [4]grace [1]ye may abound.
8 Οὐ κατ' ἐπιταγὴν λέγω, ἀλλὰ διὰ
[2]Not [3]by way of [4]command [1]I say,* but through
τῆς ἑτέρων σπουδῆς καὶ τὸ τῆς ὑμετέρας
[1]the [3]of others [2]diligence also [2]the – [4]of your
ἀγάπης γνήσιον δοκιμάζων· 9 γινώσκετε
[5]love [3]reality [1]proving; [2]ye know
γὰρ τὴν χάριν τοῦ κυρίου ἡμῶν Ἰησοῦ
[1]for the grace of the Lord of us Jesus
[Χριστοῦ], ὅτι δι' ὑμᾶς ἐπτώχευσεν
Christ, that on account of you [3]he impoverished [himself]
πλούσιος ὤν, ἵνα ὑμεῖς τῇ ἐκείνου πτωχείᾳ
[2]rich [1]being, in order that ye [1]by [3]of that one [2]poverty
πλουτήσητε. 10 καὶ γνώμην ἐν τούτῳ
might become rich. And [3]an opinion [1]in [2]this
δίδωμι· τοῦτο γὰρ ὑμῖν συμφέρει, οἵτινες
[3]I give: for this [2]for you [1]is expedient, who
οὐ μόνον τὸ ποιῆσαι ἀλλὰ καὶ τὸ θέλειν
not only the to do but also the to will
προενήρξασθε ἀπὸ πέρυσι· 11 νυνὶ δὲ καὶ
previously *ye* began from last year; but now also
=a year ago;

* That is, Paul is not issuing a command. *Cf.* I. Cor. 7. 6.

Chapter 8

Generosity Encouraged

AND now, brothers, we
want you to know
about the grace that God
has given the Macedonian
churches. 2Out of the most
severe trial, their overflowing joy and their extreme
poverty welled up in rich
generosity. 3For I testify
that they gave as much as
they were able, and even
beyond their ability. En-
tirely on their own, 4they
urgently pleaded with us
for the privilege of sharing
in this service to the saints.
5And they did not do as we
expected, but they gave
themselves first to the Lord
and then to us in keeping
with God's will. 6So we
urged Titus, since he had
earlier made a beginning, to
bring also to completion
this act of grace on your
part. 7But just as you excel
in everything—in faith, in
speech, in knowledge, in
complete earnestness and
in your love for us[l] —see
that you also excel in this
grace of giving.
8I am not commanding
you, but I want to test the
sincerity of your love by
comparing it with the earnestness of others. 9For
you know the grace of our
Lord Jesus Christ, that
though he was rich, yet for
your sakes he became
poor, so that you through
his poverty might become
rich.
10And here is my advice
about what is best for you
in this matter: Last year
you were the first not only
to give but also to have the
desire to do so. 11Now fin-

[l]7 Some manuscripts *in our love for you*

also; that just as *there was* the readiness to desire it, so *there may be* also the completion of it by your ability.

12For if the readiness is present, it is acceptable according to what *a man* has, not according to what he does not have.

13For *this* is not for the ease of others *and* for your affliction, but by way of equality—

14at this present time your abundance *being a supply* for their want, that their abundance also may become *a supply* for your want, that there may be equality;

15as it is written, "HE WHO *gathered* MUCH DID NOT HAVE TOO MUCH, AND HE WHO *gathered* LITTLE HAD NO LACK."

16But thanks be to God, who puts the same earnestness on your behalf in the heart of Titus.

17For he not only accepted our appeal, but being himself very earnest, he has gone to you of his own accord.

18And we have sent along with him the brother whose fame in *the things of* the gospel *has spread* through all the churches;

19and not only *this*, but he has also been appointed by the churches to travel with us in this gracious work, which is being administered by us for the glory of the Lord Himself, and *to show* our readiness,

20taking precaution that no one should discredit us in our administration of this generous gift;

21for we have regard for what is honorable, not only in the sight of the Lord, but also in the sight of men.

22And we have sent with

τὸ ποιῆσαι ἐπιτελέσατε, ὅπως καθάπερ ἡ
3the 4to do 1complete ye, so as as the
προθυμία τοῦ θέλειν, οὕτως καὶ τὸ
eagerness of the to will, so also the
ἐπιτελέσαι ἐκ τοῦ ἔχειν. 12 εἰ γὰρ ἡ
to complete out of the to have. For if the
=what ye have.
προθυμία πρόκειται, καθὸ ἐὰν ἔχῃ
eagerness is already there, according to whatever one has
εὐπρόσδεκτος, οὐ καθὸ οὐκ ἔχει. 13 οὐ
it is acceptable, not according to [what] one has not. not
γὰρ ἵνα ἄλλοις ἄνεσις, ὑμῖν θλῖψις,
For in order that to others [there may be] relief, to you distress,
ἀλλ' ἐξ ἰσότητος 14 ἐν τῷ νῦν καιρῷ
but by equality at the present time
τὸ ὑμῶν περίσσευμα εἰς τὸ ἐκείνων
the 2of you 1abundance [may be] for the 2of those
ὑστέρημα, ἵνα καὶ τὸ ἐκείνων περίσσευμα
1lack, in order that also the 2of those 1abundance
γένηται εἰς τὸ ὑμῶν ὑστέρημα, ὅπως
may be for the 2of you 1lack, so as
γένηται ἰσότης, 15 καθὼς γέγραπται· ὁ
there may be equality, as it has been written: He
τὸ πολὺ οὐκ ἐπλεόνασεν, καὶ ὁ τὸ
the much did not abound, and he the
ὀλίγον οὐκ ἠλαττόνησεν. 16 Χάρις δὲ
little had not less. But thanks [be]
τῷ θεῷ τῷ διδόντι τὴν αὐτὴν σπουδὴν
– to God – giving the same diligence
ὑπὲρ ὑμῶν ἐν τῇ καρδίᾳ Τίτου, 17 ὅτι
on behalf of you in the heart of Titus, because
τὴν μὲν παράκλησιν ἐδέξατο, σπουδαιότερος
3the 1indeed 4beseeching 2he received, 3more diligent
δὲ ὑπάρχων αὐθαίρετος ἐξῆλθεν πρὸς ὑμᾶς.
1and 2being of his own accord he went forth to you.
18 συνεπέμψαμεν δὲ μετ' αὐτοῦ τὸν
And we sent *with* with him the
ἀδελφὸν οὗ ὁ ἔπαινος ἐν τῷ εὐαγγελίῳ
brother of whom the praise in the gospel
διὰ πασῶν τῶν ἐκκλησιῶν, 19 οὐ μόνον δὲ
[is] through[out] all the churches, and not only [this]
ἀλλὰ καὶ χειροτονηθεὶς ὑπὸ τῶν ἐκκλησιῶν
but also 3having been elected 4by 5the 6churches
συνέκδημος ἡμῶν ἐν τῇ χάριτι ταύτῃ
1a travelling companion 2of us in this grace
τῇ διακονουμένῃ ὑφ' ἡμῶν πρὸς τὴν
– being ministered by us to 1the
αὐτοῦ τοῦ κυρίου δόξαν καὶ προθυμίαν
5[him]self 3of the 4Lord 2glory and eagerness
ἡμῶν, 20 στελλόμενοι τοῦτο, μή τις ἡμᾶς
of us, avoiding this, lest anyone 2us
μωμήσηται ἐν τῇ ἁδρότητι ταύτῃ τῇ
1should blame in this bounty –
διακονουμένῃ ὑφ' ἡμῶν· 21 προνοοῦμεν γὰρ
being ministered by us; for we provide
καλὰ οὐ μόνον ἐνώπιον κυρίου ἀλλὰ καὶ
good things not only before [the] Lord but also
ἐνώπιον ἀνθρώπων. 22 συνεπέμψαμεν δὲ
before men. And we sent with

ish the work, so that your
eager willingness to do it
may be matched by your
completion of it, according
to your means. 12For if the
willingness is there, the gift
is acceptable according to
what one has, not accord-
ing to what he does not
have.
13Our desire is not that
others might be relieved
while you are hard pressed,
but that there might be
equality. 14At the present
time your plenty will supply what they need, so that
in turn their plenty will supply what you need. Then
there will be equality, 15as
it is written: "He who gathered much did not have too
much, and he who gathered
little did not have too little."[m]

Titus Sent to Corinth

16I thank God, who put
into the heart of Titus the
same concern I have for
you. 17For Titus not only
welcomed our appeal, but
he is coming to you with
much enthusiasm and on
his own initiative. 18And
we are sending along with
him the brother who is
praised by all the churches
for his service to the gospel. 19What is more, he was
chosen by the churches to
accompany us as we carry
the offering, which we administer in order to honor
the Lord himself and to
show our eagerness to
help. 20We want to avoid
any criticism of the way we
administer this liberal gift.
21For we are taking pains to
do what is right, not only in
the eyes of the Lord but
also in the eyes of men.
22In addition, we are

[m]*15* Exodus 16:18

them our brother, whom we have often tested and found diligent in many things, but now even more diligent, because of *his* great confidence in you.

23As for Titus, *he is* my partner and fellow worker among you; as for our brethren, *they are* messengers of the churches, a glory to Christ.

24Therefore openly before the churches show them the proof of your love and of our reason for boasting about you.

Chapter 9

God Gives Most

FOR it is superfluous for me to write to you about this ministry to the saints;

2for I know your readiness, of which I boast about you to the Macedonians, *namely,* that Achaia has been prepared since last year, and your zeal has stirred up most of them.

3But I have sent the brethren, that our boasting about you may not be made empty in this case, that, as I was saying, you may be prepared;

4lest if any Macedonians come with me and find you unprepared, we (not to speak of you) should be put to shame by this confidence.

5So I thought it necessary to urge the brethren that they would go on ahead to you and arrange beforehand your previously promised bountiful gift, that the same might be ready as a bountiful gift, and not affected by covetousness.

6Now this *I say,* he who sows sparingly shall also

αὐτοῖς τὸν ἀδελφὸν ἡμῶν, ὃν ἐδοκιμάσαμεν
them the brother of us, whom [1]we proved
ἐν πολλοῖς πολλάκις σπουδαῖον ὄντα, νυνὶ
[5]in [6]many things [4]many times [3]diligent [2]being, [2]now
δὲ πολὺ σπουδαιότερον πεποιθήσει πολλῇ
[1]and much more diligent [1]in [3]confidence [2]much
τῇ εἰς ὑμᾶς. 23 εἴτε ὑπὲρ Τίτου, κοινωνὸς
– toward you. Whether as to Titus, [2]partner
ἐμὸς καὶ εἰς ὑμᾶς συνεργός· εἴτε ἀδελφοὶ
[1]my [3]and [5]for [6]you [4]fellow-worker; or brothers
ἡμῶν, ἀπόστολοι ἐκκλησιῶν, δόξα Χριστοῦ.
of us, apostles of churches, [the] glory of Christ.
24 τὴν οὖν ἔνδειξιν τῆς ἀγάπης ὑμῶν
[7]The [1]therefore [8]demonstration [9]of the [10]love [11]of you
καὶ ἡμῶν καυχήσεως ὑπὲρ ὑμῶν εἰς
[12]and [14]of us [13]boasting [15]on behalf of [16]you [17]to
αὐτοὺς ἐνδεικνύμενοι εἰς πρόσωπον τῶν
[18]them [2]showing forth [3]in [4][the] presence [5]of the
ἐκκλησιῶν.
[6]churches.

9 Περὶ μὲν γὰρ τῆς διακονίας τῆς
[3]Concerning [2]indeed [1]for the ministry –
εἰς τοὺς ἁγίους περισσόν μοί ἐστιν τὸ
to the saints [2]superfluous [3]for me [1]it is –
γράφειν ὑμῖν· 2 οἶδα γὰρ τὴν προθυμίαν
to write to you; for I know the eagerness
ὑμῶν ἣν ὑπὲρ ὑμῶν καυχῶμαι Μακε-
of you which on behalf of you I boast to Mace-
δόσιν ὅτι Ἀχαΐα παρεσκεύασται ἀπὸ
donians that Achaia has made preparations from
πέρυσι, καὶ τὸ ὑμῶν ζῆλος ἠρέθισεν
last year, =a year ago, and the [2]of you [1]zeal stirred up
τοὺς πλείονας. 3 ἔπεμψα δὲ τοὺς ἀδελφούς,
the greater number. And I sent the brothers,
ἵνα μὴ τὸ καύχημα ἡμῶν τὸ ὑπὲρ
lest the boast of us – on behalf
ὑμῶν κενωθῇ ἐν τῷ μέρει τούτῳ, ἵνα
of you should be emptied in this respect, in order that
καθὼς ἔλεγον παρεσκευασμένοι ἦτε, 4 μή
as I said *having been* prepared ye were,
πως ἐὰν ἔλθωσιν σὺν ἐμοὶ Μακεδόνες
lest if [2]come [3]with [4]me [1]Macedonians
καὶ εὕρωσιν ὑμᾶς ἀπαρασκευάστους
and find you unprepared
καταισχυνθῶμεν ἡμεῖς, ἵνα μὴ λέγωμεν
[2]should be shamed [1]we, *in order that* we say not
ὑμεῖς, ἐν τῇ ὑποστάσει ταύτῃ. 5 ἀναγκαῖον
ye, in this confidence. [2]Necessary
οὖν ἡγησάμην παρακαλέσαι τοὺς ἀδελφοὺς
[3]therefore [1]I thought [it] to beseech the brothers
ἵνα προέλθωσιν εἰς ὑμᾶς καὶ προκαταρτί-
in order that they go forward to you and arrange before-
σωσιν τὴν προεπηγγελμένην εὐλογίαν ὑμῶν,
hand [1]the [4]having been promised [2]blessing [3]of you,
ταύτην ἑτοίμην εἶναι οὕτως ὡς εὐλογίαν
this ready to be thus as a blessing
καὶ μὴ ὡς πλεονεξίαν. 6 Τοῦτο δέ,
and not as greediness. And this,
ὁ σπείρων φειδομένως φειδομένως καὶ
the [one] sowing sparingly [2]sparingly [1]also

sending with them our brother who has often proved to us in many ways that he is zealous, and now even more so because of his great confidence in you.
23As for Titus, he is my partner and fellow worker among you; as for our brothers, they are representatives of the churches and an honor to Christ.
24Therefore show these men the proof of your love and the reason for our pride in you, so that the churches can see it.

Chapter 9

THERE is no need for me to write to you about this service to the
saints. 2For I know your
eagerness to help, and I have been boasting about it to the Macedonians, telling them that since last year you in Achaia were ready to give; and your enthusiasm has stirred most of
them to action. 3But I am
sending the brothers in order that our boasting about you in this matter should not prove hollow, but that you may be ready, as I said
you would be. 4For if any
Macedonians come with me and find you unprepared, we—not to say anything about you—would be ashamed of having been so
confident. 5So I thought it
necessary to urge the brothers to visit you in advance and finish the arrangements for the generous gift you had promised. Then it will be ready as a generous gift, not as one grudgingly given.

Sowing Generously

6Remember this: Whoever sows sparingly will also

reap sparingly; and he who
sows bountifully shall also
reap bountifully.
7Let each one *do* just as
he has purposed in his
heart; not grudgingly or under compulsion; for God
loves a cheerful giver.
8And God is able to
make all grace abound to
you, that always having all
sufficiency in everything,
you may have an abun-
dance for every good deed;
9as it is written,
"HE SCATTERED ABROAD, HE GAVE TO THE POOR,
HIS RIGHTEOUSNESS ABIDES FOREVER."
10Now He who supplies
seed to the sower and bread
for food, will supply and
multiply your seed for sowing and increase the har-
vest of your righteousness;
11you will be enriched in
everything for all liberality,
which through us is pro-
ducing thanksgiving to
God.
12For the ministry of this
service is not only fully
supplying the needs of the
saints, but is also overflowing through many thanks-
givings to God.
13Because of the proof
given by this ministry they
will glorify God for *your*
obedience to your confes-
sion of the gospel of Christ,
and for the liberality of
your contribution to them
and to all,
14while they also, by
prayer on your behalf,
yearn for you because of
the surpassing grace of God
in you.
15Thanks be to God for
His indescribable gift!

θερίσει, καὶ ὁ σπείρων ἐπ' εὐλογίαις ἐπ'
[1]will reap, and the [one] sowing on(for) blessings [3]on(for)
εὐλογίαις καὶ θερίσει. **7** ἕκαστος καθὼς
[4]blessings [2]also [1]will reap. Each one as
προῄρηται τῇ καρδίᾳ, μὴ ἐκ λύπης ἢ
he chose in the(his) heart, not of grief or
ἐξ ἀνάγκης· ἱλαρὸν γὰρ δότην ἀγαπᾷ ὁ
of necessity; for [3]a cheerful [4]giver [2]loves –
θεός. **8** δυνατεῖ δὲ ὁ θεὸς πᾶσαν χάριν
[1]God. And [2]is able – [1]God [4]all [5]grace
περισσεῦσαι εἰς ὑμᾶς, ἵνα ἐν παντὶ
[3]to cause to abound toward you, in order that [5]in [6]everything
πάντοτε πᾶσαν αὐτάρκειαν ἔχοντες περισ-
[1]always [3]all [4]self-sufficiency [2]having ye may
σεύητε εἰς πᾶν ἔργον ἀγαθόν, **9** καθὼς
abound to every work good, as
γέγραπται· ἐσκόρπισεν, ἔδωκεν τοῖς πένησιν,
it has been written: He scattered, he gave to the poor,
ἡ δικαιοσύνη αὐτοῦ μένει εἰς τὸν αἰῶνα.
the righteousness of him remains unto the age.
10 ὁ δὲ ἐπιχορηγῶν σπέρμα τῷ σπείροντι
Now the [one] providing seed for the [one] sowing
καὶ ἄρτον εἰς βρῶσιν χορηγήσει καὶ
[1]both [2]bread [4]for [5]food [3]will supply and
πληθυνεῖ τὸν σπόρον ὑμῶν καὶ αὐξήσει
will multiply the seed of you and will increase
τὰ γενήματα τῆς δικαιοσύνης ὑμῶν· **11** ἐν
the fruits of the righteousness of you; in
παντὶ πλουτιζόμενοι εἰς πᾶσαν ἁπλότητα,
everything being enriched to all liberality,
ἥτις κατεργάζεται δι' ἡμῶν εὐχαριστίαν
which works out through us thanksgiving
τῷ θεῷ· **12** ὅτι ἡ διακονία τῆς λειτουργίας
– to God; because the ministry – service
ταύτης οὐ μόνον ἐστὶν προσαναπληροῦσα
of this not only is making up
τὰ ὑστερήματα τῶν ἁγίων, ἀλλὰ καὶ
the things lacking of the saints, but [is] also
περισσεύουσα διὰ πολλῶν εὐχαριστιῶν τῷ
abounding through many thanksgivings –
θεῷ· **13** διὰ τῆς δοκιμῆς τῆς διακονίας
to God; through the proof – ministry
ταύτης δοξάζοντες τὸν θεὸν ἐπὶ τῇ
of this glorifying – God on the
ὑποταγῇ τῆς ὁμολογίας ὑμῶν εἰς τὸ
submission of the confession of you to the
εὐαγγέλιον τοῦ Χριστοῦ καὶ ἁπλότητι
gospel – of Christ and [on the] liberality
τῆς κοινωνίας εἰς αὐτοὺς καὶ εἰς πάντας,
of the fellowship toward them and toward all men,
14 καὶ αὐτῶν δεήσει ὑπὲρ ὑμῶν ἐπιποθούν-
and [1]them [4]with request [5]on behalf of [6]you [2]longing
των ὑμᾶς διὰ τὴν ὑπερβάλλουσαν χάριν
after[a] [3]you on account of the excelling grace
τοῦ θεοῦ ἐφ' ὑμῖν. **15** Χάρις τῷ θεῷ
– of God upon you. Thanks – to God
ἐπὶ τῇ ἀνεκδιηγήτῳ αὐτοῦ δωρεᾷ.
for the indescribable of him gift.

reap sparingly, and whoever sows generously will
also reap generously.
7Each man should give
what he has decided in his
heart to give, not reluctant-
ly or under compulsion, for
God loves a cheerful giver.
8And God is able to make
all grace abound to you, so
that in all things at all times,
having all that you need,
you will abound in every
good work. 9As it is written:

"He has scattered
abroad his gifts to
the poor;
his righteousness
endures forever."[n]

10Now he who supplies
seed to the sower and bread
for food will also supply
and increase your store of
seed and will enlarge the
harvest of your righteousness. 11You will be made
rich in every way so that
you can be generous on every occasion, and through
us your generosity will result in thanksgiving to God.
12This service that you
perform is not only supplying the needs of God's people but is also overflowing
in many expressions of
thanks to God. 13Because
of the service by which you
have proved yourselves,
men will praise God for the
obedience that accompa-
nies your confession of the
gospel of Christ, and for
your generosity in sharing
with them and with every-
one else. 14And in their
prayers for you their hearts
will go out to you, because
of the surpassing grace God
has given you. 15Thanks be
to God for his indescribable
gift!

Chapter 10

Paul Describes Himself

NOW I, Paul, myself
urge you by the
meekness and gentleness of
Christ—I who am meek
when face to face with you,

10 Αὐτὸς δὲ ἐγὼ Παῦλος παρακαλῶ
[my]self Now I Paul beseech
ὑμᾶς διὰ τῆς πραΰτητος καὶ ἐπιεικείας
you through the meekness and forbearance
τοῦ Χριστοῦ, ὃς κατὰ πρόσωπον μὲν
– of Christ, who according to face indeed

Chapter 10

Paul's Defense of His Ministry

BY the meekness and
gentleness of Christ, I
appeal to you—I, Paul,
who am "timid" when face
to face with you, but

[n]9 Psalm 112:9

but bold toward you when absent!

2I ask that when I am present I may not be bold with the confidence with which I propose to be courageous against some, who regard us as if we walked according to the flesh.

3For though we walk in the flesh, we do not war according to the flesh,

4for the weapons of our warfare are not of the flesh, but divinely powerful for the destruction of fortresses.

5*We are* destroying speculations and every lofty thing raised up against the knowledge of God, and *we are* taking every thought captive to the obedience of Christ,

6and we are ready to punish all disobedience, whenever your obedience is complete.

7You are looking at things as they are outwardly. If anyone is confident in himself that he is Christ's, let him consider this again within himself, that just as he is Christ's, so also are we.

8For even if I should boast somewhat further about our authority, which the Lord gave for building you up and not for destroying you, I shall not be put to shame,

9for I do not wish to seem as if I would terrify you by my letters.

10For they say, "His letters are weighty and strong, but his personal presence is unimpressive, and his speech contemptible."

11Let such a person consider this, that what we are in word by letters when absent, such persons *we are* also in deed when present.

12For we are not bold to class or compare ourselves with some of those who commend themselves; but

ταπεινὸς ἐν ὑμῖν, ἀπὼν δὲ θαρρῶ εἰς
[am] humble among you, but being absent am bold toward

ὑμᾶς· 2 δέομαι δὲ τὸ μὴ παρὼν θαρρῆσαι
you: now I request – not being present to be bold

τῇ πεποιθήσει ᾗ λογίζομαι τολμῆσαι ἐπί
in the confidence which I reckon to be daring toward

τινας τοὺς λογιζομένους ἡμᾶς ὡς κατὰ
some the [ones] reckoning us as [2]according to

σάρκα περιπατοῦντας. 3 Ἐν σαρκὶ γὰρ
[3]flesh [1]walking. in flesh For

περιπατοῦντες οὐ κατὰ σάρκα στρατευόμεθα,
walking not according to flesh we war,

4 τὰ γὰρ ὅπλα τῆς στρατείας ἡμῶν
for the weapons of the warfare of us [are]

οὐ σαρκικὰ ἀλλὰ δυνατὰ τῷ θεῷ πρὸς
not fleshly but powerful – to God to

καθαίρεσιν ὀχυρωμάτων, λογισμοὺς καθαιροῦντες
overthrow of strongholds, [2]reasonings [1]overthrowing

5 καὶ πᾶν ὕψωμα ἐπαιρόμενον κατὰ
and every high thing rising up against

τῆς γνώσεως τοῦ θεοῦ, καὶ αἰχμαλωτίζοντες
the knowledge – of God, and taking captive

πᾶν νόημα εἰς τὴν ὑπακοὴν τοῦ Χριστοῦ,
every design to the obedience – of Christ,

6 καὶ ἐν ἑτοίμῳ ἔχοντες ἐκδικῆσαι πᾶσαν
and in readiness having to avenge all
=being ready

παρακοήν, ὅταν πληρωθῇ ὑμῶν ἡ ὑπακοή.
disobedience, whenever [4]is fulfilled [3]of you [1]the [2]obedience.

7 Τὰ κατὰ πρόσωπον βλέπετε. εἴ τις
[2]The things [3]according to [4]face (appearance) [1]ye look [at]. If anyone

πέποιθεν ἑαυτῷ Χριστοῦ εἶναι, τοῦτο
has persuaded himself [2]of Christ [1]to be, this

λογιζέσθω πάλιν ἐφ' ἑαυτοῦ, ὅτι καθὼς
let him reckon again as to himself, that as

αὐτὸς Χριστοῦ, οὕτως καὶ ἡμεῖς. 8 ἐάν
he [is] of Christ, so also [are] we. [2]if

τε γὰρ περισσότερόν τι καυχήσωμαι περὶ
[3]even [1]For [5]more abundantly [6]somewhat [4]I should boast concerning

τῆς ἐξουσίας ἡμῶν, ἧς ἔδωκεν ὁ κύριος
the authority of us, which [3]gave [1]the [2]Lord

εἰς οἰκοδομὴν καὶ οὐκ εἰς καθαίρεσιν
for edification and not for overthrow

ὑμῶν, οὐκ αἰσχυνθήσομαι, 9 ἵνα μὴ δόξω
of you, I shall not be shamed, in order that I may not seem

ὡσὰν ἐκφοβεῖν ὑμᾶς διὰ τῶν ἐπιστολῶν.
as though to frighten you through the epistles.

10 ὅτι αἱ ἐπιστολαὶ μέν, φησίν, βαρεῖαι
Because the(his) epistles indeed, he says, [are] weighty

καὶ ἰσχυραί, ἡ δὲ παρουσία τοῦ σώματος
and strong, but the presence of the(his) body [is]

ἀσθενὴς καὶ ὁ λόγος ἐξουθενημένος.
weak and the(his) speech *being* despised.

11 τοῦτο λογιζέσθω ὁ τοιοῦτος, ὅτι οἷοί
This let reckon such a one, that such as

ἐσμεν τῷ λόγῳ δι' ἐπιστολῶν ἀπόντες,
we are – in word through epistles being absent,

τοιοῦτοι καὶ παρόντες τῷ ἔργῳ. 12 Οὐ
such also being present – in work. [3]not

γὰρ τολμῶμεν ἐγκρῖναι ἢ συγκρῖναι
[1]For [2]we dare *to* class with or *to* compare

ἑαυτούς τισιν τῶν ἑαυτοὺς συνιστανόντων·
ourselves with some of the [ones] [2]themselves [1]commending;

"bold" when away! 2I beg
you that when I come I may
not have to be as bold as I
expect to be toward some
people who think that we
live by the standards of this
world. 3For though we live
in the world, we do not
wage war as the world
does. 4The weapons we
fight with are not the weapons of the world. On the
contrary, they have divine
power to demolish strongholds. 5We demolish arguments and every pretension
that sets itself up against
the knowledge of God, and
we take captive every
thought to make it obedient
to Christ. 6And we will be
ready to punish every act of
disobedience, once your
obedience is complete.
7You are looking only on
the surface of things.[o] If
anyone is confident that he
belongs to Christ, he
should consider again that
we belong to Christ just as
much as he. 8For even if I
boast somewhat freely
about the authority the
Lord gave us for building
you up rather than pulling
you down, I will not be
ashamed of it. 9I do not
want to seem to be trying to
frighten you with my letters. 10For some say, "His
letters are weighty and
forceful, but in person he is
unimpressive and his
speaking amounts to nothing." 11Such people should
realize that what we are in
our letters when we are absent, we will be in our actions when we are present.
12We do not dare to classify or compare ourselves
with some who commend
themselves. When they

[o]7 Or *Look at the obvious facts*

when they measure themselves by themselves, and compare themselves with themselves, they are without understanding.

13But we will not boast beyond *our* measure, but within the measure of the sphere which God apportioned to us as a measure, to reach even as far as you.

14For we are not overextending ourselves, as if we did not reach to you, for we were the first to come even as far as you in the gospel of Christ;

15not boasting beyond *our* measure, *that is,* in other men's labors, but with the hope that as your faith grows, we shall be, within our sphere, enlarged even more by you,

16so as to preach the gospel even to the regions beyond you, *and* not to boast in what has been accomplished in the sphere of another.

17But HE WHO BOASTS, LET HIM BOAST IN THE LORD.

18For not he who commends himself is approved, but whom the Lord commends.

Chapter 11

Paul Defends His Apostleship

I wish that you would bear with me in a little foolishness; but indeed you are bearing with me.

2For I am jealous for you with a godly jealousy; for I betrothed you to one husband, that to Christ I might present you *as* a pure virgin.

3But I am afraid, lest as the serpent deceived Eve by his craftiness, your minds should be led astray from the simplicity and purity *of devotion* to Christ.

4For if one comes and preaches another Jesus whom we have not preached, or you receive a different spirit which you

ἀλλὰ αὐτοὶ ἐν ἑαυτοῖς ἑαυτοὺς μετροῦντες
but they 2among 4themselves 3themselves 1measuring
καὶ συγκρίνοντες ἑαυτοὺς ἑαυτοῖς οὐ
and comparing themselves with themselves not
συνιᾶσιν. 13 ἡμεῖς δὲ οὐκ εἰς τὰ ἄμετρα
do understand. But we 2not 4immeasurably†
καυχησόμεθα, ἀλλὰ κατὰ τὸ μέτρον τοῦ
1will 3boast, but according to the measure of the
κανόνος οὗ ἐμέρισεν ἡμῖν ὁ θεὸς μέτρου,
rule which 2divided 3to us – 1God of(in) measure,
ἐφικέσθαι ἄχρι καὶ ὑμῶν. 14 οὐ γὰρ
to reach as far as even you. For not
ὡς μὴ ἐφικνούμενοι εἰς ὑμᾶς ὑπερεκτείνομεν
as not reaching to you do we overstretch
ἑαυτούς, ἄχρι γὰρ καὶ ὑμῶν ἐφθάσαμεν
ourselves, for as far as even you we came
ἐν τῷ εὐαγγελίῳ τοῦ Χριστοῦ, 15 οὐκ
in the gospel – of Christ, not
εἰς τὰ ἄμετρα καυχώμενοι ἐν ἀλλοτρίοις
immeasurably† boasting in others'†
κόποις, ἐλπίδα δὲ ἔχοντες αὐξανομένης
labours, but 2hope 1having growing
=as your faith grows
τῆς πίστεως ὑμῶν ἐν ὑμῖν μεγαλυνθῆναι
the faith of you[a] 2among 3you 1to be magnified
κατὰ τὸν κανόνα ἡμῶν εἰς περισσείαν,
according to the rule of us in abundance,
16 εἰς τὰ ὑπερέκεινα ὑμῶν εὐαγγελίσασθαι,
in the [parts] beyond you to preach good tidings,
οὐκ ἐν ἀλλοτρίῳ κανόνι εἰς τὰ ἕτοιμα
not 2in 3another's† 4rule 5in – 6things ready
καυχήσασθαι. 17 Ὁ δὲ καυχώμενος ἐν
1to boast. But the [one] boasting 2in
κυρίῳ καυχάσθω· 18 οὐ γὰρ ὁ ἑαυτὸν
3[the] Lord 1let him boast; for not the [one] himself
συνιστάνων, ἐκεῖνός ἐστιν δόκιμος, ἀλλὰ
commending, that one is approved, but
ὃν ὁ κύριος συνίστησιν.
whom the Lord commends.

11 Ὄφελον ἀνείχεσθέ μου μικρόν τι
I would that ye endured me a little [bit]
ἀφροσύνης· ἀλλὰ καὶ ἀνέχεσθέ μου.
of foolishness; but indeed ye do endure me.
2 ζηλῶ γὰρ ὑμᾶς θεοῦ ζήλῳ, ἡρμοσάμην
For I am jealous [of] you 2of God 1with a jealousy, 2I betrothed
γὰρ ὑμᾶς ἑνὶ ἀνδρὶ παρθένον ἁγνὴν
1for you to one husband 3virgin 2a pure
παραστῆσαι τῷ Χριστῷ· 3 φοβοῦμαι δὲ
1to present – to Christ; and I fear
μή πως, ὡς ὁ ὄφις ἐξηπάτησεν Εὕαν
lest somehow, as the serpent deceived Eve
ἐν τῇ πανουργίᾳ αὐτοῦ, φθαρῇ τὰ νοήματα
by the cleverness of him, 4should be seduced 1the 2thoughts
ὑμῶν ἀπὸ τῆς ἁπλότητος [καὶ τῆς
of you from the simplicity and the
ἁγνότητος] τῆς εἰς Χριστόν. 4 εἰ μὲν
purity – in Christ. 2if 3indeed
γὰρ ὁ ἐρχόμενος ἄλλον Ἰησοῦν κηρύσσει
1For the [one] coming 2another 3Jesus 1proclaims
ὃν οὐκ ἐκηρύξαμεν, ἢ πνεῦμα ἕτερον
whom we did not proclaim, or 3spirit 2a different

measure themselves by themselves and compare themselves with themselves, they are not wise.
13We, however, will not boast beyond proper limits, but will confine our boasting to the field God has assigned to us, a field that reaches even to you. 14We are not going too far in our boasting, as would be the case if we had not come to you, for we did get as far as you with the gospel of Christ. 15Neither do we go beyond our limits by boasting of work done by others.[p] Our hope is that, as your faith continues to grow, our area of activity among you will greatly expand, 16so that we can preach the gospel in the regions beyond you. For we do not want to boast about work already done in another man's territory.
17But, "Let him who boasts boast in the Lord."[q] 18For it is not the one who commends himself who is approved, but the one whom the Lord commends.

Chapter 11

Paul and the False Apostles

I HOPE you will put up with a little of my foolishness; but you are already doing that. 2I am jealous for you with a godly jealousy. I promised you to one husband, to Christ, so that I might present you as a pure virgin to him. 3But I am afraid that just as Eve was deceived by the serpent's cunning, your minds may somehow be led astray from your sincere and pure devotion to Christ. 4For if someone comes to you and preaches a Jesus other than the Jesus we preached, or if you receive a different spir-

[p] 13-15 Or *13We, however, will not boast about things that cannot be measured, but we will boast according to the standard of measurement that the God of measure has assigned us—a measurement that relates even to you. 14 . . . . 15Neither do we boast about things that cannot be measured in regard to the work done by others.*

[q] 17 Jer. 9:24

have not received, or a different gospel which you have not accepted, you bear *this* beautifully.
5 For I consider myself not in the least inferior to the most eminent apostles.
6 But even if I am unskilled in speech, yet I am not *so* in knowledge; in fact, in every way we have made *this* evident to you in all things.
7 Or did I commit a sin in humbling myself that you might be exalted, because I preached the gospel of God to you without charge?
8 I robbed other churches, taking wages *from them* to serve you;
9 and when I was present with you and was in need, I was not a burden to anyone; for when the brethren came from Macedonia, they fully supplied my need, and in everything I kept myself from being a burden to you, and will continue to do so.
10 As the truth of Christ is in me, this boasting of mine will not be stopped in the regions of Achaia.
11 Why? Because I do not love you? God knows *I do!*
12 But what I am doing, I will continue to do, that I may cut off opportunity from those who desire an opportunity to be regarded just as we are in the matter about which they are boasting.
13 For such men are false apostles, deceitful workers, disguising themselves as apostles of Christ.
14 And no wonder, for even Satan disguises himself as an angel of light.
15 Therefore it is not surprising if his servants also disguise themselves as servants of righteousness; whose end shall be according to their deeds.

λαμβάνετε ὃ οὐκ ἐλάβετε, ἢ εὐαγγέλιον
1ye receive which ye did not receive, or 3gospel
ἕτερον ὃ οὐκ ἐδέξασθε, καλῶς ἀνέχεσθε.
2a different which ye did not receive, 5[him] 4well 1ye endure.
5 λογίζομαι γὰρ μηδὲν ὑστερηκέναι τῶν
For I reckon nothing to have come behind *of* the
ὑπερλίαν ἀποστόλων. **6** εἰ δὲ καὶ ἰδιώτης
super- apostles. But if indeed unskilled [I am]
τῷ λόγῳ, ἀλλ' οὐ τῇ γνώσει, ἀλλ' ἐν
– in speech, yet not – in knowledge, but in
παντὶ φανερώσαντες ἐν πᾶσιν εἰς ὑμᾶς.
every [way] having manifested [ourselves] in all things to you.
7 Ἢ ἁμαρτίαν ἐποίησα ἐμαυτὸν ταπεινῶν
Or 2sin 1did I commit 4myself 3humbling
ἵνα ὑμεῖς ὑψωθῆτε, ὅτι δωρεὰν τὸ τοῦ
in order that ye might be exalted, because 5freely 2the –
θεοῦ εὐαγγέλιον εὐηγγελισάμην ὑμῖν;
4of God 3gospel 1I preached *good tidings* to you?
8 ἄλλας ἐκκλησίας ἐσύλησα λαβὼν ὀψώνιον
Other churches I robbed taking wages
πρὸς τὴν ὑμῶν διακονίαν, **9** καὶ παρὼν
for 1the 3of you 2ministry, and being present
πρὸς ὑμᾶς καὶ ὑστερηθεὶς οὐ κατενάρκησα
with you and lacking I was *not* an encumbrance
οὐθενός· τὸ γὰρ ὑστέρημά μου προσανε-
of no man; for the lack of me 6made
πλήρωσαν οἱ ἀδελφοὶ ἐλθόντες ἀπὸ Μακε-
up 1the 2brothers 3coming 4from 5Mace-
δονίας· καὶ ἐν παντὶ ἀβαρῆ ἐμαυτὸν
donia; and in every [way] 3unburdensome 2myself
ὑμῖν ἐτήρησα καὶ τηρήσω. **10** ἔστιν
4to you 1I kept and I will keep. 3is
ἀλήθεια Χριστοῦ ἐν ἐμοί, ὅτι ἡ καύχησις
1[The] truth 2of Christ in me, that – boasting
αὕτη οὐ φραγήσεται εἰς ἐμὲ ἐν τοῖς
this shall not be stopped in me in the
κλίμασιν τῆς Ἀχαΐας. **11** διὰ τί; ὅτι
regions – of Achaia. Why? because
οὐκ ἀγαπῶ ὑμᾶς; ὁ θεὸς οἶδεν. **12** Ὃ
I love not you? – God knows. what
δὲ ποιῶ, καὶ ποιήσω, ἵνα ἐκκόψω τὴν
But I do, also I will do, in order that I may cut off the
ἀφορμὴν τῶν θελόντων ἀφορμήν, ἵνα ἐν
occasion of the [ones] desiring an occasion, in order that where-
ᾧ καυχῶνται εὑρεθῶσιν καθὼς καὶ ἡμεῖς.
in they boast they may be found as also we.
13 οἱ γὰρ τοιοῦτοι ψευδαπόστολοι, ἐργάται
– For such [are] false apostles, 2workmen
δόλιοι, μετασχηματιζόμενοι εἰς ἀποστόλους
1deceitful, transforming themselves into apostles
Χριστοῦ. **14** καὶ οὐ θαῦμα· αὐτὸς γὰρ
of Christ. And no wonder; 3[him]self 1for
ὁ σατανᾶς μετασχηματίζεται εἰς ἄγγελον
– 2Satan transforms himself into an angel
φωτός. **15** οὐ μέγα οὖν εἰ καὶ οἱ
of light. No great thing therefore if also the
διάκονοι αὐτοῦ μετασχηματίζονται ὡς
ministers of him transform themselves as
διάκονοι δικαιοσύνης· ὧν τὸ τέλος ἔσται
ministers of righteousness; of whom the end will be
κατὰ τὰ ἔργα αὐτῶν.
according to the works of them.

it from the one you received, or a different gospel from the one you accepted, you put up with it easily enough.
5 But I do not think I am in the least inferior to those "super-apostles."
6 I may not be a trained speaker, but I do have knowledge. We have made this perfectly clear to you in every way.
7 Was it a sin for me to lower myself in order to elevate you by preaching the gospel of God to you free of charge?
8 I robbed other churches by receiving support from them so as to serve you.
9 And when I was with you and needed something, I was not a burden to anyone, for the brothers who came from Macedonia supplied what I needed. I have kept myself from being a burden to you in any way, and will continue to do so.
10 As surely as the truth of Christ is in me, nobody in the regions of Achaia will stop this boasting of mine.
11 Why? Because I do not love you? God knows I do!
12 And I will keep on doing what I am doing in order to cut the ground from under those who want an opportunity to be considered equal with us in the things they boast about.
13 For such men are false apostles, deceitful workmen, masquerading as apostles of Christ.
14 And no wonder, for Satan himself masquerades as an angel of light.
15 It is not surprising, then, if his servants masquerade as servants of righteousness. Their end will be what their actions deserve.

16Again I say, let no one think me foolish; but if *you do,* receive me even as foolish, that I also may boast a little.

17That which I am speaking, I am not speaking as the Lord would, but as in foolishness, in this confidence of boasting.

18Since many boast according to the flesh, I will boast also.

19For you, being *so* wise, bear with the foolish gladly.

20For you bear with anyone if he enslaves you, if he devours you, if he takes advantage of you, if he exalts himself, if he hits you in the face.

21To *my* shame I *must* say that we have been weak *by comparison.* But in whatever respect anyone *else* is bold (I speak in foolishness), I am just as bold myself.

22Are they Hebrews? So am I. Are they Israelites? So am I. Are they descendants of Abraham? So am I.

23Are they servants of Christ? (I speak as if insane) I more so; in far more labors, in far more imprisonments, beaten times without number, often in danger of death.

24Five times I received from the Jews thirty-nine *lashes.*

25Three times I was beaten with rods, once I was stoned, three times I was shipwrecked, a night and a day I have spent in the deep.

26*I have been* on frequent journeys, in dangers from rivers, dangers from robbers, dangers from *my* countrymen, dangers from the Gentiles, dangers in the city, dangers in the wilderness, dangers on the sea, dangers among false brethren;

27*I have been* in labor and hardship, through many sleepless nights, in hunger and thirst, often without

16 Πάλιν λέγω, μή τίς με δόξῃ ἄφρονα
Again I say, [2]not [3]anyone [4]me [1]think [6]foolish
εἶναι· εἰ δὲ μή γε, κἂν ὡς ἄφρονα
[5]to be; otherwise, even if as foolish
δέξασθέ με, ἵνα κἀγὼ μικρόν τι καυχήσ-
receive ye me, in order that I also a little [bit] may
ωμαι. 17 ὃ λαλῶ, οὐ κατὰ κύριον λαλῶ,
boast. What I speak, not according to [the] Lord I speak,
ἀλλ' ὡς ἐν ἀφροσύνῃ, ἐν ταύτῃ τῇ
but as in folly, in this –
ὑποστάσει τῆς καυχήσεως. 18 ἐπεὶ πολλοὶ
confidence – of boasting. Since many
καυχῶνται κατὰ [τὴν] σάρκα, κἀγὼ
boast according to the flesh, I also
καυχήσομαι. 19 ἡδέως γὰρ ἀνέχεσθε τῶν
will boast. For gladly ye endure –
ἀφρόνων φρόνιμοι ὄντες· 20 ἀνέχεσθε γὰρ
fools [2]prudent [1]being; for ye endure
εἴ τις ὑμᾶς καταδουλοῖ, εἴ τις κατεσθίει,
if anyone [2]you [1]enslaves, if anyone devours [you],
εἴ τις λαμβάνει, εἴ τις ἐπαίρεται, εἴ
if anyone receives [you],* if anyone lifts himself up, if
τις εἰς πρόσωπον ὑμᾶς δέρει. 21 κατὰ
anyone [3]in [4][the] face [2]you [1]beats(hits). According to
ἀτιμίαν λέγω, ὡς ὅτι ἡμεῖς ἠσθενήκαμεν·
dishonour I say, as that we have been weak;
ἐν ᾧ δ' ἄν τις τολμᾷ, ἐν ἀφροσύνῃ
but in whatever [respect] anyone dares, in folly
λέγω, τολμῶ κἀγώ. 22 Ἑβραῖοί εἰσιν;
I say, [3]dare [1]I [2]also. Hebrews are they?
κἀγώ. Ἰσραηλῖταί εἰσιν; κἀγώ. σπέρμα
I also. Israelites are they? I also. Seed
Ἀβραάμ εἰσιν; κἀγώ. 23 διάκονοι Χριστοῦ
of Abraham are they? I also. Ministers of Christ
εἰσιν; παραφρονῶν λαλῶ, ὑπὲρ ἐγώ· ἐν
are they? being out of my mind I speak, [2]beyond (more) [1]I: in
κόποις περισσοτέρως, ἐν φυλακαῖς περισ-
labours more abundantly, in prisons more
σοτέρως, ἐν πληγαῖς ὑπερβαλλόντως, ἐν
abundantly, in stripes excessively, in
θανάτοις πολλάκις. 24 ὑπὸ Ἰουδαίων
deaths many times. By Jews
πεντάκις τεσσεράκοντα παρὰ μίαν ἔλαβον,
five times forty [stripes] less one I received,
25 τρὶς ἐρραβδίσθην, ἅπαξ ἐλιθάσθην, τρὶς
thrice I was beaten with rods, once I was stoned, thrice
ἐναυάγησα, 26 νυχθήμερον ἐν τῷ βυθῷ
I was shipwrecked, a night and a day in the deep
πεποίηκα· ὁδοιπορίαις πολλάκις, κινδύνοις
I have done(been); in travels many times, in perils
ποταμῶν, κινδύνοις λῃστῶν, κινδύνοις ἐκ
of rivers, in perils of robbers, in perils of
γένους, κινδύνοις ἐξ ἐθνῶν, κινδύνοις ἐν
[my] kind, in perils of nations, in perils in
πόλει, κινδύνοις ἐν ἐρημίᾳ, κινδύνοις ἐν
a city, in perils in a desert, in perils in(at)
θαλάσσῃ, κινδύνοις ἐν ψευδαδέλφοις, 27 κόπῳ
sea; in perils among false brothers, in labour
καὶ μόχθῳ, ἐν ἀγρυπνίαις πολλάκις, ἐν
and hardship, in watchings many times, in
λιμῷ καὶ δίψει, ἐν νηστείαις πολλάκις,
famine and thirst, in fastings many times,

* ? takes [you in].

Paul Boasts About His Sufferings

16I repeat: Let no one take me for a fool. But if you do, then receive me just as you would a fool, so that I may do a little boasting. 17In this self-confident boasting I am not talking as the Lord would, but as a fool. 18Since many are boasting in the way the world does, I too will boast. 19You gladly put up with fools since you are so wise! 20In fact, you even put up with anyone who enslaves you or exploits you or takes advantage of you or pushes himself forward or slaps you in the face. 21To my shame I admit that we were too weak for that!

What anyone else dares to boast about—I am speaking as a fool—I also dare to boast about. 22Are they Hebrews? So am I. Are they Israelites? So am I. Are they Abraham's descendants? So am I. 23Are they servants of Christ? (I am out of my mind to talk like this.) I am more. I have worked much harder, been in prison more frequently, been flogged more severely, and been exposed to death again and again. 24Five times I received from the Jews the forty lashes minus one. 25Three times I was beaten with rods, once I was stoned, three times I was shipwrecked, I spent a night and a day in the open sea, 26I have been constantly on the move. I have been in danger from rivers, in danger from bandits, in danger from my own countrymen, in danger from Gentiles; in danger in the city, in danger in the country, in danger at sea; and in danger from false brothers. 27I have labored and toiled and have often gone without sleep; I have known hunger and thirst and have often gone

food, in cold and exposure.
28Apart from *such* external things, there is the daily
pressure upon me *of* concern for all the churches.
29Who is weak without
my being weak? Who is led
into sin without my intense
concern?
30If I have to boast, I will
boast of what pertains to
my weakness.
31The God and Father of
the Lord Jesus, He who is
blessed forever, knows that
I am not lying.
32In Damascus the eth-
narch under Aretas the
king was guarding the city
of the Damascenes in order
to seize me,
33and I was let down in a
basket through a window in
the wall, and *so* escaped his
hands.

Chapter 12

Paul's Vision

BOASTING is neces-
sary, though it is not
profitable; but I will go on
to visions and revelations
of the Lord.
2I know a man in Christ
who fourteen years ago—
whether in the body I do
not know, or out of the
body I do not know, God
knows—such a man was
caught up to the third
heaven.
3And I know how such a
man—whether in the body
or apart from the body I do
not know, God knows—
4was caught up into
Paradise, and heard inex-
pressible words, which a
man is not permitted to
speak.
5On behalf of such a man
will I boast; but on my own
behalf I will not boast, except in regard to *my* weaknesses.
6For if I do wish to boast
I shall not be foolish, for I
shall be speaking the truth;
but I refrain *from this,* so
that no one may credit me
with more than he sees *in*
me or hears from me.

ἐν ψύχει καὶ γυμνότητι· **28** χωρὶς τῶν
in cold and nakedness; apart from the things
παρεκτὸς ἡ ἐπίστασίς μοι ἡ καθ' ἡμέραν,
without[,] the conspiring against me – daily,
ἡ μέριμνα πασῶν τῶν ἐκκλησιῶν. **29** τίς
the care of all the churches. Who
ἀσθενεῖ, καὶ οὐκ ἀσθενῶ; τίς σκανδαλίζεται,
is weak, and I am not weak? who is offended,
καὶ οὐκ ἐγὼ πυροῦμαι; **30** εἰ καυχᾶσθαι
and ³not ¹I ²burn? If to boast
δεῖ, τὰ τῆς ἀσθενείας μου καυχήσομαι.
it behoves [me], the things of the weakness of me I will boast.
31 ὁ θεὸς καὶ πατὴρ τοῦ κυρίου Ἰησοῦ
The God and Father of the Lord Jesus
οἶδεν, ὁ ὢν εὐλογητὸς εἰς τοὺς αἰῶνας,
knows, the [one] being blessed unto the ages,
ὅτι οὐ ψεύδομαι. **32** ἐν Δαμασκῷ ὁ
that I am not lying. In Damascus the
ἐθνάρχης Ἁρέτα τοῦ βασιλέως ἐφρούρει
ethnarch of Aretas *of* the king guarded
τὴν πόλιν Δαμασκηνῶν πιάσαι με, **33** καὶ
the city of [the] Damascenes to seize me, and
διὰ θυρίδος ἐν σαργάνῃ ἐχαλάσθην διὰ
through a window in a basket I was lowered through
τοῦ τείχους καὶ ἐξέφυγον τὰς χεῖρας αὐτοῦ.
the wall and escaped the hands of him.
12 Καυχᾶσθαι δεῖ, οὐ συμφέρον μέν,
To boast it behoves [me], not expedient indeed,
ἐλεύσομαι δὲ εἰς ὀπτασίας καὶ ἀποκαλύψεις
so I will come to visions and revelations
κυρίου. **2** οἶδα ἄνθρωπον ἐν Χριστῷ
of [the] Lord. I know a man in Christ
πρὸ ἐτῶν δεκατεσσάρων, — εἴτε ἐν
before years fourteen, (whether in
σώματι οὐκ οἶδα, εἴτε ἐκτὸς τοῦ σώματος
[the] body I know not, or outside the body
οὐκ οἶδα, ὁ θεὸς οἶδεν, — ἁρπαγέντα
I know not, – God knows,) ²caught
τὸν τοιοῦτον ἕως τρίτου οὐρανοῦ. **3** καὶ
– ¹such a one to [the] third heaven. And
οἶδα τὸν τοιοῦτον ἄνθρωπον — εἴτε
I know – such a man (whether
ἐν σώματι εἴτε χωρὶς τοῦ σώματος
in [the] body or apart from the body
[οὐκ οἶδα], ὁ θεὸς οἶδεν, — **4** ὅτι
I know not, – God knows,) that
ἡρπάγη εἰς τὸν παράδεισον καὶ ἤκουσεν
he was caught into the paradise and heard
ἄρρητα ῥήματα, ἃ οὐκ ἐξὸν ἀνθρώπῳ
unspeakable words, which it is not permissible for a man
λαλῆσαι. **5** ὑπὲρ τοῦ τοιούτου καυχήσομαι,
to speak. On behalf of – such a one I will boast,
ὑπὲρ δὲ ἐμαυτοῦ οὐ καυχήσομαι εἰ
but on behalf of myself I will not boast ex-
μὴ ἐν ταῖς ἀσθενείαις. **6** ἐὰν γὰρ θελήσω
cept in the(my) weaknesses. For if I shall wish
καυχήσασθαι, οὐκ ἔσομαι ἄφρων, ἀλήθειαν
to boast, I shall not be foolish, ³truth
γὰρ ἐρῶ· φείδομαι δέ, μή τις εἰς ἐμὲ
¹for ²I will speak; but I spare, lest anyone to me
λογίσηται ὑπὲρ ὃ βλέπει με ἢ ἀκούει
reckons beyond what he sees me or hears

without food; I have been
cold and naked. 28Besides
everything else, I face daily
the pressure of my concern
for all the churches. 29Who
is weak, and I do not feel
weak? Who is led into sin,
and I do not inwardly burn?
30If I must boast, I will
boast of the things that
show my weakness. 31The
God and Father of the Lord
Jesus, who is to be praised
forever, knows that I am
not lying. 32In Damascus
the governor under King
Aretas had the city of the
Damascenes guarded in or-
der to arrest me. 33But I
was lowered in a basket
from a window in the wall
and slipped through his
hands.

Chapter 12

Paul's Vision and His Thorn

I MUST go on boasting.
Although there is noth-
ing to be gained, I will go on
to visions and revelations
from the Lord. 2I know a
man in Christ who fourteen
years ago was caught up to
the third heaven. Whether
it was in the body or out of
the body I do not know—
God knows. 3And I know
that this man—whether in
the body or apart from the
body I do not know, but
God knows— 4was caught
up to paradise. He heard inexpressible things, things
that man is not permitted to
tell. 5I will boast about a
man like that, but I will not
boast about myself, except
about my weaknesses.
6Even if I should choose to
boast, I would not be a fool,
because I would be speak-
ing the truth. But I refrain,
so no one will think more of
me than is warranted by
what I do or say.

A Thorn in the Flesh

7And because of the sur-
passing greatness of the
revelations, for this reason,
to keep me from exalting
myself, there was given me
a thorn in the flesh, a messenger of Satan to buffet
me—to keep me from ex-
alting myself!
8Concerning this I en-
treated the Lord three
times that it might depart
from me.
9And He has said to me,
"My grace is sufficient for
you, for [c]power is per-
fected in weakness." Most
gladly, therefore, I will
rather boast about my
weaknesses, that the power
of Christ may dwell in me.
10Therefore I am well
content with weaknesses,
with insults, with dis-
tresses, with persecutions,
with difficulties, for
Christ's sake; for when I
am weak, then I am strong.
11I have become foolish;
you yourselves compelled
me. Actually I should have
been commended by you,
for in no respect was I inferior to the most eminent
apostles, even though I am
a nobody.
12The signs of a true apostle were performed among
you with all perseverance,
by signs and wonders and
miracles.
13For in what respect
were you treated as inferior
to the rest of the churches,
except that I myself did not
become a burden to you?
Forgive me this wrong!
14Here for this third time I
am ready to come to you,
and I will not be a burden to
you; for I do not seek what
is yours, but you; for children are not responsible to
save up for *their* parents,
but parents for *their* children.
15And I will most gladly
spend and be expended for

[c]Later mss. read *My power*

ἐξ ἐμοῦ 7 καὶ τῇ ὑπερβολῇ τῶν ἀποκα-
of me and by the excess of the revela-

λύψεων. διὸ ἵνα μὴ ὑπεραίρωμαι, ἐδόθη
tions. Wherefore lest I should be exceedingly uplifted, there was given

μοι σκόλοψ τῇ σαρκί, ἄγγελος σατανᾶ,
to me a thorn in the flesh, a messenger of Satan,

ἵνα με κολαφίζῃ, ἵνα μὴ ὑπεραίρωμαι.
in order that [2]me [1]he might buffet, lest I should be exceedingly uplifted.

8 ὑπὲρ τούτου τρὶς τὸν κύριον παρεκάλεσα,
As to this thrice the Lord I besought,

ἵνα ἀποστῇ ἀπ' ἐμοῦ. 9 καὶ εἴρηκέν
in order that it might depart from me. And he *has* said

μοι· ἀρκεῖ σοι ἡ χάρις μου· ἡ γὰρ
to me: [4]Suffices [5]thee [1]the [2]grace [3]of me; for the(my)

δύναμις ἐν ἀσθενείᾳ τελεῖται. Ἥδιστα
power in weakness is perfected. Most gladly

οὖν μᾶλλον καυχήσομαι ἐν ταῖς ἀσθενείαις,
therefore rather I will boast in the(my) weaknesses,

ἵνα ἐπισκηνώσῃ ἐπ' ἐμὲ ἡ δύναμις τοῦ
in order that [4]might overshadow *over* [5]me [1]the [2]power –

Χριστοῦ. 10 διὸ εὐδοκῶ ἐν ἀσθενείαις,
[3]of Christ. Wherefore I am well pleased in weaknesses,

ἐν ὕβρεσιν, ἐν ἀνάγκαις, ἐν διωγμοῖς
in insults, in necessities, in persecutions

καὶ στενοχωρίαις, ὑπὲρ Χριστοῦ· ὅταν
and difficulties, on behalf of Christ; [2]whenever

γὰρ ἀσθενῶ, τότε δυνατός εἰμι.
[1]for I am weak, then [2]powerful [1]I am.

11 Γέγονα ἄφρων· ὑμεῖς με ἠναγκάσατε.
I have become foolish; ye me compelled.

ἐγὼ γὰρ ὤφειλον ὑφ' ὑμῶν συνίστασθαι.
For I ought by you to be commended.

οὐδὲν γὰρ ὑστέρησα τῶν ὑπερλίαν
For nothing I lacked of the super-

ἀποστόλων, εἰ καὶ οὐδέν εἰμι. 12 τὰ
apostles, [2]if [1]even [4]nothing [3]I am. [2]The

μὲν σημεῖα τοῦ ἀποστόλου κατειργάσθη
[1]indeed signs of the apostle were wrought

ἐν ὑμῖν ἐν πάσῃ ὑπομονῇ, σημείοις τε
among you in all endurance, [2]by signs [1]both

καὶ τέρασιν καὶ δυνάμεσιν. 13 τί γάρ
and by wonders and by powerful deeds. For what

ἐστιν ὃ ἡσσώθητε ὑπὲρ τὰς λοιπὰς
is it which ye were less than the remaining

ἐκκλησίας, εἰ μὴ ὅτι αὐτὸς ἐγὼ οὐ
churches, except that [2][my]self [1]I [5]not

κατενάρκησα ὑμῶν; χαρίσασθέ μοι τὴν
[3]encumbered [4]*of* you? Forgive ye me –

ἀδικίαν ταύτην. 14 Ἰδοὺ τρίτον τοῦτο
wrong this. Behold [2][the] third [time] [1]this [is]

ἑτοίμως ἔχω ἐλθεῖν πρὸς ὑμᾶς, καὶ
I am ready† to come to you, and

οὐ καταναρκήσω· οὐ γὰρ ζητῶ τὰ ὑμῶν
I will not encumber [you]; [3]not [1]for [2]I seek the things of you

ἀλλὰ ὑμᾶς. οὐ γὰρ ὀφείλει τὰ τέκνα
but you. For [4]not [3]ought [1]the [2]children

τοῖς γονεῦσιν θησαυρίζειν, ἀλλὰ οἱ γονεῖς
for the parents to lay up treasure, but the parents

τοῖς τέκνοις. 15 ἐγὼ δὲ ἥδιστα δαπανήσω
for the children. But I most gladly will spend

καὶ ἐκδαπανηθήσομαι ὑπὲρ τῶν ψυχῶν
and will be spent out on behalf of the souls

7To keep me from becom-
ing conceited because of
these surpassingly great
revelations, there was giv-
en me a thorn in my flesh, a
messenger of Satan, to torment me. 8Three times I
pleaded with the Lord to
take it away from me. 9But
he said to me, "My grace is
sufficient for you, for my
power is made perfect in
weakness." Therefore I
will boast all the more gladly about my weaknesses,
so that Christ's power may
rest on me. 10That is why,
for Christ's sake, I delight
in weaknesses, in insults,
in hardships, in persecu-
tions, in difficulties. For
when I am weak, then I am
strong.

Paul's Concern for the Corinthians

11I have made a fool of
myself, but you drove me
to it. I ought to have been
commended by you, for I
am not in the least inferior
to the "super-apostles,"
even though I am nothing.
12The things that mark an
apostle—signs, wonders
and miracles—were done
among you with great per-
severance. 13How were
you inferior to the other
churches, except that I was
never a burden to you? Forgive me this wrong!
14Now I am ready to visit
you for the third time, and I
will not be a burden to you,
because what I want is not
your possessions but you.
After all, children should
not have to save up for their
parents, but parents for
their children. 15So I will
very gladly spend for you

your souls. If I love you the more, am I to be loved the less?

16But be that as it may, I did not burden you myself; nevertheless, crafty fellow that I am, I took you in by deceit.

17*Certainly* I have not taken advantage of you through any of those whom I have sent to you, have I?

18I urged Titus *to go,* and sent the brother with him. Titus did not take any advantage of you, did he? Did we not conduct ourselves in the same spirit *and walk* in the same steps?

19All this time you have been thinking that we are defending ourselves to you. *Actually,* it is in the sight of God that we have been speaking in Christ; and all for your upbuilding, beloved.

20For I am afraid that perhaps when I come I may find you to be not what I wish and may be found by you to be not what you wish; that perhaps *there may be* strife, jealousy, angry tempers, disputes, slanders, gossip, arrogance, disturbances;

21I am afraid that when I come again my God may humiliate me before you, and I may mourn over many of those who have sinned in the past and not repented of the impurity, immorality and sensuality which they have practiced.

Chapter 13

Examine Yourselves

THIS is the third time I am coming to you. EVERY FACT IS TO BE CONFIRMED BY THE TESTIMONY OF TWO OR THREE WITNESSES.

2I have previously said when present the second time, and though now absent I say in advance to those who have sinned in the past and to all the rest as well, that if I come again, I will not spare *anyone,*

3since you are seeking

ὑμῶν. εἰ περισσοτέρως ὑμᾶς ἀγαπῶ,
of you. If more abundantly [2]you [1]I love,
ἧσσον ἀγαπῶμαι; 16 Ἔστω δέ, ἐγὼ οὐ
[the] less am I loved? But let it be, I not
κατεβάρησα ὑμᾶς· ἀλλὰ ὑπάρχων πανοῦργος
burdened you; but being crafty
δόλῳ ὑμᾶς ἔλαβον. 17 μή τινα ὧν
[3]with guile [2]you [1]I took. *Not* anyone of whom
ἀπέσταλκα πρὸς ὑμᾶς, 18 δι' αὐτοῦ
I have sent to you, through him
ἐπλεονέκτησα ὑμᾶς; παρεκάλεσα Τίτον καὶ
did I defraud you? I besought Titus and
συναπέστειλα τὸν ἀδελφόν· μήτι ἐπλεο-
sent with [him] the brother; *not* [2]de-
νέκτησεν ὑμᾶς Τίτος; οὐ τῷ αὐτῷ
frauded [3]you [1]Titus? [2]not [3]by the [4]same
πνεύματι περιεπατήσαμεν; οὐ τοῖς αὐτοῖς
[5]spirit [1]walked we? not in the same
ἴχνεσιν;
steps?

19 Πάλαι δοκεῖτε ὅτι ὑμῖν ἀπολογούμεθα.
Already ye think that to you we are making a defence.
κατέναντι θεοῦ ἐν Χριστῷ λαλοῦμεν· τὰ
Before God in Christ we speak; –
δὲ πάντα, ἀγαπητοί, ὑπὲρ τῆς ὑμῶν
but all things, beloved, [are] on behalf of [1]the [3]of you
οἰκοδομῆς. 20 φοβοῦμαι γὰρ μή πως ἐλθὼν
[2]edification. For I fear lest coming
οὐχ οἵους θέλω εὕρω ὑμᾶς, κἀγὼ εὑρεθῶ
[2]not [4]such as [5]I wish [1]I may find [3]you, and I am found
ὑμῖν οἷον οὐ θέλετε, μή πως ἔρις,
by you such as ye wish not, lest strife,
ζῆλος, θυμοί, ἐριθεῖαι, καταλαλιαί, ψιθυρισ-
jealousy, angers, rivalries, detractions, whisper-
μοί, φυσιώσεις, ἀκαταστασίαι· 21 μὴ πάλιν
ings, puffings up, disturbances; lest again
ἐλθόντος μου ταπεινώσῃ με ὁ θεός μου
coming me[a] [4]may humble [5]me [1]the [2]God [3]of me
=when I come
πρὸς ὑμᾶς, καὶ πενθήσω πολλοὺς τῶν
with you, and I shall mourn many of the [ones]
προημαρτηκότων καὶ μὴ μετανοησάντων
having previously sinned and not repenting
ἐπὶ τῇ ἀκαθαρσίᾳ καὶ πορνείᾳ καὶ
over the uncleanness and fornication and
ἀσελγείᾳ ᾗ ἔπραξαν. 13 Τρίτον τοῦτο
lewdness which they practised. [2][The] third [time] [1]this [is]
ἔρχομαι πρὸς ὑμᾶς· ἐπὶ στόματος
I am coming to you; at [the] mouth
δύο μαρτύρων καὶ τριῶν σταθήσεται
of two witnesses and of three shall be established
πᾶν ῥῆμα. 2 προείρηκα καὶ προλέγω,
every word. I have previously said and I say beforehand,
ὡς παρὼν τὸ δεύτερον καὶ ἀπὼν
as being present the second [time] and being absent
νῦν, τοῖς προημαρτηκόσιν καὶ τοῖς
now, to the [ones] having previously sinned and [1]to [3]the
λοιποῖς πᾶσιν, ὅτι ἐὰν ἔλθω εἰς τὸ
[4]remaining [ones] [2]all, that if I come *in the*
πάλιν οὐ φείσομαι, 3 ἐπεὶ δοκιμὴν ζητεῖτε
again I will not spare, since [2]a proof [1]ye seek

everything I have and expend myself as well. If I love you more, will you love me less? 16Be that as it may, I have not been a burden to you. Yet, crafty fellow that I am, I caught you by trickery! 17Did I exploit you through any of the men I sent you? 18I urged Titus to go to you and I sent our brother with him. Titus did not exploit you, did he? Did we not act in the same spirit and follow the same course?

19Have you been thinking all along that we have been defending ourselves to you? We have been speaking in the sight of God as those in Christ; and everything we do, dear friends, is for your strengthening. 20For I am afraid that when I come I may not find you as I want you to be, and you may not find me as you want me to be. I fear that there may be quarreling, jealousy, outbursts of anger, factions, slander, gossip, arrogance and disorder. 21I am afraid that when I come again my God will humble me before you, and I will be grieved over many who have sinned earlier and have not repented of the impurity, sexual sin and debauchery in which they have indulged.

Chapter 13

Final Warnings

THIS will be my third visit to you. "Every matter must be established by the testimony of two or three witnesses."[r] 2I already gave you a warning when I was with you the second time. I now repeat it while absent: On my return I will not spare those who sinned earlier or any of the others, 3since you are demanding proof that Christ

[r] 1 Deut. 19:15

for proof of the Christ who speaks in me, and who is not weak toward you, but mighty in you.

4For indeed He was crucified because of weakness, yet He lives because of the power of God. For we also are weak [d]in Him, yet we shall live with Him because of the power of God *directed* toward you.

5Test yourselves *to see* if you are in the faith; examine yourselves! Or do you not recognize this about yourselves, that Jesus Christ is in you—unless indeed you fail the test?

6But I trust that you will realize that we ourselves do not fail the test.

7Now we pray to God that you do no wrong; not that we ourselves may appear approved, but that you may do what is right, even though we should appear unapproved.

8For we can do nothing against the truth, but *only* for the truth.

9For we rejoice when we ourselves are weak but you are strong; this we also pray for, that you be made complete.

10For this reason I am writing these things while absent, in order that when present I may not use severity, in accordance with the authority which the Lord gave me, for building up and not for tearing down.

11Finally, brethren, rejoice, be made complete, be comforted, be like-minded, live in peace; and the God of love and peace shall be with you.

12Greet one another with a holy kiss.

13All the saints greet you.

14The grace of the Lord

[d]Some early mss. read *with Him*

τοῦ ἐν ἐμοὶ λαλοῦντος Χριστοῦ, ὃς εἰς
– [5]in [6]me [4]speaking [3]of Christ, who toward

ὑμᾶς οὐκ ἀσθενεῖ ἀλλὰ δυνατεῖ ἐν ὑμῖν.
you is not weak but is powerful in you.

4 καὶ γὰρ ἐσταυρώθη ἐξ ἀσθενείας, ἀλλὰ
For indeed he was crucified out of weakness, but

ζῇ ἐκ δυνάμεως θεοῦ. καὶ γὰρ ἡμεῖς
he lives by [the] power of God. For indeed we

ἀσθενοῦμεν ἐν αὐτῷ, ἀλλὰ ζήσομεν σὺν
are weak in him, but we shall live with

αὐτῷ ἐκ δυνάμεως θεοῦ εἰς ὑμᾶς.
him by [the] power of God toward you.

5 Ἑαυτοὺς πειράζετε εἰ ἐστὲ ἐν τῇ
[2]Yourselves [1]test if ye are in the

πίστει, ἑαυτοὺς δοκιμάζετε· ἢ οὐκ
faith, [2]yourselves [1]prove; or not

ἐπιγινώσκετε ἑαυτοὺς ὅτι Ἰησοῦς Χριστὸς
perceive ye yourselves that Jesus Christ [is]

ἐν ὑμῖν, εἰ μήτι ἀδόκιμοί ἐστε. 6 ἐλπίζω
in you, unless [2]counterfeits [1]ye are. I hope

δὲ ὅτι γνώσεσθε ὅτι ἡμεῖς οὐκ ἐσμὲν
But that ye will know that we are not

ἀδόκιμοι. 7 εὐχόμεθα δὲ πρὸς τὸν θεὸν
counterfeits. Now we pray to – God

μὴ ποιῆσαι ὑμᾶς κακὸν μηδέν, οὐχ
not to do you evil *none*, not
=that ye do no . . .

ἵνα ἡμεῖς δόκιμοι φανῶμεν, ἀλλ' ἵνα
in order that we [2]approved [1]may appear, but in order that

ὑμεῖς τὸ καλὸν ποιῆτε, ἡμεῖς δὲ ὡς
ye [2]the [3]good [1]may do, and we [2]as

ἀδόκιμοι ὦμεν. 8 οὐ γὰρ δυνάμεθά
[3]counterfeits [1]may be. For we cannot [do]

τι κατὰ τῆς ἀληθείας, ἀλλὰ ὑπὲρ τῆς
anything against the truth, but on behalf of the

ἀληθείας. 9 χαίρομεν γὰρ ὅταν ἡμεῖς
truth. For we rejoice when*ever* we

ἀσθενῶμεν, ὑμεῖς δὲ δυνατοὶ ἦτε· τοῦτο
are weak, and ye powerful are; this

καὶ εὐχόμεθα, τὴν ὑμῶν κατάρτισιν. 10 Διὰ
also we pray, the [2]of you [1]restoration. There-

τοῦτο ταῦτα ἀπὼν γράφω, ἵνα παρὼν
fore [2]these things [3]being absent [1]I write, in order that being present

μὴ ἀποτόμως χρήσωμαι κατὰ τὴν ἐξουσίαν
[2]not [3]sharply [1]I may deal according to the authority

ἣν ὁ κύριος ἔδωκέν μοι εἰς οἰκοδομὴν
which the Lord gave me for edification

καὶ οὐκ εἰς καθαίρεσιν.
and not for overthrow.

11 Λοιπόν, ἀδελφοί, χαίρετε, καταρτίζεσθε,
For the rest,† brothers, rejoice, restore yourselves,

παρακαλεῖσθε, τὸ αὐτὸ φρονεῖτε, εἰρηνεύετε,
admonish yourselves, the same thing think, be at peace,

καὶ ὁ θεὸς τῆς ἀγάπης καὶ εἰρήνης
and the God – of love and of peace

ἔσται μεθ' ὑμῶν. 12 Ἀσπάσασθε ἀλλήλους
will be with you. Greet ye one another

ἐν ἁγίῳ φιλήματι. Ἀσπάζονται ὑμᾶς οἱ
with a holy kiss. [4]greet [5]you [2]the

ἅγιοι πάντες.
[3]saints [1]All.

13 Ἡ χάρις τοῦ κυρίου Ἰησοῦ Χριστοῦ
The grace of the Lord Jesus Christ

is speaking through me. He is not weak in dealing with you, but is powerful among you. 4For to be sure, he was crucified in weakness, yet he lives by God's power. Likewise, we are weak in him, yet by God's power we will live with him to serve you.

5Examine yourselves to see whether you are in the faith; test yourselves. Do you not realize that Christ Jesus is in you—unless, of course, you fail the test? 6And I trust that you will discover that we have not failed the test. 7Now we pray to God that you will not do anything wrong. Not that people will see that we have stood the test but that you will do what is right even though we may seem to have failed. 8For we cannot do anything against the truth, but only for the truth. 9We are glad whenever we are weak but you are strong; and our prayer is for your perfection. 10This is why I write these things when I am absent, that when I come I may not have to be harsh in my use of authority—the authority the Lord gave me for building you up, not for tearing you down.

Final Greetings

11Finally, brothers, good-by. Aim for perfection, listen to my appeal, be of one mind, live in peace. And the God of love and peace will be with you.

12Greet one another with a holy kiss. 13All the saints send their greetings.

14May the grace of the

Jesus Christ, and the love
of God, and the fellowship
of the Holy Spirit, be with
you all.

καὶ ἡ ἀγάπη τοῦ θεοῦ καὶ ἡ κοινωνία
and the love – of God and the fellowship
τοῦ ἁγίου πνεύματος μετὰ πάντων ὑμῶν.
of the Holy Spirit [be] with [2]all [1]you.

Lord Jesus Christ, and the
love of God, and the fellowship of the Holy Spirit be
with you all.

Galatians

Chapter 1

Introduction

PAUL, an apostle (not
sent from men, nor
through the agency of man,
but through Jesus Christ,
and God the Father, who
raised Him from the dead),
2and all the brethren who
are with me, to the
churches of Galatia:
3Grace to you and peace
from God our Father, and
the Lord Jesus Christ,
4who gave Himself for
our sins, that He might deliver us out of this present
evil age, according to the
will of our God and Father,
5to whom *be* the glory
forevermore. Amen.

Perversion of the Gospel

6I am amazed that you
are so quickly deserting
Him who called you by the
grace of Christ, for a different gospel;
7which is *really* not another; only there are some
who are disturbing you,
and want to distort the gospel of Christ.
8But even though we, or
an angel from heaven,
should preach to you a gospel contrary to that which
we have preached to you,
let him be accursed.
9As we have said before,
so I say again now, if any
man is preaching to you a
gospel contrary to that
which you received, let him
be accursed.

ΠΡΟΣ ΓΑΛΑΤΑΣ
To Galatians

1 Παῦλος ἀπόστολος, οὐκ ἀπ' ἀνθρώπων
Paul an apostle, not from men
οὐδὲ δι' ἀνθρώπου ἀλλὰ διὰ Ἰησοῦ
nor through man but through Jesus
Χριστοῦ καὶ θεοῦ πατρὸς τοῦ ἐγείραντος
Christ and God [the] Father the [one] having raised
αὐτὸν ἐκ νεκρῶν, 2 καὶ οἱ σὺν ἐμοὶ
him out of [the] dead, and [2]the [4]with [5]me
πάντες ἀδελφοί, ταῖς ἐκκλησίαις τῆς
[1]all [3]brothers, to the churches –
Γαλατίας· 3 χάρις ὑμῖν καὶ εἰρήνη ἀπὸ
of Galatia: Grace to you and peace from
θεοῦ πατρὸς ἡμῶν καὶ κυρίου Ἰησοῦ
God Father of us and Lord Jesus
Χριστοῦ, 4 τοῦ δόντος ἑαυτὸν ὑπὲρ τῶν
Christ, the [one] having given himself on behalf of the
ἁμαρτιῶν ἡμῶν, ὅπως ἐξέληται ἡμᾶς ἐκ
sins of us, so as he might deliver us out of
τοῦ αἰῶνος τοῦ ἐνεστῶτος πονηροῦ κατὰ
the [3]age – [1]present [2]evil according to
τὸ θέλημα τοῦ θεοῦ καὶ πατρὸς ἡμῶν,
the will of the God and Father of us,
5 ᾧ ἡ δόξα εἰς τοὺς αἰῶνας τῶν
to whom the [be] glory unto the ages of the
αἰώνων· ἀμήν.
ages: Amen.

6 Θαυμάζω ὅτι οὕτως ταχέως μετατίθεσθε
I wonder that thus quickly ye are removing
ἀπὸ τοῦ καλέσαντος ὑμᾶς ἐν χάριτι
from the [one] having called you by [the] grace
Χριστοῦ εἰς ἕτερον εὐαγγέλιον, 7 ὃ οὐκ
of Christ to another gospel, which not
ἔστιν ἄλλο· εἰ μή τινές εἰσιν οἱ ταράσ-
is another; only [2]some [1]there are – troubl-
σοντες ὑμᾶς καὶ θέλοντες μεταστρέψαι
ing you and wishing to pervert
τὸ εὐαγγέλιον τοῦ Χριστοῦ. 8 ἀλλὰ
the gospel – of Christ. But
καὶ ἐὰν ἡμεῖς ἢ ἄγγελος ἐξ οὐρανοῦ
even if we or an angel out of heaven
εὐαγγελίσηται [ὑμῖν] παρ' ὃ εὐηγγελισάμεθα
should preach a gospel to you beside what we preached
ὑμῖν, ἀνάθεμα ἔστω. 9 ὡς προειρήκαμεν,
to you, [2]a curse [1]let him be. As we have previously said,
καὶ ἄρτι πάλιν λέγω, εἴ τις ὑμᾶς εὐαγ-
also now again I say, if anyone [2]you [1]preaches
γελίζεται παρ' ὃ παρελάβετε, ἀνάθεμα
[3]a gospel beside what ye received, [2]a curse
ἔστω.
[1]let him be.

Galatians

Chapter 1

PAUL, an apostle—sent
not from men nor by
man, but by Jesus Christ
and God the Father, who
raised him from the dead—
2and all the brothers with
me,

To the churches in Gala-
tia:

3Grace and peace to you
from God our Father and
the Lord Jesus Christ,
4who gave himself for our
sins to rescue us from the
present evil age, according
to the will of our God and
Father, 5to whom be glory
for ever and ever. Amen.

No Other Gospel

6I am astonished that you
are so quickly deserting the
one who called you by the
grace of Christ and are
turning to a different gospel
—7which is really no gos-
pel at all. Evidently some
people are throwing you
into confusion and are trying to pervert the gospel of
Christ. 8But even if we or
an angel from heaven
should preach a gospel other than the one we
preached to you, let him be
eternally condemned! 9As
we have already said, so
now I say again: If anybody
is preaching to you a gospel
other than what you ac-
cepted, let him be eternally
condemned!

10For am I now seeking
the favor of men, or of
God? Or am I striving to
please men? If I were still
trying to please men, I
would not be a bond-serv-
ant of Christ.

Paul Defends His Ministry

11For I would have you
know, brethren, that the
gospel which was preached
by me is not according to
man.
12For I neither received it
from man, nor was I taught
it, but *I received it* through
a revelation of Jesus
Christ.
13For you have heard of
my former manner of life in
Judaism, how I used to
persecute the church of
God beyond measure, and
tried to destroy it;
14and I was advancing in
Judaism beyond many of
my contemporaries among
my countrymen, being
more extremely zealous for
my ancestral traditions.
15But when He who had
set me apart, *even* from my
mother's womb, and called
me through His grace, was
pleased
16to reveal His Son in me,
that I might preach Him
among the Gentiles, I did
not immediately consult
with flesh and blood,
17nor did I go up to
Jerusalem to those who
were apostles before me;
but I went away to Arabia,
and returned once more to
Damascus.
18Then three years later I
went up to Jerusalem to
become acquainted with
Cephas, and stayed with
him fifteen days.
19But I did not see any
other of the apostles except
James, the Lord's brother.
20(Now in what I am writ-
ing to you, I assure you before God that I am not lying.)
21Then I went into the re-

10 Ἄρτι γὰρ ἀνθρώπους πείθω ἢ τὸν
For now men do I persuade or –
θεόν; ἢ ζητῶ ἀνθρώποις ἀρέσκειν; εἰ
God? or do I seek men to please? If
ἔτι ἀνθρώποις ἤρεσκον, Χριστοῦ δοῦλος
still men I pleased, [3]of Christ [2]a slave
οὐκ ἂν ἤμην. **11** γνωρίζω γὰρ ὑμῖν,
[1]I would not have been. For I make known to you,
ἀδελφοί, τὸ εὐαγγέλιον τὸ εὐαγγελισθὲν
brothers, the gospel – preached
ὑπ' ἐμοῦ ὅτι οὐκ ἔστιν κατὰ ἄνθρωπον·
by me that it is not according to man;
12 οὐδὲ γὰρ ἐγὼ παρὰ ἀνθρώπου παρέλαβον
for [4]not [1]I [5]from [6]man [2]received
αὐτὸ οὔτε ἐδιδάχθην, ἀλλὰ δι' ἀποκαλύψεως
[3]it nor was I taught [by man], but through a revelation
Ἰησοῦ Χριστοῦ. **13** Ἠκούσατε γὰρ τὴν
of Jesus Christ. For ye heard –
ἐμὴν ἀναστροφήν ποτε ἐν τῷ Ἰουδαϊσμῷ,
my conduct then in – Judaism,
ὅτι καθ' ὑπερβολὴν ἐδίωκον τὴν ἐκκλησίαν
that excessively† I persecuted the church
τοῦ θεοῦ καὶ ἐπόρθουν αὐτήν, **14** καὶ
– of God and wasted it, and
προέκοπτον ἐν τῷ Ἰουδαϊσμῷ ὑπὲρ πολλοὺς
progressed in – Judaism beyond many
συνηλικιώτας ἐν τῷ γένει μου, περισ-
contemporaries in the race of me, [2]abun-
σοτέρως ζηλωτὴς ὑπάρχων τῶν πατρικῶν
dantly [3]a zealot [1]being [4]of the [5]ancestral
μου παραδόσεων. **15** Ὅτε δὲ εὐδόκησεν
[7]of me [6]traditions. But when [14]was pleased
ὁ ἀφορίσας με ἐκ κοιλίας μητρός μου
[1]the [one] [2]having separated [3]me [4]from [5][the] womb [6]of mother [7]of me
καὶ καλέσας διὰ τῆς χάριτος αὐτοῦ
[8]and [9]having called [10]through [11]the [12]grace [13]of him
16 ἀποκαλύψαι τὸν υἱὸν αὐτοῦ ἐν ἐμοί,
to reveal the Son of him in me,
ἵνα εὐαγγελίζωμαι αὐτὸν ἐν τοῖς ἔθνεσιν,
in order that I might preach him among the nations,
εὐθέως οὐ προσανεθέμην σαρκὶ καὶ αἵματι,
immediately I conferred not with flesh and blood,
17 οὐδὲ ἀνῆλθον εἰς Ἱεροσόλυμα πρὸς
neither did I go up to Jerusalem to
τοὺς πρὸ ἐμοῦ ἀποστόλους, ἀλλὰ ἀπῆλθον
[1]the [3]before [4]me [2]apostles, but I went away
εἰς Ἀραβίαν, καὶ πάλιν ὑπέστρεψα εἰς
into Arabia, and again returned to
Δαμασκόν. **18** Ἔπειτα μετὰ τρία ἔτη
Damascus. Then after three years
ἀνῆλθον εἰς Ἱεροσόλυμα ἱστορῆσαι Κηφᾶν,
I went up to Jerusalem to visit Cephas,
καὶ ἐπέμεινα πρὸς αὐτὸν ἡμέρας δεκαπέντε·
and remained with him days fifteen;
19 ἕτερον δὲ τῶν ἀποστόλων οὐκ εἶδον,
but other of the apostles I saw not,
εἰ μὴ Ἰάκωβον τὸν ἀδελφὸν τοῦ κυρίου.
except James the brother of the Lord.
20 ἃ δὲ γράφω ὑμῖν, ἰδοὺ ἐνώπιον τοῦ
Now what things I write to you, behold before –
θεοῦ ὅτι οὐ ψεύδομαι. **21** ἔπειτα ἦλθον
God – I lie not. Then I went

10Am I now trying to win
the approval of men, or of
God? Or am I trying to
please men? If I were still
trying to please men, I
would not be a servant of
Christ.

Paul Called by God

11I want you to know,
brothers, that the gospel I
preached is not something
that man made up. 12I did
not receive it from any
man, nor was I taught it;
rather, I received it by revelation from Jesus Christ.
13For you have heard of
my previous way of life in
Judaism, how intensely I
persecuted the church of
God and tried to destroy it.
14I was advancing in Judaism beyond many Jews of
my own age and was ex-
tremely zealous for the traditions of my fathers. 15But
when God, who set me
apart from birth[a] and
called me by his grace, was
pleased 16to reveal his Son
in me so that I might preach
him among the Gentiles, I
did not consult any man,
17nor did I go up to Jerusalem to see those who were
apostles before I was, but I
went immediately into Arabia and later returned to
Damascus.
18Then after three years, I
went up to Jerusalem to get
acquainted with Peter[b] and
stayed with him fifteen
days. 19I saw none of the
other apostles—only
James, the Lord's brother.
20I assure you before God
that what I am writing you
is no lie. 21Later I went to
Syria and Cilicia. 22I was
personally unknown to the

[a]15 Or *from my mother's womb*
[b]18 Greek *Cephas*

gions of Syria and Cilicia.
22And I was *still* unknown
by sight to the churches of
Judea which were in Christ;
23but only, they kept
hearing, "He who once
persecuted us is now
preaching the faith which
he once tried to destroy."
24And they were glorify-
ing God because of me.

Chapter 2

The Council at Jerusalem

THEN after an interval
of fourteen years I
went up again to Jerusalem
with Barnabas, taking Titus
along also.
2And it was because of a
revelation that I went up;
and I submitted to them the
gospel which I preach
among the Gentiles, but *I*
did so in private to those
who were of reputation, for
fear that I might be run-
ning, or had run, in vain.
3But not even Titus who
was with me, though he
was a Greek, was com-
pelled to be circumcised.
4But *it was* because of
the false brethren who had
sneaked in to spy out our
liberty which we have in
Christ Jesus, in order to
bring us into bondage.
5But we did not yield in
subjection to them for even
an hour, so that the truth of
the gospel might remain
with you.
6But from those who
were of high reputation
(what they were makes no
difference to me; God
shows no partiality)—well,
those who were of reputa-
tion contributed nothing to
me.
7But on the contrary,
seeing that I had been entrusted with the gospel to
the uncircumcised, just as
Peter *had been* to the circumcised
8(for He who effectually
worked for Peter in *his*
apostleship to the circumcised effectually worked
for me also to the Gentiles),

εἰς τὰ κλίματα τῆς Συρίας καὶ τῆς
into the regions – of Syria and –
Κιλικίας. 22 ἤμην δὲ ἀγνοούμενος τῷ
of Cilicia. And I was *being* unknown –
προσώπῳ ταῖς ἐκκλησίαις τῆς Ἰουδαίας
by face to the churches – of Judæa
ταῖς ἐν Χριστῷ. 23 μόνον δὲ ἀκούοντες
– in Christ. But only hearing
ἦσαν ὅτι ὁ διώκων ἡμᾶς ποτε νῦν
they were that the [one] [2]persecuting [3]us [1]then now
εὐαγγελίζεται τὴν πίστιν ἥν ποτε ἐπόρθει,
preaches the faith which then he was destroying,
24 καὶ ἐδόξαζον ἐν ἐμοὶ τὸν θεόν.
and they glorified [2]in [3]me – [1]God.
2 Ἔπειτα διὰ δεκατεσσάρων ἐτῶν πάλιν
Then through fourteen years again
ἀνέβην εἰς Ἱεροσόλυμα μετὰ Βαρναβᾶ,
I went up to Jerusalem with Barnabas,
συμπαραλαβὼν καὶ Τίτον· 2 ἀνέβην δὲ
taking with [me] also Titus; and I went up
κατὰ ἀποκάλυψιν· καὶ ἀνεθέμην αὐτοῖς
according to a revelation; and I put before them
τὸ εὐαγγέλιον ὃ κηρύσσω ἐν τοῖς ἔθνεσιν,
the gospel which I proclaim among the nations,
κατ' ἰδίαν δὲ τοῖς δοκοῦσιν, μή πως
[2]privately [1]but to the [ones] seeming,* lest
εἰς κενὸν τρέχω ἢ ἔδραμον. 3 ἀλλ'
in vain I run or I ran. But
οὐδὲ Τίτος ὁ σὺν ἐμοί, Ἕλλην ὤν,
not Titus the [one] with me, a Greek being,
ἠναγκάσθη περιτμηθῆναι· 4 διὰ δὲ τοὺς
was compelled to be circumcised; but on account of [1]the
παρεισάκτους ψευδαδέλφους, οἵτινες παρεισ-
[3]brought in secretly [2]false brothers, who stole
ἦλθον κατασκοπῆσαι τὴν ἐλευθερίαν ἡμῶν
in to spy on the freedom of us
ἣν ἔχομεν ἐν Χριστῷ Ἰησοῦ, ἵνα ἡμᾶς
which we have in Christ Jesus, in order that [2]us
καταδουλώσουσιν· 5 οἷς οὐδὲ πρὸς ὥραν
[1]they will(might) enslave; to whom not for an hour
εἴξαμεν τῇ ὑποταγῇ, ἵνα ἡ ἀλήθεια
yielded we – in subjection, in order that the truth
τοῦ εὐαγγελίου διαμείνῃ πρὸς ὑμᾶς. 6 ἀπὸ
of the gospel might continue with you. from
δὲ τῶν δοκούντων εἶναί τι, — ὁποῖοί
But the [ones] seeming to be something, (of what kind
ποτε ἦσαν οὐδέν μοι διαφέρει· πρόσωπον
[2]then [1]they were [4]nothing [5]to me [3]matters: [8][the] face
[ὁ] θεὸς ἀνθρώπου οὐ λαμβάνει — ἐμοὶ
– [6]God [9]of a man [7]receives not,) [2]to me
γὰρ οἱ δοκοῦντες οὐδὲν προσανέθεντο,
[1]for the [ones] seeming* nothing added,
7 ἀλλὰ τοὐναντίον ἰδόντες ὅτι πεπίστευμαι
but on the contrary seeing that I have been entrusted [with]
τὸ εὐαγγέλιον τῆς ἀκροβυστίας καθὼς
the gospel of the uncircumcision as
Πέτρος τῆς περιτομῆς, 8 ὁ γὰρ ἐνεργήσας
Peter [that] of the circumcision, for the [one] operating
Πέτρῳ εἰς ἀποστολὴν τῆς περιτομῆς
in Peter to an apostleship of the circumcision
ἐνήργησεν καὶ ἐμοὶ εἰς τὰ ἔθνη, 9 καὶ
operated also in me to the nations, and

churches of Judea that are
in Christ. 23They only
heard the report: "The man
who formerly persecuted
us is now preaching the
faith he once tried to destroy." 24And they praised
God because of me.

Chapter 2

Paul Accepted by the Apostles

FOURTEEN years later
I went up again to Je-
rusalem, this time with
Barnabas. I took Titus
along also. 2I went in response to a revelation and
set before them the gospel
that I preach among the
Gentiles. But I did this privately to those who seemed
to be leaders, for fear that I
was running or had run my
race in vain. 3Yet not even
Titus, who was with me,
was compelled to be cir-
cumcised, even though he
was a Greek. 4This matter
arose because some false
brothers had infiltrated our
ranks to spy on the freedom
we have in Christ Jesus and
to make us slaves. 5We did
not give in to them for a
moment, so that the truth
of the gospel might remain
with you.
6As for those who seemed
to be important—whatever
they were makes no difference to me; God does not
judge by external appear-
ance—those men added
nothing to my message.
7On the contrary, they saw
that I had been entrusted
with the task of preaching
the gospel to the Gentiles,[c]
just as Peter had been to the
Jews.[d] 8For God, who was
at work in the ministry of
Peter as an apostle to the
Jews, was also at work in
my ministry as an apostle
to the Gentiles. 9James, Pe-

* *Cf.* the full expressions in vers. 6 (earlier) and 9.

[c]7 Greek *uncircumcised*
[d]7 Greek *circumcised*; also in verses 8 and 9

9and recognizing the
grace that had been given
to me, James and Cephas
and John, who were reput-
ed to be pillars, gave to me
and Barnabas the right
hand of fellowship, that we
might go to the Gentiles,
and they to the circum-
cised.
10*They* only *asked* us to
remember the poor—the
very thing I also was eager
to do.

Peter (Cephas) Opposed by Paul

11But when Cephas came
to Antioch, I opposed him
to his face, because he
stood condemned.
12For prior to the coming
of certain men from James,
he used to eat with the Gentiles; but when they came,
he *began* to withdraw and
hold himself aloof, fearing
the party of the circumcision.
13And the rest of the Jews
joined him in hypocrisy,
with the result that even
Barnabas was carried away
by their hypocrisy.
14But when I saw that
they were not straightfor-
ward about the truth of the
gospel, I said to Cephas in
the presence of all, "If you,
being a Jew, live like the
Gentiles and not like the
Jews, how *is it that* you
compel the Gentiles to live
like Jews?
15"We *are* Jews by na-
ture, and not sinners from
among the Gentiles;
16nevertheless knowing
that a man is not justified
by the works of the Law
but through faith in Christ
Jesus, even we have be-
lieved in Christ Jesus, that
we may be justified by faith
in Christ, and not by the
works of the Law; since by
the works of the Law shall
no flesh be justified.
17"But if, while seeking
to be justified in Christ, we

γνόντες τὴν χάριν τὴν δοθεῖσάν μοι,
knowing the grace – given to me,
Ἰάκωβος καὶ Κηφᾶς καὶ Ἰωάννης, οἱ
James and Cephas and John, the
δοκοῦντες στῦλοι εἶναι, δεξιὰς ἔδωκαν
[ones] seeming 2pillars 1to be, 5right [hands] 1gave
ἐμοὶ καὶ Βαρναβᾷ κοινωνίας, ἵνα ἡμεῖς
2to me 3and 4to Barnabas 6of fellowship, in order that we [should
εἰς τὰ ἔθνη, αὐτοὶ δὲ εἰς τὴν περιτομήν·
go] to the nations, but they to the circumcision;
10 μόνον τῶν πτωχῶν ἵνα μνημονεύωμεν,
only 3the 4poor *in order* 1that 2we might remember,
ὃ καὶ ἐσπούδασα αὐτὸ τοῦτο ποιῆσαι.
which indeed 2I was eager 1this very thing to do.
11 Ὅτε δὲ ἦλθεν Κηφᾶς εἰς Ἀντιόχειαν,
But when 2came 1Cephas to Antioch,
κατὰ πρόσωπον αὐτῷ ἀντέστην, ὅτι
against [his] face *to* him I opposed, because
κατεγνωσμένος ἦν. 12 πρὸ τοῦ γὰρ
2having been condemned 1he was. Before the for
=For before some came . . .
ἐλθεῖν τινας ἀπὸ Ἰακώβου μετὰ τῶν
to come some[b] from James 2with 3the
ἐθνῶν συνήσθιεν· ὅτε δὲ ἦλθον, ὑπέστελλεν
4nations 1he ate *with*; but when they came, he withdrew
καὶ ἀφώριζεν ἑαυτόν, φοβούμενος τοὺς
and separated himself, fearing the [ones]
ἐκ περιτομῆς· 13 καὶ συνυπεκρίθησαν αὐτῷ
of [the] circumcision; and dissembled along with him
[καὶ] οἱ λοιποὶ Ἰουδαῖοι, ὥστε καὶ
also the remaining Jews, so as even
Βαρναβᾶς συναπήχθη αὐτῶν τῇ ὑποκρίσει.
Barnabas was led away with 3of them 1the 2dissembling.
14 ἀλλ' ὅτε εἶδον ὅτι οὐκ ὀρθοποδοῦσιν
But when I saw that they walk[ed] not straight
πρὸς τὴν ἀλήθειαν τοῦ εὐαγγελίου, εἶπον
with the truth of the gospel, I said
τῷ Κηφᾷ ἔμπροσθεν πάντων· εἰ σὺ
– to Cephas in front of all: If thou
Ἰουδαῖος ὑπάρχων ἐθνικῶς καὶ οὐκ
2a Jew 1being as a Gentile and not
Ἰουδαϊκῶς ζῇς, πῶς τὰ ἔθνη ἀναγκάζεις
as a Jew livest, how 2the 3nations 1compellest thou
ἰουδαΐζειν; 15 Ἡμεῖς φύσει Ἰουδαῖοι καὶ
to judaize? We by nature Jews and
οὐκ ἐξ ἐθνῶν ἁμαρτωλοί, 16 εἰδότες δὲ
not 3of 2nations 1sinners, and knowing
ὅτι οὐ δικαιοῦται ἄνθρωπος ἐξ ἔργων
that 2is not justified 1a man by works
νόμου ἐὰν μὴ διὰ πίστεως Χριστοῦ
of law except(but) through faith of(in) Christ
Ἰησοῦ, καὶ ἡμεῖς εἰς Χριστὸν Ἰησοῦν
Jesus,* even we 2in 3Christ 4Jesus
ἐπιστεύσαμεν, ἵνα δικαιωθῶμεν ἐκ πίστεως
1believed, in order that we might be justified by faith
Χριστοῦ καὶ οὐκ ἐξ ἔργων νόμου, ὅτι
of(in) Christ* and not by works of law, because
ἐξ ἔργων νόμου οὐ δικαιωθήσεται πᾶσα
by works of law not will be justified all
=no flesh will be justified.
σάρξ. 17 εἰ δὲ ζητοῦντες δικαιωθῆναι
flesh. But if seeking to be justified

ter[e] and John, those reput-
ed to be pillars, gave me
and Barnabas the right
hand of fellowship when
they recognized the grace
given to me. They agreed
that we should go to the
Gentiles, and they to the
Jews. 10All they asked was
that we should continue to
remember the poor, the
very thing I was eager to
do.

Paul Opposes Peter

11When Peter came to
Antioch, I opposed him to
his face, because he was
clearly in the wrong. 12Be-
fore certain men came from
James, he used to eat with
the Gentiles. But when
they arrived, he began to
draw back and separate
himself from the Gentiles
because he was afraid of
those who belonged to the
circumcision group. 13The
other Jews joined him in his
hypocrisy, so that by their
hypocrisy even Barnabas
was led astray.
14When I saw that they
were not acting in line with
the truth of the gospel, I
said to Peter in front of
them all, "You are a Jew,
yet you live like a Gentile
and not like a Jew. How is
it, then, that you force Gentiles to follow Jewish customs?
15"We who are Jews by
birth and not 'Gentile sinners' 16know that a man is
not justified by observing
the law, but by faith in
Jesus Christ. So we, too,
have put our faith in Christ
Jesus that we may be justified by faith in Christ and
not by observing the law,
because by observing the
law no one will be justified.
17"If, while we seek to be
justified in Christ, it be-

* Objective genitive, as is shown by the intervening sentence see also 3. 22, 26). *Cf.* " fear of God".

[e]9 Greek *Cephas*; also in verses 11 and 14

ourselves have also been found sinners, is Christ then a minister of sin? May it never be!

18 "For if I rebuild what I have *once* destroyed, I prove myself to be a transgressor.

19 "For through the Law I died to the Law, that I might live to God.

20 "I have been crucified with Christ; and it is no longer I who live, but Christ lives in me; and the *life* which I now live in the flesh I live by faith in the Son of God, who loved me, and delivered Himself up for me.

21 "I do not nullify the grace of God; for if righteousness *comes* through the Law, then Christ died needlessly."

ἐν Χριστῷ εὑρέθημεν καὶ αὐτοὶ ἁμαρτωλοί,
in Christ we were found also [our]selves sinners,
ἆρα Χριστὸς ἁμαρτίας διάκονος; μὴ
then [is] Christ [2]of sin [1]a minister? not
γένοιτο. **18** εἰ γὰρ ἃ κατέλυσα ταῦτα
May it be. For if what things I destroyed these things
πάλιν οἰκοδομῶ, παραβάτην ἐμαυτὸν συνισ-
again I build, [3]a transgressor [2]myself [1]I con-
τάνω. **19** ἐγὼ γὰρ διὰ νόμου νόμῳ
stitute. For I through law [2]to law
ἀπέθανον ἵνα θεῷ ζήσω. **20** Χριστῷ συνεσ-
[1]died in order that to God I might live. With Christ I have
ταύρωμαι· ζῶ δὲ οὐκέτι ἐγώ, ζῇ δὲ
been co-crucified; and [2]live [3]no more [1]I, but [2]lives
ἐν ἐμοὶ Χριστός· ὃ δὲ νῦν ζῶ ἐν σαρκί,
[3]in [4]me [1]Christ; and what now I live in [the] flesh,
ἐν πίστει ζῶ τῇ τοῦ υἱοῦ τοῦ θεοῦ
[2]by [3]faith [1]I live – of(in) the Son – of God
τοῦ ἀγαπήσαντός με καὶ παραδόντος ἑαυτὸν
– loving me and giving up himself
ὑπὲρ ἐμοῦ. **21** Οὐκ ἀθετῶ τὴν χάριν
on behalf of me. I do not set aside the grace
τοῦ θεοῦ· εἰ γὰρ διὰ νόμου δικαιοσύνη,
– of God; for if through law righteousness [comes],
ἄρα Χριστὸς δωρεὰν ἀπέθανεν.
then Christ without cause died.

comes evident that we ourselves are sinners, does that mean that Christ promotes sin? Absolutely not! 18If I rebuild what I destroyed, I prove that I am a lawbreaker. 19For through the law I died to the law so that I might live for God. 20I have been crucified with Christ and I no longer live, but Christ lives in me. The life I live in the body, I live by faith in the Son of God, who loved me and gave himself for me. 21I do not set aside the grace of God, for if righteousness could be gained through the law, Christ died for nothing!"[f]

Chapter 3

Faith Brings Righteousness

YOU foolish Galatians, who has bewitched you, before whose eyes Jesus Christ was publicly portrayed *as* crucified?

2 This is the only thing I want to find out from you: did you receive the Spirit by the works of the Law, or by hearing with faith?

3 Are you so foolish? Having begun by the Spirit, are you now being perfected by the flesh?

4 Did you suffer so many things in vain—if indeed it was in vain?

5 Does He then, who provides you with the Spirit and works miracles among you, do it by the works of the Law, or by hearing with faith?

6 Even so Abraham BELIEVED GOD, AND IT WAS RECKONED TO HIM AS RIGHTEOUSNESS.

7 Therefore, be sure that it is those who are of faith who are sons of Abraham.

8 And the Scripture, foreseeing that God would justify the Gentiles by faith, preached the gospel beforehand to Abraham, *saying*, "ALL THE NATIONS SHALL BE

3 Ὦ ἀνόητοι Γαλάται, τίς ὑμᾶς
O foolish Galatians, who you
ἐβάσκανεν, οἷς κατ' ὀφθαλμοὺς Ἰησοῦς
bewitched, to whom before [the] eyes Jesus
Χριστὸς προεγράφη ἐσταυρωμένος; **2** τοῦτο
Christ was portrayed having been crucified? This
μόνον θέλω μαθεῖν ἀφ' ὑμῶν, ἐξ ἔργων
only I wish to learn from you, by works
νόμου τὸ πνεῦμα ἐλάβετε ἢ ἐξ ἀκοῆς
of law the Spirit received ye or by hearing
πίστεως; **3** οὕτως ἀνόητοί ἐστε; ἐναρξάμενοι
of faith? thus foolish are ye? having begun
πνεύματι νῦν σαρκὶ ἐπιτελεῖσθε; **4** τοσαῦτα
in [the] Spirit now in [the] flesh are ye being perfected? so many things
ἐπάθετε εἰκῇ; **5** εἴ γε καὶ εἰκῇ. ὁ
suffered ye in vain? if indeed in vain. The [one]
οὖν ἐπιχορηγῶν ὑμῖν τὸ πνεῦμα καὶ
therefore supplying to you the Spirit and
ἐνεργῶν δυνάμεις ἐν ὑμῖν ἐξ ἔργων
working powerful deeds among you [is it] by works
νόμου ἢ ἐξ ἀκοῆς πίστεως; **6** Καθὼς
of law or by hearing of faith? As
Ἀβραὰμ ἐπίστευσεν τῷ θεῷ, καὶ ἐλογίσθη
Abraham believed – God, and it was reckoned
αὐτῷ εἰς δικαιοσύνην. **7** γινώσκετε ἄρα
to him for righteousness. Know ye then
ὅτι οἱ ἐκ πίστεως, οὗτοι υἱοί εἰσιν
that the [ones] of faith, [1]these [3]sons [2]are
Ἀβραάμ. **8** προϊδοῦσα δὲ ἡ γραφὴ ὅτι
[4]of Abraham. And [3]foreseeing [1]the [2]scripture [4]that
ἐκ πίστεως δικαιοῖ τὰ ἔθνη ὁ θεός,
[9]by [10]faith [8]would justify [7]the [6]nations – [5]God,
προευηγγελίσατο τῷ Ἀβραὰμ ὅτι ἐνευλογη-
preached good tidings before – to Abraham that [6]will be

Chapter 3

Faith or Observance of the Law

YOU foolish Galatians! Who has bewitched you? Before your very eyes Jesus Christ was clearly portrayed as crucified. 2I would like to learn just one thing from you: Did you receive the Spirit by observing the law, or by believing what you heard? 3Are you so foolish? After beginning with the Spirit, are you now trying to attain your goal by human effort? 4Have you suffered so much for nothing—if it really was for nothing? 5Does God give you his Spirit and work miracles among you because you observe the law, or because you believe what you heard?

6Consider Abraham: "He believed God, and it was credited to him as righteousness."[g] 7Understand, then, that those who believe are children of Abraham. 8The Scripture foresaw that God would justify the Gentiles by faith, and announced the gospel in advance to Abraham: "All nations will be blessed

f21 Some interpreters end the quotation after verse 14.
g6 Gen. 15:6

BLESSED IN YOU.''
9So then those who are
of faith are blessed with
Abraham, the believer.
10For as many as are of
the works of the Law are
under a curse; for it is written, "CURSED IS EVERYONE
WHO DOES NOT ABIDE BY ALL
THINGS WRITTEN IN THE
BOOK OF THE LAW, TO PER-
FORM THEM."
11Now that no one is justified by the Law before God
is evident; for, "THE RIGHT-
EOUS MAN SHALL LIVE BY
FAITH."
12However, the Law is
not of faith; on the con-
trary, "HE WHO PRACTICES
THEM SHALL LIVE BY THEM."
13Christ redeemed us
from the curse of the Law,
having become a curse for
us—for it is written,
"CURSED IS EVERYONE WHO
HANGS ON A TREE"—
14in order that in Christ
Jesus the blessing of Abraham might come to the
Gentiles, so that we might
receive the promise of the
Spirit through faith.

Intent of the Law

15Brethren, I speak in
terms of human relations:
even though it is *only* a
man's covenant, yet when
it has been ratified, no one
sets it aside or adds conditions to it.
16Now the promises were
spoken to Abraham and to
his seed. He does not say,
"And to seeds," as *referring* to many, but *rather* to
one, "And to your seed,"
that is, Christ.
17What I am saying is this:
the Law, which came four
hundred and thirty years
later, does not invalidate a
covenant previously rati-
fied by God, so as to nullify
the promise.
18For if the inheritance is
based on law, it is no longer
based on a promise; but
God has granted it to Abra-

θήσονται ἐν σοὶ πάντα τὰ ἔθνη. **9** ὥστε
blessed [1]in [2]thee [3]all [4]the [5]nations. So as
οἱ ἐκ πίστεως εὐλογοῦνται σὺν τῷ πιστῷ
the[ones]of faith are blessed with the believing
Ἀβραάμ. **10** Ὅσοι γὰρ ἐξ ἔργων νόμου
Abraham. For as many as [2]of [3]works [4]of law
εἰσίν, ὑπὸ κατάραν εἰσίν· γέγραπται γὰρ
[1]are, [6]under [7]a curse [5]are; for it has been written[,]
ὅτι ἐπικατάρατος πᾶς ὃς οὐκ ἐμμένει
– Accursed everyone who continues not
πᾶσιν τοῖς γεγραμμένοις ἐν τῷ βιβλίῳ
in all the things having been written in the roll
τοῦ νόμου τοῦ ποιῆσαι αὐτά. **11** ὅτι
of the law – to do[d] them. that
δὲ ἐν νόμῳ οὐδεὶς δικαιοῦται παρὰ τῷ
Now by law no man is justified before –
θεῷ δῆλον, ὅτι ὁ δίκαιος ἐκ πίστεως
God [is] clear, because the just man by faith
ζήσεται· **12** ὁ δὲ νόμος οὐκ ἔστιν ἐκ
will live; and the law is not of
πίστεως, ἀλλ' ὁ ποιήσας αὐτὰ ζήσεται
faith, but the [one] doing them will live
ἐν αὐτοῖς. **13** Χριστὸς ἡμᾶς ἐξηγόρασεν
by them. Christ [2]us [1]redeemed
ἐκ τῆς κατάρας τοῦ νόμου γενόμενος
out of the curse of the law becoming
ὑπὲρ ἡμῶν κατάρα, ὅτι γέγραπται·
[2]on behalf of [3]us [1]a curse, because it has been written:
ἐπικατάρατος πᾶς ὁ κρεμάμενος ἐπὶ
Accursed everyone hanging on
ξύλου, **14** ἵνα εἰς τὰ ἔθνη ἡ εὐλογία
a tree, in order that [5]to [6]the [7]nations [1]the [2]blessing
τοῦ Ἀβραὰμ γένηται ἐν Ἰησοῦ Χριστῷ,
– [3]of Abraham [4]might be in Jesus Christ,
ἵνα τὴν ἐπαγγελίαν τοῦ πνεύματος λάβωμεν
in order that [2]the [3]promise [4]of the [5]Spirit [1]we might receive
διὰ τῆς πίστεως. **15** Ἀδελφοί, κατὰ
through *the* faith. Brothers, according to
ἄνθρωπον λέγω. ὅμως ἀνθρώπου κεκυρω-
man I say. Nevertheless [6]of man [7]having been
μένην διαθήκην οὐδεὶς ἀθετεῖ ἢ ἐπιδια-
ratified [5]a covenant [1]no one [2]sets aside [3]or [4]makes
τάσσεται. **16** τῷ δὲ Ἀβραὰμ ἐρρέθησαν
additions [to]. – Now to Abraham were said
αἱ ἐπαγγελίαι καὶ τῷ σπέρματι αὐτοῦ.
the promises and to the seed of him.
οὐ λέγει· καὶ τοῖς σπέρμασιν, ὡς ἐπὶ
It says not: And to the seeds, as concerning
πολλῶν, ἀλλ' ὡς ἐφ' ἑνός· καὶ τῷ
many, but as concerning one: And to the
σπέρματί σου, ὅς ἐστιν Χριστός. **17** τοῦτο δὲ
seed of thee, who is Christ. And this
λέγω· διαθήκην προκεκυρωμένην ὑπὸ
I say: [10]A covenant [11]having been previously ratified [12]by
τοῦ θεοῦ ὁ μετὰ τετρακόσια καὶ τριάκοντα
– [13]God [1]the [4]after [5]four hundred [6]and [7]thirty
ἔτη γεγονὼς νόμος οὐκ ἀκυροῖ, εἰς τὸ
[8]years [3]having come into being [2]law [9]does not annul, so as†
καταργῆσαι τὴν ἐπαγγελίαν. **18** εἰ γὰρ
to abolish the promise. For if
ἐκ νόμου ἡ κληρονομία, οὐκέτι ἐξ
[4]of [5]law [1]the [2]inheritance [3][is], no more [is it] of
ἐπαγγελίας· τῷ δὲ Ἀβραὰμ δι' ἐπαγγελίας
promise; – but [4]to Abraham [5]through [6]promise

through you."[h] 9So those
who have faith are blessed
along with Abraham, the
man of faith.
10All who rely on observ-
ing the law are under a
curse, for it is written:
"Cursed is everyone who
does not continue to do everything written in the
Book of the Law."[i]
11Clearly no one is justified
before God by the law, because, "The righteous will
live by faith."[j] 12The law
is not based on faith; on the
contrary, "The man who
does these things will live
by them."[k] 13Christ re-
deemed us from the curse
of the law by becoming a
curse for us, for it is written: "Cursed is everyone
who is hung on a tree."[l]
14He redeemed us in order
that the blessing given to
Abraham might come to
the Gentiles through Christ
Jesus, so that by faith we
might receive the promise
of the Spirit.

The Law and the Promise

15Brothers, let me take an
example from everyday
life. Just as no one can set
aside or add to a human
covenant that has been
duly established, so it is in
this case. 16The promises
were spoken to Abraham
and to his seed. The Scripture does not say "and to
seeds," meaning many
people, but "and to your
seed,"[m] meaning one person, who is Christ. 17What
I mean is this: The law, introduced 430 years later,
does not set aside the covenant previously established
by God and thus do away
with the promise. 18For if
the inheritance depends on
the law, then it no longer
depends on a promise; but
God in his grace gave it to

[h] *8* Gen. 12:3; 18:18; 22:18
[i] *10* Deut. 27:26
[j] *11* Hab. 2:4
[k] *12* Lev. 18:5
[l] *13* Deut. 21:23
[m] *16* Gen. 12:7; 13:15; 24:7

ham by means of a promise.

19 Why the Law then? It was added because of transgressions, having been ordained through angels by the agency of a mediator, until the seed should come to whom the promise had been made.

20 Now a mediator is not for one *party only*; whereas God is *only* one.

21 Is the Law then contrary to the promises of God? May it never be! For if a law had been given which was able to impart life, then righteousness would indeed have been based on law.

22 But the Scripture has shut up all men under sin, that the promise by faith in Jesus Christ might be given to those who believe.

23 But before faith came, we were kept in custody under the law, being shut up to the faith which was later to be revealed.

24 Therefore the Law has become our tutor *to lead us* to Christ, that we may be justified by faith.

25 But now that faith has come, we are no longer under a tutor.

26 For you are all sons of God through faith in Christ Jesus.

27 For all of you who were baptized into Christ have clothed yourselves with Christ.

28 There is neither Jew nor Greek, there is neither slave nor free man, there is neither male nor female; for you are all one in Christ Jesus.

29 And if you belong to Christ, then you are Abraham's offspring, heirs according to promise.

Chapter 4

Sonship in Christ

NOW I say, as long as the heir is a child, he does not differ at all from a slave although he is owner of everything,

2 but he is under guardians and managers until the

κεχάρισται ὁ θεός. **19** Τί οὖν ὁ νόμος;
[2]has given [3][it] – [1]God. Why therefore the law?

τῶν παραβάσεων χάριν προσετέθη, ἄχρις
[3]the [4]transgressions [2]by reason of [1]it was added, until

ἂν ἔλθῃ τὸ σπέρμα ᾧ ἐπήγγελται,
[3]should come [1]the [2]seed to whom it has been promised,

διαταγεὶς δι' ἀγγέλων, ἐν χειρὶ μεσίτου.
being ordained through angels, by [the] hand of a mediator.

20 ὁ δὲ μεσίτης ἑνὸς οὐκ ἔστιν, ὁ
Now the mediator [2]of one [1]is not, –

δὲ θεὸς εἷς ἐστιν. **21** ὁ οὖν νόμος κατὰ
but God [2]one [1]is. [Is] the [2]therefore [1]law against

τῶν ἐπαγγελιῶν [τοῦ θεοῦ]; μὴ γένοιτο.
the promises – of God? May it not be.

εἰ γὰρ ἐδόθη νόμος ὁ δυνάμενος ζωοποι-
For if [2]was given [1]a law – being able to make

ῆσαι, ὄντως ἐκ νόμου ἂν ἦν ἡ δικαιοσύνη·
alive, really [3]by [4]law [2]would have been – [1]righteousness;

22 ἀλλὰ συνέκλεισεν ἡ γραφὴ τὰ πάντα
but [3]shut up [1]the [2]scripture all mankind†

ὑπὸ ἁμαρτίαν ἵνα ἡ ἐπαγγελία ἐκ πίστεως
under sin in order that the promise by faith

Ἰησοῦ Χριστοῦ δοθῇ τοῖς πιστεύουσιν.
of(in) Jesus Christ might be given to the [ones] believing.

23 Πρὸ τοῦ δὲ ἐλθεῖν τὴν πίστιν ὑπὸ
before *the* But to come *the* faith[b] under
=But before faith came

νόμον ἐφρουρούμεθα συγκλειόμενοι εἰς τὴν
law we were guarded being shut up to the

μέλλουσαν πίστιν ἀποκαλυφθῆναι. **24** ὥστε
[2]being about [1]faith to be revealed. So as

ὁ νόμος παιδαγωγὸς ἡμῶν γέγονεν εἰς
the law [2]a trainer [3]of us [1]has become [up] to

Χριστόν, ἵνα ἐκ πίστεως δικαιωθῶμεν·
Christ, in order that by faith we might be justified;

25 ἐλθούσης δὲ τῆς πίστεως οὐκέτι ὑπὸ
but [3]having come [1]*the* [2]faith[a] [5]no more [6]under

παιδαγωγόν ἐσμεν. **26** Πάντες γὰρ υἱοὶ
[7]a trainer [4]we are. For all sons

θεοῦ ἐστε διὰ τῆς πίστεως ἐν Χριστῷ
of God ye are through *the* faith in Christ

Ἰησοῦ· **27** ὅσοι γὰρ εἰς Χριστὸν ἐβαπτίσ-
Jesus; for as many as [2]into [3]Christ [1]*ye* were

θητε, Χριστὸν ἐνεδύσασθε. **28** οὐκ ἔνι
baptized, [2]Christ [1]ye put on. There cannot be

Ἰουδαῖος οὐδὲ Ἕλλην, οὐκ ἔνι δοῦλος
Jew nor Greek, there cannot be slave

οὐδὲ ἐλεύθερος, οὐκ ἔνι ἄρσεν καὶ θῆλυ·
nor freeman, there cannot be male and female;

πάντες γὰρ ὑμεῖς εἷς ἐστε ἐν Χριστῷ
for [3]all [1]ye [4]one [2]are in Christ

Ἰησοῦ. **29** εἰ δὲ ὑμεῖς Χριστοῦ, ἄρα
Jesus. But if ye [are] of Christ, then

τοῦ Ἀβραὰμ σπέρμα ἐστέ, κατ' ἐπαγγελίαν
– [3]of Abraham [2]a seed [1]are ye, according to promise

κληρονόμοι. **4** Λέγω δέ, ἐφ' ὅσον χρόνον ὁ
heirs. But I say, over so long a time as the

κληρονόμος νήπιός ἐστιν, οὐδὲν διαφέρει
heir [2]an infant [1]is, [2]nothing [1]he differs [3][from]

δούλου κύριος πάντων ὤν, **2** ἀλλὰ ὑπὸ
[4]a slave [6]lord [7]of all [5]being, but [2]under

ἐπιτρόπους ἐστὶν καὶ οἰκονόμους ἄχρι τῆς
[3]guardians [1]is and stewards until the

Abraham through a promise.

19 What, then, was the purpose of the law? It was added because of transgressions until the Seed to whom the promise referred had come. The law was put into effect through angels by a mediator. 20 A mediator, however, does not represent just one party; but God is one.

21 Is the law, therefore, opposed to the promises of God? Absolutely not! For if a law had been given that could impart life, then righteousness would certainly have come by the law. 22 But the Scripture declares that the whole world is a prisoner of sin, so that what was promised, being given through faith in Jesus Christ, might be given to those who believe.

23 Before this faith came, we were held prisoners by the law, locked up until faith should be revealed. 24 So the law was put in charge to lead us to Christ[n] that we might be justified by faith. 25 Now that faith has come, we are no longer under the supervision of the law.

Sons of God

26 You are all sons of God through faith in Christ Jesus, 27 for all of you who were baptized into Christ have clothed yourselves with Christ. 28 There is neither Jew nor Greek, slave nor free, male nor female, for you are all one in Christ Jesus. 29 If you belong to Christ, then you are Abraham's seed, and heirs according to the promise.

Chapter 4

WHAT I am saying is that as long as the heir is a child, he is no different from a slave, although he owns the whole estate. 2 He is subject to guardians and trustees until the time set by his father. 3 So also, when we were

[n]24 Or *charge until Christ came*

date set by the father.
3So also we, while we
were children, were held in
bondage under the elemen-
tal things of the world.
4But when the fulness of
the time came, God sent
forth His Son, born of a
woman, born under the
Law,
5in order that He might
redeem those who were un-
der the Law, that we might
receive the adoption as
sons.
6And because you are
sons, God has sent forth
the Spirit of His Son into
our hearts, crying, "Abba!
Father!"
7Therefore you are no
longer a slave, but a son;
and if a son, then an heir
through God.
8However at that time,
when you did not know
God, you were slaves to
those which by nature are
no gods.
9But now that you have
come to know God, or
rather to be known by God,
how is it that you turn back
again to the weak and
worthless elemental things,
to which you desire to be
enslaved all over again?
10You observe days and
months and seasons and
years.
11I fear for you, that perhaps I have labored over
you in vain.
12I beg of you, brethren,
become as I *am*, for I also
have become as you *are*.
You have done me no
wrong;
13but you know that it
was because of a bodily illness that I preached the
gospel to you the first time;
14and that which was a trial to you in my bodily condition you did not despise
or loathe, but you received
me as an angel of God, as
Christ Jesus *Himself*.
15Where then is that
sense of blessing you had?
For I bear you witness, that
if possible, you would have
plucked out your eyes and

προθεσμίας τοῦ πατρός. 3 οὕτως καὶ
term previously appointed of the father. So also

ἡμεῖς, ὅτε ἦμεν νήπιοι, ὑπὸ τὰ στοιχεῖα
we, when we were infants, under the elements

τοῦ κόσμου ἤμεθα δεδουλωμένοι· 4 ὅτε
of the world we were *having been* enslaved; when

δὲ ἦλθεν τὸ πλήρωμα τοῦ χρόνου,
but came the fulness of the time,

ἐξαπέστειλεν ὁ θεὸς τὸν υἱὸν αὐτοῦ,
sent forth – God the Son of him,

γενόμενον ἐκ γυναικός, γενόμενον ὑπὸ
becoming of a woman, becoming under

νόμον, 5 ἵνα τοὺς ὑπὸ νόμον ἐξαγοράσῃ,
law, in order that [2]the ones [3]under [4]law [1]he might redeem,

ἵνα τὴν υἱοθεσίαν ἀπολάβωμεν. 6 Ὅτι δέ
in order that [2]the [3]adoption of sons [1]we might receive. And because

ἐστε υἱοί, ἐξαπέστειλεν ὁ θεὸς τὸ
ye are sons, [2]sent forth – [1]God the

πνεῦμα τοῦ υἱοῦ αὐτοῦ εἰς τὰς καρδίας
Spirit of the Son of him into the hearts

ἡμῶν, κρᾶζον· ἀββὰ ὁ πατήρ. 7 ὥστε
of us, crying: Abba – Father. So as

οὐκέτι εἶ δοῦλος ἀλλὰ υἱός· εἰ δὲ υἱός,
no more art thou a slave but a son; and if a son,

καὶ κληρονόμος διὰ θεοῦ.
also an heir through God.

8 Ἀλλὰ τότε μὲν οὐκ εἰδότες θεὸν
But then indeed not knowing God

ἐδουλεύσατε τοῖς φύσει μὴ οὖσιν θεοῖς·
ye served as slaves [1]the [5]by nature [4]not [3]being [2]gods;

9 νῦν δὲ γνόντες θεόν, μᾶλλον δὲ
but now knowing God, but rather

γνωσθέντες ὑπὸ θεοῦ, πῶς ἐπιστρέφετε
being known by God, how turn ye

πάλιν ἐπὶ τὰ ἀσθενῆ καὶ πτωχὰ στοιχεῖα,
again to the weak and poor elements,

οἷς πάλιν ἄνωθεν δουλεῦσαι θέλετε;
to which again [3]anew [2]to serve [1]ye wish?

10 ἡμέρας παρατηρεῖσθε καὶ μῆνας καὶ
[2]days [1]Ye observe and months and

καιροὺς καὶ ἐνιαυτούς. 11 φοβοῦμαι ὑμᾶς
seasons and years. I fear [for] you

μή πως εἰκῇ κεκοπίακα εἰς ὑμᾶς.
lest in vain I have laboured among you.

12 Γίνεσθε ὡς ἐγώ, ὅτι κἀγὼ ὡς
Be ye as I [am], because I also [am] as

ὑμεῖς, ἀδελφοί, δέομαι ὑμῶν. οὐδέν με
ye [are], brothers, I beg of you. Nothing me

ἠδικήσατε· 13 οἴδατε δὲ ὅτι δι' ἀσθένειαν
ye wronged; and ye know that on account of weakness

τῆς σαρκὸς εὐηγγελισάμην ὑμῖν τὸ
of the flesh I preached good tidings to you –

πρότερον, 14 καὶ τὸν πειρασμὸν ὑμῶν
formerly, and the trial of you

ἐν τῇ σαρκί μου οὐκ ἐξουθενήσατε οὐδὲ
in the flesh of me ye despised not nor

ἐξεπτύσατε, ἀλλὰ ὡς ἄγγελον θεοῦ ἐδέξασθέ
disdained *ye*, but as a messenger of God ye received

με, ὡς Χριστὸν Ἰησοῦν. 15 ποῦ οὖν
me, as Christ Jesus. Where therefore

ὁ μακαρισμὸς ὑμῶν; μαρτυρῶ γὰρ ὑμῖν
the felicitation of you?* for I witness to you

ὅτι εἰ δυνατὸν τοὺς ὀφθαλμοὺς ὑμῶν
that if possible [3]the [3]eyes [4]of you

* That is, "your felicitation [of me]".

children, we were in slavery under the basic principles of the world. 4But
when the time had fully
come, God sent his Son,
born of a woman, born un-
der law, 5to redeem those
under law, that we might
receive the full rights of
sons. 6Because you are
sons, God sent the Spirit of
his Son into our hearts, the
Spirit who calls out,
"*Abba*,[o] Father." 7So you
are no longer a slave, but a
son; and since you are a
son, God has made you
also an heir.

Paul's Concern for the Galatians

8Formerly, when you did
not know God, you were
slaves to those who by nature are not gods. 9But now
that you know God—or
rather are known by God—
how is it that you are turning back to those weak and
miserable principles? Do
you wish to be enslaved by
them all over again? 10You
are observing special days
and months and seasons
and years! 11I fear for you,
that somehow I have wast-
ed my efforts on you.
12I plead with you, brothers, become like me, for I
became like you. You have
done me no wrong. 13As
you know, it was because
of an illness that I first
preached the gospel to you.
14Even though my illness
was a trial to you, you did
not treat me with contempt
or scorn. Instead, you welcomed me as if I were an
angel of God, as if I were
Christ Jesus himself.
15What has happened to all
your joy? I can testify that,
if you could have done so,
you would have torn out
your eyes and given them

[o]6 Aramaic for *Father*

given them to me.

16Have I therefore become your enemy by telling you the truth?

17They eagerly seek you, not commendably, but they wish to shut you out, in order that you may seek them.

18But it is good always to be eagerly sought in a commendable manner, and not only when I am present with you.

19My children, with whom I am again in labor until Christ is formed in you—

20but I could wish to be present with you now and to change my tone, for I am perplexed about you.

Bond and Free

21Tell me, you who want to be under law, do you not listen to the law?

22For it is written that Abraham had two sons, one by the bondwoman and one by the free woman.

23But the son by the bondwoman was born according to the flesh, and the son by the free woman through the promise.

24This is allegorically speaking: for these *women* are two covenants, one *proceeding* from Mount Sinai bearing children who are to be slaves; she is Hagar.

25Now this Hagar is Mount Sinai in Arabia, and corresponds to the present Jerusalem, for she is in slavery with her children.

26But the Jerusalem above is free; she is our mother.

27For it is written,

"REJOICE, BARREN WOMAN WHO DOES NOT BEAR;
BREAK FORTH AND SHOUT, YOU WHO ARE NOT IN LABOR;
FOR MORE ARE THE CHILDREN OF THE DESOLATE
THAN OF THE ONE WHO HAS A HUSBAND."

28And you brethren, like Isaac, are children of promise.

29But as at that time he who was born according to

ἐξορύξαντες ἐδώκατέ μοι. 16 ὥστε ἐχθρὸς
[1]gouging out ye gave [them] to me. So that [2]an enemy

ὑμῶν γέγονα ἀληθεύων ὑμῖν; 17 ζηλοῦσιν
[3]of you [1]have I become speaking truth to you? They are zealous of

ὑμᾶς οὐ καλῶς, ἀλλὰ ἐκκλεῖσαι ὑμᾶς
you not well, but [2]to exclude [3]you

θέλουσιν, 18 ἵνα αὐτοὺς ζηλοῦτε. καλὸν δὲ
[1]wish, in order that them ye may be zealous of. But [it is] good

ζηλοῦσθαι ἐν καλῷ πάντοτε, καὶ μὴ
to be zealous in a good thing always, and not

μόνον ἐν τῷ παρεῖναί με πρὸς ὑμᾶς,
only in the to be present me[be] with you,
=when I am present

19 τέκνα μου, οὓς πάλιν ὠδίνω μέχρις οὗ
children of me,[for] whom again I travail in birth until

μορφωθῇ Χριστὸς ἐν ὑμῖν· 20 ἤθελον δὲ
[2]is formed [1]Christ in you; and I wished

παρεῖναι πρὸς ὑμᾶς ἄρτι καὶ ἀλλάξαι
to be present with you just now and to change

τὴν φωνήν μου, ὅτι ἀποροῦμαι ἐν ὑμῖν.
the voice of me, because I am perplexed in(about) you.

21 Λέγετέ μοι, οἱ ὑπὸ νόμον θέλοντες
Tell me, the [ones] [3]under [4]law [1]wishing

εἶναι, τὸν νόμον οὐκ ἀκούετε; 22 γέγραπται
[2]to be, [2]the [3]law [1]hear ye not? [2]it has been written

γὰρ ὅτι Ἀβραὰμ δύο υἱοὺς ἔσχεν, ἕνα
[1]for that Abraham two sons had, one

ἐκ τῆς παιδίσκης καὶ ἕνα ἐκ τῆς ἐλευ-
of the maidservant and one of the free

θέρας. 23 ἀλλ' ὁ [μὲν] ἐκ τῆς παιδίσκης
woman. But the [one] indeed of the maidservant

κατὰ σάρκα γεγέννηται, ὁ δὲ ἐκ τῆς
according to flesh has been born, and the [one] of the

ἐλευθέρας διὰ τῆς ἐπαγγελίας. 24 ἅτινά
free woman through the promise. Which things

ἐστιν ἀλληγορούμενα· αὗται γάρ εἰσιν
is(are) being allegorized; for these are

δύο διαθῆκαι, μία μὲν ἀπὸ ὄρους Σινά,
two covenants, one indeed from mount Sina,

εἰς δουλείαν γεννῶσα, ἥτις ἐστὶν Ἁγάρ.
to slavery bringing forth, which is Hagar.

25 τὸ δὲ Ἁγὰρ Σινὰ ὄρος ἐστὶν ἐν
[4]The [1]now [2]Hagar [6]Sina [5]mount [3]is in

τῇ Ἀραβίᾳ· συστοιχεῖ δὲ τῇ νῦν
– Arabia; and corresponds to the now

Ἰερουσαλήμ, δουλεύει γὰρ μετὰ τῶν
Jerusalem, for she serves as a slave with the

τέκνων αὐτῆς. 26 ἡ δὲ ἄνω Ἰερουσαλὴμ
children of her. But the above Jerusalem

ἐλευθέρα ἐστίν, ἥτις ἐστὶν μήτηρ ἡμῶν·
free is, who is mother of us;

27 γέγραπται γάρ· εὐφράνθητι, στεῖρα ἡ
for it has been written: Be thou glad, barren[,] the [one]

οὐ τίκτουσα, ῥῆξον καὶ βόησον, ἡ οὐκ
not bearing, break forth and shout, the [one] not

ὠδίνουσα· ὅτι πολλὰ τὰ τέκνα τῆς ἐρήμου
travailing; because many [are] the children of the desolate

μᾶλλον ἢ τῆς ἐχούσης τὸν ἄνδρα. 28 ὑμεῖς
rather than of the [one] having the husband. ye

δέ, ἀδελφοί, κατὰ Ἰσαὰκ ἐπαγγελίας τέκνα
But, brothers, [4]according to [5]Isaac [3]of promise [2]children

ἐστέ. 29 ἀλλ' ὥσπερ τότε ὁ κατὰ σάρκα
[1]are. But even as then the [one] according to flesh

to me. 16Have I now be-
come your enemy by telling
you the truth?
17Those people are zeal-
ous to win you over, but for
no good. What they want is
to alienate you ⌊from us⌋, so
that you may be zealous for
them. 18It is fine to be zealous, provided the purpose
is good, and to be so always
and not just when I am with
you. 19My dear children,
for whom I am again in the
pains of childbirth until
Christ is formed in you,
20how I wish I could be
with you now and change
my tone, because I am perplexed about you!

Hagar and Sarah

21Tell me, you who want
to be under the law, are you
not aware of what the law
says? 22For it is written that
Abraham had two sons,
one by the slave woman
and the other by the free
woman. 23His son by the
slave woman was born in
the ordinary way; but his
son by the free woman was
born as the result of a
promise.
24These things may be
taken figuratively, for the
women represent two cov-
enants. One covenant is
from Mount Sinai and
bears children who are to
be slaves: This is Hagar.
25Now Hagar stands for
Mount Sinai in Arabia and
corresponds to the present
city of Jerusalem, because
she is in slavery with her
children. 26But the Jerusalem that is above is free,
and she is our mother.
27For it is written:

"Be glad, O barren woman,
who bears no children;
break forth and cry aloud,
you who have no labor pains;
because more are the children of the desolate woman
than of her who has a husband."[p]

28Now you, brothers, like
Isaac, are children of promise. 29At that time the son
born in the ordinary way

[p]27 Isaiah 54:1

the flesh persecuted him *who was born* according to the Spirit, so it is now also.

30But what does the Scripture say?

"CAST OUT THE BOND-
WOMAN AND HER SON,
FOR THE SON OF THE
BONDWOMAN SHALL
NOT BE AN HEIR WITH
THE SON OF THE FREE
WOMAN."

31So then, brethren, we are not children of a bondwoman, but of the free woman.

Chapter 5

Walk by the Spirit

IT was for freedom that Christ set us free; therefore keep standing firm and do not be subject again to a yoke of slavery.

2Behold I, Paul, say to you that if you receive circumcision, Christ will be of no benefit to you.

3And I testify again to every man who receives circumcision, that he is under obligation to keep the whole Law.

4You have been severed from Christ, you who are seeking to be justified by law; you have fallen from grace.

5For we through the Spirit, by faith, are waiting for the hope of righteousness.

6For in Christ Jesus neither circumcision nor uncircumcision means anything, but faith working through love.

7You were running well; who hindered you from obeying the truth?

8This persuasion *did* not *come* from Him who calls you.

9A little leaven leavens the whole lump *of dough.*

10I have confidence in you in the Lord, that you will adopt no other view; but the one who is disturbing you shall bear his judgment, whoever he is.

11But I, brethren, if I still preach circumcision, why am I still persecuted? Then the stumbling block of the cross has been abolished.

12Would that those who are troubling you would even mutilate themselves.

γεννηθεὶς ἐδίωκεν τὸν κατὰ πνεῦμα, οὕτως
born persecuted the [one] according [born] to spirit, so
καὶ νῦν. 30 ἀλλὰ τί λέγει ἡ γραφή;
also now. But what says the scripture?
ἔκβαλε τὴν παιδίσκην καὶ τὸν υἱὸν αὐτῆς·
Cast out the maidservant and the son of her;
οὐ γὰρ μὴ κληρονομήσει ὁ υἱὸς τῆς
for by no means [5]shall inherit [1]the [2]son [3]of the
παιδίσκης μετὰ τοῦ υἱοῦ τῆς ἐλευθέρας.
[4]maidservant with the son of the free woman.
31 διό, ἀδελφοί, οὐκ ἐσμὲν παιδίσκης
Wherefore, brothers, we are not [2]of a maidservant
τέκνα ἀλλὰ τῆς ἐλευθέρας.
[1]children but of the free woman.

5 Τῇ ἐλευθερίᾳ ἡμᾶς Χριστὸς ἠλευθέρωσεν·
For *the* freedom [3]us [1]Christ [2]freed;
στήκετε οὖν καὶ μὴ πάλιν ζυγῷ δουλείας
stand firm therefore and not again with a yoke of slavery
ἐνέχεσθε.
be entangled.
2 Ἴδε ἐγὼ Παῦλος λέγω ὑμῖν ὅτι
Behold[,] I Paul tell you that
ἐὰν περιτέμνησθε Χριστὸς ὑμᾶς οὐδὲν
if ye are circumcised Christ [3]you [2]nothing
ὠφελήσει. 3 μαρτύρομαι δὲ πάλιν παντὶ
[1]will profit. And I testify again to every
ἀνθρώπῳ περιτεμνομένῳ ὅτι ὀφειλέτης ἐστὶν
man being circumcised that [2]a debtor [1]he is
ὅλον τὸν νόμον ποιῆσαι. 4 κατηργήθητε
[4]all [5]the [6]law [3]to do. Ye were discharged
ἀπὸ Χριστοῦ οἵτινες ἐν νόμῳ δικαιοῦσθε,
from Christ who by law are justified,
τῆς χάριτος ἐξεπέσατε. 5 ἡμεῖς γὰρ
the [2]grace [1]ye fell from. For we
πνεύματι ἐκ πίστεως ἐλπίδα δικαιοσύνης
in spirit by faith [the] hope of righteousness
ἀπεκδεχόμεθα. 6 ἐν γὰρ Χριστῷ Ἰησοῦ
eagerly expect. For in Christ Jesus
οὔτε περιτομή τι ἰσχύει οὔτε ἀκροβυστία,
neither circumcision [2]anything [1]avails nor uncircumcision,
ἀλλὰ πίστις δι' ἀγάπης ἐνεργουμένη.
but faith [2]through [3]love [1]operating.
7 Ἐτρέχετε καλῶς· τίς ὑμᾶς ἐνέκοψεν
Ye were running well: who [2]you [1]hindered
ἀληθείᾳ μὴ πείθεσθαι; 8 ἡ πεισμονὴ οὐκ
[3]by truth [2]not [4]to be persuaded? the(this) persuasion not
ἐκ τοῦ καλοῦντος ὑμᾶς. 9 μικρὰ ζύμη
of the [one] calling you. A little leaven
ὅλον τὸ φύραμα ζυμοῖ. 10 ἐγὼ πέποιθα
all the lump leavens. I trust
εἰς ὑμᾶς ἐν κυρίῳ ὅτι οὐδὲν ἄλλο φρο-
as to† you in [the] Lord that [2]nothing [3]other [1]ye
νήσετε· ὁ δὲ ταράσσων ὑμᾶς βαστάσει
will think; but the [one] troubling you shall bear
τὸ κρίμα, ὅστις ἐὰν ᾖ. 11 Ἐγὼ δέ,
the judgment, whoever he may be. [1]But [4]I,
ἀδελφοί, εἰ περιτομὴν ἔτι κηρύσσω, τί
[2]brothers, [3]if [7]circumcision [5]still [6]proclaim, why
ἔτι διώκομαι; ἄρα κατήργηται τὸ
still am I being persecuted? then has been annulled the
σκάνδαλον τοῦ σταυροῦ. 12 Ὄφελον καὶ
offence of the cross. I would that indeed
ἀποκόψονται οἱ ἀναστατοῦντες ὑμᾶς.
[4]will(might) cut themselves off [1]the [ones] [2]unsettling [3]you.

persecuted the son born by
the power of the Spirit. It is
the same now. 30But what
does the Scripture say?
"Get rid of the slave woman and her son, for the
slave woman's son will
never share in the inheritance with the free wom-
an's son."[q] 31Therefore,
brothers, we are not children of the slave woman,
but of the free woman.

Chapter 5

Freedom in Christ

IT is for freedom that
Christ has set us free.
Stand firm, then, and do
not let yourselves be burdened again by a yoke of
slavery.
2Mark my words! I, Paul,
tell you that if you let yourselves be circumcised,
Christ will be of no value to
you at all. 3Again I declare
to every man who lets himself be circumcised that he
is obligated to obey the
whole law. 4You who are
trying to be justified by law
have been alienated from
Christ; you have fallen
away from grace. 5But by
faith we eagerly await
through the Spirit the righteousness for which we
hope. 6For in Christ Jesus
neither circumcision nor
uncircumcision has any
value. The only thing that
counts is faith expressing
itself through love.
7You were running a good
race. Who cut in on you
and kept you from obeying
the truth? 8That kind of persuasion does not come
from the one who calls you.
9"A little yeast works
through the whole batch of
dough." 10I am confident in
the Lord that you will take
no other view. The one
who is throwing you into
confusion will pay the penalty, whoever he may be.
11Brothers, if I am still
preaching circumcision,
why am I still being persecuted? In that case the offense of the cross has been
abolished. 12As for those
agitators, I wish they
would go the whole way
and emasculate them-
selves!

[q]30 Gen. 21:10

13 For you were called to
freedom, brethren; only *do*
not *turn* your freedom intc
an opportunity for the
flesh, but through love
serve one another.
14 For the whole Law is
fulfilled in one word, in the
statement, "YOU SHALL
LOVE YOUR NEIGHBOR AS
YOURSELF."
15 But if you bite and devour one another, take care
lest you be consumed by
one another.
16 But I say, walk by the
Spirit, and you will not carry out the desire of the
flesh.
17 For the flesh sets its desire against the Spirit, and
the Spirit against the flesh;
for these are in opposition
to one another, so that you
may not do the things that
you please.
18 But if you are led by the
Spirit, you are not under
the Law.
19 Now the deeds of the
flesh are evident, which
are: immorality, impurity,
sensuality,
20 idolatry, sorcery, enmities, strife, jealousy, outbursts of anger, disputes,
dissensions, factions,
21 envying, drunkenness,
carousing, and things like
these, of which I forewarn
you just as I have fore-
warned you that those who
practice such things shall
not inherit the kingdom of
God.
22 But the fruit of the
Spirit is love, joy, peace,
patience, kindness, good-
ness, faithfulness,
23 gentleness, self-control;
against such things there is
no law.
24 Now those who belong
to Christ Jesus have crucified the flesh with its passions and desires.
25 If we live by the Spirit,
let us also walk by the
Spirit.
26 Let us not become
boastful, challenging one
another, envying one an-
other.

13 Ὑμεῖς γὰρ ἐπ' ἐλευθερίᾳ ἐκλήθητε,
For ye for freedom were called,
ἀδελφοί· μόνον μὴ τὴν ἐλευθερίαν εἰς
brothers; only [use] not the freedom for
ἀφορμὴν τῇ σαρκί, ἀλλὰ διὰ τῆς ἀγάπης
advantage to the flesh, but through – love
δουλεύετε ἀλλήλοις. **14** ὁ γὰρ πᾶς νόμος
serve ye as slaves one another. For the whole law
ἐν ἑνὶ λόγῳ πεπλήρωται, ἐν τῷ· ἀγα-
in one word has been summed up, in the [word]: Thou
πήσεις τὸν πλησίον σου ὡς σεαυτόν.
shalt love the neighbour of thee as thyself.
15 εἰ δὲ ἀλλήλους δάκνετε καὶ κατεσθίετε,
But if 4one another 1ye bite 2and 3ye devour,
βλέπετε μὴ ὑπ' ἀλλήλων ἀναλωθῆτε.
see lest by one another ye are destroyed.
16 Λέγω δέ, πνεύματι περιπατεῖτε καὶ
Now I say, in spirit walk ye and
ἐπιθυμίαν σαρκὸς οὐ μὴ τελέσητε. **17** ἡ
[the] lust of [the] flesh by no means ye will perform. the
γὰρ σὰρξ ἐπιθυμεῖ κατὰ τοῦ πνεύματος,
For flesh lusts against the spirit,
τὸ δὲ πνεῦμα κατὰ τῆς σαρκός, ταῦτα
and the spirit against the flesh, 2these
γὰρ ἀλλήλοις ἀντίκειται, ἵνα μὴ ἃ ἐὰν
1for 4each other 3opposes, lest whatever things
θέλητε ταῦτα ποιῆτε. **18** εἰ δὲ πνεύματι
ye wish these ye do. But if by [the] Spirit
ἄγεσθε, οὐκ ἐστὲ ὑπὸ νόμον. **19** φανερὰ δέ
ye are led, ye are not under law. Now 6manifest
ἐστιν τὰ ἔργα τῆς σαρκός, ἅτινά ἐστιν
5is(are) 1the 2works 3of the 4flesh, which is(are)
πορνεία, ἀκαθαρσία, ἀσέλγεια, **20** εἰδωλο-
fornication, uncleanness, lewdness, idola-
λατρία, φαρμακεία, ἔχθραι, ἔρις, ζῆλος,
try, sorcery, enmities, strife, jealousy,
θυμοί, ἐριθεῖαι, διχοστασίαι, αἱρέσεις,
angers, rivalries, divisions, sects,
21 φθόνοι, μέθαι, κῶμοι, καὶ τὰ ὅμοια
envyings, drunkennesses, revellings, and – like things
τούτοις, ἃ προλέγω ὑμῖν καθὼς προεῖπον,
to these, which I tell 2beforehand 1you as I previously said,
ὅτι οἱ τὰ τοιαῦτα πράσσοντες βασιλείαν
that the [ones] – 2such things 1practising 4[the] kingdom
θεοῦ οὐ κληρονομήσουσιν. **22** ὁ δὲ καρπὸς
5of God 3will not inherit. But the fruit
τοῦ πνεύματός ἐστιν ἀγάπη, χαρά, εἰρήνη,
of the Spirit is love, joy, peace,
μακροθυμία, χρηστότης, ἀγαθωσύνη, πίστις,
longsuffering, kindness, goodness, faithfulness,
23 πραΰτης, ἐγκράτεια· κατὰ τῶν τοιούτων
meekness, self-control; against – such things
οὐκ ἔστιν νόμος. **24** οἱ δὲ τοῦ Χριστοῦ
there is no law. Now the ones – of Christ
Ἰησοῦ τὴν σάρκα ἐσταύρωσαν σὺν τοῖς
Jesus 2the 3flesh 1crucified with the(its)
παθήμασιν καὶ ταῖς ἐπιθυμίαις. **25** Εἰ
passions and the(its) lusts. If
ζῶμεν πνεύματι, πνεύματι καὶ στοιχῶμεν.
we live in [the] Spirit, in [the] Spirit also let us walk.
26 μὴ γινώμεθα κενόδοξοι, ἀλλήλους
Let us not become vainglorious, one another
προκαλούμενοι, ἀλλήλοις φθονοῦντες.
provoking, one another envying.

13 You, my brothers, were
called to be free. But do not
use your freedom to in-
dulge the sinful nature[r];
rather, serve one another in
love. 14 The entire law is
summed up in a single command: "Love your neigh-
bor as yourself."[s] 15 If you
keep on biting and devouring each other, watch out
or you will be destroyed by
each other.

Life by the Spirit

16 So I say, live by the
Spirit, and you will not
gratify the desires of the
sinful nature. 17 For the sinful nature desires what is
contrary to the Spirit, and
the Spirit what is contrary
to the sinful nature. They
are in conflict with each
other, so that you do not do
what you want. 18 But if you
are led by the Spirit, you
are not under law.
19 The acts of the sinful
nature are obvious: sexual
immorality, impurity and
debauchery; 20 idolatry and
witchcraft; hatred, discord,
jealousy, fits of rage, selfish ambition, dissensions,
factions 21 and envy; drunkenness, orgies, and the
like. I warn you, as I did
before, that those who live
like this will not inherit the
kingdom of God.
22 But the fruit of the Spirit is love, joy, peace, patience, kindness, good-
ness, faithfulness, 23 gentleness and self-control.
Against such things there is
no law. 24 Those who be-
long to Christ Jesus have
crucified the sinful nature
with its passions and de-
sires. 25 Since we live by the
Spirit, let us keep in step
with the Spirit. 26 Let us not
become conceited, provok-
ing and envying each other.

[r] *13* Or *the flesh*; also in verses 16, 17, 19 and 24
[s] *14* Lev. 19:18

Chapter 6

Bear One Another's Burdens

BRETHREN, even if a
man is caught in any
trespass, you who are spiritual, restore such a one in a
spirit of gentleness; *each*
one looking to yourself,
lest you too be tempted.
2Bear one another's bur-
dens, and thus fulfill the
law of Christ.
3For if anyone thinks he
is something when he is
nothing, he deceives him-
self.
4But let each one exam-
ine his own work, and then
he will have *reason for*
boasting in regard to himself alone, and not in regard
to another.
5For each one shall bear
his own load.
6And let the one who is
taught the word share all
good things with him who
teaches.
7Do not be deceived,
God is not mocked; for
whatever a man sows, this
he will also reap.
8For the one who sows
to his own flesh shall from
the flesh reap corruption,
but the one who sows to the
Spirit shall from the Spirit
reap eternal life.
9And let us not lose heart
in doing good, for in due
time we shall reap if we do
not grow weary.
10So then, while we have
opportunity, let us do good
to all men, and especially to
those who are of the household of the faith.
11See with what large letters I am writing to you
with my own hand.
12Those who desire to
make a good showing in the
flesh try to compel you to
be circumcised, simply that
they may not be persecuted
for the cross of Christ.
13For those who [a]are circumcised do not even keep
the Law themselves, but

[a] Some ancient mss. read *have been*

6 Ἀδελφοί, ἐὰν καὶ προλημφθῇ ἄνθρω-
Brothers, if indeed [2]is overtaken [1]a

πος ἔν τινι παραπτώματι, ὑμεῖς οἱ
man in some trespass, ye the

πνευματικοὶ καταρτίζετε τὸν τοιοῦτον ἐν
spiritual [ones] restore – such a one in

πνεύματι πραΰτητος, σκοπῶν σεαυτόν, μὴ
a spirit of meekness, considering thyself, lest

καὶ σὺ πειρασθῇς. **2** Ἀλλήλων τὰ βάρη
also thou art tempted. Of one another the loads

βαστάζετε, καὶ οὕτως ἀναπληρώσετε τὸν
bear ye, and so ye will fulfil the

νόμον τοῦ Χριστοῦ. **3** εἰ γὰρ δοκεῖ
law – of Christ. For if [2]thinks

τις εἶναί τι μηδὲν ὤν, φρεναπατᾷ ἑαυτόν.
[1]anyone [3]to be [4]something [5]nothing [6]being, he deceives himself.

4 τὸ δὲ ἔργον ἑαυτοῦ δοκιμαζέτω ἕκαστος,
But the work of himself [1]let [3]prove [2]each man,

καὶ τότε εἰς ἑαυτὸν μόνον τὸ καύχημα
and then in himself alone the boast

ἕξει καὶ οὐκ εἰς τὸν ἕτερον· **5** ἕκαστος
he will have and not in the other man; [2]each man

γὰρ τὸ ἴδιον φορτίον βαστάσει. **6** Κοινωνείτω δὲ
[1]for the(his) own burden will bear. And [5]let him share

ὁ κατηχούμενος τὸν λόγον τῷ κατη-
[1]the [2]being instructed [in] [3]the [4]word [6]with the [one] in-
[one]

χοῦντι ἐν πᾶσιν ἀγαθοῖς. **7** Μὴ πλανᾶσθε,
structing in all good things. Be ye not led astray,

θεὸς οὐ μυκτηρίζεται. ὃ γὰρ ἐὰν σπείρῃ
God is not mocked. For whatever [2]may sow

ἄνθρωπος, τοῦτο καὶ θερίσει· **8** ὅτι ὁ
[1]a man, this also he will reap; because the

σπείρων εἰς τὴν σάρκα ἑαυτοῦ ἐκ τῆς
[one] sowing to the flesh of himself of the

σαρκὸς θερίσει φθοράν, ὁ δὲ σπείρων
flesh will reap corruption, but the [one] sowing

εἰς τὸ πνεῦμα ἐκ τοῦ πνεύματος θερίσει
to the spirit of the Spirit will reap

ζωὴν αἰώνιον. **9** τὸ δὲ καλὸν ποιοῦντες
life eternal. And [2]the [3]good [1]doing

μὴ ἐγκακῶμεν· καιρῷ γὰρ ἰδίῳ
let us not lose heart; for in its own time

θερίσομεν μὴ ἐκλυόμενοι. **10** Ἄρα οὖν
we shall reap not failing. Then therefore

ὡς καιρὸν ἔχομεν, ἐργαζώμεθα τὸ ἀγαθὸν
as [2]time [1]we have, let us do the good

πρὸς πάντας, μάλιστα δὲ πρὸς τοὺς
to all men, and most of all to the

οἰκείους τῆς πίστεως.
members of the family of the faith.

11 Ἴδετε πηλίκοις ὑμῖν γράμμασιν
Ye see in how large [2]to you [1]letters

ἔγραψα τῇ ἐμῇ χειρί. **12** Ὅσοι θέλουσιν
[3]I wrote – with my hand. As many as wish

εὐπροσωπῆσαι ἐν σαρκί, οὗτοι ἀναγκάζουσιν
to look well in [the] flesh, these compel

ὑμᾶς περιτέμνεσθαι, μόνον ἵνα τῷ
you to be circumcised, only in order that [3]for the

σταυρῷ τοῦ Χριστοῦ [Ἰησοῦ] μὴ
[4]cross – [5]of Christ [6]Jesus [1]not

διώκωνται. **13** οὐδὲ γὰρ οἱ περιτεμνόμενοι
[2]they are persecuted. For [4]not [1]the [ones] [2]being circumcised

αὐτοὶ νόμον φυλάσσουσιν, ἀλλὰ θέλουσιν
[3]themselves [6]law [5]keep, but they wish

Chapter 6

Doing Good to All

BROTHERS, if some-
one is caught in a sin,
you who are spiritual
should restore him gently.
But watch yourself, or you
also may be tempted. 2Car-
ry each other's burdens,
and in this way you will fulfill the law of Christ. 3If
anyone thinks he is some-
hing when he is nothing,
he deceives himself. 4Each
one should test his own actions. Then he can take
pride in himself, without
comparing himself to somebody else, 5for each one
should carry his own load.
6Anyone who receives in-
struction in the word must
share all good things with
his instructor.
7Do not be deceived: God
cannot be mocked. A man
reaps what he sows. 8The
one who sows to please his
sinful nature, from that nature[f] will reap destruction;
the one who sows to please
the Spirit, from the Spirit
will reap eternal life. 9Let
us not become weary in doing good, for at the proper
time we will reap a harvest
if we do not give up.
10Therefore, as we have opportunity, let us do good to
all people, especially to
those who belong to the
family of believers.

Not Circumcision but a New Creation

11See what large letters I
use as I write to you with
my own hand!
12Those who want to
make a good impression
outwardly are trying to
compel you to be circum-
cised. The only reason they
do this is to avoid being
persecuted for the cross of
Christ. 13Not even those
who are circumcised obey
the law, yet they want you

[f]8 Or *his flesh, from the flesh*

they desire to have you circumcised, that they may
boast in your flesh.
14But may it never be that
I should boast, except in
the cross of our Lord Jesus
Christ, through which the
world has been crucified to
me, and I to the world.
15For neither is circumcision anything, nor uncir-
cumcision, but a new creation.
16And those who will
walk by this rule, peace and
mercy *be* upon them, and
upon the Israel of God.
17From now on let no one
cause trouble for me, for I
bear on my body the brand-
marks of Jesus.
18The grace of our Lord
Jesus Christ be with your
spirit, brethren. Amen.

ὑμᾶς περιτέμνεσθαι ἵνα ἐν τῇ ὑμετέρᾳ
you to be circumcised in order that [2]in – [3]your
σαρκὶ καυχήσωνται. 14 ἐμοὶ δὲ μὴ γένοιτο
[4]flesh [1]they may boast. But to me may it not be
καυχᾶσθαι εἰ μὴ ἐν τῷ σταυρῷ τοῦ
to boast except in the cross of the
κυρίου ἡμῶν Ἰησοῦ Χριστοῦ, δι' οὗ
Lord of us Jesus Christ, through whom
ἐμοὶ κόσμος ἐσταύρωται κἀγὼ κόσμῳ.
to me [the] world has been crucified and I to [the] world.
15 οὔτε γὰρ περιτομή τί ἐστιν οὔτε
For neither circumcision [2]anything [1]is nor
ἀκροβυστία, ἀλλὰ καινὴ κτίσις. 16 καὶ
uncircumcision, but a new creation. And
ὅσοι τῷ κανόνι τούτῳ στοιχήσουσιν,
as many as by this rule will walk,
εἰρήνη ἐπ' αὐτοὺς καὶ ἔλεος, καὶ ἐπὶ τὸν
peace on them and mercy, and on the
Ἰσραὴλ τοῦ θεοῦ.
Israel – of God.
17 Τοῦ λοιποῦ κόπους μοι μηδεὶς
For the rest [3]troubles [4]me [2]no one
παρεχέτω· ἐγὼ γὰρ τὰ στίγματα τοῦ
[1]let [5]cause; for [1]I [3]the [4]brands –
Ἰησοῦ ἐν τῷ σώματί μου βαστάζω.
[5]of Jesus [6]in [7]the [8]body [9]of me [2]bear.
18 Ἡ χάρις τοῦ κυρίου ἡμῶν Ἰησοῦ
The grace of the Lord of us Jesus
Χριστοῦ μετὰ τοῦ πνεύματος ὑμῶν,
Christ with the spirit of you,
ἀδελφοί· ἀμήν.
brothers : Amen.

to be circumcised that they
may boast about your
flesh. 14May I never boast
except in the cross of our
Lord Jesus Christ, through
which[u] the world has been
crucified to me, and I to the
world. 15Neither circumcision nor uncircumcision
means anything; what
counts is a new creation.
16Peace and mercy to all
who follow this rule, even
to the Israel of God.
17Finally, let no one
cause me trouble, for I bear
on my body the marks of
Jesus.
18The grace of our Lord
Jesus Christ be with your
spirit, brothers. Amen.

Ephesians

Chapter 1

The Blessings of Redemption

PAUL, an apostle of
Christ Jesus by the will
of God, to the saints who
are [a]at Ephesus, and *who*
are faithful in Christ Jesus:
2Grace to you and peace
from God our Father and
the Lord Jesus Christ.
3Blessed *be* the God and
Father of our Lord Jesus
Christ, who has blessed us
with every spiritual
blessing in the heavenly
places in Christ,
4just as He chose us in
Him before the foundation
of the world, that we
should be holy and blame-
less before [b]Him. In love
5He predestined us to

[a] Some ancient mss. do not contain *at Ephesus*
[b] Or, *Him, in love.*

ΠΡΟΣ ΕΦΕΣΙΟΥΣ
To Ephesians

1 Παῦλος ἀπόστολος Χριστοῦ Ἰησοῦ διὰ
Paul an apostle of Christ Jesus through
θελήματος θεοῦ τοῖς ἁγίοις τοῖς οὖσιν
[the] will of God to the saints – being
[ἐν Ἐφέσῳ] καὶ πιστοῖς ἐν Χριστῷ
in Ephesus and faithful in Christ
Ἰησοῦ· 2 χάρις ὑμῖν καὶ εἰρήνη ἀπὸ
Jesus: Grace to you and peace from
θεοῦ πατρὸς ἡμῶν καὶ κυρίου Ἰησοῦ
God Father of us and Lord Jesus
Χριστοῦ.
Christ.
3 Εὐλογητὸς ὁ θεὸς καὶ πατὴρ τοῦ
Blessed the God and Father of the
κυρίου ἡμῶν Ἰησοῦ Χριστοῦ, ὁ εὐλογήσας
Lord of us Jesus Christ, the having [one] blessed
ἡμᾶς ἐν πάσῃ εὐλογίᾳ πνευματικῇ ἐν
us with every blessing spiritual in
τοῖς ἐπουρανίοις ἐν Χριστῷ, 4 καθὼς
the heavenlies in Christ, as
ἐξελέξατο ἡμᾶς ἐν αὐτῷ πρὸ καταβολῆς
he chose us in him before [the] foundation
κόσμου, εἶναι ἡμᾶς ἁγίους καὶ ἀμώμους
of [the] world, to be us holy and unblemished[b]
=that we should be . . .
κατενώπιον αὐτοῦ, ἐν ἀγάπῃ 5 προορίσας
before him, in love predestinating

Ephesians

Chapter 1

PAUL, an apostle of
Christ Jesus by the will
of God,

To the saints in Ephe-
sus,[a] the faithful[b] in Christ
Jesus:

2Grace and peace to you
from God our Father and
the Lord Jesus Christ.

Spiritual Blessings in Christ

3Praise be to the God and
Father of our Lord Jesus
Christ, who has blessed us
in the heavenly realms with
every spiritual blessing in
Christ. 4For he chose us in
him before the creation of
the world to be holy and
blameless in his sight. In
love 5he[c] predestined us to

[u] 14 Or *whom*
[a] 1 Some early manuscripts do not have *in Ephesus*.
[b] 1 Or *believers who are*
[c] 4,5 Or *sight in love. 5He*

adoption as sons through Jesus Christ to Himself, according to the kind intention of His will,

6to the praise of the glory of His grace, which He freely bestowed on us in the Beloved.

7In Him we have redemption through His blood, the forgiveness of our trespasses, according to the riches of His grace,

8which He lavished upon us. In all wisdom and insight

9He made known to us the mystery of His will, according to His kind intention which He purposed in Him

10with a view to an administration suitable to the fulness of the times, *that is*, the summing up of all things in Christ, things in the heavens and things upon the earth. In Him

11also we have obtained an inheritance, having been predestined according to His purpose who works all things after the counsel of His will,

12to the end that we who were the first to hope in [c]Christ should be to the praise of His glory.

13In Him, you also, after listening to the message of truth, the gospel of your salvation—having also believed, you were sealed in Him with the Holy Spirit of promise,

14who is given as a pledge of our inheritance, with a view to the redemption of *God's own* possession, to the praise of His glory.

15For this reason I too, having heard of the faith in the Lord Jesus which *exists* among you, and [d]your love for all the saints,

[c] I.e., the Messiah
[d] Many ancient mss. do not contain *your love*

ἡμᾶς εἰς υἱοθεσίαν διὰ Ἰησοῦ Χριστοῦ
us to adoption of sons through Jesus Christ
εἰς αὐτόν, κατὰ τὴν εὐδοκίαν τοῦ
to him[self], according to the good pleasure of the
θελήματος αὐτοῦ, **6** εἰς ἔπαινον δόξης
will of him, to [the] praise of [the] glory
τῆς χάριτος αὐτοῦ, ἧς ἐχαρίτωσεν ἡμᾶς
of the grace of him, of(with) which he favoured us
ἐν τῷ ἠγαπημένῳ, **7** ἐν ᾧ ἔχομεν τὴν
in the [one] *having been* loved, in whom we have the
ἀπολύτρωσιν διὰ τοῦ αἵματος αὐτοῦ, τὴν
redemption through the blood of him, the
ἄφεσιν τῶν παραπτωμάτων, κατὰ τὸ
forgiveness – of trespasses, according to the
πλοῦτος τῆς χάριτος αὐτοῦ, **8** ἧς ἐπερίσ-
riches of the grace of him, which he made to
σευσεν εἰς ἡμᾶς ἐν πάσῃ σοφίᾳ καὶ
abound to us in all wisdom and
φρονήσει **9** γνωρίσας ἡμῖν τὸ μυστήριον
intelligence making known to us the mystery
τοῦ θελήματος αὐτοῦ, κατὰ τὴν εὐδοκίαν
of the will of him, according to the good pleasure
αὐτοῦ, ἣν προέθετο ἐν αὐτῷ **10** εἰς
of him, which he purposed in him[self] for
οἰκονομίαν τοῦ πληρώματος τῶν καιρῶν,
a stewardship of the fulness of the times,
ἀνακεφαλαιώσασθαι τὰ πάντα ἐν τῷ
to head up – all things in –
Χριστῷ, τὰ ἐπὶ τοῖς οὐρανοῖς καὶ τὰ
Christ, the things on(in) *the* heavens and the things
ἐπὶ τῆς γῆς· ἐν αὐτῷ, **11** ἐν ᾧ καὶ
on the earth; in him, in whom also
ἐκληρώθημεν προορισθέντες κατὰ πρόθεσιν
we were chosen as [his] inheritance being predestinated according to [the] purpose
τοῦ τὰ πάντα ἐνεργοῦντος κατὰ τὴν
of the [one] – [2]all things [1]operating according to the
βουλὴν τοῦ θελήματος αὐτοῦ, **12** εἰς τὸ
counsel of the will of him, for *the*
εἶναι ἡμᾶς εἰς ἔπαινον δόξης αὐτοῦ
to be us[b] to [the] praise of [the] glory of him
=that we should be
τοὺς προηλπικότας ἐν τῷ Χριστῷ· **13** ἐν
the [ones] having previously hoped in – Christ; in
ᾧ καὶ ὑμεῖς, ἀκούσαντες τὸν λόγον
whom also ye, hearing the word
τῆς ἀληθείας, τὸ εὐαγγέλιον τῆς σωτηρίας
– of truth, the gospel of the salvation
ὑμῶν, ἐν ᾧ καὶ πιστεύσαντες ἐσφραγίσθητε
of you, in whom also believing ye were sealed
τῷ πνεύματι τῆς ἐπαγγελίας τῷ ἁγίῳ,
with [1]the [3]Spirit – [4]of promise – [2]holy,
14 ὅς ἐστιν ἀρραβὼν τῆς κληρονομίας
who is an earnest of the inheritance
ἡμῶν, εἰς ἀπολύτρωσιν τῆς περιποιήσεως,
of us, till [the] redemption of the possession,
εἰς ἔπαινον τῆς δόξης αὐτοῦ.
to [the] praise of the glory of him.
15 Διὰ τοῦτο κἀγώ, ἀκούσας τὴν καθ'
Therefore I also, hearing the [2]among
ὑμᾶς πίστιν ἐν τῷ κυρίῳ Ἰησοῦ καὶ
[3]you [1]faith in the Lord Jesus and
τὴν ἀγάπην τὴν εἰς πάντας τοὺς ἁγίους,
the love – to all the saints,

be adopted as his sons
through Jesus Christ, in accordance with his pleasure
and will— 6to the praise of
his glorious grace, which
he has freely given us in the
One he loves. 7In him we
have redemption through
his blood, the forgiveness
of sins, in accordance with
the riches of God's grace
8that he lavished on us with
all wisdom and understanding. 9And he[d] made known
to us the mystery of his will
according to his good pleasure, which he purposed in
Christ, 10to be put into effect when the times will
have reached their fulfillment—to bring all things in
heaven and on earth to-
gether under one head,
even Christ.
11In him we were also
chosen,[e] having been predestined according to the
plan of him who works out
everything in conformity
with the purpose of his will,
12in order that we, who
were the first to hope in
Christ, might be for the
praise of his glory. 13And
you also were included in
Christ when you heard the
word of truth, the gospel of
your salvation. Having believed, you were marked in
him with a seal, the promised Holy Spirit, 14who is a
deposit guaranteeing our
inheritance until the re-
demption of those who are
God's possession—to the
praise of his glory.

Thanksgiving and Prayer

15For this reason, ever
since I heard about your
faith in the Lord Jesus and
your love for all the saints,

[d] 8,9 Or *us. With all wisdom and understanding, 9he*
[e] 11 Or *were made heirs*

16do not cease giving
thanks for you, while making mention *of you* in my
prayers;
17that the God of our
Lord Jesus Christ, the Father of glory, may give to
you a spirit of wisdom and
of revelation in the knowledge of Him.
18*I pray that* the eyes of
your heart may be enlightened, so that you may
know what is the hope of
His calling, what are the
riches of the glory of His
inheritance in the saints,
19and what is the surpassing greatness of His power
toward us who believe.
These are in accordance
with the working of the
strength of His might
20which He brought about
in Christ, when He raised
Him from the dead, and
seated Him at His right
hand in the heavenly
places,
21far above all rule and
authority and power and
dominion, and every name
that is named, not only in
this age, but also in the one
to come.
22And He put all things in
subjection under His feet,
and gave Him as head over
all things to the church,
23which is His body, the
fulness of Him who fills all
in all.

16 οὐ παύομαι εὐχαριστῶν ὑπὲρ ὑμῶν
do not cease giving thanks on behalf of you
μνείαν ποιούμενος ἐπὶ τῶν προσευχῶν
mention making on(in) the prayers
μου, **17** ἵνα ὁ θεὸς τοῦ κυρίου ἡμῶν
of me, *in order* that the God of the Lord of us
Ἰησοῦ Χριστοῦ, ὁ πατὴρ τῆς δόξης,
Jesus Christ, the Father – of glory,
δώῃ ὑμῖν πνεῦμα σοφίας καὶ ἀποκαλύψεως
may give to you a spirit of wisdom and of revelation
ἐν ἐπιγνώσει αὐτοῦ, **18** πεφωτισμένους τοὺς
in a full knowledge of him, having been enlightened the
ὀφθαλμοὺς τῆς καρδίας [ὑμῶν,] εἰς τὸ
eyes of the heart of you, for *the*
εἰδέναι ὑμᾶς τίς ἐστιν ἡ ἐλπὶς τῆς
to know you[b] what is the hope of the
=that ye should know
κλήσεως αὐτοῦ, τίς ὁ πλοῦτος τῆς δόξης
calling of him, what the riches of the glory
τῆς κληρονομίας αὐτοῦ ἐν τοῖς ἁγίοις,
of the inheritance of him in the saints,
19 καὶ τί τὸ ὑπερβάλλον μέγεθος τῆς
and what the excelling greatness of the
δυνάμεως αὐτοῦ εἰς ἡμᾶς τοὺς πιστεύοντας
power of him toward us· the [ones] believing
κατὰ τὴν ἐνέργειαν τοῦ κράτους τῆς
according to the operation of the might of the
ἰσχύος αὐτοῦ, **20** ἣν ἐνήργηκεν ἐν τῷ
strength of him, which he has operated in –
Χριστῷ ἐγείρας αὐτὸν ἐκ νεκρῶν, καὶ
Christ raising him from [the] dead, and
καθίσας ἐν δεξιᾷ αὐτοῦ ἐν τοῖς ἐπου-
seating [him] at [the] right [hand] of him in the heaven-
ρανίοις **21** ὑπεράνω πάσης ἀρχῆς καὶ
lies far above all rule and
ἐξουσίας καὶ δυνάμεως καὶ κυριότητος
authority and power and lordship
καὶ παντὸς ὀνόματος ὀνομαζομένου οὐ
and every name being named not
μόνον ἐν τῷ αἰῶνι τούτῳ ἀλλὰ καὶ
only in this age but also
ἐν τῷ μέλλοντι· **22** καὶ πάντα ὑπέταξεν
in the coming; and all things subjected
ὑπὸ τοὺς πόδας αὐτοῦ, καὶ αὐτὸν ἔδωκεν
under the feet of him, and ²him ¹gave
κεφαλὴν ὑπὲρ πάντα τῇ ἐκκλησίᾳ, **23** ἥτις
[to be] head over all things to the church, which
ἐστὶν τὸ σῶμα αὐτοῦ, τὸ πλήρωμα
is the body of him, the fulness
τοῦ τὰ πάντα ἐν πᾶσιν πληρουμένου.
of the – ²all things ³with ⁴all things ¹filling.
[one]

16I have not stopped giving
thanks for you, remember-
ing you in my prayers. 17I
keep asking that the God of
our Lord Jesus Christ, the
glorious Father, may give
you the Spirit[f] of wisdom
and revelation, so that you
may know him better. 18I
pray also that the eyes of
your heart may be enlightened in order that you may
know the hope to which he
has called you, the riches of
his glorious inheritance in
the saints, 19and his incom-
parably great power for us
who believe. That power is
like the working of his
mighty strength, 20which
he exerted in Christ when
he raised him from the dead
and seated him at his right
hand in the heavenly
realms, 21far above all rule
and authority, power and
dominion, and every title
that can be given, not only
in the present age but also
in the one to come. 22And
God placed all things under
his feet and appointed him
to be head over everything
for the church, 23which is
his body, the fullness of
him who fills everything in
every way.

Chapter 2

Made Alive in Christ

AND you were dead in
your trespasses and
sins,
2in which you formerly
walked according to the
course of this world, ac-
cording to the prince of the
power of the air, of the
spirit that is now working in
the sons of disobedience.
3Among them we too all

2 Καὶ ὑμᾶς ὄντας νεκροὺς τοῖς παραπτώ-
And you being dead in the tres-
μασιν καὶ ταῖς ἁμαρτίαις ὑμῶν, **2** ἐν
passes and in the sins of you, in
αἷς ποτε περιεπατήσατε κατὰ τὸν αἰῶνα
which then ye walked according to the age
τοῦ κόσμου τούτου, κατὰ τὸν ἄρχοντα
of this world, according to the ruler
τῆς ἐξουσίας τοῦ ἀέρος, τοῦ πνεύματος
of the authority of the air, of the spirit
τοῦ νῦν ἐνεργοῦντος ἐν τοῖς υἱοῖς τῆς
– now operating in the sons –
ἀπειθείας· **3** ἐν οἷς καὶ ἡμεῖς πάντες
of disobedience; among whom also we all

Chapter 2

Made Alive in Christ

AS for you, you were
dead in your trans-
gressions and sins, 2in
which you used to live
when you followed the
ways of this world and of
the ruler of the kingdom of
the air, the spirit who is
now at work in those who
are disobedient. 3All of us

f17 *Or a spirit*

formerly lived in the lusts
of our flesh, indulging the
desires of the flesh and of
the mind, and were by na-
ture children of wrath,
even as the rest.
4But God, being rich in
mercy, because of His
great love with which He
loved us,
5even when we were
dead in our transgressions,
made us alive together
[e]with Christ (by grace you
have been saved),
6and raised us up with
Him, and seated us with
Him in the heavenly
places, in Christ Jesus,
7in order that in the ages
to come He might show the
surpassing riches of His
grace in kindness toward us
in Christ Jesus.
8For by grace you have
been saved through faith;
and that not of yourselves,
it is the gift of God;
9not as a result of works,
that no one should boast.
10For we are His work-
manship, created in Christ
Jesus for good works,
which God prepared
beforehand, that we should
walk in them.
11Therefore remember,
that formerly you, the Gentiles in the flesh, who are
called "Uncircumcision"
by the so-called "Circum-
cision," *which is* per-
formed in the flesh by human hands—
12*remember* that you
were at that time separate
from Christ, excluded from
the commonwealth of Is-
rael, and strangers to the
covenants of promise, having no hope and without
God in the world.
13But now in Christ Jesus
you who formerly were far
off have been brought near

[e] Some ancient mss. read *in Christ*

ἀνεστράφημέν ποτε ἐν ταῖς ἐπιθυμίαις
conducted ourselves then in the lusts
τῆς σαρκὸς ἡμῶν, ποιοῦντες τὰ θελήματα
of the flesh of us, doing the wishes
τῆς σαρκὸς καὶ τῶν διανοιῶν, καὶ
of the flesh and of the understandings, and
ἤμεθα τέκνα φύσει ὀργῆς ὡς καὶ οἱ
were ²children ¹by nature of wrath as also the
λοιποί· 4 ὁ δὲ θεὸς πλούσιος ὢν ἐν
rest; – but God ²rich ¹being in
ἐλέει, διὰ τὴν πολλὴν ἀγάπην αὐτοῦ
mercy, because of the much love of him
ἣν ἠγάπησεν ἡμᾶς, 5 καὶ ὄντας ἡμᾶς
[with] which he loved us, even being us =when we were
νεκροὺς τοῖς παραπτώμασιν συνεζωοποίησεν
dead – in trespasses quickened [us] with
τῷ Χριστῷ, — χάριτί ἐστε σεσωσμένοι,
– Christ, (by grace ye are *having been* saved,)
— 6 καὶ συνήγειρεν καὶ συνεκάθισεν ἐν
and raised [us] with and seated [us] with in
τοῖς ἐπουρανίοις ἐν Χριστῷ Ἰησοῦ, 7 ἵνα
the heavenlies in Christ Jesus, in order that
ἐνδείξηται ἐν τοῖς αἰῶσιν τοῖς ἐπερχομένοις
he might show forth in the ages – coming on
τὸ ὑπερβάλλον πλοῦτος τῆς χάριτος αὐτοῦ
the excelling riches of the grace of him
ἐν χρηστότητι ἐφ' ἡμᾶς ἐν Χριστῷ
in kindness toward us in Christ
Ἰησοῦ. 8 τῇ γὰρ χάριτί ἐστε σεσωσμένοι
Jesus. – For by grace ye are *having been* saved
διὰ πίστεως· καὶ τοῦτο οὐκ ἐξ ὑμῶν,
through faith; and this not of you,
θεοῦ τὸ δῶρον· 9 οὐκ ἐξ ἔργων, ἵνα μή
of God [is] the gift; not of works, lest
τις καυχήσηται. 10 αὐτοῦ γάρ ἐσμεν
anyone should boast. For of him we are
ποίημα, κτισθέντες ἐν Χριστῷ Ἰησοῦ
a product, created in Christ Jesus
ἐπὶ ἔργοις ἀγαθοῖς, οἷς προητοίμασεν
unto works good, which ²previously prepared
ὁ θεὸς ἵνα ἐν αὐτοῖς περιπατήσωμεν.
– ¹God in order that in them we might walk.
11 Διὸ μνημονεύετε ὅτι ποτὲ ὑμεῖς τὰ
Wherefore remember ye that when ye the
ἔθνη ἐν σαρκί, οἱ λεγόμενοι ἀκροβυστία
nations in [the] flesh, the [ones] *being* called uncircumcision
ὑπὸ τῆς λεγομένης περιτομῆς ἐν σαρκὶ
by the *being* called circumcision in [the] flesh
χειροποιήτου, 12 ὅτι ἦτε τῷ καιρῷ ἐκείνῳ
made by hand, that ye were at that time
χωρὶς Χριστοῦ, ἀπηλλοτριωμένοι τῆς
without Christ, having been alienated from the
πολιτείας τοῦ Ἰσραὴλ καὶ ξένοι τῶν
commonwealth – of Israel and strangers of(from) the
διαθηκῶν τῆς ἐπαγγελίας, ἐλπίδα μὴ
covenants – of promise, hope not
ἔχοντες καὶ ἄθεοι ἐν τῷ κόσμῳ. 13 νυνὶ
having and godless in the world. now
δὲ ἐν Χριστῷ Ἰησοῦ ὑμεῖς οἵ ποτε
But in Christ Jesus ye the [ones] then
ὄντες μακρὰν ἐγενήθητε ἐγγὺς ἐν τῷ
being afar became near by the

also lived among them at
one time, gratifying the
cravings of our sinful nature[g] and following its desires and thoughts. Like
the rest, we were by nature
objects of wrath. 4But because of his great love for
us, God, who is rich in mercy, 5made us alive with
Christ even when we were
dead in transgressions—it
is by grace you have been
saved. 6And God raised us
up with Christ and seated
us with him in the heavenly
realms in Christ Jesus, 7in
order that in the coming
ages he might show the incomparable riches of his
grace, expressed in his
kindness to us in Christ
Jesus. 8For it is by grace
you have been saved,
through faith—and this not
from yourselves, it is the
gift of God— 9not by
works, so that no one can
boast. 10For we are God's
workmanship, created in
Christ Jesus to do good
works, which God pre-
pared in advance for us to
do.

One in Christ

11Therefore, remember
that formerly you who are
Gentiles by birth and called
"uncircumcised" by those
who call themselves "the
circumcision" (that done in
the body by the hands of
men)— 12remember that at
that time you were separate
from Christ, excluded from
citizenship in Israel and
foreigners to the covenants
of the promise, without
hope and without God in
the world. 13But now in
Christ Jesus you who once
were far away have been

[g] 3 Or *our flesh*

by the blood of Christ.
14For He Himself is our
peace, who made both
groups into one, and broke
down the barrier of the dividing wall,
15by abolishing in His
flesh the enmity, *which is*
the Law of commandments
contained in ordinances,
that in Himself He might
make the two into one new
man, *thus* establishing
peace,
16and might reconcile
them both in one body to
God through the cross, by
it having put to death the
enmity.
17AND HE CAME AND
PREACHED PEACE TO YOU
WHO WERE FAR AWAY, AND
PEACE TO THOSE WHO WERE
NEAR;
18for through Him we
both have our access in one
Spirit to the Father.
19So then you are no
longer strangers and aliens,
but you are fellow citizens
with the saints, and are of
God's household,
20having been built upon
the foundation of the apostles and prophets, Christ
Jesus Himself being the
corner *stone*,
21in whom the whole
building, being fitted together is growing into a
holy temple in the Lord;
22in whom you also are
being built together into a
dwelling of God in the
Spirit.

Chapter 3

Paul's Stewardship

FOR this reason I, Paul,
the prisoner of Christ
Jesus for the sake of you
Gentiles—
2if indeed you have
heard of the stewardship of
God's grace which was giv-
en to me for you;
3that by revelation there
was made known to me the
mystery, as I wrote before
in brief.
4And by referring to this,
when you read you can un-
derstand my insight into
the mystery of Christ,

αἵματι τοῦ Χριστοῦ. 14 Αὐτὸς γάρ
blood – of Christ. For he
ἐστιν ἡ εἰρήνη ἡμῶν, ὁ ποιήσας τὰ
is the peace of us, the [one] having made –
ἀμφότερα ἓν καὶ τὸ μεσότοιχον τοῦ
both one and [2]the [3]middle wall –
φραγμοῦ λύσας, τὴν ἔχθραν, ἐν τῇ σαρκὶ
[4]of partition [1]having broken, the enmity, [2]in [3]the [4]flesh
αὐτοῦ 15 τὸν νόμον τῶν ἐντολῶν ἐν
[5]of him [6]the [7]law [8]of the [9]commandments [10]in
δόγμασιν καταργήσας, ἵνα τοὺς δύο κτίσῃ
[11]decrees [1]having abolished, in order that [4]the [5]two [3]he might create
ἐν αὐτῷ εἰς ἕνα καινὸν ἄνθρωπον ποιῶν
[6]in [7]him[self] [8]into [9]one [10]new [11]man [1]making
εἰρήνην, 16 καὶ ἀποκαταλλάξῃ τοὺς
[2]peace, and might reconcile –
ἀμφοτέρους ἐν ἑνὶ σώματι τῷ θεῷ διὰ
both in one body – to God through
τοῦ σταυροῦ, ἀποκτείνας τὴν ἔχθραν ἐν
the cross, killing the enmity in
αὐτῷ· 17 καὶ ἐλθὼν εὐηγγελίσατο εἰρήνην
him[self]; and coming preached peace
ὑμῖν τοῖς μακρὰν καὶ εἰρήνην τοῖς ἐγγύς·
to you the ones afar and peace to the ones near;
18 ὅτι δι' αὐτοῦ ἔχομεν τὴν προσαγωγὴν
because through him [1]we [3]have – [4]access
οἱ ἀμφότεροι ἐν ἑνὶ πνεύματι πρὸς τὸν
– [2]both by one Spirit unto the
πατέρα. 19 ἄρα οὖν οὐκέτι ἐστὲ ξένοι
Father. Then therefore no more are ye strangers
καὶ πάροικοι, ἀλλὰ ἐστὲ συμπολῖται τῶν
and sojourners, but ye are fellow-citizens of the
ἁγίων καὶ οἰκεῖοι τοῦ θεοῦ, 20 ἐποικοδομη-
saints and members of the family – of God, having been
θέντες ἐπὶ τῷ θεμελίῳ τῶν ἀποστόλων
built *on* on the foundation of the apostles
καὶ προφητῶν, ὄντος ἀκρογωνιαίου αὐτοῦ
and prophets, [4]being [5]cornerstone [3][him]self
Χριστοῦ Ἰησοῦ, 21 ἐν ᾧ πᾶσα οἰκοδομὴ
[1]Christ [2]Jesus,[a] in whom all [the] building
συναρμολογουμένη αὔξει εἰς ναὸν ἅγιον
being fitted together grows into shrine a holy
ἐν κυρίῳ, 22 ἐν ᾧ καὶ ὑμεῖς συνοικοδομεῖσθε
in [the] Lord, in whom also ye are being built together
εἰς κατοικητήριον τοῦ θεοῦ ἐν πνεύματι.
into a dwelling-place – of God in spirit.

3 Τούτου χάριν ἐγὼ Παῦλος ὁ δέσμιος
[2]*of* this [1]By reason of I Paul the prisoner
τοῦ Χριστοῦ Ἰησοῦ ὑπὲρ ὑμῶν τῶν
– of Christ Jesus on behalf of you the
ἐθνῶν 2 — εἴ γε ἠκούσατε τὴν οἰκονομίαν
nations — if indeed ye heard the stewardship
τῆς χάριτος τοῦ θεοῦ τῆς δοθείσης μοι
of the grace – of God – given to me
εἰς ὑμᾶς, 3 ὅτι κατὰ ἀποκάλυψιν ἐγνωρίσθη
for you, that by way of revelation was made known
μοι τὸ μυστήριον, καθὼς προέγραψα ἐν
to me the mystery, as I previously wrote in
ὀλίγῳ, 4 πρὸς ὃ δύνασθε ἀναγινώσκοντες
brief, as to which [2]ye can [1]reading
νοῆσαι τὴν σύνεσίν μου ἐν τῷ μυστηρίῳ
to realize the understanding of me in the mystery

brought near through the
blood of Christ.
14For he himself is our
peace, who has made the
two one and has destroyed
the barrier, the dividing
wall of hostility, 15by abolishing in his flesh the law
with its commandments
and regulations. His pur-
pose was to create in himself one new man out of the
two, thus making peace,
16and in this one body to
reconcile both of them to
God through the cross, by
which he put to death their
hostility. 17He came and
preached peace to you who
were far away and peace to
those who were near. 18For
through him we both have
access to the Father by one
Spirit.
19Consequently, you are
no longer foreigners and
aliens, but fellow citizens
with God's people and
members of God's house-
hold, 20built on the foundation of the apostles and
prophets, with Christ Jesus
himself as the chief cornerstone. 21In him the whole
building is joined together
and rises to become a holy
temple in the Lord. 22And
in him you too are being
built together to become a
dwelling in which God lives
by his Spirit.

Chapter 3

Paul the Preacher to the Gentiles

FOR this reason I, Paul,
the prisoner of Christ
Jesus for the sake of you
Gentiles—
2Surely you have heard
about the administration of
God's grace that was given
to me for you, 3that is, the
mystery made known to me
by revelation, as I have already written briefly. 4In
reading this, then, you will
be able to understand my
insight into the mystery of

5which in other generations was not made known to the sons of men, as it has now been revealed to His holy apostles and prophets in the Spirit;

6*to be specific*, that the Gentiles are fellow heirs and fellow members of the body, and fellow partakers of the promise in Christ Jesus through the gospel,

7of which I was made a minister, according to the gift of God's grace which was given to me according to the working of His power.

8To me, the very least of all saints, this grace was given, to preach to the Gentiles the unfathomable riches of Christ,

9and to bring to light what is the administration of the mystery which for ages has been hidden in God, who created all things;

10in order that the manifold wisdom of God might now be made known through the church to the rulers and the authorities in the heavenly *places*.

11*This was* in accordance with the eternal purpose which He carried out in Christ Jesus our Lord,

12in whom we have boldness and confident access through faith in Him.

13Therefore I ask you not to lose heart at my tribulations on your behalf, for they are your glory.

14For this reason, I bow my knees before the Father,

15from whom every family in heaven and on earth derives its name,

16that He would grant you, according to the riches of His glory, to be strengthened with power

τοῦ Χριστοῦ, **5** ὃ ἑτέραις γενεαῖς οὐκ
– of Christ, which in other generations not

ἐγνωρίσθη τοῖς υἱοῖς τῶν ἀνθρώπων ὡς
was made known to the sons – of men as

νῦν ἀπεκαλύφθη τοῖς ἁγίοις ἀποστόλοις
now it was revealed to the holy apostles

αὐτοῦ καὶ προφήταις ἐν πνεύματι, **6** εἶναι
of him and prophets in spirit, [3]to be

τὰ ἔθνη συγκληρονόμα καὶ σύσσωμα καὶ
[1]the [2]nations joint-heirs and a joint-body and

συμμέτοχα τῆς ἐπαγγελίας ἐν Χριστῷ
joint-sharers of the promise in Christ

Ἰησοῦ διὰ τοῦ εὐαγγελίου, **7** οὗ ἐγενήθην
Jesus through the gospel, of which I became

διάκονος κατὰ τὴν δωρεὰν τῆς χάριτος
a minister according to the gift of the grace

τοῦ θεοῦ τῆς δοθείσης μοι κατὰ τὴν
– of God – given to me according to the

ἐνέργειαν τῆς δυνάμεως αὐτοῦ. **8** ἐμοὶ
operation of the power of him. To me

τῷ ἐλαχιστοτέρῳ πάντων ἁγίων ἐδόθη
the leaster* of all saints was given

ἡ χάρις αὕτη, τοῖς ἔθνεσιν εὐαγγελίσασθαι
this grace, to the nations to preach

τὸ ἀνεξιχνίαστον πλοῦτος τοῦ Χριστοῦ,
the unsearchable riches – of Christ,

9 καὶ φωτίσαι τίς ἡ οἰκονομία τοῦ
and to bring to light what [is] the stewardship of the

μυστηρίου τοῦ ἀποκεκρυμμένου ἀπὸ τῶν
mystery – *having been* hidden from the

αἰώνων ἐν τῷ θεῷ τῷ τὰ πάντα κτίσαντι,
ages in – God [1]the [one] – [3]all things [2]having created,

10 ἵνα γνωρισθῇ νῦν ταῖς ἀρχαῖς καὶ
in order that might be made known now to the rulers and

ταῖς ἐξουσίαις ἐν τοῖς ἐπουρανίοις διὰ
to the authorities in the heavenlies through

τῆς ἐκκλησίας ἡ πολυποίκιλος σοφία τοῦ
the church the manifold wisdom –

θεοῦ, **11** κατὰ πρόθεσιν τῶν αἰώνων ἣν
of God, according to [the] purpose of the ages which

ἐποίησεν ἐν τῷ Χριστῷ Ἰησοῦ τῷ κυρίῳ
he made in – Christ Jesus the Lord

ἡμῶν, **12** ἐν ᾧ ἔχομεν τὴν παρρησίαν
of us, in whom we have – boldness

καὶ προσαγωγὴν ἐν πεποιθήσει διὰ τῆς
and access in confidence through *the*

πίστεως αὐτοῦ. **13** διὸ αἰτοῦμαι μὴ
faith of(in) him.* Wherefore I ask [you] not

ἐγκακεῖν ἐν ταῖς θλίψεσίν μου ὑπὲρ
to faint in the afflictions of me on behalf

ὑμῶν, ἥτις ἐστὶν δόξα ὑμῶν. **14** Τούτου
of you, which is glory of you. [2]*of* this

χάριν κάμπτω τὰ γόνατά μου πρὸς
[1]By reason of I bend the knees of me unto

τὸν πατέρα, **15** ἐξ οὗ πᾶσα πατριὰ
the Father, of whom every fatherhood

ἐν οὐρανοῖς καὶ ἐπὶ γῆς ὀνομάζεται,
in heavens and on earth is named,

16 ἵνα δῷ ὑμῖν κατὰ τὸ πλοῦτος τῆς
in order that he may give you according to the riches of the

δόξης αὐτοῦ δυνάμει κραταιωθῆναι διὰ
glory of him by power to become mighty through

* This is quite literal!—the apostle coins a word.

* See Gal. 2. 16.

Christ, 5which was not
made known to men in oth-
er generations as it has now
been revealed by the Spirit
to God's holy apostles and
prophets. 6This mystery is
that through the gospel the
Gentiles are heirs together
with Israel, members to-
gether of one body, and
sharers together in the
promise in Christ Jesus.
7I became a servant of
this gospel by the gift of
God's grace given me
through the working of his
power. 8Although I am less
than the least of all God's
people, this grace was giv-
en me: to preach to the
Gentiles the unsearchable
riches of Christ, 9and to
make plain to everyone the
administration of this mystery, which for ages past
was kept hidden in God,
who created all things.
10His intent was that now,
through the church, the
manifold wisdom of God
should be made known to
the rulers and authorities in
the heavenly realms, 11ac-
cording to his eternal purpose which he accom-
plished in Christ Jesus our
Lord. 12In him and through
faith in him we may ap-
proach God with freedom
and confidence. 13I ask
you, therefore, not to be
discouraged because of my
sufferings for you, which
are your glory.

A Prayer for the Ephesians

14For this reason I kneel
before the Father, 15from
whom his whole family[h] in
heaven and on earth de-
rives its name. 16I pray that
out of his glorious riches he
may strengthen you with

[h]15 Or *whom all fatherhood*

through His Spirit in the inner man;
17so that Christ may dwell
in your hearts through
faith; *and* that you, being
rooted and grounded in
love,
18may be able to com-
prehend with all the saints
what is the breadth and
length and height and
depth,
19and to know the love of
Christ which surpasses
knowledge, that you may
be filled up to all the fulness
of God.
20Now to Him who is able
to do exceeding abundantly
beyond all that we ask or
think, according to the
power that works within
us,
21to Him *be* the glory in
the church and in Christ
Jesus to all generations forever and ever. Amen.

Chapter 4

Unity of the Spirit

I, THEREFORE, the
prisoner of the Lord,
entreat you to walk in a
manner worthy of the calling with which you have
been called,
2with all humility and
gentleness, with patience,
showing forbearance to one
another in love,
3being diligent to pre-
serve the unity of the Spirit
in the bond of peace.
4*There is* one body and
one Spirit, just as also you
were called in one hope of
your calling;
5one Lord, one faith, one
baptism,
6one God and Father of
all who is over all and
through all and in all.
7But to each one of us
grace was given according
to the measure of Christ's
gift.
8 Therefore it says,
"WHEN HE ASCENDED
ON HIGH,
HE LED CAPTIVE A HOST

τοῦ πνεύματος αὐτοῦ εἰς τὸν ἔσω ἄνθρω-
the Spirit of him in the inward man,
πον, 17 κατοικῆσαι τὸν Χριστὸν διὰ τῆς
to dwell – Christ[b] through –
=that Christ may dwell
πίστεως ἐν ταῖς καρδίαις ὑμῶν, ἐν
faith in the hearts of you, in
ἀγάπῃ ἐρριζωμένοι καὶ τεθεμελιωμένοι,
love *having been* rooted and *having been* founded,
18 ἵνα ἐξισχύσητε καταλαβέσθαι σὺν πᾶσιν
in order that ye may have strength to apprehend with all
τοῖς ἁγίοις τί τὸ πλάτος καὶ μῆκος
the saints what [is] the breadth and length
καὶ ὕψος καὶ βάθος, 19 γνῶναί τε τὴν
and height and depth, and to know [1]the
ὑπερβάλλουσαν τῆς γνώσεως ἀγάπην τοῦ
[4]excelling – [5]knowledge [2]love –
Χριστοῦ, ἵνα πληρωθῆτε εἰς πᾶν τὸ
[3]of Christ, *in order* that ye may be filled to all the
πλήρωμα τοῦ θεοῦ.
fulness – of God.
20 Τῷ δὲ δυναμένῳ ὑπὲρ πάντα ποιῆσαι
Now to the [one] being able beyond all things to do
ὑπερεκπερισσοῦ ὧν αἰτούμεθα ἢ νοοῦμεν
superabundantly *of* which we ask or *we* think
κατὰ τὴν δύναμιν τὴν ἐνεργουμένην ἐν
according to the power – operating in
ἡμῖν, 21 αὐτῷ ἡ δόξα ἐν τῇ ἐκκλησίᾳ
us, to him [be] the glory in the church
καὶ ἐν Χριστῷ Ἰησοῦ εἰς πάσας τὰς
and in Christ – Jesus unto all the
γενεὰς τοῦ αἰῶνος τῶν αἰώνων· ἀμήν.
generations of the age of the ages: Amen.

4 Παρακαλῶ οὖν ὑμᾶς ἐγὼ ὁ δέσμιος
[7]beseech [6]therefore [8]you [1]I [2]the [3]prisoner
ἐν κυρίῳ ἀξίως περιπατῆσαι τῆς κλήσεως
[4]in [5][the] Lord [10]worthily [9]to walk of the calling
ἧς ἐκλήθητε, 2 μετὰ πάσης ταπεινοφροσύνης
of(with) which ye were called, with all humility
καὶ πραΰτητος, μετὰ μακροθυμίας,
and meekness, with longsuffering,
ἀνεχόμενοι ἀλλήλων ἐν ἀγάπῃ, 3 σπου-
forbearing one another in love, being
δάζοντες τηρεῖν τὴν ἑνότητα τοῦ πνεύματος
eager to keep the unity of the Spirit
ἐν τῷ συνδέσμῳ τῆς εἰρήνης· ἓν σῶμα
in the bond – of peace; [there is] one body
καὶ ἓν πνεῦμα, 4 καθὼς καὶ ἐκλήθητε
and one Spirit, as also ye were called
ἐν μιᾷ ἐλπίδι τῆς κλήσεως ὑμῶν· 5 εἷς
in one hope of the calling of you; one
κύριος, μία πίστις, ἓν βάπτισμα· 6 εἷς
Lord, one faith, one baptism; one
θεὸς καὶ πατὴρ πάντων, ὁ ἐπὶ πάντων
God and Father of all, the [one] over all
καὶ διὰ πάντων καὶ ἐν πᾶσιν. 7 Ἑνὶ
and through all and in all. [3]to [4]one
δὲ ἑκάστῳ ἡμῶν ἐδόθη ἡ χάρις κατὰ
[1]But [2]each of us was given – grace according to
τὸ μέτρον τῆς δωρεᾶς τοῦ Χριστοῦ.
the measure of the gift – of Christ.
8 διὸ λέγει· ἀναβὰς εἰς ὕψος ᾐχμαλώτευσεν
Wherefore he says: Having ascended to height he led captive

power through his Spirit in
your inner being, 17so that
Christ may dwell in your
hearts through faith. And I
pray that you, being rooted
and established in love,
18may have power, togeth-
er with all the saints, to
grasp how wide and long
and high and deep is the
love of Christ, 19and to
know this love that sur-
passes knowledge—that
you may be filled to the
measure of all the fullness
of God.
20Now to him who is able
to do immeasurably more
than all we ask or imagine,
according to his power that
is at work within us, 21to
him be glory in the church
and in Christ Jesus
throughout all generations,
for ever and ever! Amen.

Chapter 4

Unity in the Body of Christ

AS a prisoner for the
Lord, then, I urge you
to live a life worthy of the
calling you have received.
2Be completely humble and
gentle; be patient, bearing
with one another in love.
3Make every effort to keep
the unity of the Spirit
through the bond of peace.
4There is one body and one
Spirit—just as you were
called to one hope when
you were called— 5one
Lord, one faith, one bap-
tism; 6one God and Father
of all, who is over all and
through all and in all.
7But to each one of us
grace has been given as
Christ apportioned it. 8This
is why it[i] says:

"When he ascended on
high,
he led captives in his

[i]8 Or *God*

OF CAPTIVES,
AND HE GAVE GIFTS TO
MEN.''
9(Now this *expression,*
''He ascended,'' what does
it mean except that He also
had descended into the
lower parts of the earth?
10He who descended is
Himself also He who as-
cended far above all the
heavens, that He might fill
all things.)
11And He gave some
as apostles, and some *as*
prophets, and some
as evangelists, and some *as*
pastors and teachers,
12for the equipping of the
saints for the work of service, to the building up of
the body of Christ;
13until we all attain to the
unity of the faith, and of the
knowledge of the Son of
God, to a mature man, to
the measure of the stature
which belongs to the ful-
ness of Christ.
14As a result, we are no
longer to be children,
tossed here and there by
waves, and carried about
by every wind of doctrine,
by the trickery of men, by
craftiness in deceitful
scheming;
15but speaking the truth in
love, we are to grow up in
all *aspects* into Him, who is
the head, *even* Christ,
16from whom the whole
body, being fitted and held
together by that which
every joint supplies, ac-
cording to the proper working of each individual part,
causes the growth of the
body for the building up of
itself in love.

The Christian's Walk

17This I say therefore,
and affirm together with
the Lord, that you walk no
longer just as the Gentiles
also walk, in the futility of
their mind,
18being darkened in their

αἰχμαλωσίαν, ἔδωκεν δόματα τοῖς ἀνθρώποις.
captivity, he gave gifts – to men.

9 τὸ δὲ ἀνέβη τί ἐστιν εἰ μὴ ὅτι καὶ
Now the "he ascended" what is it except that also

κατέβη εἰς τὰ κατώτερα μέρη τῆς γῆς;
he descended into the lower parts of the earth?

10 ὁ καταβὰς αὐτός ἐστιν καὶ ὁ ἀναβὰς
The descending [one] himself is also the ascending [one]

ὑπεράνω πάντων τῶν οὐρανῶν, ἵνα
far above all the heavens, in order that

πληρώσῃ τὰ πάντα. 11 καὶ αὐτὸς ἔδωκεν
he might fill – all things. And he gave

τοὺς μὲν ἀποστόλους, τοὺς δὲ προφήτας,
some† apostles, some† prophets,

τοὺς δὲ εὐαγγελιστάς, τοὺς δὲ ποιμένας
some† evangelists, some† shepherds

καὶ διδασκάλους, 12 πρὸς τὸν καταρτισμὸν
and teachers, for the perfecting

τῶν ἁγίων εἰς ἔργον διακονίας, εἰς
of the saints to [the] work of ministry, to

οἰκοδομὴν τοῦ σώματος τοῦ Χριστοῦ,
building of the body – of Christ,

13 μέχρι καταντήσωμεν οἱ πάντες εἰς
until [1]we [3]arrive – [2]all at

τὴν ἑνότητα τῆς πίστεως καὶ τῆς ἐπιγνώ-
the unity of the faith and of the full know-

σεως τοῦ υἱοῦ τοῦ θεοῦ, εἰς ἄνδρα τέλειον,
ledge of the Son – of God, at [2]man [1]a complete,

εἰς μέτρον ἡλικίας τοῦ πληρώματος τοῦ
at [the] measure of [the] stature of the fulness –

Χριστοῦ, 14 ἵνα μηκέτι ὦμεν νήπιοι,
of Christ, in order that no more we may be infants,

κλυδωνιζόμενοι καὶ περιφερόμενοι παντὶ ἀνέμῳ
being blown and *being* carried round by every wind

τῆς διδασκαλίας ἐν τῇ κυβείᾳ τῶν ἀνθρώ-
– of teaching in the sleight – of

πων, ἐν πανουργίᾳ πρὸς τὴν μεθοδείαν
men, in cleverness unto the craftiness

τῆς πλάνης, 15 ἀληθεύοντες δὲ ἐν ἀγάπῃ
– of error, but speaking truth in love

αὐξήσωμεν εἰς αὐτὸν τὰ πάντα, ὅς ἐστιν
we may grow into him in all respects,† who is

ἡ κεφαλή, Χριστός, 16 ἐξ οὗ πᾶν τὸ
the head, Christ, of whom all the

σῶμα συναρμολογούμενον καὶ συμβιβαζόμενον
body being fitted together and *being* brought together

διὰ πάσης ἁφῆς τῆς ἐπιχορηγίας κατ'
through every band – of supply according to

ἐνέργειαν ἐν μέτρῳ ἑνὸς ἑκάστου μέρους
[the] operation in measure of [2]one [1]each part

τὴν αὔξησιν τοῦ σώματος ποιεῖται εἰς
[2]the [3]growth [4]of the [5]body [1]makes for

οἰκοδομὴν ἑαυτοῦ ἐν ἀγάπῃ.
building of itself in love.

17 Τοῦτο οὖν λέγω καὶ μαρτύρομαι ἐν
This therefore I say and witness in

κυρίῳ, μηκέτι ὑμᾶς περιπατεῖν καθὼς
[the] Lord, no more you to walk as

καὶ τὰ ἔθνη περιπατεῖ ἐν ματαιότητι
also the nations walks in vanity

τοῦ νοὸς αὐτῶν, 18 ἐσκοτωμένοι τῇ
of the mind of them, [1]*having been* darkened [2]in the (their)

train
and gave gifts to
men.''[j]
9(What does ''he ascend-
ed'' mean except that he
also descended to the lower, earthly regions[k]? 10He
who descended is the very
one who ascended higher
than all the heavens, in order to fill the whole universe.) 11It was he who
gave some to be apostles,
some to be prophets, some
to be evangelists, and some
to be pastors and teachers,
12to prepare God's people
for works of service, so
that the body of Christ may
be built up 13until we all
reach unity in the faith and
in the knowledge of the Son
of God and become ma-
ture, attaining to the whole
measure of the fullness of
Christ.
14Then we will no longer
be infants, tossed back and
forth by the waves, and
blown here and there by every wind of teaching and by
the cunning and craftiness
of men in their deceitful
scheming. 15Instead,
speaking the truth in love,
we will in all things grow up
into him who is the Head,
that is, Christ. 16From him
the whole body, joined and
held together by every supporting ligament, grows
and builds itself up in love,
as each part does its work.

Living as Children of Light

17So I tell you this, and
insist on it in the Lord, that
you must no longer live as
the Gentiles do, in the futility of their thinking. 18They
are darkened in their un-

[j]8 Psalm 68:18
[k]9 Or *the depths of the earth*

understanding, excluded from the life of God, because of the ignorance that is in them, because of the hardness of their heart;

19and they, having become callous, have given themselves over to sensuality, for the practice of every kind of impurity with greediness.

20But you did not learn Christ in this way,

21if indeed you have heard Him and have been taught in Him, just as truth is in Jesus,

22that, in reference to your former manner of life, you lay aside the old self, which is being corrupted in accordance with the lusts of deceit,

23and that you be renewed in the spirit of your mind,

24and put on the new self, which in *the likeness of* God has been created in righteousness and holiness of the truth.

25Therefore, laying aside falsehood, SPEAK TRUTH, EACH ONE *of you,* WITH HIS NEIGHBOR, for we are members of one another.

26BE ANGRY, AND *yet* DO NOT SIN; do not let the sun go down on your anger,

27and do not give the devil an opportunity.

28Let him who steals steal no longer; but rather let him labor, performing with his own hands what is good, in order that he may have *something* to share with him who has need.

29Let no unwholesome word proceed from your mouth, but only such *a word* as is good for edification according to the need *of the moment,* that it may give grace to those who hear.

30And do not grieve the Holy Spirit of God, by whom you were sealed for

διανοίᾳ ὄντες, ἀπηλλοτριωμένοι τῆς ζωῆς
[4]intellect [1]being, having been alienated [from] the life

τοῦ θεοῦ, διὰ τὴν ἄγνοιαν τὴν οὖσαν
– of God, through the ignorance – being

ἐν αὐτοῖς, διὰ τὴν πώρωσιν τῆς καρδίας
in them, on account of the hardness of the heart

αὐτῶν, 19 οἵτινες ἀπηλγηκότες ἑαυτοὺς
of them, who having ceased to care [2]themselves

παρέδωκαν τῇ ἀσελγείᾳ εἰς ἐργασίαν
[1]gave up – to lewdness for work

ἀκαθαρσίας πάσης ἐν πλεονεξίᾳ. 20 ὑμεῖς
[2]uncleanness [1]of all in greediness. ye

δὲ οὐχ οὕτως ἐμάθετε τὸν Χριστόν,
But not so learned – Christ,

21 εἴ γε αὐτὸν ἠκούσατε καὶ ἐν αὐτῷ
if indeed [2]him [1]ye heard and [3]by [3]him

ἐδιδάχθητε καθώς ἐστιν ἀλήθεια ἐν τῷ
[1]were taught as [2]is [1]truth in –

Ἰησοῦ, 22 ἀποθέσθαι ὑμᾶς κατὰ τὴν
Jesus, to put off you[b] as regards the(your)
=that ye put off

προτέραν ἀναστροφὴν τὸν παλαιὸν ἄνθρωπον
former conduct the old man

τὸν φθειρόμενον κατὰ τὰς ἐπιθυμίας τῆς
– being corrupted according to the lusts –

ἀπάτης, 23 ἀνανεοῦσθαι δὲ τῷ πνεύματι
of deceit, and *to* be renewed in the spirit

τοῦ νοὸς ὑμῶν 24 καὶ ἐνδύσασθαι τὸν
of the mind of you and *to* put on the

καινὸν ἄνθρωπον τὸν κατὰ θεὸν κτισθέντα
new man – [2]according to [3]God [1]created

ἐν δικαιοσύνῃ καὶ ὁσιότητι τῆς ἀληθείας.
in righteousness and holiness – of truth.

25 Διὸ ἀποθέμενοι τὸ ψεῦδος λαλεῖτε
Wherefore putting off the lie speak ye

ἀλήθειαν ἕκαστος μετὰ τοῦ πλησίον αὐτοῦ,
truth each man with the neighbour of him,

ὅτι ἐσμὲν ἀλλήλων μέλη. 26 ὀργίζεσθε
because we are of one another members. Be ye wrathful

καὶ μὴ ἁμαρτάνετε· ὁ ἥλιος μὴ
and do not sin; [3]the [4]sun [2]not

ἐπιδυέτω ἐπὶ παροργισμῷ ὑμῶν, 27 μηδὲ
[1]let [5]set *on* on provocation of you, nor

δίδοτε τόπον τῷ διαβόλῳ. 28 ὁ κλέπτων
give ye place to the devil. The [one] stealing

μηκέτι κλεπτέτω, μᾶλλον δὲ κοπιάτω
no more let him steal, but rather let him labour

ἐργαζόμενος ταῖς ἰδίαις χερσὶν τὸ ἀγαθόν,
working with the(his) own hands the good thing,

ἵνα ἔχῃ μεταδιδόναι τῷ χρείαν ἔχοντι.
in order that he may have to share [with] the [one] [2]need [1]having

29 πᾶς λόγος σαπρὸς ἐκ τοῦ στόματος
Every [2]word [1]corrupt out of the mouth

ὑμῶν μὴ ἐκπορευέσθω, ἀλλὰ εἴ τις
of you let not proceed*, but if any

ἀγαθὸς πρὸς οἰκοδομὴν τῆς χρείας, ἵνα
[is] good to improvement of the need, in order that

δῷ χάριν τοῖς ἀκούουσιν. 30 καὶ μὴ λυπεῖτε
it may give grace to the [ones] hearing. And do not grieve

τὸ πνεῦμα τὸ ἅγιον τοῦ θεοῦ, ἐν ᾧ
the Spirit – Holy – of God, by whom

ἐσφραγίσθητε εἰς ἡμέραν ἀπολυτρώσεως.
ye were sealed for a day of redemption.

* That is, " let no corrupt word proceed . . . "

derstanding and separated
from the life of God be-
cause of the ignorance that
is in them due to the hardening of their hearts.
19Having lost all sensitivi-
ty, they have given them-
selves over to sensuality so
as to indulge in every kind
of impurity, with a continu-
al lust for more.
20You, however, did not
come to know Christ that
way. 21Surely you heard of
him and were taught in him
in accordance with the
truth that is in Jesus. 22You
were taught, with regard to
your former way of life, to
put off your old self, which
is being corrupted by its deceitful desires; 23to be made
new in the attitude of your
minds; 24and to put on the
new self, created to be like
God in true righteousness
and holiness.
25Therefore each of you
must put off falsehood and
speak truthfully to his
neighbor, for we are all
members of one body.
26"In your anger do not
sin"[l]: Do not let the sun go
down while you are still angry, 27and do not give the
devil a foothold. 28He who
has been stealing must steal
no longer, but must work,
doing something useful
with his own hands, that he
may have something to
share with those in need.
29Do not let any unwhole-
some talk come out of your
mouths, but only what is
helpful for building others
up according to their
needs, that it may benefit
those who listen. 30And do
not grieve the Holy Spirit
of God, with whom you
were sealed for the day of

[l]26 Psalm 4:4

the day of redemption.
31Let all bitterness and
wrath and anger and clam-
or and slander be put away
from you, along with all
malice.
32And be kind to one an-
other, tender-hearted, forgiving each other, just as
God in Christ also has forgiven [f] you.

Chapter 5

Be Imitators of God

THEREFORE be imita-
tors of God, as be-
loved children;
2and walk in love, just as
Christ also loved [f]you, and
gave Himself up for us, an
offering and a sacrifice to
God as a fragrant aroma.
3But do not let immoral-
ity or any impurity or greed
even be named among you,
as is proper among saints;
4and *there must be no*
filthiness and silly talk, or
coarse jesting, which are
not fitting, but rather giving
of thanks.
5For this you know with
certainty, that no immoral
or impure person or covetous man, who is an idola-
ter, has an inheritance in
the kingdom of Christ and
God.
6Let no one deceive you
with empty words, for be-
cause of these things the
wrath of God comes upon
the sons of disobedience.
7Therefore do not be
partakers with them;
8for you were formerly
darkness, but now you are
light in the Lord; walk as
children of light
9(for the fruit of the light
consists in all goodness and
righteousness and truth),
10trying to learn what is
pleasing to the Lord.
11And do not participate
in the unfruitful deeds of
darkness, but instead even
expose them;
12for it is disgraceful even
to speak of the things which
are done by them in secret.
13But all things become

[f]Some ancient mss. read *us*

31 πᾶσα πικρία καὶ θυμὸς καὶ
All bitterness and anger and

ὀργὴ καὶ κραυγὴ καὶ βλασφημία ἀρθήτω
wrath and clamour and blasphemy let it be removed

ἀφ' ὑμῶν σὺν πάσῃ κακίᾳ. 32 γίνεσθε
from you with all evil. be ye

δὲ εἰς ἀλλήλους χρηστοί, εὔσπλαγχνοι,
And to one another kind, tenderhearted,

χαριζόμενοι ἑαυτοῖς καθὼς καὶ ὁ θεὸς
forgiving yourselves as also – God

ἐν Χριστῷ ἐχαρίσατο ὑμῖν. 5 Γίνεσθε
in Christ forgave you. Be ye

οὖν μιμηταὶ τοῦ θεοῦ, ὡς τέκνα
therefore imitators – of God, as children

ἀγαπητά, 2 καὶ περιπατεῖτε ἐν ἀγάπῃ,
beloved, and walk ye in love,

καθὼς καὶ ὁ Χριστὸς ἠγάπησεν ὑμᾶς
as also – Christ loved you

καὶ παρέδωκεν ἑαυτὸν ὑπὲρ ἡμῶν
and gave up himself on behalf of us

προσφορὰν καὶ θυσίαν τῷ θεῷ εἰς ὀσμὴν
an offering and a sacrifice – to God for an odour

εὐωδίας. 3 Πορνεία δὲ καὶ ἀκαθαρσία
of sweet smell. But fornication and [2]uncleanness

πᾶσα ἢ πλεονεξία μηδὲ ὀνομαζέσθω ἐν
[1]all or greediness not let it be named among

ὑμῖν, καθὼς πρέπει ἁγίοις, 4 καὶ αἰσχρότης
you, as is fitting for saints, and baseness

καὶ μωρολογία ἢ εὐτραπελία, ἃ οὐκ
and foolish talking or raillery, which things not

ἀνῆκεν, ἀλλὰ μᾶλλον εὐχαριστία. 5 τοῦτο
are becoming, but rather thanksgiving. this

γὰρ ἴστε γινώσκοντες, ὅτι πᾶς πόρνος
For be ye knowing, that every fornicator

ἢ ἀκάθαρτος ἢ πλεονέκτης, ὅ ἐστιν
or unclean man or greedy, who is

εἰδωλολάτρης, οὐκ ἔχει κληρονομίαν ἐν τῇ
an idolater, not has inheritance in the

βασιλείᾳ τοῦ Χριστοῦ καὶ θεοῦ. 6 Μηδεὶς
kingdom – of Christ and of God. [2]No man

ὑμᾶς ἀπατάτω κενοῖς λόγοις· διὰ ταῦτα
[4]you [1]let [3]deceive with empty words; because of these things

γὰρ ἔρχεται ἡ ὀργὴ τοῦ θεοῦ ἐπὶ τοὺς
for is coming the wrath – of God on the

υἱοὺς τῆς ἀπειθείας. 7 μὴ οὖν γίνεσθε
sons – of disobedience. Not therefore be ye

συμμέτοχοι αὐτῶν· 8 ἦτε γάρ ποτε σκότος,
partakers of them; for ye were then darkness,

νῦν δὲ φῶς ἐν κυρίῳ· ὡς τέκνα φωτὸς
but now light in [the] Lord; as children of light

περιπατεῖτε, 9 — ὁ γὰρ καρπὸς τοῦ
walk ye, (for the fruit of the

φωτὸς ἐν πάσῃ ἀγαθωσύνῃ καὶ δικαιοσύνῃ
light [is] in all goodness and righteousness

καὶ ἀληθείᾳ, — 10 δοκιμάζοντες τί ἐστιν
and truth,) proving what is

εὐάρεστον τῷ κυρίῳ, 11 καὶ μὴ συγκοι-
well-pleasing to the Lord, and do not have fellow-

νωνεῖτε τοῖς ἔργοις τοῖς ἀκάρποις τοῦ
ship with the [2]works – [1]unfruitful –

σκότους, μᾶλλον δὲ καὶ ἐλέγχετε, 12 τὰ
of darkness, but rather even reprove [them], [5]the

γὰρ κρυφῇ γινόμενα ὑπ' αὐτῶν αἰσχρόν
for [6]hidden things [7]being done [8]by [9]them [2]shameful

ἐστιν καὶ λέγειν· 13 τὰ δὲ πάντα ἐλεγχόμενα
[1]it is [3]even [4]to speak [of]; – but all things being reproved

redemption. 31Get rid of all
bitterness, rage and anger,
brawling and slander, along
with every form of malice.
32Be kind and compassion-
ate to one another, forgiving each other, just as in
Christ God forgave you.

Chapter 5

BE imitators of God,
therefore, as dearly
loved children 2and live a
life of love, just as Christ
loved us and gave himself
up for us as a fragrant offering and sacrifice to God.
3But among you there
must not be even a hint of
sexual immorality, or of
any kind of impurity, or of
greed, because these are
improper for God's holy
people. 4Nor should there
be obscenity, foolish talk
or coarse joking, which are
out of place, but rather
thanksgiving. 5For of this
you can be sure: No immoral, impure or greedy person
—such a man is an idola-
ter—has any inheritance in
the kingdom of Christ and
of God.[m] 6Let no one deceive you with empty
words, for because of such
things God's wrath comes
on those who are disobedient. 7Therefore do not be
partners with them.
8For you were once dark-
ness, but now you are light
in the Lord. Live as children of light 9(for the fruit
of the light consists in all
goodness, righteousness
and truth) 10and find out
what pleases the Lord.
11Have nothing to do with
the fruitless deeds of darkness, but rather expose
them. 12For it is shameful
even to mention what the
disobedient do in secret.
13But everything exposed

[m]5 Or *kingdom of the Christ and God*

visible when they are exposed by the light, for everything that becomes visible is light.
14For this reason it says,
"Awake, sleeper,
And arise from the dead,
And Christ will shine on you."
15Therefore be careful how you walk, not as unwise men, but as wise,
16making the most of your time, because the days are evil.
17So then do not be foolish, but understand what the will of the Lord is.
18And do not get drunk with wine, for that is dissipation, but be filled with the Spirit,
19speaking to one another in psalms and hymns and spiritual songs, singing and making melody with your heart to the Lord;
20always giving thanks for all things in the name of our Lord Jesus Christ to God, even the Father;
21and be subject to one another in the fear of Christ.

Marriage Like Christ and the Church

22Wives, *be subject* to your own husbands, as to the Lord.
23For the husband is the head of the wife, as Christ also is the head of the church, He Himself *being* the Savior of the body.
24But as the church is subject to Christ, so also the wives *ought to be* to their husbands in everything.
25Husbands, love your wives, just as Christ also loved the church and gave Himself up for her;
26that He might sanctify her, having cleansed her by the washing of water with the word,
27that He might present to Himself the church in all her glory, having no spot or wrinkle or any such thing;

ὑπὸ τοῦ φωτὸς φανεροῦται· 14 πᾶν γὰρ
by the light is(are) manifested; for everything
τὸ φανερούμενον φῶς ἐστιν. διὸ λέγει·
– being manifested [2]light [1]is. Wherefore he says:
ἔγειρε, ὁ καθεύδων, καὶ ἀνάστα ἐκ τῶν
Rise, the sleeping [one], and stand up out of the
νεκρῶν, καὶ ἐπιφαύσει σοι ὁ Χριστός.
dead [ones], and will shine on thee – Christ.
15 Βλέπετε οὖν ἀκριβῶς πῶς περιπατεῖτε,
See ye therefore carefully how ye walk,
μὴ ὡς ἄσοφοι ἀλλ' ὡς σοφοί, 16 ἐξαγοραζ-
not as unwise but as wise, redeem-
όμενοι τὸν καιρόν, ὅτι αἱ ἡμέραι πονηραί
ing the time, because the days evil
εἰσιν. 17 διὰ τοῦτο μὴ γίνεσθε ἄφρονες,
are. Therefore be ye not foolish,
ἀλλὰ συνίετε τί τὸ θέλημα τοῦ κυρίου.
but understand what the will of the Lord [is].
18 καὶ μὴ μεθύσκεσθε οἴνῳ, ἐν ᾧ ἐστιν
And be ye not drunk with wine, in which is
ἀσωτία, ἀλλὰ πληροῦσθε ἐν πνεύματι,
wantonness, but be filled by [the] Spirit,
19 λαλοῦντες ἑαυτοῖς ψαλμοῖς καὶ ὕμνοις
speaking to yourselves in psalms and hymns
καὶ ᾠδαῖς πνευματικαῖς, ᾄδοντες καὶ
and songs spiritual, singing and
ψάλλοντες τῇ καρδίᾳ ὑμῶν τῷ κυρίῳ,
psalming with the heart of you to the Lord,
20 εὐχαριστοῦντες πάντοτε ὑπὲρ πάντων
giving thanks always for all things
ἐν ὀνόματι τοῦ κυρίου ἡμῶν Ἰησοῦ
in [the] name of the Lord of us Jesus
Χριστοῦ τῷ θεῷ καὶ πατρί, 21 ὑποτασ-
Christ – to God even [the] Father, being
σόμενοι ἀλλήλοις ἐν φόβῳ Χριστοῦ. 22 Αἱ
subject to one another in [the] fear of Christ. The
γυναῖκες τοῖς ἰδίοις ἀνδράσιν ὡς τῷ
wives to the(ir) own husbands as to the
κυρίῳ, 23 ὅτι ἀνήρ ἐστιν κεφαλὴ τῆς
Lord, because a man is head of the
γυναικὸς ὡς καὶ ὁ Χριστὸς κεφαλὴ
woman as also – Christ [is] head
τῆς ἐκκλησίας, αὐτὸς σωτὴρ τοῦ σώματος.
of the church, [him]self Saviour of the body.
24 ἀλλὰ ὡς ἡ ἐκκλησία ὑποτάσσεται τῷ
But as the church is subject –
Χριστῷ, οὕτως καὶ αἱ γυναῖκες τοῖς
to Christ, so also the wives to the(ir)
ἀνδράσιν ἐν παντί. 25 Οἱ ἄνδρες, ἀγαπᾶτε
husbands in everything. The husbands, love ye
τὰς γυναῖκας, καθὼς καὶ ὁ Χριστὸς
the(your) wives, as also – Christ
ἠγάπησεν τὴν ἐκκλησίαν καὶ ἑαυτὸν
loved the church and himself
παρέδωκεν ὑπὲρ αὐτῆς, 26 ἵνα αὐτὴν
gave up on behalf of it, in order that it
ἁγιάσῃ καθαρίσας τῷ λουτρῷ τοῦ
he might sanctify cleansing by the washing of the
ὕδατος ἐν ῥήματι, 27 ἵνα παραστήσῃ αὐτὸς
water by word, in order that [2]might present [1]he
ἑαυτῷ ἔνδοξον τὴν ἐκκλησίαν, μὴ ἔχουσαν
[3]to himself [4]glorious [1]the [2]church, not having
σπίλον ἢ ῥυτίδα ἤ τι τῶν τοιούτων,
spot or wrinkle or any of *the* such things,

by the light becomes visible, 14for it is light that makes everything visible.
This is why it is said:
"Wake up, O sleeper,
rise from the dead,
and Christ will shine on you."
15Be very careful, then,
how you live—not as unwise but as wise, 16making
the most of every opportunity, because the days are
evil. 17Therefore do not be
foolish, but understand
what the Lord's will is.
18Do not get drunk on wine,
which leads to debauchery.
Instead, be filled with the
Spirit. 19Speak to one another with psalms, hymns
and spiritual songs. Sing
and make music in your
heart to the Lord, 20always
giving thanks to God the
Father for everything, in
the name of our Lord Jesus
Christ.
21Submit to one another
out of reverence for Christ.

Wives and Husbands

22Wives, submit to your
husbands as to the Lord.
23For the husband is the
head of the wife as Christ is
the head of the church, his
body, of which he is the
Savior. 24Now as the
church submits to Christ,
so also wives should submit to their husbands in everything.
25Husbands, love your
wives, just as Christ loved
the church and gave himself up for her 26to make her
holy, cleansing[n] her by the
washing with water
through the word, 27and to
present her to himself as a
radiant church, without
stain or wrinkle or any oth-

[n]26 Or *having cleansed*

but that she should be holy and blameless.

28 So husbands ought also to love their own wives as their own bodies. He who loves his own wife loves himself;

29 for no one ever hated his own flesh, but nourishes and cherishes it, just as Christ also *does* the church,

30 because we are members of His body.

31 FOR THIS CAUSE A MAN SHALL LEAVE HIS FATHER AND MOTHER, AND SHALL CLEAVE TO HIS WIFE; AND THE TWO SHALL BECOME ONE FLESH.

32 This mystery is great; but I am speaking with reference to Christ and the church.

33 Nevertheless let each individual among you also love his own wife even as himself; and *let* the wife *see to it* that she respect her husband.

Chapter 6

Family Relationships

CHILDREN, obey your parents in the Lord, for this is right.

2 HONOR YOUR FATHER AND MOTHER (which is the first commandment with a promise),

3 THAT IT MAY BE WELL WITH YOU, AND THAT YOU MAY LIVE LONG ON THE EARTH.

4 And, fathers, do not provoke your children to anger; but bring them up in the discipline and instruction of the Lord.

5 Slaves, be obedient to those who are your masters according to the flesh, with fear and trembling, in the sincerity of your heart, as to Christ;

6 not by way of eyeservice, as men-pleasers, but as slaves of Christ, doing the will of God from the heart.

ἀλλ' ἵνα ᾖ ἁγία καὶ ἄμωμος. **28** οὕτως
but *in order* that it might be holy and unblemished. So

ὀφείλουσιν [καὶ] οἱ ἄνδρες ἀγαπᾶν τὰς
ought also the husbands to love the

ἑαυτῶν γυναῖκας ὡς τὰ ἑαυτῶν σώματα.
of themselves wives as the of themselves bodies.

ὁ ἀγαπῶν τὴν ἑαυτοῦ γυναῖκα ἑαυτὸν
The [one] loving the of himself wife himself

ἀγαπᾷ· **29** οὐδεὶς γάρ ποτε τὴν ἑαυτοῦ
loves; for no man ever the of himself

σάρκα ἐμίσησεν, ἀλλὰ ἐκτρέφει καὶ θάλπει
flesh hated, but nourishes and cherishes

αὐτήν, καθὼς καὶ ὁ Χριστὸς τὴν ἐκ-
it, as also – Christ the

κλησίαν, **30** ὅτι μέλη ἐσμὲν τοῦ σώματος
church, because members we are of the body

αὐτοῦ. **31** ἀντὶ τούτου καταλείψει ἄνθρωπος
of him. For this [2]shall leave [1]a man

[τὸν] πατέρα καὶ [τὴν] μητέρα καὶ
the(his) father and the(his) mother and

προσκολληθήσεται πρὸς τὴν γυναῖκα αὐτοῦ,
shall cleave to the wife of him,

καὶ ἔσονται οἱ δύο εἰς σάρκα μίαν.
and [3]shall be [1]the [2]two [4]for [6]flesh [5]one.

32 τὸ μυστήριον τοῦτο μέγα ἐστίν, ἐγὼ
This mystery great is, [2]I

δὲ λέγω εἰς Χριστὸν καὶ [εἰς] τὴν
[1]but say as to Christ and as to the

ἐκκλησίαν. **33** πλὴν καὶ ὑμεῖς οἱ
church. Nevertheless also ye *the*

καθ' ἕνα ἕκαστος τὴν ἑαυτοῦ γυναῖκα
one by one† each [1]the [3]of himself [2]wife

οὕτως ἀγαπάτω ὡς ἑαυτόν, ἡ δὲ
so let him love as himself, and the

γυνὴ ἵνα φοβῆται τὸν ἄνδρα. **6** Τὰ
wife *in order* that she fears the(her) husband. The

τέκνα, ὑπακούετε τοῖς γονεῦσιν ὑμῶν
children, obey ye the parents of you

ἐν κυρίῳ· τοῦτο γάρ ἐστιν δίκαιον.
in [the] Lord; for this is right.

2 τίμα τὸν πατέρα σου καὶ τὴν μητέρα,
Honour the father of thee and the mother,

ἥτις ἐστὶν ἐντολὴ πρώτη ἐν ἐπαγγελίᾳ,
which is [2]commandment [1][the] [3]first with a promise,

3 ἵνα εὖ σοι γένηται καὶ ἔσῃ μακρο-
in order that well with thee it may be and thou mayest be long-

χρόνιος ἐπὶ τῆς γῆς. **4** Καὶ οἱ πατέρες,
timed(lived) on the earth. And the fathers,

μὴ παροργίζετε τὰ τέκνα ὑμῶν, ἀλλὰ
do not ye provoke to wrath the children of you, but

ἐκτρέφετε αὐτὰ ἐν παιδείᾳ καὶ νουθεσίᾳ
nurture them in [the] discipline and admonition

κυρίου. **5** Οἱ δοῦλοι, ὑπακούετε τοῖς
of [the] Lord. The slaves, obey ye [1]the(your)

κατὰ σάρκα κυρίοις μετὰ φόβου καὶ
[3]according to [4]flesh [2]lords with fear and

τρόμου ἐν ἁπλότητι τῆς καρδίας ὑμῶν
trembling in singleness of the heart of you

ὡς τῷ Χριστῷ, **6** μὴ κατ' ὀφθαλμοδουλίαν
as – to Christ, not by way of eye-service

ὡς ἀνθρωπάρεσκοι, ἀλλ' ὡς δοῦλοι Χριστοῦ
as men-pleasers, but as slaves of Christ

ποιοῦντες τὸ θέλημα τοῦ θεοῦ ἐκ ψυχῆς,
doing the will – of God from [the] soul,

er blemish, but holy and blameless. 28 In this same way, husbands ought to love their wives as their own bodies. He who loves his wife loves himself. 29 After all, no one ever hated his own body, but he feeds and cares for it, just as Christ does the church— 30 for we are members of his body. 31 "For this reason a man will leave his father and mother and be united to his wife, and the two will become one flesh."[o] 32 This is a profound mystery—but I am talking about Christ and the church. 33 However, each one of you also must love his wife as he loves himself, and the wife must respect her husband.

Chapter 6

Children and Parents

CHILDREN, obey your parents in the Lord, for this is right. 2 "Honor your father and mother"—which is the first commandment with a promise— 3 "that it may go well with you and that you may enjoy long life on the earth."[p]

4 Fathers, do not exasperate your children; instead, bring them up in the training and instruction of the Lord.

Slaves and Masters

5 Slaves, obey your earthly masters with respect and fear, and with sincerity of heart, just as you would obey Christ. 6 Obey them not only to win their favor when their eye is on you, but like slaves of Christ, doing the will of God from

o31 Gen. 2:24
p3 Deut. 5:16

7With good will render service, as to the Lord, and not to men,
8knowing that whatever good thing each one does, this he will receive back from the Lord, whether slave or free.
9And, masters, do the same things to them, and give up threatening, knowing that both their Master and yours is in heaven, and there is no partiality with Him.

The Armor of God

10Finally, be strong in the Lord, and in the strength of His might.
11Put on the full armor of God, that you may be able to stand firm against the schemes of the devil.
12For our struggle is not against flesh and blood, but against the rulers, against the powers, against the world forces of this darkness, against the spiritual *forces* of wickedness in the heavenly *places*.
13Therefore, take up the full armor of God, that you may be able to resist in the evil day, and having done everything, to stand firm.
14Stand firm therefore, HAVING GIRDED YOUR LOINS WITH TRUTH, and HAVING PUT ON THE BREASTPLATE OF RIGHTEOUSNESS,
15and having shod YOUR FEET WITH THE PREPARATION OF THE GOSPEL OF PEACE;
16in addition to all, taking up the shield of faith with which you will be able to extinguish all the flaming missiles of the evil *one*.
17And take THE HELMET OF SALVATION, and the sword

7 μετ᾽ εὐνοίας δουλεύοντες ὡς τῷ κυρίῳ
with goodwill serving as slaves as to the Lord
καὶ οὐκ ἀνθρώποις, **8** εἰδότες ὅτι ἕκαστος
and not to men, knowing that each man
ἐάν τι ποιήσῃ ἀγαθόν, τοῦτο κομίσεται
whatever [2]he does [1]good thing, this he will get
παρὰ κυρίου, εἴτε δοῦλος εἴτε ἐλεύθερος.
from [the] Lord, whether a slave or a freeman.
9 Καὶ οἱ κύριοι, τὰ αὐτὰ ποιεῖτε πρὸς
And the lords, the same things do ye toward
αὐτούς, ἀνιέντες τὴν ἀπειλήν, εἰδότες ὅτι
them, forbearing *the* threatening, knowing that
καὶ αὐτῶν καὶ ὑμῶν ὁ κύριός ἐστιν
both of them and of you the Lord is
ἐν οὐρανοῖς, καὶ προσωπολημψία οὐκ
in heavens, and respect of persons not
ἔστιν παρ᾽ αὐτῷ.
is with him.

10 Τοῦ λοιποῦ, ἐνδυναμοῦσθε ἐν κυρίῳ
For the rest,† be ye empowered in [the] Lord
καὶ ἐν τῷ κράτει τῆς ἰσχύος αὐτοῦ.
and in the might of the strength of him.
11 ἐνδύσασθε τὴν πανοπλίαν τοῦ θεοῦ
Put ye on the whole armour – of God
πρὸς τὸ δύνασθαι ὑμᾶς στῆναι πρὸς
for the to be able you[b] to stand against
=so that ye are able . . .
τὰς μεθοδείας τοῦ διαβόλου· **12** ὅτι οὐκ
the craftinesses of the devil; because not
ἔστιν ἡμῖν ἡ πάλη πρὸς αἷμα καὶ σάρκα,
is to us the conflict[c] against blood and flesh,
=our conflict is not
ἀλλὰ πρὸς τὰς ἀρχάς, πρὸς τὰς ἐξουσίας,
but against the rulers, against the authorities,
πρὸς τοὺς κοσμοκράτορας τοῦ σκότους
against the world rulers – darkness
τούτου, πρὸς τὰ πνευματικὰ τῆς πονηρίας
of this, against the spiritual [hosts] – of evil
ἐν τοῖς ἐπουρανίοις. **13** διὰ τοῦτο
in the heavenlies. Therefore
ἀναλάβετε τὴν πανοπλίαν τοῦ θεοῦ, ἵνα
take ye up the whole armour – of God, in order that
δυνηθῆτε ἀντιστῆναι ἐν τῇ ἡμέρᾳ τῇ
ye may be able to resist in the day –
πονηρᾷ καὶ ἅπαντα κατεργασάμενοι στῆναι.
evil and all things having wrought to stand.
14 στῆτε οὖν περιζωσάμενοι τὴν ὀσφὺν
Stand ye therefore girding round the loin[s]
ὑμῶν ἐν ἀληθείᾳ, καὶ ἐνδυσάμενοι τὸν
of you with truth, and putting on the
θώρακα τῆς δικαιοσύνης, **15** καὶ ὑπο-
breastplate – of righteousness, and shoe-
δησάμενοι τοὺς πόδας ἐν ἑτοιμασίᾳ τοῦ
ing the feet with readiness of the
εὐαγγελίου τῆς εἰρήνης, **16** ἐν πᾶσιν
gospel – of peace, in all
ἀναλαβόντες τὸν θυρεὸν τῆς πίστεως, ἐν
taking up the shield – of faith, by
ᾧ δυνήσεσθε πάντα τὰ βέλη τοῦ πονηροῦ
which ye will be able [2]all [3]the [4]darts [6]of the [7]evil one
τὰ πεπυρωμένα σβέσαι· **17** καὶ τὴν
– [5]having been equipped with fire [1]to quench; and the
περικεφαλαίαν τοῦ σωτηρίου δέξασθε, καὶ
helmet – of salvation take ye, and

your heart. 7Serve wholeheartedly, as if you were serving the Lord, not men,
8because you know that the Lord will reward everyone for whatever good he does, whether he is slave or free.
9And masters, treat your slaves in the same way. Do not threaten them, since you know that he who is both their Master and yours is in heaven, and there is no favoritism with him.

The Armor of God

10Finally, be strong in the Lord and in his mighty power. 11Put on the full armor of God so that you can take your stand against the devil's schemes. 12For our struggle is not against flesh and blood, but against the rulers, against the authorities, against the powers of this dark world and against the spiritual forces of evil in the heavenly realms. 13Therefore put on the full armor of God, so that when the day of evil comes, you may be able to stand your ground, and after you have done everything, to stand. 14Stand firm then, with the belt of truth buckled around your waist, with the breastplate of righteousness in place, 15and with your feet fitted with the readiness that comes from the gospel of peace. 16In addition to all this, take up the shield of faith, with which you can extinguish all the flaming arrows of the evil one. 17Take the helmet of salvation and the sword

of the Spirit, which is the
word of God.
18With all prayer and petition pray at all times in the
Spirit, and with this in
view, be on the alert with
all perseverance and petition for all the saints,
19and *pray* on my behalf,
that utterance may be given
to me in the opening of my
mouth, to make known
with boldness the mystery
of the gospel,
20for which I am an am-
bassador in chains; that [g]in
proclaiming it I may speak
boldly, as I ought to speak.
21But that you also may
know about my circum-
stances, how I am doing,
Tychicus, the beloved
brother and faithful min-
ister in the Lord, will make
everything known to you.
22And I have sent him to
you for this very purpose,
so that you may know
about us, and that he may
comfort your hearts.
23Peace be to the breth-
ren, and love with faith,
from God the Father and
the Lord Jesus Christ.
24Grace be with all those
who love our Lord Jesus
Christ with *a love* incorruptible.

τὴν μάχαιραν τοῦ πνεύματος, ὅ ἐστιν
the sword of the Spirit, which* is

ῥῆμα θεοῦ, **18** διὰ πάσης προσευχῆς καὶ
[the] word of God, by means of all prayer and

δεήσεως, προσευχόμενοι ἐν παντὶ καιρῷ
petition, praying at every time

ἐν πνεύματι, καὶ εἰς αὐτὸ ἀγρυπνοῦντες
in spirit, and [2]to [3]it [1]watching

ἐν πάσῃ προσκαρτερήσει καὶ δεήσει περὶ
in all perseverance and petition concerning

πάντων τῶν ἁγίων, **19** καὶ ὑπὲρ ἐμοῦ,
all the saints, and on behalf of me,

ἵνα μοι δοθῇ λόγος ἐν ἀνοίξει τοῦ
in order that to me may be given speech in opening of the

στόματός μου, ἐν παρρησίᾳ γνωρίσαι τὸ
mouth of me, in boldness to make known the

μυστήριον τοῦ εὐαγγελίου, **20** ὑπὲρ οὗ
mystery of the gospel, on behalf of which

πρεσβεύω ἐν ἁλύσει, ἵνα ἐν αὐτῷ παρ-
I am an ambassador in a chain, in order that in it I may

ρησιάσωμαι ὡς δεῖ με λαλῆσαι.
speak boldly as it behoves me to speak.

21 Ἵνα δὲ εἰδῆτε καὶ ὑμεῖς τὰ κατ'
Now in order that [3]may know [2]also [1]ye the things about

ἐμέ, τί πράσσω, πάντα γνωρίσει ὑμῖν
me, what I am doing, all things [10]will make known [11]to you

Τύχικος ὁ ἀγαπητὸς ἀδελφὸς καὶ πιστὸς
[1]Tychicus [2]the [3]beloved [4]brother [5]and [6]faithful

διάκονος ἐν κυρίῳ, **22** ὃν ἔπεμψα πρὸς
[7]minister [8]in [9][the] Lord, whom I sent to

ὑμᾶς εἰς αὐτὸ τοῦτο, ἵνα γνῶτε τὰ
you for this very thing, in order that ye may know the things

περὶ ἡμῶν καὶ παρακαλέσῃ τὰς καρδίας
concerning us and may comfort the hearts

ὑμῶν.
of you.

23 Εἰρήνη τοῖς ἀδελφοῖς καὶ ἀγάπη
Peace to the brothers and love

μετὰ πίστεως ἀπὸ θεοῦ πατρὸς καὶ
with faith from God [the] Father and

κυρίου Ἰησοῦ Χριστοῦ. **24** ἡ χάρις μετὰ
[the] Lord Jesus Christ. – Grace [be] with

πάντων τῶν ἀγαπώντων τὸν κύριον ἡμῶν
all the [ones] loving the Lord of us

Ἰησοῦν Χριστὸν ἐν ἀφθαρσίᾳ.
Jesus Christ in incorruptibility.

of the Spirit, which is the
word of God. 18And pray in
the Spirit on all occasions
with all kinds of prayers
and requests. With this in
mind, be alert and always
keep on praying for all the
saints.
19Pray also for me, that
whenever I open my
mouth, words may be given
me so that I will fearlessly
make known the mystery
of the gospel, 20for which I
am an ambassador in
chains. Pray that I may declare it fearlessly, as I
should.

Final Greetings

21Tychicus, the dear
brother and faithful servant
in the Lord, will tell you everything, so that you also
may know how I am and
what I am doing. 22I am
sending him to you for this
very purpose, that you may
know how we are, and that
he may encourage you.
23Peace to the brothers,
and love with faith from
God the Father and the
Lord Jesus Christ. 24Grace
to all who love our Lord
Jesus Christ with an undy-
ing love.

Philippians

Chapter 1

Thanksgiving

PAUL and Timothy,
bond-servants of
Christ Jesus, to all the
saints in Christ Jesus who
are in Philippi, including

ΠΡΟΣ ΦΙΛΙΠΠΗΣΙΟΥΣ
To Philippians

1 Παῦλος καὶ Τιμόθεος δοῦλοι Χριστοῦ
Paul and Timothy slaves of Christ

Ἰησοῦ πᾶσιν τοῖς ἁγίοις ἐν Χριστῷ
Jesus to all the saints in Christ

Ἰησοῦ τοῖς οὖσιν ἐν Φιλίπποις σὺν
Jesus – being in Philippi with

Philippians

Chapter 1

PAUL and Timothy, ser-
vants of Christ Jesus,
To all the saints in Christ
Jesus at Philippi, together

[g]Some ancient mss. read *I may speak it boldly*

* Neuter, agreeing with πνεῦμα, not feminine to agree with μάχαιρα.

the overseers and deacons:
2 Grace to you and peace
from God our Father and
the Lord Jesus Christ.
3 I thank my God in all
my remembrance of you,
4 always offering prayer
with joy in my every prayer
for you all,
5 in view of your participation in the gospel from
the first day until now.
6 *For I am* confident of
this very thing, that He
who began a good work in
you will perfect it until the
day of Christ Jesus.
7 For it is only right for
me to feel this way about
you all, because I have you
in my heart, since both in
my imprisonment and in
the defense and confir-
mation of the gospel, you
all are partakers of grace
with me.
8 For God is my witness,
how I long for you all with
the affection of Christ
Jesus.
9 And this I pray, that
your love may abound still
more and more in real
knowledge and all discern-
ment,
10 so that you may ap-
prove the things that are
excellent, in order to be
sincere and blameless until
the day of Christ;
11 having been filled with
the fruit of righteousness
which *comes* through Jesus
Christ, to the glory and
praise of God.

The Gospel Is Preached

12 Now I want you to
know, brethren, that my
circumstances have turned
out for the greater progress
of the gospel,
13 so that my imprison-

ἐπισκόποις καὶ διακόνοις· 2 χάρις ὑμῖν
bishops and ministers: Grace to you
καὶ εἰρήνη ἀπὸ θεοῦ πατρὸς ἡμῶν καὶ
and peace from God Father of us and
κυρίου Ἰησοῦ Χριστοῦ.
[the] Lord Jesus Christ.
3 Εὐχαριστῶ τῷ θεῷ μου ἐπὶ πάσῃ
I thank the God of me at all
τῇ μνείᾳ ὑμῶν, 4 πάντοτε ἐν πάσῃ
the remembrance of you, always in every
δεήσει μου ὑπὲρ πάντων ὑμῶν μετὰ
petition of me on behalf of all you with
χαρᾶς τὴν δέησιν ποιούμενος, 5 ἐπὶ τῇ
joy the petition making, over the
κοινωνίᾳ ὑμῶν εἰς τὸ εὐαγγέλιον ἀπὸ
fellowship of you in the gospel from
τῆς πρώτης ἡμέρας ἄχρι τοῦ νῦν,
the first day until *the* now,
6 πεποιθὼς αὐτὸ τοῦτο, ὅτι ὁ ἐναρξάμενος
being confident [of] this very thing, that the [one] having begun
ἐν ὑμῖν ἔργον ἀγαθὸν ἐπιτελέσει ἄχρι
in you work a good will complete [it] until
ἡμέρας Χριστοῦ Ἰησοῦ· 7 καθώς ἐστιν
[the] day of Christ Jesus; as it is
δίκαιον ἐμοὶ τοῦτο φρονεῖν ὑπὲρ πάντων
right for me this to think *on behalf* of all
ὑμῶν, διὰ τὸ ἔχειν με ἐν τῇ καρδίᾳ
you, because of the to have me[b] in the heart
=because I have you in the(my) heart,
ὑμᾶς, ἔν τε τοῖς δεσμοῖς μου καὶ ἐν
you, both in the bonds of me and in
τῇ ἀπολογίᾳ καὶ βεβαιώσει τοῦ εὐαγγελίου
the defence and confirmation of the gospel
συγκοινωνούς μου τῆς χάριτος πάντας
[4]partakers [7]of me [5]of the [6]grace [2]all
ὑμᾶς ὄντας. 8 μάρτυς γάρ μου ὁ θεός,
[1]you [3]being. [4]witness [1]For [5]of me – [2]God [3][is],
ὡς ἐπιποθῶ πάντας ὑμᾶς ἐν σπλάγχνοις
how I long after all you in [the] bowels
Χριστοῦ Ἰησοῦ. 9 Καὶ τοῦτο προσεύχομαι,
of Christ Jesus. And this I pray,
ἵνα ἡ ἀγάπη ὑμῶν ἔτι μᾶλλον καὶ
in order that the love of you yet more and
μᾶλλον περισσεύῃ ἐν ἐπιγνώσει καὶ πάσῃ
more may abound in full knowledge and all
αἰσθήσει, 10 εἰς τὸ δοκιμάζειν ὑμᾶς τὰ
perception, for the to prove you[b] the things
=that ye may prove
διαφέροντα, ἵνα ἦτε εἰλικρινεῖς καὶ
differing, in order that ye may be sincere and
ἀπρόσκοποι εἰς ἡμέραν Χριστοῦ, 11 πεπληρω-
unoffending in [the] day of Christ, having been
μένοι καρπὸν δικαιοσύνης τὸν διὰ Ἰησοῦ
filled [with] [the] fruit of righteousness – through Jesus
Χριστοῦ, εἰς δόξαν καὶ ἔπαινον θεοῦ.
Christ, to [the] glory and praise of God.
12 Γινώσκειν δὲ ὑμᾶς βούλομαι, ἀδελφοί,
Now [3]to know [2]you [1]I wish, brothers,
ὅτι τὰ κατ' ἐμὲ μᾶλλον εἰς προκοπὴν
that the things about me* [2]rather [3]to [4][the] advance
= my affairs
τοῦ εὐαγγελίου ἐλήλυθεν, 13 ὥστε τοὺς
[5]of the [6]gospel [1]has(ve) come, so as the

* *Cf.* ver. 27; ch. 2. 19, 20, 23; Eph. 6. 21, 22; Col. 4. 7, 8.

with the overseers[a] and
deacons:
2 Grace and peace to you
from God our Father and
the Lord Jesus Christ.

Thanksgiving and Prayer

3 I thank my God every
time I remember you. 4 In
all my prayers for all of
you, I always pray with joy
5 because of your partnership in the gospel from the
first day until now, 6 being
confident of this, that he
who began a good work in
you will carry it on to completion until the day of
Christ Jesus.
7 It is right for me to feel
this way about all of you,
since I have you in my
heart; for whether I am in
chains or defending and
confirming the gospel, all
of you share in God's grace
with me. 8 God can testify
how I long for all of you
with the affection of Christ
Jesus.
9 And this is my prayer:
that your love may abound
more and more in knowl-
edge and depth of insight,
10 so that you may be able to
discern what is best and
may be pure and blameless
until the day of Christ,
11 filled with the fruit of
righteousness that comes
through Jesus Christ—to
the glory and praise of God.

Paul's Chains Advance the Gospel

12 Now I want you to
know, brothers, that what
has happened to me has really served to advance the
gospel. 13 As a result, it has

[a] 1 Traditionally *bishops*

ment in *the cause of* Christ has become well known throughout the whole [a]praetorian guard and to everyone else,

14 and that most of the brethren, trusting in the Lord because of my imprisonment, have far more courage to speak the word of God without fear.

15 Some, to be sure, are preaching Christ even from envy and strife, but some also from good will;

16 [b]the latter *do it* out of love, knowing that I am appointed for the defense of the gospel;

17 the former proclaim Christ out of selfish ambition, rather than from pure motives, thinking to cause me distress in my imprisonment.

18 What then? Only that in every way, whether in pretense or in truth, Christ is proclaimed; and in this I rejoice, yes, and I will rejoice.

19 For I know that this shall turn out for my deliverance through your prayers and the provision of the Spirit of Jesus Christ,

20 according to my earnest expectation and hope, that I shall not be put to shame in anything, but *that* with all boldness, Christ shall even now, as always, be exalted in my body, whether by life or by death.

To Live Is Christ

21 For to me, to live is Christ, and to die is gain.

22 But if *I am* to live *on* in the flesh, this *will mean* fruitful labor for me; and I do not know which to choose.

23 But I am hard-pressed from both *directions,* having the desire to depart and be with Christ, for *that* is very much better;

24 yet to remain on in the flesh is more necessary for your sake.

25 And convinced of this, I

[a] Or, *governor's palace*

[b] Some later mss. reverse the order of vv. 16 and 17

δεσμούς μου φανεροὺς ἐν Χριστῷ γενέσθαι
bonds of me [2]manifest [3]in [4]Christ [1]*to* become

ἐν ὅλῳ τῷ πραιτωρίῳ καὶ τοῖς λοιποῖς
in all the prætorium and to [2]the [3]rest

πᾶσιν, 14 καὶ τοὺς πλείονας τῶν ἀδελφῶν
[1]all, and the majority of the brothers

ἐν κυρίῳ πεποιθότας τοῖς δεσμοῖς μου
in [the] Lord being confident in the bonds of me

περισσοτέρως τολμᾶν ἀφόβως τὸν λόγον
[2]more exceedingly [1]*to* dare [3]fearlessly [5]the [6]word

τοῦ θεοῦ λαλεῖν. 15 τινὲς μὲν καὶ διὰ
- [7]of God [4]to speak. Some indeed even because of

φθόνον καὶ ἔριν, τινὲς δὲ καὶ δι' εὐδοκίαν
envy and strife, but some also because of good-will

τὸν Χριστὸν κηρύσσουσιν· 16 οἱ μὲν ἐξ
– Christ proclaim; these† from

ἀγάπης, εἰδότες ὅτι εἰς ἀπολογίαν τοῦ
love, knowing that for defence of the

εὐαγγελίου κεῖμαι, 17 οἱ δὲ ἐξ ἐριθείας
gospel I am set, those† from rivalry

τὸν Χριστὸν καταγγέλλουσιν, οὐχ ἁγνῶς,
– [2]Christ [1]announce, not purely,

οἰόμενοι θλῖψιν ἐγείρειν τοῖς δεσμοῖς μου.
thinking [2]affliction [1]to raise to the bonds of me.

18 Τί γάρ; πλὴν ὅτι παντὶ τρόπῳ,
What then? nevertheless that in every way,

εἴτε προφάσει εἴτε ἀληθείᾳ, Χριστὸς
whether in pretence or in truth, Christ

καταγγέλλεται, καὶ ἐν τούτῳ χαίρω· ἀλλὰ
is announced, and in this I rejoice; yet

καὶ χαρήσομαι· 19 οἶδα γὰρ ὅτι τοῦτό
also I will rejoice; for I know that this

μοι ἀποβήσεται εἰς σωτηρίαν διὰ τῆς
to me will result in salvation through the

ὑμῶν δεήσεως καὶ ἐπιχορηγίας τοῦ
[2]of you [1]petition and supply of the

πνεύματος Ἰησοῦ Χριστοῦ, 20 κατὰ τὴν
spirit of Jesus Christ, according to the

ἀποκαραδοκίαν καὶ ἐλπίδα μου ὅτι ἐν
eager expectation and hope of me that in

οὐδενὶ αἰσχυνθήσομαι, ἀλλ' ἐν πάσῃ παρ-
nothing I shall be shamed, but with all bold-

ρησίᾳ ὡς πάντοτε καὶ νῦν μεγαλυνθήσεται
ness as always also now shall be magnified

Χριστὸς ἐν τῷ σώματί μου, εἴτε διὰ
Christ in the body of me, whether through

ζωῆς εἴτε διὰ θανάτου. 21 ἐμοὶ γὰρ
life or through death. For to me

τὸ ζῆν Χριστὸς καὶ τὸ ἀποθανεῖν κέρδος.
– to live [is] Christ and – to die [is] gain.

22 εἰ δὲ τὸ ζῆν ἐν σαρκί, τοῦτό μοι
But if – to live in [the] flesh, this to me

καρπὸς ἔργου, καὶ τί αἱρήσομαι οὐ
[is] fruit of [?my] work, and what I shall choose not

γνωρίζω. 23 συνέχομαι δὲ ἐκ τῶν δύο,
I perceive. But I am constrained by the two,

τὴν ἐπιθυμίαν ἔχων εἰς τὸ ἀναλῦσαι καὶ
[2]the [3]desire [1]having *for the* to depart and

σὺν Χριστῷ εἶναι, πολλῷ γὰρ μᾶλλον
[2]with [3]Christ [1]to be, for by much [this is] rather

κρεῖσσον· 24 τὸ δὲ ἐπιμένειν τῇ σαρκὶ
better; – but to remain in the flesh [is]

ἀναγκαιότερον δι' ὑμᾶς. 25 καὶ τοῦτο
more necessary on account of you. And this

become clear throughout the whole palace guard[b] and to everyone else that I am in chains for Christ. 14 Because of my chains, most of the brothers in the Lord have been encouraged to speak the word of God more courageously and fearlessly.

15 It is true that some preach Christ out of envy and rivalry, but others out of goodwill. 16 The latter do so in love, knowing that I am put here for the defense of the gospel. 17 The former preach Christ out of selfish ambition, not sincerely, supposing that they can stir up trouble for me while I am in chains.[c] 18 But what does it matter? The important thing is that in every way, whether from false motives or true, Christ is preached. And because of this I rejoice.

Yes, and I will continue to rejoice, 19 for I know that through your prayers and the help given by the Spirit of Jesus Christ, what has happened to me will turn out for my deliverance.[d] 20 I eagerly expect and hope that I will in no way be ashamed, but will have sufficient courage so that now as always Christ will be exalted in my body, whether by life or by death. 21 For to me, to live is Christ and to die is gain. 22 If I am to go on living in the body, this will mean fruitful labor for me. Yet what shall I choose? I do not know! 23 I am torn between the two: I desire to depart and be with Christ, which is better by far; 24 but it is more necessary for you that I remain in the body. 25 Convinced of this, I know

[b]13 Or *whole palace*

[c]16,17 Some late manuscripts have verses 16 and 17 in reverse order.

[d]19 Or *salvation*

know that I shall remain and continue with you all for your progress and joy in the faith,
26so that your proud confidence in me may abound in Christ Jesus through my coming to you again.
27Only conduct yourselves in a manner worthy of the gospel of Christ; so that whether I come and see you or remain absent, I may hear of you that you are standing firm in one spirit, with one mind striving together for the faith of the gospel;
28in no way alarmed by *your* opponents—which is a sign of destruction for them, but of salvation for you, and that *too*, from God.
29For to you it has been granted for Christ's sake, not only to believe in Him, but also to suffer for His sake,
30experiencing the same conflict which you saw in me, and now hear *to be* in me.

πεποιθὼς οἶδα, ὅτι μενῶ καὶ παραμενῶ
being confident I know, that I shall remain and continue

πᾶσιν ὑμῖν εἰς τὴν ὑμῶν προκοπὴν καὶ
with all you for the [6]of you [1]advance [2]and

χαρὰν τῆς πίστεως, 26 ἵνα τὸ καύχημα
[3]joy [4]of the [5]faith, in order that the boast

ὑμῶν περισσεύῃ ἐν Χριστῷ Ἰησοῦ ἐν
of you may abound in Christ Jesus in

ἐμοὶ διὰ τῆς ἐμῆς παρουσίας πάλιν
me through – my presence again

πρὸς ὑμᾶς.
with you.

27 Μόνον ἀξίως τοῦ εὐαγγελίου τοῦ
Only [2]worthily [3]of the [4]gospel –

Χριστοῦ πολιτεύεσθε, ἵνα εἴτε ἐλθὼν καὶ
[5]of Christ [1]conduct yourselves, in order that whether coming and

ἰδὼν ὑμᾶς εἴτε ἀπὼν ἀκούω τὰ περὶ
seeing you or being absent I hear the things concerning

ὑμῶν, ὅτι στήκετε ἐν ἑνὶ πνεύματι,
you, that ye stand in one spirit,

μιᾷ ψυχῇ συναθλοῦντες τῇ πίστει τοῦ
with one soul striving together in the faith of the

εὐαγγελίου, 28 καὶ μὴ πτυρόμενοι ἐν
gospel, and not being terrified in

μηδενὶ ὑπὸ τῶν ἀντικειμένων, ἥτις ἐστὶν
no(any) thing by the [ones] opposing, which is

αὐτοῖς ἔνδειξις ἀπωλείας, ὑμῶν δὲ
to them a proof of destruction, but of you

σωτηρίας, καὶ τοῦτο ἀπὸ θεοῦ· 29 ὅτι
of salvation, and this from God; because

ὑμῖν ἐχαρίσθη τὸ ὑπὲρ Χριστοῦ, οὐ
to you it was given – on behalf of Christ, not

μόνον τὸ εἰς αὐτὸν πιστεύειν ἀλλὰ καὶ
only – in him to believe but also

τὸ ὑπὲρ αὐτοῦ πάσχειν, 30 τὸν αὐτὸν
– on behalf of him to suffer, the same

ἀγῶνα ἔχοντες οἷον εἴδετε ἐν ἐμοὶ
struggle having which ye saw in me

καὶ νῦν ἀκούετε ἐν ἐμοί. 2 Εἴ τις
and now hear in me. [2]If [there is] [3]any

οὖν παράκλησις ἐν Χριστῷ, εἴ τι
[1]therefore comfort in Christ, if any

παραμύθιον ἀγάπης, εἴ τις κοινωνία
consolation of love, if any fellowship

πνεύματος, εἴ τις σπλάγχνα καὶ οἰκτιρμοί,
of spirit, if any compassions and pities,

2 πληρώσατέ μου τὴν χαρὰν ἵνα τὸ
fulfil ye of me the joy *in order* that the

αὐτὸ φρονῆτε, τὴν αὐτὴν ἀγάπην ἔχοντες,
same thing ye think, the same love having,

σύμψυχοι, τὸ ἓν φρονοῦντες, 3 μηδὲν κατ'
one in soul, the one thing thinking, [doing] nothing by way of

ἐριθείαν μηδὲ κατὰ κενοδοξίαν, ἀλλὰ τῇ
rivalry nor by way of vainglory, but –

ταπεινοφροσύνῃ ἀλλήλους ἡγούμενοι ὑπερ-
in humility [2]one another [1]deeming sur-

έχοντας ἑαυτῶν, 4 μὴ τὰ ἑαυτῶν ἕκαστοι
passing themselves, not [3]the things [4]of themselves [1]each *ones*

σκοποῦντες, ἀλλὰ καὶ τὰ ἑτέρων ἕκαστοι.
[2]looking at, but [2]also [3]the things [4]of others [1]each *ones*.

that I will remain, and I will continue with all of you for your progress and joy in the faith, 26so that through my being with you again your joy in Christ Jesus will overflow on account of me.
27Whatever happens, conduct yourselves in a manner worthy of the gospel of Christ. Then, whether I come and see you or only hear about you in my absence, I will know that you stand firm in one spirit, contending as one man for the faith of the gospel 28without being frightened in any way by those who oppose you. This is a sign to them that they will be destroyed, but that you will be saved—and that by God. 29For it has been granted to you on behalf of Christ not only to believe on him, but also to suffer for him, 30since you are going through the same struggle you saw I had, and now hear that I still have.

Chapter 2

Be Like Christ

IF therefore there is any encouragement in Christ, if there is any consolation of love, if there is any fellowship of the Spirit, if any affection and compassion,
2make my joy complete by being of the same mind, maintaining the same love, united in spirit, intent on one purpose.
3Do nothing from selfishness or empty conceit, but with humility of mind let each of you regard one another as more important than himself;
4do not *merely* look out for your own personal interests, but also for the interests of others.

Chapter 2

Imitating Christ's Humility

IF you have any encouragement from being united with Christ, if any comfort from his love, if any fellowship with the Spirit, if any tenderness and compassion, 2then make my joy complete by being like-minded, having the same love, being one in spirit and purpose. 3Do nothing out of selfish ambition or vain conceit, but in humility consider others better than yourselves. 4Each of you should look not only to your own interests, but also to the interests of others.

5Have this attitude in
yourselves which was also
in Christ Jesus,
6who, although He ex-
isted in the form of God,
did not regard equality with
God a thing to be grasped,
7but [c]emptied Himself,
taking the form of a bond-
servant, *and* being made in
the likeness of men.
8And being found in ap-
pearance as a man, He
humbled Himself by be-
coming obedient to the
point of death, even death
on a cross.
9Therefore also God
highly exalted Him, and bestowed on Him the name
which is above every
name,
10that at the name of
Jesus EVERY KNEE SHOULD
BOW, of those who are in
heaven, and on earth, and
under the earth,
11and that every tongue
should confess that Jesus
Christ is Lord, to the glory
of God the Father.
12So then, my beloved,
just as you have always
obeyed, not as in my presence only, but now much
more in my absence, work
out your salvation with fear
and trembling;
13for it is God who is at
work in you, both to will
and to work for *His* good
pleasure.
14Do all things without
grumbling or disputing;
15that you may prove
yourselves to be blameless
and innocent, children of
God above reproach in the
midst of a crooked and perverse generation, among
whom you appear as lights
in the world,
16holding fast the word of
life, so that in the day of
Christ I may have cause to
glory because I did not run
in vain nor toil in vain.
17But even if I am being
poured out as a drink offering upon the sacrifice and
service of your faith, I re-

[c] I.e., laid aside His privileges

5 τοῦτο φρονεῖτε ἐν ὑμῖν ὃ καὶ ἐν
This think ye among you which also [was] in
Χριστῷ Ἰησοῦ, **6** ὃς ἐν μορφῇ θεοῦ
Christ Jesus, who in [the] form of God
ὑπάρχων οὐχ ἁρπαγμὸν ἡγήσατο τὸ εἶναι
subsisting [2]not [3]robbery [1]deemed [it] *the* to be
ἴσα θεῷ, **7** ἀλλὰ ἑαυτὸν ἐκένωσεν μορφὴν
equal *things* with God, but himself emptied [2][the] form
δούλου λαβών, ἐν ὁμοιώματι ἀνθρώπων
[3]of a slave [1]taking, [2]in [3]likeness [4]of men
γενόμενος· καὶ σχήματι εὑρεθεὶς ὡς
[1]becoming; and [2]in fashion [1]being found as
ἄνθρωπος **8** ἐταπείνωσεν ἑαυτὸν γενόμενος
a man he humbled himself becoming
ὑπήκοος μέχρι θανάτου, θανάτου δὲ σταυροῦ.
obedient until death, and death of a cross.
9 διὸ καὶ ὁ θεὸς αὐτὸν ὑπερύψωσεν
Wherefore also – God [2]him [1]highly exalted
καὶ ἐχαρίσατο αὐτῷ τὸ ὄνομα τὸ ὑπὲρ
and gave to him the name – above
πᾶν ὄνομα, **10** ἵνα ἐν τῷ ὀνόματι Ἰησοῦ
every name, in order that in the name of Jesus
πᾶν γόνυ κάμψῃ ἐπουρανίων καὶ ἐπιγείων
every knee should bend of heavenly [beings] and earthly [beings]
καὶ καταχθονίων, **11** καὶ πᾶσα γλῶσσα
and [beings] under the earth, and every tongue
ἐξομολογήσηται ὅτι κύριος Ἰησοῦς
should acknowledge that [2]Lord [1]Jesus
Χριστὸς εἰς δόξαν θεοῦ πατρός.
[3]Christ [is] to [the] glory of God [the] Father.
12 Ὥστε, ἀγαπητοί μου, καθὼς πάντοτε
So as, beloved of me, as always
ὑπηκούσατε, μὴ ὡς ἐν τῇ παρουσίᾳ
ye obeyed, not as in the presence
μου μόνον ἀλλὰ νῦν πολλῷ μᾶλλον ἐν
of me only but now by more rather in
τῇ ἀπουσίᾳ μου, μετὰ φόβου καὶ τρόμου
the absence of me, with fear and trembling
τὴν ἑαυτῶν σωτηρίαν κατεργάζεσθε· **13** θεὸς
[1]the [2]of yourselves [3]salvation work out; [2]God
γάρ ἐστιν ὁ ἐνεργῶν ἐν ὑμῖν καὶ τὸ
[1]for is the [one] operating in you both *the*
θέλειν καὶ τὸ ἐνεργεῖν ὑπὲρ τῆς εὐδοκίας.
to will and *the* to operate on behalf of the(his) goodwill.
14 πάντα ποιεῖτε χωρὶς γογγυσμῶν καὶ
All things do ye without murmurings and
διαλογισμῶν, **15** ἵνα γένησθε ἄμεμπτοι καὶ
disputings, in order that ye may be blameless and
ἀκέραιοι, τέκνα θεοῦ ἄμωμα μέσον
harmless, children of God faultless in the midst of
γενεᾶς σκολιᾶς καὶ διεστραμμένης, ἐν
a generation crooked and *having been* perverted, among
οἷς φαίνεσθε ὡς φωστῆρες ἐν κόσμῳ,
whom ye shine as luminaries in [the] world,
16 λόγον ζωῆς ἐπέχοντες, εἰς καύχημα
a word of life holding up, for a boast
ἐμοὶ εἰς ἡμέραν Χριστοῦ, ὅτι οὐκ εἰς
to me[c] in [the] day of Christ, that not in
κενὸν ἔδραμον οὐδὲ εἰς κενὸν ἐκοπίασα.
vain I ran nor in vain laboured.
17 Ἀλλὰ εἰ καὶ σπένδομαι ἐπὶ τῇ θυσίᾳ
But if indeed I am poured out on the sacrifice
καὶ λειτουργίᾳ τῆς πίστεως ὑμῶν, χαίρω
and service of the faith of you, I rejoice

5Your attitude should be
the same as that of Christ
Jesus:
6Who, being in very
nature[e] God,
did not consider
equality with God
something to be
grasped,
7but made himself
nothing,
taking the very nature[f]
of a servant,
being made in human
likeness.
8And being found in
appearance as a
man,
he humbled himself
and became obedient
to death—
even death on a
cross!
9Therefore God exalted
him to the highest
place
and gave him the name
that is above every
name,
10that at the name of Jesus
every knee should
bow,
in heaven and on earth
and under the earth,
11and every tongue
confess that Jesus
Christ is Lord,
to the glory of God the
Father.

Shining as Stars

12Therefore, my dear
friends, as you have always
obeyed—not only in my
presence, but now much
more in my absence—con-
tinue to work out your salvation with fear and trembling, 13for it is God who
works in you to will and to
act according to his good
purpose.
14Do everything without
complaining or arguing,
15so that you may become
blameless and pure, chil-
dren of God without fault in
a crooked and depraved
generation, in which you
shine like stars in the universe 16as you hold out[g]
the word of life—in order
that I may boast on the day
of Christ that I did not run
or labor for nothing. 17But
even if I am being poured
out like a drink offering on
the sacrifice and service
coming from your faith, I

[e]6 Or *in the form of*
[f]7 Or *the form*
[g]16 Or *hold on to*

joice and share my joy with you all.

18And you too, *I urge you,* rejoice in the same way and share your joy with me.

Timothy and Epaphroditus

19But I hope in the Lord Jesus to send Timothy to you shortly, so that I also may be encouraged when I learn of your condition.

20For I have no one *else* of kindred spirit who will genuinely be concerned for your welfare.

21For they all seek after their own interests, not those of Christ Jesus.

22But you know of his proven worth that he served with me in the furtherance of the gospel like a child *serving* his father.

23Therefore I hope to send him immediately, as soon as I see how things *go* with me;

24and I trust in the Lord that I myself also shall be coming shortly.

25But I thought it necessary to send to you Epaphroditus, my brother and fellow worker and fellow soldier, who is also your messenger and minister to my need;

26because he was longing [d]for you all and was distressed because you had heard that he was sick.

27For indeed he was sick to the point of death, but God had mercy on him, and not on him only but also on me, lest I should have sorrow upon sorrow.

28Therefore I have sent him all the more eagerly in order that when you see him again you may rejoice and I may be less concerned *about you.*

29Therefore receive him in the Lord with all joy, and hold men like him in high regard;

30because he came close to death for the work of Christ, risking his life to

καὶ συγχαίρω πᾶσιν ὑμῖν· **18** τὸ δὲ αὐτὸ
and rejoice with 2all 1you; and the same

καὶ ὑμεῖς χαίρετε καὶ συγχαίρετέ μοι.
also ye rejoice and rejoice with me.

19 Ἐλπίζω δὲ ἐν κυρίῳ Ἰησοῦ Τιμόθεον
But I hope in [the] Lord Jesus 3Timothy

ταχέως πέμψαι ὑμῖν, ἵνα κἀγὼ εὐψυχῶ
4shortly 1to send 2to you, in order that I also may be of good cheer

γνοὺς τὰ περὶ ὑμῶν. **20** οὐδένα γὰρ
knowing the things concerning you. For no one

ἔχω ἰσόψυχον, ὅστις γνησίως τὰ περὶ
I have likeminded, who genuinely 2the things 3concerning

ὑμῶν μεριμνήσει· **21** οἱ πάντες γὰρ τὰ
4you 1will care for; *the* for all 3the things

ἑαυτῶν ζητοῦσιν, οὐ τὰ Χριστοῦ Ἰησοῦ.
2of themselves 1seek, not the things of Christ Jesus.

22 τὴν δὲ δοκιμὴν αὐτοῦ γινώσκετε, ὅτι
But the character of him ye know, that

ὡς πατρὶ τέκνον σὺν ἐμοὶ ἐδούλευσεν
as 3a father 1a child 2[serves] 5with 6me 4he served

εἰς τὸ εὐαγγέλιον. **23** τοῦτον μὲν οὖν
in the gospel. This one – therefore

ἐλπίζω πέμψαι ὡς ἂν ἀφίδω τὰ περὶ
I hope to send 2whenever 3I see 4the things 5concerning

ἐμὲ ἐξαυτῆς· **24** πέποιθα δὲ ἐν κυρίῳ
6me 1immediately; but I trust in [the] Lord

ὅτι καὶ αὐτὸς ταχέως ἐλεύσομαι. **25** Ἀναγ-
that 2also 3[my]self 4shortly 1I will come. 2neces-

καῖον δὲ ἡγησάμην Ἐπαφρόδιτον τὸν
sary But 1I deemed [it] 6Epaphroditus 7the

ἀδελφὸν καὶ συνεργὸν καὶ συστρατιώτην
8brother 9and 10fellow-worker 11and 12fellow-soldier

μου, ὑμῶν δὲ ἀπόστολον καὶ λειτουργὸν
13of me, 14and 16of you 15apostle 17and 18minister

τῆς χρείας μου, πέμψαι πρὸς ὑμᾶς,
19of the 20need 21of me, 3to send 4to 5you,

26 ἐπειδὴ ἐπιποθῶν ἦν πάντας ὑμᾶς, καὶ
since 2longing after 1he was 4all 3you, and

ἀδημονῶν, διότι ἠκούσατε ὅτι ἠσθένησεν.
[was] being troubled, because ye heard that he ailed.

27 καὶ γὰρ ἠσθένησεν παραπλήσιον θανάτῳ·
For indeed he ailed coming near to death;

ἀλλὰ ὁ θεὸς ἠλέησεν αὐτόν, οὐκ αὐτὸν
but – God had mercy on him, 2not 3him

δὲ μόνον ἀλλὰ καὶ ἐμέ, ἵνα μὴ λύπην
1and only but also me, lest grief

ἐπὶ λύπην σχῶ. **28** σπουδαιοτέρως οὖν
on grief I should have. More eagerly therefore

ἔπεμψα αὐτόν, ἵνα ἰδόντες αὐτὸν πάλιν
I sent him, in order that seeing him again

χαρῆτε κἀγὼ ἀλυπότερος ὦ. **29** προσδέχεσθε
ye may rejoice and 1I 3less grieved 2may be. Receive ye

οὖν αὐτὸν ἐν κυρίῳ μετὰ πάσης χαρᾶς,
therefore him in [the] Lord with all joy,

καὶ τοὺς τοιούτους ἐντίμους ἔχετε, **30** ὅτι
and – 2such *ones* 3honoured 1hold ye, because

διὰ τὸ ἔργον Χριστοῦ μέχρι θανάτου
on account of the work of Christ 2as far as 3death

ἤγγισεν παραβολευσάμενος τῇ ψυχῇ, ἵνα
1he drew near exposing the(his) life, in order that

am glad and rejoice with all of you. 18So you too should be glad and rejoice with me.

Timothy and Epaphroditus

19I hope in the Lord Jesus to send Timothy to you soon, that I also may be cheered when I receive news about you. 20I have no one else like him, who takes a genuine interest in your welfare. 21For everyone looks out for his own interests, not those of Jesus Christ. 22But you know that Timothy has proved himself, because as a son with his father he has served with me in the work of the gospel. 23I hope, therefore, to send him as soon as I see how things go with me. 24And I am confident in the Lord that I myself will come soon.

25But I think it is necessary to send back to you Epaphroditus, my brother, fellow worker and fellow soldier, who is also your messenger, whom you sent to take care of my needs. 26For he longs for all of you and is distressed because you heard he was ill. 27Indeed he was ill, and almost died. But God had mercy on him, and not on him only but also on me, to spare me sorrow upon sorrow. 28Therefore I am all the more eager to send him, so that when you see him again you may be glad and I may have less anxiety. 29Welcome him in the Lord with great joy, and honor men like him, 30because he almost died for the work of

[d] Some ancient mss. read *to see you all*

complete what was deficient in your service to me.

Chapter 3

The Goal of Life

FINALLY, my brethren, rejoice in the Lord. To write the same things *again* is no trouble to me, and it is a safeguard for you.

2Beware of the dogs, beware of the evil workers, beware of the false circumcision;

3for we are the *true* circumcision, who worship in the Spirit of God and glory in Christ Jesus and put no confidence in the flesh,

4although I myself might have confidence even in the flesh. If anyone else has a mind to put confidence in the flesh, I far more:

5circumcised the eighth day, of the nation of Israel, of the tribe of Benjamin, a Hebrew of Hebrews; as to the Law, a Pharisee;

6as to zeal, a persecutor of the church; as to the righteousness which is in the Law, found blameless.

7But whatever things were gain to me, those things I have counted as loss for the sake of Christ.

8More than that, I count all things to be loss in view of the surpassing value of knowing Christ Jesus my Lord, for whom I have suffered the loss of all things, and count them but rubbish in order that I may gain Christ,

9and may be found in Him, not having a righteousness of my own derived from *the* Law, but that which is through faith in Christ, the righteousness

ἀναπληρώσῃ τὸ ὑμῶν ὑστέρημα τῆς πρός
he might fill up [1]the [3]of you [2]lack – [5]toward
με λειτουργίας.
[6]me [4]of service.

3 Τὸ λοιπόν, ἀδελφοί μου, χαίρετε ἐν
For the rest, brothers of me, rejoice ye in
κυρίῳ. τὰ αὐτὰ γράφειν ὑμῖν ἐμοὶ μὲν
[the] Lord. [3]The [4]same things [1]to write to you for me indeed
οὐκ ὀκνηρόν, ὑμῖν δὲ ἀσφαλές.
[is] not irksome, but for you safe.
2 Βλέπετε τοὺς κύνας, βλέπετε τοὺς
Look [to] the dogs, look [to] the
κακοὺς ἐργάτας, βλέπετε τὴν κατατομήν.
evil workmen, look [to] the concision.•
3 ἡμεῖς γάρ ἐσμεν ἡ περιτομή, οἱ
For we are the circumcision, the [ones]
πνεύματι θεοῦ λατρεύοντες καὶ καυχώμενοι
[2]by [the] Spirit [3]of God [1]worshipping and boasting
ἐν Χριστῷ Ἰησοῦ καὶ οὐκ ἐν σαρκὶ
in Christ Jesus and [2]not [3]in [the] [4]flesh
πεποιθότες, **4** καίπερ ἐγὼ ἔχων πεποίθησιν
[1]trusting, even though I having trust
καὶ ἐν σαρκί. Εἴ τις δοκεῖ ἄλλος
also in [the] flesh. If any [2]thinks [1]other man
πεποιθέναι ἐν σαρκί, ἐγὼ μᾶλλον·
to trust in [the] flesh, I more:
5 περιτομῇ ὀκταήμερος, ἐκ γένους Ἰσραήλ,
in circumcision eighth day, of [the] race of Israel,
φυλῆς Βενιαμίν, Ἑβραῖος ἐξ Ἑβραίων,
[the] tribe of Benjamin, a Hebrew of Hebrew [parents],
κατὰ νόμον Φαρισαῖος, **6** κατὰ ζῆλος
according to [the] law a Pharisee, by way of zeal
διώκων τὴν ἐκκλησίαν, κατὰ δικαιοσύνην
persecuting the church, according to [the] righteousness
τὴν ἐν νόμῳ γενόμενος ἄμεμπτος. **7** ἀλλὰ
– in [the] law being blameless. But
ἅτινα ἦν μοι κέρδη, ταῦτα ἥγημαι διὰ
what things were to me gain, these I have deemed [2]on account of
τὸν Χριστὸν ζημίαν. **8** ἀλλὰ μενοῦν γε
– [3]Christ [1]loss. *But* nay rather
καὶ ἡγοῦμαι πάντα ζημίαν εἶναι διὰ
[2]also [1]I deem [3]all things [5]loss [4]to be on account of
τὸ ὑπερέχον τῆς γνώσεως Χριστοῦ Ἰησοῦ
the excellency of the knowledge of Christ Jesus
τοῦ κυρίου μου, δι' ὃν τὰ πάντα
the Lord of me, on account of whom – all things
ἐζημιώθην, καὶ ἡγοῦμαι σκύβαλα ἵνα
I suffered loss, and deem [them] refuse in order that
Χριστὸν κερδήσω **9** καὶ εὑρεθῶ ἐν αὐτῷ,
Christ I might gain and be found in him,
μὴ ἔχων ἐμὴν δικαιοσύνην τὴν ἐκ νόμου,
not having my righteousness the [one] of law,
ἀλλὰ τὴν διὰ πίστεως Χριστοῦ, τὴν
but the [one] through faith of(in) Christ,• [1]the

• The apostle uses a "studiously contemptuous paronomasia" (Ellicott). He does not use περιτομή, the proper word for "circumcision", "as this, though now abrogated in Christ, had still its spiritual aspects."

• See Gal. 2. 20.

Christ, risking his life to make up for the help you could not give me.

Chapter 3

No Confidence in the Flesh

FINALLY, my brothers, rejoice in the Lord! It is no trouble for me to write the same things to you again, and it is a safeguard for you.
2Watch out for those dogs, those men who do evil, those mutilators of the flesh. 3For it is we who are
the circumcision, we who worship by the Spirit of God, who glory in Christ Jesus, and who put no confidence in the flesh—
4though I myself have reasons for such confidence.
If anyone else thinks he has reasons to put confidence in the flesh, I have
more: 5circumcised on the
eighth day, of the people of Israel, of the tribe of Benjamin, a Hebrew of Hebrews; in regard to the law, a Pharisee; 6as for zeal, persecuting the church; as for legalistic righteousness, faultless.
7But whatever was to my profit I now consider loss for the sake of Christ.
8What is more, I consider everything a loss compared to the surpassing greatness of knowing Christ Jesus my Lord, for whose sake I have lost all things. I consider them rubbish, that I
may gain Christ 9and be
found in him, not having a righteousness of my own that comes from the law, but that which is through faith in Christ—the right-

which *comes* from God on
the basis of faith,
10that I may know Him,
and the power of His resurrection and the fellowship
of His sufferings, being
conformed to His death;
11in order that I may at-
tain to the resurrection
from the dead.
12Not that I have already
obtained *it*, or have already
become perfect, but I press
on in order that I may lay
hold of that for which also I
was laid hold of by Christ
Jesus.
13Brethren, I do not re-
gard myself as having laid
hold of *it* yet; but one thing
I do: forgetting what *lies*
behind and reaching for-
ward to what *lies* ahead,
14I press on toward the
goal for the prize of the up-
ward call of God in Christ
Jesus.
15Let us therefore, as
many as are perfect, have
this attitude; and if in anything you have a different
attitude, God will reveal
that also to you;
16however, let us keep
living by that same *standard* to which we have attained.
17Brethren, join in following my example, and ob-
serve those who walk ac-
cording to the pattern you
have in us.
18For many walk, of
whom I often told you, and
now tell you even weeping,
that they are enemies of the
cross of Christ,
19whose end is destruc-
tion, whose god is *their*
appetite, and *whose* glory
is in their shame, who set
their minds on earthly
things.
20For our citizenship is in
heaven, from which also
we eagerly wait for a Savior, the Lord Jesus Christ;
21who will transform the
body of our humble state
into conformity with the
body of His glory, by the

ἐκ θεοῦ δικαιοσύνην ἐπὶ τῇ πίστει,
[2]of [4]God [3]righteousness [based] on – faith,

10 τοῦ γνῶναι αὐτὸν καὶ τὴν δύναμιν
– to know[d] him and the power

τῆς ἀναστάσεως αὐτοῦ καὶ κοινωνίαν
of the resurrection of him and [the] fellowship

παθημάτων αὐτοῦ, συμμορφιζόμενος τῷ
of sufferings of him, being conformed to the

θανάτῳ αὐτοῦ, **11** εἴ πως καταντήσω εἰς
death of him, if [some]how I may attain *to* to

τὴν ἐξανάστασιν τὴν ἐκ νεκρῶν. **12** Οὐχ
the out-resurrection – from [the] dead. Not

ὅτι ἤδη ἔλαβον ἢ ἤδη τετελείωμαι,
that already I received or already have been perfected,

διώκω δὲ εἰ καὶ καταλάβω, ἐφ' ᾧ
but I follow if indeed I may lay hold, inasmuch as

καὶ κατελήμφθην ὑπὸ Χριστοῦ Ἰησοῦ.
also I was laid hold of by Christ Jesus.

13 ἀδελφοί, ἐγὼ ἐμαυτὸν οὔπω λογίζομαι
Brothers, [2]I [4]myself [1]not yet [3]reckon

κατειληφέναι· ἓν δέ, τὰ μὲν ὀπίσω
to have laid hold; but one thing [I do], [2]the things [3]on one hand [4]behind

ἐπιλανθανόμενος τοῖς δὲ ἔμπροσθεν ἐπεκ-
[1]forgetting [2]the things [1]on the other [4]before [3]stretching

τεινόμενος, **14** κατὰ σκοπὸν διώκω εἰς
forward to, according to a mark I follow for

τὸ βραβεῖον τῆς ἄνω κλήσεως τοῦ θεοῦ
the prize of the above calling – of God

ἐν Χριστῷ Ἰησοῦ. **15** Ὅσοι οὖν τέλειοι,
in Christ Jesus. [2]As many as [1]therefore [are] perfect,

τοῦτο φρονῶμεν· καὶ εἴ τι ἑτέρως
[2]this [1]let us think; and if anything otherwise

φρονεῖτε, καὶ τοῦτο ὁ θεὸς ὑμῖν ἀποκα-
ye think, even this – God to you will

λύψει· **16** πλὴν εἰς ὃ ἐφθάσαμεν, τῷ
reveal; nevertheless to what we arrived, by the

αὐτῷ στοιχεῖν. **17** Συμμιμηταί μου
same to walk. Fellow-imitators of me

γίνεσθε, ἀδελφοί, καὶ σκοπεῖτε τοὺς οὕτω
be ye, brothers, and mark the [ones] thus

περιπατοῦντας καθὼς ἔχετε τύπον ἡμᾶς.
walking as ye have [2]an example [1]us.

18 πολλοὶ γὰρ περιπατοῦσιν οὓς πολλάκις
For many walk [of] whom often

ἔλεγον ὑμῖν, νῦν δὲ καὶ κλαίων λέγω,
I said to you, and now also weeping I say,

τοὺς ἐχθροὺς τοῦ σταυροῦ τοῦ Χριστοῦ,
the enemies of the cross – of Christ,

19 ὧν τὸ τέλος ἀπώλεια, ὧν ὁ θεὸς
of whom the end [is] destruction, of whom the god [is]

ἡ κοιλία καὶ ἡ δόξα ἐν τῇ αἰσχύνῃ
the belly and the glory in the shame

αὐτῶν, οἱ τὰ ἐπίγεια φρονοῦντες. **20** ἡμῶν
of them, the [ones] the earthly things thinking. of us

γὰρ τὸ πολίτευμα ἐν οὐρανοῖς ὑπάρχει,
For the citizenship in heavens is,

ἐξ οὗ καὶ σωτῆρα ἀπεκδεχόμεθα κύριον
from where also [2]a Saviour [1]we await Lord

Ἰησοῦν Χριστόν, **21** ὃς μετασχηματίσει τὸ
Jesus Christ, who will change the

σῶμα τῆς ταπεινώσεως ἡμῶν σύμμορφον
body of the humiliation of us [making it] conformed

τῷ σώματι τῆς δόξης αὐτοῦ, κατὰ τὴν
to the body of the glory of him, according to the

eousness that comes from
God and is by faith. 10I
want to know Christ and
the power of his resurrection and the fellowship of
sharing in his sufferings,
becoming like him in his
death, 11and so, somehow,
to attain to the resurrection
from the dead.

Pressing on Toward the Goal

12Not that I have already
obtained all this, or have already been made perfect,
but I press on to take hold
of that for which Christ
Jesus took hold of me.
13Brothers, I do not consider myself yet to have taken
hold of it. But one thing I
do: Forgetting what is behind and straining toward
what is ahead, 14I press on
toward the goal to win the
prize for which God has
called me heavenward in
Christ Jesus.
15All of us who are ma-
ture should take such a
view of things. And if on
some point you think dif-
ferently, that too God will
make clear to you. 16Only
let us live up to what we
have already attained.
17Join with others in following my example, broth-
ers, and take note of those
who live according to the
pattern we gave you. 18For,
as I have often told you before and now say again
even with tears, many live
as enemies of the cross of
Christ. 19Their destiny is
destruction, their god is
their stomach, and their
glory is in their shame.
Their mind is on earthly
things. 20But our citizenship is in heaven. And we
eagerly await a Savior from
there, the Lord Jesus
Christ, 21who, by the power that enables him to bring
everything under his con-
trol, will transform our

exertion of the power that He has even to subject all things to Himself.

Chapter 4

Think of Excellence

THEREFORE, my beloved brethren whom I long *to see,* my joy and crown, so stand firm in the Lord, my beloved.

2I urge Euodia and I urge Syntyche to live in harmony in the Lord.

3Indeed, true comrade, I ask you also to help these women who have shared my struggle in *the cause of* the gospel, together with Clement also, and the rest of my fellow workers, whose names are in the book of life.

4Rejoice in the Lord always; again I will say, rejoice!

5Let your forbearing *spirit* be known to all men. The Lord is near.

6Be anxious for nothing, but in everything by prayer and supplication with thanksgiving let your requests be made known to God.

7And the peace of God, which surpasses all comprehension, shall guard your hearts and your minds in Christ Jesus.

8Finally, brethren, whatever is true, whatever is honorable, whatever is right, whatever is pure, whatever is lovely, whatever is of good repute, if there is any excellence and if anything worthy of praise, let your mind dwell on these things.

9The things you have learned and received and heard and seen in me, practice these things; and the God of peace shall be with you.

God's Provisions

10But I rejoiced in the Lord greatly, that now at last you have revived your concern for me; indeed,

ἐνέργειαν τοῦ δύνασθαι αὐτὸν καὶ ὑποτάξαι
operation of the to be able him[b] even to subject
=of his ability

αὐτῷ τὰ πάντα. **4** Ὥστε, ἀδελφοί μου
to him[self] – all things. So as, brothers of me

ἀγαπητοὶ καὶ ἐπιπόθητοι, χαρὰ καὶ
beloved and longed for, joy and

στέφανός μου, οὕτως στήκετε ἐν κυρίῳ, ἀγαπητοί.
crown of me, so stand in [the] Lord, beloved.

2 Εὐοδίαν παρακαλῶ καὶ Συντύχην
2Euodia 1I beseech and 2Syntyche

παρακαλῶ τὸ αὐτὸ φρονεῖν ἐν κυρίῳ.
1I beseech 4the 5same thing 3to think in [the] Lord.

3 ναὶ ἐρωτῶ καὶ σέ, γνήσιε σύζυγε,
Yes[,] I ask also thee, genuine yoke-fellow,

συλλαμβάνου αὐταῖς, αἵτινες ἐν τῷ εὐαγ-
help them, who 3in 4the 5gos-

γελίῳ συνήθλησάν μοι μετὰ καὶ Κλήμεντος
pel 1struggled with 2me with both Clement

καὶ τῶν λοιπῶν συνεργῶν μου, ὧν
and the remaining fellow-workers of me, of whom

τὰ ὀνόματα ἐν βίβλῳ ζωῆς. **4** Χαίρετε
the names [are] in [the] book of life. Rejoice ye

ἐν κυρίῳ πάντοτε· πάλιν ἐρῶ, χαίρετε.
in [the] Lord always; again I will say, rejoice.

5 τὸ ἐπιεικὲς ὑμῶν γνωσθήτω πᾶσιν
The forbearance of you let it be known to all

ἀνθρώποις. ὁ κύριος ἐγγύς. **6** μηδὲν
men. The Lord [is] near. 2Nothing

μεριμνᾶτε, ἀλλ' ἐν παντὶ τῇ προσευχῇ
1be ye anxious about, but in everything – by prayer

καὶ τῇ δεήσει μετὰ εὐχαριστίας τὰ
and – *by* petition with thanksgivings the

αἰτήματα ὑμῶν γνωριζέσθω πρὸς τὸν
requests of you let be made known to –

θεόν. **7** καὶ ἡ εἰρήνη τοῦ θεοῦ ἡ
God. And the peace – of God –

ὑπερέχουσα πάντα νοῦν φρουρήσει τὰς
surpassing all understanding will guard the

καρδίας ὑμῶν καὶ τὰ νοήματα ὑμῶν
hearts of you and the thoughts of you

ἐν Χριστῷ Ἰησοῦ. **8** Τὸ λοιπόν, ἀδελφοί,
in Christ Jesus. For the rest, brothers,

ὅσα ἐστὶν ἀληθῆ, ὅσα σεμνά, ὅσα δίκαια,
whatever things are true, whatever things grave, whatever things just,

ὅσα ἁγνά, ὅσα προσφιλῆ, ὅσα εὔφημα,
whatever things pure, whatever things lovable, • whatever things well-spoken of,

εἴ τις ἀρετὴ καὶ εἴ τις ἔπαινος, **9** ταῦτα
if any virtue and if any praise, these things

λογίζεσθε· ἃ καὶ ἐμάθετε καὶ παρελάβετε
consider ye; which things 2both 1ye 3learned and *ye* received

καὶ ἠκούσατε καὶ εἴδετε ἐν ἐμοί, ταῦτα
and *ye* heard and *ye* saw in me, these

πράσσετε· καὶ ὁ θεὸς τῆς εἰρήνης ἔσται
practise; and the God – of peace will be

μεθ' ὑμῶν.
with you.

10 Ἐχάρην δὲ ἐν κυρίῳ μεγάλως ὅτι
Now I rejoiced in [the] Lord greatly that

ἤδη ποτὲ ἀνεθάλετε τὸ ὑπὲρ ἐμοῦ φρονεῖν·
al-ready at one time ye revived the on behalf of me to think;
=now at length =your thought for me;

lowly bodies so that they will be like his glorious body.

Chapter 4

THEREFORE, my brothers, you whom I love and long for, my joy and crown, that is how you should stand firm in the Lord, dear friends!

Exhortations

2I plead with Euodia and I plead with Syntyche to agree with each other in the Lord. 3Yes, and I ask you, loyal yokefellow,[h] help these women who have contended at my side in the cause of the gospel, along with Clement and the rest of my fellow workers, whose names are in the book of life.

4Rejoice in the Lord always. I will say it again: Rejoice! 5Let your gentleness be evident to all. The Lord is near. 6Do not be anxious about anything, but in everything, by prayer and petition, with thanksgiving, present your requests to God. 7And the peace of God, which transcends all understanding, will guard your hearts and your minds in Christ Jesus.

8Finally, brothers, whatever is true, whatever is noble, whatever is right, whatever is pure, whatever is lovely, whatever is admirable—if anything is excellent or praiseworthy—think about such things. 9Whatever you have learned or received or heard from me, or seen in me—put it into practice. And the God of peace will be with you.

Thanks for Their Gifts

10I rejoice greatly in the Lord that at last you have renewed your concern for me. Indeed, you have been

[h]3 Or *loyal Syzygus*

you were concerned *be-*
fore, but you lacked opportunity.
11Not that I speak from
want; for I have learned to
be content in whatever circumstances I am.
12I know how to get along
with humble means, and I
also know how to live in
prosperity; in any and
every circumstance I have
learned the secret of being
filled and going hungry,
both of having abundance
and suffering need.
13I can do all things
through Him who
strengthens me.
14Nevertheless, you have
done well to share *with me*
in my affliction.
15And you yourselves
also know, Philippians,
that at the first preaching of
the gospel, after I departed
from Macedonia, no
church shared with me in
the matter of giving and receiving but you alone;
16for even in Thessaloni-
ca you sent *a gift* more than
once for my needs.
17Not that I seek the gift
itself, but I seek for the
profit which increases to
your account.
18But I have received
everything in full, and have
an abundance; I am amply
supplied, having received
from Epaphroditus what
you have sent, a fragrant
aroma, an acceptable sacrifice, well-pleasing to God.
19And my God shall sup-
ply all your needs according to His riches in glory in
Christ Jesus.
20Now to our God and Fa-
ther *be* the glory forever
and ever. Amen.
21Greet every saint in
Christ Jesus. The brethren
who are with me greet you.
22All the saints greet you,
especially those of Cae-
sar's household.

ἐφ' ᾧ καὶ ἐφρονεῖτε, ἠκαιρεῖσθε δέ.
as to which indeed ye thought, but ye had no opportunity.

11 οὐχ ὅτι καθ' ὑστέρησιν λέγω· ἐγὼ
Not that [2]by way of [3]lack [1]I say; [2]I

γὰρ ἔμαθον ἐν οἷς εἰμι αὐτάρκης εἶναι.
[1]for learned in what conditions I am [2]self-sufficient [1]to be.

12 οἶδα καὶ ταπεινοῦσθαι, οἶδα καὶ περισ-
I know both to be humbled, and I know to

σεύειν· ἐν παντὶ καὶ ἐν πᾶσιν μεμύημαι,
abound; in everything and in all things I have been initiated,

καὶ χορτάζεσθαι καὶ πεινᾶν, καὶ περισ-
both to be filled and to hunger, both to

σεύειν καὶ ὑστερεῖσθαι. **13** πάντα ἰσχύω
abound and to lack. [2]All things [1]I can do

ἐν τῷ ἐνδυναμοῦντί με. **14** πλὴν καλῶς
in the [one] empowering me. Nevertheless [2]well

ἐποιήσατε συγκοινωνήσαντές μου τῇ θλίψει.
[1]ye did having partnership in [3]of me [1]the [2]affliction.

15 οἴδατε δὲ καὶ ὑμεῖς, Φιλιππήσιοι, ὅτι
And [2]know [3]also [1]ye, Philippians, that

ἐν ἀρχῇ τοῦ εὐαγγελίου, ὅτε ἐξῆλθον
in [the] beginning of the gospel, when I went out

ἀπὸ Μακεδονίας, οὐδεμία μοι ἐκκλησία
from Macedonia, not one [3]me [1]church

ἐκοινώνησεν εἰς λόγον δόσεως καὶ λήμψεως
[2]shared with in matter of giving and receiving

εἰ μὴ ὑμεῖς μόνοι, **16** ὅτι καὶ ἐν
except ye only, because indeed in

Θεσσαλονίκῃ καὶ ἅπαξ καὶ δὶς εἰς τὴν
Thessalonica both once and twice to the

χρείαν μοι ἐπέμψατε. **17** οὐχ ὅτι ἐπιζητῶ
need to me[c] ye sent. Not that I seek
=to my need

τὸ δόμα, ἀλλὰ ἐπιζητῶ τὸν καρπὸν
the gift, but I seek the fruit

τὸν πλεονάζοντα εἰς λόγον ὑμῶν. **18** ἀπέχω
– increasing to account of you. I have

δὲ πάντα καὶ περισσεύω· πεπλήρωμαι
But all things and abound; I have been filled

δεξάμενος παρὰ Ἐπαφροδίτου τὰ παρ'
receiving from Epaphroditus the things from

ὑμῶν, ὀσμὴν εὐωδίας, θυσίαν δεκτήν,
you, an odour of sweet smell, a sacrifice acceptable,

εὐάρεστον τῷ θεῷ. **19** ὁ δὲ θεός μου
well-pleasing – to God. And the God of me

πληρώσει πᾶσαν χρείαν ὑμῶν κατὰ τὸ
will fill every need of you according to the

πλοῦτος αὐτοῦ ἐν δόξῃ ἐν Χριστῷ Ἰησοῦ.
riches of him in glory in Christ Jesus.

20 τῷ δὲ θεῷ καὶ πατρὶ ἡμῶν ἡ δόξα
to the Now God and Father of us [be] the glory

εἰς τοὺς αἰῶνας τῶν αἰώνων· ἀμήν.
unto the ages of the ages: Amen.

21 Ἀσπάσασθε πάντα ἅγιον ἐν Χριστῷ
Greet ye every saint in Christ

Ἰησοῦ. ἀσπάζονται ὑμᾶς οἱ σὺν ἐμοὶ
Jesus. [5]greet [6]you [1]The [3]with [4]me

ἀδελφοί. **22** ἀσπάζονται ὑμᾶς πάντες οἱ
[2]brothers. [4]greet [5]you [1]All [2]the

ἅγιοι, μάλιστα δὲ οἱ ἐκ τῆς Καίσαρος
[3]saints, but most of all the ones of [1]the [3]of Cæsar

οἰκίας.
[2]household.

concerned, but you had no
opportunity to show it. 11I
am not saying this because
I am in need, for I have
learned to be content whatever the circumstances. 12I
know what it is to be in
need, and I know what it is
to have plenty. I have
learned the secret of being
content in any and every
situation, whether well fed
or hungry, whether living
in plenty or in want. 13I can
do everything through him
who gives me strength.
14Yet it was good of you
to share in my troubles.
15Moreover, as you Philippians know, in the early
days of your acquaintance
with the gospel, when I set
out from Macedonia, not
one church shared with me
in the matter of giving and
receiving, except you only;
16for even when I was in
Thessalonica, you sent me
aid again and again when I
was in need. 17Not that I
am looking for a gift, but I
am looking for what may be
credited to your account.
18I have received full payment and even more; I am
amply supplied, now that I
have received from Epaph-
roditus the gifts you sent.
They are a fragrant offering, an acceptable sacri-
fice, pleasing to God.
19And my God will meet all
your needs according to his
glorious riches in Christ
Jesus.
20To our God and Father
be glory for ever and ever.
Amen.

Final Greetings

21Greet all the saints in
Christ Jesus. The brothers
who are with me send
greetings. 22All the saints
send you greetings, espe-
cially those who belong to
Caesar's household.

23The grace of the Lord
Jesus Christ be with your
spirit.

23 Ἡ χάρις τοῦ κυρίου Ἰησοῦ Χριστοῦ
The grace of the Lord Jesus Christ
μετὰ τοῦ πνεύματος ὑμῶν.
[be] with the spirit of you.

23The grace of the Lord
Jesus Christ be with your
spirit. Amen.[i]

Colossians

Chapter 1

Thankfulness for Spiritual Attainments

PAUL, an apostle of
Jesus Christ by the will
of God, and Timothy our
brother,
2to the saints and faithful
brethren in Christ *who are*
at Colossae: Grace to you
and peace from God our
Father.
3We give thanks to God,
the Father of our Lord
Jesus Christ, praying al-
ways for you,
4since we heard of your
faith in Christ Jesus and the
love which you have for all
the saints;
5because of the hope laid
up for you in heaven, of
which you previously
heard in the word of truth,
the gospel,
6which has come to you,
just as in all the world also
it is constantly bearing fruit
and increasing, even as *it*
has been doing in you also
since the day you heard *of*
it and understood the grace
of God in truth;
7just as you learned *it*
from Epaphras, our be-
loved fellow bond-servant,
who is a faithful servant of
Christ on [a]our behalf,
8and he also informed us
of your love in the Spirit.
9For this reason also,
since the day we heard *of it*,
we have not ceased to pray

[a] Some later mss. read *your*

ΠΡΟΣ ΚΟΛΟΣΣΑΕΙΣ
To Colossians

1 Παῦλος ἀπόστολος Χριστοῦ Ἰησοῦ διὰ
Paul an apostle of Christ Jesus through
θελήματος θεοῦ καὶ Τιμόθεος ὁ ἀδελφὸς
[the] will of God and Timothy the brother
2 τοῖς ἐν Κολοσσαῖς ἁγίοις καὶ πιστοῖς
to the in Colossae saints and faithful
ἀδελφοῖς ἐν Χριστῷ· χάρις ὑμῖν καὶ
brothers in Christ: Grace to you and
εἰρήνη ἀπὸ θεοῦ πατρὸς ἡμῶν.
peace from God Father of us.
3 Εὐχαριστοῦμεν τῷ θεῷ πατρὶ τοῦ
We give thanks – to God Father of the
κυρίου ἡμῶν Ἰησοῦ [Χριστοῦ] πάντοτε
Lord of us Jesus Christ always
περὶ ὑμῶν προσευχόμενοι, 4 ἀκούσαντες
[2]concerning [3]you [1]praying, having heard
τὴν πίστιν ὑμῶν ἐν Χριστῷ Ἰησοῦ
the faith of you in Christ Jesus
καὶ τὴν ἀγάπην ἣν ἔχετε εἰς πάντας
and the love which ye have toward all
τοὺς ἁγίους 5 διὰ τὴν ἐλπίδα τὴν
the saints because of the hope –
ἀποκειμένην ὑμῖν ἐν τοῖς οὐρανοῖς, ἣν
being laid up for you in *the* heavens, which
προηκούσατε ἐν τῷ λόγῳ τῆς ἀληθείας
ye previously heard in the word of the truth
τοῦ εὐαγγελίου 6 τοῦ παρόντος εἰς ὑμᾶς,
of the gospel – coming to you,
καθὼς καὶ ἐν παντὶ τῷ κόσμῳ ἐστὶν
as also in all the world it is
καρποφορούμενον καὶ αὐξανόμενον καθὼς
bearing fruit and growing as
καὶ ἐν ὑμῖν, ἀφ᾽ ἧς ἡμέρας ἠκούσατε
also in you, from which day ye heard
=the day on which
καὶ ἐπέγνωτε τὴν χάριν τοῦ θεοῦ ἐν
and fully knew the grace – of God in
ἀληθείᾳ· 7 καθὼς ἐμάθετε ἀπὸ Ἐπαφρᾶ
truth; as ye learned from Epaphras
τοῦ ἀγαπητοῦ συνδούλου ἡμῶν, ὅς ἐστιν
the beloved fellow-slave of us, who is
πιστὸς ὑπὲρ ὑμῶν διάκονος τοῦ Χριστοῦ,
[1]a faithful [4]on behalf of [5]you [2]minister – [3]of Christ,
8 ὁ καὶ δηλώσας ἡμῖν τὴν ὑμῶν ἀγάπην
the [one] also having shown to us [1]the [2]of you [3]love
ἐν πνεύματι.
in spirit.
9 Διὰ τοῦτο καὶ ἡμεῖς, ἀφ᾽ ἧς ἡμέρας
Therefore also we, from which day
=the day on which
ἠκούσαμεν, οὐ παυόμεθα ὑπὲρ ὑμῶν
we heard, do not cease on behalf of you

Colossians

Chapter 1

PAUL, an apostle of
Christ Jesus by the will
of God, and Timothy our
brother,

2To the holy and faithful[a]
brothers in Christ at Colos-
se:

Grace and peace to you
from God our Father.[b]

Thanksgiving and Prayer

3We always thank God,
the Father of our Lord
Jesus Christ, when we pray
for you, 4because we have
heard of your faith in Christ
Jesus and of the love you
have for all the saints—
5the faith and love that
spring from the hope that is
stored up for you in heaven
and that you have already
heard about in the word of
truth, the gospel 6that has
come to you. All over the
world this gospel is bearing
fruit and growing, just as it
has been doing among you
since the day you heard it
and understood God's
grace in all its truth. 7You
learned it from Epaphras,
our dear fellow servant,
who is a faithful minister of
Christ on our[c] behalf, 8and
who also told us of your
love in the Spirit.
9For this reason, since
the day we heard about
you, we have not stopped

[i]*23* Some manuscripts do not have *Amen.*
[a]*2* Or *believing*
[b]*2* Some manuscripts *Father and the Lord Jesus Christ*
[c]*7* Some manuscripts *your*

for you and to ask that you
may be filled with the
knowledge of His will in all
spiritual wisdom and
understanding,
10so that you may walk in
a manner worthy of the
Lord, to please *Him* in all
respects, bearing fruit in
every good work and in-
creasing in the knowledge
of God;
11strengthened with all
power, according to His
glorious might, for the attaining of all steadfastness
and patience; joyously
12giving thanks to the Father, who has qualified us
to share in the inheritance
of the saints in light.

The Incomparable Christ

13For He delivered us
from the domain of dark-
ness, and transferred us to
the kingdom of His beloved
Son,
14in whom we have re-
demption, the forgiveness
of sins.
15And He is the image of
the invisible God, the firstborn of all creation.
16For by Him all things
were created, *both* in the
heavens and on earth, visible and invisible, whether
thrones or dominions or
rulers or authorities—all
things have been created
by Him and for Him.
17And He is before all
things, and in Him all
things hold together.
18He is also head of the
body, the church; and He is
the beginning, the first-
born from the dead; so that
He Himself might come to
have first place in everything.
19For it was the *Father's*
good pleasure for all the
fulness to dwell in Him,
20and through Him to rec-
oncile all things to Himself,

προσευχόμενοι καὶ αἰτούμενοι ἵνα πληρω-
praying and asking *in order* that ye may be
θῆτε τὴν ἐπίγνωσιν τοῦ θελήματος αὐτοῦ
filled [with] the full knowledge of the will of him
ἐν πάσῃ σοφίᾳ καὶ συνέσει πνευματικῇ,
in all wisdom and understanding spiritual,
10 περιπατῆσαι ἀξίως τοῦ κυρίου εἰς
to walk worthily of the Lord to
πᾶσαν ἀρεσκείαν, ἐν παντὶ ἔργῳ ἀγαθῷ
all pleasing, in every work good
καρποφοροῦντες καὶ αὐξανόμενοι τῇ
bearing fruit and growing in the
ἐπιγνώσει τοῦ θεοῦ, 11 ἐν πάσῃ δυνάμει
full knowledge – of God, with all power
δυναμούμενοι κατὰ τὸ κράτος τῆς δόξης
being empowered according to the might of the glory
αὐτοῦ εἰς πᾶσαν ὑπομονὴν καὶ μακρο-
of him to all endurance and long-
θυμίαν, μετὰ χαρᾶς 12 εὐχαριστοῦντες τῷ
suffering, with joy giving thanks to the
πατρὶ τῷ ἱκανώσαντι ὑμᾶς εἰς τὴν μερίδα
Father – having made [2]fit [1]you for the part
τοῦ κλήρου τῶν ἁγίων ἐν τῷ φωτί·
of the lot of the saints in *the* light;
13 ὃς ἐρρύσατο ἡμᾶς ἐκ τῆς ἐξουσίας
who delivered us out of the authority
τοῦ σκότους καὶ μετέστησεν εἰς τὴν
of *the* darkness and transferred into the
βασιλείαν τοῦ υἱοῦ τῆς ἀγάπης αὐτοῦ,
kingdom of the Son of the love of him,
14 ἐν ᾧ ἔχομεν τὴν ἀπολύτρωσιν, τὴν
in whom we have *the* redemption, the
ἄφεσιν τῶν ἁμαρτιῶν· 15 ὅς ἐστιν εἰκὼν
forgiveness of the (our) sins; who is an image
τοῦ θεοῦ τοῦ ἀοράτου, πρωτότοκος πάσης
of the God – invisible, firstborn of all
κτίσεως, 16 ὅτι ἐν αὐτῷ ἐκτίσθη τὰ
creation, because in him were created –
πάντα ἐν τοῖς οὐρανοῖς καὶ ἐπὶ τῆς
all things in *the* heaven*s* and on the
γῆς, τὰ ὁρατὰ καὶ τὰ ἀόρατα, εἴτε
earth, the visible and the invisible, whether
θρόνοι εἴτε κυριότητες εἴτε ἀρχαὶ εἴτε
thrones or lordships or rulers or
ἐξουσίαι· τὰ πάντα δι' αὐτοῦ καὶ εἰς
authorities; – all things through him and for
αὐτὸν ἔκτισται· 17 καὶ αὐτός ἐστιν πρὸ
him have been created; and he is before
πάντων καὶ τὰ πάντα ἐν αὐτῷ συνέστηκεν,
all things and – all things in him consisted,
18 καὶ αὐτός ἐστιν ἡ κεφαλὴ τοῦ σώματος,
and he is the head of the body,
τῆς ἐκκλησίας· ὅς ἐστιν ἀρχή, πρωτότοκος
of the church; who is [the] beginning, firstborn
ἐκ τῶν νεκρῶν, ἵνα γένηται ἐν πᾶσιν
from the dead, in order that [4]may be [2]in [3]all things
αὐτὸς πρωτεύων, 19 ὅτι ἐν αὐτῷ εὐδόκησεν
[1]he [5]holding the first place, because in him [4]was well pleased
πᾶν τὸ πλήρωμα κατοικῆσαι 20 καὶ δι'
[1]all [2]the [3]fulness to dwell and through
αὐτοῦ ἀποκαταλλάξαι τὰ πάντα εἰς αὐτόν,
him to reconcile – all things to him[?self],

praying for you and asking
God to fill you with the
knowledge of his will
through all spiritual wisdom and understanding.
10And we pray this in order
that you may live a life worthy of the Lord and may
please him in every way:
bearing fruit in every good
work, growing in the
knowledge of God, 11being
strengthened with all power according to his glorious
might so that you may have
great endurance and pa-
tience, and joyfully 12giving
thanks to the Father, who
has qualified you[d] to share
in the inheritance of the
saints in the kingdom of
light. 13For he has rescued
us from the dominion of
darkness and brought us
into the kingdom of the Son
he loves, 14in whom we
have redemption,[e] the forgiveness of sins.

The Supremacy of Christ

15He is the image of the
invisible God, the firstborn
over all creation. 16For by
him all things were created:
things in heaven and on
earth, visible and invisible,
whether thrones or powers
or rulers or authorities; all
things were created by him
and for him. 17He is before
all things, and in him all
things hold together. 18And
he is the head of the body,
the church; he is the beginning and the firstborn from
among the dead, so that in
everything he might have
the supremacy. 19For God
was pleased to have all his
fullness dwell in him, 20and
through him to reconcile to
himself all things, whether

[d]12 Some manuscripts *us*
[e]14 A few late manuscripts *redemption through his blood*

having made peace through
the blood of His cross;
through Him, *I say*,
whether things on earth or
things in heaven.
21And although you were
formerly alienated and hostile in mind, *engaged* in evil
deeds,
22yet He has now recon-
ciled you in His fleshly
body through death, in order to present you before
Him holy and blameless
and beyond reproach—
23if indeed you continue
in the faith firmly established and steadfast, and
not moved away from the
hope of the gospel that you
have heard, which was proclaimed in all creation under heaven, and of which I,
Paul, was made a minister.
24Now I rejoice in my sufferings for your sake, and
in my flesh I do my share
on behalf of His body
(which is the church) in filling up that which is lacking
in Christ's afflictions.
25Of *this church* I was
made a minister according
to the stewardship from
God bestowed on me for
your benefit, that I might
fully carry out the *preaching of* the word of God,
26*that is,* the mystery
which has been hidden
from the *past* ages and generations; but has now been
manifested to His saints,
27to whom God willed to
make known what is the
riches of the glory of this
mystery among the Gen-
tiles, which is Christ in
you, the hope of glory.
28And we proclaim Him,
admonishing every man
and teaching every man

εἰρηνοποιήσας διὰ τοῦ αἵματος τοῦ σταυροῦ
making peace through the blood of the cross

αὐτοῦ, δι' αὐτοῦ εἴτε τὰ ἐπὶ τῆς γῆς
of him, through him whether the things on the earth

εἴτε τὰ ἐν τοῖς οὐρανοῖς. 21 Καὶ ὑμᾶς
or the things in *the* heaven*s*. And you

ποτε ὄντας ἀπηλλοτριωμένους καὶ ἐχθροὺς
then being *having been* alienated and enemies

τῇ διανοίᾳ ἐν τοῖς ἔργοις τοῖς πονηροῖς,
in *the* mind by the(your) works – evil,

22 νυνὶ δὲ ἀποκατήλλαξεν ἐν τῷ σώματι
but now he reconciled in the body

τῆς σαρκὸς αὐτοῦ διὰ τοῦ θανάτου,
of the flesh of him through the(his) death,

παραστῆσαι ὑμᾶς ἁγίους καὶ ἀμώμους
to present you holy and blameless

καὶ ἀνεγκλήτους κατενώπιον αὐτοῦ, 23 εἴ
and irreproachable before him, if

γε ἐπιμένετε τῇ πίστει τεθεμελιωμένοι
indeed ye continue in the faith having been founded

καὶ ἑδραῖοι καὶ μὴ μετακινούμενοι ἀπὸ
and steadfast and not being moved away from

τῆς ἐλπίδος τοῦ εὐαγγελίου οὗ ἠκούσατε,
the hope of the gospel which ye heard,

τοῦ κηρυχθέντος ἐν πάσῃ κτίσει τῇ
– proclaimed in all creation –

ὑπὸ τὸν οὐρανόν, οὗ ἐγενόμην ἐγὼ
under *the* heaven, of which [3]became [1]I

Παῦλος διάκονος.
[2]Paul a minister.

24 Νῦν χαίρω ἐν τοῖς παθήμασιν ὑπὲρ
Now I rejoice in the(my) sufferings on behalf of

ὑμῶν, καὶ ἀνταναπληρῶ τὰ ὑστερήματα
you, and fill up the things lacking

τῶν θλίψεων τοῦ Χριστοῦ ἐν τῇ σαρκί
of the afflictions – of Christ in the flesh

μου ὑπὲρ τοῦ σώματος αὐτοῦ, ὅ ἐστιν
of me on behalf of the body of him, which is

ἡ ἐκκλησία, 25 ἧς ἐγενόμην ἐγὼ διάκονος
the church, of which became I a minister

κατὰ τὴν οἰκονομίαν τοῦ θεοῦ τὴν
according to the stewardship – of God –

δοθεῖσάν μοι εἰς ὑμᾶς πληρῶσαι τὸν
given to me for you to fulfil the

λόγον τοῦ θεοῦ, 26 τὸ μυστήριον τὸ
word – of God, the mystery –

ἀποκεκρυμμένον ἀπὸ τῶν αἰώνων καὶ
having been hidden from the ages and

ἀπὸ τῶν γενεῶν — νῦν δὲ ἐφανερώθη
from the generations — but now was manifested

τοῖς ἁγίοις αὐτοῦ, 27 οἷς ἠθέλησεν ὁ
to the saints of him, to whom [2]wished –

θεὸς γνωρίσαι τί τὸ πλοῦτος τῆς δόξης
[1]God to make known what [is] the riches of the glory

τοῦ μυστηρίου τούτου ἐν τοῖς ἔθνεσιν,
– mystery of this among the nations,

ὅς ἐστιν Χριστὸς ἐν ὑμῖν, ἡ ἐλπὶς τῆς
who is Christ in you, the hope of the

δόξης· 28 ὃν ἡμεῖς καταγγέλλομεν νουθετοῦντες
glory; whom we announce warning

πάντα ἄνθρωπον καὶ διδάσκοντες
every man and teaching

things on earth or things in
heaven, by making peace
through his blood, shed on
the cross.
21Once you were alienat-
ed from God and were ene-
mies in your minds because
of[f] your evil behavior.
22But now he has recon-
ciled you by Christ's physical body through death to
present you holy in his
sight, without blemish and
free from accusation— 23if
you continue in your faith,
established and firm, not
moved from the hope held
out in the gospel. This is the
gospel that you heard and
that has been proclaimed to
every creature under heav-
en, and of which I, Paul,
have become a servant.

Paul's Labor for the Church

24Now I rejoice in what
was suffered for you, and I
fill up in my flesh what is
still lacking in regard to
Christ's afflictions, for the
sake of his body, which is
the church. 25I have be-
come its servant by the
commission God gave me
to present to you the word
of God in its fullness—
26the mystery that has been
kept hidden for ages and
generations, but is now disclosed to the saints. 27To
them God has chosen to
make known among the
Gentiles the glorious riches
of this mystery, which is
Christ in you, the hope of
glory.
28We proclaim him, ad-
monishing and teaching everyone with all wisdom, so

f21 Or *minds, as shown by*

with all wisdom, that we
may present every man
complete in Christ.
29And for this purpose
also I labor, striving according to His power,
which mightily works within me.

Chapter 2

You Are Built Up in Christ

FOR I want you to know
how great a struggle I
have on your behalf, and
for those who are at Laodicea, and for all those who
have not personally seen
my face,
2that their hearts may be
encouraged, having been
knit together in love, and
attaining to all the wealth
that comes from the full assurance of understanding,
resulting in a true knowledge of God's mystery,
that is, Christ *Himself,*
3in whom are hidden all
the treasures of wisdom
and knowledge.
4I say this in order that
no one may delude you
with persuasive argument.
5For even though I am
absent in body, neverthe-
less I am with you in spirit,
rejoicing to see your good
discipline and the stability
of your faith in Christ.
6As you therefore have
received Christ Jesus the
Lord, *so* walk in Him,
7having been firmly root-
ed *and now* being built up in
Him and established [b]in
your faith, just as you were
instructed, *and* overflowing with gratitude.
8See to it that no one
takes you captive through
philosophy and empty
deception, according to the
tradition of men, according
to the elementary prin-
ciples of the world, rather
than according to Christ.
9For in Him all the ful-

[b] Or, *by*

πάντα ἄνθρωπον ἐν πάσῃ σοφίᾳ,
every man in all wisdom,
ἵνα παραστήσωμεν πάντα ἄνθρωπον
in order that we may present every man
τέλειον ἐν Χριστῷ· 29 εἰς ὃ καὶ κοπιῶ
mature in Christ; for which also I labour
ἀγωνιζόμενος κατὰ τὴν ἐνέργειαν αὐτοῦ
struggling according to the operation of him
τὴν ἐνεργουμένην ἐν ἐμοὶ ἐν δυνάμει.
– operating in me in power.
2 Θέλω γὰρ ὑμᾶς εἰδέναι ἡλίκον ἀγῶνα
For I wish you to know how great a struggle
ἔχω ὑπὲρ ὑμῶν καὶ τῶν ἐν Λαοδικείᾳ
I have on behalf of you and the [ones] in Laodicea
καὶ ὅσοι οὐχ ἑόρακαν τὸ πρόσωπόν μου
and as many as have not seen the face of me
ἐν σαρκί, 2 ἵνα παρακληθῶσιν αἱ καρδίαι
in flesh, in order that [4]may be comforted [1]the [2]hearts
αὐτῶν, συμβιβασθέντες ἐν ἀγάπῃ καὶ εἰς
[3]of them, being joined together in love and for
πᾶν πλοῦτος τῆς πληροφορίας τῆς
all riches of the full assurance –
συνέσεως, εἰς ἐπίγνωσιν τοῦ μυστηρίου
of understanding, for full knowledge of the mystery
τοῦ θεοῦ, Χριστοῦ, 3 ἐν ᾧ εἰσιν πάντες
– of God, of Christ, in whom [1]are [2]all
οἱ θησαυροὶ τῆς σοφίας καὶ γνώσεως
[4]the [5]treasures – [6]of wisdom [7]and [8]of knowledge
ἀπόκρυφοι. 4 Τοῦτο λέγω ἵνα μηδεὶς
[3]hidden. This I say in order that no one
ὑμᾶς παραλογίζηται ἐν πιθανολογίᾳ. 5 εἰ
[2]you [1]may beguile with persuasive speech. if
γὰρ καὶ τῇ σαρκὶ ἄπειμι, ἀλλὰ τῷ
For indeed in the flesh I am absent, yet in the
πνεύματι σὺν ὑμῖν εἰμι, χαίρων καὶ
spirit [2]with [3]you [1]I am, rejoicing and
βλέπων ὑμῶν τὴν τάξιν καὶ τὸ στερέωμα
seeing [3]of you [1]the [2]order and the firmness
τῆς εἰς Χριστὸν πίστεως ὑμῶν.
of the [3]in [4]Christ [1]faith [2]of you.
6 Ὡς οὖν παρελάβετε τὸν Χριστὸν
As therefore ye received – Christ
Ἰησοῦν τὸν κύριον, ἐν αὐτῷ περιπατεῖτε,
Jesus the Lord, in him walk ye,
7 ἐρριζωμένοι καὶ ἐποικοδομούμενοι ἐν αὐτῷ
having been rooted and being built up in him
καὶ βεβαιούμενοι τῇ πίστει καθὼς ἐδιδάχ-
and being confirmed in the faith as ye were
θητε, περισσεύοντες ἐν εὐχαριστίᾳ.
taught, abounding in thanksgiving.
8 Βλέπετε μή τις ὑμᾶς ἔσται ὁ συλαγωγῶν
Look ye lest [2]anyone [4]you [1]there shall be – [3]robbing
διὰ τῆς φιλοσοφίας καὶ κενῆς ἀπάτης
through – philosophy and empty deceit
κατὰ τὴν παράδοσιν τῶν ἀνθρώπων, κατὰ
according to the tradition – of men, according to
τὰ στοιχεῖα τοῦ κόσμου καὶ οὐ κατὰ
the elements of the world and not according to
Χριστόν· 9 ὅτι ἐν αὐτῷ κατοικεῖ πᾶν
Christ; because in him dwells all

that we may present everyone perfect in Christ. 29To
this end I labor, struggling
with all his energy, which
so powerfully works in me.

Chapter 2

I WANT you to know
how much I am strug-
gling for you and for those
at Laodicea, and for all
who have not met me per-
sonally. 2My purpose is
that they may be encour-
aged in heart and united in
love, so that they may have
the full riches of complete
understanding, in order
that they may know the
mystery of God, namely,
Christ, 3in whom are hid-
den all the treasures of wisdom and knowledge. 4I tell
you this so that no one may
deceive you by fine-sound-
ing arguments. 5For though
I am absent from you in
body, I am present with
you in spirit and delight to
see how orderly you are
and how firm your faith in
Christ is.

Freedom From Human Regulations Through Life With Christ

6So then, just as you re-
ceived Christ Jesus as
Lord, continue to live in
him, 7rooted and built up in
him, strengthened in the
faith as you were taught,
and overflowing with
thankfulness.
8See to it that no one
takes you captive through
hollow and deceptive phi-
losophy, which depends on
human tradition and the basic principles of this world
rather than on Christ.
9For in Christ all the full-

ness of Deity dwells in
bodily form,
10and in Him you have
been made complete, and
He is the head over all rule
and authority;
11and in Him you were
also circumcised with a circumcision made without
hands, in the removal of the
body of the flesh by the circumcision of Christ;
12having been buried with
Him in baptism, in which
you were also raised up
with Him through faith in
the working of God, who
raised Him from the dead.
13And when you were
dead in your transgressions
and the uncircumcision of
your flesh, He made you
alive together with Him,
having forgiven us all our
transgressions,
14having canceled out the
certificate of debt consist-
ing of decrees against us
and which was hostile to
us; and He has taken it out
of the way, having nailed it
to the cross.
15When He had disarmed
the rulers and authorities,
He made a public display of
them, having triumphed
over them through Him.
16Therefore let no one act
as your judge in regard to
food or drink or in respect
to a festival or a new moon
or a Sabbath day—
17things which are a *mere*
shadow of what is to come;
but the substance belongs
to Christ.
18Let no one keep de-
frauding you of your prize
by delighting in self-abase-
ment and the worship of the
angels, taking his stand on
visions he has seen, inflat-
ed without cause by his
fleshly mind,
19and not holding fast to
the head, from whom the
entire body, being supplied
and held together by the

τὸ πλήρωμα τῆς θεότητος σωματικῶς,
the fulness of the Godhead bodily,

10 καὶ ἐστὲ ἐν αὐτῷ πεπληρωμένοι, ὅς
and ye are in him *having been* filled, who

ἐστιν ἡ κεφαλὴ πάσης ἀρχῆς καὶ ἐξουσίας,
is the head of all rule and authority,

11 ἐν ᾧ καὶ περιετμήθητε περιτομῇ
in whom also ye were circumcised with a circumcision

ἀχειροποιήτῳ ἐν τῇ ἀπεκδύσει τοῦ σώματος
not handwrought by the putting off of the body

τῆς σαρκός, ἐν τῇ περιτομῇ τοῦ Χριστοῦ,
of the flesh, by the circumcision – of Christ,

12 συνταφέντες αὐτῷ ἐν τῷ βαπτίσματι,
co-buried with him in the baptism,

ἐν ᾧ καὶ συνηγέρθητε διὰ τῆς πίστεως
in whom also ye were co-raised through the faith

τῆς ἐνεργείας τοῦ θεοῦ τοῦ ἐγείραντος
of(in) the operation – of God – raising

αὐτὸν ἐκ νεκρῶν· 13 καὶ ὑμᾶς νεκροὺς
him from [the] dead; and you dead

ὄντας τοῖς παραπτώμασιν καὶ τῇ ἀκρο-
being in the trespasses and in the uncir-

βυστίᾳ τῆς σαρκὸς ὑμῶν, συνεζωοποίησεν
cumcision of the flesh of you, he co-quickened

ὑμᾶς σὺν αὐτῷ, χαρισάμενος ἡμῖν πάντα
you with him, forgiving us all

τὰ παραπτώματα· 14 ἐξαλείψας τὸ καθ᾽
the trespasses; wiping out 1the 3against

ἡμῶν χειρόγραφον τοῖς δόγμασιν ὃ ἦν
4us 2handwriting – in ordinances which was

ὑπεναντίον ἡμῖν, καὶ αὐτὸ ἦρκεν ἐκ
contrary to us, and 2it 1has taken out of

τοῦ μέσου, προσηλώσας αὐτὸ τῷ σταυρῷ·
the midst(way), nailing it to the cross;

15 ἀπεκδυσάμενος τὰς ἀρχὰς καὶ τὰς
putting off the rulers and the

ἐξουσίας ἐδειγμάτισεν ἐν παρρησίᾳ,
authorities he exposed [them] with openness,

θριαμβεύσας αὐτοὺς ἐν αὐτῷ.
triumphing [over] them in it.

16 Μὴ οὖν τις ὑμᾶς κρινέτω ἐν βρώσει
2Not 3therefore 4anyone 6you 1let 5judge in eating

καὶ ἐν πόσει ἢ ἐν μέρει ἑορτῆς ἢ
and in drinking or in respect of a feast or

νεομηνίας ἢ σαββάτων, 17 ἅ ἐστιν σκιὰ
of a new moon or of sabbaths, which things is(are) a shadow

τῶν μελλόντων, τὸ δὲ σῶμα τοῦ Χριστοῦ.
of things coming, but the body [is] – of Christ.

18 μηδεὶς ὑμᾶς καταβραβευέτω θέλων ἐν
2No one 4you 1let 3give judgment against wishing [to do so] in

ταπεινοφροσύνῃ καὶ θρησκείᾳ τῶν ἀγγέλων,
humility* and worship of the angels,

ἃ ἑόρακεν ἐμβατεύων, εἰκῇ φυσιούμενος
3things which 2he has seen 1intruding into, in vain being puffed up

ὑπὸ τοῦ νοὸς τῆς σαρκὸς αὐτοῦ, 19 καὶ
by the mind of the flesh of him, and

οὐ κρατῶν τὴν κεφαλήν, ἐξ οὗ πᾶν
not holding the head, from whom all

τὸ σῶμα διὰ τῶν ἁφῶν καὶ συνδέσμων
the body 4by means of 5the (its) 6joints 7and 8bands

* Ellicott supplies " false ". *Cf.* ver. 23.

ness of the Deity lives in
bodily form, 10and you
have been given fullness in
Christ, who is the head
over every power and au-
thority. 11In him you were
also circumcised, in the
putting off of the sinful nature,[g] not with a circumcision done by the hands of
men but with the circumcision done by Christ, 12hav-
ing been buried with him in
baptism and raised with
him through your faith in
the power of God, who
raised him from the dead.
13When you were dead in
your sins and in the uncircumcision of your sinful
nature,[h] God made you[i]
alive with Christ. He forgave us all our sins, 14hav-
ing canceled the written
code, with its regulations,
that was against us and that
stood opposed to us; he
took it away, nailing it to
the cross. 15And having disarmed the powers and au-
thorities, he made a public
spectacle of them, triumphing over them by the
cross.[j]
16Therefore do not let
anyone judge you by what
you eat or drink, or with
regard to a religious festival, a New Moon celebra-
tion or a Sabbath day.
17These are a shadow of the
things that were to come;
the reality, however, is
found in Christ. 18Do not
let anyone who delights in
false humility and the worship of angels disqualify
you for the prize. Such a
person goes into great detail about what he has seen,
and his unspiritual mind
puffs him up with idle no-
tions. 19He has lost connection with the Head, from
whom the whole body, sup-
ported and held together by

g11 Or *the flesh*
h13 Or *your flesh*
i13 Some manuscripts *us*
j15 Or *them in him*

joints and ligaments, grows
with a growth which is from
God.
20If you have died with
Christ to the elementary
principles of the world,
why, as if you were living in
the world, do you submit
yourself to decrees, such
as,
21"Do not handle, do not
taste, do not touch!"
22(which all *refer to* things
destined to perish with the
using)—in accordance with
the commandments and
teachings of men?
23These are matters
which have, to be sure, the
appearance of wisdom in
self-made religion and self-
abasement and severe
treatment of the body, *but*
are of no value against
fleshly indulgence.

Chapter 3

Put On the New Self

IF then you have been
raised up with Christ,
keep seeking the things
above, where Christ is,
seated at the right hand of
God.
2Set your mind on the
things above, not on the
things that are on earth.
3For you have died and
your life is hidden with
Christ in God.
4When Christ, who is
our life, is revealed, then
you also will be revealed
with Him in glory.
5Therefore consider the
members of your earthly
body as dead to immoral-
ity, impurity, passion, evil
desire, and greed, which
amounts to idolatry.
6For it is on account of
these things that the wrath
of God will come[c],
7and in them you also
once walked, when you
were living in them.
8But now you also, put
them all aside: anger,
wrath, malice, slander, *and*
abusive speech from your
mouth.
9Do not lie to one an-
other, since you laid aside
the old self with its *evil*
practices,

[c] Some early mss. add *upon the sons of disobedience*

ἐπιχορηγούμενον καὶ συμβιβαζόμενον αὔξει
¹being supplied ²and ³*being* joined together will grow
τὴν αὔξησιν τοῦ θεοῦ.
[with] the growth – of God.
20 Εἰ ἀπεθάνετε σὺν Χριστῷ ἀπὸ τῶν στοι-
If ye died with Christ from the ele-
χείων τοῦ κόσμου, τί ὡς ζῶντες ἐν κόσμῳ
ments of the world, why as living in [the] world
δογματίζεσθε· **21** μὴ ἅψῃ μηδὲ γεύσῃ μηδὲ
are ye subject to [its] decrees: Do not touch nor taste nor
θίγῃς, **22** ἅ ἐστιν πάντα εἰς φθορὰν
handle, which things is(are) all for corruption
τῇ ἀποχρήσει, κατὰ τὰ ἐντάλματα καὶ
in the using, according to the injunctions and
διδασκαλίας τῶν ἀνθρώπων; **23** ἅτινά ἐστιν
teachings – of men? ¹which things ²is(are)
λόγον μὲν ἔχοντα σοφίας ἐν ἐθελοθρησκίᾳ
³a repute ²indeed ⁴having of wisdom in self-imposed worship
καὶ ταπεινοφροσύνῃ καὶ ἀφειδίᾳ σώματος, οὐκ
and humility and severity of [the] body, not
ἐν τιμῇ τινι πρὸς πλησμονὴν τῆς σαρκός.
in ²honour ¹any for satisfaction of the flesh.
3 Εἰ οὖν συνηγέρθητε τῷ Χριστῷ, τὰ
If therefore ye were co-raised – with Christ, the things
ἄνω ζητεῖτε, οὗ ὁ Χριστός ἐστιν ἐν
above seek, where – Christ ¹is ²at
δεξιᾷ τοῦ θεοῦ καθήμενος· **2** τὰ ἄνω
⁴[the] right [hand] – ⁵of God ³sitting; the above things
φρονεῖτε, μὴ τὰ ἐπὶ τῆς γῆς. **3** ἀπεθάνετε
mind ye, not the things on the earth. ye died
γάρ, καὶ ἡ ζωὴ ὑμῶν κέκρυπται σὺν
For, and the life of you has been hidden with
τῷ Χριστῷ ἐν τῷ θεῷ· **4** ὅταν ὁ Χριστὸς
– Christ in – God; whenever – Christ
φανερωθῇ, ἡ ζωὴ ἡμῶν, τότε καὶ ὑμεῖς
is manifested, the life of us, then also ye
σὺν αὐτῷ φανερωθήσεσθε ἐν δόξῃ.
with him will be manifested in glory.
5 Νεκρώσατε οὖν τὰ μέλη τὰ ἐπὶ
Put ye to death therefore the (your) members – on
τῆς γῆς, πορνείαν, ἀκαθαρσίαν, πάθος,
the earth, fornication, uncleanness, passion,
ἐπιθυμίαν κακήν, καὶ τὴν πλεονεξίαν ἥτις
desire bad, and – covetousness which
ἐστὶν εἰδωλολατρία, **6** δι' ἃ ἔρχεται ἡ
is idolatry, because of which things is coming the
ὀργὴ τοῦ θεοῦ· **7** ἐν οἷς καὶ ὑμεῖς
wrath – of God; in which indeed ye
περιεπατήσατέ ποτε, ὅτε ἐζῆτε ἐν τούτοις·
walked then, when ye lived in these things;
8 νυνὶ δὲ ἀπόθεσθε καὶ ὑμεῖς τὰ πάντα,
but now ¹put ³away ⁴also ²ye – all things,
ὀργήν, θυμόν, κακίαν, βλασφημίαν, αἰσχρο-
wrath, anger, malice, blasphemy, a-
λογίαν ἐκ τοῦ στόματος ὑμῶν· **9** μὴ
buse out of the mouth of you; not
ψεύδεσθε εἰς ἀλλήλους, ἀπεκδυσάμενοι τὸν
lie ye to one another, having put off the
παλαιὸν ἄνθρωπον σὺν ταῖς πράξεσιν
old man with the practices

its ligaments and sinews,
grows as God causes it to
grow.
20Since you died with
Christ to the basic principles of this world, why, as
though you still belonged to
it, do you submit to its
rules: 21"Do not handle! Do
not taste! Do not touch!"?
22These are all destined to
perish with use, because
they are based on human
commands and teachings.
23Such regulations indeed
have an appearance of wisdom, with their self-im-
posed worship, their false
humility and their harsh
treatment of the body, but
they lack any value in restraining sensual indul-
gence.

Chapter 3

Rules for Holy Living

SINCE, then, you have
been raised with
Christ, set your hearts on
things above, where Christ
is seated at the right hand of
God. 2Set your minds on
things above, not on earthly things. 3For you died,
and your life is now hidden
with Christ in God. 4When
Christ, who is your[k] life,
appears, then you also will
appear with him in glory.
5Put to death, therefore,
whatever belongs to your
earthly nature: sexual immorality, impurity, lust,
evil desires and greed,
which is idolatry. 6Because
of these, the wrath of God
is coming.[l] 7You used to
walk in these ways, in the
life you once lived. 8But
now you must rid your-
selves of all such things as
these: anger, rage, malice,
slander, and filthy language
from your lips. 9Do not lie
to each other, since you
have taken off your old self
with its practices 10and

[k] 4 Some manuscripts *our*
[l] 6 Some early manuscripts *coming on those who are disobedient*

10and have put on the new
self who is being renewed
to a true knowledge ac-
cording to the image of the
One who created him
11—*a renewal* in which
there is no *distinction between* Greek and Jew, circumcised and uncircum-
cised, barbarian, Scythian,
slave and freeman, but
Christ is all, and in all.
12And so, as those who
have been chosen of God,
holy and beloved, put on a
heart of compassion, kindness, humility, gentleness
and patience;
13bearing with one an-
other, and forgiving each
other, whoever has a com-
plaint against anyone; just
as the Lord forgave you, so
also should you.
14And beyond all these
things *put on* love, which is
the perfect bond of unity.
15And let the peace of
Christ rule in your hearts,
to which indeed you were
called in one body; and be
thankful.
16Let the word of [d]Christ
richly dwell within you,
with all wisdom teaching
and admonishing one an-
other with psalms *and*
hymns *and* spiritual songs,
singing with thankfulness
in your hearts to God.
17And whatever you do in
word or deed, *do* all in the
name of the Lord Jesus,
giving thanks through Him
to God the Father.

Family Relations

18Wives, be subject to
your husbands, as is fitting
in the Lord.
19Husbands, love your
wives, and do not be embittered against them.
20Children, be obedient to
your parents in all things,

[d]Some mss. read *the Lord;* others read *God*

αὐτοῦ, **10** καὶ ἐνδυσάμενοι τὸν νέον τὸν
of him, and having put on the new man –
ἀνακαινούμενον εἰς ἐπίγνωσιν κατ᾽ εἰκόνα
being renewed in full knowledge according to [the] image
τοῦ κτίσαντος αὐτόν, **11** ὅπου οὐκ ἔνι
of the [one] creating him, where 4have no place
Ἕλλην καὶ Ἰουδαῖος, περιτομὴ καὶ
1Greek 2and 3Jew, circumcision and
ἀκροβυστία, βάρβαρος, Σκύθης, δοῦλος,
uncircumcision, barbarian, Scythian, slave,
ἐλεύθερος, ἀλλὰ πάντα καὶ ἐν πᾶσιν
freeman, but 3all things 4and 5in 6all
Χριστός. **12** Ἐνδύσασθε οὖν, ὡς ἐκλεκτοὶ
1Christ 2[is]. Put ye on therefore, as chosen ones
τοῦ θεοῦ ἅγιοι καὶ ἠγαπημένοι, σπλάγχνα
– of God holy and having been loved, bowels
οἰκτιρμοῦ, χρηστότητα, ταπεινοφροσύνην,
of compassion, kindness, humility,
πραΰτητα, μακροθυμίαν, **13** ἀνεχόμενοι ἀλ-
meekness, long-suffering, forbearing one
λήλων καὶ χαριζόμενοι ἑαυτοῖς, ἐάν τις
another and forgiving yourselves, if anyone
πρός τινα ἔχῃ μομφήν· καθὼς καὶ ὁ
3against 4anyone 1has 2a complaint; as indeed the
κύριος ἐχαρίσατο ὑμῖν οὕτως καὶ ὑμεῖς·
Lord forgave you so also ye;
14 ἐπὶ πᾶσιν δὲ τούτοις τὴν ἀγάπην,
2over 3all 1and these things – love,
ὅ ἐστιν σύνδεσμος τῆς τελειότητος. **15** καὶ
which is [the] bond – of completeness. And
ἡ εἰρήνη τοῦ Χριστοῦ βραβευέτω ἐν ταῖς
2the 3peace – 4of Christ 1let 5rule in the
καρδίαις ὑμῶν, εἰς ἣν καὶ ἐκλήθητε
hearts of you, to which indeed ye were called
ἐν ἑνὶ σώματι· καὶ εὐχάριστοι γίνεσθε.
in one body; and thankful be ye.
16 ὁ λόγος τοῦ Χριστοῦ ἐνοικείτω ἐν
2The 3word – 4of Christ 1let 5*in*dwell in
ὑμῖν πλουσίως, ἐν πάσῃ σοφίᾳ διδάσκοντες
you richly, in all wisdom teaching
καὶ νουθετοῦντες ἑαυτούς, ψαλμοῖς ὕμνοις
and admonishing yourselves, in psalms[,] hymns[,]
ᾠδαῖς πνευματικαῖς ἐν τῇ χάριτι ᾄδοντες
[and] 2songs 1spiritual with – grace singing
ἐν ταῖς καρδίαις ὑμῶν τῷ θεῷ· **17** καὶ
in the hearts of you – to God; and
πᾶν ὅ τι ἐὰν ποιῆτε ἐν λόγῳ ἢ ἐν
every-thing whatever ye do in word or in
ἔργῳ, πάντα ἐν ὀνόματι κυρίου Ἰησοῦ,
work, all things [do] in [the] name of [the] Lord Jesus,
εὐχαριστοῦντες τῷ θεῷ πατρὶ δι᾽ αὐτοῦ.
giving thanks – to God [the] Father through him.
18 Αἱ γυναῖκες, ὑποτάσσεσθε τοῖς
The wives, be ye subject to the(your)
ἀνδράσιν, ὡς ἀνῆκεν ἐν κυρίῳ. **19** Οἱ
husbands, as is befitting in [the] Lord. The
ἄνδρες, ἀγαπᾶτε τὰς γυναῖκας καὶ μὴ
husbands, love ye the(your) wives and not
πικραίνεσθε πρὸς αὐτάς. **20** Τὰ τέκνα,
be bitter toward them. The children,
ὑπακούετε τοῖς γονεῦσιν κατὰ πάντα,
obey ye the(your) parents in all respects,

have put on the new self,
which is being renewed in
knowledge in the image of
its Creator. 11Here there is
no Greek or Jew, circum-
cised or uncircumcised,
barbarian, Scythian, slave
or free, but Christ is all, and
is in all.
12Therefore, as God's
chosen people, holy and
dearly loved, clothe yourselves with compassion,
kindness, humility, gentleness and patience. 13Bear
with each other and forgive
whatever grievances you
may have against one an-
other. Forgive as the Lord
forgave you. 14And over all
these virtues put on love,
which binds them all to-
gether in perfect unity.
15Let the peace of Christ
rule in your hearts, since as
members of one body you
were called to peace. And
be thankful. 16Let the word
of Christ dwell in you richly
as you teach and admonish
one another with all wis-
dom, and as you sing
psalms, hymns and spiritual songs with gratitude in
your hearts to God. 17And
whatever you do, whether
in word or deed, do it all in
the name of the Lord Jesus,
giving thanks to God the
Father through him.

Rules for Christian Households

18Wives, submit to your
husbands, as is fitting in the
Lord.
19Husbands, love your
wives and do not be harsh
with them.
20Children, obey your
parents in everything, for

for this is well-pleasing to the Lord.
21Fathers, do not [e]exasperate your children, that they may not lose heart.
22Slaves, in all things obey those who are your masters on earth, not with external service, as those who *merely* please men, but with sincerity of heart, fearing the Lord.
23Whatever you do, do your work heartily, as for the Lord rather than for men;
24knowing that from the Lord you will receive the reward of the inheritance. It is the Lord Christ whom you serve.
25For he who does wrong will receive the consequences of the wrong which he has done, and that without partiality.

Chapter 4

Fellow Workers

MASTERS, grant to your slaves justice and fairness, knowing that you too have a Master in heaven.
2Devote yourselves to prayer, keeping alert in it with *an attitude of* thanksgiving;
3praying at the same time for us as well, that God may open up to us a door for the word, so that we may speak forth the mystery of Christ, for which I have also been imprisoned;
4in order that I may make it clear in the way I ought to speak.
5Conduct yourselves with wisdom toward outsiders, making the most of the opportunity.
6Let your speech always be with grace, seasoned, *as it were,* with salt, so that you may know how you should respond to each person.
7As to all my affairs, Tychicus, *our* beloved brother and faithful servant

[e] Some early mss. read *provoke to anger*

τοῦτο γὰρ εὐάρεστόν ἐστιν ἐν κυρίῳ.
for this well-pleasing is in [the] Lord.
21 Οἱ πατέρες, μὴ ἐρεθίζετε τὰ τέκνα
The fathers, do not ye provoke the children
ὑμῶν, ἵνα μὴ ἀθυμῶσιν. 22 Οἱ δοῦλοι,
of you, lest they be disheartened. The slaves,
ὑπακούετε κατὰ πάντα τοῖς κατὰ σάρκα
obey ye in all respects [1]the (your) [3]according to [4][the] flesh
κυρίοις, μὴ ἐν ὀφθαλμοδουλίαις ὡς
[2]lords, not with eyeservice as
ἀνθρωπάρεσκοι, ἀλλ' ἐν ἁπλότητι καρδίας
men-pleasers, but in singleness of heart
φοβούμενοι τὸν κύριον. 23 ὃ ἐὰν ποιῆτε,
fearing the Lord. Whatever ye do,
ἐκ ψυχῆς ἐργάζεσθε ὡς τῷ κυρίῳ καὶ
from [the] soul work ye as to the Lord and
οὐκ ἀνθρώποις, 24 εἰδότες ὅτι ἀπὸ κυρίου
not to men, knowing that from [the] Lord
ἀπολήμψεσθε τὴν ἀνταπόδοσιν τῆς κλη-
ye will receive the reward of the in-
ρονομίας. τῷ κυρίῳ Χριστῷ δουλεύετε·
heritance. The Lord Christ ye serve;
25 ὁ γὰρ ἀδικῶν κομίσεται ὃ ἠδίκησεν,
for the [one] doing wrong will receive what he did wrong,
καὶ οὐκ ἔστιν προσωπολημψία. 4 Οἱ κύριοι,
and there is no respect of persons. The lords,
τὸ δίκαιον καὶ τὴν ἰσότητα τοῖς δούλοις
[2]the [3]just thing [4]and [5]the [6]equality [7]to the(your) [8]slaves
παρέχεσθε, εἰδότες ὅτι καὶ ὑμεῖς ἔχετε
[1]supply ye, knowing that also ye have
κύριον ἐν οὐρανῷ.
a Lord in heaven.
2 Τῇ προσευχῇ προσκαρτερεῖτε, γρηγο-
In *the* prayer continue ye, watch-
ροῦντες ἐν αὐτῇ ἐν εὐχαριστίᾳ, 3 προσευ-
ing in it with thanksgiving, pray-
χόμενοι ἅμα καὶ περὶ ἡμῶν, ἵνα ὁ
ing together also concerning us, *in order* that –
θεὸς ἀνοίξῃ ἡμῖν θύραν τοῦ λόγου,
God may open to us a door of the word,
λαλῆσαι τὸ μυστήριον τοῦ Χριστοῦ, δι'
to speak the mystery – of Christ, because of
ὃ καὶ δέδεμαι, 4 ἵνα φανερώσω αὐτὸ
which indeed I have been bound, in order that I may manifest it
ὡς δεῖ με λαλῆσαι. 5 Ἐν σοφίᾳ
as it behoves me to speak. In wisdom
περιπατεῖτε πρὸς τοὺς ἔξω, τὸν καιρὸν
walk ye toward the ones outside, [2]the [3]time
ἐξαγοραζόμενοι. 6 ὁ λόγος ὑμῶν πάντοτε
[1]redeeming. The speech of you [let it be] always
ἐν χάριτι, ἅλατι ἠρτυμένος, εἰδέναι πῶς
in grace, with salt *having been* seasoned, to know how
δεῖ ὑμᾶς ἑνὶ ἑκάστῳ ἀποκρίνεσθαι.
it behoves you [3]one [2]each [1]to answer.
7 Τὰ κατ' ἐμὲ πάντα γνωρίσει ὑμῖν Τύχικος
[2]The things [3]about [4]me [1]all [6]will make known [7]to you [5]Tychicus
ὁ ἀγαπητὸς ἀδελφὸς καὶ πιστὸς διάκονος
the beloved brother and faithful minister

this pleases the Lord.
21Fathers, do not embitter your children, or they will become discouraged.
22Slaves, obey your earthly masters in everything; and do it, not only when their eye is on you and to win their favor, but with sincerity of heart and reverence for the Lord.
23Whatever you do, work at it with all your heart, as working for the Lord, not for men, 24since you know that you will receive an inheritance from the Lord as a reward. It is the Lord Christ you are serving.
25Anyone who does wrong will be repaid for his wrong, and there is no favoritism.

Chapter 4

MASTERS, provide your slaves with what is right and fair, because you know that you also have a Master in heaven.

Further Instructions

2Devote yourselves to prayer, being watchful and thankful. 3And pray for us, too, that God may open a door for our message, so that we may proclaim the mystery of Christ, for which I am in chains. 4Pray that I may proclaim it clearly, as I should. 5Be wise in the way you act toward outsiders; make the most of every opportunity. 6Let your conversation be always full of grace, seasoned with salt, so that you may know how to answer everyone.

Final Greetings

7Tychicus will tell you all the news about me. He is a dear brother, a faithful min-

and fellow bond-servant in
the Lord, will bring you information.
8For I have sent him to
you for this very purpose,
that you may know *about*
our circumstances and that
he may encourage your
hearts;
9and with him Onesimus,
our faithful and beloved
brother, who is one of your
number. They will inform
you about the whole situation here.
10Aristarchus, my fellow
prisoner, sends you his
greetings; and *also* Barnabas' cousin Mark (about
whom you received in-
structions: if he comes to
you, welcome him);
11and *also* Jesus who is
called Justus; these are the
only fellow workers for the
kingdom of God who are
from the circumcision; and
they have proved to be an
encouragement to me.
12Epaphras, who is one of
your number, a bondslave
of Jesus Christ, sends you
his greetings, always labor-
ing earnestly for you in his
prayers, that you may
stand perfect and fully assured in all the will of God.
13For I bear him witness
that he has a deep concern
for you and for those who
are in Laodicea and
Hierapolis.
14Luke, the beloved
physician, sends you his
greetings, and *also* Demas.
15Greet the brethren who
are in Laodicea and also
[f]Nympha and the church
that is in her house.
16And when this letter is
read among you, have it
also read in the church of
the Laodiceans; and you,
for your part read my letter
that is coming from Laodicea.
17And say to Archippus,
"Take heed to the ministry

καὶ σύνδουλος ἐν κυρίῳ, 8 ὃν ἔπεμψα
and fellow-slave in [the] Lord, whom I sent
πρὸς ὑμᾶς εἰς αὐτὸ τοῦτο, ἵνα γνῶτε
to you for this very thing, in order that ye might know
τὰ περὶ ἡμῶν καὶ παρακαλέσῃ τὰς
the things concerning us and he might comfort the
καρδίας ὑμῶν, 9 σὺν Ὀνησίμῳ τῷ πιστῷ
hearts of you, with Onesimus the faithful
καὶ ἀγαπητῷ ἀδελφῷ, ὅς ἐστιν ἐξ ὑμῶν·
and beloved brother, who is of you;
πάντα ὑμῖν γνωρίσουσιν τὰ ὧδε.
[1]all [5]to you [4]they will make known [2]the things [3]here.
10 Ἀσπάζεται ὑμᾶς Ἀρίσταρχος ὁ
[5]greets [6]you [1]Aristarchus [2]the
συναιχμάλωτός μου, καὶ Μάρκος ὁ ἀνεψιὸς
[3]fellow-captive [4]of me, and Mark the cousin
Βαρναβᾶ, (περὶ οὗ ἐλάβετε ἐντολάς, ἐὰν
of Barnabas, (concerning whom ye received commandments, if
ἔλθῃ πρὸς ὑμᾶς, δέξασθε αὐτόν,) 11 καὶ
he comes to you, receive ye him,) and
Ἰησοῦς ὁ λεγόμενος Ἰοῦστος, οἱ ὄντες
Jesus the [one] *being* named Justus, the [ones] being
ἐκ περιτομῆς οὗτοι μόνοι συνεργοὶ εἰς
of [the] circumcision these only fellow-workers for
τὴν βασιλείαν τοῦ θεοῦ, οἵτινες ἐγενή-
the kingdom – of God, who be-
θησάν μοι παρηγορία. 12 ἀσπάζεται ὑμᾶς
came to me a comfort. [2]greets [3]you
Ἐπαφρᾶς ὁ ἐξ ὑμῶν, δοῦλος Χριστοῦ
[1]Epaphras the [one] of you, a slave of Christ
Ἰησοῦ, πάντοτε ἀγωνιζόμενος ὑπὲρ ὑμῶν
Jesus, always struggling on behalf of you
ἐν ταῖς προσευχαῖς, ἵνα σταθῆτε τέλειοι
in the prayers, in order that ye may stand complete
καὶ πεπληροφορημένοι ἐν παντὶ θελήματι
and having been fully assured in all [the] will
τοῦ Θεοῦ. 13 μαρτυρῶ γὰρ αὐτῷ ὅτι
– of God. For I bear witness to him that
ἔχει πολὺν πόνον ὑπὲρ ὑμῶν καὶ τῶν
he has much distress on behalf of you and the ones
ἐν Λαοδικείᾳ καὶ τῶν ἐν Ἱεραπόλει.
in Laodicea and the ones in Hierapolis.
14 ἀσπάζεται ὑμᾶς Λουκᾶς ὁ ἰατρὸς ὁ
[7]greets [8]you [1]Luke [2]the [4]physician –
ἀγαπητὸς καὶ Δημᾶς. 15 Ἀσπάσασθε
[3]beloved [5]and [6]Demas. Greet ye
τοὺς ἐν Λαοδικείᾳ ἀδελφοὺς καὶ Νύμφαν
[1]the [3]in [4]Laodicea [2]brothers and Nymphas
καὶ τὴν κατ᾽ οἶκον αὐτῆς ἐκκλησίαν.
and [1]the [3]at [4][the] house [5]of her [2]church.
16 καὶ ὅταν ἀναγνωσθῇ παρ᾽ ὑμῖν ἡ
And whenever is read before you the(this)
ἐπιστολή, ποιήσατε ἵνα καὶ ἐν τῇ
epistle, cause *in order* that [2]also [3]in [4]the
Λαοδικέων ἐκκλησίᾳ ἀναγνωσθῇ, καὶ τὴν
[6]of [the] Laodiceans [5]church [1]it is read, and [5]the [one]
ἐκ Λαοδικείας ἵνα καὶ ὑμεῖς ἀναγνῶτε.
[6]of [7]Laodicea [1]*in order* that [2]also [3]ye [4]read.
17 καὶ εἴπατε Ἀρχίππῳ· βλέπε τὴν
And tell Archippus: Look [to] the

ister and fellow servant in
the Lord. 8I am sending
him to you for the express
purpose that you may
know about our[m] circum-
stances and that he may encourage your hearts. 9He is
coming with Onesimus, our
faithful and dear brother,
who is one of you. They
will tell you everything that
is happening here.
10My fellow prisoner Ar-
istarchus sends you his
greetings, as does Mark,
the cousin of Barnabas.
(You have received in-
structions about him; if he
comes to you, welcome
him.) 11Jesus, who is called
Justus, also sends greet-
ings. These are the only
Jews among my fellow
workers for the kingdom of
God, and they have proved
a comfort to me. 12Epa-
phras, who is one of you
and a servant of Christ
Jesus, sends greetings. He
is always wrestling in
prayer for you, that you
may stand firm in all the
will of God, mature and fully assured. 13I vouch for
him that he is working hard
for you and for those at Laodicea and Hierapolis.
14Our dear friend Luke, the
doctor, and Demas send
greetings. 15Give my greetings to the brothers at Laodicea, and to Nympha and
the church in her house.
16After this letter has
been read to you, see that it
is also read in the church of
the Laodiceans and that
you in turn read the letter
from Laodicea.
17Tell Archippus: "See to
it that you complete the

[f]Or, *Nymphas* (masc.)

[m]8 Some manuscripts *that he may know about your*

which you have received in
the Lord, that you may fulfill it.''
18I, Paul, write this greeting with my own hand. Remember my imprisonment. Grace be with you.

διακονίαν ἣν παρέλαβες ἐν κυρίῳ, ἵνα
ministry which thou receivedst in [the] Lord, in order that
αὐτὴν πληροῖς.
[2]it [1]thou mayest fulfil.
18 Ὁ ἀσπασμὸς τῇ ἐμῇ χειρὶ Παύλου.
The greeting – by my hand[,] of Paul.
μνημονεύετέ μου τῶν δεσμῶν. ἡ χάρις
Remember ye of me the bonds. – Grace [be]
μεθ' ὑμῶν.
with you.

work you have received in
the Lord.''
18I, Paul, write this greeting in my own hand. Remember my chains. Grace be with you.

1 Thessalonians

Chapter 1

Thanksgiving for These Believers

PAUL and Silvanus and Timothy to the church of the Thessalonians in God the Father and the Lord Jesus Christ: Grace to you and peace.
2We give thanks to God always for all of you, making mention *of you* in our prayers;
3constantly bearing in mind your work of faith and labor of love and steadfastness of hope in our Lord Jesus Christ in the presence of our God and Father,
4knowing, brethren beloved by God, *His* choice of you;
5for our gospel did not come to you in word only, but also in power and in the Holy Spirit and with full conviction; just as you know what kind of men we proved to be among you for your sake.
6You also became imitators of us and of the Lord, having received the word in much tribulation with the joy of the Holy Spirit,
7so that you became an example to all the believers in Macedonia and in Achaia.

ΠΡΟΣ ΘΕΣΣΑΛΟΝΙΚΕΙΣ Α

To Thessalonians 1

1 Παῦλος καὶ Σιλουανὸς καὶ Τιμόθεος
Paul and Silvanus and Timothy
τῇ ἐκκλησίᾳ Θεσσαλονικέων ἐν θεῷ πατρὶ
to the church of [the] Thessalonians in God [the] Father
καὶ κυρίῳ Ἰησοῦ Χριστῷ· χάρις ὑμῖν
and [the] Lord Jesus Christ: Grace [be] to you
καὶ εἰρήνη.
and peace.
2 Εὐχαριστοῦμεν τῷ θεῷ πάντοτε περὶ
We give thanks – to God always concerning
πάντων ὑμῶν, μνείαν ποιούμενοι ἐπὶ τῶν
[2]all [1]you, mention making on(in) the
προσευχῶν ἡμῶν, ἀδιαλείπτως **3** μνημονεύοντες
prayers of us, unceasingly remembering
ὑμῶν τοῦ ἔργου τῆς πίστεως
of you the work – of faith
καὶ τοῦ κόπου τῆς ἀγάπης καὶ τῆς
and the labour – of love and the
ὑπομονῆς τῆς ἐλπίδος τοῦ κυρίου ἡμῶν
endurance – of hope of(in) the Lord of us
Ἰησοῦ Χριστοῦ ἔμπροσθεν τοῦ θεοῦ καὶ
Jesus Christ before the God and
πατρὸς ἡμῶν, **4** εἰδότες, ἀδελφοὶ ἠγαπημένοι
Father of us, knowing, brothers having been loved
ὑπὸ [τοῦ] θεοῦ, τὴν ἐκλογὴν ὑμῶν,
by – God, the choice of you,
5 ὅτι τὸ εὐαγγέλιον ἡμῶν οὐκ ἐγενήθη
because the gospel of us became not
εἰς ὑμᾶς ἐν λόγῳ μόνον, ἀλλὰ καὶ ἐν
to you in word only, but also in
δυνάμει καὶ ἐν πνεύματι ἁγίῳ καὶ
power and in Spirit Holy and
πληροφορίᾳ πολλῇ, καθὼς οἴδατε οἷοι
[2]assurance [1]much, as ye know what sort
ἐγενήθημεν ἐν ὑμῖν δι' ὑμᾶς. **6** καὶ
we were among you because of you. And
ὑμεῖς μιμηταὶ ἡμῶν ἐγενήθητε καὶ τοῦ
[1]ye [3]imitators [4]of us [2]became and of the
κυρίου, δεξάμενοι τὸν λόγον ἐν θλίψει
Lord, welcoming the word in [2]affliction
πολλῇ μετὰ χαρᾶς πνεύματος ἁγίου, **7** ὥστε
[1]much with joy of [2]Spirit [1][the] Holy, so as
γενέσθαι ὑμᾶς τύπον πᾶσιν τοῖς πιστεύουσιν
to become you[b] a pattern to all the [ones] believing
= so that ye became
ἐν τῇ Μακεδονίᾳ καὶ ἐν τῇ Ἀχαΐᾳ.
in – Macedonia and in – Achaia.

1 Thessalonians

Chapter 1

PAUL, Silas[a] and Timothy,
To the church of the Thessalonians in God the Father and the Lord Jesus Christ:
Grace and peace to you.[b]

Thanksgiving for the Thessalonians' Faith

2We always thank God for all of you, mentioning you in our prayers.
3We continually remember before our God and Father your work produced by faith, your labor prompted by love, and your endurance inspired by hope in our Lord Jesus Christ.
4For we know, brothers loved by God, that he has chosen you,
5because our gospel came to you not simply with words, but also with power, with the Holy Spirit and with deep conviction. You know how we lived among you for your sake.
6You became imitators of us and of the Lord; in spite of severe suffering, you welcomed the message with the joy given by the Holy Spirit.
7And so you became a model to all the believers in Macedonia and

[a]1 Greek *Silvanus*, a variant of *Silas*
[b]1 Some early manuscripts *you from God our Father and the Lord Jesus Christ*

8 For the word of the Lord has sounded forth from you, not only in Macedonia and Achaia, but also in every place your faith toward God has gone forth, so that we have no need to say anything.

9 For they themselves report about us what kind of a reception we had with you, and how you turned to God from idols to serve a living and true God,

10 and to wait for His Son from heaven, whom He raised from the dead, *that is* Jesus, who delivers us from the wrath to come.

8 ἀφ᾽ ὑμῶν γὰρ ἐξήχηται ὁ λόγος τοῦ
[2]from [3]you [1]For sounded the word of the

κυρίου οὐ μόνον ἐν τῇ Μακεδονίᾳ καὶ
Lord not only in – Macedonia and

Ἀχαΐᾳ, ἀλλ᾽ ἐν παντὶ τόπῳ ἡ πίστις
Achaia, but in every place the faith

ὑμῶν ἡ πρὸς τὸν θεὸν ἐξελήλυθεν, ὥστε
of you – toward – God has gone out, so as

μὴ χρείαν ἔχειν ἡμᾶς λαλεῖν τι· **9** αὐτοὶ
not need to have us[b] to speak anything; [2][them]selves
=so that we have no need

γὰρ περὶ ἡμῶν ἀπαγγέλλουσιν ὁποίαν
[1]for [4]concerning [5]us [3]they relate what sort of

εἴσοδον ἔσχομεν πρὸς ὑμᾶς, καὶ πῶς
entrance we had to you, and how

ἐπεστρέψατε πρὸς τὸν θεὸν ἀπὸ τῶν
ye turned to – God from *the*

εἰδώλων δουλεύειν θεῷ ζῶντι καὶ ἀληθινῷ,
idols to serve a God living and true,

10 καὶ ἀναμένειν τὸν υἱὸν αὐτοῦ ἐκ
and to await the Son of him from

τῶν οὐρανῶν, ὃν ἤγειρεν ἐκ τῶν νεκρῶν,
the heavens, whom he raised from the dead,

Ἰησοῦν τὸν ῥυόμενον ἡμᾶς ἐκ τῆς ὀργῆς
Jesus the [one] delivering us from the wrath

τῆς ἐρχομένης.
– coming.

Achaia. 8 The Lord's message rang out from you not only in Macedonia and Achaia—your faith in God has become known everywhere. Therefore we do not need to say anything about it, 9 for they themselves report what kind of reception you gave us. They tell how you turned to God from idols to serve the living and true God, 10 and to wait for his Son from heaven, whom he raised from the dead—Jesus, who rescues us from the coming wrath.

Chapter 2

Paul's Ministry

FOR you yourselves know, brethren, that our coming to you was not in vain,

2 but after we had already suffered and been mistreated in Philippi, as you know, we had the boldness in our God to speak to you the gospel of God amid much opposition.

3 For our exhortation does not *come* from error or impurity or by way of deceit;

4 but just as we have been approved by God to be entrusted with the gospel, so we speak, not as pleasing men but God, who examines our hearts.

5 For we never came with flattering speech, as you know, nor with a pretext for greed—God is witness—

6 nor did we seek glory from men, either from you or from others, even

2 Αὐτοὶ γὰρ οἴδατε, ἀδελφοί, τὴν
For [your]selves ye know, brothers, the

εἴσοδον ἡμῶν τὴν πρὸς ὑμᾶς, ὅτι οὐ
entrance of us – to you, that not

κενὴ γέγονεν, **2** ἀλλὰ προπαθόντες καὶ
in vain it has been, but having previously suffered and

ὑβρισθέντες καθὼς οἴδατε ἐν Φιλίπποις
having been insulted as ye know in Philippi

ἐπαρρησιασάμεθα ἐν τῷ θεῷ ἡμῶν λαλῆσαι
we were bold in the God of us to speak

πρὸς ὑμᾶς τὸ εὐαγγέλιον τοῦ θεοῦ ἐν
to you the gospel – of God in

πολλῷ ἀγῶνι. **3** ἡ γὰρ παράκλησις
much struggle. For the exhortation

ἡμῶν οὐκ ἐκ πλάνης οὐδὲ ἐξ ἀκαθαρσίας
of us not of error nor of uncleanness

οὐδὲ ἐν δόλῳ, **4** ἀλλὰ καθὼς δεδοκιμάσμεθα
nor in guile, but as we have been approved

ὑπὸ τοῦ θεοῦ πιστευθῆναι τὸ εὐαγγέλιον
by – God to be entrusted [with] the gospel

οὕτως λαλοῦμεν, οὐχ ὡς ἀνθρώποις ἀρέ-
so we speak, not as [2]men [1]pleas-

σκοντες, ἀλλὰ θεῷ τῷ δοκιμάζοντι τὰς
ing, but God the [one] proving the

καρδίας ἡμῶν. **5** οὔτε γάρ ποτε ἐν
hearts of us. For neither then with

λόγῳ κολακείας ἐγενήθημεν, καθὼς οἴδατε,
word of flattery were we, as ye know,

οὔτε ἐν προφάσει πλεονεξίας, θεὸς μάρτυς,
nor with pretext of covetousness, God [is] witness,

6 οὔτε ζητοῦντες ἐξ ἀνθρώπων δόξαν,
nor seeking from men glory,

οὔτε ἀφ᾽ ὑμῶν οὔτε ἀπ᾽ ἄλλων, **7** δυνάμε-
neither from you nor from others, being

Chapter 2

Paul's Ministry in Thessalonica

YOU know, brothers, that our visit to you was not a failure. 2 We had previously suffered and been insulted in Philippi, as you know, but with the help of our God we dared to tell you his gospel in spite of strong opposition. 3 For the appeal we make does not spring from error or impure motives, nor are we trying to trick you. 4 On the contrary, we speak as men approved by God to be entrusted with the gospel. We are not trying to please men but God, who tests our hearts. 5 You know we never used flattery, nor did we put on a mask to cover up greed—God is our witness. 6 We were not looking for praise from men, not from you or anyone else.

though as apostles of Christ we might have asserted our authority.

7But we proved to be [a]gentle among you, as a nursing *mother* tenderly cares for her own children.

8Having thus a fond affection for you, we were well-pleased to impart to you not only the gospel of God but also our own lives, because you had become very dear to us.

9For you recall, brethren, our labor and hardship, *how* working night and day so as not to be a burden to any of you, we proclaimed to you the gospel of God.

10You are witnesses, and *so is* God, how devoutly and uprightly and blamelessly we behaved toward you believers;

11just as you know how we *were* exhorting and encouraging and imploring each one of you as a father *would* his own children,

12so that you may walk in a manner worthy of the God who calls you into His own kingdom and glory.

13And for this reason we also constantly thank God that when you received from us the word of God's message, you accepted *it* not *as* the word of men, but *for* what it really is, the word of God, which also performs its work in you who believe.

14For you, brethren, became imitators of the churches of God in Christ Jesus that are in Judea, for you also endured the same

[a] Some ancient mss. read *babes*

νοι ἐν βάρει εἶναι ὡς Χριστοῦ ἀπόστολοι·
able [2]with [3]weight* [1]to be as [2]of Christ [1]apostles;

ἀλλὰ ἐγενήθημεν ἤπιοι ἐν μέσῳ ὑμῶν,
but we were gentle in [the] midst of you,

ὡς ἐὰν τροφὸς θάλπῃ τὰ ἑαυτῆς τέκνα·
as if a nurse should cherish [1]the [3]of herself [2]children;

8 οὕτως ὁμειρόμενοι ὑμῶν ηὐδοκοῦμεν
so longing for you we were well pleased

μεταδοῦναι ὑμῖν οὐ μόνον τὸ εὐαγγέλιον
to impart to you not only the gospel

τοῦ θεοῦ ἀλλὰ καὶ τὰς ἑαυτῶν ψυχάς,
– of God but also [1]the [3]of ourselves [2]souls,

διότι ἀγαπητοὶ ἡμῖν ἐγενήθητε. **9** μνημο-
because [3]beloved [2]to us [1]ye became. ye re-

νεύετε γάρ, ἀδελφοί, τὸν κόπον ἡμῶν
member For, brothers, the labour of us

καὶ τὸν μόχθον· νυκτὸς καὶ ἡμέρας
and the toil; night and day

ἐργαζόμενοι πρὸς τὸ μὴ ἐπιβαρῆσαί τινα
working for *the* not to put a burden on any-one

ὑμῶν ἐκηρύξαμεν εἰς ὑμᾶς τὸ εὐαγγέλιον
of you we proclaimed to you the gospel

τοῦ θεοῦ. **10** ὑμεῖς μάρτυρες καὶ ὁ
– of God. Ye [are] witnesses and –

θεός, ὡς ὁσίως καὶ δικαίως καὶ ἀμέμπτως
God, how holily and righteously and blamelessly

ὑμῖν τοῖς πιστεύουσιν ἐγενήθημεν, **11** καθά-
[2]to you [3]the [ones] [4]believing [1]we were, even

περ οἴδατε ὡς ἕνα ἕκαστον ὑμῶν ὡς
as ye know how [2]one [1]each of you as

πατὴρ τέκνα ἑαυτοῦ παρακαλοῦντες ὑμᾶς
a father children of himself exhorting you

καὶ παραμυθούμενοι **12** καὶ μαρτυρόμενοι εἰς
and consoling and witnessing for

τὸ περιπατεῖν ὑμᾶς ἀξίως τοῦ θεοῦ
the to walk you[b] worthily – of God
=that ye should walk

τοῦ καλοῦντος ὑμᾶς εἰς τὴν ἑαυτοῦ
the [one] calling you to [1]the [3]of himself

βασιλείαν καὶ δόξαν.
[2]kingdom [3]and [4]glory.

13 Καὶ διὰ τοῦτο καὶ ἡμεῖς εὐχαρισ-
And therefore also we give

τοῦμεν τῷ θεῷ ἀδιαλείπτως, ὅτι παρα-
thanks – to God unceasingly, that having

λαβόντες λόγον ἀκοῆς παρ' ἡμῶν τοῦ
received [1][the] word [3]of hearing [4]from [5]us –

θεοῦ ἐδέξασθε οὐ λόγον ἀνθρώπων ἀλλὰ
[2]of God ye welcomed [it] not [as] a word of men but

καθὼς ἀληθῶς ἐστιν λόγον θεοῦ, ὃς
as truly it is a word of God, which

καὶ ἐνεργεῖται ἐν ὑμῖν τοῖς πιστεύουσιν.
also operates in you the [ones] believing.

14 ὑμεῖς γὰρ μιμηταὶ ἐγενήθητε, ἀδελφοί,
For ye [2]imitators [1]became, brothers,

τῶν ἐκκλησιῶν τοῦ θεοῦ τῶν οὐσῶν ἐν
of the churches – of God – being in

τῇ Ἰουδαίᾳ ἐν Χριστῷ Ἰησοῦ, ὅτι τὰ
– Judæa in Christ Jesus, because [4]the

* ? dignity, authority.

As apostles of Christ we could have been a burden to you, 7but we were gentle among you, like a mother caring for her little children. 8We loved you so much that we were delighted to share with you not only the gospel of God but our lives as well, because you had become so dear to us. 9Surely you remember, brothers, our toil and hardship; we worked night and day in order not to be a burden to anyone while we preached the gospel of God to you.

10You are witnesses, and so is God, of how holy, righteous and blameless we were among you who believed. 11For you know that we dealt with each of you as a father deals with his own children, 12encouraging, comforting and urging you to live lives worthy of God, who calls you into his kingdom and glory.

13And we also thank God continually because, when you received the word of God, which you heard from us, you accepted it not as the word of men, but as it actually is, the word of God, which is at work in you who believe. 14For you, brothers, became imitators of God's churches in Judea, which are in Christ Jesus: You suffered from sufferings at the hands of your own countrymen, even as they *did* from the Jews,

15who both killed the Lord Jesus and the prophets, and drove us out. They are not pleasing to God, but hostile to all men,

16hindering us from speaking to the Gentiles that they might be saved; with the result that they always fill up the measure of their sins. But wrath has come upon them [b]to the utmost.

17But we, brethren, having been bereft of you for a short while—in person, not in spirit—were all the more eager with great desire to see your face.

18For we wanted to come to you—I, Paul, more than once—and *yet* Satan thwarted us.

19For who is our hope or joy or crown of exultation? Is it not even you, in the presence of our Lord Jesus at His coming?

20For you are our glory and joy.

Chapter 3

Encouragement of Timothy's Visit

THEREFORE when we could endure *it* no longer, we thought it best to be left behind at Athens alone;

2and we sent Timothy, our brother and God's fellow worker in the gospel of Christ, to strengthen and encourage you as to your faith,

3so that no man may be disturbed by these afflictions; for you yourselves know that we have been destined for this.

[b]Or, *forever;* or, *altogether*

αὐτὰ ἐπάθετε καὶ ὑμεῖς ὑπὸ τῶν ἰδίων
[5]same things [3]suffered [2]also [1]ye by the(your) own

συμφυλετῶν, καθὼς καὶ αὐτοὶ ὑπὸ τῶν
fellow-tribesmen, as also they by the

Ἰουδαίων, **15** τῶν καὶ τὸν κύριον
Jews, the [ones] [1]both [3]the [4]Lord

ἀποκτεινάντων Ἰησοῦν καὶ τοὺς προφήτας,
[2]killing [5]Jesus and the prophets,

καὶ ἡμᾶς ἐκδιωξάντων, καὶ θεῷ μὴ
and [2]us [1]chasing [3]out, and [3]God [1]not

ἀρεσκόντων, καὶ πᾶσιν ἀνθρώποις ἐναντίων,
[2]pleasing, and to all men contrary,

16 κωλυόντων ἡμᾶς τοῖς ἔθνεσιν λαλῆσαι
hindering us [2]to the [3]nations [1]to speak
=from speaking . . .

ἵνα σωθῶσιν, εἰς τὸ ἀναπληρῶσαι αὐτῶν
in order that they may be saved, *for the* to fill up [3]of them

τὰς ἁμαρτίας πάντοτε. ἔφθασεν δὲ ἐπ'
[1]the [2]sins always. But [3]came [4]on

αὐτοὺς ἡ ὀργὴ εἰς τέλος.
[5]them [1]the [2]wrath to [the] end.

17 Ἡμεῖς δέ, ἀδελφοί, ἀπορφανισθέντες
But we brothers, being bereaved

ἀφ' ὑμῶν πρὸς καιρὸν ὥρας προσώπῳ
from you for time of an hour in face (presence)

οὐ καρδίᾳ, περισσοτέρως ἐσπουδάσαμεν τὸ
not in heart, more abundantly were eager [2]the

πρόσωπον ὑμῶν ἰδεῖν ἐν πολλῇ ἐπιθυμίᾳ.
[3]face [4]of you [1]to see with much desire.

18 διότι ἠθελήσαμεν ἐλθεῖν πρὸς ὑμᾶς,
Wherefore we wished to come to you,

ἐγὼ μὲν Παῦλος καὶ ἅπαξ καὶ δίς,
I [2]indeed [1]Paul both once and twice (again),

καὶ ἐνέκοψεν ἡμᾶς ὁ σατανᾶς. **19** τίς
and [2]hindered [3]us – [1]Satan. what

γὰρ ἡμῶν ἐλπὶς ἢ χαρὰ ἢ στέφανος
For [is] [2]of us [1]hope or joy or crown

καυχήσεως — ἢ οὐχὶ καὶ ὑμεῖς —
of boasting — – not even ye —

ἔμπροσθεν τοῦ κυρίου ἡμῶν Ἰησοῦ
before the Lord of us Jesus

ἐν τῇ αὐτοῦ παρουσίᾳ; **20** ὑμεῖς γάρ
in(at) the [2]of him [1]presence? for ye

ἐστε ἡ δόξα ἡμῶν καὶ ἡ χαρά.
are [1]the [2]glory [3]of us [5]and [4]the [6]joy.

3 Διὸ μηκέτι στέγοντες ηὐδοκήσαμεν
Wherefore no longer bearing up we were well pleased

καταλειφθῆναι ἐν Ἀθήναις μόνοι, **2** καὶ
to be left in Athens alone, and

ἐπέμψαμεν Τιμόθεον, τὸν ἀδελφὸν ἡμῶν
we sent Timothy, the brother of us

καὶ συνεργὸν τοῦ θεοῦ ἐν τῷ εὐαγγελίῳ
and fellow-worker – of God in the gospel

τοῦ Χριστοῦ, εἰς τὸ στηρίξαι ὑμᾶς καὶ
– of Christ, *for the* to establish you and

παρακαλέσαι ὑπὲρ τῆς πίστεως ὑμῶν **3** τὸ
to exhort on behalf of the faith of you –

μηδένα σαίνεσθαι ἐν ταῖς θλίψεσιν ταύταις.
no one to be drawn aside[b] by these afflictions.

αὐτοὶ γὰρ οἴδατε ὅτι εἰς τοῦτο κείμεθα·
For [your]selves ye know that to this we are appointed;

your own countrymen the same things those churches suffered from the Jews, 15who killed the Lord Jesus and the prophets and also drove us out. They displease God and are hostile to all men 16in their effort to keep us from speaking to the Gentiles so that they may be saved. In this way they always heap up their sins to the limit. The wrath of God has come upon them at last.[c]

Paul's Longing to See the Thessalonians

17But, brothers, when we were torn away from you for a short time (in person, not in thought), out of our intense longing we made every effort to see you. 18For we wanted to come to you—certainly I, Paul, did, again and again—but Satan stopped us. 19For what is our hope, our joy, or the crown in which we will glory in the presence of our Lord Jesus when he comes? Is it not you? 20Indeed, you are our glory and joy.

Chapter 3

SO when we could stand it no longer, we thought it best to be left by ourselves in Athens. 2We sent Timothy, who is our brother and God's fellow worker[d] in spreading the gospel of Christ, to strengthen and encourage you in your faith, 3so that no one would be unsettled by these trials. You know quite well that we were destined for them. 4In fact,

[c]*16* Or *them fully*
[d]*2* Some manuscripts *brother and fellow worker;* other manuscripts *brother and God's servant*

4For indeed when we
were with you, we *kept* telling you in advance that we
were going to suffer affliction; and so it came to pass,
as you know.
5For this reason, when I
could endure *it* no longer, I
also sent to find out about
your faith, for fear that the
tempter might have tempt-
ed you, and our labor
should be in vain.
6But now that Timothy
has come to us from you,
and has brought us good
news of your faith and love,
and that you always think
kindly of us, longing to see
us just as we also long to
see you,
7for this reason, breth-
ren, in all our distress and
affliction we were comforted about you through your
faith;
8for now we *really* live, if
you stand firm in the Lord.
9For what thanks can we
render to God for you in return for all the joy with
which we rejoice before
our God on your account,
10as we night and day
keep praying most earnestly that we may see your
face, and may complete
what is lacking in your
faith?
11Now may our God and
Father Himself and Jesus
our Lord direct our way to
you;
12and may the Lord cause
you to increase and abound
in love for one another, and
for all men, just as we also
do for you;
13so that He may estab-
lish your hearts unblamable
in holiness before our God
and Father at the coming of

4 καὶ γὰρ ὅτε πρὸς ὑμᾶς ἦμεν,
for even when with you we were,
προελέγομεν ὑμῖν ὅτι μέλλομεν θλίβεσθαι,
we said before to you that we are about to be afflicted,
καθὼς καὶ ἐγένετο καὶ οἴδατε. **5** διὰ
as indeed it happened and ye know. There-
τοῦτο κἀγὼ μηκέτι στέγων ἔπεμψα εἰς
fore I also no longer bearing up sent *for*
τὸ γνῶναι τὴν πίστιν ὑμῶν, μή πως
the to know the faith of you, lest [some]how
ἐπείρασεν ὑμᾶς ὁ πειράζων καὶ εἰς
[2]tempted [4]you [1]the [one] [3]tempting and in
=the tempter
κενὸν γένηται ὁ κόπος ἡμῶν. **6** Ἄρτι
vain became the labour of us. now
δὲ ἐλθόντος Τιμοθέου πρὸς ἡμᾶς ἀφ'
But coming Timothy[a] to us from
=when Timothy came
ὑμῶν καὶ εὐαγγελισαμένου ἡμῖν τὴν πίστιν
you and announcing good news[a] to us [of] the faith
καὶ τὴν ἀγάπην ὑμῶν, καὶ ὅτι ἔχετε
and the love of you, and that ye have
μνείαν ἡμῶν ἀγαθὴν πάντοτε, ἐπιποθοῦντες
[2]remembrance [3]of us [1]good always, longing
ἡμᾶς ἰδεῖν καθάπερ καὶ ἡμεῖς ὑμᾶς,
[2]us [1]to see even as also we you,
7 διὰ τοῦτο παρεκλήθημεν, ἀδελφοί, ἐφ'
therefore we were comforted, brothers, over
ὑμῖν ἐπὶ πάσῃ τῇ ἀνάγκῃ καὶ θλίψει
you on all the distress and affliction
ἡμῶν διὰ τῆς ὑμῶν πίστεως, **8** ὅτι
of us through the [2]of you [1]faith, because
νῦν ζῶμεν ἐὰν ὑμεῖς στήκετε ἐν κυρίῳ.
now we live if ye stand in [the] Lord.
9 τίνα γὰρ εὐχαριστίαν δυνάμεθα τῷ θεῷ
For what thanks are we able – to God
ἀνταποδοῦναι περὶ ὑμῶν ἐπὶ πάσῃ τῇ
to return concerning you over all the
χαρᾷ ᾗ χαίρομεν δι' ὑμᾶς ἔμπροσθεν
joy [with] which we rejoice because of you before
τοῦ θεοῦ ἡμῶν, **10** νυκτὸς καὶ ἡμέρας
the God of us, night and day
ὑπερεκπερισσοῦ δεόμενοι εἰς τὸ ἰδεῖν ὑμῶν
exceedingly petitioning *for the* to see of you
τὸ πρόσωπον καὶ καταρτίσαι τὰ ὑστερήματα
the face and to adjust the shortcomings
τῆς πίστεως ὑμῶν; **11** Αὐτὸς δὲ ὁ θεὸς
of the faith of you? Now [him]self the God
καὶ πατὴρ ἡμῶν καὶ ὁ κύριος ἡμῶν
and Father of us and the Lord of us
Ἰησοῦς κατευθύναι τὴν ὁδὸν ἡμῶν πρὸς
Jesus may he direct the way of us to
ὑμᾶς· **12** ὑμᾶς δὲ ὁ κύριος πλεονάσαι
you; and [4]you [1]the [2]Lord [3]make [5]to abound
καὶ περισσεύσαι τῇ ἀγάπῃ εἰς ἀλλήλους
and to exceed – in love to one another
καὶ εἰς πάντας, καθάπερ καὶ ἡμεῖς
and to all men, even as also we
εἰς ὑμᾶς, **13** εἰς τὸ στηρίξαι ὑμῶν τὰς
to you, *for the* to establish of you the
καρδίας ἀμέμπτους ἐν ἁγιωσύνῃ ἔμπροσθεν
hearts blameless in holiness before
τοῦ θεοῦ καὶ πατρὸς ἡμῶν ἐν τῇ παρουσίᾳ
the God and Father of us in(at) the presence

when we were with you, we
kept telling you that we
would be persecuted. And
it turned out that way, as
you well know. 5For this
reason, when I could stand
it no longer, I sent to find
out about your faith. I was
afraid that in some way the
tempter might have tempt-
ed you and our efforts
might have been useless.

Timothy's Encouraging Report

6But Timothy has just
now come to us from you
and has brought good news
about your faith and love.
He has told us that you always have pleasant memo-
ries of us and that you long
to see us, just as we also
long to see you. 7There-
fore, brothers, in all our
distress and persecution we
were encouraged about you
because of your faith. 8For
now we really live, since
you are standing firm in the
Lord. 9How can we thank
God enough for you in re-
turn for all the joy we have
in the presence of our God
because of you? 10Night
and day we pray most ear-
nestly that we may see you
again and supply what is
lacking in your faith.
11Now may our God and
Father himself and our
Lord Jesus clear the way
for us to come to you.
12May the Lord make your
love increase and overflow
for each other and for everyone else, just as ours
does for you. 13May he
strengthen your hearts so
that you will be blameless
and holy in the presence of
our God and Father when

our Lord Jesus with all His
saints.

Chapter 4

Sanctification and Love

FINALLY then, breth-
ren, we request and
exhort you in the Lord
Jesus, that, as you received
from us *instruction* as to
how you ought to walk and
please God (just as you actually do [c]walk), that you
may excel still more.
2For you know what
commandments we gave
you [d]by *the authority of*
the Lord Jesus.
3For this is the will of
God, your sanctification;
that is, that you abstain
from sexual immorality;
4that each of you know
how to possess his own
[e]vessel in sanctification
and honor,
5not in lustful passion,
like the Gentiles who do
not know God;
6*and* that no man trans-
gress and defraud his
brother in the matter be-
cause the Lord is *the*
avenger in all these things,
just as we also told you before and solemnly warned
you.
7For God has not called
us for the purpose of im-
purity, but in sanctification.
8Consequently, he who
rejects *this* is not rejecting
man but the God who gives
His Holy Spirit to you.
9Now as to the love of
the brethren, you have no
need for *anyone* to write to
you, for you yourselves are
taught by God to love one
another;
10for indeed you do prac-
tice it toward all the brethren who are in all Mace-

[c] Or, *conduct yourselves*
[d] Lit., *through the Lord*
[e] I.e., body; or possibly, wife

τοῦ κυρίου ἡμῶν Ἰησοῦ μετὰ πάντων
of the Lord of us Jesus with all
τῶν ἁγίων αὐτοῦ.
the saints of him.

4 Λοιπὸν οὖν, ἀδελφοί, ἐρωτῶμεν ὑμᾶς
For the rest therefore, brothers, we ask you
καὶ παρακαλοῦμεν ἐν κυρίῳ Ἰησοῦ, ἵνα
and *we* beseech in [the] Lord Jesus, *in order* that
καθὼς παρελάβετε παρ' ἡμῶν τὸ πῶς
as ye received from us *the* how
δεῖ ὑμᾶς περιπατεῖν καὶ ἀρέσκειν θεῷ,
it behoves you to walk and to please God,
καθὼς καὶ περιπατεῖτε, ἵνα περισσεύητε
as indeed ye do walk, *in order* that ye abound
μᾶλλον. **2** οἴδατε γὰρ τίνας παραγγελίας
more. For ye know what injunctions
ἐδώκαμεν ὑμῖν διὰ τοῦ κυρίου Ἰησοῦ.
we gave you through the Lord Jesus.
3 Τοῦτο γάρ ἐστιν θέλημα τοῦ θεοῦ,
For this is [the] will – of God,
ὁ ἁγιασμὸς ὑμῶν, ἀπέχεσθαι ὑμᾶς ἀπὸ
the sanctification of you, to abstain you[b] from
τῆς πορνείας, **4** εἰδέναι ἕκαστον ὑμῶν
– fornication, [3]to know* [1]each one[b] [2]of you
τὸ ἑαυτοῦ σκεῦος κτᾶσθαι ἐν ἁγιασμῷ
[5]the [7]of himself [6]vessel [4]to possess in sanctification
καὶ τιμῇ, **5** μὴ ἐν πάθει ἐπιθυμίας
and honour, not in passion of lust
καθάπερ καὶ τὰ ἔθνη τὰ μὴ εἰδότα
even as indeed the nations – not knowing
τὸν θεόν, **6** τὸ μὴ ὑπερβαίνειν καὶ
God, – not to go beyond and
πλεονεκτεῖν ἐν τῷ πράγματι τὸν ἀδελφὸν
to defraud in the matter the brother
αὐτοῦ, διότι ἔκδικος κύριος περὶ πάντων
of him, because [2][the] avenger [1][the] Lord [is] concerning all
τούτων, καθὼς καὶ προείπαμεν ὑμῖν καὶ
these, as indeed we previously told you and
διεμαρτυράμεθα. **7** οὐ γὰρ ἐκάλεσεν ἡμᾶς
solemnly witnessed. For [4]not [2]called [3]us
ὁ θεὸς ἐπὶ ἀκαθαρσίᾳ ἀλλ' ἐν ἁγιασμῷ.
– [1]God to uncleanness but in sanctification.
8 τοιγαροῦν ὁ ἀθετῶν οὐκ ἄνθρωπον
Wherefore the [one] rejecting [2]not [3]man
ἀθετεῖ ἀλλὰ τὸν θεὸν τὸν καὶ διδόντα
[1]rejects but – God the [one] indeed giving
τὸ πνεῦμα αὐτοῦ τὸ ἅγιον εἰς ὑμᾶς.
the [2]Spirit [3]of him – [1]Holy to you.
9 Περὶ δὲ τῆς φιλαδελφίας οὐ χρείαν
Now concerning – brotherly love not need
ἔχετε γράφειν ὑμῖν· αὐτοὶ γὰρ ὑμεῖς
ye have [for me] to write to you; for [2][your]selves [1]ye
θεοδίδακτοί ἐστε εἰς τὸ ἀγαπᾶν ἀλλήλους·
[4]taught by God [3]are *for the* to love one another;
10 καὶ γὰρ ποιεῖτε αὐτὸ εἰς πάντας
for indeed ye do it toward all
τοὺς ἀδελφοὺς [τοὺς] ἐν ὅλῃ τῇ Μακεδο-
the brothers – in all – Macedo-

* That is, " to be able "; see note on page xviii.

our Lord Jesus comes with
all his holy ones.

Chapter 4

Living to Please God

FINALLY, brothers, we
instructed you how to
live in order to please God,
as in fact you are living.
Now we ask you and urge
you in the Lord Jesus to do
this more and more. 2For
you know what instruc-
tions we gave you by the
authority of the Lord
Jesus.
3It is God's will that you
should be sanctified: that
you should avoid sexual
immorality; 4that each of
you should learn to control
his own body[e] in a way
that is holy and honorable,
5not in passionate lust like
the heathen, who do not
know God; 6and that in this
matter no one should
wrong his brother or take
advantage of him. The
Lord will punish men for all
such sins, as we have al-
ready told you and warned
you. 7For God did not call
us to be impure, but to live
a holy life. 8Therefore, he
who rejects this instruction
does not reject man but
God, who gives you his
Holy Spirit.
9Now about brotherly
love we do not need to
write to you, for you yourselves have been taught by
God to love each other.
10And in fact, you do love
all the brothers throughout

[e]4 Or *learn to live with his own wife*; or *learn to acquire a wife*

donia. But we urge you,
brethren, to excel still
more,
11 and to make it your ambition to lead a quiet life
and attend to your own
business and work with
your hands, just as we commanded you;
12 so that you may behave
properly toward outsiders
and not be in any need.

Those Who Died in Christ

13 But we do not want you
to be uninformed, breth-
ren, about those who are
asleep, that you may not
grieve, as do the rest who
have no hope.
14 For if we believe that
Jesus died and rose again,
even so God will bring with
Him those who have fallen
asleep in Jesus.
15 For this we say to you
by the word of the Lord,
that we who are alive, and
remain until the coming of
the Lord, shall not precede
those who have fallen
asleep.
16 For the Lord Himself
will descend from heaven
with a shout, with the voice
of *the* archangel, and with
the trumpet of God; and the
dead in Christ shall rise
first.
17 Then we who are alive
and remain shall be caught
up together with them in
the clouds to meet the Lord
in the air, and thus we shall
always be with the Lord.
18 Therefore comfort one
another with these words.

νίᾳ. Παρακαλοῦμεν δὲ ὑμᾶς, ἀδελφοί,
nia. But we exhort you, brothers,
περισσεύειν μᾶλλον, 11 καὶ φιλοτιμεῖσθαι
to abound more, and to strive eagerly
ἡσυχάζειν καὶ πράσσειν τὰ ἴδια καὶ
to be quiet and to practise the (your) own things and
ἐργάζεσθαι ταῖς χερσὶν ὑμῶν, καθὼς ὑμῖν
to work with the hands of you, as [2]you
παρηγγείλαμεν, 12 ἵνα περιπατῆτε εὐσχη-
[1]we enjoined, in order that ye may walk becom-
μόνως πρὸς τοὺς ἔξω καὶ μηδενὸς
ingly toward the [ones] outside and [3]of nothing
χρείαν ἔχητε.
[2]need [1]ye may have.

13 Οὐ θέλομεν δὲ ὑμᾶς ἀγνοεῖν, ἀδελφοί,
Now we do not wish you to be ignorant, brothers,
περὶ τῶν κοιμωμένων, ἵνα μὴ λυπῆσθε
concerning the [ones] sleeping, lest ye grieve
καθὼς καὶ οἱ λοιποὶ οἱ μὴ ἔχοντες
as indeed the rest – not having
ἐλπίδα. 14 εἰ γὰρ πιστεύομεν ὅτι Ἰησοῦς
hope. For if we believe that Jesus
ἀπέθανεν καὶ ἀνέστη, οὕτως καὶ ὁ θεὸς
died and rose again, so also – [5]God
τοὺς κοιμηθέντας διὰ τοῦ Ἰησοῦ ἄξει
[1]the [ones] [2]having slept [3]through – [4]Jesus will bring
σὺν αὐτῷ. 15 Τοῦτο γὰρ ὑμῖν λέγομεν
with him. For this to you we say
ἐν λόγῳ κυρίου, ὅτι ἡμεῖς οἱ ζῶντες
by a word of [the] Lord, that we the living [ones]
οἱ περιλειπόμενοι εἰς τὴν παρουσίαν τοῦ
– remaining to the presence of the
κυρίου οὐ μὴ φθάσωμεν τοὺς κοιμηθέντας·
Lord by no means may precede the [ones] having slept;
16 ὅτι αὐτὸς ὁ κύριος ἐν κελεύσματι,
because [2][him]self [1]the [3]Lord with a word of command,
ἐν φωνῇ ἀρχαγγέλου καὶ ἐν σάλπιγγι
with a voice of an archangel and with a trumpet
θεοῦ, καταβήσεται ἀπ' οὐρανοῦ, καὶ οἱ
of God, will descend from heaven, and the
νεκροὶ ἐν Χριστῷ ἀναστήσονται πρῶτον,
dead in Christ will rise again first*ly*,
17 ἔπειτα ἡμεῖς οἱ ζῶντες οἱ περιλειπόμενοι
then we the living [ones] – remaining
ἅμα σὺν αὐτοῖς ἁρπαγησόμεθα ἐν νεφέλαις
together with them shall be seized in clouds
εἰς ἀπάντησιν τοῦ κυρίου εἰς ἀέρα·
to a meeting of the Lord in air;
καὶ οὕτως πάντοτε σὺν κυρίῳ ἐσόμεθα.
and so always with [the] Lord we shall be.
18 Ὥστε παρακαλεῖτε ἀλλήλους ἐν τοῖς λόγοις
Therefore comfort ye one another with – words
τούτοις.
these.

Macedonia. Yet we urge
you, brothers, to do so
more and more.
11 Make it your ambition
to lead a quiet life, to mind
your own business and to
work with your hands, just
as we told you, 12 so that
your daily life may win the
respect of outsiders and so
that you will not be dependent on anybody.

The Coming of the Lord

13 Brothers, we do not
want you to be ignorant
about those who fall
asleep, or to grieve like the
rest of men, who have no
hope. 14 We believe that
Jesus died and rose again
and so we believe that God
will bring with Jesus those
who have fallen asleep in
him. 15 According to the
Lord's own word, we tell
you that we who are still
alive, who are left till the
coming of the Lord, will
certainly not precede those
who have fallen asleep.
16 For the Lord himself will
come down from heaven,
with a loud command, with
the voice of the archangel
and with the trumpet call of
God, and the dead in Christ
will rise first. 17 After that,
we who are still alive and
are left will be caught up
together with them in the
clouds to meet the Lord in
the air. And so we will be
with the Lord forever.
18 Therefore encourage
each other with these
words.

Chapter 5

The Day of the Lord

NOW as to the times and the epochs, brethren, you have no need of anything to be written to you.

2For you yourselves know full well that the day of the Lord will come just like a thief in the night.

3While they are saying, "Peace and safety!" then destruction will come upon them suddenly like birth pangs upon a woman with child; and they shall not escape.

4But you, brethren, are not in darkness, that the day should overtake you like a thief;

5for you are all sons of light and sons of day. We are not of night nor of darkness;

6so then let us not sleep as others do, but let us be alert and [f] sober.

7For those who sleep do their sleeping at night, and those who get drunk get drunk at night.

8But since we are of *the* day, let us be [f]sober, having put on the breastplate of faith and love, and as a helmet, the hope of salvation.

9For God has not destined us for wrath, but for obtaining salvation through our Lord Jesus Christ,

10who died for us, that whether we are awake or asleep, we may live together with Him.

11Therefore encourage one another, and build up one another, just as you also are doing.

Christian Conduct

12But we request of you, brethren, that you appreciate those who diligently labor among you, and have charge over you in the Lord and give you instruction,

13and that you esteem them very highly in love be-

[f]Or, *self-controlled*

---

5 Περὶ δὲ τῶν χρόνων καὶ τῶν καιρῶν,
But concerning the times and the seasons,

ἀδελφοί, οὐ χρείαν ἔχετε ὑμῖν γράφεσθαι·
brothers, 2not 3need 1ye have 5to you 4to be written;

2 αὐτοὶ γὰρ ἀκριβῶς οἴδατε ὅτι ἡμέρα
for 2[your]selves 3accurately 1ye know that [the] day

κυρίου ὡς κλέπτης ἐν νυκτὶ οὕτως
of [the] Lord as a thief at night so

ἔρχεται. 3 ὅταν λέγωσιν· εἰρήνη καὶ
it comes. Whenever they say : Peace and

ἀσφάλεια, τότε αἰφνίδιος αὐτοῖς ἐφίσταται
safety, then 1sudden 4them 3comes on

ὄλεθρος ὥσπερ ἡ ὠδὶν τῇ ἐν γαστρὶ
2destruction as the birth pang to the pregnant

ἐχούσῃ, καὶ οὐ μὴ ἐκφύγωσιν. 4 ὑμεῖς
woman,† and by no means may they escape. ye

δέ, ἀδελφοί, οὐκ ἐστὲ ἐν σκότει, ἵνα
But, brothers, are not in darkness, in order that

ἡ ἡμέρα ὑμᾶς ὡς κλέπτης καταλάβῃ·
the day you as a thief should overtake;

5 πάντες γὰρ ὑμεῖς υἱοὶ φωτός ἐστε
for all ye 2sons 3of light 1are

καὶ υἱοὶ ἡμέρας. Οὐκ ἐσμὲν νυκτὸς
and sons of [the] day. We are not of [the] night

οὐδὲ σκότους· 6 ἄρα οὖν μὴ καθεύδωμεν
nor of darkness; therefore let us not sleep

ὡς οἱ λοιποί, ἀλλὰ γρηγορῶμεν καὶ
as the rest, but let us watch and

νήφωμεν. 7 οἱ γὰρ καθεύδοντες νυκτὸς
be sober. For the [ones] sleeping by night

καθεύδουσιν, καὶ οἱ μεθυσκόμενοι νυκτὸς
sleep, and the [ones] being drunk by night

μεθύουσιν· 8 ἡμεῖς δὲ ἡμέρας ὄντες
are drunk; but we of [the] day being

νήφωμεν, ἐνδυσάμενοι θώρακα πίστεως καὶ
let us be sober, putting on a breastplate of faith and

ἀγάπης καὶ περικεφαλαίαν ἐλπίδα σωτηρίας·
of love and a helmet hope of salvation;

9 ὅτι οὐκ ἔθετο ἡμᾶς ὁ θεὸς εἰς ὀργὴν
because 2did not appoint 3us – 1God to wrath

ἀλλὰ εἰς περιποίησιν σωτηρίας διὰ τοῦ
but to obtainment of salvation through the

κυρίου ἡμῶν Ἰησοῦ Χριστοῦ, 10 τοῦ
Lord of us Jesus Christ, the

ἀποθανόντος περὶ ἡμῶν, ἵνα εἴτε γρηγορ-
[one] having died concerning us, in order that whether we

ῶμεν εἴτε καθεύδωμεν ἅμα σὺν αὐτῷ
watch or *we sleep* 2together 3with 4him

ζήσωμεν. 11 Διὸ παρακαλεῖτε ἀλλήλους
1we may live. Therefore comfort ye one another

καὶ οἰκοδομεῖτε εἷς τὸν ἕνα, καθὼς καὶ
and edify ye one the one(other), as indeed

ποιεῖτε.
ye do.

12 Ἐρωτῶμεν δὲ ὑμᾶς, ἀδελφοί, εἰδέναι
Now we ask you, brothers, to know

τοὺς κοπιῶντας ἐν ὑμῖν καὶ προϊσταμένους
the [ones] labouring among you and taking the lead

ὑμῶν ἐν κυρίῳ καὶ νουθετοῦντας ὑμᾶς,
of you in [the] Lord and admonishing you,

13 καὶ ἡγεῖσθαι αὐτοὺς ὑπερεκπερισσῶς
and consider them most exceedingly

Chapter 5

NOW, brothers, about times and dates we do not need to write to you,
2for you know very well that the day of the Lord will come like a thief in the night.
3While people are saying, "Peace and safety," destruction will come on them suddenly, as labor pains on a pregnant woman, and they will not escape.
4But you, brothers, are not in darkness so that this day should surprise you like a thief.
5You are all sons of the light and sons of the day. We do not belong to the night or to the darkness.
6So then, let us not be like others, who are asleep, but let us be alert and self-controlled.
7For those who sleep, sleep at night, and those who get drunk, get drunk at night.
8But since we belong to the day, let us be self-controlled, putting on faith and love as a breastplate, and the hope of salvation as a helmet.
9For God did not appoint us to suffer wrath but to receive salvation through our Lord Jesus Christ.
10He died for us so that, whether we are awake or asleep, we may live together with him.
11Therefore encourage one another and build each other up, just as in fact you are doing.

Final Instructions

12Now we ask you, brothers, to respect those who work hard among you, who are over you in the Lord and who admonish you.
13Hold them in the highest regard in love because of

cause of their work. Live in
peace with one another.
14And we urge you,
brethren, admonish the unruly, encourage the faint-
hearted, help the weak, be
patient with all men.
15See that no one repays
another with evil for evil,
but always seek after that
which is good for one an-
other and for all men.
16Rejoice always;
17pray without ceasing;
18in everything give
thanks; for this is God's
will for you in Christ Jesus.
19Do not quench the
Spirit;
20do not despise prophet-
ic [g]utterances.
21But examine everything
carefully; hold fast to that
which is good;
22abstain from every
[h]form of evil.
23Now may the God of
peace Himself sanctify you
entirely; and may your
spirit and soul and body be
preserved complete, with-
out blame at the coming of
our Lord Jesus Christ.
24Faithful is He who calls
you, and He also will bring
it to pass.
25Brethren, pray for us[i].
26Greet all the brethren
with a holy kiss.
27I adjure you by the Lord
to have this letter read to all
the brethren.
28The grace of our Lord
Jesus Christ be with you.

ἐν ἀγάπῃ διὰ τὸ ἔργον αὐτῶν. εἰρηνεύετε
in love because of the work of them. Be at peace

ἐν ἑαυτοῖς. **14** Παρακαλοῦμεν δὲ ὑμᾶς,
among yourselves. And we exhort you,

ἀδελφοί, νουθετεῖτε τοὺς ἀτάκτους, παραμυθεῖσθε
brothers, admonish the idle, console

τοὺς ὀλιγοψύχους, ἀντέχεσθε τῶν
the faint-hearted, hold on to the [ones]

ἀσθενῶν, μακροθυμεῖτε πρὸς πάντας.
being weak, be longsuffering with all men.

15 ὁρᾶτε μή τις κακὸν ἀντὶ κακοῦ τινι
See lest anyone [3]evil [4]instead of [5]evil [2]to anyone

ἀποδῷ, ἀλλὰ πάντοτε τὸ ἀγαθὸν διώκετε
[1]returns, but always [2]the [3]good [1]follow ye

εἰς ἀλλήλους καὶ εἰς πάντας. **16** Πάντοτε
in regard to one another and in regard to all men. Always

χαίρετε, **17** ἀδιαλείπτως προσεύχεσθε, **18** ἐν
rejoice ye, unceasingly pray, in

παντὶ εὐχαριστεῖτε· τοῦτο γὰρ θέλημα
everything give thanks; for this [is] [the] will

θεοῦ ἐν Χριστῷ Ἰησοῦ εἰς ὑμᾶς. **19** τὸ
of God in Christ Jesus in regard to you. The

πνεῦμα μὴ σβέννυτε, **20** προφητείας μὴ
Spirit do not quench, prophecies not

ἐξουθενεῖτε· **21** πάντα δὲ δοκιμάζετε, τὸ
despise; and [2]all things [1]prove, the

καλὸν κατέχετε· **22** ἀπὸ παντὸς εἴδους
good hold fast; from every form

πονηροῦ ἀπέχεσθε. **23** Αὐτὸς δὲ ὁ θεὸς
of evil abstain. And [4][him]self [1]the [2]God

τῆς εἰρήνης ἁγιάσαι ὑμᾶς ὁλοτελεῖς, καὶ
– [3]of peace may he sanctify you complete, and

ὁλόκληρον ὑμῶν τὸ πνεῦμα καὶ ἡ ψυχὴ
entire of you the spirit and the soul

καὶ τὸ σῶμα ἀμέμπτως ἐν τῇ παρουσίᾳ
and the body blamelessly in(at) the presence

τοῦ κυρίου ἡμῶν Ἰησοῦ Χριστοῦ τηρηθείη.
of the Lord of us Jesus Christ may be kept.

24 πιστὸς ὁ καλῶν ὑμᾶς, ὃς καὶ ποιήσει.
Faithful [is] the [one] calling you, who indeed will do [it].

25 Ἀδελφοί, προσεύχεσθε [καὶ] περὶ ἡμῶν.
Brothers, pray ye also concerning us.

26 Ἀσπάσασθε τοὺς ἀδελφοὺς πάντας
Greet ye [2]the [3]brothers [1]all

ἐν φιλήματι ἁγίῳ. **27** Ἐνορκίζω ὑμᾶς τὸν
with kiss a holy. I adjure you [by] the

κύριον ἀναγνωσθῆναι τὴν ἐπιστολὴν πᾶσιν
Lord [3]to be read [1]the(this) [2]epistle to all

τοῖς ἀδελφοῖς.
the brothers.

28 Ἡ χάρις τοῦ κυρίου ἡμῶν Ἰησοῦ
The grace of the Lord of us Jesus

Χριστοῦ μεθ' ὑμῶν.
Christ [be] with you.

their work. Live in peace
with each other. 14And we
urge you, brothers, warn
those who are idle, encourage the timid, help the
weak, be patient with ev-
eryone. 15Make sure that
nobody pays back wrong
for wrong, but always try to
be kind to each other and to
everyone else.
16Be joyful always; 17pray
continually; 18give thanks
in all circumstances, for
this is God's will for you in
Christ Jesus.
19Do not put out the Spirit's fire; 20do not treat
prophecies with contempt.
21Test everything. Hold on
to the good. 22Avoid every
kind of evil.
23May God himself, the
God of peace, sanctify you
through and through. May
your whole spirit, soul and
body be kept blameless at
the coming of our Lord
Jesus Christ. 24The one
who calls you is faithful and
he will do it.
25Brothers, pray for us.
26Greet all the brothers
with a holy kiss. 27I charge
you before the Lord to
have this letter read to all
the brothers.
28The grace of our Lord
Jesus Christ be with you.

[g] Or, *gifts*
[h] Or, *appearance*
[i] Some mss. add *also*

2 Thessalonians

Chapter 1

Thanksgiving for Faith and Perseverance

PAUL and Silvanus and Timothy to the church of the Thessalonians in God our Father and the Lord Jesus Christ:

2Grace to you and peace from God the Father and the Lord Jesus Christ.

3We ought always to give thanks to God for you, brethren, as is *only* fitting, because your faith is greatly enlarged, and the love of each one of you toward one another grows *ever* greater;

4therefore, we ourselves speak proudly of you among the churches of God for your perseverance and faith in the midst of all your persecutions and afflictions which you endure.

5*This is* a plain indication of God's righteous judgment so that you may be considered worthy of the kingdom of God, for which indeed you are suffering.

6For after all it is *only* just for God to repay with affliction those who afflict you,

7and *to give* relief to you who are afflicted and to us as well when the Lord Jesus shall be revealed from heaven with His mighty angels in flaming fire,

8dealing out retribution to those who do not know God and to those who do not obey the gospel of our Lord Jesus.

9And these will pay the penalty of eternal destruction, away from the presence of the Lord and from the glory of His power,

10when He comes to be

ΠΡΟΣ ΘΕΣΣΑΛΟΝΙΚΕΙΣ Β

To Thessalonians 2

1 Παῦλος καὶ Σιλουανὸς καὶ Τιμόθεος
Paul and Silvanus and Timothy

τῇ ἐκκλησίᾳ Θεσσαλονικέων ἐν θεῷ πατρὶ
to the church of [the] Thessalonians in God Father

ἡμῶν καὶ κυρίῳ Ἰησοῦ Χριστῷ· **2** χάρις
of us and [the] Lord Jesus Christ: Grace [be]

ὑμῖν καὶ εἰρήνη ἀπὸ θεοῦ πατρὸς καὶ
to you and peace from God [the] Father and

κυρίου Ἰησοῦ Χριστοῦ.
[the] Lord Jesus Christ.

3 Εὐχαριστεῖν ὀφείλομεν τῷ θεῷ πάντοτε
To give thanks we ought – to God always

περὶ ὑμῶν, ἀδελφοί, καθὼς ἄξιόν ἐστιν,
concerning you, brothers, as [2]meet [1]it is,

ὅτι ὑπεραυξάνει ἡ πίστις ὑμῶν καὶ
because [4]grows exceedingly [1]the [2]faith [3]of you and

πλεονάζει ἡ ἀγάπη ἑνὸς ἑκάστου πάντων
[6]increases [1]the [2]love [4]one [3]of each [5]all

ὑμῶν εἰς ἀλλήλους, **4** ὥστε αὐτοὺς ἡμᾶς
[5]of you [7]to [8]one another, so as [our]selves us
=so that we ourselves boast

ἐν ὑμῖν ἐγκαυχᾶσθαι ἐν ταῖς ἐκκλησίαις
in you to boast[b] in the churches
in you

τοῦ θεοῦ ὑπὲρ τῆς ὑπομονῆς ὑμῶν καὶ
– of God for the [1]endurance [4]of you [3]and

πίστεως ἐν πᾶσιν τοῖς διωγμοῖς ὑμῶν
[2]faith in all the persecutions of you

καὶ ταῖς θλίψεσιν αἷς ἀνέχεσθε, **5** ἔνδειγμα
and the afflictions which ye endure, a plain token

τῆς δικαίας κρίσεως τοῦ θεοῦ, εἰς τὸ
of the just judgment – of God, for the

καταξιωθῆναι ὑμᾶς τῆς βασιλείας τοῦ
to be accounted worthy you[b] of the kingdom –
=so that ye may be accounted worthy

θεοῦ, ὑπὲρ ἧς καὶ πάσχετε, **6** εἴπερ
of God, on behalf of which indeed ye suffer, since

δίκαιον παρὰ θεῷ ἀνταποδοῦναι τοῖς
[it is] a just thing with God to repay [2]to the [ones]

θλίβουσιν ὑμᾶς θλῖψιν **7** καὶ ὑμῖν τοῖς
[3]afflicting [4]you [1]affliction and [4]to you [5]the [ones]

θλιβομένοις ἄνεσιν μεθ' ἡμῶν, ἐν τῇ
[6]being afflicted [1]rest [2]with [3]us, at the

ἀποκαλύψει τοῦ κυρίου Ἰησοῦ ἀπ'
revelation of the Lord Jesus from

οὐρανοῦ μετ' ἀγγέλων δυνάμεως αὐτοῦ
heaven with angels of power of him

8 ἐν πυρὶ φλογός, διδόντος ἐκδίκησιν τοῖς
in fire of flame, giving full vengeance to the [ones]

μὴ εἰδόσιν θεὸν καὶ τοῖς μὴ ὑπακούουσιν
not knowing God and to the [ones] not obeying

τῷ εὐαγγελίῳ τοῦ κυρίου ἡμῶν Ἰησοῦ,
the gospel of the Lord of us Jesus,

9 οἵτινες δίκην τίσουσιν ὄλεθρον αἰώνιον
who [2][the] penalty [1]will pay [4]destruction [3]eternal

ἀπὸ προσώπου τοῦ κυρίου καὶ ἀπὸ
from [the] face of the Lord and from

τῆς δόξης τῆς ἰσχύος αὐτοῦ, **10** ὅταν
the glory of the strength of him, whenever

2 Thessalonians

Chapter 1

PAUL, Silas[a] and Timothy,

To the church of the Thessalonians in God our Father and the Lord Jesus Christ:

2Grace and peace to you from God the Father and the Lord Jesus Christ.

Thanksgiving and Prayer

3We ought always to thank God for you, brothers, and rightly so, because your faith is growing more and more, and the love every one of you has for each other is increasing. 4Therefore, among God's churches we boast about your perseverance and faith in all the persecutions and trials you are enduring.

5All this is evidence that God's judgment is right, and as a result you will be counted worthy of the kingdom of God, for which you are suffering. 6God is just: He will pay back trouble to those who trouble you 7and give relief to you who are troubled, and to us as well. This will happen when the Lord Jesus is revealed from heaven in blazing fire with his powerful angels. 8He will punish those who do not know God and do not obey the gospel of our Lord Jesus. 9They will be punished with everlasting destruction and shut out from the presence of the Lord and from the majesty of his power 10on the day he

[a]*1* Greek *Silvanus*, a variant of *Silas*

glorified in His saints on
that day, and to be mar-
veled at among all who
have believed—for our testimony to you was be-
lieved.

11To this end also we pray
for you always that our
God may count you worthy
of your calling, and fulfill
every desire for goodness
and the work of faith with
power;

12in order that the name
of our Lord Jesus may be
glorified in you, and you in
Him, according to the
grace of our God and the
Lord Jesus Christ.

ἔλθῃ ἐνδοξασθῆναι ἐν τοῖς ἁγίοις αὐτοῦ
he comes to be glorified in the saints of him
καὶ θαυμασθῆναι ἐν πᾶσιν τοῖς πιστεύσασιν,
and to be admired in all the [ones] having believed,
ὅτι ἐπιστεύθη τὸ μαρτύριον ἡμῶν ἐφ'
be-cause [4]was believed [1]the [2]testimony [3]of us [5]to
ὑμᾶς, ἐν τῇ ἡμέρᾳ ἐκείνῃ. 11 Εἰς ὃ
[6]you, in that day. For which
καὶ προσευχόμεθα πάντοτε περὶ ὑμῶν,
indeed we pray always concerning you,
ἵνα ὑμᾶς ἀξιώσῃ τῆς κλήσεως ὁ θεὸς
in order that [6]you [4]may [5]deem [7]worthy [8]of the [9]calling [1]the [2]God
ἡμῶν καὶ πληρώσῃ πᾶσαν εὐδοκίαν
[3]of us and may fulfil every good pleasure
ἀγαθωσύνης καὶ ἔργον πίστεως ἐν δυνάμει,
of goodness and work of faith in power,
12 ὅπως ἐνδοξασθῇ τὸ ὄνομα τοῦ κυρίου
so as [7]may be glorified [1]the [2]name [3]of the [4]Lord
ἡμῶν Ἰησοῦ ἐν ὑμῖν, καὶ ὑμεῖς ἐν
[5]of us [6]Jesus in you, and ye in
αὐτῷ, κατὰ τὴν χάριν τοῦ θεοῦ ἡμῶν
him, according to the grace of the [1]God [4]of us
καὶ κυρίου Ἰησοῦ Χριστοῦ.
[2]and [3]Lord Jesus Christ.

comes to be glorified in his
holy people and to be marveled at among all those
who have believed. This includes you, because you
believed our testimony to
you.

11With this in mind, we
constantly pray for you,
that our God may count
you worthy of his calling,
and that by his power he
may fulfill every good purpose of yours and every act
prompted by your faith.
12We pray this so that the
name of our Lord Jesus
may be glorified in you, and
you in him, according to
the grace of our God and
the Lord Jesus Christ.[b]

Chapter 2

Man of Lawlessness

NOW we request you,
brethren, with regard
to the coming of our Lord
Jesus Christ, and our gathering together to Him,

2that you may not be
quickly shaken from your
composure or be disturbed
either by a spirit or a message or a letter as if from
us, to the effect that the day
of the Lord has come.

3Let no one in any way
deceive you, for *it will not
come* unless the [a]apostasy
comes first, and the man of
lawlessness is revealed, the
son of destruction,

4who opposes and exalts
himself above every so-
called god or object of worship, so that he takes his
seat in the temple of God,
displaying himself as being
God.

5Do you not remember
that while I was still with
you, I was telling you these
things?

6And you know what re-
strains him now, so that in

2 Ἐρωτῶμεν δὲ ὑμᾶς, ἀδελφοί, ὑπὲρ
Now we request you, brothers, by
τῆς παρουσίας τοῦ κυρίου [ἡμῶν] Ἰησοῦ
the presence of the Lord of us Jesus
Χριστοῦ καὶ ἡμῶν ἐπισυναγωγῆς ἐπ' αὐτόν,
Christ and [2]of us [1]gathering together to him,
2 εἰς τὸ μὴ ταχέως σαλευθῆναι ὑμᾶς
– – not quickly to be shaken you[b]
ἀπὸ τοῦ νοὸς μηδὲ θροεῖσθαι, μήτε
from the(your) mind nor to be disturbed, neither
διὰ πνεύματος μήτε διὰ λόγου μήτε
through a spirit nor through speech nor
δι' ἐπιστολῆς ὡς δι' ἡμῶν, ὡς ὅτι
through an epistle as through us, as that
ἐνέστηκεν ἡ ἡμέρα τοῦ κυρίου. 3 μή
[5]is come [1]the [2]day [3]of the [4]Lord. Not
τις ὑμᾶς ἐξαπατήσῃ κατὰ μηδένα τρόπον·
anyone [2]you [1]may deceive by(in) no(any) way;
ὅτι ἐὰν μὴ ἔλθῃ ἡ ἀποστασία πρῶτον
because unless [3]comes [1]the [2]apostasy [4]first*ly*
καὶ ἀποκαλυφθῇ ὁ ἄνθρωπος τῆς ἀνομίας,
and [4]is revealed [1]the [2]man – [3]of lawlessness,
ὁ υἱὸς τῆς ἀπωλείας, 4 ὁ ἀντικείμενος
the son – of perdition, the [one] setting against
καὶ ὑπεραιρόμενος ἐπὶ πάντα λεγόμενον
and exalting himself over everything *being* called
θεὸν ἢ σέβασμα, ὥστε αὐτὸν εἰς τὸν
God or object of worship, so as him in the
ναὸν τοῦ θεοῦ καθίσαι, ἀποδεικνύντα ἑαυ-
shrine – of God to sit,[b] showing him-
τὸν ὅτι ἐστὶν θεός. 5 Οὐ μνημονεύετε
self that he is a god. Do ye not remember
ὅτι ἔτι ὢν πρὸς ὑμᾶς ταῦτα ἔλεγον
that yet being with you [2]these things [1]I used to tell
ὑμῖν; 6 καὶ νῦν τὸ κατέχον οἴδατε,
[3]you? and now the [thing] restraining ye know,

Chapter 2

The Man of Lawlessness

CONCERNING the
coming of our Lord
Jesus Christ and our being
gathered to him, we ask
you, brothers, 2not to become easily unsettled or
alarmed by some prophe-
cy, report or letter sup-
posed to have come from
us, saying that the day of
the Lord has already come.
3Don't let anyone deceive
you in any way, for that
day will not come until the
rebellion occurs and the
man of lawlessness[c] is revealed, the man doomed to
destruction. 4He will op-
pose and will exalt himself
over everything that is
called God or is worshiped,
so that he sets himself up in
God's temple, proclaiming
himself to be God.

5Don't you remember
that when I was with you I
used to tell you these
things? 6And now you
know what is holding him

[a]Or, *falling away* from the faith

[b]12 Or *God and Lord, Jesus Christ*
[c]3 Some manuscripts *sin*

his time he may be re-
vealed.
7For the mystery of law-
lessness is already at work;
only he who now restrains
will do so until he is taken
out of the way.
8And then that lawless
one will be revealed whom
the Lord will slay with the
breath of His mouth and
bring to an end by the appearance of His coming;
9*that is,* the one whose
coming is in accord with
the activity of Satan, with
all power and signs and
false wonders,
10and with all the decep-
tion of wickedness for
those who perish, because
they did not receive the
love of the truth so as to be
saved.
11And for this reason God
will send upon them a
deluding influence so that
they might believe what is
false,
12in order that they all
may be judged who did not
believe the truth, but took
pleasure in wickedness.
13But we should always
give thanks to God for you,
brethren beloved by the
Lord, because God has
chosen you [b]from the beginning for salvation
through sanctification by
the Spirit and faith in the
truth.
14And it was for this He
called you through our gospel, that you may gain the
glory of our Lord Jesus
Christ.
15So then, brethren, stand
firm and hold to the traditions which you were
taught, whether by word *of
mouth* or by letter from us.
16Now may our Lord
Jesus Christ Himself and
God our Father, who has
loved us and given us eter-

[b] Some ancient mss. read *first fruits*

εἰς τὸ ἀποκαλυφθῆναι αὐτὸν ἐν τῷ
for *the* [2]to be revealed [1]him[b] in the
αὐτοῦ καιρῷ. 7 τὸ γὰρ μυστήριον ἤδη
[3]of him [1]time. For the mystery [2]already
ἐνεργεῖται τῆς ἀνομίας· μόνον ὁ κατέχων
[3]operates – [1]of lawless-ness; only the restraining [there is] [one]
ἄρτι ἕως ἐκ μέσου γένηται. 8 καὶ τότε
just now until [3]out of [4][the] midst [1]it comes. And then
ἀποκαλυφθήσεται ὁ ἄνομος, ὃν ὁ κύριος
will be revealed the lawless one, whom the Lord
[Ἰησοῦς] ἀνελεῖ τῷ πνεύματι τοῦ στό-
Jesus will destroy by the spirit of the mouth
ματος αὐτοῦ καὶ καταργήσει τῇ ἐπιφανείᾳ
of him and bring to nothing by the outshining
τῆς παρουσίας αὐτοῦ, 9 οὗ ἔστιν ἡ
of the presence of him, of whom [3]is [1]the
παρουσία κατ’ ἐνέργειαν τοῦ σατανᾶ ἐν
[2]presence according to [the] operation – of Satan with
πάσῃ δυνάμει καὶ σημείοις καὶ τέρασιν
all power and signs and wonders
ψεύδους 10 καὶ ἐν πάσῃ ἀπάτῃ ἀδικίας
of a lie and with all deceit of unright-eousness
τοῖς ἀπολλυμένοις, ἀνθ’ ὧν τὴν ἀγάπην
in the [ones] perishing, because the love
τῆς ἀληθείας οὐκ ἐδέξαντο εἰς τὸ σωθῆναι
of the truth they received not for *the* [2]to be saved
αὐτούς. 11 καὶ διὰ τοῦτο πέμπει αὐτοῖς
[1]them.[b] And therefore [2]sends [3]to them
ὁ θεὸς ἐνέργειαν πλάνης εἰς τὸ πιστεῦσαι
– [1]God an operation of error for *the* [2]to believe
αὐτοὺς τῷ ψεύδει, 12 ἵνα κριθῶσιν πάντες
[1]them[b] the lie, in or-der that [10]may be judged [1]all
οἱ μὴ πιστεύσαντες τῇ ἀληθείᾳ ἀλλὰ
[2]the [ones] [3]not [4]having believed [5]the [6]truth [7]but
εὐδοκήσαντες τῇ ἀδικίᾳ.
[8]having had pleasure – [9]in unrighteousness.
13 Ἡμεῖς δὲ ὀφείλομεν εὐχαριστεῖν τῷ
But we ought to thank –
θεῷ πάντοτε περὶ ὑμῶν, ἀδελφοὶ ἠγαπη-
God always concerning you, brothers having been
μένοι ὑπὸ κυρίου, ὅτι εἵλατο ὑμᾶς ὁ
loved by [the] Lord, because [2]chose [3]you –
θεὸς ἀπαρχὴν εἰς σωτηρίαν ἐν ἁγιασμῷ
[1]God firstfruit to salvation by sanctification
πνεύματος καὶ πίστει ἀληθείας, 14 εἰς
of spirit and faith of(in) [the] truth, to
ὃ καὶ ἐκάλεσεν ὑμᾶς διὰ τοῦ εὐαγγελίου
which also he called you through the gospel
ἡμῶν, εἰς περιποίησιν δόξης τοῦ κυρίου
of us, to obtainment of [the] glory of the Lord
ἡμῶν Ἰησοῦ Χριστοῦ. 15 Ἄρα οὖν,
of us Jesus Christ. So then,
ἀδελφοί, στήκετε, καὶ κρατεῖτε τὰς
brothers, stand, and hold the
παραδόσεις ἃς ἐδιδάχθητε εἴτε διὰ λόγου
traditions which ye were taught either through speech
εἴτε δι’ ἐπιστολῆς ἡμῶν. 16 Αὐτὸς δὲ
or through an epistle of us. And [6][him]self
ὁ κύριος ἡμῶν Ἰησοῦς Χριστὸς καὶ
[1]the [2]Lord [3]of us [4]Jesus [5]Christ and
ὁ θεὸς ὁ πατὴρ ἡμῶν, ὁ ἀγαπήσας
the God the Father of us, the [one] having loved

back, so that he may be revealed at the proper time.
7For the secret power of
lawlessness is already at
work; but the one who now
holds it back will continue
to do so till he is taken out
of the way. 8And then the
lawless one will be re-
vealed, whom the Lord
Jesus will overthrow with
the breath of his mouth and
destroy by the splendor of
his coming. 9The coming of
the lawless one will be in
accordance with the work
of Satan displayed in all
kinds of counterfeit miracles, signs and wonders,
10and in every sort of evil
that deceives those who are
perishing. They perish because they refused to love
the truth and so be saved.
11For this reason God
sends them a powerful de-
lusion so that they will believe the lie 12and so that all
will be condemned who
have not believed the truth
but have delighted in wickedness.

Stand Firm

13But we ought always to
thank God for you, broth-
ers loved by the Lord, because from the beginning
God chose you[d] to be
saved through the sanctifying work of the Spirit and
through belief in the truth.
14He called you to this
through our gospel, that
you might share in the glory
of our Lord Jesus Christ.
15So then, brothers, stand
firm and hold to the teachings[e] we passed on to you,
whether by word of mouth
or by letter.
16May our Lord Jesus
Christ himself and God our
Father, who loved us and
by his grace gave us eternal

[d] 13 Some manuscripts *because God chose you as his firstfruits*
[e] 15 Or *traditions*

nal comfort and good hope
by grace,
17 comfort and strengthen
your hearts in every good
work and word.

Chapter 3

Exhortation

FINALLY, brethren,
pray for us that the
word of the Lord may
spread rapidly and be glorified, just as *it did* also with
you;
2 and that we may be de-
livered from perverse and
evil men; for not all have
faith.
3 But the Lord is faithful,
and He will strengthen and
protect you from the evil
one.
4 And we have confi-
dence in the Lord concerning you, that you are doing
and will *continue to* do
what we command.
5 And may the Lord di-
rect your hearts into the
love of God and into the
steadfastness of Christ.
6 Now we command you,
brethren, in the name of
our Lord Jesus Christ, that
you keep aloof from every
brother who leads an unruly life and not according to
the tradition which you received from us.
7 For you yourselves
know how you ought to follow our example, because
we did not act in an undisciplined manner among you,
8 nor did we eat anyone's
bread without paying for it,
but with labor and hardship
we *kept* working night and
day so that we might not be
a burden to any of you;
9 not because we do not
have the right *to this,* but in
order to offer ourselves as a
model for you, that you

ἡμᾶς καὶ δοὺς παράκλησιν αἰωνίαν καὶ
us and having given [3]comfort [1]eternal [3]and

ἐλπίδα ἀγαθὴν ἐν χάριτι, 17 παρακαλέσαι
[5]hope [4]a good by grace, may he comfort

ὑμῶν τὰς καρδίας καὶ στηρίξαι ἐν παντὶ
of you the hearts and *may he* confirm in every

ἔργῳ καὶ λόγῳ ἀγαθῷ.
[2]work [3]and [4]word [1]good.

3 Τὸ λοιπὸν προσεύχεσθε, ἀδελφοί, περὶ
For the rest pray ye, brothers, concerning

ἡμῶν, ἵνα ὁ λόγος τοῦ κυρίου τρέχῃ
us, in order that the word of the Lord may run

καὶ δοξάζηται καθὼς καὶ πρὸς ὑμᾶς,
and be glorified as indeed with you,

2 καὶ ἵνα ῥυσθῶμεν ἀπὸ τῶν ἀτόπων
and *in order* that we may be delivered from – perverse

καὶ πονηρῶν ἀνθρώπων· οὐ γὰρ πάντων
and evil men; for [3][is] not [4]of all men

ἡ πίστις. 3 Πιστὸς δέ ἐστιν ὁ κύριος,
[1]the [2]faith. But faithful is the Lord,

ὃς στηρίξει ὑμᾶς καὶ φυλάξει ἀπὸ τοῦ
who will confirm you and will guard from the

πονηροῦ. 4 πεποίθαμεν δὲ ἐν κυρίῳ
evil [?one]. And we are persuaded in [the] Lord

ἐφ' ὑμᾶς, ὅτι ἃ παραγγέλλομεν [καὶ]
as to you, that what things we charge both

ποιεῖτε καὶ ποιήσετε. 5 Ὁ δὲ κύριος
ye do and will do. And [2]the [3]Lord

κατευθύναι ὑμῶν τὰς καρδίας εἰς τὴν
[1]may [4]direct [7]of you [5]the [6]hearts into the

ἀγάπην τοῦ θεοῦ καὶ εἰς τὴν ὑπομονὴν
love – of God and into the patience

τοῦ Χριστοῦ.
– of Christ.

6 Παραγγέλλομεν δὲ ὑμῖν, ἀδελφοί, ἐν
Now we charge you, brothers, in

ὀνόματι τοῦ κυρίου Ἰησοῦ Χριστοῦ,
[the] name of the Lord Jesus Christ,

στέλλεσθαι ὑμᾶς ἀπὸ παντὸς ἀδελφοῦ
to draw back you[b] from every brother

ἀτάκτως περιπατοῦντος καὶ μὴ κατὰ τὴν
[2]idly [1]walking and not according to the

παράδοσιν ἣν παρελάβετε παρ' ἡμῶν.
tradition which ye received from us.

7 αὐτοὶ γὰρ οἴδατε πῶς δεῖ μιμεῖσθαι
For [your]selves ye know how it behoves to imitate

ἡμᾶς, ὅτι οὐκ ἠτακτήσαμεν ἐν ὑμῖν,
us, because we were not idle among you,

8 οὐδὲ δωρεὰν ἄρτον ἐφάγομεν παρά τινος,
nor [5][as] a gift [2]bread [1]ate [3]from [4]anyone,

ἀλλ' ἐν κόπῳ καὶ μόχθῳ νυκτὸς καὶ
but by labour and struggle by night and

ἡμέρας ἐργαζόμενοι πρὸς τὸ μὴ ἐπιβαρῆσαί
by day working for *the* not to emburden

τινα ὑμῶν· 9 οὐχ ὅτι οὐκ ἔχομεν
anyone of you; not that we have not

ἐξουσίαν, ἀλλ' ἵνα ἑαυτοὺς τύπον δῶμεν
authority, but in order that [2]ourselves [3]an example [1]we might give

encouragement and good
hope, 17 encourage your
hearts and strengthen you
in every good deed and
word.

Chapter 3

Request for Prayer

FINALLY, brothers,
pray for us that the
message of the Lord may
spread rapidly and be honored, just as it was with
you. 2 And pray that we
may be delivered from
wicked and evil men, for
not everyone has faith.
3 But the Lord is faithful,
and he will strengthen and
protect you from the evil
one. 4 We have confidence
in the Lord that you are doing and will continue to do
the things we command.
5 May the Lord direct your
hearts into God's love and
Christ's perseverance.

Warning Against Idleness

6 In the name of the Lord
Jesus Christ, we command
you, brothers, to keep
away from every brother
who is idle and does not
live according to the teaching[f] you received from us.
7 For you yourselves know
how you ought to follow
our example. We were not
idle when we were with
you, 8 nor did we eat anyone's food without paying
for it. On the contrary, we
worked night and day, la-
boring and toiling so that
we would not be a burden
to any of you. 9 We did this,
not because we do not have
the right to such help, but in
order to make ourselves a

f6 Or *tradition*

might follow our example.
10For even when we were
with you, we used to give
you this order: if anyone
will not work, neither let
him eat.
11For we hear that some
among you are leading an
undisciplined life, doing no
work at all, but acting like
busybodies.
12Now such persons we
command and exhort in the
Lord Jesus Christ to work
in quiet fashion and eat
their own bread.
13But as for you, breth-
ren, do not grow weary of
doing good.
14And if anyone does not
obey our instruction in this
letter, take special note of
that man and do not asso-
ciate with him, so that he
may be put to shame.
15And *yet* do not regard
him as an enemy, but ad-
monish him as a brother.
16Now may the Lord of
peace Himself continually
grant you peace in every
circumstance. The Lord be
with you all!
17I, Paul, write this greeting with my own hand, and
this is a distinguishing mark
in every letter; this is the
way I write.
18The grace of our Lord
Jesus Christ be with you
all.

ὑμῖν εἰς τὸ μιμεῖσθαι ἡμᾶς. **10** καὶ
to you for *the* to imitate us. even

γὰρ ὅτε ἦμεν πρὸς ὑμᾶς, τοῦτο παρηγ-
For when we were with you, this we

γέλλομεν ὑμῖν, ὅτι εἴ τις οὐ θέλει
charged you, that if anyone does not wish

ἐργάζεσθαι, μηδὲ ἐσθιέτω. **11** ἀκούομεν
to work, neither let him eat. we hear [of]

γάρ τινας περιπατοῦντας ἐν ὑμῖν ἀτάκτως,
For some walking among you idly,

μηδὲν ἐργαζομένους ἀλλὰ περιεργαζομένους·
nothing working but working round;

12 τοῖς δὲ τοιούτοις παραγγέλλομεν καὶ
– and *to* such we charge and

παρακαλοῦμεν ἐν κυρίῳ Ἰησοῦ Χριστῷ
exhort in [the] Lord Jesus Christ

ἵνα μετὰ ἡσυχίας ἐργαζόμενοι τὸν
in order that [2]with [3]quietness [1]working [5]the

ἑαυτῶν ἄρτον ἐσθίωσιν. **13** Ὑμεῖς δέ,
[7]of themselves [6]bread [4]they may eat. And ye,

ἀδελφοί, μὴ ἐγκακήσητε καλοποιοῦντες
brothers, do not lose heart doing good.

14 εἰ δέ τις οὐχ ὑπακούει τῷ λόγῳ
And if anyone obeys not the word

ἡμῶν διὰ τῆς ἐπιστολῆς, τοῦτον σημειοῦσθε,
of us through the epistle, this man mark,

μὴ συναναμίγνυσθαι αὐτῷ, ἵνα ἐντραπῇ·
not to mix with* him, in order that he may be put to shame;

15 καὶ μὴ ὡς ἐχθρὸν ἡγεῖσθε, ἀλλὰ
and yet not as an enemy deem ye [him], but

νουθετεῖτε ὡς ἀδελφόν. **16** Αὐτὸς δὲ
admonish as a brother. And [4][him]self

ὁ κύριος τῆς εἰρήνης δῴη ὑμῖν τὴν
[1]the [2]Lord – [3]of peace may he give to you the (?his)

εἰρήνην διὰ παντὸς ἐν παντὶ τρόπῳ.
peace always in every way.

ὁ κύριος μετὰ πάντων ὑμῶν.
The Lord [be] with [2]all [1]you.

17 Ὁ ἀσπασμὸς τῇ ἐμῇ χειρὶ Παύλου,
The greeting – by my hand[,] of Paul,

ὅ ἐστιν σημεῖον ἐν πάσῃ ἐπιστολῇ·
which is a sign in every epistle:

οὕτως γράφω. **18** ἡ χάρις τοῦ κυρίου
thus I write. The grace of the Lord

ἡμῶν Ἰησοῦ Χριστοῦ μετὰ πάντων ὑμῶν.
of us Jesus Christ [be] with [2]all [1]you.

model for you to follow.
10For even when we were
with you, we gave you this
rule: "If a man will not
work, he shall not eat."
11We hear that some
among you are idle. They
are not busy; they are busybodies. 12Such people we
command and urge in the
Lord Jesus Christ to settle
down and earn the bread
they eat. 13And as for you,
brothers, never tire of doing what is right.
14If anyone does not obey
our instruction in this letter, take special note of
him. Do not associate with
him, in order that he may
feel ashamed. 15Yet do not
regard him as an enemy,
but warn him as a brother.

Final Greetings

16Now may the Lord of
peace himself give you
peace at all times and in every way. The Lord be with
all of you.
17I, Paul, write this greeting in my own hand, which
is the distinguishing mark
in all my letters. This is
how I write.
18The grace of our Lord
Jesus Christ be with you
all.

1 Timothy

Chapter 1

Misleadings in Doctrine and Living

PAUL, an apostle of
Christ Jesus according
to the commandment of
God our Savior, and of
Christ Jesus, *who is* our
hope;
2to Timothy, *my* true
child in *the* faith: Grace,

ΠΡΟΣ ΤΙΜΟΘΕΟΝ Α

To Timothy 1

1 Παῦλος ἀπόστολος Χριστοῦ Ἰησοῦ κατ'
Paul an apostle of Christ Jesus according to

ἐπιταγὴν θεοῦ σωτῆρος ἡμῶν καὶ Χριστοῦ
a command of God Saviour of us and of Christ

Ἰησοῦ τῆς ἐλπίδος ἡμῶν **2** Τιμοθέῳ
Jesus the hope of us to Timothy

γνησίῳ τέκνῳ ἐν πίστει· χάρις, ἔλεος,
a true child in [the] faith: Grace, mercy,

* Imperatival infinitive, as elsewhere (Phil. 3. 16, etc.).

1 Timothy

Chapter 1

PAUL, an apostle of
Christ Jesus by the
command of God our Sav-
ior and of Christ Jesus our
hope,

2To Timothy my true son
in the faith:

mercy *and* peace from God the Father and Christ Jesus our Lord.

3As I urged you upon my departure for Macedonia, remain on at Ephesus, in order that you may instruct certain men not to teach strange doctrines,

4nor to pay attention to myths and endless genealogies, which give rise to mere speculation rather than *furthering* the administration of God which is by faith.

5But the goal of our instruction is love from a pure heart and a good conscience and a sincere faith.

6For some men, straying from these things, have turned aside to fruitless discussion,

7wanting to be teachers of the Law, even though they do not understand either what they are saying or the matters about which they make confident assertions.

8But we know that the Law is good, if one uses it lawfully,

9realizing the fact that law is not made for a righteous man, but for those who are lawless and rebellious, for the ungodly and sinners, for the unholy and profane, for those who kill their fathers or mothers, for murderers

10and immoral men and homosexuals and kidnappers and liars and perjurers, and whatever else is contrary to sound teaching,

11according to the glorious gospel of the blessed God, with which I have been entrusted.

12I thank Christ Jesus our Lord, who has strengthened me, because He considered me faithful, putting me into service;

13even though I was formerly a blasphemer and a persecutor and a violent aggressor. And yet I was shown mercy, because I acted ignorantly in unbelief;

εἰρήνη ἀπὸ θεοῦ πατρὸς καὶ Χριστοῦ
peace from God [the] Father and Christ
Ἰησοῦ τοῦ κυρίου ἡμῶν.
Jesus the Lord of us.
3 Καθὼς παρεκάλεσά σε προσμεῖναι ἐν
As I besought thee to remain in
Ἐφέσῳ, πορευόμενος εἰς Μακεδονίαν, ἵνα
Ephesus, [I] going into Macedonia, in order that
παραγγείλῃς τισὶν μὴ ἑτεροδιδασκαλεῖν
thou mightest charge certain persons not to teach differently
4 μηδὲ προσέχειν μύθοις καὶ γενεαλογίαις
nor to pay attention to tales and to [2]genealogies
ἀπεράντοις, αἵτινες ἐκζητήσεις παρέχουσιν
[1]unending, which [2]questionings [1]provide
μᾶλλον ἢ οἰκονομίαν θεοῦ τὴν ἐν πίστει·
rather than a stewardship of God – in faith:
5 τὸ δὲ τέλος τῆς παραγγελίας ἐστὶν
now the end of the charge is
ἀγάπη ἐκ καθαρᾶς καρδίας καὶ συνειδήσεως
love out of a clean heart and conscience
ἀγαθῆς καὶ πίστεως ἀνυποκρίτου, 6 ὧν
a good and faith unfeigned, from which things
τινες ἀστοχήσαντες ἐξετράπησαν εἰς
some missing aim turned aside to
ματαιολογίαν, 7 θέλοντες εἶναι νομοδιδάσ-
vain talking, wishing to be law-
καλοι, μὴ νοοῦντες μήτε ἃ λέγουσιν
teachers, not understanding either what things they say
μήτε περὶ τίνων διαβεβαιοῦνται. 8 οἴδαμεν
nor concerning what things they emphatically assert. we know
δὲ ὅτι καλὸς ὁ νόμος, ἐάν τις αὐτῷ
Now that [3][is] [4]good [1]the [2]law, if anyone [2]it
νομίμως χρῆται, 9 εἰδὼς τοῦτο, ὅτι
[3]lawfully [1]uses, knowing this, that
δικαίῳ νόμος οὐ κεῖται, ἀνόμοις δὲ
[3]for a just man [1]law [2]is not laid down, but for lawless men
καὶ ἀνυποτάκτοις, ἀσεβέσι καὶ ἁμαρτωλοῖς,
and for unruly, for impious and for sinners,
ἀνοσίοις καὶ βεβήλοις, πατρολῴαις καὶ
for unholy and for profane, for parricides and
μητρολῴαις, ἀνδροφόνοις, 10 πόρνοις, ἀρ-
for matricides, for menkillers, for fornicators, for
σενοκοίταις, ἀνδραποδισταῖς, ψεύσταις, ἐπιόρ-
paederasts, for menstealers, for liars, for per-
κοις, καὶ εἴ τι ἕτερον τῇ ὑγιαινούσῃ
jurers, and if any other thing [2]*to* the [3]*being* healthful
διδασκαλίᾳ ἀντίκειται, 11 κατὰ τὸ εὐαγ-
[4]teaching [1]opposes, according to the gos-
γέλιον τῆς δόξης τοῦ μακαρίου θεοῦ,
pel of the glory of the blessed God,
ὃ ἐπιστεύθην ἐγώ. 12 Χάριν ἔχω τῷ
which [2]was entrusted [with] [1]I. Thanks I have to the
ἐνδυναμώσαντί με Χριστῷ Ἰησοῦ τῷ κυρίῳ
[one] empowering me Christ Jesus the Lord
ἡμῶν, ὅτι πιστόν με ἡγήσατο θέμενος
of us, because [3]faithful [2]me [1]he deemed putting [me]
εἰς διακονίαν, 13 τὸ πρότερον ὄντα
into [the] ministry, formerly being
βλάσφημον καὶ διώκτην καὶ ὑβριστήν·
a blasphemer and a persecutor and insolent;
ἀλλὰ ἠλεήθην, ὅτι ἀγνοῶν ἐποίησα ἐν
but I obtained mercy, because being ignorant I acted in

Grace, mercy and peace from God the Father and Chrst Jesus our Lord.

Warning Against False Teachers of the Law

3As I urged you when I
went into Macedonia, stay
there in Ephesus so that
you may command certain
men not to teach false doctrines any longer 4nor to devote themselves to myths
and endless genealogies.
These promote controver-
sies rather than God's work
—which is by faith. 5The
goal of this command is
love, which comes from a
pure heart and a good conscience and a sincere faith.
6Some have wandered
away from these and
turned to meaningless talk.
7They want to be teachers
of the law, but they do not
know what they are talking
about or what they so confidently affirm.
8We know that the law is
good if one uses it properly.
9We also know that law[a] is
made not for the righteous
but for lawbreakers and rebels, the ungodly and sinful, the unholy and irreli-
gious; for those who kill
their fathers or mothers,
for murderers, 10for adulterers and perverts, for
slave traders and liars and
perjurers—and for whatev-
er else is contrary to the
sound doctrine 11that con-
forms to the glorious gospel
of the blessed God, which
he entrusted to me.

The Lord's Grace to Paul

12I thank Christ Jesus our
Lord, who has given me
strength, that he consid-
ered me faithful, appointing
me to his service. 13Even
though I was once a blas-
phemer and a persecutor
and a violent man, I was
shown mercy because I
acted in ignorance and un-

[a]9 Or *that the law*

14and the grace of our
Lord was more than abun-
dant, with the faith and
love which are *found* in
Christ Jesus.
15It is a trustworthy
statement, deserving full
acceptance, that Christ
Jesus came into the world
to save sinners, among
whom I am foremost *of all*.
16And yet for this reason I
found mercy, in order that
in me as the foremost,
Jesus Christ might demon-
strate His perfect patience,
as an example for those
who would believe in Him
for eternal life.
17Now to the King eter-
nal, immortal, invisible, the
only God, *be* honor and
glory forever and ever.
Amen.
18This command I entrust
to you, Timothy, my son,
in accordance with the
prophecies previously
made concerning you, that
by them you may fight the
good fight,
19keeping faith and a good
conscience, which some
have rejected and suffered
shipwreck in regard to their
faith.
20Among these are Hy-
menaeus and Alexander,
whom I have delivered
over to Satan, so that they
may be taught not to blaspheme.

ἀπιστίᾳ, **14** ὑπερεπλεόνασεν δὲ ἡ χάρις
unbelief, and superabounded the grace
τοῦ κυρίου ἡμῶν μετὰ πίστεως καὶ
of the Lord of us with faith and
ἀγάπης τῆς ἐν Χριστῷ Ἰησοῦ. **15** πιστὸς
love – in Christ Jesus. Faithful [is]
ὁ λόγος καὶ πάσης ἀποδοχῆς ἄξιος,
the word and [2]of all [3]acceptance [1]worthy,
ὅτι Χριστὸς Ἰησοῦς ἦλθεν εἰς τὸν κόσμον
that Christ Jesus came into the world
ἁμαρτωλοὺς σῶσαι· ὧν πρῶτός εἰμι ἐγώ·
sinners to save; of whom first(chief) am I;
16 ἀλλὰ διὰ τοῦτο ἠλεήθην, ἵνα ἐν
but because of this I obtained mercy, in order that in
ἐμοὶ πρώτῳ ἐνδείξηται Ἰησοῦς Χριστὸς
me first might show forth Jesus Christ
τὴν ἅπασαν μακροθυμίαν, πρὸς ὑποτύπωσιν
– all longsuffering, for a pattern
τῶν μελλόντων πιστεύειν ἐπ' αὐτῷ εἰς
of the [ones] coming to believe on him to
ζωὴν αἰώνιον. **17** Τῷ δὲ βασιλεῖ τῶν
life eternal. Now to the King of the
αἰώνων, ἀφθάρτῳ ἀοράτῳ μόνῳ θεῷ, τιμὴ
ages, incorruptible invisible only God, [be] honour
καὶ δόξα εἰς τοὺς αἰῶνας τῶν αἰώνων·
and glory unto the ages of the ages:
ἀμήν. **18** Ταύτην τὴν παραγγελίαν παρα-
Amen. This – charge I com-
τίθεμαί σοι, τέκνον Τιμόθεε, κατὰ τὰς
mit to thee, child Timothy, according to the
προαγούσας ἐπὶ σὲ προφητείας, ἵνα
preceding [2]respecting [3]thee [1]prophecies, in order that
στρατεύῃ ἐν αὐταῖς τὴν καλὴν στρατείαν,
thou mightest war by them the good warfare,
19 ἔχων πίστιν καὶ ἀγαθὴν συνείδησιν,
having faith and a good conscience,
ἥν τινες ἀπωσάμενοι περὶ τὴν πίστιν
which some thrusting away [2]concerning [3]the [4]faith
ἐναυάγησαν· **20** ὧν ἐστιν Ὑμέναιος καὶ
[1]made shipwreck; of whom is Hymenæus and
Ἀλέξανδρος, οὓς παρέδωκα τῷ σατανᾷ,
Alexander, whom I delivered – to Satan,
ἵνα παιδευθῶσιν μὴ βλασφημεῖν.
in order that they may be taught not to blaspheme.

belief. 14The grace of our
Lord was poured out on me
abundantly, along with the
faith and love that are in
Christ Jesus.
15Here is a trustworthy
saying that deserves full acceptance: Christ Jesus
came into the world to save
sinners—of whom I am the
worst. 16But for that very
reason I was shown mercy
so that in me, the worst of
sinners, Christ Jesus might
display his unlimited pa-
tience as an example for
those who would believe
on him and receive eternal
life. 17Now to the King
eternal, immortal, invisible, the only God, be honor
and glory for ever and ever.
Amen.
18Timothy, my son, I give
you this instruction in
keeping with the prophe-
cies once made about you,
so that by following them
you may fight the good
fight, 19holding on to faith
and a good conscience.
Some have rejected these
and so have shipwrecked
their faith. 20Among them
are Hymenaeus and Alex-
ander, whom I have hand-
ed over to Satan to be
taught not to blaspheme.

Chapter 2

A Call to Prayer

FIRST of all, then, I urge
that entreaties *and*
prayers, petitions *and*
thanksgivings, be made on
behalf of all men,
2for kings and all who are
in authority, in order that
we may lead a tranquil and
quiet life in all godliness
and dignity.
3This is good and accept-

2 Παρακαλῶ οὖν πρῶτον πάντων
I exhort therefore first*ly* of all
ποιεῖσθαι δεήσεις, προσευχάς, ἐντεύξεις,
to be made petitions, prayers, intercessions,
εὐχαριστίας, ὑπὲρ πάντων ἀνθρώπων,
thanksgivings, on behalf of all men,
2 ὑπὲρ βασιλέων καὶ πάντων τῶν ἐν
on behalf of kings and all the [ones] [2]in
ὑπεροχῇ ὄντων, ἵνα ἤρεμον καὶ ἡσύχιον
[3]eminence [1]being, in order that [2]a tranquil [3]and [4]quiet
βίον διάγωμεν ἐν πάσῃ εὐσεβείᾳ καὶ
[5]life [1]we may lead in all piety and
σεμνότητι. **3** τοῦτο καλὸν καὶ ἀπόδεκτον
gravity. This [is] good and acceptable

Chapter 2

Instructions on Worship

I URGE, then, first of all,
that requests, prayers,
intercession and thanksgiving be made for everyone
—2for kings and all those in
authority, that we may live
peaceful and quiet lives in
all godliness and holiness.
3This is good, and pleases

able in the sight of God our Savior,

4who desires all men to be saved and to come to the knowledge of the truth.

5For there is one God, *and* one mediator also between God and men, *the* man Christ Jesus,

6who gave Himself as a ransom for all, the testimony *borne* at the proper time.

7And for this I was appointed a preacher and an apostle (I am telling the truth, I am not lying) as a teacher of the Gentiles in faith and truth.

8Therefore I want the men in every place to pray, lifting up holy hands, without wrath and dissension.

Women Instructed

9Likewise, *I want* women to adorn themselves with proper clothing, modestly and discreetly, not with braided hair and gold or pearls or costly garments;

10but rather by means of good works, as befits women making a claim to godliness.

11Let a woman quietly receive instruction with entire submissiveness.

12But I do not allow a woman to teach or exercise authority over a man, but to remain quiet.

13For it was Adam who was first created, *and* then Eve.

14And *it was* not Adam *who* was deceived, but the woman being quite deceived, fell into transgression.

15But *women* shall be preserved through the bearing of children if they continue in faith and love and sanctity with self-restraint.

Chapter 3

Overseers and Deacons

It is a trustworthy statement: if any man aspires to the office of overseer, it is a fine work he desires *to do*.

2An overseer, then, must be above reproach, the

ἐνώπιον τοῦ σωτῆρος ἡμῶν θεοῦ, 4 ὃς
before the Saviour of us God, who
πάντας ἀνθρώπους θέλει σωθῆναι καὶ εἰς
[2]all [3]men [1]wishes to be saved and [2]to
ἐπίγνωσιν ἀληθείας ἐλθεῖν. 5 εἷς γὰρ
[3]a full knowledge [4]of truth [1]to come. For [2]one
θεός, εἷς καὶ μεσίτης θεοῦ καὶ ἀνθρώπων,
[1][there is] [3]God, one also mediator of God and of men,
ἄνθρωπος Χριστὸς Ἰησοῦς, 6 ὁ δοὺς
a man Christ Jesus, the [one] having given
ἑαυτὸν ἀντίλυτρον ὑπὲρ πάντων, τὸ
himself a ransom on behalf of all, the
μαρτύριον καιροῖς ἰδίοις· 7 εἰς ὃ ἐτέθην
testimony in its own times; for which [2]was appointed
ἐγὼ κῆρυξ καὶ ἀπόστολος, ἀλήθειαν λέγω,
[1]I a herald and an apostle, [2]truth [1]I say,
οὐ ψεύδομαι, διδάσκαλος ἐθνῶν ἐν πίστει
I do not lie, a teacher of nations in faith
καὶ ἀληθείᾳ. 8 Βούλομαι οὖν προσεύχεσθαι
and truth. I desire therefore [3]to pray
τοὺς ἄνδρας ἐν παντὶ τόπῳ ἐπαίροντας
[1]the [2]men in every place lifting up
ὁσίους χεῖρας χωρὶς ὀργῆς καὶ διαλογισμοῦ.
holy hands without wrath and doubting.
9 Ὡσαύτως γυναῖκας ἐν καταστολῇ κοσμίῳ,
Similarly women in clothing orderly,
μετὰ αἰδοῦς καὶ σωφροσύνης κοσμεῖν
[3]with [4]modesty [5]and [6]sobriety [1]to adorn
ἑαυτάς, μὴ ἐν πλέγμασιν καὶ χρυσίῳ
[2]themselves, not with plaiting and gold
ἢ μαργαρίταις ἢ ἱματισμῷ πολυτελεῖ,
or pearls or raiment costly,
10 ἀλλ' ὃ πρέπει γυναιξὶν ἐπαγγελλομέναις
but what suits women professing
θεοσέβειαν, δι' ἔργων ἀγαθῶν. 11 γυνὴ
reverence, by means of [2]works [1]good. A woman
ἐν ἡσυχίᾳ μανθανέτω ἐν πάσῃ ὑποταγῇ·
in silence let learn in all subjection;
12 διδάσκειν δὲ γυναικὶ οὐκ ἐπιτρέπω,
but [3]to teach [2]a woman [1]I do not permit,
οὐδὲ αὐθεντεῖν ἀνδρός, ἀλλ' εἶναι ἐν
nor to exercise authority of(over) a man, but to be in
ἡσυχίᾳ. 13 Ἀδὰμ γὰρ πρῶτος ἐπλάσθη,
silence. For Adam first was formed,
εἶτα Εὕα. 14 καὶ Ἀδὰμ οὐκ ἠπατήθη,
then Eve. And Adam was not deceived,
ἡ δὲ γυνὴ ἐξαπατηθεῖσα ἐν παραβάσει
but the woman being deceived [2]in [3]transgression
γέγονεν· 15 σωθήσεται δὲ διὰ τῆς
[1]has become; but she will be saved through the(her)
τεκνογονίας, ἐὰν μείνωσιν ἐν πίστει καὶ
childbearing, if they remain in faith and
ἀγάπῃ καὶ ἁγιασμῷ μετὰ σωφροσύνης.
love and sanctification with sobriety.

3 Πιστὸς ὁ λόγος· εἴ τις ἐπισκοπῆς
Faithful [is] the word: If anyone [2]oversight
ὀρέγεται, καλοῦ ἔργου ἐπιθυμεῖ. 2 δεῖ
[1]aspires to, [3]a good [4]work [1]he desires. It behoves
οὖν τὸν ἐπίσκοπον ἀνεπίλημπτον εἶναι,
therefore the bishop without reproach to be,

God our Savior, 4who wants all men to be saved and to come to a knowledge of the truth. 5For there is one God and one mediator between God and men, the man Christ Jesus, 6who gave himself as a ransom for all men—the testimony given in its proper time. 7And for this purpose I was appointed a herald and an apostle—I am telling the truth, I am not lying—and a teacher of the true faith to the Gentiles.

8I want men everywhere to lift up holy hands in prayer, without anger or disputing.

9I also want women to dress modestly, with decency and propriety, not with braided hair or gold or pearls or expensive clothes, 10but with good deeds, appropriate for women who profess to worship God.

11A woman should learn in quietness and full submission. 12I do not permit a woman to teach or to have authority over a man; she must be silent. 13For Adam was formed first, then Eve. 14And Adam was not the one deceived; it was the woman who was deceived and became a sinner. 15But women[b] will be saved[c] through childbearing—if they continue in faith, love and holiness with propriety.

Chapter 3

Overseers and Deacons

HERE is a trustworthy saying: If anyone sets his heart on being an overseer,[d] he desires a noble task. 2Now the overseer must be above reproach,

b 15 Greek *she*
c 15 Or *restored*
d 1 Traditionally *bishop*; also in verse 2

husband of one wife, tem-
perate, prudent, respect-
able, hospitable, able to
teach,
3not addicted to wine or
pugnacious, but gentle, uncontentious, free from the
love of money.
4*He must be* one who
manages his own house-
hold well, keeping his children under control with all
dignity
5(but if a man does not
know how to manage his
own household, how will
he take care of the church
of God?);
6*and* not a new convert,
lest he become conceited
and fall into the condemnation incurred by the devil.
7And he must have a
good reputation with those
outside *the church,* so that
he may not fall into re-
proach and the snare of the
devil.
8Deacons likewise *must*
be men of dignity, not double-tongued, or addicted to
much wine or fond of sor-
did gain,
9*but* holding to the mystery of the faith with a clear
conscience.
10And let these also first
be tested; then let them
serve as deacons if they are
beyond reproach.
11Women *must* likewise
be dignified, not malicious
gossips, but temperate,
faithful in all things.
12Let deacons be hus-
bands of *only* one wife, *and*
good managers of *their*
children and their own
households.
13For those who have
served well as deacons obtain for themselves a high
standing and great confi-
dence in the faith that is in
Christ Jesus.
14I am writing these
things to you, hoping to
come to you before long;
15but in case I am
delayed, *I write* so that you
may know how one ought
to conduct himself in the
household of God, which is

μιᾶς γυναικὸς ἄνδρα, νηφάλιον, σώφρονα,
of one wife husband, temperate, sensible,
κόσμιον, φιλόξενον, διδακτικόν, 3 μὴ
orderly, hospitable, apt at teaching, not
πάροινον, μὴ πλήκτην, ἀλλὰ ἐπιεικῆ,
an excessive drinker, not a striker, but forbearing,
ἄμαχον, ἀφιλάργυρον, 4 τοῦ ἰδίου οἴκου
uncontentious, not avaricious, [3]the(his) [4]own [5]household
καλῶς προϊστάμενον, τέκνα ἔχοντα ἐν
[2]well [1]ruling, children having in
ὑποταγῇ μετὰ πάσης σεμνότητος, 5 (εἰ
subjection with all gravity, [2](if
δέ τις τοῦ ἰδίου οἴκου προστῆναι οὐκ
[1]but [3]anyone [7]the(his) [8]own [9]household [6]to rule [5]not*
οἶδεν, πῶς ἐκκλησίας θεοῦ ἐπιμελήσεται;)
[4]knows, how [2]a church [3]of God [1]will he care for ?)
6 μὴ νεόφυτον, ἵνα μὴ τυφωθεὶς εἰς
not a neophyte(recent convert), lest being puffed up [2]into
κρίμα ἐμπέσῃ τοῦ διαβόλου. 7 δεῖ δὲ
[3]judgment [1]he fall *in* of the devil. And it behoves
καὶ μαρτυρίαν καλὴν ἔχειν ἀπὸ τῶν
also [3]witness [2]a good [1]to have from the [ones]
ἔξωθεν, 7 ἵνα μὴ εἰς ὀνειδισμὸν ἐμπέσῃ
outside, lest [2]into [3]reproach [1]he fall *in*
καὶ παγίδα τοῦ διαβόλου. 8 Διακόνους
and a snare of the devil. [It behoves] deacons
ὡσαύτως σεμνούς, μὴ διλόγους, μὴ οἴνῳ
similarly [to be] grave, not double-tongued, not [3]wine
πολλῷ προσέχοντας, μὴ αἰσχροκερδεῖς,
[2]to much [1]*being* addicted, not fond of base gain,
9 ἔχοντας τὸ μυστήριον τῆς πίστεως ἐν
having the mystery of the faith with
καθαρᾷ συνειδήσει. 10 καὶ οὗτοι δὲ
a clean conscience. [4]Also [3]these [1]and
δοκιμαζέσθωσαν πρῶτον, εἶτα διακονείτωσαν
[2]let [5]be proved first*ly*, then let them minister
ἀνέγκλητοι ὄντες. 11 γυναῖκας ὡσαύτως
[2]irreproachable [1]being. [It behoves]* wives similarly
σεμνάς, μὴ διαβόλους, νηφαλίους, πιστὰς
[to be] grave, not slanderers, sober, faithful
ἐν πᾶσιν. 12 διάκονοι ἔστωσαν μιᾶς
in all things. [2]Deacons [1]let [3]be [5]of one
γυναικὸς ἄνδρες, τέκνων καλῶς προϊστάμενοι
[6]wife [4]husbands, [2]children [7]well [1]ruling
καὶ τῶν ἰδίων οἴκων. 13 οἱ γὰρ καλῶς
[3]and [4]the(ir) [5]own [6]households. For the [ones] [2]well
διακονήσαντες βαθμὸν ἑαυτοῖς καλὸν
[1]having ministered [6]position [4]for themselves [5]a good
περιποιοῦνται καὶ πολλὴν παρρησίαν ἐν
[3]acquire and much boldness in
πίστει τῇ ἐν Χριστῷ Ἰησοῦ. 14 Ταῦτά
faith the [one] in Christ Jesus. These things
σοι γράφω ἐλπίζων ἐλθεῖν πρὸς σὲ
to thee I write hoping to come to thee
τάχιον· 15 ἐὰν δὲ βραδύνω, ἵνα εἰδῇς
shortly; but if I delay, in order that thou mayest know
πῶς δεῖ ἐν οἴκῳ θεοῦ ἀναστρέφεσθαι,
how it behoves in [the] household of God to behave,

the husband of but one
wife, temperate, self-controlled, respectable, hospitable, able to teach, 3not
given to drunkenness, not
violent but gentle, not
quarrelsome, not a lover of
money. 4He must manage
his own family well and see
that his children obey him
with proper respect. 5(If
anyone does not know how
to manage his own family,
how can he take care of
God's church?) 6He must
not be a recent convert, or
he may become conceited
and fall under the same
judgment as the devil. 7He
must also have a good reputation with outsiders, so
that he will not fall into disgrace and into the devil's
trap.
8Deacons, likewise, are
to be men worthy of re-
spect, sincere, not indulging in much wine, and not
pursuing dishonest gain.
9They must keep hold of
the deep truths of the faith
with a clear conscience.
10They must first be tested;
and then if there is nothing
against them, let them
serve as deacons.
11In the same way, their
wives[e] are to be women
worthy of respect, not malicious talkers but temperate and trustworthy in everything.
12A deacon must be the
husband of but one wife
and must manage his chil-
dren and his household
well. 13Those who have
served well gain an excellent standing and great assurance in their faith in
Christ Jesus.
14Although I hope to
come to you soon, I am
writing you these instructions so that, 15if I am delayed, you will know how
people ought to conduct
themselves in God's house-

* That is, " cannot "; see note on page xviii.

* See verses 7 and 8.

e11 Or *way, deaconesses*

the church of the living
God, the pillar and support
of the truth.
16And by common
confession great is the mystery of godliness:

[a]He who was re-
vealed in the flesh,
Was vindicated in the
Spirit,
Beheld by angels,
Proclaimed among the
nations,
Believed on in the
world,
Taken up in glory.

Chapter 4

Apostasy

BUT the Spirit explicitly
says that in later times
some will fall away from
the faith, paying attention
to deceitful spirits and doctrines of demons,
2by means of the hypoc-
risy of liars seared in their
own conscience as with a
branding iron,
3*men* who forbid mar-
riage *and advocate* abstain-
ing from foods, which God
has created to be gratefully
shared in by those who believe and know the truth.
4For everything created
by God is good, and noth-
ing is to be rejected, if it is
received with gratitude;
5for it is sanctified by
means of the word of God
and prayer.

A Good Minister's Discipline

6In pointing out these
things to the brethren, you
will be a good servant of
Christ Jesus, *constantly*
nourished on the words of
the faith and of the sound
doctrine which you have
been following.
7But have nothing to do
with worldly fables fit only
for old women. On the
other hand, discipline yourself for the purpose of godliness;
8for bodily discipline is
only of little profit, but godliness is profitable for all
things, since it holds promise for the present life and
also for the *life* to come.
9It is a trustworthy

[a] Some later mss. read *God*

ἥτις ἐστὶν ἐκκλησία θεοῦ ζῶντος, στῦλος
which is [the] church [2]God [1]of [the] living, pillar
καὶ ἑδραίωμα τῆς ἀληθείας. **16** καὶ
and bulwark of the truth. And
ὁμολογουμένως μέγα ἐστὶν τὸ τῆς εὐσεβείας
confessedly great is the – [2]of piety
μυστήριον· ὃς ἐφανερώθη ἐν σαρκί,
[1]mystery: Who was manifested in flesh,
ἐδικαιώθη ἐν πνεύματι, ὤφθη ἀγγέλοις,
was justified in spirit, *was* seen by angels,
ἐκηρύχθη ἐν ἔθνεσιν, ἐπιστεύθη ἐν κόσμῳ,
was proclaimed among nations, *was* believed in [the] world,
ἀνελήμφθη ἐν δόξῃ.
was taken up in glory.

4 Τὸ δὲ πνεῦμα ῥητῶς λέγει ὅτι
Now the Spirit [2]in words† [1]says that
ἐν ὑστέροις καιροῖς ἀποστήσονταί τινες
in later times [2]will depart from [1]some
τῆς πίστεως, προσέχοντες πνεύμασιν
the faith, attending to [2]spirits
πλάνοις καὶ διδασκαλίαις δαιμονίων, **2** ἐν
[1]misleading and teachings of demons, [2]in
ὑποκρίσει ψευδολόγων, κεκαυστηριασμένων
[3]hypocrisy [1]of men who speak lies, having been branded on
τὴν ἰδίαν συνείδησιν, **3** κωλυόντων γαμεῖν,
the(ir) own conscience, forbidding to marry,
ἀπέχεσθαι βρωμάτων, ἃ ὁ θεὸς ἔκτισεν
[bidding] to abstain from foods, which – God created
εἰς μετάλημψιν μετὰ εὐχαριστίας τοῖς
for partaking with thanksgiving by the
πιστοῖς καὶ ἐπεγνωκόσι τὴν ἀλήθειαν.
believers and [those] having fully known the truth.
4 ὅτι πᾶν κτίσμα θεοῦ καλόν, καὶ
Because every creature of God [is] good, and
οὐδὲν ἀπόβλητον μετὰ εὐχαριστίας λαμβαν-
nothing [is] to be put away [2]with [3]thanksgiving [1]being
όμενον· **5** ἁγιάζεται γὰρ διὰ λόγου θεοῦ
received; for it is *being* sanctified through a word of God
καὶ ἐντεύξεως. **6** Ταῦτα ὑποτιθέμενος
and petition. [2]These things [1]suggesting
τοῖς ἀδελφοῖς καλὸς ἔσῃ διάκονος Χριστοῦ
[3]to the [4]brothers [6]a good [5]thou wilt be [7]minister of Christ
Ἰησοῦ, ἐντρεφόμενος τοῖς λόγοις τῆς
Jesus, being nourished by the words of the
πίστεως καὶ τῆς καλῆς διδασκαλίας ᾗ
faith and of the good teaching which
παρηκολούθηκας· **7** τοὺς δὲ βεβήλους καὶ
thou hast followed; but the profane and
γραώδεις μύθους παραιτοῦ. γύμναζε δὲ
old-womanish tales refuse. And exercise
σεαυτὸν πρὸς εὐσέβειαν. **8** ἡ γὰρ σωματικὴ
thyself to piety. – For bodily
γυμνασία πρὸς ὀλίγον ἐστὶν ὠφέλιμος·
exercise [3]for [4]a little [1]is [2]profitable;
ἡ δὲ εὐσέβεια πρὸς πάντα ὠφέλιμός
– but piety [3]for [4]all things [2]profitable
ἐστιν, ἐπαγγελίαν ἔχουσα ζωῆς τῆς νῦν
[1]is, promise having [3]life [1]of the [2]now (present)
καὶ τῆς μελλούσης. **9** πιστὸς ὁ λόγος
and of the coming. Faithful [is] the word

hold, which is the church of
the living God, the pillar
and foundation of the truth.
16Beyond all question, the
mystery of godliness is
great:

He[f] appeared in a
body,[g]
was vindicated by the
Spirit,
was seen by angels,
was preached among
the nations,
was believed on in the
world,
was taken up in glory.

Chapter 4

Instructions to Timothy

THE Spirit clearly says
that in later times
some will abandon the faith
and follow deceiving spirits
and things taught by de-
mons. 2Such teachings
come through hypocritical
liars, whose consciences
have been seared as with a
hot iron. 3They forbid people to marry and order
them to abstain from cer-
tain foods, which God created to be received with
thanksgiving by those who
believe and who know the
truth. 4For everything God
created is good, and nothing is to be rejected if it is
received with thanksgiv-
ing, 5because it is consecrated by the word of God
and prayer.
6If you point these things
out to the brothers, you will
be a good minister of Christ
Jesus, brought up in the
truths of the faith and of the
good teaching that you
have followed. 7Have nothing to do with godless
myths and old wives' tales;
rather, train yourself to be
godly. 8For physical training is of some value, but
godliness has value for all
things, holding promise for
both the present life and the
life to come.
9This is a trustworthy

[f] 16 Some manuscripts *God*
[g] 16 Or *in the flesh*

statement deserving full acceptance.
10 For it is for this we labor
and strive, because we
have fixed our hope on the
living God, who is the Savior of all men, especially of
believers.
11 Prescribe and teach
these things.
12 Let no one look down
on your youthfulness, but
rather in speech, conduct,
love, faith *and* purity, show
yourself an example of
those who believe.
13 Until I come, give at-
tention to the *public* reading *of Scripture,* to exhortation and teaching.
14 Do not neglect the spiritual gift within you, which
was bestowed upon you
through prophetic utter-
ance with the laying on of
hands by the presbytery.
15 Take pains with these
things; be *absorbed* in
them, so that your progress
may be evident to all.
16 Pay close attention to
yourself and to your teaching; persevere in these
things; for as you do this
you will insure salvation
both for yourself and for
those who hear you.

Chapter 5

Honor Widows

Do not sharply rebuke
an older man, but
rather appeal to *him* as a
father, *to* the younger men
as brothers,
2 the older women as
mothers, *and* the younger
women as sisters, in all purity.
3 Honor widows who are
widows indeed;
4 but if any widow has
children or grandchildren,
let them first learn to practice piety in regard to their
own family, and to make
some return to their par-
ents; for this is acceptable
in the sight of God.
5 Now she who is a
widow indeed, and who has
been left alone has fixed

καὶ πάσης ἀποδοχῆς ἄξιος· **10** εἰς τοῦτο
and [3]of all [2]acceptance [1]worthy; [2]to [3]this
γὰρ κοπιῶμεν καὶ ἀγωνιζόμεθα, ὅτι
[1]for we labour and struggle, because
ἠλπίκαμεν ἐπὶ θεῷ ζῶντι, ὅς ἐστιν
we have set [our] hope on [2]God [1]a living, who is
σωτὴρ πάντων ἀνθρώπων, μάλιστα πιστῶν.
[the] Saviour of all men, especially of believers.
11 Παράγγελλε ταῦτα καὶ δίδασκε.
Charge thou these things and teach.
12 μηδείς σου τῆς νεότητος καταφρονείτω,
[2]No one [5]of thee [3]the [4]youth [1]let despise,
ἀλλὰ τύπος γίνου τῶν πιστῶν ἐν λόγῳ,
but [2]a pattern [1]become thou of the believers in speech,
ἐν ἀναστροφῇ, ἐν ἀγάπῃ, ἐν πίστει,
in behaviour, in love, in faith,
ἐν ἁγνείᾳ. **13** ἕως ἔρχομαι πρόσεχε
in purity. Until I come attend
τῇ ἀναγνώσει, τῇ παρακλήσει, τῇ διδασ-
to the reading,* to the exhortation, to the teach-
καλίᾳ. **14** μὴ ἀμέλει τοῦ ἐν σοὶ
ing. Do not be neglectful [1]of the [3]in [4]thee
χαρίσματος, ὃ ἐδόθη σοι διὰ προφητείας
[2]gift, which was given to thee by means of prophecy
μετὰ ἐπιθέσεως τῶν χειρῶν τοῦ πρε-
with laying on of the hands of the body
σβυτερίου. **15** ταῦτα μελέτα, ἐν τούτοις
of elders. [2]These things [1]attend to, [3]in [4]these things
ἴσθι, ἵνα σου ἡ προκοπὴ φανερὰ ᾖ
[1]be thou, in order that of thee the advance clear may be
πᾶσιν. **16** ἔπεχε σεαυτῷ καὶ τῇ διδασκαλίᾳ,
to all men. Take heed to thyself and to the teaching,
ἐπίμενε αὐτοῖς· τοῦτο γὰρ ποιῶν καὶ
continue in them; for this doing both
σεαυτὸν σώσεις καὶ τοὺς ἀκούοντάς σου.
thyself thou wilt save and the [ones] hearing thee.

5 Πρεσβυτέρῳ μὴ ἐπιπλήξῃς, ἀλλὰ
An older man do not rebuke, but
παρακάλει ὡς πατέρα, νεωτέρους ὡς
exhort as a father, younger men as
ἀδελφούς, **2** πρεσβυτέρας ὡς μητέρας,
brothers, older women as mothers,
νεωτέρας ὡς ἀδελφὰς ἐν πάσῃ ἁγνείᾳ.
younger women as sisters with all purity.
3 Χήρας τίμα τὰς ὄντως χήρας. **4** εἰ δέ
[2]Widows [1]honour [3]the [4]real*ly* [5]widows. But if
τις χήρα τέκνα ἢ ἔκγονα ἔχει, μαν-
any widow [2]children [3]or [4]grandchildren [1]has, let
θανέτωσαν πρῶτον τὸν ἴδιον οἶκον εὐσεβεῖν
them learn firstly [2]the(ir) [3]own [4]household [1]to show piety to
καὶ ἀμοιβὰς ἀποδιδόναι τοῖς προγόνοις·
and [2]requitals [1]to return to the(ir) forebears;
τοῦτο γάρ ἐστιν ἀπόδεκτον ἐνώπιον τοῦ
for this is acceptable before
θεοῦ. **5** ἡ δὲ ὄντως χήρα καὶ μεμονωμένη
God. But the real*ly* widow and *having been* left alone

* That is, the reading aloud in public worship of the Scriptures (as nearly always in the N.T.).

saying that deserves full acceptance 10 (and for this we
labor and strive), that we
have put our hope in the living God, who is the Savior
of all men, and especially of
those who believe.
11 Command and teach
these things. 12 Don't let
anyone look down on you
because you are young, but
set an example for the believers in speech, in life, in
love, in faith and in purity.
13 Until I come, devote
yourself to the public reading of Scripture, to preaching and to teaching. 14 Do
not neglect your gift, which
was given you through a
prophetic message when
the body of elders laid their
hands on you.
15 Be diligent in these matters; give yourself wholly
to them, so that everyone
may see your progress.
16 Watch your life and doctrine closely. Persevere in
them, because if you do,
you will save both yourself
and your hearers.

Chapter 5

Advice About Widows,
Elders and Slaves

Do not rebuke an older
man harshly, but ex-
hort him as if he were your
father. Treat younger men
as brothers, 2 older women
as mothers, and younger
women as sisters, with absolute purity.
3 Give proper recognition
to those widows who are
really in need. 4 But if a widow has children or grand-
children, these should learn
first of all to put their religion into practice by caring
for their own family and so
repaying their parents and
grandparents, for this is
pleasing to God. 5 The widow who is really in need
and left all alone puts her

her hope on God, and continues in entreaties and prayers night and day.
6 But she who gives herself to wanton pleasure is dead even while she lives.
7 Prescribe these things as well, so that they may be above reproach.
8 But if anyone does not provide for his own, and especially for those of his household, he has denied the faith, and is worse than an unbeliever.
9 Let a widow be put on the list only if she is not less than sixty years old, *having been* the wife of one man,
10 having a reputation for good works; *and* if she has brought up children, if she has shown hospitality to strangers, if she has washed the saints' feet, if she has assisted those in distress, *and* if she has devoted herself to every good work.
11 But refuse *to put* younger widows *on the list*, for when they feel sensual desires in disregard of Christ, they want to get married,
12 *thus* incurring condemnation, because they have set aside their previous pledge.
13 And at the same time they also learn *to be* idle, as they go around from house to house; and not merely idle, but also gossips and busybodies, talking about things not proper *to mention*.
14 Therefore, I want younger *widows* to get married, bear children, keep house, *and* give the enemy no occasion for reproach;
15 for some have already turned aside to follow Satan.
16 If any woman who is a believer has *dependent* widows, let her assist them, and let not the church be burdened, so that it may assist those who are widows indeed.

Concerning Elders

17 Let the elders who rule well be considered worthy of double honor, especially

ἤλπικεν ἐπὶ θεὸν καὶ προσμένει ταῖς
has set [her] hope on God and continues in the

δεήσεσιν καὶ ταῖς προσευχαῖς νυκτὸς καὶ
petitions and the prayers night and

ἡμέρας· 6 ἡ δὲ σπαταλῶσα ζῶσα τέθνηκεν.
day; but the [one] living wantonly [2]living [1]has died.

7 καὶ ταῦτα παράγγελλε, ἵνα ἀνεπίλημπτοι
And these things charge thou, in order that [2]without reproach

ὦσιν. 8 εἰ δέ τις τῶν ἰδίων καὶ μάλιστα
[1]they may be. But if anyone [2]the(his) [3]own [4]and [5]especially [people]

οἰκείων οὐ προνοεῖ, τὴν πίστιν ἤρνηται
[his] [6]family [1]provides not [for], [2]the [3]faith [1]he has denied

καὶ ἔστιν ἀπίστου χείρων. 9 χήρα
and is [2]an unbeliever [1]worse [than]. A widow

καταλεγέσθω μὴ ἔλαττον ἐτῶν ἑξήκοντα
let be enrolled [2]not [3]less [than] [5]*of* years [4]sixty

γεγονυῖα, ἑνὸς ἀνδρὸς γυνή, 10 ἐν ἔργοις
[1]having become, of one man wife, [2]by [4]works

καλοῖς μαρτυρουμένη, εἰ ἐτεκνοτρόφησεν,
[3]good [1]being witnessed, if she brought up children,

εἰ ἐξενοδόχησεν, εἰ ἁγίων πόδας ἔνιψεν,
if she entertained strangers, if [3]of saints [2]feet [1]she washed,

εἰ θλιβομένοις ἐπήρκεσεν, εἰ παντὶ ἔργῳ
if [2]*being* afflicted [ones], [1]she relieved, if [3]every [4]work

ἀγαθῷ ἐπηκολούθησεν. 11 νεωτέρας δὲ
[5]good [1]she followed after. But younger

χήρας παραιτοῦ· ὅταν γὰρ καταστρηνιάσωσιν
widows refuse; for whenever they grow wanton against

τοῦ Χριστοῦ, γαμεῖν θέλουσιν, 12 ἔχουσαι
– Christ, [2]to marry [1]they wish, having

κρίμα ὅτι τὴν πρώτην πίστιν ἠθέτησαν·
judgment because [2]the(ir) [3]first [4]faith [1]they set aside;

13 ἅμα δὲ καὶ ἀργαὶ μανθάνουσιν
and at the same time also [2]idle [1]they learn [to be]

περιερχόμεναι τὰς οἰκίας, οὐ μόνον δὲ
going round the houses, [2]not [3]only [1]and

ἀργαὶ ἀλλὰ καὶ φλύαροι καὶ περίεργοι,
idle but also gossips and busybodies,

λαλοῦσαι τὰ μὴ δέοντα. 14 βούλομαι
speaking the things not proper. I will

οὖν νεωτέρας γαμεῖν, τεκνογονεῖν,
therefore younger women to marry, to bear children,

οἰκοδεσποτεῖν, μηδεμίαν ἀφορμὴν διδόναι
to be mistress of a house, [2]no [3]occasion [1]to give

τῷ ἀντικειμένῳ λοιδορίας χάριν· 15 ἤδη
to the [one] opposing [2]reproach [1]on account of; [2]already

γάρ τινες ἐξετράπησαν ὀπίσω τοῦ σατανᾶ.
[1]for some turned aside behind – Satan.

16 εἴ τις πιστὴ ἔχει χήρας, ἐπαρκείτω
If any believing woman has widows, let her relieve

αὐταῖς, καὶ μὴ βαρείσθω ἡ ἐκκλησία,
them, and not let be burdened the church,

ἵνα ταῖς ὄντως χήραις ἐπαρκέσῃ. 17 Οἱ
in order that [2]the [3]real*ly* [4]widows [1]it may relieve. [3]The

καλῶς προεστῶτες πρεσβύτεροι διπλῆς
[5]well [4]ruling [3]elders [9]of double

hope in God and continues night and day to pray and to ask God for help. 6 But the widow who lives for pleasure is dead even while she lives. 7 Give the people these instructions, too, so that no one may be open to blame. 8 If anyone does not provide for his relatives, and especially for his immediate family, he has denied the faith and is worse than an unbeliever.
9 No widow may be put on the list of widows unless she is over sixty, has been faithful to her husband,[h]
10 and is well known for her good deeds, such as bringing up children, showing hospitality, washing the feet of the saints, helping those in trouble and devoting herself to all kinds of good deeds.
11 As for younger widows, do not put them on such a list. For when their sensual desires overcome their dedication to Christ, they want to marry. 12 Thus they bring judgment on themselves, because they have broken their first pledge. 13 Besides, they get into the habit of being idle and going about from house to house. And not only do they become idlers, but also gossips and busybodies, saying things they ought not to. 14 So I counsel younger widows to marry, to have children, to manage their homes and to give the enemy no opportunity for slander. 15 Some have in fact already turned away to follow Satan.
16 If any woman who is a believer has widows in her family, she should help them and not let the church be burdened with them, so that the church can help those widows who are really in need.
17 The elders who direct the affairs of the church well are worthy of double honor, especially those

[h]9 Or *has had but one husband*

those who work hard at preaching and teaching.

18For the Scripture says, "You shall not muzzle the ox while he is threshing," and "The laborer is worthy of his wages."

19Do not receive an accusation against an elder except on the basis of two or three witnesses.

20Those who continue in sin, rebuke in the presence of all, so that the rest also may be fearful *of sinning.*

21I solemnly charge you in the presence of God and of Christ Jesus and of *His* chosen angels, to maintain these *principles* without bias, doing nothing in a *spirit of* partiality.

22Do not lay hands upon anyone *too* hastily and thus share *responsibility for* the sins of others; keep yourself free from sin.

23No longer drink water *exclusively,* but use a little wine for the sake of your stomach and your frequent ailments.

24The sins of some men are quite evident, going before them to judgment; for others, their *sins* follow after.

25Likewise also, deeds that are good are quite evident, and those which are otherwise cannot be concealed.

Chapter 6

Instructions to Those Who Minister

LET all who are under the yoke as slaves regard their own masters as worthy of all honor so that the name of God and *our* doctrine may not be spoken against.

2And let those who have believers as their masters not be disrespectful to them because they are brethren, but let them serve them all the more, because those who partake of the benefit are believers and beloved. Teach and

τιμῆς ἀξιούσθωσαν, μάλιστα οἱ κοπιῶντες
[10]honour [1]let [6]be [7]deemed [8]worthy, especially the [ones] labouring

ἐν λόγῳ καὶ διδασκαλίᾳ. 18 λέγει γὰρ
in speech and teaching. For says

ἡ γραφή· βοῦν ἀλοῶντα οὐ φιμώσεις,
the scripture: An ox threshing thou shalt not muzzle,

καί· ἄξιος ὁ ἐργάτης τοῦ μισθοῦ αὐτοῦ.
and: Worthy [is] the workman of the pay of him.

19 κατὰ πρεσβυτέρου κατηγορίαν μὴ παραδέχου,
Against an elder accusation do not receive,

ἐκτὸς εἰ μὴ ἐπὶ δύο ἢ τριῶν
except unless on [the word of] two or three

μαρτύρων. 20 Τοὺς ἁμαρτάνοντας ἐνώπιον
witnesses. The [ones] sinning [2]before

πάντων ἔλεγχε, ἵνα καὶ οἱ λοιποὶ φόβον
[3]all [1]reprove thou, in order that [3]also [1]the [2]rest [5]fear

ἔχωσιν. 21 Διαμαρτύρομαι ἐνώπιον τοῦ
[4]may have. I solemnly witness before –

θεοῦ καὶ Χριστοῦ Ἰησοῦ καὶ τῶν
God and Christ Jesus and the

ἐκλεκτῶν ἀγγέλων ἵνα ταῦτα φυλάξῃς
chosen angels in order that these things thou guard

χωρὶς προκρίματος, μηδὲν ποιῶν κατὰ
without prejudgment, [2]nothing [1]doing by way of

πρόσκλισιν. 22 χεῖρας ταχέως μηδενὶ
inclination. [3]Hands [5]quickly [4]no man

ἐπιτίθει, μηδὲ κοινώνει ἁμαρτίαις ἀλλοτρίαις·
[1]lay [2]on, nor share [2]sins [1]in others'†;

σεαυτὸν ἁγνὸν τήρει. 23 Μηκέτι
[2]thyself [3]pure [1]keep. No longer

ὑδροπότει, ἀλλὰ οἴνῳ ὀλίγῳ χρῶ διὰ
drink water, but [3]wine [2]a little [1]use on account of

τὸν στόμαχον καὶ τὰς πυκνάς σου
the(thy) stomach and the frequent [2]of thee

ἀσθενείας. 24 Τινῶν ἀνθρώπων αἱ ἁμαρτίαι
[1]weaknesses. [3]of some [4]men [1]The [2]sins

πρόδηλοί εἰσιν προάγουσαι εἰς κρίσιν,
[6]clear beforehand [5]are going before to judgment,

τισὶν δὲ καὶ ἐπακολουθοῦσιν· 25 ὡσαύτως
but some indeed they follow on; similarly

καὶ τὰ ἔργα τὰ καλὰ πρόδηλα, καὶ
also the [2]works – [1]good [are] clear beforehand, and

τὰ ἄλλως ἔχοντα κρυβῆναι οὐ δύνανται.
the [ones] [2]otherwise [1]having (being) [4]to be hidden [3]cannot.

6 Ὅσοι εἰσὶν ὑπὸ ζυγὸν δοῦλοι, τοὺς
As many as are under a yoke [being] slaves, [2]the(ir)

ἰδίους δεσπότας πάσης τιμῆς ἀξίους ἡγείσθωσαν,
[3]own [4]masters [6]of all [7]honour [5]worthy [1]let them deem,

ἵνα μὴ τὸ ὄνομα τοῦ θεοῦ καὶ
lest the name – of God and

ἡ διδασκαλία βλασφημῆται. 2 οἱ δὲ
the teaching be blasphemed. And [1]the [ones]

πιστοὺς ἔχοντες δεσπότας μὴ καταφρονείτωσαν,
[3]believing [2]having [4]masters not let them despise [them],

ὅτι ἀδελφοί εἰσιν, ἀλλὰ μᾶλλον
because brothers they are, but rather

δουλευέτωσαν, ὅτι πιστοί εἰσιν καὶ
let them serve as slaves, because [6]believing [5]are [7]and

ἀγαπητοὶ οἱ τῆς εὐεργεσίας ἀντιλαμβανόμενοι.
[8]beloved [1]the [ones] [3]of the [4]good service [2]receiving in return.

whose work is preaching
and teaching. 18For the
Scripture says, "Do not
muzzle the ox while it is
treading out the grain,"[i]
and "The worker deserves
his wages."[j] 19Do not entertain an accusation
against an elder unless it is
brought by two or three
witnesses. 20Those who sin
are to be rebuked publicly,
so that the others may take
warning.
21I charge you, in the
sight of God and Christ
Jesus and the elect angels,
to keep these instructions
without partiality, and to
do nothing out of favoritism.
22Do not be hasty in the
laying on of hands, and do
not share in the sins of others. Keep yourself pure.
23Stop drinking only wa-
ter, and use a little wine because of your stomach and
your frequent illnesses.
24The sins of some men
are obvious, reaching the
place of judgment ahead of
them; the sins of others trail
behind them. 25In the same
way, good deeds are obvi-
ous, and even those that
are not cannot be hidden.

Chapter 6

ALL who are under the yoke of slavery should consider their masters worthy of full respect, so that God's name and our teaching may not be slandered. 2Those who have believing masters are not to show less respect for them because they are brothers. Instead, they are to serve them even better, because those who benefit from their service are believers, and dear to them. These are the things you are to teach and urge on them.

[i]18 Deut. 25:4
[j]18 Luke 10:7

preach these *principles.*
[3]If anyone advocates a
different doctrine, and does
not agree with sound
words, those of our Lord
Jesus Christ, and with the
doctrine conforming to
godliness,
[4]he is conceited *and* understands nothing; but he
has a morbid interest
in controversial questions
and disputes about words,
out of which arise envy,
strife, abusive language,
evil suspicions,
[5]and constant friction
between men of depraved
mind and deprived of the
truth, who suppose that
godliness is a means of
gain.
[6]But godliness *actually*
is a means of great gain,
when accompanied by con-
tentment.
[7]For we have brought
nothing into the world, [b]so
we cannot take anything
out of it either.
[8]And if we have food and
covering, with these we
shall be content.
[9]But those who want to
get rich fall into temptation
and a snare and many foolish and harmful desires
which plunge men into ruin
and destruction.
[10]For the love of money is
a root of all sorts of evil,
and some by longing for it
have wandered away from
the faith, and pierced themselves with many a pang.
[11]But flee from these
things, you man of God;
and pursue righteousness,
godliness, faith, love,
perseverance *and* gentleness.
[12]Fight the good fight of
faith; take hold of the eternal life to which you were
called, and you made the
good confession in the

Ταῦτα δίδασκε καὶ παρακάλει. **3** εἴ
These things teach thou and exhort. If

τις ἑτεροδιδασκαλεῖ καὶ μὴ προσέρχεται
anyone teaches differently and consents not

ὑγιαίνουσιν λόγοις τοῖς τοῦ κυρίου ἡμῶν
to *being* healthy words the [words] of the Lord of us

Ἰησοῦ Χριστοῦ, καὶ τῇ κατ' εὐσέβειαν
Jesus Christ, and [1]to the [3]according to [4]piety

διδασκαλίᾳ, **4** τετύφωται, μηδὲν ἐπιστά-
[2]teaching, he has been puffed up, [2]nothing [1]under-

μενος, ἀλλὰ νοσῶν περὶ ζητήσεις καὶ
standing, but being diseased about questionings and

λογομαχίας, ἐξ ὧν γίνεται φθόνος, ἔρις,
battles of words, out of which comes envy, strife,

βλασφημίαι, ὑπόνοιαι πονηραί, **5** διαπαρα-
blasphemies, [2]suspicions [1]evil, perpetual

τριβαὶ διεφθαρμένων ἀνθρώπων τὸν νοῦν
wranglings [2]having been corrupted [1]of men the mind
=of men with corrupted mind

καὶ ἀπεστερημένων τῆς ἀληθείας, νομιζ-
and *having been* deprived of the truth, sup-

όντων πορισμὸν εἶναι τὴν εὐσέβειαν.
posing [3]gain [2]to be *the* [1]piety.*

6 ἔστιν δὲ πορισμὸς μέγας ἡ εὐσέβεια
But [4]is [6]gain [5]great *the* [1]piety

μετὰ αὐταρκείας· **7** οὐδὲν γὰρ εἰσηνέγκαμεν
[2]with [3]self-sufficiency;* for nothing we have brought *in*

εἰς τὸν κόσμον, ὅτι οὐδὲ ἐξενεγκεῖν
into the world, because neither [2]*to* carry out

τι δυνάμεθα· **8** ἔχοντες δὲ διατροφὰς καὶ
[3]anything [1]can we; but having foods and

σκεπάσματα, τούτοις ἀρκεσθησόμεθα. **9** οἱ
clothings, with these things we will be satisfied. the

δὲ βουλόμενοι πλουτεῖν ἐμπίπτουσιν εἰς
But [ones] resolving to be rich fall *in* into

πειρασμὸν καὶ παγίδα καὶ ἐπιθυμίας πολλὰς
temptation and a snare and [5]lusts [1]many

ἀνοήτους καὶ βλαβεράς, αἵτινες βυθίζουσιν
[2]foolish [3]and [4]injurious, which [1]cause [3]to sink

τοὺς ἀνθρώπους εἰς ὄλεθρον καὶ ἀπώλειαν.
– [2]men into ruin and destruction.

10 ῥίζα γὰρ πάντων τῶν κακῶν ἐστιν
For [4]a root [5]of all – [6]evils [3]is

ἡ φιλαργυρία, ἧς τινες ὀρεγόμενοι
[1]the [2]love of money,* of which some hankering after

ἀπεπλανήθησαν ἀπὸ τῆς πίστεως καὶ
wandered away from the faith and

ἑαυτοὺς περιέπειραν ὀδύναις πολλαῖς. **11** Σὺ
themselves pierced round [2]pains [1]by many. thou

δέ, ὦ ἄνθρωπε θεοῦ, ταῦτα φεῦγε· δίωκε
But, O man of God, these things flee; [2]pursue

δὲ δικαιοσύνην, εὐσέβειαν, πίστιν, ἀγάπην,
[1]and righteousness, piety, faith, love,

ὑπομονήν, πραϋπαθίαν. **12** ἀγωνίζου τὸν
endurance, meekness. Struggle the

καλὸν ἀγῶνα τῆς πίστεως, ἐπιλαβοῦ τῆς
good struggle of the faith, lay hold on *the*

αἰωνίου ζωῆς, εἰς ἣν ἐκλήθης καὶ ὡμολό-
eternal life, to which thou wast called and didst con-

γησας τὴν καλὴν ὁμολογίαν ἐνώπιον
fess the good confession before

* For order of words see note on John 1. 1.

Love of Money
[3]If anyone teaches false
doctrines and does not
agree to the sound instruction of our Lord Jesus
Christ and to godly teaching, [4]he is conceited and
understands nothing. He
has an unhealthy interest in
controversies and quarrels
about words that result in
envy, strife, malicious talk,
evil suspicions [5]and constant friction between men
of corrupt mind, who have
been robbed of the truth
and who think that godli-
ness is a means to financial
gain.
[6]But godliness with con-
tentment is great gain. [7]For
we brought nothing into the
world, and we can take
nothing out of it. [8]But if we
have food and clothing, we
will be content with that.
[9]People who want to get
rich fall into temptation and
a trap and into many foolish
and harmful desires that
plunge men into ruin and
destruction. [10]For the love
of money is a root of all
kinds of evil. Some people,
eager for money, have
wandered from the faith
and pierced themselves
with many griefs.

Paul's Charge to Timothy
[11]But you, man of God,
flee from all this, and pursue righteousness, godli-
ness, faith, love, endurance
and gentleness. [12]Fight the
good fight of the faith. Take
hold of the eternal life to
which you were called
when you made your good

[b]Later mss. read *it is clear that*

* For order of words see note on John 1. 1.

presence of many witnesses.
13I charge you in the presence of God, who gives life to all things, and of Christ Jesus, who testified the good confession before Pontius Pilate,
14that you keep the commandment without stain or reproach until the appearing of our Lord Jesus Christ,
15which He will bring about at the proper time—He who is the blessed and only Sovereign, the King of kings and Lord of lords;
16who alone possesses immortality and dwells in unapproachable light; whom no man has seen or can see. To Him *be* honor and eternal dominion! Amen.
17Instruct those who are rich in this present world not to be conceited or to fix their hope on the uncertainty of riches, but on God, who richly supplies us with all things to enjoy.
18*Instruct them* to do good, to be rich in good works, to be generous and ready to share,
19storing up for themselves the treasure of a good foundation for the future, so that they may take hold of that which is life indeed.
20O Timothy, guard what has been entrusted to you, avoiding worldly *and* empty chatter *and* the opposing arguments of what is falsely called "knowledge"—
21which some have professed and thus gone astray from the faith.
Grace be with you.

πολλῶν μαρτύρων. **13** παραγγέλλω ἐνώπιον
many witnesses. I charge before

τοῦ θεοῦ τοῦ ζῳογονοῦντος τὰ πάντα
– God the [one] quickening – all things

καὶ Χριστοῦ Ἰησοῦ τοῦ μαρτυρήσαντος
and Christ Jesus the [one] having witnessed

ἐπὶ Ποντίου Πιλάτου τὴν καλὴν ὁμολογίαν,
in the time of Pontius Pilate the good confession,

14 τηρῆσαί σε τὴν ἐντολὴν ἄσπιλον
2to keep 1thee* the(this) commandment unspotted

ἀνεπίλημπτον μέχρι τῆς ἐπιφανείας τοῦ
without reproach until the appearance of the

κυρίου ἡμῶν Ἰησοῦ Χριστοῦ, **15** ἣν
Lord of us Jesus Christ, which§

καιροῖς ἰδίοις δείξει ὁ μακάριος καὶ
7in its/his own times 6will show 1the 2blessed 3and

μόνος δυνάστης, ὁ βασιλεὺς τῶν βασιλευ-
4only 5Potentate, the King of the [ones] reign-

όντων καὶ κύριος τῶν κυριευόντων, **16** ὁ
ing and Lord of the [ones] ruling, the

μόνος ἔχων ἀθανασίαν, φῶς οἰκῶν
only [one] having immortality, 2light 1inhabiting

ἀπρόσιτον, ὃν εἶδεν οὐδεὶς ἀνθρώπων οὐδὲ
unapproachable, whom 3saw 1no one 2of men nor

ἰδεῖν δύναται· ᾧ τιμὴ καὶ κράτος αἰώνιον·
2to see 1can; to whom [be] honour and might eternal:

ἀμήν. **17** Τοῖς πλουσίοις ἐν τῷ νῦν
Amen. 1the 3rich 4in 5the 6now (present)

αἰῶνι παράγγελλε μὴ ὑψηλοφρονεῖν, μηδὲ
7age 1Charge thou not to be highminded, nor

ἠλπικέναι ἐπὶ πλούτου ἀδηλότητι, ἀλλ᾽
to have set [their] hope on 2of riches 1[the] uncertainty, but

ἐπὶ θεῷ τῷ παρέχοντι ἡμῖν πάντα
on God the [one] offering to us all things

πλουσίως εἰς ἀπόλαυσιν, **18** ἀγαθοεργεῖν,
richly for enjoyment, to work good,

πλουτεῖν ἐν ἔργοις καλοῖς, εὐμεταδότους
to be rich in 2works 1good, 2ready to impart

εἶναι, κοινωνικούς, **19** ἀποθησαυρίζοντας
1to be, generous, treasuring away

ἑαυτοῖς θεμέλιον καλὸν εἰς τὸ μέλλον,
for themselves 2foundation 1a good for the future,

ἵνα ἐπιλάβωνται τῆς ὄντως ζωῆς. **20** Ὦ
in order that they may lay hold on the real*ly* life. O

Τιμόθεε, τὴν παραθήκην φύλαξον, ἐκτρεπ-
Timothy, 2the 3deposit 1guard, turning

όμενος τὰς βεβήλους κενοφωνίας καὶ
aside from *the* profane empty utterances and

ἀντιθέσεις τῆς ψευδωνύμου γνώσεως, **21** ἥν
opposing tenets of *the* falsely named knowledge, which

τινες ἐπαγγελλόμενοι περὶ τὴν πίστιν
some promising concerning the faith

ἠστόχησαν.
missed aim.

Ἡ χάρις μεθ᾽ ὑμῶν.
– Grace [be] with you.

* "thee" is the direct object of the verb "charge" in ver. 13: "I charge . . . thee to keep . . ."
§ The antecedent to this relative pronoun is "appearance", not "Jesus Christ".

confession in the presence
of many witnesses. 13In the
sight of God, who gives life
to everything, and of Christ
Jesus, who while testifying
before Pontius Pilate made
the good confession, I
charge you 14to keep this
command without spot or
blame until the appearing
of our Lord Jesus Christ,
15which God will bring
about in his own time—
God, the blessed and only
Ruler, the King of kings
and Lord of lords, 16who
alone is immortal and who
lives in unapproachable
light, whom no one has
seen or can see. To him be
honor and might forever.
Amen.

17Command those who
are rich in this present
world not to be arrogant
nor to put their hope in
wealth, which is so uncertain, but to put their hope in
God, who richly provides
us with everything for our
enjoyment. 18Command
them to do good, to be rich
in good deeds, and to be
generous and willing to
share. 19In this way they
will lay up treasure for
themselves as a firm foundation for the coming age,
so that they may take hold
of the life that is truly life.
20Timothy, guard what
has been entrusted to your
care. Turn away from godless chatter and the opposing ideas of what is falsely
called knowledge, 21which
some have professed and in
so doing have wandered
from the faith.

Grace be with you.

Chapter 1

Timothy Charged to Guard His Trust

PAUL, an apostle of Christ Jesus by the will of God, according to the promise of life in Christ Jesus,
2to Timothy, my beloved son: Grace, mercy *and* peace from God the Father and Christ Jesus our Lord.
3I thank God, whom I serve with a clear conscience the way my forefathers did, as I constantly remember you in my prayers night and day,
4longing to see you, even as I recall your tears, so that I may be filled with joy.
5For I am mindful of the sincere faith within you, which first dwelt in your grandmother Lois, and your mother Eunice, and I am sure that *it is* in you as well.
6And for this reason I remind you to kindle afresh the gift of God which is in you through the laying on of my hands.
7For God has not given us a spirit of timidity, but of power and love and discipline.
8Therefore do not be ashamed of the testimony of our Lord, or of me His prisoner; but join with *me* in suffering for the gospel according to the power of God,
9who has saved us, and called us with a holy calling, not according to our works, but according to His own purpose and grace which was granted us in Christ Jesus from all eternity,
10but now has been re-

1 Παῦλος ἀπόστολος Χριστοῦ Ἰησοῦ διὰ
Paul an apostle of Christ Jesus through
θελήματος θεοῦ κατ' ἐπαγγελίαν ζωῆς
[the] will of God by way of a promise of life
τῆς ἐν Χριστῷ Ἰησοῦ **2** Τιμοθέῳ ἀγαπητῷ
– in Christ Jesus to Timothy beloved
τέκνῳ· χάρις, ἔλεος, εἰρήνη ἀπὸ θεοῦ
child: Grace, mercy, peace from God
πατρὸς καὶ Χριστοῦ Ἰησοῦ τοῦ κυρίου
[our] Father and Christ Jesus the Lord
ἡμῶν.
of us.
3 Χάριν ἔχω τῷ θεῷ, ᾧ λατρεύω
Thanks I have – to God, whom I worship
ἀπὸ προγόνων ἐν καθαρᾷ συνειδήσει, ὡς
from [my] forebears in a clean conscience, as
ἀδιάλειπτον ἔχω τὴν περὶ σοῦ μνείαν
unceasingly I have [1]the [3]concerning [4]thee [2]remembrance
ἐν ταῖς δεήσεσίν μου νυκτὸς καὶ ἡμέρας,
in the petitions of me night and day,
4 ἐπιποθῶν σε ἰδεῖν, μεμνημένος σου
longing [2]thee [1]to see, having been reminded [3]of thee
τῶν δακρύων, ἵνα χαρᾶς πληρωθῶ,
[1]of the [2]tears, in order that of(with) joy I may be filled,
5 ὑπόμνησιν λαβὼν τῆς ἐν σοὶ ἀνυποκρίτου
[2]recollection [1]taking [3]of the [6]in [7]thee [4]unfeigned
πίστεως, ἥτις ἐνῴκησεν πρῶτον ἐν τῇ
[5]faith, which *in*dwelt firstly in the
μάμμῃ σου Λωΐδι καὶ τῇ μητρί σου
grandmother of thee Lois and [in] the mother of thee
Εὐνίκῃ, πέπεισμαι δὲ ὅτι καὶ ἐν σοί.
Eunice, and I have been persuaded that [it dwells] also in thee.
6 Δι' ἣν αἰτίαν ἀναμιμνήσκω σε ἀναζωπυρεῖν
For which cause I remind thee to fan the flame [of]
τὸ χάρισμα τοῦ θεοῦ, ὅ ἐστιν
the gift – of God, which is
ἐν σοὶ διὰ τῆς ἐπιθέσεως τῶν χειρῶν
in thee through the laying on of the hands
μου. **7** οὐ γὰρ ἔδωκεν ἡμῖν ὁ θεὸς
of me. [3]not For [2]gave [4]to us – [1]God
πνεῦμα δειλίας, ἀλλὰ δυνάμεως καὶ ἀγάπης
a spirit of cowardice, but of power and of love
καὶ σωφρονισμοῦ. **8** μὴ οὖν ἐπαισχυνθῇς
and of self-control. [2]not [1]Therefore [3]be [4]thou ashamed [of]
τὸ μαρτύριον τοῦ κυρίου ἡμῶν μηδὲ
the testimony of the Lord of us nor
ἐμὲ τὸν δέσμιον αὐτοῦ, ἀλλὰ συγκακοπάθησον
[of] me the prisoner of him, but suffer ill with
τῷ εὐαγγελίῳ κατὰ δύναμιν
the gospel according to [the] power
θεοῦ, **9** τοῦ σώσαντος ἡμᾶς καὶ καλέσαντος
of God, of the [one] having saved us and having called
κλήσει ἁγίᾳ, οὐ κατὰ τὰ ἔργα ἡμῶν
[2]calling [1]with a holy, not according to the works of us
ἀλλὰ κατὰ ἰδίαν πρόθεσιν καὶ χάριν,
but according to [his] own purpose and grace,
τὴν δοθεῖσαν ἡμῖν ἐν Χριστῷ Ἰησοῦ
– given to us in Christ Jesus
πρὸ χρόνων αἰωνίων, **10** φανερωθεῖσαν δὲ
before times eternal, but manifested

Chapter 1

PAUL, an apostle of Christ Jesus by the will of God, according to the promise of life that is in Christ Jesus,

2To Timothy, my dear son:

Grace, mercy and peace from God the Father and Christ Jesus our Lord.

Encouragement to Be Faithful

3I thank God, whom I serve, as my forefathers did, with a clear conscience, as night and day I constantly remember you in my prayers. 4Recalling your tears, I long to see you, so that I may be filled with joy. 5I have been reminded of your sincere faith, which first lived in your grandmother Lois and in your mother Eunice and, I am persuaded, now lives in you also. 6For this reason I remind you to fan into flame the gift of God, which is in you through the laying on of my hands. 7For God did not give us a spirit of timidity, but a spirit of power, of love and of self-discipline.
8So do not be ashamed to testify about our Lord, or ashamed of me his prisoner. But join with me in suffering for the gospel, by the power of God, 9who has saved us and called us to a holy life—not because of anything we have done but because of his own purpose and grace. This grace was given us in Christ Jesus before the beginning of time,
10but it has now been re-

vealed by the appearing of
our Savior Christ Jesus,
who abolished death, and
brought life and immortality to light through the gospel,
11for which I was ap-
pointed a preacher and an
apostle and a teacher.
12For this reason I also
suffer these things, but I am
not ashamed; for I know
whom I have believed and I
am convinced that He is
able to guard what I have
entrusted to Him until that
day.
13Retain the standard of
sound words which you
have heard from me, in the
faith and love which are in
Christ Jesus.
14Guard, through the
Holy Spirit who dwells in
us, the treasure which has
been entrusted to *you*.
15You are aware of the
fact that all who are in Asia
turned away from me,
among whom are Phygelus
and Hermogenes.
16The Lord grant mercy
to the house of Onesi-
phorus for he often re-
freshed me, and was not
ashamed of my chains;
17but when he was in
Rome, he eagerly searched
for me, and found me—
18the Lord grant to him to
find mercy from the Lord
on that day—and you know
very well what services he
rendered at Ephesus.

νῦν διὰ τῆς ἐπιφανείας τοῦ σωτῆρος
now through the appearance of the Saviour

ἡμῶν Χριστοῦ Ἰησοῦ, καταργήσαντος μὲν
of us Christ Jesus, [2]abrogating [1]on one hand

τὸν θάνατον φωτίσαντος δὲ ζωὴν καὶ
– death [2]bringing to light [1]on the other life and

ἀφθαρσίαν διὰ τοῦ εὐαγγελίου, 11 εἰς ὃ
incorruption through the gospel, for which

ἐτέθην ἐγὼ κῆρυξ καὶ ἀπόστολος καὶ
[2]was appointed [1]I a herald and an apostle and

διδάσκαλος· 12 δι' ἣν αἰτίαν καὶ ταῦτα
a teacher; for which cause also these things

πάσχω, ἀλλ' οὐκ ἐπαισχύνομαι, οἶδα γὰρ
I suffer, but I am not ashamed, for I know

ᾧ πεπίστευκα, καὶ πέπεισμαι ὅτι δυνατός
whom I have believed, and I have been persuaded that [2]able

ἐστιν τὴν παραθήκην μου φυλάξαι εἰς
[1]he is [4]the [5]deposit [6]of me [3]to guard to

ἐκείνην τὴν ἡμέραν. 13 ὑποτύπωσιν ἔχε
that – day. [2]a pattern [1]Have thou

ὑγιαινόντων λόγων ὧν παρ' ἐμοῦ ἤκουσας
of *being* healthy words which [2]from [3]me [1]thou heardest

ἐν πίστει καὶ ἀγάπῃ τῇ ἐν Χριστῷ
in faith and love – in Christ

Ἰησοῦ· 14 τὴν καλὴν παραθήκην φύλαξον
Jesus; the good deposit guard

διὰ πνεύματος ἁγίου τοῦ ἐνοικοῦντος ἐν
through Spirit [the] Holy – *in*dwelling in

ἡμῖν. 15 Οἶδας τοῦτο, ὅτι ἀπεστράφησάν
us. Thou knowest this, that turned away from

με πάντες οἱ ἐν τῇ Ἀσίᾳ, ὧν ἐστιν
me all the ones in – Asia, of whom is

Φύγελος καὶ Ἑρμογένης. 16 δῴη ἔλεος
Phygelus and Hermogenes. [1]May [4]give [5]mercy

ὁ κύριος τῷ Ὀνησιφόρου οἴκῳ, ὅτι
[2]the [3]Lord [6]to the [8]of Onesiphorus [7]household, because

πολλάκις με ἀνέψυξεν καὶ τὴν ἅλυσίν
often me he refreshed and the chain

μου οὐκ ἐπαισχύνθη, 17 ἀλλὰ γενόμενος
of me was not ashamed [of], but coming to be

ἐν Ῥώμῃ σπουδαίως ἐζήτησέν με καὶ
in Rome [2]diligently [1]he [3]sought [6]me [4]and

εὗρεν· — 18 δῴη αὐτῷ ὁ κύριος εὑρεῖν
[5]found; ([1]May [4]give [5]to him [2]the [3]Lord to find

ἔλεος παρὰ κυρίου ἐν ἐκείνῃ τῇ ἡμέρᾳ·
mercy from [the] Lord in that – day;)

— καὶ ὅσα ἐν Ἐφέσῳ διηκόνησεν,
and what things in Ephesus he served,

βέλτιον σὺ γινώσκεις.
very well thou knowest.

vealed through the appearing of our Savior, Christ
Jesus, who has destroyed
death and has brought life
and immortality to light
through the gospel. 11And
of this gospel I was ap-
pointed a herald and an
apostle and a teacher.
12That is why I am suffering
as I am. Yet I am not
ashamed, because I know
whom I have believed, and
am convinced that he is
able to guard what I have
entrusted to him for that
day.
13What you heard from
me, keep as the pattern of
sound teaching, with faith
and love in Christ Jesus.
14Guard the good deposit
that was entrusted to you
—guard it with the help of
the Holy Spirit who lives in
us.
15You know that every-
one in the province of Asia
has deserted me, including
Phygelus and Hermogenes.
16May the Lord show
mercy to the household of
Onesiphorus, because he
often refreshed me and was
not ashamed of my chains.
17On the contrary, when he
was in Rome, he searched
hard for me until he found
me. 18May the Lord grant
that he will find mercy from
the Lord on that day! You
know very well in how
many ways he helped me in
Ephesus.

Chapter 2

Be Strong

YOU therefore, my son,
be strong in the grace
that is in Christ Jesus.
2And the things which
you have heard from me in
the presence of many wit-
nesses, these entrust to
faithful men, who will be

2 Σὺ οὖν, τέκνον μου, ἐνδυναμοῦ ἐν
Thou therefore, child of me, be empowered by

τῇ χάριτι τῇ ἐν Χριστῷ Ἰησοῦ, 2 καὶ
the grace – in Christ Jesus, and

ἃ ἤκουσας παρ' ἐμοῦ διὰ πολλῶν
what things thou heardest from me through many

μαρτύρων, ταῦτα παράθου πιστοῖς ἀνθρώ-
witnesses, these commit to faithful men,

Chapter 2

YOU then, my son, be
strong in the grace
that is in Christ Jesus. 2And
the things you have heard
me say in the presence of
many witnesses entrust to
reliable men who will also

able to teach others also.
3Suffer hardship with
me, as a good soldier of
Christ Jesus.
4No soldier in active service entangles himself in
the affairs of everyday life,
so that he may please the
one who enlisted him as a
soldier.
5And also if anyone com-
petes as an athlete, he does
not win the prize unless he
competes according to the
rules.
6The hard-working farm-
er ought to be the first to
receive his share of the
crops.
7Consider what I say, for
the Lord will give you
understanding in every-
thing.
8Remember Jesus
Christ, risen from the dead,
descendant of David, ac-
cording to my gospel,
9for which I suffer hard-
ship even to imprisonment
as a criminal; but the word
of God is not imprisoned.
10For this reason I endure
all things for the sake of
those who are chosen, that
they also may obtain the
salvation which is in Christ
Jesus *and* with *it* eternal
glory.
11It is a trustworthy
statement:

For if we died with
Him, we shall also
live with Him;
12 If we endure, we shall
also reign with Him;
If we deny Him, He
also will deny us;
13 If we are faithless, He
remains faithful; for
He cannot deny
Himself.

An Unashamed Workman

14Remind *them* of these
things, and solemnly
charge *them* in the presence of God not to wrangle
about words, which is useless, *and leads* to the ruin
of the hearers.
15Be diligent to present
yourself approved to God
as a workman who does not
need to be ashamed, han-
dling accurately the word
of truth.

ποις, οἵτινες ἱκανοὶ ἔσονται καὶ ἑτέρους
who [3]competent [1]will be [2]also [4]others

διδάξαι. **3** Συγκακοπάθησον ὡς καλὸς
[5]to teach. Suffer ill with* as a good

στρατιώτης Χριστοῦ Ἰησοῦ. **4** οὐδεὶς
soldier of Christ Jesus. No one

στρατευόμενος ἐμπλέκεται ταῖς τοῦ βίου
soldiering is involved [1]with the – [3]of life

πραγματείαις, ἵνα τῷ στρατολογήσαντι
[2]affairs, in order that [2]the [one] [3]having enlisted [him]

ἀρέσῃ. **5** ἐὰν δὲ καὶ ἀθλῇ τις, οὐ
[1]he may please. And if also [2]wrestles [1]anyone, not

στεφανοῦται ἐὰν μὴ νομίμως ἀθλήσῃ.
he is crowned unless [2]lawfully [1]he wrestles.

6 τὸν κοπιῶντα γεωργὸν δεῖ πρῶτον τῶν
[2]the [3]labouring [4]husbandman [1]It behoves [6]firstly [7]of the

καρπῶν μεταλαμβάνειν. **7** νόει ὃ λέγω·
[8]fruits [5]to partake. Consider what I say;

δώσει γάρ σοι ὁ κύριος σύνεσιν ἐν
for [3]will give [4]thee [1]the [2]Lord understanding in

πᾶσιν. **8** μνημόνευε Ἰησοῦν Χριστὸν
all things. Remember Jesus Christ

ἐγηγερμένον ἐκ νεκρῶν, ἐκ σπέρματος
having been raised from [the] dead, of [the] seed

Δαυίδ, κατὰ τὸ εὐαγγέλιόν μου· **9** ἐν
of David, according to the gospel of me; in

ᾧ κακοπαθῶ μέχρι δεσμῶν ὡς κακοῦργος,
which I suffer ill unto bonds as an evildoer,

ἀλλὰ ὁ λόγος τοῦ θεοῦ οὐ δέδεται.
but the word – of God has not been bound.

10 διὰ τοῦτο πάντα ὑπομένω διὰ τοὺς
Therefore all things I endure on account of the

ἐκλεκτούς, ἵνα καὶ αὐτοὶ σωτηρίας τύχωσιν
chosen ones, in order that [2]also [1]they [4]salvation [3]may obtain

τῆς ἐν Χριστῷ Ἰησοῦ μετὰ δόξης
– in Christ Jesus with glory

αἰωνίου. **11** πιστὸς ὁ λόγος· εἰ γὰρ
eternal. Faithful [is] the word: for if

συναπεθάνομεν, καὶ συζήσομεν· **12** εἰ
we died with [him], also we shall live with [him]; if

ὑπομένομεν, καὶ συμβασιλεύσομεν· εἰ
we endure, also we shall reign with [him]; if

ἀρνησόμεθα, κἀκεῖνος ἀρνήσεται ἡμᾶς· **13** εἰ
we *shall* deny, that one also will deny us; if

ἀπιστοῦμεν, ἐκεῖνος πιστὸς μένει, ἀρνή-
we disbelieve, that one [2]faithful [1]remains, [3]*to*

σασθαι γὰρ ἑαυτὸν οὐ δύναται. **14** Ταῦτα
deny [1]for [4]himself [2]he cannot. These things

ὑπομίμνησκε, διαμαρτυρόμενος ἐνώπιον τοῦ
remind thou [them] [of], solemnly witnessing before –

θεοῦ μὴ λογομαχεῖν, ἐπ' οὐδὲν χρήσιμον,
God not to fight with words, [2]for [3]nothing [1]useful,

ἐπὶ καταστροφῇ τῶν ἀκουόντων. **15** σπού-
for overthrowing of the [ones] hearing. [1]Be

δασον σεαυτὸν δόκιμον παραστῆσαι τῷ
eager [3]thyself [4]approved [2]to present –

θεῷ, ἐργάτην ἀνεπαίσχυντον, ὀρθοτομοῦντα
to God, a workman unashamed, cutting straight

τὸν λόγον τῆς ἀληθείας. **16** τὰς δὲ
the word – of truth. – But

* See 1. 8.

be qualified to teach others. 3Endure hardship with
us like a good soldier of
Christ Jesus. 4No one serving as a soldier gets in-
volved in civilian affairs—
he wants to please his commanding officer. 5Similar-
ly, if anyone competes as
an athlete, he does not receive the victor's crown
unless he competes according to the rules. 6The hard-
working farmer should be
the first to receive a share
of the crops. 7Reflect on
what I am saying, for the
Lord will give you insight
into all this.
8Remember Jesus Christ,
raised from the dead, de-
scended from David. This
is my gospel, 9for which I
am suffering even to the
point of being chained like
a criminal. But God's word
is not chained. 10Therefore
I endure everything for the
sake of the elect, that they
too may obtain the salva-
tion that is in Christ Jesus,
with eternal glory.
11Here is a trustworthy
saying:

If we died with him,
we will also live with
him;
12if we endure,
we will also reign with
him.
If we disown him,
he will also disown us;
13if we are faithless,
he will remain faithful,
for he cannot disown
himself.

A Workman Approved by God

14Keep reminding them of
these things. Warn them
before God against quarreling about words; it is of no
value, and only ruins those
who listen. 15Do your best
to present yourself to God
as one approved, a work-
man who does not need to
be ashamed and who cor-
rectly handles the word of
truth. 16Avoid godless

16But avoid worldly *and*
empty chatter, for it will
lead to further ungodliness,
17and their talk will
spread like [a]gangrene.
Among them are Hymenaeus and Philetus,
18*men* who have gone
astray from the truth saying
that the resurrection has already taken place, and thus
they upset the faith of
some.
19Nevertheless, the firm
foundation of God stands,
having this seal, "The Lord
knows those who are His,"
and, "Let everyone who
names the name of the
Lord abstain from wickedness."
20Now in a large house
there are not only gold and
silver vessels, but also vessels of wood and of earthenware, and some to honor
and some to dishonor.
21Therefore, if a man
cleanses himself from these
things, he will be a vessel
for honor, sanctified, useful to the Master, prepared
for every good work.
22Now flee from youthful
lusts, and pursue righteousness, faith, love *and* peace,
with those who call on the
Lord from a pure heart.
23But refuse foolish and
ignorant speculations,
knowing that they produce
quarrels.
24And the Lord's bond-servant must not be quarrelsome, but be kind to all,
able to teach, patient when
wronged,
25with gentleness correcting those who are in opposition, if perhaps God may
grant them repentance
leading to the knowledge of
the truth,
26and they may come to
their senses *and escape*
from the snare of the devil,

βεβήλους κενοφωνίας περιΐστασο· ἐπὶ πλεῖον
profane empty utterances shun; [3]to [4]more

γὰρ προκόψουσιν ἀσεβείας, 17 καὶ ὁ λόγος
[1]for [2]they will advance of impiety, and the word

αὐτῶν ὡς γάγγραινα νομὴν ἕξει· ὧν
of them as a canker feeding will have; of whom

ἐστιν Ὑμέναιος καὶ Φίλητος, 18 οἵτινες
is(are) Hymenæus and Philetus, who

περὶ τὴν ἀλήθειαν ἠστόχησαν, λέγοντες
concerning the truth missed aim, saying

ἀνάστασιν ἤδη γεγονέναι, καὶ ἀνατρέπουσιν
[the] resurrection already to have become, and overturn

τήν τινων πίστιν. 19 ὁ μέντοι στερεὸς
the [2]of some [1]faith. [2]the [1]However firm

θεμέλιος τοῦ θεοῦ ἕστηκεν, ἔχων τὴν
foundation – of God stands, having –

σφραγῖδα ταύτην· ἔγνω κύριος τοὺς ὄντας
seal this: [2]knew [1][The] Lord the [ones] being

αὐτοῦ, καί· ἀποστήτω ἀπὸ ἀδικίας πᾶς
of him, and: Let stand away from iniquity every-

ὁ ὀνομάζων τὸ ὄνομα κυρίου. 20 ἐν
one naming the name of [the] Lord. [1]in

μεγάλῃ δὲ οἰκίᾳ οὐκ ἔστιν μόνον σκεύη
[3]a great [2]Now [4]house there is(are) not only vessels

χρυσᾶ καὶ ἀργυρᾶ, ἀλλὰ καὶ ξύλινα
golden and silvern, but also wooden

καὶ ὀστράκινα, καὶ ἃ μὲν εἰς τιμὴν ἃ δὲ
and earthen, and some to honour others

εἰς ἀτιμίαν· 21 ἐὰν οὖν τις ἐκκαθάρῃ
to dishonour; if therefore anyone cleanses

ἑαυτὸν ἀπὸ τούτων, ἔσται σκεῦος εἰς
himself from these [latter], he will be a vessel to

τιμήν, ἡγιασμένον, εὔχρηστον τῷ δεσπότῃ,
honour, *having been* sanctified, suitable for the master,

εἰς πᾶν ἔργον ἀγαθὸν ἡτοιμασμένον.
to every work good *having been* prepared.

22 τὰς δὲ νεωτερικὰς ἐπιθυμίας φεῦγε,
Now *the* [2]youthful [3]lusts [1]flee,

δίωκε δὲ δικαιοσύνην, πίστιν, ἀγάπην,
but pursue righteousness, faith, love,

εἰρήνην μετὰ τῶν ἐπικαλουμένων τὸν
peace with the [ones] calling on the

κύριον ἐκ καθαρᾶς καρδίας. 23 τὰς δὲ
Lord out of a clean heart. – But

μωρὰς καὶ ἀπαιδεύτους ζητήσεις παραιτοῦ,
foolish and uninstructed questionings refuse,

εἰδὼς ὅτι γεννῶσιν μάχας· 24 δοῦλον δὲ
knowing that they beget fights; and [2]a slave

κυρίου οὐ δεῖ μάχεσθαι ἀλλὰ ἤπιον
[3]of [the] Lord [1]it behoves not to fight but gentle

εἶναι πρὸς πάντας, διδακτικόν, ἀνεξίκακον,
to be toward all men, apt to teach, forbearing,

25 ἐν πραΰτητι παιδεύοντα τοὺς ἀντιδιατι-
in meekness instructing the [ones] oppos-

θεμένους, μήποτε δώῃ αὐτοῖς ὁ θεὸς
ing, [if] perhaps [2]may give [3]them – [1]God

μετάνοιαν εἰς ἐπίγνωσιν ἀληθείας, 26 καὶ
repentance for a full knowledge of truth, and

ἀνανήψωσιν ἐκ τῆς τοῦ διαβόλου παγίδος,
they may return to soberness out of [1]the [3]of the [4]devil [2]snare,

chatter, because those who
indulge in it will become
more and more ungodly.
17Their teaching will spread
like gangrene. Among them
are Hymenaeus and Philetus,
18who have wandered
away from the truth. They
say that the resurrection
has already taken place,
and they destroy the faith
of some. 19Nevertheless,
God's solid foundation
stands firm, sealed with
this inscription: "The Lord
knows those who are
his,"[a] and, "Everyone
who confesses the name of
the Lord must turn away
from wickedness."
20In a large house there
are articles not only of gold
and silver, but also of wood
and clay; some are for noble purposes and some for
ignoble. 21If a man cleanses
himself from the latter, he
will be an instrument for
noble purposes, made holy,
useful to the Master and
prepared to do any good
work.
22Flee the evil desires of
youth, and pursue righteousness, faith, love and
peace, along with those
who call on the Lord out of
a pure heart. 23Don't have
anything to do with foolish
and stupid arguments, because you know they produce quarrels. 24And the
Lord's servant must not
quarrel; instead, he must be
kind to everyone, able to
teach, not resentful.
25Those who oppose him he
must gently instruct, in the
hope that God will grant
them repentance leading
them to a knowledge of the
truth, 26and that they will
come to their senses and
escape from the trap of the

[a]Or, *cancer*

[a]*19* Num. 16:5 (see Septuagint)

having been held captive by him to do his will.

Chapter 3

"Difficult Times Will Come"

BUT realize this, that in the last days difficult times will come.

2For men will be lovers of self, lovers of money, boastful, arrogant, revilers, disobedient to parents, ungrateful, unholy,

3unloving, irreconcilable, malicious gossips, without self-control, brutal, haters of good,

4treacherous, reckless, conceited, lovers of pleasure rather than lovers of God;

5holding to a form of godliness, although they have denied its power; and avoid such men as these.

6For among them are those who enter into households and captivate weak women weighed down with sins, led on by various impulses,

7always learning and never able to come to the knowledge of the truth.

8And just as Jannes and Jambres opposed Moses, so these *men* also oppose the truth, men of depraved mind, rejected as regards the faith.

9But they will not make further progress; for their folly will be obvious to all, as also that of those *two* came to be.

10But you followed my teaching, conduct, purpose, faith, patience, love, perseverance,

11persecutions, *and* sufferings, such as happened

ἐζωγρημένοι ὑπ' αὐτοῦ εἰς τὸ ἐκείνου θέλημα.
having been caught by him[,] to 1the 3of that one* 2will.

3 Τοῦτο δὲ γίνωσκε, ὅτι ἐν ἐσχάταις
And this know thou, that in [the] last
ἡμέραις ἐνστήσονται καιροὶ χαλεποί·
days 3will be at hand 2times 1grievous;
2 ἔσονται γὰρ οἱ ἄνθρωποι φίλαυτοι,
for 2will be – 1men self-lovers,
φιλάργυροι, ἀλαζόνες, ὑπερήφανοι, βλάσφημοι,
money-lovers, boasters, arrogant, blasphemers,
γονεῦσιν ἀπειθεῖς, ἀχάριστοι, ἀνόσιοι,
2to parents 1disobedient, unthankful, unholy,
3 ἄστοργοι, ἄσπονδοι, διάβολοι, ἀκρατεῖς,
without natural affection, implacable, slanderers, incontinent,
ἀνήμεροι, ἀφιλάγαθοι, 4 προδόται, προπετεῖς,
untamed, haters of good [things/men], betrayers, reckless,
τετυφωμένοι, φιλήδονοι μᾶλλον ἢ φιλόθεοι,
having been puffed up, pleasure-lovers rather than God-lovers,
5 ἔχοντες μόρφωσιν εὐσεβείας τὴν δὲ
having a form of piety but the
δύναμιν αὐτῆς ἠρνημένοι· καὶ τούτους
power of it having denied: and 2these
ἀποτρέπου. 6 ἐκ τούτων γάρ εἰσιν οἱ
3turn away 1from. 2of 3these 1For are the
ἐνδύνοντες εἰς τὰς οἰκίας καὶ αἰχμαλωτίζ-
[ones] creeping into – houses and captur-
οντες γυναικάρια σεσωρευμένα ἁμαρτίαις,
ing silly women *having been* heaped* with sins,
ἀγόμενα ἐπιθυμίαις ποικίλαις, 7 πάντοτε
being led* lusts by various, always
μανθάνοντα καὶ μηδέποτε εἰς ἐπίγνωσιν
learning* and never 3to 4a full knowledge
ἀληθείας ἐλθεῖν δυνάμενα. 8 ὃν τρόπον
5of truth 2to come 1being able.* by what way
δὲ Ἰάννης καὶ Ἰαμβρῆς ἀντέστησαν
Now Jannes and Jambres opposed
Μωϋσεῖ, οὕτως καὶ οὗτοι ἀνθίστανται τῇ
Moses, so also these oppose the
ἀληθείᾳ, ἄνθρωποι κατεφθαρμένοι τὸν νοῦν,
truth, men having been corrupted the mind, =with corrupted mind,
ἀδόκιμοι περὶ τὴν πίστιν. 9 ἀλλ' οὐ
reprobate as to the faith. But not
προκόψουσιν ἐπὶ πλεῖον· ἡ γὰρ ἄνοια
they will advance to more; =farther; for the folly
αὐτῶν ἔκδηλος ἔσται πᾶσιν, ὡς καὶ
of them very clear will be to all men, as also
ἡ ἐκείνων ἐγένετο. 10 Σὺ δὲ παρηκολού-
the [folly] of those became. But thou hast closely
θησάς μου τῇ διδασκαλίᾳ, τῇ ἀγωγῇ,
followed of me the teaching, the conduct,
τῇ προθέσει, τῇ πίστει, τῇ μακροθυμίᾳ,
the purpose, the faith, the longsuffering,
τῇ ἀγάπῃ, τῇ ὑπομονῇ, 11 τοῖς διωγμοῖς,
the love, the endurance, the persecutions,
τοῖς παθήμασιν, οἷά μοι ἐγένετο ἐν
the sufferings. which 2to me 1happened in

* That is, of God (the remoter antecedent).

* Agreeing with "silly women" (neut. pl.).

devil, who has taken them captive to do his will.

Chapter 3

Godlessness in the Last Days

BUT mark this: There
will be terrible times
in the last days. 2People
will be lovers of them-
selves, lovers of money,
boastful, proud, abusive,
disobedient to their par-
ents, ungrateful, unholy,
3without love, unforgiving,
slanderous, without self-
control, brutal, not lovers
of the good, 4treacherous,
rash, conceited, lovers of
pleasure rather than lovers
of God— 5having a form of
godliness but denying its
power. Have nothing to do
with them.
6They are the kind who
worm their way into homes
and gain control over
weak-willed women, who
are loaded down with sins
and are swayed by all kinds
of evil desires, 7always
learning but never able to
acknowledge the truth.
8Just as Jannes and Jam-
bres opposed Moses, so
also these men oppose the
truth—men of depraved
minds, who, as far as the
faith is concerned, are rejected. 9But they will not
get very far because, as in
the case of those men, their
folly will be clear to everyone.

Paul's Charge to Timothy

10You, however, know all
about my teaching, my way
of life, my purpose, faith,
patience, love, endurance,
11persecutions, sufferings
—what kinds of things hap-

to me at Antioch, at Iconium *and* at Lystra; what persecutions I endured, and
out of them all the Lord delivered me!
12 And indeed, all who desire to live godly in Christ
Jesus will be persecuted.
13 But evil men and impostors will proceed *from bad*
to worse, deceiving and being deceived.
14 You, however, con-
tinue in the things you have
learned and become con-
vinced of, knowing from
whom you have learned
them;
15 and that from childhood
you have known the sacred
writings which are able to
give you the wisdom that
leads to salvation through
faith which is in Christ
Jesus.
16 [b] All Scripture is inspired by God and profit-
able for teaching, for reproof, for correction, for
training in righteousness;
17 that the man of God
may be adequate, equipped
for every good work.

Chapter 4

"Preach the Word"

I solemnly charge *you* in
the presence of God and
of Christ Jesus, who is to
judge the living and the
dead, and by His appearing
and His kingdom:
2 preach the word; be
ready in season *and* out of
season; reprove, rebuke,
exhort, with great patience
and instruction.
3 For the time will come
when they will not endure
sound doctrine; but *wanting* to have their ears tick-
led, they will accumulate
for themselves teachers in
accordance to their own
desires;
4 and will turn away their
ears from the truth, and will
turn aside to myths.

[b] Or possibly, *Every Scripture inspired by God is also profitable*

Interlinear

Ἀντιοχείᾳ, ἐν Ἰκονίῳ, ἐν Λύστροις· οἵους
Antioch, in Iconium, in Lystra: what
διωγμοὺς ὑπήνεγκα, καὶ ἐκ πάντων με
persecutions I bore, and out of all [4]me
ἐρρύσατο ὁ κύριος. 12 καὶ πάντες δὲ
[3]delivered [1]the [2]Lord. [2]indeed [3]all [1]And
οἱ θέλοντες ζῆν εὐσεβῶς ἐν Χριστῷ
the [ones] wishing to live piously in Christ
Ἰησοῦ διωχθήσονται. 13 πονηροὶ δὲ ἄν-
Jesus will be persecuted. But evil men
θρωποι καὶ γόητες προκόψουσιν ἐπὶ τὸ
and impostors will advance to the
χεῖρον, πλανῶντες καὶ πλανώμενοι. 14 σὺ
worse, deceiving and being deceived. [2]thou
δὲ μένε ἐν οἷς ἔμαθες καὶ ἐπιστώθης,
But [1]continue in what things thou didst learn and wast assured of,
εἰδὼς παρὰ τίνων ἔμαθες, 15 καὶ ὅτι
knowing from whom* thou didst learn, and that
ἀπὸ βρέφους ἱερὰ γράμματα οἶδας, τὰ
from a babe [2]sacred [3]letters [1]thou knowest, [ones]
δυνάμενά σε σοφίσαι εἰς σωτηρίαν διὰ
being able thee to make wise to salvation through
πίστεως τῆς ἐν Χριστῷ Ἰησοῦ. 16 πᾶσα
faith – in Christ Jesus. Every
γραφὴ θεόπνευστος καὶ ὠφέλιμος πρὸς
scripture [is] God-breathed and profitable for
διδασκαλίαν, πρὸς ἐλεγμόν, πρὸς ἐπανόρ-
teaching, for reproof, for cor-
θωσιν, πρὸς παιδείαν τὴν ἐν δικαιοσύνῃ,
rection, for instruction – in righteousness,
17 ἵνα ἄρτιος ᾖ ὁ τοῦ θεοῦ ἄνθρωπος,
in order that [5]fitted [4]may be [1]the – [3]of God [2]man,
πρὸς πᾶν ἔργον ἀγαθὸν ἐξηρτισμένος.
for every work good *having been* furnished.
4 Διαμαρτύρομαι ἐνώπιον τοῦ θεοῦ καὶ
I solemnly witness before – God and
Χριστοῦ Ἰησοῦ, τοῦ μέλλοντος κρίνειν
Christ Jesus, the [one] being about to judge
ζῶντας καὶ νεκρούς, καὶ τὴν ἐπιφάνειαν
living [ones] and dead, both [by] the appearance
αὐτοῦ καὶ τὴν βασιλείαν αὐτοῦ· 2 κήρυξον
of him and [by] the kingdom of him: proclaim
τὸν λόγον, ἐπίστηθι εὐκαίρως ἀκαίρως,
the word, be attentive seasonably[,] unseasonably,
ἔλεγξον, ἐπιτίμησον, παρακάλεσον, ἐν πάσῃ
reprove, admonish, exhort, with all
μακροθυμίᾳ καὶ διδαχῇ. 3 ἔσται γὰρ
longsuffering and teaching. For there will be
καιρὸς ὅτε τῆς ὑγιαινούσης διδασκαλίας
a time when [2]the [3]*being* healthy [4]teaching
οὐκ ἀνέξονται, ἀλλὰ κατὰ τὰς ἰδίας
[1]they will not bear with, but according to the(ir) own
ἐπιθυμίας ἑαυτοῖς ἐπισωρεύσουσιν διδασ-
lusts [2]to themselves [1]they will heap up [3]teach-
κάλους κνηθόμενοι τὴν ἀκοήν, 4 καὶ ἀπὸ
ers tickling the ear, and [5]from
μὲν τῆς ἀληθείας τὴν ἀκοὴν ἀποστρέψουσιν,
[1]on one hand [6]the [7]truth [3]the [4]ear [2]will turn away,
ἐπὶ δὲ τοὺς μύθους ἐκτραπήσονται. 5 σὺ
[3]to [1]on the other *the* [4]tales [2]will be turned aside. [2]thou

* Plural.

pened to me in Antioch,
Iconium and Lystra, the
persecutions I endured.
Yet the Lord rescued me
from all of them. 12 In fact,
everyone who wants to live
a godly life in Christ Jesus
will be persecuted, 13 while
evil men and impostors will
go from bad to worse, de-
ceiving and being deceived.
14 But as for you, continue
in what you have learned
and have become con-
vinced of, because you
know those from whom
you learned it, 15 and how
from infancy you have
known the holy Scriptures,
which are able to make you
wise for salvation through
faith in Christ Jesus. 16 All
Scripture is God-breathed
and is useful for teaching,
rebuking, correcting and
training in righteousness,
17 so that the man of God
may be thoroughly
equipped for every good
work.

Chapter 4

In the presence of God
and of Christ Jesus, who
will judge the living and the
dead, and in view of his appearing and his kingdom, I
give you this charge:
2 Preach the Word; be prepared in season and out of
season; correct, rebuke and
encourage—with great pa-
tience and careful instruction. 3 For the time will
come when men will not
put up with sound doctrine.
Instead, to suit their own
desires, they will gather
around them a great num-
ber of teachers to say what
their itching ears want to
hear. 4 They will turn their
ears away from the truth
and turn aside to myths.

5But you, be sober in all things, endure hardship, do the work of an evangelist, fulfill your ministry.
6For I am already being poured out as a drink offering, and the time of my departure has come.
7I have fought the good fight, I have finished the course, I have kept the faith;
8in the future there is laid up for me the crown of righteousness, which the Lord, the righteous Judge, will award to me on that day; and not only to me, but also to all who have loved His appearing.

Personal Concerns

9Make every effort to come to me soon;
10for Demas, having loved this present world, has deserted me and gone to Thessalonica; Crescens *has gone* to Galatia, Titus to Dalmatia.
11Only Luke is with me. Pick up Mark and bring him with you, for he is useful to me for service.
12But Tychicus I have sent to Ephesus.
13When you come bring the cloak which I left at Troas with Carpus, and the books, especially the parchments.
14Alexander the coppersmith did me much harm; the Lord will repay him according to his deeds.
15Be on guard against him yourself, for he vigorously opposed our teaching.
16At my first defense no one supported me, but all deserted me; may it not be counted against them.
17But the Lord stood with me, and strengthened me, in order that through me the proclamation might be fully accomplished, and

σὺ δὲ νῆφε ἐν πᾶσιν, κακοπάθησον, ἔργον
But 1be sober in all things, suffer evil, 2[the] work

ποίησον εὐαγγελιστοῦ, τὴν διακονίαν σου
1do of an evangelist, 2the 3ministry 4of thee

πληροφόρησον. 6 Ἐγὼ γὰρ ἤδη σπένδομαι,
1fulfil. For I already am being poured out,

καὶ ὁ καιρὸς τῆς ἀναλύσεώς μου ἐφέστη-
and the time of the departure of me has

κεν. 7 τὸν καλὸν ἀγῶνα ἠγώνισμαι,
arrived. The good struggle I have struggled,

τὸν δρόμον τετέλεκα, τὴν πίστιν τετήρηκα·
the course I have finished, the faith I have kept:

8 λοιπὸν ἀπόκειταί μοι ὁ τῆς δικαιοσύνης
for the rest there is laid up for me 1the – 3of righteousness

στέφανος, ὃν ἀποδώσει μοι ὁ κύριος
2crown, which 6will render 7to me 4the 5Lord

ἐν ἐκείνῃ τῇ ἡμέρᾳ, ὁ δίκαιος κριτής,
8in 9that – 10day, 1the 2righteous 3judge,

οὐ μόνον δὲ ἐμοὶ ἀλλὰ καὶ πᾶσι τοῖς
2not 3only 1and to me but also to all the [ones]

ἠγαπηκόσι τὴν ἐπιφάνειαν αὐτοῦ.
having loved the appearance of him.

9 Σπούδασον ἐλθεῖν πρός με ταχέως·
Hasten to come to me shortly;

10 Δημᾶς γάρ με ἐγκατέλιπεν ἀγαπήσας
2Demas 1For 4me 3forsook loving

τὸν νῦν αἰῶνα, καὶ ἐπορεύθη εἰς Θεσσαλο-
the now (present) age, and went to Thessalo-

νίκην, Κρήσκης εἰς Γαλατίαν, Τίτος εἰς
nica, Crescens to Galatia, Titus to

Δαλματίαν· 11 Λουκᾶς ἐστιν μόνος μετ'
Dalmatia; Luke is alone with

ἐμοῦ. Μᾶρκον ἀναλαβὼν ἄγε μετὰ σεαυτοῦ·
me. Mark taking bring with thyself;

ἔστιν γάρ μοι εὔχρηστος εἰς διακονίαν.
2he is 1for 4to me 3useful for ministry.

12 Τύχικον δὲ ἀπέστειλα εἰς Ἔφεσον.
And Tychicus I sent to Ephesus.

13 τὸν φαιλόνην, ὃν ἀπέλιπον ἐν Τρῳάδι
The cloak, which I left in Troas

παρὰ Κάρπῳ, ἐρχόμενος φέρε, καὶ τὰ
with Carpus, coming bring thou, and the

βιβλία, μάλιστα τὰς μεμβράνας. 14 Ἀλέξ-
scrolls, especially the parchments. Alex-

ανδρος ὁ χαλκεὺς πολλά μοι κακὰ
ander the coppersmith 2many 3*to* me 4evils

ἐνεδείξατο· ἀποδώσει αὐτῷ ὁ κύριος κατὰ
1showed; 3will render 4to him 1the 2Lord according to

τὰ ἔργα αὐτοῦ· 15 ὃν καὶ σὺ φυλάσσου·
the works of him; whom also 2thou 1guard 3[against];

λίαν γὰρ ἀντέστη τοῖς ἡμετέροις λόγοις.
for greatly he opposed – our words.

16 Ἐν τῇ πρώτῃ μου ἀπολογίᾳ οὐδείς
At the first 2of me 1defence no one

μοι παρεγένετο, ἀλλὰ πάντες με ἐγκατέ-
2me 1was beside, but all men 2me 1for-

λιπον· μὴ αὐτοῖς λογισθείη· 17 ὁ δὲ
sook; not to them may it be reckoned; but the

κύριός μοι παρέστη καὶ ἐνεδυνάμωσέν με,
Lord 2me 1stood with and empowered me,

ἵνα δι' ἐμοῦ τὸ κήρυγμα πληροφορηθῇ
in order that through me the proclamation might be accomplished

5But you, keep your head in all situations, endure hardship, do the work of an evangelist, discharge all the duties of your ministry.
6For I am already being poured out like a drink offering, and the time has come for my departure. 7I have fought the good fight, I have finished the race, I have kept the faith. 8Now there is in store for me the crown of righteousness, which the Lord, the righteous Judge, will award to me on that day—and not only to me, but also to all who have longed for his appearing.

Personal Remarks

9Do your best to come to me quickly, 10for Demas, because he loved this world, has deserted me and has gone to Thessalonica. Crescens has gone to Galatia, and Titus to Dalmatia. 11Only Luke is with me. Get Mark and bring him with you, because he is helpful to me in my ministry. 12I sent Tychicus to Ephesus. 13When you come, bring the cloak that I left with Carpus at Troas, and my scrolls, especially the parchments.
14Alexander the metalworker did me a great deal of harm. The Lord will repay him for what he has done. 15You too should be on your guard against him, because he strongly opposed our message.
16At my first defense, no one came to my support, but everyone deserted me. May it not be held against them. 17But the Lord stood at my side and gave me strength, so that through me the message might be fully proclaimed and all the

that all the Gentiles might hear; and I was delivered out of the lion's mouth.

18 The Lord will deliver me from every evil deed, and will bring me safely to His heavenly kingdom; to Him *be* the glory forever and ever. Amen.

19 Greet Prisca and Aquila, and the household of Onesiphorus.

20 Erastus remained at Corinth, but Trophimus I left sick at Miletus.

21 Make every effort to come before winter. Eubulus greets you, also Pudens and Linus and Claudia and all the brethren.

22 The Lord be with your spirit. Grace be with you.

καὶ ἀκούσωσιν πάντα τὰ ἔθνη, καὶ
and [4]might hear [1]all [2]the [3]nations, and

ἐρρύσθην ἐκ στόματος λέοντος. 18 ῥύσεταί
I was delivered out of [the] mouth of [the] lion. [3]will deliver

με ὁ κύριος ἀπὸ παντὸς ἔργου πονηροῦ
[4]me [1]The [2]Lord from every work wicked

καὶ σώσει εἰς τὴν βασιλείαν αὐτοῦ τὴν
and will save to the [3]kingdom [2]of him –

ἐπουράνιον· ᾧ ἡ δόξα εἰς τοὺς αἰῶνας
[1]heavenly: to whom [be] the glory unto the ages

τῶν αἰώνων, ἀμήν.
of the ages, Amen.

19 Ἄσπασαι Πρίσκαν καὶ Ἀκύλαν καὶ
Greet Prisca and Aquila and

τὸν Ὀνησιφόρου οἶκον. 20 Ἔραστος
the [2]of Onesiphorus [1]household. Erastus

ἔμεινεν ἐν Κορίνθῳ, Τρόφιμον δὲ ἀπέλιπον
remained in Corinth, but Trophimus I left

ἐν Μιλήτῳ ἀσθενοῦντα. 21 Σπούδασον
in Miletus ailing. Hasten

πρὸ χειμῶνος ἐλθεῖν. Ἀσπάζεταί σε
before winter to come. Greets thee

Εὔβουλος καὶ Πούδης καὶ Λίνος καὶ
Eubulus and Pudens and Linus and

Κλαυδία καὶ οἱ ἀδελφοὶ πάντες.
Claudia and [2]the [3]brothers [1]all.

22 Ὁ κύριος μετὰ τοῦ πνεύματός σου.
The Lord [be] with the spirit of thee.

ἡ χάρις μεθ' ὑμῶν.
– Grace [be] with you.

Gentiles might hear it. And I was delivered from the lion's mouth. 18 The Lord will rescue me from every evil attack and will bring me safely to his heavenly kingdom. To him be glory for ever and ever. Amen.

Final Greetings

19 Greet Priscilla[b] and Aquila and the household of Onesiphorus. 20 Erastus stayed in Corinth, and I left Trophimus sick in Miletus. 21 Do your best to get here before winter. Eubulus greets you, and so do Pudens, Linus, Claudia and all the brothers.

22 The Lord be with your spirit. Grace be with you.

Titus

Chapter 1

Salutation

PAUL, a bond-servant of God, and an apostle of Jesus Christ, for the faith of those chosen of God and the knowledge of the truth which is according to godliness,

2 in the hope of eternal life, which God, who cannot lie, promised long ages ago,

3 but at the proper time manifested, *even* His word, in the proclamation with which I was entrusted according to the commandment of God our Savior;

4 to Titus, my true child in a common faith: Grace and peace from God the Father and Christ Jesus our Savior.

ΠΡΟΣ ΤΙΤΟΝ
To Titus

1 Παῦλος δοῦλος θεοῦ, ἀπόστολος δὲ
Paul a slave of God, and an apostle

Ἰησοῦ Χριστοῦ κατὰ πίστιν ἐκλεκτῶν
of Jesus Christ according to [the] faith of chosen ones

θεοῦ καὶ ἐπίγνωσιν ἀληθείας τῆς κατ'
of God and full knowledge of [the] truth – according to

εὐσέβειαν 2 ἐπ' ἐλπίδι ζωῆς αἰωνίου,
piety on(in) hope life of eternal,

ἣν ἐπηγγείλατο ὁ ἀψευδὴς θεὸς πρὸ
which [4]promised [1]the [2]unlying [3]God before

χρόνων αἰωνίων, 3 ἐφανέρωσεν δὲ καιροῖς
times eternal, but [3]manifested [2]times

ἰδίοις τὸν λόγον αὐτοῦ ἐν κηρύγματι
[1]in [its] own the word of him in a proclamation

ὃ ἐπιστεύθην ἐγὼ κατ' ἐπιταγὴν τοῦ
which [2]was entrusted [with] [1]I according to [the] command of the

σωτῆρος ἡμῶν θεοῦ, 4 Τίτῳ γνησίῳ τέκνῳ
Saviour of us God, to Titus a true child

κατὰ κοινὴν πίστιν· χάρις καὶ εἰρήνη
according to a common faith: Grace and peace

ἀπὸ θεοῦ πατρὸς καὶ Χριστοῦ Ἰησοῦ
from God [the] Father and Christ Jesus

τοῦ σωτῆρος ἡμῶν.
the Saviour of us.

Titus

Chapter 1

PAUL, a servant of God and an apostle of Jesus Christ for the faith of God's elect and the knowledge of the truth that leads to godliness—2 a faith and knowledge resting on the hope of eternal life, which God, who does not lie, promised before the beginning of time, 3 and at his appointed season he brought his word to light through the preaching entrusted to me by the command of God our Savior,

4 To Titus, my true son in our common faith:

Grace and peace from God the Father and Christ Jesus our Savior.

[b] 19 Greek *Prisca*, a variant of *Priscilla*

Qualifications of Elders

5 For this reason I left you in Crete, that you might set in order what remains, and appoint elders in every city as I directed you,

6 *namely,* if any man be above reproach, the husband of one wife, having children who believe, not accused of dissipation or rebellion.

7 For the overseer must be above reproach as God's steward, not self-willed, not quick-tempered, not addicted to wine, not pugnacious, not fond of sordid gain,

8 but hospitable, loving what is good, sensible, just, devout, self-controlled,

9 holding fast the faithful word which is in accordance with the teaching, that he may be able both to exhort in sound doctrine and to refute those who contradict.

10 For there are many rebellious men, empty talkers and deceivers, especially those of the circumcision,

11 who must be silenced because they are upsetting whole families, teaching things they should not *teach,* for the sake of sordid gain.

12 One of themselves, a prophet of their own, said, "Cretans are always liars, evil beasts, lazy gluttons."

13 This testimony is true. For this cause reprove them severely that they may be sound in the faith,

14 not paying attention to Jewish myths and commandments of men who turn away from the truth.

15 To the pure, all things are pure; but to those who are defiled and unbelieving,

5 Τούτου χάριν ἀπέλιπόν σε ἐν Κρήτῃ,
For this reason† I left thee in Crete,

ἵνα τὰ λείποντα ἐπιδιορθώσῃ, καὶ
in order that the things wanting thou shouldest set in order, and

καταστήσῃς κατὰ πόλιν πρεσβυτέρους, ὡς ἐγώ
shouldest appoint in each city elders, as I

σοι διεταξάμην, 6 εἴ τίς ἐστιν ἀνέγκλητος,
[2]thee [1]charged, if anyone is unreprovable,

μιᾶς γυναικὸς ἀνήρ, τέκνα ἔχων πιστά,
[2]of one [3]wife [1]husband, [3]children [1]having [2]believing,

μὴ ἐν κατηγορίᾳ ἀσωτίας ἢ ἀνυπότακτα.
not in accusation of profligacy or unruly.*

7 δεῖ γὰρ τὸν ἐπίσκοπον ἀνέγκλητον εἶναι
For it behoves the bishop [2]unreprovable [1]to be

ὡς θεοῦ οἰκονόμον, μὴ αὐθάδη, μὴ
as of God a steward, not self-pleasing, not

ὀργίλον, μὴ πάροινον, μὴ πλήκτην, μὴ
passionate, not given to wine, not a striker, not

αἰσχροκερδῆ, 8 ἀλλὰ φιλόξενον, φιλάγαθον,
greedy of base gain, but hospitable, a lover of good [men/things],

σώφρονα, δίκαιον, ὅσιον, ἐγκρατῆ, 9 ἀντεχόμενον
sensible, just, holy, self-controlled, holding to

τοῦ κατὰ τὴν διδαχὴν πιστοῦ
[1]the [4]according to [5]the [6]teaching [2]faithful

λόγου, ἵνα δυνατὸς ᾖ καὶ παρακαλεῖν
[3]word, in order that [2]able [1]he may be both to exhort

ἐν τῇ διδασκαλίᾳ τῇ ὑγιαινούσῃ καὶ
by the [2]teaching – [1]*being* healthy and

τοὺς ἀντιλέγοντας ἐλέγχειν. 10 Εἰσὶν γὰρ
[2]the [ones] [3]contradicting [1]to convince. For there are

πολλοὶ ἀνυπότακτοι, ματαιολόγοι καὶ
many unruly men, vain talkers and

φρεναπάται, μάλιστα οἱ ἐκ τῆς περιτομῆς,
deceivers, specially the ones of the circumcision,

11 οὓς δεῖ ἐπιστομίζειν, οἵτινες ὅλους
whom it behoves to stop the mouth, who [2]whole

οἴκους ἀνατρέπουσιν διδάσκοντες ἃ μὴ
[3]households [1]overturn teaching things which [2]not

δεῖ αἰσχροῦ κέρδους χάριν. 12 εἶπέν
[1]it behoves [4]base [5]gain [3]for the sake of. [7]Said

τις ἐξ αὐτῶν ἴδιος αὐτῶν προφήτης·
[1]a certain one [2]of [3]them [4]an own [6]of them [5]prophet:

Κρῆτες ἀεὶ ψεῦσται, κακὰ θηρία, γαστέρες
Cretans [are] always liars, evil beasts, [2]gluttons

ἀργαί. 13 ἡ μαρτυρία αὕτη ἐστὶν ἀληθής.
[1]idle. This witness is true.

δι' ἣν αἰτίαν ἔλεγχε αὐτοὺς ἀποτόμως,
For which cause reprove them severely,

ἵνα ὑγιαίνωσιν ἐν τῇ πίστει, 14 μὴ
in order that they may be healthy in the faith, not

προσέχοντες Ἰουδαϊκοῖς μύθοις καὶ
giving heed to Jewish tales and

ἐντολαῖς ἀνθρώπων ἀποστρεφομένων τὴν
commandments of men perverting the

ἀλήθειαν. 15 πάντα καθαρὰ τοῖς καθαροῖς·
truth. All things [are] clean to the clean;

τοῖς δὲ μεμιαμμένοις καὶ ἀπίστοις οὐδὲν
but to the [ones] *having been* defiled and unfaithful nothing

* In agreement with "children" (neut. pl.).

Titus' Task on Crete

5 The reason I left you in
Crete was that you might
straighten out what was left
unfinished and appoint[a] elders in every town, as I directed you. 6 An elder must
be blameless, the husband
of but one wife, a man
whose children believe and
are not open to the charge
of being wild and disobedient. 7 Since an overseer[b] is
entrusted with God's work,
he must be blameless—not
overbearing, not quick-
tempered, not given to
drunkenness, not violent,
not pursuing dishonest
gain. 8 Rather he must be
hospitable, one who loves
what is good, who is self-
controlled, upright, holy
and disciplined. 9 He must
hold firmly to the trustworthy message as it has been
taught, so that he can encourage others by sound
doctrine and refute those
who oppose it.
10 For there are many re-
bellious people, mere talkers and deceivers, especially those of the circumcision
group. 11 They must be silenced, because they are
ruining whole households
by teaching things they
ought not to teach—and
that for the sake of dishonest gain. 12 Even one of
their own prophets has
said, "Cretans are always
liars, evil brutes, lazy gluttons." 13 This testimony is
true. Therefore, rebuke
them sharply, so that they
will be sound in the faith
14 and will pay no attention
to Jewish myths or to the
commands of those who re-
ject the truth. 15 To the
pure, all things are pure,
but to those who are cor-
rupted and do not believe,

[a]5 Or *ordain*
[b]7 Traditionally *bishop*

nothing is pure, but both their mind and their conscience are defiled.
16 They profess to know God, but by *their* deeds they deny *Him*, being detestable and disobedient, and worthless for any good deed.

καθαρόν, ἀλλὰ μεμίανται αὐτῶν καὶ ὁ
[is] clean, but [8]has(ve) been defiled [7]of them [1]both [2]the
νοῦς καὶ ἡ συνείδησις. 16 θεὸν ὁμολο-
[3]mind [4]and [5]the [6]conscience. [3]God [1]they pro-
γοῦσιν εἰδέναι, τοῖς δὲ ἔργοις ἀρνοῦνται,
fess [2]to know, but by the(ir) works they deny [him],
βδελυκτοὶ ὄντες καὶ ἀπειθεῖς καὶ πρὸς
[2]abominable [1]being and disobedient and to
πᾶν ἔργον ἀγαθὸν ἀδόκιμοι.
every [2]work [1]good reprobate.

nothing is pure. In fact, both their minds and consciences are corrupted. 16 They claim to know God, but by their actions they deny him. They are detestable, disobedient and unfit for doing anything good.

Chapter 2

Duties of the Older and Younger

BUT as for you, speak the things which are fitting for sound doctrine.
2 Older men are to be temperate, dignified, sensible, sound in faith, in love, in perseverance.
3 Older women likewise are to be reverent in their behavior, not malicious gossips, nor enslaved to much wine, teaching what is good,
4 that they may encourage the young women to love their husbands, to love their children,
5 *to be* sensible, pure, workers at home, kind, being subject to their own husbands, that the word of God may not be dishonored.
6 Likewise urge the young men to be sensible;
7 in all things show yourself to be an example of good deeds, *with* purity in doctrine, dignified,
8 sound *in* speech which is beyond reproach, in order that the opponent may be put to shame, having nothing bad to say about us.
9 *Urge* bondslaves to be subject to their own masters in everything, to be well-pleasing, not argumentative,
10 not pilfering, but showing all good faith that they may adorn the doctrine of God our Savior in every respect.
11 For the grace of God has appeared, bringing salvation to all men,

2 Σὺ δὲ λάλει ἃ πρέπει τῇ ὑγιαινούσῃ
But [2]thou [1]speak things which becomes the *being* healthy
διδασκαλίᾳ. 2 Πρεσβύτας νηφαλίους εἶναι,
teaching. Aged men [2]sober [1]to be,
σεμνούς, σώφρονας, ὑγιαίνοντας τῇ πίστει,
grave, sensible, *being* healthy in the faith,
τῇ ἀγάπῃ, τῇ ὑπομονῇ· 3 πρεσβύτιδας
– in love, – in endurance; aged women
ὡσαύτως ἐν καταστήματι ἱεροπρεπεῖς, μὴ
similarly in demeanour reverent, not
διαβόλους, μηδὲ οἴνῳ πολλῷ δεδουλωμένας,
slanderers, nor [3]wine [2]by much [1]*having been* enslaved,
καλοδιδασκάλους, 4 ἵνα σωφρονίζωσιν τὰς
teachers of what is good, in order that they may train the
νέας φιλάνδρους εἶναι, φιλοτέκνους,
young women [2]lovers of [their] husbands [1]to be, child-lovers,
5 σώφρονας, ἁγνάς, οἰκουργούς, ἀγαθάς,
sensible, pure, home-workers, good,
ὑποτασσομένας τοῖς ἰδίοις ἀνδράσιν,
being subject to the(ir) own husbands,
ἵνα μὴ ὁ λόγος τοῦ θεοῦ βλασφημῆται.
lest the word – of God be blasphemed.
6 Τοὺς νεωτέρους ὡσαύτως παρακάλει
The younger men similarly exhort
σωφρονεῖν 7 περὶ πάντα, σεαυτὸν παρ-
to be sensible about all things, [2]thyself [1]show-
εχόμενος τύπον καλῶν ἔργων, ἐν τῇ
ing a pattern of good works, in the
διδασκαλίᾳ ἀφθορίαν, σεμνότητα, 8 λόγον
teaching uncorruptness, gravity, [2]speech
ὑγιῆ ἀκατάγνωστον, ἵνα ὁ ἐξ ἐναντίας
[1]healthy [3]irreprehensible, in order that the man of [the] contrary [side]
ἐντραπῇ μηδὲν ἔχων λέγειν περὶ ἡμῶν
may be put to shame [2]nothing [1]having [4]to say [5]about [6]us
φαῦλον. 9 Δούλους ἰδίοις δεσπόταις
[3]bad. Slaves to [their] own masters
ὑποτάσσεσθαι ἐν πᾶσιν, εὐαρέστους εἶναι,
to be subject in all things, well-pleasing to be,
μὴ ἀντιλέγοντας, 10 μὴ νοσφιζομένους, ἀλλὰ
not contradicting, not peculating, but
πᾶσαν πίστιν ἐνδεικνυμένους ἀγαθήν, ἵνα
[2]all [4]faith [1]showing [3]good, in order that
τὴν διδασκαλίαν τὴν τοῦ σωτῆρος ἡμῶν
[2]the [3]teaching – [4]of the [5]Saviour [6]of us
θεοῦ κοσμῶσιν ἐν πᾶσιν. 11 Ἐπεφάνη
[7]God [1]they may adorn in all things. [6]appeared
γὰρ ἡ χάρις τοῦ θεοῦ σωτήριος πᾶσιν
For [1]the [2]grace – [3]of God [4]saving to all

Chapter 2

What Must Be Taught to Various Groups

YOU must teach what is in accord with sound doctrine. 2 Teach the older men to be temperate, worthy of respect, self-controlled, and sound in faith, in love and in endurance.
3 Likewise, teach the older women to be reverent in the way they live, not to be slanderers or addicted to much wine, but to teach what is good. 4 Then they can train the younger women to love their husbands and children, 5 to be self-controlled and pure, to be busy at home, to be kind, and to be subject to their husbands, so that no one will malign the word of God.
6 Similarly, encourage the young men to be self-controlled. 7 In everything set them an example by doing what is good. In your teaching show integrity, seriousness 8 and soundness of speech that cannot be condemned, so that those who oppose you may be ashamed because they have nothing bad to say about us.
9 Teach slaves to be subject to their masters in everything, to try to please them, not to talk back to them, 10 and not to steal from them, but to show that they can be fully trusted, so that in every way they will make the teaching about God our Savior attractive.
11 For the grace of God that brings salvation has appeared to all men. 12 It

12instructing us to deny
ungodliness and worldly
desires and to live sensibly,
righteously and godly in the
present age,
13looking for the blessed
hope and the appearing of
the glory of our great God
and Savior, Christ Jesus;
14who gave Himself for
us, that He might redeem
us from every lawless deed
and purify for Himself a
people for His own possession, zealous for good
deeds.
15These things speak and
exhort and reprove with all
authority. Let no one disregard you.

Chapter 3

Godly Living

REMIND them to be
subject to rulers, to
authorities, to be obedient,
to be ready for every good
deed,
2to malign no one, to
be uncontentious, gentle,
showing every consider-
ation for all men.
3For we also once were
foolish ourselves, disobedient, deceived, enslaved to
various lusts and pleasures,
spending our life in malice
and envy, hateful, hating
one another.
4But when the kindness
of God our Savior and *His*
love for mankind appeared,
5He saved us, not on the
basis of deeds which we
have done in righteous-
ness, but according to His
mercy, by the washing of
regeneration and renewing
by the Holy Spirit,
6whom He poured out
upon us richly through
Jesus Christ our Savior,
7that being justified by
His grace we might be
made heirs according to *the*
hope of eternal life.

ἀνθρώποις, **12** παιδεύουσα ἡμᾶς, ἵνα
men, instructing us, *in order* that

ἀρνησάμενοι τὴν ἀσέβειαν καὶ τὰς κοσμικὰς
denying – impiety and – worldly

ἐπιθυμίας σωφρόνως καὶ δικαίως καὶ
lusts [2]sensibly [3]and [4]righteously [5]and

εὐσεβῶς ζήσωμεν ἐν τῷ νῦν αἰῶνι,
[6]piously [1]we might live in the now(present) age,

13 προσδεχόμενοι τὴν μακαρίαν ἐλπίδα καὶ
expecting the blessed hope and

ἐπιφάνειαν τῆς δόξης τοῦ μεγάλου θεοῦ
appearance of the glory of the great God

καὶ σωτῆρος ἡμῶν Χριστοῦ Ἰησοῦ, **14** ὃς
and Saviour of us Christ Jesus, who

ἔδωκεν ἑαυτὸν ὑπὲρ ἡμῶν ἵνα λυτρώσηται
gave himself on behalf of us in order that he might ransom

ἡμᾶς ἀπὸ πάσης ἀνομίας καὶ καθαρίσῃ
us from all iniquity and *might* cleanse

ἑαυτῷ λαὸν περιούσιον, ζηλωτὴν καλῶν ἔργων.
for himself a people [his] own possession, zealous of good works.

15 Ταῦτα λάλει καὶ παρακάλει καὶ ἔλεγχε
These things speak thou and exhort and reprove

μετὰ πάσης ἐπιταγῆς· μηδείς σου περιφρονείτω.
with all command; [2]no one [4]*of* thee [1]let [3]despise.

3 Ὑπομίμνῃσκε αὐτοὺς ἀρχαῖς ἐξουσίαις
Remind thou them [2]to rulers [3][and] [4]authorities

ὑποτάσσεσθαι, πειθαρχεῖν, πρὸς πᾶν ἔργον
[1]to be subject, to be obedient, [3]to [4]every [6]work

ἀγαθὸν ἑτοίμους εἶναι, **2** μηδένα βλασ-
[5]good [2]ready [1]to be, no one to

φημεῖν, ἀμάχους εἶναι, ἐπιεικεῖς, πᾶσαν
rail at, uncontentious to be, forbearing, [2]all

ἐνδεικνυμένους πραΰτητα πρὸς πάντας
[1]showing forth meekness to all

ἀνθρώπους. **3** Ἦμεν γάρ ποτε καὶ ἡμεῖς
men. For [3]were [4]then [2]also [1]we

ἀνόητοι, ἀπειθεῖς, πλανώμενοι, δουλεύοντες
senseless, disobedient, being deceived, serving [as slaves]

ἐπιθυμίαις καὶ ἡδοναῖς ποικίλαις, ἐν κακίᾳ
[2]lusts [3]and [4]pleasures [1]various, [2]in [3]evil

καὶ φθόνῳ διάγοντες, στυγητοί, μισοῦντες
[4]and [5]envy [1]living, hateful, hating

ἀλλήλους. **4** ὅτε δὲ ἡ χρηστότης καὶ
one another. But when the kindness and

ἡ φιλανθρωπία ἐπεφάνη τοῦ σωτῆρος ἡμῶν
the love to man [5]appeared [1]of the [3]Saviour [2]of us

θεοῦ, **5** οὐκ ἐξ ἔργων τῶν ἐν δικαιοσύνῃ
[4]God, not by works – [4]in [5]righteousness

ἃ ἐποιήσαμεν ἡμεῖς, ἀλλὰ κατὰ τὸ
[1]which [3]did [2]we, but according to the

αὐτοῦ ἔλεος ἔσωσεν ἡμᾶς διὰ λουτροῦ
of him mercy he saved us through [the] washing

παλιγγενεσίας καὶ ἀνακαινώσεως πνεύματος
of regeneration and renewal [2]Spirit

ἁγίου, **6** οὗ ἐξέχεεν ἐφ' ἡμᾶς πλουσίως
[1]of [the] Holy, which he shed on us richly

διὰ Ἰησοῦ Χριστοῦ τοῦ σωτῆρος ἡμῶν,
through Jesus Christ the Saviour of us,

7 ἵνα δικαιωθέντες τῇ ἐκείνου χάριτι
in order that being justified [1]by the [3]of that one [2]grace

κληρονόμοι γενηθῶμεν κατ' ἐλπίδα ζωῆς
heirs we might become according to a hope of life

teaches us to say "No" to
ungodliness and worldly
passions, and to live self-
controlled, upright and
godly lives in this present
age, 13while we wait for the
blessed hope—the glorious
appearing of our great God
and Savior, Jesus Christ,
14who gave himself for us
to redeem us from all wickedness and to purify for
himself a people that are his
very own, eager to do what
is good.
15These, then, are the
things you should teach.
Encourage and rebuke with
all authority. Do not let
anyone despise you.

Chapter 3

Doing What Is Good

REMIND the people to
be subject to rulers
and authorities, to be obedient, to be ready to do
whatever is good, 2to slander no one, to be peaceable
and considerate, and to
show true humility toward
all men.
3At one time we too were
foolish, disobedient, de-
ceived and enslaved by all
kinds of passions and pleasures. We lived in malice
and envy, being hated and
hating one another. 4But
when the kindness and love
of God our Savior ap-
peared, 5he saved us, not
because of righteous things
we had done, but because
of his mercy. He saved us
through the washing of re-
birth and renewal by the
Holy Spirit, 6whom he
poured out on us generously through Jesus Christ our
Savior, 7so that, having
been justified by his grace,
we might become heirs
having the hope of eternal

8This is a trustworthy
statement; and concerning
these things I want you to
speak confidently, so that
those who have believed
God may be careful to en-
gage in good deeds. These
things are good and profitable for men.
9But shun foolish contro-
versies and genealogies and
strife and disputes about
the Law; for they are un-
profitable and worthless.
10Reject a factious man
after a first and second
warning,
11knowing that such a
man is perverted and is
sinning, being self-con-
demned.

Personal Concerns

12When I send Artemas
or Tychicus to you, make
every effort to come to me
at Nicopolis, for I have decided to spend the winter
there.
13Diligently help Zenas
the lawyer and Apollos on
their way so that nothing is
lacking for them.
14And let our *people* also
learn to engage in good
deeds to meet pressing
needs, that they may not be
unfruitful.
15All who are with me
greet you. Greet those who
love us in *the* faith.
Grace be with you all.

αἰωνίου. **8** Πιστὸς ὁ λόγος, καὶ περὶ
eternal. Faithful [is] the word, and as to

τούτων βούλομαί σε διαβεβαιοῦσθαι, ἵνα
these things I wish thee to affirm confidently, in order that

φροντίζωσιν καλῶν ἔργων προΐστασθαι οἱ
4may take thought 6*of* good 7works 5to maintain 1the [ones]

πεπιστευκότες θεῷ. ταῦτά ἐστιν καλὰ
2having believed 3God. These things is(are) good

καὶ ὠφέλιμα τοῖς ἀνθρώποις· **9** μωρὰς
and profitable – to men; 2foolish

δὲ ζητήσεις καὶ γενεαλογίας καὶ ἔριν
1but questionings and genealogies and strife

καὶ μάχας νομικὰς περιΐστασο· εἰσὶν γὰρ
and 2fights 1legal shun thou; for they are

ἀνωφελεῖς καὶ μάταιοι. **10** αἱρετικὸν
unprofitable and vain. A factious

ἄνθρωπον μετὰ μίαν καὶ δευτέραν
man after one and a second

νουθεσίαν παραιτοῦ, **11** εἰδὼς ὅτι ἐξέστραπ-
admonition avoid, knowing that 2has been per-

ται ὁ τοιοῦτος καὶ ἁμαρτάνει ὢν αὐτο-
verted 1such a man and sins being self-

κατάκριτος.
condemned.

12 Ὅταν πέμψω Ἀρτεμᾶν πρὸς σὲ
Whenever I send Artemas to thee

ἢ Τύχικον, σπούδασον ἐλθεῖν πρός με
or Tychicus, hasten to come to me

εἰς Νικόπολιν· ἐκεῖ γὰρ κέκρικα παραχειμά-
in Nicopolis; for there I have decided to spend [the]

σαι. **13** Ζηνᾶν τὸν νομικὸν καὶ Ἀπολλῶν
winter. Zenas the lawyer and Apollos

σπουδαίως πρόπεμψον, ἵνα μηδὲν αὐτοῖς
urgently send forward, in order that nothing to them

λείπῃ. **14** μανθανέτωσαν δὲ καὶ οἱ ἡμέτεροι
may be lacking. And 1let 4learn 3also – 2our [people]

καλῶν ἔργων προΐστασθαι εἰς τὰς ἀναγ-
6*of* good 7works 5to maintain for – neces-

καίας χρείας, ἵνα μὴ ὦσιν ἄκαρποι.
sary wants, lest they be unfruitful.

15 Ἀσπάζονταί σε οἱ μετ' ἐμοῦ πάντες.
5greet 6thee 2the [ones] 3with 4me 1All.

ἄσπασαι τοὺς φιλοῦντας ἡμᾶς ἐν πίστει.
Greet thou the [ones] loving us in [the] faith.

Ἡ χάρις μετὰ πάντων ὑμῶν.
– Grace [be] with 2all 1you.

life. 8This is a trustworthy
saying. And I want you to
stress these things, so that
those who have trusted in
God may be careful to de-
vote themselves to doing
what is good. These things
are excellent and profitable
for everyone.
9But avoid foolish controversies and genealogies and
arguments and quarrels
about the law, because
these are unprofitable and
useless. 10Warn a divisive
person once, and then warn
him a second time. After
that, have nothing to do
with him. 11You may be
sure that such a man is
warped and sinful; he is
self-condemned.

Final Remarks

12As soon as I send Arte-
mas or Tychicus to you, do
your best to come to me at
Nicopolis, because I have
decided to winter there.
13Do everything you can to
help Zenas the lawyer and
Apollos on their way and
see that they have every-
thing they need. 14Our people must learn to devote
themselves to doing what is
good, in order that they
may provide for daily ne-
cessities and not live unproductive lives.
15Everyone with me
sends you greetings. Greet
those who love us in the
faith.
Grace be with you all.

Philemon

Chapter 1

Salutation

PAUL, a prisoner of
Christ Jesus, and Tim-
othy our brother, to Philemon our beloved *brother*
and fellow worker,
2and to Apphia our sis-
ter, and to Archippus our

ΠΡΟΣ ΦΙΛΗΜΟΝΑ

To Philemon

1 Παῦλος δέσμιος Χριστοῦ Ἰησοῦ καὶ
Paul a prisoner of Christ Jesus and

Τιμόθεος ὁ ἀδελφὸς Φιλήμονι τῷ ἀγαπητῷ
Timothy the brother to Philemon the beloved

καὶ συνεργῷ ἡμῶν **2** καὶ Ἀπφίᾳ τῇ
and a fellow-worker of us and to Apphia the

ἀδελφῇ καὶ Ἀρχίππῳ τῷ συστρατιώτῃ
sister and to Archippus the fellow-soldier

Philemon

PAUL, a prisoner of
Christ Jesus, and Tim-
othy our brother,

To Philemon our dear
friend and fellow worker,
2to Apphia our sister, to
Archippus our fellow sol-

fellow soldier, and to the
church in your house:
3Grace to you and peace
from God our Father and
the Lord Jesus Christ.

Philemon's Love and Faith

4I thank my God always,
making mention of you in
my prayers,
5because I hear of your
love, and of the faith which
you have toward the Lord
Jesus, and toward all the
saints;
6*and I pray* that the fellowship of your faith may
become effective [a]through
the knowledge of every
good thing which is in [b]you
for Christ's sake.
7For I have come to have
much joy and comfort in
your love, because the
hearts of the saints have
been refreshed through
you, brother.
8Therefore, though I
have enough confidence in
Christ to order you *to do*
that which is proper,
9yet for love's sake I
rather appeal *to you*—since
I am such a person as Paul,
the aged, and now also a
prisoner of Christ Jesus—

Plea for Onesimus, a Free Man

10I appeal to you for my
child, whom I have begot-
ten in my imprisonment,
[c]Onesimus,
11who formerly was use-
less to you, but now is useful both to you and to me.
12And I have sent him
back to you in person, that
is, *sending* my very heart,
13whom I wished to keep
with me, that in your behalf
he might minister to me in
my imprisonment for the
gospel;
14but without your con-
sent I did not want to do
anything, that your good-
ness should not be as it
were by compulsion, but of

[a]Or, *in*
[b]Some ancient mss. read *us*
[c]I.e., useful

ἡμῶν καὶ τῇ κατ' οἶκόν σου ἐκκλησίᾳ·
of us and [1]to the [3]at [4]house [5]of thee [2]church:
3 χάρις ὑμῖν καὶ εἰρήνη ἀπὸ θεοῦ πατρὸς
Grace to you and peace from God Father
ἡμῶν καὶ κυρίου Ἰησοῦ Χριστοῦ.
of us and Lord Jesus Christ.
4 Εὐχαριστῶ τῷ θεῷ μου πάντοτε μνείαν
I give thanks to the God of me always [2]mention
σου ποιούμενος ἐπὶ τῶν προσευχῶν μου,
[3]of thee [1]making at the prayers of me,
5 ἀκούων σου τὴν ἀγάπην καὶ τὴν
hearing of thee the love and the
πίστιν ἣν ἔχεις πρὸς τὸν κύριον Ἰησοῦν
faith which thou hast toward the Lord Jesus
καὶ εἰς πάντας τοὺς ἁγίους, 6 ὅπως
and to all the saints, so as
ἡ κοινωνία τῆς πίστεώς σου ἐνεργὴς
the fellowship of the faith of thee [2]operative
γένηται ἐν ἐπιγνώσει παντὸς ἀγαθοῦ τοῦ
[1]may become in a full knowledge of every good thing –
ἐν ἡμῖν εἰς Χριστόν. 7 χαρὰν γὰρ
in us for Christ. [4]joy [1]For
πολλὴν ἔσχον καὶ παράκλησιν ἐπὶ τῇ
[3]much [2]I had and consolation over the
ἀγάπῃ σου, ὅτι τὰ σπλάγχνα τῶν ἁγίων
love of thee, because the bowels of the saints
ἀναπέπαυται διὰ σοῦ, ἀδελφέ. 8 Διό,
has(ve) been refreshed through thee, brother. Wherefore,
πολλὴν ἐν Χριστῷ παρρησίαν ἔχων ἐπιτάσ-
[2]much [4]in [5]Christ [3]boldness [1]having to
σειν σοι τὸ ἀνῆκον, 9 διὰ τὴν ἀγάπην
charge thee the befitting thing, because of – love
μᾶλλον παρακαλῶ· τοιοῦτος ὢν ὡς Παῦλος
rather I beseech; such a one being as Paul
πρεσβύτης, νυνὶ δὲ καὶ δέσμιος Χριστοῦ
an old man, and now also a prisoner of Christ
Ἰησοῦ, 10 παρακαλῶ σε περὶ τοῦ ἐμοῦ
Jesus, I beseech thee concerning – my
τέκνου, ὃν ἐγέννησα ἐν τοῖς δεσμοῖς,
child, whom I begat in the(my) bonds,
Ὀνήσιμον, 11 τόν ποτέ σοι ἄχρηστον
Onesimus, the [one] then (formerly) [2]to thee [1]useless
νυνὶ δὲ καὶ σοὶ καὶ ἐμοὶ εὔχρηστον,
but now [2]both [3]to thee [4]and [5]to me [1]useful,
12 ὃν ἀνέπεμψά σοι, αὐτόν, τοῦτ' ἔστιν
whom I sent back to thee, him, this is
τὰ ἐμὰ σπλάγχνα· 13 ὃν ἐγὼ ἐβουλόμην
– my bowels; whom I resolved
πρὸς ἐμαυτὸν κατέχειν, ἵνα ὑπὲρ σοῦ
with myself to retain, in order that on behalf of thee
μοι διακονῇ ἐν τοῖς δεσμοῖς τοῦ εὐαγ-
to me he might minister in the bonds of the gos-
γελίου, 14 χωρὶς δὲ τῆς σῆς γνώμης
pel, but without – thy opinion
οὐδὲν ἠθέλησα ποιῆσαι, ἵνα μὴ ὡς κατὰ
[3]nothing [1]I was willing [2]to do, in order that not [5]as [6]by way of
ἀνάγκην τὸ ἀγαθόν σου ᾖ ἀλλὰ κατὰ
[7]necessity [1]the [3]good [2]of thee [4]might be but by way of

dier and to the church that
meets in your home:
3Grace to you and peace
from God our Father and
the Lord Jesus Christ.

Thanksgiving and Prayer

4I always thank my God
as I remember you in my
prayers, 5because I hear
about your faith in the Lord
Jesus and your love for all
the saints. 6I pray that you
may be active in sharing
your faith, so that you will
have a full understanding of
every good thing we have
in Christ. 7Your love has
given me great joy and encouragement, because you,
brother, have refreshed the
hearts of the saints.

Paul's Plea for Onesimus

8Therefore, although in
Christ I could be bold and
order you to do what you
ought to do, 9yet I appeal to
you on the basis of love. I
then, as Paul—an old man
and now also a prisoner of
Christ Jesus— 10I appeal to
you for my son Onesimus, [a]
who became my son while I
was in chains. 11Formerly
he was useless to you, but
now he has become useful
both to you and to me.
12I am sending him—who
is my very heart—back to
you. 13I would have liked to
keep him with me so that he
could take your place in
helping me while I am in
chains for the gospel. 14But
I did not want to do any-
thing without your consent,
so that any favor you do
will be spontaneous and

[a]10 *Onesimus* means *useful*.

your own free will.
15 For perhaps he was for
this reason parted *from you*
for a while, that you should
have him back forever,
16 no longer as a slave, but
more than a slave, a be-
loved brother, especially to
me, but how much more to
you, both in the flesh and in
the Lord.
17 If then you regard me a
partner, accept him as *you*
would me.
18 But if he has wronged
you in any way, or owes
you anything, charge that
to my account;
19 I, Paul, am writing this
with my own hand, I will
repay it (lest I should mention to you that you owe to
me even your own self as
well).
20 Yes, brother, let me
benefit from you in the
Lord; refresh my heart in
Christ.
21 Having confidence in
your obedience, I write to
you, since I know that you
will do even more than
what I say.
22 And at the same time
also prepare me a lodging;
for I hope that through your
prayers I shall be given to
you.
23 Epaphras, my fellow
prisoner in Christ Jesus,
greets you,
24 *as do* Mark, Aristar-
chus, Demas, Luke, my
fellow workers.
25 The grace of the Lord
Jesus Christ be with your
spirit.[d]

ἑκούσιον. **15** τάχα γὰρ διὰ τοῦτο ἐχωρίσθη
[being] voluntary. For perhaps therefore he departed

πρὸς ὥραν, ἵνα αἰώνιον αὐτὸν ἀπέχῃς,
for an hour, in order that [3]eternally [2]him [1]thou mightest receive,

16 οὐκέτι ὡς δοῦλον ἀλλὰ ὑπὲρ δοῦλον,
no longer as a slave but beyond a slave,

ἀδελφὸν ἀγαπητόν, μάλιστα ἐμοί, πόσῳ
a brother beloved, specially to me, [2]by how much

δὲ μᾶλλον σοὶ καὶ ἐν σαρκὶ καὶ ἐν
[1]and more to thee both in [the] flesh and in

κυρίῳ. **17** εἰ οὖν με ἔχεις κοινωνόν,
[the] Lord. If therefore me thou hast [as] a partner,

προσλαβοῦ αὐτὸν ὡς ἐμέ. **18** εἰ δέ
receive him as me. And if

τι ἠδίκησέν σε ἢ ὀφείλει, τοῦτο ἐμοὶ
anything he wronged thee or owes, [2]this [3]to me

ἐλλόγα· **19** ἐγὼ Παῦλος ἔγραψα τῇ ἐμῇ
[1]reckon: I Paul wrote – with my

χειρί, ἐγὼ ἀποτίσω· ἵνα μὴ λέγω σοι
hand, I will repay; lest I say to thee

ὅτι καὶ σεαυτόν μοι προσοφείλεις. **20** ναί,
that indeed [3]thyself [2]to me [1]thou owest besides. Yes,

ἀδελφέ, ἐγώ σου ὀναίμην ἐν κυρίῳ·
brother, [1]I [5]of thee [2]may [3]have [4]help in [the] Lord;

ἀνάπαυσόν μου τὰ σπλάγχνα ἐν Χριστῷ.
refresh of me the bowels in Christ.

21 Πεποιθὼς τῇ ὑπακοῇ σου ἔγραψά
Having trusted to the obedience of thee I wrote

σοι, εἰδὼς ὅτι καὶ ὑπὲρ ἃ λέγω ποιήσεις.
to thee, knowing that indeed beyond what things I say thou wilt do.

22 ἅμα δὲ καὶ ἑτοίμαζέ μοι ξενίαν·
And at the same time also prepare for me lodging;

ἐλπίζω γὰρ ὅτι διὰ τῶν προσευχῶν
for I hope that through the prayers

ὑμῶν χαρισθήσομαι ὑμῖν.
of you I shall be given to you.

23 Ἀσπάζεταί σε Ἐπαφρᾶς ὁ συναιχμά-
[8]greets [9]thee [1]Epaphras [2]the [3]fellow-

λωτός μου ἐν Χριστῷ Ἰησοῦ, **24** Μᾶρκος,
captive [4]of me [5]in [6]Christ [7]Jesus, [also] Mark,

Ἀρίσταρχος, Δημᾶς, Λουκᾶς, οἱ συνεργοί
Aristarchus, Demas, Luke, the fellow-workers

μου.
of me.

25 Ἡ χάρις τοῦ κυρίου Ἰησοῦ Χριστοῦ
The grace of the Lord Jesus Christ

μετὰ τοῦ πνεύματος ὑμῶν.
[be] with the spirit of you.

not forced. 15 Perhaps the
reason he was separated
from you for a little while
was that you might have
him back for good— 16 no
longer as a slave, but better
than a slave, as a dear
brother. He is very dear to
me but even dearer to you,
both as a man and as a
brother in the Lord.
17 So if you consider me a
partner, welcome him as
you would welcome me.
18 If he has done you any
wrong or owes you any-
thing, charge it to me. 19 I,
Paul, am writing this with
my own hand. I will pay it
back—not to mention that
you owe me your very self.
20 I do wish, brother, that I
may have some benefit
from you in the Lord; re-
fresh my heart in Christ.
21 Confident of your obedience, I write to you, knowing that you will do even
more than I ask.
22 And one thing more:
Prepare a guest room for
me, because I hope to be
restored to you in answer
to your prayers.

23 Epaphras, my fellow
prisoner in Christ Jesus,
sends you greetings. 24 And
so do Mark, Aristarchus,
Demas and Luke, my fel-
low workers.
25 The grace of the Lord
Jesus Christ be with your
spirit.

Hebrews

Chapter 1

God's Final Word in His Son

GOD, after He spoke
long ago to the fathers
in the prophets in many
portions and in many ways,

ΠΡΟΣ ΕΒΡΑΙΟΥΣ
To Hebrews

1 Πολυμερῶς καὶ πολυτρόπως πάλαι ὁ
[5]In many portions [6]and [7]in many ways [8]of old –

θεὸς λαλήσας τοῖς πατράσιν ἐν τοῖς
[1]God [2]having spoken [3]to the [4]fathers by the

Hebrews

Chapter 1

The Son Superior to Angels

IN the past God spoke to
our forefathers through
the prophets at many times
and in various ways, 2 but in

[d] Some ancient mss. add *Amen*

2 in these last days has
spoken to us in *His* Son,
whom He appointed heir of
all things, through whom
also He made the world.
3 And He is the radiance
of His glory and the exact
representation of His na-
ture, and upholds all things
by the word of His power.
When He had made purifi-
cation of sins, He sat down
at the right hand of the
Majesty on high;
4 having become as much
better than the angels, as
He has inherited a more excellent name than they.
5 For to which of the an-
gels did He ever say,
"THOU ART MY SON,
TODAY I HAVE BEGOT-
TEN THEE"?
And again,
"I WILL BE A FATHER TO
HIM,
AND HE SHALL BE A
SON TO ME"?
6 And when He again
brings the first-born into
the world, He says,
"AND LET ALL THE AN-
GELS OF GOD WORSHIP
HIM."
7 And of the angels He
says,
"WHO MAKES HIS AN-
GELS WINDS,
AND HIS MINISTERS A
FLAME OF FIRE."
8 But of the Son *He says,*
"THY THRONE, O GOD,
IS FOREVER AND EVER,
AND THE RIGHTEOUS
SCEPTER IS THE SCEP-
TER OF [a]HIS KING-
DOM.
9 "THOU HAST LOVED
RIGHTEOUSNESS AND
HATED LAWLESSNESS;
THEREFORE GOD, THY
GOD, HATH ANOINTED
THEE
WITH THE OIL OF GLAD-
NESS ABOVE THY COM-
PANIONS."
10 And,
"THOU, LORD, IN THE
BEGINNING DIDST LAY
THE FOUNDATION OF
THE EARTH,

[a] Some mss. read *Thy*

προφήταις 2 ἐπ' ἐσχάτου τῶν ἡμερῶν
prophets in [the] last – days
τούτων ἐλάλησεν ἡμῖν ἐν υἱῷ, ὃν ἔθηκεν
of these spoke to us in a Son, whom he appointed
κληρονόμον πάντων, δι' οὗ καὶ ἐποίησεν
heir of all things, through whom indeed he made
τοὺς αἰῶνας· 3 ὃς ὢν ἀπαύγασμα τῆς
the ages; who being [the] radiance of the (his)
δόξης καὶ χαρακτὴρ τῆς ὑποστάσεως αὐτοῦ,
glory and [the] representation of the reality of him,
φέρων τε τὰ πάντα τῷ ῥήματι τῆς
and bearing – all things by the word of the
δυνάμεως αὐτοῦ, καθαρισμὸν τῶν ἁμαρτιῶν
power of him, [2]cleansing – [3]of sins
ποιησάμενος ἐκάθισεν ἐν δεξιᾷ τῆς
[1]having made sat on [the] right [hand] of the
μεγαλωσύνης ἐν ὑψηλοῖς, 4 τοσούτῳ
greatness in high places, [3]by so much
κρείττων γενόμενος τῶν ἀγγέλων ὅσῳ
[2]better [1]becoming [4][than] the angels as
διαφορώτερον παρ' αὐτοὺς κεκληρονόμηκεν
[3]a more excellent [4]than [5]them [1]he has inherited
ὄνομα. 5 Τίνι γὰρ εἶπέν ποτε τῶν
[2]name. For to which [3]said he [4]ever [1]of the
ἀγγέλων· υἱός μου εἶ σύ, ἐγὼ σήμερον
[2]angels: Son of me art thou, I to-day
γεγέννηκά σε; καὶ πάλιν· ἐγὼ ἔσομαι
have begotten thee? and again: I will be
αὐτῷ εἰς πατέρα, καὶ αὐτὸς ἔσται μοι
to him for a father, and he shall be to me
εἰς υἱόν; 6 ὅταν δὲ πάλιν εἰσαγάγῃ
for a son? and whenever again he brings *in*
τὸν πρωτότοκον εἰς τὴν οἰκουμένην, λέγει·
the firstborn into the inhabited [earth], he says:
καὶ προσκυνησάτωσαν αὐτῷ πάντες ἄγγελοι
And let worship him all angels
θεοῦ. 7 καὶ πρὸς μὲν τοὺς ἀγγέλους
of God. And with regard to – the angels
λέγει· ὁ ποιῶν τοὺς ἀγγέλους αὐτοῦ
he says: The [one] making the angels of him
πνεύματα, καὶ τοὺς λειτουργοὺς αὐτοῦ
spirits, and the ministers of him
πυρὸς φλόγα· 8 πρὸς δὲ τὸν υἱόν· ὁ
[2]of fire [1]a flame; but with regard to the Son: The
θρόνος σου ὁ θεὸς εἰς τὸν αἰῶνα τοῦ
throne of thee[,] – God[,]* [is] unto the age of the
αἰῶνος, καὶ ἡ ῥάβδος τῆς εὐθύτητος
age, and the rod – of uprightness [is]
ῥάβδος τῆς βασιλείας αὐτοῦ. 9 ἠγάπησας
[the] rod of the kingdom of him. Thou lovedst
δικαιοσύνην καὶ ἐμίσησας ἀνομίαν· διὰ
righteousness and hatedst lawlessness; there-
τοῦτο ἔχρισέν σε, ὁ θεός, ὁ θεός σου
fore [4]anointed [5]thee, – [6]God,* [1]the [2]God [3]of thee
ἔλαιον ἀγαλλιάσεως παρὰ τοὺς μετόχους
[with] oil of gladness above the partners
σου. 10 καί· σὺ κατ' ἀρχάς, κύριε,
of thee. And: Thou at [the] beginnings, Lord,
τὴν γῆν ἐθεμελίωσας, καὶ ἔργα τῶν
[2]the [3]earth [1]didst found, and [4]works [5]of the

* Articular vocative; see ver. 10.

these last days he has spoken to us by his Son, whom
he appointed heir of all
things, and through whom
he made the universe. 3 The
Son is the radiance of
God's glory and the exact
representation of his being,
sustaining all things by his
powerful word. After he
had provided purification
for sins, he sat down at the
right hand of the Majesty in
heaven. 4 So he became as
much superior to the angels
as the name he has inherited is superior to theirs.
5 For to which of the an-
gels did God ever say,
"You are my Son;
today I have become
your Father[a]"[b]?
Or again,
"I will be his Father,
and he will be my
Son"[c]?
6 And again, when God
brings his firstborn into the
world, he says,
"Let all God's angels
worship him."[d]
7 In speaking of the angels
he says,
"He makes his angels
winds,
his servants flames of
fire."[e]
8 But about the Son he says,
"Your throne, O God,
will last for ever and
ever,
and righteousness will
be the scepter of
your kingdom.
9 You have loved
righteousness and
hated wickedness;
therefore God, your
God, has set you
above your
companions
by anointing you with
the oil of joy."[f]
10 He also says,
"In the beginning, O
Lord, you laid the
foundations of the
earth,

[a]5 Or *have begotten you*
[b]5 Psalm 2:7
[c]5 2 Samuel 7:14; 1 Chron. 17:13
[d]6 Deut. 32:43 (see Dead Sea Scrolls and Septuagint)
[e]7 Psalm 104:4
[f]9 Psalm 45:6,7

AND THE HEAVENS ARE THE WORKS OF THY HANDS;
11 THEY WILL PERISH, BUT THOU REMAINEST;
AND THEY ALL WILL BECOME OLD AS A GARMENT,
12 AND AS A MANTLE THOU WILT ROLL THEM UP;
AS A GARMENT THEY WILL ALSO BE CHANGED.
BUT THOU ART THE SAME,
AND THY YEARS WILL NOT COME TO AN END."
13But to which of the angels has He ever said,
"SIT AT MY RIGHT HAND,
UNTIL I MAKE THINE ENEMIES
A FOOTSTOOL FOR THY FEET"?
14Are they not all ministering spirits, sent out to render service for the sake of those who will inherit salvation?

Chapter 2

Give Heed

FOR this reason we must pay much closer attention to what we have heard, lest we drift away *from it*.
2For if the word spoken through angels proved unalterable, and every transgression and disobedience received a just recompense,
3how shall we escape if we neglect so great a salvation? After it was at the first spoken through the Lord, it was confirmed to us by those who heard,
4God also bearing witness with them, both by signs and wonders and by various miracles and by gifts of the Holy Spirit according to His own will.

Earth Subject to Man

5For He did not subject to angels the world to come, concerning which we are speaking.
6But one has testified somewhere, saying,
"WHAT IS MAN, THAT THOU REMEMBEREST HIM?
OR THE SON OF MAN, THAT THOU ART CONCERNED ABOUT HIM?
7"THOU HAST MADE HIM FOR A LITTLE WHILE LOWER THAN THE ANGELS;

χειρῶν σού εἰσιν οἱ οὐρανοί· 11 αὐτοὶ
[6]hands [7]of thee [8]are [1]the [2]heavens; they
ἀπολοῦνται, σὺ δὲ διαμένεις· καὶ πάντες
will perish, but thou remainest; and all
ὡς ἱμάτιον παλαιωθήσονται, 12 καὶ ὡσεὶ
as a garment will become old, and as
περιβόλαιον ἑλίξεις αὐτούς, ὡς ἱμάτιον
a mantle thou wilt roll up them, as a garment
καὶ ἀλλαγήσονται· σὺ δὲ ὁ αὐτὸς εἶ
also they will be changed; but thou the same art
καὶ τὰ ἔτη σου οὐκ ἐκλείψουσιν. 13 πρὸς
and the years of thee will not fail. [5]to
τίνα δὲ τῶν ἀγγέλων εἴρηκέν ποτε·
[6]which [1]But of the angels has he said at any time:
κάθου ἐκ δεξιῶν μου ἕως ἂν θῶ τοὺς
Sit at [the] right of me until I put the
ἐχθρούς σου ὑποπόδιον τῶν ποδῶν σου;
enemies of thee a footstool of the feet of thee?
14 οὐχὶ πάντες εἰσὶν λειτουργικὰ πνεύματα
[2]not [3]all [1]are they [4]ministering [5]spirits
εἰς διακονίαν ἀποστελλόμενα διὰ τοὺς
[7]for [8]service [6]being sent forth because of the [ones]
μέλλοντας κληρονομεῖν σωτηρίαν; 2 Διὰ
being about to inherit salvation ? There-
τοῦτο δεῖ περισσοτέρως προσέχειν ἡμᾶς
fore [1]it behoves [4]more abundantly [3]to give heed [2]us
τοῖς ἀκουσθεῖσιν, μήποτε παραρυῶμεν.
to the things heard, lest we drift away.
2 εἰ γὰρ ὁ δι' ἀγγέλων λαληθεὶς λόγος
For if [1]the [4]through [5]angels [3]spoken [2]word
ἐγένετο βέβαιος, καὶ πᾶσα παράβασις
was firm, and every transgression
καὶ παρακοὴ ἔλαβεν ἔνδικον μισθαποδοσίαν,
and disobedience received a just recompence,
3 πῶς ἡμεῖς ἐκφευξόμεθα τηλικαύτης
how [2]we [1]shall [3]escape [5]so great
ἀμελήσαντες σωτηρίας; ἥτις ἀρχὴν λαβοῦσα
[4]neglecting [6]a salvation ? which [2]a beginning [1]having received
λαλεῖσθαι διὰ τοῦ κυρίου, ὑπὸ τῶν
to be spoken through the Lord, by the
ἀκουσάντων εἰς ἡμᾶς ἐβεβαιώθη, 4 συνεπι-
[ones] hearing to us was confirmed, [2]bearing
μαρτυροῦντος τοῦ θεοῦ σημείοις τε καὶ
witness with – [1]God[a] [4]by signs [3]both and
τέρασιν καὶ ποικίλαις δυνάμεσιν καὶ
by wonders and *by* various powerful deeds and
πνεύματος ἁγίου μερισμοῖς κατὰ τὴν αὐτοῦ
[3]Spirit [2]of [the] Holy [1]*by* distributions according to the [2]of him
θέλησιν.
[1]will.
5 Οὐ γὰρ ἀγγέλοις ὑπέταξεν τὴν
For not to angels subjected he the
οἰκουμένην τὴν μέλλουσαν, περὶ ἧς
[2]inhabited [earth] – [1]coming, about which
λαλοῦμεν. 6 διεμαρτύρατο δέ πού τις
we speak. But [2]solemnly witnessed [3]somewhere [1]one
λέγων· τί ἐστιν ἄνθρωπος ὅτι μιμνήσκῃ
saying: What is man that thou rememberest
αὐτοῦ; ἢ υἱὸς ἀνθρώπου ὅτι ἐπισκέπτῃ
him ? or a son of man that thou observest
αὐτόν; 7 ἠλάττωσας αὐτὸν βραχύ τι παρ'
him ? Thou madest [3]less [1]him [2]a little than

and the heavens are the work of your hands.
11They will perish, but you remain;
they will all wear out like a garment.
12You will roll them up like a robe;
like a garment they will be changed.
But you remain the same,
and your years will never end."[g]

13To which of the angels did God ever say,

"Sit at my right hand
until I make your enemies
a footstool for your feet"[h]?

14Are not all angels ministering spirits sent to serve those who will inherit salvation?

Chapter 2

Warning to Pay Attention

WE must pay more careful attention, therefore, to what we have heard, so that we do not drift away. 2For if the message spoken by angels was binding, and every violation and disobedience received its just punishment, 3how shall we escape if we ignore such a great salvation? This salvation, which was first announced by the Lord, was confirmed to us by those who heard him. 4God also testified to it by signs, wonders and various miracles, and gifts of the Holy Spirit distributed according to his will.

Jesus Made Like His Brothers

5It is not to angels that he has subjected the world to come, about which we are speaking. 6But there is a place where someone has testified:

"What is man that you are mindful of him,
the son of man that you care for him?
7You made him a little[i] lower than the angels;

[g]12 Psalm 102:25-27
[h]13 Psalm 110:1
[i]7 Or *him for a little while*; also in verse 9

THOU HAST CROWNED HIM WITH GLORY AND HONOR,
[b]AND HAST APPOINTED HIM OVER THE WORKS OF THY HANDS;
8 THOU HAST PUT ALL THINGS IN SUBJECTION UNDER HIS FEET."

For in subjecting all things to him, He left nothing that is not subject to him. But now we do not yet see all things subjected to him.

Jesus Briefly Humbled

9But we do see Him who has been made for a little while lower than the angels, *namely,* Jesus, because of the suffering of death crowned with glory and honor, that by the grace of God He might taste death for everyone.

10For it was fitting for Him, for whom are all things, and through whom are all things, in bringing many sons to glory, to perfect the author of their salvation through sufferings.

11For both He who sanctifies and those who are sanctified are all from one *Father*; for which reason He is not ashamed to call them brethren,

12saying,

"I WILL PROCLAIM THY NAME TO MY BRETHREN,
IN THE MIDST OF THE CONGREGATION I WILL SING THY PRAISE."

13And again,

"I WILL PUT MY TRUST IN HIM."

And again,

"BEHOLD, I AND THE CHILDREN WHOM GOD HAS GIVEN ME."

14Since then the children share in flesh and blood, He Himself likewise also partook of the same, that through death He might render powerless him who had the power of death, that is, the devil;

15and might deliver those who through fear of death were subject to slavery all their lives.

ἀγγέλους, δόξῃ καὶ τιμῇ ἐστεφάνωσας
angels, with glory and *with* honour thou crownedst

αὐτόν, **8** πάντα ὑπέταξας ὑποκάτω τῶν
him, all things thou subjectedst underneath the

ποδῶν αὐτοῦ. ἐν τῷ γὰρ ὑποτάξαι
feet of him. 1in *the* For 2*to* subject[ing]

[αὐτῷ] τὰ πάντα οὐδὲν ἀφῆκεν αὐτῷ
4to him – 3all things 6nothing 5he left 8to him

ἀνυπότακτον. Νῦν δὲ οὔπω ὁρῶμεν
7unsubjected. But now not yet we see

αὐτῷ τὰ πάντα ὑποτεταγμένα· **9** τὸν δὲ
2to him – 1all things 3having been subjected; 3the [one] 1but

βραχύ τι παρ' ἀγγέλους ἠλαττωμένον
5a little 6than 7angels 4having been made less

βλέπομεν Ἰησοῦν διὰ τὸ πάθημα τοῦ
2we see 8Jesus because of the suffering –

θανάτου δόξῃ καὶ τιμῇ ἐστεφανωμένον,
of death with glory and *with* honour having been crowned,

ὅπως χάριτι θεοῦ ὑπὲρ παντὸς γεύσηται
so as by [the] grace of God 3on behalf of 4every man 1he might taste

θανάτου. **10** ἔπρεπεν γὰρ αὐτῷ, δι'
of 2death. For it was fitting for him, because of

ὃν τὰ πάντα καὶ δι' οὗ τὰ πάντα,
whom – all things and through whom – all things,

πολλοὺς υἱοὺς εἰς δόξαν ἀγαγόντα τὸν
10many 11sons 12to 13glory 9leading 4the

ἀρχηγὸν τῆς σωτηρίας αὐτῶν διὰ
5author 6of the 7salvation 8of them 2through

παθημάτων τελειῶσαι. **11** ὅ τε γὰρ
3sufferings 1to perfect. 3the [one] 2both 1For

ἁγιάζων καὶ οἱ ἁγιαζόμενοι ἐξ ἑνὸς
sanctifying and the [ones] being sanctified [are] 2of 3one

πάντες· δι' ἣν αἰτίαν οὐκ ἐπαισχύνεται
1all; for which cause he is not ashamed

ἀδελφοὺς αὐτοὺς καλεῖν, **12** λέγων· ἀπαγ-
3brothers 2them 1to call, saying: I will

γελῶ τὸ ὄνομά σου τοῖς ἀδελφοῖς μου,
announce the name of thee to the brothers of me,

ἐν μέσῳ ἐκκλησίας ὑμνήσω σε· **13** καὶ
in [the] midst of [the] church I will hymn thee; and

πάλιν· ἐγὼ ἔσομαι πεποιθὼς ἐπ' αὐτῷ·
again: I will be having trusted on(in) him;

καὶ πάλιν· ἰδοὺ ἐγὼ καὶ τὰ παιδία
and again: Behold[,] I and the children

ἅ μοι ἔδωκεν ὁ θεός. **14** Ἐπεὶ οὖν
whom 3to me 2gave – 1God. Since therefore

τὰ παιδία κεκοινώνηκεν αἵματος καὶ
the children has(ve) partaken of blood and

σαρκός, καὶ αὐτὸς παραπλησίως μετέσχεν
of flesh, 2also 3[him]self 4in like manner 1he shared

τῶν αὐτῶν, ἵνα διὰ τοῦ θανάτου
the same things, in order that through the(?his) death

καταργήσῃ τὸν τὸ κράτος ἔχοντα τοῦ
he might destroy 1the [one] 3the 4might 2having –

θανάτου, τοῦτ' ἔστιν τὸν διάβολον, **15** καὶ
of death, this is the devil, and

ἀπαλλάξῃ τούτους, ὅσοι φόβῳ θανάτου
release these, as many as by fear of death

διὰ παντὸς τοῦ ζῆν ἔνοχοι ἦσαν δουλείας.
through all the(ir) [time] to live 2involved in 1were slavery.

you crowned him with glory and honor
8 and put everything under his feet."[j]

In putting everything under
him, God left nothing that
is not subject to him. Yet at
present we do not see ev-
erything subject to him.
9But we see Jesus, who was
made a little lower than the
angels, now crowned with
glory and honor because he
suffered death, so that by
the grace of God he might
taste death for everyone.
10In bringing many sons
to glory, it was fitting that
God, for whom and
through whom everything
exists, should make the author of their salvation perfect through suffering.
11Both the one who makes
men holy and those who
are made holy are of the
same family. So Jesus is
not ashamed to call them
brothers. 12He says,

"I will declare your name to my brothers;
in the presence of the congregation I will sing your praises."[k]

13And again,

"I will put my trust in him."[l]

And again he says,

"Here am I, and the children God has given me."[m]

14Since the children have
flesh and blood, he too
shared in their humanity so
that by his death he might
destroy him who holds the
power of death—that is,
the devil— 15and free those
who all their lives were
held in slavery by their fear

[b] Some ancient mss. do not contain *And . . . hands*

[j] *8* Psalm 8:4-6
[k] *12* Psalm 22:22
[l] *13* Isaiah 8:17
[m] *13* Isaiah 8:18

16For assuredly He does
not give help to angels, but
He gives help to the de-
scendant of Abraham.
17Therefore, He had to be
made like His brethren in
all things, that He might
become a merciful and
faithful high priest in things
pertaining to God, to make
propitiation for the sins of
the people.
18For since He Himself
was tempted in that which
He has suffered, He is able
to come to the aid of those
who are tempted.

Chapter 3

Jesus Our High Priest

THEREFORE, holy
brethren, partakers of
a heavenly calling, con-
sider Jesus, the Apostle
and High Priest of our
confession.
2He was faithful to Him
who appointed Him, as
Moses also was in all His
house.
3For He has been count-
ed worthy of more glory
than Moses, by just so
much as the builder of the
house has more honor than
the house.
4For every house is built
by someone, but the builder of all things is God.
5Now Moses was faithful
in all His house as a servant, for a testimony of
those things which were to
be spoken later;
6but Christ *was faithful*
as a Son over His house
whose house we are, if we
hold fast our confidence
and the boast of our hope
firm until the end.
7Therefore, just as the
Holy Spirit says,
"TODAY IF YOU HEAR HIS
VOICE,
8 DO NOT HARDEN YOUR
HEARTS AS WHEN THEY
PROVOKED ME,

16 οὐ γὰρ δήπου ἀγγέλων ἐπιλαμβάνεται,
4not. 1For 2of course 5of angels 3he takes hold,
ἀλλὰ σπέρματος Ἀβραὰμ ἐπιλαμβάνεται.
but of [the] seed of Abraham he takes hold.
17 ὅθεν ὤφειλεν κατὰ πάντα τοῖς ἀδελφοῖς
Whence he owed (ought) by all means† 2to the 3brothers (his)
ὁμοιωθῆναι, ἵνα ἐλεήμων γένηται καὶ
1to become like, in order that 2a merciful 1he might become and
πιστὸς ἀρχιερεὺς τὰ πρὸς τὸν θεόν,
faithful high priest [in] the things in regard to – God,
εἰς τὸ ἱλάσκεσθαι τὰς ἁμαρτίας τοῦ
for the to make propitiation for the sins of the
λαοῦ. 18 ἐν ᾧ γὰρ πέπονθεν αὐτὸς
people. 2in 3what [way] 1For 5has suffered 4he
πειρασθείς, δύναται τοῖς πειραζομένοις
being tempted, he is able 2the [ones] 3being tempted
βοηθῆσαι.
1to help.

3 Ὅθεν, ἀδελφοὶ ἅγιοι, κλήσεως
Whence, brothers holy, 2calling
ἐπουρανίου μέτοχοι, κατανοήσατε τὸν
3of a heavenly 1sharers, consider the
ἀπόστολον καὶ ἀρχιερέα τῆς ὁμολογίας
apostle and high priest of the confession
ἡμῶν Ἰησοῦν, 2 πιστὸν ὄντα τῷ ποιήσαντι
of us[,] Jesus, faithful being to the [one] making
αὐτόν, ὡς καὶ Μωϋσῆς ἐν [ὅλῳ] τῷ
him, as also Moses in all the
οἴκῳ αὐτοῦ. 3 πλείονος γὰρ οὗτος δόξης
household of him. For 3of more 1this one 4glory
παρὰ Μωϋσῆν ἠξίωται καθ' ὅσον πλείονα
5than 6Moses 2has been counted worthy by so much as 5more
τιμὴν ἔχει τοῦ οἴκου ὁ κατασκευάσας
6honour 4has 7[than] 8the 9house 1the [one] 2having prepared
αὐτόν. 4 πᾶς γὰρ οἶκος κατασκευάζεται
3it. For every house is prepared
ὑπό τινος, ὁ δὲ πάντα κατασκευάσας
by someone, but 1the [one] 3all things 2having prepared
θεός. 5 καὶ Μωϋσῆς μὲν πιστὸς ἐν
[is] God. And Moses on one hand faithful [was] in
ὅλῳ τῷ οἴκῳ αὐτοῦ ὡς θεράπων εἰς
all the household of him as a servant for
μαρτύριον τῶν λαληθησομένων, 6 Χριστὸς
a testimony of the things being spoken [in the future], Christ
δὲ ὡς υἱὸς ἐπὶ τὸν οἶκον αὐτοῦ· οὗ
on the other as a Son over the household of him; of whom
οἶκός ἐσμεν ἡμεῖς, ἐὰν τὴν παρρησίαν
a household are we, if 2the 3confidence
καὶ τὸ καύχημα τῆς ἐλπίδος [μέχρι
4and 5the 6boast 7of the 8hope 10until
τέλους βεβαίαν] κατάσχωμεν. 7 Διό,
11[the] end 9firm 1we hold fast. Wherefore,
καθὼς λέγει τὸ πνεῦμα τὸ ἅγιον· σήμερον
as says the Spirit – Holy: To-day
ἐὰν τῆς φωνῆς αὐτοῦ ἀκούσητε, 8 μὴ
if the voice of him ye hear, not
σκληρύνητε τὰς καρδίας ὑμῶν ὡς ἐν
harden ye the hearts of you as in

of death. 16For surely it is
not angels he helps, but
Abraham's descendants.
17For this reason he had to
be made like his brothers in
every way, in order that he
might become a merciful
and faithful high priest in
service to God, and that he
might make atonement
for[n] the sins of the people.
18Because he himself suf-
fered when he was tempt-
ed, he is able to help those
who are being tempted.

Chapter 3

Jesus Greater Than Moses

THEREFORE, holy
brothers, who share in
the heavenly calling, fix
your thoughts on Jesus, the
apostle and high priest
whom we confess. 2He was
faithful to the one who appointed him, just as Moses
was faithful in all God's
house. 3Jesus has been
found worthy of greater
honor than Moses, just as
the builder of a house has
greater honor than the
house itself. 4For every
house is built by someone,
but God is the builder of everything. 5Moses was faithful as a servant in all God's
house, testifying to what
would be said in the future.
6But Christ is faithful as a
son over God's house. And
we are his house, if we hold
on to our courage and the
hope of which we boast.

Warning Against Unbelief

7So, as the Holy Spirit
says:

"Today, if you hear his
voice,
8 do not harden your
hearts
as you did in the
rebellion,

[n]17 *Or and that he might turn aside God's wrath, taking away*

AS IN THE DAY OF TRIAL
IN THE WILDERNESS,
9 WHERE YOUR FATHERS
TRIED *Me* BY TESTING
Me,
AND SAW MY WORKS
FOR FORTY YEARS.
10 "THEREFORE I WAS AN-
GRY WITH THIS GEN-
ERATION,
AND SAID, 'THEY AL-
WAYS GO ASTRAY IN
THEIR HEART;
AND THEY DID NOT
KNOW MY WAYS';
11 AS I SWORE IN MY
WRATH,
'THEY SHALL NOT ENTER
MY REST.' "

The Peril of Unbelief

12 Take care, brethren,
lest there should be in any
one of you an evil, un-
believing heart, in falling
away from the living God.
13 But encourage one an-
other day after day, as long
as it is *still* called "Today,"
lest any one of you be hardened by the deceitfulness
of sin.
14 For we have become
partakers of Christ, if we
hold fast the beginning of
our assurance firm until the
end;
15 while it is said,
"TODAY IF YOU HEAR HIS
VOICE,
DO NOT HARDEN YOUR
HEARTS, AS WHEN
THEY PROVOKED ME."
16 For who provoked *Him*
when they had heard? In-
deed, did not all those who
came out of Egypt *led* by
Moses?
17 And with whom was He
angry for forty years? Was
it not with those who
sinned, whose bodies fell in
the wilderness?
18 And to whom did He
swear that they should not
enter His rest, but to those
who were disobedient?
19 And *so* we see that they
were not able to enter because of unbelief.

τῷ παραπικρασμῷ κατὰ τὴν ἡμέραν τοῦ
the provocation in the day of the
πειρασμοῦ ἐν τῇ ἐρήμῳ, 9 οὗ ἐπείρασαν
temptation in the desert, when [4]tempted
οἱ πατέρες ὑμῶν ἐν δοκιμασίᾳ καὶ εἶδον
[1]the [2]fathers [3]of you in proving and saw
τὰ ἔργα μου τεσσεράκοντα ἔτη· 10 διὸ
the works of me forty years; wherefore
προσώχθισα τῇ γενεᾷ ταύτῃ καὶ εἶπον·
I was angry with this generation and I said:
ἀεὶ πλανῶνται τῇ καρδίᾳ· αὐτοὶ δὲ
Always they err in the heart; and they
οὐκ ἔγνωσαν τὰς ὁδούς μου, 11 ὡς
knew not the ways of me, as
ὤμοσα ἐν τῇ ὀργῇ μου· εἰ εἰσελεύσονται
I swore in the wrath of me: If they shall enter
εἰς τὴν κατάπαυσίν μου. 12 Βλέπετε,
into the rest of me. Look ye,
ἀδελφοί, μήποτε ἔσται ἔν τινι ὑμῶν
brothers, lest there shall be in anyone of you
καρδία πονηρὰ ἀπιστίας ἐν τῷ ἀποστῆναι
[2]heart [1]an evil of unbelief in *the* *to* depart[ing]
ἀπὸ θεοῦ ζῶντος, 13 ἀλλὰ παρακαλεῖτε
from God a living, but exhort
ἑαυτοὺς καθ' ἑκάστην ἡμέραν, ἄχρις οὗ
yourselves – each day, while
τὸ σήμερον καλεῖται, ἵνα μὴ σκληρυνθῇ
the to-day it is being called, lest [4]be hardened
τις ἐξ ὑμῶν ἀπάτῃ τῆς ἁμαρτίας· 14 μέτ-
[1]any-one [2]of [3]you by [the] deceit – of sin; [3]shar-
οχοι γὰρ τοῦ Χριστοῦ γεγόναμεν, ἐάνπερ
ers [1]for [4]of the [5]Christ [2]we have become, if indeed
τὴν ἀρχὴν τῆς ὑποστάσεως μέχρι τέλους
[3]the [4]beginning [5]of the [6]assurance [7]until [8][the] end
βεβαίαν κατάσχωμεν. 15 ἐν τῷ λέγεσθαι·
[9]firm [1]we hold fast. In the to be said[•]: =While it is said:
σήμερον ἐὰν τῆς φωνῆς αὐτοῦ ἀκούσητε,
To-day if the voice of him ye hear,
μὴ σκληρύνητε τὰς καρδίας ὑμῶν ὡς
do not harden the hearts of you as
ἐν τῷ παραπικρασμῷ. 16 τίνες γὰρ
in the provocation. For some
ἀκούσαντες παρεπίκραναν; ἀλλ' οὐ πάντες
hearing provoked ? yet not all
οἱ ἐξελθόντες ἐξ Αἰγύπτου διὰ
the [ones] coming *out* out of Egypt through
Μωϋσέως; 17 τίσιν δὲ προσώχθισεν τεσ-
Moses ? but with whom was he angry for-
σεράκοντα ἔτη; οὐχὶ τοῖς ἁμαρτήσασιν,
ty years ? [was it] not with the [ones] sinning,
ὧν τὰ κῶλα ἔπεσεν ἐν τῇ ἐρήμῳ;
of whom the corpses fell in the desert ?
18 τίσιν δὲ ὤμοσεν μὴ εἰσελεύσεσθαι εἰς
and to whom swore he not to enter into
τὴν κατάπαυσιν αὐτοῦ εἰ μὴ τοῖς
the rest of him except to the
ἀπειθήσασιν; 19 καὶ βλέπομεν ὅτι οὐκ
[ones] disobeying ? and we see that not
ἠδυνήθησαν εἰσελθεῖν δι' ἀπιστίαν.
they were able to enter because of disbelief.

during the time of
testing in the desert,
9 where your fathers
tested and tried me
and for forty years saw
what I did.
10 That is why I was angry
with that generation,
and I said, 'Their
hearts are always
going astray,
and they have not
known my ways.'
11 So I declared on oath in
my anger,
'They shall never enter
my rest.' "[o]

12 See to it, brothers, that
none of you has a sinful,
unbelieving heart that turns
away from the living God.
13 But encourage one another daily, as long as it is
called Today, so that none
of you may be hardened by
sin's deceitfulness. 14 We
have come to share in
Christ if we hold firmly till
the end the confidence we
had at first. 15 As has just
been said:

"Today, if you hear his
voice,
do not harden your
hearts
as you did in the
rebellion."[p]

16 Who were they who
heard and rebelled? Were
they not all those Moses led
out of Egypt? 17 And with
whom was he angry for forty years? Was it not with
those who sinned, whose
bodies fell in the desert?
18 And to whom did God
swear that they would never enter his rest if not to
those who disobeyed[q]?
19 So we see that they were
not able to enter, because
of their unbelief.

[o] *11* Psalm 95:7-11
[p] *15,7* Psalm 95:7,8
[q] *18* Or *disbelieved*

Chapter 4

The Believer's Rest

THEREFORE, let us
fear lest, while a prom-
ise remains of entering His
rest, any one of you should
seems to have come short
of it.
2For indeed we have had
good news preached to us,
just as they also; but the
word they heard did not
profit them, because it was
not united by faith in those
who heard.
3 [c]For we who have be-
lieved enter that rest, just
as He has said,
"AS I SWORE IN MY
WRATH,
THEY SHALL NOT ENTER
MY REST,"
although His works were
finished from the founda-
tion of the world.
4For He has thus said
somewhere concerning the
seventh *day*, "AND GOD
RESTED ON THE SEVENTH DAY
FROM ALL HIS WORKS";
5and again in this *pas-
sage*, "THEY SHALL NOT EN-
TER MY REST."
6Since therefore it re-
mains for some to enter it,
and those who formerly
had good news preached to
them failed to enter be-
cause of disobedience,
7He again fixes a certain
day, "Today," saying
through David after so long
a time just as has been said
before,
"TODAY IF YOU HEAR HIS
VOICE,
DO NOT HARDEN YOUR
HEARTS."
8For if Joshua had given
them rest, He would not
have spoken of another day
after that.
9There remains there-
fore a Sabbath rest for the
people of God.
10For the one who has en-
tered His rest has himself
also rested from his works,
as God did from His.

[c] Some ancient mss. read *Therefore*

4 Φοβηθῶμεν οὖν μήποτε καταλειπομένης
Let us fear therefore lest [2]being left
ἐπαγγελίας εἰσελθεῖν εἰς τὴν κατάπαυσιν
[1]a promise[a] to enter into the rest
αὐτοῦ δοκῇ τις ἐξ ὑμῶν ὑστερηκέναι.
of him [4]seems [1]anyone [2]of [3]you to have come short.
2 καὶ γάρ ἐσμεν εὐηγγελισμένοι καθάπερ
For indeed we are having had good news preached [to us] even as
κἀκεῖνοι· ἀλλ' οὐκ ὠφέλησεν ὁ λόγος
those also; but [4]did not profit [1]the [2]word
τῆς ἀκοῆς ἐκείνους μὴ συγκεκερασμένος
– [3]of hearing those not having been mixed together
τῇ πίστει τοῖς ἀκούσασιν. 3 Εἰσερχόμεθα
– with faith in the [ones] hearing. we enter
γὰρ εἰς [τὴν] κατάπαυσιν οἱ πιστεύσαντες,
For into the rest the [ones] believing,
καθὼς εἴρηκεν· ὡς ὤμοσα ἐν τῇ ὀργῇ
as he has said: As I swore in the wrath
μου· εἰ εἰσελεύσονται εἰς τὴν κατάπαυσίν
of me: If they shall enter into the rest
μου, καίτοι τῶν ἔργων ἀπὸ καταβολῆς
of me, though the works [2]from [3][the] foundation
κόσμου γενηθέντων. 4 εἴρηκεν γάρ που
[4]of [the] world [1]having come into being.[a] For he has said somewhere
περὶ τῆς ἑβδόμης οὕτως· καὶ κατέπαυσεν
concerning the seventh [day] thus: And [2]rested
ὁ θεὸς ἐν τῇ ἡμέρᾳ τῇ ἑβδόμῃ ἀπὸ
– [1]God in the [2]day – [1]seventh from
πάντων τῶν ἔργων αὐτοῦ· 5 καὶ ἐν
all the works of him; and in
τούτῳ πάλιν· εἰ εἰσελεύσονται εἰς τὴν
this [place] again: If they shall enter into the
κατάπαυσίν μου. 6 ἐπεὶ οὖν ἀπολείπεται
rest of me. Since therefore it remains
τινὰς εἰσελθεῖν εἰς αὐτήν, καὶ οἱ πρότερον
[for] some to enter into it, and the [ones] formerly
εὐαγγελισθέντες οὐκ εἰσῆλθον δι' ἀπείθειαν,
having good news preached [to them] did not enter because of disobedience,
7 πάλιν τινὰ ὁρίζει ἡμέραν, σήμερον, ἐν
again [2]a certain [1]he defines day, to-day, [3]in
Δαυὶδ λέγων μετὰ τοσοῦτον χρόνον, καθὼς
[4]David [1]saying after such a time, as
προείρηται· σήμερον ἐὰν τῆς φωνῆς αὐτοῦ
he has previously said: To-day if the voice of him
ἀκούσητε, μὴ σκληρύνητε τὰς καρδίας
ye hear, do not harden the hearts
ὑμῶν. 8 εἰ γὰρ αὐτοὺς Ἰησοῦς κατέπαυσεν,
of you. For if [3]them [1]Jesus(Joshua) [2]rested,
οὐκ ἂν περὶ ἄλλης ἐλάλει μετὰ ταῦτα
[3]not – [5]concerning [6]another [1]he [2]would [4]have spoken [8]after [9]these things
ἡμέρας. 9 ἄρα ἀπολείπεται σαββατισμὸς
[7]day. Then [2]remains [1]a sabbath rest
τῷ λαῷ τοῦ θεοῦ. 10 ὁ γὰρ εἰσελθὼν
to the people – of God. For the [one] having entered
εἰς τὴν κατάπαυσιν αὐτοῦ καὶ αὐτὸς
into the rest of him also [him]self
κατέπαυσεν ἀπὸ τῶν ἔργων αὐτοῦ,
rested from the works of him,
ὥσπερ ἀπὸ τῶν ἰδίων ὁ θεός. 11 Σπου-
as from the(his) own – God [did]. Let us

Chapter 4

A Sabbath-Rest for the People of God

THEREFORE, since the
promise of entering his
rest still stands, let us be
careful that none of you be
found to have fallen short
of it. 2For we also have had
the gospel preached to us,
just as they did; but the
message they heard was of
no value to them, because
those who heard did not
combine it with faith.[r]
3Now we who have be-
lieved enter that rest, just
as God has said,

"So I declared on oath
in my anger,
'They shall never enter
my rest.' "[s]
And yet his work has been
finished since the creation
of the world. 4For some-
where he has spoken about
the seventh day in these
words: "And on the sev-
enth day God rested from
all his work."[t] 5And again
in the passage above he
says, "They shall never enter my rest."
6It still remains that some
will enter that rest, and
those who formerly had the
gospel preached to them
did not go in, because of
their disobedience. 7There-
fore God again set a certain
day, calling it Today, when
a long time later he spoke
through David, as was said
before:

"Today, if you hear his
voice,
do not harden your
hearts."[p]

8For if Joshua had given
them rest, God would not
have spoken later about another day. 9There remains,
then, a Sabbath-rest for the
people of God; 10for anyone
who enters God's rest also
rests from his own work,
just as God did from his.

[r] 2 Many manuscripts *because they did not share in the faith of those who obeyed*
[s] 3 Psalm 95:11; also in verse 5
[t] 4 Gen. 2:2

11Let us therefore be diligent to enter that rest, lest anyone fall through *following* the same example of disobedience.
12For the word of God is living and active and sharper than any two-edged sword, and piercing as far as the division of soul and spirit, of both joints and marrow, and able to judge the thoughts and intentions of the heart.
13And there is no creature hidden from His sight, but all things are open and laid bare to the eyes of Him with whom we have to do.
14Since then we have a great high priest who has passed through the heavens, Jesus the Son of God, let us hold fast our confession.
15For we do not have a high priest who cannot sympathize with our weaknesses, but one who has been tempted in all things as *we are, yet* without sin.
16Let us therefore draw near with confidence to the throne of grace, that we may receive mercy and may find grace to help in time of need.

δάσωμεν οὖν εἰσελθεῖν εἰς ἐκείνην τὴν
be eager therefore to enter into that –
κατάπαυσιν, ἵνα μὴ ἐν τῷ αὐτῷ τις
rest, lest [3]in [4]the [5]same [1]anyone
ὑποδείγματι πέσῃ τῆς ἀπειθείας. 12 Ζῶν
[6]example [2]falls – of disobedience. [[4]is] [5]living
γὰρ ὁ λόγος τοῦ θεοῦ καὶ ἐνεργὴς
For [1]the [2]word – [3]of God and operative
καὶ τομώτερος ὑπὲρ πᾶσαν μάχαιραν
and sharper beyond every [2]sword
δίστομον καὶ διϊκνούμενος ἄχρι μερισμοῦ
[1]two-mouthed (edged) and passing through as far as division
ψυχῆς καὶ πνεύματος, ἁρμῶν τε καὶ
of soul and of spirit, [2]of joints [1]both and
μυελῶν, καὶ κριτικὸς ἐνθυμήσεων καὶ
of marrows, and able to judge of thoughts and
ἐννοιῶν καρδίας· 13 καὶ οὐκ ἔστιν κτίσις
intentions of a heart; and there is no creature
ἀφανὴς ἐνώπιον αὐτοῦ, πάντα δὲ γυμνὰ
unmanifest before him, but all things [are] naked
καὶ τετραχηλισμένα τοῖς ὀφθαλμοῖς αὐτοῦ,
and *having been* laid open to the eyes of him,
πρὸς ὃν ἡμῖν ὁ λόγος.
with whom to us [is] the word(account).° =is our account.

14 Ἔχοντες οὖν ἀρχιερέα μέγαν διεληλυ-
Having therefore high priest a great having gone
θότα τοὺς οὐρανούς, Ἰησοῦν τὸν υἱὸν
through the heavens, Jesus the Son
τοῦ θεοῦ, κρατῶμεν τῆς ὁμολογίας. 15 οὐ
– of God, let us hold the confession. [3]not
γὰρ ἔχομεν ἀρχιερέα μὴ δυνάμενον
[1]For [2]we have a high priest not being able
συμπαθῆσαι ταῖς ἀσθενείαις ἡμῶν, πεπει-
to suffer with the weaknesses of us, [2]having
ρασμένον δὲ κατὰ πάντα καθ' ὁμοιότητα
been tempted [1]but in all respects† according to [our] likeness
χωρὶς ἁμαρτίας. 16 προσερχώμεθα οὖν
apart from sin. Let us approach therefore
μετὰ παρρησίας τῷ θρόνῳ τῆς χάριτος,
with confidence *to* the throne – of grace,
ἵνα λάβωμεν ἔλεος καὶ χάριν εὕρωμεν
in order that we may receive mercy and [2]grace *we* [1]may find
εἰς εὔκαιρον βοήθειαν.
for timely help.

11Let us, therefore, make every effort to enter that rest, so that no one will fall by following their example of disobedience.
12For the word of God is living and active. Sharper than any double-edged sword, it penetrates even to dividing soul and spirit, joints and marrow; it judges the thoughts and attitudes of the heart. 13Nothing in all creation is hidden from God's sight Everything is uncovered and laid bare before the eyes of him to whom we must give account.

Jesus the Great High Priest

14Therefore, since we have a great high priest who has gone through the heavens,[u] Jesus the Son of God, let us hold firmly to the faith we profess. 15For we do not have a high priest who is unable to sympathize with our weaknesses, but we have one who has been tempted in every way, just as we are—yet was without sin. 16Let us then approach the throne of grace with confidence, so that we may receive mercy and find grace to help us in our time of need.

Chapter 5

The Perfect High Priest

FOR every high priest taken from among men is appointed on behalf of men in things pertaining to God, in order to offer both gifts and sacrifices for sins;
2he can deal gently with the ignorant and misguided, since he himself also is beset with weakness;

5 Πᾶς γὰρ ἀρχιερεὺς ἐξ ἀνθρώπων
For every high priest [2]out of [3]men
λαμβανόμενος ὑπὲρ ἀνθρώπων καθίσταται
[1]being taken on behalf of men is appointed [in]
τὰ πρὸς τὸν θεόν, ἵνα προσφέρῃ δῶρά
the things in regard to – God, in order that he may offer [2]gifts
τε καὶ θυσίας ὑπὲρ ἁμαρτιῶν, 2 μετριο-
[1]both and sacrifices on behalf of sins, [2]to feel in
παθεῖν δυνάμενος τοῖς ἀγνοοῦσιν καὶ
due measure [1]being able for the [ones] not knowing and
πλανωμένοις, ἐπεὶ καὶ αὐτὸς περίκειται
being led astray, since also he is set round [with]

Chapter 5

EVERY high priest is selected from among men and is appointed to represent them in matters related to God, to offer gifts and sacrifices for sins. 2He is able to deal gently with those who are ignorant and are going astray, since he himself is subject to weak-

[u]*14* Or *gone into heaven*

3and because of it he is
obligated to offer *sacrifices*
for sins, as for the people,
so also for himself.
4And no one takes the
honor to himself, but *receives it* when he is called
by God, even as Aaron
was.
5So also Christ did not
glorify Himself so as to
become a high priest, but
He who said to Him,

"THOU ART MY SON,
TODAY I HAVE BEGOT-
TEN THEE";

6just as He says also in
another *passage*,

"THOU ART A PRIEST FOR-
EVER
ACCORDING TO THE OR-
DER OF MEL-
CHIZEDEK."

7In the days of His flesh,
He offered up both prayers
and supplications with loud
crying and tears to the One
able to save Him from
death, and He was heard
because of His piety.
8Although He was a Son,
He learned obedience from
the things which He suf-
fered.
9And having been made
perfect, He became to all
those who obey Him the
source of eternal salvation,
10being designated by
God as a high priest according to the order of Mel-
chizedek.
11Concerning [d]him we
have much to say, and *it is*
hard to explain, since you
have become dull of hear-
ing.
12For though by this time
you ought to be teachers,
you have need again for
someone to teach you the
elementary principles of
the oracles of God, and you
have come to need milk and
not solid food.

[d] Or, *Him;* or, *this*

ἀσθένειαν, 3 καὶ δι' αὐτὴν ὀφείλει, καθὼς
weakness, and because of it he ought, as

περὶ τοῦ λαοῦ, οὕτως καὶ περὶ ἑαυτοῦ
concerning the people, so also concerning himself

προσφέρειν περὶ ἁμαρτιῶν. 4 καὶ οὐχ
to offer concerning sins. And 2not

ἑαυτῷ τις λαμβάνει τὴν τιμήν, ἀλλὰ
4to himself 1anyone 3takes the honour, but

καλούμενος ὑπὸ τοῦ θεοῦ, καθώσπερ καὶ
being called by – God, even as indeed

Ἀαρών. 5 Οὕτως καὶ ὁ Χριστὸς οὐχ
Aaron. So also – Christ 2not

ἑαυτὸν ἐδόξασεν γενηθῆναι ἀρχιερέα, ἀλλ'
3himself 1glorified to become a high priest, but

ὁ λαλήσας πρὸς αὐτόν· υἱός μου εἶ
the [one] speaking to him: Son of me art

σύ, ἐγὼ σήμερον γεγέννηκά σε· 6 καθὼς
thou, I to-day have begotten thee; as

καὶ ἐν ἑτέρῳ λέγει· σὺ ἱερεὺς εἰς τὸν
also in another [psalm] he says: Thou [art] a priest unto the

αἰῶνα κατὰ τὴν τάξιν Μελχισέδεκ. 7 ὃς
age according to the order of Melchisedec. Who

ἐν ταῖς ἡμέραις τῆς σαρκὸς αὐτοῦ δεήσεις
in the days of the flesh of him 3petitions

τε καὶ ἱκετηρίας πρὸς τὸν δυνάμενον
2both 4and 5entreaties 11to 12the [one] 13*being* able

σῴζειν αὐτὸν ἐκ θανάτου μετὰ κραυγῆς
14to save 15him 16out of 17death 6with 8crying

ἰσχυρᾶς καὶ δακρύων προσενέγκας καὶ
7strong 9and 10tears 1offering and

εἰσακουσθεὶς ἀπὸ τῆς εὐλαβείας, 8 καίπερ
being heard from(for) the(his) devoutness, though

ὢν υἱός, ἔμαθεν ἀφ' ὧν ἔπαθεν τὴν
being a Son, he learned 2from 3[the] things which 4he suffered –

ὑπακοήν, 9 καὶ τελειωθεὶς ἐγένετο πᾶσιν
1obedience, and being perfected he became to all

τοῖς ὑπακούουσιν αὐτῷ αἴτιος σωτηρίας
the [ones] obeying him [the] cause 2salvation

αἰωνίου, 10 προσαγορευθεὶς ὑπὸ τοῦ θεοῦ
1of eternal, being designated by – God

ἀρχιερεὺς κατὰ τὴν τάξιν Μελχισέδεκ.
a high priest according to the order of Melchisedec.

11 Περὶ οὗ πολὺς ἡμῖν ὁ λόγος καὶ
Concerning whom much to us the 1word 2and
=we have much to say and hard . . .

δυσερμήνευτος λέγειν, ἐπεὶ νωθροὶ γεγόνατε
4hard to interpret 3to say, since dull ye have become

ταῖς ἀκοαῖς. 12 καὶ γὰρ ὀφείλοντες
in *the* hearings. For indeed owing*

εἶναι διδάσκαλοι διὰ τὸν χρόνον, πάλιν
to be teachers because of the time, 3again

χρείαν ἔχετε τοῦ διδάσκειν ὑμᾶς τινα
2need 1ye have – 5to teach[d] 6you 4someone

τὰ στοιχεῖα τῆς ἀρχῆς τῶν λογίων
the rudiments of the beginning of the oracles

τοῦ θεοῦ, καὶ γεγόνατε χρείαν ἔχοντες
– of God, and ye have become 2need 1having

γάλακτος, οὐ στερεᾶς τροφῆς. 13 πᾶς
of milk, not of solid food. every

* That is, "ye ought . . ."

God's word all over again.
You need milk, not solid
ness. 3This is why he has to
offer sacrifices for his own
sins, as well as for the sins
of the people.
4No one takes this honor
upon himself; he must be
called by God, just as Aaron was. 5So Christ also did
not take upon himself the
glory of becoming a high
priest. But God said to him,

"You are my Son;
today I have become
your Father.[v]"[w]

6And he says in another
place,

"You are a priest
forever,
in the order of
Melchizedek."[x]

7During the days of Jesus'
life on earth, he offered up
prayers and petitions with
loud cries and tears to the
one who could save him
from death, and he was
heard because of his reverent submission. 8Although
he was a son, he learned
obedience from what he
suffered 9and, once made
perfect, he became the
source of eternal salvation
for all who obey him 10and
was designated by God to
be high priest in the order
of Melchizedek.

Warning Against Falling Away

11We have much to say
about this, but it is hard to
explain because you are
slow to learn. 12In fact,
though by this time you
ought to be teachers, you
need someone to teach you
the elementary truths of

[v]5 Or *have begotten you*
[w]5 Psalm 2:7
[x]6 Psalm 110:4

13For everyone who par-
takes *only* of milk is not accustomed to the word of
righteousness, for he is a
babe.
14But solid food is for the
mature, who because of
practice have their senses
trained to discern good and
evil.

Chapter 6

The Peril of Falling Away

THEREFORE leaving
the elementary teach-
ing about the Christ, let us
press on to maturity, not
laying again a foundation of
repentance from dead
works and of faith toward
God,
2of instruction about
washings, and laying on of
hands, and the resurrection
of the dead, and eternal
judgment.
3And this we shall do, if
God permits.
4For in the case of those
who have once been en-
lightened and have tasted
of the heavenly gift and
have been made partakers
of the Holy Spirit,
5and have tasted the
good word of God and the
powers of the age to come,
6and *then* have fallen
away, it is impossible to
renew them again to repentance, since they again
crucify to themselves the
Son of God, and put Him to
open shame.
7For ground that drinks
the rain which often falls
upon it and brings forth
vegetation useful to those
for whose sake it is also
tilled, receives a blessing
from God;
8but if it yields thorns
and thistles, it is worthless
and close to being cursed,
and it ends up being
burned.

Better Things for You

9But, beloved, we are
convinced of better things
concerning you, and things
that accompany salvation,
though we are speaking in
this way.
10For God is not unjust so

γὰρ ὁ μετέχων γάλακτος ἄπειρος λόγου
For one partaking of milk [is] without experience of [the] word
δικαιοσύνης, νήπιος γάρ ἐστιν· 14 τελείων δέ
of righteousness, for [2]an infant [1]he is; but [4]of mature men
ἐστιν ἡ στερεὰ τροφή, τῶν διὰ τὴν
[3]is *the* [1]solid [2]food, of the [ones] because of the(ir)
ἕξιν τὰ αἰσθητήρια γεγυμνασμένα ἐχόντων
condition [2]the(ir) [3]faculties *having been* [4]exercised [1]having
πρὸς διάκρισιν καλοῦ τε καὶ κακοῦ.
for distinction [2]of good [1]both and of bad.
6 Διὸ ἀφέντες τὸν τῆς ἀρχῆς τοῦ Χριστοῦ
Wherefore leaving [1]the [3]of the [4]beginning – [5]of Christ
λόγον ἐπὶ τὴν τελειότητα φερώμεθα, μὴ
[2]word [7]on to – [8]maturity [6]let us be borne, not
πάλιν θεμέλιον καταβαλλόμενοι μετανοίας
again [2]a foundation [1]laying down of repentance
ἀπὸ νεκρῶν ἔργων, καὶ πίστεως ἐπὶ
from dead works, and of faith toward
θεόν, 2 βαπτισμῶν διδαχῆς, ἐπιθέσεώς τε
God, [2]of baptisms [1]of teaching, and of laying on
χειρῶν, ἀναστάσεως νεκρῶν, καὶ κρίματος
of hands, of resurrection of dead persons, and [2]judgment
αἰωνίου. 3 καὶ τοῦτο ποιήσομεν, ἐάνπερ
[1]of eternal. And this will we do, if indeed
ἐπιτρέπῃ ὁ θεός. 4 Ἀδύνατον γὰρ τοὺς
[2]permits – [1]God. For [it is] impossible [for] the [ones]
ἅπαξ φωτισθέντας γευσαμένους τε τῆς
once being enlightened and tasting of the
δωρεᾶς τῆς ἐπουρανίου καὶ μετόχους
[2]gift – [1]heavenly and sharers
γενηθέντας πνεύματος ἁγίου 5 καὶ καλὸν
becoming Spirit of [the] Holy and [3][the] good
γευσαμένους θεοῦ ῥῆμα δυνάμεις τε
[1]tasting [4]of God [2]word and powerful deeds
μέλλοντος αἰῶνος, 6 καὶ παραπεσόντας, πάλιν
of a coming age, and falling away, again
ἀνακαινίζειν εἰς μετάνοιαν, ἀνασταυροῦντας
to renew to repentance, crucifying again
ἑαυτοῖς τὸν υἱὸν τοῦ θεοῦ καὶ παρα-
for themselves the Son – of God and putting
δειγματίζοντας. 7 γῆ γὰρ ἡ πιοῦσα
[him] to open shame. For earth – drinking
τὸν ἐπ' αὐτῆς ἐρχόμενον πολλάκις ὑετὸν
[1]the [5]upon [6]it [3]coming [4]often [2]rain
καὶ τίκτουσα βοτάνην εὔθετον ἐκείνοις
and bearing fodder suitable for those
δι' οὓς καὶ γεωργεῖται, μεταλαμβάνει
on account of whom indeed it is farmed, receives
εὐλογίας ἀπὸ τοῦ θεοῦ· 8 ἐκφέρουσα δὲ
blessing from – God; but bringing forth
ἀκάνθας καὶ τριβόλους ἀδόκιμος καὶ
thorns and thistles [it is] disapproved and
κατάρας ἐγγύς, ἧς τὸ τέλος εἰς καῦσιν.
[2]a curse [1]near, of which the end [is] for burning.
9 Πεπείσμεθα δὲ περὶ ὑμῶν, ἀγαπητοί,
But we have been persuaded concerning you, beloved,
τὰ κρείσσονα καὶ ἐχόμενα σωτηρίας, εἰ
the better things and having salvation, if
καὶ οὕτως λαλοῦμεν. 10 οὐ γὰρ ἄδικος
indeed [2]so [1]we speak. For [2]not [3]unjust

food! 13Anyone who lives
on milk, being still an infant, is not acquainted with
the teaching about right-
eousness. 14But solid food
is for the mature, who by
constant use have trained
themselves to distinguish
good from evil.

Chapter 6

THEREFORE let us
leave the elementary
teachings about Christ and
go on to maturity, not laying again the foundation of
repentance from acts that
lead to death,[y] and of faith
in God, 2instruction about
baptisms, the laying on of
hands, the resurrection of
the dead, and eternal judgment. 3And God permit-
ting, we will do so.
4It is impossible for those
who have once been en-
lightened, who have tasted
the heavenly gift, who have
shared in the Holy Spirit,
5who have tasted the goodness of the word of God and
the powers of the coming
age, 6if they fall away, to be
brought back to repen-
tance, because[z] to their
loss they are crucifying the
Son of God all over again
and subjecting him to public disgrace.
7Land that drinks in the
rain often falling on it and
that produces a crop useful
to those for whom it is
farmed receives the blessing of God. 8But land that
produces thorns and this-
tles is worthless and is in
danger of being cursed. In
the end it will be burned.
9Even though we speak
like this, dear friends, we
are confident of better
things in your case—things
that accompany salvation.
10God is not unjust; he will

y1 Or *from useless rituals*
z6 Or *repentance while*

as to forget your work and the love which you have shown toward His name, in having ministered and in still ministering to the saints.

11And we desire that each one of you show the same diligence so as to realize the full assurance of hope until the end,

12that you may not be sluggish, but imitators of those who through faith and patience inherit the promises.

13For when God made the promise to Abraham, since He could swear by no one greater, He swore by Himself,

14saying, "I WILL SURELY BLESS YOU, AND I WILL SURELY MULTIPLY YOU."

15And thus, having patiently waited, he obtained the promise.

16For men swear by one greater *than themselves*, and with them an oath *given* as confirmation is an end of every dispute.

17In the same way God, desiring even more to show to the heirs of the promise the unchangeableness of His purpose, interposed with an oath,

18in order that by two unchangeable things, in which it is impossible for God to lie, we may have strong encouragement, we who have fled for refuge in laying hold of the hope set before us.

19This hope we have as an anchor of the soul, a *hope* both sure and steadfast and one which enters within the veil,

20where Jesus has entered as a forerunner for us, having become a high priest forever according to the order of Melchizedek.

ὁ θεὸς ἐπιλαθέσθαι τοῦ ἔργου ὑμῶν
– [1]God [is] to be forgetful of the work of you

καὶ τῆς ἀγάπης ἧς ἐνεδείξασθε εἰς τὸ
and of the love which ye showed to the

ὄνομα αὐτοῦ, διακονήσαντες τοῖς ἁγίοις
name of him, having ministered to the saints

καὶ διακονοῦντες. **11** ἐπιθυμοῦμεν δὲ
and ministering. But we desire

ἕκαστον ὑμῶν τὴν αὐτὴν ἐνδείκνυσθαι
each one of you [2]the [3]same [1]to show

σπουδὴν πρὸς τὴν πληροφορίαν τῆς ἐλπίδος
eagerness to the full assurance of *the* hope

ἄχρι τέλους, **12** ἵνα μὴ νωθροὶ γένησθε,
unto [the] end, lest dull ye become,

μιμηταὶ δὲ τῶν διὰ πίστεως καὶ μακρο-
but imitators of the [ones] through faith and long-

θυμίας κληρονομούντων τὰς ἐπαγγελίας.
suffering inheriting the promises.

13 Τῷ γὰρ Ἀβραὰμ ἐπαγγειλάμενος ὁ
– For [3]to Abraham [2]making promise –

θεός, ἐπεὶ κατ' οὐδενὸς εἶχεν μείζονος
[1]God, since [3]by [5]no one [1]he had [4]greater

ὀμόσαι, ὤμοσεν καθ' ἑαυτοῦ, **14** λέγων·
to swear, swore by himself, saying:

εἰ μὴν εὐλογῶν εὐλογήσω σε καὶ πληθύνων
If surely blessing I will bless thee and multiplying

πληθυνῶ σε· **15** καὶ οὕτως μακροθυμήσας
I will multiply thee; and so being longsuffering

ἐπέτυχεν τῆς ἐπαγγελίας. **16** ἄνθρωποι γὰρ
he obtained the promise. For men

κατὰ τοῦ μείζονος ὀμνύουσιν, καὶ πάσης
by the greater swear, and [6]of all

αὐτοῖς ἀντιλογίας πέρας εἰς βεβαίωσιν ὁ
[3][is] [4]to them [7]contradiction [5]an end [8]for [9]confirmation [1]the

ὅρκος· **17** ἐν ᾧ περισσότερον βουλόμενος
[2]oath; wherein [3]more abundantly [2]resolving

ὁ θεὸς ἐπιδεῖξαι τοῖς κληρονόμοις τῆς
– [1]God to show to the heirs of the

ἐπαγγελίας τὸ ἀμετάθετον τῆς βουλῆς
promise the unchangeableness of the resolve

αὐτοῦ ἐμεσίτευσεν ὅρκῳ, **18** ἵνα διὰ
of him interposed by an oath, in order that through

δύο πραγμάτων ἀμεταθέτων, ἐν οἷς ἀδύνατον
two [2]things [1]unchangeable, in which [it was] impossible

ψεύσασθαι θεόν, ἰσχυρὰν παράκλησιν ἔχωμεν
[2]to lie [1]God,[b] [2]a strong [3]consolation [1]we may have[,]

οἱ καταφυγόντες κρατῆσαι τῆς προκειμένης
the [ones] having fled to lay hold of the [2]set before [us]

ἐλπίδος· **19** ἣν ὡς ἄγκυραν ἔχομεν τῆς
[1]hope; which as an anchor we have of the

ψυχῆς ἀσφαλῆ τε καὶ βεβαίαν καὶ
soul [2]safe [1]both and firm and

εἰσερχομένην εἰς τὸ ἐσώτερον τοῦ κατα-
entering into the inner [side] of the veil,

πετάσματος, **20** ὅπου πρόδρομος ὑπὲρ ἡμῶν
where a forerunner on behalf of us

εἰσῆλθεν Ἰησοῦς, κατὰ τὴν τάξιν Μελχισέ-
entered[,] Jesus, [6]according to [7]the [8]order [9]of Melchise-

δεκ ἀρχιερεὺς γενόμενος εἰς τὸν αἰῶνα.
dec [5]a high priest [1]becoming [2]unto [3]the [4]age.

not forget your work and
the love you have shown
him as you have helped his
people and continue to help
them. 11We want each of
you to show this same diligence to the very end, in
order to make your hope
sure. 12We do not want you
to become lazy, but to imitate those who through
faith and patience inherit
what has been promised.

The Certainty of God's Promise

13When God made his
promise to Abraham, since
there was no one greater
for him to swear by, he
swore by himself, 14saying,
"I will surely bless you and
give you many descend-
ants."[a] 15And so after
waiting patiently, Abraham
received what was prom-
ised.

16Men swear by someone
greater than themselves,
and the oath confirms what
is said and puts an end to all
argument. 17Because God
wanted to make the un-
changing nature of his purpose very clear to the heirs
of what was promised, he
confirmed it with an oath.
18God did this so that, by
two unchangeable things in
which it is impossible for
God to lie, we who have
fled to take hold of the hope
offered to us may be greatly
encouraged. 19We have this
hope as an anchor for the
soul, firm and secure. It enters the inner sanctuary behind the curtain, 20where
Jesus, who went before us,
has entered on our behalf.
He has become a high
priest forever, in the order
of Melchizedek.

[a]*14* Gen. 22:17

Chapter 7

Melchizedek's Priesthood Like Christ's

FOR this Melchizedek, king of Salem, priest of the Most High God, who met Abraham as he was returning from the slaughter of the kings and blessed him,

2to whom also Abraham apportioned a tenth part of all *the spoils*, was first of all, by the translation *of his name*, king of righteousness, and then also king of Salem, which is king of peace.

3Without father, without mother, without genealogy, having neither beginning of days nor end of life, but made like the Son of God, he abides a priest perpetually.

4Now observe how great this man was to whom Abraham, the patriarch, gave a tenth of the choicest spoils.

5And those indeed of the sons of Levi who receive the priest's office have commandment in the Law to collect a tenth from the people, that is, from their brethren, although these are descended from Abraham.

6But the one whose genealogy is not traced from them collected a tenth from Abraham, and blessed the one who had the promises.

7But without any dispute the lesser is blessed by the greater.

8And in this case mortal men receive tithes, but in that case one *receives them*, of whom it is witnessed that he lives on.

9And, so to speak, through Abraham even Levi, who received tithes, paid tithes,

10for he was still in the loins of his father when

7 Οὗτος γὰρ ὁ Μελχισέδεκ, βασιλεὺς
For this – Melchisedec, king

Σαλήμ, ἱερεὺς τοῦ θεοῦ τοῦ ὑψίστου,
of Salem, priest – [3]God [1]of the [2]most high,

ὁ συναντήσας Ἀβραὰμ ὑποστρέφοντι ἀπὸ
the [one] meeting Abraham returning from

τῆς κοπῆς τῶν βασιλέων καὶ εὐλογήσας
the slaughter of the kings and blessing

αὐτόν, 2 ᾧ καὶ δεκάτην ἀπὸ πάντων
him, to whom indeed [3]a tenth [4]from [5]all

ἐμέρισεν Ἀβραάμ, πρῶτον μὲν ἑρμηνευ-
[2]divided [1]Abraham, firstly on one hand being inter-

όμενος βασιλεὺς δικαιοσύνης, ἔπειτα δὲ καὶ
preted King of righteousness, then on the other also

βασιλεὺς Σαλήμ, ὅ ἐστιν βασιλεὺς εἰρήνης,
King of Salem, which is King of peace,

3 ἀπάτωρ, ἀμήτωρ, ἀγενεαλόγητος, μήτε
without father, without mother, without pedigree, [2]neither

ἀρχὴν ἡμερῶν μήτε ζωῆς τέλος ἔχων,
[3]beginning [4]of days [5]nor [7]of life [6]end [1]having,

ἀφωμοιωμένος δὲ τῷ υἱῷ τοῦ θεοῦ, μένει
but *having been* made like *to* the Son – of God, remains

ἱερεὺς εἰς τὸ διηνεκές. 4 Θεωρεῖτε δὲ
a priest in *the* perpetuity. Now behold ye

πηλίκος οὗτος, ᾧ δεκάτην Ἀβραὰμ
how great this man [was], to whom [5]a tenth [3]Abraham

ἔδωκεν ἐκ τῶν ἀκροθινίων ὁ πατριάρχης.
[4]gave [6]of [7]the [8]spoils [1]the [2]patriarch.

5 καὶ οἱ μὲν ἐκ τῶν υἱῶν Λευὶ τὴν
And [2]the [ones] [1]on one hand [3]of [4]the [5]sons [6]of Levi [8]the

ἱερατείαν λαμβάνοντες ἐντολὴν ἔχουσιν
[9]priesthood [7]receiving [11]a commandment [10]have

ἀποδεκατοῦν τὸν λαὸν κατὰ τὸν νόμον,
to take tithes from the people according to the law,

τοῦτ' ἔστιν τοὺς ἀδελφοὺς αὐτῶν, καίπερ
this is the brothers of them, though

ἐξεληλυθότας ἐκ τῆς ὀσφύος Ἀβραάμ·
having come forth out of the loin[s] of Abraham;

6 ὁ δὲ μὴ γενεαλογούμενος ἐξ αὐτῶν
[2]the [one] [1]on the other not counting [his] pedigree from them

δεδεκάτωκεν Ἀβραάμ, καὶ τὸν ἔχοντα
has tithed Abraham, and [2]the [one] [3]having

τὰς ἐπαγγελίας εὐλόγηκεν. 7 χωρὶς δὲ
[4]the [5]promises [1]has blessed. And without

πάσης ἀντιλογίας τὸ ἔλαττον ὑπὸ τοῦ
all(any) contradiction the less [2]by [3]the

κρείττονος εὐλογεῖται. 8 καὶ ὧδε μὲν
[4]better [1]is blessed. And here on one hand

δεκάτας ἀποθνῄσκοντες ἄνθρωποι λαμβά-
[4]tithes [1]dying [2]men [3]re-

νουσιν, ἐκεῖ δὲ μαρτυρούμενος ὅτι ζῇ.
ceive, there on the other being witnessed that he lives.

9 καὶ ὡς ἔπος εἰπεῖν, δι' Ἀβραὰμ
And as a word to say, =so to speak, through Abraham

καὶ Λευὶς ὁ δεκάτας λαμβάνων δεδε-
indeed Levi [1]the [one] [3]tithes [2]receiving has

κάτωται· 10 ἔτι γὰρ ἐν τῇ ὀσφύϊ τοῦ
been tithed; for [2]yet [3]in [4]the [5]loin[s] [6]of the(his)

Chapter 7

Melchizedek the Priest

THIS Melchizedek was
king of Salem and
priest of God Most High.
He met Abraham returning
from the defeat of the kings
and blessed him, 2and
Abraham gave him a tenth
of everything. First, his
name means "king of righteousness"; then also,
"king of Salem" means
"king of peace." 3Without
father or mother, without
genealogy, without begin-
ning of days or end of life,
like the Son of God he remains a priest forever.

4Just think how great he
was: Even the patriarch
Abraham gave him a tenth
of the plunder! 5Now the
law requires the descend-
ants of Levi who become
priests to collect a tenth
from the people—that is,
their brothers—even
though their brothers are
descended from Abraham.
6This man, however, did
not trace his descent from
Levi, yet he collected a
tenth from Abraham and
blessed him who had the
promises. 7And without
doubt the lesser person is
blessed by the greater. 8In
the one case, the tenth is
collected by men who die;
but in the other case, by
him who is declared to be
living. 9One might even say
that Levi, who collects the
tenth, paid the tenth
through Abraham, 10be-
cause when Melchizedek

Melchizedek met him.
11Now if perfection was
through the Levitical
priesthood (for on the basis
of it the people received the
Law), what further need
was there for another priest
to arise according to the order of Melchizedek, and
not be designated accord-
ing to the order of Aaron?
12For when the priest-
hood is changed, of necessity there takes place a
change of law also.
13For the one concerning
whom these things are
spoken belongs to another
tribe, from which no one
has officiated at the altar.
14For it is evident that our
Lord was descended from
Judah, a tribe with reference to which Moses spoke
nothing concerning priests.
15And this is clearer still,
if another priest arises according to the likeness of
Melchizedek,
16who has become *such*
not on the basis of a law of
physical requirement, but
according to the power of
an indestructible life.
17For it is witnessed *of
Him*,
"THOU ART A PRIEST FOR-
EVER
ACCORDING TO THE
ORDER OF MEL-
CHIZEDEK."
18For, on the one hand,
there is a setting aside of a
former commandment be-
cause of its weakness and
uselessness
19(for the Law made noth-
ing perfect), and on the
other hand there is a bringing in of a better hope,
through which we draw
near to God.
20And inasmuch as *it was*
not without an oath
21(for they indeed became
priests without an oath, but

πατρὸς ἦν ὅτε συνήντησεν αὐτῷ Μελχισέ-
[7]father [1]he was [8]when [10]met [11]him [9]Melchise-
δεκ. **11** Εἰ μὲν οὖν τελείωσις διὰ τῆς
dec. If – therefore perfection [2]through [3]the
Λευιτικῆς ἱερωσύνης ἦν, ὁ λαὸς γὰρ
[4]Levitical [5]priestly office [1]was, [4]the [5]people [1]for
ἐπ' αὐτῆς νενομοθέτηται, τίς ἔτι χρεία
[2]under* [3]it has been furnished with law, why yet need
κατὰ τὴν τάξιν Μελχισέδεκ ἕτερον
[was there for] [4]according to [5]the [6]order [7]of Melchisedec [1]another
ἀνίστασθαι ἱερέα καὶ οὐ κατὰ τὴν τάξιν
[3]to arise [2]priest and not [2]according to [3]the [4]order
'Ααρὼν λέγεσθαι; **12** μετατιθεμένης γὰρ
[5]of Aaron [1]to be said(named)? for [3]being changed
τῆς ἱερωσύνης ἐξ ἀνάγκης καὶ νόμου
[1]the [2]priestly office[a] [6]of [7]necessity [5]also [9]of law
μετάθεσις γίνεται. **13** ἐφ' ὃν γὰρ λέγεται
[8]a change [4]there occurs. [2][he] [3]with respect to [4]whom [1]For [6]is(are) said
ταῦτα, φυλῆς ἑτέρας μετέσχηκεν, ἀφ'
[5]these things, [3]tribe [2]of another [1]has partaken, from
ἧς οὐδεὶς προσέσχηκεν τῷ θυσιαστηρίῳ·
which no one has devoted himself to the altar;
14 πρόδηλον γὰρ ὅτι ἐξ 'Ιούδα ἀνατέταλκεν
for it is perfectly clear that out of Juda has risen
ὁ κύριος ἡμῶν, εἰς ἣν φυλὴν περὶ ἱερέων
the Lord of us, as to which tribe concerning priests
οὐδὲν Μωϋσῆς ἐλάλησεν. **15** καὶ περισ-
[3]nothing [1]Moses [2]spoke. And more
σότερον ἔτι κατάδηλόν ἐστιν, εἰ κατὰ
abundantly still quite clear is it, if according to
τὴν ὁμοιότητα Μελχισέδεκ ἀνίσταται ἱερεὺς
the likeness of Melchisedec arises priest
ἕτερος, **16** ὃς οὐ κατὰ νόμον ἐντολῆς
another, who not according to [the] law [2]commandment
σαρκίνης γέγονεν ἀλλὰ κατὰ δύναμιν ζωῆς
[1]of a fleshy has become but according to [the] power life
ἀκαταλύτου. **17** μαρτυρεῖται γὰρ ὅτι σὺ
of an indissoluble. For it is witnessed that Thou
ἱερεὺς εἰς τὸν αἰῶνα κατὰ τὴν τάξιν
a priest unto the age according to the order
Μελχισέδεκ. **18** ἀθέτησις μὲν γὰρ γίνεται
of Melchisedec. [4]an annulment [2]on one hand [1]For [3]there comes about
προαγούσης ἐντολῆς διὰ τὸ αὐτῆς ἀσθενὲς
of [the] preceding commandment because of [1]the [5]of it [2]weak[ness]
καὶ ἀνωφελές, **19** οὐδὲν γὰρ ἐτελείωσεν
[3]and [4]unprofitable[ness], for [4]nothing [3]perfected
ὁ νόμος, ἐπεισαγωγὴ δὲ κρείττονος ἐλπίδος,
[1]the [2]law, [2]a bringing in [1]on the other of a better hope,
δι' ἧς ἐγγίζομεν τῷ θεῷ. **20** καὶ καθ'
through which we draw near – to God. And in pro-
ὅσον οὐ χωρὶς ὁρκωμοσίας, — οἱ μὲν
portion as not without oath-taking, [3]the (they) [2]on one hand
γὰρ χωρὶς ὁρκωμοσίας εἰσὶν ἱερεῖς
[1]for [7]without [8]oath-taking [4]are [6]priests

* See note on ch. 9. 15.

met Abraham, Levi was
still in the body of his an-
cestor.

Jesus Like Melchizedek

11If perfection could have
been attained through the
Levitical priesthood (for on
the basis of it the law was
given to the people), why
was there still need for another priest to come—one
in the order of Melchize-
dek, not in the order of Aaron? 12For when there is a
change of the priesthood,
there must also be a change
of the law. 13He of whom
these things are said be-
longed to a different tribe,
and no one from that tribe
has ever served at the altar.
14For it is clear that our
Lord descended from Ju-
dah, and in regard to that
tribe Moses said nothing
about priests. 15And what
we have said is even more
clear if another priest like
Melchizedek appears,
16one who has become a
priest not on the basis of a
regulation as to his ancestry but on the basis of the
power of an indestructible
life. 17For it is declared:

"You are a priest
forever,
in the order of
Melchizedek."[b]

18The former regulation is
set aside because it was
weak and useless 19(for the
law made nothing perfect),
and a better hope is introduced, by which we draw
near to God.
20And it was not without
an oath! Others became
priests without any oath,

[b]*17,21* Psalm 110:4

He with an oath through
the One who said to Him,
"The Lord has sworn
And will not change
His mind,
'Thou art a priest forever' ");
22so much the more also
Jesus has become the guarantee of a better covenant.
23And the *former* priests,
on the one hand, existed in
greater numbers, because
they were prevented by
death from continuing,
24but He, on the other
hand, because He abides
forever, holds His priesthood permanently.
25Hence, also, He is able
to save forever those who
draw near to God through
Him, since He always lives
to make intercession for
them.
26For it was fitting that we
should have such a high
priest, holy, innocent, undefiled, separated from sinners and exalted above the
heavens;
27who does not need
daily, like those high
priests, to offer up sacrifices, first for His own sins,
and then for the *sins* of the
people, because this He did
once for all when He offered up Himself.
28For the Law appoints
men as high priests who are
weak, but the word of the
oath, which came after the
Law, *appoints* a Son, made
perfect forever.

γεγονότες, **21** ὁ δὲ μετὰ ὁρκωμοσίας διὰ
5having become, the (he) on the other with oath-taking through

τοῦ λέγοντος πρὸς αὐτόν· ὤμοσεν κύριος,
the [one] saying to him: swore [The] Lord,

καὶ οὐ μεταμεληθήσεται· σὺ ἱερεὺς εἰς
and will not change [his] mind: Thou [art] a priest unto

τὸν αἰῶνα· — **22** κατὰ τοσοῦτο καὶ
the age;) by so much indeed

κρείττονος διαθήκης γέγονεν ἔγγυος Ἰησοῦς.
4of a better 5covenant 2has become 3surety 1Jesus.

23 καὶ οἱ μὲν πλείονές εἰσιν γεγονότες
And the (they) on one hand 3many 1are 2having become

ἱερεῖς διὰ τὸ θανάτῳ κωλύεσθαι παραμέ-
4priests because of *the* 2by death 1to be prevented 3to con-
=being prevented by death from continuing;

νειν· **24** ὁ δὲ διὰ τὸ μένειν αὐτὸν εἰς
tinue; the (he) on the other because of *the* to remain him[b] unto
=because he remains

τὸν αἰῶνα ἀπαράβατον ἔχει τὴν ἱερωσύνην·
the age 4intransmissible 1has 2the 3priestly office;

25 ὅθεν καὶ σῴζειν εἰς τὸ παντελὲς
whence indeed 2to save 3to 4the 5entire
= entirely

δύναται τοὺς προσερχομένους δι' αὐτοῦ
1he is able the [ones] 1approaching 3through 4him

τῷ θεῷ, πάντοτε ζῶν εἰς τὸ ἐντυγχάνειν
– 2*to* God, always living *for the* to intercede

ὑπὲρ αὐτῶν. **26** τοιοῦτος γὰρ ἡμῖν καὶ
on behalf of them. For 1such 4to us 3indeed

ἔπρεπεν ἀρχιερεύς, ὅσιος, ἄκακος, ἀμίαντος,
4was suitable 2a high priest, holy, harmless, undefiled,

κεχωρισμένος ἀπὸ τῶν ἁμαρτωλῶν, καὶ
having been separated from – sinners, and

ὑψηλότερος τῶν οὐρανῶν γενόμενος· **27** ὃς
higher [than] the heavens becoming; who

οὐκ ἔχει καθ' ἡμέραν ἀνάγκην, ὥσπερ
has not 2daily 1necessity, as

οἱ ἀρχιερεῖς, πρότερον ὑπὲρ τῶν ἰδίων
the high priests, firstly on behalf of the(his) own

ἁμαρτιῶν θυσίας ἀναφέρειν, ἔπειτα τῶν
sins sacrifices to offer up, then the [sins]

τοῦ λαοῦ· τοῦτο γὰρ ἐποίησεν ἐφάπαξ
of the people; for this he did once for all

ἑαυτὸν ἀνενέγκας. **28** ὁ νόμος γὰρ
himself offering up. For the law

ἀνθρώπους καθίστησιν ἀρχιερεῖς ἔχοντας
2men 1appoints 5high priests 3having

ἀσθένειαν, ὁ λόγος δὲ τῆς ὁρκωμοσίας
4weakness, but the word of the oath-taking

τῆς μετὰ τὸν νόμον υἱὸν εἰς τὸν αἰῶνα
– after the law a Son [appoints] 2unto 3the 4age

τετελειωμένον.
1having been perfected.

21but he became a priest
with an oath when God said
to him:

"The Lord has sworn
and will not change his
mind:
'You are a priest
forever.' "[b]
22Because of this oath,
Jesus has become the guarantee of a better covenant.
23Now there have been
many of those priests,
since death prevented them
from continuing in office;
24but because Jesus lives
forever, he has a permanent priesthood. 25Therefore he is able to save completely[c] those who come to
God through him, because
he always lives to intercede
for them.
26Such a high priest meets
our need—one who is holy,
blameless, pure, set apart
from sinners, exalted
above the heavens. 27Unlike the other high priests,
he does not need to offer
sacrifices day after day,
first for his own sins, and
then for the sins of the people. He sacrificed for their
sins once for all when he
offered himself. 28For the
law appoints as high priests
men who are weak; but the
oath, which came after the
law, appointed the Son,
who has been made perfect
forever.

Chapter 8

A Better Ministry

NOW the main point in
what has been said *is
this*: we have such a high
priest, who has taken His
seat at the right hand of the
throne of the Majesty in the

8 Κεφάλαιον δὲ ἐπὶ τοῖς λεγομένοις,
Now a summary over(of) the things being said,

τοιοῦτον ἔχομεν ἀρχιερέα, ὃς ἐκάθισεν
2such 1we have a high priest, who sat

ἐν δεξιᾷ τοῦ θρόνου τῆς μεγαλωσύνης
at [the] right of the throne of the greatness

Chapter 8

The High Priest of a New Covenant

THE point of what we
are saying is this: We
do have such a high priest,
who sat down at the right
hand of the throne of the
Majesty in heaven, 2and

[c]25 Or *forever*

heavens,
2a minister in the sanctuary, and in the true tabernacle, which the Lord pitched, not man.
3For every high priest is appointed to offer both gifts and sacrifices; hence it is necessary that this *high priest* also have something to offer.
4Now if He were on earth, He would not be a priest at all, since there are those who offer the gifts according to the Law;
5who serve a copy and shadow of the heavenly things, just as Moses was warned *by God* when he was about to erect the tabernacle; for, "SEE," He says, "THAT YOU MAKE all things ACCORDING TO THE PATTERN WHICH WAS SHOWN YOU ON THE MOUNTAIN."
6But now He has obtained a more excellent ministry, by as much as He is also the mediator of a better covenant, which has been enacted on better promises.

A New Covenant

7For if that first *covenant* had been faultless, there would have been no occasion sought for a second.
8For finding fault with them, He says,
"BEHOLD, DAYS ARE COMING, SAYS THE LORD,
WHEN I WILL EFFECT A NEW COVENANT
WITH THE HOUSE OF ISRAEL AND WITH THE HOUSE OF JUDAH;
9 NOT LIKE THE COVENANT WHICH I MADE WITH THEIR FATHERS
ON THE DAY WHEN I TOOK THEM BY THE HAND
TO LEAD THEM OUT OF THE LAND OF EGYPT;
FOR THEY DID NOT CONTINUE IN MY COVENANT,
AND I DID NOT CARE FOR THEM, SAYS THE LORD.

ἐν τοῖς οὐρανοῖς, 2 τῶν ἁγίων λειτουργὸς
in *the* heavens, [2]of the [3]holy things [1]a minister
καὶ τῆς σκηνῆς τῆς ἀληθινῆς, ἣν ἔπηξεν
and of the [2]tabernacle – [1]true, which [3]erected
ὁ κύριος, οὐκ ἄνθρωπος. 3 Πᾶς γὰρ
[1]the [2]Lord, not man. For every
ἀρχιερεὺς εἰς τὸ προσφέρειν δῶρά τε
high priest *for the* [5]to offer [4]gifts [3]both
καὶ θυσίας καθίσταται· ὅθεν ἀναγκαῖον
[6]and [7]sacrifices [1]is appointed; whence [it is] necessary
ἔχειν τι καὶ τοῦτον ὃ προσενέγκῃ. 4 εἰ
[3]to have [4]something [2]also [1]this [priest] which he may offer. If
μὲν οὖν ἦν ἐπὶ γῆς, οὐδ' ἂν ἦν ἱερεύς,
– therefore he were on earth, he would not be a priest,
ὄντων τῶν προσφερόντων κατὰ νόμον
[there] being the [ones] offering[a] [3]according to [4]law
τὰ δῶρα· 5 οἵτινες ὑποδείγματι καὶ σκιᾷ
[1]the [2]gifts; who [2]an example [3]and [4]a shadow
λατρεύουσιν τῶν ἐπουρανίων, καθὼς
[1]serve of the heavenly things, as
κεχρημάτισται Μωϋσῆς μέλλων ἐπιτελεῖν
[2]has been warned [1]Moses being about to complete
τὴν σκηνήν· ὅρα γάρ φησιν, ποιήσεις
the tabernacle; for See[,] he says, thou shalt make
πάντα κατὰ τὸν τύπον τὸν δειχθέντα
all things according to the pattern – shown
σοι ἐν τῷ ὄρει· 6 νῦν δὲ διαφορωτέρας
to thee in the mount; but now [2]a more excellent
τέτυχεν λειτουργίας, ὅσῳ καὶ κρείττονός
[1]he has obtained ministry, by so much indeed [4]of a better
ἐστιν διαθήκης μεσίτης, ἥτις ἐπὶ κρείττοσιν
[1][as] [2]he is [5]covenant [3]mediator, which [2]on [3]better
ἐπαγγελίαις νενομοθέτηται. 7 εἰ γὰρ ἡ
[4]promises [1]has been enacted. For if –
πρώτη ἐκείνη ἦν ἄμεμπτος, οὐκ ἂν
[2]first [covenant] [1]that was faultless, [5]would not
δευτέρας ἐζητεῖτο τόπος. 8 μεμφόμενος
[4]of(for) a second [3]have been sought [1]place. finding fault [with]
γὰρ αὐτοὺς λέγει· ἰδοὺ ἡμέραι ἔρχονται,
For them he says: Behold[,] days are coming,
λέγει κύριος, καὶ συντελέσω ἐπὶ τὸν
says [the] Lord, and I will effect over the
οἶκον Ἰσραὴλ καὶ ἐπὶ τὸν οἶκον Ἰούδα
household of Israel and over the household of Juda
διαθήκην καινήν, 9 οὐ κατὰ τὴν διαθήκην
covenant a new, not according to the covenant
ἣν ἐποίησα τοῖς πατράσιν αὐτῶν ἐν
which I made with the fathers of them in
ἡμέρᾳ ἐπιλαβομένου μου τῆς χειρὸς αὐτῶν
[the] day taking =when I took me[a] the hand of them
ἐξαγαγεῖν αὐτοὺς ἐκ γῆς Αἰγύπτου, ὅτι
to lead forth them out of [the] land of Egypt, because
αὐτοὶ οὐκ ἐνέμειναν ἐν τῇ διαθήκῃ μου,
they continued not *in* in the covenant of me,
κἀγὼ ἠμέλησα αὐτῶν, λέγει κύριος. 10 ὅτι
and I disregarded them, says [the] Lord. Because

who serves in the sanctuary, the true tabernacle set up by the Lord, not by man.
3Every high priest is appointed to offer both gifts and sacrifices, and so it was necessary for this one also to have something to offer.
4If he were on earth, he would not be a priest, for there are already men who offer the gifts prescribed by the law. 5They serve at a sanctuary that is a copy and shadow of what is in heaven. This is why Moses was warned when he was about to build the tabernacle: "See to it that you make everything according to the pattern shown you on the mountain."[d] 6But the ministry Jesus has received is as superior to theirs as the covenant of which he is mediator is superior to the old one, and it is founded on better promises.
7For if there had been nothing wrong with that first covenant, no place would have been sought for another. 8But God found fault with the people and said[e]:

"The time is coming,
declares the Lord,
when I will make a new covenant
with the house of Israel
and with the house of Judah.
9It will not be like the covenant
I made with their forefathers
when I took them by the hand
to lead them out of Egypt,
because they did not remain faithful to my covenant,
and I turned away from them,
declares the Lord.

d5 Exodus 25:40
e8 Some manuscripts may be translated *fault and said to the people*.

10 "FOR THIS IS THE COVENANT THAT I WILL MAKE WITH THE HOUSE OF ISRAEL
AFTER THOSE DAYS, SAYS THE LORD:
I WILL PUT MY LAWS INTO THEIR MINDS,
AND I WILL WRITE THEM UPON THEIR HEARTS.
AND I WILL BE THEIR GOD,
AND THEY SHALL BE MY PEOPLE.
11 "AND THEY SHALL NOT TEACH EVERYONE HIS FELLOW CITIZEN,
AND EVERYONE HIS BROTHER, SAYING, 'KNOW THE LORD,'
FOR ALL SHALL KNOW ME,
FROM THE LEAST TO THE GREATEST OF THEM.
12 "FOR I WILL BE MERCIFUL TO THEIR INIQUITIES,
AND I WILL REMEMBER THEIR SINS NO MORE."
13 When He said, "A new *covenant*," He has made the first obsolete. But whatever is becoming obsolete and growing old is ready to disappear.

αὕτη ἡ διαθήκη ἣν διαθήσομαι τῷ οἴκῳ
this [is] the covenant which I will covenant with the household

Ἰσραὴλ μετὰ τὰς ἡμέρας ἐκείνας, λέγει
of Israel after those days, says

κύριος, διδοὺς νόμους μου εἰς τὴν διάνοιαν
[the] Lord, giving laws of me into the mind

αὐτῶν, καὶ ἐπὶ καρδίας αὐτῶν ἐπιγράψω
of them, and on hearts of them I will inscribe

αὐτούς, καὶ ἔσομαι αὐτοῖς εἰς θεὸν
them, and I will be to them *for* God

καὶ αὐτοὶ ἔσονταί μοι εἰς λαόν. **11** καὶ
and they shall be to me *for* a people. And

οὐ μὴ διδάξωσιν ἕκαστος τὸν πολίτην
by no means may they teach each man the citizen

αὐτοῦ καὶ ἕκαστος τὸν ἀδελφὸν αὐτοῦ,
of him and each man the brother of him,

λέγων· γνῶθι τὸν κύριον, ὅτι πάντες
saying: Know thou the Lord, because all

εἰδήσουσίν με ἀπὸ μικροῦ ἕως μεγάλου
will know me from little to great

αὐτῶν. **12** ὅτι ἵλεως ἔσομαι ταῖς ἀδικίαις
of them. Because merciful I will be to the unrighteousnesses

αὐτῶν, καὶ τῶν ἁμαρτιῶν αὐτῶν οὐ μὴ
of them, and the sins of them by no means

μνησθῶ ἔτι. **13** ἐν τῷ λέγειν καινὴν
I may remember more. In the to say• 'new'
=When he says

πεπαλαίωκεν τὴν πρώτην· τὸ δὲ παλαι-
he has made old the first; and the thing being

ούμενον καὶ γηράσκον ἐγγὺς ἀφανισμοῦ.
made old and growing aged [is] near vanishing.

13 By calling this covenant "new," he has made the first one obsolete; and what is obsolete and aging will soon disappear.

10 This is the covenant I will make with the house of Israel
after that time, declares the Lord.
I will put my laws in their minds
and write them on their hearts.
I will be their God,
and they will be my people.
11 No longer will a man teach his neighbor,
or a man his brother, saying, 'Know the Lord,'
because they will all know me,
from the least of them to the greatest.
12 For I will forgive their wickedness
and will remember their sins no more."[f]

Chapter 9

The Old and the New

NOW even the first *covenant* had regulations of divine worship and the earthly sanctuary.
2 For there was a tabernacle prepared, the outer one, in which *were* the lampstand and the table and the sacred bread; this is called the holy place.
3 And behind the second veil, there was a tabernacle which is called the Holy of Holies,
4 having a golden altar of incense and the ark of the covenant covered on all sides with gold, in which *was* a golden jar holding the manna, and Aaron's rod which budded, and the tables of the covenant.
5 And above it *were* the cherubim of glory overshadowing the mercy seat; but of these things we can-

9 Εἶχε μὲν οὖν καὶ ἡ πρώτη δικαι-
[5]had [1]So then [6]both [2]the [3]first [4][covenant] ordin-

ώματα λατρείας τό τε ἅγιον κοσμικόν.
ances of service [3]the [1]and [4]holy place [2]worldly.

2 σκηνὴ γὰρ κατεσκευάσθη ἡ πρώτη,
For a tabernacle was prepared[,] the first,

ἐν ᾗ ἥ τε λυχνία καὶ ἡ τράπεζα καὶ
in which [were] [2]the [1]both lampstand and the table and

ἡ πρόθεσις τῶν ἄρτων, ἥτις λέγεται
the setting forth of the loaves, which is called

Ἅγια· **3** μετὰ δὲ τὸ δεύτερον καταπέτασμα
Holy; and after the second veil

σκηνὴ ἡ λεγομένη Ἅγια Ἁγίων, **4** χρυσοῦν
a tabernacle the [one] *being* called Holy of Holies, [2]a golden

ἔχουσα θυμιατήριον καὶ τὴν κιβωτὸν τῆς
[1]having altar and the ark of the

διαθήκης περικεκαλυμμένην πάντοθεν χρυσίῳ,
covenant *having been* covered round on all sides with gold,

ἐν ᾗ στάμνος χρυσῆ ἔχουσα τὸ μάννα
in which [were] pot a golden having the manna

καὶ ἡ ῥάβδος Ἀαρὼν ἡ βλαστήσασα
and the rod of Aaron – budded

καὶ αἱ πλάκες τῆς διαθήκης, **5** ὑπεράνω
and the tablets of the covenant, [2]above

δὲ αὐτῆς Χερουβὶν δόξης κατασκιάζοντα
[1]and it cherubim of glory overshadowing

τὸ ἱλαστήριον· περὶ ὧν οὐκ ἔστιν νῦν
the mercy-seat; concerning which things there is not [?time] now

Chapter 9

Worship in the Earthly Tabernacle

NOW the first covenant had regulations for worship and also an earthly sanctuary. 2 A tabernacle was set up. In its first room were the lampstand, the table and the consecrated bread; this was called the Holy Place. 3 Behind the second curtain was a room called the Most Holy Place, 4 which had the golden altar of incense and the gold-covered ark of the covenant. This ark contained the gold jar of manna, Aaron's staff that had budded, and the stone tablets of the covenant. 5 Above the ark were the cherubim of the Glory, overshadowing the atonement cover.[g] But we

[f] 12 Jer. 31:31-34
[g] 5 Traditionally *the mercy seat*

not now speak in detail.

6Now when these things have been thus prepared, the priests are continually entering the outer tabernacle, performing the divine worship,

7but into the second only the high priest *enters*, once a year, not without *taking* blood, which he offers for himself and for the sins of the people committed in ignorance.

8The Holy Spirit *is* signifying this, that the way into the holy place has not yet been disclosed, while the outer tabernacle is still standing,

9which *is* a symbol for the present time. Accordingly both gifts and sacrifices are offered which cannot make the worshiper perfect in conscience,

10since they *relate* only to food and drink and various washings, regulations for the body imposed until a time of reformation.

11But when Christ appeared *as* a high priest of the good things [e]to come, *He entered* through the greater and more perfect tabernacle, not made with hands, that is to say, not of this creation;

12and not through the blood of goats and calves, but through His own blood, He entered the holy place once for all, having obtained eternal redemption.

13For if the blood of goats and bulls and the ashes of a heifer sprinkling those who have been defiled, sanctify for the cleansing of the flesh,

14how much more will the blood of Christ, who through the eternal Spirit

[e] Some ancient mss. read *that have come*

λέγειν κατὰ μέρος. **6** τούτων δὲ οὕτως
to speak in detail. These things now thus =Now when these things had

κατεσκευασμένων εἰς μὲν τὴν πρώτην
having been prepared[a] been thus prepared [6]into [1]on one hand [7]the [8]first

σκηνὴν διὰ παντὸς εἰσίασιν οἱ ἱερεῖς
[9]tabernacle [4]at all times [5]go *in* [2]the [3]priests

τὰς λατρείας ἐπιτελοῦντες, **7** εἰς δὲ τὴν
[11]the [12]services [10]accomplishing, [2]into [1]on the other [3]the

δευτέραν ἅπαξ τοῦ ἐνιαυτοῦ μόνος ὁ
[4]second [8]once [9]of(in) the [10]year [goes] [7]alone [5]the

ἀρχιερεύς, οὐ χωρὶς αἵματος ὃ προσφέρει
[6]high priest, not without blood which he offers

ὑπὲρ ἑαυτοῦ καὶ τῶν τοῦ λαοῦ ἀγνοημά-
on behalf of himself and [1]the [3]of the [4]people [2]ignor-

των, **8** τοῦτο δηλοῦντος τοῦ πνεύματος
ances, [5]this [4]showing [1]the [3]Spirit

τοῦ ἁγίου, μήπω πεφανερῶσθαι τὴν τῶν
– [2]Holy,[a] [5]not yet [6]to have been manifested [1]the [3]of the

ἁγίων ὁδὸν ἔτι τῆς πρώτης σκηνῆς
[4]holies [2]way [10]still [7]the [8]first [9]tabernacle

ἐχούσης στάσιν, **9** ἥτις παραβολὴ εἰς τὸν
[11]having[a] [12]standing, which [was] a parable for the

καιρὸν τὸν ἐνεστηκότα, καθ' ἣν δῶρά
time – present, according to which [2]gifts

τε καὶ θυσίαι προσφέρονται μὴ δυνάμεναι
[1]both and sacrifices are being offered not being able

κατὰ συνείδησιν τελειῶσαι τὸν λατρεύοντα,
in respect of conscience to perfect the [one] serving,

10 μόνον ἐπὶ βρώμασιν καὶ πόμασιν καὶ
only on foods and drinks and

διαφόροις βαπτισμοῖς, δικαιώματα σαρκὸς
various washings, ordinances of flesh

μέχρι καιροῦ διορθώσεως ἐπικείμενα.
[2]until [3]a time [4]of amendment [1]*being* imposed.

11 Χριστὸς δὲ παραγενόμενος ἀρχιερεὺς
But Christ having appeared a high priest

τῶν γενομένων ἀγαθῶν, διὰ τῆς μείζονος
[1]of the [3]having come about [2]good things, through the greater

καὶ τελειοτέρας σκηνῆς οὐ χειροποιήτου,
and more perfect tabernacle not made by hand,

τοῦτ' ἔστιν οὐ ταύτης τῆς κτίσεως,
this is not of this – creation,

12 οὐδὲ δι' αἵματος τράγων καὶ μόσχων,
nor through blood of goats and *of* calves,

διὰ δὲ τοῦ ἰδίου αἵματος εἰσῆλθεν ἐφάπαξ
but through the (his) own blood entered once for all

εἰς τὰ ἅγια, αἰωνίαν λύτρωσιν εὑράμενος.
into the holies, eternal redemption having found.

13 εἰ γὰρ τὸ αἷμα τράγων καὶ ταύρων
For if the blood of goats and *of* bulls

καὶ σποδὸς δαμάλεως ῥαντίζουσα τοὺς
and ashes of a heifer sprinkling the [ones]

κεκοινωμένους ἁγιάζει πρὸς τὴν τῆς
having been polluted sanctifies to [1]the [3]of the

σαρκὸς καθαρότητα, **14** πόσῳ μᾶλλον τὸ
[4]flesh [2]cleanness, by how much more the

αἷμα τοῦ Χριστοῦ, ὃς διὰ πνεύματος
blood – of Christ, who through [2]Spirit

cannot discuss these things in detail now.

6When everything had been arranged like this, the priests entered regularly into the outer room to carry on their ministry. 7But only the high priest entered the inner room, and that only once a year, and never without blood, which he offered for himself and for the sins the people had committed in ignorance. 8The Holy Spirit was showing by this that the way into the Most Holy Place had not yet been disclosed as long as the first tabernacle was still standing. 9This is an illustration for the present time, indicating that the gifts and sacrifices being offered were not able to clear the conscience of the worshiper. 10They are only a matter of food and drink and various ceremonial washings—external regulations applying until the time of the new order.

The Blood of Christ

11When Christ came as high priest of the good things that are already here,[h] he went through the greater and more perfect tabernacle that is not man-made, that is to say, not a part of this creation. 12He did not enter by means of the blood of goats and calves; but he entered the Most Holy Place once for all by his own blood, having obtained eternal redemption. 13The blood of goats and bulls and the ashes of a heifer sprinkled on those who are ceremonially unclean sanctify them so that they are outwardly clean. 14How much more, then, will the blood of Christ, who through the eternal Spirit offered him-

[h] *11* Some early manuscripts *are to come*

offered Himself without
blemish to God, cleanse
your conscience from dead
works to serve the living
God?
15And for this reason He
is the mediator of a new
covenant, in order that
since a death has taken
place for the redemption of
the transgressions that
were *committed* under the
first covenant, those who
have been called may re-
ceive the promise of the
eternal inheritance.
16For where a covenant
is, there must of necessity
be the death of the one who
made it.
17For a covenant is valid
only when men are dead,
[f]for it is never in force
while the one who made it
lives.
18Therefore even the first
covenant was not inaugurated without blood.
19For when every com-
mandment had been
spoken by Moses to all the
people according to the
Law, he took the blood of
the calves and the goats,
with water and scarlet wool
and hyssop, and sprinkled
both the book itself and all
the people,
20saying, "THIS IS THE
BLOOD OF THE COVENANT
WHICH GOD COMMANDED
YOU."
21And in the same way he
sprinkled both the taber-
nacle and all the vessels of
the ministry with the blood.
22And according to the
Law, *one may* almost *say*,
all things are cleansed with
blood, and without shed-
ding of blood there is no
forgiveness.
23Therefore it was neces-
sary for the copies of the
things in the heavens to be
cleansed with these, but

αἰωνίου ἑαυτὸν προσήνεγκεν ἄμωμον τῷ
[1][the] eternal [4]himself [3]offered unblemished –

θεῷ, καθαριεῖ τὴν συνείδησιν ἡμῶν ἀπὸ
to God, will cleanse the conscience of us from

νεκρῶν ἔργων εἰς τὸ λατρεύειν θεῷ
dead works *for the* to serve [2]God

ζῶντι. 15 καὶ διὰ τοῦτο διαθήκης καινῆς
[1][the] living. And therefore [4]covenant [3]of a new

μεσίτης ἐστίν, ὅπως θανάτου γενομένου
[2]mediator [1]he is, so as death having occurred[a]

εἰς ἀπολύτρωσιν τῶν ἐπὶ τῇ πρώτῃ
for redemption [1]of the [3]under * [4]the [5]first

διαθήκῃ παραβάσεων τὴν ἐπαγγελίαν
[6]covenant [2]transgressions [10]the [11]promise

λάβωσιν οἱ κεκλημένοι τῆς αἰωνίου
[9]may receive [7]the [ones] [8]having been called [12]of the [13]eternal

κληρονομίας. 16 Ὅπου γὰρ διαθήκη,
[14]inheritance. For where [there is] a covenant,

θάνατον ἀνάγκη φέρεσθαι τοῦ διαθεμένου·
[3][the] death [1][there is] necessity [2]to be offered [4]of the [one] [5]making covenant;

17 διαθήκη γὰρ ἐπὶ νεκροῖς βεβαία, ἐπεὶ
for a covenant over dead [? bodies] [is] firm, since

μήποτε ἰσχύει ὅτε ζῇ ὁ διαθέμενος.
never has it strength when [3]lives [1]the [one] [2]making covenant.

18 ὅθεν οὐδὲ ἡ πρώτη χωρὶς αἵματος
Whence neither the first [covenant] [2]without [3]blood

ἐγκεκαίνισται. 19 λαληθείσης γὰρ πάσης
[1]has been dedicated. For [3]having been spoken [1]every

ἐντολῆς κατὰ τὸν νόμον ὑπὸ Μωϋσέως
[2]commandment[a] [9]according to [10]the [11]law [4]by [5]Moses

παντὶ τῷ λαῷ, λαβὼν τὸ αἷμα τῶν
[6]to all [7]the [8]people, taking the blood of the

μόσχων καὶ τῶν τράγων μετὰ ὕδατος
calves and of the goats with water

καὶ ἐρίου κοκκίνου καὶ ὑσσώπου, αὐτό
and [2]wool [1]scarlet and hyssop, [4]it[self]

τε τὸ βιβλίον καὶ πάντα τὸν λαὸν
[2]both [3]the [4]scroll [6]and [7]all [8]the [9]people

ἐρράντισεν, 20 λέγων· τοῦτο τὸ αἷμα τῆς
[1]he sprinkled, saying: This [is] the blood of the

διαθήκης ἧς ἐνετείλατο πρὸς ὑμᾶς ὁ
covenant which [2]enjoined [3]to [4]you –

θεός. 21 καὶ τὴν σκηνὴν δὲ καὶ πάντα
[1]God. [2]both [3]the [4]tabernacle [1]And and all

τὰ σκεύη τῆς λειτουργίας τῷ αἵματι
the vessels of the service with the blood

ὁμοίως ἐρράντισεν. 22 καὶ σχεδὸν ἐν
likewise he sprinkled. And [4]almost [7]by

αἵματι πάντα καθαρίζεται κατὰ τὸν νόμον,
[8]blood [5]all things [6]is(are) cleansed [1]according to [2]the [3]law,

καὶ χωρὶς αἱματεκχυσίας οὐ γίνεται
and without bloodshedding there becomes no

ἄφεσις. 23 ἀνάγκη οὖν τὰ μὲν ὑπο-
remission. [There was] necessity therefore [2][for] [3]the [1]on one hand [4]ex-

δείγματα τῶν ἐν τοῖς οὐρανοῖς τούτοις
amples of the things in *the* heavens [2]by these

self unblemished to God,
cleanse our consciences
from acts that lead to
death,[i] so that we may
serve the living God!
15For this reason Christ is
the mediator of a new covenant, that those who are
called may receive the
promised eternal inheri-
tance—now that he has
died as a ransom to set
them free from the sins
committed under the first
covenant.
16In the case of a will,[j] it
is necessary to prove the
death of the one who made
it, 17because a will is in
force only when somebody
has died; it never takes effect while the one who
made it is living. 18This is
why even the first covenant
was not put into effect
without blood. 19When Mo-
ses had proclaimed every
commandment of the law
to all the people, he took
the blood of calves, together with water, scarlet wool
and branches of hyssop,
and sprinkled the scroll and
all the people. 20He said,
"This is the blood of the
covenant, which God has
commanded you to
keep."[k] 21In the same
way, he sprinkled with the
blood both the tabernacle
and everything used in its
ceremonies. 22In fact, the
law requires that nearly everything be cleansed with
blood, and without the
shedding of blood there is
no forgiveness.
23It was necessary, then,
for the copies of the heavenly things to be purified
with these sacrifices, but

[f]Some ancient mss. read *for is it then . . . lives?*

* It may seem strange to translate a preposition which means "on" or "over" by "under"; but ἐπί has the meaning of "during the time of" (see Mark 2. 26; I. Tim. 6. 13).

[i]14 Or *from useless rituals*
[j]16 Same Greek word as *covenant*; also in verse 17
[k]20 Exodus 24:8

the heavenly things themselves with better sacrifices than these.

24For Christ did not enter a holy place made with hands, a *mere* copy of the true one, but into heaven itself, now to appear in the presence of God for us;

25nor was it that He should offer Himself often, as the high priest enters the holy place year by year with blood not his own.

26Otherwise, He would have needed to suffer often since the foundation of the world; but now once at the consummation of the ages He has been manifested to put away sin by the sacrifice of Himself.

27And inasmuch as it is appointed for men to die once and after this *comes* judgment,

28so Christ also, having been offered once to bear the sins of many, shall appear a second time for salvation without *reference to* sin, to those who eagerly await Him.

καθαρίζεσθαι, αὐτὰ δὲ τὰ ἐπουράνια
[1]to be cleansed, [5][them]-selves [1]on the other [2][for] [3]the [4]heavenly things
κρείττοσιν θυσίαις παρὰ ταύτας. 24 οὐ
by better sacrifices than these. not
γὰρ εἰς χειροποίητα εἰσῆλθεν ἅγια Χριστός,
For into [2]made by hand [4]entered [1]holies [3]Christ,
ἀντίτυπα τῶν ἀληθινῶν, ἀλλ' εἰς αὐτὸν
figures of the true things, but into [3][it]self
τὸν οὐρανόν, νῦν ἐμφανισθῆναι τῷ προσώπῳ
[1]*the* [2]heaven, now to appear in the presence
τοῦ θεοῦ ὑπὲρ ἡμῶν· 25 οὐδ' ἵνα πολ-
– of God on behalf of us; nor *in order* that often
λάκις προσφέρῃ ἑαυτόν, ὥσπερ ὁ ἀρχιερεὺς
he should offer himself, even as the high priest
εἰσέρχεται εἰς τὰ ἅγια κατ' ἐνιαυτὸν
enters into the holies year by year†
ἐν αἵματι ἀλλοτρίῳ, 26 ἐπεὶ ἔδει αὐτὸν
with blood belonging to others, since it behoved him
πολλάκις παθεῖν ἀπὸ καταβολῆς κόσμου·
often to suffer from [the] foundation of [the] world;
νυνὶ δὲ ἅπαξ ἐπὶ συντελείᾳ τῶν αἰώνων
but now once at [the] completion of the ages
εἰς ἀθέτησιν τῆς ἁμαρτίας διὰ τῆς θυσίας
for annulment – of sin through the sacrifice
αὐτοῦ πεφανέρωται. 27 καὶ καθ' ὅσον
of him he has been manifested. And as
ἀπόκειται τοῖς ἀνθρώποις ἅπαξ ἀποθανεῖν,
it is reserved – to men once to die,
μετὰ δὲ τοῦτο κρίσις, 28 οὕτως καὶ
and after this judgment, so also
ὁ Χριστός, ἅπαξ προσενεχθεὶς εἰς τὸ
– Christ, once having been offered *for the*
πολλῶν ἀνενεγκεῖν ἁμαρτίας, ἐκ δευτέρου
[3]of many [1]to bear [2]sins, [2]a second [time]
χωρὶς ἁμαρτίας ὀφθήσεται τοῖς αὐτὸν
[3]without [4]sin [1]will appear [5]to the [ones] [7]him
ἀπεκδεχομένοις εἰς σωτηρίαν.
[6]expecting for salvation.

the heavenly things them-
selves with better sacrifices
than these. 24For Christ did
not enter a man-made sanctuary that was only a copy
of the true one; he entered
heaven itself, now to ap-
pear for us in God's presence. 25Nor did he enter
heaven to offer himself
again and again, the way
the high priest enters the
Most Holy Place every
year with blood that is not
his own. 26Then Christ
would have had to suffer
many times since the cre-
ation of the world. But now
he has appeared once for all
at the end of the ages to do
away with sin by the sacrifice of himself. 27Just as
man is destined to die once,
and after that to face judgment, 28so Christ was sacrificed once to take away the
sins of many people; and he
will appear a second time,
not to bear sin, but to bring
salvation to those who are
waiting for him.

Chapter 10

One Sacrifice of Christ Is Sufficient

FOR the Law, since it has *only* a shadow of the good things to come *and* not the very form of things, [g]can never by the same sacrifices year by year, which they offer continually, make perfect those who draw near.

2Otherwise, would they not have ceased to be offered, because the worshipers, having once been cleansed, would no longer have had consciousness of sins?

3But in those *sacrifices* there is a reminder of sins year by year.

4For it is impossible for the blood of bulls and goats to take away sins.

5Therefore, when He comes into the world, He

[g] Some ancient mss. read *they can*

10 Σκιὰν γὰρ ἔχων ὁ νόμος τῶν
For [4]a shadow [3]having [1]the [2]law of the
μελλόντων ἀγαθῶν, οὐκ αὐτὴν τὴν εἰκόνα
coming good things, not [3][it]self [1]the [2]image
τῶν πραγμάτων, κατ' ἐνιαυτὸν ταῖς αὐταῖς
of the matters, [8]every [9]year† [3]by the [4]same
θυσίαις ἃς προσφέρουσιν εἰς τὸ διηνεκὲς
[5]sacrifices [6]which [7]they offer [10]continually†
οὐδέποτε δύναται τοὺς προσερχομένους
[2]never [1]can [12]the [ones] [13]approaching
τελειῶσαι· 2 ἐπεὶ οὐκ ἂν ἐπαύσαντο
[11]*to* perfect; since would not they have ceased
προσφερόμεναι, διὰ τὸ μηδεμίαν ἔχειν
being offered, because of *the* [7]no [5]to have
ἔτι συνείδησιν ἁμαρτιῶν τοὺς λατρεύοντας
[6]still [8]conscience [9]of sins [1]the [ones] [2]serving
ἅπαξ κεκαθαρισμένους; 3 ἀλλ' ἐν αὐταῖς
[3]once [4]having been cleansed ? But in them [there
ἀνάμνησις ἁμαρτιῶν κατ' ἐνιαυτόν·
is] a remembrance of sins yearly†;
4 ἀδύνατον γὰρ αἷμα ταύρων καὶ τράγων
for [it is] impossible blood of bulls and *of* goats
ἀφαιρεῖν ἁμαρτίας. 5 Διὸ εἰσερχόμενος εἰς
to take away sins. Wherefore entering into

Chapter 10

Christ's Sacrifice Once for All

THE law is only a shad-
ow of the good things
that are coming—not the
realities themselves. For
this reason it can never, by
the same sacrifices repeated endlessly year after
year, make perfect those
who draw near to worship.
2If it could, would they not
have stopped being of-
fered? For the worshipers
would have been cleansed
once for all, and would no
longer have felt guilty for
their sins. 3But those sacrifices are an annual reminder of sins, 4because it is impossible for the blood of
bulls and goats to take
away sins.
5Therefore, when Christ
came into the world, he

says,
"SACRIFICE AND OFFER-
ING THOU HAST NOT
DESIRED,
BUT A BODY THOU
HAST PREPARED FOR
ME;
6 IN WHOLE BURNT OF-
FERINGS AND *sacri-
fices* FOR SIN THOU
HAST TAKEN NO PLEA-
SURE.
7 "THEN I SAID, 'BEHOLD,
I HAVE COME
(IN THE ROLL OF THE
BOOK IT IS WRITTEN OF
ME)
TO DO THY WILL, O
GOD.' "
8 After saying above,
"SACRIFICES AND OFFERINGS
AND WHOLE BURNT OFFER-
INGS AND *sacrifices* FOR SIN
THOU HAST NOT DESIRED,
NOR HAST THOU TAKEN PLEA-
SURE *in them*" (which are
offered according to the
Law),
9 then He said, "BEHOLD,
I HAVE COME TO DO THY
WILL." He takes away the
first in order to establish
the second.
10 By this will we have
been sanctified through the
offering of the body of
Jesus Christ once for all.
11 And every priest stands
daily ministering and offering time after time the same
sacrifices, which can never
take away sins;
12 but He, having offered
one sacrifice for sins for all
time, SAT DOWN AT THE
RIGHT HAND OF GOD,
13 waiting from that time
onward UNTIL HIS ENEMIES
BE MADE A FOOTSTOOL FOR
HIS FEET.
14 For by one offering He
has perfected for all time
those who are sanctified.
15 And the Holy Spirit also
bears witness to us; for after saying,
16 "THIS IS THE COVENANT
THAT I WILL MAKE

τὸν κόσμον λέγει· θυσίαν καὶ προσφορὰν
the world he says: Sacrifice and offering
οὐκ ἠθέλησας, σῶμα δὲ κατηρτίσω μοι·
thou didst not wish, but a body thou didst prepare for me;
6 ὁλοκαυτώματα καὶ περὶ ἁμαρτίας οὐκ
burnt offerings and concerning [sacrifices] sins not
εὐδόκησας. **7** τότε εἶπον· ἰδοὺ ἥκω,
thou wast well pleased [with]. Then I said: Behold I have come,
ἐν κεφαλίδι βιβλίου γέγραπται περὶ ἐμοῦ,
in a heading of a scroll it has been written concerning me,
τοῦ ποιῆσαι ὁ θεὸς τὸ θέλημά σου.
– to do[,][d] – God[,]* the will of thee.
8 ἀνώτερον λέγων ὅτι θυσίας καὶ προσ-
Above saying that sacrifices and offer-
φορὰς καὶ ὁλοκαυτώματα καὶ περὶ ἁμαρτίας
ings and burnt offerings and [sacrifices] concerning sins
οὐκ ἠθέλησας οὐδὲ εὐδόκησας, αἵτινες
thou didst not wish nor *thou* wast well pleased [with], which
κατὰ νόμον προσφέρονται, **9** τότε εἴρηκεν·
according to law are offered, then he *has* said:
ἰδοὺ ἥκω τοῦ ποιῆσαι τὸ θέλημά σου.
Behold I have come – to do[d] the will of thee.
ἀναιρεῖ τὸ πρῶτον ἵνα τὸ δεύτερον
He takes away the first in order that the second
στήσῃ· **10** ἐν ᾧ θελήματι ἡγιασμένοι ἐσμὲν
he may set up; by which will [2]*having been* sanctified [1]we are
διὰ τῆς προσφορᾶς τοῦ σώματος Ἰησοῦ
through the offering of the body of Jesus
Χριστοῦ ἐφάπαξ. **11** Καὶ πᾶς μὲν ἱερεὺς
Christ once for all. And [2]every [1]on one hand [3]priest
ἕστηκεν καθ' ἡμέραν λειτουργῶν καὶ τὰς
stands daily† ministering and [3]the
αὐτὰς πολλάκις προσφέρων θυσίας, αἵτινες
[4]same [1]often [2]offering [5]sacrifices, which
οὐδέποτε δύνανται περιελεῖν ἁμαρτίας· **12** οὗτος
never can *to* take away sins; [2]this [priest]
δὲ μίαν ὑπὲρ ἁμαρτιῶν προσενέγκας
[1]on the other [4]one [6]on behalf of [7]sins [3]having offered
θυσίαν εἰς τὸ διηνεκὲς ἐκάθισεν ἐν δεξιᾷ
[5]sacrifice [9]in – [10]perpetuity [8]sat at [the] right [hand]
τοῦ θεοῦ, **13** τὸ λοιπὸν ἐκδεχόμενος ἕως
– of God, henceforth expecting till
τεθῶσιν οἱ ἐχθροὶ αὐτοῦ ὑποπόδιον τῶν
[4]are put [1]the [2]enemies [3]of him a footstool of the
ποδῶν αὐτοῦ. **14** μιᾷ γὰρ προσφορᾷ
feet of him. For by one offering
τετελείωκεν εἰς τὸ διηνεκὲς τοὺς ἁγιαζ-
he has perfected in – perpetuity the [ones] being
ομένους. **15** Μαρτυρεῖ δὲ ἡμῖν καὶ
sanctified. And [5]witnesses [6]to us [4]indeed
τὸ πνεῦμα τὸ ἅγιον· μετὰ γὰρ τὸ
[1]the [3]Spirit – [2]Holy; for after *the*
εἰρηκέναι· **16** αὕτη ἡ διαθήκη ἣν δια-
to have said: =having said: This [is] the covenant which I will

* The "articular vocative"; *cf.* 1. 8, 9.

said:
"Sacrifice and offering
you did not desire,
but a body you
prepared for me;
6 with burnt offerings and
sin offerings
you were not pleased.
7 Then I said, 'Here I
am—it is written
about me in the
scroll—
I have come to do your
will, O God.' "[l]
8 First he said, "Sacrifices
and offerings, burnt offerings and sin offerings you
did not desire, nor were
you pleased with them"
(although the law required
them to be made). 9 Then he
said, "Here I am, I have
come to do your will." He
sets aside the first to establish the second. 10 And by
that will, we have been
made holy through the sacrifice of the body of Jesus
Christ once for all.
11 Day after day every
priest stands and performs
his religious duties; again
and again he offers the
same sacrifices, which can
never take away sins. 12 But
when this priest had of-
fered for all time one sacrifice for sins, he sat down at
the right hand of God.
13 Since that time he waits
for his enemies to be made
his footstool, 14 because by
one sacrifice he has made
perfect forever those who
are being made holy.
15 The Holy Spirit also
testifies to us about this.
First he says:
16 "This is the covenant I
will make with them

[l]7 Psalm 40:6-8 (see Septuagint)

WITH THEM
AFTER THOSE DAYS,
SAYS THE LORD:
I WILL PUT MY LAWS
UPON THEIR HEART,
AND UPON THEIR MIND
I WILL WRITE THEM,''
He then says,
17 "AND THEIR SINS AND
THEIR LAWLESS DEEDS
I WILL REMEMBER NO
MORE.''
18 Now where there is for-
giveness of these things,
there is no longer *any* offer-
ing for sin.

A New and Living Way

19 Since therefore, brethren, we have confidence to
enter the holy place by the
blood of Jesus,
20 by a new and living way
which He inaugurated for
us through the veil, that is,
His flesh,
21 and since *we have* a
great priest over the house
of God,
22 let us draw near with a
sincere heart in full assurance of faith, having our
hearts sprinkled *clean* from
an evil conscience and our
bodies washed with pure
water.
23 Let us hold fast the
confession of our hope
without wavering, for He
who promised is faithful;
24 and let us consider how
to stimulate one another to
love and good deeds,
25 not forsaking our own
assembling together, as is
the habit of some, but encouraging *one another*; and
all the more, as you see the
day drawing near.

Christ or Judgment

26 For if we go on sinning
willfully after receiving the
knowledge of the truth,
there no longer remains a
sacrifice for sins,
27 but a certain terrifying
expectation of judgment,
and THE FURY OF A FIRE
WHICH WILL CONSUME THE
ADVERSARIES.

θήσομαι πρὸς αὐτοὺς μετὰ τὰς ἡμέρας
covenant to them after – days
ἐκείνας, λέγει κύριος· διδοὺς νόμους μου
those, says [the] Lord: Giving laws of me
ἐπὶ καρδίας αὐτῶν, καὶ ἐπὶ τὴν διάνοιαν
on hearts of them, also on the mind
αὐτῶν ἐπιγράψω αὐτούς, 17 καὶ τῶν
of them I will inscribe them, and the
ἁμαρτιῶν αὐτῶν καὶ τῶν ἀνομιῶν αὐτῶν
sins of them and the iniquities of them
οὐ μὴ μνησθήσομαι ἔτι. 18 ὅπου δὲ
by no means I will remember still. Now where
ἄφεσις τούτων, οὐκέτι προσφορὰ περὶ
forgiveness of these [is], no longer [there is] offering concerning
ἁμαρτίας.
sins.

19 Ἔχοντες οὖν, ἀδελφοί, παρρησίαν εἰς
Having therefore, brothers, confidence for
τὴν εἴσοδον τῶν ἁγίων ἐν τῷ αἵματι
the entering of the holies by the blood
Ἰησοῦ, 20 ἣν ἐνεκαίνισεν ἡμῖν ὁδὸν
of Jesus, which he dedicated for us[,] a way
πρόσφατον καὶ ζῶσαν διὰ τοῦ κατα-
fresh and living through the veil,
πετάσματος, τοῦτ' ἔστιν τῆς σαρκὸς αὐτοῦ,
this is the flesh of him,
21 καὶ ἱερέα μέγαν ἐπὶ τὸν οἶκον τοῦ
and priest a great over the household –
θεοῦ, 22 προσερχώμεθα μετὰ ἀληθινῆς
of God, let us approach with a true
καρδίας ἐν πληροφορίᾳ πίστεως, ῥεραν-
heart in full assurance of faith, having been
τισμένοι τὰς καρδίας ἀπὸ συνειδήσεως
sprinkled [as to] the hearts from [2]conscience
πονηρᾶς καὶ λελουσμένοι τὸ σῶμα ὕδατι
[1]an evil and having been bathed [as to] the body [2]water
καθαρῷ· 23 κατέχωμεν τὴν ὁμολογίαν τῆς
[1]in clean; let us hold fast the confession of the (our)
ἐλπίδος ἀκλινῆ, πιστὸς γὰρ ὁ ἐπαγ-
hope unyieldingly, for faithful [is] the [one] pro-
γειλάμενος, 24 καὶ κατανοῶμεν ἀλλήλους
mising, and let us consider one another
εἰς παροξυσμὸν ἀγάπης καὶ καλῶν ἔργων,
to incitement of love and of good works,
25 μὴ ἐγκαταλείποντες τὴν ἐπισυναγωγὴν
not forsaking the coming together
ἑαυτῶν, καθὼς ἔθος τισίν, ἀλλὰ παρα-
of [our]selves, as custom with some [is], but ex-
καλοῦντες, καὶ τοσούτῳ μᾶλλον ὅσῳ
horting, and by so much more as
βλέπετε ἐγγίζουσαν τὴν ἡμέραν. 26 Ἑκουσίως
ye see [3]drawing near [1]the [2]day. wilfully
γὰρ ἁμαρτανόντων ἡμῶν μετὰ τὸ λαβεῖν
For sinning us[a] after *the* to receive
=when we sin wilfully =receiving
τὴν ἐπίγνωσιν τῆς ἀληθείας, οὐκέτι περὶ
the full knowledge of the truth, [5]no more [2]concerning
ἁμαρτιῶν ἀπολείπεται θυσία, 27 φοβερὰ
[3]sins [4]remains [1]a sacrifice, [3]fearful
δέ τις ἐκδοχὴ κρίσεως καὶ πυρὸς ζῆλος
[1]but [2]some expectation of judgment and [2]of fire [1]zeal
ἐσθίειν μέλλοντος τοὺς ὑπεναντίους.
[4]to consume [3]being about the adversaries.

after that time, says the
Lord.
I will put my laws in
their hearts,
and I will write them
on their minds."[m]
17 Then he adds:

"Their sins and lawless
acts
I will remember no
more."[n]

18 And where these have
been forgiven, there is no
longer any sacrifice for sin.

A Call to Persevere

19 Therefore, brothers,
since we have confidence
to enter the Most Holy
Place by the blood of Jesus,
20 by a new and living way
opened for us through the
curtain, that is, his body,
21 and since we have a great
priest over the house of
God, 22 let us draw near to
God with a sincere heart in
full assurance of faith, having our hearts sprinkled to
cleanse us from a guilty
conscience and having our
bodies washed with pure
water. 23 Let us hold un-
swervingly to the hope we
profess, for he who prom-
ised is faithful. 24 And let us
consider how we may spur
one another on toward love
and good deeds. 25 Let us
not give up meeting together, as some are in the habit
of doing, but let us encourage one another—and all
the more as you see the
Day approaching.
26 If we deliberately keep
on sinning after we have received the knowledge of
the truth, no sacrifice for
sins is left, 27 but only a
fearful expectation of judgment and of raging fire that
will consume the enemies

[m] *16* Jer. 31:33
[n] *17* Jer. 31:34

28Anyone who has set aside the Law of Moses dies without mercy on *the testimony of* two or three witnesses.
29How much severer punishment do you think he will deserve who has trampled under foot the Son of God, and has regarded as unclean the blood of the covenant by which he was sanctified, and has insulted the Spirit of grace?
30For we know Him who said, "VENGEANCE IS MINE, I WILL REPAY." And again, "THE LORD WILL JUDGE HIS PEOPLE."
31It is a terrifying thing to fall into the hands of the living God.
32But remember the former days, when, after being enlightened, you endured a great conflict of sufferings,
33partly, by being made a public spectacle through reproaches and tribulations, and partly by becoming sharers with those who were so treated.
34For you showed sympathy to the prisoners, and accepted joyfully the seizure of your property, knowing that you have for yourselves a better possession and an abiding one.
35Therefore, do not throw away your confidence, which has a great reward.
36For you have need of endurance, so that when you have done the will of God, you may receive what was promised.

37 FOR YET IN A VERY LITTLE WHILE,
HE WHO IS COMING WILL COME, AND WILL NOT DELAY.
38 BUT MY RIGHTEOUS ONE SHALL LIVE BY FAITH;
AND IF HE SHRINKS

28 ἀθετήσας τις νόμον Μωϋσέως χωρὶς
[2]Disregarding [1]anyone [3]law [4]of Moses [6]without
οἰκτιρμῶν ἐπὶ δυσὶν ἢ τρισὶν μάρτυσιν
[7]compassions [8]on [the word of] [9]two [10]or [11]three [12]witnesses
ἀποθνήσκει· **29** πόσῳ δοκεῖτε χείρονος
[5]dies; by how much think ye [2]of worse
ἀξιωθήσεται τιμωρίας ὁ τὸν υἱὸν τοῦ
[1]will be thought worthy [3]punishment [4]the [one] [6]the [7]Son –
θεοῦ καταπατήσας καὶ τὸ αἷμα τῆς
[8]of God [5]having trampled [on] and [2]the [4]blood [5]of the
διαθήκης κοινὸν ἡγησάμενος, ἐν ᾧ ἡγιάσθη,
[6]covenant [3]common [1]having deemed, by which he was sanctified,
καὶ τὸ πνεῦμα τῆς χάριτος ἐνυβρίσας.
and [2]the [3]Spirit – [4]of grace [1]having insulted.
30 οἴδαμεν γὰρ τὸν εἰπόντα· ἐμοὶ
For we know the [one] having said: To me =Vengeance
ἐκδίκησις, ἐγὼ ἀνταποδώσω· καὶ πάλιν·
vengeance,[c] is mine, I will repay; and again:
κρινεῖ κύριος τὸν λαὸν αὐτοῦ. **31** φοβερὸν
[2]will judge [[1]The] Lord the people of him. A fearful thing [it is]
τὸ ἐμπεσεῖν εἰς χεῖρας θεοῦ ζῶντος.
the to fall *in* into [the] hands [2]God [1]of a living.
32 Ἀναμιμνῄσκεσθε δὲ τὰς πρότερον ἡμέρας,
But remember ye the [2]formerly [1]days,
ἐν αἷς φωτισθέντες πολλὴν ἄθλησιν
in which being enlightened [2]a much(great) [3]struggle
ὑπεμείνατε παθημάτων, **33** τοῦτο μὲν
[1]ye endured [4]of sufferings, *this* on one hand
ὀνειδισμοῖς τε καὶ θλίψεσιν θεατριζόμενοι,
[2]to reproaches [3]both [4]and [5]to afflictions [1]being exposed,
τοῦτο δὲ κοινωνοὶ τῶν οὕτως ἀναστρεφ-
this on the other [2]sharers [3]of the [ones] [5]thus [4]liv-
ομένων γενηθέντες. **34** καὶ γὰρ τοῖς
ing [1]having become. For indeed in *the*
δεσμίοις συνεπαθήσατε, καὶ τὴν ἁρπαγὴν
bonds ye suffered together, and [4]the [5]seizure
τῶν ὑπαρχόντων ὑμῶν μετὰ χαρᾶς
[6]of the [7]possessions [8]of you [2]with [3]joy
προσεδέξασθε, γινώσκοντες ἔχειν ἑαυτοὺς
[1]ye accepted, knowing [2]to have [1][your]selves
κρείσσονα ὕπαρξιν καὶ μένουσαν. **35** Μὴ
[3]a better [6]possession [4]and [5]remaining. not
ἀποβάλητε οὖν τὴν παρρησίαν ὑμῶν, ἥτις
Cast ye away therefore the confidence of you, which
ἔχει μεγάλην μισθαποδοσίαν. **36** ὑπομονῆς
has a great recompence. [3]of endurance
γὰρ ἔχετε χρείαν ἵνα τὸ θέλημα τοῦ
For [1]ye have [2]need in order that [2]the [3]will –
θεοῦ ποιήσαντες κομίσησθε τὴν ἐπαγγελίαν.
[4]of God [1]having done ye may obtain the promise.
37 ἔτι γὰρ μικρὸν ὅσον ὅσον, ὁ ἐρχόμενος
For yet [2]little [1]a very,* the coming [one]
ἥξει καὶ οὐ χρονίσει· **38** ὁ δὲ δίκαιός
will come and will not delay; but the just man
μου ἐκ πίστεως ζήσεται, καὶ ἐὰν ὑπο-
of me by faith will live, and if he

* *Cf.* our "so so".

of God. 28Anyone who re-
jected the law of Moses
died without mercy on the
testimony of two or three
witnesses. 29How much
more severely do you think
a man deserves to be pun-
ished who has trampled the
Son of God under foot, who
has treated as an unholy
thing the blood of the covenant that sanctified him,
and who has insulted the
Spirit of grace? 30For we
know him who said, "It is
mine to avenge; I will repay,"[o] and again, "The
Lord will judge his peo-
ple."[p] 31It is a dreadful
thing to fall into the hands
of the living God.
32Remember those earlier
days after you had received
the light, when you stood
your ground in a great con-
test in the face of suffering.
33Sometimes you were
publicly exposed to insult
and persecution; at other
times you stood side by
side with those who were
so treated. 34You sympa-
thized with those in prison
and joyfully accepted the
confiscation of your property, because you knew
that you yourselves had
better and lasting possessions.
35So do not throw away
your confidence; it will be
richly rewarded. 36You
need to persevere so that
when you have done the
will of God, you will re-
ceive what he has prom-
ised. 37For in just a very little while,

"He who is coming will come and will not delay.
38 But my righteous one[q] will live by faith.
And if he shrinks back,

[o]30 Deut. 32:35
[p]30 Deut. 32:36; Psalm 135:14
[q]38 One early manuscript *But the righteous*

BACK, MY SOUL HAS NO PLEASURE IN HIM.

39But we are not of those who shrink back to destruction, but of those who have faith to the preserving of the soul.

στείληται, οὐκ εὐδοκεῖ ἡ ψυχή μου
withdraws, [4]is not well pleased [1]the [2]soul [3]of me

ἐν αὐτῷ. 39 ἡμεῖς δὲ οὐκ ἐσμὲν ὑποστολῆς
in him. But we are not of withdrawal

εἰς ἀπώλειαν, ἀλλὰ πίστεως εἰς περιποίησιν
to destruction, but of faith to possession

ψυχῆς.
of soul.

I will not be pleased with him."[r]

39But we are not of those who shrink back and are destroyed, but of those who believe and are saved.

Chapter 11

The Triumphs of Faith

NOW faith is the assurance of *things* hoped for, the conviction of things not seen.

2For by it the men of old gained approval.

3By faith we understand that the worlds were prepared by the word of God, so that what is seen was not made out of things which are visible.

4By faith Abel offered to God a better sacrifice than Cain, through which he obtained the testimony that he was righteous, God testifying about his gifts, and through faith, though he is dead, he still speaks.

5By faith Enoch was taken up so that he should not see death; AND HE WAS NOT FOUND BECAUSE GOD TOOK HIM UP; for he obtained the witness that before his being taken up he was pleasing to God.

6And without faith it is impossible to please *Him*, for he who comes to God must believe that He is, and *that* He is a rewarder of those who seek Him.

7By faith Noah, being warned *by God* about things not yet seen, in reverence prepared an ark for the salvation of his household, by which he condemned the world, and became an heir of the righteousness which is according to faith.

11 Ἔστιν δὲ πίστις ἐλπιζομένων ὑπό-
Now [2]is [1]faith [4]of things being hoped [3][the]

στασις, πραγμάτων ἔλεγχος οὐ βλεπομένων.
reality, [2]of things [1][the] proof not being seen.

2 ἐν ταύτῃ γὰρ ἐμαρτυρήθησαν οἱ
by this For [3]obtained witness [1]the

πρεσβύτεροι. 3 Πίστει νοοῦμεν κατηρτίσθαι
[2]elders. By faith we understand [4]to have been adjusted

τοὺς αἰῶνας ῥήματι θεοῦ, εἰς τὸ μὴ
[1]the [2]ages by a word of God, so as† [3]not

ἐκ φαινομένων τὸ βλεπόμενον γεγονέναι.
[5]out of [6]things appearing [1]the thing [2]being seen [4]to have become.

4 Πίστει πλείονα θυσίαν Ἅβελ παρὰ
By faith [4]a greater(? better) [5]sacrifice [1]Abel [6]than

Κάϊν προσήνεγκεν τῷ θεῷ, δι' ἧς
[7]Cain [2]offered – [3]to God, through which

ἐμαρτυρήθη εἶναι δίκαιος, μαρτυροῦντος ἐπὶ
he obtained witness to be just, [2]witnessing [3]over

τοῖς δώροις αὐτοῦ τοῦ θεοῦ, καὶ δι'
[4]the [5]gifts [6]of him – [1]God,* and through

αὐτῆς ἀποθανὼν ἔτι λαλεῖ. 5 Πίστει
it having died still he speaks. By faith

Ἐνὼχ μετετέθη τοῦ μὴ ἰδεῖν θάνατον,
Enoch was removed – not to see[d] death,

καὶ οὐχ ηὑρίσκετο διότι μετέθηκεν αὐτὸν
and was not found because [3]removed [2]him

ὁ θεός. 6 πρὸ γὰρ τῆς μεταθέσεως
– [1]God. For before the(his) removal

μεμαρτύρηται εὐαρεστηκέναι τῷ θεῷ· χωρὶς
he has obtained witness to have been well-pleasing – to God; [2]without

δὲ πίστεως ἀδύνατον εὐαρεστῆσαι· πιστεῦσαι
[1]but faith [it is] impossible to be well-pleasing [to God]; [6]to believe

γὰρ δεῖ τὸν προσερχόμενον [τῷ] θεῷ,
[1]for [3]it behoves [2]the [one] [4]approaching – [5]to God,

ὅτι ἔστιν καὶ τοῖς ἐκζητοῦσιν αὐτὸν
that he is and [3]to the [ones] [4]seeking [6]out [5]him

μισθαποδότης γίνεται. 7 Πίστει χρηματισ-
[2]a rewarder [1]becomes. By faith [2]having been warned [by

θεὶς Νῶε περὶ τῶν μηδέπω βλεπομένων,
God*] [1]Noah concerning the things not yet being seen,

εὐλαβηθεὶς κατεσκεύασεν κιβωτὸν εἰς
being devout prepared an ark for

σωτηρίαν τοῦ οἴκου αὐτοῦ, δι' ἧς
[the] salvation of the household of him, through which

κατέκρινεν τὸν κόσμον, καὶ τῆς κατὰ
he condemned the world, and [2]of the [5]according to

πίστιν δικαιοσύνης ἐγένετο κληρονόμος.
[6]faith [4]righteousness [1]became [3]heir.

* This must be understood, as the word always (or at least generally) has reference to a divine communication.

Chapter 11

By Faith

NOW faith is being sure of what we hope for and certain of what we do not see. 2This is what the ancients were commended for.

3By faith we understand that the universe was formed at God's command, so that what is seen was not made out of what was visible.

4By faith Abel offered God a better sacrifice than Cain did. By faith he was commended as a righteous man, when God spoke well of his offerings. And by faith he still speaks, even though he is dead.

5By faith Enoch was taken from this life, so that he did not experience death; he could not be found, because God had taken him away. For before he was taken, he was commended as one who pleased God. 6And without faith it is impossible to please God, because anyone who comes to him must believe that he exists and that he rewards those who earnestly seek him.

7By faith Noah, when warned about things not yet seen, in holy fear built an ark to save his family. By his faith he condemned the world and became heir of the righteousness that comes by faith.

r38 Hab. 2:3,4

8By faith Abraham, when he was called, obeyed by going out to a place which he was to receive for an inheritance; and he went out, not knowing where he was going.

9By faith he lived as an alien in the land of promise, as in a foreign *land*, dwelling in tents with Isaac and Jacob, fellow heirs of the same promise;

10for he was looking for the city which has foundations, whose architect and builder is God.

11By faith even Sarah herself received ability to conceive, even beyond the proper time of life, since she considered Him faithful who had promised;

12therefore, also, there was born of one man, and him as good as dead at that, *as many descendants* AS THE STARS OF HEAVEN IN NUMBER, AND INNUMERABLE AS THE SAND WHICH IS BY THE SEASHORE.

13All these died in faith, without receiving the promises, but having seen them and having welcomed them from a distance, and having confessed that they were strangers and exiles on the earth.

14For those who say such things make it clear that they are seeking a country of their own.

15And indeed if they had been thinking of that *country* from which they went out, they would have had opportunity to return.

16But as it is, they desire a better *country*, that is a heavenly one. Therefore God is not ashamed to be called their God; for He has prepared a city for them.

17By faith Abraham, when he was tested, offered up Isaac; and he who

8 *Πίστει καλούμενος Ἀβραὰμ ὑπήκουσεν*
By faith [2]being called [1]Abraham [11]obeyed

ἐξελθεῖν εἰς τόπον ὃν ἤμελλεν λαμβάνειν
[3]to go forth [4]to [5]a place [6]which [7]he was about [8]to receive

εἰς κληρονομίαν, καὶ ἐξῆλθεν μὴ ἐπιστάμε-
[9]for [10]an inheritance, and went forth not understand-

νος ποῦ ἔρχεται. **9** *Πίστει παρῴκησεν*
ing where he goes(went). By faith he sojourned

εἰς γῆν τῆς ἐπαγγελίας ὡς ἀλλοτρίαν,
in a land – of promise as a foreigner,

ἐν σκηναῖς κατοικήσας, μετὰ Ἰσαὰκ καὶ
in tents dwelling, with Isaac and

Ἰακὼβ τῶν συγκληρονόμων τῆς ἐπαγ-
Jacob the co-heirs of the [2]pro-

γελίας τῆς αὐτῆς· **10** *ἐξεδέχετο γὰρ τὴν*
mise – [1]same; for he expected the

τοὺς θεμελίους ἔχουσαν πόλιν, ἧς τεχνίτης
[3]the [4]foundations [2]having [1]city, of which [3]artificer

καὶ δημιουργὸς ὁ θεός. **11** *Πίστει καὶ*
[4]and [5]maker – [1]God [2][is]. By faith also

αὐτὴ Σάρρα δύναμιν εἰς καταβολὴν
[2][her]self [1]Sara [4]power [5]for [6]conception

σπέρματος ἔλαβεν καὶ παρὰ καιρὸν ἡλικίας,
[7]of seed [3]received even beyond time of age,

ἐπεὶ πιστὸν ἡγήσατο τὸν ἐπαγγειλάμενον.
since [2]faithful [1]she deemed the [one] having promised.

12 *διὸ καὶ ἀφ' ἑνὸς ἐγενήθησαν, καὶ*
Wherefore indeed from one there became, and

ταῦτα νενεκρωμένου, καθὼς τὰ ἄστρα
that too† [he] having died,* as the stars

τοῦ οὐρανοῦ τῷ πλήθει καὶ ὡς ἡ ἄμμος
of *the* heaven – in multitude and as the [2]sand

ἡ παρὰ τὸ χεῖλος τῆς θαλάσσης ἡ
– [3]by [4]the [5]lip [6]of the [7]sea –

ἀναρίθμητος. **13** *Κατὰ πίστιν ἀπέθανον*
[1]innumerable. [4]By way of [5]faith [3]died

οὗτοι πάντες, μὴ κομισάμενοι τὰς ἐπαγ-
[1]these [2]all, not having obtained the pro-

γελίας, ἀλλὰ πόρρωθεν αὐτὰς ἰδόντες καὶ
mises, but [5]from afar [4]them [1]seeing [2]and

ἀσπασάμενοι, καὶ ὁμολογήσαντες ὅτι ξένοι
[3]greeting, and confessing that [2]strangers

καὶ παρεπίδημοί εἰσιν ἐπὶ τῆς γῆς.
[3]and [4]sojourners [1]they are on the earth (? land).

14 *οἱ γὰρ τοιαῦτα λέγοντες ἐμφανίζουσιν*
For the [ones] [2]such things [1]saying make manifest

ὅτι πατρίδα ἐπιζητοῦσιν. **15** *καὶ εἰ μὲν*
that [2]a fatherland [1]they seek. And if on one hand

ἐκείνης ἐμνημόνευον ἀφ' ἧς ἐξέβησαν,
[2]that [1]they remembered from which they came out,

εἶχον ἂν καιρὸν ἀνακάμψαι· **16** *νῦν*
they might have had time(opportunity) to return; now

δὲ κρείττονος ὀρέγονται, τοῦτ' ἔστιν
on the other [2]a better [1]they aspire to, this is

ἐπουρανίου. διὸ οὐκ ἐπαισχύνεται αὐτοὺς
a heavenly. Wherefore [2]is not ashamed [of] [3]them

ὁ θεὸς θεὸς ἐπικαλεῖσθαι αὐτῶν· ἡτοίμασεν
– [1]God [5]God [4]to be called [6]of them; [2]he prepared

γὰρ αὐτοῖς πόλιν. **17** *Πίστει προσενήνοχεν*
[1]for for them a city. By faith [3]*has* offered up

Ἀβραὰμ τὸν Ἰσαὰκ πειραζόμενος, καὶ
[1]Abraham – [4]Isaac [2]being tested, and

8By faith Abraham, when called to go to a place he would later receive as his inheritance, obeyed and went, even though he did not know where he was going. 9By faith he made his home in the promised land like a stranger in a foreign country; he lived in tents, as did Isaac and Jacob, who were heirs with him of the same promise. 10For he was looking forward to the city with foundations, whose architect and builder is God.

11By faith Abraham, even though he was past age—and Sarah herself was barren—was enabled to become a father because he[s] considered him faithful who had made the promise. 12And so from this one man, and he as good as dead, came descendants as numerous as the stars in the sky and as countless as the sand on the seashore.

13All these people were still living by faith when they died. They did not receive the things promised; they only saw them and welcomed them from a distance. And they admitted that they were aliens and strangers on earth. 14People who say such things show that they are looking for a country of their own. 15If they had been thinking of the country they had left, they would have had opportunity to return. 16Instead, they were longing for a better country—a heavenly one. Therefore God is not ashamed to be called their God, for he has prepared a city for them.

17By faith Abraham, when God tested him, offered Isaac as a sacrifice.

[s] *11 Or By faith even Sarah, who was past age, was enabled to bear children because she*

had received the promises was offering up his only begotten *son;*

18*it was he* to whom it was said, "IN ISAAC YOUR DESCENDANTS SHALL BE CALLED."

19He considered that God is able to raise *men* even from the dead; from which he also received him back as a type.

20By faith Isaac blessed Jacob and Esau, even regarding things to come.

21By faith Jacob, as he was dying, blessed each of the sons of Joseph, and worshiped, *leaning* on the top of his staff.

22By faith Joseph, when he was dying, made mention of the exodus of the sons of Israel, and gave orders concerning his bones.

23By faith Moses, when he was born, was hidden for three months by his parents, because they saw he was a beautiful child; and they were not afraid of the king's edict.

24By faith Moses, when he had grown up, refused to be called the son of Pharoah's daughter;

25choosing rather to endure ill-treatment with the people of God, than to enjoy the passing pleasures of sin;

26considering the reproach of Christ greater riches than the treasures of Egypt; for he was looking to the reward.

27By faith he left Egypt, not fearing the wrath of the king; for he endured, as seeing Him who is unseen.

28By faith he kept the Passover and the sprinkling of the blood, so that he who

τὸν μονογενῆ προσέφερεν ὁ τὰς ἐπαγγελίας
6the 7only begotten (his) 5was offering up 1the [one] 3the 4promises

ἀναδεξάμενος, 18 πρὸς ὃν ἐλαλήθη ὅτι
2having undertaken, as to whom it was spoken[,] –

ἐν Ἰσαὰκ κληθήσεταί σοι σπέρμα,
In Isaac shall be called to thee a seed,° =thy seed,

19 λογισάμενος ὅτι καὶ ἐκ νεκρῶν ἐγείρειν
reckoning that 4even 6from 7dead 5to raise

δυνατὸς ὁ θεός· ὅθεν αὐτὸν καὶ ἐν
3[was] 3able – 1God; whence 5him 1indeed 3in

παραβολῇ ἐκομίσατο. 20 Πίστει καὶ περὶ
3a parable 4he obtained. By faith also 6concerning

μελλόντων εὐλόγησεν Ἰσαὰκ τὸν Ἰακὼβ
7coming things 2blessed 1Isaac – 3Jacob

καὶ τὸν Ἠσαῦ. 21 Πίστει Ἰακὼβ
4and – 5Esau. By faith Jacob

ἀποθνήσκων ἕκαστον τῶν υἱῶν Ἰωσὴφ
dying 2each 3of the 4sons 5of Joseph

εὐλόγησεν, καὶ προσεκύνησεν ἐπὶ τὸ ἄκρον
1blessed, and worshipped on the tip

τῆς ῥάβδου αὐτοῦ. 22 Πίστει Ἰωσὴφ
of the rod of him. By faith Joseph

τελευτῶν περὶ τῆς ἐξόδου τῶν υἱῶν
dying 2concerning 3the 4exodus 5of the 6sons

Ἰσραὴλ ἐμνημόνευσεν καὶ περὶ τῶν
7of Israel 1remembered and 2concerning 3the

ὀστέων αὐτοῦ ἐνετείλατο. 23 Πίστει
4bones 5of him 1gave orders. By faith

Μωϋσῆς γεννηθεὶς ἐκρύβη τρίμηνον ὑπὸ
Moses having been born was hidden three months by

τῶν πατέρων αὐτοῦ, διότι εἶδον ἀστεῖον
the parents of him, because they saw 3[to be] fine

τὸ παιδίον, καὶ οὐκ ἐφοβήθησαν τὸ
1the 2child, and they did not fear the

διάταγμα τοῦ βασιλέως. 24 Πίστει Μωϋσῆς
decree of the king. By faith Moses

μέγας γενόμενος ἠρνήσατο λέγεσθαι υἱὸς
2great 1having become denied to be said(called) son

θυγατρὸς Φαραώ, 25 μᾶλλον ἑλόμενος
of [the] daughter of Pharaoh, rather choosing

συγκακουχεῖσθαι τῷ λαῷ τοῦ θεοῦ ἢ
to be ill treated with the people – of God than

πρόσκαιρον ἔχειν ἁμαρτίας ἀπόλαυσιν,
for a time to have 2of sin 1enjoyment,

26 μείζονα πλοῦτον ἡγησάμενος τῶν
5greater 6riches 1deeming 7[than] 8the

Αἰγύπτου θησαυρῶν τὸν ὀνειδισμὸν τοῦ
10of Egypt 9treasures 2the 3reproach –

Χριστοῦ· ἀπέβλεπεν γὰρ εἰς τὴν μισθαποδοσίαν.
4of Christ; for he was looking away to the recompence.

27 Πίστει κατέλιπεν Αἴγυπτον,
By faith he left Egypt,

μὴ φοβηθεὶς τὸν θυμὸν τοῦ βασιλέως·
not fearing the anger of the king;

τὸν γὰρ ἀόρατον ὡς ὁρῶν ἐκαρτέρησεν.
for 4the 5unseen [one] 2as 3seeing 1he endured.

28 Πίστει πεποίηκεν τὸ πάσχα καὶ τὴν
By faith he *has* made the passover and the

πρόσχυσιν τοῦ αἵματος, ἵνα μὴ ὁ
affusion of the blood, lest the

ὀλεθρεύων τὰ πρωτότοκα θίγῃ αὐτῶν.
[one] destroying 2the 3firstborns 1should touch 4of them.

He who had received the
promises was about to sacrifice his one and only son,
18even though God had said
to him, "It is through Isaac
that your offspring[t] will be
reckoned."[u] 19Abraham
reasoned that God could
raise the dead, and figuratively speaking, he did receive Isaac back from
death.

20By faith Isaac blessed
Jacob and Esau in regard to
their future.

21By faith Jacob, when he
was dying, blessed each of
Joseph's sons, and worshiped as he leaned on the
top of his staff.

22By faith Joseph, when
his end was near, spoke
about the exodus of the Israelites from Egypt and
gave instructions about his
bones.

23By faith Moses' parents
hid him for three months after he was born, because
they saw he was no ordinary child, and they were
not afraid of the king's
edict.

24By faith Moses, when
he had grown up, refused to
be known as the son of
Pharaoh's daughter. 25He
chose to be mistreated
along with the people of
God rather than to enjoy
the pleasures of sin for a
short time. 26He regarded
disgrace for the sake of
Christ as of greater value
than the treasures of
Egypt, because he was
looking ahead to his reward. 27By faith he left
Egypt, not fearing the
king's anger; he persevered
because he saw him who is
invisible. 28By faith he kept
the Passover and the sprinkling of blood, so that the

t18 Greek *seed*
u18 Gen. 21:12

destroyed the first-born
might not touch them.
29By faith they passed
through the Red Sea
as though *they were passing*
through dry land;
and the Egyptians, when
they attempted it, were
drowned.
30By faith the walls of
Jericho fell down, after
they had been encircled for
seven days.
31By faith Rahab the harlot
did not perish along with
those who were disobedient,
after she had welcomed
the spies in peace.
32And what more shall I
say? For time will fail me if
I tell of Gideon, Barak,
Samson, Jephthah, of David
and Samuel and the
prophets,
33who by faith conquered
kingdoms, performed *acts
of* righteousness, obtained
promises, shut the mouths
of lions,
34quenched the power of
fire, escaped the edge of
the sword, from weakness
were made strong, became
mighty in war, put foreign
armies to flight.
35Women received *back*
their dead by resurrection;
and others were tortured,
not accepting their release,
in order that they might obtain
a better resurrection;
36and others experienced
mockings and scourgings,
yes, also chains and imprisonment.
37They were stoned, they
were sawn in two, [h]they
were tempted, they were
put to death with the
sword; they went about in
sheepskins, in goatskins,
being destitute, afflicted,
ill-treated
38(*men* of whom the
world was not worthy),
wandering in deserts and
mountains and caves and
holes in the ground.
39And all these, having
gained approval through

29 Πίστει διέβησαν τὴν ἐρυθρὰν θάλασσαν
By faith they went through the Red Sea

ὡς διὰ ξηρᾶς γῆς, ἧς πεῖραν λαβόντες
as through dry land, which [4]trial [3]taking

οἱ Αἰγύπτιοι κατεπόθησαν. 30 Πίστει
[1]the [2]Egyptians were swallowed up. By faith

τὰ τείχη Ἰεριχὼ ἔπεσαν κυκλωθέντα ἐπὶ
the walls of Jericho fell having been encircled during

ἑπτὰ ἡμέρας. 31 Πίστει Ῥαὰβ ἡ πόρνη
seven days. By faith Rahab the prostitute

οὐ συναπώλετο τοῖς ἀπειθήσασιν, δεξαμένη
did not perish with the [ones] disobeying, having received

τοὺς κατασκόπους μετ᾿ εἰρήνης. 32 Καὶ
the spies with peace. And

τί ἔτι λέγω; ἐπιλείψει με γὰρ διηγούμενον
what more may I say? [4]will fail [5]me [1]for [6]recounting

ὁ χρόνος περὶ Γεδεών, Βαράκ, Σαμψών,
[2]the [3]time concerning Gedeon, Barak, Samson,

Ἰεφθάε, Δαυίδ τε καὶ Σαμουὴλ καὶ
Jephthae, [2]David [1]both and Samuel and

τῶν προφητῶν, 33 οἳ διὰ πίστεως
the prophets, who through faith

κατηγωνίσαντο βασιλείας, ἠργάσαντο δι-
overcame kingdoms, wrought right-

καιοσύνην, ἐπέτυχον ἐπαγγελιῶν, ἔφραξαν
eousness, obtained promises, stopped

στόματα λεόντων, 34 ἔσβεσαν δύναμιν
mouths of lions, quenched [the] power

πυρός, ἔφυγον στόματα μαχαίρης, ἐδυναμώ-
of fire, escaped mouths(edges) of [the] sword, were em-

θησαν ἀπὸ ἀσθενείας, ἐγενήθησαν ἰσχυροὶ
powered from weakness, became strong

ἐν πολέμῳ, παρεμβολὰς ἔκλιναν ἀλλοτρίων.
in battle, [1]armies [3]made to yield [2]of foreigners.

35 ἔλαβον γυναῖκες ἐξ ἀναστάσεως τοὺς
[2]received [1]women [6]by [7]resurrection [3]the

νεκροὺς αὐτῶν· ἄλλοι δὲ ἐτυμπανίσθησαν,
[4]dead [5]of them; but others were beaten to death,

οὐ προσδεξάμενοι τὴν ἀπολύτρωσιν, ἵνα
not accepting – deliverance, in order that

κρείττονος ἀναστάσεως τύχωσιν· 36 ἕτεροι
[2]a better [3]resurrection [1]they might obtain; others

δὲ ἐμπαιγμῶν καὶ μαστίγων πεῖραν ἔλαβον,
and [3]of mockings [4]and [5]*of* scourgings [2]trial [1]took,

ἔτι δὲ δεσμῶν καὶ φυλακῆς· 37 ἐλιθάσ-
and more of bonds and of prison; they were

θησαν, ἐπειράσθησαν, ἐπρίσθησαν, ἐν φόνῳ
stoned, they were tried, they were sawn asunder, [2]by [3]murder

μαχαίρης ἀπέθανον, περιῆλθον ἐν μηλωταῖς,
[4]of sword [1]they died, they went about in sheepskins,

ἐν αἰγείοις δέρμασιν, ὑστερούμενοι,
in goatskins, being in want,

θλιβόμενοι, κακουχούμενοι, 38 ὧν οὐκ ἦν
being afflicted, *being* ill treated, of whom was not

ἄξιος ὁ κόσμος, ἐπὶ ἐρημίαις πλανώμενοι
worthy the world, [2]over [3]deserts [1]wandering

καὶ ὄρεσιν καὶ σπηλαίοις καὶ ταῖς ὀπαῖς
and mountains and caves and the holes

τῆς γῆς. 39 Καὶ οὗτοι πάντες μαρτυρη-
of the earth. And these all having obtained

destroyer of the firstborn
would not touch the firstborn
of Israel.
29By faith the people
passed through the Red
Sea[v] as on dry land; but
when the Egyptians tried to
do so, they were drowned.
30By faith the walls of Jericho
fell, after the people
had marched around them
for seven days.
31By faith the prostitute
Rahab, because she welcomed
the spies, was not
killed with those who were
disobedient.[w]
32And what more shall I
say? I do not have time to
tell about Gideon, Barak,
Samson, Jephthah, David,
Samuel and the prophets,
33who through faith conquered
kingdoms, administered
justice, and gained
what was promised; who
shut the mouths of lions,
34quenched the fury of the
flames, and escaped the
edge of the sword; whose
weakness was turned to
strength; and who became
powerful in battle and routed
foreign armies. 35Women
received back their
dead, raised to life again.
Others were tortured and
refused to be released, so
that they might gain a better
resurrection. 36Some
faced jeers and flogging,
while still others were
chained and put in prison.
37They were stoned[x]; they
were sawed in two; they
were put to death by the
sword. They went about in
sheepskins and goatskins,
destitute, persecuted and
mistreated—38the world
was not worthy of them.
They wandered in deserts
and mountains, and in
caves and holes in the
ground.
39These were all commended
for their faith, yet

[h] Some mss. do not contain *they were tempted*

[v] *29* That is, Sea of Reeds
[w] *31* Or *unbelieving*
[x] *37* Some early manuscripts *stoned; they were put to the test;*

their faith, did not receive what was promised,
40because God had provided something better for us, so that apart from us they should not be made perfect.

θέντες διὰ τῆς πίστεως οὐκ ἐκομίσαντο
witness through the(ir) faith obtained not
τὴν ἐπαγγελίαν, 40 τοῦ θεοῦ περὶ ἡμῶν
the promise, – God [4]concerning [5]us
κρεῖττόν τι προβλεψαμένου, ἵνα μὴ χωρὶς
[2]better [3]something [1]having foreseen,[a] in order that not without
ἡμῶν τελειωθῶσιν.
us they should be perfected.

none of them received what had been promised. 40God had planned something better for us so that only together with us would they be made perfect.

Chapter 12

Jesus, the Example

THEREFORE, since we have so great a cloud of witnesses surrounding us, let us also lay aside every encumbrance, and the sin which so easily entangles us, and let us run with endurance the race that is set before us,
2fixing our eyes on Jesus, the author and perfecter of faith, who for the joy set before Him endured the cross, despising the shame, and has sat down at the right hand of the throne of God.
3For consider Him who has endured such hostility by sinners against Himself, so that you may not grow weary and lose heart.

A Father's Discipline

4You have not yet resisted to the point of shedding blood in your striving against sin;
5and you have forgotten the exhortation which is addressed to you as sons,
"My son, do not regard lightly the discipline of the Lord,
Nor faint when you are reproved by Him;
6 For those whom the Lord loves He disciplines,
And He scourges every son whom He receives."
7It is for discipline that you endure; God deals with you as with sons; for what son is there whom *his* father does not discipline?
8But if you are without discipline, of which all have become partakers, then you are illegitimate children and not sons.
9Furthermore, we had

12 Τοιγαροῦν καὶ ἡμεῖς, τοσοῦτον ἔχοντες
So therefore [2]also [1]we, [3]such [1]having
περικείμενον ἡμῖν νέφος μαρτύρων, ὄγκον
[5]lying around [6]us [2]a cloud [4]of witnesses, [3]encumbrance
ἀποθέμενοι πάντα καὶ τὴν εὐπερίστατον
[1]putting away [2]every [4]and [5]the [7]most besetting
ἁμαρτίαν, δι' ὑπομονῆς τρέχωμεν τὸν
[6]sin, through endurance let us run [1]the
προκείμενον ἡμῖν ἀγῶνα, 2 ἀφορῶντες εἰς
[3]set before [4]us [2]contest(race), looking away to
τὸν τῆς πίστεως ἀρχηγὸν καὶ τελειωτὴν
[1]the [5]of the [6]faith [2]author [3]and [4]finisher
Ἰησοῦν, ὃς ἀντὶ τῆς προκειμένης αὐτῷ
Jesus, who against [1]the [3]set before [4]him
χαρᾶς ὑπέμεινεν σταυρὸν αἰσχύνης καταφρονήσας,
[2]joy endured a cross [2]shame [1]despising,
ἐν δεξιᾷ τε τοῦ θρόνου τοῦ
[3]at [4][the] right [hand] [1]and [5]of the [6]throne –
θεοῦ κεκάθικεν. 3 ἀναλογίσασθε γὰρ τὸν
[7]of God [2]has taken [his] seat. For consider ye [1]the [one]
τοιαύτην ὑπομεμενηκότα ὑπὸ τῶν ἁμαρτωλῶν
[3]such [2]having endured [5]by – [6]of sinners
εἰς ἑαυτὸν ἀντιλογίαν, ἵνα μὴ κάμητε
[7]against [8]himself [4]contradiction, lest ye grow weary
ταῖς ψυχαῖς ὑμῶν ἐκλυόμενοι. 4 Οὔπω
[2]in the [3]souls [4]of you [1]fainting. Not yet
μέχρις αἵματος ἀντικατέστητε πρὸς τὴν
[2]until [3]blood [1]ye resisted [5]against –
ἁμαρτίαν ἀνταγωνιζόμενοι, 5 καὶ ἐκλέλησθε
[6]sin [4]struggling *against*, and ye have forgotten
τῆς παρακλήσεως, ἥτις ὑμῖν ὡς υἱοῖς
the exhortation, which [2]with you [3]as [4]with sons
διαλέγεται· υἱέ μου, μὴ ὀλιγώρει παιδείας
[1]discourses: Son of me, do not make light of [the] discipline
κυρίου, μηδὲ ἐκλύου ὑπ' αὐτοῦ ἐλεγχόμενος·
of [the] Lord, nor faint [2]by [3]him [1]being reproved;
6 ὃν γὰρ ἀγαπᾷ κύριος παιδεύει, μαστιγοῖ
for whom [2]loves [1][the] Lord he disciplines, [2]scourges
δὲ πάντα υἱὸν ὃν παραδέχεται. 7 εἰς
[1]and every son whom he receives. For
παιδείαν ὑπομένετε· ὡς υἱοῖς ὑμῖν
discipline endure ye; [4]as [5]with sons [3]with you
προσφέρεται ὁ θεός· τίς γὰρ υἱὸς ὃν
[2]is dealing – [1]God; for what son whom [is there]
οὐ παιδεύει πατήρ; 8 εἰ δὲ χωρίς ἐστε
[2]disciplines not [1]a father ? But if [2]without [1]ye are
παιδείας, ἧς μέτοχοι γεγόνασιν πάντες,
discipline, of which [3]sharers [2]have become [1]all,
ἄρα νόθοι καὶ οὐχ υἱοί ἐστε. 9 εἶτα
then bastards and not sons ye are. Furthermore

Chapter 12

God Disciplines His Sons

THEREFORE, since we are surrounded by such a great cloud of witnesses, let us throw off everything that hinders and the sin that so easily entangles, and let us run with perseverance the race marked out for us. 2Let us fix our eyes on Jesus, the author and perfecter of our faith, who for the joy set before him endured the cross, scorning its shame, and sat down at the right hand of the throne of God. 3Consider him who endured such opposition from sinful men, so that you will not grow weary and lose heart.
4In your struggle against sin, you have not yet resisted to the point of shedding your blood. 5And you have forgotten that word of encouragement that addresses you as sons:

"My son, do not make light of the Lord's discipline,
and do not lose heart when he rebukes you,
6because the Lord disciplines those he loves,
and he punishes everyone he accepts as a son."[y]

7Endure hardship as discipline; God is treating you as sons. For what son is not disciplined by his father? 8If you are not disciplined (and everyone undergoes discipline), then you are illegitimate children and not true sons. 9Moreover, we

y6 Prov. 3:11,12

earthly fathers to discipline
us, and we respected them;
shall we not much rather be
subject to the Father of
spirits, and live?
10For they disciplined us
for a short time as seemed
best to them, but He *disciplines us* for *our* good, that
we may share His holiness.
11All discipline for the
moment seems not to be
joyful, but sorrowful; yet to
those who have been
trained by it, afterwards it
yields the peaceful fruit of
righteousness.
12Therefore, strengthen
the hands that are weak and
the knees that are feeble,
13and make straight paths
for your feet, so that *the
limb* which is lame may not
be put out of joint, but
rather be healed.
14Pursue peace with all
men, and the sanctification
without which no one will
see the Lord.
15See to it that no one
comes short of the grace of
God; that no root of bitterness springing up causes
trouble, and by it many be
defiled;
16that *there be* no immoral or godless person like
Esau, who sold his own
birthright for a *single* meal.
17For you know that even
afterwards, when he de-
sired to inherit the blessing,
he was rejected, for he
found no place for repen-
tance, though he sought for
it with tears.

Contrast of Sinai and Zion

18For you have not come
to *a mountain* that may be
touched and to a blazing
fire, and to darkness and
gloom and whirlwind,

τοὺς μὲν τῆς σαρκὸς ἡμῶν πατέρας
the – [3]of the [4]flesh [5]of us [2]fathers
εἴχομεν παιδευτὰς καὶ ἐνετρεπόμεθα· οὐ
[1]we had [6]correctors and we respected [them]: [3]not
πολὺ μᾶλλον ὑποταγησόμεθα τῷ πατρὶ
[6]much [7]more [1]shall [2]we [4]be [5]subject to the Father
τῶν πνευμάτων καὶ ζήσομεν; **10** οἱ μὲν
– of spirits and we shall live ? [2]they [3]indeed
γὰρ πρὸς ὀλίγας ἡμέρας κατὰ τὸ δοκοῦν
[1]for for a few days according to the thing seeming [good]
αὐτοῖς ἐπαίδευον, ὁ δὲ ἐπὶ τὸ συμφέρον
to them disciplined [us], but he for the(our) profit
εἰς τὸ μεταλαβεῖν τῆς ἁγιότητος αὐτοῦ.
for the to partake of the sanctity of him.
11 πᾶσα μὲν παιδεία πρὸς μὲν τὸ παρὸν
[2]All [1]on one hand [3]discipline [4]for [7]indeed [5]the [6]present
οὐ δοκεῖ χαρᾶς εἶναι ἀλλὰ λύπης, ὕστερον
seems not [2]of joy [1]to be but of grief, [2]later
δὲ καρπὸν εἰρηνικὸν τοῖς δι' αὐτῆς
[1]on the other [5]fruit [4]peaceable [7]to the [ones] [9]through [10]it
γεγυμνασμένοις ἀποδίδωσιν δικαιοσύνης.
[8]having been exercised [3]it gives back [6]of righteousness.
12 Διὸ τὰς παρειμένας χεῖρας καὶ τὰ
Wherefore [2]the [3]*having been* wearied [4]hands [5]and [6]the
παραλελυμένα γόνατα ἀνορθώσατε, **13** καὶ
[7]*having been* paralysed [8]knees [1]straighten ye, and
τροχιὰς ὀρθὰς ποιεῖτε τοῖς ποσὶν ὑμῶν,
tracks straight make for the feet of you,
ἵνα μὴ τὸ χωλὸν ἐκτραπῇ, ἰαθῇ δὲ
lest the lame be turned aside, [3]may be cured [1]but
μᾶλλον. **14** Εἰρήνην διώκετε μετὰ πάντων,
[2]rather. Peace follow with all men,
καὶ τὸν ἁγιασμόν, οὗ χωρὶς οὐδεὶς
and – sanctification, [2]which [1]without no one
ὄψεται τὸν κύριον, **15** ἐπισκοποῦντες μή
will see the Lord, observing not(lest)
τις ὑστερῶν ἀπὸ τῆς χάριτος τοῦ θεοῦ,
anyone fail*ing* from the grace – of God,
μή τις ῥίζα πικρίας ἄνω φύουσα ἐνοχλῇ
not (lest) any root of bitterness [2]up [1]growing disturb
καὶ διὰ ταύτης μιανθῶσιν οἱ πολλοί,
and through this [2]be defiled *the* [1]many,
16 μή τις πόρνος ἢ βέβηλος ὡς Ἠσαῦ,
not(lest) any fornicator or profane man as Esau,
ὃς ἀντὶ βρώσεως μιᾶς ἀπέδοτο τὰ
who against [2]eating [1]one gave up the
πρωτοτόκια ἑαυτοῦ. **17** ἴστε γὰρ ὅτι
rights of the firstborn of himself. For ye know that
καὶ μετέπειτα θέλων κληρονομῆσαι τὴν
indeed afterwards wishing to inherit the
εὐλογίαν ἀπεδοκιμάσθη, μετανοίας γὰρ
blessing he was rejected, for [4]of repentance
τόπον οὐχ εὗρεν, καίπερ μετὰ δακρύων
[3]place [2]not [1]he found, though with tears
ἐκζητήσας αὐτήν. **18** Οὐ γὰρ προσεληλύθατε
seeking out it. For [3]not [1]ye [2]have [4]approached
ψηλαφωμένῳ καὶ κεκαυμένῳ πυρὶ καὶ
to [a mountain] being felt and having been ignited with fire and
γνόφῳ καὶ ζόφῳ καὶ θυέλλῃ **19** καὶ
to darkness and *to* deep gloom and *to* whirlwind and

have all had human fathers
who disciplined us and we
respected them for it. How
much more should we sub-
mit to the Father of our
spirits and live! 10Our fathers disciplined us for a little while as they thought
best; but God disciplines us
for our good, that we may
share in his holiness. 11No
discipline seems pleasant at
the time, but painful. Later
on, however, it produces a
harvest of righteousness
and peace for those who
have been trained by it.
12Therefore, strengthen
your feeble arms and weak
knees. 13"Make level paths
for your feet,"[z] so that the
lame may not be disabled,
but rather healed.

Warning Against Refusing God

14Make every effort to
live in peace with all men
and to be holy; without holiness no one will see the
Lord. 15See to it that no one
misses the grace of God
and that no bitter root
grows up to cause trouble
and defile many. 16See that
no one is sexually immoral,
or is godless like Esau, who
for a single meal sold his
inheritance rights as the
oldest son. 17Afterward, as
you know, when he wanted
to inherit this blessing, he
was rejected. He could
bring about no change of
mind, though he sought the
blessing with tears.
18You have not come to a
mountain that can be
touched and that is burning
with fire; to darkness,
gloom and storm; 19to a

[z]*13* Prov. 4:26

19and to the blast of a
trumpet and the sound of
words which *sound was
such that* those who heard
begged that no further
word should be spoken to
them.
20For they could not bear
the command, "IF EVEN A
BEAST TOUCHES THE MOUN-
TAIN, IT WILL BE STONED."
21And so terrible was the
sight, *that* Moses said, "I
AM FULL OF FEAR and trem-
bling."
22But you have come to
Mount Zion and to the city
of the living God, the heavenly Jerusalem, and to
myriads of angels,
23to the general assembly
and church of the first-born
who are enrolled in heaven,
and to God, the Judge of
all, and to the spirits of
righteous men made per-
fect,
24and to Jesus, the mediator of a new covenant, and
to the sprinkled blood,
which speaks better than
the blood of Abel.

The Unshaken Kingdom

25See to it that you do not
refuse Him who is speak-
ing. For if those did not escape when they refused
him who warned *them* on
earth, much less *shall* we
escape who turn away from
Him who *warns* from
heaven.
26And His voice shook
the earth then, but now He
has promised, saying,
"YET ONCE MORE I WILL
SHAKE NOT ONLY THE EARTH,
BUT ALSO THE HEAVEN."
27And this *expression*,
"Yet once more," denotes
the removing of those
things which can be shak-
en, as of created things, in
order that those things
which cannot be shaken
may remain.
28Therefore, since we re-
ceive a kingdom which cannot be shaken, let us show
gratitude, by which we may
offer to God an acceptable
service with reverence and
awe;
29for our God is a con-
suming fire.

σάλπιγγος ἤχῳ καὶ φωνῇ ῥημάτων, ἧς
[2]of trumpet [1]*to* a sound and *to* a voice of words, which

οἱ ἀκούσαντες παρῃτήσαντο μὴ προστεθῆναι
the [ones] hearing entreated not to be added

αὐτοῖς λόγον· 20 οὐκ ἔφερον γὰρ τὸ
to them a word; [3]not [2]they bore [1]for the thing

διαστελλόμενον· κἂν θηρίον θίγῃ τοῦ ὄρους,
being charged: If even a beast touches the mountain,

λιθοβοληθήσεται· 21 καί, οὕτω φοβερὸν ἦν
it shall be stoned; and, so fearful was

τὸ φανταζόμενον, Μωϋσῆς εἶπεν· ἔκφοβός
the thing appearing, Moses said: [2]Terrified

εἰμι καὶ ἔντρομος· 22 ἀλλὰ προσεληλύθατε
[1]I am and trembling; but ye have approached

Σιὼν ὄρει καὶ πόλει θεοῦ ζῶντος,
[2]Zion [1]*to* mount and *to* a city [2]God [1]of [the] living,

Ἰερουσαλὴμ ἐπουρανίῳ, καὶ μυριάσιν
[2]Jerusalem [1]*to* a heavenly, and *to* myriads

ἀγγέλων, 23 πανηγύρει καὶ ἐκκλησίᾳ
of angels, *to* an assembly and a church

πρωτοτόκων ἀπογεγραμμένων ἐν οὐρανοῖς,
of firstborn [ones] *having been* enrolled in heavens,

καὶ κριτῇ θεῷ πάντων, καὶ πνεύμασι
and [2]judge [1]*to* God of all men, and *to* spirits

δικαίων τετελειωμένων, 24 καὶ διαθήκης
of just men *having been* made perfect, and [4]covenant

νέας μεσίτῃ Ἰησοῦ, καὶ αἵματι ῥαντισμοῦ
[3]of a new [2]mediator [1]*to* Jesus, and *to* blood of sprinkling

κρεῖττον λαλοῦντι παρὰ τὸν Ἄβελ.
[2]a better thing [1]speaking than – Abel.

25 Βλέπετε μὴ παραιτήσησθε τὸν λαλοῦντα·
Look ye [that] [2]not [1]ye refuse the [one] speaking;

εἰ γὰρ ἐκεῖνοι οὐκ ἐξέφυγον ἐπὶ γῆς
for if those escaped not [4]on [5]earth

παραιτησάμενοι τὸν χρηματίζοντα, πολὺ
[1]refusing [2]the [one] [3]warning, much

μᾶλλον ἡμεῖς οἱ τὸν ἀπ' οὐρανῶν
more we* [1]the [ones] [3]the [one] [4][warning] [5]from [6]heavens

ἀποστρεφόμενοι· 26 οὗ ἡ φωνὴ τὴν γῆν
[2]turning from; of whom the voice [3]the [4]earth

ἐσάλευσεν τότε, νῦν δὲ ἐπήγγελται λέγων·
[2]shook [1]then, but now he has promised saying:

ἔτι ἅπαξ ἐγὼ σείσω οὐ μόνον τὴν
Yet once I will shake not only the

γῆν ἀλλὰ καὶ τὸν οὐρανόν. 27 τὸ δὲ
earth but also *the* heaven. Now the [phrase]

ἔτι ἅπαξ δηλοῖ τὴν τῶν σαλευομένων
'Yet once' declares [1]the [3]of the things [4]being shaken

μετάθεσιν ὡς πεποιημένων, ἵνα μείνῃ τὰ
[2]removal as of things having been made, in order that [4]may remain [1]the things

μὴ σαλευόμενα. 28 Διὸ βασιλείαν ἀσάλευτος
[2]not [3]being shaken. Wherefore [3]kingdom [2]an unshakable

παραλαμβάνοντες ἔχωμεν χάριν, δι' ἧς
[1]receiving let us have grace, through which

λατρεύωμεν εὐαρέστως τῷ θεῷ, μετὰ
we may serve [2]well-pleasingly – [1]God, with

εὐλαβείας καὶ δέους· 29 καὶ γὰρ ὁ θεὸς
devoutness and awe; for indeed the God

ἡμῶν πῦρ καταναλίσκον.
of us [is] fire a consuming.

* That is, "much more [shall] we [not escape]"; or, putting it in another way, "much less shall we escape."

trumpet blast or to such a
voice speaking words that
those who heard it begged
that no further word be
spoken to them, 20because
they could not bear what
was commanded: "If even
an animal touches the
mountain, it must be
stoned."[a] 21The sight was
so terrifying that Moses
said, "I am trembling with
fear."[b]
22But you have come to
Mount Zion, to the heavenly Jerusalem, the city of the
living God. You have come
to thousands upon thou-
sands of angels in joyful assembly, 23to the church of
the firstborn, whose names
are written in heaven. You
have come to God, the
judge of all men, to the spirits of righteous men made
perfect, 24to Jesus the mediator of a new covenant,
and to the sprinkled blood
that speaks a better word
than the blood of Abel.
25See to it that you do not
refuse him who speaks. If
they did not escape when
they refused him who
warned them on earth, how
much less will we, if we
turn away from him who
warns us from heaven? 26At
that time his voice shook
the earth, but now he has
promised, "Once more I
will shake not only the
earth but also the heav-
ens."[c] 27The words "once
more" indicate the remov-
ing of what can be shaken
—that is, created things—
so that what cannot be
shaken may remain.
28Therefore, since we are
receiving a kingdom that
cannot be shaken, let us be
thankful, and so worship
God acceptably with reverence and awe, 29for our
"God is a consuming
fire."[d]

[a]*20* Exodus 19:12,13
[b]*21* Deut. 9:19
[c]*26* Haggai 2:6
[d]*29* Deut. 4:24

Chapter 13

The Changeless Christ

LET love of the brethren continue.

2Do not neglect to show hospitality to strangers, for by this some have entertained angels without knowing it.

3Remember the prisoners, as though in prison with them, and those who are ill-treated, since you yourselves also are in the body.

4*Let* marriage *be held* in honor among all, and let the *marriage* bed *be* undefiled; for fornicators and adulterers God will judge.

5Let your character be free from the love of money, being content with what you have; for He Himself has said, "I WILL NEVER DESERT YOU, NOR WILL I EVER FORSAKE YOU,"

6so that we confidently say,

"THE LORD IS MY HELPER, I WILL NOT BE AFRAID.
WHAT SHALL MAN DO TO ME?"

7Remember those who led you, who spoke the word of God to you; and considering the result of their conduct, imitate their faith.

8Jesus Christ *is* the same yesterday and today, *yes* and forever.

9Do not be carried away by varied and strange teachings; for it is good for the heart to be strengthened by grace, not by foods, through which those who were thus occupied were not benefited.

10We have an altar, from which those who serve the tabernacle have no right to eat.

11For the bodies of those animals whose blood is brought into the holy place by the high priest *as an offering* for sin, are burned outside the camp.

12Therefore Jesus also, that He might sanctify the

13 Ἡ φιλαδελφία μενέτω. 2 τῆς
– [2]brotherly love [1]Let *it* [3]remain. –
φιλοξενίας μὴ ἐπιλανθάνεσθε· διὰ ταύτης
of hospitality Be ye not forgetful; [2]through [3]this
γὰρ ἔλαθόν τινες ξενίσαντες ἀγγέλους.
[1]for [5]unconsciously† [4]some [6]entertaining(ed) [7]angels.
3 μιμνήσκεσθε τῶν δεσμίων ὡς συνδεδεμένοι,
Be ye mindful of the prisoners as *having been* bound with [them],
τῶν κακουχουμένων ὡς καὶ αὐτοὶ ὄντες
of the [ones] *being* ill treated as also [your]selves being
ἐν σώματι. 4 Τίμιος ὁ γάμος ἐν πᾶσιν
in [the] body. [4]honourable – [2]marriage in all [1][Let] [3][be]
καὶ ἡ κοίτη ἀμίαντος· πόρνους γὰρ
and the bed undefiled; for fornicators
καὶ μοιχοὺς κρινεῖ ὁ θεός. 5 Ἀφιλάργυρος
and adulterers [2]will judge – [1]God. [5]without love of money
ὁ τρόπος, ἀρκούμενοι τοῖς παροῦσιν·
[1][Let] [2]the (your) [3]way of life [4][be], being satisfied with the things present;
αὐτὸς γὰρ εἴρηκεν· οὐ μή σε ἀνῶ οὐδʼ
for he has said: By no means thee will I leave nor
οὐ μή σε ἐγκαταλίπω· 6 ὥστε θαρροῦντας
by no(any) means thee I forsake; so as being of good cheer
ἡμᾶς λέγειν· κύριος ἐμοὶ βοηθός, οὐ
us to say[b]: [The] Lord to me[c] [is] a helper, not
φοβηθήσομαι· τί ποιήσει μοι ἄνθρωπος;
I will fear; what [1]will [3]do [4]to me [2]man ?
7 Μνημονεύετε τῶν ἡγουμένων ὑμῶν,
Remember the [ones] leading of you,
οἵτινες ἐλάλησαν ὑμῖν τὸν λόγον τοῦ
who spoke to you the word –
θεοῦ, ὧν ἀναθεωροῦντες τὴν ἔκβασιν τῆς
of God, [6]of whom [1]looking at [2]the [3]result [4]of the
ἀναστροφῆς μιμεῖσθε τὴν πίστιν. 8 Ἰησοῦς
[5]conduct imitate ye the(ir) faith. Jesus
Χριστὸς ἐχθὲς καὶ σήμερον ὁ αὐτὸς
Christ [4]yesterday [5]and [6]to-day [1][is] [2]the [3]same
καὶ εἰς τοὺς αἰῶνας. 9 Διδαχαῖς ποικίλαις
and unto the ages. [5]teachings [2]by various
καὶ ξέναις μὴ παραφέρεσθε· καλὸν γὰρ
[3]and [4]strange [1]Do not be carried away; for [it is] good
χάριτι βεβαιοῦσθαι τὴν καρδίαν, οὐ
[4]by grace [3]to be confirmed [1]the [2]heart,[b] not
βρώμασιν, ἐν οἷς οὐκ ὠφελήθησαν οἱ
by foods, by which [3]were not profited [1]the
περιπατοῦντες. 10 ἔχομεν θυσιαστήριον ἐξ
[2][ones] walking. We have an altar of
οὗ φαγεῖν οὐκ ἔχουσιν ἐξουσίαν οἱ τῇ
which [7]to eat [5]have not [6]authority [1]the [ones] [3]the
σκηνῇ λατρεύοντες. 11 ὧν γὰρ εἰσφέρεται
[4]tabernacle [2]serving. For [3]of what [7]is brought *in*
ζῴων τὸ αἷμα περὶ ἁμαρτίας εἰς τὰ
[4]animals [1]the [2]blood [5]concerning [6]sins into the
ἅγια διὰ τοῦ ἀρχιερέως, τούτων τὰ
holies through the high priest, of these the
σώματα κατακαίεται ἔξω τῆς παρεμβολῆς.
bodies is(are) burned outside the camp.
12 διὸ καὶ Ἰησοῦς, ἵνα ἁγιάσῃ διὰ
Wherefore indeed Jesus, in order that he might sanctify [3]through

Chapter 13

Concluding Exhortations

KEEP on loving each
other as brothers.
2Do not forget to entertain
strangers, for by so doing
some people have enter-
tained angels without
knowing it. 3Remember
those in prison as if you
were their fellow prisoners,
and those who are mistreated as if you yourselves
were suffering.
4Marriage should be hon-
ored by all, and the mar-
riage bed kept pure, for
God will judge the adulter-
er and all the sexually immoral. 5Keep your lives
free from the love of money
and be content with what
you have, because God has
said,

"Never will I leave you;
never will I forsake
you."[e]

6So we say with confi-
dence,

"The Lord is my helper;
I will not be afraid.
What can man do to
me?"[f]

7Remember your leaders,
who spoke the word of God
to you. Consider the out-
come of their way of life
and imitate their faith.
8Jesus Christ is the same
yesterday and today and
forever.
9Do not be carried away
by all kinds of strange
teachings. It is good for our
hearts to be strengthened
by grace, not by ceremonial foods, which are of no
value to those who eat
them. 10We have an altar
from which those who min-
ister at the tabernacle have
no right to eat.
11The high priest carries
the blood of animals into
the Most Holy Place as a
sin offering, but the bodies
are burned outside the
camp. 12And so Jesus also
suffered outside the city

[e]5 Deut. 31:6
[f]6 Psalm 118:6,7

people through His own
blood, suffered outside the
gate.
13 Hence, let us go out to
Him outside the camp,
bearing His reproach.
14 For here we do not have
a lasting city, but we are
seeking *the city* which is to
come.

God-pleasing Sacrifices

15 Through Him then, let
us continually offer up a
sacrifice of praise to God,
that is, the fruit of lips that
give thanks to His name.
16 And do not neglect do-
ing good and sharing; for
with such sacrifices God is
pleased.
17 Obey your leaders, and
submit *to them*; for they
keep watch over your
souls, as those who will
give an account. Let them
do this with joy and not
with grief, for this would be
unprofitable for you.
18 Pray for us, for we are
sure that we have a good
conscience, desiring to
conduct ourselves honor-
ably in all things.
19 And I urge *you* all the
more to do this, that I may
be restored to you the
sooner.

Benediction

20 Now the God of peace,
who brought up from the
dead the great Shepherd of
the sheep through the
blood of the eternal cov-
enant, *even* Jesus our
Lord,
21 equip you in every good
thing to do His will, working in us that which is pleasing in His sight, through
Jesus Christ, to whom *be*
the glory forever and ever.

τοῦ ἰδίου αἵματος τὸν λαόν, ἔξω τῆς
4the(his) 5own 6blood 1the 2people, outside the
πύλης ἔπαθεν. 13 τοίνυν ἐξερχώμεθα πρὸς
gate suffered. So let us go forth to
αὐτὸν ἔξω τῆς παρεμβολῆς τὸν ὀνειδισμὸν
him outside the camp the reproach
αὐτοῦ φέροντες· 14 οὐ γὰρ ἔχομεν ὧδε
of him bearing; for 2not 1we have here
μένουσαν πόλιν, ἀλλὰ τὴν μέλλουσαν
a continuing city, but the [one] coming
ἐπιζητοῦμεν. 15 Δι' αὐτοῦ οὖν ἀναφέρωμεν
we seek. Through him therefore let us offer up
θυσίαν αἰνέσεως διὰ παντὸς τῷ θεῷ,
a sacrifice of praise always – to God,
τοῦτ' ἔστιν καρπὸν χειλέων ὁμολογούντων
this is fruit of lips confessing
τῷ ὀνόματι αὐτοῦ. 16 τῆς δὲ εὐποιΐας
to the name of him. But of the doing good
καὶ κοινωνίας μὴ ἐπιλανθάνεσθε· τοιαύταις
and sharing be ye not forgetful; 2with such
γὰρ θυσίαις εὐαρεστεῖται ὁ θεός. 17 Πεί-
1for sacrifices 3is well pleased – 1God. Obey
θεσθε τοῖς ἡγουμένοις ὑμῶν καὶ ὑπείκετε·
ye the [ones] leading of you and submit to [them];
αὐτοὶ γὰρ ἀγρυπνοῦσιν ὑπὲρ τῶν ψυχῶν
for they watch on behalf of the souls
ὑμῶν ὡς λόγον ἀποδώσοντες· ἵνα μετὰ
of you as 2account 1rendering*; in order that with
χαρᾶς τοῦτο ποιῶσιν καὶ μὴ στενάζ-
joy 2this 1they may do and not groan-
οντες· ἀλυσιτελὲς γὰρ ὑμῖν τοῦτο.
ing; for profitless to you this [would be].
18 Προσεύχεσθε περὶ ἡμῶν· πειθόμεθα
Pray ye concerning us; 2we are persuaded
γὰρ ὅτι καλὴν συνείδησιν ἔχομεν, ἐν
1for that a good conscience we have, 4in
πᾶσιν καλῶς θέλοντες ἀναστρέφεσθαι.
5all [respects] 3well 1wishing 2to behave.
19 περισσοτέρως δὲ παρακαλῶ τοῦτο
And more abundantly I beseech [you] this
ποιῆσαι, ἵνα τάχιον ἀποκατασταθῶ ὑμῖν.
to do, in order that sooner I may be restored to you.
20 Ὁ δὲ θεὸς τῆς εἰρήνης, ὁ ἀναγαγὼν
Now the God – of peace, the having led up [one]
ἐκ νεκρῶν τὸν ποιμένα τῶν προβάτων
out of [the] dead the 2shepherd 3of the 4sheep
τὸν μέγαν ἐν αἵματι διαθήκης αἰωνίου,
the 1great in (? with) blood 2covenant 1of an eternal,
τὸν κύριον ἡμῶν Ἰησοῦν, 21 καταρτίσαι
the Lord of us Jesus, *may he* adjust
ὑμᾶς ἐν παντὶ ἀγαθῷ εἰς τὸ ποιῆσαι
you in every good thing *for the* to do
τὸ θέλημα αὐτοῦ, ποιῶν ἐν ἡμῖν τὸ
the will of him, doing in us the [thing]
εὐάρεστον ἐνώπιον αὐτοῦ διὰ Ἰησοῦ
wellpleasing before him through Jesus
Χριστοῦ, ᾧ ἡ δόξα εἰς τοὺς αἰῶνας
Christ, to whom [be] the glory unto the ages

* In the future.

gate to make the people
holy through his own
blood. 13 Let us, then, go to
him outside the camp,
bearing the disgrace he
bore. 14 For here we do not
have an enduring city, but
we are looking for the city
that is to come.
15 Through Jesus, there-
fore, let us continually offer to God a sacrifice of
praise—the fruit of lips that
confess his name. 16 And do
not forget to do good and to
share with others, for with
such sacrifices God is
pleased.
17 Obey your leaders and
submit to their authority.
They keep watch over you
as men who must give an
account. Obey them so that
their work will be a joy, not
a burden, for that would be
of no advantage to you.
18 Pray for us. We are sure
that we have a clear con-
science and desire to live
honorably in every way. 19 I
particularly urge you to
pray so that I may be re-
stored to you soon.
20 May the God of peace,
who through the blood of
the eternal covenant
brought back from the dead
our Lord Jesus, that great
Shepherd of the sheep,
21 equip you with every-
thing good for doing his
will, and may he work in us
what is pleasing to him,
through Jesus Christ, to
whom be glory for ever and

Amen.
22But I urge you, brethren, bear with this word of exhortation, for I have written to you briefly.
23Take notice that our brother Timothy has been released, with whom, if he comes soon, I shall see you.
24Greet all of your leaders and all the saints. Those from Italy greet you.
25Grace be with you all.

τῶν αἰώνων· ἀμήν. 22 Παρακαλῶ δὲ
of the ages: Amen. And I beseech
ὑμᾶς, ἀδελφοί, ἀνέχεσθε τοῦ λόγου τῆς
you, brothers, endure the word –
παρακλήσεως· καὶ γὰρ διὰ βραχέων
of beseeching; for indeed through few [words]
ἐπέστειλα ὑμῖν. 23 Γινώσκετε τὸν ἀδελφὸν
I wrote to you. Know ye the brother
ἡμῶν Τιμόθεον ἀπολελυμένον, μεθ' οὗ
of us Timothy having been released, with whom
ἐὰν τάχιον ἔρχηται ὄψομαι ὑμᾶς.
if sooner I come I will see you.
24 Ἀσπάσασθε πάντας τοὺς ἡγουμένους
Greet ye all the [ones] leading
ὑμῶν καὶ πάντας τοὺς ἁγίους. Ἀσπάζονται
of you and all the saints. 4greet
ὑμᾶς οἱ ἀπὸ τῆς Ἰταλίας.
5you 1The [ones] 2from – 3Italy.
25 Ἡ χάρις μετὰ πάντων ὑμῶν.
– Grace [be] with all you.

ever. Amen.
22Brothers, I urge you to bear with my word of exhortation, for I have written you only a short letter.
23I want you to know that our brother Timothy has been released. If he arrives soon, I will come with him to see you.
24Greet all your leaders and all God's people. Those from Italy send you their greetings.
25Grace be with you all.

James

Chapter 1

Testing Your Faith

JAMES, a bond-servant of God and of the Lord Jesus Christ, to the twelve tribes who are dispersed abroad, greetings.
2Consider it all joy, my brethren, when you encounter various trials,
3knowing that the testing of your faith produces endurance.
4And let endurance have *its* perfect result, that you may be perfect and complete, lacking in nothing.
5But if any of you lacks wisdom, let him ask of God, who gives to all men generously and without reproach, and it will be given to him.
6But let him ask in faith without any doubting, for the one who doubts is like the surf of the sea driven and tossed by the wind.
7For let not that man expect that he will receive anything from the Lord,

ΙΑΚΩΒΟΥ ΕΠΙΣΤΟΛΗ

2Of James 1Epistle

1 Ἰάκωβος θεοῦ καὶ κυρίου Ἰησοῦ
James 2of God 3and 4of [the] Lord 5Jesus
Χριστοῦ δοῦλος ταῖς δώδεκα φυλαῖς ταῖς
6Christ 1a slave to the twelve tribes –
ἐν τῇ διασπορᾷ χαίρειν.
in the dispersion greeting.*
2 Πᾶσαν χαρὰν ἡγήσασθε, ἀδελφοί μου,
All joy deem [it], brothers of me,
ὅταν πειρασμοῖς περιπέσητε ποικίλοις,
whenever 3trials 1ye fall 2into various,
3 γινώσκοντες ὅτι τὸ δοκίμιον ὑμῶν τῆς
knowing that the approved part 3of you 1of the
=that which is approved in your faith
πίστεως κατεργάζεται ὑπομονήν. 4 ἡ δὲ
2faith works endurance. – And
ὑπομονὴ ἔργον τέλειον ἐχέτω, ἵνα ἦτε
endurance 3work 2perfect 1let it have, in order that ye may be
τέλειοι καὶ ὁλόκληροι, ἐν μηδενὶ λειπόμενοι.
perfect and entire, in nothing wanting.
5 Εἰ δέ τις ὑμῶν λείπεται σοφίας, αἰτείτω
if But anyone of you wants wisdom, let him ask
παρὰ τοῦ διδόντος θεοῦ πᾶσιν ἁπλῶς
from 2the [one] 3giving 1God to all men unreservedly
καὶ μὴ ὀνειδίζοντος, καὶ δοθήσεται αὐτῷ.
and not reproaching, and it will be given to him.
6 αἰτείτω δὲ ἐν πίστει, μηδὲν διακριν-
But let him ask in faith, nothing doubt-
όμενος· ὁ γὰρ διακρινόμενος ἔοικεν κλύδωνι
ing; for the [one] doubting is like a wave
θαλάσσης ἀνεμιζομένῳ καὶ ῥιπιζομένῳ.
of [the] sea *being* driven by wind and *being* tossed.
7 μὴ γὰρ οἰέσθω ὁ ἄνθρωπος ἐκεῖνος
For let not 3suppose 1that 2man
ὅτι λήμψεταί τι παρὰ τοῦ κυρίου, 8 ἀνὴρ
that he will receive anything from the Lord, a man

* See note on Phil. 3.16 in Introduction.

James

Chapter 1

JAMES, a servant of God and of the Lord Jesus Christ,

To the twelve tribes scattered among the nations:

Greetings.

Trials and Temptations

2Consider it pure joy, my
brothers, whenever you
face trials of many kinds,
3because you know that the
testing of your faith devel-
ops perseverance. 4Perse-
verance must finish its
work so that you may be
mature and complete, not
lacking anything. 5If any of
you lacks wisdom, he
should ask God, who gives
generously to all without
finding fault, and it will be
given to him. 6But when he
asks, he must believe and
not doubt, because he who
doubts is like a wave of the
sea, blown and tossed by
the wind. 7That man should
not think he will receive
anything from the Lord;

8 *being* a double-minded
man, unstable in all his
ways.
9 But let the brother of
humble circumstances
glory in his high position;
10 and *let* the rich man
glory in his humiliation, because like flowering grass
he will pass away.
11 For the sun rises with a
scorching wind, and with-
ers the grass; and its flower
falls off, and the beauty of
its appearance is de-
stroyed; so too the rich man
in the midst of his pursuits
will fade away.
12 Blessed is a man who
perseveres under trial; for
once he has been ap-
proved, he will receive the
crown of life, which *the*
Lord has promised to those
who love Him.
13 Let no one say when he
is tempted, "I am being
tempted by God"; for God
cannot be tempted by evil,
and He Himself does not
tempt anyone.
14 But each one is tempted
when he is carried away
and enticed by his own lust.
15 Then when lust has conceived, it gives birth to sin;
and when sin is accom-
plished, it brings forth
death.
16 Do not be deceived, my
beloved brethren.
17 Every good thing be-
stowed and every perfect
gift is from above, coming
down from the Father of
lights, with whom there is
no variation, or shifting
shadow.
18 In the exercise of His
will He brought us forth by
the word of truth, so that
we might be, as it were, the
first fruits among His creatures.
19 [a]*This* you know, my beloved brethren. But let

[a] Or, *Know* this

δίψυχος, ἀκατάστατος ἐν πάσαις ταῖς
two-souled, unsettled in all the
ὁδοῖς αὐτοῦ. 9 Καυχάσθω δὲ ὁ ἀδελφὸς
ways of him. But let [4]boast [1]the [3]brother
ὁ ταπεινὸς ἐν τῷ ὕψει αὐτοῦ, 10 ὁ δὲ
– [2]humble in the height of him, and the
πλούσιος ἐν τῇ ταπεινώσει αὐτοῦ, ὅτι
rich one in the humiliation of him, because
ὡς ἄνθος χόρτου παρελεύσεται. 11 ἀνέτειλεν
as a flower of grass he will pass away. [4]rose
γὰρ ὁ ἥλιος σὺν τῷ καύσωνι καὶ ἐξήρανεν
[1]For [2]the [3]sun with the hot wind and dried
τὸν χόρτον, καὶ τὸ ἄνθος αὐτοῦ ἐξέπεσεν
the grass, and the flower of it fell out
καὶ ἡ εὐπρέπεια τοῦ προσώπου αὐτοῦ
and the comeliness of the appearance of it
ἀπώλετο· οὕτως καὶ ὁ πλούσιος ἐν ταῖς
perished; thus also the rich man in the
πορείαις αὐτοῦ μαρανθήσεται. 12 Μακάριος
goings of him will fade away. Blessed
ἀνὴρ ὃς ὑπομένει πειρασμόν, ὅτι δόκιμος
[the] man who endures trial, because [2]approved
γενόμενος λήμψεται τὸν στέφανον τῆς
[1]having become he will receive the crown –
ζωῆς, ὃν ἐπηγγείλατο τοῖς ἀγαπῶσιν αὐτόν.
of life, which he promised to the [ones] loving him.
13 Μηδεὶς πειραζόμενος λεγέτω ὅτι ἀπὸ
[2]no man [3]being tempted [1]Let [4]say[,] – From
θεοῦ πειράζομαι· ὁ γὰρ θεὸς ἀπείραστός
God I am tempted; – for God [2]untempted
ἐστιν κακῶν, πειράζει δὲ αὐτὸς οὐδένα.
[1]is of(with) evil things, and [2]tempts [1]he no man.
14 ἕκαστος δὲ πειράζεται ὑπὸ τῆς ἰδίας
But each man is tempted by the(his) own
ἐπιθυμίας ἐξελκόμενος καὶ δελεαζόμενος·
lusts being drawn out and *being* enticed;
15 εἶτα ἡ ἐπιθυμία συλλαβοῦσα τίκτει
then – lust having conceived bears
ἁμαρτίαν, ἡ δὲ ἁμαρτία ἀποτελεσθεῖσα
sin, – and sin having been fully formed
ἀποκύει θάνατον. 16 Μὴ πλανᾶσθε, ἀδελφοί
brings forth death. Do not err, [2]brothers
μου ἀγαπητοί.
[3]of me [1]beloved.
17 Πᾶσα δόσις ἀγαθὴ καὶ πᾶν δώρημα
Every [2]giving [1]good and every [2]gift
τέλειον ἄνωθέν ἐστιν καταβαῖνον ἀπὸ τοῦ
[1]perfect [4]from above [3]is coming down from the
πατρὸς τῶν φώτων, παρ' ᾧ οὐκ ἔνι
Father of the lights, with whom [5]has no place
παραλλαγὴ ἢ τροπῆς ἀποσκίασμα. 18 βου-
[1]change [2]or [4]of turning [3]shadow. Having
ληθεὶς ἀπεκύησεν ἡμᾶς λόγῳ ἀληθείας,
purposed he brought forth us by a word of truth,
εἰς τὸ εἶναι ἡμᾶς ἀπαρχήν τινα τῶν
for the to be =that we should be us[b] [2]firstfruit [1]a certain [3]of the
αὐτοῦ κτισμάτων.
[5]of him [4]creatures.
19 Ἴστε, ἀδελφοί μου ἀγαπητοί. ἔστω
Know ye, [2]brothers [3]of me [1]beloved. [2]let be

8 he is a double-minded
man, unstable in all he
does.
9 The brother in humble
circumstances ought to
take pride in his high position. 10 But the one who is
rich should take pride in his
low position, because he
will pass away like a wild
flower. 11 For the sun rises
with scorching heat and
withers the plant; its blos-
som falls and its beauty is
destroyed. In the same
way, the rich man will fade
away even while he goes
about his business.
12 Blessed is the man who
perseveres under trial, because when he has stood
the test, he will receive the
crown of life that God has
promised to those who love
him.
13 When tempted, no one
should say, "God is tempting me." For God cannot
be tempted by evil, nor
does he tempt anyone;
14 but each one is tempted
when, by his own evil de-
sire, he is dragged away
and enticed. 15 Then, after
desire has conceived, it
gives birth to sin; and sin,
when it is full-grown, gives
birth to death.
16 Don't be deceived, my
dear brothers. 17 Every
good and perfect gift is
from above, coming down
from the Father of the
heavenly lights, who does
not change like shifting
shadows. 18 He chose to
give us birth through the
word of truth, that we
might be a kind of firstfruits
of all he created.

Listening and Doing

19 My dear brothers, take
note of this: Everyone

everyone be quick to hear,
slow to speak *and* slow to
anger;
20 for the anger of man
does not achieve the righteousness of God.
21 Therefore putting aside
all filthiness and *all* that remains of wickedness, in
humility receive the word
implanted, which is able to
save your souls.
22 But prove yourselves
doers of the word, and not
merely hearers who delude
themselves.
23 For if anyone is a hearer
of the word and not a doer,
he is like a man who looks
at his natural face in a mirror;
24 for *once* he has looked
at himself and gone away,
he has immediately forgotten what kind of person he
was.
25 But one who looks in-
tently at the perfect law,
the *law* of liberty, and
abides by it, not having
become a forgetful hearer
but an effectual doer, this
man shall be blessed in
what he does.
26 If anyone thinks himself
to be religious, and yet
does not bridle his tongue
but deceives his *own* heart,
this man's religion is
worthless.
27 This is pure and un-
defiled religion in the sight
of *our* God and Father, to
visit orphans and widows
in their distress, *and* to
keep oneself unstained by
the world.

δὲ πᾶς ἄνθρωπος ταχὺς εἰς τὸ ἀκοῦσαι,
[1]But every man swift *for the* to hear,

βραδὺς εἰς τὸ λαλῆσαι, βραδὺς εἰς ὀργήν·
slow *for the* to speak, slow to wrath;

20 ὀργὴ γὰρ ἀνδρὸς δικαιοσύνην θεοῦ
for [the] wrath of a man [2][the] righteousness [3]of God

οὐκ ἐργάζεται. **21** διὸ ἀποθέμενοι πᾶσαν
[1]works not. Wherefore putting away all

ῥυπαρίαν καὶ περισσείαν κακίας ἐν πραΰ-
filthiness and superfluity of evil in meek-

τητι δέξασθε τὸν ἔμφυτον λόγον τὸν
ness receive ye the implanted word –

δυνάμενον σῶσαι τὰς ψυχὰς ὑμῶν. **22** γίν-
being able to save the souls of you. be-

εσθε δὲ ποιηταὶ λόγου, καὶ μὴ ἀκροαταὶ
come ye And doers of [the] word, and not hearers

μόνον παραλογιζόμενοι ἑαυτούς. **23** ὅτι
only misleading yourselves. Because

εἴ τις ἀκροατὴς λόγου ἐστὶν καὶ οὐ
if anyone [2]a hearer [3]of [the] word [1]is and not

ποιητής, οὗτος ἔοικεν ἀνδρὶ κατανοοῦντι
a doer, this one is like a man perceiving

τὸ πρόσωπον τῆς γενέσεως αὐτοῦ ἐν
the face of the birth of him in

ἐσόπτρῳ· **24** κατενόησεν γὰρ ἑαυτὸν καὶ
a mirror; for he perceived himself and

ἀπελήλυθεν, καὶ εὐθέως ἐπελάθετο ὁποῖος
has gone away, and straightway forgot what sort

ἦν. **25** ὁ δὲ παρακύψας εἰς νόμον
he was. But the [one] having looked *into* into [2]law

τέλειον τὸν τῆς ἐλευθερίας καὶ παραμείνας,
[3]perfect [1]the – of freedom and remaining,

οὐκ ἀκροατὴς ἐπιλησμονῆς γενόμενος ἀλλὰ
not [2]a hearer [3]of forgetfulness* [1]becoming but

ποιητὴς ἔργου, οὗτος μακάριος ἐν τῇ
a doer of [the] work, this one [2]blessed [3]in [4]the

ποιήσει αὐτοῦ ἔσται. **26** Εἴ τις δοκεῖ
[5]doing [6]of him [1]will be. If anyone thinks

θρησκὸς εἶναι, μὴ χαλιναγωγῶν γλῶσσαν
[2]religious [1]to be, not bridling tongue

ἑαυτοῦ ἀλλὰ ἀπατῶν καρδίαν ἑαυτοῦ,
of himself but deceiving heart of himself,

τούτου μάταιος ἡ θρησκεία. **27** θρησκεία
of this one vain the religion. Religion

καθαρὰ καὶ ἀμίαντος παρὰ τῷ θεῷ
clean and undefiled before the God

καὶ πατρὶ αὕτη ἐστίν, ἐπισκέπτεσθαι
and Father [2]this [1]is, to visit

ὀρφανοὺς καὶ χήρας ἐν τῇ θλίψει αὐτῶν,
orphans and widows in the affliction of them,

ἄσπιλον ἑαυτὸν τηρεῖν ἀπὸ τοῦ κόσμου.
unspotted himself to keep from the world.

should be quick to listen,
slow to speak and slow to
become angry, 20 for man's
anger does not bring about
the righteous life that God
desires. 21 Therefore, get
rid of all moral filth and the
evil that is so prevalent and
humbly accept the word
planted in you, which can
save you.
22 Do not merely listen to
the word, and so deceive
yourselves. Do what it
says. 23 Anyone who listens
to the word but does not do
what it says is like a man
who looks at his face in a
mirror 24 and, after looking
at himself, goes away and
immediately forgets what
he looks like. 25 But the man
who looks intently into the
perfect law that gives freedom, and continues to do
this, not forgetting what he
has heard, but doing it—he
will be blessed in what he
does.
26 If anyone considers
himself religious and yet
does not keep a tight rein
on his tongue, he deceives
himself and his religion is
worthless. 27 Religion that
God our Father accepts as
pure and faultless is this: to
look after orphans and widows in their distress and to
keep oneself from being
polluted by the world.

Chapter 2

The Sin of Partiality

MY brethren, do not
hold your faith in our
glorious Lord Jesus Christ
with *an attitude of* personal
favoritism.
2 For if a man comes into
your assembly with a gold

2 Ἀδελφοί μου, μὴ ἐν προσωπολημψίαις
Brothers of me, not in respects of persons

ἔχετε τὴν πίστιν τοῦ κυρίου ἡμῶν Ἰησοῦ
have ye the faith of the Lord of us Jesus

Χριστοῦ τῆς δόξης. **2** ἐὰν γὰρ εἰσέλθῃ
Christ[,] *of* the glory.* For if [there] enters

εἰς συναγωγὴν ὑμῶν ἀνὴρ χρυσοδακτύλιος
into a synagogue of you a man gold-fingered

Chapter 2

Favoritism Forbidden

MY brothers, as believ-
ers in our glorious
Lord Jesus Christ, don't
show favoritism. 2 Suppose
a man comes into your
meeting wearing a gold ring

* Genitive of quality: "a forgetful hearer."

* That is, taking "the glory" as in apposition to "Jesus Christ"; see Luke 2. 32*b*.

[b] Or, *there is one God*

ring and dressed in fine
clothes, and there also
comes in a poor man in
dirty clothes,
3 and you pay special at-
tention to the one who is
wearing the fine clothes,
and say, "You sit here in a
good place," and you say
to the poor man, "You
stand over there, or sit
down by my footstool,"
4 have you not made dis-
tinctions among your-
selves, and become judges
with evil motives?
5 Listen, my beloved
brethren: did not God
choose the poor of this
world *to be* rich in faith and
heirs of the kingdom which
He promised to those who
love Him?
6 But you have dishon-
ored the poor man. Is it not
the rich who oppress you
and personally drag you
into court?
7 Do they not blaspheme
the fair name by which you
have been called?
8 If, however, you are
fulfilling the royal law, according to the Scripture,
"YOU SHALL LOVE YOUR
NEIGHBOR AS YOURSELF,"
you are doing well.
9 But if you show partiality, you are committing sin
and are convicted by the
law as transgressors.
10 For whoever keeps the
whole law and yet stumbles
in one *point,* he has become
guilty of all.
11 For He who said, "DO
NOT COMMIT ADULTERY,"
also said, "DO NOT COMMIT
MURDER." Now if you do
not commit adultery, but
do commit murder, you
have become a transgres-
sor of the law.
12 So speak and so act, as
those who are to be judged
by *the* law of liberty.
13 For judgment *will be*
merciless to one who has
shown no mercy; mercy triumphs over judgment.

Faith and Works

14 What use is it, my

ἐν ἐσθῆτι λαμπρᾷ, εἰσέλθῃ δὲ καὶ πτωχὸς
in [2]clothing [1]splendid, and [there] enters also a poor man
ἐν ῥυπαρᾷ ἐσθῆτι, 3 ἐπιβλέψητε δὲ ἐπὶ
in shabby clothing, and ye look *on* on
τὸν φοροῦντα τὴν ἐσθῆτα τὴν λαμπρὰν
the [one] wearing the clothing – splendid
καὶ εἴπητε· σὺ κάθου ὧδε καλῶς, καὶ
and say: [2]thou [1]Sit here well, and
τῷ πτωχῷ εἴπητε· σὺ στῆθι ἐκεῖ ἢ
to the poor man ye say: [2]thou [1]Stand there or
κάθου ὑπὸ τὸ ὑποπόδιόν μου, 4 οὐ
sit under the footstool of me, not
διεκρίθητε ἐν ἑαυτοῖς καὶ ἐγένεσθε κριταὶ
did ye discriminate among yourselves and became judges
διαλογισμῶν πονηρῶν; 5 Ἀκούσατε, ἀδελφοί
[2]thoughts [1]of evil ?§ Hear ye, brothers
μου ἀγαπητοί. οὐχ ὁ θεὸς ἐξελέξατο
of me beloved. [2]not – [3]God [1]Chose
τοὺς πτωχοὺς τῷ κόσμῳ πλουσίους ἐν
the poor in the world rich in
πίστει καὶ κληρονόμους τῆς βασιλείας
faith and heirs of the kingdom
ἧς ἐπηγγείλατο τοῖς ἀγαπῶσιν αὐτόν;
which he promised to the [ones] loving him?
6 ὑμεῖς δὲ ἠτιμάσατε τὸν πτωχόν. οὐχ
But ye dishonoured the poor man. [Do] not
οἱ πλούσιοι καταδυναστεύουσιν ὑμῶν, καὶ
the rich men oppress you, and
αὐτοὶ ἕλκουσιν ὑμᾶς εἰς κριτήρια; 7 οὐκ
they drag you to tribunals ? [Do] not
αὐτοὶ βλασφημοῦσιν τὸ καλὸν ὄνομα τὸ
they blaspheme the good name –
ἐπικληθὲν ἐφ' ὑμᾶς; 8 εἰ μέντοι νόμον
called *on* on you ? If indeed [3]law
τελεῖτε βασιλικὸν κατὰ τὴν γραφήν·
[1]ye fulfil [2]a royal according to the scripture:
ἀγαπήσεις τὸν πλησίον σου ὡς σεαυτόν,
Thou shalt love the neighbour of thee as thyself,
καλῶς ποιεῖτε· 9 εἰ δὲ προσωποληπτεῖτε,
[2]well [1]ye do; but if ye respect persons,
ἁμαρτίαν ἐργάζεσθε, ἐλεγχόμενοι ὑπὸ τοῦ
[2]sin [1]ye work, being reproved by the
νόμου ὡς παραβάται. 10 ὅστις γὰρ
law as transgressors. For [1][he] who
ὅλον τὸν νόμον τηρήσῃ, πταίσῃ δὲ ἐν
[3]all [4]the [5]law [2]keeps, yet stumbles in
ἑνί, γέγονεν πάντων ἔνοχος. 11 ὁ γὰρ
one thing, he has become [2]of all [1]guilty. For the [one]
εἰπών· μὴ μοιχεύσῃς, εἶπεν καί· μή
saying: Do not commit adultery, said also: not
φονεύσῃς· εἰ δὲ οὐ μοιχεύεις, φονεύεις
Do murder; now if thou dost not commit adultery, [2]murderest
δέ, γέγονας παραβάτης νόμου. 12 οὕτως
[1]but, thou hast become a transgressor of [the] law. So
λαλεῖτε καὶ οὕτως ποιεῖτε ὡς διὰ νόμου
speak ye and so do ye as [3]through [4]a law
ἐλευθερίας μέλλοντες κρίνεσθαι. 13 ἡ γὰρ
[5]of freedom [1]being about [2]to be judged. For the
κρίσις ἀνέλεος τῷ μὴ ποιήσαντι ἔλεος·
judgment [will be] unmerciful to the [one] not do(show)ing mercy;
κατακαυχᾶται ἔλεος κρίσεως. 14 Τί τὸ
[2]exults over [1]mercy *of* judgment. What [is] the

§ Genitive of quality: "evil-thinking judges."

and fine clothes, and a poor
man in shabby clothes also
comes in. 3 If you show special attention to the man
wearing fine clothes and
say, "Here's a good seat
for you," but say to the
poor man, "You stand
there" or "Sit on the floor
by my feet," 4 have you not
discriminated among your-
selves and become judges
with evil thoughts?
5 Listen, my dear broth-
ers: Has not God chosen
those who are poor in the
eyes of the world to be rich
in faith and to inherit the
kingdom he promised those
who love him? 6 But you
have insulted the poor. Is it
not the rich who are ex-
ploiting you? Are they not
the ones who are dragging
you into court? 7 Are they
not the ones who are slan-
dering the noble name of
him to whom you belong?
8 If you really keep the
royal law found in Scrip-
ture, "Love your neighbor
as yourself,"[a] you are doing right. 9 But if you show
favoritism, you sin and are
convicted by the law as
lawbreakers. 10 For whoever keeps the whole law and
yet stumbles at just one
point is guilty of breaking
all of it. 11 For he who said,
"Do not commit adul-
tery,"[b] also said, "Do not
murder."[c] If you do not
commit adultery but do
commit murder, you have
become a lawbreaker.
12 Speak and act as those
who are going to be judged
by the law that gives freedom, 13 because judgment
without mercy will be
shown to anyone who has
not been merciful. Mercy
triumphs over judgment!

Faith and Deeds

14 What good is it, my

[a] *8* Lev. 19:18
[b] *11* Exodus 20:14; Deut. 5:18
[c] *11* Exodus 20:13; Deut. 5:17

brethren, if a man says he has faith, but he has no works? Can that faith save him?

15If a brother or sister is without clothing and in need of daily food,

16and one of you says to them, "Go in peace, be warmed and be filled," and yet you do not give them what is necessary for *their* body, what use is that?

17Even so faith, if it has no works, is dead, *being* by itself.

18But someone may *well* say, "You have faith, and I have works; show me your faith without the works, and I will show you my faith by my works."

19You believe that [b]God is one. You do well; the demons also believe, and shudder.

20But are you willing to recognize, you foolish fellow, that faith without works is useless?

21Was not Abraham our father justified by works, when he offered up Isaac his son on the altar?

22You see that faith was working with his works, and as a result of the works, faith was perfected;

23and the Scripture was fulfilled which says, "AND ABRAHAM BELIEVED GOD, AND IT WAS RECKONED TO HIM AS RIGHTEOUSNESS," and he was called the friend of God.

24You see that a man is justified by works, and not by faith alone.

25And in the same way was not Rahab the harlot also justified by works, when she received the messengers and sent them out

ὄφελος, ἀδελφοί μου, ἐὰν πίστιν λέγῃ
profit, brothers of me, if [4]faith [2]says
τις ἔχειν ἔργα δὲ μὴ ἔχῃ; μὴ δύναται
[1]any-one [3]to have [8]works [5]but [7]not [6]has? *not* can
ἡ πίστις σῶσαι αὐτόν; 15 ἐὰν ἀδελφὸς
the faith *to* save him? If a brother
ἢ ἀδελφὴ γυμνοὶ ὑπάρχωσιν καὶ λειπόμενοι
or a sister [2]naked [1]are and lacking
τῆς ἐφημέρου τροφῆς, 16 εἴπῃ δέ τις
of the daily food, and [4]says [1]any-one
αὐτοῖς ἐξ ὑμῶν· ὑπάγετε ἐν εἰρήνῃ,
[5]to them [2]of [3]you: Go ye in peace,
θερμαίνεσθε καὶ χορτάζεσθε, μὴ δῶτε
be warmed and filled, [4]not [2]ye give
δὲ αὐτοῖς τὰ ἐπιτήδεια τοῦ σώματος,
[1]but [3]them the necessaries of the body,
τί τὸ ὄφελος; 17 οὕτως καὶ ἡ πίστις,
what [is] the profit? So indeed – faith,
ἐὰν μὴ ἔχῃ ἔργα, νεκρά ἐστιν καθ'
if it has not works, [2]dead [1]is by
ἑαυτήν. 18 ἀλλ' ἐρεῖ τις· σὺ πίστιν
itself. But [2]will say [1]someone: Thou [2]faith
ἔχεις, κἀγὼ ἔργα ἔχω· δεῖξόν μοι τὴν
[1]hast, and I [2]works [1]have; show me the
πίστιν σου χωρὶς τῶν ἔργων, κἀγώ
faith of thee without the works, and I
σοι δείξω ἐκ τῶν ἔργων μου τὴν πίστιν.
thee will show [4]by [5]the [6]works [3]of me [1]the [2]faith.
19 σὺ πιστεύεις ὅτι εἷς ἐστιν ὁ θεός;
Thou believest that [3]one [2]is – [1]God?
καλῶς ποιεῖς· καὶ τὰ δαιμόνια πιστεύουσιν
[2]well [1]thou doest; also the demons believe
καὶ φρίσσουσιν. 20 θέλεις δὲ γνῶναι,
and shudder. But art thou willing to know,
ὦ ἄνθρωπε κενέ, ὅτι ἡ πίστις χωρὶς
O [2]man [1]vain, that – faith without
τῶν ἔργων ἀργή ἐστιν; 21 Ἀβραὰμ ὁ
– works barren is? Abraham the
πατὴρ ἡμῶν οὐκ ἐξ ἔργων ἐδικαιώθη,
father of us not by works was justified,
ἀνενέγκας Ἰσαὰκ τὸν υἱὸν αὐτοῦ ἐπὶ
offering up Isaac the son of him on
τὸ θυσιαστήριον; 22 βλέπεις ὅτι ἡ πίστις
the altar? Thou seest that – faith
συνήργει τοῖς ἔργοις αὐτοῦ, καὶ ἐκ
worked with the works of him, and by
τῶν ἔργων ἡ πίστις ἐτελειώθη, 23 καὶ
the works the faith was perfected, and
ἐπληρώθη ἡ γραφὴ ἡ λέγουσα· ἐπίστευσεν
was fulfilled the scripture – saying: believed
δὲ Ἀβραὰμ τῷ θεῷ, καὶ ἐλογίσθη αὐτῷ
And Abraham – God, and it was reckoned to him
εἰς δικαιοσύνην, καὶ φίλος θεοῦ ἐκλήθη.
for righteousness, and [3]friend [2]of God [1]he was called.
24 ὁρᾶτε ὅτι ἐξ ἔργων δικαιοῦται ἄνθρωπος
Ye see that by works [2]is justified [1]a man
καὶ οὐκ ἐκ πίστεως μόνον. 25 ὁμοίως
and not by faith only. likewise
δὲ καὶ Ῥαὰβ ἡ πόρνη οὐκ ἐξ ἔργων
And also Rahab the prostitute not by works
ἐδικαιώθη, ὑποδεξαμένη τοὺς ἀγγέλους καὶ
was justified, entertaining the messengers and

brothers, if a man claims to
have faith but has no
deeds? Can such faith save
him? 15Suppose a brother
or sister is without clothes
and daily food. 16If one of
you says to him, "Go, I
wish you well; keep warm
and well fed," but does
nothing about his physical
needs, what good is it? 17In
the same way, faith by itself, if it is not accompanied by action, is dead.
18But someone will say,
"You have faith; I have
deeds."
Show me your faith with-
out deeds, and I will show
you my faith by what I do.
19You believe that there is
one God. Good! Even the
demons believe that—and
shudder.
20You foolish man, do
you want evidence that
faith without deeds is useless[d]? 21Was not our ances-
tor Abraham considered
righteous for what he did
when he offered his son
Isaac on the altar? 22You
see that his faith and his actions were working together, and his faith was made
complete by what he did.
23And the scripture was fulfilled that says, "Abraham
believed God, and it was
credited to him as right-
eousness,"[e] and he was
called God's friend. 24You
see that a person is justified
by what he does and not by
faith alone.
25In the same way, was
not even Rahab the prostitute considered righteous
for what she did when she
gave lodging to the spies
and sent them off in a dif-

[d]20 Some early manuscripts *dead*
[e]23 Gen. 15:6

by another way?
26For just as the body
without *the* spirit is dead,
so also faith without works
is dead.

Chapter 3

The Tongue Is a Fire

LET not many *of you*
become teachers, my
brethren, knowing that as
such we shall incur a strict-
er judgment.
2For we all stumble in
many *ways*. If anyone does
not stumble in what he
says, he is a perfect man,
able to bridle the whole
body as well.
3Now if we put the bits
into the horses' mouths so
that they may obey us, we
direct their entire body as
well.
4Behold, the ships also,
though they are so great
and are driven by strong
winds, are still directed by
a very small rudder,
wherever the inclination of
the pilot desires.
5So also the tongue is a
small part of the body, and
yet it boasts of great things.
Behold, how great a forest
is set aflame by such a
small fire!
6And the tongue is a fire,
the *very* world of iniquity;
the tongue is set among our
members as that which
defiles the entire body, and
sets on fire the course of
our life, and is set on fire by
hell.
7For every species of
beasts and birds, of reptiles
and creatures of the sea, is
tamed, and has been tamed
by the human race.
8But no one can tame the
tongue; *it is* a restless evil
and full of deadly poison.
9With it we bless *our*
Lord and Father; and with
it we curse men, who have
been made in the likeness
of God;

ἑτέρᾳ ὁδῷ ἐκβαλοῦσα; 26 ὥσπερ γὰρ τὸ
by a different way sending [them] forth ? For as the
σῶμα χωρὶς πνεύματος νεκρόν ἐστιν, οὕτως
body without spirit [2]dead [1]is, so
καὶ ἡ πίστις χωρὶς ἔργων νεκρά ἐστιν.
also – faith without works [2]dead [1]is.

3 Μὴ πολλοὶ διδάσκαλοι γίνεσθε, ἀδελφοί
[2]not [3]many [4]teachers [1]Become ye, brothers
μου, εἰδότες ὅτι μεῖζον κρίμα λημψόμεθα.
of me, knowing that greater judgment we shall receive.
2 πολλὰ γὰρ πταίομεν ἅπαντες· εἴ τις
For [in] many [respects] we stumble all; if anyone
ἐν λόγῳ οὐ πταίει, οὗτος τέλειος ἀνήρ,
[2]in [3]word [1]stumbles not, this [is] a perfect man,
δυνατὸς χαλιναγωγῆσαι καὶ ὅλον τὸ σῶμα.
able [2]to bridle [1]indeed all the body.
3 εἰ δὲ τῶν ἵππων τοὺς χαλινοὺς εἰς
Now if – [6]of horses – [2]bridles [3]into
τὰ στόματα βάλλομεν εἰς τὸ πείθεσθαι
[4]the [5]mouths [1]we put for the to obey
=to make them obey us,
αὐτοὺς ἡμῖν, καὶ ὅλον τὸ σῶμα αὐτῶν
them[b] *to* us, and [2]all [3]the [4]body [5]of them
μετάγομεν. 4 ἰδοὺ καὶ τὰ πλοῖα, τηλικαῦτα
[1]we direct. Behold also the ships, [2]so great
ὄντα καὶ ὑπὸ ἀνέμων σκληρῶν ἐλαυνόμενα,
being [3]and [5]by [7]winds [6]hard(strong) [4]*being* driven,
μετάγεται ὑπὸ ἐλαχίστου πηδαλίου ὅπου
is(are) directed by a very little helm where
ἡ ὁρμὴ τοῦ εὐθύνοντος βούλεται· 5 οὕτως
the impulse of the [one] steering resolves; so
καὶ ἡ γλῶσσα μικρὸν μέλος ἐστὶν καὶ
also the tongue [2]a little [3]member [1]is and
μεγάλα αὐχεῖ. ἰδοὺ ἡλίκον πῦρ ἡλίκην
great things boasts. Behold how little a fire [2]how great
ὕλην ἀνάπτει· 6 καὶ ἡ γλῶσσα πῦρ,
[3]wood [1]kindles; and the tongue [is] a fire,
ὁ κόσμος τῆς ἀδικίας, ἡ γλῶσσα καθίστα-
the world – of iniquity, the tongue is
ται ἐν τοῖς μέλεσιν ἡμῶν, ἡ σπιλοῦσα
set among the members of us, – spotting
ὅλον τὸ σῶμα καὶ φλογίζουσα τὸν
all the body and inflaming the
τροχὸν τῆς γενέσεως καὶ φλογιζομένη
course – of nature and being inflamed
ὑπὸ τῆς γεέννης. 7 πᾶσα γὰρ φύσις
by – gehenna. For every nature
θηρίων τε καὶ πετεινῶν, ἑρπετῶν τε
[2]of beasts [1]both and of birds, [2]of reptiles [1]both
καὶ ἐναλίων δαμάζεται καὶ δεδάμασται
and of marine creatures is tamed and has been tamed
τῇ φύσει τῇ ἀνθρωπίνῃ, 8 τὴν δὲ
by *the* [2]nature – [1]human, but the
γλῶσσαν οὐδεὶς δαμάσαι δύναται ἀνθρώπων·
tongue [1]no one [4]to tame [3]is able [2]of men;
ἀκατάστατον κακόν, μεστὴ ἰοῦ θανατηφόρου.
an unruly evil, full [2]poison [1]of death-dealing.
9 ἐν αὐτῇ εὐλογοῦμεν τὸν κύριον καὶ
By this we bless the Lord and
πατέρα, καὶ ἐν αὐτῇ καταρώμεθα τοὺς
Father, and by this we curse –
ἀνθρώπους τοὺς καθ' ὁμοίωσιν θεοῦ
men – [2]according to [3]likeness [4]of God

ferent direction? 26As the
body without the spirit is
dead, so faith without
deeds is dead.

Chapter 3

Taming the Tongue

NOT many of you
should presume to be
teachers, my brothers, because you know that we
who teach will be judged
more strictly. 2We all stumble in many ways. If any-
one is never at fault in what
he says, he is a perfect
man, able to keep his whole
body in check.
3When we put bits into
the mouths of horses to
make them obey us, we can
turn the whole animal. 4Or
take ships as an example.
Although they are so large
and are driven by strong
winds, they are steered by
a very small rudder
wherever the pilot wants to
go. 5Likewise the tongue is
a small part of the body, but
it makes great boasts. Consider what a great forest is
set on fire by a small spark.
6The tongue also is a fire, a
world of evil among the
parts of the body. It corrupts the whole person,
sets the whole course of his
life on fire, and is itself set
on fire by hell.
7All kinds of animals,
birds, reptiles and crea-
tures of the sea are being
tamed and have been
tamed by man, 8but no man
can tame the tongue. It is a
restless evil, full of deadly
poison.
9With the tongue we
praise our Lord and Fa-
ther, and with it we curse
men, who have been made

10from the same mouth
come *both* blessing and
cursing. My brethren,
these things ought not to be
this way.
11Does a fountain send
out from the same opening
both fresh and bitter *water*?
12Can a fig tree, my brethren, produce olives, or a
vine produce figs? Neither
can salt water produce
fresh.

Wisdom from Above

13Who among you is wise
and understanding? Let
him show by his good be-
havior his deeds in the gentleness of wisdom.
14But if you have bitter
jealousy and selfish ambition in your heart, do not be
arrogant and *so* lie against
the truth.
15This wisdom is not that
which comes down from
above, but is earthly, natural, demonic.
16For where jealousy and
selfish ambition exist, there
is disorder and every evil
thing.
17But the wisdom from
above is first pure, then
peaceable, gentle, reasonable, full of mercy and good
fruits, unwavering, without
hypocrisy.
18And the seed whose
fruit is righteousness is
sown in peace by those
who make peace.

Chapter 4

Things to Avoid

WHAT is the source of
quarrels and con-
flicts among you? Is not the
source your pleasures that
wage war in your mem-
bers?
2You lust and do not
have; *so* you commit murder. And you are envious
and cannot obtain; *so* you
fight and quarrel. You do
not have because you do
not ask.
3You ask and do not re-
ceive, because you ask
with wrong motives, so

γεγονότας· 10 ἐκ τοῦ αὐτοῦ στόματος ἐξέρχεται
[1]having become; out of the same mouth comes forth
εὐλογία καὶ κατάρα. οὐ χρή, ἀδελφοί
blessing and cursing. It is not fitting, brothers
μου, ταῦτα οὕτως γίνεσθαι. 11 μήτι
of me, these things so to be. *Not*
ἡ πηγὴ ἐκ τῆς αὐτῆς ὀπῆς βρύει τὸ
the fountain out of the same hole sends forth the
γλυκὺ καὶ τὸ πικρόν; 12 μὴ δύναται,
sweet and the bitter? *Not* can,
ἀδελφοί μου, συκῆ ἐλαίας ποιῆσαι ἢ
brothers of me, a fig-tree [2]olives [1]*to* produce or
ἄμπελος σῦκα; οὔτε ἁλυκὸν γλυκὺ
a vine figs? neither [1]salt [4]sweet
ποιῆσαι ὕδωρ. 13 Τίς σοφὸς καὶ ἐπιστήμων
[3]*to* make [2]water. Who [is] wise and knowing
ἐν ὑμῖν; δειξάτω ἐκ τῆς καλῆς ἀναστροφῆς
among you? let him show by the(his) good conduct
τὰ ἔργα αὐτοῦ ἐν πραΰτητι σοφίας.
the works of him in meekness of wisdom.*
14 εἰ δὲ ζῆλον πικρὸν ἔχετε καὶ ἐριθείαν
But if [3]jealousy [2]bitter [1]ye have and rivalry
ἐν τῇ καρδίᾳ ὑμῶν, μὴ κατακαυχᾶσθε
in the heart of you, do not exult over
καὶ ψεύδεσθε κατὰ τῆς ἀληθείας. 15 οὐκ
and lie against the truth. [4]not
ἔστιν αὕτη ἡ σοφία ἄνωθεν κατερχομένη,
[3]is [1]This – [2]wisdom [6]from above [5]coming down,
ἀλλὰ ἐπίγειος, ψυχική, δαιμονιώδης· 16 ὅπου
but [is] earthly, natural, demon-like; [2]where
γὰρ ζῆλος καὶ ἐριθεία, ἐκεῖ ἀκαταστασία
[1]for jealousy and rivalry [are], there [is] tumult
καὶ πᾶν φαῦλον πρᾶγμα. 17 ἡ δὲ ἄνωθεν
and every worthless practice. But [1]the [3]from above
σοφία πρῶτον μὲν ἁγνή ἐστιν, ἔπειτα
[2]wisdom [5]firstly – [6]pure [4]is, then
εἰρηνική, ἐπιεικής, εὐπειθής, μεστὴ ἐλέους
peaceable, forbearing, compliant, full of mercy
καὶ καρπῶν ἀγαθῶν, ἀδιάκριτος, ἀνυπό-
and [2]fruits [1]of good, without uncertainty, un-
κριτος. 18 καρπὸς δὲ δικαιοσύνης ἐν
feigned. And [the] fruit of righteousness [2]in
εἰρήνῃ σπείρεται τοῖς ποιοῦσιν εἰρήνην.
[3]peace [1]is sown for the [ones] making peace.

4 Πόθεν πόλεμοι καὶ πόθεν μάχαι ἐν
Whence wars and whence fights among
ὑμῖν; οὐκ ἐντεῦθεν, ἐκ τῶν ἡδονῶν
you? not thence, out of the pleasures
ὑμῶν τῶν στρατευομένων ἐν τοῖς μέλεσιν
of you – soldiering in the members
ὑμῶν; 2 ἐπιθυμεῖτε, καὶ οὐκ ἔχετε·
of you? Ye desire, and have not;
φονεύετε καὶ ζηλοῦτε, καὶ οὐ δύνασθε
ye murder and are jealous, and are not able
ἐπιτυχεῖν· μάχεσθε καὶ πολεμεῖτε. οὐκ
to obtain; ye fight and ye war. not
ἔχετε διὰ τὸ μὴ αἰτεῖσθαι ὑμᾶς· 3 αἰτεῖτε
Ye have be- *the* not to ask you[b]; ye ask
cause of
=because ye ask not;
καὶ οὐ λαμβάνετε, διότι κακῶς αἰτεῖσθε,
and receive not, because [2]ill [1]ye ask,

* Genitive of quality : " a wise meekness."

in God's likeness. 10Out of
the same mouth come
praise and cursing. My
brothers, this should not
be. 11Can both fresh water
and salt[f] water flow from
the same spring? 12My
brothers, can a fig tree bear
olives, or a grapevine bear
figs? Neither can a salt
spring produce fresh water.

Two Kinds of Wisdom

13Who is wise and under-
standing among you? Let
him show it by his good life,
by deeds done in the humility that comes from wis-
dom. 14But if you harbor
bitter envy and selfish ambition in your hearts, do not
boast about it or deny the
truth. 15Such "wisdom"
does not come down from
heaven but is earthly, unspiritual, of the devil. 16For
where you have envy and
selfish ambition, there you
find disorder and every evil
practice.
17But the wisdom that
comes from heaven is first
of all pure; then peace-lov-
ing, considerate, submis-
sive, full of mercy and good
fruit, impartial and sincere.
18Peacemakers who sow in
peace raise a harvest of
righteousness.

Chapter 4

Submit Yourselves to God

WHAT causes fights
and quarrels among
you? Don't they come from
your desires that battle
within you? 2You want
something but don't get it.
You kill and covet, but you
cannot have what you
want. You quarrel and
fight. You do not have, because you do not ask God.
3When you ask, you do not
receive, because you ask
with wrong motives, that

[f] 11 Greek *bitter* (see also verse 14)

that you may spend *it* on your pleasures.

4You adulteresses, do you not know that friendship with the world is hostility toward God? Therefore whoever wishes to be a friend of the world makes himself an enemy of God.

5Or do you think that the Scripture speaks to no purpose: "[c]He jealously desires the Spirit which He has made to dwell in us"?

6But He gives a greater grace. Therefore *it* says, "GOD IS OPPOSED TO THE PROUD, BUT GIVES GRACE TO THE HUMBLE."

7Submit therefore to God. Resist the devil and he will flee from you.

8Draw near to God and He will draw near to you. Cleanse your hands, you sinners; and purify your hearts, you double-minded.

9Be miserable and mourn and weep; let your laughter be turned into mourning, and your joy to gloom.

10Humble yourselves in the presence of the Lord, and He will exalt you.

11Do not speak against one another, brethren. He who speaks against a brother, or judges his brother, speaks against the law, and judges the law; but if you judge the law, you are not a doer of the law, but a judge *of it*.

12There is *only* one Lawgiver and Judge, the One who is able to save and to destroy; but who are you who judge your neighbor?

13Come now, you who say, "Today or tomorrow, we shall go to such and such a city, and spend a year there and engage in business and make a profit."

14Yet you do not know

[c] Or, *The Spirit which He has made to dwell in us jealously desires us*

ἵνα ἐν ταῖς ἡδοναῖς ὑμῶν δαπανήσητε.
in order that in the pleasures of you ye may spend.

4 μοιχαλίδες, οὐκ οἴδατε ὅτι ἡ φιλία
Adulteresses, know ye not that the friendship

τοῦ κόσμου ἔχθρα τοῦ θεοῦ ἐστιν; ὃς
of the world [2]enmity – [3]of God [1]is? Who-

ἐὰν οὖν βουληθῇ φίλος εἶναι τοῦ κόσμου,
ever therefore [1]resolves [3]a friend [2]to be of the world,

ἐχθρὸς τοῦ θεοῦ καθίσταται. 5 ἢ δοκεῖτε
[2]an enemy – [3]of God [1]is constituted. Or think ye

ὅτι κενῶς ἡ γραφὴ λέγει· πρὸς φθόνον
that vainly the scripture says: [8]to [9]envy

ἐπιποθεῖ τὸ πνεῦμα ὃ κατῴκισεν ἐν
[7]yearns [1]The [2]Spirit [3]which [4]dwelt [5]in

ἡμῖν; 6 μείζονα δὲ δίδωσιν χάριν· διὸ
[6]you? But [2]greater [1]he gives [3]grace; wherefore

λέγει· ὁ θεὸς ὑπερηφάνοις ἀντιτάσσεται,
it* says: – God [2]arrogant men [1]resists,

ταπεινοῖς δὲ δίδωσιν χάριν. 7 ὑποτάγητε
but to humble men he gives grace. Be ye subject

οὖν τῷ θεῷ· ἀντίστητε δὲ τῷ διαβόλῳ,
therefore – to God; but oppose the devil,

καὶ φεύξεται ἀφ' ὑμῶν· 8 ἐγγίσατε τῷ
and he will flee from you; draw near –

θεῷ, καὶ ἐγγίσει ὑμῖν. καθαρίσατε
to God, and he will draw near to you. Cleanse ye

χεῖρας, ἁμαρτωλοί, καὶ ἁγνίσατε καρδίας,
hands, sinners, and purify hearts,

δίψυχοι. 9 ταλαιπωρήσατε καὶ πενθήσατε
two-souled (double-minded). Be ye distressed and mourn

καὶ κλαύσατε· ὁ γέλως ὑμῶν εἰς πένθος
and weep; the laughter of you to mourning

μετατραπήτω καὶ ἡ χαρὰ εἰς κατήφειαν.
let it be turned and the joy to dejection.

10 ταπεινώθητε ἐνώπιον κυρίου, καὶ ὑψώσει
Be ye humbled before [the] Lord, and he will exalt

ὑμᾶς. 11 Μὴ καταλαλεῖτε ἀλλήλων, ἀδελφοί.
you. Speak not against one another, brothers.

ὁ καταλαλῶν ἀδελφοῦ ἢ κρίνων τὸν
The [one] speaking against a brother or judging the

ἀδελφὸν αὐτοῦ καταλαλεῖ νόμου καὶ κρίνει
brother of him speaks against law and judges

νόμον· εἰ δὲ νόμον κρίνεις, οὐκ εἶ
law; and if law thou judgest, thou art not

ποιητὴς νόμου ἀλλὰ κριτής. 12 εἷς ἐστιν
a doer of law but a judge. One is

νομοθέτης καὶ κριτής, ὁ δυνάμενος
lawgiver and judge, the [one] being able

σῶσαι καὶ ἀπολέσαι· σὺ δὲ τίς εἶ, ὁ
to save and to destroy; [4]thou [1]and [3]who [2]art, the

κρίνων τὸν πλησίον;
[one] judging the(thy) neighbour?

13 Ἄγε νῦν οἱ λέγοντες· σήμερον ἢ
Come now the [ones] saying: To-day or

αὔριον πορευσόμεθα εἰς τήνδε τὴν πόλιν
to-morrow we will go into this – city

καὶ ποιήσομεν ἐκεῖ ἐνιαυτὸν καὶ ἐμπορευ-
and we will do there a year and *we will*

σόμεθα καὶ κερδήσομεν· 14 οἵτινες οὐκ
trade and *we will* make a profit; who not

* That is, " the scripture" (as ver. 5).

you may spend what you get on your pleasures.

4You adulterous people, don't you know that friendship with the world is hatred toward God? Anyone who chooses to be a friend of the world becomes an enemy of God. 5Or do you think Scripture says without reason that the spirit he caused to live in us envies intensely?[g] 6But he gives us more grace. That is why Scripture says:

"God opposes the proud
but gives grace to the humble."[h]

7Submit yourselves, then, to God. Resist the devil, and he will flee from you. 8Come near to God and he will come near to you. Wash your hands, you sinners, and purify your hearts, you double-minded. 9Grieve, mourn and wail. Change your laughter to mourning and your joy to gloom. 10Humble yourselves before the Lord, and he will lift you up.

11Brothers, do not slander one another. Anyone who speaks against his brother or judges him speaks against the law and judges it. When you judge the law, you are not keeping it, but sitting in judgment on it. 12There is only one Lawgiver and Judge, the one who is able to save and destroy. But you—who are you to judge your neighbor?

Boasting About Tomorrow

13Now listen, you who say, "Today or tomorrow we will go to this or that city, spend a year there, carry on business and make money." 14Why, you do

[g]5 Or *that God jealously longs for the spirit that he made to live in us*; or *that the Spirit he caused to live in us longs jealously*
[h]6 Prov. 3:34

what your life will be like tomorrow. You are *just* a vapor that appears for a little while and then vanishes away.

15Instead, *you ought* to say, "If the Lord wills, we shall live and also do this or that."

16But as it is, you boast in your arrogance; all such boasting is evil.

17Therefore, to one who knows *the* right thing to do, and does not do it, to him it is sin.

Chapter 5

Misuse of Riches

COME now, you rich, weep and howl for your miseries which are coming upon you.

2Your riches have rotted and your garments have become moth-eaten.

3Your gold and your silver have rusted; and their rust will be a witness against you and will consume your flesh like fire. It is in the last days that you have stored up your treasure!

4Behold, the pay of the laborers who mowed your fields, *and* which has been withheld by you, cries out *against you;* and the outcry of those who did the harvesting has reached the ears of the Lord of Sabaoth.

5You have lived luxuriously on the earth and led a life of wanton pleasure; you have fattened your hearts in a day of slaughter.

6You have condemned and put to death the righteous *man;* he does not resist you.

Exhortation

7Be patient, therefore, brethren, until the coming of the Lord. Behold, the farmer waits for the precious produce of the soil, being patient about it, until it gets the early and late

ἐπίστασθε τῆς αὔριον ποία ἡ ζωὴ ὑμῶν.
ye know [5]of the [6]morrow [1]what [2]the [3]life [4]of you [will be].
ἀτμὶς γάρ ἐστε ἡ πρὸς ὀλίγον φαινομένη,
For [2]a vapour [1]ye are – [4]for [5]a little while [3]appearing,
ἔπειτα καὶ ἀφανιζομένη· 15 ἀντὶ τοῦ
thereafter indeed disappearing; instead of *the*
λέγειν ὑμᾶς· ἐὰν ὁ κύριος θελήσῃ, καὶ
to say you[b]: If the Lord wills, both
=your saying:
ζήσομεν καὶ ποιήσομεν τοῦτο ἢ ἐκεῖνο.
we will live and *we will* do this or that.
16 νῦν δὲ καυχᾶσθε ἐν ταῖς ἀλαζονείαις
But now ye boast in the vauntings
ὑμῶν· πᾶσα καύχησις τοιαύτη πονηρά
of you; all [2]boasting [1]such [4]evil
ἐστιν. 17 εἰδότι οὖν καλὸν ποιεῖν καὶ
[3]is. [2]to [one] knowing* [1]Therefore [4]good [3]to do and
μὴ ποιοῦντι, ἁμαρτία αὐτῷ ἐστιν.
not doing, [3]sin [1]to him [2]it is.
5 Ἄγε νῦν οἱ πλούσιοι, κλαύσατε
Come now *the* rich men, weep ye
ὀλολύζοντες ἐπὶ ταῖς ταλαιπωρίαις ὑμῶν
crying aloud over the hardships of you
ταῖς ἐπερχομέναις. 2 ὁ πλοῦτος ὑμῶν
– coming upon. The riches of you
σέσηπεν, καὶ τὰ ἱμάτια ὑμῶν σητόβρωτα
have become corrupted, and the garments of you moth-eaten
γέγονεν, 3 ὁ χρυσὸς ὑμῶν καὶ ὁ ἄργυρος
have become, the gold of you and the silver
κατίωται, καὶ ὁ ἰὸς αὐτῶν εἰς μαρτύριον
has become rusted over, and the poison of them for a testimony
ὑμῖν ἔσται καὶ φάγεται τὰς σάρκας
to(against) you will be and will eat the fleshes
ὑμῶν ὡς πῦρ. ἐθησαυρίσατε ἐν ἐσχάταις
of you as fire. Ye treasured in [the] last
ἡμέραις. 4 ἰδοὺ ὁ μισθὸς τῶν ἐργατῶν
days. Behold[,] the wages of the workmen
τῶν ἀμησάντων τὰς χώρας ὑμῶν ὁ
– having reaped the lands of you –
ἀφυστερημένος ἀφ' ὑμῶν κράζει, καὶ αἱ
being kept back from(by) you cries, and the
βοαὶ τῶν θερισάντων εἰς τὰ ὦτα κυρίου
cries of the [ones] having reaped [2]into [3]the [4]ears [5]of [the] Lord
σαβαὼθ εἰσελήλυθαν. 5 ἐτρυφήσατε ἐπὶ
[6]of hosts [1]have entered. Ye lived daintily on
τῆς γῆς καὶ ἐσπαταλήσατε, ἐθρέψατε τὰς
the earth and lived riotously, ye nourished the
καρδίας ὑμῶν ἐν ἡμέρᾳ σφαγῆς. 6 κατε-
hearts of you in a day of slaughter. Ye
δικάσατε, ἐφονεύσατε τὸν δίκαιον· οὐκ
condemned, ye murdered the righteous man; not
ἀντιτάσσεται ὑμῖν.
he resists you.
7 Μακροθυμήσατε οὖν, ἀδελφοί, ἕως τῆς
Be ye longsuffering therefore, brothers, until the
παρουσίας τοῦ κυρίου. ἰδοὺ ὁ γεωργὸς
presence of the Lord. Behold[,] the farmer
ἐκδέχεται τὸν τίμιον καρπὸν τῆς γῆς,
awaits the precious fruit of the earth,
μακροθυμῶν ἐπ' αὐτῷ ἕως λάβῃ πρόϊμον
being longsuffering over it until he receives early

* See note on page xviii.

not even know what will
happen tomorrow. What is
your life? You are a mist
that appears for a little
while and then vanishes.
15Instead, you ought to say,
"If it is the Lord's will, we
will live and do this or
that." 16As it is, you boast
and brag. All such boasting
is evil. 17Anyone, then,
who knows the good he
ought to do and doesn't do
it, sins.

Chapter 5

Warning to Rich Oppressors

NOW listen, you rich
people, weep and
wail because of the misery
that is coming upon you.
2Your wealth has rotted,
and moths have eaten your
clothes. 3Your gold and silver are corroded. Their
corrosion will testify
against you and eat your
flesh like fire. You have
hoarded wealth in the last
days. 4Look! The wages
you failed to pay the workmen who mowed your
fields are crying out against
you. The cries of the harvesters have reached the
ears of the Lord Almighty.
5You have lived on earth in
luxury and self-indulgence.
You have fattened your-
selves in the day of slaughter.[i] 6You have con-
demned and murdered in-
nocent men, who were not
opposing you.

Patience in Suffering

7Be patient, then, broth-
ers, until the Lord's coming. See how the farmer
waits for the land to yield
its valuable crop and how
patient he is for the autumn

[i]5 Or *yourselves as in a day of feasting*

rains.
8You too be patient; strengthen your hearts, for the coming of the Lord is at hand.
9Do not complain, brethren, against one another, that you yourselves may not be judged; behold, the Judge is standing right at the door.
10As an example, brethren, of suffering and patience, take the prophets who spoke in the name of the Lord.
11Behold, we count those blessed who endured. You have heard of the endurance of Job and have seen the outcome of the Lord's dealings, that the Lord is full of compassion and *is* merciful.
12But above all, my brethren, do not swear, either by heaven or by earth or with any other oath; but let your yes be yes, and your no, no; so that you may not fall under judgment.
13Is anyone among you suffering? Let him pray. Is anyone cheerful? Let him sing praises.
14Is anyone among you sick? Let him call for the elders of the church, and let them pray over him, anointing him with oil in the name of the Lord;
15and the prayer offered in faith will [d]restore the one who is sick, and the Lord will raise him up, and if he has committed sins, they will be forgiven him.
16Therefore, confess your sins to one another, and pray for one another, so that you may be healed. The effective prayer of a righteous man can accomplish much.
17Elijah was a man with a nature like ours, and he prayed earnestly that it might not rain; and it did

καὶ ὄψιμον. 8 μακροθυμήσατε καὶ ὑμεῖς,
and latter [rain]. Be [3]longsuffering [2]also [1]ye,
στηρίξατε τὰς καρδίας ὑμῶν, ὅτι ἡ
establish the hearts of you, because the
παρουσία τοῦ κυρίου ἤγγικεν. 9 μὴ
presence of the Lord has drawn near. not
στενάζετε, ἀδελφοί, κατ' ἀλλήλων ἵνα μὴ
Murmur ye, brothers, against one another lest
κριθῆτε· ἰδοὺ ὁ κριτὴς πρὸ τῶν θυρῶν
ye be judged; behold[,] the judge [2]before [3]the [4]doors
ἕστηκεν. 10 ὑπόδειγμα λάβετε, ἀδελφοί,
[1]stands. [5]an example [1]Take ye, [2]brothers,
τῆς κακοπαθίας καὶ τῆς μακροθυμίας
– [6]of suffering ill [7]and – [8]of longsuffering
τοὺς προφήτας, οἳ ἐλάλησαν ἐν τῷ
[3]the [4]prophets, who spoke in the
ὀνόματι κυρίου. 11 ἰδοὺ μακαρίζομεν τοὺς
name of [the] Lord. Behold we count blessed the
ὑπομείναντας· τὴν ὑπομονὴν Ἰὼβ ἠκούσατε,
[ones] enduring; [2]the [3]endurance [4]of Job [1]ye heard [of],
καὶ τὸ τέλος κυρίου εἴδετε, ὅτι πολύ-
and [2]the [3]end [4]of [the] Lord [1]ye saw, that [4]very
σπλαγχνός ἐστιν ὁ κύριος καὶ οἰκτίρμων.
compassionate [3]is [1]the [2]Lord and pitiful.
12 Πρὸ πάντων δέ, ἀδελφοί μου, μὴ
[2]before [3]all things [1]But, brothers of me, not
ὀμνύετε, μήτε τὸν οὐρανὸν μήτε τὴν
swear ye, neither by *the* heaven nor by the
γῆν μήτε ἄλλον τινὰ ὅρκον· ἤτω δὲ
earth nor [2]other [1]any oath; but let be
ὑμῶν τὸ ναὶ ναί, καὶ τὸ οὒ οὔ, ἵνα μὴ
of you the Yes yes, and the No no, lest
ὑπὸ κρίσιν πέσητε. 13 Κακοπαθεῖ τις
[2]under [3]judgment [1]ye fall. Suffers ill anyone
ἐν ὑμῖν; προσευχέσθω· εὐθυμεῖ τις;
among you? let him pray; is cheerful anyone?
ψαλλέτω. 14 ἀσθενεῖ τις ἐν ὑμῖν;
let him sing a psalm. Is weak anyone among you?
προσκαλεσάσθω τοὺς πρεσβυτέρους τῆς
let him summon the elders of the
ἐκκλησίας, καὶ προσευξάσθωσαν ἐπ' αὐτὸν
church, and let them pray over him
ἀλείψαντες ἐλαίῳ ἐν τῷ ὀνόματι τοῦ
having anointed [him] with oil in the name of the
κυρίου. 15 καὶ ἡ εὐχὴ τῆς πίστεως
Lord. And the prayer – of faith
σώσει τὸν κάμνοντα, καὶ ἐγερεῖ αὐτὸν
will heal the [one] being sick, and [3]will raise [4]him
ὁ κύριος· κἂν ἁμαρτίας ᾖ πεποιηκώς,
[1]the [2]Lord; and if [3]sins [1]he may be [2]having done,
ἀφεθήσεται αὐτῷ. 16 ἐξομολογεῖσθε οὖν
it will be forgiven him. Confess ye therefore
ἀλλήλοις τὰς ἁμαρτίας, καὶ προσεύχεσθε
to one another the(your) sins, and pray ye
ὑπὲρ ἀλλήλων, ὅπως ἰαθῆτε. πολὺ
on behalf of one another, so as ye may be cured. [5]much(very)
ἰσχύει δέησις δικαίου ἐνεργουμένη.
[4]is [6]strong [1]*a* petition [2]of a righteous man [3]being made effective.
17 Ἠλίας ἄνθρωπος ἦν ὁμοιοπαθὴς ἡμῖν,
Elias [2]a man [1]was of like feeling to us,

and spring rains. 8You too, be patient and stand firm, because the Lord's coming is near. 9Don't grumble against each other, brothers, or you will be judged. The Judge is standing at the door!
10Brothers, as an example of patience in the face of suffering, take the prophets who spoke in the name of the Lord. 11As you know, we consider blessed those who have persevered. You have heard of Job's perseverance and have seen what the Lord finally brought about. The Lord is full of compassion and mercy.
12Above all, my brothers, do not swear—not by heaven or by earth or by anything else. Let your "Yes" be yes, and your "No," no, or you will be condemned.

The Prayer of Faith

13Is any one of you in trouble? He should pray. Is anyone happy? Let him sing songs of praise. 14Is any one of you sick? He should call the elders of the church to pray over him and anoint him with oil in the name of the Lord. 15And the prayer offered in faith will make the sick person well; the Lord will raise him up. If he has sinned, he will be forgiven. 16Therefore confess your sins to each other and pray for each other so that you may be healed. The prayer of a righteous man is powerful and effective.
17Elijah was a man just like us. He prayed earnestly that it would not rain,

[d]Or, *save*

not rain on the earth for three years and six months.
18And he prayed again, and the sky poured rain, and the earth produced its fruit.
19My brethren, if any among you strays from the truth, and one turns him back,
20let him know that he who turns a sinner from the error of his way will save his soul from death, and will cover a multitude of sins.

καὶ προσευχῇ προσηύξατο τοῦ μὴ βρέξαι,
and [2]in prayer [1]he prayed – not to rain,[a]
=that it should not rain,
καὶ οὐκ ἔβρεξεν ἐπὶ τῆς γῆς ἐνιαυτοὺς
and it rained not on the earth [2]years
τρεῖς καὶ μῆνας ἕξ· 18 καὶ πάλιν προσ-
[1]three and [2]months [1]six; and again he
ηύξατο, καὶ ὁ οὐρανὸς ὑετὸν ἔδωκεν καὶ
prayed, and the heaven [2]rain [1]gave and
ἡ γῆ ἐβλάστησεν τὸν καρπὸν αὐτῆς.
the earth brought forth the fruit of it.
19 Ἀδελφοί μου, ἐάν τις ἐν ὑμῖν πλανηθῇ
Brothers of me, if anyone among you errs
ἀπὸ τῆς ἀληθείας καὶ ἐπιστρέψῃ τις
from the truth and [2]turns [1]anyone
αὐτόν, 20 γινώσκετε ὅτι ὁ ἐπιστρέψας
him, know ye that the [one] turning
ἁμαρτωλὸν ἐκ πλάνης ὁδοῦ •αὐτοῦ σώσει
a sinner out of [the] error of way of him will save
ψυχὴν αὐτοῦ ἐκ θανάτου καὶ καλύψει
soul of him out of death and will hide
πλῆθος ἁμαρτιῶν.
a multitude of sins.

and it did not rain on the land for three and a half years. 18Again he prayed, and the heavens gave rain, and the earth produced its crops.
19My brothers, if one of you should wander from the truth and someone should bring him back,
20remember this: Whoever turns a sinner from the error of his way will save him from death and cover over a multitude of sins.

1 Peter

Chapter 1

A Living Hope, and a Sure Salvation

PETER, an apostle of Jesus Christ, to those who reside as aliens, scattered throughout Pontus, Galatia, Cappadocia, Asia, and Bithynia, who are chosen
2according to the foreknowledge of God the Father, by the sanctifying work of the Spirit, that you may obey Jesus Christ and be sprinkled with His blood: May grace and peace be yours in fullest measure.
3Blessed be the God and Father of our Lord Jesus Christ, who according to His great mercy has caused us to be born again to a living hope through the resurrection of Jesus Christ from the dead,
4to *obtain* an inheritance *which is* imperishable and undefiled and will not fade away, reserved in heaven for you,
5who are protected by the power of God through faith for a salvation ready to be revealed in the last

ΠΕΤΡΟΥ Α

Of Peter 1

1 Πέτρος ἀπόστολος Ἰησοῦ Χριστοῦ
Peter an apostle of Jesus Christ
ἐκλεκτοῖς παρεπιδήμοις διασπορᾶς Πόντου,
to [the] chosen sojourners of [the] dispersion of Pontus,
Γαλατίας, Καππαδοκίας, Ἀσίας καὶ
of Galatia, *of* Cappadocia, *of* Asia and
Βιθυνίας, 2 κατὰ πρόγνωσιν θεοῦ πατρός,
of Bithynia, according to [the] foreknowledge of God Father,
ἐν ἁγιασμῷ πνεύματος, εἰς ὑπακοὴν καὶ
in sanctification of spirit, to obedience and
ῥαντισμὸν αἵματος Ἰησοῦ Χριστοῦ· χάρις
sprinkling of [the] blood of Jesus Christ: Grace
ὑμῖν καὶ εἰρήνη πληθυνθείη.
to you and peace *may it* be multiplied.
3 Εὐλογητὸς ὁ θεὸς καὶ πατὴρ τοῦ
Blessed [be] the God and Father of the
κυρίου ἡμῶν Ἰησοῦ Χριστοῦ, ὁ κατὰ τὸ
Lord of us Jesus Christ, the [one] according to the
πολὺ αὐτοῦ ἔλεος ἀναγεννήσας ἡμᾶς εἰς
much (great) of him mercy having regenerated us to
ἐλπίδα ζῶσαν δι' ἀναστάσεως Ἰησοῦ
[2]hope [1]a living through [the] resurrection of Jesus
Χριστοῦ ἐκ νεκρῶν, 4 εἰς κληρονομίαν
Christ from [the] dead, to an inheritance
ἄφθαρτον καὶ ἀμίαντον καὶ ἀμάραντον,
incorruptible and undefiled and unfading,
τετηρημένην ἐν οὐρανοῖς εἰς ὑμᾶς 5 τοὺς
having been kept in heavens for you the [ones]
ἐν δυνάμει θεοῦ φρουρουμένους διὰ πίστεως
[2]by [3][the] power [4]of God [1]being guarded through faith
εἰς σωτηρίαν ἑτοίμην ἀποκαλυφθῆναι ἐν
to a salvation ready to be revealed at

1 Peter

Chapter 1

PETER, an apostle of Jesus Christ,
To God's elect, strangers in the world, scattered throughout Pontus, Galatia, Cappadocia, Asia and Bithynia, 2who have been chosen according to the foreknowledge of God the Father, through the sanctifying work of the Spirit, for obedience to Jesus Christ and sprinkling by his blood:

Grace and peace be yours in abundance.

Praise to God for a Living Hope

3Praise be to the God and Father of our Lord Jesus Christ! In his great mercy he has given us new birth into a living hope through the resurrection of Jesus Christ from the dead, 4and into an inheritance that can never perish, spoil or fade —kept in heaven for you, 5who through faith are shielded by God's power until the coming of the salvation that is ready to be revealed in the last time.

time.
6In this you greatly re-
joice, even though now for
a little while, if necessary,
you have been distressed
by various trials,
7that the proof of your
faith, *being* more precious
than gold which is perishable, even though tested by
fire, may be found to result
in praise and glory and hon-
or at the revelation of Jesus
Christ;
8and though you have
not seen Him, you love
Him, and though you do
not see Him now, but be-
lieve in Him, you greatly
rejoice with joy inexpressible and full of glory,
9obtaining as the out-
come of your faith the salvation of [a]your souls.
10As to this salvation, the
prophets who prophesied
of the grace that *would
come* to you made careful
search and inquiry,
11seeking to know what
person or time the Spirit of
Christ within them was indicating as He predicted
the sufferings of Christ and
the glories to follow.
12It was revealed to them
that they were not serving
themselves, but you, in
these things which now
have been announced to
you through those who
preached the gospel to you
by the Holy Spirit sent
from heaven—things into
which angels long to look.
13Therefore, gird your
minds for action, keep sober *in spirit,* fix your hope
completely on the grace to
be brought to you at the
revelation of Jesus Christ.
14As obedient children,
do not be conformed to the
former lusts *which were
yours* in your ignorance,
15but like the Holy One
who called you, be holy

καιρῷ ἐσχάτῳ. 6 ἐν ᾧ ἀγαλλιᾶσθε,
[2]time [1][the] last. In which ye exult,
ὀλίγον ἄρτι εἰ δέον λυπηθέντες ἐν
a little [while] yet if necessary grieving by
ποικίλοις πειρασμοῖς, 7 ἵνα τὸ δοκίμιον
manifold trials, in order that the proving
ὑμῶν τῆς πίστεως πολυτιμότερον χρυσίου
[3]of you [1]of the [2]faith[,] much more precious [than] [2]gold
τοῦ ἀπολλυμένου, διὰ πυρὸς δὲ δοκιμαζ-
– [1]of perishing, [3]through [4]fire [1]yet [2]being
ομένου, εὑρεθῇ εἰς ἔπαινον καὶ δόξαν
proved, may be found to praise and glory
καὶ τιμὴν ἐν ἀποκαλύψει Ἰησοῦ Χριστοῦ·
and honour at [the] revelation of Jesus Christ;
8 ὃν οὐκ ἰδόντες ἀγαπᾶτε, εἰς ὃν ἄρτι
whom not having seen ye love, in whom yet
μὴ ὁρῶντες πιστεύοντες δὲ ἀγαλλιᾶσθε
not seeing [2]believing [1]but ye exult
χαρᾷ ἀνεκλαλήτῳ καὶ δεδοξασμένῃ,
with joy unspeakable and *having been* glorified,
9 κομιζόμενοι τὸ τέλος τῆς πίστεως
obtaining the end of the(your) faith
σωτηρίαν ψυχῶν. 10 περὶ ἧς σωτηρίας
[the] salvation of [your] souls. Concerning which salvation
ἐξεζήτησαν καὶ ἐξηρεύνησαν προφῆται οἱ
[9]sought out [10]and [11]searched out [1]prophets [2]the
περὶ τῆς εἰς ὑμᾶς χάριτος προφητεύσαντες,
[4]concerning [5]the [7]for [8]you [6]grace [3][ones] prophesying,
11 ἐρευνῶντες εἰς τίνα ἢ ποῖον καιρὸν
searching for what or what sort of time
ἐδήλου τὸ ἐν αὐτοῖς πνεῦμα Χριστοῦ
[6]made clear [1]the [4]in [5]them [3]Spirit [2]of Christ
προμαρτυρόμενον τὰ εἰς Χριστὸν παθήματα
[7]forewitnessing [8]the [10]for [11]Christ [9]sufferings
καὶ τὰς μετὰ ταῦτα δόξας. 12 οἷς
[12]and [13]the [15]after [16]these [14]glories. To whom
ἀπεκαλύφθη ὅτι οὐχ ἑαυτοῖς ὑμῖν δὲ
it was revealed that not to themselves [2]to you [1]but
διηκόνουν αὐτά, ἃ νῦν ἀνηγγέλη ὑμῖν
they ministered the same things, which now were announced to you
διὰ τῶν εὐαγγελισαμένων ὑμᾶς ἐν
through the [ones] having evangelized you by
πνεύματι ἁγίῳ ἀποσταλέντι ἀπ' οὐρανοῦ,
[2]Spirit [1][the] Holy sent forth from heaven,
εἰς ἃ ἐπιθυμοῦσιν ἄγγελοι παρακύψαι.
into [1]which things [3]long [2]angels [4]to look into.
13 Διὸ ἀναζωσάμενοι τὰς ὀσφύας τῆς
Wherefore girding up the loins of the
διανοίας ὑμῶν, νήφοντες, τελείως ἐλπίσατε
mind of you, being sober, perfectly hope
ἐπὶ τὴν φερομένην ὑμῖν χάριν ἐν
on [1]the [3]being brought [4]to you [2]grace at
ἀποκαλύψει Ἰησοῦ Χριστοῦ. 14 ὡς τέκνα
[the] revelation of Jesus Christ. As children
ὑπακοῆς, μὴ συσχηματιζόμενοι ταῖς πρότε-
of obedience,* not fashioning yourselves to the [6]form-
ρον ἐν τῇ ἀγνοίᾳ ὑμῶν ἐπιθυμίαις, 15 ἀλλὰ
erly [2]in [3]the [4]ignorance [5]of you [1]longings, but
κατὰ τὸν καλέσαντα ὑμᾶς ἅγιον καὶ
according to [1]the [3]having called [4]you [2]holy [one] [7]also

6In this you greatly rejoice,
though now for a little
while you may have had to
suffer grief in all kinds of
trials. 7These have come so
that your faith—of greater
worth than gold, which perishes even though refined
by fire—may be proved
genuine and may result in
praise, glory and honor
when Jesus Christ is re-
vealed. 8Though you have
not seen him, you love him;
and even though you do not
see him now, you believe in
him and are filled with an
inexpressible and glorious
joy, 9for you are receiving
the goal of your faith, the
salvation of your souls.
10Concerning this salva-
tion, the prophets, who
spoke of the grace that was
to come to you, searched
intently and with the greatest care, 11trying to find out
the time and circumstances
to which the Spirit of Christ
in them was pointing when
he predicted the sufferings
of Christ and the glories
that would follow. 12It was
revealed to them that they
were not serving them-
selves but you, when they
spoke of the things that
have now been told you by
those who have preached
the gospel to you by the
Holy Spirit sent from heav-
en. Even angels long to
look into these things.

Be Holy

13Therefore, prepare
your minds for action; be
self-controlled; set your
hope fully on the grace to
be given you when Jesus
Christ is revealed. 14As
obedient children, do not
conform to the evil desires
you had when you lived in
ignorance. 15But just as he
who called you is holy, so

[a] Some ancient mss. do not contain *your*

* Genitive of quality: "obedient children."

yourselves also in all *your* behavior;
16because it is written, "YOU SHALL BE HOLY, FOR I AM HOLY."
17And if you address as Father the One who impartially judges according to each man's work, conduct yourselves in fear during the time of your stay *upon earth*;
18knowing that you were not redeemed with perishable things like silver or gold from your futile way of life inherited from your forefathers,
19but with precious blood, as of a lamb unblemished and spotless, *the blood* of Christ.
20For He was foreknown before the foundation of the world, but has appeared in these last times for the sake of you
21who through Him are believers in God, who raised Him from the dead and gave Him glory, so that your faith and hope are in God.
22Since you have in obedience to the truth purified your souls for a sincere love of the brethren, fervently love one another from [b]the heart,
23for you have been born again not of seed which is perishable but imperishable, *that is,* through the living and abiding word of God.
24For,

"ALL FLESH IS LIKE GRASS,
AND ALL ITS GLORY LIKE THE FLOWER OF GRASS.
THE GRASS WITHERS,
AND THE FLOWER FALLS OFF,
25 BUT THE WORD OF THE LORD ABIDES FOREVER."

And this is the word which was preached to you.

αὐτοὶ ἅγιοι ἐν πάσῃ ἀναστροφῇ γενήθητε,
[6][your]-selves [8]holy [9]in [10]all [11]conduct [5]become ye,
16 διότι γέγραπται· [ὅτι] ἅγιοι ἔσεσθε,
because it has been written: – Holy ye shall be,
ὅτι ἐγὼ ἅγιος. 17 καὶ εἰ πατέρα
because I [am] holy. And if [2]Father
ἐπικαλεῖσθε τὸν ἀπροσωπολήμπτως κρίνοντα
[1]ye invoke [as] [3]the [one] [5]without respect to persons [4]judging
κατὰ τὸ ἑκάστου ἔργον, ἐν φόβῳ τὸν
according to the [2]of each man [1]work, [2]in [3]fear [4]the
τῆς παροικίας ὑμῶν χρόνον ἀναστράφητε,
[6]of the [7]sojourning [8]of you [5]time [1]pass,
18 εἰδότες ὅτι οὐ φθαρτοῖς, ἀργυρίῳ ἢ
knowing that not with corruptible things, silver or
χρυσίῳ, ἐλυτρώθητε ἐκ τῆς ματαίας ὑμῶν
gold, ye were redeemed from the vain [2]of you
ἀναστροφῆς πατροπαραδότου, 19 ἀλλὰ τιμίῳ
[1]conduct delivered from [your] fathers, but with precious
αἵματι ὡς ἀμνοῦ ἀμώμου καὶ ἀσπίλου
blood[,] as of a lamb unblemished and unspotted[,]
Χριστοῦ, 20 προεγνωσμένου μὲν πρὸ κατα-
of Christ, *having been* foreknown on one hand from [the]
βολῆς κόσμου, φανερωθέντος δὲ ἐπ' ἐσχάτου
foundation of [the] world, manifested on the other in [the] last
τῶν χρόνων δι' ὑμᾶς 21 τοὺς δι' αὐτοῦ
of the times because of you the ones through him
πιστοὺς εἰς θεὸν τὸν ἐγείραντα αὐτὸν
believing in God the [one] having raised him
ἐκ νεκρῶν καὶ δόξαν αὐτῷ δόντα, ὥστε
from [the] dead and [2]glory [3]to him [1]having given, so as
τὴν πίστιν ὑμῶν καὶ ἐλπίδα εἶναι εἰς
the [1]faith [4]of you [2]and [3]hope to be in
θεόν. 22 Τὰς ψυχὰς ὑμῶν ἡγνικότες
God. [2]The [3]souls [4]of you [1]having purified
ἐν τῇ ὑπακοῇ τῆς ἀληθείας εἰς φιλαδελφίαν
by – obedience of(to) the truth to [2]brotherly love
ἀνυπόκριτον, ἐκ καρδίας ἀλλήλους ἀγαπήσατε
[1]unfeigned, [4]from [5][the] heart [2]one another [1]love ye
ἐκτενῶς, 23 ἀναγεγεννημένοι οὐκ ἐκ σπορᾶς
[3]earnestly, having been regenerated not by [2]seed
φθαρτῆς ἀλλὰ ἀφθάρτου, διὰ λόγου ζῶντος
[1]corruptible but incorruptible, through [4]word [1][the] living
θεοῦ καὶ μένοντος. 24 διότι πᾶσα σὰρξ
[5]of God [2]and [3]remaining. Because all flesh [is]
ὡς χόρτος, καὶ πᾶσα δόξα αὐτῆς ὡς
as grass, and all [the] glory of it as
ἄνθος χόρτου· ἐξηράνθη ὁ χόρτος, καὶ
a flower of grass; was dried the grass, and
τὸ ἄνθος ἐξέπεσεν· 25 τὸ δὲ ῥῆμα κυρίου
the flower fell out; but the word of [the] Lord
μένει εἰς τὸν αἰῶνα. τοῦτο δέ ἐστιν
remains unto the age. And this is
τὸ ῥῆμα τὸ εὐαγγελισθὲν εἰς ὑμᾶς.
the word – preached [as good news] to you.

be holy in all you do; 16for it is written: "Be holy, because I am holy."[a]
17Since you call on a Father who judges each man's work impartially, live your lives as strangers here in reverent fear. 18For you know that it was not with perishable things such as silver or gold that you were redeemed from the empty way of life handed down to you from your forefathers,
19but with the precious blood of Christ, a lamb without blemish or defect.
20He was chosen before the creation of the world, but was revealed in these last times for your sake.
21Through him you believe in God, who raised him from the dead and glorified him, and so your faith and hope are in God.
22Now that you have purified yourselves by obeying the truth so that you have sincere love for your brothers, love one another deeply, from the heart.[b]
23For you have been born again, not of perishable seed, but of imperishable, through the living and enduring word of God. 24For,

"All men are like grass,
and all their glory is like the flowers of the field;
the grass withers and the flowers fall,
25 but the word of the Lord stands forever."[c]

And this is the word that was preached to you.

Chapter 2

As Newborn Babes

THEREFORE, putting aside all malice and all guile and hypocrisy and envy and all slander,
2like newborn babes, long for the pure milk of the

2 Ἀποθέμενοι οὖν πᾶσαν κακίαν καὶ
Putting away therefore all malice and
πάντα δόλον καὶ ὑποκρίσεις καὶ φθόνους
all guile and hypocrisies and envies
καὶ πάσας καταλαλιάς, 2 ὡς ἀρτιγέννητα
and all detractions, as newborn
βρέφη τὸ λογικὸν ἄδολον γάλα ἐπιποθήσατε,
babes [2]the [3]spiritual [4]pure [5]milk [1]desire ye,

Chapter 2

THEREFORE, rid yourselves of all malice and all deceit, hypocrisy, envy, and slander of every kind.
2Like newborn babies, crave pure spiritual milk,

[b]Some mss. read *a clean heart*

[a]16 Lev. 11:44,45; 19:2; 20:7
[b]22 Some early manuscripts *from a pure heart*
[c]25 Isaiah 40:6-8

word, that by it you may
grow in respect to salva-
tion,
3 if you have tasted the
kindness of the Lord.

As Living Stones

4 And coming to Him as
to a living stone, rejected
by men, but choice and precious in the sight of God,
5 you also, as living
stones, are being built up as
a spiritual house for a holy
priesthood, to offer up spiritual sacrifices acceptable
to God through Jesus
Christ.
6 For *this* is contained in
Scripture:
"BEHOLD I LAY IN ZION
A CHOICE STONE, A
PRECIOUS CORNER
stone,
AND HE WHO BELIEVES
IN HIM SHALL NOT BE
DISAPPOINTED."
7 This precious value,
then, is for you who be-
lieve. But for those who
disbelieve,
"THE STONE WHICH THE
BUILDERS REJECTED,
THIS BECAME THE VERY
CORNER *stone*,"
8 and,
"A STONE OF STUMBLING
AND A ROCK OF OF-
FENSE";
for they stumble because
they are disobedient to the
word, and to this *doom*
they were also appointed.
9 But you are A CHOSEN
RACE, A royal PRIESTHOOD, A
HOLY NATION, A PEOPLE FOR
God's OWN POSSESSION, that
you may proclaim the ex-
cellencies of Him who has
called you out of darkness
into His marvelous light;
10 for you once were NOT A
PEOPLE, but now you are
THE PEOPLE OF GOD; you had
NOT RECEIVED MERCY, but
now you have RECEIVED
MERCY.
11 Beloved, I urge you as
aliens and strangers to abstain from fleshly lusts,
which wage war against the
soul.
12 Keep your behavior ex-
cellent among the Gentiles,
so that in the thing in which

ἵνα ἐν αὐτῷ αὐξηθῆτε εἰς σωτηρίαν,
in order that by it ye may grow to salvation,
3 εἰ ἐγεύσασθε ὅτι χρηστὸς ὁ κύριος.
if ye tasted that [3]good [1]the [2]Lord [is].
4 πρὸς ὃν προσερχόμενοι, λίθον ζῶντα,
to whom approaching, [2]stone [1]a living,
ὑπὸ ἀνθρώπων μὲν ἀποδεδοκιμασμένον παρὰ
by men on one hand *having been* rejected [3]by
δὲ θεῷ ἐκλεκτὸν ἔντιμον, 5 καὶ
[1]on the other [4]God [2]chosen[,] precious, [2]also
αὐτοὶ ὡς λίθοι ζῶντες οἰκοδομεῖσθε οἶκος
[1][your]selves [3]as [5]stones [4]living are being built [2]house
πνευματικὸς εἰς ἱεράτευμα ἅγιον, ἀνενέγκαι
[1]a spiritual for [2]priesthood [1]a holy, to offer
πνευματικὰς θυσίας εὐπροσδέκτους θεῷ διὰ
spiritual sacrifices acceptable to God through
Ἰησοῦ Χριστοῦ· 6 διότι περιέχει ἐν γραφῇ·
Jesus Christ; because it is contained in scripture:
ἰδοὺ τίθημι ἐν Σιὼν λίθον ἐκλεκτὸν
Behold I lay in Sion [4]stone [1]a chosen
ἀκρογωνιαῖον ἔντιμον, καὶ ὁ πιστεύων
[3]corner foundation [2]precious, and the [one] believing
ἐπ' αὐτῷ οὐ μὴ καταισχυνθῇ. 7 ὑμῖν
on it(him) by no means will be shamed. To you =Yours
οὖν ἡ τιμὴ τοῖς πιστεύουσιν· ἀπιστοῦσιν
therefore [3][is] [4]the [5]honour [1]the [ones] [2]believing[c]; [2]to unbelieving [ones]
therefore who believe is the honour;
δὲ λίθος ὃν ἀπεδοκίμασαν οἱ οἰκοδομοῦντες,
[1]but a stone which [3]rejected [1]the [ones] [2]building,
οὗτος ἐγενήθη εἰς κεφαλὴν γωνίας 8 καὶ
this came to be for head of [the] corner and
λίθος προσκόμματος καὶ πέτρα σκανδάλου·
a stone of stumbling and a rock of offence;
οἳ προσκόπτουσιν τῷ λόγῳ ἀπειθοῦντες,
who stumble at the word disobeying,
9 εἰς ὃ καὶ ἐτέθησαν· ὑμεῖς δὲ γένος
to which indeed they were appointed; but ye [are] [2]race
ἐκλεκτόν, βασίλειον ἱεράτευμα, ἔθνος ἅγιον,
[1]a chosen, a royal priesthood, nation a holy,
λαὸς εἰς περιποίησιν, ὅπως τὰς ἀρετὰς
a people for possession, so as [2]the [3]virtues
ἐξαγγείλητε τοῦ ἐκ σκότους ὑμᾶς καλέ-
[1]ye may tell out [4]of the [one] [7]out of [8]darkness [6]you [5]having
σαντος εἰς τὸ θαυμαστὸν αὐτοῦ φῶς·
called into the marvellous [2]of him [1]light;
10 οἵ ποτε οὐ λαός, νῦν δὲ λαὸς θεοῦ,
who then [were] not a people, but [are] now a people of God,
οἱ οὐκ ἠλεημένοι, νῦν δὲ ἐλεηθέντες.
the [ones] not having been pitied, but now pitied.
11 Ἀγαπητοί, παρακαλῶ ὡς παροίκους
Beloved, I exhort [you] as sojourners
καὶ παρεπιδήμους ἀπέχεσθαι τῶν σαρκικῶν
and aliens to abstain from – fleshly
ἐπιθυμιῶν, αἵτινες στρατεύονται κατὰ τῆς
lusts, which war against the
ψυχῆς· 12 τὴν ἀναστροφὴν ὑμῶν ἐν τοῖς
soul; [2]the [3]conduct [4]of you [5]among [6]the
ἔθνεσιν ἔχοντες καλήν, ἵνα ἐν ᾧ κατα-
[7]nations [1]having [8]good, in order that while they

so that by it you may grow
up in your salvation, 3 now
that you have tasted that
the Lord is good.

The Living Stone and a Chosen People

4 As you come to him, the
living Stone—rejected by
men but chosen by God and
precious to him— 5 you
also, like living stones, are
being built into a spiritual
house to be a holy priesthood, offering spiritual sacrifices acceptable to God
through Jesus Christ. 6 For
in Scripture it says:
"See, I lay a stone in
Zion,
a chosen and precious
cornerstone,
and the one who trusts in
him
will never be put to
shame."[d]
7 Now to you who believe,
this stone is precious. But
to those who do not be-
lieve,
"The stone the builders
rejected
has become the
capstone,[e]"[f]
8 and,
"A stone that causes
men to stumble
and a rock that makes
them fall."[g]
They stumble because they
disobey the message—
which is also what they
were destined for.
9 But you are a chosen
people, a royal priesthood,
a holy nation, a people belonging to God, that you
may declare the praises of
him who called you out of
darkness into his wonderful
light. 10 Once you were not
a people, but now you are
the people of God; once
you had not received mer-
cy, but now you have re-
ceived mercy.
11 Dear friends, I urge
you, as aliens and strangers
in the world, to abstain
from sinful desires, which
war against your soul.
12 Live such good lives
among the pagans that,
though they accuse you of

[d]6 Isaiah 28:16
[e]7 Or *cornerstone*
[f]7 Psalm 118:22
[g]8 Isaiah 8:14

they slander you as evil-
doers, they may on account
of your good deeds, as they
observe *them,* glorify God
in the day of [c] visitation.

Honor Authority

13Submit yourselves for
the Lord's sake to every
human institution, whether
to a king as the one in authority,
14or to governors as sent
by him for the punishment
of evildoers and the praise
of those who do right.
15For such is the will of
God that by doing right you
may silence the ignorance
of foolish men.
16*Act* as free men, and do
not use your freedom as a
covering for evil, but *use it*
as bondslaves of God.
17Honor all men; love the
brotherhood, fear God,
honor the king.
18Servants, be submis-
sive to your masters with
all respect, not only to
those who are good and
gentle, but also to those
who are unreasonable.
19For this *finds* favor, if
for the sake of conscience
toward God a man bears up
under sorrows when suffering unjustly.
20For what credit is there
if, when you sin and are
harshly treated, you endure
it with patience? But if
when you do what is right
and suffer *for it* you patiently endure it, this *finds*
favor with God.

Christ Is Our Example

21For you have been
called for this purpose,
since Christ also suffered
for you, leaving you an example for you to follow in
His steps,
22WHO COMMITTED NO SIN,
NOR WAS ANY DECEIT FOUND
IN HIS MOUTH;
23and while being reviled,
He did not revile in return;
while suffering, He uttered
no threats, but kept en-
trusting *Himself* to Him
who judges righteously;

[c] I.e., Christ's coming again in judgment

λαλοῦσιν ὑμῶν ὡς κακοποιῶν, ἐκ τῶν
speak against you as evildoers, by the (your)
καλῶν ἔργων ἐποπτεύοντες δοξάσωσιν τὸν
good works observing they may glorify –
θεὸν ἐν ἡμέρᾳ ἐπισκοπῆς.
God in a day of visitation.
13 Ὑποτάγητε πάσῃ ἀνθρωπίνῃ κτίσει
Submit to every human ordinance
διὰ τὸν κύριον· εἴτε βασιλεῖ ὡς ὑπερέχοντι,
because of the Lord: whether to a king as being supreme,
14 εἴτε ἡγεμόσιν ὡς δι' αὐτοῦ πεμπομένοις
or to governors as through him being sent
εἰς ἐκδίκησιν κακοποιῶν ἔπαινον δὲ
for vengeance of(on) evildoers [2]praise [1]but
ἀγαθοποιῶν· 15 ὅτι οὕτως ἐστὶν τὸ
of welldoers; because so is the
θέλημα τοῦ θεοῦ, ἀγαθοποιοῦντας φιμοῦν
will – of God, doing good to silence
τὴν τῶν ἀφρόνων ἀνθρώπων ἀγνωσίαν·
[1]the – [3]of foolish [4]men [2]ignorance;
16 ὡς ἐλεύθεροι, καὶ μὴ ὡς ἐπικάλυμμα
as free, and not [3]as [4]a cloak
ἔχοντες τῆς κακίας τὴν ἐλευθερίαν, ἀλλ'
[1]having *the* [5]of evil *the* [2]freedom, but
ὡς θεοῦ δοῦλοι. 17 πάντας τιμήσατε,
as of God slaves. [2]All men [1]honour ye,
τὴν ἀδελφότητα ἀγαπᾶτε, τὸν θεὸν
[2]the [3]brotherhood [1]love, – [2]God
φοβεῖσθε, τὸν βασιλέα τιμᾶτε. 18 Οἱ
[1]fear, [2]the [3]king [1]honour. –
οἰκέται, ὑποτασσόμενοι ἐν παντὶ φόβῳ
House servants, submitting yourselves in all fear
τοῖς δεσπόταις, οὐ μόνον τοῖς ἀγαθοῖς
to the(your) masters, not only to the good
καὶ ἐπιεικέσιν ἀλλὰ καὶ τοῖς σκολιοῖς.
and forbearing but also to the perverse.
19 τοῦτο γὰρ χάρις εἰ διὰ συνείδησιν
For this [is] a favour if because of conscience
θεοῦ ὑποφέρει τις λύπας πάσχων ἀδίκως.
of God [2]bears [1]anyone griefs suffering unjustly.
20 ποῖον γὰρ κλέος εἰ ἁμαρτάνοντες καὶ
For what glory [is it] if sinning and
κολαφιζόμενοι ὑπομενεῖτε; ἀλλ' εἰ ἀγαθο-
being buffeted ye endure? but if doing
ποιοῦντες καὶ πάσχοντες ὑπομενεῖτε, τοῦτο
good and suffering ye endure, this [is]
χάρις παρὰ θεῷ. 21 εἰς τοῦτο γὰρ
a favour with God. [2]to [3]this [1]For
ἐκλήθητε, ὅτι καὶ Χριστὸς ἔπαθεν ὑπὲρ
ye were called, because indeed Christ suffered on behalf of
ὑμῶν, ὑμῖν ὑπολιμπάνων ὑπογραμμὸν ἵνα
you, [2]to you [1]leaving behind an example in order that
ἐπακολουθήσητε τοῖς ἴχνεσιν αὐτοῦ· 22 ὃς
ye should follow the steps of him; who
ἁμαρτίαν οὐκ ἐποίησεν οὐδὲ εὑρέθη δόλος
[3]sin [2]not [1]did nor was [2]found [1]guile
ἐν τῷ στόματι αὐτοῦ· 23 ὃς λοιδορούμενος
in the mouth of him; who being reviled
οὐκ ἀντελοιδόρει, πάσχων οὐκ ἠπείλει,
reviled not in return, suffering he threatened not,
παρεδίδου δὲ τῷ κρίνοντι δικαίως· 24 ὃς
but delivered [himself] to the [one] judging righteously; who

doing wrong, they may see
your good deeds and glorify God on the day he visits
us.

Submission to Rulers and Masters

13Submit yourselves for
the Lord's sake to every
authority instituted among
men: whether to the king,
as the supreme authority,
14or to governors, who are
sent by him to punish those
who do wrong and to com-
mend those who do right.
15For it is God's will that by
doing good you should si-
lence the ignorant talk of
foolish men. 16Live as free
men, but do not use your
freedom as a cover-up for
evil; live as servants of
God. 17Show proper re-
spect to everyone: Love
the brotherhood of believers, fear God, honor the
king.
18Slaves, submit your-
selves to your masters with
all respect, not only to
those who are good and
considerate, but also to
those who are harsh. 19For
it is commendable if a man
bears up under the pain of
unjust suffering because he
is conscious of God. 20But
how is it to your credit if
you receive a beating for
doing wrong and endure it?
But if you suffer for doing
good and you endure it, this
is commendable before
God. 21To this you were
called, because Christ suffered for you, leaving you
an example, that you
should follow in his steps.

22"He committed no sin,
and no deceit was
found in his
mouth."[h]

23When they hurled their
insults at him, he did not
retaliate; when he suffered,
he made no threats. In-
stead, he entrusted himself
to him who judges justly.

[h] 22 Isaiah 53:9

24and He Himself bore
our sins in His body on the
cross, that we might die to
sin and live to righteousness; for by His wounds
you were healed.
25For you were continual-
ly straying like sheep, but
now you have returned to
the Shepherd and Guardian
of your souls.

Chapter 3

Godly Living

IN the same way, you
wives, be submissive to
your own husbands so that
even if any *of them* are
disobedient to the word,
they may be won without a
word by the behavior of
their wives,
2as they observe your
chaste and respectful be-
havior.
3And let not your adorn-
ment be *merely* external—
braiding the hair, and wearing gold jewelry, or putting
on dresses;
4but *let it be* the hidden
person of the heart, with
the imperishable quality of
a gentle and quiet spirit,
which is precious in the
sight of God.
5For in this way in for-
mer times the holy women
also, who hoped in God,
used to adorn themselves,
being submissive to their
own husbands.
6Thus Sarah obeyed
Abraham, calling him lord,
and you have become her
children if you do what is
right without being frightened by any fear.
7You husbands likewise,
live with *your wives* in an
understanding way, as with
a weaker vessel, since she
is a woman; and grant her
honor as a fellow heir of the
grace of life, so that your
prayers may not be hin-
dered.
8To sum up, let all be
harmonious, sympathetic,

τὰς ἁμαρτίας ἡμῶν αὐτὸς ἀνήνεγκεν ἐν
3the 4sins 5of us 1[him]self 2carried up in
τῷ σώματι αὐτοῦ ἐπὶ τὸ ξύλον, ἵνα
the body of him onto the tree, in order that
ταῖς ἁμαρτίαις ἀπογενόμενοι τῇ δικαιοσύνῃ
– 2to sins 1dying – 4to righteousness
ζήσωμεν· οὗ τῷ μώλωπι ἰάθητε.
3we might live; 3of whom 1by the 2bruise ye were cured.
25 ἦτε γὰρ ὡς πρόβατα πλανώμενοι,
2ye were 1For 4as 5sheep 3wandering,
ἀλλὰ ἐπεστράφητε νῦν ἐπὶ τὸν ποιμένα
but ye turned now to the shepherd
καὶ ἐπίσκοπον τῶν ψυχῶν ὑμῶν.
and bishop of the souls of you.
3 Ὁμοίως γυναῖκες, ὑποτασσόμεναι τοῖς
Likewise wives, submitting yourselves to the (your)
ἰδίοις ἀνδράσιν, ἵνα καὶ εἴ τινες ἀπειθοῦσιν
own husbands, in order that even if any disobey
τῷ λόγῳ, διὰ τῆς τῶν γυναικῶν ἀναστροφῆς
the word, through 1the 3of the(ir) 4wives 2conduct
ἄνευ λόγου κερδηθήσονται, **2** ἐποπτεύσαντες
without a word they will(may) be gained, observing
τὴν ἐν φόβῳ ἁγνὴν ἀναστροφὴν ὑμῶν.
1the 5in 6fear 2pure 3conduct 4of you.
3 ὧν ἔστω οὐχ ὁ ἔξωθεν ἐμπλοκῆς
Of whom let it be not 1the 2outward 4of plaiting
τριχῶν καὶ περιθέσεως χρυσίων ἢ ἐνδύσεως
5of hairs 6and 7of putting round(on) 8of gold [ornaments] 9or 10of clothing
ἱματίων κόσμος, **4** ἀλλ' ὁ κρυπτὸς τῆς
11of(with) garments 3adorning, but 1the 2hidden 4of the
καρδίας ἄνθρωπος ἐν τῷ ἀφθάρτῳ τοῦ
5heart 3man in(?by) the incorruptible [adorning] of the
πραέος καὶ ἡσυχίου πνεύματος, ὅ ἐστιν
meek and quiet spirit, which is
ἐνώπιον τοῦ θεοῦ πολυτελές. **5** οὕτως
before – God of great value. so
γάρ ποτε καὶ αἱ ἅγιαι γυναῖκες αἱ
For then indeed the holy women –
ἐλπίζουσαι εἰς θεὸν ἐκόσμουν ἑαυτάς,
hoping in God adorned themselves,
ὑποτασσόμεναι τοῖς ἰδίοις ἀνδράσιν, **6** ὡς
submitting themselves to the(ir) own husbands, as
Σάρρα ὑπήκουσεν τῷ Ἀβραάμ, κύριον
Sara obeyed – Abraham, 3lord
αὐτὸν καλοῦσα· ἧς ἐγενήθητε τέκνα
2him 1calling; of whom ye became children
ἀγαθοποιοῦσαι καὶ μὴ φοβούμεναι μηδεμίαν
doing good and not fearing no(any)
πτόησιν. **7** Οἱ ἄνδρες ὁμοίως, συνοικοῦντες
terror. – Husbands likewise, dwelling together
κατὰ γνῶσιν ὡς ἀσθενεστέρῳ σκεύει τῷ
according to knowledge as with a weaker vessel the
γυναικείῳ, ἀπονέμοντες τιμὴν ὡς καὶ
female, assigning honour as indeed
συγκληρονόμοις χάριτος ζωῆς, εἰς τὸ μὴ
co-heirs of [the] grace of life, *for the* not
ἐγκόπτεσθαι τὰς προσευχὰς ὑμῶν. **8** Τὸ δὲ
to be hindered the prayers of you.[b] Now the
τέλος πάντες ὁμόφρονες, συμπαθεῖς,
end[,] [be ye] all of one mind, sympathetic,

24He himself bore our sins
in his body on the tree, so
that we might die to sins
and live for righteousness;
by his wounds you have
been healed. 25For you
were like sheep going
astray, but now you have
returned to the Shepherd
and Overseer of your souls.

Chapter 3

Wives and Husbands

WIVES, in the same
way be submissive
to your husbands so that, if
any of them do not believe
the word, they may be won
over without words by the
behavior of their wives,
2when they see the purity
and reverence of your
lives. 3Your beauty should
not come from outward
adornment, such as braided
hair and the wearing of gold
jewelry and fine clothes.
4Instead, it should be that
of your inner self, the unfading beauty of a gentle
and quiet spirit, which is of
great worth in God's sight.
5For this is the way the holy
women of the past who put
their hope in God used to
make themselves beautiful.
They were submissive to
their own husbands, 6like
Sarah, who obeyed Abra-
ham and called him her
master. You are her daughters if you do what is right
and do not give way to fear.
7Husbands, in the same
way be considerate as you
live with your wives, and
treat them with respect as
the weaker partner and as
heirs with you of the gracious gift of life, so that
nothing will hinder your
prayers.

Suffering for Doing Good

8Finally, all of you, live in
harmony with one another;
be sympathetic, love as

brotherly, kindhearted,
and humble in spirit;
9not returning evil for
evil, or insult for insult, but
giving a blessing instead;
for you were called for the
very purpose that you
might inherit a blessing.
10For,
"LET HIM WHO MEANS TO
LOVE LIFE AND SEE
GOOD DAYS
REFRAIN HIS TONGUE
FROM EVIL AND HIS
LIPS FROM SPEAKING
GUILE.
11"AND LET HIM TURN
AWAY FROM EVIL AND
DO GOOD;
LET HIM SEEK PEACE
AND PURSUE IT.
12"FOR THE EYES OF THE
LORD ARE UPON THE
RIGHTEOUS,
AND HIS EARS ATTEND
TO THEIR PRAYER,
BUT THE FACE OF THE
LORD IS AGAINST
THOSE WHO DO EVIL."
13And who is there to
harm you if you prove zealous for what is good?
14But even if you should
suffer for the sake of righteousness, *you are* blessed.
AND DO NOT FEAR THEIR IN-
TIMIDATION, AND DO NOT BE
TROUBLED,
15but [d]sanctify Christ as
Lord in your hearts, always
being ready to make a defense to everyone who asks
you to give an account for
the hope that is in you, yet
with gentleness and reverence;
16and keep a good con-
science so that in the thing
in which you are slandered,
those who revile your good
behavior in Christ may be
put to shame.
17For it is better, if God
should will it so, that you
suffer for doing what is
right rather than for doing
what is wrong.
18For Christ also died for
sins once for all, *the* just for
the unjust, in order that He
might bring us to God, hav-

[d] I.e., set apart

φιλάδελφοι, εὔσπλαγχνοι, ταπεινόφρονες,
loving [the] brothers, compassionate, humble-minded,
9 μὴ ἀποδιδόντες κακὸν ἀντὶ κακοῦ ἢ
not giving back evil instead of evil or
λοιδορίαν ἀντὶ λοιδορίας, τοὐναντίον δὲ
reviling instead of reviling, but on the contrary
εὐλογοῦντες, ὅτι εἰς τοῦτο ἐκλήθητε ἵνα
blessing, because to this ye were called in order that
εὐλογίαν κληρονομήσητε. 10 ὁ γὰρ θέλων
blessing ye might inherit. For the [one] wishing
ζωὴν ἀγαπᾶν καὶ ἰδεῖν ἡμέρας ἀγαθάς,
[2]life [1]to love and to see [2]days [1]good,
παυσάτω τὴν γλῶσσαν ἀπὸ κακοῦ καὶ
let him restrain the(his) tongue from evil and
χείλη τοῦ μὴ λαλῆσαι δόλον, 11 ἐκκλινάτω
[his] lips – not to speak[d] guile, [2]let him turn aside
δὲ ἀπὸ κακοῦ καὶ ποιησάτω ἀγαθόν,
[1]and from evil and let him do good,
ζητησάτω εἰρήνην καὶ διωξάτω αὐτήν·
let him seek peace and pursue it;
12 ὅτι ὀφθαλμοὶ κυρίου ἐπὶ δικαίους καὶ
because [the] eyes of [the] Lord [are] on [the] righteous and
ὦτα αὐτοῦ εἰς δέησιν αὐτῶν, πρόσωπον
[the] ears of him [open] to [the] petition of them, [2][the] face
δὲ κυρίου ἐπὶ ποιοῦντας κακά.
[1]but of [the] Lord [is] against [ones] doing evil things.

13 Καὶ τίς ὁ κακώσων ὑμᾶς ἐὰν τοῦ
And who [is] the [one] harming you if [3]of the
ἀγαθοῦ ζηλωταὶ γένησθε; 14 ἀλλ' εἰ καὶ
[4]good [2]zealots [1]ye become ? but if indeed
πάσχοιτε διὰ δικαιοσύνην, μακάριοι. τὸν
ye suffer because of righteousness, blessed [are ye]. [3]the
δὲ φόβον αὐτῶν μὴ φοβηθῆτε μηδὲ
[1]But [4]fear [5]of them [2]fear ye not nor
ταραχθῆτε, 15 κύριον δὲ τὸν Χριστὸν
be ye troubled, [1]but [4][as] [5]Lord – [3]Christ
ἁγιάσατε ἐν ταῖς καρδίαις ὑμῶν, ἕτοιμοι
[2]sanctify in the hearts of you, ready
ἀεὶ πρὸς ἀπολογίαν παντὶ τῷ αἰτοῦντι
always for defence to every one asking
ὑμᾶς λόγον περὶ τῆς ἐν ὑμῖν ἐλπίδος,
you a word concerning [1]the [3]in [4]you [2]hope,
16 ἀλλὰ μετὰ πραΰτητος καὶ φόβου,
but with meekness and fear,
συνείδησιν ἔχοντες ἀγαθήν, ἵνα ἐν ᾧ
[3]conscience [1]having [2]a good, in order that while
καταλαλεῖσθε καταισχυνθῶσιν οἱ ἐπηρεάζοντες
ye are spoken against [3]may be shamed [by] [1]the [ones] [2]abusing [you]
ὑμῶν τὴν ἀγαθὴν ἐν Χριστῷ
[7]of you [4]the [5]good [8]in [9]Christ
ἀναστροφήν. 17 κρεῖττον γὰρ ἀγαθοποιοῦντας,
[6]conduct. For [it is] better doing good,
εἰ θέλοι τὸ θέλημα τοῦ θεοῦ,
if [4]wills [1]the [2]will – [3]of God,
πάσχειν ἢ κακοποιοῦντας. 18 ὅτι καὶ
to suffer than doing evil. Because indeed
Χριστὸς ἅπαξ περὶ ἁμαρτιῶν ἀπέθανεν,
Christ once [2]concerning [3]sins [1]died,
δίκαιος ὑπὲρ ἀδίκων, ἵνα ὑμᾶς προσαγάγῃ
a righteous man on behalf of unrighteous ones, in order that [2]you [1]he might bring

brothers, be compassion-
ate and humble. 9Do not repay evil with evil or insult
with insult, but with blessing, because to this you
were called so that you may
inherit a blessing. 10For,
"Whoever would love
life
and see good days
must keep his tongue
from evil
and his lips from
deceitful speech.
11He must turn from evil
and do good;
he must seek peace and
pursue it.
12For the eyes of the Lord
are on the righteous
and his ears are
attentive to their
prayer,
but the face of the Lord
is against those who
do evil."[i]
13Who is going to harm
you if you are eager to do
good? 14But even if you
should suffer for what is
right, you are blessed. "Do
not fear what they fear[j]; do
not be frightened."[k] 15But
in your hearts set apart
Christ as Lord. Always be
prepared to give an answer
to everyone who asks you
to give the reason for the
hope that you have. But do
this with gentleness and respect, 16keeping a clear
conscience, so that those
who speak maliciously
against your good behavior
in Christ may be ashamed
of their slander. 17It is better, if it is God's will, to
suffer for doing good than
for doing evil. 18For Christ
died for sins once for all,
the righteous for the un-
righteous, to bring you to

[i] 12 Psalm 34:12-16
[j] 14 Or *not fear their threats*
[k] 14 Isaiah 8:12

ing been put to death in the flesh, but made alive in the spirit;
19 in which also He went and made proclamation to the spirits *now* in prison,
20 who once were disobedient, when the patience of God kept waiting in the days of Noah, during the construction of the ark, in which a few, that is, eight persons, were brought safely through *the* water.
21 And corresponding to that, baptism now saves you—not the removal of dirt from the flesh, but an appeal to God for a good conscience—through the resurrection of Jesus Christ,
22 who is at the right hand of God, having gone into heaven, after angels and authorities and powers had been subjected to Him.

Chapter 4

Keep Fervent in Your Love

THEREFORE, since Christ has [e]suffered in the flesh, arm yourselves also with the same purpose, because he who has suffered in the flesh has ceased from sin,
2 so as to live the rest of the time in the flesh no longer for the lusts of men, but for the will of God.
3 For the time already past is sufficient *for you* to have carried out the desire of the Gentiles, having pursued a course of sensuality, lusts, drunkenness, carousals, drinking parties and abominable idolatries.
4 And in *all* this, they are surprised that you do not run with *them* into the same excess of dissipation, and they malign *you*;
5 but they shall give account to Him who is ready to judge the living and the dead.
6 For the gospel has for this purpose been preached even to those who are dead, that though they are

[e]I.e., suffered death

τῷ θεῷ, θανατωθεὶς μὲν σαρκὶ ζωοποιηθεὶς
– to God, being put to death on one hand in [the] flesh[,] quickened
δὲ πνεύματι· 19 ἐν ᾧ καὶ τοῖς ἐν
on the other in [the] spirit; in which indeed [3]to the [4]in
φυλακῇ πνεύμασιν πορευθεὶς ἐκήρυξεν,
[5]prison [2]spirits [1]going he proclaimed,
20 ἀπειθήσασίν ποτε ὅτε ἀπεξεδέχετο ἡ
to disobeying ones then when [4]waited [1]the
τοῦ θεοῦ μακροθυμία ἐν ἡμέραις Νῶε
– [3]of God [2]longsuffering in [the] days of Noe
κατασκευαζομένης κιβωτοῦ, εἰς ἣν ὀλίγοι,
[2]being prepared [1]an ark,[a] in which a few,
τοῦτ' ἔστιν ὀκτὼ ψυχαί, διεσώθησαν δι'
this is eight souls, were quite saved through
ὕδατος. 21 ὃ καὶ ὑμᾶς ἀντίτυπον νῦν
water. [1]Which [3]also [6]us [2]figure [4]now
σῴζει βάπτισμα, οὐ σαρκὸς ἀπόθεσις
[5]saves [even] baptism, not [3]of [the] flesh [1]a putting away
ῥύπου ἀλλὰ συνειδήσεως ἀγαθῆς ἐπερώτημα
[2]of [the] filth but [3]conscience [2]of a good [1]an answer
εἰς θεόν, δι' ἀναστάσεως Ἰησοῦ Χριστοῦ,
toward God, through [the] resurrection of Jesus Christ,
22 ὅς ἐστιν ἐν δεξιᾷ θεοῦ, πορευθεὶς
who is at [the] right [hand] of God, having gone
εἰς οὐρανόν, ὑποταγέντων αὐτῷ ἀγγέλων
into heaven, [6]being subjected [7]to him [1]angels
καὶ ἐξουσιῶν καὶ δυνάμεων.
[2]and [3]authorities [4]and [5]powers[a].
4 Χριστοῦ οὖν παθόντος σαρκὶ καὶ ὑμεῖς
[2]Christ [1]therefore having suffered[a] in [the] flesh [2]also [1]ye
τὴν αὐτὴν ἔννοιαν ὁπλίσασθε, ὅτι ὁ
[4]the [5]same [6]mind [3]arm yourselves [with], because the [one]
παθὼν σαρκὶ πέπαυται ἁμαρτίας, 2 εἰς
having suffered in [the] flesh has ceased from sin, for
τὸ μηκέτι ἀνθρώπων ἐπιθυμίαις ἀλλὰ
the [1]no longer [9]of men [8]in [the] lusts [10]but
θελήματι θεοῦ τὸν ἐπίλοιπον ἐν σαρκὶ
[11]in [the] will [12]of God [3]the [4]remaining [6]in [7][the] flesh
βιῶσαι χρόνον. 3 ἀρκετὸς γὰρ ὁ παρεληλυ-
[2]to live [5]time. For [5]sufficient [1]the [3]having passed
θὼς χρόνος τὸ βούλημα τῶν ἐθνῶν
away [2]time [4][is] [7]the [8]purpose [9]of the [10]nations
κατειργάσθαι, πεπορευμένους ἐν ἀσελγείαις,
[6]to have worked out, having gone [on] in licentiousnesses,
ἐπιθυμίαις, οἰνοφλυγίαις, κώμοις, πότοις
lusts, debaucheries, carousals, drinking bouts
καὶ ἀθεμίτοις εἰδωλολατρίαις. 4 ἐν ᾧ
and unlawful idolatries. While
ξενίζονται μὴ συντρεχόντων ὑμῶν εἰς
they are surprised [2]not [3]running with [1]you[a] to
τὴν αὐτὴν τῆς ἀσωτίας ἀνάχυσιν, βλασ-
the same – [2]of profligacy [1]excess, blas-
φημοῦντες· 5 οἳ ἀποδώσουσιν λόγον τῷ
pheming; who will render account to the [one]
ἑτοίμως ἔχοντι κρῖναι ζῶντας καὶ νεκρούς.
readily having =who is ready to judge living and dead.
6 εἰς τοῦτο γὰρ καὶ νεκροῖς εὐηγγελίσθη,
[2]for [3]this [1]For indeed [2]to dead men [1]good news was preached,

God. He was put to death in the body but made alive by the Spirit, 19 through whom[l] also he went and preached to the spirits in prison 20 who disobeyed long ago when God waited patiently in the days of Noah while the ark was being built. In it only a few people, eight in all, were saved through water, 21 and this water symbolizes baptism that now saves you also—not the removal of dirt from the body but the pledge[m] of a good conscience toward God. It saves you by the resurrection of Jesus Christ, 22 who has gone into heaven and is at God's right hand—with angels, authorities and powers in submission to him.

Chapter 4

Living for God

THEREFORE, since Christ suffered in his body, arm yourselves also with the same attitude, because he who has suffered in his body is done with sin. 2 As a result, he does not live the rest of his earthly life for evil human desires, but rather for the will of God. 3 For you have spent enough time in the past doing what pagans choose to do—living in debauchery, lust, drunkenness, orgies, carousing and detestable idolatry. 4 They think it strange that you do not plunge with them into the same flood of dissipation, and they heap abuse on you. 5 But they will have to give account to him who is ready to judge the living and the dead. 6 For this is the reason the gospel was preached even to those who are now dead, so that

[l]*18,19* Or *alive in the spirit,* *19through which*
[m]*21* Or *response*

judged in the flesh as men, they may live in the spirit according to *the will of* God.
7The end of all things is at hand; therefore, be of sound judgment and sober *spirit* for the purpose of prayer.
8Above all, keep fervent in your love for one another, because love covers a multitude of sins.
9Be hospitable to one another without complaint.
10As each one has received a *special* gift, employ it in serving one another, as good stewards of the manifold grace of God.
11Whoever speaks, *let him speak,* as it were, the utterances of God; whoever serves, *let him do so* as by the strength which God supplies; so that in all things God may be glorified through Jesus Christ, to whom belongs the glory and dominion forever and ever. Amen.

Share the Sufferings of Christ

12Beloved, do not be surprised at the fiery ordeal among you, which comes upon you for your testing, as though some strange thing were happening to you;
13but to the degree that you share the sufferings of Christ, keep on rejoicing; so that also at the revelation of His glory, you may rejoice with exultation.
14If you are reviled for the name of Christ, you are blessed, because the Spirit of glory and of God rests upon you.
15By no means let any of you suffer as a murderer, or thief, or evildoer, or a troublesome meddler;
16but if *anyone suffers* as a Christian, let him not feel ashamed, but in that name let him glorify God.

ἵνα κριθῶσι μὲν κατὰ ἀνθρώπους
in order that [2]they might be judged [1]on one hand according to men
σαρκί, ζῶσι δὲ κατὰ θεὸν πνεύματι.
in [the] flesh, [2]might live [1]on the other according to God in [the] spirit.
7 Πάντων δὲ τὸ τέλος ἤγγικεν.
Now of all things the end has drawn near.
σωφρονήσατε οὖν καὶ νήψατε εἰς
Be ye soberminded therefore and be *ye* sober unto
προσευχάς· **8** πρὸ πάντων τὴν εἰς ἑαυτοὺς
prayers; before all things – [4]to [5]yourselves
ἀγάπην ἐκτενῆ ἔχοντες, ὅτι ἀγάπη
[3]love [2]fervent [1]having, because love
καλύπτει πλῆθος ἁμαρτιῶν· **9** φιλόξενοι εἰς
covers a multitude of sins; [be] hospitable to
ἀλλήλους ἄνευ γογγυσμοῦ· **10** ἕκαστος καθὼς
one another without murmuring; each one as
ἔλαβεν χάρισμα, εἰς ἑαυτοὺς αὐτὸ διακον-
he received a gift, [3]to [4]yourselves [2]it [1]minister-
οῦντες ὡς καλοὶ οἰκονόμοι ποικίλης χάριτος
ing as good stewards of [the] manifold grace
θεοῦ· **11** εἴ τις λαλεῖ, ὡς λόγια θεοῦ·
of God; if anyone speaks, as [the] oracles of God;
εἴ τις διακονεῖ, ὡς ἐξ ἰσχύος ἧς χορηγεῖ
if anyone ministers, as by strength which [2]supplies
ὁ θεός· ἵνα ἐν πᾶσιν δοξάζηται ὁ θεὸς
– [1]God; in order that in all things [2]may be glorified – [1]God
διὰ Ἰησοῦ Χριστοῦ, ᾧ ἐστιν ἡ δόξα
through Jesus Christ, to whom = whose is[c] the glory
καὶ τὸ κράτος εἰς τοὺς αἰῶνας τῶν
and the might unto the ages of the
αἰώνων· ἀμήν.
ages: Amen.
12 Ἀγαπητοί, μὴ ξενίζεσθε τῇ ἐν ὑμῖν
Beloved, be not surprised [at] [1]the [4]among [5]you
πυρώσει πρὸς πειρασμὸν ὑμῖν γινομένῃ,
[2]fiery trial [6]for [7]trial [8]to you [3]happening,
ὡς ξένου ὑμῖν συμβαίνοντος, **13** ἀλλὰ
as a surprising thing [2]to you [1]occurring[a], but
καθὸ κοινωνεῖτε τοῖς τοῦ Χριστοῦ
[2]as [3]ye share [4]the – [6]of Christ
παθήμασιν χαίρετε, ἵνα καὶ ἐν τῇ ἀπο-
[5]sufferings [1]rejoice, in order that also at the reve-
καλύψει τῆς δόξης αὐτοῦ χαρῆτε ἀγαλ-
lation of the glory of him ye may rejoice exult-
λιώμενοι. **14** εἰ ὀνειδίζεσθε ἐν ὀνόματι
ing. If ye are reproached in [the] name
Χριστοῦ, μακάριοι, ὅτι τὸ τῆς δόξης
of Christ, blessed [are ye], because [1]the – [2]of glory
καὶ τὸ τοῦ θεοῦ πνεῦμα ἐφ' ὑμᾶς
[4]and [5]*the*(?that) – [6]of God [3]spirit [8]on [9]you
ἀναπαύεται. **15** μὴ γάρ τις ὑμῶν πασχέτω
[7]rests. [3]Not [1]for [4]anyone [5]of you [2]let [6]suffer
ὡς φονεὺς ἢ κλέπτης ἢ κακοποιὸς ἢ
as a murderer or a thief or an evildoer or
ὡς ἀλλοτριεπίσκοπος· **16** εἰ δὲ ὡς
as a pryer into other men's affairs; but if as
Χριστιανός, μὴ αἰσχυνέσθω, δοξαζέτω δὲ
a Christian, let him not be shamed, but let him glorify
τὸν θεὸν ἐν τῷ ὀνόματι τούτῳ. **17** ὅτι
– God by this name. Because

they might be judged according to men in regard to the body, but live according to God in regard to the spirit.
7The end of all things is near. Therefore be clear minded and self-controlled so that you can pray.
8Above all, love each other deeply, because love covers over a multitude of sins.
9Offer hospitality to one another without grumbling.
10Each one should use whatever gift he has received to serve others, faithfully administering God's grace in its various forms.
11If anyone speaks, he should do it as one speaking the very words of God. If anyone serves, he should do it with the strength God provides, so that in all things God may be praised through Jesus Christ. To him be the glory and the power for ever and ever. Amen.

Suffering for Being a Christian

12Dear friends, do not be surprised at the painful trial you are suffering, as though something strange were happening to you.
13But rejoice that you participate in the sufferings of Christ, so that you may be overjoyed when his glory is revealed.
14If you are insulted because of the name of Christ, you are blessed, for the Spirit of glory and of God rests on you.
15If you suffer, it should not be as a murderer or thief or any other kind of criminal, or even as a meddler.
16However, if you suffer as a Christian, do not be ashamed, but praise God that you bear that name.

17For *it is* time for judgment to begin with the
household of God; and if *it*
begins with us first, what
will be the outcome for
those who do not obey the
gospel of God?
18AND IF IT IS WITH DIF-
FICULTY THAT THE RIGHT-
EOUS IS SAVED, WHAT WILL
BECOME OF THE GODLESS MAN
AND THE SINNER?
19Therefore, let those
also who suffer according
to the will of God entrust
their souls to a faithful
Creator in doing what is
right.

[ὁ] καιρὸς τοῦ ἄρξασθαι τὸ κρίμα ἀπὸ
the time [?has come] – to begin[d] the judgment from
τοῦ οἴκου τοῦ θεοῦ· εἰ δὲ πρῶτον ἀφ'
the household – of God; and if firstly from
ἡμῶν, τί τὸ τέλος τῶν ἀπειθούντων
us, what [will be] the end of the [ones] disobeying
τῷ τοῦ θεοῦ εὐαγγελίῳ; 18 καὶ εἰ ὁ
the – [2]of God [1]gospel? and if the
δίκαιος μόλις σῴζεται, ὁ [δὲ] ἀσεβὴς
righteous man scarcely is saved, [3]the – [4]impious
καὶ ἁμαρτωλὸς ποῦ φανεῖται; 19 ὥστε
[5]and [6]sinner [1]where [2]will [7]appear ? so as
καὶ οἱ πάσχοντες κατὰ τὸ θέλημα τοῦ
indeed the [ones] suffering according to the will –
θεοῦ πιστῷ κτίστῃ παρατιθέσθωσαν τὰς
of God [5]to a faithful [6]Creator [1]let them commit [2]the
ψυχὰς αὐτῶν ἐν ἀγαθοποιΐᾳ.
[3]souls [4]of them in welldoing.

17For it is time for judgment
to begin with the family of
God; and if it begins with
us, what will the outcome
be for those who do not
obey the gospel of God?
18And,

"If it is hard for the
righteous to be
saved,
what will become of
the ungodly and the
sinner?"[n]

19So then, those who suf-
fer according to God's will
should commit themselves
to their faithful Creator and
continue to do good.

Chapter 5

Serve God Willingly

THEREFORE, I exhort
the elders among you,
as *your* fellow elder and
witness of the sufferings of
Christ, and a partaker also
of the glory that is to be revealed,
2shepherd the flock of
God among you, exercising
oversight not under com-
pulsion, but voluntarily,
according to *the will of*
God; and not for sordid
gain, but with eagerness;
3nor yet as lording it over
those allotted to your
charge, but proving to be
examples to the flock.
4And when the Chief
Shepherd appears, you will
receive the unfading crown
of glory.
5You younger men, like-
wise, be subject to your elders; and all of you, clothe
yourselves with humility
toward one another, for
GOD IS OPPOSED TO THE
PROUD, BUT GIVES GRACE TO
THE HUMBLE.
6Humble yourselves,
therefore, under the mighty
hand of God, that He may
exalt you at the proper
time,
7casting all your anxiety
upon Him, because He

5 Πρεσβυτέρους οὖν ἐν ὑμῖν παρακαλῶ
Elders therefore among you I exhort
ὁ συμπρεσβύτερος καὶ μάρτυς τῶν τοῦ
the co-elder and witness [1]of the –
Χριστοῦ παθημάτων, ὁ καὶ τῆς μελλούσης
[3]of Christ [2]sufferings, [1]the [3]also [4]of the [6]*being* about
ἀποκαλύπτεσθαι δόξης κοινωνός· 2 ποιμάνατε
[7]to be revealed [5]glory [2]sharer : shepherd
τὸ ἐν ὑμῖν ποίμνιον τοῦ θεοῦ, μὴ
[1]the [4]among [5]you [2]flock – [3]of God, not
ἀναγκαστῶς ἀλλὰ ἑκουσίως κατὰ θεόν,
by way of compulsion but willingly according to God,
μηδὲ αἰσχροκερδῶς ἀλλὰ προθύμως, 3 μηδ'
nor from eagerness for base gain but eagerly, nor
ὡς κατακυριεύοντες τῶν κλήρων ἀλλὰ
as exercising lordship over the lots* but
τύποι γινόμενοι τοῦ ποιμνίου· 4 καὶ
[2]examples [1]becoming of the flock; and
φανερωθέντος τοῦ ἀρχιποίμενος κομιεῖσθε
appearing the chief shepherd[a] ye will receive
=when the chief shepherd appears
τὸν ἀμαράντινον τῆς δόξης στέφανον.
the unfading – [2]of glory [1]crown.
5 Ὁμοίως, νεώτεροι, ὑποτάγητε πρεσβυτέ-
Likewise, younger men, submit yourselves to older
ροις· πάντες δὲ ἀλλήλοις τὴν ταπεινοφρο-
men; and all [3]to one another – [2]humil-
σύνην ἐγκομβώσασθε, ὅτι ὁ θεὸς ὑπερηφάνοις
ity [1]gird ye on, because – God [2]arrogant men
ἀντιτάσσεται, ταπεινοῖς δὲ δίδωσιν χάριν.
[1]resists, but to humble men he gives grace.
6 Ταπεινώθητε οὖν ὑπὸ τὴν κραταιὰν
Be ye humbled therefore under the mighty
χεῖρα τοῦ θεοῦ, ἵνα ὑμᾶς ὑψώσῃ ἐν
hand – of God, in order that [2]you [1]he may exalt in
καιρῷ, 7 πᾶσαν τὴν μέριμναν ὑμῶν
time, [2]all [3]the [4]anxiety [5]of you
ἐπιρίψαντες ἐπ' αὐτόν, ὅτι αὐτῷ μέλει
[1]casting on him, because [2]to him [1]it matters

Chapter 5

To Elders and Young Men

TO the elders among
you, I appeal as a fel-
low elder, a witness of
Christ's sufferings and one
who also will share in the
glory to be revealed: 2Be
shepherds of God's flock
that is under your care,
serving as overseers—not
because you must, but be-
cause you are willing, as
God wants you to be; not
greedy for money, but ea-
ger to serve; 3not lording it
over those entrusted to
you, but being examples to
the flock. 4And when the
Chief Shepherd appears,
you will receive the crown
of glory that will never fade
away.
5Young men, in the same
way be submissive to those
who are older. All of you,
clothe yourselves with humility toward one another,
because,

"God opposes the proud
but gives grace to the
humble."[o]

6Humble yourselves,
therefore, under God's
mighty hand, that he may
lift you up in due time.
7Cast all your anxiety on
him because he cares for
you.

* That is, the various spheres assigned to the elders.

[n] *18* Prov. 11:31
[o] *5* Prov. 3:34

cares for you.
8Be of sober *spirit,* be on
the alert. Your adversary,
the devil, prowls about like
a roaring lion, seeking
someone to devour.
9But resist him, firm in
your faith, knowing that the
same experiences of suffering are being accomplished
by your brethren who are in
the world.
10And after you have suf-
fered for a little while, the
God of all grace, who called
you to His eternal glory in
Christ, will Himself per-
fect, confirm, strengthen
and establish you.
11To Him *be* dominion
forever and ever. Amen.
12Through Silvanus, our
faithful brother (for so I regard *him*), I have written to
you briefly, exhorting and
testifying that this is the
true grace of God. Stand
firm in it!
13[f]She who is in Bab-
ylon, chosen together with
you, sends you greetings,
and *so does* my son, Mark.
14Greet one another with
a kiss of love.
Peace be to you all who
are in Christ.

περὶ ὑμῶν. **8** Νήψατε, γρηγορήσατε. ὁ
concerning you. Be ye sober, watch ye. The
ἀντίδικος ὑμῶν διάβολος ὡς λέων ὠρυόμενος
adversary of you [the] devil as a lion roaring
περιπατεῖ ζητῶν τινα καταπιεῖν· **9** ᾧ
walks about seeking whom to devour; whom
ἀντίστητε στερεοὶ τῇ πίστει, εἰδότες τὰ
oppose firm in the faith, knowing the
αὐτὰ τῶν παθημάτων τῇ ἐν τῷ κόσμῳ
same *of the* sufferings [2]in the [5]in [6]the [7]world
things
ὑμῶν ἀδελφότητι ἐπιτελεῖσθαι. **10** Ὁ δὲ
[4]of you [3]brotherhood [1]to be accomplished. [2]the [1]Now
θεὸς πάσης χάριτος, ὁ καλέσας ὑμᾶς
God of all grace, the [one] having called you
εἰς τὴν αἰώνιον αὐτοῦ δόξαν ἐν Χριστῷ,
to the [1]eternal [3]of him [2]glory in Christ,
ὀλίγον παθόντας αὐτὸς καταρτίσει, στηρίξει,
[1][you] [3]a little [2]having suffered [him]self will adjust, confirm,
σθενώσει, θεμελιώσει. **11** αὐτῷ τὸ κράτος
strengthen, found. To him [is][c] the might
=His is*
εἰς τοὺς αἰῶνας τῶν αἰώνων· ἀμήν.
unto the ages of the ages: Amen.
12 Διὰ Σιλουανοῦ ὑμῖν τοῦ πιστοῦ
Through Silvanus to you the faithful
ἀδελφοῦ, ὡς λογίζομαι, δι' ὀλίγων ἔγραψα,
brother, as I reckon, by means of a few [words] I wrote,
παρακαλῶν καὶ ἐπιμαρτυρῶν ταύτην εἶναι
exhorting and witnessing this to be
ἀληθῆ χάριν τοῦ θεοῦ, εἰς ἣν στῆτε.
[the] true grace – of God, in which ye stand.
13 Ἀσπάζεται ὑμᾶς ἡ ἐν Βαβυλῶνι
[10]greets [11]you [1]The [3]in [4]Babylon
συνεκλεκτὴ καὶ Μᾶρκος ὁ υἱός μου.
[2]co-chosen [? church] [5]and [6]Mark [7]the [8]son [9]of me.
14 ἀσπάσασθε ἀλλήλους ἐν φιλήματι ἀγάπης.
Greet ye one another with a kiss of love.
Εἰρήνη ὑμῖν πᾶσιν τοῖς ἐν Χριστῷ.
Peace to you all the ones in Christ.

8Be self-controlled and
alert. Your enemy the devil
prowls around like a roaring lion looking for someone to devour. 9Resist him,
standing firm in the faith,
because you know that
your brothers throughout
the world are undergoing
the same kind of sufferings.
10And the God of all
grace, who called you to his
eternal glory in Christ, after you have suffered a little while, will himself restore you and make you
strong, firm and steadfast.
11To him be the power for
ever and ever. Amen.

Final Greetings

12With the help of Silas,[p]
whom I regard as a faithful
brother, I have written to
you briefly, encouraging
you and testifying that this
is the true grace of God.
Stand fast in it.
13She who is in Babylon,
chosen together with you,
sends you her greetings,
and so does my son Mark.
14Greet one another with a
kiss of love.
Peace to all of you who
are in Christ.

2 Peter

Chapter 1

Growth in Christian Virtue

[a]SIMON Peter, a bond-
servant and apostle
of Jesus Christ, to those
who have received a faith
of the same kind as ours, by
the righteousness of our
God and Savior, Jesus
Christ:
2Grace and peace be
multiplied to you in the
knowledge of God and of
Jesus our Lord;
3seeing that His divine
power has granted to us

ΠΕΤΡΟΥ Β
Of Peter 2

1 Συμεὼν Πέτρος δοῦλος καὶ ἀπόστολος
Symeon Peter a slave and an apostle
Ἰησοῦ Χριστοῦ τοῖς ἰσότιμον ἡμῖν
of Jesus Christ [1]to the [ones] [3]equally precious [5]with us
λαχοῦσιν πίστιν ἐν δικαιοσύνῃ τοῦ θεοῦ
[2]having obtained [4]faith in [the] righteousness of the God
ἡμῶν καὶ σωτῆρος Ἰησοῦ Χριστοῦ·
of us and Saviour Jesus Christ:
2 χάρις ὑμῖν καὶ εἰρήνη πληθυνθείη ἐν
Grace to you and peace *may it* be multiplied by
ἐπιγνώσει τοῦ θεοῦ καὶ Ἰησοῦ τοῦ
a full knowledge – of God and of Jesus the
κυρίου ἡμῶν.
Lord of us.
3 Ὡς τὰ πάντα ἡμῖν τῆς θείας δυνάμεως
As – all things to us the divine power
=his divine power has given us all things . . .

2 Peter

Chapter 1

SIMON Peter, a servant
and apostle of Jesus
Christ,
To those who through the
righteousness of our God
and Savior Jesus Christ
have received a faith as
precious as ours:
2Grace and peace be
yours in abundance
through the knowledge of
God and of Jesus our Lord.

Making One's Calling and Election Sure

3His divine power has
given us everything we

[f]Some mss. read *The church which*
[a]Most early mss. read *Simeon*

* *Cf.* 4. 11 (a statement of fact, not a wish).

[p]*12* Greek *Silvanus,* a variant of *Silas*

everything pertaining to life
and godliness, through the
true knowledge of Him
who called us by His own
glory and excellence.
4For by these He has
granted to us His precious
and magnificent promises,
in order that by them you
might become partakers of
the divine nature, having
escaped the corruption that
is in the world by lust.
5Now for this very rea-
son also, applying all diligence, in your faith supply
moral excellence, and in
your moral excellence,
knowledge;
6and in *your* knowledge,
self-control, and in *your*
self-control, perseverance,
and in *your* perseverance,
godliness;
7and in *your* godliness,
brotherly kindness, and in
your brotherly kindness,
love.
8For if these *qualities* are
yours and are increasing,
they render you neither
useless nor unfruitful in the
true knowledge of our Lord
Jesus Christ.
9For he who lacks these
qualities is blind *or* short-
sighted, having forgotten
his purification from his
former sins.
10Therefore, brethren, be
all the more diligent to
make certain about His
calling and choosing you;
for as long as you practice
these things, you will never
stumble;
11for in this way the en-
trance into the eternal kingdom of our Lord and Savior
Jesus Christ will be abundantly supplied to you.
12Therefore, I shall al-
ways be ready to remind
you of these things, even
though you *already* know
them, and have been established in the truth which is
present with *you*.

αὐτοῦ τὰ πρὸς ζωὴν καὶ εὐσέβειαν δεδωρημένης
of him – [belong-ing] to life and piety having given[a]

διὰ τῆς ἐπιγνώσεως τοῦ καλέσαντος ἡμᾶς
through the full knowledge of the [one] having called us

ἰδίᾳ δόξῃ καὶ ἀρετῇ, 4 δι' ὧν τὰ τίμια
to [his] own glory and virtue, through which *the* [3]precious things

καὶ μέγιστα ἡμῖν ἐπαγγέλματα δεδώρηται,
[4]and [5]very great [2]to us [6]promises [1]he has given,

ἵνα διὰ τούτων γένησθε θείας κοινωνοὶ
in order that through these ye might become [2]of a divine [1]sharers

φύσεως, ἀποφυγόντες τῆς ἐν τῷ κόσμῳ
[3]nature, escaping from [1]the [3]in [4]the [5]world

ἐν ἐπιθυμίᾳ φθορᾶς. 5 καὶ αὐτὸ τοῦτο
[6]by [7]lust [2]corruption. [2]also [3]for this very thing (reason)

δὲ σπουδὴν πᾶσαν παρεισενέγκαντες
[1]But [6]diligence [5]all [4]bringing in

ἐπιχορηγήσατε ἐν τῇ πίστει ὑμῶν τὴν
supply in the faith of you –

ἀρετήν, ἐν δὲ τῇ ἀρετῇ τὴν γνῶσιν,
virtue, and in – virtue – knowledge,

6 ἐν δὲ τῇ γνώσει τὴν ἐγκράτειαν,
and in – knowledge – self-control,

ἐν δὲ τῇ ἐγκρατείᾳ τὴν ὑπομονήν, ἐν
and in – self-control – endurance, [2]in

δὲ τῇ ὑπομονῇ τὴν εὐσέβειαν, 7 ἐν δὲ
[1]and – endurance – piety, and in

τῇ εὐσεβείᾳ τὴν φιλαδελφίαν, ἐν δὲ
– piety – brotherly friendship, and in

τῇ φιλαδελφίᾳ τὴν ἀγάπην. 8 ταῦτα
– brotherly friendship – love. these things

γὰρ ὑμῖν ὑπάρχοντα καὶ πλεονάζοντα
For [2]in you [1]being and abounding

οὐκ ἀργοὺς οὐδὲ ἀκάρπους καθίστησιν
[3]not [4]barren [5]nor [6]unfruitful [1]makes [2][you]

εἰς τὴν τοῦ κυρίου ἡμῶν Ἰησοῦ Χριστοῦ
in [1]the [3]of the [4]Lord [5]of us [6]Jesus [7]Christ

ἐπίγνωσιν· 9 ᾧ γὰρ μὴ πάρεστιν ταῦτα,
[2]full knowledge; for [he] in whom [3]not [2]is(are) [4]present [1]these things.

τυφλός ἐστιν μυωπάζων, λήθην λαβὼν
[2]blind [1]is being short-sighted, forgetfulness taking =being forgetful

τοῦ καθαρισμοῦ τῶν πάλαι αὐτοῦ ἁμαρτιῶν.
of the cleansing of the [3]in time past [2]of him [1]sins.

10 διὸ μᾶλλον, ἀδελφοί, σπουδάσατε
Wherefore rather, brothers, be ye diligent

βεβαίαν ὑμῶν τὴν κλῆσιν καὶ ἐκλογὴν
[2]firm [7]of you [3]the [4]calling [5]and [6]choice

ποιεῖσθαι· ταῦτα γὰρ ποιοῦντες οὐ μὴ
[1]to make; for these things doing by no means

πταίσητέ ποτε. 11 οὕτως γὰρ πλουσίως
ye will fail ever. For so [3]richly

ἐπιχορηγηθήσεται ὑμῖν ἡ εἴσοδος εἰς τὴν
[1]will be supplied [2]to you the entrance into the

αἰώνιον βασιλείαν τοῦ κυρίου ἡμῶν καὶ
eternal kingdom of the Lord of us and

σωτῆρος Ἰησοῦ Χριστοῦ.
Saviour Jesus Christ.

12 Διὸ μελλήσω ἀεὶ ὑμᾶς ὑπομιμνήσκειν
Wherefore I *will* intend always you to remind

περὶ τούτων, καίπερ εἰδότας καὶ
concerning these things, though knowing and

ἐστηριγμένους ἐν τῇ παρούσῃ ἀληθείᾳ.
having been confirmed in the present truth.

need for life and godliness
through our knowledge of
him who called us by his
own glory and goodness.
4Through these he has giv-
en us his very great and
precious promises, so that
through them you may par-
ticipate in the divine nature
and escape the corruption
in the world caused by evil
desires.
5For this very reason,
make every effort to add to
your faith goodness; and to
goodness, knowledge; 6and
to knowledge, self-control;
and to self-control, perseverance; and to persever-
ance, godliness; 7and to
godliness, brotherly kindness; and to brotherly kindness, love. 8For if you possess these qualities in increasing measure, they will
keep you from being inef-
fective and unproductive in
your knowledge of our
Lord Jesus Christ. 9But if
anyone does not have
them, he is nearsighted and
blind, and has forgotten
that he has been cleansed
from his past sins.
10Therefore, my broth-
ers, be all the more eager to
make your calling and election sure. For if you do
these things, you will never
fall, 11and you will receive
a rich welcome into the
eternal kingdom of our
Lord and Savior Jesus
Christ.

Prophecy of Scripture

12So I will always remind
you of these things, even
though you know them and
are firmly established in the
truth you now have. 13I

13And I consider it right,
as long as I am in this *earth-*
ly dwelling, to stir you up
by way of reminder,
14knowing that the laying
aside of my *earthly* dwelling is imminent, as also our
Lord Jesus Christ has made
clear to me.
15And I will also be diligent that at any time after
my departure you may be
able to call these things to
mind.

Eyewitnesses

16For we did not follow
cleverly devised tales when
we made known to you the
power and coming of our
Lord Jesus Christ, but we
were eyewitnesses of His
majesty.
17For when He received
honor and glory from God
the Father, such an utterance as this was made to
Him by the Majestic Glory,
"This is My beloved Son
with whom I am well-
pleased"—
18and we ourselves heard
this utterance made from
heaven when we were with
Him on the holy mountain.
19And *so* we have the prophetic word *made* more
sure, to which you do well
to pay attention as to a
lamp shining in a dark
place, until the day dawns
and the morning star arises
in your hearts.
20But knows this first
of all, that no prophecy of
Scripture is *a matter* of
one's own interpretation,
21for no prophecy was
ever made by an act of human will, but men moved
by the Holy Spirit spoke
from God.

13 δίκαιον δὲ ἡγοῦμαι, ἐφ' ὅσον εἰμι
And [2]right [1]I deem [it], so long as† I am
ἐν τούτῳ τῷ σκηνώματι, διεγείρειν ὑμᾶς
in this – tabernacle, to rouse you
ἐν ὑπομνήσει, **14** εἰδὼς ὅτι ταχινή ἐστιν
by a reminder, knowing that soon is
ἡ ἀπόθεσις τοῦ σκηνώματός μου, καθὼς
the putting off of the tabernacle of me, as
καὶ ὁ κύριος ἡμῶν Ἰησοῦς Χριστὸς
indeed the Lord of us Jesus Christ
ἐδήλωσέν μοι· **15** σπουδάσω δὲ καὶ
made clear to me; and I will be diligent also
ἑκάστοτε ἔχειν ὑμᾶς μετὰ τὴν ἐμὴν
[6]always [7]to have [2]you [3]after – [4]my
ἔξοδον τὴν τούτων μνήμην ποιεῖσθαι.
[5]exodus [8]the [10]of these things [9]memory [1]to cause.
16 οὐ γὰρ σεσοφισμένοις μύθοις ἐξακολου-
For not [3]having been cleverly devised [2]fables [1]follow-
θήσαντες ἐγνωρίσαμεν ὑμῖν τὴν τοῦ κυρίου
ing we made known to you [1]the [5]of the [6]Lord
ἡμῶν Ἰησοῦ Χριστοῦ δύναμιν καὶ
[7]of us [8]Jesus [9]Christ [2]power [3]and
παρουσίαν, ἀλλ' ἐπόπται γενηθέντες τῆς
[4]presence, but [2]eyewitnesses [1]having become [3]of the
ἐκείνου μεγαλειότητος. **17** λαβὼν γὰρ
[5]of that one [4]majesty. For receiving
παρὰ θεοῦ πατρὸς τιμὴν καὶ δόξαν
from God [the] Father honour and glory
φωνῆς ἐνεχθείσης αὐτῷ τοιᾶσδε ὑπὸ τῆς
[2]a voice [3]being borne[a] [4]to him [1]such by the
μεγαλοπρεποῦς δόξης· ὁ υἱός μου ὁ
magnificent glory: The Son of me the
ἀγαπητός μου οὗτός ἐστιν, εἰς ὃν ἐγὼ
beloved of me this is, in whom I
εὐδόκησα, — **18** καὶ ταύτην τὴν φωνὴν
was wellpleased,— and this – voice
ἡμεῖς ἠκούσαμεν ἐξ οὐρανοῦ ἐνεχθεῖσαν
we heard [2]out of [3]heaven [1]being borne
σὺν αὐτῷ ὄντες ἐν τῷ ἁγίῳ ὄρει. **19** καὶ
[5]with [6]him [4]being in the holy mountain. And
ἔχομεν βεβαιότερον τὸν προφητικὸν λόγον,
we have more firm the prophetic word,
ᾧ καλῶς ποιεῖτε προσέχοντες ὡς λύχνῳ
to which [2]well [1]ye do taking heed as to a lamp
φαίνοντι ἐν αὐχμηρῷ τόπῳ, ἕως οὗ
shining in a murky place, until
ἡμέρα διαυγάσῃ καὶ φωσφόρος ἀνατείλῃ
day dawns and [the] daystar rises
ἐν ταῖς καρδίαις ὑμῶν· **20** τοῦτο πρῶτον
in the hearts of you; [2]this [3]firstly
γινώσκοντες, ὅτι πᾶσα προφητεία γραφῆς
[1]knowing, that every =no ... is ... prophecy of scripture
ἰδίας ἐπιλύσεως οὐ γίνεται· **21** οὐ γὰρ
of [its] own solution not becomes; for not
θελήματι ἀνθρώπου ἠνέχθη προφητεία
by will of man [2]was borne [1]prophecy
ποτέ, ἀλλὰ ὑπὸ πνεύματος ἁγίου φερόμενοι
at any time, but [6]by [8]Spirit [7][the] Holy [5]being borne
ἐλάλησαν ἀπὸ θεοῦ ἄνθρωποι.
[2]spoke [3]from [4]God [1]men.

think it is right to refresh
your memory as long as I
live in the tent of this body,
14because I know that I will
soon put it aside, as our
Lord Jesus Christ has made
clear to me. 15And I will
make every effort to see
that after my departure you
will always be able to remember these things.
16We did not follow clev-
erly invented stories when
we told you about the power and coming of our Lord
Jesus Christ, but we were
eyewitnesses of his majesty. 17For he received honor
and glory from God the Father when the voice came
to him from the Majestic
Glory, saying, "This is my
Son, whom I love; with him
I am well pleased."[a] 18We
ourselves heard this voice
that came from heaven
when we were with him on
the sacred mountain.
19And we have the word
of the prophets made more
certain, and you will do
well to pay attention to it,
as to a light shining in a
dark place, until the day
dawns and the morning star
rises in your hearts.
20Above all, you must un-
derstand that no prophecy
of Scripture came about by
the prophet's own interpretation. 21For prophecy never had its origin in the will
of man, but men spoke
from God as they were carried along by the Holy Spirit.

[a] *17* Matt. 17:5; Mark 9:7; Luke 9:35

Chapter 2

The Rise of False Prophets

BUT false prophets also arose among the people, just as there will also be false teachers among you, who will secretly introduce destructive heresies, even denying the Master who bought them, bringing swift destruction upon themselves.

2And many will follow their sensuality, and because of them the way of the truth will be maligned;

3and in *their* greed they will exploit you with false words; their judgment from long ago is not idle, and their destruction is not asleep.

4For if God did not spare angels when they sinned, but cast them into hell and committed them to pits of darkness, reserved for judgment;

5and did not spare the ancient world, but preserved Noah, a preacher of righteousness, with seven others, when He brought a flood upon the world of the ungodly;

6and *if* He condemned the cities of Sodom and Gomorrah to destruction by reducing *them* to ashes, having made them an example to those who would live ungodly thereafter;

7and *if* He rescued righteous Lot, oppressed by the sensual conduct of unprincipled men

8(for by what he saw and heard *that* righteous man, while living among them, felt *his* righteous soul tormented day after day with *their* lawless deeds),

9*then* the Lord knows how to rescue the godly from temptation, and to keep the unrighteous under punishment for the day of judgment,

10and especially those

2 Ἐγένοντο δὲ καὶ ψευδοπροφῆται ἐν
But there were also false prophets among

τῷ λαῷ, ὡς καὶ ἐν ὑμῖν ἔσονται
the people, as indeed among you there will be

ψευδοδιδάσκαλοι, οἵτινες παρεισάξουσιν
false teachers, who will secretly bring in

αἱρέσεις ἀπωλείας, καὶ τὸν ἀγοράσαντα
opinions of destruction,* and [2]the [4]having bought

αὐτοὺς δεσπότην ἀρνούμενοι, ἐπάγοντες
[5]them [3]Master [1]denying, bringing on

ἑαυτοῖς ταχινὴν ἀπώλειαν· **2** καὶ πολλοὶ
themselves swift destruction; and many

ἐξακολουθήσουσιν αὐτῶν ταῖς ἀσελγείαις,
will follow [3]of them [1]the [2]licentiousness*es*,

δι' οὓς ἡ ὁδὸς τῆς ἀληθείας βλασφημη-
because of whom the way of *the* truth will be

θήσεται· **3** καὶ ἐν πλεονεξίᾳ πλαστοῖς
blasphemed; and by covetousness with fabricated

λόγοις ὑμᾶς ἐμπορεύσονται· οἷς τὸ κρίμα
words [2]you [1]they will make merchandise of; for whom the judgment

ἔκπαλαι οὐκ ἀργεῖ, καὶ ἡ ἀπώλεια
of old lingers not, and the destruction

αὐτῶν οὐ νυστάζει. **4** εἰ γὰρ ὁ θεὸς
of them slumbers not. For if – God

ἀγγέλων ἁμαρτησάντων οὐκ ἐφείσατο, ἀλλὰ
[2]angels [3]sinning [1]spared not, but

σιροῖς ζόφου ταρταρώσας παρέδωκεν
[2]in pits [3]of gloom [1]consigning to Tartarus [4]delivered [them]

εἰς κρίσιν τηρουμένους, **5** καὶ ἀρχαίου
[6]to [7]judgment [5]being kept, and [2][the] ancient

κόσμου οὐκ ἐφείσατο, ἀλλὰ ὄγδοον Νῶε
[3]world [1]spared not, but [2][the] eighth man [3]Noe

δικαιοσύνης κήρυκα ἐφύλαξεν, κατακλυσμὸν
[5]of righteousness [4]a herald [1]guarded, [2]a flood

κόσμῳ ἀσεβῶν ἐπάξας, **6** καὶ πόλεις
[4]a world [5]of impious men [1]bringing [3]on, and [3][the] cities

Σοδόμων καὶ Γομόρρας τεφρώσας
[4]of Sodom [5]and [6]Gomorra [1]covering [them] with ashes

καταστροφῇ κατέκρινεν, ὑπόδειγμα μελ-
[7]by an overthrow [2]condemned, [8]an example [9]of men

λόντων ἀσεβεῖν τεθεικώς, **7** καὶ δίκαιον
intending [4]to live impiously [1]having set(made), and [2]righteous

Λὼτ καταπονούμενον ὑπὸ τῆς τῶν ἀθέσμων
[3]Lot [4]*being* oppressed [5]by [6]the [10]of the [11]lawless

ἐν ἀσελγείᾳ ἀναστροφῆς ἐρρύσατο· **8** βλέμ-
[8]in [9]licentiousness [7]conduct [1]delivered; [2]in

ματι γὰρ καὶ ἀκοῇ ὁ δίκαιος ἐγκατοικῶν
seeing [1]for and in hearing the (that) righteous man dwelling

ἐν αὐτοῖς ἡμέραν ἐξ ἡμέρας ψυχὴν
among them day after† day [2][his] [4]soul

δικαίαν ἀνόμοις ἔργοις ἐβασάνιζεν·
[3]righteous [5]with [their] lawless [6]works [1]tormented;

9 οἶδεν κύριος εὐσεβεῖς ἐκ πειρασμοῦ
[2]knows* [1][the] Lord [4]pious men [5]out of [6]trial

ῥύεσθαι, ἀδίκους δὲ εἰς ἡμέραν κρίσεως
[3]to deliver, [3]unjust men [1]but [5]for [6]a day [7]of judgment

κολαζομένους τηρεῖν, **10** μάλιστα δὲ τοὺς
[4]being punished [2]to keep, and most of all [1]the

* Genitive of quality : " destructive opinions."

* That is, " the Lord can deliver "; see note on page xviii.

Chapter 2

False Teachers and Their Destruction

BUT there were also false prophets among the people, just as there will be false teachers among you. They will secretly introduce destructive heresies, even denying the sovereign Lord who bought them—bringing swift destruction on themselves. 2Many will follow their shameful ways and will bring the way of truth into disrepute. 3In their greed these teachers will exploit you with stories they have made up. Their condemnation has long been hanging over them, and their destruction has not been sleeping.

4For if God did not spare angels when they sinned, but sent them to hell,[b] putting them into gloomy dungeons[c] to be held for judgment; 5if he did not spare the ancient world when he brought the flood on its ungodly people, but protected Noah, a preacher of righteousness, and seven others; 6if he condemned the cities of Sodom and Gomorrah by burning them to ashes, and made them an example of what is going to happen to the ungodly; 7and if he rescued Lot, a righteous man, who was distressed by the filthy lives of lawless men 8(for that righteous man, living among them day after day, was tormented in his righteous soul by the lawless deeds he saw and heard)— 9if this is so, then the Lord knows how to rescue godly men from trials and to hold the unrighteous for the day of judgment, while continuing their punishment.[d] 10This is especially true of

[b]4 Greek *Tartarus*
[c]4 Some manuscripts *into chains of darkness*
[d]9 Or *unrighteous for punishment until the day of judgment*

who indulge the flesh in *its*
corrupt desires and despise
authority. Daring, self-
willed, they do not tremble
when they revile angelic
majesties,
11whereas angels who are
greater in might and power
do not bring a reviling judgment against them before
the Lord.
12But these, like unrea-
soning animals, born as
creatures of instinct to be
captured and killed, reviling where they have no
knowledge, will in the destruction of those creatures
also be destroyed,
13suffering wrong as the
wages of doing wrong.
They count it a pleasure to
revel in the daytime. They
are stains and blemishes,
reveling in their [b]decep-
tions, as they carouse with
you,
14having eyes full of adultery and that never cease
from sin, enticing unstable
souls, having a heart
trained in greed, accursed
children;
15forsaking the right way
they have gone astray, having followed the way of Balaam, the *son* of Beor, who
loved the wages of unrighteousness,
16but he received a
rebuke for his own trans-
gression; *for* a dumb donkey, speaking with a voice
of a man, restrained the
madness of the prophet.
17These are springs with-
out water, and mists driven
by a storm, for whom the
black darkness has been reserved.
18For speaking out arro-
gant *words* of vanity they
entice by fleshly desires,
by sensuality, those who
barely escape from the
ones who live in error,
19promising them free-

ὀπίσω σαρκὸς ἐν ἐπιθυμίᾳ μιασμοῦ
[3]after [4]flesh [5]in [6]lust [7]of defilement*

πορευομένους καὶ κυριότητος καταφρονοῦντας.
[2][ones] going [8]and [10]dominion [9]despising.

τολμηταὶ αὐθάδεις, δόξας οὐ τρέμουσιν
[2]darers [1]Self-satisfied, glories they do not tremble [at]

βλασφημοῦντες, **11** ὅπου ἄγγελοι ἰσχύϊ καὶ
blaspheming, where angels [3]in strength [4]and

δυνάμει μείζονες ὄντες οὐ φέρουσιν κατ'
[5]in power [2]greater [1]being do not bring against

αὐτῶν παρὰ κυρίῳ βλάσφημον κρίσιν.
them before [the] Lord railing judgment.

12 οὗτοι δέ, ὡς ἄλογα ζῷα γεγεννημένα
But these men, [1]as [4]without reason [3]animals [2]having been born

φυσικὰ εἰς ἅλωσιν καὶ φθοράν, ἐν οἷς
[1]natural for capture and corruption, [2]in [3]things which

ἀγνοοῦσιν βλασφημοῦντες, ἐν τῇ φθορᾷ
[4]they are ignorant [of] [1]railing, in the corruption

αὐτῶν καὶ φθαρήσονται, **13** ἀδικούμενοι
of them indeed they will be corrupted, suffering wrong

μισθὸν ἀδικίας· ἡδονὴν ἡγούμενοι τὴν
[as] wages of wrong; [5][to be] pleasure [1]deeming –

ἐν ἡμέρᾳ τρυφήν, σπίλοι καὶ μῶμοι
[2]in [4][the] day [3]luxury, spots and blemishes

ἐντρυφῶντες ἐν ταῖς ἀπάταις αὐτῶν
revelling in the deceits of them

συνευωχούμενοι ὑμῖν, **14** ὀφθαλμοὺς ἔχοντες
feasting along with you, [2]eyes [1]having

μεστοὺς μοιχαλίδος καὶ ἀκαταπαύστους
full of an adulteress and not ceasing from

ἁμαρτίας, δελεάζοντες ψυχὰς ἀστηρίκτους,
sin, alluring [2]souls [1]unsteady,

καρδίαν γεγυμνασμένην πλεονεξίας ἔχοντες,
[2]a heart [3]*having been* exercised [4]of(in) covetousness [1]having,

κατάρας τέκνα· **15** καταλείποντες εὐθεῖαν
[2]of curse [1]children; forsaking a straight

ὁδὸν ἐπλανήθησαν, ἐξακολουθήσαντες τῇ
way they erred, following the

ὁδῷ τοῦ Βαλαὰμ τοῦ Βεώρ, ὃς μισθὸν
way – of Balaam the [son] of Beor, who [3][the] wages

ἀδικίας ἠγάπησεν, **16** ἔλεγξιν δὲ ἔσχεν
[3]of wrong [1]loved, and [2]reproof [1]had

ἰδίας παρανομίας· ὑποζύγιον ἄφωνον ἐν
of [his] own transgression; [2]ass [1]a dumb [4]with

ἀνθρώπου φωνῇ φθεγξάμενον ἐκώλυσεν
[6]of a man [5]voice [3]speaking restrained

τὴν τοῦ προφήτου παραφρονίαν. **17** οὗτοί
[1]the [3]of the [4]prophet [2]madness. These men

εἰσιν πηγαὶ ἄνυδροι καὶ ὁμίχλαι ὑπὸ
are [2]springs [1]waterless and mists [2]by

λαίλαπος ἐλαυνόμεναι, οἷς ὁ ζόφος τοῦ
[3]storm [1]being driven, for whom the gloom of *the*

σκότους τετήρηται. **18** ὑπέρογκα γὰρ
darkness has been kept. For [2]immoderate [words]

ματαιότητος φθεγγόμενοι δελεάζουσιν ἐν
[3]of vanity [1]speaking they allure by

ἐπιθυμίαις σαρκὸς ἀσελγείαις τοὺς ὀλίγως
[the] lusts of [the] flesh in excesses the [ones] almost

ἀποφεύγοντας τοὺς ἐν πλάνῃ ἀναστρε-
escaping [1]the [ones] [3]in [4]error [2]liv-

φομένους, **19** ἐλευθερίαν αὐτοῖς ἐπαγγελ-
ing, [3]freedom [2]*to* them [1]promis-

* Genitive of quality: " defiling lust."

those who follow the cor-
rupt desire of the sinful nature[e] and despise authority.
Bold and arrogant, these
men are not afraid to slander celestial beings; 11yet
even angels, although they
are stronger and more powerful, do not bring slanderous accusations against
such beings in the presence
of the Lord. 12But these
men blaspheme in matters
they do not understand.
They are like brute beasts,
creatures of instinct, born
only to be caught and de-
stroyed, and like beasts
they too will perish.
13They will be paid back
with harm for the harm
they have done. Their idea
of pleasure is to carouse in
broad daylight. They are
blots and blemishes, reveling in their pleasures while
they feast with you.[f]
14With eyes full of adultery,
they never stop sinning;
they seduce the unstable;
they are experts in greed—
an accursed brood! 15They
have left the straight way
and wandered off to follow
the way of Balaam son of
Beor, who loved the wages
of wickedness. 16But he
was rebuked for his wrongdoing by a donkey—a
beast without speech—
who spoke with a man's
voice and restrained the
prophet's madness.
17These men are springs
without water and mists
driven by a storm. Blackest
darkness is reserved for
them. 18For they mouth
empty, boastful words and,
by appealing to the lustful
desires of sinful human nature, they entice people
who are just escaping from
those who live in error.
19They promise them free-

[b] Some ancient mss. read *love feasts*, (cf. Jude 12)

[e]10 Or *the flesh*
[f]13 Some manuscripts *in their love feasts*

dom while they themselves
are slaves of corruption; for
by what a man is over-
come, by this he is en-
slaved.
20For if after they have
escaped the defilements of
the world by the knowledge
of the Lord and Savior
Jesus Christ, they are again
entangled in them and are
overcome, the last state
has become worse for them
than the first.
21For it would be better
for them not to have known
the way of righteousness,
than having known it, to
turn away from the holy
commandment delivered to
them.
22It has happened to them
according to the true proverb, "A DOG RETURNS TO ITS
OWN VOMIT," and, "A sow,
after washing, *returns* to
wallowing in the mire."

Chapter 3

Purpose of This Letter

THIS is now, beloved,
the second letter I am
writing to you in which I am
stirring up your sincere
mind by way of reminder,
2that you should remem-
ber the words spoken
beforehand by the holy
prophets and the com-
mandment of the Lord and
Savior *spoken* by your
apostles.

The Coming Day of the Lord

3Know this first of all,
that in the last days mockers will come with *their*
mocking, following after
their own lusts,
4and saying, "Where is
the promise of His coming?
For *ever* since the fathers
fell asleep, all continues
just as it was from the beginning of creation."
5For when they maintain
this, it escapes their notice
that by the word of God *the*
heavens existed long ago

λόμενοι, αὐτοὶ δοῦλοι ὑπάρχοντες τῆς
ing, [them]selves [2]slaves [1]being –
φθορᾶς· ᾧ γάρ τις ἥττηται, τούτῳ
of corruption; for by whom anyone has been defeated, to this man
δεδούλωται. 20 εἰ γὰρ ἀποφυγόντες τὰ
he has been enslaved. For if having escaped the
μιάσματα τοῦ κόσμου ἐν ἐπιγνώσει τοῦ
defilements of the world by a full knowledge of the
κυρίου καὶ σωτῆρος Ἰησοῦ Χριστοῦ,
Lord and Saviour Jesus Christ,
τούτοις δὲ πάλιν ἐμπλακέντες ἡττῶνται,
yet by these again having been entangled have been defeated,
γέγονεν αὐτοῖς τὰ ἔσχατα χείρονα τῶν
[3]have become [4]to them [1]the [2]last things worse [than] the
πρώτων. 21 κρεῖττον γὰρ ἦν αὐτοῖς
first. For better it was for them
μὴ ἐπεγνωκέναι τὴν ὁδὸν τῆς δικαιοσύνης,
not to have fully known the way – of righteousness,
ἢ ἐπιγνοῦσιν ὑποστρέψαι ἐκ τῆς παρα-
than fully knowing to turn from [1]the [4]de-
δοθείσης αὐτοῖς ἁγίας ἐντολῆς. 22 συμβέ-
livered [5]to them [2]holy [3]commandment. [5]has
βηκεν αὐτοῖς τὸ τῆς ἀληθοῦς παροιμίας·
happened [6]to them [1]The thing [2]of the [3]true [4]proverb:
κύων ἐπιστρέψας ἐπὶ τὸ ἴδιον ἐξέραμα,
[The] dog turning upon the(its) own vomit,
καί· ὗς λουσαμένη εἰς κυλισμὸν βορβόρου.
and: [The] sow washed to wallowing of mud.

3 Ταύτην ἤδη, ἀγαπητοί, δευτέραν ὑμῖν
[1]This [6]now, [4]beloved, [2]second [7]to you
γράφω ἐπιστολήν, ἐν αἷς διεγείρω ὑμῶν
[5]I write [3]epistle, in [both] which I rouse [4]of you
ἐν ὑπομνήσει τὴν εἰλικρινῆ διάνοιαν,
[5]by [6]reminder [1]the [2]sincere [3]mind,
2 μνησθῆναι τῶν προειρημένων ῥημάτων
to remember the [2]having been previously spoken [1]words
ὑπὸ τῶν ἁγίων προφητῶν καὶ τῆς τῶν
by the holy prophets and [1]the [3]of the
ἀποστόλων ὑμῶν ἐντολῆς τοῦ κυρίου καὶ
[4]apostles [5]of you [2]commandment of the Lord and
σωτῆρος, 3 τοῦτο πρῶτον γινώσκοντες, ὅτι
Saviour, [2]this [3]first*ly* [1]knowing, that
ἐλεύσονται ἐπ' ἐσχάτων τῶν ἡμερῶν ἐν
there will come during [the] last of the days [3]in
ἐμπαιγμονῇ ἐμπαῖκται κατὰ τὰς ἰδίας
[4]mocking [1]mockers [5]according to [6]the(ir) [7]own
ἐπιθυμίας αὐτῶν πορευόμενοι 4 καὶ λέγοντες·
[8]lusts *of them* [2]going and saying:
ποῦ ἐστιν ἡ ἐπαγγελία τῆς παρουσίας
Where is the promise of the presence
αὐτοῦ; ἀφ' ἧς γὰρ οἱ πατέρες ἐκοι-
of him? [2]from [3]which [day] [1]for the fathers fell
=for from the day when . . .
μήθησαν, πάντα οὕτως διαμένει ἀπ'
asleep, all things so remain*s* from
ἀρχῆς κτίσεως. 5 λανθάνει γὰρ αὐτοὺς
[the] beginning of creation. For [2]is concealed [from] [3]them
τοῦτο θέλοντας ὅτι οὐρανοὶ ἦσαν ἔκπαλαι
[1]this wishing* that heavens were of old

* That is, they wish it to be so.

dom, while they them-
selves are slaves of depravity—for a man is a slave to
whatever has mastered
him. 20If they have escaped
the corruption of the world
by knowing our Lord and
Savior Jesus Christ and are
again entangled in it and
overcome, they are worse
off at the end than they
were at the beginning. 21It
would have been better for
them not to have known the
way of righteousness, than
to have known it and then
to turn their backs on the
sacred command that was
passed on to them. 22Of
them the proverbs are true:
"A dog returns to its vomit,"[g] and, "A sow that is
washed goes back to her
wallowing in the mud."

Chapter 3

The Day of the Lord

DEAR friends, this is
now my second letter
to you. I have written both
of them as reminders to
stimulate you to whole-
some thinking. 2I want you
to recall the words spoken
in the past by the holy
prophets and the command
given by our Lord and Savior through your apostles.
3First of all, you must understand that in the last
days scoffers will come,
scoffing and following their
own evil desires. 4They will
say, "Where is this 'com-
ing' he promised? Ever
since our fathers died, everything goes on as it has
since the beginning of creation." 5But they deliberately forget that long ago by
God's word the heavens
existed and the earth was

[g]22 Prov. 26:11

and *the* earth was formed
out of water and by water,
6through which the
world at that time was destroyed, being flooded with
water.
7But the present heavens
and earth by His word are
being reserved for fire,
kept for the day of judg-
ment and destruction of
ungodly men.
8But do not let this one
fact escape your notice, beloved, that with the Lord
one day is as a thousand
years, and a thousand
years as one day.
9The Lord is not slow
about His promise, as some
count slowness, but is patient toward you, not wishing for any to perish but for
all to come to repentance.

A New Heaven and Earth

10But the day of the Lord
will come like a thief, in
which the heavens will pass
away with a roar and the
elements will be destroyed
with intense heat, and the
earth and its works will be
[c]burned up.
11Since all these things
are to be destroyed in this
way, what sort of people
ought you to be in holy conduct and godliness,
12looking for and hasten-
ing the coming of the day of
God, on account of which
the heavens will be de-
stroyed by burning, and the
elements will melt with intense heat!
13But according to His
promise we are looking for
new heavens and a new
earth, in which righteousness dwells.
14Therefore, beloved,
since you look for these

καὶ γῆ ἐξ ὕδατος καὶ δι᾽ ὕδατος
and earth by water and through water
συνεστῶσα τῷ τοῦ θεοῦ λόγῳ, 6 δι᾽
[1]having been held together [2]by the – [4]of God [3]word, through
ὧν ὁ τότε κόσμος ὕδατι κατακλυσθεὶς
which things the then§ world [2]by water [1]being inundated
ἀπώλετο· 7 οἱ δὲ νῦν οὐρανοὶ καὶ ἡ
perished; but the now heavens and the
γῆ τῷ αὐτῷ λόγῳ τεθησαυρισμένοι εἰσὶν
earth by the same word [2]*having been* stored up [1]are
πυρὶ τηρούμενοι εἰς ἡμέραν κρίσεως καὶ
[3]for fire [1]being kept in a day of judgment and
ἀπωλείας τῶν ἀσεβῶν ἀνθρώπων. 8 ᾿Εν
destruction of *the* impious men. [2]one
δὲ τοῦτο μὴ λανθανέτω ὑμᾶς, ἀγαπητοί,
But [1]this [3]thing let not be concealed [from] you, beloved,
ὅτι μία ἡμέρα παρὰ κυρίῳ ὡς χίλια
that one day with [the] Lord [is] as a thousand
ἔτη καὶ χίλια ἔτη ὡς ἡμέρα μία. 9 οὐ
years and a thousand years as [2]day [1]one. [3]not
βραδύνει κύριος τῆς ἐπαγγελίας, ὥς τινες
[2]is [4]slow [1][The] Lord of the (his) promise, as some
βραδύτητα ἡγοῦνται, ἀλλὰ μακροθυμεῖ εἰς
[2]slowness [1]deem, but is longsuffering toward
ὑμᾶς, μὴ βουλόμενός τινας ἀπολέσθαι
you, not purposing any to perish
ἀλλὰ πάντας εἰς μετάνοιαν χωρῆσαι.
but all men [2]to [3]repentance [1]to come.
10 ῞Ηξει δὲ ἡμέρα κυρίου ὡς κλέπτης,
But will come [the] day of [the] Lord as a thief,
ἐν ᾗ οἱ οὐρανοὶ ῥοιζηδὸν παρελεύσονται,
in which the heavens [2]with rushing sound [1]will pass away,
στοιχεῖα δὲ καυσούμενα λυθήσεται, καὶ
and [the] elements burning will be dissolved, and
γῆ καὶ τὰ ἐν αὐτῇ ἔργα εὑρεθήσεται.
[the] earth and [1]the [3]in [4]it [2]works will be discovered.
11 Τούτων οὕτως πάντων λυομένων
[2]these things [3]thus [1]All [4]being dissolved*
ποταποὺς δεῖ ὑπάρχειν [ὑμᾶς] ἐν ἁγίαις
what sort of men it behoves [2]to be [1]you in holy
ἀναστροφαῖς καὶ εὐσεβείαις, 12 προσδοκῶντας
conduct* and piety,* awaiting
καὶ σπεύδοντας τὴν παρουσίαν τῆς τοῦ
and hastening the presence [1]of the –
θεοῦ ἡμέρας, δι᾽ ἣν οὐρανοὶ πυρούμενοι
[2]of God [1]day, on account of which [the] heavens being set on fire
λυθήσονται καὶ στοιχεῖα καυσούμενα
will be dissolved and [the] elements burning
τήκεται. 13 καινοὺς δὲ οὐρανοὺς καὶ
melts. But new heavens and
γῆν καινὴν κατὰ τὸ ἐπάγγελμα αὐτοῦ
[2]earth [1]a new according to the promise of him
προσδοκῶμεν, ἐν οἷς δικαιοσύνη κατοικεῖ.
we await, in which righteousness dwells.
14 Διό, ἀγαπητοί, ταῦτα προσδοκῶντες
Wherefore, beloved, [2]these things [1]awaiting

formed out of water and by
water. 6By these waters
also the world of that time
was deluged and de-
stroyed. 7By the same
word the present heavens
and earth are reserved for
fire, being kept for the day
of judgment and destruc-
tion of ungodly men.
8But do not forget this
one thing, dear friends:
With the Lord a day is like
a thousand years, and a
thousand years are like a
day. 9The Lord is not slow
in keeping his promise, as
some understand slowness.
He is patient with you, not
wanting anyone to perish,
but everyone to come to repentance.
10But the day of the Lord
will come like a thief. The
heavens will disappear with
a roar; the elements will be
destroyed by fire, and the
earth and everything in it
will be laid bare.[h]
11Since everything will be
destroyed in this way, what
kind of people ought you to
be? You ought to live holy
and godly lives 12as you
look forward to the day of
God and speed its com-
ing.[i] That day will bring
about the destruction of the
heavens by fire, and the elements will melt in the
heat. 13But in keeping with
his promise we are looking
forward to a new heaven
and a new earth, the home
of righteousness.
14So then, dear friends,
since you are looking for-

[c] Some ancient mss. read *discovered*

§ This is allowable English : *cf.* "the then Prime Minister."

* The Greek plurals cannot be literally reproduced in English.

[h] *10* Some manuscripts *be burned up*

[i] *12* Or *as you wait eagerly for the day of God to come*

things, be diligent to be found by Him in peace, spotless and blameless,

15and regard the patience of our Lord *to be* salvation; just as also our beloved brother Paul, according to the wisdom given him, wrote to you,

16as also in all *his* letters, speaking in them of these things, in which are some things hard to understand, which the untaught and unstable distort, as *they do* also the rest of the Scriptures, to their own destruction.

17You therefore, beloved, knowing this beforehand, be on your guard lest, being carried away by the error of unprincipled men, you fall from your own steadfastness,

18but grow in the grace and knowledge of our Lord and Savior Jesus Christ. To Him *be* the glory, both now and to the day of eternity. Amen.

σπουδάσατε ἄσπιλοι καὶ ἀμώμητοι αὐτῷ
be diligent [5]spotless [6]and [7]unblemished [3]by him

εὑρεθῆναι ἐν εἰρήνῃ, 15 καὶ τὴν τοῦ
[1]to be found [2]in [4]peace, and [2]the [4]of the

κυρίου ἡμῶν μακροθυμίαν σωτηρίαν ἡγεῖσθε,
[5]Lord [6]of us [3]longsuffering [7]salvation [1]deem,

καθὼς καὶ ὁ ἀγαπητὸς ἡμῶν ἀδελφὸς
as indeed the beloved [2]of us [1]brother

Παῦλος κατὰ τὴν δοθεῖσαν αὐτῷ σοφίαν
Paul according to [1]the [3]given [4]to him [2]wisdom

ἔγραψεν ὑμῖν, 16 ὡς καὶ ἐν πάσαις
wrote to you, as also in all [his]

ἐπιστολαῖς λαλῶν ἐν αὐταῖς περὶ τούτων,
epistles speaking in them concerning these things,

ἐν αἷς ἐστιν δυσνόητά τινα, ἃ οἱ
in which is(are) [2]hard to understand [1]some things, which the

ἀμαθεῖς καὶ ἀστήρικτοι στρεβλοῦσιν ὡς
unlearned and unsteady twist as

καὶ τὰς λοιπὰς γραφὰς πρὸς τὴν ἰδίαν
also the remaining scriptures to the(ir) own

αὐτῶν ἀπώλειαν. 17 Ὑμεῖς οὖν, ἀγαπητοί,
of them destruction. Ye therefore, beloved,

προγινώσκοντες φυλάσσεσθε ἵνα μὴ τῇ
knowing before guard lest [2]by the

τῶν ἀθέσμων πλάνῃ συναπαχθέντες ἐκπέ-
[4]of the [5]lawless [3]error [1]being led away *with* ye fall

σητε τοῦ ἰδίου στηριγμοῦ, 18 αὐξάνετε
from the(your) own stability, [2]grow ye

δὲ ἐν χάριτι καὶ γνώσει τοῦ κυρίου
[1]but in grace and knowledge of the Lord

ἡμῶν καὶ σωτῆρος Ἰησοῦ Χριστοῦ.
of us and Saviour Jesus Christ.

αὐτῷ ἡ δόξα καὶ νῦν καὶ εἰς
To him[c] [is] the glory both now and unto
=His is* =for ever.

ἡμέραν αἰῶνος.
a day of age.§

ward to this, make every
effort to be found spotless,
blameless and at peace
with him. 15Bear in mind
that our Lord's patience
means salvation, just as our
dear brother Paul also
wrote you with the wisdom
that God gave him. 16He
writes the same way in all
his letters, speaking in
them of these matters. His
letters contain some things
that are hard to understand,
which ignorant and
unstable people distort, as
they do the other Scriptures,
to their own destruction.

17Therefore, dear friends,
since you already know
this, be on your guard so
that you may not be carried
away by the error of lawless
men and fall from your
secure position. 18But grow
in the grace and knowledge
of our Lord and Savior
Jesus Christ. To him be glory
both now and forever!
Amen.

1 John

Chapter 1

Introduction
The Incarnate Word

WHAT was from the beginning, what we have heard, what we have seen with our eyes, what we beheld and our hands handled, concerning the Word of Life—

2and the life was manifested, and we have seen and bear witness and proclaim to you the eternal life, which was with the Father and was manifested to us—

3what we have seen and heard we proclaim to you

ΙΩΑΝΝΟΥ Α
Of John 1

1 Ὃ ἦν ἀπ' ἀρχῆς, ὃ ἀκηκόαμεν,
What was from [the] beginning, what we have heard,

ὃ ἑωράκαμεν τοῖς ὀφθαλμοῖς ἡμῶν, ὃ
what we have seen with the eyes of us, what

ἐθεασάμεθα καὶ αἱ χεῖρες ἡμῶν ἐψηλάφησαν,
we beheld and the hands of us touched,

περὶ τοῦ λόγου τῆς ζωῆς, — 2 καὶ
concerning the word – of life, — and

ἡ ζωὴ ἐφανερώθη, καὶ ἑωράκαμεν καὶ
the life was manifested, and we have seen and

μαρτυροῦμεν καὶ ἀπαγγέλλομεν ὑμῖν τὴν
we bear witness and *we* announce to you the

ζωὴν τὴν αἰώνιον, ἥτις ἦν πρὸς τὸν
life – eternal, which was with the

πατέρα καὶ ἐφανερώθη ἡμῖν, — 3 ὃ
Father and was manifested to us, — what

ἑωράκαμεν καὶ ἀκηκόαμεν, ἀπαγγέλλομεν
we have seen and *we* have heard, we announce

1 John

Chapter 1

The Word of Life

THAT which was from
the beginning, which
we have heard, which we
have seen with our eyes,
which we have looked at
and our hands have
touched—this we proclaim
concerning the Word of
life. 2The life appeared; we
have seen it and testify to
it, and we proclaim to you
the eternal life, which was
with the Father and has appeared
to us. 3We proclaim
to you what we have seen

* See note on I. Pet. 5. 11. § ? "An age-lasting (*i.e.* eternal) day."

also, that you also may
have fellowship with us;
and indeed our fellowship
is with the Father, and with
His Son Jesus Christ.
4 And these things we
write, so that our joy may
be made complete.

God Is Light

5 And this is the message
we have heard from Him
and announce to you, that
God is light, and in Him
there is no darkness at all.
6 If we say that we have
fellowship with Him and
yet walk in the darkness,
we lie and do not practice
the truth;
7 but if we walk in the
light as He Himself is in the
light, we have fellowship
with one another, and the
blood of Jesus His Son
cleanses us from all sin.
8 If we say that we have
no sin, we are deceiving
ourselves, and the truth is
not in us.
9 If we confess our sins,
He is faithful and righteous
to forgive us our sins and to
cleanse us from all unrighteousness.
10 If we say that we have
not sinned, we make Him a
liar, and His word is not in
us.

Chapter 2

Christ Is Our Advocate

MY little children, I am
writing these things
to you that you may not sin.
And if anyone sins, we
have an [a]Advocate with
the Father, Jesus Christ the
righteous;
2 and He Himself is the
propitiation for our sins;
and not for ours only, but

[a]Gr., *Paracletos*, one called alongside to help

καὶ ὑμῖν, ἵνα καὶ ὑμεῖς κοινωνίαν ἔχητε
also to you, in order that [2]also [1]ye [4]fellowship [3]may have
μεθ᾽ ἡμῶν. καὶ ἡ κοινωνία δὲ ἡ ἡμετέρα
with us. [2]indeed *the* [4]fellowship [1]And – [3]our
μετὰ τοῦ πατρὸς καὶ μετὰ τοῦ υἱοῦ
[is] with the Father and with the Son
αὐτοῦ Ἰησοῦ Χριστοῦ. 4 καὶ ταῦτα
of him Jesus Christ. And these things
γράφομεν ἡμεῖς ἵνα ἡ χαρὰ ἡμῶν ᾖ
write we in order that the joy of us may be
πεπληρωμένη.
having been fulfilled.
5 Καὶ ἔστιν αὕτη ἡ ἀγγελία ἣν
And [2]is [1]this the message which
ἀκηκόαμεν ἀπ᾽ αὐτοῦ καὶ ἀναγγέλλομεν
we have heard from him and *we* announce
ὑμῖν, ὅτι ὁ θεὸς φῶς ἐστιν καὶ σκοτία
to you, that – God [2]light [1]is and [5]darkness
ἐν αὐτῷ οὐκ ἔστιν οὐδεμία. 6 Ἐὰν
[1]in [2]him [4]not [3]is *none*. If
εἴπωμεν ὅτι κοινωνίαν ἔχομεν μετ᾽ αὐτοῦ
we say that [2]fellowship [1]we have with him
καὶ ἐν τῷ σκότει περιπατῶμεν, ψευδόμεθα
and [2]in [3]the [4]darkness [1]*we* walk, we lie
καὶ οὐ ποιοῦμεν τὴν ἀλήθειαν· 7 ἐὰν
and are not doing the truth; [2]if
δὲ ἐν τῷ φωτὶ περιπατῶμεν ὡς αὐτός
[1]but [4]in [5]the [6]light [3]we walk as he
ἐστιν ἐν τῷ φωτί, κοινωνίαν ἔχομεν
is in the light, [2]fellowship [1]we have
μετ᾽ ἀλλήλων καὶ τὸ αἷμα Ἰησοῦ τοῦ
with each other and the blood of Jesus the
υἱοῦ αὐτοῦ καθαρίζει ἡμᾶς ἀπὸ πάσης
Son of him cleanses us from all
ἁμαρτίας. 8 ἐὰν εἴπωμεν ὅτι ἁμαρτίαν
sin. If we say that sin
οὐκ ἔχομεν, ἑαυτοὺς πλανῶμεν καὶ ἡ
we have not, [2]ourselves [1]we deceive and the
ἀλήθεια οὐκ ἔστιν ἐν ἡμῖν. 9 ἐὰν
truth is not in us. If
ὁμολογῶμεν τὰς ἁμαρτίας ἡμῶν, πιστός
we confess the sins of us, faithful
ἐστιν καὶ δίκαιος, ἵνα ἀφῇ ἡμῖν τὰς
he is and righteous, in order that he may forgive us the
ἁμαρτίας καὶ καθαρίσῃ ἡμᾶς ἀπὸ πάσης
sins and *he* may cleanse us from all
ἀδικίας. 10 ἐὰν εἴπωμεν ὅτι οὐχ
iniquity. If we say that not
ἡμαρτήκαμεν, ψεύστην ποιοῦμεν αὐτὸν
we have sinned, a liar we make him
καὶ ὁ λόγος αὐτοῦ οὐκ ἔστιν ἐν ἡμῖν.
and the word of him is not in us.
2 Τεκνία μου, ταῦτα γράφω ὑμῖν ἵνα
Little children of me, these things I write to you in order that
μὴ ἁμάρτητε. καὶ ἐάν τις ἁμάρτῃ,
ye sin not. And if anyone sins,
παράκλητον ἔχομεν πρὸς τὸν πατέρα,
an advocate we have with the Father,
Ἰησοῦν Χριστὸν δίκαιον· 2 καὶ αὐτὸς
Jesus Christ [the] righteous; and he
ἱλασμός ἐστιν περὶ τῶν ἁμαρτιῶν ἡμῶν,
[3]a propitiation [1]is concerning the sins of us,
οὐ περὶ τῶν ἡμετέρων δὲ μόνον ἀλλὰ
[2]not [3]concerning – [4]ours [1]but only but

and heard, so that you also
may have fellowship with
us. And our fellowship is
with the Father and with
his Son, Jesus Christ. 4 We
write this to make our[a] joy
complete.

Walking in the Light

5 This is the message we
have heard from him and
declare to you: God is light;
in him there is no darkness
at all. 6 If we claim to have
fellowship with him yet
walk in the darkness, we lie
and do not live by the truth.
7 But if we walk in the light,
as he is in the light, we have
fellowship with one another, and the blood of Jesus,
his Son, purifies us from
all[b] sin.
8 If we claim to be without
sin, we deceive ourselves
and the truth is not in us. 9 If
we confess our sins, he is
faithful and just and will
forgive us our sins and purify us from all unrighteousness. 10 If we claim we have
not sinned, we make him
out to be a liar and his word
has no place in our lives.

Chapter 2

MY dear children, I
write this to you so
that you will not sin. But if
anybody does sin, we have
one who speaks to the Fa-
ther in our defense—Jesus
Christ, the Righteous One.
2 He is the atoning sacrifice
for our sins, and not only
for ours but also for[c] the

[a]4 Some manuscripts *your*
[b]7 Or *every*
[c]2 Or *He is the one who turns aside God's wrath, taking away our sins, and not only ours but also*

also for *those of* the whole world.
3And by this we know that we have come to know Him, if we keep His commandments.
4The one who says, "I have come to know Him," and does not keep His commandments, is a liar, and the truth is not in him;
5but whoever keeps His word, in him the love of God has truly been perfected. By this we know that we are in Him:
6the one who says he abides in Him ought himself to walk in the same manner as He walked.
7Beloved, I am not writing a new commandment to you, but an old commandment which you have had from the beginning; the old commandment is the word which you have heard.
8On the other hand, I am writing a new commandment to you, which is true in Him and in you, because the darkness is passing away, and the true light is already shining.
9The one who says he is in the light and *yet* hates his brother is in the darkness until now.
10The one who loves his brother abides in the light and there is no cause for stumbling in him.
11But the one who hates his brother is in the darkness and walks in the darkness, and does not know where he is going because the darkness has blinded his eyes.
12I am writing to you, little children, because your sins are forgiven you for

καὶ περὶ ὅλου τοῦ κόσμου. 3 καὶ ἐν
also concerning all the world. And by
τούτῳ γινώσκομεν ὅτι ἐγνώκαμεν αὐτόν,
this we know that we have known him,
ἐὰν τὰς ἐντολὰς αὐτοῦ τηρῶμεν. 4 ὁ
if 2the 3commandments 4of him 1we keep. The [one]
λέγων ὅτι Ἔγνωκα αὐτόν, καὶ τὰς ἐντολὰς
saying[,] – I have known him, and 3the 4commandments
αὐτοῦ μὴ τηρῶν, ψεύστης ἐστίν, καὶ
5of him 1not 2keeping, 2a liar 1is, and
ἐν τούτῳ ἡ ἀλήθεια οὐκ ἔστιν· 5 ὃς δ'
in this man the truth is not; but who-
ἂν τηρῇ αὐτοῦ τὸν λόγον, ἀληθῶς ἐν
ever keeps 3of him 1the 2word, truly in
τούτῳ ἡ ἀγάπη τοῦ θεοῦ τετελείωται.
this man the love – of God has been perfected.
ἐν τούτῳ γινώσκομεν ὅτι ἐν αὐτῷ ἐσμεν.
By this we know that 2in 3him 1we are.
6 ὁ λέγων ἐν αὐτῷ μένειν ὀφείλει καθὼς
The [one] saying in him to remain ought as
ἐκεῖνος περιεπάτησεν καὶ αὐτὸς οὕτως
that [one]* walked also [him]self so
περιπατεῖν.
to walk.
7 Ἀγαπητοί, οὐκ ἐντολὴν καινὴν γράφω
Beloved, 2not 4commandment 3a new 1I write
ὑμῖν, ἀλλ' ἐντολὴν παλαιὰν ἣν εἴχετε
to you, but 2commandment 1an old which ye had
ἀπ' ἀρχῆς· ἡ ἐντολὴ ἡ παλαιά ἐστιν
from [the] beginning; the 2commandment – 1old is
ὁ λόγος ὃν ἠκούσατε. 8 πάλιν ἐντολὴν
the word which ye heard. Again 2commandment
καινὴν γράφω ὑμῖν, ὅ ἐστιν ἀληθὲς
1a new I write to you, what is true
ἐν αὐτῷ καὶ ἐν ὑμῖν, ὅτι ἡ σκοτία
in him and in you, because the darkness
παράγεται καὶ τὸ φῶς τὸ ἀληθινὸν
is passing and the 2light – 1true
ἤδη φαίνει. 9 ὁ λέγων ἐν τῷ φωτὶ
already shines. The [one] saying in the light
εἶναι καὶ τὸν ἀδελφὸν αὐτοῦ μισῶν
to be and the brother of him hating
ἐν τῇ σκοτίᾳ ἐστὶν ἕως ἄρτι. 10 ὁ
in the darkness is until now. The
ἀγαπῶν τὸν ἀδελφὸν αὐτοῦ ἐν τῷ φωτὶ
[one] loving the brother of him in the light
μένει, καὶ σκάνδαλον ἐν αὐτῷ οὐκ ἔστιν·
remains, and offence in him is not;
11 ὁ δὲ μισῶν τὸν ἀδελφὸν αὐτοῦ ἐν
but the [one] hating the brother of him in
τῇ σκοτίᾳ ἐστὶν καὶ ἐν τῇ σκοτίᾳ
the darkness is and in the darkness
περιπατεῖ, καὶ οὐκ οἶδεν ποῦ ὑπάγει,
walks, and knows not where he is going,
ὅτι ἡ σκοτία ἐτύφλωσεν τοὺς ὀφθαλμοὺς
because the darkness blinded the eyes
αὐτοῦ. 12 Γράφω ὑμῖν, τεκνία, ὅτι
of him. I write to you, little children, because
ἀφέωνται ὑμῖν αἱ ἁμαρτίαι διὰ τὸ ὄνομα
have been forgiven *to* you the (your) sins on account of the name

sins of the whole world.
3We know that we have come to know him if we obey his commands. 4The man who says, "I know him," but does not do what he commands is a liar, and the truth is not in him. 5But if anyone obeys his word, God's love[d] is truly made complete in him. This is how we know we are in him: 6Whoever claims to live in him must walk as Jesus did.
7Dear friends, I am not writing you a new command but an old one, which you have had since the beginning. This old command is the message you have heard. 8Yet I am writing you a new command; its truth is seen in him and you, because the darkness is passing and the true light is already shining.
9Anyone who claims to be in the light but hates his brother is still in the darkness. 10Whoever loves his brother lives in the light, and there is nothing in him[e] to make him stumble. 11But whoever hates his brother is in the darkness and walks around in the darkness; he does not know where he is going, because the darkness has blinded him.

12I write to you, dear children,
because your sins have been forgiven on

*** In a number of places John uses this demonstrative adjective as a substitute for "Christ": "the remoter antecedent." See also John 2. 21.**

[d]5 Or *word, love for God*
[e]10 Or *it*

His name's sake.
13I am writing to you, fathers, because you know
Him who has been from the
beginning. I am writing to
you, young men, because
you have overcome the evil
one. I have written to you,
children, because you
know the Father.
14I have written to you,
fathers, because you know
Him who has been from the
beginning. I have written to
you, young men, because
you are strong, and the
word of God abides in you,
and you have overcome the
evil one.

Do Not Love the World

15Do not love the world,
nor the things in the
world. If anyone loves the
world, the love of the Father is not in him.
16For all that is in the
world, the lust of the flesh
and the lust of the eyes and
the boastful pride of life, is
not from the Father, but is
from the world.
17And the world is pass-
ing away, and *also* its lusts;
but the one who does the
will of God abides forever.
18Children, it is the last
hour; and just as you heard
that antichrist is coming,
even now many antichrists
have arisen; from this we
know that it is the last hour.
19They went out from us,
but they were not *really* of
us; for if they had been of
us, they would have re-
mained with us; but *they*
went out, in order that it
might be shown that they
all are not of us.
20But you have an anoint-
ing from the Holy One, and
you all know.
21I have not written to
you because you do not
know the truth, but be-
cause you do know it, and
because no lie is of the

αὐτοῦ. **13** γράφω ὑμῖν, πατέρες, ὅτι
of him. I write to you, fathers, because
ἐγνώκατε τὸν ἀπ' ἀρχῆς. γράφω ὑμῖν,
ye have known the [one] from [the] beginning. I write to you,
νεανίσκοι, ὅτι νενικήκατε τὸν πονηρόν.
young men, because ye have overcome the evil one.
14 ἔγραψα ὑμῖν, παιδία, ὅτι ἐγνώκατε
I wrote to you, young children, because ye have known
τὸν πατέρα. ἔγραψα ὑμῖν, πατέρες,
the Father. I wrote to you, fathers,
ὅτι ἐγνώκατε τὸν ἀπ' ἀρχῆς. ἔγραψα
because ye have known the [one] from [the] beginning. I wrote
ὑμῖν, νεανίσκοι, ὅτι ἰσχυροί ἐστε καὶ
to you, young men, because strong ye are and
ὁ λόγος τοῦ θεοῦ ἐν ὑμῖν μένει καὶ
the word – of God in you remains and
νενικήκατε τὸν πονηρόν. **15** Μὴ ἀγαπᾶτε
ye have overcome the evil one. Love ye not
τὸν κόσμον μηδὲ τὰ ἐν τῷ κόσμῳ.
the world nor the things in the world.
ἐάν τις ἀγαπᾷ τὸν κόσμον, οὐκ ἔστιν
If anyone loves the world, [5]not [6]is
ἡ ἀγάπη τοῦ πατρὸς ἐν αὐτῷ· **16** ὅτι
[1]the [2]love [3]of the [4]Father in him; because
πᾶν τὸ ἐν τῷ κόσμῳ, ἡ ἐπιθυμία τῆς
all that which† [is] in the world, the lust of the
σαρκὸς καὶ ἡ ἐπιθυμία τῶν ὀφθαλμῶν
flesh and the lust of the eyes
καὶ ἡ ἀλαζονεία τοῦ βίου, οὐκ ἔστιν
and the vainglory – of life, is not
ἐκ τοῦ πατρός, ἀλλὰ ἐκ τοῦ κόσμου
of the Father, but of the world
ἐστίν. **17** καὶ ὁ κόσμος παράγεται καὶ
is. And the world is passing away and
ἡ ἐπιθυμία αὐτοῦ· ὁ δὲ ποιῶν τὸ θέλημα
the lust of it; but the [one] doing the will
τοῦ θεοῦ μένει εἰς τὸν αἰῶνα.
– of God remains unto the age.
18 Παιδία, ἐσχάτη ὥρα ἐστίν, καὶ
Young children, a last hour it is, and
καθὼς ἠκούσατε ὅτι ἀντίχριστος ἔρχεται,
as ye heard that antichrist is coming,
καὶ νῦν ἀντίχριστοι πολλοὶ γεγόνασιν·
even now [2]antichrists [1]many have arisen;
ὅθεν γινώσκομεν ὅτι ἐσχάτη ὥρα ἐστίν.
whence we know that a last hour it is.
19 ἐξ ἡμῶν ἐξῆλθαν, ἀλλ' οὐκ ἦσαν
From us they went out, but they were not
ἐξ ἡμῶν· εἰ γὰρ ἐξ ἡμῶν ἦσαν, μεμενή-
of us; for if of us they were, they would
κεισαν ἂν μεθ' ἡμῶν· ἀλλ' ἵνα φανερω-
have remained with us; but in order that it might be
θῶσιν ὅτι οὐκ εἰσὶν πάντες ἐξ ἡμῶν.
manifested that they are not all of us.
20 καὶ ὑμεῖς χρῖσμα ἔχετε ἀπὸ τοῦ
And ye an anointing have from the
ἁγίου, καὶ οἴδατε πάντες. **21** οὐκ ἔγραψα
Holy One, and [1]ye [3]know [2]all. I wrote not
ὑμῖν ὅτι οὐκ οἴδατε τὴν ἀλήθειαν, ἀλλ'
to you because ye know not the truth, but
ὅτι οἴδατε αὐτήν, καὶ ὅτι πᾶν ψεῦδος
because ye know it, and because every lie
=no lie is . . .

account of his name.
13I write to you, fathers,
because you have
known him who is
from the beginning.
I write to you, young
men,
because you have
overcome the evil
one.
I write to you, dear
children,
because you have
known the Father.
14I write to you, fathers,
because you have
known him who is
from the beginning.
I write to you, young
men,
because you are
strong,
and the word of God
lives in you,
and you have
overcome the evil
one.

Do Not Love the World

15Do not love the world or
anything in the world. If
anyone loves the world, the
love of the Father is not in
him. 16For everything in
the world—the cravings of
sinful man, the lust of his
eyes and the boasting of
what he has and does—
comes not from the Father
but from the world. 17The
world and its desires pass
away, but the man who
does the will of God lives
forever.

Warning Against Antichrists

18Dear children, this is
the last hour; and as you
have heard that the anti-
christ is coming, even now
many antichrists have
come. This is how we know
it is the last hour. 19They
went out from us, but they
did not really belong to us.
For if they had belonged to
us, they would have re-
mained with us; but their
going showed that none of
them belonged to us.
20But you have an anoint-
ing from the Holy One, and
all of you know the truth.[f]
21I do not write to you because you do not know the
truth, but because you do
know it and because no lie
comes from the truth.

[f]20 Some manuscripts *and you know all things*

truth.
22Who is the liar but the
one who denies that Jesus
is the Christ? This is the
antichrist, the one who denies the Father and the
Son.
23Whoever denies the
Son does not have the Fa-
ther; the one who confesses
the Son has the Father also.
24As for you, let that
abide in you which you
heard from the beginning.
If what you heard from the
beginning abides in you,
you also will abide in the
Son and in the Father.

The Promise Is Eternal Life

25And this is the promise
which He Himself made to
us: eternal life.
26These things I have
written to you concerning
those who are trying to deceive you.
27And as for you, the
anointing which you re-
ceived from Him abides in
you, and you have no need
for anyone to teach you;
but as His anointing teaches you about all things, and
is true and is not a lie, and
just as it has taught you,
you abide in Him.
28And now, little chil-
dren, abide in Him, so that
when He appears, we may
have confidence and not
shrink away from Him in
shame at His coming.
29If you know that He is
righteous, you know that
everyone also who prac-
tices righteousness is born
of Him.

Chapter 3

Children of God Love One Another

SEE how great a love the
Father has bestowed
upon us, that we should be
called children of God; and
such we are. For this reason the world does not

ἐκ τῆς ἀληθείας οὐκ ἔστιν. **22** Τίς
of the truth is not. Who
ἐστιν ὁ ψεύστης εἰ μὴ ὁ ἀρνούμενος
is the liar except the [one] denying
ὅτι Ἰησοῦς οὐκ ἔστιν ὁ χριστός; οὗτός
that Jesus *not* is the Christ? this
ἐστιν ὁ ἀντίχριστος, ὁ ἀρνούμενος τὸν
is the antichrist, the [one] denying the
πατέρα καὶ τὸν υἱόν. **23** πᾶς ὁ ἀρνούμενος
Father and the Son. Everyone denying
τὸν υἱὸν οὐδὲ τὸν πατέρα ἔχει· ὁ
the Son [2]neither [3]the [4]Father [1]has; the
ὁμολογῶν τὸν υἱὸν καὶ τὸν πατέρα ἔχει.
[one] confessing the Son [2]also [3]the [4]Father [1]has.
24 ὑμεῖς ὃ ἠκούσατε ἀπ' ἀρχῆς, ἐν
[2]Ye [1]what heard from [the] beginning, in
ὑμῖν μενέτω. ἐὰν ἐν ὑμῖν μείνῃ ὃ ἀπ'
you let it remain. If [6]in [7]you [5]remains [1]what [3]from
ἀρχῆς ἠκούσατε, καὶ ὑμεῖς ἐν τῷ υἱῷ
[4][the] beginning [2]ye heard, [3]both [1]ye [4]in [5]the [6]Son
καὶ [ἐν] τῷ πατρὶ μενεῖτε. **25** καὶ
[7]and [8]in [9]the [10]Father [2]will remain. And
αὕτη ἐστὶν ἡ ἐπαγγελία ἣν αὐτὸς ἐπηγ-
this is the promise which he pro-
γείλατο ἡμῖν, τὴν ζωὴν τὴν αἰώνιον.
mised us, the life – eternal.
26 Ταῦτα ἔγραψα ὑμῖν περὶ τῶν πλανών-
These things I wrote to you concern-ing the [ones] leading
των ὑμᾶς. **27** καὶ ὑμεῖς τὸ χρῖσμα
[2]astray [1]you. And [4]ye [1]the [2]anointing
ὃ ἐλάβετε ἀπ' αὐτοῦ μένει ἐν ὑμῖν,
[3]which received from him remains in you,
καὶ οὐ χρείαν ἔχετε ἵνα τις διδάσκῃ
and [2]no [3]need [1]ye have *in order that* anyone should teach
ὑμᾶς· ἀλλ' ὡς τὸ αὐτοῦ χρῖσμα διδάσκει
you; but as the [2]of him [1]anointing teaches
ὑμᾶς περὶ πάντων, καὶ ἀληθές ἐστιν
you concerning all things, and [2]true [1]is
καὶ οὐκ ἔστιν ψεῦδος, καὶ καθὼς ἐδίδαξεν
and is not a lie, and as he/it taught
ὑμᾶς, μένετε ἐν αὐτῷ.
you, remain ye in him.
28 Καὶ νῦν, τεκνία, μένετε ἐν αὐτῷ,
And now, little children, remain ye in him,
ἵνα ἐὰν φανερωθῇ σχῶμεν παρρησίαν καὶ
in order that if he is manifested we may have confidence and
μὴ αἰσχυνθῶμεν ἀπ' αὐτοῦ ἐν τῇ παρουσίᾳ
not be shamed from him in the presence
αὐτοῦ. **29** ἐὰν εἰδῆτε ὅτι δίκαιός ἐστιν,
of him. If ye know that [2]righteous [1]he is,
γινώσκετε ὅτι καὶ πᾶς ὁ ποιῶν τὴν
know ye that also every one doing –
δικαιοσύνην ἐξ αὐτοῦ γεγέννηται.
righteousness [2]of [3]him [1]has been born.
3 Ἴδετε ποταπὴν ἀγάπην δέδωκεν ἡμῖν
See ye what manner of love [3]has given [4]to us
ὁ πατὴρ ἵνα τέκνα θεοῦ κληθῶμεν,
[1]the [2]Father in order that [2]children [3]of God [1]we may be called,
καὶ ἐσμέν. διὰ τοῦτο ὁ κόσμος οὐ
and we are. Therefore the world [2]not

22Who is the liar? It is the
man who denies that Jesus
is the Christ. Such a man is
the antichrist—he denies
the Father and the Son.
23No one who denies the
Son has the Father; whoever acknowledges the Son
has the Father also.
24See that what you have
heard from the beginning
remains in you. If it does,
you also will remain in the
Son and in the Father.
25And this is what he promised us—even eternal life.
26I am writing these
things to you about those
who are trying to lead you
astray. 27As for you, the
anointing you received
from him remains in you,
and you do not need any-
one to teach you. But as his
anointing teaches you
about all things and as that
anointing is real, not counterfeit—just as it has taught
you, remain in him.

Children of God

28And now, dear chil-
dren, continue in him, so
that when he appears we
may be confident and un-
ashamed before him at his
coming.
29If you know that he is
righteous, you know that
everyone who does what is
right has been born of him.

Chapter 3

HOW great is the love
the Father has lav-
ished on us, that we should
be called children of God!
And that is what we are!
The reason the world does

know us, because it did not
know Him.
2Beloved, now we are
children of God, and it has
not appeared as yet what
we shall be. We know that,
when He appears, we shall
be like Him, because we
shall see Him just as He is.
3And everyone who has
this hope *fixed* on Him
purifies himself, just as He
is pure.
4Everyone who prac-
tices sin also practices lawlessness; and sin is lawlessness.
5And you know that He
appeared in order to take
away sins; and in Him there
is no sin.
6No one who abides in
Him sins; no one who sins
has seen Him or knows
Him.
7Little children, let no
one deceive you; the one
who practices righteous-
ness is righteous, just as He
is righteous;
8the one who practices
sin is of the devil; for the
devil has sinned from the
beginning. The Son of God
appeared for this purpose,
that He might destroy the
works of the devil.
9No one who is born of
God practices sin, because
His seed abides in him; and
he cannot sin, because he is
born of God.
10By this the children of
God and the children of the
devil are obvious: anyone
who does not practice
righteousness is not of
God, nor the one who does
not love his brother.
11For this is the message

γινώσκει ἡμᾶς, ὅτι οὐκ ἔγνω αὐτόν.
[1]knows [2]us, because it knew not him.

2 ἀγαπητοί, νῦν τέκνα θεοῦ ἐσμεν, καὶ
Beloved, [2]now [3]children [4]of God [1]we are, and

οὔπω ἐφανερώθη τί ἐσόμεθα. οἴδαμεν
not yet was it manifested what we shall be. We know

ὅτι ἐὰν φανερωθῇ ὅμοιοι αὐτῷ ἐσόμεθα,
that if he(?it) is manifested like him we shall be,

ὅτι ὀψόμεθα αὐτὸν καθώς ἐστιν. 3 καὶ
because we shall see him as he is. And

πᾶς ὁ ἔχων τὴν ἐλπίδα ταύτην ἐπ'
everyone having this hope on

αὐτῷ ἁγνίζει ἑαυτὸν καθὼς ἐκεῖνος ἁγνός
him purifies himself as that one* [2]pure

ἐστιν. 4 πᾶς ὁ ποιῶν τὴν ἁμαρτίαν
[1]is. Everyone doing – sin

καὶ τὴν ἀνομίαν ποιεῖ, καὶ ἡ ἁμαρτία
[2]also – [3]lawlessness [1]does, and – sin

ἐστὶν ἡ ἀνομία. 5 καὶ οἴδατε ὅτι ἐκεῖνος
is – lawlessness. And ye know that that one*

ἐφανερώθη ἵνα τὰς ἁμαρτίας ἄρῃ, καὶ
was manifested in order that – sins he might bear, and

ἁμαρτία ἐν αὐτῷ οὐκ ἔστιν. 6 πᾶς ὁ
sin [2]in [3]him [1]is not. Everyone

ἐν αὐτῷ μένων οὐχ ἁμαρτάνει· πᾶς ὁ
[2]in [3]him [1]remaining sins not; everyone

ἁμαρτάνων οὐχ ἑώρακεν αὐτὸν οὐδὲ
sinning has not seen him nor

ἔγνωκεν αὐτόν. 7 Τεκνία, μηδεὶς πλανάτω
has known him. Little children, [2]no man [1]let [3]lead [5]astray

ὑμᾶς· ὁ ποιῶν τὴν δικαιοσύνην δίκαιός
[4]you; the [one] doing – righteousness [2]righteous

ἐστιν, καθὼς ἐκεῖνος δίκαιός ἐστιν· 8 ὁ
[1]is, as that one* [2]righteous [1]is; the

ποιῶν τὴν ἁμαρτίαν ἐκ τοῦ διαβόλου
[one] doing – sin [2]of [3]the [4]devil

ἐστίν, ὅτι ἀπ' ἀρχῆς ὁ διάβολος ἁμαρτάνει.
[1]is, because [4]from [5][the] beginning [1]the [2]devil [3]sins.

εἰς τοῦτο ἐφανερώθη ὁ υἱὸς τοῦ θεοῦ,
For this was manifested the Son – of God,

ἵνα λύσῃ τὰ ἔργα τοῦ διαβόλου.
in order that he might undo the works of the devil.

9 Πᾶς ὁ γεγεννημένος ἐκ τοῦ θεοῦ
Everyone having been begotten of – God

ἁμαρτίαν οὐ ποιεῖ, ὅτι σπέρμα αὐτοῦ
[3]sin [2]not [1]does, because seed of him

ἐν αὐτῷ μένει· καὶ οὐ δύναται ἁμαρτάνειν,
in him remains; and he cannot *to* sin,

ὅτι ἐκ τοῦ θεοῦ γεγέννηται. 10 ἐν
because of – God he has been begotten. By

τούτῳ φανερά ἐστιν τὰ τέκνα τοῦ θεοῦ
this [2]manifest [1]is(are) the children – of God

καὶ τὰ τέκνα τοῦ διαβόλου· πᾶς ὁ
and the children of the devil; everyone

μὴ ποιῶν δικαιοσύνην οὐκ ἔστιν ἐκ
not doing righteousness is not of

τοῦ θεοῦ, καὶ ὁ μὴ ἀγαπῶν τὸν ἀδελφὸν
– God, and the [one] not loving the brother

αὐτοῦ. 11 ὅτι αὕτη ἐστὶν ἡ ἀγγελία
of him. Because this is the message

not know us is that it did
not know him. 2Dear
friends, now we are chil-
dren of God, and what we
will be has not yet been
made known. But we know
that when he appears,[g] we
shall be like him, for we
shall see him as he is. 3Ev-
eryone who has this hope in
him purifies himself, just as
he is pure.
4Everyone who sins
breaks the law; in fact, sin
is lawlessness. 5But you
know that he appeared so
that he might take away our
sins. And in him is no sin.
6No one who lives in him
keeps on sinning. No one
who continues to sin has either seen him or known
him.
7Dear children, do not let
anyone lead you astray. He
who does what is right is
righteous, just as he is
righteous. 8He who does
what is sinful is of the devil,
because the devil has been
sinning from the beginning.
The reason the Son of God
appeared was to destroy
the devil's work. 9No one
who is born of God will
continue to sin, because
God's seed remains in him;
he cannot go on sinning,
because he has been born
of God. 10This is how we
know who the children of
God are and who the chil-
dren of the devil are: Anyone who does not do what
is right is not a child of God;
nor is anyone who does not
love his brother.

Love One Another

11This is the message you

* See ch. 2. 6.

g2 Or *when it is made known*

which you have heard from
the beginning, that we
should love one another;
12 not as Cain, *who* was of
the evil one, and slew his
brother. And for what reason did he slay him? Be-
cause his deeds were evil,
and his brother's were
righteous.
13 Do not marvel, breth-
ren, if the world hates you.
14 We know that we have
passed out of death into
life, because we love the
brethren. He who does not
love abides in death.
15 Everyone who hates his
brother is a murderer; and
you know that no murderer
has eternal life abiding in
him.
16 We know love by this,
that He laid down His life
for us; and we ought to lay
down our lives for the
brethren.
17 But whoever has the
world's goods, and beholds
his brother in need and
closes his heart against
him, how does the love of
God abide in him?
18 Little children, let us
not love with word or with
tongue, but in deed and
truth.
19 We shall know by this
that we are of the truth, and
shall assure our heart before Him,
20 in whatever our heart
condemns us; for God is
greater than our heart, and
knows all things.
21 Beloved, if our heart

ἣν ἠκούσατε ἀπ' ἀρχῆς, ἵνα ἀγαπῶμεν
which ye heard from [the] beginning, *in order* that we should love

ἀλλήλους· 12 οὐ καθὼς Κάϊν ἐκ τοῦ
one another; not as Cain [2]of [3]the

πονηροῦ ἦν καὶ ἔσφαξεν τὸν ἀδελφὸν
[4]evil one [1]was and slew the brother

αὐτοῦ· καὶ χάριν τίνος ἔσφαξεν αὐτόν;
of him; and for the sake of what slew he him?

ὅτι τὰ ἔργα αὐτοῦ πονηρὰ ἦν, τὰ δὲ
because the works of him [2]evil [1]was(were), but the [works]

τοῦ ἀδελφοῦ αὐτοῦ δίκαια. 13 μὴ
of the brother of him righteous. not

θαυμάζετε, ἀδελφοί, εἰ μισεῖ ὑμᾶς ὁ
Marvel ye, brothers, if [3]hates [4]you [1]the

κόσμος. 14 ἡμεῖς οἴδαμεν ὅτι μεταβεβή-
[2]world. We know that we have re-

καμεν ἐκ τοῦ θανάτου εἰς τὴν ζωήν,
moved out of *the* death into *the* life,

ὅτι ἀγαπῶμεν τοὺς ἀδελφούς· ὁ μὴ
because we love the brothers; the [one] not

ἀγαπῶν μένει ἐν τῷ θανάτῳ. 15 πᾶς
loving remains in – death. Every-

ὁ μισῶν τὸν ἀδελφὸν αὐτοῦ ἀνθρωποκτόνος
one hating the brother of him [2]a murderer

ἐστίν, καὶ οἴδατε ὅτι πᾶς ἀνθρωποκτόνος
[1]is, and ye know that every murderer
=no murderer has . . .

οὐκ ἔχει ζωὴν αἰώνιον ἐν αὐτῷ μένουσαν.
has not life eternal in him remaining.

16 ἐν τούτῳ ἐγνώκαμεν τὴν ἀγάπην, ὅτι
By this we have known – love, because

ἐκεῖνος ὑπὲρ ἡμῶν τὴν ψυχὴν αὐτοῦ
that one* on behalf of us the life of him

ἔθηκεν· καὶ ἡμεῖς ὀφείλομεν ὑπὲρ τῶν
laid down; and we ought on behalf of the

ἀδελφῶν τὰς ψυχὰς θεῖναι. 17 ὃς δ'
brothers the(our) lives to lay down. Who-

ἂν ἔχῃ τὸν βίον τοῦ κόσμου καὶ θεωρῇ
ever has the means of life of the world and beholds

τὸν ἀδελφὸν αὐτοῦ χρείαν ἔχοντα καὶ
the brother of him [2]need [1]having and

κλείσῃ τὰ σπλάγχνα αὐτοῦ ἀπ' αὐτοῦ,
shuts the bowels of him from him,

πῶς ἡ ἀγάπη τοῦ θεοῦ μένει ἐν αὐτῷ;
how [2]the [3]love – [4]of God [1]remains in him?

18 Τεκνία, μὴ ἀγαπῶμεν λόγῳ μηδὲ τῇ
Little children, let us not love in word nor in *the*

γλώσσῃ, ἀλλὰ ἐν ἔργῳ καὶ ἀληθείᾳ.
tongue, but in work and truth.

19 ἐν τούτῳ γνωσόμεθα ὅτι ἐκ τῆς ἀληθείας
By this we shall know that [2]of [3]the [4]truth

ἐσμέν, καὶ ἔμπροσθεν αὐτοῦ πείσομεν
[1]we are, and before him shall persuade

τὴν καρδίαν ἡμῶν 20 ὅτι ἐὰν καταγινώσκῃ
the heart of us that if [4]blames [us]

ἡμῶν ἡ καρδία, ὅτι μείζων ἐστὶν ὁ
[3]of us [1]the [2]heart, that greater is –

θεὸς τῆς καρδίας ἡμῶν καὶ γινώσκει
God [than] the heart of us and knows

πάντα. 21 Ἀγαπητοί, ἐὰν ἡ καρδία
all things. Beloved, if the(our) heart

* See ch. 2. 6, 3. 3, 5, 7.

heard from the beginning:
We should love one anoth-
er. 12 Do not be like Cain,
who belonged to the evil
one and murdered his
brother. And why did he
murder him? Because his
own actions were evil and
his brother's were right-
eous. 13 Do not be sur-
prised, my brothers, if the
world hates you. 14 We
know that we have passed
from death to life, because
we love our brothers. Anyone who does not love re-
mains in death. 15 Anyone
who hates his brother is a
murderer, and you know
that no murderer has eternal life in him.
16 This is how we know
what love is: Jesus Christ
laid down his life for us.
And we ought to lay down
our lives for our brothers.
17 If anyone has material
possessions and sees his
brother in need but has no
pity on him, how can the
love of God be in him?
18 Dear children, let us not
love with words or tongue
but with actions and in
truth. 19 This then is how we
know that we belong to the
truth, and how we set our
hearts at rest in his presence 20 whenever our hearts
condemn us. For God is
greater than our hearts, and
he knows everything.
21 Dear friends, if our

does not condemn us, we have confidence before God;
22and whatever we ask we receive from Him, because we keep His commandments and do the things that are pleasing in His sight.
23And this is His commandment, that we believe in the name of His Son Jesus Christ, and love one another, just as He commanded us.
24And the one who keeps His commandments abides in Him, and He in him. And we know by this that He abides in us, by the Spirit whom He has given us.

μὴ καταγινώσκῃ, παρρησίαν ἔχομεν πρὸς
does not blame [us], confidence we have with
τὸν θεόν, 22 καὶ ὃ ἐὰν αἰτῶμεν λαμβάν-
– God, and whatever we ask we re-
ομεν ἀπ' αὐτοῦ, ὅτι τὰς ἐντολὰς αὐτοῦ
ceive from him, because [2]the [3]commandments [4]of him
τηροῦμεν καὶ τὰ ἀρεστὰ ἐνώπιον αὐτοῦ
[1]we keep and [2]the things [3]pleasing [4]before [5]him
ποιοῦμεν. 23 καὶ αὕτη ἐστὶν ἡ ἐντολὴ
[1]*we* do. And this is the commandment
αὐτοῦ, ἵνα πιστεύσωμεν τῷ ὀνόματι τοῦ
of him, *in order* that we should believe the name of the
υἱοῦ αὐτοῦ Ἰησοῦ Χριστοῦ καὶ ἀγαπῶμεν
Son of him Jesus Christ and love
ἀλλήλους καθὼς ἔδωκεν ἐντολὴν ἡμῖν.
one another as he gave commandment to us.
24 καὶ ὁ τηρῶν τὰς ἐντολὰς αὐτοῦ ἐν
And the keeping [one] the commandments of him in
αὐτῷ μένει καὶ αὐτὸς ἐν αὐτῷ· καὶ
him remains and he in him; and
ἐν τούτῳ γινώσκομεν ὅτι μένει ἐν ἡμῖν,
by this we know that he remains in us,
ἐκ τοῦ πνεύματος οὗ ἡμῖν ἔδωκεν.
by the Spirit whom to us he gave.

hearts do not condemn us, we have confidence before God 22and receive from him anything we ask, because we obey his commands and do what pleases him. 23And this is his command: to believe in the name of his Son, Jesus Christ, and to love one another as he commanded us. 24Those who obey his commands live in him, and he in them. And this is how we know that he lives in us: We know it by the Spirit he gave us.

Chapter 4

Testing the Spirits

BELOVED, do not believe every spirit, but test the spirits to see whether they are from God; because many false prophets have gone out into the world.
2By this you know the Spirit of God: every spirit that confesses that Jesus Christ has come in the flesh is from God;
3and every spirit that does not confess Jesus is not from God; and this is the *spirit* of the antichrist, of which you have heard that it is coming, and now it is already in the world.
4You are from God, little children, and have overcome them; because greater is He who is in you than he who is in the world.
5They are from the world; therefore they speak *as* from the world, and the world listens to them.

4 Ἀγαπητοί, μὴ παντὶ πνεύματι
Beloved, [2]not [3]every [4]spirit
πιστεύετε, ἀλλὰ δοκιμάζετε τὰ πνεύματα
[1]believe ye, but prove the spirits
εἰ ἐκ τοῦ θεοῦ ἐστιν, ὅτι πολλοὶ
if of – God they are, because many
ψευδοπροφῆται ἐξεληλύθασιν εἰς τὸν
false prophets have gone forth into the
κόσμον. 2 ἐν τούτῳ γινώσκετε τὸ πνεῦμα
world. By this know ye the Spirit
τοῦ θεοῦ· πᾶν πνεῦμα ὃ ὁμολογεῖ Ἰησοῦν
– of God: every spirit which confesses Jesus
Χριστὸν ἐν σαρκὶ ἐληλυθότα ἐκ τοῦ
Christ [2]in [3][the] flesh [1]having come [5]of –
θεοῦ ἐστιν, 3 καὶ πᾶν πνεῦμα ὃ μὴ
[6]God [4]is, and every spirit which not
ὁμολογεῖ τὸν Ἰησοῦν ἐκ τοῦ θεοῦ οὐκ
confesses – Jesus [3]of – [4]God [2]not
ἔστιν· καὶ τοῦτό ἐστιν τὸ τοῦ ἀντιχρίστου,
[1]is; and this is the [spirit] of the antichrist,
ὃ ἀκηκόατε ὅτι ἔρχεται, καὶ νῦν ἐν
which ye have heard that it is coming, and [2]now [4]in
τῷ κόσμῳ ἐστὶν ἤδη. 4 ὑμεῖς ἐκ τοῦ
[5]the [6]world [1]is [3]already. Ye of –
θεοῦ ἐστε, τεκνία, καὶ νενικήκατε αὐτούς,
God are, little children, and have overcome them,
ὅτι μείζων ἐστὶν ὁ ἐν ὑμῖν ἢ ὁ ἐν
because greater is the [one] in you than the [one] in
τῷ κόσμῳ. 5 αὐτοὶ ἐκ τοῦ κόσμου
the world. [1]They [3]of [4]the [5]world
εἰσίν· διὰ τοῦτο ἐκ τοῦ κόσμου λαλοῦσιν
[2]are; therefore [2]of [3]the [4]world [1]they speak
καὶ ὁ κόσμος αὐτῶν ἀκούει. 6 ἡμεῖς
and the world them hears. [1]We

Chapter 4

Test the Spirits

DEAR friends, do not believe every spirit, but test the spirits to see whether they are from God, because many false prophets have gone out into the world. 2This is how you can recognize the Spirit of God: Every spirit that acknowledges that Jesus Christ has come in the flesh is from God, 3but every spirit that does not acknowledge Jesus is not from God. This is the spirit of the antichrist, which you have heard is coming and even now is already in the world.
4You, dear children, are from God and have overcome them, because the one who is in you is greater than the one who is in the world. 5They are from the world and therefore speak from the viewpoint of the world, and the world listens to them. 6We are from

6We are from God; he
who knows God listens to
us; he who is not from God
does not listen to us. By
this we know the spirit of
truth and the spirit of error.

God Is Love

7Beloved, let us love one
another, for love is from
God; and everyone who
loves is born of God and
knows God.
8The one who does not
love does not know God,
for God is love.
9By this the love of God
was manifested in us, that
God has sent His only be-
gotten Son into the world
so that we might live
through Him.
10In this is love, not that
we loved God, but that He
loved us and sent His Son
to be the propitiation for
our sins.
11Beloved, if God so
loved us, we also ought to
love one another.
12No one has beheld God
at any time; if we love one
another, God abides in us,
and His love is perfected in
us.
13By this we know that
we abide in Him and He in
us, because He has given
us of His Spirit.
14And we have beheld
and bear witness that the
Father has sent the Son *to
be* the Savior of the world.
15Whoever confesses that
Jesus is the Son of God,
God abides in him, and he
in God.
16And we have come to
know and have believed
the love which God has for

ἐκ τοῦ θεοῦ ἐσμεν· ὁ γινώσκων τὸν
[3]of – [4]God [2]are; the [one] knowing –
θεὸν ἀκούει ἡμῶν, ὃς οὐκ ἔστιν ἐκ
God hears us, [he] who is not of
τοῦ θεοῦ οὐκ ἀκούει ἡμῶν. ἐκ τούτου
– God hears not us. From this
γινώσκομεν τὸ πνεῦμα τῆς ἀληθείας καὶ
we know the spirit – of truth and
τὸ πνεῦμα τῆς πλάνης.
the spirit – of error.
7 Ἀγαπητοί, ἀγαπῶμεν ἀλλήλους, ὅτι
Beloved, let us love one another, because
ἡ ἀγάπη ἐκ τοῦ θεοῦ ἐστιν, καὶ πᾶς ὁ
– love [2]of – [3]God [1]is, and everyone
ἀγαπῶν ἐκ τοῦ θεοῦ γεγέννηται καὶ
loving [2]of – [3]God [1]has been begotten and
γινώσκει τὸν θεόν. 8 ὁ μὴ ἀγαπῶν
knows – God. The [one] not loving
οὐκ ἔγνω τὸν θεόν, ὅτι ὁ θεὸς ἀγάπη
knew not – God, because – God [2]love
ἐστίν. 9 ἐν τούτῳ ἐφανερώθη ἡ ἀγάπη
[1]is. By this was manifested the love
τοῦ θεοῦ ἐν ἡμῖν, ὅτι τὸν υἱὸν αὐτοῦ
– of God in(to) us, because [3]the [5]Son [6]of him
τὸν μονογενῆ ἀπέσταλκεν ὁ θεὸς εἰς
– [4]only begotten [2]has sent – [1]God into
τὸν κόσμον ἵνα ζήσωμεν δι' αὐτοῦ.
the world in order that we might live through him.
10 ἐν τούτῳ ἐστὶν ἡ ἀγάπη, οὐχ ὅτι
In this is – love, not that
ἡμεῖς ἠγαπήκαμεν τὸν θεόν, ἀλλ' ὅτι
we have loved – God, but that
αὐτὸς ἠγάπησεν ἡμᾶς καὶ ἀπέστειλεν τὸν
he loved us and sent the
υἱὸν αὐτοῦ ἱλασμὸν περὶ τῶν ἁμαρτιῶν
Son of him a propitiation concerning the sins
ἡμῶν. 11 ἀγαπητοί, εἰ οὕτως ὁ θεὸς
of us. Beloved, if so – God
ἠγάπησεν ἡμᾶς, καὶ ἡμεῖς ὀφείλομεν
loved us, [2]also [1]we [3]ought
ἀλλήλους ἀγαπᾶν. 12 θεὸν οὐδεὶς πώποτε
[5]one another [4]to love. [4]God [1]no man [2]ever
τεθέαται· ἐὰν ἀγαπῶμεν ἀλλήλους, ὁ θεὸς
[3]has beheld; if we love one another, – God
ἐν ἡμῖν μένει καὶ ἡ ἀγάπη αὐτοῦ
in us remains and the love of him
τετελειωμένη ἐν ἡμῖν ἐστιν. 13 Ἐν
[2]*having been* perfected [3]in [4]us [1]is. By
τούτῳ γινώσκομεν ὅτι ἐν αὐτῷ μένομεν
this we know that in him we remain
καὶ αὐτὸς ἐν ἡμῖν, ὅτι ἐκ τοῦ πνεύματος
and he in us, because [3]of [4]the [5]Spirit
αὐτοῦ δέδωκεν ἡμῖν. 14 καὶ ἡμεῖς
[6]of him [1]he has given [2]us. And we
τεθεάμεθα καὶ μαρτυροῦμεν ὅτι ὁ πατὴρ
have beheld and bear witness that the Father
ἀπέσταλκεν τὸν υἱὸν σωτῆρα τοῦ κόσμου.
has sent the Son [as] Saviour of the world.
15 ὃς ἐὰν ὁμολογήσῃ ὅτι Ἰησοῦς ἐστιν
Whoever confesses that Jesus is
ὁ υἱὸς τοῦ θεοῦ, ὁ θεὸς ἐν αὐτῷ μένει
the Son – of God, – God in him remains
καὶ αὐτὸς ἐν τῷ θεῷ. 16 καὶ ἡμεῖς
and he in – God. And we
ἐγνώκαμεν καὶ πεπιστεύκαμεν τὴν ἀγάπην
have known and have believed the love

God, and whoever knows
God listens to us; but whoever is not from God does
not listen to us. This is how
we recognize the Spirit[h] of
truth and the spirit of falsehood.

God's Love and Ours

7Dear friends, let us love
one another, for love
comes from God. Every-
one who loves has been
born of God and knows
God. 8Whoever does not
love does not know God,
because God is love. 9This
is how God showed his love
among us: He sent his one
and only Son[i] into the
world that we might live
through him. 10This is love:
not that we loved God, but
that he loved us and sent
his Son as an atoning sacrifice for[j] our sins. 11Dear
friends, since God so loved
us, we also ought to love
one another. 12No one has
ever seen God; but if we
love one another, God lives
in us and his love is made
complete in us.
13We know that we live in
him and he in us, because
he has given us of his Spirit.
14And we have seen and
testify that the Father has
sent his Son to be the Savior of the world. 15If anyone acknowledges that
Jesus is the Son of God,
God lives in him and he in
God. 16And so we know
and rely on the love God
has for us.

[h]6 Or *spirit*
[i]9 Or *his only begotten Son*
[j]10 Or *as the one who would turn aside his wrath, taking away*

us. God is love, and the one who abides in love abides in God, and God abides in him.
[17]By this, love is perfected with us, that we may have confidence in the day of judgment; because as He is, so also are we in this world.
[18]There is no fear in love; but perfect love casts out fear, because fear involves punishment, and the one who fears is not perfected in love.
[19]We love, because He first loved us.
[20]If someone says, "I love God," and hates his brother, he is a liar; for the one who does not love his brother whom he has seen, cannot love God whom he has not seen.
[21]And this commandment we have from Him, that the one who loves God should love his brother also.

ἣν ἔχει ὁ θεὸς ἐν ἡμῖν. Ὁ θεὸς ἀγάπη
which [2]has – [1]God in(to) us. – God [3]love

ἐστίν, καὶ ὁ μένων ἐν τῇ ἀγάπῃ ἐν
[1]is, and the remaining [one] in – love [3]in

τῷ θεῷ μένει καὶ ὁ θεὸς ἐν αὐτῷ
– [4]God [1]remains and – God [2]in [3]him

μένει. 17 Ἐν τούτῳ τετελείωται ἡ ἀγάπη
[1]remains. By this [2]has been perfected – [1]love

μεθ' ἡμῶν, ἵνα παρρησίαν ἔχωμεν ἐν
with us, in order that [2]confidence [1]we may have in

τῇ ἡμέρᾳ τῆς κρίσεως, ὅτι καθὼς ἐκεῖνός
the day – of judgment, because as that one*

ἐστιν καὶ ἡμεῖς ἐσμεν ἐν τῷ κόσμῳ
is [3]also [1]we [2]are in – world

τούτῳ. 18 φόβος οὐκ ἔστιν ἐν τῇ ἀγάπῃ,
this. Fear is not in – love,

ἀλλ' ἡ τελεία ἀγάπη ἔξω βάλλει τὸν
but – perfect love [2]out [1]casts *the*

φόβον, ὅτι ὁ φόβος κόλασιν ἔχει, ὁ δὲ
fear, because – fear [2]punishment [1]has, and the

φοβούμενος οὐ τετελείωται ἐν τῇ ἀγάπῃ.
[one] fearing has not been perfected in – love.

19 ἡμεῖς ἀγαπῶμεν, ὅτι αὐτὸς πρῶτος
We love, because he first

ἠγάπησεν ἡμᾶς. 20 ἐάν τις εἴπῃ ὅτι
loved us. If anyone says[,] –

ἀγαπῶ τὸν θεόν, καὶ τὸν ἀδελφὸν αὐτοῦ
I love – God, and [2]the [3]brother [4]of him

μισῇ, ψεύστης ἐστίν· ὁ γὰρ μὴ ἀγαπῶν
[1]hates, [2]a liar [1]he is; for the [one] not loving

τὸν ἀδελφὸν αὐτοῦ ὃν ἑώρακεν, τὸν
the brother of him whom he has seen, –

θεὸν ὃν οὐχ ἑώρακεν οὐ δύναται ἀγαπᾶν.
[3]God [4]whom [5]he has not seen [1]*he* cannot [2]*to* love.

21 καὶ ταύτην τὴν ἐντολὴν ἔχομεν ἀπ'
And this – commandment we have from

αὐτοῦ, ἵνα ὁ ἀγαπῶν τὸν θεὸν ἀγαπᾷ
him, in order that the [one] loving – God loves

καὶ τὸν ἀδελφὸν αὐτοῦ.
also the brother of him.

God is love. Whoever lives in love lives in God, and God in him. [17]In this way, love is made complete among us so that we will have confidence on the day of judgment, because in this world we are like him. [18]There is no fear in love. But perfect love drives out fear, because fear has to do with punishment. The one who fears is not made perfect in love.
[19]We love because he first loved us. [20]If anyone says, "I love God," yet hates his brother, he is a liar. For anyone who does not love his brother, whom he has seen, cannot love God, whom he has not seen. [21]And he has given us this command: Whoever loves God must also love his brother.

Chapter 5

Overcoming the World

WHOEVER believes that Jesus is the [b]Christ is born of God; and whoever loves the Father loves the *child* born of Him.
[2]By this we know that we love the children of God, when we love God and observe His commandments.
[3]For this is the love of God, that we keep His commandments; and His commandments are not

5 Πᾶς ὁ πιστεύων ὅτι Ἰησοῦς ἐστιν
Everyone believing that Jesus is

ὁ χριστὸς ἐκ τοῦ θεοῦ γεγέννηται, καὶ
the Christ [2]of – [3]God [1]has been begotten, and

πᾶς ὁ ἀγαπῶν τὸν γεννήσαντα ἀγαπᾷ
everyone loving the [one] begetting loves

τὸν γεγεννημένον ἐξ αὐτοῦ. 2 ἐν τούτῳ
the [one] having been begotten of him. By this

γινώσκομεν ὅτι ἀγαπῶμεν τὰ τέκνα τοῦ
we know that we love the children –

θεοῦ, ὅταν τὸν θεὸν ἀγαπῶμεν καὶ τὰς
of God, when*ever* – [2]God [1]we love and [2]the

ἐντολὰς αὐτοῦ ποιῶμεν. 3 αὕτη γάρ
[3]commandments [4]of him [1]*we* do. For this

ἐστιν ἡ ἀγάπη τοῦ θεοῦ, ἵνα τὰς ἐντολὰς
is the love – of God, *in order* that [2]the [3]commandments

αὐτοῦ τηρῶμεν· καὶ αἱ ἐντολαὶ αὐτοῦ
[4]of him [1]we keep; and the commandments of him

Chapter 5

Faith in the Son of God

EVERYONE who believes that Jesus is the Christ is born of God, and everyone who loves the father loves his child as well. [2]This is how we know that we love the children of God: by loving God and carrying out his commands. [3]This is love for God: to obey his commands. And his commands

[b] I.e., Messiah

* See ch. 2. 6, 3. 3, 5, 7, 16.

burdensome.
4For whatever is born of
God overcomes the world;
and this is the victory that
has overcome the world—
our faith.
5And who is the one who
overcomes the world, but
he who believes that Jesus
is the Son of God?
6This is the one who
came by water and blood,
Jesus Christ; not with the
water only, but with the
water and with the blood.
7And it is the Spirit who
bears witness, because the
Spirit is the truth.
8For there are three that
bear witness, [c]the Spirit
and the water and the
blood; and the three are in
agreement.
9If we receive the wit-
ness of men, the witness of
God is greater; for the witness of God is this, that He
has borne witness concerning His Son.
10The one who believes in
the Son of God has the witness in himself; the one
who does not believe God
has made Him a liar, be-
cause he has not believed in
the witness that God has
borne concerning His Son.
11And the witness is this,
that God has given us eternal life, and this life is in
His Son.
12He who has the Son has
the life; he who does not
have the Son of God does
not have the life.

This Is Written That You May Know

13These things I have
written to you who believe

[c] A few late mss. read *in heaven, the Father, the Word, and the Holy Spirit, and these three are one. And there are three that bear witness on earth, the Spirit*

βαρεῖαι οὐκ εἰσίν, 4 ὅτι πᾶν τὸ γεγεν-
heavy are not, because everything having
νημένον ἐκ τοῦ θεοῦ νικᾷ τὸν κόσμον·
been begotten of – God overcomes the world;
καὶ αὕτη ἐστὶν ἡ νίκη ἡ νικήσασα τὸν
and this is the victory – overcoming the
κόσμον, ἡ πίστις ἡμῶν. 5 Τίς ἐστιν
world, the faith of us. [2]Who [3]is
[δὲ] ὁ νικῶν τὸν κόσμον εἰ μὴ ὁ
[1]and the overcoming [one] the world except the
πιστεύων ὅτι Ἰησοῦς ἐστιν ὁ υἱὸς τοῦ
[one] believing that Jesus is the Son –
θεοῦ; 6 οὗτός ἐστιν ὁ ἐλθὼν δι' ὕδατος
of God ? This is the coming [one] through water
καὶ αἵματος, Ἰησοῦς Χριστός· οὐκ ἐν
and blood, Jesus Christ; not by
τῷ ὕδατι μόνον, ἀλλ' ἐν τῷ ὕδατι καὶ
the water only, but by the water and
ἐν τῷ αἵματι· καὶ τὸ πνεῦμά ἐστιν τὸ
by the blood; and the Spirit is the
μαρτυροῦν, ὅτι τὸ πνεῦμά ἐστιν ἡ ἀλήθεια.
[one] bearing witness, because the Spirit is the truth.
7 ὅτι τρεῖς εἰσιν οἱ μαρτυροῦντες, 8 τὸ
Because three there are the [ones] bearing witness, the
πνεῦμα καὶ τὸ ὕδωρ καὶ τὸ αἷμα, καὶ
Spirit and the water and the blood, and
οἱ τρεῖς εἰς τὸ ἕν εἰσιν. 9 εἰ τὴν
the three [2]in *the* [3]one [1]are. If [3]the
μαρτυρίαν τῶν ἀνθρώπων λαμβάνομεν, ἡ
[2]witness – [4]of men [1]we receive, the
μαρτυρία τοῦ θεοῦ μείζων ἐστίν, ὅτι
witness – of God [2]greater [1]is, because
αὕτη ἐστὶν ἡ μαρτυρία τοῦ θεοῦ, ὅτι
this is the witness – of God, because
μεμαρτύρηκεν περὶ τοῦ υἱοῦ αὐτοῦ. 10 ὁ
he has borne witness concerning the Son of him. The
πιστεύων εἰς τὸν υἱὸν τοῦ θεοῦ ἔχει
[one] believing in the Son – of God has
τὴν μαρτυρίαν ἐν αὐτῷ. ὁ μὴ πιστεύων
the witness in him. The [one] not believing
τῷ θεῷ ψεύστην πεποίηκεν αὐτόν, ὅτι
– God [3]a liar [1]has made [2]him, because
οὐ πεπίστευκεν εἰς τὴν μαρτυρίαν ἣν
he has not believed in the witness which
μεμαρτύρηκεν ὁ θεὸς περὶ τοῦ υἱοῦ
[2]has borne witness – [1]God concerning the Son
αὐτοῦ. 11 καὶ αὕτη ἐστὶν ἡ μαρτυρία,
of him. And this is the witness,
ὅτι ζωὴν αἰώνιον ἔδωκεν ὁ θεὸς ἡμῖν,
that [5]life [4]eternal [2]gave – [1]God [3]to us,
καὶ αὕτη ἡ ζωὴ ἐν τῷ υἱῷ αὐτοῦ
and this – life [2]in [3]the [4]Son [5]of him
ἐστιν. 12 ὁ ἔχων τὸν υἱὸν ἔχει τὴν
[1]is. The [one] having the Son has *the*
ζωήν· ὁ μὴ ἔχων τὸν υἱὸν τοῦ θεοῦ
life; the [one] not having the Son – of God
τὴν ζωὴν οὐκ ἔχει.
the life has not.
13 Ταῦτα ἔγραψα ὑμῖν ἵνα εἰδῆτε ὅτι
These things I wrote to you in order that ye may know that

are not burdensome, 4for
everyone born of God
overcomes the world. This
is the victory that has overcome the world, even our
faith. 5Who is it that overcomes the world? Only he
who believes that Jesus is
the Son of God.
6This is the one who came
by water and blood—Jesus
Christ. He did not come by
water only, but by water
and blood. And it is the
Spirit who testifies, be-
cause the Spirit is the truth.
7For there are three that
testify: 8the[k] Spirit, the water and the blood; and the
three are in agreement.
9We accept man's testimo-
ny, but God's testimony is
greater because it is the testimony of God, which he
has given about his Son.
10Anyone who believes in
the Son of God has this testimony in his heart. Any-
one who does not believe
God has made him out to be
a liar, because he has not
believed the testimony God
has given about his Son.
11And this is the testimony:
God has given us eternal
life, and this life is in his
Son. 12He who has the Son
has life; he who does not
have the Son of God does
not have life.

Concluding Remarks

13I write these things to
you who believe in the

[k]7,8 Late manuscripts of the Vulgate *testify in heaven: the Father, the Word and the Holy Spirit, and these three are one. 8And there are three that testify on earth: the* (not found in any Greek manuscript before the sixteenth century)

in the name of the Son of God, in order that you may know that you have eternal life.

14And this is the confidence which we have before Him, that, if we ask anything according to His will, He hears us.

15And if we know that He hears us *in* whatever we ask, we know that we have the requests which we have asked from Him.

16If anyone sees his brother committing a sin not *leading* to death, he shall ask and *God* will for him give life to those who commit sin not *leading* to death. There is a sin *leading* to death; I do not say that he should make request for this.

17All unrighteousness is sin, and there is a sin not *leading* to death.

18We know that no one who is born of God sins; but He who was born of God keeps him and the evil one does not touch him.

19We know that we are of God, and the whole world lies in *the power of* the evil one.

20And we know that the Son of God has come, and has given us understanding, in order that we might know Him who is true, and we are in Him who is true, in His Son Jesus Christ. This is the true God and eternal life.

21Little children, guard yourselves from idols.

ζωὴν ἔχετε αἰώνιον, τοῖς πιστεύουσιν
[3]life [1]ye have [2]eternal, to the [ones] believing

εἰς τὸ ὄνομα τοῦ υἱοῦ τοῦ θεοῦ. **14** Καὶ
in the name of the Son – of God. And

αὕτη ἐστὶν ἡ παρρησία ἣν ἔχομεν πρὸς
this is the confidence which we have toward

αὐτόν, ὅτι ἐάν τι αἰτώμεθα κατὰ τὸ
him, that if [2]anything [1]we ask according to the

θέλημα αὐτοῦ ἀκούει ἡμῶν. **15** καὶ
will of him he hears us. And

ἐὰν οἴδαμεν ὅτι ἀκούει ἡμῶν ὃ ἐὰν
if we know that he hears us whatever

αἰτώμεθα, οἴδαμεν ὅτι ἔχομεν τὰ αἰτήματα
we ask, we know that we have the requests

ἃ ᾐτήκαμεν ἀπ' αὐτοῦ. **16** Ἐάν τις
which we have asked from him. If anyone

ἴδῃ τὸν ἀδελφὸν αὐτοῦ ἁμαρτάνοντα
sees the brother of him sinning

ἁμαρτίαν μὴ πρὸς θάνατον, αἰτήσει, καὶ
a sin not unto death, he shall ask, and

δώσει αὐτῷ ζωήν, τοῖς ἁμαρτάνουσιν
he will give to him life, to the [ones] sinning

μὴ πρὸς θάνατον. ἔστιν ἁμαρτία πρὸς
not unto death. There is a sin unto

θάνατον· οὐ περὶ ἐκείνης λέγω ἵνα
death; not concerning that do I say *in order* that

ἐρωτήσῃ. **17** πᾶσα ἀδικία ἁμαρτία ἐστίν,
he should inquire. All iniquity [2]sin [1]is,

καὶ ἔστιν ἁμαρτία οὐ πρὸς θάνατον.
and there is a sin not unto death.

18 Οἴδαμεν ὅτι πᾶς ὁ γεγεννημένος ἐκ
We know that everyone having been begotten of

τοῦ θεοῦ οὐχ ἁμαρτάνει, ἀλλ' ὁ γεννηθεὶς
– God sins not, but the [one] begotten

ἐκ τοῦ θεοῦ τηρεῖ αὐτόν, καὶ ὁ πονηρὸς
of – God keeps him, and the evil one

οὐχ ἅπτεται αὐτοῦ. **19** οἴδαμεν ὅτι ἐκ
does not touch him. We know that of

τοῦ θεοῦ ἐσμεν, καὶ ὁ κόσμος ὅλος ἐν
– God we are, and the [2]world [1]whole in

τῷ πονηρῷ κεῖται. **20** οἴδαμεν δὲ ὅτι
the evil one lies. [2]we know [1]And that

ὁ υἱὸς τοῦ θεοῦ ἥκει, καὶ δέδωκεν
the Son – of God is come, and has given

ἡμῖν διάνοιαν ἵνα γινώσκωμεν τὸν
to us an understanding in order that we might know the

ἀληθινόν· καὶ ἐσμὲν ἐν τῷ ἀληθινῷ,
true [one]; and we are in the true [one],

ἐν τῷ υἱῷ αὐτοῦ Ἰησοῦ Χριστῷ. οὗτός
in the Son of him Jesus Christ. This

ἐστιν ὁ ἀληθινὸς θεὸς καὶ ζωὴ αἰώνιος.
is the true God and life eternal.

21 Τεκνία, φυλάξατε ἑαυτὰ ἀπὸ τῶν
Little children, guard yourselves from *the*

εἰδώλων.
idols.

name of the Son of God so that you may know that you have eternal life. 14This is the confidence we have in approaching God: that if we ask anything according to his will, he hears us. 15And if we know that he hears us—whatever we ask—we know that we have what we asked of him.

16If anyone sees his brother commit a sin that does not lead to death, he should pray and God will give him life. I refer to those whose sin does not lead to death. There is a sin that leads to death. I am not saying that he should pray about that. 17All wrongdoing is sin, and there is sin that does not lead to death.

18We know that anyone born of God does not continue to sin; the one who was born of God keeps him safe, and the evil one cannot harm him. 19We know that we are children of God, and that the whole world is under the control of the evil one. 20We know also that the Son of God has come and has given us understanding, so that we may know him who is true. And we are in him who is true—even in his Son Jesus Christ. He is the true God and eternal life.

21Dear children, keep yourselves from idols.

2 John

Chapter 1

Walk According to His Commandments

THE elder to the chosen lady and her children, whom I love in truth; and not only I, but also all who know the truth,

2for the sake of the truth which abides in us and will be with us forever:

3Grace, mercy *and* peace will be with us, from God the Father and from Jesus Christ, the Son of the Father, in truth and love.

4I was very glad to find *some* of your children walking in truth, just as we have received commandment *to do* from the Father.

5And now I ask you, lady, not as writing to you a new commandment, but the one which we have had from the beginning, that we love one another.

6And this is love, that we walk according to His commandments. This is the commandment, just as you have heard from the beginning, that you should walk in it.

7For many deceivers have gone out into the world, those who do not acknowledge Jesus Christ *as* coming in the flesh. This is the deceiver and the antichrist.

8Watch yourselves, that you might not lose what we have accomplished, but that you may receive a full reward.

9Anyone who goes too far and does not abide in the teaching of Christ, does not have God; the one who abides in the teaching, he

ΙΩΑΝΝΟΥ Β

Of John 2

1 Ὁ πρεσβύτερος ἐκλεκτῇ κυρίᾳ καὶ
The elder to [the] chosen lady and

τοῖς τέκνοις αὐτῆς, οὓς ἐγὼ ἀγαπῶ ἐν
to the children of her, whom I love in

ἀληθείᾳ, καὶ οὐκ ἐγὼ μόνος ἀλλὰ καὶ
truth, and not I alone but also

πάντες οἱ ἐγνωκότες τὴν ἀλήθειαν, 2 διὰ
all the [ones] having known the truth, because of

τὴν ἀλήθειαν τὴν μένουσαν ἐν ἡμῖν,
the truth – remaining among us,

καὶ μεθ' ἡμῶν ἔσται εἰς τὸν αἰῶνα.
and with us will be unto the age.

3 ἔσται μεθ' ἡμῶν χάρις ἔλεος εἰρήνη
[4]will be [5]with [6]us [1]Grace[,] [2]mercy[,] [3]peace

παρὰ θεοῦ πατρός, καὶ παρὰ Ἰησοῦ
from God [the] Father, and from Jesus

Χριστοῦ τοῦ υἱοῦ τοῦ πατρός, ἐν ἀληθείᾳ
Christ the Son of the Father, in truth

καὶ ἀγάπῃ.
and love.

4 Ἐχάρην λίαν ὅτι εὕρηκα ἐκ τῶν
I rejoiced greatly because I have found [some] of the

τέκνων σου περιπατοῦντας ἐν ἀληθείᾳ,
children of thee walking in truth,

καθὼς ἐντολὴν ἐλάβομεν παρὰ τοῦ πατρός.
as commandment we received from the Father.

5 καὶ νῦν ἐρωτῶ σε, κυρία, οὐχ ὡς
And now I request thee, lady, not as

ἐντολὴν γράφων σοι καινήν, ἀλλὰ ἣν
[3]commandment [1]writing [4]to thee [2]a new, but which

εἴχομεν ἀπ' ἀρχῆς, ἵνα ἀγαπῶμεν
we had from [the] beginning, *in order that* we should love

ἀλλήλους. 6 καὶ αὕτη ἐστὶν ἡ ἀγάπη,
one another. And this is – love,

ἵνα περιπατῶμεν κατὰ τὰς ἐντολὰς
in order that we should walk according to the commandments

αὐτοῦ· αὕτη ἡ ἐντολή ἐστιν, καθὼς
of him; this [2]the [3]commandment [1]is, as

ἠκούσατε ἀπ' ἀρχῆς, ἵνα ἐν αὐτῇ
ye heard from [the] beginning, *in order that* [2]in [3]it

περιπατῆτε. 7 ὅτι πολλοὶ πλάνοι ἐξῆλθον
[1]ye should walk. Because many deceivers went forth

εἰς τὸν κόσμον, οἱ μὴ ὁμολογοῦντες
into the world, the [ones] not confessing

Ἰησοῦν Χριστὸν ἐρχόμενον ἐν σαρκί·
Jesus Christ coming in [the] flesh;

οὗτός ἐστιν ὁ πλάνος καὶ ὁ ἀντίχριστος.
this is the deceiver and the antichrist.

8 βλέπετε ἑαυτούς, ἵνα μὴ ἀπολέσητε
See yourselves, lest ye lose

ἃ ἠργασάμεθα, ἀλλὰ μισθὸν πλήρη
[the] things which we wrought, but [2]reward [1]a full

ἀπολάβητε. 9 πᾶς ὁ προάγων καὶ μὴ
[1]ye may receive. Everyone going forward and not

μένων ἐν τῇ διδαχῇ τοῦ Χριστοῦ θεὸν
remaining in the teaching – of Christ [2]God

οὐκ ἔχει· ὁ μένων ἐν τῇ διδαχῇ, οὗτος
[3]not [1]has; the [one] remaining in the teaching, this one

2 John

THE elder,

To the chosen lady and her children, whom I love in the truth—and not I only, but also all who know the truth— 2because of the truth, which lives in us and will be with us forever:

3Grace, mercy and peace from God the Father and from Jesus Christ, the Father's Son, will be with us in truth and love.

4It has given me great joy to find some of your children walking in the truth, just as the Father commanded us. 5And now, dear lady, I am not writing you a new command but one we have had from the beginning. I ask that we love one another. 6And this is love: that we walk in obedience to his commands. As you have heard from the beginning, his command is that you walk in love.

7Many deceivers, who do not acknowledge Jesus Christ as coming in the flesh, have gone out into the world. Any such person is the deceiver and the antichrist. 8Watch out that you do not lose what you have worked for, but that you may be rewarded fully. 9Anyone who runs ahead and does not continue in the teaching of Christ does not have God; whoever continues in the teaching

has both the Father and the
Son.
10If anyone comes to you
and does not bring this
teaching, do not receive
him into *your* house, and do
not give him a greeting;
11for the one who gives
him a greeting participates
in his evil deeds.
12Having many things to
write to you, I do not want
to *do so* with paper and ink;
but I hope to come to you
and speak face to face, that
your joy may be made full.
13The children of your
chosen sister greet you.

καὶ τὸν πατέρα καὶ τὸν υἱὸν ἔχει.
[2]both [3]the [4]Father [5]and [6]the [7]Son [1]has.

10 εἴ τις ἔρχεται πρὸς ὑμᾶς καὶ ταύτην
If anyone comes to you and this

τὴν διδαχὴν οὐ φέρει, μὴ λαμβάνετε
– teaching brings not, do not ye receive

αὐτὸν εἰς οἰκίαν, καὶ χαίρειν αὐτῷ μὴ
him into [your] house, and [4]to rejoice [3]him [2]not

λέγετε· 11 ὁ λέγων γὰρ αὐτῷ χαίρειν
[1]tell ye*; [2]the [one] [3]telling [1]for him to rejoice

κοινωνεῖ τοῖς ἔργοις αὐτοῦ τοῖς πονηροῖς.
shares in the [2]works [3]of him – [1]evil.

12 Πολλὰ ἔχων ὑμῖν γράφειν οὐκ
[2]Many things [1]having [4]to you [3]to write [6]not

ἐβουλήθην διὰ χάρτου καὶ μέλανος, ἀλλὰ
[5]I purpose by means of paper and ink, but

ἐλπίζω γενέσθαι πρὸς ὑμᾶς καὶ στόμα
I am hoping to be with you and [3]mouth

πρὸς στόμα λαλῆσαι, ἵνα ἡ χαρὰ ἡμῶν
[2]to [4]mouth [1]to speak, in order that the joy of us

πεπληρωμένη ᾖ. 13 Ἀσπάζεταί σε τὰ
having been fulfilled may be. [7]greet*s* [8]thee [1]The

τέκνα τῆς ἀδελφῆς σου τῆς ἐκλεκτῆς.
[2]children [3]of the [5]sister [6]of thee – [4]chosen.

has both the Father and the
Son. 10If anyone comes to
you and does not bring this
teaching, do not take him
into your house or wel-
come him. 11Anyone who
welcomes him shares in his
wicked work.
12I have much to write to
you, but I do not want to
use paper and ink. Instead,
I hope to visit you and talk
with you face to face, so
that our joy may be com-
plete.
13The children of your
chosen sister send their
greetings.

3 John

Chapter 1

You Walk in the Truth

THE elder to the beloved
Gaius, whom I love in
truth.
2Beloved, I pray that in
all respects you may prosper and be in good health,
just as your soul prospers.
3For I was very glad
when brethren came and
bore witness to your truth,
that is, how you are walking in truth.
4I have no greater joy
than this, to hear of my
children walking in the
truth.
5Beloved, you are acting
faithfully in whatever you
accomplish for the breth-
ren, and especially *when
they are* strangers;
6and they bear witness to

ΙΩΑΝΝΟΥ Γ
Of John 3

1 Ὁ πρεσβύτερος Γαΐῳ τῷ ἀγαπητῷ,
The elder to Gaius the beloved,

ὃν ἐγὼ ἀγαπῶ ἐν ἀληθείᾳ.
whom I love in truth.

2 Ἀγαπητέ, περὶ πάντων εὔχομαί σε
Beloved, concerning all things I pray thee =that

εὐοδοῦσθαι καὶ ὑγιαίνειν, καθὼς εὐοδοῦταί
to prosper and to be in health, as [4]prospers
thou mayest prosper . . .

σου ἡ ψυχή. 3 ἐχάρην γὰρ λίαν ἐρχομένων
[3]of thee [1]the [2]soul. For I rejoiced greatly coming =when [some]

ἀδελφῶν καὶ μαρτυρούντων σου τῇ
brothers and bearing witness[a] of thee in the
brothers came and bore witness

ἀληθείᾳ, καθὼς σὺ ἐν ἀληθείᾳ περιπατεῖς.
truth, as thou in truth walkest.

4 μειζοτέραν τούτων οὐκ ἔχω χαράν, ἵνα
[3]greater [4][than] [5]these things [1]I have no [2]joy, *in order* that

ἀκούω τὰ ἐμὰ τέκνα ἐν τῇ ἀληθείᾳ
I hear – my children [2]in [3]the [4]truth

περιπατοῦντα. 5 Ἀγαπητέ, πιστὸν ποιεῖς
[1]walking. Beloved, faithfully thou doest

ὃ ἐὰν ἐργάσῃ εἰς τοὺς ἀδελφοὺς καὶ
whatever thou workest for the brothers and

τοῦτο ξένους, 6 οἳ ἐμαρτύρησάν σου τῇ
this strangers, who bore witness of thee –

* That is, "do not greet him."

3 John

THE elder,
To my dear friend Ga-
ius, whom I love in the
truth.
2Dear friend, I pray that
you may enjoy good health
and that all may go well
with you, even as your soul
is getting along well. 3It
gave me great joy to have
some brothers come and
tell about your faithfulness
to the truth and how you
continue to walk in the
truth. 4I have no greater joy
than to hear that my children are walking in the
truth.
5Dear friend, you are
faithful in what you are doing for the brothers, even
though they are strangers
to you. 6They have told the

your love before the
church; and you will do
well to send them on their
way in a manner worthy of
God.
7For they went out for
the sake of the Name, ac-
cepting nothing from the
Gentiles.
8Therefore we ought to
support such men, that we
may be fellow workers with
the truth.
9I wrote something to
the church; but Diotrephes,
who loves to be first among
them, does not accept what
we say.
10For this reason, if I
come, I will call attention
to his deeds which he does,
unjustly accusing us with
wicked words; and not satisfied with this, neither
does he himself receive the
brethren, and he forbids
those who desire *to do so,*
and puts *them* out of the
church.
11Beloved, do not imitate
what is evil, but what is
good. The one who does
good is of God; the one who
does evil has not seen God.
12Demetrius has received
a *good* testimony from
everyone, and from the
truth itself; and we also
bear witness, and you
know that our witness is
true.
13I had many things to
write to you, but I am not
willing to write *them* to you
with pen and ink;
14but I hope to see you
shortly, and we shall speak
face to face. Peace *be* to
you. The friends greet you.
Greet the friends by name.

ἀγάπῃ ἐνώπιον ἐκκλησίας, οὓς καλῶς
in love before [the] church, whom well

ποιήσεις προπέμψας ἀξίως τοῦ θεοῦ·
thou wilt do sending forward worthily – of God;

7 ὑπὲρ γὰρ τοῦ ὀνόματος ἐξῆλθαν μηδὲν
for on behalf of the name they went forth [2]nothing

λαμβάνοντες ἀπὸ τῶν ἐθνικῶν. **8** ἡμεῖς
[1]taking from the Gentiles. We

οὖν ὀφείλομεν ὑπολαμβάνειν τοὺς τοιούτους,
therefore ought to entertain – such men,

ἵνα συνεργοὶ γινώμεθα τῇ ἀληθείᾳ.
in order that [2]co-workers [1]we may become in the truth.

9 Ἔγραψά τι τῇ ἐκκλησίᾳ· ἀλλ᾽ ὁ
I wrote something to the church; but the [one]

φιλοπρωτεύων αὐτῶν Διοτρέφης οὐκ
loving to be first of them Diotrephes not

ἐπιδέχεται ἡμᾶς. **10** διὰ τοῦτο, ἐὰν
receives us. Therefore, if

ἔλθω, ὑπομνήσω αὐτοῦ τὰ ἔργα ἃ ποιεῖ
I come, I will remember [3]of him [1]the [2]works which he does

λόγοις πονηροῖς φλυαρῶν ἡμᾶς, καὶ μὴ
[4]words [3]with evil [1]prating against [2]us, and not

ἀρκούμενος ἐπὶ τούτοις οὔτε αὐτὸς
being satisfied on(with) these [2]neither [1]he

ἐπιδέχεται τοὺς ἀδελφοὺς καὶ τοὺς
[3]receives the brothers and the

βουλομένους κωλύει καὶ ἐκ τῆς ἐκκλησίας
[ones] purposing he prevents and [2]out of [3]the [4]church

ἐκβάλλει.
[1]puts *out.*

11 Ἀγαπητέ, μὴ μιμοῦ τὸ κακὸν ἀλλὰ
Beloved, imitate not the bad but

τὸ ἀγαθόν. ὁ ἀγαθοποιῶν ἐκ τοῦ θεοῦ
the good. The [one] doing good [2]of – [3]God

ἐστιν· ὁ κακοποιῶν οὐχ ἑώρακεν τὸν
[1]is; the [one] doing ill has not seen –

θεόν. **12** Δημητρίῳ μεμαρτύρηται ὑπὸ
God. To Demetrius witness has been borne by

πάντων καὶ ὑπὸ αὐτῆς τῆς ἀληθείας·
all and by [3][it]self [1]the [2]truth;

καὶ ἡμεῖς δὲ μαρτυροῦμεν, καὶ οἶδας
[3]also [2]we [1]and bear witness, and thou knowest

ὅτι ἡ μαρτυρία ἡμῶν ἀληθής ἐστιν.
that the witness of us [2]true [1]is.

13 Πολλὰ εἶχον γράψαι σοι, ἀλλ᾽ οὐ
[2]Many things [1]I had to write to thee, but not

θέλω διὰ μέλανος καὶ καλάμου σοι
I wish [3]by means of [4]ink [5]and [6]pen [2]to thee

γράφειν· **14** ἐλπίζω δὲ εὐθέως σε ἰδεῖν,
[1]to write; but I am hoping [3]immediately [2]thee [1]to see,

καὶ στόμα πρὸς στόμα λαλήσομεν.
and [2]mouth [3]to [4]mouth [1]we will speak.

15 Εἰρήνη σοι. ἀσπάζονταί σε οἱ φίλοι.
Peace to thee. [3]greet [4]thee [1]The [2]friends.

ἀσπάζου τοὺς φίλους κατ᾽ ὄνομα.
Greet thou the friends by name.

church about your love.
You will do well to send
them on their way in a manner worthy of God. 7It was
for the sake of the Name
that they went out, receiving no help from the pa-
gans. 8We ought therefore
to show hospitality to such
men so that we may work
together for the truth.
9I wrote to the church,
but Diotrephes, who loves
to be first, will have nothing to do with us. 10So if I
come, I will call attention
to what he is doing, gossip-
ing maliciously about us.
Not satisfied with that, he
refuses to welcome the
brothers. He also stops
those who want to do so
and puts them out of the
church.
11Dear friend, do not imitate what is evil but what is
good. Anyone who does
what is good is from God.
Anyone who does what is
evil has not seen God.
12Demetrius is well spoken
of by everyone—and even
by the truth itself. We also
speak well of him, and you
know that our testimony is
true.
13I have much to write
you, but I do not want to do
so with pen and ink. 14I
hope to see you soon, and
we will talk face to face.

Peace to you. The friends
here send their greetings.
Greet the friends there by
name.

Jude

Chapter 1

The Warnings of History to the Ungodly

JUDE, a bond-servant of Jesus Christ, and brother of James, to those who are the called, beloved in God the Father, and kept for Jesus Christ:

2May mercy and peace and love be multiplied to you.

3Beloved, while I was making every effort to write you about our common salvation, I felt the necessity to write to you appealing that you contend earnestly for the faith which was once for all delivered to the saints.

4For certain persons have crept in unnoticed, those who were long beforehand marked out of this condemnation, ungodly persons who turn the grace of our God into licentiousness and deny our only Master and Lord, Jesus Christ.

5Now I desire to remind you, though you know all things once for all, that [a]the Lord, after saving a people out of the land of Egypt, subsequently destroyed those who did not believe.

6And angels who did not keep their own domain, but abandoned their proper abode, He has kept in eternal bonds under darkness for the judgment of the great day.

7Just as Sodom and Gomorrah and the cities around them, since they in the same way as these indulged in gross immorality and went after strange flesh, are exhibited as an example, in undergoing the punishment of eternal fire.

8Yet in the same manner these men, also by dreaming, defile the flesh, and reject authority, and revile angelic majesties.

[a] Some ancient mss. read *Jesus*

ΙΟΥΔΑ
Of Jude

1 Ἰούδας Ἰησοῦ Χριστοῦ δοῦλος, ἀδελφὸς
Jude of Jesus Christ a slave, [2]brother
δὲ Ἰακώβου, τοῖς ἐν θεῷ πατρὶ
[1]and of James, [1]to the [ones] [4]by [5]God [6][the] Father
ἠγαπημένοις καὶ Ἰησοῦ Χριστῷ
[3]having been loved [7]and [9]for Jesus [10]Christ
τετηρημένοις κλητοῖς. 2 ἔλεος ὑμῖν καὶ
[8]having been kept [2]called. Mercy to you and
εἰρήνη καὶ ἀγάπη πληθυνθείη.
peace and love may *it* be multiplied.
3 Ἀγαπητοί, πᾶσαν σπουδὴν ποιούμενος
Beloved, [2]all [3]haste [1]making
γράφειν ὑμῖν περὶ τῆς κοινῆς ἡμῶν
to write to you concerning the common [2]of us
σωτηρίας, ἀνάγκην ἔσχον γράψαι ὑμῖν
[1]salvation, necessity I had to write to you
παρακαλῶν ἐπαγωνίζεσθαι τῇ ἅπαξ
exhorting to contend for [1]the [3]once
παραδοθείσῃ τοῖς ἁγίοις πίστει. 4 παρεισε-
[4]delivered [5]to the [6]saints [2]faith. [3]crept
δύησαν γάρ τινες ἄνθρωποι, οἱ πάλαι
in For [1]certain [2]men, the [ones] of old
προγεγραμμένοι εἰς τοῦτο τὸ κρίμα,
having been previously written for this – judgment,
ἀσεβεῖς, τὴν τοῦ θεοῦ ἡμῶν χάριτα
impious men, [2]the [4]of the [5]God [6]of us [3]grace
μετατιθέντες εἰς ἀσέλγειαν καὶ τὸν μόνον
[1]making [7]a pretext for wantonness and [8]the [9]only
δεσπότην καὶ κύριον ἡμῶν Ἰησοῦν Χριστὸν
[4]Master [5]and [6]Lord [7]of us [8]Jesus [9]Christ
ἀρνούμενοι. 5 Ὑπομνῆσαι δὲ ὑμᾶς βούλομαι,
[1]denying. But [2]to remind [3]you [1]I purpose,
εἰδότας ἅπαξ πάντα, ὅτι κύριος λαὸν
[2]knowing [1]once all things, that [the] Lord [2][the] people
ἐκ γῆς Αἰγύπτου σώσας τὸ δεύτερον
[3]out of [4][the] land [5]of Egypt [1]having saved in the second place
τοὺς μὴ πιστεύσαντας ἀπώλεσεν, 6 ἀγγέλους
[2]the [ones] [3]not [4]believing [1]destroyed, [2]angels
τε τοὺς μὴ τηρήσαντας τὴν ἑαυτῶν
[1]and – not having kept the [3]of themselves
ἀρχὴν ἀλλὰ ἀπολιπόντας τὸ ἴδιον
[1]rule but having deserted the(ir) own
οἰκητήριον εἰς κρίσιν μεγάλης ἡμέρας
habitation [6]for [7][the] judgment [8]of [the] great [9]day
δεσμοῖς ἀϊδίοις ὑπὸ ζόφον τετήρηκεν·
[3]bonds [2]in everlasting [4]under [5]gloom [1]he has kept;
7 ὡς Σόδομα καὶ Γόμορρα καὶ αἱ περὶ
as Sodom and Gomorra and [1]the [3]round
αὐτὰς πόλεις, τὸν ὅμοιον τρόπον τούτοις
[4]them [2]cities, in the like manner to these
ἐκπορνεύσασαι καὶ ἀπελθοῦσαι ὀπίσω σαρκὸς
committing fornication and going away after [2]flesh
ἑτέρας, πρόκεινται δεῖγμα πυρὸς αἰωνίου
[1]different, are set forth an example [4]fire [3]of eternal
δίκην ὑπέχουσαι. 8 Ὁμοίως μέντοι καὶ
[2]vengeance [1]undergoing. Likewise indeed also
οὗτοι ἐνυπνιαζόμενοι σάρκα μὲν μιαίνουσιν,
these dreaming [ones] [2]flesh [1]on one hand [3]defile,
κυριότητα δὲ ἀθετοῦσιν, δόξας δὲ
[2]lordship [1]on the other [3]despise, and [2]glories

Jude

JUDE, a servant of Jesus Christ and a brother of James,

To those who have been called, who are loved by God the Father and kept by[a] Jesus Christ:

2Mercy, peace and love be yours in abundance.

The Sin and Doom of Godless Men

3Dear friends, although I
was very eager to write to
you about the salvation we
share, I felt I had to write
and urge you to contend for
the faith that was once for
all entrusted to the saints.
4For certain men whose
condemnation was written
about[b] long ago have secretly slipped in among
you. They are godless men,
who change the grace of
our God into a license for
immorality and deny Jesus
Christ our only Sovereign
and Lord.
5Though you already
know all this, I want to remind you that the Lord[c]
delivered his people out of
Egypt, but later destroyed
those who did not believe.
6And the angels who did
not keep their positions of
authority but abandoned
their own home—these he
has kept in darkness,
bound with everlasting
chains for judgment on the
great Day. 7In a similar
way, Sodom and Gomorrah
and the surrounding towns
gave themselves up to sexual immorality and perversion. They serve as an example of those who suffer
the punishment of eternal
fire.
8In the very same way,
these dreamers pollute
their own bodies, reject authority and slander celestial

[a] *1* Or *for*; or *in*
[b] *4* Or *men who were marked out for condemnation*
[c] *5* Some early manuscripts *Jesus*

9But Michael the archangel, when he disputed with the devil and argued about the body of Moses, did not dare pronounce against him a railing judgment, but said, "The Lord rebuke you."

10But these men revile the things which they do not understand; and the things which they know by instinct, like unreasoning animals, by these things they are destroyed.

11Woe to them! For they have gone the way of Cain, and for pay they have rushed headlong into the error of Balaam, and perished in the rebellion of Korah.

12These men are those who are hidden reefs in your love feasts when they feast with you without fear, caring for themselves; clouds without water, carried along by winds; autumn trees without fruit, doubly dead, uprooted;

13wild waves of the sea, casting up their own shame like foam; wandering stars, for whom the black darkness has been reserved forever.

14And about these also Enoch, *in* the seventh *generation* from Adam, prophesied, saying, "Behold, the Lord came with many thousands of His holy ones,

15to execute judgment upon all, and to convict all the ungodly of all their ungodly deeds which they have done in an ungodly way, and of all the harsh things which ungodly sinners have spoken against Him."

16These are grumblers, finding fault, following after their *own* lusts; they speak arrogantly, flattering people for the sake of *gain-*

βλασφημοῦσιν. 9 Ὁ δὲ Μιχαὴλ ὁ ἀρχάγ-
[1]rail at. – But Michael the arch-
γελος, ὅτε τῷ διαβόλῳ διακρινόμενος
angel, when [3]with the [4]devil [1]contending
διελέγετο περὶ τοῦ Μωϋσέως σώματος,
he argued about [1]the [3]of Moses [2]body,
οὐκ ἐτόλμησεν κρίσιν ἐπενεγκεῖν βλασφημίας,
durst not [2]a judgment [1]*to* bring *on* of railing,
ἀλλὰ εἶπεν· ἐπιτιμήσαι σοι κύριος. 10 οὗτοι
but said : [2]rebuke [3]thee [1][The] Lord. these men
δὲ ὅσα μὲν οὐκ οἴδασιν βλασφημοῦσιν,
But what things on one hand they know not they rail at,
ὅσα δὲ φυσικῶς ὡς τὰ ἄλογα ζῷα
what things on the other [6]naturally [2]as [3]the [4]without reason [5]animals
ἐπίστανται, ἐν τούτοις φθείρονται. 11 οὐαὶ
[1]they understand, by these they are corrupted. Woe
αὐτοῖς, ὅτι τῇ ὁδῷ τοῦ Κάϊν ἐπορεύθησαν,
to them, because in the way – of Cain they went,
καὶ τῇ πλάνῃ τοῦ Βαλαὰμ μισθοῦ
and [2]to the [3]error – [4]of Balaam [5]of(for) reward
ἐξεχύθησαν, καὶ τῇ ἀντιλογίᾳ τοῦ Κόρε
[1]gave themselves up, and [2]in the [3]dispute – [4]of Korah
ἀπώλοντο. 12 Οὗτοί εἰσιν οἱ ἐν ταῖς
[1]perished. These men are [1]the [2]in [4]the
ἀγάπαις ὑμῶν σπιλάδες συνευωχούμενοι
[6]love feasts [5]of you [3]rocks feasting together
ἀφόβως, ἑαυτοὺς ποιμαίνοντες, νεφέλαι
without fear, [2]themselves [1]feeding, [2]clouds
ἄνυδροι ὑπὸ ἀνέμων παραφερόμεναι, δένδρα
[1]waterless [4]by [5]winds [3]*being* carried away, [2]trees
φθινοπωρινὰ ἄκαρπα δὶς ἀποθανόντα
[1]autumn without fruit twice dying
ἐκριζωθέντα, 13 κύματα ἄγρια θαλάσσης
having been uprooted, [2]waves [1]fierce [3]of [the] sea
ἐπαφρίζοντα τὰς ἑαυτῶν αἰσχύνας, ἀστέρες
[4]foaming up [5]the [7]of themselves [6]shames, [2]stars
πλανῆται, οἷς ὁ ζόφος τοῦ σκότους
[1]wandering, for whom the gloom – of darkness
εἰς αἰῶνα τετήρηται. 14 Ἐπροφήτευσεν
unto [the] age has been kept. [7]prophesied
δὲ καὶ τούτοις ἕβδομος ἀπὸ Ἀδὰμ
[1]And [2]also [8]to these men [4][the] seventh [5]from [6]Adam
Ἐνὼχ λέγων· ἰδοὺ ἦλθεν κύριος ἐν
[3]Enoch saying : Behold came [the] Lord with
ἁγίαις μυριάσιν αὐτοῦ, 15 ποιῆσαι κρίσιν
saints ten thousands of him, to do judgment
κατὰ πάντων καὶ ἐλέγξαι πάντας τοὺς
against all men and to rebuke all the
ἀσεβεῖς περὶ πάντων τῶν ἔργων ἀσεβείας
impious concerning all the works of impiety
αὐτῶν ὧν ἠσέβησαν καὶ περὶ πάντων
of them which they impiously did and concerning all
τῶν σκληρῶν ὧν ἐλάλησαν κατ᾽ αὐτοῦ
the hard things which [3]spoke [4]against [5]him
ἁμαρτωλοὶ ἀσεβεῖς. 16 Οὗτοί εἰσιν γογ-
[2]sinners [1]impious. These men are [1]mur-
γυσταὶ μεμψίμοιροι, κατὰ τὰς ἐπιθυμίας
murers [1]querulous, [2]according to [3]the [4]lusts
αὐτῶν πορευόμενοι, καὶ τὸ στόμα αὐτῶν
[5]of them [1]going, and the mouth of them
λαλεῖ ὑπέρογκα, θαυμάζοντες πρόσωπα
speaks arrogant things, admiring faces

beings. 9But even the archangel Michael, when he
was disputing with the devil about the body of Moses,
did not dare to bring a slanderous accusation against
him, but said, "The Lord
rebuke you!" 10Yet these
men speak abusively
against whatever they do
not understand; and what
things they do understand
by instinct, like unreasoning animals—these are the
very things that destroy
them.
11Woe to them! They
have taken the way of Cain;
they have rushed for profit
into Balaam's error; they
have been destroyed in Korah's rebellion.
12These men are blemish-
es at your love feasts, eating with you without the
slightest qualm—shep-
herds who feed only them-
selves. They are clouds
without rain, blown along
by the wind; autumn trees,
without fruit and uprooted
—twice dead. 13They are
wild waves of the sea,
foaming up their shame;
wandering stars, for whom
blackest darkness has been
reserved forever.
14Enoch, the seventh
from Adam, prophesied
about these men: "See, the
Lord is coming with thou-
sands upon thousands of
his holy ones 15to judge everyone, and to convict all
the ungodly of all the ungodly acts they have done
in the ungodly way, and of
all the harsh words ungodly
sinners have spoken
against him." 16These men
are grumblers and fault-
finders; they follow their
own evil desires; they boast
about themselves and flat-

ing an advantage.

Keep Yourselves in the Love of God

17But you, beloved, ought
to remember the words that
were spoken beforehand by
the apostles of our Lord
Jesus Christ,
18that they were saying to
you, "In the last time there
shall be mockers, following
after their own ungodly
lusts."
19These are the ones who
cause divisions, worldly-
minded, devoid of the
Spirit.
20But you, beloved,
building yourselves up on
your most holy faith; praying in the Holy Spirit;
21keep yourselves in the
love of God, waiting anx-
iously for the mercy of our
Lord Jesus Christ to eternal life.
22And have mercy on
some, who are doubting;
23save others, snatching
them out of the fire; and on
some have mercy with fear,
hating even the garment
polluted by the flesh.
24Now to Him who is able
to keep you from stum-
bling, and to make you
stand in the presence of His
glory blameless with great
joy,
25to the only God our
Savior, through Jesus
Christ our Lord, *be* glory,
majesty, dominion and au-
thority, before all time and
now and forever. Amen.

ὠφελείας χάριν.
[2]advantage [1]for the sake of.

17 Ὑμεῖς δέ, ἀγαπητοί, μνήσθητε τῶν
But ye, beloved, be mindful of the
ῥημάτων τῶν προειρημένων ὑπὸ τῶν
words – previously spoken by the
ἀποστόλων τοῦ κυρίου ἡμῶν Ἰησοῦ
apostles of the Lord of us Jesus
Χριστοῦ, 18 ὅτι ἔλεγον ὑμῖν· ἐπ' ἐσχάτου
Christ, because they told you: At [the] last
τοῦ χρόνου ἔσονται ἐμπαῖκται κατὰ τὰς
of the time will be mockers [2]according to [3]the
ἑαυτῶν ἐπιθυμίας πορευόμενοι τῶν ἀσεβειῶν.
[5]of themselves [4]lusts [1]going – [6]of impious things.
19 Οὗτοί εἰσιν οἱ ἀποδιορίζοντες, ψυχικοί,
These men are the [ones] making separations, natural,
πνεῦμα μὴ ἔχοντες. 20 ὑμεῖς δέ, ἀγαπητοί,
[3]spirit [1]not [2]having. But ye, beloved,
ἐποικοδομοῦντες ἑαυτοὺς τῇ ἁγιωτάτῃ ὑμῶν
building up yourselves in the most holy [3]of you
πίστει, ἐν πνεύματι ἁγίῳ προσευχόμενοι,
[1]faith, [2]in [4]Spirit [3][the] Holy [1]praying.
21 ἑαυτοὺς ἐν ἀγάπῃ θεοῦ τηρήσατε,
[2]yourselves [3]in [4][the] love [5]of God [1]keep,
προσδεχόμενοι τὸ ἔλεος τοῦ κυρίου ἡμῶν
awaiting the mercy of the Lord of us
Ἰησοῦ Χριστοῦ εἰς ζωὴν αἰώνιον. 22 καὶ
Jesus Christ to life eternal. And
οὓς μὲν ἐλεᾶτε διακρινομένους 23 σῴζετε
some [2]pity ye [1][who are] wavering [2]save
ἐκ πυρὸς ἁρπάζοντες, οὓς δὲ ἐλεᾶτε
[3]out of [4]fire [1]seizing, others pity
ἐν φόβῳ, μισοῦντες καὶ τὸν ἀπὸ τῆς
with fear, hating even [1]the [4]from [5]the
σαρκὸς ἐσπιλωμένον χιτῶνα.
[6]flesh [3]*having been* spotted [2]tunic.

24 Τῷ δὲ δυναμένῳ φυλάξαι ὑμᾶς
Now to the [one] *being* able to guard you
ἀπταίστους καὶ στῆσαι κατενώπιον τῆς
without stumbling and to set [you] before the
δόξης αὐτοῦ ἀμώμους ἐν ἀγαλλιάσει,
glory of him unblemished with exultation,
25 μόνῳ θεῷ σωτῆρι ἡμῶν διὰ Ἰησοῦ
to [the] only God Saviour of us through Jesus
Χριστοῦ τοῦ κυρίου ἡμῶν δόξα μεγαλωσύνη
Christ the Lord of us [be] glory[,] greatness[,]
κράτος καὶ ἐξουσία πρὸ παντὸς τοῦ
might[,] and authority before all the
αἰῶνος καὶ νῦν καὶ εἰς πάντας τοὺς
age and now and unto all the
αἰῶνας· ἀμήν.
ages: Amen.

ter others for their own advantage.

A Call to Persevere

17But, dear friends, re-
member what the apostles
of our Lord Jesus Christ
foretold.
18They said to
you, "In the last times
there will be scoffers who
will follow their own un-
godly desires."
19These are
the men who divide you,
who follow mere natural in-
stincts and do not have the
Spirit.
20But you, dear friends,
build yourselves up in your
most holy faith and pray in
the Holy Spirit.
21Keep
yourselves in God's love as
you wait for the mercy of
our Lord Jesus Christ to
bring you to eternal life.
22Be merciful to those
who doubt;
23snatch others
from the fire and save
them; to others show mer-
cy, mixed with fear—hat-
ing even the clothing
stained by corrupted flesh.

Doxology

24To him who is able to
keep you from falling and
to present you before his
glorious presence without
fault and with great joy—
25to the only God our Savior be glory, majesty, power and authority, through
Jesus Christ our Lord, before all ages, now and forevermore! Amen.

Revelation

Chapter 1

The Revelation of Jesus Christ

THE Revelation of Jesus Christ, which God gave Him to show to His bond-servants, the things which must shortly take place; and He sent and communicated *it* by His angel to His bond-servant John,

2who bore witness to the word of God and to the testimony of Jesus Christ, *even* to all that he saw.

3Blessed is he who reads and those who hear the words of the prophecy, and heed the things which are written in it; for the time is near.

Message to the Seven Churches

4John to the seven churches that are in Asia: Grace to you and peace, from Him who is and who was and who is to come; and from the seven Spirits who are before His throne;

5and from Jesus Christ, the faithful witness, the first-born of the dead, and the ruler of the kings of the earth. To Him who loves us, and released us from our sins by His blood,

6and He has made us *to be* a kingdom, priests to His God and Father; to Him *be* the glory and the dominion forever and ever. Amen.

7BEHOLD, HE IS COMING WITH THE CLOUDS, and every eye will see Him, even those who pierced Him; and all the tribes of the earth will mourn over Him. Even so. Amen.

8"I am the Alpha and the Omega," says the Lord

ΑΠΟΚΑΛΥΨΙΣ ΙΩΑΝΝΟΥ

A Revelation of John

1 Ἀποκάλυψις Ἰησοῦ Χριστοῦ, ἣν
A revelation of Jesus Christ, which
ἔδωκεν αὐτῷ ὁ θεός, δεῖξαι τοῖς δούλοις
[2]gave [3]to him – [1]God, to show to the slaves
αὐτοῦ ἃ δεῖ γενέσθαι ἐν τάχει, καὶ
of him things which it behoves to occur with speed, and
ἐσήμανεν ἀποστείλας διὰ τοῦ ἀγγέλου
he signified sending through the angel
αὐτοῦ τῷ δούλῳ αὐτοῦ Ἰωάννῃ, **2** ὃς
of him to the slave of him John, who
ἐμαρτύρησεν τὸν λόγον τοῦ θεοῦ καὶ
bore witness [of] the word – of God and
τὴν μαρτυρίαν Ἰησοῦ Χριστοῦ, ὅσα εἶδεν.
the witness of Jesus Christ, as many things as he saw.
3 Μακάριος ὁ ἀναγινώσκων καὶ οἱ
Blessed [is] the [one] reading and the
ἀκούοντες τοὺς λόγους τῆς προφητείας
[ones] hearing the words of the prophecy
καὶ τηροῦντες τὰ ἐν αὐτῇ γεγραμμένα·
and keeping the things [2]in [3]it [1]having been written;
ὁ γὰρ καιρὸς ἐγγύς.
[2]the [1]for time [is] near.
4 Ἰωάννης ταῖς ἑπτὰ ἐκκλησίαις ταῖς
John to the seven churches –
ἐν τῇ Ἀσίᾳ· χάρις ὑμῖν καὶ εἰρήνη
in – Asia: Grace to you and peace
ἀπὸ ὁ ὢν καὶ ὁ ἦν καὶ ὁ ἐρχόμενος,
from the being [one] and the was [one who] and the [one] coming,
=the one who is
καὶ ἀπὸ τῶν ἑπτὰ πνευμάτων ἃ ἐνώπιον
and from the seven spirits which [are] before
τοῦ θρόνου αὐτοῦ, **5** καὶ ἀπὸ Ἰησοῦ
the throne of him, and from Jesus
Χριστοῦ, ὁ μάρτυς ὁ πιστός, ὁ πρωτότοκος
Christ, the [2]witness – [1]faithful, the firstborn
τῶν νεκρῶν καὶ ὁ ἄρχων τῶν βασιλέων
of the dead and the ruler of the kings
τῆς γῆς. Τῷ ἀγαπῶντι ἡμᾶς καὶ λύσαντι
of the earth. To the [one] loving us and having loosed
ἡμᾶς ἐκ τῶν ἁμαρτιῶν ἡμῶν ἐν τῷ
us out of the sins of us by the
αἵματι αὐτοῦ, **6** καὶ ἐποίησεν ἡμᾶς
blood of him, and made us
βασιλείαν, ἱερεῖς τῷ θεῷ καὶ πατρὶ
a kingdom, priests to the God and Father
αὐτοῦ, αὐτῷ ἡ δόξα καὶ τὸ κράτος
of him, to him[c] [is] the glory and the might
= his is
εἰς τοὺς αἰῶνας τῶν αἰώνων· ἀμήν.
unto the ages of the ages: Amen.
7 Ἰδοὺ ἔρχεται μετὰ τῶν νεφελῶν,
Behold he comes with the clouds,
καὶ ὄψεται αὐτὸν πᾶς ὀφθαλμὸς καὶ
and [3]will see [4]him [1]every [2]eye and
οἵτινες αὐτὸν ἐξεκέντησαν, καὶ κόψονται
[those] who [2]him [1]pierced, and [6]will wail
ἐπ' αὐτὸν πᾶσαι αἱ φυλαὶ τῆς γῆς.
[7]over [8]him [1]all [2]the [3]tribes [4]of the [5]land.
ναί, ἀμήν.
Yes, amen.
8 Ἐγώ εἰμι τὸ ἄλφα καὶ τὸ ὦ, λέγει
I am the alpha and the omega, says

Revelation

Chapter 1

Prologue

THE revelation of Jesus Christ, which God gave him to show his servants what must soon take place. He made it known by sending his angel to his servant John, 2who testifies to everything he saw—that is, the word of God and the testimony of Jesus Christ. 3Blessed is the one who reads the words of this prophecy, and blessed are those who hear it and take to heart what is written in it, because the time is near.

Greetings and Doxology

4John,

To the seven churches in the province of Asia:

Grace and peace to you from him who is, and who was, and who is to come, and from the seven spirits[a] before his throne, 5and from Jesus Christ, who is the faithful witness, the firstborn from the dead, and the ruler of the kings of the earth.

To him who loves us and has freed us from our sins by his blood, 6and has made us to be a kingdom and priests to serve his God and Father—to him be glory and power for ever and ever! Amen.

7Look, he is coming with the clouds,
and every eye will see him,
even those who pierced him;
and all the peoples of the earth will mourn because of him.
So shall it be! Amen.

8"I am the Alpha and the Omega," says the Lord

[a]4 Or *the sevenfold Spirit*

God, "who is and who was
and who is to come, the Almighty."

The Patmos Vision

9 I, John, your brother
and fellow partaker in the
tribulation and kingdom
and perseverance *which
are* in Jesus, was on the island called Patmos, be-
cause of the word of God
and the testimony of Jesus.
10 I was [a]in the Spirit on
the Lord's day, and I heard
behind me a loud voice like
the sound of a trumpet,
11 saying, "Write in a
book what you see, and
send *it* to the seven
churches: to Ephesus and
to Smyrna and to Per-
gamum and to Thyatira and
to Sardis and to Phila-
delphia and to Laodicea."
12 And I turned to see the
voice that was speaking
with me. And having
turned I saw seven golden
lampstands;
13 and in the middle of the
lampstands one like [b]a son
of man, clothed in a robe
reaching to the feet, and
girded across His breast
with a golden girdle.
14 And His head and His
hair were white like white
wool, like snow; and His
eyes were like a flame of
fire;
15 and His feet *were* like
burnished bronze, when it
has been caused to glow in
a furnace, and His voice
was like the sound of many
waters.
16 And in His right hand
He held seven stars; and
out of His mouth came a
sharp two-edged sword;
and His face was like the

κύριος ὁ θεός, ὁ ὢν καὶ ὁ ἦν
[the] Lord – God, the [one] being =the one who is and the [one who] was

καὶ ὁ ἐρχόμενος, ὁ παντοκράτωρ.
and the [one] coming, the Almighty.

9 Ἐγὼ Ἰωάννης, ὁ ἀδελφὸς ὑμῶν καὶ
I John, the brother of you and

συγκοινωνὸς ἐν τῇ θλίψει καὶ βασιλείᾳ
co-sharer in the affliction and kingdom

καὶ ὑπομονῇ ἐν Ἰησοῦ, ἐγενόμην ἐν
and endurance in Jesus, came to be in

τῇ νήσῳ τῇ καλουμένῃ Πάτμῳ διὰ
the island – *being* called Patmos on account of

τὸν λόγον τοῦ θεοῦ καὶ τὴν μαρτυρίαν
the word – of God and the witness

Ἰησοῦ. **10** ἐγενόμην ἐν πνεύματι ἐν
of Jesus. I came to be in [the] spirit on

τῇ κυριακῇ ἡμέρᾳ, καὶ ἤκουσα ὀπίσω
the imperial* day, and heard behind

μου φωνὴν μεγάλην ὡς σάλπιγγος
me [2]voice [1]a great(loud) as of a trumpet

11 λεγούσης· ὃ βλέπεις γράψον εἰς βιβλίον
saying: What thou seest write in a scroll

καὶ πέμψον ταῖς ἑπτὰ ἐκκλησίαις, εἰς
and send to the seven churches, to

Ἔφεσον καὶ εἰς Σμύρναν καὶ εἰς Πέργαμον
Ephesus and to Smyrna and to Pergamum

καὶ εἰς Θυάτιρα καὶ εἰς Σάρδεις καὶ
and to Thyatira and to Sardis and

εἰς Φιλαδέλφειαν καὶ εἰς Λαοδίκειαν.
to Philadelphia and to Laodicea.

12 Καὶ ἐπέστρεψα βλέπειν τὴν φωνὴν
And I turned to see the voice

ἥτις ἐλάλει μετ᾽ ἐμοῦ· καὶ ἐπιστρέψας
which spoke with me; and having turned

εἶδον ἑπτὰ λυχνίας χρυσᾶς, **13** καὶ ἐν
I saw seven [2]lampstands [1]golden, and in

μέσῳ τῶν λυχνιῶν ὅμοιον υἱὸν ἀνθρώπου,
[the] midst of the lampstands [one] like a son of man,*

ἐνδεδυμένον ποδήρη καὶ περιεζωσμένον
having been clothed to the feet and *having been* girdled round

πρὸς τοῖς μαστοῖς ζώνην χρυσᾶν· **14** ἡ
at the breasts [2]girdle [1][with] a golden; [2]the

δὲ κεφαλὴ αὐτοῦ καὶ αἱ τρίχες λευκαὶ
[1]and head of him and the hair*s* white

ὡς ἔριον λευκὸν ὡς χιών, καὶ οἱ ὀφθαλμοὶ
as wool white as snow, and the eyes

αὐτοῦ ὡς φλὸξ πυρός, **15** καὶ οἱ πόδες
of him as a flame of fire, and the feet

αὐτοῦ ὅμοιοι χαλκολιβάνῳ ὡς ἐν καμίνῳ
of him like *to* burnished brass as [2]in [3]a furnace

πεπυρωμένης, καὶ ἡ φωνὴ αὐτοῦ ὡς
[1]having been fired, and the voice of him as

φωνὴ ὑδάτων πολλῶν, **16** καὶ ἔχων ἐν
a sound waters of many, and having in

τῇ δεξιᾷ χειρὶ αὐτοῦ ἀστέρας ἑπτά,
the right hand of him [2]stars [1]seven,

καὶ ἐκ τοῦ στόματος αὐτοῦ ῥομφαία
and out of the mouth of him [4]sword

δίστομος ὀξεῖα ἐκπορευομένη, καὶ ἡ ὄψις
[3]two-mouthed(edged) [2]a sharp [1]proceeding, and the face

God, "who is, and who
was, and who is to come,
the Almighty."

One Like a Son of Man

9 I, John, your brother and
companion in the suffering
and kingdom and patient
endurance that are ours in
Jesus, was on the island of
Patmos because of the
word of God and the testimony of Jesus. 10 On the
Lord's Day I was in the
Spirit, and I heard behind
me a loud voice like a trumpet, 11 which said: "Write
on a scroll what you see
and send it to the seven
churches: to Ephesus,
Smyrna, Pergamum, Thya-
tira, Sardis, Philadelphia
and Laodicea."
12 I turned around to see
the voice that was speaking
to me. And when I turned I
saw seven golden lamp-
stands, 13 and among the
lampstands was someone
"like a son of man,"[b]
dressed in a robe reaching
down to his feet and with a
golden sash around his
chest. 14 His head and hair
were white like wool, as
white as snow, and his eyes
were like blazing fire. 15 His
feet were like bronze glow-
ing in a furnace, and his
voice was like the sound of
rushing waters. 16 In his
right hand he held seven
stars, and out of his mouth
came a sharp double-edged
sword. His face was like

[a] Or, *in spirit*
[b] Or, *the Son of Man*

* See I. Cor. 11. 20.
* Anarthrous; see also ch. 14. 14 and John 5. 27, and *cf.* Heb. 2. 6.

[b] *13* Daniel 7:13

sun shining in its strength.
17And when I saw Him, I fell at His feet as a dead man. And He laid His right hand upon me, saying, "Do not be afraid; I am the first and the last,
18and the living One; and I was dead, and behold, I am alive forevermore, and I have the keys of death and of Hades.
19"Write therefore the things which you have seen, and the things which are, and the things which shall take place after these things.
20"As for the mystery of the seven stars which you saw in My right hand, and the seven golden lampstands: the seven stars are the angels of the seven churches, and the seven lampstands are the seven churches.

αὐτοῦ ὡς ὁ ἥλιος φαίνει ἐν τῇ δυνάμει
of him as the sun shines in the power
αὐτοῦ. 17 Καὶ ὅτε εἶδον αὐτόν, ἔπεσα
of it. And when I saw him, I fell
πρὸς τοὺς πόδας αὐτοῦ ὡς νεκρός· καὶ
at the feet of him as dead; and
ἔθηκεν τὴν δεξιὰν αὐτοῦ ἐπ' ἐμὲ λέγων·
he placed the right [hand] of him on me saying:
μὴ φοβοῦ· ἐγώ εἰμι ὁ πρῶτος καὶ
Fear not: I am the first and
ὁ ἔσχατος 18 καὶ ὁ ζῶν, καὶ ἐγενόμην
the last and the living [one], and I became
νεκρὸς καὶ ἰδοὺ ζῶν εἰμι εἰς τοὺς
dead and behold [2]living [1]I am unto the
αἰῶνας τῶν αἰώνων, καὶ ἔχω τὰς κλεῖς
ages of the ages, and I have the keys
τοῦ θανάτου καὶ τοῦ ᾅδου. 19 γράψον
– of death and – of hades. Write thou
οὖν ἃ εἶδες καὶ ἃ εἰσὶν καὶ ἃ
therefore [the] things which thou sawest and [the] things which are and [the] things which
μέλλει γενέσθαι μετὰ ταῦτα. 20 τὸ
(is)are *about* to occur after these things. The
μυστήριον τῶν ἑπτὰ ἀστέρων οὓς εἶδες
mystery of the seven stars which thou sawest
ἐπὶ τῆς· δεξιᾶς μου, καὶ τὰς ἑπτὰ
on the right [hand] of me, and the seven
λυχνίας τὰς χρυσᾶς· οἱ ἑπτὰ ἀστέρες
[2]lampstands – [1]golden: the seven stars
ἄγγελοι τῶν ἑπτὰ ἐκκλησιῶν εἰσιν, καὶ
messengers* of the seven churches are, and
αἱ λυχνίαι αἱ ἑπτὰ ἑπτὰ ἐκκλησίαι εἰσίν.
the [2]lampstands – [1]seven [4]seven [5]churches [3]are.

the sun shining in all its brilliance.
17When I saw him, I fell at
his feet as though dead.
Then he placed his right
hand on me and said: "Do
not be afraid. I am the First
and the Last. 18I am the
Living One; I was dead,
and behold I am alive for
ever and ever! And I hold
the keys of death and Ha-
des.
19"Write, therefore, what
you have seen, what is now
and what will take place later. 20The mystery of the
seven stars that you saw in
my right hand and of the
seven golden lampstands is
this: The seven stars are the
angels[c] of the seven
churches, and the seven
lampstands are the seven
churches.

Chapter 2

Message to Ephesus

"TO the angel of the church in Ephesus write:
The One who holds the seven stars in His right hand, the One who walks among the seven golden lampstands, says this:
2'I know your deeds and your toil and perseverance, and that you cannot endure evil men, and you put to the test those who call themselves apostles, and they are not, and you found them *to be* false:
3and you have persevered and have endured for My name's sake, and have not grown weary.
4'But I have *this* against you, that you have left your

2 Τῷ ἀγγέλῳ τῆς ἐν Ἐφέσῳ ἐκκλησίας
To the messenger [1]of the [3]in [4]Ephesus [2]church
γράψον·
write thou:
Τάδε λέγει ὁ κρατῶν τοὺς ἑπτὰ
These things says the [one] holding the seven
ἀστέρας ἐν τῇ δεξιᾷ αὐτοῦ, ὁ περιπατῶν
stars in the right [hand] of him, the [one] walking
ἐν μέσῳ τῶν ἑπτὰ λυχνιῶν τῶν
in [the] midst of the seven [2]lampstands –
χρυσῶν· 2 οἶδα τὰ ἔργα σου καὶ τὸν
[1]golden: I know the works of thee and the
κόπον καὶ τὴν ὑπομονήν σου, καὶ ὅτι
labour and the endurance of thee, and that
οὐ δύνῃ βαστάσαι κακούς, καὶ ἐπείρασας
thou canst not *to* bear bad men, and didst try
τοὺς λέγοντας ἑαυτοὺς ἀποστόλους καὶ
the [ones] say(call)ing themselves apostles and
οὐκ εἰσίν, καὶ εὗρες αὐτοὺς ψευδεῖς·
are not, and didst find them liars;
3 καὶ ὑπομονὴν ἔχεις, καὶ ἐβάστασας
and [2]endurance [1]thou hast, and didst bear
διὰ τὸ ὄνομά μου, καὶ οὐ κεκοπίακας.
because of the name of me, and hast not grown weary.
4 ἀλλὰ ἔχω κατὰ σοῦ ὅτι τὴν ἀγάπην
But I have against thee that [3]the [4]love

Chapter 2

To the Church in Ephesus

"TO the angel[d] of the
church in Ephesus
write:
These are the words
of him who holds the
seven stars in his right
hand and walks among
the seven golden lamp-
stands: 2I know your
deeds, your hard work
and your perseverance.
I know that you cannot
tolerate wicked men,
that you have tested
those who claim to be
apostles but are not,
and have found them
false. 3You have perse-
vered and have endured
hardships for my name,
and have not grown
weary.
4Yet I hold this
against you: You have

* This, of course, is the prime meaning of the word: whether these beings were "messengers" from the churches, or supernatural beings, "angels" as usually understood, is a matter of exegesis.

c20 Or *messengers*
d1 Or *messenger*; also in verses 8, 12 and 18

ve.
member therefore
where you have
and repent and do
ds you did at first; or
am coming to you,
I remove your lamp-
out of its place—
you repent.
t this you do have,
u hate the deeds of
icolaitans, which I
te.
who has an ear, let
ear what the Spirit
the churches. To
ho overcomes, I will
o eat of the tree of
hich is in the Para-
God.'

ge to Smyrna

nd to the angel of the
in Smyrna write:
first and the last,
vas dead, and has
o life, says this:
now your tribulation
our poverty (but you
ch), and the blas-
by those who say
re Jews and are not,
e a synagogue of Sa-

o not fear what you
out to suffer. Behold,
evil is about to cast
of you into prison,
ou may be tested, and
will have tribulation
ays. Be faithful until
, and I will give you
own of life.
e who has an ear, let
ear what the Spirit
to the churches. He
overcomes shall not
urt by the second
.'

age to Pergamum

And to the angel of the
h in Pergamum write:

σου τὴν πρώτην ἀφῆκας. **5** μνημόνευε
[6]of thee – [5]first [1]thou didst leave. Remember

οὖν πόθεν πέπτωκας, καὶ μετανόησον
therefore whence thou hast fallen, and repent

καὶ τὰ πρῶτα ἔργα ποίησον· εἰ δὲ
and [2]the [3]first [4]works [1]do; and if

μή, ἔρχομαί σοι καὶ κινήσω τὴν λυχνίαν
not, I am coming to thee and will move the lampstand

σου ἐκ τοῦ τόπου αὐτῆς, ἐὰν μὴ
of thee out of the place of it, unless

μετανοήσῃς. **6** ἀλλὰ τοῦτο ἔχεις, ὅτι
thou repentest. But this thou hast, that

μισεῖς τὰ ἔργα τῶν Νικολαϊτῶν, ἃ
thou hatest the works of the Nicolaitans, which

κἀγὼ μισῶ. **7** Ὁ ἔχων οὖς ἀκουσάτω
I also hate. The [one] having an ear let him hear

τί τὸ πνεῦμα λέγει ταῖς ἐκκλησίαις.
what the Spirit says to the churches.

Τῷ νικῶντι δώσω αὐτῷ φαγεῖν ἐκ
To the [one] overcoming I will give *to him* to eat of

τοῦ ξύλου τῆς ζωῆς, ὅ ἐστιν ἐν τῷ
the tree – of life, which is in the

παραδείσῳ τοῦ θεοῦ.
paradise – of God.

8 Καὶ τῷ ἀγγέλῳ τῆς ἐν Σμύρνῃ
And to the messenger [1]of the [3]in [4]Smyrna

ἐκκλησίας γράψον·
[2]church write thou:

Τάδε λέγει ὁ πρῶτος καὶ ὁ ἔσχατος,
These things says the first and the last,

ὃς ἐγένετο νεκρὸς καὶ ἔζησεν· **9** οἶδά
who became dead and lived [again]: I know

σου τὴν θλῖψιν καὶ τὴν πτωχείαν, ἀλλὰ
[6]of thee [1]the [2]affliction [3]and [4]the [5]poverty, but

πλούσιος εἶ, καὶ τὴν βλασφημίαν ἐκ
rich thou art, and the railing of

τῶν λεγόντων Ἰουδαίους εἶναι ἑαυτούς,
the [ones] say(call)ing [3]Jews [2]to be [1]themselves,

καὶ οὐκ εἰσὶν ἀλλὰ συναγωγὴ τοῦ σατανᾶ.
and they are not but a synagogue – of Satan.

10 μὴ φοβοῦ ἃ μέλλεις πάσχειν. ἰδοὺ
Do not fear [the] things which thou art about to suffer. Behold[,]

μέλλει βάλλειν ὁ διάβολος ἐξ ὑμῶν
[3]is about [4]to cast [1]the [2]devil [some] of you

εἰς φυλακὴν ἵνα πειρασθῆτε, καὶ ἕξετε
into prison in order that ye may be tried, and ye will have

θλῖψιν ἡμερῶν δέκα. γίνου πιστὸς ἄχρι
affliction [2]days [1]ten. Be thou faithful until

θανάτου, καὶ δώσω σοι τὸν στέφανον
death, and I will give thee the crown

τῆς ζωῆς. **11** Ὁ ἔχων οὖς ἀκουσάτω
– of life. The [one] having an ear let him hear

τί τὸ πνεῦμα λέγει ταῖς ἐκκλησίαις.
what the Spirit says to the churches.

Ὁ νικῶν οὐ μὴ ἀδικηθῇ ἐκ τοῦ θανάτου
The [one] over-coming by no means will be hurt by the [2]death

τοῦ δευτέρου.
– [1]second.

12 Καὶ τῷ ἀγγέλῳ τῆς ἐν Περγάμῳ
And to the messenger [1]of the [3]in [4]Pergamum

ἐκκλησίας γράψον·
[2]church write thou:

forsaken your first love.
5Remember the height
from which you have
fallen! Repent and do
the things you did at
first. If you do not re-
pent, I will come to you
and remove your lamp-
stand from its place.
6But you have this in
your favor: You hate
the practices of the Nic-
olaitans, which I also
hate.
7He who has an ear,
let him hear what the
Spirit says to the
churches. To him who
overcomes, I will give
the right to eat from the
tree of life, which is in
the paradise of God.

To the Church in Smyrna

8"To the angel of the
church in Smyrna write:

These are the words
of him who is the First
and the Last, who died
and came to life again.
9I know your afflictions
and your poverty—yet
you are rich! I know the
slander of those who
say they are Jews and
are not, but are a syna-
gogue of Satan. 10Do
not be afraid of what
you are about to suffer.
I tell you, the devil will
put some of you in pris-
on to test you, and you
will suffer persecution
for ten days. Be faith-
ful, even to the point of
death, and I will give
you the crown of life.
11He who has an ear,
let him hear what the
Spirit says to the
churches. He who over-
comes will not be hurt
at all by the second
death.

To the Church in Pergamum

12"To the angel of the
church in Pergamum write:

The One who has the
sharp two-edged sword
says this:
13 'I know where you
dwell, where Satan's
throne is; and you hold fast
My name, and did not deny
My faith, even in the days
of Antipas, My witness,
My faithful one, who was
killed among you, where
Satan dwells.
14 'But I have a few things
against you, because you
have there some who hold
the teaching of Balaam,
who kept teaching Balak to
put a stumbling block be-
fore the sons of Israel, to
eat things sacrificed to
idols, and to commit *acts of*
immorality.
15 'Thus you also have
some who in the same way
hold the teaching of the
Nicolaitans.
16 'Repent therefore; or
else I am coming to you
quickly, and I will make
war against them with the
sword of My mouth.
17 'He who has an ear, let
him hear what the Spirit
says to the churches. To
him who overcomes, to
him I will give *some* of the
hidden manna, and I will
give him a white stone, and
a new name written on the
stone which no one knows
but he who receives it.'

Message to Thyatira

18 "And to the angel of the
church in Thyatira write:
The Son of God, who has
eyes like a flame of fire, and
His feet are like burnished
bronze, says this:
19 'I know your deeds, and
your love and faith and service and perseverance, and
that your deeds of late are
greater than at first.

Τάδε λέγει ὁ ἔχων τὴν ῥομφαίαν τὴν
These things says the having [one] the [3]sword –
δίστομον τὴν ὀξεῖαν· **13** οἶδα ποῦ κατοικεῖς·
[1]two-mouthed (edged) – [2]sharp: I know where thou dwellest;
ὅπου ὁ θρόνος τοῦ σατανᾶ· καὶ κρατεῖς
where the throne – of Satan [is]; and thou holdest
τὸ ὄνομά μου, καὶ οὐκ ἠρνήσω τὴν
the name of me, and didst not deny the
πίστιν μου καὶ ἐν ταῖς ἡμέραις Ἀντιπᾶς
faith of me even in the days of Antipas
ὁ μάρτυς μου ὁ πιστός μου, ὃς
[1]the [3]witness [4]of me *the* [2]faithful *of me,* who
ἀπεκτάνθη παρʼ ὑμῖν, ὅπου ὁ σατανᾶς
was killed among you, where – Satan
κατοικεῖ. **14** ἀλλʼ ἔχω κατὰ σοῦ ὀλίγα,
dwells. But I have against thee a few things,
ὅτι ἔχεις ἐκεῖ κρατοῦντας τὴν διδαχὴν
because thou hast there [ones] holding the teaching
Βαλαάμ, ὃς ἐδίδασκεν τῷ Βαλὰκ βαλεῖν
of Balaam, who taught – Balak to cast
σκάνδαλον ἐνώπιον τῶν υἱῶν Ἰσραήλ,
a stumbling-block before the sons of Israel,
φαγεῖν εἰδωλόθυτα καὶ πορνεῦσαι. **15** οὕτως
to eat idol sacrifices and to commit fornication. So
ἔχεις καὶ σὺ κρατοῦντας τὴν διδαχὴν
[2]hast [3]also [1]thou [ones] holding the teaching
τῶν Νικολαϊτῶν ὁμοίως. **16** μετανόησον
of the Nicolaitans likewise. Repent thou
οὖν· εἰ δὲ μή, ἔρχομαί σοι ταχὺ καὶ
therefore; otherwise, I am coming to thee quickly and
πολεμήσω μετʼ αὐτῶν ἐν τῇ ῥομφαίᾳ
will fight with them with the sword
τοῦ στόματός μου. **17** Ὁ ἔχων οὖς
of the mouth of me. The [one] having an ear
ἀκουσάτω τί τὸ πνεῦμα λέγει ταῖς
let him hear what the Spirit says to the
ἐκκλησίαις. Τῷ νικῶντι δώσω αὐτῷ
churches. To the [one] overcoming I will give *to him*
τοῦ μάννα τοῦ κεκρυμμένου, καὶ δώσω
of the [2]manna – [1]*having been* hidden, and I will give
αὐτῷ ψῆφον λευκήν, καὶ ἐπὶ τὴν ψῆφον
him [2]stone [1]a white, and on the stone
ὄνομα καινὸν γεγραμμένον, ὃ οὐδεὶς οἶδεν
[2]name [1]a new *having been* written, which no man knows
εἰ μὴ ὁ λαμβάνων.
except the [one] receiving [it].
18 Καὶ τῷ ἀγγέλῳ τῆς ἐν Θυατίροις
And to the messenger [1]of the [3]in [4]Thyatira
ἐκκλησίας γράψον·
[2]church write thou:
Τάδε λέγει ὁ υἱὸς τοῦ θεοῦ, ὁ ἔχων
These things says the Son – of God, the having [one]
τοὺς ὀφθαλμοὺς [αὐτοῦ] ὡς φλόγα πυρός,
the eyes of him as a flame of fire,
καὶ οἱ πόδες αὐτοῦ ὅμοιοι χαλκολιβάνῳ·
and the feet of him like *to* burnished brass:
19 οἶδά σου τὰ ἔργα καὶ τὴν ἀγάπην
I know of thee the works and the love
καὶ τὴν πίστιν καὶ τὴν διακονίαν καὶ
and the faith and the ministry and
τὴν ὑπομονήν σου, καὶ τὰ ἔργα σου
the endurance *of thee,* and the [2]works [3]of thee
τὰ ἔσχατα πλείονα τῶν πρώτων. **20** ἀλλὰ
the [1]last more [than] the first. But

These are the words
of him who has the
sharp, double-edged
sword. 13 I know where
you live—where Satan
has his throne. Yet you
remain true to my
name. You did not re-
nounce your faith in
me, even in the days of
Antipas, my faithful
witness, who was put to
death in your city—
where Satan lives.
14 Nevertheless, I
have a few things
against you: You have
people there who hold
to the teaching of Ba-
laam, who taught Balak
to entice the Israelites
to sin by eating food
sacrificed to idols and
by committing sexual
immorality. 15 Likewise
you also have those
who hold to the teach-
ing of the Nicolaitans.
16 Repent therefore!
Otherwise, I will soon
come to you and will
fight against them with
the sword of my mouth.
17 He who has an ear,
let him hear what the
Spirit says to the
churches. To him who
overcomes, I will give
some of the hidden
manna. I will also give
him a white stone with a
new name written on it,
known only to him who
receives it.

To the Church in Thyatira

18 "To the angel of the
church in Thyatira write:

These are the words
of the Son of God,
whose eyes are like
blazing fire and whose
feet are like burnished
bronze. 19 I know your
deeds, your love and
faith, your service and
perseverance, and that
you are now doing more
than you did at first.

20 'But I have *this* against you, that you tolerate the woman Jezebel, who calls herself a prophetess, and she teaches and leads My bond-servants astray, so that they commit *acts of* immorality and eat things sacrificed to idols.

21 'And I gave her time to repent; and she does not want to repent of her immorality.

22 'Behold, I will cast her upon a bed *of sickness*, and those who commit adultery with her into great tribulation, unless they repent of [c]her deeds.

23 'And I will kill her children with pestilence; and all the churches will know that I am He who searches the minds and hearts; and I will give to each one of you according to your deeds.

24 'But I say to you, the rest who are in Thyatira, who do not hold this teaching, who have not known the deep things of Satan, as they call them—I place no other burden on you.

25 'Nevertheless what you have, hold fast until I come.

26 'And he who overcomes, and he who keeps My deeds until the end, TO HIM I WILL GIVE AUTHORITY OVER THE NATIONS;

27 AND HE SHALL RULE THEM WITH A ROD OF IRON, AS THE VESSELS OF THE POTTER ARE BROKEN TO PIECES, as I also have received *authority* from My Father;

28 and I will give him the morning star.

29 'He who has an ear, let him hear what the Spirit says to the churches.'

ἔχω κατὰ σοῦ ὅτι ἀφεῖς τὴν γυναῖκα
I have against thee that thou permittest the woman
Ἰεζάβελ, ἡ λέγουσα ἑαυτὴν προφῆτιν,
Jezabel, the [one] say(call)ing herself a prophetess,
καὶ διδάσκει καὶ πλανᾷ τοὺς ἐμοὺς
and she teaches and deceives – my
δούλους πορνεῦσαι καὶ φαγεῖν εἰδωλόθυτα·
slaves to commit fornication and to eat idol sacrifices;
21 καὶ ἔδωκα αὐτῇ χρόνον ἵνα μετανοήσῃ,
and I gave her time in order that she might repent,
καὶ οὐ θέλει μετανοῆσαι ἐκ τῆς πορνείας
and she wishes not to repent of the fornication
αὐτῆς. **22** ἰδοὺ βάλλω αὐτὴν εἰς κλίνην,
of her. Behold[,] I am casting her into a bed,
καὶ τοὺς μοιχεύοντας μετ' αὐτῆς εἰς
and the [ones] committing adultery with her into
θλῖψιν μεγάλην, ἐὰν μὴ μετανοήσουσιν
²affliction ¹great, unless they shall repent
ἐκ τῶν ἔργων αὐτῆς· **23** καὶ τὰ τέκνα
of the works of her; and the children
αὐτῆς ἀποκτενῶ ἐν θανάτῳ· καὶ γνώσονται
of her I will kill with death; and ⁴will know
πᾶσαι αἱ ἐκκλησίαι ὅτι ἐγώ εἰμι ὁ
¹all ²the ³churches that I am the [one]
ἐρευνῶν νεφροὺς καὶ καρδίας, καὶ δώσω
searching kidneys and hearts, and I will give
ὑμῖν ἑκάστῳ κατὰ τὰ ἔργα ὑμῶν.
to you each one according to the works of you.
24 ὑμῖν δὲ λέγω τοῖς λοιποῖς τοῖς ἐν
But to you I say *to* the rest – in
Θυατίροις, ὅσοι οὐκ ἔχουσιν τὴν διδαχὴν
Thyatira, as many as have not – teaching
ταύτην, οἵτινες οὐκ ἔγνωσαν τὰ βαθέα
this, who knew not the deep things
τοῦ σατανᾶ, ὡς λέγουσιν· οὐ βάλλω
– of Satan, as they say: I am not casting
ἐφ' ὑμᾶς ἄλλο βάρος· **25** πλὴν ὃ ἔχετε
on you another burden; nevertheless what ye have
κρατήσατε ἄχρι οὗ ἂν ἥξω. **26** Καὶ
hold until I shall come. And
ὁ νικῶν καὶ ὁ τηρῶν ἄχρι τέλους τὰ
the [one] overcoming and the [one] keeping until [the] end the
ἔργα μου, δώσω αὐτῷ ἐξουσίαν ἐπὶ
works of me, I will give him authority over
τῶν ἐθνῶν, **27** καὶ ποιμανεῖ αὐτοὺς ἐν
the nations, and he will shepherd them with
ῥάβδῳ σιδηρᾷ, ὡς τὰ σκεύη τὰ κεραμικὰ
²staff ¹an iron, as *the* ²vessels – ¹clay
συντρίβεται, ὡς κἀγὼ εἴληφα παρὰ
is(are) broken, as I also have received from
τοῦ πατρός μου, **28** καὶ δώσω αὐτῷ τὸν
the Father of me, and I will give him the
ἀστέρα τὸν πρωϊνόν. **29** Ὁ ἔχων οὖς
²star – ¹morning. The [one] having an ear
ἀκουσάτω τί τὸ πνεῦμα λέγει ταῖς
let him hear what the Spirit says to the
ἐκκλησίαις
churches.

20 Nevertheless, I
have this against you:
You tolerate that wom-
an Jezebel, who calls
herself a prophetess. By
her teaching she mis-
leads my servants into
sexual immorality and
the eating of food sacri-
ficed to idols. 21 I have
given her time to repent
of her immorality, but
she is unwilling. 22 So I
will cast her on a bed of
suffering, and I will
make those who com-
mit adultery with her
suffer intensely, unless
they repent of her ways.
23 I will strike her children dead. Then all the
churches will know that
I am he who searches
hearts and minds, and I
will repay each of you
according to your
deeds. 24 Now I say to
the rest of you in Thya-
tira, to you who do not
hold to her teaching and
have not learned Sa-
tan's so-called deep se-
crets (I will not impose
any other burden on
you): 25 Only hold on to
what you have until I
come.
26 To him who over-
comes and does my will
to the end, I will give
authority over the na-
tions—

27 'He will rule them
with an iron
scepter;
he will dash them
to pieces like
pottery'[e]—

just as I have received
authority from my Fa-
ther. 28 I will also give
him the morning star.
29 He who has an ear, let
him hear what the Spirit
says to the churches.

[c] Some mss. read *their*

[e] 27 Psalm 2:9

Chapter 3

Message to Sardis

"AND to the angel of
the church in Sar-
dis write:
He who has the seven
Spirits of God, and the
seven stars, says this: 'I
know your deeds, that you
have a name that you are
alive, but you are dead.
2'Wake up, and strength-
en the things that remain,
which were about to die;
for I have not found your
deeds completed in the
sight of My God.
3'Remember therefore
what you have received
and heard; and keep *it*, and
repent. If therefore you will
not wake up, I will come
like a thief, and you will not
know at what hour I will
come upon you.
4'But you have a few
people in Sardis who have
not soiled their garments;
and they will walk with Me
in white; for they are
worthy.
5'He who overcomes
shall thus be clothed in
white garments; and I will
not erase his name from the
book of life, and I will confess his name before My
Father, and before His angels.
6'He who has an ear, let
him hear what the Spirit
says to the churches.'

Message to Philadelphia

7"And to the angel of the
church in Philadelphia
write:
He who is holy, who is
true, who has the key of
David, who opens and no
one will shut, and who
shuts and no one opens,
says this:
8'I know your [d]deeds.
Behold, I have put before
you an open door which no
one can shut, because you
have a little power,
and have kept My word,
and have not denied My
name.
9'Behold, I will cause
those of the synagogue of

[d]Or, *deeds (behold . . . shut), that you*

Chapter 3

3 Καὶ τῷ ἀγγέλῳ τῆς ἐν Σάρδεσιν
And to the messenger [1]of the [3]in [4]Sardis

ἐκκλησίας γράψον·
[2]church write thou:

Τάδε λέγει ὁ ἔχων τὰ ἑπτὰ πνεύματα
These things says the having [one] the seven Spirits

τοῦ θεοῦ καὶ τοὺς ἑπτὰ ἀστέρας· οἶδά
– of God and the seven stars: I know

σου τὰ ἔργα, ὅτι ὄνομα ἔχεις ὅτι ζῇς,
[2]of thee [1]the [3]works, that a name thou hast that thou livest,

καὶ νεκρὸς εἶ. **2** γίνου γρηγορῶν, καὶ
and [yet] [2]dead [1]thou art. Be thou watching, and

στήρισον τὰ λοιπὰ ἃ ἔμελλον ἀποθανεῖν·
establish the things remaining which were about to die;

οὐ γὰρ εὕρηκά σου ἔργα πεπληρωμένα
for I have not found of thee works *having been* fulfilled

ἐνώπιον τοῦ θεοῦ μου· **3** μνημόνευε οὖν
before the God of me; remember therefore

πῶς εἴληφας καὶ ἤκουσας, καὶ τήρει
how thou hast received and didst hear, and keep

καὶ μετανόησον. ἐὰν οὖν μὴ γρηγορήσῃς,
and repent. If therefore thou dost not watch,

ἥξω ὡς κλέπτης, καὶ οὐ μὴ γνῷς ποίαν
I will come as a thief, and by no means thou knowest at what

ὥραν ἥξω ἐπὶ σέ. **4** ἀλλὰ ἔχεις ὀλίγα
hour I will come on thee. But thou hast a few

ὀνόματα ἐν Σάρδεσιν ἃ οὐκ ἐμόλυναν τὰ
names in Sardis which did not defile the

ἱμάτια αὐτῶν, καὶ περιπατήσουσιν μετ'
garments of them, and they shall walk with

ἐμοῦ ἐν λευκοῖς, ὅτι ἄξιοί εἰσιν. **5** Ὁ
me in white [garments], because [2]worthy [1]they are. The [one]

νικῶν οὕτως περιβαλεῖται ἐν ἱματίοις
overcoming [2]thus [1]shall be clothed in [2]garments

λευκοῖς, καὶ οὐ μὴ ἐξαλείψω τὸ ὄνομα
[1]white, and by no means will I blot *out* the name

αὐτοῦ ἐκ τῆς βίβλου τῆς ζωῆς, καὶ
of him out of the scroll – of life, and

ὁμολογήσω τὸ ὄνομα αὐτοῦ ἐνώπιον τοῦ
I will confess the name of him before the

πατρός μου καὶ ἐνώπιον τῶν ἀγγέλων
Father of me and before the angels

αὐτοῦ. **6** Ὁ ἔχων οὖς ἀκουσάτω τί τὸ
of him. The [one] having an ear let him hear what the

πνεῦμα λέγει ταῖς ἐκκλησίαις.
Spirit says to the churches.

7 Καὶ τῷ ἀγγέλῳ τῆς ἐν Φιλαδελφείᾳ
And to the messenger [1]of the [3]in [4]Philadelphia

ἐκκλησίας γράψον·
[2]church write thou:

Τάδε λέγει ὁ ἅγιος, ὁ ἀληθινός, ὁ
These things says the holy [one], the true [one], the [one]

ἔχων τὴν κλεῖν Δαυίδ, ὁ ἀνοίγων καὶ
having the key of David, the [one] opening and

οὐδεὶς κλείσει, καὶ κλείων καὶ οὐδεὶς
no one shall shut, and shutting and no one

ἀνοίγει· **8** οἶδά σου τὰ ἔργα· ἰδοὺ
opens: I know of thee the works; behold[,]

δέδωκα ἐνώπιόν σου θύραν ἠνεῳγμένην,
I have given before thee a door *having been* opened,

Chapter 3

To the Church in Sardis

"TO the angel[f] of the
church in Sardis
write:
These are the words
of him who holds the
seven spirits[g] of God
and the seven stars. I
know your deeds; you
have a reputation of be-
ing alive, but you are
dead. 2Wake up!
Strengthen what re-
mains and is about to
die, for I have not found
your deeds complete in
the sight of my God.
3Remember, therefore,
what you have received
and heard; obey it, and
repent. But if you do
not wake up, I will
come like a thief, and
you will not know at
what time I will come to
you.
4Yet you have a few
people in Sardis who
have not soiled their
clothes. They will walk
with me, dressed in
white, for they are wor-
thy. 5He who over-
comes will, like them,
be dressed in white. I
will never blot out his
name from the book of
life, but will acknowl-
edge his name before
my Father and his an-
gels. 6He who has an
ear, let him hear what
the Spirit says to the
churches.

To the Church in Philadelphia

7"To the angel of the
church in Philadelphia
write:
These are the words
of him who is holy and
true, who holds the key
of David. What he
opens no one can shut,
and what he shuts no
one can open. 8I know
your deeds. See, I have
placed before you an
open door that no one
can shut. I know that
you have little strength,
yet you have kept my
word and have not de-
nied my name. 9I will
make those who are of
the synagogue of Satan,

[f]1 Or *messenger;* also in verses 7 and 14
[g]1 Or *the sevenfold Spirit*

Satan, who say that they are Jews, and are not, but lie—behold, I will make them to come and bow down at your feet, and to know that I have loved you.

10 'Because you have kept the word of My perseverance, I also will keep you from the hour of testing, that *hour* which is about to come upon the whole world, to test those who dwell upon the earth.

11 'I am coming quickly; hold fast what you have, in order that no one take your crown.

12 'He who overcomes, I will make him a pillar in the temple of My God, and he will not go out from it anymore; and I will write upon him the name of My God, and the name of the city of My God, the new Jerusalem, which comes down out of heaven from My God, and My new name.

13 'He who has an ear, let him hear what the Spirit says to the churches.'

Message to Laodicea

14 "And to the angel of the church in Laodicea write:

The Amen, the faithful and true Witness, the [e] Beginning of the creation of God, says this:

15 'I know your deeds,

[e] I.e., origin or source

ἣν οὐδεὶς δύναται κλεῖσαι αὐτήν· ὅτι
which no one can *to* shut *it;* because

μικρὰν ἔχεις δύναμιν, καὶ ἐτήρησάς μου
²a little ¹thou hast power, and didst keep of me

τὸν λόγον καὶ οὐκ ἠρνήσω τὸ ὄνομά
the word and didst not deny the name

μου. 9 ἰδοὺ διδῶ ἐκ τῆς συναγωγῆς
of me. Behold[,] I may (will) give [some] of the synagogue

τοῦ σατανᾶ, τῶν λεγόντων ἑαυτοὺς
– of Satan, the [ones] say(call)ing themselves

Ἰουδαίους εἶναι, καὶ οὐκ εἰσὶν ἀλλὰ
Jews to be, and they are not but

ψεύδονται· ἰδοὺ ποιήσω αὐτοὺς ἵνα
they lie; behold[,] I will make them *in order* that

ἥξουσιν καὶ προσκυνήσουσιν ἐνώπιον τῶν
they shall come and *they* shall worship before the

ποδῶν σου, καὶ γνῶσιν ὅτι ἐγὼ ἠγάπησά
feet of thee, and *they* shall know that I loved

σε. 10 ὅτι ἐτήρησας τὸν λόγον τῆς
thee. Because thou didst keep the word of the

ὑπομονῆς μου, κἀγώ σε τηρήσω ἐκ
endurance of me, I also ²thee ¹will keep out of

τῆς ὥρας τοῦ πειρασμοῦ τῆς μελλούσης
the hour – of trial – *being* about

ἔρχεσθαι ἐπὶ τῆς οἰκουμένης ὅλης, πειράσαι
to come on ²the ³inhabited [earth] ¹all, to try

τοὺς κατοικοῦντας ἐπὶ τῆς γῆς. 11 ἔρχομαι
the [ones] dwelling on the earth. I am coming

ταχύ· κράτει ὃ ἔχεις, ἵνα μηδεὶς λάβῃ
quickly; hold what thou hast, in order that no one takes

τὸν στέφανόν σου. 12 Ὁ νικῶν, ποιήσω
the crown of thee. The [one] overcoming, I will make

αὐτὸν στῦλον ἐν τῷ ναῷ τοῦ θεοῦ
him a pillar in the shrine of the God

μου, καὶ ἔξω οὐ μὴ ἐξέλθῃ ἔτι, καὶ
of me, and out by no means he will go forth [any] longer, and

γράψω ἐπ' αὐτὸν τὸ ὄνομα τοῦ θεοῦ
I will write on him the name of the God

μου καὶ τὸ ὄνομα τῆς πόλεως τοῦ
of me and the name of the city of the

θεοῦ μου, τῆς καινῆς Ἰερουσαλὴμ ἡ
God of me, *of* the new Jerusalem –

καταβαίνουσα ἐκ τοῦ οὐρανοῦ ἀπὸ τοῦ
descending out of – heaven from the

θεοῦ μου, καὶ τὸ ὄνομά μου τὸ καινόν.
God of me, and ¹the ³name ⁴of me – ²new.

13 Ὁ ἔχων οὖς ἀκουσάτω τί τὸ πνεῦμα
The [one] having an ear let him hear what the Spirit

λέγει ταῖς ἐκκλησίαις.
says to the churches.

14 Καὶ τῷ ἀγγέλῳ τῆς ἐν Λαοδικείᾳ
And to the messenger ¹of the ³in ⁴Laodicea

ἐκκλησίας γράψον·
²church write thou:

Τάδε λέγει ὁ ἀμήν, ὁ μάρτυς ὁ
These things says the Amen, the ⁴witness –

πιστὸς καὶ ἀληθινός, ἡ ἀρχὴ τῆς κτίσεως
¹faithful ²and ³true, the chief of the creation

τοῦ θεοῦ· 15 οἶδά σου τὰ ἔργα, ὅτι
– of God: I know of thee the works, that

who claim to be Jews though they are not, but are liars—I will make them come and fall down at your feet and acknowledge that I have loved you. 10 Since you have kept my command to endure patiently, I will also keep you from the hour of trial that is going to come upon the whole world to test those who live on the earth.

11 I am coming soon. Hold on to what you have, so that no one will take your crown. 12 Him who overcomes I will make a pillar in the temple of my God. Never again will he leave it. I will write on him the name of my God and the name of the city of my God, the new Jerusalem, which is coming down out of heaven from my God; and I will also write on him my new name. 13 He who has an ear, let him hear what the Spirit says to the churches.

To the Church in Laodicea

14 "To the angel of the church in Laodicea write:

These are the words of the Amen, the faithful and true witness, the ruler of God's creation. 15 I know your deeds,

that you are neither cold
nor hot; I would that you
were cold or hot.
16'So because you are
lukewarm, and neither hot
nor cold, I will spit you out
of My mouth.
17'Because you say, "I
am rich, and have become
wealthy, and have need of
nothing," and you do not
know that you are
wretched and miserable
and poor and blind and
naked,
18I advise you to buy from
Me gold refined by fire,
that you may become rich,
and white garments, that
you may clothe yourself,
and *that* the shame of your
nakedness may not be re-
vealed; and eye salve to
anoint your eyes, that you
may see.
19'Those whom I love, I
reprove and discipline; be
zealous therefore, and repent.
20'Behold, I stand at the
door and knock; if anyone
hears My voice and opens
the door, I will come in to
him, and will dine with him,
and he with Me.
21'He who overcomes, I
will grant to him to sit down
with Me on My throne, as I
also overcame and sat
down with My Father on
His throne.
22'He who has an ear, let
him hear what the Spirit
says to the churches.' "

οὔτε ψυχρὸς εἶ οὔτε ζεστός. ὄφελον
neither cold art thou nor hot. I would that†

ψυχρὸς ἦς ἢ ζεστός. 16 οὕτως ὅτι
cold thou wast or hot. So because

χλιαρὸς εἶ, καὶ οὔτε ζεστὸς οὔτε ψυχρός,
lukewarm thou art, and neither hot nor cold,

μέλλω σε ἐμέσαι ἐκ τοῦ στόματός μου.
I am about* [2]thee [1]to vomit out of the mouth of me.

17 ὅτι λέγεις ὅτι πλούσιός εἰμι καὶ
Because thou sayest[,] – [2]rich [1]I am and

πεπλούτηκα καὶ οὐδὲν χρείαν ἔχω, καὶ
I have become rich and [2]no [3]need [1]*I* have, and

οὐκ οἶδας ὅτι σὺ εἶ ὁ ταλαίπωρος
knowest not that thou art the [one] wretched

καὶ ἐλεεινὸς καὶ πτωχὸς καὶ τυφλὸς
and pitiable and poor and blind

καὶ γυμνός, 18 συμβουλεύω σοι ἀγοράσαι
and naked, I counsel thee to buy

παρ' ἐμοῦ χρυσίον πεπυρωμένον ἐκ πυρὸς
from me gold *having been* refined *by fire* by fire

ἵνα πλουτήσῃς, καὶ ἱμάτια λευκὰ ἵνα
in order that thou mayest be rich, and [2]garments [1]white in order that

περιβάλῃ καὶ μὴ φανερωθῇ ἡ αἰσχύνη
thou mayest be clothed and [6]may not be manifested [1]the [2]shame

τῆς γυμνότητός σου, καὶ κολλύριον
[3]of the [4]nakedness [5]of thee, and eyesalve

ἐγχρῖσαι τοὺς ὀφθαλμούς σου ἵνα βλέπῃς.
to anoint the eyes of thee in order that thou mayest see.

19 ἐγὼ ὅσους ἐὰν φιλῶ ἐλέγχω καὶ
[2]I [1]as many as love I rebuke and

παιδεύω· ζήλευε οὖν καὶ μετανόησον.
I chasten; be hot therefore and repent thou.

20 Ἰδοὺ ἕστηκα ἐπὶ τὴν θύραν καὶ
Behold[,] I stand at the door and

κρούω· ἐάν τις ἀκούσῃ τῆς φωνῆς μου
I knock; if anyone hears the voice of me

καὶ ἀνοίξῃ τὴν θύραν, εἰσελεύσομαι πρὸς
and opens the door, I will enter to

αὐτὸν καὶ δειπνήσω μετ' αὐτοῦ καὶ
him and *I* will dine with him and

αὐτὸς μετ' ἐμοῦ. 21 Ὁ νικῶν, δώσω
he with me. The [one] overcoming, I will give

αὐτῷ καθίσαι μετ' ἐμοῦ ἐν τῷ θρόνῳ
him to sit with me in the throne

μου, ὡς κἀγὼ ἐνίκησα καὶ ἐκάθισα
of me, as I also overcame and sat

μετὰ τοῦ πατρός μου ἐν τῷ θρόνῳ
with the Father of me in the throne

αὐτοῦ. 22 Ὁ ἔχων οὖς ἀκουσάτω τί
of him. The [one] having an ear let him hear what

τὸ πνεῦμα λέγει ταῖς ἐκκλησίαις.
the Spirit says to the churches.

that you are neither
cold nor hot. I wish you
were either one or the
other! 16So, because
you are lukewarm—
neither hot nor cold—I
am about to spit you out
of my mouth. 17You
say, 'I am rich; I have
acquired wealth and do
not need a thing.' But
you do not realize that
you are wretched, piti-
ful, poor, blind and na-
ked. 18I counsel you to
buy from me gold re-
fined in the fire, so you
can become rich; and
white clothes to wear,
so you can cover your
shameful nakedness;
and salve to put on your
eyes, so you can see.
19Those whom I love I
rebuke and discipline.
So be earnest, and re-
pent. 20Here I am! I
stand at the door and
knock. If anyone hears
my voice and opens the
door, I will come in and
eat with him, and he
with me.
21To him who over-
comes, I will give the
right to sit with me on
my throne, just as I
overcame and sat down
with my Father on his
throne. 22He who has an
ear, let him hear what
the Spirit says to the
churches."

Chapter 4

Scene in Heaven

AFTER these things I
looked, and behold, a
door *standing* open in
heaven, and the first voice
which I had heard, like *the*
sound of a trumpet speak-

4 Μετὰ ταῦτα εἶδον, καὶ ἰδοὺ θύρα
After these things I saw, and behold[,] a door

ἠνεῳγμένη ἐν τῷ οὐρανῷ, καὶ ἡ φωνὴ
having been opened in – heaven, and the [2]voice

ἡ πρώτη ἣν ἤκουσα ὡς σάλπιγγος
– [1]first which I heard as of a trumpet

Chapter 4

The Throne in Heaven

AFTER this I looked, and
there before me was a
door standing open in heav-
en. And the voice I had first
heard speaking to me like a

* As so often (see also ch. 1. 19, 2. 10), this verb does not necessarily connote imminence, but only simple futurity.

ing with me, said, "Come
up here, and I will show
you what must take place
after these things."
2Immediately I was [f] in
the Spirit; and behold, a
throne was standing in
heaven, and One sitting on
the throne.
3And He who was sitting
was like a jasper stone and
a sardius in appearance;
and *there was* a rainbow
around the throne, like an
emerald in appearance.
4And around the throne
were twenty-four thrones;
and upon the thrones *I saw*
twenty-four elders sitting,
clothed in white garments,
and golden crowns on their
heads.

The Throne and Worship of the Creator

5And from the throne
proceed flashes of lightning
and sounds and peals of
thunder. And *there were*
seven lamps of fire burning
before the throne, which
are the seven Spirits of
God;
6and before the throne
there was, as it were, a sea
of glass like crystal; and in
the center and around the
throne, four living crea-
tures full of eyes in front
and behind.
7And the first creature
was like a lion, and the second creature like a calf, and
the third creature had a
face like that of a man, and
the fourth creature *was* like
a flying eagle.
8And the four living
creatures, each one of them
having six wings, are full of
eyes around and within;
and day and night they do
not cease to say,

λαλούσης μετ' ἐμοῦ, λέγων· ἀνάβα ὧδε,
speaking with me, saying: Come up here,

καὶ δείξω σοι ἃ δεῖ γενέσθαι μετὰ
and I will show thee things which it behoves to occur after

ταῦτα. εὐθέως ἐγενόμην ἐν πνεύματι·
these things. Immediately I became in spirit;

2 καὶ ἰδοὺ θρόνος ἔκειτο ἐν τῷ οὐρανῷ,
and behold[,] a throne was set in – heaven,

καὶ ἐπὶ τὸν θρόνον καθήμενος, **3** καὶ
and on the throne a sitting [one], and

ὁ καθήμενος ὅμοιος ὁράσει λίθῳ ἰάσπιδι
the [one] sitting [was] like in appearance [4]stone [1]*to* a jasper

καὶ σαρδίῳ, καὶ ἶρις κυκλόθεν τοῦ
[2]and [3]a sardius, and [there was] a rainbow round the

θρόνου ὅμοιος ὁράσει σμαραγδίνῳ. **4** καὶ
throne like in appearance *to* an emerald. And

κυκλόθεν τοῦ θρόνου θρόνους εἴκοσι
round the throne [I saw] [2]thrones [1]twenty-

τέσσαρας, καὶ ἐπὶ τοὺς θρόνους εἴκοσι
four, and on the thrones twenty-

τέσσαρας πρεσβυτέρους καθημένους περι-
four elders sitting *having been*

βεβλημένους ἐν ἱματίοις λευκοῖς, καὶ ἐπὶ
clothed in garments white, and on

τὰς κεφαλὰς αὐτῶν στεφάνους χρυσοῦς
the heads of them [2]crowns [1]golden.

5 καὶ ἐκ τοῦ θρόνου ἐκπορεύονται ἀστραπαὶ
And out of the throne come forth lightnings

καὶ φωναὶ καὶ βρονταί· καὶ ἑπτὰ λαμπάδες
and voices* and thunders; and seven lamps

πυρὸς καιόμεναι ἐνώπιον τοῦ θρόνου, ἅ
of fire [are] burning before the throne, which

εἰσιν τὰ ἑπτὰ πνεύματα τοῦ θεοῦ· **6** καὶ
are the seven Spirits – of God; and

ἐνώπιον τοῦ θρόνου ὡς θάλασσα ὑαλίνη
before the throne as [2]sea [1]a glassy

ὁμοία κρυστάλλῳ· καὶ ἐν μέσῳ τοῦ
like *to* crystal; and in [the] midst of the

θρόνου καὶ κύκλῳ τοῦ θρόνου τέσσερα
throne and round the throne four

ζῷα γέμοντα ὀφθαλμῶν ἔμπροσθεν καὶ
living creatures filling(full) of eyes before and

ὄπισθεν. **7** καὶ τὸ ζῷον τὸ πρῶτον
behind. And the [2]living creature – [1]first

ὅμοιον λέοντι, καὶ τὸ δεύτερον ζῷον
[was] like *to* a lion, and the second living creature

ὅμοιον μόσχῳ, καὶ τὸ τρίτον ζῷον ἔχων
like *to* a calf, and the third living creature having

τὸ πρόσωπον ὡς ἀνθρώπου, καὶ τὸ
the(its) face as of a man, and the

τέταρτον ζῷον ὅμοιον ἀετῷ πετομένῳ.
fourth living creature like eagle *to* a flying.

8 καὶ τὰ τέσσερα ζῷα, ἓν καθ' ἓν
And the four living creatures, one by one

αὐτῶν ἔχων ἀνὰ πτέρυγας ἕξ, κυκλόθεν
of them having each [2]wings [1]six, around

καὶ ἔσωθεν γέμουσιν ὀφθαλμῶν· καὶ
and within are full of eyes; and

ἀνάπαυσιν οὐκ ἔχουσιν ἡμέρας καὶ νυκτὸς
respite they have not day and night

trumpet said, "Come up
here, and I will show you
what must take place after
this." 2At once I was in the
Spirit, and there before me
was a throne in heaven with
someone sitting on it. 3And
the one who sat there had
the appearance of jasper
and carnelian. A rainbow,
resembling an emerald, encircled the throne. 4Sur-
rounding the throne were
twenty-four other thrones,
and seated on them were
twenty-four elders. They
were dressed in white and
had crowns of gold on their
heads. 5From the throne
came flashes of lightning,
rumblings and peals of
thunder. Before the throne,
seven lamps were blazing.
These are the seven spir-
its[h] of God. 6Also before
the throne there was what
looked like a sea of glass,
clear as crystal.

In the center, around the
throne, were four living
creatures, and they were
covered with eyes, in front
and in back. 7The first living creature was like a lion,
the second was like an ox,
the third had a face like a
man, the fourth was like a
flying eagle. 8Each of the
four living creatures had
six wings and was covered
with eyes all around, even
under his wings. Day and
night they never stop saying:

[f] Or, *in spirit*

* Or "sounds"; and so elsewhere.

[h] 5 Or *the sevenfold Spirit*

"HOLY, HOLY, HOLY, *is*
THE LORD GOD, THE
ALMIGHTY, who was
and who is and who
is to come."
9And when the living
creatures give glory and
honor and thanks to Him
who sits on the throne, to
Him who lives forever and
ever,
10the twenty-four elders
will fall down before Him
who sits on the throne, and
will worship Him who lives
forever and ever, and will
cast their crowns before
the throne, saying,
11"Worthy art Thou, our
Lord and our God, to
receive glory and
honor and power; for
Thou didst create all
things, and because
of Thy will they existed,
and were
created."

Chapter 5

The Book with Seven Seals

AND I saw in the right
hand of Him who sat
on the throne a book written
inside and on the back,
sealed up with seven seals.
2And I saw a strong angel
proclaiming with a loud
voice, "Who is worthy to
open the book and to break
its seals?"
3And no one in heaven,
or on the earth, or under
the earth, was able to open
the book, or to look into it.
4And I *began* to weep
greatly, because no one
was found worthy to open
the book, or to look into it;
5and one of the elders
*said to me, "Stop weeping;
behold, the Lion that is

λέγοντες· ἅγιος ἅγιος ἅγιος κύριος ὁ
saying: Holy[,] holy[,] holy[,] Lord –

θεὸς ὁ παντοκράτωρ, ὁ ἦν καὶ ὁ ὢν
God the Almighty, the [one who] was and the [one] being = the one who is

καὶ ὁ ἐρχόμενος. 9 Καὶ ὅταν δώσουσιν
and the coming [one]. And whenever [3]shall give

τὰ ζῷα δόξαν καὶ τιμὴν καὶ εὐχαριστίαν
[1]the [2]living creatures glory and honour and thanks

τῷ καθημένῳ ἐπὶ τῷ θρόνῳ τῷ ζῶντι
to the [one] sitting on the throne[,] to the [one] living

εἰς τοὺς αἰῶνας τῶν αἰώνων, 10 πεσοῦνται
unto the ages of the ages, [4]will fall

οἱ εἴκοσι τέσσαρες πρεσβύτεροι ἐνώπιον
[1]the [2]twenty-four [3]elders before

τοῦ καθημένου ἐπὶ τοῦ θρόνου, καὶ
the [one] sitting on the throne, and

προσκυνήσουσιν τῷ ζῶντι εἰς τοὺς αἰῶνας
they will worship the [one] living unto the ages

τῶν αἰώνων, καὶ βαλοῦσιν τοὺς στεφάνους
of the ages, and will cast the crowns

αὐτῶν ἐνώπιον τοῦ θρόνου, λέγοντες·
of them before the throne, saying:

11 ἄξιος εἶ, ὁ κύριος καὶ ὁ θεὸς ἡμῶν,
Worthy art thou, the Lord and the God of us,

λαβεῖν τὴν δόξαν καὶ τὴν τιμὴν καὶ
to receive the glory and the honour and

τὴν δύναμιν, ὅτι σὺ ἔκτισας τὰ πάντα,
the power, because thou createdst – all things,*

καὶ διὰ τὸ θέλημά σου ἦσαν καὶ
and on account of the will of thee they were and

ἐκτίσθησαν.
they were created.

5 Καὶ εἶδον ἐπὶ τὴν δεξιὰν τοῦ
And I saw on the right [hand] of the [one]

καθημένου ἐπὶ τοῦ θρόνου βιβλίον
sitting on the throne a scroll

γεγραμμένον ἔσωθεν καὶ ὄπισθεν,
having been written within and on the reverse side,

κατεσφραγισμένον σφραγῖσιν ἑπτά. 2 καὶ
having been sealed with [2]seals [1]seven. And

εἶδον ἄγγελον ἰσχυρὸν κηρύσσοντα ἐν
I saw angel a strong proclaiming in

φωνῇ μεγάλῃ· τίς ἄξιος ἀνοῖξαι τὸ
[2]voice [1]a great(loud): Who [is] worthy to open the

βιβλίον καὶ λῦσαι τὰς σφραγῖδας αὐτοῦ;
scroll and to loosen the seals of it ?

3 καὶ οὐδεὶς ἐδύνατο ἐν τῷ οὐρανῷ
And no one was able in – heaven

οὐδὲ ἐπὶ τῆς γῆς οὐδὲ ὑποκάτω τῆς
nor on the earth nor underneath the

γῆς ἀνοῖξαι τὸ βιβλίον οὔτε βλέπειν
earth to open the scroll nor to see(look at)

αὐτό. 4 καὶ ἔκλαιον πολύ, ὅτι οὐδεὶς
it. And I wept much, because no one

ἄξιος εὑρέθη ἀνοῖξαι τὸ βιβλίον οὔτε
worthy was found to open the scroll nor

βλέπειν αὐτό. 5 καὶ εἷς ἐκ τῶν πρεσ-
to look at it. And one of the el-

βυτέρων λέγει μοι· μὴ κλαῖε· ἰδοὺ
ders says to me: Weep not; behold[,]

* τὰ πάντα = the universe.

"Holy, holy, holy
is the Lord God Almighty,
who was, and is, and is to
come."

9Whenever the living creatures
give glory, honor and
thanks to him who sits on
the throne and who lives
for ever and ever, 10the
twenty-four elders fall
down before him who sits
on the throne, and worship
him who lives for ever and
ever. They lay their crowns
before the throne and say:

11"You are worthy, our
Lord and God,
to receive glory and
honor and power,
for you created all
things,
and by your will they
were created
and have their being."

Chapter 5

The Scroll and the Lamb

THEN I saw in the right
hand of him who sat on
the throne a scroll with
writing on both sides and
sealed with seven seals.
2And I saw a mighty angel
proclaiming in a loud voice,
"Who is worthy to break
the seals and open the
scroll?" 3But no one in
heaven or on earth or under
the earth could open the
scroll or even look inside it.
4I wept and wept because
no one was found who was
worthy to open the scroll or
look inside. 5Then one of
the elders said to me, "Do
not weep! See, the Lion of

from the tribe of Judah, the
Root of David, has over-
come so as to open the
book and its seven seals."
6And I saw [g]between the
throne (with the four living
creatures) and the elders a
Lamb standing, as if slain,
having seven horns and
seven eyes, which are the
seven Spirits of God, sent
out into all the earth.
7And He came, and He
took *it* out of the right hand
of Him who sat on the
throne.
8And when He had taken
the book, the four living
creatures and the twenty-
four elders fell down before
the Lamb, having each one
a harp, and golden bowls
full of incense, which are
the prayers of the saints.
9And they *sang a new
song, saying,
"Worthy art Thou to
take the book, and to
break its seals; for
Thou wast slain, and
didst purchase for
God with Thy blood
men from every tribe
and tongue and
people and nation.
10"And Thou hast made
them *to be* a kingdom
and priests to our
God; and they will
reign upon the
earth."

Angels Exalt the Lamb

11And I looked, and I
heard the voice of many angels around the throne and
the living creatures and the
elders; and the number of
them was myriads of myr-
iads, and thousands of
thousands,
12saying with a loud
voice,
"Worthy is the Lamb
that was slain to re-
ceive power and

[g] Lit., *in the middle of the throne and of the four living creatures, and in the middle of the elders*

ἐνίκησεν ὁ λέων ὁ ἐκ τῆς φυλῆς Ἰούδα,
[10]overcame [1]the [2]Lion – [3]of [4]the [5]tribe [6]Juda,

ἡ ῥίζα Δαυίδ, ἀνοῖξαι τὸ βιβλίον καὶ
[7]the [8]root [9]of David, to open the scroll and

τὰς ἑπτὰ σφραγῖδας αὐτοῦ. **6** Καὶ εἶδον
the seven seals of it. And I saw

ἐν μέσῳ τοῦ θρόνου καὶ τῶν τεσσάρων
in [the] midst of the throne and of the four

ζῴων καὶ ἐν μέσῳ τῶν πρεσβυτέρων
living creatures and in [the] midst of the elders

ἀρνίον ἑστηκὸς ὡς ἐσφαγμένον, ἔχων
a Lamb standing as having been slain, having

κέρατα ἑπτὰ καὶ ὀφθαλμοὺς ἑπτά, οἵ
[2]horns [1]seven and [2]eyes [1]seven, which

εἰσιν τὰ ἑπτὰ πνεύματα τοῦ θεοῦ
are the seven Spirits – of God

ἀπεσταλμένοι εἰς πᾶσαν τὴν γῆν. **7** καὶ
having been sent forth into all the earth. And

ἦλθεν καὶ εἴληφεν ἐκ τῆς δεξιᾶς τοῦ
he came and has taken out of the right [hand] of the

καθημένου ἐπὶ τοῦ θρόνου. **8** Καὶ ὅτε
[one] sitting on the throne. And when

ἔλαβεν τὸ βιβλίον, τὰ τέσσερα ζῷα
he took the scroll, the four living creatures

καὶ οἱ εἴκοσι τέσσαρες πρεσβύτεροι ἔπεσαν
and the twenty-four elders fell

ἐνώπιον τοῦ ἀρνίου, ἔχοντες ἕκαστος
before the Lamb, having each one

κιθάραν καὶ φιάλας χρυσᾶς γεμούσας
a harp and [2]bowls [1]golden *being* full

θυμιαμάτων, αἵ εἰσιν αἱ προσευχαὶ τῶν
of incense*s*, which are the prayers of the

ἁγίων. **9** καὶ ᾄδουσιν ᾠδὴν καινὴν
saints. And they sing [2]song [1]a new

λέγοντες· ἄξιος εἶ λαβεῖν τὸ βιβλίον
saying: Worthy art thou to receive the scroll

καὶ ἀνοῖξαι τὰς σφραγῖδας αὐτοῦ, ὅτι
and to open the seals of it, because

ἐσφάγης καὶ ἠγόρασας τῷ θεῷ ἐν τῷ
thou wast slain and didst purchase – to God by the

αἵματί σου ἐκ πάσης φυλῆς καὶ γλώσσης
blood of thee out of every tribe and tongue

καὶ λαοῦ καὶ ἔθνους, **10** καὶ ἐποίησας
and people and nation, and didst make

αὐτοὺς τῷ θεῷ ἡμῶν βασιλείαν καὶ
them to the God of us a kingdom and

ἱερεῖς, καὶ βασιλεύσουσιν ἐπὶ τῆς γῆς.
priests, and they will reign on(? over) the earth.

11 καὶ εἶδον, καὶ ἤκουσα φωνὴν ἀγγέλων
And I saw, and I heard a sound [2]angels

πολλῶν κύκλῳ τοῦ θρόνου καὶ τῶν
[1]of many round the throne and the

ζῴων καὶ τῶν πρεσβυτέρων, καὶ ἦν
living creatures and the elders, and [4]was

ὁ ἀριθμὸς αὐτῶν μυριάδες μυριάδων καὶ
[1]the [2]number [3]of them myriads of myriads and

χιλιάδες χιλιάδων, **12** λέγοντες φωνῇ
thousands of thousands, saying [2]voice

μεγάλῃ· ἄξιός ἐστιν τὸ ἀρνίον τὸ
[1]with a great (loud): Worthy is the Lamb –

ἐσφαγμένον λαβεῖν τὴν δύναμιν καὶ πλοῦτον
having been slain to receive the power and riches

the tribe of Judah, the Root
of David, has triumphed.
He is able to open the scroll
and its seven seals."
6Then I saw a Lamb,
looking as if it had been
slain, standing in the center
of the throne, encircled by
the four living creatures
and the elders. He had sev-
en horns and seven eyes,
which are the seven spir-
its[i] of God sent out into all
the earth. 7He came and
took the scroll from the
right hand of him who sat
on the throne. 8And when
he had taken it, the four living creatures and the twenty-four elders fell down before the Lamb. Each one
had a harp and they were
holding golden bowls full of
incense, which are the
prayers of the saints. 9And
they sang a new song:

"You are worthy to take
the scroll
and to open its seals,
because you were slain,
and with your blood
you purchased men
for God
from every tribe and
language and people
and nation.
10You have made them to
be a kingdom and
priests to serve our
God,
and they will reign on
the earth."

11Then I looked and
heard the voice of many angels, numbering thousands
upon thousands, and ten
thousand times ten thou-
sand. They encircled the
throne and the living creatures and the elders. 12In a
loud voice they sang:

"Worthy is the Lamb,
who was slain,
to receive power and

6 Or *the sevenfold Spirit*

riches and wisdom
and might and honor
and glory and
blessing."
13And every created thing
which is in heaven and on
the earth and under the
earth and on the sea, and all
things in them, I heard saying,
"To Him who sits on
the throne, and to the
Lamb, *be* blessing
and honor and glory
and dominion for-
ever and ever."
14And the four living
creatures kept saying,
"Amen." And the elders
fell down and worshiped.

καὶ σοφίαν καὶ ἰσχὺν καὶ τιμὴν καὶ
and wisdom and strength and honour and
δόξαν καὶ εὐλογίαν. 13 καὶ πᾶν κτίσμα
glory and blessing. And every creature
ὃ ἐν τῷ οὐρανῷ καὶ ἐπὶ τῆς γῆς καὶ
which [2]in – [3]heaven [4]and [5]on [6]the [7]earth [8]and
ὑποκάτω τῆς γῆς καὶ ἐπὶ τῆς θαλάσσης
[9]underneath [10]the [11]earth [12]and [13]on [14]the [15]sea
[ἐστίν], καὶ τὰ ἐν αὐτοῖς πάντα, ἤκουσα
[1]is, and – [2]in [3]them [1]all things, I heard
λέγοντας· τῷ καθημένῳ ἐπὶ τῷ θρόνῳ
saying: To the [one] sitting on the throne
καὶ τῷ ἀρνίῳ ἡ εὐλογία καὶ ἡ τιμὴ
and to the Lamb the blessing and the honour
καὶ ἡ δόξα καὶ τὸ κράτος εἰς τοὺς
and the glory and the might unto the
αἰῶνας τῶν αἰώνων. 14 καὶ τὰ τέσσερα
ages of the ages. And the four
ζῷα ἔλεγον· ἀμήν, καὶ οἱ πρεσβύτεροι
living creatures said: Amen, and the elders
ἔπεσαν καὶ προσεκύνησαν.
fell and worshipped.

wealth and wisdom
and strength
and honor and glory and
praise!"
13Then I heard every
creature in heaven and on
earth and under the earth
and on the sea, and all that
is in them, singing:
"To him who sits on the
throne and to the
Lamb
be praise and honor and
glory and power,
for ever and ever!"
14The four living creatures
said, "Amen," and the el-
ders fell down and wor-
shiped.

Chapter 6

The Book Opened
The First Seal—False Christ

AND I saw when the
Lamb broke one of
the seven seals, and I heard
one of the four living creatures saying as with a voice
of thunder, "Come."
2And I looked, and be-
hold, a white horse, and he
who sat on it had a bow;
and a crown was given to
him; and he went out con-
quering, and to conquer.

The Second Seal—War

3And when He broke the
second seal, I heard the
second living creature saying, "Come."
4And another, a red
horse, went out; and to him
who sat on it, it was granted
to take peace from the
earth, and that *men* should
slay one another; and a
great sword was given to
him.

The Third Seal—Famine

5And when He broke the
third seal, I heard the third
living creature saying,
"Come." And I looked,
and behold, a black horse;
and he who sat on it had a

6 Καὶ εἶδον ὅτε ἤνοιξεν τὸ ἀρνίον
And I saw when [3]opened [1]the [2]Lamb
μίαν ἐκ τῶν ἑπτὰ σφραγίδων, καὶ ἤκουσα
one of the seven seals, and I heard
ἑνὸς ἐκ τῶν τεσσάρων ζῴων λέγοντος
one of the four living creatures saying
ὡς φωνῇ βροντῆς· ἔρχου. 2 καὶ εἶδον,
as with a sound of thunder: Come. And I saw,
καὶ ἰδοὺ ἵππος λευκός, καὶ ὁ καθήμενος
and behold[,] [2]horse [1]a white, and the [one] sitting
ἐπ᾽ αὐτὸν ἔχων τόξον, καὶ ἐδόθη αὐτῷ
on it having a bow, and [2]was given [3]to him
στέφανος, καὶ ἐξῆλθεν νικῶν καὶ ἵνα
[1]a crown, and he went forth overcoming and in order that
νικήσῃ. 3 Καὶ ὅτε ἤνοιξεν τὴν σφραγῖδα
he might overcome. And when he opened the [2]seal
τὴν δευτέραν, ἤκουσα τοῦ δευτέρου ζῴου
– [1]second, I heard the second living creature
λέγοντος· ἔρχου. 4 καὶ ἐξῆλθεν ἄλλος
saying: Come. And [4]went forth [1]another
ἵππος πυρρός, καὶ τῷ καθημένῳ ἐπ᾽
[3]horse[,] [2]red, and to the [one] sitting on
αὐτὸν ἐδόθη αὐτῷ λαβεῖν τὴν εἰρήνην
it was given *to him* to take – peace
ἐκ τῆς γῆς καὶ ἵνα ἀλλήλους σφάξουσιν,
out of the earth and *in order* that [2]one another [1]they shall slay,
καὶ ἐδόθη αὐτῷ μάχαιρα μεγάλη. 5 Καὶ
and [3]was given [4]to him [2]sword [1]a great. And
ὅτε ἤνοιξεν τὴν σφραγῖδα τὴν τρίτην,
when he opened the [2]seal – [1]third,
ἤκουσα τοῦ τρίτου ζῴου λέγοντος· ἔρχου.
I heard the third living creature saying: Come.
καὶ εἶδον, καὶ ἰδοὺ ἵππος μέλας, καὶ
And I saw, and behold[,] [2]horse [1]a black, and
ὁ καθήμενος ἐπ᾽ αὐτὸν ἔχων ζυγὸν
the [one] sitting on it having a balance

Chapter 6

The Seals

I WATCHED as the
Lamb opened the first of
the seven seals. Then I
heard one of the four living
creatures say in a voice like
thunder, "Come!" 2I
looked, and there before
me was a white horse! Its
rider held a bow, and he
was given a crown, and he
rode out as a conqueror
bent on conquest.
3When the Lamb opened
the second seal, I heard the
second living creature say,
"Come!" 4Then another
horse came out, a fiery red
one. Its rider was given
power to take peace from
the earth and to make men
slay each other. To him
was given a large sword.
5When the Lamb opened
the third seal, I heard the
third living creature say,
"Come!" I looked, and
there before me was a black
horse! Its rider was holding

pair of scales in his hand.
6And I heard as it were a
voice in the center of the
four living creatures saying, "A [h]quart of wheat for
a [i]denarius, and three
quarts of barley for a
denarius; and do not harm
the oil and the wine."

The Fourth Seal—Death

7And when He broke the
fourth seal, I heard the
voice of the fourth living
creature saying, "Come."
8And I looked, and be-
hold, an ashen horse; and
he who sat on it had the
name Death; and Hades
was following with him.
And authority was given to
them over a fourth of the
earth, to kill with sword
and with famine and with
pestilence and by the wild
beasts of the earth.

The Fifth Seal—Martyrs

9And when He broke the
fifth seal, I saw underneath
the altar the souls of those
who had been slain because
of the word of God, and because of the testimony
which they had maintained;
10and they cried out with
a loud voice, saying, "How
long, O Lord, holy and
true, wilt Thou refrain from
judging and avenging our
blood on those who dwell
on the earth?"
11And there was given to
each of them a white robe;
and they were told that
they should rest for a little
while longer, until *the number of* their fellow servants
and their brethren who
were to be killed even as
they had been, should be
completed also.

The Sixth Seal—Terror

12And I looked when He
broke the sixth seal, and
there was a great earth-

[h]Gr., *choenix;* i.e., a dry measure almost equal to a quart
[i]The denarius was equivalent to one day's wage

ἐν τῇ χειρὶ αὐτοῦ. **6** καὶ ἤκουσα ὡς
in the hand of him. And I heard as
φωνὴν ἐν μέσῳ τῶν τεσσάρων ζῴων
a voice in [the] midst of the four living creatures
λέγουσαν· χοῖνιξ σίτου δηναρίου, καὶ τρεῖς
saying: A chœnix of wheat of(for) a denarius, and three
χοίνικες κριθῶν δηναρίου· καὶ τὸ ἔλαιον
chœnixes of barley of(for) a denarius; and [3]the [3]oil
καὶ τὸν οἶνον μὴ ἀδικήσῃς. **7** Καὶ
[4]and [5]the [6]wine [1]do not harm. And
ὅτε ἤνοιξεν τὴν σφραγῖδα τὴν τετάρτην,
when he opened the [2]seal – [1]fourth,
ἤκουσα φωνὴν τοῦ τετάρτου ζῴου λέγοντος·
I heard [the] voice of the fourth living creature saying:
ἔρχου. **8** καὶ εἶδον, καὶ ἰδοὺ ἵππος
Come. And I saw, and behold[,] [2]horse
χλωρός, καὶ ὁ καθήμενος ἐπάνω αὐτοῦ,
[1]a pale green, and the [one] sitting upon it,
ὄνομα αὐτῷ [ὁ] θάνατος, καὶ ὁ ᾅδης
name to him[c] – death, and – hades
ἠκολούθει μετ' αὐτοῦ, καὶ ἐδόθη αὐτοῖς
followed with him, and [2]was given [3]to them
ἐξουσία ἐπὶ τὸ τέταρτον τῆς γῆς,
[1]authority over the fourth [part] of the earth,
ἀποκτεῖναι ἐν ῥομφαίᾳ καὶ ἐν λιμῷ
to kill with sword and with famine
καὶ ἐν θανάτῳ καὶ ὑπὸ τῶν θηρίων
and with death and by the wild beasts
τῆς γῆς. **9** Καὶ ὅτε ἤνοιξεν τὴν πέμπτην
of the earth. And when he opened the fifth
σφραγῖδα, εἶδον ὑποκάτω τοῦ θυσιαστηρίου
seal, I saw underneath the altar
τὰς ψυχὰς τῶν ἐσφαγμένων διὰ τὸν
the souls of the [ones] having been slain on account of the
λόγον τοῦ θεοῦ καὶ διὰ τὴν μαρτυρίαν
word – of God and on account of the witness
ἣν εἶχον. **10** καὶ ἔκραξαν φωνῇ μεγάλῃ
which they had. And they cried [2]voice [1]with a great(loud)
λέγοντες· ἕως πότε, ὁ δεσπότης ὁ ἅγιος
saying: Until when, *the* Master – holy
καὶ ἀληθινός, οὐ κρίνεις καὶ ἐκδικεῖς
and true, judgest thou not and avengest
τὸ αἷμα ἡμῶν ἐκ τῶν κατοικούντων
the blood of us of the [ones] dwelling
ἐπὶ τῆς γῆς; **11** καὶ ἐδόθη αὐτοῖς ἑκάστῳ
on the earth? And [3]was given [4]to them [5]each one
στολὴ λευκή, καὶ ἐρρέθη αὐτοῖς ἵνα
[2]robe [1]a white, and it was said to them *in order* that
ἀναπαύσωνται ἔτι χρόνον μικρόν, ἕως
they should rest yet [2]time [1]a little, until
πληρωθῶσιν καὶ οἱ σύνδουλοι αὐτῶν καὶ
should be fulfilled also the fellow-slaves of them and
οἱ ἀδελφοὶ αὐτῶν οἱ μέλλοντες ἀποκτέν-
the brothers of them the [ones] *being* about to be
νεσθαι ὡς καὶ αὐτοί. **12** Καὶ εἶδον
killed as also they. And I saw
ὅτε ἤνοιξεν τὴν σφραγῖδα τὴν ἕκτην,
when he opened the [2]seal – [1]sixth,
καὶ σεισμὸς μέγας ἐγένετο, καὶ ὁ ἥλιος
and [2]earthquake [1]a great occurred, and the sun

a pair of scales in his hand.
6Then I heard what sound-
ed like a voice among the
four living creatures, saying, "A quart[j] of wheat for
a day's wages,[k] and three
quarts of barley for a day's
wages,[l] and do not damage
the oil and the wine!"
7When the Lamb opened
the fourth seal, I heard the
voice of the fourth living
creature say, "Come!" 8I
looked, and there before
me was a pale horse! Its rider was named Death, and
Hades was following close
behind him. They were giv-
en power over a fourth of
the earth to kill by sword,
famine and plague, and by
the wild beasts of the earth.
9When he opened the fifth
seal, I saw under the altar
the souls of those who had
been slain because of the
word of God and the testimony they had maintained.
10They called out in a loud
voice, "How long, Sover-
eign Lord, holy and true,
until you judge the inhabitants of the earth and
avenge our blood?" 11Then
each of them was given a
white robe, and they were
told to wait a little longer,
until the number of their
fellow servants and brothers who were to be killed as
they had been was com-
pleted.
12I watched as he opened
the sixth seal. There was a
great earthquake. The sun

[j]6 Greek *a choinix* (probably about a liter)
[k]6 Greek *a denarius*
[l]6 Greek *a denarius*

quake; and the sun became
black as sackcloth *made* of
hair, and the whole moon
became like blood;
13and the stars of the sky
fell to the earth, as a fig tree
casts its unripe figs when
shaken by a great wind.
14And the sky was split
apart like a scroll when it is
rolled up; and every mountain and island were moved
out of their places.
15And the kings of the
earth and the great men and
the [j]commanders and the
rich and the strong and
every slave and free man,
hid themselves in the caves
and among the rocks of the
mountains;
16and they *said to the
mountains and to the
rocks, "Fall on us and hide
us from the presence of
Him who sits on the throne,
and from the wrath of the
Lamb;
17for the great day of their
wrath has come; and who is
able to stand?"

Chapter 7

An Interlude

AFTER this I saw four
angels standing at the
four corners of the earth,
holding back the four winds
of the earth, so that no wind
should blow on the earth or
on the sea or on any tree.
2And I saw another angel
ascending from the rising of
the sun, having the seal of
the living God; and he cried
out with a loud voice to the
four angels to whom it was
granted to harm the earth
and the sea,
3saying, "Do not harm
the earth or the sea or the

[j]I.e., chiliarchs, in command of one thousand troops

ἐγένετο μέλας ὡς σάκκος τρίχινος, καὶ
became black as sackcloth made of hair, and

ἡ σελήνη ὅλη ἐγένετο ὡς αἷμα, 13 καὶ
the 2moon 1whole became as blood, and

οἱ ἀστέρες τοῦ οὐρανοῦ ἔπεσαν εἰς τὴν
the stars – of heaven fell to the

γῆν, ὡς συκῆ βάλλει τοὺς ὀλύνθους
earth, as a fig-tree casts the unripe figs

αὐτῆς ὑπὸ ἀνέμου μεγάλου σειομένη,
of it 2by 4wind 3a great(strong) 1being shaken,

14 καὶ ὁ οὐρανὸς ἀπεχωρίσθη ὡς βιβλίον
and the heaven departed as a scroll

ἑλισσόμενον, καὶ πᾶν ὄρος καὶ νῆσος
being rolled up, and every mountain and island

ἐκ τῶν τόπων αὐτῶν ἐκινήθησαν. 15 καὶ
out of the places of them were moved. And

οἱ βασιλεῖς τῆς γῆς καὶ οἱ μεγιστᾶνες
the kings of the earth and the great men

καὶ οἱ χιλίαρχοι καὶ οἱ πλούσιοι καὶ
and the chiliarchs and the rich men and

οἱ ἰσχυροὶ καὶ πᾶς δοῦλος καὶ ἐλεύθερος
the strong men and every slave and free man

ἔκρυψαν ἑαυτοὺς εἰς τὰ σπήλαια καὶ
hid themselves in the caves and

εἰς τὰς πέτρας τῶν ὀρέων, 16 καὶ
in the rocks of the mountains, and

λέγουσιν τοῖς ὄρεσιν καὶ ταῖς πέτραις·
they say to the mountains and to the rocks:

πέσετε ἐφ' ἡμᾶς καὶ κρύψατε ἡμᾶς
Fall ye on us and hide us

ἀπὸ προσώπου τοῦ καθημένου ἐπὶ τοῦ
from [the] face of the [one] sitting on the

θρόνου καὶ ἀπὸ τῆς ὀργῆς τοῦ ἀρνίου,
throne and from the wrath of the Lamb,

17 ὅτι ἦλθεν ἡ ἡμέρα ἡ μεγάλη τῆς
because 7came 1the 3day – 2great 4of the

ὀργῆς αὐτῶν, καὶ τίς δύναται σταθῆναι;
5wrath 6of them, and who can *to* stand?

7 Μετὰ τοῦτο εἶδον τέσσαρας ἀγγέλους
After this I saw four angels

ἑστῶτας ἐπὶ τὰς τέσσαρας γωνίας τῆς
standing on the four corners of the

γῆς, κρατοῦντας τοὺς τέσσαρας ἀνέμους
earth, holding the four winds

τῆς γῆς, ἵνα μὴ πνέῃ ἄνεμος ἐπὶ τῆς
of the earth, in order that 3not 2should 4blow 1wind on the

γῆς μήτε ἐπὶ τῆς θαλάσσης μήτε ἐπὶ
earth nor on the sea nor on

πᾶν δένδρον. 2 καὶ εἶδον ἄλλον ἄγγελον
every(any) tree. And I saw another angel

ἀναβαίνοντα ἀπὸ ἀνατολῆς ἡλίου, ἔχοντα
coming up from [the] rising of [the] sun, having

σφραγῖδα θεοῦ ζῶντος, καὶ ἔκραξεν φωνῇ
a seal God of [the] living, and he cried 2voice

μεγάλῃ τοῖς τέσσαρσιν ἀγγέλοις οἷς
1with a great(loud) to the four angels to whom

ἐδόθη αὐτοῖς ἀδικῆσαι τὴν γῆν καὶ
it was given *to them* to harm the earth and

τὴν θάλασσαν, 3 λέγων· μὴ ἀδικήσητε
the sea, saying: Do not harm

τὴν γῆν μήτε τὴν θάλασσαν μήτε τὰ
the earth nor the sea nor the

turned black like sackcloth
made of goat hair, the
whole moon turned blood
red, 13and the stars in the
sky fell to earth, as late figs
drop from a fig tree when
shaken by a strong wind.
14The sky receded like a
scroll, rolling up, and every
mountain and island was
removed from its place.
15Then the kings of the
earth, the princes, the generals, the rich, the mighty,
and every slave and every
free man hid in caves and
among the rocks of the
mountains. 16They called
to the mountains and the
rocks, "Fall on us and hide
us from the face of him who
sits on the throne and from
the wrath of the Lamb!
17For the great day of their
wrath has come, and who
can stand?"

Chapter 7

144,000 Sealed

AFTER this I saw four
angels standing at the
four corners of the earth,
holding back the four winds
of the earth to prevent any
wind from blowing on the
land or on the sea or on any
tree. 2Then I saw another
angel coming up from the
east, having the seal of the
living God. He called out in
a loud voice to the four angels who had been given
power to harm the land and
the sea: 3"Do not harm the
land or the sea or the trees

trees, until we have sealed the bond-servants of our God on their foreheads."

A Remnant of Israel—144,000

4 And I heard the number of those who were sealed, one hundred and forty-four thousand sealed from every tribe of the sons of Israel:

5 from the tribe of Judah, twelve thousand *were* sealed, from the tribe of Reuben twelve thousand, from the tribe of Gad twelve thousand,

6 from the tribe of Asher twelve thousand, from the tribe of Naphtali twelve thousand, from the tribe of Manasseh twelve thousand,

7 from the tribe of Simeon twelve thousand, from the tribe of Levi twelve thousand, from the tribe of Issachar twelve thousand,

8 from the tribe of Zebulun twelve thousand, from the tribe of Joseph twelve thousand, from the tribe of Benjamin, twelve thousand *were* sealed.

A Multitude from the Tribulation

9 After these things I looked, and behold, a great multitude, which no one could count, from every nation and *all* tribes and peoples and tongues, standing before the throne and before the Lamb, clothed in white robes, and palm branches *were* in their hands;

10 and they cry out with a loud voice, saying,

"Salvation to our God who sits on the throne, and to the Lamb."

11 And all the angels were standing around the throne and *around* the elders and the four living creatures; and they fell on their faces before the throne and worshiped God,

12 saying,

"Amen, blessing and glo-

δένδρα, ἄχρι σφραγίσωμεν τοὺς δούλους
trees, until we *may* seal the slaves

τοῦ θεοῦ ἡμῶν ἐπὶ τῶν μετώπων αὐτῶν.
of the God of us on the foreheads of them.

4 Καὶ ἤκουσα τὸν ἀριθμὸν τῶν ἐσφραγισ-
And I heard the number of the [ones] *having been*

μένων, ἑκατὸν τεσσεράκοντα τέσσαρες
sealed, a hundred [and] forty-four

χιλιάδες ἐσφραγισμένοι ἐκ πάσης φυλῆς
thousand*s* *having been* sealed out of every tribe

υἱῶν Ἰσραήλ· 5 ἐκ φυλῆς Ἰούδα δώδεκα
of sons of Israel: of [the] tribe Juda twelve

χιλιάδες ἐσφραγισμένοι, ἐκ φυλῆς Ῥουβὴν
thousand*s* *having been* sealed, of [the] tribe Reuben

δώδεκα χιλιάδες, ἐκ φυλῆς Γὰδ δώδεκα
twelve thousand*s*, of [the] tribe Gad twelve

χιλιάδες, 6 ἐκ φυλῆς Ἀσὴρ δώδεκα
thousand*s*, of [the] tribe Aser twelve

χιλιάδες, ἐκ φυλῆς Νεφθαλὶμ δώδεκα
thousand*s*, of [the] tribe Nephthalim twelve

χιλιάδες, ἐκ φυλῆς Μανασσῆ δώδεκα
thousand*s*, of [the] tribe Manasse twelve

χιλιάδες, 7 ἐκ φυλῆς Συμεὼν δώδεκα
thousand*s*, of [the] tribe Symeon twelve

χιλιάδες, ἐκ φυλῆς Λευὶ δώδεκα χιλιάδες,
thousand*s*, of [the] tribe Levi twelve thousand*s*,

ἐκ φυλῆς Ἰσσαχὰρ δώδεκα χιλιάδες,
of [the] tribe Issachar twelve thousand*s*,

8 ἐκ φυλῆς Ζαβουλὼν δώδεκα χιλιάδες,
of [the] tribe Zabulon twelve thousand*s*,

ἐκ φυλῆς Ἰωσὴφ δώδεκα χιλιάδες, ἐκ
of [the] tribe Joseph twelve thousand*s*, of

φυλῆς Βενιαμὶν δώδεκα χιλιάδες ἐσφραγισ-
[the] tribe Benjamin twelve thousand*s* *having been*

μένοι. 9 Μετὰ ταῦτα εἶδον, καὶ ἰδοὺ ὄχλος
sealed. After these things I saw, and behold[,] [2]crowd

πολύς, ὃν ἀριθμῆσαι αὐτὸν οὐδεὶς ἐδύνατο,
[1]a much (great), which [3]to number *it* [1]no one [2]was able,

ἐκ παντὸς ἔθνους καὶ φυλῶν καὶ λαῶν
out of every nation and tribe*s* and people*s*

καὶ γλωσσῶν, ἑστῶτες ἐνώπιον τοῦ θρόνου
and tongue*s*, standing before the throne

καὶ ἐνώπιον τοῦ ἀρνίου, περιβεβλημένους
and before the Lamb, *having been* clothed [with]

στολὰς λευκάς, καὶ φοίνικες ἐν ταῖς
[2]robes [1]white, and palms in the

χερσὶν αὐτῶν· 10 καὶ κράζουσιν φωνῇ
hands of them; and they cry [2]voice

μεγάλῃ λέγοντες· ἡ σωτηρία τῷ θεῷ
[1]with a great(loud) saying: – Salvation to the God[c]

ἡμῶν τῷ καθημένῳ ἐπὶ τῷ θρόνῳ καὶ
of us – sitting on the throne and

τῷ ἀρνίῳ. 11 καὶ πάντες οἱ ἄγγελοι
to the Lamb.[c] And all the angels

εἱστήκεισαν κύκλῳ τοῦ θρόνου καὶ τῶν
stood round the throne and the

πρεσβυτέρων καὶ τῶν τεσσάρων ζῴων,
elders and the four living creatures,

καὶ ἔπεσαν ἐνώπιον τοῦ θρόνου ἐπὶ
and fell before the throne on

τὰ πρόσωπα αὐτῶν καὶ προσεκύνησαν
the faces of them and worshipped

τῷ θεῷ, 12 λέγοντες· ἀμήν, ἡ εὐλογία
– God, saying: Amen, – blessing

until we put a seal on the foreheads of the servants of our God." 4 Then I heard the number of those who were sealed: 144,000 from all the tribes of Israel.

5 From the tribe of Judah 12,000 were sealed,
from the tribe of Reuben 12,000,
from the tribe of Gad 12,000,
6 from the tribe of Asher 12,000,
from the tribe of Naphtali 12,000,
from the tribe of Manasseh 12,000,
7 from the tribe of Simeon 12,000,
from the tribe of Levi 12,000,
from the tribe of Issachar 12,000,
8 from the tribe of Zebulun 12,000,
from the tribe of Joseph 12,000,
from the tribe of Benjamin 12,000.

The Great Multitude in White Robes

9 After this I looked and there before me was a great multitude that no one could count, from every nation, tribe, people and language, standing before the throne and in front of the Lamb. They were wearing white robes and were holding palm branches in their hands. 10 And they cried out in a loud voice:

"Salvation belongs to our God,
who sits on the throne,
and to the Lamb."

11 All the angels were standing around the throne and around the elders and the four living creatures. They fell down on their faces before the throne and worshiped God, 12 saying:

"Amen!
Praise and glory

ry and wisdom and thanksgiving and honor and power and might, *be* to our God forever and ever. Amen."

13And one of the elders answered, saying to me, "These who are clothed in the white robes, who are they, and from where have they come?"

14And I said to him, "My lord, you know." And he said to me, "These are the ones who come out of the great tribulation, and they have washed their robes and made them white in the blood of the Lamb.

15"For this reason, they are before the throne of God; and they serve Him day and night in His temple; and He who sits on the throne shall spread His tabernacle over them.

16"They shall hunger no more, neither thirst anymore; neither shall the sun beat down on them, nor any heat;

17for the Lamb in the center of the throne shall be their shepherd, and shall guide them to springs of the water of life; and God shall wipe every tear from their eyes."

καὶ ἡ δόξα καὶ ἡ σοφία καὶ ἡ εὐχαριστία
and – glory and – wisdom and – thanks
καὶ ἡ τιμὴ καὶ ἡ δύναμις καὶ ἡ ἰσχὺς
and – honour and – power and – strength
τῷ θεῷ ἡμῶν εἰς τοὺς αἰῶνας τῶν
to the God[c] of us unto the ages of the
αἰώνων· ἀμήν. 13 Καὶ ἀπεκρίθη εἷς
ages: Amen. And [5]answered [1]one
ἐκ τῶν πρεσβυτέρων λέγων μοι· οὗτοι
[2]of [3]the [4]elders saying to me: These
οἱ περιβεβλημένοι τὰς στολὰς τὰς
the [ones] *having been* clothed [with] the [2]robes –
λευκὰς τίνες εἰσὶν καὶ πόθεν ἦλθον;
[1]white who are they and whence came they?
14 καὶ εἴρηκα αὐτῷ· κύριέ μου, σὺ
And I *have* said to him: Lord of me, thou
οἶδας. καὶ εἶπέν μοι· οὗτοί εἰσιν οἱ
knowest. And he told me: These are the
ἐρχόμενοι ἐκ τῆς θλίψεως τῆς μεγάλης
[ones] coming out of the [2]affliction – [1]great
καὶ ἔπλυναν τὰς στολὰς αὐτῶν καὶ
and washed the robes of them and
ἐλεύκαναν αὐτὰς ἐν τῷ αἵματι τοῦ
whitened them in the blood of the
ἀρνίου. 15 διὰ τοῦτό εἰσιν ἐνώπιον τοῦ
Lamb. Therefore are they before the
θρόνου τοῦ θεοῦ, καὶ λατρεύουσιν αὐτῷ
throne – of God, and serve him
ἡμέρας καὶ νυκτὸς ἐν τῷ ναῷ αὐτοῦ,
day and night in the shrine of him,
καὶ ὁ καθήμενος ἐπὶ τοῦ θρόνου σκηνώσει
and the [one] sitting on the throne will spread [his] tent
ἐπ' αὐτούς. 16 οὐ πεινάσουσιν ἔτι οὐδὲ
over them. They will not hunger longer nor
διψήσουσιν ἔτι, οὐδὲ μὴ πέσῃ ἐπ' αὐτοὺς
will they thirst longer, neither *not* fall on them
ὁ ἥλιος οὐδὲ πᾶν καῦμα, 17 ὅτι τὸ
the sun nor every(any) heat, because the
ἀρνίον τὸ ἀνὰ μέσον τοῦ θρόνου ποιμανεῖ
Lamb – in the midst of the throne will shepherd
αὐτοὺς καὶ ὁδηγήσει αὐτοὺς ἐπὶ ζωῆς
them and will lead them upon [3]of life
πηγὰς ὑδάτων· καὶ ἐξαλείψει ὁ θεὸς
[1]fountains [2]of waters; and [2]will wipe off – [1]God
πᾶν δάκρυον ἐκ τῶν ὀφθαλμῶν αὐτῶν.
every tear out of the eyes of them.

and wisdom and thanks
and honor
and power and strength
be to our God for ever
and ever.
Amen!"

13Then one of the elders asked me, "These in white robes—who are they, and where did they come from?"

14I answered, "Sir, you know."

And he said, "These are they who have come out of the great tribulation; they have washed their robes and made them white in the blood of the Lamb.

15Therefore,

"they are before the
throne of God
and serve him day and
night in his temple;
and he who sits on the
throne will spread
his tent over them.

16Never again will they
hunger;
never again will they
thirst.
The sun will not beat
upon them,
nor any scorching heat.

17For the Lamb at the
center of the throne
will be their
shepherd;
he will lead them to
springs of living
water.
And God will wipe away
every tear from their
eyes."

Chapter 8

The Seventh Seal—the Trumpets

AND when He broke the seventh seal, there was silence in heaven for about half an hour.

2And I saw the seven angels who stand before God; and seven trumpets were given to them.

3And another angel came and stood at the altar, holding a golden censer; and much incense was given to

8 Καὶ ὅταν ἤνοιξεν τὴν σφραγῖδα τὴν
And when*ever* he opened the [2]seal –
ἑβδόμην, ἐγένετο σιγὴ ἐν τῷ οὐρανῷ
[1]seventh, occurred a silence in – heaven
ὡς ἡμιώρον. 2 Καὶ εἶδον τοὺς ἑπτὰ
about a half-hour. And I saw the seven
ἀγγέλους οἳ ἐνώπιον τοῦ θεοῦ ἑστήκασιν,
angels who before – God stood,
καὶ ἐδόθησαν αὐτοῖς ἑπτὰ σάλπιγγες.
and there were given to them seven trumpets.
3 Καὶ ἄλλος ἄγγελος ἦλθεν καὶ ἐστάθη
And another angel came and stood
ἐπὶ τοῦ θυσιαστηρίου ἔχων λιβανωτὸν
on the altar having [2]censer
χρυσοῦν, καὶ ἐδόθη αὐτῷ θυμιάματα πολλά,
[1]a golden, and there was given to him incense*s* many (much),

Chapter 8

The Seventh Seal and the Golden Censer

WHEN he opened the seventh seal, there was silence in heaven for about half an hour.

2And I saw the seven angels who stand before God, and to them were given seven trumpets.

3Another angel, who had a golden censer, came and stood at the altar. He was given much incense to of-him, that he might add it to the prayers of all the saints upon the golden altar which was before the throne.

4And the smoke of the incense, with the prayers of the saints, went up before God out of the angel's hand.

5And the angel took the censer; and he filled it with the fire of the altar and threw it to the earth; and there followed peals of thunder and sounds and flashes of lightning and an earthquake.

6And the seven angels who had the seven trumpets prepared themselves to sound them.

7And the first sounded, and there came hail and fire, mixed with blood, and they were thrown to the earth; and a third of the earth was burned up, and a third of the trees were burned up, and all the green grass was burned up.

8And the second angel sounded, and *something* like a great mountain burning with fire was thrown into the sea; and a third of the sea became blood;

9and a third of the creatures, which were in the sea and had life, died; and a third of the ships were destroyed.

10And the third angel sounded, and a great star fell from heaven, burning like a torch, and it fell on a third of the rivers and on the springs of waters;

11and the name of the star

ἵνα δώσει ταῖς προσευχαῖς τῶν ἁγίων
in order that he will give [it] with the prayers of [3]the [4]saints

πάντων ἐπὶ τὸ θυσιαστήριον τὸ χρυσοῦν
[1]all on the [2]altar – [1]golden

τὸ ἐνώπιον τοῦ θρόνου. **4** καὶ ἀνέβη
– before the throne. And went up

ὁ καπνὸς τῶν θυμιαμάτων ταῖς προσευχαῖς
the smoke of the incenses with the prayers

τῶν ἁγίων ἐκ χειρὸς τοῦ ἀγγέλου ἐνώπιον
of the saints out of [the] hand of the angel before

τοῦ θεοῦ. **5** καὶ εἴληφεν ὁ ἄγγελος
– God. And [3]has taken [1]the [2]angel

τὸν λιβανωτόν, καὶ ἐγέμισεν αὐτὸν ἐκ
the censer, and filled it from

τοῦ πυρὸς τοῦ θυσιαστηρίου καὶ ἔβαλεν
the fire of the altar and cast

εἰς τὴν γῆν· καὶ ἐγένοντο βρονταὶ καὶ
into the earth; and there occurred thunders and

φωναὶ καὶ ἀστραπαὶ καὶ σεισμός.
sounds and lightnings and an earthquake.

6 Καὶ οἱ ἑπτὰ ἄγγελοι οἱ ἔχοντες
And the seven angels – having

τὰς ἑπτὰ σάλπιγγας ἡτοίμασαν αὑτοὺς
the seven trumpets prepared themselves

ἵνα σαλπίσωσιν. **7** Καὶ ὁ πρῶτος
in order that they might trumpet. And the first

ἐσάλπισεν· καὶ ἐγένετο χάλαζα καὶ πῦρ
trumpeted; and there occurred hail and fire

μεμιγμένα ἐν αἵματι καὶ ἐβλήθη εἰς
having been mixed in (with) blood and it was cast to

τὴν γῆν· καὶ τὸ τρίτον τῆς γῆς
the earth; and the third [part] of the earth

κατεκάη, καὶ τὸ τρίτον τῶν δένδρων
was burnt down(up), and the third [part] of the trees

κατεκάη, καὶ πᾶς χόρτος χλωρὸς κατεκάη.
was burnt down(up), and all [2]grass [1]green was burnt down(up).

8 Καὶ ὁ δεύτερος ἄγγελος ἐσάλπισεν·
And the second angel trumpeted;

καὶ ὡς ὄρος μέγα πυρὶ καιόμενον ἐβλήθη
and as [2]mountain [1]a great [4]with fire [3]burning was cast

εἰς τὴν θάλασσαν· καὶ ἐγένετο τὸ τρίτον
into the sea; and [5]became [1]the [2]third [part]

τῆς θαλάσσης αἷμα, **9** καὶ ἀπέθανεν τὸ
[3]of the [4]sea [6]blood, and [10]died [1]the

τρίτον τῶν κτισμάτων τῶν ἐν τῇ θαλάσσῃ,
[2]third [part] [3]of the [4]creatures – [5]in [6]the [7]sea,

τὰ ἔχοντα ψυχάς, καὶ τὸ τρίτον τῶν
– [8]having [9]souls, and the third [part] of the

πλοίων διεφθάρησαν. **10** Καὶ ὁ τρίτος
ships were destroyed. And the third

ἄγγελος ἐσάλπισεν· καὶ ἔπεσεν ἐκ τοῦ
angel trumpeted; and fell out of –

οὐρανοῦ ἀστὴρ μέγας καιόμενος ὡς
heaven star a great burning as

λαμπάς, καὶ ἔπεσεν ἐπὶ τὸ τρίτον τῶν
a lamp, and it fell onto the third [part] of the

ποταμῶν καὶ ἐπὶ τὰς πηγὰς τῶν ὑδάτων.
rivers and onto the fountains of the waters.

11 καὶ τὸ ὄνομα τοῦ ἀστέρος λέγεται
And the name of the star is said(called)

fer, with the prayers of all
the saints, on the golden altar before the throne. 4The
smoke of the incense, to-
gether with the prayers of
the saints, went up before
God from the angel's hand.
5Then the angel took the
censer, filled it with fire
from the altar, and hurled it
on the earth; and there
came peals of thunder,
rumblings, flashes of lightning and an earthquake.

The Trumpets

6Then the seven angels
who had the seven trum-
pets prepared to sound
them.
7The first angel sounded
his trumpet, and there
came hail and fire mixed
with blood, and it was
hurled down upon the
earth. A third of the earth
was burned up, a third of
the trees were burned up,
and all the green grass was
burned up.
8The second angel sound-
ed his trumpet, and some-
thing like a huge mountain,
all ablaze, was thrown into
the sea. A third of the sea
turned into blood, 9a third
of the living creatures in the
sea died, and a third of the
ships were destroyed.
10The third angel sounded
his trumpet, and a great
star, blazing like a torch,
fell from the sky on a third
of the rivers and on the
springs of water— 11the
name of the star is Worm-

is called Wormwood; and a
third of the waters became
wormwood; and many men
died from the waters, be-
cause they were made bit-
ter.
12 And the fourth angel
sounded, and a third of the
sun and a third of the moon
and a third of the stars were
smitten, so that a third of
them might be darkened
and the day might not shine
for a third of it, and the
night in the same way.
13 And I looked, and I
heard an eagle flying in
midheaven, saying with a
loud voice, "Woe, woe,
woe, to those who dwell on
the earth, because of the remaining blasts of the trumpet of the three angels who
are about to sound!"

ὁ Ἄψινθος. καὶ ἐγένετο τὸ τρίτον τῶν
– Wormwood. And [5]became [1]the [2]third [part] [3]of the
ὑδάτων εἰς ἄψινθον, καὶ πολλοὶ τῶν
[4]waters *into* wormwood, and many of the
ἀνθρώπων ἀπέθανον ἐκ τῶν ὑδάτων ὅτι
men died from the waters because
ἐπικράνθησαν. 12 Καὶ ὁ τέταρτος ἄγγελος
they were made bitter. And the fourth angel
ἐσάλπισεν· καὶ ἐπλήγη τὸ τρίτον τοῦ
trumpeted; and [5]was struck [1]the [2]third [part] [3]of the
ἡλίου καὶ τὸ τρίτον τῆς σελήνης καὶ
[4]sun and the third [part] of the moon and
τὸ τρίτον τῶν ἀστέρων, ἵνα σκοτισθῇ
the third [part] of the stars, in order that [4]might be darkened
τὸ τρίτον αὐτῶν καὶ ἡ ἡμέρα μὴ φάνῃ
[1]the [2]third [part] [3]of them and the day might not appear
τὸ τρίτον αὐτῆς, καὶ ἡ νὺξ ὁμοίως.
the third [part] of it, and the night likewise.

13 Καὶ εἶδον, καὶ ἤκουσα ἑνὸς ἀετοῦ
And I saw, and I heard one eagle
πετομένου ἐν μεσουρανήματι λέγοντος φωνῇ
flying in mid-heaven saying [2]voice
μεγάλῃ· οὐαὶ οὐαὶ οὐαὶ τοὺς κατοικοῦν-
[1]with a great(loud): Woe[,] woe[,] woe to the [ones] dwell-
τας ἐπὶ τῆς γῆς ἐκ τῶν λοιπῶν φωνῶν
ing on the earth from the remaining voices
τῆς σάλπιγγος τῶν τριῶν ἀγγέλων τῶν
of the trumpet of the three angels –
μελλόντων σαλπίζειν.
being about to trumpet.

wood.[m] A third of the waters turned bitter, and
many people died from the
waters that had become bitter.
12 The fourth angel sounded his trumpet, and a third
of the sun was struck, a
third of the moon, and a
third of the stars, so that a
third of them turned dark.
A third of the day was without light, and also a third of
the night.
13 As I watched, I heard
an eagle that was flying in
midair call out in a loud
voice: "Woe! Woe! Woe to
the inhabitants of the earth,
because of the trumpet
blasts about to be sounded
by the other three angels!"

Chapter 9

The Fifth Trumpet—the Bottomless Pit

AND the fifth angel
sounded, and I saw a
star from heaven which had
fallen to the earth; and the
key of the bottomless pit
was given to him.
2 And he opened the bot-
tomless pit; and smoke
went up out of the pit, like
the smoke of a great fur-
nace; and the sun and the
air were darkened by the
smoke of the pit.
3 And out of the smoke
came forth locusts upon the
earth; and power was given
them, as the scorpions of
the earth have power.
4 And they were told that
they should not hurt the
grass of the earth, nor any
green thing, nor any tree,
but only the men who do

9 Καὶ ὁ πέμπτος ἄγγελος ἐσάλπισεν·
And the fifth angel trumpeted;
καὶ εἶδον ἀστέρα ἐκ τοῦ οὐρανοῦ πεπτω-
and I saw a star out of – heaven having
κότα εἰς τὴν γῆν, καὶ ἐδόθη αὐτῷ
fallen onto the earth, and was given to it
ἡ κλεὶς τοῦ φρέατος τῆς ἀβύσσου. 2 καὶ
the key of the shaft of the abyss. And
ἤνοιξεν τὸ φρέαρ τῆς ἀβύσσου· καὶ
he opened the shaft of the abyss; and
ἀνέβη καπνὸς ἐκ τοῦ φρέατος ὡς
went up a smoke out of the shaft as
καπνὸς καμίνου μεγάλης, καὶ ἐσκοτώθη
smoke [2]furnace [1]of a great, and [6]was darkened
ὁ ἥλιος καὶ ὁ ἀὴρ ἐκ τοῦ καπνοῦ
[1]the [2]sun [3]and [4]the [5]air by the smoke
τοῦ φρέατος. 3 καὶ ἐκ τοῦ καπνοῦ
of the shaft. And out of the smoke
ἐξῆλθον ἀκρίδες εἰς τὴν γῆν, καὶ ἐδόθη
came forth locusts to the earth, and [2]was given
αὐτοῖς ἐξουσία ὡς ἔχουσιν ἐξουσίαν οἱ
[3]to them [1]authority as [5]have [6]authority [1]the
σκορπίοι τῆς γῆς. 4 καὶ ἐρρέθη αὐτοῖς
[2]scorpions [3]of the [4]earth. And it was said to them
ἵνα μὴ ἀδικήσουσιν τὸν χόρτον τῆς
in order that they shall not harm the grass of the
γῆς οὐδὲ πᾶν χλωρὸν οὐδὲ πᾶν δένδρον,
earth nor every (any) greenstuff nor every (any) tree,
εἰ μὴ τοὺς ἀνθρώπους οἵτινες οὐκ ἔχουσιν
except the men who have not

Chapter 9

THE fifth angel sounded
his trumpet, and I saw
a star that had fallen from
the sky to the earth. The
star was given the key to
the shaft of the Abyss.
2 When he opened the
Abyss, smoke rose from it
like the smoke from a gi-
gantic furnace. The sun and
sky were darkened by the
smoke from the Abyss.
3 And out of the smoke locusts came down upon the
earth and were given power
like that of scorpions of the
earth. 4 They were told not
to harm the grass of the
earth or any plant or tree,
but only those people who

[m] 11 That is, Bitterness

not have the seal of God on
their foreheads.
5And they were not per-
mitted to kill anyone, but to
torment for five months;
and their torment was like
the torment of a scorpion
when it stings a man.
6And in those days men
will seek death and will not
find it; and they will long to
die and death flees from
them.
7And the appearance of
the locusts was like horses
prepared for battle; and on
their heads, as it were,
crowns like gold, and their
faces were like the faces of
men.
8And they had hair like
the hair of women, and
their teeth were like *the
teeth* of lions.
9And they had breast-
plates like breastplates of
iron; and the sound of their
wings was like the sound of
chariots, of many horses
rushing to battle.
10And they have tails like
scorpions, and stings; and
in their tails is their power
to hurt men for five
months.
11They have as king over
them, the angel of the
abyss; his name in Hebrew
is [k]Abaddon, and in the
Greek he has the name
Apollyon.
12The first woe is past; behold, two woes are still
coming after these things.

The Sixth Trumpet—Army from the East

13And the sixth angel
sounded, and I heard a
voice from the [l]four horns
of the golden altar which is
before God,
14one saying to the sixth

[k] I.e., destruction
[l] Some ancient mss. do not contain *four*

τὴν σφραγῖδα τοῦ θεοῦ ἐπὶ τῶν μετώπων.
the seal – of God on the(ir) foreheads.

5 καὶ ἐδόθη αὐτοῖς ἵνα μὴ ἀποκτείνωσιν
And it was given to them *in order that* they should not kill

αὐτούς, ἀλλ' ἵνα βασανισθήσονται μῆνας
them, but *in order that* they shall be tormented [2]months

πέντε· καὶ ὁ βασανισμὸς αὐτῶν ὡς
[1]five; and the torment of them [is] as

βασανισμὸς σκορπίου, ὅταν παίσῃ ἄνθρωπον.
[the] torment of a scorpion, whenever it stings a man.

6 καὶ ἐν ταῖς ἡμέραις ἐκείναις ζητήσουσιν
And in those days [2]will seek

οἱ ἄνθρωποι τὸν θάνατον καὶ οὐ μὴ
– [1]men – death and by no means

εὑρήσουσιν αὐτόν, καὶ ἐπιθυμήσουσιν
will they find it, and they will long

ἀποθανεῖν καὶ φεύγει ὁ θάνατος ἀπ'
to die and [2]flees – [1]death from

αὐτῶν. **7** καὶ τὰ ὁμοιώματα τῶν ἀκρίδων
them. And the likeness*es* of the locusts

ὅμοιοι ἵπποις ἡτοιμασμένοις εἰς πόλεμον,
like *to* horses *having been* prepared for war,

καὶ ἐπὶ τὰς κεφαλὰς αὐτῶν ὡς στέφανοι
and on the heads of them as crowns

ὅμοιοι χρυσῷ, καὶ τὰ πρόσωπα αὐτῶν
like *to* gold, and the faces of them

ὡς πρόσωπα ἀνθρώπων, **8** καὶ εἶχον
as faces of men, and they had

τρίχας ὡς τρίχας γυναικῶν, καὶ οἱ
hair*s* as hair*s* of women, and the

ὀδόντες αὐτῶν ὡς λεόντων ἦσαν, **9** καὶ
teeth of them [2]as [3]of lions [1]were, and

εἶχον θώρακας ὡς θώρακας σιδηροῦς,
they had breastplates as [2]breastplates [1]iron,

καὶ ἡ φωνὴ τῶν πτερύγων αὐτῶν ὡς
and the sound of the wings of them as

φωνὴ ἁρμάτων ἵππων πολλῶν τρεχόντων
sound [4]chariots [3]of horses [1]of many running

εἰς πόλεμον. **10** καὶ ἔχουσιν οὐρὰς ὁμοίας
to war. And they have tails like

σκορπίοις καὶ κέντρα, καὶ ἐν ταῖς οὐραῖς
to scorpions and stings, and [6]with [7]the [8]tails

αὐτῶν ἡ ἐξουσία αὐτῶν ἀδικῆσαι τοὺς
[9]of them [1]the [2]authority [3]of them [4][is] to harm –

ἀνθρώπους μῆνας πέντε. **11** ἔχουσιν ἐπ'
[5]men [11]months [10]five. They have over

αὐτῶν βασιλέα τὸν ἄγγελον τῆς ἀβύσσου,
them a king the angel of the abyss,

ὄνομα αὐτῷ Ἑβραϊστὶ Ἀβαδδών, καὶ
name to him[c] in Hebrew Abaddon, and

ἐν τῇ Ἑλληνικῇ ὄνομα ἔχει Ἀπολλύων.
in the Greek [2][the] name [1]he has Apollyon.

12 Ἡ οὐαὶ ἡ μία ἀπῆλθεν· ἰδοὺ ἔρχεται
The [2]woe – [1]one(first) passed away; behold [4]come*s*

ἔτι δύο οὐαὶ μετὰ ταῦτα.
[1]yet [2]two [3]woes after these things.

13 Καὶ ὁ ἕκτος ἄγγελος ἐσάλπισεν·
And the sixth angel trumpeted;

καὶ ἤκουσα φωνὴν μίαν ἐκ τῶν τεσσάρων
and I heard [2]voice [1]one out of the four

κεράτων τοῦ θυσιαστηρίου τοῦ χρυσοῦ
horns of the [2]altar – [1]golden

τοῦ ἐνώπιον τοῦ θεοῦ, **14** λέγοντα τῷ
– before – God, saying to the

did not have the seal of God
on their foreheads. 5They
were not given power to kill
them, but only to torture
them for five months. And
the agony they suffered
was like that of the sting of
a scorpion when it strikes a
man. 6During those days
men will seek death, but
will not find it; they will
long to die, but death will
elude them.
7The locusts looked like
horses prepared for battle.
On their heads they wore
something like crowns of
gold, and their faces resembled human faces. 8Their
hair was like women's hair,
and their teeth were like lions' teeth. 9They had
breastplates like breast-
plates of iron, and the
sound of their wings was
like the thundering of many
horses and chariots rushing
into battle. 10They had tails
and stings like scorpions,
and in their tails they had
power to torment people
for five months. 11They had
as king over them the angel
of the Abyss, whose name
in Hebrew is Abaddon, and
in Greek, Apollyon.[n]
12The first woe is past;
two other woes are yet to
come.
13The sixth angel sounded
his trumpet, and I heard a
voice coming from the
horns[o] of the golden altar
that is before God. 14It said
to the sixth angel who had

[n] *11 Abaddon* and *Apollyon* mean *Destroyer.*
[o] *13* That is, projections

angel who had the trumpet,
"Release the four angels
who are bound at the great
river Euphrates."
15 And the four angels,
who had been prepared for
the hour and day and
month and year, were
released, so that they might
kill a third of mankind.
16 And the number of the
armies of the horsemen
was two hundred million; I
heard the number of them.
17 And this is how I saw in
the vision the horses and
those who sat on them: *the
riders* had breastplates *the
color* of fire and of hyacinth
and of brimstone; and the
heads of the horses are like
the heads of lions; and out
of their mouths proceed
fire and smoke and brim-
stone.
18 A third of mankind was
killed by these three
plagues, by the fire and the
smoke and the brimstone,
which proceeded out of
their mouths.
19 For the power of the
horses is in their mouths
and in their tails; for their
tails are like serpents and
have heads; and with them
they do harm.
20 And the rest of man-
kind, who were not killed
by these plagues, did not
repent of the works of their
hands, so as not to worship
demons, and the idols of
gold and of silver and
of brass and of stone and of
wood, which can neither
see nor hear nor walk;

ἕκτῳ ἀγγέλῳ, ὁ ἔχων τὴν σάλπιγγα·
sixth angel, – having the trumpet:
λῦσον τοὺς τέσσαρας ἀγγέλους τοὺς
Loose the four angels –
δεδεμένους ἐπὶ τῷ ποταμῷ τῷ μεγάλῳ
having been bound at the [2]river – [1]great
Εὐφράτῃ. **15** καὶ ἐλύθησαν οἱ τέσσαρες
Euphrates. And were loosed the four
ἄγγελοι οἱ ἡτοιμασμένοι εἰς τὴν ὥραν
angels – *having been* prepared for the hour
καὶ ἡμέραν καὶ μῆνα καὶ ἐνιαυτόν,
and day and month and year,
ἵνα ἀποκτείνωσιν τὸ τρίτον τῶν ἀνθρώπων.
in order that they should kill the third [part] – of men.
16 καὶ ὁ ἀριθμὸς τῶν στρατευμάτων τοῦ
And the number of the bodies of soldiers of the
ἱππικοῦ δισμυριάδες μυριάδων· ἤκουσα τὸν
cavalry [was] two myriads of myriads; I heard the
ἀριθμὸν αὐτῶν. **17** καὶ οὕτως εἶδον
number of them. And thus I saw
τοὺς ἵππους ἐν τῇ ὁράσει καὶ τοὺς
the horses in the vision and the
καθημένους ἐπ' αὐτῶν, ἔχοντας θώρακας
[ones] sitting on them, having breastplates
πυρίνους καὶ ὑακινθίνους καὶ θειώδεις·
fire-coloured and dusky red and sulphurous;
καὶ αἱ κεφαλαὶ τῶν ἵππων ὡς κεφαλαὶ
and the heads of the horses as heads
λεόντων, καὶ ἐκ τῶν στομάτων αὐτῶν
of lions, and out of the mouths of them
ἐκπορεύεται πῦρ καὶ καπνὸς καὶ θεῖον.
proceed*s* fire and smoke and sulphur.
18 ἀπὸ τῶν τριῶν πληγῶν τούτων ἀπεκτάν-
From *the* [2]three [3]plagues [1]these were
θησαν τὸ τρίτον τῶν ἀνθρώπων, ἐκ
killed the third [part] – of men, by
τοῦ πυρὸς καὶ τοῦ καπνοῦ καὶ τοῦ
the fire and the smoke and the
θείου τοῦ ἐκπορευομένου ἐκ τῶν στομάτων
sulphur – proceeding out of the mouths
αὐτῶν. **19** ἡ γὰρ ἐξουσία τῶν ἵππων
of them. For the authority of the horses
ἐν τῷ στόματι αὐτῶν ἐστιν καὶ ἐν
[2]in [3]the [4]mouth [5]of them [1]is and in
ταῖς οὐραῖς αὐτῶν· αἱ γὰρ οὐραὶ αὐτῶν
the tails of them; for the tails of them
ὅμοιαι ὄφεσιν, ἔχουσαι κεφαλάς, καὶ ἐν
[are] like *to* serpents, having heads, and with
αὐταῖς ἀδικοῦσιν. **20** καὶ οἱ λοιποὶ τῶν
them they do harm. And the rest –
ἀνθρώπων, οἳ οὐκ ἀπεκτάνθησαν ἐν ταῖς
of men, who were not killed by –
πληγαῖς ταύταις, οὐδὲ μετενόησαν ἐκ
plagues these, not even repented of
τῶν ἔργων τῶν χειρῶν αὐτῶν, ἵνα μὴ
the works of the hands of them, in order not that
προσκυνήσουσιν τὰ δαιμόνια καὶ τὰ εἴδωλα
they will worship – demons and – idols
τὰ χρυσᾶ καὶ τὰ ἀργυρᾶ καὶ τὰ χαλκᾶ
– golden and – silver and – bronze
καὶ τὰ λίθινα καὶ τὰ ξύλινα, ἃ οὔτε
and – stone and – wooden, which [2]neither
βλέπειν δύνανται οὔτε ἀκούειν οὔτε
[3]*to* see [1]can nor *to* hear nor

the trumpet, "Release the
four angels who are bound
at the great river Euphrates." 15 And the four angels
who had been kept ready
for this very hour and day
and month and year were
released to kill a third of
mankind. 16 The number of
the mounted troops was
two hundred million. I
heard their number.
17 The horses and riders I
saw in my vision looked
like this: Their breastplates
were fiery red, dark blue,
and yellow as sulfur. The
heads of the horses resembled the heads of lions, and
out of their mouths came
fire, smoke and sulfur. 18 A
third of mankind was killed
by the three plagues of fire,
smoke and sulfur that came
out of their mouths. 19 The
power of the horses was in
their mouths and in their
tails; for their tails were like
snakes, having heads with
which they inflict injury.
20 The rest of mankind
that were not killed by
these plagues still did not
repent of the work of their
hands; they did not stop
worshiping demons, and
idols of gold, silver,
bronze, stone and wood—
idols that cannot see or

21 and they did not repent of their murders nor of their sorceries nor of their immorality nor of their thefts.

Chapter 10

The Angel and the Little Book

AND I saw another strong angel coming down out of heaven, clothed with a cloud; and the rainbow was upon his head, and his face was like the sun, and his feet like pillars of fire;

2 and he had in his hand a little book which was open. And he placed his right foot on the sea and his left on the land;

3 and he cried out with a loud voice, as when a lion roars; and when he had cried out, the seven peals of thunder uttered their voices.

4 And when the seven peals of thunder had spoken, I was about to write; and I heard a voice from heaven saying, "Seal up the things which the seven peals of thunder have spoken, and do not write them."

5 And the angel whom I saw standing on the sea and on the land lifted up his right hand to heaven,

6 and swore by Him who lives forever and ever, WHO CREATED HEAVEN AND THE THINGS IN IT, AND THE EARTH AND THE THINGS IN IT, AND THE SEA AND THE THINGS IN IT, that there shall be delay no longer,

7 but in the days of the voice of the seventh angel, when he is about to sound, then the mystery of God is

περιπατεῖν, 21 καὶ οὐ μετενόησαν ἐκ τῶν
to walk, and they repented not of the
φόνων αὐτῶν οὔτε ἐκ τῶν φαρμακειῶν
murders of them nor of the sorceries
αὐτῶν οὔτε ἐκ τῆς πορνείας αὐτῶν
of them nor of the fornication of them
οὔτε ἐκ τῶν κλεμμάτων αὐτῶν.
nor of the thefts of them.

Chapter 10

10 Καὶ εἶδον ἄλλον ἄγγελον ἰσχυρὸν
And I saw another [2]angel [1]strong
καταβαίνοντα ἐκ τοῦ οὐρανοῦ, περιβεβλημέ-
coming down out of – heaven, *having been* clothed
νον νεφέλην, καὶ ἡ ἶρις ἐπὶ τὴν κεφαλὴν
[with] a cloud, and the rainbow on the head
αὐτοῦ, καὶ τὸ πρόσωπον αὐτοῦ ὡς ὁ
of him, and the face of him as the
ἥλιος, καὶ οἱ πόδες αὐτοῦ ὡς στῦλοι
sun, and the feet of him as pillars
πυρός, 2 καὶ ἔχων ἐν τῇ χειρὶ αὐτοῦ
of fire, and having in the hand of him
βιβλαρίδιον ἠνεῳγμένον. καὶ ἔθηκεν τὸν
a little scroll *having been* opened. And he placed [1]the
πόδα αὐτοῦ τὸν δεξιὸν ἐπὶ τῆς θαλάσσης,
[3]foot [4]of him – [2]right on the sea,
τὸν δὲ εὐώνυμον ἐπὶ τῆς γῆς, 3 καὶ
and the left on the land, and
ἔκραξεν φωνῇ μεγάλῃ ὥσπερ λέων μυκᾶται.
cried [2]voice [1]with a great(loud) as a lion roars.
καὶ ὅτε ἔκραξεν, ἐλάλησαν αἱ ἑπτὰ
And when he cried, [4]spoke(uttered) [1]the [2]seven
βρονταὶ τὰς ἑαυτῶν φωνάς. 4 Καὶ ὅτε
[3]thunders [5]the [7]of them*selves* [6]voices. And when
ἐλάλησαν αἱ ἑπτὰ βρονταί, ἤμελλον
spoke the seven thunders, I was about
γράφειν· καὶ ἤκουσα φωνὴν ἐκ τοῦ
to write; and I heard a voice out of –
οὐρανοῦ λέγουσαν· σφράγισον ἃ ἐλάλησαν
heaven saying: Seal thou [the] things which [4]spoke
αἱ ἑπτὰ βρονταί, καὶ μὴ αὐτὰ γράψῃς.
[1]the [2]seven [3]thunders, and [2]not [3]them *thou mayest* [1]write.
5 Καὶ ὁ ἄγγελος, ὃν εἶδον ἑστῶτα
And the angel, whom I saw standing
ἐπὶ τῆς θαλάσσης καὶ ἐπὶ τῆς γῆς,
on the sea and on the land,
ἦρεν τὴν χεῖρα αὐτοῦ τὴν δεξιὰν εἰς
lifted [1]the [3]hand [4]of him – [2]right to
τὸν οὐρανόν, 6 καὶ ὤμοσεν ἐν τῷ ζῶντι
– heaven, and swore by the [one] living
εἰς τοὺς αἰῶνας τῶν αἰώνων, ὃς ἔκτισεν
unto the ages of the ages, who created
τὸν οὐρανὸν καὶ τὰ ἐν αὐτῷ καὶ τὴν
the heaven and the things in it and the
γῆν καὶ τὰ ἐν αὐτῇ καὶ τὴν θάλασσαν
earth and the things in it and the sea
καὶ τὰ ἐν αὐτῇ, ὅτι χρόνος οὐκέτι
and the things in it, that time [2]no longer
ἔσται, 7 ἀλλ' ἐν ταῖς ἡμέραις τῆς
[1]shall be, but in the days of the
φωνῆς τοῦ ἑβδόμου ἀγγέλου, ὅταν μέλλῃ
voice of the seventh angel, whenever he is about
σαλπίζειν, καὶ ἐτελέσθη τὸ μυστήριον
to trumpet, even was finished the mystery

hear or walk. 21 Nor did
they repent of their mur-
ders, their magic arts, their
sexual immorality or their
thefts.

Chapter 10

The Angel and the Little Scroll

THEN I saw another
mighty angel coming
down from heaven. He was
robed in a cloud, with a
rainbow above his head; his
face was like the sun, and
his legs were like fiery pillars. 2 He was holding a little scroll, which lay open in
his hand. He planted his
right foot on the sea and his
left foot on the land, 3 and
he gave a loud shout like
the roar of a lion. When he
shouted, the voices of the
seven thunders spoke.
4 And when the seven thunders spoke, I was about to
write; but I heard a voice
from heaven say, "Seal up
what the seven thunders
have said and do not write
it down."
5 Then the angel I had
seen standing on the sea
and on the land raised his
right hand to heaven. 6 And
he swore by him who lives
for ever and ever, who created the heavens and all
that is in them, the earth
and all that is in it, and the
sea and all that is in it, and
said, "There will be no
more delay! 7 But in the
days when the seventh an-
gel is about to sound his
trumpet, the mystery of

finished, as He preached to
His servants the prophets.
8And the voice which I
heard from heaven, *I heard*
again speaking with me,
and saying, "Go, take the
book which is open in the
hand of the angel who
stands on the sea and on the
land."
9And I went to the angel,
telling him to give me the
little book. And he *said to
me, "Take it, and eat it;
and it will make your stomach bitter, but in your
mouth it will be sweet as
honey."
10And I took the little
book out of the angel's
hand and ate it, and it was
in my mouth sweet as
honey; and when I had eat-
en it, my stomach was
made bitter.
11And they *said to me,
"You must prophesy again
concerning many peoples
and nations and tongues
and kings."

Chapter 11

The Two Witnesses

AND there was given me
a measuring rod like a
staff; and someone said,
"Rise and measure the
temple of God, and the altar, and those who worship
in it.
2"And leave out the
court which is outside the
temple, and do not measure
it, for it has been given to
the nations; and they will
tread under foot the holy
city for forty-two months.
3"And I will grant *au-
thority* to my two wit-
nesses, and they will
prophesy for twelve hun-
dred and sixty days,
clothed in sackcloth."
4These are the two olive
trees and the two lamp-
stands that stand before the

τοῦ θεοῦ, ὡς εὐηγγέλισεν τοὺς ἑαυτοῦ
– of God, as he preached [to] the [2]of him*self*

δούλους τοὺς προφήτας. **8** Καὶ ἡ φωνὴ
[1]slaves the prophets. And the voice

ἣν ἤκουσα ἐκ τοῦ οὐρανοῦ, πάλιν
which I heard out of – heaven, again

λαλοῦσαν μετ' ἐμοῦ καὶ λέγουσαν· ὕπαγε
speaking with me and saying: Go thou

λάβε τὸ βιβλίον τὸ ἠνεῳγμένον ἐν τῇ
take the scroll – *having been* opened in the

χειρὶ τοῦ ἀγγέλου τοῦ ἑστῶτος ἐπὶ
hand of the angel – standing on

τῆς θαλάσσης καὶ ἐπὶ τῆς γῆς. **9** καὶ
the sea and on the land. And

ἀπῆλθα πρὸς τὸν ἄγγελον, λέγων αὐτῷ
I went away toward the angel, telling him

δοῦναί μοι τὸ βιβλαρίδιον. καὶ λέγει
to give me the little scroll. And he says

μοι· λάβε καὶ κατάφαγε αὐτό, καὶ
to me: Take and devour it, and

πικρανεῖ σου τὴν κοιλίαν, ἀλλ' ἐν τῷ
it will embitter [3]of thee [1]the [2]stomach, but in the

στόματί σου ἔσται γλυκὺ ὡς μέλι.
mouth of thee it will be sweet as honey.

10 καὶ ἔλαβον τὸ βιβλαρίδιον ἐκ τῆς
And I took the little scroll out of the

χειρὸς τοῦ ἀγγέλου καὶ κατέφαγον αὐτό,
hand of the angel and devoured it,

καὶ ἦν ἐν τῷ στόματί μου ὡς μέλι
and it was in the mouth of me as [2]honey

γλυκύ· καὶ ὅτε ἔφαγον αὐτό, ἐπικράνθη
[1]sweet; and when I ate it, [4]was made bitter

ἡ κοιλία μου. **11** καὶ λέγουσίν μοι·
[1]the [2]stomach [3]of me. And they say to me:

δεῖ σε πάλιν προφητεῦσαι ἐπὶ λαοῖς
It behoves thee again to prophesy before peoples

καὶ ἔθνεσιν καὶ γλώσσαις καὶ βασιλεῦσιν
and nations and tongues and [2]kings

πολλοῖς. **11** Καὶ ἐδόθη μοι κάλαμος ὅμοιος
[1]many. And was given to me a reed like

ῥάβδῳ, λέγων· ἔγειρε καὶ μέτρησον τὸν ναὸν
to a staff, saying: Rise and measure the shrine

τοῦ θεοῦ καὶ τὸ θυσιαστήριον καὶ τοὺς
of God and the altar and the

προσκυνοῦντας ἐν αὐτῷ. **2** καὶ τὴν
[ones] worshipping in it. And the

αὐλὴν τὴν ἔξωθεν τοῦ ναοῦ ἔκβαλε
[2]court – [1]outside of the shrine cast *out*

ἔξωθεν καὶ μὴ αὐτὴν μετρήσῃς, ὅτι
outside and [3]not [2]it *thou mayest* [1]measure, because

ἐδόθη τοῖς ἔθνεσιν, καὶ τὴν πόλιν τὴν
it was given to the nations, and the [2]city –

ἁγίαν πατήσουσιν μῆνας τεσσεράκοντα
[1]holy they will trample [3]months [1]forty-

[καὶ] δύο. **3** καὶ δώσω τοῖς δυσὶν
and [2]two. And I will give to the two

μάρτυσίν μου, καὶ προφητεύσουσιν ἡμέρας
witnesses of me, and they will prophesy [5]days

χιλίας διακοσίας ἑξήκοντα περιβεβλημένοι
[1]a thousand [2]two hundred [3][and] [4]sixty *having been* clothed

σάκκους. **4** οὗτοί εἰσιν αἱ δύο ἐλαῖαι
[in] sackclothes. These are the two olive-trees

καὶ αἱ δύο λυχνίαι αἱ ἐνώπιον τοῦ
and the two lampstands – [3]before [4]the

God will be accomplished,
just as he announced to his
servants the prophets."
8Then the voice that I had
heard from heaven spoke
to me once more: "Go,
take the scroll that lies
open in the hand of the angel who is standing on the
sea and on the land."
9So I went to the angel
and asked him to give me
the little scroll. He said to
me, "Take it and eat it. It
will turn your stomach
sour, but in your mouth it
will be as sweet as honey."
10I took the little scroll
from the angel's hand and
ate it. It tasted as sweet as
honey in my mouth, but
when I had eaten it, my
stomach turned sour.
11Then I was told, "You
must prophesy again about
many peoples, nations, languages and kings."

Chapter 11

The Two Witnesses

I WAS given a reed like a
measuring rod and was
told, "Go and measure the
temple of God and the al-
tar, and count the worshipers there. 2But exclude the
outer court; do not measure
it, because it has been giv-
en to the Gentiles. They
will trample on the holy
city for 42 months. 3And I
will give power to my two
witnesses, and they will
prophesy for 1,260 days,
clothed in sackcloth."
4These are the two olive
trees and the two lamp-
stands that stand before the

Lord of the earth.
5And if anyone desires to
harm them, fire proceeds
out of their mouth and devours their enemies; and if
anyone would desire to
harm them, in this manner
he must be killed.
6These have the power
to shut up the sky, in order
that rain may not fall during
the days of their prophesying; and they have power
over the waters to turn
them into blood, and to
smite the earth with every
plague, as often as they desire.
7And when they have
finished their testimony,
the beast that comes up out
of the abyss will make war
with them, and overcome
them and kill them.
8And their dead [m]bodies
will lie in the street of the
great city which [n]mystical-
ly is called Sodom and
Egypt, where also their
Lord was crucified.
9And those from the peo-
ples and tribes and tongues
and nations *will* look at
their dead [m]bodies for three
and a half days, and will not
permit their dead bodies to
be laid in a tomb.
10And those who dwell on
the earth *will* rejoice over
them and make merry; and
they will send gifts to one
another, because these two
prophets tormented those
who dwell on the earth.
11And after the three and
a half days the breath of life
from God came into them,
and they stood on their
feet; and great fear fell

[m] Some ancient mss. read *body*
[n] Lit., *spiritually*

κυρίου τῆς γῆς ἑστῶτες. 5 καὶ εἴ τις
[4]Lord [5]of the [6]earth [1]standing. And if anyone
αὐτοὺς θέλει ἀδικῆσαι, πῦρ ἐκπορεύεται
[2]them [1]wishes [3]to harm, fire proceeds
ἐκ τοῦ στόματος αὐτῶν καὶ κατεσθίει
out of the mouth of them and devours
τοὺς ἐχθροὺς αὐτῶν· καὶ εἴ τις θελήσῃ
the enemies of them; and if anyone should wish
αὐτοὺς ἀδικῆσαι, οὕτως δεῖ αὐτὸν
[2]them [1]to harm, thus it behoves him
ἀποκτανθῆναι. 6 οὗτοι ἔχουσιν τὴν ἐξουσίαν
to be killed. These have the authority
κλεῖσαι τὸν οὐρανόν, ἵνα μὴ ὑετὸς
to shut – heaven, in order that [3]not [1]rain
βρέχῃ τὰς ἡμέρας τῆς προφητείας αὐτῶν,
[2]may [4]rain(fall) the days of the prophecy of them,
καὶ ἐξουσίαν ἔχουσιν ἐπὶ τῶν ὑδάτων
and authority they have over the waters
στρέφειν αὐτὰ εἰς αἷμα καὶ πατάξαι
to turn them into blood and to strike
τὴν γῆν ἐν πάσῃ πληγῇ ὁσάκις ἐὰν
the earth with every [kind of] plague as often as
θελήσωσιν. 7 Καὶ ὅταν τελέσωσιν τὴν
they may wish. And whenever they finish the
μαρτυρίαν αὐτῶν, τὸ θηρίον τὸ ἀναβαῖνον
witness of them, the beast – coming up
ἐκ τῆς ἀβύσσου ποιήσει μετ' αὐτῶν
out of the abyss [1]will make [3]with [4]them
πόλεμον καὶ νικήσει αὐτοὺς καὶ ἀποκτενεῖ
[2]war and will overcome them and will kill
αὐτούς. 8 καὶ τὸ πτῶμα αὐτῶν ἐπὶ
them. And the corpse of them on
τῆς πλατείας τῆς πόλεως τῆς μεγάλης,
the open street of the [2]city – [1]great,
ἥτις καλεῖται πνευματικῶς Σόδομα καὶ
which is called spiritually Sodom and
Αἴγυπτος, ὅπου καὶ ὁ κύριος αὐτῶν
Egypt, where indeed the Lord of them
ἐσταυρώθη. 9 καὶ βλέπουσιν ἐκ τῶν
was crucified. And [10]see [1][some] of [2]the
λαῶν καὶ φυλῶν καὶ γλωσσῶν καὶ
[3]peoples [4]and [5]tribes [6]and [7]tongues [8]and
ἐθνῶν τὸ πτῶμα αὐτῶν ἡμέρας τρεῖς
[9]nations the corpse of them [4]days [1]three
καὶ ἥμισυ, καὶ τὰ πτώματα αὐτῶν
[2]and [3]a half, and [2]the [3]corpses [4]of them
οὐκ ἀφίουσιν τεθῆναι εἰς μνῆμα. 10 καὶ
[1]they do not allow to be placed in a tomb. And
οἱ κατοικοῦντες ἐπὶ τῆς γῆς χαίρουσιν
the [ones] dwelling on the earth rejoice
ἐπ' αὐτοῖς καὶ εὐφραίνονται, καὶ δῶρα
over them and are glad, and [2]gifts
πέμψουσιν ἀλλήλοις, ὅτι οὗτοι οἱ δύο
[1]they will send to one another, because these – two
προφῆται ἐβασάνισαν τοὺς κατοικοῦντας
prophets tormented the [ones] dwelling
ἐπὶ τῆς γῆς. 11 Καὶ μετὰ [τὰς] τρεῖς
on the earth. And after the [1]three
ἡμέρας καὶ ἥμισυ πνεῦμα ζωῆς ἐκ τοῦ
[4]days [2]and [3]a half a spirit of life out of –
θεοῦ εἰσῆλθεν ἐν αὐτοῖς, καὶ ἔστησαν
God entered in[to] them, and they stood
ἐπὶ τοὺς πόδας αὐτῶν, καὶ φόβος μέγας
on the feet of them, and [2]fear [1]great

Lord of the earth. 5If anyone tries to harm them, fire
comes from their mouths
and devours their enemies.
This is how anyone who
wants to harm them must
die. 6These men have pow-
er to shut up the sky so that
it will not rain during the
time they are prophesying;
and they have power to
turn the waters into blood
and to strike the earth with
every kind of plague as often as they want.
7Now when they have fin-
ished their testimony, the
beast that comes up from
the Abyss will attack them,
and overpower and kill
them. 8Their bodies will lie
in the street of the great
city, which is figuratively
called Sodom and Egypt,
where also their Lord was
crucified. 9For three and a
half days men from every
people, tribe, language and
nation will gaze on their
bodies and refuse them
burial. 10The inhabitants of
the earth will gloat over
them and will celebrate by
sending each other gifts,
because these two prophets
had tormented those who
live on the earth.
11But after the three and a
half days a breath of life
from God entered them,
and they stood on their
feet, and terror struck

upon those who were be-
holding them.
12And they heard a loud
voice from heaven saying
to them, "Come up here."
And they went up into
heaven in the cloud, and
their enemies beheld them.
13And in that hour there
was a great earthquake,
and a tenth of the city fell;
and seven thousand people
were killed in the earth-
quake, and the rest were
terrified and gave glory to
the God of heaven.
14The second woe is past;
behold, the third woe is
coming quickly.

The Seventh Trumpet—Christ's Reign Foreseen

15And the seventh angel
sounded; and there arose
loud voices in heaven, saying,
"The kingdom of the
world has become *the kingdom* of our Lord, and of
His [o]Christ; and He will
reign forever and ever."
16And the twenty-four el-
ders, who sit on their
thrones before God, fell on
their faces and worshiped
God,
17saying,
"We give Thee thanks, O
Lord God, the Almighty,
who art and who wast, be-
cause Thou hast taken Thy
great power and hast begun
to reign.
18"And the nations were
enraged, and Thy wrath
came, and the time *came*
for the dead to be judged,
and *the time* to give their
reward to Thy bond-serv-
ants the prophets and to the
saints and to those who fear
Thy name, the small and

[o]I.e., Messiah

ἐπέπεσεν ἐπὶ τοὺς θεωροῦντας αὐτούς.
fell *on* on the [ones] beholding them.
12 καὶ ἤκουσαν φωνῆς μεγάλης ἐκ τοῦ
And they heard 2voice 1a great(loud) out of –
οὐρανοῦ λεγούσης αὐτοῖς· ἀνάβατε ὧδε·
heaven saying to them: Come ye up here;
καὶ ἀνέβησαν εἰς τὸν οὐρανὸν ἐν τῇ
and they went up to – heaven in the
νεφέλῃ, καὶ ἐθεώρησαν αὐτοὺς οἱ ἐχθροὶ
cloud, and 4beheld 5them 1the 2enemies
αὐτῶν. **13** Καὶ ἐν ἐκείνῃ τῇ ὥρᾳ ἐγένετο
3of them. And in that – hour 3occurred
σεισμὸς μέγας, καὶ τὸ δέκατον τῆς
2earthquake 1a great, and the tenth [part] of the
πόλεως ἔπεσεν, καὶ ἀπεκτάνθησαν ἐν τῷ
city fell, and 5were killed 6in 7the
σεισμῷ ὀνόματα ἀνθρώπων χιλιάδες ἑπτά,
8earthquake 3names 4of men 2thousands 1seven,
καὶ οἱ λοιποὶ ἔμφοβοι ἐγένοντο καὶ
and the rest 2terrified 1became and
ἔδωκαν δόξαν τῷ θεῷ τοῦ οὐρανοῦ.
gave glory to the God – of heaven.
14 Ἡ οὐαὶ ἡ δευτέρα ἀπῆλθεν· ἰδοὺ
The 2woe – 1second passed away; behold[,]
ἡ οὐαὶ ἡ τρίτη ἔρχεται ταχύ.
the 2woe – 1third is coming quickly.
15 Καὶ ὁ ἕβδομος ἄγγελος ἐσάλπισεν·
And the seventh angel trumpeted;
καὶ ἐγένοντο φωναὶ μεγάλαι ἐν τῷ
and there were voices great(loud) in –
οὐρανῷ, λέγοντες· ἐγένετο ἡ βασιλεία
heaven, saying: 3became 1The 2kingdom
τοῦ κόσμου τοῦ κυρίου ἡμῶν καὶ τοῦ
3of the 4world of the Lord of us and of the
6[the kingdom]
χριστοῦ αὐτοῦ, καὶ βασιλεύσει εἰς τοὺς
Christ of him, and he shall reign unto the
αἰῶνας τῶν αἰώνων. **16** καὶ οἱ εἴκοσι
ages of the ages. And the twenty-
τέσσαρες πρεσβύτεροι, οἱ ἐνώπιον τοῦ
four elders, – 2before –
θεοῦ καθήμενοι ἐπὶ τοὺς θρόνους αὐτῶν,
3God 1sitting on the thrones of them,
ἔπεσαν ἐπὶ τὰ πρόσωπα αὐτῶν καὶ
fell on the faces of them and
προσεκύνησαν τῷ θεῷ, **17** λέγοντες·
worshipped – God, saying:
εὐχαριστοῦμέν σοι, κύριε ὁ θεὸς ὁ
We thank thee, [O] Lord – God the
παντοκράτωρ, ὁ ὢν καὶ ὁ ἦν, ὅτι
Almighty, the [one] being and the was, beca
=the one who is [one who]
εἴληφας τὴν δύναμίν σου τὴν μεγάλη
thou hast taken 1the 3power 4of thee – 2great
καὶ ἐβασίλευσας· **18** καὶ τὰ ἔθνη ὠργίσ-
and didst reign; and the nations were
θησαν, καὶ ἦλθεν ἡ ὀργή σου καὶ ὁ
wrathful, and 4came 1the 2wrath 3of thee and the
καιρὸς τῶν νεκρῶν κριθῆναι καὶ δοῦναι
time of the dead to be judged and to give
τὸν μισθὸν τοῖς δούλοις σου τοῖς προφήταις
the reward to the slaves of thee *to* the prophets
καὶ τοῖς ἁγίοις καὶ τοῖς φοβουμένοις
and to the saints and to the [ones] fearing
τὸ ὄνομά σου, τοῖς μικροῖς καὶ τοῖς
the name of thee, to the small and to the

those who saw them.
12Then they heard a loud
voice from heaven saying
to them, "Come up here."
And they went up to heav-
en in a cloud, while their
enemies looked on.
13At that very hour there
was a severe earthquake
and a tenth of the city collapsed. Seven thousand
people were killed in the
earthquake, and the survi-
vors were terrified and
gave glory to the God of
heaven.
14The second woe has
passed; the third woe is
coming soon.

The Seventh Trumpet

15The seventh angel
sounded his trumpet, and
there were loud voices in
heaven, which said:

"The kingdom of the
world has become
the kingdom of our
Lord and of his
Christ,
and he will reign for
ever and ever."
16And the twenty-four el-
ders, who were seated on
their thrones before God,
fell on their faces and worshiped God, 17saying:

"We give thanks to you,
Lord God Almighty,
the One who is and
who was,
because you have taken
your great power
and have begun to
reign.
18The nations were angry;
and your wrath has
come.
The time has come for
judging the dead,
and for rewarding y
servants the
prophets
and your saints and
those who reverence
your name,

the great, and to destroy
those who destroy the
earth.''
19And the temple of God
which is in heaven was
opened; and the ark of His
covenant appeared in His
temple, and there were
flashes of lightning and
sounds and peals of thun-
der and an earthquake and
a great hailstorm.

Chapter 12

The Woman, Israel

AND a great sign ap-
peared in heaven: a
woman clothed with the
sun, and the moon under
her feet, and on her head a
crown of twelve stars;
2and she was with child;
and she *cried out, being in
labor and in pain to give
birth.

The Red Dragon, Satan

3And another sign ap-
peared in heaven: and be-
hold, a great red dragon
having seven heads and ten
horns, and on his heads
were seven diadems.
4And his tail *swept
away a third of the stars of
heaven, and threw them to
the earth. And the dragon
stood before the woman
who was about to give
birth, so that when she
gave birth he might devour
her child.

The Male Child, Christ

5And she gave birth to a
son, a male *child*, who is to
rule all the nations with a
rod of iron; and her child
was caught up to God and
to His throne.
6And the woman fled
into the wilderness where
she *had a place prepared
by God, so that there she
might be nourished for one
thousand two hundred and
sixty days.

μεγάλοις, καὶ διαφθεῖραι τοὺς διαφθείροντας
great, and to destroy the [ones] destroying

τὴν γῆν. **19** καὶ ἠνοίγη ὁ ναὸς τοῦ
the earth. And was opened the shrine –

θεοῦ ὁ ἐν τῷ οὐρανῷ, καὶ ὤφθη ἡ
of God – in – heaven, and was seen the

κιβωτὸς τῆς διαθήκης αὐτοῦ ἐν τῷ
ark of the covenant of him in the

ναῷ αὐτοῦ, καὶ ἐγένοντο ἀστραπαὶ καὶ
shrine of him, and occurred lightnings and

φωναὶ καὶ βρονταὶ καὶ σεισμὸς καὶ
voices and thunders and an earthquake and

χάλαζα μεγάλη.
[2]hail [1]a great.

12 Καὶ σημεῖον μέγα ὤφθη ἐν τῷ
And [2]sign [1]a great was seen in –

οὐρανῷ, γυνὴ περιβεβλημένη τὸν ἥλιον,
heaven, a woman *having been* clothed [with] the sun,

καὶ ἡ σελήνη ὑποκάτω τῶν ποδῶν αὐτῆς,
and the moon underneath the feet of her,

καὶ ἐπὶ τῆς κεφαλῆς αὐτῆς στέφανος
and on the head of her a crown

ἀστέρων δώδεκα, **2** καὶ ἐν γαστρὶ ἔχουσα,
[2]stars [1]of twelve, and in womb having,
=being pregnant,

καὶ κράζει ὠδίνουσα καὶ βασανιζομένη
and she cries suffering birth-pains and being distressed

τεκεῖν. **3** καὶ ὤφθη ἄλλο σημεῖον
to bear. And was seen another sign

ἐν τῷ οὐρανῷ, καὶ ἰδοὺ δράκων μέγας
in – heaven, and behold[,] [3]dragon [1]a great

πυρρός, ἔχων κεφαλὰς ἑπτὰ καὶ κέρατα
[2]red, having [2]heads [1]seven and [2]horns

δέκα καὶ ἐπὶ τὰς κεφαλὰς αὐτοῦ ἑπτὰ
[1]ten and on the heads of him seven

διαδήματα, **4** καὶ ἡ οὐρὰ αὐτοῦ σύρει
diadems, and the tail of him draws

τὸ τρίτον τῶν ἀστέρων τοῦ οὐρανοῦ,
the third [part] of the stars – of heaven,

καὶ ἔβαλεν αὐτοὺς εἰς τὴν γῆν. Καὶ
and cast them to the earth. And

ὁ δράκων ἕστηκεν ἐνώπιον τῆς γυναικὸς
the dragon stood before the woman

τῆς μελλούσης τεκεῖν, ἵνα ὅταν τέκῃ
– *being* about to bear, in order that whenever she bears

τὸ τέκνον αὐτῆς καταφάγῃ. **5** καὶ
[2]the [3]child [4]of her [1]he might devour. And

ἔτεκεν υἱὸν ἄρσεν, ὃς μέλλει ποιμαίνειν
she bore a son[,] a male, who is about to shepherd

πάντα τὰ ἔθνη ἐν ῥάβδῳ σιδηρᾷ· καὶ
all the nations with [2]staff [1]an iron; and

ἡρπάσθη τὸ τέκνον αὐτῆς πρὸς τὸν
[4]was seized [1]the [2]child [3]of her to –

θεὸν καὶ πρὸς τὸν θρόνον αὐτοῦ. **6** καὶ
God and to the throne of him. And

ἡ γυνὴ ἔφυγεν εἰς τὴν ἔρημον, ὅπου
the woman fled into the desert, where

ἔχει ἐκεῖ τόπον ἡτοιμασμένον ἀπὸ
she has *there* a place *having been* prepared from

τοῦ θεοῦ, ἵνα ἐκεῖ τρέφωσιν αὐτὴν
– God, in order that there they might nourish her

ἡμέρας χιλίας διακοσίας ἑξήκοντα.
[5]days [1]a thousand [2]two hundred [3][and] [4]sixty.

both small and great—
and for destroying those
who destroy the
earth.''
19Then God's temple in
heaven was opened, and
within his temple was seen
the ark of his covenant.
And there came flashes of
lightning, rumblings, peals
of thunder, an earthquake
and a great hailstorm.

Chapter 12

The Woman and the Dragon

A GREAT and wondrous
sign appeared in heav-
en: a woman clothed with
the sun, with the moon under her feet and a crown of
twelve stars on her head.
2She was pregnant and
cried out in pain as she was
about to give birth. 3Then
another sign appeared in
heaven: an enormous red
dragon with seven heads
and ten horns and seven
crowns on his heads. 4His
tail swept a third of the
stars out of the sky and
flung them to the earth. The
dragon stood in front of the
woman who was about to
give birth, so that he might
devour her child the mo-
ment it was born. 5She gave
birth to a son, a male child,
who will rule all the nations
with an iron scepter. And
her child was snatched up
to God and to his throne.
6The woman fled into the
desert to a place prepared
for her by God, where she
might be taken care of for
1,260 days.

The Angel, Michael

7 And there was war in
heaven, Michael and his
angels waging war with the
dragon. And the dragon
and his angels waged war,
8 and they were not
strong enough, and there
was no longer a place found
for them in heaven.
9 And the great dragon
was thrown down, the ser-
pent of old who is called the
devil and Satan, who de-
ceives the whole world; he
was thrown down to the
earth, and his angels were
thrown down with him.
10 And I heard a loud
voice in heaven, saying,
"Now the salvation, and
the power, and the king-
dom of our God and the authority of His Christ have
come, for the accuser of
our brethren has been
thrown down, who accuses
them before our God day
and night.
11 "And they overcame
him because of the blood of
the Lamb and because of
the word of their testi-
mony, and they did not
love their life even to
death.
12 "For this reason, re-
joice, O heavens and you
who dwell in them. Woe to
the earth and the sea, because the devil has come
down to you, having great
wrath, knowing that he has
only a short time."
13 And when the dragon
saw that he was thrown
down to the earth, he persecuted the woman who
gave birth to the male *child*.
14 And the two wings of
the great eagle were given
to the woman, in order that
she might fly into the wil-

7 Καὶ ἐγένετο πόλεμος ἐν τῷ οὐρανῷ,
And occurred war in – heaven,
ὁ Μιχαὴλ καὶ οἱ ἄγγελοι αὐτοῦ τοῦ
– Michael and the angels of him –
πολεμῆσαι μετὰ τοῦ δράκοντος. καὶ ὁ
to make war[d] with the dragon. And the
δράκων ἐπολέμησεν καὶ οἱ ἄγγελοι αὐτοῦ,
dragon warred and the angels of him,
8 καὶ οὐκ ἴσχυσεν, οὐδὲ τόπος εὑρέθη
and prevailed not, not even place was found
αὐτῶν ἔτι ἐν τῷ οὐρανῷ. **9** καὶ ἐβλήθη
of them still in – heaven. And *was cast*
ὁ δράκων ὁ μέγας, ὁ ὄφις ὁ ἀρχαῖος,
[1]the [3]dragon – [2]great, [4]the [6]serpent – [5]old,
ὁ καλούμενος Διάβολος καὶ ὁ Σατανᾶς,
– *being* called Devil and the Satan,
ὁ πλανῶν τὴν οἰκουμένην ὅλην, ἐβλήθη
the [one] deceiving the [2]inhabited [earth] [1]whole, was cast
εἰς τὴν γῆν, καὶ οἱ ἄγγελοι αὐτοῦ μετ'
to the earth, and the angels of him with
αὐτοῦ ἐβλήθησαν. **10** καὶ ἤκουσα φωνὴν
him were cast. And I heard [2]voice
μεγάλην ἐν τῷ οὐρανῷ λέγουσαν ἄρτι
[1]a great(loud) in – heaven saying: Now
ἐγένετο ἡ σωτηρία καὶ ἡ δύναμις καὶ
became the salvation and the power and
ἡ βασιλεία τοῦ θεοῦ ἡμῶν καὶ ἡ ἐξουσία
the kingdom of the God of us and the authority
τοῦ χριστοῦ αὐτοῦ, ὅτι ἐβλήθη ὁ κατήγωρ
of the Christ of him, because [6]was cast [1]the [2]accuser
τῶν ἀδελφῶν ἡμῶν, ὁ κατηγορῶν αὐτοὺς
[3]of the [4]brothers [5]of us, the [one] accusing them
ἐνώπιον τοῦ θεοῦ ἡμῶν ἡμέρας καὶ
before the God of us day and
νυκτός. **11** καὶ αὐτοὶ ἐνίκησαν αὐτὸν
night. And they overcame him
διὰ τὸ αἷμα τοῦ ἀρνίου καὶ διὰ τὸν
because of the blood of the Lamb and because of the
λόγον τῆς μαρτυρίας αὐτῶν, καὶ οὐκ
word of the witness of them, and not
ἠγάπησαν τὴν ψυχὴν αὐτῶν ἄχρι θανάτου.
they loved the life of them until death.
12 διὰ τοῦτο εὐφραίνεσθε, οὐρανοὶ καὶ
Therefore be ye glad, heavens and
οἱ ἐν αὐτοῖς σκηνοῦντες· οὐαὶ τὴν
the [ones] [2]in [3]them [1]tabernacling; woe [to] the
γῆν καὶ τὴν θάλασσαν, ὅτι κατέβη ὁ
earth and the sea, because [3]came down [1]the
διάβολος πρὸς ὑμᾶς ἔχων θυμὸν μέγαν,
[2]devil to you having [2]anger [1]great,
εἰδὼς ὅτι ὀλίγον καιρὸν ἔχει. **13** Καὶ
knowing that [2]few(short) [3]time [1]he has. And
ὅτε εἶδεν ὁ δράκων ὅτι ἐβλήθη εἰς
when [3]saw [1]the [2]dragon that he was cast to
τὴν γῆν, ἐδίωξεν τὴν γυναῖκα ἥτις
the earth, he pursued the woman who
ἔτεκεν τὸν ἄρσενα. **14** καὶ ἐδόθησαν
bore the male. And were given
τῇ γυναικὶ αἱ δύο πτέρυγες τοῦ ἀετοῦ
to the woman the two wings of the [2]eagle
τοῦ μεγάλου, ἵνα πέτηται εἰς τὴν ἔρημον
– [1]great, in order that she might fly to the desert

7 And there was war in
heaven. Michael and his
angels fought against the
dragon, and the dragon and
his angels fought back.
8 But he was not strong
enough, and they lost their
place in heaven. 9 The great
dragon was hurled down—
that ancient serpent called
the devil, or Satan, who
leads the whole world
astray. He was hurled to
the earth, and his angels
with him.
10 Then I heard a loud
voice in heaven say:

"Now have come the
salvation and the
power and the
kingdom of our
God,
and the authority of his
Christ.
For the accuser of our
brothers,
who accuses them
before our God day
and night,
has been hurled down.
11 They overcame him
by the blood of the
Lamb
and by the word of
their testimony;
they did not love their
lives so much
as to shrink from
death.
12 Therefore rejoice, you
heavens
and you who dwell in
them!
But woe to the earth and
the sea,
because the devil has
gone down to you!
He is filled with fury,
because he knows that
his time is short."
13 When the dragon saw
that he had been hurled to
the earth, he pursued the
woman who had given birth
to the male child. 14 The
woman was given the two
wings of a great eagle, so
that she might fly to the

derness to her place, where she *was nourished for a time and times and half a time, from the presence of the serpent.
15And the serpent poured water like a river out of his mouth after the woman, so that he might cause her to be swept away with the flood.
16And the earth helped the woman, and the earth opened its mouth and drank up the river which the dragon poured out of his mouth.
17And the dragon was enraged with the woman, and went off to make war with the rest of her offspring, who keep the commandments of God and hold to the testimony of Jesus.

εἰς τὸν τόπον αὐτῆς, ὅπου τρέφεται
to the place of her, where she is nourished
ἐκεῖ καιρὸν καὶ καιροὺς καὶ ἥμισυ καιροῦ
there a time and times and half of a time
ἀπὸ προσώπου τοῦ ὄφεως. **15** καὶ ἔβαλεν
from [the] face of the serpent. And [3]cast
ὁ ὄφις ἐκ τοῦ στόματος αὐτοῦ ὀπίσω
[1]the [2]serpent out of the mouth of him behind
τῆς γυναικὸς ὕδωρ ὡς ποταμόν, ἵνα
the woman water as a river, in order that
αὐτὴν ποταμοφόρητον ποιήσῃ. **16** καὶ
[2]her [3]carried off by [the] river [1]he might make. And
ἐβοήθησεν ἡ γῆ τῇ γυναικί, καὶ ἤνοιξεν
[3]helped [1]the [2]earth the woman, and [3]opened
ἡ γῆ τὸ στόμα αὐτῆς καὶ κατέπιεν
[1]the [2]earth the mouth of it and swallowed
τὸν ποταμὸν ὃν ἔβαλεν ὁ δράκων ἐκ
the river which [3]cast [1]the [2]dragon out of
τοῦ στόματος αὐτοῦ. **17** καὶ ὠργίσθη
the mouth of him. And [3]was enraged
ὁ δράκων ἐπὶ τῇ γυναικί, καὶ ἀπῆλθεν
[1]the [2]dragon over the woman, and went away
ποιῆσαι πόλεμον μετὰ τῶν λοιπῶν τοῦ
to make war with the rest of the
σπέρματος αὐτῆς, τῶν τηρούντων τὰς
seed of her, the [ones] keeping the
ἐντολὰς τοῦ θεοῦ καὶ ἐχόντων τὴν
commandments – of God and having the
μαρτυρίαν Ἰησοῦ· (18) καὶ ἐστάθη ἐπὶ τὴν
witness of Jesus; and he stood on the
ἄμμον τῆς θαλάσσης.
sand of the sea.

place prepared for her in the desert, where she would be taken care of for a time, times and half a time, out of the serpent's reach.
15Then from his mouth the serpent spewed water like a river, to overtake the woman and sweep her away with the torrent. 16But the earth helped the woman by opening its mouth and swallowing the river that the dragon had spewed out of his mouth. 17Then the dragon was enraged at the woman and went off to make war against the rest of her offspring—those who obey God's commandments and hold to the testimony of Jesus.

Chapter 13

The Beast from the Sea

AND he stood on the sand of the seashore.
And I saw a beast coming up out of the sea, having ten horns and seven heads, and on his horns *were* ten diadems, and on his heads *were* blasphemous names.
2And the beast which I saw was like a leopard, and his feet were *like those* of a bear, and his mouth like the mouth of a lion. And the dragon gave him his power and his throne and great authority.
3And *I saw* one of his heads as if it had been slain, and his fatal wound was healed. And the whole

13 Καὶ εἶδον ἐκ τῆς θαλάσσης θηρίον
And I saw [3]out of [4]the [5]sea [1]a beast
ἀναβαῖνον, ἔχον κέρατα δέκα καὶ κεφαλὰς
[2]coming up, having [2]horns [1]ten and [2]heads
ἑπτά, καὶ ἐπὶ τῶν κεράτων αὐτοῦ δέκα
[1]seven, and on the horns of it* ten
διαδήματα, καὶ ἐπὶ τὰς κεφαλὰς αὐτοῦ
diadems, and on the heads of it
ὀνόματα βλασφημίας. **2** καὶ τὸ θηρίον
names of blasphemy. And the beast
ὃ εἶδον ἦν ὅμοιον παρδάλει, καὶ οἱ
which I saw was like *to* a leopard, and the
πόδες αὐτοῦ ὡς ἄρκου, καὶ τὸ στόμα
feet of it as of a bear, and the mouth
αὐτοῦ ὡς στόμα λέοντος. καὶ ἔδωκεν
of it as [the] mouth of a lion. And [5]gave
αὐτῷ ὁ δράκων τὴν δύναμιν αὐτοῦ καὶ
[4]to it [1]the [2]dragon the power of it and
τὸν θρόνον αὐτοῦ καὶ ἐξουσίαν μεγάλην.
the throne of it and [2]authority [1]great.
3 καὶ μίαν ἐκ τῶν κεφαλῶν αὐτοῦ ὡς
And one of the heads of it as
ἐσφαγμένην εἰς θάνατον, καὶ ἡ πληγὴ
having been slain to death, and the stroke
τοῦ θανάτου αὐτοῦ ἐθεραπεύθη. καὶ
of the death of it was healed. And

1And the dragon[p] stood on the shore of the sea.

The Beast out of the Sea

And I saw a beast coming out of the sea. He had ten horns and seven heads, with ten crowns on his horns, and on each head a blasphemous name. 2The beast I saw resembled a leopard, but had feet like those of a bear and a mouth like that of a lion. The dragon gave the beast his power and his throne and great authority. 3One of the heads of the beast seemed to have had a fatal wound, but the fatal wound had been healed. The whole world

* αὐτοῦ, of course, may be neuter or masculine—"of it" or "of him". δράκων being masculine (=Satan), we have kept to the masculine. But θηρίον is neuter. Yet if it stands for a person, as ἀρνίον certainly does, it too should be treated, as to the pronoun, as a masculine. However, not to enter the province of interpretation, we have rendered αὐτοῦ by "of it", though it will be seen that αὐτόν (him) is used in ver. 8, τίς (who?) in ver. 4, and ὅς (who) in ver. 14. See also ch. 17. 11.

[p] 1 Some late manuscripts *And I*

earth was amazed *and followed* after the beast;
4and they worshiped the
dragon, because he gave
his authority to the beast;
and they worshiped the
beast, saying, "Who is like
the beast, and who is able
to wage war with him?"
5And there was given to
him a mouth speaking arrogant words and blasphe-
mies; and authority to act
for forty-two months was
given to him.
6And he opened his
mouth in blasphemies
against God, to blaspheme
His name and His taber-
nacle, *that is,* those who
dwell in heaven.
7And it was given to him
to make war with the saints
and to overcome them; and
authority over every tribe
and people and tongue and
nation was given to him.
8And all who dwell on
the earth will worship him,
everyone whose name has
not been [p]written from the
foundation of the world in
the book of life of the Lamb
who has been slain.
9If anyone has an ear, let
him hear.
10If anyone [q]*is destined*
for captivity, to captivity
he goes; if anyone kills with
the sword, with the sword
he must be killed. Here is
the perseverance and the
faith of the saints.

The Beast from the Earth

11And I saw another beast
coming up out of the earth;
and he had two horns like a
lamb, and he spoke as a
dragon.
12And he exercises all the
authority of the first beast
in his presence. And he

ἐθαυμάσθη ὅλη ἡ γῆ ὀπίσω τοῦ θηρίου,
[4]wondered [1]all [2]the [3]earth after the beast,
4 καὶ προσεκύνησαν τῷ δράκοντι, ὅτι
and they worshipped the dragon, because
ἔδωκεν τὴν ἐξουσίαν τῷ θηρίῳ, καὶ
he gave the authority to the beast, and
προσεκύνησαν τῷ θηρίῳ λέγοντες· τίς
they worshipped the beast saying: Who
ὅμοιος τῷ θηρίῳ, καὶ τίς δύναται
[is] like *to* the beast, and who can
πολεμῆσαι μετ' αὐτοῦ; 5 καὶ ἐδόθη αὐτῷ
to make war with it? And was given to it
στόμα λαλοῦν μεγάλα καὶ βλασφημίας,
a mouth speaking great things and blasphemies,
καὶ ἐδόθη αὐτῷ ἐξουσία ποιῆσαι μῆνας
and was given to it authority to act [2]months
τεσσεράκοντα [καὶ] δύο. 6 καὶ ἤνοιξεν
[1]forty-two. And it opened
τὸ στόμα αὐτοῦ εἰς βλασφημίας πρὸς
the mouth of it in blasphemies against
τὸν θεόν, βλασφημῆσαι τὸ ὄνομα αὐτοῦ
– God, to blaspheme the name of him
καὶ τὴν σκηνὴν αὐτοῦ, τοὺς ἐν τῷ
and the tabernacle of him, [1]the [ones] [3]in –
οὐρανῷ σκηνοῦντας. 7 καὶ ἐδόθη αὐτῷ
[4]heaven [2]tabernacling. And it was given to it
ποιῆσαι πόλεμον μετὰ τῶν ἁγίων καὶ
to make war with the saints and
νικῆσαι αὐτούς, καὶ ἐδόθη αὐτῷ ἐξουσία
to overcome them, and [2]was given [3]to it [1]authority
ἐπὶ πᾶσαν φυλὴν καὶ λαὸν καὶ γλῶσσαν
over every tribe and people and tongue
καὶ ἔθνος. 8 καὶ προσκυνήσουσιν αὐτὸν
and nation. And [7]will worship [8]him
πάντες οἱ κατοικοῦντες ἐπὶ τῆς γῆς,
[1]all [2]the [ones] [3]dwelling [4]on [5]the [6]earth,
οὗ οὐ γέγραπται τὸ ὄνομα αὐτοῦ ἐν
[3]of whom [4]has not been written [1]the [2]name *of him* in
τῷ βιβλίῳ τῆς ζωῆς τοῦ ἀρνίου τοῦ
the scroll – of life of the Lamb –
ἐσφαγμένου ἀπὸ καταβολῆς κόσμου.
having been slain from [the] foundation of [the] world.
9 Εἴ τις ἔχει οὖς ἀκουσάτω. 10 εἴ
If anyone has an ear let him hear. If
τις εἰς αἰχμαλωσίαν, εἰς αἰχμαλωσίαν
anyone [is] for captivity, to captivity
ὑπάγει· εἴ τις ἐν μαχαίρῃ ἀποκτενεῖ,
he goes; if anyone by a sword will kill,
δεῖ αὐτὸν ἐν μαχαίρῃ ἀποκτανθῆναι.
it behoves him by a sword to be killed.
Ὧδέ ἐστιν ἡ ὑπομονὴ καὶ ἡ πίστις
Here is the endurance and the faith
τῶν ἁγίων.
of the saints.
11 Καὶ εἶδον ἄλλο θηρίον ἀναβαῖνον
And I saw another beast coming up
ἐκ τῆς γῆς, καὶ εἶχεν κέρατα δύο
out of the earth, and it had [2]horns [1]two
ὅμοια ἀρνίῳ, καὶ ἐλάλει ὡς δράκων.
like *to* a lamb, and spoke as a dragon.
12 καὶ τὴν ἐξουσίαν τοῦ πρώτου θηρίου
And [3]the [4]authority [5]of the [6]first [7]beast
πᾶσαν ποιεῖ ἐνώπιον αὐτοῦ. καὶ ποιεῖ
[2]all [1]it does(exercises) before it. And it makes

was astonished and fol-
lowed the beast. 4Men worshiped the dragon because
he had given authority to
the beast, and they also
worshiped the beast and
asked, "Who is like the
beast? Who can make war
against him?"
5The beast was given a
mouth to utter proud words
and blasphemies and to exercise his authority for forty-two months. 6He opened
his mouth to blaspheme
God, and to slander his
name and his dwelling
place and those who live in
heaven. 7He was given
power to make war against
the saints and to conquer
them. And he was given authority over every tribe,
people, language and na-
tion. 8All inhabitants of the
earth will worship the beast
—all whose names have
not been written in the
book of life belonging to the
Lamb that was slain from
the creation of the world.[q]
9He who has an ear, let
him hear.

10If anyone is to go into
captivity,
into captivity he will
go.
If anyone is to be killed[r]
with the sword,
with the sword he will
be killed.

This calls for patient endurance and faithfulness on
the part of the saints.

The Beast out of the Earth

11Then I saw another
beast, coming out of the
earth. He had two horns
like a lamb, but he spoke
like a dragon. 12He exer-
cised all the authority of the
first beast on his behalf,

[p] Or, *written in the book . . . slain from the foundation of the world*
[q] Or, leads *into captivity*

[q]8 Or *written from the creation of the world in the book of life belonging to the Lamb that was slain*
[r]10 Some manuscripts *anyone kills*

makes the earth and those who dwell in it to worship the first beast, whose fatal wound was healed.
13And he performs great signs, so that he even makes fire come down out of heaven to the earth in the presence of men.
14And he deceives those who dwell on the earth because of the signs which it was given him to perform in the presence of the beast, telling those who dwell on the earth to make an image to the beast who *had the wound of the sword and has come to life.
15And there was given to him to give breath to the image of the beast, that the image of the beast might even [r]speak and cause as many as do not worship the image of the beast to be killed.
16And he causes all, the small and the great, and the rich and the poor, and the free men and the slaves, to be given a mark on their right hand, or on their forehead.
17and *he provides* that no one should be able to buy or to sell, except the one who has the mark, *either* the name of the beast or the number of his name.
18Here is wisdom. Let him who has understanding calculate the number of the beast, for the number is that of a man; and his number is [s]six hundred and sixty-six.

τὴν γῆν καὶ τοὺς ἐν αὐτῇ κατοικοῦντας
the earth and 1the [ones] 3in 4it 2dwelling

ἵνα προσκυνήσουσιν τὸ θηρίον τὸ πρῶτον,
in order that they shall worship the 2beast – 1first,

οὗ ἐθεραπεύθη ἡ πληγὴ τοῦ θανάτου
of which 4was healed 1the 2stroke – 3of death

αὐτοῦ. **13** καὶ ποιεῖ σημεῖα μεγάλα,
of it. And it does 2signs 1great,

ἵνα καὶ πῦρ ποιῇ ἐκ τοῦ οὐρανοῦ
in order that 2even 4fire 1it 3makes 6out of – 7heaven

καταβαίνειν εἰς τὴν γῆν ἐνώπιον τῶν
5to come down onto the earth before –

ἀνθρώπων. **14** καὶ πλανᾷ τοὺς κατοι-
men. And it deceives the [ones] dwell-

κοῦντας ἐπὶ τῆς γῆς διὰ τὰ σημεῖα
ing on the earth because of the signs

ἃ ἐδόθη αὐτῷ ποιῆσαι ἐνώπιον τοῦ
which it was given to it to do before the

θηρίου, λέγων τοῖς κατοικοῦσιν ἐπὶ τῆς
beast, telling *to* the [ones] dwelling on the

γῆς ποιῆσαι εἰκόνα τῷ θηρίῳ, ὃς ἔχει
earth to make an image to the beast, who has

τὴν πληγὴν τῆς μαχαίρης καὶ ἔζησεν.
the stroke of the sword and lived [again].

15 καὶ ἐδόθη αὐτῷ δοῦναι πνεῦμα τῇ
And it was given to it to give spirit to the

εἰκόνι τοῦ θηρίου, ἵνα καὶ λαλήσῃ ἡ
image of the beast, in order that 6even 5might 7speak 1the

εἰκὼν τοῦ θηρίου, καὶ ποιήσῃ [ἵνα]
2image 3of the 4beast, and might make *in order that*

ὅσοι ἐὰν μὴ προσκυνήσωσιν τῇ εἰκόνι
as many as might not worship the image

τοῦ θηρίου ἀποκτανθῶσιν. **16** καὶ ποιεῖ
of the beast should be killed. And it makes

πάντας, τοὺς μικροὺς καὶ τοὺς μεγάλους,
all men, the small and the great,

καὶ τοὺς πλουσίους καὶ τοὺς πτωχούς,
both the rich and the poor,

καὶ τοὺς ἐλευθέρους καὶ τοὺς δούλους,
both the free men and the slaves,

ἵνα δῶσιν αὐτοῖς χάραγμα ἐπὶ τῆς
in order that they should give to them a mark on the

χειρὸς αὐτῶν τῆς δεξιᾶς ἢ ἐπὶ τὸ
2hand 3of them – 1right or on the

μέτωπον αὐτῶν, **17** [καὶ] ἵνα μή τις
forehead of them, and lest anyone

δύνηται ἀγοράσαι ἢ πωλῆσαι εἰ μὴ
could *to* buy or *to* sell except

ὁ ἔχων τὸ χάραγμα τὸ ὄνομα τοῦ
the [one] having the mark[,] the name of the

θηρίου ἢ τὸν ἀριθμὸν τοῦ ὀνόματος
beast or the number of the name

αὐτοῦ. **18** Ὧδε ἡ σοφία ἐστίν. ὁ ἔχων
of it. Here – 2wisdom 1is. The [one] having

νοῦν ψηφισάτω τὸν ἀριθμὸν τοῦ θηρίου·
reason let him count the number of the beast;

ἀριθμὸς γὰρ ἀνθρώπου ἐστίν. καὶ ὁ
for 2[the] 3number 4of a man 1it is. And the

ἀριθμὸς αὐτοῦ ἑξακόσιοι ἑξήκοντα ἕξ.
number of it [is] six hundreds [and] sixty-six.

and made the earth and its inhabitants worship the first beast, whose fatal wound had been healed.
13And he performed great and miraculous signs, even causing fire to come down from heaven to earth in full view of men.
14Because of the signs he was given power to do on behalf of the first beast, he deceived the inhabitants of the earth. He ordered them to set up an image in honor of the beast who was wounded by the sword and yet lived.
15He was given power to give breath to the image of the first beast, so that it could speak and cause all who refused to worship the image to be killed.
16He also forced everyone, small and great, rich and poor, free and slave, to receive a mark on his right hand or on his forehead,
17so that no one could buy or sell unless he had the mark, which is the name of the beast or the number of his name.
18This calls for wisdom. If anyone has insight, let him calculate the number of the beast, for it is man's number. His number is 666.

[r] Some ancient mss. read *speak, and he will cause*
[s] Some mss. read 616

Chapter 14

The Lamb and the 144,000 on Mount Zion

AND I looked, and behold, the Lamb *was* standing on Mount Zion, and with Him one hundred and forty-four thousand, having His name and the name of His Father written on their foreheads.

2And I heard a voice from heaven, like the sound of many waters and like the sound of loud thunder, and the voice which I heard *was* like *the sound* of harpists playing on their harps.

3And they *sang a new song before the throne and before the four living creatures and the elders; and no one could learn the song except the one hundred and forty-four thousand who had been purchased from the earth.

4These are the ones who have not been defiled with women, for they [1]have kept themselves chaste. These *are* the ones who follow the Lamb wherever He goes. These have been purchased from among men as first fruits to God and to the Lamb.

5And no lie was found in their mouth; they are blameless.

Vision of the Angel with the Gospel

6And I saw another angel flying in midheaven, having an eternal gospel to preach to those who live on the earth, and to every nation and tribe and tongue and people;

7and he said with a loud voice, "Fear God, and give Him glory, because the hour of His judgment has come; and worship Him who made the heaven and the earth and sea and springs of waters."

[1]Lit., *are chaste men*

14 Καὶ εἶδον, καὶ ἰδοὺ τὸ ἀρνίον
And I saw, and behold[,] the Lamb

ἑστὸς ἐπὶ τὸ ὄρος Σιών, καὶ μετ' αὐτοῦ
standing on the mount Sion, and with him

ἑκατὸν τεσσεράκοντα τέσσαρες χιλιάδες
a hundred [and] forty-four thousands

ἔχουσαι τὸ ὄνομα αὐτοῦ καὶ τὸ ὄνομα
having the name of him and the name

τοῦ πατρὸς αὐτοῦ γεγραμμένον ἐπὶ τῶν
of the Father of him *having been* written on the

μετώπων αὐτῶν. **2** καὶ ἤκουσα φωνὴν
foreheads of them. And I heard a sound

ἐκ τοῦ οὐρανοῦ ὡς φωνὴν ὑδάτων πολλῶν
out of – heaven as a sound [2]waters [1]of many

καὶ ὡς φωνὴν βροντῆς μεγάλης, καὶ
and as a sound [2]thunder [1]of great(loud), and

ἡ φωνὴ ἣν ἤκουσα ὡς κιθαρῳδῶν
the sound which I heard [was] as of harpers

κιθαριζόντων ἐν ταῖς κιθάραις αὐτῶν.
harping with the harps of them.

3 καὶ ᾄδουσιν ᾠδὴν καινὴν ἐνώπιον τοῦ
And they sing [2]song [1]a new before the

θρόνου καὶ ἐνώπιον τῶν τεσσάρων ζῴων
throne and before the four living creatures

καὶ τῶν πρεσβυτέρων· καὶ οὐδεὶς ἐδύνατο
and the elders; and no man could

μαθεῖν τὴν ᾠδὴν εἰ μὴ αἱ ἑκατὸν
to learn the song except the hundred

τεσσεράκοντα τέσσαρες χιλιάδες, οἱ
[and] forty-four thousands, the

ἠγορασμένοι ἀπὸ τῆς γῆς. **4** οὗτοί εἰσιν
[ones] *having been* purchased from the earth. These are

οἳ μετὰ γυναικῶν οὐκ ἐμολύνθησαν·
[those] who [2]with [3]women [1]were not defiled;

παρθένοι γάρ εἰσιν. οὗτοι οἱ ἀκολουθοῦντες
for [2]celibates [1]they are. These [are] the [ones] following

τῷ ἀρνίῳ ὅπου ἂν ὑπάγῃ. οὗτοι ἠγοράσ-
the Lamb wherever he may go. These were

θησαν ἀπὸ τῶν ἀνθρώπων ἀπαρχὴ τῷ
purchased from – men firstfruit –

θεῷ καὶ τῷ ἀρνίῳ, **5** καὶ ἐν τῷ στόματι
to God and to the Lamb, and in the mouth

αὐτῶν οὐχ εὑρέθη ψεῦδος· ἄμωμοί εἰσιν.
of them was not found a lie; [2]unblemished [1]they are.

6 Καὶ εἶδον ἄλλον ἄγγελον πετόμενον
And I saw another angel flying

ἐν μεσουρανήματι, ἔχοντα εὐαγγέλιον
in mid-heaven, having [2]gospel

αἰώνιον εὐαγγελίσαι ἐπὶ τοὺς καθημένους
[1]an eternal to preach over the [ones] sitting

ἐπὶ τῆς γῆς καὶ ἐπὶ πᾶν ἔθνος καὶ
on the earth and over every nation and

φυλὴν καὶ γλῶσσαν καὶ λαόν, **7** λέγων
tribe and tongue and people, saying

ἐν φωνῇ μεγάλῃ· φοβήθητε τὸν θεὸν
in [2]voice [1]a great(loud): Fear ye – God

καὶ δότε αὐτῷ δόξαν, ὅτι ἦλθεν ἡ ὥρα
and give [2]to him [1]glory, because came the hour

τῆς κρίσεως αὐτοῦ, καὶ προσκυνήσατε
of the judgment of him, and worship

τῷ ποιήσαντι τὸν οὐρανὸν καὶ τὴν γῆν
the [one] having made the heaven and the earth

καὶ θάλασσαν καὶ πηγὰς ὑδάτων. **8** Καὶ
and sea and fountains of waters. And

Chapter 14

The Lamb and the 144,000

THEN I looked, and there before me was the Lamb, standing on Mount Zion, and with him 144,000 who had his name and his Father's name written on their foreheads. 2And I heard a sound from heaven like the roar of rushing waters and like a loud peal of thunder. The sound I heard was like that of harpists playing their harps. 3And they sang a new song before the throne and before the four living creatures and the elders. No one could learn the song except the 144,000 who had been redeemed from the earth. 4These are those who did not defile themselves with women, for they kept themselves pure. They follow the Lamb wherever he goes. They were purchased from among men and offered as firstfruits to God and the Lamb. 5No lie was found in their mouths; they are blameless.

The Three Angels

6Then I saw another angel flying in midair, and he had the eternal gospel to proclaim to those who live on the earth—to every nation, tribe, language and people. 7He said in a loud voice, "Fear God and give him glory, because the hour of his judgment has come. Worship him who made the heavens, the earth, the sea and the springs of water."

8And another angel, a
second one, followed, saying, "Fallen, fallen is Babylon the great, she who has
made all the nations drink
of the wine of the passion of
her immorality."

Doom for Worshipers of the Beast

9And another angel, a
third one, followed them,
saying with a loud voice,
"If anyone worships the
beast and his image, and receives a mark on his forehead or upon his hand,
10he also will drink of the
wine of the wrath of God,
which is mixed in full
strength in the cup of His
anger; and he will be tormented with fire and brimstone in the presence of the
holy angels and in the presence of the Lamb.
11"And the smoke of
their torment goes up forever and ever; and they
have no rest day and night,
those who worship the
beast and his image, and
whoever receives the mark
of his name."
12Here is the persever-
ance of the saints who keep
the commandments of God
and their faith in Jesus.
13And I heard a voice
from heaven, saying,
"Write, 'Blessed are the
dead who die in the Lord
from now on!' " "Yes,"
says the Spirit, "that they
may rest from their labors,
for their deeds follow with
them."

The Reapers

14And I looked, and be-
hold, a white cloud, and sitting on the cloud *was* one
like [u]a son of man, having a
golden crown on His head,

ἄλλος ἄγγελος δεύτερος ἠκολούθησεν λέγων·
another angel a second followed saying:
ἔπεσεν ἔπεσεν Βαβυλὼν ἡ μεγάλη, ἣ
Fell[,] fell Babylon the great, which
ἐκ τοῦ οἴνου τοῦ θυμοῦ τῆς πορνείας
of the wine of the anger of the fornication
αὐτῆς πεπότικεν πάντα τὰ ἔθνη. 9 Καὶ
of her has made to drink all the nations. And
ἄλλος ἄγγελος τρίτος ἠκολούθησεν αὐτοῖς
another angel a third followed them
λέγων ἐν φωνῇ μεγάλῃ· εἴ τις προσκυνεῖ
saying in [2]voice [1]a great(loud): If anyone worships
τὸ θηρίον καὶ τὴν εἰκόνα αὐτοῦ, καὶ
the beast and the image of it, and
λαμβάνει χάραγμα ἐπὶ τοῦ μετώπου αὐτοῦ
receives a mark on the forehead of him
ἢ ἐπὶ τὴν χεῖρα αὐτοῦ, 10 καὶ αὐτὸς
or on the hand of him, even he
πίεται ἐκ τοῦ οἴνου τοῦ θυμοῦ τοῦ
shall drink of the wine of the anger –
θεοῦ τοῦ κεκερασμένου ἀκράτου ἐν τῷ
of God – *having been* mixed undiluted in the
ποτηρίῳ τῆς ὀργῆς αὐτοῦ, καὶ βασανισθήσε-
cup of the wrath of him, and will be torment-
ται ἐν πυρὶ καὶ θείῳ ἐνώπιον ἀγγέλων
ed by fire and sulphur before [2]angels
ἁγίων καὶ ἐνώπιον τοῦ ἀρνίου. 11 Καὶ
[1]holy and before the Lamb. And
ὁ καπνὸς τοῦ βασανισμοῦ αὐτῶν εἰς
the smoke of the torment of them unto
αἰῶνας αἰώνων ἀναβαίνει, καὶ οὐκ ἔχουσιν
ages of ages goes up, and they have not
ἀνάπαυσιν ἡμέρας καὶ νυκτὸς οἱ προσκυ-
rest day and night the [ones] wor-
νοῦντες τὸ θηρίον καὶ τὴν εἰκόνα αὐτοῦ,
shipping the beast and the image of it,
καὶ εἴ τις λαμβάνει τὸ χάραγμα τοῦ
and if anyone receives the mark of the
ὀνόματος αὐτοῦ. 12 Ὧδε ἡ ὑπομονὴ
name of it. [1]Here [3]the [4]endurance
τῶν ἁγίων ἐστίν, οἱ τηροῦντες τὰς
[5]of the [6]saints [2]is, the [ones] keeping the
ἐντολὰς τοῦ θεοῦ καὶ τὴν πίστιν Ἰησοῦ.
command-ments – of God and the faith of Jesus.
13 Καὶ ἤκουσα φωνῆς ἐκ τοῦ οὐρανοῦ
And I heard a voice out of – heaven
λεγούσης· γράψον· μακάριοι οἱ νεκροὶ
saying: Write thou: Blessed [are] the dead
οἱ ἐν κυρίῳ ἀποθνήσκοντες ἀπ' ἄρτι.
[1]the [ones] [3]in [4][the] Lord [2]dying from now.
ναί, λέγει τὸ πνεῦμα, ἵνα ἀναπαήσονται
Yes, says the Spirit, in order that they shall rest
ἐκ τῶν κόπων αὐτῶν· τὰ γὰρ ἔργα
from the labours of them; for the works
αὐτῶν ἀκολουθεῖ μετ' αὐτῶν.
of them follows with them.
14 Καὶ εἶδον, καὶ ἰδοὺ νεφέλη λευκή,
And I saw, and behold[,] [2]cloud [1]a white,
καὶ ἐπὶ τὴν νεφέλην καθήμενον ὅμοιον
and on the cloud [one] sitting like
υἱὸν ἀνθρώπου, ἔχων ἐπὶ τῆς κεφαλῆς
a son of man,* having on the head

8A second angel followed
and said, "Fallen! Fallen is
Babylon the Great, which
made all the nations drink
the maddening wine of her
adulteries."
9A third angel followed
them and said in a loud
voice: "If anyone worships
the beast and his image and
receives his mark on the
forehead or on the hand,
10he, too, will drink of the
wine of God's fury, which
has been poured full
strength into the cup of his
wrath. He will be tormented with burning sulfur in
the presence of the holy angels and of the Lamb.
11And the smoke of their
torment rises for ever and
ever. There is no rest day
or night for those who worship the beast and his image, or for anyone who receives the mark of his
name." 12This calls for patient endurance on the part
of the saints who obey
God's commandments and
remain faithful to Jesus.
13Then I heard a voice
from heaven say, "Write:
Blessed are the dead who
die in the Lord from now
on."
"Yes," says the Spirit,
"they will rest from their
labor, for their deeds will
follow them."

The Harvest of the Earth

14I looked, and there be-
fore me was a white cloud,
and seated on the cloud
was one "like a son of
man"[s] with a crown of
gold on his head and a

[u]Or, *the Son of Man*

* See also ch. 1. 13 and John 5. 27.

[s]14 Daniel 7:13

and a sharp sickle in His
hand.
15And another angel came
out of the temple, crying
out with a loud voice to
Him who sat on the cloud,
"Put in your sickle and
reap, because the hour to
reap has come, because the
harvest of the earth is
ripe."
16And He who sat on the
cloud swung His sickle
over the earth; and the
earth was reaped.
17And another angel came
out of the temple which is
in heaven, and he also had a
sharp sickle.
18And another angel, the
one who has power over
fire, came out from the altar; and he called with a
loud voice to him who had
the sharp sickle, saying,
"Put in your sharp sickle,
and gather the clusters
from the vine of the earth,
because her grapes are
ripe."
19And the angel swung his
sickle to the earth, and
gathered *the clusters from*
the vine of the earth, and
threw them into the great
wine press of the wrath of
God.
20And the wine press was
trodden outside the city,
and blood came out from
the wine press, up to the
horses' bridles, for a distance of [v]two hundred
miles.

Chapter 15

A Scene of Heaven

AND I saw another sign
in heaven, great and
marvelous, seven angels
who had seven plagues,
which are the last, because
in them the wrath of God is
finished.
2And I saw, as it were, a
sea of glass mixed with fire,

[v]Lit., *sixteen hundred stadia*. A stadion was about six hundred feet.

αὐτοῦ στέφανον χρυσοῦν καὶ ἐν τῇ χειρὶ
of him crown a golden and in the hand
αὐτοῦ δρέπανον ὀξύ. 15 καὶ ἄλλος ἄγγελος
of him sickle a sharp. And another angel
ἐξῆλθεν ἐκ τοῦ ναοῦ, κράζων ἐν φωνῇ
went forth out of the shrine, crying in [2]voice
μεγάλῃ τῷ καθημένῳ ἐπὶ τῆς νεφέλης·
[1]a great (loud) to the [one] sitting on the cloud:
πέμψον τὸ δρέπανόν σου καὶ θέρισον,
Send(Thrust) the sickle of thee and reap thou,
ὅτι ἦλθεν ἡ ὥρα θερίσαι, ὅτι ἐξηράνθη
because came the hour to reap, because was dried
ὁ θερισμὸς τῆς γῆς. 16 καὶ ἔβαλεν
the harvest of the earth. And [6]thrust
ὁ καθήμενος ἐπὶ τῆς νεφέλης τὸ δρέπανον
[1]the [2]sitting [one] [3]on [4]the [5]cloud the sickle
αὐτοῦ ἐπὶ τὴν γῆν, καὶ ἐθερίσθη ἡ
of him over the earth, and [3]was reaped [1]the
γῆ. 17 Καὶ ἄλλος ἄγγελος ἐξῆλθεν ἐκ
[2]earth. And another angel went forth out of
τοῦ ναοῦ τοῦ ἐν τῷ οὐρανῷ, ἔχων καὶ
the shrine – in – heaven, [3]having [2]also
αὐτὸς δρέπανον ὀξύ. 18 καὶ ἄλλος ἄγγελος
[1]he [5]sickle [4]a sharp. And another angel
ἐξῆλθεν ἐκ τοῦ θυσιαστηρίου, [ὁ] ἔχων
went forth out of the altar, the [one] having
ἐξουσίαν ἐπὶ τοῦ πυρός, καὶ ἐφώνησεν
authority over the fire, and he spoke
φωνῇ μεγάλῃ τῷ ἔχοντι τὸ δρέπανον
[2]voice [1]in a great (loud) to the [one] having the [3]sickle
τὸ ὀξὺ λέγων· πέμψον σου τὸ δρέπανον
– [2]sharp saying: Send(Thrust) [4]of thee [1]the [3]sickle
τὸ ὀξὺ καὶ τρύγησον τοὺς βότρυας τῆς
– [2]sharp and gather the clusters of the
ἀμπέλου τῆς γῆς, ὅτι ἤκμασαν αἱ
vine of the earth, because [4]ripened [1]the
σταφυλαὶ αὐτῆς. 19 καὶ ἔβαλεν ὁ ἄγγελος
[2]grapes [3]of it. And [3]thrust [1]the [2]angel
τὸ δρέπανον αὐτοῦ εἰς τὴν γῆν, καὶ
the sickle of him into the earth, and
ἐτρύγησεν τὴν ἄμπελον τῆς γῆς καὶ
gathered the vine of the earth and
ἔβαλεν εἰς τὴν ληνὸν τοῦ θυμοῦ τοῦ
cast into the [1]winepress [3]of the [4]anger –
θεοῦ τὸν μέγαν. 20 καὶ ἐπατήθη ἡ
[5]of God – [2]great. And [3]was trodden [1]the
ληνὸς ἔξωθεν τῆς πόλεως, καὶ ἐξῆλθεν
winepress outside the city, and [2]went *out*
αἷμα ἐκ τῆς ληνοῦ ἄχρι τῶν χαλινῶν
[1]blood out of the winepress as far as the bridles
τῶν ἵππων, ἀπὸ σταδίων χιλίων ἑξακοσίων.
of the horses, from [3]furlongs [1]a thousand [2]six hundred.

15 Καὶ εἶδον ἄλλο σημεῖον ἐν τῷ
And I saw another sign in –
οὐρανῷ μέγα καὶ θαυμαστόν, ἀγγέλους
heaven[,] great and wonderful, [2]angels
ἑπτὰ ἔχοντας πληγὰς ἑπτὰ τὰς ἐσχάτας,
[1]seven having [2]plagues [1]seven the last,
ὅτι ἐν αὐταῖς ἐτελέσθη ὁ θυμὸς τοῦ
because in them [4]was finished [1]the [2]anger –
θεοῦ. 2 Καὶ εἶδον ὡς θάλασσαν ὑαλίνην
[3]of God. And I saw as [2]sea [1]a glassy

sharp sickle in his hand.
15Then another angel came
out of the temple and called
in a loud voice to him who
was sitting on the cloud,
"Take your sickle and
reap, because the time to
reap has come, for the harvest of the earth is ripe."
16So he who was seated on
the cloud swung his sickle
over the earth, and the
earth was harvested.
17Another angel came out
of the temple in heaven,
and he too had a sharp sickle. 18Still another angel,
who had charge of the fire,
came from the altar and
called in a loud voice to him
who had the sharp sickle,
"Take your sharp sickle
and gather the clusters of
grapes from the earth's
vine, because its grapes are
ripe." 19The angel swung
his sickle on the earth,
gathered its grapes and
threw them into the great
winepress of God's wrath.
20They were trampled in
the winepress outside the
city, and blood flowed out
of the press, rising as high
as the horses' bridles for a
distance of 1,600 stadia.[r]

Chapter 15

Seven Angels With Seven Plagues

I SAW in heaven another
great and marvelous
sign: seven angels with the
seven last plagues—last,
because with them God's
wrath is completed. 2And I
saw what looked like a sea
of glass mixed with fire

[r]*20* That is, about 180 miles (about 300 kilometers)

and those who had come
off victorious from the
beast and from his image
and from the number of his
name, standing on the sea
of glass, holding harps of
God.
3And they *sang the
song of Moses the bond-
servant of God and the
song of the Lamb, saying,
"Great and marvelous
are Thy works,
O Lord God, the Al-
mighty;
Righteous and true
are Thy ways,
Thou King of the [w]na-
tions.
4"Who will not fear, O
Lord, and glorify
Thy name?
For Thou alone art
holy;
For ALL THE NATIONS
WILL COME AND WOR-
SHIP BEFORE THEE,
For Thy righteous
acts have been re-
vealed."
5After these things I
looked, and the temple of
the tabernacle of testimony
in heaven was opened,
6and the seven angels
who had the seven plagues
came out of the temple,
clothed in [x]linen, clean *and*
bright, and girded around
their breasts with golden
girdles.
7And one of the four liv-
ing creatures gave to the
seven angels seven golden
bowls full of the wrath of
God, who lives forever and
ever.
8And the temple was
filled with smoke from the
glory of God and from His
power; and no one was able
to enter the temple until the
seven plagues of the seven
angels were finished.

Chapter 16

Six Bowls of Wrath

AND I heard a loud voice
from the temple, say-
ing to the seven angels,
"Go and pour out the seven

[w] Some ancient mss. read *ages*
[x] Some mss. read *stone*

μεμιγμένην πυρί, καὶ τοὺς νικῶντας
having been mixed with fire, and the [ones] overcoming

ἐκ τοῦ θηρίου καὶ ἐκ τῆς εἰκόνος αὐτοῦ
of the beast and of the image of it

καὶ ἐκ τοῦ ἀριθμοῦ τοῦ ὀνόματος αὐτοῦ
and of the number of the name of it

ἑστῶτας ἐπὶ τὴν θάλασσαν τὴν ὑαλίνην,
standing on the [2]sea – [1]glassy,

ἔχοντας κιθάρας τοῦ θεοῦ. 3 καὶ ᾄδουσιν
having harps – of God. And they sing

τὴν ᾠδὴν Μωϋσέως τοῦ δούλου τοῦ
the song of Moses the slave –

θεοῦ καὶ τὴν ᾠδὴν τοῦ ἀρνίου, λέγοντες·
of God and the song of the Lamb, saying:

μεγάλα καὶ θαυμαστὰ τὰ ἔργα σου,
Great and wonderful the works of thee,

κύριε ὁ θεὸς ὁ παντοκράτωρ· δίκαιαι
[O] Lord – God the Almighty; righteous

καὶ ἀληθιναὶ αἱ ὁδοί σου, ὁ βασιλεὺς
and true the ways of thee, the king

τῶν ἐθνῶν· 4 τίς οὐ μὴ φοβηθῇ, κύριε,
of the nations; who will not fear, [O] Lord,

καὶ δοξάσει τὸ ὄνομά σου; ὅτι μόνος
and *will* glorify the name of thee? because [thou] only

ὅσιος, ὅτι πάντα τὰ ἔθνη ἥξουσιν καὶ
[art] holy, because all the nations will come and

προσκυνήσουσιν ἐνώπιόν σου, ὅτι τὰ
will worship before thee, because the

δικαιώματά σου ἐφανερώθησαν. 5 Καὶ
ordinances of thee were made manifest. And

μετὰ ταῦτα εἶδον, καὶ ἠνοίγη ὁ ναὸς
after these things I saw, and was opened the shrine

τῆς σκηνῆς τοῦ μαρτυρίου ἐν τῷ οὐρανῷ,
of the tabernacle of the testimony in – heaven,

6 καὶ ἐξῆλθον οἱ ἑπτὰ ἄγγελοι οἱ ἔχοντες
and [8]came forth [1]the [2]seven [3]angels – [4]having

τὰς ἑπτὰ πληγὰς ἐκ τοῦ ναοῦ, ἐνδεδυμένοι
[5]the [6]seven [7]plagues out of the shrine, *having been* clothed [in]

λίνον καθαρὸν λαμπρὸν καὶ περιεζωσμένοι
[3]linen [1]clean [2]bright and *having been* girdled

περὶ τὰ στήθη ζώνας χρυσᾶς. 7 καὶ
round the breasts [with] [2]girdles [1]golden. And

ἓν ἐκ τῶν τεσσάρων ζῴων ἔδωκεν τοῖς
one of the four living creatures gave to the

ἑπτὰ ἀγγέλοις ἑπτὰ φιάλας χρυσᾶς
seven angels seven [2]bowls [1]golden

γεμούσας τοῦ θυμοῦ τοῦ θεοῦ τοῦ ζῶντος
being filled of(with) the anger – of God – living

εἰς τοὺς αἰῶνας τῶν αἰώνων. 8 καὶ
unto the ages of the ages. And

ἐγεμίσθη ὁ ναὸς καπνοῦ ἐκ τῆς δόξης
was filled the shrine of(with) smoke of the glory

τοῦ θεοῦ καὶ ἐκ τῆς δυνάμεως αὐτοῦ,
— of God and of the power of him,

καὶ οὐδεὶς ἐδύνατο εἰσελθεῖν εἰς τὸν
and no one could *to* enter into the

ναὸν ἄχρι τελεσθῶσιν αἱ ἑπτὰ πληγαὶ
shrine until should be finished the seven plagues

τῶν ἑπτὰ ἀγγέλων. 16 Καὶ ἤκουσα
of the seven angels. And I heard

μεγάλης φωνῆς ἐκ τοῦ ναοῦ λεγούσης τοῖς
a great(loud) voice out of the shrine saying to the

ἑπτὰ ἀγγέλοις· ὑπάγετε καὶ ἐκχέετε τὰς ἑπτὰ
seven angels: Go ye and pour out the seven

and, standing beside the
sea, those who had been
victorious over the beast
and his image and over the
number of his name. They
held harps given them by
God 3and sang the song of
Moses the servant of God
and the song of the Lamb:
"Great and marvelous
are your deeds,
Lord God Almighty.
Just and true are your
ways,
King of the ages.
4Who will not fear you, O
Lord,
and bring glory to your
name?
For you alone are holy.
All nations will come
and worship before
you,
for your righteous acts
have been
revealed."
5After this I looked and in
heaven the temple, that
is, the tabernacle of the
Testimony, was opened.
6Out of the temple came,
the seven angels with the
seven plagues. They were
dressed in clean, shining
linen and wore golden
sashes around their chests.
7Then one of the four living
creatures gave to the seven
angels seven golden bowls
filled with the wrath of
God, who lives for ever and
ever. 8And the temple was
filled with smoke from the
glory of God and from his
power, and no one could
enter the temple until the
seven plagues of the seven
angels were completed.

Chapter 16

The Seven Bowls of God's Wrath

THEN I heard a loud
voice from the temple
saying to the seven angels,
"Go, pour out the seven

bowls of the wrath of God
into the earth.''
2And the first *angel* went
and poured out his bowl
into the earth; and it
became a loathsome and
malignant sore upon the
men who had the mark of
the beast and who wor-
shiped his image.
3And the second *angel*
poured out his bowl into
the sea, and it became
blood like *that* of a dead
man; and every living
[y]thing in the sea died.
4And the third *angel*
poured out his bowl into
the rivers and the springs of
waters; and [z]they became
blood.
5And I heard the angel of
the waters saying, "Righteous art Thou, who art and
who wast, O Holy One, be-
cause Thou didst judge
these things;
6for they poured out the
blood of saints and prophets, and Thou hast given
them blood to drink. They
deserve it."
7And I heard the altar
saying, "Yes, O Lord God,
the Almighty, true and
righteous are Thy judg-
ments."
8And the fourth *angel*
poured out his bowl upon
the sun; and it was given to
it to scorch men with fire.
9And men were scorched
with fierce heat; and they
blasphemed the name of
God who has the power
over these plagues; and
they did not repent, so as to
give Him glory.
10And the fifth *angel*
poured out his bowl upon
the throne of the beast; and
his kingdom became dark-

φιάλας τοῦ θυμοῦ τοῦ θεοῦ εἰς τὴν γῆν.
bowls of the anger – of God onto the earth.
2 Καὶ ἀπῆλθεν ὁ πρῶτος καὶ ἐξέχεεν τὴν
And [2]went away [1]the [3]first and poured out the
φιάλην αὐτοῦ εἰς τὴν γῆν· καὶ ἐγένετο
bowl of him onto the earth; and [5]came
ἕλκος κακὸν καὶ πονηρὸν ἐπὶ τοὺς ἀνθρώπους
[4]sore [1]a bad [2]and [3]evil on the men
τοὺς ἔχοντας τὸ χάραγμα τοῦ θηρίου καὶ
– having the mark of the beast and
τοὺς προσκυνοῦντας τῇ εἰκόνι αὐτοῦ. 3 Καὶ
– worshipping the image of it. And
ὁ δεύτερος ἐξέχεεν τὴν φιάλην αὐτοῦ
the second poured out the bowl of him
εἰς τὴν θάλασσαν· καὶ ἐγένετο αἷμα
onto the sea; and it became blood
ὡς νεκροῦ, καὶ πᾶσα ψυχὴ ζωῆς ἀπέθανεν,
as of a dead man, and every soul of life died,
τὰ ἐν τῇ θαλάσσῃ. 4 Καὶ ὁ τρίτος
the things in the sea. And the third
ἐξέχεεν τὴν φιάλην αὐτοῦ εἰς τοὺς
poured out the bowl of him onto the
ποταμοὺς καὶ τὰς πηγὰς τῶν ὑδάτων·
rivers and the fountains of the waters;
καὶ ἐγένετο αἷμα. 5 Καὶ ἤκουσα τοῦ
and it became blood. And I heard the
ἀγγέλου τῶν ὑδάτων λέγοντος· δίκαιος
angel of the waters saying: Righteous
εἶ, ὁ ὢν καὶ ὁ ἦν, ὁ ὅσιος, ὅτι
art thou, the being [one] and the [one who] was, the holy [one], because
=the one who is
ταῦτα ἔκρινας, 6 ὅτι αἷμα ἁγίων
[2]these things [1]thou judgedst, because [3][the] blood [4]of saints
καὶ προφητῶν ἐξέχεαν, καὶ αἷμα αὐτοῖς
[4]and [5]of prophets [1]they shed, and blood to them
δέδωκας πεῖν· ἄξιοί εἰσιν. 7 Καὶ ἤκουσα
thou hast given to drink; [2]worthy [1]they are. And I heard
τοῦ θυσιαστηρίου λέγοντος· ναί, κύριε
the altar saying: Yes, [O] Lord
ὁ θεὸς ὁ παντοκράτωρ, ἀληθιναὶ καὶ
– God the Almighty, true and
δίκαιαι αἱ κρίσεις σου. 8 Καὶ ὁ τέταρτος
righteous the judgments of thee. And the fourth
ἐξέχεεν τὴν φιάλην αὐτοῦ ἐπὶ τὸν ἥλιον·
poured out the bowl of him onto the sun;
καὶ ἐδόθη αὐτῷ καυματίσαι τοὺς
and it was given to him to burn –
ἀνθρώπους ἐν πυρί. 9 καὶ ἐκαυματίσθησαν
men with fire. And [2]were burnt [with]
οἱ ἄνθρωποι καῦμα μέγα, καὶ ἐβλασ-
– [1]men [4]heat [3]great, and they blas-
φήμησαν τὸ ὄνομα τοῦ θεοῦ τοῦ ἔχοντος
phemed the name – of God the [one] having
τὴν ἐξουσίαν ἐπὶ τὰς πληγὰς ταύτας,
the authority over these plagues,
καὶ οὐ μετενόησαν δοῦναι αὐτῷ δόξαν.
and they repented not to give [2]to him [1]glory.
10 Καὶ ὁ πέμπτος ἐξέχεεν τὴν φιάλην
And the fifth poured out the bowl
αὐτοῦ ἐπὶ τὸν θρόνον τοῦ θηρίου· καὶ
of him onto the throne of the beast; and
ἐγένετο ἡ βασιλεία αὐτοῦ ἐσκοτωμένη,
[4]became [1]the [2]kingdom [3]of it *having been* darkened,

bowls of God's wrath on
the earth."
2The first angel went and
poured out his bowl on the
land, and ugly and painful
sores broke out on the people who had the mark of the
beast and worshiped his
image.
3The second angel poured
out his bowl on the sea, and
it turned into blood like that
of a dead man, and every
living thing in the sea died.
4The third angel poured
out his bowl on the rivers
and springs of water, and
they became blood. 5Then I
heard the angel in charge of
the waters say:

"You are just in these
judgments,
you who are and who
were, the Holy One,
because you have so
judged;
6for they have shed the
blood of your saints
and prophets,
and you have given
them blood to drink
as they deserve."

7And I heard the altar respond:

"Yes, Lord God
Almighty,
true and just are your
judgments."

8The fourth angel poured
out his bowl on the sun, and
the sun was given power to
scorch people with fire.
9They were seared by the
intense heat and they
cursed the name of God,
who had control over these
plagues, but they refused to
repent and glorify him.
10The fifth angel poured
out his bowl on the throne
of the beast, and his kingdom was plunged into dark-

[y] Lit., *soul.* Some ancient mss. read *thing, the things in the sea.*
[z] Some ancient mss. read *it became*

ened; and they gnawed
their tongues because of
pain,
11and they blasphemed
the God of heaven because
of their pains and their
sores; and they did not repent of their deeds.
12And the sixth *angel*
poured out his bowl upon
the great river, the Euphrates; and its water was dried
up, that the way might be
prepared for the kings from
the east.

Armageddon

13And I saw *coming* out
of the mouth of the dragon
and out of the mouth of the
beast and out of the mouth
of the false prophet, three
unclean spirits like frogs;
14for they are spirits of
demons, performing signs,
which go out to the kings of
the whole world, to gather
them together for the war
of the great day of God, the
Almighty.
15("Behold, I am coming
like a thief. Blessed is the
one who stays awake and
keeps his garments, lest he
walk about naked and men
see his shame.")
16And they gathered them
together to the place which
in Hebrew is called [a]Har-
Magedon.

Seventh Bowl of Wrath

17And the seventh *angel*
poured out his bowl upon
the air; and a loud voice
came out of the temple
from the throne, saying,
"It is done."
18And there were flashes
of lightning and sounds and
peals of thunder; and there
was a great earthquake,
such as there had not been
since man came to be upon
the earth, so great an earthquake *was it, and* so
mighty.
19And the great city was
split into three parts, and

[a] Some authorities read *Armageddon*

καὶ ἐμασῶντο τὰς γλώσσας αὐτῶν ἐκ
and they(men) gnawed the tongues of them from
τοῦ πόνου, **11** καὶ ἐβλασφήμησαν τὸν θεὸν
the pain, and *they* blasphemed the God
τοῦ οὐρανοῦ ἐκ τῶν πόνων αὐτῶν καὶ
– of heaven from the pains of them and
ἐκ τῶν ἑλκῶν αὐτῶν, καὶ οὐ μετενόησαν
from the sores of them, and they repented not
ἐκ τῶν ἔργων αὐτῶν. **12** Καὶ ὁ ἕκτος
of the works of them. And the sixth
ἐξέχεεν τὴν φιάλην αὐτοῦ ἐπὶ τὸν ποταμὸν
poured out the bowl of him onto the [2]river
τὸν μέγαν Εὐφράτην· καὶ ἐξηράνθη τὸ
– [1]great Euphrates; and [4]was dried [1]the
ὕδωρ αὐτοῦ, ἵνα ἑτοιμασθῇ ἡ ὁδὸς τῶν
[2]water [3]of it, in order that [8]might be prepared [1]the [2]way [3]of the
βασιλέων τῶν ἀπὸ ἀνατολῆς ἡλίου. **13** Καὶ
[4]kings – [5]from [6][the] rising [7]of [the] sun. And
εἶδον ἐκ τοῦ στόματος τοῦ δράκοντος
I saw out of the mouth of the dragon
καὶ ἐκ τοῦ στόματος τοῦ θηρίου καὶ
and out of the mouth of the beast and
ἐκ τοῦ στόματος τοῦ ψευδοπροφήτου
out of the mouth of the false prophet
πνεύματα τρία ἀκάθαρτα ὡς βάτραχοι·
[3]spirits [1]three [2]unclean [coming] as frogs;
14 εἰσὶν γὰρ πνεύματα δαιμονίων ποιοῦντα
for they are spirits of demons doing
σημεῖα, ἃ ἐκπορεύεται ἐπὶ τοὺς βασιλεῖς
signs, which go*es* forth unto the kings
τῆς οἰκουμένης ὅλης, συναγαγεῖν αὐτοὺς
of the [2]inhabited [earth] [1]whole, to assemble them
εἰς τὸν πόλεμον τῆς ἡμέρας τῆς μεγάλης
to the war of the [2]day – [1]great
τοῦ θεοῦ τοῦ παντοκράτορος. **15** Ἰδοὺ
– of God *of* the Almighty. Behold
ἔρχομαι ὡς κλέπτης· μακάριος ὁ γρηγορῶν
I am coming as a thief: blessed [is] the [one] watching
καὶ τηρῶν τὰ ἱμάτια αὐτοῦ, ἵνα μὴ
and keeping the garments of him, lest
γυμνὸς περιπατῇ καὶ βλέπωσιν τὴν
naked he walk and they(men) see the
ἀσχημοσύνην αὐτοῦ. **16** Καὶ συνήγαγεν
shame of him. And [t]he[y] assembled
αὐτοὺς εἰς τὸν τόπον τὸν καλούμενον
them in the place – *being* called
Ἑβραϊστὶ Ἁρμαγεδών. **17** Καὶ ὁ ἕβδομος
in Hebrew Harmagedon. And the seventh
ἐξέχεεν τὴν φιάλην αὐτοῦ ἐπὶ τὸν ἀέρα·
poured out the bowl of him on the air;
καὶ ἐξῆλθεν φωνὴ μεγάλη ἐκ τοῦ ναοῦ
and [3]came *out* [2]voice [1]a great(loud) out of the shrine
ἀπὸ τοῦ θρόνου λέγουσα· γέγονεν. **18** καὶ
from the throne saying: It has occurred. And
ἐγένοντο ἀστραπαὶ καὶ φωναὶ καὶ βρονταί,
there were lightnings and voices and thunders,
καὶ σεισμὸς ἐγένετο μέγας, οἷος οὐκ
and [2]earthquake [3]occurred [1]a great, such as not
ἐγένετο ἀφ᾽ οὗ ἄνθρωπος ἐγένετο ἐπὶ
did occur from when† man was on
τῆς γῆς, τηλικοῦτος σεισμὸς οὕτω μέγας.
the earth, such an earthquake so great.
19 καὶ ἐγένετο ἡ πόλις ἡ μεγάλη εἰς
And [4]became [1]the [3]city – [2]great into

ness. Men gnawed their
tongues in agony 11and
cursed the God of heaven
because of their pains and
their sores, but they re-
fused to repent of what
they had done.
12The sixth angel poured
out his bowl on the great
river Euphrates, and its
water was dried up to prepare the way for the kings
from the East. 13Then I saw
three evil[u] spirits that
looked like frogs; they
came out of the mouth of
the dragon, out of the
mouth of the beast and out
of the mouth of the false
prophet. 14They are spirits
of demons performing mi-
raculous signs, and they go
out to the kings of the
whole world, to gather
them for the battle on the
great day of God Almighty.
15"Behold, I come like a
thief! Blessed is he who
stays awake and keeps his
clothes with him, so that he
may not go naked and be
shamefully exposed."
16Then they gathered the
kings together to the place
that in Hebrew is called Armageddon.
17The seventh angel
poured out his bowl into
the air, and out of the temple came a loud voice from
the throne, saying, "It is
done!" 18Then there came
flashes of lightning, rumblings, peals of thunder and
a severe earthquake. No
earthquake like it has ever
occurred since man has
been on earth, so tremen-
dous was the quake. 19The
great city split into three

[u] *13* Greek *unclean*

the cities of the nations fell. And Babylon the great was remembered before God, to give her the cup of the wine of His fierce wrath.
20 And every island fled away, and the mountains were not found.
21 And huge hailstones, about [b]one hundred pounds each, *came down from heaven upon men; and men blasphemed God because of the plague of the hail, because its plague *was extremely severe.

τρία μέρη, καὶ αἱ πόλεις τῶν ἐθνῶν
three parts, and the cities of the nations
ἔπεσαν. καὶ Βαβυλὼν ἡ μεγάλη ἐμνήσθη
fell. And Babylon the great was remembered
ἐνώπιον τοῦ θεοῦ δοῦναι αὐτῇ τὸ ποτήριον
before – God to give to her/it* the cup
τοῦ οἴνου τοῦ θυμοῦ τῆς ὀργῆς αὐτοῦ.
of the wine of the anger of the wrath of him.
20 καὶ πᾶσα νῆσος ἔφυγεν, καὶ ὄρη
And every island fled, and mountains
οὐχ εὑρέθησαν. 21 καὶ χάλαζα μεγάλη
were not found. And [2]hail [1]a great
ὡς ταλαντιαία καταβαίνει ἐκ τοῦ οὐρανοῦ
as a talent in size comes down out of – heaven
ἐπὶ τοὺς ἀνθρώπους· καὶ ἐβλασφήμησαν
on – men; and [2]blasphemed
οἱ ἄνθρωποι τὸν θεὸν ἐκ τῆς πληγῆς
– [1]men – God from the plague
τῆς χαλάζης, ὅτι μεγάλη ἐστὶν ἡ πληγὴ
of the hail, because [6]great [4]is [1]the [2]plague
αὐτῆς σφόδρα.
[3]of it [5]exceeding.

parts, and the cities of the nations collapsed. God remembered Babylon the Great and gave her the cup filled with the wine of the fury of his wrath. 20 Every island fled away and the mountains could not be found. 21 From the sky huge hailstones of about a hundred pounds each fell upon men. And they cursed God on account of the plague of hail, because the plague was so terrible.

Chapter 17

The Doom of Babylon

AND one of the seven angels who had the seven bowls came and spoke with me, saying, "Come here, I shall show you the judgment of the great harlot who sits on many waters,
2 with whom the kings of the earth committed *acts of* immorality, and those who dwell on the earth were made drunk with the wine of her immorality."
3 And he carried me away [c]in the Spirit into a wilderness; and I saw a woman sitting on a scarlet beast, full of blasphemous names, having seven heads and ten horns.
4 And the woman was clothed in purple and scarlet, and adorned with gold and precious stones and pearls, having in her hand a gold cup full of abominations and of the unclean things of her immorality,
5 and upon her forehead a name *was* written, a mys-

17 Καὶ ἦλθεν εἷς ἐκ τῶν ἑπτὰ ἀγγέλων
And came one of the seven angels
τῶν ἐχόντων τὰς ἑπτὰ φιάλας, καὶ
– having the seven bowls, and
ἐλάλησεν μετ' ἐμοῦ λέγων· δεῦρο, δείξω
spoke with me saying: Come, I will show
σοι τὸ κρίμα τῆς πόρνης τῆς μεγάλης
thee the judgment of the [2]harlot – [1]great
τῆς καθημένης ἐπὶ ὑδάτων πολλῶν, 2 μεθ'
– sitting on [2]waters [1]many, with
ἧς ἐπόρνευσαν οἱ βασιλεῖς τῆς γῆς,
whom [5]practised fornication [1]the [2]kings [3]of the [4]earth,
καὶ ἐμεθύσθησαν οἱ κατοικοῦντες τὴν γῆν
and [5]became drunk [1]the [2]dwelling [on] [ones] [3]the [4]earth
ἐκ τοῦ οἴνου τῆς πορνείας αὐτῆς. 3 καὶ
from the wine of the fornication of her. And
ἀπήνεγκέν με εἰς ἔρημον ἐν πνεύματι.
he carried away me into a desert in spirit.
καὶ εἶδον γυναῖκα καθημένην ἐπὶ θηρίον
And I saw a woman sitting on [2]beast
κόκκινον, γέμοντα ὀνόματα βλασφημίας,
[1]a scarlet, *being* filled [with] names of blasphemy,
ἔχοντα κεφαλὰς ἑπτὰ καὶ κέρατα δέκα.
having [2]heads [1]seven and [2]horns [1]ten.
4 καὶ ἡ γυνὴ ἦν περιβεβλημένη πορφυροῦν
And the woman was *having been* clothed [in] purple
καὶ κόκκινον, καὶ κεχρυσωμένη χρυσίῳ
and scarlet, and *having been* gilded with gold
καὶ λίθῳ τιμίῳ καὶ μαργαρίταις, ἔχουσα
and [2]stone [1]precious and pearls, having
ποτήριον χρυσοῦν ἐν τῇ χειρὶ αὐτῆς
[2]cup [1]a golden in the hand of her
γέμον βδελυγμάτων καὶ τὰ ἀκάθαρτα
being filled of(with) abominations and the unclean things
τῆς πορνείας αὐτῆς, 5 καὶ ἐπὶ τὸ
of the fornication of her, and on the
μέτωπον αὐτῆς ὄνομα γεγραμμένον,
forehead of her a name *having been* written,

Chapter 17

The Woman on the Beast

ONE of the seven angels who had the seven bowls came and said to me, "Come, I will show you the punishment of the great prostitute, who sits on many waters. 2 With her the kings of the earth committed adultery and the inhabitants of the earth were intoxicated with the wine of her adulteries."
3 Then the angel carried me away in the Spirit into a desert. There I saw a woman sitting on a scarlet beast that was covered with blasphemous names and had seven heads and ten horns. 4 The woman was dressed in purple and scarlet, and was glittering with gold, precious stones and pearls. She held a golden cup in her hand, filled with abominable things and the filth of her adulteries. 5 This title was written on her forehead:

[b] Lit., *the weight of a talent*
[c] Or, *in spirit*

* Even in English a city is often personified as feminine.

tery, "BABYLON THE
GREAT, THE MOTHER
OF HARLOTS AND OF
THE ABOMINATIONS
OF THE EARTH."
6And I saw the woman
drunk with the blood of the
saints, and with the blood
of the witnesses of Jesus.
And when I saw her, I wondered greatly.
7And the angel said to
me, "Why do you wonder?
I shall tell you the mystery
of the woman and of the
beast that carries her,
which has the seven heads
and the ten horns.
8"The beast that you
saw was and is not, and is
about to come up out of the
abyss and [d]to go to de-
struction. And those who
dwell on the earth will wonder, whose name has not
been written in the book of
life from the foundation of
the world, when they see
the beast, that he was and is
not and will come.
9"Here is the mind
which has wisdom. The
seven heads are seven
mountains on which the
woman sits,
10and they are seven
kings; five have fallen, one
is, the other has not yet
come; and when he comes,
he must remain a little
while.
11"And the beast which
was and is not, is himself
also an eighth, and is *one* of
the seven, and he goes to
destruction.
12"And the ten horns
which you saw are ten
kings, who have not yet received a kingdom, but they
receive authority as kings
with the beast for one hour.

μυστήριον, ΒΑΒΥΛΩΝ Η ΜΕΓΑΛΗ,
a mystery, BABYLON THE GREAT,
Η ΜΗΤΗΡ ΤΩΝ ΠΟΡΝΩΝ ΚΑΙ
The Mother of the Harlots and
ΤΩΝ ΒΔΕΛΥΓΜΑΤΩΝ ΤΗΣ ΓΗΣ.
of the Abominations of the Earth.
6 καὶ εἶδον τὴν γυναῖκα μεθύουσαν ἐκ
And I saw the woman *being* drunk from
τοῦ αἵματος τῶν ἁγίων καὶ ἐκ τοῦ
the blood of the saints and from the
αἵματος τῶν μαρτύρων Ἰησοῦ. Καὶ
blood of the witnesses of Jesus. And
ἐθαύμασα ἰδὼν αὐτὴν θαῦμα μέγα. 7 καὶ
[2]I wondered [1]seeing [3]her [4][with] [6]wonder [5]a great. And
εἶπέν μοι ὁ ἄγγελος· διὰ τί ἐθαύμασας;
[3]said [4]to me [1]the [2]angel: Why didst thou wonder?
ἐγὼ ἐρῶ σοι τὸ μυστήριον τῆς γυναικὸς
I will tell thee the mystery of the woman
καὶ τοῦ θηρίου τοῦ βαστάζοντος αὐτὴν
and of the beast – carrying her
τοῦ ἔχοντος τὰς ἑπτὰ κεφαλὰς καὶ τὰ
– having the seven heads and the
δέκα κέρατα. 8 Τὸ θηρίον ὃ εἶδες ἦν
ten horns. The beast which thou sawest was
καὶ οὐκ ἔστιν, καὶ μέλλει ἀναβαίνειν
and is not, and is about to come up
ἐκ τῆς ἀβύσσου καὶ εἰς ἀπώλειαν ὑπάγει·
out of the abyss and [2]to [3]destruction [1]goes;
καὶ θαυμασθήσονται οἱ κατοικοῦντες ἐπὶ
and [6]will wonder [1]the [ones] [2]dwelling [3]on
τῆς γῆς, ὧν οὐ γέγραπται τὸ ὄνομα
[4]the [5]earth, of whom [3]has not been written [1]the [2]name
ἐπὶ τὸ βιβλίον τῆς ζωῆς ἀπὸ καταβολῆς
on the scroll – of life from [the] foundation
κόσμου, βλεπόντων τὸ θηρίον ὅτι ἦν
of [the] world, seeing the beast that it was
καὶ οὐκ ἔστιν καὶ παρέσται. 9 ὧδε
and is not and is present. Here [is]
ὁ νοῦς ὁ ἔχων σοφίαν. αἱ ἑπτὰ
the mind – having wisdom. The seven
κεφαλαὶ ἑπτὰ ὄρη εἰσίν, ὅπου ἡ γυνὴ
heads [2]seven [3]mountains [1]are, where the woman
κάθηται ἐπ' αὐτῶν, καὶ βασιλεῖς ἑπτά
sits on them, and [3]kings [2]seven
εἰσιν· 10 οἱ πέντε ἔπεσαν, ὁ εἷς ἔστιν,
[1]are: the five fell, the one is,
ὁ ἄλλος οὔπω ἦλθεν, καὶ ὅταν ἔλθῃ
the other not yet came, and whenever he comes
ὀλίγον αὐτὸν δεῖ μεῖναι. 11 καὶ τὸ
[4]a little [while] [2]him [1]it behoves [3]to remain. And the
θηρίον ὃ ἦν καὶ οὐκ ἔστιν, καὶ αὐτὸς
beast which was and is not, even he
ὄγδοός ἐστιν, καὶ ἐκ τῶν ἑπτά ἐστιν,
[2]an eighth [1]is, and [2]of [3]the [4]seven [1]is,
καὶ εἰς ἀπώλειαν ὑπάγει. 12 καὶ τὰ
and to destruction goes. And the
δέκα κέρατα ἃ εἶδες δέκα βασιλεῖς
ten horns which thou sawest [2]ten [3]kings
εἰσιν, οἵτινες βασιλείαν οὔπω ἔλαβον,
[1]are, who a kingdom not yet received,
ἀλλὰ ἐξουσίαν ὡς βασιλεῖς μίαν ὥραν
but [2]authority [3]as [4]kings [5]one [6]hour
λαμβάνουσιν μετὰ τοῦ θηρίου. 13 οὗτοι
[1]receive with the beast. These

MYSTERY
BABYLON THE GREAT
THE MOTHER OF PROSTITUTES
AND OF THE ABOMINATIONS
OF THE EARTH.
6I saw that the woman was
drunk with the blood of the
saints, the blood of those
who bore testimony to
Jesus.
When I saw her, I was
greatly astonished. 7Then
the angel said to me: "Why
are you astonished? I will
explain to you the mystery
of the woman and of the
beast she rides, which has
the seven heads and ten
horns. 8The beast, which
you saw, once was, now is
not, and will come up out of
the Abyss and go to his destruction. The inhabitants
of the earth whose names
have not been written in the
book of life from the creation of the world will be
astonished when they see
the beast, because he once
was, now is not, and yet
will come.
9"This calls for a mind
with wisdom. The seven
heads are seven hills on
which the woman sits.
10They are also seven
kings. Five have fallen, one
is, the other has not yet
come; but when he does
come, he must remain for a
little while. 11The beast
who once was, and now is
not, is an eighth king. He
belongs to the seven and is
going to his destruction.
12"The ten horns you saw
are ten kings who have not
yet received a kingdom,
but who for one hour will
receive authority as kings
along with the beast.

[d]Some ancient mss. read *he goes*

[13]"These have one pur-
pose and they give their
power and authority to the
beast.

Victory for the Lamb

[14]"These will wage war
against the Lamb, and the
Lamb will overcome them,
because He is Lord of lords
and King of kings, and
those who are with Him *are
the* called and chosen and
faithful."
[15]And he *said to me,
"The waters which you
saw where the harlot sits,
are peoples and multitudes
and nations and tongues.
[16]"And the ten horns
which you saw, and the
beast, these will hate the
harlot and will make her
desolate and naked, and
will eat her flesh and will
burn her up with fire.
[17]"For God has put it in
their hearts to execute His
purpose by having a com-
mon purpose, and by giving
their kingdom to the beast,
until the words of God
should be fulfilled.
[18]"And the woman whom
you saw is the great city,
which reigns over the kings
of the earth."

μίαν γνώμην ἔχουσιν, καὶ τὴν δύναμιν
one mind have, and the power

καὶ ἐξουσίαν αὐτῶν τῷ θηρίῳ διδόασιν.
and authority of them to the beast they give.

14 οὗτοι μετὰ τοῦ ἀρνίου πολεμήσουσιν
These [2]with [3]the [4]Lamb [1]will make war

καὶ τὸ ἀρνίον νικήσει αὐτούς, ὅτι κύριος
and the Lamb will overcome them, because [2]Lord

κυρίων ἐστὶν καὶ βασιλεὺς βασιλέων, καὶ
[3]of lords [1]he is and King of kings, and

οἱ μετ' αὐτοῦ κλητοὶ καὶ ἐκλεκτοὶ καὶ
the [ones] with him [are] called and chosen and

πιστοί. 15 Καὶ λέγει μοι· τὰ ὕδατα
faithful. And he says to me: The waters

ἃ εἶδες, οὗ ἡ πόρνη κάθηται, λαοὶ
which thou sawest, where the harlot sits, peoples

καὶ ὄχλοι εἰσὶν καὶ ἔθνη καὶ γλῶσσαι.
and crowds are and nations and tongues.

16 καὶ τὰ δέκα κέρατα ἃ εἶδες καὶ
And the ten horns which thou sawest and

τὸ θηρίον, οὗτοι μισήσουσιν τὴν πόρνην,
the beast, these will hate the harlot,

καὶ ἠρημωμένην ποιήσουσιν αὐτὴν καὶ
and [3]*having been* desolated [1]will make [2]her and

γυμνήν, καὶ τὰς σάρκας αὐτῆς φάγονται,
naked, and [2]the [3]flesh*es* [4]of her [1]will eat,

καὶ αὐτὴν κατακαύσουσιν [ἐν] πυρί· 17 ὁ
and [2]her [1]will consume with fire; –

γὰρ θεὸς ἔδωκεν εἰς τὰς καρδίας αὐτῶν
for God gave into the hearts of them

ποιῆσαι τὴν γνώμην αὐτοῦ, καὶ ποιῆσαι
to do the mind of him, and to make

μίαν γνώμην καὶ δοῦναι τὴν βασιλείαν
one mind and to give the kingdom

αὐτῶν τῷ θηρίῳ, ἄχρι τελεσθήσονται οἱ
of them to the beast, until [4]shall be accomplished [1]the

λόγοι τοῦ θεοῦ. 18 καὶ ἡ γυνὴ ἣν
[2]words – [3]of God. And the woman whom

εἶδες ἔστιν ἡ πόλις ἡ μεγάλη ἡ ἔχουσα
thou sawest is the [2]city – [1]great – having

βασιλείαν ἐπὶ τῶν βασιλέων τῆς γῆς.
a kingdom over the kings of the earth.

[13]They have one purpose
and will give their power
and authority to the beast.
[14]They will make war
against the Lamb, but the
Lamb will overcome them
because he is Lord of lords
and King of kings—and
with him will be his called,
chosen and faithful followers."
[15]Then the angel said to
me, "The waters you saw,
where the prostitute sits,
are peoples, multitudes,
nations and languages.
[16]The beast and the ten
horns you saw will hate the
prostitute. They will bring
her to ruin and leave her
naked; they will eat her
flesh and burn her with fire.
[17]For God has put it into
their hearts to accomplish
his purpose by agreeing to
give the beast their power
to rule, until God's words
are fulfilled. [18]The woman
you saw is the great city
that rules over the kings of
the earth."

Chapter 18

Babylon Is Fallen

AFTER these things I
saw another angel
coming down from heaven,
having great authority, and
the earth was illumined
with his glory.
[2]And he cried out with a
mighty voice, saying,
"Fallen, fallen is Babylon
the great! And she has
become a dwelling place of
demons and a prison of
every unclean spirit, and a
prison of every unclean and
hateful bird.
[3]"For all the nations
[e]have drunk of the wine of
the passion of her immoral-

18 Μετὰ ταῦτα εἶδον ἄλλον ἄγγελον
After these things I saw another angel

καταβαίνοντα ἐκ τοῦ οὐρανοῦ, ἔχοντα
coming down out of – heaven, having

ἐξουσίαν μεγάλην, καὶ ἡ γῆ ἐφωτίσθη
[2]authority [1]great, and the earth was enlightened

ἐκ τῆς δόξης αὐτοῦ. 2 καὶ ἔκραξεν
from the glory of him. And he cried

ἐν ἰσχυρᾷ φωνῇ λέγων· ἔπεσεν ἔπεσεν
in a strong voice saying: Fell[,] fell

Βαβυλὼν ἡ μεγάλη, καὶ ἐγένετο κατοικητή-
Babylon the great, and became a dwelling-

ριον δαιμονίων καὶ φυλακὴ παντὸς
place of demons and a prison of every

πνεύματος ἀκαθάρτου καὶ φυλακὴ παντὸς
[2]spirit [1]unclean and a prison of every

ὀρνέου ἀκαθάρτου καὶ μεμισημένου, 3 ὅτι
[4]bird [1]unclean [2]and [3]*having been* hated, because

ἐκ τοῦ οἴνου τοῦ θυμοῦ τῆς πορνείας
[8]of [9]the [7]wine [6]of the [5]anger [10]of the [11]fornication

Chapter 18

The Fall of Babylon

AFTER this I saw anoth-
er angel coming down
from heaven. He had great
authority, and the earth
was illuminated by his
splendor. [2]With a mighty
voice he shouted:

"Fallen! Fallen is
Babylon the Great!
She has become a
home for demons
and a haunt for every
evil[v] spirit,
a haunt for every
unclean and
detestable bird.
[3]For all the nations have
drunk
the maddening wine of
her adulteries.

[e]Many ancient mss. read *have fallen by*

[v]2 Greek *unclean*

ity, and the kings of the earth have committed *acts of* immorality with her, and the merchants of the earth have become rich by the wealth of her sensuality."
4And I heard another voice from heaven, saying, "Come out of her, my people, that you may not participate in her sins and that you may not receive of her plagues;
5for her sins have piled up as high as heaven, and God has remembered her iniquities.
6"Pay her back even as she has paid, and give back *to her* double according to her deeds; in the cup which she has mixed, mix twice as much for her.
7"To the degree that she glorified herself and lived sensuously, to the same degree give her torment and mourning; for she says in her heart, 'I SIT *as* A QUEEN AND I AM NOT A WIDOW, and will never see mourning.'
8"For this reason in one day her plagues will come, pestilence and mourning and famine, and she will be burned up with fire; for the Lord God who judges her is strong.

Lament for Babylon

9"And the kings of the earth, who committed *acts of* immorality and lived sensuously with her, will weep and lament over her when they see the smoke of her burning,
10standing at a distance because of the fear of her torment, saying, 'Woe, woe, the great city, Babylon, the strong city! For in

αὐτῆς πέπωκαν πάντα τὰ ἔθνη, καὶ
12of her 4have drunk 1all 2the 3nations, and
οἱ βασιλεῖς τῆς γῆς μετ' αὐτῆς ἐπόρνευσαν,
the kings of the earth with her practised fornication,
καὶ οἱ ἔμποροι τῆς γῆς ἐκ τῆς δυνάμεως
and the merchants of the earth 2from 3the 4power
τοῦ στρήνους αὐτῆς ἐπλούτησαν. **4** Καὶ
5of the 6luxury 7of her 1became rich. And
ἤκουσα ἄλλην φωνὴν ἐκ τοῦ οὐρανοῦ
I heard another voice out of – heaven
λέγουσαν· ἐξέλθατε ὁ λαός μου ἐξ αὐτῆς,
saying: Come ye *out*[,] the people of me[,] out of her,
ἵνα μὴ συγκοινωνήσητε ταῖς ἁμαρτίαις
lest ye share in the sins
αὐτῆς, καὶ ἐκ τῶν πληγῶν αὐτῆς ἵνα
of her, and 3of 4the 5plagues 6of her 1lest
μὴ λάβητε· **5** ὅτι ἐκολλήθησαν αὐτῆς αἱ
2ye receive; because 4joined together 3of her 1the
ἁμαρτίαι ἄχρι τοῦ οὐρανοῦ, καὶ ἐμνημό-
2sins up to – heaven, and 2remem-
νευσεν ὁ θεὸς τὰ ἀδικήματα αὐτῆς.
bered – 1God the misdeeds of her.
6 ἀπόδοτε αὐτῇ ὡς καὶ αὐτὴ ἀπέδωκεν,
Give ye back to her as indeed she gave back,
καὶ διπλώσατε τὰ διπλᾶ κατὰ τὰ ἔργα
and double ye the double according to the works
αὐτῆς· ἐν τῷ ποτηρίῳ ᾧ ἐκέρασεν
of her; in the cup in which she mixed
κεράσατε αὐτῇ διπλοῦν· **7** ὅσα ἐδόξασεν
mix ye to her double; by what things she glorified
αὐτὴν καὶ ἐστρηνίασεν, τοσοῦτον δότε
her[self] and luxuriated, by so much give ye
αὐτῇ βασανισμὸν καὶ πένθος. ὅτι ἐν
to her torment and sorrow. Because in
τῇ καρδίᾳ αὐτῆς λέγει ὅτι κάθημαι
the heart of her she says[,] – I sit
βασίλισσα καὶ χήρα οὐκ εἰμὶ καὶ πένθος
a queen and a widow I am not and sorrow
οὐ μὴ ἴδω· **8** διὰ τοῦτο ἐν μιᾷ ἡμέρᾳ
by no means I see; therefore in one day
ἥξουσιν αἱ πληγαὶ αὐτῆς, θάνατος καὶ
will come the plagues of her, death and
πένθος καὶ λιμός, καὶ ἐν πυρὶ κατακαυ-
sorrow and famine, and with fire she will be
θήσεται· ὅτι ἰσχυρὸς κύριος ὁ θεὸς ὁ
consumed; because strong [is] [the] Lord – God the
κρίνας αὐτήν. **9** καὶ κλαύσουσιν καὶ
[one] judging her. And 4will weep 6and
κόψονται ἐπ' αὐτὴν οἱ βασιλεῖς τῆς
7wail 8over 9her 1the 2kings 3of the
γῆς οἱ μετ' αὐτῆς πορνεύσαντες καὶ
4earth 10the [ones] 12with 13her 11having practised fornication and
στρηνιάσαντες, ὅταν βλέπωσιν τὸν καπνὸν
having luxuriated, when*ever* they see the smoke
τῆς πυρώσεως αὐτῆς, **10** ἀπὸ μακρόθεν
of the burning of her, 2from 3afar
ἑστηκότες διὰ τὸν φόβον τοῦ βασανισμοῦ
1standing because of the fear of the torment
αὐτῆς, λέγοντες· οὐαὶ οὐαί, ἡ πόλις
of her, saying: Woe[,] woe, the 2city
ἡ μεγάλη, Βαβυλὼν ἡ πόλις ἡ ἰσχυρά,
– 1great, Babylon the 2city – 1strong,

The kings of the earth
committed adultery
with her,
and the merchants of
the earth grew rich
from her excessive
luxuries."
4Then I heard another voice from heaven say:

"Come out of her, my
people,
so that you will not
share in her sins,
so that you will not
receive any of her
plagues;
5for her sins are piled up
to heaven,
and God has
remembered her
crimes.
6Give back to her as she
has given;
pay her back double
for what she has
done.
Mix her a double
portion from her
own cup.
7Give her as much torture
and grief
as the glory and luxury
she gave herself.
In her heart she boasts,
'I sit as queen; I am not
a widow,
and I will never
mourn.'
8Therefore in one day her
plagues will
overtake her:
death, mourning and
famine.
She will be consumed by
fire,
for mighty is the Lord
God who judges her.

9"When the kings of the earth who committed adultery with her and shared her luxury see the smoke of her burning, they will weep and mourn over her. 10Terrified at her torment, they will stand far off and cry:

" 'Woe! Woe, O great
city,
O Babylon, city of
power!

one hour your judgment has come.'
11"And the merchants of the earth weep and mourn over her, because no one buys their cargoes any more;
12cargoes of gold and silver and precious stones and pearls and fine linen and purple and silk and scarlet, and every *kind of* citron wood and every article of ivory and every article *made* from very costly wood and bronze and iron and marble,
13and cinnamon and spice and incense and perfume and frankincense and wine and olive oil and fine flour and wheat and cattle and sheep, and *cargoes* of horses and chariots and slaves and human lives.
14"And the fruit you long for has gone from you, and all things that were luxurious and splendid have passed away from you and *men* will no longer find them.
15"The merchants of these things, who became rich from her, will stand at a distance because of the fear of her torment, weeping and mourning,
16saying, 'Woe, woe, the great city, she who was clothed in fine linen and purple and scarlet, and adorned with gold and precious stones and pearls;
17for in one hour such great wealth has been laid waste!' And every shipmaster and every passenger and sailor, and as many

ὅτι μιᾷ ὥρᾳ ἦλθεν ἡ κρίσις σου. 11 καὶ
because in one hour came the judgment of thee. And
οἱ ἔμποροι τῆς γῆς κλαίουσιν καὶ
the merchants of the earth weep and
πενθοῦσιν ἐπ' αὐτήν, ὅτι τὸν γόμον
sorrow over her, because [4]the [5]cargo
αὐτῶν οὐδεὶς ἀγοράζει οὐκέτι, 12 γόμον
[6]of them [1]no one [3]buys [2]any more, cargo
χρυσοῦ καὶ ἀργύρου καὶ λίθου τιμίου
of gold and of silver and [2]stone [1]of valuable
καὶ μαργαριτῶν καὶ βυσσίνου καὶ πορφύρας
and of pearls and of fine linen and of purple
καὶ σηρικοῦ καὶ κοκκίνου, καὶ πᾶν
and of silk and of scarlet, and all
ξύλον θύϊνον καὶ πᾶν σκεῦος ἐλεφάντινον
[2]wood [1]thyine and every [2]vessel [1]ivory
καὶ πᾶν σκεῦος ἐκ ξύλου τιμιωτάτου
and every vessel of [2]wood [1]very valuable
καὶ χαλκοῦ καὶ σιδήρου καὶ μαρμάρου,
and of bronze and of iron and of marble,
13 καὶ κιννάμωμον καὶ ἄμωμον καὶ
and cinnamon and spice and
θυμιάματα καὶ μύρον καὶ λίβανον καὶ
incenses and ointment and frankincense and
οἶνον καὶ ἔλαιον καὶ σεμίδαλιν καὶ σῖτον
wine and oil and fine meal and corn
καὶ κτήνη καὶ πρόβατα, καὶ ἵππων
and beasts of burden and sheep, and of horses
καὶ ῥεδῶν καὶ σωμάτων, καὶ ψυχὰς
and of carriages and of bodies, and souls
ἀνθρώπων. 14 καὶ ἡ ὀπώρα σου τῆς
of men. And the fruit [5]of thee [1]of the
ἐπιθυμίας τῆς ψυχῆς ἀπῆλθεν ἀπὸ σοῦ,
[2]lust [3]of the [4]soul went away from thee,
καὶ πάντα τὰ λιπαρὰ καὶ τὰ λαμπρὰ
and all the sumptuous things and the bright things
ἀπώλετο ἀπὸ σοῦ, καὶ οὐκέτι οὐ μὴ
perished from thee, and no more by no(any) means
αὐτὰ εὑρήσουσιν. 15 οἱ ἔμποροι τούτων,
[2]them [1]shall they find. The merchants of these things,
οἱ πλουτήσαντες ἀπ' αὐτῆς, ἀπὸ μακρόθεν
the [ones] having been rich from her, [2]from [3]afar
στήσονται διὰ τὸν φόβον τοῦ βασανισμοῦ
[1]will stand because of the fear of the torment
αὐτῆς κλαίοντες καὶ πενθοῦντες, 16 λέγοντες·
of her weeping and sorrowing, saying:
οὐαὶ οὐαί, ἡ πόλις ἡ μεγάλη, ἡ περι-
Woe[,] woe, the [2]city – [1]great, – *having*
βεβλημένη βύσσινον καὶ πορφυροῦν καὶ
been clothed [with] fine linen and purple and
κόκκινον, καὶ κεχρυσωμένη ἐν χρυσίῳ
scarlet, and *having been* gilded with gold
καὶ λίθῳ τιμίῳ καὶ μαργαρίτῃ, 17 ὅτι
and [2]stone [1]valuable and pearl, because
μιᾷ ὥρᾳ ἠρημώθη ὁ τοσοῦτος πλοῦτος.
in one hour [3]was made desolate [1]such great [2]wealth.
καὶ πᾶς κυβερνήτης καὶ πᾶς ὁ ἐπὶ
And every steersman and [1]every [2]one [4]to
τόπον πλέων καὶ ναῦται καὶ ὅσοι τὴν
[5]a place [3]sailing and sailors and as many as [2]the

In one hour your doom
has come!'

11"The merchants of the
earth will weep and mourn
over her because no one
buys their cargoes any
more—12cargoes of gold,
silver, precious stones and
pearls; fine linen, purple,
silk and scarlet cloth; every
sort of citron wood, and articles of every kind made of
ivory, costly wood,
bronze, iron and marble;
13cargoes of cinnamon and
spice, of incense, myrrh
and frankincense, of wine
and olive oil, of fine flour
and wheat; cattle and
sheep; horses and car-
riages; and bodies and
souls of men.
14"They will say, 'The
fruit you longed for is gone
from you. All your riches
and splendor have van-
ished, never to be recov-
ered.' 15The merchants
who sold these things and
gained their wealth from
her will stand far off, terrified at her torment. They
will weep and mourn 16and
cry out:

"'Woe! Woe, O great
city,
dressed in fine linen,
purple and scarlet,
and glittering with
gold, precious
stones and pearls!
17In one hour such great
wealth has been
brought to ruin!'

"Every sea captain, and
all who travel by ship, the
sailors, and all who earn

as make their living by the
sea, stood at a distance,
18and were crying out as
they saw the smoke of her
burning, saying, 'What *city*
is like the great city?'
19"And they threw dust
on their heads and were
crying out, weeping and
mourning, saying, 'Woe,
woe, the great city, in
which all who had ships at
sea became rich by her
wealth, for in one hour she
has been laid waste!'
20"Rejoice over her, O
heaven, and you saints and
apostles and prophets, because God has pronounced
judgment for you against
her."
21And a strong angel took
up a stone like a great millstone and threw it into the
sea, saying, "Thus will
Babylon, the great city, be
thrown down with vio-
lence, and will not be found
any longer.
22And the sound of harp-
ists and musicians and
flute-players and trumpeters will not be heard in you
any longer; and no craftsman of any craft will be
found in you any longer;
and the sound of a mill will
not be heard in you any
longer;
23and the light of a lamp
will not shine in you any
longer; and the voice of the
bridegroom and bride will
not be heard in you any
longer; for your merchants
were the great men of the
earth, because all the nations were deceived by
your sorcery.
24"And in her was found
the blood of prophets and
of saints and of all who
have been slain on the
earth."

θάλασσαν ἐργάζονται, ἀπὸ μακρόθεν ἔστησαν
[2]sea [1]work, [2]from [3]afar [1]stood

18 καὶ ἔκραζον βλέποντες τὸν καπνὸν
and cried out seeing the smoke

τῆς πυρώσεως αὐτῆς λέγοντες· τίς ὁμοία
of the burning of her saying: Who(What) [is] like

τῇ πόλει τῇ μεγάλῃ; **19** καὶ ἔβαλον
to the [2]city – [1]great ? And they cast

χοῦν ἐπὶ τὰς κεφαλὰς αὐτῶν καὶ ἔκραζον
dust on the heads of them and cried out

κλαίοντες καὶ πενθοῦντες, λέγοντες· οὐαὶ
weeping and sorrowing, saying: Woe[,]

οὐαί, ἡ πόλις ἡ μεγάλη, ἐν ᾗ ἐπλούτησαν
woe, the [2]city – [1]great, by which [8]were rich

πάντες οἱ ἔχοντες τὰ πλοῖα ἐν τῇ
[1]all [2]the [ones] [3]having [4]the [5]ships [6]in [7]the

θαλάσσῃ ἐκ τῆς τιμιότητος αὐτῆς, ὅτι
[8]sea from the worth of her, because

μιᾷ ὥρᾳ ἠρημώθη. **20** Εὐφραίνου ἐπ'
in one hour she was made desolate. Be thou glad over

αὐτῇ, οὐρανὲ καὶ οἱ ἅγιοι καὶ οἱ ἀπό-
her, heaven and *the* saints and *the* apost-

στολοι καὶ οἱ προφῆται, ὅτι ἔκρινεν ὁ
les and *the* prophets, because [2]judged –

θεὸς τὸ κρίμα ὑμῶν ἐξ αὐτῆς. **21** Καὶ
[1]God the judgment of you by her. And

ἦρεν εἷς ἄγγελος ἰσχυρὸς λίθον ὡς
[4]lifted [1]one [3]angel [2]strong a stone as

μύλινον μέγαν, καὶ ἔβαλεν εἰς τὴν θά-
[2]millstone [1]a great, and threw into the sea

λασσαν λέγων· οὕτως ὁρμήματι βληθήσεται
saying: Thus with a rush [5]shall be thrown

Βαβυλὼν ἡ μεγάλη πόλις, καὶ οὐ μὴ
[1]Babylon [2]the [3]great [4]city, and by no means

εὑρεθῇ ἔτι. **22** καὶ φωνὴ κιθαρῳδῶν
[shall] be found longer. And sound of harpers

καὶ μουσικῶν καὶ αὐλητῶν καὶ σαλπιστῶν
and of musicians and of flutists and of trumpeters

οὐ μὴ ἀκουσθῇ ἐν σοὶ ἔτι, καὶ πᾶς
by no means [shall] be heard in thee longer, and every

τεχνίτης πάσης τέχνης οὐ μὴ εὑρεθῇ
craftsman of every craft by no means [shall] be found

ἐν σοὶ ἔτι, καὶ φωνὴ μύλου οὐ μὴ
in thee longer, and sound of a mill by no means

ἀκουσθῇ ἐν σοὶ ἔτι, **23** καὶ φῶς
[shall] be heard in thee longer, and light

λύχνου οὐ μὴ φάνῃ ἐν σοὶ ἔτι, καὶ
of a lamp by no means [shall] shine in thee longer, and

φωνὴ νυμφίου καὶ νύμφης οὐ μὴ
voice of bridegroom and of bride by no means

ἀκουσθῇ ἐν σοὶ ἔτι· ὅτι [οἱ] ἔμποροί
[shall] be heard in thee longer; because the merchants

σου ἦσαν οἱ μεγιστᾶνες τῆς γῆς, ὅτι
of thee were the great ones of the earth, because

ἐν τῇ φαρμακείᾳ σου ἐπλανήθησαν πάντα
by the sorcery of thee [4]were deceived [1]all

τὰ ἔθνη, **24** καὶ ἐν αὐτῇ αἷμα προφητῶν
[2]the [3]nations, and in her [2]blood [3]of prophets

καὶ ἁγίων εὑρέθη καὶ πάντων τῶν
[4]and [5]of saints [1]was found and of all the [ones]

ἐσφαγμένων ἐπὶ τῆς γῆς.
having been slain on the earth.

their living from the sea,
will stand far off. 18When
they see the smoke of her
burning, they will exclaim,
'Was there ever a city like
this great city?' 19They will
throw dust on their heads,
and with weeping and
mourning cry out:

" 'Woe! Woe, O great
city,
where all who had
ships on the sea
became rich through
her wealth!
In one hour she has been
brought to ruin!
0Rejoice over her, O
heaven!
Rejoice, saints and
apostles and
prophets!
God has judged her for
the way she treated
you.' "

21Then a mighty angel
picked up a boulder the size
of a large millstone and
threw it into the sea, and
said:

"With such violence
the great city of
Babylon will be
thrown down,
never to be found
again.
22The music of harpists
and musicians, flute
players and
trumpeters,
will never be heard in
you again.
No workman of any
trade
will ever be found in
you again.
The sound of a millstone
will never be heard in
you again.
23The light of a lamp
will never shine in you
again.
The voice of bridegroom
and bride
will never be heard in
you again.
Your merchants were
the world's great
men.
By your magic spell all
the nations were led
astray.
24In her was found the
blood of prophets
and of the saints,
and of all who have
been killed on the
earth."

Chapter 19

The Fourfold Hallelujah

AFTER these things I
heard, as it were, a
loud voice of a great multitude in heaven, saying,
"Hallelujah! Salvation
and glory and power belong
to our God;
2BECAUSE HIS JUDGMENTS
ARE TRUE AND RIGHTEOUS;
for He has judged the great
harlot who was corrupting
the earth with her immorality, and HE HAS AVENGED
THE BLOOD OF HIS BOND-
SERVANTS ON HER."
3And a second time they
said, "Hallelujah! HER
SMOKE RISES UP FOREVER AND
EVER."
4And the twenty-four el-
ders and the four living
creatures fell down and
worshiped God who sits on
the throne saying, "Amen.
Hallelujah!"
5And a voice came from
the throne, saying,
"Give praise to our God,
all you His bond-servants,
you who fear Him, the
small and the great."
6And I heard, as it were,
the voice of a great multitude and as the sound of
many waters and as the
sound of mighty peals of
thunder, saying,
"Hallelujah! For the
Lord our God, the Al-
mighty, reigns.

Marriage of the Lamb

7"Let us rejoice and be
glad and give the glory to
Him, for the marriage of
the Lamb has come and His
bride has made herself
ready."
8And it was given to her
to clothe herself in fine
linen, bright *and* clean; for
the fine linen is the righteous acts of the saints.
9And he *said to me,
"Write, 'Blessed are those

19 Μετὰ ταῦτα ἤκουσα ὡς φωνὴν
After these things I heard as [2]voice

μεγάλην ὄχλου πολλοῦ ἐν τῷ οὐρανῷ
[1]a great (loud) [4]crowd [3]of a much (great) in – heaven

λεγόντων· ἀλληλουϊά· ἡ σωτηρία καὶ ἡ
saying: Halleluia: The salvation and the

δόξα καὶ ἡ δύναμις τοῦ θεοῦ ἡμῶν,
glory and the power of the God of us,

2 ὅτι ἀληθιναὶ καὶ δίκαιαι αἱ κρίσεις
because true and righteous the judgments

αὐτοῦ· ὅτι ἔκρινεν τὴν πόρνην τὴν
of him; because he judged the [2]harlot –

μεγάλην ἥτις ἔφθειρεν τὴν γῆν ἐν τῇ
[1]great who defiled the earth with the

πορνείᾳ αὐτῆς, καὶ ἐξεδίκησεν τὸ αἷμα
fornication of her, and *he* avenged the blood

τῶν δούλων αὐτοῦ ἐκ χειρὸς αὐτῆς.
of the slaves of him out of [the] hand of her.

3 καὶ δεύτερον εἴρηκαν· ἀλληλουϊά· καὶ
And secondly they *have* said: Halleluia; and

ὁ καπνὸς αὐτῆς ἀναβαίνει εἰς τοὺς
the smoke of her goes up unto the

αἰῶνας τῶν αἰώνων. **4** καὶ ἔπεσαν οἱ
ages of the ages. And [8]fell [1]the

πρεσβύτεροι οἱ εἴκοσι τέσσαρες καὶ τὰ
[3]elders – [2]twenty-four [4]and [5]the

τέσσερα ζῷα, καὶ προσεκύνησαν τῷ θεῷ
[6]four [7]living creatures, and worshipped – God

τῷ καθημένῳ ἐπὶ τῷ θρόνῳ λέγοντες·
– sitting on the throne saying:

ἀμὴν ἀλληλουϊά. **5** καὶ φωνὴ ἀπὸ τοῦ
Amen[,] halleluia. And a voice [2]from [3]the

θρόνου ἐξῆλθεν λέγουσα· αἰνεῖτε τῷ θεῷ
[4]throne [1]came out saying: Praise ye the God

ἡμῶν, πάντες οἱ δοῦλοι αὐτοῦ, οἱ
of us, all the slaves of him, the

φοβούμενοι αὐτόν, οἱ μικροὶ καὶ οἱ
[ones] fearing him, the small and the

μεγάλοι. **6** Καὶ ἤκουσα ὡς φωνὴν ὄχλου
great. And I heard as a sound [2]crowd

πολλοῦ καὶ ὡς φωνὴν ὑδάτων πολλῶν
[1]of a much(great) and as a sound [2]waters [1]of many

καὶ ὡς φωνὴν βροντῶν ἰσχυρῶν, λεγόντων·
and as a sound [2]thunders [1]of strong (loud), saying:

ἀλληλουϊά, ὅτι ἐβασίλευσεν κύριος ὁ θεὸς
Halleluia, because [7]reigned [1][the] Lord [2]the [3]God

ἡμῶν ὁ παντοκράτωρ. **7** χαίρωμεν καὶ
[4]of us [5]the [6]Almighty. Let us rejoice and

ἀγαλλιῶμεν, καὶ δώσομεν τὴν δόξαν αὐτῷ,
let us exult, and we will give the glory to him,

ὅτι ἦλθεν ὁ γάμος τοῦ ἀρνίου, καὶ
because [5]came [1]the [2]marriage [3]of the [4]Lamb, and

ἡ γυνὴ αὐτοῦ ἡτοίμασεν ἑαυτήν, **8** καὶ
the wife of him prepared herself, and

ἐδόθη αὐτῇ ἵνα περιβάληται βύσσινον
it was given to her *in order* that she might be clothed [with] [3]fine linen

λαμπρὸν καθαρόν· τὸ γὰρ βύσσινον τὰ
[1]bright [2]clean; for the fine linen [2]the

δικαιώματα τῶν ἁγίων ἐστίν. **9** Καὶ
[3]righteous deeds [4]of the [5]saints [1]is. And

λέγει μοι· γράψον· μακάριοι οἱ εἰς τὸ
he tells me: Write thou; blessed [1]the [ones] [2]to [4]the

Chapter 19

Hallelujah!

AFTER this I heard what
sounded like the roar
of a great multitude in
heaven shouting:
"Hallelujah!
Salvation and glory and
power belong to our
God,
2 for true and just are his
judgments.
He has condemned the
great prostitute
who corrupted the
earth by her
adulteries.
He has avenged on her
the blood of his
servants."
3And again they shouted:
"Hallelujah!
The smoke from her
goes up for ever and
ever."
4The twenty-four elders
and the four living crea-
tures fell down and wor-
shiped God, who was seat-
ed on the throne. And they
cried:
"Amen, Hallelujah!"
5Then a voice came from
the throne, saying:
"Praise our God,
all you his servants,
you who fear him,
both small and great!"
6Then I heard what
sounded like a great multitude, like the roar of rushing waters and like loud
peals of thunder, shouting:
"Hallelujah!
For our Lord God
Almighty reigns.
7Let us rejoice and be
glad
and give him glory!
For the wedding of the
Lamb has come,
and his bride has made
herself ready.
8Fine linen, bright and
clean,
was given her to
wear."
(Fine linen stands for the
righteous acts of the
saints.)
9Then the angel said to
me, "Write: 'Blessed are

who are invited to the marriage supper of the Lamb.' " And he *said to me, "These are true words of God."
10And I fell at his feet to worship him. And he *said to me, "Do not do that; I am a fellow servant of yours and your brethren who hold the testimony of Jesus; worship God. For the testimony of Jesus is the spirit of prophecy."

The Coming of Christ

11And I saw heaven opened; and behold, a white horse, and He who sat upon it *is* called Faithful and True; and in righteousness He judges and wages war.
12And His eyes *are* a flame of fire, and upon His head *are* many diadems; and He has a name written *upon Him* which no one knows except Himself.
13And *He is* clothed with a robe dipped in blood; and His name is called The Word of God.
14And the armies which are in heaven, clothed in fine linen, white *and* clean, were following Him on white horses.
15And from His mouth comes a sharp sword, so that with it He may smite the nations; and He will rule them with a rod of iron; and He treads the wine press of the fierce wrath of God, the Almighty.
16And on His robe and on His thigh He has a name written, "KING OF KINGS, AND LORD OF LORDS."

δεῖπνον τοῦ γάμου τοῦ ἀρνίου κεκλημένοι.
[5]supper [6]of the [7]marriage [8]of the [9]Lamb [2]*having been* called.

καὶ λέγει μοι· οὗτοι οἱ λόγοι ἀληθινοὶ
And he says to me: [1]These – [2]words [5]true

τοῦ θεοῦ εἰσιν. **10** καὶ ἔπεσα ἔμπροσθεν
– [3]of God [4]are. And I fell before

τῶν ποδῶν αὐτοῦ προσκυνῆσαι αὐτῷ.
the feet of him to worship him.

καὶ λέγει μοι· ὅρα μή· σύνδουλός σού
And he says to me: See thou [do it] not; [2]a fellow-slave [3]of thee

εἰμι καὶ τῶν ἀδελφῶν σου τῶν ἐχόντων
[1]I am and of the brothers of thee – having

τὴν μαρτυρίαν Ἰησοῦ· τῷ θεῷ προσκύνησον.
the witness of Jesus; – [2]God [1]worship thou.

ἡ γὰρ μαρτυρία Ἰησοῦ ἐστιν τὸ πνεῦμα
For the witness of Jesus is the spirit

τῆς προφητείας.
– of prophecy.

11 Καὶ εἶδον τὸν οὐρανὸν ἠνεῳγμένον,
And I saw – heaven *having been* opened,

καὶ ἰδοὺ ἵππος λευκός, καὶ ὁ καθήμενος
and behold[,] [2]horse [1]a white, and the [one] sitting

ἐπ' αὐτὸν πιστὸς καλούμενος καὶ ἀληθινός,
on it [2]faithful [1]*being* called and true,

καὶ ἐν δικαιοσύνῃ κρίνει καὶ πολεμεῖ.
and in righteousness he judges and makes war.

12 οἱ δὲ ὀφθαλμοὶ αὐτοῦ φλὸξ πυρός,
And the eyes of him [are as] a flame of fire,

καὶ ἐπὶ τὴν κεφαλὴν αὐτοῦ διαδήματα
and on the head of him [2]diadems

πολλά, ἔχων ὄνομα γεγραμμένον ὃ οὐδεὶς
[1]many, having a name *having been* written which no one

οἶδεν εἰ μὴ αὐτός, **13** καὶ περιβεβλημένος
knows except [him]self, and *having been* clothed [with]

ἱμάτιον βεβαμμένον αἵματι, καὶ κέκληται
a garment *having been* dipped in blood, and [4]has been called

τὸ ὄνομα αὐτοῦ ὁ λόγος τοῦ θεοῦ.
[1]the [2]name [3]of him The Word – of God.

14 καὶ τὰ στρατεύματα τὰ ἐν τῷ οὐρανῷ
And the armies – in – heaven

ἠκολούθει αὐτῷ ἐφ' ἵπποις λευκοῖς, ἐνδεδυμένοι
followed him on [2]horses [1]white, *having been* dressed [in]

βύσσινον λευκὸν καθαρόν. **15** καὶ ἐκ
[3]fine linen [1]white [2]clean. And out of

τοῦ στόματος αὐτοῦ ἐκπορεύεται ῥομφαία
the mouth of him proceeds [2]sword

ὀξεῖα, ἵνα ἐν αὐτῇ πατάξῃ τὰ ἔθνη·
[1]a sharp, in order that with it he may smite the nations;

καὶ αὐτὸς ποιμανεῖ αὐτοὺς ἐν ῥάβδῳ
and he will shepherd them with [2]staff

σιδηρᾷ· καὶ αὐτὸς πατεῖ τὴν ληνὸν
[1]an iron; and he treads the winepress

τοῦ οἴνου τοῦ θυμοῦ τῆς ὀργῆς τοῦ
of the wine of the anger[,] of the wrath –

θεοῦ τοῦ παντοκράτορος. **16** καὶ ἔχει
of God *of* the Almighty. And he has

ἐπὶ τὸ ἱμάτιον καὶ ἐπὶ τὸν μηρὸν
on the garment and on the thigh

αὐτοῦ ὄνομα γεγραμμένον· ΒΑΣΙΛΕΥΣ
of him a name *having been* written: KING

ΒΑΣΙΛΕΩΝ ΚΑΙ ΚΥΡΙΟΣ ΚΥΡΙΩΝ.
OF KINGS AND LORD OF LORDS.

those who are invited to the wedding supper of the Lamb!' " And he added, "These are the true words of God."
10At this I fell at his feet to worship him. But he said to me, "Do not do it! I am a fellow servant with you and with your brothers who hold to the testimony of Jesus. Worship God! For the testimony of Jesus is the spirit of prophecy."

The Rider on the White Horse

11I saw heaven standing open and there before me was a white horse, whose rider is called Faithful and True. With justice he judges and makes war.
12His eyes are like blazing fire, and on his head are many crowns. He has a name written on him that no one knows but he himself.
13He is dressed in a robe dipped in blood, and his name is the Word of God.
14The armies of heaven were following him, riding on white horses and dressed in fine linen, white and clean.
15Out of his mouth comes a sharp sword with which to strike down the nations. "He will rule them with an iron scepter."[w] He treads the winepress of the fury of the wrath of God Almighty.
16On his robe and on his thigh he has this name written:

KING OF KINGS AND LORD OF LORDS.

[w]*15* Psalm 2:9

17And I saw an angel standing in the sun; and he cried out with a loud voice, saying to all the birds which fly in midheaven, "Come, assemble for the great supper of God;

18in order that you may eat the flesh of kings and the flesh of [f]commanders and the flesh of mighty men and the flesh of horses and of those who sit on them and the flesh of all men, both free men and slaves, and small and great."

19And I saw the beast and the kings of the earth and their armies, assembled to make war against Him who sat upon the horse, and against His army.

Doom of the Beast and False Prophet

20And the beast was seized, and with him the false prophet who performed the signs in his presence, by which he deceived those who had received the mark of the beast and those who worshiped his image; these two were thrown alive into the lake of fire which burns with brimstone.

21And the rest were killed with the sword which came from the mouth of Him who sat upon the horse, and all the birds were filled with their flesh.

17 Καὶ εἶδον ἕνα ἄγγελον ἑστῶτα ἐν
And I saw one angel standing in
τῷ ἡλίῳ, καὶ ἔκραξεν ἐν φωνῇ μεγάλῃ
the sun, and he cried out in [2]voice [1]a great (loud)
λέγων πᾶσιν τοῖς ὀρνέοις τοῖς πετομένοις
saying to all the birds – flying
ἐν μεσουρανήματι· δεῦτε συνάχθητε εἰς
in mid-heaven: Come *ye*[,] assemble ye to
τὸ δεῖπνον τὸ μέγα τοῦ θεοῦ, **18** ἵνα
the [2]supper – [1]great – of God, in order that
φάγητε σάρκας βασιλέων καὶ σάρκας
ye may eat flesh*es* of kings and flesh*es*
χιλιάρχων καὶ σάρκας ἰσχυρῶν καὶ σάρκας
of chiliarchs and flesh*es* of strong men and flesh*es*
ἵππων καὶ τῶν καθημένων ἐπ' αὐτῶν,
of horses and of the [ones] sitting on them,
καὶ σάρκας πάντων ἐλευθέρων τε καὶ
and flesh*es* of all [2]free men [1]both and
δούλων καὶ μικρῶν καὶ μεγάλων. **19** Καὶ
slaves both small and great. And
εἶδον τὸ θηρίον καὶ τοὺς βασιλεῖς τῆς
I saw the beast and the kings of the
γῆς καὶ τὰ στρατεύματα αὐτῶν συνηγμένα
earth and the armies of them *having been* assembled
ποιῆσαι τὸν πόλεμον μετὰ τοῦ καθημένου
to make the war with the [one] sitting
ἐπὶ τοῦ ἵππου καὶ μετὰ τοῦ στρατεύματος
on the horse and with the army
αὐτοῦ. **20** καὶ ἐπιάσθη τὸ θηρίον καὶ
of him. And [3]was seized [1]the [2]beast and
μετ' αὐτοῦ ὁ ψευδοπροφήτης ὁ ποιήσας
with it the false prophet the [one] having done
τὰ σημεῖα ἐνώπιον αὐτοῦ, ἐν οἷς ἐπλάνη-
the signs before it, by which he de-
σεν τοὺς λαβόντας τὸ χάραγμα τοῦ
ceived the [ones] having received the mark of the
θηρίου καὶ τοὺς προσκυνοῦντας τῇ εἰκόνι
beast and the [ones] worshipping the image
αὐτοῦ· ζῶντες ἐβλήθησαν οἱ δύο εἰς
of it; [4]living [3]were cast [1]the [2]two into
τὴν λίμνην τοῦ πυρὸς τῆς καιομένης
the lake – of fire – burning*
ἐν θείῳ. **21** καὶ οἱ λοιποὶ ἀπεκτάνθησαν
with sulphur. And the rest were killed
ἐν τῇ ῥομφαίᾳ τοῦ καθημένου ἐπὶ τοῦ
with the sword of the [one] sitting on the
ἵππου τῇ ἐξελθούσῃ ἐκ τοῦ στόματος
horse – proceeding§ out of the mouth
αὐτοῦ, καὶ πάντα τὰ ὄρνεα ἐχορτάσθησαν
of him, and all the birds were filled
ἐκ τῶν σαρκῶν αὐτῶν.
by the flesh*es* of them.

17And I saw an angel
standing in the sun, who
cried in a loud voice to all
the birds flying in midair,
"Come, gather together for
the great supper of God,
18so that you may eat the
flesh of kings, generals,
and mighty men, of horses
and their riders, and the
flesh of all people, free and
slave, small and great."
19Then I saw the beast
and the kings of the earth
and their armies gathered
together to make war
against the rider on the
horse and his army. 20But
the beast was captured,
and with him the false
prophet who had per-
formed the miraculous
signs on his behalf. With
these signs he had deluded
those who had received the
mark of the beast and worshiped his image. The two
of them were thrown alive
into the fiery lake of burning sulfur. 21The rest of
them were killed with the
sword that came out of the
mouth of the rider on the
horse, and all the birds
gorged themselves on their
flesh.

Chapter 20

Satan Bound

AND I saw an angel coming down from heaven, having the key of the abyss and a great chain in his hand.

20 Καὶ εἶδον ἄγγελον καταβαίνοντα ἐκ
And I saw an angel coming down out of
τοῦ οὐρανοῦ, ἔχοντα τὴν κλεῖν τῆς
– heaven, having the key of the
ἀβύσσου καὶ ἅλυσιν μεγάλην ἐπὶ τὴν χεῖρα
abyss and [2]chain [1]a great on the hand

Chapter 20

The Thousand Years

AND I saw an angel coming down out of heaven, having the key to the Abyss and holding in his hand a great chain. 2He

* Feminine, agreeing with λίμνη, not with the neuter πῦρ.
§ Agreeing, of course, with ῥομφαίᾳ.

[f]I.e., chiliarchs, in command of one thousand troops

2And he laid hold of the
dragon, the serpent of old,
who is the devil and Satan,
and bound him for a thou-
sand years,
3and threw him into the
abyss, and shut *it* and
sealed *it* over him, so that
he should not deceive the
nations any longer, until
the thousand years were
completed; after these
things he must be released
for a short time.
4And I saw thrones, and
they sat upon them, and
judgment was given to
them. And I *saw* the souls
of those who had been be-
headed because of the testimony of Jesus and because
of the word of God, and
those who had not wor-
shiped the beast or his image, and had not received
the mark upon their fore-
head and upon their hand;
and they came to life and
reigned with Christ for a
thousand years.
5The rest of the dead did
not come to life until the
thousand years were com-
pleted. This is the first
resurrection.
6Blessed and holy is the
one who has a part in the
first resurrection; over
these the second death has
no power, but they will be
priests of God and of Christ
and will reign with Him for
a thousand years.

Satan Freed, Doomed

7And when the thousand
years are completed, Satan
will be released from his
prison,
8and will come out to de-
ceive the nations which are
in the four corners of the
earth, Gog and Magog, to
gather them together for
the war; the number of

αὐτοῦ. **2** καὶ ἐκράτησεν τὸν δράκοντα,
of him. And he laid hold [of] the dragon,

ὁ ὄφις ὁ ἀρχαῖος, ὅς ἐστιν Διάβολος
the [2]serpent – [1]old, who is Devil

καὶ ὁ Σατανᾶς, καὶ ἔδησεν αὐτὸν χίλια
and – Satan, and bound him a thousand

ἔτη, **3** καὶ ἔβαλεν αὐτὸν εἰς τὴν ἄβυσσον,
years, and cast him into the abyss,

καὶ ἔκλεισεν καὶ ἐσφράγισεν ἐπάνω αὐτοῦ,
and shut and sealed over him,

ἵνα μὴ πλανήσῃ ἔτι τὰ ἔθνη, ἄχρι
in order that he should not deceive longer the nations, until

τελεσθῇ τὰ χίλια ἔτη· μετὰ ταῦτα
[4]are finished [1]the [2]thousand [3]years; after these things

δεῖ λυθῆναι αὐτὸν μικρὸν χρόνον.
it behoves [2]to be loosed [1]him a little time.

4 Καὶ εἶδον θρόνους, καὶ ἐκάθισαν ἐπ᾽
And I saw thrones, and they sat on

αὐτούς, καὶ κρίμα ἐδόθη αὐτοῖς, καὶ
them, and judgment was given to them, and

τὰς ψυχὰς τῶν πεπελεκισμένων διὰ τὴν
the souls of the [ones] having been beheaded because of the

μαρτυρίαν Ἰησοῦ καὶ διὰ τὸν λόγον
witness of Jesus and because of the word

τοῦ θεοῦ, καὶ οἵτινες οὐ προσεκύνησαν
– of God, and who did not worship

τὸ θηρίον οὐδὲ τὴν εἰκόνα αὐτοῦ καὶ
the beast nor the image of it and

οὐκ ἔλαβον τὸ χάραγμα ἐπὶ τὸ μέτωπον
did not receive the mark on the forehead

καὶ ἐπὶ τὴν χεῖρα αὐτῶν· καὶ ἔζησαν
and on the hand of them; and they lived [again]

καὶ ἐβασίλευσαν μετὰ τοῦ Χριστοῦ χίλια
and reigned with – Christ a thousand

ἔτη. **5** οἱ λοιποὶ τῶν νεκρῶν οὐκ ἔζησαν
years. The rest of the dead did not live [again]

ἄχρι τελεσθῇ τὰ χίλια ἔτη. Αὕτη ἡ
until were finished the thousand years. This [is] the

ἀνάστασις ἡ πρώτη. **6** μακάριος καὶ
[2]resurrection – [1]first. Blessed and

ἅγιος ὁ ἔχων μέρος ἐν τῇ ἀναστάσει
holy [is] the [one] having part in the [2]resurrection

τῇ πρώτῃ· ἐπὶ τούτων ὁ δεύτερος θάνατος
– [1]first; over these the second death

οὐκ ἔχει ἐξουσίαν, ἀλλ᾽ ἔσονται ἱερεῖς
has not authority, but they will be priests

τοῦ θεοῦ καὶ τοῦ Χριστοῦ, καὶ βασιλεύ-
– of God and – of Christ, and will

σουσιν μετ᾽ αὐτοῦ [τὰ] χίλια ἔτη.
reign with him the thousand years.

7 Καὶ ὅταν τελεσθῇ τὰ χίλια ἔτη,
And whenever are finished the thousand years,

λυθήσεται ὁ σατανᾶς ἐκ τῆς φυλακῆς
[2]will be loosed – [1]Satan out of the prison

αὐτοῦ, **8** καὶ ἐξελεύσεται πλανῆσαι τὰ
of him, and will go forth to deceive the

ἔθνη τὰ ἐν ταῖς τέσσαρσιν γωνίαις τῆς
nations – in the four corners of the

γῆς, τὸν Γὼγ καὶ Μαγώγ, συναγαγεῖν
earth, – Gog and Magog, to assemble

αὐτοὺς εἰς τὸν πόλεμον, ὧν ὁ ἀριθμὸς
them to the war, of whom the number

seized the dragon, that ancient serpent, who is the
devil, or Satan, and bound
him for a thousand years.
3He threw him into the
Abyss, and locked and
sealed it over him, to keep
him from deceiving the nations anymore until the
thousand years were end-
ed. After that, he must be
set free for a short time.
4I saw thrones on which
were seated those who had
been given authority to
judge. And I saw the souls
of those who had been be-
headed because of their
testimony for Jesus and because of the word of God.
They had not worshiped
the beast or his image and
had not received his mark
on their foreheads or their
hands. They came to life
and reigned with Christ a
thousand years. 5(The rest
of the dead did not come to
life until the thousand years
were ended.) This is the
first resurrection. 6Blessed
and holy are those who
have part in the first resurrection. The second death
has no power over them,
but they will be priests of
God and of Christ and will
reign with him for a thousand years.

Satan's Doom

7When the thousand
years are over, Satan will
be released from his prison
8and will go out to deceive
the nations in the four corners of the earth—Gog and
Magog—to gather them for
battle. In number they are

them is like the sand of the
seashore.
9And they came up on
the broad plain of the earth
and surrounded the camp
of the saints and the be-
loved city, and fire came
down from heaven and de-
voured them.
10And the devil who de-
ceived them was thrown
into the lake of fire and
brimstone, where the beast
and the false prophet are
also; and they will be tormented day and night for-
ever and ever.

Judgment at the Throne of God

11And I saw a great white
throne and Him who sat
upon it, from whose pres-
ence earth and heaven fled
away, and no place was
found for them.
12And I saw the dead, the
great and the small, standing before the throne, and
books were opened; and
another book was opened,
which is *the book* of life;
and the dead were judged
from the things which were
written in the books, ac-
cording to their deeds.
13And the sea gave up the
dead which were in it, and
death and Hades gave up
the dead which were in
them; and they were
judged, every one *of them*
according to their deeds.
14And death and Hades
were thrown into the lake
of fire. This is the second
death, the lake of fire.
15And if anyone's name
was not found written in
the book of life, he was
thrown into the lake of fire.

αὐτῶν ὡς ἡ ἄμμος τῆς θαλάσσης. **9** καὶ
of them [is] as the sand of the sea. And

ἀνέβησαν ἐπὶ τὸ πλάτος τῆς γῆς, καὶ
they went up over the breadth of the land, and

ἐκύκλευσαν τὴν παρεμβολὴν τῶν ἁγίων
encircled the camp of the saints

καὶ τὴν πόλιν τὴν ἠγαπημένην· καὶ
and the [2]city – *having been* [1]loved; and

κατέβη πῦρ ἐκ τοῦ οὐρανοῦ καὶ κατέφαγεν
[2]came down [1]fire out of – heaven and devoured

αὐτούς· **10** καὶ ὁ διάβολος ὁ πλανῶν αὐτοὺς
them; and the Devil – deceiving them

ἐβλήθη εἰς τὴν λίμνην τοῦ πυρὸς καὶ
was cast into the lake – of fire and

θείου, ὅπου καὶ τὸ θηρίον καὶ ὁ
sulphur, where [were] also the beast and the

ψευδοπροφήτης, καὶ βασανισθήσονται ἡμέρας
false prophet, and they will be tormented day

καὶ νυκτὸς εἰς τοὺς αἰῶνας τῶν αἰώνων.
and night unto the ages of the ages.

11 Καὶ εἶδον θρόνον μέγαν λευκὸν καὶ
And I saw [3]throne [1]a great [2]white and

τὸν καθήμενον ἐπ' αὐτὸν οὗ ἀπὸ τοῦ
the [one] sitting on it [4]of whom [1]from [2]the

προσώπου ἔφυγεν ἡ γῆ καὶ ὁ οὐρανός,
[3]face [6]fled [1]the [2]earth [3]and [4]the [5]heaven,

καὶ τόπος οὐχ εὑρέθη αὐτοῖς. **12** καὶ
and a place was not found for them. And

εἶδον τοὺς νεκρούς, τοὺς μεγάλους καὶ
I saw the dead, the great and

τοὺς μικρούς, ἑστῶτας ἐνώπιον τοῦ θρόνου,
the small, standing before the throne,

καὶ βιβλία ἠνοίχθησαν· καὶ ἄλλο βιβλίον
and scrolls were opened; and another scroll

ἠνοίχθη, ὅ ἐστιν τῆς ζωῆς· καὶ ἐκρίθησαν
was opened, which is [the – scroll] of life; and [3]were judged

οἱ νεκροὶ ἐκ τῶν γεγραμμένων ἐν τοῖς
[1]the [2]dead by the things *having been* written in the

βιβλίοις κατὰ τὰ ἔργα αὐτῶν. **13** καὶ
scrolls according to the works of them. And

ἔδωκεν ἡ θάλασσα τοὺς νεκροὺς τοὺς
[3]gave [1]the [2]sea the dead –

ἐν αὐτῇ, καὶ ὁ θάνατος καὶ ὁ ᾅδης
in it, and – death and – hades

ἔδωκαν τοὺς νεκροὺς τοὺς ἐν αὐτοῖς,
gave the dead – in them,

καὶ ἐκρίθησαν ἕκαστος κατὰ τὰ ἔργα
and they were judged each one according to the works

αὐτῶν. **14** καὶ ὁ θάνατος καὶ ὁ ᾅδης
of them. And – death and – hades

ἐβλήθησαν εἰς τὴν λίμνην τοῦ πυρός.
were cast into the lake – of fire.

οὗτος ὁ θάνατος ὁ δεύτερός ἐστιν, ἡ
This [2]the [4]death – [3]second [1]is, the

λίμνη τοῦ πυρός. **15** καὶ εἴ τις οὐχ
lake – of fire. And if anyone not

εὑρέθη ἐν τῇ βίβλῳ τῆς ζωῆς γεγραμ-
was found [2]in [3]the [4]scroll – [5]of life [1]*having been*

μένος, ἐβλήθη εἰς τὴν λίμνην τοῦ πυρός.
written, he was cast into the lake – of fire.

like the sand on the sea-
shore. 9They marched
across the breadth of the
earth and surrounded the
camp of God's people, the
city he loves. But fire came
down from heaven and de-
voured them. 10And the
devil, who deceived them,
was thrown into the lake of
burning sulfur, where the
beast and the false prophet
had been thrown. They will
be tormented day and night
for ever and ever.

The Dead Are Judged

11Then I saw a great white
throne and him who was
seated on it. Earth and sky
fled from his presence, and
there was no place for
them. 12And I saw the
dead, great and small,
standing before the throne,
and books were opened.
Another book was opened,
which is the book of life.
The dead were judged ac-
cording to what they had
done as recorded in the
books. 13The sea gave up
the dead that were in it, and
death and Hades gave up
the dead that were in them,
and each person was
judged according to what
he had done. 14Then death
and Hades were thrown
into the lake of fire. The
lake of fire is the second
death. 15If anyone's name
was not found written in
the book of life, he was
thrown into the lake of fire.

Chapter 21

The New Heaven and Earth

AND I saw a new heaven and a new earth; for the first heaven and the first earth passed away, and there is no longer *any* sea.

2And I saw the holy city, new Jerusalem, coming down out of heaven from God, made ready as a bride adorned for her husband.

3And I heard a loud voice from the throne, saying, "Behold, the tabernacle of God is among men, and He shall dwell among them, and they shall be His people, and God Himself shall be among them,[g]

4and He shall wipe away every tear from their eyes; and there shall no longer be *any* death; there shall no longer be *any* mourning, or crying, or pain; the first things have passed away."

5And He who sits on the throne said, "Behold, I am making all things new." And He *said, "Write, for these words are faithful and true."

6And He said to me, "It is done. I am the Alpha and the Omega, the beginning and the end. I will give to the one who thirsts from the spring of the water of life without cost.

7"He who overcomes shall inherit these things, and I will be his God and he will be My son.

8"But for the cowardly and unbelieving and abominable and murderers and immoral persons and sorcerers and idolaters and all liars, their part *will be* in the lake that burns with fire and brimstone, which is the second death."

[g] Some ancient mss. add, and be *their God*

21 Καὶ εἶδον οὐρανὸν καινὸν καὶ γῆν
And I saw [2]heaven [1]a new and [2]earth
καινήν· ὁ γὰρ πρῶτος οὐρανὸς καὶ ἡ
[1]a new; for the first heaven and the
πρώτη γῆ ἀπῆλθαν, καὶ ἡ θάλασσα
first earth passed away, and the sea
οὐκ ἔστιν ἔτι. **2** καὶ τὴν πόλιν τὴν
is not longer. And [2]the [4]city –
ἁγίαν Ἰερουσαλὴμ καινὴν εἶδον κατα-
[3]holy [6]Jerusalem [5]new [1]I saw coming
βαίνουσαν ἐκ τοῦ οὐρανοῦ ἀπὸ τοῦ θεοῦ,
down out of – heaven from – God,
ἡτοιμασμένην ὡς νύμφην κεκοσμημένην
having been prepared as a bride *having been* adorned
τῷ ἀνδρὶ αὐτῆς. **3** καὶ ἤκουσα φωνῆς
for the husband of her. And I heard [2]voice
μεγάλης ἐκ τοῦ θρόνου λεγούσης· ἰδοὺ
[1]a great(loud) out of the throne saying: Behold[,]
ἡ σκηνὴ τοῦ θεοῦ μετὰ τῶν ἀνθρώπων,
the tabernacle – of God [is] with – men,
καὶ σκηνώσει μετ' αὐτῶν, καὶ αὐτοὶ
and he will tabernacle with them, and they
λαοὶ αὐτοῦ ἔσονται, καὶ αὐτὸς ὁ θεὸς
[2]peoples [3]of him [1]will be, and [2][him]self – [1]God
μετ' αὐτῶν ἔσται, **4** καὶ ἐξαλείψει πᾶν
with them will be, and will wipe off every
δάκρυον ἐκ τῶν ὀφθαλμῶν αὐτῶν, καὶ
tear out of the eyes of them, and
ὁ θάνατος οὐκ ἔσται ἔτι, οὔτε πένθος
– death will not be longer, nor sorrow
οὔτε κραυγὴ οὔτε πόνος οὐκ ἔσται ἔτι·
nor clamour nor pain will *not* be longer;
ὅτι τὰ πρῶτα ἀπῆλθαν. **5** καὶ εἶπεν
because the first things passed away. And [6]said
ὁ καθήμενος ἐπὶ τῷ θρόνῳ· ἰδοὺ καινὰ
[1]the [one] [2]sitting [3]on [4]the [5]throne: Behold [3]new
ποιῶ πάντα. καὶ λέγει· γράψον, ὅτι
[1]I make [2]all things. And he says: Write thou, because
οὗτοι οἱ λόγοι πιστοὶ καὶ ἀληθινοί εἰσιν.
these – words faithful and true are.
6 καὶ εἶπέν μοι· γέγοναν. ἐγὼ τὸ ἄλφα
And he said to me: It has occurred.* I [am] the alpha
καὶ τὸ ὦ, ἡ ἀρχὴ καὶ τὸ τέλος. ἐγὼ
and the omega, the beginning and the end. [3]I
τῷ διψῶντι δώσω ἐκ τῆς πηγῆς
[1]to the [one] [2]thirsting [4]will give out of the fountain
τοῦ ὕδατος τῆς ζωῆς δωρεάν. **7** ὁ νικῶν
of the water – of life freely. The over- [one] coming
κληρονομήσει ταῦτα, καὶ ἔσομαι αὐτῷ
shall inherit these things, and I will be to him
θεὸς καὶ αὐτὸς ἔσται μοι υἱός. **8** τοῖς δὲ
God and he shall be to me a son. But for the
δειλοῖς καὶ ἀπίστοις καὶ ἐβδελυγμένοις
cowardly and unbelieving and *having become* foul
καὶ φονεῦσιν καὶ πόρνοις καὶ φαρμακοῖς
and murderers and fornicators and sorcerers
καὶ εἰδωλολάτραις καὶ πᾶσιν τοῖς ψευδέσιν
and idolaters and all the false [ones]
τὸ μέρος αὐτῶν ἐν τῇ λίμνῃ τῇ καιομένῃ
the part of them in the lake – burning
πυρὶ καὶ θείῳ, ὅ ἐστιν ὁ θάνατος ὁ
with fire and *with* sulphur, which is the [2]death
δεύτερος.
[1]second [, shall be].

* Collective neuter plural; *cf.* ch. 16. 17.

Chapter 21

The New Jerusalem

THEN I saw a new heav-
en and a new earth, for
the first heaven and the
first earth had passed
away, and there was no
longer any sea. 2I saw the
Holy City, the new Jerusalem, coming down out of
heaven from God, prepared
as a bride beautifully
dressed for her husband.
3And I heard a loud voice
from the throne saying,
"Now the dwelling of God
is with men, and he will live
with them. They will be his
people, and God himself
will be with them and be
their God. 4He will wipe
every tear from their eyes.
There will be no more
death or mourning or cry-
ing or pain, for the old order of things has passed
away."

5He who was seated on
the throne said, "I am making everything new!" Then
he said, "Write this down,
for these words are trustworthy and true."

6He said to me: "It is
done. I am the Alpha and
the Omega, the Beginning
and the End. To him who is
thirsty I will give to drink
without cost from the
spring of the water of life.
7He who overcomes will inherit all this, and I will be
his God and he will be my
son. 8But the cowardly, the
unbelieving, the vile, the
murderers, the sexually immoral, those who practice
magic arts, the idolaters
and all liars—their place
will be in the fiery lake of
burning sulfur. This is the
second death."

9 And one of the seven angels who had the seven bowls full of the seven last plagues, came and spoke with me, saying, "Come here, I shall show you the bride, the wife of the Lamb."

The New Jerusalem

10 And he carried me away [h]in the Spirit to a great and high mountain, and showed me the holy city, Jerusalem, coming down out of heaven from God,

11 having the glory of God. Her brilliance was like a very costly stone, as a stone of crystal-clear jasper.

12 It had a great and high wall, with twelve gates, and at the gates twelve angels; and names *were* written on them, which are *those* of the twelve tribes of the sons of Israel.

13 *There were* three gates on the east and three gates on the north and three gates on the south and three gates on the west.

14 And the wall of the city had twelve foundation stones, and on them *were* the twelve names of the twelve apostles of the Lamb.

15 And the one who spoke with me had a gold measuring rod to measure the city, and its gates and its wall.

16 And the city is laid out as a square, and its length is as great as the width; and he measured the city with the rod, [i]fifteen hundred miles; its length and width and height are equal.

17 And he measured its

[h] Or, *in spirit*
[i] Lit., *twelve thousand stadia;* a stadion was about 600 ft.

9 Καὶ ἦλθεν εἷς ἐκ τῶν ἑπτὰ ἀγγέλων
And came one of the seven angels
τῶν ἐχόντων τὰς ἑπτὰ φιάλας, τῶν
– having the seven bowls, –
γεμόντων τῶν ἑπτὰ πληγῶν τῶν ἐσχάτων,
being filled of(with) the seven [2]plagues – [1]last,
καὶ ἐλάλησεν μετ' ἐμοῦ λέγων· δεῦρο,
and spoke with me saying: Come,
δείξω σοι τὴν νύμφην τὴν γυναῖκα
I will show thee the bride[,] the wife
τοῦ ἀρνίου. 10 καὶ ἀπήνεγκέν με ἐν
of the Lamb. And he bore away me in
πνεύματι ἐπὶ ὄρος μέγα καὶ ὑψηλόν,
spirit onto [4]mountain [1]a great [2]and [3]high,
καὶ ἔδειξέν μοι τὴν πόλιν τὴν ἁγίαν
and showed me the [2]city – [1]holy
Ἰερουσαλὴμ καταβαίνουσαν ἐκ τοῦ οὐρανοῦ
Jerusalem coming down out of – heaven
ἀπὸ τοῦ θεοῦ, 11 ἔχουσαν τὴν δόξαν
from – God, having the glory
τοῦ θεοῦ· ὁ φωστὴρ αὐτῆς ὅμοιος λίθῳ
– of God; the light of it [was] like *to* a stone
τιμιωτάτῳ, ὡς λίθῳ ἰάσπιδι κρυσταλλίζοντι·
very valuable, as [2]stone [1]*to* a jasper *being* clear as crystal;
12 ἔχουσα τεῖχος μέγα καὶ ὑψηλόν,
having [4]wall [1]a great [2]and [3]high,
ἔχουσα πυλῶνας δώδεκα, καὶ ἐπὶ τοῖς
having [2]gates [1]twelve, and at the
πυλῶσιν ἀγγέλους δώδεκα, καὶ ὀνόματα
gates [2]angels [1]twelve, and names
ἐπιγεγραμμένα, ἅ ἐστιν τῶν δώδεκα
having been inscribed, which is(are) of the twelve
φυλῶν υἱῶν Ἰσραήλ. 13 ἀπὸ ἀνατολῆς
tribes of sons of Israel. From east
πυλῶνες τρεῖς, καὶ ἀπὸ βορρᾶ πυλῶνες
[2]gates [1]three, and from north [2]gates
τρεῖς, καὶ ἀπὸ νότου πυλῶνες τρεῖς,
[1]three, and from south [2]gates [1]three,
καὶ ἀπὸ δυσμῶν πυλῶνες τρεῖς. 14 καὶ
and from west [2]gates [1]three. And
τὸ τεῖχος τῆς πόλεως ἔχων θεμελίους
the wall of the city having [2]foundations
δώδεκα, καὶ ἐπ' αὐτῶν δώδεκα ὀνόματα
[1]twelve, and on them twelve names
τῶν δώδεκα ἀποστόλων τοῦ ἀρνίου. 15 Καὶ
of the twelve apostles of the Lamb. And
ὁ λαλῶν μετ' ἐμοῦ εἶχεν μέτρον κάλαμον
the [one] speaking with me had [2]measure [3]reed
χρυσοῦν, ἵνα μετρήσῃ τὴν πόλιν καὶ
[1]a golden, in order that he might measure the city and
τοὺς πυλῶνας αὐτῆς καὶ τὸ τεῖχος αὐτῆς.
the gates of it and the wall of it.
16 καὶ ἡ πόλις τετράγωνος κεῖται, καὶ
And the city [2]square [1]lies, and
τὸ μῆκος αὐτῆς ὅσον τὸ πλάτος. καὶ
the length of it [is] as much as the breadth. And
ἐμέτρησεν τὴν πόλιν τῷ καλάμῳ ἐπὶ
he measured the city with the reed at
σταδίων δώδεκα χιλιάδων· τὸ μῆκος καὶ
[2]furlongs [1]twelve [3]thousands; the length and
τὸ πλάτος καὶ τὸ ὕψος αὐτῆς ἴσα ἐστίν.
the breadth and the height of it [2]equal [1]is(are).
17 καὶ ἐμέτρησεν τὸ τεῖχος αὐτῆς ἑκατὸν
And he measured the wall of it *of* a hundred

9 One of the seven angels
who had the seven bowls
full of the seven last
plagues came and said to
me, "Come, I will show
you the bride, the wife of
the Lamb." 10 And he car-
ried me away in the Spirit
to a mountain great and
high, and showed me the
Holy City, Jerusalem, coming down out of heaven
from God. 11 It shone with
the glory of God, and its
brilliance was like that of a
very precious jewel, like a
jasper, clear as crystal. 12 It
had a great, high wall with
twelve gates, and with
twelve angels at the gates.
On the gates were written
the names of the twelve
tribes of Israel. 13 There
were three gates on the
east, three on the north,
three on the south and
three on the west. 14 The
wall of the city had twelve
foundations, and on them
were the names of the
twelve apostles of the
Lamb.
15 The angel who talked
with me had a measuring
rod of gold to measure the
city, its gates and its walls.
16 The city was laid out like
a square, as long as it was
wide. He measured the city
with the rod and found it to
be 12,000 stadia[x] in length,
and as wide and high as it is
long. 17 He measured its

[x] *16* That is, about 1,400 miles (about 2,200 kilometers)

wall, [j]seventy-two yards, *according to* human measurements, which are *also* angelic *measurements*.

18And the material of the wall was jasper; and the city was pure gold, like clear glass.

19The foundation stones of the city wall were adorned with every kind of precious stone. The first foundation stone was jasper; the second, sapphire; the third, chalcedony; the fourth, emerald;

20the fifth, sardonyx; the sixth, sardius; the seventh, chrysolite; the eighth, beryl; the ninth, topaz; the tenth, chrysoprase; the eleventh, jacinth; the twelfth, amethyst.

21And the twelve gates were twelve pearls; each one of the gates was a single pearl. And the street of the city was pure gold, like transparent glass.

22And I saw no temple in it, for the Lord God, the Almighty, and the Lamb, are its temple.

23And the city has no need of the sun or of the moon to shine upon it, for the glory of God has illumined it, and its lamp *is* the Lamb.

24And the nations shall walk by its light, and the kings of the earth shall bring their glory into it.

25And in the daytime (for there shall be no night there) its gates shall never be closed;

26and they shall bring the glory and the honor of the nations into it;

27and nothing unclean

[j] Lit., *one hundred forty-four cubits*

τεσσεράκοντα τεσσάρων πηχῶν, μέτρον
[and] forty-four cubits, a measure

ἀνθρώπου, ὅ ἐστιν ἀγγέλου. **18** καὶ
of a man, which is of an angel. And

ἡ ἐνδώμησις τοῦ τείχους αὐτῆς ἴασπις,
the coping of the wall of it [was] jasper,

καὶ ἡ πόλις χρυσίον καθαρὸν ὅμοιον
and the city [was] [2]gold [1]clean(pure) like

ὑάλῳ καθαρῷ. **19** οἱ θεμέλιοι τοῦ τείχους
[2]glass [1]*to* clean(pure). The foundations of the wall

τῆς πόλεως παντὶ λίθῳ τιμίῳ κεκοσμημένοι·
of the city [2]with every [4]stone [3]precious [1]*having been* adorned;

ὁ θεμέλιος ὁ πρῶτος ἴασπις, ὁ δεύτερος
the foundation – first jasper, the second

σάπφιρος, ὁ τρίτος χαλκηδών, ὁ τέταρτος
sapphire, the third chalcedony, the fourth

σμάραγδος, **20** ὁ πέμπτος σαρδόνυξ, ὁ
emerald, the fifth sardonyx, the

ἕκτος σάρδιον, ὁ ἕβδομος χρυσόλιθος,
sixth sardius, the seventh chrysolite,

ὁ ὄγδοος βήρυλλος, ὁ ἔνατος τοπάζιον,
the eighth beryl, the ninth topaz,

ὁ δέκατος χρυσόπρασος, ὁ ἑνδέκατος
the tenth chrysoprasus, the eleventh

ὑάκινθος, ὁ δωδέκατος ἀμέθυστος. **21** καὶ
hyacinth, the twelfth amethyst. And

οἱ δώδεκα πυλῶνες δώδεκα μαργαρῖται·
the twelve gates [were] twelve pearls;

ἀνὰ εἷς ἕκαστος τῶν πυλώνων ἦν ἐξ
respectively† [2]one [1]each of the gates was of

ἑνὸς μαργαρίτου. καὶ ἡ πλατεῖα τῆς
one pearl. And the street of the

πόλεως χρυσίον καθαρὸν ὡς ὕαλος διαυγής.
city [was] [2]gold [1]clean(pure) as [2]glass [1]transparent.

22 Καὶ ναὸν οὐκ εἶδον ἐν αὐτῇ· ὁ γὰρ
And a shrine I saw not in it; for the

κύριος ὁ θεὸς ὁ παντοκράτωρ ναὸς αὐτῆς
Lord – God the Almighty shrine of it

ἐστιν, καὶ τὸ ἀρνίον. **23** καὶ ἡ πόλις
is, and the Lamb. And the city

οὐ χρείαν ἔχει τοῦ ἡλίου οὐδὲ τῆς
not need has of the sun nor of the

σελήνης, ἵνα φαίνωσιν αὐτῇ· ἡ γὰρ
moon, in order that they might shine in it; for the

δόξα τοῦ θεοῦ ἐφώτισεν αὐτήν, καὶ
glory – of God enlightened it, and

ὁ λύχνος αὐτῆς τὸ ἀρνίον. **24** καὶ
the lamp of it [is] the Lamb. And

περιπατήσουσιν τὰ ἔθνη διὰ τοῦ φωτὸς
[3]shall walk about [1]the [2]nations through the light

αὐτῆς, καὶ οἱ βασιλεῖς τῆς γῆς φέρουσιν
of it, and the kings of the earth bring

τὴν δόξαν αὐτῶν εἰς αὐτήν· **25** καὶ οἱ
the glory of them into it; and the

πυλῶνες αὐτῆς οὐ μὴ κλεισθῶσιν ἡμέρας,
gates of it by no means may be shut by day,

νὺξ γὰρ οὐκ ἔσται ἐκεῖ· **26** καὶ οἴσουσιν
for night shall not be there; and they will bring

τὴν δόξαν καὶ τὴν τιμὴν τῶν ἐθνῶν
the glory and the honour of the nations

εἰς αὐτήν. **27** καὶ οὐ μὴ εἰσέλθῃ εἰς
into it. And by no means may enter into

wall and it was 144 cubits[y] thick,[z] by man's measurement, which the angel was using. 18The wall was made of jasper, and the city of pure gold, as pure as glass. 19The foundations of the city walls were decorated with every kind of precious stone. The first foundation was jasper, the second sapphire, the third chalcedony, the fourth emerald, 20the fifth sardonyx, the sixth carnelian, the seventh chrysolite, the eighth beryl, the ninth topaz, the tenth chrysoprase, the eleventh jacinth, and the twelfth amethyst.[a] 21The twelve gates were twelve pearls, each gate made of a single pearl. The great street of the city was of pure gold, like transparent glass.

22I did not see a temple in the city, because the Lord God Almighty and the Lamb are its temple. 23The city does not need the sun or the moon to shine on it, for the glory of God gives it light, and the Lamb is its lamp. 24The nations will walk by its light, and the kings of the earth will bring their splendor into it. 25On no day will its gates ever be shut, for there will be no night there. 26The glory and honor of the nations will be brought into it. 27Nothing impure will ever enter it,

[y] *17* That is, about 200 feet (about 65 meters)

[z] *17* Or *high*

[a] *20* The precise identification of some of these precious stones is uncertain.

and no one who practices
abomination and lying,
shall ever come into it, but
only those whose names
are written in the Lamb's
book of life.

Chapter 22

The River and the Tree of Life

AND he showed me a river of the water of life,
clear as crystal, coming
from the throne of God and
of [k]the Lamb,
2in the middle of its
street. And on either side of
the river was the tree of
life, bearing twelve [l] *kinds
of* fruit, yielding its fruit
every month; and the
leaves of the tree were for
the healing of the nations.
3And there shall no
longer be any curse; and
the throne of God and of
the Lamb shall be in it, and
His bond-servants shall
serve Him;
4and they shall see His
face, and His name *shall be*
on their foreheads.
5And there shall no
longer be *any* night; and
they shall not have need of
the light of a lamp nor the
light of the sun, because the
Lord God shall illumine
them; and they shall reign
forever and ever.
6And he said to me,
"These words are faithful
and true"; and the Lord,
the God of the spirits of the
prophets, sent His angel to
show to His bond-servants
the things which must
shortly take place.
7"And behold, I am
coming quickly. Blessed is
he who heeds the words of
the prophecy of this
book."
8And I, John, am the one
who heard and saw these

[k] Or, *the Lamb. In the middle of its street, and on either side of the river, was*

[l] Or, crops of *fruit*

αὐτὴν πᾶν κοινὸν καὶ [ὁ] ποιῶν
it every(any) profane thing and the [one] making
βδέλυγμα καὶ ψεῦδος, εἰ μὴ οἱ γεγραμ-
an abomination and a lie, except the [ones] *having been*
μένοι ἐν τῷ βιβλίῳ τῆς ζωῆς τοῦ ἀρνίου.
written in the scroll – of life of the Lamb.
22 Καὶ ἔδειξέν μοι ποταμὸν ὕδατος
And he showed me a river of water
ζωῆς λαμπρὸν ὡς κρύσταλλον, ἐκπορευόμε-
of life bright as crystal, proceed-
νον ἐκ τοῦ θρόνου τοῦ θεοῦ καὶ τοῦ
ing out of the throne – of God and of the
ἀρνίου. 2 ἐν μέσῳ τῆς πλατείας αὐτῆς
Lamb. In [the] midst of the street of it
καὶ τοῦ ποταμοῦ ἐντεῦθεν καὶ ἐκεῖθεν
and of the river hence and thence
ξύλον ζωῆς ποιοῦν καρποὺς δώδεκα,
a tree of life producing fruits twelve,
κατὰ μῆνα ἕκαστον ἀποδιδοῦν τὸν καρπὸν
according to [2]month [1]each rendering the fruit
αὐτοῦ, καὶ τὰ φύλλα τοῦ ξύλου εἰς
of it, and the leaves of the tree [will be] for
θεραπείαν τῶν ἐθνῶν. 3 καὶ πᾶν κατάθεμα
healing of the nations. And every curse
=no curse will be any
οὐκ ἔσται ἔτι. καὶ ὁ θρόνος τοῦ θεοῦ
will not be longer. And the throne – of God
καὶ τοῦ ἀρνίου ἐν αὐτῇ ἔσται, καὶ οἱ
and of the Lamb [2]in [3]it [1]will be, and the
δοῦλοι αὐτοῦ λατρεύσουσιν αὐτῷ, 4 καὶ
slaves of him will do service to him, and
ὄψονται τὸ πρόσωπον αὐτοῦ, καὶ τὸ
they will see the face of him, and the
ὄνομα αὐτοῦ ἐπὶ τῶν μετώπων αὐτῶν.
name of him [will be] on the foreheads of them.
5 καὶ νὺξ οὐκ ἔσται ἔτι, καὶ οὐκ
And night will not be longer, and not
ἔχουσιν χρείαν φωτὸς λύχνου καὶ φωτὸς
they have need of light of lamp and of light
ἡλίου, ὅτι κύριος ὁ θεὸς φωτίσει ἐπ'
of sun, because [the] Lord – God will shed light on
αὐτούς, καὶ βασιλεύσουσιν εἰς τοὺς
them, and they will reign unto the
αἰῶνας τῶν αἰώνων.
ages of the ages.
6 Καὶ εἶπέν μοι· οὗτοι οἱ λόγοι πιστοὶ
And he said to me: These – words [are] faithful
καὶ ἀληθινοί, καὶ ὁ κύριος ὁ θεὸς τῶν
and true, and the Lord the God of the
πνευμάτων τῶν προφητῶν ἀπέστειλεν τὸν
spirits of the prophets sent the
ἄγγελον αὐτοῦ δεῖξαι τοῖς δούλοις αὐτοῦ
angel of him to show to the slaves of him
ἃ δεῖ γενέσθαι ἐν τάχει. 7 καὶ ἰδοὺ
things which it behoves to occur quickly. And behold
ἔρχομαι ταχύ. μακάριος ὁ τηρῶν τοὺς
I am coming quickly. Blessed [is] the [one] keeping the
λόγους τῆς προφητείας τοῦ βιβλίου τούτου.
words of the prophecy of this scroll.
8 Κἀγὼ Ἰωάννης ὁ ἀκούων καὶ βλέπων
And I John [am] the [one] hearing and seeing
ταῦτα. καὶ ὅτε ἤκουσα καὶ ἔβλεψα,
these things. And when I heard and I saw,

nor will anyone who does
what is shameful or deceitful, but only those whose
names are written in the
Lamb's book of life.

Chapter 22

The River of Life

THEN the angel showed
me the river of the wa-
ter of life, as clear as crystal, flowing from the throne
of God and of the Lamb
2down the middle of the
great street of the city. On
each side of the river stood
the tree of life, bearing
twelve crops of fruit, yielding its fruit every month.
And the leaves of the tree
are for the healing of the
nations. 3No longer will
there be any curse. The
throne of God and of the
Lamb will be in the city,
and his servants will serve
him. 4They will see his
face, and his name will be
on their foreheads. 5There
will be no more night. They
will not need the light of a
lamp or the light of the sun,
for the Lord God will give
them light. And they will
reign for ever and ever.
6The angel said to me,
"These words are trust-
worthy and true. The Lord,
the God of the spirits of the
prophets, sent his angel to
show his servants the
things that must soon take
place."

Jesus Is Coming

7"Behold, I am coming
soon! Blessed is he who
keeps the words of the
prophecy in this book."
8I, John, am the one who
heard and saw these things.

things. And when I heard
and saw, I fell down to worship at the feet of the angel
who showed me these
things.
9And he *said to me,
"Do not do that; I am a fellow servant of yours and of
your brethren the prophets
and of those who heed the
words of this book; wor-
ship God."

The Final Message

10And he *said to me,
"Do not seal up the words
of the prophecy of this
book, for the time is near.
11"Let the one who does
wrong, still do wrong; and
let the one who is filthy,
still be filthy; and let the
one who is righteous, still
practice righteousness; and
let the one who is holy, still
keep himself holy."
12"Behold, I am coming
quickly, and My reward *is*
with Me, to render to every
man according to what he
has done.
13"I am the Alpha and
the Omega, the first and the
last, the beginning and the
end."
14Blessed are those who
wash their robes, that they
may have the right to the
tree of life, and may enter
by the gates into the city.
15Outside are the dogs
and the sorcerers and the
immoral persons and the
murderers and the idola-
ters, and everyone who
loves and practices lying.
16"I, Jesus, have sent My
angel to testify to you these
things for the churches. I
am the root and the off-
spring of David, the bright
morning star."
17And the Spirit and the
bride say, "Come." And
let the one who hears say,
"Come." And let the one

ἔπεσα προσκυνῆσαι ἔμπροσθεν τῶν ποδῶν
I fell to worship before the feet

τοῦ ἀγγέλου τοῦ δεικνύοντός μοι ταῦτα.
of the angel – showing me these things.

9 καὶ λέγει μοι· ὅρα μή· σύνδουλός
And he tells me: See thou [do] not; [2]a fellow-slave

σού εἰμι καὶ τῶν ἀδελφῶν σου τῶν
[3]of thee [1]I am and of the brothers of thee the

προφητῶν καὶ τῶν τηρούντων τοὺς λόγους
prophets and of the [ones] keeping the words

τοῦ βιβλίου τούτου· τῷ θεῷ προσκύνησον.
of this scroll: – [2]God [1]worship thou.

10 Καὶ λέγει μοι· μὴ σφραγίσῃς τοὺς
And he tells me: Seal not the

λόγους τῆς προφητείας τοῦ βιβλίου τούτου·
words of the prophecy of this scroll;

ὁ καιρὸς γὰρ ἐγγύς ἐστιν 11 ὁ ἀδικῶν
[2]the [3]time [1]for [5]near [4]is. The [one] acting unjustly

ἀδικησάτω ἔτι, καὶ ὁ ῥυπαρὸς ῥυπανθήτω
let him act unjustly still, and the filthy [one] let him act filthily

ἔτι, καὶ ὁ δίκαιος δικαιοσύνην ποιησάτω
still, and the righteous [one] [2]righteousness [1]let him do

ἔτι, καὶ ὁ ἅγιος ἁγιασθήτω ἔτι.
still, and the holy [one] let him be hallowed still.

12 Ἰδοὺ ἔρχομαι ταχύ, καὶ ὁ μισθός
Behold I am coming quickly, and the reward

μου μετ' ἐμοῦ, ἀποδοῦναι ἑκάστῳ ὡς
of me [is] with me, to render to each man as

τὸ ἔργον ἐστὶν αὐτοῦ. 13 ἐγὼ τὸ ἄλφα
the work [2]is [1]of him. I [am] the alpha

καὶ τὸ ὦ, ὁ πρῶτος καὶ ὁ ἔσχατος,
and the omega, the first and the last,

ἡ ἀρχὴ καὶ τὸ τέλος. 14 μακάριοι οἱ
the beginning and the end. Blessed [are] the [ones]

πλύνοντες τὰς στολὰς αὐτῶν, ἵνα ἔσται
washing the robes of them, in order that [4]will be

ἡ ἐξουσία αὐτῶν ἐπὶ τὸ ξύλον τῆς
[1]the [3]authority [2]of them over the tree –

ζωῆς καὶ τοῖς πυλῶσιν εἰσέλθωσιν εἰς
of life and [3]by the [4]gates [1]they may enter into

τὴν πόλιν. 15 ἔξω οἱ κύνες καὶ οἱ φαρμακοὶ
the city. Outside [are] the dogs and the sorcerers

καὶ οἱ πόρνοι καὶ οἱ φονεῖς καὶ οἱ
and the fornicators and the murderers and the

εἰδωλολάτραι καὶ πᾶς φιλῶν καὶ ποιῶν
idolaters and everyone loving and making

ψεῦδος.
a lie.

16 Ἐγὼ Ἰησοῦς ἔπεμψα τὸν ἄγγελόν
I Jesus sent the angel

μου μαρτυρῆσαι ὑμῖν ταῦτα ἐπὶ ταῖς
of me to witness to you these things over(in) the

ἐκκλησίαις. ἐγώ εἰμι ἡ ῥίζα καὶ τὸ
churches. I am the root and the

γένος Δαυίδ, ὁ ἀστὴρ ὁ λαμπρὸς ὁ
offspring of David, the [2]star – [1]bright –

πρωϊνός.
[3]morning.

17 Καὶ τὸ πνεῦμα καὶ ἡ νύμφη λέγουσιν·
And the Spirit and the bride say:

ἔρχου. καὶ ὁ ἀκούων εἰπάτω· ἔρχου.
Come. And the [one] hearing let him say: Come.

And when I had heard and
seen them, I fell down to
worship at the feet of the
angel who had been show-
ing them to me.
9But he
said to me, "Do not do it! I
am a fellow servant with
you and with your brothers
the prophets and of all who
keep the words of this
book. Worship God!"
10Then he told me, "Do
not seal up the words of the
prophecy of this book, because the time is near.
11Let him who does wrong
continue to do wrong; let
him who is vile continue to
be vile; let him who does
right continue to do right;
and let him who is holy continue to be holy."

12"Behold, I am coming
soon! My reward is with
me, and I will give to everyone according to what he
has done.
13I am the Alpha
and the Omega, the First
and the Last, the Beginning
and the End.
14"Blessed are those who
wash their robes, that they
may have the right to the
tree of life and may go
through the gates into the
city.
15Outside are the
dogs, those who practice
magic arts, the sexually immoral, the murderers, the
idolaters and everyone who
loves and practices falsehood.
16"I, Jesus, have sent my
angel to give you[b] this testimony for the churches. I
am the Root and the Off-
spring of David, and the
bright Morning Star."

17The Spirit and the bride
say, "Come!" And let him
who hears say, "Come!"

[b]16 The Greek is plural.

who is thirsty come; let the
one who wishes take the
water of life without cost.
18I testify to everyone
who hears the words of the
prophecy of this book: if
anyone adds to them, God
shall add to him the plagues
which are written in this
book;
19and if anyone takes
away from the words of the
book of this prophecy, God
shall take away his part
from the tree of life and
from the holy city, which
are written in this book.
20He who testifies to
these things says, "Yes, I
am coming quickly."
Amen. Come, Lord Jesus.
21The grace of the Lord
Jesus be with [m]all. Amen.

καὶ ὁ διψῶν ἐρχέσθω, ὁ θέλων λαβέτω
And the thirsting [one] let him come, the wishing [one] let him take

ὕδωρ ζωῆς δωρεάν.
[the] water of life freely.

18 Μαρτυρῶ ἐγὼ παντὶ τῷ ἀκούοντι
[2]witness [1]I to everyone hearing

τοὺς λόγους τῆς προφητείας τοῦ βιβλίου
the words of the prophecy – [3]scroll

τούτου· ἐάν τις ἐπιθῇ ἐπ' αὐτά, ἐπιθήσει
[1]of this: If anyone adds upon(to) them,* [2]will add

ὁ θεὸς ἐπ' αὐτὸν τὰς πληγὰς τὰς
– [1]God upon him the plagues –

γεγραμμένας ἐν τῷ βιβλίῳ τούτῳ· **19** καὶ
having been written in this scroll; and

ἐάν τις ἀφέλῃ ἀπὸ τῶν λόγων τοῦ
if anyone takes away from the words of the

βιβλίου τῆς προφητείας ταύτης, ἀφελεῖ
scroll of this prophecy, [2]will take away

ὁ θεὸς τὸ μέρος αὐτοῦ ἀπὸ τοῦ ξύλου
– [1]God the part of him from the tree

τῆς ζωῆς καὶ ἐκ τῆς πόλεως τῆς ἁγίας,
– of life and out of the [2]city – [1]holy,

τῶν γεγραμμένων ἐν τῷ βιβλίῳ τούτῳ.
of the things *having been* written in this scroll.

20 Λέγει ὁ μαρτυρῶν ταῦτα· ναί, ἔρχομαι
Says the witnessing [one] these things: Yes, I am coming

ταχύ. Ἀμήν, ἔρχου κύριε Ἰησοῦ.
quickly. Amen, come[,] Lord Jesus.

21 Ἡ χάρις τοῦ κυρίου Ἰησοῦ μετὰ
The grace of the Lord Jesus [be] with

πάντων.
all.

Whoever is thirsty, let him
come; and whoever wishes,
let him take the free gift of
the water of life.

18I warn everyone who
hears the words of the
prophecy of this book: If
anyone adds anything to
them, God will add to him
the plagues described in
this book. 19And if anyone
takes words away from this
book of prophecy, God will
take away from him his
share in the tree of life and
in the holy city, which are
described in this book.
20He who testifies to
these things says, "Yes, I
am coming soon."
Amen. Come, Lord
Jesus.
21The grace of the Lord
Jesus be with God's peo-
ple. Amen.

[m] Some ancient mss. read *the saints*

*** Neuter plural; see last clause of ver. 19.**